The New Jersey Municipal Data Book

2008 Maywood Public Library
459 Maywood Avenue
Maywood, NJ 07607

State & Municipal Profiles Series

The New Jersey Municipal Data Book

2008

State & Municipal Profiles Series

 information publications

Woodside, California

Titles from Information Publications

State & Municipal Profiles Series

Almanac of the 50 States

California Cities, Towns & Counties *Connecticut Municipal Profiles*
Florida Cities, Towns & Counties *Massachusetts Municipal Profiles*
The New Jersey Municipal Data Book *North Carolina Cities, Towns & Counties*

American Profiles Series

Asian Americans: A Statistical Sourcebook and Guide to Government Data
Black Americans: A Statistical Sourcebook and Guide to Government Data
Hispanic Americans: A Statistical Sourcebook and Guide to Government Data

Essential Topics Series

*Energy, Transportation & the Environment:
A Statistical Sourcebook and Guide to Government Data*

ISBN 978-0-911273-40-3 Paper
ISBN 978-0-911273-41-0 CD
The New Jersey Municipal Data Book 2008

©2008 Information Publications, Inc.
Printed in the United States of America

All rights reserved. No part of this book may be reproduced or transmitted in any form or by any means, including but not limited to electronic or mechanical photocopying, recording, or any information storage and retrieval system without written permission from the publisher.

Information Publications, Inc.
2995 Woodside Rd., Suite 400-182
Woodside, CA 94062-2446

www.informationpublications.com
info@informationpublications.com

Toll Free Phone 877.544.INFO (4636)
Toll Free Fax 877.544.4635

Direct Dial Phone 650.568.6170
Direct Dial Fax 650.568.6150

Table of Contents

Detailed Table of Contents..vi-x
Map of New Jersey...xi
Introduction & Explanation of the Categories xv
Disclaimer...xx
Municipal Profiles 3-568
County Profiles..571-591
Appendices
    Appendix A   State of New Jersey Overview 595-602
    Appendix B   List of Municipalities by County 603-605
    Appendix C   2006 American Community Survey Data for Selected Municipalities 607-613
    Appendix D   Supplemental School District Data 615-623
    Appendix E   Comparative Tables for Counties.......................................625
    Appendix F   Comparative Tables for Municipalities.................................627-646
    Appendix G   Federal and State Representatives.....................................647-648
Order Forms

Detailed Table of Contents

Municipal Profiles

Aberdeen Township, Monmouth County	3
Absecon City, Atlantic County	4
Alexandria Township, Hunterdon County	5
Allamuchy Township, Warren County	6
Allendale Borough, Bergen County	7
Allenhurst Borough, Monmouth County	8
Allentown Borough, Monmouth County	9
Alloway Township, Salem County	10
Alpha Borough, Warren County	11
Alpine Borough, Bergen County	12
Andover Borough, Sussex County	13
Andover Township, Sussex County	14
Asbury Park City, Monmouth County	15
Atlantic City, Atlantic County	16
Atlantic Highlands Borough, Monmouth County	17
Audubon Borough, Camden County	18
Audubon Park Borough, Camden County	19
Avalon Borough, Cape May County	20
Avon-by-the-Sea Borough, Monmouth County	21
Barnegat Light Borough, Ocean County	22
Barnegat Township, Ocean County	23
Barrington Borough, Camden County	24
Bass River Township, Burlington County	25
Bay Head Borough, Ocean County	26
Bayonne City, Hudson County	27
Beach Haven Borough, Ocean County	28
Beachwood Borough, Ocean County	29
Bedminster Township, Somerset County	30
Belleville Township, Essex County	31
Bellmawr Borough, Camden County	32
Belmar Borough, Monmouth County	33
Belvidere Town, Warren County	34
Bergenfield Borough, Bergen County	35
Berkeley Heights Township, Union County	36
Berkeley Township, Ocean County	37
Berlin Borough, Camden County	38
Berlin Township, Camden County	39
Bernards Township, Somerset County	40
Bernardsville Borough, Somerset County	41
Bethlehem Township, Hunterdon County	42
Beverly City, Burlington County	43
Blairstown Township, Warren County	44
Bloomfield Township, Essex County	45
Bloomingdale Borough, Passaic County	46
Bloomsbury Borough, Hunterdon County	47
Bogota Borough, Bergen County	48
Boonton Town, Morris County	49
Boonton Township, Morris County	50
Bordentown City, Burlington County	51
Bordentown Township, Burlington County	52
Bound Brook Borough, Somerset County	53
Bradley Beach Borough, Monmouth County	54
Branchburg Township, Somerset County	55
Branchville Borough, Sussex County	56
Brick Township, Ocean County	57
Bridgeton City, Cumberland County	58
Bridgewater Township, Somerset County	59
Brielle Borough, Monmouth County	60
Brigantine City, Atlantic County	61
Brooklawn Borough, Camden County	62
Buena Borough, Atlantic County	63
Buena Vista Township, Atlantic County	64
Burlington City, Burlington County	65
Burlington Township, Burlington County	66
Butler Borough, Morris County	67
Byram Township, Sussex County	68
Caldwell Borough, Essex County	69
Califon Borough, Hunterdon County	70
Camden City, Camden County	71
Cape May City, Cape May County	72
Cape May Point Borough, Cape May County	73
Carlstadt Borough, Bergen County	74
Carneys Point Township, Salem County	75
Carteret Borough, Middlesex County	76
Cedar Grove Township, Essex County	77
Chatham Borough, Morris County	78
Chatham Township, Morris County	79
Cherry Hill Township, Camden County	80
Chesilhurst Borough, Camden County	81
Chester Borough, Morris County	82
Chester Township, Morris County	83
Chesterfield Township, Burlington County	84
Cinnaminson Township, Burlington County	85
Clark Township, Union County	86
Clayton Borough, Gloucester County	87
Clementon Borough, Camden County	88
Cliffside Park Borough, Bergen County	89
Clifton City, Passaic County	90
Clinton Town, Hunterdon County	91
Clinton Township, Hunterdon County	92
Closter Borough, Bergen County	93
Collingswood Borough, Camden County	94
Colts Neck Township, Monmouth County	95
Commercial Township, Cumberland County	96
Corbin City, Atlantic County	97
Cranbury Township, Middlesex County	98
Cranford Township, Union County	99
Cresskill Borough, Bergen County	100
Deal Borough, Monmouth County	101
Deerfield Township, Cumberland County	102
Delanco Township, Burlington County	103
Delaware Township, Hunterdon County	104
Delran Township, Burlington County	105
Demarest Borough, Bergen County	106
Dennis Township, Cape May County	107
Denville Township, Morris County	108
Deptford Township, Gloucester County	109
Dover Town, Morris County	110
Dover Township, Ocean County	*see Toms River*
Downe Township, Cumberland County	111
Dumont Borough, Bergen County	112
Dunellen Borough, Middlesex County	113
Eagleswood Township, Ocean County	114
East Amwell Township, Hunterdon County	115
East Brunswick Township, Middlesex County	116
East Greenwich Township, Gloucester County	117
East Hanover Township, Morris County	118
East Newark Borough, Hudson County	119
East Orange City, Essex County	120
East Rutherford Borough, Bergen County	121
East Windsor Township, Mercer County	122
Eastampton Township, Burlington County	123

Detailed Table of Contents

Municipal Profiles (con't)

- Eatontown Borough, Monmouth County 124
- Edgewater Borough, Bergen County 125
- Edgewater Park Township, Burlington County 126
- Edison Township, Middlesex County 127
- Egg Harbor City, Atlantic County 128
- Egg Harbor Township, Atlantic County 129
- Elizabeth City, Union County 130
- Elk Township, Gloucester County 131
- Elmer Borough, Salem County 132
- Elmwood Park Borough, Bergen County 133
- Elsinboro Township, Salem County 134
- Emerson Borough, Bergen County 135
- Englewood City, Bergen County 136
- Englewood Cliffs Borough, Bergen County 137
- Englishtown Borough, Monmouth County 138
- Essex Fells Borough, Essex County 139
- Estell Manor City, Atlantic County 140
- Evesham Township, Burlington County 141
- Ewing Township, Mercer County 142
- Fair Haven Borough, Monmouth County 143
- Fair Lawn Borough, Bergen County 144
- Fairfield Township, Cumberland County 145
- Fairfield Township, Essex County 146
- Fairview Borough, Bergen County 147
- Fanwood Borough, Union County 148
- Far Hills Borough, Somerset County 149
- Farmingdale Borough, Monmouth County 150
- Fieldsboro Borough, Burlington County 151
- Flemington Borough, Hunterdon County 152
- Florence Township, Burlington County 153
- Florham Park Borough, Morris County 154
- Folsom Borough, Atlantic County 155
- Fort Lee Borough, Bergen County 156
- Frankford Township, Sussex County 157
- Franklin Borough, Sussex County 158
- Franklin Lakes Borough, Bergen County 159
- Franklin Township, Gloucester County 160
- Franklin Township, Hunterdon County 161
- Franklin Township, Somerset County 162
- Franklin Township, Warren County 163
- Fredon Township, Sussex County 164
- Freehold Borough, Monmouth County 165
- Freehold Township, Monmouth County 166
- Frelinghuysen Township, Warren County 167
- Frenchtown Borough, Hunterdon County 168
- Galloway Township, Atlantic County 169
- Garfield City, Bergen County 170
- Garwood Borough, Union County 171
- Gibbsboro Borough, Camden County 172
- Glassboro Borough, Gloucester County 173
- Glen Gardner Borough, Hunterdon County 174
- Glen Ridge Borough, Essex County 175
- Glen Rock Borough, Bergen County 176
- Gloucester City, Camden County 177
- Gloucester Township, Camden County 178
- Green Brook Township, Somerset County 179
- Green Township, Sussex County 180
- Greenwich Township, Cumberland County 181
- Greenwich Township, Gloucester County 182
- Greenwich Township, Warren County 183
- Guttenberg Town, Hudson County 184
- Hackensack City, Bergen County 185
- Hackettstown Town, Warren County 186
- Haddon Heights Borough, Camden County 187
- Haddon Township, Camden County 188
- Haddonfield Borough, Camden County 189
- Hainesport Township, Burlington County 190
- Haledon Borough, Passaic County 191
- Hamburg Borough, Sussex County 192
- Hamilton Township, Atlantic County 193
- Hamilton Township, Mercer County 194
- Hammonton Town, Atlantic County 195
- Hampton Borough, Hunterdon County 196
- Hampton Township, Sussex County 197
- Hanover Township, Morris County 198
- Harding Township, Morris County 199
- Hardwick Township, Warren County 200
- Hardyston Township, Sussex County 201
- Harmony Township, Warren County 202
- Harrington Park Borough, Bergen County 203
- Harrison Town, Hudson County 204
- Harrison Township, Gloucester County 205
- Harvey Cedars Borough, Ocean County 206
- Hasbrouck Heights Borough, Bergen County 207
- Haworth Borough, Bergen County 208
- Hawthorne Borough, Passaic County 209
- Hazlet Township, Monmouth County 210
- Helmetta Borough, Middlesex County 211
- High Bridge Borough, Hunterdon County 212
- Highland Park Borough, Middlesex County 213
- Highlands Borough, Monmouth County 214
- Hightstown Borough, Mercer County 215
- Hillsborough Township, Somerset County 216
- Hillsdale Borough, Bergen County 217
- Hillside Township, Union County 218
- Hi-Nella Borough, Camden County 219
- Hoboken City, Hudson County 220
- Ho-Ho-Kus Borough, Bergen County 221
- Holland Township, Hunterdon County 222
- Holmdel Township, Monmouth County 223
- Hopatcong Borough, Sussex County 224
- Hope Township, Warren County 225
- Hopewell Borough, Mercer County 226
- Hopewell Township, Cumberland County 227
- Hopewell Township, Mercer County 228
- Howell Township, Monmouth County 229
- Independence Township, Warren County 230
- Interlaken Borough, Monmouth County 231
- Irvington Township, Essex County 232
- Island Heights Borough, Ocean County 233
- Jackson Township, Ocean County 234
- Jamesburg Borough, Middlesex County 235
- Jefferson Township, Morris County 236
- Jersey City, Hudson County 237
- Keansburg Borough, Monmouth County 238
- Kearny Town, Hudson County 239
- Kenilworth Borough, Union County 240
- Keyport Borough, Monmouth County 241
- Kingwood Township, Hunterdon County 242
- Kinnelon Borough, Morris County 243
- Knowlton Township, Warren County 244
- Lacey Township, Ocean County 245

The New Jersey Municipal Data Book

Detailed Table of Contents

Municipal Profiles (con't)

Lafayette Township, Sussex County	246
Lake Como Borough, Monmouth County	247
Lakehurst Borough, Ocean County	248
Lakewood Township, Ocean County	249
Lambertville City, Hunterdon County	250
Laurel Springs Borough, Camden County	251
Lavallette Borough, Ocean County	252
Lawnside Borough, Camden County	253
Lawrence Township, Cumberland County	254
Lawrence Township, Mercer County	255
Lebanon Borough, Hunterdon County	256
Lebanon Township, Hunterdon County	257
Leonia Borough, Bergen County	258
Liberty Township, Warren County	259
Lincoln Park Borough, Morris County	260
Linden City, Union County	261
Lindenwold Borough, Camden County	262
Linwood City, Atlantic County	263
Little Egg Harbor Township, Ocean County	264
Little Falls Township, Passaic County	265
Little Ferry Borough, Bergen County	266
Little Silver Borough, Monmouth County	267
Livingston Township, Essex County	268
Loch Arbour Village, Monmouth County	269
Lodi Borough, Bergen County	270
Logan Township, Gloucester County	271
Long Beach Township, Ocean County	272
Long Branch City, Monmouth County	273
Long Hill Township, Morris County	274
Longport Borough, Atlantic County	275
Lopatcong Township, Warren County	276
Lower Alloways Creek Township, Salem County	277
Lower Township, Cape May County	278
Lumberton Township, Burlington County	279
Lyndhurst Township, Bergen County	280
Madison Borough, Morris County	281
Magnolia Borough, Camden County	282
Mahwah Township, Bergen County	283
Manalapan Township, Monmouth County	284
Manasquan Borough, Monmouth County	285
Manchester Township, Ocean County	286
Mannington Township, Salem County	287
Mansfield Township, Burlington County	288
Mansfield Township, Warren County	289
Mantoloking Borough, Ocean County	290
Mantua Township, Gloucester County	291
Manville Borough, Somerset County	292
Maple Shade Township, Burlington County	293
Maplewood Township, Essex County	294
Margate City, Atlantic County	295
Marlboro Township, Monmouth County	296
Matawan Borough, Monmouth County	297
Maurice River Township, Cumberland County	298
Maywood Borough, Bergen County	299
Medford Lakes Borough, Burlington County	300
Medford Township, Burlington County	301
Mendham Borough, Morris County	302
Mendham Township, Morris County	303
Merchantville Borough, Camden County	304
Metuchen Borough, Middlesex County	305
Middle Township, Cape May County	306
Middlesex Borough, Middlesex County	307
Middletown Township, Monmouth County	308
Midland Park Borough, Bergen County	309
Milford Borough, Hunterdon County	310
Millburn Township, Essex County	311
Millstone Borough, Somerset County	312
Millstone Township, Monmouth County	313
Milltown Borough, Middlesex County	314
Millville City, Cumberland County	315
Mine Hill Township, Morris County	316
Monmouth Beach Borough, Monmouth County	317
Monroe Township, Gloucester County	318
Monroe Township, Middlesex County	319
Montague Township, Sussex County	320
Montclair Township, Essex County	321
Montgomery Township, Somerset County	322
Montvale Borough, Bergen County	323
Montville Township, Morris County	324
Moonachie Borough, Bergen County	325
Moorestown Township, Burlington County	326
Morris Plains Borough, Morris County	327
Morris Township, Morris County	328
Morristown Town, Morris County	329
Mount Arlington Borough, Morris County	330
Mount Ephraim Borough, Camden County	331
Mount Holly Township, Burlington County	332
Mount Laurel Township, Burlington County	333
Mount Olive Township, Morris County	334
Mountain Lakes Borough, Morris County	335
Mountainside Borough, Union County	336
Mullica Township, Atlantic County	337
National Park Borough, Gloucester County	338
Neptune City Borough, Monmouth County	339
Neptune Township, Monmouth County	340
Netcong Borough, Morris County	341
New Brunswick City, Middlesex County	342
New Hanover Township, Burlington County	343
New Milford Borough, Bergen County	344
New Providence Borough, Union County	345
Newark City, Essex County	346
Newfield Borough, Gloucester County	347
Newton Town, Sussex County	348
North Arlington Borough, Bergen County	349
North Bergen Township, Hudson County	350
North Brunswick Township, Middlesex County	351
North Caldwell Borough, Essex County	352
North Haledon Borough, Passaic County	353
North Hanover Township, Burlington County	354
North Plainfield Borough, Somerset County	355
North Wildwood City, Cape May County	356
Northfield City, Atlantic County	357
Northvale Borough, Bergen County	358
Norwood Borough, Bergen County	359
Nutley Township, Essex County	360
Oakland Borough, Bergen County	361
Oaklyn Borough, Camden County	362
Ocean City, Cape May County	363
Ocean Gate Borough, Ocean County	364
Ocean Township, Monmouth County	365
Ocean Township, Ocean County	366
Oceanport Borough, Monmouth County	367

The New Jersey Municipal Data Book

Detailed Table of Contents

Municipal Profiles (con't)

Ogdensburg Borough, Sussex County....................368
Old Bridge Township, Middlesex County.................369
Old Tappan Borough, Bergen County...................370
Oldmans Township, Salem County......................371
Oradell Borough, Bergen County.......................372
Orange City Township, Essex County..................373
Oxford Township, Warren County......................374
Palisades Park Borough, Bergen County................375
Palmyra Borough, Burlington County...................376
Paramus Borough, Bergen County.....................377
Park Ridge Borough, Bergen County....................378
Parsippany-Troy Hills Township, Morris County........379
Passaic City, Passaic County.........................380
Paterson City, Passaic County.......................381
Paulsboro Borough, Gloucester County................382
Peapack & Gladstone Borough, Somerset County......383
Pemberton Borough, Burlington County................384
Pemberton Township, Burlington County...............385
Pennington Borough, Mercer County..................386
Penns Grove Borough, Salem County.................387
Pennsauken Township, Camden County...............388
Pennsville Township, Salem County..................389
Pequannock Township, Morris County................390
Perth Amboy City, Middlesex County.................391
Phillipsburg Town, Warren County....................392
Pilesgrove Township, Salem County..................393
Pine Beach Borough, Ocean County..................394
Pine Hill Borough, Camden County...................395
Pine Valley Borough, Camden County................396
Piscataway Township, Middlesex County..............397
Pitman Borough, Gloucester County..................398
Pittsgrove Township, Salem County..................399
Plainfield City, Union County........................400
Plainsboro Township, Middlesex County..............401
Pleasantville City, Atlantic County....................402
Plumsted Township, Ocean County...................403
Pohatcong Township, Warren County.................404
Point Pleasant Beach Borough, Ocean County........405
Point Pleasant Borough, Ocean County...............406
Pompton Lakes Borough, Passaic County.............407
Port Republic City, Atlantic County...................408
Princeton Borough, Mercer County...................409
Princeton Township, Mercer County..................410
Prospect Park Borough, Passaic County..............411
Quinton Township, Salem County....................412
Rahway City, Union County.........................413
Ramsey Borough, Bergen County....................414
Randolph Township, Morris County...................415
Raritan Borough, Somerset County..................416
Raritan Township, Hunterdon County.................417
Readington Township, Hunterdon County.............418
Red Bank Borough, Monmouth County...............419
Ridgefield Borough, Bergen County..................420
Ridgefield Park Village, Bergen County...............421
Ridgewood Village, Bergen County..................422
Ringwood Borough, Passaic County.................423
River Edge Borough, Bergen County.................424
River Vale Township, Bergen County.................425
Riverdale Borough, Morris County...................426
Riverside Township, Burlington County...............427
Riverton Borough, Burlington County................428

Robbinsville Township, Mercer County................429
Rochelle Park Township, Bergen County.............430
Rockaway Borough, Morris County..................431
Rockaway Township, Morris County.................432
Rockleigh Borough, Bergen County..................433
Rocky Hill Borough, Somerset County...............434
Roosevelt Borough, Monmouth County..............435
Roseland Borough, Essex County...................436
Roselle Borough, Union County.....................437
Roselle Park Borough, Union County................438
Roxbury Township, Morris County..................439
Rumson Borough, Monmouth County................440
Runnemede Borough, Camden County..............441
Rutherford Borough, Bergen County................442
Saddle Brook Township, Bergen County.............443
Saddle River Borough, Bergen County..............444
Salem City, Salem County.........................445
Sandyston Township, Sussex County...............446
Sayreville Borough, Middlesex County..............447
Scotch Plains Township, Union County.............448
Sea Bright Borough, Monmouth County.............449
Sea Girt Borough, Monmouth County...............450
Sea Isle City, Cape May County...................451
Seaside Heights Borough, Ocean County...........452
Seaside Park Borough, Ocean County..............453
Secaucus Town, Hudson County..................454
Shamong Township, Burlington County............455
Shiloh Borough, Cumberland County...............456
Ship Bottom Borough, Ocean County..............457
Shrewsbury Borough, Monmouth County..........458
Shrewsbury Township, Monmouth County.........459
Somerdale Borough, Camden County.............460
Somers Point City, Atlantic County................461
Somerville Borough, Somerset County............462
South Amboy City, Middlesex County.............463
South Belmar Borough, Monmouth County..... see Lake Como
South Bound Brook Borough, Somerset County....464
South Brunswick Township, Middlesex County....465
South Hackensack Township, Bergen County.....466
South Harrison Township, Gloucester County.....467
South Orange Village Township, Essex County....468
South Plainfield Borough, Middlesex County......469
South River Borough, Middlesex County..........470
South Toms River Borough, Ocean County........471
Southampton Township, Burlington County.......472
Sparta Township, Sussex County................473
Spotswood Borough, Middlesex County..........474
Spring Lake Borough, Monmouth County.........475
Spring Lake Heights Borough, Monmouth County..476
Springfield Township, Burlington County.........477
Springfield Township, Union County..............478
Stafford Township, Ocean County................479
Stanhope Borough, Sussex County...............480
Stillwater Township, Sussex County..............481
Stockton Borough, Hunterdon County............482
Stone Harbor Borough, Cape May County........483
Stow Creek Township, Cumberland County.......484
Stratford Borough, Camden County..............485
Summit City, Union County.....................486
Surf City Borough, Ocean County...............487
Sussex Borough, Sussex County................488

The New Jersey Municipal Data Book

Detailed Table of Contents

Municipal Profiles (con't)

Swedesboro Borough, Gloucester County 489
Tabernacle Township, Burlington County 490
Tavistock Borough, Camden County 491
Teaneck Township, Bergen County 492
Tenafly Borough, Bergen County 493
Teterboro Borough, Bergen County 494
Tewksbury Township, Hunterdon County 495
Tinton Falls Borough, Monmouth County 496
Toms River Township, Ocean County 497
Totowa Borough, Passaic County 498
Trenton City, Mercer County 499
Tuckerton Borough, Ocean County 500
Union Beach Borough, Monmouth County 501
Union City, Hudson County 502
Union Township, Hunterdon County 503
Union Township, Union County 504
Upper Deerfield Township, Cumberland County 505
Upper Freehold Township, Monmouth County 506
Upper Pittsgrove Township, Salem County 507
Upper Saddle River Borough, Bergen County 508
Upper Township, Cape May County 509
Ventnor City, Atlantic County 510
Vernon Township, Sussex County 511
Verona Township, Essex County 512
Victory Gardens Borough, Morris County 513
Vineland City, Cumberland County 514
Voorhees Township, Camden County 515
Waldwick Borough, Bergen County 516
Wall Township, Monmouth County 517
Wallington Borough, Bergen County 518
Walpack Township, Sussex County 519
Wanaque Borough, Passaic County 520
Wantage Township, Sussex County 521
Warren Township, Somerset County 522
Washington Borough, Warren County 523
Washington Township, Bergen County 524
Washington Township, Burlington County 525
Washington Township, Gloucester County 526
Washington Township, Mercer County . . . . see Robbinsville
Washington Township, Morris County 527
Washington Township, Warren County 528
Watchung Borough, Somerset County 529
Waterford Township, Camden County 530
Wayne Township, Passaic County 531
Weehawken Township, Hudson County 532
Wenonah Borough, Gloucester County 533
West Amwell Township, Hunterdon County 534
West Caldwell Township, Essex County 535
West Cape May Borough, Cape May County 536
West Deptford Township, Gloucester County 537
West Long Branch Borough, Monmouth County 538
West Milford Township, Passaic County 539
West New York Town, Hudson County 540
West Orange Township, Essex County 541
West Paterson Borough, Passaic County 542
West Wildwood Borough, Cape May County 543
West Windsor Township, Mercer County 544
Westampton Township, Burlington County 545
Westfield Town, Union County 546
Westville Borough, Gloucester County 547
Westwood Borough, Bergen County 548
Weymouth Township, Atlantic County 549
Wharton Borough, Morris County 550
White Township, Warren County 551
Wildwood City, Cape May County 552
Wildwood Crest Borough, Cape May County 553
Willingboro Township, Burlington County 554
Winfield Township, Union County 555
Winslow Township, Camden County 556
Woodbine Borough, Cape May County 557
Woodbridge Township, Middlesex County 558
Woodbury City, Gloucester County 559
Woodbury Heights Borough, Gloucester County 560
Woodcliff Lake Borough, Bergen County 561
Woodland Township, Burlington County 562
Woodlynne Borough, Camden County 563
Wood-Ridge Borough, Bergen County 564
Woodstown Borough, Salem County 565
Woolwich Township, Gloucester County 566
Wrightstown Borough, Burlington County 567
Wyckoff Township, Bergen County 568

County Profiles

Atlantic County 571
Bergen County 572
Burlington County 573
Camden County 574
Cape May County 575
Cumberland County 576
Essex County 577
Gloucester County 578
Hudson County 579
Hunterdon County 580
Mercer County 581
Middlesex County 582
Monmouth County 583
Morris County 584
Ocean County 585
Passaic County 586
Salem County 587
Somerset County 588
Sussex County 589
Union County 590
Warren County 591

New Jersey Counties

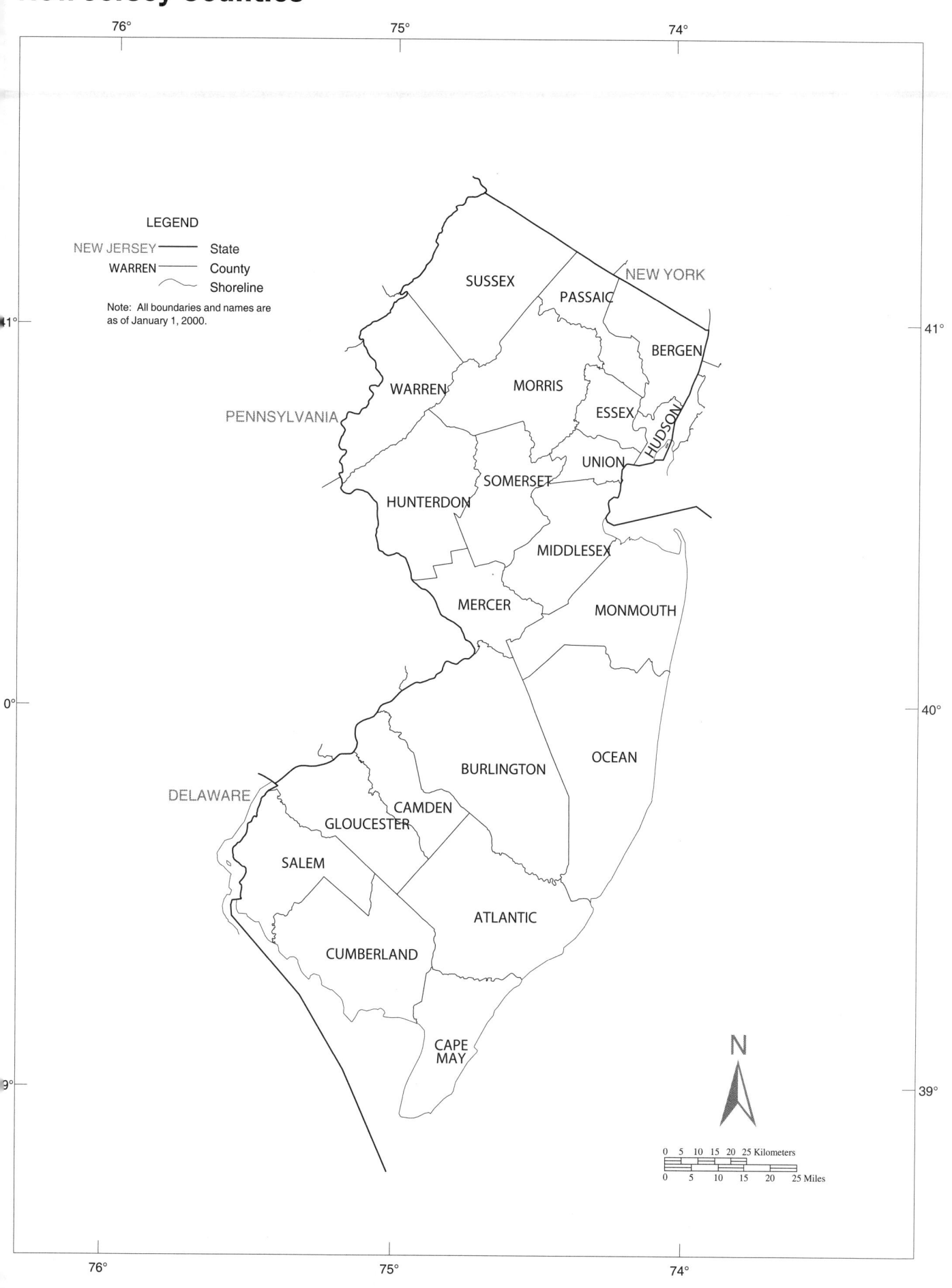

The New Jersey Municipal Data Book

2008

State & Municipal Profiles Series

State & Municipal Profiles Series

Introduction

The New Jersey Municipal Data Book is an annual reference book published by Information Publications since 1981. It is part of the **State & Municipal Profiles Series**, which also includes the **Almanac of the 50 States**, as well as municipal and county profile books on California, Connecticut, Florida, Massachusetts, and North Carolina.

Drawing from a variety of established sources, **The New Jersey Municipal Data Book** is designed to provide concise yet comprehensive profiles for all 566 municipalities and 21 counties in New Jersey. The book contains one page for every municipality and county in the state. (Our use of the term "municipality" in New Jersey encompasses the categories of "township," "town," "city," "borough," and "village.") Pages in the **Municipal Profiles** and **County Profiles** sections are arranged alphabetically. To aid in finding information about a specific place, as well as in making comparisons, each page has the same format, organizing the data into nine categories: **Demographics & Socioeconomic Characteristics**, **General Information**, **Government**, **Housing & Construction**, **Public Library**, **Public Safety**, **Public School District**, **Municipal Finance** or **County Finance**, and **Taxes**. Following the **Municipal Profiles** and **County Profiles**, there are seven appendices.

Some changes in municipality names should be noted. In 2005, South Belmar Borough in Monmouth County changed its name to Lake Como. In 2006, Dover Township in Ocean County changed its name to Toms River. In 2008, Washington Township in Mercer County changed its name to Robbinsville. These name changes are reflected in this edition.

Introduction to the Data

The information in this volume has been obtained from a variety of sources. To aid researchers with questions about the methodology behind the data collection or the terms used, we have identified the source for each piece of data. These questions can best be answered by the original data collectors, who are cited in the **explanation of the categories**.

Information Publications conducted mail, phone, email, and online surveys in February, March, and April of 2008 in order to obtain the most recent names of **government officials**, **police chiefs**, **fire chiefs**, **librarians**, and **school superintendents**. Information gathered from the surveys is used to supplement other sources to provide complete and up-to-date information.

Almost all the information was originally collected by an agency of the state or federal government. Using such information assures a high level of accuracy, reliability, and comprehensiveness. However, not all the information collected by government agencies has been published, nor is it necessarily readily available. Many government agencies collect information largely for their own internal use, and the data remains in the original materials used for collection. We have selected the most appropriate items from the available information.

Our goal is to provide accurate, reliable, and useful information for all 566 municipalities and 21 counties in New Jersey. Data in the profiles is the latest available for all local governing bodies as of April 15, 2008. The dates of the information are indicated in the headings or data items.

The notation "NA" stands for "not available." Although we strive to obtain all available data, there are several reasons data may not be available. Many agencies only provide data for places of a certain size or population, so data is not available for many smaller municipalities. Other times, "NA" indicates that the information was never sent to the data-collecting agency, or was not available from the agency at press time. Reporting is often voluntary, and some places have chosen not to report. Finally, sometimes the category or descriptor simply does not apply to a given place (for example, in the case of towns without police or fire chiefs).

Readers should also note that the numbers for subcategories do not always add up to the total shown. In some cases, this is due to rounding error in the original data collection. Other times, only certain subgroups of a larger category are presented.

Explanation of the Categories

Municipal Profiles Section

Demographics & Socioeconomic Characteristics

Municipal information in this category, with a few exceptions, comes from the 2000 US Census (the data shown here has been revised from the original data published by the Bureau of Census). The exceptions are the **1980** and **1990 population** figures, which are from their respective Decennial Censuses; the **2006 population estimates**, which come from the US Census Bureau's Population Estimates division; and the **labor force** and **unemployment rate** for 2006, which come from the New Jersey Department of Labor and Workforce Development. **Population density** for 2006 was calculated by Information Publications based on the 2006 population estimates, and the **land area** figure from 2000.

Race, as used by the Bureau of the Census, is not meant to denote any scientific or biological concept of race. Terms used here match the categories used by the Census for data collection, and represent the self-categorization of respondents. It should also be noted that **Hispanic origin** is not a racial category. Persons may be of any race, and be of Hispanic origin as well.

Introduction

Educational attainment applies to persons who are 25 years or older. College graduates are persons with at least a four-year degree.

Income and **poverty** information as reported in the 2000 US Census is from 1999.

A **household** includes all persons occupying a housing unit. A **family household** includes a householder and one or more other persons living in the same household who are related to the householder by birth, marriage, or adoption. The number of family households always equals the number of families in a given place. However, a family household may also include nonrelatives living with the family. A **nonfamily household** includes a householder living alone or with nonrelatives only. Not all persons live in households. For example, some are members of the armed forces, inmates of institutions, or live in group quarters. As a result, the total number of persons in a city or town can be greater than the number of persons living in all households in that town. The subgroups listed were selected for potential interest and do not represent a full breakdown of all types of households. Readers should also note that there is overlap among types of households. For example, the same household may have both members under 18 years of age and members over 65 years of age.

Total civilian labor force includes all persons at least 16 years of age who are not members of the armed forces, and are either employed or unemployed. **Self-employed workers** refers to workers who own non-incorporated businesses.

The American Community Survey (ACS), which surveys a monthly sample of the US population, is beginning to track much of the information previously only measured by the Decennial Census. Currently, the ACS provides data for the United States, each state, and cities and counties with populations over 65,000. Beginning with the 2007 ACS, coverage will expand to all places with populations greater than 20,000. By 2010, the Bureau of the Census hopes to use the ACS to track all the information currently collected in the long form of the Decennial Census. The 2006 ACS provided data for 20 of New Jersey's 566 municipalities, as well as all 21 counties. For those municipalities currently tracked by the ACS, we have provided that data in **Appendix C**. (ACS data for counties appears in the profiles in place of 2000 Census data.) You can find more information about the ACS at http://www.census.gov/acs/www.

General Information

The **address** and **telephone number** shown are for the central location of municipal business (i.e., the city hall or city administrative office), and were obtained from surveys done by Information Publications. Other information such as the **website** was also obtained from the surveys. Some municipalities do not have their own websites, but have pages on their county's website. In these cases, the notation "(county website)" is used. **Form of government** comes from the Center for Government Services at Rutgers University, supplemented by our surveys. Readers who are interested in the different forms of municipal government in New Jersey should refer to the New Jersey League of Municipalities' guide at www.njslom.com/types.html. **Year of incorporation** represents the date of a municipality's creation in its present form. Dates are taken from *The Story of New Jersey's Civil Boundaries, 1606-1968*, by John P. Snyder, with updates by the Center for Government Services at Rutgers.

Land area and **water area** are from the 2000 US Census. It should be noted that land area measurement as reported by the 2000 US Census is given in square meters. It has been converted into square miles in the profiles, using a conversion factor of 2,589,988 square meters per square mile.

Government

State legislative district comes from the Municipal and County Government section of New Jersey's official website: http://www.state.nj.us. **US congressional district** information comes from the Census Bureau's "110th Congressional Districts" summary file, and was also verified by our surveys.

All names of **local officials** are from our surveys.

Housing and Construction

Housing unit data for 2000 comes from the 2000 US Census. A **housing unit** is defined as a house, apartment, mobile home or trailer, group of rooms, or single room occupied as a separate living quarter or, if vacant, intended as a separate living quarter. Separate living quarters are those in which the occupants live and eat separately from any other persons in the building, and which have direct access from the outside of the building or through a common hall.

A **single-family unit** is defined as a housing unit which does not share the building with any other housing units, and is not attached to any other structure. In Census terminology, it is defined as a single, detached unit. **Single-family home** is equivalent to the Census term "specified owner-occupied unit," and refers to single-family houses on less than ten acres without a business or medical office on the property.

A housing unit is **owner-occupied** if the owner or co-owner lives in the unit, even if the unit is mortgaged or not fully paid for. All other housing units are considered **renter-occupied**.

Introduction

Value is the Census respondent's estimate of how much the house would sell for if it were on the market. **Median value** represents the middle value of the distribution of these estimates, such that half the houses have higher values than the median and half have lower values. **Median rent** is defined in a similar fashion.

Statistics on **permits for new residential construction** for 2006 and 2007 come from the US Bureau of the Census' Manufacturing, Mining, and Construction Statistics division. Places that issue building permits are asked to report monthly to the Bureau. Figures for 2007 are the year-to-date totals from December 2007, and may differ from the annual estimates, which were not available at press time. Figures for 2006 are the annual averages, but readers are cautioned that estimates are updated periodically on the Census' website, so the data presented here may differ slightly from the most recent information.

Data from 2007 for **real property valuation** and **average property value & tax** comes from the New Jersey Division of Local Government Services, Department of Community Affairs.

Public Library

The name of the **library director** was obtained from our surveys. All **library statistics** come from "New Jersey Public Library Statistics, 2006." Information was obtained from the website for the New Jersey State Library, under the section for the Library Development Bureau. **Full-time staff** refers only to professionally-certified staff who work more than 35 hours per week, and does not include all employees.

The New Jersey State Library does not provide separate statistics for branches of county libraries. For municipalities whose library is a branch of a county library, the appropriate county page is listed. For municipalities whose library is the main library for the county, the county system statistics are listed.

Public Safety

Data on **number of officers, violent crimes, property crimes, domestic violence**, and **arson** come from the "Crime in the United States" reports for 2005 and 2006, published by the Uniform Crime Reports division of the Federal Bureau of Investigation and the New Jersey State Police. **Violent crime** is defined as **murder, rape, robbery**, and **aggravated assault**. **Property crime** is defined as **burglary, larceny**, and **motor vehicle theft**. **Crime rates** are defined as crimes per 1,000 residents.

Names of **police chiefs** and **fire chiefs** were obtained using our surveys.

Public School District

The municipal profiles provide information for the principal school district in each municipality. If a governing body does not maintain a school district, data is given for the system it uses. If only an elementary school system is maintained, that is the information provided. For districts that do not contain any regular public schools, the school system used by residents of that district is provided if it is available. New Jersey also has several regional public school districts. Information about these districts can be found in **Appendix D**.

The **name, address, telephone number, superintendent**, and **grade plan** of public school districts were obtained from the New Jersey School Directory, published by the New Jersey Department of Education. This information was supplemented by our surveys.

All other school information is for the school year 2006-07 except where indicated. The information comes from the "New Jersey Report Card" for 2006-07, except for **Adequate Yearly Progress (AYP), Highly-Qualified Teachers (HQT)**, and **attendance rate** for 2005-06, which come from the annual **No Child Left Behind (NCLB)** report.

Grade plan shows the range of grades available in the schools within the district. "K" denotes kindergarten, and "9-12" indicates a four-year high school. A grade plan of "K-12" means that the school district contains at least one of each of the following types of schools: an elementary school with kindergarten through sixth grade, a junior high school with seventh and eighth grades, and a four-year high school. **Number of schools** refers only to regular elementary and high schools in the district, and not vocational or special service schools.

Enrollment includes all regular day school students enrolled for all grades in the district. **Enrollment** and **grade 12 enrollment** are grouped by school districts and reflect the total enrollment of all schools within the district.

Assessment tests are a key element of New Jersey's participation in the federal **No Child Left Behind (NCLB)** program. The profiles show the percentage of students scoring at the proficient or advanced level for **math** and **language arts** on the following tests: the **New Jersey Assessment of Skills and Knowledge (NJASK)** for third graders, the **Grade Eight Proficiency Assessment (GEPA)**, and the **High School Proficiency Assessment (HSPA)**. In addition, the **NCLB** program sets goals for **highly-qualified teachers** in single subjects and across all subjects. It also determines **Adequate Yearly Progress (AYP)**, an overall indicator of whether the district needs to improve to meet federal goals.

The New Jersey Municipal Data Book — xvii

Introduction

New Jersey's Department of Education does not calculate figures for **graduation rate** and **SAT results** at the district level. As a result, only districts that contain a single high school have available data for these categories.

The goals of education are complex, and standardized tests measure the degree of attainment of only a few of those goals. Standardized test scores should not be the only criterion used to evaluate an educational program. Readers must realize that only a small amount of the information that is required for a total evaluation is provided in the district profiles, and for a more in-depth look should talk with the districts directly and do extensive research of all data available from the schools, the districts, and the New Jersey Department of Education.

Municipal Finance

Information in this section is obtained from the New Jersey Department of Community Affairs. While most municipalities in New Jersey operate on calendar year budgets (January 1-December 31), approximately 50 municipalities operate on a state fiscal year (July 1-June 30). Municipalities that do so are indicated as such in their profiles.

State aid refers to funds received from the state to provide relief for property taxes, and is taken from the report "CY2008/SFY2009 State Aid." State aid information is taken from the governor's proposed budget for 2008 (or fiscal year 2009, for those municipalities using a fiscal year schedule), and figures may differ from the final budget adopted by the state legislature.

General budget information refers to property tax levies paid by residents of a municipality. Data in this section is distilled from the Abstract of Ratables and the New Jersey Property Tax Information report. **County levies** represent the municipality's share of the budget for county-administered programs (such as health departments and libraries). The **school levy** represents taxes raised to support local schools. The **municipal levy** refers to taxes that go to funding municipal government and debt service.

For a more detailed explanation, users of this data may find it helpful to contact the Department of Community Affairs, Division of Local Government Services.

Taxes

The information shown under this heading was obtained from the New Jersey Department of the Treasury, Division of Taxation's "Tables of Equalized Valuations" for 2005, 2006, and 2007, from the Abstracts of Ratables for those years. **County equalization ratio** is computed by the state for the purpose of apportioning state school aid and for equalizing county taxes. It is computed during the final months of the year, and is used for the following year (ratios appear under the year in which they are used). Data shown for **state equalized value** is after any tax court appeals.

County Profiles Section

All the information on the county pages is derived from the same sources as the municipal pages, with a few exceptions, notes, and additions.

Unlike counties in many states, New Jersey counties contain no unincorporated areas. Since the counties are essentially collections of municipalities, many agencies do not report separate county data. In these cases, the information presented here was obtained by adding the corresponding figures (where applicable) for the municipalities contained in the counties. Data obtained in this manner is marked as such in the profiles.

Demographics & Socioeconomic Characteristics

All information in this section comes from the 2006 ACS, with a few exceptions. **Population** figures for 1990, 2000, and 2007 come from the 1990 and 2000 Censuses, and the Census Bureau's Population Estimates Division, respectively. **Population density** is calculated from the 2007 estimate.

Civilian labor force projections come from the New Jersey Department of Labor's Planning & Analysis division.

General Information

The **number of municipalities** and **address** of the county (county seat) are updated annually from our own surveys. **Form of government**, **class**, and **number of freeholders** information comes from the New Jersey Association of Counties.

Government & Voters

All names of **county officials** come from our surveys.

Registered voters data is compiled from information provided by the Office of the Attorney General, New Jersey Division of Elections. Numbers do not add up to the total because not all party affiliations are shown, only Democratic, Republican, and Unaffiliated.

County School District

The **county superintendent** (a state rather than county official), **address**, and **phone number** were obtained from our own surveys and the New Jersey Department of Education. The **number of districts** comes from the New Jersey School Directory.

Introduction

Housing & Construction

Housing Unit data comes from the 2006 ACS.

Real property parcels and **valuation** are not provided separately for counties. Information on the pages is obtained by adding the corresponding figures for the municipalities contained in each county.

Public Safety

County police officers data (including officers in the sheriff's and prosecutors' departments) comes from the same "Crime in the United States" report as the rest of the crime data.

Public Library

Several counties do not have their own library (that is, one specified as a "county library"). In this case, **library statistics** shown are obtained from adding the figures for the municipalities in those counties that provide statistics. For these counties, **number of libraries** refers to the number listed in the library directory and reporting statistics.

State Income Tax

Information in this section was obtained from the New Jersey Department of Taxation's 2005 "Statistics of Income" report.

County Finance

Much of the financial data presented here is not reported separately for counties. For these data items, figures shown are the sum of the municipalities in each county. These items are marked in the profiles.

Appendices

The appendices supplement the information that appears on the individual profile pages. Information in the appendices comes from the same source as the corresponding item on the profile page unless otherwise noted below.

Appendix A is the profile for the state of New Jersey, taken from the 2008 edition of the ***Almanac of the 50 States*** (ISBN: 978-0-929960-46-3, paper; 978-0-929960-47-0, cloth), also published by Information Publications. Please refer to that volume for similar information on each of the 50 States, the District of Columbia, and the United States in summary.

Appendix B lists New Jersey's municipalities by county.

Appendix C gives ACS data for the 20 municipalities tracked in 2006.

Appendix D provides data for other school districts not shown in the municipal profiles.

Appendix E provides comparative tables for counties in New Jersey.

Appendix F provides comparative tables for municipalities in New Jersey.

Appendix G lists New Jersey's representatives in the US Congress and the New Jersey Legislature.

Introduction

Abbreviations

Actg	Acting
Admin	Administrator
Assoc	Associates
Avg	Average
AYP	Adequate Yearly Progress
Bd Sec	Board Secretary
Chr	Chairperson
CMPTRA	Consolidated Municipal Property Tax Relief Aid
CFO	Chief Financial Officer
Coord	Coordinator
(County)	Services provided by County
DCA	Department of Community Affairs (New Jersey state agency)
Dep	Deputy
Dev	Development
Dir	Director
Dist	District
FY	Fiscal year ended in June 30
GEPA	Grade Eight Proficiency Assessment
H'holds	Households
HSPA	High School Proficiency Assessment
Int	Interim
Mgr	Manager
Muni	Municipal
NA	Not Available or Not Applicable
NJASK	New Jersey Assessment of Skills and Knowledge
(State)	Services provided by State
Superint	Superintendent
Svcs	Services
Treas	Treasurer

Disclaimer

The New Jersey Municipal Data Book contains thousands of pieces of information. Reasonable precautions, along with a good deal of care, were taken in its preparation. Despite our efforts, it is possible that some of the information contained in this book may not be accurate. Some errors may be due to errors in the original source materials, and others may have been made by the compilers of this volume. An incorrect spelling may occur, a figure may be inverted, and similar mistakes may exist. The compilers, editors, typist, printers, and others working on this volume are all human, and in a work of this magnitude the possibility of error can never be fully eliminated. If any piece of information is believed to be inaccurate, please contact the publisher. We are eager to eliminate any errors from future editions and we will be pleased to check a piece of information. The publisher is also aware that some users may apply the data in this book to various remunerative projects. Although we have taken reasonable, responsible measures to insure accuracy, we cannot take responsibility for liability or losses suffered by users of the data. The information provided here is believed to be correct at the time of publication. No other guarantees are made or implied.

The publisher assumes no liability for losses incurred by users, and warrants only that diligence and due care were used in the production of this volume.

A Final Word

In order to continue to meet its goals, ***The New Jersey Municipal Data Book*** is revised and updated on an annual basis. The best suggestions for improvement in a ready-reference source such as this come from the regular users of the work. Therefore, we actively solicit your comments and ideas. If you know how this book could become more useful to you, please contact us.

The Editors
The New Jersey Municipal Data Book
Information Publications, Inc.
2995 Woodside Road, Suite 400-182
Woodside, CA 94062

www.informationpublications.com
info@informationpublications.com

Toll Free Phone: 877-544-4636
Toll Free Fax: 877-544-4635

The New Jersey Municipal Data Book

2008

State & Municipal Profiles Series

State &
Municipal
Profiles
Series

Monmouth County
Aberdeen Township

Demographics & Socio-Economic Characteristics
(2000 US Census, except as noted)

Population
- 1980*............................17,235
- 1990*............................17,038
- 2000............................17,454
  - Male............................8,506
  - Female..........................8,948
- 2006 (estimate)*..................18,382
  - Population density.............3,318.1

Race & Hispanic Origin, 2000
Race
- White............................13,758
- Black/African American............2,098
- American Indian/Alaska Native........24
- Asian..............................962
- Native Hawaiian/Pacific Islander......1
- Other race........................306
- Two or more races.................305
- Hispanic origin, total...........1,225
  - Mexican..........................90
  - Puerto Rican....................648
  - Cuban............................96
  - Other Hispanic..................391

Age & Nativity, 2000
- Under 5 years....................1,211
- 18 years and over...............13,185
- 21 years and over...............12,708
- 65 years and over................1,811
- 85 years and over..................129
- Median age........................37.0
- Native-born.....................15,392
- Foreign-born.....................1,995

Educational Attainment, 2000
- Population 25 years and over....12,263
- Less than 9th grade...............3.1%
- High school grad or higher.......87.9%
- Bachelor's degree or higher......34.4%
- Graduate degree..................11.4%

Income & Poverty, 1999
- Per capita income..............$28,984
- Median household income........$68,125
- Median family income...........$76,648
- Persons in poverty................807
- H'holds receiving public assistance...102
- H'holds receiving social security...1,432

Households, 2000
- Total households................6,421
  - With persons under 18..........2,416
  - With persons over 65...........1,299
  - Family households..............4,774
  - Single-person households.......1,300
- Persons per household............2.70
- Persons per family...............3.14

Labor & Employment
- Total civilian labor force, 2006**....10,473
  - Unemployment rate...............3.4%
- Total civilian labor force, 2000......9,742
  - Unemployment rate...............3.5%

Employed persons 16 years and over by occupation, 2000
- Managers & professionals.........3,963
- Service occupations..............1,120
- Sales & office occupations.......2,712
- Farming, fishing & forestry..........8
- Construction & maintenance........647
- Production & transportation.......947
- Self-employed persons.............396

‡ Joint library with Matawan Borough
* US Census Bureau
** New Jersey Department of Labor

See Introduction for an explanation of all data sources.

General Information
Township of Aberdeen
1 Aberdeen Sq
Aberdeen, NJ 07747
732-583-4200
- Website...............www.aberdeennj.org
- Year of incorporation...............1979
- Land/water area (sq. miles).....5.54/2.22
- Form of government........Council-Manager

Government
Legislative Districts
- US Congressional.....................6
- State Legislative...................13

Local Officials, 2008
- Mayor.....................David Sobel
- Manager.............James Lauro (Actg)
- Clerk...................Karen Ventura
- Finance Dir..............Angela Morin
- Tax Assessor............Holly Reycraft
- Tax Collector.............Marie Taylor
- Attorney................Dan McCarthy
- Building.................John Quinn
- Comm Dev/Planning................NA
- Engineering.............David Samuel
- Public Works............James Lauro
- Police Chief.............John Powers
- Fire/Emergency Dir.................NA

Housing & Construction
Housing Units, 2000*
- Total............................6,558
- Median rent.......................$817
- Median SF home value.........$160,800

Permits for New Residential Construction
	Units	Value
Total, 2007	15	$1,693,577
Single family	15	$1,693,577
Total, 2006	16	$1,563,075
Single family	16	$1,563,075

Real Property Valuation, 2007
	Parcels	Valuation
Total	6,787	$841,892,360
Vacant	460	14,668,230
Residential	6,133	711,414,730
Commercial	165	87,610,300
Industrial	4	11,849,700
Apartments	7	15,392,900
Farm land	13	94,800
Farm homestead	5	861,700

Average Property Value & Tax, 2007
- Residential value..............$116,044
- Property tax.....................$5,880
- Tax credit/rebate...............$1,132

Public Library
Matawan-Aberdeen Public Library‡
165 Main St
Matawan, NJ 07747
732-583-9100
- Director.....................Susan Pike

Library statistics, 2006
- Population served................26,364
- Full-time/total staff................3/6

	Total	Per capita
Holdings	96,193	3.65
Revenues	$957,222	$36.31
Expenditures	$837,766	$31.78
Annual visits	104,471	3.96
Internet terminals/annual users		14/15,294

Taxes
	2005	2006	2007
General tax rate per $100	4.76	5.004	5.067
County equalization ratio	51.95	45.23	40.32
Net valuation taxable	$845,098,132	$846,250,890	$842,941,776
State equalized value	$1,868,446,014	$2,099,959,424	$2,220,059,326

Public Safety
Number of officers, 2006.............32

Crime	2005	2006
Total crimes	259	281
Violent	23	36
Murder	0	0
Rape	2	4
Robbery	4	12
Aggravated assault	17	20
Non-violent	236	245
Burglary	33	40
Larceny	187	191
Vehicle theft	16	14
Domestic violence	222	211
Arson	2	4
Total crime rate	14.0	15.3
Violent	1.2	2.0
Non-violent	12.8	13.4

Public School District
(for school year 2006-07 except as noted)

Matawan-Aberdeen Regional School District
One Crest Way
Aberdeen, NJ 07747
732-705-4003
- Superintendent........Richard O'Malley
- Number of schools...................14
- Grade plan.........................K-12
- Enrollment.......................3,889
- Attendance rate, '05-06..........95.0%
- Dropout rate......................0.4%
- Students per teacher..............10.8
- Per pupil expenditure..........$14,180
- Median faculty salary..........$58,220
- Median administrator salary...$115,224
- Grade 12 enrollment................232
- High school graduation rate......98.2%

Assessment test results
(percent scoring at proficient or advanced level)
	Language	Math
NJASK-Grade 3	87.7%	87.5%
GEPA-Grade 8	76.4%	70.5%
HSPA-High School	90.4%	70.8%

SAT score averages
Pct tested	Math	Verbal	Writing
82%	478	469	467

Teacher Qualifications
- Avg. years of experience.............9
- Highly-qualified teachers
  one subject/all subjects......99.0%/99.0%
- With emergency credentials........0.0%

No Child Left Behind
- AYP, 2005-06............Meets Standards

Municipal Finance
State Aid Programs, 2008
- Total aid....................$1,851,845
- CMPTRA......................716,960
- Energy tax receipts.........1,128,991
- Garden State Trust..............5,894

General Budget, 2007
- Total tax levy..............$42,709,431
- County levy.................5,333,322
  - County taxes..............5,019,571
  - County library...................0
  - County health....................0
  - County open space.........313,751
- School levy................30,385,869
- Muni. levy..................6,990,240
- Misc. revenues..............7,064,657

©2008 Information Publications, Inc. All rights reserved. Photocopying prohibited. For additional copies, contact the publisher at www.informationpublications.com or (877)544-INFO (4636)

The New Jersey Municipal Data Book

Absecon City
Atlantic County

Demographics & Socio-Economic Characteristics
(2000 US Census, except as noted)

Population
- 1980* 6,859
- 1990* 7,298
- 2000 7,638
  - Male 3,660
  - Female 3,978
- 2006 (estimate)* 8,065
- Population density 1,410.0

Race & Hispanic Origin, 2000
Race
- White 6,363
- Black/African American 459
- American Indian/Alaska Native 13
- Asian 570
- Native Hawaiian/Pacific Islander 0
- Other race 115
- Two or more races 118
- Hispanic origin, total 288
  - Mexican 30
  - Puerto Rican 111
  - Cuban 19
  - Other Hispanic 128

Age & Nativity, 2000
- Under 5 years 460
- 18 years and over 5,842
- 21 years and over 5,672
- 65 years and over 1,231
- 85 years and over 165
  - Median age 40.3
- Native-born 6,894
- Foreign-born 799

Educational Attainment, 2000
- Population 25 years and over 5,357
- Less than 9th grade 3.2%
- High school grad or higher 86.0%
- Bachelor's degree or higher 22.4%
- Graduate degree 7.3%

Income & Poverty, 1999
- Per capita income $23,615
- Median household income $55,745
- Median family income $61,563
- Persons in poverty 364
- H'holds receiving public assistance 30
- H'holds receiving social security 836

Households, 2000
- Total households 2,773
  - With persons under 18 996
  - With persons over 65 777
  - Family households 2,084
  - Single-person households 532
- Persons per household 2.69
- Persons per family 3.08

Labor & Employment
- Total civilian labor force, 2006** 4,385
  - Unemployment rate 6.1%
- Total civilian labor force, 2000 4,009
  - Unemployment rate 6.5%

Employed persons 16 years and over by occupation, 2000
- Managers & professionals 1,042
- Service occupations 1,097
- Sales & office occupations 1,087
- Farming, fishing & forestry 4
- Construction & maintenance 280
- Production & transportation 239
- Self-employed persons 197

* US Census Bureau
** New Jersey Department of Labor

General Information
City of Absecon
Municipal Complex
500 Mill Rd
Absecon, NJ 08201
609 641 0663
- Website .... absecon-newjersey.org
- Year of incorporation 1902
- Land/water area (sq. miles) 5.72/1.21
- Form of government .... City

Government
Legislative Districts
- US Congressional 2
- State Legislative 2

Local Officials, 2008
- Mayor .... Peter C. Elco
- Administrator .... Terrence Dolan
- Clerk .... Carie A. Crone (Actg)
- Finance Dir. .... Jessica Thompson
- Tax Assessor .... Brian Conover
- Tax Collector .... Agnes Bambrick
- Attorney .... Michael Blee
- Building .... Michael O'Hagan
- Planning .... Remington & Vernick
- Engineering .... Remington & Vernick
- Public Works .... Lloyd Jones
- Police Chief .... Charles J. Smith
- Emerg/Fire Director .... Butch Stewart

Housing & Construction
Housing Units, 2000*
- Total 2,902
- Median rent $792
- Median SF home value $123,000

Permits for New Residential Construction

	Units	Value
Total, 2007	165	$14,236,542
Single family	92	$8,804,375
Total, 2006	68	$7,358,333
Single family	56	$6,658,333

Real Property Valuation, 2007

	Parcels	Valuation
Total	3,759	$475,352,800
Vacant	426	20,262,800
Residential	3,138	364,638,800
Commercial	195	90,451,200
Industrial	0	0
Apartments	0	0
Farm land	0	0
Farm homestead	0	0

Average Property Value & Tax, 2007
- Residential value $116,201
- Property tax $4,435
- Tax credit/rebate $891

Public Library
Absecon Public Library
305 New Jersey Ave
Absecon, NJ 08201
609-646-2228
- Director .... Barbara Wilson

Library statistics, 2006
- Population served 7,638
- Full-time/total staff 0/1

	Total	Per capita
Holdings	22,510	2.95
Revenues	$252,157	$33.01
Expenditures	$194,094	$25.41
Annual visits	18,787	2.46
Internet terminals/annual users		7/10,021

Taxes

	2005	2006	2007
General tax rate per $100	3.694	3.778	3.817
County equalization ratio	72.9	63.39	53.87
Net valuation taxable	$445,470,853	$452,747,300	$476,112,407
State equalized value	$702,746,258	$841,301,889	$969,680,928

Public Safety
Number of officers, 2006 25

Crime	2005	2006
Total crimes	377	319
Violent	38	35
Murder	0	1
Rape	1	3
Robbery	10	14
Aggravated assault	27	17
Non-violent	339	284
Burglary	61	41
Larceny	253	231
Vehicle theft	25	12
Domestic violence	77	70
Arson	0	2
Total crime rate	47.7	39.9
Violent	4.8	4.4
Non-violent	42.9	35.5

Public School District
(for school year 2006-07 except as noted)

Absecon City School District
800 Irelan Ave
Absecon, NJ 08201
609-641-5375
- Superintendent .... James Giaquinto
- Number of schools 2
- Grade plan K-8
- Enrollment 847
- Attendance rate, '05-06 .... 95.4%
- Dropout rate .... NA
- Students per teacher 11.0
- Per pupil expenditure $10,244
- Median faculty salary $52,035
- Median administrator salary $88,162
- Grade 12 enrollment .... NA
- High school graduation rate .... NA

Assessment test results
(percent scoring at proficient or advanced level)

	Language	Math
NJASK-Grade 3	80.5%	89.1%
GEPA-Grade 8	75.3%	67.0%
HSPA-High School	NA	NA

SAT score averages

Pct tested	Math	Verbal	Writing
NA	NA	NA	NA

Teacher Qualifications
- Avg. years of experience 8
- Highly-qualified teachers
  - one subject/all subjects 98.5%/98.5%
- With emergency credentials 0.0%

No Child Left Behind
- AYP, 2005-06 .... Meets Standards

Municipal Finance
State Aid Programs, 2008
- Total aid $929,793
  - CMPTRA 85,803
  - Energy tax receipts 836,880
  - Garden State Trust 3,773

General Budget, 2007
- Total tax levy $18,171,073
  - County levy 2,450,553
    - County taxes 2,164,465
    - County library 0
    - County health 109,195
    - County open space 176,893
  - School levy 9,748,529
  - Muni. levy 5,971,991
  - Misc. revenues 3,923,545

Hunterdon County
Alexandria Township

Demographics & Socio-Economic Characteristics
(2000 US Census, except as noted)

Population
- 1980*...2,798
- 1990*...3,594
- 2000..4,698
  - Male...2,353
  - Female...2,345
- 2006 (estimate)*.................................5,089
  - Population density.............................184.8

Race & Hispanic Origin, 2000
Race
- White..4,558
- Black/African American.............................37
- American Indian/Alaska Native.......................5
- Asian..34
- Native Hawaiian/Pacific Islander....................2
- Other race..21
- Two or more races.................................41
- Hispanic origin, total............................81
  - Mexican..17
  - Puerto Rican.....................................30
  - Cuban...6
  - Other Hispanic...................................28

Age & Nativity, 2000
- Under 5 years....................................331
- 18 years and over...............................3,378
- 21 years and over...............................3,259
- 65 years and over.................................568
- 85 years and over.................................124
- Median age.......................................40.2
- Native-born.....................................4,448
- Foreign-born.....................................250

Educational Attainment, 2000
- Population 25 years and over...................3,150
- Less than 9th grade..............................3.4%
- High school grad or higher......................93.2%
- Bachelor's degree or higher.....................39.7%
- Graduate degree.................................16.0%

Income & Poverty, 1999
- Per capita income............................$34,622
- Median household income......................$92,730
- Median family income.........................$93,619
- Persons in poverty...............................229
- H'holds receiving public assistance................8
- H'holds receiving social security................319

Households, 2000
- Total households..............................1,535
- With persons under 18............................679
- With persons over 65.............................289
- Family households............................1,291
- Single-person households.........................207
- Persons per household............................2.95
- Persons per family...............................3.25

Labor & Employment
- Total civilian labor force, 2006**............2,647
- Unemployment rate...............................5.7%
- Total civilian labor force, 2000..............2,351
- Unemployment rate...............................4.0%

Employed persons 16 years and over by occupation, 2000
- Managers & professionals......................1,115
- Service occupations..............................187
- Sales & office occupations.......................633
- Farming, fishing & forestry.......................28
- Construction & maintenance.......................153
- Production & transportation.....................142
- Self-employed persons............................234

* US Census Bureau
** New Jersey Department of Labor

See Introduction for an explanation of all data sources.

General Information
Township of Alexandria
21 Hog Hollow Rd
Pittstown, NJ 08867
908-996-7071
- Website...........................www.alexandria-nj.us
- Year of incorporation...........................1765
- Land/water area (sq. miles)..............27.54/0.10
- Form of government.........................Township

Government
Legislative Districts
- US Congressional...................................7
- State Legislative.................................23

Local Officials, 2008
- Mayor.........................Harry Fuerstenberger
- Manager/Admin....................................NA
- Clerk..................................Ellen Kluber
- Finance Dir.........................William Hance
- Tax Assessor......................Eloise Hagaman
- Tax Collector..........................Jack Earley
- Attorney..........................Valerie Kimson
- Building......................Guenther Majewski
- Comm Dev/Planning................................NA
- Engineering..................Gerald D. Philkill
- Public Works Foreman.............Glenn Griffith
- Police Chief.....................................NA
- Fire/Emergency Dir...............................NA

Housing & Construction
Housing Units, 2000*
- Total..1,598
- Median rent...................................$1,021
- Median SF home value........................$274,100

Permits for New Residential Construction
	Units	Value
Total, 2007	14	$3,406,200
Single family	14	$3,406,200
Total, 2006	40	$9,079,396
Single family	40	$9,079,396

Real Property Valuation, 2007
	Parcels	Valuation
Total	2,340	$785,041,168
Vacant	237	33,421,700
Residential	1,431	613,108,800
Commercial	32	21,479,488
Industrial	3	2,534,800
Apartments	1	418,900
Farm land	383	3,972,780
Farm homestead	253	110,104,700

Average Property Value & Tax, 2007
- Residential value...........................$429,462
- Property tax..................................$8,780
- Tax credit/rebate.............................$1,256

Public Library
No public municipal library

Library statistics, 2006
- Population served................................NA
- Full-time/total staff.........................NA/NA

	Total	Per capita
Holdings	NA	NA
Revenues	NA	NA
Expenditures	NA	NA
Annual visits	NA	NA
Internet terminals/annual users	NA/NA	

Taxes
	2005	2006	2007
General tax rate per $100	1.88	2	2.05
County equalization ratio	105.02	91.81	88.04
Net valuation taxable	$741,419,296	$764,932,037	$787,045,773
State equalized value	$742,012,906	$849,522,252	$913,782,965

Public Safety
- Number of officers, 2006...........................0

Crime
	2005	2006
Total crimes	19	22
Violent	2	2
Murder	0	0
Rape	0	0
Robbery	1	0
Aggravated assault	1	2
Non-violent	17	20
Burglary	1	5
Larceny	13	15
Vehicle theft	3	0
Domestic violence	4	1
Arson	0	1
Total crime rate	3.8	4.4
Violent	0.4	0.4
Non-violent	3.4	4.0

Public School District
(for school year 2006-07 except as noted)

Alexandria Township School District
557 County Rd 513
Pittstown, NJ 08867
908-996-6811

- Superintendent..............Matthew Jennings
- Number of schools.................................2
- Grade plan.....................................K-8
- Enrollment......................................654
- Attendance rate, '05-06.......................95.4%
- Dropout rate....................................NA
- Students per teacher............................9.7
- Per pupil expenditure........................$12,638
- Median faculty salary........................$57,424
- Median administrator salary.................$101,850
- Grade 12 enrollment.............................NA
- High school graduation rate....................NA

Assessment test results
(percent scoring at proficient or advanced level)

	Language	Math
NJASK-Grade 3	95.4%	89.1%
GEPA-Grade 8	87.3%	83.5%
HSPA-High School	NA	NA

SAT score averages
Pct tested	Math	Verbal	Writing
NA	NA	NA	NA

Teacher Qualifications
- Avg. years of experience..........................13
- Highly-qualified teachers
  - one subject/all subjects...............100%/100%
- With emergency credentials.....................0.0%

No Child Left Behind
- AYP, 2005-06......................Meets Standards

Municipal Finance
State Aid Programs, 2008
- Total aid...................................$408,453
  - CMPTRA.....................................48,227
  - Energy tax receipts.......................346,778
  - Garden State Trust.........................13,448

General Budget, 2007
- Total tax levy..........................$16,089,851
  - County levy..............................2,967,444
    - County taxes...........................2,483,408
    - County library...........................216,112
    - County health..................................0
    - County open space........................267,924
  - School levy.............................11,475,443
  - Muni. levy...............................1,646,963
  - Misc. revenues...........................2,215,605

©2008 Information Publications, Inc. All rights reserved. Photocopying prohibited. For additional copies, contact the publisher at www.informationpublications.com or (877)544-INFO (4636)

The New Jersey Municipal Data Book

Allamuchy Township — Warren County

Demographics & Socio-Economic Characteristics
(2000 US Census, except as noted)

Population
- 1980*..2,560
- 1990*..3,484
- 2000..3,877
  - Male...1,800
  - Female..2,077
- 2006 (estimate)*...................................4,093
- Population density..................................199.3

Race & Hispanic Origin, 2000
Race
- White...3,702
- Black/African American..............................36
- American Indian/Alaska Native.......................2
- Asian..72
- Native Hawaiian/Pacific Islander....................0
- Other race..27
- Two or more races..................................38
- Hispanic origin, total.............................104
  - Mexican...15
  - Puerto Rican......................................28
  - Cuban..9
  - Other Hispanic....................................52

Age & Nativity, 2000
- Under 5 years.......................................229
- 18 years and over.................................3,142
- 21 years and over.................................3,072
- 65 years and over...................................637
- 85 years and over....................................60
  - Median age..44.1
- Native-born.......................................3,493
- Foreign-born..384

Educational Attainment, 2000
- Population 25 years and over......................3,003
- Less than 9th grade................................1.0%
- High school grad or higher........................94.5%
- Bachelor's degree or higher.......................43.8%
- Graduate degree...................................15.2%

Income & Poverty, 1999
- Per capita income...............................$43,552
- Median household income.........................$70,107
- Median family income............................$89,653
- Persons in poverty..................................71
- H'holds receiving public assistance.................42
- H'holds receiving social security..................420

Households, 2000
- Total households.................................1,692
  - With persons under 18.............................423
  - With persons over 65..............................442
  - Family households...............................1,134
  - Single-person households..........................482
- Persons per household..............................2.28
- Persons per family.................................2.80

Labor & Employment
- Total civilian labor force, 2006**...............2,449
  - Unemployment rate................................2.1%
- Total civilian labor force, 2000.................2,144
  - Unemployment rate................................1.7%

Employed persons 16 years and over by occupation, 2000
- Managers & professionals.........................1,033
- Service occupations................................145
- Sales & office occupations.........................616
- Farming, fishing & forestry.........................19
- Construction & maintenance........................115
- Production & transportation.......................179
- Self-employed persons.............................138

* US Census Bureau
** New Jersey Department of Labor

General Information
Township of Allamuchy
292 Alphano Rd
PO Box A
Allamuchy, NJ 07820
908-852-5132
- Website.......................www.allamuchynj.org
- Year of incorporation...........................1873
- Land/water area (sq. miles).............20.54/0.23
- Form of government.............Small Municipality

Government
Legislative Districts
- US Congressional....................................5
- State Legislative..................................23

Local Officials, 2008
- Mayor......................Robert Resker
- Manager..................Anne Marie Tracy
- Clerk....................Anne Marie Tracy
- Finance Dir................Jim Kozimor
- Tax Assessor............Michael Schmidt
- Tax Collector................Betty Drake
- Attorney..................Edward Wacks
- Building................Charles Cutler
- Planning..................Alfia Schemm
- Engineering...............Paul Sterbenz
- Public Works.............Edward Tracy
- Police Chief.........................NA
- Emerg/Fire Director.......Daniel Bulka

Housing & Construction
Housing Units, 2000*
- Total...1,774
- Median rent......................................$1,075
- Median SF home value..........................$192,500

Permits for New Residential Construction

	Units	Value
Total, 2007	6	$1,299,600
Single family	6	$1,299,600
Total, 2006	180	$11,966,352
Single family	180	$11,966,352

Real Property Valuation, 2007

	Parcels	Valuation
Total	2,351	$521,272,215
Vacant	377	20,292,700
Residential	1,765	459,370,600
Commercial	19	17,944,600
Industrial	1	977,300
Apartments	0	0
Farm land	120	1,342,915
Farm homestead	69	21,344,100

Average Property Value & Tax, 2007
- Residential value...............................$262,113
- Property tax......................................$5,376
- Tax credit/rebate................................$1,064

Public Library
No public municipal library

Library statistics, 2006
- Population served...................................NA
- Full-time/total staff............................NA/NA

	Total	Per capita
Holdings	NA	NA
Revenues	NA	NA
Expenditures	NA	NA
Annual visits	NA	NA

Internet terminals/annual users....NA/NA

Public Safety
Number of officers, 2006.............................0

Crime	2005	2006
Total crimes	25	40
Violent	3	3
Murder	0	0
Rape	0	0
Robbery	0	1
Aggravated assault	3	2
Non-violent	22	37
Burglary	2	11
Larceny	19	23
Vehicle theft	1	3
Domestic violence	19	0
Arson	0	4
Total crime rate	6.2	10.0
Violent	0.7	0.7
Non-violent	5.5	9.2

Public School District
(for school year 2006-07 except as noted)

Allamuchy Township School District
Allamuchy Township School, Box J
Allamuchy, NJ 07820
908-852-1894

- Superintendent..........Timothy Frederiks
- Number of schools...................................1
- Grade plan.......................................K-8
- Enrollment......................................356
- Attendance rate, '05-06........................94.9%
- Dropout rate.....................................NA
- Students per teacher............................9.8
- Per pupil expenditure........................$12,997
- Median faculty salary.........................$40,075
- Median administrator salary..................$83,000
- Grade 12 enrollment..............................NA
- High school graduation rate......................NA

Assessment test results
(percent scoring at proficient or advanced level)

	Language	Math
NJASK-Grade 3	92.9%	100.0%
GEPA-Grade 8	93.7%	71.9%
HSPA-High School	NA	NA

SAT score averages

Pct tested	Math	Verbal	Writing
NA	NA	NA	NA

Teacher Qualifications
- Avg. years of experience............................6
- Highly-qualified teachers
  - one subject/all subjects...............100%/100%
- With emergency credentials.......................0.0%

No Child Left Behind
- AYP, 2005-06.....................Meets Standards

Municipal Finance
State Aid Programs, 2008
- Total aid.....................................$482,388
  - CMPTRA...0
  - Energy tax receipts..........................421,014
  - Garden State Trust............................61,374

General Budget, 2007
- Total tax levy.............................$10,714,828
  - County levy................................4,048,356
    - County taxes............................3,304,984
    - County library............................345,148
    - County health..................................0
    - County open space.........................398,224
  - School levy................................5,779,162
  - Muni. levy...................................887,310
- Misc. revenues...............................2,766,765

Taxes	2005	2006	2007
General tax rate per $100	1.91	1.94	2.06
County equalization ratio	95.72	86.71	78.95
Net valuation taxable	$492,508,822	$507,768,165	$522,369,304
State equalized value	$567,995,412	$644,337,810	$683,212,000

Bergen County

Allendale Borough

Demographics & Socio-Economic Characteristics
(2000 US Census, except as noted)

Population
1980*	5,901
1990*	5,900
2000	6,699
Male	3,245
Female	3,454
2006 (estimate)*	6,713
Population density	2,151.6

Race & Hispanic Origin, 2000
Race
White	6,195
Black/African American	26
American Indian/Alaska Native	4
Asian	408
Native Hawaiian/Pacific Islander	0
Other race	31
Two or more races	35
Hispanic origin, total	170
Mexican	12
Puerto Rican	41
Cuban	40
Other Hispanic	77

Age & Nativity, 2000
Under 5 years	478
18 years and over	4,663
21 years and over	4,528
65 years and over	945
85 years and over	224
Median age	39.5
Native-born	5,933
Foreign-born	766

Educational Attainment, 2000
Population 25 years and over	4,376
Less than 9th grade	2.7%
High school grad or higher	94.8%
Bachelor's degree or higher	62.5%
Graduate degree	22.6%

Income & Poverty, 1999
Per capita income	$47,772
Median household income	$105,704
Median family income	$113,390
Persons in poverty	117
H'holds receiving public assistance	11
H'holds receiving social security	484

Households, 2000
Total households	2,110
With persons under 18	1,028
With persons over 65	461
Family households	1,796
Single-person households	277
Persons per household	3.03
Persons per family	3.33

Labor & Employment
Total civilian labor force, 2006**	3,252
Unemployment rate	2.7%
Total civilian labor force, 2000	3,079
Unemployment rate	2.7%

Employed persons 16 years and over by occupation, 2000
Managers & professionals	1,583
Service occupations	216
Sales & office occupations	913
Farming, fishing & forestry	0
Construction & maintenance	138
Production & transportation	145
Self-employed persons	298

* US Census Bureau
** New Jersey Department of Labor

See Introduction for an explanation of all data sources.

General Information
Borough of Allendale
500 W Crescent Ave
Allendale, NJ 07401
201-818-4400

Website	www.allendale.org
Year of incorporation	1894
Land/water area (sq. miles)	3.12/0.03
Form of government	Borough

Government
Legislative Districts
US Congressional	5
State Legislative	39

Local Officials, 2008
Mayor	Vince Barra
Borough Admin	Leslie Shenkler
Clerk	Gwen McCarthy
Finance Dir	Paula Favata
Tax Assessor	Angela Mattiace
Tax Collector	Paula Favata
Attorney	David Bole
Building	John Wittekind
Comm Dev/Planning	NA
Engineering	John Yakimik
Public Works	George Higbie
Police Chief	Robert Herndon
Emerg/Fire Director	Dave Walters

Housing & Construction
Housing Units, 2000*
Total	2,143
Median rent	$1,778
Median SF home value	$421,800

Permits for New Residential Construction
	Units	Value
Total, 2007	14	$3,179,716
Single family	8	$3,094,716
Total, 2006	1	$1,862,800
Single family	1	$1,862,800

Real Property Valuation, 2007
	Parcels	Valuation
Total	2,234	$1,294,930,400
Vacant	60	19,933,000
Residential	2,106	1,120,804,400
Commercial	49	90,089,700
Industrial	13	63,135,200
Apartments	0	0
Farm land	5	16,200
Farm homestead	1	951,900

Average Property Value & Tax, 2007
Residential value	$532,395
Property tax	$13,023
Tax credit/rebate	$1,446

Public Library
Lee Memorial Library
500 W Crescent Ave
Allendale, NJ 07401
201-327-4338

Director.....................Carol Cannon

Library statistics, 2006
Population served	6,699
Full-time/total staff	1/5

	Total	Per capita
Holdings	62,414	9.32
Revenues	$592,849	$88.50
Expenditures	$514,380	$76.78
Annual visits	68,263	10.19
Internet terminals/annual users	5/15,900	

Taxes
	2005	2006	2007
General tax rate per $100	2.18	2.36	2.45
County equalization ratio	88.21	80.51	71.56
Net valuation taxable	$1,283,268,177	$1,279,103,400	$1,297,519,683
State equalized value	$1,593,923,956	$1,790,140,296	$1,844,857,600

Public Safety
Number of officers, 2006		14
Crime	**2005**	**2006**
Total crimes	59	63
Violent	0	4
Murder	0	0
Rape	0	1
Robbery	0	2
Aggravated assault	0	1
Non-violent	59	59
Burglary	6	16
Larceny	52	41
Vehicle theft	1	2
Domestic violence	4	5
Arson	2	1
Total crime rate	8.7	9.3
Violent	0.0	0.6
Non-violent	8.7	8.7

Public School District
(for school year 2006-07 except as noted)

Allendale School District
100 Brookside Ave
Allendale, NJ 07401
201-327-2020

Superintendent	Jerilyn Caprio
Number of schools	2
Grade plan	K-8
Enrollment	1,032
Attendance rate, '05-06	96.4%
Dropout rate	NA
Students per teacher	12.5
Per pupil expenditure	$12,497
Median faculty salary	$54,335
Median administrator salary	$111,750
Grade 12 enrollment	NA
High school graduation rate	NA

Assessment test results
(percent scoring at proficient or advanced level)
	Language	Math
NJASK-Grade 3	93.7%	97.3%
GEPA-Grade 8	86.7%	95.4%
HSPA-High School	NA	NA

SAT score averages
Pct tested	Math	Verbal	Writing
NA	NA	NA	NA

Teacher Qualifications
Avg. years of experience	8
Highly-qualified teachers one subject/all subjects	98.5%/98.5%
With emergency credentials	0.0%

No Child Left Behind
AYP, 2005-06............Meets Standards

Municipal Finance
State Aid Programs, 2008
Total aid	$1,285,734
CMPTRA	0
Energy tax receipts	1,285,734
Garden State Trust	0

General Budget, 2007
Total tax levy	$31,738,481
County levy	3,284,593
County taxes	3,103,132
County library	0
County health	0
County open space	181,461
School levy	20,436,880
Muni. levy	8,017,009
Misc. revenues	3,650,740

The New Jersey Municipal Data Book

Allenhurst Borough

Monmouth County

Demographics & Socio-Economic Characteristics
(2000 US Census, except as noted)

Population
1980*	912
1990*	759
2000	718
Male	370
Female	348
2006 (estimate)*	701
Population density	2,696.2

Race & Hispanic Origin, 2000
Race
- White 699
- Black/African American 6
- American Indian/Alaska Native 2
- Asian 3
- Native Hawaiian/Pacific Islander 0
- Other race 1
- Two or more races 7
- Hispanic origin, total 18
  - Mexican 3
  - Puerto Rican 3
  - Cuban 0
  - Other Hispanic 12

Age & Nativity, 2000
- Under 5 years 40
- 18 years and over 582
- 21 years and over 569
- 65 years and over 134
- 85 years and over 20
- Median age 42.5
- Native-born 700
- Foreign-born 23

Educational Attainment, 2000
- Population 25 years and over 556
- Less than 9th grade 2.3%
- High school grad or higher 96.0%
- Bachelor's degree or higher 57.7%
- Graduate degree 21.2%

Income & Poverty, 1999
- Per capita income $42,710
- Median household income $85,000
- Median family income $109,180
- Persons in poverty 27
- H'holds receiving public assistance 2
- H'holds receiving social security 96

Households, 2000
- Total households 285
- With persons under 18 74
- With persons over 65 90
- Family households 189
- Single-person households 71
- Persons per household 2.52
- Persons per family 3.08

Labor & Employment
- Total civilian labor force, 2006** 398
- Unemployment rate 2.7%
- Total civilian labor force, 2000 370
- Unemployment rate 3.5%

Employed persons 16 years and over by occupation, 2000
- Managers & professionals 181
- Service occupations 32
- Sales & office occupations 123
- Farming, fishing & forestry 0
- Construction & maintenance 7
- Production & transportation 14
- Self-employed persons 41

* US Census Bureau
** New Jersey Department of Labor

General Information
Borough of Allenhurst
125 Corlies Ave
Allenhurst, NJ 07711
732-531-2757

- Website .... www.allenhurstnj.org
- Year of incorporation 1897
- Land/water area (sq. miles) 0.26/0.02
- Form of government .... Commission

Government
Legislative Districts
- US Congressional 6
- State Legislative 11

Local Officials, 2008
- Mayor .... David J. McLaughlin
- Manager .... Lori L. Osborn
- Clerk .... Lori L. Osborn
- Finance Dir .... Chris Brown
- Tax Assessor .... Peter Barnett
- Tax Collector .... Edward Mazzocco
- Attorney .... William O'Hagan
- Building .... NA
- Comm Dev/Planning .... NA
- Engineering .... Peter Avakian
- Public Works .... Doug Caron
- Police Chief .... Robert Richter
- Emerg/Fire Director .... Frank Manfredi

Housing & Construction
Housing Units, 2000*
- Total 370
- Median rent $815
- Median SF home value $359,000

Permits for New Residential Construction
	Units	Value
Total, 2007	1	$1,275,000
Single family	1	$1,275,000
Total, 2006	0	$0
Single family	0	$0

Real Property Valuation, 2007
	Parcels	Valuation
Total	335	$589,069,100
Vacant	7	5,478,200
Residential	297	543,093,400
Commercial	26	32,915,300
Industrial	1	3,666,100
Apartments	4	3,916,100
Farm land	0	0
Farm homestead	0	0

Average Property Value & Tax, 2007
- Residential value $1,828,597
- Property tax $10,582
- Tax credit/rebate $1,204

Public Library
No public municipal library

Library statistics, 2006
- Population served .... NA
- Full-time/total staff .... NA/NA

	Total	Per capita
Holdings	NA	NA
Revenues	NA	NA
Expenditures	NA	NA
Annual visits	NA	NA
Internet terminals/annual users	NA/NA	

Taxes
	2005	2006	2007
General tax rate per $100	1.329	1.477	0.579
County equalization ratio	70.66	50.8	115.39
Net valuation taxable	$209,922,567	$210,679,200	$589,208,759
State equalized value	$413,233,400	$510,560,989	$560,997,604

Public Safety
Number of officers, 2006 9

Crime	2005	2006
Total crimes	24	18
Violent	2	2
Murder	0	0
Rape	1	0
Robbery	0	1
Aggravated assault	1	1
Non-violent	22	16
Burglary	1	2
Larceny	21	13
Vehicle theft	0	1
Domestic violence	8	5
Arson	0	0
Total crime rate	33.6	25.5
Violent	2.8	2.8
Non-violent	30.8	22.7

Public School District
(for school year 2006-07 except as noted)

Allenhurst School District
125 Corlies Ave
Allenhurst, NJ 07711

No schools in district

- Per pupil expenditure .... NA
- Median faculty salary .... NA
- Median administrator salary .... NA
- Grade 12 enrollment .... NA
- High school graduation rate .... NA

Assessment test results
(percent scoring at proficient or advanced level)
	Language	Math
NJASK-Grade 3	NA	NA
GEPA-Grade 8	NA	NA
HSPA-High School	NA	NA

SAT score averages
Pct tested	Math	Verbal	Writing
NA	NA	NA	NA

Teacher Qualifications
- Avg. years of experience .... NA
- Highly-qualified teachers one subject/all subjects .... NA/NA
- With emergency credentials .... NA

No Child Left Behind
- AYP, 2005-06 .... NA

Municipal Finance
State Aid Programs, 2008
- Total aid $212,607
- CMPTRA 0
- Energy tax receipts 212,607
- Garden State Trust 0

General Budget, 2007
- Total tax levy $3,409,821
- County levy 1,365,636
- County taxes 1,219,554
- County library 69,822
- County health 0
- County open space 76,260
- School levy 257,516
- Muni. levy 1,786,668
- Misc. revenues 1,957,649

Monmouth County

Allentown Borough

Demographics & Socio-Economic Characteristics
(2000 US Census, except as noted)

Population
- 1980* 1,962
- 1990* 1,828
- 2000 1,882
  - Male 890
  - Female 992
- 2006 (estimate)* 1,847
- Population density 3,027.9

Race & Hispanic Origin, 2000
Race
- White 1,706
- Black/African American 121
- American Indian/Alaska Native 11
- Asian 12
- Native Hawaiian/Pacific Islander ... 0
- Other race 11
- Two or more races 21
- Hispanic origin, total 36
  - Mexican 2
  - Puerto Rican 24
  - Cuban 3
  - Other Hispanic 7

Age & Nativity, 2000
- Under 5 years 136
- 18 years and over 1,379
- 21 years and over 1,327
- 65 years and over 184
- 85 years and over 22
- Median age 38.5
- Native-born 1,827
- Foreign-born 55

Educational Attainment, 2000
- Population 25 years and over ... 1,269
- Less than 9th grade 1.7%
- High school grad or higher 92.5%
- Bachelor's degree or higher .. 41.1%
- Graduate degree 15.7%

Income & Poverty, 1999
- Per capita income $29,455
- Median household income .. $71,193
- Median family income $79,843
- Persons in poverty 44
- H'holds receiving public assistance ... 15
- H'holds receiving social security ... 155

Households, 2000
- Total households 708
  - With persons under 18 271
  - With persons over 65 136
  - Family households 527
  - Single-person households ... 151
- Persons per household 2.66
- Persons per family 3.13

Labor & Employment
- Total civilian labor force, 2006** ... 1,162
  - Unemployment rate 3.7%
- Total civilian labor force, 2000 ... 1,073
  - Unemployment rate 3.3%

Employed persons 16 years and over by occupation, 2000
- Managers & professionals 488
- Service occupations 122
- Sales & office occupations 276
- Farming, fishing & forestry 1
- Construction & maintenance ... 65
- Production & transportation ... 86
- Self-employed persons 64

‡ Branch of county library
* US Census Bureau
** New Jersey Department of Labor

See Introduction for an explanation of all data sources.

General Information
Borough of Allentown
8 N Main St
PO Box 487
Allentown, NJ 08501
609-259-3151

- Website .... NA
- Year of incorporation 1889
- Land/water area (sq. miles) ... 0.61/0.02
- Form of government .... Borough

Government
Legislative Districts
- US Congressional 4
- State Legislative 30

Local Officials, 2008
- Mayor .... Stuart Fierstein
- Manager/Admin .... NA
- Clerk .... Julie Martin
- Finance Dir .... Robert Benick
- Tax Assessor .... Victoria Butchon
- Tax Collector .... Barbara Pater
- Attorney .... Donald Driggers
- Building .... (Washington Twp, Mercer Co)
- Comm Dev/Planning .... NA
- Engineering .... Hatch Mott McDonald
- Public Works .... NA
- Police Chief .... Harvey Morrell
- Emerg/Fire Director .... Brad Carter

Housing & Construction
Housing Units, 2000*
- Total 718
- Median rent $792
- Median SF home value $167,100

Permits for New Residential Construction

	Units	Value
Total, 2007	0	$0
Single family	0	$0
Total, 2006	7	$1,294,500
Single family	7	$1,294,500

Real Property Valuation, 2007

	Parcels	Valuation
Total	659	$101,337,350
Vacant	30	509,600
Residential	584	89,274,450
Commercial	41	8,788,900
Industrial	0	0
Apartments	2	2,760,100
Farm land	2	4,300
Farm homestead	0	0

Average Property Value & Tax, 2007
- Residential value $152,867
- Property tax $6,469
- Tax credit/rebate $1,101

Public Library
Allentown Branch Library‡
16 S Main St
Allentown, NJ 08501
609-259-7565

Branch Librarian .... Nancy Stein

Library statistics, 2006
see Monmouth County profile
for library system statistics

Public Safety
Number of officers, 2006 6

Crime	2005	2006
Total crimes	16	24
Violent	0	3
Murder	0	0
Rape	0	0
Robbery	0	0
Aggravated assault	0	3
Non-violent	16	21
Burglary	1	3
Larceny	14	17
Vehicle theft	1	1
Domestic violence	4	3
Arson	0	0
Total crime rate	8.5	12.9
Violent	0.0	1.6
Non-violent	8.5	11.3

Public School District
(for school year 2006-07 except as noted)

Upper Freehold Regional School District
27 High St
Allentown, NJ 08501
609-259-7292

- Superintendent .... Richard Fitzpatrick
- Number of schools 4
- Grade plan K-12
- Enrollment 2,280
- Attendance rate, '05-06 .... 95.1%
- Dropout rate 0.2%
- Students per teacher 11.8
- Per pupil expenditure $11,552
- Median faculty salary $51,966
- Median administrator salary .. $101,891
- Grade 12 enrollment 265
- High school graduation rate ... 98.9%

Assessment test results
(percent scoring at proficient or advanced level)

	Language	Math
NJASK-Grade 3	93.3%	97.0%
GEPA-Grade 8	80.0%	82.5%
HSPA-High School	93.9%	84.3%

SAT score averages

Pct tested	Math	Verbal	Writing
81%	511	512	496

Teacher Qualifications
- Avg. years of experience 8
- Highly-qualified teachers
  - one subject/all subjects ... 99.0%/99.0%
- With emergency credentials 0.7%

No Child Left Behind
- AYP, 2005-06 .... Meets Standards

Municipal Finance
State Aid Programs, 2008
- Total aid $103,437
  - CMPTRA 0
  - Energy tax receipts 103,437
  - Garden State Trust 0

General Budget, 2007
- Total tax levy $4,329,720
  - County levy 551,701
    - County taxes 484,469
    - County library 27,734
    - County health 9,228
    - County open space 30,270
  - School levy 2,699,785
  - Muni. levy 1,078,234
- Misc. revenues 915,997

Taxes	2005	2006	2007
General tax rate per $100	3.843	4.148	4.232
County equalization ratio	66.54	58.39	50.66
Net valuation taxable	$101,991,312	$100,801,400	$102,316,950
State equalized value	$174,672,567	$200,091,295	$217,651,291

The New Jersey Municipal Data Book

Alloway Township — Salem County

Demographics & Socio-Economic Characteristics
(2000 US Census, except as noted)

Population
- 1980[1] 2,600
- 1990* 2,795
- 2000 2,774
  - Male 1,411
  - Female 1,363
- 2006 (estimate)* 3,066
- Population density 93.3

Race & Hispanic Origin, 2000
Race
- White 2,516
- Black/African American 191
- American Indian/Alaska Native .. 15
- Asian 12
- Native Hawaiian/Pacific Islander . 0
- Other race 11
- Two or more races 29
- Hispanic origin, total 66
  - Mexican 3
  - Puerto Rican 3
  - Cuban 1
  - Other Hispanic 59

Age & Nativity, 2000
- Under 5 years 181
- 18 years and over 1,995
- 21 years and over 1,891
- 65 years and over 343
- 85 years and over 37
- Median age 36.7
- Native-born 2,726
- Foreign-born 48

Educational Attainment, 2000
- Population 25 years and over .. 1,812
- Less than 9th grade 3.4%
- High school grad or higher 87.4%
- Bachelor's degree or higher ... 20.3%
- Graduate degree 6.6%

Income & Poverty, 1999
- Per capita income $22,935
- Median household income $56,528
- Median family income $65,132
- Persons in poverty 226
- H'holds receiving public assistance . 16
- H'holds receiving social security .. 235

Households, 2000
- Total households 948
  - With persons under 18 373
  - With persons over 65 239
  - Family households 742
  - Single-person households 177
- Persons per household 2.80
- Persons per family 3.19

Labor & Employment
- Total civilian labor force, 2006** .. 1,445
  - Unemployment rate 5.4%
- Total civilian labor force, 2000 .. 1,465
  - Unemployment rate 9.4%

Employed persons 16 years and over by occupation, 2000
- Managers & professionals 417
- Service occupations 159
- Sales & office occupations 311
- Farming, fishing & forestry ... 24
- Construction & maintenance 218
- Production & transportation ... 199
- Self-employed persons 112

* US Census Bureau
** New Jersey Department of Labor

General Information
Township of Alloway
PO Box 425
Alloway, NJ 08001
856-935-4080

- Website .... (county website)
- Year of incorporation 1884
- Land/water area (sq. miles) ... 32.85/0.33
- Form of government .... Township

Government
Legislative Districts
- US Congressional 2
- State Legislative 3

Local Officials, 2008
- Mayor .... Joseph G. Fedora
- Manager/Admin .... NA
- Clerk .... Mary Lou Rutherford
- Finance Dir .... Marie Stout
- Tax Assessor .... Lisa Perella
- Tax Collector .... Thomas Freeman
- Attorney .... John G. Hoffman
- Building .... Harold Underwood
- Planning .... Patricia Paruszewski
- Engineering .... Carl Gaskill
- Public Works .... Kenneth McKelrey
- Police Chief .... NA
- Emerg/Fire Director ..... Jeffery Pompper

Housing & Construction
Housing Units, 2000*
- Total 995
- Median rent $700
- Median SF home value $133,300

Permits for New Residential Construction

	Units	Value
Total, 2007	18	$2,990,000
Single family	18	$2,990,000
Total, 2006	10	$2,070,000
Single family	10	$2,070,000

Real Property Valuation, 2007

	Parcels	Valuation
Total	2,165	$197,001,600
Vacant	399	8,072,100
Residential	1,058	141,414,500
Commercial	29	9,287,900
Industrial	0	0
Apartments	0	0
Farm land	459	4,910,700
Farm homestead	220	33,316,400

Average Property Value & Tax, 2007
- Residential value $136,722
- Property tax $4,501
- Tax credit/rebate $909

Public Library
No public municipal library

Library statistics, 2006
- Population served .... NA
- Full-time/total staff .... NA/NA

	Total	Per capita
Holdings	NA	NA
Revenues	NA	NA
Expenditures	NA	NA
Annual visits	NA	NA
Internet terminals/annual users	NA/NA	

Taxes

	2005	2006	2007
General tax rate per $100	2.906	3.157	3.293
County equalization ratio	89.69	77.63	72.89
Net valuation taxable	$187,580,464	$190,910,500	$197,526,284
State equalized value	$241,633,987	$262,450,918	$280,436,022

Public Safety
- Number of officers, 2006 0

Crime	2005	2006
Total crimes	33	32
Violent	2	2
Murder	0	0
Rape	0	0
Robbery	0	0
Aggravated assault	2	2
Non-violent	31	30
Burglary	18	8
Larceny	11	19
Vehicle theft	2	3
Domestic violence	9	4
Arson	1	0
Total crime rate	11.3	10.7
Violent	0.7	0.7
Non-violent	10.6	10.0

Public School District
(for school year 2006-07 except as noted)

Alloway Township School District
43 Cedar St, Box 327
Alloway, NJ 08001
856-935-1622

- Superintendent .... Robert Bazzel
- Number of schools 1
- Grade plan K-8
- Enrollment 482
- Attendance rate, '05-06 .... 95.6%
- Dropout rate .... NA
- Students per teacher 12.1
- Per pupil expenditure $10,395
- Median faculty salary $49,632
- Median administrator salary ... $85,890
- Grade 12 enrollment .... NA
- High school graduation rate ... NA

Assessment test results
(percent scoring at proficient or advanced level)

	Language	Math
NJASK-Grade 3	78.8%	84.6%
GEPA-Grade 8	80.0%	84.0%
HSPA-High School	NA	NA

SAT score averages

Pct tested	Math	Verbal	Writing
NA	NA	NA	NA

Teacher Qualifications
- Avg. years of experience 12
- Highly-qualified teachers
  - one subject/all subjects 100%/97.0%
- With emergency credentials 0.0%

No Child Left Behind
- AYP, 2005-06 .... Meets Standards

Municipal Finance
State Aid Programs, 2008
- Total aid $424,931
  - CMPTRA 0
  - Energy tax receipts 410,147
  - Garden State Trust 14,596

General Budget, 2007
- Total tax levy $6,503,380
  - County levy 2,552,670
    - County taxes 2,498,216
    - County library 0
    - County health 0
    - County open space 54,455
  - School levy 3,555,660
  - Muni. levy 395,050
- Misc. revenues 1,428,950

Warren County
Alpha Borough

Demographics & Socio-Economic Characteristics
(2000 US Census, except as noted)

Population
- 1980* 2,644
- 1990* 2,530
- 2000 2,482
  - Male 1,208
  - Female 1,274
- 2006 (estimate)* 2,437
  - Population density 1,433.5

Race & Hispanic Origin, 2000
Race
- White 2,409
- Black/African American 7
- American Indian/Alaska Native 1
- Asian 30
- Native Hawaiian/Pacific Islander 0
- Other race 16
- Two or more races 19
- Hispanic origin, total 47
  - Mexican 15
  - Puerto Rican 12
  - Cuban 1
  - Other Hispanic 19

Age & Nativity, 2000
- Under 5 years 144
- 18 years and over 1,876
- 21 years and over 1,812
- 65 years and over 434
- 85 years and over 45
  - Median age 37.7
- Native-born 2,433
- Foreign-born 49

Educational Attainment, 2000
- Population 25 years and over 1,729
- Less than 9th grade 6.2%
- High school grad or higher 80.6%
- Bachelor's degree or higher 11.9%
- Graduate degree 4.4%

Income & Poverty, 1999
- Per capita income $20,104
- Median household income $42,209
- Median family income $45,435
- Persons in poverty 187
- H'holds receiving public assistance 26
- H'holds receiving social security 375

Households, 2000
- Total households 989
  - With persons under 18 336
  - With persons over 65 317
  - Family households 688
  - Single-person households 266
- Persons per household 2.50
- Persons per family 3.05

Labor & Employment
- Total civilian labor force, 2006** 1,443
  - Unemployment rate 6.3%
- Total civilian labor force, 2000 1,268
  - Unemployment rate 5.7%

Employed persons 16 years and over by occupation, 2000
- Managers & professionals 255
- Service occupations 212
- Sales & office occupations 397
- Farming, fishing & forestry 0
- Construction & maintenance 144
- Production & transportation 188
- Self-employed persons 66

* US Census Bureau
** New Jersey Department of Labor

See Introduction for an explanation of all data sources.

General Information
Borough of Alpha
1001 East Blvd
Alpha, NJ 08865
908-454-0088
- Website .... www.alphaboro.org
- Year of incorporation 1911
- Land/water area (sq. miles) 1.70/0.04
- Form of government .... Borough

Government
Legislative Districts
- US Congressional 5
- State Legislative 23

Local Officials, 2008
- Mayor .... Edward Z. Hanics Jr
- Manager/Admin .... NA
- Clerk .... Laurie Courter-Barton
- Finance Dir .... Lorraine Russetti
- Tax Assessor .... Kathy Degan
- Tax Collector .... Carrie Emery
- Attorney .... Christopher Troxell
- Building .... Kevin Duddy
- Comm Dev/Planning .... NA
- Engineering .... Stanley Schrek
- Senior Pub Works Repairer ... Charles Olah
- Police Chief .... NA
- Emerg/Fire Director .... Carl Gercie Jr

Housing & Construction
Housing Units, 2000*
- Total 1,034
- Median rent $710
- Median SF home value $117,200

Permits for New Residential Construction

	Units	Value
Total, 2007	3	$456,650
Single family	3	$456,650
Total, 2006	3	$584,150
Single family	3	$584,150

Real Property Valuation, 2007

	Parcels	Valuation
Total	943	$206,623,467
Vacant	52	5,411,100
Residential	800	144,173,900
Commercial	52	28,283,600
Industrial	15	20,844,400
Apartments	9	6,665,100
Farm land	12	236,067
Farm homestead	3	1,009,300

Average Property Value & Tax, 2007
- Residential value $180,801
- Property tax $4,995
- Tax credit/rebate $1,009

Public Library
W.H. Walters Free Library
1001 East Blvd
Alpha, NJ 08865
908-454-1445
- Director .... Myrna Minardi

Library statistics, 2006
- Population served 2,482
- Full-time/total staff 0/0

	Total	Per capita
Holdings	NA	NA
Revenues	NA	NA
Expenditures	NA	NA
Annual visits	NA	NA
Internet terminals/annual users	NA/NA	

Taxes

	2005	2006	2007
General tax rate per $100	2.54	2.7	2.77
County equalization ratio	106.73	97.07	90.16
Net valuation taxable	$195,072,549	$197,353,641	$207,028,137
State equalized value	$200,960,697	$219,257,802	$240,776,316

Public Safety
- Number of officers, 2006 0

Crime

	2005	2006
Total crimes	49	44
Violent	9	13
Murder	0	0
Rape	0	0
Robbery	0	0
Aggravated assault	9	13
Non-violent	40	31
Burglary	7	3
Larceny	31	28
Vehicle theft	2	0
Domestic violence	9	4
Arson	0	0
Total crime rate	19.8	17.9
Violent	3.6	5.3
Non-violent	16.1	12.6

Public School District
(for school year 2006-07 except as noted)

Alpha School District
817 North Boulevard
Alpha, NJ 08865
908-454-5000

- Chief School Admin .... Donna Medea
- Number of schools 1
- Grade plan K-8
- Enrollment 278
- Attendance rate, '05-06 .... 95.9%
- Dropout rate .... NA
- Students per teacher 8.5
- Per pupil expenditure $10,798
- Median faculty salary $47,160
- Median administrator salary $83,000
- Grade 12 enrollment .... NA
- High school graduation rate .... NA

Assessment test results
(percent scoring at proficient or advanced level)

	Language	Math
NJASK-Grade 3	85.3%	85.3%
GEPA-Grade 8	79.4%	64.7%
HSPA-High School	NA	NA

SAT score averages

Pct tested	Math	Verbal	Writing
NA	NA	NA	NA

Teacher Qualifications
- Avg. years of experience 10
- Highly-qualified teachers
  - one subject/all subjects 96.5%/96.5%
- With emergency credentials 0.0%

No Child Left Behind
- AYP, 2005-06 .... Meets Standards

Municipal Finance
State Aid Programs, 2008
- Total aid $177,445
- CMPTRA 0
- Energy tax receipts 177,445
- Garden State Trust 0

General Budget, 2007
- Total tax levy $5,719,319
- County levy 1,288,025
  - County taxes 1,149,534
  - County library 0
  - County health 0
  - County open space 138,491
- School levy 2,765,358
- Muni. levy 1,665,936
- Misc. revenues 1,009,142

Alpine Borough   Bergen County

Demographics & Socio-Economic Characteristics
(2000 US Census, except as noted)

Population
1980*	1,549
1990*	1,716
2000	2,183
Male	1,104
Female	1,079
2006 (estimate)*	2,429
Population density	381.9

Race & Hispanic Origin, 2000
Race
White	1,689
Black/African American	33
American Indian/Alaska Native	5
Asian	417
Native Hawaiian/Pacific Islander	1
Other race	7
Two or more races	31
Hispanic origin, total	55
Mexican	1
Puerto Rican	16
Cuban	1
Other Hispanic	37

Age & Nativity, 2000
Under 5 years	104
18 years and over	1,644
21 years and over	1,594
65 years and over	322
85 years and over	26
Median age	44.2
Native-born	1,589
Foreign-born	594

Educational Attainment, 2000
Population 25 years and over	1,530
Less than 9th grade	2.2%
High school grad or higher	93.6%
Bachelor's degree or higher	62.8%
Graduate degree	28.0%

Income & Poverty, 1999
Per capita income	$76,995
Median household income	$130,740
Median family income	$134,068
Persons in poverty	135
H'holds receiving public assistance	0
H'holds receiving social security	165

Households, 2000
Total households	708
With persons under 18	274
With persons over 65	210
Family households	623
Single-person households	70
Persons per household	3.08
Persons per family	3.24

Labor & Employment
Total civilian labor force, 2006**	1,105
Unemployment rate	2.9%
Total civilian labor force, 2000	1,037
Unemployment rate	2.6%

Employed persons 16 years and over by occupation, 2000
Managers & professionals	591
Service occupations	62
Sales & office occupations	278
Farming, fishing & forestry	0
Construction & maintenance	40
Production & transportation	39
Self-employed persons	93

* US Census Bureau
** New Jersey Department of Labor

General Information
Borough of Alpine
100 Church St
Alpine, NJ 07620
201-784-2900

Website	www.alpinenj07620.org
Year of incorporation	1903
Land/water area (sq. miles)	6.36/2.82
Form of government	Borough

Government
Legislative Districts
US Congressional	5
State Legislative	39

Local Officials, 2008
Mayor	Paul Tomasko
Manager/Admin	NA
Clerk	Gail Warming-Tanno
Finance Dir	Irene Kateris
Tax Assessor	Stuart Stolarz
Tax Collector	NA
Attorney	Terry Paul Bottinelli
Building	James Taormina
Comm Dev/Planning	NA
Engineering	Gary VanderVeer
Public Works	Ralph Wehmann
Police Chief	Thomas Blake
Fire Chief	H. Josh Schneeweiss

Housing & Construction
Housing Units, 2000*
Total	730
Median rent	$1,844
Median SF home value	$1,000,001

Permits for New Residential Construction
	Units	Value
Total, 2007	17	$26,659,435
Single family	17	$26,659,435
Total, 2006	20	$17,404,392
Single family	20	$17,404,392

Real Property Valuation, 2007
	Parcels	Valuation
Total	739	$1,800,791,500
Vacant	72	99,925,400
Residential	647	1,605,454,300
Commercial	20	95,411,800
Industrial	0	0
Apartments	0	0
Farm land	0	0
Farm homestead	0	0

Average Property Value & Tax, 2007
Residential value	$2,481,382
Property tax	$15,130
Tax credit/rebate	$1,194

Public Library
No public municipal library

Library statistics, 2006
Population served	NA
Full-time/total staff	NA/NA

	Total	Per capita
Holdings	NA	NA
Revenues	NA	NA
Expenditures	NA	NA
Annual visits	NA	NA
Internet terminals/annual users	NA/NA	

Taxes
	2005	2006	2007
General tax rate per $100	0.55	0.58	0.61
County equalization ratio	136.87	115.04	97.65
Net valuation taxable	$1,767,890,565	$1,774,526,700	$1,801,859,730
State equalized value	$1,536,761,618	$1,818,295,163	$2,012,002,345

Public Safety
Number of officers, 2006 12

Crime	2005	2006
Total crimes	28	9
Violent	9	4
Murder	0	0
Rape	0	0
Robbery	0	0
Aggravated assault	9	4
Non-violent	19	5
Burglary	12	2
Larceny	6	3
Vehicle theft	1	0
Domestic violence	6	5
Arson	0	1
Total crime rate	12.0	3.8
Violent	3.8	1.7
Non-violent	8.1	2.1

Public School District
(for school year 2006-07 except as noted)

Alpine School District
500 Hillside Ave
Alpine, NJ 07620
201-768-6804

Superintendent	Kathleen Semergieff
Number of schools	1
Grade plan	K-8
Enrollment	136
Attendance rate, '05-06	96.1%
Dropout rate	NA
Students per teacher	6.7
Per pupil expenditure	$25,260
Median faculty salary	$46,575
Median administrator salary	$86,850
Grade 12 enrollment	NA
High school graduation rate	NA

Assessment test results
(percent scoring at proficient or advanced level)
	Language	Math
NJASK-Grade 3	100.0%	94.2%
GEPA-Grade 8	93.3%	86.7%
HSPA-High School	NA	NA

SAT score averages
Pct tested	Math	Verbal	Writing
NA	NA	NA	NA

Teacher Qualifications
Avg. years of experience	8
Highly-qualified teachers one subject/all subjects	100%/100%
With emergency credentials	8.7%

No Child Left Behind
AYP, 2005-06 . . . . Meets Standards

Municipal Finance
State Aid Programs, 2008
Total aid	$448,834
CMPTRA	0
Energy tax receipts	440,989
Garden State Trust	7,845

General Budget, 2007
Total tax levy	$10,986,357
County levy	3,344,402
County taxes	3,159,660
County library	0
County health	0
County open space	184,742
School levy	4,881,191
Muni. levy	2,760,764
Misc. revenues	2,355,517

Sussex County

Andover Borough

Demographics & Socio-Economic Characteristics
(2000 US Census, except as noted)

Population
1980*	892
1990*	700
2000	658
Male	335
Female	323
2006 (estimate)*	654
Population density	447.9

Race & Hispanic Origin, 2000
Race
White	610
Black/African American	15
American Indian/Alaska Native	5
Asian	15
Native Hawaiian/Pacific Islander	1
Other race	8
Two or more races	4
Hispanic origin, total	17
Mexican	4
Puerto Rican	2
Cuban	0
Other Hispanic	11

Age & Nativity, 2000
Under 5 years	30
18 years and over	515
21 years and over	492
65 years and over	65
85 years and over	5
Median age	38.3
Native-born	622
Foreign-born	36

Educational Attainment, 2000
Population 25 years and over	480
Less than 9th grade	5.4%
High school grad or higher	84.2%
Bachelor's degree or higher	20.0%
Graduate degree	6.5%

Income & Poverty, 1999
Per capita income	$25,914
Median household income	$60,000
Median family income	$69,688
Persons in poverty	18
H'holds receiving public assistance	1
H'holds receiving social security	55

Households, 2000
Total households	261
With persons under 18	85
With persons over 65	50
Family households	181
Single-person households	65
Persons per household	2.52
Persons per family	2.98

Labor & Employment
Total civilian labor force, 2006**	497
Unemployment rate	5.9%
Total civilian labor force, 2000	442
Unemployment rate	4.3%

Employed persons 16 years and over by occupation, 2000
Managers & professionals	117
Service occupations	44
Sales & office occupations	127
Farming, fishing & forestry	10
Construction & maintenance	61
Production & transportation	64
Self-employed persons	14

* US Census Bureau
** New Jersey Department of Labor

See Introduction for an explanation of all data sources.

General Information
Borough of Andover
137 Main St
Andover, NJ 07821
973-786-6688
Email	andover@tellurtan.net
Year of incorporation	1904
Land/water area (sq. miles)	1.46/0.01
Form of government	Borough

Government
Legislative Districts
US Congressional	5
State Legislative	24

Local Officials, 2008
Mayor	John A. Morgan
Manager/Admin	NA
Clerk	Beth Brothman
Finance Dir.	Jessica M. Caruso
Tax Assessor	Joseph Ferraris
Tax Collector	NA
Attorney	Frank McGovern
Building	Brendon O'Connor
Planning	Ken Nelson
Engineering	Harold Pellow
Public Works	NA
Police Chief	NA
Emerg/Fire Director	Frank Greenhalgh

Housing & Construction
Housing Units, 2000*
Total	273
Median rent	$804
Median SF home value	$154,800

Permits for New Residential Construction
	Units	Value
Total, 2007	0	$0
Single family	0	$0
Total, 2006	0	$0
Single family	0	$0

Real Property Valuation, 2007
	Parcels	Valuation
Total	303	$45,181,500
Vacant	45	1,521,300
Residential	192	29,165,300
Commercial	47	12,511,500
Industrial	1	150,200
Apartments	2	968,100
Farm land	11	113,400
Farm homestead	5	751,700

Average Property Value & Tax, 2007
Residential value	$151,863
Property tax	$4,677
Tax credit/rebate	$963

Public Library
No public municipal library

Library statistics, 2006
Population served	NA
Full-time/total staff	NA/NA

	Total	Per capita
Holdings	NA	NA
Revenues	NA	NA
Expenditures	NA	NA
Annual visits	NA	NA
Internet terminals/annual users	NA/NA	

Public Safety
Number of officers, 2006 0

Crime	2005	2006
Total crimes	18	12
Violent	2	1
Murder	0	0
Rape	0	0
Robbery	0	1
Aggravated assault	2	0
Non-violent	16	11
Burglary	4	5
Larceny	11	5
Vehicle theft	1	1
Domestic violence	3	0
Arson	1	0
Total crime rate	27.3	18.2
Violent	3.0	1.5
Non-violent	24.2	16.6

Public School District
(for school year 2006-07 except as noted)

Andover Regional School District
707 Limecrest Rd
Newton, NJ 07860
973-383-3746

Chief School Admin	Jerry A. Clymer
Number of schools	4
Grade plan	K-8
Enrollment	709
Attendance rate, '05-06	95.7%
Dropout rate	NA
Students per teacher	10.0
Per pupil expenditure	$12,452
Median faculty salary	$58,441
Median administrator salary	$94,982
Grade 12 enrollment	NA
High school graduation rate	NA

Assessment test results
(percent scoring at proficient or advanced level)

	Language	Math
NJASK-Grade 3	87.0%	97.4%
GEPA-Grade 8	93.5%	89.6%
HSPA-High School	NA	NA

SAT score averages
Pct tested	Math	Verbal	Writing
NA	NA	NA	NA

Teacher Qualifications
Avg. years of experience	11
Highly-qualified teachers one subject/all subjects	100%/100%
With emergency credentials	0.0%

No Child Left Behind
AYP, 2005-06 . . . . Meets Standards

Municipal Finance
State Aid Programs, 2008
Total aid	$152,619
CMPTRA	0
Energy tax receipts	152,466
Garden State Trust	153

General Budget, 2007
Total tax levy	$1,403,990
County levy	313,455
County taxes	256,118
County library	21,835
County health	8,446
County open space	27,056
School levy	903,024
Muni. levy	187,512
Misc. revenues	555,836

Taxes
	2005	2006	2007
General tax rate per $100	3.02	3.27	3.08
County equalization ratio	65.89	59.96	59.34
Net valuation taxable	$45,423,685	$45,238,300	$45,587,731
State equalized value	$75,756,646	$76,653,224	$76,700,557

The New Jersey Municipal Data Book

Andover Township
Sussex County

Demographics & Socio-Economic Characteristics
(2000 US Census, except as noted)

Population
1980*	4,506
1990*	5,438
2000	6,033
Male	2,889
Female	3,144
2006 (estimate)*	6,552
Population density	324.7

Race & Hispanic Origin, 2000
Race
White	5,698
Black/African American	112
American Indian/Alaska Native	5
Asian	139
Native Hawaiian/Pacific Islander	2
Other race	36
Two or more races	41
Hispanic origin, total	136
Mexican	17
Puerto Rican	57
Cuban	12
Other Hispanic	50

Age & Nativity, 2000
Under 5 years	389
18 years and over	4,522
21 years and over	4,392
65 years and over	950
85 years and over	241
Median age	40.2
Native-born	5,587
Foreign-born	446

Educational Attainment, 2000
Population 25 years and over	4,298
Less than 9th grade	8.7%
High school grad or higher	84.2%
Bachelor's degree or higher	28.6%
Graduate degree	8.8%

Income & Poverty, 1999
Per capita income	$29,180
Median household income	$75,748
Median family income	$78,439
Persons in poverty	186
H'holds receiving public assistance	33
H'holds receiving social security	375

Households, 2000
Total households	1,889
With persons under 18	787
With persons over 65	331
Family households	1,500
Single-person households	304
Persons per household	2.80
Persons per family	3.16

Labor & Employment
Total civilian labor force, 2006**	3,209
Unemployment rate	2.8%
Total civilian labor force, 2000	2,879
Unemployment rate	2.2%

Employed persons 16 years and over by occupation, 2000
Managers & professionals	1,288
Service occupations	271
Sales & office occupations	804
Farming, fishing & forestry	0
Construction & maintenance	200
Production & transportation	254
Self-employed persons	176

* US Census Bureau
** New Jersey Department of Labor

General Information
Township of Andover
134 Newton Sparta Rd
Newton, NJ 07860
973-383-4280

Website	www.andovertwp.org
Year of incorporation	1864
Land/water area (sq. miles)	20.18/0.57
Form of government	Township

Government
Legislative Districts
US Congressional	5
State Legislative	24

Local Officials, 2008
Mayor	Gail Phoebus
Manager	Jayme Alfano
Clerk	Vita Thompson
Finance Dir	Tim Day
Tax Assessor	Jack Marchione
Tax Collector	Daryn Cashin
Attorney	Fred Semrau
Building	James Cutler
Planning	Linda Paolucci
Engineering	Joseph Golden
Public Works	Darren Dickinson
Police Chief	Phillip Coleman
Emerg/Fire Director	Eric Danielson

Housing & Construction
Housing Units, 2000*
Total	1,968
Median rent	$1,033
Median SF home value	$164,600

Permits for New Residential Construction
	Units	Value
Total, 2007	25	$4,246,043
Single family	25	$4,246,043
Total, 2006	37	$5,075,869
Single family	37	$5,075,869

Real Property Valuation, 2007
	Parcels	Valuation
Total	2,573	$616,071,170
Vacant	219	14,274,900
Residential	2,003	486,203,200
Commercial	123	84,839,600
Industrial	12	6,829,200
Apartments	1	1,700,000
Farm land	161	1,226,770
Farm homestead	54	20,997,500

Average Property Value & Tax, 2007
Residential value	$246,573
Property tax	$7,138
Tax credit/rebate	$1,081

Public Library
No public municipal library

Library statistics, 2006
Population served	NA
Full-time/total staff	NA/NA

	Total	Per capita
Holdings	NA	NA
Revenues	NA	NA
Expenditures	NA	NA
Annual visits	NA	NA
Internet terminals/annual users	NA/NA	

Taxes
	2005	2006	2007
General tax rate per $100	2.67	2.81	2.9
County equalization ratio	87.38	78.52	70.58
Net valuation taxable	$592,774,536	$599,891,370	$617,159,865
State equalized value	$754,934,457	$851,211,838	$896,801,359

Public Safety
Number of officers, 2006 ... 12

Crime	2005	2006
Total crimes	80	57
Violent	1	3
Murder	0	0
Rape	0	0
Robbery	0	0
Aggravated assault	1	3
Non-violent	79	54
Burglary	5	9
Larceny	68	42
Vehicle theft	6	3
Domestic violence	48	36
Arson	0	0
Total crime rate	12.3	8.7
Violent	0.2	0.5
Non-violent	12.2	8.3

Public School District
(for school year 2006-07 except as noted)

Andover Regional School District
707 Limecrest Rd
Newton, NJ 07860
973-383-3746

Chief School Admin	Jerry A. Clymer
Number of schools	4
Grade plan	K-8
Enrollment	709
Attendance rate, '05-06	95.7%
Dropout rate	NA
Students per teacher	10.0
Per pupil expenditure	$12,452
Median faculty salary	$58,441
Median administrator salary	$94,982
Grade 12 enrollment	NA
High school graduation rate	NA

Assessment test results
(percent scoring at proficient or advanced level)
	Language	Math
NJASK-Grade 3	87.0%	97.4%
GEPA-Grade 8	93.5%	89.6%
HSPA-High School	NA	NA

SAT score averages
Pct tested	Math	Verbal	Writing
NA	NA	NA	NA

Teacher Qualifications
Avg. years of experience	11
Highly-qualified teachers one subject/all subjects	100%/100%
With emergency credentials	0.0%

No Child Left Behind
AYP, 2005-06 ... Meets Standards

Municipal Finance
State Aid Programs, 2008
Total aid	$557,902
CMPTRA	105,207
Energy tax receipts	394,727
Garden State Trust	57,968

General Budget, 2007
Total tax levy	$17,866,641
County levy	3,558,364
County taxes	2,907,468
County library	247,869
County health	95,867
County open space	307,160
School levy	9,868,316
Muni. levy	4,439,960
Misc. revenues	2,905,385

Monmouth County
Asbury Park City

Demographics & Socio-Economic Characteristics
(2000 US Census, except as noted)

Population
1980*	17,015
1990*	16,799
2000	16,930
Male	7,943
Female	8,987
2006 (estimate)*	16,546
Population density	11,570.6

Race & Hispanic Origin, 2000
Race
White	4,194
Black/African American	10,515
American Indian/Alaska Native	55
Asian	119
Native Hawaiian/Pacific Islander	12
Other race	1,098
Two or more races	937
Hispanic origin, total	2,637
Mexican	956
Puerto Rican	1,021
Cuban	35
Other Hispanic	625

Age & Nativity, 2000
Under 5 years	1,539
18 years and over	11,841
21 years and over	11,132
65 years and over	1,891
85 years and over	305
Median age	30.6
Native-born	13,761
Foreign-born	3,169

Educational Attainment, 2000
Population 25 years and over	9,936
Less than 9th grade	9.9%
High school grad or higher	67.6%
Bachelor's degree or higher	11.2%
Graduate degree	3.5%

Income & Poverty, 1999
Per capita income	$13,516
Median household income	$23,081
Median family income	$26,370
Persons in poverty	5,006
H'holds receiving public assistance	707
H'holds receiving social security	1,675

Households, 2000
Total households	6,754
With persons under 18	2,490
With persons over 65	1,622
Family households	3,587
Single-person households	2,658
Persons per household	2.46
Persons per family	3.36

Labor & Employment
Total civilian labor force, 2006**	7,518
Unemployment rate	10.7%
Total civilian labor force, 2000	7,094
Unemployment rate	11.6%

Employed persons 16 years and over by occupation, 2000
Managers & professionals	1,324
Service occupations	1,554
Sales & office occupations	1,806
Farming, fishing & forestry	20
Construction & maintenance	590
Production & transportation	978
Self-employed persons	318

* US Census Bureau
** New Jersey Department of Labor

See Introduction for an explanation of all data sources.

General Information
City of Asbury Park
1 Municipal Plz
Asbury Park, NJ 07712
732-775-2100

Website	www.cityofasburypark.com
Year of incorporation	1897
Land/water area (sq. miles)	1.43/0.17
Form of government	Municipal Mgr 1923

Government
Legislative Districts
US Congressional	6
State Legislative	11

Local Officials, 2008
Mayor	Kevin G. Sanders
Manager	Terence J. Reidy
Clerk	Stephen M. Kay
Finance Dir	Greg Mayers
Tax Assessor	Mary Lou Hartman
Tax Collector	Dorothy Ruth
Attorney	Frederick C. Raffetto
Building	William Gray
Planning	Don Sammet
Engineering	Brian Grant
Public Works	NA
Police Chief	Mark Kinmon
Emerg/Fire Director	Kevin Keddy

Housing & Construction
Housing Units, 2000*
Total	7,744
Median rent	$615
Median SF home value	$92,800

Permits for New Residential Construction
	Units	Value
Total, 2007	46	$1,247,748
Single family	8	$1,031,660
Total, 2006	442	$3,508,415
Single family	5	$1,277,864

Real Property Valuation, 2007
	Parcels	Valuation
Total	3,726	$421,209,400
Vacant	386	18,508,400
Residential	2,808	253,717,300
Commercial	378	84,723,500
Industrial	3	694,100
Apartments	151	63,566,100
Farm land	0	0
Farm homestead	0	0

Average Property Value & Tax, 2007
Residential value	$90,355
Property tax	$4,177
Tax credit/rebate	$870

Public Library
Asbury Park Public Library
500 First Ave
Asbury Park, NJ 07712
732-774-4221

Director............Robert Stewart

Library statistics, 2006
Population served	16,930
Full-time/total staff	1/8

	Total	Per capita
Holdings	127,086	7.51
Revenues	$567,481	$33.52
Expenditures	$560,274	$33.09
Annual visits	45,285	2.67
Internet terminals/annual users	8/38,936	

Public Safety
Number of officers, 2006 82

Crime	2005	2006
Total crimes	1,313	1,305
Violent	346	387
Murder	3	8
Rape	10	7
Robbery	148	194
Aggravated assault	185	178
Non-violent	967	918
Burglary	288	284
Larceny	547	541
Vehicle theft	132	93
Domestic violence	420	424
Arson	4	11
Total crime rate	78.1	78.5
Violent	20.6	23.3
Non-violent	57.5	55.2

Public School District
(for school year 2006-07 except as noted)

Asbury Park School District
407 Lake Ave
Asbury Park, NJ 07712
732-776-2606

Superintendent	James T. Parham (Actg)
Number of schools	4
Grade plan	K-12
Enrollment	1,920
Attendance rate, '05-06	90.4%
Dropout rate	6.3%
Students per teacher	6.3
Per pupil expenditure	$18,337
Median faculty salary	$55,425
Median administrator salary	$93,142
Grade 12 enrollment	84
High school graduation rate	63.5%

Assessment test results
(percent scoring at proficient or advanced level)
	Language	Math
NJASK-Grade 3	56.0%	73.1%
GEPA-Grade 8	28.5%	22.3%
HSPA-High School	45.6%	30.3%

SAT score averages
Pct tested	Math	Verbal	Writing
81%	380	361	353

Teacher Qualifications
Avg. years of experience	8
Highly-qualified teachers one subject/all subjects	100%/100%
With emergency credentials	0.0%

No Child Left Behind
AYP, 2005-06 .... Needs Improvement

Municipal Finance
State Aid Programs, 2008
Total aid	$8,656,813
CMPTRA	7,117,859
Energy tax receipts	1,538,954
Garden State Trust	0

General Budget, 2007
Total tax levy	$19,556,090
County levy	3,278,274
County taxes	3,031,150
County library	0
County health	57,738
County open space	189,386
School levy	5,766,200
Muni. levy	10,511,616
Misc. revenues	24,983,765

Taxes
	2005	2006	2007
General tax rate per $100	4.146	4.323	4.623
County equalization ratio	50.16	40.37	34.22
Net valuation taxable	$415,169,666	$427,795,000	$423,063,224
State equalized value	$1,028,411,360	$1,252,320,449	$1,386,045,083

Atlantic City

Atlantic County

Demographics & Socio-Economic Characteristics
(2000 US Census, except as noted)

Population
1980*	40,199
1990*	37,986
2000	40,517
Male	19,852
Female	20,665
2006 (estimate)*	39,958
Population density	3,520.5

Race & Hispanic Origin, 2000
Race
White	10,809
Black/African American	17,892
American Indian/Alaska Native	193
Asian	4,213
Native Hawaiian/Pacific Islander	24
Other race	5,575
Two or more races	1,811
Hispanic origin, total	10,107
Mexican	2,199
Puerto Rican	3,635
Cuban	238
Other Hispanic	4,035

Age & Nativity, 2000
Under 5 years	3,041
18 years and over	30,090
21 years and over	28,568
65 years and over	5,734
85 years and over	744
Median age	34.7
Native-born	30,508
Foreign-born	10,009

Educational Attainment, 2000
Population 25 years and over	26,521
Less than 9th grade	11.9%
High school grad or higher	61.8%
Bachelor's degree or higher	10.4%
Graduate degree	3.2%

Income & Poverty, 1999
Per capita income	$15,402
Median household income	$26,969
Median family income	$31,997
Persons in poverty	9,427
H'holds receiving public assistance	1,208
H'holds receiving social security	4,821

Households, 2000
Total households	15,848
With persons under 18	5,260
With persons over 65	4,445
Family households	8,708
Single-person households	5,902
Persons per household	2.46
Persons per family	3.26

Labor & Employment
Total civilian labor force, 2006**	17,648
Unemployment rate	8.4%
Total civilian labor force, 2000	17,683
Unemployment rate	12.9%

Employed persons 16 years and over by occupation, 2000
Managers & professionals	2,114
Service occupations	7,477
Sales & office occupations	3,430
Farming, fishing & forestry	30
Construction & maintenance	758
Production & transportation	1,599
Self-employed persons	492

* US Census Bureau
** New Jersey Department of Labor

General Information
City of Atlantic
1301 Bacharach Blvd
Atlantic City, NJ 08401
609-347-5300
Website.......... www.cityofatlanticcity.org
Year of incorporation 1854
Land/water area (sq. miles) 11.35/6.00
Form of government .... Mayor-Council

Government
Legislative Districts
US Congressional	2
State Legislative	2

Local Officials, 2008
Mayor	Scott Evans
Manager	Carol Fredericks
Clerk	Rosemary Adams
Finance Dir	JoAnne Shepherd
Tax Assessor	Novalette Hopkins
Tax Collector	Patricia Gallo
Attorney	Kathleen M. Kissane
Building	Wally Shields
Planning	William Crane
Engineering	William Rafferty
Public Works	Richard Norwood
Police Chief	John Mooney
Emerg/Fire Director	Dennis Brooks

Housing & Construction
Housing Units, 2000*
Total	20,219
Median rent	$561
Median SF home value	$87,500

Permits for New Residential Construction
	Units	Value
Total, 2007	70	$14,218,624
Single family	52	$13,762,925
Total, 2006	272	$16,489,593
Single family	81	$11,352,145

Real Property Valuation, 2007
	Parcels	Valuation
Total	15,379	$8,150,513,500
Vacant	2,446	415,502,100
Residential	11,039	908,196,200
Commercial	1,692	6,741,345,100
Industrial	11	3,987,700
Apartments	191	81,482,400
Farm land	0	0
Farm homestead	0	0

Average Property Value & Tax, 2007
Residential value	$82,272
Property tax	$3,065
Tax credit/rebate	$708

Public Library
Atlantic City Public Library
1 N Tennessee Ave
Atlantic City, NJ 08401
609-345-2269
Director .... Maureen Sherr Frank

Library statistics, 2006
Population served	40,517
Full-time/total staff	5/27

	Total	Per capita
Holdings	122,078	3.01
Revenues	$3,590,211	$88.61
Expenditures	$2,704,263	$66.74
Annual visits	335,000	8.27
Internet terminals/annual users	38/75,299	

Public Safety
Number of officers, 2006 317

Crime	2005	2006
Total crimes	5,708	5,357
Violent	772	822
Murder	9	18
Rape	44	46
Robbery	385	375
Aggravated assault	334	383
Non-violent	4,936	4,535
Burglary	558	510
Larceny	4,224	3,821
Vehicle theft	154	204
Domestic violence	1,794	1,618
Arson	15	8
Total crime rate	140.7	132.7
Violent	19.0	20.4
Non-violent	121.6	112.3

Public School District
(for school year 2006-07 except as noted)

Atlantic City School District
1300 Atlantic Ave, 5th Fl
Atlantic City, NJ 08401
609-343-7200

Superintendent	Fredrick Nickles
Number of schools	10
Grade plan	K-12
Enrollment	6,939
Attendance rate, '05-06	92.2%
Dropout rate	6.4%
Students per teacher	10.2
Per pupil expenditure	$15,997
Median faculty salary	$61,072
Median administrator salary	$102,750
Grade 12 enrollment	572
High school graduation rate	76.7%

Assessment test results
(percent scoring at proficient or advanced level)
	Language	Math
NJASK-Grade 3	64.2%	72.9%
GEPA-Grade 8	39.0%	33.4%
HSPA-High School	66.1%	47.0%

SAT score averages
Pct tested	Math	Verbal	Writing
52%	454	432	421

Teacher Qualifications
Avg. years of experience	10
Highly-qualified teachers one subject/all subjects	99.0%/99.0%
With emergency credentials	0.4%

No Child Left Behind
AYP, 2005-06 .... Needs Improvement

Municipal Finance
State Aid Programs, 2008
Total aid	$7,584,254
CMPTRA	0
Energy tax receipts	7,582,967
Garden State Trust	1,287

General Budget, 2007
Total tax levy	$303,840,678
County levy	45,355,731
County taxes	41,670,886
County library	0
County health	0
County open space	3,684,845
School levy	105,019,963
Muni. levy	153,464,985
Misc. revenues	39,702,098

Taxes	2005	2006	2007
General tax rate per $100	3.502	3.696	3.726
County equalization ratio	73.2	64.81	44.42
Net valuation taxable	$7,820,776,556	$7,915,330,200	$8,155,061,595
State equalized value	$12,067,237,395	$17,825,942,534	$22,213,031,746

Monmouth County
Atlantic Highlands Borough

Demographics & Socio-Economic Characteristics
(2000 US Census, except as noted)

Population
- 1980* 4,950
- 1990* 4,629
- 2000 4,705
  - Male 2,274
  - Female 2,431
- 2006 (estimate)* 4,614
  - Population density 3,721.0

Race & Hispanic Origin, 2000
Race
- White 4,440
- Black/African American 108
- American Indian/Alaska Native 3
- Asian 58
- Native Hawaiian/Pacific Islander ... 0
- Other race 48
- Two or more races 48
- Hispanic origin, total 165
  - Mexican 32
  - Puerto Rican 45
  - Cuban 13
  - Other Hispanic 75

Age & Nativity, 2000
- Under 5 years 285
- 18 years and over 3,700
- 21 years and over 3,585
- 65 years and over 665
- 85 years and over 69
  - Median age 40.2
- Native-born 4,410
- Foreign-born 295

Educational Attainment, 2000
- Population 25 years and over 3,366
- Less than 9th grade 4.0%
- High school grad or higher 91.5%
- Bachelor's degree or higher 36.7%
- Graduate degree 11.6%

Income & Poverty, 1999
- Per capita income $34,798
- Median household income $64,955
- Median family income $79,044
- Persons in poverty 231
- H'holds receiving public assistance 10
- H'holds receiving social security 518

Households, 2000
- Total households 1,969
  - With persons under 18 567
  - With persons over 65 508
  - Family households 1,259
  - Single-person households 585
- Persons per household 2.39
- Persons per family 3.00

Labor & Employment
- Total civilian labor force, 2006** 2,778
  - Unemployment rate 5.9%
- Total civilian labor force, 2000 2,583
  - Unemployment rate 5.9%
- *Employed persons 16 years and over by occupation, 2000*
  - Managers & professionals 1,131
  - Service occupations 367
  - Sales & office occupations 663
  - Farming, fishing & forestry 0
  - Construction & maintenance 157
  - Production & transportation 112
  - Self-employed persons 180

* US Census Bureau
** New Jersey Department of Labor

See Introduction for an explanation of all data sources.

General Information
Borough of Atlantic Highlands
100 First Ave
Atlantic Highlands, NJ 07716
732-291-1444

- Website .... www.ahnj.com
- Year of incorporation 1887
- Land/water area (sq. miles) 1.24/3.27
- Form of government .... Borough

Government
Legislative Districts
- US Congressional 6
- State Legislative 11

Local Officials, 2008
- Mayor .... Frederick J. Rast III
- Administrator .... Adam Hubeny
- Clerk .... Dwayne Harris
- CFO .... Gerard Gagliano (Actg)
- Tax Assessor .... Eldo Magnani
- Tax Collector .... Judith Wierchinski
- Attorney .... Bernard Reilly
- Building .... Theresa Radigan
- Planning .... William Kuzman (Chr)
- Engineering .... Robert W. Bucco Jr
- Public Works .... Robert Dougherty
- Police Chief .... Jerry Vasto
- Emerg/Fire Director .... Beau Marios

Housing & Construction
Housing Units, 2000*
- Total 2,056
- Median rent $812
- Median SF home value $187,700

Permits for New Residential Construction

	Units	Value
Total, 2007	3	$1,199,000
Single family	3	$1,199,000
Total, 2006	1	$300,000
Single family	1	$300,000

Real Property Valuation, 2007

	Parcels	Valuation
Total	1,826	$631,062,000
Vacant	95	8,673,500
Residential	1,629	551,795,300
Commercial	90	55,898,300
Industrial	4	3,077,000
Apartments	8	11,617,900
Farm land	0	0
Farm homestead	0	0

Average Property Value & Tax, 2007
- Residential value $338,733
- Property tax $7,281
- Tax credit/rebate $1,138

Public Library
Atlantic Highlands Public Library
100 First Ave
Atlantic Highlands, NJ 07716
732-291-1956

- Director .... Marilyn Scherfen

Library statistics, 2006
- Population served 4,705
- Full-time/total staff 0/1

	Total	Per capita
Holdings	21,223	4.51
Revenues	$89,817	$19.09
Expenditures	$88,673	$18.85
Annual visits	12,345	2.62

- Internet terminals/annual users 2/1,707

Public Safety
- Number of officers, 2006 15

Crime	2005	2006
Total crimes	78	63
Violent	6	5
Murder	0	0
Rape	0	0
Robbery	0	2
Aggravated assault	6	3
Non-violent	72	58
Burglary	14	3
Larceny	57	55
Vehicle theft	1	0
Domestic violence	33	49
Arson	1	0
Total crime rate	16.6	13.6
Violent	1.3	1.1
Non-violent	15.4	12.5

Public School District
(for school year 2006-07 except as noted)

Atlantic Highlands School District
140 First Ave
Atlantic Highlands, NJ 07716
732-291-2020

- Superintendent .... Christopher Rooney
- Number of schools 1
- Grade plan K-6
- Enrollment 293
- Attendance rate, '05-06 .... 95.4%
- Dropout rate .... NA
- Students per teacher 8.8
- Per pupil expenditure $13,246
- Median faculty salary $45,150
- Median administrator salary ... $51,200
- Grade 12 enrollment .... NA
- High school graduation rate .... NA

Assessment test results
(percent scoring at proficient or advanced level)

	Language	Math
NJASK-Grade 3	88.9%	86.1%
GEPA-Grade 8	NA	NA
HSPA-High School	NA	NA

SAT score averages

Pct tested	Math	Verbal	Writing
NA	NA	NA	NA

Teacher Qualifications
- Avg. years of experience 9
- Highly-qualified teachers
  - one subject/all subjects 100%/100%
- With emergency credentials 0.0%

No Child Left Behind
- AYP, 2005-06 .... Meets Standards

Municipal Finance
State Aid Programs, 2008
- Total aid $322,492
  - CMPTRA 0
  - Energy tax receipts 322,492
  - Garden State Trust 0

General Budget, 2007
- Total tax levy $13,599,932
  - County levy 2,265,223
    - County taxes 1,989,132
    - County library 113,881
    - County health 37,891
    - County open space 124,320
  - School levy 7,588,786
  - Muni. levy 3,745,923
- Misc. revenues 3,220,012

Taxes

	2005	2006	2007
General tax rate per $100	2.128	2.157	2.15
County equalization ratio	95.34	82.98	76.41
Net valuation taxable	$612,995,415	$618,802,400	$632,709,049
State equalized value	$738,726,699	$811,643,298	$878,731,135

The New Jersey Municipal Data Book

Audubon Borough
Camden County

Demographics & Socio-Economic Characteristics
(2000 US Census, except as noted)

Population
1980*	9,533
1990*	9,205
2000	9,182
Male	4,391
Female	4,791
2006 (estimate)*	8,981
Population density	6,027.5

Race & Hispanic Origin, 2000
Race
White	8,938
Black/African American	48
American Indian/Alaska Native	10
Asian	82
Native Hawaiian/Pacific Islander	1
Other race	44
Two or more races	59
Hispanic origin, total	139
Mexican	21
Puerto Rican	68
Cuban	9
Other Hispanic	41

Age & Nativity, 2000
Under 5 years	507
18 years and over	6,907
21 years and over	6,613
65 years and over	1,456
85 years and over	192
Median age	38.1
Native-born	8,935
Foreign-born	247

Educational Attainment, 2000
Population 25 years and over	6,289
Less than 9th grade	4.0%
High school grad or higher	87.4%
Bachelor's degree or higher	25.1%
Graduate degree	6.3%

Income & Poverty, 1999
Per capita income	$24,942
Median household income	$49,250
Median family income	$59,115
Persons in poverty	502
H'holds receiving public assistance	50
H'holds receiving social security	1,159

Households, 2000
Total households	3,673
With persons under 18	1,207
With persons over 65	1,096
Family households	2,388
Single-person households	1,113
Persons per household	2.50
Persons per family	3.16

Labor & Employment
Total civilian labor force, 2006**	5,173
Unemployment rate	1.8%
Total civilian labor force, 2000	4,752
Unemployment rate	1.7%

Employed persons 16 years and over by occupation, 2000
Managers & professionals	1,640
Service occupations	675
Sales & office occupations	1,364
Farming, fishing & forestry	6
Construction & maintenance	494
Production & transportation	493
Self-employed persons	211

* US Census Bureau
** New Jersey Department of Labor

General Information
Borough of Audubon
606 W Nicholson Rd
Audubon, NJ 08106
856-547-0711
Website...... www.boroughofaudubon.com
Year of incorporation............1905
Land/water area (sq. miles).......1.49/0.02
Form of government............ Commission

Government
Legislative Districts
US Congressional	1
State Legislative	5

Local Officials, 2008
Mayor	Chris Tassi Jr
Manager	David Taraschi
Clerk	Nancy Doman
Finance Dir	Jack Bruno
Tax Assessor	Douglas Kolton
Tax Collector	Dottie Samartino
Attorney	Joe Nardi
Building	Duane Wallace
Comm Dev/Planning	NA
Engineering	Michael Angelastro
Public Works	David Taraschi
Police Chief	Thomas Tassi
Emerg/Fire Director	John Carpenter

Housing & Construction
Housing Units, 2000*
Total	3,813
Median rent	$598
Median SF home value	$107,200

Permits for New Residential Construction
	Units	Value
Total, 2007	2	$437,300
Single family	0	$286,300
Total, 2006	7	$460,086
Single family	4	$459,236

Real Property Valuation, 2007
	Parcels	Valuation
Total	3,212	$352,680,750
Vacant	45	1,136,700
Residential	2,995	293,651,150
Commercial	155	49,638,300
Industrial	1	140,000
Apartments	16	8,114,600
Farm land	0	0
Farm homestead	0	0

Average Property Value & Tax, 2007
Residential value	$98,047
Property tax	$5,105
Tax credit/rebate	$951

Public Library
Audubon Public Library
239 Oakland Ave
Audubon, NJ 08106
856-547-8686
Admin Coord............ Kathy Ostberg

Library statistics, 2006
Population served	9,182
Full-time/total staff	0/0

	Total	Per capita
Holdings	24,608	2.68
Revenues	$227,914	$24.82
Expenditures	$142,210	$15.49
Annual visits	21,050	2.29
Internet terminals/annual users		5/2,588

Public Safety
Number of officers, 2006...............22

Crime	2005	2006
Total crimes	239	262
Violent	12	8
Murder	0	0
Rape	0	1
Robbery	4	4
Aggravated assault	8	3
Non-violent	227	254
Burglary	32	37
Larceny	190	210
Vehicle theft	5	7
Domestic violence	49	49
Arson	1	3
Total crime rate	26.4	29.0
Violent	1.3	0.9
Non-violent	25.0	28.1

Public School District
(for school year 2006-07 except as noted)

Audubon School District
350 Edgewood Ave
Audubon, NJ 08106
856-547-1325

Superintendent	Donald Borden
Number of schools	3
Grade plan	K-12
Enrollment	1,568
Attendance rate, '05-06	97.8%
Dropout rate	0.7%
Students per teacher	11.0
Per pupil expenditure	$11,215
Median faculty salary	$53,600
Median administrator salary	$102,752
Grade 12 enrollment	174
High school graduation rate	93.3%

Assessment test results
(percent scoring at proficient or advanced level)
	Language	Math
NJASK-Grade 3	88.9%	91.1%
GEPA-Grade 8	83.6%	78.7%
HSPA-High School	89.5%	84.2%

SAT score averages
Pct tested	Math	Verbal	Writing
62%	514	489	477

Teacher Qualifications
Avg. years of experience...............12
Highly-qualified teachers
  one subject/all subjects......100%/99.0%
With emergency credentials..........0.0%

No Child Left Behind
AYP, 2005-06............Meets Standards

Municipal Finance
State Aid Programs, 2008
Total aid	$958,545
CMPTRA	190,873
Energy tax receipts	767,672
Garden State Trust	0

General Budget, 2007
Total tax levy	$18,383,803
County levy	4,572,210
County taxes	4,433,653
County library	0
County health	0
County open space	138,558
School levy	9,917,593
Muni. levy	3,894,000
Misc. revenues	4,775,000

Taxes
	2005	2006	2007
General tax rate per $100	4.597	5.029	5.208
County equalization ratio	70.14	61.07	51.16
Net valuation taxable	$345,523,565	$345,377,650	$353,050,643
State equalized value	$565,782,815	$675,502,642	$738,350,119

Camden County

Audubon Park Borough

Demographics & Socio-Economic Characteristics
(2000 US Census, except as noted)

Population
1980*	1,274
1990*	1,150
2000	1,102
Male	492
Female	610
2006 (estimate)*	1,071
Population density	7,140.0

Race & Hispanic Origin, 2000
Race
- White 1,090
- Black/African American 4
- American Indian/Alaska Native 1
- Asian 2
- Native Hawaiian/Pacific Islander 0
- Other race 1
- Two or more races 4
- Hispanic origin, total 7
  - Mexican 2
  - Puerto Rican 0
  - Cuban 0
  - Other Hispanic 5

Age & Nativity, 2000
- Under 5 years 45
- 18 years and over 868
- 21 years and over 843
- 65 years and over 202
- 85 years and over 18
- Median age 41.9
- Native-born 1,092
- Foreign-born 10

Educational Attainment, 2000
- Population 25 years and over 809
- Less than 9th grade 5.4%
- High school grad or higher 71.8%
- Bachelor's degree or higher 3.2%
- Graduate degree 0.4%

Income & Poverty, 1999
- Per capita income $16,926
- Median household income $34,643
- Median family income $41,029
- Persons in poverty 97
- H'holds receiving public assistance 25
- H'holds receiving social security 170

Households, 2000
- Total households 496
- With persons under 18 128
- With persons over 65 165
- Family households 302
- Single-person households 175
- Persons per household 2.22
- Persons per family 2.88

Labor & Employment
- Total civilian labor force, 2006** 566
- Unemployment rate 4.1%
- Total civilian labor force, 2000 518
- Unemployment rate 3.7%

Employed persons 16 years and over by occupation, 2000
- Managers & professionals 79
- Service occupations 88
- Sales & office occupations 178
- Farming, fishing & forestry 0
- Construction & maintenance 43
- Production & transportation 111
- Self-employed persons 15

‡ Branch of county library
* US Census Bureau
** New Jersey Department of Labor

See Introduction for an explanation of all data sources.

General Information
Borough of Audubon Park
20 Road C, Second Floor
Audubon Park, NJ 08106
856-547-5236

Website	audubonparknj.org
Year of incorporation	1947
Land/water area (sq. miles)	0.15/0.02
Form of government	Borough

Government
Legislative Districts
- US Congressional 1
- State Legislative 6

Local Officials, 2008
- Mayor .... Lawrence E. Pennock
- Manager/Admin .... NA
- Clerk .... Dawn M. Pennock
- Finance Dir .... Dawn Thompson
- Tax Assessor .... Stephen Kessler
- Tax Collector .... Andrea Penny
- Attorney .... Stuart Platt
- Building .... DCA
- Comm Dev/Planning .... NA
- Engineering .... Remington & Vernick
- Public Works .... Ken Whalen
- Police Chief .... NA
- Emerg/Fire Director .... David Laird

Housing & Construction
Housing Units, 2000*
- Total 499
- Median rent $474
- Median SF home value $47,400

Permits for New Residential Construction
	Units	Value
Total, 2007	0	$0
Single family	0	$0
Total, 2006	0	$0
Single family	0	$0

Real Property Valuation, 2007
	Parcels	Valuation
Total	1	$9,267,500
Vacant	0	0
Residential	0	0
Commercial	0	0
Industrial	0	0
Apartments	1	9,267,500
Farm land	0	0
Farm homestead	0	0

Average Property Value & Tax, 2007
- Residential value .... NA
- Property tax .... NA
- Tax credit/rebate $641

Public Library
Audubon Park Library‡
20 Road C
Audubon Park, NJ 08106
856-547-9583

Librarian .... Dorathea Zeoli

Library statistics, 2006
see Camden County profile for library system statistics

Public Safety
Number of officers, 2006 0

Crime	2005	2006
Total crimes	15	33
Violent	1	1
Murder	0	0
Rape	0	0
Robbery	0	0
Aggravated assault	1	1
Non-violent	14	32
Burglary	5	8
Larceny	9	21
Vehicle theft	0	3
Domestic violence	0	0
Arson	0	0
Total crime rate	13.8	30.6
Violent	0.9	0.9
Non-violent	12.9	29.6

Public School District
(for school year 2006-07 except as noted)

Audubon Park School District
20 Rd C
Audubon Park, NJ 08106
856-547-6825
No schools in district - sends students to Audubon Borough schools

- Per pupil expenditure .... NA
- Median faculty salary .... NA
- Median administrator salary .... NA
- Grade 12 enrollment .... NA
- High school graduation rate .... NA

Assessment test results
(percent scoring at proficient or advanced level)
	Language	Math
NJASK-Grade 3	NA	NA
GEPA-Grade 8	NA	NA
HSPA-High School	NA	NA

SAT score averages
Pct tested	Math	Verbal	Writing
NA	NA	NA	NA

Teacher Qualifications
- Avg. years of experience .... NA
- Highly-qualified teachers
  - one subject/all subjects .... NA/NA
- With emergency credentials .... NA

No Child Left Behind
- AYP, 2005-06 .... NA

Municipal Finance
State Aid Programs, 2008
- Total aid $28,121
- CMPTRA 0
- Energy tax receipts 28,121
- Garden State Trust 0

General Budget, 2007
- Total tax levy $668,792
- County levy 66,304
  - County taxes 60,229
  - County library 4,193
  - County health 0
  - County open space 1,882
- School levy 122,417
- Muni. levy 480,071
- Misc. revenues 384,170

Taxes	2005	2006	2007
General tax rate per $100	6.1	6.56	7.192
County equalization ratio	100	100	100
Net valuation taxable	$9,301,243	$9,267,500	$9,300,056
State equalized value	$9,301,243	$9,299,122	$9,300,056

The New Jersey Municipal Data Book

Avalon Borough
Cape May County

Demographics & Socio-Economic Characteristics
(2000 US Census, except as noted)

Population
- 1980* 2,162
- 1990* 1,809
- 2000 2,143
  - Male 1,043
  - Female 1,100
- 2006 (estimate)* 2,125
  - Population density 504.8

Race & Hispanic Origin, 2000
Race
- White 2,115
- Black/African American 3
- American Indian/Alaska Native 0
- Asian 12
- Native Hawaiian/Pacific Islander 1
- Other race 1
- Two or more races 11
- Hispanic origin, total 12
  - Mexican 5
  - Puerto Rican 3
  - Cuban 0
  - Other Hispanic 4

Age & Nativity, 2000
- Under 5 years 61
- 18 years and over 1,841
- 21 years and over 1,816
- 65 years and over 701
- 85 years and over 52
  - Median age 56.0
- Native-born 2,106
- Foreign-born 37

Educational Attainment, 2000
- Population 25 years and over 1,780
- Less than 9th grade 0.3%
- High school grad or higher 93.1%
- Bachelor's degree or higher 37.9%
- Graduate degree 11.0%

Income & Poverty, 1999
- Per capita income $50,016
- Median household income $59,196
- Median family income $72,750
- Persons in poverty 93
- H'holds receiving public assistance 0
- H'holds receiving social security 475

Households, 2000
- Total households 1,045
  - With persons under 18 147
  - With persons over 65 479
  - Family households 669
  - Single-person households 349
- Persons per household 2.05
- Persons per family 2.56

Labor & Employment
- Total civilian labor force, 2006** 1,095
  - Unemployment rate 2.8%
- Total civilian labor force, 2000 884
  - Unemployment rate 3.3%

Employed persons 16 years and over by occupation, 2000
- Managers & professionals 355
- Service occupations 109
- Sales & office occupations 257
- Farming, fishing & forestry 5
- Construction & maintenance 73
- Production & transportation 56
- Self-employed persons 95

* US Census Bureau
** New Jersey Department of Labor

General Information
Borough of Avalon
3100 Dune Dr
Avalon, NJ 08202
609-967-8200

- Website .... www.avalonboro.org
- Year of incorporation 1892
- Land/water area (sq. miles) 4.21/0.67
- Form of government .... Mayor-Council

Government
Legislative Districts
- US Congressional 2
- State Legislative 1

Local Officials, 2008
- Mayor .... Martin Pagliughi
- Manager .... Andrew Bednarek
- Clerk .... Amy Kleuskens
- Finance Dir .... James Craft
- Tax Assessor .... Jeffrey Hesley
- Tax Collector .... Connie DiCola
- Attorney .... Stephen D. Barse
- Building .... Salvatore DeSimone
- Comm Dev/Planning .... NA
- Engineering .... Thomas Thorton
- Public Works .... Harry deButts
- Police Chief .... David P. Dean
- Emerg/Fire Director .... Ed Dean

Housing & Construction
Housing Units, 2000*
- Total 5,281
- Median rent $719
- Median SF home value $443,300

Permits for New Residential Construction

	Units	Value
Total, 2007	79	$56,061,685
Single family	67	$52,533,535
Total, 2006	93	$51,378,624
Single family	77	$48,085,574

Real Property Valuation, 2007

	Parcels	Valuation
Total	5,527	$8,642,823,000
Vacant	240	338,797,900
Residential	5,141	8,118,508,300
Commercial	146	185,516,800
Industrial	0	0
Apartments	0	0
Farm land	0	0
Farm homestead	0	0

Average Property Value & Tax, 2007
- Residential value $1,579,169
- Property tax $5,460
- Tax credit/rebate $1,017

Public Library
Avalon Free Public Library
235 32nd Street
Avalon, NJ 08202
609-967-7155

- Director .... Norman Gluckman

Library statistics, 2006
- Population served 2,143
- Full-time/total staff 2/4

	Total	Per capita
Holdings	37,145	17.33
Revenues	$2,043,092	$953.38
Expenditures	$1,804,467	$842.03
Annual visits	25,000	11.67
Internet terminals/annual users		18/10,630

Public Safety
- Number of officers, 2006 19

Crime	2005	2006
Total crimes	217	311
Violent	2	6
Murder	0	0
Rape	0	1
Robbery	0	0
Aggravated assault	2	5
Non-violent	215	305
Burglary	31	45
Larceny	183	256
Vehicle theft	1	4
Domestic violence	2	2
Arson	0	1
Total crime rate	100.3	145.8
Violent	0.9	2.8
Non-violent	99.4	143.0

Public School District
(for school year 2006-07 except as noted)

Avalon School District
235 32nd St
Avalon, NJ 08202
609-967-7544

- Chief School Admin ..... David Rauenzahn
- Number of schools 1
- Grade plan K-8
- Enrollment 88
- Attendance rate, '05-06 .... 93.9%
- Dropout rate .... NA
- Students per teacher 5.2
- Per pupil expenditure $27,993
- Median faculty salary $67,621
- Median administrator salary $52,894
- Grade 12 enrollment .... NA
- High school graduation rate .... NA

Assessment test results
(percent scoring at proficient or advanced level)

	Language	Math
NJASK-Grade 3	NA	NA
GEPA-Grade 8	NA	NA
HSPA-High School	NA	NA

SAT score averages

Pct tested	Math	Verbal	Writing
NA	NA	NA	NA

Teacher Qualifications
- Avg. years of experience 19
- Highly-qualified teachers
  - one subject/all subjects 100%/100%
- With emergency credentials 0.0%

No Child Left Behind
- AYP, 2005-06 .... Meets Standards

Municipal Finance
State Aid Programs, 2008
- Total aid $463,850
- CMPTRA 0
- Energy tax receipts 458,646
- Garden State Trust 5,204

General Budget, 2007
- Total tax levy $29,885,464
- County levy 13,374,372
- County taxes 12,543,910
- County library 0
- County health 0
- County open space 830,462
- School levy 3,150,092
- Muni. levy 13,361,000
- Misc. revenues 5,254,749

Taxes

	2005	2006	2007
General tax rate per $100	0.46	0.32	0.35
County equalization ratio	101.87	126.23	104.31
Net valuation taxable	$5,463,821,704	$8,508,952,600	$8,644,312,225
State equalized value	$6,685,209,475	$8,158,822,719	$8,651,232,019

Monmouth County

Avon-by-the-Sea Borough

Demographics & Socio-Economic Characteristics
(2000 US Census, except as noted)

Population
- 1980*..................................2,337
- 1990*..................................2,165
- 2000..................................2,244
  - Male................................1,084
  - Female..............................1,160
- 2006 (estimate)*......................2,166
- Population density.................5,037.2

Race & Hispanic Origin, 2000
Race
- White.................................2,180
- Black/African American................12
- American Indian/Alaska Native.........10
- Asian..................................20
- Native Hawaiian/Pacific Islander.......0
- Other race............................14
- Two or more races......................8
- Hispanic origin, total................54
  - Mexican..............................46
  - Puerto Rican..........................2
  - Cuban.................................0
  - Other Hispanic........................6

Age & Nativity, 2000
- Under 5 years.........................112
- 18 years and over...................1,831
- 21 years and over...................1,784
- 65 years and over.....................501
- 85 years and over......................68
- Median age............................43.9
- Native-born........................2,161
- Foreign-born..........................76

Educational Attainment, 2000
- Population 25 years and over........1,746
- Less than 9th grade..................0.8%
- High school grad or higher..........92.6%
- Bachelor's degree or higher.........48.0%
- Graduate degree.....................21.2%

Income & Poverty, 1999
- Per capita income................$41,238
- Median household income..........$60,192
- Median family income.............$80,605
- Persons in poverty...................61
- H'holds receiving public assistance...9
- H'holds receiving social security...389

Households, 2000
- Total households...................1,043
  - With persons under 18.............210
  - With persons over 65..............376
  - Family households.................535
  - Single-person households..........429
- Persons per household...............2.15
- Persons per family..................3.04

Labor & Employment
- Total civilian labor force, 2006**..1,292
  - Unemployment rate.................4.2%
- Total civilian labor force, 2000....1,198
  - Unemployment rate.................3.7%

Employed persons 16 years and over by occupation, 2000
- Managers & professionals............584
- Service occupations.................132
- Sales & office occupations..........306
- Farming, fishing & forestry...........4
- Construction & maintenance..........72
- Production & transportation.........56
- Self-employed persons..............112

* US Census Bureau
** New Jersey Department of Labor

See Introduction for an explanation of all data sources.

General Information
Borough of Avon-by-the-Sea
301 Main St
Avon By the Sea, NJ 07717
732-502-4510
- Email..................avonboro@aol.com
- Year of incorporation................1900
- Land/water area (sq. miles).....0.43/0.12
- Form of government............Commission

Government
Legislative Districts
- US Congressional........................6
- State Legislative......................11

Local Officials, 2008
- Mayor....................Robert Mahon
- Administrator........Timothy Gallagher
- Clerk................Timothy Gallagher
- Finance Dir..............John Antonides
- Tax Assessor...............Tim Anfuso
- Tax Collector...........Kerry McGrath
- Attorney.................Barry Cooke
- Building...............Paul Orlando
- Comm Dev/Planning..............NA
- Engineering............Charles Rooney
- Public Works....................NA
- Police Chief............Terry Mahon
- Emerg/Fire Director......Scott Hauselt

Housing & Construction
Housing Units, 2000*
- Total................................1,387
- Median rent..........................$789
- Median SF home value............$370,100

Permits for New Residential Construction

	Units	Value
Total, 2007	22	$4,224,072
Single family	11	$3,399,072
Total, 2006	7	$3,099,500
Single family	7	$3,099,500

Real Property Valuation, 2007

	Parcels	Valuation
Total	1,023	$311,080,900
Vacant	17	2,746,800
Residential	945	283,865,500
Commercial	51	18,678,600
Industrial	2	843,400
Apartments	8	4,946,600
Farm land	0	0
Farm homestead	0	0

Average Property Value & Tax, 2007
- Residential value.................$300,387
- Property tax........................$7,988
- Tax credit/rebate..................$1,242

Public Library
Avon Free Public Library
Garfield & Fifth Aves
Avon-by-the-Sea, NJ 07717
732-502-4525
- Director..............Sheila M. Watson

Library statistics, 2006
- Population served..................2,244
- Full-time/total staff.................1/1

	Total	Per capita
Holdings	24,464	10.90
Revenues	$263,880	$117.59
Expenditures	$264,105	$117.69
Annual visits	20,000	8.91
Internet terminals/annual users	7/4,500	

Public Safety
- Number of officers, 2006..............12

Crime	2005	2006
Total crimes	64	118
Violent	3	4
Murder	0	0
Rape	0	1
Robbery	2	1
Aggravated assault	1	2
Non-violent	61	114
Burglary	13	20
Larceny	48	93
Vehicle theft	0	1
Domestic violence	8	10
Arson	0	0
Total crime rate	28.7	53.9
Violent	1.3	1.8
Non-violent	27.3	52.1

Public School District
(for school year 2006-07 except as noted)

Avon Borough School District
Lincoln and 5th Aves
Avon, NJ 07717
732-775-4328

- Superintendent..............Helen Payne
- Number of schools......................1
- Grade plan..........................K-8
- Enrollment..........................140
- Attendance rate, '05-06.............94.3%
- Dropout rate..........................NA
- Students per teacher..................9.1
- Per pupil expenditure............$16,219
- Median faculty salary............$46,412
- Median administrator salary......$92,585
- Grade 12 enrollment...................NA
- High school graduation rate...........NA

Assessment test results
(percent scoring at proficient or advanced level)

	Language	Math
NJASK-Grade 3	85.7%	85.7%
GEPA-Grade 8	93.3%	100.0%
HSPA-High School	NA	NA

SAT score averages

Pct tested	Math	Verbal	Writing
NA	NA	NA	NA

Teacher Qualifications
- Avg. years of experience...............6
- Highly-qualified teachers
  - one subject/all subjects......100%/100%
- With emergency credentials..........0.0%

No Child Left Behind
- AYP, 2005-06..........Meets Standards

Municipal Finance
State Aid Programs, 2008
- Total aid........................$177,770
- CMPTRA...............................0
- Energy tax receipts..............177,770
- Garden State Trust....................0

General Budget, 2007
- Total tax levy................$8,273,886
  - County levy...................2,384,989
    - County taxes................2,205,203
    - County library....................0
    - County health................42,005
    - County open space...........137,781
  - School levy...................3,054,497
  - Muni. levy....................2,834,400
  - Misc. revenues................1,516,731

Taxes

	2005	2006	2007
General tax rate per $100	2.348	2.526	2.66
County equalization ratio	47.22	41.69	34
Net valuation taxable	$305,369,343	$307,753,800	$311,136,658
State equalized value	$732,476,237	$905,226,078	$1,036,646,561

Barnegat Light Borough
Ocean County

Demographics & Socio-Economic Characteristics
(2000 US Census, except as noted)

Population
1980*	619
1990*	675
2000	764
Male	389
Female	375
2006 (estimate)*	833
Population density	1,156.9

Race & Hispanic Origin, 2000
Race
- White ... 751
- Black/African American ... 4
- American Indian/Alaska Native ... 0
- Asian ... 2
- Native Hawaiian/Pacific Islander ... 2
- Other race ... 3
- Two or more races ... 2
- Hispanic origin, total ... 6
  - Mexican ... 3
  - Puerto Rican ... 1
  - Cuban ... 0
  - Other Hispanic ... 2

Age & Nativity, 2000
- Under 5 years ... 25
- 18 years and over ... 654
- 21 years and over ... 641
- 65 years and over ... 262
- 85 years and over ... 23
- Median age ... 54.9
- Native-born ... 747
- Foreign-born ... 25

Educational Attainment, 2000
- Population 25 years and over ... 610
- Less than 9th grade ... 2.0%
- High school grad or higher ... 92.1%
- Bachelor's degree or higher ... 38.9%
- Graduate degree ... 17.4%

Income & Poverty, 1999
- Per capita income ... $34,599
- Median household income ... $52,361
- Median family income ... $66,406
- Persons in poverty ... 36
- H'holds receiving public assistance ... 3
- H'holds receiving social security ... 202

Households, 2000
- Total households ... 371
- With persons under 18 ... 61
- With persons over 65 ... 182
- Family households ... 230
- Single-person households ... 129
- Persons per household ... 2.05
- Persons per family ... 2.60

Labor & Employment
- Total civilian labor force, 2006** ... 307
- Unemployment rate ... 3.4%
- Total civilian labor force, 2000 ... 300
- Unemployment rate ... 2.7%

Employed persons 16 years and over by occupation, 2000
- Managers & professionals ... 119
- Service occupations ... 38
- Sales & office occupations ... 68
- Farming, fishing & forestry ... 19
- Construction & maintenance ... 33
- Production & transportation ... 15
- Self-employed persons ... 55

* US Census Bureau
** New Jersey Department of Labor

General Information
Borough of Barnegat Light
10 W 10th St
Barnegat Light, NJ 08006
609-494-9196

- Website ... www.barnlight.com
- Year of incorporation ... 1948
- Land/water area (sq. miles) ... 0.72/0.14
- Form of government ... Borough

Government
Legislative Districts
- US Congressional ... 3
- State Legislative ... 9

Local Officials, 2008
- Mayor ... Kirk Larson
- Manager ... Gail Wetmore
- Clerk ... Gail Wetmore
- Finance Dir ... T.C. Kay
- Tax Assessor ... Bernard Haney
- Tax Collector ... NA
- Attorney ... Terry Brady
- Building ... Frank Zappavigna
- Comm Dev/Planning ... NA
- Engineering ... Frank Little
- Public Works ... NA
- Police Chief ... Michael Bradley
- Emerg/Fire Director ... Keith Anderson

Housing & Construction
Housing Units, 2000*
- Total ... 1,207
- Median rent ... $772
- Median SF home value ... $299,400

Permits for New Residential Construction
	Units	Value
Total, 2007	7	$2,595,000
Single family	7	$2,595,000
Total, 2006	5	$2,318,000
Single family	5	$2,318,000

Real Property Valuation, 2007
	Parcels	Valuation
Total	1,290	$1,062,293,500
Vacant	70	40,850,500
Residential	1,173	976,830,300
Commercial	45	43,455,900
Industrial	0	0
Apartments	2	1,156,800
Farm land	0	0
Farm homestead	0	0

Average Property Value & Tax, 2007
- Residential value ... $832,762
- Property tax ... $6,031
- Tax credit/rebate ... $1,052

Public Library
No public municipal library

Library statistics, 2006
- Population served ... NA
- Full-time/total staff ... NA/NA

	Total	Per capita
Holdings	NA	NA
Revenues	NA	NA
Expenditures	NA	NA
Annual visits	NA	NA
Internet terminals/annual users	NA/NA	

Taxes
	2005	2006	2007
General tax rate per $100	0.809	0.706	0.725
County equalization ratio	102.12	101.86	94.11
Net valuation taxable	$881,983,000	$1,049,534,600	$1,062,628,253
State equalized value	$1,014,239,880	$1,115,566,192	$1,227,143,276

Public Safety
Number of officers, 2006 ... 0

Crime	2005	2006
Total crimes	22	37
Violent	1	0
Murder	0	0
Rape	1	0
Robbery	0	0
Aggravated assault	0	0
Non-violent	21	37
Burglary	1	1
Larceny	20	36
Vehicle theft	0	0
Domestic violence	9	7
Arson	0	0
Total crime rate	27.0	45.0
Violent	1.2	0.0
Non-violent	25.8	45.0

Public School District
(for school year 2006-07 except as noted)

Long Beach Island School District
200 Barnegat Ave
Surf City, NJ 08008
609-494-2341

- Superintendent ... Robert A. Garguilo
- Number of schools ... 10
- Grade plan ... K-6
- Enrollment ... 248
- Attendance rate, '05-06 ... 94.3%
- Dropout rate ... NA
- Students per teacher ... 6.9
- Per pupil expenditure ... $21,956
- Median faculty salary ... $94,335
- Median administrator salary ... $68,857
- Grade 12 enrollment ... NA
- High school graduation rate ... NA

Assessment test results
(percent scoring at proficient or advanced level)
	Language	Math
NJASK-Grade 3	100.0%	90.0%
GEPA-Grade 8	NA	NA
HSPA-High School	NA	NA

SAT score averages
Pct tested	Math	Verbal	Writing
NA	NA	NA	NA

Teacher Qualifications
- Avg. years of experience ... 19
- Highly-qualified teachers
  one subject/all subjects ... 100%/100%
- With emergency credentials ... 0.0%

No Child Left Behind
AYP, 2005-06 ... Meets Standards

Municipal Finance
State Aid Programs, 2008
- Total aid ... $102,288
- CMPTRA ... 0
- Energy tax receipts ... 99,337
- Garden State Trust ... 2,951

General Budget, 2007
- Total tax levy ... $7,696,133
- County levy ... 3,368,023
- County taxes ... 2,889,740
- County library ... 342,487
- County health ... 0
- County open space ... 135,796
- School levy ... 2,896,110
- Muni. levy ... 1,432,000
- Misc. revenues ... 1,168,815

Ocean County
Barnegat Township

Demographics & Socio-Economic Characteristics
(2000 US Census, except as noted)

Population
- 1980* 8,702
- 1990* 12,235
- 2000 15,270
  - Male 7,358
  - Female 7,912
- 2006 (estimate)* 21,192
- Population density 611.2

Race & Hispanic Origin, 2000
Race
- White 14,468
- Black/African American 338
- American Indian/Alaska Native 14
- Asian 152
- Native Hawaiian/Pacific Islander 0
- Other race 107
- Two or more races 191
- Hispanic origin, total 590
  - Mexican 39
  - Puerto Rican 281
  - Cuban 68
  - Other Hispanic 202

Age & Nativity, 2000
- Under 5 years 947
- 18 years and over 11,137
- 21 years and over 10,637
- 65 years and over 2,739
- 85 years and over 223
- Median age 39.0
- Native-born 14,656
- Foreign-born 629

Educational Attainment, 2000
- Population 25 years and over 10,068
- Less than 9th grade 3.1%
- High school grad or higher 84.8%
- Bachelor's degree or higher 15.8%
- Graduate degree 4.3%

Income & Poverty, 1999
- Per capita income $19,307
- Median household income $48,572
- Median family income $56,093
- Persons in poverty 944
- H'holds receiving public assistance ... 122
- H'holds receiving social security 2,164

Households, 2000
- Total households 5,493
  - With persons under 18 2,090
  - With persons over 65 1,879
  - Family households 4,192
  - Single-person households 1,110
- Persons per household 2.76
- Persons per family 3.19

Labor & Employment
- Total civilian labor force, 2006** 6,512
  - Unemployment rate 4.5%
- Total civilian labor force, 2000 6,589
  - Unemployment rate 4.4%

Employed persons 16 years and over by occupation, 2000
- Managers & professionals 1,692
- Service occupations 1,150
- Sales & office occupations 1,864
- Farming, fishing & forestry 0
- Construction & maintenance 755
- Production & transportation 841
- Self-employed persons 355

‡ Branch of county library
* US Census Bureau
** New Jersey Department of Labor

See Introduction for an explanation of all data sources.

General Information
Township of Barnegat
900 W Bay Ave
Barnegat, NJ 08005
609-698-0080

- Website .... www.ci.barnegat.nj.us
- Year of incorporation 1977
- Land/water area (sq. miles) 34.67/6.16
- Form of government .... Township

Government
Legislative Districts
- US Congressional 3
- State Legislative 9

Local Officials, 2008
- Mayor .... Jeffrey Melchiondo
- Administrator .... David Breeden
- Clerk .... Veronica Jasina
- Finance Dir .... David Breeden
- Tax Assessor .... Ellen Kelleher
- Tax Collector .... Effie E. Pressley
- Attorney .... Jerry J. Dasti
- Construction Official .... Louis Fischer
- Comm Dev/Planning .... NA
- Engineering .... John Hess
- Public Works .... Edward L. Richard Jr
- Police Chief .... Arthur Drexler
- Emerg/Fire Director .... Kevin Kadlubowski

Housing & Construction
Housing Units, 2000*
- Total 6,066
- Median rent $898
- Median SF home value $119,200

Permits for New Residential Construction

	Units	Value
Total, 2007	176	$26,861,703
Single family	176	$26,861,703
Total, 2006	300	$32,081,057
Single family	300	$32,081,057

Real Property Valuation, 2007

	Parcels	Valuation
Total	11,555	$2,784,671,800
Vacant	3,844	233,013,700
Residential	7,485	2,337,695,000
Commercial	188	158,395,300
Industrial	15	7,258,300
Apartments	2	45,669,300
Farm land	12	77,900
Farm homestead	9	2,562,300

Average Property Value & Tax, 2007
- Residential value $312,284
- Property tax $4,977
- Tax credit/rebate $966

Public Library
Barnegat Branch Library‡
112 Burr St
Barnegat, NJ 08005
609-698-3331

- Branch Librarian .... Lydia Lloyd

Library statistics, 2006
see Ocean County profile for library system statistics

Public Safety
- Number of officers, 2006 40

Crime	2005	2006
Total crimes	250	239
Violent	41	30
Murder	0	0
Rape	1	1
Robbery	4	3
Aggravated assault	36	26
Non-violent	209	209
Burglary	56	51
Larceny	151	152
Vehicle theft	2	6
Domestic violence	222	207
Arson	3	5
Total crime rate	13.0	11.8
Violent	2.1	1.5
Non-violent	10.9	10.3

Public School District
(for school year 2006-07 except as noted)

Barnegat Township School District
550 Barnegat Blvd. North
Barnegat, NJ 08005
609-698-5800

- Superintendent .... Thomas C. Mc Mahon
- Number of schools 5
- Grade plan K-12
- Enrollment 3,050
- Attendance rate, '05-06 .... 93.4%
- Dropout rate 0.1%
- Students per teacher 11.1
- Per pupil expenditure $11,908
- Median faculty salary $46,238
- Median administrator salary $82,750
- Grade 12 enrollment 2
- High school graduation rate 100.0%

Assessment test results
(percent scoring at proficient or advanced level)

	Language	Math
NJASK-Grade 3	85.1%	95.5%
GEPA-Grade 8	83.3%	84.3%
HSPA-High School	88.7%	80.0%

SAT score averages

Pct tested	Math	Verbal	Writing
NA	NA	NA	NA

Teacher Qualifications
- Avg. years of experience 8
- Highly-qualified teachers
  - one subject/all subjects 100%/100%
- With emergency credentials 0.5%

No Child Left Behind
- AYP, 2005-06 .... Meets Standards

Municipal Finance
State Aid Programs, 2008
- Total aid $1,363,858
  - CMPTRA 330,064
  - Energy tax receipts 981,405
  - Garden State Trust 37,953

General Budget, 2007
- Total tax levy $44,478,890
  - County levy 7,839,822
    - County taxes 6,460,315
    - County library 765,694
    - County health 310,216
    - County open space 303,598
  - School levy 27,060,015
  - Muni. levy 9,579,053
  - Misc. revenues 8,271,817

Taxes	2005	2006	2007
General tax rate per $100	3.649	3.672	1.594
County equalization ratio	56.67	48.33	110.49
Net valuation taxable	$914,600,898	$984,159,400	$2,790,603,086
State equalized value	$2,638,018,166	$2,347,659,432	$2,627,539,081

©2008 Information Publications, Inc. All rights reserved. Photocopying prohibited. For additional copies, contact the publisher at www.informationpublications.com or (877)544-INFO (4636)

Barrington Borough
Camden County

Demographics & Socio-Economic Characteristics
(2000 US Census, except as noted)

Population
1980*	7,418
1990*	6,774
2000	7,084
Male	3,376
Female	3,708
2006 (estimate)*	7,004
Population density	4,350.3

Race & Hispanic Origin, 2000
Race
White	6,490
Black/African American	295
American Indian/Alaska Native	17
Asian	102
Native Hawaiian/Pacific Islander	3
Other race	76
Two or more races	101
Hispanic origin, total	201
Mexican	25
Puerto Rican	122
Cuban	10
Other Hispanic	44

Age & Nativity, 2000
Under 5 years	410
18 years and over	5,588
21 years and over	5,366
65 years and over	1,250
85 years and over	133
Median age	38.2
Native-born	6,825
Foreign-born	227

Educational Attainment, 2000
Population 25 years and over	5,030
Less than 9th grade	4.7%
High school grad or higher	86.2%
Bachelor's degree or higher	25.8%
Graduate degree	5.9%

Income & Poverty, 1999
Per capita income	$24,434
Median household income	$45,148
Median family income	$59,706
Persons in poverty	134
H'holds receiving public assistance	43
H'holds receiving social security	1,001

Households, 2000
Total households	3,028
With persons under 18	842
With persons over 65	968
Family households	1,832
Single-person households	1,016
Persons per household	2.34
Persons per family	3.04

Labor & Employment
Total civilian labor force, 2006**	4,069
Unemployment rate	3.4%
Total civilian labor force, 2000	3,733
Unemployment rate	3.0%

Employed persons 16 years and over by occupation, 2000
Managers & professionals	1,432
Service occupations	450
Sales & office occupations	1,187
Farming, fishing & forestry	6
Construction & maintenance	291
Production & transportation	256
Self-employed persons	248

* US Census Bureau
** New Jersey Department of Labor

General Information
Borough of Barrington
229 Trenton Ave
Barrington, NJ 08007
856-547-0706

Website	www.barringtonboro.com
Year of incorporation	1917
Land/water area (sq. miles)	1.61/0.00
Form of government	Borough

Government
Legislative Districts
US Congressional	1
State Legislative	5

Local Officials, 2008
Mayor	John Rink
Manager/Admin	NA
Clerk	Terry Shannon
Finance Dir	Denise Moules
Tax Assessor	Steven Kessler
Tax Collector	Kristy Emmett
Attorney	Timothy Higgins
Building	John Szczerbinski
Comm Dev/Planning	NA
Engineering	Greg Fusco
Public Works	Mike Ciocco
Police Chief	Joseph Eisenhardt
Emerg/Fire Director	Jason Houck

Housing & Construction
Housing Units, 2000*
Total	3,164
Median rent	$607
Median SF home value	$111,200

Permits for New Residential Construction
	Units	Value
Total, 2007	5	$902,250
Single family	5	$902,250
Total, 2006	2	$328,250
Single family	2	$328,250

Real Property Valuation, 2007
	Parcels	Valuation
Total	2,167	$271,098,700
Vacant	51	1,328,300
Residential	2,022	217,142,600
Commercial	75	19,133,900
Industrial	11	16,268,600
Apartments	7	16,921,300
Farm land	0	0
Farm homestead	1	304,000

Average Property Value & Tax, 2007
Residential value	$107,487
Property tax	$6,132
Tax credit/rebate	$1,056

Public Library
No public municipal library

Library statistics, 2006
Population served	NA
Full-time/total staff	NA/NA

	Total	Per capita
Holdings	NA	NA
Revenues	NA	NA
Expenditures	NA	NA
Annual visits	NA	NA
Internet terminals/annual users	NA/NA	

Taxes
	2005	2006	2007
General tax rate per $100	4.984	5.336	5.705
County equalization ratio	73.86	61.83	54.44
Net valuation taxable	$269,369,449	$271,762,900	$271,426,258
State equalized value	$435,661,409	$499,563,406	$537,369,357

Public Safety
Number of officers, 2006 ... 15

Crime	2005	2006
Total crimes	92	73
Violent	11	11
Murder	0	0
Rape	0	1
Robbery	0	2
Aggravated assault	11	8
Non-violent	81	62
Burglary	24	11
Larceny	50	41
Vehicle theft	7	10
Domestic violence	83	59
Arson	0	1
Total crime rate	13.1	10.4
Violent	1.6	1.6
Non-violent	11.5	8.8

Public School District
(for school year 2006-07 except as noted)

Barrington Borough School District
311 Reading Ave
Barrington, NJ 08007
856-547-8467

Superintendent	Loyola Garcia
Number of schools	2
Grade plan	K-8
Enrollment	599
Attendance rate, '05-06	94.6%
Dropout rate	NA
Students per teacher	11.1
Per pupil expenditure	$13,547
Median faculty salary	$45,500
Median administrator salary	$94,636
Grade 12 enrollment	NA
High school graduation rate	NA

Assessment test results
(percent scoring at proficient or advanced level)
	Language	Math
NJASK-Grade 3	79.7%	90.7%
GEPA-Grade 8	81.7%	78.0%
HSPA-High School	NA	NA

SAT score averages
Pct tested	Math	Verbal	Writing
NA	NA	NA	NA

Teacher Qualifications
Avg. years of experience	13
Highly-qualified teachers one subject/all subjects	100%/100%
With emergency credentials	0.0%

No Child Left Behind
AYP, 2005-06 ... Meets Standards

Municipal Finance
State Aid Programs, 2008
Total aid	$771,742
CMPTRA	225,694
Energy tax receipts	546,048
Garden State Trust	0

General Budget, 2007
Total tax levy	$15,483,512
County levy	3,545,530
County taxes	3,219,998
County library	224,673
County health	0
County open space	100,859
School levy	8,747,834
Muni. levy	3,190,148
Misc. revenues	2,453,000

Burlington County
Bass River Township

Demographics & Socio-Economic Characteristics
(2000 US Census, except as noted)

Population
1980*	1,334
1990*	1,580
2000	1,510
Male	768
Female	742
2006 (estimate)*	1,570
Population density	20.7

Race & Hispanic Origin, 2000
Race
White	1,493
Black/African American	1
American Indian/Alaska Native	1
Asian	2
Native Hawaiian/Pacific Islander	0
Other race	2
Two or more races	11
Hispanic origin, total	33
Mexican	0
Puerto Rican	17
Cuban	10
Other Hispanic	6

Age & Nativity, 2000
Under 5 years	66
18 years and over	1,105
21 years and over	1,048
65 years and over	161
85 years and over	9
Median age	38.1
Native-born	1,504
Foreign-born	48

Educational Attainment, 2000
Population 25 years and over	1,011
Less than 9th grade	4.5%
High school grad or higher	80.5%
Bachelor's degree or higher	17.9%
Graduate degree	4.8%

Income & Poverty, 1999
Per capita income	$20,382
Median household income	$47,469
Median family income	$51,167
Persons in poverty	81
H'holds receiving public assistance	13
H'holds receiving social security	161

Households, 2000
Total households	548
With persons under 18	215
With persons over 65	122
Family households	410
Single-person households	106
Persons per household	2.76
Persons per family	3.15

Labor & Employment
Total civilian labor force, 2006**	932
Unemployment rate	4.1%
Total civilian labor force, 2000	804
Unemployment rate	3.9%

Employed persons 16 years and over by occupation, 2000
Managers & professionals	178
Service occupations	122
Sales & office occupations	215
Farming, fishing & forestry	5
Construction & maintenance	171
Production & transportation	82
Self-employed persons	75

* US Census Bureau
** New Jersey Department of Labor

See Introduction for an explanation of all data sources.

General Information
Township of Bass River
PO Box 307
New Gretna, NJ 08224
609-296-3337

Website	www.basriver-nj.org
Year of incorporation	1864
Land/water area (sq. miles)	75.88/2.37
Form of government	Commission

Government
Legislative Districts
US Congressional	3
State Legislative	9

Local Officials, 2008
Mayor	T. Richard Bethea
Manager/Admin	NA
Clerk	Amanda Somes
Finance Dir	Kathleen Phelan
Tax Assessor	Jay Renwick
Tax Collector	Linda Ash
Attorney	Matt McCrink
Building	John Ewert
Comm Dev/Planning	NA
Engineering	Kris Kluk
Public Works	NA
Police Chief	NA
Emerg/Fire Director	Kemp Wetmore

Housing & Construction
Housing Units, 2000*
Total	602
Median rent	$650
Median SF home value	$98,800

Permits for New Residential Construction
	Units	Value
Total, 2007	4	$474,545
Single family	4	$474,545
Total, 2006	8	$1,156,357
Single family	8	$1,156,357

Real Property Valuation, 2007
	Parcels	Valuation
Total	1,091	$73,472,301
Vacant	455	4,812,800
Residential	528	56,004,701
Commercial	47	10,214,700
Industrial	0	0
Apartments	0	0
Farm land	47	478,600
Farm homestead	14	1,961,500

Average Property Value & Tax, 2007
Residential value	$106,949
Property tax	$3,702
Tax credit/rebate	$793

Public Library
Bass River Library
11 N Maple Ave
North Gretna, NJ 08224
609-296-6942

Branch Librarian........Sheila Daugherty

Library statistics, 2006
Population served	1,510
Full-time/total staff	NA/0

	Total	Per capita
Holdings	NA	NA
Revenues	NA	NA
Expenditures	NA	NA
Annual visits	NA	NA
Internet terminals/annual users	NA/NA	

Taxes
	2005	2006	2007
General tax rate per $100	3.26	3.254	3.47
County equalization ratio	65.51	55.7	42.15
Net valuation taxable	$72,146,105	$71,868,900	$73,975,271
State equalized value	$129,526,221	$171,165,987	$192,336,654

Public Safety
Number of officers, 2006 0

Crime
	2005	2006
Total crimes	39	43
Violent	3	2
Murder	0	0
Rape	0	0
Robbery	0	0
Aggravated assault	3	2
Non-violent	36	41
Burglary	10	11
Larceny	22	28
Vehicle theft	4	2
Domestic violence	22	4
Arson	1	3
Total crime rate	24.9	27.5
Violent	1.9	1.3
Non-violent	23.0	26.2

Public School District
(for school year 2006-07 except as noted)

Bass River Township School District
11 North Maple Ave, PO Box 304
New Gretna, NJ 08224
609-296-4230

Superintendent	Lawrence Mathis
Number of schools	1
Grade plan	K-6
Enrollment	127
Attendance rate, '05-06	94.8%
Dropout rate	NA
Students per teacher	8.5
Per pupil expenditure	$15,833
Median faculty salary	$45,934
Median administrator salary	$79,119
Grade 12 enrollment	NA
High school graduation rate	NA

Assessment test results
(percent scoring at proficient or advanced level)
	Language	Math
NJASK-Grade 3	100.0%	100.0%
GEPA-Grade 8	NA	NA
HSPA-High School	NA	NA

SAT score averages
Pct tested	Math	Verbal	Writing
NA	NA	NA	NA

Teacher Qualifications
Avg. years of experience	11
Highly-qualified teachers one subject/all subjects	100%/100%
With emergency credentials	0.0%

No Child Left Behind
AYP, 2005-06 .... Meets Standards

Municipal Finance
State Aid Programs, 2008
Total aid	$347,662
CMPTRA	0
Energy tax receipts	148,655
Garden State Trust	100,250

General Budget, 2007
Total tax levy	$2,560,554
County levy	737,977
County taxes	611,515
County library	56,116
County health	0
County open space	70,345
School levy	1,822,577
Muni. levy	0
Misc. revenues	1,351,000

Bay Head Borough — Ocean County

Demographics & Socio-Economic Characteristics
(2000 US Census, except as noted)

Population
- 1980*..............................1,340
- 1990*..............................1,226
- 2000..............................1,238
  - Male...............................587
  - Female............................651
- 2006 (estimate)*.....................1,260
- Population density..................2,135.6

Race & Hispanic Origin, 2000
Race
- White............................1,213
- Black/African American................2
- American Indian/Alaska Native.........1
- Asian.................................7
- Native Hawaiian/Pacific Islander......0
- Other race...........................6
- Two or more races....................9
- Hispanic origin, total..............16
  - Mexican...........................0
  - Puerto Rican......................0
  - Cuban.............................1
  - Other Hispanic...................15

Age & Nativity, 2000
- Under 5 years.......................39
- 18 years and over................1,047
- 21 years and over................1,024
- 65 years and over..................312
- 85 years and over...................32
  - Median age......................51.5
- Native-born.....................1,269
- Foreign-born.......................23

Educational Attainment, 2000
- Population 25 years and over....1,029
- Less than 9th grade...............1.3%
- High school grad or higher.......97.2%
- Bachelor's degree or higher......52.8%
- Graduate degree..................19.9%

Income & Poverty, 1999
- Per capita income...............$49,639
- Median household income.........$77,790
- Median family income............$93,055
- Persons in poverty..................39
- H'holds receiving public assistance...4
- H'holds receiving social security...243

Households, 2000
- Total households....................584
  - With persons under 18...........103
  - With persons over 65............223
  - Family households...............350
  - Single-person households........207
- Persons per household..............2.12
- Persons per family.................2.73

Labor & Employment
- Total civilian labor force, 2006**...624
  - Unemployment rate...............5.1%
- Total civilian labor force, 2000....630
  - Unemployment rate...............4.8%

Employed persons 16 years and over by occupation, 2000
- Managers & professionals...........285
- Service occupations.................52
- Sales & office occupations.........168
- Farming, fishing & forestry..........0
- Construction & maintenance..........73
- Production & transportation.........22
- Self-employed persons...............97

‡ Branch of county library
* US Census Bureau
** New Jersey Department of Labor

General Information
Borough of Bay Head
PO Box 248
Bay Head, NJ 08742
732-892-0636

- Website................www.bayheadnj.org
- Year of incorporation................1886
- Land/water area (sq. miles).......0.59/0.11
- Form of government................Borough

Government
Legislative Districts
- US Congressional......................4
- State Legislative....................10

Local Officials, 2008
- Mayor................William W. Curtis
- Manager/Admin......................NA
- Clerk.................Patricia Applegate
- Finance Dir...............April J. Yezzi
- Tax Assessor...........Mary Anne Clear
- Tax Collector.........Michael Campbell
- Attorney............Kenneth Fitzsimmons
- Building...............Douglas Applegate
- Comm Dev/Planning.................NA
- Engineering............William England
- Public Works............Charles Tillson
- Police Chief..........Charles B. Grace Jr
- Emerg/Fire Director.......William Boyle

Housing & Construction
Housing Units, 2000*
- Total..............................1,053
- Median rent.......................$817
- Median SF home value..........$450,700

Permits for New Residential Construction

	Units	Value
Total, 2007	2	$612,002
Single family	2	$612,002
Total, 2006	8	$3,540,206
Single family	8	$3,540,206

Real Property Valuation, 2007

	Parcels	Valuation
Total	1,051	$947,926,300
Vacant	56	18,294,000
Residential	945	879,385,000
Commercial	49	49,694,000
Industrial	0	0
Apartments	1	553,300
Farm land	0	0
Farm homestead	0	0

Average Property Value & Tax, 2007
- Residential value................$930,566
- Property tax......................$9,659
- Tax credit/rebate.................$1,056

Public Library
Bay Head Reading Center‡
136 Meadow Ave
Bay Head, NJ 08742
732-892-0662

- Director................Virginia Berkman

Library statistics, 2006
see Ocean County profile for library system statistics

Public Safety
- Number of officers, 2006................8

Crime	2005	2006
Total crimes	47	51
Violent	0	1
Murder	0	0
Rape	0	0
Robbery	0	0
Aggravated assault	0	1
Non-violent	47	50
Burglary	6	10
Larceny	39	39
Vehicle theft	2	1
Domestic violence	0	3
Arson	0	0
Total crime rate	37.2	40.5
Violent	0.0	0.8
Non-violent	37.2	39.7

Public School District
(for school year 2006-07 except as noted)

Bay Head School District
145 Grove St
Bay Head, NJ 08742
732-892-0668

- Superintendent...............John Ravally
- Number of schools....................1
- Grade plan.........................K-8
- Enrollment..........................93
- Attendance rate, '05-06............95.6%
- Dropout rate........................NA
- Students per teacher................7.9
- Per pupil expenditure............$16,793
- Median faculty salary............$40,246
- Median administrator salary......$54,055
- Grade 12 enrollment.................NA
- High school graduation rate.........NA

Assessment test results
(percent scoring at proficient or advanced level)

	Language	Math
NJASK-Grade 3	91.6%	100.0%
GEPA-Grade 8	83.3%	75.0%
HSPA-High School	NA	NA

SAT score averages

Pct tested	Math	Verbal	Writing
NA	NA	NA	NA

Teacher Qualifications
- Avg. years of experience..............8
- Highly-qualified teachers
  - one subject/all subjects......91.5%/91.5%
- With emergency credentials..........0.0%

No Child Left Behind
- AYP, 2005-06............Meets Standards

Municipal Finance
State Aid Programs, 2008
- Total aid.......................$215,725
  - CMPTRA...........................0
  - Energy tax receipts............215,725
  - Garden State Trust................0

General Budget, 2007
- Total tax levy................$9,842,116
  - County levy..................4,933,544
    - County taxes...............4,065,460
    - County library...............481,829
    - County health................195,210
    - County open space............191,044
  - School levy...................2,502,548
  - Muni. levy....................2,406,024
- Misc. revenues..................1,647,803

Taxes

	2005	2006	2007
General tax rate per $100	0.898	0.953	1.039
County equalization ratio	78.79	68.79	59.69
Net valuation taxable	$932,904,536	$938,069,700	$948,161,485
State equalized value	$1,356,163,012	$1,571,835,250	$1,677,090,483

Hudson County

Bayonne City

Demographics & Socio-Economic Characteristics
(2000 US Census, except as noted)

Population
- 1980* 65,047
- 1990* 61,444
- 2000 61,842
  - Male 29,269
  - Female 32,573
- 2006 (estimate)* 58,844
- Population density 10,451.9

Race & Hispanic Origin, 2000
Race
- White 48,631
- Black/African American 3,416
- American Indian/Alaska Native 106
- Asian 2,562
- Native Hawaiian/Pacific Islander 30
- Other race 4,611
- Two or more races 2,486
- Hispanic origin, total 11,015
  - Mexican 631
  - Puerto Rican 4,244
  - Cuban 454
  - Other Hispanic 5,686

Age & Nativity, 2000
- Under 5 years 3,603
- 18 years and over 48,170
- 21 years and over 46,048
- 65 years and over 10,237
- 85 years and over 1,141
  - Median age 38.1
- Native-born 49,372
- Foreign-born 12,470

Educational Attainment, 2000
- Population 25 years and over 43,359
- Less than 9th grade 7.8%
- High school grad or higher 78.8%
- Bachelor's degree or higher 20.9%
- Graduate degree 6.7%

Income & Poverty, 1999
- Per capita income $21,553
- Median household income $41,566
- Median family income $52,413
- Persons in poverty 6,262
- H'holds receiving public assistance .. 855
- H'holds receiving social security .. 8,406

Households, 2000
- Total households 25,545
  - With persons under 18 7,795
  - With persons over 65 8,001
  - Family households 16,022
  - Single-person households 8,390
- Persons per household 2.42
- Persons per family 3.10

Labor & Employment
- Total civilian labor force, 2006** .. 29,176
  - Unemployment rate 5.5%
- Total civilian labor force, 2000 ... 29,496
  - Unemployment rate 6.5%

Employed persons 16 years and over by occupation, 2000
- Managers & professionals 8,811
- Service occupations 3,896
- Sales & office occupations 8,835
- Farming, fishing & forestry 18
- Construction & maintenance 2,144
- Production & transportation 3,861
- Self-employed persons 849

---

* US Census Bureau
** New Jersey Department of Labor
§ State Fiscal Year July 1–June 30

See Introduction for an explanation of all data sources.

General Information
City of Bayonne
Municipal Building
630 Avenue C
Bayonne, NJ 07002
201-858-6000

- Website .... www.bayonnenj.org
- Year of incorporation 1869
- Land/water area (sq. miles) 5.63/5.63
- Form of government .... Mayor-Council

Government
Legislative Districts
- US Congressional 10, 13
- State Legislative 31

Local Officials, 2008
- Mayor .... Terrence Malloy
- Manager .... Peter Cresci
- Clerk .... Robert Sloan
- Finance Dir .... Janet Convery
- Tax Assessor .... Joseph Nichols
- Tax Collector .... Joanne Sisk
- Attorney .... John Coffey
- Building .... Michael Feurer
- Planning .... John Fussa
- Engineering .... William England
- Public Works .... Frank Carine
- Police Chief .... Robert Kubert
- Emerg/Fire Director ...... Thomas Lynch

Housing & Construction
Housing Units, 2000*
- Total 26,826
- Median rent $681
- Median SF home value $155,600

Permits for New Residential Construction
	Units	Value
Total, 2007	247	$32,767,021
Single family	32	$3,077,351
Total, 2006	134	$12,621,345
Single family	50	$4,874,593

Real Property Valuation, 2007
	Parcels	Valuation
Total	13,146	$2,379,359,200
Vacant	448	83,967,600
Residential	11,022	1,495,742,100
Commercial	1,189	346,656,800
Industrial	141	340,326,900
Apartments	346	112,665,800
Farm land	0	0
Farm homestead	0	0

Average Property Value & Tax, 2007
- Residential value $135,705
- Property tax $7,730
- Tax credit/rebate $1,059

Public Library
Bayonne Free Public Library
697 Ave C
Bayonne, NJ 07002
201-858-6973

- Director .... Sneh Bains

Library statistics, 2006
- Population served 61,842
- Full-time/total staff 7/24

	Total	Per capita
Holdings	287,090	4.64
Revenues	$2,028,219	$32.80
Expenditures	$2,066,368	$33.41
Annual visits	168,796	2.73
Internet terminals/annual users	39/42,610	

Public Safety
- Number of officers, 2006 227

Crime
	2005	2006
Total crimes	1,158	1,057
Violent	220	194
Murder	2	1
Rape	7	4
Robbery	79	87
Aggravated assault	132	102
Non-violent	938	863
Burglary	191	188
Larceny	605	575
Vehicle theft	142	100
Domestic violence	370	357
Arson	1	9
Total crime rate	19.1	17.6
Violent	3.6	3.2
Non-violent	15.4	14.4

Public School District
(for school year 2006-07 except as noted)

Bayonne School District
669 Ave A
Bayonne, NJ 07002
201-858-5817

- Superintendent .... Patricia McGeehan
- Number of schools 12
- Grade plan K-12
- Enrollment 8,740
- Attendance rate, '05-06 .... 93.8%
- Dropout rate 1.5%
- Students per teacher 12.0
- Per pupil expenditure $10,985
- Median faculty salary $53,000
- Median administrator salary $108,079
- Grade 12 enrollment 570
- High school graduation rate 96.3%

Assessment test results
(percent scoring at proficient or advanced level)
	Language	Math
NJASK-Grade 3	85.3%	89.8%
GEPA-Grade 8	75.9%	69.3%
HSPA-High School	81.8%	71.0%

SAT score averages
Pct tested	Math	Verbal	Writing
74%	459	442	444

Teacher Qualifications
- Avg. years of experience 11
- Highly-qualified teachers
  one subject/all subjects 100%/100%
- With emergency credentials 0.4%

No Child Left Behind
- AYP, 2005-06 .... Meets Standards

Municipal Finance§
State Aid Programs, 2008
- Total aid $10,751,651
- CMPTRA 6,405,830
- Energy tax receipts 4,345,821
- Garden State Trust 0

General Budget, 2007
- Total tax levy $135,654,861
- County levy 23,408,830
- County taxes 22,834,053
- County library 0
- County health 0
- County open space 574,777
- School levy 59,871,453
- Muni. levy 52,374,579
- Misc. revenues 84,210,618

Taxes
	2005	2006	2007
General tax rate per $100	5.186	5.251	5.697
County equalization ratio	55.99	48.73	42.22
Net valuation taxable	$2,365,566,270	$2,373,915,900	$2,381,422,330
State equalized value	$4,854,435,194	$5,625,098,505	$6,321,742,280

©2008 Information Publications, Inc. All rights reserved. Photocopying prohibited. For additional copies, contact the publisher at www.informationpublications.com or (877)544-INFO (4636)

The New Jersey Municipal Data Book

Beach Haven Borough

Ocean County

Demographics & Socio-Economic Characteristics
(2000 US Census, except as noted)

Population
1980*	1,714
1990*	1,475
2000	1,278
Male	595
Female	683
2006 (estimate)*	1,366
Population density	1,393.9

Race & Hispanic Origin, 2000
Race
White	1,263
Black/African American	1
American Indian/Alaska Native	0
Asian	7
Native Hawaiian/Pacific Islander	0
Other race	1
Two or more races	6
Hispanic origin, total	60
Mexican	52
Puerto Rican	2
Cuban	1
Other Hispanic	5

Age & Nativity, 2000
Under 5 years	62
18 years and over	1,059
21 years and over	1,032
65 years and over	354
85 years and over	43
Median age	48.6
Native-born	1,226
Foreign-born	54

Educational Attainment, 2000
Population 25 years and over	942
Less than 9th grade	2.8%
High school grad or higher	90.2%
Bachelor's degree or higher	35.6%
Graduate degree	14.1%

Income & Poverty, 1999
Per capita income	$30,267
Median household income	$48,355
Median family income	$68,036
Persons in poverty	47
H'holds receiving public assistance	12
H'holds receiving social security	264

Households, 2000
Total households	586
With persons under 18	119
With persons over 65	261
Family households	347
Single-person households	205
Persons per household	2.17
Persons per family	2.80

Labor & Employment
Total civilian labor force, 2006**	545
Unemployment rate	7.7%
Total civilian labor force, 2000	557
Unemployment rate	7.0%

Employed persons 16 years and over by occupation, 2000
Managers & professionals	208
Service occupations	79
Sales & office occupations	130
Farming, fishing & forestry	0
Construction & maintenance	64
Production & transportation	37
Self-employed persons	52

* US Census Bureau
** New Jersey Department of Labor

General Information
Borough of Beach Haven
300 Engleside Ave
Beach Haven, NJ 08008
609-492-0111

Website	www.beachhaven-nj.gov
Year of incorporation	1890
Land/water area (sq. miles)	0.98/1.34
Form of government	Commission

Government

Legislative Districts
US Congressional	3
State Legislative	9

Local Officials, 2008
Mayor	Thomas J. Stewart
Administrator	Richard Crane
Clerk	Judith Howard
Finance Dir	Diane Marshall
Tax Assessor	Tracy Hafner
Tax Collector	Sharon Voisine
Attorney	Jerry Dasti
Building	Frank Zappavigna
Comm Dev/Planning	NA
Engineering	Frank Little
Public Works	Kim England
Police Dir	Louis Taranto
Emerg/Fire Director	Stanley Markoski

Housing & Construction

Housing Units, 2000*
Total	2,555
Median rent	$697
Median SF home value	$286,300

Permits for New Residential Construction
	Units	Value
Total, 2007	27	$8,619,481
Single family	27	$8,619,481
Total, 2006	33	$8,630,449
Single family	33	$8,630,449

Real Property Valuation, 2007
	Parcels	Valuation
Total	2,663	$1,623,265,992
Vacant	341	55,679,700
Residential	2,197	1,444,938,500
Commercial	113	108,759,692
Industrial	0	0
Apartments	12	13,888,100
Farm land	0	0
Farm homestead	0	0

Average Property Value & Tax, 2007
Residential value	$657,687
Property tax	$6,572
Tax credit/rebate	$1,157

Public Library
Beach Haven Public Library
Third St & Beach Ave
Beach Haven, NJ 08008
609-492-7081

Director	Virginia Donnelly

Library statistics, 2006
Population served	1,278
Full-time/total staff	0/0

	Total	Per capita
Holdings	32,823	25.68
Revenues	$171,075	$133.86
Expenditures	$148,469	$116.17
Annual visits	10,000	7.82
Internet terminals/annual users	3/4,343	

Public Safety
Number of officers, 2006 10

Crime	2005	2006
Total crimes	133	133
Violent	4	4
Murder	0	0
Rape	0	1
Robbery	0	0
Aggravated assault	4	3
Non-violent	129	129
Burglary	8	11
Larceny	120	114
Vehicle theft	1	4
Domestic violence	14	15
Arson	0	0
Total crime rate	100.4	98.4
Violent	3.0	3.0
Non-violent	97.4	95.4

Public School District
(for school year 2006-07 except as noted)

Beach Haven Borough School District
Beach Ave at Eighth St
Beach Haven, NJ 08008
609-492-7411

Superintendent	Patricia P. Daggy
Number of schools	1
Grade plan	K-6
Enrollment	65
Attendance rate, '05-06	94.9%
Dropout rate	NA
Students per teacher	5.5
Per pupil expenditure	$20,062
Median faculty salary	$40,023
Median administrator salary	$104,500
Grade 12 enrollment	NA
High school graduation rate	NA

Assessment test results
(percent scoring at proficient or advanced level)
	Language	Math
NJASK-Grade 3	NA	NA
GEPA-Grade 8	NA	NA
HSPA-High School	NA	NA

SAT score averages
Pct tested	Math	Verbal	Writing
NA	NA	NA	NA

Teacher Qualifications
Avg. years of experience	11
Highly-qualified teachers one subject/all subjects	100%/100%
With emergency credentials	0.0%

No Child Left Behind
AYP, 2005-06 .... Meets Standards

Municipal Finance

State Aid Programs, 2008
Total aid	$232,632
CMPTRA	0
Energy tax receipts	232,632
Garden State Trust	0

General Budget, 2007
Total tax levy	$16,225,611
County levy	5,515,498
County taxes	5,267,954
County library	0
County health	0
County open space	247,544
School levy	5,453,140
Muni. levy	5,256,973
Misc. revenues	3,320,075

Taxes
	2005	2006	2007
General tax rate per $100	0.945	0.977	1
County equalization ratio	102.57	86.85	78.97
Net valuation taxable	$1,569,221,700	$1,600,295,592	$1,623,718,636
State equalized value	$1,806,818,307	$2,027,082,428	$2,105,856,006

Ocean County
Beachwood Borough

Demographics & Socio-Economic Characteristics
(2000 US Census, except as noted)

Population
1980*	7,687
1990*	9,324
2000	10,375
Male	5,111
Female	5,264
2006 (estimate)*	10,744
Population density	3,892.8

Race & Hispanic Origin, 2000
Race
White	9,925
Black/African American	101
American Indian/Alaska Native	13
Asian	117
Native Hawaiian/Pacific Islander	6
Other race	115
Two or more races	98
Hispanic origin, total	438
Mexican	106
Puerto Rican	196
Cuban	53
Other Hispanic	83

Age & Nativity, 2000
Under 5 years	720
18 years and over	7,415
21 years and over	7,038
65 years and over	896
85 years and over	69
Median age	35.2
Native-born	9,928
Foreign-born	388

Educational Attainment, 2000
Population 25 years and over	6,636
Less than 9th grade	1.6%
High school grad or higher	87.4%
Bachelor's degree or higher	13.2%
Graduate degree	3.4%

Income & Poverty, 1999
Per capita income	$21,247
Median household income	$59,022
Median family income	$64,190
Persons in poverty	462
H'holds receiving public assistance	9
H'holds receiving social security	714

Households, 2000
Total households	3,475
With persons under 18	1,584
With persons over 65	678
Family households	2,817
Single-person households	521
Persons per household	2.98
Persons per family	3.31

Labor & Employment
Total civilian labor force, 2006**	5,485
Unemployment rate	5.2%
Total civilian labor force, 2000	5,538
Unemployment rate	4.7%

Employed persons 16 years and over by occupation, 2000
Managers & professionals	1,354
Service occupations	978
Sales & office occupations	1,518
Farming, fishing & forestry	0
Construction & maintenance	769
Production & transportation	656
Self-employed persons	245

‡ Branch of county library
* US Census Bureau
** New Jersey Department of Labor

See Introduction for an explanation of all data sources.

General Information
Borough of Beachwood
1600 Pinewald Rd
Beachwood, NJ 08722
732-286-6000

Website	www.beachwoodusa.com
Year of incorporation	1917
Land/water area (sq. miles)	2.76/0.00
Form of government	Borough

Government
Legislative Districts
US Congressional	3
State Legislative	9

Local Officials, 2008
Mayor	Ronald W. Jones Jr
Manager	NA
Clerk	Elizabeth Mastropasqua
Finance Dir	John Mauder
Tax Assessor	Denise Siegal
Tax Collector	Jeanette Larrison
Attorney	William Hiering Jr
Building	Wayne Gibson
Comm Dev/Planning	NA
Engineering	James Oris
Public Works Supervisor	John Behrens
Police Chief	William Cairns
Emerg/Fire Director	Roger Hull

Housing & Construction
Housing Units, 2000*
Total	3,623
Median rent	$926
Median SF home value	$114,400

Permits for New Residential Construction
	Units	Value
Total, 2007	21	$2,528,700
Single family	19	$2,393,200
Total, 2006	23	$1,878,547
Single family	23	$1,878,547

Real Property Valuation, 2007
	Parcels	Valuation
Total	4,122	$1,008,575,700
Vacant	363	22,217,100
Residential	3,678	951,081,700
Commercial	76	33,412,600
Industrial	1	224,900
Apartments	4	1,639,400
Farm land	0	0
Farm homestead	0	0

Average Property Value & Tax, 2007
Residential value	$258,587
Property tax	$3,580
Tax credit/rebate	$753

Public Library
Beachwood Branch Library‡
126 Beachwood Blvd
Beachwood, NJ 08722
732-244-4573

Branch Librarian	NA

Library statistics, 2006
see Ocean County profile for library system statistics

Public Safety
Number of officers, 2006	18

Crime
	2005	2006
Total crimes	210	249
Violent	16	10
Murder	0	0
Rape	0	0
Robbery	5	4
Aggravated assault	11	6
Non-violent	194	239
Burglary	30	29
Larceny	155	204
Vehicle theft	9	6
Domestic violence	111	114
Arson	2	3
Total crime rate	19.6	23.2
Violent	1.5	0.9
Non-violent	18.1	22.3

Public School District
(for school year 2006-07 except as noted)

Toms River Regional School District
1144 Hooper Ave
Toms River, NJ 08753
732-505-5510

Superintendent	Michael J. Ritacco
Number of schools	72
Grade plan	K-12
Enrollment	17,631
Attendance rate, '05-06	93.5%
Dropout rate	3.5%
Students per teacher	13.3
Per pupil expenditure	$10,065
Median faculty salary	$47,174
Median administrator salary	$111,050
Grade 12 enrollment	1,315
High school graduation rate	NA

Assessment test results
(percent scoring at proficient or advanced level)
	Language	Math
NJASK-Grade 3	94.0%	95.0%
GEPA-Grade 8	81.0%	73.6%
HSPA-High School	87.0%	70.9%

SAT score averages
Pct tested	Math	Verbal	Writing
NA	NA	NA	NA

Teacher Qualifications
Avg. years of experience	9
Highly-qualified teachers one subject/all subjects	99.5%/99.0%
With emergency credentials	0.0%

No Child Left Behind
AYP, 2005-06	Meets Standards

Municipal Finance
State Aid Programs, 2008
Total aid	$852,758
CMPTRA	298,627
Energy tax receipts	553,325
Garden State Trust	0

General Budget, 2007
Total tax levy	$13,973,847
County levy	3,039,484
County taxes	2,504,675
County library	296,845
County health	120,265
County open space	117,699
School levy	5,960,790
Muni. levy	4,973,573
Misc. revenues	3,334,332

Taxes
	2005	2006	2007
General tax rate per $100	3.107	3.275	1.385
County equalization ratio	57.19	48.56	103.16
Net valuation taxable	$407,618,972	$412,302,200	$1,009,421,076
State equalized value	$839,413,040	$966,649,776	$1,033,798,776

The New Jersey Municipal Data Book

Bedminster Township
Somerset County

Demographics & Socio-Economic Characteristics
(2000 US Census, except as noted)

Population
- 1980* 2,469
- 1990* 7,086
- 2000 8,302
  - Male 3,836
  - Female 4,466
- 2006 (estimate)* 8,449
- Population density 319.2

Race & Hispanic Origin, 2000
Race
- White 7,476
- Black/African American 145
- American Indian/Alaska Native 9
- Asian 532
- Native Hawaiian/Pacific Islander 2
- Other race 69
- Two or more races 69
- Hispanic origin, total 319
  - Mexican 32
  - Puerto Rican 53
  - Cuban 22
  - Other Hispanic 212

Age & Nativity, 2000
- Under 5 years 482
- 18 years and over 6,822
- 21 years and over 6,710
- 65 years and over 890
- 85 years and over 64
- Median age 39.3
- Native-born 7,079
- Foreign-born 1,223

Educational Attainment, 2000
- Population 25 years and over 6,508
- Less than 9th grade 1.5%
- High school grad or higher 96.2%
- Bachelor's degree or higher 60.4%
- Graduate degree 22.6%

Income & Poverty, 1999
- Per capita income $53,549
- Median household income $71,550
- Median family income $96,890
- Persons in poverty 254
- H'holds receiving public assistance .. 15
- H'holds receiving social security ... 733

Households, 2000
- Total households 4,235
  - With persons under 18 902
  - With persons over 65 667
  - Family households 2,100
  - Single-person households 1,862
- Persons per household 1.96
- Persons per family 2.76

Labor & Employment
- Total civilian labor force, 2006** ... 5,766
  - Unemployment rate 2.7%
- Total civilian labor force, 2000 .. 5,117
  - Unemployment rate 2.4%

Employed persons 16 years and over by occupation, 2000
- Managers & professionals 2,924
- Service occupations 345
- Sales & office occupations 1,369
- Farming, fishing & forestry 19
- Construction & maintenance 115
- Production & transportation 223
- Self-employed persons 320

‡ Joint library with Far Hills Borough
* US Census Bureau
** New Jersey Department of Labor

General Information
Township of Bedminster
One Miller Lane
Bedminster, NJ 07921
908-212-7000

- Website .... www.bedminster.us
- Year of incorporation 1749
- Land/water area (sq. miles) ... 26.47/0.00
- Form of government .... Township

Government
Legislative Districts
- US Congressional 7
- State Legislative 16

Local Officials, 2008
- Mayor .... Robert F. Holtaway
- Manager .... Susan S. Stanbury
- Clerk .... Judith A. Sullivan
- Finance Dir .... June G. Enos
- Tax Assessor .... Edward Kerwin Jr
- Tax Collector ...... Deborah Giordano
- Attorney .... John Belardo
- Building .... Joseph Alicino
- Comm Dev/Planning .... NA
- Engineering .... Paul Ferriero
- Public Works .... John Mantz
- Police Chief .... William Stephens
- Emerg/Fire Director .... Adam Segal

Housing & Construction
Housing Units, 2000*
- Total 4,467
- Median rent $1,430
- Median SF home value $228,000

Permits for New Residential Construction

	Units	Value
Total, 2007	6	$4,431,500
Single family	6	$4,431,500
Total, 2006	1	$750,000
Single family	1	$750,000

Real Property Valuation, 2007

	Parcels	Valuation
Total	4,788	$2,604,283,756
Vacant	87	14,943,900
Residential	4,049	1,570,628,976
Commercial	130	546,437,200
Industrial	1	450,000
Apartments	0	0
Farm land	309	3,319,380
Farm homestead	212	468,504,300

Average Property Value & Tax, 2007
- Residential value $478,557
- Property tax $5,333
- Tax credit/rebate $696

Public Library
Clarence Dillon Public Library‡
2336 Lamington Rd
Bedminster, NJ 07921
908-234-2325

- Director .... Nanette E. Geiger

Library statistics, 2006
- Population served 9,161
- Full-time/total staff 2/3

	Total	Per capita
Holdings	120,691	13.17
Revenues	$1,012,359	$110.51
Expenditures	$852,310	$93.04
Annual visits	85,403	9.32
Internet terminals/annual users	22/5,023	

Public Safety
- Number of officers, 2006 17

Crime	2005	2006
Total crimes	69	77
Violent	1	3
Murder	0	0
Rape	0	1
Robbery	0	0
Aggravated assault	1	2
Non-violent	68	74
Burglary	14	17
Larceny	52	52
Vehicle theft	2	5
Domestic violence	54	57
Arson	0	1
Total crime rate	8.2	9.2
Violent	0.1	0.4
Non-violent	8.1	8.8

Public School District
(for school year 2006-07 except as noted)

Bedminster Township School District
234 Somerville Rd
Bedminster, NJ 07921
908-234-0768

- Superintendent .... Andrew Rinko
- Number of schools 1
- Grade plan K-8
- Enrollment 582
- Attendance rate, '05-06 .... 96.3%
- Dropout rate .... NA
- Students per teacher 8.7
- Per pupil expenditure $15,803
- Median faculty salary $54,000
- Median administrator salary ... $112,000
- Grade 12 enrollment .... NA
- High school graduation rate .... NA

Assessment test results
(percent scoring at proficient or advanced level)

	Language	Math
NJASK-Grade 3	95.8%	98.6%
GEPA-Grade 8	87.9%	92.4%
HSPA-High School	NA	NA

SAT score averages

Pct tested	Math	Verbal	Writing
NA	NA	NA	NA

Teacher Qualifications
- Avg. years of experience 8
- Highly-qualified teachers
  - one subject/all subjects ... 100%/100%
- With emergency credentials 0.0%

No Child Left Behind
- AYP, 2005-06 .... Meets Standards

Municipal Finance
State Aid Programs, 2008
- Total aid $1,087,053
  - CMPTRA 0
  - Energy tax receipts 1,086,407
  - Garden State Trust 646

General Budget, 2007
- Total tax levy $29,097,456
  - County levy 8,144,830
  - County taxes 7,340,954
  - County library 0
  - County health 0
  - County open space 803,876
  - School levy 14,428,609
  - Muni. levy 6,524,018
  - Misc. revenues 3,772,844

Taxes	2005	2006	2007
General tax rate per $100	1.2	1.14	1.12
County equalization ratio	95.9	98.05	97.56
Net valuation taxable	$2,219,874,678	$2,435,033,000	$2,611,247,886
State equalized value	$2,471,195,233	$2,681,962,293	$2,720,607,723

Essex County
Belleville Township

Demographics & Socio-Economic Characteristics
(2000 US Census, except as noted)

Population
- 1980*.........................35,367
- 1990*.........................34,213
- 2000..........................35,928
  - Male........................17,330
  - Female......................18,598
- 2006 (estimate)*..............34,444
- Population density...........10,312.6

Race & Hispanic Origin, 2000
Race
- White.........................24,950
- Black/African American.........1,926
- American Indian/Alaska Native....60
- Asian..........................4,062
- Native Hawaiian/Pacific Islander..26
- Other race....................3,532
- Two or more races.............1,372
- Hispanic origin, total........8,507
  - Mexican........................158
  - Puerto Rican.................3,430
  - Cuban...........................454
  - Other Hispanic...............4,465

Age & Nativity, 2000
- Under 5 years..................2,133
- 18 years and over.............28,082
- 21 years and over.............26,925
- 65 years and over..............4,806
- 85 years and over................612
- Median age......................36.2
- Native-born...................26,290
- Foreign-born...................9,638

Educational Attainment, 2000
- Population 25 years and over..25,114
- Less than 9th grade.............8.5%
- High school grad or higher....78.2%
- Bachelor's degree or higher...21.7%
- Graduate degree................5.9%

Income & Poverty, 1999
- Per capita income............$22,093
- Median household income......$48,576
- Median family income.........$55,212
- Persons in poverty.............2,939
- H'holds receiving public assistance..321
- H'holds receiving social security..3,351

Households, 2000
- Total households..............13,731
  - With persons under 18.......4,469
  - With persons over 65........3,543
  - Family households...........9,091
  - Single-person households....3,828
- Persons per household...........2.60
- Persons per family..............3.23

Labor & Employment
- Total civilian labor force, 2006**...18,443
  - Unemployment rate.............5.5%
- Total civilian labor force, 2000....18,387
  - Unemployment rate.............6.6%

Employed persons 16 years and over by occupation, 2000
- Managers & professionals.......5,282
- Service occupations............2,578
- Sales & office occupations.....5,453
- Farming, fishing & forestry........0
- Construction & maintenance.....1,398
- Production & transportation....2,467
- Self-employed persons............619

* US Census Bureau
** New Jersey Department of Labor

See Introduction for an explanation of all data sources.

General Information
Township of Belleville
152 Washington Ave
Belleville, NJ 07109
973-450-3302
- Website.............www.bellevillenj.org
- Year of incorporation............1981
- Land/water area (sq. miles)...3.34/0.07
- Form of government......Council-Manager

Government
Legislative Districts
- US Congressional..................8
- State Legislative................28

Local Officials, 2008
- Mayor................Raymond Kimble
- Manager.............Victor Canning
- Clerk...............Kelly Cavanaugh
- Finance Dir..........Arthur Minsky
- Tax Assessor....William Merdinger
- Tax Collector.....................NA
- Attorney............Thom Murphy
- Building..........Frank DeLorenzo
- Comm Dev/Planning................NA
- Engineering............Tom Herits
- Public Works.....................NA
- Police Chief.......Joseph Rotonda
- Emerg/Fire Director...Robert Caruso

Housing & Construction
Housing Units, 2000*
- Total.........................14,144
- Median rent....................$752
- Median SF home value.......$147,500

Permits for New Residential Construction

	Units	Value
Total, 2007	99	$9,028,397
Single family	65	$5,528,417
Total, 2006	177	$16,791,268
Single family	37	$3,296,748

Real Property Valuation, 2007

	Parcels	Valuation
Total	9,515	$3,414,017,200
Vacant	389	68,248,200
Residential	8,348	2,539,284,500
Commercial	506	343,468,600
Industrial	132	178,613,900
Apartments	140	284,402,000
Farm land	0	0
Farm homestead	0	0

Average Property Value & Tax, 2007
- Residential value.............$304,179
- Property tax....................$6,870
- Tax credit/rebate..............$1,101

Public Library
Belleville Public Public Library
221 Washington Ave
Belleville, NJ 07109
973-450-3434
- Director..................Joan Taub

Library statistics, 2006
- Population served.............35,928
- Full-time/total staff............4/11

	Total	Per capita
Holdings	112,650	3.14
Revenues	$1,117,164	$31.09
Expenditures	$1,105,990	$30.78
Annual visits	58,964	1.64

Internet terminals/annual users...41/18,832

Taxes

	2005	2006	2007
General tax rate per $100	15.07	15.89	2.26
County equalization ratio	18.46	15.28	101.6
Net valuation taxable	$432,613,316	$435,220,350	$3,418,293,147
State equalized value	$2,831,238,979	$3,345,910,882	$3,620,819,591

Public Safety
- Number of officers, 2006..........111

Crime	2005	2006
Total crimes	1,054	1,014
Violent	126	132
Murder	1	0
Rape	7	3
Robbery	49	59
Aggravated assault	69	70
Non-violent	928	882
Burglary	164	163
Larceny	501	502
Vehicle theft	263	217
Domestic violence	105	57
Arson	4	2
Total crime rate	29.8	29.1
Violent	3.6	3.8
Non-violent	26.2	25.3

Public School District
(for school year 2006-07 except as noted)

Belleville School District
102 Passaic Ave
Belleville, NJ 07109
973-450-3500

- Superintendent........Edward A. Kliszus
- Number of schools....................9
- Grade plan........................K-12
- Enrollment......................4,481
- Attendance rate, '05-06..........96.0%
- Dropout rate.....................1.0%
- Students per teacher.............11.6
- Per pupil expenditure.........$11,321
- Median faculty salary.........$56,315
- Median administrator salary..$123,609
- Grade 12 enrollment..............399
- High school graduation rate.....87.0%

Assessment test results
(percent scoring at proficient or advanced level)

	Language	Math
NJASK-Grade 3	77.0%	80.9%
GEPA-Grade 8	68.6%	52.1%
HSPA-High School	76.4%	63.2%

SAT score averages

Pct tested	Math	Verbal	Writing
61%	459	449	442

Teacher Qualifications
- Avg. years of experience...........9
- Highly-qualified teachers
  - one subject/all subjects....99.5%/99.5%
- With emergency credentials.......0.7%

No Child Left Behind
- AYP, 2005-06.........Needs Improvement

Municipal Finance
State Aid Programs, 2008
- Total aid..................$7,824,788
  - CMPTRA...................5,134,549
  - Energy tax receipts......2,690,239
  - Garden State Trust..............0

General Budget, 2007
- Total tax levy............$77,204,801
  - County levy.............13,244,826
    - County taxes..........12,903,978
    - County library................0
    - County health.................0
    - County open space........340,848
  - School levy.............31,691,984
  - Muni. levy..............32,267,991
- Misc. revenues............18,964,696

©2008 Information Publications, Inc. All rights reserved. Photocopying prohibited. For additional copies, contact the publisher at www.informationpublications.com or (877) 544-INFO (4636)

The New Jersey Municipal Data Book 31

Bellmawr Borough

Camden County

Demographics & Socio-Economic Characteristics
(2000 US Census, except as noted)

Population
1980*	13,721
1990*	12,603
2000	11,262
Male	5,531
Female	5,731
2006 (estimate)*	11,193
Population density	3,694.1

Race & Hispanic Origin, 2000
Race
White	10,450
Black/African American	133
American Indian/Alaska Native	7
Asian	344
Native Hawaiian/Pacific Islander	2
Other race	173
Two or more races	153
Hispanic origin, total	394
Mexican	115
Puerto Rican	202
Cuban	1
Other Hispanic	76

Age & Nativity, 2000
Under 5 years	571
18 years and over	8,922
21 years and over	8,522
65 years and over	1,969
85 years and over	127
Median age	40.1
Native-born	10,415
Foreign-born	847

Educational Attainment, 2000
Population 25 years and over	7,925
Less than 9th grade	6.0%
High school grad or higher	74.5%
Bachelor's degree or higher	10.4%
Graduate degree	2.8%

Income & Poverty, 1999
Per capita income	$19,863
Median household income	$44,653
Median family income	$53,839
Persons in poverty	446
H'holds receiving public assistance	50
H'holds receiving social security	1,690

Households, 2000
Total households	4,446
With persons under 18	1,356
With persons over 65	1,441
Family households	3,136
Single-person households	1,124
Persons per household	2.53
Persons per family	3.02

Labor & Employment
Total civilian labor force, 2006**	6,401
Unemployment rate	4.5%
Total civilian labor force, 2000	5,899
Unemployment rate	4.2%

Employed persons 16 years and over by occupation, 2000
Managers & professionals	1,322
Service occupations	761
Sales & office occupations	1,864
Farming, fishing & forestry	4
Construction & maintenance	672
Production & transportation	1,029
Self-employed persons	234

‡ Branch of county library
* US Census Bureau
** New Jersey Department of Labor

General Information
Borough of Bellmawr
21 E Browning Rd
PO Box 368
Bellmawr, NJ 08099
856-933-1313

Website	www.bellmawr.com
Year of incorporation	1926
Land/water area (sq. miles)	3.03/0.10
Form of government	Borough

Government
Legislative Districts
US Congressional	1
State Legislative	5

Local Officials, 2008
Mayor	Frank Filipek
Manager/Admin	NA
Clerk	Charles Sauter
Finance Dir	Maria Fasulo
Tax Assessor	John Dymond
Tax Collector	Margaret Sandrock
Attorney	Robert L. Messick
Building	William Glover
Comm Dev/Planning	NA
Engineering	Greg Sullivan
Public Works	Joseph Ciano Jr
Police Chief	William Walsh
Fire Chief	J. Burleigh/T. Calhoun

Housing & Construction
Housing Units, 2000*
Total	4,561
Median rent	$523
Median SF home value	$95,800

Permits for New Residential Construction
	Units	Value
Total, 2007	22	$924,236
Single family	11	$915,910
Total, 2006	25	$892,550
Single family	10	$881,195

Real Property Valuation, 2007
	Parcels	Valuation
Total	3,660	$429,111,500
Vacant	96	4,180,700
Residential	3,389	296,793,900
Commercial	111	41,060,700
Industrial	55	58,522,900
Apartments	9	28,553,300
Farm land	0	0
Farm homestead	0	0

Average Property Value & Tax, 2007
Residential value	$87,576
Property tax	$4,599
Tax credit/rebate	$913

Public Library
Bellmawr Branch Library‡
35 E Browning Rd
Bellmawr, NJ 08031
856-931-1400

Branch librarian: Deborah Stefano

Library statistics, 2006
see Camden County profile for library system statistics

Public Safety
Number of officers, 2006: 24

Crime	2005	2006
Total crimes	262	270
Violent	11	17
Murder	0	0
Rape	0	1
Robbery	6	4
Aggravated assault	5	12
Non-violent	251	253
Burglary	55	46
Larceny	177	182
Vehicle theft	19	25
Domestic violence	44	74
Arson	0	0
Total crime rate	23.4	24.2
Violent	1.0	1.5
Non-violent	22.4	22.7

Public School District
(for school year 2006-07 except as noted)

Bellmawr Borough School District
256 Anderson Ave
Bellmawr, NJ 08031
856-931-3620

Superintendent	Annette Castiglione
Number of schools	3
Grade plan	K-8
Enrollment	1,076
Attendance rate, '05-06	96.0%
Dropout rate	NA
Students per teacher	12.4
Per pupil expenditure	$10,567
Median faculty salary	$56,505
Median administrator salary	$90,615
Grade 12 enrollment	NA
High school graduation rate	NA

Assessment test results
(percent scoring at proficient or advanced level)
	Language	Math
NJASK-Grade 3	79.3%	77.0%
GEPA-Grade 8	85.0%	76.8%
HSPA-High School	NA	NA

SAT score averages
Pct tested	Math	Verbal	Writing
NA	NA	NA	NA

Teacher Qualifications
Avg. years of experience	10
Highly-qualified teachers one subject/all subjects	100%/100%
With emergency credentials	0.0%

No Child Left Behind
AYP, 2005-06: Meets Standards

Municipal Finance
State Aid Programs, 2008
Total aid	$1,445,778
CMPTRA	442,766
Energy tax receipts	1,003,012
Garden State Trust	0

General Budget, 2007
Total tax levy	$22,568,836
County levy	5,509,673
County taxes	5,004,390
County library	348,732
County health	0
County open space	156,550
School levy	10,890,982
Muni. levy	6,168,181
Misc. revenues	5,153,170

Taxes	2005	2006	2007
General tax rate per $100	4.651	5.02	5.251
County equalization ratio	75.48	63.66	54.99
Net valuation taxable	$426,409,790	$428,087,200	$429,807,409
State equalized value	$669,823,735	$779,290,022	$860,811,163

Monmouth County | Belmar Borough

Demographics & Socio-Economic Characteristics
(2000 US Census, except as noted)

Population
- 1980*.....................................6,771
- 1990*.....................................5,877
- 2000.....................................6,045
  - Male.....................................3,020
  - Female...................................3,025
- 2006 (estimate)*.........................5,923
- Population density...................5,806.9

Race & Hispanic Origin, 2000
Race
- White....................................5,533
- Black/African American..................209
- American Indian/Alaska Native............11
- Asian......................................62
- Native Hawaiian/Pacific Islander..........0
- Other race...............................120
- Two or more races........................110
- Hispanic origin, total...................414
  - Mexican..................................198
  - Puerto Rican..............................86
  - Cuban......................................6
  - Other Hispanic...........................124

Age & Nativity, 2000
- Under 5 years............................293
- 18 years and over.......................5,007
- 21 years and over.......................4,850
- 65 years and over.........................952
- 85 years and over.........................113
- Median age...............................38.5
- Native-born.............................5,524
- Foreign-born..............................521

Educational Attainment, 2000
- Population 25 years and over...........4,553
- Less than 9th grade......................4.7%
- High school grad or higher..............89.3%
- Bachelor's degree or higher.............34.0%
- Graduate degree.........................11.9%

Income & Poverty, 1999
- Per capita income.....................$29,456
- Median household income...............$44,896
- Median family income..................$61,250
- Persons in poverty.......................520
- H'holds receiving public assistance......76
- H'holds receiving social security.......763

Households, 2000
- Total households......................2,946
  - With persons under 18..................564
  - With persons over 65...................726
  - Family households...................1,318
  - Single-person households.............1,305
- Persons per household...................2.05
- Persons per family......................2.92

Labor & Employment
- Total civilian labor force, 2006**....3,746
  - Unemployment rate.....................4.9%
- Total civilian labor force, 2000......3,492
  - Unemployment rate.....................4.8%

Employed persons 16 years and over by occupation, 2000
- Managers & professionals..............1,333
- Service occupations.....................461
- Sales & office occupations..............924
- Farming, fishing & forestry...............0
- Construction & maintenance..............314
- Production & transportation.............292
- Self-employed persons...................234

* US Census Bureau
** New Jersey Department of Labor

See Introduction for an explanation of all data sources.

General Information
Borough of Belmar
PO Box A
Belmar, NJ 07719
732-681-1176
- Website....................www.belmar.com
- Year of incorporation..................1890
- Land/water area (sq. miles)......1.02/0.67
- Form of government......Small Municipality

Government
Legislative Districts
- US Congressional............................6
- State Legislative..........................11

Local Officials, 2008
- Mayor....................Kenneth Pringle
- Manager....................Robbin Kirk
- Clerk..................Margaret Plummer
- Finance Dir................Robbin Kirk
- Tax Assessor............Edward Mullane
- Tax Collector..............Robbin Kirk
- Attorney....................Karl Kemm
- Building................Patrick McMahon
- Comm Dev/Planning..................NA
- Engineering................Tom Rospos
- Public Works............Andy Meuerle
- Police Chief...................Jack Hill
- Emerg/Fire Director......John Rizzitello

Housing & Construction
Housing Units, 2000*
- Total...............................3,996
- Median rent...........................$779
- Median SF home value..............$186,700

Permits for New Residential Construction

	Units	Value
Total, 2007	19	$3,265,900
Single family	19	$3,088,900
Total, 2006	24	$5,485,495
Single family	24	$5,485,495

Real Property Valuation, 2007

	Parcels	Valuation
Total	2,837	$1,004,904,300
Vacant	109	21,349,400
Residential	2,531	847,873,700
Commercial	166	104,438,700
Industrial	0	0
Apartments	31	31,242,500
Farm land	0	0
Farm homestead	0	0

Average Property Value & Tax, 2007
- Residential value..................$334,996
- Property tax.........................$5,775
- Tax credit/rebate.....................$983

Public Library
Belmar Public Library
517 Tenth Ave
Belmar, NJ 07719
732-681-0775
- Director............Natalie Gallagher

Library statistics, 2006
- Population served....................6,045
- Full-time/total staff...................0/1

	Total	Per capita
Holdings	31,550	5.22
Revenues	NA	NA
Expenditures	NA	NA
Annual visits	12,000	1.99
Internet terminals/annual users	4/5,400	

Taxes

	2005	2006	2007
General tax rate per $100	1.589	1.666	1.724
County equalization ratio	85.86	72.06	61.62
Net valuation taxable	$992,515,029	$999,285,400	$1,005,169,363
State equalized value	$1,377,345,308	$1,621,990,735	$1,749,141,325

Public Safety
- Number of officers, 2006.................21

Crime	2005	2006
Total crimes	433	368
Violent	29	35
Murder	0	0
Rape	0	0
Robbery	5	3
Aggravated assault	24	32
Non-violent	404	333
Burglary	77	37
Larceny	314	281
Vehicle theft	13	15
Domestic violence	122	112
Arson	1	0
Total crime rate	71.8	61.7
Violent	4.8	5.9
Non-violent	67.0	55.9

Public School District
(for school year 2006-07 except as noted)

Belmar School District
1101 Main St
Belmar, NJ 07719
732-681-2388

- Superintendent..........Paul S. Shappirio
- Number of schools..........................1
- Grade plan..............................K-8
- Enrollment...............................534
- Attendance rate, '05-06................94.5%
- Dropout rate.............................NA
- Students per teacher.....................9.8
- Per pupil expenditure................$13,401
- Median faculty salary................$52,800
- Median administrator salary..........$97,813
- Grade 12 enrollment......................NA
- High school graduation rate..............NA

Assessment test results
(percent scoring at proficient or advanced level)

	Language	Math
NJASK-Grade 3	94.0%	90.2%
GEPA-Grade 8	63.7%	70.1%
HSPA-High School	NA	NA

SAT score averages

Pct tested	Math	Verbal	Writing
NA	NA	NA	NA

Teacher Qualifications
- Avg. years of experience.................11
- Highly-qualified teachers
  - one subject/all subjects.......100%/100%
- With emergency credentials.............0.0%

No Child Left Behind
- AYP, 2005-06............Meets Standards

Municipal Finance
State Aid Programs, 2008
- Total aid.........................$522,258
  - CMPTRA............................66,121
  - Energy tax receipts..............456,137
  - Garden State Trust....................0

General Budget, 2007
- Total tax levy.................$17,329,064
  - County levy.....................4,257,624
    - County taxes..................3,936,675
    - County library......................0
    - County health..................74,986
    - County open space.............245,963
  - School levy.....................6,918,701
  - Muni. levy......................6,152,739
  - Misc. revenues..................6,129,321

The New Jersey Municipal Data Book

Belvidere Town — Warren County

Demographics & Socio-Economic Characteristics
(2000 US Census, except as noted)

Population
1980*	2,475
1990*	2,669
2000	2,771
Male	1,328
Female	1,443
2006 (estimate)*	2,701
Population density	2,046.2

Race & Hispanic Origin, 2000
Race
White	2,716
Black/African American	14
American Indian/Alaska Native	1
Asian	14
Native Hawaiian/Pacific Islander	0
Other race	7
Two or more races	19
Hispanic origin, total	64
Mexican	1
Puerto Rican	28
Cuban	12
Other Hispanic	23

Age & Nativity, 2000
Under 5 years	201
18 years and over	1,991
21 years and over	1,903
65 years and over	356
85 years and over	57
Median age	36.4
Native-born	2,703
Foreign-born	68

Educational Attainment, 2000
Population 25 years and over	1,823
Less than 9th grade	2.7%
High school grad or higher	84.0%
Bachelor's degree or higher	26.2%
Graduate degree	7.7%

Income & Poverty, 1999
Per capita income	$23,231
Median household income	$52,792
Median family income	$62,212
Persons in poverty	93
H'holds receiving public assistance	27
H'holds receiving social security	304

Households, 2000
Total households	1,088
With persons under 18	416
With persons over 65	266
Family households	717
Single-person households	310
Persons per household	2.54
Persons per family	3.17

Labor & Employment
Total civilian labor force, 2006**	1,659
Unemployment rate	5.5%
Total civilian labor force, 2000	1,454
Unemployment rate	4.6%

Employed persons 16 years and over by occupation, 2000
Managers & professionals	490
Service occupations	192
Sales & office occupations	369
Farming, fishing & forestry	1
Construction & maintenance	116
Production & transportation	219
Self-employed persons	107

* US Census Bureau
** New Jersey Department of Labor

General Information
Town of Belvidere
691 Water St
Belvidere, NJ 07823
908-475-5331

Website	www.belviderenj.com
Year of incorporation	1845
Land/water area (sq. miles)	1.32/0.02
Form of government	Town

Government
Legislative Districts
US Congressional	5
State Legislative	23

Local Officials, 2008
Mayor	Charles J. Liegel Sr
Manager	Teresa A. DeMont
Clerk	Teresa A. DeMont
Finance Dir	Cathy Gangaware
Tax Assessor	David Gill
Tax Collector	Rita Kelly
Attorney	Brian Smith
Building	Charles O'Connor
Planning	Maser Consulting
Engineering	Maser Consulting
Public Works	John Snyder
Police Chief	Kent Sweigert
Emerg/Fire Director	James Christine

Housing & Construction
Housing Units, 2000*
Total	1,165
Median rent	$575
Median SF home value	$124,200

Permits for New Residential Construction
	Units	Value
Total, 2007	2	$361,000
Single family	2	$361,000
Total, 2006	1	$125,000
Single family	1	$125,000

Real Property Valuation, 2007
	Parcels	Valuation
Total	1,031	$144,808,700
Vacant	78	2,725,600
Residential	833	100,123,800
Commercial	89	14,722,600
Industrial	12	24,150,800
Apartments	8	2,488,700
Farm land	8	39,900
Farm homestead	3	557,300

Average Property Value & Tax, 2007
Residential value	$120,432
Property tax	$5,269
Tax credit/rebate	$983

Public Library
Belvidere Public Library
301 Second St
Belvidere, NJ 07823
908-475-3941

Director: Teresa Aicher

Library statistics, 2006
Population served	2,771
Full-time/total staff	0/1

	Total	Per capita
Holdings	24,175	8.72
Revenues	$113,159	$40.84
Expenditures	$122,322	$44.14
Annual visits	12,924	4.66
Internet terminals/annual users		2/302

Public Safety
Number of officers, 2006: 6

Crime	2005	2006
Total crimes	15	20
Violent	4	2
Murder	0	0
Rape	0	0
Robbery	0	0
Aggravated assault	4	2
Non-violent	11	18
Burglary	3	3
Larceny	7	14
Vehicle theft	1	1
Domestic violence	32	34
Arson	0	0
Total crime rate	5.4	7.3
Violent	1.4	0.7
Non-violent	4.0	6.6

Public School District
(for school year 2006-07 except as noted)

Belvidere School District
809 Oxford St
Belvidere, NJ 07823
908-475-6600

Superintendent	Dirk Swaneveld
Number of schools	3
Grade plan	K-12
Enrollment	924
Attendance rate, '05-06	93.9%
Dropout rate	2.2%
Students per teacher	10.6
Per pupil expenditure	$10,323
Median faculty salary	$43,900
Median administrator salary	$86,600
Grade 12 enrollment	140
High school graduation rate	93.8%

Assessment test results
(percent scoring at proficient or advanced level)
	Language	Math
NJASK-Grade 3	97.1%	91.2%
GEPA-Grade 8	75.0%	69.6%
HSPA-High School	88.7%	73.0%

SAT score averages
Pct tested	Math	Verbal	Writing
66%	477	475	467

Teacher Qualifications
Avg. years of experience	9
Highly-qualified teachers one subject/all subjects	100%/96.5%
With emergency credentials	0.0%

No Child Left Behind
AYP, 2005-06: Meets Standards

Municipal Finance
State Aid Programs, 2008
Total aid	$533,784
CMPTRA	0
Energy tax receipts	527,262
Garden State Trust	6,522

General Budget, 2007
Total tax levy	$6,394,202
County levy	1,480,768
County taxes	1,321,516
County library	0
County health	0
County open space	159,251
School levy	3,347,000
Muni. levy	1,566,434
Misc. revenues	1,371,623

Taxes
	2005	2006	2007
General tax rate per $100	3.92	4.15	4.38
County equalization ratio	71.27	64.04	55.61
Net valuation taxable	$145,090,423	$144,076,800	$146,136,632
State equalized value	$226,562,185	$260,569,019	$291,293,290

Bergen County

Bergenfield Borough

Demographics & Socio-Economic Characteristics
(2000 US Census, except as noted)

Population
1980*	25,568
1990*	24,458
2000	26,247
Male	12,534
Female	13,713
2006 (estimate)*	26,194
Population density	9,032.4

Race & Hispanic Origin, 2000

Race
- White 16,510
- Black/African American 1,812
- American Indian/Alaska Native 63
- Asian 5,357
- Native Hawaiian/Pacific Islander 4
- Other race 1,698
- Two or more races 803

Hispanic origin, total 4,474
- Mexican 220
- Puerto Rican 926
- Cuban 247
- Other Hispanic 3,081

Age & Nativity, 2000
- Under 5 years 1,779
- 18 years and over 19,726
- 21 years and over 18,881
- 65 years and over 3,556
- 85 years and over 387
- Median age 37.6
- Native-born 17,810
- Foreign-born 8,437

Educational Attainment, 2000
- Population 25 years and over 17,831
- Less than 9th grade 4.9%
- High school grad or higher 86.6%
- Bachelor's degree or higher 32.3%
- Graduate degree 9.9%

Income & Poverty, 1999
- Per capita income $24,706
- Median household income $62,172
- Median family income $71,187
- Persons in poverty 919
- H'holds receiving public assistance ... 105
- H'holds receiving social security .. 2,593

Households, 2000
- Total households 8,981
-   With persons under 18 3,542
-   With persons over 65 2,656
-   Family households 6,750
-   Single-person households 1,868
- Persons per household 2.92
- Persons per family 3.41

Labor & Employment
- Total civilian labor force, 2006** .. 14,085
-   Unemployment rate 3.7%
- Total civilian labor force, 2000 .. 13,731
-   Unemployment rate 3.6%

Employed persons 16 years and over by occupation, 2000
- Managers & professionals 5,040
- Service occupations 1,898
- Sales & office occupations 3,875
- Farming, fishing & forestry 0
- Construction & maintenance 933
- Production & transportation 1,495
- Self-employed persons 606

* US Census Bureau
** New Jersey Department of Labor
§ State Fiscal Year July 1–June 30

See Introduction for an explanation of all data sources.

General Information
Borough of Bergenfield
198 N Washington Ave
Bergenfield, NJ 07621
201-387-4055

- Website .... www.bergenfield.com
- Year of incorporation 1894
- Land/water area (sq. miles) 2.90/0.00
- Form of government .... Borough

Government

Legislative Districts
- US Congressional 5
- State Legislative 37

Local Officials, 2008
- Mayor .... Timothy J. Driscoll
- Manager .... Catherine Navarro-Steinel
- Clerk .... Catherine Navarro-Steinel
- Finance Dir .... Robert Gilman
- Tax Assessor .... Art Carlson
- Tax Collector .... Barbara Kozay
- Attorney .... Dennis Oury
- Building .... Dennis Mulligan
- Planning .... Louis Castellucci
- Engineering .... AFR Group
- Public Works .... Edward Kneisler
- Police Chief .... Bruce Carlson
- Emerg/Fire Director .... Thomas A. Lodato

Housing & Construction

Housing Units, 2000*
- Total 9,147
- Median rent $855
- Median SF home value $184,400

Permits for New Residential Construction

	Units	Value
Total, 2007	11	$4,074,565
Single family	9	$3,892,365
Total, 2006	17	$3,601,835
Single family	17	$3,601,835

Real Property Valuation, 2007

	Parcels	Valuation
Total	7,295	$2,392,852,755
Vacant	63	10,769,100
Residential	6,876	2,079,827,755
Commercial	258	195,395,400
Industrial	50	33,554,200
Apartments	48	73,306,300
Farm land	0	0
Farm homestead	0	0

Average Property Value & Tax, 2007
- Residential value $302,476
- Property tax $8,804
- Tax credit/rebate $1,365

Public Library
Bergenfield Public Library
50 W Clinton Ave
Bergenfield, NJ 07621
201-387-4040

Director .... Mary Riskind

Library statistics, 2006
- Population served 26,247
- Full-time/total staff 6/19

	Total	Per capita
Holdings	167,795	6.39
Revenues	$1,765,444	$67.26
Expenditures	$1,775,147	$67.63
Annual visits	244,023	9.30
Internet terminals/annual users		14/23,280

Taxes

	2005	2006	2007
General tax rate per $100	2.57	2.75	2.92
County equalization ratio	102.68	89.49	78.37
Net valuation taxable	$2,422,312,290	$2,398,213,755	$2,393,894,036
State equalized value	$2,706,796,614	$3,061,286,059	$3,276,229,832

Public Safety
Number of officers, 2006 46

Crime	2005	2006
Total crimes	212	254
Violent	20	15
Murder	0	0
Rape	0	0
Robbery	12	5
Aggravated assault	8	10
Non-violent	192	239
Burglary	22	50
Larceny	153	168
Vehicle theft	17	21
Domestic violence	192	176
Arson	1	3
Total crime rate	8.1	9.7
Violent	0.8	0.6
Non-violent	7.3	9.2

Public School District
(for school year 2006-07 except as noted)

Bergenfield School District
100 S Prospect Ave
Bergenfield, NJ 07621
201-385-8202

- Superintendent .... Michael Kuchar
- Number of schools 7
- Grade plan K-12
- Enrollment 3,619
- Attendance rate, '05-06 .... 96.1%
- Dropout rate 2.7%
- Students per teacher 11.8
- Per pupil expenditure $13,438
- Median faculty salary $55,995
- Median administrator salary ... $125,699
- Grade 12 enrollment 277
- High school graduation rate 87.8%

Assessment test results
(percent scoring at proficient or advanced level)

	Language	Math
NJASK-Grade 3	89.9%	94.9%
GEPA-Grade 8	70.2%	70.7%
HSPA-High School	92.2%	77.1%

SAT score averages

Pct tested	Math	Verbal	Writing
80%	471	463	455

Teacher Qualifications
- Avg. years of experience 8
- Highly-qualified teachers
    one subject/all subjects 100%/100%
- With emergency credentials 0.0%

No Child Left Behind
AYP, 2005-06 .... Meets Standards

Municipal Finance§

State Aid Programs, 2008
- Total aid $2,421,756
-   CMPTRA 914,532
-   Energy tax receipts 1,507,224
-   Garden State Trust 0

General Budget, 2007
- Total tax levy $69,676,538
-   County levy 5,556,359
-     County taxes 5,250,004
-     County library 0
-     County health 0
-     County open space 306,355
-   School levy 40,614,139
-   Muni. levy 23,506,040
-   Misc. revenues 6,224,071

©2008 Information Publications, Inc. All rights reserved. Photocopying prohibited. For additional copies, contact the publisher at www.informationpublications.com or (877)544-INFO (4636)

Berkeley Heights Township

Union County

Demographics & Socio-Economic Characteristics
(2000 US Census, except as noted)

Population
- 1980*...................................12,549
- 1990*...................................11,980
- 2000....................................13,407
  - Male..................................6,389
  - Female.................................7,018
- 2006 (estimate)*........................13,575
- Population density.....................2,168.5

Race & Hispanic Origin, 2000
Race
- White...................................12,019
- Black/African American....................149
- American Indian/Alaska Native..............11
- Asian...................................1,055
- Native Hawaiian/Pacific Islander............0
- Other race.................................82
- Two or more races..........................91
- Hispanic origin, total....................494
  - Mexican..................................37
  - Puerto Rican.............................93
  - Cuban....................................45
  - Other Hispanic..........................319

Age & Nativity, 2000
- Under 5 years...........................1,070
- 18 years and over.......................9,812
- 21 years and over.......................9,560
- 65 years and over.......................2,200
- 85 years and over.........................354
- Median age...............................39.7
- Native-born............................11,552
- Foreign-born............................1,855

Educational Attainment, 2000
- Population 25 years and over............9,267
- Less than 9th grade......................3.5%
- High school grad or higher..............92.5%
- Bachelor's degree or higher.............52.3%
- Graduate degree.........................23.2%

Income & Poverty, 1999
- Per capita income.....................$43,981
- Median household income..............$107,716
- Median family income.................$118,862
- Persons in poverty........................278
- H'holds receiving public assistance........12
- H'holds receiving social security......1,282

Households, 2000
- Total households........................4,479
  - With persons under 18.................1,910
  - With persons over 65..................1,249
  - Family households.....................3,719
  - Single-person households................661
- Persons per household....................2.89
- Persons per family.......................3.21

Labor & Employment
- Total civilian labor force, 2006**......6,618
  - Unemployment rate......................2.2%
- Total civilian labor force, 2000........6,312
  - Unemployment rate......................2.2%

Employed persons 16 years and over by occupation, 2000
- Managers & professionals................3,494
- Service occupations.......................541
- Sales & office occupations..............1,649
- Farming, fishing & forestry.................0
- Construction & maintenance................297
- Production & transportation...............193
- Self-employed persons.....................464

* US Census Bureau
** New Jersey Department of Labor

General Information
Township of Berkeley Heights
29 Park Ave
Berkeley Heights, NJ 07922
908-464-2700

- Website........www.berkeleyheightstwp.com
- Year of incorporation..................1951
- Land/water area (sq. miles).......6.26/0.01
- Form of government...Mayor-Council-Admin

Government
Legislative Districts
- US Congressional.........................7
- State Legislative.......................21

Local Officials, 2008
- Mayor..................David A. Cohen
- Administrator..............Jack Conway
- Clerk..................Patricia Rapach
- Finance Dir.............Tracy Tedesco
- Tax Assessor.............Stan Belenky
- Tax Collector........Rachele Sanfilippo
- Attorney................Thomas Scrivo
- Building..............Robin Greenwald
- Comm Dev/Planning................NA
- Municipal Engineer.......Jack D'Agostaro
- Public Works......Jack D'Agostaro (Actg)
- Police Chief.................David Zager
- Emerg/Fire Director...Anthony Padovano

Housing & Construction
Housing Units, 2000*
- Total....................................4,562
- Median rent.............................$1,248
- Median SF home value..................$324,900

Permits for New Residential Construction

	Units	Value
Total, 2007	15	$4,367,823
Single family	15	$4,367,823
Total, 2006	27	$5,726,528
Single family	24	$5,576,528

Real Property Valuation, 2007

	Parcels	Valuation
Total	4,666	$1,823,659,020
Vacant	143	24,938,000
Residential	4,375	1,323,139,300
Commercial	110	279,462,800
Industrial	35	190,184,000
Apartments	2	5,934,500
Farm land	1	420
Farm homestead	0	0

Average Property Value & Tax, 2007
- Residential value....................$302,432
- Property tax...........................$9,086
- Tax credit/rebate......................$1,275

Public Library
Berkeley Heights Public Library
290 Plainfield Ave
Berkeley Heights, NJ 07922
908-464-9333

- Director.............Stephanie Bakos

Library statistics, 2006
- Population served......................13,407
- Full-time/total staff......................4/7

	Total	Per capita
Holdings	93,198	6.95
Revenues	$998,892	$74.51
Expenditures	$990,883	$73.91
Annual visits	155,400	11.59
Internet terminals/annual users		16/31,848

Taxes	2005	2006	2007
General tax rate per $100	2.717	2.958	3.005
County equalization ratio	67.34	57.49	55.97
Net valuation taxable	$1,837,988,047	$1,821,418,020	$1,824,842,728
State equalized value	$2,944,549,899	$3,255,565,575	$3,429,114,197

Public Safety
Number of officers, 2006................26

Crime	2005	2006
Total crimes	64	91
Violent	2	5
Murder	0	0
Rape	0	0
Robbery	0	1
Aggravated assault	2	4
Non-violent	62	86
Burglary	4	8
Larceny	52	76
Vehicle theft	6	2
Domestic violence	66	50
Arson	1	0
Total crime rate	4.7	6.7
Violent	0.1	0.4
Non-violent	4.6	6.3

Public School District
(for school year 2006-07 except as noted)

Berkeley Heights School District
345 Plainfield Ave
Berkeley Heights, NJ 07922
908-464-1718

- Superintendent............Judith Rattner
- Number of schools............................6
- Grade plan................................K-12
- Enrollment...............................2,848
- Attendance rate, '05-06..................96.1%
- Dropout rate..............................0.5%
- Students per teacher......................10.8
- Per pupil expenditure..................$13,232
- Median faculty salary..................$58,053
- Median administrator salary...........$113,575
- Grade 12 enrollment........................249
- High school graduation rate..............97.2%

Assessment test results
(percent scoring at proficient or advanced level)

	Language	Math
NJASK-Grade 3	95.1%	94.1%
GEPA-Grade 8	90.3%	84.2%
HSPA-High School	94.5%	89.8%

SAT score averages

Pct tested	Math	Verbal	Writing
99%	576	559	557

Teacher Qualifications
- Avg. years of experience....................8
- Highly-qualified teachers
  - one subject/all subjects.....99.5%/99.5%
- With emergency credentials................0.0%

No Child Left Behind
- AYP, 2005-06............Meets Standards

Municipal Finance
State Aid Programs, 2008
- Total aid..........................$2,082,551
  - CMPTRA............................823,974
  - Energy tax receipts............1,258,577
  - Garden State Trust....................0

General Budget, 2007
- Total tax levy....................$54,821,462
  - County levy....................11,526,421
    - County taxes.................11,030,926
    - County library....................0
    - County health.....................0
    - County open space............495,495
  - School levy....................33,437,645
  - Muni. levy......................9,857,396
- Misc. revenues.....................6,374,739

Ocean County   Berkeley Township

Demographics & Socio-Economic Characteristics
(2000 US Census, except as noted)

Population
- 1980*.................................23,151
- 1990*.................................37,319
- 2000.................................39,991
  - Male..............................17,765
  - Female...........................22,226
- 2006 (estimate)*..................42,577
  - Population density................992.5

Race & Hispanic Origin, 2000
Race
- White..............................38,833
- Black/African American............519
- American Indian/Alaska Native......16
- Asian.................................181
- Native Hawaiian/Pacific Islander.....4
- Other race..........................173
- Two or more races..................265
- Hispanic origin, total..............932
  - Mexican..........................228
  - Puerto Rican......................354
  - Cuban..............................78
  - Other Hispanic....................272

Age & Nativity, 2000
- Under 5 years....................1,089
- 18 years and over................35,433
- 21 years and over................34,738
- 65 years and over................20,806
- 85 years and over.................2,376
- Median age.........................66.3
- Native-born......................37,308
- Foreign-born......................2,680

Educational Attainment, 2000
- Population 25 years and over....34,037
- Less than 9th grade................7.4%
- High school grad or higher........72.4%
- Bachelor's degree or higher......10.3%
- Graduate degree....................2.8%

Income & Poverty, 1999
- Per capita income...............$22,198
- Median household income.........$32,134
- Median family income............$40,208
- Persons in poverty................2,157
- H'holds receiving public assistance....296
- H'holds receiving social security....14,125

Households, 2000
- Total households.................19,828
  - With persons under 18............2,450
  - With persons over 65............13,931
  - Family households...............12,175
  - Single-person households.........7,110
- Persons per household..............1.99
- Persons per family.................2.52

Labor & Employment
- Total civilian labor force, 2006**....12,749
  - Unemployment rate................6.0%
- Total civilian labor force, 2000....11,892
  - Unemployment rate................9.6%

Employed persons 16 years and over by occupation, 2000
- Managers & professionals..........2,945
- Service occupations...............1,557
- Sales & office occupations........3,571
- Farming, fishing & forestry...........0
- Construction & maintenance........1,381
- Production & transportation.......1,302
- Self-employed persons...............607

‡ Branch of county library
* US Census Bureau
** New Jersey Department of Labor

See Introduction for an explanation of all data sources.

General Information
Township of Berkeley
627 Pinewald Keswick Rd
PO Box B
Bayville, NJ 08721
732-244-7400
- Website....................twp.berkeley.nj.us
- Year of incorporation................1875
- Land/water area (sq. miles)....42.90/12.90
- Form of government...........Mayor-Council

Government
Legislative Districts
- US Congressional.......................3
- State Legislative......................9

Local Officials, 2008
- Mayor...................Jason J. Varano
- Manager...............Leonard Roeber
- Clerk..................Beverly M. Carle
- Finance Dir............Frederick Ebenau
- Tax Assessor..............Eric Zanetti
- Tax Collector..............Gerry Dorso
- Attorney..............Patrick Sheehan
- Building.............William I. Schultz
- Planning..................David Roberts
- Engineering.............Chris Theodos
- Public Works..........Steven J. Seiler
- Police Chief.............John Weinlein
- Emerg/Fire Director.........Tom Raneri

Housing & Construction
Housing Units, 2000*
- Total..............................22,288
- Median rent..........................$774
- Median SF home value.............$102,100

Permits for New Residential Construction

	Units	Value
Total, 2007	78	$11,041,411
Single family	78	$11,041,411
Total, 2006	102	$14,913,168
Single family	99	$14,895,668

Real Property Valuation, 2007

	Parcels	Valuation
Total	26,343	$2,653,505,990
Vacant	3,443	49,339,700
Residential	22,666	2,447,836,590
Commercial	200	119,958,300
Industrial	20	11,321,600
Apartments	9	24,756,300
Farm land	3	22,700
Farm homestead	2	270,800

Average Property Value & Tax, 2007
- Residential value................$107,998
- Property tax......................$3,365
- Tax credit/rebate.................$1,024

Public Library
Berkeley Branch Library‡
30 Station Rd
Bayville, NJ 08721
732-269-2144
- Branch Librarian........Heather Andolsen

Library statistics, 2006
see Ocean County profile
for library system statistics

Public Safety
Number of officers, 2006...............70

Crime	2005	2006
Total crimes	769	735
Violent	62	46
Murder	0	0
Rape	2	3
Robbery	12	8
Aggravated assault	48	35
Non-violent	707	689
Burglary	144	167
Larceny	538	511
Vehicle theft	25	11
Domestic violence	460	477
Arson	14	13
Total crime rate	18.1	17.3
Violent	1.5	1.1
Non-violent	16.6	16.2

Public School District
(for school year 2006-07 except as noted)

Berkeley Township School District
53 Central Parkway
Bayville, NJ 08721
732-269-2233
- Superintendent..........Joseph H. Vicari
- Number of schools.....................4
- Grade plan.........................K-6
- Enrollment......................1,908
- Attendance rate, '05-06............94.8%
- Dropout rate.........................NA
- Students per teacher...............10.0
- Per pupil expenditure...........$13,454
- Median faculty salary...........$50,545
- Median administrator salary....$100,000
- Grade 12 enrollment..................NA
- High school graduation rate..........NA

Assessment test results
(percent scoring at proficient or advanced level)

	Language	Math
NJASK-Grade 3	90.2%	92.6%
GEPA-Grade 8	NA	NA
HSPA-High School	NA	NA

SAT score averages

Pct tested	Math	Verbal	Writing
NA	NA	NA	NA

Teacher Qualifications
- Avg. years of experience..............7
- Highly-qualified teachers
  - one subject/all subjects......100%/100%
- With emergency credentials.........0.0%

No Child Left Behind
- AYP, 2005-06........Needs Improvement

Municipal Finance
State Aid Programs, 2008
- Total aid......................$5,573,395
  - CMPTRA........................160,517
  - Energy tax receipts..........5,269,752
  - Garden State Trust.............74,221

General Budget, 2007
- Total tax levy................$82,792,754
  - County levy................18,515,856
    - County taxes..............15,257,885
    - County library.............1,808,334
    - County health...............732,636
    - County open space...........717,001
  - School levy................41,914,581
  - Muni. levy.................22,362,316
  - Misc. revenues.............14,726,554

Taxes

	2005	2006	2007
General tax rate per $100	2.83	2.958	3.117
County equalization ratio	58.55	51.2	44.55
Net valuation taxable	$2,606,388,907	$2,625,562,640	$2,656,968,666
State equalized value	$5,090,603,334	$5,897,441,977	$6,350,044,809

The New Jersey Municipal Data Book

Berlin Borough

Camden County

Demographics & Socio-Economic Characteristics
(2000 US Census, except as noted)

Population
1980*	5,786
1990*	5,672
2000	6,149
Male	3,045
Female	3,104
2006 (estimate)*	7,910
Population density	2,209.5

Race & Hispanic Origin, 2000
Race
White	5,784
Black/African American	134
American Indian/Alaska Native	13
Asian	104
Native Hawaiian/Pacific Islander	4
Other race	30
Two or more races	80
Hispanic origin, total	130
Mexican	8
Puerto Rican	50
Cuban	21
Other Hispanic	51

Age & Nativity, 2000
Under 5 years	335
18 years and over	4,636
21 years and over	4,438
65 years and over	837
85 years and over	91
Median age	38.2
Native-born	5,896
Foreign-born	253

Educational Attainment, 2000
Population 25 years and over	4,222
Less than 9th grade	5.4%
High school grad or higher	84.2%
Bachelor's degree or higher	24.4%
Graduate degree	6.3%

Income & Poverty, 1999
Per capita income	$24,675
Median household income	$60,286
Median family income	$68,704
Persons in poverty	212
H'holds receiving public assistance	29
H'holds receiving social security	654

Households, 2000
Total households	2,205
With persons under 18	817
With persons over 65	581
Family households	1,660
Single-person households	432
Persons per household	2.76
Persons per family	3.19

Labor & Employment
Total civilian labor force, 2006**	3,755
Unemployment rate	4.3%
Total civilian labor force, 2000	3,471
Unemployment rate	4.6%

Employed persons 16 years and over by occupation, 2000
Managers & professionals	1,212
Service occupations	466
Sales & office occupations	971
Farming, fishing & forestry	0
Construction & maintenance	318
Production & transportation	343
Self-employed persons	130

* US Census Bureau
** New Jersey Department of Labor

General Information
Borough of Berlin
59 S White Horse Pike
Berlin, NJ 08009
856-767-7777

Website	www.berlinnj.org
Year of incorporation	1927
Land/water area (sq. miles)	3.58/0.00
Form of government	Borough

Government
Legislative Districts
US Congressional	1
State Legislative	6

Local Officials, 2008
Mayor	Joseph Keskes
Manager	Charleen Santora
Clerk	Charleen Santora
Finance Dir	Karen Wingert
Tax Assessor	Blackwell Albertson
Tax Collector	Lisa Eggert
Attorney	George Botcheos
Building	Anthony Saccomanno
Planning	Valerie Tarus
Engineering	Pennoni Associates
Public Works	Dave Watson
Police Chief	Robert Carrara
Emerg/Fire Director	Paul Miller

Housing & Construction
Housing Units, 2000*
Total	2,275
Median rent	$642
Median SF home value	$135,800

Permits for New Residential Construction
	Units	Value
Total, 2007	17	$1,748,735
Single family	17	$1,748,735
Total, 2006	20	$2,114,315
Single family	20	$2,114,315

Real Property Valuation, 2007
	Parcels	Valuation
Total	2,933	$401,664,940
Vacant	287	11,325,600
Residential	2,470	323,181,200
Commercial	145	56,977,400
Industrial	10	6,539,940
Apartments	14	3,326,800
Farm land	5	69,100
Farm homestead	2	244,900

Average Property Value & Tax, 2007
Residential value	$130,836
Property tax	$5,661
Tax credit/rebate	$1,019

Public Library
M. Fleche Memorial Library
49 S White Horse Pike
Berlin, NJ 08009
856-767-2448

Director ..... Mary Rencic

Library statistics, 2006
Population served	6,149
Full-time/total staff	0/0

	Total	Per capita
Holdings	29,415	4.78
Revenues	$80,180	$13.04
Expenditures	$105,165	$17.10
Annual visits	10,712	1.74
Internet terminals/annual users		3/584

Taxes
	2005	2006	2007
General tax rate per $100	3.924	4.192	4.328
County equalization ratio	72.12	64.03	55.88
Net valuation taxable	$388,627,543	$393,147,240	$404,749,492
State equalized value	$606,946,030	$707,038,122	$791,590,520

Public Safety
Number of officers, 2006 18

Crime	2005	2006
Total crimes	198	223
Violent	5	8
Murder	0	0
Rape	0	0
Robbery	4	5
Aggravated assault	1	3
Non-violent	193	215
Burglary	25	35
Larceny	157	170
Vehicle theft	11	10
Domestic violence	48	31
Arson	1	2
Total crime rate	26.1	28.4
Violent	0.7	1.0
Non-violent	25.4	27.4

Public School District
(for school year 2006-07 except as noted)

Berlin Borough School District
215 South Franklin Ave
Berlin, NJ 08009
856-767-6785

Superintendent	Leonard Binowski
Number of schools	1
Grade plan	K-8
Enrollment	813
Attendance rate, '05-06	95.3%
Dropout rate	NA
Students per teacher	12.1
Per pupil expenditure	$10,180
Median faculty salary	$50,475
Median administrator salary	$98,864
Grade 12 enrollment	NA
High school graduation rate	NA

Assessment test results
(percent scoring at proficient or advanced level)
	Language	Math
NJASK-Grade 3	96.6%	96.6%
GEPA-Grade 8	88.6%	74.7%
HSPA-High School	NA	NA

SAT score averages
Pct tested	Math	Verbal	Writing
NA	NA	NA	NA

Teacher Qualifications
Avg. years of experience	9
Highly-qualified teachers one subject/all subjects	100%/100%
With emergency credentials	0.0%

No Child Left Behind
AYP, 2005-06 ..... Meets Standards

Municipal Finance
State Aid Programs, 2008
Total aid	$810,395
CMPTRA	150,627
Energy tax receipts	659,767
Garden State Trust	1

General Budget, 2007
Total tax levy	$17,513,725
County levy	5,049,555
County taxes	4,583,023
County library	321,987
County health	0
County open space	144,544
School levy	9,457,290
Muni. levy	3,006,881
Misc. revenues	3,498,024

Camden County

Berlin Township

Demographics & Socio-Economic Characteristics
(2000 US Census, except as noted)

Population
- 1980* 5,348
- 1990* 5,466
- 2000 5,290
  - Male 2,632
  - Female 2,658
- 2006 (estimate)* 5,405
- Population density 1,663.1

Race & Hispanic Origin, 2000
Race
- White 4,362
- Black/African American 628
- American Indian/Alaska Native 9
- Asian 143
- Native Hawaiian/Pacific Islander ... 4
- Other race 64
- Two or more races 80
- Hispanic origin, total 254
  - Mexican 146
  - Puerto Rican 72
  - Cuban 6
  - Other Hispanic 30

Age & Nativity, 2000
- Under 5 years 352
- 18 years and over 3,926
- 21 years and over 3,722
- 65 years and over 663
- 85 years and over 69
- Median age 35.9
- Native-born 5,015
- Foreign-born 275

Educational Attainment, 2000
- Population 25 years and over ... 3,495
- Less than 9th grade 5.6%
- High school grad or higher 76.7%
- Bachelor's degree or higher ... 15.1%
- Graduate degree 4.3%

Income & Poverty, 1999
- Per capita income $22,178
- Median household income $54,448
- Median family income $61,042
- Persons in poverty 312
- H'holds receiving public assistance ... 37
- H'holds receiving social security 565

Households, 2000
- Total households 1,893
  - With persons under 18 736
  - With persons over 65 510
  - Family households 1,368
  - Single-person households 427
- Persons per household 2.78
- Persons per family 3.28

Labor & Employment
- Total civilian labor force, 2006** ... 3,002
  - Unemployment rate 3.1%
- Total civilian labor force, 2000 ... 2,774
  - Unemployment rate 3.6%

Employed persons 16 years and over by occupation, 2000
- Managers & professionals 728
- Service occupations 518
- Sales & office occupations 695
- Farming, fishing & forestry 0
- Construction & maintenance 422
- Production & transportation 310
- Self-employed persons 75

‡ Branch of county library
* US Census Bureau
** New Jersey Department of Labor
§ State Fiscal Year July 1–June 30

See Introduction for an explanation of all data sources.

General Information
Township of Berlin
170 Bate Ave
West Berlin, NJ 08091
856-767-1854

- Website .... www.berlintwp.com
- Year of incorporation 1910
- Land/water area (sq. miles) 3.25/0.00
- Form of government ... Small Municipality

Government
Legislative Districts
- US Congressional 1
- State Legislative 6

Local Officials, 2008
- Mayor .... Phyllis Jeffries-Magazzu
- Manager/Admin .... NA
- Clerk .... Jamey Eggers
- Finance Dir .... Lori Campisano
- Tax Assessor .... Anthony Colavecchio
- Tax Collector .... NA
- Attorney .... Donafaye Zoll
- Building .... Mike DePalma
- Comm Dev/Planning .... NA
- Engineering .... Charles Riebel Jr
- Public Works .... NA
- Police Chief .... Michael Hayden
- Emerg/Fire Director ..... Joseph Jackson

Housing & Construction
Housing Units, 2000*
- Total 2,009
- Median rent $590
- Median SF home value $109,600

Permits for New Residential Construction

	Units	Value
Total, 2007	23	$3,657,844
Single family	23	$3,657,844
Total, 2006	15	$934,235
Single family	15	$934,235

Real Property Valuation, 2007

	Parcels	Valuation
Total	2,356	$338,944,800
Vacant	270	10,810,400
Residential	1,682	173,496,100
Commercial	341	118,941,200
Industrial	50	31,533,000
Apartments	3	3,955,600
Farm land	8	42,100
Farm homestead	2	166,400

Average Property Value & Tax, 2007
- Residential value $103,125
- Property tax $4,639
- Tax credit/rebate $955

Public Library
Berlin Township Library‡
201 Veteran's Ave
West Berlin, NJ 08901
856-767-0439

- Director .... Mary Holt

Library statistics, 2006
see Camden County profile for library system statistics

Taxes

	2005	2006	2007
General tax rate per $100	4.111	4.381	4.499
County equalization ratio	82.14	73.26	63.03
Net valuation taxable	$328,956,262	$332,937,700	$339,541,019
State equalized value	$449,025,747	$528,862,022	$583,476,357

Public Safety
Number of officers, 2006 19

Crime

Crime	2005	2006
Total crimes	232	202
Violent	21	15
Murder	1	0
Rape	6	0
Robbery	4	3
Aggravated assault	10	12
Non-violent	211	187
Burglary	22	31
Larceny	178	144
Vehicle theft	11	12
Domestic violence	49	54
Arson	2	7
Total crime rate	43.2	37.4
Violent	3.9	2.8
Non-violent	39.3	34.6

Public School District
(for school year 2006-07 except as noted)

Berlin Township School District
225 Grove Ave
West Berlin, NJ 08091
856-767-9480

- Superintendent .... Brian J. Betze
- Number of schools 2
- Grade plan K-8
- Enrollment 615
- Attendance rate, '05-06 .... 97.8%
- Dropout rate .... NA
- Students per teacher 8.3
- Per pupil expenditure $13,217
- Median faculty salary $49,738
- Median administrator salary ... $91,327
- Grade 12 enrollment .... NA
- High school graduation rate ...... NA

Assessment test results
(percent scoring at proficient or advanced level)

	Language	Math
NJASK-Grade 3	81.8%	78.2%
GEPA-Grade 8	63.1%	71.4%
HSPA-High School	NA	NA

SAT score averages

Pct tested	Math	Verbal	Writing
NA	NA	NA	NA

Teacher Qualifications
- Avg. years of experience 10
- Highly-qualified teachers
  - one subject/all subjects ... 100%/100%
- With emergency credentials 0.0%

No Child Left Behind
- AYP, 2005-06 .... Meets Standards

Municipal Finance§
State Aid Programs, 2008
- Total aid $1,554,441
- CMPTRA 0
- Energy tax receipts 1,554,121
- Garden State Trust 0

General Budget, 2007
- Total tax levy $15,272,941
- County levy 3,784,890
  - County taxes 3,438,002
  - County library 239,413
  - County health 0
  - County open space 107,476
- School levy 7,815,485
- Muni. levy 3,672,566
- Misc. revenues 3,389,350

Bernards Township
Somerset County

Demographics & Socio-Economic Characteristics
(2000 US Census, except as noted)

Population
1980*	12,920
1990*	17,199
2000	24,575
Male	11,945
Female	12,630
2006 (estimate)*	27,140
Population density	1,130.8

Race & Hispanic Origin, 2000
Race
White	21,921
Black/African American	354
American Indian/Alaska Native	13
Asian	1,928
Native Hawaiian/Pacific Islander	3
Other race	98
Two or more races	258
Hispanic origin, total	646
Mexican	60
Puerto Rican	105
Cuban	82
Other Hispanic	399

Age & Nativity, 2000
Under 5 years	1,962
18 years and over	17,770
21 years and over	17,403
65 years and over	3,063
85 years and over	383
Median age	39.2
Native-born	21,499
Foreign-born	3,076

Educational Attainment, 2000
Population 25 years and over	16,950
Less than 9th grade	1.8%
High school grad or higher	95.8%
Bachelor's degree or higher	67.4%
Graduate degree	30.6%

Income & Poverty, 1999
Per capita income	$56,521
Median household income	$107,204
Median family income	$135,806
Persons in poverty	319
H'holds receiving public assistance	55
H'holds receiving social security	1,927

Households, 2000
Total households	9,242
With persons under 18	3,549
With persons over 65	2,004
Family households	6,484
Single-person households	2,442
Persons per household	2.58
Persons per family	3.17

Labor & Employment
Total civilian labor force, 2006**	14,105
Unemployment rate	2.6%
Total civilian labor force, 2000	12,279
Unemployment rate	2.7%

Employed persons 16 years and over by occupation, 2000
Managers & professionals	7,651
Service occupations	629
Sales & office occupations	2,835
Farming, fishing & forestry	0
Construction & maintenance	379
Production & transportation	452
Self-employed persons	713

* US Census Bureau
** New Jersey Department of Labor

General Information
Township of Bernards
1 Collyer Ln
Basking Ridge, NJ 07920
908-766-2510

Website	www.bernards.org
Year of incorporation	1760
Land/water area (sq. miles)	24.00/0.01
Form of government	Township

Government
Legislative Districts
US Congressional	11
State Legislative	16

Local Officials, 2008
Mayor	John Carpenter
Manager	Bruce McArthur
Clerk	Denise Szabo
Finance Dir	Bruce McArthur
Tax Assessor	Marcia Sudano
Tax Collector	Peggy Warren
Attorney	John Belardo
Building	Dennis Bettler
Planning	Peter Messina
Engineering	Peter Messina
Public Works	Pat Monaco
Police Chief	Dennis Mott
Fire Chief	Brandon Watt (Basking Ridge)

Housing & Construction
Housing Units, 2000*
Total	9,485
Median rent	$1,494
Median SF home value	$380,500

Permits for New Residential Construction
	Units	Value
Total, 2007	22	$9,124,910
Single family	22	$9,124,910
Total, 2006	21	$9,127,000
Single family	21	$9,127,000

Real Property Valuation, 2007
	Parcels	Valuation
Total	10,042	$7,138,231,800
Vacant	304	38,810,400
Residential	9,489	6,211,176,500
Commercial	160	848,521,100
Industrial	7	7,748,900
Apartments	2	8,540,100
Farm land	51	336,800
Farm homestead	29	23,098,000

Average Property Value & Tax, 2007
Residential value	$654,998
Property tax	$9,965
Tax credit/rebate	$1,156

Public Library
Bernards Township Library
32 S Maple Ave
Basking Ridge, NJ 07920
908-204-3031

Director .... Anne Meany

Library statistics, 2006
Population served	24,575
Full-time/total staff	8/15

	Total	Per capita
Holdings	143,340	5.83
Revenues	$2,161,669	$87.96
Expenditures	$1,934,879	$78.73
Annual visits	212,876	8.66
Internet terminals/annual users	19/151,892	

Taxes
	2005	2006	2007
General tax rate per $100	1.55	1.49	1.53
County equalization ratio	108.69	108.55	100.71
Net valuation taxable	$6,406,611,095	$7,017,642,325	$7,145,579,652
State equalized value	$6,423,955,776	$6,964,618,232	$7,202,420,728

Public Safety
Number of officers, 2006 38

Crime	2005	2006
Total crimes	168	172
Violent	2	8
Murder	0	1
Rape	0	3
Robbery	0	0
Aggravated assault	2	4
Non-violent	166	164
Burglary	36	42
Larceny	124	115
Vehicle theft	6	7
Domestic violence	119	123
Arson	2	3
Total crime rate	6.2	6.4
Violent	0.1	0.3
Non-violent	6.2	6.1

Public School District
(for school year 2006-07 except as noted)

Bernards Township School District
101 Peachtree Rd
Basking Ridge, NJ 07920
908-204-2600

Superintendent	Valerie A. Goger
Number of schools	6
Grade plan	K-12
Enrollment	5,315
Attendance rate, '05-06	96.3%
Dropout rate	0.3%
Students per teacher	10.9
Per pupil expenditure	$12,460
Median faculty salary	$53,641
Median administrator salary	$106,917
Grade 12 enrollment	358
High school graduation rate	98.6%

Assessment test results
(percent scoring at proficient or advanced level)
	Language	Math
NJASK-Grade 3	96.5%	97.7%
GEPA-Grade 8	96.8%	93.8%
HSPA-High School	98.7%	94.8%

SAT score averages
Pct tested	Math	Verbal	Writing
103%	594	570	567

Teacher Qualifications
Avg. years of experience	6
Highly-qualified teachers one subject/all subjects	100%/100%
With emergency credentials	0.6%

No Child Left Behind
AYP, 2005-06 .... Meets Standards

Municipal Finance
State Aid Programs, 2008
Total aid	$2,408,717
CMPTRA	90,040
Energy tax receipts	2,318,677
Garden State Trust	0

General Budget, 2007
Total tax levy	$108,709,902
County levy	21,582,647
County taxes	19,452,477
County library	0
County health	0
County open space	2,130,170
School levy	68,260,463
Muni. levy	18,866,792
Misc. revenues	20,819,977

Somerset County
Bernardsville Borough

Demographics & Socio-Economic Characteristics
(2000 US Census, except as noted)

Population
1980*	6,715
1990*	6,597
2000	7,345
Male	3,599
Female	3,746
2006 (estimate)*	7,688
Population density	594.6

Race & Hispanic Origin, 2000
Race
White	6,900
Black/African American	18
American Indian/Alaska Native	11
Asian	194
Native Hawaiian/Pacific Islander	0
Other race	114
Two or more races	108
Hispanic origin, total	439
Mexican	28
Puerto Rican	21
Cuban	10
Other Hispanic	380

Age & Nativity, 2000
Under 5 years	557
18 years and over	5,430
21 years and over	5,280
65 years and over	933
85 years and over	76
Median age	40.0
Native-born	6,428
Foreign-born	917

Educational Attainment, 2000
Population 25 years and over	5,129
Less than 9th grade	2.3%
High school grad or higher	92.3%
Bachelor's degree or higher	59.6%
Graduate degree	24.3%

Income & Poverty, 1999
Per capita income	$69,854
Median household income	$104,162
Median family income	$126,601
Persons in poverty	202
H'holds receiving public assistance	21
H'holds receiving social security	732

Households, 2000
Total households	2,723
With persons under 18	1,010
With persons over 65	669
Family households	2,050
Single-person households	573
Persons per household	2.69
Persons per family	3.12

Labor & Employment
Total civilian labor force, 2006**	4,304
Unemployment rate	1.5%
Total civilian labor force, 2000	3,831
Unemployment rate	1.4%

Employed persons 16 years and over by occupation, 2000
Managers & professionals	1,999
Service occupations	477
Sales & office occupations	905
Farming, fishing & forestry	0
Construction & maintenance	190
Production & transportation	208
Self-employed persons	382

* US Census Bureau
** New Jersey Department of Labor

General Information
Borough of Bernardsville
166 Mine Brook Road
Bernardsville, NJ 07924
908-766-3000

Website	www.bernardsvilleboro.org
Year of incorporation	1924
Land/water area (sq. miles)	12.93/0.01
Form of government	Borough

Government
Legislative Districts
US Congressional	7
State Legislative	16

Local Officials, 2008
Mayor	Lee Honecker
Manager	Ralph Maresca Jr
Clerk	Sandra Jones
Finance Dir	Ralph Maresca Jr
Tax Assessor	Marcia Sudano
Tax Collector	Antonietta Marino
Attorney	John Pidgeon
Building	Len Perre
Planning	Michael Mondok
Engineering	Paul Ferriero
Public Works	John Macdowall
Police Chief	Kevin Valentine
Emerg/Fire Director	Jerry Negri Jr

Housing & Construction
Housing Units, 2000*
Total	2,807
Median rent	$1,039
Median SF home value	$409,700

Permits for New Residential Construction
	Units	Value
Total, 2007	15	$11,739,800
Single family	15	$11,739,800
Total, 2006	10	$6,612,905
Single family	10	$6,612,905

Real Property Valuation, 2007
	Parcels	Valuation
Total	3,012	$2,672,330,480
Vacant	152	40,959,700
Residential	2,494	2,294,001,600
Commercial	167	182,741,600
Industrial	26	20,673,500
Apartments	12	8,889,300
Farm land	101	509,780
Farm homestead	60	124,555,000

Average Property Value & Tax, 2007
Residential value	$946,968
Property tax	$12,689
Tax credit/rebate	$1,150

Public Library
Bernardsville Public Library
1 Anderson Hill Rd
Bernardsville, NJ 07924
908-766-0118

Director . . . . Karen Brodsky

Library statistics, 2006
Population served	7,345
Full-time/total staff	4/6

	Total	Per capita
Holdings	101,058	13.76
Revenues	$970,101	$132.08
Expenditures	$900,262	$122.57
Annual visits	197,286	26.86
Internet terminals/annual users	39/84,382	

Taxes
	2005	2006	2007
General tax rate per $100	1.41	1.33	1.34
County equalization ratio	111.04	108.75	104.29
Net valuation taxable	$2,342,570,600	$2,588,197,080	$2,678,361,185
State equalized value	$2,376,555,341	$2,549,311,975	$2,644,066,717

Public Safety
Number of officers, 2006 18

Crime	2005	2006
Total crimes	74	68
Violent	1	2
Murder	0	0
Rape	0	1
Robbery	0	0
Aggravated assault	1	1
Non-violent	73	66
Burglary	15	7
Larceny	57	58
Vehicle theft	1	1
Domestic violence	36	52
Arson	0	0
Total crime rate	9.7	8.9
Violent	0.1	0.3
Non-violent	9.6	8.7

Public School District
(for school year 2006-07 except as noted)

Somerset Hills Regional School District
25 Olcott Ave
Bernardsville, NJ 07924
908-630-3011

Superintendent	Peter Miller
Number of schools	9
Grade plan	K-12
Enrollment	2,022
Attendance rate, '05-06	96.0%
Dropout rate	0.3%
Students per teacher	11.0
Per pupil expenditure	$15,675
Median faculty salary	$61,868
Median administrator salary	$132,115
Grade 12 enrollment	181
High school graduation rate	98.9%

Assessment test results
(percent scoring at proficient or advanced level)
	Language	Math
NJASK-Grade 3	94.4%	99.3%
GEPA-Grade 8	89.5%	86.2%
HSPA-High School	97.2%	92.7%

SAT score averages
Pct tested	Math	Verbal	Writing
91%	575	561	558

Teacher Qualifications
Avg. years of experience	10
Highly-qualified teachers one subject/all subjects	100%/100%
With emergency credentials	0.0%

No Child Left Behind
AYP, 2005-06 . . . . Meets Standards

Municipal Finance
State Aid Programs, 2008
Total aid	$879,323
CMPTRA	37,268
Energy tax receipts	842,055
Garden State Trust	0

General Budget, 2007
Total tax levy	$35,887,759
County levy	7,800,663
County taxes	7,030,645
County library	0
County health	0
County open space	770,018
School levy	20,259,574
Muni. levy	7,827,522
Misc. revenues	4,527,643

Bethlehem Township
Hunterdon County

Demographics & Socio-Economic Characteristics
(2000 US Census, except as noted)

Population
- 1980* ... 3,045
- 1990* ... 3,104
- 2000 ... 3,820
  - Male ... 1,921
  - Female ... 1,899
- 2006 (estimate)* ... 4,008
- Population density ... 192.3

Race & Hispanic Origin, 2000
Race
- White ... 3,725
- Black/African American ... 33
- American Indian/Alaska Native ... 4
- Asian ... 39
- Native Hawaiian/Pacific Islander ... 2
- Other race ... 1
- Two or more races ... 16
- Hispanic origin, total ... 62
  - Mexican ... 5
  - Puerto Rican ... 25
  - Cuban ... 8
  - Other Hispanic ... 24

Age & Nativity, 2000
- Under 5 years ... 283
- 18 years and over ... 2,693
- 21 years and over ... 2,598
- 65 years and over ... 249
- 85 years and over ... 27
  - Median age ... 38.8
- Native-born ... 3,634
- Foreign-born ... 186

Educational Attainment, 2000
- Population 25 years and over ... 2,499
- Less than 9th grade ... 3.6%
- High school grad or higher ... 92.3%
- Bachelor's degree or higher ... 45.3%
- Graduate degree ... 18.6%

Income & Poverty, 1999
- Per capita income ... $35,298
- Median household income ... $88,048
- Median family income ... $92,768
- Persons in poverty ... 40
- H'holds receiving public assistance ... 7
- H'holds receiving social security ... 221

Households, 2000
- Total households ... 1,266
  - With persons under 18 ... 575
  - With persons over 65 ... 188
  - Family households ... 1,093
  - Single-person households ... 131
- Persons per household ... 3.02
- Persons per family ... 3.26

Labor & Employment
- Total civilian labor force, 2006** ... 2,275
  - Unemployment rate ... 2.0%
- Total civilian labor force, 2000 ... 2,028
  - Unemployment rate ... 1.4%

Employed persons 16 years and over by occupation, 2000
- Managers & professionals ... 958
- Service occupations ... 172
- Sales & office occupations ... 538
- Farming, fishing & forestry ... 15
- Construction & maintenance ... 236
- Production & transportation ... 80
- Self-employed persons ... 124

* US Census Bureau
** New Jersey Department of Labor

General Information
Township of Bethlehem
405 Mine Rd
Asbury, NJ 08802
908-735-4107

- Website ... www.bethlehemnj.org
- Year of incorporation ... 1730
- Land/water area (sq. miles) ... 20.84/0.00
- Form of government ... Township

Government
Legislative Districts
- US Congressional ... 7
- State Legislative ... 23

Local Officials, 2008
- Mayor ... John Graefe
- Manager ... Diane Pflugfelder
- Clerk ... Diane Pflugfelder
- Finance Dir ... Edward P. Rees
- Tax Assessor ... Eloise Hagaman
- Tax Collector ... Steve Davis
- Attorney ... Robert Kenny
- Building ... NA
- Comm Dev/Planning ... NA
- Engineering ... Robert O'Brien
- Public Works ... Steve Douglas
- Police Chief ... NA
- Fire/Emergency Dir ... NA

Housing & Construction
Housing Units, 2000*
- Total ... 1,303
- Median rent ... $750
- Median SF home value ... $278,400

Permits for New Residential Construction

	Units	Value
Total, 2007	1	$72,360
Single family	1	$72,360
Total, 2006	2	$321,400
Single family	2	$321,400

Real Property Valuation, 2007

	Parcels	Valuation
Total	1,794	$526,352,628
Vacant	153	7,322,000
Residential	1,268	447,447,700
Commercial	24	21,090,800
Industrial	7	8,333,000
Apartments	0	0
Farm land	214	1,946,328
Farm homestead	128	40,212,800

Average Property Value & Tax, 2007
- Residential value ... $349,327
- Property tax ... $9,708
- Tax credit/rebate ... $1,294

Public Library
No public municipal library

Library statistics, 2006
- Population served ... NA
- Full-time/total staff ... NA/NA

	Total	Per capita
Holdings	NA	NA
Revenues	NA	NA
Expenditures	NA	NA
Annual visits	NA	NA
Internet terminals/annual users	NA/NA	

Taxes

	2005	2006	2007
General tax rate per $100	2.65	2.7	2.78
County equalization ratio	83.14	78.47	74.59
Net valuation taxable	$522,659,062	$522,301,828	$527,063,675
State equalized value	$610,654,354	$670,498,896	$693,553,785

Public Safety
Number of officers, 2006 ... 0

Crime	2005	2006
Total crimes	20	14
Violent	0	1
Murder	0	0
Rape	0	0
Robbery	0	0
Aggravated assault	0	1
Non-violent	20	13
Burglary	7	4
Larceny	11	5
Vehicle theft	2	4
Domestic violence	5	1
Arson	1	0
Total crime rate	5.0	3.5
Violent	0.0	0.3
Non-violent	5.0	3.3

Public School District
(for school year 2006-07 except as noted)

Bethlehem Township School District
940 Iron Bridge Rd
Asbury, NJ 08802
908-537-4044

- Superintendent ... Carol Conger (Int)
- Number of schools ... 2
- Grade plan ... K-8
- Enrollment ... 622
- Attendance rate, '05-06 ... 96.4%
- Dropout rate ... NA
- Students per teacher ... 9.4
- Per pupil expenditure ... $12,844
- Median faculty salary ... $48,891
- Median administrator salary ... $104,878
- Grade 12 enrollment ... NA
- High school graduation rate ... NA

Assessment test results
(percent scoring at proficient or advanced level)

	Language	Math
NJASK-Grade 3	93.3%	93.3%
GEPA-Grade 8	87.1%	85.7%
HSPA-High School	NA	NA

SAT score averages

Pct tested	Math	Verbal	Writing
NA	NA	NA	NA

Teacher Qualifications
- Avg. years of experience ... 9
- Highly-qualified teachers
  - one subject/all subjects ... 100%/100%
- With emergency credentials ... 2.1%

No Child Left Behind
- AYP, 2005-06 ... Meets Standards

Municipal Finance
State Aid Programs, 2008
- Total aid ... $290,918
  - CMPTRA ... 0
  - Energy tax receipts ... 279,603
  - Garden State Trust ... 11,315

General Budget, 2007
- Total tax levy ... $14,646,743
  - County levy ... 2,348,852
    - County taxes ... 1,965,758
    - County library ... 171,058
    - County health ... 0
    - County open space ... 212,037
  - School levy ... 10,553,340
  - Muni. levy ... 1,744,551
- Misc. revenues ... 1,704,843

Burlington County

Beverly City

Demographics & Socio-Economic Characteristics
(2000 US Census, except as noted)

Population
1980*	2,919
1990*	2,973
2000	2,661
Male	1,251
Female	1,410
2006 (estimate)*	2,651
Population density	4,570.7

Race & Hispanic Origin, 2000
Race
White	1,721
Black/African American	765
American Indian/Alaska Native	3
Asian	24
Native Hawaiian/Pacific Islander	0
Other race	38
Two or more races	110
Hispanic origin, total	122
Mexican	6
Puerto Rican	88
Cuban	3
Other Hispanic	25

Age & Nativity, 2000
Under 5 years	172
18 years and over	1,907
21 years and over	1,784
65 years and over	314
85 years and over	33
Median age	35.0
Native-born	2,596
Foreign-born	65

Educational Attainment, 2000
Population 25 years and over	1,689
Less than 9th grade	4.5%
High school grad or higher	77.0%
Bachelor's degree or higher	11.2%
Graduate degree	4.6%

Income & Poverty, 1999
Per capita income	$17,760
Median household income	$45,054
Median family income	$49,519
Persons in poverty	302
H'holds receiving public assistance	25
H'holds receiving social security	256

Households, 2000
Total households	960
With persons under 18	381
With persons over 65	244
Family households	694
Single-person households	207
Persons per household	2.77
Persons per family	3.23

Labor & Employment
Total civilian labor force, 2006**	1,603
Unemployment rate	9.5%
Total civilian labor force, 2000	1,368
Unemployment rate	8.4%

Employed persons 16 years and over by occupation, 2000
Managers & professionals	276
Service occupations	288
Sales & office occupations	311
Farming, fishing & forestry	0
Construction & maintenance	126
Production & transportation	252
Self-employed persons	62

‡ Joint library with Edgewater Park
* US Census Bureau
** New Jersey Department of Labor

See Introduction for an explanation of all data sources.

General Information
City of Beverly
446 Broad St
Beverly, NJ 08010
609-387-1881

Website	beverlycitynj.com
Year of incorporation	1857
Land/water area (sq. miles)	0.58/0.20
Form of government	City

Government
Legislative Districts
US Congressional	3
State Legislative	7

Local Officials, 2008
Mayor	Jean C. Wetherill
Manager	Barbara A. Sheipe
Clerk	Barbara A. Sheipe
Finance Dir	Victoria Boras
Tax Assessor	Joseph Robinson
Tax Collector	Victoria Boras
Attorney	Skip Reale
Building	Daniel McGonigle
Comm Dev/Planning	NA
Engineering	William Kirchner
Public Works	Daniel Schoen
Public Safety Dir	Michael Morton
Emerg/Fire Director	Ray Rodarmel

Housing & Construction
Housing Units, 2000*
Total	1,042
Median rent	$645
Median SF home value	$94,300

Permits for New Residential Construction
	Units	Value
Total, 2007	5	$296,400
Single family	5	$296,400
Total, 2006	1	$62,188
Single family	1	$62,188

Real Property Valuation, 2007
	Parcels	Valuation
Total	985	$83,299,800
Vacant	60	709,500
Residential	862	75,064,400
Commercial	45	4,595,300
Industrial	13	2,130,200
Apartments	5	800,400
Farm land	0	0
Farm homestead	0	0

Average Property Value & Tax, 2007
Residential value	$87,082
Property tax	$4,483
Tax credit/rebate	$919

Public Library
Beverly Public Library‡
441 Cooper St
Beverly, NJ 08010
609-387-1259

Director	Tracey Hall

Library statistics, 2006
Population served	2,661
Full-time/total staff	NA/0

	Total	Per capita
Holdings	NA	NA
Revenues	NA	NA
Expenditures	NA	NA
Annual visits	NA	NA
Internet terminals/annual users	NA/NA	

Taxes
	2005	2006	2007
General tax rate per $100	4.658	4.963	5.15
County equalization ratio	79.2	69.77	61.91
Net valuation taxable	$83,097,206	$82,852,900	$83,395,044
State equalized value	$119,101,628	$133,931,508	$149,646,052

Public Safety
Number of officers, 2006		6

Crime	2005	2006
Total crimes	68	82
Violent	14	15
Murder	0	0
Rape	2	5
Robbery	3	0
Aggravated assault	9	10
Non-violent	54	67
Burglary	20	18
Larceny	28	38
Vehicle theft	6	11
Domestic violence	80	48
Arson	0	1
Total crime rate	25.3	30.7
Violent	5.2	5.6
Non-violent	20.1	25.1

Public School District
(for school year 2006-07 except as noted)

Beverly City School District
601 Bentley Ave
Beverly, NJ 08010
609-387-2200

Superintendent	Glenn T. Gray
Number of schools	1
Grade plan	K-8
Enrollment	277
Attendance rate, '05-06	94.1%
Dropout rate	NA
Students per teacher	9.5
Per pupil expenditure	$12,708
Median faculty salary	$44,288
Median administrator salary	$107,330
Grade 12 enrollment	2
High school graduation rate	NA

Assessment test results
(percent scoring at proficient or advanced level)
	Language	Math
NJASK-Grade 3	58.6%	71.4%
GEPA-Grade 8	56.0%	68.0%
HSPA-High School	NA	NA

SAT score averages
Pct tested	Math	Verbal	Writing
NA	NA	NA	NA

Teacher Qualifications
Avg. years of experience	10
Highly-qualified teachers one subject/all subjects	100%/100%
With emergency credentials	4.2%

No Child Left Behind
AYP, 2005-06	Meets Standards

Municipal Finance
State Aid Programs, 2008
Total aid	$213,181
CMPTRA	0
Energy tax receipts	213,181
Garden State Trust	0

General Budget, 2007
Total tax levy	$4,293,066
County levy	567,908
County taxes	470,593
County library	43,184
County health	0
County open space	54,131
School levy	2,527,439
Muni. levy	1,197,719
Misc. revenues	1,609,410

Blairstown Township — Warren County

Demographics & Socio-Economic Characteristics
(2000 US Census, except as noted)

Population
1980*	4,360
1990*	5,331
2000	5,747
Male	2,866
Female	2,881
2006 (estimate)*	5,982
Population density	192.8

Race & Hispanic Origin, 2000
Race
- White 5,642
- Black/African American 15
- American Indian/Alaska Native 8
- Asian 32
- Native Hawaiian/Pacific Islander 1
- Other race 16
- Two or more races 33

Hispanic origin, total 114
- Mexican 6
- Puerto Rican 35
- Cuban 15
- Other Hispanic 58

Age & Nativity, 2000
- Under 5 years 335
- 18 years and over 4,278
- 21 years and over 4,110
- 65 years and over 713
- 85 years and over 79
- Median age 40.4
- Native-born 5,450
- Foreign-born 298

Educational Attainment, 2000
- Population 25 years and over 3,957
- Less than 9th grade 5.1%
- High school grad or higher 86.7%
- Bachelor's degree or higher 29.8%
- Graduate degree 12.7%

Income & Poverty, 1999
- Per capita income $27,775
- Median household income $64,809
- Median family income $71,214
- Persons in poverty 261
- H'holds receiving public assistance 27
- H'holds receiving social security 582

Households, 2000
- Total households 2,040
- With persons under 18 773
- With persons over 65 519
- Family households 1,638
- Single-person households 312
- Persons per household 2.81
- Persons per family 3.14

Labor & Employment
- Total civilian labor force, 2006** 3,428
- Unemployment rate 4.6%
- Total civilian labor force, 2000 2,994
- Unemployment rate 3.9%

Employed persons 16 years and over by occupation, 2000
- Managers & professionals 1,274
- Service occupations 208
- Sales & office occupations 641
- Farming, fishing & forestry 17
- Construction & maintenance 387
- Production & transportation 350
- Self-employed persons 221

‡ Branch of county library
* US Census Bureau
** New Jersey Department of Labor

General Information
Township of Blairstown
106 Route 94
Blairstown, NJ 07825
908-362-6663

- Website ..... www.blairstown-nj.org
- Year of incorporation 1845
- Land/water area (sq. miles) 31.02/0.75
- Form of government ..... Township

Government
Legislative Districts
- US Congressional 5
- State Legislative 23

Local Officials, 2008
- Mayor ..... Stephen J. Lance
- Manager/Admin ..... NA
- Clerk ..... Phyllis E. Pizzaia
- Finance Dir ..... Barbara Emery
- Tax Assessor ..... Lydia Schmidt
- Tax Collector ..... Rita Kelley
- Attorney ..... Robert Benbrook
- Building ..... Ralph Price
- Comm Dev/Planning ..... NA
- Engineering ..... Norton B. Rodman
- Public Works ..... Robert DePuy
- Police Chief ..... Tom Krisak
- Fire Chief ..... William Weinbrecht

Housing & Construction
Housing Units, 2000*
- Total 2,136
- Median rent $882
- Median SF home value $207,600

Permits for New Residential Construction
	Units	Value
Total, 2007	13	$3,505,053
Single family	13	$3,505,053
Total, 2006	26	$5,302,139
Single family	26	$5,302,139

Real Property Valuation, 2007
	Parcels	Valuation
Total	2,776	$906,921,100
Vacant	209	26,456,500
Residential	1,849	687,372,600
Commercial	125	80,708,800
Industrial	9	16,024,600
Apartments	0	0
Farm land	368	2,120,200
Farm homestead	216	94,238,400

Average Property Value & Tax, 2007
- Residential value $378,504
- Property tax $6,234
- Tax credit/rebate $1,093

Public Library
C.D. Hofman Library‡
4 Lambert Rd
Blairstown, NJ 07825
908-362-8335

Branch Librarian ..... Marilyn Grandin

Library statistics, 2006
see Warren County profile
for library system statistics

Public Safety
Number of officers, 2006 6

Crime	2005	2006
Total crimes	40	68
Violent	3	8
Murder	0	0
Rape	0	1
Robbery	0	1
Aggravated assault	3	6
Non-violent	37	60
Burglary	7	12
Larceny	30	46
Vehicle theft	0	2
Domestic violence	13	13
Arson	0	0
Total crime rate	6.7	11.4
Violent	0.5	1.3
Non-violent	6.2	10.0

Public School District
(for school year 2006-07 except as noted)

Blairstown Township School District
1 Sunset Hill Rd, PO Box E
Blairstown, NJ 07825
908-362-6111

- Chief School Admin ..... W. Michael Feeney
- Number of schools 1
- Grade plan K-6
- Enrollment 736
- Attendance rate, '05-06 ..... 95.6%
- Dropout rate ..... NA
- Students per teacher 12.2
- Per pupil expenditure $10,424
- Median faculty salary $60,570
- Median administrator salary $93,275
- Grade 12 enrollment ..... NA
- High school graduation rate ..... NA

Assessment test results
(percent scoring at proficient or advanced level)

	Language	Math
NJASK-Grade 3	92.9%	94.0%
GEPA-Grade 8	NA	NA
HSPA-High School	NA	NA

SAT score averages
Pct tested	Math	Verbal	Writing
NA	NA	NA	NA

Teacher Qualifications
- Avg. years of experience 17
- Highly-qualified teachers one subject/all subjects 100%/100%
- With emergency credentials 0.0%

No Child Left Behind
AYP, 2005-06 ..... Meets Standards

Municipal Finance
State Aid Programs, 2008
- Total aid $3,200,528
- CMPTRA 0
- Energy tax receipts 3,167,609
- Garden State Trust 32,919

General Budget, 2007
- Total tax levy $14,976,492
- County levy 5,451,136
- County taxes 4,450,520
- County library 464,586
- County health 0
- County open space 536,030
- School levy 9,207,243
- Muni. levy 318,112
- Misc. revenues 4,918,037

Taxes	2005	2006	2007
General tax rate per $100	2.87	2.99	1.65
County equalization ratio	66	59.07	102
Net valuation taxable	$462,054,641	$466,498,694	$909,363,531
State equalized value	$782,215,407	$876,015,592	$955,090,645

Essex County / Bloomfield Township

Demographics & Socio-Economic Characteristics
(2000 US Census, except as noted)

Population
- 1980* 47,792
- 1990* 45,061
- 2000 47,683
  - Male 22,695
  - Female 24,988
- 2006 (estimate)* 45,372
  - Population density 8,528.6

Race & Hispanic Origin, 2000
Race
- White 33,421
- Black/African American 5,573
- American Indian/Alaska Native 91
- Asian 3,998
- Native Hawaiian/Pacific Islander 31
- Other race 3,061
- Two or more races 1,508
- Hispanic origin, total 6,901
  - Mexican 160
  - Puerto Rican 2,724
  - Cuban 377
  - Other Hispanic 3,640

Age & Nativity, 2000
- Under 5 years 2,820
- 18 years and over 37,644
- 21 years and over 36,087
- 65 years and over 6,827
- 85 years and over 871
- Median age 37.1
- Native-born 36,791
- Foreign-born 10,892

Educational Attainment, 2000
- Population 25 years and over 33,673
- Less than 9th grade 6.1%
- High school grad or higher 83.5%
- Bachelor's degree or higher 31.8%
- Graduate degree 9.9%

Income & Poverty, 1999
- Per capita income $26,049
- Median household income $53,289
- Median family income $64,945
- Persons in poverty 2,772
- H'holds receiving public assistance ... 339
- H'holds receiving social security ... 5,146

Households, 2000
- Total households 19,017
  - With persons under 18 5,796
  - With persons over 65 5,034
  - Family households 12,069
  - Single-person households 5,789
- Persons per household 2.49
- Persons per family 3.16

Labor & Employment
- Total civilian labor force, 2006** ... 26,240
  - Unemployment rate 4.6%
- Total civilian labor force, 2000 ... 26,092
  - Unemployment rate 5.1%

Employed persons 16 years and over by occupation, 2000
- Managers & professionals 9,624
- Service occupations 2,968
- Sales & office occupations 7,522
- Farming, fishing & forestry 15
- Construction & maintenance 1,635
- Production & transportation 3,006
- Self-employed persons 840

* US Census Bureau
** New Jersey Department of Labor

See Introduction for an explanation of all data sources.

General Information
Township of Bloomfield
1 Municipal Plaza
Bloomfield, NJ 07003
973-680-4000

- Website .... www.bloomfieldtwpnj.com
- Year of incorporation 1981
- Land/water area (sq. miles) 5.32/0.01
- Form of government .... Special Charter

Government

Legislative Districts
- US Congressional 8
- State Legislative 28

Local Officials, 2008
- Mayor .... Raymond J. McCarthy
- Administrator .... Louise M. Palagano
- Clerk .... Louise M. Palagano
- Finance Dir .... Robert Renna
- Tax Assessor .... Joseph Pisauro
- Tax Collector .... Cindy Prochilo
- Attorney .... Brian Aloia
- Building .... Carl Graziano
- Comm Dev/Planning ...... Glenn Domenick
- Engineering .... Paul Lasek
- Public Works .... Gerald MacIntyre
- Police Chief .... Michael A. Sisco
- Emerg/Fire Director .... Joseph Intile

Housing & Construction

Housing Units, 2000*
- Total 19,508
- Median rent $768
- Median SF home value $164,800

Permits for New Residential Construction

	Units	Value
Total, 2007	31	$5,179,879
Single family	29	$4,974,129
Total, 2006	46	$7,881,632
Single family	42	$7,470,132

Real Property Valuation, 2007

	Parcels	Valuation
Total	12,588	$2,079,718,500
Vacant	133	9,879,000
Residential	11,657	1,636,108,400
Commercial	670	291,284,000
Industrial	40	33,789,600
Apartments	88	108,657,500
Farm land	0	0
Farm homestead	0	0

Average Property Value & Tax, 2007
- Residential value $140,354
- Property tax $7,648
- Tax credit/rebate $1,197

Public Library
Bloomfield Public Library
90 Broad St
Bloomfield, NJ 07003
973-566-6200

- Director .... Gian Hasija

Library statistics, 2006
- Population served 47,683
- Full-time/total staff 8/15

	Total	Per capita
Holdings	181,465	3.81
Revenues	$1,599,370	$33.54
Expenditures	$1,373,720	$28.81
Annual visits	108,624	2.28
Internet terminals/annual users	28/70,523	

Taxes

	2005	2006	2007
General tax rate per $100	4.79	5.11	5.45
County equalization ratio	57.17	49.13	42.66
Net valuation taxable	$2,101,703,005	$2,083,516,600	$2,082,553,700
State equalized value	$4,277,840,434	$4,887,217,357	$5,226,945,976

Public Safety
- Number of officers, 2006 138

Crime

	2005	2006
Total crimes	1,797	1,478
Violent	143	134
Murder	0	1
Rape	4	4
Robbery	89	86
Aggravated assault	50	43
Non-violent	1,654	1,344
Burglary	228	192
Larceny	998	895
Vehicle theft	428	257
Domestic violence	141	177
Arson	8	5
Total crime rate	38.4	32.0
Violent	3.1	2.9
Non-violent	35.3	29.1

Public School District
(for school year 2006-07 except as noted)

Bloomfield Township School District
155 Broad St
Bloomfield, NJ 07003
973-680-8501

- Superintendent .... Frank DiGesere
- Number of schools 10
- Grade plan K-12
- Enrollment 5,561
- Attendance rate, '05-06 .... 94.1%
- Dropout rate 4.8%
- Students per teacher 10.7
- Per pupil expenditure $11,416
- Median faculty salary $46,558
- Median administrator salary $100,574
- Grade 12 enrollment 376
- High school graduation rate 83.2%

Assessment test results
(percent scoring at proficient or advanced level)

	Language	Math
NJASK-Grade 3	82.2%	86.9%
GEPA-Grade 8	71.1%	56.9%
HSPA-High School	84.9%	58.7%

SAT score averages

Pct tested	Math	Verbal	Writing
86%	456	456	448

Teacher Qualifications
- Avg. years of experience 7
- Highly-qualified teachers
  - one subject/all subjects 100%/100%
- With emergency credentials 0.0%

No Child Left Behind
- AYP, 2005-06 .... Meets Standards

Municipal Finance

State Aid Programs, 2008
- Total aid $7,760,915
  - CMPTRA 4,731,960
  - Energy tax receipts 3,028,955
  - Garden State Trust 0

General Budget, 2007
- Total tax levy $113,477,129
  - County levy 19,163,642
    - County taxes 18,670,727
    - County library 0
    - County health 0
    - County open space 492,915
  - School levy 53,645,952
  - Muni. levy 40,667,535
- Misc. revenues 18,693,732

©2008 Information Publications, Inc. All rights reserved.

The New Jersey Municipal Data Book

Bloomingdale Borough
Passaic County

Demographics & Socio-Economic Characteristics
(2000 US Census, except as noted)

Population
1980*	7,867
1990*	7,530
2000	7,610
Male	3,763
Female	3,847
2006 (estimate)*	7,604
Population density	864.1

Race & Hispanic Origin, 2000
Race
White	7,271
Black/African American	32
American Indian/Alaska Native	9
Asian	167
Native Hawaiian/Pacific Islander	0
Other race	51
Two or more races	80
Hispanic origin, total	332
Mexican	93
Puerto Rican	100
Cuban	21
Other Hispanic	118

Age & Nativity, 2000
Under 5 years	509
18 years and over	5,914
21 years and over	5,698
65 years and over	903
85 years and over	117
Median age	37.9
Native-born	6,839
Foreign-born	771

Educational Attainment, 2000
Population 25 years and over	5,442
Less than 9th grade	3.4%
High school grad or higher	87.6%
Bachelor's degree or higher	25.7%
Graduate degree	7.7%

Income & Poverty, 1999
Per capita income	$27,736
Median household income	$67,885
Median family income	$75,433
Persons in poverty	251
H'holds receiving public assistance	46
H'holds receiving social security	604

Households, 2000
Total households	2,847
With persons under 18	974
With persons over 65	583
Family households	2,077
Single-person households	623
Persons per household	2.63
Persons per family	3.09

Labor & Employment
Total civilian labor force, 2006**	4,935
Unemployment rate	3.1%
Total civilian labor force, 2000	4,546
Unemployment rate	3.1%

Employed persons 16 years and over by occupation, 2000
Managers & professionals	1,649
Service occupations	589
Sales & office occupations	1,243
Farming, fishing & forestry	0
Construction & maintenance	325
Production & transportation	599
Self-employed persons	206

* US Census Bureau
** New Jersey Department of Labor

General Information
Borough of Bloomingdale
101 Hamburg Turnpike
Bloomingdale, NJ 07403
973-838-0778
Website..........www.bloomingdalenj.net
Year of incorporation 1918
Land/water area (sq. miles) 8.80/0.41
Form of government .... Borough

Government
Legislative Districts
US Congressional	5, 11
State Legislative	26

Local Officials, 2008
Mayor	William Steenstra
Administrator	Ted Ehrenburg
Clerk	Jane McCarthy
Treasurer	Sherry Gallagher
Tax Assessor	Brian Townsend
Tax Collector	Dale Mathews
Attorney	Joseph MacMahon
Building	Daniel Hagberg
Comm Dev/Planning	NA
Engineering	James Floystrop
Public Works	Albert Gallagher
Police Chief	Joseph Borell
Emerg/Fire Director	John D'Amato

Housing & Construction
Housing Units, 2000*
Total	2,940
Median rent	$899
Median SF home value	$177,000

Permits for New Residential Construction
	Units	Value
Total, 2007	2	$221,300
Single family	2	$221,300
Total, 2006	0	$105,000
Single family	0	$105,000

Real Property Valuation, 2007
	Parcels	Valuation
Total	2,719	$420,321,264
Vacant	132	12,842,600
Residential	2,463	362,868,800
Commercial	102	32,801,200
Industrial	1	6,000
Apartments	8	11,245,500
Farm land	10	64,264
Farm homestead	3	492,900

Average Property Value & Tax, 2007
Residential value	$147,349
Property tax	$7,954
Tax credit/rebate	$1,282

Public Library
Bloomingdale Public Library
101 Hamburg Turnpike
Bloomingdale, NJ 07403
973-838-0077
Director .... Theresa J. Rubin

Library statistics, 2006
Population served	7,610
Full-time/total staff	0/2

	Total	Per capita
Holdings	27,094	3.56
Revenues	$323,223	$42.47
Expenditures	$306,129	$40.23
Annual visits	23,306	3.06
Internet terminals/annual users		4/3,516

Public Safety
Number of officers, 2006 16

Crime	2005	2006
Total crimes	50	75
Violent	3	1
Murder	0	0
Rape	0	0
Robbery	0	0
Aggravated assault	3	1
Non-violent	47	74
Burglary	6	14
Larceny	39	50
Vehicle theft	2	10
Domestic violence	85	55
Arson	0	1
Total crime rate	6.5	9.8
Violent	0.4	0.1
Non-violent	6.1	9.7

Public School District
(for school year 2006-07 except as noted)

Bloomingdale School District
Captolene Ave
Bloomingdale, NJ 07403
973-838-3282

Chief School Admin	Fredda Rosenberg
Number of schools	3
Grade plan	K-8
Enrollment	605
Attendance rate, '05-06	96.3%
Dropout rate	NA
Students per teacher	9.5
Per pupil expenditure	$15,207
Median faculty salary	$49,350
Median administrator salary	$115,000
Grade 12 enrollment	1
High school graduation rate	NA

Assessment test results
(percent scoring at proficient or advanced level)
	Language	Math
NJASK-Grade 3	75.9%	87.1%
GEPA-Grade 8	77.9%	80.8%
HSPA-High School	NA	NA

SAT score averages
Pct tested	Math	Verbal	Writing
NA	NA	NA	NA

Teacher Qualifications
Avg. years of experience	7
Highly-qualified teachers one subject/all subjects	100%/100%
With emergency credentials	0.0%

No Child Left Behind
AYP, 2005-06 .... Meets Standards

Municipal Finance
State Aid Programs, 2008
Total aid	$642,315
CMPTRA	146,170
Energy tax receipts	472,056
Garden State Trust	21,261

General Budget, 2007
Total tax levy	$22,706,284
County levy	4,801,086
County taxes	4,703,845
County library	0
County health	0
County open space	97,241
School levy	12,122,702
Muni. levy	5,782,496
Misc. revenues	2,645,203

Taxes	2005	2006	2007
General tax rate per $100	4.58	4.94	5.4
County equalization ratio	54.91	48.94	43.36
Net valuation taxable	$421,434,459	$420,693,199	$420,614,373
State equalized value	$861,124,763	$970,554,566	$1,023,968,862

Hunterdon County

Bloomsbury Borough

Demographics & Socio-Economic Characteristics
(2000 US Census, except as noted)

Population
1980*	864
1990*	890
2000	886
Male	427
Female	459
2006 (estimate)*	881
Population density	968.1

Race & Hispanic Origin, 2000
Race
- White . . . 870
- Black/African American . . . 3
- American Indian/Alaska Native . . . 2
- Asian . . . 3
- Native Hawaiian/Pacific Islander . . . 0
- Other race . . . 1
- Two or more races . . . 7
- Hispanic origin, total . . . 13
  - Mexican . . . 1
  - Puerto Rican . . . 2
  - Cuban . . . 2
  - Other Hispanic . . . 8

Age & Nativity, 2000
- Under 5 years . . . 102
- 18 years and over . . . 622
- 21 years and over . . . 605
- 65 years and over . . . 89
- 85 years and over . . . 7
- Median age . . . 35.5
- Native-born . . . 861
- Foreign-born . . . 25

Educational Attainment, 2000
- Population 25 years and over . . . 581
- Less than 9th grade . . . 0.9%
- High school grad or higher . . . 93.6%
- Bachelor's degree or higher . . . 33.0%
- Graduate degree . . . 11.7%

Income & Poverty, 1999
- Per capita income . . . $26,392
- Median household income . . . $64,375
- Median family income . . . $67,500
- Persons in poverty . . . 34
- H'holds receiving public assistance . . . 4
- H'holds receiving social security . . . 64

Households, 2000
- Total households . . . 322
  - With persons under 18 . . . 151
  - With persons over 65 . . . 62
  - Family households . . . 252
  - Single-person households . . . 51
- Persons per household . . . 2.74
- Persons per family . . . 3.11

Labor & Employment
- Total civilian labor force, 2006** . . . 543
  - Unemployment rate . . . 5.5%
- Total civilian labor force, 2000 . . . 472
  - Unemployment rate . . . 3.2%

Employed persons 16 years and over by occupation, 2000
- Managers & professionals . . . 185
- Service occupations . . . 66
- Sales & office occupations . . . 116
- Farming, fishing & forestry . . . 0
- Construction & maintenance . . . 56
- Production & transportation . . . 34
- Self-employed persons . . . 31

* US Census Bureau
** New Jersey Department of Labor

See Introduction for an explanation of all data sources.

General Information
Borough of Bloomsbury
91 Brunswick Ave
Bloomsbury, NJ 08804
908-479-4200
- Website . . . bloomsburynewjersey.com
- Year of incorporation . . . 1905
- Land/water area (sq. miles) . . . 0.91/0.00
- Form of government . . . Borough

Government
Legislative Districts
- US Congressional . . . 7
- State Legislative . . . 23

Local Officials, 2008
- Mayor . . . Mark R. Peck
- Administrator . . . Lisa A. Burd
- Clerk . . . Lisa A. Burd
- Finance Dir . . . Kim Francisco
- Tax Assessor . . . Eloise Hagaman
- Tax Collector . . . Jane Heater
- Attorney . . . William Edleston
- Building . . . NA
- Comm Dev/Planning . . . NA
- Engineering . . . Robert Zederbaum
- Public Works . . . NA
- Police Chief . . . NA
- Emerg/Fire Director . . . Peter Horsch

Housing & Construction
Housing Units, 2000*
- Total . . . 342
- Median rent . . . $875
- Median SF home value . . . $172,800

Permits for New Residential Construction
	Units	Value
Total, 2007	0	$0
Single family	0	$0
Total, 2006	0	$0
Single family	0	$0

Real Property Valuation, 2007
	Parcels	Valuation
Total	386	$121,889,400
Vacant	34	832,500
Residential	315	95,540,300
Commercial	22	18,905,700
Industrial	5	4,850,500
Apartments	3	1,203,900
Farm land	6	124,400
Farm homestead	1	432,100

Average Property Value & Tax, 2007
- Residential value . . . $303,710
- Property tax . . . $5,527
- Tax credit/rebate . . . $980

Public Library
No public municipal library

Library statistics, 2006
- Population served . . . NA
- Full-time/total staff . . . NA/NA

	Total	Per capita
Holdings	NA	NA
Revenues	NA	NA
Expenditures	NA	NA
Annual visits	NA	NA
Internet terminals/annual users	NA/NA	

Taxes
	2005	2006	2007
General tax rate per $100	3.37	1.75	1.82
County equalization ratio	59.87	106.92	102.32
Net valuation taxable	$59,307,022	$121,930,500	$122,071,027
State equalized value	$100,299,378	$109,765,900	$118,291,511

Public Safety
Number of officers, 2006 . . . 0

Crime	2005	2006
Total crimes	21	19
Violent	2	2
Murder	0	0
Rape	0	0
Robbery	0	0
Aggravated assault	2	2
Non-violent	19	17
Burglary	2	1
Larceny	14	14
Vehicle theft	3	2
Domestic violence	3	1
Arson	0	0
Total crime rate	23.5	21.4
Violent	2.2	2.3
Non-violent	21.3	19.2

Public School District
(for school year 2006-07 except as noted)

Bloomsbury School District
20 Main St, PO Box 375
Bloomsbury, NJ 08804
908-479-4414

- Chief School Admin . . . Michael Slattery
- Number of schools . . . 1
- Grade plan . . . K-8
- Enrollment . . . 154
- Attendance rate, '05-06 . . . 96.2%
- Dropout rate . . . NA
- Students per teacher . . . 7.8
- Per pupil expenditure . . . $10,964
- Median faculty salary . . . $43,549
- Median administrator salary . . . $81,150
- Grade 12 enrollment . . . NA
- High school graduation rate . . . NA

Assessment test results
(percent scoring at proficient or advanced level)
	Language	Math
NJASK-Grade 3	93.8%	100.1%
GEPA-Grade 8	92.9%	78.6%
HSPA-High School	NA	NA

SAT score averages
Pct tested	Math	Verbal	Writing
NA	NA	NA	NA

Teacher Qualifications
- Avg. years of experience . . . 9
- Highly-qualified teachers
  one subject/all subjects . . . 100%/100%
- With emergency credentials . . . 0.0%

No Child Left Behind
- AYP, 2005-06 . . . Meets Standards

Municipal Finance
State Aid Programs, 2008
- Total aid . . . $49,061
  - CMPTRA . . . 0
  - Energy tax receipts . . . 48,322
  - Garden State Trust . . . 739

General Budget, 2007
- Total tax levy . . . $2,221,679
  - County levy . . . 397,622
    - County taxes . . . 332,771
    - County library . . . 28,954
    - County health . . . 0
    - County open space . . . 35,897
  - School levy . . . 1,547,229
  - Muni. levy . . . 276,828
- Misc. revenues . . . 335,271

The New Jersey Municipal Data Book

Bogota Borough — Bergen County

Demographics & Socio-Economic Characteristics
(2000 US Census, except as noted)

Population
1980*	8,344
1990*	7,824
2000	8,249
Male	3,917
Female	4,332
2006 (estimate)*	8,108
Population density	10,668.4

Race & Hispanic Origin, 2000
Race
- White: 6,246
- Black/African American: 473
- American Indian/Alaska Native: 12
- Asian: 639
- Native Hawaiian/Pacific Islander: 5
- Other race: 558
- Two or more races: 316
- Hispanic origin, total: 1,759
  - Mexican: 83
  - Puerto Rican: 422
  - Cuban: 220
  - Other Hispanic: 1,034

Age & Nativity, 2000
- Under 5 years: 538
- 18 years and over: 6,161
- 21 years and over: 5,891
- 65 years and over: 915
- 85 years and over: 93
- Median age: 36.5
- Native-born: 6,437
- Foreign-born: 1,812

Educational Attainment, 2000
- Population 25 years and over: 5,542
- Less than 9th grade: 5.0%
- High school grad or higher: 84.4%
- Bachelor's degree or higher: 28.4%
- Graduate degree: 9.2%

Income & Poverty, 1999
- Per capita income: $25,505
- Median household income: $59,813
- Median family income: $69,841
- Persons in poverty: 331
- H'holds receiving public assistance: 68
- H'holds receiving social security: 647

Households, 2000
- Total households: 2,874
  - With persons under 18: 1,129
  - With persons over 65: 694
  - Family households: 2,126
  - Single-person households: 628
- Persons per household: 2.85
- Persons per family: 3.38

Labor & Employment
- Total civilian labor force, 2006**: 4,861
  - Unemployment rate: 6.9%
- Total civilian labor force, 2000: 4,585
  - Unemployment rate: 6.7%

Employed persons 16 years and over by occupation, 2000
- Managers & professionals: 1,471
- Service occupations: 637
- Sales & office occupations: 1,377
- Farming, fishing & forestry: 0
- Construction & maintenance: 372
- Production & transportation: 422
- Self-employed persons: 132

* US Census Bureau
** New Jersey Department of Labor

General Information
Borough of Bogota
375 Larch Ave
Bogota, NJ 07603
201-342-1736

- Website: www.bogotaonline.org
- Year of incorporation: 1894
- Land/water area (sq. miles): 0.76/0.06
- Form of government: Borough

Government
Legislative Districts
- US Congressional: 9
- State Legislative: 37

Local Officials, 2008
- Mayor: Patrick McHale
- Manager: Patrick O'Brien
- Clerk: Fran Garlicki
- Finance Dir: Helen Hegel
- Tax Assessor: Edward Hynes
- Tax Collector: Betty Wiemer
- Attorney: Joseph Managhan
- Building: Daniel Howell
- Planning: Dan Schnipp
- Engineering: Vincent De Nave
- Public Works: Don Viviani
- Police Chief: Frank Gurnari
- Emerg/Fire Director: Lou Kern

Housing & Construction
Housing Units, 2000*
- Total: 2,915
- Median rent: $819
- Median SF home value: $166,700

Permits for New Residential Construction
	Units	Value
Total, 2007	4	$666,940
Single family	4	$666,940
Total, 2006	7	$1,088,360
Single family	7	$1,088,360

Real Property Valuation, 2007
	Parcels	Valuation
Total	2,203	$473,659,075
Vacant	53	2,839,700
Residential	2,021	395,385,875
Commercial	91	36,218,400
Industrial	13	14,550,200
Apartments	25	24,664,900
Farm land	0	0
Farm homestead	0	0

Average Property Value & Tax, 2007
- Residential value: $195,639
- Property tax: $7,286
- Tax credit/rebate: $1,131

Public Library
Bogota Public Library
375 Larch Ave
Bogota, NJ 07603
201-488-7185

- Director: Jonna Davis

Library statistics, 2006
- Population served: 8,249
- Full-time/total staff: 1/2

	Total	Per capita
Holdings	37,208	4.51
Revenues	$228,012	$27.64
Expenditures	$211,209	$25.60
Annual visits	34,320	4.16
Internet terminals/annual users	4/4,966	

Taxes
	2005	2006	2007
General tax rate per $100	3.29	3.4	3.73
County equalization ratio	70.79	63.07	54.72
Net valuation taxable	$472,605,507	$472,577,200	$474,040,356
State equalized value	$749,334,877	$864,064,997	$906,905,826

Public Safety
- Number of officers, 2006: 15

Crime
	2005	2006
Total crimes	97	91
Violent	7	5
Murder	0	0
Rape	0	0
Robbery	3	2
Aggravated assault	4	3
Non-violent	90	86
Burglary	20	14
Larceny	57	69
Vehicle theft	13	3
Domestic violence	37	25
Arson	0	0
Total crime rate	11.8	11.2
Violent	0.9	0.6
Non-violent	11.0	10.6

Public School District
(for school year 2006-07 except as noted)

Bogota School District
1 Henry C. Luthin Place
Bogota, NJ 07603
201-441-4800

- Superintendent: Charles R. Smith (Int)
- Number of schools: 3
- Grade plan: K-12
- Enrollment: 1,182
- Attendance rate, '05-06: 95.9%
- Dropout rate: 1.4%
- Students per teacher: 11.6
- Per pupil expenditure: $13,002
- Median faculty salary: $51,122
- Median administrator salary: $101,536
- Grade 12 enrollment: 93
- High school graduation rate: 93.8%

Assessment test results
(percent scoring at proficient or advanced level)
	Language	Math
NJASK-Grade 3	80.4%	83.8%
GEPA-Grade 8	66.7%	56.9%
HSPA-High School	72.7%	53.3%

SAT score averages
Pct tested	Math	Verbal	Writing
77%	447	449	458

Teacher Qualifications
- Avg. years of experience: 9
- Highly-qualified teachers one subject/all subjects: 100%/100%
- With emergency credentials: 0.0%

No Child Left Behind
- AYP, 2005-06: Meets Standards

Municipal Finance
State Aid Programs, 2008
- Total aid: $729,831
  - CMPTRA: 246,699
  - Energy tax receipts: 483,132
  - Garden State Trust: 0

General Budget, 2007
- Total tax levy: $17,654,977
  - County tax levy: 1,596,170
    - County taxes: 1,508,354
    - County library: 0
    - County health: 0
    - County open space: 87,816
  - School levy: 11,385,570
  - Muni. levy: 4,673,237
- Misc. revenues: 2,143,220

Morris County | Boonton Town

Demographics & Socio-Economic Characteristics
(2000 US Census, except as noted)

Population
- 1980*..........................8,620
- 1990*..........................8,343
- 2000..........................8,496
  - Male..........................4,214
  - Female..........................4,282
- 2006 (estimate)*..........................8,600
  - Population density..........................3,659.6

Race & Hispanic Origin, 2000
Race
- White..........................7,052
- Black/African American..........................337
- American Indian/Alaska Native..........................18
- Asian..........................660
- Native Hawaiian/Pacific Islander..........................1
- Other race..........................187
- Two or more races..........................241
- Hispanic origin, total..........................582
  - Mexican..........................46
  - Puerto Rican..........................140
  - Cuban..........................19
  - Other Hispanic..........................377

Age & Nativity, 2000
- Under 5 years..........................621
- 18 years and over..........................6,633
- 21 years and over..........................6,418
- 65 years and over..........................1,147
- 85 years and over..........................158
  - Median age..........................36.9
- Native-born..........................7,112
- Foreign-born..........................1,384

Educational Attainment, 2000
- Population 25 years and over..........................6,081
- Less than 9th grade..........................6.4%
- High school grad or higher..........................86.1%
- Bachelor's degree or higher..........................32.9%
- Graduate degree..........................9.4%

Income & Poverty, 1999
- Per capita income..........................$29,919
- Median household income..........................$65,322
- Median family income..........................$75,147
- Persons in poverty..........................559
- H'holds receiving public assistance..........................94
- H'holds receiving social security..........................865

Households, 2000
- Total households..........................3,272
  - With persons under 18..........................1,000
  - With persons over 65..........................813
  - Family households..........................2,159
  - Single-person households..........................861
- Persons per household..........................2.55
- Persons per family..........................3.11

Labor & Employment
- Total civilian labor force, 2006**..........................5,238
  - Unemployment rate..........................6.3%
- Total civilian labor force, 2000..........................4,792
  - Unemployment rate..........................6.0%

Employed persons 16 years and over by occupation, 2000
- Managers & professionals..........................1,845
- Service occupations..........................515
- Sales & office occupations..........................1,265
- Farming, fishing & forestry..........................0
- Construction & maintenance..........................327
- Production & transportation..........................552
- Self-employed persons..........................181

* US Census Bureau
** New Jersey Department of Labor

See Introduction for an explanation of all data sources.

General Information
Town of Boonton
100 Washington St
Boonton, NJ 07005
973-402-9410

- Website..........................www.boonton.org
- Year of incorporation..........................1866
- Land/water area (sq. miles)..........................2.35/0.12
- Form of government..........................Town

Government
Legislative Districts
- US Congressional..........................11
- State Legislative..........................25

Local Officials, 2008
- Mayor..........................Cyril Wekilsky
- Manager..........................Terry McCue
- Clerk..........................Cynthia Oravits
- Finance Dir..........................Terry McCue
- Tax Assessor..........................Paul Parsons
- Tax Collector..........................NA
- Attorney..........................John Dorsey
- Building..........................Russell Heiney
- Comm Dev/Planning..........................NA
- Engineering..........................John Miller
- Superintendent..........................Michael Petonak
- Police Chief..........................Michael Beltran
- Emerg/Fire Director..........................Peter Herbert

Housing & Construction
Housing Units, 2000*
- Total..........................3,352
- Median rent..........................$897
- Median SF home value..........................$212,000

Permits for New Residential Construction

	Units	Value
Total, 2007	23	$2,677,058
Single family	23	$2,677,058
Total, 2006	23	$3,361,789
Single family	23	$3,361,789

Real Property Valuation, 2007

	Parcels	Valuation
Total	2,725	$568,591,300
Vacant	110	4,056,200
Residential	2,362	438,059,900
Commercial	197	80,898,000
Industrial	39	36,017,800
Apartments	15	9,339,000
Farm land	1	1,700
Farm homestead	1	218,700

Average Property Value & Tax, 2007
- Residential value..........................$185,475
- Property tax..........................$7,450
- Tax credit/rebate..........................$1,141

Public Library
Boonton-Holmes Library
621 Main St
Boonton, NJ 07005
973-334-2980

- Director..........................Lesley Karczewski

Library statistics, 2006
- Population served..........................8,496
- Full-time/total staff..........................2/4

	Total	Per capita
Holdings	28,928	3.40
Revenues	$402,533	$47.38
Expenditures	$362,688	$42.69
Annual visits	28,000	3.30
Internet terminals/annual users		6/14,900

Taxes

	2005	2006	2007
General tax rate per $100	3.31	3.71	4.02
County equalization ratio	57.79	49.92	46.22
Net valuation taxable	$565,312,920	$563,994,900	$572,176,168
State equalized value	$1,132,437,740	$1,224,079,147	$1,320,683,084

Public Safety
- Number of officers, 2006..........................22

Crime	2005	2006
Total crimes	97	67
Violent	11	9
Murder	0	0
Rape	0	0
Robbery	2	0
Aggravated assault	9	9
Non-violent	86	58
Burglary	18	4
Larceny	64	46
Vehicle theft	4	8
Domestic violence	69	68
Arson	2	1
Total crime rate	11.5	7.8
Violent	1.3	1.1
Non-violent	10.2	6.8

Public School District
(for school year 2006-07 except as noted)

Boonton Town School District
434 Lathrop Ave
Boonton, NJ 07005
973-335-3994

- Superintendent..........................Juanita A. Petty (Int)
- Number of schools..........................4
- Grade plan..........................K-12
- Enrollment..........................1,273
- Attendance rate, '05-06..........................94.9%
- Dropout rate..........................NA
- Students per teacher..........................9.1
- Per pupil expenditure..........................$14,070
- Median faculty salary..........................$51,030
- Median administrator salary..........................$112,741
- Grade 12 enrollment..........................155
- High school graduation rate..........................99.3%

Assessment test results
(percent scoring at proficient or advanced level)

	Language	Math
NJASK-Grade 3	90.3%	93.9%
GEPA-Grade 8	62.9%	61.9%
HSPA-High School	88.2%	71.8%

SAT score averages

Pct tested	Math	Verbal	Writing
75%	516	479	480

Teacher Qualifications
- Avg. years of experience..........................7
- Highly-qualified teachers
  - one subject/all subjects..........................100%/100%
- With emergency credentials..........................0.0%

No Child Left Behind
- AYP, 2005-06..........................Meets Standards

Municipal Finance
State Aid Programs, 2008
- Total aid..........................$982,404
  - CMPTRA..........................331,812
  - Energy tax receipts..........................643,997
  - Garden State Trust..........................62

General Budget, 2007
- Total tax levy..........................$22,983,842
  - County levy..........................2,988,108
    - County taxes..........................2,390,229
    - County library..........................0
    - County health..........................0
    - County open space..........................597,879
  - School levy..........................13,812,452
  - Muni. levy..........................6,183,282
- Misc. revenues..........................4,186,047

The New Jersey Municipal Data Book

Boonton Township
Morris County

Demographics & Socio-Economic Characteristics
(2000 US Census, except as noted)

Population
- 1980* 3,273
- 1990* 3,566
- 2000 4,287
  - Male 2,128
  - Female 2,159
- 2006 (estimate)* 4,396
- Population density 522.1

Race & Hispanic Origin, 2000
Race
- White 3,987
- Black/African American 51
- American Indian/Alaska Native 2
- Asian 175
- Native Hawaiian/Pacific Islander 0
- Other race 27
- Two or more races 45
- Hispanic origin, total 92
  - Mexican 11
  - Puerto Rican 34
  - Cuban 7
  - Other Hispanic 40

Age & Nativity, 2000
- Under 5 years 247
- 18 years and over 3,221
- 21 years and over 3,124
- 65 years and over 638
- 85 years and over 99
  - Median age 41.6
- Native-born 3,932
- Foreign-born 355

Educational Attainment, 2000
- Population 25 years and over 3,047
- Less than 9th grade 1.6%
- High school grad or higher 93.1%
- Bachelor's degree or higher 45.9%
- Graduate degree 17.0%

Income & Poverty, 1999
- Per capita income $45,014
- Median household income $91,753
- Median family income $102,944
- Persons in poverty 55
- H'holds receiving public assistance .. 11
- H'holds receiving social security .. 340

Households, 2000
- Total households 1,476
  - With persons under 18 567
  - With persons over 65 383
  - Family households 1,157
  - Single-person households 258
- Persons per household 2.78
- Persons per family 3.18

Labor & Employment
- Total civilian labor force, 2006** .. 2,428
  - Unemployment rate 3.7%
- Total civilian labor force, 2000 .. 2,198
  - Unemployment rate 3.0%

Employed persons 16 years and over by occupation, 2000
- Managers & professionals 1,163
- Service occupations 133
- Sales & office occupations 615
- Farming, fishing & forestry 0
- Construction & maintenance 133
- Production & transportation 88
- Self-employed persons 204

* US Census Bureau
** New Jersey Department of Labor

General Information
Township of Boonton
155 Powerville Rd
Boonton, NJ 07005
973-402-4002
- Website .... www.boontontownship.com
- Year of incorporation 1867
- Land/water area (sq. miles) 8.42/0.16
- Form of government .... Township

Government
Legislative Districts
- US Congressional 11
- State Legislative 25

Local Officials, 2008
- Mayor .... Douglas Spender
- Manager .... Barbara Shepard
- Clerk .... Barbara Shepard
- Finance Dir .... Norman Eckstein
- Tax Assessor .... Mark Burek
- Tax Collector .... Norman Eckstein
- Attorney .... John P. Jansen
- Building .... Edward Bucceri
- Planning .... William Denzler
- Engineering ...... R. Henry Huelsebusch
- Public Works .... NA
- Police Chief .... John Speirs
- Emerg/Fire Director .... Ian Perrson

Housing & Construction
Housing Units, 2000*
- Total 1,510
- Median rent $1,077
- Median SF home value $322,600

Permits for New Residential Construction

	Units	Value
Total, 2007	39	$16,405,988
Single family	39	$16,405,988
Total, 2006	27	$7,463,515
Single family	27	$7,463,515

Real Property Valuation, 2007

	Parcels	Valuation
Total	1,719	$1,138,879,200
Vacant	130	29,126,600
Residential	1,498	1,049,570,100
Commercial	11	16,901,200
Industrial	7	18,460,900
Apartments	1	571,000
Farm land	43	264,400
Farm homestead	29	23,985,000

Average Property Value & Tax, 2007
- Residential value $703,049
- Property tax $9,736
- Tax credit/rebate $1,170

Public Library
No public municipal library

Library statistics, 2006
- Population served .... NA
- Full-time/total staff .... NA/NA

	Total	Per capita
Holdings	NA	NA
Revenues	NA	NA
Expenditures	NA	NA
Annual visits	NA	NA
Internet terminals/annual users	NA/NA	

Public Safety
- Number of officers, 2006 13

Crime	2005	2006
Total crimes	32	28
Violent	4	3
Murder	0	0
Rape	1	0
Robbery	0	0
Aggravated assault	3	3
Non-violent	28	25
Burglary	7	6
Larceny	20	17
Vehicle theft	1	2
Domestic violence	30	32
Arson	0	0
Total crime rate	7.3	6.4
Violent	0.9	0.7
Non-violent	6.4	5.7

Public School District
(for school year 2006-07 except as noted)

Boonton Township School District
11 Valley Rd
Boonton Township, NJ 07005
973-334-4162
- Superintendent .... Roseann Humphrey
- Number of schools 1
- Grade plan K-8
- Enrollment 525
- Attendance rate, '05-06 .... 96.3%
- Dropout rate .... NA
- Students per teacher 11.2
- Per pupil expenditure $13,158
- Median faculty salary $52,095
- Median administrator salary ... $135,949
- Grade 12 enrollment .... NA
- High school graduation rate .... NA

Assessment test results
(percent scoring at proficient or advanced level)

	Language	Math
NJASK-Grade 3	86.2%	86.2%
GEPA-Grade 8	98.4%	88.9%
HSPA-High School	NA	NA

SAT score averages

Pct tested	Math	Verbal	Writing
NA	NA	NA	NA

Teacher Qualifications
- Avg. years of experience 11
- Highly-qualified teachers
  - one subject/all subjects ... 97.0%/97.0%
- With emergency credentials 0.0%

No Child Left Behind
- AYP, 2005-06 .... Meets Standards

Municipal Finance
State Aid Programs, 2008
- Total aid $248,355
  - CMPTRA 0
  - Energy tax receipts 248,355
  - Garden State Trust 0

General Budget, 2007
- Total tax levy $15,784,943
  - County levy 2,548,655
    - County taxes 2,038,715
    - County library 0
    - County health 0
    - County open space 509,940
  - School levy 10,163,910
  - Muni. levy 3,072,377
- Misc. revenues 1,944,056

Taxes	2005	2006	2007
General tax rate per $100	2.8	2.87	1.39
County equalization ratio	61.82	55.72	107.17
Net valuation taxable	$515,119,321	$522,586,895	$1,139,792,181
State equalized value	$924,478,322	$1,042,311,280	$1,095,989,135

Burlington County / Bordentown City

Demographics & Socio-Economic Characteristics
(2000 US Census, except as noted)

Population
- 1980* 4,441
- 1990* 4,341
- 2000 3,969
  - Male 1,881
  - Female 2,088
- 2006 (estimate)* 3,953
  - Population density 4,296.7

Race & Hispanic Origin, 2000
Race
- White 3,225
- Black/African American 519
- American Indian/Alaska Native 2
- Asian 76
- Native Hawaiian/Pacific Islander 1
- Other race 32
- Two or more races 114
- Hispanic origin, total 112
  - Mexican 6
  - Puerto Rican 67
  - Cuban 5
  - Other Hispanic 34

Age & Nativity, 2000
- Under 5 years 204
- 18 years and over 3,139
- 21 years and over 3,019
- 65 years and over 556
- 85 years and over 71
- Median age 37.9
- Native-born 3,896
- Foreign-born 73

Educational Attainment, 2000
- Population 25 years and over 2,837
- Less than 9th grade 3.2%
- High school grad or higher 85.7%
- Bachelor's degree or higher 26.7%
- Graduate degree 7.8%

Income & Poverty, 1999
- Per capita income $25,882
- Median household income $47,279
- Median family income $59,872
- Persons in poverty 266
- H'holds receiving public assistance ... 32
- H'holds receiving social security ... 413

Households, 2000
- Total households 1,757
  - With persons under 18 482
  - With persons over 65 420
  - Family households 990
  - Single-person households 627
- Persons per household 2.23
- Persons per family 2.93

Labor & Employment
- Total civilian labor force, 2006** ... 2,726
  - Unemployment rate 4.2%
- Total civilian labor force, 2000 ... 2,352
  - Unemployment rate 3.8%

Employed persons 16 years and over by occupation, 2000
- Managers & professionals 763
- Service occupations 412
- Sales & office occupations 677
- Farming, fishing & forestry 0
- Construction & maintenance 192
- Production & transportation 219
- Self-employed persons 169

‡ Branch of county library
* US Census Bureau
** New Jersey Department of Labor

See Introduction for an explanation of all data sources.

General Information
City of Bordentown
324 Farnsworth Ave
Bordentown, NJ 08505
609-298-0604
- Email .... btownch@verizon.net
- Year of incorporation 1867
- Land/water area (sq. miles) ... 0.92/0.05
- Form of government .... Commission

Government
Legislative Districts
- US Congressional 4
- State Legislative 30

Local Officials, 2008
- Mayor .... John W. Collom
- Manager/Admin .... NA
- Clerk .... Patricia D. Ryan
- Finance Dir .... Patricia D. Ryan
- Tax Assessor .... William Tantum
- Tax Collector .... NA
- Attorney .... Richard W. Hunt
- Building .... DCA
- Comm Dev/Planning .... NA
- Engineering .... Michael Filmyer
- Public Works .... Robert E. Erickson
- Police Chief ...... Matthew J. Simmons III
- Emerg/Fire Director ...... Peter J. Sedor

Housing & Construction
Housing Units, 2000*
- Total 1,884
- Median rent $736
- Median SF home value $110,200

Permits for New Residential Construction

	Units	Value
Total, 2007	1	$13,000
Single family	1	$13,000
Total, 2006	0	$0
Single family	0	$0

Real Property Valuation, 2007

	Parcels	Valuation
Total	1,409	$180,040,460
Vacant	83	3,065,000
Residential	1,193	128,491,960
Commercial	107	25,673,300
Industrial	7	9,089,600
Apartments	19	13,720,600
Farm land	0	0
Farm homestead	0	0

Average Property Value & Tax, 2007
- Residential value $107,705
- Property tax $5,438
- Tax credit/rebate $996

Public Library
Bordentown Branch Library‡
18 E Union St
Bordentown, NJ 08505
609-298-0622
- Branch Librarian .... Isabelle Addis

Library statistics, 2006
see Burlington County profile for library system statistics

Public Safety
- Number of officers, 2006 12

Crime	2005	2006
Total crimes	75	42
Violent	6	4
Murder	0	0
Rape	2	0
Robbery	2	2
Aggravated assault	2	2
Non-violent	69	38
Burglary	11	8
Larceny	51	25
Vehicle theft	7	5
Domestic violence	17	12
Arson	0	0
Total crime rate	18.7	10.5
Violent	1.5	1.0
Non-violent	17.2	9.5

Public School District
(for school year 2006-07 except as noted)

Bordentown Regional School District
318 Ward Ave
Bordentown, NJ 08505
609-298-0025

- Superintendent .... Albert Monillas
- Number of schools 15
- Grade plan K-12
- Enrollment 2,276
- Attendance rate, '05-06 .... 95.6%
- Dropout rate 1.3%
- Students per teacher 11.6
- Per pupil expenditure $13,418
- Median faculty salary $51,839
- Median administrator salary $90,143
- Grade 12 enrollment 156
- High school graduation rate 94.5%

Assessment test results
(percent scoring at proficient or advanced level)

	Language	Math
NJASK-Grade 3	90.7%	91.9%
GEPA-Grade 8	78.0%	76.9%
HSPA-High School	87.7%	68.1%

SAT score averages

Pct tested	Math	Verbal	Writing
76%	479	486	469

Teacher Qualifications
- Avg. years of experience 9
- Highly-qualified teachers
  - one subject/all subjects ... 100%/100%
- With emergency credentials 0.0%

No Child Left Behind
- AYP, 2005-06 .... Meets Standards

Municipal Finance
State Aid Programs, 2008
- Total aid $324,270
  - CMPTRA 0
  - Energy tax receipts 324,145
  - Garden State Trust 125

General Budget, 2007
- Total tax levy $9,099,564
  - County levy 1,329,620
    - County taxes 1,101,220
    - County library 101,251
    - County health 0
    - County open space 127,149
  - School levy 5,141,110
  - Muni. levy 2,628,834
- Misc. revenues 2,143,467

Taxes	2005	2006	2007
General tax rate per $100	4.302	4.934	5.051
County equalization ratio	66.28	62.07	55.03
Net valuation taxable	$188,104,625	$179,400,260	$180,225,288
State equalized value	$303,052,401	$326,199,956	$363,535,908

©2008 Information Publications, Inc. All rights reserved. Photocopying prohibited. For additional copies, contact the publisher at www.informationpublications.com or (877)544-INFO (4636)

The New Jersey Municipal Data Book

Bordentown Township

Burlington County

Demographics & Socio-Economic Characteristics
(2000 US Census, except as noted)

Population
1980*	7,170
1990*	7,683
2000	8,380
Male	4,081
Female	4,299
2006 (estimate)*	10,469
Population density	1,230.2

Race & Hispanic Origin, 2000
Race
White	7,486
Black/African American	421
American Indian/Alaska Native	17
Asian	278
Native Hawaiian/Pacific Islander	0
Other race	57
Two or more races	121
Hispanic origin, total	254
Mexican	15
Puerto Rican	121
Cuban	9
Other Hispanic	109

Age & Nativity, 2000
Under 5 years	556
18 years and over	6,394
21 years and over	6,166
65 years and over	980
85 years and over	73
Median age	37.6
Native-born	7,768
Foreign-born	612

Educational Attainment, 2000
Population 25 years and over	5,863
Less than 9th grade	3.7%
High school grad or higher	87.0%
Bachelor's degree or higher	23.9%
Graduate degree	7.5%

Income & Poverty, 1999
Per capita income	$26,934
Median household income	$60,131
Median family income	$71,627
Persons in poverty	234
H'holds receiving public assistance	18
H'holds receiving social security	808

Households, 2000
Total households	3,293
With persons under 18	1,138
With persons over 65	714
Family households	2,305
Single-person households	775
Persons per household	2.53
Persons per family	3.03

Labor & Employment
Total civilian labor force, 2006**	5,636
Unemployment rate	3.8%
Total civilian labor force, 2000	4,833
Unemployment rate	3.4%

Employed persons 16 years and over by occupation, 2000
Managers & professionals	1,622
Service occupations	650
Sales & office occupations	1,567
Farming, fishing & forestry	10
Construction & maintenance	405
Production & transportation	416
Self-employed persons	123

* US Census Bureau
** New Jersey Department of Labor

General Information
Township of Bordentown
1 Municipal Dr
Bordentown, NJ 08505
609-298-2800
Website: www.bordentowntownship.com
Year of incorporation: 1852
Land/water area (sq. miles): 8.51/0.77
Form of government: Township

Government
Legislative Districts
US Congressional	4
State Legislative	30

Local Officials, 2008
Mayor	George A. Chidley
Manager	Leonard M. Klepner
Clerk	Colleen Eckert
Finance Dir.	David Kocian
Tax Assessor	William Tantum
Tax Collector	Mary Picariello
Attorney	Gregory Sullivan
Building	Dan McGonigle
Planning	Werner Nitschmann
Engineering	Fred Turek
Public Works	Dean Buhrer
Police Chief	Frank Nucera Jr
Fire/Emergency Dir.	NA

Housing & Construction
Housing Units, 2000*
Total	3,436
Median rent	$698
Median SF home value	$136,000

Permits for New Residential Construction
	Units	Value
Total, 2007	1	$23,750
Single family	1	$23,750
Total, 2006	1	$176,500
Single family	1	$176,500

Real Property Valuation, 2007
	Parcels	Valuation
Total	3,942	$696,080,640
Vacant	224	35,599,100
Residential	3,475	502,616,250
Commercial	186	118,175,260
Industrial	19	20,537,830
Apartments	6	17,901,800
Farm land	23	200,300
Farm homestead	9	1,050,100

Average Property Value & Tax, 2007
Residential value	$144,566
Property tax	$5,935
Tax credit/rebate	$1,023

Public Library
No public municipal library

Library statistics, 2006
Population served	NA
Full-time/total staff	NA/NA

	Total	Per capita
Holdings	NA	NA
Revenues	NA	NA
Expenditures	NA	NA
Annual visits	NA	NA
Internet terminals/annual users	NA/NA	

Taxes
	2005	2006	2007
General tax rate per $100	3.492	3.815	4.108
County equalization ratio	65.18	58.86	52.47
Net valuation taxable	$643,689,731	$672,799,540	$698,418,058
State equalized value	$1,093,594,514	$1,284,793,375	$1,400,932,234

Public Safety
Number of officers, 2006: 22

Crime	2005	2006
Total crimes	187	189
Violent	15	18
Murder	0	0
Rape	1	1
Robbery	8	8
Aggravated assault	6	9
Non-violent	172	171
Burglary	31	32
Larceny	125	112
Vehicle theft	16	27
Domestic violence	61	37
Arson	0	0
Total crime rate	18.8	18.3
Violent	1.5	1.7
Non-violent	17.2	16.6

Public School District
(for school year 2006-07 except as noted)

Bordentown Regional School District
318 Ward Ave
Bordentown, NJ 08505
609-298-0025

Superintendent	Albert Monillas
Number of schools	15
Grade plan	K-12
Enrollment	2,276
Attendance rate, '05-06	95.6%
Dropout rate	1.3%
Students per teacher	11.6
Per pupil expenditure	$13,418
Median faculty salary	$51,839
Median administrator salary	$90,143
Grade 12 enrollment	156
High school graduation rate	94.5%

Assessment test results
(percent scoring at proficient or advanced level)
	Language	Math
NJASK-Grade 3	90.7%	91.9%
GEPA-Grade 8	78.0%	76.9%
HSPA-High School	87.7%	68.1%

SAT score averages
Pct tested	Math	Verbal	Writing
76%	479	486	469

Teacher Qualifications
Avg. years of experience	9
Highly-qualified teachers one subject/all subjects	100%/100%
With emergency credentials	0.0%

No Child Left Behind
AYP, 2005-06: Meets Standards

Municipal Finance
State Aid Programs, 2008
Total aid	$1,157,611
CMPTRA	341,968
Energy tax receipts	800,384
Garden State Trust	15,259

General Budget, 2007
Total tax levy	$28,674,167
County levy	5,621,134
County taxes	4,659,926
County library	426,557
County health	0
County open space	534,651
School levy	19,360,095
Muni. levy	3,692,938
Misc. revenues	5,167,866

Somerset County
Bound Brook Borough

Demographics & Socio-Economic Characteristics
(2000 US Census, except as noted)

Population
- 1980* 9,710
- 1990* 9,487
- 2000 10,155
  - Male 5,251
  - Female 4,904
- 2006 (estimate)* 10,225
  - Population density 5,979.5

Race & Hispanic Origin, 2000
Race
- White 8,385
- Black/African American 256
- American Indian/Alaska Native 31
- Asian 292
- Native Hawaiian/Pacific Islander 7
- Other race 880
- Two or more races 304
- Hispanic origin, total 3,541
  - Mexican 706
  - Puerto Rican 246
  - Cuban 43
  - Other Hispanic 2,546

Age & Nativity, 2000
- Under 5 years 699
- 18 years and over 7,950
- 21 years and over 7,569
- 65 years and over 1,268
- 85 years and over 120
- Median age 34.2
- Native-born 6,535
- Foreign-born 3,656

Educational Attainment, 2000
- Population 25 years and over 7,006
- Less than 9th grade 13.5%
- High school grad or higher 75.9%
- Bachelor's degree or higher 23.9%
- Graduate degree 7.5%

Income & Poverty, 1999
- Per capita income $22,395
- Median household income $46,858
- Median family income $51,346
- Persons in poverty 1,109
- H'holds receiving public assistance ... 55
- H'holds receiving social security ... 994

Households, 2000
- Total households 3,615
  - With persons under 18 1,257
  - With persons over 65 931
  - Family households 2,461
  - Single-person households 834
- Persons per household 2.81
- Persons per family 3.21

Labor & Employment
- Total civilian labor force, 2006** ... 6,489
  - Unemployment rate 5.4%
- Total civilian labor force, 2000 ... 5,723
  - Unemployment rate 4.7%

Employed persons 16 years and over by occupation, 2000
- Managers & professionals 1,406
- Service occupations 1,028
- Sales & office occupations 1,367
- Farming, fishing & forestry 25
- Construction & maintenance 479
- Production & transportation 1,151
- Self-employed persons 241

* US Census Bureau
** New Jersey Department of Labor

See Introduction for an explanation of all data sources.

General Information
Borough of Bound Brook
230 Hamilton St
Bound Brook, NJ 08805
732-356-0833
- Website .... www.boundbrooknj.net
- Year of incorporation 1891
- Land/water area (sq. miles) ... 1.71/0.00
- Form of government .... Borough

Government
Legislative Districts
- US Congressional 7
- State Legislative 16

Local Officials, 2008
- Mayor .... Carey Pilato
- Manager .... (vacant)
- Clerk .... Donna Marie Godleski
- Finance Dir .... Randy Bahr
- Tax Assessor .... Gary Toth
- Tax Collector .... Randy Bahr
- Attorney .... James O'Donahue
- Building .... Michael Wright
- Planning .... Scarlet Doyle
- Engineering .... T&M Associates
- Public Works .... Tom Miller
- Police Chief .... Tom White
- Emerg/Fire Director ...... James Knight

Housing & Construction
Housing Units, 2000*
- Total 3,802
- Median rent $853
- Median SF home value $157,600

Permits for New Residential Construction

	Units	Value
Total, 2007	86	$7,045,425
Single family	50	$3,070,427
Total, 2006	50	$5,696,850
Single family	2	$396,850

Real Property Valuation, 2007

	Parcels	Valuation
Total	2,600	$423,469,700
Vacant	46	3,086,800
Residential	2,308	340,292,000
Commercial	220	59,082,200
Industrial	1	763,300
Apartments	25	20,245,400
Farm land	0	0
Farm homestead	0	0

Average Property Value & Tax, 2007
- Residential value $147,440
- Property tax $7,455
- Tax credit/rebate $1,215

Public Library
Bound Brook Memorial Library
402 E High St
Bound Brook, NJ 08805
732-356-0043
- Director .... Hannah Kerwin

Library statistics, 2006
- Population served .... NA
- Full-time/total staff .... NA/NA

	Total	Per capita
Holdings	NA	NA
Revenues	NA	NA
Expenditures	NA	NA
Annual visits	NA	NA
Internet terminals/annual users	NA/NA	

Public Safety
- Number of officers, 2006 22

Crime	2005	2006
Total crimes	250	257
Violent	27	33
Murder	0	0
Rape	3	1
Robbery	13	19
Aggravated assault	11	13
Non-violent	223	224
Burglary	54	64
Larceny	150	148
Vehicle theft	19	12
Domestic violence	221	216
Arson	0	0
Total crime rate	24.6	25.3
Violent	2.7	3.2
Non-violent	21.9	22.0

Public School District
(for school year 2006-07 except as noted)

Bound Brook Borough School District
West 2nd St, LaMonte Bldg
Bound Brook, NJ 08805
732-652-7920
- Superintendent .... Edward C. Hoffman
- Number of schools 5
- Grade plan K-12
- Enrollment 1,465
- Attendance rate, '05-06 .... 94.4%
- Dropout rate 2.5%
- Students per teacher 11.3
- Per pupil expenditure $13,512
- Median faculty salary $53,400
- Median administrator salary ... $108,360
- Grade 12 enrollment 100
- High school graduation rate 86.8%

Assessment test results
(percent scoring at proficient or advanced level)

	Language	Math
NJASK-Grade 3	75.7%	76.4%
GEPA-Grade 8	44.1%	46.4%
HSPA-High School	77.1%	65.6%

SAT score averages

Pct tested	Math	Verbal	Writing
64%	460	458	437

Teacher Qualifications
- Avg. years of experience 7
- Highly-qualified teachers
  - one subject/all subjects ... 99.0%/99.0%
- With emergency credentials 0.0%

No Child Left Behind
- AYP, 2005-06 .... Meets Standards

Municipal Finance
State Aid Programs, 2008
- Total aid $1,430,514
  - CMPTRA 705,408
  - Energy tax receipts 725,106
  - Garden State Trust 0

General Budget, 2007
- Total tax levy $21,581,098
  - County levy 3,071,779
    - County taxes 2,484,351
    - County library 315,381
    - County health 0
    - County open space 272,047
  - School levy 12,431,343
  - Muni. levy 6,077,977
- Misc. revenues 5,581,628

Taxes	2005	2006	2007
General tax rate per $100	4.51	4.83	5.06
County equalization ratio	63.29	55.71	47.05
Net valuation taxable	$426,121,949	$423,045,100	$426,823,567
State equalized value	$764,893,105	$903,475,366	$946,073,591

The New Jersey Municipal Data Book

Bradley Beach Borough
Monmouth County

Demographics & Socio-Economic Characteristics
(2000 US Census, except as noted)

Population
- 1980* 4,772
- 1990* 4,475
- 2000 4,793
  - Male 2,385
  - Female 2,408
- 2006 (estimate)* 4,784
- Population density 8,108.5

Race & Hispanic Origin, 2000
Race
- White 4,225
- Black/African American 185
- American Indian/Alaska Native 8
- Asian 70
- Native Hawaiian/Pacific Islander 1
- Other race 192
- Two or more races 112
- Hispanic origin, total 615
  - Mexican 248
  - Puerto Rican 213
  - Cuban 19
  - Other Hispanic 135

Age & Nativity, 2000
- Under 5 years 265
- 18 years and over 3,931
- 21 years and over 3,792
- 65 years and over 590
- 85 years and over 83
- Median age 36.9
- Native-born 4,258
- Foreign-born 535

Educational Attainment, 2000
- Population 25 years and over 3,544
- Less than 9th grade 4.8%
- High school grad or higher 81.8%
- Bachelor's degree or higher 25.2%
- Graduate degree 10.0%

Income & Poverty, 1999
- Per capita income $25,438
- Median household income $40,878
- Median family income $49,688
- Persons in poverty 439
- H'holds receiving public assistance ... 11
- H'holds receiving social security ... 511

Households, 2000
- Total households 2,297
  - With persons under 18 478
  - With persons over 65 450
  - Family households 1,086
  - Single-person households 977
- Persons per household 2.09
- Persons per family 2.91

Labor & Employment
- Total civilian labor force, 2006** ... 2,918
  - Unemployment rate 6.3%
- Total civilian labor force, 2000 .. 2,714
  - Unemployment rate 6.5%
- *Employed persons 16 years and over by occupation, 2000*
  - Managers & professionals 825
  - Service occupations 431
  - Sales & office occupations 759
  - Farming, fishing & forestry 0
  - Construction & maintenance 247
  - Production & transportation 275
  - Self-employed persons 153

* US Census Bureau
** New Jersey Department of Labor

General Information
Borough of Bradley Beach
701 Main St
Bradley Beach, NJ 07720
732-776-2999
- Website .... www.bradleybeachonline.com
- Year of incorporation 1893
- Land/water area (sq. miles) ... 0.59/0.02
- Form of government ..... Small Municipality

Government
Legislative Districts
- US Congressional 6
- State Legislative 11

Local Officials, 2008
- Mayor .... Stephen Schueler
- Business Admin .... Phyllis Quixley
- Clerk .... Mary Ann Solinski
- Finance Dir .... Joyce Wilkins
- Tax Assessor .... Ed Mullane
- Tax Collector .... Joyce Wilkins
- Attorney .... Michael DuPont
- Building .... Donald Clare
- Comm Dev/Planning .... NA
- Engineering .... Philip R. Kavanuagh
- Public Works .... Richard Bianchi
- Police Chief .... Leonard Guida
- Emerg/Fire Director .... Nicole Zech

Housing & Construction
Housing Units, 2000*
- Total 3,132
- Median rent $729
- Median SF home value $161,200

Permits for New Residential Construction

	Units	Value
Total, 2007	50	$6,349,105
Single family	20	$2,868,390
Total, 2006	52	$4,950,967
Single family	22	$2,989,537

Real Property Valuation, 2007

	Parcels	Valuation
Total	2,050	$1,118,334,200
Vacant	53	10,444,100
Residential	1,851	980,111,700
Commercial	102	67,587,200
Industrial	4	1,774,900
Apartments	40	58,416,300
Farm land	0	0
Farm homestead	0	0

Average Property Value & Tax, 2007
- Residential value $529,504
- Property tax $6,026
- Tax credit/rebate $1,071

Public Library
Bradley Beach Public Library
511 Fourth Ave
Bradley Beach, NJ 07720
732-776-2995
- Director .... Karen J. Klapperstuck

Library statistics, 2006
- Population served 4,793
- Full-time/total staff 0/1

	Total	Per capita
Holdings	34,646	7.23
Revenues	$318,654	$66.48
Expenditures	$187,643	$39.15
Annual visits	16,379	3.42
Internet terminals/annual users	8/10,264	

Taxes

	2005	2006	2007
General tax rate per $100	2.483	1.092	1.139
County equalization ratio	62.26	125.68	106.45
Net valuation taxable	$445,169,128	$1,115,000,500	$1,118,702,991
State equalized value	$880,999,660	$1,047,805,007	$1,138,274,977

Public Safety
- Number of officers, 2006 15

Crime	2005	2006
Total crimes	232	194
Violent	11	6
Murder	0	0
Rape	0	0
Robbery	5	3
Aggravated assault	6	3
Non-violent	221	188
Burglary	77	44
Larceny	141	140
Vehicle theft	3	4
Domestic violence	113	105
Arson	1	0
Total crime rate	48.3	40.6
Violent	2.3	1.3
Non-violent	46.0	39.3

Public School District
(for school year 2006-07 except as noted)

Bradley Beach School District
515 Brinley Ave
Bradley Beach, NJ 07720
732-775-4413

- Superintendent .... Wayne W. Turner
- Number of schools 1
- Grade plan K-8
- Enrollment 264
- Attendance rate, '05-06 .... 95.4%
- Dropout rate .... NA
- Students per teacher 7.9
- Per pupil expenditure $17,726
- Median faculty salary $60,378
- Median administrator salary ... $81,747
- Grade 12 enrollment .... NA
- High school graduation rate .... NA

Assessment test results
(percent scoring at proficient or advanced level)

	Language	Math
NJASK-Grade 3	90.5%	71.4%
GEPA-Grade 8	75.0%	78.1%
HSPA-High School	NA	NA

SAT score averages

Pct tested	Math	Verbal	Writing
NA	NA	NA	NA

Teacher Qualifications
- Avg. years of experience 19
- Highly-qualified teachers
  - one subject/all subjects ... 92.5%/92.5%
- With emergency credentials 0.0%

No Child Left Behind
- AYP, 2005-06 .... Meets Standards

Municipal Finance
State Aid Programs, 2008
- Total aid $374,121
  - CMPTRA 0
  - Energy tax receipts 374,121
  - Garden State Trust 0

General Budget, 2007
- Total tax levy $12,731,933
  - County levy 2,732,330
    - County taxes 2,526,277
    - County library 0
    - County health 48,164
    - County open space 157,889
  - School levy 5,214,836
  - Muni. levy 4,784,767
- Misc. revenues 2,174,710

54 The New Jersey Municipal Data Book

Somerset County
Branchburg Township

Demographics & Socio-Economic Characteristics
(2000 US Census, except as noted)

Population
- 1980* 7,846
- 1990* 10,888
- 2000 14,566
  - Male 7,148
  - Female 7,418
- 2006 (estimate)* 15,049
- Population density 742.8

Race & Hispanic Origin, 2000
Race
- White 13,174
- Black/African American 284
- American Indian/Alaska Native 15
- Asian 898
- Native Hawaiian/Pacific Islander 4
- Other race 57
- Two or more races 134
- Hispanic origin, total 392
  - Mexican 20
  - Puerto Rican 137
  - Cuban 51
  - Other Hispanic 184

Age & Nativity, 2000
- Under 5 years 1,269
- 18 years and over 10,583
- 21 years and over 10,303
- 65 years and over 1,206
- 85 years and over 98
  - Median age 37.5
- Native-born 12,997
- Foreign-born 1,565

Educational Attainment, 2000
- Population 25 years and over 9,954
- Less than 9th grade 1.8%
- High school grad or higher 94.8%
- Bachelor's degree or higher 53.7%
- Graduate degree 23.0%

Income & Poverty, 1999
- Per capita income $41,241
- Median household income $96,864
- Median family income $110,268
- Persons in poverty 282
- H'holds receiving public assistance ... 63
- H'holds receiving social security 942

Households, 2000
- Total households 5,272
  - With persons under 18 2,148
  - With persons over 65 898
  - Family households 4,065
  - Single-person households 990
- Persons per household 2.76
- Persons per family 3.19

Labor & Employment
- Total civilian labor force, 2006** ... 9,047
  - Unemployment rate 2.4%
- Total civilian labor force, 2000 ... 8,018
  - Unemployment rate 2.1%
- *Employed persons 16 years and over by occupation, 2000*
  - Managers & professionals 4,376
  - Service occupations 453
  - Sales & office occupations 1,984
  - Farming, fishing & forestry 0
  - Construction & maintenance 521
  - Production & transportation 516
- Self-employed persons 392

* US Census Bureau
** New Jersey Department of Labor

See Introduction for an explanation of all data sources.

General Information
Township of Branchburg
1077 US Highway 202 N
Branchburg, NJ 08876
908-526-1300

- Website .... www.branchburg.nj.us
- Year of incorporation 1845
- Land/water area (sq. miles) 20.26/0.00
- Form of government .... Township

Government
Legislative Districts
- US Congressional 7
- State Legislative 16

Local Officials, 2008
- Mayor .... John Sanford
- Administrator .... Gregory Bonin
- Township Clerk .... Sharon Brienza
- CFO .... Diane Schubach
- Tax Assessor .... Frances Kuczynski
- Tax Collector .... Diane Wynn
- Attorney .... Mark S. Anderson
- Code Enforcement ...... John Tamburini
- Planning .... James Melitski (Chr)
- Township Engineer .... Douglas Ball
- Public Works .... Bruce Kosensky
- Police Chief .... Brian Fitzgerald
- Emerg/Fire Director ..... James McAleer

Housing & Construction
Housing Units, 2000*
- Total 5,405
- Median rent $1,036
- Median SF home value $278,000

Permits for New Residential Construction

	Units	Value
Total, 2007	31	$2,814,104
Single family	7	$2,314,104
Total, 2006	15	$3,399,708
Single family	15	$3,399,708

Real Property Valuation, 2007

	Parcels	Valuation
Total	5,450	$3,104,800,700
Vacant	158	24,572,100
Residential	4,788	2,282,796,800
Commercial	146	202,426,400
Industrial	189	529,423,800
Apartments	1	27,851,200
Farm land	108	1,443,400
Farm homestead	60	36,287,000

Average Property Value & Tax, 2007
- Residential value $478,359
- Property tax $8,630
- Tax credit/rebate $1,213

Public Library
No public municipal library

Library statistics, 2006
- Population served .... NA
- Full-time/total staff .... NA/NA

	Total	Per capita
Holdings	NA	NA
Revenues	NA	NA
Expenditures	NA	NA
Annual visits	NA	NA
Internet terminals/annual users	NA/NA

Taxes

	2005	2006	2007
General tax rate per $100	1.94	1.82	1.81
County equalization ratio	106.66	105.88	99.91
Net valuation taxable	$2,638,596,002	$2,990,720,700	$3,109,676,947
State equalized value	$2,776,592,657	$3,082,222,556	$3,198,787,059

Public Safety
- Number of officers, 2006 26

Crime

	2005	2006
Total crimes	121	114
Violent	1	3
Murder	0	0
Rape	0	1
Robbery	0	1
Aggravated assault	1	1
Non-violent	120	111
Burglary	30	28
Larceny	84	78
Vehicle theft	6	5
Domestic violence	105	84
Arson	0	0
Total crime rate	8.1	7.6
Violent	0.1	0.2
Non-violent	8.0	7.4

Public School District
(for school year 2006-07 except as noted)

Branchburg Township School District
240 Baird Rd
Branchburg, NJ 08876
908-722-3265

- Superintendent .... Kenneth J. Knops
- Number of schools 4
- Grade plan K-8
- Enrollment 1,949
- Attendance rate, '05-06 .... 96.6%
- Dropout rate .... NA
- Students per teacher 9.5
- Per pupil expenditure $14,516
- Median faculty salary $51,535
- Median administrator salary ... $113,033
- Grade 12 enrollment .... NA
- High school graduation rate .... NA

Assessment test results
(percent scoring at proficient or advanced level)

	Language	Math
NJASK-Grade 3	91.6%	95.5%
GEPA-Grade 8	90.4%	87.9%
HSPA-High School	NA	NA

SAT score averages

Pct tested	Math	Verbal	Writing
NA	NA	NA	NA

Teacher Qualifications
- Avg. years of experience 8
- Highly-qualified teachers
  - one subject/all subjects 99.0%/99.0%
- With emergency credentials 0.0%

No Child Left Behind
- AYP, 2005-06 .... Meets Standards

Municipal Finance
State Aid Programs, 2008
- Total aid $3,492,850
- CMPTRA 0
- Energy tax receipts 3,476,642
- Garden State Trust 16,208

General Budget, 2007
- Total tax levy $56,101,969
- County levy 10,559,831
  - County taxes 8,540,433
  - County library 1,084,187
  - County health 0
  - County open space 935,211
- School levy 37,313,467
- Muni. levy 8,228,671
- Misc. revenues 8,422,695

The New Jersey Municipal Data Book

Branchville Borough
Sussex County

Demographics & Socio-Economic Characteristics
(2000 US Census, except as noted)

Population
- 1980* 870
- 1990* 851
- 2000 845
  - Male 394
  - Female 451
- 2006 (estimate)* 839
  - Population density 1,422.0

Race & Hispanic Origin, 2000
Race
- White 832
- Black/African American 1
- American Indian/Alaska Native ... 3
- Asian 3
- Native Hawaiian/Pacific Islander ... 0
- Other race 1
- Two or more races 5
- Hispanic origin, total 11
  - Mexican 7
  - Puerto Rican 1
  - Cuban 0
  - Other Hispanic 3

Age & Nativity, 2000
- Under 5 years 29
- 18 years and over 642
- 21 years and over 615
- 65 years and over 153
- 85 years and over 15
  - Median age 41.7
- Native-born 829
- Foreign-born 18

Educational Attainment, 2000
- Population 25 years and over 613
- Less than 9th grade 3.8%
- High school grad or higher 85.2%
- Bachelor's degree or higher ... 18.3%
- Graduate degree 6.9%

Income & Poverty, 1999
- Per capita income $22,748
- Median household income $45,855
- Median family income $60,909
- Persons in poverty 37
- H'holds receiving public assistance ... 8
- H'holds receiving social security ... 134

Households, 2000
- Total households 354
  - With persons under 18 107
  - With persons over 65 119
  - Family households 225
  - Single-person households 114
- Persons per household 2.37
- Persons per family 3.03

Labor & Employment
- Total civilian labor force, 2006** ... 486
  - Unemployment rate 6.1%
- Total civilian labor force, 2000 ... 435
  - Unemployment rate 4.4%

Employed persons 16 years and over by occupation, 2000
- Managers & professionals 122
- Service occupations 54
- Sales & office occupations 122
- Farming, fishing & forestry 2
- Construction & maintenance 57
- Production & transportation 59
- Self-employed persons 27

* US Census Bureau
** New Jersey Department of Labor

General Information
Borough of Branchville
PO Box 840
Branchville, NJ 07826
973-948-4626

- Website .... (county website)
- Year of incorporation 1898
- Land/water area (sq. miles) ... 0.59/0.00
- Form of government .... Borough

Government
Legislative Districts
- US Congressional 5
- State Legislative 24

Local Officials, 2008
- Mayor .... Gerald Van Gorden
- Manager/Admin .... NA
- Clerk .... Kate Leissler
- Finance Dir .... Jessica Caruso
- Tax Assessor .... Katherine Kieb
- Tax Collector .... Beverly Bathgate
- Attorney .... Thomas Bain
- Building .... Wesley Powers
- Comm Dev/Planning .... NA
- Engineering .... Harold Pellow
- Public Works .... NA
- Police Chief .... NA
- Emerg/Fire Director ...... Brian Geimer

Housing & Construction
Housing Units, 2000*
- Total 377
- Median rent $671
- Median SF home value $149,600

Permits for New Residential Construction

	Units	Value
Total, 2007	0	$0
Single family	0	$0
Total, 2006	1	$290,000
Single family	1	$290,000

Real Property Valuation, 2007

	Parcels	Valuation
Total	384	$161,006,950
Vacant	44	2,693,750
Residential	275	80,641,600
Commercial	57	75,629,900
Industrial	0	0
Apartments	4	1,567,000
Farm land	2	5,500
Farm homestead	2	469,200

Average Property Value & Tax, 2007
- Residential value $292,819
- Property tax $4,028
- Tax credit/rebate $835

Public Library
No public municipal library

Library statistics, 2006
- Population served .... NA
- Full-time/total staff .... NA/NA

	Total	Per capita
Holdings	NA	NA
Revenues	NA	NA
Expenditures	NA	NA
Annual visits	NA	NA
Internet terminals/annual users	NA/NA	

Public Safety
- Number of officers, 2006 0

Crime	2005	2006
Total crimes	26	10
Violent	4	2
Murder	0	0
Rape	0	0
Robbery	0	0
Aggravated assault	4	2
Non-violent	22	8
Burglary	3	1
Larceny	18	6
Vehicle theft	1	1
Domestic violence	2	1
Arson	0	0
Total crime rate	30.7	11.8
Violent	4.7	2.4
Non-violent	25.9	9.5

Public School District
(for school year 2006-07 except as noted)

Branchville Borough School District
4 Pines Rd
Branchville, NJ 07826

No schools in district

- Per pupil expenditure .... NA
- Median faculty salary .... NA
- Median administrator salary .... NA
- Grade 12 enrollment .... NA
- High school graduation rate .... NA

Assessment test results
(percent scoring at proficient or advanced level)

	Language	Math
NJASK-Grade 3	NA	NA
GEPA-Grade 8	NA	NA
HSPA-High School	NA	NA

SAT score averages

Pct tested	Math	Verbal	Writing
NA	NA	NA	NA

Teacher Qualifications
- Avg. years of experience .... NA
- Highly-qualified teachers
  - one subject/all subjects ..... NA/NA
- With emergency credentials ..... NA

No Child Left Behind
- AYP, 2005-06 .... NA

Municipal Finance
State Aid Programs, 2008
- Total aid $56,836
- CMPTRA 0
- Energy tax receipts 56,836
- Garden State Trust 0

General Budget, 2007
- Total tax levy $2,218,257
- County levy 563,242
- County taxes 476,439
- County library 40,293
- County health 15,295
- County open space 50,558
- School levy 1,655,016
- Muni. levy 0
- Misc. revenues 1,337,577

Taxes	2005	2006	2007
General tax rate per $100	2.29	1.25	1.38
County equalization ratio	69.95	117.59	105.07
Net valuation taxable	$100,787,356	$189,094,500	$161,257,058
State equalized value	$160,642,901	$180,259,182	$171,025,405

Ocean County / Brick Township

Demographics & Socio-Economic Characteristics[†]
(2000 US Census, except as noted)

Population
1980*	53,629
1990*	66,473
2000	76,119
Male	36,155
Female	39,964
2006 (estimate)*	78,232
Population density	2,982.5

Race & Hispanic Origin, 2000
Race
White	72,932
Black/African American	751
American Indian/Alaska Native	76
Asian	904
Native Hawaiian/Pacific Islander	12
Other race	650
Two or more races	794
Hispanic origin, total	2,930
Mexican	491
Puerto Rican	1,229
Cuban	200
Other Hispanic	1,010

Age & Nativity, 2000
Under 5 years	4,721
18 years and over	57,965
21 years and over	55,790
65 years and over	12,963
85 years and over	1,671
Median age	39.4
Native-born	71,816
Foreign-born	4,303

Educational Attainment, 2000
Population 25 years and over	52,965
Less than 9th grade	3.3%
High school grad or higher	86.6%
Bachelor's degree or higher	19.4%
Graduate degree	5.6%

Income & Poverty, 1999
Per capita income	$24,462
Median household income	$52,092
Median family income	$61,446
Persons in poverty	3,411
H'holds receiving public assistance	420
H'holds receiving social security	10,004

Households, 2000
Total households	29,511
With persons under 18	9,995
With persons over 65	9,081
Family households	20,788
Single-person households	7,367
Persons per household	2.56
Persons per family	3.07

Labor & Employment
Total civilian labor force, 2006**	40,883
Unemployment rate	4.5%
Total civilian labor force, 2000	37,840
Unemployment rate	4.1%

Employed persons 16 years and over by occupation, 2000
Managers & professionals	11,269
Service occupations	5,427
Sales & office occupations	11,236
Farming, fishing & forestry	80
Construction & maintenance	4,211
Production & transportation	4,049
Self-employed persons	1,820

[†] see Appendix C for American Community Survey data
[‡] Branch of county library
[*] US Census Bureau
[**] New Jersey Department of Labor

See Introduction for an explanation of all data sources.

General Information
Township of Brick
401 Chambersbridge Rd
Brick, NJ 08723
732-262-1000

Website	www.twp.brick.nj.us
Year of incorporation	1850
Land/water area (sq. miles)	26.23/6.03
Form of government	Mayor-Council

Government
Legislative Districts
US Congressional	4
State Legislative	10

Local Officials, 2008
Mayor	Stephen C. Acropolis
Manager	Scott Pezarras
Clerk	Virginia A. Lampman
Finance Dir	Scott Pezarras
Tax Assessor	Fred Millman
Tax Collector	JoAnne Lambusta
Attorney	George Gilmore
Building	Daniel Newman Jr
Planning	Michael Fowler
Engineering	James Priolo
Public Works	Robert Russo
Police Chief	Nils R. Bergquist
Fire/Emergency Dir	NA

Housing & Construction
Housing Units, 2000*
Total	32,689
Median rent	$820
Median SF home value	$136,800

Permits for New Residential Construction
	Units	Value
Total, 2007	103	$21,195,983
Single family	103	$21,195,983
Total, 2006	111	$21,688,780
Single family	111	$21,688,780

Real Property Valuation, 2007
	Parcels	Valuation
Total	32,640	$4,676,831,200
Vacant	1,415	79,395,400
Residential	30,468	4,067,300,200
Commercial	720	464,922,800
Industrial	22	10,645,300
Apartments	14	54,471,600
Farm land	0	0
Farm homestead	1	95,900

Average Property Value & Tax, 2007
Residential value	$133,493
Property tax	$4,775
Tax credit/rebate	$907

Public Library
Brick Branch Library[‡]
301 Chambers Bridge Rd
Brick, NJ 08723
732-477-4513

Branch Librarian.............Eleanor Clark

Library statistics, 2006
see Ocean County profile for library system statistics

Public Safety
Number of officers, 2006............127

Crime	2005	2006
Total crimes	1,385	1,545
Violent	44	80
Murder	0	0
Rape	0	3
Robbery	6	19
Aggravated assault	38	58
Non-violent	1,341	1,465
Burglary	192	303
Larceny	1,103	1,101
Vehicle theft	46	61
Domestic violence	774	830
Arson	2	0
Total crime rate	17.6	19.8
Violent	0.6	1.0
Non-violent	17.1	18.7

Public School District
(for school year 2006-07 except as noted)

Brick Township School District
101 Hendrickson Ave
Brick, NJ 08724
732-785-3000

Superintendent	Melindo Persi (Int)
Number of schools	12
Grade plan	K-12
Enrollment	10,714
Attendance rate, '05-06	93.9%
Dropout rate	2.1%
Students per teacher	11.6
Per pupil expenditure	$10,925
Median faculty salary	$47,785
Median administrator salary	$106,463
Grade 12 enrollment	814
High school graduation rate	NA

Assessment test results
(percent scoring at proficient or advanced level)
	Language	Math
NJASK-Grade 3	87.3%	90.1%
GEPA-Grade 8	82.9%	70.9%
HSPA-High School	88.8%	75.5%

SAT score averages
Pct tested	Math	Verbal	Writing
NA	NA	NA	NA

Teacher Qualifications
Avg. years of experience	9
Highly-qualified teachers one subject/all subjects	99.5%/99.5%
With emergency credentials	1.4%

No Child Left Behind
AYP, 2005-06............Meets Standards

Municipal Finance
State Aid Programs, 2008
Total aid	$6,915,588
CMPTRA	1,846,837
Energy tax receipts	5,067,719
Garden State Trust	1,032

General Budget, 2007
Total tax levy	$167,508,722
County levy	37,669,605
County taxes	31,041,237
County library	3,679,069
County health	1,490,551
County open space	1,458,748
School levy	87,119,475
Muni. levy	42,719,642
Misc. revenues	29,410,997

Taxes
	2005	2006	2007
General tax rate per $100	3.233	3.398	3.578
County equalization ratio	51.8	44.38	38.58
Net valuation taxable	$4,630,699,335	$4,655,477,500	$4,682,741,915
State equalized value	$10,434,203,098	$12,073,730,213	$12,889,743,222

Bridgeton City

Cumberland County

Demographics & Socio-Economic Characteristics
(2000 US Census, except as noted)

Population
1980*	18,795
1990*	18,942
2000	22,771
Male	12,899
Female	9,872
2006 (estimate)*	24,389
Population density	3,921.1

Race & Hispanic Origin, 2000
Race
White	8,854
Black/African American	9,528
American Indian/Alaska Native	271
Asian	159
Native Hawaiian/Pacific Islander	20
Other race	3,112
Two or more races	827
Hispanic origin, total	5,576
Mexican	3,264
Puerto Rican	1,558
Cuban	62
Other Hispanic	692

Age & Nativity, 2000
Under 5 years	1,658
18 years and over	16,843
21 years and over	15,857
65 years and over	2,485
85 years and over	342
Median age	31.5
Native-born	19,942
Foreign-born	2,829

Educational Attainment, 2000
Population 25 years and over	14,198
Less than 9th grade	14.6%
High school grad or higher	57.6%
Bachelor's degree or higher	7.3%
Graduate degree	2.6%

Income & Poverty, 1999
Per capita income	$10,917
Median household income	$26,923
Median family income	$30,502
Persons in poverty	4,880
H'holds receiving public assistance	515
H'holds receiving social security	1,840

Households, 2000
Total households	6,182
With persons under 18	2,665
With persons over 65	1,735
Family households	4,181
Single-person households	1,691
Persons per household	2.96
Persons per family	3.49

Labor & Employment
Total civilian labor force, 2006**	8,500
Unemployment rate	9.4%
Total civilian labor force, 2000	7,850
Unemployment rate	13.5%

Employed persons 16 years and over by occupation, 2000
Managers & professionals	1,301
Service occupations	1,607
Sales & office occupations	1,468
Farming, fishing & forestry	340
Construction & maintenance	436
Production & transportation	1,642
Self-employed persons	175

* US Census Bureau
** New Jersey Department of Labor
§ State Fiscal Year July 1–June 30

General Information
City of Bridgeton
181 E Commerce St
Bridgeton, NJ 08302
856-455-3230

Website	www.cityofbridgeton.com
Year of incorporation	1865
Land/water area (sq. miles)	6.22/0.23
Form of government	Mayor-Council

Government

Legislative Districts
US Congressional	2
State Legislative	3

Local Officials, 2008
Mayor	James Begley
Manager	Arch Liston
Clerk	Darlene Richmond
Finance Dir	Terry Delp
Tax Assessor	Kevin Maloney
Tax Collector	Mary Pierce
Attorney	Theodore Baker
Building	Robert Mixner
Planning	Sandra Zapolski
Engineering	J. Michael Fralinger
Public Works	Roy Burlew
Police Chief	Mark Ott
Emerg/Fire Director	Dave Schoch

Housing & Construction

Housing Units, 2000*
Total	6,795
Median rent	$602
Median SF home value	$71,500

Permits for New Residential Construction
	Units	Value
Total, 2007	93	$8,409,451
Single family	93	$8,409,451
Total, 2006	176	$17,872,408
Single family	176	$17,872,408

Real Property Valuation, 2007
	Parcels	Valuation
Total	5,680	$354,249,800
Vacant	677	5,486,400
Residential	4,416	240,247,400
Commercial	480	69,871,700
Industrial	45	22,873,900
Apartments	53	15,544,600
Farm land	6	43,800
Farm homestead	3	182,000

Average Property Value & Tax, 2007
Residential value	$54,408
Property tax	$2,440
Tax credit/rebate	$764

Public Library
Bridgeton Public Library
150 E Commerce St
Bridgeton, NJ 08302
856-451-2620

Director................ Gail S. Robinson

Library statistics, 2006
Population served	22,771
Full-time/total staff	1/5

	Total	Per capita
Holdings	62,294	2.74
Revenues	$375,523	$16.49
Expenditures	$351,540	$15.44
Annual visits	56,000	2.46
Internet terminals/annual users	8/12,870	

Public Safety
Number of officers, 2006		67

Crime	2005	2006
Total crimes	1,298	1,400
Violent	322	359
Murder	5	0
Rape	18	21
Robbery	125	156
Aggravated assault	174	182
Non-violent	976	1,041
Burglary	228	289
Larceny	672	666
Vehicle theft	76	86
Domestic violence	586	617
Arson	2	3
Total crime rate	57.1	58.4
Violent	14.2	15.0
Non-violent	42.9	43.4

Public School District
(for school year 2006-07 except as noted)

Bridgeton School District
Bank St, PO Box 657
Bridgeton, NJ 08302
856-455-8030

Superintendent	H. Victor Gilson
Number of schools	8
Grade plan	K-12
Enrollment	4,577
Attendance rate, '05-06	92.7%
Dropout rate	8.8%
Students per teacher	8.8
Per pupil expenditure	$14,369
Median faculty salary	$44,500
Median administrator salary	$85,906
Grade 12 enrollment	180
High school graduation rate	77.0%

Assessment test results
(percent scoring at proficient or advanced level)
	Language	Math
NJASK-Grade 3	52.4%	68.3%
GEPA-Grade 8	43.0%	42.6%
HSPA-High School	66.2%	32.8%

SAT score averages
Pct tested	Math	Verbal	Writing
44%	414	421	418

Teacher Qualifications
Avg. years of experience	7
Highly-qualified teachers one subject/all subjects	100%/100%
With emergency credentials	1.0%

No Child Left Behind
AYP, 2005-06 .... Needs Improvement

Municipal Finance §

State Aid Programs, 2008
Total aid	$5,105,511
CMPTRA	3,890,635
Energy tax receipts	1,210,813
Garden State Trust	4,063

General Budget, 2007
Total tax levy	$16,045,276
County levy	4,992,246
County taxes	4,729,053
County library	0
County health	212,588
County open space	50,606
School levy	3,373,058
Muni. levy	7,679,972
Misc. revenues	12,143,680

Taxes
	2005	2006	2007
General tax rate per $100	4.082	4.272	4.487
County equalization ratio	92.65	81.85	73.09
Net valuation taxable	$362,228,210	$352,619,600	$357,843,234
State equalized value	$442,551,265	$486,398,952	$553,670,763

Somerset County
Bridgewater Township

Demographics & Socio-Economic Characteristics
(2000 US Census, except as noted)

Population
- 1980* 29,175
- 1990* 32,509
- 2000 42,940
  - Male 20,636
  - Female 22,304
- 2006 (estimate)* 44,818
  - Population density 1,381.1

Race & Hispanic Origin, 2000
Race
- White 36,527
- Black/African American 931
- American Indian/Alaska Native 33
- Asian 4,525
- Native Hawaiian/Pacific Islander 5
- Other race 381
- Two or more races 538
- Hispanic origin, total 2,056
  - Mexican 194
  - Puerto Rican 352
  - Cuban 143
  - Other Hispanic 1,367

Age & Nativity, 2000
- Under 5 years 3,295
- 18 years and over 31,922
- 21 years and over 30,977
- 65 years and over 5,443
- 85 years and over 778
- Median age 38.2
- Native-born 36,128
- Foreign-born 6,754

Educational Attainment, 2000
- Population 25 years and over 29,686
- Less than 9th grade 3.2%
- High school grad or higher 92.0%
- Bachelor's degree or higher 49.9%
- Graduate degree 22.0%

Income & Poverty, 1999
- Per capita income $39,555
- Median household income $88,308
- Median family income $99,832
- Persons in poverty 885
- H'holds receiving public assistance ... 138
- H'holds receiving social security .. 3,435

Households, 2000
- Total households 15,561
  - With persons under 18 6,121
  - With persons over 65 3,523
  - Family households 11,890
  - Single-person households 3,083
- Persons per household 2.71
- Persons per family 3.14

Labor & Employment
- Total civilian labor force, 2006** .. 25,057
  - Unemployment rate 3.0%
- Total civilian labor force, 2000 .. 23,028
  - Unemployment rate 2.8%
- *Employed persons 16 years and over by occupation, 2000*
  - Managers & professionals 12,020
  - Service occupations 1,705
  - Sales & office occupations 5,808
  - Farming, fishing & forestry 18
  - Construction & maintenance 1,514
  - Production & transportation 1,323
- Self-employed persons 1,045

‡ Main library for county
* US Census Bureau
** New Jersey Department of Labor

See Introduction for an explanation of all data sources.

General Information
Township of Bridgewater
700 Garretson Rd
Bridgewater, NJ 08807
908-725-6300

- Website .... www.bridgewaternj.gov
- Year of incorporation 1749
- Land/water area (sq. miles) 32.45/0.09
- Form of government .... Mayor-Council

Government
Legislative Districts
- US Congressional 7, 11
- State Legislative 16

Local Officials, 2008
- Mayor .... Patricia Flannery
- Manager .... James Naples
- Clerk .... Linda Doyle
- Treasurer .... Natasha Turchan
- Tax Assessor .... Anthony DiRado
- Tax Collector .... Dawn Murdock
- Attorney .... William Savo
- Construction Official ..... Steve Rodzinak
- Planner .... Scarlett Doyle
- Engineering .... Chip Mills
- Public Works Dir .... John Langel
- Police Chief .... Richard Borden
- Fire Chief .... (6 districts)

Housing & Construction
Housing Units, 2000*
- Total 15,879
- Median rent $1,096
- Median SF home value $268,100

Permits for New Residential Construction

	Units	Value
Total, 2007	46	$9,408,590
Single family	26	$6,169,035
Total, 2006	172	$27,363,680
Single family	32	$9,202,520

Real Property Valuation, 2007

	Parcels	Valuation
Total	15,916	$9,168,735,500
Vacant	765	139,533,300
Residential	14,665	6,852,458,800
Commercial	379	1,757,447,900
Industrial	47	364,458,400
Apartments	13	48,401,800
Farm land	37	122,100
Farm homestead	10	6,313,200

Average Property Value & Tax, 2007
- Residential value $467,378
- Property tax $7,909
- Tax credit/rebate $1,143

Public Library
Somerset County Library‡
1 Vogt Dr
Bridgewater, NJ 08807
908-526-4016

- Branch Director .... James M. Hecht

County Library statistics, 2006
- Population served 176,402
- Full-time/total staff 53/128

	Total	Per capita
Holdings	979,932	5.56
Revenues	$12,643,845	$71.68
Expenditures	$12,702,699	$72.01
Annual visits	1,060,418	6.01
Internet terminals/annual users	.	113/213,510

Public Safety
Number of officers, 2006 77

Crime	2005	2006
Total crimes	616	676
Violent	20	17
Murder	0	0
Rape	2	0
Robbery	6	8
Aggravated assault	12	9
Non-violent	596	659
Burglary	85	99
Larceny	479	531
Vehicle theft	32	29
Domestic violence	132	144
Arson	6	4
Total crime rate	13.9	15.2
Violent	0.5	0.4
Non-violent	13.4	14.8

Public School District
(for school year 2006-07 except as noted)

Bridgewater-Raritan Regional School Dist.
836 Newmans Ln, PO Box 6030
Bridgewater, NJ 08807
908-685-2777

- Superintendent .... Michael Schilder
- Number of schools 22
- Grade plan K-12
- Enrollment 9,176
- Attendance rate, '05-06 .... 96.1%
- Dropout rate 0.5%
- Students per teacher 10.4
- Per pupil expenditure $13,025
- Median faculty salary $51,364
- Median administrator salary $120,072
- Grade 12 enrollment 644
- High school graduation rate 98.6%

Assessment test results
(percent scoring at proficient or advanced level)

	Language	Math
NJASK-Grade 3	86.9%	94.2%
GEPA-Grade 8	88.6%	83.9%
HSPA-High School	93.3%	87.2%

SAT score averages

Pct tested	Math	Verbal	Writing
94%	568	529	529

Teacher Qualifications
- Avg. years of experience 7
- Highly-qualified teachers
  one subject/all subjects 99.5%/99.5%
- With emergency credentials 0.3%

No Child Left Behind
- AYP, 2005-06 .... Meets Standards

Municipal Finance
State Aid Programs, 2008
- Total aid $8,152,547
- CMPTRA 1,930,733
- Energy tax receipts 6,215,691
- Garden State Trust 6,123

General Budget, 2007
- Total tax levy $155,319,789
- County levy 33,999,517
  - County taxes 27,494,142
  - County library 3,492,423
  - County health 0
  - County open space 3,012,952
- School levy 100,637,326
- Muni. levy 20,682,946
- Misc. revenues 19,569,732

Taxes	2005	2006	2007
General tax rate per $100	1.69	1.64	1.7
County equalization ratio	94.21	97.82	91.98
Net valuation taxable	$8,450,016,633	$9,058,616,300	$9,178,040,920
State equalized value	$9,234,990,856	$9,941,810,714	$9,676,888,191

The New Jersey Municipal Data Book

Brielle Borough
Monmouth County

Demographics & Socio-Economic Characteristics
(2000 US Census, except as noted)

Population
- 1980* 4,068
- 1990* 4,406
- 2000 4,893
  - Male 2,336
  - Female 2,557
- 2006 (estimate)* 4,852
- Population density 2,725.8

Race & Hispanic Origin, 2000
Race
- White 4,553
- Black/African American 172
- American Indian/Alaska Native 3
- Asian 33
- Native Hawaiian/Pacific Islander 0
- Other race 79
- Two or more races 53
- Hispanic origin, total 162
  - Mexican 88
  - Puerto Rican 31
  - Cuban 11
  - Other Hispanic 32

Age & Nativity, 2000
- Under 5 years 348
- 18 years and over 3,733
- 21 years and over 3,631
- 65 years and over 868
- 85 years and over 77
  - Median age 42.9
- Native-born 4,734
- Foreign-born 159

Educational Attainment, 2000
- Population 25 years and over 3,533
- Less than 9th grade 1.8%
- High school grad or higher 94.8%
- Bachelor's degree or higher 44.7%
- Graduate degree 14.7%

Income & Poverty, 1999
- Per capita income $35,785
- Median household income $68,368
- Median family income $82,867
- Persons in poverty 193
- H'holds receiving public assistance 24
- H'holds receiving social security 693

Households, 2000
- Total households 1,938
  - With persons under 18 640
  - With persons over 65 633
  - Family households 1,414
  - Single-person households 456
- Persons per household 2.52
- Persons per family 3.00

Labor & Employment
- Total civilian labor force, 2006** 2,476
  - Unemployment rate 3.5%
- Total civilian labor force, 2000 2,297
  - Unemployment rate 3.5%
- *Employed persons 16 years and over by occupation, 2000*
  - Managers & professionals 1,241
  - Service occupations 225
  - Sales & office occupations 484
  - Farming, fishing & forestry 16
  - Construction & maintenance 107
  - Production & transportation 144
- Self-employed persons 229

* US Census Bureau
** New Jersey Department of Labor

General Information
Borough of Brielle
601 Union Ln
Brielle, NJ 08730
732-528-6600

- Website .... www.briellenj.com
- Year of incorporation 1919
- Land/water area (sq. miles) 1.78/0.59
- Form of government .... Borough

Government
Legislative Districts
- US Congressional 4
- State Legislative 11

Local Officials, 2008
- Mayor .... Thomas B. Nichol
- Manager .... Thomas Nolan
- Clerk .... Thomas Nolan
- Finance Dir .... Stephen Mayer
- Tax Assessor .... Mary Lou Hartman
- Tax Collector .... Colleen Castronova
- Attorney .... Nicholas Montenegro
- Building .... Albert Ratz Jr
- Comm Dev/Planning .... NA
- Engineering .... Alan Hilla Jr
- Public Works .... William Burkhardt Jr
- Police Chief .... Michael Palmer
- Emerg/Fire Director ..... Thomas B. Nichol

Housing & Construction
Housing Units, 2000*
- Total 2,123
- Median rent $1,090
- Median SF home value $285,000

Permits for New Residential Construction

	Units	Value
Total, 2007	17	$4,712,792
Single family	17	$4,712,792
Total, 2006	29	$7,888,791
Single family	29	$7,888,791

Real Property Valuation, 2007

	Parcels	Valuation
Total	2,090	$1,703,450,200
Vacant	96	43,966,400
Residential	1,908	1,522,792,700
Commercial	83	122,709,300
Industrial	0	0
Apartments	3	13,981,800
Farm land	0	0
Farm homestead	0	0

Average Property Value & Tax, 2007
- Residential value $798,109
- Property tax $8,876
- Tax credit/rebate $1,125

Public Library
Brielle Public Library
610 South St
Brielle, NJ 08730
732-528-9381

- Director .... Kerri DiBrienza

Library statistics, 2006
- Population served 4,893
- Full-time/total staff 1/1

	Total	Per capita
Holdings	36,609	7.48
Revenues	$208,916	$42.70
Expenditures	$215,266	$43.99
Annual visits	30,000	6.13
Internet terminals/annual users		6/12,812

Public Safety
- Number of officers, 2006 15

Crime	2005	2006
Total crimes	53	51
Violent	6	5
Murder	0	0
Rape	0	1
Robbery	1	1
Aggravated assault	5	3
Non-violent	47	46
Burglary	15	25
Larceny	28	20
Vehicle theft	4	1
Domestic violence	25	16
Arson	0	0
Total crime rate	10.8	10.5
Violent	1.2	1.0
Non-violent	9.6	9.4

Public School District
(for school year 2006-07 except as noted)

Brielle Borough School District
605 Union Lane
Brielle, NJ 08730
732-528-6400

- Superintendent .... Christine Carlson
- Number of schools 1
- Grade plan K-8
- Enrollment 704
- Attendance rate, '05-06 .... 95.8%
- Dropout rate .... NA
- Students per teacher 11.7
- Per pupil expenditure $10,121
- Median faculty salary $47,920
- Median administrator salary $95,366
- Grade 12 enrollment .... NA
- High school graduation rate .... NA

Assessment test results
(percent scoring at proficient or advanced level)

	Language	Math
NJASK-Grade 3	88.2%	100.0%
GEPA-Grade 8	85.5%	87.1%
HSPA-High School	NA	NA

SAT score averages

Pct tested	Math	Verbal	Writing
NA	NA	NA	NA

Teacher Qualifications
- Avg. years of experience 9
- Highly-qualified teachers
  - one subject/all subjects 100%/100%
- With emergency credentials 0.0%

No Child Left Behind
- AYP, 2005-06 .... Meets Standards

Municipal Finance
State Aid Programs, 2008
- Total aid $353,870
  - CMPTRA 0
  - Energy tax receipts 353,870
  - Garden State Trust 0

General Budget, 2007
- Total tax levy $18,950,931
  - County levy 4,014,533
    - County taxes 3,585,219
    - County library 205,283
    - County health 0
    - County open space 224,031
  - School levy 10,373,298
  - Muni. levy 4,563,100
  - Misc. revenues 2,396,924

Taxes	2005	2006	2007
General tax rate per $100	2.83	2.894	1.113
County equalization ratio	53.03	47.36	114.03
Net valuation taxable	$606,638,971	$611,796,200	$1,703,970,532
State equalized value	$1,280,909,989	$1,485,900,588	$1,557,746,952

Atlantic County — Brigantine City

Demographics & Socio-Economic Characteristics
(2000 US Census, except as noted)

Population
1980*	8,318
1990*	11,354
2000	12,594
Male	6,138
Female	6,456
2006 (estimate)*	12,886
Population density	2,004.0

Race & Hispanic Origin, 2000
Race
White	10,472
Black/African American	496
American Indian/Alaska Native	23
Asian	720
Native Hawaiian/Pacific Islander	6
Other race	588
Two or more races	289
Hispanic origin, total	1,185
Mexican	171
Puerto Rican	526
Cuban	29
Other Hispanic	459

Age & Nativity, 2000
Under 5 years	701
18 years and over	9,973
21 years and over	9,689
65 years and over	2,090
85 years and over	161
Median age	40.7
Native-born	11,045
Foreign-born	1,549

Educational Attainment, 2000
Population 25 years and over	9,314
Less than 9th grade	3.0%
High school grad or higher	84.5%
Bachelor's degree or higher	23.8%
Graduate degree	8.5%

Income & Poverty, 1999
Per capita income	$23,950
Median household income	$44,639
Median family income	$51,679
Persons in poverty	1,185
H'holds receiving public assistance	113
H'holds receiving social security	1,711

Households, 2000
Total households	5,473
With persons under 18	1,449
With persons over 65	1,536
Family households	3,338
Single-person households	1,678
Persons per household	2.30
Persons per family	2.89

Labor & Employment
Total civilian labor force, 2006**	7,365
Unemployment rate	4.3%
Total civilian labor force, 2000	6,713
Unemployment rate	4.6%

Employed persons 16 years and over by occupation, 2000
Managers & professionals	1,844
Service occupations	2,159
Sales & office occupations	1,652
Farming, fishing & forestry	29
Construction & maintenance	373
Production & transportation	350
Self-employed persons	295

‡ Branch of county library
* US Census Bureau
** New Jersey Department of Labor

See Introduction for an explanation of all data sources.

General Information
City of Brigantine
1417 W Brigantine Ave
Brigantine, NJ 08203
609-266-7600

Website	www.brigantinebeachnj.com
Year of incorporation	1924
Land/water area (sq. miles)	6.43/3.36
Form of government	Council-Manager

Government

Legislative Districts
US Congressional	2
State Legislative	2

Local Officials, 2008
Mayor	Philip Guenther
Manager	James Barber
Clerk	Lynn Sweeney
Finance Dir	Christian Johansen
Tax Assessor	Barbara Saccoccia
Tax Collector	Dana Wineland
Attorney	Timothy Maguire
Building	Rich Stevens
Comm Dev/Planning	NA
Engineering	Edward Stinson
Public Works	Ernie Purdy
Police Chief	Arthur L. Gordy
Emerg/Fire Director	Stanley Cwiklinski

Housing & Construction

Housing Units, 2000*
Total	9,304
Median rent	$792
Median SF home value	$144,400

Permits for New Residential Construction
	Units	Value
Total, 2007	25	$9,135,530
Single family	25	$9,135,530
Total, 2006	78	$22,410,120
Single family	70	$20,632,720

Real Property Valuation, 2007
	Parcels	Valuation
Total	8,800	$4,665,552,000
Vacant	252	122,550,100
Residential	8,424	4,443,305,200
Commercial	117	95,193,900
Industrial	0	0
Apartments	7	4,502,800
Farm land	0	0
Farm homestead	0	0

Average Property Value & Tax, 2007
Residential value	$527,458
Property tax	$5,007
Tax credit/rebate	$974

Public Library
Brigantine Branch Library‡
201 15th St
Brigantine, NJ 08203
609-266-0110

Branch Librarian: Sue Wick

Library statistics, 2006
see Atlantic County profile for library system statistics

Public Safety
Number of officers, 2006	37

Crime
	2005	2006
Total crimes	220	234
Violent	12	8
Murder	1	0
Rape	1	0
Robbery	4	3
Aggravated assault	6	5
Non-violent	208	226
Burglary	30	51
Larceny	170	169
Vehicle theft	8	6
Domestic violence	202	158
Arson	1	2
Total crime rate	17.2	18.2
Violent	0.9	0.6
Non-violent	16.3	17.6

Public School District
(for school year 2006-07 except as noted)

Brigantine City School District
301 E. Evans Blvd, PO Box 947
Brigantine, NJ 08203
609-266-7671

Superintendent	Robert A. Previti
Number of schools	2
Grade plan	K-8
Enrollment	885
Attendance rate, '05-06	94.4%
Dropout rate	NA
Students per teacher	9.8
Per pupil expenditure	$15,417
Median faculty salary	$68,623
Median administrator salary	$112,661
Grade 12 enrollment	NA
High school graduation rate	NA

Assessment test results
(percent scoring at proficient or advanced level)
	Language	Math
NJASK-Grade 3	88.9%	90.0%
GEPA-Grade 8	79.8%	79.8%
HSPA-High School	NA	NA

SAT score averages
Pct tested	Math	Verbal	Writing
NA	NA	NA	NA

Teacher Qualifications
Avg. years of experience	15
Highly-qualified teachers one subject/all subjects	100%/100%
With emergency credentials	0.0%

No Child Left Behind
AYP, 2005-06 .... Meets Standards

Municipal Finance

State Aid Programs, 2008
Total aid	$877,612
CMPTRA	80,580
Energy tax receipts	788,284
Garden State Trust	8,748

General Budget, 2007
Total tax levy	$44,310,585
County levy	12,905,996
County taxes	10,235,501
County library	1,291,608
County health	526,298
County open space	852,588
School levy	15,021,496
Muni. levy	16,383,093
Misc. revenues	5,346,126

Taxes
	2005	2006	2007
General tax rate per $100	3.365	0.909	0.95
County equalization ratio	43.06	139.47	109.55
Net valuation taxable	$1,180,618,094	$4,716,824,700	$4,667,422,755
State equalized value	$3,311,691,708	$4,307,470,826	$4,547,420,248

©2008 Information Publications, Inc. All rights reserved. Photocopying prohibited. For additional copies, contact the publisher at www.informationpublications.com or (877)544-INFO (4636)

The New Jersey Municipal Data Book

Brooklawn Borough
Camden County

Demographics & Socio-Economic Characteristics
(2000 US Census, except as noted)

Population
1980*	2,133
1990*	1,805
2000	2,354
Male	1,109
Female	1,245
2006 (estimate)*	2,294
Population density	4,880.9

Race & Hispanic Origin, 2000
Race
White	2,125
Black/African American	101
American Indian/Alaska Native	2
Asian	25
Native Hawaiian/Pacific Islander	0
Other race	56
Two or more races	45
Hispanic origin, total	111
Mexican	7
Puerto Rican	73
Cuban	0
Other Hispanic	31

Age & Nativity, 2000
Under 5 years	165
18 years and over	1,746
21 years and over	1,670
65 years and over	310
85 years and over	40
Median age	35.2
Native-born	2,283
Foreign-born	71

Educational Attainment, 2000
Population 25 years and over	1,525
Less than 9th grade	4.5%
High school grad or higher	80.1%
Bachelor's degree or higher	7.9%
Graduate degree	3.5%

Income & Poverty, 1999
Per capita income	$18,295
Median household income	$39,600
Median family income	$47,891
Persons in poverty	170
H'holds receiving public assistance	12
H'holds receiving social security	249

Households, 2000
Total households	961
With persons under 18	345
With persons over 65	246
Family households	601
Single-person households	297
Persons per household	2.45
Persons per family	3.09

Labor & Employment
Total civilian labor force, 2006**	1,371
Unemployment rate	3.4%
Total civilian labor force, 2000	1,263
Unemployment rate	3.2%

Employed persons 16 years and over by occupation, 2000
Managers & professionals	239
Service occupations	259
Sales & office occupations	352
Farming, fishing & forestry	5
Construction & maintenance	155
Production & transportation	212
Self-employed persons	48

* US Census Bureau
** New Jersey Department of Labor

General Information
Borough of Brooklawn
301 Christiana St
Brooklawn, NJ 08030
856-456-0750

Website	www.brooklawn.us
Year of incorporation	1924
Land/water area (sq. miles)	0.47/0.05
Form of government	Borough

Government

Legislative Districts
US Congressional	1
State Legislative	5

Local Officials, 2008
Mayor	John Soubasis
Manager/Admin	NA
Clerk	Barbara Lewis
Finance Dir	Barbara Lewis
Tax Assessor	Anthony Leone
Tax Collector	Maria S. Branson
Attorney	Timothy Higgins
Building	Christopher Mecca
Comm Dev/Planning	NA
Engineering	Chuck Reibel
Public Works	Donna Domico
Police Chief	Francis McKinney
Emerg/Fire Director	A. Sam Cilurso

Housing & Construction

Housing Units, 2000*
Total	1,025
Median rent	$622
Median SF home value	$79,300

Permits for New Residential Construction
	Units	Value
Total, 2007	0	$0
Single family	0	$0
Total, 2006	0	$0
Single family	0	$0

Real Property Valuation, 2007
	Parcels	Valuation
Total	803	$78,666,800
Vacant	33	458,300
Residential	687	52,298,600
Commercial	76	24,059,500
Industrial	3	819,700
Apartments	4	1,030,700
Farm land	0	0
Farm homestead	0	0

Average Property Value & Tax, 2007
Residential value	$76,126
Property tax	$3,073
Tax credit/rebate	$739

Public Library
No public municipal library

Library statistics, 2006
Population served	NA
Full-time/total staff	NA/NA

	Total	Per capita
Holdings	NA	NA
Revenues	NA	NA
Expenditures	NA	NA
Annual visits	NA	NA
Internet terminals/annual users	NA/NA	

Taxes
	2005	2006	2007
General tax rate per $100	3.793	3.964	4.037
County equalization ratio	87.63	78.51	64.93
Net valuation taxable	$78,043,592	$78,001,000	$78,842,199
State equalized value	$99,405,925	$120,339,285	$138,648,907

Public Safety
Number of officers, 2006 ... 7

Crime	2005	2006
Total crimes	204	248
Violent	27	6
Murder	0	1
Rape	4	1
Robbery	15	2
Aggravated assault	8	2
Non-violent	177	242
Burglary	14	30
Larceny	150	196
Vehicle theft	13	16
Domestic violence	17	21
Arson	0	0
Total crime rate	87.7	107.1
Violent	11.6	2.6
Non-violent	76.1	104.5

Public School District
(for school year 2006-07 except as noted)

Brooklawn School District
301 Haakon Rd
Brooklawn, NJ 08030
856-456-4039

Superintendent	John Kellmayer
Number of schools	1
Grade plan	K-8
Enrollment	316
Attendance rate, '05-06	94.9%
Dropout rate	NA
Students per teacher	11.3
Per pupil expenditure	$9,557
Median faculty salary	$47,066
Median administrator salary	$86,008
Grade 12 enrollment	NA
High school graduation rate	NA

Assessment test results
(percent scoring at proficient or advanced level)
	Language	Math
NJASK-Grade 3	82.1%	79.4%
GEPA-Grade 8	78.4%	75.6%
HSPA-High School	NA	NA

SAT score averages
Pct tested	Math	Verbal	Writing
NA	NA	NA	NA

Teacher Qualifications
Avg. years of experience	10
Highly-qualified teachers one subject/all subjects	100%/100%
With emergency credentials	0.0%

No Child Left Behind
AYP, 2005-06 ... Meets Standards

Municipal Finance

State Aid Programs, 2008
Total aid	$178,660
CMPTRA	0
Energy tax receipts	178,660
Garden State Trust	0

General Budget, 2007
Total tax levy	$3,182,535
County levy	859,015
County taxes	780,308
County library	54,322
County health	0
County open space	24,386
School levy	1,158,805
Muni. levy	1,164,714
Misc. revenues	1,398,471

Atlantic County — Buena Borough

Demographics & Socio-Economic Characteristics
(2000 US Census, except as noted)

Population
1980*	3,642
1990*	4,441
2000	3,873
Male	1,887
Female	1,986
2006 (estimate)*	3,804
Population density	499.9

Race & Hispanic Origin, 2000
Race
- White 2,993
- Black/African American 296
- American Indian/Alaska Native 20
- Asian 17
- Native Hawaiian/Pacific Islander 1
- Other race 408
- Two or more races 138

Hispanic origin, total 916
- Mexican 175
- Puerto Rican 660
- Cuban 8
- Other Hispanic 73

Age & Nativity, 2000
- Under 5 years 245
- 18 years and over 2,876
- 21 years and over 2,715
- 65 years and over 613
- 85 years and over 59
- Median age 36.2
- Native-born 3,626
- Foreign-born 247

Educational Attainment, 2000
- Population 25 years and over ... 2,552
- Less than 9th grade 17.4%
- High school grad or higher 62.3%
- Bachelor's degree or higher 8.8%
- Graduate degree 2.5%

Income & Poverty, 1999
- Per capita income $16,717
- Median household income $35,679
- Median family income $44,352
- Persons in poverty 725
- H'holds receiving public assistance ... 28
- H'holds receiving social security ... 513

Households, 2000
- Total households 1,454
-   With persons under 18 525
-   With persons over 65 475
-   Family households 978
-   Single-person households 407
- Persons per household 2.64
- Persons per family 3.23

Labor & Employment
- Total civilian labor force, 2006** ... 1,907
-   Unemployment rate 6.4%
- Total civilian labor force, 2000 ... 1,779
-   Unemployment rate 8.3%

Employed persons 16 years and over by occupation, 2000
- Managers & professionals 353
- Service occupations 296
- Sales & office occupations 401
- Farming, fishing & forestry ... 103
- Construction & maintenance ... 190
- Production & transportation .. 288
- Self-employed persons 80

* US Census Bureau
** New Jersey Department of Labor

See Introduction for an explanation of all data sources.

General Information
Borough of Buena
616 Central Ave
Minotola, NJ 08341
856-697-9393

- Website .... buenaboro.org
- Year of incorporation 1948
- Land/water area (sq. miles) ... 7.61/0.00
- Form of government .... Borough

Government

Legislative Districts
- US Congressional 2
- State Legislative 1

Local Officials, 2008
- Mayor .... Joseph Baruffi
- Manager/Admin .... NA
- Clerk .... Maryann Coraluzzo
- Finance Dir .... Nancy Brunini
- Tax Assessor .... Dennis Deklerk
- Tax Collector ..... Mary Ann Coraluzzo
- Attorney .... Robert DeSanto
- Building .... David Zappariello
- Comm Dev/Planning .... NA
- Engineering ..... Remington & Vernick
- Public Works .... John Brunini
- Police Chief .... Douglas Adams
- Fire/Emergency Dir .... NA

Housing & Construction

Housing Units, 2000*
- Total 1,553
- Median rent $639
- Median SF home value $98,100

Permits for New Residential Construction
	Units	Value
Total, 2007	2	$272,500
Single family	2	$272,500
Total, 2006	8	$1,090,000
Single family	8	$1,090,000

Real Property Valuation, 2007
	Parcels	Valuation
Total	1,802	$293,647,700
Vacant	206	9,554,900
Residential	1,222	219,281,700
Commercial	102	29,807,300
Industrial	3	5,409,800
Apartments	8	8,243,600
Farm land	160	1,718,200
Farm homestead	101	19,632,200

Average Property Value & Tax, 2007
- Residential value $180,585
- Property tax $4,093
- Tax credit/rebate $865

Public Library
No public municipal library

Library statistics, 2006
- Population served .... NA
- Full-time/total staff .... NA/NA

	Total	Per capita
Holdings	NA	NA
Revenues	NA	NA
Expenditures	NA	NA
Annual visits	NA	NA
Internet terminals/annual users	NA/NA	

Taxes
	2005	2006	2007
General tax rate per $100	3.773	4.129	2.267
County equalization ratio	75.35	65.87	106.57
Net valuation taxable	$146,766,272	$147,789,000	$295,454,759
State equalized value	$222,812,012	$274,762,119	$299,654,407

Public Safety
Number of officers, 2006 9

Crime	2005	2006
Total crimes	162	136
Violent	25	22
Murder	0	0
Rape	4	1
Robbery	0	1
Aggravated assault	21	20
Non-violent	137	114
Burglary	43	45
Larceny	92	66
Vehicle theft	2	3
Domestic violence	44	56
Arson	0	1
Total crime rate	41.9	35.3
Violent	6.5	5.7
Non-violent	35.5	29.6

Public School District
(for school year 2006-07 except as noted)

Buena Regional School District
Harding Highway, PO Box 309
Buena, NJ 08310
856-697-0800

- Superintendent .... Walter Whitaker
- Number of schools 12
- Grade plan K-12
- Enrollment 2,594
- Attendance rate, '05-06 .... 91.6%
- Dropout rate 1.8%
- Students per teacher 12.0
- Per pupil expenditure $12,313
- Median faculty salary $54,469
- Median administrator salary .. $98,839
- Grade 12 enrollment 221
- High school graduation rate ... 89.6%

Assessment test results
(percent scoring at proficient or advanced level)

	Language	Math
NJASK-Grade 3	76.9%	84.2%
GEPA-Grade 8	61.7%	59.6%
HSPA-High School	81.2%	61.8%

SAT score averages
Pct tested	Math	Verbal	Writing
46%	479	475	472

Teacher Qualifications
- Avg. years of experience 12
- Highly-qualified teachers
  - one subject/all subjects ... 99.5%/99.5%
- With emergency credentials 0.0%

No Child Left Behind
AYP, 2005-06 .... Meets Standards

Municipal Finance

State Aid Programs, 2008
- Total aid $349,357
-   CMPTRA 0
-   Energy tax receipts 349,357
-   Garden State Trust 0

General Budget, 2007
- Total tax levy $6,696,652
-   County levy 856,761
-     County taxes 681,966
-     County library 84,541
-     County health 34,448
-     County open space 55,805
-   School levy 3,988,253
-   Muni. levy 1,851,638
-   Misc. revenues 1,608,597

Buena Vista Township
Atlantic County

Demographics & Socio-Economic Characteristics
(2000 US Census, except as noted)

Population
- 1980" 6,959
- 1990* 7,655
- 2000 7,436
  - Male 3,622
  - Female 3,814
- 2006 (estimate)* 7,487
- Population density 181.0

Race & Hispanic Origin, 2000
Race
- White 5,751
- Black/African American 1,167
- American Indian/Alaska Native 16
- Asian 17
- Native Hawaiian/Pacific Islander ... 1
- Other race 303
- Two or more races 181
- Hispanic origin, total 689
  - Mexican 63
  - Puerto Rican 513
  - Cuban 7
  - Other Hispanic 106

Age & Nativity, 2000
- Under 5 years 409
- 18 years and over 5,598
- 21 years and over 5,317
- 65 years and over 1,138
- 85 years and over 120
  - Median age 39.0
- Native-born 7,174
- Foreign-born 262

Educational Attainment, 2000
- Population 25 years and over .. 5,007
- Less than 9th grade 9.7%
- High school grad or higher 70.3%
- Bachelor's degree or higher ... 12.2%
- Graduate degree 3.8%

Income & Poverty, 1999
- Per capita income $18,382
- Median household income $43,770
- Median family income $50,403
- Persons in poverty 890
- H'holds receiving public assistance 47
- H'holds receiving social security 861

Households, 2000
- Total households 2,648
  - With persons under 18 935
  - With persons over 65 818
  - Family households 1,973
  - Single-person households 555
- Persons per household 2.77
- Persons per family 3.20

Labor & Employment
- Total civilian labor force, 2006** 3,983
  - Unemployment rate 4.6%
- Total civilian labor force, 2000 3,719
  - Unemployment rate 6.7%

Employed persons 16 years and over by occupation, 2000
- Managers & professionals 683
- Service occupations 599
- Sales & office occupations 938
- Farming, fishing & forestry 40
- Construction & maintenance 550
- Production & transportation 658
- Self-employed persons 195

* US Census Bureau
** New Jersey Department of Labor

General Information
Township of Buena Vista
890 Harding Hwy
PO Box 605
Buena, NJ 08310
856-697-2100

- Website .... www.buenavistatownship.org
- Year of incorporation 1867
- Land/water area (sq. miles) 41.36/0.16
- Form of government .... Township

Government
Legislative Districts
- US Congressional 2
- State Legislative 1

Local Officials, 2008
- Mayor .... Chuck Chiarello
- Manager .... Ronald Trebing
- Clerk .... Linda Gonzales (Actg)
- Finance Dir .... Ronald Trebing
- Tax Assessor .... Bernadette Leonardi
- Tax Collector .... Terence S. Graff
- Attorney .... Mark Stein
- Building .... David S. Scheidegg
- Comm Dev/Planning .... NA
- Engineering .... David S. Scheidegg
- Public Works .... Richard Calareso
- Police Chief .... NA
- Fire/Emergency Dir .... NA

Housing & Construction
Housing Units, 2000*
- Total 2,827
- Median rent $740
- Median SF home value $96,100

Permits for New Residential Construction

	Units	Value
Total, 2007	19	$2,907,206
Single family	19	$2,907,206
Total, 2006	9	$1,224,947
Single family	9	$1,224,947

Real Property Valuation, 2007

	Parcels	Valuation
Total	6,021	$273,824,600
Vacant	3,142	17,043,300
Residential	2,387	214,573,600
Commercial	88	22,353,700
Industrial	15	6,281,100
Apartments	0	0
Farm land	278	2,149,700
Farm homestead	111	11,423,200

Average Property Value & Tax, 2007
- Residential value $90,471
- Property tax $3,642
- Tax credit/rebate $872

Public Library
No public municipal library

Library statistics, 2006
- Population served .... NA
- Full-time/total staff .... NA/NA

	Total	Per capita
Holdings	NA	NA
Revenues	NA	NA
Expenditures	NA	NA
Annual visits	NA	NA
Internet terminals/annual users	NA/NA	

Taxes

	2005	2006	2007
General tax rate per $100	3.626	4.054	4.026
County equalization ratio	66.2	57.84	52.14
Net valuation taxable	$262,577,992	$267,848,900	$274,598,634
State equalized value	$453,973,015	$514,538,404	$581,649,299

Public Safety
Number of officers, 2006 0

Crime

	2005	2006
Total crimes	164	184
Violent	25	20
Murder	0	0
Rape	2	1
Robbery	2	4
Aggravated assault	21	15
Non-violent	139	164
Burglary	42	59
Larceny	74	94
Vehicle theft	23	11
Domestic violence	77	20
Arson	5	1
Total crime rate	21.7	24.4
Violent	3.3	2.7
Non-violent	18.4	21.8

Public School District
(for school year 2006-07 except as noted)

Buena Regional School District
Harding Highway, PO Box 309
Buena, NJ 08310
856-697-0800

- Superintendent .... Walter Whitaker
- Number of schools 12
- Grade plan K-12
- Enrollment 2,594
- Attendance rate, '05-06 .... 91.6%
- Dropout rate 1.8%
- Students per teacher 12.0
- Per pupil expenditure $12,313
- Median faculty salary $54,469
- Median administrator salary $98,839
- Grade 12 enrollment 221
- High school graduation rate 89.6%

Assessment test results
(percent scoring at proficient or advanced level)

	Language	Math
NJASK-Grade 3	76.9%	84.2%
GEPA-Grade 8	61.7%	59.6%
HSPA-High School	81.2%	61.8%

SAT score averages

Pct tested	Math	Verbal	Writing
46%	479	475	472

Teacher Qualifications
- Avg. years of experience 12
- Highly-qualified teachers
  one subject/all subjects 99.5%/99.5%
- With emergency credentials 0.0%

No Child Left Behind
- AYP, 2005-06 .... Meets Standards

Municipal Finance
State Aid Programs, 2008
- Total aid $890,069
  - CMPTRA 73,168
  - Energy tax receipts 788,175
  - Garden State Trust 28,726

General Budget, 2007
- Total tax levy $11,054,532
  - County levy 1,620,774
    - County taxes 1,290,081
    - County library 159,943
    - County health 65,173
    - County open space 105,578
  - School levy 7,801,418
  - Muni. levy 1,632,340
- Misc. revenues 2,821,613

64 The New Jersey Municipal Data Book

Burlington County | Burlington City

Demographics & Socio-Economic Characteristics
(2000 US Census, except as noted)

Population
- 1980*........................10,246
- 1990*.........................9,835
- 2000..........................9,736
  - Male........................4,618
  - Female......................5,118
- 2006 (estimate)*..............9,715
- Population density........3,238.3

Race & Hispanic Origin, 2000
Race
- White.........................6,638
- Black/African American........2,592
- American Indian/Alaska Native...26
- Asian...........................125
- Native Hawaiian/Pacific Islander..1
- Other race.....................126
- Two or more races..............228
- Hispanic origin, total.........332
  - Mexican.......................32
  - Puerto Rican.................193
  - Cuban...........................7
  - Other Hispanic...............100

Age & Nativity, 2000
- Under 5 years..................618
- 18 years and over............7,408
- 21 years and over............7,072
- 65 years and over............1,636
- 85 years and over..............189
  - Median age..................38.1
- Native-born..................9,129
- Foreign-born...................607

Educational Attainment, 2000
- Population 25 years and over...6,646
- Less than 9th grade...........6.7%
- High school grad or higher...77.6%
- Bachelor's degree or higher..12.1%
- Graduate degree...............3.7%

Income & Poverty, 1999
- Per capita income..........$20,208
- Median household income....$43,115
- Median family income.......$47,969
- Persons in poverty.............776
- H'holds receiving public assistance...156
- H'holds receiving social security...1,357

Households, 2000
- Total households.............3,898
  - With persons under 18......1,270
  - With persons over 65.......1,254
  - Family households..........2,521
  - Single-person households...1,167
- Persons per household.........2.48
- Persons per family............3.09

Labor & Employment
- Total civilian labor force, 2006**......5,810
  - Unemployment rate...........5.9%
- Total civilian labor force, 2000......5,004
  - Unemployment rate...........5.6%

Employed persons 16 years and over by occupation, 2000
- Managers & professionals....1,161
- Service occupations............794
- Sales & office occupations..1,414
- Farming, fishing & forestry.....7
- Construction & maintenance...459
- Production & transportation...888
- Self-employed persons..........153

‡ Joint library with Burlington Township
* US Census Bureau
** New Jersey Department of Labor

See Introduction for an explanation of all data sources.

General Information
City of Burlington
525 High St
Burlington, NJ 08016
609-386-0200

- Website..............www.burlingtonnj.us
- Year of incorporation.............1693
- Land/water area (sq. miles).....3.00/0.72
- Form of government.........Mayor-Council

Government
Legislative Districts
- US Congressional.................4
- State Legislative................7

Local Officials, 2008
- Mayor..................James Fazzone
- Manager...................Eric Berry
- Clerk.................Cindy Crivaro
- Finance Dir........Kenneth MacMillan
- Tax Assessor..........Dennis Bianchini
- Tax Collector..........Lynette Miller
- Attorney...............Andrew Bayer
- Building..............Howard Wilkins
- Comm Dev/Planning................NA
- Engineering............Jeffrey Taylor
- Public Works.....................NA
- Police Chief..........John Lazzarotti
- Emerg/Fire Director........Ron Devlin

Housing & Construction
Housing Units, 2000*
- Total.........................4,181
- Median rent...................$620
- Median SF home value.......$97,600

Permits for New Residential Construction

	Units	Value
Total, 2007	2	$289,835
Single family	2	$289,835
Total, 2006	6	$733,440
Single family	6	$733,440

Real Property Valuation, 2007

	Parcels	Valuation
Total	3,832	$434,313,200
Vacant	250	7,740,400
Residential	3,225	306,394,100
Commercial	330	80,890,500
Industrial	10	25,946,900
Apartments	17	13,341,300
Farm land	0	0
Farm homestead	0	0

Average Property Value & Tax, 2007
- Residential value..........$95,006
- Property tax................$3,455
- Tax credit/rebate............$819

Public Library
Library Company of Burlington‡
23 W Union St
Burlington, NJ 08016
609-386-1273

- Director...........Sharon K. Vincz

Library statistics, 2006
- Population served.............9,736
- Full-time/total staff............0/1

	Total	Per capita
Holdings	64,243	6.60
Revenues	$151,647	$15.58
Expenditures	$135,118	$13.88
Annual visits	21,638	2.22
Internet terminals/annual users	12/7,852	

Taxes

	2005	2006	2007
General tax rate per $100	3.257	3.416	3.64
County equalization ratio	81.92	69.49	61.89
Net valuation taxable	$437,853,174	$435,366,000	$436,665,516
State equalized value	$630,095,228	$706,093,128	$757,416,989

Public Safety
- Number of officers, 2006.........32

Crime

	2005	2006
Total crimes	210	234
Violent	49	55
Murder	0	2
Rape	4	5
Robbery	16	23
Aggravated assault	29	25
Non-violent	161	179
Burglary	40	46
Larceny	93	116
Vehicle theft	28	17
Domestic violence	130	109
Arson	1	1
Total crime rate	21.4	23.9
Violent	5.0	5.6
Non-violent	16.4	18.3

Public School District
(for school year 2006-07 except as noted)

Burlington City School District
518 Locust Ave
Burlington, NJ 08016
609-387-5874

- Superintendent........Edward F. Gola Jr
- Number of schools................5
- Grade plan....................K-12
- Enrollment..................1,881
- Attendance rate, '05-06.....93.6%
- Dropout rate.................2.1%
- Students per teacher..........9.4
- Per pupil expenditure.....$15,266
- Median faculty salary.....$51,656
- Median administrator salary...$107,903
- Grade 12 enrollment...........131
- High school graduation rate..85.3%

Assessment test results
(percent scoring at proficient or advanced level)

	Language	Math
NJASK-Grade 3	61.1%	69.3%
GEPA-Grade 8	51.7%	48.8%
HSPA-High School	69.1%	50.7%

SAT score averages

Pct tested	Math	Verbal	Writing
56%	456	438	424

Teacher Qualifications
- Avg. years of experience........8
- Highly-qualified teachers
  - one subject/all subjects....100%/100%
- With emergency credentials....0.0%

No Child Left Behind
- AYP, 2005-06.........Meets Standards

Municipal Finance
State Aid Programs, 2008
- Total aid................$5,971,008
  - CMPTRA........................0
  - Energy tax receipts....5,971,008
  - Garden State Trust............0

General Budget, 2007
- Total tax levy.........$15,880,483
  - County levy...........2,977,875
    - County taxes........2,467,592
    - County library........226,439
    - County health.............0
    - County open space.....283,843
  - School levy...........8,159,671
  - Muni. levy............4,742,938
- Misc. revenues.........10,639,191

©2008 Information Publications, Inc. All rights reserved. Photocopying prohibited. For additional copies, contact the publisher at www.informationpublications.com or (877)544-INFO (4636)

The New Jersey Municipal Data Book   65

Burlington Township
Burlington County

Demographics & Socio-Economic Characteristics
(2000 US Census, except as noted)

Population
1980*	11,527
1990*	12,454
2000	20,294
Male	9,620
Female	10,674
2006 (estimate)*	21,787
Population density	1,617.4

Race & Hispanic Origin, 2000
Race
White	13,742
Black/African American	4,971
American Indian/Alaska Native	33
Asian	757
Native Hawaiian/Pacific Islander	6
Other race	296
Two or more races	489
Hispanic origin, total	814
Mexican	84
Puerto Rican	401
Cuban	28
Other Hispanic	301

Age & Nativity, 2000
Under 5 years	1,819
18 years and over	14,775
21 years and over	14,289
65 years and over	2,558
85 years and over	536
Median age	35.6
Native-born	18,695
Foreign-born	1,599

Educational Attainment, 2000
Population 25 years and over	13,724
Less than 9th grade	5.0%
High school grad or higher	85.1%
Bachelor's degree or higher	26.0%
Graduate degree	7.2%

Income & Poverty, 1999
Per capita income	$24,754
Median household income	$61,663
Median family income	$70,958
Persons in poverty	969
H'holds receiving public assistance	163
H'holds receiving social security	1,550

Households, 2000
Total households	7,112
With persons under 18	3,081
With persons over 65	1,313
Family households	5,280
Single-person households	1,521
Persons per household	2.72
Persons per family	3.18

Labor & Employment
Total civilian labor force, 2006**	12,219
Unemployment rate	4.2%
Total civilian labor force, 2000	10,552
Unemployment rate	3.9%

Employed persons 16 years and over by occupation, 2000
Managers & professionals	3,796
Service occupations	1,429
Sales & office occupations	2,857
Farming, fishing & forestry	43
Construction & maintenance	684
Production & transportation	1,336
Self-employed persons	314

‡ Joint library with Burlington City
* US Census Bureau
** New Jersey Department of Labor

General Information
Burlington Township
PO Box 340
Burlington, NJ 08016
609-386-4444

Website	www.twp.burlington.nj.us
Year of incorporation	1677
Land/water area (sq. miles)	13.47/0.50
Form of government	Mayor-Council

Government
Legislative Districts
US Congressional	3, 4
State Legislative	7

Local Officials, 2008
Mayor	Stephen M. George
Manager	Kevin J. McLernon
Clerk	Anthony J. Carnivale Jr
Finance Dir	Dawn M. Hubbard
Tax Assessor	Gil Goble
Tax Collector	Dolores Coolidge
Attorney	Kenneth S. Domzalski
Building	Henry Freck
Planning	Eileen Liss
Engineering	Robert L. Schreibel
Public Works	John Pinto
Police Chief	Walter J. Corter
Emerg/Fire Director	William Diamond

Housing & Construction
Housing Units, 2000*
Total	7,348
Median rent	$621
Median SF home value	$151,600

Permits for New Residential Construction
	Units	Value
Total, 2007	52	$6,085,876
Single family	52	$6,085,876
Total, 2006	40	$4,744,231
Single family	40	$4,744,231

Real Property Valuation, 2007
	Parcels	Valuation
Total	7,217	$2,369,033,538
Vacant	338	67,750,650
Residential	6,576	1,660,867,238
Commercial	182	386,969,200
Industrial	41	190,490,200
Apartments	7	55,990,000
Farm land	64	1,781,250
Farm homestead	9	5,185,000

Average Property Value & Tax, 2007
Residential value	$253,007
Property tax	$5,634
Tax credit/rebate	$971

Public Library
Library Company of Burlington‡
23 W Union St
Burlington, NJ 08016
609-386-1273

Director	Sharon K. Vincz

Library statistics, 2006
Population served	9,736
Full-time/total staff	0/1

	Total	Per capita
Holdings	64,243	6.60
Revenues	$151,647	$15.58
Expenditures	$135,118	$13.88
Annual visits	21,638	2.22
Internet terminals/annual users	12/7,852	

Public Safety
Number of officers, 2006 43

Crime	2005	2006
Total crimes	469	478
Violent	21	34
Murder	0	1
Rape	4	7
Robbery	14	14
Aggravated assault	3	12
Non-violent	448	444
Burglary	52	60
Larceny	363	357
Vehicle theft	33	27
Domestic violence	143	147
Arson	2	3
Total crime rate	21.3	21.8
Violent	1.0	1.6
Non-violent	20.4	20.3

Public School District
(for school year 2006-07 except as noted)

Burlington Township School District
PO Box 428
Burlington, NJ 08016
609-387-3955

Superintendent	Christopher Manno
Number of schools	3
Grade plan	K-12
Enrollment	3,404
Attendance rate, '05-06	95.6%
Dropout rate	0.6%
Students per teacher	12.7
Per pupil expenditure	$10,913
Median faculty salary	$46,750
Median administrator salary	$96,410
Grade 12 enrollment	239
High school graduation rate	98.8%

Assessment test results
(percent scoring at proficient or advanced level)
	Language	Math
NJASK-Grade 3	80.5%	84.3%
GEPA-Grade 8	75.2%	74.2%
HSPA-High School	87.1%	82.8%

SAT score averages
Pct tested	Math	Verbal	Writing
87%	473	467	464

Teacher Qualifications
Avg. years of experience	6
Highly-qualified teachers one subject/all subjects	100%/100%
With emergency credentials	0.0%

No Child Left Behind
AYP, 2005-06	Meets Standards

Municipal Finance
State Aid Programs, 2008
Total aid	$5,470,151
CMPTRA	0
Energy tax receipts	5,470,151
Garden State Trust	0

General Budget, 2007
Total tax levy	$52,838,777
County levy	11,340,755
County taxes	9,397,004
County library	862,446
County health	0
County open space	1,081,305
School levy	34,641,833
Muni. levy	6,856,189
Misc. revenues	18,225,837

Taxes
	2005	2006	2007
General tax rate per $100	1.867	2.02	2.23
County equalization ratio	114.58	96.67	87.88
Net valuation taxable	$2,341,425,856	$2,360,497,260	$2,372,999,223
State equalized value	$2,422,081,159	$2,690,343,660	$2,924,371,920

Morris County
Butler Borough

Demographics & Socio-Economic Characteristics
(2000 US Census, except as noted)
Population
1980*	7,616
1990*	7,392
2000	7,420
Male	3,655
Female	3,765
2006 (estimate)*	8,074
Population density	3,881.7

Race & Hispanic Origin, 2000
Race
- White 7,041
- Black/African American 46
- American Indian/Alaska Native 15
- Asian 137
- Native Hawaiian/Pacific Islander 1
- Other race 110
- Two or more races 70
- Hispanic origin, total 379
  - Mexican 109
  - Puerto Rican 89
  - Cuban 38
  - Other Hispanic 143

Age & Nativity, 2000
- Under 5 years 467
- 18 years and over 5,813
- 21 years and over 5,609
- 65 years and over 983
- 85 years and over 96
- Median age 37.5
- Native-born 6,690
- Foreign-born 730

Educational Attainment, 2000
- Population 25 years and over 5,293
- Less than 9th grade 4.9%
- High school grad or higher 85.8%
- Bachelor's degree or higher 24.1%
- Graduate degree 7.4%

Income & Poverty, 1999
- Per capita income $27,113
- Median household income $57,455
- Median family income $66,199
- Persons in poverty 372
- H'holds receiving public assistance 33
- H'holds receiving social security 703

Households, 2000
- Total households 2,868
  - With persons under 18 934
  - With persons over 65 725
  - Family households 2,025
  - Single-person households 691
- Persons per household 2.58
- Persons per family 3.09

Labor & Employment
- Total civilian labor force, 2006** 4,544
  - Unemployment rate 3.1%
- Total civilian labor force, 2000 4,156
  - Unemployment rate 3.0%

Employed persons 16 years and over by occupation, 2000
- Managers & professionals 1,419
- Service occupations 518
- Sales & office occupations 1,233
- Farming, fishing & forestry 4
- Construction & maintenance 378
- Production & transportation 481
- Self-employed persons 179

* US Census Bureau
** New Jersey Department of Labor

See Introduction for an explanation of all data sources.

General Information
Borough of Butler
1 Ace Rd
Butler, NJ 07405
973-838-7200

- Website .... www.butlerborough.com
- Year of incorporation 1901
- Land/water area (sq. miles) 2.08/0.02
- Form of government .... Borough

Government
Legislative Districts
- US Congressional 11
- State Legislative 26

Local Officials, 2008
- Mayor .... Joseph Heywang
- Manager .... James Lampmann
- Clerk .... Carol Ashley
- Finance Dir .... James Kozimor
- Tax Assessor .... Shawn Hopkins
- Tax Collector .... Cora Wright
- Attorney .... Martin Murphy
- Building .... Daniel Hagberg
- Comm Dev/Planning .... NA
- Engineering .... Paul Darmolfaski
- Public Works .... Ed Becker
- Police Chief .... Ed Card
- Emerg/Fire Director .... Earl Dean

Housing & Construction
Housing Units, 2000*
- Total 2,923
- Median rent $796
- Median SF home value $187,500

Permits for New Residential Construction
	Units	Value
Total, 2007	38	$3,755,350
Single family	38	$3,755,350
Total, 2006	58	$4,216,854
Single family	38	$3,414,460

Real Property Valuation, 2007
	Parcels	Valuation
Total	2,554	$728,296,100
Vacant	76	10,799,500
Residential	2,315	585,016,500
Commercial	133	91,864,700
Industrial	16	21,111,700
Apartments	13	19,503,000
Farm land	1	700
Farm homestead	0	0

Average Property Value & Tax, 2007
- Residential value $252,707
- Property tax $6,585
- Tax credit/rebate $1,100

Public Library
Butler Public Library
1 Ace Rd
Butler, NJ 07405
973-838-3262

- Director .... Deborah Maynard

Library statistics, 2006
- Population served 7,420
- Full-time/total staff 1/1

	Total	Per capita
Holdings	39,152	5.28
Revenues	$314,829	$42.43
Expenditures	$287,938	$38.81
Annual visits	45,949	6.19
Internet terminals/annual users		3/4,284

Public Safety
Number of officers, 2006 17

Crime	2005	2006
Total crimes	105	164
Violent	5	9
Murder	0	0
Rape	2	0
Robbery	0	0
Aggravated assault	3	9
Non-violent	100	155
Burglary	43	45
Larceny	56	95
Vehicle theft	1	15
Domestic violence	69	69
Arson	3	0
Total crime rate	12.9	20.3
Violent	0.6	1.1
Non-violent	12.3	19.2

Public School District
(for school year 2006-07 except as noted)

Butler School District
HS Annex Bldg, Bartholdi Ave
Butler, NJ 07405
973-492-2032

- Superintendent .... Rene Rovtar
- Number of schools 3
- Grade plan K-12
- Enrollment 1,189
- Attendance rate, '05-06 .... 95.2%
- Dropout rate 1.6%
- Students per teacher 9.9
- Per pupil expenditure $14,676
- Median faculty salary $54,630
- Median administrator salary $113,800
- Grade 12 enrollment 113
- High school graduation rate 90.4%

Assessment test results
(percent scoring at proficient or advanced level)
	Language	Math
NJASK-Grade 3	83.8%	83.8%
GEPA-Grade 8	77.9%	66.7%
HSPA-High School	85.1%	71.9%

SAT score averages
Pct tested	Math	Verbal	Writing
76%	487	488	487

Teacher Qualifications
- Avg. years of experience 8
- Highly-qualified teachers
  - one subject/all subjects 100%/100%
- With emergency credentials 0.0%

No Child Left Behind
- AYP, 2005-06 .... Meets Standards

Municipal Finance
State Aid Programs, 2008
- Total aid $1,177,268
  - CMPTRA 110,070
  - Energy tax receipts 1,067,198
  - Garden State Trust 0

General Budget, 2007
- Total tax levy $18,994,468
  - County levy 2,518,905
    - County taxes 2,014,906
    - County library 0
    - County health 0
    - County open space 503,999
  - School levy 11,320,369
  - Muni. levy 5,155,194
- Misc. revenues 4,727,086

Taxes
	2005	2006	2007
General tax rate per $100	2.35	2.5	2.61
County equalization ratio	89.51	78.89	69.69
Net valuation taxable	$707,936,070	$718,235,000	$728,881,233
State equalized value	$897,371,112	$1,031,250,586	$1,038,339,621

Byram Township
Sussex County

Demographics & Socio-Economic Characteristics
(2000 US Census, except as noted)

Population
1980*	7,502
1990*	8,048
2000	8,254
Male	4,098
Female	4,156
2006 (estimate)*	8,656
Population density	410.8

Race & Hispanic Origin, 2000
Race
White	7,905
Black/African American	80
American Indian/Alaska Native	5
Asian	116
Native Hawaiian/Pacific Islander	5
Other race	53
Two or more races	90
Hispanic origin, total	243
Mexican	20
Puerto Rican	75
Cuban	29
Other Hispanic	119

Age & Nativity, 2000
Under 5 years	644
18 years and over	5,874
21 years and over	5,633
65 years and over	501
85 years and over	40
Median age	36.3
Native-born	7,730
Foreign-born	505

Educational Attainment, 2000
Population 25 years and over	5,364
Less than 9th grade	1.2%
High school grad or higher	94.1%
Bachelor's degree or higher	32.2%
Graduate degree	9.4%

Income & Poverty, 1999
Per capita income	$30,710
Median household income	$81,532
Median family income	$89,500
Persons in poverty	143
H'holds receiving public assistance	31
H'holds receiving social security	411

Households, 2000
Total households	2,833
With persons under 18	1,302
With persons over 65	383
Family households	2,317
Single-person households	395
Persons per household	2.91
Persons per family	3.24

Labor & Employment
Total civilian labor force, 2006**	5,228
Unemployment rate	4.5%
Total civilian labor force, 2000	4,632
Unemployment rate	3.3%

Employed persons 16 years and over by occupation, 2000
Managers & professionals	1,994
Service occupations	455
Sales & office occupations	1,271
Farming, fishing & forestry	5
Construction & maintenance	408
Production & transportation	345
Self-employed persons	184

‡ Branch of county library
* US Census Bureau
** New Jersey Department of Labor

General Information
Township of Byram
10 Mansfield Dr
Stanhope, NJ 07874
973-347-2500

Website	byramtwp.org
Year of incorporation	1798
Land/water area (sq. miles)	21.07/1.11
Form of government	Council-Manager

Government
Legislative Districts
US Congressional	11
State Legislative	24

Local Officials, 2008
Mayor	Eskil Danielson
Manager	Joseph Sabatini
Clerk	Doris Flynn
Finance Dir	Lisa Spring
Tax Assessor	Penny Holenstein
Tax Collector	Lisa Spring
Attorney	Thomas Collins
Building	Richard O'Connor
Planning	Christopher Hellwig
Engineering	Harold Pellow
Public Works	Adolf Steyh
Police Chief	Raymond Rafferty
Emerg/Fire Director	Paul Conklin

Housing & Construction
Housing Units, 2000*
Total	3,078
Median rent	$953
Median SF home value	$175,300

Permits for New Residential Construction
	Units	Value
Total, 2007	15	$4,886,041
Single family	15	$4,886,041
Total, 2006	16	$3,643,307
Single family	16	$3,643,307

Real Property Valuation, 2007
	Parcels	Valuation
Total	4,014	$529,060,730
Vacant	556	10,889,000
Residential	3,173	464,460,700
Commercial	111	43,859,100
Industrial	8	1,594,000
Apartments	3	643,600
Farm land	127	274,230
Farm homestead	36	7,340,100

Average Property Value & Tax, 2007
Residential value	$147,024
Property tax	$6,961
Tax credit/rebate	$1,133

Public Library
E. Louise Child Branch Library‡
21 Sparta Rd
Stanhope, NJ 07874
973-770-1000

Branch Librarian . . . . Victoria Larson

Library statistics, 2006
see Sussex County profile
for library system statistics

Public Safety
Number of officers, 2006 15

Crime	2005	2006
Total crimes	97	54
Violent	1	2
Murder	0	0
Rape	0	1
Robbery	0	0
Aggravated assault	1	1
Non-violent	96	52
Burglary	10	17
Larceny	84	34
Vehicle theft	2	1
Domestic violence	43	57
Arson	1	2
Total crime rate	11.2	6.2
Violent	0.1	0.2
Non-violent	11.1	6.0

Public School District
(for school year 2006-07 except as noted)

Byram Township School District
12 Mansfield Dr
Stanhope, NJ 07874
973-347-6663

Superintendent	Joseph Pezak
Number of schools	2
Grade plan	K-8
Enrollment	1,183
Attendance rate, '05-06	95.8%
Dropout rate	NA
Students per teacher	12.4
Per pupil expenditure	$10,146
Median faculty salary	$48,750
Median administrator salary	$99,750
Grade 12 enrollment	NA
High school graduation rate	NA

Assessment test results
(percent scoring at proficient or advanced level)
	Language	Math
NJASK-Grade 3	87.7%	90.1%
GEPA-Grade 8	93.1%	84.7%
HSPA-High School	NA	NA

SAT score averages
Pct tested	Math	Verbal	Writing
NA	NA	NA	NA

Teacher Qualifications
Avg. years of experience	7
Highly-qualified teachers one subject/all subjects	100%/100%
With emergency credentials	0.0%

No Child Left Behind
AYP, 2005-06 . . . . Meets Standards

Municipal Finance
State Aid Programs, 2008
Total aid	$726,309
CMPTRA	156,657
Energy tax receipts	493,927
Garden State Trust	75,725

General Budget, 2007
Total tax levy	$25,079,989
County levy	4,689,802
County taxes	3,831,946
County library	326,685
County health	126,356
County open space	404,815
School levy	14,240,439
Muni. levy	6,149,748
Misc. revenues	2,995,712

Taxes
	2005	2006	2007
General tax rate per $100	4.34	4.56	4.74
County equalization ratio	55.93	50.56	45.88
Net valuation taxable	$519,353,941	$525,051,030	$529,747,749
State equalized value	$1,027,203,206	$1,145,148,933	$1,205,287,953

Essex County

Caldwell Borough

Demographics & Socio-Economic Characteristics
(2000 US Census, except as noted)

Population
1980*	7,624
1990*	7,549
2000	7,584
Male	3,423
Female	4,161
2006 (estimate)*	7,373
Population density	6,195.8

Race & Hispanic Origin, 2000
Race
White	6,918
Black/African American	172
American Indian/Alaska Native	8
Asian	308
Native Hawaiian/Pacific Islander	5
Other race	91
Two or more races	82
Hispanic origin, total	352
Mexican	29
Puerto Rican	103
Cuban	26
Other Hispanic	194

Age & Nativity, 2000
Under 5 years	379
18 years and over	6,215
21 years and over	5,885
65 years and over	1,350
85 years and over	226
Median age	39.1
Native-born	6,656
Foreign-born	928

Educational Attainment, 2000
Population 25 years and over	5,547
Less than 9th grade	2.8%
High school grad or higher	91.2%
Bachelor's degree or higher	44.0%
Graduate degree	18.2%

Income & Poverty, 1999
Per capita income	$34,630
Median household income	$61,250
Median family income	$81,989
Persons in poverty	347
H'holds receiving public assistance	64
H'holds receiving social security	1,043

Households, 2000
Total households	3,311
With persons under 18	796
With persons over 65	998
Family households	1,814
Single-person households	1,257
Persons per household	2.17
Persons per family	2.93

Labor & Employment
Total civilian labor force, 2006**	4,418
Unemployment rate	2.3%
Total civilian labor force, 2000	4,430
Unemployment rate	2.8%

Employed persons 16 years and over by occupation, 2000
Managers & professionals	2,257
Service occupations	368
Sales & office occupations	1,284
Farming, fishing & forestry	0
Construction & maintenance	201
Production & transportation	197
Self-employed persons	218

* US Census Bureau
** New Jersey Department of Labor

See Introduction for an explanation of all data sources.

General Information
Borough of Caldwell
1 Provost Sq
Caldwell, NJ 07006
973-226-6100

Website	www.caldwell-nj.com
Year of incorporation	1892
Land/water area (sq. miles)	1.19/0.00
Form of government	Borough

Government
Legislative Districts
US Congressional	
State Legislative	27

Local Officials, 2008
Mayor	Susan Gartland
Manager	Maureen Ruane
Clerk	Maureen Ruane
Finance Dir	Maureen Ruane
Tax Assessor	Jack Kelly
Tax Collector	NA
Attorney	Stuart Koenig
Building	Paul Milani
Comm Dev/Planning	NA
Engineering	Anthony Marucci
Public Works	Mario Bifalco
Police Chief	Kurt Dombrowsi
Emerg/Fire Director	Anthony Grenci

Housing & Construction
Housing Units, 2000*
Total	3,396
Median rent	$905
Median SF home value	$228,800

Permits for New Residential Construction
	Units	Value
Total, 2007	1	$54,500
Single family	1	$54,500
Total, 2006	5	$1,391,137
Single family	3	$825,573

Real Property Valuation, 2007
	Parcels	Valuation
Total	2,141	$1,023,089,600
Vacant	28	7,083,500
Residential	1,896	815,602,600
Commercial	189	121,848,700
Industrial	0	0
Apartments	28	78,554,800
Farm land	0	0
Farm homestead	0	0

Average Property Value & Tax, 2007
Residential value	$430,170
Property tax	$9,101
Tax credit/rebate	$1,324

Public Library
Caldwell Public Library
268 Bloomfield Ave
Caldwell, NJ 07006
973-226-2837

Director: Karen Kleppe Lembo

Library statistics, 2006
Population served	7,584
Full-time/total staff	2/5

	Total	Per capita
Holdings	41,545	5.48
Revenues	$411,813	$54.30
Expenditures	$395,556	$52.16
Annual visits	63,518	8.38
Internet terminals/annual users		9/9,360

Taxes
	2005	2006	2007
General tax rate per $100	1.88	2.04	2.12
County equalization ratio	117.23	104.22	92.55
Net valuation taxable	$1,034,280,810	$1,023,566,400	$1,028,111,010
State equalized value	$1,022,825,168	$1,110,981,864	$1,135,132,533

Public Safety
Number of officers, 2006 ... 22

Crime
	2005	2006
Total crimes	70	51
Violent	1	2
Murder	0	0
Rape	0	1
Robbery	1	0
Aggravated assault	0	1
Non-violent	69	49
Burglary	23	9
Larceny	43	37
Vehicle theft	3	3
Domestic violence	36	42
Arson	0	0
Total crime rate	9.2	6.8
Violent	0.1	0.3
Non-violent	9.1	6.5

Public School District
(for school year 2006-07 except as noted)

Caldwell-West Caldwell School District
Harrison Bldg, Gray St
West Caldwell, NJ 07006
973-228-6979

Superintendent	Daniel Gerardi
Number of schools	12
Grade plan	K-12
Enrollment	2,638
Attendance rate, '05-06	96.6%
Dropout rate	0.1%
Students per teacher	11.6
Per pupil expenditure	$12,831
Median faculty salary	$52,270
Median administrator salary	$107,824
Grade 12 enrollment	190
High school graduation rate	100.0%

Assessment test results
(percent scoring at proficient or advanced level)
	Language	Math
NJASK-Grade 3	93.0%	91.2%
GEPA-Grade 8	80.0%	82.2%
HSPA-High School	96.3%	87.9%

SAT score averages
Pct tested	Math	Verbal	Writing
93%	541	529	535

Teacher Qualifications
Avg. years of experience	8
Highly-qualified teachers one subject/all subjects	100%/100%
With emergency credentials	0.0%

No Child Left Behind
AYP, 2005-06 ... Meets Standards

Municipal Finance
State Aid Programs, 2008
Total aid	$809,996
CMPTRA	129,904
Energy tax receipts	679,913
Garden State Trust	179

General Budget, 2007
Total tax levy	$21,751,194
County levy	4,379,232
County taxes	4,266,688
County library	0
County health	0
County open space	112,544
School levy	10,923,559
Muni. levy	6,448,402
Misc. revenues	5,421,268

The New Jersey Municipal Data Book

Califon Borough
Hunterdon County

Demographics & Socio-Economic Characteristics
(2000 US Census, except as noted)

Population
1980*	1,023
1990*	1,073
2000	1,055
Male	504
Female	551
2006 (estimate)*	1,052
Population density	1,084.5

Race & Hispanic Origin, 2000
Race
White	1,041
Black/African American	0
American Indian/Alaska Native	0
Asian	8
Native Hawaiian/Pacific Islander	0
Other race	0
Two or more races	6
Hispanic origin, total	5
Mexican	3
Puerto Rican	1
Cuban	1
Other Hispanic	0

Age & Nativity, 2000
Under 5 years	67
18 years and over	772
21 years and over	746
65 years and over	112
85 years and over	8
Median age	39.1
Native-born	1,015
Foreign-born	40

Educational Attainment, 2000
Population 25 years and over	735
Less than 9th grade	3.3%
High school grad or higher	93.2%
Bachelor's degree or higher	42.4%
Graduate degree	14.8%

Income & Poverty, 1999
Per capita income	$31,064
Median household income	$76,657
Median family income	$85,963
Persons in poverty	45
H'holds receiving public assistance	2
H'holds receiving social security	75

Households, 2000
Total households	401
With persons under 18	151
With persons over 65	85
Family households	302
Single-person households	85
Persons per household	2.63
Persons per family	3.11

Labor & Employment
Total civilian labor force, 2006**	602
Unemployment rate	0.0%
Total civilian labor force, 2000	549
Unemployment rate	0.9%

Employed persons 16 years and over by occupation, 2000
Managers & professionals	264
Service occupations	44
Sales & office occupations	133
Farming, fishing & forestry	0
Construction & maintenance	60
Production & transportation	43
Self-employed persons	43

‡ Branch of county library
* US Census Bureau
** New Jersey Department of Labor

General Information
Borough of Califon
39 Academy St
PO Box 368
Califon, NJ 07830
908-832-7850

Website	www.califonborough-nj.org
Year of incorporation	1918
Land/water area (sq. miles)	0.97/0.01
Form of government	Borough

Government
Legislative Districts
US Congressional	7
State Legislative	24

Local Officials, 2008
Mayor	Walter Burnett
Manager	Laura Eidsvaag
Clerk	Laura Eidsvaag
Finance Dir	Bonnie Holborow
Tax Assessor	Eloise Hagaman
Tax Collector	Bonnie Holbrow
Attorney	J. Peter Jost
Building	NA
Comm Dev/Planning	NA
Engineering	Donald Scott
Public Works	NA
Police Chief	NA
Emerg/Fire Director	Michael Yaple

Housing & Construction
Housing Units, 2000*
Total	410
Median rent	$883
Median SF home value	$220,900

Permits for New Residential Construction
	Units	Value
Total, 2007	2	$507,300
Single family	2	$507,300
Total, 2006	0	$0
Single family	0	$0

Real Property Valuation, 2007
	Parcels	Valuation
Total	504	$161,798,808
Vacant	62	3,199,100
Residential	384	140,743,600
Commercial	30	14,999,300
Industrial	1	396,100
Apartments	2	475,700
Farm land	19	27,508
Farm homestead	6	1,957,500

Average Property Value & Tax, 2007
Residential value	$365,900
Property tax	$8,352
Tax credit/rebate	$1,353

Public Library
Bunnvale Library‡
23 Bunnvale Rd
Califon, NJ 07830
908-638-8884

Branch Librarian .... Marie Taluba

Library statistics, 2006
see Hunterdon County profile for library system statistics

Public Safety
Number of officers, 2006	0

Crime	2005	2006
Total crimes	10	5
Violent	1	0
Murder	0	0
Rape	0	0
Robbery	0	0
Aggravated assault	1	0
Non-violent	9	5
Burglary	1	2
Larceny	8	3
Vehicle theft	0	0
Domestic violence	1	0
Arson	0	0
Total crime rate	9.5	4.7
Violent	0.9	0.0
Non-violent	8.5	4.7

Public School District
(for school year 2006-07 except as noted)

Califon School District
6 School St
Califon, NJ 07830
908-832-2828

Chief School Admin	Kathleen Prystash
Number of schools	1
Grade plan	K-8
Enrollment	141
Attendance rate, '05-06	96.8%
Dropout rate	NA
Students per teacher	7.8
Per pupil expenditure	$14,013
Median faculty salary	$44,800
Median administrator salary	$92,263
Grade 12 enrollment	NA
High school graduation rate	NA

Assessment test results
(percent scoring at proficient or advanced level)
	Language	Math
NJASK-Grade 3	NA	NA
GEPA-Grade 8	93.3%	93.4%
HSPA-High School	NA	NA

SAT score averages
Pct tested	Math	Verbal	Writing
NA	NA	NA	NA

Teacher Qualifications
Avg. years of experience	10
Highly-qualified teachers one subject/all subjects	100%/94.0%
With emergency credentials	0.0%

No Child Left Behind
AYP, 2005-06	Meets Standards

Municipal Finance
State Aid Programs, 2008
Total aid	$107,521
CMPTRA	0
Energy tax receipts	107,459
Garden State Trust	62

General Budget, 2007
Total tax levy	$3,721,124
County levy	542,124
County taxes	453,705
County library	39,481
County health	0
County open space	48,939
School levy	2,541,269
Muni. levy	637,730
Misc. revenues	348,300

Taxes	2005	2006	2007
General tax rate per $100	4.1	2.3	2.29
County equalization ratio	62.96	105.74	100.13
Net valuation taxable	$89,443,444	$161,171,008	$163,022,880
State equalized value	$147,014,208	$158,016,090	$163,688,986

Camden County

Camden City

Demographics & Socio-Economic Characteristics[†]
(2000 US Census, except as noted)

Population
1980*	84,910
1990*	87,492
2000	79,904
Male	38,784
Female	41,120
2006 (estimate)*	79,318
Population density	8,993.0

Race & Hispanic Origin, 2000
Race
White	13,454
Black/African American	42,628
American Indian/Alaska Native	435
Asian	1,958
Native Hawaiian/Pacific Islander	59
Other race	18,239
Two or more races	3,131
Hispanic origin, total	31,019
Mexican	1,908
Puerto Rican	23,051
Cuban	206
Other Hispanic	5,854

Age & Nativity, 2000
Under 5 years	7,302
18 years and over	52,230
21 years and over	47,879
65 years and over	6,090
85 years and over	577
Median age	27.2
Native-born	72,804
Foreign-born	7,100

Educational Attainment, 2000
Population 25 years and over	42,746
Less than 9th grade	17.7%
High school grad or higher	51.0%
Bachelor's degree or higher	5.4%
Graduate degree	1.9%

Income & Poverty, 1999
Per capita income	$9,815
Median household income	$23,421
Median family income	$24,612
Persons in poverty	26,786
H'holds receiving public assistance	3,948
H'holds receiving social security	5,714

Households, 2000
Total households	24,177
With persons under 18	12,530
With persons over 65	4,818
Family households	17,434
Single-person households	5,439
Persons per household	3.12
Persons per family	3.62

Labor & Employment
Total civilian labor force, 2006**	27,653
Unemployment rate	10.7%
Total civilian labor force, 2000	27,304
Unemployment rate	15.9%

Employed persons 16 years and over by occupation, 2000
Managers & professionals	3,850
Service occupations	5,858
Sales & office occupations	5,763
Farming, fishing & forestry	68
Construction & maintenance	1,528
Production & transportation	5,906
Self-employed persons	637

[†] see Appendix C for American Community Survey data
* US Census Bureau
** New Jersey Department of Labor
§ State Fiscal Year July 1–June 30

See Introduction for an explanation of all data sources.

General Information
City of Camden
PO Box 95120
Camden, NJ 08101
856-757-7000

Website	www.ci.camden.nj.us
Year of incorporation	1828
Land/water area (sq. miles)	8.82/1.56
Form of government	Mayor-Council

Government
Legislative Districts
US Congressional	1
State Legislative	5

Local Officials, 2008
Mayor	Gwendolyn A. Faison
Manager	Christine Jones-Tucker
Clerk	Luis Pastoriza
Finance Dir	Thelma Reese (Actg)
Tax Assessor	Frank Librizzi
Tax Collector	Sherry Garton
Attorney	Lewis Wilson
Building	Roberto Scouler
Planning	Ed William
Engineering	Remington & Vernick
Public Works	Anthony Falconero
Police Chief	NA
Emerg/Fire Director	Joseph Marini

Housing & Construction
Housing Units, 2000*
Total	29,769
Median rent	$522
Median SF home value	$40,700

Permits for New Residential Construction
	Units	Value
Total, 2007	286	$27,699,290
Single family	53	$3,215,342
Total, 2006	173	$16,484,876
Single family	18	$2,680,626

Real Property Valuation, 2007
	Parcels	Valuation
Total	26,364	$768,592,257
Vacant	4,615	19,062,180
Residential	20,108	527,807,860
Commercial	1,430	132,268,913
Industrial	89	57,999,750
Apartments	122	31,453,554
Farm land	0	0
Farm homestead	0	0

Average Property Value & Tax, 2007
Residential value	$26,249
Property tax	$1,206
Tax credit/rebate	$490

Public Library
Camden Free Public Library
418 Federal St
Camden, NJ 08103
856-757-7650

Director.............. Theresa M. Gorman

Library statistics, 2006
Population served	79,904
Full-time/total staff	6/21

	Total	Per capita
Holdings	205,994	2.58
Revenues	$1,284,986	$16.08
Expenditures	$1,300,496	$16.28
Annual visits	144,047	1.80
Internet terminals/annual users	51/77,814	

Taxes
	2005	2006	2007
General tax rate per $100	4.473	4.638	4.597
County equalization ratio	81.66	74.56	67.58
Net valuation taxable	$801,235,072	$769,528,617	$794,027,569
State equalized value	$1,074,617,854	$1,166,062,898	$1,276,806,619

Public Safety
Number of officers, 2006 423

Crime	2005	2006
Total crimes	6,016	6,515
Violent	1,686	1,698
Murder	34	32
Rape	47	66
Robbery	704	775
Aggravated assault	901	825
Non-violent	4,330	4,817
Burglary	1,021	1,179
Larceny	2,354	2,458
Vehicle theft	955	1,180
Domestic violence	2,297	2,373
Arson	142	132
Total crime rate	75.2	81.4
Violent	21.1	21.2
Non-violent	54.2	60.2

Public School District
(for school year 2006-07 except as noted)

Camden City School District
201 N Front St
Camden, NJ 08102
856-966-2040

Superintendent	Bessie LeFra Young
Number of schools	32
Grade plan	K-12
Enrollment	15,244
Attendance rate, '05-06	92.7%
Dropout rate	16.6%
Students per teacher	8.8
Per pupil expenditure	$13,314
Median faculty salary	$51,964
Median administrator salary	$105,373
Grade 12 enrollment	465
High school graduation rate	NA

Assessment test results
(percent scoring at proficient or advanced level)
	Language	Math
NJASK-Grade 3	48.7%	54.2%
GEPA-Grade 8	23.8%	14.5%
HSPA-High School	48.0%	22.1%

SAT score averages
Pct tested	Math	Verbal	Writing
NA	NA	NA	NA

Teacher Qualifications
Avg. years of experience	12
Highly-qualified teachers one subject/all subjects	95.0%/95.0%
With emergency credentials	0.7%

No Child Left Behind
AYP, 2005-06 .... Needs Improvement

Municipal Finance[§]
State Aid Programs, 2008
Total aid	$53,345,640
CMPTRA	44,980,957
Energy tax receipts	8,364,385
Garden State Trust	298

General Budget, 2007
Total tax levy	$36,494,872
County levy	8,923,776
County taxes	8,650,887
County library	0
County health	0
County open space	272,889
School levy	7,305,715
Muni. levy	20,265,382
Misc. revenues	138,256,051

©2008 Information Publications, Inc. All rights reserved.

The New Jersey Municipal Data Book

Cape May City — Cape May County

Demographics & Socio-Economic Characteristics
(2000 US Census, except as noted)

Population
1980*	4,853
1990*	4,668
2000	4,034
Male	1,987
Female	2,047
2006 (estimate)*	3,809
Population density	1,535.9

Race & Hispanic Origin, 2000
Race
White	3,684
Black/African American	212
American Indian/Alaska Native	8
Asian	16
Native Hawaiian/Pacific Islander	2
Other race	51
Two or more races	61
Hispanic origin, total	153
Mexican	49
Puerto Rican	61
Cuban	11
Other Hispanic	32

Age & Nativity, 2000
Under 5 years	167
18 years and over	3,375
21 years and over	3,133
65 years and over	1,148
85 years and over	143
Median age	47.4
Native-born	3,787
Foreign-born	247

Educational Attainment, 2000
Population 25 years and over	2,942
Less than 9th grade	2.6%
High school grad or higher	87.6%
Bachelor's degree or higher	30.8%
Graduate degree	11.8%

Income & Poverty, 1999
Per capita income	$29,902
Median household income	$33,462
Median family income	$46,250
Persons in poverty	336
H'holds receiving public assistance	53
H'holds receiving social security	904

Households, 2000
Total households	1,821
With persons under 18	348
With persons over 65	863
Family households	1,035
Single-person households	717
Persons per household	2.02
Persons per family	2.69

Labor & Employment
Total civilian labor force, 2006**	1,817
Unemployment rate	7.3%
Total civilian labor force, 2000	1,494
Unemployment rate	8.8%

Employed persons 16 years and over by occupation, 2000
Managers & professionals	459
Service occupations	286
Sales & office occupations	454
Farming, fishing & forestry	12
Construction & maintenance	81
Production & transportation	71
Self-employed persons	205

‡ Branch of county library
* US Census Bureau
** New Jersey Department of Labor

General Information
City of Cape May
643 Washington St
Cape May, NJ 08204
609-884-9530

Website	www.capemaycity.org
Year of incorporation	1869
Land/water area (sq. miles)	2.48/0.32
Form of government	Council-Manager

Government
Legislative Districts
US Congressional	2
State Legislative	1

Local Officials, 2008
Mayor	Jerome Inderwies
Manager	Luciano Corea
Clerk	Diane Weldon
Finance Dir	Bruce MacLeod
Tax Assessor	Michael Jones
Tax Collector	Bruce MacLeod
Attorney	Anthony Monzo
Building	William Callahan
Planning	Mary Rothwell
Engineering	Remington & Vernick
Public Works	Robert Smith
Police Chief	Diane Sorantino
Emerg/Fire Director	Jerome Inderwies Jr

Housing & Construction
Housing Units, 2000*
Total	4,064
Median rent	$564
Median SF home value	$212,900

Permits for New Residential Construction
	Units	Value
Total, 2007	19	$4,849,515
Single family	11	$4,178,880
Total, 2006	6	$1,366,030
Single family	6	$1,366,030

Real Property Valuation, 2007
	Parcels	Valuation
Total	3,874	$2,203,301,400
Vacant	167	45,603,600
Residential	3,309	1,678,813,200
Commercial	274	351,105,400
Industrial	0	0
Apartments	124	127,779,200
Farm land	0	0
Farm homestead	0	0

Average Property Value & Tax, 2007
Residential value	$507,348
Property tax	$3,873
Tax credit/rebate	$965

Public Library
Cape May Branch Library‡
110 Ocean St
Cape May, NJ 08204
609-884-9568

Branch Librarian — Linda Smith

Library statistics, 2006
see Cape May County profile for library system statistics

Public Safety
Number of officers, 2006 — 22

Crime	2005	2006
Total crimes	218	291
Violent	4	7
Murder	0	0
Rape	0	0
Robbery	0	2
Aggravated assault	4	5
Non-violent	214	284
Burglary	22	20
Larceny	190	260
Vehicle theft	2	4
Domestic violence	42	72
Arson	1	3
Total crime rate	56.5	77.4
Violent	1.0	1.9
Non-violent	55.5	75.5

Public School District
(for school year 2006-07 except as noted)

Cape May City School District
921 Lafayette St
Cape May, NJ 08204
609-884-8485

Chief School Admin	Victoria Zelenak
Number of schools	1
Grade plan	K-6
Enrollment	167
Attendance rate, '05-06	93.8%
Dropout rate	NA
Students per teacher	7.8
Per pupil expenditure	$18,515
Median faculty salary	$51,225
Median administrator salary	$85,493
Grade 12 enrollment	NA
High school graduation rate	NA

Assessment test results
(percent scoring at proficient or advanced level)
	Language	Math
NJASK-Grade 3	78.9%	89.4%
GEPA-Grade 8	NA	NA
HSPA-High School	NA	NA

SAT score averages
Pct tested	Math	Verbal	Writing
NA	NA	NA	NA

Teacher Qualifications
Avg. years of experience	16
Highly-qualified teachers one subject/all subjects	100%/100%
With emergency credentials	0.0%

No Child Left Behind
AYP, 2005-06 — Meets Standards

Municipal Finance
State Aid Programs, 2008
Total aid	$426,027
CMPTRA	0
Energy tax receipts	423,326
Garden State Trust	2,701

General Budget, 2007
Total tax levy	$16,823,973
County levy	4,766,314
County taxes	3,787,789
County library	727,783
County health	0
County open space	250,742
School levy	6,029,860
Muni. levy	6,027,799
Misc. revenues	7,311,261

Taxes
	2005	2006	2007
General tax rate per $100	0.76	0.77	0.77
County equalization ratio	109.35	97.57	88.56
Net valuation taxable	$2,111,729,697	$2,174,583,300	$2,204,049,457
State equalized value	$2,164,322,740	$2,456,304,828	$2,659,813,227

Cape May County
Cape May Point Borough

Demographics & Socio-Economic Characteristics
(2000 US Census, except as noted)

Population
1980*	255
1990*	248
2000	241
Male	118
Female	123
2006 (estimate)*	230
Population density	793.1

Race & Hispanic Origin, 2000
Race
- White 229
- Black/African American 5
- American Indian/Alaska Native 0
- Asian 1
- Native Hawaiian/Pacific Islander 0
- Other race 0
- Two or more races 6
- Hispanic origin, total 4
  - Mexican 3
  - Puerto Rican 0
  - Cuban 0
  - Other Hispanic 1

Age & Nativity, 2000
- Under 5 years 5
- 18 years and over 225
- 21 years and over 224
- 65 years and over 115
- 85 years and over 18
- Median age 64.2
- Native-born 226
- Foreign-born 12

Educational Attainment, 2000
- Population 25 years and over 215
- Less than 9th grade 1.9%
- High school grad or higher 91.6%
- Bachelor's degree or higher 54.9%
- Graduate degree 17.7%

Income & Poverty, 1999
- Per capita income $52,689
- Median household income $55,313
- Median family income $69,750
- Persons in poverty 4
- H'holds receiving public assistance 0
- H'holds receiving social security 89

Households, 2000
- Total households 133
  - With persons under 18 11
  - With persons over 65 81
  - Family households 78
  - Single-person households 47
- Persons per household 1.81
- Persons per family 2.27

Labor & Employment
- Total civilian labor force, 2006** 62
  - Unemployment rate 0.0%
- Total civilian labor force, 2000 55
  - Unemployment rate 5.5%

Employed persons 16 years and over by occupation, 2000
- Managers & professionals 23
- Service occupations 4
- Sales & office occupations 25
- Farming, fishing & forestry 0
- Construction & maintenance 0
- Production & transportation 0
- Self-employed persons 4

* US Census Bureau
** New Jersey Department of Labor

See Introduction for an explanation of all data sources.

General Information
Borough of Cape May Point
215 Lighthouse Ave
PO Box 490
Cape May Point, NJ 08212
609-884-8468

- Website .... www.cmpnj.com
- Year of incorporation 1878
- Land/water area (sq. miles) 0.29/0.02
- Form of government .... Commission

Government
Legislative Districts
- US Congressional 2
- State Legislative 1

Local Officials, 2008
- Mayor .... Malcolm Fraser
- Manager/Admin .... Connie Mahon
- Clerk .... Connie Mahon
- Finance Dir .... Francine Springer
- Tax Assessor .... Mike Jones
- Tax Collector .... Susan Jackson
- Attorney .... George Neidig
- Building .... Jim James
- Planning .... Sally Birdsall
- Engineering .... Bruce Graham
- Public Works .... Malcom Fraser
- Police Chief .... Diane Sorantino
- Emerg/Fire Director .... Robert Shepanski

Housing & Construction
Housing Units, 2000*
- Total 501
- Median rent $850
- Median SF home value $301,400

Permits for New Residential Construction
	Units	Value
Total, 2007	4	$1,122,800
Single family	4	$1,122,800
Total, 2006	5	$1,591,700
Single family	5	$1,591,700

Real Property Valuation, 2007
	Parcels	Valuation
Total	670	$284,947,200
Vacant	72	20,300,100
Residential	597	264,237,000
Commercial	1	410,100
Industrial	0	0
Apartments	0	0
Farm land	0	0
Farm homestead	0	0

Average Property Value & Tax, 2007
- Residential value $442,608
- Property tax $3,326
- Tax credit/rebate $966

Public Library
No public municipal library

Library statistics, 2006
- Population served .... NA
- Full-time/total staff .... NA/NA

	Total	Per capita
Holdings	NA	NA
Revenues	NA	NA
Expenditures	NA	NA
Annual visits	NA	NA
Internet terminals/annual users	NA/NA	

Taxes
	2005	2006	2007
General tax rate per $100	0.75	0.75	0.76
County equalization ratio	71.53	60.58	55.71
Net valuation taxable	$280,937,095	$283,297,300	$284,974,513
State equalized value	$463,745,617	$508,550,336	$542,577,199

Public Safety
Number of officers, 2006 0

Crime
	2005	2006
Total crimes	16	29
Violent	0	0
Murder	0	0
Rape	0	0
Robbery	0	0
Aggravated assault	0	0
Non-violent	16	29
Burglary	8	4
Larceny	8	25
Vehicle theft	0	0
Domestic violence	0	0
Arson	0	0
Total crime rate	66.9	122.9
Violent	0.0	0.0
Non-violent	66.9	122.9

Public School District
(for school year 2006-07 except as noted)

Cape May Point School District
921 Lafayette St
Cape May, NJ 08204

No schools in district - sends students to Cape May City schools

- Per pupil expenditure .... NA
- Median faculty salary .... NA
- Median administrator salary .... NA
- Grade 12 enrollment .... NA
- High school graduation rate .... NA

Assessment test results
(percent scoring at proficient or advanced level)
	Language	Math
NJASK-Grade 3	NA	NA
GEPA-Grade 8	NA	NA
HSPA-High School	NA	NA

SAT score averages
Pct tested	Math	Verbal	Writing
NA	NA	NA	NA

Teacher Qualifications
- Avg. years of experience .... NA
- Highly-qualified teachers
  - one subject/all subjects .... NA/NA
- With emergency credentials .... NA

No Child Left Behind
- AYP, 2005-06 .... NA

Municipal Finance
State Aid Programs, 2008
- Total aid $33,211
- CMPTRA 0
- Energy tax receipts 33,146
- Garden State Trust 65

General Budget, 2007
- Total tax levy $2,141,271
- County levy 974,195
  - County taxes 774,195
  - County library 148,751
  - County health 0
  - County open space 51,249
- School levy 27,620
- Muni. levy 1,139,456
- Misc. revenues 331,999

Carlstadt Borough
Bergen County

Demographics & Socio-Economic Characteristics
(2000 US Census, except as noted)

Population
1980*	6,166
1990*	5,510
2000	5,917
Male	2,869
Female	3,048
2006 (estimate)*	6,037
Population density	1,528.4

Race & Hispanic Origin, 2000
Race
White	5,260
Black/African American	81
American Indian/Alaska Native	5
Asian	366
Native Hawaiian/Pacific Islander	1
Other race	126
Two or more races	78
Hispanic origin, total	473
Mexican	27
Puerto Rican	97
Cuban	64
Other Hispanic	285

Age & Nativity, 2000
Under 5 years	303
18 years and over	4,790
21 years and over	4,621
65 years and over	904
85 years and over	86
Median age	38.9
Native-born	4,704
Foreign-born	1,213

Educational Attainment, 2000
Population 25 years and over	4,306
Less than 9th grade	7.8%
High school grad or higher	80.0%
Bachelor's degree or higher	21.0%
Graduate degree	5.7%

Income & Poverty, 1999
Per capita income	$28,713
Median household income	$55,058
Median family income	$62,040
Persons in poverty	357
H'holds receiving public assistance	60
H'holds receiving social security	688

Households, 2000
Total households	2,393
With persons under 18	670
With persons over 65	672
Family households	1,593
Single-person households	631
Persons per household	2.47
Persons per family	3.04

Labor & Employment
Total civilian labor force, 2006**	3,551
Unemployment rate	3.3%
Total civilian labor force, 2000	3,332
Unemployment rate	3.3%

Employed persons 16 years and over by occupation, 2000
Managers & professionals	1,175
Service occupations	400
Sales & office occupations	1,034
Farming, fishing & forestry	0
Construction & maintenance	259
Production & transportation	355
Self-employed persons	155

* US Census Bureau
** New Jersey Department of Labor

General Information
Borough of Carlstadt
500 Madison St
Carlstadt, NJ 07072
201-939-2850

Website	www.carlstadtnj.us
Year of incorporation	1894
Land/water area (sq. miles)	3.95/0.28
Form of government	Borough

Government
Legislative Districts
US Congressional	9
State Legislative	36

Local Officials, 2008
Mayor	William Jay Roseman
Administrator	Jane Fontana
Clerk	Claire Foy
Finance Dir	Domenick Giancaspro
Tax Assessor	Joyce Ranone
Tax Collector	Christopher Assenheimer
Attorney	Jay Fahy
Building	Mark Sadomis
Comm Dev/Planning	NA
Engineering	Paul Sarlo
Public Works	Paul Ritchie
Police Chief	Thomas Nielsen
Fire Chief	Daniel Eckert

Housing & Construction
Housing Units, 2000*
Total	2,473
Median rent	$839
Median SF home value	$201,900

Permits for New Residential Construction
	Units	Value
Total, 2007	23	$2,093,289
Single family	3	$466,622
Total, 2006	35	$3,355,109
Single family	3	$439,866

Real Property Valuation, 2007
	Parcels	Valuation
Total	2,091	$972,917,677
Vacant	93	15,548,680
Residential	1,546	242,047,507
Commercial	143	190,698,410
Industrial	294	518,931,180
Apartments	15	5,691,900
Farm land	0	0
Farm homestead	0	0

Average Property Value & Tax, 2007
Residential value	$156,564
Property tax	$5,166
Tax credit/rebate	$883

Public Library
William Dermody Public Library
420 Hackensack St
Carlstadt, NJ 07072
201-438-8866

Director .... Mary Disanza

Library statistics, 2006
Population served	5,917
Full-time/total staff	1/6

	Total	Per capita
Holdings	29,547	4.99
Revenues	$662,367	$111.94
Expenditures	$528,875	$89.38
Annual visits	18,655	3.15
Internet terminals/annual users	6/7,573	

Taxes
	2005	2006	2007
General tax rate per $100	2.78	3.06	3.3
County equalization ratio	58.53	54.15	46.51
Net valuation taxable	$1,055,036,099	$980,697,377	$975,202,440
State equalized value	$1,948,358,447	$2,111,467,636	$2,351,192,723

Public Safety
Number of officers, 2006 31

Crime	2005	2006
Total crimes	209	169
Violent	8	7
Murder	0	0
Rape	0	1
Robbery	3	2
Aggravated assault	5	4
Non-violent	201	162
Burglary	19	17
Larceny	150	111
Vehicle theft	32	34
Domestic violence	73	53
Arson	0	0
Total crime rate	34.7	28.1
Violent	1.3	1.2
Non-violent	33.4	26.9

Public School District
(for school year 2006-07 except as noted)

Carlstadt School District
550 Washington St
Carlstadt, NJ 07072
201-672-3000

Superintendent	Steven Kollinock
Number of schools	1
Grade plan	K-8
Enrollment	550
Attendance rate, '05-06	95.0%
Dropout rate	NA
Students per teacher	11.5
Per pupil expenditure	$14,343
Median faculty salary	$62,950
Median administrator salary	$121,000
Grade 12 enrollment	NA
High school graduation rate	NA

Assessment test results
(percent scoring at proficient or advanced level)
	Language	Math
NJASK-Grade 3	81.4%	84.1%
GEPA-Grade 8	80.0%	66.7%
HSPA-High School	NA	NA

SAT score averages
Pct tested	Math	Verbal	Writing
NA	NA	NA	NA

Teacher Qualifications
Avg. years of experience	12
Highly-qualified teachers one subject/all subjects	100%/100%
With emergency credentials	NA

No Child Left Behind
AYP, 2005-06 .... Meets Standards

Municipal Finance
State Aid Programs, 2008
Total aid	$1,314,518
CMPTRA	87,721
Energy tax receipts	1,226,797
Garden State Trust	0

General Budget, 2007
Total tax levy	$32,177,376
County levy	3,779,077
County taxes	3,567,458
County library	0
County health	0
County open space	211,619
School levy	14,925,588
Muni. levy	13,472,711
Misc. revenues	4,388,301

Salem County

Carneys Point Township

Demographics & Socio-Economic Characteristics
(2000 US Census, except as noted)

Population
1980*	8,396
1990*	8,443
2000	7,684
Male	3,667
Female	4,017
2006 (estimate)*	7,981
Population density	456.1

Race & Hispanic Origin, 2000
Race
- White: 6,034
- Black/African American: 1,250
- American Indian/Alaska Native: 21
- Asian: 70
- Native Hawaiian/Pacific Islander: 3
- Other race: 161
- Two or more races: 145
- Hispanic origin, total: 306
  - Mexican: 42
  - Puerto Rican: 182
  - Cuban: 6
  - Other Hispanic: 76

Age & Nativity, 2000
- Under 5 years: 467
- 18 years and over: 5,927
- 21 years and over: 5,621
- 65 years and over: 1,243
- 85 years and over: 152
- Median age: 38.7
- Native-born: 7,385
- Foreign-born: 299

Educational Attainment, 2000
- Population 25 years and over: 5,240
- Less than 9th grade: 7.6%
- High school grad or higher: 77.6%
- Bachelor's degree or higher: 14.1%
- Graduate degree: 3.8%

Income & Poverty, 1999
- Per capita income: $19,978
- Median household income: $41,007
- Median family income: $52,213
- Persons in poverty: 808
- H'holds receiving public assistance: 116
- H'holds receiving social security: 931

Households, 2000
- Total households: 3,121
  - With persons under 18: 1,003
  - With persons over 65: 847
  - Family households: 2,052
  - Single-person households: 916
- Persons per household: 2.42
- Persons per family: 2.99

Labor & Employment
- Total civilian labor force, 2006**: 3,766
  - Unemployment rate: 6.9%
- Total civilian labor force, 2000: 3,669
  - Unemployment rate: 8.3%

Employed persons 16 years and over by occupation, 2000
- Managers & professionals: 849
- Service occupations: 472
- Sales & office occupations: 902
- Farming, fishing & forestry: 13
- Construction & maintenance: 354
- Production & transportation: 773
- Self-employed persons: 130

‡ Joint library with Penns Grove
* US Census Bureau
** New Jersey Department of Labor

See Introduction for an explanation of all data sources.

General Information
Township of Carneys Point
303 Harding Hwy
Carneys Point, NJ 08069
856-299-0070

Website	NA
Year of incorporation	1977
Land/water area (sq. miles)	17.50/0.25
Form of government	Township

Government
Legislative Districts
- US Congressional: 2
- State Legislative: 3

Local Officials, 2008
- Mayor: Wayne D. Pelura
- Manager: Marie Stout
- Clerk: June Proffitt
- Finance Dir: Marie Stout
- Tax Assessor: Sandra Elliott
- Tax Collector: Thomas Freeman
- Attorney: John Jordan
- Building: Louis Palena
- Comm Dev/Planning: NA
- Engineering: Brian Mitchell
- Public Works: Eugene Gilbert
- Police Chief: Edmond Spinelli Jr
- Emerg/Fire Director: Mike Hanna

Housing & Construction
Housing Units, 2000*
- Total: 3,330
- Median rent: $607
- Median SF home value: $89,700

Permits for New Residential Construction
	Units	Value
Total, 2007	33	$3,040,969
Single family	28	$2,798,545
Total, 2006	44	$3,822,498
Single family	44	$3,822,498

Real Property Valuation, 2007
	Parcels	Valuation
Total	3,325	$344,805,305
Vacant	452	9,919,400
Residential	2,453	202,364,425
Commercial	165	64,767,810
Industrial	11	43,344,200
Apartments	8	15,198,000
Farm land	162	1,951,220
Farm homestead	74	7,260,250

Average Property Value & Tax, 2007
- Residential value: $82,954
- Property tax: $3,529
- Tax credit/rebate: $818

Public Library
Penns Grove-Carneys Point Library‡
222 S Broad St
Penns Grove, NJ 08069
856-299-4255

Director: Barbara Hunt

Library statistics, 2006
- Population served: 12,570
- Full-time/total staff: NA/0

	Total	Per capita
Holdings	NA	NA
Revenues	NA	NA
Expenditures	NA	NA
Annual visits	NA	NA
Internet terminals/annual users	NA/NA	

Taxes
	2005	2006	2007
General tax rate per $100	3.743	4.052	4.255
County equalization ratio	79.45	70.97	65.49
Net valuation taxable	$337,316,561	$341,895,005	$345,609,329
State equalized value	$475,294,577	$522,905,263	$603,189,253

Public Safety
Number of officers, 2006: 20

Crime
	2005	2006
Total crimes	217	199
Violent	24	25
Murder	1	1
Rape	0	0
Robbery	6	9
Aggravated assault	17	15
Non-violent	193	174
Burglary	47	55
Larceny	134	108
Vehicle theft	12	11
Domestic violence	88	65
Arson	1	2
Total crime rate	27.8	25.0
Violent	3.1	3.1
Non-violent	24.7	21.9

Public School District
(for school year 2006-07 except as noted)

Penns Grove-Carneys Pt. Reg. School Dist.
100 Iona Ave
Penns Grove, NJ 08069
856-299-4250

- Superintendent: Joseph A. Massare
- Number of schools: 10
- Grade plan: K-12
- Enrollment: 2,393
- Attendance rate, '05-06: 93.0%
- Dropout rate: 4.3%
- Students per teacher: 11.3
- Per pupil expenditure: $12,045
- Median faculty salary: $52,275
- Median administrator salary: $90,926
- Grade 12 enrollment: 120
- High school graduation rate: 85.8%

Assessment test results
(percent scoring at proficient or advanced level)
	Language	Math
NJASK-Grade 3	71.8%	83.0%
GEPA-Grade 8	44.0%	45.1%
HSPA-High School	75.7%	58.3%

SAT score averages
Pct tested	Math	Verbal	Writing
71%	427	419	412

Teacher Qualifications
- Avg. years of experience: 12
- Highly-qualified teachers one subject/all subjects: 99.5%/99.5%
- With emergency credentials: 0.0%

No Child Left Behind
- AYP, 2005-06: Meets Standards

Municipal Finance
State Aid Programs, 2008
- Total aid: $904,626
  - CMPTRA: 239,591
  - Energy tax receipts: 661,605
  - Garden State Trust: 3,430

General Budget, 2007
- Total tax levy: $14,703,563
  - County levy: 5,039,953
    - County taxes: 4,932,452
    - County library: 0
    - County health: 0
    - County open space: 107,501
  - School levy: 7,707,906
  - Muni. levy: 1,955,705
- Misc. revenues: 7,553,465

The New Jersey Municipal Data Book

Carteret Borough
Middlesex County

Demographics & Socio-Economic Characteristics
(2000 US Census, except as noted)

Population
1980*	20,598
1990*	19,025
2000	20,709
Male	10,050
Female	10,659
2006 (estimate)*	22,264
Population density	5,106.4

Race & Hispanic Origin, 2000
Race
White	14,239
Black/African American	1,975
American Indian/Alaska Native	49
Asian	1,722
Native Hawaiian/Pacific Islander	7
Other race	1,918
Two or more races	799
Hispanic origin, total	4,839
Mexican	184
Puerto Rican	2,216
Cuban	244
Other Hispanic	2,195

Age & Nativity, 2000
Under 5 years	1,276
18 years and over	15,481
21 years and over	14,723
65 years and over	3,099
85 years and over	332
Median age	37.0
Native-born	15,866
Foreign-born	4,843

Educational Attainment, 2000
Population 25 years and over	13,745
Less than 9th grade	9.3%
High school grad or higher	74.9%
Bachelor's degree or higher	12.8%
Graduate degree	3.7%

Income & Poverty, 1999
Per capita income	$18,967
Median household income	$47,148
Median family income	$54,609
Persons in poverty	2,253
H'holds receiving public assistance	248
H'holds receiving social security	2,356

Households, 2000
Total households	7,039
With persons under 18	2,807
With persons over 65	2,213
Family households	5,212
Single-person households	1,544
Persons per household	2.88
Persons per family	3.38

Labor & Employment
Total civilian labor force, 2006**	10,758
Unemployment rate	8.3%
Total civilian labor force, 2000	9,972
Unemployment rate	9.4%

Employed persons 16 years and over by occupation, 2000
Managers & professionals	1,953
Service occupations	1,348
Sales & office occupations	3,016
Farming, fishing & forestry	8
Construction & maintenance	808
Production & transportation	1,903
Self-employed persons	264

* US Census Bureau
** New Jersey Department of Labor

General Information
Borough of Carteret
61 Cooke Ave
Carteret, NJ 07008
732-541-3800

Website	www.ci.carteret.nj.us
Year of incorporation	1922
Land/water area (sq. miles)	4.36/0.63
Form of government	Borough

Government
Legislative Districts
US Congressional	13
State Legislative	19

Local Officials, 2008
Mayor	Daniel J. Reiman
Manager/Admin	NA
Clerk	Kathleen Barney
Finance Dir	Patrick DeBlasio
Tax Assessor	Charles Heck
Tax Collector	NA
Attorney	Robert Bergen
Building	Anthony Neibert
Comm Dev/Planning	Kathleen Shaw
Engineering	John P. Dupont
Public Works	Ted Surick
Police Chief	John Pieczyski
Emerg/Fire Director	Brian O'Connor

Housing & Construction
Housing Units, 2000*
Total	7,320
Median rent	$741
Median SF home value	$135,500

Permits for New Residential Construction
	Units	Value
Total, 2007	284	$16,855,618
Single family	26	$5,012,640
Total, 2006	228	$6,490,482
Single family	38	$5,016,535

Real Property Valuation, 2007
	Parcels	Valuation
Total	5,572	$976,964,674
Vacant	232	22,441,250
Residential	5,063	607,248,124
Commercial	162	109,199,400
Industrial	102	216,767,200
Apartments	13	21,308,700
Farm land	0	0
Farm homestead	0	0

Average Property Value & Tax, 2007
Residential value	$119,938
Property tax	$5,959
Tax credit/rebate	$1,044

Public Library
Carteret Public Library
100 Cooke Ave
Carteret, NJ 07008
732-541-3830

Director... Cheryl A. Smith

Library statistics, 2006
Population served	20,709
Full-time/total staff	2/6

	Total	Per capita
Holdings	57,607	2.78
Revenues	$716,854	$34.62
Expenditures	$586,244	$28.31
Annual visits	146,227	7.06
Internet terminals/annual users	18/19,364	

Taxes
	2005	2006	2007
General tax rate per $100	4.42	4.62	4.97
County equalization ratio	58.92	48.39	41.22
Net valuation taxable	$977,494,346	$978,141,500	$978,370,983
State equalized value	$2,020,033,780	$2,374,704,570	$2,447,487,115

Public Safety
Number of officers, 2006... 63

Crime	2005	2006
Total crimes	431	418
Violent	56	58
Murder	1	3
Rape	7	3
Robbery	20	21
Aggravated assault	28	31
Non-violent	375	360
Burglary	61	61
Larceny	256	275
Vehicle theft	58	24
Domestic violence	332	285
Arson	4	0
Total crime rate	20.0	19.5
Violent	2.6	2.7
Non-violent	17.4	16.8

Public School District
(for school year 2006-07 except as noted)

Carteret Borough School District
599 Roosevelt Ave
Carteret, NJ 07008
732-541-8960

Superintendent	Kevin W. Ahearn
Number of schools	5
Grade plan	K-12
Enrollment	3,873
Attendance rate, '05-06	93.5%
Dropout rate	2.5%
Students per teacher	12.4
Per pupil expenditure	$10,961
Median faculty salary	$53,120
Median administrator salary	$103,168
Grade 12 enrollment	190
High school graduation rate	90.0%

Assessment test results
(percent scoring at proficient or advanced level)
	Language	Math
NJASK-Grade 3	77.8%	86.6%
GEPA-Grade 8	61.0%	61.8%
HSPA-High School	80.7%	70.1%

SAT score averages
Pct tested	Math	Verbal	Writing
76%	472	441	432

Teacher Qualifications
Avg. years of experience	8
Highly-qualified teachers one subject/all subjects	98.0%/98.0%
With emergency credentials	0.0%

No Child Left Behind
AYP, 2005-06... Meets Standards

Municipal Finance
State Aid Programs, 2008
Total aid	$3,270,950
CMPTRA	1,527,960
Energy tax receipts	1,742,990
Garden State Trust	0

General Budget, 2007
Total tax levy	$48,612,938
County levy	6,912,569
County taxes	6,188,276
County library	0
County health	0
County open space	724,293
School levy	24,224,455
Muni. levy	17,475,914
Misc. revenues	17,992,965

Essex County

Cedar Grove Township

Demographics & Socio-Economic Characteristics
(2000 US Census, except as noted)

Population
1980*	12,600
1990*	12,053
2000	12,300
Male	5,722
Female	6,578
2006 (estimate)*	12,848
Population density	3,044.5

Race & Hispanic Origin, 2000
Race
White	11,076
Black/African American	368
American Indian/Alaska Native	6
Asian	667
Native Hawaiian/Pacific Islander	3
Other race	57
Two or more races	123
Hispanic origin, total	393
Mexican	23
Puerto Rican	112
Cuban	55
Other Hispanic	203

Age & Nativity, 2000
Under 5 years	666
18 years and over	9,934
21 years and over	9,667
65 years and over	2,766
85 years and over	539
Median age	44.0
Native-born	10,951
Foreign-born	1,349

Educational Attainment, 2000
Population 25 years and over	9,264
Less than 9th grade	3.7%
High school grad or higher	88.4%
Bachelor's degree or higher	41.3%
Graduate degree	14.0%

Income & Poverty, 1999
Per capita income	$36,558
Median household income	$78,863
Median family income	$94,475
Persons in poverty	230
H'holds receiving public assistance	22
H'holds receiving social security	1,529

Households, 2000
Total households	4,403
With persons under 18	1,321
With persons over 65	1,521
Family households	3,240
Single-person households	1,017
Persons per household	2.57
Persons per family	3.05

Labor & Employment
Total civilian labor force, 2006**	6,272
Unemployment rate	1.2%
Total civilian labor force, 2000	5,938
Unemployment rate	1.1%

Employed persons 16 years and over by occupation, 2000
Managers & professionals	3,036
Service occupations	530
Sales & office occupations	1,751
Farming, fishing & forestry	0
Construction & maintenance	218
Production & transportation	338
Self-employed persons	348

* US Census Bureau
** New Jersey Department of Labor

See Introduction for an explanation of all data sources.

General Information
Township of Cedar Grove
525 Pompton Ave
Cedar Grove, NJ 07009
973-239-1410

Website	www.cedargrovenj.org
Year of incorporation	1908
Land/water area (sq. miles)	4.22/0.13
Form of government	Council-Manager

Government
Legislative Districts
US Congressional	8
State Legislative	40

Local Officials, 2008
Mayor	Peter H. Tanella
Manager	Thomas Tucci
Clerk	Kathleen Stutz
Finance Dir.	William Homa
Tax Assessor	Richard Hamilton
Tax Collector	NA
Attorney	Thomas Scrivo
Building	John D'Ascensio
Comm Dev/Planning	John D'Ascensio
Engineering	Alex Palumbo
Public Works	NA
Police Chief	Jeffrey Rowe
Emerg/Fire Director	Alec Spinella

Housing & Construction
Housing Units, 2000*
Total	4,470
Median rent	$973
Median SF home value	$237,600

Permits for New Residential Construction
	Units	Value
Total, 2007	41	$7,349,160
Single family	20	$4,847,863
Total, 2006	54	$10,341,230
Single family	27	$7,125,277

Real Property Valuation, 2007
	Parcels	Valuation
Total	4,236	$330,358,000
Vacant	144	8,501,000
Residential	3,888	271,131,100
Commercial	153	27,924,200
Industrial	43	15,208,800
Apartments	6	7,288,500
Farm land	1	2,400
Farm homestead	1	302,000

Average Property Value & Tax, 2007
Residential value	$69,795
Property tax	$7,579
Tax credit/rebate	$1,147

Public Library
Cedar Grove Public Library
One Municipal Plaza
Cedar Grove, NJ 07009
973-239-1447

Director............Catherine Wolverton

Library statistics, 2006
Population served	12,300
Full-time/total staff	3/5

	Total	Per capita
Holdings	52,695	4.28
Revenues	$804,558	$65.41
Expenditures	$646,021	$52.52
Annual visits	42,275	3.44
Internet terminals/annual users	5/2,593	

Taxes
	2005	2006	2007
General tax rate per $100	10.5	10.96	10.86
County equalization ratio	17.49	15.13	14.45
Net valuation taxable	$316,579,600	$325,012,300	$330,583,600
State equalized value	$2,092,396,563	$2,249,448,169	$2,411,597,863

Public Safety
Number of officers, 2006 32

Crime
	2005	2006
Total crimes	197	219
Violent	12	8
Murder	0	0
Rape	2	0
Robbery	1	0
Aggravated assault	9	8
Non-violent	185	211
Burglary	26	36
Larceny	148	168
Vehicle theft	11	7
Domestic violence	49	63
Arson	0	4
Total crime rate	15.7	17.2
Violent	1.0	0.6
Non-violent	14.7	16.6

Public School District
(for school year 2006-07 except as noted)

Cedar Grove Township School District
520 Pompton Ave
Cedar Grove, NJ 07009
973-239-1550

Superintendent	Gene Polles
Number of schools	4
Grade plan	K-12
Enrollment	1,577
Attendance rate, '05-06	95.8%
Dropout rate	0.5%
Students per teacher	10.6
Per pupil expenditure	$14,095
Median faculty salary	$53,300
Median administrator salary	$119,100
Grade 12 enrollment	108
High school graduation rate	97.2%

Assessment test results
(percent scoring at proficient or advanced level)
	Language	Math
NJASK-Grade 3	92.3%	98.3%
GEPA-Grade 8	90.2%	78.6%
HSPA-High School	94.0%	79.3%

SAT score averages
Pct tested	Math	Verbal	Writing
92%	487	473	474

Teacher Qualifications
Avg. years of experience	8
Highly-qualified teachers one subject/all subjects	100%/100%
With emergency credentials	0.0%

No Child Left Behind
AYP, 2005-06 .... Meets Standards

Municipal Finance
State Aid Programs, 2008
Total aid	$1,345,845
CMPTRA	268,608
Energy tax receipts	1,071,550
Garden State Trust	0

General Budget, 2007
Total tax levy	$35,897,876
County levy	9,027,546
County taxes	8,795,573
County library	0
County health	0
County open space	231,972
School levy	20,656,214
Muni. levy	6,214,117
Misc. revenues	6,058,803

Chatham Borough

Morris County

Demographics & Socio-Economic Characteristics
(2000 US Census, except as noted)

Population
1980*	8,537
1990*	8,007
2000	8,460
Male	4,037
Female	4,423
2006 (estimate)*	8,390
Population density	3,481.3

Race & Hispanic Origin, 2000
Race
White	8,104
Black/African American	12
American Indian/Alaska Native	5
Asian	238
Native Hawaiian/Pacific Islander	1
Other race	42
Two or more races	58
Hispanic origin, total	223
Mexican	22
Puerto Rican	29
Cuban	17
Other Hispanic	155

Age & Nativity, 2000
Under 5 years	871
18 years and over	6,068
21 years and over	5,924
65 years and over	1,098
85 years and over	148
Median age	36.9
Native-born	7,629
Foreign-born	831

Educational Attainment, 2000
Population 25 years and over	5,723
Less than 9th grade	1.5%
High school grad or higher	96.6%
Bachelor's degree or higher	66.7%
Graduate degree	28.3%

Income & Poverty, 1999
Per capita income	$53,027
Median household income	$101,991
Median family income	$119,635
Persons in poverty	188
H'holds receiving public assistance	7
H'holds receiving social security	747

Households, 2000
Total households	3,159
With persons under 18	1,271
With persons over 65	766
Family households	2,384
Single-person households	673
Persons per household	2.67
Persons per family	3.14

Labor & Employment
Total civilian labor force, 2006**	4,595
Unemployment rate	2.5%
Total civilian labor force, 2000	4,197
Unemployment rate	2.1%

Employed persons 16 years and over by occupation, 2000
Managers & professionals	2,567
Service occupations	298
Sales & office occupations	986
Farming, fishing & forestry	0
Construction & maintenance	102
Production & transportation	155
Self-employed persons	244

‡ Joint library with Chatham Township
* US Census Bureau
** New Jersey Department of Labor

General Information
Chatham Borough
54 Fairmount Ave
Chatham, NJ 07928
973-635-0674

Website	www.chathamborough.org
Year of incorporation	1897
Land/water area (sq. miles)	2.41/0.00
Form of government	Borough

Government
Legislative Districts
US Congressional	11
State Legislative	26

Local Officials, 2008
Mayor	V. Nelson Vaughan III
Manager	Robert J. Falzarano
Clerk	Susan Caljean
Finance Dir	Dorothy Klein
Tax Assessor	Pat Aceto
Tax Collector	Madeline Polidor-LeBoeuf
Attorney	Joseph J. Bell
Building	William Jankowski
Planning	H.H. Montague
Engineering	Vincent DeNave
Public Works	Robert Venezia
Police Chief	John Drake
Emerg/Fire Director	Peter Gloglolich

Housing & Construction
Housing Units, 2000*
Total	3,232
Median rent	$1,082
Median SF home value	$376,900

Permits for New Residential Construction
	Units	Value
Total, 2007	10	$3,162,260
Single family	10	$3,162,260
Total, 2006	10	$2,484,716
Single family	10	$2,484,716

Real Property Valuation, 2007
	Parcels	Valuation
Total	2,989	$2,043,381,200
Vacant	59	13,555,600
Residential	2,691	1,751,080,200
Commercial	194	217,881,000
Industrial	29	21,490,500
Apartments	15	39,373,700
Farm land	1	200
Farm homestead	0	0

Average Property Value & Tax, 2007
Residential value	$650,717
Property tax	$9,885
Tax credit/rebate	$1,274

Public Library
Library Of The Chathams‡
214 Main St
Chatham, NJ 07928
973-635-0603

Director	Diane R. O'Brien

Library statistics, 2006
Population served	18,546
Full-time/total staff	6/15

	Total	Per capita
Holdings	99,093	5.34
Revenues	$1,522,852	$82.11
Expenditures	$1,378,140	$74.31
Annual visits	224,952	12.13
Internet terminals/annual users	18/34,999	

Public Safety
Number of officers, 2006	24

Crime	2005	2006
Total crimes	75	98
Violent	3	5
Murder	0	0
Rape	1	1
Robbery	0	3
Aggravated assault	2	1
Non-violent	72	93
Burglary	16	22
Larceny	46	66
Vehicle theft	10	5
Domestic violence	15	14
Arson	0	0
Total crime rate	8.9	11.6
Violent	0.4	0.6
Non-violent	8.5	11.0

Public School District
(for school year 2006-07 except as noted)

School District of the Chathams
58 Meyersville Rd
Chatham, NJ 07928
973-635-5656

Superintendent	James O'Neill
Number of schools	12
Grade plan	K-12
Enrollment	3,490
Attendance rate, '05-06	96.2%
Dropout rate	0.5%
Students per teacher	11.6
Per pupil expenditure	$12,674
Median faculty salary	$53,760
Median administrator salary	$124,125
Grade 12 enrollment	218
High school graduation rate	98.1%

Assessment test results
(percent scoring at proficient or advanced level)
	Language	Math
NJASK-Grade 3	96.6%	98.6%
GEPA-Grade 8	90.5%	91.8%
HSPA-High School	97.9%	94.5%

SAT score averages
Pct tested	Math	Verbal	Writing
94%	583	581	577

Teacher Qualifications
Avg. years of experience	8
Highly-qualified teachers one subject/all subjects	100%/100%
With emergency credentials	0.0%

No Child Left Behind
AYP, 2005-06	Meets Standards

Municipal Finance
State Aid Programs, 2008
Total aid	$719,306
CMPTRA	100,046
Energy tax receipts	616,957
Garden State Trust	0

General Budget, 2007
Total tax levy	$31,066,307
County levy	5,315,228
County taxes	4,251,613
County library	0
County health	0
County open space	1,063,615
School levy	19,086,691
Muni. levy	6,664,388
Misc. revenues	7,051,367

Taxes	2005	2006	2007
General tax rate per $100	1.39	1.5	1.52
County equalization ratio	110.74	99.75	92.06
Net valuation taxable	$2,031,217,435	$2,033,203,200	$2,045,037,166
State equalized value	$2,036,308,206	$2,210,239,856	$2,328,969,406

Morris County — Chatham Township

Demographics & Socio-Economic Characteristics
(2000 US Census, except as noted)

Population
- 1980* 8,883
- 1990* 9,361
- 2000 10,086
  - Male 4,803
  - Female 5,283
- 2006 (estimate)* 10,279
  - Population density 1,101.7

Race & Hispanic Origin, 2000
Race
- White 9,452
- Black/African American 45
- American Indian/Alaska Native 6
- Asian 485
- Native Hawaiian/Pacific Islander 1
- Other race 15
- Two or more races 82
- Hispanic origin, total 197
  - Mexican 27
  - Puerto Rican 26
  - Cuban 22
  - Other Hispanic 122

Age & Nativity, 2000
- Under 5 years 768
- 18 years and over 7,392
- 21 years and over 7,209
- 65 years and over 1,366
- 85 years and over 185
- Median age 40.1
- Native-born 8,874
- Foreign-born 1,212

Educational Attainment, 2000
- Population 25 years and over 7,013
- Less than 9th grade 1.0%
- High school grad or higher 96.6%
- Bachelor's degree or higher 65.7%
- Graduate degree 31.7%

Income & Poverty, 1999
- Per capita income $65,497
- Median household income $106,208
- Median family income $131,609
- Persons in poverty 271
- H'holds receiving public assistance 13
- H'holds receiving social security 911

Households, 2000
- Total households 3,920
  - With persons under 18 1,380
  - With persons over 65 922
  - Family households 2,772
  - Single-person households 1,030
- Persons per household 2.54
- Persons per family 3.11

Labor & Employment
- Total civilian labor force, 2006** 5,453
  - Unemployment rate 1.4%
- Total civilian labor force, 2000 4,995
  - Unemployment rate 1.3%

Employed persons 16 years and over by occupation, 2000
- Managers & professionals 3,132
- Service occupations 255
- Sales & office occupations 1,296
- Farming, fishing & forestry 0
- Construction & maintenance 134
- Production & transportation 111
- Self-employed persons 361

‡ Joint library with Chatham Borough
* US Census Bureau
** New Jersey Department of Labor

See Introduction for an explanation of all data sources.

General Information
Township of Chatham
58 Meyersville Rd
Chatham, NJ 07928
973-635-4600

- Website .... www.chathamtownship.org
- Year of incorporation 1806
- Land/water area (sq. miles) 9.33/0.02
- Form of government .... Township

Government

Legislative Districts
- US Congressional 11
- State Legislative 21

Local Officials, 2008
- Mayor .... Kevin R. Tubbs
- Manager .... Thomas Ciccarone
- Clerk .... Joy Wiley
- Finance Dir .... Thomas Ciccarone
- Tax Assessor .... Glen Sherman
- Tax Collector .... Mary Ellen Babyack
- Attorney .... Carl Woodward
- Building .... Greg Impink
- Planning .... Banisch Associates
- Engineering .... John Ruschke
- Public Works .... Joseph Barilla
- Police Chief .... Elizabeth Goeckel
- Fire Chief .... Kevin Doherty

Housing & Construction

Housing Units, 2000*
- Total 4,019
- Median rent $1,371
- Median SF home value $449,000

Permits for New Residential Construction

	Units	Value
Total, 2007	30	$12,021,884
Single family	30	$12,021,884
Total, 2006	57	$24,294,233
Single family	57	$24,294,233

Real Property Valuation, 2007

	Parcels	Valuation
Total	3,965	$2,793,728,099
Vacant	252	51,091,100
Residential	3,638	2,538,114,699
Commercial	31	122,146,200
Industrial	4	13,725,100
Apartments	3	54,660,000
Farm land	23	479,200
Farm homestead	14	13,511,800

Average Property Value & Tax, 2007
- Residential value $698,693
- Property tax $10,424
- Tax credit/rebate $1,186

Public Library
Library Of The Chathams‡
214 Main St
Chatham, NJ 07928
973-635-0603

- Director .... Diane R. O'Brien

Library statistics, 2006
- Population served 18,546
- Full-time/total staff 6/15

	Total	Per capita
Holdings	99,093	5.34
Revenues	$1,522,852	$82.11
Expenditures	$1,378,140	$74.31
Annual visits	224,952	12.13

- Internet terminals/annual users 18/34,999

Taxes

	2005	2006	2007
General tax rate per $100	1.32	1.44	1.5
County equalization ratio	114.3	101.01	90.52
Net valuation taxable	$2,734,636,563	$2,756,256,400	$2,794,861,217
State equalized value	$2,707,292,905	$3,046,142,630	$3,215,640,193

Public Safety
- Number of officers, 2006 24

Crime

	2005	2006
Total crimes	40	46
Violent	3	0
Murder	0	0
Rape	1	0
Robbery	0	0
Aggravated assault	2	0
Non-violent	37	46
Burglary	3	15
Larceny	31	31
Vehicle theft	3	0
Domestic violence	43	29
Arson	1	0
Total crime rate	3.9	4.5
Violent	0.3	0.0
Non-violent	3.6	4.5

Public School District
(for school year 2006-07 except as noted)

School District of the Chathams
58 Meyersville Rd
Chatham, NJ 07928
973-635-5656

- Superintendent .... James O'Neill
- Number of schools 12
- Grade plan K-12
- Enrollment 3,490
- Attendance rate, '05-06 .... 96.2%
- Dropout rate 0.5%
- Students per teacher 11.6
- Per pupil expenditure $12,674
- Median faculty salary $53,760
- Median administrator salary $124,125
- Grade 12 enrollment 218
- High school graduation rate 98.1%

Assessment test results
(percent scoring at proficient or advanced level)

	Language	Math
NJASK-Grade 3	96.6%	98.6%
GEPA-Grade 8	90.5%	91.8%
HSPA-High School	97.9%	94.5%

SAT score averages

Pct tested	Math	Verbal	Writing
94%	583	581	577

Teacher Qualifications
- Avg. years of experience 8
- Highly-qualified teachers one subject/all subjects 100%/100%
- With emergency credentials 0.0%

No Child Left Behind
- AYP, 2005-06 .... Meets Standards

Municipal Finance

State Aid Programs, 2008
- Total aid $1,121,528
  - CMPTRA 46,340
  - Energy tax receipts 1,075,172
  - Garden State Trust 16

General Budget, 2007
- Total tax levy $41,698,790
  - County levy 7,365,568
    - County taxes 5,891,653
    - County library 0
    - County health 0
    - County open space 1,473,915
  - School levy 25,881,446
  - Muni. levy 8,451,777
- Misc. revenues 4,392,616

Cherry Hill Township
Camden County

Demographics & Socio-Economic Characteristics[†]
(2000 US Census, except as noted)

Population
1980*	68,785
1990*	69,348
2000	69,965
Male	33,450
Female	36,515
2006 (estimate)*	71,586
Population density	2,952.0

Race & Hispanic Origin, 2000
Race
White	59,240
Black/African American	3,121
American Indian/Alaska Native	71
Asian	6,205
Native Hawaiian/Pacific Islander	24
Other race	491
Two or more races	813
Hispanic origin, total	1,778
Mexican	252
Puerto Rican	823
Cuban	96
Other Hispanic	607

Age & Nativity, 2000
Under 5 years	3,928
18 years and over	53,495
21 years and over	51,739
65 years and over	12,570
85 years and over	1,814
Median age	41.8
Native-born	61,245
Foreign-born	8,720

Educational Attainment, 2000
Population 25 years and over	49,401
Less than 9th grade	2.8%
High school grad or higher	91.0%
Bachelor's degree or higher	46.2%
Graduate degree	19.1%

Income & Poverty, 1999
Per capita income	$32,658
Median household income	$69,421
Median family income	$80,766
Persons in poverty	2,725
H'holds receiving public assistance	452
H'holds receiving social security	8,124

Households, 2000
Total households	26,227
With persons under 18	8,930
With persons over 65	8,218
Family households	19,399
Single-person households	5,900
Persons per household	2.61
Persons per family	3.08

Labor & Employment
Total civilian labor force, 2006**	39,008
Unemployment rate	3.4%
Total civilian labor force, 2000	35,499
Unemployment rate	3.7%

Employed persons 16 years and over by occupation, 2000
Managers & professionals	18,091
Service occupations	3,249
Sales & office occupations	9,710
Farming, fishing & forestry	23
Construction & maintenance	1,259
Production & transportation	1,865
Self-employed persons	2,383

[†] see Appendix C for American Community Survey data
* US Census Bureau
** New Jersey Department of Labor
§ State Fiscal Year July 1–June 30

General Information
Township of Cherry Hill
820 Mercer St
PO Box 5002
Cherry Hill, NJ 08034
856-665-6500

Website	www.cherryhill-nj.com
Year of incorporation	1961
Land/water area (sq. miles)	24.25/0.11
Form of government	Mayor-Council

Government
Legislative Districts
US Congressional	3
State Legislative	6

Local Officials, 2008
Mayor	Bernie Platt
Manager	Maris Kukainis
Clerk	Nancy L. Saffos
Finance Dir.	Peggy Bustard
Tax Assessor	Thomas Glock
Tax Collector	Carol Redmond
Attorney	Lisa Kmiec
Building	Anthony Saccamanno
Planning	David Benedetti
Engineering	Remington & Vernick
Public Works	Steven Musilli
Police Chief	Clarence Jones
Emerg/Fire Director	Robert Giorgio

Housing & Construction
Housing Units, 2000*
Total	27,074
Median rent	$793
Median SF home value	$154,900

Permits for New Residential Construction
	Units	Value
Total, 2007	27	$7,110,470
Single family	27	$7,110,470
Total, 2006	129	$14,840,150
Single family	129	$14,840,150

Real Property Valuation, 2007
	Parcels	Valuation
Total	26,499	$4,607,890,500
Vacant	1,686	59,213,100
Residential	23,650	3,304,555,800
Commercial	911	1,024,620,900
Industrial	223	116,132,100
Apartments	15	99,629,800
Farm land	8	188,300
Farm homestead	6	3,550,500

Average Property Value & Tax, 2007
Residential value	$139,842
Property tax	$7,003
Tax credit/rebate	$1,183

Public Library
Cherry Hill Public Library
1100 Kings Highway N
Cherry Hill, NJ 08034
856-667-0300

Director: Manuel A. Paredes

Library statistics, 2006
Population served	69,965
Full-time/total staff	11/34

	Total	Per capita
Holdings	158,931	2.27
Revenues	$2,825,743	$40.39
Expenditures	$2,932,985	$41.92
Annual visits	428,058	6.12
Internet terminals/annual users	88/81,692	

Taxes
	2005	2006	2007
General tax rate per $100	4.479	4.88	5.008
County equalization ratio	66.47	54.38	50.1
Net valuation taxable	$4,588,818,942	$4,587,684,000	$4,616,705,857
State equalized value	$8,438,431,302	$9,166,284,744	$9,954,618,292

Public Safety
Number of officers, 2006	134

Crime	2005	2006
Total crimes	2,140	2,376
Violent	102	107
Murder	1	1
Rape	5	4
Robbery	46	40
Aggravated assault	50	62
Non-violent	2,038	2,269
Burglary	265	266
Larceny	1,664	1,890
Vehicle theft	109	113
Domestic violence	429	460
Arson	0	5
Total crime rate	29.8	33.1
Violent	1.4	1.5
Non-violent	28.3	31.6

Public School District
(for school year 2006-07 except as noted)

Cherry Hill Township School District
45 Ranoldo Terrace, Malberg Bldg
Cherry Hill, NJ 08034
856-429-5600

Superintendent	David Campbell
Number of schools	18
Grade plan	K-12
Enrollment	11,479
Attendance rate, '05-06	94.7%
Dropout rate	0.4%
Students per teacher	11.7
Per pupil expenditure	$13,367
Median faculty salary	$53,520
Median administrator salary	$112,315
Grade 12 enrollment	934
High school graduation rate	NA

Assessment test results
(percent scoring at proficient or advanced level)
	Language	Math
NJASK-Grade 3	91.3%	96.2%
GEPA-Grade 8	85.9%	85.2%
HSPA-High School	94.2%	87.4%

SAT score averages
Pct tested	Math	Verbal	Writing
NA	NA	NA	NA

Teacher Qualifications
Avg. years of experience	9
Highly-qualified teachers one subject/all subjects	99.5%/99.5%
With emergency credentials	0.6%

No Child Left Behind
AYP, 2005-06 ... Meets Standards

Municipal Finance[§]
State Aid Programs, 2008
Total aid	$11,243,823
CMPTRA	4,223,385
Energy tax receipts	7,020,438
Garden State Trust	0

General Budget, 2007
Total tax levy	$231,181,972
County levy	60,924,667
County taxes	59,077,045
County library	0
County health	0
County open space	1,847,623
School levy	140,769,493
Muni. levy	29,487,812
Misc. revenues	25,195,442

Camden County

Chesilhurst Borough

Demographics & Socio-Economic Characteristics
(2000 US Census, except as noted)

Population
- 1980*....................1,590
- 1990*....................1,526
- 2000......................1,520
  - Male.....................760
  - Female..................760
- 2006 (estimate)*.....1,879
- Population density.....1,092.4

Race & Hispanic Origin, 2000
Race
- White......................568
- Black/African American....851
- American Indian/Alaska Native....3
- Asian.......................5
- Native Hawaiian/Pacific Islander....0
- Other race.................44
- Two or more races..........49
- Hispanic origin, total.....62
  - Mexican....................6
  - Puerto Rican...............45
  - Cuban.......................2
  - Other Hispanic..............9

Age & Nativity, 2000
- Under 5 years..............66
- 18 years and over........1,172
- 21 years and over........1,120
- 65 years and over..........229
- 85 years and over...........21
- Median age................42.1
- Native-born..............1,486
- Foreign-born................34

Educational Attainment, 2000
- Population 25 years and over....1,060
- Less than 9th grade........9.3%
- High school grad or higher....65.7%
- Bachelor's degree or higher....9.5%
- Graduate degree...........4.1%

Income & Poverty, 1999
- Per capita income......$15,252
- Median household income....$41,786
- Median family income....$50,263
- Persons in poverty.........214
- H'holds receiving public assistance....20
- H'holds receiving social security....196

Households, 2000
- Total households...........493
  - With persons under 18....171
  - With persons over 65.....165
  - Family households........345
  - Single-person households....124
- Persons per household.....2.81
- Persons per family........3.32

Labor & Employment
- Total civilian labor force, 2006**....709
  - Unemployment rate........8.2%
- Total civilian labor force, 2000....651
  - Unemployment rate........8.6%

Employed persons 16 years and over by occupation, 2000
- Managers & professionals....150
- Service occupations........115
- Sales & office occupations....152
- Farming, fishing & forestry....4
- Construction & maintenance....73
- Production & transportation....101
- Self-employed persons......26

* US Census Bureau
** New Jersey Department of Labor

See Introduction for an explanation of all data sources.

General Information
Borough of Chesilhurst
201 Grant Ave
Chesilhurst, NJ 08089
856-767-4153

- Website............www.chesilhurstgov.org
- Year of incorporation.............1887
- Land/water area (sq. miles)....1.72/0.00
- Form of government...........Borough

Government

Legislative Districts
- US Congressional..............1
- State Legislative..............6

Local Officials, 2008
- Mayor..................Michael Blunt
- Manager/Admin................NA
- Clerk..............Sylvia VanNockay
- Finance Dir............Terry Henry
- Tax Assessor........Theresa Stalgiano
- Tax Collector......Jennifer DellaValle
- Attorney...........Harvey Johnson
- Building......................NA
- Comm Dev/Planning............NA
- Engineering..........Steven Bach
- Public Works.................NA
- Police Chief......Sheldon Fortune
- Emerg/Fire Director..........NA

Housing & Construction

Housing Units, 2000*
- Total.......................535
- Median rent...............$817
- Median SF home value....$93,300

Permits for New Residential Construction

	Units	Value
Total, 2007	14	$1,341,650
Single family	14	$1,341,650
Total, 2006	7	$349,858
Single family	7	$349,858

Real Property Valuation, 2007

	Parcels	Valuation
Total	797	$46,330,836
Vacant	327	3,845,900
Residential	448	39,444,536
Commercial	18	2,337,800
Industrial	2	481,700
Apartments	2	220,900
Farm land	0	0
Farm homestead	0	0

Average Property Value & Tax, 2007
- Residential value.........$88,046
- Property tax...............$3,562
- Tax credit/rebate............$828

Public Library
No public municipal library

Library statistics, 2006
- Population served.............NA
- Full-time/total staff........NA/NA

	Total	Per capita
Holdings	NA	NA
Revenues	NA	NA
Expenditures	NA	NA
Annual visits	NA	NA
Internet terminals/annual users	NA/NA	

Taxes

	2005	2006	2007
General tax rate per $100	3.463	3.837	4.047
County equalization ratio	84.42	77.29	65.47
Net valuation taxable	$44,806,765	$45,209,736	$46,536,124
State equalized value	$57,972,267	$69,272,242	$78,945,662

Public Safety
Number of officers, 2006..........10

Crime

	2005	2006
Total crimes	45	56
Violent	7	2
Murder	0	0
Rape	0	0
Robbery	3	0
Aggravated assault	4	2
Non-violent	38	54
Burglary	10	21
Larceny	25	31
Vehicle theft	3	2
Domestic violence	20	7
Arson	0	0
Total crime rate	24.8	30.0
Violent	3.9	1.1
Non-violent	21.0	29.0

Public School District
(for school year 2006-07 except as noted)

Chesilhurst Borough School District
511 Edwards Ave
Chesilhurst, NJ 08089
856-767-5451

- Chief School Admin........Abdi Gass
- Number of schools...............1
- Grade plan....................K-6
- Enrollment....................118
- Attendance rate, '05-06......94.6%
- Dropout rate..................NA
- Students per teacher..........8.9
- Per pupil expenditure......$14,752
- Median faculty salary......$49,023
- Median administrator salary....$95,608
- Grade 12 enrollment............NA
- High school graduation rate....NA

Assessment test results
(percent scoring at proficient or advanced level)

	Language	Math
NJASK-Grade 3	NA	NA
GEPA-Grade 8	NA	NA
HSPA-High School	NA	NA

SAT score averages

Pct tested	Math	Verbal	Writing
NA	NA	NA	NA

Teacher Qualifications
- Avg. years of experience........23
- Highly-qualified teachers
  - one subject/all subjects....91.5%/91.5%
- With emergency credentials......0.0%

No Child Left Behind
- AYP, 2005-06.........Meets Standards

Municipal Finance

State Aid Programs, 2008
- Total aid...............$123,240
  - CMPTRA........................0
  - Energy tax receipts.......123,057
  - Garden State Trust............0

General Budget, 2007
- Total tax levy..........$1,882,877
  - County levy..............500,075
    - County taxes..........454,257
    - County library.........31,623
    - County health..............0
    - County open space......14,196
  - School levy..............817,488
  - Muni. levy...............565,314
- Misc. revenues..........1,959,283

Chester Borough

Morris County

Demographics & Socio-Economic Characteristics
(2000 US Census, except as noted)

Population
1980*	1,433
1990*	1,214
2000	1,635
Male	819
Female	816
2006 (estimate)*	1,651
Population density	1,072.1

Race & Hispanic Origin, 2000
Race
White	1,548
Black/African American	13
American Indian/Alaska Native	0
Asian	28
Native Hawaiian/Pacific Islander	0
Other race	33
Two or more races	13
Hispanic origin, total	112
Mexican	59
Puerto Rican	1
Cuban	4
Other Hispanic	48

Age & Nativity, 2000
Under 5 years	120
18 years and over	1,229
21 years and over	1,192
65 years and over	223
85 years and over	34
Median age	39.1
Native-born	1,434
Foreign-born	201

Educational Attainment, 2000
Population 25 years and over	1,138
Less than 9th grade	3.5%
High school grad or higher	90.2%
Bachelor's degree or higher	48.3%
Graduate degree	19.9%

Income & Poverty, 1999
Per capita income	$42,564
Median household income	$80,398
Median family income	$106,260
Persons in poverty	84
H'holds receiving public assistance	4
H'holds receiving social security	172

Households, 2000
Total households	609
With persons under 18	218
With persons over 65	172
Family households	427
Single-person households	145
Persons per household	2.66
Persons per family	3.15

Labor & Employment
Total civilian labor force, 2006**	902
Unemployment rate	4.2%
Total civilian labor force, 2000	836
Unemployment rate	5.0%

Employed persons 16 years and over by occupation, 2000
Managers & professionals	394
Service occupations	108
Sales & office occupations	187
Farming, fishing & forestry	0
Construction & maintenance	51
Production & transportation	54
Self-employed persons	44

‡ Joint library with Chester Township
* US Census Bureau
** New Jersey Department of Labor

General Information
Borough of Chester
300 Main St
Chester, NJ 07930
908-879-5361

Website	www.chesterborough.org
Year of incorporation	1930
Land/water area (sq. miles)	1.54/0.00
Form of government	Borough

Government
Legislative Districts
US Congressional	11
State Legislative	24

Local Officials, 2008
Mayor	Dennis Verbaro
Manager	Valerie A. Egan
Clerk	Valerie A. Egan
Finance Dir	Vidya Nayak
Tax Assessor	Mark Whitt
Tax Collector	Ana Hopler
Attorney	Brian Mason
Building	Steven Freedman
Planning	Frank Banisch
Engineering	Paul Ferriero
Public Works	Paul Kapral
Police Chief	Neil Logan
Emerg/Fire Director	Steven Feller

Housing & Construction
Housing Units, 2000*
Total	627
Median rent	$802
Median SF home value	$313,600

Permits for New Residential Construction
	Units	Value
Total, 2007	16	$1,452,900
Single family	7	$743,300
Total, 2006	3	$962,400
Single family	3	$962,400

Real Property Valuation, 2007
	Parcels	Valuation
Total	663	$446,750,700
Vacant	44	7,114,300
Residential	460	241,279,800
Commercial	140	192,169,300
Industrial	0	0
Apartments	3	2,214,500
Farm land	11	75,400
Farm homestead	5	3,897,400

Average Property Value & Tax, 2007
Residential value	$527,263
Property tax	$9,772
Tax credit/rebate	$1,283

Public Library
Chester Library‡
250 West Main St
Chester, NJ 07930
908-879-7612

Director: Susan Persak

Library statistics, 2006
Population served	8,917
Full-time/total staff	1/1

	Total	Per capita
Holdings	63,338	7.10
Revenues	$773,816	$86.78
Expenditures	$565,589	$63.43
Annual visits	134,118	15.04
Internet terminals/annual users	11/20,000	

Taxes
	2005	2006	2007
General tax rate per $100	1.92	1.81	1.86
County equalization ratio	119.17	109.16	101.23
Net valuation taxable	$370,787,766	$419,032,500	$448,851,355
State equalized value	$376,587,209	$415,951,417	$459,134,619

Public Safety
Number of officers, 2006		8

Crime	2005	2006
Total crimes	21	24
Violent	0	2
Murder	0	0
Rape	0	0
Robbery	0	0
Aggravated assault	0	2
Non-violent	21	22
Burglary	2	2
Larceny	19	20
Vehicle theft	0	0
Domestic violence	2	1
Arson	0	0
Total crime rate	12.7	14.5
Violent	0.0	1.2
Non-violent	12.7	13.3

Public School District
(for school year 2006-07 except as noted)

Chester Township School District
415 Route 24
Chester, NJ 07930
908-879-7383

Superintendent	Michael Roth
Number of schools	6
Grade plan	K-8
Enrollment	1,388
Attendance rate, '05-06	95.2%
Dropout rate	NA
Students per teacher	10.9
Per pupil expenditure	$12,974
Median faculty salary	$56,654
Median administrator salary	$109,964
Grade 12 enrollment	NA
High school graduation rate	NA

Assessment test results
(percent scoring at proficient or advanced level)
	Language	Math
NJASK-Grade 3	92.9%	95.8%
GEPA-Grade 8	93.2%	90.0%
HSPA-High School	NA	NA

SAT score averages
Pct tested	Math	Verbal	Writing
NA	NA	NA	NA

Teacher Qualifications
Avg. years of experience	10
Highly-qualified teachers one subject/all subjects	99.0%/99.0%
With emergency credentials	1.1%

No Child Left Behind
AYP, 2005-06	Meets Standards

Municipal Finance
State Aid Programs, 2008
Total aid	$168,688
CMPTRA	0
Energy tax receipts	168,688
Garden State Trust	0

General Budget, 2007
Total tax levy	$8,318,969
County levy	1,063,954
County taxes	851,076
County library	0
County health	0
County open space	212,878
School levy	4,377,746
Muni. levy	2,877,269
Misc. revenues	1,451,655

Morris County
Chester Township

Demographics & Socio-Economic Characteristics
(2000 US Census, except as noted)

Population
1980*	5,198
1990*	5,958
2000	7,282
Male	3,586
Female	3,696
2006 (estimate)*	7,890
Population density	269.0

Race & Hispanic Origin, 2000
Race
- White 6,927
- Black/African American 84
- American Indian/Alaska Native 1
- Asian 174
- Native Hawaiian/Pacific Islander 4
- Other race 19
- Two or more races 73
- Hispanic origin, total 188
  - Mexican 12
  - Puerto Rican 49
  - Cuban 21
  - Other Hispanic 106

Age & Nativity, 2000
- Under 5 years 532
- 18 years and over 5,064
- 21 years and over 4,919
- 65 years and over 664
- 85 years and over 77
- Median age 39.6
- Native-born 6,616
- Foreign-born 666

Educational Attainment, 2000
- Population 25 years and over 4,789
- Less than 9th grade 1.4%
- High school grad or higher 96.3%
- Bachelor's degree or higher 63.7%
- Graduate degree 30.7%

Income & Poverty, 1999
- Per capita income $55,353
- Median household income $117,298
- Median family income $133,586
- Persons in poverty 163
- H'holds receiving public assistance 0
- H'holds receiving social security 396

Households, 2000
- Total households 2,323
  - With persons under 18 1,111
  - With persons over 65 399
  - Family households 2,013
  - Single-person households 240
- Persons per household 3.05
- Persons per family 3.29

Labor & Employment
- Total civilian labor force, 2006** 3,805
  - Unemployment rate 2.3%
- Total civilian labor force, 2000 3,500
  - Unemployment rate 2.1%

Employed persons 16 years and over by occupation, 2000
- Managers & professionals 2,113
- Service occupations 197
- Sales & office occupations 816
- Farming, fishing & forestry 8
- Construction & maintenance 207
- Production & transportation 86
- Self-employed persons 323

‡ Joint library with Chester Borough
* US Census Bureau
** New Jersey Department of Labor

See Introduction for an explanation of all data sources.

General Information
Township of Chester
1 Parker Rd
Chester, NJ 07930
908-879-5100

- Website .... www.chestertownship.org
- Year of incorporation 1799
- Land/water area (sq. miles) 29.33/0.01
- Form of government .... Small Municipality

Government
Legislative Districts
- US Congressional 11
- State Legislative 24

Local Officials, 2008
- Mayor .... William Cogger
- Manager .... Carol Isemann
- Clerk .... Carol Isemann
- Finance Dir .... Theresa Vervaet
- Tax Assessor .... Maureen Kaman
- Tax Collector .... Toni Theesfeld
- Attorney .... John Suminski
- Building .... Jim Fania
- Planning .... Sarah Jane Noll
- Engineering .... Peter Turek
- Public Works .... Marc Cook
- Police Chief .... Adam Schuler
- Emerg/Fire Director .... Steve Feller

Housing & Construction
Housing Units, 2000*
- Total 2,377
- Median rent $1,315
- Median SF home value $407,900

Permits for New Residential Construction
	Units	Value
Total, 2007	10	$4,780,800
Single family	10	$4,780,800
Total, 2006	8	$2,408,200
Single family	8	$2,408,200

Real Property Valuation, 2007
	Parcels	Valuation
Total	3,018	$2,258,409,233
Vacant	159	33,925,400
Residential	2,508	2,072,231,633
Commercial	81	52,360,000
Industrial	9	3,493,000
Apartments	0	0
Farm land	167	1,224,000
Farm homestead	94	95,175,200

Average Property Value & Tax, 2007
- Residential value $832,977
- Property tax $13,163
- Tax credit/rebate $1,371

Public Library
Chester Library‡
250 West Main St
Chester, NJ 07930
908-879-7612

- Director .... Susan Persak

Library statistics, 2006
- Population served 8,917
- Full-time/total staff 1/1

	Total	Per capita
Holdings	63,338	7.10
Revenues	$773,816	$86.78
Expenditures	$565,589	$63.43
Annual visits	134,118	15.04
Internet terminals/annual users	11/20,000	

Taxes
	2005	2006	2007
General tax rate per $100	3.11	1.5	1.59
County equalization ratio	58.27	119.44	106.18
Net valuation taxable	$982,730,899	$2,270,555,200	$2,260,529,892
State equalized value	$1,868,309,694	$2,140,667,996	$2,219,508,222

Public Safety
- Number of officers, 2006 16

Crime
	2005	2006
Total crimes	49	52
Violent	1	1
Murder	0	0
Rape	0	0
Robbery	0	0
Aggravated assault	1	1
Non-violent	48	51
Burglary	2	3
Larceny	46	47
Vehicle theft	0	1
Domestic violence	33	25
Arson	0	0
Total crime rate	6.3	6.6
Violent	0.1	0.1
Non-violent	6.2	6.5

Public School District
(for school year 2006-07 except as noted)

Chester Township School District
415 Route 24
Chester, NJ 07930
908-879-7383

- Superintendent .... Michael Roth
- Number of schools 6
- Grade plan K-8
- Enrollment 1,388
- Attendance rate, '05-06 .... 95.2%
- Dropout rate .... NA
- Students per teacher 10.9
- Per pupil expenditure $12,974
- Median faculty salary $56,654
- Median administrator salary $109,964
- Grade 12 enrollment .... NA
- High school graduation rate .... NA

Assessment test results
(percent scoring at proficient or advanced level)
	Language	Math
NJASK-Grade 3	92.9%	95.8%
GEPA-Grade 8	93.2%	90.0%
HSPA-High School	NA	NA

SAT score averages
Pct tested	Math	Verbal	Writing
NA	NA	NA	NA

Teacher Qualifications
- Avg. years of experience 10
- Highly-qualified teachers
  - one subject/all subjects 99.0%/99.0%
- With emergency credentials 1.1%

No Child Left Behind
- AYP, 2005-06 .... Meets Standards

Municipal Finance
State Aid Programs, 2008
- Total aid $1,141,590
- CMPTRA 5,835
- Energy tax receipts 1,114,981
- Garden State Trust 20,774

General Budget, 2007
- Total tax levy $35,720,634
- County levy 5,073,909
  - County taxes 4,058,592
  - County library 0
  - County health 0
  - County open space 1,015,317
- School levy 23,652,028
- Muni. levy 6,994,698
- Misc. revenues 6,145,471

Chesterfield Township
Burlington County

Demographics & Socio-Economic Characteristics
(2000 US Census, except as noted)

Population
1980*	3,867
1990*	5,152
2000	5,955
Male	4,619
Female	1,336
2006 (estimate)*	6,451
Population density	301.3

Race & Hispanic Origin, 2000
Race
White	2,960
Black/African American	2,225
American Indian/Alaska Native	40
Asian	38
Native Hawaiian/Pacific Islander	5
Other race	503
Two or more races	184
Hispanic origin, total	735
Mexican	43
Puerto Rican	478
Cuban	27
Other Hispanic	187

Age & Nativity, 2000
Under 5 years	183
18 years and over	5,250
21 years and over	4,581
65 years and over	299
85 years and over	25
Median age	24.6
Native-born	5,752
Foreign-born	203

Educational Attainment, 2000
Population 25 years and over	2,790
Less than 9th grade	2.6%
High school grad or higher	78.5%
Bachelor's degree or higher	26.6%
Graduate degree	7.5%

Income & Poverty, 1999
Per capita income	$17,193
Median household income	$85,428
Median family income	$91,267
Persons in poverty	46
H'holds receiving public assistance	11
H'holds receiving social security	233

Households, 2000
Total households	899
With persons under 18	374
With persons over 65	209
Family households	744
Single-person households	115
Persons per household	2.91
Persons per family	3.19

Labor & Employment
Total civilian labor force, 2006**	1,630
Unemployment rate	3.9%
Total civilian labor force, 2000	1,396
Unemployment rate	3.5%

Employed persons 16 years and over by occupation, 2000
Managers & professionals	663
Service occupations	154
Sales & office occupations	296
Farming, fishing & forestry	17
Construction & maintenance	111
Production & transportation	106
Self-employed persons	104

* US Census Bureau
** New Jersey Department of Labor

General Information
Township of Chesterfield
300 Bordentown Chesterfield Rd
Chesterfield, NJ 08515
609-298-2311
Website	www.chesterfieldtwp.com
Year of incorporation	1688
Land/water area (sq. miles)	21.41/0.09
Form of government	Township

Government
Legislative Districts
US Congressional	4
State Legislative	30

Local Officials, 2008
Mayor	Lawrence H. Durr
Manager/Admin	NA
Clerk	Bonnie Haines
Finance Dir	Caryn Hoyer
Tax Assessor	William Tantum
Tax Collector	Janice Jones
Attorney	John Gillespie
Building	Raymond Verner
Comm Dev/Planning	NA
Engineering	Nancy W. Jamanow
Public Works	G. Lebak
Police Chief	Kyle Wilson
Emerg/Fire Director	B. Wilson

Housing & Construction
Housing Units, 2000*
Total	924
Median rent	$940
Median SF home value	$197,500

Permits for New Residential Construction
	Units	Value
Total, 2007	179	$27,437,120
Single family	175	$27,393,052
Total, 2006	203	$27,643,323
Single family	191	$27,557,483

Real Property Valuation, 2007
	Parcels	Valuation
Total	2,114	$672,641,600
Vacant	648	82,590,600
Residential	1,080	496,199,700
Commercial	46	29,990,500
Industrial	0	0
Apartments	1	336,700
Farm land	230	9,730,800
Farm homestead	109	53,793,300

Average Property Value & Tax, 2007
Residential value	$462,568
Property tax	$7,205
Tax credit/rebate	$1,173

Public Library
Crosswicks Public Library
483 Main St
Crosswicks, NJ 08515
609-298-0510
Director	Alice Bumbera

Library statistics, 2006
Population served	5,955
Full-time/total staff	NA/0

	Total	Per capita
Holdings	NA	NA
Revenues	NA	NA
Expenditures	NA	NA
Annual visits	NA	NA
Internet terminals/annual users	NA/NA	

Public Safety
Number of officers, 2006 ... 10

Crime	2005	2006
Total crimes	29	37
Violent	0	1
Murder	0	1
Rape	0	0
Robbery	0	0
Aggravated assault	0	0
Non-violent	29	36
Burglary	4	10
Larceny	25	23
Vehicle theft	0	3
Domestic violence	5	6
Arson	0	0
Total crime rate	4.7	6.0
Violent	0.0	0.2
Non-violent	4.7	5.8

Public School District
(for school year 2006-07 except as noted)

Chesterfield Township School District
295 Bordentown-Chesterfield Rd
Chesterfield, NJ 08515
609-298-6900
Chief School Admin	Contance Bauer
Number of schools	1
Grade plan	K-6
Enrollment	348
Attendance rate, '05-06	95.5%
Dropout rate	NA
Students per teacher	11.0
Per pupil expenditure	$11,977
Median faculty salary	$46,910
Median administrator salary	$105,390
Grade 12 enrollment	NA
High school graduation rate	NA

Assessment test results
(percent scoring at proficient or advanced level)
	Language	Math
NJASK-Grade 3	88.6%	88.6%
GEPA-Grade 8	NA	NA
HSPA-High School	NA	NA

SAT score averages
Pct tested	Math	Verbal	Writing
NA	NA	NA	NA

Teacher Qualifications
Avg. years of experience	12
Highly-qualified teachers one subject/all subjects	100%/100%
With emergency credentials	0.0%

No Child Left Behind
AYP, 2005-06 ... Meets Standards

Municipal Finance
State Aid Programs, 2008
Total aid	$671,706
CMPTRA	44,539
Energy tax receipts	627,167
Garden State Trust	0

General Budget, 2007
Total tax levy	$10,491,446
County levy	2,525,472
County taxes	2,092,691
County library	192,039
County health	0
County open space	240,743
School levy	7,687,101
Muni. levy	278,872
Misc. revenues	3,139,599

Taxes
	2005	2006	2007
General tax rate per $100	3.104	3.25	1.56
County equalization ratio	66.28	61.1	112.05
Net valuation taxable	$264,289,512	$284,269,385	$673,598,296
State equalized value	$432,552,393	$493,032,223	$601,851,461

Burlington County

Cinnaminson Township

Demographics & Socio-Economic Characteristics
(2000 US Census, except as noted)

Population
1980*	16,072
1990*	14,583
2000	14,595
Male	7,121
Female	7,474
2006 (estimate)*	15,449
Population density	2,032.8

Race & Hispanic Origin, 2000
Race
- White 13,334
- Black/African American 742
- American Indian/Alaska Native 24
- Asian 274
- Native Hawaiian/Pacific Islander 1
- Other race 72
- Two or more races 148

Hispanic origin, total 224
- Mexican 24
- Puerto Rican 126
- Cuban 19
- Other Hispanic 55

Age & Nativity, 2000
- Under 5 years 701
- 18 years and over 11,012
- 21 years and over 10,576
- 65 years and over 2,794
- 85 years and over 219
- Median age 42.0
- Native-born 13,935
- Foreign-born 660

Educational Attainment, 2000
- Population 25 years and over 10,127
- Less than 9th grade 2.7%
- High school grad or higher 89.7%
- Bachelor's degree or higher 28.8%
- Graduate degree 9.3%

Income & Poverty, 1999
- Per capita income $27,790
- Median household income $68,474
- Median family income $75,920
- Persons in poverty 353
- H'holds receiving public assistance 67
- H'holds receiving social security 1,825

Households, 2000
- Total households 5,057
- With persons under 18 1,834
- With persons over 65 1,838
- Family households 4,143
- Single-person households 786
- Persons per household 2.85
- Persons per family 3.18

Labor & Employment
- Total civilian labor force, 2006** 8,631
- Unemployment rate 4.1%
- Total civilian labor force, 2000 7,431
- Unemployment rate 4.1%

Employed persons 16 years and over by occupation, 2000
- Managers & professionals 2,791
- Service occupations 652
- Sales & office occupations 2,426
- Farming, fishing & forestry 4
- Construction & maintenance 521
- Production & transportation 736
- Self-employed persons 462

‡ Branch of county library
* US Census Bureau
** New Jersey Department of Labor

See Introduction for an explanation of all data sources.

General Information
Township of Cinnaminson
PO Box 2100
Cinnaminson, NJ 08077
856-829-6000

Website	www.cinnaminsonnj.org
Year of incorporation	1860
Land/water area (sq. miles)	7.60/0.46
Form of government	Township

Government
Legislative Districts
- US Congressional 3
- State Legislative 7

Local Officials, 2008
Mayor	W. Ben Young
Manager	John Ostrowski
Clerk	Pamela McCartney
Finance Dir	John Ostrowski
Tax Assessor	James Mancini
Tax Collector	Sandra Root
Attorney	John Gillespie
Building	Edward Schaefer
Comm Dev/Planning	NA
Engineering	Remington & Vernick
Public Works	W. Ben Young
Police Chief	Michael Wallace
Emerg/Fire Director	Robert Yearly

Housing & Construction
Housing Units, 2000*
- Total 5,147
- Median rent $916
- Median SF home value $158,900

Permits for New Residential Construction
	Units	Value
Total, 2007	94	$7,017,900
Single family	42	$3,261,203
Total, 2006	70	$5,208,634
Single family	60	$4,365,040

Real Property Valuation, 2007
	Parcels	Valuation
Total	5,973	$946,069,650
Vacant	264	10,257,600
Residential	5,412	765,962,750
Commercial	182	104,312,900
Industrial	102	64,783,100
Apartments	1	95,200
Farm land	7	95,400
Farm homestead	5	562,700

Average Property Value & Tax, 2007
- Residential value $141,504
- Property tax $5,899
- Tax credit/rebate $1,076

Public Library
Cinnaminson Branch Library‡
1619 Riverton Rd
Cinnaminson, NJ 08077
856-829-9340

Branch Librarian .... NA

Library statistics, 2006
see Burlington County profile for library system statistics

Public Safety
Number of officers, 2006 32

Crime
	2005	2006
Total crimes	331	368
Violent	32	25
Murder	0	1
Rape	2	2
Robbery	12	12
Aggravated assault	18	10
Non-violent	299	343
Burglary	44	57
Larceny	228	256
Vehicle theft	27	30
Domestic violence	72	70
Arson	2	1
Total crime rate	21.9	24.3
Violent	2.1	1.7
Non-violent	19.8	22.6

Public School District
(for school year 2006-07 except as noted)

Cinnaminson Township School District
2195 Riverton Road, Box 224
Cinnaminson, NJ 08077
856-829-7600

Superintendent	Salvatore Illuzzi
Number of schools	4
Grade plan	K-12
Enrollment	2,526
Attendance rate, '05-06	95.1%
Dropout rate	1.0%
Students per teacher	10.6
Per pupil expenditure	$12,821
Median faculty salary	$54,194
Median administrator salary	$103,233
Grade 12 enrollment	227
High school graduation rate	97.5%

Assessment test results
(percent scoring at proficient or advanced level)

	Language	Math
NJASK-Grade 3	92.5%	96.0%
GEPA-Grade 8	87.1%	75.9%
HSPA-High School	97.7%	85.7%

SAT score averages
Pct tested	Math	Verbal	Writing
87%	522	503	486

Teacher Qualifications
- Avg. years of experience 8
- Highly-qualified teachers one subject/all subjects 100%/100%
- With emergency credentials 0.0%

No Child Left Behind
AYP, 2005-06 .... Meets Standards

Municipal Finance
State Aid Programs, 2008
- Total aid $2,474,145
- CMPTRA 347,852
- Energy tax receipts 2,115,737
- Garden State Trust 10,556

General Budget, 2007
- Total tax levy $39,541,116
- County levy 7,352,499
-   County taxes 6,092,541
-   County library 559,080
-   County health 0
-   County open space 700,878
- School levy 26,445,873
- Muni. levy 5,742,744
- Misc. revenues 6,360,060

Taxes
	2005	2006	2007
General tax rate per $100	3.756	4.007	4.17
County equalization ratio	66.18	59.85	54.33
Net valuation taxable	$926,809,520	$940,113,200	$948,449,306
State equalized value	$1,548,553,918	$1,732,929,062	$1,857,054,524

Clark Township
Union County

Demographics & Socio-Economic Characteristics
(2000 US Census, except as noted)

Population
1980*	16,699
1990*	14,629
2000	14,597
Male	6,934
Female	7,663
2006 (estimate)*	14,650
Population density	3,375.6

Race & Hispanic Origin, 2000
Race
White	13,956
Black/African American	44
American Indian/Alaska Native	2
Asian	402
Native Hawaiian/Pacific Islander	0
Other race	92
Two or more races	101
Hispanic origin, total	535
Mexican	21
Puerto Rican	99
Cuban	97
Other Hispanic	318

Age & Nativity, 2000
Under 5 years	759
18 years and over	11,562
21 years and over	11,209
65 years and over	3,163
85 years and over	381
Median age	42.7
Native-born	12,976
Foreign-born	1,621

Educational Attainment, 2000
Population 25 years and over	10,839
Less than 9th grade	5.3%
High school grad or higher	88.1%
Bachelor's degree or higher	28.2%
Graduate degree	8.6%

Income & Poverty, 1999
Per capita income	$29,883
Median household income	$65,019
Median family income	$77,291
Persons in poverty	248
H'holds receiving public assistance	28
H'holds receiving social security	2,069

Households, 2000
Total households	5,637
With persons under 18	1,681
With persons over 65	2,150
Family households	4,124
Single-person households	1,361
Persons per household	2.56
Persons per family	3.07

Labor & Employment
Total civilian labor force, 2006**	7,447
Unemployment rate	2.1%
Total civilian labor force, 2000	7,098
Unemployment rate	2.0%

Employed persons 16 years and over by occupation, 2000
Managers & professionals	2,572
Service occupations	749
Sales & office occupations	2,402
Farming, fishing & forestry	0
Construction & maintenance	596
Production & transportation	636
Self-employed persons	370

* US Census Bureau
** New Jersey Department of Labor

General Information
Township of Clark
430 Westfield Ave
Clark, NJ 07066
732-388-3600

Website	www.ourclark.com
Year of incorporation	1864
Land/water area (sq. miles)	4.34/0.14
Form of government	Mayor-Council

Government
Legislative Districts
US Congressional	7
State Legislative	22

Local Officials, 2008
Mayor	Salvatore F. Bonaccorso
Manager	John Laezza
Clerk	Edith L. Merkel
Finance Dir	Terry O'Neill
Tax Assessor	Michael Ross
Tax Collector	Tom Grady
Attorney	Joseph Triarsi
Building	Michael Khoda
Planning	Grotto Engineering Assoc
Engineering	Richard O'Connor
Public Works	Joseph Bonaccorso
Police Chief	Dennis Connell
Emerg/Fire Director	Robert Venturella

Housing & Construction
Housing Units, 2000*
Total	5,709
Median rent	$941
Median SF home value	$217,500

Permits for New Residential Construction
	Units	Value
Total, 2007	23	$5,865,368
Single family	23	$5,865,368
Total, 2006	18	$3,991,524
Single family	18	$3,991,524

Real Property Valuation, 2007
	Parcels	Valuation
Total	5,138	$718,587,000
Vacant	113	11,266,600
Residential	4,798	568,202,500
Commercial	199	89,218,600
Industrial	22	31,597,100
Apartments	6	18,302,200
Farm land	0	0
Farm homestead	0	0

Average Property Value & Tax, 2007
Residential value	$118,425
Property tax	$7,881
Tax credit/rebate	$1,293

Public Library
Clark Public Library
303 Westfield Ave
Clark, NJ 07066
732-388-5999

Director: Maureen Baker Wilkinson

Library statistics, 2006
Population served	14,597
Full-time/total staff	4/7

	Total	Per capita
Holdings	78,981	5.41
Revenues	$893,406	$61.20
Expenditures	$748,043	$51.25
Annual visits	162,403	11.13
Internet terminals/annual users	18/17,285	

Taxes
	2005	2006	2007
General tax rate per $100	6.478	6.559	6.655
County equalization ratio	34.19	31.39	28.83
Net valuation taxable	$712,884,989	$711,498,000	$719,004,044
State equalized value	$2,187,434,762	$2,468,371,990	$2,773,813,416

Public Safety
Number of officers, 2006 40

Crime	2005	2006
Total crimes	218	215
Violent	3	11
Murder	0	0
Rape	0	0
Robbery	1	1
Aggravated assault	2	10
Non-violent	215	204
Burglary	13	15
Larceny	187	169
Vehicle theft	15	20
Domestic violence	34	34
Arson	0	1
Total crime rate	14.8	14.7
Violent	0.2	0.8
Non-violent	14.6	13.9

Public School District
(for school year 2006-07 except as noted)

Clark Township School District
365 Westfield Ave, 2nd Fl
Clark, NJ 07066
732-574-9600

Superintendent	Vito A. Gagliardi (Int)
Number of schools	4
Grade plan	K-12
Enrollment	2,373
Attendance rate, '05-06	95.9%
Dropout rate	NA
Students per teacher	11.4
Per pupil expenditure	$12,492
Median faculty salary	$50,310
Median administrator salary	$111,800
Grade 12 enrollment	202
High school graduation rate	100.0%

Assessment test results
(percent scoring at proficient or advanced level)

	Language	Math
NJASK-Grade 3	89.2%	92.2%
GEPA-Grade 8	85.1%	88.5%
HSPA-High School	96.0%	88.9%

SAT score averages
Pct tested	Math	Verbal	Writing
81%	501	485	487

Teacher Qualifications
Avg. years of experience	8
Highly-qualified teachers one subject/all subjects	100%/100%
With emergency credentials	0.0%

No Child Left Behind
AYP, 2005-06 .... Meets Standards

Municipal Finance
State Aid Programs, 2008
Total aid	$2,291,642
CMPTRA	852,498
Energy tax receipts	1,439,144
Garden State Trust	0

General Budget, 2007
Total tax levy	$47,848,474
County levy	8,795,886
County taxes	8,417,867
County library	0
County health	0
County open space	378,019
School levy	26,808,105
Muni. levy	12,244,483
Misc. revenues	5,852,065

Gloucester County

Clayton Borough

Demographics & Socio-Economic Characteristics
(2000 US Census, except as noted)

Population
1980*	6,013
1990*	6,155
2000	7,139
Male	3,415
Female	3,724
2006 (estimate)*	7,469
Population density	1,040.3

Race & Hispanic Origin, 2000
Race
White	5,656
Black/African American	1,146
American Indian/Alaska Native	30
Asian	47
Native Hawaiian/Pacific Islander	2
Other race	68
Two or more races	190
Hispanic origin, total	234
Mexican	25
Puerto Rican	147
Cuban	5
Other Hispanic	57

Age & Nativity, 2000
Under 5 years	551
18 years and over	5,061
21 years and over	4,779
65 years and over	688
85 years and over	50
Median age	33.6
Native-born	6,840
Foreign-born	299

Educational Attainment, 2000
Population 25 years and over	4,430
Less than 9th grade	3.7%
High school grad or higher	83.7%
Bachelor's degree or higher	18.8%
Graduate degree	3.6%

Income & Poverty, 1999
Per capita income	$20,006
Median household income	$53,219
Median family income	$63,097
Persons in poverty	209
H'holds receiving public assistance	25
H'holds receiving social security	592

Households, 2000
Total households	2,464
With persons under 18	1,073
With persons over 65	538
Family households	1,886
Single-person households	485
Persons per household	2.89
Persons per family	3.31

Labor & Employment
Total civilian labor force, 2006**	4,518
Unemployment rate	5.4%
Total civilian labor force, 2000	3,800
Unemployment rate	4.6%

Employed persons 16 years and over by occupation, 2000
Managers & professionals	955
Service occupations	460
Sales & office occupations	1,065
Farming, fishing & forestry	8
Construction & maintenance	468
Production & transportation	671
Self-employed persons	112

‡ Branch of county library
* US Census Bureau
** New Jersey Department of Labor

See Introduction for an explanation of all data sources.

General Information
Borough of Clayton
125 N Delsea Dr
Clayton, NJ 08312
856-881-2882

Website	claytonnj.com
Year of incorporation	1887
Land/water area (sq. miles)	7.18/0.17
Form of government	Borough

Government
Legislative Districts
US Congressional	2
State Legislative	3

Local Officials, 2008
Mayor	Melissa Hoffman
Manager	Sue Miller
Clerk	Christine Newcomb
Finance Dir	Donna Nestore
Tax Assessor	(vacant)
Tax Collector	Donna Nestore
Attorney	Timothy Scaffidi
Building	Jerry Myers
Comm Dev/Planning	NA
Engineering	Sickels & Associates
Public Works	Richard Middleton
Police Chief	Dennis Marchei
Fire Chief	John Kinsley

Housing & Construction
Housing Units, 2000*
Total	2,680
Median rent	$544
Median SF home value	$96,300

Permits for New Residential Construction
	Units	Value
Total, 2007	19	$2,436,678
Single family	19	$2,436,678
Total, 2006	8	$1,099,600
Single family	8	$1,099,600

Real Property Valuation, 2007
	Parcels	Valuation
Total	3,144	$275,828,775
Vacant	544	8,467,400
Residential	2,450	233,501,400
Commercial	78	13,659,200
Industrial	14	11,762,375
Apartments	9	6,222,700
Farm land	34	391,100
Farm homestead	15	1,824,600

Average Property Value & Tax, 2007
Residential value	$95,467
Property tax	$4,491
Tax credit/rebate	$910

Public Library
Glassboro Public Library‡
2 Center St
Glassboro, NJ 08028
856-881-0001

Director .... Carol Wolf

Library statistics, 2006
see Gloucester County profile for library system statistics

Taxes
	2005	2006	2007
General tax rate per $100	4.205	4.504	4.704
County equalization ratio	77.43	68.88	60.83
Net valuation taxable	$265,695,237	$271,559,075	$276,490,876
State equalized value	$385,736,407	$447,118,911	$492,423,155

Public Safety
Number of officers, 2006 18

Crime
	2005	2006
Total crimes	259	238
Violent	25	14
Murder	0	0
Rape	2	0
Robbery	12	4
Aggravated assault	11	10
Non-violent	234	224
Burglary	44	22
Larceny	172	197
Vehicle theft	18	5
Domestic violence	116	110
Arson	0	0
Total crime rate	34.9	32.0
Violent	3.4	1.9
Non-violent	31.5	30.1

Public School District
(for school year 2006-07 except as noted)

Clayton School District
300 W Chestnut St
Clayton, NJ 08312
856-881-8700

Superintendent	Cleve Bryan
Number of schools	3
Grade plan	K-12
Enrollment	1,289
Attendance rate, '05-06	93.9%
Dropout rate	3.0%
Students per teacher	11.7
Per pupil expenditure	$10,401
Median faculty salary	$44,651
Median administrator salary	$84,038
Grade 12 enrollment	70
High school graduation rate	87.4%

Assessment test results
(percent scoring at proficient or advanced level)
	Language	Math
NJASK-Grade 3	78.1%	83.4%
GEPA-Grade 8	65.1%	49.5%
HSPA-High School	82.4%	70.6%

SAT score averages
Pct tested	Math	Verbal	Writing
55%	481	459	454

Teacher Qualifications
Avg. years of experience	6
Highly-qualified teachers one subject/all subjects	100%/100%
With emergency credentials	0.0%

No Child Left Behind
AYP, 2005-06 .... Meets Standards

Municipal Finance
State Aid Programs, 2008
Total aid	$626,158
CMPTRA	130,420
Energy tax receipts	490,970
Garden State Trust	4,768

General Budget, 2007
Total tax levy	$13,005,814
County levy	2,701,631
County taxes	2,326,749
County library	192,714
County health	0
County open space	182,168
School levy	6,971,433
Muni. levy	3,332,750
Misc. revenues	3,444,049

Clementon Borough

Camden County

Demographics & Socio-Economic Characteristics
(2000 US Census, except as noted)

Population
1980*	5,764
1990*	5,601
2000	4,986
Male	2,407
Female	2,579
2006 (estimate)*	4,922
Population density	2,604.2

Race & Hispanic Origin, 2000
Race
White	4,100
Black/African American	577
American Indian/Alaska Native	11
Asian	46
Native Hawaiian/Pacific Islander	9
Other race	117
Two or more races	126
Hispanic origin, total	206
Mexican	31
Puerto Rican	90
Cuban	3
Other Hispanic	82

Age & Nativity, 2000
Under 5 years	361
18 years and over	3,752
21 years and over	3,563
65 years and over	554
85 years and over	60
Median age	35.3
Native-born	4,817
Foreign-born	169

Educational Attainment, 2000
Population 25 years and over	3,358
Less than 9th grade	3.4%
High school grad or higher	77.4%
Bachelor's degree or higher	11.0%
Graduate degree	2.6%

Income & Poverty, 1999
Per capita income	$18,510
Median household income	$42,207
Median family income	$50,963
Persons in poverty	570
H'holds receiving public assistance	72
H'holds receiving social security	473

Households, 2000
Total households	1,978
With persons under 18	660
With persons over 65	438
Family households	1,246
Single-person households	583
Persons per household	2.52
Persons per family	3.13

Labor & Employment
Total civilian labor force, 2006**	2,948
Unemployment rate	9.1%
Total civilian labor force, 2000	2,700
Unemployment rate	8.3%

Employed persons 16 years and over by occupation, 2000
Managers & professionals	643
Service occupations	436
Sales & office occupations	737
Farming, fishing & forestry	0
Construction & maintenance	299
Production & transportation	362
Self-employed persons	126

* US Census Bureau
** New Jersey Department of Labor

General Information
Borough of Clementon
101 Gibbsboro Rd
Clementon, NJ 08021
856-783-0284

Website	www.clementonborough.com
Year of incorporation	1925
Land/water area (sq. miles)	1.89/0.06
Form of government	Borough

Government

Legislative Districts
US Congressional	1
State Legislative	4

Local Officials, 2008
Mayor	Mark E. Armbruster
Manager/Admin	NA
Clerk	Jenai Johnson
Finance Dir	Jodi Kahn
Tax Assessor	Charles E. Warrington
Tax Collector	Joann Watson
Attorney	George Botcheos
Building	Albert O. Hallworth
Planning	Joseph Feldman
Engineering	Churchill Consulting
Public Works	Melvin Applegate
Police Chief	David Kunkel
Emerg/Fire Director	John Busch

Housing & Construction

Housing Units, 2000*
Total	2,206
Median rent	$604
Median SF home value	$85,300

Permits for New Residential Construction
	Units	Value
Total, 2007	9	$728,924
Single family	9	$728,924
Total, 2006	9	$876,310
Single family	9	$876,310

Real Property Valuation, 2007
	Parcels	Valuation
Total	1,887	$171,265,680
Vacant	168	3,227,600
Residential	1,627	134,331,980
Commercial	84	26,063,300
Industrial	0	0
Apartments	6	7,536,100
Farm land	1	3,600
Farm homestead	1	103,100

Average Property Value & Tax, 2007
Residential value	$82,577
Property tax	$3,987
Tax credit/rebate	$842

Public Library
Clementon Memorial Library
195 Gibbsboro Rd
Clementon, NJ 08021
856-783-3233

Director.................... Dale Swanson

Library statistics, 2006
Population served	4,986
Full-time/total staff	NA/0

	Total	Per capita
Holdings	NA	NA
Revenues	NA	NA
Expenditures	NA	NA
Annual visits	NA	NA
Internet terminals/annual users	NA/NA	

Taxes
	2005	2006	2007
General tax rate per $100	4.251	4.49	4.829
County equalization ratio	88.21	78.15	65.38
Net valuation taxable	$171,035,857	$170,981,430	$171,674,606
State equalized value	$218,855,863	$261,969,974	$283,586,307

Public Safety
Number of officers, 2006		17
Crime	2005	2006
Total crimes	272	244
Violent	41	36
Murder	0	0
Rape	2	0
Robbery	13	12
Aggravated assault	26	24
Non-violent	231	208
Burglary	49	38
Larceny	152	154
Vehicle theft	30	16
Domestic violence	151	148
Arson	3	2
Total crime rate	54.9	49.4
Violent	8.3	7.3
Non-violent	46.6	42.1

Public School District
(for school year 2006-07 except as noted)

Clementon Borough School District
Audubon Ave
Clementon, NJ 08021
856-783-2300

Superintendent	John F. Bigley (Int)
Number of schools	1
Grade plan	K-8
Enrollment	559
Attendance rate, '05-06	93.8%
Dropout rate	NA
Students per teacher	10.8
Per pupil expenditure	$10,946
Median faculty salary	$46,966
Median administrator salary	$80,872
Grade 12 enrollment	NA
High school graduation rate	NA

Assessment test results
(percent scoring at proficient or advanced level)
	Language	Math
NJASK-Grade 3	82.2%	87.5%
GEPA-Grade 8	68.2%	61.9%
HSPA-High School	NA	NA

SAT score averages
Pct tested	Math	Verbal	Writing
NA	NA	NA	NA

Teacher Qualifications
Avg. years of experience	11
Highly-qualified teachers one subject/all subjects	100%/100%
With emergency credentials	0.0%

No Child Left Behind
AYP, 2005-06 .... Meets Standards

Municipal Finance

State Aid Programs, 2008
Total aid	$314,401
CMPTRA	0
Energy tax receipts	314,368
Garden State Trust	33

General Budget, 2007
Total tax levy	$8,289,775
County levy	1,850,724
County taxes	1,681,118
County library	117,057
County health	0
County open space	52,549
School levy	3,825,680
Muni. levy	2,613,372
Misc. revenues	2,046,008

Bergen County

Cliffside Park Borough

Demographics & Socio-Economic Characteristics
(2000 US Census, except as noted)

Population
- 1980* 21,464
- 1990* 20,393
- 2000 23,007
  - Male 11,091
  - Female 11,916
- 2006 (estimate)* 22,970
  - Population density 23,927.1

Race & Hispanic Origin, 2000
Race
- White 17,911
- Black/African American 422
- American Indian/Alaska Native 58
- Asian 2,772
- Native Hawaiian/Pacific Islander 5
- Other race 1,144
- Two or more races 695
- Hispanic origin, total 4,177
  - Mexican 89
  - Puerto Rican 578
  - Cuban 565
  - Other Hispanic 2,945

Age & Nativity, 2000
- Under 5 years 1,129
- 18 years and over 19,126
- 21 years and over 18,527
- 65 years and over 4,229
- 85 years and over 498
  - Median age 39.8
- Native-born 13,054
- Foreign-born 9,953

Educational Attainment, 2000
- Population 25 years and over 17,382
- Less than 9th grade 11.1%
- High school grad or higher 78.7%
- Bachelor's degree or higher 32.7%
- Graduate degree 13.1%

Income & Poverty, 1999
- Per capita income $28,516
- Median household income $46,288
- Median family income $54,915
- Persons in poverty 2,462
- H'holds receiving public assistance . 162
- H'holds receiving social security . 2,916

Households, 2000
- Total households 10,027
  - With persons under 18 2,393
  - With persons over 65 3,185
  - Family households 6,041
  - Single-person households 3,390
- Persons per household 2.29
- Persons per family 2.95

Labor & Employment
- Total civilian labor force, 2006** .. 12,387
  - Unemployment rate 4.5%
- Total civilian labor force, 2000 .. 11,674
  - Unemployment rate 4.5%

Employed persons 16 years and over by occupation, 2000
- Managers & professionals 3,919
- Service occupations 1,604
- Sales & office occupations 3,323
- Farming, fishing & forestry 5
- Construction & maintenance 943
- Production & transportation 1,354
- Self-employed persons 893

* US Census Bureau
** New Jersey Department of Labor

See Introduction for an explanation of all data sources.

General Information
Borough of Cliffside Park
525 Palisade Ave
Cliffside Park, NJ 07010
201-945-3456

- Website .... www.cliffsideparknj.gov
- Year of incorporation 1895
- Land/water area (sq. miles) 0.96/0.00
- Form of government .... Borough

Government
Legislative Districts
- US Congressional 9
- State Legislative 38

Local Officials, 2008
- Mayor .... Gerald A. Calabrese
- Manager .... Martin A. Gobbo
- Clerk .... Martin A. Gobbo
- Finance Dir .... Frank Berado
- Tax Assessor .... Frank Bucino
- Tax Collector .... NA
- Attorney .... Chris Diktas
- Building .... John Candelmo
- Comm Dev/Planning .... NA
- Engineering .... Stephen Boswell
- Public Works .... NA
- Police Chief .... Donald Keane
- Emerg/Fire Director .... Al Deleone

Housing & Construction
Housing Units, 2000*
- Total 10,375
- Median rent $864
- Median SF home value $227,500

Permits for New Residential Construction

	Units	Value
Total, 2007	118	$8,218,791
Single family	28	$5,587,818
Total, 2006	98	$12,613,883
Single family	42	$8,305,476

Real Property Valuation, 2007

	Parcels	Valuation
Total	6,832	$2,453,102,200
Vacant	106	9,532,300
Residential	6,305	2,090,836,700
Commercial	252	141,369,500
Industrial	9	6,232,400
Apartments	160	205,131,300
Farm land	0	0
Farm homestead	0	0

Average Property Value & Tax, 2007
- Residential value $331,616
- Property tax $6,751
- Tax credit/rebate $1,129

Public Library
Cliffside Park Public Library
505 Palisade Ave
Cliffside Park, NJ 07010
201-945-2867

- Director .... Ana Chelariu

Library statistics, 2006
- Population served 23,007
- Full-time/total staff 3/12

	Total	Per capita
Holdings	69,808	3.03
Revenues	$975,014	$42.38
Expenditures	$815,381	$35.44
Annual visits	102,030	4.43
Internet terminals/annual users	18/31,063	

Taxes

	2005	2006	2007
General tax rate per $100	1.86	1.98	2.04
County equalization ratio	97.35	85.33	73.59
Net valuation taxable	$2,416,716,438	$2,426,853,300	$2,456,887,669
State equalized value	$2,832,200,209	$3,302,324,421	$3,577,652,310

Public Safety
- Number of officers, 2006 48

Crime

	2005	2006
Total crimes	263	230
Violent	30	15
Murder	0	0
Rape	0	0
Robbery	4	5
Aggravated assault	26	10
Non-violent	233	215
Burglary	47	55
Larceny	173	138
Vehicle theft	13	22
Domestic violence	84	89
Arson	0	0
Total crime rate	11.4	10.0
Violent	1.3	0.7
Non-violent	10.1	9.3

Public School District
(for school year 2006-07 except as noted)

Cliffside Park School District
525 Palisade Ave
Cliffside Park, NJ 07010
201-313-2310

- Superintendent ...... Michael J. Romagnino
- Number of schools 6
- Grade plan K-12
- Enrollment 2,617
- Attendance rate, '05-06 .... 93.9%
- Dropout rate 0.5%
- Students per teacher 12.1
- Per pupil expenditure $10,963
- Median faculty salary $54,335
- Median administrator salary $123,360
- Grade 12 enrollment 257
- High school graduation rate 96.3%

Assessment test results
(percent scoring at proficient or advanced level)

	Language	Math
NJASK-Grade 3	82.5%	90.9%
GEPA-Grade 8	70.3%	74.7%
HSPA-High School	88.9%	72.0%

SAT score averages

Pct tested	Math	Verbal	Writing
83%	459	447	438

Teacher Qualifications
- Avg. years of experience 9
- Highly-qualified teachers
  - one subject/all subjects 100%/100%
- With emergency credentials 0.6%

No Child Left Behind
- AYP, 2005-06 .... Meets Standards

Municipal Finance
State Aid Programs, 2008
- Total aid $1,444,312
  - CMPTRA 526,913
  - Energy tax receipts 917,399
  - Garden State Trust 0

General Budget, 2007
- Total tax levy $50,015,364
  - County levy 6,076,095
    - County taxes 5,741,179
    - County library 0
    - County health 0
    - County open space 334,916
  - School levy 24,210,468
  - Muni. levy 19,728,802
- Misc. revenues 9,825,787

The New Jersey Municipal Data Book
89

Clifton City
Passaic County

Demographics & Socio-Economic Characteristics[†]
(2000 US Census, except as noted)

Population
1980*	74,388
1990*	71,742
2000	78,672
Male	37,560
Female	41,112
2006 (estimate)*	79,606
Population density	7,044.8

Race & Hispanic Origin, 2000
Race
White	59,960
Black/African American	2,277
American Indian/Alaska Native	192
Asian	5,066
Native Hawaiian/Pacific Islander	27
Other race	7,553
Two or more races	3,597
Hispanic origin, total	15,608
Mexican	1,591
Puerto Rican	3,923
Cuban	510
Other Hispanic	9,584

Age & Nativity, 2000
Under 5 years	4,700
18 years and over	61,700
21 years and over	59,327
65 years and over	13,829
85 years and over	2,037
Median age	38.8
Native-born	55,680
Foreign-born	22,992

Educational Attainment, 2000
Population 25 years and over	55,730
Less than 9th grade	8.8%
High school grad or higher	78.6%
Bachelor's degree or higher	23.6%
Graduate degree	7.6%

Income & Poverty, 1999
Per capita income	$23,638
Median household income	$50,619
Median family income	$60,688
Persons in poverty	4,932
H'holds receiving public assistance	593
H'holds receiving social security	10,239

Households, 2000
Total households	30,244
With persons under 18	9,459
With persons over 65	10,261
Family households	20,352
Single-person households	8,448
Persons per household	2.59
Persons per family	3.20

Labor & Employment
Total civilian labor force, 2006**	41,018
Unemployment rate	4.9%
Total civilian labor force, 2000	39,232
Unemployment rate	4.9%

Employed persons 16 years and over by occupation, 2000
Managers & professionals	12,055
Service occupations	4,374
Sales & office occupations	11,520
Farming, fishing & forestry	11
Construction & maintenance	3,146
Production & transportation	6,211
Self-employed persons	1,623

[†] see Appendix C for American Community Survey data
* US Census Bureau
** New Jersey Department of Labor

General Information
City of Clifton
900 Clifton Ave
Clifton, NJ 07013
973-470-5800

Website	www.cliftonnj.org
Year of incorporation	1917
Land/water area (sq. miles)	11.30/0.10
Form of government	Municipal Mgr 1923

Government
Legislative Districts
US Congressional	8
State Legislative	34

Local Officials, 2008
Mayor	James Anzaldi
Manager	Albert Greco
Clerk	Richard C. Moran
CFO	Kimberly Kientz
Tax Assessor	Jon Whiting
Tax Collector	Luisa Castillo
Attorney	Matthew Priore
Building	Joseph Lotorto
Planning	Dennis Kirwan
Engineering	James Yellen
Public Works	Vincent Cahill
Police Chief	Robert Ferreri
Emerg/Fire Dir	Jeffrey Adams (Actg)

Housing & Construction
Housing Units, 2000*
Total	31,060
Median rent	$784
Median SF home value	$181,600

Permits for New Residential Construction
	Units	Value
Total, 2007	71	$6,638,048
Single family	19	$3,242,996
Total, 2006	60	$6,657,446
Single family	19	$3,841,395

Real Property Valuation, 2007
	Parcels	Valuation
Total	23,128	$5,273,159,500
Vacant	419	48,668,900
Residential	21,075	3,710,979,000
Commercial	1,093	738,047,400
Industrial	421	641,444,900
Apartments	118	133,743,700
Farm land	1	11,300
Farm homestead	1	264,300

Average Property Value & Tax, 2007
Residential value	$176,089
Property tax	$7,362
Tax credit/rebate	$1,174

Public Library
Clifton Public Library
292 Piaget Ave
Clifton, NJ 07011
973-772-5500

Director	Christine R. Zembicki

Library statistics, 2006
Population served	78,672
Full-time/total staff	8/26

	Total	Per capita
Holdings	217,173	2.76
Revenues	$3,152,679	$40.07
Expenditures	$2,919,978	$37.12
Annual visits	331,380	4.21
Internet terminals/annual users	19/113,510	

Taxes
	2005	2006	2007
General tax rate per $100	3.74	3.95	4.19
County equalization ratio	65.2	58.23	50.71
Net valuation taxable	$5,272,195,890	$5,254,875,900	$5,279,398,981
State equalized value	$9,054,088,769	$10,369,828,950	$11,121,668,444

Public Safety
Number of officers, 2006 158

Crime	2005	2006
Total crimes	2,073	2,131
Violent	170	179
Murder	2	1
Rape	9	2
Robbery	85	78
Aggravated assault	74	98
Non-violent	1,903	1,952
Burglary	305	361
Larceny	1,293	1,296
Vehicle theft	305	295
Domestic violence	527	591
Arson	3	1
Total crime rate	25.9	26.7
Violent	2.1	2.2
Non-violent	23.8	24.4

Public School District
(for school year 2006-07 except as noted)

Clifton School District
745 Clifton Ave, PO Box 2209
Clifton, NJ 07015
973-470-2260

Superintendent	Anthony Barbary (Int)
Number of schools	17
Grade plan	K-12
Enrollment	10,388
Attendance rate, '05-06	95.1%
Dropout rate	5.1%
Students per teacher	11.4
Per pupil expenditure	$11,946
Median faculty salary	$52,130
Median administrator salary	$109,935
Grade 12 enrollment	746
High school graduation rate	84.8%

Assessment test results
(percent scoring at proficient or advanced level)
	Language	Math
NJASK-Grade 3	77.0%	85.6%
GEPA-Grade 8	68.3%	59.8%
HSPA-High School	80.5%	68.2%

SAT score averages
Pct tested	Math	Verbal	Writing
72%	482	460	461

Teacher Qualifications
Avg. years of experience	10
Highly-qualified teachers one subject/all subjects	100%/99.5%
With emergency credentials	0.3%

No Child Left Behind
AYP, 2005-06	Meets Standards

Municipal Finance
State Aid Programs, 2008
Total aid	$12,868,621
CMPTRA	5,513,249
Energy tax receipts	7,355,372
Garden State Trust	0

General Budget, 2007
Total tax levy	$220,721,860
County levy	52,102,257
County taxes	51,048,024
County library	0
County health	0
County open space	1,054,233
School levy	109,600,671
Muni. levy	59,018,932
Misc. revenues	33,126,602

Hunterdon County — Clinton Town

Demographics & Socio-Economic Characteristics
(2000 US Census, except as noted)

Population
- 1980* 1,910
- 1990* 2,054
- 2000 2,632
  - Male 1,284
  - Female 1,348
- 2006 (estimate)* 2,605
- Population density 1,901.5

Race & Hispanic Origin, 2000
Race
- White 2,423
- Black/African American 35
- American Indian/Alaska Native 12
- Asian 98
- Native Hawaiian/Pacific Islander 0
- Other race 36
- Two or more races 28
- Hispanic origin, total 108
  - Mexican 15
  - Puerto Rican 18
  - Cuban 6
  - Other Hispanic 69

Age & Nativity, 2000
- Under 5 years 200
- 18 years and over 1,938
- 21 years and over 1,892
- 65 years and over 248
- 85 years and over 18
- Median age 36.7
- Native-born 2,349
- Foreign-born 283

Educational Attainment, 2000
- Population 25 years and over 1,852
- Less than 9th grade 2.9%
- High school grad or higher 93.6%
- Bachelor's degree or higher 49.1%
- Graduate degree 20.6%

Income & Poverty, 1999
- Per capita income $37,463
- Median household income $78,121
- Median family income $88,671
- Persons in poverty 74
- H'holds receiving public assistance 4
- H'holds receiving social security 206

Households, 2000
- Total households 1,068
  - With persons under 18 388
  - With persons over 65 196
  - Family households 724
  - Single-person households 281
- Persons per household 2.46
- Persons per family 3.00

Labor & Employment
- Total civilian labor force, 2006** 1,706
  - Unemployment rate 2.6%
- Total civilian labor force, 2000 1,526
  - Unemployment rate 1.8%

Employed persons 16 years and over by occupation, 2000
- Managers & professionals 873
- Service occupations 171
- Sales & office occupations 329
- Farming, fishing & forestry 4
- Construction & maintenance 57
- Production & transportation 65
- Self-employed persons 130

‡ Branch of county library
* US Census Bureau
** New Jersey Department of Labor

See Introduction for an explanation of all data sources.

General Information
Town of Clinton
PO Box 5194
Clinton, NJ 08809
908-735-8616

- Website .... www.clintonnj.gov
- Year of incorporation 1865
- Land/water area (sq. miles) 1.37/0.04
- Form of government .... Town

Government
Legislative Districts
- US Congressional 7
- State Legislative 23

Local Officials, 2008
- Mayor .... Christine Schaumburg
- Manager .... Robert Cutter
- Clerk .... Cecilia Covino
- Finance Dir .... Kathleen Olsen
- Tax Assessor .... Ann Marie Obiedzinski
- Tax Collector .... NA
- Attorney .... Richard Cushing
- Building .... John Leonard
- Comm Dev/Planning ..... Diane Laudenbach
- Engineering .... Robert J. Clerico
- Public Works .... NA
- Police Chief .... Richard Brett Matheis
- Emerg/Fire Director ..... Scott Wintermute

Housing & Construction
Housing Units, 2000*
- Total 1,095
- Median rent $862
- Median SF home value $222,100

Permits for New Residential Construction

	Units	Value
Total, 2007	0	$4,820
Single family	0	$4,820
Total, 2006	0	$0
Single family	0	$0

Real Property Valuation, 2007

	Parcels	Valuation
Total	1,031	$417,943,900
Vacant	39	4,204,500
Residential	856	321,272,600
Commercial	123	84,349,200
Industrial	0	0
Apartments	8	7,829,100
Farm land	4	73,800
Farm homestead	1	214,700

Average Property Value & Tax, 2007
- Residential value $375,131
- Property tax $8,588
- Tax credit/rebate $1,263

Public Library
North County Branch Library‡
65 Halstead St
Clinton, NJ 08809
908-730-6262

- Branch Librarian ...... Barbara Riesenfeld

Library statistics, 2006
see Hunterdon County profile
for library system statistics

Public Safety
- Number of officers, 2006 10

Crime

	2005	2006
Total crimes	23	20
Violent	2	2
Murder	0	0
Rape	1	0
Robbery	1	1
Aggravated assault	0	1
Non-violent	21	18
Burglary	4	1
Larceny	16	17
Vehicle theft	1	0
Domestic violence	10	3
Arson	0	0
Total crime rate	8.7	7.6
Violent	0.8	0.8
Non-violent	8.0	6.9

Public School District
(for school year 2006-07 except as noted)

Clinton Town School District
10 School St
Clinton, NJ 08809
908-735-8512

- Superintendent .... John Alfieri
- Number of schools 1
- Grade plan K-8
- Enrollment 554
- Attendance rate, '05-06 .... 95.6%
- Dropout rate .... NA
- Students per teacher 10.4
- Per pupil expenditure $11,751
- Median faculty salary $52,230
- Median administrator salary $112,455
- Grade 12 enrollment .... NA
- High school graduation rate .... NA

Assessment test results
(percent scoring at proficient or advanced level)

	Language	Math
NJASK-Grade 3	76.4%	89.3%
GEPA-Grade 8	85.5%	88.4%
HSPA-High School	NA	NA

SAT score averages

Pct tested	Math	Verbal	Writing
NA	NA	NA	NA

Teacher Qualifications
- Avg. years of experience 14
- Highly-qualified teachers
  - one subject/all subjects 100%/100%
- With emergency credentials 4.0%

No Child Left Behind
- AYP, 2005-06 .... Meets Standards

Municipal Finance
State Aid Programs, 2008
- Total aid $145,677
  - CMPTRA 0
  - Energy tax receipts 145,677
  - Garden State Trust 0

General Budget, 2007
- Total tax levy $9,591,636
  - County levy 1,505,157
    - County taxes 1,259,660
    - County library 109,611
    - County health 0
    - County open space 135,887
  - School levy 6,338,678
  - Muni. levy 1,747,801
- Misc. revenues 1,872,825

Taxes

	2005	2006	2007
General tax rate per $100	2.44	2.3	2.29
County equalization ratio	98.92	102.18	92.55
Net valuation taxable	$359,205,736	$401,556,800	$418,956,082
State equalized value	$382,296,441	$414,151,268	$435,917,385

©2008 Information Publications, Inc. All rights reserved.

Clinton Township
Hunterdon County

Demographics & Socio-Economic Characteristics
(2000 US Census, except as noted)

Population
1980*	7,345
1990*	10,816
2000	12,957
Male	7,023
Female	5,934
2006 (estimate)*	14,082
Population density	469.4

Race & Hispanic Origin, 2000
Race
White	11,365
Black/African American	902
American Indian/Alaska Native	26
Asian	304
Native Hawaiian/Pacific Islander	9
Other race	206
Two or more races	145
Hispanic origin, total	507
Mexican	36
Puerto Rican	253
Cuban	46
Other Hispanic	172

Age & Nativity, 2000
Under 5 years	852
18 years and over	9,559
21 years and over	9,081
65 years and over	951
85 years and over	120
Median age	36.4
Native-born	12,039
Foreign-born	918

Educational Attainment, 2000
Population 25 years and over	8,100
Less than 9th grade	1.8%
High school grad or higher	93.0%
Bachelor's degree or higher	50.5%
Graduate degree	22.1%

Income & Poverty, 1999
Per capita income	$37,264
Median household income	$96,570
Median family income	$106,448
Persons in poverty	105
H'holds receiving public assistance	10
H'holds receiving social security	658

Households, 2000
Total households	4,129
With persons under 18	1,782
With persons over 65	655
Family households	3,255
Single-person households	717
Persons per household	2.82
Persons per family	3.23

Labor & Employment
Total civilian labor force, 2006**	6,949
Unemployment rate	4.5%
Total civilian labor force, 2000	6,170
Unemployment rate	3.4%

Employed persons 16 years and over by occupation, 2000
Managers & professionals	3,542
Service occupations	411
Sales & office occupations	1,339
Farming, fishing & forestry	0
Construction & maintenance	296
Production & transportation	370
Self-employed persons	423

* US Census Bureau
** New Jersey Department of Labor

General Information
Township of Clinton
1225 Route 31 South
Lebanon, NJ 08833
908-735-8800

Website	www.township.clinton.nj.us
Year of incorporation	1841
Land/water area (sq. miles)	30.00/3.93
Form of government	Small Municipality

Government
Legislative Districts
US Congressional	7
State Legislative	23

Local Officials, 2008
Mayor	Nick Corcodilos
Manager	Marvin Joss
Clerk	Donna Burham
Finance Dir	Kathleen Colognato
Tax Assessor	NA
Tax Collector	Patricia Centofanti
Attorney	Kristina P. Hadinger
Building	Michael Wright
Comm Dev/Planning	NA
Engineering	Cathleen F. Marcelli
Public Works	NA
Police Dir	Robert Manney
Emerg/Fire Director	Marc Strauss

Housing & Construction
Housing Units, 2000*
Total	4,234
Median rent	$1,062
Median SF home value	$283,900

Permits for New Residential Construction
	Units	Value
Total, 2007	6	$2,306,644
Single family	6	$2,306,644
Total, 2006	15	$3,466,454
Single family	15	$3,466,454

Real Property Valuation, 2007
	Parcels	Valuation
Total	5,153	$2,577,401,416
Vacant	185	20,364,500
Residential	4,328	2,080,587,600
Commercial	265	221,664,300
Industrial	8	162,969,600
Apartments	4	18,005,800
Farm land	228	2,861,516
Farm homestead	135	70,948,100

Average Property Value & Tax, 2007
Residential value	$482,083
Property tax	$9,594
Tax credit/rebate	$1,253

Public Library
No public municipal library

Library statistics, 2006
Population served	NA
Full-time/total staff	NA/NA

	Total	Per capita
Holdings	NA	NA
Revenues	NA	NA
Expenditures	NA	NA
Annual visits	NA	NA
Internet terminals/annual users	NA/NA	

Taxes
	2005	2006	2007
General tax rate per $100	2.35	1.9	2
County equalization ratio	85.24	98.46	92.88
Net valuation taxable	$1,996,746,013	$2,568,797,400	$2,590,473,113
State equalized value	$2,323,148,357	$2,601,331,262	$2,683,123,925

Public Safety
Number of officers, 2006 23

Crime
	2005	2006
Total crimes	68	81
Violent	4	3
Murder	0	0
Rape	0	0
Robbery	0	0
Aggravated assault	4	3
Non-violent	64	78
Burglary	12	12
Larceny	47	62
Vehicle theft	5	4
Domestic violence	61	58
Arson	2	0
Total crime rate	4.9	5.8
Violent	0.3	0.2
Non-violent	4.6	5.6

Public School District
(for school year 2006-07 except as noted)

Clinton Township School District
128 Cokesbury Rd, PO Box 362
Lebanon, NJ 08833
908-735-8320

Superintendent	Elizabeth Nastus
Number of schools	3
Grade plan	K-8
Enrollment	1,805
Attendance rate, '05-06	96.1%
Dropout rate	NA
Students per teacher	11.0
Per pupil expenditure	$11,532
Median faculty salary	$48,910
Median administrator salary	$115,296
Grade 12 enrollment	NA
High school graduation rate	NA

Assessment test results
(percent scoring at proficient or advanced level)
	Language	Math
NJASK-Grade 3	92.2%	95.1%
GEPA-Grade 8	84.6%	82.1%
HSPA-High School	NA	NA

SAT score averages
Pct tested	Math	Verbal	Writing
NA	NA	NA	NA

Teacher Qualifications
Avg. years of experience	8
Highly-qualified teachers one subject/all subjects	100%/100%
With emergency credentials	0.0%

No Child Left Behind
AYP, 2005-06 .... Meets Standards

Municipal Finance
State Aid Programs, 2008
Total aid	$1,378,032
CMPTRA	246,379
Energy tax receipts	1,084,845
Garden State Trust	46,808

General Budget, 2007
Total tax levy	$51,551,278
County levy	9,253,928
County taxes	7,744,961
County library	673,476
County health	0
County open space	835,491
School levy	36,753,863
Muni. levy	5,543,487
Misc. revenues	6,778,792

Bergen County

Closter Borough

Demographics & Socio-Economic Characteristics
(2000 US Census, except as noted)

Population
- 1980* 8,164
- 1990* 8,094
- 2000 8,383
  - Male 4,130
  - Female 4,253
- 2006 (estimate)* 8,730
  - Population density 2,753.9

Race & Hispanic Origin, 2000
Race
- White 6,314
- Black/African American 78
- American Indian/Alaska Native 8
- Asian 1,807
- Native Hawaiian/Pacific Islander 0
- Other race 68
- Two or more races 108
- Hispanic origin, total 343
  - Mexican 24
  - Puerto Rican 69
  - Cuban 55
  - Other Hispanic 195

Age & Nativity, 2000
- Under 5 years 546
- 18 years and over 6,038
- 21 years and over 5,839
- 65 years and over 1,102
- 85 years and over 108
- Median age 39.6
- Native-born 6,264
- Foreign-born 2,119

Educational Attainment, 2000
- Population 25 years and over 5,687
- Less than 9th grade 2.9%
- High school grad or higher 93.1%
- Bachelor's degree or higher 49.9%
- Graduate degree 19.6%

Income & Poverty, 1999
- Per capita income $37,065
- Median household income $83,918
- Median family income $94,543
- Persons in poverty 229
- H'holds receiving public assistance 0
- H'holds receiving social security 759

Households, 2000
- Total households 2,789
  - With persons under 18 1,254
  - With persons over 65 763
  - Family households 2,321
  - Single-person households 391
- Persons per household 2.98
- Persons per family 3.30

Labor & Employment
- Total civilian labor force, 2006** ... 4,145
  - Unemployment rate 2.1%
- Total civilian labor force, 2000 3,918
  - Unemployment rate 1.8%

Employed persons 16 years and over by occupation, 2000
- Managers & professionals 1,972
- Service occupations 274
- Sales & office occupations 1,216
- Farming, fishing & forestry 0
- Construction & maintenance 198
- Production & transportation 186
- Self-employed persons 323

* US Census Bureau
** New Jersey Department of Labor

See Introduction for an explanation of all data sources.

General Information
Borough of Closter
295 Closter Dock Rd
Closter, NJ 07624
201-784-0600

- Website .... www.closterboro.com
- Year of incorporation 1904
- Land/water area (sq. miles) 3.17/0.12
- Form of government .... Borough

Government
Legislative Districts
- US Congressional 5
- State Legislative 39

Local Officials, 2008
- Mayor .... Sophie Heymann
- Manager .... John DiStefano (Actg)
- Clerk .... Loretta Castano
- Finance Dir .... Joseph Luppino
- Tax Assessor .... Angela Mattiace
- Tax Collector .... Norma Ketler
- Attorney .... Edward T. Rogan
- Building .... Keith Sager
- Comm Dev/Planning .... NA
- Engineering .... Steven Boswell
- Public Works .... Bill Dahle (Actg)
- Police Chief .... David Berrian
- Emerg/Fire Director .... Brian Pierro

Housing & Construction
Housing Units, 2000*
- Total 2,865
- Median rent $1,184
- Median SF home value $346,000

Permits for New Residential Construction

	Units	Value
Total, 2007	20	$10,237,553
Single family	20	$10,237,553
Total, 2006	30	$13,766,520
Single family	30	$13,766,520

Real Property Valuation, 2007

	Parcels	Valuation
Total	2,946	$2,367,586,100
Vacant	92	40,014,800
Residential	2,677	2,088,854,600
Commercial	160	214,440,600
Industrial	8	18,309,800
Apartments	1	1,005,700
Farm land	4	30,500
Farm homestead	4	4,930,100

Average Property Value & Tax, 2007
- Residential value $780,972
- Property tax $12,196
- Tax credit/rebate $1,517

Public Library
Closter Public Library
280 High St
Closter, NJ 07624
201-768-4197

- Director .... Ruth Rando

Library statistics, 2006
- Population served 8,383
- Full-time/total staff 2/5

	Total	Per capita
Holdings	50,342	6.01
Revenues	$729,814	$87.06
Expenditures	$618,015	$73.72
Annual visits	70,100	8.36

- Internet terminals/annual users ... 17/49,500

Public Safety
- Number of officers, 2006 23

Crime

	2005	2006
Total crimes	64	73
Violent	2	1
Murder	0	0
Rape	0	0
Robbery	0	0
Aggravated assault	2	1
Non-violent	62	72
Burglary	13	18
Larceny	46	52
Vehicle theft	3	2
Domestic violence	29	40
Arson	0	0
Total crime rate	7.4	8.4
Violent	0.2	0.1
Non-violent	7.2	8.3

Public School District
(for school year 2006-07 except as noted)

Closter School District
340 Homans Ave
Closter, NJ 07624
201-768-3001

- Superintendent .... Joanne Newberry
- Number of schools 2
- Grade plan K-8
- Enrollment 1,183
- Attendance rate, '05-06 .... 96.6%
- Dropout rate .... NA
- Students per teacher 11.9
- Per pupil expenditure $12,092
- Median faculty salary $72,663
- Median administrator salary $110,733
- Grade 12 enrollment .... NA
- High school graduation rate .... NA

Assessment test results
(percent scoring at proficient or advanced level)

	Language	Math
NJASK-Grade 3	94.3%	96.0%
GEPA-Grade 8	97.4%	87.4%
HSPA-High School	NA	NA

SAT score averages

Pct tested	Math	Verbal	Writing
NA	NA	NA	NA

Teacher Qualifications
- Avg. years of experience 11
- Highly-qualified teachers
  - one subject/all subjects 100%/100%
- With emergency credentials 0.0%

No Child Left Behind
- AYP, 2005-06 .... Meets Standards

Municipal Finance
State Aid Programs, 2008
- Total aid $1,846,239
- CMPTRA 0
- Energy tax receipts 1,832,750
- Garden State Trust 0

General Budget, 2007
- Total tax levy $37,059,375
  - County levy 4,037,073
    - County taxes 3,814,010
    - County library 0
    - County health 0
    - County open space 223,062
  - School levy 24,276,360
  - Muni. levy 8,745,942
- Misc. revenues 4,908,854

Taxes

	2005	2006	2007
General tax rate per $100	2.79	1.49	1.57
County equalization ratio	66.55	117.92	106.66
Net valuation taxable	$1,172,622,035	$2,363,028,100	$2,373,108,216
State equalized value	$1,958,613,721	$2,220,960,019	$2,277,023,699

The New Jersey Municipal Data Book

Collingswood Borough
Camden County

Demographics & Socio-Economic Characteristics
(2000 US Census, except as noted)

Population
1980*	15,838
1990*	15,289
2000	14,326
Male	6,732
Female	7,594
2006 (estimate)*	13,961
Population density	7,629.0

Race & Hispanic Origin, 2000
Race
White	12,388
Black/African American	955
American Indian/Alaska Native	48
Asian	395
Native Hawaiian/Pacific Islander	3
Other race	346
Two or more races	191
Hispanic origin, total	812
Mexican	112
Puerto Rican	450
Cuban	9
Other Hispanic	241

Age & Nativity, 2000
Under 5 years	785
18 years and over	11,209
21 years and over	10,708
65 years and over	2,066
85 years and over	357
Median age	37.1
Native-born	13,511
Foreign-born	826

Educational Attainment, 2000
Population 25 years and over	10,095
Less than 9th grade	3.0%
High school grad or higher	87.5%
Bachelor's degree or higher	30.3%
Graduate degree	10.2%

Income & Poverty, 1999
Per capita income	$24,358
Median household income	$43,175
Median family income	$57,987
Persons in poverty	866
H'holds receiving public assistance	126
H'holds receiving social security	1,710

Households, 2000
Total households	6,263
With persons under 18	1,733
With persons over 65	1,641
Family households	3,461
Single-person households	2,291
Persons per household	2.27
Persons per family	3.05

Labor & Employment
Total civilian labor force, 2006**	8,625
Unemployment rate	5.0%
Total civilian labor force, 2000	7,926
Unemployment rate	4.6%

Employed persons 16 years and over by occupation, 2000
Managers & professionals	3,207
Service occupations	803
Sales & office occupations	2,379
Farming, fishing & forestry	0
Construction & maintenance	606
Production & transportation	563
Self-employed persons	347

* US Census Bureau
** New Jersey Department of Labor

General Information
Borough of Collingswood
678 Haddon Ave
Collingswood, NJ 08108
856-854-0720

Website	www.collingswood.com
Year of incorporation	1888
Land/water area (sq. miles)	1.83/0.09
Form of government	Commission

Government
Legislative Districts
US Congressional	1
State Legislative	6

Local Officials, 2008
Mayor	M. James Maley Jr
Manager	Bradford Stokes
Clerk	Alice Marks
Finance Dir	Sandra Powell
Tax Assessor	John Dymond
Tax Collector	Keith Hastings
Attorney	Joseph Nardi III
Building	William Joseph
Comm Dev/Planning	John Kane
Engineering	Remington & Vernick
Public Works	Carl Jubb Jr
Police Chief	Thomas Garrity
Emerg/Fire Director	John Amet

Housing & Construction
Housing Units, 2000*
Total	6,866
Median rent	$688
Median SF home value	$101,200

Permits for New Residential Construction
	Units	Value
Total, 2007	0	$0
Single family	0	$0
Total, 2006	0	$0
Single family	0	$0

Real Property Valuation, 2007
	Parcels	Valuation
Total	4,452	$479,756,900
Vacant	198	3,258,300
Residential	3,915	402,555,600
Commercial	299	55,417,400
Industrial	0	0
Apartments	40	18,525,600
Farm land	0	0
Farm homestead	0	0

Average Property Value & Tax, 2007
Residential value	$102,824
Property tax	$5,485
Tax credit/rebate	$979

Public Library
Collingswood Public Library
771 Haddon Ave
Collingswood, NJ 08108
856-858-0649

Director: Kathleen Liu

Library statistics, 2006
Population served	14,326
Full-time/total staff	0/0

	Total	Per capita
Holdings	67,709	4.73
Revenues	$545,651	$38.09
Expenditures	$504,519	$35.22
Annual visits	64,000	4.47
Internet terminals/annual users	11/9,627	

Taxes
	2005	2006	2007
General tax rate per $100	4.516	5.081	5.335
County equalization ratio	71.82	59.55	50.18
Net valuation taxable	$482,118,388	$478,689,900	$481,828,181
State equalized value	$809,602,667	$956,366,647	$1,069,383,628

Public Safety
Number of officers, 2006: 37

Crime	2005	2006
Total crimes	445	433
Violent	29	23
Murder	0	0
Rape	1	1
Robbery	7	7
Aggravated assault	21	15
Non-violent	416	410
Burglary	110	66
Larceny	274	315
Vehicle theft	32	29
Domestic violence	130	157
Arson	2	0
Total crime rate	31.5	30.7
Violent	2.1	1.6
Non-violent	29.4	29.1

Public School District
(for school year 2006-07 except as noted)

Collingswood Borough School District
200 Lees Ave
Collingswood, NJ 08108
856-962-5732

Superintendent	Scott A. Oswald
Number of schools	7
Grade plan	K-12
Enrollment	1,899
Attendance rate, '05-06	94.5%
Dropout rate	1.5%
Students per teacher	9.7
Per pupil expenditure	$14,316
Median faculty salary	$52,650
Median administrator salary	$100,976
Grade 12 enrollment	206
High school graduation rate	90.2%

Assessment test results
(percent scoring at proficient or advanced level)
	Language	Math
NJASK-Grade 3	86.0%	82.2%
GEPA-Grade 8	81.8%	79.3%
HSPA-High School	86.9%	72.9%

SAT score averages
Pct tested	Math	Verbal	Writing
61%	483	486	482

Teacher Qualifications
Avg. years of experience	10
Highly-qualified teachers one subject/all subjects	100%/100%
With emergency credentials	0.0%

No Child Left Behind
AYP, 2005-06: Meets Standards

Municipal Finance
State Aid Programs, 2008
Total aid	$1,530,145
CMPTRA	661,950
Energy tax receipts	868,195
Garden State Trust	0

General Budget, 2007
Total tax levy	$25,700,950
County levy	6,443,356
County taxes	6,247,769
County library	0
County health	0
County open space	195,587
School levy	12,666,194
Muni. levy	6,591,400
Misc. revenues	9,393,496

Monmouth County

Colts Neck Township

Demographics & Socio-Economic Characteristics
(2000 US Census, except as noted)

Population
1980*	7,888
1990*	8,559
2000	12,331
Male	6,448
Female	5,883
2006 (estimate)*	11,587
Population density	368.7

Race & Hispanic Origin, 2000
Race
White	10,544
Black/African American	973
American Indian/Alaska Native	28
Asian	447
Native Hawaiian/Pacific Islander	1
Other race	179
Two or more races	159
Hispanic origin, total	520
Mexican	113
Puerto Rican	186
Cuban	15
Other Hispanic	206

Age & Nativity, 2000
Under 5 years	1,019
18 years and over	8,731
21 years and over	8,116
65 years and over	1,003
85 years and over	88
Median age	33.2
Native-born	11,271
Foreign-born	1,060

Educational Attainment, 2000
Population 25 years and over	7,254
Less than 9th grade	2.2%
High school grad or higher	95.0%
Bachelor's degree or higher	47.5%
Graduate degree	19.3%

Income & Poverty, 1999
Per capita income	$46,795
Median household income	$109,190
Median family income	$117,980
Persons in poverty	308
H'holds receiving public assistance	21
H'holds receiving social security	747

Households, 2000
Total households	3,513
With persons under 18	1,813
With persons over 65	697
Family households	3,195
Single-person households	262
Persons per household	3.17
Persons per family	3.33

Labor & Employment
Total civilian labor force, 2006**	4,994
Unemployment rate	3.7%
Total civilian labor force, 2000	4,692
Unemployment rate	3.6%

Employed persons 16 years and over by occupation, 2000
Managers & professionals	2,373
Service occupations	442
Sales & office occupations	1,183
Farming, fishing & forestry	8
Construction & maintenance	259
Production & transportation	259
Self-employed persons	375

‡ Branch of county library
* US Census Bureau
** New Jersey Department of Labor

See Introduction for an explanation of all data sources.

General Information
Township of Colts Neck
124 Cedar Dr
Colts Neck, NJ 07722
732-462-5470

Website	www.colts-neck.nj.us
Year of incorporation	1962
Land/water area (sq. miles)	31.43/0.68
Form of government	Township

Government
Legislative Districts
US Congressional	4
State Legislative	12

Local Officials, 2008
Mayor	Thomas E. Hennessey Jr
Manager	Robert Bowden
Clerk	Robert Bowden
Finance Dir	John Antonides
Tax Assessor	Eldo Magnani
Tax Collector	John Antonides
Attorney	John Bennett
Building	Henry Salerno
Planning	Timothy Anfuso
Engineering	Schoor De Palma
Public Works	Edward Thompson
Police Chief	Kevin Sauter
Emerg/Fire Director	Morgan Savage

Housing & Construction
Housing Units, 2000*
Total	3,614
Median rent	$974
Median SF home value	$425,500

Permits for New Residential Construction
	Units	Value
Total, 2007	12	$6,935,801
Single family	12	$6,935,801
Total, 2006	11	$4,994,905
Single family	11	$4,994,905

Real Property Valuation, 2007
	Parcels	Valuation
Total	3,763	$1,413,647,950
Vacant	162	24,759,000
Residential	3,033	1,206,627,700
Commercial	66	71,775,300
Industrial	0	0
Apartments	0	0
Farm land	296	3,712,550
Farm homestead	206	106,773,400

Average Property Value & Tax, 2007
Residential value	$405,496
Property tax	$12,775
Tax credit/rebate	$1,343

Public Library
Colts Neck Branch Library‡
1 Winthrop Rd
Colts Neck, NJ 07722
732-431-5656

Branch Librarian......Virginia Lyons

Library statistics, 2006
see Monmouth County profile for library system statistics

Public Safety
Number of officers, 2006.....22

Crime
	2005	2006
Total crimes	132	95
Violent	9	2
Murder	0	0
Rape	0	0
Robbery	0	1
Aggravated assault	9	1
Non-violent	123	93
Burglary	19	15
Larceny	102	76
Vehicle theft	2	2
Domestic violence	30	40
Arson	1	4
Total crime rate	11.3	8.2
Violent	0.8	0.2
Non-violent	10.5	8.0

Public School District
(for school year 2006-07 except as noted)

Colts Neck Township School District
70 Conover Rd
Colts Neck, NJ 07722
732-946-0055

Superintendent	Robert Mahon (Int)
Number of schools	3
Grade plan	K-8
Enrollment	1,561
Attendance rate, '05-06	95.6%
Dropout rate	NA
Students per teacher	10.1
Per pupil expenditure	$13,375
Median faculty salary	$51,705
Median administrator salary	$115,995
Grade 12 enrollment	NA
High school graduation rate	NA

Assessment test results
(percent scoring at proficient or advanced level)
	Language	Math
NJASK-Grade 3	91.7%	92.3%
GEPA-Grade 8	91.5%	91.9%
HSPA-High School	NA	NA

SAT score averages
Pct tested	Math	Verbal	Writing
NA	NA	NA	NA

Teacher Qualifications
Avg. years of experience	7
Highly-qualified teachers one subject/all subjects	100%/100%
With emergency credentials	0.0%

No Child Left Behind
AYP, 2005-06.....Meets Standards

Municipal Finance
State Aid Programs, 2008
Total aid	$2,283,189
CMPTRA	0
Energy tax receipts	2,254,801
Garden State Trust	0

General Budget, 2007
Total tax levy	$44,575,710
County levy	8,929,318
County taxes	7,974,498
County library	456,518
County health	0
County open space	498,302
School levy	30,978,781
Muni. levy	4,667,611
Misc. revenues	5,947,984

Taxes
	2005	2006	2007
General tax rate per $100	3.017	3.07	3.151
County equalization ratio	51.2	46.59	42.66
Net valuation taxable	$1,365,818,868	$1,391,529,100	$1,414,928,678
State equalized value	$2,931,570,869	$3,263,252,356	$3,389,698,633

©2008 Information Publications, Inc. All rights reserved. Photocopying prohibited. For additional copies, contact the publisher at www.informationpublications.com or (877)544-INFO (4636)

The New Jersey Municipal Data Book   95

Commercial Township
Cumberland County

Demographics & Socio-Economic Characteristics
(2000 US Census, except as noted)

Population
- 1900* 1,671
- 1990* 5,026
- 2000 5,259
  - Male 2,590
  - Female 2,669
- 2006 (estimate)* 5,419
- Population density 166.9

Race & Hispanic Origin, 2000
Race
- White 4,364
- Black/African American 706
- American Indian/Alaska Native 22
- Asian 12
- Native Hawaiian/Pacific Islander ... 1
- Other race 53
- Two or more races 101
- Hispanic origin, total 203
  - Mexican 29
  - Puerto Rican 126
  - Cuban 1
  - Other Hispanic 47

Age & Nativity, 2000
- Under 5 years 373
- 18 years and over 3,773
- 21 years and over 3,534
- 65 years and over 648
- 85 years and over 58
  - Median age 34.0
- Native-born 5,200
- Foreign-born 59

Educational Attainment, 2000
- Population 25 years and over 3,281
- Less than 9th grade 10.3%
- High school grad or higher 63.2%
- Bachelor's degree or higher 6.3%
- Graduate degree 1.3%

Income & Poverty, 1999
- Per capita income $14,663
- Median household income $34,960
- Median family income $37,500
- Persons in poverty 827
- H'holds receiving public assistance ... 107
- H'holds receiving social security ... 565

Households, 2000
- Total households 1,873
  - With persons under 18 791
  - With persons over 65 490
  - Family households 1,368
  - Single-person households 400
- Persons per household 2.80
- Persons per family 3.22

Labor & Employment
- Total civilian labor force, 2006** ... 2,615
  - Unemployment rate 6.8%
- Total civilian labor force, 2000 ... 2,362
  - Unemployment rate 9.1%

Employed persons 16 years and over by occupation, 2000
- Managers & professionals 367
- Service occupations 420
- Sales & office occupations 421
- Farming, fishing & forestry 58
- Construction & maintenance 289
- Production & transportation 593
- Self-employed persons 137

* US Census Bureau
** New Jersey Department of Labor

General Information
Township of Commercial
Township Hall
1768 Main St
Port Norris, NJ 08349
856-785-3100

- Website .... (county website)
- Year of incorporation 1874
- Land/water area (sq. miles) 32.46/2.04
- Form of government .... Township

Government
Legislative Districts
- US Congressional 2
- State Legislative 3

Local Officials, 2008
- Mayor .... George W. Garrison
- Manager .... Judson Moore
- Clerk .... Hannah E. Nichols
- Finance Dir .... Judson Moore
- Tax Assessor .... Ruth Benz
- Tax Collector .... Grace Robinson
- Attorney .... Thomas E. Seeley
- Building .... David Dean
- Comm Dev/Planning .... NA
- Engineering .... Remington & Vernick
- Public Works .... John Barnes
- Police Chief .... NA
- Fire/Emergency Dir .... NA

Housing & Construction
Housing Units, 2000*
- Total 2,171
- Median rent $689
- Median SF home value $66,100

Permits for New Residential Construction

	Units	Value
Total, 2007	11	$1,229,539
Single family	11	$1,229,539
Total, 2006	9	$998,110
Single family	9	$998,110

Real Property Valuation, 2007

	Parcels	Valuation
Total	4,045	$115,561,725
Vacant	1,775	9,275,275
Residential	2,110	94,833,900
Commercial	63	4,139,050
Industrial	18	5,914,700
Apartments	1	62,400
Farm land	55	546,000
Farm homestead	23	790,400

Average Property Value & Tax, 2007
- Residential value $44,831
- Property tax $1,759
- Tax credit/rebate $681

Public Library
Commercial Township Free Public Library
1628 Main St
Port Norris, NJ 08349
856-785-1900

- Librarian .... NA

Library statistics, 2006
- Population served .... NA
- Full-time/total staff .... NA/NA

	Total	Per capita
Holdings	NA	NA
Revenues	NA	NA
Expenditures	NA	NA
Annual visits	NA	NA
Internet terminals/annual users	NA/NA	

Taxes

	2005	2006	2007
General tax rate per $100	3.545	3.825	3.926
County equalization ratio	73.36	63.45	57.02
Net valuation taxable	$116,304,201	$115,588,325	$116,782,824
State equalized value	$183,300,553	$204,051,705	$231,561,392

Public Safety
Number of officers, 2006 0

Crime	2005	2006
Total crimes	182	217
Violent	18	30
Murder	0	0
Rape	0	0
Robbery	4	6
Aggravated assault	14	24
Non-violent	164	187
Burglary	50	73
Larceny	95	102
Vehicle theft	19	12
Domestic violence	124	30
Arson	5	5
Total crime rate	33.8	40.2
Violent	3.3	5.6
Non-violent	30.4	34.6

Public School District
(for school year 2006-07 except as noted)

Commercial Township School District
1308 North Ave, PO Box 650
Port Norris, NJ 08349
856-785-0840

- Superintendent .... Barry Ballard
- Number of schools 2
- Grade plan K-8
- Enrollment 717
- Attendance rate, '05-06 .... 93.5%
- Dropout rate .... NA
- Students per teacher 10.7
- Per pupil expenditure $11,356
- Median faculty salary $46,900
- Median administrator salary ... $93,989
- Grade 12 enrollment .... NA
- High school graduation rate ..... NA

Assessment test results
(percent scoring at proficient or advanced level)

	Language	Math
NJASK-Grade 3	83.1%	94.3%
GEPA-Grade 8	73.7%	48.7%
HSPA-High School	NA	NA

SAT score averages

Pct tested	Math	Verbal	Writing
NA	NA	NA	NA

Teacher Qualifications
- Avg. years of experience 8
- Highly-qualified teachers
  - one subject/all subjects 100%/100%
- With emergency credentials 0.0%

No Child Left Behind
- AYP, 2005-06 .... Meets Standards

Municipal Finance
State Aid Programs, 2008
- Total aid $634,027
  - CMPTRA 118,794
  - Energy tax receipts 379,130
  - Garden State Trust 136,103

General Budget, 2007
- Total tax levy $4,581,826
  - County levy 2,027,013
    - County taxes 1,920,127
    - County library 0
    - County health 86,334
    - County open space 20,552
  - School levy 1,637,784
  - Muni. levy 917,029
- Misc. revenues 2,478,428

Atlantic County

Corbin City

Demographics & Socio-Economic Characteristics
(2000 US Census, except as noted)

Population
- 1980* 254
- 1990* 412
- 2000 468
  - Male 232
  - Female 236
- 2006 (estimate)* 530
  - Population density 67.2

Race & Hispanic Origin, 2000
Race
- White 440
- Black/African American 13
- American Indian/Alaska Native 4
- Asian 6
- Native Hawaiian/Pacific Islander 0
- Other race 3
- Two or more races 2
- Hispanic origin, total 14
  - Mexican 3
  - Puerto Rican 3
  - Cuban 5
  - Other Hispanic 3

Age & Nativity, 2000
- Under 5 years 38
- 18 years and over 328
- 21 years and over 317
- 65 years and over 49
- 85 years and over 1
  - Median age 36.5
- Native-born 453
- Foreign-born 15

Educational Attainment, 2000
- Population 25 years and over 325
- Less than 9th grade 4.0%
- High school grad or higher 84.6%
- Bachelor's degree or higher 20.6%
- Graduate degree 4.9%

Income & Poverty, 1999
- Per capita income $21,321
- Median household income $47,083
- Median family income $56,000
- Persons in poverty 23
- H'holds receiving public assistance 4
- H'holds receiving social security 32

Households, 2000
- Total households 172
  - With persons under 18 71
  - With persons over 65 37
  - Family households 121
  - Single-person households 39
- Persons per household 2.72
- Persons per family 3.21

Labor & Employment
- Total civilian labor force, 2006** 253
  - Unemployment rate 4.0%
- Total civilian labor force, 2000 231
  - Unemployment rate 3.5%

Employed persons 16 years and over by occupation, 2000
- Managers & professionals 76
- Service occupations 60
- Sales & office occupations 31
- Farming, fishing & forestry 0
- Construction & maintenance 28
- Production & transportation 28
- Self-employed persons 20

* US Census Bureau
** New Jersey Department of Labor

See Introduction for an explanation of all data sources.

General Information
City of Corbin
316 Route 50
Corbin City, NJ 08270
609-628-2673
- Email .... corbincity@plexi.com
- Year of incorporation 1922
- Land/water area (sq. miles) 7.89/1.10
- Form of government .... City

Government
Legislative Districts
- US Congressional 2
- State Legislative 2

Local Officials, 2008
- Mayor .... Carol Foster
- Manager .... Joanne Siedlecki
- Clerk .... Joanne Siedlecki
- Finance Dir .... James Nicola
- Tax Assessor .... Bernadette Leonardi
- Tax Collector .... Beverly Totton
- Attorney .... Richard Russell
- Building .... NA
- Comm Dev/Planning .... NA
- Engineering .... David Scheidegg
- Public Works .... NA
- Police Chief .... NA
- Fire/Emergency Dir .... NA

Housing & Construction
Housing Units, 2000*
- Total 204
- Median rent $792
- Median SF home value $150,000

Permits for New Residential Construction

	Units	Value
Total, 2007	3	$290,850
Single family	3	$290,850
Total, 2006	2	$115,993
Single family	2	$115,993

Real Property Valuation, 2007

	Parcels	Valuation
Total	317	$29,424,800
Vacant	76	1,753,500
Residential	210	24,908,900
Commercial	15	2,398,900
Industrial	0	0
Apartments	0	0
Farm land	13	105,500
Farm homestead	3	258,000

Average Property Value & Tax, 2007
- Residential value $118,154
- Property tax $3,957
- Tax credit/rebate $853

Public Library
No public municipal library

Library statistics, 2006
- Population served .... NA
- Full-time/total staff .... NA/NA

	Total	Per capita
Holdings	NA	NA
Revenues	NA	NA
Expenditures	NA	NA
Annual visits	NA	NA
Internet terminals/annual users	NA/NA	

Taxes

	2005	2006	2007
General tax rate per $100	3.396	3.162	3.349
County equalization ratio	100.38	104.08	62.9
Net valuation taxable	$29,278,025	$29,936,500	$29,499,474
State equalized value	$28,130,308	$47,707,801	$67,423,724

Public Safety
Number of officers, 2006 0

Crime

	2005	2006
Total crimes	11	15
Violent	1	1
Murder	0	0
Rape	0	0
Robbery	0	0
Aggravated assault	1	1
Non-violent	10	14
Burglary	2	5
Larceny	7	8
Vehicle theft	1	1
Domestic violence	2	1
Arson	0	0
Total crime rate	21.0	28.2
Violent	1.9	1.9
Non-violent	19.0	26.4

Public School District
(for school year 2006-07 except as noted)

Corbin City School District
501 Atlantic Ave, Suite 1
Ocean City, NJ 08226

No schools in district - sends students to Upper Township and Ocean City schools

- Per pupil expenditure .... NA
- Median faculty salary .... NA
- Median administrator salary .... NA
- Grade 12 enrollment .... NA
- High school graduation rate .... NA

Assessment test results
(percent scoring at proficient or advanced level)

	Language	Math
NJASK-Grade 3	NA	NA
GEPA-Grade 8	NA	NA
HSPA-High School	NA	NA

SAT score averages

Pct tested	Math	Verbal	Writing
NA	NA	NA	NA

Teacher Qualifications
- Avg. years of experience .... NA
- Highly-qualified teachers
  - one subject/all subjects .... NA/NA
- With emergency credentials .... NA

No Child Left Behind
- AYP, 2005-06 .... NA

Municipal Finance
State Aid Programs, 2008
- Total aid $150,750
- CMPTRA 0
- Energy tax receipts 70,085
- Garden State Trust 80,665

General Budget, 2007
- Total tax levy $987,863
  - County levy 144,105
    - County taxes 114,715
    - County library 14,215
    - County health 5,792
    - County open space 9,383
  - School levy 759,100
  - Muni. levy 84,658
- Misc. revenues 530,592

Cranbury Township
Middlesex County

Demographics & Socio-Economic Characteristics
(2000 US Census, except as noted)

Population
1980*	1,927
1990*	2,500
2000	3,227
Male	1,558
Female	1,669
2006 (estimate)*	3,899
Population density	290.8

Race & Hispanic Origin, 2000
Race
White	2,865
Black/African American	73
American Indian/Alaska Native	0
Asian	239
Native Hawaiian/Pacific Islander	0
Other race	7
Two or more races	43
Hispanic origin, total	55
Mexican	4
Puerto Rican	8
Cuban	6
Other Hispanic	37

Age & Nativity, 2000
Under 5 years	214
18 years and over	2,245
21 years and over	2,191
65 years and over	363
85 years and over	64
Median age	39.6
Native-born	2,857
Foreign-born	370

Educational Attainment, 2000
Population 25 years and over	2,142
Less than 9th grade	3.4%
High school grad or higher	93.5%
Bachelor's degree or higher	62.7%
Graduate degree	27.5%

Income & Poverty, 1999
Per capita income	$50,698
Median household income	$111,680
Median family income	$128,410
Persons in poverty	51
H'holds receiving public assistance	2
H'holds receiving social security	261

Households, 2000
Total households	1,091
With persons under 18	517
With persons over 65	236
Family households	877
Single-person households	178
Persons per household	2.92
Persons per family	3.31

Labor & Employment
Total civilian labor force, 2006**	1,709
Unemployment rate	2.1%
Total civilian labor force, 2000	1,551
Unemployment rate	1.8%

Employed persons 16 years and over by occupation, 2000
Managers & professionals	920
Service occupations	122
Sales & office occupations	360
Farming, fishing & forestry	0
Construction & maintenance	32
Production & transportation	89
Self-employed persons	114

* US Census Bureau
** New Jersey Department of Labor

General Information
Township of Cranbury
23A N Main St
Cranbury, NJ 08512
609-395-0900

Website	www.cranburytownship.org
Year of incorporation	1872
Land/water area (sq. miles)	13.41/0.04
Form of government	Township

Government
Legislative Districts
US Congressional	12
State Legislative	14

Local Officials, 2008
Mayor	David J. Stout
Manager	Christine Smeltzer
Clerk	Kathleen Cunningham
Finance Dir	Denise Marabello
Tax Assessor	Steve Benner
Tax Collector	NA
Attorney	Trishka Waterbury
Building	Greg Farrington
Comm Dev/Planning	NA
Engineering	Cathleen Marcelli
Public Works	Thomas C. Witt
Police Chief	Jay Hansen
Emerg/Fire Director	Sam Distasio

Housing & Construction
Housing Units, 2000*
Total	1,121
Median rent	$756
Median SF home value	$361,000

Permits for New Residential Construction
	Units	Value
Total, 2007	0	$0
Single family	0	$0
Total, 2006	25	$3,525,955
Single family	25	$3,525,955

Real Property Valuation, 2007
	Parcels	Valuation
Total	1,517	$1,853,927,100
Vacant	73	29,857,600
Residential	1,160	780,884,700
Commercial	96	243,145,200
Industrial	38	762,437,400
Apartments	1	1,025,800
Farm land	100	2,866,400
Farm homestead	49	33,710,000

Average Property Value & Tax, 2007
Residential value	$673,776
Property tax	$9,872
Tax credit/rebate	$1,110

Public Library
Cranbury Public Library
23 N Main St
Cranbury, NJ 08512
609-655-0555

Director	Marilynn Mullen

Library statistics, 2006
Population served	3,227
Full-time/total staff	2/2

	Total	Per capita
Holdings	27,098	8.40
Revenues	$435,675	$135.01
Expenditures	$350,592	$108.64
Annual visits	58,936	18.26
Internet terminals/annual users	29/22,000	

Taxes
	2005	2006	2007
General tax rate per $100	3.6	3.84	1.47
County equalization ratio	49.7	42.31	102.11
Net valuation taxable	$588,192,697	$619,376,965	$1,856,220,613
State equalized value	$1,390,197,818	$1,751,591,280	$1,830,984,675

Public Safety
Number of officers, 2006	17

Crime	2005	2006
Total crimes	62	79
Violent	3	8
Murder	0	0
Rape	0	1
Robbery	1	2
Aggravated assault	2	5
Non-violent	59	71
Burglary	13	15
Larceny	32	51
Vehicle theft	14	5
Domestic violence	6	6
Arson	0	0
Total crime rate	16.7	20.0
Violent	0.8	2.0
Non-violent	15.9	18.0

Public School District
(for school year 2006-07 except as noted)

Cranbury Township School District
23 N Main St
Cranbury, NJ 08512
609-395-1700

Superintendent	John Haney
Number of schools	1
Grade plan	K-8
Enrollment	637
Attendance rate, '05-06	96.0%
Dropout rate	NA
Students per teacher	10.2
Per pupil expenditure	$15,722
Median faculty salary	$58,294
Median administrator salary	$107,566
Grade 12 enrollment	NA
High school graduation rate	NA

Assessment test results
(percent scoring at proficient or advanced level)
	Language	Math
NJASK-Grade 3	98.6%	94.4%
GEPA-Grade 8	95.9%	93.2%
HSPA-High School	NA	NA

SAT score averages
Pct tested	Math	Verbal	Writing
NA	NA	NA	NA

Teacher Qualifications
Avg. years of experience	12
Highly-qualified teachers one subject/all subjects	100%/100%
With emergency credentials	3.2%

No Child Left Behind
AYP, 2005-06	Meets Standards

Municipal Finance
State Aid Programs, 2008
Total aid	$570,595
CMPTRA	0
Energy tax receipts	568,540
Garden State Trust	2,055

General Budget, 2007
Total tax levy	$27,198,077
County levy	5,246,310
County taxes	4,696,620
County library	0
County health	0
County open space	549,690
School levy	15,097,326
Muni. levy	6,854,441
Misc. revenues	5,756,733

Union County — Cranford Township

Demographics & Socio-Economic Characteristics
(2000 US Census, except as noted)

Population
- 1980* 24,573
- 1990* 22,633
- 2000 22,578
  - Male 10,724
  - Female 11,854
- 2006 (estimate)* 22,369
  - Population density 4,640.9

Race & Hispanic Origin, 2000
Race
- White 21,156
- Black/African American 583
- American Indian/Alaska Native 9
- Asian 485
- Native Hawaiian/Pacific Islander 5
- Other race 151
- Two or more races 189
- Hispanic origin, total 879
  - Mexican 47
  - Puerto Rican 241
  - Cuban 198
  - Other Hispanic 393

Age & Nativity, 2000
- Under 5 years 1,465
- 18 years and over 17,316
- 21 years and over 16,793
- 65 years and over 4,048
- 85 years and over 615
  - Median age 40.4
- Native-born 20,613
- Foreign-born 1,965

Educational Attainment, 2000
- Population 25 years and over 16,204
- Less than 9th grade 2.9%
- High school grad or higher 91.5%
- Bachelor's degree or higher 43.0%
- Graduate degree 16.0%

Income & Poverty, 1999
- Per capita income $33,283
- Median household income $76,338
- Median family income $86,624
- Persons in poverty 553
- H'holds receiving public assistance 54
- H'holds receiving social security 2,438

Households, 2000
- Total households 8,397
  - With persons under 18 2,902
  - With persons over 65 2,509
  - Family households 6,225
  - Single-person households 1,842
- Persons per household 2.62
- Persons per family 3.09

Labor & Employment
- Total civilian labor force, 2006** 12,535
  - Unemployment rate 2.6%
- Total civilian labor force, 2000 12,149
  - Unemployment rate 4.1%

Employed persons 16 years and over by occupation, 2000
- Managers & professionals 5,895
- Service occupations 1,065
- Sales & office occupations 3,161
- Farming, fishing & forestry 0
- Construction & maintenance 798
- Production & transportation 727
- Self-employed persons 584

* US Census Bureau
** New Jersey Department of Labor

See Introduction for an explanation of all data sources.

General Information
Township of Cranford
8 Springfield Ave
Cranford, NJ 07016
908-709-7200
- Website .... www.cranford.com/township
- Year of incorporation 1871
- Land/water area (sq. miles) 4.82/0.02
- Form of government .... Township

Government
Legislative Districts
- US Congressional 7
- State Legislative 21

Local Officials, 2008
- Mayor .... Robert I. Puhak
- Manager .... Marlena Schmid
- Clerk .... Tara Rowley
- Finance Dir .... Thomas Grady
- Tax Assessor .... Peter Barnett
- Tax Collector .... Thomas Grady
- Attorney .... Carl Woodward III
- Building .... Richard Belluscio
- Comm Dev/Planning .... NA
- Engineering .... Richard Marsden
- Public Works .... Wayne Rozman
- Police Chief .... Eric G. Mason
- Emerg/Fire Director .... Leonard Dolan III

Housing & Construction
Housing Units, 2000*
- Total 8,560
- Median rent $867
- Median SF home value $233,600

Permits for New Residential Construction
	Units	Value
Total, 2007	28	$3,726,397
Single family	23	$3,419,897
Total, 2006	29	$3,294,076
Single family	29	$3,294,076

Real Property Valuation, 2007
	Parcels	Valuation
Total	7,902	$1,644,650,800
Vacant	102	10,160,700
Residential	7,461	1,345,807,100
Commercial	287	233,950,900
Industrial	42	48,125,100
Apartments	9	6,501,800
Farm land	1	105,200
Farm homestead	0	0

Average Property Value & Tax, 2007
- Residential value $180,379
- Property tax $8,041
- Tax credit/rebate $1,206

Public Library
Cranford Public Library
224 Walnut Ave
Cranford, NJ 07016
908-709-7272
- Director .... John Malar

Library statistics, 2006
- Population served 22,578
- Full-time/total staff 5/11

	Total	Per capita
Holdings	129,555	5.74
Revenues	$1,287,003	$57.00
Expenditures	$1,279,206	$56.66
Annual visits	180,224	7.98
Internet terminals/annual users	9/16,961	

Public Safety
- Number of officers, 2006 51

Crime	2005	2006
Total crimes	333	290
Violent	13	5
Murder	0	1
Rape	2	0
Robbery	4	3
Aggravated assault	7	1
Non-violent	320	285
Burglary	45	31
Larceny	258	247
Vehicle theft	17	7
Domestic violence	99	106
Arson	0	1
Total crime rate	14.7	12.9
Violent	0.6	0.2
Non-violent	14.1	12.7

Public School District
(for school year 2006-07 except as noted)

Cranford Township School District
132 Thomas St
Cranford, NJ 07016
908-709-6202

- Superintendent .... Lawrence S. Feinsod
- Number of schools 7
- Grade plan K-12
- Enrollment 3,699
- Attendance rate, '05-06 .... 95.9%
- Dropout rate 0.1%
- Students per teacher 10.7
- Per pupil expenditure $12,686
- Median faculty salary $54,717
- Median administrator salary $110,860
- Grade 12 enrollment 279
- High school graduation rate 99.3%

Assessment test results
(percent scoring at proficient or advanced level)

	Language	Math
NJASK-Grade 3	89.5%	93.6%
GEPA-Grade 8	92.2%	87.5%
HSPA-High School	95.3%	87.6%

SAT score averages
Pct tested	Math	Verbal	Writing
99%	551	532	535

Teacher Qualifications
- Avg. years of experience 9
- Highly-qualified teachers
  - one subject/all subjects 100%/100%
- With emergency credentials 0.0%

No Child Left Behind
- AYP, 2005-06 .... Meets Standards

Municipal Finance
State Aid Programs, 2008
- Total aid $3,729,776
- CMPTRA 602,938
- Energy tax receipts 3,126,838
- Garden State Trust 0

General Budget, 2007
- Total tax levy $73,424,024
- County levy 13,883,998
- County taxes 13,285,752
- County library 0
- County health 0
- County open space 598,247
- School levy 41,071,892
- Muni. levy 18,468,134
- Misc. revenues 9,444,530

Taxes

	2005	2006	2007
General tax rate per $100	3.923	4.191	4.458
County equalization ratio	48.22	43.85	41.48
Net valuation taxable	$1,674,054,231	$1,658,492,700	$1,647,063,669
State equalized value	$3,617,230,404	$4,001,321,019	$4,193,673,827

©2008 Information Publications, Inc. All rights reserved. Photocopying prohibited. For additional copies, contact the publisher at www.informationpublications.com or (877)544-INFO (4636)

The New Jersey Municipal Data Book

Cresskill Borough
Bergen County

Demographics & Socio-Economic Characteristics
(2000 US Census, except as noted)

Population
1980*	7,609
1990*	7,558
2000	7,746
Male	3,726
Female	4,020
2006 (estimate)*	8,437
Population density	3,942.5

Race & Hispanic Origin, 2000
Race
White	6,046
Black/African American	71
American Indian/Alaska Native	3
Asian	1,444
Native Hawaiian/Pacific Islander	0
Other race	50
Two or more races	132
Hispanic origin, total	309
Mexican	7
Puerto Rican	71
Cuban	79
Other Hispanic	152

Age & Nativity, 2000
Under 5 years	530
18 years and over	5,710
21 years and over	5,563
65 years and over	1,308
85 years and over	177
Median age	40.9
Native-born	5,848
Foreign-born	1,898

Educational Attainment, 2000
Population 25 years and over	5,408
Less than 9th grade	2.6%
High school grad or higher	92.3%
Bachelor's degree or higher	50.1%
Graduate degree	17.6%

Income & Poverty, 1999
Per capita income	$41,573
Median household income	$84,692
Median family income	$96,245
Persons in poverty	232
H'holds receiving public assistance	36
H'holds receiving social security	807

Households, 2000
Total households	2,630
With persons under 18	1,113
With persons over 65	873
Family households	2,163
Single-person households	418
Persons per household	2.91
Persons per family	3.26

Labor & Employment
Total civilian labor force, 2006**	3,965
Unemployment rate	2.5%
Total civilian labor force, 2000	3,731
Unemployment rate	2.3%

Employed persons 16 years and over by occupation, 2000
Managers & professionals	1,955
Service occupations	284
Sales & office occupations	982
Farming, fishing & forestry	0
Construction & maintenance	291
Production & transportation	132
Self-employed persons	274

* US Census Bureau
** New Jersey Department of Labor

General Information
Borough of Cresskill
67 Union Ave
Cresskill, NJ 07626
201-569-5400

Website	www.cresskillboro.com
Year of incorporation	1894
Land/water area (sq. miles)	2.14/0.00
Form of government	Borough

Government
Legislative Districts
US Congressional	5
State Legislative	39

Local Officials, 2008
Mayor	Benedict Romeo
Manager/Admin	Andrew Vaccaro
Clerk	Barbara Nasuto
Finance Dir	Harold Laufeld
Tax Assessor	James Anzevino
Tax Collector	Harold Laufeld
Attorney	Robert Quinn
Building	Edward Rossi
Comm Dev/Planning	NA
Engineering	Paul Azzolina
Public Works	NA
Police Chief	Stephen Lillis
Fire Chief	Joseph Spina

Housing & Construction
Housing Units, 2000*
Total	2,702
Median rent	$1,571
Median SF home value	$281,100

Permits for New Residential Construction
	Units	Value
Total, 2007	11	$4,552,750
Single family	11	$4,552,750
Total, 2006	90	$9,366,762
Single family	14	$6,587,385

Real Property Valuation, 2007
	Parcels	Valuation
Total	2,899	$1,797,281,500
Vacant	99	29,687,100
Residential	2,710	1,614,496,200
Commercial	82	136,072,200
Industrial	3	11,685,200
Apartments	5	5,340,800
Farm land	0	0
Farm homestead	0	0

Average Property Value & Tax, 2007
Residential value	$595,755
Property tax	$11,848
Tax credit/rebate	$1,345

Public Library
Cresskill Public Library
53 Union Ave
Cresskill, NJ 07626
201-567-3521

Director .... Alice Chi

Library statistics, 2006
Population served	7,746
Full-time/total staff	2/4

	Total	Per capita
Holdings	59,925	7.74
Revenues	$696,200	$89.88
Expenditures	$691,765	$89.31
Annual visits	79,300	10.24
Internet terminals/annual users	11/20,592	

Taxes
	2005	2006	2007
General tax rate per $100	1.79	1.87	1.99
County equalization ratio	100.53	87.6	77.03
Net valuation taxable	$1,706,514,983	$1,773,432,200	$1,797,946,077
State equalized value	$1,948,076,465	$2,303,050,977	$2,528,486,659

Public Safety
Number of officers, 2006		25

Crime	2005	2006
Total crimes	55	28
Violent	1	1
Murder	0	0
Rape	0	0
Robbery	0	0
Aggravated assault	1	1
Non-violent	54	27
Burglary	4	8
Larceny	50	18
Vehicle theft	0	1
Domestic violence	1	0
Arson	2	0
Total crime rate	6.7	3.3
Violent	0.1	0.1
Non-violent	6.6	3.2

Public School District
(for school year 2006-07 except as noted)

Cresskill School District
1 Lincoln Dr
Cresskill, NJ 07626
201-567-5919

Superintendent	Charles Khoury
Number of schools	3
Grade plan	K-12
Enrollment	1,741
Attendance rate, '05-06	96.3%
Dropout rate	0.4%
Students per teacher	13.0
Per pupil expenditure	$12,273
Median faculty salary	$64,391
Median administrator salary	$119,500
Grade 12 enrollment	124
High school graduation rate	99.2%

Assessment test results
(percent scoring at proficient or advanced level)
	Language	Math
NJASK-Grade 3	93.6%	97.8%
GEPA-Grade 8	86.5%	81.2%
HSPA-High School	96.3%	87.5%

SAT score averages
Pct tested	Math	Verbal	Writing
94%	563	542	553

Teacher Qualifications
Avg. years of experience	9
Highly-qualified teachers one subject/all subjects	100%/100%
With emergency credentials	0.0%

No Child Left Behind
AYP, 2005-06 .... Meets Standards

Municipal Finance
State Aid Programs, 2008
Total aid	$1,070,809
CMPTRA	25,316
Energy tax receipts	1,045,493
Garden State Trust	0

General Budget, 2007
Total tax levy	$35,755,730
County levy	4,213,276
County taxes	3,979,473
County library	0
County health	0
County open space	233,803
School levy	21,537,369
Muni. levy	10,005,085
Misc. revenues	3,746,307

Monmouth County

Deal Borough

Demographics & Socio-Economic Characteristics
(2000 US Census, except as noted)

Population
- 1980* 1,952
- 1990* 1,179
- 2000 1,070
  - Male 535
  - Female 535
- 2006 (estimate)* 1,044
  - Population density 855.7

Race & Hispanic Origin, 2000
Race
- White 1,010
- Black/African American 13
- American Indian/Alaska Native 1
- Asian 3
- Native Hawaiian/Pacific Islander 0
- Other race 29
- Two or more races 14
- Hispanic origin, total 54
  - Mexican 10
  - Puerto Rican 7
  - Cuban 2
  - Other Hispanic 35

Age & Nativity, 2000
- Under 5 years 53
- 18 years and over 851
- 21 years and over 818
- 65 years and over 286
- 85 years and over 25
- Median age 44.6
- Native-born 935
- Foreign-born 135

Educational Attainment, 2000
- Population 25 years and over 756
- Less than 9th grade 2.2%
- High school grad or higher 88.6%
- Bachelor's degree or higher 26.9%
- Graduate degree 8.2%

Income & Poverty, 1999
- Per capita income $38,510
- Median household income $58,472
- Median family income $65,313
- Persons in poverty 120
- H'holds receiving public assistance ... 3
- H'holds receiving social security .. 191

Households, 2000
- Total households 434
  - With persons under 18 96
  - With persons over 65 194
  - Family households 290
  - Single-person households 126
- Persons per household 2.46
- Persons per family 3.02

Labor & Employment
- Total civilian labor force, 2006** ... 387
  - Unemployment rate 2.8%
- Total civilian labor force, 2000 ... 359
  - Unemployment rate 3.1%

Employed persons 16 years and over by occupation, 2000
- Managers & professionals 131
- Service occupations 51
- Sales & office occupations 139
- Farming, fishing & forestry 0
- Construction & maintenance 15
- Production & transportation 12
- Self-employed persons 35

* US Census Bureau
** New Jersey Department of Labor

See Introduction for an explanation of all data sources.

General Information
Borough of Deal
PO Box 56
Deal, NJ 07723
732-531-1454

- Website .... www.dealborough.com
- Year of incorporation 1898
- Land/water area (sq. miles) ... 1.22/0.08
- Form of government .... Commission

Government
Legislative Districts
- US Congressional 6
- State Legislative 11

Local Officials, 2008
- Mayor .... Harry Franco
- Manager .... James Rogers
- Clerk .... James Rogers
- Finance Dir .... Thomas Seaman
- Tax Assessor .... Peter Barnett
- Tax Collector .... Theresa Davis
- Attorney .... Martin Barger
- Building .... William Doolittle
- Comm Dev/Planning .... NA
- Engineering .... Leon Avakian
- Public Works .... Brendan Kelly
- Police Chief .... Michael Sylvester
- Emerg/Fire Director .... Richard Fronapfel

Housing & Construction
Housing Units, 2000*
- Total 953
- Median rent $950
- Median SF home value $553,800

Permits for New Residential Construction

	Units	Value
Total, 2007	6	$770,500
Single family	6	$770,500
Total, 2006	3	$31,500
Single family	3	$31,500

Real Property Valuation, 2007

	Parcels	Valuation
Total	931	$1,105,840,600
Vacant	52	38,658,800
Residential	859	1,051,405,900
Commercial	16	13,305,400
Industrial	0	0
Apartments	4	2,470,500
Farm land	0	0
Farm homestead	0	0

Average Property Value & Tax, 2007
- Residential value $1,223,988
- Property tax $13,298
- Tax credit/rebate $1,323

Public Library
No public municipal library

Library statistics, 2006
- Population served .... NA
- Full-time/total staff .... NA/NA

	Total	Per capita
Holdings	NA	NA
Revenues	NA	NA
Expenditures	NA	NA
Annual visits	NA	NA
Internet terminals/annual users	NA/NA	

Taxes

	2005	2006	2007
General tax rate per $100	0.821	0.999	1.087
County equalization ratio	87.02	58.2	48.99
Net valuation taxable	$1,093,026,348	$1,101,444,300	$1,106,427,167
State equalized value	$1,878,052,144	$2,249,013,616	$2,651,846,696

Public Safety
- Number of officers, 2006 16

Crime

	2005	2006
Total crimes	35	43
Violent	2	3
Murder	0	0
Rape	0	0
Robbery	1	0
Aggravated assault	1	3
Non-violent	33	40
Burglary	6	5
Larceny	27	35
Vehicle theft	0	0
Domestic violence	6	4
Arson	0	0
Total crime rate	33.2	41.2
Violent	1.9	2.9
Non-violent	31.3	38.4

Public School District
(for school year 2006-07 except as noted)

Deal Borough School District
201 Roseld Ave
Deal, NJ 07723
732-531-0480

- Superintendent .... Anthony F. Moro Jr
- Number of schools 1
- Grade plan K-8
- Enrollment 116
- Attendance rate, '05-06 .... 95.5%
- Dropout rate .... NA
- Students per teacher 8.4
- Per pupil expenditure $15,004
- Median faculty salary $43,120
- Median administrator salary .. $131,527
- Grade 12 enrollment .... NA
- High school graduation rate .... NA

Assessment test results
(percent scoring at proficient or advanced level)

	Language	Math
NJASK-Grade 3	NA	NA
GEPA-Grade 8	84.6%	92.3%
HSPA-High School	NA	NA

SAT score averages

Pct tested	Math	Verbal	Writing
NA	NA	NA	NA

Teacher Qualifications
- Avg. years of experience 10
- Highly-qualified teachers
  - one subject/all subjects ... 100%/100%
- With emergency credentials 0.0%

No Child Left Behind
- AYP, 2005-06 .... Meets Standards

Municipal Finance
State Aid Programs, 2008
- Total aid $479,456
  - CMPTRA 0
  - Energy tax receipts 479,456
  - Garden State Trust 0

General Budget, 2007
- Total tax levy $12,020,713
  - County levy 6,087,898
    - County taxes 5,436,951
    - County library 311,246
    - County health 0
    - County open space 339,700
  - School levy 1,748,681
  - Muni. levy 4,184,135
- Misc. revenues 2,840,166

Deerfield Township
Cumberland County

Demographics & Socio-Economic Characteristics
(2000 US Census, except as noted)

Population
1980*	2,523
1990*	2,933
2000	2,927
Male	1,425
Female	1,502
2006 (estimate)*	3,231
Population density	191.9

Race & Hispanic Origin, 2000
Race
White	2,289
Black/African American	382
American Indian/Alaska Native	45
Asian	30
Native Hawaiian/Pacific Islander	0
Other race	89
Two or more races	92
Hispanic origin, total	174
Mexican	27
Puerto Rican	104
Cuban	1
Other Hispanic	42

Age & Nativity, 2000
Under 5 years	160
18 years and over	2,154
21 years and over	2,037
65 years and over	412
85 years and over	39
Median age	38.8
Native-born	2,841
Foreign-born	86

Educational Attainment, 2000
Population 25 years and over	1,912
Less than 9th grade	12.2%
High school grad or higher	73.4%
Bachelor's degree or higher	10.6%
Graduate degree	2.6%

Income & Poverty, 1999
Per capita income	$18,468
Median household income	$45,365
Median family income	$47,225
Persons in poverty	268
H'holds receiving public assistance	12
H'holds receiving social security	334

Households, 2000
Total households	1,013
With persons under 18	412
With persons over 65	304
Family households	785
Single-person households	178
Persons per household	2.86
Persons per family	3.22

Labor & Employment
Total civilian labor force, 2006**	1,573
Unemployment rate	4.8%
Total civilian labor force, 2000	1,402
Unemployment rate	6.1%

Employed persons 16 years and over by occupation, 2000
Managers & professionals	275
Service occupations	224
Sales & office occupations	357
Farming, fishing & forestry	11
Construction & maintenance	146
Production & transportation	303
Self-employed persons	60

* US Census Bureau
** New Jersey Department of Labor

General Information
Township of Deerfield
PO Box 350
Rosenhayn, NJ 08352
856-455-3200

Website	www.deerfieldtownship.org
Year of incorporation	1748
Land/water area (sq. miles)	16.84/0.00
Form of government	Township

Government
Legislative Districts
US Congressional	2
State Legislative	3

Local Officials, 2008
Mayor	Carol Musso
Manager	Karen Seifrit
Clerk	Karen Seifrit
Finance Dir	Ruth Moynihan
Tax Assessor	Donald Seifrit
Tax Collector	Ruth Moynihan
Attorney	Michael Testa
Building	Theodore Cooper
Comm Dev/Planning	NA
Engineering	J. Michael Fralinger
Public Works	Michael Laurella
Police Chief	NA
Fire/Emergency Dir	NA

Housing & Construction
Housing Units, 2000*
Total	1,065
Median rent	$646
Median SF home value	$99,500

Permits for New Residential Construction
	Units	Value
Total, 2007	12	$1,441,237
Single family	12	$1,441,237
Total, 2006	16	$2,093,642
Single family	16	$2,093,642

Real Property Valuation, 2007
	Parcels	Valuation
Total	1,710	$180,798,800
Vacant	285	7,198,700
Residential	941	124,957,400
Commercial	70	16,178,400
Industrial	2	8,193,600
Apartments	0	0
Farm land	253	2,636,500
Farm homestead	159	21,634,200

Average Property Value & Tax, 2007
Residential value	$133,265
Property tax	$3,901
Tax credit/rebate	$924

Public Library
No public municipal library

Library statistics, 2006
Population served	NA
Full-time/total staff	NA/NA

	Total	Per capita
Holdings	NA	NA
Revenues	NA	NA
Expenditures	NA	NA
Annual visits	NA	NA
Internet terminals/annual users	NA/NA	

Taxes
	2005	2006	2007
General tax rate per $100	2.866	2.968	2.931
County equalization ratio	104.81	100.84	94.01
Net valuation taxable	$171,360,347	$174,553,500	$181,724,786
State equalized value	$169,932,911	$186,636,081	$244,065,846

Public Safety
Number of officers, 2006 0

Crime	2005	2006
Total crimes	46	47
Violent	7	4
Murder	0	0
Rape	0	0
Robbery	0	1
Aggravated assault	7	3
Non-violent	39	43
Burglary	19	17
Larceny	18	20
Vehicle theft	2	6
Domestic violence	22	1
Arson	2	2
Total crime rate	14.6	14.7
Violent	2.2	1.3
Non-violent	12.4	13.4

Public School District
(for school year 2006-07 except as noted)

Deerfield Township School District
Morton Ave, PO Box 375
Rosenhayn, NJ 08352
856-451-6610

Chief School Admin	Edythe Austermuhl
Number of schools	1
Grade plan	K-8
Enrollment	373
Attendance rate, '05-06	94.6%
Dropout rate	NA
Students per teacher	10.8
Per pupil expenditure	$12,304
Median faculty salary	$43,100
Median administrator salary	$88,750
Grade 12 enrollment	NA
High school graduation rate	NA

Assessment test results
(percent scoring at proficient or advanced level)
	Language	Math
NJASK-Grade 3	64.0%	80.0%
GEPA-Grade 8	71.1%	75.0%
HSPA-High School	NA	NA

SAT score averages
Pct tested	Math	Verbal	Writing
NA	NA	NA	NA

Teacher Qualifications
Avg. years of experience	11
Highly-qualified teachers one subject/all subjects	100%/100%
With emergency credentials	0.0%

No Child Left Behind
AYP, 2005-06 . . . . Meets Standards

Municipal Finance
State Aid Programs, 2008
Total aid	$327,991
CMPTRA	0
Energy tax receipts	327,116
Garden State Trust	875

General Budget, 2007
Total tax levy	$5,319,676
County levy	1,923,942
County taxes	1,822,483
County library	0
County health	81,951
County open space	19,508
School levy	3,377,237
Muni. levy	18,498
Misc. revenues	1,756,502

Burlington County
Delanco Township

Demographics & Socio-Economic Characteristics
(2000 US Census, except as noted)

Population
1980*	3,730
1990*	3,316
2000	3,237
Male	1,568
Female	1,669
2006 (estimate)*	4,224
Population density	1,696.4

Race & Hispanic Origin, 2000
Race
White	3,104
Black/African American	62
American Indian/Alaska Native	8
Asian	13
Native Hawaiian/Pacific Islander	0
Other race	13
Two or more races	37
Hispanic origin, total	63
Mexican	13
Puerto Rican	42
Cuban	2
Other Hispanic	6

Age & Nativity, 2000
Under 5 years	184
18 years and over	2,430
21 years and over	2,326
65 years and over	430
85 years and over	36
Median age	37.0
Native-born	3,076
Foreign-born	161

Educational Attainment, 2000
Population 25 years and over	2,213
Less than 9th grade	4.7%
High school grad or higher	85.2%
Bachelor's degree or higher	14.8%
Graduate degree	4.7%

Income & Poverty, 1999
Per capita income	$21,096
Median household income	$50,106
Median family income	$56,985
Persons in poverty	305
H'holds receiving public assistance	36
H'holds receiving social security	268

Households, 2000
Total households	1,227
With persons under 18	444
With persons over 65	325
Family households	892
Single-person households	280
Persons per household	2.64
Persons per family	3.09

Labor & Employment
Total civilian labor force, 2006**	2,019
Unemployment rate	6.3%
Total civilian labor force, 2000	1,731
Unemployment rate	6.0%

Employed persons 16 years and over by occupation, 2000
Managers & professionals	426
Service occupations	223
Sales & office occupations	528
Farming, fishing & forestry	3
Construction & maintenance	178
Production & transportation	269
Self-employed persons	80

* US Census Bureau
** New Jersey Department of Labor

See Introduction for an explanation of all data sources.

General Information
Township of Delanco
770 Coopertown Rd
Delanco, NJ 08075
856-461-0561

Website	www.delancotownship.com
Year of incorporation	1926
Land/water area (sq. miles)	2.49/0.90
Form of government	Township

Government
Legislative Districts
US Congressional	3
State Legislative	7

Local Officials, 2008
Mayor	Fernand Ouellette
Manager	Steven Corcoran
Clerk	Janice Lohr
Finance Dir	Robert Hudnell
Tax Assessor	Joseph Robinson
Tax Collector	Lynn Davis
Attorney	William Kearns
Building	Edward Schaefer
Comm Dev/Planning	NA
Engineering	David Denton
Public Works	John Fenimore
Police Chief	Edmund Parsons
Emerg/Fire Director	Keith Mohrmann

Housing & Construction
Housing Units, 2000*
Total	1,285
Median rent	$615
Median SF home value	$111,600

Permits for New Residential Construction
	Units	Value
Total, 2007	135	$12,583,519
Single family	135	$12,583,519
Total, 2006	111	$10,301,535
Single family	111	$10,301,535

Real Property Valuation, 2007
	Parcels	Valuation
Total	1,976	$461,247,800
Vacant	355	15,464,700
Residential	1,551	373,804,400
Commercial	46	42,074,500
Industrial	11	27,120,000
Apartments	4	1,730,000
Farm land	6	50,300
Farm homestead	3	1,003,900

Average Property Value & Tax, 2007
Residential value	$241,189
Property tax	$4,739
Tax credit/rebate	$956

Public Library
Delanco Public Library
1303 Burlington Ave
Delanco, NJ 08075
856-461-6850

Director .... Katharina Radcliffe

Library statistics, 2006
Population served	3,237
Full-time/total staff	0/0

	Total	Per capita
Holdings	32,664	10.09
Revenues	$46,567	$14.39
Expenditures	$64,393	$19.89
Annual visits	4,042	1.25
Internet terminals/annual users	2/2,020	

Public Safety
Number of officers, 2006	10

Crime
	2005	2006
Total crimes	63	90
Violent	4	4
Murder	0	0
Rape	0	0
Robbery	1	1
Aggravated assault	3	3
Non-violent	59	86
Burglary	12	20
Larceny	42	61
Vehicle theft	5	5
Domestic violence	21	39
Arson	0	1
Total crime rate	17.0	22.7
Violent	1.1	1.0
Non-violent	15.9	21.7

Public School District
(for school year 2006-07 except as noted)

Delanco Township School District
1301 Burlington Ave
Delanco, NJ 08075
856-461-1905

Superintendent	Michael Livengood
Number of schools	2
Grade plan	K-8
Enrollment	366
Attendance rate, '05-06	94.9%
Dropout rate	NA
Students per teacher	10.1
Per pupil expenditure	$12,498
Median faculty salary	$58,800
Median administrator salary	$92,570
Grade 12 enrollment	NA
High school graduation rate	NA

Assessment test results
(percent scoring at proficient or advanced level)
	Language	Math
NJASK-Grade 3	70.8%	79.2%
GEPA-Grade 8	76.2%	71.5%
HSPA-High School	NA	NA

SAT score averages
Pct tested	Math	Verbal	Writing
NA	NA	NA	NA

Teacher Qualifications
Avg. years of experience	16
Highly-qualified teachers one subject/all subjects	100%/100%
With emergency credentials	0.0%

No Child Left Behind
AYP, 2005-06 .... Meets Standards

Municipal Finance
State Aid Programs, 2008
Total aid	$336,329
CMPTRA	0
Energy tax receipts	336,324
Garden State Trust	5

General Budget, 2007
Total tax levy	$9,072,347
County levy	1,712,837
County taxes	1,419,285
County library	130,248
County health	0
County open space	163,303
School levy	4,826,282
Muni. levy	2,533,228
Misc. revenues	2,257,081

Taxes
	2005	2006	2007
General tax rate per $100	3.596	3.887	1.97
County equalization ratio	73.26	64.38	114.25
Net valuation taxable	$203,136,315	$214,307,200	$461,699,048
State equalized value	$315,527,050	$380,508,303	$436,330,855

The New Jersey Municipal Data Book

Delaware Township
Hunterdon County

Demographics & Socio-Economic Characteristics
(2000 US Census, except as noted)

Population
1980*	3,816
1990*	4,512
2000	4,478
Male	2,226
Female	2,252
2006 (estimate)*	4,730
Population density	128.7

Race & Hispanic Origin, 2000
Race
White	4,375
Black/African American	18
American Indian/Alaska Native	2
Asian	46
Native Hawaiian/Pacific Islander	1
Other race	11
Two or more races	25
Hispanic origin, total	51
Mexican	3
Puerto Rican	15
Cuban	12
Other Hispanic	21

Age & Nativity, 2000
Under 5 years	220
18 years and over	3,429
21 years and over	3,301
65 years and over	530
85 years and over	43
Median age	42.4
Native-born	4,279
Foreign-born	202

Educational Attainment, 2000
Population 25 years and over	3,163
Less than 9th grade	1.9%
High school grad or higher	91.1%
Bachelor's degree or higher	39.1%
Graduate degree	17.8%

Income & Poverty, 1999
Per capita income	$38,285
Median household income	$80,756
Median family income	$90,842
Persons in poverty	154
H'holds receiving public assistance	13
H'holds receiving social security	374

Households, 2000
Total households	1,643
With persons under 18	573
With persons over 65	367
Family households	1,303
Single-person households	243
Persons per household	2.72
Persons per family	3.06

Labor & Employment
Total civilian labor force, 2006**	2,780
Unemployment rate	2.2%
Total civilian labor force, 2000	2,482
Unemployment rate	1.8%

Employed persons 16 years and over by occupation, 2000
Managers & professionals	1,124
Service occupations	302
Sales & office occupations	587
Farming, fishing & forestry	5
Construction & maintenance	235
Production & transportation	184
Self-employed persons	291

* US Census Bureau
** New Jersey Department of Labor

General Information
Township of Delaware
PO Box 500
Sergeantsville, NJ 08557
609-397-3240

Website	www.delawaretwpnj.org
Year of incorporation	1838
Land/water area (sq. miles)	36.74/0.28
Form of government	Township

Government
Legislative Districts
US Congressional	12
State Legislative	23

Local Officials, 2008
Mayor	Susan Lockwood
Manager/Admin	NA
Clerk	Judith Allen
Finance Dir	Linda Zengel
Tax Assessor	Michelle Trivigno
Tax Collector	Brigid Pfenninger
Attorney	Kristina Hadinger
Building	Phillip Izzo
Comm Dev/Planning	NA
Engineering	Peter Turek
Public Works	Jay Trstensky
Police Chief	Bruce Must
Emerg/Fire Director	Sean Conway

Housing & Construction
Housing Units, 2000*
Total	1,701
Median rent	$1,130
Median SF home value	$275,900

Permits for New Residential Construction
	Units	Value
Total, 2007	9	$2,799,263
Single family	9	$2,799,263
Total, 2006	17	$4,406,569
Single family	17	$4,406,569

Real Property Valuation, 2007
	Parcels	Valuation
Total	2,637	$889,927,920
Vacant	129	11,832,320
Residential	1,285	580,165,800
Commercial	34	18,552,800
Industrial	10	8,724,800
Apartments	2	1,065,700
Farm land	705	6,573,000
Farm homestead	472	263,013,500

Average Property Value & Tax, 2007
Residential value	$479,897
Property tax	$9,780
Tax credit/rebate	$1,281

Public Library
No public municipal library

Library statistics, 2006
Population served	NA
Full-time/total staff	NA/NA

	Total	Per capita
Holdings	NA	NA
Revenues	NA	NA
Expenditures	NA	NA
Annual visits	NA	NA
Internet terminals/annual users	NA/NA	

Taxes
	2005	2006	2007
General tax rate per $100	1.8	1.89	2.04
County equalization ratio	103.74	96.91	85.21
Net valuation taxable	$876,960,532	$886,605,720	$891,383,319
State equalized value	$871,383,676	$967,603,697	$1,035,053,448

Public Safety
Number of officers, 2006 7

Crime
	2005	2006
Total crimes	32	39
Violent	0	2
Murder	0	0
Rape	0	0
Robbery	0	0
Aggravated assault	0	2
Non-violent	32	37
Burglary	13	21
Larceny	17	16
Vehicle theft	2	0
Domestic violence	6	18
Arson	0	1
Total crime rate	6.8	8.3
Violent	0.0	0.4
Non-violent	6.8	7.8

Public School District
(for school year 2006-07 except as noted)

Delaware Township School District
501 Rosemont-Ringoes Rd, PO Box 1000
Sergeantsville, NJ 08557
609-397-3179

Superintendent	Richard Wiener
Number of schools	1
Grade plan	K-8
Enrollment	484
Attendance rate, '05-06	97.7%
Dropout rate	NA
Students per teacher	9.3
Per pupil expenditure	$15,856
Median faculty salary	$54,465
Median administrator salary	$99,000
Grade 12 enrollment	NA
High school graduation rate	NA

Assessment test results
(percent scoring at proficient or advanced level)
	Language	Math
NJASK-Grade 3	72.9%	89.8%
GEPA-Grade 8	95.4%	87.5%
HSPA-High School	NA	NA

SAT score averages
Pct tested	Math	Verbal	Writing
NA	NA	NA	NA

Teacher Qualifications
Avg. years of experience	10
Highly-qualified teachers one subject/all subjects	97.5%/97.5%
With emergency credentials	0.0%

No Child Left Behind
AYP, 2005-06 .... Meets Standards

Municipal Finance
State Aid Programs, 2008
Total aid	$364,816
CMPTRA	0
Energy tax receipts	354,203
Garden State Trust	10,613

General Budget, 2007
Total tax levy	$18,165,960
County levy	3,484,087
County taxes	2,915,839
County library	253,733
County health	0
County open space	314,515
School levy	12,159,250
Muni. levy	2,522,624
Misc. revenues	1,855,627

Burlington County
Delran Township

Demographics & Socio-Economic Characteristics
(2000 US Census, except as noted)

Population
1980*	14,811
1990*	13,178
2000	15,536
Male	7,646
Female	7,890
2006 (estimate)*	17,283
Population density	2,602.9

Race & Hispanic Origin, 2000
Race
White	12,875
Black/African American	1,464
American Indian/Alaska Native	27
Asian	435
Native Hawaiian/Pacific Islander	25
Other race	253
Two or more races	457
Hispanic origin, total	505
Mexican	51
Puerto Rican	253
Cuban	7
Other Hispanic	194

Age & Nativity, 2000
Under 5 years	970
18 years and over	11,722
21 years and over	11,197
65 years and over	1,672
85 years and over	132
Median age	36.7
Native-born	13,931
Foreign-born	1,605

Educational Attainment, 2000
Population 25 years and over	10,463
Less than 9th grade	3.9%
High school grad or higher	88.2%
Bachelor's degree or higher	27.3%
Graduate degree	8.1%

Income & Poverty, 1999
Per capita income	$25,312
Median household income	$58,526
Median family income	$67,895
Persons in poverty	637
H'holds receiving public assistance	140
H'holds receiving social security	1,249

Households, 2000
Total households	5,816
With persons under 18	2,175
With persons over 65	1,233
Family households	4,330
Single-person households	1,222
Persons per household	2.67
Persons per family	3.11

Labor & Employment
Total civilian labor force, 2006**	10,068
Unemployment rate	3.3%
Total civilian labor force, 2000	8,665
Unemployment rate	3.0%

Employed persons 16 years and over by occupation, 2000
Managers & professionals	3,206
Service occupations	858
Sales & office occupations	2,442
Farming, fishing & forestry	7
Construction & maintenance	738
Production & transportation	1,152
Self-employed persons	267

* US Census Bureau
** New Jersey Department of Labor

See Introduction for an explanation of all data sources.

General Information
Township of Delran
900 S Chester Ave
Delran, NJ 08075
856-461-7734

Website	www.delrantownship.org
Year of incorporation	1880
Land/water area (sq. miles)	6.64/0.61
Form of government	Mayor-Council

Government
Legislative Districts
US Congressional	3
State Legislative	7

Local Officials, 2008
Mayor	Joseph Stellwag
Manager	Jeffrey Hatcher
Clerk	Jamey Eggers
Finance Dir	Teresa Leisse
Tax Assessor	Tom Davis
Tax Collector	Donna Ibbetson
Attorney	Brian Guest
Building	Hugh McCurley
Comm Dev/Planning	NA
Engineering	Pennoni Associates
Public Works	Ed Bart
Police Chief	Al Parente
Emerg/Fire Director	Joseph Bennett Sr

Housing & Construction
Housing Units, 2000*
Total	5,936
Median rent	$698
Median SF home value	$145,600

Permits for New Residential Construction
	Units	Value
Total, 2007	5	$684,200
Single family	5	$684,200
Total, 2006	35	$6,412,980
Single family	35	$6,412,980

Real Property Valuation, 2007
	Parcels	Valuation
Total	5,504	$1,548,007,300
Vacant	171	11,987,800
Residential	5,129	1,199,464,900
Commercial	169	268,014,700
Industrial	5	2,869,100
Apartments	2	62,667,200
Farm land	17	179,900
Farm homestead	11	2,823,700

Average Property Value & Tax, 2007
Residential value	$233,908
Property tax	$6,148
Tax credit/rebate	$1,068

Public Library
No public municipal library

Library statistics, 2006
Population served	NA
Full-time/total staff	NA/NA

	Total	Per capita
Holdings	NA	NA
Revenues	NA	NA
Expenditures	NA	NA
Annual visits	NA	NA
Internet terminals/annual users	NA/NA	

Taxes
	2005	2006	2007
General tax rate per $100	2.249	2.405	2.63
County equalization ratio	115.24	98.94	88.78
Net valuation taxable	$1,513,499,343	$1,530,562,200	$1,549,963,948
State equalized value	$1,529,714,315	$1,726,126,454	$1,842,850,095

Public Safety
Number of officers, 2006	32

Crime	2005	2006
Total crimes	293	259
Violent	39	20
Murder	0	0
Rape	2	0
Robbery	18	8
Aggravated assault	19	12
Non-violent	254	239
Burglary	46	43
Larceny	198	183
Vehicle theft	10	13
Domestic violence	174	106
Arson	3	2
Total crime rate	16.9	14.9
Violent	2.3	1.1
Non-violent	14.7	13.7

Public School District
(for school year 2006-07 except as noted)

Delran Township School District
52 Hartford Rd
Delran, NJ 08075
856-461-6800

Superintendent	George Sharp
Number of schools	4
Grade plan	K-12
Enrollment	2,817
Attendance rate, '05-06	95.3%
Dropout rate	NA
Students per teacher	12.2
Per pupil expenditure	$11,867
Median faculty salary	$51,200
Median administrator salary	$106,062
Grade 12 enrollment	171
High school graduation rate	97.8%

Assessment test results
(percent scoring at proficient or advanced level)
	Language	Math
NJASK-Grade 3	93.4%	91.8%
GEPA-Grade 8	76.9%	70.3%
HSPA-High School	92.6%	78.1%

SAT score averages
Pct tested	Math	Verbal	Writing
90%	483	471	461

Teacher Qualifications
Avg. years of experience	9
Highly-qualified teachers one subject/all subjects	99.5%/99.5%
With emergency credentials	0.0%

No Child Left Behind
AYP, 2005-06	Meets Standards

Municipal Finance
State Aid Programs, 2008
Total aid	$1,641,385
CMPTRA	474,554
Energy tax receipts	1,166,628
Garden State Trust	203

General Budget, 2007
Total tax levy	$40,736,344
County levy	7,356,887
County taxes	6,096,224
County library	559,419
County health	0
County open space	701,244
School levy	24,363,457
Muni. levy	9,016,000
Misc. revenues	5,758,200

©2008 Information Publications, Inc. All rights reserved. Photocopying prohibited. For additional copies, contact the publisher at www.informationpublications.com or (877)544-INFO (4636)

The New Jersey Municipal Data Book

Demarest Borough — Bergen County

Demographics & Socio-Economic Characteristics
(2000 US Census, except as noted)

Population
- 1980 4,963
- 1990* 4,800
- 2000 4,845
  - Male 2,376
  - Female 2,469
- 2006 (estimate)* 5,106
- Population density 2,466.7

Race & Hispanic Origin, 2000
Race
- White 3,744
- Black/African American 24
- American Indian/Alaska Native 1
- Asian 981
- Native Hawaiian/Pacific Islander 1
- Other race 23
- Two or more races 71
- Hispanic origin, total 167
  - Mexican 14
  - Puerto Rican 27
  - Cuban 48
  - Other Hispanic 78

Age & Nativity, 2000
- Under 5 years 297
- 18 years and over 3,444
- 21 years and over 3,320
- 65 years and over 698
- 85 years and over 67
- Median age 41.1
- Native-born 3,661
- Foreign-born 1,184

Educational Attainment, 2000
- Population 25 years and over 3,251
- Less than 9th grade 2.9%
- High school grad or higher 94.4%
- Bachelor's degree or higher 58.9%
- Graduate degree 24.1%

Income & Poverty, 1999
- Per capita income $51,939
- Median household income $103,286
- Median family income $113,144
- Persons in poverty 79
- H'holds receiving public assistance 14
- H'holds receiving social security 448

Households, 2000
- Total households 1,601
  - With persons under 18 752
  - With persons over 65 487
  - Family households 1,387
  - Single-person households 186
- Persons per household 3.02
- Persons per family 3.27

Labor & Employment
- Total civilian labor force, 2006** ... 2,413
  - Unemployment rate 4.0%
- Total civilian labor force, 2000 2,267
  - Unemployment rate 3.9%

Employed persons 16 years and over by occupation, 2000
- Managers & professionals 1,344
- Service occupations 186
- Sales & office occupations 502
- Farming, fishing & forestry 0
- Construction & maintenance 75
- Production & transportation 72
- Self-employed persons 208

* US Census Bureau
** New Jersey Department of Labor

General Information
Borough of Demarest
118 Serpentine Rd
Demarest, NJ 07627
201-768-0167

- Website .... www.demarestnj.net
- Year of incorporation 1903
- Land/water area (sq. miles) 2.07/0.00
- Form of government .... Borough

Government

Legislative Districts
- US Congressional 5
- State Legislative 39

Local Officials, 2008
- Mayor .... Jim Carroll
- Manager/Admin .... NA
- Clerk .... Susan Jarsiewicz
- Finance Dir .... Maureen Neville
- Tax Assessor .... George Reggo
- Tax Collector .... Maureen Neville
- Attorney .... Gregg Paster
- Building .... Edward Rossi
- Comm Dev/Planning .... NA
- Engineering .... AFR Group
- Public Works .... John Crosman
- Police Chief .... James Powderly III
- Emerg/Fire Director .... Al Bolduc

Housing & Construction

Housing Units, 2000*
- Total 1,634
- Median rent $2,001
- Median SF home value $360,300

Permits for New Residential Construction
	Units	Value
Total, 2007	19	$11,957,201
Single family	19	$11,957,201
Total, 2006	33	$15,071,074
Single family	33	$15,071,074

Real Property Valuation, 2007
	Parcels	Valuation
Total	1,686	$1,142,715,200
Vacant	76	25,416,600
Residential	1,601	1,078,919,200
Commercial	8	37,029,400
Industrial	0	0
Apartments	1	1,350,000
Farm land	0	0
Farm homestead	0	0

Average Property Value & Tax, 2007
- Residential value $673,903
- Property tax $13,874
- Tax credit/rebate $1,525

Public Library
Demarest Public Library
90 Hardenburgh Ave
Demarest, NJ 07627
201-768-8714

- Director .... Edna Ortega

Library statistics, 2006
- Population served 4,845
- Full-time/total staff 0/2

	Total	Per capita
Holdings	32,262	6.66
Revenues	$258,783	$53.41
Expenditures	$207,048	$42.73
Annual visits	14,450	2.98
Internet terminals/annual users	5/8,000	

Taxes
	2005	2006	2007
General tax rate per $100	1.96	2	2.06
County equalization ratio	101.92	93.78	83
Net valuation taxable	$1,113,022,663	$1,125,453,900	$1,143,304,777
State equalized value	$1,186,844,384	$1,356,579,708	$1,382,516,291

Public Safety
- Number of officers, 2006 14

Crime
	2005	2006
Total crimes	42	46
Violent	1	0
Murder	0	0
Rape	0	0
Robbery	0	0
Aggravated assault	1	0
Non-violent	41	46
Burglary	3	3
Larceny	38	43
Vehicle theft	0	0
Domestic violence	6	6
Arson	0	0
Total crime rate	8.5	9.2
Violent	0.2	0.0
Non-violent	8.3	9.2

Public School District
(for school year 2006-07 except as noted)

Demarest School District
568 Piermont Rd
Demarest, NJ 07627
201-768-6060

- Superintendent .... Gregg Hauser (Int)
- Number of schools 3
- Grade plan K-8
- Enrollment 708
- Attendance rate, '05-06 .... 96.7%
- Dropout rate .... NA
- Students per teacher 10.8
- Per pupil expenditure $14,535
- Median faculty salary $58,940
- Median administrator salary $123,480
- Grade 12 enrollment .... NA
- High school graduation rate .... NA

Assessment test results
(percent scoring at proficient or advanced level)
	Language	Math
NJASK-Grade 3	97.8%	97.8%
GEPA-Grade 8	93.4%	92.4%
HSPA-High School	NA	NA

SAT score averages
Pct tested	Math	Verbal	Writing
NA	NA	NA	NA

Teacher Qualifications
- Avg. years of experience 10
- Highly-qualified teachers
  - one subject/all subjects 98.0%/98.0%
- With emergency credentials 0.0%

No Child Left Behind
- AYP, 2005-06 .... Meets Standards

Municipal Finance

State Aid Programs, 2008
- Total aid $539,951
  - CMPTRA 21,090
  - Energy tax receipts 518,861
  - Garden State Trust 0

General Budget, 2007
- Total tax levy $23,537,563
  - County levy 2,500,624
    - County taxes 2,362,811
    - County library 0
    - County health 0
    - County open space 137,813
  - School levy 16,190,738
  - Muni. levy 4,846,201
  - Misc. revenues 2,496,636

Cape May County — Dennis Township

Demographics & Socio-Economic Characteristics
(2000 US Census, except as noted)

Population
1980*	3,989
1990*	5,574
2000	6,492
Male	3,188
Female	3,304
2006 (estimate)*	5,907
Population density	96.3

Race & Hispanic Origin, 2000
Race
White	6,325
Black/African American	62
American Indian/Alaska Native	6
Asian	28
Native Hawaiian/Pacific Islander	1
Other race	40
Two or more races	30
Hispanic origin, total	98
Mexican	45
Puerto Rican	34
Cuban	6
Other Hispanic	13

Age & Nativity, 2000
Under 5 years	429
18 years and over	4,656
21 years and over	4,442
65 years and over	798
85 years and over	162
Median age	37.4
Native-born	6,351
Foreign-born	152

Educational Attainment, 2000
Population 25 years and over	4,275
Less than 9th grade	5.2%
High school grad or higher	83.2%
Bachelor's degree or higher	20.5%
Graduate degree	5.1%

Income & Poverty, 1999
Per capita income	$21,455
Median household income	$56,595
Median family income	$61,445
Persons in poverty	346
H'holds receiving public assistance	38
H'holds receiving social security	533

Households, 2000
Total households	2,159
With persons under 18	970
With persons over 65	460
Family households	1,738
Single-person households	333
Persons per household	2.91
Persons per family	3.24

Labor & Employment
Total civilian labor force, 2006**	4,076
Unemployment rate	4.0%
Total civilian labor force, 2000	3,362
Unemployment rate	4.8%

Employed persons 16 years and over by occupation, 2000
Managers & professionals	968
Service occupations	557
Sales & office occupations	769
Farming, fishing & forestry	6
Construction & maintenance	574
Production & transportation	328
Self-employed persons	249

* US Census Bureau
** New Jersey Department of Labor

See Introduction for an explanation of all data sources.

General Information
Township of Dennis
571 Petersburg Rd
Dennisville, NJ 08214
609-861-9700

Website	www.dennistwp.org
Year of incorporation	1827
Land/water area (sq. miles)	61.35/2.94
Form of government	Township

Government
Legislative Districts
US Congressional	2
State Legislative	1

Local Officials, 2008
Mayor	John Murphy
Manager	Joseph J. Alessandrine Jr
Clerk	Jacqueline B. Justice
Finance Dir.	Glenn O. Clarke
Tax Assessor	Patricia Sutton
Tax Collector	Michele T. Heim
Attorney	Jeffrey A. April
Building	James P. Cannon
Comm Dev/Planning	NA
Engineering	Andrew Previti
Public Works	Clarence F. Ryan
Police Chief	NA
Fire/Emergency Dir.	NA

Housing & Construction
Housing Units, 2000*
Total	2,327
Median rent	$981
Median SF home value	$135,500

Permits for New Residential Construction
	Units	Value
Total, 2007	13	$2,350,020
Single family	13	$2,350,020
Total, 2006	13	$2,390,018
Single family	13	$2,390,018

Real Property Valuation, 2007
	Parcels	Valuation
Total	4,512	$1,026,226,400
Vacant	602	64,571,800
Residential	3,482	800,446,500
Commercial	166	143,388,500
Industrial	0	0
Apartments	0	0
Farm land	203	1,549,100
Farm homestead	59	16,270,500

Average Property Value & Tax, 2007
Residential value	$230,646
Property tax	$2,439
Tax credit/rebate	$723

Public Library
No public municipal library

Library statistics, 2006
Population served	NA
Full-time/total staff	NA/NA

	Total	Per capita
Holdings	NA	NA
Revenues	NA	NA
Expenditures	NA	NA
Annual visits	NA	NA
Internet terminals/annual users	NA/NA	

Taxes
	2005	2006	2007
General tax rate per $100	2.27	1.02	1.06
County equalization ratio	61.4	134.56	111.01
Net valuation taxable	$393,439,189	$1,021,979,900	$1,028,766,249
State equalized value	$751,268,262	$923,078,987	$1,028,766,249

Public Safety
Number of officers, 2006 … 0

Crime
	2005	2006
Total crimes	108	141
Violent	11	8
Murder	0	0
Rape	1	0
Robbery	0	2
Aggravated assault	10	6
Non-violent	97	133
Burglary	41	43
Larceny	41	86
Vehicle theft	15	4
Domestic violence	32	6
Arson	0	0
Total crime rate	17.3	23.2
Violent	1.8	1.3
Non-violent	15.6	21.9

Public School District
(for school year 2006-07 except as noted)

Dennis Township School District
601 Hagen Rd
Cape May Court House, NJ 08210
609-861-0549

Superintendent	George Papp
Number of schools	2
Grade plan	K-8
Enrollment	716
Attendance rate, '05-06	93.9%
Dropout rate	NA
Students per teacher	9.2
Per pupil expenditure	$13,438
Median faculty salary	$62,687
Median administrator salary	$86,872
Grade 12 enrollment	NA
High school graduation rate	NA

Assessment test results
(percent scoring at proficient or advanced level)
	Language	Math
NJASK-Grade 3	87.0%	88.3%
GEPA-Grade 8	83.3%	84.6%
HSPA-High School	NA	NA

SAT score averages
Pct tested	Math	Verbal	Writing
NA	NA	NA	NA

Teacher Qualifications
Avg. years of experience	14
Highly-qualified teachers one subject/all subjects	100%/100%
With emergency credentials	0.0%

No Child Left Behind
AYP, 2005-06 … Meets Standards

Municipal Finance
State Aid Programs, 2008
Total aid	$1,939,277
CMPTRA	0
Energy tax receipts	1,730,063
Garden State Trust	195,436

General Budget, 2007
Total tax levy	$10,879,425
County levy	1,760,206
County taxes	1,398,733
County library	268,862
County health	0
County open space	92,611
School levy	7,819,870
Muni. levy	1,299,348
Misc. revenues	3,646,408

©2008 Information Publications, Inc. All rights reserved.

Denville Township — Morris County

Demographics & Socio-Economic Characteristics
(2000 US Census, except as noted)

Population
- 1980* 14,380
- 1990* 13,812
- 2000 15,824
  - Male 7,617
  - Female 8,207
- 2006 (estimate)* 16,671
- Population density 1,376.6

Race & Hispanic Origin, 2000
Race
- White 14,659
- Black/African American 181
- American Indian/Alaska Native ... 12
- Asian 734
- Native Hawaiian/Pacific Islander ... 5
- Other race 70
- Two or more races 163
- Hispanic origin, total 418
  - Mexican 30
  - Puerto Rican 115
  - Cuban 55
  - Other Hispanic 218

Age & Nativity, 2000
- Under 5 years 1,147
- 18 years and over 12,047
- 21 years and over 11,689
- 65 years and over 2,376
- 85 years and over 487
- Median age 39.7
- Native-born 14,151
- Foreign-born 1,673

Educational Attainment, 2000
- Population 25 years and over 11,319
- Less than 9th grade 2.0%
- High school grad or higher ... 92.3%
- Bachelor's degree or higher ... 44.0%
- Graduate degree 17.0%

Income & Poverty, 1999
- Per capita income $38,607
- Median household income ... $76,778
- Median family income $90,651
- Persons in poverty 436
- H'holds receiving public assistance ... 49
- H'holds receiving social security ... 1,656

Households, 2000
- Total households 5,990
  - With persons under 18 2,074
  - With persons over 65 1,624
  - Family households 4,315
  - Single-person households ... 1,416
- Persons per household 2.59
- Persons per family 3.11

Labor & Employment
- Total civilian labor force, 2006** ... 8,814
  - Unemployment rate 3.0%
- Total civilian labor force, 2000 ... 8,054
  - Unemployment rate 2.8%

Employed persons 16 years and over by occupation, 2000
- Managers & professionals ... 3,821
- Service occupations 559
- Sales & office occupations ... 2,297
- Farming, fishing & forestry 6
- Construction & maintenance ... 599
- Production & transportation ... 548
- Self-employed persons 507

* US Census Bureau
** New Jersey Department of Labor

General Information
Township of Denville
1 Saint Marys Pl
Denville, NJ 07834
973-625-8300

- Website .... www.denvillenj.org
- Year of incorporation 1913
- Land/water area (sq. miles) ... 12.11/0.52
- Form of government .... Mayor-Council

Government

Legislative Districts
- US Congressional 11
- State Legislative 25

Local Officials, 2008
- Mayor .... Philip Ted Hussa
- Manager .... Marie A. Goble
- Clerk .... Donna Costello
- Finance Dir .... Marie Goble
- Tax Assessor .... Ginny Klein
- Tax Collector .... Annemarie Hopler
- Attorney .... John Dorsey
- Building .... Walter Stefanacci
- Planning .... Bill Denzler
- Engineering .... Nick Rosania
- Public Works .... Joe Lowell
- Police Chief ..... Christopher Wagner
- Emerg/Fire Director ... George Petersen

Housing & Construction

Housing Units, 2000*
- Total 6,178
- Median rent $1,129
- Median SF home value $228,300

Permits for New Residential Construction

	Units	Value
Total, 2007	31	$6,417,400
Single family	15	$3,441,400
Total, 2006	46	$9,745,444
Single family	36	$7,887,444

Real Property Valuation, 2007

	Parcels	Valuation
Total	7,068	$2,253,211,400
Vacant	726	51,305,900
Residential	5,918	1,819,429,300
Commercial	354	299,050,900
Industrial	38	70,322,400
Apartments	3	8,173,600
Farm land	17	86,900
Farm homestead	12	4,842,400

Average Property Value & Tax, 2007
- Residential value $307,634
- Property tax $7,533
- Tax credit/rebate $1,079

Public Library
Denville Public Library
121 Diamond Spring Rd
Denville, NJ 07834
973-627-6555

- Director .... Elizabeth L. Kanouse

Library statistics, 2006
- Population served 15,824
- Full-time/total staff 4/8

	Total	Per capita
Holdings	67,484	4.26
Revenues	$1,038,704	$65.64
Expenditures	$790,326	$49.94
Annual visits	127,031	8.03
Internet terminals/annual users		8/26,132

Taxes

	2005	2006	2007
General tax rate per $100	2.24	2.32	2.45
County equalization ratio	83.08	74.34	67.78
Net valuation taxable	$2,146,959,541	$2,210,435,200	$2,258,051,846
State equalized value	$2,888,027,362	$3,265,798,617	$3,487,392,842

Public Safety
- Number of officers, 2006 32

Crime	2005	2006
Total crimes	205	190
Violent	6	6
Murder	0	0
Rape	1	1
Robbery	1	1
Aggravated assault	4	4
Non-violent	199	184
Burglary	28	33
Larceny	159	140
Vehicle theft	12	11
Domestic violence	64	67
Arson	1	1
Total crime rate	12.7	11.5
Violent	0.4	0.4
Non-violent	12.3	11.2

Public School District
(for school year 2006-07 except as noted)

Denville Township School District
501 Openaki Rd
Denville, NJ 07834
973-983-6500

- Superintendent .... Drucilla Clark
- Number of schools 3
- Grade plan K-8
- Enrollment 1,945
- Attendance rate, '05-06 .... 96.2%
- Dropout rate .... NA
- Students per teacher 11.8
- Per pupil expenditure $11,767
- Median faculty salary $48,464
- Median administrator salary ... $107,938
- Grade 12 enrollment .... NA
- High school graduation rate .... NA

Assessment test results
(percent scoring at proficient or advanced level)

	Language	Math
NJASK-Grade 3	93.6%	90.9%
GEPA-Grade 8	88.0%	81.2%
HSPA-High School	NA	NA

SAT score averages

Pct tested	Math	Verbal	Writing
NA	NA	NA	NA

Teacher Qualifications
- Avg. years of experience 7
- Highly-qualified teachers
  - one subject/all subjects ... 100%/100%
- With emergency credentials 0.9%

No Child Left Behind
- AYP, 2005-06 .... Meets Standards

Municipal Finance

State Aid Programs, 2008
- Total aid $2,336,910
  - CMPTRA 161,844
  - Energy tax receipts 2,162,911
  - Garden State Trust 12,155

General Budget, 2007
- Total tax levy $55,292,282
  - County levy 7,985,805
    - County taxes 6,387,965
    - County library 0
    - County health 0
    - County open space ... 1,597,840
  - School levy 36,944,449
  - Muni. levy 10,362,028
  - Misc. revenues 9,007,651

Gloucester County
Deptford Township

Demographics & Socio-Economic Characteristics
(2000 US Census, except as noted)

Population
1980*	23,473
1990*	24,137
2000	26,763
Male	12,911
Female	13,852
2006 (estimate)*	30,216
Population density	1,726.6

Race & Hispanic Origin, 2000
Race
- White 22,330
- Black/African American 3,314
- American Indian/Alaska Native....... 56
- Asian 410
- Native Hawaiian/Pacific Islander 9
- Other race 266
- Two or more races 378

Hispanic origin, total 766
- Mexican 114
- Puerto Rican 421
- Cuban 25
- Other Hispanic 206

Age & Nativity, 2000
- Under 5 years 1,668
- 18 years and over 20,383
- 21 years and over 19,533
- 65 years and over 4,012
- 85 years and over 421
- Median age 37.3
- Native-born 25,646
- Foreign-born 1,117

Educational Attainment, 2000
- Population 25 years and over 18,448
- Less than 9th grade 4.5%
- High school grad or higher 80.0%
- Bachelor's degree or higher 15.2%
- Graduate degree 4.2%

Income & Poverty, 1999
- Per capita income $21,477
- Median household income $50,147
- Median family income $56,642
- Persons in poverty 1,535
- H'holds receiving public assistance 140
- H'holds receiving social security 2,935

Households, 2000
- Total households 10,013
- With persons under 18 3,572
- With persons over 65 2,648
- Family households 7,083
- Single-person households 2,435
- Persons per household 2.62
- Persons per family 3.12

Labor & Employment
- Total civilian labor force, 2006** 16,174
- Unemployment rate 3.5%
- Total civilian labor force, 2000 13,829
- Unemployment rate 5.5%

Employed persons 16 years and over by occupation, 2000
- Managers & professionals 3,508
- Service occupations 1,752
- Sales & office occupations 3,886
- Farming, fishing & forestry 5
- Construction & maintenance 1,612
- Production & transportation 2,305
- Self-employed persons 446

* US Census Bureau
** New Jersey Department of Labor

See Introduction for an explanation of all data sources.

General Information
Township of Deptford
1011 Cooper St
Deptford, NJ 08096
856-845-5300

Website	www.deptford-nj.org
Year of incorporation	1695
Land/water area (sq. miles)	17.50/0.08
Form of government	Council-Manager

Government
Legislative Districts
- US Congressional 1
- State Legislative 5

Local Officials, 2008
Mayor	Paul Medany
Manager	Denise Rose
Clerk	Dina Zawadski
Finance Dir	Joanne Strange
Tax Assessor	Joseph Harasta
Tax Collector	NA
Attorney	Harvey C. Johnson
Building	William Coughlin
Comm Dev/Planning	NA
Engineering	Federici & Akin
Public Works	NA
Police Chief	John Marolt
Emerg/Fire Director	Steve Hubbs

Housing & Construction
Housing Units, 2000*
- Total 10,647
- Median rent $664
- Median SF home value $106,000

Permits for New Residential Construction
	Units	Value
Total, 2007	48	$7,048,367
Single family	48	$7,048,367
Total, 2006	99	$7,855,056
Single family	99	$7,855,056

Real Property Valuation, 2007
	Parcels	Valuation
Total	12,099	$1,678,906,860
Vacant	1,728	45,052,400
Residential	9,800	1,104,654,300
Commercial	337	459,953,760
Industrial	28	10,001,000
Apartments	14	52,722,000
Farm land	132	389,600
Farm homestead	60	6,133,800

Average Property Value & Tax, 2007
- Residential value $112,656
- Property tax $4,178
- Tax credit/rebate $910

Public Library
Johnson Memorial Library
670 Ward Dr
Deptford, NJ 08096
856-848-9149

Director .... Arn Ellsworth Winter

Library statistics, 2006
- Population served 26,763
- Full-time/total staff 3/11

	Total	Per capita
Holdings	72,511	2.71
Revenues	$845,100	$31.58
Expenditures	$706,544	$26.40
Annual visits	127,021	4.75
Internet terminals/annual users	10/24,228	

Taxes
	2005	2006	2007
General tax rate per $100	3.279	3.57	3.709
County equalization ratio	80.88	68	59.46
Net valuation taxable	$1,606,111,389	$1,648,843,860	$1,681,506,598
State equalized value	$2,361,928,513	$2,775,914,850	$2,871,054,992

Public Safety
Number of officers, 2006 70

Crime	2005	2006
Total crimes	1,469	1,549
Violent	99	109
Murder	1	1
Rape	1	1
Robbery	30	37
Aggravated assault	67	70
Non-violent	1,370	1,440
Burglary	230	209
Larceny	1,062	1,157
Vehicle theft	78	74
Domestic violence	320	355
Arson	12	13
Total crime rate	50.8	52.1
Violent	3.4	3.7
Non-violent	47.3	48.4

Public School District
(for school year 2006-07 except as noted)

Deptford Township School District
2022 Good Intent Rd
Deptford, NJ 08096
856-232-2700

- Superintendent .... Joseph F. Conataro
- Number of schools 8
- Grade plan K-12
- Enrollment 4,274
- Attendance rate, '05-06 .... 94.6%
- Dropout rate 3.1%
- Students per teacher 11.9
- Per pupil expenditure $11,011
- Median faculty salary $52,800
- Median administrator salary $97,438
- Grade 12 enrollment 239
- High school graduation rate 89.5%

Assessment test results
(percent scoring at proficient or advanced level)
	Language	Math
NJASK-Grade 3	81.9%	87.5%
GEPA-Grade 8	73.2%	67.6%
HSPA-High School	84.3%	75.5%

SAT score averages
Pct tested	Math	Verbal	Writing
65%	479	457	451

Teacher Qualifications
- Avg. years of experience 9
- Highly-qualified teachers one subject/all subjects 100%/99.0%
- With emergency credentials 0.0%

No Child Left Behind
AYP, 2005-06 .... Meets Standards

Municipal Finance
State Aid Programs, 2008
- Total aid $2,848,599
- CMPTRA 811,542
- Energy tax receipts 2,035,303
- Garden State Trust 1,754

General Budget, 2007
- Total tax levy $62,360,684
- County levy 15,597,104
- County taxes 14,464,611
- County library 0
- County health 0
- County open space 1,132,492
- School levy 33,173,662
- Muni. levy 13,589,918
- Misc. revenues 11,743,985

The New Jersey Municipal Data Book

Dover Town
Morris County

Demographics & Socio-Economic Characteristics
(2000 US Census, except as noted)

Population
1980*	14,681
1990*	15,115
2000	18,188
Male	9,377
Female	8,811
2006 (estimate)*	18,387
Population density	6,860.8

Race & Hispanic Origin, 2000
Race
White	12,631
Black/African American	1,242
American Indian/Alaska Native	62
Asian	450
Native Hawaiian/Pacific Islander	5
Other race	2,909
Two or more races	889
Hispanic origin, total	10,539
Mexican	1,557
Puerto Rican	2,413
Cuban	98
Other Hispanic	6,471

Age & Nativity, 2000
Under 5 years	1,278
18 years and over	13,976
21 years and over	13,203
65 years and over	1,922
85 years and over	310
Median age	33.7
Native-born	10,400
Foreign-born	7,788

Educational Attainment, 2000
Population 25 years and over	12,011
Less than 9th grade	16.8%
High school grad or higher	66.9%
Bachelor's degree or higher	12.5%
Graduate degree	4.4%

Income & Poverty, 1999
Per capita income	$18,056
Median household income	$53,423
Median family income	$57,141
Persons in poverty	2,381
H'holds receiving public assistance	183
H'holds receiving social security	1,446

Households, 2000
Total households	5,436
With persons under 18	2,242
With persons over 65	1,277
Family households	3,918
Single-person households	1,156
Persons per household	3.29
Persons per family	3.55

Labor & Employment
Total civilian labor force, 2006**	10,518
Unemployment rate	8.5%
Total civilian labor force, 2000	9,523
Unemployment rate	7.4%

Employed persons 16 years and over by occupation, 2000
Managers & professionals	1,713
Service occupations	1,845
Sales & office occupations	2,262
Farming, fishing & forestry	0
Construction & maintenance	789
Production & transportation	2,207
Self-employed persons	296

* US Census Bureau
** New Jersey Department of Labor

General Information
Town of Dover
37 N Sussex St
Dover, NJ 07801
973-366-2200

Website	www.dover.nj.us
Year of incorporation	1869
Land/water area (sq. miles)	2.68/0.03
Form of government	Town

Government
Legislative Districts
US Congressional	11
State Legislative	25

Local Officials, 2008
Mayor	James Dodd
Manager	Bibi Stewart Garvin
Clerk	Margaret Verga
Finance Dir	Kelly Toohey
Tax Assessor	Therese dePierro
Tax Collector	Kunjesh Trivedi
Attorney	David Pennella
Building	Robert Young
Planning	Mike Hantson
Engineering	Mike Hantson
Public Works	Luis Acevedo
Police Chief	Harold Valentine
Emerg/Fire Director	Richard Mattison

Housing & Construction
Housing Units, 2000*
Total	5,568
Median rent	$870
Median SF home value	$150,500

Permits for New Residential Construction
	Units	Value
Total, 2007	5	$567,175
Single family	5	$567,175
Total, 2006	1	$86,530
Single family	1	$86,530

Real Property Valuation, 2007
	Parcels	Valuation
Total	4,158	$682,497,000
Vacant	134	7,111,100
Residential	3,611	480,512,600
Commercial	330	111,733,400
Industrial	55	61,061,800
Apartments	28	22,078,100
Farm land	0	0
Farm homestead	0	0

Average Property Value & Tax, 2007
Residential value	$133,069
Property tax	$5,147
Tax credit/rebate	$975

Public Library
Dover Free Public Library
32 E Clinton St
Dover, NJ 07801
973-361-0172

Director: Robert F. Tambini

Library statistics, 2006
Population served	18,188
Full-time/total staff	2/4

	Total	Per capita
Holdings	59,931	3.30
Revenues	$598,370	$32.90
Expenditures	$576,458	$31.69
Annual visits	53,820	2.96
Internet terminals/annual users	9/32,119	

Taxes
	2005	2006	2007
General tax rate per $100	3.64	3.78	3.87
County equalization ratio	57.37	51.17	43.52
Net valuation taxable	$686,483,971	$681,246,600	$685,128,983
State equalized value	$1,341,575,085	$1,568,401,820	$1,687,809,761

Public Safety
Number of officers, 2006 34

Crime	2005	2006
Total crimes	504	419
Violent	62	64
Murder	0	0
Rape	4	2
Robbery	25	30
Aggravated assault	33	32
Non-violent	442	355
Burglary	163	85
Larceny	249	240
Vehicle theft	30	30
Domestic violence	102	116
Arson	0	1
Total crime rate	27.3	22.7
Violent	3.4	3.5
Non-violent	23.9	19.3

Public School District
(for school year 2006-07 except as noted)

Dover Town School District
100 Grace St
Dover, NJ 07801
973-989-2000

Superintendent	Robert Becker
Number of schools	5
Grade plan	K-12
Enrollment	2,876
Attendance rate, '05-06	95.3%
Dropout rate	2.3%
Students per teacher	12.2
Per pupil expenditure	$11,651
Median faculty salary	$52,822
Median administrator salary	$93,630
Grade 12 enrollment	186
High school graduation rate	94.2%

Assessment test results
(percent scoring at proficient or advanced level)
	Language	Math
NJASK-Grade 3	77.4%	80.8%
GEPA-Grade 8	67.7%	54.2%
HSPA-High School	83.5%	67.5%

SAT score averages
Pct tested	Math	Verbal	Writing
44%	461	457	460

Teacher Qualifications
Avg. years of experience	10
Highly-qualified teachers one subject/all subjects	99.5%/99.5%
With emergency credentials	0.0%

No Child Left Behind
AYP, 2005-06 . . . . Meets Standards

Municipal Finance
State Aid Programs, 2008
Total aid	$1,578,685
CMPTRA	802,606
Energy tax receipts	776,061
Garden State Trust	18

General Budget, 2007
Total tax levy	$26,501,867
County levy	3,779,574
County taxes	3,023,303
County library	0
County health	0
County open space	756,271
School levy	12,909,172
Muni. levy	9,813,121
Misc. revenues	8,348,070

Cumberland County

Downe Township

Demographics & Socio-Economic Characteristics
(2000 US Census, except as noted)

Population
1980*	1,803
1990*	1,702
2000	1,631
Male	846
Female	785
2006 (estimate)*	1,675
Population density	33.0

Race & Hispanic Origin, 2000
Race
White	1,485
Black/African American	79
American Indian/Alaska Native	24
Asian	3
Native Hawaiian/Pacific Islander	0
Other race	16
Two or more races	24
Hispanic origin, total	55
Mexican	4
Puerto Rican	49
Cuban	0
Other Hispanic	2

Age & Nativity, 2000
Under 5 years	91
18 years and over	1,247
21 years and over	1,201
65 years and over	309
85 years and over	13
Median age	42.3
Native-born	1,607
Foreign-born	24

Educational Attainment, 2000
Population 25 years and over	1,151
Less than 9th grade	9.9%
High school grad or higher	71.2%
Bachelor's degree or higher	7.8%
Graduate degree	2.2%

Income & Poverty, 1999
Per capita income	$17,366
Median household income	$34,667
Median family income	$39,375
Persons in poverty	213
H'holds receiving public assistance	23
H'holds receiving social security	255

Households, 2000
Total households	658
With persons under 18	216
With persons over 65	232
Family households	439
Single-person households	180
Persons per household	2.48
Persons per family	3.03

Labor & Employment
Total civilian labor force, 2006**	791
Unemployment rate	5.3%
Total civilian labor force, 2000	704
Unemployment rate	6.8%

Employed persons 16 years and over by occupation, 2000
Managers & professionals	110
Service occupations	117
Sales & office occupations	168
Farming, fishing & forestry	13
Construction & maintenance	84
Production & transportation	164
Self-employed persons	42

* US Census Bureau
** New Jersey Department of Labor

See Introduction for an explanation of all data sources.

General Information
Township of Downe
288 Main St
Newport, NJ 08345
856-447-3100

Website	www.downetwpnj.org
Year of incorporation	1722
Land/water area (sq. miles)	50.76/3.47
Form of government	Township

Government
Legislative Districts
US Congressional	2
State Legislative	3

Local Officials, 2008
Mayor	Renee Blizzard
Manager/Admin	NA
Clerk	Diane Patterson (Actg)
Finance Dir	Lois R. Buttner
Tax Assessor	Doris Sanza
Tax Collector	Jennifer Hernandez
Attorney	Tom Farnoly
Building	NA
Comm Dev/Planning	NA
Engineering	Pennoni Associates
Public Works	E. Beardsworth/R. Thomas
Police Chief	NA
Fire/Emergency Dir	NA

Housing & Construction
Housing Units, 2000*
Total	1,134
Median rent	$581
Median SF home value	$74,500

Permits for New Residential Construction
	Units	Value
Total, 2007	12	$812,673
Single family	12	$812,673
Total, 2006	3	$48,650
Single family	3	$48,650

Real Property Valuation, 2007
	Parcels	Valuation
Total	1,769	$76,066,000
Vacant	664	7,922,900
Residential	939	57,412,100
Commercial	51	6,850,500
Industrial	3	67,200
Apartments	1	123,500
Farm land	53	277,900
Farm homestead	58	3,411,900

Average Property Value & Tax, 2007
Residential value	$61,007
Property tax	$2,160
Tax credit/rebate	$765

Public Library
No public municipal library

Library statistics, 2006
Population served	NA
Full-time/total staff	NA/NA

	Total	Per capita
Holdings	NA	NA
Revenues	NA	NA
Expenditures	NA	NA
Annual visits	NA	NA
Internet terminals/annual users	NA/NA	

Taxes
	2005	2006	2007
General tax rate per $100	3.367	3.475	3.543
County equalization ratio	74.11	57.96	52.07
Net valuation taxable	$76,737,907	$75,872,800	$76,357,897
State equalized value	$132,398,045	$146,030,867	$162,203,349

Public Safety
Number of officers, 2006		0

Crime	2005	2006
Total crimes	22	35
Violent	2	4
Murder	0	0
Rape	0	0
Robbery	0	0
Aggravated assault	2	4
Non-violent	20	31
Burglary	6	13
Larceny	12	17
Vehicle theft	2	1
Domestic violence	13	5
Arson	1	3
Total crime rate	13.2	20.9
Violent	1.2	2.4
Non-violent	12.0	18.5

Public School District
(for school year 2006-07 except as noted)

Downe Township School District
220 Main St
Newport, NJ 08345
856-447-3878

Superintendent/Principal	Dina Elliott
Number of schools	1
Grade plan	K-8
Enrollment	194
Attendance rate, '05-06	94.0%
Dropout rate	NA
Students per teacher	7.2
Per pupil expenditure	$16,390
Median faculty salary	$59,416
Median administrator salary	$62,000
Grade 12 enrollment	NA
High school graduation rate	NA

Assessment test results
(percent scoring at proficient or advanced level)

	Language	Math
NJASK-Grade 3	70.0%	65.0%
GEPA-Grade 8	66.7%	41.7%
HSPA-High School	NA	NA

SAT score averages
Pct tested	Math	Verbal	Writing
NA	NA	NA	NA

Teacher Qualifications
Avg. years of experience	20
Highly-qualified teachers one subject/all subjects	100%/94.5%
With emergency credentials	0.0%

No Child Left Behind
AYP, 2005-06 .... Meets Standards

Municipal Finance
State Aid Programs, 2008
Total aid	$602,399
CMPTRA	0
Energy tax receipts	232,755
Garden State Trust	369,644

General Budget, 2007
Total tax levy	$2,703,466
County levy	1,460,695
County taxes	1,383,692
County library	0
County health	62,197
County open space	14,806
School levy	1,242,771
Muni. levy	0
Misc. revenues	1,264,250

Dumont Borough   Bergen County

Demographics & Socio-Economic Characteristics
(2000 US Census, except as noted)

Population
1980*	18,334
1990*	17,187
2000	17,503
Male	8,416
Female	9,087
2006 (estimate)*	17,365
Population density	8,726.1

Race & Hispanic Origin, 2000
Race
White	14,663
Black/African American	261
American Indian/Alaska Native	17
Asian	1,918
Native Hawaiian/Pacific Islander	1
Other race	339
Two or more races	304
Hispanic origin, total	1,463
Mexican	59
Puerto Rican	419
Cuban	160
Other Hispanic	825

Age & Nativity, 2000
Under 5 years	1,173
18 years and over	13,239
21 years and over	12,787
65 years and over	2,702
85 years and over	309
Median age	38.4
Native-born	14,250
Foreign-born	3,253

Educational Attainment, 2000
Population 25 years and over	12,229
Less than 9th grade	3.6%
High school grad or higher	88.5%
Bachelor's degree or higher	27.4%
Graduate degree	8.2%

Income & Poverty, 1999
Per capita income	$26,489
Median household income	$65,490
Median family income	$73,880
Persons in poverty	459
H'holds receiving public assistance	119
H'holds receiving social security	2,009

Households, 2000
Total households	6,370
With persons under 18	2,345
With persons over 65	2,000
Family households	4,757
Single-person households	1,422
Persons per household	2.75
Persons per family	3.24

Labor & Employment
Total civilian labor force, 2006**	9,630
Unemployment rate	2.9%
Total civilian labor force, 2000	9,072
Unemployment rate	2.9%

Employed persons 16 years and over by occupation, 2000
Managers & professionals	3,319
Service occupations	1,154
Sales & office occupations	2,776
Farming, fishing & forestry	10
Construction & maintenance	766
Production & transportation	784
Self-employed persons	356

* US Census Bureau
** New Jersey Department of Labor

General Information
Borough of Dumont
50 Washington Ave
Dumont, NJ 07628
201-387-5022

Website	www.dumontboro.org
Year of incorporation	1898
Land/water area (sq. miles)	1.99/0.00
Form of government	Borough

Government
Legislative Districts
US Congressional	5
State Legislative	39

Local Officials, 2008
Mayor	Matthew McHale
Manager	John Perkins
Clerk	Susan Connelly
Finance Dir.	Rosemarie Giotis
Tax Assessor	James Anzevino
Tax Collector	Barbara Kozay
Attorney	Gregg Paster
Building	Steve Cavadias
Comm Dev/Planning	NA
Engineering	T&M Associates
Public Works	William Ebenhack
Police Chief	Brian Venezio
Emerg/Fire Director	James Molinaro

Housing & Construction
Housing Units, 2000*
Total	6,465
Median rent	$882
Median SF home value	$195,000

Permits for New Residential Construction
	Units	Value
Total, 2007	7	$2,003,980
Single family	7	$2,003,980
Total, 2006	6	$920,300
Single family	6	$920,300

Real Property Valuation, 2007
	Parcels	Valuation
Total	5,171	$2,080,927,000
Vacant	15	1,141,800
Residential	4,975	1,903,953,900
Commercial	144	99,752,100
Industrial	11	6,762,200
Apartments	25	69,306,500
Farm land	1	10,500
Farm homestead	0	0

Average Property Value & Tax, 2007
Residential value	$382,704
Property tax	$8,518
Tax credit/rebate	$1,371

Public Library
Dixon Homestead Library
180 Washington Ave
Dumont, NJ 07628
201-384-2030

Director... Carolyn M. Blowers

Library statistics, 2006
Population served	17,503
Full-time/total staff	2/7

	Total	Per capita
Holdings	50,361	2.88
Revenues	$702,572	$40.14
Expenditures	$665,669	$38.03
Annual visits	96,911	5.54
Internet terminals/annual users	9/17,341	

Taxes
	2005	2006	2007
General tax rate per $100	1.94	2.12	2.23
County equalization ratio	124.38	106.18	95.16
Net valuation taxable	$2,083,517,734	$2,077,344,700	$2,084,122,878
State equalized value	$1,962,250,644	$2,186,281,418	$2,276,190,963

Public Safety
Number of officers, 2006 33

Crime
	2005	2006
Total crimes	157	181
Violent	8	10
Murder	0	0
Rape	0	2
Robbery	1	0
Aggravated assault	7	8
Non-violent	149	171
Burglary	15	17
Larceny	133	147
Vehicle theft	1	7
Domestic violence	136	157
Arson	0	1
Total crime rate	8.9	10.4
Violent	0.5	0.6
Non-violent	8.5	9.8

Public School District
(for school year 2006-07 except as noted)

Dumont School District
25 Depew St
Dumont, NJ 07628
201-387-3082

Superintendent	James Montesano
Number of schools	5
Grade plan	K-12
Enrollment	2,679
Attendance rate, '05-06	95.5%
Dropout rate	NA
Students per teacher	11.7
Per pupil expenditure	$12,509
Median faculty salary	$75,980
Median administrator salary	$122,811
Grade 12 enrollment	193
High school graduation rate	100.0%

Assessment test results
(percent scoring at proficient or advanced level)
	Language	Math
NJASK-Grade 3	87.8%	93.1%
GEPA-Grade 8	81.7%	74.7%
HSPA-High School	91.0%	79.2%

SAT score averages
Pct tested	Math	Verbal	Writing
81%	497	475	481

Teacher Qualifications
Avg. years of experience	14
Highly-qualified teachers one subject/all subjects	100%/100%
With emergency credentials	0.0%

No Child Left Behind
AYP, 2005-06 .... Meets Standards

Municipal Finance
State Aid Programs, 2008
Total aid	$1,738,370
CMPTRA	533,787
Energy tax receipts	1,204,583
Garden State Trust	0

General Budget, 2007
Total tax levy	$46,387,397
County levy	3,981,585
County taxes	3,762,286
County library	0
County health	0
County open space	219,299
School levy	29,200,116
Muni. levy	13,205,697
Misc. revenues	4,280,023

Middlesex County

Dunellen Borough

Demographics & Socio-Economic Characteristics
(2000 US Census, except as noted)

Population
1980*	6,593
1990*	6,528
2000	6,823
Male	3,428
Female	3,395
2006 (estimate)*	6,940
Population density	6,673.1

Race & Hispanic Origin, 2000
Race
White	5,736
Black/African American	250
American Indian/Alaska Native	17
Asian	243
Native Hawaiian/Pacific Islander	1
Other race	435
Two or more races	141
Hispanic origin, total	1,010
Mexican	71
Puerto Rican	121
Cuban	29
Other Hispanic	789

Age & Nativity, 2000
Under 5 years	503
18 years and over	5,124
21 years and over	4,917
65 years and over	773
85 years and over	91
Median age	35.8
Native-born	5,715
Foreign-born	1,108

Educational Attainment, 2000
Population 25 years and over	4,715
Less than 9th grade	3.0%
High school grad or higher	86.0%
Bachelor's degree or higher	22.2%
Graduate degree	6.2%

Income & Poverty, 1999
Per capita income	$26,529
Median household income	$59,205
Median family income	$67,188
Persons in poverty	224
H'holds receiving public assistance	24
H'holds receiving social security	550

Households, 2000
Total households	2,451
With persons under 18	918
With persons over 65	559
Family households	1,711
Single-person households	575
Persons per household	2.75
Persons per family	3.30

Labor & Employment
Total civilian labor force, 2006**	4,110
Unemployment rate	7.1%
Total civilian labor force, 2000	3,779
Unemployment rate	7.8%

Employed persons 16 years and over by occupation, 2000
Managers & professionals	1,233
Service occupations	444
Sales & office occupations	909
Farming, fishing & forestry	11
Construction & maintenance	363
Production & transportation	524
Self-employed persons	220

* US Census Bureau
** New Jersey Department of Labor
§ State Fiscal Year July 1–June 30

See Introduction for an explanation of all data sources.

General Information
Borough of Dunellen
355 North Ave
Dunellen, NJ 08812
732-968-3033

Website	www.dunellen.com
Year of incorporation	1887
Land/water area (sq. miles)	1.04/0.00
Form of government	Borough

Government
Legislative Districts
US Congressional	6
State Legislative	22

Local Officials, 2008
Mayor	Robert Seader
Manager	William Robins
Clerk	William Robins
Finance Dir	Scott Olsen
Tax Assessor	Richard Gianchiglia
Tax Collector	Eileen Leonard
Attorney	John Bruder
Building	Scott Luthman
Comm Dev/Planning	NA
Engineering	CME Associates
Public Works	Jerry Schafer
Police Chief	Gerard Cappella
Emerg/Fire Director	William Scott

Housing & Construction
Housing Units, 2000*
Total	2,520
Median rent	$811
Median SF home value	$155,800

Permits for New Residential Construction
	Units	Value
Total, 2007	27	$1,803,982
Single family	7	$692,870
Total, 2006	28	$1,947,704
Single family	8	$836,592

Real Property Valuation, 2007
	Parcels	Valuation
Total	2,078	$143,257,100
Vacant	38	554,000
Residential	1,931	123,925,600
Commercial	96	13,659,400
Industrial	6	3,669,600
Apartments	7	1,448,500
Farm land	0	0
Farm homestead	0	0

Average Property Value & Tax, 2007
Residential value	$64,177
Property tax	$6,613
Tax credit/rebate	$1,058

Public Library
Dunellen Free Public Library
New Market Rd
Dunellen, NJ 08812
732-968-4585

Director....................Joan F. Henry

Library statistics, 2006
Population served	6,823
Full-time/total staff	1/3

	Total	Per capita
Holdings	40,425	5.92
Revenues	$263,212	$38.58
Expenditures	$273,564	$40.09
Annual visits	24,536	3.60
Internet terminals/annual users		9/8,622

Taxes
	2005	2006	2007
General tax rate per $100	8.45	9.31	10.31
County equalization ratio	28.79	25.05	22.36
Net valuation taxable	$144,169,538	$143,133,775	$143,903,300
State equalized value	$575,527,098	$640,946,411	$713,722,855

Public Safety
Number of officers, 2006 15

Crime
	2005	2006
Total crimes	161	147
Violent	20	7
Murder	0	0
Rape	0	0
Robbery	6	3
Aggravated assault	14	4
Non-violent	141	140
Burglary	19	19
Larceny	109	115
Vehicle theft	13	6
Domestic violence	83	83
Arson	0	2
Total crime rate	23.0	21.0
Violent	2.9	1.0
Non-violent	20.2	20.0

Public School District
(for school year 2006-07 except as noted)

Dunellen School District
High St & Lehigh St
Dunellen, NJ 08812
732-968-3226

Superintendent	Pio Pennisi
Number of schools	3
Grade plan	K-12
Enrollment	1,091
Attendance rate, '05-06	94.5%
Dropout rate	1.3%
Students per teacher	10.7
Per pupil expenditure	$10,279
Median faculty salary	$45,961
Median administrator salary	$102,105
Grade 12 enrollment	76
High school graduation rate	92.2%

Assessment test results
(percent scoring at proficient or advanced level)
	Language	Math
NJASK-Grade 3	82.4%	85.5%
GEPA-Grade 8	70.3%	63.6%
HSPA-High School	81.9%	69.9%

SAT score averages
Pct tested	Math	Verbal	Writing
68%	470	474	473

Teacher Qualifications
Avg. years of experience	8
Highly-qualified teachers one subject/all subjects	100%/100%
With emergency credentials	0.0%

No Child Left Behind
AYP, 2005-06 .... Meets Standards

Municipal Finance§
State Aid Programs, 2008
Total aid	$662,567
CMPTRA	196,852
Energy tax receipts	465,715
Garden State Trust	0

General Budget, 2007
Total tax levy	$14,827,418
County levy	1,866,167
County taxes	1,670,617
County library	0
County health	0
County open space	195,550
School levy	8,829,075
Muni. levy	4,132,176
Misc. revenues	2,304,708

The New Jersey Municipal Data Book

Eagleswood Township
Ocean County

Demographics & Socio-Economic Characteristics
(2000 US Census, except as noted)

Population
- 1980* 1,009
- 1990* 1,476
- 2000 1,441
  - Male 726
  - Female 715
- 2006 (estimate)* 1,614
- Population density 98.6

Race & Hispanic Origin, 2000
Race
- White 1,426
- Black/African American 1
- American Indian/Alaska Native 4
- Asian 3
- Native Hawaiian/Pacific Islander .. 0
- Other race 0
- Two or more races 7
- Hispanic origin, total 16
  - Mexican 1
  - Puerto Rican 8
  - Cuban 4
  - Other Hispanic 3

Age & Nativity, 2000
- Under 5 years 73
- 18 years and over 1,085
- 21 years and over 1,038
- 65 years and over 207
- 85 years and over 16
  - Median age 39.4
- Native-born 1,413
- Foreign-born 28

Educational Attainment, 2000
- Population 25 years and over ... 974
- Less than 9th grade 4.4%
- High school grad or higher ... 75.8%
- Bachelor's degree or higher .. 10.1%
- Graduate degree 2.4%

Income & Poverty, 1999
- Per capita income $20,617
- Median household income $38,625
- Median family income $49,453
- Persons in poverty 51
- H'holds receiving public assistance .. 10
- H'holds receiving social security .. 194

Households, 2000
- Total households 546
  - With persons under 18 190
  - With persons over 65 156
  - Family households 395
  - Single-person households 122
- Persons per household 2.64
- Persons per family 3.11

Labor & Employment
- Total civilian labor force, 2006** .. 713
  - Unemployment rate 4.4%
- Total civilian labor force, 2000 .. 717
  - Unemployment rate 3.8%

Employed persons 16 years and over by occupation, 2000
- Managers & professionals 131
- Service occupations 105
- Sales & office occupations 186
- Farming, fishing & forestry 4
- Construction & maintenance 183
- Production & transportation 81
- Self-employed persons 104

* US Census Bureau
** New Jersey Department of Labor

General Information
Township of Eagleswood
146 Division St
PO Box 409
West Creek, NJ 08092
609-296-3040
Email ... ekennedy_eagleswood@comcast.net
- Year of incorporation 1874
- Land/water area (sq. miles) .. 16.37/2.49
- Form of government .... Township

Government
Legislative Districts
- US Congressional 3
- State Legislative 9

Local Officials, 2008
- Mayor .... Wayne Thomas
- Administrator ..... Elaine B. Kennedy
- Clerk .... Elaine B. Kennedy
- Finance Dir ...... Tracey L. Peschko
- Tax Assessor .... Fred Millman
- Tax Collector ..... Barbara Stover
- Attorney .... Tom Monahan
- Building .... Robert Gaestel
- Comm Dev/Planning .... NA
- Engineering .... Jack Mallon
- Public Works .... Richard Lombardo
- Police Chief .... NA
- Emerg/Fire Director ..... Ed Nickel

Housing & Construction
Housing Units, 2000*
- Total 693
- Median rent $678
- Median SF home value $115,700

Permits for New Residential Construction
	Units	Value
Total, 2007	17	$3,706,181
Single family	17	$3,706,181
Total, 2006	18	$4,029,407
Single family	18	$4,029,407

Real Property Valuation, 2007
	Parcels	Valuation
Total	1,187	$278,783,400
Vacant	408	43,644,500
Residential	672	197,300,400
Commercial	81	33,120,400
Industrial	4	3,967,600
Apartments	1	436,900
Farm land	20	48,300
Farm homestead	1	265,300

Average Property Value & Tax, 2007
- Residential value $293,560
- Property tax $4,585
- Tax credit/rebate $897

Public Library
No public municipal library

Library statistics, 2006
- Population served .... NA
- Full-time/total staff .... NA/NA

	Total	Per capita
Holdings	NA	NA
Revenues	NA	NA
Expenditures	NA	NA
Annual visits	NA	NA
Internet terminals/annual users	NA/NA	

Public Safety
Number of officers, 2006 0

Crime	2005	2006
Total crimes	60	29
Violent	2	4
Murder	0	0
Rape	0	0
Robbery	1	0
Aggravated assault	1	4
Non-violent	58	25
Burglary	3	3
Larceny	52	18
Vehicle theft	3	4
Domestic violence	19	1
Arson	1	0
Total crime rate	39.1	18.5
Violent	1.3	2.6
Non-violent	37.8	16.0

Public School District
(for school year 2006-07 except as noted)

Eagleswood Township School District
511 Route 9, Box 355
West Creek, NJ 08092
609-597-3663

- Superintendent .... Deborah Snyder
- Number of schools 1
- Grade plan K-6
- Enrollment 140
- Attendance rate, '05-06 ...... 95.1%
- Dropout rate .... NA
- Students per teacher 7.6
- Per pupil expenditure $11,293
- Median faculty salary $43,083
- Median administrator salary .. $78,025
- Grade 12 enrollment .... NA
- High school graduation rate ..... NA

Assessment test results
(percent scoring at proficient or advanced level)

	Language	Math
NJASK-Grade 3	90.5%	100.0%
GEPA-Grade 8	NA	NA
HSPA-High School	NA	NA

SAT score averages
Pct tested	Math	Verbal	Writing
NA	NA	NA	NA

Teacher Qualifications
- Avg. years of experience 9
- Highly-qualified teachers
  - one subject/all subjects ... 100%/100%
- With emergency credentials ... 15.0%

No Child Left Behind
- AYP, 2005-06 .... Meets Standards

Municipal Finance
State Aid Programs, 2008
- Total aid $250,475
  - CMPTRA 0
  - Energy tax receipts 222,457
  - Garden State Trust 10,534

General Budget, 2007
- Total tax levy $4,360,870
  - County levy 916,888
    - County taxes 755,535
    - County library 89,559
    - County health 36,284
    - County open space 35,510
  - School levy 2,704,727
  - Muni. levy 739,255
  - Misc. revenues 1,178,659

Taxes
	2005	2006	2007
General tax rate per $100	3.358	1.436	1.562
County equalization ratio	61.79	118.4	94.43
Net valuation taxable	$99,006,855	$271,355,000	$279,203,605
State equalized value	$219,527,395	$305,145,407	$302,035,914

Hunterdon County

East Amwell Township

Demographics & Socio-Economic Characteristics
(2000 US Census, except as noted)

Population
1980*	3,468
1990*	4,332
2000	4,455
Male	2,265
Female	2,190
2006 (estimate)*	4,557
Population density	158.9

Race & Hispanic Origin, 2000
Race
- White 4,320
- Black/African American 32
- American Indian/Alaska Native .. 6
- Asian 41
- Native Hawaiian/Pacific Islander .. 1
- Other race 21
- Two or more races 34

Hispanic origin, total 68
- Mexican 15
- Puerto Rican 6
- Cuban 6
- Other Hispanic 41

Age & Nativity, 2000
- Under 5 years 269
- 18 years and over 3,328
- 21 years and over 3,218
- 65 years and over 455
- 85 years and over 52
- Median age 40.8
- Native-born 4,189
- Foreign-born 266

Educational Attainment, 2000
- Population 25 years and over ... 3,135
- Less than 9th grade 1.8%
- High school grad or higher .. 92.2%
- Bachelor's degree or higher .. 39.6%
- Graduate degree 15.9%

Income & Poverty, 1999
- Per capita income $37,187
- Median household income .. $85,664
- Median family income $90,000
- Persons in poverty 74
- H'holds receiving public assistance .. 45
- H'holds receiving social security .. 382

Households, 2000
- Total households 1,581
-   With persons under 18 606
-   With persons over 65 336
-   Family households 1,306
-   Single-person households .. 210
- Persons per household 2.80
- Persons per family 3.07

Labor & Employment
- Total civilian labor force, 2006** .. 2,732
-   Unemployment rate 3.3%
- Total civilian labor force, 2000 .. 2,426
-   Unemployment rate 2.5%

Employed persons 16 years and over by occupation, 2000
- Managers & professionals .. 1,144
- Service occupations 137
- Sales & office occupations .. 534
- Farming, fishing & forestry .. 20
- Construction & maintenance .. 262
- Production & transportation .. 269
- Self-employed persons 248

* US Census Bureau
** New Jersey Department of Labor

See Introduction for an explanation of all data sources.

General Information
Township of East Amwell
1070 Route 202
Ringoes, NJ 08551
908-782-8536

Website	www.eastamwelltownship.com
Year of incorporation	1846
Land/water area (sq. miles)	28.68/0.04
Form of government	Township

Government
Legislative Districts
- US Congressional 12
- State Legislative 23

Local Officials, 2008
Mayor	C. Larry Tatsch
Administrator	Timothy L. Matheny
Clerk	Teresa Stahl
Finance Dir	Jane Luhrs
Tax Assessor	Marianne Busher
Tax Collector	Mary Hyland
Attorney	Richard Cushing
Building	Stewart Doddy
Planning	Frank Banisch
Engineering	Dennis O'Neal
Public Works	George Howell
Police Chief	NA
Emerg/Fire Director	Robert Jason

Housing & Construction
Housing Units, 2000*
- Total 1,624
- Median rent $913
- Median SF home value ... $252,500

Permits for New Residential Construction
	Units	Value
Total, 2007	9	$2,799,238
Single family	9	$2,799,238
Total, 2006	9	$3,749,578
Single family	9	$3,749,578

Real Property Valuation, 2007
	Parcels	Valuation
Total	2,135	$785,043,981
Vacant	171	14,327,800
Residential	1,216	518,694,600
Commercial	60	103,801,561
Industrial	0	0
Apartments	5	2,188,600
Farm land	428	5,014,720
Farm homestead	255	141,016,700

Average Property Value & Tax, 2007
- Residential value $448,478
- Property tax $7,851
- Tax credit/rebate $1,221

Public Library
No public municipal library

Library statistics, 2006
- Population served .... NA
- Full-time/total staff ..... NA/NA

	Total	Per capita
Holdings	NA	NA
Revenues	NA	NA
Expenditures	NA	NA
Annual visits	NA	NA
Internet terminals/annual users	NA/NA	

Public Safety
Number of officers, 2006 0

Crime	2005	2006
Total crimes	15	20
Violent	1	0
Murder	0	0
Rape	0	0
Robbery	0	0
Aggravated assault	1	0
Non-violent	14	20
Burglary	3	8
Larceny	10	11
Vehicle theft	1	1
Domestic violence	9	3
Arson	0	0
Total crime rate	3.3	4.4
Violent	0.2	0.0
Non-violent	3.1	4.4

Public School District
(for school year 2006-07 except as noted)

East Amwell Township School District
43 Wertsville Rd, PO Box 680
Ringoes, NJ 08551
908-782-6464

Superintendent	Edward Stoloski
Number of schools	1
Grade plan	K-8
Enrollment	497
Attendance rate, '05-06	96.5%
Dropout rate	NA
Students per teacher	10.5
Per pupil expenditure	$13,108
Median faculty salary	$53,885
Median administrator salary	$102,250
Grade 12 enrollment	NA
High school graduation rate	NA

Assessment test results
(percent scoring at proficient or advanced level)

	Language	Math
NJASK-Grade 3	92.4%	96.2%
GEPA-Grade 8	77.1%	77.0%
HSPA-High School	NA	NA

SAT score averages
Pct tested	Math	Verbal	Writing
NA	NA	NA	NA

Teacher Qualifications
- Avg. years of experience 8
- Highly-qualified teachers
  - one subject/all subjects .. 100%/100%
- With emergency credentials 2.7%

No Child Left Behind
AYP, 2005-06 .... Meets Standards

Municipal Finance
State Aid Programs, 2008
- Total aid $331,358
-   CMPTRA 0
-   Energy tax receipts 304,028
-   Garden State Trust 27,330

General Budget, 2007
- Total tax levy $13,764,532
-   County levy 2,825,274
-     County taxes 2,364,466
-     County library 205,743
-     County health 0
-     County open space .. 255,065
-   School levy 9,535,968
-   Muni. levy 1,403,289
-   Misc. revenues 2,011,378

Taxes
	2005	2006	2007
General tax rate per $100	1.67	1.78	1.76
County equalization ratio	111.31	101.14	92.59
Net valuation taxable	$784,572,366	$783,040,722	$786,307,681
State equalized value	$752,154,507	$808,202,098	$827,017,335

The New Jersey Municipal Data Book

East Brunswick Township
Middlesex County

Demographics & Socio-Economic Characteristics
(2000 US Census, except as noted)

Population
- 1980* 37,711
- 1990* 43,548
- 2000 46,756
  - Male 22,692
  - Female 24,064
- 2006 (estimate)* 47,649
- Population density 2,170.8

Race & Hispanic Origin, 2000
Race
- White 36,265
- Black/African American 1,321
- American Indian/Alaska Native 42
- Asian 7,607
- Native Hawaiian/Pacific Islander 5
- Other race 526
- Two or more races 990
- Hispanic origin, total 1,957
  - Mexican 160
  - Puerto Rican 718
  - Cuban 189
  - Other Hispanic 890

Age & Nativity, 2000
- Under 5 years 2,768
- 18 years and over 34,588
- 21 years and over 33,305
- 65 years and over 5,429
- 85 years and over 480
  - Median age 39.1
- Native-born 35,774
- Foreign-born 10,982

Educational Attainment, 2000
- Population 25 years and over 31,652
- Less than 9th grade 3.2%
- High school grad or higher 92.1%
- Bachelor's degree or higher 47.1%
- Graduate degree 19.5%

Income & Poverty, 1999
- Per capita income $33,286
- Median household income $75,956
- Median family income $86,863
- Persons in poverty 1,321
- H'holds receiving public assistance 186
- H'holds receiving social security 3,764

Households, 2000
- Total households 16,372
  - With persons under 18 6,916
  - With persons over 65 3,836
  - Family households 13,074
  - Single-person households 2,815
  - Persons per household 2.84
  - Persons per family 3.23

Labor & Employment
- Total civilian labor force, 2006** ... 27,119
  - Unemployment rate 3.5%
- Total civilian labor force, 2000 25,008
  - Unemployment rate 3.5%

Employed persons 16 years and over by occupation, 2000
- Managers & professionals 11,965
- Service occupations 1,840
- Sales & office occupations 7,210
- Farming, fishing & forestry 0
- Construction & maintenance 1,364
- Production & transportation 1,757
- Self-employed persons 1,276

* US Census Bureau
** New Jersey Department of Labor

General Information
Township of East Brunswick
PO Box 1081
East Brunswick, NJ 08816
732-390-6810

- Website .... www.eastbrunswick.org
- Year of incorporation 1860
- Land/water area (sq. miles) 21.95/0.43
- Form of government .... Mayor-Council

Government
Legislative Districts
- US Congressional 12
- State Legislative 18

Local Officials, 2008
- Mayor .... William Neary
- Manager .... James White
- Clerk .... Nennette Perry
- Finance Dir .... L. Mason Neely
- Tax Assessor .... Frank Colon
- Tax Collector .... Michelle O'Hara
- Attorney .... Michael Baker
- Building .... Edward Grobelny
- Planning .... Leslie McGowan
- Engineering .... CME Associates
- Public Works .... Thomas Williams
- Police Chief .... Barry Roberson
- Fire/Emergency Dir .... NA

Housing & Construction
Housing Units, 2000*
- Total 16,640
- Median rent $877
- Median SF home value $212,800

Permits for New Residential Construction

	Units	Value
Total, 2007	16	$2,873,400
Single family	16	$2,873,400
Total, 2006	12	$2,424,500
Single family	12	$2,424,500

Real Property Valuation, 2007

	Parcels	Valuation
Total	16,940	$2,015,368,900
Vacant	737	18,878,000
Residential	15,395	1,515,720,500
Commercial	617	349,214,100
Industrial	107	96,603,700
Apartments	13	32,110,300
Farm land	49	259,900
Farm homestead	22	2,582,400

Average Property Value & Tax, 2007
- Residential value $98,482
- Property tax $7,789
- Tax credit/rebate $1,160

Public Library
East Brunswick Public Library
2 Jean Walling Civic Center
East Brunswick, NJ 08816
732-390-6950

- Director .... Carol Nersinger

Library statistics, 2006
- Population served 46,756
- Full-time/total staff 13/27

	Total	Per capita
Holdings	174,871	3.74
Revenues	$4,375,752	$93.59
Expenditures	$4,331,929	$92.65
Annual visits	517,563	11.07
Internet terminals/annual users	27/68,536	

Taxes

	2005	2006	2007
General tax rate per $100	6.96	7.35	7.91
County equalization ratio	31.62	28.41	26.23
Net valuation taxable	$2,024,791,877	$2,022,361,800	$2,019,089,899
State equalized value	$7,127,039,342	$7,714,221,594	$8,045,895,380

Public Safety
- Number of officers, 2006 93

Crime	2005	2006
Total crimes	876	932
Violent	51	37
Murder	0	0
Rape	7	0
Robbery	12	9
Aggravated assault	32	28
Non-violent	825	895
Burglary	112	137
Larceny	671	717
Vehicle theft	42	41
Domestic violence	248	239
Arson	6	2
Total crime rate	18.1	19.3
Violent	1.1	0.8
Non-violent	17.1	18.5

Public School District
(for school year 2006-07 except as noted)

East Brunswick Township School District
760 Route #18
East Brunswick, NJ 08816
732-613-6705

- Superintendent .... Jo Ann Magistro
- Number of schools 11
- Grade plan K-12
- Enrollment 8,968
- Attendance rate, '05-06 .... 96.3%
- Dropout rate 0.4%
- Students per teacher 12.6
- Per pupil expenditure $13,427
- Median faculty salary $62,509
- Median administrator salary $109,363
- Grade 12 enrollment 769
- High school graduation rate 98.9%

Assessment test results
(percent scoring at proficient or advanced level)

	Language	Math
NJASK-Grade 3	90.9%	95.5%
GEPA-Grade 8	83.3%	82.9%
HSPA-High School	96.0%	90.3%

SAT score averages

Pct tested	Math	Verbal	Writing
97%	581	537	544

Teacher Qualifications
- Avg. years of experience 11
- Highly-qualified teachers
  - one subject/all subjects 100%/100%
- With emergency credentials 0.2%

No Child Left Behind
- AYP, 2005-06 .... Meets Standards

Municipal Finance
State Aid Programs, 2008
- Total aid $5,356,238
- CMPTRA 1,390,080
- Energy tax receipts 3,958,591
- Garden State Trust 0

General Budget, 2007
- Total tax levy $159,684,960
- County levy 21,977,468
- County taxes 19,672,395
- County library 0
- County health 0
- County open space 2,305,073
- School levy 108,989,388
- Muni. levy 28,718,104
- Misc. revenues 34,535,421

Gloucester County

East Greenwich Township

Demographics & Socio-Economic Characteristics
(2000 US Census, except as noted)

Population
- 1980* 4,144
- 1990* 5,258
- 2000 5,430
  - Male 2,591
  - Female 2,839
- 2006 (estimate)* 6,788
  - Population density 460.2

Race & Hispanic Origin, 2000
Race
- White 5,141
- Black/African American 177
- American Indian/Alaska Native 7
- Asian 35
- Native Hawaiian/Pacific Islander 0
- Other race 13
- Two or more races 57
- Hispanic origin, total 76
  - Mexican 15
  - Puerto Rican 40
  - Cuban 7
  - Other Hispanic 14

Age & Nativity, 2000
- Under 5 years 311
- 18 years and over 4,070
- 21 years and over 3,891
- 65 years and over 811
- 85 years and over 120
  - Median age 40.7
- Native-born 5,241
- Foreign-born 189

Educational Attainment, 2000
- Population 25 years and over 3,661
- Less than 9th grade 3.6%
- High school grad or higher 88.1%
- Bachelor's degree or higher 23.9%
- Graduate degree 7.0%

Income & Poverty, 1999
- Per capita income $25,345
- Median household income $65,701
- Median family income $74,455
- Persons in poverty 203
- H'holds receiving public assistance 11
- H'holds receiving social security 558

Households, 2000
- Total households 1,901
  - With persons under 18 732
  - With persons over 65 507
  - Family households 1,516
  - Single-person households 330
- Persons per household 2.77
- Persons per family 3.12

Labor & Employment
- Total civilian labor force, 2006** 3,167
  - Unemployment rate 4.0%
- Total civilian labor force, 2000 2,672
  - Unemployment rate 3.0%

Employed persons 16 years and over by occupation, 2000
- Managers & professionals 1,051
- Service occupations 237
- Sales & office occupations 683
- Farming, fishing & forestry 9
- Construction & maintenance 260
- Production & transportation 351
- Self-employed persons 103

* US Census Bureau
** New Jersey Department of Labor

See Introduction for an explanation of all data sources.

General Information
Township of East Greenwich
159 Democrat Rd
Mickleton, NJ 08056
856-423-0654
- Website .... county website)
- Year of incorporation 1881
- Land/water area (sq. miles) 14.75/0.22
- Form of government .... Township

Government
Legislative Districts
- US Congressional 1
- State Legislative 3

Local Officials, 2008
- Mayor .... Frederick J. Grant
- Manager/Admin .... NA
- Clerk .... Susan Costill
- Finance Dir .... Robert E. Scharle
- Tax Assessor .... NA
- Tax Collector .... Gail Capasso
- Attorney .... Timothy W. Chell
- Building .... James Sabetta
- Planning .... Bach Associates
- Engineering .... Remington & Vernick
- Public Works .... Joseph Schweigart
- Police Chief .... William Giordano
- Emerg/Fire Director .... Nelson Wiest

Housing & Construction
Housing Units, 2000*
- Total 1,971
- Median rent $706
- Median SF home value $155,000

Permits for New Residential Construction

	Units	Value
Total, 2007	204	$33,545,270
Single family	199	$33,417,943
Total, 2006	173	$29,625,267
Single family	108	$27,970,017

Real Property Valuation, 2007

	Parcels	Valuation
Total	3,728	$489,597,100
Vacant	759	25,575,800
Residential	2,555	404,065,600
Commercial	64	27,419,700
Industrial	23	12,534,600
Apartments	7	1,799,600
Farm land	221	2,597,600
Farm homestead	99	15,604,200

Average Property Value & Tax, 2007
- Residential value $158,127
- Property tax $6,460
- Tax credit/rebate $1,076

Public Library
East Greenwich Public Library
535 Kings Highway
Mickleton, NJ 08056
856-423-3480
- Director .... Carol Baughman

Library statistics, 2006
- Population served 5,430
- Full-time/total staff 0/1

	Total	Per capita
Holdings	20,391	3.76
Revenues	$65,267	$12.02
Expenditures	$56,472	$10.40
Annual visits	13,500	2.49
Internet terminals/annual users	6/7,000	

Public Safety
- Number of officers, 2006 18

Crime	2005	2006
Total crimes	94	109
Violent	10	5
Murder	0	0
Rape	1	2
Robbery	2	1
Aggravated assault	7	2
Non-violent	84	104
Burglary	17	31
Larceny	60	69
Vehicle theft	7	4
Domestic violence	43	26
Arson	1	1
Total crime rate	15.4	17.1
Violent	1.6	0.8
Non-violent	13.7	16.3

Public School District
(for school year 2006-07 except as noted)

East Greenwich Township School District
535 Kings Highway
Mickleton, NJ 08056
856-423-0412
- Superintendent .... Joseph P. Conroy
- Number of schools 2
- Grade plan K-6
- Enrollment 758
- Attendance rate, '05-06 .... 96.1%
- Dropout rate .... NA
- Students per teacher 11.3
- Per pupil expenditure $11,578
- Median faculty salary $53,253
- Median administrator salary $89,106
- Grade 12 enrollment .... NA
- High school graduation rate .... NA

Assessment test results
(percent scoring at proficient or advanced level)

	Language	Math
NJASK-Grade 3	90.3%	94.0%
GEPA-Grade 8	NA	NA
HSPA-High School	NA	NA

SAT score averages

Pct tested	Math	Verbal	Writing
NA	NA	NA	NA

Teacher Qualifications
- Avg. years of experience 14
- Highly-qualified teachers
  one subject/all subjects 100%/100%
- With emergency credentials 0.0%

No Child Left Behind
- AYP, 2005-06 .... Meets Standards

Municipal Finance
State Aid Programs, 2008
- Total aid $2,071,705
  - CMPTRA 0
  - Energy tax receipts 2,068,324
  - Garden State Trust 3,381

General Budget, 2007
- Total tax levy $20,038,604
  - County levy 5,207,367
    - County taxes 4,484,699
    - County library 371,484
    - County health 0
    - County open space 351,185
  - School levy 13,225,289
  - Muni. levy 1,605,947
- Misc. revenues 4,822,518

Taxes	2005	2006	2007
General tax rate per $100	3.751	4.026	4.086
County equalization ratio	70.55	62.8	55.75
Net valuation taxable	$419,994,197	$456,088,450	$490,492,524
State equalized value	$668,780,568	$818,998,322	$971,547,882

East Hanover Township
Morris County

Demographics & Socio-Economic Characteristics
(2000 US Census, except as noted)

Population
1980*	9,319
1990*	9,926
2000	11,393
Male	5,520
Female	5,873
2006 (estimate)*	11,633
Population density	1,425.6

Race & Hispanic Origin, 2000
Race
White	9,921
Black/African American	66
American Indian/Alaska Native	3
Asian	1,269
Native Hawaiian/Pacific Islander	0
Other race	27
Two or more races	107
Hispanic origin, total	312
Mexican	22
Puerto Rican	71
Cuban	53
Other Hispanic	166

Age & Nativity, 2000
Under 5 years	713
18 years and over	8,828
21 years and over	8,511
65 years and over	1,662
85 years and over	138
Median age	40.7
Native-born	9,274
Foreign-born	2,119

Educational Attainment, 2000
Population 25 years and over	8,147
Less than 9th grade	4.9%
High school grad or higher	88.1%
Bachelor's degree or higher	33.4%
Graduate degree	13.4%

Income & Poverty, 1999
Per capita income	$32,129
Median household income	$82,133
Median family income	$88,348
Persons in poverty	192
H'holds receiving public assistance	23
H'holds receiving social security	1,214

Households, 2000
Total households	3,843
With persons under 18	1,407
With persons over 65	1,163
Family households	3,214
Single-person households	521
Persons per household	2.96
Persons per family	3.26

Labor & Employment
Total civilian labor force, 2006**	6,513
Unemployment rate	3.5%
Total civilian labor force, 2000	5,952
Unemployment rate	3.1%

Employed persons 16 years and over by occupation, 2000
Managers & professionals	2,553
Service occupations	748
Sales & office occupations	1,528
Farming, fishing & forestry	0
Construction & maintenance	474
Production & transportation	462
Self-employed persons	317

* US Census Bureau
** New Jersey Department of Labor

General Information
Township of East Hanover
411 Ridgedale Ave
East Hanover, NJ 07936
973-428-3000

Website	www.easthanovertownship.com
Year of incorporation	1928
Land/water area (sq. miles)	8.16/0.00
Form of government	Small Municipality

Government
Legislative Districts
US Congressional	11
State Legislative	26

Local Officials, 2008
Mayor	Joseph Pannullo
Manager	C. Richard Paduch
Clerk	Marilyn J. Snow
Finance Dir	Smruti Amin
Tax Assessor	Stan Belenky
Tax Collector	Carole Reardon
Attorney	Matthew O'Donnell
Building	Thomas Pershouse
Comm Dev/Planning	NA
Engineering	Lawrence Palmer
Public Works	Marc Macaluso
Police Chief	Stanley Hansen
Emerg/Fire Director	Raymond Serra

Housing & Construction
Housing Units, 2000*
Total	3,895
Median rent	$1,504
Median SF home value	$322,800

Permits for New Residential Construction
	Units	Value
Total, 2007	16	$2,996,508
Single family	16	$2,996,508
Total, 2006	23	$4,299,742
Single family	23	$4,299,742

Real Property Valuation, 2007
	Parcels	Valuation
Total	4,351	$2,443,935,800
Vacant	171	28,357,400
Residential	3,912	1,398,387,900
Commercial	177	858,164,200
Industrial	91	159,026,300
Apartments	0	0
Farm land	0	0
Farm homestead	0	0

Average Property Value & Tax, 2007
Residential value	$357,461
Property tax	$6,594
Tax credit/rebate	$1,074

Public Library
East Hanover Township Library
415 Ridgedale Ave
East Hanover, NJ 07936
973-428-3075

Director.................Gayle Carlson

Library statistics, 2006
Population served	11,393
Full-time/total staff	1/5

	Total	Per capita
Holdings	78,700	6.91
Revenues	$1,211,967	$106.38
Expenditures	$780,262	$68.49
Annual visits	100,000	8.78
Internet terminals/annual users	13/10,000	

Taxes
	2005	2006	2007
General tax rate per $100	1.67	1.78	1.85
County equalization ratio	82.17	75.27	71.28
Net valuation taxable	$2,459,779,889	$2,439,426,400	$2,446,386,012
State equalized value	$3,267,941,928	$3,424,519,698	$3,630,082,392

Public Safety
Number of officers, 2006 33

Crime	2005	2006
Total crimes	241	273
Violent	11	11
Murder	0	0
Rape	0	0
Robbery	2	3
Aggravated assault	9	8
Non-violent	230	262
Burglary	15	21
Larceny	197	219
Vehicle theft	18	22
Domestic violence	69	65
Arson	1	0
Total crime rate	20.9	23.5
Violent	1.0	0.9
Non-violent	19.9	22.6

Public School District
(for school year 2006-07 except as noted)

East Hanover Township School District
20 School Ave
East Hanover, NJ 07936
973-887-2112

Superintendent	Larry Santos
Number of schools	3
Grade plan	K-8
Enrollment	1,147
Attendance rate, '05-06	95.9%
Dropout rate	NA
Students per teacher	10.6
Per pupil expenditure	$13,515
Median faculty salary	$55,020
Median administrator salary	$103,435
Grade 12 enrollment	NA
High school graduation rate	NA

Assessment test results
(percent scoring at proficient or advanced level)
	Language	Math
NJASK-Grade 3	93.7%	99.2%
GEPA-Grade 8	89.1%	79.7%
HSPA-High School	NA	NA

SAT score averages
Pct tested	Math	Verbal	Writing
NA	NA	NA	NA

Teacher Qualifications
Avg. years of experience	10
Highly-qualified teachers one subject/all subjects	100%/98.5%
With emergency credentials	0.0%

No Child Left Behind
AYP, 2005-06 .... Meets Standards

Municipal Finance
State Aid Programs, 2008
Total aid	$3,378,458
CMPTRA	0
Energy tax receipts	3,378,250
Garden State Trust	208

General Budget, 2007
Total tax levy	$45,125,987
County levy	8,174,546
County taxes	6,537,231
County library	0
County health	0
County open space	1,637,315
School levy	24,436,880
Muni. levy	12,514,561
Misc. revenues	6,886,122

Hudson County

East Newark Borough

Demographics & Socio-Economic Characteristics
(2000 US Census, except as noted)

Population
1980*	1,923
1990*	2,157
2000	2,377
Male	1,211
Female	1,166
2006 (estimate)*	2,217
Population density	22,170.0

Race & Hispanic Origin, 2000
Race
White	1,593
Black/African American	40
American Indian/Alaska Native	12
Asian	60
Native Hawaiian/Pacific Islander	1
Other race	499
Two or more races	172
Hispanic origin, total	1,130
Mexican	48
Puerto Rican	124
Cuban	59
Other Hispanic	899

Age & Nativity, 2000
Under 5 years	161
18 years and over	1,761
21 years and over	1,657
65 years and over	181
85 years and over	23
Median age	32.3
Native-born	1,104
Foreign-born	1,273

Educational Attainment, 2000
Population 25 years and over	1,495
Less than 9th grade	22.9%
High school grad or higher	60.9%
Bachelor's degree or higher	13.2%
Graduate degree	5.0%

Income & Poverty, 1999
Per capita income	$16,415
Median household income	$44,352
Median family income	$46,375
Persons in poverty	298
H'holds receiving public assistance	18
H'holds receiving social security	152

Households, 2000
Total households	767
With persons under 18	351
With persons over 65	137
Family households	605
Single-person households	123
Persons per household	3.10
Persons per family	3.40

Labor & Employment
Total civilian labor force, 2006**	1,107
Unemployment rate	4.4%
Total civilian labor force, 2000	1,122
Unemployment rate	6.4%

Employed persons 16 years and over by occupation, 2000
Managers & professionals	163
Service occupations	184
Sales & office occupations	278
Farming, fishing & forestry	4
Construction & maintenance	150
Production & transportation	271
Self-employed persons	29

* US Census Bureau
** New Jersey Department of Labor

See Introduction for an explanation of all data sources.

General Information
Borough of East Newark
34 Sherman Ave
East Newark, NJ 07029
973-481-2902

Website	www.boroughofeastnewark.com
Year of incorporation	1895
Land/water area (sq. miles)	0.10/0.02
Form of government	Borough

Government

Legislative Districts
US Congressional	13
State Legislative	32

Local Officials, 2008
Mayor	Joseph R. Smith
Manager/Admin	NA
Clerk	Robert Knapp
Finance Dir	Elizabeth Higgins
Tax Assessor	Denis McGuire
Tax Collector	Anthony Blasi
Attorney	Neil Marotta
Building	Mark Sadonis
Comm Dev/Planning	NA
Engineering	CME Associates
Public Works	NA
Police Chief	Kenneth Sheehan
Emerg/Fire Director	Robert Tomasko

Housing & Construction

Housing Units, 2000*
Total	799
Median rent	$725
Median SF home value	$126,300

Permits for New Residential Construction
	Units	Value
Total, 2007	0	$0
Single family	0	$0
Total, 2006	2	$134,000
Single family	0	$0

Real Property Valuation, 2007
	Parcels	Valuation
Total	381	$39,694,600
Vacant	7	558,400
Residential	334	25,228,900
Commercial	22	2,762,500
Industrial	6	9,650,500
Apartments	12	1,494,300
Farm land	0	0
Farm homestead	0	0

Average Property Value & Tax, 2007
Residential value	$75,536
Property tax	$5,645
Tax credit/rebate	$914

Public Library
No public municipal library

Library statistics, 2006
Population served	NA
Full-time/total staff	NA/NA

	Total	Per capita
Holdings	NA	NA
Revenues	NA	NA
Expenditures	NA	NA
Annual visits	NA	NA
Internet terminals/annual users	NA/NA	

Taxes
	2005	2006	2007
General tax rate per $100	6.978	7.116	7.474
County equalization ratio	31.18	28.34	24.42
Net valuation taxable	$38,962,213	$39,310,900	$39,714,673
State equalized value	$137,481,344	$161,003,505	$187,082,278

Public Safety
Number of officers, 2006 ... 6

Crime
	2005	2006
Total crimes	38	30
Violent	7	10
Murder	0	1
Rape	0	1
Robbery	1	1
Aggravated assault	6	7
Non-violent	31	20
Burglary	4	3
Larceny	11	11
Vehicle theft	16	6
Domestic violence	15	4
Arson	0	0
Total crime rate	16.5	13.3
Violent	3.0	4.4
Non-violent	13.4	8.8

Public School District
(for school year 2006-07 except as noted)

East Newark School District
501-11 N Third St
East Newark, NJ 07029
973-481-6803

Chief School Admin	Salvatore Montagna
Number of schools	1
Grade plan	K-8
Enrollment	213
Attendance rate, '05-06	95.2%
Dropout rate	NA
Students per teacher	13.9
Per pupil expenditure	$11,663
Median faculty salary	$39,800
Median administrator salary	$54,314
Grade 12 enrollment	NA
High school graduation rate	NA

Assessment test results
(percent scoring at proficient or advanced level)
	Language	Math
NJASK-Grade 3	57.2%	73.9%
GEPA-Grade 8	83.3%	75.0%
HSPA-High School	NA	NA

SAT score averages
Pct tested	Math	Verbal	Writing
NA	NA	NA	NA

Teacher Qualifications
Avg. years of experience	10
Highly-qualified teachers one subject/all subjects	100%/100%
With emergency credentials	7.1%

No Child Left Behind
AYP, 2005-06 ... Meets Standards

Municipal Finance

State Aid Programs, 2008
Total aid	$136,950
CMPTRA	0
Energy tax receipts	136,950
Garden State Trust	0

General Budget, 2007
Total tax levy	$2,967,905
County levy	715,548
County taxes	698,184
County library	0
County health	0
County open space	17,364
School levy	1,058,876
Muni. levy	1,193,482
Misc. revenues	2,045,425

©2008 Information Publications, Inc. All rights reserved.

East Orange City

Essex County

Demographics & Socio-Economic Characteristics[†]
(2000 US Census, except as noted)

Population
1980*	77,025
1990*	73,552
2000	69,824
Male	31,429
Female	38,395
2006 (estimate)*	67,247
Population density	17,111.2

Race & Hispanic Origin, 2000
Race
White	2,683
Black/African American	62,462
American Indian/Alaska Native	177
Asian	302
Native Hawaiian/Pacific Islander	51
Other race	1,496
Two or more races	2,653
Hispanic origin, total	3,284
Mexican	196
Puerto Rican	1,248
Cuban	138
Other Hispanic	1,702

Age & Nativity, 2000
Under 5 years	5,535
18 years and over	50,188
21 years and over	47,327
65 years and over	7,845
85 years and over	879
Median age	33.0
Native-born	57,145
Foreign-born	12,759

Educational Attainment, 2000
Population 25 years and over	43,509
Less than 9th grade	7.5%
High school grad or higher	72.4%
Bachelor's degree or higher	15.0%
Graduate degree	4.5%

Income & Poverty, 1999
Per capita income	$16,488
Median household income	$32,346
Median family income	$38,562
Persons in poverty	13,159
H'holds receiving public assistance	2,415
H'holds receiving social security	6,691

Households, 2000
Total households	26,024
With persons under 18	10,289
With persons over 65	6,072
Family households	16,079
Single-person households	8,584
Persons per household	2.63
Persons per family	3.37

Labor & Employment
Total civilian labor force, 2006**	30,252
Unemployment rate	7.6%
Total civilian labor force, 2000	31,605
Unemployment rate	13.3%

Employed persons 16 years and over by occupation, 2000
Managers & professionals	6,740
Service occupations	6,079
Sales & office occupations	8,823
Farming, fishing & forestry	9
Construction & maintenance	1,612
Production & transportation	4,136
Self-employed persons	821

[†] see Appendix C for American Community Survey data
* US Census Bureau
** New Jersey Department of Labor
§ State Fiscal Year July 1–June 30

General Information
City of East Orange
44 City Hall Plz
East Orange, NJ 07017
973-266-5100

Website	www.eastorange-nj.org
Year of incorporation	1899
Land/water area (sq. miles)	3.93/0.00
Form of government	City

Government
Legislative Districts
US Congressional	10
State Legislative	34

Local Officials, 2008
Mayor	Robert L. Bowser
Manager	Reginald Lewis
Clerk	Cynthia Brown
Finance Dir	Soe Myint
Tax Assessor	Barbara Williams
Tax Collector	Annmarie Corbitt
Attorney	Jason Holt
Building	Lloyd Abdul Raheem
Planning	Ernest Freeman
Engineering	Michael Johnson
Public Works	Michael Johnson
Police Chief	Ronald Borgo (Actg)
Emerg/Fire Director	Dean Spann

Housing & Construction
Housing Units, 2000*
Total	28,485
Median rent	$650
Median SF home value	$122,000

Permits for New Residential Construction
	Units	Value
Total, 2007	131	$12,628,500
Single family	40	$5,162,150
Total, 2006	106	$8,659,704
Single family	12	$1,912,158

Real Property Valuation, 2007
	Parcels	Valuation
Total	10,245	$3,512,420,900
Vacant	541	58,912,800
Residential	8,662	2,075,185,000
Commercial	679	551,170,300
Industrial	39	59,001,300
Apartments	324	768,151,500
Farm land	0	0
Farm homestead	0	0

Average Property Value & Tax, 2007
Residential value	$239,573
Property tax	$5,785
Tax credit/rebate	$1,034

Public Library
East Orange Public Library
21 S Arlington Ave
East Orange, NJ 07018
973-266-5607

Director..............Carolyn Ryan Reed

Library statistics, 2006
Population served	69,824
Full-time/total staff	13/49

	Total	Per capita
Holdings	398,347	5.71
Revenues	$4,801,697	$68.77
Expenditures	$4,046,248	$57.95
Annual visits	376,630	5.39
Internet terminals/annual users		91/75,771

Taxes
	2005	2006	2007
General tax rate per $100	27.09	27.21	2.42
County equalization ratio	15.63	13.23	126.9
Net valuation taxable	$304,103,330	$300,518,000	$3,519,868,772
State equalized value	$2,298,589,040	$2,740,463,385	$3,159,862,968

Public Safety
Number of officers, 2006		266

Crime	2005	2006
Total crimes	4,591	3,181
Violent	1,068	721
Murder	14	9
Rape	31	25
Robbery	553	373
Aggravated assault	470	314
Non-violent	3,523	2,460
Burglary	878	593
Larceny	1,648	1,229
Vehicle theft	997	638
Domestic violence	768	564
Arson	41	50
Total crime rate	66.6	46.6
Violent	15.5	10.6
Non-violent	51.1	36.1

Public School District
(for school year 2006-07 except as noted)

East Orange School District
715 Park Ave
East Orange, NJ 07017
973-266-5760

Superintendent	Clarence C. Hoover III
Number of schools	20
Grade plan	K-12
Enrollment	10,240
Attendance rate, '05-06	93.2%
Dropout rate	2.9%
Students per teacher	9.3
Per pupil expenditure	$16,066
Median faculty salary	$76,523
Median administrator salary	$120,471
Grade 12 enrollment	429
High school graduation rate	NA

Assessment test results
(percent scoring at proficient or advanced level)
	Language	Math
NJASK-Grade 3	68.4%	76.8%
GEPA-Grade 8	44.8%	31.0%
HSPA-High School	62.3%	37.3%

SAT score averages
Pct tested	Math	Verbal	Writing
NA	NA	NA	NA

Teacher Qualifications
Avg. years of experience	10
Highly-qualified teachers one subject/all subjects	98.0%/98.0%
With emergency credentials	0.1%

No Child Left Behind
AYP, 2005-06..............Meets Standards

Municipal Finance[§]

State Aid Programs, 2008
Total aid	$25,431,942
CMPTRA	20,972,823
Energy tax receipts	4,459,117
Garden State Trust	2

General Budget, 2007
Total tax levy	$84,995,189
County levy	10,950,423
County taxes	10,668,658
County library	0
County health	0
County open space	281,765
School levy	19,339,336
Muni. levy	54,705,430
Misc. revenues	71,321,009

Bergen County
East Rutherford Borough

Demographics & Socio-Economic Characteristics
(2000 US Census, except as noted)

Population
1980*	7,849
1990*	7,902
2000	8,716
Male	4,241
Female	4,475
2006 (estimate)*	8,931
Population density	2,344.1

Race & Hispanic Origin, 2000
Race
White	6,945
Black/African American	324
American Indian/Alaska Native	10
Asian	932
Native Hawaiian/Pacific Islander	4
Other race	280
Two or more races	221
Hispanic origin, total	928
Mexican	42
Puerto Rican	221
Cuban	91
Other Hispanic	574

Age & Nativity, 2000
Under 5 years	475
18 years and over	7,027
21 years and over	6,803
65 years and over	1,250
85 years and over	168
Median age	37.9
Native-born	6,202
Foreign-born	2,514

Educational Attainment, 2000
Population 25 years and over	6,434
Less than 9th grade	9.0%
High school grad or higher	78.5%
Bachelor's degree or higher	25.5%
Graduate degree	10.0%

Income & Poverty, 1999
Per capita income	$28,072
Median household income	$50,163
Median family income	$59,583
Persons in poverty	832
H'holds receiving public assistance	55
H'holds receiving social security	980

Households, 2000
Total households	3,644
With persons under 18	1,004
With persons over 65	952
Family households	2,156
Single-person households	1,216
Persons per household	2.35
Persons per family	3.05

Labor & Employment
Total civilian labor force, 2006**	4,966
Unemployment rate	5.2%
Total civilian labor force, 2000	4,809
Unemployment rate	5.5%

Employed persons 16 years and over by occupation, 2000
Managers & professionals	1,557
Service occupations	647
Sales & office occupations	1,402
Farming, fishing & forestry	12
Construction & maintenance	285
Production & transportation	643
Self-employed persons	188

* US Census Bureau
** New Jersey Department of Labor

See Introduction for an explanation of all data sources.

General Information
Borough of East Rutherford
1 Everett Pl
East Rutherford, NJ 07073
201-933-3444

Website	www.eastrutherfordnj.net
Year of incorporation	1894
Land/water area (sq. miles)	3.81/0.34
Form of government	Borough

Government
Legislative Districts
US Congressional	9
State Legislative	36

Local Officials, 2008
Mayor	James Cassella
Manager/Admin	NA
Clerk	Danielle Lorenc
Finance Dir	Anthony Bianchi
Tax Assessor	Dennis McGuire
Tax Collector	Linda Ramsaier
Attorney	Peter Melchionne
Dir of Inspections	Frank Recanati
Planning/Zoning	John Giancaspro
Engineering	Glenn Beckmeyer
Public Works Superint	Alan DeRosa
Police Chief	Larry Minda (Dep)
Fire Chief	Paul DeRosa

Housing & Construction
Housing Units, 2000*
Total	3,771
Median rent	$817
Median SF home value	$196,200

Permits for New Residential Construction
	Units	Value
Total, 2007	622	$71,654,975
Single family	0	$489,000
Total, 2006	1	$189,500
Single family	1	$189,500

Real Property Valuation, 2007
	Parcels	Valuation
Total	2,286	$927,843,831
Vacant	69	21,905,600
Residential	1,916	279,467,660
Commercial	171	273,181,971
Industrial	94	292,189,000
Apartments	36	61,099,600
Farm land	0	0
Farm homestead	0	0

Average Property Value & Tax, 2007
Residential value	$145,860
Property tax	$3,761
Tax credit/rebate	$785

Public Library
East Rutherford Mem Library
143 Boiling Springs Ave
East Rutherford, NJ 07073
201-939-3930

Director: Karen S. DiNardo

Library statistics, 2006
Population served	8,716
Full-time/total staff	1/3

	Total	Per capita
Holdings	30,757	3.53
Revenues	$523,159	$60.02
Expenditures	$388,110	$44.53
Annual visits	12,582	1.44
Internet terminals/annual users	3/3,588	

Public Safety
Number of officers, 2006: 34

Crime	2005	2006
Total crimes	438	407
Violent	15	16
Murder	0	1
Rape	0	0
Robbery	3	3
Aggravated assault	12	12
Non-violent	423	391
Burglary	42	39
Larceny	304	292
Vehicle theft	77	60
Domestic violence	37	56
Arson	1	0
Total crime rate	50.0	45.4
Violent	1.7	1.8
Non-violent	48.3	43.6

Public School District
(for school year 2006-07 except as noted)

East Rutherford School District
Uhland and Grove Streets
East Rutherford, NJ 07073
201-804-3100

Superintendent	Gayle Strauss
Number of schools	2
Grade plan	K-8
Enrollment	730
Attendance rate, '05-06	94.9%
Dropout rate	NA
Students per teacher	9.5
Per pupil expenditure	$12,735
Median faculty salary	$65,558
Median administrator salary	$122,520
Grade 12 enrollment	NA
High school graduation rate	NA

Assessment test results
(percent scoring at proficient or advanced level)
	Language	Math
NJASK-Grade 3	79.5%	88.6%
GEPA-Grade 8	71.6%	74.1%
HSPA-High School	NA	NA

SAT score averages
Pct tested	Math	Verbal	Writing
NA	NA	NA	NA

Teacher Qualifications
Avg. years of experience	11
Highly-qualified teachers one subject/all subjects	100%/100%
With emergency credentials	0.0%

No Child Left Behind
AYP, 2005-06: Meets Standards

Municipal Finance
State Aid Programs, 2008
Total aid	$1,867,980
CMPTRA	96,640
Energy tax receipts	1,768,038
Garden State Trust	3,302

General Budget, 2007
Total tax levy	$23,975,674
County levy	3,015,088
County taxes	2,846,922
County library	0
County health	0
County open space	168,167
School levy	15,813,924
Muni. levy	5,146,662
Misc. revenues	12,861,695

Taxes
	2005	2006	2007
General tax rate per $100	2.5	2.69	2.58
County equalization ratio	65.53	58.14	56.11
Net valuation taxable	$882,647,583	$879,975,231	$929,872,429
State equalized value	$1,518,141,698	$1,570,443,342	$1,694,247,878

The New Jersey Municipal Data Book

East Windsor Township — Mercer County

Demographics & Socio-Economic Characteristics
(2000 US Census, except as noted)

Population
1980*	21,041
1990*	22,353
2000	24,919
Male	12,153
Female	12,766
2006 (estimate)*	26,926
Population density	1,720.5

Race & Hispanic Origin, 2000
Race
White	18,545
Black/African American	2,217
American Indian/Alaska Native	49
Asian	2,380
Native Hawaiian/Pacific Islander	31
Other race	1,148
Two or more races	549
Hispanic origin, total	3,559
Mexican	282
Puerto Rican	515
Cuban	96
Other Hispanic	2,666

Age & Nativity, 2000
Under 5 years	1,915
18 years and over	18,935
21 years and over	18,221
65 years and over	2,062
85 years and over	402
Median age	35.6
Native-born	19,155
Foreign-born	5,764

Educational Attainment, 2000
Population 25 years and over	17,196
Less than 9th grade	4.0%
High school grad or higher	88.6%
Bachelor's degree or higher	42.0%
Graduate degree	15.5%

Income & Poverty, 1999
Per capita income	$28,695
Median household income	$63,616
Median family income	$73,461
Persons in poverty	1,312
H'holds receiving public assistance	67
H'holds receiving social security	1,451

Households, 2000
Total households	9,448
With persons under 18	3,451
With persons over 65	1,485
Family households	6,557
Single-person households	2,320
Persons per household	2.61
Persons per family	3.12

Labor & Employment
Total civilian labor force, 2006**	17,151
Unemployment rate	3.1%
Total civilian labor force, 2000	14,352
Unemployment rate	3.1%

Employed persons 16 years and over by occupation, 2000
Managers & professionals	6,312
Service occupations	1,332
Sales & office occupations	4,026
Farming, fishing & forestry	19
Construction & maintenance	498
Production & transportation	1,721
Self-employed persons	476

‡ Branch of county library
* US Census Bureau
** New Jersey Department of Labor

General Information
Township of East Windsor
16 Lanning Blvd
East Windsor, NJ 08520
609-443-4000

Website	www.east-windsor.nj.us
Year of incorporation	1797
Land/water area (sq. miles)	15.65/0.05
Form of government	Council-Manager

Government
Legislative Districts
US Congressional	4
State Legislative	12

Local Officials, 2008
Mayor	Janice Mironov
Manager	Alan M. Fisher
Clerk	Cindy A. Dye
Finance Dir.	Margaret Gorman
Tax Assessor	H. Rick Kline
Tax Collector	Lois A. Burns
Attorney	David Orron
Building	Stanley Rodefeld
Planning	Richard Coppola
Engineering	Raymond Jordan
Public Works	William Askenstedt
Police Chief	William Spain
Fire/Emergency Dir.	NA

Housing & Construction
Housing Units, 2000*
Total	9,880
Median rent	$791
Median SF home value	$152,600

Permits for New Residential Construction
	Units	Value
Total, 2007	36	$4,246,765
Single family	36	$4,246,765
Total, 2006	66	$7,630,450
Single family	66	$7,630,450

Real Property Valuation, 2007
	Parcels	Valuation
Total	8,363	$1,409,090,180
Vacant	421	25,567,600
Residential	7,609	1,019,171,600
Commercial	151	230,785,700
Industrial	11	52,532,300
Apartments	19	73,589,000
Farm land	117	1,469,980
Farm homestead	35	5,974,000

Average Property Value & Tax, 2007
Residential value	$134,111
Property tax	$6,787
Tax credit/rebate	$1,077

Public Library
Hickory Corner Branch Library‡
138 Hickory Corner Rd
East Windsor, NJ 08520
609-448-1330

Branch Librarian — Marilyn Fischer

Library statistics, 2006
see Mercer County profile for library system statistics

Public Safety
Number of officers, 2006 — 48

Crime
	2005	2006
Total crimes	390	397
Violent	32	41
Murder	0	1
Rape	3	3
Robbery	9	8
Aggravated assault	20	29
Non-violent	358	356
Burglary	63	73
Larceny	266	257
Vehicle theft	29	26
Domestic violence	150	194
Arson	4	7
Total crime rate	14.5	14.8
Violent	1.2	1.5
Non-violent	13.3	13.2

Public School District
(for school year 2006-07 except as noted)

East Windsor Regional School District
25A Leshin Lane
Hightstown, NJ 08520
609-443-7717

Superintendent	Ronald Bolandi
Number of schools	12
Grade plan	K-12
Enrollment	5,032
Attendance rate, '05-06	95.7%
Dropout rate	1.6%
Students per teacher	11.7
Per pupil expenditure	$14,597
Median faculty salary	$65,340
Median administrator salary	$108,015
Grade 12 enrollment	312
High school graduation rate	90.2%

Assessment test results
(percent scoring at proficient or advanced level)
	Language	Math
NJASK-Grade 3	85.1%	89.5%
GEPA-Grade 8	79.7%	76.1%
HSPA-High School	82.5%	72.2%

SAT score averages
Pct tested	Math	Verbal	Writing
86%	536	517	508

Teacher Qualifications
Avg. years of experience	17
Highly-qualified teachers one subject/all subjects	100%/100%
With emergency credentials	0.0%

No Child Left Behind
AYP, 2005-06 — Needs Improvement

Municipal Finance
State Aid Programs, 2008
Total aid	$4,528,183
CMPTRA	422,999
Energy tax receipts	4,104,875
Garden State Trust	309

General Budget, 2007
Total tax levy	$71,393,268
County levy	15,784,538
County taxes	13,597,568
County library	1,254,460
County health	0
County open space	932,509
School levy	48,384,159
Muni. levy	7,224,571
Misc. revenues	12,627,984

Taxes
	2005	2006	2007
General tax rate per $100	4.52	4.83	5.07
County equalization ratio	59.85	51.49	45.5
Net valuation taxable	$1,363,476,665	$1,393,251,480	$1,410,709,636
State equalized value	$2,648,041,688	$3,063,907,037	$3,129,455,594

Burlington County

Eastampton Township

Demographics & Socio-Economic Characteristics
(2000 US Census, except as noted)

Population
1980*	3,814
1990*	4,962
2000	6,202
Male	3,085
Female	3,117
2006 (estimate)*	6,697
Population density	1,164.7

Race & Hispanic Origin, 2000
Race
White	4,853
Black/African American	730
American Indian/Alaska Native	14
Asian	336
Native Hawaiian/Pacific Islander	0
Other race	89
Two or more races	180
Hispanic origin, total	293
Mexican	28
Puerto Rican	149
Cuban	17
Other Hispanic	99

Age & Nativity, 2000
Under 5 years	443
18 years and over	4,371
21 years and over	4,185
65 years and over	444
85 years and over	26
Median age	34.9
Native-born	5,705
Foreign-born	497

Educational Attainment, 2000
Population 25 years and over	3,945
Less than 9th grade	2.7%
High school grad or higher	90.1%
Bachelor's degree or higher	29.6%
Graduate degree	8.6%

Income & Poverty, 1999
Per capita income	$24,534
Median household income	$66,406
Median family income	$71,765
Persons in poverty	179
H'holds receiving public assistance	28
H'holds receiving social security	321

Households, 2000
Total households	2,226
With persons under 18	995
With persons over 65	338
Family households	1,639
Single-person households	478
Persons per household	2.78
Persons per family	3.29

Labor & Employment
Total civilian labor force, 2006**	4,014
Unemployment rate	2.8%
Total civilian labor force, 2000	3,453
Unemployment rate	2.5%

Employed persons 16 years and over by occupation, 2000
Managers & professionals	1,200
Service occupations	442
Sales & office occupations	1,021
Farming, fishing & forestry	8
Construction & maintenance	251
Production & transportation	446
Self-employed persons	141

* US Census Bureau
** New Jersey Department of Labor

See Introduction for an explanation of all data sources.

General Information
Township of Eastampton
12 Manorhouse Ct
Eastampton, NJ 08060
609-267-5723

Website	www.eastampton.com
Year of incorporation	1880
Land/water area (sq. miles)	5.75/0.08
Form of government	Council-Manager

Government
Legislative Districts
US Congressional	3
State Legislative	8

Local Officials, 2008
Mayor	Keith Nagler
Manager	Scott Carew
Clerk	Linda M. Lovins
Finance Dir	D. Lavacca
Tax Assessor	Harry Renwick
Tax Collector	Doris LaVacca
Attorney	Eileen Fahey
Building	Stephen Murray
Planning	Linda M. Lovins
Engineering	Nancy Jamanow
Public Works	Richard Parks
Police Chief	Gerald Mingin
Emerg/Fire Director	Phillip Polios

Housing & Construction
Housing Units, 2000*
Total	2,312
Median rent	$722
Median SF home value	$143,100

Permits for New Residential Construction
	Units	Value
Total, 2007	27	$4,761,299
Single family	23	$4,149,913
Total, 2006	6	$728,970
Single family	6	$728,970

Real Property Valuation, 2007
	Parcels	Valuation
Total	1,866	$520,414,100
Vacant	169	9,364,100
Residential	1,598	437,165,100
Commercial	36	29,141,000
Industrial	4	2,655,000
Apartments	4	36,900,000
Farm land	38	462,300
Farm homestead	17	4,726,600

Average Property Value & Tax, 2007
Residential value	$273,617
Property tax	$6,278
Tax credit/rebate	$1,113

Public Library
No public municipal library

Library statistics, 2006
Population served	NA
Full-time/total staff	NA/NA

	Total	Per capita
Holdings	NA	NA
Revenues	NA	NA
Expenditures	NA	NA
Annual visits	NA	NA
Internet terminals/annual users	NA/NA	

Taxes
	2005	2006	2007
General tax rate per $100	4.187	2.207	2.297
County equalization ratio	66.18	121.51	105.93
Net valuation taxable	$250,161,950	$520,362,400	$521,083,404
State equalized value	$426,897,526	$491,879,139	$524,699,210

Public Safety
Number of officers, 2006 17

Crime
	2005	2006
Total crimes	111	79
Violent	11	13
Murder	0	0
Rape	2	1
Robbery	1	4
Aggravated assault	8	8
Non-violent	100	66
Burglary	12	11
Larceny	78	46
Vehicle theft	10	9
Domestic violence	40	51
Arson	0	0
Total crime rate	16.5	11.7
Violent	1.6	1.9
Non-violent	14.8	9.8

Public School District
(for school year 2006-07 except as noted)

Eastampton Township School District
1 Student Dr
Eastampton, NJ 08060
609-267-9172

Superintendent	Robert Krastek
Number of schools	1
Grade plan	K-8
Enrollment	455
Attendance rate, '05-06	93.7%
Dropout rate	NA
Students per teacher	10.2
Per pupil expenditure	$10,701
Median faculty salary	$48,000
Median administrator salary	$96,122
Grade 12 enrollment	NA
High school graduation rate	NA

Assessment test results
(percent scoring at proficient or advanced level)
	Language	Math
NJASK-Grade 3	75.7%	78.5%
GEPA-Grade 8	87.0%	84.7%
HSPA-High School	NA	NA

SAT score averages
Pct tested	Math	Verbal	Writing
NA	NA	NA	NA

Teacher Qualifications
Avg. years of experience	9
Highly-qualified teachers one subject/all subjects	100%/100%
With emergency credentials	0.0%

No Child Left Behind
AYP, 2005-06 .... Meets Standards

Municipal Finance
State Aid Programs, 2008
Total aid	$510,963
CMPTRA	67,719
Energy tax receipts	443,244
Garden State Trust	0

General Budget, 2007
Total tax levy	$11,956,164
County levy	2,058,439
County taxes	1,705,673
County library	156,519
County health	0
County open space	196,247
School levy	6,936,755
Muni. levy	2,960,969
Misc. revenues	2,308,913

Eatontown Borough — Monmouth County

Demographics & Socio-Economic Characteristics
(2000 US Census, except as noted)

Population
1980*	12,703
1990*	13,800
2000	14,008
Male	6,813
Female	7,195
2006 (estimate)*	14,022
Population density	2,368.6

Race & Hispanic Origin, 2000
Race
White	10,267
Black/African American	1,626
American Indian/Alaska Native	48
Asian	1,305
Native Hawaiian/Pacific Islander	5
Other race	323
Two or more races	434
Hispanic origin, total	928
Mexican	158
Puerto Rican	378
Cuban	35
Other Hispanic	357

Age & Nativity, 2000
Under 5 years	958
18 years and over	10,796
21 years and over	10,441
65 years and over	1,867
85 years and over	288
Median age	36.6
Native-born	11,691
Foreign-born	2,307

Educational Attainment, 2000
Population 25 years and over	9,877
Less than 9th grade	3.7%
High school grad or higher	89.1%
Bachelor's degree or higher	33.5%
Graduate degree	13.4%

Income & Poverty, 1999
Per capita income	$26,965
Median household income	$53,833
Median family income	$69,397
Persons in poverty	777
H'holds receiving public assistance	110
H'holds receiving social security	1,206

Households, 2000
Total households	5,780
With persons under 18	1,783
With persons over 65	1,232
Family households	3,447
Single-person households	1,951
Persons per household	2.35
Persons per family	3.08

Labor & Employment
Total civilian labor force, 2006**	8,062
Unemployment rate	4.0%
Total civilian labor force, 2000	7,511
Unemployment rate	4.4%

Employed persons 16 years and over by occupation, 2000
Managers & professionals	3,215
Service occupations	958
Sales & office occupations	2,046
Farming, fishing & forestry	0
Construction & maintenance	384
Production & transportation	579
Self-employed persons	288

* US Census Bureau
** New Jersey Department of Labor

General Information
Borough of Eatontown
47 Broad St
Eatontown, NJ 07724
732-389-7621

Website	www.eatontownnj.com
Year of incorporation	1926
Land/water area (sq. miles)	5.92/0.01
Form of government	Borough

Government
Legislative Districts
US Congressional	12
State Legislative	11

Local Officials, 2008
Mayor	Gerald Tarantolo
Manager/Admin	NA
Clerk	Karen Siano
Finance Dir	Lesley Connolly
Tax Assessor	Thomas Lenahan
Tax Collector	Patricia DePonti
Attorney	Gene Anthony
Building	Wallace Englehart
Comm Dev/Planning	NA
Engineering	Edward Broberg
Public Works	Nate Albert
Police Chief	George Jackson
Emerg/Fire Director	William Mego

Housing & Construction
Housing Units, 2000*
Total	6,341
Median rent	$766
Median SF home value	$178,200

Permits for New Residential Construction
	Units	Value
Total, 2007	89	$8,408,866
Single family	17	$2,347,366
Total, 2006	26	$4,429,828
Single family	26	$4,429,828

Real Property Valuation, 2007
	Parcels	Valuation
Total	3,207	$2,483,299,100
Vacant	173	50,434,200
Residential	2,765	1,103,387,000
Commercial	196	938,918,200
Industrial	42	213,318,200
Apartments	23	176,808,300
Farm land	6	16,300
Farm homestead	2	416,900

Average Property Value & Tax, 2007
Residential value	$398,917
Property tax	$6,439
Tax credit/rebate	$996

Public Library
Eatontown Public Library
33 Broad St
Eatontown, NJ 07724
732-389-2665

Director	Amy Garibay

Library statistics, 2006
Population served	14,008
Full-time/total staff	NA/0

	Total	Per capita
Holdings	NA	NA
Revenues	NA	NA
Expenditures	NA	NA
Annual visits	NA	NA
Internet terminals/annual users	NA/NA	

Taxes
	2005	2006	2007
General tax rate per $100	3.322	1.441	1.615
County equalization ratio	62.61	124.46	111.25
Net valuation taxable	$1,069,828,539	$2,626,436,100	$2,490,880,992
State equalized value	$2,066,502,876	$2,368,717,720	$2,419,254,321

Public Safety
Number of officers, 2006	35

Crime
	2005	2006
Total crimes	545	639
Violent	23	36
Murder	0	0
Rape	4	4
Robbery	8	16
Aggravated assault	11	16
Non-violent	522	603
Burglary	32	50
Larceny	473	536
Vehicle theft	17	17
Domestic violence	54	47
Arson	2	0
Total crime rate	38.5	45.4
Violent	1.6	2.6
Non-violent	36.9	42.8

Public School District
(for school year 2006-07 except as noted)

Eatontown School District
67 Wyckoff Rd
Eatontown, NJ 07724
732-542-1310

Superintendent	Barbara Struble
Number of schools	4
Grade plan	K-8
Enrollment	1,173
Attendance rate, '05-06	95.8%
Dropout rate	NA
Students per teacher	9.5
Per pupil expenditure	$14,825
Median faculty salary	$61,650
Median administrator salary	$125,000
Grade 12 enrollment	NA
High school graduation rate	NA

Assessment test results
(percent scoring at proficient or advanced level)
	Language	Math
NJASK-Grade 3	88.8%	90.4%
GEPA-Grade 8	82.3%	77.9%
HSPA-High School	NA	NA

SAT score averages
Pct tested	Math	Verbal	Writing
NA	NA	NA	NA

Teacher Qualifications
Avg. years of experience	17
Highly-qualified teachers one subject/all subjects	99.0%/99.0%
With emergency credentials	0.0%

No Child Left Behind
AYP, 2005-06	Meets Standards

Municipal Finance
State Aid Programs, 2008
Total aid	$1,879,717
CMPTRA	513,294
Energy tax receipts	1,366,421
Garden State Trust	2

General Budget, 2007
Total tax levy	$40,207,931
County levy	5,996,154
County taxes	5,354,889
County library	306,610
County health	0
County open space	334,656
School levy	22,460,302
Muni. levy	11,751,475
Misc. revenues	8,398,882

Bergen County
Edgewater Borough

Demographics & Socio-Economic Characteristics
(2000 US Census, except as noted)

Population
1980*	4,628
1990*	5,001
2000	7,677
Male	3,739
Female	3,938
2006 (estimate)*	9,628
Population density	11,327.1

Race & Hispanic Origin, 2000
Race
White	5,153
Black/African American	270
American Indian/Alaska Native	16
Asian	1,775
Native Hawaiian/Pacific Islander	3
Other race	226
Two or more races	234
Hispanic origin, total	802
Mexican	71
Puerto Rican	169
Cuban	102
Other Hispanic	460

Age & Nativity, 2000
Under 5 years	430
18 years and over	6,494
21 years and over	6,362
65 years and over	687
85 years and over	67
Median age	36.3
Native-born	4,954
Foreign-born	2,723

Educational Attainment, 2000
Population 25 years and over	6,124
Less than 9th grade	2.8%
High school grad or higher	90.8%
Bachelor's degree or higher	51.4%
Graduate degree	18.6%

Income & Poverty, 1999
Per capita income	$42,650
Median household income	$63,455
Median family income	$72,692
Persons in poverty	662
H'holds receiving public assistance	51
H'holds receiving social security	551

Households, 2000
Total households	3,836
With persons under 18	800
With persons over 65	551
Family households	1,973
Single-person households	1,499
Persons per household	2.00
Persons per family	2.70

Labor & Employment
Total civilian labor force, 2006**	5,114
Unemployment rate	4.0%
Total civilian labor force, 2000	4,817
Unemployment rate	4.0%

Employed persons 16 years and over by occupation, 2000
Managers & professionals	2,494
Service occupations	342
Sales & office occupations	1,203
Farming, fishing & forestry	0
Construction & maintenance	202
Production & transportation	385
Self-employed persons	174

* US Census Bureau
** New Jersey Department of Labor
§ State Fiscal Year July 1–June 30

See Introduction for an explanation of all data sources.

General Information
Borough of Edgewater
916 River Rd
Edgewater, NJ 07020
201-943-1700

Website	www.edgewaternj.org
Year of incorporation	1899
Land/water area (sq. miles)	0.85/1.57
Form of government	Borough

Government
Legislative Districts
US Congressional	9
State Legislative	38

Local Officials, 2008
Mayor	Nancy Merse
Manager	Greg Franz
Clerk	Barbara Rae
Finance Dir	Joseph Iannaconi Jr
Tax Assessor	Art Carlson
Tax Collector	Joseph Iannaconi Jr
Attorney	Philip Boggia
Building	John Candelmo
Planning	John Candelmo
Engineering	Neglia Engineering
Public Works Superint	Thomas Quinton
Police Chief	Donald Martin
Emerg/Fire Director	Joseph Chevalier

Housing & Construction
Housing Units, 2000*
Total	4,277
Median rent	$1,209
Median SF home value	$283,900

Permits for New Residential Construction
	Units	Value
Total, 2007	75	$7,076,424
Single family	8	$2,183,724
Total, 2006	55	$7,359,454
Single family	1	$25,000

Real Property Valuation, 2007
	Parcels	Valuation
Total	3,117	$1,115,902,900
Vacant	194	27,174,800
Residential	2,753	588,285,400
Commercial	109	236,662,300
Industrial	12	16,900,800
Apartments	49	246,879,600
Farm land	0	0
Farm homestead	0	0

Average Property Value & Tax, 2007
Residential value	$213,689
Property tax	$6,325
Tax credit/rebate	$922

Public Library
Edgewater Free Public Library
49 Hudson Ave
Edgewater, NJ 07020
201-224-6144

Director	Linda Corona

Library statistics, 2006
Population served	7,677
Full-time/total staff	1/4

	Total	Per capita
Holdings	28,007	3.65
Revenues	$568,023	$73.99
Expenditures	$491,433	$64.01
Annual visits	40,494	5.27
Internet terminals/annual users	7/34,200	

Taxes
	2005	2006	2007
General tax rate per $100	2.72	2.84	2.96
County equalization ratio	56.17	55.45	42.38
Net valuation taxable	$1,062,824,270	$1,095,842,800	$1,116,344,757
State equalized value	$1,916,725,464	$2,586,322,619	$2,753,039,045

Public Safety
Number of officers, 2006	29

Crime
	2005	2006
Total crimes	166	194
Violent	8	16
Murder	0	0
Rape	0	0
Robbery	4	5
Aggravated assault	4	11
Non-violent	158	178
Burglary	16	30
Larceny	125	135
Vehicle theft	17	13
Domestic violence	45	40
Arson	0	0
Total crime rate	17.7	20.1
Violent	0.9	1.7
Non-violent	16.9	18.5

Public School District
(for school year 2006-07 except as noted)

Edgewater School District
251 Undercliff Ave
Edgewater, NJ 07020
201-945-4106

Superintendent	Ted I. Blumstein
Number of schools	1
Grade plan	K-6
Enrollment	424
Attendance rate, '05-06	95.7%
Dropout rate	NA
Students per teacher	10.3
Per pupil expenditure	$16,909
Median faculty salary	$50,689
Median administrator salary	$94,560
Grade 12 enrollment	NA
High school graduation rate	NA

Assessment test results
(percent scoring at proficient or advanced level)
	Language	Math
NJASK-Grade 3	93.8%	100.0%
GEPA-Grade 8	NA	NA
HSPA-High School	NA	NA

SAT score averages
Pct tested	Math	Verbal	Writing
NA	NA	NA	NA

Teacher Qualifications
Avg. years of experience	9
Highly-qualified teachers one subject/all subjects	100%/100%
With emergency credentials	0.0%

No Child Left Behind
AYP, 2005-06	Meets Standards

Municipal Finance §
State Aid Programs, 2008
Total aid	$807,804
CMPTRA	352,899
Energy tax receipts	454,905
Garden State Trust	0

General Budget, 2007
Total tax levy	$33,042,984
County levy	4,912,556
County taxes	4,642,108
County library	0
County health	0
County open space	270,448
School levy	12,131,790
Muni. levy	15,998,638
Misc. revenues	9,753,188

The New Jersey Municipal Data Book

Edgewater Park Township

Burlington County

Demographics & Socio-Economic Characteristics
(2000 US Census, except as noted)

Population
1980*	9,273
1990*	8,388
2000	7,864
Male	3,789
Female	4,075
2006 (estimate)*	7,968
Population density	2,738.1

Race & Hispanic Origin, 2000
Race
White	5,353
Black/African American	1,683
American Indian/Alaska Native	13
Asian	256
Native Hawaiian/Pacific Islander	1
Other race	252
Two or more races	306
Hispanic origin, total	519
Mexican	70
Puerto Rican	211
Cuban	4
Other Hispanic	234

Age & Nativity, 2000
Under 5 years	462
18 years and over	6,053
21 years and over	5,773
65 years and over	1,025
85 years and over	58
Median age	37.9
Native-born	7,188
Foreign-born	676

Educational Attainment, 2000
Population 25 years and over	5,527
Less than 9th grade	3.5%
High school grad or higher	85.8%
Bachelor's degree or higher	19.6%
Graduate degree	4.1%

Income & Poverty, 1999
Per capita income	$22,920
Median household income	$48,936
Median family income	$52,016
Persons in poverty	677
H'holds receiving public assistance	95
H'holds receiving social security	973

Households, 2000
Total households	3,152
With persons under 18	1,044
With persons over 65	782
Family households	2,099
Single-person households	868
Persons per household	2.49
Persons per family	3.03

Labor & Employment
Total civilian labor force, 2006**	5,049
Unemployment rate	5.3%
Total civilian labor force, 2000	4,322
Unemployment rate	4.8%

Employed persons 16 years and over by occupation, 2000
Managers & professionals	1,384
Service occupations	578
Sales & office occupations	1,105
Farming, fishing & forestry	0
Construction & maintenance	389
Production & transportation	658
Self-employed persons	192

‡ Joint library with Beverly City
* US Census Bureau
** New Jersey Department of Labor

General Information
Township of Edgewater Park
400 Delanco Rd
Edgewater Park, NJ 08010
609-877-2050

Website	www.edgewaterpark-nj.com
Year of incorporation	1924
Land/water area (sq. miles)	2.91/0.13
Form of government	Township

Government
Legislative Districts
US Congressional	3
State Legislative	7

Local Officials, 2008
Mayor	Judy Hall
Manager	Linda Dougherty
Clerk	Linda Dougherty
Finance Dir.	Frank VanGelder
Tax Assessor	Leo Midure
Tax Collector	Tanyika Johns
Attorney	William Kearns
Building	Jim Scott
Comm Dev/Planning	NA
Engineering	Remington & Vernick
Public Works	Aubrey Painter
Public Safety Dir	Robert Brian
Emerg/Fire Director	(Beverly Fire Dept)

Housing & Construction
Housing Units, 2000*
Total	3,301
Median rent	$661
Median SF home value	$119,800

Permits for New Residential Construction
	Units	Value
Total, 2007	0	$21,400
Single family	0	$21,400
Total, 2006	0	$260,087
Single family	0	$260,087

Real Property Valuation, 2007
	Parcels	Valuation
Total	2,543	$310,184,000
Vacant	65	3,086,800
Residential	2,388	237,589,700
Commercial	58	33,838,100
Industrial	9	4,442,100
Apartments	9	30,490,400
Farm land	10	134,700
Farm homestead	4	602,200

Average Property Value & Tax, 2007
Residential value	$99,579
Property tax	$4,009
Tax credit/rebate	$852

Public Library
Beverly Public Library‡
441 Cooper St
Beverly, NJ 08010
609-387-1259

Director	Tracey Hall

Library statistics, 2006
Population served	2,661
Full-time/total staff	NA/0

	Total	Per capita
Holdings	NA	NA
Revenues	NA	NA
Expenditures	NA	NA
Annual visits	NA	NA
Internet terminals/annual users	NA/NA	

Taxes
	2005	2006	2007
General tax rate per $100	3.47	3.695	4.03
County equalization ratio	67.76	62.82	54.09
Net valuation taxable	$311,021,411	$309,653,200	$310,588,619
State equalized value	$495,099,349	$572,933,783	$636,679,491

Public Safety
Number of officers, 2006 ... 14

Crime	2005	2006
Total crimes	218	224
Violent	16	23
Murder	0	0
Rape	3	5
Robbery	6	8
Aggravated assault	7	10
Non-violent	202	201
Burglary	26	52
Larceny	152	127
Vehicle theft	24	22
Domestic violence	157	105
Arson	0	1
Total crime rate	27.0	27.9
Violent	2.0	2.9
Non-violent	25.0	25.1

Public School District
(for school year 2006-07 except as noted)

Edgewater Park Township School District
25 Washington Ave
Edgewater Park, NJ 08010
609-877-2124

Superintendent	Scott Streckenbein
Number of schools	2
Grade plan	K-8
Enrollment	846
Attendance rate, '05-06	94.7%
Dropout rate	NA
Students per teacher	10.0
Per pupil expenditure	$12,558
Median faculty salary	$55,600
Median administrator salary	$103,000
Grade 12 enrollment	NA
High school graduation rate	NA

Assessment test results
(percent scoring at proficient or advanced level)
	Language	Math
NJASK-Grade 3	84.4%	81.1%
GEPA-Grade 8	66.6%	60.5%
HSPA-High School	NA	NA

SAT score averages
Pct tested	Math	Verbal	Writing
NA	NA	NA	NA

Teacher Qualifications
Avg. years of experience	14
Highly-qualified teachers one subject/all subjects	98.5%/98.5%
With emergency credentials	0.0%

No Child Left Behind
AYP, 2005-06 ... Meets Standards

Municipal Finance
State Aid Programs, 2008
Total aid	$775,860
CMPTRA	164,170
Energy tax receipts	611,690
Garden State Trust	0

General Budget, 2007
Total tax levy	$12,504,338
County levy	2,423,278
County taxes	2,008,019
County library	184,268
County health	0
County open space	230,992
School levy	7,158,917
Muni. levy	2,922,143
Misc. revenues	2,706,690

Middlesex County
Edison Township

Demographics & Socio-Economic Characteristics[†]
(2000 US Census, except as noted)

Population
1980*	70,193
1990*	88,680
2000	97,687
Male	47,926
Female	49,761
2006 (estimate)*	99,523
Population density	3,304.2

Race & Hispanic Origin, 2000
Race
White	58,116
Black/African American	6,728
American Indian/Alaska Native	132
Asian	28,597
Native Hawaiian/Pacific Islander	37
Other race	1,973
Two or more races	2,104
Hispanic origin, total	6,226
Mexican	546
Puerto Rican	2,095
Cuban	590
Other Hispanic	2,995

Age & Nativity, 2000
Under 5 years	6,299
18 years and over	75,365
21 years and over	72,264
65 years and over	11,668
85 years and over	1,247
Median age	36.3
Native-born	65,336
Foreign-born	32,351

Educational Attainment, 2000
Population 25 years and over	67,649
Less than 9th grade	4.4%
High school grad or higher	87.6%
Bachelor's degree or higher	42.3%
Graduate degree	17.2%

Income & Poverty, 1999
Per capita income	$30,148
Median household income	$69,746
Median family income	$77,976
Persons in poverty	4,606
H'holds receiving public assistance	455
H'holds receiving social security	7,681

Households, 2000
Total households	35,136
With persons under 18	12,887
With persons over 65	7,991
Family households	25,881
Single-person households	7,419
Persons per household	2.72
Persons per family	3.19

Labor & Employment
Total civilian labor force, 2006**	56,337
Unemployment rate	3.6%
Total civilian labor force, 2000	52,409
Unemployment rate	4.1%

Employed persons 16 years and over by occupation, 2000
Managers & professionals	23,944
Service occupations	4,449
Sales & office occupations	14,077
Farming, fishing & forestry	13
Construction & maintenance	2,626
Production & transportation	5,144
Self-employed persons	1,684

[†] see Appendix C for American Community Survey data
* US Census Bureau
** New Jersey Department of Labor
§ State Fiscal Year July 1–June 30

See Introduction for an explanation of all data sources.

General Information
Township of Edison
100 Municipal Blvd
Edison, NJ 08817
732-248-7200

Website	www.edisonnj.org
Year of incorporation	1954
Land/water area (sq. miles)	30.12/0.57
Form of government	Mayor-Council

Government
Legislative Districts
US Congressional	6, 7
State Legislative	18

Local Officials, 2008
Mayor	Jun H. Choi
Manager	Anthony Cancro
Clerk	Reina Murphy
Finance Dir	David Hollberg
Tax Assessor	Victoria Riddle
Tax Collector	Marilyn Chetrancold
Attorney	Jeffrey Lehrer
Building	Edward Wheeler
Planning	Brandy Forbes
Engineering	John Medina
Public Works	Jeff Roderman
Police Chief	Ronald Gerba (Actg)
Emerg/Fire Director	Norman Jensen

Housing & Construction
Housing Units, 2000*
Total	36,018
Median rent	$913
Median SF home value	$186,900

Permits for New Residential Construction
	Units	Value
Total, 2007	94	$16,468,381
Single family	40	$14,782,381
Total, 2006	338	$19,490,628
Single family	19	$15,625,996

Real Property Valuation, 2007
	Parcels	Valuation
Total	27,313	$7,329,545,300
Vacant	1,193	167,916,500
Residential	24,863	4,322,860,900
Commercial	867	1,105,731,700
Industrial	310	1,278,726,600
Apartments	74	454,295,000
Farm land	6	14,600
Farm homestead	0	0

Average Property Value & Tax, 2007
Residential value	$173,867
Property tax	$6,467
Tax credit/rebate	$1,059

Public Library
Edison Public Library
340 Plainfield Ave
Edison, NJ 08817
732-287-2298

Director	Judith Mansbach

Library statistics, 2006
Population served	97,687
Full-time/total staff	1/3

	Total	Per capita
Holdings	301,585	3.09
Revenues	$5,426,350	$55.55
Expenditures	$5,347,834	$54.74
Annual visits	532,867	5.45
Internet terminals/annual users	26/50,625	

Taxes
	2005	2006	2007
General tax rate per $100	3.35	3.59	3.72
County equalization ratio	65.26	58.05	52.93
Net valuation taxable	$7,276,174,542	$7,291,812,000	$7,339,891,295
State equalized value	$12,534,323,070	$13,787,645,360	$15,385,939,240

Public Safety
Number of officers, 2006 204

Crime	2005	2006
Total crimes	2,696	2,618
Violent	234	295
Murder	0	1
Rape	6	15
Robbery	71	86
Aggravated assault	157	193
Non-violent	2,462	2,323
Burglary	470	369
Larceny	1,720	1,686
Vehicle theft	272	268
Domestic violence	357	364
Arson	18	12
Total crime rate	26.9	26.1
Violent	2.3	2.9
Non-violent	24.6	23.1

Public School District
(for school year 2006-07 except as noted)

Edison Township School District
312 Pierson Ave
Edison, NJ 08837
732-452-4900

Superintendent	John DiMuzio (Actg)
Number of schools	17
Grade plan	K-12
Enrollment	13,690
Attendance rate, '05-06	96.1%
Dropout rate	0.6%
Students per teacher	10.8
Per pupil expenditure	$12,601
Median faculty salary	$65,627
Median administrator salary	$109,600
Grade 12 enrollment	1,040
High school graduation rate	NA

Assessment test results
(percent scoring at proficient or advanced level)
	Language	Math
NJASK-Grade 3	91.0%	94.3%
GEPA-Grade 8	87.3%	81.1%
HSPA-High School	92.3%	84.6%

SAT score averages
Pct tested	Math	Verbal	Writing
NA	NA	NA	NA

Teacher Qualifications
Avg. years of experience	8
Highly-qualified teachers one subject/all subjects	99.5%/99.5%
With emergency credentials	0.1%

No Child Left Behind
AYP, 2005-06 .... Needs Improvement

Municipal Finance[§]
State Aid Programs, 2008
Total aid	$19,999,703
CMPTRA	0
Energy tax receipts	19,970,443
Garden State Trust	29,260

General Budget, 2007
Total tax levy	$273,027,107
County levy	39,626,085
County taxes	35,471,397
County library	0
County health	0
County open space	4,154,688
School levy	163,798,816
Muni. levy	69,602,206
Misc. revenues	37,758,695

©2008 Information Publications, Inc. All rights reserved. Photocopying prohibited. For additional copies, contact the publisher at www.informationpublications.com or (877)544-INFO (4636)

The New Jersey Municipal Data Book

Egg Harbor City — Atlantic County

Demographics & Socio-Economic Characteristics
(2000 US Census, except as noted)

Population
1980*	4,618
1990*	4,583
2000	4,545
Male	2,197
Female	2,348
2006 (estimate)*	4,454
Population density	400.9

Race & Hispanic Origin, 2000
Race
White	3,036
Black/African American	645
American Indian/Alaska Native	17
Asian	57
Native Hawaiian/Pacific Islander	4
Other race	613
Two or more races	173
Hispanic origin, total	1,116
Mexican	77
Puerto Rican	880
Cuban	10
Other Hispanic	149

Age & Nativity, 2000
Under 5 years	305
18 years and over	3,261
21 years and over	3,070
65 years and over	633
85 years and over	57
Median age	34.9
Native-born	4,286
Foreign-born	259

Educational Attainment, 2000
Population 25 years and over	2,928
Less than 9th grade	8.5%
High school grad or higher	70.0%
Bachelor's degree or higher	10.2%
Graduate degree	2.5%

Income & Poverty, 1999
Per capita income	$15,151
Median household income	$32,956
Median family income	$40,040
Persons in poverty	588
H'holds receiving public assistance	33
H'holds receiving social security	534

Households, 2000
Total households	1,658
With persons under 18	645
With persons over 65	459
Family households	1,150
Single-person households	413
Persons per household	2.70
Persons per family	3.20

Labor & Employment
Total civilian labor force, 2006**	2,352
Unemployment rate	8.7%
Total civilian labor force, 2000	2,170
Unemployment rate	9.7%

Employed persons 16 years and over by occupation, 2000
Managers & professionals	297
Service occupations	455
Sales & office occupations	579
Farming, fishing & forestry	0
Construction & maintenance	242
Production & transportation	387
Self-employed persons	49

‡ Branch of county library
* US Census Bureau
** New Jersey Department of Labor

General Information
City of Egg Harbor
500 London Ave
Egg Harbor City, NJ 08215
609-965-0081

Website	www.eggharborcity.org
Year of incorporation	1858
Land/water area (sq. miles)	11.11/0.43
Form of government	City

Government
Legislative Districts
US Congressional	2
State Legislative	2

Local Officials, 2008
Mayor	Joseph A. Kuehner Jr
Manager	Thomas Henshaw
Clerk	Lillian DeBow
Finance Dir	Betty Wenzel
Tax Assessor	Gregory Busa
Tax Collector	Beverly Totten
Attorney	James Carroll
Building	Wayne Gibson
Planner	Tim Michel
Engineering	Remington & Vernick
Public Works	NA
Police Chief	John McColgan
Emerg/Fire Director	Russell Fenton

Housing & Construction
Housing Units, 2000*
Total	1,770
Median rent	$615
Median SF home value	$86,800

Permits for New Residential Construction
	Units	Value
Total, 2007	12	$1,166,589
Single family	12	$1,166,589
Total, 2006	14	$1,456,544
Single family	14	$1,456,544

Real Property Valuation, 2007
	Parcels	Valuation
Total	2,508	$297,327,800
Vacant	1,103	7,940,600
Residential	1,229	231,678,700
Commercial	149	42,528,400
Industrial	16	8,236,700
Apartments	11	6,943,400
Farm land	0	0
Farm homestead	0	0

Average Property Value & Tax, 2007
Residential value	$188,510
Property tax	$4,673
Tax credit/rebate	$935

Public Library
Egg Harbor City Branch Library‡
134 Philadelphia Ave
Egg Harbor City, NJ 08215
609-804-1063

Branch Librarian: Molly Montee

Library statistics, 2006
see Atlantic County profile for library system statistics

Public Safety
Number of officers, 2006: 13

Crime	2005	2006
Total crimes	108	106
Violent	15	13
Murder	1	0
Rape	0	0
Robbery	5	6
Aggravated assault	9	7
Non-violent	93	93
Burglary	19	28
Larceny	71	63
Vehicle theft	3	2
Domestic violence	47	30
Arson	0	0
Total crime rate	24.0	23.6
Violent	3.3	2.9
Non-violent	20.7	20.7

Public School District
(for school year 2006-07 except as noted)

Egg Harbor City School District
527 Philadelphia Ave
Egg Harbor City, NJ 08215
609-965-1034

Superintendent	John Gilly III
Number of schools	2
Grade plan	K-8
Enrollment	520
Attendance rate, '05-06	93.7%
Dropout rate	NA
Students per teacher	8.8
Per pupil expenditure	$15,312
Median faculty salary	$43,063
Median administrator salary	$80,000
Grade 12 enrollment	NA
High school graduation rate	NA

Assessment test results
(percent scoring at proficient or advanced level)
	Language	Math
NJASK-Grade 3	59.1%	63.6%
GEPA-Grade 8	56.6%	59.3%
HSPA-High School	NA	NA

SAT score averages
Pct tested	Math	Verbal	Writing
NA	NA	NA	NA

Teacher Qualifications
Avg. years of experience	7
Highly-qualified teachers one subject/all subjects	100%/100%
With emergency credentials	0.0%

No Child Left Behind
AYP, 2005-06: Meets Standards

Municipal Finance
State Aid Programs, 2008
Total aid	$348,081
CMPTRA	0
Energy tax receipts	347,974
Garden State Trust	107

General Budget, 2007
Total tax levy	$7,428,643
County levy	917,972
County taxes	730,358
County library	90,741
County health	36,975
County open space	59,898
School levy	3,309,361
Muni. levy	3,201,310
Misc. revenues	3,075,354

Taxes
	2005	2006	2007
General tax rate per $100	5.183	2.309	2.479
County equalization ratio	65.8	131.9	100.88
Net valuation taxable	$125,448,242	$295,460,100	$299,694,731
State equalized value	$224,535,962	$295,187,653	$328,777,953

Atlantic County
Egg Harbor Township

Demographics & Socio-Economic Characteristics
(2000 US Census, except as noted)

Population
1980*	19,381
1990*	24,544
2000	30,726
Male	14,934
Female	15,792
2006 (estimate)*	38,793
Population density	576.0

Race & Hispanic Origin, 2000
Race
White	24,404
Black/African American	3,185
American Indian/Alaska Native	66
Asian	1,552
Native Hawaiian/Pacific Islander	15
Other race	868
Two or more races	636
Hispanic origin, total	2,076
Mexican	213
Puerto Rican	1,098
Cuban	44
Other Hispanic	721

Age & Nativity, 2000
Under 5 years	2,278
18 years and over	22,142
21 years and over	21,198
65 years and over	2,815
85 years and over	274
Median age	36.0
Native-born	28,047
Foreign-born	2,572

Educational Attainment, 2000
Population 25 years and over	20,071
Less than 9th grade	5.4%
High school grad or higher	82.8%
Bachelor's degree or higher	19.0%
Graduate degree	5.5%

Income & Poverty, 1999
Per capita income	$22,328
Median household income	$52,550
Median family income	$60,032
Persons in poverty	1,637
H'holds receiving public assistance	245
H'holds receiving social security	2,411

Households, 2000
Total households	11,199
With persons under 18	4,617
With persons over 65	2,167
Family households	8,106
Single-person households	2,467
Persons per household	2.74
Persons per family	3.23

Labor & Employment
Total civilian labor force, 2006**	21,510
Unemployment rate	4.8%
Total civilian labor force, 2000	16,367
Unemployment rate	4.2%

Employed persons 16 years and over by occupation, 2000
Managers & professionals	4,188
Service occupations	4,276
Sales & office occupations	4,058
Farming, fishing & forestry	16
Construction & maintenance	1,708
Production & transportation	1,437
Self-employed persons	803

‡ Branch of county library
* US Census Bureau
** New Jersey Department of Labor

See Introduction for an explanation of all data sources.

General Information
Egg Harbor Township
3515 Bargaintown Rd
Egg Harbor Township, NJ 08234
609-926-4000

Website	www.ehtgov.org
Year of incorporation	1693
Land/water area (sq. miles)	67.35/7.61
Form of government	Township

Government
Legislative Districts
US Congressional	2
State Legislative	2

Local Officials, 2008
Mayor	James McCollough
Manager	Peter J. Miller
Clerk	Eileen M. Tedesco
Finance Dir	Charlene Canale
Tax Assessor	Maryanne Lavner
Tax Collector	Sharon Miller
Attorney	Marc Friedman
Building	Pat Natchionne
Planning	Theresa Wilbert
Township Engineer	James Mott
Public Works	Al Simerson
Police Chief	Blaze Catania
Emerg/Fire Director	Bill Danz Jr

Housing & Construction
Housing Units, 2000*
Total	12,067
Median rent	$700
Median SF home value	$131,300

Permits for New Residential Construction
	Units	Value
Total, 2007	335	$34,774,721
Single family	335	$34,774,721
Total, 2006	616	$58,813,683
Single family	573	$58,315,183

Real Property Valuation, 2007
	Parcels	Valuation
Total	19,448	$2,415,980,000
Vacant	5,243	159,294,300
Residential	13,209	1,800,348,500
Commercial	902	444,702,400
Industrial	0	0
Apartments	21	8,452,000
Farm land	56	399,800
Farm homestead	17	2,783,000

Average Property Value & Tax, 2007
Residential value	$136,332
Property tax	$4,880
Tax credit/rebate	$880

Public Library
Egg Harbor Township Branch Library‡
1 Swift Ave
Egg Harbor Township, NJ 08234
609-927-8664

Branch Librarian........William D. Paulin

Library statistics, 2006
see Atlantic County profile for library system statistics

Taxes
	2005	2006	2007
General tax rate per $100	3.245	3.359	3.579
County equalization ratio	68.23	57.29	50.97
Net valuation taxable	$2,174,128,643	$2,281,667,500	$2,422,334,498
State equalized value	$3,794,953,121	$4,483,497,977	$5,080,876,657

Public Safety
Number of officers, 2006 95

Crime	2005	2006
Total crimes	1,240	1,290
Violent	72	88
Murder	3	7
Rape	2	6
Robbery	27	35
Aggravated assault	40	40
Non-violent	1,168	1,202
Burglary	231	283
Larceny	892	888
Vehicle theft	45	31
Domestic violence	460	400
Arson	20	13
Total crime rate	33.6	33.9
Violent	2.0	2.3
Non-violent	31.7	31.6

Public School District
(for school year 2006-07 except as noted)

Egg Harbor Township School District
13 Swift Dr
Egg Harbor Township, NJ 08234
609-646-7911

Superintendent	Philip Heery
Number of schools	5
Grade plan	K-12
Enrollment	4,951
Attendance rate, '05-06	94.5%
Dropout rate	1.9%
Students per teacher	11.9
Per pupil expenditure	$11,010
Median faculty salary	$46,950
Median administrator salary	$87,772
Grade 12 enrollment	519
High school graduation rate	91.2%

Assessment test results
(percent scoring at proficient or advanced level)
	Language	Math
NJASK-Grade 3	83.6%	85.5%
GEPA-Grade 8	66.6%	66.7%
HSPA-High School	83.1%	68.6%

SAT score averages
Pct tested	Math	Verbal	Writing
61%	486	477	468

Teacher Qualifications
Avg. years of experience	8
Highly-qualified teachers one subject/all subjects	99.5%/99.5%
With emergency credentials	0.0%

No Child Left Behind
AYP, 2005-06 .... Meets Standards

Municipal Finance
State Aid Programs, 2008
Total aid	$6,965,260
CMPTRA	0
Energy tax receipts	6,933,042
Garden State Trust	15,439

General Budget, 2007
Total tax levy	$86,700,985
County taxes	14,650,893
County taxes	11,666,184
County library	1,443,581
County health	588,223
County open space	952,905
School levy	61,189,264
Muni. levy	10,860,828
Misc. revenues	22,362,057

Elizabeth City
Union County

Demographics & Socio-Economic Characteristics[†]
(2000 US Census, except as noted)

Population
1980*	106,201
1990*	110,002
2000	120,568
Male	59,674
Female	60,894
2006 (estimate)*	126,179
Population density	10,325.6

Race & Hispanic Origin, 2000
Race
White	67,250
Black/African American	24,090
American Indian/Alaska Native	580
Asian	2,830
Native Hawaiian/Pacific Islander	55
Other race	18,702
Two or more races	7,061
Hispanic origin, total	59,627
Mexican	1,612
Puerto Rican	12,989
Cuban	7,069
Other Hispanic	37,957

Age & Nativity, 2000
Under 5 years	9,266
18 years and over	88,888
21 years and over	83,630
65 years and over	12,041
85 years and over	1,556
Median age	32.6
Native-born	67,593
Foreign-born	52,975

Educational Attainment, 2000
Population 25 years and over	75,912
Less than 9th grade	18.1%
High school grad or higher	61.7%
Bachelor's degree or higher	12.1%
Graduate degree	4.2%

Income & Poverty, 1999
Per capita income	$15,114
Median household income	$35,175
Median family income	$38,370
Persons in poverty	20,963
H'holds receiving public assistance	2,532
H'holds receiving social security	8,924

Households, 2000
Total households	40,482
With persons under 18	16,813
With persons over 65	9,034
Family households	28,170
Single-person households	9,944
Persons per household	2.91
Persons per family	3.45

Labor & Employment
Total civilian labor force, 2006**	55,660
Unemployment rate	6.8%
Total civilian labor force, 2000	52,403
Unemployment rate	9.0%

Employed persons 16 years and over by occupation, 2000
Managers & professionals	8,698
Service occupations	8,488
Sales & office occupations	12,356
Farming, fishing & forestry	44
Construction & maintenance	4,539
Production & transportation	13,546
Self-employed persons	1,774

[†] see Appendix C for American Community Survey data
* US Census Bureau
** New Jersey Department of Labor
§ State Fiscal Year July 1–June 30

General Information
City of Elizabeth
50 Winfield Scott Plz
Elizabeth, NJ 07201
908-820-4000

Website	www.elizabethnj.org
Year of incorporation	1855
Land/water area (sq. miles)	12.22/1.43
Form of government	Mayor-Council

Government
Legislative Districts
US Congressional	10, 13
State Legislative	20

Local Officials, 2008
Mayor	J. Christian Bollwage
Manager	Bridget S. Zellner
Clerk	Yolanda M. Roberts
Finance Dir.	Robert Mack
Tax Assessor	Enrico Emma
Tax Collector	Robert A. Mack
Attorney	William Holzapfel
Building	Michael Mazza
Comm Dev/Planning	NA
Engineering	Ernesto Marticorena
Public Works	John F. Papetti Jr
Police Chief	Ronald Simon
Emerg/Fire Director	Edward Sisk

Housing & Construction
Housing Units, 2000*
Total	42,838
Median rent	$681
Median SF home value	$143,000

Permits for New Residential Construction
	Units	Value
Total, 2007	341	$23,004,410
Single family	6	$406,700
Total, 2006	433	$34,406,218
Single family	16	$2,827,400

Real Property Valuation, 2007
	Parcels	Valuation
Total	18,289	$903,635,400
Vacant	1,129	50,421,400
Residential	14,536	492,296,600
Commercial	1,853	181,956,800
Industrial	176	77,715,200
Apartments	595	101,245,400
Farm land	0	0
Farm homestead	0	0

Average Property Value & Tax, 2007
Residential value	$33,867
Property tax	$6,043
Tax credit/rebate	$974

Public Library
Elizabeth Free Public Library
11 South Broad St
Elizabeth, NJ 07202
908-354-6060

Director	Dorothy M. Key

Library statistics, 2006
Population served	120,568
Full-time/total staff	17/45

	Total	Per capita
Holdings	343,505	2.85
Revenues	$3,669,889	$30.44
Expenditures	$3,671,366	$30.45
Annual visits	414,090	3.43
Internet terminals/annual users	111/13,159	

Taxes
	2005	2006	2007
General tax rate per $100	15.604	16.813	17.844
County equalization ratio	14.29	12.23	10.98
Net valuation taxable	$909,344,204	$908,000,600	$905,207,567
State equalized value	$6,883,756,276	$8,271,743,551	$9,212,942,198

Public Safety
Number of officers, 2006		357

Crime	2005	2006
Total crimes	5,974	5,772
Violent	834	905
Murder	17	17
Rape	18	35
Robbery	544	539
Aggravated assault	255	314
Non-violent	5,140	4,867
Burglary	652	682
Larceny	3,033	2,948
Vehicle theft	1,455	1,237
Domestic violence	762	873
Arson	5	11
Total crime rate	47.9	45.9
Violent	6.7	7.2
Non-violent	41.2	38.7

Public School District
(for school year 2006-07 except as noted)

Elizabeth School District
500 N Broad St
Elizabeth, NJ 07207
908-436-5010

Superintendent	Pablo Munoz
Number of schools	30
Grade plan	K-12
Enrollment	21,214
Attendance rate, '05-06	92.7%
Dropout rate	7.2%
Students per teacher	9.0
Per pupil expenditure	$16,102
Median faculty salary	$52,756
Median administrator salary	$102,506
Grade 12 enrollment	1,001
High school graduation rate	74.4%

Assessment test results
(percent scoring at proficient or advanced level)
	Language	Math
NJASK-Grade 3	74.5%	80.2%
GEPA-Grade 8	45.3%	33.5%
HSPA-High School	61.2%	37.0%

SAT score averages
Pct tested	Math	Verbal	Writing
50%	404	395	391

Teacher Qualifications
Avg. years of experience	7
Highly-qualified teachers one subject/all subjects	98.5%/98.5%
With emergency credentials	0.6%

No Child Left Behind
AYP, 2005-06	Needs Improvement

Municipal Finance[§]
State Aid Programs, 2008
Total aid	$33,816,764
CMPTRA	18,133,640
Energy tax receipts	15,683,123
Garden State Trust	1

General Budget, 2007
Total tax levy	$161,525,031
County tax	28,739,316
County taxes	27,482,564
County library	0
County health	0
County open space	1,256,752
School levy	38,651,708
Muni. levy	94,134,006
Misc. revenues	92,325,235

Gloucester County — Elk Township

Demographics & Socio-Economic Characteristics
(2000 US Census, except as noted)

Population
1980*	3,187
1990*	3,806
2000	3,514
Male	1,722
Female	1,792
2006 (estimate)*	3,867
Population density	197.0

Race & Hispanic Origin, 2000
Race
White	2,884
Black/African American	501
American Indian/Alaska Native	20
Asian	15
Native Hawaiian/Pacific Islander	0
Other race	48
Two or more races	46
Hispanic origin, total	103
Mexican	34
Puerto Rican	57
Cuban	2
Other Hispanic	10

Age & Nativity, 2000
Under 5 years	213
18 years and over	2,558
21 years and over	2,432
65 years and over	443
85 years and over	44
Median age	38.2
Native-born	3,444
Foreign-born	70

Educational Attainment, 2000
Population 25 years and over	2,349
Less than 9th grade	6.0%
High school grad or higher	78.6%
Bachelor's degree or higher	13.8%
Graduate degree	5.2%

Income & Poverty, 1999
Per capita income	$18,621
Median household income	$51,047
Median family income	$55,472
Persons in poverty	297
H'holds receiving public assistance	8
H'holds receiving social security	393

Households, 2000
Total households	1,263
With persons under 18	489
With persons over 65	326
Family households	959
Single-person households	248
Persons per household	2.74
Persons per family	3.16

Labor & Employment
Total civilian labor force, 2006**	1,914
Unemployment rate	5.2%
Total civilian labor force, 2000	1,641
Unemployment rate	4.7%

Employed persons 16 years and over by occupation, 2000
Managers & professionals	479
Service occupations	273
Sales & office occupations	367
Farming, fishing & forestry	11
Construction & maintenance	223
Production & transportation	211
Self-employed persons	130

‡ Branch of county library
* US Census Bureau
** New Jersey Department of Labor

See Introduction for an explanation of all data sources.

General Information
Township of Elk
667 Whig Lane Rd
Monroeville, NJ 08343
856-881-6525

Website	www.elktownshipnj.gov
Year of incorporation	1891
Land/water area (sq. miles)	19.63/0.08
Form of government	Township

Government
Legislative Districts
US Congressional	2
State Legislative	3

Local Officials, 2008
Mayor	Philip A. Barbaro Jr
Manager/Admin	NA
Clerk	Debbie Pine
Finance Dir	Steve Considine
Tax Assessor	Darlene Campbell
Tax Collector	Susan DeFrancesco
Attorney	Brian J. Duffield
Building	Anthony Dariano Sr
Planning	Leah Furey
Engineering	J. Michael Fralinger
Public Works	Steven Alexander
Police Chief	Charles DeFalco
Emerg/Fire Director	Dennis Marchei

Housing & Construction
Housing Units, 2000*
Total	1,347
Median rent	$715
Median SF home value	$127,900

Permits for New Residential Construction
	Units	Value
Total, 2007	19	$2,344,457
Single family	19	$2,344,457
Total, 2006	15	$1,724,898
Single family	15	$1,724,898

Real Property Valuation, 2007
	Parcels	Valuation
Total	2,255	$380,163,100
Vacant	517	23,642,500
Residential	1,315	301,100,300
Commercial	58	25,429,300
Industrial	1	1,137,400
Apartments	0	0
Farm land	261	4,295,700
Farm homestead	103	24,557,900

Average Property Value & Tax, 2007
Residential value	$229,660
Property tax	$4,613
Tax credit/rebate	$945

Public Library
Glassboro Public Library‡
2 Center St
Glassboro, NJ 08028
856-881-0001

Director.......Carol Wolf

Library statistics, 2006
see Gloucester County profile for library system statistics

Public Safety
Number of officers, 2006....11

Crime
	2005	2006
Total crimes	78	132
Violent	3	11
Murder	0	0
Rape	0	3
Robbery	0	3
Aggravated assault	3	5
Non-violent	75	121
Burglary	17	29
Larceny	48	86
Vehicle theft	10	6
Domestic violence	63	51
Arson	5	2
Total crime rate	21.2	34.8
Violent	0.8	2.9
Non-violent	20.4	31.9

Public School District
(for school year 2006-07 except as noted)

Elk Township School District
98 Unionville Rd
Glassboro, NJ 08028
856-881-4551

Superintendent	Robert Suessmuth (Int)
Number of schools	1
Grade plan	K-6
Enrollment	371
Attendance rate, '05-06	95.7%
Dropout rate	NA
Students per teacher	9.9
Per pupil expenditure	$12,088
Median faculty salary	$43,102
Median administrator salary	$71,644
Grade 12 enrollment	NA
High school graduation rate	NA

Assessment test results
(percent scoring at proficient or advanced level)
	Language	Math
NJASK-Grade 3	73.4%	71.4%
GEPA-Grade 8	NA	NA
HSPA-High School	NA	NA

SAT score averages
Pct tested	Math	Verbal	Writing
NA	NA	NA	NA

Teacher Qualifications
Avg. years of experience	12
Highly-qualified teachers one subject/all subjects	100%/100%
With emergency credentials	0.0%

No Child Left Behind
AYP, 2005-06........Meets Standards

Municipal Finance
State Aid Programs, 2008
Total aid	$361,001
CMPTRA	0
Energy tax receipts	361,001
Garden State Trust	0

General Budget, 2007
Total tax levy	$7,799,917
County levy	1,933,146
County taxes	1,664,888
County library	137,900
County health	0
County open space	130,358
School levy	4,170,033
Muni. levy	1,696,738
Misc. revenues	2,505,685

Taxes
	2005	2006	2007
General tax rate per $100	3.572	3.643	2.046
County equalization ratio	78.03	70.95	117.17
Net valuation taxable	$184,143,896	$195,826,000	$381,289,205
State equalized value	$259,540,375	$315,856,551	$363,807,941

©2008 Information Publications, Inc. All rights reserved. Photocopying prohibited. For additional copies, contact the publisher at www.informationpublications.com or (877)544-INFO (4636)

Elmer Borough
Salem County

Demographics & Socio-Economic Characteristics
(2000 US Census, except as noted)

Population
1980*	1,569
1990*	1,571
2000	1,384
Male	671
Female	713
2006 (estimate)*	1,370
Population density	1,574.7

Race & Hispanic Origin, 2000
Race
White	1,346
Black/African American	9
American Indian/Alaska Native	0
Asian	7
Native Hawaiian/Pacific Islander	0
Other race	10
Two or more races	12
Hispanic origin, total	21
Mexican	0
Puerto Rican	15
Cuban	0
Other Hispanic	6

Age & Nativity, 2000
Under 5 years	75
18 years and over	1,046
21 years and over	982
65 years and over	214
85 years and over	24
Median age	36.7
Native-born	1,368
Foreign-born	16

Educational Attainment, 2000
Population 25 years and over	920
Less than 9th grade	3.7%
High school grad or higher	85.2%
Bachelor's degree or higher	14.8%
Graduate degree	3.8%

Income & Poverty, 1999
Per capita income	$21,356
Median household income	$46,172
Median family income	$58,438
Persons in poverty	73
H'holds receiving public assistance	12
H'holds receiving social security	150

Households, 2000
Total households	524
With persons under 18	194
With persons over 65	146
Family households	385
Single-person households	117
Persons per household	2.61
Persons per family	3.06

Labor & Employment
Total civilian labor force, 2006**	767
Unemployment rate	3.4%
Total civilian labor force, 2000	757
Unemployment rate	5.8%

Employed persons 16 years and over by occupation, 2000
Managers & professionals	181
Service occupations	91
Sales & office occupations	209
Farming, fishing & forestry	2
Construction & maintenance	80
Production & transportation	150
Self-employed persons	39

* US Census Bureau
** New Jersey Department of Labor

General Information
Borough of Elmer
120 S Main St
PO Box 882
Elmer, NJ 08318
856-358-4010

Website	www.elmerboroughnj.com
Year of incorporation	1893
Land/water area (sq. miles)	0.87/0.01
Form of government	Borough

Government
Legislative Districts
US Congressional	2
State Legislative	3

Local Officials, 2008
Mayor	Joseph P. Stemberger
Manager/Admin	NA
Clerk	Beverly S. Richards
Finance Dir	Darla J. Timberman
Tax Assessor	James Milliken
Tax Collector	Joanne Marone
Attorney	Charles J. Girard
Building	Pittsgrove Township
Comm Dev/Planning	NA
Engineering	John Schweppenheiser
Public Works	NA
Police Captain	Patrick Bryan
Fire Chief	Benjamin Hitzelberger Jr

Housing & Construction
Housing Units, 2000*
Total	557
Median rent	$643
Median SF home value	$103,900

Permits for New Residential Construction
	Units	Value
Total, 2007	3	$152,001
Single family	3	$152,001
Total, 2006	0	$0
Single family	0	$0

Real Property Valuation, 2007
	Parcels	Valuation
Total	631	$104,282,400
Vacant	67	1,351,900
Residential	480	80,908,400
Commercial	60	21,264,800
Industrial	0	0
Apartments	0	0
Farm land	19	97,100
Farm homestead	5	660,200

Average Property Value & Tax, 2007
Residential value	$168,183
Property tax	$3,729
Tax credit/rebate	$850

Public Library
Elmer Public Library
120 S Main St
Elmer, NJ 08318
856-358-2014

Director	Linda Fritz

Library statistics, 2006
Population served	1,384
Full-time/total staff	0/0

	Total	Per capita
Holdings	11,120	8.03
Revenues	$3,500	$2.53
Expenditures	$25,154	$18.17
Annual visits	5,697	4.12
Internet terminals/annual users	5/4,000	

Taxes
	2005	2006	2007
General tax rate per $100	3.934	2.184	2.218
County equalization ratio	74.96	120.92	117.33
Net valuation taxable	$58,002,872	$103,731,800	$105,518,388
State equalized value	$87,091,399	$89,789,370	$104,780,191

Public Safety
Number of officers, 2006		1

Crime	2005	2006
Total crimes	22	37
Violent	0	2
Murder	0	0
Rape	0	0
Robbery	0	0
Aggravated assault	0	2
Non-violent	22	35
Burglary	9	7
Larceny	13	26
Vehicle theft	0	2
Domestic violence	9	11
Arson	0	0
Total crime rate	16.0	26.8
Violent	0.0	1.5
Non-violent	16.0	25.4

Public School District
(for school year 2006-07 except as noted)

Elmer Borough School District
207 Front St, PO Box 596
Elmer, NJ 08318
856-358-6761

Chief School Admin	Stephen E. Berkowitz
Number of schools	1
Grade plan	K-6
Enrollment	81
Attendance rate, '05-06	95.8%
Dropout rate	NA
Students per teacher	11.6
Per pupil expenditure	$12,702
Median faculty salary	$37,947
Median administrator salary	$98,980
Grade 12 enrollment	NA
High school graduation rate	NA

Assessment test results
(percent scoring at proficient or advanced level)
	Language	Math
NJASK-Grade 3	100.0%	100.0%
GEPA-Grade 8	NA	NA
HSPA-High School	NA	NA

SAT score averages
Pct tested	Math	Verbal	Writing
NA	NA	NA	NA

Teacher Qualifications
Avg. years of experience	4
Highly-qualified teachers one subject/all subjects	100%/100%
With emergency credentials	0.0%

No Child Left Behind
AYP, 2005-06	Meets Standards

Municipal Finance
State Aid Programs, 2008
Total aid	$84,326
CMPTRA	0
Energy tax receipts	84,326
Garden State Trust	0

General Budget, 2007
Total tax levy	$2,339,856
County levy	851,557
County taxes	833,392
County library	0
County health	0
County open space	18,166
School levy	1,093,693
Muni. levy	394,606
Misc. revenues	703,105

Bergen County

Elmwood Park Borough

Demographics & Socio-Economic Characteristics
(2000 US Census, except as noted)

Population
1980*	18,377
1990*	17,623
2000	18,925
Male	9,042
Female	9,883
2006 (estimate)*	18,805
Population density	7,096.2

Race & Hispanic Origin, 2000
Race
- White ... 15,619
- Black/African American ... 409
- American Indian/Alaska Native ... 21
- Asian ... 1,477
- Native Hawaiian/Pacific Islander ... 1
- Other race ... 841
- Two or more races ... 557
- Hispanic origin, total ... 2,535
  - Mexican ... 43
  - Puerto Rican ... 535
  - Cuban ... 237
  - Other Hispanic ... 1,720

Age & Nativity, 2000
- Under 5 years ... 1,084
- 18 years and over ... 14,971
- 21 years and over ... 14,380
- 65 years and over ... 3,115
- 85 years and over ... 386
- Median age ... 38.5
- Native-born ... 13,217
- Foreign-born ... 5,708

Educational Attainment, 2000
- Population 25 years and over ... 13,537
- Less than 9th grade ... 7.7%
- High school grad or higher ... 80.0%
- Bachelor's degree or higher ... 20.6%
- Graduate degree ... 6.0%

Income & Poverty, 1999
- Per capita income ... $22,588
- Median household income ... $52,319
- Median family income ... $59,131
- Persons in poverty ... 1,212
- H'holds receiving public assistance ... 140
- H'holds receiving social security ... 2,336

Households, 2000
- Total households ... 7,089
  - With persons under 18 ... 2,275
  - With persons over 65 ... 2,311
  - Family households ... 5,077
  - Single-person households ... 1,645
- Persons per household ... 2.66
- Persons per family ... 3.17

Labor & Employment
- Total civilian labor force, 2006** ... 10,559
  - Unemployment rate ... 4.9%
- Total civilian labor force, 2000 ... 9,945
  - Unemployment rate ... 4.9%

Employed persons 16 years and over by occupation, 2000
- Managers & professionals ... 2,680
- Service occupations ... 1,145
- Sales & office occupations ... 3,345
- Farming, fishing & forestry ... 0
- Construction & maintenance ... 871
- Production & transportation ... 1,421
- Self-employed persons ... 496

* US Census Bureau
** New Jersey Department of Labor

See Introduction for an explanation of all data sources.

General Information
Borough of Elmwood Park
182 Market St
Elmwood Park, NJ 07407
201-796-1457

- Website ... www.elmwoodparknj.us
- Year of incorporation ... 1973
- Land/water area (sq. miles) ... 2.65/0.11
- Form of government ... Borough

Government
Legislative Districts
- US Congressional ... 9
- State Legislative ... 38

Local Officials, 2008
- Mayor ... Richard A. Mola
- Manager/Admin ... NA
- Clerk ... Keith Kazmark
- Finance Dir ... Roy Riggitano
- Tax Assessor ... Pasquale Aceto
- Tax Collector ... Frank Santora
- Attorney ... Brian Giblin
- Building ... John Buonanno
- Planning ... Ronald Vicari
- Engineering ... Peter Ten Kate
- Public Works ... Scott Karcz
- Police Chief ... Donald Ingrasselino
- Emerg/Fire Director ... Ray Appel

Housing & Construction
Housing Units, 2000*
- Total ... 7,242
- Median rent ... $897
- Median SF home value ... $184,100

Permits for New Residential Construction
	Units	Value
Total, 2007	17	$2,075,500
Single family	3	$612,500
Total, 2006	101	$2,376,643
Single family	1	$130,000

Real Property Valuation, 2007
	Parcels	Valuation
Total	5,001	$2,047,328,400
Vacant	64	23,822,600
Residential	4,636	1,534,921,200
Commercial	223	297,067,700
Industrial	58	123,075,400
Apartments	20	68,441,500
Farm land	0	0
Farm homestead	0	0

Average Property Value & Tax, 2007
- Residential value ... $331,087
- Property tax ... $7,092
- Tax credit/rebate ... $1,095

Public Library
Elmwood Park Public Library
210 Lee St
Elmwood Park, NJ 07407
201-796-8888

- Director ... Bobbie Protono

Library statistics, 2006
- Population served ... 18,925
- Full-time/total staff ... 2/5

	Total	Per capita
Holdings	77,113	4.07
Revenues	$761,118	$40.22
Expenditures	$708,200	$37.42
Annual visits	51,538	2.72
Internet terminals/annual users	8/13,250	

Taxes
	2005	2006	2007
General tax rate per $100	1.87	2.01	2.15
County equalization ratio	106.05	90.26	83.77
Net valuation taxable	$2,044,940,201	$2,039,625,500	$2,049,282,597
State equalized value	$2,265,610,681	$2,436,746,485	$2,561,114,697

Public Safety
Number of officers, 2006 ... 46

Crime	2005	2006
Total crimes	420	399
Violent	25	32
Murder	1	0
Rape	0	0
Robbery	10	16
Aggravated assault	14	16
Non-violent	395	367
Burglary	62	59
Larceny	282	277
Vehicle theft	51	31
Domestic violence	226	231
Arson	0	0
Total crime rate	22.1	21.1
Violent	1.3	1.7
Non-violent	20.8	19.4

Public School District
(for school year 2006-07 except as noted)

Elmwood Park School District
465 Boulevard
Elmwood Park, NJ 07407
201-794-2979

- Superintendent ... Joseph Casapulla
- Number of schools ... 5
- Grade plan ... K-12
- Enrollment ... 2,142
- Attendance rate, '05-06 ... 95.6%
- Dropout rate ... NA
- Students per teacher ... 15.4
- Per pupil expenditure ... $12,731
- Median faculty salary ... $48,554
- Median administrator salary ... $103,916
- Grade 12 enrollment ... 167
- High school graduation rate ... 96.0%

Assessment test results
(percent scoring at proficient or advanced level)
	Language	Math
NJASK-Grade 3	78.2%	85.9%
GEPA-Grade 8	73.8%	58.3%
HSPA-High School	82.0%	68.0%

SAT score averages
Pct tested	Math	Verbal	Writing
72%	468	453	470

Teacher Qualifications
- Avg. years of experience ... 8
- Highly-qualified teachers
  one subject/all subjects ... 100%/100%
- With emergency credentials ... 1.0%

No Child Left Behind
- AYP, 2005-06 ... Meets Standards

Municipal Finance
State Aid Programs, 2008
- Total aid ... $1,873,051
- CMPTRA ... 702,140
- Energy tax receipts ... 1,170,911
- Garden State Trust ... 0

General Budget, 2007
- Total tax levy ... $43,975,400
  - County levy ... 4,471,188
    - County taxes ... 4,224,267
    - County library ... 0
    - County health ... 0
    - County open space ... 246,922
  - School levy ... 25,741,716
  - Muni. levy ... 13,762,497
- Misc. revenues ... 8,809,212

The New Jersey Municipal Data Book

Elsinboro Township
Salem County

Demographics & Socio-Economic Characteristics
(2000 US Census, except as noted)

Population
1980*	1,290
1990*	1,170
2000	1,092
Male	518
Female	574
2006 (estimate)*	1,073
Population density	87.4

Race & Hispanic Origin, 2000
Race
White	1,038
Black/African American	39
American Indian/Alaska Native	2
Asian	0
Native Hawaiian/Pacific Islander	0
Other race	3
Two or more races	10
Hispanic origin, total	7
Mexican	0
Puerto Rican	5
Cuban	0
Other Hispanic	2

Age & Nativity, 2000
Under 5 years	52
18 years and over	861
21 years and over	847
65 years and over	216
85 years and over	17
Median age	43.6
Native-born	1,085
Foreign-born	7

Educational Attainment, 2000
Population 25 years and over	814
Less than 9th grade	4.8%
High school grad or higher	83.9%
Bachelor's degree or higher	16.5%
Graduate degree	6.9%

Income & Poverty, 1999
Per capita income	$25,415
Median household income	$50,972
Median family income	$59,688
Persons in poverty	19
H'holds receiving public assistance	5
H'holds receiving social security	170

Households, 2000
Total households	468
With persons under 18	129
With persons over 65	158
Family households	325
Single-person households	123
Persons per household	2.33
Persons per family	2.80

Labor & Employment
Total civilian labor force, 2006**	572
Unemployment rate	1.5%
Total civilian labor force, 2000	559
Unemployment rate	2.9%

Employed persons 16 years and over by occupation, 2000
Managers & professionals	162
Service occupations	77
Sales & office occupations	142
Farming, fishing & forestry	5
Construction & maintenance	67
Production & transportation	90
Self-employed persons	36

* US Census Bureau
** New Jersey Department of Labor

General Information
Township of Elsinboro
619 Salem Fort Elfsborg Rd
Salem, NJ 08079
856-935-2200

Website	NA
Year of incorporation	1701
Land/water area (sq. miles)	12.27/1.06
Form of government	Township

Government
Legislative Districts
US Congressional	2
State Legislative	3

Local Officials, 2008
Mayor	John Elk
Manager/Admin	NA
Clerk	Betty Jean Eby
Finance Dir	John Willadsen
Tax Assessor	R. Shidner
Tax Collector	Joanne Marone
Attorney	M. Hoffman
Building	Wayne Serfass
Planning	David Faulhaber
Engineering	Albert Fralinger Jr
Public Works	NA
Police Chief	Lee Peterson
Emerg/Fire Director	Shawn Love

Housing & Construction
Housing Units, 2000*
Total	530
Median rent	$639
Median SF home value	$110,100

Permits for New Residential Construction
	Units	Value
Total, 2007	0	$0
Single family	0	$0
Total, 2006	1	$209,000
Single family	1	$209,000

Real Property Valuation, 2007
	Parcels	Valuation
Total	844	$57,697,100
Vacant	156	1,458,000
Residential	540	47,158,400
Commercial	10	2,656,100
Industrial	0	0
Apartments	0	0
Farm land	94	1,004,200
Farm homestead	44	5,420,400

Average Property Value & Tax, 2007
Residential value	$90,032
Property tax	$3,713
Tax credit/rebate	$882

Public Library
No public municipal library

Library statistics, 2006
Population served	NA
Full-time/total staff	NA/NA

	Total	Per capita
Holdings	NA	NA
Revenues	NA	NA
Expenditures	NA	NA
Annual visits	NA	NA
Internet terminals/annual users	NA/NA	

Taxes
	2005	2006	2007
General tax rate per $100	3.732	3.882	4.125
County equalization ratio	74.16	70.18	59.64
Net valuation taxable	$57,069,015	$56,983,700	$57,848,345
State equalized value	$81,318,061	$95,718,123	$102,505,511

Public Safety
Number of officers, 2006		0

Crime	2005	2006
Total crimes	21	25
Violent	0	1
Murder	0	0
Rape	0	0
Robbery	0	0
Aggravated assault	0	1
Non-violent	21	24
Burglary	8	9
Larceny	12	14
Vehicle theft	1	1
Domestic violence	4	7
Arson	0	0
Total crime rate	19.5	23.2
Violent	0.0	0.9
Non-violent	19.5	22.2

Public School District
(for school year 2006-07 except as noted)

Elsinboro Township School District
631 Salem-Fort Elfsborg Rd
Salem, NJ 08079
856-935-3817

Chief School Admin	Calvin Ferguson
Number of schools	1
Grade plan	K-8
Enrollment	108
Attendance rate, '05-06	95.4%
Dropout rate	NA
Students per teacher	9.9
Per pupil expenditure	$12,663
Median faculty salary	$41,316
Median administrator salary	$75,920
Grade 12 enrollment	NA
High school graduation rate	NA

Assessment test results
(percent scoring at proficient or advanced level)
	Language	Math
NJASK-Grade 3	NA	NA
GEPA-Grade 8	75.0%	56.3%
HSPA-High School	NA	NA

SAT score averages
Pct tested	Math	Verbal	Writing
NA	NA	NA	NA

Teacher Qualifications
Avg. years of experience	13
Highly-qualified teachers one subject/all subjects	100%/100%
With emergency credentials	0.0%

No Child Left Behind
AYP, 2005-06 .... Meets Standards

Municipal Finance
State Aid Programs, 2008
Total aid	$133,497
CMPTRA	0
Energy tax receipts	126,243
Garden State Trust	7,254

General Budget, 2007
Total tax levy	$2,386,030
County levy	912,503
County taxes	893,038
County library	0
County health	0
County open space	19,465
School levy	1,248,487
Muni. levy	225,040
Misc. revenues	477,547

Bergen County — Emerson Borough

Demographics & Socio-Economic Characteristics
(2000 US Census, except as noted)

Population
- 1980* 7,793
- 1990* 6,930
- 2000 7,197
  - Male 3,432
  - Female 3,765
- 2006 (estimate)* 7,318
- Population density 3,267.0

Race & Hispanic Origin, 2000
Race
- White 6,450
- Black/African American 61
- American Indian/Alaska Native 4
- Asian 568
- Native Hawaiian/Pacific Islander 0
- Other race 63
- Two or more races 51
- Hispanic origin, total 332
  - Mexican 22
  - Puerto Rican 65
  - Cuban 62
  - Other Hispanic 183

Age & Nativity, 2000
- Under 5 years 500
- 18 years and over 5,527
- 21 years and over 5,357
- 65 years and over 1,351
- 85 years and over 262
  - Median age 41.1
- Native-born 6,072
- Foreign-born 1,125

Educational Attainment, 2000
- Population 25 years and over 5,166
- Less than 9th grade 4.3%
- High school grad or higher 89.0%
- Bachelor's degree or higher 40.3%
- Graduate degree 12.3%

Income & Poverty, 1999
- Per capita income $31,506
- Median household income $74,556
- Median family income $80,468
- Persons in poverty 166
- H'holds receiving public assistance 0
- H'holds receiving social security 759

Households, 2000
- Total households 2,373
  - With persons under 18 907
  - With persons over 65 770
  - Family households 1,964
  - Single-person households 344
- Persons per household 2.91
- Persons per family 3.23

Labor & Employment
- Total civilian labor force, 2006** 3,603
  - Unemployment rate 1.8%
- Total civilian labor force, 2000 3,413
  - Unemployment rate 1.8%

Employed persons 16 years and over by occupation, 2000
- Managers & professionals 1,598
- Service occupations 395
- Sales & office occupations 1,031
- Farming, fishing & forestry 0
- Construction & maintenance 174
- Production & transportation 152
- Self-employed persons 286

* US Census Bureau
** New Jersey Department of Labor

See Introduction for an explanation of all data sources.

General Information
Borough of Emerson
1 Municipal Pl
Emerson, NJ 07630
201-262-6086

- Website .... www.emersonnj.org
- Year of incorporation 1909
- Land/water area (sq. miles) 2.24/0.18
- Form of government .... Borough

Government
Legislative Districts
- US Congressional 5
- State Legislative 39

Local Officials, 2008
- Mayor .... Louis J. Lamatina
- Manager .... Joseph Scarpa
- Clerk .... Carol Dray
- Finance Dir .... Nancy Burns
- Tax Assessor .... Claire Psoto
- Tax Collector .... Barbara Kozay
- Attorney .... Phillip Boggia
- Building .... Michael Sartori
- Planning .... Burgis Associates
- Engineering .... Job & Job Engineering
- Public Works .... Joseph Solimando
- Police Chief .... Michael Saudino
- Emerg/Fire Director .... Thomas Carlos

Housing & Construction
Housing Units, 2000*
- Total 2,398
- Median rent $1,096
- Median SF home value $260,600

Permits for New Residential Construction

	Units	Value
Total, 2007	27	$4,206,886
Single family	12	$2,540,218
Total, 2006	48	$6,108,728
Single family	10	$1,805,728

Real Property Valuation, 2007

	Parcels	Valuation
Total	2,495	$1,364,647,300
Vacant	78	19,367,100
Residential	2,274	1,180,119,000
Commercial	131	159,993,400
Industrial	10	4,886,000
Apartments	0	0
Farm land	1	5,100
Farm homestead	1	276,700

Average Property Value & Tax, 2007
- Residential value $518,855
- Property tax $9,250
- Tax credit/rebate $1,343

Public Library
Emerson Public Library
20 Palisade Ave
Emerson, NJ 07630
201-261-5604

- Director .... Jodi L. Fulgione

Library statistics, 2006
- Population served 7,197
- Full-time/total staff 1/2

	Total	Per capita
Holdings	36,681	5.10
Revenues	$405,909	$56.40
Expenditures	$359,801	$49.99
Annual visits	39,876	5.54
Internet terminals/annual users	6/10,832	

Taxes

	2005	2006	2007
General tax rate per $100	3.42	3.54	1.79
County equalization ratio	62.71	55.99	105.25
Net valuation taxable	$647,381,792	$651,457,250	$1,365,915,507
State equalized value	$1,156,245,387	$1,299,592,448	$1,346,013,280

Public Safety
- Number of officers, 2006 18

Crime

	2005	2006
Total crimes	54	48
Violent	4	4
Murder	0	0
Rape	0	0
Robbery	2	0
Aggravated assault	2	4
Non-violent	50	44
Burglary	10	7
Larceny	38	36
Vehicle theft	2	1
Domestic violence	31	34
Arson	0	1
Total crime rate	7.4	6.5
Violent	0.5	0.5
Non-violent	6.8	6.0

Public School District
(for school year 2006-07 except as noted)

Emerson School District
Administration Building, Main St
Emerson, NJ 07630
201-262-2828

- Superintendent .... Vincent Taffaro
- Number of schools 3
- Grade plan K-12
- Enrollment 1,168
- Attendance rate, '05-06 .... 96.1%
- Dropout rate 0.7%
- Students per teacher 12.2
- Per pupil expenditure $13,030
- Median faculty salary $51,750
- Median administrator salary $116,433
- Grade 12 enrollment 70
- High school graduation rate 100.0%

Assessment test results
(percent scoring at proficient or advanced level)

	Language	Math
NJASK-Grade 3	89.8%	92.1%
GEPA-Grade 8	84.5%	78.9%
HSPA-High School	93.8%	84.4%

SAT score averages

Pct tested	Math	Verbal	Writing
96%	487	501	489

Teacher Qualifications
- Avg. years of experience 6
- Highly-qualified teachers
  - one subject/all subjects 100%/100%
- With emergency credentials 0.0%

No Child Left Behind
- AYP, 2005-06 .... Meets Standards

Municipal Finance
State Aid Programs, 2008
- Total aid $755,300
  - CMPTRA 106,522
  - Energy tax receipts 630,589
  - Garden State Trust 0

General Budget, 2007
- Total tax levy $24,351,823
  - County levy 2,364,892
    - County taxes 2,234,745
    - County library 0
    - County health 0
    - County open space 130,147
  - School levy 15,039,240
  - Muni. levy 6,947,691
- Misc. revenues 3,129,845

©2008 Information Publications, Inc. All rights reserved. Photocopying prohibited. For additional copies, contact the publisher at www.informationpublications.com or (877)544-INFO (4636)

The New Jersey Municipal Data Book

Englewood City — Bergen County

Demographics & Socio-Economic Characteristics
(2000 US Census, except as noted)

Population
1980*	23,701
1990*	24,850
2000	26,203
Male	12,318
Female	13,885
2006 (estimate)*	27,824
Population density	5,655.3

Race & Hispanic Origin, 2000
Race
White	11,134
Black/African American	10,215
American Indian/Alaska Native	71
Asian	1,366
Native Hawaiian/Pacific Islander	12
Other race	2,226
Two or more races	1,179
Hispanic origin, total	5,703
Mexican	251
Puerto Rican	666
Cuban	257
Other Hispanic	4,529

Age & Nativity, 2000
Under 5 years	1,814
18 years and over	19,947
21 years and over	19,112
65 years and over	3,491
85 years and over	439
Median age	37.4
Native-born	18,124
Foreign-born	8,079

Educational Attainment, 2000
Population 25 years and over	18,010
Less than 9th grade	6.8%
High school grad or higher	82.7%
Bachelor's degree or higher	36.7%
Graduate degree	16.5%

Income & Poverty, 1999
Per capita income	$35,275
Median household income	$58,379
Median family income	$67,194
Persons in poverty	2,295
H'holds receiving public assistance	289
H'holds receiving social security	2,478

Households, 2000
Total households	9,273
With persons under 18	3,342
With persons over 65	2,559
Family households	6,486
Single-person households	2,299
Persons per household	2.79
Persons per family	3.29

Labor & Employment
Total civilian labor force, 2006**	13,524
Unemployment rate	4.6%
Total civilian labor force, 2000	13,298
Unemployment rate	6.0%

Employed persons 16 years and over by occupation, 2000
Managers & professionals	4,826
Service occupations	2,005
Sales & office occupations	3,403
Farming, fishing & forestry	18
Construction & maintenance	698
Production & transportation	1,545
Self-employed persons	721

* US Census Bureau
** New Jersey Department of Labor

General Information
City of Englewood
PO Box 228
Englewood, NJ 07631
201-871-6637
Website: www.cityofenglewood.org
Year of incorporation: 1899
Land/water area (sq. miles): 4.92/0.01
Form of government: Special Charter

Government
Legislative Districts
US Congressional	9
State Legislative	37

Local Officials, 2008
Mayor	Michael Wildes
Manager	Robert Casey
Clerk	Lenore Schiavelli
Finance Dir.	Howard Feinstein
Tax Assessor	Claire Psota
Tax Collector	Tamara Beamer
Attorney	William Bailey
Building	Piero Abballe
Comm Dev/Planning	NA
Engineering	Kenneth Albert
Public Works	Clyde Sweatt
Police Chief	David Bowman
Emerg/Fire Director	Robert Moran

Housing & Construction
Housing Units, 2000*
Total	9,614
Median rent	$825
Median SF home value	$212,400

Permits for New Residential Construction
	Units	Value
Total, 2007	527	$56,141,883
Single family	15	$8,721,868
Total, 2006	238	$32,895,182
Single family	19	$10,563,696

Real Property Valuation, 2007
	Parcels	Valuation
Total	7,478	$4,982,474,400
Vacant	119	27,778,700
Residential	6,661	3,737,817,100
Commercial	514	750,996,800
Industrial	133	318,166,500
Apartments	51	147,715,300
Farm land	0	0
Farm homestead	0	0

Average Property Value & Tax, 2007
Residential value	$561,150
Property tax	$10,143
Tax credit/rebate	$1,110

Public Library
Englewood Public Library
31 Engle St
Englewood, NJ 07631
201-568-2215
Director: Donald Jacobsen

Library statistics, 2006
Population served	26,203
Full-time/total staff	10/25

	Total	Per capita
Holdings	105,372	4.02
Revenues	$2,561,536	$97.76
Expenditures	$2,572,093	$98.16
Annual visits	207,387	7.91
Internet terminals/annual users	9/36,326	

Taxes
	2005	2006	2007
General tax rate per $100	4.02	4.16	1.84
County equalization ratio	54.25	48.68	105.85
Net valuation taxable	$2,044,264,194	$2,058,940,800	$4,992,356,340
State equalized value	$4,199,392,346	$4,605,699,341	$5,091,446,856

Public Safety
Number of officers, 2006: 80

Crime	2005	2006
Total crimes	651	651
Violent	74	67
Murder	1	1
Rape	5	3
Robbery	26	19
Aggravated assault	42	44
Non-violent	577	584
Burglary	141	177
Larceny	368	371
Vehicle theft	68	36
Domestic violence	279	299
Arson	1	0
Total crime rate	24.7	24.8
Violent	2.8	2.6
Non-violent	21.9	22.3

Public School District
(for school year 2006-07 except as noted)

Englewood City School District
12 Tenafly Rd
Englewood, NJ 07631
201-862-6234

Superintendent	Richard Segall (Int)
Number of schools	6
Grade plan	K-12
Enrollment	2,694
Attendance rate, '05-06	93.2%
Dropout rate	0.4%
Students per teacher	9.0
Per pupil expenditure	$18,328
Median faculty salary	$55,277
Median administrator salary	$106,649
Grade 12 enrollment	228
High school graduation rate	96.2%

Assessment test results
(percent scoring at proficient or advanced level)
	Language	Math
NJASK-Grade 3	74.2%	79.6%
GEPA-Grade 8	57.4%	45.4%
HSPA-High School	81.1%	60.2%

SAT score averages
Pct tested	Math	Verbal	Writing
92%	472	456	459

Teacher Qualifications
Avg. years of experience	9
Highly-qualified teachers one subject/all subjects	97.0%/97.0%
With emergency credentials	0.0%

No Child Left Behind
AYP, 2005-06: Meets Standards

Municipal Finance
State Aid Programs, 2008
Total aid	$3,465,110
CMPTRA	824,419
Energy tax receipts	2,640,691
Garden State Trust	0

General Budget, 2007
Total tax levy	$91,385,333
County levy	8,596,284
County taxes	8,121,384
County library	0
County health	0
County open space	474,900
School levy	44,212,899
Muni. levy	38,576,150
Misc. revenues	14,006,179

Bergen County

Englewood Cliffs Borough

Demographics & Socio-Economic Characteristics
(2000 US Census, except as noted)

Population
1980*	5,698
1990*	5,634
2000	5,322
Male	2,508
Female	2,814
2006 (estimate)*	5,793
Population density	2,771.8

Race & Hispanic Origin, 2000
Race
White	3,557
Black/African American	73
American Indian/Alaska Native	2
Asian	1,580
Native Hawaiian/Pacific Islander	0
Other race	38
Two or more races	72
Hispanic origin, total	260
Mexican	10
Puerto Rican	24
Cuban	96
Other Hispanic	130

Age & Nativity, 2000
Under 5 years	304
18 years and over	4,221
21 years and over	4,098
65 years and over	1,171
85 years and over	106
Median age	44.8
Native-born	3,261
Foreign-born	2,061

Educational Attainment, 2000
Population 25 years and over	3,921
Less than 9th grade	4.6%
High school grad or higher	92.7%
Bachelor's degree or higher	52.5%
Graduate degree	23.7%

Income & Poverty, 1999
Per capita income	$57,399
Median household income	$106,478
Median family income	$113,187
Persons in poverty	136
H'holds receiving public assistance	20
H'holds receiving social security	660

Households, 2000
Total households	1,818
With persons under 18	599
With persons over 65	775
Family households	1,560
Single-person households	228
Persons per household	2.90
Persons per family	3.16

Labor & Employment
Total civilian labor force, 2006**	2,743
Unemployment rate	3.5%
Total civilian labor force, 2000	2,577
Unemployment rate	3.4%

Employed persons 16 years and over by occupation, 2000
Managers & professionals	1,421
Service occupations	135
Sales & office occupations	760
Farming, fishing & forestry	0
Construction & maintenance	79
Production & transportation	94
Self-employed persons	269

* US Census Bureau
** New Jersey Department of Labor

See Introduction for an explanation of all data sources.

General Information
Borough of Englewood Cliffs
10 Kahn Ter
Englewood Cliffs, NJ 07632
201-569-5252

Website	www.englewoodcliffsnj.net
Year of incorporation	1895
Land/water area (sq. miles)	2.09/1.29
Form of government	Borough

Government
Legislative Districts
US Congressional	9
State Legislative	37

Local Officials, 2008
Mayor	Joseph Parisi Jr
Manager	Debra L. Fehre
Clerk	Debra L. Fehre
Finance Dir	Joseph Iannaconi Jr
Tax Assessor	George Reggo
Tax Collector	Joseph Iannaconi Jr
Attorney	Michael Kates
Building	Paul Renaud
Comm Dev/Planning	NA
Engineering	Stephen Boswell
Public Works	Rodney Bialko
Police Chief	Thomas Bauernschmidt
Emerg/Fire Director	George Drimones

Housing & Construction
Housing Units, 2000*
Total	1,889
Median rent	$2,001
Median SF home value	$507,100

Permits for New Residential Construction
	Units	Value
Total, 2007	29	$23,524,544
Single family	29	$23,524,544
Total, 2006	25	$14,937,145
Single family	25	$14,937,145

Real Property Valuation, 2007
	Parcels	Valuation
Total	2,108	$2,045,749,300
Vacant	68	36,930,800
Residential	1,925	1,367,120,100
Commercial	113	639,342,300
Industrial	1	1,383,600
Apartments	1	972,500
Farm land	0	0
Farm homestead	0	0

Average Property Value & Tax, 2007
Residential value	$710,192
Property tax	$8,219
Tax credit/rebate	$1,129

Public Library
No public municipal library

Library statistics, 2006
Population served	NA
Full-time/total staff	NA/NA

	Total	Per capita
Holdings	NA	NA
Revenues	NA	NA
Expenditures	NA	NA
Annual visits	NA	NA
Internet terminals/annual users	NA/NA	

Taxes
	2005	2006	2007
General tax rate per $100	1.02	1.08	1.16
County equalization ratio	89.91	79.01	65.89
Net valuation taxable	$2,021,066,288	$2,033,170,200	$2,047,021,897
State equalized value	$2,557,987,961	$3,086,976,346	$3,244,889,689

Public Safety
Number of officers, 2006 24

Crime	2005	2006
Total crimes	101	101
Violent	5	3
Murder	0	0
Rape	1	0
Robbery	0	0
Aggravated assault	4	3
Non-violent	96	98
Burglary	18	22
Larceny	74	73
Vehicle theft	4	3
Domestic violence	24	18
Arson	0	0
Total crime rate	17.9	17.6
Violent	0.9	0.5
Non-violent	17.0	17.1

Public School District
(for school year 2006-07 except as noted)

Englewood Cliffs School District
143 Charlotte Place
Englewood Cliffs, NJ 07632
201-567-7292

Superintendent	Philomena T. Pezzano
Number of schools	2
Grade plan	K-8
Enrollment	421
Attendance rate, '05-06	96.2%
Dropout rate	NA
Students per teacher	8.2
Per pupil expenditure	$18,167
Median faculty salary	$55,585
Median administrator salary	$141,617
Grade 12 enrollment	NA
High school graduation rate	NA

Assessment test results
(percent scoring at proficient or advanced level)
	Language	Math
NJASK-Grade 3	100.1%	98.0%
GEPA-Grade 8	90.3%	67.7%
HSPA-High School	NA	NA

SAT score averages
Pct tested	Math	Verbal	Writing
NA	NA	NA	NA

Teacher Qualifications
Avg. years of experience	10
Highly-qualified teachers one subject/all subjects	100%/100%
With emergency credentials	0.0%

No Child Left Behind
AYP, 2005-06 .... Meets Standards

Municipal Finance
State Aid Programs, 2008
Total aid	$882,587
CMPTRA	102,723
Energy tax receipts	778,295
Garden State Trust	1,569

General Budget, 2007
Total tax levy	$23,691,120
County levy	5,531,638
County taxes	5,217,560
County library	0
County health	0
County open space	314,078
School levy	8,932,706
Muni. levy	9,226,776
Misc. revenues	3,413,203

©2008 Information Publications, Inc. All rights reserved. Photocopying prohibited. For additional copies, contact the publisher at www.informationpublications.com or (877)544-INFO (4636)

The New Jersey Municipal Data Book

Englishtown Borough
Monmouth County

Demographics & Socio-Economic Characteristics
(2000 US Census, except as noted)

Population
1980*	976
1990*	1,268
2000	1,764
Male	843
Female	921
2006 (estimate)*	1,841
Population density	3,229.8

Race & Hispanic Origin, 2000
Race
White	1,559
Black/African American	73
American Indian/Alaska Native	2
Asian	79
Native Hawaiian/Pacific Islander	0
Other race	29
Two or more races	22
Hispanic origin, total	110
Mexican	14
Puerto Rican	49
Cuban	16
Other Hispanic	31

Age & Nativity, 2000
Under 5 years	161
18 years and over	1,251
21 years and over	1,204
65 years and over	194
85 years and over	52
Median age	34.9
Native-born	1,556
Foreign-born	208

Educational Attainment, 2000
Population 25 years and over	1,162
Less than 9th grade	7.2%
High school grad or higher	81.6%
Bachelor's degree or higher	18.8%
Graduate degree	5.9%

Income & Poverty, 1999
Per capita income	$23,438
Median household income	$57,557
Median family income	$73,750
Persons in poverty	126
H'holds receiving public assistance	13
H'holds receiving social security	177

Households, 2000
Total households	643
With persons under 18	269
With persons over 65	161
Family households	416
Single-person households	183
Persons per household	2.74
Persons per family	3.51

Labor & Employment
Total civilian labor force, 2006**	947
Unemployment rate	3.4%
Total civilian labor force, 2000	881
Unemployment rate	3.5%

Employed persons 16 years and over by occupation, 2000
Managers & professionals	266
Service occupations	133
Sales & office occupations	230
Farming, fishing & forestry	1
Construction & maintenance	113
Production & transportation	107
Self-employed persons	47

* US Census Bureau
** New Jersey Department of Labor

General Information
Borough of Englishtown
15 Main St
Englishtown, NJ 07726
732-446-9235

Website	www.englishtownnj.com
Year of incorporation	1888
Land/water area (sq. miles)	0.57/0.01
Form of government	Borough

Government
Legislative Districts
US Congressional	12
State Legislative	12

Local Officials, 2008
Mayor	Thomas E. Reynolds
Manager	Laurie Finger
Clerk	Peter Gorbatuk
Finance Dir	Laurie Finger
Tax Assessor	Sharon Hartman
Tax Collector	Janice Garcia
Attorney	Stuart Moskovitz
Building	Bob Ward
Comm Dev/Planning	NA
Engineering	Thomas Herits
Public Works	NA
Police Chief	John Niziolek
Emerg/Fire Director	Ralph Kirkland

Housing & Construction
Housing Units, 2000*
Total	680
Median rent	$772
Median SF home value	$150,600

Permits for New Residential Construction
	Units	Value
Total, 2007	14	$1,369,807
Single family	14	$1,369,807
Total, 2006	30	$2,938,916
Single family	30	$2,938,916

Real Property Valuation, 2007
	Parcels	Valuation
Total	673	$100,674,600
Vacant	31	1,454,000
Residential	605	80,571,800
Commercial	30	14,729,700
Industrial	5	2,975,900
Apartments	2	743,200
Farm land	0	0
Farm homestead	0	0

Average Property Value & Tax, 2007
Residential value	$133,507
Property tax	$5,286
Tax credit/rebate	$1,027

Public Library
No public municipal library

Library statistics, 2006
Population served	NA
Full-time/total staff	NA/NA

	Total	Per capita
Holdings	NA	NA
Revenues	NA	NA
Expenditures	NA	NA
Annual visits	NA	NA
Internet terminals/annual users	NA/NA	

Taxes
	2005	2006	2007
General tax rate per $100	3.691	3.861	3.96
County equalization ratio	55.21	49.83	44.22
Net valuation taxable	$95,237,609	$95,721,600	$101,845,431
State equalized value	$191,125,043	$218,018,531	$238,835,137

Public Safety
Number of officers, 2006 ... 8

Crime	2005	2006
Total crimes	19	16
Violent	1	0
Murder	0	0
Rape	0	0
Robbery	0	0
Aggravated assault	1	0
Non-violent	18	16
Burglary	0	3
Larceny	18	11
Vehicle theft	0	2
Domestic violence	3	8
Arson	1	0
Total crime rate	10.5	8.9
Violent	0.6	0.0
Non-violent	9.9	8.9

Public School District
(for school year 2006-07 except as noted)

Manalapan-Englishtown Reg. School Dist.
54 Main St
Englishtown, NJ 07726
732-786-2500

Superintendent	John J. Marciante Jr
Number of schools	14
Grade plan	K-8
Enrollment	5,446
Attendance rate, '05-06	95.7%
Dropout rate	NA
Students per teacher	12.2
Per pupil expenditure	$11,340
Median faculty salary	$50,888
Median administrator salary	$92,939
Grade 12 enrollment	NA
High school graduation rate	NA

Assessment test results
(percent scoring at proficient or advanced level)
	Language	Math
NJASK-Grade 3	92.8%	93.7%
GEPA-Grade 8	91.8%	85.3%
HSPA-High School	NA	NA

SAT score averages
Pct tested	Math	Verbal	Writing
NA	NA	NA	NA

Teacher Qualifications
Avg. years of experience	9
Highly-qualified teachers one subject/all subjects	100%/100%
With emergency credentials	0.0%

No Child Left Behind
AYP, 2005-06 ... Meets Standards

Municipal Finance
State Aid Programs, 2008
Total aid	$114,230
CMPTRA	0
Energy tax receipts	114,230
Garden State Trust	0

General Budget, 2007
Total tax levy	$4,032,300
County levy	628,254
County taxes	551,685
County library	31,584
County health	10,509
County open space	34,475
School levy	2,604,810
Muni. levy	799,236
Misc. revenues	1,150,819

Essex County / Essex Fells Borough

Demographics & Socio-Economic Characteristics
(2000 US Census, except as noted)

Population
1980*	2,363
1990*	2,139
2000	2,162
Male	1,064
Female	1,098
2006 (estimate)*	2,071
Population density	1,468.8

Race & Hispanic Origin, 2000
Race
White	2,096
Black/African American	10
American Indian/Alaska Native	4
Asian	22
Native Hawaiian/Pacific Islander	0
Other race	3
Two or more races	27
Hispanic origin, total	26
Mexican	1
Puerto Rican	3
Cuban	4
Other Hispanic	18

Age & Nativity, 2000
Under 5 years	198
18 years and over	1,520
21 years and over	1,484
65 years and over	318
85 years and over	27
Median age	40.3
Native-born	2,004
Foreign-born	158

Educational Attainment, 2000
Population 25 years and over	1,438
Less than 9th grade	1.2%
High school grad or higher	97.1%
Bachelor's degree or higher	72.4%
Graduate degree	32.0%

Income & Poverty, 1999
Per capita income	$77,434
Median household income	$148,173
Median family income	$175,000
Persons in poverty	23
H'holds receiving public assistance	3
H'holds receiving social security	219

Households, 2000
Total households	737
With persons under 18	304
With persons over 65	222
Family households	605
Single-person households	111
Persons per household	2.93
Persons per family	3.28

Labor & Employment
Total civilian labor force, 2006**	1,028
Unemployment rate	2.5%
Total civilian labor force, 2000	954
Unemployment rate	1.2%

Employed persons 16 years and over by occupation, 2000
Managers & professionals	617
Service occupations	43
Sales & office occupations	247
Farming, fishing & forestry	0
Construction & maintenance	23
Production & transportation	13
Self-employed persons	110

* US Census Bureau
** New Jersey Department of Labor

See Introduction for an explanation of all data sources.

General Information
Borough of Essex Fells
255 Roseland Ave
Essex Fells, NJ 07021
973-226-3400

Website	www.essexfellsboro.com
Year of incorporation	1902
Land/water area (sq. miles)	1.41/0.00
Form of government	Borough

Government
Legislative Districts
US Congressional	11
State Legislative	27

Local Officials, 2008
Mayor	Edward P. Abbot
Manager	Amey Upchurch
Clerk	Francine T. Paserchia
Finance Dir	Joe DeIorio
Tax Assessor	Jack Kelly
Tax Collector	Richard Mondelli
Attorney	Martin Murphy
Building	Robert Young
Comm Dev/Planning	NA
Engineering	Frank Ziccelli
Public Works	Roger Kerr
Police Chief	Kelly J. Reilly
Emerg/Fire Director	James Egan

Housing & Construction
Housing Units, 2000*
Total	761
Median rent	$1,656
Median SF home value	$584,100

Permits for New Residential Construction
	Units	Value
Total, 2007	42	$10,164,295
Single family	2	$1,854,025
Total, 2006	2	$2,171,050
Single family	2	$2,171,050

Real Property Valuation, 2007
	Parcels	Valuation
Total	786	$814,952,500
Vacant	32	9,147,000
Residential	748	783,758,100
Commercial	6	22,047,400
Industrial	0	0
Apartments	0	0
Farm land	0	0
Farm homestead	0	0

Average Property Value & Tax, 2007
Residential value	$1,047,805
Property tax	$15,585
Tax credit/rebate	$1,287

Public Library
No public municipal library

Library statistics, 2006
Population served	NA
Full-time/total staff	NA/NA

	Total	Per capita
Holdings	NA	NA
Revenues	NA	NA
Expenditures	NA	NA
Annual visits	NA	NA
Internet terminals/annual users	NA/NA	

Taxes
	2005	2006	2007
General tax rate per $100	1.4	1.47	1.49
County equalization ratio	116.82	100.15	92.56
Net valuation taxable	$809,115,363	$811,698,850	$815,247,863
State equalized value	$807,903,508	$877,238,805	$909,637,586

Public Safety
Number of officers, 2006 13

Crime
	2005	2006
Total crimes	16	16
Violent	1	0
Murder	0	0
Rape	0	0
Robbery	0	0
Aggravated assault	1	0
Non-violent	15	16
Burglary	5	2
Larceny	10	13
Vehicle theft	0	1
Domestic violence	6	5
Arson	0	2
Total crime rate	7.5	7.6
Violent	0.5	0.0
Non-violent	7.0	7.6

Public School District
(for school year 2006-07 except as noted)

Essex Fells School District
102 Hawthorne Rd
Essex Fells, NJ 07021
973-226-0505

Superintendent	Raymond Hyman
Number of schools	1
Grade plan	K-6
Enrollment	281
Attendance rate, '05-06	93.0%
Dropout rate	NA
Students per teacher	10.3
Per pupil expenditure	$11,701
Median faculty salary	$45,641
Median administrator salary	$83,181
Grade 12 enrollment	NA
High school graduation rate	NA

Assessment test results
(percent scoring at proficient or advanced level)
	Language	Math
NJASK-Grade 3	93.7%	100.0%
GEPA-Grade 8	NA	NA
HSPA-High School	NA	NA

SAT score averages
Pct tested	Math	Verbal	Writing
NA	NA	NA	NA

Teacher Qualifications
Avg. years of experience	4
Highly-qualified teachers one subject/all subjects	100%/100%
With emergency credentials	0.0%

No Child Left Behind
AYP, 2005-06 .... Meets Standards

Municipal Finance
State Aid Programs, 2008
Total aid	$243,846
CMPTRA	0
Energy tax receipts	243,846
Garden State Trust	0

General Budget, 2007
Total tax levy	$12,125,955
County levy	3,453,329
County taxes	3,364,563
County library	0
County health	0
County open space	88,765
School levy	6,058,616
Muni. levy	2,614,010
Misc. revenues	2,401,302

©2008 Information Publications, Inc. All rights reserved.

Estell Manor City
Atlantic County

Demographics & Socio-Economic Characteristics
(2000 US Census, except as noted)

Population
1980*	848
1990*	1,404
2000	1,585
Male	800
Female	785
2006 (estimate)*	1,720
Population density	32.1

Race & Hispanic Origin, 2000
Race
White	1,493
Black/African American	57
American Indian/Alaska Native	7
Asian	5
Native Hawaiian/Pacific Islander	0
Other race	2
Two or more races	21
Hispanic origin, total	15
Mexican	1
Puerto Rican	10
Cuban	0
Other Hispanic	4

Age & Nativity, 2000
Under 5 years	111
18 years and over	1,107
21 years and over	1,053
65 years and over	153
85 years and over	13
Median age	36.6
Native-born	1,522
Foreign-born	70

Educational Attainment, 2000
Population 25 years and over	1,008
Less than 9th grade	4.1%
High school grad or higher	84.8%
Bachelor's degree or higher	17.0%
Graduate degree	4.9%

Income & Poverty, 1999
Per capita income	$19,469
Median household income	$54,653
Median family income	$56,548
Persons in poverty	77
H'holds receiving public assistance	10
H'holds receiving social security	133

Households, 2000
Total households	528
With persons under 18	234
With persons over 65	116
Family households	433
Single-person households	73
Persons per household	2.95
Persons per family	3.27

Labor & Employment
Total civilian labor force, 2006**	811
Unemployment rate	6.3%
Total civilian labor force, 2000	729
Unemployment rate	5.8%

Employed persons 16 years and over by occupation, 2000
Managers & professionals	238
Service occupations	111
Sales & office occupations	155
Farming, fishing & forestry	2
Construction & maintenance	105
Production & transportation	76
Self-employed persons	46

* US Census Bureau
** New Jersey Department of Labor

General Information
City of Estell Manor
PO Box 102
Estell Manor, NJ 08319
609-476-2692

Website	NA
Year of incorporation	1925
Land/water area (sq. miles)	53.57/1.34
Form of government	Small Municipality

Government
Legislative Districts
US Congressional	2
State Legislative	2

Local Officials, 2008
Mayor	Joseph Venezia
Manager	NA
Clerk	Kimberly Hodson
Finance Dir	Judson Moore
Tax Assessor	James Mancini
Tax Collector	Deborah Hample
Attorney	Alfred Scerni
Building	Charles Kane
Comm Dev/Planning	NA
Engineering	J. Michael Fralinger
Public Works	Chuck Cole
Police Chief	NA
Emerg/Fire Director	Jeff Cornew

Housing & Construction
Housing Units, 2000*
Total	546
Median rent	$838
Median SF home value	$123,500

Permits for New Residential Construction
	Units	Value
Total, 2007	7	$527,593
Single family	7	$527,593
Total, 2006	10	$1,061,967
Single family	10	$1,061,967

Real Property Valuation, 2007
	Parcels	Valuation
Total	1,551	$115,969,600
Vacant	749	9,916,200
Residential	721	95,807,700
Commercial	6	3,379,300
Industrial	5	1,573,300
Apartments	1	700,000
Farm land	50	1,675,700
Farm homestead	19	2,917,400

Average Property Value & Tax, 2007
Residential value	$133,412
Property tax	$3,328
Tax credit/rebate	$803

Public Library
No public municipal library

Library statistics, 2006
Population served	NA
Full-time/total staff	NA/NA

	Total	Per capita
Holdings	NA	NA
Revenues	NA	NA
Expenditures	NA	NA
Annual visits	NA	NA
Internet terminals/annual users	NA/NA	

Taxes
	2005	2006	2007
General tax rate per $100	2.408	2.487	2.495
County equalization ratio	82.52	69.28	58.29
Net valuation taxable	$114,052,299	$116,131,100	$116,367,942
State equalized value	$164,625,143	$199,663,203	$213,030,539

Public Safety
Number of officers, 2006		0

Crime	2005	2006
Total crimes	20	24
Violent	3	3
Murder	0	0
Rape	0	0
Robbery	0	0
Aggravated assault	3	3
Non-violent	17	21
Burglary	5	9
Larceny	10	10
Vehicle theft	2	2
Domestic violence	11	6
Arson	0	0
Total crime rate	11.7	13.9
Violent	1.8	1.7
Non-violent	10.0	12.2

Public School District
(for school year 2006-07 except as noted)

Estell Manor City School District
128 Cape May Ave
Estell Manor, NJ 08319
609-476-2267

Superintendent	John Cressey
Number of schools	1
Grade plan	K-8
Enrollment	218
Attendance rate, '05-06	95.3%
Dropout rate	NA
Students per teacher	10.6
Per pupil expenditure	$11,965
Median faculty salary	$50,784
Median administrator salary	$91,027
Grade 12 enrollment	NA
High school graduation rate	NA

Assessment test results
(percent scoring at proficient or advanced level)
	Language	Math
NJASK-Grade 3	85.2%	96.3%
GEPA-Grade 8	86.4%	72.7%
HSPA-High School	NA	NA

SAT score averages
Pct tested	Math	Verbal	Writing
NA	NA	NA	NA

Teacher Qualifications
Avg. years of experience	15
Highly-qualified teachers one subject/all subjects	100%/100%
With emergency credentials	0.0%

No Child Left Behind
AYP, 2005-06	Meets Standards

Municipal Finance
State Aid Programs, 2008
Total aid	$467,449
CMPTRA	0
Energy tax receipts	244,430
Garden State Trust	223,019

General Budget, 2007
Total tax levy	$2,903,214
County levy	614,146
County taxes	488,984
County library	60,536
County health	24,667
County open space	39,959
School levy	2,090,870
Muni. levy	198,198
Misc. revenues	1,145,603

Burlington County
Evesham Township

Demographics & Socio-Economic Characteristics
(2000 US Census, except as noted)

Population
1980*	21,659
1990*	35,309
2000	42,275
Male	20,498
Female	21,777
2006 (estimate)*	46,711
Population density	1,581.3

Race & Hispanic Origin, 2000
Race
White	38,579
Black/African American	1,313
American Indian/Alaska Native	31
Asian	1,721
Native Hawaiian/Pacific Islander	8
Other race	203
Two or more races	420
Hispanic origin, total	829
Mexican	136
Puerto Rican	330
Cuban	81
Other Hispanic	282

Age & Nativity, 2000
Under 5 years	3,090
18 years and over	30,790
21 years and over	29,702
65 years and over	3,750
85 years and over	368
Median age	36.0
Native-born	39,688
Foreign-born	2,740

Educational Attainment, 2000
Population 25 years and over	28,565
Less than 9th grade	1.5%
High school grad or higher	93.3%
Bachelor's degree or higher	39.7%
Graduate degree	12.3%

Income & Poverty, 1999
Per capita income	$29,494
Median household income	$67,010
Median family income	$77,245
Persons in poverty	1,174
H'holds receiving public assistance	123
H'holds receiving social security	3,011

Households, 2000
Total households	15,712
With persons under 18	6,297
With persons over 65	2,733
Family households	11,346
Single-person households	3,584
Persons per household	2.68
Persons per family	3.21

Labor & Employment
Total civilian labor force, 2006**	28,024
Unemployment rate	3.0%
Total civilian labor force, 2000	23,374
Unemployment rate	2.6%

Employed persons 16 years and over by occupation, 2000
Managers & professionals	10,930
Service occupations	2,200
Sales & office occupations	7,092
Farming, fishing & forestry	8
Construction & maintenance	1,158
Production & transportation	1,382
Self-employed persons	1,228

‡ Branch of county library
* US Census Bureau
** New Jersey Department of Labor

See Introduction for an explanation of all data sources.

General Information
Township of Evesham
984 Tuckerton Rd
Marlton, NJ 08053
856-983-2900

Website	www.evesham-nj.gov
Year of incorporation	1688
Land/water area (sq. miles)	29.54/0.17
Form of government	Council-Manager

Government
Legislative Districts
US Congressional	3
State Legislative	8

Local Officials, 2008
Mayor	Randy Brown
Manager	Thomas Czerniecki
Clerk	Carmela Bonfrisco
Finance Dir	Eileen Zaharchak
Tax Assessor	Blackwell Albertson
Tax Collector	Kathie Sanders
Attorney	William Ruggierio
Building	Carlos Martinez
Comm Dev/Planning	NA
Engineering	Chris Rehmann
Public Works	William Cromie
Police Chief	Joseph Cornely
Emerg/Fire Director	Ted Lowden

Housing & Construction
Housing Units, 2000*
Total	16,324
Median rent	$886
Median SF home value	$157,000

Permits for New Residential Construction
	Units	Value
Total, 2007	25	$4,741,246
Single family	25	$4,741,246
Total, 2006	30	$6,516,132
Single family	30	$6,516,132

Real Property Valuation, 2007
	Parcels	Valuation
Total	16,473	$2,815,359,200
Vacant	695	18,227,500
Residential	15,106	2,230,968,600
Commercial	495	433,279,600
Industrial	16	18,546,600
Apartments	18	106,365,100
Farm land	96	691,900
Farm homestead	47	7,279,900

Average Property Value & Tax, 2007
Residential value	$147,710
Property tax	$6,363
Tax credit/rebate	$1,066

Public Library
Evesham Branch Library‡
984 Tuckerton Rd
Marlton, NJ 08053
856-983-1444

Branch Librarian........ Susan Szymanik

Library statistics, 2006
see Burlington County profile
for library system statistics

Public Safety
Number of officers, 2006 75

Crime
	2005	2006
Total crimes	695	765
Violent	47	42
Murder	1	0
Rape	9	6
Robbery	8	8
Aggravated assault	29	28
Non-violent	648	723
Burglary	98	92
Larceny	528	607
Vehicle theft	22	24
Domestic violence	399	354
Arson	10	8
Total crime rate	14.8	16.3
Violent	1.0	0.9
Non-violent	13.8	15.4

Public School District
(for school year 2006-07 except as noted)

Evesham Township School District
25 S Maple Ave
Marlton, NJ 08053
856-983-1800

Superintendent	Patricia Lucas
Number of schools	9
Grade plan	K-8
Enrollment	5,060
Attendance rate, '05-06	95.3%
Dropout rate	NA
Students per teacher	10.6
Per pupil expenditure	$12,461
Median faculty salary	$49,991
Median administrator salary	$99,400
Grade 12 enrollment	NA
High school graduation rate	NA

Assessment test results
(percent scoring at proficient or advanced level)
	Language	Math
NJASK-Grade 3	89.9%	93.7%
GEPA-Grade 8	86.2%	79.1%
HSPA-High School	NA	NA

SAT score averages
Pct tested	Math	Verbal	Writing
NA	NA	NA	NA

Teacher Qualifications
Avg. years of experience	10
Highly-qualified teachers one subject/all subjects	100%/100%
With emergency credentials	0.3%

No Child Left Behind
AYP, 2005-06 .... Meets Standards

Municipal Finance
State Aid Programs, 2008
Total aid	$4,133,186
CMPTRA	959,727
Energy tax receipts	3,104,412
Garden State Trust	2,895

General Budget, 2007
Total tax levy	$121,634,577
County levy	22,404,940
County taxes	18,565,663
County library	1,703,689
County health	0
County open space	2,135,588
School levy	82,908,709
Muni. levy	16,320,928
Misc. revenues	14,612,879

Taxes
	2005	2006	2007
General tax rate per $100	3.885	4.148	4.31
County equalization ratio	65.2	59.26	52.85
Net valuation taxable	$2,770,634,123	$2,799,540,400	$2,823,669,826
State equalized value	$4,675,386,640	$5,305,923,983	$5,861,448,256

Ewing Township — Mercer County

Demographics & Socio-Economic Characteristics
(2000 US Census, except as noted)

Population
1980*	34,842
1990*	34,185
2000	35,707
Male	17,203
Female	18,504
2006 (estimate)*	36,916
Population density	2,408.1

Race & Hispanic Origin, 2000
Race
- White ... 24,645
- Black/African American ... 8,863
- American Indian/Alaska Native ... 55
- Asian ... 811
- Native Hawaiian/Pacific Islander ... 22
- Other race ... 653
- Two or more races ... 658
- Hispanic origin, total ... 1,586
  - Mexican ... 97
  - Puerto Rican ... 900
  - Cuban ... 72
  - Other Hispanic ... 517

Age & Nativity, 2000
- Under 5 years ... 1,623
- 18 years and over ... 29,263
- 21 years and over ... 25,573
- 65 years and over ... 5,631
- 85 years and over ... 761
- Median age ... 37.0
- Native-born ... 32,778
- Foreign-born ... 2,929

Educational Attainment, 2000
- Population 25 years and over ... 23,114
- Less than 9th grade ... 4.7%
- High school grad or higher ... 84.1%
- Bachelor's degree or higher ... 29.1%
- Graduate degree ... 12.0%

Income & Poverty, 1999
- Per capita income ... $24,268
- Median household income ... $57,274
- Median family income ... $67,618
- Persons in poverty ... 1,964
- H'holds receiving public assistance ... 155
- H'holds receiving social security ... 4,007

Households, 2000
- Total households ... 12,551
  - With persons under 18 ... 3,645
  - With persons over 65 ... 3,978
  - Family households ... 8,211
  - Single-person households ... 3,480
- Persons per household ... 2.45
- Persons per family ... 3.00

Labor & Employment
- Total civilian labor force, 2006** ... 21,047
  - Unemployment rate ... 3.8%
- Total civilian labor force, 2000 ... 18,364
  - Unemployment rate ... 4.6%

Employed persons 16 years and over by occupation, 2000
- Managers & professionals ... 6,765
- Service occupations ... 2,785
- Sales & office occupations ... 5,269
- Farming, fishing & forestry ... 26
- Construction & maintenance ... 1,013
- Production & transportation ... 1,664
- Self-employed persons ... 686

‡ Branch of county library
* US Census Bureau
** New Jersey Department of Labor
§ State Fiscal Year July 1–June 30

General Information
Township of Ewing
2 Jake Garzio Dr
Ewing, NJ 08628
609-883-2900

- Website ... www.ewingtwp.net
- Year of incorporation ... 1834
- Land/water area (sq. miles) ... 15.33/0.27
- Form of government ... Mayor-Council

Government
Legislative Districts
- US Congressional ... 12
- State Legislative ... 15

Local Officials, 2008
- Mayor ... Jack Ball
- Manager ... David Thompson
- Clerk ... Stephen Elliott
- Finance Dir. ... John Barrett
- Tax Assessor ... Jeff Burd
- Tax Collector ... Thomas Hespe
- Attorney ... Michael Hartsough
- Building ... William Erney
- Planning ... Richard Owen
- Engineering ... Robert Mannix
- Public Works ... Angelo Capuano
- Police Chief ... Robert Coulton
- Fire/Emergency Dir. ... NA

Housing & Construction
Housing Units, 2000*
- Total ... 12,924
- Median rent ... $720
- Median SF home value ... $133,100

Permits for New Residential Construction
	Units	Value
Total, 2007	4	$814,100
Single family	4	$814,100
Total, 2006	7	$4,177,050
Single family	7	$4,177,050

Real Property Valuation, 2007
	Parcels	Valuation
Total	11,625	$1,806,799,700
Vacant	448	16,219,600
Residential	10,551	1,293,637,300
Commercial	585	414,021,700
Industrial	19	16,415,000
Apartments	19	65,985,700
Farm land	2	58,700
Farm homestead	1	461,700

Average Property Value & Tax, 2007
- Residential value ... $122,640
- Property tax ... $5,322
- Tax credit/rebate ... $1,003

Public Library
Ewing Branch Library‡
61 Scotch Rd
West Trenton, NJ 08628
609-882-3130

- Branch Librarian ... Jacquelyn Huff

Library statistics, 2006
see Mercer County profile for library system statistics

Taxes
	2005	2006	2007
General tax rate per $100	3.94	4.26	4.34
County equalization ratio	68.6	60.82	58.53
Net valuation taxable	$1,782,975,217	$1,789,314,800	$1,816,428,761
State equalized value	$2,931,560,699	$3,066,541,943	$3,526,171,879

Public Safety
- Number of officers, 2006 ... 82

Crime	2005	2006
Total crimes	1,039	894
Violent	121	114
Murder	1	0
Rape	9	8
Robbery	52	57
Aggravated assault	59	49
Non-violent	918	780
Burglary	165	173
Larceny	678	559
Vehicle theft	75	48
Domestic violence	218	218
Arson	9	13
Total crime rate	28.0	24.0
Violent	3.3	3.1
Non-violent	24.8	20.9

Public School District
(for school year 2006-07 except as noted)

Ewing Township School District
1331 Lower Ferry Rd
Ewing, NJ 08618
609-538-9800

- Superintendent ... Raymond Broach
- Number of schools ... 5
- Grade plan ... K-12
- Enrollment ... 3,861
- Attendance rate, '05-06 ... 95.4%
- Dropout rate ... 1.1%
- Students per teacher ... 11.3
- Per pupil expenditure ... $12,798
- Median faculty salary ... $55,912
- Median administrator salary ... $111,937
- Grade 12 enrollment ... 242
- High school graduation rate ... 97.2%

Assessment test results
(percent scoring at proficient or advanced level)

	Language	Math
NJASK-Grade 3	83.2%	83.3%
GEPA-Grade 8	73.3%	54.8%
HSPA-High School	82.4%	62.1%

SAT score averages
Pct tested	Math	Verbal	Writing
77%	461	458	465

Teacher Qualifications
- Avg. years of experience ... 10
- Highly-qualified teachers one subject/all subjects ... 100%/100%
- With emergency credentials ... 0.0%

No Child Left Behind
- AYP, 2005-06 ... Meets Standards

Municipal Finance§
State Aid Programs, 2008
- Total aid ... $12,437,070
  - CMPTRA ... 9,252,262
  - Energy tax receipts ... 3,184,094
  - Garden State Trust ... 714

General Budget, 2007
- Total tax levy ... $78,820,967
  - County levy ... 16,155,158
    - County taxes ... 13,918,208
    - County library ... 1,283,339
    - County health ... 0
    - County open space ... 953,611
  - School levy ... 46,961,137
  - Muni. levy ... 15,704,673
- Misc. revenues ... 29,807,669

Monmouth County
Fair Haven Borough

Demographics & Socio-Economic Characteristics
(2000 US Census, except as noted)

Population
1980*	5,679
1990*	5,270
2000	5,937
Male	2,877
Female	3,060
2006 (estimate)*	5,885
Population density	3,524.0

Race & Hispanic Origin, 2000
Race
White	5,573
Black/African American	243
American Indian/Alaska Native	2
Asian	58
Native Hawaiian/Pacific Islander	0
Other race	13
Two or more races	48
Hispanic origin, total	79
Mexican	10
Puerto Rican	8
Cuban	14
Other Hispanic	47

Age & Nativity, 2000
Under 5 years	537
18 years and over	3,976
21 years and over	3,858
65 years and over	614
85 years and over	65
Median age	37.4
Native-born	5,655
Foreign-born	282

Educational Attainment, 2000
Population 25 years and over	3,747
Less than 9th grade	1.4%
High school grad or higher	97.1%
Bachelor's degree or higher	61.8%
Graduate degree	26.4%

Income & Poverty, 1999
Per capita income	$44,018
Median household income	$97,220
Median family income	$109,760
Persons in poverty	139
H'holds receiving public assistance	7
H'holds receiving social security	424

Households, 2000
Total households	1,998
With persons under 18	980
With persons over 65	438
Family households	1,658
Single-person households	304
Persons per household	2.97
Persons per family	3.33

Labor & Employment
Total civilian labor force, 2006**	2,938
Unemployment rate	3.0%
Total civilian labor force, 2000	2,728
Unemployment rate	2.9%

Employed persons 16 years and over by occupation, 2000
Managers & professionals	1,474
Service occupations	183
Sales & office occupations	717
Farming, fishing & forestry	5
Construction & maintenance	164
Production & transportation	107
Self-employed persons	298

* US Census Bureau
** New Jersey Department of Labor

See Introduction for an explanation of all data sources.

General Information
Borough of Fair Haven
748 River Rd
Fair Haven, NJ 07704
732-747-0241

Website	www.fairhavennj.net
Year of incorporation	1912
Land/water area (sq. miles)	1.67/0.01
Form of government	Borough

Government
Legislative Districts
US Congressional	12
State Legislative	12

Local Officials, 2008
Mayor	Michael Halfacre
Manager	Mary Howell
Clerk	Allyson M. Cinquegrana
Finance Dir.	Denise Jawidzik
Tax Assessor	Stephen Walters
Tax Collector	Dale Connor
Attorney	Salvatore Alfieri
Building	Paul Reinhold
Comm Dev/Planning	NA
Engineering	Richard Gardella
Public Works	Richard Gardella
Police Chief	Darryl Breckenridge
Emerg/Fire Director	Larry Hartman

Housing & Construction
Housing Units, 2000*
Total	2,037
Median rent	$1,219
Median SF home value	$305,900

Permits for New Residential Construction
	Units	Value
Total, 2007	13	$3,675,664
Single family	13	$3,675,664
Total, 2006	15	$4,274,410
Single family	15	$4,274,410

Real Property Valuation, 2007
	Parcels	Valuation
Total	2,125	$1,123,152,300
Vacant	50	9,753,800
Residential	2,012	1,076,615,700
Commercial	63	36,782,800
Industrial	0	0
Apartments	0	0
Farm land	0	0
Farm homestead	0	0

Average Property Value & Tax, 2007
Residential value	$535,097
Property tax	$11,596
Tax credit/rebate	$1,327

Public Library
Fair Haven Public Library
748 River Rd
Fair Haven, NJ 07704
732-747-5031

Director .... Donna Powers

Library statistics, 2006
Population served	5,937
Full-time/total staff	NA/0

	Total	Per capita
Holdings	NA	NA
Revenues	NA	NA
Expenditures	NA	NA
Annual visits	NA	NA
Internet terminals/annual users	NA/NA	

Public Safety
Number of officers, 2006 15

Crime
	2005	2006
Total crimes	47	43
Violent	0	5
Murder	0	0
Rape	0	0
Robbery	0	1
Aggravated assault	0	4
Non-violent	47	38
Burglary	5	3
Larceny	42	35
Vehicle theft	0	0
Domestic violence	6	3
Arson	0	0
Total crime rate	7.9	7.3
Violent	0.0	0.8
Non-violent	7.9	6.4

Public School District
(for school year 2006-07 except as noted)

Fair Haven Borough School District
224 Hance Rd
Fair Haven, NJ 07704
732-747-2294

Superintendent	Kathleen Cronin
Number of schools	2
Grade plan	K-8
Enrollment	991
Attendance rate, '05-06	95.7%
Dropout rate	NA
Students per teacher	12.1
Per pupil expenditure	$10,355
Median faculty salary	$47,240
Median administrator salary	$111,764
Grade 12 enrollment	NA
High school graduation rate	NA

Assessment test results
(percent scoring at proficient or advanced level)
	Language	Math
NJASK-Grade 3	93.7%	93.7%
GEPA-Grade 8	92.9%	93.0%
HSPA-High School	NA	NA

SAT score averages
Pct tested	Math	Verbal	Writing
NA	NA	NA	NA

Teacher Qualifications
Avg. years of experience	9
Highly-qualified teachers one subject/all subjects	100%/100%
With emergency credentials	0.0%

No Child Left Behind
AYP, 2005-06 .... Meets Standards

Municipal Finance
State Aid Programs, 2008
Total aid	$582,413
CMPTRA	62,000
Energy tax receipts	520,413
Garden State Trust	0

General Budget, 2007
Total tax levy	$24,348,699
County levy	4,066,578
County taxes	3,631,741
County library	207,906
County health	0
County open space	226,930
School levy	14,768,199
Muni. levy	5,513,922
Misc. revenues	2,120,057

Taxes
	2005	2006	2007
General tax rate per $100	2.014	2.102	2.168
County equalization ratio	96.68	84.01	74.44
Net valuation taxable	$1,104,975,059	$1,113,795,300	$1,123,605,985
State equalized value	$1,315,289,917	$1,496,562,873	$1,574,377,872

Fair Lawn Borough
Bergen County

Demographics & Socio-Economic Characteristics
(2000 US Census, except as noted)

Population
1980*	32,229
1990*	30,548
2000	31,637
Male	15,039
Female	16,598
2006 (estimate)*	31,246
Population density	6,043.7

Race & Hispanic Origin, 2000
Race
White	28,960
Black/African American	234
American Indian/Alaska Native	13
Asian	1,558
Native Hawaiian/Pacific Islander	1
Other race	434
Two or more races	437
Hispanic origin, total	1,744
Mexican	55
Puerto Rican	456
Cuban	171
Other Hispanic	1,062

Age & Nativity, 2000
Under 5 years	1,673
18 years and over	24,423
21 years and over	23,584
65 years and over	5,919
85 years and over	711
Median age	41.8
Native-born	23,161
Foreign-born	8,476

Educational Attainment, 2000
Population 25 years and over	22,452
Less than 9th grade	3.3%
High school grad or higher	89.9%
Bachelor's degree or higher	44.8%
Graduate degree	17.6%

Income & Poverty, 1999
Per capita income	$32,273
Median household income	$72,127
Median family income	$81,220
Persons in poverty	1,161
H'holds receiving public assistance	86
H'holds receiving social security	3,823

Households, 2000
Total households	11,806
With persons under 18	4,135
With persons over 65	4,163
Family households	8,906
Single-person households	2,516
Persons per household	2.67
Persons per family	3.12

Labor & Employment
Total civilian labor force, 2006**	16,752
Unemployment rate	3.8%
Total civilian labor force, 2000	16,156
Unemployment rate	2.7%

Employed persons 16 years and over by occupation, 2000
Managers & professionals	7,563
Service occupations	1,428
Sales & office occupations	4,602
Farming, fishing & forestry	0
Construction & maintenance	912
Production & transportation	1,222
Self-employed persons	1,046

* US Census Bureau
** New Jersey Department of Labor

General Information
Borough of Fair Lawn
8-01 Fair Lawn Ave
Fair Lawn, NJ 07410
201-796-1700

Website	www.fairlawn.org
Year of incorporation	1924
Land/water area (sq. miles)	5.17/0.05
Form of government	Council-Manager

Government
Legislative Districts
US Congressional	9
State Legislative	38

Local Officials, 2008
Mayor	Steven Weinstein
Manager	Thomas Metzler
Clerk	Joanne Kwasniewski
Finance Dir.	Barry Eccleston
Tax Assessor	Timothy Henderson
Tax Collector	Alice Lee
Attorney	Bruce Rosenberg
Building	Dennis Kolano
Comm Dev/Planning	NA
Engineering	Kenneth Garrison
Public Works	NA
Police Chief	Erik Rose
Emerg/Fire Director	Peter Yuskaitis

Housing & Construction
Housing Units, 2000*
Total	12,006
Median rent	$923
Median SF home value	$218,000

Permits for New Residential Construction
	Units	Value
Total, 2007	11	$1,882,157
Single family	11	$1,882,157
Total, 2006	12	$2,630,371
Single family	9	$2,049,121

Real Property Valuation, 2007
	Parcels	Valuation
Total	10,819	$5,065,801,300
Vacant	136	30,195,800
Residential	10,204	4,171,669,200
Commercial	400	498,913,900
Industrial	66	220,147,700
Apartments	13	144,874,700
Farm land	0	0
Farm homestead	0	0

Average Property Value & Tax, 2007
Residential value	$408,827
Property tax	$8,276
Tax credit/rebate	$1,287

Public Library
Maurice M. Pine Library
10-01 Fair Lawn Ave
Fair Lawn, NJ 07410
201-796-3400

Director... Timothy H. Murphy

Library statistics, 2006
Population served	31,637
Full-time/total staff	6/17

	Total	Per capita
Holdings	199,857	6.32
Revenues	$2,216,092	$70.05
Expenditures	$2,199,840	$69.53
Annual visits	176,523	5.58
Internet terminals/annual users	10/16,038	

Taxes
	2005	2006	2007
General tax rate per $100	3.89	4.26	2.03
County equalization ratio	57.16	50.67	101.25
Net valuation taxable	$2,297,274,817	$2,294,112,200	$5,074,119,673
State equalized value	$4,533,796,757	$4,988,285,128	$5,331,774,972

Public Safety
Number of officers, 2006		59

Crime	2005	2006
Total crimes	398	491
Violent	35	38
Murder	0	0
Rape	2	3
Robbery	19	11
Aggravated assault	14	24
Non-violent	363	453
Burglary	48	60
Larceny	290	373
Vehicle theft	25	20
Domestic violence	143	143
Arson	2	5
Total crime rate	12.6	15.6
Violent	1.1	1.2
Non-violent	11.5	14.4

Public School District
(for school year 2006-07 except as noted)

Fair Lawn School District
37-01 Fair Lawn Ave
Fair Lawn, NJ 07410
201-794-5510

Superintendent	Bruce Watson
Number of schools	9
Grade plan	K-12
Enrollment	4,733
Attendance rate, '05-06	96.0%
Dropout rate	0.9%
Students per teacher	11.3
Per pupil expenditure	$14,632
Median faculty salary	$63,525
Median administrator salary	$126,840
Grade 12 enrollment	353
High school graduation rate	97.0%

Assessment test results
(percent scoring at proficient or advanced level)
	Language	Math
NJASK-Grade 3	85.9%	92.4%
GEPA-Grade 8	90.5%	82.2%
HSPA-High School	95.8%	82.4%

SAT score averages
Pct tested	Math	Verbal	Writing
94%	534	500	510

Teacher Qualifications
Avg. years of experience	12
Highly-qualified teachers one subject/all subjects	100%/100%
With emergency credentials	0.0%

No Child Left Behind
AYP, 2005-06 ... Meets Standards

Municipal Finance
State Aid Programs, 2008
Total aid	$4,814,819
CMPTRA	775,574
Energy tax receipts	4,039,245
Garden State Trust	0

General Budget, 2007
Total tax levy	$102,715,604
County levy	9,172,174
County taxes	8,667,502
County library	0
County health	0
County open space	504,673
School levy	64,546,304
Muni. levy	28,997,125
Misc. revenues	13,139,404

Cumberland County

Fairfield Township

Demographics & Socio-Economic Characteristics
(2000 US Census, except as noted)

Population
1980*	5,693
1990*	5,699
2000	6,283
Male	3,736
Female	2,547
2006 (estimate)*	6,783
Population density	160.4

Race & Hispanic Origin, 2000
Race
White	2,602
Black/African American	2,980
American Indian/Alaska Native	319
Asian	35
Native Hawaiian/Pacific Islander	2
Other race	150
Two or more races	195
Hispanic origin, total	557
Mexican	123
Puerto Rican	149
Cuban	0
Other Hispanic	285

Age & Nativity, 2000
Under 5 years	279
18 years and over	5,037
21 years and over	4,823
65 years and over	670
85 years and over	53
Median age	36.8
Native-born	6,165
Foreign-born	118

Educational Attainment, 2000
Population 25 years and over	4,491
Less than 9th grade	8.2%
High school grad or higher	63.3%
Bachelor's degree or higher	5.1%
Graduate degree	1.5%

Income & Poverty, 1999
Per capita income	$17,547
Median household income	$37,891
Median family income	$41,326
Persons in poverty	551
H'holds receiving public assistance	67
H'holds receiving social security	591

Households, 2000
Total households	1,751
With persons under 18	660
With persons over 65	484
Family households	1,322
Single-person households	358
Persons per household	2.78
Persons per family	3.19

Labor & Employment
Total civilian labor force, 2006**	2,495
Unemployment rate	9.1%
Total civilian labor force, 2000	2,288
Unemployment rate	12.3%

Employed persons 16 years and over by occupation, 2000
Managers & professionals	398
Service occupations	460
Sales & office occupations	433
Farming, fishing & forestry	7
Construction & maintenance	176
Production & transportation	532
Self-employed persons	101

* US Census Bureau
** New Jersey Department of Labor

See Introduction for an explanation of all data sources.

General Information
Township of Fairfield
PO Box 240
Fairton, NJ 08320
856-451-9284

Website	www.fairfieldtwp-nj.com
Year of incorporation	1697
Land/water area (sq. miles)	42.29/1.51
Form of government	Township

Government

Legislative Districts
US Congressional	2
State Legislative	3

Local Officials, 2008
Mayor	Marion Kennedy Jr
Manager	R. J. DeVillasanta
Clerk	R. J. DeVillasanta
Finance Dir	Judson Moore
Tax Assessor	Michelle Sharp
Tax Collector	Heddi Sutherland
Attorney	John Carr
Building	Milt Truxton
Comm Dev/Planning	NA
Engineering	Uzo Ahiarakwe
Public Works	NA
Police Chief	NA
Fire/Emergency Dir	NA

Housing & Construction

Housing Units, 2000*
Total	1,915
Median rent	$596
Median SF home value	$84,100

Permits for New Residential Construction
	Units	Value
Total, 2007	10	$1,561,825
Single family	10	$1,561,825
Total, 2006	7	$994,913
Single family	7	$994,913

Real Property Valuation, 2007
	Parcels	Valuation
Total	2,673	$164,915,900
Vacant	736	9,386,100
Residential	1,601	130,982,500
Commercial	84	13,554,300
Industrial	0	0
Apartments	0	0
Farm land	188	3,084,300
Farm homestead	64	7,908,700

Average Property Value & Tax, 2007
Residential value	$83,418
Property tax	$2,851
Tax credit/rebate	$745

Public Library
No public municipal library

Library statistics, 2006
Population served	NA
Full-time/total staff	NA/NA

	Total	Per capita
Holdings	NA	NA
Revenues	NA	NA
Expenditures	NA	NA
Annual visits	NA	NA
Internet terminals/annual users	NA/NA	

Taxes
	2005	2006	2007
General tax rate per $100	2.676	3.007	3.421
County equalization ratio	91.45	78.11	68.06
Net valuation taxable	$159,109,561	$161,019,200	$165,821,170
State equalized value	$203,699,348	$237,567,843	$284,265,923

Public Safety
Number of officers, 2006 ... 0

Crime
	2005	2006
Total crimes	100	156
Violent	12	20
Murder	0	1
Rape	0	1
Robbery	1	2
Aggravated assault	11	16
Non-violent	88	136
Burglary	33	55
Larceny	43	72
Vehicle theft	12	9
Domestic violence	61	5
Arson	1	1
Total crime rate	15.0	23.0
Violent	1.8	3.0
Non-violent	13.2	20.1

Public School District
(for school year 2006-07 except as noted)

Fairfield Township School District
375 Gouldtown-Woodruff Rd
Bridgeton, NJ 08302
856-453-1882

Superintendent	John Klug
Number of schools	1
Grade plan	K-8
Enrollment	566
Attendance rate, '05-06	96.2%
Dropout rate	NA
Students per teacher	10.0
Per pupil expenditure	$12,761
Median faculty salary	$46,455
Median administrator salary	$77,737
Grade 12 enrollment	NA
High school graduation rate	NA

Assessment test results
(percent scoring at proficient or advanced level)
	Language	Math
NJASK-Grade 3	63.6%	53.0%
GEPA-Grade 8	43.9%	45.7%
HSPA-High School	NA	NA

SAT score averages
Pct tested	Math	Verbal	Writing
NA	NA	NA	NA

Teacher Qualifications
Avg. years of experience	14
Highly-qualified teachers one subject/all subjects	100%/100%
With emergency credentials	0.0%

No Child Left Behind
AYP, 2005-06 ... Meets Standards

Municipal Finance

State Aid Programs, 2008
Total aid	$540,577
CMPTRA	90,701
Energy tax receipts	412,006
Garden State Trust	37,870

General Budget, 2007
Total tax levy	$5,667,200
County levy	2,406,361
County taxes	2,279,412
County library	0
County health	102,540
County open space	24,409
School levy	2,577,324
Muni. levy	683,514
Misc. revenues	2,495,067

Fairfield Township — Essex County

Demographics & Socio-Economic Characteristics
(2000 US Census, except as noted)

Population
1980*	7,987
1990*	7,615
2000	7,063
Male	3,454
Female	3,609
2006 (estimate)*	7,707
Population density	737.5

Race & Hispanic Origin, 2000
Race
White	6,754
Black/African American	37
American Indian/Alaska Native	7
Asian	199
Native Hawaiian/Pacific Islander	0
Other race	28
Two or more races	38
Hispanic origin, total	244
Mexican	33
Puerto Rican	68
Cuban	32
Other Hispanic	111

Age & Nativity, 2000
Under 5 years	390
18 years and over	5,506
21 years and over	5,300
65 years and over	1,065
85 years and over	118
Median age	40.7
Native-born	6,174
Foreign-born	889

Educational Attainment, 2000
Population 25 years and over	5,028
Less than 9th grade	4.9%
High school grad or higher	86.9%
Bachelor's degree or higher	34.8%
Graduate degree	11.6%

Income & Poverty, 1999
Per capita income	$32,099
Median household income	$83,120
Median family income	$90,998
Persons in poverty	195
H'holds receiving public assistance	8
H'holds receiving social security	776

Households, 2000
Total households	2,296
With persons under 18	837
With persons over 65	703
Family households	1,982
Single-person households	251
Persons per household	3.04
Persons per family	3.29

Labor & Employment
Total civilian labor force, 2006**	3,873
Unemployment rate	3.3%
Total civilian labor force, 2000	3,652
Unemployment rate	2.7%

Employed persons 16 years and over by occupation, 2000
Managers & professionals	1,500
Service occupations	341
Sales & office occupations	1,136
Farming, fishing & forestry	0
Construction & maintenance	307
Production & transportation	270
Self-employed persons	255

* US Census Bureau
** New Jersey Department of Labor

General Information
Township of Fairfield
230 Fairfield Rd
Fairfield, NJ 07004
973-882-2700

Website	www.fairfieldnj.org
Year of incorporation	1964
Land/water area (sq. miles)	10.45/0.00
Form of government	Small Municipality

Government
Legislative Districts
US Congressional	11
State Legislative	27

Local Officials, 2008
Mayor	Rocco Palmieri
Manager	Joseph Catenaro
Clerk	Denise D. Cafone
Finance Dir	Joseph John McClusky
Tax Assessor	E. Romeo Longo
Tax Collector	Marita Shatzel
Attorney	David Paris
Building	Phil Cheff
Comm Dev/Planning	NA
Engineering	Lawrence Gonnello
Public Works	Ron Karl
Police Chief	Charles Voelker Jr
Emerg/Fire Director	Gene Iandolo

Housing & Construction
Housing Units, 2000*
Total	2,326
Median rent	$988
Median SF home value	$274,800

Permits for New Residential Construction
	Units	Value
Total, 2007	7	$2,617,850
Single family	7	$2,617,850
Total, 2006	9	$3,295,308
Single family	9	$3,295,308

Real Property Valuation, 2007
	Parcels	Valuation
Total	3,414	$1,580,634,900
Vacant	265	20,315,800
Residential	2,465	650,134,500
Commercial	398	418,904,900
Industrial	276	479,097,500
Apartments	1	11,701,000
Farm land	7	46,600
Farm homestead	2	434,600

Average Property Value & Tax, 2007
Residential value	$263,709
Property tax	$6,934
Tax credit/rebate	$1,095

Public Library
A.P. Costa Memorial Library
261 Hollywood Ave
Fairfield, NJ 07004
973-227-3575

Director	John J. Helle

Library statistics, 2006
Population served	7,063
Full-time/total staff	1/5

	Total	Per capita
Holdings	77,082	10.91
Revenues	$903,577	$127.93
Expenditures	$644,670	$91.27
Annual visits	39,784	5.63
Internet terminals/annual users	4/3,756	

Taxes
	2005	2006	2007
General tax rate per $100	2.44	2.52	2.63
County equalization ratio	69.77	60.84	54.56
Net valuation taxable	$1,544,958,000	$1,561,994,800	$1,585,913,000
State equalized value	$2,539,378,698	$2,868,924,895	$3,026,369,270

Public Safety
Number of officers, 2006 39

Crime
	2005	2006
Total crimes	325	386
Violent	16	13
Murder	0	0
Rape	0	0
Robbery	2	3
Aggravated assault	14	10
Non-violent	309	373
Burglary	34	44
Larceny	255	300
Vehicle theft	20	29
Domestic violence	44	73
Arson	0	0
Total crime rate	41.5	49.8
Violent	2.0	1.7
Non-violent	39.5	48.1

Public School District
(for school year 2006-07 except as noted)

Fairfield Township School District
15 Knoll Rd
Fairfield, NJ 07004
973-227-5586

Superintendent	Mary Kildow
Number of schools	2
Grade plan	K-6
Enrollment	708
Attendance rate, '05-06	96.0%
Dropout rate	NA
Students per teacher	11.3
Per pupil expenditure	$12,643
Median faculty salary	$47,100
Median administrator salary	$98,424
Grade 12 enrollment	NA
High school graduation rate	NA

Assessment test results
(percent scoring at proficient or advanced level)
	Language	Math
NJASK-Grade 3	92.4%	93.5%
GEPA-Grade 8	NA	NA
HSPA-High School	NA	NA

SAT score averages
Pct tested	Math	Verbal	Writing
NA	NA	NA	NA

Teacher Qualifications
Avg. years of experience	8
Highly-qualified teachers one subject/all subjects	100%/100%
With emergency credentials	0.0%

No Child Left Behind
AYP, 2005-06 .... Meets Standards

Municipal Finance
State Aid Programs, 2008
Total aid	$1,441,765
CMPTRA	234,215
Energy tax receipts	1,185,043
Garden State Trust	22,507

General Budget, 2007
Total tax levy	$41,701,226
County levy	11,458,024
County taxes	11,163,675
County library	0
County health	0
County open space	294,348
School levy	20,560,570
Muni. levy	9,682,632
Misc. revenues	7,313,112

Bergen County
Fairview Borough

Demographics & Socio-Economic Characteristics
(2000 US Census, except as noted)
Population
- 1980* 10,519
- 1990* 10,733
- 2000 13,255
  - Male 6,844
  - Female 6,411
- 2006 (estimate)* 13,628
  - Population density 16,032.9

Race & Hispanic Origin, 2000
Race
- White 9,605
- Black/African American 226
- American Indian/Alaska Native 51
- Asian 659
- Native Hawaiian/Pacific Islander 4
- Other race 1,712
- Two or more races 998
- Hispanic origin, total 4,911
  - Mexican 149
  - Puerto Rican 452
  - Cuban 562
  - Other Hispanic 3,748

Age & Nativity, 2000
- Under 5 years 852
- 18 years and over 10,456
- 21 years and over 9,843
- 65 years and over 1,824
- 85 years and over 191
- Median age 34.5
- Native-born 6,841
- Foreign-born 6,414

Educational Attainment, 2000
- Population 25 years and over 8,859
- Less than 9th grade 19.6%
- High school grad or higher 65.4%
- Bachelor's degree or higher 16.5%
- Graduate degree 4.0%

Income & Poverty, 1999
- Per capita income $18,835
- Median household income $40,393
- Median family income $46,365
- Persons in poverty 1,557
- H'holds receiving public assistance ... 221
- H'holds receiving social security 1,364

Households, 2000
- Total households 4,861
  - With persons under 18 1,600
  - With persons over 65 1,395
  - Family households 3,178
  - Single-person households 1,362
- Persons per household 2.73
- Persons per family 3.31

Labor & Employment
- Total civilian labor force, 2006** 6,446
  - Unemployment rate 7.2%
- Total civilian labor force, 2000 6,053
  - Unemployment rate 7.0%

Employed persons 16 years and over by occupation, 2000
- Managers & professionals 1,345
- Service occupations 894
- Sales & office occupations 1,770
- Farming, fishing & forestry 0
- Construction & maintenance 656
- Production & transportation 964
- Self-employed persons 269

---

* US Census Bureau
** New Jersey Department of Labor

See Introduction for an explanation of all data sources.

General Information
Borough of Fairview
59 Anderson Ave
Fairview, NJ 07022
201-943-3300

- Website .... NA
- Year of incorporation 1894
- Land/water area (sq. miles) 0.85/0.00
- Form of government .... Borough

Government
Legislative Districts
- US Congressional 9
- State Legislative 32

Local Officials, 2008
- Mayor .... Vincent Bellucci Jr
- Manager .... Diane Testa
- Clerk .... Diane Testa
- Finance Dir .... Joseph Rutch
- Tax Assessor .... George Reggo
- Tax Collector .... Eugene Pedoto
- Attorney .... John Schettino
- Building .... Thomas Leonardi
- Comm Dev/Planning .... NA
- Engineering .... Boswell Engineering
- Public Works .... Paul Juliano
- Police Chief .... John Pinzone
- Emerg/Fire Director .... David Masso

Housing & Construction
Housing Units, 2000*
- Total 4,988
- Median rent $846
- Median SF home value $179,900

Permits for New Residential Construction
	Units	Value
Total, 2007	48	$7,412,352
Single family	5	$846,068
Total, 2006	48	$6,464,172
Single family	4	$497,424

Real Property Valuation, 2007
	Parcels	Valuation
Total	2,587	$619,574,500
Vacant	74	6,899,600
Residential	2,075	388,905,900
Commercial	203	111,008,700
Industrial	112	45,829,800
Apartments	123	66,930,500
Farm land	0	0
Farm homestead	0	0

Average Property Value & Tax, 2007
- Residential value $187,425
- Property tax $7,106
- Tax credit/rebate $1,138

Public Library
Fairview Free Public Library
213 Anderson Ave
Fairview, NJ 07022
201-943-6244
- Director .... Roger M. Verdi

Library statistics, 2006
- Population served 13,255
- Full-time/total staff 1/1

	Total	Per capita
Holdings	23,057	1.74
Revenues	$405,337	$30.58
Expenditures	$306,777	$23.14
Annual visits	40,000	3.02
Internet terminals/annual users	6/19,556	

Public Safety
- Number of officers, 2006 31

Crime	2005	2006
Total crimes	333	307
Violent	55	54
Murder	0	0
Rape	3	3
Robbery	28	25
Aggravated assault	24	26
Non-violent	278	253
Burglary	127	113
Larceny	133	119
Vehicle theft	18	21
Domestic violence	204	202
Arson	8	1
Total crime rate	24.6	22.6
Violent	4.1	4.0
Non-violent	20.5	18.7

Public School District
(for school year 2006-07 except as noted)

Fairview School District
130 Hamilton Ave
Fairview, NJ 07022
201-943-1699

- Superintendent .... Louis DeLisio
- Number of schools 3
- Grade plan K-8
- Enrollment 1,028
- Attendance rate, '05-06 .... 94.9%
- Dropout rate .... NA
- Students per teacher 11.8
- Per pupil expenditure $11,976
- Median faculty salary $45,301
- Median administrator salary ... $113,679
- Grade 12 enrollment .... NA
- High school graduation rate .... NA

Assessment test results
(percent scoring at proficient or advanced level)

	Language	Math
NJASK-Grade 3	75.7%	76.8%
GEPA-Grade 8	70.5%	68.8%
HSPA-High School	NA	NA

SAT score averages
Pct tested	Math	Verbal	Writing
NA	NA	NA	NA

Teacher Qualifications
- Avg. years of experience 9
- Highly-qualified teachers
  one subject/all subjects 100%/100%
- With emergency credentials 0.0%

No Child Left Behind
- AYP, 2005-06 .... Meets Standards

Municipal Finance
State Aid Programs, 2008
- Total aid $1,271,144
  - CMPTRA 531,551
  - Energy tax receipts 739,593
  - Garden State Trust 0

General Budget, 2007
- Total tax levy $23,504,351
  - County levy 2,283,688
    - County taxes 2,157,066
    - County library 0
    - County health 0
    - County open space 126,622
  - School levy 11,426,217
  - Muni. levy 9,794,446
- Misc. revenues 4,281,871

Taxes
	2005	2006	2007
General tax rate per $100	3.43	3.64	3.8
County equalization ratio	63.78	56.2	49.42
Net valuation taxable	$612,105,473	$616,266,200	$619,922,889
State equalized value	$1,089,155,646	$1,247,382,324	$1,300,882,604

The New Jersey Municipal Data Book

Fanwood Borough
Union County

Demographics & Socio-Economic Characteristics
(2000 US Census, except as noted)

Population
1980*	7,767
1990*	7,115
2000	7,174
Male	3,422
Female	3,752
2006 (estimate)*	7,211
Population density	5,381.3

Race & Hispanic Origin, 2000
Race
White	6,335
Black/African American	369
American Indian/Alaska Native	7
Asian	315
Native Hawaiian/Pacific Islander	2
Other race	57
Two or more races	89
Hispanic origin, total	268
Mexican	13
Puerto Rican	105
Cuban	26
Other Hispanic	124

Age & Nativity, 2000
Under 5 years	608
18 years and over	5,323
21 years and over	5,183
65 years and over	1,055
85 years and over	136
Median age	38.6
Native-born	6,316
Foreign-born	858

Educational Attainment, 2000
Population 25 years and over	4,999
Less than 9th grade	1.9%
High school grad or higher	95.0%
Bachelor's degree or higher	51.0%
Graduate degree	18.3%

Income & Poverty, 1999
Per capita income	$34,804
Median household income	$85,233
Median family income	$99,232
Persons in poverty	243
H'holds receiving public assistance	44
H'holds receiving social security	709

Households, 2000
Total households	2,574
With persons under 18	1,042
With persons over 65	727
Family households	2,053
Single-person households	463
Persons per household	2.76
Persons per family	3.13

Labor & Employment
Total civilian labor force, 2006**	3,857
Unemployment rate	2.9%
Total civilian labor force, 2000	3,756
Unemployment rate	4.7%

Employed persons 16 years and over by occupation, 2000
Managers & professionals	1,984
Service occupations	214
Sales & office occupations	1,004
Farming, fishing & forestry	0
Construction & maintenance	181
Production & transportation	195
Self-employed persons	179

* US Census Bureau
** New Jersey Department of Labor

General Information
Borough of Fanwood
75 N Martine Ave
Fanwood, NJ 07023
908-322-8236

Website	visitfanwood.com
Year of incorporation	1895
Land/water area (sq. miles)	1.34/0.00
Form of government	Borough

Government
Legislative Districts
US Congressional	7
State Legislative	22

Local Officials, 2008
Mayor	Colleen Mahr
Manager	Eleanor McGovern
Clerk	Eleanor McGovern
Finance Dir	Fred Tomkins
Tax Assessor	Michael Ross
Tax Collector	Colleen Huehn
Attorney	Dennis Estis
Building	Bruce Helmstetter
Planning	Greg Cummings
Engineering	Kupper Associates
Public Works	Clinton Dicksen
Police Chief	Donald Domanoski
Emerg/Fire Director	David Ziegler

Housing & Construction
Housing Units, 2000*
Total	2,615
Median rent	$1,077
Median SF home value	$224,300

Permits for New Residential Construction
	Units	Value
Total, 2007	9	$1,785,604
Single family	9	$1,785,604
Total, 2006	29	$5,351,821
Single family	11	$1,926,221

Real Property Valuation, 2007
	Parcels	Valuation
Total	2,622	$225,443,500
Vacant	52	1,727,600
Residential	2,480	208,944,400
Commercial	72	12,284,500
Industrial	18	2,487,000
Apartments	0	0
Farm land	0	0
Farm homestead	0	0

Average Property Value & Tax, 2007
Residential value	$84,252
Property tax	$8,677
Tax credit/rebate	$1,317

Public Library
Fanwood Memorial Library
14 Tillotson Rd
Fanwood, NJ 07023
908-322-6400

Director .... Dan Weiss

Library statistics, 2006
Population served	7,174
Full-time/total staff	2/4

	Total	Per capita
Holdings	49,789	6.94
Revenues	$454,622	$63.37
Expenditures	$450,473	$62.79
Annual visits	51,893	7.23
Internet terminals/annual users	8/6,328	

Public Safety
Number of officers, 2006 21

Crime
	2005	2006
Total crimes	87	64
Violent	5	2
Murder	1	0
Rape	0	0
Robbery	2	0
Aggravated assault	2	2
Non-violent	82	62
Burglary	17	12
Larceny	54	50
Vehicle theft	11	0
Domestic violence	19	14
Arson	1	0
Total crime rate	12.0	8.9
Violent	0.7	0.3
Non-violent	11.3	8.6

Public School District
(for school year 2006-07 except as noted)

Scotch Plains-Fanwood School District
Evergreen Ave & Cedar St
Scotch Plains, NJ 07076
908-232-6161

Superintendent	Margaret W. Hayes
Number of schools	16
Grade plan	K-12
Enrollment	5,333
Attendance rate, '05-06	96.1%
Dropout rate	0.1%
Students per teacher	12.0
Per pupil expenditure	$12,673
Median faculty salary	$55,269
Median administrator salary	$116,675
Grade 12 enrollment	340
High school graduation rate	100.0%

Assessment test results
(percent scoring at proficient or advanced level)
	Language	Math
NJASK-Grade 3	93.6%	96.1%
GEPA-Grade 8	88.9%	85.7%
HSPA-High School	93.4%	87.8%

SAT score averages
Pct tested	Math	Verbal	Writing
105%	550	522	518

Teacher Qualifications
Avg. years of experience	8
Highly-qualified teachers one subject/all subjects	99.5%/99.5%
With emergency credentials	0.3%

No Child Left Behind
AYP, 2005-06 .... Meets Standards

Municipal Finance
State Aid Programs, 2008
Total aid	$929,079
CMPTRA	76,660
Energy tax receipts	852,419
Garden State Trust	0

General Budget, 2007
Total tax levy	$23,226,574
County levy	3,951,736
County taxes	3,781,928
County library	0
County health	0
County open space	169,808
School levy	14,701,841
Muni. levy	4,572,997
Misc. revenues	3,752,821

Taxes
	2005	2006	2007
General tax rate per $100	9.378	9.872	10.299
County equalization ratio	24.03	21.19	19.95
Net valuation taxable	$223,765,836	$224,513,400	$225,534,430
State equalized value	$1,006,593,954	$1,125,480,420	$1,178,572,373

Somerset County
Far Hills Borough

Demographics & Socio-Economic Characteristics
(2000 US Census, except as noted)

Population
1980*	677
1990*	657
2000	859
Male	404
Female	455
2006 (estimate)*	928
Population density	190.9

Race & Hispanic Origin, 2000
Race
- White 825
- Black/African American 7
- American Indian/Alaska Native 1
- Asian 18
- Native Hawaiian/Pacific Islander 0
- Other race 0
- Two or more races 8
- Hispanic origin, total 31
- Mexican 6
- Puerto Rican 0
- Cuban 0
- Other Hispanic 25

Age & Nativity, 2000
- Under 5 years 52
- 18 years and over 701
- 21 years and over 688
- 65 years and over 142
- 85 years and over 12
- Median age 44.6
- Native-born 756
- Foreign-born 100

Educational Attainment, 2000
- Population 25 years and over 669
- Less than 9th grade 2.1%
- High school grad or higher 94.8%
- Bachelor's degree or higher 58.1%
- Graduate degree 23.5%

Income & Poverty, 1999
- Per capita income $81,535
- Median household income $112,817
- Median family income $149,095
- Persons in poverty 21
- H'holds receiving public assistance 0
- H'holds receiving social security 104

Households, 2000
- Total households 368
- With persons under 18 91
- With persons over 65 97
- Family households 253
- Single-person households 94
- Persons per household 2.33
- Persons per family 2.76

Labor & Employment
- Total civilian labor force, 2006** 496
- Unemployment rate 2.6%
- Total civilian labor force, 2000 444
- Unemployment rate 2.5%

Employed persons 16 years and over by occupation, 2000
- Managers & professionals 240
- Service occupations 57
- Sales & office occupations 91
- Farming, fishing & forestry 4
- Construction & maintenance 30
- Production & transportation 11
- Self-employed persons 49

‡ Joint library with Bedminster Township
* US Census Bureau
** New Jersey Department of Labor

See Introduction for an explanation of all data sources.

General Information
Borough of Far Hills
PO Box 249
Far Hills, NJ 07931
908-234-0611
Email .... farhillsborough@patmedia.net
Year of incorporation 1921
Land/water area (sq. miles) 4.86/0.06
Form of government .... Borough

Government
Legislative Districts
- US Congressional 7
- State Legislative 16

Local Officials, 2008
- Mayor .... Carl J. Torsilieri
- Manager/Admin .... NA
- Clerk .... Robin Collins
- Finance Dir .... Debra Stern
- Tax Assessor .... Edward Kerwin
- Tax Collector .... Deborah Giordano
- Attorney .... Maryann Nergaard
- Building .... Joseph Alicino
- Planning .... David Banisch
- Engineering .... Paul Ferriero
- Public Works .... NA
- Police Chief .... Kenneth Hartman
- Emerg/Fire Director .... Kevin Sullivan

Housing & Construction
Housing Units, 2000*
- Total 386
- Median rent $1,208
- Median SF home value $393,300

Permits for New Residential Construction
	Units	Value
Total, 2007	0	$0
Single family	0	$0
Total, 2006	3	$8,400,000
Single family	3	$8,400,000

Real Property Valuation, 2007
	Parcels	Valuation
Total	457	$477,528,950
Vacant	20	10,497,800
Residential	310	334,123,100
Commercial	28	32,742,900
Industrial	0	0
Apartments	1	429,000
Farm land	55	382,650
Farm homestead	43	99,353,500

Average Property Value & Tax, 2007
- Residential value $1,227,979
- Property tax $11,529
- Tax credit/rebate $871

Public Library
Clarence Dillon Public Library‡
2336 Lamington Rd
Bedminster, NJ 07921
908-234-2325
Director .... Nanette E. Geiger

Library statistics, 2006
- Population served 9,161
- Full-time/total staff 2/3

	Total	Per capita
Holdings	120,691	13.17
Revenues	$1,012,359	$110.51
Expenditures	$852,310	$93.04
Annual visits	85,403	9.32
Internet terminals/annual users	22/5,023	

Public Safety
Number of officers, 2006 6

Crime	2005	2006
Total crimes	10	13
Violent	0	2
Murder	0	0
Rape	0	0
Robbery	0	0
Aggravated assault	0	2
Non-violent	10	11
Burglary	4	2
Larceny	5	9
Vehicle theft	1	0
Domestic violence	6	6
Arson	0	0
Total crime rate	10.9	14.1
Violent	0.0	2.2
Non-violent	10.9	12.0

Public School District
(for school year 2006-07 except as noted)

Somerset Hills Regional School District
25 Olcott Ave
Bernardsville, NJ 07924
908-630-3011

- Superintendent .... Peter Miller
- Number of schools 9
- Grade plan K-12
- Enrollment 2,022
- Attendance rate, '05-06 .... 96.0%
- Dropout rate 0.3%
- Students per teacher 11.0
- Per pupil expenditure $15,675
- Median faculty salary $61,868
- Median administrator salary $132,115
- Grade 12 enrollment 181
- High school graduation rate 98.9%

Assessment test results
(percent scoring at proficient or advanced level)
	Language	Math
NJASK-Grade 3	94.4%	99.3%
GEPA-Grade 8	89.5%	86.2%
HSPA-High School	97.2%	92.7%

SAT score averages
Pct tested	Math	Verbal	Writing
91%	575	561	558

Teacher Qualifications
- Avg. years of experience 10
- Highly-qualified teachers one subject/all subjects 100%/100%
- With emergency credentials 0.0%

No Child Left Behind
AYP, 2005-06 .... Meets Standards

Municipal Finance
State Aid Programs, 2008
- Total aid $83,753
- CMPTRA 0
- Energy tax receipts 83,753
- Garden State Trust 0

General Budget, 2007
- Total tax levy $4,486,401
- County levy 1,387,423
- County taxes 1,250,488
- County library 0
- County health 0
- County open space 136,935
- School levy 1,635,950
- Muni. levy 1,463,027
- Misc. revenues 626,150

Taxes
	2005	2006	2007
General tax rate per $100	0.96	0.92	0.94
County equalization ratio	104.32	106.14	104.84
Net valuation taxable	$434,723,333	$469,017,158	$477,863,541
State equalized value	$438,759,924	$447,691,277	$485,037,139

Farmingdale Borough
Monmouth County

Demographics & Socio-Economic Characteristics
(2000 US Census, except as noted)

Population
- 1980* 1,348
- 1990* 1,462
- 2000 1,587
  - Male 802
  - Female 785
- 2006 (estimate)* 1,563
  - Population density 2,949.1

Race & Hispanic Origin, 2000
Race
- White 1,486
- Black/African American 18
- American Indian/Alaska Native ... 0
- Asian 37
- Native Hawaiian/Pacific Islander ... 0
- Other race 33
- Two or more races 13
- Hispanic origin, total 61
  - Mexican 12
  - Puerto Rican 27
  - Cuban 0
  - Other Hispanic 22

Age & Nativity, 2000
- Under 5 years 102
- 18 years and over 1,159
- 21 years and over 1,117
- 65 years and over 143
- 85 years and over 7
- Median age 34.7
- Native-born 1,496
- Foreign-born 91

Educational Attainment, 2000
- Population 25 years and over ... 1,041
- Less than 9th grade 2.2%
- High school grad or higher ... 88.5%
- Bachelor's degree or higher ... 19.0%
- Graduate degree 6.3%

Income & Poverty, 1999
- Per capita income $21,667
- Median household income ... $48,889
- Median family income $59,625
- Persons in poverty 90
- H'holds receiving public assistance ... 20
- H'holds receiving social security ... 120

Households, 2000
- Total households 625
  - With persons under 18 244
  - With persons over 65 105
  - Family households 406
  - Single-person households 181
- Persons per household 2.54
- Persons per family 3.21

Labor & Employment
- Total civilian labor force, 2006** ... 915
  - Unemployment rate 2.4%
- Total civilian labor force, 2000 ... 860
  - Unemployment rate 3.1%

Employed persons 16 years and over by occupation, 2000
- Managers & professionals 274
- Service occupations 121
- Sales & office occupations 230
- Farming, fishing & forestry 0
- Construction & maintenance ... 114
- Production & transportation ... 94
- Self-employed persons 40

* US Census Bureau
** New Jersey Department of Labor

General Information
Borough of Farmingdale
11 Asbury Ave
PO Box 58
Farmingdale, NJ 07727
732-938-4077

- Email ...... farmingdale.borough@verizon.net
- Year of incorporation 1903
- Land/water area (sq. miles) 0.53/0.00
- Form of government .... Borough

Government
Legislative Districts
- US Congressional 4
- State Legislative 30

Local Officials, 2008
- Mayor .... John P. Morgan
- Borough Admin .... Donna M. Phalps
- Clerk .... Lorene Wright
- Finance Dir .... Robbin Kirk
- Tax Assessor .... Thomas Glock
- Tax Collector .... Robbin Kirk
- Attorney .... John O. Bennett III
- Building .... Chester Phillips
- Comm Dev/Planning .... NA
- Engineering .... Matt Shafai
- Public Works .... Richard Dusch
- Police Chief .... NA
- Emerg/Fire Director ... William Lewis

Housing & Construction
Housing Units, 2000*
- Total 638
- Median rent $780
- Median SF home value ... $154,100

Permits for New Residential Construction

	Units	Value
Total, 2007	2	$121,167
Single family	2	$121,167
Total, 2006	6	$349,000
Single family	6	$349,000

Real Property Valuation, 2007

	Parcels	Valuation
Total	419	$149,209,200
Vacant	25	2,192,700
Residential	351	110,413,000
Commercial	35	19,617,700
Industrial	3	2,742,800
Apartments	3	13,507,100
Farm land	1	14,200
Farm homestead	1	721,700

Average Property Value & Tax, 2007
- Residential value $315,724
- Property tax $5,416
- Tax credit/rebate $1,033

Public Library
No public municipal library

Library statistics, 2006
- Population served .... NA
- Full-time/total staff .... NA/NA

	Total	Per capita
Holdings	NA	NA
Revenues	NA	NA
Expenditures	NA	NA
Annual visits	NA	NA
Internet terminals/annual users	NA/NA	

Taxes

	2005	2006	2007
General tax rate per $100	1.725	1.76	1.716
County equalization ratio	103.57	100.29	100.19
Net valuation taxable	$150,594,944	$148,431,800	$151,181,169
State equalized value	$150,159,482	$150,439,213	$155,811,746

Public Safety
Number of officers, 2006 0

Crime	2005	2006
Total crimes	12	27
Violent	3	2
Murder	0	0
Rape	0	0
Robbery	0	1
Aggravated assault	3	1
Non-violent	9	25
Burglary	2	3
Larceny	6	17
Vehicle theft	1	5
Domestic violence	8	2
Arson	0	0
Total crime rate	7.6	17.2
Violent	1.9	1.3
Non-violent	5.7	15.9

Public School District
(for school year 2006-07 except as noted)

Farmingdale Borough School District
Academy St, PO Box 706
Farmingdale, NJ 07727
732-938-9611

- Superintendent .... Cheri-Ellen Crowl
- Number of schools 1
- Grade plan K-8
- Enrollment 150
- Attendance rate, '05-06 .... 94.1%
- Dropout rate .... NA
- Students per teacher 8.6
- Per pupil expenditure $14,498
- Median faculty salary $67,759
- Median administrator salary ... $58,311
- Grade 12 enrollment .... NA
- High school graduation rate ..... NA

Assessment test results
(percent scoring at proficient or advanced level)

	Language	Math
NJASK-Grade 3	90.5%	100.0%
GEPA-Grade 8	90.0%	90.0%
HSPA-High School	NA	NA

SAT score averages

Pct tested	Math	Verbal	Writing
NA	NA	NA	NA

Teacher Qualifications
- Avg. years of experience 17
- Highly-qualified teachers
  - one subject/all subjects ... 100%/100%
- With emergency credentials 0.0%

No Child Left Behind
- AYP, 2005-06 .... Meets Standards

Municipal Finance
State Aid Programs, 2008
- Total aid $96,109
  - CMPTRA 0
  - Energy tax receipts 96,109
  - Garden State Trust 0

General Budget, 2007
- Total tax levy $2,593,379
  - County levy 416,866
  - County taxes 366,065
  - County library 20,956
  - County health 6,973
  - County open space 22,872
  - School levy 1,965,299
  - Muni. levy 211,213
  - Misc. revenues 578,409

Burlington County
Fieldsboro Borough

Demographics & Socio-Economic Characteristics
(2000 US Census, except as noted)

Population
1980*	597
1990*	579
2000	522
Male	245
Female	277
2006 (estimate)*	577
Population density	2,137.0

Race & Hispanic Origin, 2000
Race
White	426
Black/African American	83
American Indian/Alaska Native	1
Asian	0
Native Hawaiian/Pacific Islander	0
Other race	2
Two or more races	10
Hispanic origin, total	13
Mexican	0
Puerto Rican	5
Cuban	1
Other Hispanic	7

Age & Nativity, 2000
Under 5 years	39
18 years and over	390
21 years and over	378
65 years and over	65
85 years and over	3
Median age	35.4
Native-born	508
Foreign-born	20

Educational Attainment, 2000
Population 25 years and over	351
Less than 9th grade	1.7%
High school grad or higher	88.6%
Bachelor's degree or higher	27.6%
Graduate degree	5.4%

Income & Poverty, 1999
Per capita income	$23,908
Median household income	$58,958
Median family income	$66,607
Persons in poverty	10
H'holds receiving public assistance	0
H'holds receiving social security	34

Households, 2000
Total households	189
With persons under 18	76
With persons over 65	45
Family households	139
Single-person households	33
Persons per household	2.76
Persons per family	3.17

Labor & Employment
Total civilian labor force, 2006**	362
Unemployment rate	7.0%
Total civilian labor force, 2000	303
Unemployment rate	4.0%

Employed persons 16 years and over by occupation, 2000
Managers & professionals	84
Service occupations	39
Sales & office occupations	99
Farming, fishing & forestry	0
Construction & maintenance	18
Production & transportation	51
Self-employed persons	8

* US Census Bureau
** New Jersey Department of Labor

See Introduction for an explanation of all data sources.

General Information
Borough of Fieldsboro
204 Washington St
Fieldsboro, NJ 08505
609-298-6344

Website	www.fieldsboro.us
Year of incorporation	1850
Land/water area (sq. miles)	0.27/0.00
Form of government	Borough

Government
Legislative Districts
US Congressional	4
State Legislative	30

Local Officials, 2008
Mayor	Edward Tyler Sr
Manager/Admin	NA
Clerk	Patrice Hansell
Finance Dir	Peter Federico
Tax Assessor	Walter Kosul
Tax Collector	Lan Chen Shen
Attorney	Kenneth Domzalski
Building	DCA
Comm Dev/Planning	NA
Engineering	Birdsall Engineering
Public Works	Roger Redwanski
Police Chief	Joseph Conlin
Fire/Emergency Dir	NA

Housing & Construction
Housing Units, 2000*
Total	204
Median rent	$1,050
Median SF home value	$103,900

Permits for New Residential Construction
	Units	Value
Total, 2007	0	$0
Single family	0	$0
Total, 2006	2	$330,000
Single family	2	$330,000

Real Property Valuation, 2007
	Parcels	Valuation
Total	243	$28,938,000
Vacant	34	815,900
Residential	201	18,971,100
Commercial	7	1,285,100
Industrial	1	7,865,900
Apartments	0	0
Farm land	0	0
Farm homestead	0	0

Average Property Value & Tax, 2007
Residential value	$94,384
Property tax	$4,642
Tax credit/rebate	$893

Public Library
No public municipal library

Library statistics, 2006
Population served	NA
Full-time/total staff	NA/NA

	Total	Per capita
Holdings	NA	NA
Revenues	NA	NA
Expenditures	NA	NA
Annual visits	NA	NA
Internet terminals/annual users	NA/NA	

Taxes
	2005	2006	2007
General tax rate per $100	3.637	4.334	4.92
County equalization ratio	74.25	57.55	48.62
Net valuation taxable	$28,596,674	$28,892,800	$28,961,828
State equalized value	$49,690,137	$59,452,878	$64,459,366

Public Safety
Number of officers, 2006 0

Crime	2005	2006
Total crimes	10	7
Violent	3	2
Murder	0	0
Rape	0	0
Robbery	0	1
Aggravated assault	3	1
Non-violent	7	5
Burglary	2	1
Larceny	5	4
Vehicle theft	0	0
Domestic violence	2	1
Arson	0	0
Total crime rate	17.1	12.0
Violent	5.1	3.4
Non-violent	11.9	8.6

Public School District
(for school year 2006-07 except as noted)

Bordentown Regional School District
318 Ward Ave
Bordentown, NJ 08505
609-298-0025

Superintendent	Albert Monillas
Number of schools	15
Grade plan	K-12
Enrollment	2,276
Attendance rate, '05-06	95.6%
Dropout rate	1.3%
Students per teacher	11.6
Per pupil expenditure	$13,418
Median faculty salary	$51,839
Median administrator salary	$90,143
Grade 12 enrollment	156
High school graduation rate	94.5%

Assessment test results
(percent scoring at proficient or advanced level)
	Language	Math
NJASK-Grade 3	90.7%	91.9%
GEPA-Grade 8	78.0%	76.9%
HSPA-High School	87.7%	68.1%

SAT score averages
Pct tested	Math	Verbal	Writing
76%	479	486	469

Teacher Qualifications
Avg. years of experience	9
Highly-qualified teachers one subject/all subjects	100%/100%
With emergency credentials	0.0%

No Child Left Behind
AYP, 2005-06 .... Meets Standards

Municipal Finance
State Aid Programs, 2008
Total aid	$48,714
CMPTRA	0
Energy tax receipts	48,714
Garden State Trust	0

General Budget, 2007
Total tax levy	$1,424,454
County levy	260,917
County taxes	216,207
County library	19,840
County health	0
County open space	24,870
School levy	888,409
Muni. levy	275,128
Misc. revenues	441,437

The New Jersey Municipal Data Book

Flemington Borough

Hunterdon County

Demographics & Socio-Economic Characteristics
(2000 US Census, except as noted)

Population
1980*	4,132
1990*	4,047
2000	4,200
Male	2,038
Female	2,162
2006 (estimate)*	4,267
Population density	3,987.9

Race & Hispanic Origin, 2000
Race
White	3,684
Black/African American	134
American Indian/Alaska Native	13
Asian	131
Native Hawaiian/Pacific Islander	7
Other race	132
Two or more races	99
Hispanic origin, total	461
Mexican	143
Puerto Rican	40
Cuban	3
Other Hispanic	275

Age & Nativity, 2000
Under 5 years	296
18 years and over	3,267
21 years and over	3,134
65 years and over	510
85 years and over	87
Median age	34.9
Native-born	3,618
Foreign-born	582

Educational Attainment, 2000
Population 25 years and over	2,942
Less than 9th grade	5.6%
High school grad or higher	82.6%
Bachelor's degree or higher	27.4%
Graduate degree	11.2%

Income & Poverty, 1999
Per capita income	$23,769
Median household income	$39,886
Median family income	$51,582
Persons in poverty	281
H'holds receiving public assistance	72
H'holds receiving social security	496

Households, 2000
Total households	1,804
With persons under 18	518
With persons over 65	406
Family households	998
Single-person households	680
Persons per household	2.26
Persons per family	3.00

Labor & Employment
Total civilian labor force, 2006**	2,532
Unemployment rate	3.6%
Total civilian labor force, 2000	2,259
Unemployment rate	2.9%

Employed persons 16 years and over by occupation, 2000
Managers & professionals	694
Service occupations	439
Sales & office occupations	640
Farming, fishing & forestry	37
Construction & maintenance	165
Production & transportation	219
Self-employed persons	130

* US Census Bureau
** New Jersey Department of Labor

General Information
Borough of Flemington
38 Park Ave
Flemington, NJ 08822
908-782-8840

Website	www.historicflemington.com
Year of incorporation	1910
Land/water area (sq. miles)	1.07/0.00
Form of government	Borough

Government
Legislative Districts
US Congressional	7
State Legislative	23

Local Officials, 2008
Mayor	Robert B. Hauck
Manager/Admin	NA
Clerk	Diane Schottman
Finance Dir	William Hance
Tax Assessor	Edward Kerwin
Tax Collector	Cathrine Park
Attorney	Barry Goodman
Building	Jeffrey Klein
Comm Dev/Planning	NA
Engineering	Robert J. Clerico
Public Works	Michael Campion
Police Chief	George Becker
Emerg/Fire Director	Paul Klinski

Housing & Construction
Housing Units, 2000*
Total	1,876
Median rent	$828
Median SF home value	$163,300

Permits for New Residential Construction
	Units	Value
Total, 2007	37	$1,567,083
Single family	0	$0
Total, 2006	22	$762,300
Single family	0	$0

Real Property Valuation, 2007
	Parcels	Valuation
Total	1,135	$517,456,800
Vacant	36	4,926,100
Residential	864	258,214,800
Commercial	223	209,805,200
Industrial	2	3,257,100
Apartments	10	41,253,600
Farm land	0	0
Farm homestead	0	0

Average Property Value & Tax, 2007
Residential value	$298,860
Property tax	$6,796
Tax credit/rebate	$1,098

Public Library
Flemington Free Public Library
118 Main St
Flemington, NJ 08822
908-782-5733

Director	Shawn Armington

Library statistics, 2006
Population served	4,200
Full-time/total staff	1/3

	Total	Per capita
Holdings	53,979	12.85
Revenues	$270,392	$64.38
Expenditures	$258,656	$61.58
Annual visits	38,542	9.18
Internet terminals/annual users	11/14,400	

Public Safety
Number of officers, 2006	16

Crime	2005	2006
Total crimes	127	96
Violent	5	13
Murder	0	0
Rape	0	0
Robbery	0	6
Aggravated assault	5	7
Non-violent	122	83
Burglary	18	12
Larceny	96	69
Vehicle theft	8	2
Domestic violence	18	24
Arson	0	3
Total crime rate	30.2	23.0
Violent	1.2	3.1
Non-violent	29.0	19.9

Public School District
(for school year 2006-07 except as noted)

Flemington-Raritan Regional School Dist.
50 Court St
Flemington, NJ 08822
908-284-7575

Superintendent	Jack Farr
Number of schools	12
Grade plan	K-8
Enrollment	3,587
Attendance rate, '05-06	96.2%
Dropout rate	NA
Students per teacher	10.5
Per pupil expenditure	$12,736
Median faculty salary	$49,870
Median administrator salary	$108,184
Grade 12 enrollment	NA
High school graduation rate	NA

Assessment test results
(percent scoring at proficient or advanced level)
	Language	Math
NJASK-Grade 3	93.9%	96.4%
GEPA-Grade 8	89.1%	83.7%
HSPA-High School	NA	NA

SAT score averages
Pct tested	Math	Verbal	Writing
NA	NA	NA	NA

Teacher Qualifications
Avg. years of experience	11
Highly-qualified teachers one subject/all subjects	99.5%/99.5%
With emergency credentials	0.0%

No Child Left Behind
AYP, 2005-06	Meets Standards

Municipal Finance
State Aid Programs, 2008
Total aid	$306,869
CMPTRA	0
Energy tax receipts	306,869
Garden State Trust	0

General Budget, 2007
Total tax levy	$11,906,212
County levy	1,714,987
County taxes	1,548,008
County library	0
County health	0
County open space	166,979
School levy	7,689,929
Muni. levy	2,501,296
Misc. revenues	2,235,825

Taxes	2005	2006	2007
General tax rate per $100	2.39	2.38	2.28
County equalization ratio	98.62	97.24	94.63
Net valuation taxable	$440,812,963	$480,096,900	$523,552,384
State equalized value	$510,969,008	$510,237,181	$538,349,030

Burlington County
Florence Township

Demographics & Socio-Economic Characteristics
(2000 US Census, except as noted)

Population
1980*	9,084
1990*	10,266
2000	10,746
Male	5,140
Female	5,606
2006 (estimate)*	11,637
Population density	1,198.5

Race & Hispanic Origin, 2000
Race
White	9,190
Black/African American	1,047
American Indian/Alaska Native	19
Asian	253
Native Hawaiian/Pacific Islander	1
Other race	70
Two or more races	166
Hispanic origin, total	253
Mexican	23
Puerto Rican	126
Cuban	11
Other Hispanic	93

Age & Nativity, 2000
Under 5 years	660
18 years and over	8,039
21 years and over	7,680
65 years and over	1,277
85 years and over	123
Median age	36.9
Native-born	10,059
Foreign-born	687

Educational Attainment, 2000
Population 25 years and over	7,210
Less than 9th grade	5.1%
High school grad or higher	85.5%
Bachelor's degree or higher	19.9%
Graduate degree	6.8%

Income & Poverty, 1999
Per capita income	$23,529
Median household income	$56,843
Median family income	$67,412
Persons in poverty	654
H'holds receiving public assistance	86
H'holds receiving social security	1,082

Households, 2000
Total households	4,149
With persons under 18	1,501
With persons over 65	949
Family households	2,892
Single-person households	1,037
Persons per household	2.58
Persons per family	3.10

Labor & Employment
Total civilian labor force, 2006**	6,613
Unemployment rate	5.6%
Total civilian labor force, 2000	5,661
Unemployment rate	4.9%

Employed persons 16 years and over by occupation, 2000
Managers & professionals	1,770
Service occupations	684
Sales & office occupations	1,544
Farming, fishing & forestry	6
Construction & maintenance	482
Production & transportation	895
Self-employed persons	174

* US Census Bureau
** New Jersey Department of Labor

See Introduction for an explanation of all data sources.

General Information
Township of Florence
Municipal Complex
711 Broad St
Florence, NJ 08518
609-499-2525

Website	www.florence-nj.com
Year of incorporation	1872
Land/water area (sq. miles)	9.71/0.42
Form of government	Mayor-Council

Government
Legislative Districts
US Congressional	4
State Legislative	7

Local Officials, 2008
Mayor	William E. Berry
Manager	Richard A. Brook
Clerk	Joy M. Weiler
Finance Dir	Sandra A. Blacker
Tax Assessor	Dennis Bianchini
Tax Collector	Ann Schubert
Attorney	William J. Kearns Jr
Building	Thomas Layou
Planning	Nancy Erlston
Engineering	Dante Guzzi
Public Works	Richard Pendle
Police Chief	Stephen C. Fazekas
Emerg/Fire Director	Edward Kensler

Housing & Construction
Housing Units, 2000*
Total	4,391
Median rent	$680
Median SF home value	$115,900

Permits for New Residential Construction
	Units	Value
Total, 2007	23	$3,521,208
Single family	23	$3,521,208
Total, 2006	46	$3,756,800
Single family	22	$2,601,800

Real Property Valuation, 2007
	Parcels	Valuation
Total	4,957	$595,721,950
Vacant	420	24,597,600
Residential	4,276	500,277,850
Commercial	129	24,346,500
Industrial	21	33,154,800
Apartments	9	6,279,200
Farm land	70	2,238,700
Farm homestead	32	4,827,300

Average Property Value & Tax, 2007
Residential value	$117,248
Property tax	$4,486
Tax credit/rebate	$930

Public Library
Florence Township Public Library
1350 Hornberger Ave
Roebling, NJ 08554
609-499-0143

Director: LaVonna Lawrence

Library statistics, 2006
Population served	10,746
Full-time/total staff	0/3

	Total	Per capita
Holdings	27,123	2.52
Revenues	$111,763	$10.40
Expenditures	$104,632	$9.74
Annual visits	9,367	0.87
Internet terminals/annual users	5/4,100	

Taxes
	2005	2006	2007
General tax rate per $100	3.557	3.764	3.83
County equalization ratio	71.72	62.65	54.28
Net valuation taxable	$540,769,035	$554,961,750	$597,221,853
State equalized value	$863,158,875	$1,024,118,144	$1,173,258,263

Public Safety
Number of officers, 2006		25

Crime	2005	2006
Total crimes	143	126
Violent	12	10
Murder	1	0
Rape	1	0
Robbery	1	3
Aggravated assault	9	7
Non-violent	131	116
Burglary	43	38
Larceny	74	60
Vehicle theft	14	18
Domestic violence	117	129
Arson	2	2
Total crime rate	12.7	11.0
Violent	1.1	0.9
Non-violent	11.6	10.1

Public School District
(for school year 2006-07 except as noted)

Florence Township School District
201 Cedar St
Florence, NJ 08518
609-499-4600

Superintendent	Louis Talarico
Number of schools	3
Grade plan	K-12
Enrollment	1,376
Attendance rate, '05-06	93.3%
Dropout rate	1.5%
Students per teacher	11.3
Per pupil expenditure	$12,612
Median faculty salary	$54,770
Median administrator salary	$112,544
Grade 12 enrollment	111
High school graduation rate	90.0%

Assessment test results
(percent scoring at proficient or advanced level)
	Language	Math
NJASK-Grade 3	80.1%	83.1%
GEPA-Grade 8	70.0%	62.4%
HSPA-High School	87.9%	75.0%

SAT score averages
Pct tested	Math	Verbal	Writing
67%	505	496	479

Teacher Qualifications
Avg. years of experience	11
Highly-qualified teachers one subject/all subjects	90.0%/90.0%
With emergency credentials	0.0%

No Child Left Behind
AYP, 2005-06 ... Meets Standards

Municipal Finance
State Aid Programs, 2008
Total aid	$1,731,104
CMPTRA	667,919
Energy tax receipts	1,063,185
Garden State Trust	0

General Budget, 2007
Total tax levy	$22,849,311
County levy	4,684,098
County taxes	3,881,431
County library	356,183
County health	0
County open space	446,484
School levy	14,541,615
Muni. levy	3,623,598
Misc. revenues	6,604,438

Florham Park Borough — Morris County

Demographics & Socio-Economic Characteristics
(2000 US Census, except as noted)

Population
- 1980: 9,359
- 1990*: 8,521
- 2000: 8,857
  - Male: 4,095
  - Female: 4,762
- 2006 (estimate)*: 12,605
- Population density: 1,696.5

Race & Hispanic Origin, 2000
Race
- White: 8,326
- Black/African American: 88
- American Indian/Alaska Native: 1
- Asian: 343
- Native Hawaiian/Pacific Islander: 5
- Other race: 34
- Two or more races: 60
- Hispanic origin, total: 190
  - Mexican: 14
  - Puerto Rican: 30
  - Cuban: 28
  - Other Hispanic: 118

Age & Nativity, 2000
- Under 5 years: 542
- 18 years and over: 6,935
- 21 years and over: 6,756
- 65 years and over: 1,806
- 85 years and over: 261
- Median age: 43.8
- Native-born: 7,927
- Foreign-born: 930

Educational Attainment, 2000
- Population 25 years and over: 6,484
- Less than 9th grade: 2.9%
- High school grad or higher: 92.2%
- Bachelor's degree or higher: 57.7%
- Graduate degree: 24.4%

Income & Poverty, 1999
- Per capita income: $42,133
- Median household income: $88,706
- Median family income: $102,047
- Persons in poverty: 507
- H'holds receiving public assistance: 52
- H'holds receiving social security: 1,044

Households, 2000
- Total households: 3,239
  - With persons under 18: 1,040
  - With persons over 65: 1,067
  - Family households: 2,474
  - Single-person households: 671
- Persons per household: 2.62
- Persons per family: 3.05

Labor & Employment
- Total civilian labor force, 2006**: 4,728
  - Unemployment rate: 2.7%
- Total civilian labor force, 2000: 4,399
  - Unemployment rate: 3.3%

Employed persons 16 years and over by occupation, 2000
- Managers & professionals: 2,346
- Service occupations: 451
- Sales & office occupations: 1,074
- Farming, fishing & forestry: 0
- Construction & maintenance: 213
- Production & transportation: 172
- Self-employed persons: 246

* US Census Bureau
** New Jersey Department of Labor

General Information
Borough of Florham Park
111 Ridgedale Ave
Florham Park, NJ 07932
973-410-5300
- Website: www.florhamparkboro.net
- Year of incorporation: 1899
- Land/water area (sq. miles): 7.43/0.02
- Form of government: Borough

Government
Legislative Districts
- US Congressional: 11
- State Legislative: 26

Local Officials, 2008
- Mayor: R. Scott Eveland
- Manager: Nancy C. Gage
- Clerk: Sheila A. Williams
- Finance Dir: NA
- Tax Assessor: Lisa Baratto
- Tax Collector: Rosemary Schumacher
- Attorney: Joseph Bell
- Building: Stephen Jones
- Planning: Robert Michaels
- Engineering: Michael Sgaramella
- Public Works: Carl F. Ganger Jr
- Police Chief: Patrick Montuore
- Emerg/Fire Director: Robert Young

Housing & Construction
Housing Units, 2000*
- Total: 3,342
- Median rent: $917
- Median SF home value: $322,400

Permits for New Residential Construction

	Units	Value
Total, 2007	25	$8,360,931
Single family	25	$8,360,931
Total, 2006	25	$6,447,699
Single family	25	$6,447,699

Real Property Valuation, 2007

	Parcels	Valuation
Total	3,368	$3,329,588,500
Vacant	84	66,582,200
Residential	3,058	1,977,590,900
Commercial	201	894,240,000
Industrial	19	228,460,100
Apartments	4	161,878,700
Farm land	1	119,800
Farm homestead	1	716,800

Average Property Value & Tax, 2007
- Residential value: $646,717
- Property tax: $7,505
- Tax credit/rebate: $1,142

Public Library
Florham Park Public Library
107 Ridgedale Ave
Florham Park, NJ 07932
973-377-2694
- Director: Barbara M. McConville

Library statistics, 2006
- Population served: 8,857
- Full-time/total staff: 2/7

	Total	Per capita
Holdings	46,067	5.20
Revenues	$677,600	$76.50
Expenditures	$608,635	$68.72
Annual visits	89,556	10.11
Internet terminals/annual users	15/15,548	

Taxes

	2005	2006	2007
General tax rate per $100	2.25	1.15	1.17
County equalization ratio	56.21	111.61	106.18
Net valuation taxable	$1,589,186,314	$3,297,260,500	$3,334,145,253
State equalized value	$2,948,397,614	$3,109,902,314	$3,279,776,603

Public Safety
- Number of officers, 2006: 30

Crime

	2005	2006
Total crimes	115	110
Violent	2	6
Murder	0	0
Rape	0	1
Robbery	0	1
Aggravated assault	2	4
Non-violent	113	104
Burglary	12	10
Larceny	97	88
Vehicle theft	4	6
Domestic violence	39	41
Arson	2	0
Total crime rate	9.2	8.7
Violent	0.2	0.5
Non-violent	9.0	8.2

Public School District
(for school year 2006-07 except as noted)

Florham Park School District
67-71 Ridgedale Ave, PO Box 39
Florham Park, NJ 07932
973-822-3888

- Superintendent: William Ronzitti
- Number of schools: 3
- Grade plan: K-8
- Enrollment: 970
- Attendance rate, '05-06: 95.9%
- Dropout rate: NA
- Students per teacher: 9.4
- Per pupil expenditure: $14,110
- Median faculty salary: $48,430
- Median administrator salary: $103,990
- Grade 12 enrollment: NA
- High school graduation rate: NA

Assessment test results
(percent scoring at proficient or advanced level)

	Language	Math
NJASK-Grade 3	92.2%	94.8%
GEPA-Grade 8	93.1%	83.2%
HSPA-High School	NA	NA

SAT score averages

Pct tested	Math	Verbal	Writing
NA	NA	NA	NA

Teacher Qualifications
- Avg. years of experience: 8
- Highly-qualified teachers
  - one subject/all subjects: 98.5%/98.5%
- With emergency credentials: 1.5%

No Child Left Behind
- AYP, 2005-06: Meets Standards

Municipal Finance
State Aid Programs, 2008
- Total aid: $1,396,107
  - CMPTRA: 181,726
  - Energy tax receipts: 1,214,306
  - Garden State Trust: 75

General Budget, 2007
- Total tax levy: $38,693,096
  - County levy: 7,400,716
    - County taxes: 5,914,912
    - County library: 0
    - County health: 0
    - County open space: 1,485,805
  - School levy: 20,789,808
  - Muni. levy: 10,502,572
- Misc. revenues: 4,864,582

Atlantic County
Folsom Borough

Demographics & Socio-Economic Characteristics
(2000 US Census, except as noted)

Population
1980*	1,892
1990*	2,181
2000	1,972
Male	967
Female	1,005
2006 (estimate)*	1,948
Population density	235.6

Race & Hispanic Origin, 2000
Race
- White ... 1,809
- Black/African American ... 87
- American Indian/Alaska Native ... 3
- Asian ... 17
- Native Hawaiian/Pacific Islander ... 3
- Other race ... 31
- Two or more races ... 22

Hispanic origin, total ... 68
- Mexican ... 9
- Puerto Rican ... 50
- Cuban ... 5
- Other Hispanic ... 4

Age & Nativity, 2000
- Under 5 years ... 102
- 18 years and over ... 1,481
- 21 years and over ... 1,399
- 65 years and over ... 193
- 85 years and over ... 20
- Median age ... 37.5
- Native-born ... 1,919
- Foreign-born ... 53

Educational Attainment, 2000
Population 25 years and over ... 1,301
- Less than 9th grade ... 4.3%
- High school grad or higher ... 83.0%
- Bachelor's degree or higher ... 16.4%
- Graduate degree ... 4.5%

Income & Poverty, 1999
- Per capita income ... $20,617
- Median household income ... $56,406
- Median family income ... $59,231
- Persons in poverty ... 111
- H'holds receiving public assistance ... 26
- H'holds receiving social security ... 151

Households, 2000
- Total households ... 671
  - With persons under 18 ... 286
  - With persons over 65 ... 133
  - Family households ... 552
  - Single-person households ... 92
- Persons per household ... 2.93
- Persons per family ... 3.18

Labor & Employment
- Total civilian labor force, 2006** ... 1,187
  - Unemployment rate ... 2.6%
- Total civilian labor force, 2000 ... 1,084
  - Unemployment rate ... 3.3%

Employed persons 16 years and over by occupation, 2000
- Managers & professionals ... 251
- Service occupations ... 153
- Sales & office occupations ... 327
- Farming, fishing & forestry ... 2
- Construction & maintenance ... 147
- Production & transportation ... 168
- Self-employed persons ... 36

‡ Branch of county library
* US Census Bureau
** New Jersey Department of Labor

See Introduction for an explanation of all data sources.

General Information
Borough of Folsom
Route 54
1700 12th St
Folsom, NJ 08037
609-561-3178

- Website ... NA
- Year of incorporation ... 1906
- Land/water area (sq. miles) ... 8.27/0.19
- Form of government ... Borough

Government
Legislative Districts
- US Congressional ... 2
- State Legislative ... 9

Local Officials, 2008
- Mayor ... Thomas Ballistreri
- Manager/Admin ... NA
- Clerk ... Gail Macera
- Finance Dir ... Dawn Stollenwerk
- Tax Assessor ... Joseph Ingemi
- Tax Collector ... NA
- Attorney ... Michael Fitzgerald
- Building ... Patrick Newton
- Comm Dev/Planning ... NA
- Engineering ... Pollistina & Associates
- Public Works ... NA
- Police Chief ... NA
- Emerg/Fire Director ... Larry Smith

Housing & Construction
Housing Units, 2000*
- Total ... 702
- Median rent ... $883
- Median SF home value ... $104,700

Permits for New Residential Construction
	Units	Value
Total, 2007	3	$883,000
Single family	3	$883,000
Total, 2006	3	$468,000
Single family	3	$468,000

Real Property Valuation, 2007
	Parcels	Valuation
Total	1,268	$103,358,100
Vacant	493	4,542,900
Residential	655	76,338,900
Commercial	42	10,155,900
Industrial	11	10,383,200
Apartments	0	0
Farm land	56	192,000
Farm homestead	11	1,745,200

Average Property Value & Tax, 2007
- Residential value ... $117,243
- Property tax ... $2,990
- Tax credit/rebate ... $648

Public Library
Hammonton Branch Library‡
451 Egg Harbor Rd
Hammonton, NJ 08037
609-561-2264

- Branch Manager ... David Munn

Library statistics, 2006
see Atlantic County profile for library system statistics

Public Safety
Number of officers, 2006 ... 0

Crime	2005	2006
Total crimes	35	38
Violent	4	4
Murder	0	0
Rape	0	0
Robbery	1	0
Aggravated assault	3	4
Non-violent	31	34
Burglary	5	9
Larceny	22	21
Vehicle theft	4	4
Domestic violence	16	4
Arson	1	0
Total crime rate	17.7	19.3
Violent	2.0	2.0
Non-violent	15.7	17.2

Public School District
(for school year 2006-07 except as noted)

Folsom School District
1357 Mays Landing Rd
Folsom, NJ 08037
609-561-8666

- Superintendent ... Jean Rishel
- Number of schools ... 1
- Grade plan ... K-8
- Enrollment ... 392
- Attendance rate, '05-06 ... 95.0%
- Dropout rate ... NA
- Students per teacher ... 11.0
- Per pupil expenditure ... $10,721
- Median faculty salary ... $42,864
- Median administrator salary ... $68,525
- Grade 12 enrollment ... NA
- High school graduation rate ... NA

Assessment test results
(percent scoring at proficient or advanced level)
	Language	Math
NJASK-Grade 3	87.8%	95.1%
GEPA-Grade 8	66.7%	83.3%
HSPA-High School	NA	NA

SAT score averages
Pct tested	Math	Verbal	Writing
NA	NA	NA	NA

Teacher Qualifications
- Avg. years of experience ... 7
- Highly-qualified teachers one subject/all subjects ... 96.5%/96.5%
- With emergency credentials ... 0.0%

No Child Left Behind
AYP, 2005-06 ... Meets Standards

Municipal Finance
State Aid Programs, 2008
- Total aid ... $173,229
- CMPTRA ... 0
- Energy tax receipts ... 171,616
- Garden State Trust ... 1,613

General Budget, 2007
- Total tax levy ... $2,645,317
- County levy ... 526,421
  - County taxes ... 419,077
  - County library ... 51,918
  - County health ... 21,155
  - County open space ... 34,271
- School levy ... 1,647,919
- Muni. levy ... 470,977
- Misc. revenues ... 1,061,859

Taxes
	2005	2006	2007
General tax rate per $100	2.387	2.4	2.55
County equalization ratio	73.51	69.53	60.93
Net valuation taxable	$101,736,617	$102,913,900	$103,743,473
State equalized value	$146,320,462	$169,334,970	$188,343,365

©2008 Information Publications, Inc. All rights reserved. Photocopying prohibited. For additional copies, contact the publisher at www.informationpublications.com or (877) 544-INFO (4636)

The New Jersey Municipal Data Book

Fort Lee Borough

Bergen County

Demographics & Socio-Economic Characteristics
(2000 US Census, except as noted)

Population
1980*	32,449
1990*	31,997
2000	35,461
Male	16,569
Female	18,892
2006 (estimate)*	37,008
Population density	14,627.7

Race & Hispanic Origin, 2000
Race
- White ... 22,253
- Black/African American ... 615
- American Indian/Alaska Native ... 25
- Asian ... 11,146
- Native Hawaiian/Pacific Islander ... 20
- Other race ... 600
- Two or more races ... 802

Hispanic origin, total ... 2,791
- Mexican ... 78
- Puerto Rican ... 562
- Cuban ... 425
- Other Hispanic ... 1,726

Age & Nativity, 2000
- Under 5 years ... 1,870
- 18 years and over ... 29,261
- 21 years and over ... 28,499
- 65 years and over ... 7,151
- 85 years and over ... 901
- Median age ... 41.6
- Native-born ... 19,597
- Foreign-born ... 15,864

Educational Attainment, 2000
- Population 25 years and over ... 27,490
- Less than 9th grade ... 4.7%
- High school grad or higher ... 89.5%
- Bachelor's degree or higher ... 48.2%
- Graduate degree ... 18.5%

Income & Poverty, 1999
- Per capita income ... $37,899
- Median household income ... $58,161
- Median family income ... $72,140
- Persons in poverty ... 2,807
- H'holds receiving public assistance ... 188
- H'holds receiving social security ... 4,843

Households, 2000
- Total households ... 16,544
- With persons under 18 ... 3,909
- With persons over 65 ... 5,452
- Family households ... 9,402
- Single-person households ... 6,448
- Persons per household ... 2.14
- Persons per family ... 2.88

Labor & Employment
- Total civilian labor force, 2006** ... 19,183
- Unemployment rate ... 3.0%
- Total civilian labor force, 2000 ... 17,802
- Unemployment rate ... 3.4%

Employed persons 16 years and over by occupation, 2000
- Managers & professionals ... 8,870
- Service occupations ... 1,430
- Sales & office occupations ... 5,324
- Farming, fishing & forestry ... 0
- Construction & maintenance ... 561
- Production & transportation ... 1,020
- Self-employed persons ... 1,160

* US Census Bureau
** New Jersey Department of Labor

General Information
Borough of Fort Lee
309 Main St
Fort Lee, NJ 07024
201-592-3546

- Website ... www.fortleenj.org
- Year of incorporation ... 1904
- Land/water area (sq. miles) ... 2.53/0.35
- Form of government ... Borough

Government
Legislative Districts
- US Congressional ... 9
- State Legislative ... 38

Local Officials, 2008
- Mayor ... Mark J. Sokolich
- Administrator ... Peggy Thomas
- Clerk ... Neil Grant
- Finance Dir ... Joseph Iannaconi Jr
- Tax Assessor ... Kevin Hartley
- Tax Collector ... Joseph Iannaconi Jr
- Attorney ... J. Sheldon Cohen
- Building ... Eric Swanson
- Planning ... Ray Levy
- Engineering ... Steven Boswell
- Public Works ... Anthony Lione
- Police Chief ... Tom Ripoli
- Emerg/Fire Director ... Stephan Ferraro

Housing & Construction
Housing Units, 2000*
- Total ... 17,446
- Median rent ... $1,101
- Median SF home value ... $287,000

Permits for New Residential Construction
	Units	Value
Total, 2007	31	$9,192,950
Single family	13	$5,646,950
Total, 2006	33	$9,524,095
Single family	23	$7,622,095

Real Property Valuation, 2007
	Parcels	Valuation
Total	9,107	$6,004,593,320
Vacant	117	130,801,900
Residential	8,498	3,525,098,500
Commercial	413	926,872,600
Industrial	9	10,229,700
Apartments	70	1,411,590,620
Farm land	0	0
Farm homestead	0	0

Average Property Value & Tax, 2007
- Residential value ... $414,815
- Property tax ... $7,130
- Tax credit/rebate ... $944

Public Library
Fort Lee Public Library
320 Main St
Fort Lee, NJ 07024
201-592-3614

- Director ... Rita Altomara

Library statistics, 2006
- Population served ... 35,461
- Full-time/total staff ... 7/23

	Total	Per capita
Holdings	151,118	4.26
Revenues	$1,979,139	$55.81
Expenditures	$1,646,559	$46.43
Annual visits	324,696	9.16

Internet terminals/annual users ... 10/24,484

Public Safety
Number of officers, 2006 ... 106

Crime	2005	2006
Total crimes	406	375
Violent	28	28
Murder	0	1
Rape	1	0
Robbery	12	5
Aggravated assault	15	22
Non-violent	378	347
Burglary	67	67
Larceny	278	260
Vehicle theft	33	20
Domestic violence	72	74
Arson	2	7
Total crime rate	10.9	10.1
Violent	0.8	0.8
Non-violent	10.1	9.3

Public School District
(for school year 2006-07 except as noted)

Fort Lee School District
255 Whiteman St
Fort Lee, NJ 07024
201-585-4610

- Superintendent ... Joanne Calabro
- Number of schools ... 6
- Grade plan ... K-12
- Enrollment ... 3,454
- Attendance rate, '05-06 ... 95.0%
- Dropout rate ... 0.3%
- Students per teacher ... 12.0
- Per pupil expenditure ... $13,274
- Median faculty salary ... $60,137
- Median administrator salary ... $113,100
- Grade 12 enrollment ... 285
- High school graduation rate ... 97.0%

Assessment test results
(percent scoring at proficient or advanced level)

	Language	Math
NJASK-Grade 3	88.5%	96.2%
GEPA-Grade 8	86.3%	84.9%
HSPA-High School	90.6%	82.6%

SAT score averages
Pct tested	Math	Verbal	Writing
93%	546	499	500

Teacher Qualifications
- Avg. years of experience ... 13
- Highly-qualified teachers one subject/all subjects ... 96.5%/96.5%
- With emergency credentials ... 0.0%

No Child Left Behind
AYP, 2005-06 ... Meets Standards

Municipal Finance
State Aid Programs, 2008
- Total aid ... $2,210,379
- CMPTRA ... 511,209
- Energy tax receipts ... 1,698,795
- Garden State Trust ... 375

General Budget, 2007
- Total tax levy ... $103,362,954
- County levy ... 10,918,080
-   County taxes ... 10,309,537
-   County library ... 0
-   County health ... 0
-   County open space ... 608,543
- School levy ... 43,433,482
- Muni. levy ... 49,011,392
- Misc. revenues ... 10,937,547

Taxes
	2005	2006	2007
General tax rate per $100	1.59	1.66	1.72
County equalization ratio	107.7	102.2	99.27
Net valuation taxable	$5,809,064,016	$5,929,867,820	$6,013,133,358
State equalized value	$5,684,015,671	$5,982,132,760	$6,354,548,620

Sussex County

Frankford Township

Demographics & Socio-Economic Characteristics
(2000 US Census, except as noted)

Population
1980*	4,654
1990*	5,114
2000	5,420
Male	2,664
Female	2,756
2006 (estimate)*	5,680
Population density	166.5

Race & Hispanic Origin, 2000
Race
White	5,320
Black/African American	21
American Indian/Alaska Native	3
Asian	21
Native Hawaiian/Pacific Islander	0
Other race	27
Two or more races	28
Hispanic origin, total	96
Mexican	13
Puerto Rican	41
Cuban	17
Other Hispanic	25

Age & Nativity, 2000
Under 5 years	267
18 years and over	4,067
21 years and over	3,885
65 years and over	703
85 years and over	149
Median age	40.8
Native-born	5,254
Foreign-born	165

Educational Attainment, 2000
Population 25 years and over	3,731
Less than 9th grade	3.9%
High school grad or higher	88.8%
Bachelor's degree or higher	25.2%
Graduate degree	7.8%

Income & Poverty, 1999
Per capita income	$25,051
Median household income	$64,444
Median family income	$69,449
Persons in poverty	269
H'holds receiving public assistance	46
H'holds receiving social security	498

Households, 2000
Total households	1,839
With persons under 18	727
With persons over 65	390
Family households	1,473
Single-person households	303
Persons per household	2.81
Persons per family	3.17

Labor & Employment
Total civilian labor force, 2006**	3,104
Unemployment rate	3.8%
Total civilian labor force, 2000	2,779
Unemployment rate	3.2%

Employed persons 16 years and over by occupation, 2000
Managers & professionals	1,000
Service occupations	449
Sales & office occupations	639
Farming, fishing & forestry	10
Construction & maintenance	302
Production & transportation	291
Self-employed persons	262

‡ Main library for county
* US Census Bureau
** New Jersey Department of Labor

See Introduction for an explanation of all data sources.

General Information
Township of Frankford
151 State Hwy 206
Augusta, NJ 07822
973-948-5566

Website	www.frankfordtownship.com
Year of incorporation	1797
Land/water area (sq. miles)	34.11/1.31
Form of government	Township

Government
Legislative Districts
US Congressional	5
State Legislative	24

Local Officials, 2008
Mayor	Robert McDowell
Manager	Louanne Cular
Clerk	Louanne Cular
Finance Dir	Gail Magura
Tax Assessor	John Dyksen
Tax Collector	Stephen Lance
Attorney	Kevin Benbrook
Building	Jeff Fette
Planning	NA
Engineering	Harold Pellow
Public Works	NA
Police Chief	NA
Emerg/Fire Director	Mike Seo

Housing & Construction
Housing Units, 2000*
Total	2,295
Median rent	$675
Median SF home value	$179,100

Permits for New Residential Construction
	Units	Value
Total, 2007	19	$4,460,767
Single family	19	$4,460,767
Total, 2006	20	$4,467,720
Single family	20	$4,467,720

Real Property Valuation, 2007
	Parcels	Valuation
Total	3,321	$434,662,364
Vacant	467	17,333,700
Residential	2,134	329,339,764
Commercial	97	36,519,500
Industrial	10	2,989,600
Apartments	2	485,500
Farm land	380	2,405,300
Farm homestead	231	45,589,000

Average Property Value & Tax, 2007
Residential value	$158,532
Property tax	$5,669
Tax credit/rebate	$1,019

Public Library
Sussex County Library‡
125 Morris Turnpike
Newton, NJ 07860
973-948-3660

Director ... Stan Pollakoff

County Library statistics, 2006
Population served	126,086
Full-time/total staff	13/56

	Total	Per capita
Holdings	321,551	2.55
Revenues	$4,742,094	$37.61
Expenditures	$4,673,761	$37.07
Annual visits	483,391	3.83
Internet terminals/annual users	55/68,344	

Taxes
	2005	2006	2007
General tax rate per $100	3.28	3.44	3.58
County equalization ratio	66.9	58.66	52.99
Net valuation taxable	$424,539,664	$430,306,126	$436,270,916
State equalized value	$723,729,397	$813,812,418	$905,648,411

Public Safety
Number of officers, 2006 ... 0

Crime
	2005	2006
Total crimes	59	84
Violent	2	8
Murder	0	0
Rape	0	1
Robbery	0	0
Aggravated assault	2	7
Non-violent	57	76
Burglary	6	13
Larceny	44	53
Vehicle theft	7	10
Domestic violence	11	9
Arson	0	0
Total crime rate	10.4	14.8
Violent	0.4	1.4
Non-violent	10.1	13.4

Public School District
(for school year 2006-07 except as noted)

Frankford Township School District
4 Pines Rd
Branchville, NJ 07826
973-948-3727

Superintendent/Principal	Harry O. Tachovsky
Number of schools	1
Grade plan	K-8
Enrollment	734
Attendance rate, '05-06	95.5%
Dropout rate	NA
Students per teacher	10.3
Per pupil expenditure	$13,066
Median faculty salary	$69,839
Median administrator salary	$104,500
Grade 12 enrollment	NA
High school graduation rate	NA

Assessment test results
(percent scoring at proficient or advanced level)
	Language	Math
NJASK-Grade 3	83.1%	83.1%
GEPA-Grade 8	90.0%	85.6%
HSPA-High School	NA	NA

SAT score averages
Pct tested	Math	Verbal	Writing
NA	NA	NA	NA

Teacher Qualifications
Avg. years of experience	17
Highly-qualified teachers one subject/all subjects	100%/100%
With emergency credentials	0.0%

No Child Left Behind
AYP, 2005-06 ... Meets Standards

Municipal Finance
State Aid Programs, 2008
Total aid	$595,288
CMPTRA	91,287
Energy tax receipts	474,616
Garden State Trust	16,319

General Budget, 2007
Total tax levy	$15,599,579
County levy	3,342,730
County taxes	2,731,272
County library	232,835
County health	90,031
County open space	288,592
School levy	10,608,505
Muni. levy	1,648,344
Misc. revenues	1,878,695

Franklin Borough

Sussex County

Demographics & Socio-Economic Characteristics
(2000 US Census, except as noted)

Population
1980*	4,486
1990*	4,977
2000	5,160
Male	2,444
Female	2,716
2006 (estimate)*	5,210
Population density	1,160.4

Race & Hispanic Origin, 2000
Race
- White 4,907
- Black/African American 32
- American Indian/Alaska Native 18
- Asian 76
- Native Hawaiian/Pacific Islander 0
- Other race 63
- Two or more races 64

Hispanic origin, total 228
- Mexican 16
- Puerto Rican 96
- Cuban 12
- Other Hispanic 104

Age & Nativity, 2000
- Under 5 years 357
- 18 years and over 3,741
- 21 years and over 3,579
- 65 years and over 603
- 85 years and over 85
- Median age 36.7
- Native-born 4,805
- Foreign-born 382

Educational Attainment, 2000
- Population 25 years and over 3,325
- Less than 9th grade 3.6%
- High school grad or higher 86.8%
- Bachelor's degree or higher 15.3%
- Graduate degree 4.7%

Income & Poverty, 1999
- Per capita income $19,386
- Median household income $44,985
- Median family income $52,682
- Persons in poverty 360
- H'holds receiving public assistance 35
- H'holds receiving social security 581

Households, 2000
- Total households 1,898
- With persons under 18 751
- With persons over 65 472
- Family households 1,325
- Single-person households 457
- Persons per household 2.69
- Persons per family 3.22

Labor & Employment
- Total civilian labor force, 2006** 2,889
- Unemployment rate 5.1%
- Total civilian labor force, 2000 2,547
- Unemployment rate 3.6%

Employed persons 16 years and over by occupation, 2000
- Managers & professionals 626
- Service occupations 369
- Sales & office occupations 703
- Farming, fishing & forestry 0
- Construction & maintenance 302
- Production & transportation 456
- Self-employed persons 156

‡ Branch of county library
* US Census Bureau
** New Jersey Department of Labor

General Information
Borough of Franklin
46 Main St
Franklin, NJ 07416
973-827-9280

- Website .... www.franklinboro.com
- Year of incorporation 1913
- Land/water area (sq. miles) 4.49/0.06
- Form of government .... Borough

Government
Legislative Districts
- US Congressional 5
- State Legislative 24

Local Officials, 2008
- Mayor .... Paul Crowley
- Manager .... Richard R. Wolak
- Clerk .... Patricia Leasure
- Finance Dir .... Grant Rome
- Tax Assessor .... Scott Holzhauer
- Tax Collector .... Terry Beshada
- Attorney .... John Ursin
- Building .... Anthony Piechowski
- Planning .... Jim Kilduff
- Engineering .... George Unverzagt
- Public Works .... Mike Gunderman
- Police Chief .... Joseph Kistle
- Emerg/Fire Director .... Jim Nidelko

Housing & Construction
Housing Units, 2000*
- Total 1,997
- Median rent $771
- Median SF home value $123,000

Permits for New Residential Construction
	Units	Value
Total, 2007	10	$1,235,912
Single family	10	$1,235,912
Total, 2006	14	$1,700,801
Single family	14	$1,700,801

Real Property Valuation, 2007
	Parcels	Valuation
Total	1,740	$240,607,000
Vacant	139	5,977,900
Residential	1,427	165,345,500
Commercial	117	56,514,700
Industrial	10	6,506,000
Apartments	12	3,588,200
Farm land	20	155,700
Farm homestead	15	2,519,000

Average Property Value & Tax, 2007
- Residential value $116,411
- Property tax $5,244
- Tax credit/rebate $961

Public Library
Franklin Branch Library‡
103 Main St
Franklin, NJ 07416
973-827-6555

Branch Librarian .... Carol Crowley

Library statistics, 2006
see Sussex County profile for library system statistics

Public Safety
Number of officers, 2006 13

Crime	2005	2006
Total crimes	118	96
Violent	2	2
Murder	0	0
Rape	0	0
Robbery	0	1
Aggravated assault	2	1
Non-violent	116	94
Burglary	13	18
Larceny	99	74
Vehicle theft	4	2
Domestic violence	78	101
Arson	0	2
Total crime rate	22.5	18.3
Violent	0.4	0.4
Non-violent	22.2	18.0

Public School District
(for school year 2006-07 except as noted)

Franklin Borough School District
50 Washington Ave
Franklin, NJ 07416
973-827-9775

- Chief School Admin .... Thomas N. Turner
- Number of schools 1
- Grade plan K-8
- Enrollment 489
- Attendance rate, '05-06 .... 95.2%
- Dropout rate .... NA
- Students per teacher 8.0
- Per pupil expenditure $14,403
- Median faculty salary $46,525
- Median administrator salary $106,089
- Grade 12 enrollment .... NA
- High school graduation rate .... NA

Assessment test results
(percent scoring at proficient or advanced level)

	Language	Math
NJASK-Grade 3	87.3%	95.2%
GEPA-Grade 8	78.6%	67.9%
HSPA-High School	NA	NA

SAT score averages
Pct tested	Math	Verbal	Writing
NA	NA	NA	NA

Teacher Qualifications
- Avg. years of experience 6
- Highly-qualified teachers
  - one subject/all subjects 100%/100%
- With emergency credentials 0.0%

No Child Left Behind
AYP, 2005-06 .... Meets Standards

Municipal Finance
State Aid Programs, 2008
- Total aid $748,191
- CMPTRA 79,685
- Energy tax receipts 657,309
- Garden State Trust 7,108

General Budget, 2007
- Total tax levy $10,947,479
- County levy 2,022,193
- County taxes 1,652,351
- County library 140,869
- County health 54,434
- County open space 174,539
- School levy 5,960,868
- Muni. levy 2,964,418
- Misc. revenues 2,819,753

Taxes	2005	2006	2007
General tax rate per $100	3.98	4.23	4.51
County equalization ratio	63.09	55	48.94
Net valuation taxable	$243,330,078	$240,111,400	$243,017,024
State equalized value	$442,418,324	$493,006,684	$521,630,999

Bergen County

Franklin Lakes Borough

Demographics & Socio-Economic Characteristics
(2000 US Census, except as noted)

Population
1980*	8,769
1990*	9,873
2000	10,422
Male	5,146
Female	5,276
2006 (estimate)*	11,340
Population density	1,200.0

Race & Hispanic Origin, 2000
Race
- White 9,521
- Black/African American 96
- American Indian/Alaska Native 11
- Asian 660
- Native Hawaiian/Pacific Islander 1
- Other race 43
- Two or more races 90
- Hispanic origin, total 286
  - Mexican 11
  - Puerto Rican 62
  - Cuban 60
  - Other Hispanic 153

Age & Nativity, 2000
- Under 5 years 703
- 18 years and over 7,433
- 21 years and over 7,209
- 65 years and over 1,164
- 85 years and over 104
- Median age 40.7
- Native-born 9,191
- Foreign-born 1,231

Educational Attainment, 2000
- Population 25 years and over 6,885
- Less than 9th grade 1.7%
- High school grad or higher 94.7%
- Bachelor's degree or higher 52.9%
- Graduate degree 21.5%

Income & Poverty, 1999
- Per capita income $59,763
- Median household income $132,373
- Median family income $142,930
- Persons in poverty 331
- H'holds receiving public assistance 17
- H'holds receiving social security 798

Households, 2000
- Total households 3,322
- With persons under 18 1,508
- With persons over 65 803
- Family households 2,960
- Single-person households 287
- Persons per household 3.13
- Persons per family 3.34

Labor & Employment
- Total civilian labor force, 2006** 5,197
- Unemployment rate 2.3%
- Total civilian labor force, 2000 4,900
- Unemployment rate 2.3%

Employed persons 16 years and over by occupation, 2000
- Managers & professionals 2,601
- Service occupations 286
- Sales & office occupations 1,442
- Farming, fishing & forestry 0
- Construction & maintenance 221
- Production & transportation 235
- Self-employed persons 483

* US Census Bureau
** New Jersey Department of Labor

See Introduction for an explanation of all data sources.

General Information
Borough of Franklin Lakes
480 De Korte Dr
Franklin Lakes, NJ 07417
201-891-0048

Website	www.franklinlakes.org
Year of incorporation	1922
Land/water area (sq. miles)	9.45/0.38
Form of government	Borough

Government
Legislative Districts
- US Congressional 5
- State Legislative 40

Local Officials, 2008
Mayor	Maura R. DeNicola
Manager	Gregory C. Hart
Clerk	Sally T. Bleeker
CFOr	William G. Pike (Int)
Tax Assessor	Michael Leposky
Tax Collector	Philip Moore
Attorney	William Smith
Building	Frank Horesta
Planning	Frank Conte
Engineering	Boswell Engineering
Public Works	Brian Peterson
Police Chief	Irving Conklin
Emerg/Fire Director	Chuck Bohny

Housing & Construction
Housing Units, 2000*
- Total 3,395
- Median rent $1,313
- Median SF home value $609,400

Permits for New Residential Construction
	Units	Value
Total, 2007	47	$27,865,718
Single family	32	$26,889,368
Total, 2006	136	$32,151,640
Single family	36	$25,642,640

Real Property Valuation, 2007
	Parcels	Valuation
Total	3,699	$4,892,940,000
Vacant	165	80,998,400
Residential	3,447	4,379,627,600
Commercial	55	384,240,500
Industrial	15	23,568,000
Apartments	1	18,139,400
Farm land	11	21,200
Farm homestead	5	6,344,900

Average Property Value & Tax, 2007
- Residential value $1,270,560
- Property tax $14,060
- Tax credit/rebate $1,335

Public Library
Franklin Lakes Public Library
470 DeKorte Dr
Franklin Lakes, NJ 07417
201-891-2224

Director .... Geraldine McMahon

Library statistics, 2006
- Population served 10,422
- Full-time/total staff 5/10

	Total	Per capita
Holdings	105,840	10.16
Revenues	$1,475,156	$141.54
Expenditures	$1,221,414	$117.20
Annual visits	165,814	15.91
Internet terminals/annual users	34/29,714	

Taxes
	2005	2006	2007
General tax rate per $100	2.28	2.37	1.11
County equalization ratio	59.76	54.75	109.74
Net valuation taxable	$2,194,474,587	$2,199,599,502	$4,894,273,619
State equalized value	$4,008,172,762	$4,411,116,101	$4,648,883,011

Public Safety
Number of officers, 2006 23

Crime	2005	2006
Total crimes	110	117
Violent	1	1
Murder	0	0
Rape	0	1
Robbery	0	0
Aggravated assault	1	0
Non-violent	109	116
Burglary	17	17
Larceny	91	98
Vehicle theft	1	1
Domestic violence	31	44
Arson	1	0
Total crime rate	9.8	10.4
Violent	0.1	0.1
Non-violent	9.7	10.3

Public School District
(for school year 2006-07 except as noted)

Franklin Lakes School District
490 Pulis Ave
Franklin Lakes, NJ 07417
201-891-1856

- Superintendent .... Roger Bayersdorfer
- Number of schools 4
- Grade plan K-8
- Enrollment 1,501
- Attendance rate, '05-06 .... 96.3%
- Dropout rate .... NA
- Students per teacher 8.3
- Per pupil expenditure $15,061
- Median faculty salary $50,000
- Median administrator salary ... $112,455
- Grade 12 enrollment .... NA
- High school graduation rate .... NA

Assessment test results
(percent scoring at proficient or advanced level)

	Language	Math
NJASK-Grade 3	95.0%	96.3%
GEPA-Grade 8	87.6%	87.2%
HSPA-High School	NA	NA

SAT score averages
Pct tested	Math	Verbal	Writing
NA	NA	NA	NA

Teacher Qualifications
- Avg. years of experience 7
- Highly-qualified teachers
  - one subject/all subjects 100%/100%
- With emergency credentials 0.0%

No Child Left Behind
AYP, 2005-06 .... Meets Standards

Municipal Finance
State Aid Programs, 2008
- Total aid $2,043,043
- CMPTRA 0
- Energy tax receipts 2,037,074
- Garden State Trust 0

General Budget, 2007
- Total tax levy $54,160,366
- County levy 8,087,997
- County taxes 7,641,425
- County library 0
- County health 0
- County open space 446,572
- School levy 38,073,388
- Muni. levy 7,998,981
- Misc. revenues 7,187,732

Franklin Township
Gloucester County

Demographics & Socio-Economic Characteristics
(2000 US Census, except as noted)

Population
1980*	12,396
1990*	14,482
2000	15,466
Male	7,723
Female	7,743
2006 (estimate)*	16,853
Population density	300.9

Race & Hispanic Origin, 2000
Race
White	13,954
Black/African American	1,030
American Indian/Alaska Native	48
Asian	63
Native Hawaiian/Pacific Islander	2
Other race	193
Two or more races	176
Hispanic origin, total	543
Mexican	86
Puerto Rican	365
Cuban	13
Other Hispanic	79

Age & Nativity, 2000
Under 5 years	956
18 years and over	11,185
21 years and over	10,543
65 years and over	1,480
85 years and over	110
Median age	36.4
Native-born	15,111
Foreign-born	355

Educational Attainment, 2000
Population 25 years and over	9,811
Less than 9th grade	4.8%
High school grad or higher	81.8%
Bachelor's degree or higher	14.9%
Graduate degree	3.4%

Income & Poverty, 1999
Per capita income	$20,277
Median household income	$55,169
Median family income	$60,518
Persons in poverty	778
H'holds receiving public assistance	103
H'holds receiving social security	1,412

Households, 2000
Total households	5,225
With persons under 18	2,333
With persons over 65	1,085
Family households	4,190
Single-person households	831
Persons per household	2.94
Persons per family	3.29

Labor & Employment
Total civilian labor force, 2006**	9,289
Unemployment rate	7.0%
Total civilian labor force, 2000	7,856
Unemployment rate	6.1%

Employed persons 16 years and over by occupation, 2000
Managers & professionals	1,949
Service occupations	1,105
Sales & office occupations	1,884
Farming, fishing & forestry	41
Construction & maintenance	1,291
Production & transportation	1,105
Self-employed persons	481

* US Census Bureau
** New Jersey Department of Labor

General Information
Township of Franklin
1571 Delsea Dr
Franklinville, NJ 08322
856-694-1234

Website	www.franklintownship.com
Year of incorporation	1820
Land/water area (sq. miles)	56.01/0.42
Form of government	Township

Government
Legislative Districts
US Congressional	2
State Legislative	4

Local Officials, 2008
Mayor	David Ferrucci
Township Admin.	William Krebs
Clerk	Carolyn K. Toy
Finance Dir.	Frances Carder
Tax Assessor	Timothy Mead
Tax Collector	Lawrence Nightlinger Jr
Attorney	Samuel J. Ragonese
Building	Steven Rickerschauser
Planning	Patricia Knobloch
Engineering	J. Michael Fralinger
Public Works	William Nese
Police Chief	Michael DiGiorgio
Fire/Emergency Dir.	NA

Housing & Construction
Housing Units, 2000*
Total	5,461
Median rent	$710
Median SF home value	$111,700

Permits for New Residential Construction
	Units	Value
Total, 2007	60	$10,750,760
Single family	60	$10,750,760
Total, 2006	91	$16,095,346
Single family	91	$16,095,346

Real Property Valuation, 2007
	Parcels	Valuation
Total	7,889	$753,217,000
Vacant	1,232	28,786,900
Residential	5,338	624,421,300
Commercial	301	59,315,300
Industrial	0	0
Apartments	8	1,985,700
Farm land	709	5,327,000
Farm homestead	301	33,380,800

Average Property Value & Tax, 2007
Residential value	$116,652
Property tax	$4,516
Tax credit/rebate	$915

Public Library
Franklin Township Free Public Library
1584 Coles Mill Rd
Franklinville, NJ 08322
856-694-2833

Director	Denise Saia

Library statistics, 2006
Population served	15,466
Full-time/total staff	2/2

	Total	Per capita
Holdings	49,791	3.22
Revenues	$490,135	$31.69
Expenditures	$420,494	$27.19
Annual visits	67,432	4.36
Internet terminals/annual users	8/9,004	

Taxes
	2005	2006	2007
General tax rate per $100	3.396	3.619	3.872
County equalization ratio	75.47	65.97	56.52
Net valuation taxable	$706,202,585	$732,343,700	$755,794,876
State equalized value	$1,070,490,503	$1,298,628,506	$1,453,303,993

Public Safety
Number of officers, 2006 29

Crime	2005	2006
Total crimes	352	351
Violent	22	22
Murder	1	1
Rape	2	0
Robbery	7	4
Aggravated assault	12	17
Non-violent	330	329
Burglary	119	114
Larceny	191	200
Vehicle theft	20	15
Domestic violence	183	187
Arson	6	1
Total crime rate	21.5	21.1
Violent	1.3	1.3
Non-violent	20.1	19.7

Public School District
(for school year 2006-07 except as noted)

Franklin Township School District
3228 Coles Mill Rd
Franklinville, NJ 08322
856-629-9500

Superintendent	Michael G. Kozak
Number of schools	3
Grade plan	K-6
Enrollment	1,525
Attendance rate, '05-06	95.1%
Dropout rate	NA
Students per teacher	13.5
Per pupil expenditure	$10,053
Median faculty salary	$58,000
Median administrator salary	$91,450
Grade 12 enrollment	NA
High school graduation rate	NA

Assessment test results
(percent scoring at proficient or advanced level)
	Language	Math
NJASK-Grade 3	86.8%	88.6%
GEPA-Grade 8	NA	NA
HSPA-High School	NA	NA

SAT score averages
Pct tested	Math	Verbal	Writing
NA	NA	NA	NA

Teacher Qualifications
Avg. years of experience	17
Highly-qualified teachers one subject/all subjects	100%/100%
With emergency credentials	0.0%

No Child Left Behind
AYP, 2005-06 .... Meets Standards

Municipal Finance
State Aid Programs, 2008
Total aid	$1,873,172
CMPTRA	391,746
Energy tax receipts	1,466,212
Garden State Trust	15,214

General Budget, 2007
Total tax levy	$29,259,639
County levy	7,360,664
County taxes	6,826,178
County library	0
County health	0
County open space	534,487
School levy	16,298,536
Muni. levy	5,600,439
Misc. revenues	5,237,382

Hunterdon County

Franklin Township

Demographics & Socio-Economic Characteristics
(2000 US Census, except as noted)

Population
- 1980*........................2,294
- 1990*........................2,851
- 2000.........................2,990
  - Male.......................1,482
  - Female.....................1,508
- 2006 (estimate)*.............3,152
  - Population density........137.8

Race & Hispanic Origin, 2000
Race
- White........................2,916
- Black/African American..........12
- American Indian/Alaska Native....7
- Asian...........................23
- Native Hawaiian/Pacific Islander..0
- Other race.....................10
- Two or more races..............22
- Hispanic origin, total.........67
  - Mexican......................13
  - Puerto Rican.................20
  - Cuban..........................7
  - Other Hispanic...............27

Age & Nativity, 2000
- Under 5 years.................174
- 18 years and over............2,244
- 21 years and over............2,183
- 65 years and over.............361
- 85 years and over..............33
  - Median age..................41.6
- Native-born.................2,785
- Foreign-born..................205

Educational Attainment, 2000
- Population 25 years and over..2,112
- Less than 9th grade..........2.2%
- High school grad or higher..93.5%
- Bachelor's degree or higher.44.5%
- Graduate degree.............16.2%

Income & Poverty, 1999
- Per capita income..........$39,668
- Median household income....$91,364
- Median family income.......$96,320
- Persons in poverty..............49
- H'holds receiving public assistance....5
- H'holds receiving social security....258

Households, 2000
- Total households............1,091
  - With persons under 18.....403
  - With persons over 65......260
  - Family households.........890
  - Single-person households..155
- Persons per household........2.74
- Persons per family...........3.04

Labor & Employment
- Total civilian labor force, 2006**....1,881
  - Unemployment rate..........4.0%
- Total civilian labor force, 2000....1,668
  - Unemployment rate..........3.0%

Employed persons 16 years and over by occupation, 2000
- Managers & professionals......831
- Service occupations...........118
- Sales & office occupations....374
- Farming, fishing & forestry.....4
- Construction & maintenance....148
- Production & transportation...143
- Self-employed persons.........194

* US Census Bureau
** New Jersey Department of Labor

See Introduction for an explanation of all data sources.

General Information
Township of Franklin
202 Sidney Rd
Pittstown, NJ 08867
908-735-5215

- Website....................(county website)
- Year of incorporation................1845
- Land/water area (sq. miles).....22.88/0.04
- Form of government................Township

Government
Legislative Districts
- US Congressional..................12
- State Legislative.................23

Local Officials, 2008
- Mayor................Steven M. Tarshis
- Manager/Admin......................NA
- Clerk..................Ursula Stryker
- Finance Dir..........Ronald Mathews
- Tax Assessor..............Mary Mastro
- Tax Collector........Linda Swackhamer
- Attorney...........William J. Caldwell
- Building............Mark Fornaciari
- Planning..................Carl Hintz
- Engineering.....C. Richard Roseberry
- Public Works............Alan Dilley
- Police Chief........Kenneth Mandoli
- Emerg/Fire Director...Bradley Patkochis

Housing & Construction
Housing Units, 2000*
- Total..........................1,125
- Median rent.....................$892
- Median SF home value........$283,500

Permits for New Residential Construction

	Units	Value
Total, 2007	53	$7,847,295
Single family	11	$2,597,295
Total, 2006	9	$1,754,138
Single family	9	$1,754,138

Real Property Valuation, 2007

	Parcels	Valuation
Total	1,618	$546,333,822
Vacant	70	6,839,800
Residential	876	376,527,500
Commercial	22	38,788,000
Industrial	6	3,712,400
Apartments	3	1,113,400
Farm land	387	4,178,822
Farm homestead	254	115,173,900

Average Property Value & Tax, 2007
- Residential value............$435,134
- Property tax..................$9,887
- Tax credit/rebate.............$1,343

Public Library
No public municipal library

Library statistics, 2006
- Population served..................NA
- Full-time/total staff...........NA/NA

	Total	Per capita
Holdings	NA	NA
Revenues	NA	NA
Expenditures	NA	NA
Annual visits	NA	NA
Internet terminals/annual users	NA/NA	

Public Safety
Number of officers, 2006...........6

Crime	2005	2006
Total crimes	33	27
Violent	1	0
Murder	0	0
Rape	0	0
Robbery	0	0
Aggravated assault	1	0
Non-violent	32	27
Burglary	5	2
Larceny	24	23
Vehicle theft	3	2
Domestic violence	9	3
Arson	0	1
Total crime rate	10.5	8.6
Violent	0.3	0.0
Non-violent	10.2	8.6

Public School District
(for school year 2006-07 except as noted)

Franklin Township School District
226 Quakertown Rd, PO Box 368
Quakertown, NJ 08868
908-735-7929

- Chief School Admin.........Karen Lewis
- Number of schools................1
- Grade plan......................K-8
- Enrollment.....................352
- Attendance rate, '05-06.......94.0%
- Dropout rate....................NA
- Students per teacher...........9.9
- Per pupil expenditure.......$13,478
- Median faculty salary.......$65,137
- Median administrator salary.$83,000
- Grade 12 enrollment.............NA
- High school graduation rate.....NA

Assessment test results
(percent scoring at proficient or advanced level)

	Language	Math
NJASK-Grade 3	94.9%	89.7%
GEPA-Grade 8	87.0%	82.6%
HSPA-High School	NA	NA

SAT score averages

Pct tested	Math	Verbal	Writing
NA	NA	NA	NA

Teacher Qualifications
- Avg. years of experience.........18
- Highly-qualified teachers
  - one subject/all subjects...100%/100%
- With emergency credentials......0.0%

No Child Left Behind
- AYP, 2005-06..........Meets Standards

Municipal Finance
State Aid Programs, 2008
- Total aid..................$292,206
  - CMPTRA..........................0
  - Energy tax receipts.......290,366
  - Garden State Trust..........1,840

General Budget, 2007
- Total tax levy...........$12,436,169
  - County levy..............2,269,956
    - County taxes...........1,899,726
    - County library..........165,313
    - County health................0
    - County open space.......204,917
  - School levy..............8,469,448
  - Muni. levy...............1,696,765
- Misc. revenues............1,783,666

Taxes

	2005	2006	2007
General tax rate per $100	2.06	2.22	2.28
County equalization ratio	95.95	85.95	80.3
Net valuation taxable	$528,248,963	$534,932,543	$547,311,702
State equalized value	$571,203,463	$629,194,556	$666,832,630

The New Jersey Municipal Data Book

Franklin Township
Somerset County

Demographics & Socio-Economic Characteristics
(2000 US Census, except as noted)

Population
1980*	31,358
1990*	42,780
2000	50,903
Male	24,353
Female	26,550
2006 (estimate)*	60,273
Population density	1,288.7

Race & Hispanic Origin, 2000
Race
White	28,052
Black/African American	13,223
American Indian/Alaska Native	93
Asian	6,486
Native Hawaiian/Pacific Islander	21
Other race	1,811
Two or more races	1,217
Hispanic origin, total	4,127
Mexican	522
Puerto Rican	1,372
Cuban	206
Other Hispanic	2,027

Age & Nativity, 2000
Under 5 years	3,733
18 years and over	39,361
21 years and over	38,095
65 years and over	5,805
85 years and over	943
Median age	36.1
Native-born	39,092
Foreign-born	11,811

Educational Attainment, 2000
Population 25 years and over	36,111
Less than 9th grade	4.6%
High school grad or higher	88.2%
Bachelor's degree or higher	43.3%
Graduate degree	16.0%

Income & Poverty, 1999
Per capita income	$31,209
Median household income	$67,923
Median family income	$78,177
Persons in poverty	2,535
H'holds receiving public assistance	350
H'holds receiving social security	3,694

Households, 2000
Total households	19,355
With persons under 18	6,560
With persons over 65	3,699
Family households	12,989
Single-person households	4,975
Persons per household	2.58
Persons per family	3.14

Labor & Employment
Total civilian labor force, 2006**	33,818
Unemployment rate	4.2%
Total civilian labor force, 2000	27,856
Unemployment rate	3.5%

Employed persons 16 years and over by occupation, 2000
Managers & professionals	13,889
Service occupations	2,450
Sales & office occupations	6,833
Farming, fishing & forestry	18
Construction & maintenance	1,384
Production & transportation	2,312
Self-employed persons	913

* US Census Bureau
** New Jersey Department of Labor
§ State Fiscal Year July 1–June 30

General Information
Township of Franklin
475 Demott Ln
Somerset, NJ 08873
732-873-2500

Website	www.franklintwpnj.org
Year of incorporation	1798
Land/water area (sq. miles)	46.77/0.07
Form of government	Council-Manager

Government
Legislative Districts
US Congressional	6, 12
State Legislative	17

Local Officials, 2008
Mayor	Brian D. Levine
Manager	Kenneth Daly
Clerk	Ann Marie McCarthy
Finance Dir	Vandana Khurana
Tax Assessor	Stan Belenky
Tax Collector	Carol Langone
Attorney	Leslie G. London
Building	Vincent Lupo
Planning	Mark Healy
Engineering	Thomas Zilinek
Public Works	Thomas Zilinek
Police Chief	Craig Novick
Emerg/Fire Director	John Hauss

Housing & Construction
Housing Units, 2000*
Total	19,789
Median rent	$897
Median SF home value	$169,700

Permits for New Residential Construction
	Units	Value
Total, 2007	184	$19,021,992
Single family	154	$18,839,991
Total, 2006	344	$34,134,970
Single family	344	$34,134,970

Real Property Valuation, 2007
	Parcels	Valuation
Total	21,109	$8,757,206,280
Vacant	1,377	138,567,850
Residential	18,711	6,629,723,030
Commercial	473	991,258,400
Industrial	164	667,004,600
Apartments	26	266,447,700
Farm land	234	2,638,900
Farm homestead	124	61,565,800

Average Property Value & Tax, 2007
Residential value	$355,258
Property tax	$6,588
Tax credit/rebate	$1,109

Public Library
Franklin Township Library
485 DeMott Lane
Somerset, NJ 08873
732-873-8700

Director ... January Adams

Library statistics, 2006
Population served	50,903
Full-time/total staff	9/14

	Total	Per capita
Holdings	142,924	2.81
Revenues	$2,543,900	$49.98
Expenditures	$1,752,576	$34.43
Annual visits	126,104	2.48
Internet terminals/annual users	13/25,735	

Taxes
	2005	2006	2007
General tax rate per $100	1.93	1.83	1.86
County equalization ratio	109.36	106.85	102.56
Net valuation taxable	$7,453,186,258	$8,527,935,840	$8,770,370,572
State equalized value	$7,694,803,075	$8,327,912,573	$8,993,072,290

Public Safety
Number of officers, 2006 ... 116

Crime	2005	2006
Total crimes	954	950
Violent	93	88
Murder	1	1
Rape	9	5
Robbery	44	45
Aggravated assault	39	37
Non-violent	861	862
Burglary	218	190
Larceny	573	569
Vehicle theft	70	103
Domestic violence	458	471
Arson	14	12
Total crime rate	16.8	16.3
Violent	1.6	1.5
Non-violent	15.1	14.7

Public School District
(for school year 2006-07 except as noted)

Franklin Township School District
1755 Amwell Rd
Somerset, NJ 08873
732-873-2400

Superintendent	Edward Seto
Number of schools	9
Grade plan	K-12
Enrollment	7,275
Attendance rate, '05-06	94.6%
Dropout rate	NA
Students per teacher	10.7
Per pupil expenditure	$15,283
Median faculty salary	$54,505
Median administrator salary	$113,264
Grade 12 enrollment	396
High school graduation rate	96.8%

Assessment test results
(percent scoring at proficient or advanced level)
	Language	Math
NJASK-Grade 3	81.4%	89.4%
GEPA-Grade 8	68.9%	64.0%
HSPA-High School	84.0%	67.5%

SAT score averages
Pct tested	Math	Verbal	Writing
82%	487	473	470

Teacher Qualifications
Avg. years of experience	6
Highly-qualified teachers one subject/all subjects	100%/100%
With emergency credentials	0.2%

No Child Left Behind
AYP, 2005-06 ... Needs Improvement

Municipal Finance§
State Aid Programs, 2008
Total aid	$5,983,889
CMPTRA	1,440,161
Energy tax receipts	4,447,348
Garden State Trust	96,380

General Budget, 2007
Total tax levy	$162,649,672
County levy	25,979,059
County taxes	23,414,652
County library	0
County health	0
County open space	2,564,407
School levy	104,258,808
Muni. levy	32,411,805
Misc. revenues	22,672,488

Warren County
Franklin Township

Demographics & Socio-Economic Characteristics
(2000 US Census, except as noted)

Population
- 1980*..2,341
- 1990*..2,404
- 2000..2,768
  - Male..1,403
  - Female.......................................1,365
- 2006 (estimate)*..........................3,189
- Population density....................132.9

Race & Hispanic Origin, 2000
Race
- White..2,686
- Black/African American................23
- American Indian/Alaska Native........2
- Asian..24
- Native Hawaiian/Pacific Islander......0
- Other race..3
- Two or more races........................30
- Hispanic origin, total......................55
  - Mexican...8
  - Puerto Rican................................18
  - Cuban..3
  - Other Hispanic............................26

Age & Nativity, 2000
- Under 5 years...............................195
- 18 years and over......................1,970
- 21 years and over......................1,903
- 65 years and over.........................281
- 85 years and over...........................20
- Median age..................................38.2
- Native-born...............................2,666
- Foreign-born................................102

Educational Attainment, 2000
- Population 25 years and over....1,818
- Less than 9th grade.....................3.7%
- High school grad or higher......87.0%
- Bachelor's degree or higher....21.5%
- Graduate degree........................6.7%

Income & Poverty, 1999
- Per capita income..................$27,224
- Median household income...$69,115
- Median family income..........$72,763
- Persons in poverty........................86
- H'holds receiving public assistance....25
- H'holds receiving social security....189

Households, 2000
- Total households........................972
  - With persons under 18.............415
  - With persons over 65...............211
  - Family households..................750
  - Single-person households.......181
- Persons per household..............2.84
- Persons per family....................3.28

Labor & Employment
- Total civilian labor force, 2006**....1,665
  - Unemployment rate................3.1%
- Total civilian labor force, 2000....1,463
  - Unemployment rate................2.7%
- *Employed persons 16 years and over by occupation, 2000*
  - Managers & professionals........408
  - Service occupations.................191
  - Sales & office occupations.......385
  - Farming, fishing & forestry........17
  - Construction & maintenance...224
  - Production & transportation....198
- Self-employed persons................82

‡ Branch of county library
* US Census Bureau
** New Jersey Department of Labor

See Introduction for an explanation of all data sources.

General Information
Township of Franklin
2093 Rt 57
PO Box 547
Broadway, NJ 08808
908-689-3994

- Website........www.franklintwpwarren.org
- Year of incorporation..................1839
- Land/water area (sq. miles).....23.99/0.04
- Form of government..............Township

Government
Legislative Districts
- US Congressional...........................5
- State Legislative............................23

Local Officials, 2008
- Mayor......................Bonnie Butler
- Manager/Admin.........................NA
- Clerk...................Denise L. Cicerelle
- Finance Dir..............Dawn Stanchina
- Tax Assessor............Eloise Hagaman
- Tax Collector...........Karin Kneafsey
- Attorney..............James Broscious
- Building................Walter Van Lieu
- Comm Dev/Planning...................NA
- Engineering............Michael Finelli
- Public Works................Ronnie Read
- Police Chief...............................NA
- Emerg/Fire Director....Raymond Read

Housing & Construction
Housing Units, 2000*
- Total.......................................1,019
- Median rent................................$725
- Median SF home value..........$176,200

Permits for New Residential Construction
	Units	Value
Total, 2007	1	$161,500
Single family	1	$161,500
Total, 2006	4	$2,051,400
Single family	4	$2,051,400

Real Property Valuation, 2007
	Parcels	Valuation
Total	1,655	$409,570,025
Vacant	124	6,937,700
Residential	945	288,425,300
Commercial	46	32,616,800
Industrial	15	28,866,100
Apartments	1	306,300
Farm land	382	5,121,825
Farm homestead	142	47,296,000

Average Property Value & Tax, 2007
- Residential value...................$308,851
- Property tax...........................$7,784
- Tax credit/rebate..................$1,179

Public Library
Franklin Branch Library‡
1502 Rte 57 West
Washington, NJ 07882
908-689-7922

- Branch Librarian............Chris Reedell

Library statistics, 2006
see Warren County profile
for library system statistics

Public Safety
- Number of officers, 2006................0

Crime	2005	2006
Total crimes	28	36
Violent	3	2
Murder	0	0
Rape	0	0
Robbery	0	0
Aggravated assault	3	2
Non-violent	25	34
Burglary	6	9
Larceny	15	24
Vehicle theft	4	1
Domestic violence	14	0
Arson	0	1
Total crime rate	8.8	11.3
Violent	0.9	0.6
Non-violent	7.8	10.7

Public School District
(for school year 2006-07 except as noted)

Franklin Township School District
52 Asbury Broadway Rd
Washington, NJ 07882
908-689-2958

- Chief School Admin..........Paul Rinaldi
- Number of schools........................1
- Grade plan................................K-6
- Enrollment.............................400
- Attendance rate, '05-06............95.6%
- Dropout rate...............................NA
- Students per teacher..................12.0
- Per pupil expenditure...........$10,434
- Median faculty salary............$47,905
- Median administrator salary...$86,749
- Grade 12 enrollment....................NA
- High school graduation rate.........NA

Assessment test results
(percent scoring at proficient or advanced level)

	Language	Math
NJASK-Grade 3	81.8%	76.4%
GEPA-Grade 8	NA	NA
HSPA-High School	NA	NA

SAT score averages
Pct tested	Math	Verbal	Writing
NA	NA	NA	NA

Teacher Qualifications
- Avg. years of experience..............14
- Highly-qualified teachers
  - one subject/all subjects......100%/100%
- With emergency credentials.........0.0%

No Child Left Behind
- AYP, 2005-06............Meets Standards

Municipal Finance
State Aid Programs, 2008
- Total aid....................................$285,085
- CMPTRA..0
- Energy tax receipts................275,078
- Garden State Trust..................10,007

General Budget, 2007
- Total tax levy..................$10,346,515
- County levy......................2,820,515
  - County taxes................2,302,581
  - County library..................240,477
  - County health.............................0
  - County open space..........277,457
- School levy.......................6,798,688
- Muni. levy...........................727,312
- Misc. revenues.................1,508,993

Taxes
	2005	2006	2007
General tax rate per $100	2.23	2.35	2.53
County equalization ratio	107.01	98.36	89.32
Net valuation taxable	$399,556,586	$404,414,025	$410,536,965
State equalized value	$406,218,571	$453,823,161	$471,304,589

Fredon Township
Sussex County

Demographics & Socio-Economic Characteristics
(2000 US Census, except as noted)

Population
1980*	2,281
1990*	2,763
2000	2,860
Male	1,399
Female	1,461
2006 (estimate)*	3,361
Population density	189.2

Race & Hispanic Origin, 2000
Race
White	2,779
Black/African American	15
American Indian/Alaska Native	7
Asian	24
Native Hawaiian/Pacific Islander	0
Other race	16
Two or more races	19
Hispanic origin, total	62
Mexican	9
Puerto Rican	16
Cuban	12
Other Hispanic	25

Age & Nativity, 2000
Under 5 years	197
18 years and over	2,099
21 years and over	2,017
65 years and over	266
85 years and over	27
Median age	39.3
Native-born	2,721
Foreign-born	139

Educational Attainment, 2000
Population 25 years and over	1,946
Less than 9th grade	2.8%
High school grad or higher	92.9%
Bachelor's degree or higher	34.0%
Graduate degree	10.9%

Income & Poverty, 1999
Per capita income	$31,430
Median household income	$75,710
Median family income	$84,038
Persons in poverty	62
H'holds receiving public assistance	6
H'holds receiving social security	210

Households, 2000
Total households	982
With persons under 18	401
With persons over 65	194
Family households	818
Single-person households	131
Persons per household	2.89
Persons per family	3.18

Labor & Employment
Total civilian labor force, 2006**	1,835
Unemployment rate	1.6%
Total civilian labor force, 2000	1,645
Unemployment rate	1.1%

Employed persons 16 years and over by occupation, 2000
Managers & professionals	678
Service occupations	234
Sales & office occupations	434
Farming, fishing & forestry	5
Construction & maintenance	144
Production & transportation	132
Self-employed persons	171

* US Census Bureau
** New Jersey Department of Labor

General Information
Township of Fredon
443 State Route 94 S
Newton, NJ 07860
973-383-7025

Website	www.twp.fredon.nj.us
Year of incorporation	1904
Land/water area (sq. miles)	17.76/0.19
Form of government	Township

Government
Legislative Districts
US Congressional	5
State Legislative	24

Local Officials, 2008
Mayor	Sandra Coltelli
Manager/Admin	NA
Clerk	Joanne Charner
Finance Dir	Patrick Bailey
Tax Assessor	Kathleen Kieb
Tax Collector	Gisela Boltzer
Attorney	William Hinkes
Building	John de Jager
Comm Dev/Planning	NA
Engineering	Harold Pellow
Public Works	Donald Nelson
Police Chief	NA
Emerg/Fire Director	Joel Sparling

Housing & Construction
Housing Units, 2000*
Total	1,019
Median rent	$708
Median SF home value	$199,700

Permits for New Residential Construction
	Units	Value
Total, 2007	10	$2,262,145
Single family	10	$2,262,145
Total, 2006	21	$3,930,155
Single family	21	$3,930,155

Real Property Valuation, 2007
	Parcels	Valuation
Total	1,527	$278,199,600
Vacant	106	4,738,000
Residential	1,068	227,203,400
Commercial	36	12,813,100
Industrial	5	3,912,700
Apartments	0	0
Farm land	197	1,967,300
Farm homestead	115	27,565,100

Average Property Value & Tax, 2007
Residential value	$215,358
Property tax	$7,479
Tax credit/rebate	$1,103

Public Library
No public municipal library

Library statistics, 2006
Population served	NA
Full-time/total staff	NA/NA

	Total	Per capita
Holdings	NA	NA
Revenues	NA	NA
Expenditures	NA	NA
Annual visits	NA	NA
Internet terminals/annual users	NA/NA	

Taxes
	2005	2006	2007
General tax rate per $100	3.08	3.27	3.48
County equalization ratio	65.7	57.85	54.13
Net valuation taxable	$263,630,328	$271,876,400	$278,728,130
State equalized value	$455,713,618	$502,876,944	$551,964,804

Public Safety
Number of officers, 2006 0

Crime	2005	2006
Total crimes	29	22
Violent	2	1
Murder	0	0
Rape	0	0
Robbery	0	0
Aggravated assault	2	1
Non-violent	27	21
Burglary	4	8
Larceny	23	13
Vehicle theft	0	0
Domestic violence	4	0
Arson	0	0
Total crime rate	8.9	6.6
Violent	0.6	0.3
Non-violent	8.3	6.3

Public School District
(for school year 2006-07 except as noted)

Fredon Township School District
459 Route 94
Newton, NJ 07860
973-383-4151

Superintendent	Sal Constantino
Number of schools	1
Grade plan	K-6
Enrollment	331
Attendance rate, '05-06	95.6%
Dropout rate	NA
Students per teacher	11.4
Per pupil expenditure	$11,130
Median faculty salary	$46,200
Median administrator salary	$83,201
Grade 12 enrollment	NA
High school graduation rate	NA

Assessment test results
(percent scoring at proficient or advanced level)
	Language	Math
NJASK-Grade 3	80.7%	100.0%
GEPA-Grade 8	NA	NA
HSPA-High School	NA	NA

SAT score averages
Pct tested	Math	Verbal	Writing
NA	NA	NA	NA

Teacher Qualifications
Avg. years of experience	7
Highly-qualified teachers one subject/all subjects	100%/100%
With emergency credentials	0.0%

No Child Left Behind
AYP, 2005-06 ..... Meets Standards

Municipal Finance
State Aid Programs, 2008
Total aid	$266,730
CMPTRA	0
Energy tax receipts	253,391
Garden State Trust	13,339

General Budget, 2007
Total tax levy	$9,679,413
County levy	2,094,344
County taxes	1,711,254
County library	145,884
County health	56,413
County open space	180,793
School levy	6,223,069
Muni. levy	1,362,000
Misc. revenues	1,471,000

Monmouth County
Freehold Borough

Demographics & Socio-Economic Characteristics
(2000 US Census, except as noted)

Population
1980*	10,020
1990*	10,742
2000	10,976
Male	5,656
Female	5,320
2006 (estimate)*	11,394
Population density	5,697.0

Race & Hispanic Origin, 2000
Race
- White ... 7,795
- Black/African American ... 1,738
- American Indian/Alaska Native ... 60
- Asian ... 269
- Native Hawaiian/Pacific Islander ... 2
- Other race ... 729
- Two or more races ... 383

Hispanic origin, total ... 3,081
- Mexican ... 1,903
- Puerto Rican ... 627
- Cuban ... 31
- Other Hispanic ... 520

Age & Nativity, 2000
- Under 5 years ... 858
- 18 years and over ... 8,258
- 21 years and over ... 7,788
- 65 years and over ... 1,171
- 85 years and over ... 169
- Median age ... 33.0
- Native-born ... 8,720
- Foreign-born ... 2,256

Educational Attainment, 2000
- Population 25 years and over ... 7,148
- Less than 9th grade ... 10.7%
- High school grad or higher ... 76.0%
- Bachelor's degree or higher ... 19.7%
- Graduate degree ... 4.6%

Income & Poverty, 1999
- Per capita income ... $19,910
- Median household income ... $48,654
- Median family income ... $53,374
- Persons in poverty ... 1,314
- H'holds receiving public assistance ... 108
- H'holds receiving social security ... 931

Households, 2000
- Total households ... 3,695
- With persons under 18 ... 1,436
- With persons over 65 ... 898
- Family households ... 2,570
- Single-person households ... 898
- Persons per household ... 2.96
- Persons per family ... 3.39

Labor & Employment
- Total civilian labor force, 2006** ... 6,223
-    Unemployment rate ... 6.3%
- Total civilian labor force, 2000 ... 5,833
-    Unemployment rate ... 7.0%

Employed persons 16 years and over by occupation, 2000
- Managers & professionals ... 1,410
- Service occupations ... 1,374
- Sales & office occupations ... 1,378
- Farming, fishing & forestry ... 36
- Construction & maintenance ... 542
- Production & transportation ... 683
- Self-employed persons ... 228

* US Census Bureau
** New Jersey Department of Labor

See Introduction for an explanation of all data sources.

General Information
Freehold Borough
51 W Main St
Freehold, NJ 07728
732-462-1410

Website	www.freeholdboro.org
Year of incorporation	1919
Land/water area (sq. miles)	2.00/0.00
Form of government	Borough

Government
Legislative Districts
- US Congressional ... 4
- State Legislative ... 12

Local Officials, 2008
Mayor	Michael Wilson
Manager	Joseph Bellina
Clerk	Traci L. DiBenedetto
Finance Dir	Nancy Forman
Tax Assessor	Mitchell Elias
Tax Collector	Edward Lewis
Attorney	Kerry Higgins
Building	Henry Stryker
Comm Dev/Planning	NA
Engineering	Jim Kovacs
Public Works	Bobby Holmes
Police Chief	Mitchell E. Roth
Emerg/Fire Director	William Maushardt

Housing & Construction
Housing Units, 2000*
- Total ... 3,821
- Median rent ... $821
- Median SF home value ... $137,500

Permits for New Residential Construction
	Units	Value
Total, 2007	16	$1,216,932
Single family	11	$1,216,432
Total, 2006	16	$1,682,162
Single family	16	$1,682,162

Real Property Valuation, 2007
	Parcels	Valuation
Total	3,301	$1,071,145,000
Vacant	88	13,574,000
Residential	2,944	761,011,000
Commercial	254	238,891,500
Industrial	3	34,727,100
Apartments	12	22,941,400
Farm land	0	0
Farm homestead	0	0

Average Property Value & Tax, 2007
- Residential value ... $258,496
- Property tax ... $5,272
- Tax credit/rebate ... $1,000

Public Library
Freehold Public Library
28 1/2 E Main St
Freehold, NJ 07728
732-462-5135

Director ... Barbara Greenberg

Library statistics, 2006
- Population served ... 10,976
- Full-time/total staff ... 1/3

	Total	Per capita
Holdings	26,723	2.43
Revenues	$332,192	$30.27
Expenditures	$312,538	$28.47
Annual visits	25,230	2.30
Internet terminals/annual users	6/13,570	

Public Safety
Number of officers, 2006 ... 35

Crime	2005	2006
Total crimes	340	309
Violent	30	49
Murder	0	0
Rape	0	1
Robbery	11	26
Aggravated assault	19	22
Non-violent	310	260
Burglary	59	35
Larceny	234	211
Vehicle theft	17	14
Domestic violence	232	211
Arson	3	3
Total crime rate	29.5	27.0
Violent	2.6	4.3
Non-violent	26.9	22.7

Public School District
(for school year 2006-07 except as noted)

Freehold Borough School District
280 Park Ave
Freehold, NJ 07728
732-761-2102

Superintendent	Elizabeth O'Connell
Number of schools	3
Grade plan	K-8
Enrollment	1,359
Attendance rate, '05-06	94.8%
Dropout rate	NA
Students per teacher	12.5
Per pupil expenditure	$10,459
Median faculty salary	$55,195
Median administrator salary	$97,007
Grade 12 enrollment	NA
High school graduation rate	NA

Assessment test results
(percent scoring at proficient or advanced level)
	Language	Math
NJASK-Grade 3	69.1%	76.6%
GEPA-Grade 8	64.4%	44.8%
HSPA-High School	NA	NA

SAT score averages
Pct tested	Math	Verbal	Writing
NA	NA	NA	NA

Teacher Qualifications
- Avg. years of experience ... 14
- Highly-qualified teachers
  - one subject/all subjects ... 100%/100%
- With emergency credentials ... 1.3%

No Child Left Behind
AYP, 2005-06 ... Meets Standards

Municipal Finance
State Aid Programs, 2008
- Total aid ... $1,600,115
- CMPTRA ... 756,158
- Energy tax receipts ... 843,957
- Garden State Trust ... 0

General Budget, 2007
- Total tax levy ... $22,046,491
- County levy ... 2,992,874
-   County taxes ... 2,816,800
-   County library ... 0
-   County health ... 0
-   County open space ... 176,074
- School levy ... 11,931,281
- Muni. levy ... 7,122,336
- Misc. revenues ... 6,162,284

Taxes
	2005	2006	2007
General tax rate per $100	1.815	1.949	2.04
County equalization ratio	119	100.99	92.47
Net valuation taxable	$1,085,562,930	$1,074,863,600	$1,080,991,278
State equalized value	$1,074,921,210	$1,172,895,348	$1,242,464,230

Freehold Township
Monmouth County

Demographics & Socio-Economic Characteristics
(2000 US Census, except as noted)

Population
1980*	19,202
1990*	24,710
2000	31,537
Male	15,588
Female	15,949
2006 (estimate)*	33,953
Population density	883.0

Race & Hispanic Origin, 2000
Race
White	27,466
Black/African American	1,616
American Indian/Alaska Native	44
Asian	1,623
Native Hawaiian/Pacific Islander	5
Other race	374
Two or more races	409
Hispanic origin, total	1,637
Mexican	328
Puerto Rican	607
Cuban	133
Other Hispanic	569

Age & Nativity, 2000
Under 5 years	2,137
18 years and over	23,564
21 years and over	22,722
65 years and over	3,781
85 years and over	613
Median age	38.3
Native-born	28,008
Foreign-born	3,529

Educational Attainment, 2000
Population 25 years and over	21,808
Less than 9th grade	3.6%
High school grad or higher	88.8%
Bachelor's degree or higher	37.5%
Graduate degree	13.1%

Income & Poverty, 1999
Per capita income	$31,505
Median household income	$77,185
Median family income	$89,845
Persons in poverty	1,155
H'holds receiving public assistance	113
H'holds receiving social security	2,726

Households, 2000
Total households	10,814
With persons under 18	4,266
With persons over 65	2,468
Family households	8,279
Single-person households	2,163
Persons per household	2.76
Persons per family	3.21

Labor & Employment
Total civilian labor force, 2006**	18,127
Unemployment rate	3.5%
Total civilian labor force, 2000	15,970
Unemployment rate	2.8%

Employed persons 16 years and over by occupation, 2000
Managers & professionals	7,117
Service occupations	1,422
Sales & office occupations	5,002
Farming, fishing & forestry	24
Construction & maintenance	1,031
Production & transportation	934
Self-employed persons	787

* US Census Bureau
** New Jersey Department of Labor

General Information
Freehold Township
1 Municipal Plz
Freehold, NJ 07728
732-294-2000

Website	www.twp.freehold.nj.us
Year of incorporation	1693
Land/water area (sq. miles)	38.45/0.08
Form of government	Township

Government
Legislative Districts
US Congressional	4, 12
State Legislative	12

Local Officials, 2008
Mayor	Eugene B. Golub
Manager	Thomas E. Antus
Clerk	Romeo Cascaes
Finance Dir.	Debrah Defeo
Tax Assessor	Helen Ward
Tax Collector	MaryLou Angelo
Attorney	Duane O. Davison
Building	Drew Ricciardi
Comm Dev/Planning	NA
Engineering	Joseph Mavuro
Public Works	Tim White
Police Chief	Ernest Schriefer
Emerg/Fire Director	Tom Luongo

Housing & Construction
Housing Units, 2000*
Total	11,032
Median rent	$904
Median SF home value	$227,500

Permits for New Residential Construction
	Units	Value
Total, 2007	33	$9,843,333
Single family	16	$9,559,263
Total, 2006	101	$11,373,264
Single family	16	$8,187,109

Real Property Valuation, 2007
	Parcels	Valuation
Total	12,435	$3,007,501,000
Vacant	603	49,811,400
Residential	11,192	2,205,318,600
Commercial	360	633,230,100
Industrial	26	71,697,200
Apartments	2	30,948,600
Farm land	171	1,764,500
Farm homestead	81	14,730,600

Average Property Value & Tax, 2007
Residential value	$196,935
Property tax	$6,834
Tax credit/rebate	$1,048

Public Library
No public municipal library

Library statistics, 2006
Population served	NA
Full-time/total staff	NA/NA

	Total	Per capita
Holdings	NA	NA
Revenues	NA	NA
Expenditures	NA	NA
Annual visits	NA	NA
Internet terminals/annual users	NA/NA	

Taxes
	2005	2006	2007
General tax rate per $100	3.161	3.343	3.471
County equalization ratio	61.49	54.78	49.75
Net valuation taxable	$2,975,359,174	$2,982,974,600	$3,044,471,360
State equalized value	$5,431,469,832	$6,037,954,660	$6,427,750,216

Public Safety
Number of officers, 2006		70

Crime	2005	2006
Total crimes	1,035	957
Violent	56	36
Murder	0	0
Rape	18	8
Robbery	12	11
Aggravated assault	26	17
Non-violent	979	921
Burglary	89	76
Larceny	854	831
Vehicle theft	36	14
Domestic violence	300	283
Arson	2	4
Total crime rate	30.6	28.3
Violent	1.7	1.1
Non-violent	28.9	27.2

Public School District
(for school year 2006-07 except as noted)

Freehold Township School District
384 W Main St
Freehold, NJ 07728
732-462-8400

Superintendent	William Setaro
Number of schools	8
Grade plan	K-8
Enrollment	4,586
Attendance rate, '05-06	95.5%
Dropout rate	NA
Students per teacher	12.0
Per pupil expenditure	$12,529
Median faculty salary	$49,620
Median administrator salary	$108,370
Grade 12 enrollment	NA
High school graduation rate	NA

Assessment test results
(percent scoring at proficient or advanced level)
	Language	Math
NJASK-Grade 3	91.7%	96.8%
GEPA-Grade 8	92.4%	85.0%
HSPA-High School	NA	NA

SAT score averages
Pct tested	Math	Verbal	Writing
NA	NA	NA	NA

Teacher Qualifications
Avg. years of experience	7
Highly-qualified teachers one subject/all subjects	100%/100%
With emergency credentials	0.4%

No Child Left Behind
AYP, 2005-06 .... Meets Standards

Municipal Finance
State Aid Programs, 2008
Total aid	$10,051,673
CMPTRA	1,452,061
Energy tax receipts	8,564,434
Garden State Trust	35,178

General Budget, 2007
Total tax levy	$105,650,699
County levy	16,481,442
County taxes	14,719,371
County library	842,405
County health	0
County open space	919,666
School levy	75,818,210
Muni. levy	13,351,047
Misc. revenues	25,935,294

Warren County
Frelinghuysen Township

Demographics & Socio-Economic Characteristics
(2000 US Census, except as noted)

Population
1980*	1,435
1990*	1,779
2000	2,083
Male	1,028
Female	1,055
2006 (estimate)*	2,218
Population density	94.7

Race & Hispanic Origin, 2000
Race
- White 2,037
- Black/African American ... 7
- American Indian/Alaska Native .. 1
- Asian 8
- Native Hawaiian/Pacific Islander .. 4
- Other race 10
- Two or more races 16

Hispanic origin, total 55
- Mexican 1
- Puerto Rican 17
- Cuban 16
- Other Hispanic 21

Age & Nativity, 2000
- Under 5 years 132
- 18 years and over 1,540
- 21 years and over 1,487
- 65 years and over 230
- 85 years and over 43
- Median age 40.3
- Native-born 1,986
- Foreign-born 97

Educational Attainment, 2000
- Population 25 years and over .. 1,438
- Less than 9th grade 4.0%
- High school grad or higher .. 89.6%
- Bachelor's degree or higher .. 33.4%
- Graduate degree 12.7%

Income & Poverty, 1999
- Per capita income $28,792
- Median household income .. $72,434
- Median family income $78,464
- Persons in poverty 46
- H'holds receiving public assistance .. 11
- H'holds receiving social security .. 146

Households, 2000
- Total households 722
- With persons under 18 .. 287
- With persons over 65 .. 133
- Family households 578
- Single-person households .. 105
- Persons per household .. 2.81
- Persons per family 3.13

Labor & Employment
- Total civilian labor force, 2006** .. 1,221
- Unemployment rate 3.2%
- Total civilian labor force, 2000 .. 1,082
- Unemployment rate 3.3%

Employed persons 16 years and over by occupation, 2000
- Managers & professionals .. 450
- Service occupations 135
- Sales & office occupations .. 252
- Farming, fishing & forestry .. 4
- Construction & maintenance .. 126
- Production & transportation .. 79
- Self-employed persons .. 90

* US Census Bureau
** New Jersey Department of Labor

See Introduction for an explanation of all data sources.

General Information
Township of Frelinghuysen
PO Box 417
Johnsonburg, NJ 07846
908-852-4121

- Website .... www.freylinghuysen-nj.us
- Year of incorporation 1848
- Land/water area (sq. miles) 23.43/0.12
- Form of government .... Township

Government
Legislative Districts
- US Congressional 5
- State Legislative 23

Local Officials, 2008
- Mayor .... Thomas K. Charles
- Manager/Admin .... NA
- Clerk .... Brenda Kleber
- Finance Dir .... Gene Marie McCartney
- Tax Assessor .... David Gill
- Tax Collector .... Donna Clouse
- Attorney .... Edward Wacks
- Building .... Richard O'Connor
- Comm Dev/Planning .... NA
- Engineering .... Paul Sterbenz
- Public Works .... NA
- Police Chief .... NA
- Fire/Emergency Dir .... NA

Housing & Construction
Housing Units, 2000*
- Total 755
- Median rent $817
- Median SF home value $211,000

Permits for New Residential Construction
	Units	Value
Total, 2007	13	$3,708,991
Single family	13	$3,708,991
Total, 2006	13	$3,009,524
Single family	13	$3,009,524

Real Property Valuation, 2007
	Parcels	Valuation
Total	1,330	$273,850,278
Vacant	109	7,533,700
Residential	597	186,195,600
Commercial	25	8,171,878
Industrial	0	0
Apartments	0	0
Farm land	403	2,350,000
Farm homestead	196	69,599,100

Average Property Value & Tax, 2007
- Residential value $322,566
- Property tax $6,981
- Tax credit/rebate $1,137

Public Library
No public municipal library

Library statistics, 2006
- Population served .... NA
- Full-time/total staff .... NA/NA

	Total	Per capita
Holdings	NA	NA
Revenues	NA	NA
Expenditures	NA	NA
Annual visits	NA	NA
Internet terminals/annual users	NA/NA	

Taxes
	2005	2006	2007
General tax rate per $100	2.05	2.13	2.17
County equalization ratio	105.55	96.98	87.8
Net valuation taxable	$265,076,647	$267,488,578	$274,503,413
State equalized value	$273,331,251	$305,380,159	$308,626,907

Public Safety
Number of officers, 2006 0

Crime
	2005	2006
Total crimes	14	19
Violent	0	1
Murder	0	0
Rape	0	0
Robbery	0	0
Aggravated assault	0	1
Non-violent	14	18
Burglary	3	3
Larceny	10	13
Vehicle theft	1	2
Domestic violence	11	0
Arson	0	0
Total crime rate	6.4	8.7
Violent	0.0	0.5
Non-violent	6.4	8.2

Public School District
(for school year 2006-07 except as noted)

Frelinghuysen Township School District
180 Route 94, PO Box 421
Johnsonburg, NJ 07846
908-362-6319

- Chief School Admin .... Dwight Klett
- Number of schools 1
- Grade plan K-6
- Enrollment 203
- Attendance rate, '05-06 .... 96.1%
- Dropout rate .... NA
- Students per teacher 10.0
- Per pupil expenditure $11,875
- Median faculty salary $45,340
- Median administrator salary ... $86,375
- Grade 12 enrollment .... NA
- High school graduation rate .... NA

Assessment test results
(percent scoring at proficient or advanced level)
	Language	Math
NJASK-Grade 3	95.4%	90.9%
GEPA-Grade 8	NA	NA
HSPA-High School	NA	NA

SAT score averages
Pct tested	Math	Verbal	Writing
NA	NA	NA	NA

Teacher Qualifications
- Avg. years of experience 12
- Highly-qualified teachers
  one subject/all subjects 100%/100%
- With emergency credentials 0.0%

No Child Left Behind
AYP, 2005-06 .... Meets Standards

Municipal Finance
State Aid Programs, 2008
- Total aid $214,524
- CMPTRA 0
- Energy tax receipts 195,270
- Garden State Trust 19,254

General Budget, 2007
- Total tax levy $5,940,824
- County levy 1,915,430
- County taxes 1,563,610
- County library 163,350
- County health 0
- County open space 188,470
- School levy 3,631,377
- Muni. levy 394,017
- Misc. revenues 986,497

©2008 Information Publications, Inc. All rights reserved. Photocopying prohibited. For additional copies, contact the publisher at www.informationpublications.com or (877)544-INFO (4636)

Frenchtown Borough
Hunterdon County

Demographics & Socio-Economic Characteristics
(2000 US Census, except as noted)

Population
1980*	1,573
1990*	1,528
2000	1,488
Male	721
Female	767
2006 (estimate)*	1,491
Population density	1,164.8

Race & Hispanic Origin, 2000
Race
White	1,428
Black/African American	6
American Indian/Alaska Native	3
Asian	18
Native Hawaiian/Pacific Islander	0
Other race	20
Two or more races	13
Hispanic origin, total	39
Mexican	2
Puerto Rican	5
Cuban	0
Other Hispanic	32

Age & Nativity, 2000
Under 5 years	94
18 years and over	1,153
21 years and over	1,102
65 years and over	146
85 years and over	12
Median age	38.0
Native-born	1,385
Foreign-born	103

Educational Attainment, 2000
Population 25 years and over	1,051
Less than 9th grade	3.0%
High school grad or higher	85.6%
Bachelor's degree or higher	32.4%
Graduate degree	13.1%

Income & Poverty, 1999
Per capita income	$27,765
Median household income	$52,109
Median family income	$62,132
Persons in poverty	49
H'holds receiving public assistance	9
H'holds receiving social security	120

Households, 2000
Total households	613
With persons under 18	199
With persons over 65	107
Family households	376
Single-person households	177
Persons per household	2.38
Persons per family	2.99

Labor & Employment
Total civilian labor force, 2006**	967
Unemployment rate	3.1%
Total civilian labor force, 2000	862
Unemployment rate	3.2%

Employed persons 16 years and over by occupation, 2000
Managers & professionals	356
Service occupations	78
Sales & office occupations	199
Farming, fishing & forestry	0
Construction & maintenance	104
Production & transportation	97
Self-employed persons	99

* US Census Bureau
** New Jersey Department of Labor

General Information
Borough of Frenchtown
Borough Hall
29 2nd St
Frenchtown, NJ 08825
908-996-4524

Website	www.frenchtown.com/newsite
Year of incorporation	1867
Land/water area (sq. miles)	1.28/0.06
Form of government	Borough

Government
Legislative Districts
US Congressional	12
State Legislative	23

Local Officials, 2008
Mayor	Ronald Sworen
Manager/Admin	NA
Clerk	Brenda Shepherd
Finance Dir	Diane Laudenbach
Tax Assessor	Curtis Schick
Tax Collector	Diane Laudenbach
Attorney	Douglas Cole
Building	DCA
Comm Dev/Planning	NA
Engineering	Robert J. Clerico
Public Works	NA
Police Chief	Allan Kurylka
Emerg/Fire Director	Gerald Hoffman

Housing & Construction
Housing Units, 2000*
Total	630
Median rent	$755
Median SF home value	$165,900

Permits for New Residential Construction
	Units	Value
Total, 2007	1	$106,000
Single family	1	$106,000
Total, 2006	1	$163,000
Single family	1	$163,000

Real Property Valuation, 2007
	Parcels	Valuation
Total	548	$148,104,079
Vacant	45	2,554,500
Residential	418	108,089,500
Commercial	61	26,662,500
Industrial	6	3,726,350
Apartments	10	6,119,880
Farm land	6	52,749
Farm homestead	2	898,600

Average Property Value & Tax, 2007
Residential value	$259,495
Property tax	$6,750
Tax credit/rebate	$1,102

Public Library
Frenchtown Public Library
29 Second St
Frenchtown, NJ 08825
908-996-4788

Director: Sara Heil

Library statistics, 2006
Population served	1,488
Full-time/total staff	NA/0

	Total	Per capita
Holdings	NA	NA
Revenues	NA	NA
Expenditures	NA	NA
Annual visits	NA	NA
Internet terminals/annual users	NA/NA	

Taxes
	2005	2006	2007
General tax rate per $100	2.25	2.42	2.61
County equalization ratio	105.49	90.27	82.37
Net valuation taxable	$149,912,746	$149,618,555	$149,049,848
State equalized value	$156,714,140	$177,616,197	$189,878,132

Public Safety
Number of officers, 2006: 2

Crime	2005	2006
Total crimes	26	26
Violent	1	1
Murder	1	0
Rape	0	0
Robbery	0	0
Aggravated assault	0	1
Non-violent	25	25
Burglary	5	2
Larceny	24	23
Vehicle theft	3	0
Domestic violence	9	4
Arson	0	0
Total crime rate	17.2	17.3
Violent	0.7	0.7
Non-violent	16.5	16.6

Public School District
(for school year 2006-07 except as noted)

Frenchtown Borough School District
902 Harrison St
Frenchtown, NJ 08825
908-996-2751

Chief School Admin	Erik Falkenstein
Number of schools	1
Grade plan	K-8
Enrollment	141
Attendance rate, '05-06	96.0%
Dropout rate	NA
Students per teacher	7.3
Per pupil expenditure	$14,895
Median faculty salary	$48,950
Median administrator salary	$74,760
Grade 12 enrollment	NA
High school graduation rate	NA

Assessment test results
(percent scoring at proficient or advanced level)
	Language	Math
NJASK-Grade 3	77.8%	83.3%
GEPA-Grade 8	NA	NA
HSPA-High School	NA	NA

SAT score averages
Pct tested	Math	Verbal	Writing
NA	NA	NA	NA

Teacher Qualifications
Avg. years of experience	12
Highly-qualified teachers one subject/all subjects	100%/100%
With emergency credentials	0.0%

No Child Left Behind
AYP, 2005-06: Meets Standards

Municipal Finance
State Aid Programs, 2008
Total aid	$116,714
CMPTRA	0
Energy tax receipts	79,097
Garden State Trust	37,617

General Budget, 2007
Total tax levy	$3,877,350
County levy	603,052
County taxes	504,675
County library	43,916
County health	0
County open space	54,462
School levy	2,466,831
Muni. levy	807,467
Misc. revenues	635,124

Atlantic County / Galloway Township

Demographics & Socio-Economic Characteristics
(2000 US Census, except as noted)

Population
1980*	12,176
1990*	23,330
2000	31,209
Male	14,984
Female	16,225
2006 (estimate)*	36,205
Population density	400.1

Race & Hispanic Origin, 2000
Race
- White 24,081
- Black/African American 3,058
- American Indian/Alaska Native 75
- Asian 2,498
- Native Hawaiian/Pacific Islander 15
- Other race 807
- Two or more races 675

Hispanic origin, total 1,924
- Mexican 126
- Puerto Rican 1,048
- Cuban 69
- Other Hispanic 681

Age & Nativity, 2000
- Under 5 years 2,030
- 18 years and over 23,147
- 21 years and over 20,991
- 65 years and over 2,830
- 85 years and over 237
- Median age 34.0
- Native-born 27,665
- Foreign-born 3,494

Educational Attainment, 2000
- Population 25 years and over 18,733
- Less than 9th grade 3.0%
- High school grad or higher 87.3%
- Bachelor's degree or higher 22.8%
- Graduate degree 7.3%

Income & Poverty, 1999
- Per capita income $21,048
- Median household income $51,592
- Median family income $57,156
- Persons in poverty 1,907
- H'holds receiving public assistance 206
- H'holds receiving social security 2,344

Households, 2000
- Total households 10,772
- With persons under 18 4,451
- With persons over 65 2,106
- Family households 7,681
- Single-person households 2,317
- Persons per household 2.70
- Persons per family 3.18

Labor & Employment
- Total civilian labor force, 2006** 19,407
- Unemployment rate 5.2%
- Total civilian labor force, 2000 16,928
- Unemployment rate 10.1%

Employed persons 16 years and over by occupation, 2000
- Managers & professionals 4,380
- Service occupations 4,332
- Sales & office occupations 4,193
- Farming, fishing & forestry 0
- Construction & maintenance 1,244
- Production & transportation 1,067
- Self-employed persons 661

‡ Branch of county library
* US Census Bureau
** New Jersey Department of Labor

See Introduction for an explanation of all data sources.

General Information
Township of Galloway
300 E Jimmie Leeds Rd
Galloway, NJ 08205
609-652-3700

- Website ..... www.gallowaytwp-nj.gov
- Year of incorporation 1774
- Land/water area (sq. miles) 90.49/24.31
- Form of government ..... Council-Manager

Government
Legislative Districts
- US Congressional 2
- State Legislative 2

Local Officials, 2008
- Mayor ..... Tom Bassford
- Manager ..... Jill A. Gougher
- Clerk ..... Lisa Tilton (Actg)
- Finance Dir ..... Jill A. Gougher
- Tax Assessor ..... David Jackson
- Tax Collector ..... Albert Stanley
- Attorney ..... Michael Blee
- Building ..... Richard Roesch
- Planning ..... Pamela Alleyne
- Engineering ..... Kevin Dixon
- Public Works ..... Stephen Bonanni
- Police Chief ..... Peter Romanelli
- Emerg/Fire Director ..... Rodney Calimer

Housing & Construction
Housing Units, 2000*
- Total 11,406
- Median rent $811
- Median SF home value $130,000

Permits for New Residential Construction
	Units	Value
Total, 2007	116	$13,537,835
Single family	116	$13,537,835
Total, 2006	226	$23,877,809
Single family	226	$23,877,809

Real Property Valuation, 2007
	Parcels	Valuation
Total	17,918	$1,895,052,000
Vacant	4,172	62,172,400
Residential	12,947	1,575,075,500
Commercial	419	191,445,400
Industrial	2	11,426,300
Apartments	16	39,586,300
Farm land	256	1,319,800
Farm homestead	106	14,026,300

Average Property Value & Tax, 2007
- Residential value $121,742
- Property tax $4,163
- Tax credit/rebate $870

Public Library
Galloway Township Branch Library‡
306 E Jimmie Leeds Rd
Absecon, NJ 08201
609-652-2352
- Branch Librarian ..... Katherine Ostrum

Library statistics, 2006
see Atlantic County profile for library system statistics

Public Safety
- Number of officers, 2006 73

Crime	2005	2006
Total crimes	778	861
Violent	83	90
Murder	0	0
Rape	5	6
Robbery	26	26
Aggravated assault	52	58
Non-violent	695	771
Burglary	173	200
Larceny	490	535
Vehicle theft	32	36
Domestic violence	711	656
Arson	5	4
Total crime rate	22.2	24.0
Violent	2.4	2.5
Non-violent	19.8	21.5

Public School District
(for school year 2006-07 except as noted)

Galloway Township School District
101 S Reeds Rd
Galloway, NJ 08205
609-748-1250

- Superintendent ..... Douglas Groff
- Number of schools 7
- Grade plan K-8
- Enrollment 3,791
- Attendance rate, '05-06 ..... 95.2%
- Dropout rate ..... NA
- Students per teacher 10.1
- Per pupil expenditure $11,667
- Median faculty salary $47,600
- Median administrator salary $93,358
- Grade 12 enrollment ..... NA
- High school graduation rate ..... NA

Assessment test results
(percent scoring at proficient or advanced level)
	Language	Math
NJASK-Grade 3	85.1%	91.3%
GEPA-Grade 8	76.0%	66.1%
HSPA-High School	NA	NA

SAT score averages
Pct tested	Math	Verbal	Writing
NA	NA	NA	NA

Teacher Qualifications
- Avg. years of experience 9
- Highly-qualified teachers one subject/all subjects 100%/100%
- With emergency credentials 0.0%

No Child Left Behind
- AYP, 2005-06 ..... Needs Improvement

Municipal Finance
State Aid Programs, 2008
- Total aid $3,456,120
- CMPTRA 575,664
- Energy tax receipts 2,723,466
- Garden State Trust 14,417

General Budget, 2007
- Total tax levy $64,983,858
- County levy 11,065,509
- County taxes 8,798,708
- County library 1,096,358
- County health 446,739
- County open space 723,704
- School levy 42,369,034
- Muni. levy 11,549,314
- Misc. revenues 10,377,373

Taxes
	2005	2006	2007
General tax rate per $100	3.239	3.369	3.42
County equalization ratio	69.53	61.12	52.53
Net valuation taxable	$1,767,441,446	$1,826,386,100	$1,900,451,760
State equalized value	$2,891,756,293	$3,483,028,296	$3,908,699,451

Garfield City
Bergen County

Demographics & Socio-Economic Characteristics
(2000 US Census, except as noted)

Population
1980*	26,803
1990*	26,727
2000	29,786
Male	14,514
Female	15,272
2006 (estimate)*	29,644
Population density	13,917.4

Race & Hispanic Origin, 2000
Race
White	24,456
Black/African American	887
American Indian/Alaska Native	99
Asian	800
Native Hawaiian/Pacific Islander	2
Other race	2,414
Two or more races	1,128
Hispanic origin, total	5,989
Mexican	469
Puerto Rican	1,348
Cuban	130
Other Hispanic	4,042

Age & Nativity, 2000
Under 5 years	1,809
18 years and over	23,124
21 years and over	22,039
65 years and over	4,185
85 years and over	479
Median age	35.6
Native-born	18,150
Foreign-born	11,636

Educational Attainment, 2000
Population 25 years and over	20,271
Less than 9th grade	13.5%
High school grad or higher	70.3%
Bachelor's degree or higher	14.0%
Graduate degree	3.8%

Income & Poverty, 1999
Per capita income	$19,530
Median household income	$42,748
Median family income	$51,654
Persons in poverty	2,305
H'holds receiving public assistance	253
H'holds receiving social security	3,264

Households, 2000
Total households	11,250
With persons under 18	3,748
With persons over 65	3,242
Family households	7,426
Single-person households	3,077
Persons per household	2.64
Persons per family	3.26

Labor & Employment
Total civilian labor force, 2006**	15,886
Unemployment rate	6.4%
Total civilian labor force, 2000	15,594
Unemployment rate	7.6%

Employed persons 16 years and over by occupation, 2000
Managers & professionals	2,954
Service occupations	2,237
Sales & office occupations	4,059
Farming, fishing & forestry	69
Construction & maintenance	2,107
Production & transportation	2,986
Self-employed persons	543

* US Census Bureau
** New Jersey Department of Labor

General Information
City of Garfield
111 Outwater Ln
Garfield, NJ 07026
973-340-2001

Website	www.garfieldnj.org
Year of incorporation	1917
Land/water area (sq. miles)	2.13/0.06
Form of government	Municipal Mgr 1923

Government
Legislative Districts
US Congressional	9
State Legislative	36

Local Officials, 2008
Mayor	Frank Calandriello
Manager	Thomas J. Duch
Clerk	Andrew J. Pavlica
Finance Dir	Roy Riggitano
Tax Assessor	Kurt Hielle
Tax Collector	Rosemarie Cokinos
Attorney	Joseph Rotolo
Building	Nicholas Melfi
Comm Dev/Planning	NA
Engineering	Kevin J. Boswell
Public Works	Sam Garofalo
Police Chief	Robert Andrezzi
Emerg/Fire Director	Stephen Semancik

Housing & Construction
Housing Units, 2000*
Total	11,698
Median rent	$777
Median SF home value	$161,500

Permits for New Residential Construction
	Units	Value
Total, 2007	19	$1,662,955
Single family	7	$528,000
Total, 2006	13	$1,248,503
Single family	1	$141,500

Real Property Valuation, 2007
	Parcels	Valuation
Total	6,260	$1,184,444,600
Vacant	138	11,812,800
Residential	5,470	890,072,700
Commercial	456	152,907,900
Industrial	79	81,162,600
Apartments	117	48,488,600
Farm land	0	0
Farm homestead	0	0

Average Property Value & Tax, 2007
Residential value	$162,719
Property tax	$6,018
Tax credit/rebate	$986

Public Library
Garfield Public Library
500 Midland Ave
Garfield, NJ 07026
973-478-3800

Director .... MacArthur Nickles

Library statistics, 2006
Population served	29,786
Full-time/total staff	3/8

	Total	Per capita
Holdings	85,045	2.86
Revenues	$912,932	$30.65
Expenditures	$909,993	$30.55
Annual visits	89,800	3.01
Internet terminals/annual users	8/36,642	

Public Safety
Number of officers, 2006 61

Crime
	2005	2006
Total crimes	665	527
Violent	73	62
Murder	1	0
Rape	0	1
Robbery	40	28
Aggravated assault	32	33
Non-violent	592	465
Burglary	140	122
Larceny	381	276
Vehicle theft	71	67
Domestic violence	184	230
Arson	0	0
Total crime rate	22.3	17.7
Violent	2.4	2.1
Non-violent	19.8	15.6

Public School District
(for school year 2006-07 except as noted)

Garfield School District
125 Outwater Lane
Garfield, NJ 07026
973-340-5000

Superintendent	Nicholas Perrapato
Number of schools	11
Grade plan	K-12
Enrollment	4,591
Attendance rate, '05-06	93.7%
Dropout rate	4.1%
Students per teacher	11.3
Per pupil expenditure	$13,656
Median faculty salary	$52,755
Median administrator salary	$121,150
Grade 12 enrollment	293
High school graduation rate	88.1%

Assessment test results
(percent scoring at proficient or advanced level)
	Language	Math
NJASK-Grade 3	80.7%	88.6%
GEPA-Grade 8	67.8%	67.6%
HSPA-High School	71.1%	60.3%

SAT score averages
Pct tested	Math	Verbal	Writing
69%	460	430	436

Teacher Qualifications
Avg. years of experience	9
Highly-qualified teachers one subject/all subjects	100%/100%
With emergency credentials	0.0%

No Child Left Behind
AYP, 2005-06 .... Meets Standards

Municipal Finance
State Aid Programs, 2008
Total aid	$3,233,042
CMPTRA	1,845,777
Energy tax receipts	1,387,264
Garden State Trust	1

General Budget, 2007
Total tax levy	$43,830,042
County levy	4,612,306
County taxes	4,355,892
County library	0
County health	0
County open space	256,414
School levy	21,189,604
Muni. levy	18,028,132
Misc. revenues	10,331,285

Taxes
	2005	2006	2007
General tax rate per $100	3.32	3.57	3.7
County equalization ratio	62.2	53.35	46.67
Net valuation taxable	$1,183,265,460	$1,186,470,900	$1,185,151,116
State equalized value	$2,217,929,634	$2,543,044,099	$2,785,014,461

Union County

Garwood Borough

Demographics & Socio-Economic Characteristics
(2000 US Census, except as noted)

Population
1980*	4,752
1990*	4,227
2000	4,153
Male	2,005
Female	2,148
2006 (estimate)*	4,233
Population density	6,413.6

Race & Hispanic Origin, 2000
Race
White	3,983
Black/African American	15
American Indian/Alaska Native	0
Asian	55
Native Hawaiian/Pacific Islander	0
Other race	64
Two or more races	36
Hispanic origin, total	207
Mexican	30
Puerto Rican	15
Cuban	30
Other Hispanic	132

Age & Nativity, 2000
Under 5 years	231
18 years and over	3,322
21 years and over	3,215
65 years and over	716
85 years and over	75
Median age	38.3
Native-born	3,718
Foreign-born	435

Educational Attainment, 2000
Population 25 years and over	3,090
Less than 9th grade	4.1%
High school grad or higher	86.5%
Bachelor's degree or higher	27.6%
Graduate degree	11.2%

Income & Poverty, 1999
Per capita income	$26,944
Median household income	$52,571
Median family income	$64,053
Persons in poverty	210
H'holds receiving public assistance	11
H'holds receiving social security	572

Households, 2000
Total households	1,731
With persons under 18	487
With persons over 65	527
Family households	1,125
Single-person households	496
Persons per household	2.40
Persons per family	2.96

Labor & Employment
Total civilian labor force, 2006**	2,501
Unemployment rate	2.7%
Total civilian labor force, 2000	2,382
Unemployment rate	2.6%

Employed persons 16 years and over by occupation, 2000
Managers & professionals	893
Service occupations	243
Sales & office occupations	743
Farming, fishing & forestry	0
Construction & maintenance	245
Production & transportation	196
Self-employed persons	118

* US Census Bureau
** New Jersey Department of Labor

See Introduction for an explanation of all data sources.

General Information
Borough of Garwood
403 South Ave
Garwood, NJ 07027
908-789-0710

Website	www.garwood.org
Year of incorporation	1903
Land/water area (sq. miles)	0.66/0.00
Form of government	Borough

Government
Legislative Districts
US Congressional	7
State Legislative	21

Local Officials, 2008
Mayor	Dennis McCarthy
Manager	Christina M. Ariemma
Clerk	Christina M. Ariemma
Finance Dir	Sue Wright
Tax Assessor	Annmarie Switzer
Tax Collector	Loretta J. Glogorski
Attorney	Robert Renaud
Building	Richard Belluscio
Comm Dev/Planning	NA
Engineering	Donald Guarriello
Public Works	Fred Corbitt
Police Chief	William Legg
Emerg/Fire Director	Ed Silver

Housing & Construction
Housing Units, 2000*
Total	1,782
Median rent	$913
Median SF home value	$181,500

Permits for New Residential Construction
	Units	Value
Total, 2007	61	$5,133,840
Single family	22	$3,679,295
Total, 2006	72	$8,069,145
Single family	47	$7,500,965

Real Property Valuation, 2007
	Parcels	Valuation
Total	1,457	$181,845,300
Vacant	42	3,729,900
Residential	1,265	127,568,600
Commercial	119	40,993,100
Industrial	23	7,353,700
Apartments	8	2,200,000
Farm land	0	0
Farm homestead	0	0

Average Property Value & Tax, 2007
Residential value	$100,845
Property tax	$6,965
Tax credit/rebate	$1,125

Public Library
Garwood Public Library
411 Third Ave
Garwood, NJ 07027
908-789-1670

Director.....Carol A. Lombardo

Library statistics, 2006
Population served	4,153
Full-time/total staff	1/1

	Total	Per capita
Holdings	31,180	7.51
Revenues	$189,404	$45.61
Expenditures	$124,666	$30.02
Annual visits	7,400	1.78
Internet terminals/annual users		4/170

Taxes
	2005	2006	2007
General tax rate per $100	6.533	6.694	6.907
County equalization ratio	33.62	29.71	30.77
Net valuation taxable	$179,687,144	$181,754,300	$181,931,178
State equalized value	$525,862,289	$590,779,485	$641,968,335

Public Safety
Number of officers, 2006.....14

Crime	2005	2006
Total crimes	65	52
Violent	4	3
Murder	0	0
Rape	2	0
Robbery	1	1
Aggravated assault	1	2
Non-violent	61	49
Burglary	10	11
Larceny	48	37
Vehicle theft	3	1
Domestic violence	9	6
Arson	0	0
Total crime rate	15.6	12.5
Violent	1.0	0.7
Non-violent	14.6	11.8

Public School District
(for school year 2006-07 except as noted)

Garwood School District
500 East St
Garwood, NJ 07027
908-789-0165

Superintendent	Teresa Quigley (Actg)
Number of schools	2
Grade plan	K-8
Enrollment	407
Attendance rate, '05-06	95.4%
Dropout rate	NA
Students per teacher	12.2
Per pupil expenditure	$11,217
Median faculty salary	$50,267
Median administrator salary	$84,492
Grade 12 enrollment	NA
High school graduation rate	NA

Assessment test results
(percent scoring at proficient or advanced level)
	Language	Math
NJASK-Grade 3	79.2%	89.6%
GEPA-Grade 8	87.5%	72.5%
HSPA-High School	NA	NA

SAT score averages
Pct tested	Math	Verbal	Writing
NA	NA	NA	NA

Teacher Qualifications
Avg. years of experience	11
Highly-qualified teachers one subject/all subjects	96.5%/96.5%
With emergency credentials	0.0%

No Child Left Behind
AYP, 2005-06.....Meets Standards

Municipal Finance
State Aid Programs, 2008
Total aid	$374,033
CMPTRA	0
Energy tax receipts	374,033
Garden State Trust	0

General Budget, 2007
Total tax levy	$12,565,752
County levy	2,102,318
County taxes	2,011,903
County library	0
County health	0
County open space	90,416
School levy	6,053,295
Muni. levy	4,410,139
Misc. revenues	2,209,106

Gibbsboro Borough

Camden County

Demographics & Socio-Economic Characteristics
(2000 US Census, except as noted)

Population
1980*	2,510
1990*	2,383
2000	2,435
Male	1,211
Female	1,224
2006 (estimate)*	2,451
Population density	1,114.1

Race & Hispanic Origin, 2000
Race
White	2,289
Black/African American	68
American Indian/Alaska Native	10
Asian	26
Native Hawaiian/Pacific Islander	0
Other race	18
Two or more races	24
Hispanic origin, total	58
Mexican	17
Puerto Rican	16
Cuban	0
Other Hispanic	25

Age & Nativity, 2000
Under 5 years	140
18 years and over	1,819
21 years and over	1,732
65 years and over	330
85 years and over	20
Median age	38.6
Native-born	2,334
Foreign-born	101

Educational Attainment, 2000
Population 25 years and over	1,650
Less than 9th grade	2.7%
High school grad or higher	84.7%
Bachelor's degree or higher	23.3%
Graduate degree	6.6%

Income & Poverty, 1999
Per capita income	$26,035
Median household income	$57,326
Median family income	$63,864
Persons in poverty	101
H'holds receiving public assistance	10
H'holds receiving social security	272

Households, 2000
Total households	829
With persons under 18	333
With persons over 65	222
Family households	665
Single-person households	138
Persons per household	2.91
Persons per family	3.28

Labor & Employment
Total civilian labor force, 2006**	1,437
Unemployment rate	4.0%
Total civilian labor force, 2000	1,319
Unemployment rate	3.9%

Employed persons 16 years and over by occupation, 2000
Managers & professionals	515
Service occupations	98
Sales & office occupations	388
Farming, fishing & forestry	0
Construction & maintenance	145
Production & transportation	121
Self-employed persons	58

* US Census Bureau
** New Jersey Department of Labor

General Information
Borough of Gibbsboro
49 Kirkwood Rd
Gibbsboro, NJ 08026
856-783-6655

Website	www.gibbsborotownhall.com
Year of incorporation	1924
Land/water area (sq. miles)	2.20/0.04
Form of government	Borough

Government
Legislative Districts
US Congressional	1
State Legislative	6

Local Officials, 2008
Mayor	Edward Campbell III
Manager/Admin	NA
Clerk	Anne Levy
Finance Dir	Deborah Jackson
Tax Assessor	Lawrence O. Vituscka
Tax Collector	Carolyn Halbert
Attorney	John Jehl
Building	John White
Comm Dev/Planning	NA
Engineering	Greg Fusco
Public Works	Wally Pratz
Police Chief	Joseph Mingori
Emerg/Fire Director	George Haaf

Housing & Construction
Housing Units, 2000*
Total	847
Median rent	$782
Median SF home value	$117,500

Permits for New Residential Construction
	Units	Value
Total, 2007	2	$284,450
Single family	2	$284,450
Total, 2006	2	$483,045
Single family	2	$483,045

Real Property Valuation, 2007
	Parcels	Valuation
Total	1,038	$179,918,400
Vacant	120	8,384,100
Residential	799	128,116,700
Commercial	104	30,713,900
Industrial	11	12,284,600
Apartments	1	225,000
Farm land	2	24,700
Farm homestead	1	169,400

Average Property Value & Tax, 2007
Residential value	$160,358
Property tax	$6,253
Tax credit/rebate	$1,040

Public Library
Gibbsboro Public Library
49 Kirkwood Rd
Gibbsboro, NJ 08026
856-435-3656

Director.................... Jodie A Favat

Library statistics, 2006
Population served	2,435
Full-time/total staff	NA/0

	Total	Per capita
Holdings	NA	NA
Revenues	NA	NA
Expenditures	NA	NA
Annual visits	NA	NA
Internet terminals/annual users	NA/NA	

Taxes
	2005	2006	2007
General tax rate per $100	3.345	3.665	3.9
County equalization ratio	88.9	78	66.95
Net valuation taxable	$183,861,193	$184,170,200	$180,413,454
State equalized value	$235,719,478	$275,634,801	$286,079,816

Public Safety
Number of officers, 2006 6

Crime
	2005	2006
Total crimes	49	54
Violent	3	5
Murder	0	0
Rape	0	0
Robbery	1	2
Aggravated assault	2	3
Non-violent	46	49
Burglary	15	17
Larceny	29	31
Vehicle theft	2	1
Domestic violence	6	22
Arson	1	5
Total crime rate	19.8	21.9
Violent	1.2	2.0
Non-violent	18.6	19.9

Public School District
(for school year 2006-07 except as noted)

Gibbsboro School District
37 Kirkwood Rd
Gibbsboro, NJ 08026
856-783-1140

Superintendent	James Lavender
Number of schools	1
Grade plan	K-8
Enrollment	292
Attendance rate, '05-06	96.4%
Dropout rate	NA
Students per teacher	9.3
Per pupil expenditure	$13,654
Median faculty salary	$51,143
Median administrator salary	$85,495
Grade 12 enrollment	NA
High school graduation rate	NA

Assessment test results
(percent scoring at proficient or advanced level)
	Language	Math
NJASK-Grade 3	57.1%	76.2%
GEPA-Grade 8	73.8%	76.7%
HSPA-High School	NA	NA

SAT score averages
Pct tested	Math	Verbal	Writing
NA	NA	NA	NA

Teacher Qualifications
Avg. years of experience	16
Highly-qualified teachers one subject/all subjects	96.0%/92.0%
With emergency credentials	0.0%

No Child Left Behind
AYP, 2005-06 .... Meets Standards

Municipal Finance
State Aid Programs, 2008
Total aid	$278,353
CMPTRA	0
Energy tax receipts	278,353
Garden State Trust	0

General Budget, 2007
Total tax levy	$7,035,502
County levy	1,905,783
County taxes	1,731,124
County library	120,544
County health	0
County open space	54,114
School levy	3,925,661
Muni. levy	1,204,058
Misc. revenues	1,363,150

Gloucester County

Glassboro Borough

Demographics & Socio-Economic Characteristics
(2000 US Census, except as noted)

Population
1980*	14,574
1990*	15,614
2000	19,068
Male	9,126
Female	9,942
2006 (estimate)*	19,360
Population density	2,102.1

Race & Hispanic Origin, 2000
Race
White	14,212
Black/African American	3,712
American Indian/Alaska Native	32
Asian	441
Native Hawaiian/Pacific Islander	17
Other race	282
Two or more races	372
Hispanic origin, total	728
Mexican	62
Puerto Rican	468
Cuban	28
Other Hispanic	170

Age & Nativity, 2000
Under 5 years	1,216
18 years and over	14,859
21 years and over	12,445
65 years and over	1,866
85 years and over	176
Median age	27.1
Native-born	18,310
Foreign-born	758

Educational Attainment, 2000
Population 25 years and over	9,943
Less than 9th grade	5.9%
High school grad or higher	82.1%
Bachelor's degree or higher	24.0%
Graduate degree	7.8%

Income & Poverty, 1999
Per capita income	$18,113
Median household income	$44,992
Median family income	$55,246
Persons in poverty	2,525
H'holds receiving public assistance	153
H'holds receiving social security	1,508

Households, 2000
Total households	6,225
With persons under 18	2,225
With persons over 65	1,386
Family households	4,049
Single-person households	1,472
Persons per household	2.66
Persons per family	3.17

Labor & Employment
Total civilian labor force, 2006**	10,255
Unemployment rate	6.4%
Total civilian labor force, 2000	10,552
Unemployment rate	19.2%

Employed persons 16 years and over by occupation, 2000
Managers & professionals	2,903
Service occupations	1,479
Sales & office occupations	2,348
Farming, fishing & forestry	6
Construction & maintenance	675
Production & transportation	1,114
Self-employed persons	236

‡ Branch of county library
* US Census Bureau
** New Jersey Department of Labor

See Introduction for an explanation of all data sources.

General Information
Borough of Glassboro
1 S Main St
Glassboro, NJ 08028
856-881-9230

Website	www.glassboroonline.com
Year of incorporation	1920
Land/water area (sq. miles)	9.21/0.01
Form of government	Borough

Government
Legislative Districts
US Congressional	1
State Legislative	4

Local Officials, 2008
Mayor	Leo McCabe
Manager	Joseph Brigandi Jr
Clerk	Patricia A. Frontino
Finance Dir	Josephine Myers
Tax Assessor	Thomas Colavecchio
Tax Collector	Rosemary A. Turner
Attorney	Timothy Scaffidi
Building	R. Angelo Martilini
Planning	R. Angelo Martilini
Engineering	Mark Brunermer
Public Works	Russell Clark
Police Chief	Alex Fanfarillo
Emerg/Fire Director	Ralph Johnson

Housing & Construction
Housing Units, 2000*
Total	6,555
Median rent	$567
Median SF home value	$114,100

Permits for New Residential Construction
	Units	Value
Total, 2007	57	$5,708,569
Single family	57	$5,708,569
Total, 2006	71	$7,146,467
Single family	71	$7,146,467

Real Property Valuation, 2007
	Parcels	Valuation
Total	6,059	$666,516,600
Vacant	1,009	21,787,800
Residential	4,707	503,148,100
Commercial	256	103,127,300
Industrial	9	8,641,200
Apartments	32	27,974,100
Farm land	34	147,000
Farm homestead	12	1,691,100

Average Property Value & Tax, 2007
Residential value	$106,980
Property tax	$5,242
Tax credit/rebate	$998

Public Library
Glassboro Public Library‡
2 Center St
Glassboro, NJ 08028
856-881-0001

Branch Librarian............. Carol Wolf

Library statistics, 2006
see Gloucester County profile
for library system statistics

Public Safety
Number of officers, 2006 45

Crime	2005	2006
Total crimes	789	815
Violent	67	77
Murder	0	0
Rape	12	14
Robbery	30	26
Aggravated assault	25	37
Non-violent	722	738
Burglary	152	133
Larceny	540	579
Vehicle theft	30	26
Domestic violence	276	195
Arson	4	6
Total crime rate	41.1	42.2
Violent	3.5	4.0
Non-violent	37.6	38.3

Public School District
(for school year 2006-07 except as noted)

Glassboro School District
Beach Admin Bldg, Joseph L Bowe Blvd
Glassboro, NJ 08028
856-881-0123

Superintendent	Leonard Fitts (Int)
Number of schools	5
Grade plan	K-12
Enrollment	2,423
Attendance rate, '05-06	94.8%
Dropout rate	1.6%
Students per teacher	11.1
Per pupil expenditure	$12,548
Median faculty salary	$54,031
Median administrator salary	$104,797
Grade 12 enrollment	141
High school graduation rate	86.4%

Assessment test results
(percent scoring at proficient or advanced level)
	Language	Math
NJASK-Grade 3	66.1%	77.8%
GEPA-Grade 8	60.3%	56.6%
HSPA-High School	82.4%	72.3%

SAT score averages
Pct tested	Math	Verbal	Writing
68%	484	463	448

Teacher Qualifications
Avg. years of experience	11
Highly-qualified teachers one subject/all subjects	99.5%/99.5%
With emergency credentials	0.0%

No Child Left Behind
AYP, 2005-06 .... Meets Standards

Municipal Finance
State Aid Programs, 2008
Total aid	$3,015,526
CMPTRA	1,240,123
Energy tax receipts	1,773,087
Garden State Trust	2,316

General Budget, 2007
Total tax levy	$32,863,578
County levy	6,263,804
County taxes	5,394,643
County library	446,808
County health	0
County open space	422,353
School levy	16,861,704
Muni. levy	9,738,070
Misc. revenues	10,430,768

Taxes
	2005	2006	2007
General tax rate per $100	4.373	4.687	4.901
County equalization ratio	82.32	72.17	64.01
Net valuation taxable	$642,433,197	$653,071,600	$670,666,018
State equalized value	$890,166,547	$1,024,845,459	$1,136,140,926

The New Jersey Municipal Data Book

Glen Gardner Borough

Hunterdon County

Demographics & Socio-Economic Characteristics
(2000 US Census, except as noted)

Population
1980*	834
1990*	1,665
2000	1,902
Male	929
Female	973
2006 (estimate)*	1,992
Population density	1,276.9

Race & Hispanic Origin, 2000
Race
White	1,820
Black/African American	17
American Indian/Alaska Native	2
Asian	28
Native Hawaiian/Pacific Islander	2
Other race	11
Two or more races	22
Hispanic origin, total	65
Mexican	9
Puerto Rican	23
Cuban	7
Other Hispanic	26

Age & Nativity, 2000
Under 5 years	135
18 years and over	1,421
21 years and over	1,374
65 years and over	145
85 years and over	17
Median age	35.4
Native-born	1,810
Foreign-born	92

Educational Attainment, 2000
Population 25 years and over	1,304
Less than 9th grade	3.0%
High school grad or higher	91.0%
Bachelor's degree or higher	35.3%
Graduate degree	11.5%

Income & Poverty, 1999
Per capita income	$28,647
Median household income	$59,917
Median family income	$75,369
Persons in poverty	84
H'holds receiving public assistance	11
H'holds receiving social security	148

Households, 2000
Total households	805
With persons under 18	275
With persons over 65	123
Family households	474
Single-person households	275
Persons per household	2.33
Persons per family	3.07

Labor & Employment
Total civilian labor force, 2006**	1,212
Unemployment rate	2.5%
Total civilian labor force, 2000	1,079
Unemployment rate	2.0%

Employed persons 16 years and over by occupation, 2000
Managers & professionals	486
Service occupations	134
Sales & office occupations	269
Farming, fishing & forestry	5
Construction & maintenance	112
Production & transportation	51
Self-employed persons	47

* US Census Bureau
** New Jersey Department of Labor

General Information
Borough of Glen Gardner
PO Box 307
Glen Gardner, NJ 08826
908-537-4748

Website	www.glengardnernj.org
Year of incorporation	1919
Land/water area (sq. miles)	1.56/0.00
Form of government	Borough

Government
Legislative Districts
US Congressional	7
State Legislative	23

Local Officials, 2008
Mayor	Stanley Kovach
Manager/Admin	NA
Clerk	Marilyn Hodgson
Finance Dir	Nancy Smith
Tax Assessor	Robert Vance
Tax Collector	Diane Laudenbach
Attorney	J. Peter Jost
Building	Charles Herring
Planning	Judy Bass
Engineering	Robert J. Clerico
Public Works	John Jordan
Police Chief	NA
Fire Chief	Steve Apgar

Housing & Construction
Housing Units, 2000*
Total	829
Median rent	$866
Median SF home value	$170,700

Permits for New Residential Construction
	Units	Value
Total, 2007	1	$121,500
Single family	1	$121,500
Total, 2006	0	$0
Single family	0	$0

Real Property Valuation, 2007
	Parcels	Valuation
Total	795	$139,203,541
Vacant	43	1,363,104
Residential	706	128,664,600
Commercial	17	4,920,800
Industrial	1	568,600
Apartments	4	1,205,200
Farm land	15	50,937
Farm homestead	9	2,430,300

Average Property Value & Tax, 2007
Residential value	$183,350
Property tax	$4,909
Tax credit/rebate	$877

Public Library
No public municipal library

Library statistics, 2006
Population served	NA
Full-time/total staff	NA/NA

	Total	Per capita
Holdings	NA	NA
Revenues	NA	NA
Expenditures	NA	NA
Annual visits	NA	NA
Internet terminals/annual users	NA/NA	

Taxes
	2005	2006	2007
General tax rate per $100	2.47	2.68	2.68
County equalization ratio	83.96	76.49	67.36
Net valuation taxable	$139,551,793	$138,740,940	$139,490,475
State equalized value	$170,392,910	$188,826,566	$198,131,648

Public Safety
Number of officers, 2006 0

Crime	2005	2006
Total crimes	8	14
Violent	0	0
Murder	0	0
Rape	0	0
Robbery	0	0
Aggravated assault	0	0
Non-violent	8	14
Burglary	4	6
Larceny	21	7
Vehicle theft	0	1
Domestic violence	6	2
Arson	0	0
Total crime rate	4.0	7.0
Violent	0.0	0.0
Non-violent	4.0	7.0

Public School District
(for school year 2006-07 except as noted)

Glen Gardner Borough School District
PO Box 158
Glen Gardner, NJ 08826

No schools in district

Per pupil expenditure	NA
Median faculty salary	NA
Median administrator salary	NA
Grade 12 enrollment	NA
High school graduation rate	NA

Assessment test results
(percent scoring at proficient or advanced level)
	Language	Math
NJASK-Grade 3	NA	NA
GEPA-Grade 8	NA	NA
HSPA-High School	NA	NA

SAT score averages
Pct tested	Math	Verbal	Writing
NA	NA	NA	NA

Teacher Qualifications
Avg. years of experience	NA
Highly-qualified teachers one subject/all subjects	NA/NA
With emergency credentials	NA

No Child Left Behind
AYP, 2005-06 .... NA

Municipal Finance
State Aid Programs, 2008
Total aid	$108,853
CMPTRA	0
Energy tax receipts	108,687
Garden State Trust	166

General Budget, 2007
Total tax levy	$3,734,449
County levy	687,841
County taxes	575,655
County library	50,093
County health	0
County open space	62,093
School levy	2,419,658
Muni. levy	626,950
Misc. revenues	778,461

Essex County

Glen Ridge Borough

Demographics & Socio-Economic Characteristics
(2000 US Census, except as noted)

Population
1980*	7,855
1990*	7,076
2000	7,271
Male	3,540
Female	3,731
2006 (estimate)*	6,908
Population density	5,396.9

Race & Hispanic Origin, 2000
Race
White	6,484
Black/African American	362
American Indian/Alaska Native	11
Asian	243
Native Hawaiian/Pacific Islander	0
Other race	72
Two or more races	99
Hispanic origin, total	251
Mexican	22
Puerto Rican	63
Cuban	36
Other Hispanic	130

Age & Nativity, 2000
Under 5 years	679
18 years and over	5,039
21 years and over	4,885
65 years and over	757
85 years and over	102
Median age	37.8
Native-born	6,617
Foreign-born	654

Educational Attainment, 2000
Population 25 years and over	4,727
Less than 9th grade	2.2%
High school grad or higher	96.2%
Bachelor's degree or higher	65.8%
Graduate degree	31.0%

Income & Poverty, 1999
Per capita income	$48,456
Median household income	$105,638
Median family income	$120,650
Persons in poverty	219
H'holds receiving public assistance	36
H'holds receiving social security	520

Households, 2000
Total households	2,458
With persons under 18	1,170
With persons over 65	555
Family households	1,978
Single-person households	410
Persons per household	2.95
Persons per family	3.33

Labor & Employment
Total civilian labor force, 2006**	3,755
Unemployment rate	3.0%
Total civilian labor force, 2000	3,551
Unemployment rate	2.8%

Employed persons 16 years and over by occupation, 2000
Managers & professionals	2,125
Service occupations	205
Sales & office occupations	924
Farming, fishing & forestry	0
Construction & maintenance	117
Production & transportation	82
Self-employed persons	224

* US Census Bureau
** New Jersey Department of Labor

See Introduction for an explanation of all data sources.

General Information
Borough of Glen Ridge
825 Bloomfield Ave
Glen Ridge, NJ 07028
973-748-8400

Website	www.glenridgenj.org
Year of incorporation	1895
Land/water area (sq. miles)	1.28/0.00
Form of government	Borough

Government
Legislative Districts
US Congressional	8
State Legislative	34

Local Officials, 2008
Mayor	Carl Bergmanson
Manager	Michael Rohal
Clerk	Michael Rohal
Finance Dir	Cindy Goldberg
Tax Assessor	William Merdinger
Tax Collector	Donna Altschuler
Attorney	John Malyska
Building	Ronald Young
Planning	Michael Zichelli
Engineering	Michael Rohal
Public Works	Jay Weisenbach
Police Chief	John Magnier
Emerg/Fire Director	Bob Hayes

Housing & Construction
Housing Units, 2000*
Total	2,490
Median rent	$1,058
Median SF home value	$264,700

Permits for New Residential Construction
	Units	Value
Total, 2007	2	$43,800
Single family	2	$43,800
Total, 2006	0	$0
Single family	0	$0

Real Property Valuation, 2007
	Parcels	Valuation
Total	2,265	$234,550,600
Vacant	10	130,000
Residential	2,232	220,588,900
Commercial	19	8,142,700
Industrial	0	0
Apartments	4	5,689,000
Farm land	0	0
Farm homestead	0	0

Average Property Value & Tax, 2007
Residential value	$98,830
Property tax	$15,424
Tax credit/rebate	$1,473

Public Library
Glen Ridge Public Library
240 Ridgewood Ave
Glen Ridge, NJ 07028
973-748-5482

Director................John A. Sitnik

Library statistics, 2006
Population served	7,271
Full-time/total staff	2/9

	Total	Per capita
Holdings	46,013	6.33
Revenues	$659,329	$90.68
Expenditures	$672,588	$92.50
Annual visits	85,960	11.82
Internet terminals/annual users	9/8,903	

Public Safety
Number of officers, 2006 26

Crime	2005	2006
Total crimes	261	215
Violent	16	5
Murder	1	0
Rape	2	2
Robbery	2	2
Aggravated assault	11	1
Non-violent	245	210
Burglary	46	46
Larceny	164	153
Vehicle theft	35	11
Domestic violence	18	15
Arson	3	1
Total crime rate	36.6	30.6
Violent	2.2	0.7
Non-violent	34.4	29.9

Public School District
(for school year 2006-07 except as noted)

Glen Ridge School District
12 High St
Glen Ridge, NJ 07028
973-429-8302

Superintendent	Daniel Fishbein
Number of schools	4
Grade plan	K-12
Enrollment	1,824
Attendance rate, '05-06	96.3%
Dropout rate	NA
Students per teacher	11.7
Per pupil expenditure	$12,134
Median faculty salary	$58,448
Median administrator salary	$122,469
Grade 12 enrollment	106
High school graduation rate	100.0%

Assessment test results
(percent scoring at proficient or advanced level)
	Language	Math
NJASK-Grade 3	92.0%	96.0%
GEPA-Grade 8	79.5%	83.8%
HSPA-High School	95.5%	92.7%

SAT score averages
Pct tested	Math	Verbal	Writing
95%	573	561	550

Teacher Qualifications
Avg. years of experience	8
Highly-qualified teachers one subject/all subjects	100%/100%
With emergency credentials	0.0%

No Child Left Behind
AYP, 2005-06 ....Meets Standards

Municipal Finance
State Aid Programs, 2008
Total aid	$481,176
CMPTRA	99,934
Energy tax receipts	381,242
Garden State Trust	0

General Budget, 2007
Total tax levy	$36,618,588
County levy	5,535,961
County taxes	5,393,691
County library	0
County health	0
County open space	142,271
School levy	23,017,558
Muni. levy	8,065,069
Misc. revenues	3,679,492

Taxes
	2005	2006	2007
General tax rate per $100	14.27	15.06	15.61
County equalization ratio	19.89	18.1	16.64
Net valuation taxable	$233,220,100	$233,908,600	$234,629,485
State equalized value	$1,288,508,840	$1,405,786,305	$1,520,173,506

The New Jersey Municipal Data Book — 175

Glen Rock Borough — Bergen County

Demographics & Socio-Economic Characteristics
(2000 US Census, except as noted)

Population
1980*	11,497
1990*	10,883
2000	11,546
Male	5,622
Female	5,924
2006 (estimate)*	11,396
Population density	4,189.7

Race & Hispanic Origin, 2000
Race
White	10,399
Black/African American	209
American Indian/Alaska Native	18
Asian	748
Native Hawaiian/Pacific Islander	2
Other race	71
Two or more races	99
Hispanic origin, total	314
Mexican	37
Puerto Rican	99
Cuban	57
Other Hispanic	121

Age & Nativity, 2000
Under 5 years	962
18 years and over	8,151
21 years and over	7,945
65 years and over	1,579
85 years and over	193
Median age	39.5
Native-born	10,270
Foreign-born	1,276

Educational Attainment, 2000
Population 25 years and over	7,714
Less than 9th grade	1.3%
High school grad or higher	96.0%
Bachelor's degree or higher	61.1%
Graduate degree	24.3%

Income & Poverty, 1999
Per capita income	$45,091
Median household income	$104,192
Median family income	$111,280
Persons in poverty	278
H'holds receiving public assistance	7
H'holds receiving social security	1,135

Households, 2000
Total households	3,977
With persons under 18	1,785
With persons over 65	1,121
Family households	3,322
Single-person households	586
Persons per household	2.89
Persons per family	3.22

Labor & Employment
Total civilian labor force, 2006**	6,080
Unemployment rate	2.8%
Total civilian labor force, 2000	5,757
Unemployment rate	3.0%

Employed persons 16 years and over by occupation, 2000
Managers & professionals	3,501
Service occupations	289
Sales & office occupations	1,426
Farming, fishing & forestry	0
Construction & maintenance	159
Production & transportation	208
Self-employed persons	374

* US Census Bureau
** New Jersey Department of Labor

General Information
Borough of Glen Rock
Harding Plaza
Municipal Building
Glen Rock, NJ 07452
201-670-3956

Website	glenrocknj.net
Year of incorporation	1894
Land/water area (sq. miles)	2.72/0.01
Form of government	Borough

Government
Legislative Districts
US Congressional	5
State Legislative	35

Local Officials, 2008
Mayor	John VanKeuren
Manager	Lenora Benjamin
Clerk	Jacqueline Scalia
Finance Dir	Lenora Benjamin
Tax Assessor	Steven Rubenstein
Tax Collector	Patricia McCormick
Attorney	Robert Garibaldi Jr
Building	Brian Frugis
Comm Dev/Planning	NA
Engineering	Stantec Consulting Services
Public Works	Bob Tirserio
Police Chief	Steven Cherry
Emerg/Fire Director	Pete Flannery

Housing & Construction
Housing Units, 2000*
Total	4,024
Median rent	$1,188
Median SF home value	$316,900

Permits for New Residential Construction
	Units	Value
Total, 2007	8	$2,883,157
Single family	8	$2,883,157
Total, 2006	6	$1,934,380
Single family	6	$1,934,380

Real Property Valuation, 2007
	Parcels	Valuation
Total	4,009	$2,280,657,400
Vacant	60	13,634,300
Residential	3,842	2,074,105,200
Commercial	100	165,440,900
Industrial	7	27,477,000
Apartments	0	0
Farm land	0	0
Farm homestead	0	0

Average Property Value & Tax, 2007
Residential value	$539,850
Property tax	$12,028
Tax credit/rebate	$1,506

Public Library
Glen Rock Public Library
315 Rock Rd
Glen Rock, NJ 07452
201-670-3970

Director	Roz Pelcyger

Library statistics, 2006
Population served	11,546
Full-time/total staff	3/10

	Total	Per capita
Holdings	96,401	8.35
Revenues	$1,015,967	$87.99
Expenditures	$929,547	$80.51
Annual visits	189,276	16.39
Internet terminals/annual users	11/20,900	

Public Safety
Number of officers, 2006: 21

Crime	2005	2006
Total crimes	61	74
Violent	2	1
Murder	0	0
Rape	1	0
Robbery	0	1
Aggravated assault	1	0
Non-violent	59	73
Burglary	8	15
Larceny	51	53
Vehicle theft	0	5
Domestic violence	5	5
Arson	0	0
Total crime rate	5.3	6.5
Violent	0.2	0.1
Non-violent	5.1	6.4

Public School District
(for school year 2006-07 except as noted)

Glen Rock School District
620 Harristown Rd
Glen Rock, NJ 07452
201-445-7700

Superintendent	George Connelly
Number of schools	6
Grade plan	K-12
Enrollment	2,473
Attendance rate, '05-06	95.4%
Dropout rate	NA
Students per teacher	10.6
Per pupil expenditure	$14,633
Median faculty salary	$57,311
Median administrator salary	$115,316
Grade 12 enrollment	172
High school graduation rate	100.0%

Assessment test results
(percent scoring at proficient or advanced level)
	Language	Math
NJASK-Grade 3	94.6%	97.8%
GEPA-Grade 8	92.4%	84.2%
HSPA-High School	96.6%	91.9%

SAT score averages
Pct tested	Math	Verbal	Writing
107%	571	532	540

Teacher Qualifications
Avg. years of experience	9
Highly-qualified teachers one subject/all subjects	100%/100%
With emergency credentials	0.0%

No Child Left Behind
AYP, 2005-06	Meets Standards

Municipal Finance
State Aid Programs, 2008
Total aid	$1,340,407
CMPTRA	308,590
Energy tax receipts	1,031,817
Garden State Trust	0

General Budget, 2007
Total tax levy	$50,844,877
County levy	4,518,986
County taxes	4,270,313
County library	0
County health	0
County open space	248,673
School levy	35,647,959
Muni. levy	10,677,932
Misc. revenues	4,780,876

Taxes
	2005	2006	2007
General tax rate per $100	2.54	2.66	2.23
County equalization ratio	90.76	82.24	92.08
Net valuation taxable	$1,822,099,032	$1,835,057,000	$2,282,055,921
State equalized value	$2,215,587,344	$2,454,731,801	$2,576,375,827

Camden County
Gloucester City

Demographics & Socio-Economic Characteristics
(2000 US Census, except as noted)

Population
1980*	13,121
1990*	12,649
2000	11,484
Male	5,594
Female	5,890
2006 (estimate)*	11,482
Population density	5,219.1

Race & Hispanic Origin, 2000
Race
White	11,155
Black/African American	79
American Indian/Alaska Native	21
Asian	78
Native Hawaiian/Pacific Islander	4
Other race	74
Two or more races	73
Hispanic origin, total	216
Mexican	15
Puerto Rican	142
Cuban	10
Other Hispanic	49

Age & Nativity, 2000
Under 5 years	736
18 years and over	8,435
21 years and over	7,953
65 years and over	1,582
85 years and over	136
Median age	36.4
Native-born	11,366
Foreign-born	109

Educational Attainment, 2000
Population 25 years and over	7,438
Less than 9th grade	6.7%
High school grad or higher	72.4%
Bachelor's degree or higher	8.2%
Graduate degree	1.7%

Income & Poverty, 1999
Per capita income	$16,912
Median household income	$36,855
Median family income	$46,038
Persons in poverty	1,155
H'holds receiving public assistance	148
H'holds receiving social security	1,458

Households, 2000
Total households	4,213
With persons under 18	1,556
With persons over 65	1,248
Family households	2,840
Single-person households	1,145
Persons per household	2.72
Persons per family	3.32

Labor & Employment
Total civilian labor force, 2006**	5,949
Unemployment rate	8.6%
Total civilian labor force, 2000	5,482
Unemployment rate	8.5%

Employed persons 16 years and over by occupation, 2000
Managers & professionals	1,010
Service occupations	769
Sales & office occupations	1,500
Farming, fishing & forestry	0
Construction & maintenance	550
Production & transportation	1,188
Self-employed persons	203

* US Census Bureau
** New Jersey Department of Labor

See Introduction for an explanation of all data sources.

General Information
City of Gloucester
512 Monmouth St
Gloucester City, NJ 08030
856-456-0205

Website	www.cityofgloucester.org
Year of incorporation	1868
Land/water area (sq. miles)	2.20/0.63
Form of government	Special Charter

Government
Legislative Districts
US Congressional	1
State Legislative	5

Local Officials, 2008
Mayor	William P. James
Manager	Paul Kain
Clerk	Paul Kain
Finance Dir	Frank Robertson
Tax Assessor	John Dymond
Tax Collector	Joanne Marone
Attorney	John Kearney
Building	Robert Scouler
Planning	Regina Dunphy
Engineering	Remington & Vernick
Public Works	James Johnson
Police Chief	William Crothers
Emerg/Fire Director	Brian Hagan

Housing & Construction
Housing Units, 2000*
Total	4,604
Median rent	$625
Median SF home value	$79,500

Permits for New Residential Construction
	Units	Value
Total, 2007	55	$5,748,889
Single family	55	$5,748,889
Total, 2006	18	$1,105,904
Single family	18	$1,105,904

Real Property Valuation, 2007
	Parcels	Valuation
Total	4,224	$349,375,400
Vacant	292	8,568,400
Residential	3,612	255,443,700
Commercial	272	73,618,500
Industrial	29	7,091,700
Apartments	19	4,653,100
Farm land	0	0
Farm homestead	0	0

Average Property Value & Tax, 2007
Residential value	$70,721
Property tax	$2,917
Tax credit/rebate	$752

Public Library
Gloucester City Library
50 N Railroad Ave
Gloucester City, NJ 08030
856-456-4181

Director ... Elizabeth Egan

Library statistics, 2006
Population served	11,484
Full-time/total staff	1/4

	Total	Per capita
Holdings	68,295	5.95
Revenues	$528,438	$46.02
Expenditures	$524,052	$45.63
Annual visits	72,960	6.35
Internet terminals/annual users	37/25,688	

Taxes
	2005	2006	2007
General tax rate per $100	3.632	3.923	4.125
County equalization ratio	89.74	78.46	65.95
Net valuation taxable	$359,186,253	$347,356,800	$352,666,849
State equalized value	$457,795,377	$530,576,891	$610,162,041

Public Safety
Number of officers, 2006 ... 30

Crime
	2005	2006
Total crimes	294	334
Violent	27	33
Murder	1	1
Rape	5	3
Robbery	9	16
Aggravated assault	12	13
Non-violent	267	301
Burglary	49	55
Larceny	195	219
Vehicle theft	23	27
Domestic violence	228	256
Arson	0	0
Total crime rate	25.3	28.8
Violent	2.3	2.8
Non-violent	23.0	26.0

Public School District
(for school year 2006-07 except as noted)

Gloucester City School District
520 Cumberland St
Gloucester City, NJ 08030
856-456-9394

Superintendent	Paul Spaventa
Number of schools	3
Grade plan	K-12
Enrollment	2,106
Attendance rate, '05-06	94.3%
Dropout rate	1.8%
Students per teacher	8.4
Per pupil expenditure	$17,130
Median faculty salary	$48,412
Median administrator salary	$107,525
Grade 12 enrollment	137
High school graduation rate	96.5%

Assessment test results
(percent scoring at proficient or advanced level)
	Language	Math
NJASK-Grade 3	72.7%	80.4%
GEPA-Grade 8	43.7%	45.6%
HSPA-High School	77.9%	67.8%

SAT score averages
Pct tested	Math	Verbal	Writing
47%	476	461	469

Teacher Qualifications
Avg. years of experience	9
Highly-qualified teachers one subject/all subjects	100%/100%
With emergency credentials	0.0%

No Child Left Behind
AYP, 2005-06 ... Meets Standards

Municipal Finance
State Aid Programs, 2008
Total aid	$3,168,429
CMPTRA	1,093,525
Energy tax receipts	2,074,904
Garden State Trust	0

General Budget, 2007
Total tax levy	$14,544,987
County levy	3,695,794
County taxes	3,583,724
County library	0
County health	0
County open space	112,069
School levy	3,244,193
Muni. levy	7,605,000
Misc. revenues	7,960,762

Gloucester Township
Camden County

Demographics & Socio-Economic Characteristics[†]
(2000 US Census, except as noted)

Population
1980*	45,156
1990*	53,797
2000	64,350
Male	31,309
Female	33,041
2006 (estimate)*	65,687
Population density	2,828.9

Race & Hispanic Origin, 2000
Race
White	53,484
Black/African American	7,432
American Indian/Alaska Native	100
Asian	1,688
Native Hawaiian/Pacific Islander	16
Other race	715
Two or more races	915
Hispanic origin, total	1,962
Mexican	248
Puerto Rican	1,160
Cuban	81
Other Hispanic	473

Age & Nativity, 2000
Under 5 years	4,405
18 years and over	47,057
21 years and over	44,616
65 years and over	6,052
85 years and over	536
Median age	34.6
Native-born	61,187
Foreign-born	3,128

Educational Attainment, 2000
Population 25 years and over	41,473
Less than 9th grade	2.8%
High school grad or higher	85.8%
Bachelor's degree or higher	22.0%
Graduate degree	6.1%

Income & Poverty, 1999
Per capita income	$22,604
Median household income	$54,280
Median family income	$62,992
Persons in poverty	3,934
H'holds receiving public assistance	523
H'holds receiving social security	4,983

Households, 2000
Total households	23,150
With persons under 18	9,456
With persons over 65	4,351
Family households	16,878
Single-person households	4,948
Persons per household	2.75
Persons per family	3.24

Labor & Employment
Total civilian labor force, 2006**	37,704
Unemployment rate	2.7%
Total civilian labor force, 2000	34,739
Unemployment rate	4.9%

Employed persons 16 years and over by occupation, 2000
Managers & professionals	11,214
Service occupations	4,410
Sales & office occupations	10,334
Farming, fishing & forestry	0
Construction & maintenance	3,332
Production & transportation	3,753
Self-employed persons	1,485

[†] see Appendix C for American Community Survey data
[‡] Branch of county library
[*] US Census Bureau
[**] New Jersey Department of Labor
[§] State Fiscal Year July 1–June 30

General Information
Gloucester Township
1261 Chews Landing Rd
PO Box 8
Blackwood, NJ 08012
856-228-4000

Website	www.glotwp.com
Year of incorporation	1695
Land/water area (sq. miles)	23.22/0.10
Form of government	Mayor-Council

Government
Legislative Districts
US Congressional	1
State Legislative	4

Local Officials, 2008
Mayor	Cindy Rau-Hatton
Manager	Thomas Cardis
Clerk	Rosemary Di Josie
Finance Dir	Dorothea Jones
Tax Assessor	Charles G. Palumbo Jr
Tax Collector	Sandra Ferguson
Attorney	David Carlamere
Building	Bernie Shepherd
Planning	Kenneth Lechner
Engineering	Remington & Vernick
Public Works	Gabe Busa
Police Chief	Edward Smith
Fire/Emergency Dir	NA

Housing & Construction
Housing Units, 2000*
Total	24,257
Median rent	$706
Median SF home value	$116,100

Permits for New Residential Construction
	Units	Value
Total, 2007	7	$765,506
Single family	7	$765,506
Total, 2006	20	$646,057
Single family	20	$646,057

Real Property Valuation, 2007
	Parcels	Valuation
Total	21,505	$2,419,124,100
Vacant	1,229	24,462,900
Residential	19,624	2,125,453,500
Commercial	493	148,503,800
Industrial	33	33,918,700
Apartments	26	82,508,000
Farm land	70	506,900
Farm homestead	30	3,770,300

Average Property Value & Tax, 2007
Residential value	$108,335
Property tax	$5,454
Tax credit/rebate	$1,037

Public Library
Gloucester Township Branch Library[‡]
15 S Black Horse Pike
Blackwood, NJ 08012
856-228-0022

Branch Librarian . . . . Ann Ackroyd

Library statistics, 2006
see Camden County profile
for library system statistics

Taxes
	2005	2006	2007
General tax rate per $100	4.658	4.88	5.035
County equalization ratio	72.87	60.84	54.89
Net valuation taxable	$2,376,365,270	$2,387,157,200	$2,425,179,677
State equalized value	$3,905,925,822	$4,355,545,598	$4,764,364,192

Public Safety
Number of officers, 2006 109

Crime	2005	2006
Total crimes	1,779	1,831
Violent	195	178
Murder	0	0
Rape	18	24
Robbery	52	49
Aggravated assault	125	105
Non-violent	1,584	1,653
Burglary	356	362
Larceny	1,114	1,171
Vehicle theft	114	120
Domestic violence	573	585
Arson	12	21
Total crime rate	26.8	27.5
Violent	2.9	2.7
Non-violent	23.9	24.8

Public School District
(for school year 2006-07 except as noted)

Gloucester Township School District
17 Erial Rd
Blackwood, NJ 08012
856-227-1400

Superintendent	Thomas D. Seddon
Number of schools	11
Grade plan	K-8
Enrollment	7,773
Attendance rate, '05-06	95.2%
Dropout rate	NA
Students per teacher	12.0
Per pupil expenditure	$10,325
Median faculty salary	$51,400
Median administrator salary	$92,500
Grade 12 enrollment	NA
High school graduation rate	NA

Assessment test results
(percent scoring at proficient or advanced level)
	Language	Math
NJASK-Grade 3	87.9%	92.1%
GEPA-Grade 8	73.3%	63.0%
HSPA-High School	NA	NA

SAT score averages
Pct tested	Math	Verbal	Writing
NA	NA	NA	NA

Teacher Qualifications
Avg. years of experience	13
Highly-qualified teachers one subject/all subjects	100%/100%
With emergency credentials	0.2%

No Child Left Behind
AYP, 2005-06 . . . . Meets Standards

Municipal Finance[§]
State Aid Programs, 2008
Total aid	$6,389,976
CMPTRA	2,337,350
Energy tax receipts	4,052,371
Garden State Trust	255

General Budget, 2007
Total tax levy	$122,091,982
County levy	31,165,109
County taxes	28,307,821
County library	1,972,021
County health	0
County open space	885,267
School levy	65,695,227
Muni. levy	25,231,647
Misc. revenues	16,559,180

Somerset County

Green Brook Township

Demographics & Socio-Economic Characteristics
(2000 US Census, except as noted)

Population
1980*	4,640
1990*	4,460
2000	5,654
Male	2,704
Female	2,950
2006 (estimate)*	6,854
Population density	1,496.5

Race & Hispanic Origin, 2000
Race
White	5,000
Black/African American	95
American Indian/Alaska Native	4
Asian	452
Native Hawaiian/Pacific Islander	2
Other race	40
Two or more races	61
Hispanic origin, total	231
Mexican	7
Puerto Rican	65
Cuban	48
Other Hispanic	111

Age & Nativity, 2000
Under 5 years	371
18 years and over	4,278
21 years and over	4,160
65 years and over	884
85 years and over	157
Median age	39.9
Native-born	4,912
Foreign-born	742

Educational Attainment, 2000
Population 25 years and over	3,984
Less than 9th grade	6.9%
High school grad or higher	88.3%
Bachelor's degree or higher	39.7%
Graduate degree	14.9%

Income & Poverty, 1999
Per capita income	$37,290
Median household income	$80,644
Median family income	$87,744
Persons in poverty	130
H'holds receiving public assistance	14
H'holds receiving social security	490

Households, 2000
Total households	1,893
With persons under 18	735
With persons over 65	449
Family households	1,508
Single-person households	301
Persons per household	2.84
Persons per family	3.20

Labor & Employment
Total civilian labor force, 2006**	3,308
Unemployment rate	3.1%
Total civilian labor force, 2000	2,939
Unemployment rate	3.0%

Employed persons 16 years and over by occupation, 2000
Managers & professionals	1,326
Service occupations	220
Sales & office occupations	802
Farming, fishing & forestry	0
Construction & maintenance	242
Production & transportation	261
Self-employed persons	187

* US Census Bureau
** New Jersey Department of Labor

See Introduction for an explanation of all data sources.

General Information
Township of Green Brook
111 Greenbrook Rd
Green Brook, NJ 08812
732-968-1023

Website	www.greenbrooktwp.org
Year of incorporation	1932
Land/water area (sq. miles)	4.58/0.00
Form of government	Township

Government
Legislative Districts
US Congressional	7
State Legislative	22

Local Officials, 2008
Mayor	Kenneth Herrmann
Manager	Kathryn Kitchener
Clerk	Kathryn Kitchener
Finance Dir	Raymond S. Murray
Tax Assessor	Rosalie Lauerman
Tax Collector	Raymond S. Murray
Attorney	Robert Rusignola
Building	Thomas Carisone
Comm Dev/Planning	NA
Engineering	C. Richard Roseberry
Public Works	C. Richard Roseberry
Police Chief	Martin Rasmussen
Emerg/Fire Director	Geno Panella

Housing & Construction
Housing Units, 2000*
Total	1,916
Median rent	$1,148
Median SF home value	$242,500

Permits for New Residential Construction
	Units	Value
Total, 2007	2	$340,000
Single family	2	$340,000
Total, 2006	3	$544,904
Single family	3	$544,904

Real Property Valuation, 2007
	Parcels	Valuation
Total	2,700	$1,454,772,900
Vacant	172	24,438,200
Residential	2,335	1,198,628,800
Commercial	175	211,668,100
Industrial	9	13,671,500
Apartments	8	6,365,200
Farm land	1	1,100
Farm homestead	0	0

Average Property Value & Tax, 2007
Residential value	$513,331
Property tax	$10,032
Tax credit/rebate	$1,222

Public Library
No public municipal library

Library statistics, 2006
Population served	NA
Full-time/total staff	NA/NA

	Total	Per capita
Holdings	NA	NA
Revenues	NA	NA
Expenditures	NA	NA
Annual visits	NA	NA
Internet terminals/annual users	NA/NA	

Taxes
	2005	2006	2007
General tax rate per $100	1.64	1.81	1.96
County equalization ratio	121.51	107.68	98.87
Net valuation taxable	$1,430,231,789	$1,442,878,300	$1,455,709,427
State equalized value	$1,328,224,173	$1,460,288,372	$1,526,975,444

Public Safety
Number of officers, 2006 22

Crime
	2005	2006
Total crimes	155	156
Violent	7	10
Murder	0	0
Rape	1	3
Robbery	2	0
Aggravated assault	4	7
Non-violent	148	146
Burglary	23	35
Larceny	115	97
Vehicle theft	10	14
Domestic violence	71	67
Arson	1	0
Total crime rate	23.2	23.3
Violent	1.0	1.5
Non-violent	22.2	21.8

Public School District
(for school year 2006-07 except as noted)

Green Brook Township School District
132 Jefferson Ave
Green Brook, NJ 08812
732-968-1171

Superintendent	Stephanie Bilenker
Number of schools	2
Grade plan	K-8
Enrollment	969
Attendance rate, '05-06	95.9%
Dropout rate	NA
Students per teacher	10.4
Per pupil expenditure	$13,020
Median faculty salary	$46,185
Median administrator salary	$112,367
Grade 12 enrollment	NA
High school graduation rate	NA

Assessment test results
(percent scoring at proficient or advanced level)
	Language	Math
NJASK-Grade 3	96.0%	96.8%
GEPA-Grade 8	94.9%	89.1%
HSPA-High School	NA	NA

SAT score averages
Pct tested	Math	Verbal	Writing
NA	NA	NA	NA

Teacher Qualifications
Avg. years of experience	7
Highly-qualified teachers one subject/all subjects	100%/100%
With emergency credentials	1.2%

No Child Left Behind
AYP, 2005-06 .... Meets Standards

Municipal Finance
State Aid Programs, 2008
Total aid	$733,353
CMPTRA	0
Energy tax receipts	733,249
Garden State Trust	104

General Budget, 2007
Total tax levy	$28,450,060
County levy	4,987,310
County taxes	4,033,436
County library	512,116
County health	0
County open space	441,759
School levy	18,694,126
Muni. levy	4,768,624
Misc. revenues	2,638,194

©2008 Information Publications, Inc. All rights reserved. Photocopying prohibited. For additional copies, contact the publisher at www.informationpublications.com or (877)544-INFO (4636)

Green Township
Sussex County

Demographics & Socio-Economic Characteristics
(2000 US Census, except as noted)

Population
1980*	2,450
1990*	2,709
2000	3,220
Male	1,647
Female	1,573
2006 (estimate)*	3,558
Population density	219.9

Race & Hispanic Origin, 2000
Race
White	3,107
Black/African American	30
American Indian/Alaska Native	1
Asian	31
Native Hawaiian/Pacific Islander	0
Other race	9
Two or more races	42
Hispanic origin, total	103
Mexican	6
Puerto Rican	40
Cuban	12
Other Hispanic	45

Age & Nativity, 2000
Under 5 years	254
18 years and over	2,227
21 years and over	2,137
65 years and over	193
85 years and over	19
Median age	36.3
Native-born	2,948
Foreign-born	264

Educational Attainment, 2000
Population 25 years and over	2,079
Less than 9th grade	2.2%
High school grad or higher	93.9%
Bachelor's degree or higher	34.2%
Graduate degree	10.7%

Income & Poverty, 1999
Per capita income	$34,127
Median household income	$84,847
Median family income	$89,788
Persons in poverty	52
H'holds receiving public assistance	0
H'holds receiving social security	150

Households, 2000
Total households	1,046
With persons under 18	499
With persons over 65	144
Family households	890
Single-person households	115
Persons per household	3.07
Persons per family	3.34

Labor & Employment
Total civilian labor force, 2006**	1,946
Unemployment rate	3.8%
Total civilian labor force, 2000	1,729
Unemployment rate	2.8%

Employed persons 16 years and over by occupation, 2000
Managers & professionals	788
Service occupations	117
Sales & office occupations	480
Farming, fishing & forestry	4
Construction & maintenance	158
Production & transportation	134
Self-employed persons	57

* US Census Bureau
** New Jersey Department of Labor

General Information
Township of Green
PO Box 65
150 Kennedy Rd
Tranquility, NJ 07879
908-852-9333

Website	www.greentwp.com
Year of incorporation	1824
Land/water area (sq. miles)	16.18/0.13
Form of government	Township

Government
Legislative Districts
US Congressional	5
State Legislative	24

Local Officials, 2008
Mayor	Roger Michaud
Manager	A. Denise Stagnari
Clerk	A. Denise Stagnari
Finance Dir.	Linda Padula
Tax Assessor	Penny Holenstein
Tax Collector	Victoria Trogani
Attorney	William Hinkes
Building	Edward Vanderberg
Comm Dev/Planning	NA
Engineering	John Miller
Public Works	Watson Perigo Jr
Police Chief	NA
Emerg/Fire Director	Richard Porzilli

Housing & Construction
Housing Units, 2000*
Total	1,069
Median rent	$968
Median SF home value	$182,500

Permits for New Residential Construction
	Units	Value
Total, 2007	32	$6,886,540
Single family	32	$6,886,540
Total, 2006	20	$4,898,076
Single family	20	$4,898,076

Real Property Valuation, 2007
	Parcels	Valuation
Total	1,512	$536,628,300
Vacant	97	16,190,900
Residential	1,108	455,212,900
Commercial	25	17,278,100
Industrial	1	6,142,000
Apartments	0	0
Farm land	188	1,551,800
Farm homestead	93	40,252,600

Average Property Value & Tax, 2007
Residential value	$412,544
Property tax	$8,639
Tax credit/rebate	$1,237

Public Library
No public municipal library

Library statistics, 2006
Population served	NA
Full-time/total staff	NA/NA

	Total	Per capita
Holdings	NA	NA
Revenues	NA	NA
Expenditures	NA	NA
Annual visits	NA	NA
Internet terminals/annual users	NA/NA	

Public Safety
Number of officers, 2006 0

Crime	2005	2006
Total crimes	28	22
Violent	0	2
Murder	0	0
Rape	0	0
Robbery	0	0
Aggravated assault	0	2
Non-violent	28	20
Burglary	5	8
Larceny	22	11
Vehicle theft	1	1
Domestic violence	7	0
Arson	0	0
Total crime rate	8.0	6.2
Violent	0.0	0.6
Non-violent	8.0	5.6

Public School District
(for school year 2006-07 except as noted)

Green Township School District
PO Box 14
Greendell, NJ 07839
973-300-3800

Superintendent	Timothy Frederiks
Number of schools	1
Grade plan	K-8
Enrollment	515
Attendance rate, '05-06	95.3%
Dropout rate	NA
Students per teacher	10.8
Per pupil expenditure	$11,865
Median faculty salary	$55,819
Median administrator salary	$63,188
Grade 12 enrollment	NA
High school graduation rate	NA

Assessment test results
(percent scoring at proficient or advanced level)
	Language	Math
NJASK-Grade 3	88.3%	96.1%
GEPA-Grade 8	95.3%	84.4%
HSPA-High School	NA	NA

SAT score averages
Pct tested	Math	Verbal	Writing
NA	NA	NA	NA

Teacher Qualifications
Avg. years of experience	7
Highly-qualified teachers one subject/all subjects	100%/100%
With emergency credentials	0.0%

No Child Left Behind
AYP, 2005-06 .... Meets Standards

Municipal Finance
State Aid Programs, 2008
Total aid	$182,978
CMPTRA	0
Energy tax receipts	175,745
Garden State Trust	7,233

General Budget, 2007
Total tax levy	$11,255,465
County levy	2,183,282
County taxes	1,783,895
County library	152,078
County health	58,814
County open space	188,495
School levy	6,838,391
Muni. levy	2,233,792
Misc. revenues	1,390,707

Taxes
	2005	2006	2007
General tax rate per $100	1.85	2.02	2.1
County equalization ratio	122.74	108.17	100.1
Net valuation taxable	$522,299,256	$525,549,300	$537,484,284
State equalized value	$482,850,380	$525,971,726	$565,608,983

Cumberland County

Greenwich Township

Demographics & Socio-Economic Characteristics
(2000 US Census, except as noted)

Population
- 1980* 973
- 1990* 911
- 2000 847
  - Male 420
  - Female 427
- 2006 (estimate)* 893
  - Population density 49.2

Race & Hispanic Origin, 2000
Race
- White 762
- Black/African American 43
- American Indian/Alaska Native 22
- Asian 2
- Native Hawaiian/Pacific Islander 0
- Other race 1
- Two or more races 17
- Hispanic origin, total 13
  - Mexican 4
  - Puerto Rican 1
  - Cuban 0
  - Other Hispanic 8

Age & Nativity, 2000
- Under 5 years 47
- 18 years and over 661
- 21 years and over 629
- 65 years and over 126
- 85 years and over 13
  - Median age 43.4
- Native-born 838
- Foreign-born 4

Educational Attainment, 2000
- Population 25 years and over 627
- Less than 9th grade 3.8%
- High school grad or higher 86.3%
- Bachelor's degree or higher 22.0%
- Graduate degree 7.2%

Income & Poverty, 1999
- Per capita income $22,233
- Median household income $52,188
- Median family income $56,111
- Persons in poverty 67
- H'holds receiving public assistance 6
- H'holds receiving social security 94

Households, 2000
- Total households 326
  - With persons under 18 104
  - With persons over 65 92
  - Family households 245
  - Single-person households 71
- Persons per household 2.60
- Persons per family 3.05

Labor & Employment
- Total civilian labor force, 2006** 516
  - Unemployment rate 3.3%
- Total civilian labor force, 2000 460
  - Unemployment rate 4.3%

Employed persons 16 years and over by occupation, 2000
- Managers & professionals 185
- Service occupations 52
- Sales & office occupations 98
- Farming, fishing & forestry 5
- Construction & maintenance 39
- Production & transportation 61
- Self-employed persons 61

* US Census Bureau
** New Jersey Department of Labor

See Introduction for an explanation of all data sources.

General Information
Township of Greenwich
PO Box 64
Greenwich, NJ 08323
856-455-4677

- Website ....(county website)
- Year of incorporation 1748
- Land/water area (sq. miles) 18.16/0.72
- Form of government ....Township

Government
Legislative Districts
- US Congressional 2
- State Legislative 3

Local Officials, 2008
- Mayor ....Theodore Kiefer
- Manager/Admin ....NA
- Clerk ....Elaine Hancock
- Finance Dir ....Susan Cummins
- Tax Assessor ....Lois Mazza
- Tax Collector ....Elizabeth Wallendar
- Attorney ....Thomas Seeley
- Building ....Gordon Gross
- Planning ....Dean Roork
- Engineering ....Alexander Churchill
- Public Works ....NA
- Police Chief ....NA
- Emerg/Fire Director ....Wade McFarland

Housing & Construction
Housing Units, 2000*
- Total 361
- Median rent $742
- Median SF home value $112,000

Permits for New Residential Construction

	Units	Value
Total, 2007	5	$493,989
Single family	5	$493,989
Total, 2006	4	$459,988
Single family	4	$459,988

Real Property Valuation, 2007

	Parcels	Valuation
Total	647	$62,357,100
Vacant	116	3,593,500
Residential	301	41,867,300
Commercial	10	2,872,200
Industrial	0	0
Apartments	0	0
Farm land	158	3,305,400
Farm homestead	62	10,718,700

Average Property Value & Tax, 2007
- Residential value $144,865
- Property tax $4,839
- Tax credit/rebate $935

Public Library
No public municipal library

Library statistics, 2006
- Population served ....NA
- Full-time/total staff ....NA/NA

	Total	Per capita
Holdings	NA	NA
Revenues	NA	NA
Expenditures	NA	NA
Annual visits	NA	NA

Internet terminals/annual users ....NA/NA

Taxes

	2005	2006	2007
General tax rate per $100	2.809	3.03	3.344
County equalization ratio	119.27	106.96	91.24
Net valuation taxable	$61,732,103	$61,565,600	$62,572,212
State equalized value	$57,715,130	$67,706,004	$72,063,366

Public Safety
Number of officers, 2006 0

Crime

	2005	2006
Total crimes	5	12
Violent	1	0
Murder	0	0
Rape	0	0
Robbery	0	0
Aggravated assault	1	0
Non-violent	4	12
Burglary	1	2
Larceny	2	7
Vehicle theft	1	3
Domestic violence	1	0
Arson	0	0
Total crime rate	5.7	13.7
Violent	1.1	0.0
Non-violent	4.6	13.7

Public School District
(for school year 2006-07 except as noted)

Greenwich Township School District
839 Ye Greate St
Greenwich, NJ 08323
856-451-5513

- Superintendent ....Nancy Nosta
- Number of schools 1
- Grade plan K-8
- Enrollment 78
- Attendance rate, '05-06 ....93.8%
- Dropout rate ....NA
- Students per teacher 7.5
- Per pupil expenditure $15,066
- Median faculty salary $46,318
- Median administrator salary $75,445
- Grade 12 enrollment ....NA
- High school graduation rate ....NA

Assessment test results
(percent scoring at proficient or advanced level)

	Language	Math
NJASK-Grade 3	90.9%	63.6%
GEPA-Grade 8	NA	NA
HSPA-High School	NA	NA

SAT score averages

Pct tested	Math	Verbal	Writing
NA	NA	NA	NA

Teacher Qualifications
- Avg. years of experience 18
- Highly-qualified teachers
  - one subject/all subjects 100%/100%
- With emergency credentials 0.0%

No Child Left Behind
- AYP, 2005-06 ....Meets Standards

Municipal Finance
State Aid Programs, 2008
- Total aid $99,421
- CMPTRA 0
- Energy tax receipts 70,637
- Garden State Trust 28,784

General Budget, 2007
- Total tax levy $2,090,074
- County levy 682,556
  - County taxes 646,580
  - County library 0
  - County health 29,059
  - County open space 6,917
- School levy 1,170,371
- Muni. levy 237,147
- Misc. revenues 472,226

Greenwich Township
Gloucester County

Demographics & Socio-Economic Characteristics
(2000 US Census, except as noted)

Population
1980*	5,404
1990*	5,102
2000	4,879
Male	2,382
Female	2,497
2006 (estimate)*	4,972
Population density	533.5

Race & Hispanic Origin, 2000
Race
White	4,613
Black/African American	162
American Indian/Alaska Native	5
Asian	33
Native Hawaiian/Pacific Islander	1
Other race	13
Two or more races	52
Hispanic origin, total	75
Mexican	19
Puerto Rican	21
Cuban	3
Other Hispanic	32

Age & Nativity, 2000
Under 5 years	281
18 years and over	3,767
21 years and over	3,594
65 years and over	884
85 years and over	92
Median age	40.1
Native-born	4,702
Foreign-born	177

Educational Attainment, 2000
Population 25 years and over	3,394
Less than 9th grade	5.2%
High school grad or higher	86.9%
Bachelor's degree or higher	17.4%
Graduate degree	2.9%

Income & Poverty, 1999
Per capita income	$24,791
Median household income	$53,651
Median family income	$60,565
Persons in poverty	174
H'holds receiving public assistance	21
H'holds receiving social security	700

Households, 2000
Total households	1,866
With persons under 18	640
With persons over 65	642
Family households	1,393
Single-person households	413
Persons per household	2.61
Persons per family	3.05

Labor & Employment
Total civilian labor force, 2006**	2,870
Unemployment rate	4.0%
Total civilian labor force, 2000	2,424
Unemployment rate	3.1%

Employed persons 16 years and over by occupation, 2000
Managers & professionals	666
Service occupations	264
Sales & office occupations	652
Farming, fishing & forestry	10
Construction & maintenance	312
Production & transportation	446
Self-employed persons	82

‡ Branch of county library
* US Census Bureau
** New Jersey Department of Labor

General Information
Township of Greenwich
420 Washington St
Gibbstown, NJ 08027
856-423-1038

Website	www.greenwichtwp.com
Year of incorporation	1695
Land/water area (sq. miles)	9.32/2.74
Form of government	Small Municipality

Government
Legislative Districts
US Congressional	1
State Legislative	3

Local Officials, 2008
Mayor	George Shivery Jr
Manager	Horace Spoto
Clerk	Lori Biermann
Finance Dir	Merrie Schmidt
Tax Assessor	Brian Schneider
Tax Collector	Barbara Hoffmann
Attorney	Thomas Ward
Building	Bob DeAngelo
Planning	Raymond Shivers
Engineering	Joseph Schiavo
Public Works	John Daly (Int)
Police Chief	Jeffrey Godfrey
Emerg/Fire Director	Ken Chew

Housing & Construction
Housing Units, 2000*
Total	1,944
Median rent	$778
Median SF home value	$114,400

Permits for New Residential Construction
	Units	Value
Total, 2007	8	$879,854
Single family	8	$879,854
Total, 2006	9	$988,400
Single family	9	$988,400

Real Property Valuation, 2007
	Parcels	Valuation
Total	2,159	$545,853,101
Vacant	199	8,603,087
Residential	1,821	185,070,050
Commercial	60	27,491,800
Industrial	19	322,704,264
Apartments	3	410,300
Farm land	48	719,400
Farm homestead	9	854,200

Average Property Value & Tax, 2007
Residential value	$101,598
Property tax	$3,543
Tax credit/rebate	$816

Public Library
Greenwich Branch Library‡
415 Swedesboro Rd
Gibbstown, NJ 08027
856-423-0684

Branch Librarian..........Pat Woodruff

Library statistics, 2006
see Gloucester County profile for library system statistics

Public Safety
Number of officers, 2006................18

Crime
	2005	2006
Total crimes	140	144
Violent	5	3
Murder	0	0
Rape	1	0
Robbery	0	1
Aggravated assault	4	2
Non-violent	135	141
Burglary	33	24
Larceny	97	114
Vehicle theft	5	3
Domestic violence	61	79
Arson	0	1
Total crime rate	28.0	28.9
Violent	1.0	0.6
Non-violent	27.0	28.3

Public School District
(for school year 2006-07 except as noted)

Greenwich Township School District
415 Swedesboro Rd
Gibbstown, NJ 08027
856-224-4920

Superintendent	Francine Marteski
Number of schools	2
Grade plan	K-8
Enrollment	541
Attendance rate, '05-06	95.4%
Dropout rate	NA
Students per teacher	9.6
Per pupil expenditure	$16,045
Median faculty salary	$68,395
Median administrator salary	$89,753
Grade 12 enrollment	NA
High school graduation rate	NA

Assessment test results
(percent scoring at proficient or advanced level)
	Language	Math
NJASK-Grade 3	85.2%	98.2%
GEPA-Grade 8	77.4%	80.7%
HSPA-High School	NA	NA

SAT score averages
Pct tested	Math	Verbal	Writing
NA	NA	NA	NA

Teacher Qualifications
Avg. years of experience	16
Highly-qualified teachers one subject/all subjects	100%/100%
With emergency credentials	0.0%

No Child Left Behind
AYP, 2005-06............Meets Standards

Municipal Finance
State Aid Programs, 2008
Total aid	$583,276
CMPTRA	0
Energy tax receipts	583,244
Garden State Trust	32

General Budget, 2007
Total tax levy	$21,471,689
County levy	5,721,282
County taxes	4,927,396
County library	408,110
County health	0
County open space	385,777
School levy	8,531,261
Muni. levy	7,219,145
Misc. revenues	3,908,200

Taxes
	2005	2006	2007
General tax rate per $100	3.326	3.292	3.488
County equalization ratio	77.3	69.98	62.19
Net valuation taxable	$588,372,774	$544,612,501	$615,649,387
State equalized value	$840,772,755	$966,782,679	$931,714,968

Warren County

Greenwich Township

Demographics & Socio-Economic Characteristics
(2000 US Census, except as noted)

Population
1980*	1,738
1990*	1,899
2000	4,365
Male	2,154
Female	2,211
2006 (estimate)*	5,229
Population density	495.6

Race & Hispanic Origin, 2000
Race
White	4,071
Black/African American	108
American Indian/Alaska Native	12
Asian	97
Native Hawaiian/Pacific Islander	3
Other race	25
Two or more races	49
Hispanic origin, total	166
Mexican	10
Puerto Rican	64
Cuban	4
Other Hispanic	88

Age & Nativity, 2000
Under 5 years	527
18 years and over	2,897
21 years and over	2,823
65 years and over	270
85 years and over	27
Median age	33.9
Native-born	4,111
Foreign-born	254

Educational Attainment, 2000
Population 25 years and over	2,763
Less than 9th grade	2.6%
High school grad or higher	91.6%
Bachelor's degree or higher	39.0%
Graduate degree	11.1%

Income & Poverty, 1999
Per capita income	$32,886
Median household income	$87,613
Median family income	$92,579
Persons in poverty	106
H'holds receiving public assistance	20
H'holds receiving social security	226

Households, 2000
Total households	1,421
With persons under 18	752
With persons over 65	197
Family households	1,224
Single-person households	162
Persons per household	3.07
Persons per family	3.34

Labor & Employment
Total civilian labor force, 2006**	2,439
Unemployment rate	2.7%
Total civilian labor force, 2000	2,132
Unemployment rate	2.3%

Employed persons 16 years and over by occupation, 2000
Managers & professionals	1,012
Service occupations	192
Sales & office occupations	570
Farming, fishing & forestry	0
Construction & maintenance	148
Production & transportation	161
Self-employed persons	84

* US Census Bureau
** New Jersey Department of Labor

See Introduction for an explanation of all data sources.

General Information
Township of Greenwich
321 Greenwich St
Stewartsville, NJ 08886
908-859-0909

Website	greenwichtownship.com
Year of incorporation	1738
Land/water area (sq. miles)	10.55/0.00
Form of government	Township

Government
Legislative Districts
US Congressional	5
State Legislative	23

Local Officials, 2008
Mayor	Elaine Emiliani
Manager	Kim Viscomi
Clerk	Kim Viscomi
Finance Dir	Gregory Della Pia
Tax Assessor	Eloise Hagman
Tax Collector	Gordon Kobler
Attorney	J. Peter Jost
Building	DCA
Comm Dev/Planning	NA
Engineering	Michael Finelli
Public Works	John Howell
Police Chief	Richard Guzzo
Emerg/Fire Director	Joseph Mecsey III

Housing & Construction
Housing Units, 2000*
Total	1,477
Median rent	$871
Median SF home value	$233,300

Permits for New Residential Construction
	Units	Value
Total, 2007	0	$0
Single family	0	$0
Total, 2006	2	$716,000
Single family	2	$716,000

Real Property Valuation, 2007
	Parcels	Valuation
Total	2,046	$591,363,390
Vacant	77	4,047,000
Residential	1,757	470,971,990
Commercial	50	87,616,600
Industrial	5	14,947,300
Apartments	0	0
Farm land	108	2,201,200
Farm homestead	49	11,579,300

Average Property Value & Tax, 2007
Residential value	$267,193
Property tax	$6,710
Tax credit/rebate	$1,055

Public Library
uses Phillipsburg Public Library
200 Frost Ave
Phillipsburg, NJ 08865
908-454-3712

Director............Ann DeRenzis

Library statistics, 2006
Population served	15,166
Full-time/total staff	4/12

	Total	Per capita
Holdings	117,311	7.74
Revenues	$1,302,209	$85.86
Expenditures	$1,363,522	$89.91
Annual visits	128,204	8.45
Internet terminals/annual users	15/25,376	

Taxes
	2005	2006	2007
General tax rate per $100	2.34	2.5	2.52
County equalization ratio	87.62	75.82	73.24
Net valuation taxable	$574,611,201	$577,371,990	$592,987,564
State equalized value	$757,862,307	$789,966,140	$827,204,783

Public Safety
Number of officers, 2006 11

Crime
	2005	2006
Total crimes	99	133
Violent	3	7
Murder	0	0
Rape	1	1
Robbery	1	2
Aggravated assault	1	4
Non-violent	96	126
Burglary	9	12
Larceny	86	109
Vehicle theft	1	5
Domestic violence	59	53
Arson	1	0
Total crime rate	19.0	25.4
Violent	0.6	1.3
Non-violent	18.4	24.1

Public School District
(for school year 2006-07 except as noted)

Greenwich Township School District
642 S Main St
Stewartsville, NJ 08886
908-859-2022

Superintendent	Kevin Brennan
Number of schools	2
Grade plan	K-8
Enrollment	986
Attendance rate, '05-06	95.6%
Dropout rate	NA
Students per teacher	11.1
Per pupil expenditure	$9,446
Median faculty salary	$42,435
Median administrator salary	$95,950
Grade 12 enrollment	NA
High school graduation rate	NA

Assessment test results
(percent scoring at proficient or advanced level)
	Language	Math
NJASK-Grade 3	93.4%	94.3%
GEPA-Grade 8	81.4%	73.2%
HSPA-High School	NA	NA

SAT score averages
Pct tested	Math	Verbal	Writing
NA	NA	NA	NA

Teacher Qualifications
Avg. years of experience	5
Highly-qualified teachers one subject/all subjects	100%/100%
With emergency credentials	0.0%

No Child Left Behind
AYP, 2005-06 .... Meets Standards

Municipal Finance
State Aid Programs, 2008
Total aid	$395,139
CMPTRA	20,150
Energy tax receipts	374,793
Garden State Trust	196

General Budget, 2007
Total tax levy	$14,892,597
County levy	4,944,010
County taxes	4,036,089
County library	421,548
County health	0
County open space	486,373
School levy	7,597,576
Muni. levy	2,351,011
Misc. revenues	1,455,225

Guttenberg Town   Hudson County

Demographics & Socio-Economic Characteristics
(2000 US Census, except as noted)

Population
1980*	7,340
1990*	8,268
2000	10,807
Male	5,205
Female	5,602
2006 (estimate)*	10,717
Population density	56,405.3

Race & Hispanic Origin, 2000
Race
White	7,022
Black/African American	412
American Indian/Alaska Native	41
Asian	789
Native Hawaiian/Pacific Islander	1
Other race	1,775
Two or more races	767
Hispanic origin, total	5,871
Mexican	233
Puerto Rican	608
Cuban	1,203
Other Hispanic	3,827

Age & Nativity, 2000
Under 5 years	695
18 years and over	8,520
21 years and over	8,175
65 years and over	1,273
85 years and over	170
Median age	35.5
Native-born	5,434
Foreign-born	5,259

Educational Attainment, 2000
Population 25 years and over	7,566
Less than 9th grade	11.9%
High school grad or higher	75.0%
Bachelor's degree or higher	29.8%
Graduate degree	13.4%

Income & Poverty, 1999
Per capita income	$27,931
Median household income	$44,515
Median family income	$47,440
Persons in poverty	1,377
H'holds receiving public assistance	128
H'holds receiving social security	969

Households, 2000
Total households	4,493
With persons under 18	1,344
With persons over 65	964
Family households	2,620
Single-person households	1,576
Persons per household	2.38
Persons per family	3.13

Labor & Employment
Total civilian labor force, 2006**	5,513
Unemployment rate	4.6%
Total civilian labor force, 2000	5,596
Unemployment rate	6.7%

Employed persons 16 years and over by occupation, 2000
Managers & professionals	1,798
Service occupations	714
Sales & office occupations	1,548
Farming, fishing & forestry	0
Construction & maintenance	331
Production & transportation	828
Self-employed persons	276

* US Census Bureau
** New Jersey Department of Labor
§ State Fiscal Year July 1–June 30

General Information
Town of Guttenberg
6808 Park Ave
Guttenberg, NJ 07093
201-868-2315

Website	www.guttenbergnj.org
Year of incorporation	1859
Land/water area (sq. miles)	0.19/0.04
Form of government	Town

Government
Legislative Districts
US Congressional	13
State Legislative	33

Local Officials, 2008
Mayor	David Delle Donna
Manager	Linda Martin
Clerk	Linda Martin
Finance Dir	Nicholas Goldsack
Tax Assessor	James Terhune
Tax Collector	Nicholas Goldsack
Attorney	Charles Daglian
Building	Franco Zanardelli
Comm Dev/Planning	NA
Engineering	Wendell Bibbs
Public Works	Michael Ronchi
Police Chief	Michael Caliguiro
Public Safety Dir	Nicholas Lordo

Housing & Construction
Housing Units, 2000*
Total	4,650
Median rent	$794
Median SF home value	$150,200

Permits for New Residential Construction
	Units	Value
Total, 2007	43	$3,625,709
Single family	4	$616,929
Total, 2006	46	$4,551,789
Single family	8	$756,072

Real Property Valuation, 2007
	Parcels	Valuation
Total	2,616	$407,592,400
Vacant	56	3,218,800
Residential	2,297	319,510,000
Commercial	128	37,033,600
Industrial	61	13,082,300
Apartments	74	34,747,700
Farm land	0	0
Farm homestead	0	0

Average Property Value & Tax, 2007
Residential value	$139,099
Property tax	$7,248
Tax credit/rebate	$989

Public Library
No public municipal library

Library statistics, 2006
Population served	NA
Full-time/total staff	NA/NA

	Total	Per capita
Holdings	NA	NA
Revenues	NA	NA
Expenditures	NA	NA
Annual visits	NA	NA
Internet terminals/annual users	NA/NA	

Taxes
	2005	2006	2007
General tax rate per $100	4.704	5.102	5.394
County equalization ratio	52.61	46.61	38.2
Net valuation taxable	$405,269,784	$405,518,500	$407,727,414
State equalized value	$869,491,062	$1,061,731,929	$1,149,902,010

Public Safety
Number of officers, 2006 21

Crime	2005	2006
Total crimes	237	238
Violent	57	49
Murder	0	0
Rape	0	2
Robbery	25	28
Aggravated assault	32	19
Non-violent	180	189
Burglary	72	75
Larceny	87	90
Vehicle theft	21	24
Domestic violence	64	62
Arson	2	3
Total crime rate	21.5	21.9
Violent	5.2	4.5
Non-violent	16.3	17.4

Public School District
(for school year 2006-07 except as noted)

Guttenberg School District
301 69th St
Guttenberg, NJ 07093
201-861-3100

Superintendent	Thomas Roberts (Int)
Number of schools	1
Grade plan	K-8
Enrollment	937
Attendance rate, '05-06	95.0%
Dropout rate	NA
Students per teacher	13.8
Per pupil expenditure	$9,169
Median faculty salary	$42,832
Median administrator salary	$107,180
Grade 12 enrollment	NA
High school graduation rate	NA

Assessment test results
(percent scoring at proficient or advanced level)
	Language	Math
NJASK-Grade 3	80.0%	83.0%
GEPA-Grade 8	70.4%	56.8%
HSPA-High School	NA	NA

SAT score averages
Pct tested	Math	Verbal	Writing
NA	NA	NA	NA

Teacher Qualifications
Avg. years of experience	7
Highly-qualified teachers one subject/all subjects	100%/100%
With emergency credentials	0.0%

No Child Left Behind
AYP, 2005-06 .... Meets Standards

Municipal Finance§
State Aid Programs, 2008
Total aid	$922,964
CMPTRA	607,758
Energy tax receipts	315,206
Garden State Trust	0

General Budget, 2007
Total tax levy	$21,990,135
County levy	4,412,715
County taxes	4,305,561
County library	0
County health	0
County open space	107,154
School levy	8,618,259
Muni. levy	8,959,161
Misc. revenues	3,900,847

Bergen County

Hackensack City

Demographics & Socio-Economic Characteristics
(2000 US Census, except as noted)

Population
1980*	36,039
1990*	37,049
2000	42,677
Male	21,199
Female	21,478
2006 (estimate)*	43,671
Population density	10,599.8

Race & Hispanic Origin, 2000
Race
White	22,451
Black/African American	10,518
American Indian/Alaska Native	191
Asian	3,181
Native Hawaiian/Pacific Islander	23
Other race	4,144
Two or more races	2,169
Hispanic origin, total	11,061
Mexican	340
Puerto Rican	1,371
Cuban	298
Other Hispanic	9,052

Age & Nativity, 2000
Under 5 years	2,465
18 years and over	34,906
21 years and over	33,607
65 years and over	5,329
85 years and over	768
Median age	36.2
Native-born	28,231
Foreign-born	14,446

Educational Attainment, 2000
Population 25 years and over	31,518
Less than 9th grade	8.5%
High school grad or higher	79.7%
Bachelor's degree or higher	29.1%
Graduate degree	10.7%

Income & Poverty, 1999
Per capita income	$26,856
Median household income	$49,316
Median family income	$56,953
Persons in poverty	3,867
H'holds receiving public assistance	417
H'holds receiving social security	4,019

Households, 2000
Total households	18,113
With persons under 18	4,503
With persons over 65	3,924
Family households	9,549
Single-person households	7,206
Persons per household	2.26
Persons per family	3.08

Labor & Employment
Total civilian labor force, 2006**	24,540
Unemployment rate	5.4%
Total civilian labor force, 2000	23,543
Unemployment rate	6.8%

Employed persons 16 years and over by occupation, 2000
Managers & professionals	7,817
Service occupations	3,262
Sales & office occupations	6,534
Farming, fishing & forestry	4
Construction & maintenance	1,344
Production & transportation	2,992
Self-employed persons	926

* US Census Bureau
** New Jersey Department of Labor

See Introduction for an explanation of all data sources.

General Information
City of Hackensack
65 Central Ave
Hackensack, NJ 07601
201-646-3980

Website	www.hackensack.org
Year of incorporation	1921
Land/water area (sq. miles)	4.12/0.19
Form of government	Municipal Mgr 1923

Government
Legislative Districts
US Congressional	9
State Legislative	37

Local Officials, 2008
Mayor	Jorge E. Meneses
Manager	Stephen Lo Iacono
Clerk	Debra Heck
Finance Dir	Margaret Cherone
Tax Assessor	Arthur Carlson
Tax Collector	Elisa Coccia
Attorney	Joseph C. Zisa
Building	Joseph Mellone
Comm Dev/Planning	NA
Engineering	Vincent DeNave
Public Works	Jesse D'Amore
Police Chief	Charles Zisa
Emerg/Fire Director	Joel Thornton

Housing & Construction
Housing Units, 2000*
Total	18,945
Median rent	$848
Median SF home value	$187,300

Permits for New Residential Construction
	Units	Value
Total, 2007	17	$1,413,300
Single family	3	$463,300
Total, 2006	14	$658,500
Single family	4	$164,000

Real Property Valuation, 2007
	Parcels	Valuation
Total	9,891	$6,274,127,300
Vacant	226	52,587,500
Residential	8,202	2,749,255,400
Commercial	1,020	2,007,826,000
Industrial	236	342,569,200
Apartments	207	1,121,889,200
Farm land	0	0
Farm homestead	0	0

Average Property Value & Tax, 2007
Residential value	$335,193
Property tax	$6,640
Tax credit/rebate	$1,058

Public Library
Johnson Free Public Library
274 Main St
Hackensack, NJ 07601
201-343-4169

Director	Sharon Castanteen

Library statistics, 2006
Population served	42,677
Full-time/total staff	7/22

	Total	Per capita
Holdings	172,274	4.04
Revenues	$2,120,192	$49.68
Expenditures	$2,112,449	$49.50
Annual visits	126,432	2.96
Internet terminals/annual users	10/24,407	

Taxes
	2005	2006	2007
General tax rate per $100	4.69	5.01	1.99
County equalization ratio	51.29	45.7	108.12
Net valuation taxable	$2,276,491,440	$2,259,646,600	$6,298,631,089
State equalized value	$4,981,381,707	$5,778,410,390	$5,955,241,382

Public Safety
Number of officers, 2006	112

Crime	2005	2006
Total crimes	1,194	1,237
Violent	134	147
Murder	0	0
Rape	5	5
Robbery	39	61
Aggravated assault	90	81
Non-violent	1,060	1,090
Burglary	59	83
Larceny	874	885
Vehicle theft	127	122
Domestic violence	386	250
Arson	0	1
Total crime rate	27.3	28.3
Violent	3.1	3.4
Non-violent	24.3	24.9

Public School District
(for school year 2006-07 except as noted)

Hackensack School District
355 State St
Hackensack, NJ 07601
201-646-7830

Superintendent	Joseph Montesano
Number of schools	7
Grade plan	K-12
Enrollment	4,881
Attendance rate, '05-06	94.7%
Dropout rate	1.2%
Students per teacher	11.6
Per pupil expenditure	$14,301
Median faculty salary	$74,521
Median administrator salary	$125,015
Grade 12 enrollment	412
High school graduation rate	87.8%

Assessment test results
(percent scoring at proficient or advanced level)
	Language	Math
NJASK-Grade 3	80.0%	86.5%
GEPA-Grade 8	60.9%	64.3%
HSPA-High School	79.2%	68.6%

SAT score averages
Pct tested	Math	Verbal	Writing
77%	462	444	437

Teacher Qualifications
Avg. years of experience	9
Highly-qualified teachers one subject/all subjects	94.0%/94.0%
With emergency credentials	0.0%

No Child Left Behind
AYP, 2005-06	Meets Standards

Municipal Finance
State Aid Programs, 2008
Total aid	$5,251,140
CMPTRA	1,962,461
Energy tax receipts	3,288,679
Garden State Trust	0

General Budget, 2007
Total tax levy	$124,776,739
County levy	10,476,289
County taxes	9,887,410
County library	0
County health	0
County open space	588,879
School levy	56,010,195
Muni. levy	58,290,255
Misc. revenues	17,871,944

Hackettstown Town
Warren County

Demographics & Socio-Economic Characteristics
(2000 US Census, except as noted)

Population
1980*	8,850
1990*	8,120
2000	10,403
Male	5,006
Female	5,397
2006 (estimate)*	9,478
Population density	2,561.6

Race & Hispanic Origin, 2000
Race
White	9,389
Black/African American	227
American Indian/Alaska Native	13
Asian	303
Native Hawaiian/Pacific Islander	6
Other race	208
Two or more races	257
Hispanic origin, total	833
Mexican	79
Puerto Rican	188
Cuban	48
Other Hispanic	518

Age & Nativity, 2000
Under 5 years	658
18 years and over	8,043
21 years and over	7,536
65 years and over	1,270
85 years and over	208
Median age	35.4
Native-born	9,100
Foreign-born	1,303

Educational Attainment, 2000
Population 25 years and over	6,994
Less than 9th grade	3.6%
High school grad or higher	87.1%
Bachelor's degree or higher	24.5%
Graduate degree	6.8%

Income & Poverty, 1999
Per capita income	$24,742
Median household income	$51,955
Median family income	$64,383
Persons in poverty	475
H'holds receiving public assistance	86
H'holds receiving social security	1,013

Households, 2000
Total households	4,134
With persons under 18	1,327
With persons over 65	918
Family households	2,532
Single-person households	1,311
Persons per household	2.41
Persons per family	3.10

Labor & Employment
Total civilian labor force, 2006**	6,374
Unemployment rate	2.9%
Total civilian labor force, 2000	5,820
Unemployment rate	4.7%

Employed persons 16 years and over by occupation, 2000
Managers & professionals	1,855
Service occupations	813
Sales & office occupations	1,584
Farming, fishing & forestry	11
Construction & maintenance	620
Production & transportation	665
Self-employed persons	160

* US Census Bureau
** New Jersey Department of Labor

General Information
Town of Hackettstown
215 W Stiger St
Hackettstown, NJ 07840
908-852-3130
Website	www.hackettstown.net
Year of incorporation	1853
Land/water area (sq. miles)	3.70/0.00
Form of government	Special Charter

Government
Legislative Districts
US Congressional	5
State Legislative	23

Local Officials, 2008
Mayor	Michael B. Lavery
Manager	William Kuster Jr
Clerk	William Kuster Jr
Finance Dir	Danette Dyer
Tax Assessor	Bernard Murdoch
Tax Collector	Regina McKenna
Attorney	Thomas Thorp
Building	Richard O'Connor
Comm Dev/Planning	NA
Engineering	Paul Sterbenz
Public Works	Thomas Kitchen
Police Chief	Leonard Kunz
Emerg/Fire Director	Barry Mayberry

Housing & Construction
Housing Units, 2000*
Total	4,347
Median rent	$719
Median SF home value	$154,000

Permits for New Residential Construction
	Units	Value
Total, 2007	54	$6,005,510
Single family	37	$5,004,991
Total, 2006	62	$4,046,550
Single family	9	$1,346,544

Real Property Valuation, 2007
	Parcels	Valuation
Total	2,776	$598,531,402
Vacant	182	17,758,600
Residential	2,265	384,305,622
Commercial	265	110,782,930
Industrial	30	53,337,350
Apartments	34	32,346,900
Farm land	0	0
Farm homestead	0	0

Average Property Value & Tax, 2007
Residential value	$169,671
Property tax	$6,738
Tax credit/rebate	$1,142

Public Library
Hackettstown Free Public Library
110 Church St
Hackettstown, NJ 07840
908-852-4936
Director	J. Rona Mosler

Library statistics, 2006
Population served	10,403
Full-time/total staff	1/4

	Total	Per capita
Holdings	38,863	3.74
Revenues	$341,036	$32.78
Expenditures	$371,872	$35.75
Annual visits	51,932	4.99
Internet terminals/annual users		4/4,135

Taxes
	2005	2006	2007
General tax rate per $100	3.68	3.83	3.98
County equalization ratio	76.71	69.27	61.47
Net valuation taxable	$586,384,815	$587,260,832	$601,497,001
State equalized value	$846,520,593	$958,703,599	$1,062,500,742

Public Safety
Number of officers, 2006 ... 21

Crime	2005	2006
Total crimes	144	247
Violent	9	8
Murder	0	0
Rape	1	0
Robbery	1	0
Aggravated assault	7	8
Non-violent	135	239
Burglary	11	26
Larceny	116	204
Vehicle theft	8	9
Domestic violence	142	136
Arson	0	1
Total crime rate	15.4	26.3
Violent	1.0	0.9
Non-violent	14.5	25.5

Public School District
(for school year 2006-07 except as noted)

Hackettstown School District
315 Washington Ave, PO Box 465
Hackettstown, NJ 07840
908-850-6500

Superintendent	Robert Gratz
Number of schools	4
Grade plan	K-12
Enrollment	1,890
Attendance rate, '05-06	95.2%
Dropout rate	0.5%
Students per teacher	10.7
Per pupil expenditure	$12,863
Median faculty salary	$58,943
Median administrator salary	$107,255
Grade 12 enrollment	230
High school graduation rate	96.6%

Assessment test results
(percent scoring at proficient or advanced level)
	Language	Math
NJASK-Grade 3	93.0%	93.8%
GEPA-Grade 8	80.7%	74.8%
HSPA-High School	93.7%	79.8%

SAT score averages
Pct tested	Math	Verbal	Writing
83%	492	490	488

Teacher Qualifications
Avg. years of experience	12
Highly-qualified teachers one subject/all subjects	100%/100%
With emergency credentials	0.0%

No Child Left Behind
AYP, 2005-06 ... Meets Standards

Municipal Finance
State Aid Programs, 2008
Total aid	$811,162
CMPTRA	215,052
Energy tax receipts	588,565
Garden State Trust	7,545

General Budget, 2007
Total tax levy	$23,886,044
County taxes	5,491,972
County taxes	4,900,794
County library	0
County health	0
County open space	591,178
School levy	13,824,080
Muni. levy	4,569,992
Misc. revenues	3,871,525

Camden County | Haddon Heights Borough

Demographics & Socio-Economic Characteristics
(2000 US Census, except as noted)

Population
1980*	8,361
1990*	7,860
2000	7,547
Male	3,554
Female	3,993
2006 (estimate)*	7,365
Population density	4,751.6

Race & Hispanic Origin, 2000
Race
White	7,394
Black/African American	30
American Indian/Alaska Native	8
Asian	49
Native Hawaiian/Pacific Islander	3
Other race	20
Two or more races	43
Hispanic origin, total	79
Mexican	17
Puerto Rican	27
Cuban	3
Other Hispanic	32

Age & Nativity, 2000
Under 5 years	464
18 years and over	5,731
21 years and over	5,541
65 years and over	1,373
85 years and over	154
Median age	40.6
Native-born	7,325
Foreign-born	222

Educational Attainment, 2000
Population 25 years and over	5,366
Less than 9th grade	2.6%
High school grad or higher	90.7%
Bachelor's degree or higher	38.1%
Graduate degree	13.4%

Income & Poverty, 1999
Per capita income	$28,198
Median household income	$58,424
Median family income	$73,460
Persons in poverty	211
H'holds receiving public assistance	7
H'holds receiving social security	1,041

Households, 2000
Total households	3,039
With persons under 18	989
With persons over 65	1,012
Family households	2,039
Single-person households	867
Persons per household	2.48
Persons per family	3.09

Labor & Employment
Total civilian labor force, 2006**	4,189
Unemployment rate	3.6%
Total civilian labor force, 2000	3,863
Unemployment rate	3.3%

Employed persons 16 years and over by occupation, 2000
Managers & professionals	1,830
Service occupations	432
Sales & office occupations	1,022
Farming, fishing & forestry	0
Construction & maintenance	242
Production & transportation	211
Self-employed persons	232

* US Census Bureau
** New Jersey Department of Labor

See Introduction for an explanation of all data sources.

General Information
Borough of Haddon Heights
625 Station Ave
Haddon Heights, NJ 08035
856-547-7164

Website	www.haddonhts.com
Year of incorporation	1904
Land/water area (sq. miles)	1.55/0.00
Form of government	Borough

Government
Legislative Districts
US Congressional	1
State Legislative	5

Local Officials, 2008
Mayor	Scott M. Alexander
Manager	Joan Moreland
Clerk	Joan Moreland
Finance Dir	Ernest Merlino
Tax Assessor	Thomas Colavecchio
Tax Collector	Andrea Penny
Attorney	Salvatore Sciliano
Building	(vacant)
Comm Dev/Planning	NA
Engineering	Todd Day
Public Works	Richard Edelen
Police Chief	Richard Kinkler
Emerg/Fire Director	Nicholas Scardino

Housing & Construction
Housing Units, 2000*
Total	3,136
Median rent	$586
Median SF home value	$139,800

Permits for New Residential Construction
	Units	Value
Total, 2007	133	$8,946,663
Single family	70	$6,887,563
Total, 2006	3	$299,600
Single family	3	$299,600

Real Property Valuation, 2007
	Parcels	Valuation
Total	2,716	$824,250,100
Vacant	19	1,584,700
Residential	2,511	732,517,900
Commercial	171	82,034,800
Industrial	2	517,600
Apartments	13	7,595,100
Farm land	0	0
Farm homestead	0	0

Average Property Value & Tax, 2007
Residential value	$291,724
Property tax	$7,494
Tax credit/rebate	$1,176

Public Library
Haddon Heights Public Library
608 Station Ave
Haddon Heights, NJ 08035
856-547-7132

Director: Robert J. Hunter

Library statistics, 2006
Population served	7,547
Full-time/total staff	1/3

	Total	Per capita
Holdings	54,698	7.25
Revenues	$303,923	$40.27
Expenditures	$311,006	$41.21
Annual visits	49,112	6.51
Internet terminals/annual users	8/17,550	

Public Safety
Number of officers, 2006: 17

Crime
	2005	2006
Total crimes	120	143
Violent	3	5
Murder	0	0
Rape	1	1
Robbery	0	2
Aggravated assault	2	2
Non-violent	117	138
Burglary	13	19
Larceny	101	117
Vehicle theft	3	2
Domestic violence	17	23
Arson	0	3
Total crime rate	16.1	19.3
Violent	0.4	0.7
Non-violent	15.7	18.6

Public School District
(for school year 2006-07 except as noted)

Haddon Heights School District
316A 7th Ave, Admin Bldg
Haddon Heights, NJ 08035
856-547-1412

Superintendent	Nancy Hacker
Number of schools	4
Grade plan	K-12
Enrollment	1,266
Attendance rate, '05-06	93.6%
Dropout rate	1.1%
Students per teacher	10.3
Per pupil expenditure	$13,879
Median faculty salary	$55,170
Median administrator salary	$84,498
Grade 12 enrollment	175
High school graduation rate	95.5%

Assessment test results
(percent scoring at proficient or advanced level)
	Language	Math
NJASK-Grade 3	90.2%	96.7%
GEPA-Grade 8	85.2%	82.1%
HSPA-High School	87.4%	77.6%

SAT score averages
Pct tested	Math	Verbal	Writing
80%	497	498	491

Teacher Qualifications
Avg. years of experience	15
Highly-qualified teachers one subject/all subjects	100%/100%
With emergency credentials	0.0%

No Child Left Behind
AYP, 2005-06: Meets Standards

Municipal Finance
State Aid Programs, 2008
Total aid	$899,235
CMPTRA	125,439
Energy tax receipts	773,796
Garden State Trust	0

General Budget, 2007
Total tax levy	$21,191,117
County levy	5,005,931
County taxes	4,854,226
County library	0
County health	
County open space	151,705
School levy	11,388,114
Muni. levy	4,797,072
Misc. revenues	2,379,123

Taxes
	2005	2006	2007
General tax rate per $100	4.574	5.02	2.569
County equalization ratio	69.72	60.01	108.69
Net valuation taxable	$400,081,674	$401,025,100	$824,910,879
State equalized value	$666,691,675	$752,643,482	$800,748,238

Haddon Township
Camden County

Demographics & Socio-Economic Characteristics
(2000 US Census, except as noted)

Population
1980*	15,875
1990*	14,837
2000	14,651
Male	6,876
Female	7,775
2006 (estimate)*	14,484
Population density	5,384.4

Race & Hispanic Origin, 2000
Race
White	13,980
Black/African American	173
American Indian/Alaska Native	8
Asian	294
Native Hawaiian/Pacific Islander	6
Other race	82
Two or more races	108
Hispanic origin, total	226
Mexican	39
Puerto Rican	114
Cuban	19
Other Hispanic	54

Age & Nativity, 2000
Under 5 years	801
18 years and over	11,340
21 years and over	10,972
65 years and over	2,929
85 years and over	386
Median age	40.7
Native-born	14,084
Foreign-born	576

Educational Attainment, 2000
Population 25 years and over	10,348
Less than 9th grade	2.9%
High school grad or higher	89.5%
Bachelor's degree or higher	30.6%
Graduate degree	9.7%

Income & Poverty, 1999
Per capita income	$25,610
Median household income	$51,076
Median family income	$65,269
Persons in poverty	607
H'holds receiving public assistance	81
H'holds receiving social security	2,214

Households, 2000
Total households	6,207
With persons under 18	1,804
With persons over 65	2,224
Family households	3,889
Single-person households	2,048
Persons per household	2.36
Persons per family	3.05

Labor & Employment
Total civilian labor force, 2006**	8,116
Unemployment rate	3.6%
Total civilian labor force, 2000	7,474
Unemployment rate	3.5%

Employed persons 16 years and over by occupation, 2000
Managers & professionals	3,000
Service occupations	883
Sales & office occupations	2,112
Farming, fishing & forestry	0
Construction & maintenance	633
Production & transportation	586
Self-employed persons	373

‡ Branch of county library
* US Census Bureau
** New Jersey Department of Labor

General Information
Township of Haddon
135 Haddon Ave
Westmont, NJ 08108
856-854-1176

Website	www.haddontwp.com
Year of incorporation	1865
Land/water area (sq. miles)	2.69/0.11
Form of government	Commission

Government
Legislative Districts
US Congressional	1
State Legislative	6

Local Officials, 2008
Mayor	Randall W. Teague
Manager/Admin	NA
Township Clerk	Denise P. Adams
CFO	Denise P. Adams
Tax Assessor	Martin G. Blaskey III
Tax Collector	Jennifer Dellavalle
Attorney	Richard F. Klineburger III
Construction Official	Lawrence Orcutt
Comm Dev/Planning	NA
Engineering	Key Engineers
Public Works Mgr	Thomas Cella
Police Chief	Mark Cavallo (Actg)
Fire Chief	John Medes

Housing & Construction
Housing Units, 2000*
Total	6,423
Median rent	$690
Median SF home value	$122,200

Permits for New Residential Construction
	Units	Value
Total, 2007	24	$1,395,013
Single family	4	$507,013
Total, 2006	24	$1,378,138
Single family	4	$490,138

Real Property Valuation, 2007
	Parcels	Valuation
Total	5,159	$680,085,400
Vacant	122	2,677,100
Residential	4,730	562,685,200
Commercial	270	78,238,900
Industrial	20	4,323,300
Apartments	17	32,160,900
Farm land	0	0
Farm homestead	0	0

Average Property Value & Tax, 2007
Residential value	$118,961
Property tax	$6,100
Tax credit/rebate	$1,082

Public Library
Haddon Township Branch Library‡
15 MacArthur Blvd
Westmont, NJ 08108
856-854-2752

Branch Librarian............Nan Rosenthal

Library statistics, 2006
see Camden County profile
for library system statistics

Public Safety
Number of officers, 2006 30

Crime
	2005	2006
Total crimes	315	427
Violent	24	29
Murder	0	0
Rape	0	1
Robbery	12	19
Aggravated assault	12	9
Non-violent	291	398
Burglary	42	51
Larceny	237	332
Vehicle theft	12	15
Domestic violence	139	123
Arson	4	2
Total crime rate	21.6	29.3
Violent	1.6	2.0
Non-violent	19.9	27.3

Public School District
(for school year 2006-07 except as noted)

Haddon Township School District
500 Rhoads Ave
Westmont, NJ 08108
856-869-7700

Superintendent	Mark Raivetz
Number of schools	7
Grade plan	K-12
Enrollment	2,135
Attendance rate, '05-06	95.5%
Dropout rate	0.7%
Students per teacher	12.5
Per pupil expenditure	$12,576
Median faculty salary	$57,510
Median administrator salary	$89,500
Grade 12 enrollment	189
High school graduation rate	98.5%

Assessment test results
(percent scoring at proficient or advanced level)
	Language	Math
NJASK-Grade 3	89.5%	90.2%
GEPA-Grade 8	76.6%	78.7%
HSPA-High School	85.4%	75.8%

SAT score averages
Pct tested	Math	Verbal	Writing
82%	504	504	489

Teacher Qualifications
Avg. years of experience	12
Highly-qualified teachers one subject/all subjects	100%/99.0%
With emergency credentials	0.0%

No Child Left Behind
AYP, 2005-06 .... Meets Standards

Municipal Finance
State Aid Programs, 2008
Total aid	$1,618,049
CMPTRA	555,680
Energy tax receipts	1,062,369
Garden State Trust	0

General Budget, 2007
Total tax levy	$34,898,379
County levy	8,753,067
County taxes	7,949,342
County library	554,709
County health	0
County open space	249,016
School levy	19,506,700
Muni. levy	6,638,612
Misc. revenues	5,138,988

Taxes
	2005	2006	2007
General tax rate per $100	4.373	4.842	5.129
County equalization ratio	71.2	62.39	54.66
Net valuation taxable	$680,072,447	$681,710,800	$680,543,342
State equalized value	$1,090,034,376	$1,247,693,816	$1,351,173,731

Camden County — Haddonfield Borough

Demographics & Socio-Economic Characteristics
(2000 US Census, except as noted)

Population
1980*	12,337
1990*	11,628
2000	11,659
Male	5,536
Female	6,123
2006 (estimate)*	11,515
Population density	4,068.9

Race & Hispanic Origin, 2000
Race
- White 11,247
- Black/African American 148
- American Indian/Alaska Native 15
- Asian 131
- Native Hawaiian/Pacific Islander ... 3
- Other race 37
- Two or more races 78

Hispanic origin, total 170
- Mexican 22
- Puerto Rican 54
- Cuban 24
- Other Hispanic 70

Age & Nativity, 2000
- Under 5 years 743
- 18 years and over 8,488
- 21 years and over 8,250
- 65 years and over 1,850
- 85 years and over 222
- Median age 41.3
- Native-born 11,290
- Foreign-born 370

Educational Attainment, 2000
- Population 25 years and over ... 8,091
- Less than 9th grade 1.0%
- High school grad or higher 95.1%
- Bachelor's degree or higher ... 64.8%
- Graduate degree 28.9%

Income & Poverty, 1999
- Per capita income $43,170
- Median household income ... $86,872
- Median family income $103,597
- Persons in poverty 250
- H'holds receiving public assistance .. 33
- H'holds receiving social security .. 1,338

Households, 2000
- Total households 4,496
- With persons under 18 1,620
- With persons over 65 1,297
- Family households 3,253
- Single-person households 1,085
- Persons per household 2.57
- Persons per family 3.09

Labor & Employment
- Total civilian labor force, 2006** .. 6,373
- Unemployment rate 2.9%
- Total civilian labor force, 2000 .. 5,872
- Unemployment rate 2.8%

Employed persons 16 years and over by occupation, 2000
- Managers & professionals 3,855
- Service occupations 355
- Sales & office occupations 1,169
- Farming, fishing & forestry 5
- Construction & maintenance 76
- Production & transportation ... 245
- Self-employed persons 545

* US Census Bureau
** New Jersey Department of Labor

See Introduction for an explanation of all data sources.

General Information
Borough of Haddonfield
242 Kings Highway E
PO Box 3005
Haddonfield, NJ 08033
856-429-4700

- Website .... www.haddonfieldnj.org
- Year of incorporation 1875
- Land/water area (sq. miles) ... 2.83/0.03
- Form of government .... Commission

Government
Legislative Districts
- US Congressional 1
- State Legislative 6

Local Officials, 2008
- Mayor .... Letitia G. Colombi
- Manager .... Sharon McCullough
- Clerk .... Deanna Speck
- Finance Dir .... Terry W. Henry
- Tax Assessor .... Thomas Colavecchio
- Tax Collector .... Terry W. Henry
- Attorney .... Mario Iavicoli
- Building .... Steven P. Walko
- Comm Dev/Planning .... NA
- Engineering .... Remington & Vernick
- Public Works .... E. Dave Watson
- Police Chief .... Richard W. Tsonis
- Emerg/Fire Director ...... Joseph Riggs Jr

Housing & Construction
Housing Units, 2000*
- Total 4,620
- Median rent $732
- Median SF home value $225,300

Permits for New Residential Construction
	Units	Value
Total, 2007	12	$4,819,302
Single family	12	$4,819,302
Total, 2006	18	$5,457,288
Single family	18	$5,457,288

Real Property Valuation, 2007
	Parcels	Valuation
Total	4,452	$1,035,564,900
Vacant	60	2,849,400
Residential	4,096	920,345,300
Commercial	285	106,420,600
Industrial	0	0
Apartments	11	5,949,600
Farm land	0	0
Farm homestead	0	0

Average Property Value & Tax, 2007
- Residential value $224,694
- Property tax $10,991
- Tax credit/rebate $1,314

Public Library
Haddonfield Public Library
60 N Haddon Ave
Haddonfield, NJ 08033
856-429-1304

Director .... Susan Briant

Library statistics, 2006
- Population served 11,659
- Full-time/total staff 4/6

	Total	Per capita
Holdings	85,180	7.31
Revenues	$996,915	$85.51
Expenditures	$963,795	$82.67
Annual visits	120,467	10.33
Internet terminals/annual users	9/18,391	

Taxes
	2005	2006	2007
General tax rate per $100	4.45	4.762	4.892
County equalization ratio	64.91	58.15	51.87
Net valuation taxable	$1,018,820,904	$1,027,068,300	$1,038,588,443
State equalized value	$1,752,056,585	$1,983,430,626	$2,141,295,069

Public Safety
Number of officers, 2006 23

Crime
	2005	2006
Total crimes	246	280
Violent	9	12
Murder	0	0
Rape	0	2
Robbery	0	6
Aggravated assault	9	4
Non-violent	237	268
Burglary	39	40
Larceny	197	223
Vehicle theft	1	5
Domestic violence	47	21
Arson	4	11
Total crime rate	21.2	24.2
Violent	0.8	1.0
Non-violent	20.4	23.1

Public School District
(for school year 2006-07 except as noted)

Haddonfield Borough School District
One Lincoln Ave
Haddonfield, NJ 08033
856-429-4130

- Superintendent .... Alan Fegley
- Number of schools 5
- Grade plan K-12
- Enrollment 2,406
- Attendance rate, '05-06 .... 95.2%
- Dropout rate .... NA
- Students per teacher 12.2
- Per pupil expenditure $12,029
- Median faculty salary $62,900
- Median administrator salary ... $111,250
- Grade 12 enrollment 194
- High school graduation rate 98.5%

Assessment test results
(percent scoring at proficient or advanced level)
	Language	Math
NJASK-Grade 3	93.1%	97.2%
GEPA-Grade 8	94.1%	92.7%
HSPA-High School	99.0%	93.2%

SAT score averages
Pct tested	Math	Verbal	Writing
106%	562	566	556

Teacher Qualifications
- Avg. years of experience 13
- Highly-qualified teachers
  - one subject/all subjects 100%/100%
- With emergency credentials 0.0%

No Child Left Behind
AYP, 2005-06 .... Meets Standards

Municipal Finance
State Aid Programs, 2008
- Total aid $1,293,324
- CMPTRA 346,489
- Energy tax receipts 946,834
- Garden State Trust 1

General Budget, 2007
- Total tax levy $50,804,185
- County levy 13,187,441
  - County taxes 12,787,801
  - County library 0
  - County health 0
  - County open space 399,640
- School levy 29,543,527
- Muni. levy 8,073,217
- Misc. revenues 5,130,501

©2008 Information Publications, Inc. All rights reserved. Photocopying prohibited. For additional copies, contact the publisher at www.informationpublications.com or (877) 544-INFO (4636)

Hainesport Township
Burlington County

Demographics & Socio-Economic Characteristics
(2000 US Census, except as noted)

Population
1980*	3,236
1990*	3,249
2000	4,126
Male	2,018
Female	2,108
2006 (estimate)*	6,161
Population density	944.9

Race & Hispanic Origin, 2000
Race
White	3,882
Black/African American	110
American Indian/Alaska Native	4
Asian	70
Native Hawaiian/Pacific Islander	0
Other race	21
Two or more races	39
Hispanic origin, total	88
Mexican	9
Puerto Rican	63
Cuban	6
Other Hispanic	10

Age & Nativity, 2000
Under 5 years	321
18 years and over	3,042
21 years and over	2,936
65 years and over	485
85 years and over	41
Median age	38.4
Native-born	4,007
Foreign-born	119

Educational Attainment, 2000
Population 25 years and over	2,784
Less than 9th grade	0.9%
High school grad or higher	88.6%
Bachelor's degree or higher	24.7%
Graduate degree	7.7%

Income & Poverty, 1999
Per capita income	$28,091
Median household income	$66,417
Median family income	$72,005
Persons in poverty	121
H'holds receiving public assistance	9
H'holds receiving social security	385

Households, 2000
Total households	1,477
With persons under 18	569
With persons over 65	355
Family households	1,150
Single-person households	259
Persons per household	2.78
Persons per family	3.16

Labor & Employment
Total civilian labor force, 2006**	2,700
Unemployment rate	3.3%
Total civilian labor force, 2000	2,307
Unemployment rate	2.7%

Employed persons 16 years and over by occupation, 2000
Managers & professionals	843
Service occupations	278
Sales & office occupations	662
Farming, fishing & forestry	4
Construction & maintenance	191
Production & transportation	266
Self-employed persons	84

* US Census Bureau
** New Jersey Department of Labor

General Information
Township of Hainesport
One Hainesport Centre
PO Box 477
Hainesport, NJ 08036
609-267-2730
Website: www.hainesporttownship.com
Year of incorporation: 1924
Land/water area (sq. miles): 6.52/0.20
Form of government: Township

Government
Legislative Districts
US Congressional	3
State Legislative	8

Local Officials, 2008
Mayor	William Boettcher III
Manager	Paul Tuliano Jr
Clerk	Paul Tuliano Jr
Finance Dir	Dawn Robertson
Tax Assessor	Edward Burek
Tax Collector	Sharon Deviney
Attorney	Ted Costa
Building	M. Gene Blair
Planning	Paula Tiver
Engineering	Richard Alaimo & Assoc
Public Works	Jay Jones Jr
Police Chief	NA
Emerg/Fire Director	William Wiley

Housing & Construction
Housing Units, 2000*
Total	1,555
Median rent	$744
Median SF home value	$144,400

Permits for New Residential Construction
	Units	Value
Total, 2007	2	$258,127
Single family	2	$258,127
Total, 2006	5	$2,396,505
Single family	5	$2,396,505

Real Property Valuation, 2007
	Parcels	Valuation
Total	2,585	$432,805,400
Vacant	232	8,893,800
Residential	2,174	352,740,900
Commercial	83	35,102,400
Industrial	31	30,836,700
Apartments	2	247,500
Farm land	39	221,700
Farm homestead	24	4,762,400

Average Property Value & Tax, 2007
Residential value	$162,649
Property tax	$5,534
Tax credit/rebate	$942

Public Library
No public municipal library

Library statistics, 2006
Population served	NA
Full-time/total staff	NA/NA

	Total	Per capita
Holdings	NA	NA
Revenues	NA	NA
Expenditures	NA	NA
Annual visits	NA	NA
Internet terminals/annual users	NA/NA	

Taxes
	2005	2006	2007
General tax rate per $100	3.103	3.255	3.41
County equalization ratio	67.34	60.69	53.19
Net valuation taxable	$414,129,405	$423,804,600	$433,693,880
State equalized value	$682,368,438	$797,777,678	$884,705,919

Public Safety
Number of officers, 2006: 0

Crime	2005	2006
Total crimes	134	138
Violent	7	10
Murder	0	0
Rape	0	1
Robbery	2	1
Aggravated assault	5	8
Non-violent	127	128
Burglary	17	15
Larceny	100	102
Vehicle theft	10	11
Domestic violence	19	8
Arson	0	0
Total crime rate	21.9	22.6
Violent	1.1	1.6
Non-violent	20.8	20.9

Public School District
(for school year 2006-07 except as noted)

Hainesport Township School District
211 Broad St, PO Box 538
Hainesport, NJ 08036
609-265-8050

Superintendent	Mark Silverstein
Number of schools	1
Grade plan	K-8
Enrollment	666
Attendance rate, '05-06	95.3%
Dropout rate	NA
Students per teacher	10.7
Per pupil expenditure	$11,525
Median faculty salary	$45,249
Median administrator salary	$79,945
Grade 12 enrollment	NA
High school graduation rate	NA

Assessment test results
(percent scoring at proficient or advanced level)
	Language	Math
NJASK-Grade 3	86.7%	96.0%
GEPA-Grade 8	78.0%	74.6%
HSPA-High School	NA	NA

SAT score averages
Pct tested	Math	Verbal	Writing
NA	NA	NA	NA

Teacher Qualifications
Avg. years of experience	9
Highly-qualified teachers one subject/all subjects	100%/100%
With emergency credentials	2.0%

No Child Left Behind
AYP, 2005-06: Meets Standards

Municipal Finance
State Aid Programs, 2008
Total aid	$484,750
CMPTRA	56,641
Energy tax receipts	427,090
Garden State Trust	1,019

General Budget, 2007
Total tax levy	$14,755,296
County levy	3,424,873
County taxes	2,837,977
County library	260,427
County health	0
County open space	326,468
School levy	9,369,913
Muni. levy	1,960,510
Misc. revenues	2,398,126

Passaic County
Haledon Borough

Demographics & Socio-Economic Characteristics
(2000 US Census, except as noted)

Population
1980*	6,607
1990*	6,951
2000	8,252
Male	3,894
Female	4,358
2006 (estimate)*	8,358
Population density	7,205.2

Race & Hispanic Origin, 2000
Race
White	6,073
Black/African American	585
American Indian/Alaska Native	14
Asian	377
Native Hawaiian/Pacific Islander	2
Other race	833
Two or more races	368
Hispanic origin, total	1,865
Mexican	66
Puerto Rican	729
Cuban	48
Other Hispanic	1,022

Age & Nativity, 2000
Under 5 years	576
18 years and over	6,144
21 years and over	5,847
65 years and over	1,163
85 years and over	191
Median age	34.6
Native-born	6,097
Foreign-born	2,155

Educational Attainment, 2000
Population 25 years and over	5,393
Less than 9th grade	12.2%
High school grad or higher	77.1%
Bachelor's degree or higher	18.5%
Graduate degree	6.1%

Income & Poverty, 1999
Per capita income	$19,099
Median household income	$45,599
Median family income	$49,014
Persons in poverty	872
H'holds receiving public assistance	78
H'holds receiving social security	725

Households, 2000
Total households	2,820
With persons under 18	1,090
With persons over 65	744
Family households	1,975
Single-person households	660
Persons per household	2.83
Persons per family	3.41

Labor & Employment
Total civilian labor force, 2006**	4,512
Unemployment rate	7.5%
Total civilian labor force, 2000	4,168
Unemployment rate	7.2%

Employed persons 16 years and over by occupation, 2000
Managers & professionals	1,083
Service occupations	567
Sales & office occupations	1,200
Farming, fishing & forestry	0
Construction & maintenance	371
Production & transportation	645
Self-employed persons	198

* US Census Bureau
** New Jersey Department of Labor

General Information
Borough of Haledon
510 Belmont Ave
Haledon, NJ 07508
973-595-7766

Website	www.haledonboronj.com
Year of incorporation	1908
Land/water area (sq. miles)	1.16/0.00
Form of government	Borough

Government
Legislative Districts
US Congressional	8
State Legislative	35

Local Officials, 2008
Mayor	Domenick Stampone
Manager	William Close
Clerk	Allan Susen
Finance Dir	William Close
Tax Assessor	Brian Townsend
Tax Collector	Theresa Bosland
Attorney	Andrew Oddo
Building Inspector	Jim Booth
Comm Dev/Planning	NA
Engineering	Stephen Boswell
Superintendent	Angelo Passafaro
Police Chief	Louis Mercuro
Emerg/Fire Director	Scott Wilson

Housing & Construction
Housing Units, 2000*
Total	2,906
Median rent	$826
Median SF home value	$164,100

Permits for New Residential Construction
	Units	Value
Total, 2007	69	$2,220,054
Single family	7	$1,148,720
Total, 2006	57	$1,556,400
Single family	5	$910,400

Real Property Valuation, 2007
	Parcels	Valuation
Total	1,859	$323,054,900
Vacant	66	4,029,100
Residential	1,630	260,764,400
Commercial	128	36,531,100
Industrial	27	13,211,300
Apartments	8	8,519,000
Farm land	0	0
Farm homestead	0	0

Average Property Value & Tax, 2007
Residential value	$159,978
Property tax	$7,977
Tax credit/rebate	$1,215

Public Library
Haledon Free Public Library
404 Morrissee Ave
Haledon, NJ 07508
973-790-3808

Director	Judie Erk

Library statistics, 2006
Population served	8,252
Full-time/total staff	NA/0

	Total	Per capita
Holdings	NA	NA
Revenues	NA	NA
Expenditures	NA	NA
Annual visits	NA	NA
Internet terminals/annual users	NA/NA	

Public Safety
Number of officers, 2006	16

Crime
	2005	2006
Total crimes	125	111
Violent	12	13
Murder	0	0
Rape	0	0
Robbery	6	7
Aggravated assault	6	6
Non-violent	113	98
Burglary	36	27
Larceny	56	60
Vehicle theft	21	11
Domestic violence	76	60
Arson	1	1
Total crime rate	14.8	13.2
Violent	1.4	1.5
Non-violent	13.4	11.7

Public School District
(for school year 2006-07 except as noted)

Haledon School District
70 Church St
Haledon, NJ 07508
973-956-2582

Chief School Admin	Raymond Kwak
Number of schools	1
Grade plan	K-8
Enrollment	1,033
Attendance rate, '05-06	94.7%
Dropout rate	NA
Students per teacher	11.9
Per pupil expenditure	$11,226
Median faculty salary	$47,200
Median administrator salary	$92,530
Grade 12 enrollment	NA
High school graduation rate	NA

Assessment test results
(percent scoring at proficient or advanced level)
	Language	Math
NJASK-Grade 3	82.7%	64.6%
GEPA-Grade 8	67.9%	68.8%
HSPA-High School	NA	NA

SAT score averages
Pct tested	Math	Verbal	Writing
NA	NA	NA	NA

Teacher Qualifications
Avg. years of experience	7
Highly-qualified teachers one subject/all subjects	95.5%/95.5%
With emergency credentials	0.0%

No Child Left Behind
AYP, 2005-06	Meets Standards

Municipal Finance
State Aid Programs, 2008
Total aid	$673,697
CMPTRA	121,526
Energy tax receipts	552,171
Garden State Trust	0

General Budget, 2007
Total tax levy	$16,219,699
County levy	3,237,627
County taxes	3,172,236
County library	0
County health	0
County open space	65,391
School levy	8,380,007
Muni. levy	4,602,065
Misc. revenues	4,009,015

Taxes
	2005	2006	2007
General tax rate per $100	4.37	4.82	4.99
County equalization ratio	63.64	55.93	49.79
Net valuation taxable	$324,795,464	$322,117,200	$325,297,777
State equalized value	$580,717,797	$649,461,511	$713,660,847

Hamburg Borough
Sussex County

Demographics & Socio-Economic Characteristics
(2000 US Census, except as noted)

Population
1980*	1,832
1990*	2,566
2000	3,105
Male	1,489
Female	1,616
2006 (estimate)*	3,554
Population density	3,063.8

Race & Hispanic Origin, 2000
Race
White	2,892
Black/African American	23
American Indian/Alaska Native	9
Asian	71
Native Hawaiian/Pacific Islander	0
Other race	52
Two or more races	58
Hispanic origin, total	131
Mexican	7
Puerto Rican	70
Cuban	6
Other Hispanic	48

Age & Nativity, 2000
Under 5 years	229
18 years and over	2,274
21 years and over	2,194
65 years and over	252
85 years and over	14
Median age	35.0
Native-born	2,925
Foreign-born	180

Educational Attainment, 2000
Population 25 years and over	2,060
Less than 9th grade	3.3%
High school grad or higher	88.8%
Bachelor's degree or higher	19.8%
Graduate degree	6.1%

Income & Poverty, 1999
Per capita income	$24,651
Median household income	$58,246
Median family income	$64,773
Persons in poverty	142
H'holds receiving public assistance	7
H'holds receiving social security	199

Households, 2000
Total households	1,173
With persons under 18	466
With persons over 65	188
Family households	844
Single-person households	273
Persons per household	2.65
Persons per family	3.14

Labor & Employment
Total civilian labor force, 2006**	1,938
Unemployment rate	4.6%
Total civilian labor force, 2000	1,726
Unemployment rate	3.9%

Employed persons 16 years and over by occupation, 2000
Managers & professionals	594
Service occupations	215
Sales & office occupations	443
Farming, fishing & forestry	4
Construction & maintenance	170
Production & transportation	233
Self-employed persons	76

* US Census Bureau
** New Jersey Department of Labor

General Information
Borough of Hamburg
16 Wallkill Ave
Hamburg, NJ 07419
973-827-9230

Website	www.hamburgnj.org
Year of incorporation	1920
Land/water area (sq. miles)	1.16/0.01
Form of government	Borough

Government
Legislative Districts
US Congressional	5
State Legislative	24

Local Officials, 2008
Mayor	Paul Marino
Manager/Admin	NA
Clerk	Doreen Schott
Finance Dir	Charles Wood
Tax Assessor	John Dyksen
Tax Collector	Regina Flammer
Attorney	Richard Clemack
Building	Hardyston Township
Comm Dev/Planning	NA
Engineering	John Ruschke
Public Works	NA
Police Captain	Jan Wright (Actg)
Emerg/Fire Director	Daniel Shane

Housing & Construction
Housing Units, 2000*
Total	1,233
Median rent	$864
Median SF home value	$124,500

Permits for New Residential Construction
	Units	Value
Total, 2007	7	$477,036
Single family	7	$477,036
Total, 2006	9	$613,333
Single family	9	$613,333

Real Property Valuation, 2007
	Parcels	Valuation
Total	1,532	$208,492,850
Vacant	145	5,635,450
Residential	1,327	179,462,200
Commercial	54	19,514,500
Industrial	3	3,375,700
Apartments	1	331,500
Farm land	1	4,500
Farm homestead	1	169,000

Average Property Value & Tax, 2007
Residential value	$135,264
Property tax	$4,917
Tax credit/rebate	$916

Public Library
No public municipal library

Library statistics, 2006
Population served	NA
Full-time/total staff	NA/NA

	Total	Per capita
Holdings	NA	NA
Revenues	NA	NA
Expenditures	NA	NA
Annual visits	NA	NA
Internet terminals/annual users	NA/NA	

Taxes
	2005	2006	2007
General tax rate per $100	3.16	3.43	3.64
County equalization ratio	79.54	68.02	59.44
Net valuation taxable	$205,165,577	$206,794,350	$208,795,218
State equalized value	$301,625,370	$348,276,694	$383,139,037

Public Safety
Number of officers, 2006 8

Crime	2005	2006
Total crimes	39	65
Violent	1	2
Murder	0	0
Rape	0	1
Robbery	0	0
Aggravated assault	1	1
Non-violent	38	63
Burglary	9	22
Larceny	29	39
Vehicle theft	0	2
Domestic violence	59	59
Arson	0	0
Total crime rate	11.1	18.2
Violent	0.3	0.6
Non-violent	10.8	17.7

Public School District
(for school year 2006-07 except as noted)

Hamburg Borough School District
30 Linwood Ave
Hamburg, NJ 07419
973-827-7570

Chief School Admin	Robert N. McCann
Number of schools	1
Grade plan	K-8
Enrollment	338
Attendance rate, '05-06	94.9%
Dropout rate	NA
Students per teacher	9.6
Per pupil expenditure	$14,153
Median faculty salary	$49,675
Median administrator salary	$93,875
Grade 12 enrollment	NA
High school graduation rate	NA

Assessment test results
(percent scoring at proficient or advanced level)

	Language	Math
NJASK-Grade 3	71.9%	71.9%
GEPA-Grade 8	87.5%	68.7%
HSPA-High School	NA	NA

SAT score averages
Pct tested	Math	Verbal	Writing
NA	NA	NA	NA

Teacher Qualifications
Avg. years of experience	9
Highly-qualified teachers one subject/all subjects	100%/100%
With emergency credentials	0.0%

No Child Left Behind
AYP, 2005-06 . . . . Meets Standards

Municipal Finance
State Aid Programs, 2008
Total aid	$196,187
CMPTRA	0
Energy tax receipts	195,481
Garden State Trust	706

General Budget, 2007
Total tax levy	$7,590,572
County levy	1,430,648
County taxes	1,168,959
County library	99,654
County health	38,537
County open space	123,499
School levy	4,677,265
Muni. levy	1,482,659
Misc. revenues	1,147,977

Atlantic County
Hamilton Township

Demographics & Socio-Economic Characteristics
(2000 US Census, except as noted)

Population
1980*	9,499
1990*	16,012
2000	20,499
Male	10,217
Female	10,282
2006 (estimate)*	24,423
Population density	219.5

Race & Hispanic Origin, 2000
Race
White	14,646
Black/African American	3,949
American Indian/Alaska Native	60
Asian	675
Native Hawaiian/Pacific Islander	10
Other race	682
Two or more races	477
Hispanic origin, total	1,621
Mexican	91
Puerto Rican	960
Cuban	34
Other Hispanic	536

Age & Nativity, 2000
Under 5 years	1,431
18 years and over	14,946
21 years and over	14,202
65 years and over	1,683
85 years and over	182
Median age	34.5
Native-born	19,152
Foreign-born	1,347

Educational Attainment, 2000
Population 25 years and over	13,351
Less than 9th grade	4.7%
High school grad or higher	80.4%
Bachelor's degree or higher	19.3%
Graduate degree	5.0%

Income & Poverty, 1999
Per capita income	$21,309
Median household income	$50,259
Median family income	$54,899
Persons in poverty	1,280
H'holds receiving public assistance	130
H'holds receiving social security	1,318

Households, 2000
Total households	7,148
With persons under 18	2,976
With persons over 65	1,241
Family households	5,039
Single-person households	1,586
Persons per household	2.72
Persons per family	3.21

Labor & Employment
Total civilian labor force, 2006**	11,268
Unemployment rate	4.8%
Total civilian labor force, 2000	10,275
Unemployment rate	5.2%

Employed persons 16 years and over by occupation, 2000
Managers & professionals	2,918
Service occupations	2,553
Sales & office occupations	2,507
Farming, fishing & forestry	31
Construction & maintenance	904
Production & transportation	828
Self-employed persons	341

* US Census Bureau
** New Jersey Department of Labor

See Introduction for an explanation of all data sources.

General Information
Township of Hamilton
6101 13th St
Mays Landing, NJ 08330
609-625-1511

Website	www.townshipofhamilton.com
Year of incorporation	1813
Land/water area (sq. miles)	111.28/1.71
Form of government	Township

Government
Legislative Districts
US Congressional	2
State Legislative	2

Local Officials, 2008
Mayor	Charles Pritchard
Manager	Edward Sasdelli
Clerk	Joan Anderson
Finance Dir	Richard Tuthill
Tax Assessor	Gerard Mead
Tax Collector	Renee DeSalvo
Attorney	Randolph Lafferty
Building	Warren Dagrosa
Planning	Philip Sartorio
Engineering	Robert Smith
Public Works	William Montag
Police Chief	Jay McKeen
Fire/Emergency Dir	NA

Housing & Construction
Housing Units, 2000*
Total	7,567
Median rent	$806
Median SF home value	$105,700

Permits for New Residential Construction
	Units	Value
Total, 2007	98	$13,173,447
Single family	98	$13,173,447
Total, 2006	192	$18,426,606
Single family	172	$17,442,406

Real Property Valuation, 2007
	Parcels	Valuation
Total	13,907	$1,262,807,300
Vacant	5,235	69,736,600
Residential	8,202	836,779,600
Commercial	233	286,493,500
Industrial	11	15,803,100
Apartments	14	44,455,500
Farm land	160	1,974,700
Farm homestead	52	7,564,300

Average Property Value & Tax, 2007
Residential value	$102,295
Property tax	$3,823
Tax credit/rebate	$804

Public Library
No public municipal library

Library statistics, 2006
Population served	NA
Full-time/total staff	NA/NA

	Total	Per capita
Holdings	NA	NA
Revenues	NA	NA
Expenditures	NA	NA
Annual visits	NA	NA
Internet terminals/annual users	NA/NA	

Taxes
	2005	2006	2007
General tax rate per $100	3.355	3.593	3.738
County equalization ratio	68.52	58.28	49.16
Net valuation taxable	$1,194,829,436	$1,248,435,800	$1,266,509,452
State equalized value	$2,050,153,459	$2,543,665,795	$2,700,855,719

Public Safety
Number of officers, 2006 79

Crime
	2005	2006
Total crimes	1,126	1,171
Violent	78	59
Murder	1	1
Rape	7	5
Robbery	18	18
Aggravated assault	52	35
Non-violent	1,048	1,112
Burglary	124	199
Larceny	868	863
Vehicle theft	56	50
Domestic violence	722	772
Arson	18	9
Total crime rate	47.5	49.0
Violent	3.3	2.5
Non-violent	44.2	46.5

Public School District
(for school year 2006-07 except as noted)

Hamilton Township School District
1876 Dr. Dennis Foreman Drive
Mays Landing, NJ 08330
609-476-6300

Superintendent	Frederick Donatucci
Number of schools	3
Grade plan	K-8
Enrollment	3,225
Attendance rate, '05-06	94.3%
Dropout rate	NA
Students per teacher	12.3
Per pupil expenditure	$10,271
Median faculty salary	$45,702
Median administrator salary	$81,654
Grade 12 enrollment	NA
High school graduation rate	NA

Assessment test results
(percent scoring at proficient or advanced level)
	Language	Math
NJASK-Grade 3	74.5%	83.7%
GEPA-Grade 8	73.6%	73.3%
HSPA-High School	NA	NA

SAT score averages
Pct tested	Math	Verbal	Writing
NA	NA	NA	NA

Teacher Qualifications
Avg. years of experience	9
Highly-qualified teachers one subject/all subjects	100%/100%
With emergency credentials	0.0%

No Child Left Behind
AYP, 2005-06 .... Needs Improvement

Municipal Finance
State Aid Programs, 2008
Total aid	$3,782,678
CMPTRA	130,952
Energy tax receipts	3,418,852
Garden State Trust	138,161

General Budget, 2007
Total tax levy	$47,335,843
County levy	7,907,151
County taxes	6,291,166
County library	781,585
County health	318,477
County open space	515,923
School levy	27,989,563
Muni. levy	11,439,130
Misc. revenues	10,567,870

The New Jersey Municipal Data Book

Hamilton Township — Mercer County

Demographics & Socio-Economic Characteristics[†]
(2000 US Census, except as noted)

Population
1980*	82,801
1990*	86,553
2000	87,109
Male	41,530
Female	45,579
2006 (estimate)*	90,559
Population density	2,295.5

Race & Hispanic Origin, 2000
Race
White	74,173
Black/African American	7,112
American Indian/Alaska Native	121
Asian	2,234
Native Hawaiian/Pacific Islander	31
Other race	1,908
Two or more races	1,530
Hispanic origin, total	4,471
Mexican	221
Puerto Rican	2,409
Cuban	113
Other Hispanic	1,728

Age & Nativity, 2000
Under 5 years	5,006
18 years and over	66,909
21 years and over	64,219
65 years and over	13,623
85 years and over	1,520
Median age	39.1
Native-born	78,943
Foreign-born	8,311

Educational Attainment, 2000
Population 25 years and over	61,062
Less than 9th grade	5.1%
High school grad or higher	83.0%
Bachelor's degree or higher	22.5%
Graduate degree	7.2%

Income & Poverty, 1999
Per capita income	$25,441
Median household income	$57,110
Median family income	$66,986
Persons in poverty	3,619
H'holds receiving public assistance	686
H'holds receiving social security	9,939

Households, 2000
Total households	33,523
With persons under 18	11,338
With persons over 65	9,655
Family households	23,681
Single-person households	8,222
Persons per household	2.58
Persons per family	3.10

Labor & Employment
Total civilian labor force, 2006**	52,321
Unemployment rate	2.2%
Total civilian labor force, 2000	46,420
Unemployment rate	3.7%

Employed persons 16 years and over by occupation, 2000
Managers & professionals	16,451
Service occupations	6,001
Sales & office occupations	13,647
Farming, fishing & forestry	60
Construction & maintenance	3,744
Production & transportation	4,813
Self-employed persons	1,942

[†] see Appendix C for American Community Survey data
* US Census Bureau
** New Jersey Department of Labor
§ State Fiscal Year July 1–June 30

General Information
Township of Hamilton
2090 Greenwood Ave
Hamilton, NJ 08609
609-890-3500

Website	www.hamiltonnj.com
Year of incorporation	1842
Land/water area (sq. miles)	39.45/0.92
Form of government	Mayor-Council

Government
Legislative Districts
US Congressional	4
State Legislative	14

Local Officials, 2008
Mayor	John F. Bencivengo
Manager	William Guhl
Municipal Clerk	Jean Chianese
Finance Dir.	NA
Tax Assessor	Donald Kosul
Tax Collector	Michele Rossi
Attorney	Lindsay L. Burbage
Building	Ray Lumio
Planning	Allen Schectel
Engineering	NA
Public Works	Richard Balgowan
Police Chief	James W. Collins
Fire/Emergency Dir.	NA

Housing & Construction
Housing Units, 2000*
Total	34,535
Median rent	$739
Median SF home value	$136,700

Permits for New Residential Construction
	Units	Value
Total, 2007	240	$20,003,880
Single family	210	$18,386,851
Total, 2006	390	$19,272,292
Single family	148	$8,596,517

Real Property Valuation, 2007
	Parcels	Valuation
Total	31,633	$5,112,892,858
Vacant	1,219	67,692,359
Residential	28,571	3,816,408,000
Commercial	1,535	958,845,904
Industrial	62	98,156,400
Apartments	57	155,900,800
Farm land	125	2,171,145
Farm homestead	64	13,718,250

Average Property Value & Tax, 2007
Residential value	$133,757
Property tax	$4,739
Tax credit/rebate	$960

Public Library
Hamilton Township Public Library
1 Justice Samuel A. Alito Jr Way
Hamilton, NJ 08619
609-581-4060

Director: George Conwell

Library statistics, 2006
Population served	87,109
Full-time/total staff	8/27

	Total	Per capita
Holdings	273,114	3.14
Revenues	$2,629,247	$30.18
Expenditures	$2,732,940	$31.37
Annual visits	450,000	5.17
Internet terminals/annual users	19/42,630	

Taxes
	2005	2006	2007
General tax rate per $100	3.35	3.42	3.55
County equalization ratio	70.72	63.85	54.97
Net valuation taxable	$4,964,076,086	$5,041,520,430	$5,128,624,286
State equalized value	$7,774,590,581	$9,189,543,234	$9,953,326,876

Public Safety
Number of officers, 2006		182

Crime	2005	2006
Total crimes	1,876	2,117
Violent	172	209
Murder	2	1
Rape	9	9
Robbery	93	109
Aggravated assault	68	90
Non-violent	1,704	1,908
Burglary	387	441
Larceny	1,138	1,282
Vehicle theft	179	185
Domestic violence	633	532
Arson	3	10
Total crime rate	20.8	23.5
Violent	1.9	2.3
Non-violent	18.9	21.2

Public School District
(for school year 2006-07 except as noted)

Hamilton Township School District
90 Park Ave
Hamilton Square, NJ 08690
609-631-4100

Superintendent	Neil Bencivengo
Number of schools	23
Grade plan	K-12
Enrollment	13,208
Attendance rate, '05-06	94.2%
Dropout rate	1.5%
Students per teacher	12.0
Per pupil expenditure	$11,446
Median faculty salary	$52,829
Median administrator salary	$95,720
Grade 12 enrollment	961
High school graduation rate	NA

Assessment test results
(percent scoring at proficient or advanced level)
	Language	Math
NJASK-Grade 3	84.8%	85.3%
GEPA-Grade 8	68.2%	64.2%
HSPA-High School	83.3%	68.5%

SAT score averages
Pct tested	Math	Verbal	Writing
NA	NA	NA	NA

Teacher Qualifications
Avg. years of experience	9
Highly-qualified teachers one subject/all subjects	100%/100%
With emergency credentials	0.1%

No Child Left Behind
AYP, 2005-06 .... Meets Standards

Municipal Finance[§]

State Aid Programs, 2008
Total aid	$24,641,331
CMPTRA	4,255,218
Energy tax receipts	20,385,207
Garden State Trust	906

General Budget, 2007
Total tax levy	$181,714,274
County levy	43,650,316
County taxes	40,848,329
County library	0
County health	0
County open space	2,801,987
School levy	96,671,335
Muni. levy	41,392,623
Misc. revenues	39,210,293

Atlantic County
Hammonton Town

Demographics & Socio-Economic Characteristics
(2000 US Census, except as noted)

Population
- 1980* 12,298
- 1990* 12,208
- 2000 12,604
  - Male 6,105
  - Female 6,499
- 2006 (estimate)* 13,572
- Population density 328.9

Race & Hispanic Origin, 2000
Race
- White 11,073
- Black/African American 219
- American Indian/Alaska Native 18
- Asian 144
- Native Hawaiian/Pacific Islander 3
- Other race 987
- Two or more races 160
- Hispanic origin, total 1,876
  - Mexican 685
  - Puerto Rican 994
  - Cuban 11
  - Other Hispanic 186

Age & Nativity, 2000
- Under 5 years 754
- 18 years and over 9,730
- 21 years and over 9,292
- 65 years and over 2,265
- 85 years and over 355
- Median age 38.7
- Native-born 11,581
- Foreign-born 1,023

Educational Attainment, 2000
- Population 25 years and over 8,696
- Less than 9th grade 12.1%
- High school grad or higher 72.5%
- Bachelor's degree or higher 16.2%
- Graduate degree 4.6%

Income & Poverty, 1999
- Per capita income $19,889
- Median household income $43,197
- Median family income $52,205
- Persons in poverty 1,119
- H'holds receiving public assistance ... 103
- H'holds receiving social security ... 1,565

Households, 2000
- Total households 4,619
  - With persons under 18 1,564
  - With persons over 65 1,513
  - Family households 3,269
  - Single-person households 1,103
- Persons per household 2.65
- Persons per family 3.14

Labor & Employment
- Total civilian labor force, 2006** ... 6,768
  - Unemployment rate 7.2%
- Total civilian labor force, 2000 ... 6,249
  - Unemployment rate 8.9%

Employed persons 16 years and over by occupation, 2000
- Managers & professionals 1,459
- Service occupations 1,069
- Sales & office occupations 1,689
- Farming, fishing & forestry 97
- Construction & maintenance 577
- Production & transportation 803
- Self-employed persons 327

‡ Branch of county library
* US Census Bureau
** New Jersey Department of Labor

See Introduction for an explanation of all data sources.

General Information
Town of Hammonton
100 Central Ave
Hammonton, NJ 08037
609-567-4300

- Website .... www.townofhammonton.org
- Year of incorporation 1866
- Land/water area (sq. miles) ... 41.26/0.21
- Form of government .... Town

Government
Legislative Districts
- US Congressional 2
- State Legislative 9

Local Officials, 2008
- Mayor .... John DiDonato
- Manager .... Susanne Oddo
- Clerk .... Susanne Oddo
- Finance Dir .... Rosemarie Jacobs
- Tax Assessor .... Mary Joan Wyatt
- Tax Collector .... Rosemarie Jacobs
- Attorney .... Brian Howell
- Building .... John Aloisio
- Comm Dev/Planning .... NA
- Engineering .. Adams, Rehmann & Heggan
- Public Works .... NA
- Police Chief .... Frank Ingemi
- Emerg/Fire Director ... Frank Domenico

Housing & Construction
Housing Units, 2000*
- Total 4,843
- Median rent $689
- Median SF home value $125,200

Permits for New Residential Construction
	Units	Value
Total, 2007	27	$3,782,375
Single family	27	$3,782,375
Total, 2006	81	$11,353,150
Single family	81	$11,353,150

Real Property Valuation, 2007
	Parcels	Valuation
Total	6,266	$812,750,900
Vacant	755	19,674,500
Residential	4,476	590,584,400
Commercial	399	144,151,300
Industrial	28	21,031,700
Apartments	12	7,732,900
Farm land	425	5,889,800
Farm homestead	171	23,686,300

Average Property Value & Tax, 2007
- Residential value $132,187
- Property tax $4,371
- Tax credit/rebate $938

Public Library
Hammonton West Branch‡
451 S Egg Harbor Rd
Hammonton, NJ 08037
609-561-2264

- Branch Librarian .... Dave Munn

Library statistics, 2006
see Atlantic County profile for library system statistics

Public Safety
- Number of officers, 2006 33

Crime	2005	2006
Total crimes	270	228
Violent	32	34
Murder	0	2
Rape	1	2
Robbery	8	6
Aggravated assault	23	24
Non-violent	238	194
Burglary	62	35
Larceny	163	140
Vehicle theft	13	19
Domestic violence	221	276
Arson	3	2
Total crime rate	20.3	16.8
Violent	2.4	2.5
Non-violent	17.9	14.3

Public School District
(for school year 2006-07 except as noted)

Hammonton Town School District
566 Old Forks Rd, Box 631
Hammonton, NJ 08037
609-567-7000

- Superintendent ..... Mary Lou DeFrancisco
- Number of schools 4
- Grade plan K-12
- Enrollment 3,326
- Attendance rate, '05-06 .... 93.1%
- Dropout rate 3.3%
- Students per teacher 12.8
- Per pupil expenditure $9,267
- Median faculty salary $47,881
- Median administrator salary ... $92,974
- Grade 12 enrollment 316
- High school graduation rate 89.7%

Assessment test results
(percent scoring at proficient or advanced level)

	Language	Math
NJASK-Grade 3	84.1%	87.6%
GEPA-Grade 8	85.1%	75.9%
HSPA-High School	84.7%	69.1%

SAT score averages
Pct tested	Math	Verbal	Writing
56%	518	508	493

Teacher Qualifications
- Avg. years of experience 8
- Highly-qualified teachers
  - one subject/all subjects ... 99.0%/97.0%
- With emergency credentials 2.0%

No Child Left Behind
- AYP, 2005-06 .... Needs Improvement

Municipal Finance
State Aid Programs, 2008
- Total aid $1,640,711
  - CMPTRA 531,116
  - Energy tax receipts 1,056,223
  - Garden State Trust 46,329

General Budget, 2007
- Total tax levy $26,998,978
  - County levy 4,187,875
    - County taxes 3,333,784
    - County library 413,088
    - County health 168,323
    - County open space 272,679
  - School levy 16,642,570
  - Muni. levy 6,168,533
  - Misc. revenues 6,148,895

Taxes	2005	2006	2007
General tax rate per $100	3.223	3.328	3.307
County equalization ratio	81.86	68.71	60.28
Net valuation taxable	$756,627,824	$783,368,300	$816,529,774
State equalized value	$1,101,190,255	$1,303,830,020	$1,463,460,806

Hampton Borough
Hunterdon County

Demographics & Socio-Economic Characteristics
(2000 US Census, except as noted)

Population
1980*	1,614
1990*	1,515
2000	1,546
Male	798
Female	748
2006 (estimate)*	1,658
Population density	1,076.6

Race & Hispanic Origin, 2000
Race
White	1,407
Black/African American	77
American Indian/Alaska Native	6
Asian	15
Native Hawaiian/Pacific Islander	0
Other race	12
Two or more races	29
Hispanic origin, total	44
Mexican	3
Puerto Rican	26
Cuban	2
Other Hispanic	13

Age & Nativity, 2000
Under 5 years	126
18 years and over	1,148
21 years and over	1,086
65 years and over	170
85 years and over	15
Median age	34.7
Native-born	1,476
Foreign-born	70

Educational Attainment, 2000
Population 25 years and over	972
Less than 9th grade	2.8%
High school grad or higher	86.9%
Bachelor's degree or higher	22.0%
Graduate degree	6.6%

Income & Poverty, 1999
Per capita income	$22,440
Median household income	$51,111
Median family income	$64,583
Persons in poverty	121
H'holds receiving public assistance	21
H'holds receiving social security	150

Households, 2000
Total households	559
With persons under 18	218
With persons over 65	138
Family households	378
Single-person households	155
Persons per household	2.58
Persons per family	3.20

Labor & Employment
Total civilian labor force, 2006**	870
Unemployment rate	5.2%
Total civilian labor force, 2000	779
Unemployment rate	4.4%

Employed persons 16 years and over by occupation, 2000
Managers & professionals	247
Service occupations	130
Sales & office occupations	185
Farming, fishing & forestry	2
Construction & maintenance	95
Production & transportation	86
Self-employed persons	38

* US Census Bureau
** New Jersey Department of Labor

General Information
Borough of Hampton
PO Box 418
Hampton, NJ 08827
908-537-2329

Website	(county website)
Year of incorporation	1909
Land/water area (sq. miles)	1.54/0.00
Form of government	Borough

Government
Legislative Districts
US Congressional	7
State Legislative	23

Local Officials, 2008
Mayor	Rob Walton
Manager/Admin	NA
Clerk	Cathy Drummond
Finance Dir	Kathleen Olsen
Tax Assessor	Robert Vance
Tax Collector	Diane Laudenbach
Attorney	Richard Cushing
Building	NA
Comm Dev/Planning	NA
Engineering	William Burr
Public Works	John Spiridigliozzi
Police Chief	NA
Emerg/Fire Director	Howard Eick

Housing & Construction
Housing Units, 2000*
Total	574
Median rent	$543
Median SF home value	$165,200

Permits for New Residential Construction
	Units	Value
Total, 2007	0	$0
Single family	0	$0
Total, 2006	5	$904,778
Single family	5	$904,778

Real Property Valuation, 2007
	Parcels	Valuation
Total	551	$147,043,335
Vacant	60	5,311,801
Residential	443	128,480,585
Commercial	18	5,839,050
Industrial	2	1,011,500
Apartments	3	2,745,800
Farm land	18	107,199
Farm homestead	7	3,547,400

Average Property Value & Tax, 2007
Residential value	$293,396
Property tax	$6,632
Tax credit/rebate	$1,126

Public Library
No public municipal library

Library statistics, 2006
Population served	NA
Full-time/total staff	NA/NA

	Total	Per capita
Holdings	NA	NA
Revenues	NA	NA
Expenditures	NA	NA
Annual visits	NA	NA
Internet terminals/annual users	NA/NA	

Taxes
	2005	2006	2007
General tax rate per $100	4.34	2.22	2.27
County equalization ratio	62.18	123.53	97.59
Net valuation taxable	$67,942,703	$143,203,760	$148,166,403
State equalized value	$113,256,714	$129,499,366	$144,902,607

Public Safety
Number of officers, 2006	0

Crime	2005	2006
Total crimes	14	26
Violent	1	3
Murder	0	0
Rape	0	0
Robbery	0	0
Aggravated assault	1	3
Non-violent	13	23
Burglary	1	11
Larceny	5	10
Vehicle theft	2	2
Domestic violence	6	2
Arson	0	2
Total crime rate	8.8	16.2
Violent	0.6	1.9
Non-violent	8.2	14.3

Public School District
(for school year 2006-07 except as noted)

Hampton Borough School District
32-41 South St
Hampton, NJ 08827
908-537-4101

Chief School Admin	Joanna Hughes
Number of schools	1
Grade plan	K-8
Enrollment	187
Attendance rate, '05-06	95.3%
Dropout rate	NA
Students per teacher	8.2
Per pupil expenditure	$14,193
Median faculty salary	$44,600
Median administrator salary	$96,975
Grade 12 enrollment	NA
High school graduation rate	NA

Assessment test results
(percent scoring at proficient or advanced level)
	Language	Math
NJASK-Grade 3	86.6%	93.3%
GEPA-Grade 8	75.0%	71.5%
HSPA-High School	NA	NA

SAT score averages
Pct tested	Math	Verbal	Writing
NA	NA	NA	NA

Teacher Qualifications
Avg. years of experience	14
Highly-qualified teachers one subject/all subjects	93.0%/93.0%
With emergency credentials	5.3%

No Child Left Behind
AYP, 2005-06 .... Meets Standards

Municipal Finance
State Aid Programs, 2008
Total aid	$61,657
CMPTRA	0
Energy tax receipts	60,448
Garden State Trust	1,209

General Budget, 2007
Total tax levy	$3,349,016
County levy	504,896
County taxes	422,548
County library	36,770
County health	0
County open space	45,578
School levy	2,391,957
Muni. levy	452,162
Misc. revenues	607,451

Sussex County

Hampton Township

Demographics & Socio-Economic Characteristics
(2000 US Census, except as noted)

Population
1980*	3,916
1990*	4,438
2000	4,943
Male	2,413
Female	2,530
2006 (estimate)*	5,213
Population density	211.7

Race & Hispanic Origin, 2000
Race
White	4,809
Black/African American	48
American Indian/Alaska Native	1
Asian	33
Native Hawaiian/Pacific Islander	1
Other race	15
Two or more races	36
Hispanic origin, total	94
Mexican	7
Puerto Rican	38
Cuban	13
Other Hispanic	36

Age & Nativity, 2000
Under 5 years	276
18 years and over	3,632
21 years and over	3,503
65 years and over	547
85 years and over	63
Median age	39.8
Native-born	4,766
Foreign-born	177

Educational Attainment, 2000
Population 25 years and over	3,373
Less than 9th grade	2.1%
High school grad or higher	91.4%
Bachelor's degree or higher	27.3%
Graduate degree	7.1%

Income & Poverty, 1999
Per capita income	$25,353
Median household income	$60,698
Median family income	$67,386
Persons in poverty	101
H'holds receiving public assistance	32
H'holds receiving social security	466

Households, 2000
Total households	1,857
With persons under 18	720
With persons over 65	400
Family households	1,413
Single-person households	384
Persons per household	2.65
Persons per family	3.10

Labor & Employment
Total civilian labor force, 2006**	2,911
Unemployment rate	3.5%
Total civilian labor force, 2000	2,596
Unemployment rate	2.6%

Employed persons 16 years and over by occupation, 2000
Managers & professionals	941
Service occupations	324
Sales & office occupations	641
Farming, fishing & forestry	13
Construction & maintenance	326
Production & transportation	283
Self-employed persons	183

* US Census Bureau
** New Jersey Department of Labor

See Introduction for an explanation of all data sources.

General Information
Township of Hampton
1 Municipal Complex Rd
Newton, NJ 07860
973-383-5570
Email.... administrator@hamptontwp-nj.org
Year of incorporation 1864
Land/water area (sq. miles) 24.62/0.69
Form of government .... Township

Government
Legislative Districts
US Congressional	5
State Legislative	24

Local Officials, 2008
Mayor	Philip Yetter
Manager	Eileen Klose
Clerk	Kathleen Armstrong
Finance Dir.	Jessica Caruso
Tax Assessor	John Dyksen
Tax Collector	Kelly Hahn
Attorney	Stephen Roseman
Building	John deJager
Planning	Harold Pellow
Engineering	Harold Pellow
Public Works	Daniel Bayles
Police Chief	NA
Emerg/Fire Director	David Gunderman

Housing & Construction
Housing Units, 2000*
Total	2,026
Median rent	$953
Median SF home value	$149,500

Permits for New Residential Construction
	Units	Value
Total, 2007	5	$817,696
Single family	5	$817,696
Total, 2006	16	$3,112,528
Single family	16	$3,112,528

Real Property Valuation, 2007
	Parcels	Valuation
Total	2,778	$383,792,425
Vacant	467	8,518,000
Residential	1,884	278,836,900
Commercial	67	66,591,500
Industrial	2	335,000
Apartments	0	0
Farm land	235	2,041,025
Farm homestead	123	27,470,000

Average Property Value & Tax, 2007
Residential value	$152,619
Property tax	$5,395
Tax credit/rebate	$988

Public Library
No public municipal library

Library statistics, 2006
Population served	NA
Full-time/total staff	NA/NA

	Total	Per capita
Holdings	NA	NA
Revenues	NA	NA
Expenditures	NA	NA
Annual visits	NA	NA
Internet terminals/annual users	NA/NA	

Public Safety
Number of officers, 2006 0

Crime
	2005	2006
Total crimes	72	72
Violent	5	5
Murder	0	0
Rape	0	1
Robbery	0	0
Aggravated assault	5	4
Non-violent	67	67
Burglary	6	9
Larceny	60	55
Vehicle theft	1	3
Domestic violence	5	1
Arson	0	0
Total crime rate	13.9	13.8
Violent	1.0	1.0
Non-violent	12.9	12.9

Public School District
(for school year 2006-07 except as noted)

Hampton Township School District
One School Rd
Newton, NJ 07860
973-383-5300

Chief School Admin	Everett C. Burns
Number of schools	1
Grade plan	K-6
Enrollment	439
Attendance rate, '05-06	95.8%
Dropout rate	NA
Students per teacher	10.0
Per pupil expenditure	$13,923
Median faculty salary	$52,440
Median administrator salary	$93,000
Grade 12 enrollment	NA
High school graduation rate	NA

Assessment test results
(percent scoring at proficient or advanced level)
	Language	Math
NJASK-Grade 3	95.6%	94.1%
GEPA-Grade 8	NA	NA
HSPA-High School	NA	NA

SAT score averages
Pct tested	Math	Verbal	Writing
NA	NA	NA	NA

Teacher Qualifications
Avg. years of experience	12
Highly-qualified teachers one subject/all subjects	100%/100%
With emergency credentials	2.8%

No Child Left Behind
AYP, 2005-06 .... Meets Standards

Municipal Finance
State Aid Programs, 2008
Total aid	$528,739
CMPTRA	78,859
Energy tax receipts	406,148
Garden State Trust	43,732

General Budget, 2007
Total tax levy	$13,596,516
County levy	3,032,951
County taxes	2,478,164
County library	211,271
County health	81,715
County open space	261,801
School levy	8,795,855
Muni. levy	1,767,710
Misc. revenues	1,907,465

Taxes
	2005	2006	2007
General tax rate per $100	3.22	3.43	3.54
County equalization ratio	66.38	57.4	51.59
Net valuation taxable	$369,027,457	$372,289,805	$384,661,546
State equalized value	$642,904,977	$722,673,955	$775,737,736

The New Jersey Municipal Data Book

Hanover Township — Morris County

Demographics & Socio-Economic Characteristics
(2000 US Census, except as noted)

Population
1980*	11,846
1990*	11,538
2000	12,898
Male	6,273
Female	6,625
2006 (estimate)*	13,737
Population density	1,288.6

Race & Hispanic Origin, 2000
Race
White	11,452
Black/African American	140
American Indian/Alaska Native	7
Asian	1,123
Native Hawaiian/Pacific Islander	1
Other race	76
Two or more races	99
Hispanic origin, total	452
Mexican	44
Puerto Rican	63
Cuban	56
Other Hispanic	289

Age & Nativity, 2000
Under 5 years	828
18 years and over	9,956
21 years and over	9,658
65 years and over	1,921
85 years and over	173
Median age	40.1
Native-born	10,868
Foreign-born	2,030

Educational Attainment, 2000
Population 25 years and over	9,272
Less than 9th grade	4.6%
High school grad or higher	89.5%
Bachelor's degree or higher	41.5%
Graduate degree	15.3%

Income & Poverty, 1999
Per capita income	$37,661
Median household income	$84,115
Median family income	$93,937
Persons in poverty	152
H'holds receiving public assistance	23
H'holds receiving social security	1,449

Households, 2000
Total households	4,745
With persons under 18	1,631
With persons over 65	1,363
Family households	3,619
Single-person households	930
Persons per household	2.71
Persons per family	3.13

Labor & Employment
Total civilian labor force, 2006**	7,583
Unemployment rate	1.8%
Total civilian labor force, 2000	6,941
Unemployment rate	1.5%

Employed persons 16 years and over by occupation, 2000
Managers & professionals	3,150
Service occupations	638
Sales & office occupations	2,050
Farming, fishing & forestry	0
Construction & maintenance	510
Production & transportation	486
Self-employed persons	308

* US Census Bureau
** New Jersey Department of Labor

General Information
Township of Hanover
1000 Route 10
PO Box 250
Whippany, NJ 07981
973-428-2500

Website	www.hanovertownship.com
Year of incorporation	1720
Land/water area (sq. miles)	10.66/0.03
Form of government	Township

Government

Legislative Districts
US Congressional	11
State Legislative	26

Local Officials, 2008
Mayor	Ronald Francioli
Manager	Joseph Giorgio
Clerk	Joseph Giorgio
Finance Dir.	Silvio Esposito
Tax Assessor	John Dyksen
Tax Collector	Michael Zambito
Attorney	John Dorsey
Building	Steven Kaplan
Planning	Kimberly B. Howard
Engineering	Gerardo Maceira
Public Works	Brian Foran
Police Chief	Stephen Gallagher
Fire Chiefs	J. Cortright/J. Davidson

Housing & Construction

Housing Units, 2000*
Total	4,818
Median rent	$1,098
Median SF home value	$286,100

Permits for New Residential Construction
	Units	Value
Total, 2007	35	$6,830,200
Single family	35	$6,830,200
Total, 2006	52	$9,981,946
Single family	52	$9,981,946

Real Property Valuation, 2007
	Parcels	Valuation
Total	5,487	$2,019,385,733
Vacant	382	75,065,500
Residential	4,737	1,123,936,422
Commercial	213	546,826,011
Industrial	146	244,676,100
Apartments	6	28,868,800
Farm land	1	3,800
Farm homestead	2	9,100

Average Property Value & Tax, 2007
Residential value	$237,169
Property tax	$5,795
Tax credit/rebate	$975

Public Library
Whippanong Library
1000 Route 10
Whippany, NJ 07981
973-428-2460

Director . . . . Sulekha Das

Library statistics, 2006
Population served	12,898
Full-time/total staff	2/3

	Total	Per capita
Holdings	52,728	4.09
Revenues	$437,651	$33.93
Expenditures	$446,861	$34.65
Annual visits	77,000	5.97
Internet terminals/annual users	9/24,333	

Taxes
	2005	2006	2007
General tax rate per $100	2.18	2.34	2.45
County equalization ratio	66.94	56.88	52.19
Net valuation taxable	$2,026,835,617	$2,014,007,733	$2,031,454,261
State equalized value	$3,563,353,757	$3,872,058,359	$4,107,354,947

Public Safety
Number of officers, 2006 31

Crime	2005	2006
Total crimes	183	184
Violent	7	10
Murder	0	0
Rape	0	0
Robbery	2	4
Aggravated assault	5	6
Non-violent	176	174
Burglary	27	20
Larceny	137	144
Vehicle theft	12	10
Domestic violence	59	60
Arson	2	3
Total crime rate	13.5	13.4
Violent	0.5	0.7
Non-violent	13.0	12.7

Public School District
(for school year 2006-07 except as noted)

Hanover Township School District
61 Highland Ave
Whippany, NJ 07981
973-515-2404

Superintendent	Scott Pepper
Number of schools	4
Grade plan	K-8
Enrollment	1,553
Attendance rate, '05-06	96.3%
Dropout rate	NA
Students per teacher	10.4
Per pupil expenditure	$13,508
Median faculty salary	$55,821
Median administrator salary	$121,630
Grade 12 enrollment	NA
High school graduation rate	NA

Assessment test results
(percent scoring at proficient or advanced level)
	Language	Math
NJASK-Grade 3	93.3%	97.2%
GEPA-Grade 8	89.5%	90.1%
HSPA-High School	NA	NA

SAT score averages
Pct tested	Math	Verbal	Writing
NA	NA	NA	NA

Teacher Qualifications
Avg. years of experience	10
Highly-qualified teachers one subject/all subjects	100%/100%
With emergency credentials	0.0%

No Child Left Behind
AYP, 2005-06 . . . . Meets Standards

Municipal Finance

State Aid Programs, 2008
Total aid	$3,019,839
CMPTRA	1,030,841
Energy tax receipts	1,988,706
Garden State Trust	292

General Budget, 2007
Total tax levy	$49,638,163
County levy	9,395,613
County taxes	7,515,091
County library	0
County health	0
County open space	1,880,522
School levy	27,975,871
Muni. levy	12,266,680
Misc. revenues	9,222,993

Morris County / Harding Township

Demographics & Socio-Economic Characteristics
(2000 US Census, except as noted)

Population
1980*	3,236
1990*	3,640
2000	3,180
Male	1,540
Female	1,640
2006 (estimate)*	3,363
Population density	164.5

Race & Hispanic Origin, 2000
Race
White	3,091
Black/African American	13
American Indian/Alaska Native	0
Asian	34
Native Hawaiian/Pacific Islander	1
Other race	7
Two or more races	34
Hispanic origin, total	57
Mexican	3
Puerto Rican	2
Cuban	10
Other Hispanic	42

Age & Nativity, 2000
Under 5 years	199
18 years and over	2,379
21 years and over	2,321
65 years and over	521
85 years and over	56
Median age	44.5
Native-born	2,984
Foreign-born	196

Educational Attainment, 2000
Population 25 years and over	2,265
Less than 9th grade	0.7%
High school grad or higher	97.5%
Bachelor's degree or higher	66.0%
Graduate degree	31.9%

Income & Poverty, 1999
Per capita income	$72,689
Median household income	$111,297
Median family income	$128,719
Persons in poverty	36
H'holds receiving public assistance	9
H'holds receiving social security	342

Households, 2000
Total households	1,180
With persons under 18	393
With persons over 65	361
Family households	941
Single-person households	208
Persons per household	2.69
Persons per family	3.03

Labor & Employment
Total civilian labor force, 2006**	1,503
Unemployment rate	2.5%
Total civilian labor force, 2000	1,369
Unemployment rate	2.3%

Employed persons 16 years and over by occupation, 2000
Managers & professionals	821
Service occupations	109
Sales & office occupations	313
Farming, fishing & forestry	0
Construction & maintenance	72
Production & transportation	23
Self-employed persons	129

* US Census Bureau
** New Jersey Department of Labor

General Information
Township of Harding
PO Box 666
New Vernon, NJ 07976
973-267-8000

Website	www.hardingnj.org
Year of incorporation	1922
Land/water area (sq. miles)	20.44/0.04
Form of government	Township

Government
Legislative Districts
US Congressional	11
State Legislative	21

Local Officials, 2008
Mayor	Loius Lanzerotti
Manager	Gail McKane
Clerk	Gail McKane
Finance Dir.	Himanshu Shah
Tax Assessor	Pat Aceto
Tax Collector	Kathy Silber
Attorney	Maryann Nergaard
Building	Mary Ellen Balady
Planning	Susan Kimball
Engineering	Paul Fox
Public Works	Tracy Toribio
Police Chief	Kevin Gaffney
Emerg/Fire Director	Kenneth Noetzli

Housing & Construction
Housing Units, 2000*
Total	1,243
Median rent	$1,125
Median SF home value	$665,400

Permits for New Residential Construction
	Units	Value
Total, 2007	9	$16,077,000
Single family	9	$16,077,000
Total, 2006	10	$13,506,559
Single family	10	$13,506,559

Real Property Valuation, 2007
	Parcels	Valuation
Total	1,887	$1,965,313,981
Vacant	195	63,092,100
Residential	1,400	1,649,478,963
Commercial	43	70,990,600
Industrial	3	9,641,900
Apartments	0	0
Farm land	155	1,836,418
Farm homestead	91	170,274,000

Average Property Value & Tax, 2007
Residential value	$1,220,492
Property tax	$12,573
Tax credit/rebate	$1,017

Public Library
Harding Township Library
21 Blue Mill Rd
New Vernon, NJ 07976
973-267-8000

Director: Anne N. Thomas

Library statistics, 2006
Population served	3,180
Full-time/total staff	0/0

	Total	Per capita
Holdings	7,383	2.32
Revenues	$76,062	$23.92
Expenditures	$76,543	$24.07
Annual visits	8,782	2.76
Internet terminals/annual users	0/0	

Taxes
	2005	2006	2007
General tax rate per $100	0.93	0.94	1.04
County equalization ratio	94.72	87.05	78.32
Net valuation taxable	$1,952,896,363	$1,949,507,371	$1,966,563,766
State equalized value	$2,243,419,142	$2,490,359,978	$2,697,523,596

Public Safety
Number of officers, 2006		15

Crime	2005	2006
Total crimes	28	17
Violent	0	0
Murder	0	0
Rape	0	0
Robbery	0	0
Aggravated assault	0	0
Non-violent	28	17
Burglary	2	9
Larceny	26	7
Vehicle theft	0	1
Domestic violence	9	6
Arson	1	0
Total crime rate	8.5	5.1
Violent	0.0	0.0
Non-violent	8.5	5.1

Public School District
(for school year 2006-07 except as noted)

Harding Township School District
Lee's Hill Rd, PO Box 248
New Vernon, NJ 07976
973-267-6398

Superintendent	Dennis Pallozzi
Number of schools	1
Grade plan	K-8
Enrollment	317
Attendance rate, '05-06	96.3%
Dropout rate	NA
Students per teacher	7.9
Per pupil expenditure	$18,153
Median faculty salary	$47,200
Median administrator salary	$111,800
Grade 12 enrollment	NA
High school graduation rate	NA

Assessment test results
(percent scoring at proficient or advanced level)
	Language	Math
NJASK-Grade 3	93.6%	95.9%
GEPA-Grade 8	93.1%	92.9%
HSPA-High School	NA	NA

SAT score averages
Pct tested	Math	Verbal	Writing
NA	NA	NA	NA

Teacher Qualifications
Avg. years of experience	6
Highly-qualified teachers one subject/all subjects	100%/100%
With emergency credentials	0.0%

No Child Left Behind
AYP, 2005-06 .... Meets Standards

Municipal Finance
State Aid Programs, 2008
Total aid	$517,871
CMPTRA	0
Energy tax receipts	517,453
Garden State Trust	418

General Budget, 2007
Total tax levy	$20,258,077
County levy	6,001,635
County taxes	4,800,758
County library	0
County health	0
County open space	1,200,877
School levy	8,563,173
Muni. levy	5,693,268
Misc. revenues	3,469,085

Hardwick Township
Warren County

Demographics & Socio-Economic Characteristics
(2000 US Census, except as noted)

Population
1980*	947
1990*	1,235
2000	1,464
Male	731
Female	733
2006 (estimate)*	1,631
Population density	44.7

Race & Hispanic Origin, 2000
Race
- White ... 1,421
- Black/African American ... 9
- American Indian/Alaska Native ... 1
- Asian ... 6
- Native Hawaiian/Pacific Islander ... 0
- Other race ... 13
- Two or more races ... 14
- Hispanic origin, total ... 34
  - Mexican ... 2
  - Puerto Rican ... 11
  - Cuban ... 1
  - Other Hispanic ... 20

Age & Nativity, 2000
- Under 5 years ... 92
- 18 years and over ... 1,075
- 21 years and over ... 1,035
- 65 years and over ... 141
- 85 years and over ... 13
- Median age ... 39.4
- Native-born ... 1,398
- Foreign-born ... 65

Educational Attainment, 2000
- Population 25 years and over ... 994
- Less than 9th grade ... 2.0%
- High school grad or higher ... 92.1%
- Bachelor's degree or higher ... 29.8%
- Graduate degree ... 9.6%

Income & Poverty, 1999
- Per capita income ... $30,038
- Median household income ... $72,167
- Median family income ... $76,111
- Persons in poverty ... 38
- H'holds receiving public assistance ... 4
- H'holds receiving social security ... 102

Households, 2000
- Total households ... 502
  - With persons under 18 ... 206
  - With persons over 65 ... 98
  - Family households ... 410
  - Single-person households ... 70
- Persons per household ... 2.85
- Persons per family ... 3.15

Labor & Employment
- Total civilian labor force, 2006** ... 889
  - Unemployment rate ... 2.9%
- Total civilian labor force, 2000 ... 784
  - Unemployment rate ... 3.1%

Employed persons 16 years and over by occupation, 2000
- Managers & professionals ... 328
- Service occupations ... 89
- Sales & office occupations ... 200
- Farming, fishing & forestry ... 8
- Construction & maintenance ... 80
- Production & transportation ... 55
- Self-employed persons ... 68

* US Census Bureau
** New Jersey Department of Labor

General Information
Township of Hardwick
40 Spring Valley Rd
Hardwick, NJ 07825
908-362-6528

- Website ... www.hardwick-nj.us
- Year of incorporation ... 1750
- Land/water area (sq. miles) ... 36.48/1.44
- Form of government ... Township

Government
Legislative Districts
- US Congressional ... 5
- State Legislative ... 23

Local Officials, 2008
- Mayor ... Kevin Duffy
- Manager/Admin ... NA
- Clerk ... Judith Fisher
- Finance Dir ... Gregory Della Pia
- Tax Assessor ... David Gill
- Tax Collector ... Donna Clouse
- Attorney ... Michael Lavery
- Building ... David Peck
- Comm Dev/Planning ... NA
- Engineering ... Ted Rodman
- Public Works ... Thomas Campbell
- Police Chief ... NA
- Fire/Emergency Dir ... NA

Housing & Construction
Housing Units, 2000*
- Total ... 530
- Median rent ... $775
- Median SF home value ... $196,700

Permits for New Residential Construction
	Units	Value
Total, 2007	7	$1,345,869
Single family	7	$1,345,869
Total, 2006	8	$1,518,970
Single family	8	$1,518,970

Real Property Valuation, 2007
	Parcels	Valuation
Total	933	$153,832,200
Vacant	93	6,877,000
Residential	450	110,028,500
Commercial	3	1,506,200
Industrial	1	627,000
Apartments	0	0
Farm land	253	1,056,100
Farm homestead	133	33,737,400

Average Property Value & Tax, 2007
- Residential value ... $246,597
- Property tax ... $7,204
- Tax credit/rebate ... $1,228

Public Library
No public municipal library

Library statistics, 2006
- Population served ... NA
- Full-time/total staff ... NA/NA

	Total	Per capita
Holdings	NA	NA
Revenues	NA	NA
Expenditures	NA	NA
Annual visits	NA	NA
Internet terminals/annual users	NA/NA	

Taxes
	2005	2006	2007
General tax rate per $100	2.81	2.93	2.93
County equalization ratio	76.68	70.84	65.49
Net valuation taxable	$149,347,090	$151,348,250	$154,155,426
State equalized value	$210,823,108	$231,479,311	$251,027,594

Public Safety
- Number of officers, 2006 ... 0

Crime
	2005	2006
Total crimes	10	8
Violent	0	0
Murder	0	0
Rape	0	0
Robbery	0	0
Aggravated assault	0	0
Non-violent	10	8
Burglary	5	3
Larceny	5	5
Vehicle theft	0	0
Domestic violence	10	0
Arson	0	0
Total crime rate	6.2	5.0
Violent	0.0	0.0
Non-violent	6.2	5.0

Public School District
(for school year 2006-07 except as noted)

Hardwick Township School District
2551 Belvidere Rd
Phillipsburg, NJ 08865

No schools in district - sends students to Blairstown schools

- Per pupil expenditure ... NA
- Median faculty salary ... NA
- Median administrator salary ... NA
- Grade 12 enrollment ... NA
- High school graduation rate ... NA

Assessment test results
(percent scoring at proficient or advanced level)
	Language	Math
NJASK-Grade 3	NA	NA
GEPA-Grade 8	NA	NA
HSPA-High School	NA	NA

SAT score averages
Pct tested	Math	Verbal	Writing
NA	NA	NA	NA

Teacher Qualifications
- Avg. years of experience ... NA
- Highly-qualified teachers one subject/all subjects ... NA/NA
- With emergency credentials ... NA

No Child Left Behind
- AYP, 2005-06 ... NA

Municipal Finance
State Aid Programs, 2008
- Total aid ... $183,756
  - CMPTRA ... 0
  - Energy tax receipts ... 147,818
  - Garden State Trust ... 35,938

General Budget, 2007
- Total tax levy ... $4,503,234
  - County levy ... 1,433,870
    - County taxes ... 1,169,924
    - County library ... 122,550
    - County health ... 0
    - County open space ... 141,396
  - School levy ... 2,788,462
  - Muni. levy ... 280,902
- Misc. revenues ... 743,551

Sussex County

Hardyston Township

Demographics & Socio-Economic Characteristics
(2000 US Census, except as noted)

Population
1980*	4,553
1990*	5,275
2000	6,171
Male	3,038
Female	3,133
2006 (estimate)*	8,283
Population density	258.1

Race & Hispanic Origin, 2000
Race
White	5,897
Black/African American	52
American Indian/Alaska Native	10
Asian	97
Native Hawaiian/Pacific Islander	0
Other race	30
Two or more races	85
Hispanic origin, total	199
Mexican	10
Puerto Rican	105
Cuban	10
Other Hispanic	74

Age & Nativity, 2000
Under 5 years	424
18 years and over	4,588
21 years and over	4,436
65 years and over	630
85 years and over	54
Median age	38.4
Native-born	5,848
Foreign-born	296

Educational Attainment, 2000
Population 25 years and over	4,267
Less than 9th grade	2.8%
High school grad or higher	90.4%
Bachelor's degree or higher	26.7%
Graduate degree	10.4%

Income & Poverty, 1999
Per capita income	$28,457
Median household income	$65,511
Median family income	$72,199
Persons in poverty	285
H'holds receiving public assistance	35
H'holds receiving social security	503

Households, 2000
Total households	2,319
With persons under 18	869
With persons over 65	465
Family households	1,715
Single-person households	500
Persons per household	2.66
Persons per family	3.12

Labor & Employment
Total civilian labor force, 2006**	3,769
Unemployment rate	5.1%
Total civilian labor force, 2000	3,340
Unemployment rate	3.8%

Employed persons 16 years and over by occupation, 2000
Managers & professionals	1,160
Service occupations	409
Sales & office occupations	851
Farming, fishing & forestry	11
Construction & maintenance	404
Production & transportation	378
Self-employed persons	178

* US Census Bureau
** New Jersey Department of Labor

See Introduction for an explanation of all data sources.

General Information
Township of Hardyston
149 Wheatsworth Rd
Hardyston, NJ 07419
973-823-7020

Website	www.hardyston.com
Year of incorporation	1762
Land/water area (sq. miles)	32.09/0.55
Form of government	Special Charter

Government
Legislative Districts
US Congressional	5
State Legislative	24

Local Officials, 2008
Mayor	James G. Armstrong
Manager	Marianne Smith
Clerk	Jane Bakalarczyk
Finance Dir	Grant Rome
Tax Assessor	Scott Holzhauer
Tax Collector	Terry Beshada
Attorney	Fred Semrau
Building	Keith Utter
Planning	Anne-Marie Wilhelm
Engineering	Robert Guerin
Public Works	Robert F. Schultz
Police Chief	Bret Alemy
Emerg/Fire Director	William Hickerson

Housing & Construction
Housing Units, 2000*
Total	2,690
Median rent	$740
Median SF home value	$152,300

Permits for New Residential Construction
	Units	Value
Total, 2007	12	$2,052,700
Single family	12	$2,052,700
Total, 2006	110	$12,540,100
Single family	99	$11,649,100

Real Property Valuation, 2007
	Parcels	Valuation
Total	4,334	$641,087,300
Vacant	677	26,103,700
Residential	3,345	525,192,800
Commercial	119	57,790,200
Industrial	22	11,877,300
Apartments	4	9,688,000
Farm land	119	1,134,900
Farm homestead	48	9,300,400

Average Property Value & Tax, 2007
Residential value	$157,528
Property tax	$5,273
Tax credit/rebate	$991

Public Library
No public municipal library

Library statistics, 2006
Population served	NA
Full-time/total staff	NA/NA

	Total	Per capita
Holdings	NA	NA
Revenues	NA	NA
Expenditures	NA	NA
Annual visits	NA	NA
Internet terminals/annual users	NA/NA	

Public Safety
Number of officers, 2006	19

Crime	2005	2006
Total crimes	79	109
Violent	2	10
Murder	0	0
Rape	1	0
Robbery	0	3
Aggravated assault	1	7
Non-violent	77	99
Burglary	19	20
Larceny	52	75
Vehicle theft	6	4
Domestic violence	78	72
Arson	0	0
Total crime rate	10.4	13.8
Violent	0.3	1.3
Non-violent	10.1	12.5

Public School District
(for school year 2006-07 except as noted)

Hardyston Township School District
183 Wheatsworth Rd
Hamburg, NJ 07419
973-823-7000

Chief School Admin	Dennis Tobin (Int)
Number of schools	2
Grade plan	K-8
Enrollment	766
Attendance rate, '05-06	95.5%
Dropout rate	NA
Students per teacher	11.4
Per pupil expenditure	$11,563
Median faculty salary	$52,333
Median administrator salary	$90,158
Grade 12 enrollment	NA
High school graduation rate	NA

Assessment test results
(percent scoring at proficient or advanced level)
	Language	Math
NJASK-Grade 3	82.9%	89.7%
GEPA-Grade 8	81.6%	81.5%
HSPA-High School	NA	NA

SAT score averages
Pct tested	Math	Verbal	Writing
NA	NA	NA	NA

Teacher Qualifications
Avg. years of experience	13
Highly-qualified teachers one subject/all subjects	100%/100%
With emergency credentials	0.0%

No Child Left Behind
AYP, 2005-06	Meets Standards

Municipal Finance
State Aid Programs, 2008
Total aid	$837,921
CMPTRA	81,115
Energy tax receipts	516,743
Garden State Trust	45,342

General Budget, 2007
Total tax levy	$21,502,407
County levy	5,085,073
County taxes	4,154,871
County library	354,216
County health	137,053
County open space	438,932
School levy	12,049,979
Muni. levy	4,367,355
Misc. revenues	4,334,057

Taxes
	2005	2006	2007
General tax rate per $100	3.29	3.35	3.35
County equalization ratio	63.66	56.37	51.33
Net valuation taxable	$570,828,703	$601,256,000	$642,411,016
State equalized value	$1,012,646,271	$1,172,782,482	$1,264,052,296

Harmony Township — Warren County

Demographics & Socio-Economic Characteristics
(2000 US Census, except as noted)

Population
1980*	2,592
1990*	2,653
2000	2,729
Male	1,349
Female	1,380
2006 (estimate)*	2,860
Population density	120.1

Race & Hispanic Origin, 2000
Race
White	2,672
Black/African American	19
American Indian/Alaska Native	2
Asian	11
Native Hawaiian/Pacific Islander	0
Other race	5
Two or more races	20
Hispanic origin, total	35
Mexican	1
Puerto Rican	22
Cuban	2
Other Hispanic	10

Age & Nativity, 2000
Under 5 years	163
18 years and over	2,071
21 years and over	2,005
65 years and over	379
85 years and over	51
Median age	40.1
Native-born	2,690
Foreign-born	39

Educational Attainment, 2000
Population 25 years and over	1,936
Less than 9th grade	4.0%
High school grad or higher	84.5%
Bachelor's degree or higher	16.0%
Graduate degree	5.3%

Income & Poverty, 1999
Per capita income	$25,776
Median household income	$60,977
Median family income	$64,196
Persons in poverty	122
H'holds receiving public assistance	18
H'holds receiving social security	280

Households, 2000
Total households	1,010
With persons under 18	370
With persons over 65	263
Family households	787
Single-person households	180
Persons per household	2.68
Persons per family	3.05

Labor & Employment
Total civilian labor force, 2006**	1,652
Unemployment rate	2.4%
Total civilian labor force, 2000	1,457
Unemployment rate	2.3%

Employed persons 16 years and over by occupation, 2000
Managers & professionals	414
Service occupations	184
Sales & office occupations	419
Farming, fishing & forestry	4
Construction & maintenance	202
Production & transportation	200
Self-employed persons	102

* US Census Bureau
** New Jersey Department of Labor

General Information
Township of Harmony
3003 Belvidere Rd
Phillipsburg, NJ 08865
908-213-1600

Website	www.harmonytwp-nj.gov
Year of incorporation	1839
Land/water area (sq. miles)	23.81/0.33
Form of government	Township

Government
Legislative Districts
US Congressional	5
State Legislative	23

Local Officials, 2008
Mayor	Brian Tipton
Manager/Admin	NA
Clerk	Kelley D. Smith
Finance Dir.	Dawn Stanchina
Tax Assessor	Richard Motyka
Tax Collector	Joseph Hriczak
Attorney	Sieglinde K. Rath
Building	DCA
Comm Dev/Planning	NA
Engineering	Nevitt S. Duveneck
Public Works	James Fox
Police Chief	NA
Emerg/Fire Director	Wesley Garrison

Housing & Construction
Housing Units, 2000*
Total	1,076
Median rent	$745
Median SF home value	$156,000

Permits for New Residential Construction
	Units	Value
Total, 2007	4	$671,411
Single family	4	$671,411
Total, 2006	6	$630,867
Single family	6	$630,867

Real Property Valuation, 2007
	Parcels	Valuation
Total	1,637	$491,850,300
Vacant	236	10,508,700
Residential	977	196,800,400
Commercial	37	19,910,400
Industrial	7	234,455,400
Apartments	0	0
Farm land	274	3,774,200
Farm homestead	106	26,401,200

Average Property Value & Tax, 2007
Residential value	$206,096
Property tax	$4,460
Tax credit/rebate	$922

Public Library
No public municipal library

Library statistics, 2006
Population served	NA
Full-time/total staff	NA/NA

	Total	Per capita
Holdings	NA	NA
Revenues	NA	NA
Expenditures	NA	NA
Annual visits	NA	NA
Internet terminals/annual users	NA/NA	

Taxes
	2005	2006	2007
General tax rate per $100	1.85	2.1	2.17
County equalization ratio	92.28	72.54	72.49
Net valuation taxable	$522,265,386	$497,661,100	$492,525,925
State equalized value	$719,968,825	$687,170,348	$709,597,937

Public Safety
Number of officers, 2006 … 0

Crime
	2005	2006
Total crimes	14	20
Violent	0	0
Murder	0	0
Rape	0	0
Robbery	0	0
Aggravated assault	0	0
Non-violent	14	20
Burglary	4	12
Larceny	7	7
Vehicle theft	3	1
Domestic violence	12	0
Arson	0	0
Total crime rate	5.0	7.1
Violent	0.0	0.0
Non-violent	5.0	7.1

Public School District
(for school year 2006-07 except as noted)

Harmony Township School District
2551 Belvidere Rd
Phillipsburg, NJ 08865
908-859-1001

Chief School Admin	Jason Kornegay
Number of schools	1
Grade plan	K-8
Enrollment	305
Attendance rate, '05-06	96.1%
Dropout rate	NA
Students per teacher	9.1
Per pupil expenditure	$13,568
Median faculty salary	$53,733
Median administrator salary	$72,160
Grade 12 enrollment	NA
High school graduation rate	NA

Assessment test results
(percent scoring at proficient or advanced level)
	Language	Math
NJASK-Grade 3	100.0%	100.0%
GEPA-Grade 8	77.8%	73.0%
HSPA-High School	NA	NA

SAT score averages
Pct tested	Math	Verbal	Writing
NA	NA	NA	NA

Teacher Qualifications
Avg. years of experience	13
Highly-qualified teachers one subject/all subjects	100%/100%
With emergency credentials	0.0%

No Child Left Behind
AYP, 2005-06 … Meets Standards

Municipal Finance
State Aid Programs, 2008
Total aid	$572,479
CMPTRA	0
Energy tax receipts	240,648
Garden State Trust	331,831

General Budget, 2007
Total tax levy	$10,658,671
County levy	4,163,106
County taxes	3,397,984
County library	355,246
County health	0
County open space	409,876
School levy	5,479,598
Muni. levy	1,015,967
Misc. revenues	1,834,726

Bergen County

Harrington Park Borough

Demographics & Socio-Economic Characteristics
(2000 US Census, except as noted)

Population
1980*	4,532
1990*	4,623
2000	4,740
Male	2,305
Female	2,435
2006 (estimate)*	4,916
Population density	2,643.0

Race & Hispanic Origin, 2000
Race
White	3,959
Black/African American	32
American Indian/Alaska Native	2
Asian	695
Native Hawaiian/Pacific Islander	0
Other race	30
Two or more races	22
Hispanic origin, total	122
Mexican	6
Puerto Rican	46
Cuban	13
Other Hispanic	57

Age & Nativity, 2000
Under 5 years	344
18 years and over	3,384
21 years and over	3,279
65 years and over	606
85 years and over	41
Median age	40.2
Native-born	3,959
Foreign-born	781

Educational Attainment, 2000
Population 25 years and over	3,114
Less than 9th grade	1.3%
High school grad or higher	96.1%
Bachelor's degree or higher	58.4%
Graduate degree	21.9%

Income & Poverty, 1999
Per capita income	$39,017
Median household income	$100,302
Median family income	$105,223
Persons in poverty	138
H'holds receiving public assistance	5
H'holds receiving social security	421

Households, 2000
Total households	1,563
With persons under 18	716
With persons over 65	430
Family households	1,344
Single-person households	191
Persons per household	3.03
Persons per family	3.31

Labor & Employment
Total civilian labor force, 2006**	2,434
Unemployment rate	2.7%
Total civilian labor force, 2000	2,299
Unemployment rate	2.9%

Employed persons 16 years and over by occupation, 2000
Managers & professionals	1,217
Service occupations	112
Sales & office occupations	676
Farming, fishing & forestry	0
Construction & maintenance	100
Production & transportation	127
Self-employed persons	153

* US Census Bureau
** New Jersey Department of Labor

See Introduction for an explanation of all data sources.

General Information
Borough of Harrington Park
85 Harriot Ave
PO Box 174
Harrington Park, NJ 07640
201-768-1700

Website	www.hpboro.net
Year of incorporation	1904
Land/water area (sq. miles)	1.86/0.21
Form of government	Borough

Government
Legislative Districts
US Congressional	5
State Legislative	39

Local Officials, 2008
Mayor	Paul Hoelscher
Manager/Admin	NA
Clerk	Susan Nelson
Finance Dir	Anne Murphy
Tax Assessor	Raymond Damiano
Tax Collector	Anne Murphy
Attorney	John Dineen
Building	Nick Lepore
Comm Dev/Planning	NA
Engineering	Michael Neglia
Public Works	Mark Kiernan
Police Chief	David Moppert
Emerg/Fire Director	Russell Lowe

Housing & Construction
Housing Units, 2000*
Total	1,583
Median rent	$1,281
Median SF home value	$349,700

Permits for New Residential Construction
	Units	Value
Total, 2007	11	$3,938,256
Single family	11	$3,938,256
Total, 2006	14	$4,615,883
Single family	14	$4,615,883

Real Property Valuation, 2007
	Parcels	Valuation
Total	1,666	$1,073,207,200
Vacant	70	22,888,400
Residential	1,568	1,012,540,900
Commercial	28	37,777,900
Industrial	0	0
Apartments	0	0
Farm land	0	0
Farm homestead	0	0

Average Property Value & Tax, 2007
Residential value	$645,753
Property tax	$10,891
Tax credit/rebate	$1,495

Public Library
Harrington Park Public Library
10 Herring St
Harrington Park, NJ 07640
201-768-5675

Director..........Judith Heldman

Library statistics, 2006
Population served	4,740
Full-time/total staff	1/1

	Total	Per capita
Holdings	34,745	7.33
Revenues	$338,441	$71.40
Expenditures	$291,754	$61.55
Annual visits	24,000	5.06
Internet terminals/annual users	4/15,000	

Taxes
	2005	2006	2007
General tax rate per $100	3.27	1.65	1.69
County equalization ratio	62.1	110.83	101.58
Net valuation taxable	$515,032,901	$1,070,895,300	$1,074,000,773
State equalized value	$953,235,056	$1,055,002,891	$1,109,707,811

Public Safety
Number of officers, 2006.............12

Crime	2005	2006
Total crimes	22	11
Violent	0	0
Murder	0	0
Rape	0	0
Robbery	0	0
Aggravated assault	0	0
Non-violent	22	11
Burglary	2	1
Larceny	20	10
Vehicle theft	0	0
Domestic violence	17	10
Arson	0	0
Total crime rate	4.5	2.2
Violent	0.0	0.0
Non-violent	4.5	2.2

Public School District
(for school year 2006-07 except as noted)

Harrington Park School District
191 Harriot Ave
Harrington Park, NJ 07640
201-768-5700

Superintendent	Adam Fried
Number of schools	1
Grade plan	K-8
Enrollment	704
Attendance rate, '05-06	96.7%
Dropout rate	NA
Students per teacher	12.5
Per pupil expenditure	$11,932
Median faculty salary	$51,627
Median administrator salary	$107,000
Grade 12 enrollment	NA
High school graduation rate	NA

Assessment test results
(percent scoring at proficient or advanced level)
	Language	Math
NJASK-Grade 3	93.4%	93.4%
GEPA-Grade 8	92.1%	89.5%
HSPA-High School	NA	NA

SAT score averages
Pct tested	Math	Verbal	Writing
NA	NA	NA	NA

Teacher Qualifications
Avg. years of experience	6
Highly-qualified teachers one subject/all subjects	98.0%/98.0%
With emergency credentials	0.0%

No Child Left Behind
AYP, 2005-06.............Meets Standards

Municipal Finance
State Aid Programs, 2008
Total aid	$532,659
CMPTRA	0
Energy tax receipts	512,402
Garden State Trust	0

General Budget, 2007
Total tax levy	$18,112,856
County levy	1,915,067
County taxes	1,809,272
County library	0
County health	0
County open space	105,795
School levy	12,487,283
Muni. levy	3,710,506
Misc. revenues	2,074,603

The New Jersey Municipal Data Book

Harrison Town   Hudson County

Demographics & Socio-Economic Characteristics
(2000 US Census, except as noted)

Population
1980*	12,242
1990*	13,425
2000	14,424
Male	7,352
Female	7,072
2006 (estimate)*	13,942
Population density	11,427.9

Race & Hispanic Origin, 2000
Race
White	9,534
Black/African American	142
American Indian/Alaska Native	57
Asian	1,715
Native Hawaiian/Pacific Islander	4
Other race	2,302
Two or more races	670
Hispanic origin, total	5,333
Mexican	139
Puerto Rican	605
Cuban	438
Other Hispanic	4,151

Age & Nativity, 2000
Under 5 years	931
18 years and over	11,320
21 years and over	10,725
65 years and over	1,481
85 years and over	132
Median age	34.1
Native-born	6,346
Foreign-born	8,078

Educational Attainment, 2000
Population 25 years and over	9,737
Less than 9th grade	17.0%
High school grad or higher	69.3%
Bachelor's degree or higher	20.9%
Graduate degree	10.1%

Income & Poverty, 1999
Per capita income	$18,490
Median household income	$41,350
Median family income	$48,489
Persons in poverty	1,791
H'holds receiving public assistance	164
H'holds receiving social security	1,148

Households, 2000
Total households	5,136
With persons under 18	1,883
With persons over 65	1,165
Family households	3,638
Single-person households	1,154
Persons per household	2.81
Persons per family	3.27

Labor & Employment
Total civilian labor force, 2006**	7,168
Unemployment rate	5.4%
Total civilian labor force, 2000	7,287
Unemployment rate	7.7%

Employed persons 16 years and over by occupation, 2000
Managers & professionals	1,578
Service occupations	1,434
Sales & office occupations	1,637
Farming, fishing & forestry	3
Construction & maintenance	680
Production & transportation	1,394
Self-employed persons	487

* US Census Bureau
** New Jersey Department of Labor

General Information
Town of Harrison
318 Harrison Ave
Harrison, NJ 07029
973-268-2425

Website	www.townofharrison.com
Year of incorporation	1869
Land/water area (sq. miles)	1.22/0.09
Form of government	Town

Government
Legislative Districts
US Congressional	13
State Legislative	32

Local Officials, 2008
Mayor	Raymond McDonough
Manager/Admin	NA
Clerk	Paul Zarbetski
Finance Dir	Elizabeth Higgins
Tax Assessor	Albert Cifelli
Tax Collector	Margaret A. Powell
Attorney	Paul Zarbetski
Building	Rocco Russomano
Comm Dev/Planning	NA
Engineering	Rocco Rossomano
Public Works	Ronald F. Catrambone
Police Chief	Derek Kearns
Emerg/Fire Director	Thomas Dolaghan

Housing & Construction
Housing Units, 2000*
Total	5,254
Median rent	$723
Median SF home value	$135,000

Permits for New Residential Construction
	Units	Value
Total, 2007	519	$6,837,800
Single family	21	$976,300
Total, 2006	200	$18,470,695
Single family	144	$14,175,580

Real Property Valuation, 2007
	Parcels	Valuation
Total	2,446	$472,953,265
Vacant	109	16,068,690
Residential	1,938	269,926,765
Commercial	256	61,596,530
Industrial	70	107,866,430
Apartments	73	17,494,850
Farm land	0	0
Farm homestead	0	0

Average Property Value & Tax, 2007
Residential value	$139,281
Property tax	$6,985
Tax credit/rebate	$990

Public Library
Harrison Public Library
415 Harrison Ave
Harrison, NJ 07029
973-483-2366

Director .... Ellen Lucas

Library statistics, 2006
Population served	14,424
Full-time/total staff	NA/0

	Total	Per capita
Holdings	NA	NA
Revenues	NA	NA
Expenditures	NA	NA
Annual visits	NA	NA
Internet terminals/annual users	NA/NA	

Taxes
	2005	2006	2007
General tax rate per $100	4.424	4.626	5.016
County equalization ratio	52.07	46.41	39.44
Net valuation taxable	$480,599,440	$480,878,765	$473,338,579
State equalized value	$1,035,551,476	$1,219,701,441	$1,335,280,219

Public Safety
Number of officers, 2006 50

Crime
	2005	2006
Total crimes	454	406
Violent	68	47
Murder	2	1
Rape	1	3
Robbery	29	27
Aggravated assault	36	16
Non-violent	386	359
Burglary	56	60
Larceny	226	188
Vehicle theft	104	111
Domestic violence	79	71
Arson	1	0
Total crime rate	32.1	28.9
Violent	4.8	3.3
Non-violent	27.3	25.5

Public School District
(for school year 2006-07 except as noted)

Harrison School District
430 William St
Harrison, NJ 07029
973-483-4627

Superintendent	Anthony Comprelli
Number of schools	3
Grade plan	K-12
Enrollment	1,874
Attendance rate, '05-06	94.9%
Dropout rate	NA
Students per teacher	11.1
Per pupil expenditure	$14,309
Median faculty salary	$67,955
Median administrator salary	$111,961
Grade 12 enrollment	165
High school graduation rate	99.4%

Assessment test results
(percent scoring at proficient or advanced level)
	Language	Math
NJASK-Grade 3	79.5%	88.2%
GEPA-Grade 8	72.2%	47.7%
HSPA-High School	83.6%	71.4%

SAT score averages
Pct tested	Math	Verbal	Writing
57%	447	438	423

Teacher Qualifications
Avg. years of experience	12
Highly-qualified teachers one subject/all subjects	100%/100%
With emergency credentials	0.0%

No Child Left Behind
AYP, 2005-06 .... Meets Standards

Municipal Finance
State Aid Programs, 2008
Total aid	$9,803,567
CMPTRA	1,646,201
Energy tax receipts	8,157,366
Garden State Trust	0

General Budget, 2007
Total tax levy	$23,738,944
County levy	5,150,833
County taxes	5,025,707
County library	0
County health	0
County open space	125,125
School levy	8,566,552
Muni. levy	10,021,559
Misc. revenues	22,867,235

Gloucester County

Harrison Township

Demographics & Socio-Economic Characteristics
(2000 US Census, except as noted)

Population
1980*	3,585
1990*	4,715
2000	8,788
Male	4,360
Female	4,428
2006 (estimate)*	11,849
Population density	619.4

Race & Hispanic Origin, 2000
Race
White	8,363
Black/African American	260
American Indian/Alaska Native	11
Asian	64
Native Hawaiian/Pacific Islander	0
Other race	36
Two or more races	54
Hispanic origin, total	156
Mexican	18
Puerto Rican	79
Cuban	12
Other Hispanic	47

Age & Nativity, 2000
Under 5 years	757
18 years and over	5,866
21 years and over	5,620
65 years and over	582
85 years and over	61
Median age	35.1
Native-born	8,609
Foreign-born	179

Educational Attainment, 2000
Population 25 years and over	5,469
Less than 9th grade	1.9%
High school grad or higher	91.1%
Bachelor's degree or higher	38.5%
Graduate degree	10.8%

Income & Poverty, 1999
Per capita income	$28,645
Median household income	$77,143
Median family income	$84,379
Persons in poverty	278
H'holds receiving public assistance	23
H'holds receiving social security	516

Households, 2000
Total households	2,848
With persons under 18	1,466
With persons over 65	433
Family households	2,324
Single-person households	435
Persons per household	3.06
Persons per family	3.44

Labor & Employment
Total civilian labor force, 2006**	5,164
Unemployment rate	4.4%
Total civilian labor force, 2000	4,374
Unemployment rate	3.5%

Employed persons 16 years and over by occupation, 2000
Managers & professionals	1,951
Service occupations	289
Sales & office occupations	1,206
Farming, fishing & forestry	48
Construction & maintenance	454
Production & transportation	271
Self-employed persons	193

* US Census Bureau
** New Jersey Department of Labor

See Introduction for an explanation of all data sources.

General Information
Township of Harrison
114 Bridgeton Pike
Mullica Hill, NJ 08062
856-478-4111

Website	www.harrisontwp.us
Year of incorporation	1845
Land/water area (sq. miles)	19.13/0.05
Form of government	Township

Government
Legislative Districts
US Congressional	2
State Legislative	3

Local Officials, 2008
Mayor	Louis J. Manzo
Manager	Carole Rieck
Clerk	Diane Malloy
Finance Dir.	Yvonne Bullock
Tax Assessor	Timothy Mead
Tax Collector	Michelle Mitchell
Attorney	Brian J. Duffield
Building	Jeffrey Kier
Planning	Susanne Rhudy
Engineering	J. Michael Fralinger
Public Works	Mike Micklasavage
Police Chief	Frank Rodgers
Fire/Emergency Dir.	NA

Housing & Construction
Housing Units, 2000*
Total	2,939
Median rent	$590
Median SF home value	$181,900

Permits for New Residential Construction
	Units	Value
Total, 2007	69	$22,186,421
Single family	69	$22,186,421
Total, 2006	123	$34,023,922
Single family	123	$34,023,922

Real Property Valuation, 2007
	Parcels	Valuation
Total	4,529	$762,961,100
Vacant	641	31,226,000
Residential	3,426	664,202,700
Commercial	107	40,081,600
Industrial	0	0
Apartments	3	4,531,500
Farm land	242	3,193,000
Farm homestead	110	19,726,300

Average Property Value & Tax, 2007
Residential value	$193,419
Property tax	$7,459
Tax credit/rebate	$1,109

Public Library
No public municipal library

Library statistics, 2006
Population served	NA
Full-time/total staff	NA/NA

	Total	Per capita
Holdings	NA	NA
Revenues	NA	NA
Expenditures	NA	NA
Annual visits	NA	NA
Internet terminals/annual users	NA/NA	

Public Safety
Number of officers, 2006		16
Crime	**2005**	**2006**
Total crimes	245	176
Violent	10	5
Murder	0	0
Rape	0	1
Robbery	0	3
Aggravated assault	10	1
Non-violent	235	171
Burglary	35	39
Larceny	195	126
Vehicle theft	5	6
Domestic violence	97	78
Arson	5	4
Total crime rate	22.5	15.6
Violent	0.9	0.4
Non-violent	21.6	15.1

Public School District
(for school year 2006-07 except as noted)

Harrison Township School District
120 N Main St
Mullica Hill, NJ 08062
856-478-2016

Superintendent	Patricia Hoey
Number of schools	2
Grade plan	K-6
Enrollment	1,465
Attendance rate, '05-06	96.1%
Dropout rate	NA
Students per teacher	12.7
Per pupil expenditure	$9,610
Median faculty salary	$48,432
Median administrator salary	$93,726
Grade 12 enrollment	NA
High school graduation rate	NA

Assessment test results
(percent scoring at proficient or advanced level)
	Language	Math
NJASK-Grade 3	90.9%	88.2%
GEPA-Grade 8	NA	NA
HSPA-High School	NA	NA

SAT score averages
Pct tested	Math	Verbal	Writing
NA	NA	NA	NA

Teacher Qualifications
Avg. years of experience	8
Highly-qualified teachers one subject/all subjects	100%/100%
With emergency credentials	0.0%

No Child Left Behind
AYP, 2005-06	Meets Standards

Municipal Finance
State Aid Programs, 2008
Total aid	$736,534
CMPTRA	107,688
Energy tax receipts	628,846
Garden State Trust	0

General Budget, 2007
Total tax levy	$29,512,467
County levy	8,163,053
County taxes	7,030,320
County library	582,294
County health	0
County open space	550,440
School levy	18,594,331
Muni. levy	2,755,083
Misc. revenues	5,193,364

Taxes
	2005	2006	2007
General tax rate per $100	3.727	3.773	3.857
County equalization ratio	69.67	62.43	55.57
Net valuation taxable	$647,137,264	$705,936,500	$765,311,619
State equalized value	$1,036,580,593	$1,272,895,814	$1,435,410,436

Harvey Cedars Borough

Ocean County

Demographics & Socio-Economic Characteristics
(2000 US Census, except as noted)

Population
1980*	363
1990*	362
2000	359
Male	182
Female	177
2006 (estimate)*	389
Population density	707.3

Race & Hispanic Origin, 2000
Race
- White ... 348
- Black/African American ... 2
- American Indian/Alaska Native ... 1
- Asian ... 1
- Native Hawaiian/Pacific Islander ... 0
- Other race ... 7
- Two or more races ... 0

Hispanic origin, total ... 13
- Mexican ... 12
- Puerto Rican ... 0
- Cuban ... 0
- Other Hispanic ... 1

Age & Nativity, 2000
- Under 5 years ... 11
- 18 years and over ... 307
- 21 years and over ... 299
- 65 years and over ... 109
- 85 years and over ... 4
- Median age ... 53.7
- Native-born ... 339
- Foreign-born ... 14

Educational Attainment, 2000
- Population 25 years and over ... 308
- Less than 9th grade ... 1.9%
- High school grad or higher ... 95.1%
- Bachelor's degree or higher ... 46.1%
- Graduate degree ... 14.3%

Income & Poverty, 1999
- Per capita income ... $36,757
- Median household income ... $61,875
- Median family income ... $69,722
- Persons in poverty ... 18
- H'holds receiving public assistance ... 6
- H'holds receiving social security ... 102

Households, 2000
- Total households ... 167
- With persons under 18 ... 31
- With persons over 65 ... 76
- Family households ... 112
- Single-person households ... 49
- Persons per household ... 2.15
- Persons per family ... 2.61

Labor & Employment
- Total civilian labor force, 2006** ... 138
- Unemployment rate ... 0.0%
- Total civilian labor force, 2000 ... 134
- Unemployment rate ... 0.0%

Employed persons 16 years and over by occupation, 2000
- Managers & professionals ... 56
- Service occupations ... 20
- Sales & office occupations ... 36
- Farming, fishing & forestry ... 0
- Construction & maintenance ... 18
- Production & transportation ... 4
- Self-employed persons ... 24

* US Census Bureau
** New Jersey Department of Labor

General Information
Borough of Harvey Cedars
7606 Long Beach Blvd
PO Box 3185
Harvey Cedars, NJ 08008
609-361-6000

- Website ... www.harveycedars.org
- Year of incorporation ... 1894
- Land/water area (sq. miles) ... 0.55/0.65
- Form of government ... Commission

Government
Legislative Districts
- US Congressional ... 3
- State Legislative ... 9

Local Officials, 2008
- Mayor ... Jonathan Oldham
- Manager/Admin ... NA
- Clerk ... Daina Dale
- Finance Dir ... Sharon Sulecki
- Tax Assessor ... Bernard Haney
- Tax Collector ... Sharon Sulecki
- Attorney ... John Cerefice
- Building ... Frank Zappavigna
- Comm Dev/Planning ... NA
- Engineering ... Frank Little
- Public Works ... J. Lloyd Vosseller
- Police Chief ... Jerry Falkowski
- Emerg/Fire Director ... Sean Marti

Housing & Construction
Housing Units, 2000*
- Total ... 1,205
- Median rent ... $870
- Median SF home value ... $456,500

Permits for New Residential Construction
	Units	Value
Total, 2007	7	$2,690,400
Single family	7	$2,690,400
Total, 2006	11	$4,070,950
Single family	11	$4,070,950

Real Property Valuation, 2007
	Parcels	Valuation
Total	1,253	$1,362,325,000
Vacant	46	31,069,300
Residential	1,183	1,316,938,800
Commercial	24	14,316,900
Industrial	0	0
Apartments	0	0
Farm land	0	0
Farm homestead	0	0

Average Property Value & Tax, 2007
- Residential value ... $1,113,220
- Property tax ... $7,745
- Tax credit/rebate ... $1,268

Public Library
No public municipal library

Library statistics, 2006
- Population served ... NA
- Full-time/total staff ... NA/NA

	Total	Per capita
Holdings	NA	NA
Revenues	NA	NA
Expenditures	NA	NA
Annual visits	NA	NA
Internet terminals/annual users	NA/NA	

Taxes
	2005	2006	2007
General tax rate per $100	0.83	0.717	0.696
County equalization ratio	102.83	109.21	101.2
Net valuation taxable	$1,048,636,368	$1,356,109,000	$1,362,664,038
State equalized value	$1,231,950,620	$1,340,369,101	$1,406,102,117

Public Safety
Number of officers, 2006 ... 9

Crime	2005	2006
Total crimes	15	19
Violent	0	0
Murder	0	0
Rape	0	0
Robbery	0	0
Aggravated assault	0	0
Non-violent	15	19
Burglary	2	0
Larceny	13	19
Vehicle theft	0	0
Domestic violence	4	6
Arson	0	0
Total crime rate	39.5	49.2
Violent	0.0	0.0
Non-violent	39.5	49.2

Public School District
(for school year 2006-07 except as noted)

Long Beach Island School District
200 Barnegat Ave
Surf City, NJ 08008
609-494-2341

- Superintendent ... Robert A. Garguilo
- Number of schools ... 10
- Grade plan ... K-6
- Enrollment ... 248
- Attendance rate, '05-06 ... 94.3%
- Dropout rate ... NA
- Students per teacher ... 6.9
- Per pupil expenditure ... $21,956
- Median faculty salary ... $94,335
- Median administrator salary ... $68,857
- Grade 12 enrollment ... NA
- High school graduation rate ... NA

Assessment test results
(percent scoring at proficient or advanced level)

	Language	Math
NJASK-Grade 3	100.0%	90.0%
GEPA-Grade 8	NA	NA
HSPA-High School	NA	NA

SAT score averages
Pct tested	Math	Verbal	Writing
NA	NA	NA	NA

Teacher Qualifications
- Avg. years of experience ... 19
- Highly-qualified teachers one subject/all subjects ... 100%/100%
- With emergency credentials ... 0.0%

No Child Left Behind
AYP, 2005-06 ... Meets Standards

Municipal Finance
State Aid Programs, 2008
- Total aid ... $112,557
- CMPTRA ... 0
- Energy tax receipts ... 112,557
- Garden State Trust ... 0

General Budget, 2007
- Total tax levy ... $9,480,193
- County levy ... 4,008,451
- County taxes ... 3,439,150
- County library ... 407,664
- County health ... 0
- County open space ... 161,638
- School levy ... 2,925,193
- Muni. levy ... 2,546,549
- Misc. revenues ... 1,002,060

Bergen County
Hasbrouck Heights Borough

Demographics & Socio-Economic Characteristics
(2000 US Census, except as noted)

Population
1980*	12,166
1990*	11,488
2000	11,662
Male	5,605
Female	6,057
2006 (estimate)*	11,621
Population density	7,696.0

Race & Hispanic Origin, 2000
Race
White	10,247
Black/African American	200
American Indian/Alaska Native	5
Asian	776
Native Hawaiian/Pacific Islander	1
Other race	255
Two or more races	178
Hispanic origin, total	964
Mexican	28
Puerto Rican	241
Cuban	184
Other Hispanic	511

Age & Nativity, 2000
Under 5 years	671
18 years and over	9,076
21 years and over	8,752
65 years and over	1,986
85 years and over	235
Median age	40.1
Native-born	9,685
Foreign-born	1,977

Educational Attainment, 2000
Population 25 years and over	8,311
Less than 9th grade	5.4%
High school grad or higher	86.9%
Bachelor's degree or higher	29.9%
Graduate degree	8.1%

Income & Poverty, 1999
Per capita income	$29,626
Median household income	$64,529
Median family income	$75,032
Persons in poverty	492
H'holds receiving public assistance	45
H'holds receiving social security	1,438

Households, 2000
Total households	4,521
With persons under 18	1,475
With persons over 65	1,469
Family households	3,144
Single-person households	1,185
Persons per household	2.58
Persons per family	3.16

Labor & Employment
Total civilian labor force, 2006**	6,305
Unemployment rate	4.1%
Total civilian labor force, 2000	5,916
Unemployment rate	3.9%

Employed persons 16 years and over by occupation, 2000
Managers & professionals	2,456
Service occupations	595
Sales & office occupations	1,805
Farming, fishing & forestry	6
Construction & maintenance	351
Production & transportation	473
Self-employed persons	195

* US Census Bureau
** New Jersey Department of Labor

See Introduction for an explanation of all data sources.

General Information
Borough of Hasbrouck Heights
320 Boulevard
Hasbrouck Heights, NJ 07604
201-288-0195

Website	www.hasbrouck-heights.nj.us
Year of incorporation	1894
Land/water area (sq. miles)	1.51/0.00
Form of government	Borough

Government
Legislative Districts
US Congressional	9
State Legislative	38

Local Officials, 2008
Mayor	Rose Heck
Manager	Michael Kronyak
Clerk	Rose Marie Sees
Finance Dir	Michael Kronyak
Tax Assessor	George Reggo
Tax Collector	Conchita Parker
Attorney	Ralph W. Chandless Jr
Building	Nicholas Melfi
Comm Dev/Planning	NA
Engineering	Kenneth Job
Public Works	William Spindler
Police Chief	Michael Colaneri
Emerg/Fire Director	Michael Ratkowski

Housing & Construction
Housing Units, 2000*
Total	4,617
Median rent	$874
Median SF home value	$215,300

Permits for New Residential Construction
	Units	Value
Total, 2007	11	$2,522,977
Single family	11	$2,522,977
Total, 2006	23	$6,053,242
Single family	23	$6,053,242

Real Property Valuation, 2007
	Parcels	Valuation
Total	3,625	$1,852,638,400
Vacant	105	12,969,500
Residential	3,295	1,439,494,900
Commercial	189	307,638,600
Industrial	12	20,988,000
Apartments	24	71,547,400
Farm land	0	0
Farm homestead	0	0

Average Property Value & Tax, 2007
Residential value	$436,873
Property tax	$8,249
Tax credit/rebate	$1,270

Public Library
Hasbrouck Heights Public Library
320 Boulevard
Hasbrouck Heights, NJ 07604
201-288-0488

Director	Mimi Hui

Library statistics, 2006
Population served	11,662
Full-time/total staff	3/7

	Total	Per capita
Holdings	55,010	4.72
Revenues	$799,208	$68.53
Expenditures	$801,586	$68.73
Annual visits	56,048	4.81
Internet terminals/annual users	26/34,208	

Taxes
	2005	2006	2007
General tax rate per $100	3.52	1.78	1.89
County equalization ratio	60.64	113.7	104.81
Net valuation taxable	$875,710,063	$1,854,140,700	$1,853,773,480
State equalized value	$1,617,491,805	$1,770,175,523	$1,888,501,013

Public Safety
Number of officers, 2006	32

Crime	2005	2006
Total crimes	194	177
Violent	4	0
Murder	0	0
Rape	0	0
Robbery	4	0
Aggravated assault	0	0
Non-violent	190	177
Burglary	22	31
Larceny	148	128
Vehicle theft	20	18
Domestic violence	70	121
Arson	1	0
Total crime rate	16.6	15.2
Violent	0.3	0.0
Non-violent	16.3	15.2

Public School District
(for school year 2006-07 except as noted)

Hasbrouck Heights School District
379 Boulevard
Hasbrouck Heights, NJ 07604
201-393-8145

Superintendent	Joseph Luongo
Number of schools	4
Grade plan	K-12
Enrollment	1,556
Attendance rate, '05-06	96.1%
Dropout rate	0.9%
Students per teacher	10.9
Per pupil expenditure	$12,724
Median faculty salary	$51,885
Median administrator salary	$101,442
Grade 12 enrollment	117
High school graduation rate	99.2%

Assessment test results
(percent scoring at proficient or advanced level)
	Language	Math
NJASK-Grade 3	94.0%	96.0%
GEPA-Grade 8	83.2%	86.4%
HSPA-High School	93.8%	93.8%

SAT score averages
Pct tested	Math	Verbal	Writing
89%	532	505	506

Teacher Qualifications
Avg. years of experience	10
Highly-qualified teachers one subject/all subjects	100%/100%
With emergency credentials	0.0%

No Child Left Behind
AYP, 2005-06	Meets Standards

Municipal Finance
State Aid Programs, 2008
Total aid	$1,391,389
CMPTRA	304,831
Energy tax receipts	1,086,558
Garden State Trust	0

General Budget, 2007
Total tax levy	$35,001,222
County levy	3,194,166
County taxes	3,016,781
County library	0
County health	0
County open space	177,386
School levy	19,902,335
Muni. levy	11,904,721
Misc. revenues	4,654,137

The New Jersey Municipal Data Book

Haworth Borough

Bergen County

Demographics & Socio-Economic Characteristics
(2000 US Census, except as noted)

Population
1980*	3,509
1990*	3,384
2000	3,390
Male	1,661
Female	1,729
2006 (estimate)*	3,433
Population density	1,751.5

Race & Hispanic Origin, 2000
Race
White	2,981
Black/African American	41
American Indian/Alaska Native	0
Asian	312
Native Hawaiian/Pacific Islander	0
Other race	25
Two or more races	31
Hispanic origin, total	92
Mexican	1
Puerto Rican	12
Cuban	28
Other Hispanic	51

Age & Nativity, 2000
Under 5 years	232
18 years and over	2,411
21 years and over	2,349
65 years and over	474
85 years and over	51
Median age	41.1
Native-born	2,857
Foreign-born	533

Educational Attainment, 2000
Population 25 years and over	2,259
Less than 9th grade	1.6%
High school grad or higher	93.9%
Bachelor's degree or higher	57.0%
Graduate degree	23.9%

Income & Poverty, 1999
Per capita income	$45,615
Median household income	$101,836
Median family income	$112,500
Persons in poverty	68
H'holds receiving public assistance	13
H'holds receiving social security	304

Households, 2000
Total households	1,134
With persons under 18	519
With persons over 65	336
Family households	971
Single-person households	145
Persons per household	2.98
Persons per family	3.25

Labor & Employment
Total civilian labor force, 2006**	1,722
Unemployment rate	3.8%
Total civilian labor force, 2000	1,628
Unemployment rate	3.6%

Employed persons 16 years and over by occupation, 2000
Managers & professionals	928
Service occupations	84
Sales & office occupations	443
Farming, fishing & forestry	0
Construction & maintenance	67
Production & transportation	47
Self-employed persons	141

* US Census Bureau
** New Jersey Department of Labor

General Information
Borough of Haworth
300 Haworth Ave
Haworth, NJ 07641
201-384-4785

Website	www.haworthnj.org
Year of incorporation	1904
Land/water area (sq. miles)	1.96/0.40
Form of government	Borough

Government

Legislative Districts
US Congressional	5
State Legislative	39

Local Officials, 2008
Mayor	John DeRienzo
Manager	Ann Fay
Clerk	Ann Fay
Finance Dir	NA
Tax Assessor	Neil Rubenstein
Tax Collector	Dawn Wheeler
Attorney	Peter Scandariato
Building	Harry Kraus
Comm Dev/Planning	NA
Engineering	Schwanewede/Hals Eng.
Public Works	Martin Mahon
Police Chief	Patrick O'Dea
Emerg/Fire Director	Robert Hennion

Housing & Construction

Housing Units, 2000*
Total	1,146
Median rent	$1,625
Median SF home value	$378,400

Permits for New Residential Construction
	Units	Value
Total, 2007	12	$5,331,922
Single family	12	$5,331,922
Total, 2006	11	$5,012,919
Single family	11	$5,012,919

Real Property Valuation, 2007
	Parcels	Valuation
Total	1,216	$750,426,300
Vacant	54	17,828,700
Residential	1,118	654,232,100
Commercial	44	78,365,500
Industrial	0	0
Apartments	0	0
Farm land	0	0
Farm homestead	0	0

Average Property Value & Tax, 2007
Residential value	$585,181
Property tax	$13,345
Tax credit/rebate	$1,516

Public Library
Haworth Municipal Library
300 Haworth Ave
Haworth, NJ 07641
201-384-1020

Director: Elizabeth Rosenberg

Library statistics, 2006
Population served	3,390
Full-time/total staff	1/3

	Total	Per capita
Holdings	26,372	7.78
Revenues	$295,593	$87.20
Expenditures	$292,266	$86.21
Annual visits	25,600	7.55
Internet terminals/annual users	6/15,000	

Public Safety
Number of officers, 2006		12
Crime	**2005**	**2006**
Total crimes	4	8
Violent	1	0
Murder	0	0
Rape	0	0
Robbery	0	0
Aggravated assault	1	0
Non-violent	3	8
Burglary	1	4
Larceny	2	4
Vehicle theft	0	0
Domestic violence	3	3
Arson	0	0
Total crime rate	1.2	2.3
Violent	0.3	0.0
Non-violent	0.9	2.3

Public School District
(for school year 2006-07 except as noted)

Haworth School District
205 Valley Rd
Haworth, NJ 07641
201-501-7077

Superintendent	David Eichenholtz
Number of schools	1
Grade plan	K-8
Enrollment	528
Attendance rate, '05-06	95.6%
Dropout rate	NA
Students per teacher	10.8
Per pupil expenditure	$12,878
Median faculty salary	$51,638
Median administrator salary	$144,120
Grade 12 enrollment	NA
High school graduation rate	NA

Assessment test results
(percent scoring at proficient or advanced level)
	Language	Math
NJASK-Grade 3	97.1%	100.0%
GEPA-Grade 8	94.1%	85.1%
HSPA-High School	NA	NA

SAT score averages
Pct tested	Math	Verbal	Writing
NA	NA	NA	NA

Teacher Qualifications
Avg. years of experience	7
Highly-qualified teachers one subject/all subjects	100%/100%
With emergency credentials	0.0%

No Child Left Behind
AYP, 2005-06 .... Meets Standards

Municipal Finance

State Aid Programs, 2008
Total aid	$747,014
CMPTRA	0
Energy tax receipts	727,744
Garden State Trust	0

General Budget, 2007
Total tax levy	$17,118,989
County levy	1,684,734
County taxes	1,591,958
County library	0
County health	0
County open space	92,776
School levy	10,707,054
Muni. levy	4,727,201
Misc. revenues	1,805,955

Taxes
	2005	2006	2007
General tax rate per $100	2.1	2.16	2.29
County equalization ratio	99.81	88.31	81
Net valuation taxable	$733,076,067	$742,422,500	$750,686,547
State equalized value	$830,116,710	$916,849,843	$967,304,448

Passaic County

Hawthorne Borough

Demographics & Socio-Economic Characteristics
(2000 US Census, except as noted)

Population
- 1980* 18,200
- 1990* 17,084
- 2000 18,218
  - Male 8,686
  - Female 9,532
- 2006 (estimate)* 18,166
- Population density 5,342.9

Race & Hispanic Origin, 2000
Race
- White 17,080
- Black/African American 137
- American Indian/Alaska Native 25
- Asian 344
- Native Hawaiian/Pacific Islander 3
- Other race 287
- Two or more races 342
- Hispanic origin, total 1,354
  - Mexican 55
  - Puerto Rican 345
  - Cuban 99
  - Other Hispanic 855

Age & Nativity, 2000
- Under 5 years 1,155
- 18 years and over 14,252
- 21 years and over 13,797
- 65 years and over 2,817
- 85 years and over 347
  - Median age 38.2
- Native-born 15,684
- Foreign-born 2,534

Educational Attainment, 2000
- Population 25 years and over 13,122
- Less than 9th grade 6.4%
- High school grad or higher 84.3%
- Bachelor's degree or higher 25.6%
- Graduate degree 7.9%

Income & Poverty, 1999
- Per capita income $26,551
- Median household income $55,340
- Median family income $65,451
- Persons in poverty 619
- H'holds receiving public assistance 59
- H'holds receiving social security 2,140

Households, 2000
- Total households 7,260
  - With persons under 18 2,216
  - With persons over 65 2,095
  - Family households 4,933
  - Single-person households 1,922
- Persons per household 2.50
- Persons per family 3.07

Labor & Employment
- Total civilian labor force, 2006** ... 10,771
  - Unemployment rate 2.9%
- Total civilian labor force, 2000 9,925
  - Unemployment rate 2.9%

Employed persons 16 years and over by occupation, 2000
- Managers & professionals 3,462
- Service occupations 1,387
- Sales & office occupations 3,090
- Farming, fishing & forestry 13
- Construction & maintenance 826
- Production & transportation 858
- Self-employed persons 574

* US Census Bureau
** New Jersey Department of Labor

See Introduction for an explanation of all data sources.

General Information
Borough of Hawthorne
445 Lafayette Ave
Hawthorne, NJ 07506
973-427-5555

- Website .... www.hawthornenj.org
- Year of incorporation 1898
- Land/water area (sq. miles) 3.40/0.02
- Form of government .... Mayor-Council

Government
Legislative Districts
- US Congressional 9
- State Legislative 35

Local Officials, 2008
- Mayor .... Patrick J. Botbyl
- Manager .... Eric Maurer
- Clerk .... Jean Mele
- Finance Dir .... Mary Jeanne Hewitt
- Tax Assessor .... Tim Henderson
- Tax Collector .... Barbara Crowley
- Attorney .... Michael Pasquale
- Building .... John Pallotta
- Comm Dev/Planning .... NA
- Engineering .... Stephen Boswell
- Public Works .... NA
- Police Chief .... Robert Scully (Actg)
- Emerg/Fire Director ..... Joseph Speranza

Housing & Construction
Housing Units, 2000*
- Total 7,419
- Median rent $949
- Median SF home value $198,600

Permits for New Residential Construction

	Units	Value
Total, 2007	6	$933,650
Single family	4	$873,650
Total, 2006	89	$7,632,960
Single family	89	$7,632,960

Real Property Valuation, 2007

	Parcels	Valuation
Total	5,975	$1,223,567,650
Vacant	225	15,201,600
Residential	5,346	978,314,050
Commercial	276	122,246,400
Industrial	109	84,517,200
Apartments	19	23,288,400
Farm land	0	0
Farm homestead	0	0

Average Property Value & Tax, 2007
- Residential value $182,999
- Property tax $7,805
- Tax credit/rebate $1,194

Public Library
Louis Bay 2nd Library
345 Lafayette Ave
Hawthorne, NJ 07506
973-427-5745

- Director .... Thomas Frawley

Library statistics, 2006
- Population served 18,218
- Full-time/total staff 2/11

	Total	Per capita
Holdings	102,697	5.64
Revenues	$1,043,024	$57.25
Expenditures	$1,087,002	$59.67
Annual visits	84,506	4.64
Internet terminals/annual users		6/18,382

Taxes

	2005	2006	2007
General tax rate per $100	3.87	4.09	4.27
County equalization ratio	58.68	52.74	47.59
Net valuation taxable	$1,217,455,045	$1,221,228,650	$1,224,345,290
State equalized value	$2,308,409,262	$2,566,988,859	$2,724,053,068

Public Safety
Number of officers, 2006 31

Crime

	2005	2006
Total crimes	289	259
Violent	10	10
Murder	0	1
Rape	0	0
Robbery	1	3
Aggravated assault	9	6
Non-violent	279	249
Burglary	54	42
Larceny	207	191
Vehicle theft	18	16
Domestic violence	107	100
Arson	0	0
Total crime rate	15.7	14.2
Violent	0.5	0.5
Non-violent	15.2	13.6

Public School District
(for school year 2006-07 except as noted)

Hawthorne School District
445 Lafayette Ave
Hawthorne, NJ 07506
973-423-6401

- Chief School Admin .... Richard Spirito
- Number of schools 5
- Grade plan K-12
- Enrollment 2,382
- Attendance rate, '05-06 .... 95.5%
- Dropout rate .... NA
- Students per teacher 10.6
- Per pupil expenditure $12,729
- Median faculty salary $47,030
- Median administrator salary $108,135
- Grade 12 enrollment 160
- High school graduation rate 100.0%

Assessment test results
(percent scoring at proficient or advanced level)

	Language	Math
NJASK-Grade 3	84.4%	84.9%
GEPA-Grade 8	73.8%	72.5%
HSPA-High School	88.6%	77.1%

SAT score averages

Pct tested	Math	Verbal	Writing
86%	496	498	488

Teacher Qualifications
- Avg. years of experience 8
- Highly-qualified teachers
  - one subject/all subjects 99.0%/99.0%
- With emergency credentials 0.0%

No Child Left Behind
- AYP, 2005-06 .... Meets Standards

Municipal Finance
State Aid Programs, 2008
- Total aid $1,884,670
  - CMPTRA 499,568
  - Energy tax receipts 1,385,102
  - Garden State Trust 0

General Budget, 2007
- Total tax levy $52,216,005
  - County levy 12,792,879
    - County taxes 12,534,404
    - County library 0
    - County health 0
    - County open space 258,474
  - School levy 28,276,801
  - Muni. levy 11,146,325
- Misc. revenues 6,281,490

©2008 Information Publications, Inc. All rights reserved.

The New Jersey Municipal Data Book

Hazlet Township
Monmouth County

Demographics & Socio-Economic Characteristics
(2000 US Census, except as noted)

Population
- 1980* 23,013
- 1990* 21,976
- 2000 21,378
  - Male 10,217
  - Female 11,161
- 2006 (estimate)* 20,936
- Population density 3,725.3

Race & Hispanic Origin, 2000
Race
- White 19,918
- Black/African American 235
- American Indian/Alaska Native 12
- Asian 725
- Native Hawaiian/Pacific Islander ... 1
- Other race 242
- Two or more races 245
- Hispanic origin, total 1,254
  - Mexican 137
  - Puerto Rican 564
  - Cuban 107
  - Other Hispanic 446

Age & Nativity, 2000
- Under 5 years 1,400
- 18 years and over 15,932
- 21 years and over 15,259
- 65 years and over 2,879
- 85 years and over 294
  - Median age 38.5
- Native-born 19,719
- Foreign-born 1,659

Educational Attainment, 2000
- Population 25 years and over ... 14,567
- Less than 9th grade 3.7%
- High school grad or higher 83.8%
- Bachelor's degree or higher 19.2%
- Graduate degree 6.0%

Income & Poverty, 1999
- Per capita income $25,262
- Median household income $65,697
- Median family income $71,361
- Persons in poverty 727
- H'holds receiving public assistance ... 108
- H'holds receiving social security ... 2,274

Households, 2000
- Total households 7,244
  - With persons under 18 2,925
  - With persons over 65 2,054
  - Family households 5,799
  - Single-person households 1,253
- Persons per household 2.92
- Persons per family 3.32

Labor & Employment
- Total civilian labor force, 2006** ... 11,529
  - Unemployment rate 4.5%
- Total civilian labor force, 2000 ... 10,746
  - Unemployment rate 4.6%
- *Employed persons 16 years and over by occupation, 2000*
  - Managers & professionals 3,424
  - Service occupations 1,320
  - Sales & office occupations .. 3,265
  - Farming, fishing & forestry 25
  - Construction & maintenance .. 1,082
  - Production & transportation . 1,138
- Self-employed persons 373

‡ Branch of county library
* US Census Bureau
** New Jersey Department of Labor

General Information
Township of Hazlet
1766 Union Avenue
PO Box 371
Hazlet, NJ 07730
732-264-1700
- Website .... www.hazlettwp.org
- Year of incorporation 1967
- Land/water area (sq. miles) ... 5.62/0.04
- Form of government .... Township

Government
Legislative Districts
- US Congressional 6
- State Legislative 13

Local Officials, 2008
- Mayor .... James C. DiNardo
- Manager .... Michael F. Muscillo
- Clerk .... Evelyn A. Grandi
- Finance Dir ..... Catherine M. Campbell
- Tax Assessor ...... Elizabeth Cusumano
- Tax Collector ..... Patricia A. McCarthy
- Attorney .... Daniel J. McCarthy
- Building .... Dennis Pino
- Planning .... Jeffrey Tyler
- Engineering .... Greg Valesi
- Public Works .... David Rooke
- Police Chief .... James Broderick
- Emerg/Fire Director ..... Tito Acevedo

Housing & Construction
Housing Units, 2000*
- Total 7,406
- Median rent $510
- Median SF home value $173,700

Permits for New Residential Construction

	Units	Value
Total, 2007	22	$3,650,952
Single family	22	$3,650,952
Total, 2006	22	$3,068,644
Single family	22	$3,068,644

Real Property Valuation, 2007

	Parcels	Valuation
Total	6,798	$1,066,264,300
Vacant	204	10,088,000
Residential	6,225	843,287,700
Commercial	361	195,193,400
Industrial	7	17,690,400
Apartments	0	0
Farm land	1	4,800
Farm homestead	0	0

Average Property Value & Tax, 2007
- Residential value $135,468
- Property tax $6,145
- Tax credit/rebate $1,082

Public Library
Hazlet Township Library‡
251 Middle Rd
Hazlet, NJ 07730
732-264-7164
- Branch Librarian ...... Beth Henderson

Library statistics, 2006
see Monmouth County profile for library system statistics

Public Safety
- Number of officers, 2006 46

Crime	2005	2006
Total crimes	242	301
Violent	7	9
Murder	0	0
Rape	0	2
Robbery	3	0
Aggravated assault	4	7
Non-violent	235	292
Burglary	30	51
Larceny	187	220
Vehicle theft	18	21
Domestic violence	148	151
Arson	2	0
Total crime rate	11.4	14.3
Violent	0.3	0.4
Non-violent	11.1	13.9

Public School District
(for school year 2006-07 except as noted)

Hazlet Township School District
421 Middle Rd
Hazlet, NJ 07730
732-264-8402
- Superintendent .... William George
- Number of schools 8
- Grade plan K-12
- Enrollment 3,378
- Attendance rate, '05-06 .... 95.1%
- Dropout rate 0.2%
- Students per teacher 11.3
- Per pupil expenditure $12,701
- Median faculty salary $50,120
- Median administrator salary ... $107,977
- Grade 12 enrollment 215
- High school graduation rate ... 99.5%

Assessment test results
(percent scoring at proficient or advanced level)

	Language	Math
NJASK-Grade 3	86.7%	92.4%
GEPA-Grade 8	88.3%	83.3%
HSPA-High School	92.0%	89.9%

SAT score averages

Pct tested	Math	Verbal	Writing
87%	505	483	481

Teacher Qualifications
- Avg. years of experience 10
- Highly-qualified teachers
  - one subject/all subjects ... 100%/100%
- With emergency credentials 0.0%

No Child Left Behind
- AYP, 2005-06 .... Meets Standards

Municipal Finance
State Aid Programs, 2008
- Total aid $2,416,612
  - CMPTRA 766,720
  - Energy tax receipts 1,649,892
  - Garden State Trust 0

General Budget, 2007
- Total tax levy $48,406,375
  - County levy 6,635,087
    - County taxes 5,925,630
    - County library 339,222
    - County health 0
    - County open space 370,235
  - School levy 30,629,438
  - Muni. levy 11,141,850
  - Misc. revenues 6,556,644

Taxes	2005	2006	2007
General tax rate per $100	4.105	4.373	4.537
County equalization ratio	55.61	49.49	43.46
Net valuation taxable	$1,057,465,395	$1,064,593,600	$1,067,070,090
State equalized value	$2,136,725,389	$2,450,492,919	$2,663,803,542

Middlesex County
Helmetta Borough

Demographics & Socio-Economic Characteristics
(2000 US Census, except as noted)

Population
1980*	955
1990*	1,211
2000	1,825
Male	905
Female	920
2006 (estimate)*	2,023
Population density	2,380.0

Race & Hispanic Origin, 2000
Race
White	1,700
Black/African American	44
American Indian/Alaska Native	4
Asian	44
Native Hawaiian/Pacific Islander	1
Other race	16
Two or more races	16
Hispanic origin, total	97
Mexican	4
Puerto Rican	43
Cuban	2
Other Hispanic	48

Age & Nativity, 2000
Under 5 years	124
18 years and over	1,422
21 years and over	1,358
65 years and over	113
85 years and over	12
Median age	35.8
Native-born	1,659
Foreign-born	166

Educational Attainment, 2000
Population 25 years and over	1,308
Less than 9th grade	4.2%
High school grad or higher	88.8%
Bachelor's degree or higher	18.4%
Graduate degree	3.2%

Income & Poverty, 1999
Per capita income	$26,668
Median household income	$60,125
Median family income	$64,659
Persons in poverty	61
H'holds receiving public assistance	11
H'holds receiving social security	116

Households, 2000
Total households	746
With persons under 18	256
With persons over 65	89
Family households	495
Single-person households	191
Persons per household	2.45
Persons per family	3.01

Labor & Employment
Total civilian labor force, 2006**	1,271
Unemployment rate	4.8%
Total civilian labor force, 2000	1,141
Unemployment rate	3.9%

Employed persons 16 years and over by occupation, 2000
Managers & professionals	319
Service occupations	168
Sales & office occupations	344
Farming, fishing & forestry	0
Construction & maintenance	110
Production & transportation	156
Self-employed persons	40

* US Census Bureau
** New Jersey Department of Labor

General Information
Borough of Helmetta
60 Main St
PO Box 378
Helmetta, NJ 08828
732-521-4946

Website	www.helmettaboro.com
Year of incorporation	1888
Land/water area (sq. miles)	0.85/0.05
Form of government	Borough

Government

Legislative Districts
US Congressional	12
State Legislative	18

Local Officials, 2008
Mayor	Nancy Martin
Manager	William Schmeling
Clerk	Sandra Bohinski
Finance Dir	Lori Russo
Tax Assessor	Kenneth Pacera
Tax Collector	Denise Jawidzik
Attorney	David Clark
Building	Robert Simonelli
Comm Dev/Planning	NA
Engineering	Terence M. Vogt
Public Works	Darren Doran
Police Chief	Cully Lewis
Emerg/Fire Director	Vincent Amobile

Housing & Construction

Housing Units, 2000*
Total	769
Median rent	$1,051
Median SF home value	$148,300

Permits for New Residential Construction
	Units	Value
Total, 2007	3	$512,000
Single family	3	$512,000
Total, 2006	0	$0
Single family	0	$0

Real Property Valuation, 2007
	Parcels	Valuation
Total	927	$250,335,900
Vacant	42	2,387,500
Residential	868	238,202,600
Commercial	12	6,167,700
Industrial	5	3,578,100
Apartments	0	0
Farm land	0	0
Farm homestead	0	0

Average Property Value & Tax, 2007
Residential value	$274,427
Property tax	$5,219
Tax credit/rebate	$945

Public Library
No public municipal library

Library statistics, 2006
Population served	NA
Full-time/total staff	NA/NA

	Total	Per capita
Holdings	NA	NA
Revenues	NA	NA
Expenditures	NA	NA
Annual visits	NA	NA
Internet terminals/annual users	NA/NA	

Public Safety
Number of officers, 2006 ... 3

Crime	2005	2006
Total crimes	9	8
Violent	3	3
Murder	0	0
Rape	0	0
Robbery	0	0
Aggravated assault	3	3
Non-violent	6	5
Burglary	1	0
Larceny	3	5
Vehicle theft	2	0
Domestic violence	0	4
Arson	0	0
Total crime rate	4.4	3.9
Violent	1.5	1.5
Non-violent	3.0	2.4

Public School District
(for school year 2006-07 except as noted)

Helmetta School District
60 Main St, PO Box 287
Helmetta, NJ 08828

No schools in district

Per pupil expenditure	NA
Median faculty salary	NA
Median administrator salary	NA
Grade 12 enrollment	NA
High school graduation rate	NA

Assessment test results
(percent scoring at proficient or advanced level)
	Language	Math
NJASK-Grade 3	NA	NA
GEPA-Grade 8	NA	NA
HSPA-High School	NA	NA

SAT score averages
Pct tested	Math	Verbal	Writing
NA	NA	NA	NA

Teacher Qualifications
Avg. years of experience	NA
Highly-qualified teachers one subject/all subjects	NA/NA
With emergency credentials	NA

No Child Left Behind
AYP, 2005-06	NA

Municipal Finance

State Aid Programs, 2008
Total aid	$105,144
CMPTRA	0
Energy tax receipts	105,144
Garden State Trust	0

General Budget, 2007
Total tax levy	$4,766,672
County levy	717,226
County taxes	642,077
County library	0
County health	0
County open space	75,148
School levy	2,987,666
Muni. levy	1,061,780
Misc. revenues	899,974

Taxes
	2005	2006	2007
General tax rate per $100	6.24	7.05	1.91
County equalization ratio	34.95	29.66	101.71
Net valuation taxable	$63,787,570	$64,824,500	$250,640,757
State equalized value	$215,062,610	$245,724,858	$252,075,852

See Introduction for an explanation of all data sources.

High Bridge Borough
Hunterdon County

Demographics & Socio-Economic Characteristics
(2000 US Census, except as noted)

Population
1980*	3,435
1990*	3,886
2000	3,776
Male	1,830
Female	1,946
2006 (estimate)*	3,763
Population density	1,561.4

Race & Hispanic Origin, 2000
Race
- White 3,634
- Black/African American 30
- American Indian/Alaska Native 13
- Asian 54
- Native Hawaiian/Pacific Islander 1
- Other race 17
- Two or more races 27

Hispanic origin, total 80
- Mexican 11
- Puerto Rican 39
- Cuban 4
- Other Hispanic 26

Age & Nativity, 2000
- Under 5 years 326
- 18 years and over 2,732
- 21 years and over 2,636
- 65 years and over 246
- 85 years and over 26
- Median age 36.1
- Native-born 3,531
- Foreign-born 245

Educational Attainment, 2000
- Population 25 years and over 2,530
- Less than 9th grade 1.9%
- High school grad or higher 92.4%
- Bachelor's degree or higher 39.1%
- Graduate degree 12.1%

Income & Poverty, 1999
- Per capita income $29,276
- Median household income $68,719
- Median family income $75,357
- Persons in poverty 120
- H'holds receiving public assistance 9
- H'holds receiving social security 202

Households, 2000
- Total households 1,428
- With persons under 18 587
- With persons over 65 187
- Family households 1,051
- Single-person households 298
- Persons per household 2.64
- Persons per family 3.10

Labor & Employment
- Total civilian labor force, 2006** 2,565
- Unemployment rate 3.5%
- Total civilian labor force, 2000 2,273
- Unemployment rate 2.7%

Employed persons 16 years and over by occupation, 2000
- Managers & professionals 892
- Service occupations 310
- Sales & office occupations 642
- Farming, fishing & forestry 0
- Construction & maintenance 212
- Production & transportation 156
- Self-employed persons 142

* US Census Bureau
** New Jersey Department of Labor

General Information
Borough of High Bridge
71 Main St
High Bridge, NJ 08829
908-638-6455

- Website .... www.highbridge.org
- Year of incorporation 1898
- Land/water area (sq. miles) 2.41/0.02
- Form of government .... Borough

Government
Legislative Districts
- US Congressional 7
- State Legislative 23

Local Officials, 2008
- Mayor .... Mark Desire
- Borough Admin .... Douglas Walker
- Clerk .... Diane Seals
- Finance Dir .... Bonnie Fleming
- Tax Assessor .... Pat Spychala
- Tax Collector .... Bonnie Fleming
- Attorney .... Barry Goodman
- Building .... Al Hopping
- Comm Dev/Planning .... NA
- Engineering .... H. Clay McEldowney
- Public Works .... Mark Banks
- Police Chief .... Edward Spinks
- Fire Chief .... Jeff Smith

Housing & Construction
Housing Units, 2000*
- Total 1,478
- Median rent $788
- Median SF home value $163,300

Permits for New Residential Construction
	Units	Value
Total, 2007	2	$354,540
Single family	2	$354,540
Total, 2006	3	$473,184
Single family	3	$473,184

Real Property Valuation, 2007
	Parcels	Valuation
Total	1,475	$379,471,300
Vacant	86	4,152,200
Residential	1,334	350,188,600
Commercial	28	10,530,400
Industrial	8	9,719,500
Apartments	8	3,782,200
Farm land	8	14,200
Farm homestead	3	1,084,200

Average Property Value & Tax, 2007
- Residential value $262,732
- Property tax $7,839
- Tax credit/rebate $1,153

Public Library
High Bridge Public Library
71 Main St
High Bridge, NJ 08829
908-638-8231

- Director .... Teresa Streets

Library statistics, 2006
- Population served 3,776
- Full-time/total staff 0/0

	Total	Per capita
Holdings	12,259	3.25
Revenues	$25,629	$6.79
Expenditures	$24,612	$6.52
Annual visits	6,507	1.72
Internet terminals/annual users		1/1,050

Taxes
	2005	2006	2007
General tax rate per $100	2.39	2.59	2.99
County equalization ratio	105.25	95.83	85.71
Net valuation taxable	$381,159,200	$378,812,600	$380,517,106
State equalized value	$381,770,032	$415,999,654	$434,422,294

Public Safety
Number of officers, 2006 6

Crime	2005	2006
Total crimes	41	42
Violent	1	4
Murder	0	0
Rape	1	0
Robbery	0	0
Aggravated assault	0	4
Non-violent	40	38
Burglary	1	4
Larceny	8	32
Vehicle theft	4	2
Domestic violence	6	52
Arson	0	0
Total crime rate	10.8	11.1
Violent	0.3	1.1
Non-violent	10.5	10.1

Public School District
(for school year 2006-07 except as noted)

High Bridge Borough School District
50 Thomas St
High Bridge, NJ 08829
908-638-4103

- Superintendent .... Patricia Ash
- Number of schools 2
- Grade plan K-8
- Enrollment 432
- Attendance rate, '05-06 .... 96.2%
- Dropout rate .... NA
- Students per teacher 8.9
- Per pupil expenditure $12,952
- Median faculty salary $52,156
- Median administrator salary $88,247
- Grade 12 enrollment .... NA
- High school graduation rate .... NA

Assessment test results
(percent scoring at proficient or advanced level)

	Language	Math
NJASK-Grade 3	84.4%	90.7%
GEPA-Grade 8	84.0%	88.0%
HSPA-High School	NA	NA

SAT score averages
Pct tested	Math	Verbal	Writing
NA	NA	NA	NA

Teacher Qualifications
- Avg. years of experience 13
- Highly-qualified teachers one subject/all subjects 100%/100%
- With emergency credentials 0.0%

No Child Left Behind
AYP, 2005-06 .... Meets Standards

Municipal Finance
State Aid Programs, 2008
- Total aid $210,778
- CMPTRA 0
- Energy tax receipts 185,957
- Garden State Trust 24,821

General Budget, 2007
- Total tax levy $11,353,092
- County levy 1,477,091
- County taxes 1,236,154
- County library 107,562
- County health 0
- County open space 133,375
- School levy 7,022,209
- Muni. levy 2,853,792
- Misc. revenues 3,357,208

Middlesex County

Highland Park Borough

Demographics & Socio-Economic Characteristics
(2000 US Census, except as noted)

Population
1980*	13,396
1990*	13,279
2000	13,999
Male	6,758
Female	7,241
2006 (estimate)*	14,175
Population density	7,703.8

Race & Hispanic Origin, 2000
Race
White	10,087
Black/African American	1,111
American Indian/Alaska Native	16
Asian	1,908
Native Hawaiian/Pacific Islander	12
Other race	503
Two or more races	362
Hispanic origin, total	1,145
Mexican	247
Puerto Rican	287
Cuban	46
Other Hispanic	565

Age & Nativity, 2000
Under 5 years	836
18 years and over	10,955
21 years and over	10,579
65 years and over	1,672
85 years and over	220
Median age	34.7
Native-born	9,914
Foreign-born	4,085

Educational Attainment, 2000
Population 25 years and over	9,801
Less than 9th grade	2.3%
High school grad or higher	91.1%
Bachelor's degree or higher	59.5%
Graduate degree	35.2%

Income & Poverty, 1999
Per capita income	$28,767
Median household income	$53,250
Median family income	$71,267
Persons in poverty	1,181
H'holds receiving public assistance	141
H'holds receiving social security	1,279

Households, 2000
Total households	5,899
With persons under 18	1,729
With persons over 65	1,266
Family households	3,412
Single-person households	1,857
Persons per household	2.37
Persons per family	3.06

Labor & Employment
Total civilian labor force, 2006**	8,671
Unemployment rate	4.2%
Total civilian labor force, 2000	7,846
Unemployment rate	3.8%

Employed persons 16 years and over by occupation, 2000
Managers & professionals	4,646
Service occupations	616
Sales & office occupations	1,502
Farming, fishing & forestry	0
Construction & maintenance	258
Production & transportation	526
Self-employed persons	318

* US Census Bureau
** New Jersey Department of Labor

See Introduction for an explanation of all data sources.

General Information
Borough of Highland Park
221 So 5th Ave
PO Box 1330
Highland Park, NJ 08904
732-572-3400

Website	www.hpboro.com
Year of incorporation	1905
Land/water area (sq. miles)	1.84/0.00
Form of government	Borough

Government
Legislative Districts
US Congressional	6
State Legislative	17

Local Officials, 2008
Mayor	Meryl Frank
Manager	Karen Waldron
Clerk	Joan Hullings
Finance Dir	Kathleen Kovach
Tax Assessor	Thomas Mancuso
Tax Collector	Kathleen Kovach
Attorney	Edwin Schmierer
Building	Scott Luthman
Comm Dev/Planning	NA
Engineering	David Samuel
Public Works	Donald Rish
Police Chief	Stephen Rizco
Emerg/Fire Director	Hector Malave

Housing & Construction
Housing Units, 2000*
Total	6,071
Median rent	$848
Median SF home value	$183,300

Permits for New Residential Construction
	Units	Value
Total, 2007	54	$7,443,287
Single family	7	$1,019,956
Total, 2006	57	$7,960,086
Single family	7	$1,126,755

Real Property Valuation, 2007
	Parcels	Valuation
Total	3,210	$530,409,800
Vacant	76	3,073,900
Residential	2,842	392,449,400
Commercial	194	49,407,300
Industrial	10	4,750,900
Apartments	88	80,728,300
Farm land	0	0
Farm homestead	0	0

Average Property Value & Tax, 2007
Residential value	$138,089
Property tax	$8,353
Tax credit/rebate	$1,214

Public Library
Highland Park Public Library
31 N Fifth Ave
Highland Park, NJ 08904
732-572-2750

Director	Jane Stanley

Library statistics, 2006
Population served	13,999
Full-time/total staff	4/8

	Total	Per capita
Holdings	69,714	4.98
Revenues	$930,574	$66.47
Expenditures	$947,076	$67.65
Annual visits	181,645	12.98
Internet terminals/annual users	15/23,962	

Taxes
	2005	2006	2007
General tax rate per $100	5.39	5.72	6.05
County equalization ratio	46.73	41.78	37.28
Net valuation taxable	$532,483,063	$534,753,800	$530,719,837
State equalized value	$1,274,492,731	$1,434,769,489	$1,485,219,891

Public Safety
Number of officers, 2006	28

Crime	2005	2006
Total crimes	222	243
Violent	15	16
Murder	1	0
Rape	1	1
Robbery	9	5
Aggravated assault	4	10
Non-violent	207	227
Burglary	30	32
Larceny	172	180
Vehicle theft	5	15
Domestic violence	109	77
Arson	2	0
Total crime rate	15.7	17.0
Violent	1.1	1.1
Non-violent	14.6	15.9

Public School District
(for school year 2006-07 except as noted)

Highland Park School District
435 Mansfield St
Highland Park, NJ 08904
732-572-6990

Superintendent	David Ottaviano
Number of schools	4
Grade plan	K-12
Enrollment	1,545
Attendance rate, '05-06	94.9%
Dropout rate	0.2%
Students per teacher	10.0
Per pupil expenditure	$15,006
Median faculty salary	$56,330
Median administrator salary	$115,640
Grade 12 enrollment	115
High school graduation rate	98.3%

Assessment test results
(percent scoring at proficient or advanced level)
	Language	Math
NJASK-Grade 3	85.3%	85.1%
GEPA-Grade 8	65.1%	57.4%
HSPA-High School	87.5%	81.0%

SAT score averages
Pct tested	Math	Verbal	Writing
91%	563	554	536

Teacher Qualifications
Avg. years of experience	7
Highly-qualified teachers one subject/all subjects	100%/100%
With emergency credentials	0.0%

No Child Left Behind
AYP, 2005-06	Meets Standards

Municipal Finance
State Aid Programs, 2008
Total aid	$1,256,412
CMPTRA	542,141
Energy tax receipts	714,271
Garden State Trust	0

General Budget, 2007
Total tax levy	$32,104,393
County levy	4,101,615
County taxes	3,671,857
County library	0
County health	0
County open space	429,758
School levy	20,144,926
Muni. levy	7,857,852
Misc. revenues	5,076,552

Highlands Borough
Monmouth County

Demographics & Socio-Economic Characteristics
(2000 US Census, except as noted)

Population
1980*	5,187
1990*	4,849
2000	5,097
Male	2,554
Female	2,543
2006 (estimate)*	4,987
Population density	6,561.8

Race & Hispanic Origin, 2000
Race
White	4,847
Black/African American	81
American Indian/Alaska Native	17
Asian	51
Native Hawaiian/Pacific Islander	0
Other race	30
Two or more races	71
Hispanic origin, total	207
Mexican	22
Puerto Rican	100
Cuban	21
Other Hispanic	64

Age & Nativity, 2000
Under 5 years	259
18 years and over	4,140
21 years and over	3,998
65 years and over	576
85 years and over	70
Median age	38.6
Native-born	4,789
Foreign-born	308

Educational Attainment, 2000
Population 25 years and over	3,791
Less than 9th grade	1.0%
High school grad or higher	87.9%
Bachelor's degree or higher	26.4%
Graduate degree	9.2%

Income & Poverty, 1999
Per capita income	$29,369
Median household income	$45,692
Median family income	$50,985
Persons in poverty	625
H'holds receiving public assistance	44
H'holds receiving social security	646

Households, 2000
Total households	2,450
With persons under 18	542
With persons over 65	450
Family households	1,194
Single-person households	1,021
Persons per household	2.08
Persons per family	2.90

Labor & Employment
Total civilian labor force, 2006**	3,122
Unemployment rate	5.9%
Total civilian labor force, 2000	2,905
Unemployment rate	5.7%

Employed persons 16 years and over by occupation, 2000
Managers & professionals	955
Service occupations	454
Sales & office occupations	771
Farming, fishing & forestry	23
Construction & maintenance	293
Production & transportation	242
Self-employed persons	256

* US Census Bureau
** New Jersey Department of Labor
§ State Fiscal Year July 1–June 30

General Information
Borough of Highlands
171 Bay Ave
Highlands, NJ 07732
732-872-1224

Website	www.highlandsnj.com
Year of incorporation	1900
Land/water area (sq. miles)	0.76/0.56
Form of government	Small Municipality

Government
Legislative Districts
US Congressional	6
State Legislative	11

Local Officials, 2008
Mayor	Anna C. Little
Manager/Admin	NA
Borough Clerk	Nina Light Flannery
CFO	Stephen Pfeffer
Tax Assessor	Charles Heck
Tax Collector	Patrick DeBlaso
Attorney	Joseph W. Oxley
Building	Edward Wheeler
Comm Dev/Planning	NA
Engineering	Robert Bucco
Public Works	NA
Police Chief	Joseph Blewett
Fire Chief	Kevin Branin

Housing & Construction
Housing Units, 2000*
Total	2,820
Median rent	$760
Median SF home value	$139,300

Permits for New Residential Construction
	Units	Value
Total, 2007	1	$48,000
Single family	1	$48,000
Total, 2006	10	$1,502,000
Single family	10	$1,502,000

Real Property Valuation, 2007
	Parcels	Valuation
Total	2,518	$535,903,800
Vacant	156	6,532,800
Residential	2,253	477,469,900
Commercial	100	47,140,200
Industrial	0	0
Apartments	9	4,760,900
Farm land	0	0
Farm homestead	0	0

Average Property Value & Tax, 2007
Residential value	$211,926
Property tax	$5,511
Tax credit/rebate	$1,004

Public Library
No public municipal library

Library statistics, 2006
Population served	NA
Full-time/total staff	NA/NA

	Total	Per capita
Holdings	NA	NA
Revenues	NA	NA
Expenditures	NA	NA
Annual visits	NA	NA
Internet terminals/annual users	NA/NA	

Taxes
	2005	2006	2007
General tax rate per $100	2.382	2.517	2.601
County equalization ratio	97.91	83.59	72.55
Net valuation taxable	$532,068,848	$533,838,400	$536,206,909
State equalized value	$636,522,129	$736,155,437	$798,253,973

Public Safety
Number of officers, 2006 13

Crime
	2005	2006
Total crimes	94	86
Violent	8	7
Murder	1	0
Rape	1	0
Robbery	1	0
Aggravated assault	5	7
Non-violent	86	79
Burglary	14	16
Larceny	70	60
Vehicle theft	2	3
Domestic violence	129	108
Arson	0	1
Total crime rate	18.5	17.2
Violent	1.6	1.4
Non-violent	17.0	15.8

Public School District
(for school year 2006-07 except as noted)

Highlands Borough School District
360 Navesink Ave
Highlands, NJ 07732
732-872-1476

Superintendent	Maryann Galassetti
Number of schools	1
Grade plan	K-6
Enrollment	197
Attendance rate, '05-06	93.8%
Dropout rate	NA
Students per teacher	7.0
Per pupil expenditure	$15,399
Median faculty salary	$46,440
Median administrator salary	$90,000
Grade 12 enrollment	NA
High school graduation rate	NA

Assessment test results
(percent scoring at proficient or advanced level)
	Language	Math
NJASK-Grade 3	100.0%	100.0%
GEPA-Grade 8	NA	NA
HSPA-High School	NA	NA

SAT score averages
Pct tested	Math	Verbal	Writing
NA	NA	NA	NA

Teacher Qualifications
Avg. years of experience	8
Highly-qualified teachers one subject/all subjects	100%/100%
With emergency credentials	0.0%

No Child Left Behind
AYP, 2005-06 .... Meets Standards

Municipal Finance §
State Aid Programs, 2008
Total aid	$333,794
CMPTRA	0
Energy tax receipts	332,766
Garden State Trust	1,028

General Budget, 2007
Total tax levy	$13,944,927
County levy	1,989,965
County taxes	1,777,164
County library	101,741
County health	0
County open space	111,060
School levy	7,062,614
Muni. levy	4,892,347
Misc. revenues	2,913,224

Mercer County
Hightstown Borough

Demographics & Socio-Economic Characteristics
(2000 US Census, except as noted)

Population
1980*	4,581
1990*	5,126
2000	5,216
Male	2,651
Female	2,565
2006 (estimate)*	5,300
Population density	4,308.9

Race & Hispanic Origin, 2000
Race
White	3,992
Black/African American	444
American Indian/Alaska Native	19
Asian	119
Native Hawaiian/Pacific Islander	4
Other race	503
Two or more races	135
Hispanic origin, total	1,046
Mexican	69
Puerto Rican	135
Cuban	12
Other Hispanic	830

Age & Nativity, 2000
Under 5 years	379
18 years and over	4,042
21 years and over	3,873
65 years and over	562
85 years and over	141
Median age	35.5
Native-born	4,115
Foreign-born	1,101

Educational Attainment, 2000
Population 25 years and over	3,671
Less than 9th grade	8.0%
High school grad or higher	82.1%
Bachelor's degree or higher	39.5%
Graduate degree	17.4%

Income & Poverty, 1999
Per capita income	$28,605
Median household income	$64,299
Median family income	$72,092
Persons in poverty	380
H'holds receiving public assistance	25
H'holds receiving social security	426

Households, 2000
Total households	2,001
With persons under 18	658
With persons over 65	423
Family households	1,300
Single-person households	559
Persons per household	2.60
Persons per family	3.15

Labor & Employment
Total civilian labor force, 2006**	2,832
Unemployment rate	3.4%
Total civilian labor force, 2000	3,076
Unemployment rate	3.0%

Employed persons 16 years and over by occupation, 2000
Managers & professionals	1,257
Service occupations	405
Sales & office occupations	690
Farming, fishing & forestry	15
Construction & maintenance	207
Production & transportation	411
Self-employed persons	100

‡ Branch of county library
* US Census Bureau
** New Jersey Department of Labor

See Introduction for an explanation of all data sources.

General Information
Borough of Hightstown
148 N Main St
Hightstown, NJ 08520
609-490-5100

Website	www.hightstownborough.com
Year of incorporation	1853
Land/water area (sq. miles)	1.23/0.02
Form of government	Borough

Government
Legislative Districts
US Congressional	4
State Legislative	12

Local Officials, 2008
Mayor	Robert Patten
Manager	Candace Gallagher
Clerk	Candace Gallagher
Finance Dir	George Lang
Tax Assessor	Ken Pacera
Tax Collector	Nancy Martin
Attorney	Frederick C. Raffetto
Building	George Chin
Comm Dev/Planning	Tamara Lee
Engineering	Carmela Roberts
Public Works	Larry Blake
Police Chief	James Eufemia
Emerg/Fire Director	John Archer

Housing & Construction
Housing Units, 2000*
Total	2,081
Median rent	$820
Median SF home value	$141,300

Permits for New Residential Construction
	Units	Value
Total, 2007	22	$3,823,765
Single family	22	$3,823,765
Total, 2006	21	$2,940,875
Single family	21	$2,940,875

Real Property Valuation, 2007
	Parcels	Valuation
Total	1,635	$217,054,600
Vacant	139	4,246,900
Residential	1,385	164,513,800
Commercial	100	38,822,400
Industrial	6	1,979,500
Apartments	5	7,492,000
Farm land	0	0
Farm homestead	0	0

Average Property Value & Tax, 2007
Residential value	$118,783
Property tax	$7,192
Tax credit/rebate	$1,164

Public Library
Hightstown Mem Library‡
114 Franklin St
Hightstown, NJ 08520
609-448-1474

Branch Librarian .... Linda Chorewiak

Library statistics, 2006
see Mercer County profile for library system statistics

Public Safety
Number of officers, 2006		13

Crime	2005	2006
Total crimes	112	125
Violent	14	17
Murder	0	0
Rape	0	3
Robbery	6	6
Aggravated assault	8	8
Non-violent	98	108
Burglary	17	25
Larceny	79	77
Vehicle theft	2	6
Domestic violence	41	66
Arson	2	1
Total crime rate	21.0	23.6
Violent	2.6	3.2
Non-violent	18.4	20.4

Public School District
(for school year 2006-07 except as noted)

East Windsor Regional School District
25A Leshin Lane
Hightstown, NJ 08520
609-443-7717

Superintendent	Ronald Bolandi
Number of schools	12
Grade plan	K-12
Enrollment	5,032
Attendance rate, '05-06	95.7%
Dropout rate	1.6%
Students per teacher	11.7
Per pupil expenditure	$14,597
Median faculty salary	$65,340
Median administrator salary	$108,015
Grade 12 enrollment	312
High school graduation rate	90.2%

Assessment test results
(percent scoring at proficient or advanced level)
	Language	Math
NJASK-Grade 3	85.1%	89.5%
GEPA-Grade 8	79.7%	76.1%
HSPA-High School	82.5%	72.2%

SAT score averages
Pct tested	Math	Verbal	Writing
86%	536	517	508

Teacher Qualifications
Avg. years of experience	17
Highly-qualified teachers one subject/all subjects	100%/100%
With emergency credentials	0.0%

No Child Left Behind
AYP, 2005-06 .... Needs Improvement

Municipal Finance
State Aid Programs, 2008
Total aid	$545,528
CMPTRA	177,780
Energy tax receipts	367,748
Garden State Trust	0

General Budget, 2007
Total tax levy	$13,248,509
County levy	2,502,707
County taxes	2,155,966
County library	198,893
County health	0
County open space	147,848
School levy	7,604,138
Muni. levy	3,141,664
Misc. revenues	2,644,076

Taxes	2005	2006	2007
General tax rate per $100	5.31	5.7	6.06
County equalization ratio	59.87	51.05	44.47
Net valuation taxable	$215,287,797	$215,855,800	$218,806,857
State equalized value	$421,719,485	$487,461,972	$523,267,394

The New Jersey Municipal Data Book 215

Hillsborough Township
Somerset County

Demographics & Socio-Economic Characteristics
(2000 US Census, except as noted)

Population
1980*	19,061
1990*	28,808
2000	36,634
Male	18,091
Female	18,543
2006 (estimate)*	38,110
Population density	696.8

Race & Hispanic Origin, 2000
Race
White	31,491
Black/African American	1,379
American Indian/Alaska Native	32
Asian	2,679
Native Hawaiian/Pacific Islander	23
Other race	468
Two or more races	562
Hispanic origin, total	1,740
Mexican	203
Puerto Rican	436
Cuban	133
Other Hispanic	968

Age & Nativity, 2000
Under 5 years	2,898
18 years and over	25,963
21 years and over	24,938
65 years and over	2,508
85 years and over	257
Median age	35.7
Native-born	32,233
Foreign-born	4,421

Educational Attainment, 2000
Population 25 years and over	23,743
Less than 9th grade	2.6%
High school grad or higher	92.7%
Bachelor's degree or higher	46.6%
Graduate degree	16.2%

Income & Poverty, 1999
Per capita income	$33,091
Median household income	$83,290
Median family income	$93,933
Persons in poverty	1,140
H'holds receiving public assistance	87
H'holds receiving social security	1,867

Households, 2000
Total households	12,649
With persons under 18	5,843
With persons over 65	1,740
Family households	9,797
Single-person households	2,249
Persons per household	2.88
Persons per family	3.31

Labor & Employment
Total civilian labor force, 2006**	22,108
Unemployment rate	3.2%
Total civilian labor force, 2000	20,181
Unemployment rate	2.0%

Employed persons 16 years and over by occupation, 2000
Managers & professionals	10,534
Service occupations	1,632
Sales & office occupations	5,063
Farming, fishing & forestry	92
Construction & maintenance	1,133
Production & transportation	1,326
Self-employed persons	862

‡ Branch of county library
* US Census Bureau
** New Jersey Department of Labor

General Information
Township of Hillsborough
379 S Branch Rd
Hillsborough, NJ 08844
908-369-4313

Website	www.hillsborough-nj.org
Year of incorporation	1771
Land/water area (sq. miles)	54.69/0.10
Form of government	Township

Government
Legislative Districts
US Congressional	7
State Legislative	16

Local Officials, 2008
Mayor	Anthony Ferrera
Manager	Kevin Davis
Clerk	Kevin Davis
Finance Dir.	Ronald Zilinski
Tax Assessor	Debra Blaney
Tax Collector	Ronald Zilinski
Attorney	Albert Cruz
Building	Ron Skobo
Planning	Robert Ringleheim
Engineering	William White
Public Works	Buck Sixt
Police Chief	Paul Kaminsky
Fire/Emergency Dir.	NA

Housing & Construction
Housing Units, 2000*
Total	12,854
Median rent	$931
Median SF home value	$238,600

Permits for New Residential Construction
	Units	Value
Total, 2007	183	$36,723,690
Single family	156	$32,209,104
Total, 2006	114	$16,577,025
Single family	37	$14,344,977

Real Property Valuation, 2007
	Parcels	Valuation
Total	14,346	$3,685,168,000
Vacant	1,275	71,723,900
Residential	12,082	3,092,768,800
Commercial	345	286,934,200
Industrial	121	130,420,400
Apartments	9	41,824,100
Farm land	342	4,128,700
Farm homestead	172	57,367,900

Average Property Value & Tax, 2007
Residential value	$257,070
Property tax	$7,522
Tax credit/rebate	$1,117

Public Library
Hillsborough Branch Library‡
379 S Branch Rd
Hillsborough, NJ 08844
908-369-2200

Branch Librarian............Edward Hoag

Library statistics, 2006
see Somerset County profile for library system statistics

Public Safety
Number of officers, 2006.............55

Crime	2005	2006
Total crimes	368	368
Violent	18	21
Murder	0	0
Rape	1	5
Robbery	4	5
Aggravated assault	13	11
Non-violent	350	347
Burglary	60	80
Larceny	274	251
Vehicle theft	16	16
Domestic violence	390	341
Arson	9	2
Total crime rate	9.7	9.7
Violent	0.5	0.6
Non-violent	9.2	9.2

Public School District
(for school year 2006-07 except as noted)

Hillsborough Township School District
379 S Branch Rd
Hillsborough, NJ 08844
908-369-0030

Superintendent	Edward J. Forsthoffer III
Number of schools	9
Grade plan	K-12
Enrollment	7,559
Attendance rate, '05-06	95.8%
Dropout rate	0.5%
Students per teacher	10.2
Per pupil expenditure	$11,964
Median faculty salary	$57,831
Median administrator salary	$109,725
Grade 12 enrollment	577
High school graduation rate	98.4%

Assessment test results
(percent scoring at proficient or advanced level)
	Language	Math
NJASK-Grade 3	92.7%	96.2%
GEPA-Grade 8	90.7%	83.5%
HSPA-High School	96.5%	91.3%

SAT score averages
Pct tested	Math	Verbal	Writing
92%	550	520	524

Teacher Qualifications
Avg. years of experience	10
Highly-qualified teachers one subject/all subjects	100%/100%
With emergency credentials	0.4%

No Child Left Behind
AYP, 2005-06............Meets Standards

Municipal Finance
State Aid Programs, 2008
Total aid	$4,206,364
CMPTRA	708,037
Energy tax receipts	3,473,004
Garden State Trust	25,323

General Budget, 2007
Total tax levy	$108,077,862
County levy	19,540,079
County taxes	15,803,245
County library	2,006,253
County health	0
County open space	1,730,582
School levy	72,347,059
Muni. levy	16,190,724
Misc. revenues	12,705,698

Taxes
	2005	2006	2007
General tax rate per $100	2.74	2.82	2.93
County equalization ratio	76.1	70.09	64.06
Net valuation taxable	$3,603,640,564	$3,622,804,700	$3,693,852,115
State equalized value	$5,141,447,516	$5,664,669,359	$6,056,883,688

Bergen County
Hillsdale Borough

Demographics & Socio-Economic Characteristics
(2000 US Census, except as noted)

Population
1980*	10,495
1990*	9,750
2000	10,087
Male	4,915
Female	5,172
2006 (estimate)*	10,053
Population density	3,373.5

Race & Hispanic Origin, 2000
Race
White	9,321
Black/African American	86
American Indian/Alaska Native	7
Asian	512
Native Hawaiian/Pacific Islander	4
Other race	87
Two or more races	70
Hispanic origin, total	429
Mexican	76
Puerto Rican	70
Cuban	55
Other Hispanic	228

Age & Nativity, 2000
Under 5 years	736
18 years and over	7,465
21 years and over	7,235
65 years and over	1,493
85 years and over	146
Median age	39.5
Native-born	8,744
Foreign-born	1,343

Educational Attainment, 2000
Population 25 years and over	6,903
Less than 9th grade	2.4%
High school grad or higher	92.4%
Bachelor's degree or higher	45.8%
Graduate degree	17.0%

Income & Poverty, 1999
Per capita income	$34,651
Median household income	$82,904
Median family income	$90,861
Persons in poverty	334
H'holds receiving public assistance	51
H'holds receiving social security	1,021

Households, 2000
Total households	3,502
With persons under 18	1,405
With persons over 65	1,041
Family households	2,849
Single-person households	551
Persons per household	2.87
Persons per family	3.20

Labor & Employment
Total civilian labor force, 2006**	5,506
Unemployment rate	2.7%
Total civilian labor force, 2000	5,207
Unemployment rate	2.8%

Employed persons 16 years and over by occupation, 2000
Managers & professionals	2,326
Service occupations	553
Sales & office occupations	1,612
Farming, fishing & forestry	0
Construction & maintenance	382
Production & transportation	186
Self-employed persons	348

* US Census Bureau
** New Jersey Department of Labor

See Introduction for an explanation of all data sources.

General Information
Borough of Hillsdale
380 Hillsdale Ave
Hillsdale, NJ 07642
201-666-4800

Website	www.hillsdalenj.org
Year of incorporation	1923
Land/water area (sq. miles)	2.98/0.00
Form of government	Borough

Government
Legislative Districts
US Congressional	5
State Legislative	39

Local Officials, 2008
Mayor	John Sapanara
Manager	Harold Karns
Clerk	Robert Sandt
Finance Dir	Harold Karns
Tax Assessor	Richard Mohr
Tax Collector	Marilyn Feigle
Attorney	Elizabeth Randall
Building	Keith Durie
Comm Dev/Planning	NA
Engineering	Christopher Statile
Public Works	Keith Durie
Police Chief	Elwood Stalter
Emerg/Fire Director	Terence Beutel

Housing & Construction
Housing Units, 2000*
Total	3,547
Median rent	$926
Median SF home value	$291,800

Permits for New Residential Construction
	Units	Value
Total, 2007	11	$2,837,300
Single family	1	$687,300
Total, 2006	4	$1,401,150
Single family	4	$1,401,150

Real Property Valuation, 2007
	Parcels	Valuation
Total	3,479	$1,957,694,200
Vacant	66	12,213,500
Residential	3,296	1,819,107,700
Commercial	99	108,183,300
Industrial	12	14,315,500
Apartments	2	1,995,300
Farm land	2	13,100
Farm homestead	2	1,865,800

Average Property Value & Tax, 2007
Residential value	$552,145
Property tax	$9,846
Tax credit/rebate	$1,334

Public Library
Hillsdale Public Library
509 Hillsdale Ave
Hillsdale, NJ 07642
201-358-5072

Director... David J. Franz

Library statistics, 2006
Population served	10,087
Full-time/total staff	3/4

	Total	Per capita
Holdings	65,922	6.54
Revenues	$645,173	$63.96
Expenditures	$647,357	$64.18
Annual visits	85,000	8.43
Internet terminals/annual users	18/30,000	

Taxes
	2005	2006	2007
General tax rate per $100	3.52	3.8	1.79
County equalization ratio	55.21	48.6	100.7
Net valuation taxable	$847,398,387	$846,424,800	$1,964,439,900
State equalized value	$1,743,618,080	$1,932,943,252	$1,981,023,836

Public Safety
Number of officers, 2006 ... 20

Crime	2005	2006
Total crimes	59	92
Violent	2	3
Murder	0	0
Rape	0	0
Robbery	0	0
Aggravated assault	2	3
Non-violent	57	89
Burglary	7	7
Larceny	50	81
Vehicle theft	0	1
Domestic violence	14	18
Arson	0	0
Total crime rate	5.8	9.1
Violent	0.2	0.3
Non-violent	5.6	8.8

Public School District
(for school year 2006-07 except as noted)

Hillsdale School District
32 Ruckman Rd
Hillsdale, NJ 07642
201-664-0282

Superintendent	Anthony S. DeNorchia
Number of schools	3
Grade plan	K-8
Enrollment	1,455
Attendance rate, '05-06	96.8%
Dropout rate	NA
Students per teacher	12.3
Per pupil expenditure	$11,053
Median faculty salary	$51,851
Median administrator salary	$118,650
Grade 12 enrollment	NA
High school graduation rate	NA

Assessment test results
(percent scoring at proficient or advanced level)
	Language	Math
NJASK-Grade 3	92.2%	91.6%
GEPA-Grade 8	87.2%	82.2%
HSPA-High School	NA	NA

SAT score averages
Pct tested	Math	Verbal	Writing
NA	NA	NA	NA

Teacher Qualifications
Avg. years of experience	7
Highly-qualified teachers one subject/all subjects	100%/100%
With emergency credentials	0.0%

No Child Left Behind
AYP, 2005-06 ... Meets Standards

Municipal Finance
State Aid Programs, 2008
Total aid	$1,520,542
CMPTRA	192,253
Energy tax receipts	1,325,986
Garden State Trust	0

General Budget, 2007
Total tax levy	$35,030,189
County levy	3,549,699
County taxes	3,354,162
County library	0
County health	0
County open space	195,537
School levy	24,647,345
Muni. levy	6,833,145
Misc. revenues	4,386,144

©2008 Information Publications, Inc. All rights reserved. Photocopying prohibited. For additional copies, contact the publisher at www.informationpublications.com or (877)544-INFO (4636)

The New Jersey Municipal Data Book

Hillside Township
Union County

Demographics & Socio-Economic Characteristics
(2000 US Census, except as noted)

Population
1980*	21,440
1990*	21,044
2000	21,747
Male	10,199
Female	11,548
2006 (estimate)*	21,684
Population density	7,772.0

Race & Hispanic Origin, 2000
Race
White	8,705
Black/African American	10,122
American Indian/Alaska Native	50
Asian	751
Native Hawaiian/Pacific Islander	17
Other race	1,144
Two or more races	958
Hispanic origin, total	3,153
Mexican	56
Puerto Rican	832
Cuban	402
Other Hispanic	1,863

Age & Nativity, 2000
Under 5 years	1,390
18 years and over	16,185
21 years and over	15,321
65 years and over	2,410
85 years and over	253
Median age	35.7
Native-born	15,788
Foreign-born	5,959

Educational Attainment, 2000
Population 25 years and over	14,279
Less than 9th grade	10.0%
High school grad or higher	76.1%
Bachelor's degree or higher	18.5%
Graduate degree	5.6%

Income & Poverty, 1999
Per capita income	$21,724
Median household income	$59,136
Median family income	$64,635
Persons in poverty	1,147
H'holds receiving public assistance	279
H'holds receiving social security	1,849

Households, 2000
Total households	7,161
With persons under 18	3,081
With persons over 65	1,808
Family households	5,579
Single-person households	1,288
Persons per household	3.04
Persons per family	3.45

Labor & Employment
Total civilian labor force, 2006**	12,046
Unemployment rate	7.4%
Total civilian labor force, 2000	11,436
Unemployment rate	7.0%

Employed persons 16 years and over by occupation, 2000
Managers & professionals	2,935
Service occupations	1,567
Sales & office occupations	3,210
Farming, fishing & forestry	9
Construction & maintenance	969
Production & transportation	1,943
Self-employed persons	295

* US Census Bureau
** New Jersey Department of Labor
§ State Fiscal Year July 1–June 30

General Information
Township of Hillside
Liberty & Hillside Aves
Hillside, NJ 07205
973-926-3000

Website	NA
Year of incorporation	1913
Land/water area (sq. miles)	2.79/0.00
Form of government	Mayor-Council

Government
Legislative Districts
US Congressional	10
State Legislative	29

Local Officials, 2008
Mayor	Karen McCoy Oliver
Manager/Admin	NA
Clerk	Janet Vlaisavljevic
Finance Dir	Marie Pardo
Tax Assessor	Benard Murdoch
Tax Collector	Joe Skelly
Attorney	Christine Burgess
Building	Larry Ditzel
Comm Dev/Planning	NA
Engineering	Victor Vinegra
Public Works	Scott Anderson
Police Chief	Robert Quinlan
Emerg/Fire Director	Dominick Naples

Housing & Construction
Housing Units, 2000*
Total	7,388
Median rent	$797
Median SF home value	$135,200

Permits for New Residential Construction
	Units	Value
Total, 2007	9	$997,000
Single family	5	$708,000
Total, 2006	25	$2,839,290
Single family	11	$1,541,000

Real Property Valuation, 2007
	Parcels	Valuation
Total	6,284	$919,309,144
Vacant	184	7,465,800
Residential	5,647	696,949,494
Commercial	256	70,259,200
Industrial	174	133,210,350
Apartments	23	11,424,300
Farm land	0	0
Farm homestead	0	0

Average Property Value & Tax, 2007
Residential value	$123,419
Property tax	$7,516
Tax credit/rebate	$1,210

Public Library
Hillside Free Public Library
John F Kennedy Plaza
Hillside, NJ 07205
973-923-4413

Director	Miriam Bein

Library statistics, 2006
Population served	21,747
Full-time/total staff	2/6

	Total	Per capita
Holdings	106,488	4.90
Revenues	$822,344	$37.81
Expenditures	$799,438	$36.76
Annual visits	47,600	2.19
Internet terminals/annual users	20/16,320	

Taxes
	2005	2006	2007
General tax rate per $100	5.163	5.812	6.09
County equalization ratio	57.47	51.13	44.93
Net valuation taxable	$911,322,839	$916,214,627	$919,869,035
State equalized value	$1,741,492,144	$2,039,883,506	$2,335,016,834

Public Safety
Number of officers, 2006 74

Crime	2005	2006
Total crimes	905	756
Violent	109	102
Murder	0	1
Rape	11	10
Robbery	62	53
Aggravated assault	36	38
Non-violent	796	654
Burglary	152	129
Larceny	473	374
Vehicle theft	171	151
Domestic violence	351	258
Arson	4	3
Total crime rate	41.3	34.8
Violent	5.0	4.7
Non-violent	36.4	30.1

Public School District
(for school year 2006-07 except as noted)

Hillside Township School District
195 Virginia St
Hillside, NJ 07205
908-352-7664

Superintendent	Raymond J. Bandlow
Number of schools	6
Grade plan	K-12
Enrollment	3,207
Attendance rate, '05-06	93.7%
Dropout rate	4.2%
Students per teacher	12.3
Per pupil expenditure	$13,132
Median faculty salary	$57,110
Median administrator salary	$108,625
Grade 12 enrollment	171
High school graduation rate	76.4%

Assessment test results
(percent scoring at proficient or advanced level)
	Language	Math
NJASK-Grade 3	76.9%	80.5%
GEPA-Grade 8	57.9%	41.7%
HSPA-High School	71.2%	37.9%

SAT score averages
Pct tested	Math	Verbal	Writing
80%	394	406	393

Teacher Qualifications
Avg. years of experience	8
Highly-qualified teachers one subject/all subjects	98.5%/98.5%
With emergency credentials	3.0%

No Child Left Behind
AYP, 2005-06 .... Meets Standards

Municipal Finance§
State Aid Programs, 2008
Total aid	$5,253,121
CMPTRA	3,171,462
Energy tax receipts	2,081,659
Garden State Trust	0

General Budget, 2007
Total tax levy	$56,017,015
County levy	7,245,057
County taxes	6,933,141
County library	0
County health	0
County open space	311,916
School levy	24,321,784
Muni. levy	24,450,174
Misc. revenues	13,406,306

Camden County
Hi-Nella Borough

Demographics & Socio-Economic Characteristics
(2000 US Census, except as noted)

Population
1980*	1,250
1990*	1,045
2000	1,029
Male	485
Female	544
2006 (estimate)*	1,007
Population density	4,378.3

Race & Hispanic Origin, 2000
Race
- White 731
- Black/African American 198
- American Indian/Alaska Native 0
- Asian 32
- Native Hawaiian/Pacific Islander 0
- Other race 45
- Two or more races 23
- Hispanic origin, total 71
  - Mexican 12
  - Puerto Rican 42
  - Cuban 5
  - Other Hispanic 12

Age & Nativity, 2000
- Under 5 years 78
- 18 years and over 772
- 21 years and over 735
- 65 years and over 141
- 85 years and over 11
- Median age 31.8
- Native-born 965
- Foreign-born 68

Educational Attainment, 2000
- Population 25 years and over 696
- Less than 9th grade 2.4%
- High school grad or higher 79.2%
- Bachelor's degree or higher 13.8%
- Graduate degree 3.9%

Income & Poverty, 1999
- Per capita income $19,285
- Median household income $34,948
- Median family income $38,393
- Persons in poverty 126
- H'holds receiving public assistance 12
- H'holds receiving social security 112

Households, 2000
- Total households 472
  - With persons under 18 142
  - With persons over 65 105
  - Family households 260
  - Single-person households 172
- Persons per household 2.18
- Persons per family 2.83

Labor & Employment
- Total civilian labor force, 2006** 601
  - Unemployment rate 9.7%
- Total civilian labor force, 2000 539
  - Unemployment rate 8.2%

Employed persons 16 years and over by occupation, 2000
- Managers & professionals 117
- Service occupations 73
- Sales & office occupations 190
- Farming, fishing & forestry 0
- Construction & maintenance 40
- Production & transportation 75
- Self-employed persons 9

* US Census Bureau
** New Jersey Department of Labor

See Introduction for an explanation of all data sources.

General Information
Borough of Hi-Nella
100 Wykagyl Rd
Hi Nella, NJ 08083
856-784-6237

- Website .... NA
- Year of incorporation 1929
- Land/water area (sq. miles) 0.23/0.00
- Form of government .... Borough

Government
Legislative Districts
- US Congressional 1
- State Legislative 5

Local Officials, 2008
- Mayor .... Merideth Dobbs
- Manager/Admin .... NA
- Clerk .... Phyllis Twisler
- Finance Dir .... William Hales Jr
- Tax Assessor .... Richard Arrowood
- Tax Collector .... Janice Gattone
- Attorney .... Robert Messick
- Building .... DCA
- Comm Dev/Planning .... NA
- Engineering .... Churchill Consulting
- Public Works .... Gary Vonder Lieth
- Police Chief .... Dominic Palese
- Emerg/Fire Director .... Brian Cunningham

Housing & Construction
Housing Units, 2000*
- Total 495
- Median rent $650
- Median SF home value $96,700

Permits for New Residential Construction
	Units	Value
Total, 2007	0	$0
Single family	0	$0
Total, 2006	0	$0
Single family	0	$0

Real Property Valuation, 2007
	Parcels	Valuation
Total	145	$22,764,000
Vacant	3	34,300
Residential	126	11,718,400
Commercial	12	4,754,800
Industrial	0	0
Apartments	2	6,104,900
Farm land	1	11,600
Farm homestead	1	140,000

Average Property Value & Tax, 2007
- Residential value $93,373
- Property tax $5,228
- Tax credit/rebate $1,073

Public Library
No public municipal library

Library statistics, 2006
- Population served .... NA
- Full-time/total staff .... NA/NA

	Total	Per capita
Holdings	NA	NA
Revenues	NA	NA
Expenditures	NA	NA
Annual visits	NA	NA
Internet terminals/annual users	NA/NA	

Taxes
	2005	2006	2007
General tax rate per $100	5.636	5.841	5.72
County equalization ratio	73.17	65.03	58.42
Net valuation taxable	$23,147,047	$23,085,000	$22,807,808
State equalized value	$35,594,413	$39,563,203	$42,521,882

Public Safety
Number of officers, 2006 5

Crime	2005	2006
Total crimes	43	23
Violent	6	9
Murder	0	0
Rape	0	0
Robbery	1	3
Aggravated assault	5	6
Non-violent	37	14
Burglary	11	5
Larceny	23	8
Vehicle theft	3	1
Domestic violence	9	2
Arson	0	0
Total crime rate	42.2	22.7
Violent	5.9	8.9
Non-violent	36.3	13.8

Public School District
(for school year 2006-07 except as noted)

Hi Nella School District
801 Preston Ave
Somerdale, NJ 08083

No schools in district - sends students to Oaklyn schools

- Per pupil expenditure .... NA
- Median faculty salary .... NA
- Median administrator salary .... NA
- Grade 12 enrollment .... NA
- High school graduation rate .... NA

Assessment test results
(percent scoring at proficient or advanced level)

	Language	Math
NJASK-Grade 3	NA	NA
GEPA-Grade 8	NA	NA
HSPA-High School	NA	NA

SAT score averages
Pct tested	Math	Verbal	Writing
NA	NA	NA	NA

Teacher Qualifications
- Avg. years of experience .... NA
- Highly-qualified teachers one subject/all subjects .... NA/NA
- With emergency credentials .... NA

No Child Left Behind
- AYP, 2005-06 .... NA

Municipal Finance
State Aid Programs, 2008
- Total aid $68,341
  - CMPTRA 0
  - Energy tax receipts 68,341
  - Garden State Trust 0

General Budget, 2007
- Total tax levy $1,304,413
  - County levy 271,958
    - County taxes 246,767
    - County library 17,386
    - County health 0
    - County open space 7,805
  - School levy 727,714
  - Muni. levy 304,741
- Misc. revenues 400,142

©2008 Information Publications, Inc. All rights reserved.

Hoboken City — Hudson County

Demographics & Socio-Economic Characteristics
(2000 US Census, except as noted)

Population
1980*	42,460
1990*	33,397
2000	38,577
Male	19,654
Female	18,923
2006 (estimate)*	39,853
Population density	31,135.2

Race & Hispanic Origin, 2000
Race
White	31,178
Black/African American	1,644
American Indian/Alaska Native	60
Asian	1,661
Native Hawaiian/Pacific Islander	21
Other race	2,942
Two or more races	1,071
Hispanic origin, total	7,783
Mexican	359
Puerto Rican	4,660
Cuban	560
Other Hispanic	2,204

Age & Nativity, 2000
Under 5 years	1,232
18 years and over	34,543
21 years and over	33,399
65 years and over	3,483
85 years and over	392
Median age	30.4
Native-born	33,081
Foreign-born	5,588

Educational Attainment, 2000
Population 25 years and over	28,637
Less than 9th grade	8.4%
High school grad or higher	83.3%
Bachelor's degree or higher	59.4%
Graduate degree	18.7%

Income & Poverty, 1999
Per capita income	$43,195
Median household income	$62,550
Median family income	$67,500
Persons in poverty	4,124
H'holds receiving public assistance	472
H'holds receiving social security	3,118

Households, 2000
Total households	19,418
With persons under 18	2,498
With persons over 65	2,819
Family households	6,842
Single-person households	8,126
Persons per household	1.92
Persons per family	2.73

Labor & Employment
Total civilian labor force, 2006**	28,139
Unemployment rate	2.8%
Total civilian labor force, 2000	26,850
Unemployment rate	4.4%

Employed persons 16 years and over by occupation, 2000
Managers & professionals	15,655
Service occupations	1,687
Sales & office occupations	6,635
Farming, fishing & forestry	5
Construction & maintenance	495
Production & transportation	1,184
Self-employed persons	852

* US Census Bureau
** New Jersey Department of Labor
§ State Fiscal Year July 1–June 30

General Information
City of Hoboken
94 Washington St
Hoboken, NJ 07030
201-420-2000

Website	www.hobokennj.org
Year of incorporation	1855
Land/water area (sq. miles)	1.28/0.70
Form of government	Mayor-Council

Government
Legislative Districts
US Congressional	13
State Legislative	33

Local Officials, 2008
Mayor	David Roberts
Business Admin	Richard England
Clerk	James J. Farina
Finance Dir	George D. DeStefano
Tax Assessor	Sal Bonaccorsi
Tax Collector	Louis Picardo
Attorney	Steven Kleinman
Building	Alfred N. Arezzo
Comm Dev/Planning	Fred M. Bado
Engineering	Wendell Bibbs
Environmental Svcs Dir	Joseph Peluso
Police Chief	Carmen LaBruno
Emerg/Fire Director	John Cassesa

Housing & Construction
Housing Units, 2000*
Total	19,915
Median rent	$1,002
Median SF home value	$428,900

Permits for New Residential Construction
	Units	Value
Total, 2007	434	$90,542,078
Single family	0	$0
Total, 2006	879	$128,772,827
Single family	0	$390,000

Real Property Valuation, 2007
	Parcels	Valuation
Total	13,375	$2,817,503,000
Vacant	673	60,492,100
Residential	11,323	1,875,359,700
Commercial	963	475,425,100
Industrial	47	45,659,400
Apartments	369	360,566,700
Farm land	0	0
Farm homestead	0	0

Average Property Value & Tax, 2007
Residential value	$165,624
Property tax	$5,780
Tax credit/rebate	$820

Public Library
Hoboken Public Library
500 Park Ave
Hoboken, NJ 07030
201-420-2346

Director	Lina Podles

Library statistics, 2006
Population served	38,577
Full-time/total staff	4/18

	Total	Per capita
Holdings	88,276	2.29
Revenues	$1,755,910	$45.52
Expenditures	$1,718,405	$44.54
Annual visits	128,972	3.34
Internet terminals/annual users	27/17,061	

Taxes
	2005	2006	2007
General tax rate per $100	3.287	3.434	3.49
County equalization ratio	43.16	38.01	34.45
Net valuation taxable	$2,581,437,395	$2,721,640,900	$2,818,798,604
State equalized value	$6,791,469,074	$7,901,663,779	$9,459,177,444

Public Safety
Number of officers, 2006		153

Crime	2005	2006
Total crimes	1,521	1,194
Violent	118	116
Murder	1	2
Rape	2	0
Robbery	56	46
Aggravated assault	59	68
Non-violent	1,403	1,078
Burglary	391	281
Larceny	847	681
Vehicle theft	165	116
Domestic violence	180	186
Arson	5	0
Total crime rate	37.9	29.9
Violent	2.9	2.9
Non-violent	34.9	27.0

Public School District
(for school year 2006-07 except as noted)

Hoboken School District
1115 Clinton St
Hoboken, NJ 07030
201-356-3601

Superintendent	John Raslowsky
Number of schools	6
Grade plan	K-12
Enrollment	1,891
Attendance rate, '05-06	92.4%
Dropout rate	0.8%
Students per teacher	7.9
Per pupil expenditure	$16,040
Median faculty salary	$81,682
Median administrator salary	$124,019
Grade 12 enrollment	161
High school graduation rate	NA

Assessment test results
(percent scoring at proficient or advanced level)
	Language	Math
NJASK-Grade 3	78.5%	84.2%
GEPA-Grade 8	73.5%	57.2%
HSPA-High School	88.5%	75.3%

SAT score averages
Pct tested	Math	Verbal	Writing
81%	405	398	394

Teacher Qualifications
Avg. years of experience	15
Highly-qualified teachers one subject/all subjects	100%/100%
With emergency credentials	0.0%

No Child Left Behind
AYP, 2005-06	Meets Standards

Municipal Finance §
State Aid Programs, 2008
Total aid	$14,917,026
CMPTRA	12,223,817
Energy tax receipts	2,693,209
Garden State Trust	0

General Budget, 2007
Total tax levy	$98,367,509
County levy	34,281,954
County taxes	33,448,931
County library	0
County health	0
County open space	833,023
School levy	34,100,000
Muni. levy	29,985,555
Misc. revenues	48,990,848

Bergen County — Ho-Ho-Kus Borough

Demographics & Socio-Economic Characteristics
(2000 US Census, except as noted)

Population
1980*	4,129
1990*	3,935
2000	4,060
Male	1,944
Female	2,116
2006 (estimate)*	4,095
Population density	2,353.4

Race & Hispanic Origin, 2000
Race
White	3,762
Black/African American	24
American Indian/Alaska Native	4
Asian	212
Native Hawaiian/Pacific Islander	8
Other race	15
Two or more races	35
Hispanic origin, total	80
Mexican	5
Puerto Rican	16
Cuban	21
Other Hispanic	38

Age & Nativity, 2000
Under 5 years	343
18 years and over	2,942
21 years and over	2,877
65 years and over	618
85 years and over	58
Median age	41.1
Native-born	3,700
Foreign-born	360

Educational Attainment, 2000
Population 25 years and over	2,776
Less than 9th grade	1.3%
High school grad or higher	97.7%
Bachelor's degree or higher	68.3%
Graduate degree	22.6%

Income & Poverty, 1999
Per capita income	$63,594
Median household income	$129,900
Median family income	$144,588
Persons in poverty	83
H'holds receiving public assistance	0
H'holds receiving social security	381

Households, 2000
Total households	1,433
With persons under 18	574
With persons over 65	416
Family households	1,199
Single-person households	209
Persons per household	2.82
Persons per family	3.11

Labor & Employment
Total civilian labor force, 2006**	2,029
Unemployment rate	0.5%
Total civilian labor force, 2000	1,915
Unemployment rate	0.3%

Employed persons 16 years and over by occupation, 2000
Managers & professionals	1,175
Service occupations	81
Sales & office occupations	524
Farming, fishing & forestry	0
Construction & maintenance	62
Production & transportation	67
Self-employed persons	151

* US Census Bureau
** New Jersey Department of Labor

See Introduction for an explanation of all data sources.

General Information
Borough of Ho-Ho-Kus
333 Warren Ave
Ho Ho Kus, NJ 07423
201-652-4400

Website	www.ho-ho-kusboro.com
Year of incorporation	1908
Land/water area (sq. miles)	1.74/0.01
Form of government	Borough

Government
Legislative Districts
US Congressional	5
State Legislative	39

Local Officials, 2008
Mayor	Thomas W. Randall
Manager	Catherine Henderson
Clerk	Laura Borchers
Finance Dir.	Catherine Henderson
Tax Assessor	Marie Merolla
Tax Collector	NA
Attorney	David Bole
Building	Lawrence Scorzelli
Planning	Joe Clementi
Engineering	Schwanewede/Hals Eng.
Public Works	Michael Frank
Police Chief	Gregory Kallenberg
Emerg/Fire Dir.	Christopher Raimondi

Housing & Construction
Housing Units, 2000*
Total	1,465
Median rent	$1,479
Median SF home value	$456,600

Permits for New Residential Construction
	Units	Value
Total, 2007	6	$1,730,974
Single family	6	$1,730,974
Total, 2006	9	$3,209,937
Single family	9	$3,209,937

Real Property Valuation, 2007
	Parcels	Valuation
Total	1,526	$1,358,322,500
Vacant	52	15,391,100
Residential	1,430	1,283,535,800
Commercial	43	41,253,400
Industrial	1	18,142,200
Apartments	0	0
Farm land	0	0
Farm homestead	0	0

Average Property Value & Tax, 2007
Residential value	$897,577
Property tax	$11,956
Tax credit/rebate	$1,357

Public Library
Worth-Pinkham Memorial Library
91 Warren Ave
Ho-Ho-Kus, NJ 07423
201-445-8078

Director .... Sandra Witkowski

Library statistics, 2006
Population served	4,060
Full-time/total staff	0/1

	Total	Per capita
Holdings	23,693	5.84
Revenues	$392,992	$96.80
Expenditures	$278,494	$68.59
Annual visits	9,300	2.29
Internet terminals/annual users	3/408	

Public Safety
Number of officers, 2006 15

Crime
	2005	2006
Total crimes	31	14
Violent	1	0
Murder	0	0
Rape	0	0
Robbery	0	0
Aggravated assault	1	0
Non-violent	30	14
Burglary	5	3
Larceny	25	11
Vehicle theft	0	0
Domestic violence	2	3
Arson	0	0
Total crime rate	7.6	3.4
Violent	0.2	0.0
Non-violent	7.3	3.4

Public School District
(for school year 2006-07 except as noted)

Ho-Ho-Kus School District
70 Lloyd Rd
Ho-Ho-Kus, NJ 07423
201-652-4555

Superintendent	Loretta Bellina
Number of schools	1
Grade plan	K-8
Enrollment	670
Attendance rate, '05-06	95.7%
Dropout rate	NA
Students per teacher	12.0
Per pupil expenditure	$12,693
Median faculty salary	$62,460
Median administrator salary	$128,798
Grade 12 enrollment	NA
High school graduation rate	NA

Assessment test results
(percent scoring at proficient or advanced level)
	Language	Math
NJASK-Grade 3	100.0%	100.0%
GEPA-Grade 8	90.3%	89.1%
HSPA-High School	NA	NA

SAT score averages
Pct tested	Math	Verbal	Writing
NA	NA	NA	NA

Teacher Qualifications
Avg. years of experience	10
Highly-qualified teachers one subject/all subjects	100%/100%
With emergency credentials	0.0%

No Child Left Behind
AYP, 2005-06 .... Meets Standards

Municipal Finance
State Aid Programs, 2008
Total aid	$382,812
CMPTRA	0
Energy tax receipts	382,812
Garden State Trust	0

General Budget, 2007
Total tax levy	$18,103,770
County levy	2,437,448
County taxes	2,303,185
County library	0
County health	0
County open space	134,263
School levy	10,424,388
Muni. levy	5,241,934
Misc. revenues	2,129,822

Taxes
	2005	2006	2007
General tax rate per $100	2.47	1.27	1.34
County equalization ratio	62.07	114.1	101.4
Net valuation taxable	$667,161,897	$1,356,486,900	$1,359,069,432
State equalized value	$1,167,387,396	$1,338,294,571	$1,367,956,293

©2008 Information Publications, Inc. All rights reserved. Photocopying prohibited. For additional copies, contact the publisher at www.informationpublications.com or (877)544-INFO (4636)

Holland Township — Hunterdon County

Demographics & Socio-Economic Characteristics
(2000 US Census, except as noted)

Population
1980*	4,593
1990*	4,892
2000	5,124
Male	2,532
Female	2,592
2006 (estimate)*	5,310
Population density	224.1

Race & Hispanic Origin, 2000
Race
- White 5,026
- Black/African American 22
- American Indian/Alaska Native .. 2
- Asian 22
- Native Hawaiian/Pacific Islander .. 0
- Other race 20
- Two or more races 32
- Hispanic origin, total 87
  - Mexican 21
  - Puerto Rican 21
  - Cuban 10
  - Other Hispanic 35

Age & Nativity, 2000
- Under 5 years 290
- 18 years and over 3,856
- 21 years and over 3,715
- 65 years and over 741
- 85 years and over 74
- Median age 41.2
- Native-born 4,990
- Foreign-born 134

Educational Attainment, 2000
- Population 25 years and over .. 3,557
- Less than 9th grade 3.1%
- High school grad or higher .. 90.9%
- Bachelor's degree or higher . 24.3%
- Graduate degree 8.3%

Income & Poverty, 1999
- Per capita income $28,581
- Median household income ... $68,083
- Median family income $71,925
- Persons in poverty 111
- H'holds receiving public assistance .. 47
- H'holds receiving social security .. 549

Households, 2000
- Total households 1,881
  - With persons under 18 665
  - With persons over 65 501
  - Family households 1,523
  - Single-person households . 291
- Persons per household 2.72
- Persons per family 3.06

Labor & Employment
- Total civilian labor force, 2006** .. 3,019
  - Unemployment rate 4.0%
- Total civilian labor force, 2000 .. 2,677
  - Unemployment rate 2.9%

Employed persons 16 years and over by occupation, 2000
- Managers & professionals ... 958
- Service occupations 302
- Sales & office occupations .. 729
- Farming, fishing & forestry .. 9
- Construction & maintenance .. 327
- Production & transportation . 274
- Self-employed persons 198

* US Census Bureau
** New Jersey Department of Labor

General Information
Township of Holland
61 Church Rd
Milford, NJ 08848
908-995-4847

- Website .... hollandtownship.org
- Year of incorporation 1874
- Land/water area (sq. miles) .. 23.70/0.39
- Form of government .... Township

Government
Legislative Districts
- US Congressional 7
- State Legislative 23

Local Officials, 2008
- Mayor .... Bernard O'Brien
- Manager/Admin .... NA
- Clerk .... Catherine M. Miller
- Finance Dir .... Michael Balogh
- Tax Assessor ...... Michelle Trivigno
- Tax Collector .... Michael Balogh
- Attorney .... Richard Dieterly
- Building .... DCA
- Planning .... BettyAnn Bechtold
- Engineering .... Gerald Philkill
- Public Works .... Alan Turdo
- Police Chief ...... David Van Gilson
- Emerg/Fire Director ... Skip LaVigna

Housing & Construction
Housing Units, 2000*
- Total 1,942
- Median rent $905
- Median SF home value $199,000

Permits for New Residential Construction
	Units	Value
Total, 2007	6	$952,075
Single family	6	$952,075
Total, 2006	11	$1,116,446
Single family	11	$1,116,446

Real Property Valuation, 2007
	Parcels	Valuation
Total	2,452	$765,504,700
Vacant	168	15,993,100
Residential	1,859	646,038,300
Commercial	22	16,192,600
Industrial	8	17,736,700
Apartments	1	409,900
Farm land	231	2,402,600
Farm homestead	163	66,731,500

Average Property Value & Tax, 2007
- Residential value $352,507
- Property tax $6,429
- Tax credit/rebate $1,100

Public Library
Holland Township Library
129 Spring Mills Rd
Milford, NJ 08848
908-995-4767

- Director .... Donna Longcor

Library statistics, 2006
- Population served 9,822
- Full-time/total staff 0/0

	Total	Per capita
Holdings	27,723	2.82
Revenues	$70,383	$7.17
Expenditures	$61,701	$6.28
Annual visits	23,284	2.37
Internet terminals/annual users	2/2,540	

Public Safety
- Number of officers, 2006 7

Crime
	2005	2006
Total crimes	19	20
Violent	1	1
Murder	0	0
Rape	0	0
Robbery	0	0
Aggravated assault	1	1
Non-violent	18	19
Burglary	15	5
Larceny	21	14
Vehicle theft	4	0
Domestic violence	38	6
Arson	1	0
Total crime rate	3.6	3.8
Violent	0.2	0.2
Non-violent	3.4	3.6

Public School District
(for school year 2006-07 except as noted)

Holland Township School District
714 Milford-Warren Glen Rd
Milford, NJ 08848
908-995-2401

- Superintendent .... Eugene Costa
- Number of schools 2
- Grade plan K-8
- Enrollment 718
- Attendance rate, '05-06 ..... 95.8%
- Dropout rate .... NA
- Students per teacher 10.3
- Per pupil expenditure $12,236
- Median faculty salary $50,170
- Median administrator salary .. $89,250
- Grade 12 enrollment .... NA
- High school graduation rate .. NA

Assessment test results
(percent scoring at proficient or advanced level)
	Language	Math
NJASK-Grade 3	84.4%	93.5%
GEPA-Grade 8	92.0%	89.1%
HSPA-High School	NA	NA

SAT score averages
Pct tested	Math	Verbal	Writing
NA	NA	NA	NA

Teacher Qualifications
- Avg. years of experience 12
- Highly-qualified teachers
  - one subject/all subjects ... 100%/100%
- With emergency credentials 0.0%

No Child Left Behind
- AYP, 2005-06 .... Meets Standards

Municipal Finance
State Aid Programs, 2008
- Total aid $2,915,234
- CMPTRA 0
- Energy tax receipts 2,898,243
- Garden State Trust 16,991

General Budget, 2007
- Total tax levy $13,994,283
- County levy 2,913,114
- County taxes 2,437,997
- County library 212,127
- County health 0
- County open space 262,990
- School levy 11,081,170
- Muni. levy 0
- Misc. revenues 5,866,129

Taxes
	2005	2006	2007
General tax rate per $100	1.68	1.8	1.83
County equalization ratio	100.38	94.24	87.57
Net valuation taxable	$762,806,228	$759,879,300	$767,370,480
State equalized value	$770,122,391	$833,097,146	$855,366,393

Monmouth County — Holmdel Township

Demographics & Socio-Economic Characteristics
(2000 US Census, except as noted)

Population
1980*	8,447
1990*	11,532
2000	15,781
Male	7,557
Female	8,224
2006 (estimate)*	16,834
Population density	936.8

Race & Hispanic Origin, 2000
Race
White	12,657
Black/African American	102
American Indian/Alaska Native	4
Asian	2,753
Native Hawaiian/Pacific Islander	1
Other race	82
Two or more races	182
Hispanic origin, total	387
Mexican	30
Puerto Rican	105
Cuban	78
Other Hispanic	174

Age & Nativity, 2000
Under 5 years	917
18 years and over	11,279
21 years and over	10,871
65 years and over	1,926
85 years and over	378
Median age	40.8
Native-born	12,811
Foreign-born	2,970

Educational Attainment, 2000
Population 25 years and over	10,400
Less than 9th grade	3.6%
High school grad or higher	91.1%
Bachelor's degree or higher	54.8%
Graduate degree	28.1%

Income & Poverty, 1999
Per capita income	$47,898
Median household income	$112,879
Median family income	$122,785
Persons in poverty	518
H'holds receiving public assistance	42
H'holds receiving social security	972

Households, 2000
Total households	4,947
With persons under 18	2,393
With persons over 65	1,043
Family households	4,330
Single-person households	549
Persons per household	3.09
Persons per family	3.35

Labor & Employment
Total civilian labor force, 2006**	7,760
Unemployment rate	2.5%
Total civilian labor force, 2000	7,210
Unemployment rate	2.6%

Employed persons 16 years and over by occupation, 2000
Managers & professionals	4,506
Service occupations	394
Sales & office occupations	1,582
Farming, fishing & forestry	0
Construction & maintenance	279
Production & transportation	262
Self-employed persons	379

‡ Branch of county library
* US Census Bureau
** New Jersey Department of Labor

See Introduction for an explanation of all data sources.

General Information
Township of Holmdel
PO Box 410
Holmdel, NJ 07733
732-946-2820

Website	www.holmdeltownship-nj.com
Year of incorporation	1857
Land/water area (sq. miles)	17.97/0.12
Form of government	Township

Government
Legislative Districts
US Congressional	12
State Legislative	13

Local Officials, 2008
Mayor	Serena DiMaso
Administrator	Christopher Schultz
Clerk	Maureen Doloughty
Finance Dir.	Joseph Annecharico
Tax Assessor	Eldo Magnani
Tax Collector	Adeline Schmidt
Attorney	Duane Davison
Building	Django Wiegers
Comm Dev/Planning	NA
Engineering	Edward Broberg
Public Works	Jeffrey Smith
Police Chief	Raymond Wilson
Emerg/Fire Director	Tom Savage

Housing & Construction
Housing Units, 2000*
Total	5,137
Median rent	$1,512
Median SF home value	$404,200

Permits for New Residential Construction
	Units	Value
Total, 2007	24	$15,663,070
Single family	24	$15,663,070
Total, 2006	21	$6,320,928
Single family	16	$6,273,528

Real Property Valuation, 2007
	Parcels	Valuation
Total	5,908	$4,612,078,500
Vacant	173	66,876,000
Residential	5,421	3,994,163,600
Commercial	205	415,843,400
Industrial	7	104,124,500
Apartments	3	8,819,200
Farm land	68	1,145,700
Farm homestead	31	21,106,100

Average Property Value & Tax, 2007
Residential value	$736,476
Property tax	$11,175
Tax credit/rebate	$1,214

Public Library
Holmdel Public Library‡
4 Crawford's Corner Rd
Holmdel, NJ 07733
732-946-4118

Branch Librarian — Karen Nealis

Library statistics, 2006
see Monmouth County profile for library system statistics

Public Safety
Number of officers, 2006 — 43

Crime	2005	2006
Total crimes	240	236
Violent	7	7
Murder	1	0
Rape	0	2
Robbery	2	1
Aggravated assault	4	4
Non-violent	233	229
Burglary	29	25
Larceny	198	196
Vehicle theft	6	8
Domestic violence	79	98
Arson	1	2
Total crime rate	14.2	13.9
Violent	0.4	0.4
Non-violent	13.7	13.5

Public School District
(for school year 2006-07 except as noted)

Holmdel Township School District
4 Crawford's Corner Rd, PO Box 407
Holmdel, NJ 07733
732-946-1800

Superintendent	Barbara Duncan
Number of schools	4
Grade plan	K-12
Enrollment	3,482
Attendance rate, '05-06	95.9%
Dropout rate	0.1%
Students per teacher	12.0
Per pupil expenditure	$12,888
Median faculty salary	$67,500
Median administrator salary	$109,164
Grade 12 enrollment	290
High school graduation rate	100.0%

Assessment test results
(percent scoring at proficient or advanced level)
	Language	Math
NJASK-Grade 3	95.0%	92.8%
GEPA-Grade 8	93.1%	89.9%
HSPA-High School	94.7%	91.2%

SAT score averages
Pct tested	Math	Verbal	Writing
108%	607	579	576

Teacher Qualifications
Avg. years of experience	10
Highly-qualified teachers one subject/all subjects	99.5%/99.5%
With emergency credentials	0.0%

No Child Left Behind
AYP, 2005-06 — Meets Standards

Municipal Finance
State Aid Programs, 2008
Total aid	$2,704,712
CMPTRA	262,526
Energy tax receipts	2,436,285
Garden State Trust	825

General Budget, 2007
Total tax levy	$70,115,056
County levy	12,134,583
County taxes	10,837,006
County library	620,408
County health	0
County open space	677,169
School levy	47,667,768
Muni. levy	10,312,706
Misc. revenues	10,236,490

Taxes
	2005	2006	2007
General tax rate per $100	3.238	3.3	1.518
County equalization ratio	55.03	50.75	103.03
Net valuation taxable	$2,033,008,578	$2,026,614,684	$4,621,043,569
State equalized value	$4,005,928,233	$4,461,653,247	$4,608,624,489

©2008 Information Publications, Inc. All rights reserved.

Hopatcong Borough — Sussex County

Demographics & Socio-Economic Characteristics
(2000 US Census, except as noted)

Population
1980*	15,531
1990*	15,586
2000	15,888
Male	8,022
Female	7,866
2006 (estimate)*	15,884
Population density	1,449.3

Race & Hispanic Origin, 2000
Race
White	14,792
Black/African American	310
American Indian/Alaska Native	18
Asian	286
Native Hawaiian/Pacific Islander	0
Other race	226
Two or more races	256
Hispanic origin, total	952
Mexican	45
Puerto Rican	352
Cuban	72
Other Hispanic	483

Age & Nativity, 2000
Under 5 years	1,148
18 years and over	11,687
21 years and over	11,159
65 years and over	1,073
85 years and over	102
Median age	35.7
Native-born	14,915
Foreign-born	1,036

Educational Attainment, 2000
Population 25 years and over	10,653
Less than 9th grade	2.1%
High school grad or higher	89.3%
Bachelor's degree or higher	19.4%
Graduate degree	4.5%

Income & Poverty, 1999
Per capita income	$26,698
Median household income	$65,799
Median family income	$73,277
Persons in poverty	480
H'holds receiving public assistance	123
H'holds receiving social security	972

Households, 2000
Total households	5,656
With persons under 18	2,325
With persons over 65	826
Family households	4,239
Single-person households	1,054
Persons per household	2.81
Persons per family	3.24

Labor & Employment
Total civilian labor force, 2006**	10,418
Unemployment rate	5.7%
Total civilian labor force, 2000	9,207
Unemployment rate	4.3%

Employed persons 16 years and over by occupation, 2000
Managers & professionals	2,862
Service occupations	903
Sales & office occupations	2,962
Farming, fishing & forestry	0
Construction & maintenance	972
Production & transportation	1,114
Self-employed persons	337

‡ Branch of county library
* US Census Bureau
** New Jersey Department of Labor

General Information
Borough of Hopatcong
111 River Styx Rd
Hopatcong, NJ 07843
973-770-1200

Website	www.hopatcong.org
Year of incorporation	1901
Land/water area (sq. miles)	10.96/1.38
Form of government	Borough

Government

Legislative Districts
US Congressional	11
State Legislative	24

Local Officials, 2008
Mayor	Sylvia Petillo
Manager	Joseph Moskovitz
Clerk	Lorraine Stark
Finance Dir	Kelleyanne McGann
Tax Assessor	Therese dePierro
Tax Collector	Regina Thomas
Attorney	John Ursin
Building	William O'Connor
Comm Dev/Planning	NA
Engineering	John Ruschke
Public Works	Ron Jobeless
Police Chief	John Swanson
Emerg/Fire Director	Chris Steinmetz

Housing & Construction

Housing Units, 2000*
Total	6,190
Median rent	$915
Median SF home value	$141,300

Permits for New Residential Construction
	Units	Value
Total, 2007	18	$2,564,155
Single family	18	$2,564,155
Total, 2006	25	$3,919,682
Single family	25	$3,919,682

Real Property Valuation, 2007
	Parcels	Valuation
Total	7,182	$2,075,125,500
Vacant	1,008	44,950,700
Residential	6,068	1,916,714,600
Commercial	79	108,771,800
Industrial	1	486,800
Apartments	0	0
Farm land	20	1,906,200
Farm homestead	6	2,295,400

Average Property Value & Tax, 2007
Residential value	$315,938
Property tax	$5,303
Tax credit/rebate	$961

Public Library
E. Louise Childs Branch Library‡
21 Sparta Rd
Stanhope, NJ 07874
973-770-1000

Branch Librarian .... Victoria Larson

Library statistics, 2006
see Sussex County profile for library system statistics

Public Safety
Number of officers, 2006 28

Crime
	2005	2006
Total crimes	139	152
Violent	7	5
Murder	0	0
Rape	2	0
Robbery	0	1
Aggravated assault	5	4
Non-violent	132	147
Burglary	26	17
Larceny	101	125
Vehicle theft	5	5
Domestic violence	182	225
Arson	1	0
Total crime rate	8.7	9.5
Violent	0.4	0.3
Non-violent	8.2	9.2

Public School District
(for school year 2006-07 except as noted)

Hopatcong Borough School District
2 Windsor Ave, PO Box 1029
Hopatcong, NJ 07843
973-398-8801

Chief School Admin	Wayne Threlkeld
Number of schools	5
Grade plan	K-12
Enrollment	2,492
Attendance rate, '05-06	93.4%
Dropout rate	0.6%
Students per teacher	11.0
Per pupil expenditure	$12,083
Median faculty salary	$61,930
Median administrator salary	$113,613
Grade 12 enrollment	170
High school graduation rate	96.5%

Assessment test results
(percent scoring at proficient or advanced level)
	Language	Math
NJASK-Grade 3	84.7%	84.6%
GEPA-Grade 8	72.3%	71.8%
HSPA-High School	86.2%	69.5%

SAT score averages
Pct tested	Math	Verbal	Writing
74%	486	461	453

Teacher Qualifications
Avg. years of experience	8
Highly-qualified teachers one subject/all subjects	100%/100%
With emergency credentials	0.0%

No Child Left Behind
AYP, 2005-06 .... Meets Standards

Municipal Finance

State Aid Programs, 2008
Total aid	$1,219,457
CMPTRA	573,885
Energy tax receipts	645,534
Garden State Trust	38

General Budget, 2007
Total tax levy	$34,855,782
County levy	6,854,550
County taxes	5,755,801
County library	490,703
County health	0
County open space	608,046
School levy	19,278,562
Muni. levy	8,722,670
Misc. revenues	5,466,234

Taxes
	2005	2006	2007
General tax rate per $100	3.64	3.83	1.68
County equalization ratio	66.42	57.97	119.78
Net valuation taxable	$874,871,569	$878,966,200	$2,076,503,853
State equalized value	$1,509,179,867	$1,727,633,748	$1,874,404,348

Warren County
Hope Township

Demographics & Socio-Economic Characteristics
(2000 US Census, except as noted)

Population
- 1980*............................1,468
- 1990*............................1,719
- 2000............................1,891
  - Male............................947
  - Female..........................944
- 2006 (estimate)*.................1,974
- Population density...............106.7

Race & Hispanic Origin, 2000
Race
- White............................1,858
- Black/African American.............8
- American Indian/Alaska Native......0
- Asian..............................8
- Native Hawaiian/Pacific Islander...0
- Other race.........................1
- Two or more races.................16
- Hispanic origin, total............28
  - Mexican..........................2
  - Puerto Rican.....................6
  - Cuban............................0
  - Other Hispanic..................20

Age & Nativity, 2000
- Under 5 years....................122
- 18 years and over...............1,391
- 21 years and over...............1,342
- 65 years and over.................208
- 85 years and over..................20
- Median age.......................39.5
- Native-born.....................1,813
- Foreign-born......................78

Educational Attainment, 2000
- Population 25 years and over....1,312
- Less than 9th grade..............2.2%
- High school grad or higher......90.9%
- Bachelor's degree or higher.....26.9%
- Graduate degree..................8.1%

Income & Poverty, 1999
- Per capita income..............$27,902
- Median household income........$61,319
- Median family income...........$68,750
- Persons in poverty................36
- H'holds receiving public assistance...10
- H'holds receiving social security...171

Households, 2000
- Total households.................697
  - With persons under 18..........267
  - With persons over 65...........155
  - Family households..............539
  - Single-person households......137
- Persons per household............2.71
- Persons per family...............3.12

Labor & Employment
- Total civilian labor force, 2006**...1,131
  - Unemployment rate..............4.6%
- Total civilian labor force, 2000....989
  - Unemployment rate..............4.2%

Employed persons 16 years and over by occupation, 2000
- Managers & professionals.........342
- Service occupations..............113
- Sales & office occupations.......275
- Farming, fishing & forestry........5
- Construction & maintenance.......108
- Production & transportation......104
- Self-employed persons.............60

* US Census Bureau
** New Jersey Department of Labor

See Introduction for an explanation of all data sources.

General Information
Township of Hope
PO Box 284
Hope, NJ 07844
908-459-5011

- Email..............townclerk@hopetwp-nj.us
- Year of incorporation...............1839
- Land/water area (sq. miles).....18.50/0.18
- Form of government..............Township

Government
Legislative Districts
- US Congressional....................5
- State Legislative..................23

Local Officials, 2008
- Mayor..............Timothy McDonough
- Manager/Admin......................NA
- Clerk..................Mary Pat Quinn
- Finance Dir..........Kathleen Reinalda
- Tax Assessor..........Richard Motyka
- Tax Collector..........Stephen Lance
- Attorney............Michael Selvaggi
- Building................Ralph Price
- Comm Dev/Planning.................NA
- Engineering............Ted Rodman
- Public Works.........Donald Whitmore
- Police Chief......................NA
- Emerg/Fire Director........Chad Koonz

Housing & Construction
Housing Units, 2000*
- Total..............................747
- Median rent......................$711
- Median SF home value.........$179,500

Permits for New Residential Construction

	Units	Value
Total, 2007	7	$1,253,350
Single family	7	$1,253,350
Total, 2006	5	$1,201,000
Single family	5	$1,201,000

Real Property Valuation, 2007

	Parcels	Valuation
Total	1,146	$314,073,614
Vacant	134	14,930,000
Residential	649	232,661,200
Commercial	30	17,588,500
Industrial	1	357,600
Apartments	1	523,900
Farm land	216	1,776,714
Farm homestead	115	46,235,700

Average Property Value & Tax, 2007
- Residential value...............$365,048
- Property tax......................$6,311
- Tax credit/rebate................$1,088

Public Library
No public municipal library

Library statistics, 2006
- Population served..................NA
- Full-time/total staff............NA/NA

	Total	Per capita
Holdings	NA	NA
Revenues	NA	NA
Expenditures	NA	NA
Annual visits	NA	NA
Internet terminals/annual users	NA/NA	

Taxes

	2005	2006	2007
General tax rate per $100	3.24	3.47	1.73
County equalization ratio	63.4	56.78	111
Net valuation taxable	$139,629,354	$140,870,300	$315,370,245
State equalized value	$245,912,917	$284,305,818	$304,984,132

Public Safety
Number of officers, 2006...............0

Crime

	2005	2006
Total crimes	19	21
Violent	1	0
Murder	0	0
Rape	0	0
Robbery	0	0
Aggravated assault	1	0
Non-violent	18	21
Burglary	1	8
Larceny	14	7
Vehicle theft	3	6
Domestic violence	9	2
Arson	1	0
Total crime rate	9.7	10.7
Violent	0.5	0.0
Non-violent	9.2	10.7

Public School District
(for school year 2006-07 except as noted)

Hope Township School District
Hope Township School, PO Box 293
Hope, NJ 07844
908-459-4242

- Superintendent........Alfred Annunziata
- Number of schools..................1
- Grade plan.......................K-8
- Enrollment.......................228
- Attendance rate, '05-06.........96.3%
- Dropout rate......................NA
- Students per teacher............11.5
- Per pupil expenditure.........$12,260
- Median faculty salary.........$47,370
- Median administrator salary...$68,000
- Grade 12 enrollment..............NA
- High school graduation rate......NA

Assessment test results
(percent scoring at proficient or advanced level)

	Language	Math
NJASK-Grade 3	88.0%	92.0%
GEPA-Grade 8	82.1%	75.0%
HSPA-High School	NA	NA

SAT score averages

Pct tested	Math	Verbal	Writing
NA	NA	NA	NA

Teacher Qualifications
- Avg. years of experience...........10
- Highly-qualified teachers
  - one subject/all subjects...100%/100%
- With emergency credentials......0.0%

No Child Left Behind
- AYP, 2005-06..........Meets Standards

Municipal Finance
State Aid Programs, 2008
- Total aid....................$231,003
  - CMPTRA..........................0
  - Energy tax receipts.........211,498
  - Garden State Trust..........19,505

General Budget, 2007
- Total tax levy.............$5,452,327
  - County levy...............1,740,625
    - County taxes...........1,421,114
    - County library..........148,349
    - County health...............0
    - County open space........171,162
  - School levy..............3,252,759
  - Muni. levy................458,943
  - Misc. revenues..........1,110,819

©2008 Information Publications, Inc. All rights reserved. Photocopying prohibited. For additional copies, contact the publisher at www.informationpublications.com or (877)544-INFO (4636)

The New Jersey Municipal Data Book 225

Hopewell Borough

Mercer County

Demographics & Socio-Economic Characteristics
(2000 US Census, except as noted)

Population
1980	2,001
1990*	1,968
2000	2,035
Male	986
Female	1,049
2006 (estimate)*	2,022
Population density	2,930.4

Race & Hispanic Origin, 2000
Race
White	1,942
Black/African American	22
American Indian/Alaska Native	10
Asian	20
Native Hawaiian/Pacific Islander	0
Other race	25
Two or more races	16
Hispanic origin, total	47
Mexican	6
Puerto Rican	3
Cuban	0
Other Hispanic	38

Age & Nativity, 2000
Under 5 years	118
18 years and over	1,503
21 years and over	1,457
65 years and over	215
85 years and over	33
Median age	39.7
Native-born	1,878
Foreign-born	157

Educational Attainment, 2000
Population 25 years and over	1,417
Less than 9th grade	3.4%
High school grad or higher	89.6%
Bachelor's degree or higher	53.9%
Graduate degree	28.8%

Income & Poverty, 1999
Per capita income	$38,413
Median household income	$77,270
Median family income	$91,205
Persons in poverty	43
H'holds receiving public assistance	0
H'holds receiving social security	174

Households, 2000
Total households	813
With persons under 18	305
With persons over 65	167
Family households	562
Single-person households	204
Persons per household	2.50
Persons per family	3.01

Labor & Employment
Total civilian labor force, 2006**	1,134
Unemployment rate	1.0%
Total civilian labor force, 2000	1,228
Unemployment rate	1.0%

Employed persons 16 years and over by occupation, 2000
Managers & professionals	672
Service occupations	122
Sales & office occupations	243
Farming, fishing & forestry	0
Construction & maintenance	112
Production & transportation	67
Self-employed persons	95

* US Census Bureau
** New Jersey Department of Labor

General Information
Borough of Hopewell
4 Columbia Ave
PO Box 128
Hopewell, NJ 08525
609-466-2636

Website	www.hopewellboro-nj.us
Year of incorporation	1891
Land/water area (sq. miles)	0.69/0.00
Form of government	Borough

Government
Legislative Districts
US Congressional	12
State Legislative	15

Local Officials, 2008
Mayor	David R. Nettles
Manager	Michele Hovan
Clerk	Michele Hovan
Finance Dir	Judie McGrorey
Tax Assessor	Christopher Fuges
Tax Collector	Donna Griffiths
Attorney	Edmond Konin
Building	Robert Ward
Planning	Carl Lindbloom
Engineering	Dennis O'Neal
Public Works	Herbert Ruehle
Police Chief	George Meyer
Fire/Emergency Dir	NA

Housing & Construction
Housing Units, 2000*
Total	836
Median rent	$843
Median SF home value	$221,900

Permits for New Residential Construction
	Units	Value
Total, 2007	0	$0
Single family	0	$0
Total, 2006	1	$45,000
Single family	1	$45,000

Real Property Valuation, 2007
	Parcels	Valuation
Total	776	$361,440,500
Vacant	29	4,323,900
Residential	666	301,240,200
Commercial	70	50,635,300
Industrial	2	857,700
Apartments	3	2,322,900
Farm land	3	28,000
Farm homestead	3	2,032,500

Average Property Value & Tax, 2007
Residential value	$453,322
Property tax	$8,666
Tax credit/rebate	$1,295

Public Library
Hopewell Public Library
13 E Broad St
Hopewell, NJ 08525
609-466-1625

Director	Jennifer T. Spencer

Library statistics, 2006
Population served	2,035
Full-time/total staff	0/0

	Total	Per capita
Holdings	17,047	8.38
Revenues	$125,205	$61.53
Expenditures	$112,732	$55.40
Annual visits	14,062	6.91
Internet terminals/annual users	5/2,240	

Taxes
	2005	2006	2007
General tax rate per $100	3.79	1.78	1.92
County equalization ratio	59.19	118.64	105.87
Net valuation taxable	$155,969,562	$362,812,400	$363,186,950
State equalized value	$306,483,714	$344,339,682	$350,391,670

Public Safety
Number of officers, 2006	0

Crime	2005	2006
Total crimes	26	12
Violent	0	0
Murder	0	0
Rape	0	0
Robbery	0	0
Aggravated assault	0	0
Non-violent	26	12
Burglary	7	5
Larceny	18	7
Vehicle theft	1	0
Domestic violence	1	18
Arson	0	0
Total crime rate	12.7	5.9
Violent	0.0	0.0
Non-violent	12.7	5.9

Public School District
(for school year 2006-07 except as noted)

Hopewell Valley Regional School District
425 S Main St
Pennington, NJ 08534
609-737-4000

Chief School Admin	Judith Ferguson
Number of schools	18
Grade plan	K-12
Enrollment	4,036
Attendance rate, '05-06	96.2%
Dropout rate	0.5%
Students per teacher	10.6
Per pupil expenditure	$15,143
Median faculty salary	$109,814
Median administrator salary	$61,343
Grade 12 enrollment	284
High school graduation rate	97.9%

Assessment test results
(percent scoring at proficient or advanced level)
	Language	Math
NJASK-Grade 3	93.5%	92.9%
GEPA-Grade 8	88.7%	83.5%
HSPA-High School	97.1%	90.0%

SAT score averages
Pct tested	Math	Verbal	Writing
96%	562	557	585

Teacher Qualifications
Avg. years of experience	10
Highly-qualified teachers one subject/all subjects	100%/100%
With emergency credentials	0.0%

No Child Left Behind
AYP, 2005-06	Meets Standards

Municipal Finance
State Aid Programs, 2008
Total aid	$150,832
CMPTRA	0
Energy tax receipts	150,817
Garden State Trust	15

General Budget, 2007
Total tax levy	$6,943,008
County levy	1,609,979
County taxes	1,506,664
County library	0
County health	0
County open space	103,315
School levy	4,061,883
Muni. levy	1,271,146
Misc. revenues	1,240,878

Cumberland County
Hopewell Township

Demographics & Socio-Economic Characteristics
(2000 US Census, except as noted)

Population
1980*	4,365
1990*	4,215
2000	4,434
Male	2,103
Female	2,331
2006 (estimate)*	4,756
Population density	159.1

Race & Hispanic Origin, 2000
Race
White	3,862
Black/African American	306
American Indian/Alaska Native	103
Asian	25
Native Hawaiian/Pacific Islander	1
Other race	64
Two or more races	73
Hispanic origin, total	159
Mexican	55
Puerto Rican	86
Cuban	0
Other Hispanic	18

Age & Nativity, 2000
Under 5 years	210
18 years and over	3,430
21 years and over	3,290
65 years and over	906
85 years and over	129
Median age	42.4
Native-born	4,321
Foreign-born	111

Educational Attainment, 2000
Population 25 years and over	3,177
Less than 9th grade	7.1%
High school grad or higher	83.2%
Bachelor's degree or higher	18.8%
Graduate degree	7.6%

Income & Poverty, 1999
Per capita income	$22,783
Median household income	$49,767
Median family income	$59,675
Persons in poverty	279
H'holds receiving public assistance	16
H'holds receiving social security	577

Households, 2000
Total households	1,628
With persons under 18	549
With persons over 65	539
Family households	1,206
Single-person households	372
Persons per household	2.58
Persons per family	3.03

Labor & Employment
Total civilian labor force, 2006**	2,503
Unemployment rate	3.0%
Total civilian labor force, 2000	2,284
Unemployment rate	3.9%

Employed persons 16 years and over by occupation, 2000
Managers & professionals	713
Service occupations	408
Sales & office occupations	484
Farming, fishing & forestry	29
Construction & maintenance	169
Production & transportation	391
Self-employed persons	161

* US Census Bureau
** New Jersey Department of Labor

See Introduction for an explanation of all data sources.

General Information
Township of Hopewell
590 Shiloh Pike
Bridgeton, NJ 08302
856-455-1230

Website	hopewelltwp-nj.com
Year of incorporation	1748
Land/water area (sq. miles)	29.90/0.88
Form of government	Township

Government
Legislative Districts
US Congressional	2
State Legislative	3

Local Officials, 2008
Mayor	Bruce Hankins Jr
Manager	Ted Ritter
Clerk	Ted Ritter
Finance Dir	Terry Delp
Tax Assessor	Lois Mazza
Tax Collector	Liz Wallender
Attorney	T. Henry Ritter
Building	Gordon Gross
Planning	Donna Hickman
Engineering	Steve Nardelli
Public Works	Ken Hildreth
Police Chief	NA
Emerg/Fire Director	D. Maxwell Dilks

Housing & Construction
Housing Units, 2000*
Total	1,683
Median rent	$495
Median SF home value	$97,000

Permits for New Residential Construction
	Units	Value
Total, 2007	16	$1,828,385
Single family	16	$1,828,385
Total, 2006	18	$1,959,814
Single family	18	$1,959,814

Real Property Valuation, 2007
	Parcels	Valuation
Total	2,388	$228,827,300
Vacant	242	4,953,600
Residential	1,430	173,613,900
Commercial	50	13,690,000
Industrial	0	0
Apartments	2	415,400
Farm land	471	6,805,600
Farm homestead	193	29,348,800

Average Property Value & Tax, 2007
Residential value	$125,054
Property tax	$4,693
Tax credit/rebate	$923

Public Library
No public municipal library

Library statistics, 2006
Population served	NA
Full-time/total staff	NA/NA

	Total	Per capita
Holdings	NA	NA
Revenues	NA	NA
Expenditures	NA	NA
Annual visits	NA	NA
Internet terminals/annual users	NA/NA	

Public Safety
Number of officers, 2006		0
Crime	**2005**	**2006**
Total crimes	51	97
Violent	7	5
Murder	0	0
Rape	0	0
Robbery	1	0
Aggravated assault	6	5
Non-violent	44	92
Burglary	13	33
Larceny	29	42
Vehicle theft	2	17
Domestic violence	10	0
Arson	1	0
Total crime rate	10.9	20.5
Violent	1.5	1.1
Non-violent	9.4	19.5

Public School District
(for school year 2006-07 except as noted)

Hopewell Township School District
122 Sewall Rd
Bridgeton, NJ 08302
856-451-9203

Chief School Admin	Terry Van Zoeren
Number of schools	1
Grade plan	K-8
Enrollment	540
Attendance rate, '05-06	95.7%
Dropout rate	NA
Students per teacher	12.7
Per pupil expenditure	$10,752
Median faculty salary	$65,098
Median administrator salary	$90,600
Grade 12 enrollment	NA
High school graduation rate	NA

Assessment test results
(percent scoring at proficient or advanced level)
	Language	Math
NJASK-Grade 3	86.8%	86.8%
GEPA-Grade 8	80.6%	81.9%
HSPA-High School	NA	NA

SAT score averages
Pct tested	Math	Verbal	Writing
NA	NA	NA	NA

Teacher Qualifications
Avg. years of experience	16
Highly-qualified teachers one subject/all subjects	100%/100%
With emergency credentials	0.0%

No Child Left Behind
AYP, 2005-06	Meets Standards

Municipal Finance
State Aid Programs, 2008
Total aid	$276,150
CMPTRA	0
Energy tax receipts	266,539
Garden State Trust	9,611

General Budget, 2007
Total tax levy	$8,615,156
County levy	3,166,242
County taxes	2,999,339
County library	0
County health	134,811
County open space	32,091
School levy	5,102,776
Muni. levy	346,138
Misc. revenues	1,724,716

Taxes
	2005	2006	2007
General tax rate per $100	3.23	3.497	3.755
County equalization ratio	92.02	82.65	72.16
Net valuation taxable	$224,987,536	$225,910,000	$229,567,880
State equalized value	$272,217,224	$313,892,520	$360,758,358

©2008 Information Publications, Inc. All rights reserved. Photocopying prohibited. For additional copies, contact the publisher at www.informationpublications.com or (877) 544-INFO (4636)

The New Jersey Municipal Data Book 227

Hopewell Township — Mercer County

Demographics & Socio-Economic Characteristics
(2000 US Census, except as noted)

Population
1980*	10,893
1990*	11,590
2000	16,105
Male	8,208
Female	7,897
2006 (estimate)*	17,968
Population density	309.2

Race & Hispanic Origin, 2000
Race
White	14,220
Black/African American	939
American Indian/Alaska Native	20
Asian	639
Native Hawaiian/Pacific Islander	4
Other race	107
Two or more races	176
Hispanic origin, total	395
Mexican	36
Puerto Rican	152
Cuban	50
Other Hispanic	157

Age & Nativity, 2000
Under 5 years	1,076
18 years and over	11,833
21 years and over	11,413
65 years and over	1,845
85 years and over	130
Median age	39.1
Native-born	14,862
Foreign-born	1,243

Educational Attainment, 2000
Population 25 years and over	10,956
Less than 9th grade	1.2%
High school grad or higher	93.0%
Bachelor's degree or higher	55.8%
Graduate degree	27.7%

Income & Poverty, 1999
Per capita income	$43,947
Median household income	$93,640
Median family income	$101,579
Persons in poverty	173
H'holds receiving public assistance	15
H'holds receiving social security	1,334

Households, 2000
Total households	5,498
With persons under 18	2,310
With persons over 65	1,279
Family households	4,429
Single-person households	878
Persons per household	2.77
Persons per family	3.11

Labor & Employment
Total civilian labor force, 2006**	7,162
Unemployment rate	2.6%
Total civilian labor force, 2000	7,738
Unemployment rate	2.1%

Employed persons 16 years and over by occupation, 2000
Managers & professionals	4,625
Service occupations	638
Sales & office occupations	1,534
Farming, fishing & forestry	23
Construction & maintenance	422
Production & transportation	334
Self-employed persons	540

‡ Branch of county library
* US Census Bureau
** New Jersey Department of Labor

General Information
Township of Hopewell
201 Washington Crossing Rd
Titusville, NJ 08560
609-737-0605

Website	www.hopewelltwp.org
Year of incorporation	1700
Land/water area (sq. miles)	58.11/0.54
Form of government	Township

Government
Legislative Districts
US Congressional	12
State Legislative	15

Local Officials, 2008
Mayor	Vanessa Sandom
Administrator	Paul Pogorzelski
Clerk	Annette Bielawski
Finance Dir	Elaine Borges
Tax Assessor	Antoinette Sost
Tax Collector	Alice Anne Pareti
Attorney	Steven Goodell
Building	Chris Rose
Comm Dev/Planning	NA
Engineering	Paul Pogorzelski
Public Works	NA
Police Chief	George Meyer
Fire/Emergency Dir	NA

Housing & Construction
Housing Units, 2000*
Total	5,629
Median rent	$925
Median SF home value	$252,600

Permits for New Residential Construction
	Units	Value
Total, 2007	6	$1,824,500
Single family	6	$1,824,500
Total, 2006	16	$2,518,530
Single family	16	$2,518,530

Real Property Valuation, 2007
	Parcels	Valuation
Total	7,307	$4,552,451,800
Vacant	376	75,740,200
Residential	5,895	3,237,955,500
Commercial	172	582,520,300
Industrial	30	378,220,600
Apartments	6	5,831,600
Farm land	518	5,714,700
Farm homestead	310	266,468,900

Average Property Value & Tax, 2007
Residential value	$564,774
Property tax	$10,501
Tax credit/rebate	$1,300

Public Library
Hopewell Township Branch Library‡
245 Pennington/Titusville Rd
Pennington, NJ 08534
609-737-2610

Branch Librarian........Andrea Merrick

Library statistics, 2006
see Mercer County profile for library system statistics

Public Safety
Number of officers, 2006 ... 32

Crime	2005	2006
Total crimes	107	124
Violent	14	6
Murder	0	0
Rape	3	0
Robbery	0	2
Aggravated assault	11	4
Non-violent	93	118
Burglary	19	28
Larceny	67	86
Vehicle theft	7	4
Domestic violence	44	90
Arson	0	1
Total crime rate	6.1	7.0
Violent	0.8	0.3
Non-violent	5.3	6.7

Public School District
(for school year 2006-07 except as noted)

Hopewell Valley Regional School District
425 S Main St
Pennington, NJ 08534
609-737-4000

Chief School Admin	Judith Ferguson
Number of schools	18
Grade plan	K-12
Enrollment	4,036
Attendance rate, '05-06	96.2%
Dropout rate	0.5%
Students per teacher	10.6
Per pupil expenditure	$15,143
Median faculty salary	$109,814
Median administrator salary	$61,343
Grade 12 enrollment	284
High school graduation rate	97.9%

Assessment test results
(percent scoring at proficient or advanced level)
	Language	Math
NJASK-Grade 3	93.5%	92.9%
GEPA-Grade 8	88.7%	83.5%
HSPA-High School	97.1%	90.0%

SAT score averages
Pct tested	Math	Verbal	Writing
96%	562	557	585

Teacher Qualifications
Avg. years of experience	10
Highly-qualified teachers one subject/all subjects	100%/100%
With emergency credentials	0.0%

No Child Left Behind
AYP, 2005-06 .... Meets Standards

Municipal Finance
State Aid Programs, 2008
Total aid	$2,228,571
CMPTRA	226,293
Energy tax receipts	1,949,261
Garden State Trust	53,017

General Budget, 2007
Total tax levy	$84,748,062
County levy	21,258,758
County taxes	18,312,271
County library	1,689,302
County health	0
County open space	1,257,185
School levy	51,179,753
Muni. levy	12,309,551
Misc. revenues	7,584,179

Taxes
	2005	2006	2007
General tax rate per $100	3.32	1.87	1.86
County equalization ratio	67.45	112.67	108.87
Net valuation taxable	$2,369,199,280	$4,588,936,100	$4,558,163,334
State equalized value	$4,016,272,724	$4,219,728,189	$4,372,990,697

Monmouth County
Howell Township

Demographics & Socio-Economic Characteristics
(2000 US Census, except as noted)

Population
- 1980*..................................25,065
- 1990*..................................38,987
- 2000..................................48,903
  - Male..............................23,864
  - Female...........................25,039
- 2006 (estimate)*....................50,548
- Population density................829.9

Race & Hispanic Origin, 2000
Race
- White................................44,008
- Black/African American..........1,739
- American Indian/Alaska Native....58
- Asian..................................1,749
- Native Hawaiian/Pacific Islander....5
- Other race............................633
- Two or more races..................711
- Hispanic origin, total.............2,610
  - Mexican............................229
  - Puerto Rican....................1,252
  - Cuban...............................202
  - Other Hispanic....................927

Age & Nativity, 2000
- Under 5 years......................3,910
- 18 years and over...............33,815
- 21 years and over...............32,333
- 65 years and over................4,295
- 85 years and over..................451
- Median age..........................35.7
- Native-born........................44,543
- Foreign-born........................4,360

Educational Attainment, 2000
- Population 25 years and over....30,878
- Less than 9th grade................3.3%
- High school grad or higher......88.2%
- Bachelor's degree or higher.....29.0%
- Graduate degree....................8.7%

Income & Poverty, 1999
- Per capita income...............$26,143
- Median household income.....$68,069
- Median family income..........$74,623
- Persons in poverty................2,049
- H'holds receiving public assistance....196
- H'holds receiving social security....3,473

Households, 2000
- Total households.................16,063
  - With persons under 18........7,962
  - With persons over 65..........3,249
  - Family households.............13,006
  - Single-person households......2,466
- Persons per household............3.04
- Persons per family.................3.42

Labor & Employment
- Total civilian labor force, 2006**....26,900
  - Unemployment rate...............3.8%
- Total civilian labor force, 2000....24,937
  - Unemployment rate...............4.2%

Employed persons 16 years and over by occupation, 2000
- Managers & professionals........9,175
- Service occupations...............3,020
- Sales & office occupations......7,350
- Farming, fishing & forestry.........67
- Construction & maintenance....2,016
- Production & transportation....2,258
- Self-employed persons............1,221

‡ Branch of county library
* US Census Bureau
** New Jersey Department of Labor

See Introduction for an explanation of all data sources.

General Information
Township of Howell
251 Preventorium Rd
PO Box 580
Howell, NJ 07731
732-938-4500

- Website..............www.twp.howell.nj.us
- Year of incorporation...............1801
- Land/water area (sq. miles).....60.91/0.09
- Form of government........Council-Manager

Government
Legislative Districts
- US Congressional......................4
- State Legislative.....................30

Local Officials, 2008
- Mayor..................Joseph M. Di Bella
- Manager................Helene Schlegel
- Clerk.........................Bruce Davis
- Finance Dir..........Jeffrey L. Fillatreault
- Tax Assessor...........Thomas P. Lenahan
- Tax Collector............Susan Davison
- Attorney.............Ernest Bongiovanni
- Building....................Chet Philips
- Planning..................Ernie Peters
- Engineering..........William Nunziato
- Public Works..........Jeffrey Cramer
- Police Chief............Ronald T. Carter
- Emerg/Fire Director....Robert H. Hotmar

Housing & Construction
Housing Units, 2000*
- Total...............................16,572
- Median rent..........................$816
- Median SF home value..........$172,400

Permits for New Residential Construction

	Units	Value
Total, 2007	110	$16,904,248
Single family	110	$16,904,248
Total, 2006	88	$14,243,515
Single family	88	$14,243,515

Real Property Valuation, 2007

	Parcels	Valuation
Total	22,574	$6,846,805,200
Vacant	5,215	249,995,100
Residential	16,163	5,667,270,700
Commercial	443	703,025,300
Industrial	66	115,926,300
Apartments	0	0
Farm land	403	2,510,100
Farm homestead	284	108,077,700

Average Property Value & Tax, 2007
- Residential value................$351,149
- Property tax.......................$6,609
- Tax credit/rebate................$1,112

Public Library
Howell Public Library‡
318 Old Tavern Rd
Howell, NJ 07731
732-938-2300

- Branch Librarian.........Stephenie Acosta

Library statistics, 2006
see Monmouth County profile
for library system statistics

Public Safety
- Number of officers, 2006..............94

Crime	2005	2006
Total crimes	668	535
Violent	46	59
Murder	1	0
Rape	6	1
Robbery	5	11
Aggravated assault	34	47
Non-violent	622	476
Burglary	116	94
Larceny	468	348
Vehicle theft	38	34
Domestic violence	297	292
Arson	4	6
Total crime rate	13.3	10.6
Violent	0.9	1.2
Non-violent	12.4	9.4

Public School District
(for school year 2006-07 except as noted)

Howell Township School District
200 Squankum-Yellowbrook Rd, PO Box 579
Howell, NJ 07731
732-751-2480

- Superintendent..............Enid Golden
- Number of schools....................13
- Grade plan..........................K-8
- Enrollment........................7,265
- Attendance rate, '05-06..........95.5%
- Dropout rate..........................NA
- Students per teacher..............11.3
- Per pupil expenditure..........$12,852
- Median faculty salary..........$48,400
- Median administrator salary...$115,814
- Grade 12 enrollment.................NA
- High school graduation rate.......NA

Assessment test results
(percent scoring at proficient or advanced level)

	Language	Math
NJASK-Grade 3	93.4%	96.8%
GEPA-Grade 8	85.7%	86.6%
HSPA-High School	NA	NA

SAT score averages

Pct tested	Math	Verbal	Writing
NA	NA	NA	NA

Teacher Qualifications
- Avg. years of experience.............9
- Highly-qualified teachers
  one subject/all subjects......100%/100%
- With emergency credentials........0.5%

No Child Left Behind
- AYP, 2005-06............Meets Standards

Municipal Finance
State Aid Programs, 2008
- Total aid......................$9,992,997
  - CMPTRA............................927
  - Energy tax receipts.........9,985,366
  - Garden State Trust.............6,704

General Budget, 2007
- Total tax levy...............$129,037,902
  - County levy.................18,278,517
    - County taxes..............16,050,285
    - County library................918,969
    - County health................305,788
    - County open space..........1,003,474
  - School levy.................91,188,255
  - Muni. levy..................19,571,130
  - Misc. revenues.............26,586,732

Taxes	2005	2006	2007
General tax rate per $100	3.778	4.062	1.883
County equalization ratio	57.56	50.08	102.18
Net valuation taxable	$2,900,931,838	$2,939,678,340	$6,855,681,063
State equalized value	$5,792,595,523	$6,558,866,149	$7,052,914,135

©2008 Information Publications, Inc. All rights reserved. Photocopying prohibited. For additional copies, contact the publisher at www.informationpublications.com or (877)544-INFO (4636)

The New Jersey Municipal Data Book

Independence Township
Warren County

Demographics & Socio-Economic Characteristics
(2000 US Census, except as noted)

Population
- 1980* 2,829
- 1990* 3,940
- 2000 5,603
  - Male 2,710
  - Female 2,893
- 2006 (estimate)* 5,770
- Population density 290.8

Race & Hispanic Origin, 2000
Race
- White 5,322
- Black/African American 65
- American Indian/Alaska Native 3
- Asian 97
- Native Hawaiian/Pacific Islander 0
- Other race 44
- Two or more races 72
- Hispanic origin, total 211
  - Mexican 17
  - Puerto Rican 54
  - Cuban 17
  - Other Hispanic 123

Age & Nativity, 2000
- Under 5 years 364
- 18 years and over 4,104
- 21 years and over 3,969
- 65 years and over 451
- 85 years and over 42
- Median age 36.8
- Native-born 5,193
- Foreign-born 410

Educational Attainment, 2000
- Population 25 years and over 3,811
- Less than 9th grade 2.3%
- High school grad or higher 91.3%
- Bachelor's degree or higher 35.7%
- Graduate degree 9.9%

Income & Poverty, 1999
- Per capita income $30,555
- Median household income $67,247
- Median family income $79,819
- Persons in poverty 158
- H'holds receiving public assistance ... 37
- H'holds receiving social security ... 384

Households, 2000
- Total households 2,146
  - With persons under 18 819
  - With persons over 65 354
  - Family households 1,490
  - Single-person households 525
- Persons per household 2.61
- Persons per family 3.18

Labor & Employment
- Total civilian labor force, 2006** ... 3,630
  - Unemployment rate 1.4%
- Total civilian labor force, 2000 3,191
  - Unemployment rate 1.2%

Employed persons 16 years and over by occupation, 2000
- Managers & professionals 1,258
- Service occupations 466
- Sales & office occupations 834
- Farming, fishing & forestry 0
- Construction & maintenance 313
- Production & transportation 281
- Self-employed persons 150

‡ Branch of county library
* US Census Bureau
** New Jersey Department of Labor

General Information
Township of Independence
286-B Route 46
Great Meadows, NJ 07838
908-637-4133
- Website .... www.independencenj.com
- Year of incorporation 1782
- Land/water area (sq. miles) 19.84/0.05
- Form of government .... Township

Government
Legislative Districts
- US Congressional 5
- State Legislative 23

Local Officials, 2008
- Mayor .... Robert M. Giordano
- Manager .... Deborah Hrebenak
- Clerk .... Deborah Hrebenak
- Finance Dir .... Kevin Lifer
- Tax Assessor .... Kathleen Degan
- Tax Collector .... Patricia Noll
- Attorney .... William Edleston
- Building .... Richard O'Connor
- Planning .... Kathy Dossena
- Engineering .... Michael Finelli
- Public Works .... Alan Shimchook
- Police Chief .... Dennis Riley
- Emerg/Fire Director ..... Cheryl Holowath

Housing & Construction
Housing Units, 2000*
- Total 2,210
- Median rent $720
- Median SF home value $169,500

Permits for New Residential Construction

	Units	Value
Total, 2007	13	$3,740,951
Single family	13	$3,740,951
Total, 2006	11	$2,841,283
Single family	11	$2,841,283

Real Property Valuation, 2007

	Parcels	Valuation
Total	2,362	$686,618,244
Vacant	131	13,043,100
Residential	1,876	595,614,900
Commercial	54	28,206,800
Industrial	6	3,861,200
Apartments	9	15,911,600
Farm land	194	2,082,644
Farm homestead	92	27,898,000

Average Property Value & Tax, 2007
- Residential value $316,826
- Property tax $6,131
- Tax credit/rebate $1,032

Public Library
Northeast Branch Library‡
63 US Hwy 46
Hackettstown, NJ 07840
908-813-3858
- Branch Librarian .... Patricia Optiz

Library statistics, 2006
see Warren County profile for library system statistics

Public Safety
- Number of officers, 2006 8

Crime	2005	2006
Total crimes	53	71
Violent	2	2
Murder	0	0
Rape	0	0
Robbery	0	0
Aggravated assault	2	2
Non-violent	51	69
Burglary	10	8
Larceny	40	60
Vehicle theft	1	1
Domestic violence	66	61
Arson	0	0
Total crime rate	9.1	12.3
Violent	0.3	0.3
Non-violent	8.8	12.0

Public School District
(for school year 2006-07 except as noted)
Great Meadows Regional School District
Po Box 74
Great Meadows, NJ 07838
908-637-6576
- Superintendent .... Jason Bing
- Number of schools 6
- Grade plan K-8
- Enrollment 1,009
- Attendance rate, '05-06 .... 95.9%
- Dropout rate .... NA
- Students per teacher 10.9
- Per pupil expenditure $11,977
- Median faculty salary $55,135
- Median administrator salary ... $86,100
- Grade 12 enrollment .... NA
- High school graduation rate .... NA

Assessment test results
(percent scoring at proficient or advanced level)

	Language	Math
NJASK-Grade 3	83.3%	94.5%
GEPA-Grade 8	74.3%	73.6%
HSPA-High School	NA	NA

SAT score averages

Pct tested	Math	Verbal	Writing
NA	NA	NA	NA

Teacher Qualifications
- Avg. years of experience 16
- Highly-qualified teachers
  - one subject/all subjects ... 100%/100%
- With emergency credentials 0.0%

No Child Left Behind
- AYP, 2005-06 .... Meets Standards

Municipal Finance
State Aid Programs, 2008
- Total aid $372,766
  - CMPTRA 66,361
  - Energy tax receipts 299,747
  - Garden State Trust 6,658

General Budget, 2007
- Total tax levy $13,315,496
  - County levy 4,430,591
    - County taxes 3,615,128
    - County library 378,619
    - County health 0
    - County open space 436,843
  - School levy 7,401,041
  - Muni. levy 1,483,864
- Misc. revenues 2,417,568

Taxes	2005	2006	2007
General tax rate per $100	1.73	1.85	1.94
County equalization ratio	119.14	104.97	94.69
Net valuation taxable	$682,095,974	$685,510,734	$688,072,010
State equalized value	$649,800,871	$725,473,572	$755,813,516

Monmouth County / Interlaken Borough

Demographics & Socio-Economic Characteristics
(2000 US Census, except as noted)

Population
1980*	1,037
1990*	910
2000	900
Male	435
Female	465
2006 (estimate)*	881
Population density	2,517.1

Race & Hispanic Origin, 2000
Race
White	888
Black/African American	0
American Indian/Alaska Native	0
Asian	2
Native Hawaiian/Pacific Islander	1
Other race	0
Two or more races	9
Hispanic origin, total	10
Mexican	2
Puerto Rican	5
Cuban	0
Other Hispanic	3

Age & Nativity, 2000
Under 5 years	36
18 years and over	739
21 years and over	724
65 years and over	205
85 years and over	21
Median age	47.6
Native-born	861
Foreign-born	39

Educational Attainment, 2000
Population 25 years and over	705
Less than 9th grade	1.0%
High school grad or higher	97.7%
Bachelor's degree or higher	53.5%
Graduate degree	21.7%

Income & Poverty, 1999
Per capita income	$47,307
Median household income	$82,842
Median family income	$104,618
Persons in poverty	27
H'holds receiving public assistance	0
H'holds receiving social security	144

Households, 2000
Total households	386
With persons under 18	86
With persons over 65	152
Family households	261
Single-person households	106
Persons per household	2.33
Persons per family	2.86

Labor & Employment
Total civilian labor force, 2006**	506
Unemployment rate	4.3%
Total civilian labor force, 2000	465
Unemployment rate	3.0%

Employed persons 16 years and over by occupation, 2000
Managers & professionals	246
Service occupations	36
Sales & office occupations	126
Farming, fishing & forestry	0
Construction & maintenance	23
Production & transportation	20
Self-employed persons	58

* US Census Bureau
** New Jersey Department of Labor

See Introduction for an explanation of all data sources.

General Information
Borough of Interlaken
100 Grassmere Ave
Interlaken, NJ 07712
732-531-7405

Website	NA
Year of incorporation	1922
Land/water area (sq. miles)	0.35/0.04
Form of government	Borough

Government
Legislative Districts
US Congressional	6
State Legislative	11

Local Officials, 2008
Mayor	Robert Wolf
Manager	Aime Sweeney
Clerk	Aime Sweeney
Finance Dir.	Aime Sweeney
Tax Assessor	Ed Mullane
Tax Collector	Eleanor Cottrell
Attorney	Dennis Crawford
Building	Paul Vitale
Planning	James Watt
Engineering	Peter Avakian
Public Works	Norman Cottrell
Police Chief	James Lanza
Fire/Emergency Dir.	NA

Housing & Construction
Housing Units, 2000*
Total	397
Median rent	$1,333
Median SF home value	$280,600

Permits for New Residential Construction
	Units	Value
Total, 2007	5	$116,665
Single family	5	$116,665
Total, 2006	15	$350,000
Single family	15	$350,000

Real Property Valuation, 2007
	Parcels	Valuation
Total	407	$198,325,100
Vacant	13	1,773,900
Residential	394	196,551,200
Commercial	0	0
Industrial	0	0
Apartments	0	0
Farm land	0	0
Farm homestead	0	0

Average Property Value & Tax, 2007
Residential value	$498,861
Property tax	$7,005
Tax credit/rebate	$1,019

Public Library
Interlaken Municipal Library
100 Grassmere Ave
Interlaken, NJ 07712
732-531-7405

Librarian	Vicki LaBella

Library statistics, 2006
Population served	NA
Full-time/total staff	NA/NA

	Total	Per capita
Holdings	NA	NA
Revenues	NA	NA
Expenditures	NA	NA
Annual visits	NA	NA
Internet terminals/annual users	NA/NA	

Public Safety
Number of officers, 2006 6

Crime	2005	2006
Total crimes	9	3
Violent	0	0
Murder	0	0
Rape	0	0
Robbery	0	0
Aggravated assault	0	0
Non-violent	9	3
Burglary	6	1
Larceny	3	2
Vehicle theft	0	0
Domestic violence	0	1
Arson	0	0
Total crime rate	10.1	3.4
Violent	0.0	0.0
Non-violent	10.1	3.4

Public School District
(for school year 2006-07 except as noted)

Interlaken Borough School District
100 Grassmere Ave
Interlaken, NJ 07712

No schools in district - sends students to Asbury Park schools

Per pupil expenditure	NA
Median faculty salary	NA
Median administrator salary	NA
Grade 12 enrollment	NA
High school graduation rate	NA

Assessment test results
(percent scoring at proficient or advanced level)
	Language	Math
NJASK-Grade 3	NA	NA
GEPA-Grade 8	NA	NA
HSPA-High School	NA	NA

SAT score averages
Pct tested	Math	Verbal	Writing
NA	NA	NA	NA

Teacher Qualifications
Avg. years of experience	NA
Highly-qualified teachers one subject/all subjects	NA/NA
With emergency credentials	NA

No Child Left Behind
AYP, 2005-06	NA

Municipal Finance
State Aid Programs, 2008
Total aid	$123,563
CMPTRA	0
Energy tax receipts	123,563
Garden State Trust	0

General Budget, 2007
Total tax levy	$2,785,676
County levy	764,184
County taxes	682,474
County library	39,069
County health	0
County open space	42,641
School levy	456,042
Muni. levy	1,565,450
Misc. revenues	544,684

Taxes
	2005	2006	2007
General tax rate per $100	1.214	1.292	1.405
County equalization ratio	94.11	78.84	69.95
Net valuation taxable	$196,919,396	$197,301,900	$198,387,185
State equalized value	$249,770,923	$282,129,903	$293,572,667

Irvington Township

Essex County

Demographics & Socio-Economic Characteristics
(2000 US Census, except as noted)

Population
1980*	61,493
1990*	61,018
2000	60,695
Male	28,353
Female	32,342
2006 (estimate)*	58,024
Population density	19,602.7

Race & Hispanic Origin, 2000
Race
White	5,446
Black/African American	49,566
American Indian/Alaska Native	146
Asian	669
Native Hawaiian/Pacific Islander	59
Other race	2,234
Two or more races	2,575
Hispanic origin, total	5,086
Mexican	357
Puerto Rican	2,083
Cuban	105
Other Hispanic	2,541

Age & Nativity, 2000
Under 5 years	4,891
18 years and over	43,691
21 years and over	41,138
65 years and over	4,576
85 years and over	507
Median age	31.5
Native-born	45,937
Foreign-born	14,678

Educational Attainment, 2000
Population 25 years and over	37,143
Less than 9th grade	7.6%
High school grad or higher	72.0%
Bachelor's degree or higher	12.1%
Graduate degree	2.7%

Income & Poverty, 1999
Per capita income	$16,874
Median household income	$36,575
Median family income	$41,098
Persons in poverty	10,420
H'holds receiving public assistance	1,778
H'holds receiving social security	4,020

Households, 2000
Total households	22,032
With persons under 18	9,079
With persons over 65	3,679
Family households	14,403
Single-person households	6,453
Persons per household	2.74
Persons per family	3.39

Labor & Employment
Total civilian labor force, 2006**	28,338
Unemployment rate	7.0%
Total civilian labor force, 2000	29,740
Unemployment rate	12.5%

Employed persons 16 years and over by occupation, 2000
Managers & professionals	5,480
Service occupations	5,654
Sales & office occupations	8,445
Farming, fishing & forestry	4
Construction & maintenance	1,547
Production & transportation	4,878
Self-employed persons	698

* US Census Bureau
** New Jersey Department of Labor
§ State Fiscal Year July 1–June 30

General Information
Township of Irvington
1 Civic Square
Irvington, NJ 07111
973-399-8111

Website	www.irvington.net
Year of incorporation	1982
Land/water area (sq. miles)	2.96/0.00
Form of government	Mayor-Council

Government
Legislative Districts
US Congressional	10
State Legislative	28

Local Officials, 2008
Mayor	Wayne Smith
Manager	Wayne Bradley
Clerk	Harold Wiener
Finance Dir.	Faheem Ra'Oof
Tax Assessor	James Gibbs
Tax Collector	Beverly Baytops
Attorney	Marvin Braker
Building	Nagy Sileem
Planning	Wayne Bradley
Engineering	John Wiggins
Public Works	Luis Mollinedo
Police Chief	Michael Chase
Emerg/Fire Director	Gary Shumlich

Housing & Construction
Housing Units, 2000*
Total	24,116
Median rent	$678
Median SF home value	$112,200

Permits for New Residential Construction
	Units	Value
Total, 2007	50	$3,722,622
Single family	2	$300,697
Total, 2006	112	$7,776,179
Single family	11	$1,390,700

Real Property Valuation, 2007
	Parcels	Valuation
Total	9,541	$3,232,617,800
Vacant	399	48,053,200
Residential	7,954	2,052,731,300
Commercial	685	486,137,900
Industrial	173	172,177,200
Apartments	330	473,518,200
Farm land	0	0
Farm homestead	0	0

Average Property Value & Tax, 2007
Residential value	$258,075
Property tax	$5,849
Tax credit/rebate	$893

Public Library
Irvington Public Library
Civic Square
Irvington, NJ 07111
973-372-6400

Director .... Joan E. Whittaker

Library statistics, 2006
Population served	60,695
Full-time/total staff	8/20

	Total	Per capita
Holdings	190,095	3.13
Revenues	$1,632,349	$26.89
Expenditures	$1,635,925	$26.95
Annual visits	242,465	3.99
Internet terminals/annual users	33/43,973	

Taxes
	2005	2006	2007
General tax rate per $100	23.82	25	2.27
County equalization ratio	15.23	12.71	133.52
Net valuation taxable	$263,815,483	$262,646,850	$3,242,943,457
State equalized value	$2,075,652,895	$2,419,805,930	$2,904,343,383

Public Safety
Number of officers, 2006	190

Crime	2005	2006
Total crimes	4,706	4,488
Violent	1,397	1,321
Murder	28	21
Rape	23	23
Robbery	728	681
Aggravated assault	618	596
Non-violent	3,309	3,167
Burglary	1,018	924
Larceny	1,251	1,289
Vehicle theft	1,040	954
Domestic violence	899	807
Arson	4	20
Total crime rate	78.8	76.2
Violent	23.4	22.4
Non-violent	55.4	53.8

Public School District
(for school year 2006-07 except as noted)

Irvington Township School District
1 University Place
Irvington, NJ 07111
973-399-6800

Superintendent	Ethel W. Davion
Number of schools	9
Grade plan	K-12
Enrollment	6,134
Attendance rate, '05-06	92.1%
Dropout rate	1.2%
Students per teacher	10.6
Per pupil expenditure	$15,367
Median faculty salary	$59,741
Median administrator salary	$102,107
Grade 12 enrollment	297
High school graduation rate	86.0%

Assessment test results
(percent scoring at proficient or advanced level)
	Language	Math
NJASK-Grade 3	62.5%	65.3%
GEPA-Grade 8	35.0%	22.9%
HSPA-High School	61.6%	20.3%

SAT score averages
Pct tested	Math	Verbal	Writing
58%	369	375	379

Teacher Qualifications
Avg. years of experience	10
Highly-qualified teachers one subject/all subjects	100%/100%
With emergency credentials	0.2%

No Child Left Behind
AYP, 2005-06 .... Needs Improvement

Municipal Finance§
State Aid Programs, 2008
Total aid	$13,433,146
CMPTRA	10,382,037
Energy tax receipts	3,051,109
Garden State Trust	0

General Budget, 2007
Total tax levy	$73,501,770
County levy	9,627,544
County taxes	9,380,099
County library	0
County health	0
County open space	247,446
School levy	17,459,529
Muni. levy	46,414,697
Misc. revenues	40,639,513

Ocean County
Island Heights Borough

Demographics & Socio-Economic Characteristics
(2000 US Census, except as noted)

Population
1980*	1,575
1990*	1,470
2000	1,751
Male	843
Female	908
2006 (estimate)*	1,877
Population density	3,128.3

Race & Hispanic Origin, 2000
Race
White	1,712
Black/African American	2
American Indian/Alaska Native	8
Asian	11
Native Hawaiian/Pacific Islander	0
Other race	1
Two or more races	17
Hispanic origin, total	24
Mexican	0
Puerto Rican	16
Cuban	4
Other Hispanic	4

Age & Nativity, 2000
Under 5 years	84
18 years and over	1,359
21 years and over	1,308
65 years and over	303
85 years and over	31
Median age	43.0
Native-born	1,663
Foreign-born	86

Educational Attainment, 2000
Population 25 years and over	1,175
Less than 9th grade	1.4%
High school grad or higher	90.8%
Bachelor's degree or higher	33.4%
Graduate degree	12.8%

Income & Poverty, 1999
Per capita income	$26,975
Median household income	$61,125
Median family income	$72,596
Persons in poverty	71
H'holds receiving public assistance	8
H'holds receiving social security	235

Households, 2000
Total households	705
With persons under 18	218
With persons over 65	212
Family households	498
Single-person households	171
Persons per household	2.48
Persons per family	2.97

Labor & Employment
Total civilian labor force, 2006**	842
Unemployment rate	5.0%
Total civilian labor force, 2000	856
Unemployment rate	4.7%

Employed persons 16 years and over by occupation, 2000
Managers & professionals	351
Service occupations	89
Sales & office occupations	202
Farming, fishing & forestry	0
Construction & maintenance	119
Production & transportation	55
Self-employed persons	79

‡ Branch of county library
* US Census Bureau
** New Jersey Department of Labor

See Introduction for an explanation of all data sources.

General Information
Borough of Island Heights
PO Box AH
Island Heights, NJ 08732
732-270-6415
Website .... www.islandheightsboro.com
Year of incorporation 1887
Land/water area (sq. miles) 0.60/0.27
Form of government .... Small Municipality

Government
Legislative Districts
US Congressional 3
State Legislative 10

Local Officials, 2008
Mayor	David Siddons
Manager	Adrian Fanning
Clerk	Eleanor Rogalski
Finance Dir	Adrian Fanning
Tax Assessor	Victoria Mickiewicz
Tax Collector	Wendy Prior
Attorney	Robert Grietz
Building	Ken Anderson
Comm Dev/Planning	NA
Engineering	Michael O'Donnell
Public Works	Jay Price
Police Chief	NA
Emerg/Fire Director	Robert Wilber Jr

Housing & Construction
Housing Units, 2000*
Total	807
Median rent	$830
Median SF home value	$167,400

Permits for New Residential Construction
	Units	Value
Total, 2007	9	$696,213
Single family	9	$696,213
Total, 2006	10	$773,570
Single family	10	$773,570

Real Property Valuation, 2007
	Parcels	Valuation
Total	904	$347,145,100
Vacant	64	14,163,100
Residential	809	309,770,900
Commercial	30	22,721,800
Industrial	0	0
Apartments	1	489,300
Farm land	0	0
Farm homestead	0	0

Average Property Value & Tax, 2007
Residential value	$382,906
Property tax	$5,606
Tax credit/rebate	$956

Public Library
Island Heights Branch Library‡
Summit & Central
Island Heights, NJ 08732
732-270-6266
Branch Librarian .... Emily Holman

Library statistics, 2006
see Ocean County profile
for library system statistics

Public Safety
Number of officers, 2006 5
Crime	2005	2006
Total crimes	17	16
Violent	0	0
Murder	0	0
Rape	0	0
Robbery	0	0
Aggravated assault	0	0
Non-violent	17	16
Burglary	2	4
Larceny	10	11
Vehicle theft	5	1
Domestic violence	2	16
Arson	1	0
Total crime rate	9.2	8.6
Violent	0.0	0.0
Non-violent	9.2	8.6

Public School District
(for school year 2006-07 except as noted)

Island Heights School District
115 Summit Ave, PO Box 329
Island Heights, NJ 08732
732-929-1222

Superintendent	John Lichtenberg
Number of schools	1
Grade plan	K-6
Enrollment	114
Attendance rate, '05-06	95.6%
Dropout rate	NA
Students per teacher	8.8
Per pupil expenditure	$15,919
Median faculty salary	$42,495
Median administrator salary	$75,343
Grade 12 enrollment	NA
High school graduation rate	NA

Assessment test results
(percent scoring at proficient or advanced level)
	Language	Math
NJASK-Grade 3	100.0%	100.0%
GEPA-Grade 8	NA	NA
HSPA-High School	NA	NA

SAT score averages
Pct tested	Math	Verbal	Writing
NA	NA	NA	NA

Teacher Qualifications
Avg. years of experience	13
Highly-qualified teachers one subject/all subjects	100%/100%
With emergency credentials	0.0%

No Child Left Behind
AYP, 2005-06 .... Meets Standards

Municipal Finance
State Aid Programs, 2008
Total aid	$123,464
CMPTRA	0
Energy tax receipts	123,464
Garden State Trust	0

General Budget, 2007
Total tax levy	$5,084,756
County levy	1,217,651
County taxes	1,003,382
County library	118,930
County health	48,184
County open space	47,155
School levy	2,539,147
Muni. levy	1,327,958
Misc. revenues	1,041,562

Taxes	2005	2006	2007
General tax rate per $100	1.361	1.444	1.464
County equalization ratio	135.67	100.89	88.53
Net valuation taxable	$343,054,532	$342,070,700	$347,331,640
State equalized value	$340,028,280	$386,587,938	$416,677,362

The New Jersey Municipal Data Book 233

©2008 Information Publications, Inc. All rights reserved. Photocopying prohibited. For additional copies, contact the publisher at www.informationpublications.com or (877)544-INFO (4636)

Jackson Township
Ocean County

Demographics & Socio-Economic Characteristics
(2000 US Census, except as noted)

Population
1980*	25,644
1990*	33,233
2000	42,816
Male	20,911
Female	21,905
2006 (estimate)*	52,305
Population density	522.7

Race & Hispanic Origin, 2000
Race
White	39,073
Black/African American	1,670
American Indian/Alaska Native	57
Asian	882
Native Hawaiian/Pacific Islander	3
Other race	414
Two or more races	717
Hispanic origin, total	2,474
Mexican	201
Puerto Rican	1,316
Cuban	161
Other Hispanic	796

Age & Nativity, 2000
Under 5 years	3,515
18 years and over	30,114
21 years and over	28,764
65 years and over	4,009
85 years and over	456
Median age	35.2
Native-born	40,097
Foreign-born	2,713

Educational Attainment, 2000
Population 25 years and over	27,385
Less than 9th grade	3.6%
High school grad or higher	86.9%
Bachelor's degree or higher	23.1%
Graduate degree	6.0%

Income & Poverty, 1999
Per capita income	$23,981
Median household income	$65,218
Median family income	$71,045
Persons in poverty	1,573
H'holds receiving public assistance	193
H'holds receiving social security	3,181

Households, 2000
Total households	14,176
With persons under 18	6,676
With persons over 65	2,750
Family households	11,264
Single-person households	2,267
Persons per household	2.99
Persons per family	3.38

Labor & Employment
Total civilian labor force, 2006**	27,135
Unemployment rate	4.4%
Total civilian labor force, 2000	21,325
Unemployment rate	4.3%

Employed persons 16 years and over by occupation, 2000
Managers & professionals	7,163
Service occupations	2,825
Sales & office occupations	5,568
Farming, fishing & forestry	26
Construction & maintenance	2,508
Production & transportation	2,320
Self-employed persons	915

‡ Branch of county library
* US Census Bureau
** New Jersey Department of Labor

General Information
Township of Jackson
95 W Veterans Hwy
Jackson, NJ 08527
732-928-1200

Website	www.jacksontwpnj.net
Year of incorporation	1844
Land/water area (sq. miles)	100.06/0.75
Form of government	Township

Government
Legislative Districts
US Congressional	4
State Legislative	30

Local Officials, 2008
Mayor	Mark A. Seda
Manager	Philip Del Turco
Clerk	Ann Marie Eden
Finance Dir	Sharon Pinkava
Tax Assessor	Dennis Raftery
Tax Collector	Michael Campbell
Attorney	George Gilmore
Building	Barry Olejarz
Planning	Jeff Purpuro
Engineering	Daniel Burke
Public Works	Fred Rasiewicz
Police Chief	NA
Emerg/Fire Director	Barry Olejarz

Housing & Construction
Housing Units, 2000*
Total	14,640
Median rent	$863
Median SF home value	$156,300

Permits for New Residential Construction
	Units	Value
Total, 2007	37	$6,095,405
Single family	37	$6,095,405
Total, 2006	146	$18,951,911
Single family	146	$18,951,911

Real Property Valuation, 2007
	Parcels	Valuation
Total	19,900	$2,958,607,250
Vacant	2,807	94,868,650
Residential	16,640	2,550,024,600
Commercial	218	252,420,000
Industrial	52	18,118,100
Apartments	10	30,853,100
Farm land	108	741,300
Farm homestead	65	11,581,500

Average Property Value & Tax, 2007
Residential value	$153,344
Property tax	$5,892
Tax credit/rebate	$1,054

Public Library
Jackson Branch Library‡
2nd Jackson Rd
Jackson, NJ 08527
732-928-4400

Branch Librarian .... John Glace

Library statistics, 2006
see Ocean County profile for library system statistics

Public Safety
Number of officers, 2006 86

Crime	2005	2006
Total crimes	575	612
Violent	42	31
Murder	0	0
Rape	5	1
Robbery	11	8
Aggravated assault	26	22
Non-violent	533	581
Burglary	122	105
Larceny	373	438
Vehicle theft	38	38
Domestic violence	389	383
Arson	8	18
Total crime rate	11.1	11.8
Violent	0.8	0.6
Non-violent	10.3	11.2

Public School District
(for school year 2006-07 except as noted)

Jackson Township School District
151 Don Connor Blvd
Jackson, NJ 08527
732-833-4600

Superintendent	Thomas Gialanella
Number of schools	10
Grade plan	K-12
Enrollment	9,682
Attendance rate, '05-06	94.5%
Dropout rate	0.8%
Students per teacher	12.2
Per pupil expenditure	$11,585
Median faculty salary	$48,400
Median administrator salary	$124,319
Grade 12 enrollment	684
High school graduation rate	96.9%

Assessment test results
(percent scoring at proficient or advanced level)
	Language	Math
NJASK-Grade 3	92.4%	97.4%
GEPA-Grade 8	85.0%	83.8%
HSPA-High School	87.0%	75.8%

SAT score averages
Pct tested	Math	Verbal	Writing
73%	499	484	477

Teacher Qualifications
Avg. years of experience	8
Highly-qualified teachers one subject/all subjects	99.5%/99.5%
With emergency credentials	0.2%

No Child Left Behind
AYP, 2005-06 .... Meets Standards

Municipal Finance
State Aid Programs, 2008
Total aid	$4,396,809
CMPTRA	1,120,247
Energy tax receipts	3,182,885
Garden State Trust	83,805

General Budget, 2007
Total tax levy	$113,867,261
County levy	21,917,145
County taxes	18,060,632
County library	2,140,551
County health	867,229
County open space	848,733
School levy	67,524,186
Muni. levy	24,425,930
Misc. revenues	15,427,704

Taxes
	2005	2006	2007
General tax rate per $100	3.457	3.774	3.843
County equalization ratio	51.63	46.89	41.96
Net valuation taxable	$2,661,659,878	$2,822,880,550	$2,963,469,271
State equalized value	$5,676,391,295	$6,732,766,452	$7,403,229,738

Middlesex County

Jamesburg Borough

Demographics & Socio-Economic Characteristics
(2000 US Census, except as noted)

Population
- 1980* 4,114
- 1990* 5,294
- 2000 6,025
  - Male 2,935
  - Female 3,090
- 2006 (estimate)* 6,429
- Population density 7,653.6

Race & Hispanic Origin, 2000
Race
- White 4,990
- Black/African American 532
- American Indian/Alaska Native 12
- Asian 134
- Native Hawaiian/Pacific Islander 0
- Other race 229
- Two or more races 128
- Hispanic origin, total 606
  - Mexican 119
  - Puerto Rican 180
  - Cuban 26
  - Other Hispanic 281

Age & Nativity, 2000
- Under 5 years 457
- 18 years and over 4,541
- 21 years and over 4,364
- 65 years and over 646
- 85 years and over 117
  - Median age 35.4
- Native-born 5,344
- Foreign-born 681

Educational Attainment, 2000
- Population 25 years and over 4,089
- Less than 9th grade 5.5%
- High school grad or higher 82.9%
- Bachelor's degree or higher 20.2%
- Graduate degree 5.0%

Income & Poverty, 1999
- Per capita income $23,325
- Median household income $59,461
- Median family income $67,887
- Persons in poverty 206
- H'holds receiving public assistance . 65
- H'holds receiving social security .. 424

Households, 2000
- Total households 2,176
  - With persons under 18 843
  - With persons over 65 402
  - Family households 1,551
  - Single-person households 487
- Persons per household 2.70
- Persons per family 3.18

Labor & Employment
- Total civilian labor force, 2006** .. 3,680
  - Unemployment rate 4.6%
- Total civilian labor force, 2000 ... 3,327
  - Unemployment rate 4.3%

Employed persons 16 years and over by occupation, 2000
- Managers & professionals 855
- Service occupations 429
- Sales & office occupations 980
- Farming, fishing & forestry 0
- Construction & maintenance 324
- Production & transportation 595
- Self-employed persons 127

* US Census Bureau
** New Jersey Department of Labor

See Introduction for an explanation of all data sources.

General Information
Borough of Jamesburg
131 Perrineville Rd
Jamesburg, NJ 08831
732-521-2222

- Website .... www.jamesburgborough.org
- Year of incorporation 1887
- Land/water area (sq. miles) 0.84/0.00
- Form of government .... Borough

Government
Legislative Districts
- US Congressional 12
- State Legislative 14

Local Officials, 2008
- Mayor .... Anthony La Mantia
- Business Admin .... Denise Jawidzik
- Clerk .... Gretchen McCarthy
- Finance Dir .... Denise Jawidzik
- Tax Assessor .... Ken Pacera
- Tax Collector .... Denise Jawidzik
- Attorney .... Frederick Raffetto
- Building .... NA
- Comm Dev/Planning .... NA
- Engineering .... Alan Dittenhofer
- Public Works .... Joseph Intravartola
- Police Chief .... Martin Horvath
- Fire Chief .... Dwayne Fitzpatrick

Housing & Construction
Housing Units, 2000*
- Total 2,240
- Median rent $777
- Median SF home value $139,300

Permits for New Residential Construction

	Units	Value
Total, 2007	3	$321,996
Single family	3	$321,996
Total, 2006	0	$6,000
Single family	0	$6,000

Real Property Valuation, 2007

	Parcels	Valuation
Total	1,801	$239,906,300
Vacant	114	2,941,300
Residential	1,569	194,587,500
Commercial	103	33,062,400
Industrial	1	925,000
Apartments	14	8,390,100
Farm land	0	0
Farm homestead	0	0

Average Property Value & Tax, 2007
- Residential value $124,020
- Property tax $5,670
- Tax credit/rebate $1,019

Public Library
Jamesburg Public Library
229 Gatzmer Ave
Jamesburg, NJ 08831
732-521-0440

- Director .... Cynthia Yasher

Library statistics, 2006
- Population served 6,025
- Full-time/total staff 0/1

	Total	Per capita
Holdings	26,822	4.45
Revenues	$160,015	$26.56
Expenditures	$155,538	$25.82
Annual visits	27,724	4.60

- Internet terminals/annual users ... 2/2,555

Public Safety
- Number of officers, 2006 13

Crime	2005	2006
Total crimes	64	72
Violent	11	12
Murder	0	0
Rape	2	3
Robbery	1	3
Aggravated assault	8	6
Non-violent	53	60
Burglary	13	20
Larceny	36	33
Vehicle theft	4	7
Domestic violence	32	39
Arson	0	0
Total crime rate	9.8	11.0
Violent	1.7	1.8
Non-violent	8.1	9.2

Public School District
(for school year 2006-07 except as noted)

Jamesburg School District
13 Augusta St
Jamesburg, NJ 08831
732-521-0303

- Superintendent .... Gail S. Verona
- Number of schools 2
- Grade plan K-8
- Enrollment 658
- Attendance rate, '05-06 .... 94.9%
- Dropout rate .... NA
- Students per teacher 11.3
- Per pupil expenditure $11,619
- Median faculty salary $44,852
- Median administrator salary $86,280
- Grade 12 enrollment .... NA
- High school graduation rate .... NA

Assessment test results
(percent scoring at proficient or advanced level)

	Language	Math
NJASK-Grade 3	78.0%	83.0%
GEPA-Grade 8	50.0%	60.4%
HSPA-High School	NA	NA

SAT score averages

Pct tested	Math	Verbal	Writing
NA	NA	NA	NA

Teacher Qualifications
- Avg. years of experience 11
- Highly-qualified teachers
  one subject/all subjects ... 90.5%/90.5%
- With emergency credentials 0.0%

No Child Left Behind
- AYP, 2005-06 .... Meets Standards

Municipal Finance
State Aid Programs, 2008
- Total aid $466,775
  - CMPTRA 114,646
  - Energy tax receipts 352,129
  - Garden State Trust 0

General Budget, 2007
- Total tax levy $11,025,309
  - County levy 1,488,182
    - County taxes 1,332,255
    - County library 0
    - County health 0
    - County open space 155,927
  - School levy 6,587,474
  - Muni. levy 2,949,653
- Misc. revenues 2,400,973

Taxes

	2005	2006	2007
General tax rate per $100	4.32	4.39	4.58
County equalization ratio	60.8	53.62	46.52
Net valuation taxable	$239,196,175	$238,571,800	$241,151,778
State equalized value	$446,095,067	$514,239,424	$556,841,356

The New Jersey Municipal Data Book

Jefferson Township — Morris County

Demographics & Socio-Economic Characteristics
(2000 US Census, except as noted)

Population
1980*	16,413
1990*	17,825
2000	19,717
Male	9,775
Female	9,942
2006 (estimate)*	21,963
Population density	540.6

Race & Hispanic Origin, 2000
Race
- White: 18,955
- Black/African American: 163
- American Indian/Alaska Native: 32
- Asian: 211
- Native Hawaiian/Pacific Islander: 10
- Other race: 122
- Two or more races: 224
- Hispanic origin, total: 672
  - Mexican: 50
  - Puerto Rican: 244
  - Cuban: 53
  - Other Hispanic: 325

Age & Nativity, 2000
- Under 5 years: 1,452
- 18 years and over: 14,407
- 21 years and over: 13,861
- 65 years and over: 1,690
- 85 years and over: 158
- Median age: 37.2
- Native-born: 18,474
- Foreign-born: 1,243

Educational Attainment, 2000
- Population 25 years and over: 13,398
- Less than 9th grade: 2.6%
- High school grad or higher: 89.6%
- Bachelor's degree or higher: 27.8%
- Graduate degree: 7.1%

Income & Poverty, 1999
- Per capita income: $27,950
- Median household income: $68,837
- Median family income: $76,974
- Persons in poverty: 468
- H'holds receiving public assistance: 33
- H'holds receiving social security: 1,371

Households, 2000
- Total households: 7,131
- With persons under 18: 2,907
- With persons over 65: 1,281
- Family households: 5,446
- Single-person households: 1,316
- Persons per household: 2.76
- Persons per family: 3.17

Labor & Employment
- Total civilian labor force, 2006**: 12,079
- Unemployment rate: 3.4%
- Total civilian labor force, 2000: 11,023
- Unemployment rate: 3.1%

Employed persons 16 years and over by occupation, 2000
- Managers & professionals: 4,036
- Service occupations: 1,132
- Sales & office occupations: 3,210
- Farming, fishing & forestry: 9
- Construction & maintenance: 1,326
- Production & transportation: 968
- Self-employed persons: 447

* US Census Bureau
** New Jersey Department of Labor

General Information
Township of Jefferson
1033 Weldon Rd
Lake Hopatcong, NJ 07849
973-697-1500

- Website: www.jeffersontownship.net
- Year of incorporation: 1804
- Land/water area (sq. miles): 40.63/2.41
- Form of government: Mayor-Council

Government
Legislative Districts
- US Congressional: 11
- State Legislative: 25

Local Officials, 2008
- Mayor: Russell Felter
- Manager: James Leach
- Clerk: Lydia Magnotti
- Finance Dir: Bill Eagen
- Tax Assessor: Shawn Hopkins
- Tax Collector: Elizabeth Recksiek
- Attorney: Lawrence Cohen
- Building: Tom Mahoney
- Comm Dev/Planning: NA
- Engineering: Hatch Mott McDonald
- Public Works: Jeff Elam
- Police Chief: John Palko
- Fire Chief: Andy Schmidt

Housing & Construction
Housing Units, 2000*
- Total: 7,527
- Median rent: $847
- Median SF home value: $180,400

Permits for New Residential Construction
	Units	Value
Total, 2007	41	$6,004,268
Single family	41	$6,004,268
Total, 2006	53	$6,121,288
Single family	48	$6,120,238

Real Property Valuation, 2007
	Parcels	Valuation
Total	8,903	$3,230,039,800
Vacant	748	84,932,800
Residential	7,851	2,912,854,700
Commercial	211	191,001,800
Industrial	11	6,382,900
Apartments	27	24,933,900
Farm land	36	259,800
Farm homestead	19	9,673,900

Average Property Value & Tax, 2007
- Residential value: $371,351
- Property tax: $6,299
- Tax credit/rebate: $1,081

Public Library
Jefferson Township Municipal Library
1031 Weldon Rd
Oak Ridge, NJ 07438
973-208-6115

- Director: Seth Stephens

Library statistics, 2006
- Population served: 19,717
- Full-time/total staff: 1/7

	Total	Per capita
Holdings	55,920	2.84
Revenues	$1,747,517	$88.63
Expenditures	$684,380	$34.71
Annual visits	100,957	5.12
Internet terminals/annual users	15/15,750	

Taxes
	2005	2006	2007
General tax rate per $100	3.48	1.6	1.7
County equalization ratio	58.82	118.78	106.15
Net valuation taxable	$1,385,310,610	$3,203,336,300	$3,234,361,311
State equalized value	$2,643,722,538	$3,022,155,884	$3,201,431,082

Public Safety
- Number of officers, 2006: 39

Crime	2005	2006
Total crimes	285	250
Violent	22	14
Murder	0	0
Rape	3	1
Robbery	0	6
Aggravated assault	19	7
Non-violent	263	236
Burglary	77	67
Larceny	183	158
Vehicle theft	3	11
Domestic violence	99	104
Arson	2	2
Total crime rate	13.4	11.6
Violent	1.0	0.6
Non-violent	12.4	10.9

Public School District
(for school year 2006-07 except as noted)

Jefferson Township School District
28 Bowling Green Parkway
Lake Hopatcong, NJ 07849
973-663-5780

- Superintendent: Kathleen Fuchs
- Number of schools: 8
- Grade plan: K-12
- Enrollment: 3,635
- Attendance rate, '05-06: 94.6%
- Dropout rate: 1.5%
- Students per teacher: 11.8
- Per pupil expenditure: $12,707
- Median faculty salary: $48,980
- Median administrator salary: $107,917
- Grade 12 enrollment: 269
- High school graduation rate: 95.2%

Assessment test results
(percent scoring at proficient or advanced level)
	Language	Math
NJASK-Grade 3	92.1%	96.3%
GEPA-Grade 8	77.1%	80.1%
HSPA-High School	90.5%	83.7%

SAT score averages
Pct tested	Math	Verbal	Writing
69%	503	488	480

Teacher Qualifications
- Avg. years of experience: 9
- Highly-qualified teachers one subject/all subjects: 100%/100%
- With emergency credentials: 0.9%

No Child Left Behind
- AYP, 2005-06: Meets Standards

Municipal Finance
State Aid Programs, 2008
- Total aid: $2,633,757
- CMPTRA: 168,787
- Energy tax receipts: 2,238,360
- Garden State Trust: 33,816

General Budget, 2007
- Total tax levy: $54,858,723
- County levy: 7,286,770
- County taxes: 5,826,245
- County library: 0
- County health: 0
- County open space: 1,460,525
- School levy: 33,924,113
- Muni. levy: 13,647,840
- Misc. revenues: 7,641,177

Hudson County — Jersey City

Demographics & Socio-Economic Characteristics†
(2000 US Census, except as noted)

Population
- 1980* 223,532
- 1990* 228,537
- 2000 240,055
  - Male 117,144
  - Female 122,911
- 2006 (estimate)* 241,789
- Population density 16,205.7

Race & Hispanic Origin, 2000
Race
- White 81,637
- Black/African American 67,994
- American Indian/Alaska Native 1,071
- Asian 38,881
- Native Hawaiian/Pacific Islander 181
- Other race 36,280
- Two or more races 14,011
- Hispanic origin, total 67,952
  - Mexican 2,495
  - Puerto Rican 29,777
  - Cuban 1,860
  - Other Hispanic 33,820

Age & Nativity, 2000
- Under 5 years 16,631
- 18 years and over 180,652
- 21 years and over 170,621
- 65 years and over 23,438
- 85 years and over 2,805
- Median age 32.4
- Native-born 158,501
- Foreign-born 81,554

Educational Attainment, 2000
- Population 25 years and over 155,460
- Less than 9th grade 10.6%
- High school grad or higher 72.6%
- Bachelor's degree or higher 27.5%
- Graduate degree 9.3%

Income & Poverty, 1999
- Per capita income $19,410
- Median household income $37,862
- Median family income $41,639
- Persons in poverty 44,075
- H'holds receiving public assistance 5,977
- H'holds receiving social security 17,981

Households, 2000
- Total households 88,632
  - With persons under 18 31,837
  - With persons over 65 17,802
  - Family households 55,636
  - Single-person households 25,921
- Persons per household 2.67
- Persons per family 3.37

Labor & Employment
- Total civilian labor force, 2006** 113,225
  - Unemployment rate 6.0%
- Total civilian labor force, 2000 114,909
  - Unemployment rate 10.0%

Employed persons 16 years and over by occupation, 2000
- Managers & professionals 34,111
- Service occupations 16,436
- Sales & office occupations 31,502
- Farming, fishing & forestry 81
- Construction & maintenance 5,313
- Production & transportation 16,005
- Self-employed persons 3,448

† see Appendix C for American Community Survey data
* US Census Bureau
** New Jersey Department of Labor
§ State Fiscal Year July 1–June 30

See Introduction for an explanation of all data sources.

General Information
City of Jersey
280 Grove St
Jersey City, NJ 07302
201-547-5000

- Website .... www.cityofjerseycity.com
- Year of incorporation 1820
- Land/water area (sq. miles) 14.92/6.20
- Form of government .... Mayor-Council

Government
Legislative Districts
- US Congressional 9-10, 13
- State Legislative 31-33

Local Officials, 2008
- Mayor .... Jerramiah T. Healy
- Manager .... Brian O'Reilly
- Clerk .... Robert Byrne
- Finance Dir .... Paul Soyka
- Tax Assessor .... Eduardo Toloza
- Tax Collector .... Maureen Cosgrove
- Attorney .... William Matsikoudis
- Building .... Raymond Meyer
- Planning .... Robert Cotter
- Engineering .... William Goble
- Public Works .... John M. Yurchak
- Police Chief .... Thomas J. Comey
- Fire Chief .... William C. Sinnott

Housing & Construction
Housing Units, 2000*
- Total 93,648
- Median rent $675
- Median SF home value $125,000

Permits for New Residential Construction

	Units	Value
Total, 2007	1,480	$282,277,288
Single family	41	$7,789,922
Total, 2006	2,422	$151,232,624
Single family	5	$2,440,417

Real Property Valuation, 2007

	Parcels	Valuation
Total	46,126	$5,697,281,578
Vacant	6,771	346,505,428
Residential	33,532	3,122,714,174
Commercial	3,469	1,354,389,526
Industrial	677	468,631,900
Apartments	1,677	405,040,550
Farm land	0	0
Farm homestead	0	0

Average Property Value & Tax, 2007
- Residential value $93,126
- Property tax $5,167
- Tax credit/rebate $858

Public Library
Jersey City Public Library
472 Jersey Ave
Jersey City, NJ 07302
201-547-4500

- Director .... Priscilla Gardner

Library statistics, 2006
- Population served 240,055
- Full-time/total staff 21/110

	Total	Per capita
Holdings	457,963	1.91
Revenues	$8,550,374	$35.62
Expenditures	$8,108,875	$33.78
Annual visits	471,053	1.96
Internet terminals/annual users	175/153,413	

Taxes

	2005	2006	2007
General tax rate per $100	4.605	5.175	5.549
County equalization ratio	44.01	34.59	28.71
Net valuation taxable	$5,470,850,530	$5,666,397,426	$5,716,019,239
State equalized value	$15,816,277,913	$19,758,887,061	$21,830,688,572

Public Safety
- Number of officers, 2006 870

Crime	2005	2006
Total crimes	11,987	10,589
Violent	3,180	2,923
Murder	38	22
Rape	43	60
Robbery	1,667	1,573
Aggravated assault	1,432	1,268
Non-violent	8,807	7,666
Burglary	2,219	
Larceny	4,726	4,496
Vehicle theft	1,862	1,499
Domestic violence	2,347	1,823
Arson	73	97
Total crime rate	50.1	44.2
Violent	13.3	12.2
Non-violent	36.8	32.0

Public School District
(for school year 2006-07 except as noted)

Jersey City School District
346 Claremont Ave
Jersey City, NJ 07305
201-915-6202

- State District Superint .... Charles T. Epps Jr
- Number of schools 37
- Grade plan K-12
- Enrollment 27,791
- Attendance rate, '05-06 .... 93.1%
- Dropout rate 8.1%
- Students per teacher 9.1
- Per pupil expenditure $15,044
- Median faculty salary $50,092
- Median administrator salary $111,402
- Grade 12 enrollment 1,380
- High school graduation rate .... NA

Assessment test results
(percent scoring at proficient or advanced level)

	Language	Math
NJASK-Grade 3	69.9%	75.8%
GEPA-Grade 8	51.6%	47.1%
HSPA-High School	65.4%	48.4%

SAT score averages

Pct tested	Math	Verbal	Writing
NA	NA	NA	NA

Teacher Qualifications
- Avg. years of experience 7
- Highly-qualified teachers
  - one subject/all subjects 99.5%/99.0%
- With emergency credentials 0.8%

No Child Left Behind
- AYP, 2005-06 .... Meets Standards

Municipal Finance§
State Aid Programs, 2008
- Total aid $78,681,196
  - CMPTRA 40,060,703
  - Energy tax receipts 38,590,455
  - Garden State Trust 30,038

General Budget, 2007
- Total tax levy $317,147,041
  - County levy 82,661,082
    - County taxes 80,635,800
    - County library 0
    - County health 0
    - County open space 2,025,282
  - School levy 88,885,960
  - Muni. levy 145,600,000
- Misc. revenues 285,339,523

©2008 Information Publications, Inc. All rights reserved. Photocopying prohibited. For additional copies, contact the publisher at www.informationpublications.com or (877)544-INFO (4636)

The New Jersey Municipal Data Book

Keansburg Borough
Monmouth County

Demographics & Socio-Economic Characteristics
(2000 US Census, except as noted)

Population
1980*	10,613
1990*	11,069
2000	10,732
Male	5,237
Female	5,495
2006 (estimate)*	10,573
Population density	9,789.8

Race & Hispanic Origin, 2000
Race
White	10,014
Black/African American	229
American Indian/Alaska Native	11
Asian	132
Native Hawaiian/Pacific Islander	7
Other race	187
Two or more races	152
Hispanic origin, total	853
Mexican	61
Puerto Rican	473
Cuban	70
Other Hispanic	249

Age & Nativity, 2000
Under 5 years	755
18 years and over	7,814
21 years and over	7,407
65 years and over	1,207
85 years and over	152
Median age	34.4
Native-born	9,950
Foreign-born	782

Educational Attainment, 2000
Population 25 years and over	6,854
Less than 9th grade	6.7%
High school grad or higher	69.8%
Bachelor's degree or higher	9.5%
Graduate degree	2.8%

Income & Poverty, 1999
Per capita income	$17,417
Median household income	$36,383
Median family income	$45,438
Persons in poverty	1,874
H'holds receiving public assistance	138
H'holds receiving social security	1,052

Households, 2000
Total households	3,872
With persons under 18	1,525
With persons over 65	859
Family households	2,563
Single-person households	1,059
Persons per household	2.71
Persons per family	3.35

Labor & Employment
Total civilian labor force, 2006**	5,556
Unemployment rate	7.6%
Total civilian labor force, 2000	5,159
Unemployment rate	7.5%

Employed persons 16 years and over by occupation, 2000
Managers & professionals	1,001
Service occupations	808
Sales & office occupations	1,461
Farming, fishing & forestry	15
Construction & maintenance	678
Production & transportation	810
Self-employed persons	217

---

* US Census Bureau
** New Jersey Department of Labor
§ State Fiscal Year July 1–June 30

General Information
Borough of Keansburg
29 Church St
Keansburg, NJ 07734
732-787-0215

Website	keansburgboro.com
Year of incorporation	1917
Land/water area (sq. miles)	1.08/15.75
Form of government	Council-Manager

Government
Legislative Districts
US Congressional	6
State Legislative	13

Local Officials, 2008
Mayor	Lisa Strydio
Manager	Terence Wall
Clerk	Thomas Cusick
Finance Dir	Glenn Cullen
Tax Assessor	Michael Frangella
Tax Collector	Thomas Cusick
Attorney	John O. Bennett III
Building	Robert Burlew
Comm Dev/Planning	NA
Engineering	Rick Brown
Public Works	Dennis O'Keefe
Police Chief	Raymond O'Hare
Emerg/Fire Director	James Merkel

Housing & Construction
Housing Units, 2000*
Total	4,269
Median rent	$718
Median SF home value	$99,000

Permits for New Residential Construction
	Units	Value
Total, 2007	19	$2,238,000
Single family	19	$2,168,000
Total, 2006	5	$455,551
Single family	5	$455,551

Real Property Valuation, 2007
	Parcels	Valuation
Total	3,317	$774,747,900
Vacant	99	6,144,100
Residential	3,042	669,815,700
Commercial	125	62,573,100
Industrial	3	2,850,300
Apartments	48	33,364,700
Farm land	0	0
Farm homestead	0	0

Average Property Value & Tax, 2007
Residential value	$220,189
Property tax	$3,884
Tax credit/rebate	$825

Public Library
Keansburg Public Library
55 Shore Blvd
Keansburg, NJ 07734
732-787-0636

Director	Ellen O'Brien

Library statistics, 2006
Population served	NA
Full-time/total staff	NA/NA

	Total	Per capita
Holdings	NA	NA
Revenues	NA	NA
Expenditures	NA	NA
Annual visits	NA	NA
Internet terminals/annual users	NA/NA	

Taxes
	2005	2006	2007
General tax rate per $100	4.591	4.747	1.764
County equalization ratio	54.34	45.49	106.32
Net valuation taxable	$276,085,830	$277,074,590	$775,164,574
State equalized value	$606,915,432	$721,170,835	$789,365,656

Public Safety
Number of officers, 2006	33

Crime	2005	2006
Total crimes	309	369
Violent	40	65
Murder	0	0
Rape	4	3
Robbery	7	6
Aggravated assault	29	56
Non-violent	269	304
Burglary	40	57
Larceny	212	235
Vehicle theft	17	12
Domestic violence	587	613
Arson	1	1
Total crime rate	28.8	34.7
Violent	3.7	6.1
Non-violent	25.0	28.6

Public School District
(for school year 2006-07 except as noted)

Keansburg Borough School District
100 Palmer Place
Keansburg, NJ 07734
732-787-2007

Superintendent	Barbara A. Trzeszkowski
Number of schools	4
Grade plan	K-12
Enrollment	1,915
Attendance rate, '05-06	92.0%
Dropout rate	0.8%
Students per teacher	6.7
Per pupil expenditure	$19,976
Median faculty salary	$46,120
Median administrator salary	$96,600
Grade 12 enrollment	116
High school graduation rate	97.5%

Assessment test results
(percent scoring at proficient or advanced level)
	Language	Math
NJASK-Grade 3	75.7%	84.2%
GEPA-Grade 8	47.9%	57.7%
HSPA-High School	85.1%	71.1%

SAT score averages
Pct tested	Math	Verbal	Writing
63%	455	432	427

Teacher Qualifications
Avg. years of experience	6
Highly-qualified teachers one subject/all subjects	100%/100%
With emergency credentials	0.0%

No Child Left Behind
AYP, 2005-06	Meets Standards

Municipal Finance §
State Aid Programs, 2008
Total aid	$2,156,306
CMPTRA	1,589,642
Energy tax receipts	566,664
Garden State Trust	0

General Budget, 2007
Total tax levy	$13,671,805
County levy	1,971,663
County taxes	1,760,841
County library	100,801
County health	0
County open space	110,021
School levy	4,473,434
Muni. levy	7,226,708
Misc. revenues	5,396,015

Hudson County
Kearny Town

Demographics & Socio-Economic Characteristics
(2000 US Census, except as noted)

Population
1980*	35,735
1990*	34,874
2000	40,513
Male	20,901
Female	19,612
2006 (estimate)*	38,008
Population density	4,158.4

Race & Hispanic Origin, 2000
Race
White	30,687
Black/African American	1,609
American Indian/Alaska Native	148
Asian	2,228
Native Hawaiian/Pacific Islander	27
Other race	4,068
Two or more races	1,746
Hispanic origin, total	11,075
Mexican	375
Puerto Rican	2,237
Cuban	847
Other Hispanic	7,616

Age & Nativity, 2000
Under 5 years	2,328
18 years and over	31,814
21 years and over	30,154
65 years and over	4,407
85 years and over	506
Median age	34.7
Native-born	25,038
Foreign-born	15,475

Educational Attainment, 2000
Population 25 years and over	27,690
Less than 9th grade	12.6%
High school grad or higher	70.9%
Bachelor's degree or higher	17.4%
Graduate degree	6.6%

Income & Poverty, 1999
Per capita income	$20,886
Median household income	$47,757
Median family income	$54,596
Persons in poverty	3,262
H'holds receiving public assistance	400
H'holds receiving social security	3,358

Households, 2000
Total households	13,539
With persons under 18	5,100
With persons over 65	3,276
Family households	9,809
Single-person households	2,958
Persons per household	2.81
Persons per family	3.28

Labor & Employment
Total civilian labor force, 2006**	18,525
Unemployment rate	5.5%
Total civilian labor force, 2000	19,045
Unemployment rate	6.8%

Employed persons 16 years and over by occupation, 2000
Managers & professionals	4,747
Service occupations	2,658
Sales & office occupations	5,261
Farming, fishing & forestry	15
Construction & maintenance	2,044
Production & transportation	3,016
Self-employed persons	757

* US Census Bureau
** New Jersey Department of Labor
§ State Fiscal Year July 1–June 30

See Introduction for an explanation of all data sources.

General Information
Town of Kearny
402 Kearny Ave
Kearny, NJ 07032
201-955-7400

Website	www.kearnyusa.com
Year of incorporation	1899
Land/water area (sq. miles)	9.14/1.05
Form of government	Town

Government
Legislative Districts
US Congressional	9, 13
State Legislative	32

Local Officials, 2008
Mayor	Alberto Santos
Manager	Joseph D'Arco
Clerk	Jill E. Waller (Actg)
Finance Dir	Shuaib Firozvi
Tax Assessor	Gerard Pontrelli
Tax Collector	Sharon Curran
Attorney	Gregory Castano
Building	Michael Martello
Comm Dev/Planning	NA
Engineering	Joseph Neglia
Public Works	Gerard Kerr
Police Chief	John Dowie
Fire Chief	Steven Dyl (Actg)

Housing & Construction
Housing Units, 2000*
Total	13,872
Median rent	$769
Median SF home value	$158,200

Permits for New Residential Construction
	Units	Value
Total, 2007	11	$1,155,750
Single family	1	$227,000
Total, 2006	15	$1,392,070
Single family	1	$266,700

Real Property Valuation, 2007
	Parcels	Valuation
Total	8,124	$1,063,848,200
Vacant	183	16,500,400
Residential	7,091	666,130,000
Commercial	490	104,965,500
Industrial	222	241,456,200
Apartments	138	34,796,100
Farm land	0	0
Farm homestead	0	0

Average Property Value & Tax, 2007
Residential value	$93,940
Property tax	$7,774
Tax credit/rebate	$1,160

Public Library
Kearny Public Library
318 Kearny Ave
Kearny, NJ 07032
201-998-2666

Director	Julie McCarthy

Library statistics, 2006
Population served	40,513
Full-time/total staff	4/13

	Total	Per capita
Holdings	84,175	2.08
Revenues	$1,151,051	28.41
Expenditures	$1,004,216	24.79
Annual visits	64,320	1.59
Internet terminals/annual users	20/36,363	

Taxes
	2005	2006	2007
General tax rate per $100	7.329	7.91	8.276
County equalization ratio	38.41	32.61	28.1
Net valuation taxable	$1,058,747,069	$1,056,765,200	$1,066,043,901
State equalized value	$3,246,694,477	$3,763,223,911	$4,079,804,747

Public Safety
Number of officers, 2006	118

Crime	2005	2006
Total crimes	1,197	1,091
Violent	116	104
Murder	0	1
Rape	6	1
Robbery	39	44
Aggravated assault	71	58
Non-violent	1,081	987
Burglary	151	152
Larceny	665	617
Vehicle theft	265	218
Domestic violence	298	276
Arson	10	14
Total crime rate	30.3	28.1
Violent	2.9	2.7
Non-violent	27.4	25.5

Public School District
(for school year 2006-07 except as noted)

Kearny School District
100 Davis Ave
Kearny, NJ 07032
201-955-5021

Superintendent	Robert Mooney
Number of schools	7
Grade plan	K-12
Enrollment	5,492
Attendance rate, '05-06	94.5%
Dropout rate	3.9%
Students per teacher	11.7
Per pupil expenditure	$12,447
Median faculty salary	$55,752
Median administrator salary	$112,955
Grade 12 enrollment	382
High school graduation rate	88.4%

Assessment test results
(percent scoring at proficient or advanced level)
	Language	Math
NJASK-Grade 3	84.9%	89.1%
GEPA-Grade 8	73.7%	73.1%
HSPA-High School	83.5%	71.1%

SAT score averages
Pct tested	Math	Verbal	Writing
62%	469	446	438

Teacher Qualifications
Avg. years of experience	11
Highly-qualified teachers one subject/all subjects	99.0%/99.0%
With emergency credentials	0.9%

No Child Left Behind
AYP, 2005-06	Meets Standards

Municipal Finance§
State Aid Programs, 2008
Total aid	$21,584,844
CMPTRA	2,267,539
Energy tax receipts	19,316,266
Garden State Trust	1,039

General Budget, 2007
Total tax levy	$88,216,889
County levy	15,858,207
County taxes	15,470,599
County library	0
County health	0
County open space	387,607
School levy	43,223,408
Muni. levy	29,135,274
Misc. revenues	38,078,683

Kenilworth Borough

Union County

Demographics & Socio-Economic Characteristics
(2000 US Census, except as noted)

Population
1980*	8,221
1990*	7,574
2000	7,675
Male	3,723
Female	3,952
2006 (estimate)*	7,741
Population density	3,617.3

Race & Hispanic Origin, 2000
Race
White	7,007
Black/African American	184
American Indian/Alaska Native	19
Asian	221
Native Hawaiian/Pacific Islander	0
Other race	138
Two or more races	106
Hispanic origin, total	663
Mexican	71
Puerto Rican	117
Cuban	93
Other Hispanic	382

Age & Nativity, 2000
Under 5 years	423
18 years and over	6,079
21 years and over	5,864
65 years and over	1,399
85 years and over	144
Median age	39.7
Native-born	6,322
Foreign-born	1,353

Educational Attainment, 2000
Population 25 years and over	5,574
Less than 9th grade	7.8%
High school grad or higher	80.0%
Bachelor's degree or higher	15.5%
Graduate degree	4.1%

Income & Poverty, 1999
Per capita income	$24,343
Median household income	$59,929
Median family income	$66,500
Persons in poverty	157
H'holds receiving public assistance	13
H'holds receiving social security	1,060

Households, 2000
Total households	2,854
With persons under 18	908
With persons over 65	1,009
Family households	2,117
Single-person households	611
Persons per household	2.69
Persons per family	3.15

Labor & Employment
Total civilian labor force, 2006**	4,198
Unemployment rate	4.8%
Total civilian labor force, 2000	3,992
Unemployment rate	4.6%

Employed persons 16 years and over by occupation, 2000
Managers & professionals	1,161
Service occupations	619
Sales & office occupations	1,194
Farming, fishing & forestry	8
Construction & maintenance	402
Production & transportation	426
Self-employed persons	198

* US Census Bureau
** New Jersey Department of Labor

General Information
Borough of Kenilworth
567 Boulevard
Kenilworth, NJ 07033
908-276-9090

Website	www.kenilworthnj.com
Year of incorporation	1907
Land/water area (sq. miles)	2.14/0.00
Form of government	Borough

Government
Legislative Districts
US Congressional	7
State Legislative	20

Local Officials, 2008
Mayor	Kathy Fiamingo
Manager/Admin	NA
Clerk	Hedy Lipke
Finance Dir	Nancy Nichols
Tax Assessor	Paul Parsons
Tax Collector	Nancy Nichols
Attorney	Harvey Fruchter
Building	Jerry Egor
Comm Dev/Planning	NA
Engineering	PMK Group
Public Works	NA
Police Chief	William Dowd
Emerg/Fire Director	Lou Giordino

Housing & Construction
Housing Units, 2000*
Total	2,926
Median rent	$967
Median SF home value	$175,900

Permits for New Residential Construction
	Units	Value
Total, 2007	14	$1,628,652
Single family	6	$786,002
Total, 2006	24	$3,340,699
Single family	14	$2,204,249

Real Property Valuation, 2007
	Parcels	Valuation
Total	2,960	$879,802,700
Vacant	123	7,721,600
Residential	2,507	437,504,000
Commercial	176	84,092,700
Industrial	154	350,484,400
Apartments	0	0
Farm land	0	0
Farm homestead	0	0

Average Property Value & Tax, 2007
Residential value	$174,513
Property tax	$5,965
Tax credit/rebate	$1,042

Public Library
Kenilworth Free Public Library
548 Boulevard
Kenilworth, NJ 07033
908-276-2451

Director.................Dale Spindel

Library statistics, 2006
Population served	7,675
Full-time/total staff	1/5

	Total	Per capita
Holdings	42,269	5.51
Revenues	$536,715	$69.93
Expenditures	$490,871	$63.96
Annual visits	53,543	6.98
Internet terminals/annual users	8/7,966	

Taxes
	2005	2006	2007
General tax rate per $100	3.029	3.231	3.418
County equalization ratio	59.37	51.83	48.85
Net valuation taxable	$871,435,353	$877,740,900	$880,223,723
State equalized value	$1,538,551,118	$1,797,277,119	$1,895,730,588

Public Safety
Number of officers, 2006 ... 30

Crime	2005	2006
Total crimes	163	145
Violent	5	1
Murder	0	0
Rape	0	0
Robbery	2	1
Aggravated assault	3	0
Non-violent	158	144
Burglary	7	9
Larceny	129	126
Vehicle theft	22	9
Domestic violence	51	37
Arson	0	0
Total crime rate	21.0	18.7
Violent	0.6	0.1
Non-violent	20.4	18.6

Public School District
(for school year 2006-07 except as noted)

Kenilworth School District
426 Boulevard
Kenilworth, NJ 07033
908-276-1644

Superintendent	Lloyd M. Leschuk
Number of schools	2
Grade plan	K-12
Enrollment	1,325
Attendance rate, '05-06	95.1%
Dropout rate	NA
Students per teacher	11.7
Per pupil expenditure	$11,523
Median faculty salary	$54,445
Median administrator salary	$110,029
Grade 12 enrollment	110
High school graduation rate	100.0%

Assessment test results
(percent scoring at proficient or advanced level)
	Language	Math
NJASK-Grade 3	88.0%	97.0%
GEPA-Grade 8	83.7%	81.6%
HSPA-High School	88.3%	81.0%

SAT score averages
Pct tested	Math	Verbal	Writing
73%	475	454	459

Teacher Qualifications
Avg. years of experience	9
Highly-qualified teachers one subject/all subjects	100%/100%
With emergency credentials	0.0%

No Child Left Behind
AYP, 2005-06 .... Meets Standards

Municipal Finance
State Aid Programs, 2008
Total aid	$1,183,187
CMPTRA	233,212
Energy tax receipts	949,975
Garden State Trust	0

General Budget, 2007
Total tax levy	$30,084,420
County levy	6,375,554
County taxes	6,101,291
County library	0
County health	0
County open space	274,263
School levy	15,094,519
Muni. levy	8,614,346
Misc. revenues	4,112,444

Monmouth County

Keyport Borough

Demographics & Socio-Economic Characteristics
(2000 US Census, except as noted)

Population
- 1980* 7,413
- 1990* 7,586
- 2000 7,568
  - Male 3,648
  - Female 3,920
- 2006 (estimate)* 7,471
  - Population density 5,298.6

Race & Hispanic Origin, 2000
Race
- White 6,447
- Black/African American 531
- American Indian/Alaska Native 9
- Asian 168
- Native Hawaiian/Pacific Islander ... 3
- Other race 224
- Two or more races 186
- Hispanic origin, total 839
  - Mexican 151
  - Puerto Rican 385
  - Cuban 29
  - Other Hispanic 274

Age & Nativity, 2000
- Under 5 years 443
- 18 years and over 5,919
- 21 years and over 5,677
- 65 years and over 1,219
- 85 years and over 199
  - Median age 38.1
- Native-born 6,750
- Foreign-born 818

Educational Attainment, 2000
- Population 25 years and over ... 5,345
- Less than 9th grade 5.9%
- High school grad or higher ... 82.9%
- Bachelor's degree or higher .. 15.9%
- Graduate degree 6.6%

Income & Poverty, 1999
- Per capita income $23,288
- Median household income $43,869
- Median family income $58,176
- Persons in poverty 587
- H'holds receiving public assistance ... 90
- H'holds receiving social security .. 1,055

Households, 2000
- Total households 3,264
  - With persons under 18 921
  - With persons over 65 1,013
  - Family households 1,797
  - Single-person households . 1,253
- Persons per household 2.31
- Persons per family 3.11

Labor & Employment
- Total civilian labor force, 2006** .. 4,295
  - Unemployment rate 5.1%
- Total civilian labor force, 2000 ... 3,986
  - Unemployment rate 4.8%

Employed persons 16 years and over by occupation, 2000
- Managers & professionals ... 1,233
- Service occupations 624
- Sales & office occupations .. 1,176
- Farming, fishing & forestry 11
- Construction & maintenance ... 315
- Production & transportation .. 434
- Self-employed persons 156

* US Census Bureau
** New Jersey Department of Labor

See Introduction for an explanation of all data sources.

General Information
Borough of Keyport
70 W Front St
Keyport, NJ 07735
732-739-3900

- Website .... www.keyportonline.com
- Year of incorporation 1908
- Land/water area (sq. miles) 1.41/0.01
- Form of government .... Borough

Government
Legislative Districts
- US Congressional 6
- State Legislative 13

Local Officials, 2008
- Mayor .... Robert J. Bergen
- Manager .... Peter R. Valesi
- Clerk .... Valerie T. Heilweil
- Finance Dir .... K. Stencel /T. Fallon
- Tax Assessor .... Scott Pezzaras
- Tax Collector .... Keri R. Stencel
- Attorney .... John Wisniewski
- Building .... Robert Burlew
- Comm Dev/Planning .... NA
- Engineering .... Donald Norbut
- Public Works .... George Sappah
- Police Chief .... Thomas Mitchell
- Emerg/Fire Director ..... William Vaughn

Housing & Construction
Housing Units, 2000*
- Total 3,400
- Median rent $673
- Median SF home value $141,100

Permits for New Residential Construction

	Units	Value
Total, 2007	14	$1,391,666
Single family	14	$1,391,666
Total, 2006	24	$2,928,391
Single family	24	$2,928,391

Real Property Valuation, 2007

	Parcels	Valuation
Total	2,312	$328,971,850
Vacant	140	5,522,400
Residential	1,934	236,930,650
Commercial	213	65,063,600
Industrial	6	6,218,500
Apartments	19	15,236,700
Farm land	0	0
Farm homestead	0	0

Average Property Value & Tax, 2007
- Residential value $122,508
- Property tax $5,574
- Tax credit/rebate $994

Public Library
Keyport Public Library
Third St & Broad St
Keyport, NJ 07735
732-264-0543

Director .... Jacqueline LaPolla

Library statistics, 2006
- Population served 7,568
- Full-time/total staff 0/2

	Total	Per capita
Holdings	43,997	5.81
Revenues	$274,380	$36.26
Expenditures	$191,293	$25.28
Annual visits	22,805	3.01

Internet terminals/annual users 5/4,818

Public Safety
- Number of officers, 2006 18

Crime	2005	2006
Total crimes	143	172
Violent	12	11
Murder	0	0
Rape	3	1
Robbery	4	6
Aggravated assault	5	4
Non-violent	131	161
Burglary	15	24
Larceny	106	121
Vehicle theft	10	16
Domestic violence	53	59
Arson	3	8
Total crime rate	18.9	22.9
Violent	1.6	1.5
Non-violent	17.3	21.5

Public School District
(for school year 2006-07 except as noted)

Keyport School District
335 BRd St
Keyport, NJ 07735
732-264-2840

- Superintendent .... C. Dan Blachford
- Number of schools 2
- Grade plan K-12
- Enrollment 1,166
- Attendance rate, '05-06 .... 93.0%
- Dropout rate 0.8%
- Students per teacher 10.3
- Per pupil expenditure $13,339
- Median faculty salary $56,745
- Median administrator salary ... $87,390
- Grade 12 enrollment 98
- High school graduation rate 91.6%

Assessment test results
(percent scoring at proficient or advanced level)

	Language	Math
NJASK-Grade 3	83.6%	85.2%
GEPA-Grade 8	68.0%	44.9%
HSPA-High School	76.8%	57.8%

SAT score averages

Pct tested	Math	Verbal	Writing
60%	423	402	420

Teacher Qualifications
- Avg. years of experience 13
- Highly-qualified teachers
  - one subject/all subjects 100%/100%
- With emergency credentials 6.7%

No Child Left Behind
- AYP, 2005-06 .... Meets Standards

Municipal Finance
State Aid Programs, 2008
- Total aid $782,554
  - CMPTRA 237,647
  - Energy tax receipts 544,907
  - Garden State Trust 0

General Budget, 2007
- Total tax levy $15,065,226
  - County levy 1,834,601
    - County taxes 1,726,712
    - County library 0
    - County health 0
    - County open space 107,889
  - School levy 8,481,567
  - Muni. levy 4,749,057
- Misc. revenues 3,868,009

Taxes

	2005	2006	2007
General tax rate per $100	4.178	4.397	4.55
County equalization ratio	57.17	50.77	46.25
Net valuation taxable	$328,694,446	$327,591,500	$331,110,697
State equalized value	$647,418,645	$710,648,220	$787,274,527

The New Jersey Municipal Data Book

Kingwood Township
Hunterdon County

Demographics & Socio-Economic Characteristics
(2000 US Census, except as noted)

Population
1980*	2,772
1990*	3,325
2000	3,782
Male	1,910
Female	1,872
2006 (estimate)*	4,043
Population density	114.8

Race & Hispanic Origin, 2000
Race
White	3,692
Black/African American	23
American Indian/Alaska Native	3
Asian	29
Native Hawaiian/Pacific Islander	0
Other race	7
Two or more races	28
Hispanic origin, total	70
Mexican	7
Puerto Rican	22
Cuban	16
Other Hispanic	25

Age & Nativity, 2000
Under 5 years	262
18 years and over	2,750
21 years and over	2,653
65 years and over	399
85 years and over	35
Median age	38.8
Native-born	3,621
Foreign-born	161

Educational Attainment, 2000
Population 25 years and over	2,618
Less than 9th grade	4.3%
High school grad or higher	89.1%
Bachelor's degree or higher	26.5%
Graduate degree	9.5%

Income & Poverty, 1999
Per capita income	$30,219
Median household income	$71,551
Median family income	$81,642
Persons in poverty	108
H'holds receiving public assistance	19
H'holds receiving social security	346

Households, 2000
Total households	1,340
With persons under 18	550
With persons over 65	291
Family households	1,042
Single-person households	236
Persons per household	2.82
Persons per family	3.21

Labor & Employment
Total civilian labor force, 2006**	2,387
Unemployment rate	3.8%
Total civilian labor force, 2000	2,115
Unemployment rate	2.8%

Employed persons 16 years and over by occupation, 2000
Managers & professionals	749
Service occupations	383
Sales & office occupations	460
Farming, fishing & forestry	9
Construction & maintenance	326
Production & transportation	128
Self-employed persons	238

* US Census Bureau
** New Jersey Department of Labor

General Information
Township of Kingwood
PO Box 199
Baptistown, NJ 08803
908-996-4276

Website	www.kingwoodtownship.com
Year of incorporation	1749
Land/water area (sq. miles)	35.23/0.59
Form of government	Township

Government
Legislative Districts
US Congressional	12
State Legislative	23

Local Officials, 2008
Mayor	Margaret E. Augustine
Manager/Admin	NA
Clerk	Mary MacConnell
Finance Dir	Diane Laudenbach
Tax Assessor	David Gill
Tax Collector	Diane Laudenbach
Attorney	Judith Kopen
Building	Mark Fornaciari
Comm Dev/Planning	NA
Engineering	Thomas Decker
Public Works	Jack Search
Police Chief	NA
Fire Chief	Jack Search

Housing & Construction
Housing Units, 2000*
Total	1,422
Median rent	$787
Median SF home value	$231,700

Permits for New Residential Construction
	Units	Value
Total, 2007	16	$3,186,264
Single family	16	$3,186,264
Total, 2006	19	$3,666,199
Single family	19	$3,666,199

Real Property Valuation, 2007
	Parcels	Valuation
Total	2,176	$697,488,567
Vacant	157	29,392,700
Residential	1,150	486,985,900
Commercial	51	36,682,000
Industrial	4	11,539,200
Apartments	4	2,262,500
Farm land	527	6,256,967
Farm homestead	283	124,369,300

Average Property Value & Tax, 2007
Residential value	$426,626
Property tax	$6,903
Tax credit/rebate	$1,107

Public Library
No public municipal library

Library statistics, 2006
Population served	NA
Full-time/total staff	NA/NA

	Total	Per capita
Holdings	NA	NA
Revenues	NA	NA
Expenditures	NA	NA
Annual visits	NA	NA
Internet terminals/annual users	NA/NA	

Taxes
	2005	2006	2007
General tax rate per $100	3.08	3.08	1.62
County equalization ratio	57.91	57.19	97.61
Net valuation taxable	$334,549,335	$350,903,102	$699,110,769
State equalized value	$596,770,130	$663,528,579	$708,082,819

Public Safety
Number of officers, 2006	0

Crime
	2005	2006
Total crimes	28	19
Violent	3	1
Murder	0	0
Rape	0	0
Robbery	0	0
Aggravated assault	3	1
Non-violent	25	18
Burglary	7	3
Larceny	11	11
Vehicle theft	0	4
Domestic violence	9	2
Arson	0	0
Total crime rate	7.0	4.7
Violent	0.7	0.2
Non-violent	6.2	4.5

Public School District
(for school year 2006-07 except as noted)

Kingwood Township School District
880 County Rd 519
Frenchtown, NJ 08825
908-996-2941

Chief School Admin	Laura Hartner
Number of schools	1
Grade plan	K-8
Enrollment	488
Attendance rate, '05-06	96.1%
Dropout rate	NA
Students per teacher	9.4
Per pupil expenditure	$12,482
Median faculty salary	$50,861
Median administrator salary	$87,000
Grade 12 enrollment	NA
High school graduation rate	NA

Assessment test results
(percent scoring at proficient or advanced level)
	Language	Math
NJASK-Grade 3	98.2%	98.1%
GEPA-Grade 8	91.7%	85.0%
HSPA-High School	NA	NA

SAT score averages
Pct tested	Math	Verbal	Writing
NA	NA	NA	NA

Teacher Qualifications
Avg. years of experience	12
Highly-qualified teachers one subject/all subjects	97.5%/97.5%
With emergency credentials	0.0%

No Child Left Behind
AYP, 2005-06	Meets Standards

Municipal Finance
State Aid Programs, 2008
Total aid	$366,639
CMPTRA	0
Energy tax receipts	316,698
Garden State Trust	49,941

General Budget, 2007
Total tax levy	$11,312,548
County levy	2,381,397
County taxes	1,992,972
County library	173,423
County health	0
County open space	215,003
School levy	7,725,351
Muni. levy	1,205,800
Misc. revenues	1,926,734

Morris County / Kinnelon Borough

Demographics & Socio-Economic Characteristics
(2000 US Census, except as noted)

Population
1980*	7,770
1990*	8,470
2000	9,365
Male	4,673
Female	4,692
2006 (estimate)*	9,681
Population density	541.1

Race & Hispanic Origin, 2000
Race
White	8,953
Black/African American	54
American Indian/Alaska Native	4
Asian	266
Native Hawaiian/Pacific Islander	9
Other race	22
Two or more races	57
Hispanic origin, total	218
Mexican	10
Puerto Rican	54
Cuban	49
Other Hispanic	105

Age & Nativity, 2000
Under 5 years	702
18 years and over	6,556
21 years and over	6,358
65 years and over	841
85 years and over	66
Median age	39.6
Native-born	8,465
Foreign-born	900

Educational Attainment, 2000
Population 25 years and over	6,182
Less than 9th grade	1.4%
High school grad or higher	96.4%
Bachelor's degree or higher	57.4%
Graduate degree	25.2%

Income & Poverty, 1999
Per capita income	$45,796
Median household income	$105,991
Median family income	$110,593
Persons in poverty	244
H'holds receiving public assistance	28
H'holds receiving social security	572

Households, 2000
Total households	3,062
With persons under 18	1,440
With persons over 65	586
Family households	2,685
Single-person households	287
Persons per household	3.06
Persons per family	3.27

Labor & Employment
Total civilian labor force, 2006**	5,109
Unemployment rate	2.2%
Total civilian labor force, 2000	4,664
Unemployment rate	1.8%

Employed persons 16 years and over by occupation, 2000
Managers & professionals	2,701
Service occupations	302
Sales & office occupations	1,169
Farming, fishing & forestry	0
Construction & maintenance	214
Production & transportation	192
Self-employed persons	353

* US Census Bureau
** New Jersey Department of Labor

See Introduction for an explanation of all data sources.

General Information
Borough of Kinnelon
130 Kinnelon Rd
Kinnelon, NJ 07405
973-838-5401

Website	www.kinnelonnj.org
Year of incorporation	1922
Land/water area (sq. miles)	17.89/0.93
Form of government	Borough

Government
Legislative Districts
US Congressional	11
State Legislative	26

Local Officials, 2008
Mayor	Glenn L. Sisco
Manager	(vacant)
Clerk	Elizabeth M. Sebrowski
Finance Dir	Jennifer Stillman
Tax Assessor	Robert Edgar
Tax Collector	Lisa Kimkowski
Attorney	Edward J. Buzak
Building	Russell Heiney
Comm Dev/Planning	NA
Engineering	Paul Darmofalski
Public Works	John Whitehead
Police Chief	John Finkle
Emerg/Fire Director	Alan Bresett

Housing & Construction
Housing Units, 2000*
Total	3,123
Median rent	$1,538
Median SF home value	$354,000

Permits for New Residential Construction
	Units	Value
Total, 2007	20	$6,286,064
Single family	20	$6,286,064
Total, 2006	26	$7,695,405
Single family	26	$7,695,405

Real Property Valuation, 2007
	Parcels	Valuation
Total	3,841	$1,640,695,300
Vacant	342	44,023,500
Residential	3,387	1,512,760,000
Commercial	95	62,329,400
Industrial	0	0
Apartments	2	18,360,100
Farm land	11	65,700
Farm homestead	4	3,156,600

Average Property Value & Tax, 2007
Residential value	$447,041
Property tax	$11,585
Tax credit/rebate	$1,284

Public Library
Kinnelon Public Library
132 Kinnelon Rd
Kinnelon, NJ 07405
973-838-1321

Director: Barbara Owens

Library statistics, 2006
Population served	9,365
Full-time/total staff	4/8

	Total	Per capita
Holdings	76,007	8.12
Revenues	$820,748	$87.64
Expenditures	$716,797	$76.54
Annual visits	98,500	10.52
Internet terminals/annual users	20/14,700	

Taxes
	2005	2006	2007
General tax rate per $100	2.39	2.49	2.6
County equalization ratio	81.1	74.48	68.13
Net valuation taxable	$1,587,429,281	$1,614,971,600	$1,642,274,479
State equalized value	$2,131,349,733	$2,372,089,516	$2,433,680,128

Public Safety
Number of officers, 2006		16

Crime	2005	2006
Total crimes	75	70
Violent	2	1
Murder	0	0
Rape	0	0
Robbery	0	0
Aggravated assault	2	1
Non-violent	73	69
Burglary	22	26
Larceny	48	38
Vehicle theft	3	5
Domestic violence	20	40
Arson	0	0
Total crime rate	7.9	7.3
Violent	0.2	0.1
Non-violent	7.7	7.2

Public School District
(for school year 2006-07 except as noted)

Kinnelon Borough School District
109 Kiel Ave
Kinnelon, NJ 07405
973-838-1418

Superintendent	James Opiekun
Number of schools	4
Grade plan	K-12
Enrollment	2,194
Attendance rate, '05-06	96.0%
Dropout rate	0.1%
Students per teacher	12.2
Per pupil expenditure	$12,857
Median faculty salary	$63,620
Median administrator salary	$118,500
Grade 12 enrollment	176
High school graduation rate	99.5%

Assessment test results
(percent scoring at proficient or advanced level)

	Language	Math
NJASK-Grade 3	96.9%	99.4%
GEPA-Grade 8	94.5%	94.6%
HSPA-High School	97.5%	91.9%

SAT score averages
Pct tested	Math	Verbal	Writing
106%	532	519	510

Teacher Qualifications
Avg. years of experience	9
Highly-qualified teachers one subject/all subjects	98.5%/98.5%
With emergency credentials	0.0%

No Child Left Behind
AYP, 2005-06: Meets Standards

Municipal Finance
State Aid Programs, 2008
Total aid	$1,077,229
CMPTRA	67,867
Energy tax receipts	651,845
Garden State Trust	312,256

General Budget, 2007
Total tax levy	$42,559,729
County levy	5,761,287
County taxes	4,608,527
County library	0
County health	0
County open space	1,152,759
School levy	29,180,377
Muni. levy	7,618,065
Misc. revenues	3,731,744

Knowlton Township
Warren County

Demographics & Socio-Economic Characteristics
(2000 US Census, except as noted)

Population
1980*	2,074
1990*	2,543
2000	2,977
Male	1,502
Female	1,475
2006 (estimate)*	3,180
Population density	128.3

Race & Hispanic Origin, 2000
Race
White	2,901
Black/African American	12
American Indian/Alaska Native	2
Asian	19
Native Hawaiian/Pacific Islander	0
Other race	14
Two or more races	29
Hispanic origin, total	55
Mexican	8
Puerto Rican	24
Cuban	7
Other Hispanic	16

Age & Nativity, 2000
Under 5 years	208
18 years and over	2,154
21 years and over	2,069
65 years and over	333
85 years and over	41
Median age	38.0
Native-born	2,887
Foreign-born	129

Educational Attainment, 2000
Population 25 years and over	2,021
Less than 9th grade	4.0%
High school grad or higher	87.1%
Bachelor's degree or higher	26.8%
Graduate degree	6.5%

Income & Poverty, 1999
Per capita income	$24,631
Median household income	$63,409
Median family income	$72,130
Persons in poverty	103
H'holds receiving public assistance	8
H'holds receiving social security	240

Households, 2000
Total households	1,028
With persons under 18	432
With persons over 65	228
Family households	816
Single-person households	154
Persons per household	2.87
Persons per family	3.21

Labor & Employment
Total civilian labor force, 2006**	1,899
Unemployment rate	5.5%
Total civilian labor force, 2000	1,655
Unemployment rate	4.6%

Employed persons 16 years and over by occupation, 2000
Managers & professionals	553
Service occupations	245
Sales & office occupations	346
Farming, fishing & forestry	13
Construction & maintenance	192
Production & transportation	230
Self-employed persons	109

* US Census Bureau
** New Jersey Department of Labor

General Information
Township of Knowlton
628 Route 94
Columbia, NJ 07832
908-496-4816

Website	knowlton-nj.com
Year of incorporation	1763
Land/water area (sq. miles)	24.78/0.53
Form of government	Township

Government
Legislative Districts
US Congressional	5
State Legislative	23

Local Officials, 2008
Mayor	Frank Van Horn
Manager/Admin	NA
Clerk	Lisa Patton
Finance Dir	Gregory Della Pia
Tax Assessor	Richard Motyka
Tax Collector	Evan Howell
Attorney	Richard Cushing
Building	DCA
Comm Dev/Planning	NA
Engineering	Ted Rodman
Public Works	Ramon Cowell
Police Chief	NA
Emerg/Fire Director	Dave Fisher

Housing & Construction
Housing Units, 2000*
Total	1,135
Median rent	$739
Median SF home value	$180,300

Permits for New Residential Construction
	Units	Value
Total, 2007	10	$2,483,488
Single family	10	$2,483,488
Total, 2006	10	$2,581,408
Single family	10	$2,581,408

Real Property Valuation, 2007
	Parcels	Valuation
Total	1,630	$254,250,640
Vacant	173	7,542,800
Residential	933	188,221,300
Commercial	61	21,066,700
Industrial	0	0
Apartments	3	665,700
Farm land	321	2,861,540
Farm homestead	139	33,892,600

Average Property Value & Tax, 2007
Residential value	$207,196
Property tax	$6,369
Tax credit/rebate	$1,114

Public Library
No public municipal library

Library statistics, 2006
Population served	NA
Full-time/total staff	NA/NA

	Total	Per capita
Holdings	NA	NA
Revenues	NA	NA
Expenditures	NA	NA
Annual visits	NA	NA
Internet terminals/annual users	NA/NA	

Taxes
	2005	2006	2007
General tax rate per $100	2.79	2.97	3.08
County equalization ratio	79.18	72.37	65.06
Net valuation taxable	$242,420,098	$246,921,740	$254,975,680
State equalized value	$334,973,191	$380,349,267	$410,014,544

Public Safety
Number of officers, 2006 0

Crime
	2005	2006
Total crimes	43	42
Violent	6	6
Murder	0	0
Rape	0	0
Robbery	0	0
Aggravated assault	6	6
Non-violent	37	36
Burglary	8	6
Larceny	24	29
Vehicle theft	5	1
Domestic violence	24	3
Arson	1	0
Total crime rate	13.7	13.3
Violent	1.9	1.9
Non-violent	11.8	11.4

Public School District
(for school year 2006-07 except as noted)

Knowlton Township School District
Knowlton Township Elementary, PO Box 227
Delaware, NJ 07833
908-475-5118

Superintendent	Sharon Mooney
Number of schools	1
Grade plan	K-6
Enrollment	320
Attendance rate, '05-06	95.7%
Dropout rate	NA
Students per teacher	9.7
Per pupil expenditure	$12,019
Median faculty salary	$53,945
Median administrator salary	$74,153
Grade 12 enrollment	NA
High school graduation rate	NA

Assessment test results
(percent scoring at proficient or advanced level)
	Language	Math
NJASK-Grade 3	93.1%	88.6%
GEPA-Grade 8	NA	NA
HSPA-High School	NA	NA

SAT score averages
Pct tested	Math	Verbal	Writing
NA	NA	NA	NA

Teacher Qualifications
Avg. years of experience	15
Highly-qualified teachers one subject/all subjects	100%/100%
With emergency credentials	0.0%

No Child Left Behind
AYP, 2005-06 .... Meets Standards

Municipal Finance
State Aid Programs, 2008
Total aid	$332,996
CMPTRA	0
Energy tax receipts	291,329
Garden State Trust	41,667

General Budget, 2007
Total tax levy	$7,837,407
County levy	2,396,520
County taxes	1,956,155
County library	204,462
County health	0
County open space	235,904
School levy	4,814,560
Muni. levy	626,327
Misc. revenues	1,490,472

Ocean County / Lacey Township

Demographics & Socio-Economic Characteristics
(2000 US Census, except as noted)

Population
1980*	14,161
1990*	22,141
2000	25,346
Male	12,343
Female	13,003
2006 (estimate)*	26,300
Population density	313.1

Race & Hispanic Origin, 2000
Race
White	24,800
Black/African American	91
American Indian/Alaska Native	38
Asian	139
Native Hawaiian/Pacific Islander	2
Other race	103
Two or more races	173
Hispanic origin, total	545
Mexican	78
Puerto Rican	216
Cuban	49
Other Hispanic	202

Age & Nativity, 2000
Under 5 years	1,565
18 years and over	18,863
21 years and over	18,094
65 years and over	3,854
85 years and over	360
Median age	38.9
Native-born	24,671
Foreign-born	675

Educational Attainment, 2000
Population 25 years and over	17,180
Less than 9th grade	3.5%
High school grad or higher	86.1%
Bachelor's degree or higher	19.5%
Graduate degree	6.0%

Income & Poverty, 1999
Per capita income	$23,136
Median household income	$55,938
Median family income	$61,298
Persons in poverty	1,140
H'holds receiving public assistance	107
H'holds receiving social security	2,941

Households, 2000
Total households	9,336
With persons under 18	3,480
With persons over 65	2,719
Family households	7,245
Single-person households	1,714
Persons per household	2.71
Persons per family	3.08

Labor & Employment
Total civilian labor force, 2006**	13,698
Unemployment rate	4.9%
Total civilian labor force, 2000	12,542
Unemployment rate	4.3%

Employed persons 16 years and over by occupation, 2000
Managers & professionals	3,584
Service occupations	1,975
Sales & office occupations	3,519
Farming, fishing & forestry	0
Construction & maintenance	1,719
Production & transportation	1,209
Self-employed persons	555

‡ Branch of county library
* US Census Bureau
** New Jersey Department of Labor

See Introduction for an explanation of all data sources.

General Information
Township of Lacey
818 W Lacey Rd
Forked River, NJ 08731
609-693-1100

Website	www.laceytownship.org
Year of incorporation	1871
Land/water area (sq. miles)	84.00/14.52
Form of government	Township

Government

Legislative Districts
US Congressional	3
State Legislative	9

Local Officials, 2008
Mayor	David Most
Manager	John Adams
Clerk	Veronica Laureigh
Finance Dir	John Adams
Tax Assessor	Theresa Poznanski
Tax Collector	Joe Regatts
Attorney	George Gilmore
Building	Frank Crandall
Planning	John Curtin
Engineering	James Stanton
Public Works	Casey Parker
Police Chief	William Nally
Fire/Emergency Dir	NA

Housing & Construction

Housing Units, 2000*
Total	10,580
Median rent	$915
Median SF home value	$131,900

Permits for New Residential Construction
	Units	Value
Total, 2007	39	$8,104,601
Single family	39	$8,104,601
Total, 2006	35	$7,501,426
Single family	35	$7,501,426

Real Property Valuation, 2007
	Parcels	Valuation
Total	15,495	$1,743,182,100
Vacant	3,941	42,485,300
Residential	11,240	1,503,942,000
Commercial	256	126,610,300
Industrial	40	65,983,700
Apartments	1	1,719,300
Farm land	10	914,900
Farm homestead	7	1,526,600

Average Property Value & Tax, 2007
Residential value	$133,855
Property tax	$4,436
Tax credit/rebate	$863

Public Library
Lacey Branch Library‡
10 E Lacey Rd
Forked River, NJ 08731
609-693-8566

Branch Librarian: Kathlyn Lanzim

Library statistics, 2006
see Ocean County profile for library system statistics

Public Safety
Number of officers, 2006: 44

Crime
	2005	2006
Total crimes	528	641
Violent	19	18
Murder	0	1
Rape	0	0
Robbery	3	1
Aggravated assault	16	16
Non-violent	509	623
Burglary	58	94
Larceny	438	516
Vehicle theft	13	13
Domestic violence	274	302
Arson	1	1
Total crime rate	20.1	24.4
Violent	0.7	0.7
Non-violent	19.4	23.8

Public School District
(for school year 2006-07 except as noted)

Lacey Township School District
200 Western Blvd, PO Box 216
Lanoka Harbor, NJ 08734
609-971-2002

Superintendent	Richard P. Starodub
Number of schools	6
Grade plan	K-12
Enrollment	5,005
Attendance rate, '05-06	93.0%
Dropout rate	0.7%
Students per teacher	12.6
Per pupil expenditure	$10,998
Median faculty salary	$50,539
Median administrator salary	$94,450
Grade 12 enrollment	357
High school graduation rate	96.3%

Assessment test results
(percent scoring at proficient or advanced level)
	Language	Math
NJASK-Grade 3	87.6%	92.1%
GEPA-Grade 8	71.8%	64.7%
HSPA-High School	87.9%	79.3%

SAT score averages
Pct tested	Math	Verbal	Writing
61%	503	474	476

Teacher Qualifications
Avg. years of experience	12
Highly-qualified teachers one subject/all subjects	99.5%/99.5%
With emergency credentials	0.0%

No Child Left Behind
AYP, 2005-06: Meets Standards

Municipal Finance

State Aid Programs, 2008
Total aid	$12,295,373
CMPTRA	0
Energy tax receipts	11,978,205
Garden State Trust	245,350

General Budget, 2007
Total tax levy	$57,873,096
County levy	12,988,865
County taxes	10,703,306
County library	1,268,595
County health	513,959
County open space	503,005
School levy	39,648,961
Muni. levy	5,235,270
Misc. revenues	19,337,576

Taxes
	2005	2006	2007
General tax rate per $100	2.976	3.123	3.315
County equalization ratio	55.82	47.49	41.69
Net valuation taxable	$1,690,296,493	$1,717,585,500	$1,746,120,974
State equalized value	$3,559,268,252	$4,123,116,637	$4,359,804,907

Lafayette Township   Sussex County

Demographics & Socio-Economic Characteristics
(2000 US Census, except as noted)

Population
1980*	1,614
1990*	1,902
2000	2,300
Male	1,154
Female	1,146
2006 (estimate)*	2,524
Population density	140.1

Race & Hispanic Origin, 2000
Race
- White ... 2,232
- Black/African American ... 24
- American Indian/Alaska Native ... 2
- Asian ... 18
- Native Hawaiian/Pacific Islander ... 0
- Other race ... 8
- Two or more races ... 16
- Hispanic origin, total ... 54
  - Mexican ... 0
  - Puerto Rican ... 21
  - Cuban ... 11
  - Other Hispanic ... 22

Age & Nativity, 2000
- Under 5 years ... 150
- 18 years and over ... 1,669
- 21 years and over ... 1,611
- 65 years and over ... 213
- 85 years and over ... 13
- Median age ... 38.9
- Native-born ... 2,177
- Foreign-born ... 122

Educational Attainment, 2000
- Population 25 years and over ... 1,509
- Less than 9th grade ... 2.7%
- High school grad or higher ... 91.8%
- Bachelor's degree or higher ... 33.3%
- Graduate degree ... 11.3%

Income & Poverty, 1999
- Per capita income ... $30,491
- Median household income ... $82,805
- Median family income ... $87,650
- Persons in poverty ... 85
- H'holds receiving public assistance ... 14
- H'holds receiving social security ... 143

Households, 2000
- Total households ... 771
  - With persons under 18 ... 314
  - With persons over 65 ... 150
  - Family households ... 648
  - Single-person households ... 93
- Persons per household ... 2.95
- Persons per family ... 3.20

Labor & Employment
- Total civilian labor force, 2006** ... 1,411
  - Unemployment rate ... 5.2%
- Total civilian labor force, 2000 ... 1,270
  - Unemployment rate ... 4.4%

Employed persons 16 years and over by occupation, 2000
- Managers & professionals ... 491
- Service occupations ... 134
- Sales & office occupations ... 302
- Farming, fishing & forestry ... 16
- Construction & maintenance ... 167
- Production & transportation ... 104
- Self-employed persons ... 90

* US Census Bureau
** New Jersey Department of Labor

General Information
Township of Lafayette
33 Morris Farm Rd
Lafayette, NJ 07848
973-383-1817

- Website ... (county website)
- Year of incorporation ... 1845
- Land/water area (sq. miles) ... 18.02/0.03
- Form of government ... Township

Government
Legislative Districts
- US Congressional ... 5
- State Legislative ... 24

Local Officials, 2008
- Mayor ... Richard Hughes
- Manager/Admin ... NA
- Clerk ... Anna Rose Fedish
- Finance Dir ... Gail Magura
- Tax Assessor ... Maureen Kaman
- Tax Collector ... Linda L. Pettenger
- Attorney ... Roy Kurnos
- Building ... Charles O'Connor
- Comm Dev/Planning ... NA
- Engineering ... Michael Finelli
- Public Works ... W. Macko
- Police Chief ... NA
- Emerg/Fire Director ... Sam Cifelli

Housing & Construction
Housing Units, 2000*
- Total ... 799
- Median rent ... $815
- Median SF home value ... $221,100

Permits for New Residential Construction
	Units	Value
Total, 2007	4	$1,509,000
Single family	4	$1,509,000
Total, 2006	3	$1,586,600
Single family	3	$1,586,600

Real Property Valuation, 2007
	Parcels	Valuation
Total	1,369	$471,120,100
Vacant	94	17,732,000
Residential	712	298,542,000
Commercial	53	45,127,600
Industrial	18	44,689,900
Apartments	0	0
Farm land	335	2,772,600
Farm homestead	157	62,256,000

Average Property Value & Tax, 2007
- Residential value ... $415,188
- Property tax ... $7,116
- Tax credit/rebate ... $1,147

Public Library
No public municipal library

Library statistics, 2006
- Population served ... NA
- Full-time/total staff ... NA/NA

	Total	Per capita
Holdings	NA	NA
Revenues	NA	NA
Expenditures	NA	NA
Annual visits	NA	NA
Internet terminals/annual users	NA/NA	

Public Safety
- Number of officers, 2006 ... 0

Crime	2005	2006
Total crimes	21	27
Violent	3	2
Murder	0	0
Rape	0	1
Robbery	0	0
Aggravated assault	3	1
Non-violent	18	25
Burglary	7	5
Larceny	10	17
Vehicle theft	1	3
Domestic violence	10	0
Arson	0	0
Total crime rate	8.5	10.8
Violent	1.2	0.8
Non-violent	7.3	10.0

Public School District
(for school year 2006-07 except as noted)

Lafayette Township School District
178 Beaver Run Rd
Lafayette, NJ 07848
973-875-3344

- Chief School Admin ... Keith Neuhs
- Number of schools ... 1
- Grade plan ... K-8
- Enrollment ... 313
- Attendance rate, '05-06 ... 96.2%
- Dropout rate ... NA
- Students per teacher ... 9.5
- Per pupil expenditure ... $12,458
- Median faculty salary ... $47,311
- Median administrator salary ... $77,487
- Grade 12 enrollment ... NA
- High school graduation rate ... NA

Assessment test results
(percent scoring at proficient or advanced level)

	Language	Math
NJASK-Grade 3	100.0%	100.0%
GEPA-Grade 8	95.8%	93.8%
HSPA-High School	NA	NA

SAT score averages
Pct tested	Math	Verbal	Writing
NA	NA	NA	NA

Teacher Qualifications
- Avg. years of experience ... 8
- Highly-qualified teachers
  - one subject/all subjects ... 100%/100%
- With emergency credentials ... 0.0%

No Child Left Behind
- AYP, 2005-06 ... Meets Standards

Municipal Finance
State Aid Programs, 2008
- Total aid ... $192,045
  - CMPTRA ... 0
  - Energy tax receipts ... 181,444
  - Garden State Trust ... 10,601

General Budget, 2007
- Total tax levy ... $8,095,178
  - County levy ... 1,875,175
    - County taxes ... 1,532,160
    - County library ... 130,619
    - County health ... 50,515
    - County open space ... 161,881
  - School levy ... 5,670,616
  - Muni. levy ... 549,388
- Misc. revenues ... 1,492,600

Taxes
	2005	2006	2007
General tax rate per $100	3.37	1.6	1.72
County equalization ratio	60.37	121.33	102.7
Net valuation taxable	$206,450,276	$466,370,500	$472,307,991
State equalized value	$378,321,928	$455,321,428	$475,390,307

Monmouth County

Lake Como Borough

Demographics & Socio-Economic Characteristics
(2000 US Census, except as noted)

Population
1980*	1,566
1990*	1,482
2000	1,806
Male	913
Female	893
2006 (estimate)*	1,752
Population density	7,008.0

Race & Hispanic Origin, 2000
Race
White	1,484
Black/African American	140
American Indian/Alaska Native	8
Asian	23
Native Hawaiian/Pacific Islander	1
Other race	106
Two or more races	44
Hispanic origin, total	183
Mexican	110
Puerto Rican	37
Cuban	1
Other Hispanic	35

Age & Nativity, 2000
Under 5 years	113
18 years and over	1,413
21 years and over	1,350
65 years and over	234
85 years and over	31
Median age	35.8
Native-born	1,666
Foreign-born	140

Educational Attainment, 2000
Population 25 years and over	1,253
Less than 9th grade	2.1%
High school grad or higher	87.5%
Bachelor's degree or higher	25.2%
Graduate degree	6.6%

Income & Poverty, 1999
Per capita income	$27,111
Median household income	$47,566
Median family income	$56,538
Persons in poverty	134
H'holds receiving public assistance	14
H'holds receiving social security	171

Households, 2000
Total households	824
With persons under 18	215
With persons over 65	191
Family households	391
Single-person households	339
Persons per household	2.19
Persons per family	3.10

Labor & Employment
Total civilian labor force, 2006**	1,141
Unemployment rate	4.8%
Total civilian labor force, 2000	1,051
Unemployment rate	4.2%

Employed persons 16 years and over by occupation, 2000
Managers & professionals	346
Service occupations	166
Sales & office occupations	241
Farming, fishing & forestry	6
Construction & maintenance	110
Production & transportation	138
Self-employed persons	49

* US Census Bureau
** New Jersey Department of Labor
§ State Fiscal Year July 1–June 30

See Introduction for an explanation of all data sources.

General Information
Borough of Lake Como
1740 Main St
PO Box 569
Lake Como, NJ 07719
732-681-3232

Website	lakecomonj.org
Year of incorporation	1924
Land/water area (sq. miles)	0.25/0.01
Form of government	Borough

Government
Legislative Districts
US Congressional	6
State Legislative	11

Local Officials, 2008
Mayor	Michael Ryan
Manager	Louise Mekosh
Clerk	Louise Mekosh
Finance Dir.	Louise Mekosh
Tax Assessor	Mary Lou Hartman
Tax Collector	Esther Kiss
Attorney	William Gallagher Jr
Building	John Rowe
Planning	Mark Fessler
Engineering	William Birdsall
Public Works	Brendan Maas
Police Chief	Rosman Cash
Emerg/Fire Director	Dave Keyes

Housing & Construction
Housing Units, 2000*
Total	1,107
Median rent	$811
Median SF home value	$124,300

Permits for New Residential Construction
	Units	Value
Total, 2007	3	$476,899
Single family	3	$476,899
Total, 2006	5	$442,350
Single family	5	$442,350

Real Property Valuation, 2007
	Parcels	Valuation
Total	983	$374,328,000
Vacant	67	11,192,000
Residential	877	336,665,100
Commercial	36	23,260,700
Industrial	2	759,200
Apartments	1	2,451,000
Farm land	0	0
Farm homestead	0	0

Average Property Value & Tax, 2007
Residential value	$383,883
Property tax	$4,955
Tax credit/rebate	$920

Public Library
No public municipal library

Library statistics, 2006
Population served	NA
Full-time/total staff	NA/NA

	Total	Per capita
Holdings	NA	NA
Revenues	NA	NA
Expenditures	NA	NA
Annual visits	NA	NA
Internet terminals/annual users	NA/NA	

Taxes
	2005	2006	2007
General tax rate per $100	3.987	1.204	1.291
County equalization ratio	43.04	123.98	105.45
Net valuation taxable	$106,097,865	$369,619,400	$374,523,408
State equalized value	$293,899,903	$350,708,160	$376,064,471

Public Safety
Number of officers, 2006 ... 9

Crime
	2005	2006
Total crimes	36	57
Violent	2	6
Murder	0	0
Rape	0	0
Robbery	1	3
Aggravated assault	1	3
Non-violent	34	51
Burglary	9	7
Larceny	24	41
Vehicle theft	1	3
Domestic violence	14	10
Arson	0	0
Total crime rate	20.0	32.4
Violent	1.1	3.4
Non-violent	18.9	29.0

Public School District
(for school year 2006-07 except as noted)

Lake Como School District
Borough Hall, F Street, Box 569
Belmar, NJ 07719

No schools in district - sends students to Belmar Elementary and Manasquan High School

Per pupil expenditure	NA
Median faculty salary	NA
Median administrator salary	NA
Grade 12 enrollment	NA
High school graduation rate	NA

Assessment test results
(percent scoring at proficient or advanced level)
	Language	Math
NJASK-Grade 3	NA	NA
GEPA-Grade 8	NA	NA
HSPA-High School	NA	NA

SAT score averages
Pct tested	Math	Verbal	Writing
NA	NA	NA	NA

Teacher Qualifications
Avg. years of experience	NA
Highly-qualified teachers one subject/all subjects	NA/NA
With emergency credentials	NA

No Child Left Behind
AYP, 2005-06 ... NA

Municipal Finance§
State Aid Programs, 2008
Total aid	$124,823
CMPTRA	0
Energy tax receipts	124,823
Garden State Trust	0

General Budget, 2007
Total tax levy	$4,834,473
County levy	973,340
County taxes	854,721
County library	48,932
County health	16,281
County open space	53,406
School levy	2,545,601
Muni. levy	1,315,532
Misc. revenues	1,884,455

©2008 Information Publications, Inc. All rights reserved. Photocopying prohibited. For additional copies, contact the publisher at www.informationpublications.com or (877)544-INFO (4636)

The New Jersey Municipal Data Book

Lakehurst Borough
Ocean County

Demographics & Socio-Economic Characteristics
(2000 US Census, except as noted)

Population
1980*	2,908
1990*	3,078
2000	2,522
Male	1,301
Female	1,221
2006 (estimate)*	2,674
Population density	2,906.5

Race & Hispanic Origin, 2000
Race
White	2,124
Black/African American	198
American Indian/Alaska Native	16
Asian	59
Native Hawaiian/Pacific Islander	2
Other race	69
Two or more races	54
Hispanic origin, total	201
Mexican	50
Puerto Rican	94
Cuban	6
Other Hispanic	51

Age & Nativity, 2000
Under 5 years	207
18 years and over	1,751
21 years and over	1,666
65 years and over	201
85 years and over	15
Median age	32.3
Native-born	2,291
Foreign-born	231

Educational Attainment, 2000
Population 25 years and over	1,558
Less than 9th grade	5.3%
High school grad or higher	73.3%
Bachelor's degree or higher	7.5%
Graduate degree	3.1%

Income & Poverty, 1999
Per capita income	$18,390
Median household income	$43,567
Median family income	$48,833
Persons in poverty	179
H'holds receiving public assistance	35
H'holds receiving social security	192

Households, 2000
Total households	870
With persons under 18	405
With persons over 65	151
Family households	662
Single-person households	172
Persons per household	2.90
Persons per family	3.33

Labor & Employment
Total civilian labor force, 2006**	1,170
Unemployment rate	7.2%
Total civilian labor force, 2000	1,173
Unemployment rate	6.1%

Employed persons 16 years and over by occupation, 2000
Managers & professionals	225
Service occupations	298
Sales & office occupations	236
Farming, fishing & forestry	5
Construction & maintenance	195
Production & transportation	142
Self-employed persons	72

‡ Branch of county library
* US Census Bureau
** New Jersey Department of Labor

General Information
Borough of Lakehurst
5 Union Ave
Lakehurst, NJ 08733
732-657-4141

Website	www.lakehurstnj.org
Year of incorporation	1921
Land/water area (sq. miles)	0.92/0.09
Form of government	Borough

Government
Legislative Districts
US Congressional	4
State Legislative	9

Local Officials, 2008
Mayor	Timothy J. Borsetti
Manager	Norbert B. MacLean Jr
Clerk	Bernadette Dugan
Finance Dir	Christine Thorne
Tax Assessor	Matcene Hopkins
Tax Collector	Marie C. Bell
Attorney	Sean Gertner
Building	(county)
Comm Dev/Planning	NA
Engineering	Alan Dittenhofer
Public Works	David Winton
Police Chief	Eric Higgins
Emerg/Fire Director	Vern Spoon

Housing & Construction
Housing Units, 2000*
Total	961
Median rent	$833
Median SF home value	$89,300

Permits for New Residential Construction
	Units	Value
Total, 2007	2	$161,000
Single family	2	$161,000
Total, 2006	16	$1,365,000
Single family	16	$1,365,000

Real Property Valuation, 2007
	Parcels	Valuation
Total	795	$184,783,100
Vacant	44	3,551,300
Residential	690	151,488,000
Commercial	59	29,174,800
Industrial	0	0
Apartments	2	569,000
Farm land	0	0
Farm homestead	0	0

Average Property Value & Tax, 2007
Residential value	$219,548
Property tax	$3,625
Tax credit/rebate	$755

Public Library
Manchester Branch Library‡
21 Colonial Dr
Lakehurst, NJ 08733
732-657-7600

Branch Librarian ... Louise Innella

Library statistics, 2006
see Ocean County profile for library system statistics

Public Safety
Number of officers, 2006 ... 9

Crime	2005	2006
Total crimes	44	36
Violent	9	8
Murder	0	0
Rape	3	2
Robbery	2	3
Aggravated assault	4	3
Non-violent	35	28
Burglary	2	5
Larceny	27	22
Vehicle theft	6	1
Domestic violence	52	41
Arson	0	0
Total crime rate	16.4	13.4
Violent	3.3	3.0
Non-violent	13.0	10.4

Public School District
(for school year 2006-07 except as noted)

Lakehurst School District
301 Union Ave
Lakehurst, NJ 08733
732-657-5741

Superintendent	Kevin Carroll
Number of schools	1
Grade plan	K-8
Enrollment	469
Attendance rate, '05-06	95.0%
Dropout rate	NA
Students per teacher	10.9
Per pupil expenditure	$12,211
Median faculty salary	$47,270
Median administrator salary	$101,189
Grade 12 enrollment	NA
High school graduation rate	NA

Assessment test results
(percent scoring at proficient or advanced level)

	Language	Math
NJASK-Grade 3	71.7%	68.7%
GEPA-Grade 8	52.1%	68.7%
HSPA-High School	NA	NA

SAT score averages
Pct tested	Math	Verbal	Writing
NA	NA	NA	NA

Teacher Qualifications
Avg. years of experience	8
Highly-qualified teachers one subject/all subjects	100%/100%
With emergency credentials	0.0%

No Child Left Behind
AYP, 2005-06 ... Meets Standards

Municipal Finance
State Aid Programs, 2008
Total aid	$188,773
CMPTRA	0
Energy tax receipts	188,773
Garden State Trust	0

General Budget, 2007
Total tax levy	$3,082,796
County tax	549,887
County taxes	453,112
County library	53,714
County health	21,760
County open space	21,300
School levy	1,032,404
Muni. levy	1,500,505
Misc. revenues	2,067,464

Taxes	2005	2006	2007
General tax rate per $100	3.815	1.575	1.652
County equalization ratio	60.5	123.74	105.53
Net valuation taxable	$75,035,610	$184,219,800	$186,708,124
State equalized value	$150,764,738	$176,471,589	$186,523,525

Ocean County | Lakewood Township

Demographics & Socio-Economic Characteristics†
(2000 US Census, except as noted)

Population
1980*	38,464
1990*	45,048
2000	60,352
Male	28,845
Female	31,507
2006 (estimate)*	69,606
Population density	2,804.4

Race & Hispanic Origin, 2000
Race
White	47,542
Black/African American	7,270
American Indian/Alaska Native	105
Asian	836
Native Hawaiian/Pacific Islander	19
Other race	2,783
Two or more races	1,797
Hispanic origin, total	8,935
Mexican	2,825
Puerto Rican	3,730
Cuban	214
Other Hispanic	2,166

Age & Nativity, 2000
Under 5 years	7,169
18 years and over	41,166
21 years and over	39,014
65 years and over	11,429
85 years and over	2,147
Median age	30.6
Native-born	52,031
Foreign-born	8,321

Educational Attainment, 2000
Population 25 years and over	35,168
Less than 9th grade	8.4%
High school grad or higher	78.6%
Bachelor's degree or higher	21.0%
Graduate degree	8.2%

Income & Poverty, 1999
Per capita income	$16,700
Median household income	$35,634
Median family income	$43,806
Persons in poverty	11,440
H'holds receiving public assistance	969
H'holds receiving social security	8,186

Households, 2000
Total households	19,876
With persons under 18	7,019
With persons over 65	7,763
Family households	13,355
Single-person households	5,674
Persons per household	2.92
Persons per family	3.64

Labor & Employment
Total civilian labor force, 2006**	24,704
Unemployment rate	4.9%
Total civilian labor force, 2000	21,234
Unemployment rate	7.5%

Employed persons 16 years and over by occupation, 2000
Managers & professionals	6,553
Service occupations	3,266
Sales & office occupations	5,137
Farming, fishing & forestry	43
Construction & maintenance	1,657
Production & transportation	2,985
Self-employed persons	974

---

† see Appendix C for American Community Survey data
‡ Branch of county library
* US Census Bureau
** New Jersey Department of Labor

See Introduction for an explanation of all data sources.

General Information
Township of Lakewood
231 3rd St
Lakewood, NJ 08701
732-364-2500

Website	www.lakewood.nj.us
Year of incorporation	1892
Land/water area (sq. miles)	24.82/0.30
Form of government	Township

Government
Legislative Districts
US Congressional	4
State Legislative	30

Local Officials, 2008
Mayor	Ray Coles
Manager	Frank Edwards
Clerk	Bernadette Standowski
Finance Dir	William Reiker
Tax Assessor	Linda Solakian
Tax Collector	Patricia Tomassini
Attorney	Steven Secare
Building	Edward Mack
Comm Dev/Planning	NA
Engineering	Birdsall Engineering
Public Works Dir	John Franklin
Police Chief	Robert Lawson
Emerg/Fire Director	NA

Housing & Construction
Housing Units, 2000*
Total	21,214
Median rent	$849
Median SF home value	$126,400

Permits for New Residential Construction
	Units	Value
Total, 2007	423	$17,428,614
Single family	167	$16,316,614
Total, 2006	185	$22,278,056
Single family	185	$22,278,056

Real Property Valuation, 2007
	Parcels	Valuation
Total	23,330	$7,719,622,990
Vacant	3,762	516,913,990
Residential	18,719	5,488,354,800
Commercial	543	729,287,500
Industrial	178	602,049,000
Apartments	94	377,306,100
Farm land	23	60,800
Farm homestead	11	5,650,800

Average Property Value & Tax, 2007
Residential value	$293,327
Property tax	$4,700
Tax credit/rebate	$1,075

Public Library
Lakewood Branch Library‡
301 Lexington Ave
Lakewood, NJ 08701
732-363-1435

Director........Jeff Kesper

Library statistics, 2006
see Ocean County profile for library system statistics

Public Safety
Number of officers, 2006.......132

Crime
	2005	2006
Total crimes	1,636	1,887
Violent	164	225
Murder	0	4
Rape	13	10
Robbery	81	138
Aggravated assault	70	73
Non-violent	1,472	1,662
Burglary	345	573
Larceny	1,005	953
Vehicle theft	122	136
Domestic violence	1,023	1,077
Arson	20	8
Total crime rate	24.5	27.4
Violent	2.5	3.3
Non-violent	22.1	24.1

Public School District
(for school year 2006-07 except as noted)

Lakewood Township School District
655 Princeton Ave
Lakewood, NJ 08701
732-905-3633

Superintendent	Edward Luick
Number of schools	6
Grade plan	K-12
Enrollment	5,452
Attendance rate, '05-06	91.5%
Dropout rate	3.8%
Students per teacher	10.0
Per pupil expenditure	$17,506
Median faculty salary	$47,751
Median administrator salary	$105,444
Grade 12 enrollment	255
High school graduation rate	64.4%

Assessment test results
(percent scoring at proficient or advanced level)
	Language	Math
NJASK-Grade 3	69.7%	82.8%
GEPA-Grade 8	38.3%	32.9%
HSPA-High School	67.3%	49.6%

SAT score averages
Pct tested	Math	Verbal	Writing
38%	457	432	433

Teacher Qualifications
Avg. years of experience	6
Highly-qualified teachers one subject/all subjects	100%/100%
With emergency credentials	0.5%

No Child Left Behind
AYP, 2005-06........Needs Improvement

Municipal Finance
State Aid Programs, 2008
Total aid	$6,455,998
CMPTRA	2,239,256
Energy tax receipts	4,216,506
Garden State Trust	236

General Budget, 2007
Total tax levy	$123,949,188
County levy	23,923,057
County taxes	19,709,664
County library	2,338,511
County health	947,299
County open space	927,583
School levy	64,756,770
Muni. levy	35,269,361
Misc. revenues	27,642,648

Taxes
	2005	2006	2007
General tax rate per $100	3.447	1.518	1.603
County equalization ratio	55.24	111.97	99.73
Net valuation taxable	$2,876,116,816	$7,520,812,300	$7,735,617,454
State equalized value	$6,411,317,022	$7,556,744,207	$7,951,462,176

Lambertville City — Hunterdon County

Demographics & Socio-Economic Characteristics
(2000 US Census, except as noted)

Population
1980*	4,044
1990*	3,927
2000	3,868
Male	1,882
Female	1,986
2006 (estimate)*	3,808
Population density	3,369.9

Race & Hispanic Origin, 2000
Race
White	3,661
Black/African American	75
American Indian/Alaska Native	13
Asian	41
Native Hawaiian/Pacific Islander	2
Other race	35
Two or more races	41
Hispanic origin, total	120
Mexican	69
Puerto Rican	19
Cuban	5
Other Hispanic	27

Age & Nativity, 2000
Under 5 years	145
18 years and over	3,274
21 years and over	3,156
65 years and over	589
85 years and over	62
Median age	42.8
Native-born	3,671
Foreign-born	197

Educational Attainment, 2000
Population 25 years and over	3,082
Less than 9th grade	4.1%
High school grad or higher	87.9%
Bachelor's degree or higher	37.5%
Graduate degree	18.5%

Income & Poverty, 1999
Per capita income	$36,267
Median household income	$52,647
Median family income	$80,669
Persons in poverty	230
H'holds receiving public assistance	31
H'holds receiving social security	482

Households, 2000
Total households	1,860
With persons under 18	365
With persons over 65	445
Family households	940
Single-person households	721
Persons per household	2.06
Persons per family	2.82

Labor & Employment
Total civilian labor force, 2006**	2,837
Unemployment rate	3.7%
Total civilian labor force, 2000	2,509
Unemployment rate	2.4%

Employed persons 16 years and over by occupation, 2000
Managers & professionals	1,099
Service occupations	319
Sales & office occupations	614
Farming, fishing & forestry	13
Construction & maintenance	212
Production & transportation	192
Self-employed persons	251

* US Census Bureau
** New Jersey Department of Labor

General Information
City of Lambertville
18 York St
Lambertville, NJ 08530
609-397-0110

Website	www.lambertvillenj.org
Year of incorporation	1872
Land/water area (sq. miles)	1.13/0.12
Form of government	Small Municipality

Government
Legislative Districts
US Congressional	12
State Legislative	23

Local Officials, 2008
Mayor	David DelVecchio
Manager/Admin	NA
Clerk	Loretta Buckelew
Finance Dir	Linda Monteverde
Tax Assessor	Richard Carmosino
Tax Collector	Bonnie Eick
Attorney	Phillip Faherty III
Building	Ken Rogers
Comm Dev/Planning	NA
Engineering	Robert J. Clerico
Public Works	Paul Cronce
Police Dir	Bruce Cocuzza
Emerg/Fire Director	Matt Hartigan

Housing & Construction
Housing Units, 2000*
Total	1,961
Median rent	$811
Median SF home value	$170,500

Permits for New Residential Construction
	Units	Value
Total, 2007	17	$3,638,744
Single family	17	$3,638,744
Total, 2006	1	$168,635
Single family	1	$168,635

Real Property Valuation, 2007
	Parcels	Valuation
Total	2,049	$717,916,362
Vacant	248	12,609,598
Residential	1,557	561,320,700
Commercial	188	111,651,900
Industrial	11	10,326,600
Apartments	33	20,540,600
Farm land	10	128,264
Farm homestead	2	1,338,700

Average Property Value & Tax, 2007
Residential value	$360,910
Property tax	$5,392
Tax credit/rebate	$934

Public Library
Lambertville Public Library
6 Lilly St
Lambertville, NJ 08530
609-397-0275

Director: Harold Dunn

Library statistics, 2006
Population served	3,868
Full-time/total staff	0/0

	Total	Per capita
Holdings	21,137	5.46
Revenues	$222,997	$57.65
Expenditures	$169,448	$43.81
Annual visits	15,288	3.95
Internet terminals/annual users	8/7,808	

Taxes
	2005	2006	2007
General tax rate per $100	1.66	1.51	1.5
County equalization ratio	92.68	96.85	96.17
Net valuation taxable	$567,008,832	$652,181,283	$719,369,163
State equalized value	$634,948,300	$734,220,003	$768,621,386

Public Safety
Number of officers, 2006: 10

Crime
	2005	2006
Total crimes	89	68
Violent	8	10
Murder	0	0
Rape	0	0
Robbery	0	2
Aggravated assault	8	8
Non-violent	81	58
Burglary	9	16
Larceny	16	41
Vehicle theft	0	1
Domestic violence	12	27
Arson	0	0
Total crime rate	23.0	17.7
Violent	2.1	2.6
Non-violent	20.9	15.1

Public School District
(for school year 2006-07 except as noted)

Lambertville School District
200 N Main St
Lambertville, NJ 08530
609-397-0183

Chief School Admin	Todd Fay
Number of schools	1
Grade plan	K-6
Enrollment	165
Attendance rate, '05-06	94.6%
Dropout rate	NA
Students per teacher	9.3
Per pupil expenditure	$15,245
Median faculty salary	$57,419
Median administrator salary	$69,920
Grade 12 enrollment	NA
High school graduation rate	NA

Assessment test results
(percent scoring at proficient or advanced level)
	Language	Math
NJASK-Grade 3	91.7%	87.5%
GEPA-Grade 8	NA	NA
HSPA-High School	NA	NA

SAT score averages
Pct tested	Math	Verbal	Writing
NA	NA	NA	NA

Teacher Qualifications
Avg. years of experience	18
Highly-qualified teachers one subject/all subjects	100%/100%
With emergency credentials	0.0%

No Child Left Behind
AYP, 2005-06: Meets Standards

Municipal Finance
State Aid Programs, 2008
Total aid	$267,753
CMPTRA	0
Energy tax receipts	267,536
Garden State Trust	217

General Budget, 2007
Total tax levy	$10,746,534
County levy	2,315,871
County taxes	2,090,389
County library	0
County health	0
County open space	225,482
School levy	7,047,964
Muni. levy	1,382,699
Misc. revenues	2,684,976

Camden County
Laurel Springs Borough

Demographics & Socio-Economic Characteristics
(2000 US Census, except as noted)

Population
1980*	2,249
1990*	2,341
2000	1,970
Male	983
Female	987
2006 (estimate)*	1,923
Population density	4,091.5

Race & Hispanic Origin, 2000
Race
- White 1,859
- Black/African American 54
- American Indian/Alaska Native 5
- Asian 19
- Native Hawaiian/Pacific Islander 0
- Other race 14
- Two or more races 19
- Hispanic origin, total 32
  - Mexican 4
  - Puerto Rican 10
  - Cuban 2
  - Other Hispanic 16

Age & Nativity, 2000
- Under 5 years 106
- 18 years and over 1,495
- 21 years and over 1,411
- 65 years and over 281
- 85 years and over 22
- Median age 36.9
- Native-born 1,929
- Foreign-born 41

Educational Attainment, 2000
- Population 25 years and over 1,333
- Less than 9th grade 2.7%
- High school grad or higher 87.0%
- Bachelor's degree or higher 22.5%
- Graduate degree 6.7%

Income & Poverty, 1999
- Per capita income $23,254
- Median household income $52,500
- Median family income $58,854
- Persons in poverty 72
- H'holds receiving public assistance 10
- H'holds receiving social security 242

Households, 2000
- Total households 762
  - With persons under 18 262
  - With persons over 65 204
  - Family households 534
  - Single-person households 199
- Persons per household 2.59
- Persons per family 3.16

Labor & Employment
- Total civilian labor force, 2006** 1,154
  - Unemployment rate 4.0%
- Total civilian labor force, 2000 1,059
  - Unemployment rate 4.0%

Employed persons 16 years and over by occupation, 2000
- Managers & professionals 359
- Service occupations 150
- Sales & office occupations 288
- Farming, fishing & forestry 0
- Construction & maintenance 95
- Production & transportation 125
- Self-employed persons 43

* US Census Bureau
** New Jersey Department of Labor

See Introduction for an explanation of all data sources.

General Information
Borough of Laurel Springs
135 Broadway
Laurel Springs, NJ 08021
856-784-0500

- Website .... www.laurelsprings-nj.com
- Year of incorporation 1913
- Land/water area (sq. miles) 0.47/0.00
- Form of government .... Borough

Government
Legislative Districts
- US Congressional 1
- State Legislative 4

Local Officials, 2008
- Mayor .... Jack Severson
- Manager/Admin .... NA
- Clerk .... Barbara M. Hawk
- Finance Dir .... D. Ciminera
- Tax Assessor .... Richard Arrowood
- Tax Collector .... Janice M. Gattone
- Attorney .... George Botcheos
- Building .... Albert Hallworth
- Planning .... Eric Hafer
- Engineering .... Melanie Adamson
- Public Works .... Eric P. Warner
- Police Chief .... Michael Wolcott
- Emerg/Fire Director .... Ken Cheeseman

Housing & Construction
Housing Units, 2000*
- Total 806
- Median rent $605
- Median SF home value $110,200

Permits for New Residential Construction
	Units	Value
Total, 2007	2	$317,792
Single family	2	$317,792
Total, 2006	2	$301,284
Single family	2	$301,284

Real Property Valuation, 2007
	Parcels	Valuation
Total	684	$78,502,200
Vacant	14	337,000
Residential	629	67,947,800
Commercial	38	8,377,100
Industrial	0	0
Apartments	3	1,840,300
Farm land	0	0
Farm homestead	0	0

Average Property Value & Tax, 2007
- Residential value $108,025
- Property tax $6,039
- Tax credit/rebate $1,037

Public Library
No public municipal library

Library statistics, 2006
- Population served .... NA
- Full-time/total staff .... NA/NA

	Total	Per capita
Holdings	NA	NA
Revenues	NA	NA
Expenditures	NA	NA
Annual visits	NA	NA
Internet terminals/annual users	NA/NA	

Taxes
	2005	2006	2007
General tax rate per $100	4.383	5.076	5.591
County equalization ratio	77.14	66.83	60.07
Net valuation taxable	$85,110,694	$79,987,300	$82,550,551
State equalized value	$127,354,024	$137,605,448	$150,398,463

Public Safety
Number of officers, 2006 7

Crime	2005	2006
Total crimes	71	56
Violent	17	2
Murder	1	0
Rape	2	0
Robbery	2	0
Aggravated assault	12	2
Non-violent	54	54
Burglary	12	18
Larceny	37	35
Vehicle theft	5	1
Domestic violence	22	15
Arson	0	0
Total crime rate	36.5	28.9
Violent	8.7	1.0
Non-violent	27.7	27.8

Public School District
(for school year 2006-07 except as noted)

Laurel Springs School District
623 Grand Ave
Laurel Springs, NJ 08021
856-783-1086

- Superintendent .... Albert Brown
- Number of schools 1
- Grade plan K-6
- Enrollment 181
- Attendance rate, '05-06 .... 95.7%
- Dropout rate .... NA
- Students per teacher 13.6
- Per pupil expenditure $10,595
- Median faculty salary $43,723
- Median administrator salary $34,979
- Grade 12 enrollment .... NA
- High school graduation rate .... NA

Assessment test results
(percent scoring at proficient or advanced level)
	Language	Math
NJASK-Grade 3	100.0%	94.1%
GEPA-Grade 8	NA	NA
HSPA-High School	NA	NA

SAT score averages
Pct tested	Math	Verbal	Writing
NA	NA	NA	NA

Teacher Qualifications
- Avg. years of experience 13
- Highly-qualified teachers
  one subject/all subjects 100%/100%
- With emergency credentials 0.0%

No Child Left Behind
- AYP, 2005-06 .... Meets Standards

Municipal Finance
State Aid Programs, 2008
- Total aid $206,861
  - CMPTRA 0
  - Energy tax receipts 206,861
  - Garden State Trust 0

General Budget, 2007
- Total tax levy $4,614,666
  - County levy 931,758
    - County taxes 844,807
    - County library 60,011
    - County health 0
    - County open space 26,940
  - School levy 2,463,924
  - Muni. levy 1,218,984
- Misc. revenues 1,244,116

Lavallette Borough
Ocean County

Demographics & Socio-Economic Characteristics
(2000 US Census, except as noted)

Population
1980*	2,072
1990*	2,299
2000	2,665
Male	1,220
Female	1,445
2006 (estimate)*	2,752
Population density	3,440.0

Race & Hispanic Origin, 2000
Race
White	2,615
Black/African American	7
American Indian/Alaska Native	3
Asian	4
Native Hawaiian/Pacific Islander	0
Other race	17
Two or more races	19
Hispanic origin, total	43
Mexican	19
Puerto Rican	3
Cuban	10
Other Hispanic	11

Age & Nativity, 2000
Under 5 years	89
18 years and over	2,316
21 years and over	2,250
65 years and over	970
85 years and over	162
Median age	56.4
Native-born	2,578
Foreign-born	87

Educational Attainment, 2000
Population 25 years and over	2,168
Less than 9th grade	5.1%
High school grad or higher	85.1%
Bachelor's degree or higher	26.5%
Graduate degree	10.7%

Income & Poverty, 1999
Per capita income	$28,588
Median household income	$43,846
Median family income	$57,778
Persons in poverty	201
H'holds receiving public assistance	34
H'holds receiving social security	613

Households, 2000
Total households	1,208
With persons under 18	197
With persons over 65	588
Family households	742
Single-person households	417
Persons per household	2.09
Persons per family	2.66

Labor & Employment
Total civilian labor force, 2006**	1,058
Unemployment rate	3.0%
Total civilian labor force, 2000	1,062
Unemployment rate	2.7%

Employed persons 16 years and over by occupation, 2000
Managers & professionals	417
Service occupations	101
Sales & office occupations	310
Farming, fishing & forestry	0
Construction & maintenance	128
Production & transportation	77
Self-employed persons	81

‡ Branch of county library
* US Census Bureau
** New Jersey Department of Labor

General Information
Borough of Lavallette
1306 Grand Central
PO Box 67
Lavallette, NJ 08735
732-793-7477

Website	lavallette.org
Year of incorporation	1887
Land/water area (sq. miles)	0.80/0.12
Form of government	Borough

Government
Legislative Districts
US Congressional	3
State Legislative	10

Local Officials, 2008
Mayor	Walter LaCicero
Manager	Christopher Parlow
Clerk	Christopher Parlow
Finance Dir.	Michele Burk
Tax Assessor	Scott Pezarras
Tax Collector	Chrissa Sierfeld
Attorney	Philip George
Building	Jim Erdman
Comm Dev/Planning	NA
Engineering	Mike O'Donnell
Public Works	Gary Schlosser
Police Chief	Colin Grant
Emerg/Fire Director	Michael Phillips

Housing & Construction
Housing Units, 2000*
Total	3,210
Median rent	$786
Median SF home value	$323,100

Permits for New Residential Construction
	Units	Value
Total, 2007	10	$1,921,188
Single family	10	$1,921,188
Total, 2006	14	$2,819,208
Single family	14	$2,819,208

Real Property Valuation, 2007
	Parcels	Valuation
Total	2,658	$1,799,654,160
Vacant	53	27,933,400
Residential	2,530	1,728,313,700
Commercial	67	38,413,960
Industrial	0	0
Apartments	8	4,993,100
Farm land	0	0
Farm homestead	0	0

Average Property Value & Tax, 2007
Residential value	$683,128
Property tax	$5,439
Tax credit/rebate	$1,069

Public Library
Upper Shores Branch Library‡
112 Jersey City Ave
Lavallette, NJ 08735
732-793-3996

Branch Librarian...... June Schneider

Library statistics, 2006
see Ocean County profile for library system statistics

Public Safety
Number of officers, 2006 12

Crime	2005	2006
Total crimes	30	32
Violent	0	1
Murder	0	0
Rape	0	0
Robbery	0	0
Aggravated assault	0	1
Non-violent	30	31
Burglary	2	7
Larceny	28	24
Vehicle theft	0	0
Domestic violence	5	2
Arson	0	0
Total crime rate	10.9	11.6
Violent	0.0	0.4
Non-violent	10.9	11.3

Public School District
(for school year 2006-07 except as noted)

Lavallette Borough School District
105 Brooklyn Ave
Lavallette, NJ 08735
732-793-7722

Superintendent	Peter Morris
Number of schools	1
Grade plan	K-8
Enrollment	143
Attendance rate, '05-06	94.2%
Dropout rate	NA
Students per teacher	7.5
Per pupil expenditure	$15,368
Median faculty salary	$43,181
Median administrator salary	$103,750
Grade 12 enrollment	NA
High school graduation rate	NA

Assessment test results
(percent scoring at proficient or advanced level)
	Language	Math
NJASK-Grade 3	93.8%	100.0%
GEPA-Grade 8	83.3%	100.0%
HSPA-High School	NA	NA

SAT score averages
Pct tested	Math	Verbal	Writing
NA	NA	NA	NA

Teacher Qualifications
Avg. years of experience	11
Highly-qualified teachers one subject/all subjects	100%/100%
With emergency credentials	0.0%

No Child Left Behind
AYP, 2005-06 .... Meets Standards

Municipal Finance
State Aid Programs, 2008
Total aid	$193,246
CMPTRA	0
Energy tax receipts	193,246
Garden State Trust	0

General Budget, 2007
Total tax levy	$14,345,534
County levy	6,956,083
County taxes	5,732,191
County library	679,320
County health	275,223
County open space	269,349
School levy	3,057,182
Muni. levy	4,332,269
Misc. revenues	2,117,681

Taxes	2005	2006	2007
General tax rate per $100	0.741	0.754	0.797
County equalization ratio	108.93	93.72	80.48
Net valuation taxable	$1,776,114,173	$1,785,831,960	$1,801,656,626
State equalized value	$1,895,128,226	$2,221,296,139	$2,395,159,594

Camden County
Lawnside Borough

Demographics & Socio-Economic Characteristics
(2000 US Census, except as noted)

Population
1980*	3,042
1990*	2,841
2000	2,692
Male	1,224
Female	1,468
2006 (estimate)*	2,800
Population density	2,000.0

Race & Hispanic Origin, 2000
Race
White	47
Black/African American	2,520
American Indian/Alaska Native	27
Asian	14
Native Hawaiian/Pacific Islander	2
Other race	13
Two or more races	69
Hispanic origin, total	64
Mexican	8
Puerto Rican	40
Cuban	3
Other Hispanic	13

Age & Nativity, 2000
Under 5 years	108
18 years and over	2,065
21 years and over	1,968
65 years and over	507
85 years and over	59
Median age	42.4
Native-born	2,561
Foreign-born	163

Educational Attainment, 2000
Population 25 years and over	1,856
Less than 9th grade	6.8%
High school grad or higher	79.0%
Bachelor's degree or higher	18.8%
Graduate degree	7.0%

Income & Poverty, 1999
Per capita income	$18,831
Median household income	$45,192
Median family income	$55,197
Persons in poverty	289
H'holds receiving public assistance	48
H'holds receiving social security	419

Households, 2000
Total households	1,026
With persons under 18	331
With persons over 65	396
Family households	701
Single-person households	291
Persons per household	2.62
Persons per family	3.23

Labor & Employment
Total civilian labor force, 2006**	1,484
Unemployment rate	7.8%
Total civilian labor force, 2000	1,356
Unemployment rate	7.2%

Employed persons 16 years and over by occupation, 2000
Managers & professionals	392
Service occupations	225
Sales & office occupations	405
Farming, fishing & forestry	0
Construction & maintenance	41
Production & transportation	195
Self-employed persons	26

* US Census Bureau
** New Jersey Department of Labor
§ State Fiscal Year July 1–June 30

See Introduction for an explanation of all data sources.

General Information
Borough of Lawnside
4 N Douglas Ave
Lawnside, NJ 08045
856-573-6200

Website	www.lawnsidenj.org
Year of incorporation	1926
Land/water area (sq. miles)	1.40/0.00
Form of government	Borough

Government
Legislative Districts
US Congressional	1
State Legislative	5

Local Officials, 2008
Mayor	Mark Bryant
Manager	Dwight Wilson
Clerk	Sylvia VanNockay
Finance Dir	John A. Bruno Jr
Tax Assessor	Thomas Colavecchio
Tax Collector	Jessie Harris
Attorney	Allen Zeller
Building	Mengste Thomas El
Comm Dev/Planning	NA
Engineering	SmithCo Group
Public Works	Alex Barr
Public Safety Dir	John Cunningham
Fire Chief	Michael Harper

Housing & Construction
Housing Units, 2000*
Total	1,110
Median rent	$566
Median SF home value	$99,900

Permits for New Residential Construction
	Units	Value
Total, 2007	6	$1,218,300
Single family	6	$1,218,300
Total, 2006	20	$4,448,900
Single family	20	$4,448,900

Real Property Valuation, 2007
	Parcels	Valuation
Total	1,276	$154,160,500
Vacant	236	3,744,000
Residential	971	96,116,300
Commercial	63	39,808,600
Industrial	1	11,250,000
Apartments	5	3,241,600
Farm land	0	0
Farm homestead	0	0

Average Property Value & Tax, 2007
Residential value	$98,987
Property tax	$4,194
Tax credit/rebate	$945

Public Library
No public municipal library

Library statistics, 2006
Population served	NA
Full-time/total staff	NA/NA

	Total	Per capita
Holdings	NA	NA
Revenues	NA	NA
Expenditures	NA	NA
Annual visits	NA	NA
Internet terminals/annual users	NA/NA	

Taxes
	2005	2006	2007
General tax rate per $100	3.564	4.005	4.237
County equalization ratio	92.5	76.68	74.96
Net valuation taxable	$144,107,889	$147,697,000	$154,372,482
State equalized value	$187,934,128	$197,228,657	$238,077,281

Public Safety
Number of officers, 2006	10

Crime	2005	2006
Total crimes	125	117
Violent	16	15
Murder	0	0
Rape	0	0
Robbery	8	4
Aggravated assault	8	11
Non-violent	109	102
Burglary	7	13
Larceny	96	88
Vehicle theft	6	1
Domestic violence	5	3
Arson	0	1
Total crime rate	45.5	42.1
Violent	5.8	5.4
Non-violent	39.7	36.7

Public School District
(for school year 2006-07 except as noted)

Lawnside Borough School District
426 Charleston Ave
Lawnside, NJ 08045
856-546-4850

Superintendent	Cassandra Brown
Number of schools	1
Grade plan	K-8
Enrollment	304
Attendance rate, '05-06	94.6%
Dropout rate	NA
Students per teacher	10.1
Per pupil expenditure	$14,219
Median faculty salary	$51,423
Median administrator salary	$76,217
Grade 12 enrollment	NA
High school graduation rate	NA

Assessment test results
(percent scoring at proficient or advanced level)
	Language	Math
NJASK-Grade 3	66.6%	80.6%
GEPA-Grade 8	21.4%	33.3%
HSPA-High School	NA	NA

SAT score averages
Pct tested	Math	Verbal	Writing
NA	NA	NA	NA

Teacher Qualifications
Avg. years of experience	16
Highly-qualified teachers one subject/all subjects	100%/100%
With emergency credentials	0.0%

No Child Left Behind
AYP, 2005-06 .... Meets Standards

Municipal Finance §
State Aid Programs, 2008
Total aid	$651,697
CMPTRA	0
Energy tax receipts	651,697
Garden State Trust	0

General Budget, 2007
Total tax levy	$6,540,430
County levy	1,451,814
County taxes	1,318,354
County library	92,110
County health	0
County open space	41,350
School levy	3,822,385
Muni. levy	1,266,232
Misc. revenues	2,742,000

Lawrence Township — Cumberland County

Demographics & Socio-Economic Characteristics
(2000 US Census, except as noted)

Population
- 1980* 2,166
- 1990* 2,433
- 2000 2,721
  - Male 1,356
  - Female 1,365
- 2006 (estimate)* 2,944
- Population density 78.6

Race & Hispanic Origin, 2000
Race
- White 2,228
- Black/African American 283
- American Indian/Alaska Native 29
- Asian 7
- Native Hawaiian/Pacific Islander 5
- Other race 93
- Two or more races 76
- Hispanic origin, total 191
  - Mexican 77
  - Puerto Rican 79
  - Cuban 2
  - Other Hispanic 33

Age & Nativity, 2000
- Under 5 years 168
- 18 years and over 1,946
- 21 years and over 1,854
- 65 years and over 287
- 85 years and over 21
  - Median age 35.7
- Native-born 2,613
- Foreign-born 108

Educational Attainment, 2000
- Population 25 years and over 1,801
- Less than 9th grade 7.9%
- High school grad or higher 75.2%
- Bachelor's degree or higher 11.0%
- Graduate degree 2.7%

Income & Poverty, 1999
- Per capita income $17,654
- Median household income $46,083
- Median family income $48,456
- Persons in poverty 242
- H'holds receiving public assistance 36
- H'holds receiving social security 291

Households, 2000
- Total households 920
  - With persons under 18 402
  - With persons over 65 228
  - Family households 712
  - Single-person households 164
- Persons per household 2.90
- Persons per family 3.27

Labor & Employment
- Total civilian labor force, 2006** 1,377
  - Unemployment rate 6.1%
- Total civilian labor force, 2000 1,276
  - Unemployment rate 8.4%

Employed persons 16 years and over by occupation, 2000
- Managers & professionals 249
- Service occupations 163
- Sales & office occupations 246
- Farming, fishing & forestry 12
- Construction & maintenance 183
- Production & transportation 316
- Self-employed persons 99

* US Census Bureau
** New Jersey Department of Labor

General Information
Township of Lawrence
357 Main St
Cedarville, NJ 08311
856-447-4554

- Email .... lawrencemayor@comcast.net
- Year of incorporation 1885
- Land/water area (sq. miles) 37.47/0.98
- Form of government .... Township

Government
Legislative Districts
- US Congressional 2
- State Legislative 3

Local Officials, 2008
- Mayor .... Thomas Sheppard
- Manager/Admin .... NA
- Clerk .... Ruth Dawson
- Finance Dir .... Teresa Delp
- Tax Assessor .... Donald Seifrit
- Tax Collector .... Ruth Dawson
- Attorney .... Tom Seeley
- Building .... David Dean
- Comm Dev/Planning .... NA
- Engineering .... Albert Fralinger Jr
- Public Works .... Michael Day
- Police Chief .... NA
- Emerg/Fire Director ...... Brian Scarlato

Housing & Construction
Housing Units, 2000*
- Total 1,023
- Median rent $680
- Median SF home value $91,500

Permits for New Residential Construction

	Units	Value
Total, 2007	7	$733,000
Single family	7	$733,000
Total, 2006	13	$1,559,500
Single family	13	$1,559,500

Real Property Valuation, 2007

	Parcels	Valuation
Total	3,299	$114,670,000
Vacant	1,881	8,298,700
Residential	1,089	90,326,300
Commercial	31	2,941,400
Industrial	2	3,134,900
Apartments	1	80,000
Farm land	183	1,200,900
Farm homestead	112	8,687,800

Average Property Value & Tax, 2007
- Residential value $82,443
- Property tax $3,136
- Tax credit/rebate $781

Public Library
No public municipal library

Library statistics, 2006
- Population served .... NA
- Full-time/total staff .... NA/NA

	Total	Per capita
Holdings	NA	NA
Revenues	NA	NA
Expenditures	NA	NA
Annual visits	NA	NA
Internet terminals/annual users	NA/NA	

Public Safety
- Number of officers, 2006 0

Crime	2005	2006
Total crimes	74	84
Violent	9	9
Murder	0	0
Rape	0	1
Robbery	1	0
Aggravated assault	8	8
Non-violent	65	75
Burglary	22	23
Larceny	37	46
Vehicle theft	6	6
Domestic violence	36	11
Arson	1	0
Total crime rate	25.8	29.2
Violent	3.1	3.1
Non-violent	22.7	26.0

Public School District
(for school year 2006-07 except as noted)

Lawrence Township School District
225 Main St
Cedarville, NJ 08311
856-447-4237

- Principal/Chief School Admin ...... Ralph Scazafabo
- Number of schools 1
- Grade plan K-8
- Enrollment 474
- Attendance rate, '05-06 .... 95.0%
- Dropout rate .... NA
- Students per teacher 12.2
- Per pupil expenditure $11,321
- Median faculty salary $45,987
- Median administrator salary $72,583
- Grade 12 enrollment .... NA
- High school graduation rate .... NA

Assessment test results
(percent scoring at proficient or advanced level)

	Language	Math
NJASK-Grade 3	66.7%	84.5%
GEPA-Grade 8	49.1%	51.9%
HSPA-High School	NA	NA

SAT score averages

Pct tested	Math	Verbal	Writing
NA	NA	NA	NA

Teacher Qualifications
- Avg. years of experience 9
- Highly-qualified teachers
  - one subject/all subjects 100%/100%
- With emergency credentials 0.0%

No Child Left Behind
- AYP, 2005-06 .... Meets Standards

Municipal Finance
State Aid Programs, 2008
- Total aid $312,200
  - CMPTRA 0
  - Energy tax receipts 205,994
  - Garden State Trust 106,206

General Budget, 2007
- Total tax levy $4,395,026
  - County levy 1,810,825
    - County taxes 1,715,289
    - County library 0
    - County health 77,167
    - County open space 18,369
  - School levy 1,902,201
  - Muni. levy 682,000
- Misc. revenues 1,534,837

Taxes

	2005	2006	2007
General tax rate per $100	3.397	3.683	3.806
County equalization ratio	82.61	74.04	63.09
Net valuation taxable	$108,372,677	$110,364,000	$115,535,323
State equalized value	$146,370,444	$175,878,864	$207,925,634

Mercer County
Lawrence Township

Demographics & Socio-Economic Characteristics
(2000 US Census, except as noted)

Population
1980*	19,724
1990*	25,787
2000	29,159
Male	13,650
Female	15,509
2006 (estimate)*	32,081
Population density	1,449.0

Race & Hispanic Origin, 2000
Race
White	23,101
Black/African American	2,707
American Indian/Alaska Native	23
Asian	2,306
Native Hawaiian/Pacific Islander	31
Other race	523
Two or more races	468
Hispanic origin, total	1,344
Mexican	180
Puerto Rican	365
Cuban	42
Other Hispanic	757

Age & Nativity, 2000
Under 5 years	1,678
18 years and over	22,836
21 years and over	20,879
65 years and over	3,953
85 years and over	524
Median age	36.7
Native-born	24,062
Foreign-born	5,097

Educational Attainment, 2000
Population 25 years and over	19,151
Less than 9th grade	3.7%
High school grad or higher	89.2%
Bachelor's degree or higher	50.5%
Graduate degree	24.0%

Income & Poverty, 1999
Per capita income	$33,120
Median household income	$67,959
Median family income	$82,704
Persons in poverty	1,311
H'holds receiving public assistance	100
H'holds receiving social security	2,771

Households, 2000
Total households	10,797
With persons under 18	3,595
With persons over 65	2,724
Family households	7,239
Single-person households	2,892
Persons per household	2.49
Persons per family	3.05

Labor & Employment
Total civilian labor force, 2006**	18,146
Unemployment rate	2.0%
Total civilian labor force, 2000	16,554
Unemployment rate	10.0%

Employed persons 16 years and over by occupation, 2000
Managers & professionals	8,020
Service occupations	1,571
Sales & office occupations	3,748
Farming, fishing & forestry	0
Construction & maintenance	673
Production & transportation	884
Self-employed persons	826

‡ Main library for county
* US Census Bureau
** New Jersey Department of Labor

See Introduction for an explanation of all data sources.

General Information
Township of Lawrence
2207 Lawrenceville Rd
PO Box 6006
Lawrenceville, NJ 08648
609-844-7000

Website	www.lawrencetwp.com
Year of incorporation	1816
Land/water area (sq. miles)	22.14/0.04
Form of government	Council-Manager

Government
Legislative Districts
US Congressional	12
State Legislative	15

Local Officials, 2008
Mayor	Mark W. Holmes
Manager	Richard Krawczun
Clerk	Kathleen Norcia
Finance Dir	Richard Krawczun
Tax Assessor	Geoffrey Acolia
Tax Collector	Alice Fish
Attorney	Kevin Nerwenski
Building	Anthony Cermele
Comm Dev/Planning	NA
Engineering	James Parvesse
Public Works	Greg Whitehead
Police Chief	Daniel Posluszny
Fire/Emergency Dir	NA

Housing & Construction
Housing Units, 2000*
Total	11,180
Median rent	$935
Median SF home value	$177,900

Permits for New Residential Construction
	Units	Value
Total, 2007	19	$5,517,480
Single family	19	$5,517,480
Total, 2006	55	$6,471,852
Single family	55	$6,471,852

Real Property Valuation, 2007
	Parcels	Valuation
Total	11,155	$2,691,710,223
Vacant	852	47,768,700
Residential	9,710	1,596,163,750
Commercial	404	858,168,773
Industrial	36	44,638,700
Apartments	21	129,072,600
Farm land	86	632,500
Farm homestead	46	15,265,200

Average Property Value & Tax, 2007
Residential value	$165,173
Property tax	$6,264
Tax credit/rebate	$989

Public Library
Mercer County Library‡
2751 Brunswick Pike
Lawrenceville, NJ 08648
609-689-6916

Director . . . . Ellen Brown

County Library statistics, 2006
Population served	143,288
Full-time/total staff	47/114

	Total	Per capita
Holdings	790,563	5.52
Revenues	$11,142,128	$77.76
Expenditures	$11,142,128	$77.76
Annual visits	1,125,704	7.86
Internet terminals/annual users	123/740,529	

Taxes
	2005	2006	2007
General tax rate per $100	3.56	3.65	3.8
County equalization ratio	64.33	60.67	53.15
Net valuation taxable	$2,660,737,130	$2,681,365,023	$2,695,162,162
State equalized value	$4,385,589,468	$5,048,432,000	$5,625,236,030

Public Safety
Number of officers, 2006	69

Crime	2005	2006
Total crimes	1,121	1,074
Violent	57	50
Murder	0	0
Rape	2	2
Robbery	18	27
Aggravated assault	37	21
Non-violent	1,064	1,024
Burglary	117	128
Larceny	891	849
Vehicle theft	56	47
Domestic violence	241	198
Arson	3	7
Total crime rate	35.7	34.2
Violent	1.8	1.6
Non-violent	33.9	32.6

Public School District
(for school year 2006-07 except as noted)

Lawrence Township School District
2565 Princeton Pike
Lawrenceville, NJ 08648
609-671-5405

Chief School Admin	Philip J. Meara
Number of schools	7
Grade plan	K-12
Enrollment	4,005
Attendance rate, '05-06	94.6%
Dropout rate	0.7%
Students per teacher	10.5
Per pupil expenditure	$14,806
Median faculty salary	$54,575
Median administrator salary	$113,501
Grade 12 enrollment	362
High school graduation rate	95.3%

Assessment test results
(percent scoring at proficient or advanced level)
	Language	Math
NJASK-Grade 3	91.0%	92.0%
GEPA-Grade 8	72.9%	66.0%
HSPA-High School	87.3%	77.2%

SAT score averages
Pct tested	Math	Verbal	Writing
90%	527	507	500

Teacher Qualifications
Avg. years of experience	9
Highly-qualified teachers one subject/all subjects	100%/100%
With emergency credentials	0.0%

No Child Left Behind
AYP, 2005-06 . . . . Meets Standards

Municipal Finance
State Aid Programs, 2008
Total aid	$5,118,156
CMPTRA	803,283
Energy tax receipts	4,310,551
Garden State Trust	4,322

General Budget, 2007
Total tax levy	$102,211,008
County levy	25,821,093
County taxes	22,243,169
County library	2,052,257
County health	0
County open space	1,525,667
School levy	57,523,812
Muni. levy	18,866,104
Misc. revenues	20,878,428

Lebanon Borough — Hunterdon County

Demographics & Socio-Economic Characteristics
(2000 US Census, except as noted)

Population
- 1980*...................................820
- 1990*.................................1,036
- 2000.................................1,065
  - Male.................................511
  - Female.............................554
- 2006 (estimate)*....................1,830
- Population density..............2,103.4

Race & Hispanic Origin, 2000
Race
- White..............................1,016
- Black/African American...............7
- American Indian/Alaska Native......2
- Asian..................................33
- Native Hawaiian/Pacific Islander....0
- Other race............................4
- Two or more races...................3
- Hispanic origin, total...............22
  - Mexican..............................4
  - Puerto Rican.......................14
  - Cuban................................1
  - Other Hispanic......................3

Age & Nativity, 2000
- Under 5 years........................81
- 18 years and over..................808
- 21 years and over..................786
- 65 years and over..................124
- 85 years and over...................13
- Median age.........................39.3
- Native-born........................997
- Foreign-born........................68

Educational Attainment, 2000
- Population 25 years and over......764
- Less than 9th grade................1.4%
- High school grad or higher......93.2%
- Bachelor's degree or higher.....39.7%
- Graduate degree..................13.2%

Income & Poverty, 1999
- Per capita income..............$34,066
- Median household income......$68,542
- Median family income..........$83,436
- Persons in poverty..................38
- H'holds receiving public assistance...4
- H'holds receiving social security....90

Households, 2000
- Total households...................458
  - With persons under 18............147
  - With persons over 65..............96
  - Family households................287
  - Single-person households.......151
- Persons per household.............2.33
- Persons per family.................2.97

Labor & Employment
- Total civilian labor force, 2006**....759
  - Unemployment rate................5.9%
- Total civilian labor force, 2000......657
  - Unemployment rate................3.8%

Employed persons 16 years and over by occupation, 2000
- Managers & professionals..........270
- Service occupations.................54
- Sales & office occupations........206
- Farming, fishing & forestry...........0
- Construction & maintenance.......54
- Production & transportation......48
- Self-employed persons..............42

* US Census Bureau
** New Jersey Department of Labor

General Information
Borough of Lebanon
6 High St
Lebanon, NJ 08833
908-236-2425

- Website................www.lebanonboro.com
- Year of incorporation.................1926
- Land/water area (sq. miles).......0.87/0.00
- Form of government................Borough

Government

Legislative Districts
- US Congressional.......................7
- State Legislative......................23

Local Officials, 2008
- Mayor................Mark E. Paradis
- Manager/Admin....................NA
- Clerk...................Karen Romano
- Finance Dir..............Kay Winzenried
- Tax Assessor............Curtis Schick
- Tax Collector..........Kay Winzenried
- Attorney................Joseph Novak
- Building.........................NA
- Planning................Karen Romano
- Engineering............Paul Ferriero
- Public Works....................NA
- Police Chief.....................NA
- Emerg/Fire Director....Albert Bross IV

Housing & Construction

Housing Units, 2000*
- Total.............................477
- Median rent......................$969
- Median SF home value..........$168,100

Permits for New Residential Construction

	Units	Value
Total, 2007	35	$1,447,135
Single family	35	$1,447,135
Total, 2006	46	$1,917,746
Single family	46	$1,917,746

Real Property Valuation, 2007

	Parcels	Valuation
Total	670	$342,466,124
Vacant	132	25,286,100
Residential	467	173,037,900
Commercial	57	123,971,600
Industrial	6	18,021,700
Apartments	1	1,301,000
Farm land	6	5,824
Farm homestead	1	842,000

Average Property Value & Tax, 2007
- Residential value................$371,538
- Property tax......................$5,705
- Tax credit/rebate...................$950

Public Library
No public municipal library

Library statistics, 2006
- Population served....................NA
- Full-time/total staff..............NA/NA

	Total	Per capita
Holdings	NA	NA
Revenues	NA	NA
Expenditures	NA	NA
Annual visits	NA	NA
Internet terminals/annual users	NA/NA	

Taxes

	2005	2006	2007
General tax rate per $100	3	3.05	1.54
County equalization ratio	59.08	51.52	96.5
Net valuation taxable	$150,007,459	$166,822,064	$343,851,747
State equalized value	$252,537,810	$308,114,103	$322,136,886

Public Safety
Number of officers, 2006...............0

Crime	2005	2006
Total crimes	26	21
Violent	1	1
Murder	0	0
Rape	0	0
Robbery	0	1
Aggravated assault	1	0
Non-violent	25	20
Burglary	5	3
Larceny	73	14
Vehicle theft	3	3
Domestic violence	43	2
Arson	1	0
Total crime rate	16.6	12.0
Violent	0.6	0.6
Non-violent	16.0	11.4

Public School District
(for school year 2006-07 except as noted)

Lebanon Borough School District
6 Maple St
Lebanon, NJ 08833
908-735-8320

- Superintendent..........Elizabeth Nastas
- Number of schools.....................1
- Grade plan...........................K-6
- Enrollment...........................81
- Attendance rate, '05-06............96.4%
- Dropout rate.........................NA
- Students per teacher.................6.3
- Per pupil expenditure............$17,374
- Median faculty salary.............$41,568
- Median administrator salary......$57,612
- Grade 12 enrollment..................NA
- High school graduation rate..........NA

Assessment test results
(percent scoring at proficient or advanced level)

	Language	Math
NJASK-Grade 3	94.5%	94.5%
GEPA-Grade 8	NA	NA
HSPA-High School	NA	NA

SAT score averages

Pct tested	Math	Verbal	Writing
NA	NA	NA	NA

Teacher Qualifications
- Avg. years of experience..............10
- Highly-qualified teachers
  - one subject/all subjects......100%/100%
- With emergency credentials..........0.0%

No Child Left Behind
AYP, 2005-06............Meets Standards

Municipal Finance

State Aid Programs, 2008
- Total aid.......................$109,753
- CMPTRA..............................0
- Energy tax receipts.............109,753
- Garden State Trust..................0

General Budget, 2007
- Total tax levy................$5,280,050
- County levy...................1,184,635
  - County taxes.................991,591
  - County library................86,287
  - County health......................0
  - County open space...........106,957
- School levy...................3,522,819
- Muni. levy......................572,395
- Misc. revenues................1,089,726

256 — The New Jersey Municipal Data Book

Hunterdon County
Lebanon Township

Demographics & Socio-Economic Characteristics
(2000 US Census, except as noted)

Population
- 1980* 5,459
- 1990* 5,679
- 2000 5,816
  - Male 2,869
  - Female 2,947
- 2006 (estimate)* 6,292
- Population density 198.5

Race & Hispanic Origin, 2000
Race
- White 5,640
- Black/African American 47
- American Indian/Alaska Native 6
- Asian 54
- Native Hawaiian/Pacific Islander 1
- Other race 22
- Two or more races 46
- Hispanic origin, total 100
  - Mexican 18
  - Puerto Rican 27
  - Cuban 9
  - Other Hispanic 46

Age & Nativity, 2000
- Under 5 years 352
- 18 years and over 4,332
- 21 years and over 4,180
- 65 years and over 680
- 85 years and over 100
- Median age 40.3
- Native-born 5,639
- Foreign-born 177

Educational Attainment, 2000
- Population 25 years and over 4,028
- Less than 9th grade 1.4%
- High school grad or higher 94.1%
- Bachelor's degree or higher 37.0%
- Graduate degree 12.7%

Income & Poverty, 1999
- Per capita income $30,793
- Median household income $77,662
- Median family income $86,145
- Persons in poverty 112
- H'holds receiving public assistance 22
- H'holds receiving social security 400

Households, 2000
- Total households 1,963
  - With persons under 18 791
  - With persons over 65 354
  - Family households 1,556
  - Single-person households 305
- Persons per household 2.79
- Persons per family 3.15

Labor & Employment
- Total civilian labor force, 2006** 3,648
  - Unemployment rate 6.2%
- Total civilian labor force, 2000 3,213
  - Unemployment rate 4.5%

Employed persons 16 years and over by occupation, 2000
- Managers & professionals 1,344
- Service occupations 305
- Sales & office occupations 788
- Farming, fishing & forestry 12
- Construction & maintenance 323
- Production & transportation 296
- Self-employed persons 222

‡ Branch of county library
* US Census Bureau
** New Jersey Department of Labor

See Introduction for an explanation of all data sources.

General Information
Lebanon Township
530 W Hill Rd
Glen Gardner, NJ 08826
908-638-8523

- Website .... www.lebanontownship.net
- Year of incorporation 1731
- Land/water area (sq. miles) 31.69/0.04
- Form of government .... Township

Government
Legislative Districts
- US Congressional 7
- State Legislative 23

Local Officials, 2008
- Mayor .... George Piazza
- Manager/Admin .... NA
- Clerk .... Karen J. Sandorse
- Finance Dir .... Gregory Della Pia
- Tax Assessor .... Mary Mastro
- Tax Collector .... Mary Hyland
- Attorney .... Eric Bernstein
- Building .... NA
- Comm Dev/Planning .... NA
- Engineering .... Steve Risse
- Public Works .... Paul R. Jones
- Police Chief .... Chris Mattson
- Emerg/Fire Director ...... Warren Gadriel

Housing & Construction
Housing Units, 2000*
- Total 2,020
- Median rent $871
- Median SF home value $233,400

Permits for New Residential Construction

	Units	Value
Total, 2007	4	$658,036
Single family	4	$658,036
Total, 2006	9	$3,030,770
Single family	9	$3,030,770

Real Property Valuation, 2007

	Parcels	Valuation
Total	2,816	$746,924,845
Vacant	198	13,153,100
Residential	2,037	617,869,700
Commercial	72	34,995,900
Industrial	5	3,410,900
Apartments	4	1,857,800
Farm land	288	2,000,945
Farm homestead	212	73,636,500

Average Property Value & Tax, 2007
- Residential value $307,473
- Property tax $8,209
- Tax credit/rebate $1,217

Public Library
Bunnvale Library‡
3 Bunnvale Rd
Califon, NJ 07830
908-638-8884

- Branch Librarian .... Maria Taluba

Library statistics, 2006
see Hunterdon County profile for library system statistics

Public Safety
- Number of officers, 2006 9

Crime	2005	2006
Total crimes	88	58
Violent	3	1
Murder	0	0
Rape	1	0
Robbery	1	0
Aggravated assault	1	1
Non-violent	85	57
Burglary	2	17
Larceny	19	34
Vehicle theft	4	6
Domestic violence	3	23
Arson	0	0
Total crime rate	14.0	9.2
Violent	0.5	0.2
Non-violent	13.5	9.0

Public School District
(for school year 2006-07 except as noted)

Lebanon Township School District
70 Bunnvale Rd
Califon, NJ 07830
908-638-4521

- Superintendent .... Judith Burd
- Number of schools 2
- Grade plan K-8
- Enrollment 829
- Attendance rate, '05-06 .... 96.0%
- Dropout rate .... NA
- Students per teacher 9.3
- Per pupil expenditure $13,993
- Median faculty salary $50,460
- Median administrator salary $106,128
- Grade 12 enrollment .... NA
- High school graduation rate .... NA

Assessment test results
(percent scoring at proficient or advanced level)

	Language	Math
NJASK-Grade 3	95.3%	98.8%
GEPA-Grade 8	94.0%	90.0%
HSPA-High School	NA	NA

SAT score averages

Pct tested	Math	Verbal	Writing
NA	NA	NA	NA

Teacher Qualifications
- Avg. years of experience 11
- Highly-qualified teachers one subject/all subjects 100%/100%
- With emergency credentials 0.0%

No Child Left Behind
- AYP, 2005-06 .... Meets Standards

Municipal Finance
State Aid Programs, 2008
- Total aid $2,919,053
- CMPTRA 0
- Energy tax receipts 2,890,060
- Garden State Trust 28,993

General Budget, 2007
- Total tax levy $19,970,746
  - County levy 3,796,499
    - County taxes 3,177,297
    - County library 276,484
    - County health 0
    - County open space 342,718
  - School levy 15,777,064
  - Muni. levy 397,183
  - Misc. revenues 4,273,639

Taxes	2005	2006	2007
General tax rate per $100	2.53	2.64	2.67
County equalization ratio	75.68	71.15	65.5
Net valuation taxable	$728,557,848	$739,744,421	$748,039,373
State equalized value	$967,540,303	$1,051,310,156	$1,091,515,762

Leonia Borough — Bergen County

Demographics & Socio-Economic Characteristics
(2000 US Census, except as noted)

Population
- 1980* 8,027
- 1990* 8,365
- 2000 8,914
  - Male 4,289
  - Female 4,625
- 2006 (estimate)* 8,799
- Population density 5,827.2

Race & Hispanic Origin, 2000
Race
- White 5,860
- Black/African American 202
- American Indian/Alaska Native 8
- Asian 2,323
- Native Hawaiian/Pacific Islander 1
- Other race 285
- Two or more races 235
- Hispanic origin, total 1,135
  - Mexican 44
  - Puerto Rican 171
  - Cuban 204
  - Other Hispanic 716

Age & Nativity, 2000
- Under 5 years 513
- 18 years and over 6,725
- 21 years and over 6,484
- 65 years and over 1,223
- 85 years and over 155
- Median age 39.9
- Native-born 5,719
- Foreign-born 3,195

Educational Attainment, 2000
- Population 25 years and over 6,221
- Less than 9th grade 2.4%
- High school grad or higher 92.7%
- Bachelor's degree or higher 49.9%
- Graduate degree 20.4%

Income & Poverty, 1999
- Per capita income $35,352
- Median household income $72,440
- Median family income $84,591
- Persons in poverty 574
- H'holds receiving public assistance 37
- H'holds receiving social security 872

Households, 2000
- Total households 3,271
  - With persons under 18 1,257
  - With persons over 65 915
  - Family households 2,437
  - Single-person households 722
- Persons per household 2.72
- Persons per family 3.20

Labor & Employment
- Total civilian labor force, 2006** 4,996
  - Unemployment rate 2.8%
- Total civilian labor force, 2000 4,700
  - Unemployment rate 2.7%

Employed persons 16 years and over by occupation, 2000
- Managers & professionals 2,335
- Service occupations 499
- Sales & office occupations 1,209
- Farming, fishing & forestry 18
- Construction & maintenance 212
- Production & transportation 299
- Self-employed persons 413

* US Census Bureau
** New Jersey Department of Labor

General Information
Borough of Leonia
312 Broad Ave
Leonia, NJ 07605
201-592-5780

- Website .... www.leonianj.gov
- Year of incorporation 1894
- Land/water area (sq. miles) 1.51/0.12
- Form of government .... Borough

Government
Legislative Districts
- US Congressional 9
- State Legislative 37

Local Officials, 2008
- Mayor .... Mary Heveran
- Manager .... Jack Terhune
- Clerk .... Fran Lehmann
- Finance Dir. .... Myrna Becker
- Tax Assessor .... Tim Henderson
- Tax Collector .... Mike Apicella
- Attorney .... Brian T. Giblin
- Building .... Jack Peters
- Comm Dev/Planning .... NA
- Engineering .... Katherine Elliott
- Public Works .... Tony Saitta
- Police Chief .... Jay Ziegler
- Emerg/Fire Director .... Ron Chace

Housing & Construction
Housing Units, 2000*
- Total 3,343
- Median rent $892
- Median SF home value $282,500

Permits for New Residential Construction

	Units	Value
Total, 2007	5	$1,399,999
Single family	5	$1,399,999
Total, 2006	3	$852,100
Single family	3	$852,100

Real Property Valuation, 2007

	Parcels	Valuation
Total	2,583	$715,064,300
Vacant	47	4,239,800
Residential	2,443	623,636,900
Commercial	58	39,037,500
Industrial	5	13,685,700
Apartments	30	34,464,400
Farm land	0	0
Farm homestead	0	0

Average Property Value & Tax, 2007
- Residential value $255,275
- Property tax $9,686
- Tax credit/rebate $1,370

Public Library
Leonia Public Library
227 Fort Lee Rd
Leonia, NJ 07605
201-592-5770

- Director .... Deborah Bigelow

Library statistics, 2006
- Population served 8,914
- Full-time/total staff 3/10

	Total	Per capita
Holdings	46,108	5.17
Revenues	$803,446	$90.13
Expenditures	$799,135	$89.65
Annual visits	161,884	18.16
Internet terminals/annual users	5/25,598	

Public Safety
- Number of officers, 2006 19

Crime	2005	2006
Total crimes	81	86
Violent	9	4
Murder	0	0
Rape	0	0
Robbery	1	2
Aggravated assault	8	2
Non-violent	72	82
Burglary	18	24
Larceny	48	54
Vehicle theft	6	4
Domestic violence	13	18
Arson	0	2
Total crime rate	9.1	9.7
Violent	1.0	0.5
Non-violent	8.1	9.3

Public School District
(for school year 2006-07 except as noted)

Leonia School District
570 Grand Ave
Leonia, NJ 07605
201-302-5200

- Superintendent .... Bernard Josefsberg
- Number of schools 3
- Grade plan K-12
- Enrollment 1,732
- Attendance rate, '05-06 .... 95.4%
- Dropout rate 0.5%
- Students per teacher 8.8
- Per pupil expenditure $13,319
- Median faculty salary $46,592
- Median administrator salary $102,079
- Grade 12 enrollment 143
- High school graduation rate 96.5%

Assessment test results
(percent scoring at proficient or advanced level)

	Language	Math
NJASK-Grade 3	82.7%	87.0%
GEPA-Grade 8	82.2%	87.7%
HSPA-High School	89.4%	81.4%

SAT score averages

Pct tested	Math	Verbal	Writing
92%	538	508	505

Teacher Qualifications
- Avg. years of experience 7
- Highly-qualified teachers
  - one subject/all subjects 100%/100%
- With emergency credentials 0.0%

No Child Left Behind
- AYP, 2005-06 .... Meets Standards

Municipal Finance
State Aid Programs, 2008
- Total aid $1,297,619
  - CMPTRA 50,705
  - Energy tax receipts 1,246,914
  - Garden State Trust 0

General Budget, 2007
- Total tax levy $27,150,730
  - County levy 2,724,860
    - County taxes 2,574,925
    - County library 0
    - County health 0
    - County open space 149,935
  - School levy 15,842,431
  - Muni. levy 8,583,439
  - Misc. revenues 3,370,397

Taxes	2005	2006	2007
General tax rate per $100	3.46	3.59	3.8
County equalization ratio	61.88	54.1	47.79
Net valuation taxable	$717,001,996	$716,961,000	$715,534,888
State equalized value	$1,325,327,165	$1,500,763,043	$1,529,692,786

Warren County
Liberty Township

Demographics & Socio-Economic Characteristics
(2000 US Census, except as noted)

Population
1980*	1,730
1990*	2,493
2000	2,765
Male	1,373
Female	1,392
2006 (estimate)*	2,954
Population density	250.3

Race & Hispanic Origin, 2000
Race
White	2,693
Black/African American	10
American Indian/Alaska Native	3
Asian	16
Native Hawaiian/Pacific Islander	0
Other race	15
Two or more races	28
Hispanic origin, total	74
Mexican	14
Puerto Rican	15
Cuban	13
Other Hispanic	32

Age & Nativity, 2000
Under 5 years	195
18 years and over	1,981
21 years and over	1,915
65 years and over	234
85 years and over	30
Median age	37.6
Native-born	2,556
Foreign-born	170

Educational Attainment, 2000
Population 25 years and over	1,806
Less than 9th grade	3.4%
High school grad or higher	88.3%
Bachelor's degree or higher	25.7%
Graduate degree	8.7%

Income & Poverty, 1999
Per capita income	$24,743
Median household income	$62,535
Median family income	$68,529
Persons in poverty	95
H'holds receiving public assistance	11
H'holds receiving social security	220

Households, 2000
Total households	980
With persons under 18	413
With persons over 65	171
Family households	751
Single-person households	172
Persons per household	2.79
Persons per family	3.23

Labor & Employment
Total civilian labor force, 2006**	1,623
Unemployment rate	4.8%
Total civilian labor force, 2000	1,424
Unemployment rate	4.4%

Employed persons 16 years and over by occupation, 2000
Managers & professionals	472
Service occupations	154
Sales & office occupations	300
Farming, fishing & forestry	20
Construction & maintenance	201
Production & transportation	215
Self-employed persons	78

* US Census Bureau
** New Jersey Department of Labor

See Introduction for an explanation of all data sources.

General Information
Township of Liberty
349 Mountain Lake Rd
Great Meadows, NJ 07838
908-637-4579

Website	www.libertytownship.org
Year of incorporation	1926
Land/water area (sq. miles)	11.80/0.21
Form of government	Township

Government
Legislative Districts
US Congressional	5
State Legislative	23

Local Officials, 2008
Mayor	John Inscho
Manager	Willa Reilly
Clerk	Willa Reilly
Finance Dir	Kevin Lifer
Tax Assessor	Lydia Zdrodowski
Tax Collector	Kristine Blanchard
Attorney	Michael Lavery
Building	Ralph Price
Comm Dev/Planning	NA
Engineering	Thomas Quinn
Public Works	Steve Romanowitch
Police Chief	NA
Emerg/Fire Director	Ken Lunden

Housing & Construction
Housing Units, 2000*
Total	1,088
Median rent	$686
Median SF home value	$169,600

Permits for New Residential Construction
	Units	Value
Total, 2007	4	$411,500
Single family	4	$411,500
Total, 2006	11	$2,504,000
Single family	11	$2,504,000

Real Property Valuation, 2007
	Parcels	Valuation
Total	1,570	$266,301,600
Vacant	260	7,023,700
Residential	1,013	227,954,600
Commercial	27	6,968,400
Industrial	0	0
Apartments	1	308,800
Farm land	179	729,400
Farm homestead	90	23,316,700

Average Property Value & Tax, 2007
Residential value	$227,807
Property tax	$6,488
Tax credit/rebate	$1,130

Public Library
No public municipal library

Library statistics, 2006
Population served	NA
Full-time/total staff	NA/NA

	Total	Per capita
Holdings	NA	NA
Revenues	NA	NA
Expenditures	NA	NA
Annual visits	NA	NA
Internet terminals/annual users	NA/NA	

Taxes
	2005	2006	2007
General tax rate per $100	2.53	2.68	2.85
County equalization ratio	94.04	83.67	77.45
Net valuation taxable	$259,912,044	$264,298,500	$267,055,571
State equalized value	$310,639,469	$342,027,932	$373,047,554

Public Safety
Number of officers, 2006	0

Crime	2005	2006
Total crimes	13	24
Violent	5	2
Murder	1	0
Rape	0	0
Robbery	0	0
Aggravated assault	4	2
Non-violent	8	22
Burglary	1	8
Larceny	6	11
Vehicle theft	1	3
Domestic violence	18	3
Arson	0	0
Total crime rate	4.4	8.1
Violent	1.7	0.7
Non-violent	2.7	7.4

Public School District
(for school year 2006-07 except as noted)

Great Meadows Regional School District
PO BOX 74
Great Meadows, NJ 07838
908-637-6576

Superintendent	Jason Bing
Number of schools	6
Grade plan	K-8
Enrollment	1,009
Attendance rate, '05-06	95.9%
Dropout rate	NA
Students per teacher	10.9
Per pupil expenditure	$11,977
Median faculty salary	$55,135
Median administrator salary	$86,100
Grade 12 enrollment	NA
High school graduation rate	NA

Assessment test results
(percent scoring at proficient or advanced level)
	Language	Math
NJASK-Grade 3	83.3%	94.5%
GEPA-Grade 8	74.3%	73.6%
HSPA-High School	NA	NA

SAT score averages
Pct tested	Math	Verbal	Writing
NA	NA	NA	NA

Teacher Qualifications
Avg. years of experience	16
Highly-qualified teachers one subject/all subjects	100%/100%
With emergency credentials	0.0%

No Child Left Behind
AYP, 2005-06	Meets Standards

Municipal Finance
State Aid Programs, 2008
Total aid	$246,001
CMPTRA	0
Energy tax receipts	181,777
Garden State Trust	64,224

General Budget, 2007
Total tax levy	$7,605,459
County levy	2,104,939
County taxes	1,718,362
County library	179,488
County health	0
County open space	207,089
School levy	4,631,778
Muni. levy	868,742
Misc. revenues	1,492,636

Lincoln Park Borough
Morris County

Demographics & Socio-Economic Characteristics
(2000 US Census, except as noted)

Population
- 1980*..8,806
- 1990*..10,978
- 2000..10,930
  - Male..5,239
  - Female..5,691
- 2006 (estimate)*...........................10,856
- Population density.......................1,613.1

Race & Hispanic Origin, 2000
Race
- White..9,845
- Black/African American................191
- American Indian/Alaska Native.....13
- Asian..578
- Native Hawaiian/Pacific Islander.....1
- Other race..142
- Two or more races.........................160
- Hispanic origin, total....................633
  - Mexican..41
  - Puerto Rican................................214
  - Cuban...75
  - Other Hispanic...........................303

Age & Nativity, 2000
- Under 5 years.................................632
- 18 years and over.......................8,716
- 21 years and over.......................8,466
- 65 years and over.......................1,622
- 85 years and over..........................266
  - Median age...................................39.6
- Native-born..................................9,449
- Foreign-born................................1,481

Educational Attainment, 2000
- Population 25 years and over...8,139
- Less than 9th grade......................4.5%
- High school grad or higher.....86.3%
- Bachelor's degree or higher....32.9%
- Graduate degree..........................11.0%

Income & Poverty, 1999
- Per capita income..................$30,389
- Median household income.....$69,050
- Median family income..........$77,307
- Persons in poverty........................286
- H'holds receiving public assistance......37
- H'holds receiving social security......890

Households, 2000
- Total households.......................4,026
  - With persons under 18.........1,251
  - With persons over 65..............853
  - Family households...............2,707
  - Single-person households...1,072
- Persons per household................2.54
- Persons per family.......................3.14

Labor & Employment
- Total civilian labor force, 2006**.....6,590
  - Unemployment rate..................3.5%
- Total civilian labor force, 2000.....6,021
  - Unemployment rate..................3.2%

Employed persons 16 years and over by occupation, 2000
- Managers & professionals......2,484
- Service occupations....................482
- Sales & office occupations....1,731
- Farming, fishing & forestry........11
- Construction & maintenance...492
- Production & transportation...629
- Self-employed persons...............340

* US Census Bureau
** New Jersey Department of Labor

General Information
Borough of Lincoln Park
34 Chapel Hill Rd
Lincoln Park, NJ 07035
973-694-6100
- Website................www.linconpark.org
- Year of incorporation................1922
- Land/water area (sq. miles).....6.73/0.24
- Form of government.........Mayor-Council

Government
Legislative Districts
- US Congressional...............................11
- State Legislative..................................26

Local Officials, 2008
- Mayor.........................David Runfeldt
- Manager...................Joseph Maiella
- Clerk..................Annette Maida-Smith
- Finance Dir............Joseph Maiella (Int)
- Tax Assessor..............Tom Lenhardt
- Tax Collector..........Kristen Runfeldt
- Attorney.....................Edward Buzak
- Building.................Salvatore Marino
- Planning..................Joseph Maiella
- Engineering............Joseph Maiella
- Public Works.........Tom Piorkowski
- Police Chief....................Sean Cannig
- Emerg/Fire Director..........Sal Marino

Housing & Construction
Housing Units, 2000*
- Total..4,110
- Median rent.......................................$947
- Median SF home value............$194,300

Permits for New Residential Construction

	Units	Value
Total, 2007	3	$425,414
Single family	3	$425,414
Total, 2006	6	$787,938
Single family	6	$787,938

Real Property Valuation, 2007

	Parcels	Valuation
Total	3,859	$737,480,300
Vacant	135	4,327,000
Residential	3,588	618,197,100
Commercial	75	49,887,600
Industrial	26	38,831,800
Apartments	2	22,954,100
Farm land	19	329,700
Farm homestead	14	2,953,000

Average Property Value & Tax, 2007
- Residential value....................$172,446
- Property tax................................$6,616
- Tax credit/rebate.......................$1,060

Public Library
Lincoln Park Public Library
12 Boonton Turnpike
Lincoln Park, NJ 07035
973-694-8283
- Director..............Francis R. Kaiser Jr

Library statistics, 2006
- Population served....................10,930
- Full-time/total staff........................1/2

	Total	Per capita
Holdings	61,301	5.61
Revenues	$521,892	$47.75
Expenditures	$400,277	$36.62
Annual visits	49,731	4.55
Internet terminals/annual users	12/13,357	

Public Safety
Number of officers, 2006..............25

Crime	2005	2006
Total crimes	130	87
Violent	5	8
Murder	0	0
Rape	1	2
Robbery	0	1
Aggravated assault	4	5
Non-violent	125	79
Burglary	28	13
Larceny	93	62
Vehicle theft	4	4
Domestic violence	45	42
Arson	2	0
Total crime rate	11.9	8.0
Violent	0.5	0.7
Non-violent	11.5	7.2

Public School District
(for school year 2006-07 except as noted)

Lincoln Park Borough School District
92 Ryerson Rd
Lincoln Park, NJ 07035
973-696-5500
- Superintendent..........James W. Grube
- Number of schools..............................2
- Grade plan.....................................K-8
- Enrollment...................................934
- Attendance rate, '05-06..............96.1%
- Dropout rate.....................................NA
- Students per teacher..................10.2
- Per pupil expenditure............$13,768
- Median faculty salary............$57,285
- Median administrator salary....$115,416
- Grade 12 enrollment.....................NA
- High school graduation rate.......NA

Assessment test results
(percent scoring at proficient or advanced level)

	Language	Math
NJASK-Grade 3	89.0%	97.0%
GEPA-Grade 8	76.2%	72.5%
HSPA-High School	NA	NA

SAT score averages

Pct tested	Math	Verbal	Writing
NA	NA	NA	NA

Teacher Qualifications
- Avg. years of experience................10
- Highly-qualified teachers
  one subject/all subjects......100%/100%
- With emergency credentials..........2.7%

No Child Left Behind
- AYP, 2005-06...............Meets Standards

Municipal Finance
State Aid Programs, 2008
- Total aid......................................$1,189,377
- CMPTRA..393,927
- Energy tax receipts.....................734,242
- Garden State Trust........................61,208

General Budget, 2007
- Total tax levy.............................$28,318,639
- County levy....................................3,788,138
  - County taxes................................3,029,701
  - County library...0
  - County health..0
  - County open space..........................758,436
- School levy..................................15,185,165
- Muni. levy......................................9,345,336
- Misc. revenues..............................6,616,589

Taxes

	2005	2006	2007
General tax rate per $100	3.5	3.65	3.84
County equalization ratio	59.3	52.27	46.33
Net valuation taxable	$745,330,899	$737,713,200	$738,166,918
State equalized value	$1,425,924,812	$1,592,990,457	$1,704,661,433

Union County
Linden City

Demographics & Socio-Economic Characteristics
(2000 US Census, except as noted)

Population
1980*	37,836
1990*	36,701
2000	39,394
Male	18,703
Female	20,691
2006 (estimate)*	39,874
Population density	3,688.6

Race & Hispanic Origin, 2000
Race
- White ... 26,031
- Black/African American ... 8,981
- American Indian/Alaska Native ... 56
- Asian ... 925
- Native Hawaiian/Pacific Islander ... 15
- Other race ... 1,923
- Two or more races ... 1,463

Hispanic origin, total ... 5,674
- Mexican ... 153
- Puerto Rican ... 1,512
- Cuban ... 593
- Other Hispanic ... 3,416

Age & Nativity, 2000
- Under 5 years ... 2,345
- 18 years and over ... 30,548
- 21 years and over ... 29,186
- 65 years and over ... 6,426
- 85 years and over ... 881
- Median age ... 38.0
- Native-born ... 29,043
- Foreign-born ... 10,351

Educational Attainment, 2000
- Population 25 years and over ... 27,238
- Less than 9th grade ... 8.7%
- High school grad or higher ... 78.2%
- Bachelor's degree or higher ... 14.1%
- Graduate degree ... 4.5%

Income & Poverty, 1999
- Per capita income ... $21,314
- Median household income ... $46,345
- Median family income ... $54,903
- Persons in poverty ... 2,490
- H'holds receiving public assistance ... 389
- H'holds receiving social security ... 4,896

Households, 2000
- Total households ... 15,052
- With persons under 18 ... 4,980
- With persons over 65 ... 4,786
- Family households ... 10,087
- Single-person households ... 4,207
- Persons per household ... 2.60
- Persons per family ... 3.21

Labor & Employment
- Total civilian labor force, 2006** ... 21,010
- Unemployment rate ... 5.4%
- Total civilian labor force, 2000 ... 19,892
- Unemployment rate ... 5.6%

Employed persons 16 years and over by occupation, 2000
- Managers & professionals ... 4,311
- Service occupations ... 2,805
- Sales & office occupations ... 6,071
- Farming, fishing & forestry ... 11
- Construction & maintenance ... 1,723
- Production & transportation ... 3,851
- Self-employed persons ... 654

* US Census Bureau
** New Jersey Department of Labor

See Introduction for an explanation of all data sources.

General Information
City of Linden
301 N Wood Ave
Linden, NJ 07036
908-474-8452

Website	www.linden-nj.org
Year of incorporation	1925
Land/water area (sq. miles)	10.81/0.41
Form of government	City

Government
Legislative Districts
- US Congressional ... 7, 10, 13
- State Legislative ... 22

Local Officials, 2008
Mayor	Richard J. Gerbounka
Manager/Admin	NA
Clerk	Joseph C. Bodek
Finance Dir	Alexis Zack
Tax Assessor	Michael Frangella
Tax Collector	Stacey L. Carron
Attorney	Edward J. Kologi
Building	Thomas Caverly
Comm Dev/Planning	NA
Engineering	George Vercik
Public Works	John Mesler III
Police Chief	Michael F. Boyle
Emerg/Fire Director	Robert Pakulski

Housing & Construction
Housing Units, 2000*
- Total ... 15,567
- Median rent ... $795
- Median SF home value ... $148,800

Permits for New Residential Construction
	Units	Value
Total, 2007	49	$4,114,211
Single family	31	$3,489,687
Total, 2006	119	$5,704,938
Single family	41	$4,421,038

Real Property Valuation, 2007
	Parcels	Valuation
Total	11,717	$2,857,002,000
Vacant	475	36,702,400
Residential	10,006	1,408,485,900
Commercial	914	454,435,100
Industrial	230	888,980,500
Apartments	92	68,398,100
Farm land	0	0
Farm homestead	0	0

Average Property Value & Tax, 2007
- Residential value ... $140,764
- Property tax ... $6,191
- Tax credit/rebate ... $1,036

Public Library
Linden Free Public Library
31 E Henry St
Linden, NJ 07036
908-298-3830

Director ... Dennis P. Purves Jr

Library statistics, 2006
- Population served ... 39,394
- Full-time/total staff ... 6/21

	Total	Per capita
Holdings	87,925	2.23
Revenues	$1,887,190	$47.91
Expenditures	$1,917,420	$48.67
Annual visits	95,000	2.41
Internet terminals/annual users	14/34,034	

Public Safety
Number of officers, 2006 ... 133

Crime	2005	2006
Total crimes	1,573	1,450
Violent	107	133
Murder	0	4
Rape	2	3
Robbery	61	67
Aggravated assault	44	59
Non-violent	1,466	1,317
Burglary	172	186
Larceny	925	919
Vehicle theft	369	212
Domestic violence	247	282
Arson	3	2
Total crime rate	39.3	36.2
Violent	2.7	3.3
Non-violent	36.6	32.9

Public School District
(for school year 2006-07 except as noted)

Linden School District
2 E Gibbons St
Linden, NJ 07036
908-486-5818

Superintendent	Joseph E. Martino
Number of schools	11
Grade plan	K-12
Enrollment	6,206
Attendance rate, '05-06	94.4%
Dropout rate	1.7%
Students per teacher	10.8
Per pupil expenditure	$14,259
Median faculty salary	$53,412
Median administrator salary	$112,136
Grade 12 enrollment	454
High school graduation rate	91.0%

Assessment test results
(percent scoring at proficient or advanced level)

	Language	Math
NJASK-Grade 3	76.6%	79.2%
GEPA-Grade 8	61.6%	58.7%
HSPA-High School	75.5%	50.5%

SAT score averages
Pct tested	Math	Verbal	Writing
59%	408	412	415

Teacher Qualifications
- Avg. years of experience ... 8
- Highly-qualified teachers one subject/all subjects ... 99.0%/99.0%
- With emergency credentials ... 0.3%

No Child Left Behind
AYP, 2005-06 ... Meets Standards

Municipal Finance
State Aid Programs, 2008
- Total aid ... $23,429,585
- CMPTRA ... 0
- Energy tax receipts ... 23,429,585
- Garden State Trust ... 0

General Budget, 2007
- Total tax levy ... $125,867,397
- County levy ... 20,607,509
- County taxes ... 19,721,612
- County library ... 0
- County health ... 0
- County open space ... 885,897
- School levy ... 70,107,550
- Muni. levy ... 35,152,339
- Misc. revenues ... 50,646,088

Taxes
	2005	2006	2007
General tax rate per $100	3.771	4.029	4.399
County equalization ratio	61.24	53.95	49.47
Net valuation taxable	$2,937,112,324	$2,889,715,300	$2,861,742,166
State equalized value	$4,892,740,836	$5,846,754,481	$6,360,695,672

Lindenwold Borough
Camden County

Demographics & Socio-Economic Characteristics
(2000 US Census, except as noted)

Population
1980*	18,196
1990*	18,734
2000	17,414
Male	8,312
Female	9,102
2006 (estimate)*	17,160
Population density	4,355.3

Race & Hispanic Origin, 2000
Race
White	10,695
Black/African American	4,915
American Indian/Alaska Native	83
Asian	614
Native Hawaiian/Pacific Islander	10
Other race	564
Two or more races	533
Hispanic origin, total	1,316
Mexican	203
Puerto Rican	587
Cuban	30
Other Hispanic	496

Age & Nativity, 2000
Under 5 years	1,258
18 years and over	13,299
21 years and over	12,619
65 years and over	1,539
85 years and over	132
Median age	33.3
Native-born	16,160
Foreign-born	1,254

Educational Attainment, 2000
Population 25 years and over	11,593
Less than 9th grade	7.0%
High school grad or higher	77.6%
Bachelor's degree or higher	13.3%
Graduate degree	3.7%

Income & Poverty, 1999
Per capita income	$18,659
Median household income	$36,080
Median family income	$40,931
Persons in poverty	2,047
H'holds receiving public assistance	267
H'holds receiving social security	1,565

Households, 2000
Total households	7,465
With persons under 18	2,422
With persons over 65	1,230
Family households	4,301
Single-person households	2,558
Persons per household	2.32
Persons per family	3.00

Labor & Employment
Total civilian labor force, 2006**	10,532
Unemployment rate	8.4%
Total civilian labor force, 2000	9,721
Unemployment rate	8.0%

Employed persons 16 years and over by occupation, 2000
Managers & professionals	2,106
Service occupations	1,783
Sales & office occupations	2,897
Farming, fishing & forestry	10
Construction & maintenance	922
Production & transportation	1,228
Self-employed persons	235

‡ Branch of county library
* US Census Bureau
** New Jersey Department of Labor

General Information
Borough of Lindenwold
2001 Egg Harbor Rd
Lindenwold, NJ 08021
856-783-2121

Website	www.lindenwoldnj.gov
Year of incorporation	1929
Land/water area (sq. miles)	3.94/0.03
Form of government	Borough

Government
Legislative Districts
US Congressional	1
State Legislative	4

Local Officials, 2008
Mayor	Frank DeLucca Jr
Manager	Frank DeLucca Jr
Clerk	Jane Barber
Finance Dir	Dawn Thompson
Tax Assessor	Thomas Glock
Tax Collector	Margie Schieber
Attorney	John Kearney
Building	Albert Hallworth
Comm Dev/Planning	NA
Engineering	Remington & Vernick
Public Works	Robert Lodovici
Police Chief	Michael McCarthy
Emerg/Fire Director	NA

Housing & Construction
Housing Units, 2000*
Total	8,244
Median rent	$615
Median SF home value	$84,000

Permits for New Residential Construction
	Units	Value
Total, 2007	142	$9,096,401
Single family	10	$965,792
Total, 2006	104	$1,235,817
Single family	12	$1,234,817

Real Property Valuation, 2007
	Parcels	Valuation
Total	4,524	$428,945,200
Vacant	325	5,291,800
Residential	4,029	282,747,700
Commercial	142	36,424,700
Industrial	3	1,411,100
Apartments	25	103,069,900
Farm land	0	0
Farm homestead	0	0

Average Property Value & Tax, 2007
Residential value	$70,178
Property tax	$4,262
Tax credit/rebate	$940

Public Library
Lindenwold Public Library‡
310 E Linden Ave
Lindenwold, NJ 08021
856-784-5602
Branch Librarian.. B. Roach/M. Cavanaugh

Library statistics, 2006
see Camden County profile
for library system statistics

Public Safety
Number of officers, 2006 41

Crime	2005	2006
Total crimes	748	839
Violent	124	163
Murder	2	1
Rape	8	8
Robbery	48	89
Aggravated assault	66	65
Non-violent	624	676
Burglary	251	235
Larceny	310	356
Vehicle theft	63	85
Domestic violence	389	406
Arson	5	10
Total crime rate	43.2	48.6
Violent	7.2	9.4
Non-violent	36.1	39.2

Public School District
(for school year 2006-07 except as noted)

Lindenwold Borough School District
1017 E Linden Ave
Lindenwold, NJ 08021
856-784-4071

Superintendent	Geraldine Carroll
Number of schools	4
Grade plan	K-12
Enrollment	2,328
Attendance rate, '05-06	91.3%
Dropout rate	9.2%
Students per teacher	9.6
Per pupil expenditure	$12,918
Median faculty salary	$45,597
Median administrator salary	$91,548
Grade 12 enrollment	136
High school graduation rate	75.8%

Assessment test results
(percent scoring at proficient or advanced level)
	Language	Math
NJASK-Grade 3	71.6%	76.2%
GEPA-Grade 8	53.3%	43.9%
HSPA-High School	79.0%	56.5%

SAT score averages
Pct tested	Math	Verbal	Writing
52%	445	430	436

Teacher Qualifications
Avg. years of experience	7
Highly-qualified teachers one subject/all subjects	99.5%/99.5%
With emergency credentials	0.0%

No Child Left Behind
AYP, 2005-06 .... Meets Standards

Municipal Finance
State Aid Programs, 2008
Total aid	$2,443,620
CMPTRA	1,549,825
Energy tax receipts	893,696
Garden State Trust	99

General Budget, 2007
Total tax levy	$26,099,341
County levy	5,117,338
County taxes	4,648,159
County library	323,815
County health	0
County open space	145,365
School levy	14,311,515
Muni. levy	6,670,488
Misc. revenues	5,407,726

Taxes	2005	2006	2007
General tax rate per $100	5.07	5.747	6.074
County equalization ratio	81.63	67.74	58.98
Net valuation taxable	$428,699,889	$428,583,700	$429,742,466
State equalized value	$632,860,775	$727,555,991	$870,163,298

Atlantic County
Linwood City

Demographics & Socio-Economic Characteristics
(2000 US Census, except as noted)

Population
1980*	6,144
1990*	6,866
2000	7,172
Male	3,343
Female	3,829
2006 (estimate)*	7,354
Population density	1,920.1

Race & Hispanic Origin, 2000
Race
White	6,828
Black/African American	76
American Indian/Alaska Native	8
Asian	173
Native Hawaiian/Pacific Islander	0
Other race	16
Two or more races	71
Hispanic origin, total	130
Mexican	13
Puerto Rican	64
Cuban	2
Other Hispanic	51

Age & Nativity, 2000
Under 5 years	375
18 years and over	5,291
21 years and over	5,163
65 years and over	1,345
85 years and over	231
Median age	42.8
Native-born	6,877
Foreign-born	318

Educational Attainment, 2000
Population 25 years and over	5,111
Less than 9th grade	3.0%
High school grad or higher	90.5%
Bachelor's degree or higher	37.9%
Graduate degree	15.0%

Income & Poverty, 1999
Per capita income	$32,159
Median household income	$60,000
Median family income	$71,415
Persons in poverty	275
H'holds receiving public assistance	28
H'holds receiving social security	905

Households, 2000
Total households	2,647
With persons under 18	976
With persons over 65	878
Family households	1,966
Single-person households	590
Persons per household	2.65
Persons per family	3.13

Labor & Employment
Total civilian labor force, 2006**	3,613
Unemployment rate	3.7%
Total civilian labor force, 2000	3,300
Unemployment rate	4.0%

Employed persons 16 years and over by occupation, 2000
Managers & professionals	1,420
Service occupations	536
Sales & office occupations	806
Farming, fishing & forestry	0
Construction & maintenance	274
Production & transportation	133
Self-employed persons	264

* US Census Bureau
** New Jersey Department of Labor

See Introduction for an explanation of all data sources.

General Information
City of Linwood
400 W Poplar Ave
Linwood, NJ 08221
609-927-4108

Website	www.linwoodcity.org
Year of incorporation	1931
Land/water area (sq. miles)	3.83/0.31
Form of government	City

Government
Legislative Districts
US Congressional	2
State Legislative	2

Local Officials, 2008
Mayor	Richard DePamphilis III
Manager/Admin	NA
Clerk	Leigh Ann Napoli
Finance Dir	F. Bonnie Tiemann
Tax Assessor	Arthur Amonette
Tax Collector	Carl Wentzell
Attorney	Joseph Youngblood Jr
Building	James Galentino
Comm Dev/Planning	NA
Engineering	Dixon Associates
Public Works	Hank Kolakowski
Police Chief	James Baker
Emerg/Fire Director	Demetrios Foster

Housing & Construction
Housing Units, 2000*
Total	2,751
Median rent	$714
Median SF home value	$165,100

Permits for New Residential Construction
	Units	Value
Total, 2007	16	$4,922,659
Single family	16	$4,922,659
Total, 2006	15	$3,580,413
Single family	15	$3,580,413

Real Property Valuation, 2007
	Parcels	Valuation
Total	3,016	$772,374,100
Vacant	137	14,714,500
Residential	2,728	666,666,400
Commercial	147	90,209,200
Industrial	0	0
Apartments	0	0
Farm land	2	34,600
Farm homestead	2	749,400

Average Property Value & Tax, 2007
Residential value	$244,475
Property tax	$7,929
Tax credit/rebate	$1,162

Public Library
Linwood Public Library
301 Davis Ave
Linwood, NJ 08221
609-926-7991

Director	Maria Moss

Library statistics, 2006
Population served	7,172
Full-time/total staff	0/2

	Total	Per capita
Holdings	46,329	6.46
Revenues	$356,277	$49.68
Expenditures	$309,708	$43.18
Annual visits	21,316	2.97
Internet terminals/annual users	7/4,518	

Taxes
	2005	2006	2007
General tax rate per $100	3.03	3.187	3.244
County equalization ratio	87.01	74.78	66.18
Net valuation taxable	$751,545,247	$758,330,300	$773,023,780
State equalized value	$1,005,008,354	$1,146,565,765	$1,242,408,683

Public Safety
Number of officers, 2006	20

Crime	2005	2006
Total crimes	110	94
Violent	4	9
Murder	0	0
Rape	0	1
Robbery	0	3
Aggravated assault	4	5
Non-violent	106	85
Burglary	39	30
Larceny	64	48
Vehicle theft	3	7
Domestic violence	86	87
Arson	0	4
Total crime rate	14.8	12.7
Violent	0.5	1.2
Non-violent	14.3	11.5

Public School District
(for school year 2006-07 except as noted)

Linwood City School District
Belhaven Ave Middle School
Linwood, NJ 08221
609-926-6703

Superintendent	Thomas Baruffi
Number of schools	2
Grade plan	K-8
Enrollment	998
Attendance rate, '05-06	94.9%
Dropout rate	NA
Students per teacher	11.1
Per pupil expenditure	$11,489
Median faculty salary	$51,353
Median administrator salary	$93,150
Grade 12 enrollment	NA
High school graduation rate	NA

Assessment test results
(percent scoring at proficient or advanced level)
	Language	Math
NJASK-Grade 3	98.9%	100.0%
GEPA-Grade 8	92.7%	88.4%
HSPA-High School	NA	NA

SAT score averages
Pct tested	Math	Verbal	Writing
NA	NA	NA	NA

Teacher Qualifications
Avg. years of experience	8
Highly-qualified teachers one subject/all subjects	100%/100%
With emergency credentials	0.0%

No Child Left Behind
AYP, 2005-06	Meets Standards

Municipal Finance
State Aid Programs, 2008
Total aid	$683,090
CMPTRA	92,383
Energy tax receipts	590,707
Garden State Trust	0

General Budget, 2007
Total tax levy	$25,072,170
County tax	3,236,614
County taxes	2,858,345
County library	0
County health	144,379
County open space	233,890
School levy	15,479,914
Muni. levy	6,355,642
Misc. revenues	4,002,200

The New Jersey Municipal Data Book

Little Egg Harbor Township
Ocean County

Demographics & Socio-Economic Characteristics
(2000 US Census, except as noted)

Population
1980*	8,183
1990*	13,333
2000	15,945
Male	7,655
Female	8,290
2006 (estimate)*	20,283
Population density	413.0

Race & Hispanic Origin, 2000
Race
White	15,342
Black/African American	126
American Indian/Alaska Native	41
Asian	96
Native Hawaiian/Pacific Islander	1
Other race	156
Two or more races	183
Hispanic origin, total	520
Mexican	79
Puerto Rican	253
Cuban	19
Other Hispanic	169

Age & Nativity, 2000
Under 5 years	931
18 years and over	12,091
21 years and over	11,618
65 years and over	2,821
85 years and over	271
Median age	39.9
Native-born	15,525
Foreign-born	494

Educational Attainment, 2000
Population 25 years and over	10,971
Less than 9th grade	3.5%
High school grad or higher	81.0%
Bachelor's degree or higher	15.1%
Graduate degree	4.5%

Income & Poverty, 1999
Per capita income	$20,619
Median household income	$45,628
Median family income	$51,580
Persons in poverty	1,028
H'holds receiving public assistance	107
H'holds receiving social security	2,299

Households, 2000
Total households	6,179
With persons under 18	2,065
With persons over 65	1,916
Family households	4,442
Single-person households	1,389
Persons per household	2.55
Persons per family	2.98

Labor & Employment
Total civilian labor force, 2006**	7,438
Unemployment rate	5.7%
Total civilian labor force, 2000	7,505
Unemployment rate	5.2%

Employed persons 16 years and over by occupation, 2000
Managers & professionals	1,875
Service occupations	1,571
Sales & office occupations	1,985
Farming, fishing & forestry	26
Construction & maintenance	943
Production & transportation	711
Self-employed persons	432

‡ Branch of county library
* US Census Bureau
** New Jersey Department of Labor

General Information
Township of Little Egg Harbor
665 Radio Rd
Little Egg Harbor Twp, NJ 08087
609-296-7241

Website	www.leht.com
Year of incorporation	1740
Land/water area (sq. miles)	49.11/24.07
Form of government	Township

Government
Legislative Districts
US Congressional	3
State Legislative	9

Local Officials, 2008
Mayor	Scott Stites
Manager	Raymond Urezzio
Clerk	Diana K. McCracken
Finance Dir	Raymond Urezzio
Tax Assessor	Joseph Sorrentino
Tax Collector	Dayna Cook
Attorney	G. Gilmore & Monahan
Building	Jay Haines
Comm Dev/Planning	NA
Engineering	CMX
Public Works	Anthony Savino
Police Chief	Mark Siino
Fire/Emergency Dir	NA

Housing & Construction
Housing Units, 2000*
Total	7,931
Median rent	$817
Median SF home value	$98,800

Permits for New Residential Construction
	Units	Value
Total, 2007	106	$12,746,800
Single family	100	$12,206,800
Total, 2006	143	$16,710,523
Single family	143	$16,710,523

Real Property Valuation, 2007
	Parcels	Valuation
Total	11,582	$3,117,188,616
Vacant	1,576	160,884,400
Residential	9,802	2,804,394,189
Commercial	178	145,989,800
Industrial	2	566,100
Apartments	2	3,060,000
Farm land	17	73,427
Farm homestead	5	2,220,700

Average Property Value & Tax, 2007
Residential value	$286,185
Property tax	$3,951
Tax credit/rebate	$882

Public Library
Little Egg Harbor Branch Library‡
290 Mathistown Rd
Little Egg Harbor, NJ 08087
609-294-1197

Branch Librarian .... Kathy Erickson

Library statistics, 2006
see Ocean County profile
for library system statistics

Public Safety
Number of officers, 2006 41

Crime	2005	2006
Total crimes	462	491
Violent	27	31
Murder	0	0
Rape	2	2
Robbery	0	5
Aggravated assault	25	24
Non-violent	435	460
Burglary	76	83
Larceny	347	362
Vehicle theft	12	15
Domestic violence	275	287
Arson	2	4
Total crime rate	23.9	24.8
Violent	1.4	1.6
Non-violent	22.5	23.2

Public School District
(for school year 2006-07 except as noted)

Little Egg Harbor Township School District
307 Frog Pond Rd
Little Egg Harbor, NJ 08087
609-296-1719

Superintendent	Frank Kasyan
Number of schools	2
Grade plan	K-6
Enrollment	1,712
Attendance rate, '05-06	93.0%
Dropout rate	NA
Students per teacher	11.1
Per pupil expenditure	$11,772
Median faculty salary	$47,300
Median administrator salary	$84,500
Grade 12 enrollment	NA
High school graduation rate	NA

Assessment test results
(percent scoring at proficient or advanced level)
	Language	Math
NJASK-Grade 3	84.2%	82.3%
GEPA-Grade 8	NA	NA
HSPA-High School	NA	NA

SAT score averages
Pct tested	Math	Verbal	Writing
NA	NA	NA	NA

Teacher Qualifications
Avg. years of experience	9
Highly-qualified teachers one subject/all subjects	100%/100%
With emergency credentials	0.0%

No Child Left Behind
AYP, 2005-06 .... Meets Standards

Municipal Finance
State Aid Programs, 2008
Total aid	$1,857,216
CMPTRA	315,118
Energy tax receipts	1,355,607
Garden State Trust	184,674

General Budget, 2007
Total tax levy	$43,118,588
County levy	8,911,944
County taxes	7,343,788
County library	870,404
County health	352,638
County open space	345,114
School levy	21,238,708
Muni. levy	12,967,936
Misc. revenues	5,943,733

Taxes	2005	2006	2007
General tax rate per $100	3.312	1.318	1.381
County equalization ratio	60.58	130.54	108.8
Net valuation taxable	$1,142,744,520	$3,034,192,460	$3,123,347,088
State equalized value	$2,215,909,482	$2,794,768,299	$3,046,131,766

Passaic County / Little Falls Township

Demographics & Socio-Economic Characteristics
(2000 US Census, except as noted)

Population
- 1980* 11,496
- 1990* 11,294
- 2000 10,855
  - Male 5,134
  - Female 5,721
- 2006 (estimate)* 11,829
  - Population density 4,301.5

Race & Hispanic Origin, 2000
Race
- White 10,001
- Black/African American 71
- American Indian/Alaska Native 7
- Asian 456
- Native Hawaiian/Pacific Islander 2
- Other race 144
- Two or more races 174
- Hispanic origin, total 579
  - Mexican 56
  - Puerto Rican 166
  - Cuban 66
  - Other Hispanic 291

Age & Nativity, 2000
- Under 5 years 556
- 18 years and over 8,888
- 21 years and over 8,604
- 65 years and over 1,938
- 85 years and over 213
  - Median age 40.6
- Native-born 9,369
- Foreign-born 1,486

Educational Attainment, 2000
- Population 25 years and over 8,178
- Less than 9th grade 6.0%
- High school grad or higher 85.3%
- Bachelor's degree or higher 34.7%
- Graduate degree 12.3%

Income & Poverty, 1999
- Per capita income $33,242
- Median household income $58,857
- Median family income $70,223
- Persons in poverty 493
- H'holds receiving public assistance 61
- H'holds receiving social security 1,491

Households, 2000
- Total households 4,687
  - With persons under 18 1,139
  - With persons over 65 1,474
  - Family households 2,871
  - Single-person households 1,552
- Persons per household 2.32
- Persons per family 2.99

Labor & Employment
- Total civilian labor force, 2006** 6,326
  - Unemployment rate 4.5%
- Total civilian labor force, 2000 5,821
  - Unemployment rate 4.4%

Employed persons 16 years and over by occupation, 2000
- Managers & professionals 2,430
- Service occupations 531
- Sales & office occupations 1,804
- Farming, fishing & forestry 0
- Construction & maintenance 349
- Production & transportation 452
- Self-employed persons 291

* US Census Bureau
** New Jersey Department of Labor

See Introduction for an explanation of all data sources.

General Information
Township of Little Falls
225 Main St
Little Falls, NJ 07424
973-256-0170

- Website .... www.lfnj.com
- Year of incorporation 1868
- Land/water area (sq. miles) 2.75/0.07
- Form of government .... Mayor-Council

Government

Legislative Districts
- US Congressional 8
- State Legislative 40

Local Officials, 2008
- Mayor .... Eugene Kulick
- Manager .... William Wilk
- Clerk .... William Wilk
- Finance Dir .... Kathy Albanese
- Tax Assessor .... E. Romeo Longo
- Tax Collector .... NA
- Attorney .... Joseph Trapanese
- Building .... William Cullen
- Comm Dev/Planning .... NA
- Engineering .... Robert Schilling
- Public Works .... NA
- Police Chief .... Gerald Hunter
- Emerg/Fire Director .... Jack Sweezy Jr

Housing & Construction

Housing Units, 2000*
- Total 4,797
- Median rent $909
- Median SF home value $212,300

Permits for New Residential Construction

	Units	Value
Total, 2007	8	$942,250
Single family	2	$597,900
Total, 2006	11	$1,003,005
Single family	11	$1,003,005

Real Property Valuation, 2007

	Parcels	Valuation
Total	4,066	$723,933,100
Vacant	175	16,968,300
Residential	3,665	541,871,900
Commercial	174	95,431,400
Industrial	43	29,034,200
Apartments	9	40,627,300
Farm land	0	0
Farm homestead	0	0

Average Property Value & Tax, 2007
- Residential value $147,850
- Property tax $6,964
- Tax credit/rebate $1,131

Public Library
Little Falls Public Library
8 Warren St
Little Falls, NJ 07424
973-256-2784

Director .... Patricia A. Pelak

Library statistics, 2006
- Population served 10,855
- Full-time/total staff 2/5

	Total	Per capita
Holdings	53,979	4.97
Revenues	$584,475	$53.84
Expenditures	$475,433	$43.80
Annual visits	51,428	4.74
Internet terminals/annual users		10/14,883

Public Safety
- Number of officers, 2006 23

Crime	2005	2006
Total crimes	362	446
Violent	26	25
Murder	0	0
Rape	6	6
Robbery	3	4
Aggravated assault	17	15
Non-violent	336	421
Burglary	53	73
Larceny	254	320
Vehicle theft	29	28
Domestic violence	178	129
Arson	0	0
Total crime rate	30.3	37.5
Violent	2.2	2.1
Non-violent	28.1	35.4

Public School District
(for school year 2006-07 except as noted)

Little Falls Township School District
560 Main St, School #3
Little Falls, NJ 07424
973-256-1034

- Chief School Admin .... Bruce deLyon
- Number of schools 3
- Grade plan K-8
- Enrollment 882
- Attendance rate, '05-06 .... 95.6%
- Dropout rate .... NA
- Students per teacher 11.1
- Per pupil expenditure $12,655
- Median faculty salary $56,548
- Median administrator salary $101,290
- Grade 12 enrollment .... NA
- High school graduation rate .... NA

Assessment test results
(percent scoring at proficient or advanced level)

	Language	Math
NJASK-Grade 3	93.4%	86.6%
GEPA-Grade 8	80.2%	74.8%
HSPA-High School	NA	NA

SAT score averages

Pct tested	Math	Verbal	Writing
NA	NA	NA	NA

Teacher Qualifications
- Avg. years of experience 7
- Highly-qualified teachers
  one subject/all subjects 100%/100%
- With emergency credentials 0.0%

No Child Left Behind
- AYP, 2005-06 .... Meets Standards

Municipal Finance

State Aid Programs, 2008
- Total aid $1,656,501
  - CMPTRA 424,620
  - Energy tax receipts 1,221,221
  - Garden State Trust 9,203

General Budget, 2007
- Total tax levy $34,217,242
  - County levy 9,304,255
    - County taxes 9,116,028
    - County library 0
    - County health 0
    - County open space 188,227
  - School levy 16,345,348
  - Muni. levy 8,567,639
- Misc. revenues 4,330,842

Taxes	2005	2006	2007
General tax rate per $100	4.12	4.39	4.72
County equalization ratio	46.6	42.99	38.75
Net valuation taxable	$724,283,752	$721,434,900	$726,417,800
State equalized value	$1,684,772,626	$1,865,145,936	$1,953,786,856

Little Ferry Borough

Bergen County

Demographics & Socio-Economic Characteristics
(2000 US Census, except as noted)

Population
1980*	9,399
1990*	9,989
2000	10,800
Male	5,261
Female	5,539
2006 (estimate)*	10,715
Population density	7,003.3

Race & Hispanic Origin, 2000
Race
White	7,426
Black/African American	509
American Indian/Alaska Native	16
Asian	1,847
Native Hawaiian/Pacific Islander	6
Other race	621
Two or more races	375
Hispanic origin, total	1,641
Mexican	43
Puerto Rican	344
Cuban	199
Other Hispanic	1,055

Age & Nativity, 2000
Under 5 years	687
18 years and over	8,616
21 years and over	8,314
65 years and over	1,342
85 years and over	133
Median age	37.1
Native-born	7,443
Foreign-born	3,357

Educational Attainment, 2000
Population 25 years and over	7,762
Less than 9th grade	5.7%
High school grad or higher	81.5%
Bachelor's degree or higher	24.1%
Graduate degree	8.0%

Income & Poverty, 1999
Per capita income	$24,210
Median household income	$49,958
Median family income	$59,176
Persons in poverty	677
H'holds receiving public assistance	65
H'holds receiving social security	1,017

Households, 2000
Total households	4,366
With persons under 18	1,300
With persons over 65	1,002
Family households	2,785
Single-person households	1,364
Persons per household	2.47
Persons per family	3.16

Labor & Employment
Total civilian labor force, 2006**	6,401
Unemployment rate	4.6%
Total civilian labor force, 2000	6,021
Unemployment rate	4.6%

Employed persons 16 years and over by occupation, 2000
Managers & professionals	1,979
Service occupations	676
Sales & office occupations	1,920
Farming, fishing & forestry	0
Construction & maintenance	413
Production & transportation	758
Self-employed persons	246

* US Census Bureau
** New Jersey Department of Labor

General Information
Borough of Little Ferry
215-217 Liberty St
Little Ferry, NJ 07643
201-641-9234

Website	www.littleferrynj.org
Year of incorporation	1894
Land/water area (sq. miles)	1.53/0.16
Form of government	Borough

Government
Legislative Districts
US Congressional	9
State Legislative	38

Local Officials, 2008
Mayor	Mauro Raguseo
Manager	Kenneth Gabbert
Clerk	Barbara Maldonado
Finance Dir.	Leonard Nicolosi
Tax Assessor	George Reggo
Tax Collector	Frank Berardo
Attorney	Joseph Monaghan
Building	Richard Bolan
Planning	NA
Engineering	Kenneth Job
Public Works	William Holly
Police Chief	Ralph Verdi
Emerg/Fire Director	Marty Loesner

Housing & Construction
Housing Units, 2000*
Total	4,449
Median rent	$822
Median SF home value	$192,800

Permits for New Residential Construction
	Units	Value
Total, 2007	1	$241,000
Single family	1	$241,000
Total, 2006	1	$200,000
Single family	1	$200,000

Real Property Valuation, 2007
	Parcels	Valuation
Total	2,543	$1,226,544,600
Vacant	38	10,351,700
Residential	2,238	797,532,900
Commercial	164	154,249,500
Industrial	78	151,755,800
Apartments	25	112,654,700
Farm land	0	0
Farm homestead	0	0

Average Property Value & Tax, 2007
Residential value	$356,360
Property tax	$7,310
Tax credit/rebate	$1,165

Public Library
Little Ferry Public Library
239 Liberty St
Little Ferry, NJ 07643
201-641-3721

Director .... Cheryl Ashley

Library statistics, 2006
Population served	10,800
Full-time/total staff	1/4

	Total	Per capita
Holdings	29,967	2.77
Revenues	$454,512	$42.08
Expenditures	$334,966	$31.02
Annual visits	26,576	2.46
Internet terminals/annual users	8/6,123	

Taxes
	2005	2006	2007
General tax rate per $100	1.78	1.93	2.06
County equalization ratio	125.09	113.5	101.35
Net valuation taxable	$1,235,795,240	$1,224,881,300	$1,233,156,597
State equalized value	$1,088,806,379	$1,214,969,161	$1,326,896,819

Public Safety
Number of officers, 2006 28

Crime	2005	2006
Total crimes	105	120
Violent	10	5
Murder	0	0
Rape	2	1
Robbery	3	0
Aggravated assault	5	4
Non-violent	95	115
Burglary	8	23
Larceny	67	71
Vehicle theft	20	21
Domestic violence	80	95
Arson	1	0
Total crime rate	9.7	11.1
Violent	0.9	0.5
Non-violent	8.8	10.7

Public School District
(for school year 2006-07 except as noted)

Little Ferry School District
130 Liberty St
Little Ferry, NJ 07643
201-641-6192

Superintendent	Frank R. Scarafile
Number of schools	2
Grade plan	K-8
Enrollment	975
Attendance rate, '05-06	96.9%
Dropout rate	NA
Students per teacher	12.5
Per pupil expenditure	$11,687
Median faculty salary	$59,643
Median administrator salary	$112,570
Grade 12 enrollment	NA
High school graduation rate	NA

Assessment test results
(percent scoring at proficient or advanced level)
	Language	Math
NJASK-Grade 3	84.4%	85.5%
GEPA-Grade 8	71.6%	69.0%
HSPA-High School	NA	NA

SAT score averages
Pct tested	Math	Verbal	Writing
NA	NA	NA	NA

Teacher Qualifications
Avg. years of experience	14
Highly-qualified teachers one subject/all subjects	100%/100%
With emergency credentials	0.0%

No Child Left Behind
AYP, 2005-06 .... Meets Standards

Municipal Finance
State Aid Programs, 2008
Total aid	$1,202,838
CMPTRA	415,717
Energy tax receipts	787,121
Garden State Trust	0

General Budget, 2007
Total tax levy	$25,296,840
County levy	2,219,579
County taxes	2,097,396
County library	0
County health	0
County open space	122,183
School levy	14,624,293
Muni. levy	8,452,968
Misc. revenues	4,757,253

Monmouth County
Little Silver Borough

Demographics & Socio-Economic Characteristics
(2000 US Census, except as noted)

Population
- 1980*......................................5,548
- 1990*......................................5,721
- 2000......................................6,170
  - Male....................................2,979
  - Female..................................3,191
- 2006 (estimate)*...........................6,089
- Population density.......................2,198.2

Race & Hispanic Origin, 2000
Race
- White......................................5,994
- Black/African American........................19
- American Indian/Alaska Native.................10
- Asian...93
- Native Hawaiian/Pacific Islander...............1
- Other race....................................12
- Two or more races.............................41
- Hispanic origin, total........................81
  - Mexican....................................16
  - Puerto Rican...............................14
  - Cuban......................................11
  - Other Hispanic.............................40

Age & Nativity, 2000
- Under 5 years................................452
- 18 years and over..........................4,479
- 21 years and over..........................4,344
- 65 years and over............................967
- 85 years and over.............................97
- Median age..................................41.1
- Native-born................................5,810
- Foreign-born.................................360

Educational Attainment, 2000
- Population 25 years and over...............4,199
- Less than 9th grade.........................0.5%
- High school grad or higher.................96.8%
- Bachelor's degree or higher................60.5%
- Graduate degree............................22.0%

Income & Poverty, 1999
- Per capita income.......................$46,798
- Median household income..................$94,094
- Median family income....................$104,033
- Persons in poverty............................48
- H'holds receiving public assistance...........21
- H'holds receiving social security............659

Households, 2000
- Total households...........................2,232
  - With persons under 18.....................869
  - With persons over 65......................666
  - Family households.......................1,810
  - Single-person households..................375
- Persons per household.......................2.76
- Persons per family..........................3.13

Labor & Employment
- Total civilian labor force, 2006**.........3,175
  - Unemployment rate........................3.1%
- Total civilian labor force, 2000...........2,934
  - Unemployment rate........................2.7%

Employed persons 16 years and over by occupation, 2000
- Managers & professionals..................1,694
- Service occupations..........................166
- Sales & office occupations..................810
- Farming, fishing & forestry....................5
- Construction & maintenance..................126
- Production & transportation..................53
- Self-employed persons.......................288

* US Census Bureau
** New Jersey Department of Labor

See Introduction for an explanation of all data sources.

General Information
Borough of Little Silver
480 Prospect Ave
Little Silver, NJ 07739
732-842-2400

- Website..................www.littlesilver.org
- Year of incorporation.....................1923
- Land/water area (sq. miles).........2.77/0.60
- Form of government...................Borough

Government
Legislative Districts
- US Congressional.............................12
- State Legislative............................12

Local Officials, 2008
- Mayor....................Suzanne Castleman
- Manager...................Michael Biehl
- Clerk.....................Michael Biehl
- Finance Dir..............Lynn Marie Gale
- Tax Assessor............J. Stephen Walters
- Tax Collector............Lynn Marie Gale
- Attorney.............John O. Bennett III
- Building.................Stanley Sickels
- Comm Dev/Planning....................NA
- Engineering..............Gregory Blash
- Public Works...............John Clark
- Police Chief............Shannon Giblin
- Emerg/Fire Director.......Chris Beronio

Housing & Construction
Housing Units, 2000*
- Total.................................2,288
- Median rent..........................$1,125
- Median SF home value...............$300,400

Permits for New Residential Construction

	Units	Value
Total, 2007	14	$6,242,963
Single family	14	$6,242,963
Total, 2006	13	$4,150,691
Single family	13	$4,150,691

Real Property Valuation, 2007

	Parcels	Valuation
Total	2,520	$1,245,276,800
Vacant	96	13,882,900
Residential	2,275	1,144,025,300
Commercial	144	83,976,300
Industrial	0	0
Apartments	0	0
Farm land	3	15,800
Farm homestead	2	3,376,500

Average Property Value & Tax, 2007
- Residential value....................$503,909
- Property tax.........................$10,680
- Tax credit/rebate.....................$1,304

Public Library
Little Silver Public Library
484 Prospect Ave
Little Silver, NJ 07739
732-747-9649

Director................Susan M. Edwards

Library statistics, 2006
- Population served........................6,170
- Full-time/total staff.......................1/1

	Total	Per capita
Holdings	32,434	5.26
Revenues	$257,200	$41.69
Expenditures	$259,842	$42.11
Annual visits	25,095	4.07
Internet terminals/annual users		4/2,129

Taxes

	2005	2006	2007
General tax rate per $100	2.012	2.086	2.12
County equalization ratio	94.03	84.94	77.88
Net valuation taxable	$1,225,631,503	$1,235,213,600	$1,246,314,064
State equalized value	$1,442,937,960	$1,586,968,655	$1,651,284,812

Public Safety
- Number of officers, 2006....................15

Crime

	2005	2006
Total crimes	90	63
Violent	2	0
Murder	0	0
Rape	1	0
Robbery	0	0
Aggravated assault	1	0
Non-violent	88	63
Burglary	9	12
Larceny	78	49
Vehicle theft	1	2
Domestic violence	15	0
Arson	0	0
Total crime rate	14.5	10.3
Violent	0.3	0.0
Non-violent	14.2	10.3

Public School District
(for school year 2006-07 except as noted)

Little Silver Borough School District
124 Willow Dr
Little Silver, NJ 07739
732-741-2188

- Superintendent.........Carolyn M. Kossack
- Number of schools..........................2
- Grade plan...............................K-8
- Enrollment..............................788
- Attendance rate, '05-06................96.1%
- Dropout rate..............................NA
- Students per teacher......................9.7
- Per pupil expenditure.................$12,748
- Median faculty salary.................$42,525
- Median administrator salary..........$100,500
- Grade 12 enrollment.......................NA
- High school graduation rate..............NA

Assessment test results
(percent scoring at proficient or advanced level)

	Language	Math
NJASK-Grade 3	97.6%	97.6%
GEPA-Grade 8	95.4%	91.8%
HSPA-High School	NA	NA

SAT score averages

Pct tested	Math	Verbal	Writing
NA	NA	NA	NA

Teacher Qualifications
- Avg. years of experience....................7
- Highly-qualified teachers
  - one subject/all subjects.......100%/100%
- With emergency credentials...............0.0%

No Child Left Behind
- AYP, 2005-06.............Meets Standards

Municipal Finance
State Aid Programs, 2008
- Total aid.........................$759,001
- CMPTRA.............................65,058
- Energy tax receipts...............693,943
- Garden State Trust......................0

General Budget, 2007
- Total tax levy.................$26,414,284
- County taxes...................4,316,462
  - County taxes.................3,854,916
  - County library................220,680
  - County health......................0
  - County open space............240,865
- School levy.....................16,265,747
- Muni. levy.......................5,832,075
- Misc. revenues...................3,782,244

The New Jersey Municipal Data Book

Livingston Township
Essex County

Demographics & Socio-Economic Characteristics
(2000 US Census, except as noted)

Population
1980*	28,040
1990*	26,609
2000	27,391
Male	13,322
Female	14,069
2006 (estimate)*	28,413
Population density	2,047.0

Race & Hispanic Origin, 2000
Race
White	22,637
Black/African American	328
American Indian/Alaska Native	14
Asian	3,982
Native Hawaiian/Pacific Islander	3
Other race	190
Two or more races	237
Hispanic origin, total	695
Mexican	39
Puerto Rican	128
Cuban	88
Other Hispanic	440

Age & Nativity, 2000
Under 5 years	1,917
18 years and over	20,107
21 years and over	19,495
65 years and over	4,221
85 years and over	420
Median age	40.6
Native-born	22,237
Foreign-born	5,154

Educational Attainment, 2000
Population 25 years and over	18,769
Less than 9th grade	2.2%
High school grad or higher	94.0%
Bachelor's degree or higher	57.7%
Graduate degree	26.7%

Income & Poverty, 1999
Per capita income	$47,218
Median household income	$98,869
Median family income	$108,049
Persons in poverty	480
H'holds receiving public assistance	56
H'holds receiving social security	2,779

Households, 2000
Total households	9,300
With persons under 18	4,003
With persons over 65	2,911
Family households	7,936
Single-person households	1,207
Persons per household	2.93
Persons per family	3.21

Labor & Employment
Total civilian labor force, 2006**	14,655
Unemployment rate	3.0%
Total civilian labor force, 2000	13,724
Unemployment rate	2.1%

Employed persons 16 years and over by occupation, 2000
Managers & professionals	7,514
Service occupations	988
Sales & office occupations	3,984
Farming, fishing & forestry	0
Construction & maintenance	524
Production & transportation	420
Self-employed persons	927

* US Census Bureau
** New Jersey Department of Labor

General Information
Township of Livingston
357 S Livingston Ave
Livingston, NJ 07039
973-992-5000

Website	www.livingstonnj.org
Year of incorporation	1813
Land/water area (sq. miles)	13.88/0.19
Form of government	Council-Manager

Government
Legislative Districts
US Congressional	8, 11
State Legislative	27

Local Officials, 2008
Mayor	Gary Schneiderman
Manager	Michele Meade
Clerk	Glenn Turtletaub
Finance Dir	William Nadolny Jr
Tax Assessor	Lidia Dumytsch
Tax Collector	Vibha Desai
Attorney	Sharon Weiner
Building	Martin Chiarolanzio
Planning	Jackie Hollis
Engineering	Robert Schaefer
Public Works	Robert Schaefer
Police Chief	Michael Erb
Emerg/Fire Director	Christopher Mullin

Housing & Construction
Housing Units, 2000*
Total	9,457
Median rent	$1,244
Median SF home value	$290,200

Permits for New Residential Construction
	Units	Value
Total, 2007	19	$19,086,501
Single family	19	$19,086,501
Total, 2006	89	$47,265,513
Single family	89	$47,265,513

Real Property Valuation, 2007
	Parcels	Valuation
Total	10,516	$965,732,700
Vacant	368	18,823,400
Residential	9,812	777,972,000
Commercial	291	152,816,100
Industrial	43	16,022,800
Apartments	0	0
Farm land	1	6,000
Farm homestead	1	92,400

Average Property Value & Tax, 2007
Residential value	$79,289
Property tax	$11,153
Tax credit/rebate	$1,258

Public Library
R.L. Rockwood Memorial Library
10 Robert H. Harp Dr
Livingston, NJ 07039
973-992-4600

Director............Barbara Jean Sikora

Library statistics, 2006
Population served	27,391
Full-time/total staff	13/26

	Total	Per capita
Holdings	189,456	6.92
Revenues	$2,935,280	$107.16
Expenditures	$2,744,038	$100.18
Annual visits	281,772	10.29
Internet terminals/annual users	10/12,407	

Public Safety
Number of officers, 2006 74

Crime
	2005	2006
Total crimes	598	544
Violent	15	30
Murder	0	1
Rape	1	1
Robbery	3	8
Aggravated assault	11	20
Non-violent	583	514
Burglary	46	43
Larceny	504	439
Vehicle theft	33	32
Domestic violence	84	88
Arson	2	1
Total crime rate	21.5	19.6
Violent	0.5	1.1
Non-violent	20.9	18.5

Public School District
(for school year 2006-07 except as noted)

Livingston Township School District
11 Foxcroft Dr
Livingston, NJ 07039
973-535-8000

Superintendent	Brad Draeger
Number of schools	9
Grade plan	K-12
Enrollment	5,534
Attendance rate, '05-06	96.6%
Dropout rate	0.1%
Students per teacher	11.0
Per pupil expenditure	$14,490
Median faculty salary	$70,200
Median administrator salary	$109,556
Grade 12 enrollment	440
High school graduation rate	100.0%

Assessment test results
(percent scoring at proficient or advanced level)
	Language	Math
NJASK-Grade 3	95.0%	94.3%
GEPA-Grade 8	95.7%	93.9%
HSPA-High School	98.3%	92.8%

SAT score averages
Pct tested	Math	Verbal	Writing
99%	591	562	566

Teacher Qualifications
Avg. years of experience	9
Highly-qualified teachers one subject/all subjects	100%/100%
With emergency credentials	0.0%

No Child Left Behind
AYP, 2005-06 .... Meets Standards

Municipal Finance
State Aid Programs, 2008
Total aid	$4,018,825
CMPTRA	829,914
Energy tax receipts	3,178,101
Garden State Trust	0

General Budget, 2007
Total tax levy	$136,011,178
County levy	30,077,022
County taxes	29,303,730
County library	0
County health	0
County open space	773,292
School levy	81,093,043
Muni. levy	24,841,113
Misc. revenues	14,725,802

Taxes
	2005	2006	2007
General tax rate per $100	12.63	12.94	14.07
County equalization ratio	16.2	14.7	12.6
Net valuation taxable	$952,120,200	$951,511,100	$966,964,700
State equalized value	$6,477,008,163	$7,553,097,297	$7,936,586,971

Monmouth County — Loch Arbour Village

Demographics & Socio-Economic Characteristics
(2000 US Census, except as noted)

Population
1980*	369
1990*	380
2000	280
Male	144
Female	136
2006 (estimate)*	274
Population density	2,740.0

Race & Hispanic Origin, 2000
Race
White	266
Black/African American	6
American Indian/Alaska Native	0
Asian	2
Native Hawaiian/Pacific Islander	0
Other race	1
Two or more races	5
Hispanic origin, total	2
Mexican	0
Puerto Rican	1
Cuban	0
Other Hispanic	1

Age & Nativity, 2000
Under 5 years	18
18 years and over	231
21 years and over	225
65 years and over	44
85 years and over	6
Median age	43.0
Native-born	273
Foreign-born	2

Educational Attainment, 2000
Population 25 years and over	200
Less than 9th grade	0.0%
High school grad or higher	100.0%
Bachelor's degree or higher	50.0%
Graduate degree	20.0%

Income & Poverty, 1999
Per capita income	$34,037
Median household income	$68,542
Median family income	$74,250
Persons in poverty	13
H'holds receiving public assistance	0
H'holds receiving social security	24

Households, 2000
Total households	120
With persons under 18	28
With persons over 65	30
Family households	77
Single-person households	33
Persons per household	2.33
Persons per family	2.88

Labor & Employment
Total civilian labor force, 2006**	172
Unemployment rate	6.3%
Total civilian labor force, 2000	162
Unemployment rate	7.4%

Employed persons 16 years and over by occupation, 2000
Managers & professionals	89
Service occupations	10
Sales & office occupations	34
Farming, fishing & forestry	0
Construction & maintenance	12
Production & transportation	5
Self-employed persons	18

* US Census Bureau
** New Jersey Department of Labor

General Information
Village of Loch Arbour
550 Main St
Loch Arbour, NJ 07711
732-531-4740

Website	www.locharbournj.us
Year of incorporation	1957
Land/water area (sq. miles)	0.10/0.04
Form of government	Village

Government
Legislative Districts
US Congressional	6
State Legislative	11

Local Officials, 2008
Mayor	Betty McBain
Manager/Admin	NA
Clerk	Lorraine Carafa
Finance Dir	Lorraine Carafa
Tax Assessor	Eldo Magnani
Tax Collector	Lorraine Carafa
Attorney	Kenneth Fitzsimmons
Building	Alan Decker
Comm Dev/Planning	NA
Engineering	Peter Avakian
Public Works	NA
Police Chief	Antonio Amodio
Fire/Emergency Dir	Frank Manfredi

Housing & Construction
Housing Units, 2000*
Total	156
Median rent	$755
Median SF home value	$322,400

Permits for New Residential Construction
	Units	Value
Total, 2007	0	$0
Single family	0	$0
Total, 2006	0	$0
Single family	0	$0

Real Property Valuation, 2007
	Parcels	Valuation
Total	147	$73,122,600
Vacant	5	1,233,400
Residential	135	68,026,900
Commercial	6	3,598,900
Industrial	0	0
Apartments	1	263,400
Farm land	0	0
Farm homestead	0	0

Average Property Value & Tax, 2007
Residential value	$503,903
Property tax	$8,509
Tax credit/rebate	$1,035

Public Library
served by Monmouth County Library
125 Symmes Dr
Manalapan, NJ 07726
732-431-7235

Director............Ken Sheinbaum

Library statistics, 2006
Population served	399,613
Full-time/total staff	36/117

	Total	Per capita
Holdings	1,366,533	3.42
Revenues	$13,614,168	$34.07
Expenditures	$11,921,555	$29.83
Annual visits	2,235,563	5.59
Internet terminals/annual users	78/253,864	

Public Safety
Number of officers, 2006	0

Crime	2005	2006
Total crimes	10	18
Violent	2	0
Murder	0	0
Rape	0	0
Robbery	0	0
Aggravated assault	2	0
Non-violent	8	18
Burglary	2	4
Larceny	6	14
Vehicle theft	0	0
Domestic violence	0	0
Arson	0	0
Total crime rate	35.8	65.5
Violent	7.2	0.0
Non-violent	28.7	65.5

Public School District
(for school year 2006-07 except as noted)

Ocean Township School District
163 Monmouth Rd
Oakhurst, NJ 07755
732-531-5600

Superintendent	Thomas M. Pagano
Number of schools	10
Grade plan	K-12
Enrollment	4,318
Attendance rate, '05-06	95.6%
Dropout rate	0.1%
Students per teacher	11.4
Per pupil expenditure	$13,410
Median faculty salary	$62,280
Median administrator salary	$108,750
Grade 12 enrollment	326
High school graduation rate	99.1%

Assessment test results
(percent scoring at proficient or advanced level)
	Language	Math
NJASK-Grade 3	87.5%	90.7%
GEPA-Grade 8	81.6%	83.5%
HSPA-High School	91.1%	84.2%

SAT score averages
Pct tested	Math	Verbal	Writing
96%	525	502	496

Teacher Qualifications
Avg. years of experience	11
Highly-qualified teachers one subject/all subjects	100%/100%
With emergency credentials	0.0%

No Child Left Behind
AYP, 2005-06............Meets Standards

Municipal Finance
State Aid Programs, 2008
Total aid	$39,390
CMPTRA	0
Energy tax receipts	39,390
Garden State Trust	0

General Budget, 2007
Total tax levy	$1,235,120
County levy	486,381
County taxes	434,375
County library	24,866
County health	
County open space	27,140
School levy	300,000
Muni. levy	448,739
Misc. revenues	373,294

Taxes	2005	2006	2007
General tax rate per $100	1.454	1.576	1.689
County equalization ratio	72.33	52.12	40.63
Net valuation taxable	$71,891,574	$72,907,200	$73,146,872
State equalized value	$137,934,716	$179,473,339	$187,038,594

Lodi Borough
Bergen County

Demographics & Socio-Economic Characteristics
(2000 US Census, except as noted)

Population
1980*	23,956
1990*	22,355
2000	23,971
Male	11,378
Female	12,593
2006 (estimate)*	24,310
Population density	10,756.6

Race & Hispanic Origin, 2000
Race
White	18,736
Black/African American	852
American Indian/Alaska Native	40
Asian	2,124
Native Hawaiian/Pacific Islander	8
Other race	1,498
Two or more races	713
Hispanic origin, total	4,309
Mexican	212
Puerto Rican	912
Cuban	178
Other Hispanic	3,007

Age & Nativity, 2000
Under 5 years	1,533
18 years and over	18,865
21 years and over	18,157
65 years and over	3,564
85 years and over	425
Median age	36.4
Native-born	16,840
Foreign-born	7,131

Educational Attainment, 2000
Population 25 years and over	17,017
Less than 9th grade	11.7%
High school grad or higher	75.8%
Bachelor's degree or higher	18.7%
Graduate degree	5.1%

Income & Poverty, 1999
Per capita income	$21,667
Median household income	$43,421
Median family income	$51,959
Persons in poverty	1,921
H'holds receiving public assistance	227
H'holds receiving social security	2,742

Households, 2000
Total households	9,528
With persons under 18	3,002
With persons over 65	2,619
Family households	6,100
Single-person households	2,871
Persons per household	2.50
Persons per family	3.16

Labor & Employment
Total civilian labor force, 2006**	13,217
Unemployment rate	4.8%
Total civilian labor force, 2000	12,425
Unemployment rate	4.7%

Employed persons 16 years and over by occupation, 2000
Managers & professionals	3,251
Service occupations	1,501
Sales & office occupations	4,050
Farming, fishing & forestry	5
Construction & maintenance	1,083
Production & transportation	1,949
Self-employed persons	435

* US Census Bureau
** New Jersey Department of Labor
§ State Fiscal Year July 1–June 30

General Information
Borough of Lodi
1 Memorial Drive, Suite 1
Lodi, NJ 07644
973-365-4005

Website	www.lodi-nj.org
Year of incorporation	1894
Land/water area (sq. miles)	2.26/0.01
Form of government	Municipal Mgr 1923

Government
Legislative Districts
US Congressional	9
State Legislative	38

Local Officials, 2008
Mayor	Karen Viscana
Manager	Tony Luna
Clerk	Debra A. Cannizzo
Finance Dir	George F. Fenn
Tax Assessor	George Reggo
Tax Collector	Gary Stramandino
Attorney	Scott G. Sproviero
Building	Joel Lavin
Planning Rep	Tony Luna
Engineering	Thomas Solfaro
Public Works	Gerald Woods
Police Chief	Vincent Caruso
Emerg/Fire Director	Robert Cassiello

Housing & Construction
Housing Units, 2000*
Total	9,908
Median rent	$811
Median SF home value	$172,600

Permits for New Residential Construction
	Units	Value
Total, 2007	11	$1,566,750
Single family	7	$961,650
Total, 2006	17	$2,077,500
Single family	11	$1,700,000

Real Property Valuation, 2007
	Parcels	Valuation
Total	5,024	$1,948,349,700
Vacant	83	12,173,700
Residential	4,426	1,410,476,800
Commercial	309	253,309,900
Industrial	115	134,837,300
Apartments	91	137,552,000
Farm land	0	0
Farm homestead	0	0

Average Property Value & Tax, 2007
Residential value	$318,680
Property tax	$8,707
Tax credit/rebate	$1,268

Public Library
Lodi Memorial Library
1 Memorial Dr
Lodi, NJ 07644
973-365-4044

Director ... Anthony P. Taormina

Library statistics, 2006
Population served	23,971
Full-time/total staff	2/8

	Total	Per capita
Holdings	95,368	3.98
Revenues	$1,047,985	$43.72
Expenditures	$1,006,245	$41.98
Annual visits	62,088	2.59
Internet terminals/annual users	17/29,743	

Public Safety
Number of officers, 2006 ... 40

Crime	2005	2006
Total crimes	449	353
Violent	52	41
Murder	2	0
Rape	0	0
Robbery	20	9
Aggravated assault	30	32
Non-violent	397	312
Burglary	78	64
Larceny	251	195
Vehicle theft	68	53
Domestic violence	177	207
Arson	1	1
Total crime rate	18.5	14.5
Violent	2.1	1.7
Non-violent	16.3	12.8

Public School District
(for school year 2006-07 except as noted)

Lodi School District
8 Hunter St
Lodi, NJ 07644
973-778-4620

Superintendent	Frank Quatrone
Number of schools	7
Grade plan	K-12
Enrollment	3,169
Attendance rate, '05-06	95.0%
Dropout rate	1.3%
Students per teacher	11.9
Per pupil expenditure	$12,903
Median faculty salary	$54,470
Median administrator salary	$115,075
Grade 12 enrollment	226
High school graduation rate	94.2%

Assessment test results
(percent scoring at proficient or advanced level)
	Language	Math
NJASK-Grade 3	84.9%	88.8%
GEPA-Grade 8	62.8%	52.2%
HSPA-High School	81.8%	69.1%

SAT score averages
Pct tested	Math	Verbal	Writing
73%	476	445	458

Teacher Qualifications
Avg. years of experience	12
Highly-qualified teachers one subject/all subjects	99.0%/99.0%
With emergency credentials	0.0%

No Child Left Behind
AYP, 2005-06 ... Meets Standards

Municipal Finance§
State Aid Programs, 2008
Total aid	$2,441,076
CMPTRA	1,276,807
Energy tax receipts	1,164,269
Garden State Trust	0

General Budget, 2007
Total tax levy	$53,285,094
County levy	4,244,791
County taxes	4,010,583
County library	0
County health	0
County open space	234,208
School levy	32,197,863
Muni. levy	16,842,440
Misc. revenues	6,067,389

Taxes
	2005	2006	2007
General tax rate per $100	2.4	2.58	2.74
County equalization ratio	108.9	94.05	83.79
Net valuation taxable	$1,931,260,753	$1,931,641,400	$1,950,189,705
State equalized value	$2,053,440,460	$2,307,340,572	$2,413,760,901

Gloucester County

Logan Township

Demographics & Socio-Economic Characteristics
(2000 US Census, except as noted)

Population
- 1980* 3,078
- 1990* 5,147
- 2000 6,032
  - Male 2,974
  - Female 3,058
- 2006 (estimate)* 6,177
- Population density 273.1

Race & Hispanic Origin, 2000
Race
- White 4,946
- Black/African American 815
- American Indian/Alaska Native 8
- Asian 107
- Native Hawaiian/Pacific Islander 1
- Other race 73
- Two or more races 82
- Hispanic origin, total 165
  - Mexican 34
  - Puerto Rican 97
  - Cuban 11
  - Other Hispanic 23

Age & Nativity, 2000
- Under 5 years 514
- 18 years and over 4,095
- 21 years and over 3,906
- 65 years and over 372
- 85 years and over 40
- Median age 33.6
- Native-born 5,813
- Foreign-born 219

Educational Attainment, 2000
- Population 25 years and over 3,740
- Less than 9th grade 2.3%
- High school grad or higher 89.5%
- Bachelor's degree or higher 25.0%
- Graduate degree 7.6%

Income & Poverty, 1999
- Per capita income $26,853
- Median household income $67,148
- Median family income $70,771
- Persons in poverty 257
- H'holds receiving public assistance 16
- H'holds receiving social security 372

Households, 2000
- Total households 2,001
  - With persons under 18 1,020
  - With persons over 65 277
  - Family households 1,610
  - Single-person households 314
- Persons per household 3.00
- Persons per family 3.38

Labor & Employment
- Total civilian labor force, 2006** ... 3,702
  - Unemployment rate 2.3%
- Total civilian labor force, 2000 3,138
  - Unemployment rate 1.9%

Employed persons 16 years and over by occupation, 2000
- Managers & professionals 1,157
- Service occupations 335
- Sales & office occupations 923
- Farming, fishing & forestry 20
- Construction & maintenance 199
- Production & transportation 443
- Self-employed persons 116

‡ Branch of county library
* US Census Bureau
** New Jersey Department of Labor

See Introduction for an explanation of all data sources.

General Information
Township of Logan
125 Main St
PO Box 314
Bridgeport, NJ 08014
856-467-3424

- Website .... www.logan-twp.org
- Year of incorporation 1878
- Land/water area (sq. miles) 22.62/4.21
- Form of government .... Small Municipality

Government
Legislative Districts
- US Congressional 1
- State Legislative 3

Local Officials, 2008
- Mayor .... Frank W. Minor
- Manager .... NA
- Clerk .... Linda L. Oswald
- Finance Dir .... Robert Best
- Tax Assessor .... Horace Spoto
- Tax Collector .... NA
- Attorney .... Brian Duffield
- Building .... Charles Bastow
- Comm Dev/Planning .... Beth Walls
- Engineering .... Annina Hogan
- Public Works .... Dave McCormick
- Police Chief .... James Schmidt
- Emerg/Fire Director .... NA

Housing & Construction
Housing Units, 2000*
- Total 2,077
- Median rent $764
- Median SF home value $114,200

Permits for New Residential Construction

	Units	Value
Total, 2007	19	$7,111,800
Single family	19	$7,111,800
Total, 2006	0	$714,950
Single family	0	$714,950

Real Property Valuation, 2007

	Parcels	Valuation
Total	2,966	$616,218,590
Vacant	525	13,986,800
Residential	2,048	212,717,300
Commercial	151	346,504,900
Industrial	8	34,662,590
Apartments	1	127,200
Farm land	184	3,208,600
Farm homestead	49	5,011,200

Average Property Value & Tax, 2007
- Residential value $103,829
- Property tax $3,275
- Tax credit/rebate $646

Public Library
Logan Township Branch Library‡
101 Beckett Rd
Swedesboro, NJ 08085
856-241-0202

Branch Librarian .... Anne Woonick

Library statistics, 2006
see Gloucester County profile
for library system statistics

Public Safety
- Number of officers, 2006 20

Crime	2005	2006
Total crimes	112	118
Violent	5	10
Murder	0	1
Rape	2	1
Robbery	1	0
Aggravated assault	2	8
Non-violent	107	108
Burglary	19	21
Larceny	82	76
Vehicle theft	6	11
Domestic violence	45	55
Arson	0	0
Total crime rate	18.3	19.0
Violent	0.8	1.6
Non-violent	17.5	17.4

Public School District
(for school year 2006-07 except as noted)

Logan Township School District
110 School Lane
Logan Twp, NJ 08085
856-467-5133

- Superintendent .... John Herbst
- Number of schools 2
- Grade plan K-8
- Enrollment 927
- Attendance rate, '05-06 .... 96.0%
- Dropout rate .... NA
- Students per teacher 10.4
- Per pupil expenditure $12,468
- Median faculty salary $54,508
- Median administrator salary $94,500
- Grade 12 enrollment .... NA
- High school graduation rate .... NA

Assessment test results
(percent scoring at proficient or advanced level)

	Language	Math
NJASK-Grade 3	90.8%	87.2%
GEPA-Grade 8	85.5%	83.3%
HSPA-High School	NA	NA

SAT score averages

Pct tested	Math	Verbal	Writing
NA	NA	NA	NA

Teacher Qualifications
- Avg. years of experience 15
- Highly-qualified teachers
  - one subject/all subjects 100%/100%
- With emergency credentials 0.0%

No Child Left Behind
AYP, 2005-06 .... Meets Standards

Municipal Finance
State Aid Programs, 2008
- Total aid $642,832
  - CMPTRA 51,792
  - Energy tax receipts 590,910
  - Garden State Trust 130

General Budget, 2007
- Total tax levy $19,492,463
  - County levy 5,744,363
    - County taxes 4,947,280
    - County library 409,755
    - County health 0
    - County open space 387,328
  - School levy 11,727,680
  - Muni. levy 2,020,420
- Misc. revenues 7,649,574

Taxes	2005	2006	2007
General tax rate per $100	2.835	2.977	3.155
County equalization ratio	83.08	75.46	63.95
Net valuation taxable	$590,278,043	$609,237,590	$617,982,578
State equalized value	$782,239,654	$954,687,780	$1,089,528,489

Long Beach Township
Ocean County

Demographics & Socio-Economic Characteristics
(2000 US Census, except as noted)

Population
1980*	3,488
1990*	3,407
2000	3,329
Male	1,579
Female	1,750
2006 (estimate)*	3,498
Population density	658.8

Race & Hispanic Origin, 2000
Race
- White ... 3,280
- Black/African American ... 8
- American Indian/Alaska Native ... 1
- Asian ... 12
- Native Hawaiian/Pacific Islander ... 0
- Other race ... 11
- Two or more races ... 17
- Hispanic origin, total ... 70
  - Mexican ... 53
  - Puerto Rican ... 14
  - Cuban ... 0
  - Other Hispanic ... 3

Age & Nativity, 2000
- Under 5 years ... 88
- 18 years and over ... 2,940
- 21 years and over ... 2,884
- 65 years and over ... 1,214
- 85 years and over ... 111
- Median age ... 57.3
- Native-born ... 3,203
- Foreign-born ... 122

Educational Attainment, 2000
- Population 25 years and over ... 2,847
- Less than 9th grade ... 2.0%
- High school grad or higher ... 92.0%
- Bachelor's degree or higher ... 36.7%
- Graduate degree ... 12.8%

Income & Poverty, 1999
- Per capita income ... $33,404
- Median household income ... $48,697
- Median family income ... $59,833
- Persons in poverty ... 171
- H'holds receiving public assistance ... 41
- H'holds receiving social security ... 842

Households, 2000
- Total households ... 1,664
  - With persons under 18 ... 224
  - With persons over 65 ... 857
  - Family households ... 1,039
  - Single-person households ... 562
- Persons per household ... 2.00
- Persons per family ... 2.50

Labor & Employment
- Total civilian labor force, 2006** ... 1,337
  - Unemployment rate ... 5.5%
- Total civilian labor force, 2000 ... 1,351
  - Unemployment rate ... 5.0%

Employed persons 16 years and over by occupation, 2000
- Managers & professionals ... 429
- Service occupations ... 205
- Sales & office occupations ... 413
- Farming, fishing & forestry ... 0
- Construction & maintenance ... 111
- Production & transportation ... 125
- Self-employed persons ... 141

‡ Branch of county library
* US Census Bureau
** New Jersey Department of Labor

General Information
Township of Long Beach
6805 Long Beach Blvd
Brant Beach, NJ 08008
609-361-1000

- Website ... www.longbeachtownship.com
- Year of incorporation ... 1899
- Land/water area (sq. miles) ... 5.31/16.69
- Form of government ... Commission

Government
Legislative Districts
- US Congressional ... 3
- State Legislative ... 9

Local Officials, 2008
- Mayor ... DiAnne C. Gove
- Administrator ... Bonnie Leonetti
- Clerk ... Bonnie Leonetti
- Finance Dir ... Elizabeth Jones
- Tax Assessor ... Tracy A. Hafner
- Tax Collector ... Deborah Hample
- Attorney ... Shackleton & Hazeltine
- Building ... Ron Pingaro
- Comm Dev/Planning ... NA
- Engineering ... Frank Little
- Public Works ... NA
- Police Chief ... Michael Bradley
- Fire/Emergency Dir ... NA

Housing & Construction
Housing Units, 2000*
- Total ... 9,023
- Median rent ... $766
- Median SF home value ... $334,400

Permits for New Residential Construction
	Units	Value
Total, 2007	65	$29,352,215
Single family	65	$29,352,215
Total, 2006	112	$47,935,608
Single family	108	$46,835,608

Real Property Valuation, 2007
	Parcels	Valuation
Total	8,992	$7,279,902,100
Vacant	1,020	246,077,300
Residential	7,803	6,868,844,500
Commercial	160	157,261,400
Industrial	0	0
Apartments	9	7,718,900
Farm land	0	0
Farm homestead	0	0

Average Property Value & Tax, 2007
- Residential value ... $880,283
- Property tax ... $7,201
- Tax credit/rebate ... $1,134

Public Library
Long Beach Island Branch Library‡
217 S Central Ave
Surf City, NJ 08008
609-494-2480

Branch Librarian ... Linda Feaster

Library statistics, 2006
see Ocean County profile for library system statistics

Public Safety
- Number of officers, 2006 ... 40

Crime	2005	2006
Total crimes	234	228
Violent	6	5
Murder	0	0
Rape	4	0
Robbery	1	0
Aggravated assault	1	5
Non-violent	228	223
Burglary	18	24
Larceny	206	199
Vehicle theft	4	0
Domestic violence	15	9
Arson	0	0
Total crime rate	67.8	65.9
Violent	1.7	1.4
Non-violent	66.1	64.4

Public School District
(for school year 2006-07 except as noted)

Long Beach Island School District
200 Barnegat Ave
Surf City, NJ 08008
609-494-2341

- Superintendent ... Robert A. Garguilo
- Number of schools ... 10
- Grade plan ... K-6
- Enrollment ... 248
- Attendance rate, '05-06 ... 94.3%
- Dropout rate ... NA
- Students per teacher ... 6.9
- Per pupil expenditure ... $21,956
- Median faculty salary ... $94,335
- Median administrator salary ... $68,857
- Grade 12 enrollment ... NA
- High school graduation rate ... NA

Assessment test results
(percent scoring at proficient or advanced level)
	Language	Math
NJASK-Grade 3	100.0%	90.0%
GEPA-Grade 8	NA	NA
HSPA-High School	NA	NA

SAT score averages
Pct tested	Math	Verbal	Writing
NA	NA	NA	NA

Teacher Qualifications
- Avg. years of experience ... 19
- Highly-qualified teachers
  - one subject/all subjects ... 100%/100%
- With emergency credentials ... 0.0%

No Child Left Behind
- AYP, 2005-06 ... Meets Standards

Municipal Finance
State Aid Programs, 2008
- Total aid ... $724,137
  - CMPTRA ... 0
  - Energy tax receipts ... 724,051
  - Garden State Trust ... 86

General Budget, 2007
- Total tax levy ... $59,566,061
  - County levy ... 26,039,787
    - County taxes ... 22,342,052
    - County library ... 2,647,862
    - County health ... 0
    - County open space ... 1,049,873
  - School levy ... 18,706,274
  - Muni. levy ... 14,820,000
- Misc. revenues ... 5,802,000

Taxes	2005	2006	2007
General tax rate per $100	0.781	0.798	0.819
County equalization ratio	113.33	94.83	83.41
Net valuation taxable	$7,073,611,662	$7,139,888,400	$7,281,862,420
State equalized value	$7,459,255,153	$8,562,182,884	$8,626,414,887

Monmouth County
Long Branch City

Demographics & Socio-Economic Characteristics
(2000 US Census, except as noted)

Population
- 1980*..29,819
- 1990*..28,658
- 2000...31,340
  - Male...15,210
  - Female.......................................16,130
- 2006 (estimate)*..............................32,314
  - Population density........................6,190.4

Race & Hispanic Origin, 2000
Race
- White..21,320
- Black/African American..........5,847
- American Indian/Alaska Native......113
- Asian..513
- Native Hawaiian/Pacific Islander.......15
- Other race....................................2,220
- Two or more races.......................1,312
- Hispanic origin, total.................6,477
  - Mexican....................................1,448
  - Puerto Rican.............................2,778
  - Cuban...84
  - Other Hispanic.........................2,167

Age & Nativity, 2000
- Under 5 years...............................2,183
- 18 years and over.......................23,890
- 21 years and over.......................22,628
- 65 years and over.........................4,036
- 85 years and over...........................495
  - Median age..................................34.7
- Native-born................................25,176
- Foreign-born................................6,164

Educational Attainment, 2000
- Population 25 years and over........20,774
- Less than 9th grade........................8.3%
- High school grad or higher...........76.3%
- Bachelor's degree or higher..........20.2%
- Graduate degree.............................7.2%

Income & Poverty, 1999
- Per capita income......................$20,532
- Median household income.........$38,651
- Median family income...............$42,825
- Persons in poverty.......................5,208
- H'holds receiving public assistance.....551
- H'holds receiving social security......3,119

Households, 2000
- Total households.........................12,594
  - With persons under 18..............3,885
  - With persons over 65................3,027
  - Family households...................7,248
  - Single-person households........4,295
- Persons per household...................2.47
- Persons per family..........................3.19

Labor & Employment
- Total civilian labor force, 2006**....16,156
  - Unemployment rate.....................5.2%
- Total civilian labor force, 2000......15,398
  - Unemployment rate.....................7.4%

Employed persons 16 years and over by occupation, 2000
- Managers & professionals...........4,077
- Service occupations.....................2,925
- Sales & office occupations..........4,016
- Farming, fishing & forestry..............22
- Construction & maintenance......1,503
- Production & transportation.......1,720
- Self-employed persons................1,002

* US Census Bureau
** New Jersey Department of Labor

See Introduction for an explanation of all data sources.

General Information
City of Long Branch
344 Broadway
Long Branch, NJ 07740
732-222-7000
- Website..................www.longbranch.org
- Year of incorporation..................1903
- Land/water area (sq. miles).......5.22/0.97
- Form of government..........Mayor-Council

Government
Legislative Districts
- US Congressional..............................6
- State Legislative..............................11

Local Officials, 2008
- Mayor...................Adam Schneider
- Manager..............Howard Woolley Jr
- Clerk........................Irene Joline
- Finance Dir..........Ronald Mehlhorn Sr
- Tax Assessor..........William Fitzpatrick
- Tax Collector..........Ed Mazzacco
- Attorney..................James Aaron
- Building......................Kevin Hayes
- Planning.....................Jacob Jones
- Engineering..........Birdsall Engineering
- Public Works............Fred Migliaccio
- Police Chief............Anthony Tomaine
- Emerg/Fire Director.......John Zambrano

Housing & Construction
Housing Units, 2000*
- Total..13,983
- Median rent.......................$727
- Median SF home value..........$135,300

Permits for New Residential Construction

	Units	Value
Total, 2007	238	$31,088,875
Single family	22	$3,763,875
Total, 2006	7	$1,010,100
Single family	7	$1,010,100

Real Property Valuation, 2007

	Parcels	Valuation
Total	9,431	$5,065,303,440
Vacant	517	183,581,300
Residential	8,248	3,989,142,800
Commercial	506	516,906,240
Industrial	6	11,657,100
Apartments	152	360,517,500
Farm land	1	4,500
Farm homestead	1	3,494,000

Average Property Value & Tax, 2007
- Residential value................$484,015
- Property tax.......................$6,517
- Tax credit/rebate....................$975

Public Library
Long Branch Public Library
328 Broadway
Long Branch, NJ 07740
732-222-3900
- Director....................Ingrid Bruck

Library statistics, 2006
- Population served.................31,340
- Full-time/total staff.................3/16

	Total	Per capita
Holdings	98,577	3.15
Revenues	$1,212,466	$38.69
Expenditures	$1,087,828	$34.71
Annual visits	120,878	3.86

- Internet terminals/annual users...33/34,999

Taxes

	2005	2006	2007
General tax rate per $100	2.354	2.442	1.347
County equalization ratio	83.52	66.89	110.33
Net valuation taxable	$2,386,074,565	$2,491,582,200	$5,071,576,657
State equalized value	$3,567,161,855	$4,511,755,907	$4,966,421,513

Public Safety
- Number of officers, 2006..............99

Crime	2005	2006
Total crimes	959	978
Violent	138	174
Murder	0	4
Rape	1	2
Robbery	51	76
Aggravated assault	86	92
Non-violent	821	804
Burglary	186	230
Larceny	596	538
Vehicle theft	39	36
Domestic violence	385	449
Arson	3	0
Total crime rate	30.4	30.5
Violent	4.4	5.4
Non-violent	26.0	25.1

Public School District
(for school year 2006-07 except as noted)

Long Branch School District
540 Broadway
Long Branch, NJ 07740
732-571-2868

- Superintendent........Joseph M. Ferraina
- Number of schools........................9
- Grade plan...........................K-12
- Enrollment............................4,854
- Attendance rate, '05-06.............91.3%
- Dropout rate...........................2.2%
- Students per teacher..................8.4
- Per pupil expenditure............$16,896
- Median faculty salary..............$49,295
- Median administrator salary....$109,243
- Grade 12 enrollment....................223
- High school graduation rate........90.9%

Assessment test results
(percent scoring at proficient or advanced level)

	Language	Math
NJASK-Grade 3	78.3%	86.6%
GEPA-Grade 8	57.9%	48.8%
HSPA-High School	72.7%	44.4%

SAT score averages

Pct tested	Math	Verbal	Writing
56%	446	429	423

Teacher Qualifications
- Avg. years of experience..................7
- Highly-qualified teachers
  - one subject/all subjects......99.5%/99.5%
- With emergency credentials............0.5%

No Child Left Behind
- AYP, 2005-06.........Needs Improvement

Municipal Finance
State Aid Programs, 2008
- Total aid.........................$5,477,497
  - CMPTRA......................3,050,129
  - Energy tax receipts...........2,427,368
  - Garden State Trust...................0

General Budget, 2007
- Total tax levy....................$68,290,475
  - County levy......................11,804,248
    - County taxes...................11,110,059
    - County library.........................0
    - County health..........................0
    - County open space.............694,190
  - School levy......................29,772,875
  - Muni. levy.......................26,713,351
- Misc. revenues..................15,178,693

The New Jersey Municipal Data Book   273

Long Hill Township
Morris County

Demographics & Socio-Economic Characteristics
(2000 US Census, except as noted)

Population
1980*	7,275
1990*	7,826
2000	8,777
Male	4,258
Female	4,519
2006 (estimate)*	8,785
Population density	727.2

Race & Hispanic Origin, 2000
Race
White	8,141
Black/African American	34
American Indian/Alaska Native	15
Asian	420
Native Hawaiian/Pacific Islander	3
Other race	49
Two or more races	115
Hispanic origin, total	303
Mexican	26
Puerto Rican	41
Cuban	32
Other Hispanic	204

Age & Nativity, 2000
Under 5 years	680
18 years and over	6,470
21 years and over	6,292
65 years and over	1,109
85 years and over	98
Median age	39.2
Native-born	7,785
Foreign-born	992

Educational Attainment, 2000
Population 25 years and over	5,995
Less than 9th grade	1.9%
High school grad or higher	93.8%
Bachelor's degree or higher	49.3%
Graduate degree	18.9%

Income & Poverty, 1999
Per capita income	$42,613
Median household income	$84,532
Median family income	$103,037
Persons in poverty	286
H'holds receiving public assistance	14
H'holds receiving social security	801

Households, 2000
Total households	3,139
With persons under 18	1,202
With persons over 65	782
Family households	2,458
Single-person households	570
Persons per household	2.79
Persons per family	3.19

Labor & Employment
Total civilian labor force, 2006**	4,994
Unemployment rate	3.1%
Total civilian labor force, 2000	4,559
Unemployment rate	2.8%

Employed persons 16 years and over by occupation, 2000
Managers & professionals	2,143
Service occupations	529
Sales & office occupations	1,222
Farming, fishing & forestry	14
Construction & maintenance	198
Production & transportation	325
Self-employed persons	228

* US Census Bureau
** New Jersey Department of Labor

General Information
Township of Long Hill
915 Valley Rd
Gillette, NJ 07933
908-647-8000

Website	www.longhillnj.us
Year of incorporation	1993
Land/water area (sq. miles)	12.08/0.00
Form of government	Township

Government
Legislative Districts
US Congressional	11
State Legislative	21

Local Officials, 2008
Mayor	George Vitureira
Township Admin	Richard Sheola
Clerk	Richard Sheola (Actg)
Finance Dir	Richard Sheola
Tax Assessor	Brett Trout
Tax Collector	Joan Donat
Attorney	John Pidgeon
Building	Tom Yotka
Planning	Dawn Wolfe
Engineering	Justin Lizza
Public Works	Justin Lizza
Police Chief	Dan Hedden
Emergency Mgmt Dir	Ken Fullagar

Housing & Construction
Housing Units, 2000*
Total	3,206
Median rent	$1,024
Median SF home value	$297,000

Permits for New Residential Construction
	Units	Value
Total, 2007	8	$2,462,810
Single family	8	$2,462,810
Total, 2006	2	$475,000
Single family	2	$475,000

Real Property Valuation, 2007
	Parcels	Valuation
Total	3,301	$1,273,967,800
Vacant	242	20,688,800
Residential	2,890	1,123,401,600
Commercial	116	104,085,000
Industrial	21	16,541,200
Apartments	7	6,691,600
Farm land	18	40,000
Farm homestead	7	2,519,600

Average Property Value & Tax, 2007
Residential value	$388,651
Property tax	$9,678
Tax credit/rebate	$1,299

Public Library
Long Hill Township Public Library
917 Valley Rd
Gillette, NJ 07980
908-647-2088

Director: Mary Martin

Library statistics, 2006
Population served	8,777
Full-time/total staff	3/4

	Total	Per capita
Holdings	57,134	6.51
Revenues	$603,906	$68.81
Expenditures	$490,658	$55.90
Annual visits	82,872	9.44
Internet terminals/annual users	20/21,060	

Public Safety
Number of officers, 2006: 29

Crime
	2005	2006
Total crimes	65	53
Violent	6	1
Murder	0	0
Rape	2	0
Robbery	0	0
Aggravated assault	4	1
Non-violent	59	52
Burglary	1	9
Larceny	58	43
Vehicle theft	0	0
Domestic violence	38	35
Arson	0	0
Total crime rate	7.4	6.0
Violent	0.7	0.1
Non-violent	6.7	5.9

Public School District
(for school year 2006-07 except as noted)

Long Hill Township School District
759 Valley Rd
Gillette, NJ 07933
908-647-1200

Superintendent	Kenneth Gross
Number of schools	3
Grade plan	K-8
Enrollment	1,065
Attendance rate, '05-06	95.6%
Dropout rate	NA
Students per teacher	10.6
Per pupil expenditure	$11,520
Median faculty salary	$52,113
Median administrator salary	$89,566
Grade 12 enrollment	NA
High school graduation rate	NA

Assessment test results
(percent scoring at proficient or advanced level)
	Language	Math
NJASK-Grade 3	83.7%	95.2%
GEPA-Grade 8	96.7%	91.7%
HSPA-High School	NA	NA

SAT score averages
Pct tested	Math	Verbal	Writing
NA	NA	NA	NA

Teacher Qualifications
Avg. years of experience	8
Highly-qualified teachers one subject/all subjects	99.0%/99.0%
With emergency credentials	0.0%

No Child Left Behind
AYP, 2005-06: Meets Standards

Municipal Finance
State Aid Programs, 2008
Total aid	$1,704,867
CMPTRA	0
Energy tax receipts	1,704,665
Garden State Trust	202

General Budget, 2007
Total tax levy	$31,823,990
County levy	4,332,208
County taxes	3,465,404
County library	0
County health	0
County open space	866,804
School levy	18,694,076
Muni. levy	8,797,706
Misc. revenues	5,675,692

Taxes
	2005	2006	2007
General tax rate per $100	2.3	2.4	2.5
County equalization ratio	85.97	77.01	70.65
Net valuation taxable	$1,264,002,788	$1,266,429,330	$1,278,011,246
State equalized value	$1,641,348,900	$1,796,620,576	$1,873,950,682

Atlantic County
Longport Borough

Demographics & Socio-Economic Characteristics
(2000 US Census, except as noted)

Population
1980*	1,249
1990*	1,224
2000	1,054
Male	489
Female	565
2006 (estimate)*	1,088
Population density	2,863.2

Race & Hispanic Origin, 2000
Race
White	1,039
Black/African American	1
American Indian/Alaska Native	0
Asian	12
Native Hawaiian/Pacific Islander	0
Other race	0
Two or more races	2
Hispanic origin, total	5
Mexican	1
Puerto Rican	3
Cuban	0
Other Hispanic	1

Age & Nativity, 2000
Under 5 years	34
18 years and over	934
21 years and over	927
65 years and over	364
85 years and over	47
Median age	56.6
Native-born	1,022
Foreign-born	32

Educational Attainment, 2000
Population 25 years and over	900
Less than 9th grade	2.8%
High school grad or higher	86.9%
Bachelor's degree or higher	39.0%
Graduate degree	15.8%

Income & Poverty, 1999
Per capita income	$50,884
Median household income	$51,324
Median family income	$68,194
Persons in poverty	39
H'holds receiving public assistance	0
H'holds receiving social security	244

Households, 2000
Total households	544
With persons under 18	65
With persons over 65	261
Family households	317
Single-person households	204
Persons per household	1.94
Persons per family	2.53

Labor & Employment
Total civilian labor force, 2006**	549
Unemployment rate	3.7%
Total civilian labor force, 2000	505
Unemployment rate	4.0%

Employed persons 16 years and over by occupation, 2000
Managers & professionals	247
Service occupations	87
Sales & office occupations	113
Farming, fishing & forestry	0
Construction & maintenance	18
Production & transportation	20
Self-employed persons	48

‡ Branch of county library
* US Census Bureau
** New Jersey Department of Labor

See Introduction for an explanation of all data sources.

General Information
Borough of Longport
2305 Atlantic Ave
Longport, NJ 08403
609-823-2731

Website	NA
Year of incorporation	1898
Land/water area (sq. miles)	0.38/1.24
Form of government	Commission

Government
Legislative Districts
US Congressional	2
State Legislative	2

Local Officials, 2008
Mayor	Mary C. Garvin
Manager/Admin	NA
Clerk	Thomas Hiltner
Finance Dir	Maria Mento
Tax Assessor	Jeffrey Hesley
Tax Collector	Thomas Hiltner
Attorney	Thomas Subranni
Building	James Agnesino
Comm Dev/Planning	NA
Engineering	Richard Carter
Public Works	William Trinkle
Police Chief	A. Scott Porter
Emerg/Fire Director	Levon Clayton

Housing & Construction
Housing Units, 2000*
Total	1,574
Median rent	$909
Median SF home value	$267,300

Permits for New Residential Construction
	Units	Value
Total, 2007	28	$14,731,682
Single family	28	$14,731,682
Total, 2006	23	$9,586,650
Single family	23	$9,586,650

Real Property Valuation, 2007
	Parcels	Valuation
Total	1,659	$1,549,477,300
Vacant	83	69,253,600
Residential	1,568	1,476,492,700
Commercial	8	3,731,000
Industrial	0	0
Apartments	0	0
Farm land	0	0
Farm homestead	0	0

Average Property Value & Tax, 2007
Residential value	$941,641
Property tax	$6,542
Tax credit/rebate	$1,024

Public Library
Longport Branch Library‡
2305 Atlantic Ave
Longport, NJ 08403
609-487-0272

Director............Kathy Gindin

Library statistics, 2006
see Atlantic County profile for library system statistics

Public Safety
Number of officers, 2006	13

Crime	2005	2006
Total crimes	11	33
Violent	0	0
Murder	0	0
Rape	0	0
Robbery	0	0
Aggravated assault	0	0
Non-violent	11	33
Burglary	2	15
Larceny	9	17
Vehicle theft	0	1
Domestic violence	3	3
Arson	0	0
Total crime rate	10.2	30.3
Violent	0.0	0.0
Non-violent	10.2	30.3

Public School District
(for school year 2006-07 except as noted)

Longport School District
2305 Atlantic Ave
Longport, NJ 08403

No schools in district

Per pupil expenditure	NA
Median faculty salary	NA
Median administrator salary	NA
Grade 12 enrollment	NA
High school graduation rate	NA

Assessment test results
(percent scoring at proficient or advanced level)
	Language	Math
NJASK-Grade 3	NA	NA
GEPA-Grade 8	NA	NA
HSPA-High School	NA	NA

SAT score averages
Pct tested	Math	Verbal	Writing
NA	NA	NA	NA

Teacher Qualifications
Avg. years of experience	NA
Highly-qualified teachers one subject/all subjects	NA/NA
With emergency credentials	NA

No Child Left Behind
AYP, 2005-06	NA

Municipal Finance
State Aid Programs, 2008
Total aid	$135,221
CMPTRA	0
Energy tax receipts	135,221
Garden State Trust	0

General Budget, 2007
Total tax levy	$10,766,760
County levy	5,136,285
County taxes	4,088,762
County library	506,643
County health	206,445
County open space	334,434
School levy	965,223
Muni. levy	4,665,253
Misc. revenues	1,610,715

Taxes
	2005	2006	2007
General tax rate per $100	0.67	0.7	0.695
County equalization ratio	124.96	105.98	92.72
Net valuation taxable	$1,528,140,594	$1,528,220,900	$1,549,659,019
State equalized value	$1,441,914,129	$1,648,403,159	$1,848,538,274

©2008 Information Publications, Inc. All rights reserved. Photocopying prohibited. For additional copies, contact the publisher at www.informationpublications.com or (877)544-INFO (4636)

Lopatcong Township
Warren County

Demographics & Socio-Economic Characteristics
(2000 US Census, except as noted)

Population
1980*	4,998
1990*	5,052
2000	5,765
Male	2,655
Female	3,110
2006 (estimate)*	8,439
Population density	1,191.9

Race & Hispanic Origin, 2000
Race
White	5,550
Black/African American	65
American Indian/Alaska Native	4
Asian	94
Native Hawaiian/Pacific Islander	0
Other race	28
Two or more races	24
Hispanic origin, total	115
Mexican	6
Puerto Rican	50
Cuban	16
Other Hispanic	43

Age & Nativity, 2000
Under 5 years	385
18 years and over	4,351
21 years and over	4,227
65 years and over	1,279
85 years and over	269
Median age	41.3
Native-born	5,502
Foreign-born	263

Educational Attainment, 2000
Population 25 years and over	4,137
Less than 9th grade	7.0%
High school grad or higher	82.5%
Bachelor's degree or higher	22.4%
Graduate degree	7.0%

Income & Poverty, 1999
Per capita income	$24,333
Median household income	$50,918
Median family income	$65,545
Persons in poverty	350
H'holds receiving public assistance	28
H'holds receiving social security	736

Households, 2000
Total households	2,143
With persons under 18	735
With persons over 65	746
Family households	1,524
Single-person households	562
Persons per household	2.55
Persons per family	3.09

Labor & Employment
Total civilian labor force, 2006**	2,928
Unemployment rate	2.2%
Total civilian labor force, 2000	2,578
Unemployment rate	1.9%

Employed persons 16 years and over by occupation, 2000
Managers & professionals	1,086
Service occupations	331
Sales & office occupations	621
Farming, fishing & forestry	14
Construction & maintenance	242
Production & transportation	235
Self-employed persons	124

* US Census Bureau
** New Jersey Department of Labor

General Information
Township of Lopatcong
232 S 3rd St
Phillipsburg, NJ 08865
908-859-3355

Website	www.lopatcongtwp.com
Year of incorporation	1863
Land/water area (sq. miles)	7.08/0.06
Form of government	Small Municipality

Government
Legislative Districts
US Congressional	5
State Legislative	23

Local Officials, 2008
Mayor	Douglas Steinhardt
Manager	M. Beth Dilts
Clerk	M. Beth Dilts
Finance Dir	Mary Dobes
Tax Assessor	Kathleen Degan
Tax Collector	Rachel Edinger
Attorney	Michael Lavery
Building	John Fritts
Comm Dev/Planning	NA
Engineering	Paul Sterbenz
Public Works Dir	Steve Hockman
Police Chief	Scott Marinelli
Emerg/Fire Director	Pat Rivoli

Housing & Construction
Housing Units, 2000*
Total	2,429
Median rent	$624
Median SF home value	$156,600

Permits for New Residential Construction
	Units	Value
Total, 2007	29	$3,630,571
Single family	29	$3,630,571
Total, 2006	45	$5,348,174
Single family	43	$5,105,674

Real Property Valuation, 2007
	Parcels	Valuation
Total	3,394	$1,016,716,858
Vacant	524	60,018,600
Residential	2,624	772,071,256
Commercial	135	133,529,311
Industrial	12	20,708,500
Apartments	2	18,230,400
Farm land	69	694,191
Farm homestead	28	11,464,600

Average Property Value & Tax, 2007
Residential value	$295,451
Property tax	$5,742
Tax credit/rebate	$1,005

Public Library
No public municipal library

Library statistics, 2006
Population served	NA
Full-time/total staff	NA/NA

	Total	Per capita
Holdings	NA	NA
Revenues	NA	NA
Expenditures	NA	NA
Annual visits	NA	NA
Internet terminals/annual users	NA/NA	

Taxes
	2005	2006	2007
General tax rate per $100	3.09	1.88	1.95
County equalization ratio	71.03	115	104.47
Net valuation taxable	$539,276,816	$1,009,864,216	$1,018,383,086
State equalized value	$858,037,893	$967,659,558	$1,009,314,254

Public Safety
Number of officers, 2006	14

Crime	2005	2006
Total crimes	103	99
Violent	3	11
Murder	0	1
Rape	0	0
Robbery	0	4
Aggravated assault	3	6
Non-violent	100	88
Burglary	21	19
Larceny	73	67
Vehicle theft	6	2
Domestic violence	78	66
Arson	0	0
Total crime rate	12.8	12.0
Violent	0.4	1.3
Non-violent	12.4	10.7

Public School District
(for school year 2006-07 except as noted)

Lopatcong Township School District
263 Route 57
Phillipsburg, NJ 08865
908-859-0800

Superintendent	Michael Rossi
Number of schools	2
Grade plan	K-8
Enrollment	912
Attendance rate, '05-06	96.2%
Dropout rate	NA
Students per teacher	11.1
Per pupil expenditure	$10,756
Median faculty salary	$52,482
Median administrator salary	$84,496
Grade 12 enrollment	NA
High school graduation rate	NA

Assessment test results
(percent scoring at proficient or advanced level)
	Language	Math
NJASK-Grade 3	89.8%	94.9%
GEPA-Grade 8	77.0%	73.3%
HSPA-High School	NA	NA

SAT score averages
Pct tested	Math	Verbal	Writing
NA	NA	NA	NA

Teacher Qualifications
Avg. years of experience	9
Highly-qualified teachers one subject/all subjects	98.5%/98.5%
With emergency credentials	0.0%

No Child Left Behind
AYP, 2005-06 .... Meets Standards

Municipal Finance
State Aid Programs, 2008
Total aid	$1,227,162
CMPTRA	26,712
Energy tax receipts	1,197,646
Garden State Trust	2,804

General Budget, 2007
Total tax levy	$19,791,645
County levy	5,956,864
County taxes	4,861,154
County library	508,738
County health	0
County open space	586,972
School levy	11,802,165
Muni. levy	2,032,617
Misc. revenues	4,060,972

Salem County
Lower Alloways Creek Township

Demographics & Socio-Economic Characteristics
(2000 US Census, except as noted)

Population
- 1980* 1,547
- 1990* 1,858
- 2000 1,851
  - Male 894
  - Female 957
- 2006 (estimate)* 1,914
  - Population density 40.9

Race & Hispanic Origin, 2000
Race
- White 1,784
- Black/African American 40
- American Indian/Alaska Native 2
- Asian 12
- Native Hawaiian/Pacific Islander 0
- Other race 3
- Two or more races 10
- Hispanic origin, total 9
  - Mexican 1
  - Puerto Rican 4
  - Cuban 2
  - Other Hispanic 2

Age & Nativity, 2000
- Under 5 years 121
- 18 years and over 1,400
- 21 years and over 1,338
- 65 years and over 258
- 85 years and over 30
  - Median age 39.5
- Native-born 1,837
- Foreign-born 14

Educational Attainment, 2000
- Population 25 years and over 1,284
- Less than 9th grade 6.2%
- High school grad or higher 82.4%
- Bachelor's degree or higher 11.7%
- Graduate degree 2.2%

Income & Poverty, 1999
- Per capita income $21,962
- Median household income $55,078
- Median family income $59,653
- Persons in poverty 135
- H'holds receiving public assistance . 6
- H'holds receiving social security . 208

Households, 2000
- Total households 693
  - With persons under 18 246
  - With persons over 65 178
  - Family households 538
  - Single-person households 126
- Persons per household 2.67
- Persons per family 3.00

Labor & Employment
- Total civilian labor force, 2006** . 986
  - Unemployment rate 2.6%
- Total civilian labor force, 2000 .. 947
  - Unemployment rate 3.0%

Employed persons 16 years and over by occupation, 2000
- Managers & professionals 244
- Service occupations 171
- Sales & office occupations 201
- Farming, fishing & forestry 8
- Construction & maintenance 119
- Production & transportation 176
- Self-employed persons 44

* US Census Bureau
** New Jersey Department of Labor

See Introduction for an explanation of all data sources.

General Information
Township of Lower Alloways Creek
501 Locust Island Rd
PO Box 157
Hancock's Bridge, NJ 08038
856-935-1549

- Website .... (county website)
- Year of incorporation 1767
- Land/water area (sq. miles) 46.78/25.80
- Form of government .... Township

Government
Legislative Districts
- US Congressional 2
- State Legislative 3

Local Officials, 2008
- Mayor .... Ellen Pompper
- Manager/Admin .... NA
- Clerk .... Ronald L. Campbell Sr
- Finance Dir .... Kevin Clour
- Tax Assessor .... Joseph Harasta
- Tax Collector ..... D. Michelle Mitchell
- Attorney .... George Rosenberger
- Building .... Wayne Serfass
- Comm Dev/Planning .... NA
- Engineering ...... J. Michael Fralinger
- Public Works .... Jack Lynch
- Police Chief .... Lee Peterson
- Emerg/Fire Director ..... Lee Peterson

Housing & Construction
Housing Units, 2000*
- Total 730
- Median rent $640
- Median SF home value $118,000

Permits for New Residential Construction

	Units	Value
Total, 2007	3	$594,000
Single family	3	$594,000
Total, 2006	2	$355,000
Single family	2	$355,000

Real Property Valuation, 2007

	Parcels	Valuation
Total	1,270	$204,615,810
Vacant	181	2,469,000
Residential	501	59,410,500
Commercial	10	1,527,200
Industrial	1	111,214,100
Apartments	0	0
Farm land	389	4,205,910
Farm homestead	188	25,789,100

Average Property Value & Tax, 2007
- Residential value $123,657
- Property tax $1,392
- Tax credit/rebate $475

Public Library
No public municipal library

Library statistics, 2006
- Population served .... NA
- Full-time/total staff .... NA/NA

	Total	Per capita
Holdings	NA	NA
Revenues	NA	NA
Expenditures	NA	NA
Annual visits	NA	NA

Internet terminals/annual users .... NA/NA

Public Safety
Number of officers, 2006 12

Crime	2005	2006
Total crimes	13	16
Violent	3	1
Murder	0	0
Rape	0	0
Robbery	0	0
Aggravated assault	3	1
Non-violent	10	15
Burglary	4	3
Larceny	6	10
Vehicle theft	0	2
Domestic violence	10	22
Arson	0	0
Total crime rate	6.8	8.3
Violent	1.6	0.5
Non-violent	5.3	7.8

Public School District
(for school year 2006-07 except as noted)

Lower Alloways Creek Township Dist.
967 Main Street-Canton
Salem, NJ 08079
856-935-2707

- Chief School Admin .... Fred Pratta
- Number of schools 1
- Grade plan K-8
- Enrollment 236
- Attendance rate, '05-06 .... 95.8%
- Dropout rate .... NA
- Students per teacher 8.9
- Per pupil expenditure $14,819
- Median faculty salary $56,930
- Median administrator salary .. $62,508
- Grade 12 enrollment .... NA
- High school graduation rate ...... NA

Assessment test results
(percent scoring at proficient or advanced level)

	Language	Math
NJASK-Grade 3	94.8%	94.8%
GEPA-Grade 8	72.2%	72.2%
HSPA-High School	NA	NA

SAT score averages

Pct tested	Math	Verbal	Writing
NA	NA	NA	NA

Teacher Qualifications
- Avg. years of experience 22
- Highly-qualified teachers
  - one subject/all subjects ... 100%/100%
- With emergency credentials 0.0%

No Child Left Behind
AYP, 2005-06 .... Meets Standards

Municipal Finance
State Aid Programs, 2008
- Total aid $7,755,239
  - CMPTRA 0
  - Energy tax receipts 7,702,174
  - Garden State Trust 53,065

General Budget, 2007
- Total tax levy $2,310,262
  - County levy 2,310,262
    - County taxes 2,260,980
    - County library 0
    - County health 0
    - County open space 49,281
  - School levy 0
  - Muni. levy 0
- Misc. revenues 11,806,568

Taxes	2005	2006	2007
General tax rate per $100	1.136	1.072	1.127
County equalization ratio	89.36	92.84	83.83
Net valuation taxable	$204,829,688	$204,281,210	$205,160,269
State equalized value	$220,626,549	$244,288,066	$226,589,322

Lower Township
Cape May County

Demographics & Socio-Economic Characteristics
(2000 US Census, except as noted)

Population
1980*	17,105
1990*	20,820
2000	22,945
Male	10,888
Female	12,057
2006 (estimate)*	20,785
Population density	736.5

Race & Hispanic Origin, 2000
Race
White	22,088
Black/African American	319
American Indian/Alaska Native	52
Asian	121
Native Hawaiian/Pacific Islander	5
Other race	150
Two or more races	210
Hispanic origin, total	432
Mexican	74
Puerto Rican	250
Cuban	30
Other Hispanic	78

Age & Nativity, 2000
Under 5 years	1,177
18 years and over	17,504
21 years and over	16,815
65 years and over	4,740
85 years and over	543
Median age	41.8
Native-born	22,293
Foreign-born	655

Educational Attainment, 2000
Population 25 years and over	16,099
Less than 9th grade	4.3%
High school grad or higher	77.0%
Bachelor's degree or higher	13.1%
Graduate degree	3.4%

Income & Poverty, 1999
Per capita income	$19,786
Median household income	$38,977
Median family income	$45,058
Persons in poverty	1,742
H'holds receiving public assistance	219
H'holds receiving social security	3,693

Households, 2000
Total households	9,328
With persons under 18	2,894
With persons over 65	3,361
Family households	6,379
Single-person households	2,535
Persons per household	2.43
Persons per family	2.95

Labor & Employment
Total civilian labor force, 2006**	12,787
Unemployment rate	8.4%
Total civilian labor force, 2000	10,530
Unemployment rate	9.9%

Employed persons 16 years and over by occupation, 2000
Managers & professionals	2,269
Service occupations	2,290
Sales & office occupations	2,623
Farming, fishing & forestry	137
Construction & maintenance	1,298
Production & transportation	869
Self-employed persons	669

‡ Branch of county library
* US Census Bureau
** New Jersey Department of Labor

General Information
Township of Lower
2600 Bayshore Rd
Villas, NJ 08251
609-886-2005

Website	townshipoflower.org
Year of incorporation	1723
Land/water area (sq. miles)	28.22/2.85
Form of government	Council-Manager

Government
Legislative Districts
US Congressional	2
State Legislative	1

Local Officials, 2008
Mayor	Walt Craig
Manager	Joseph Jackson
Clerk	Claudia R. Kammer
CFO/Treasurer	Lauren Read
Tax Assessor	Arthur Amonette
Tax Collector	Susan Jackson
Attorney	Paul Baldini
Construction	Gary Playford
Planning	Jay Dillworth (Chr)
Engineering	Paul Kelly
Public Works	Gary Douglass
Police Chief	Edward Donohue
Fire Safety	Dave Perry

Housing & Construction
Housing Units, 2000*
Total	13,924
Median rent	$687
Median SF home value	$95,900

Permits for New Residential Construction
	Units	Value
Total, 2007	246	$27,652,387
Single family	36	$4,452,387
Total, 2006	68	$16,861,895
Single family	46	$7,363,768

Real Property Valuation, 2007
	Parcels	Valuation
Total	15,213	$4,696,123,800
Vacant	819	139,128,300
Residential	13,932	4,221,414,400
Commercial	348	310,577,500
Industrial	0	0
Apartments	4	13,262,500
Farm land	88	1,188,000
Farm homestead	22	10,553,100

Average Property Value & Tax, 2007
Residential value	$303,280
Property tax	$3,078
Tax credit/rebate	$808

Public Library
Lower Cape Branch Library‡
2600 Bayshore Rd
Villas, NJ 08251
609-886-8999

Branch Librarian.......... Edward Carson

Library statistics, 2006
see Cape May County profile for library system statistics

Public Safety
Number of officers, 2006 ... 45

Crime	2005	2006
Total crimes	565	526
Violent	34	43
Murder	0	0
Rape	3	2
Robbery	8	6
Aggravated assault	23	35
Non-violent	531	483
Burglary	149	119
Larceny	359	348
Vehicle theft	23	16
Domestic violence	442	454
Arson	1	4
Total crime rate	25.7	24.5
Violent	1.5	2.0
Non-violent	24.1	22.5

Public School District
(for school year 2006-07 except as noted)

Lower Township School District
834 Seashore Rd
Cape May, NJ 08204
609-884-9400

Superintendent	Joseph Cirrinicione
Number of schools	4
Grade plan	K-6
Enrollment	1,952
Attendance rate, '05-06	93.9%
Dropout rate	NA
Students per teacher	12.0
Per pupil expenditure	$13,113
Median faculty salary	$68,573
Median administrator salary	$103,262
Grade 12 enrollment	NA
High school graduation rate	NA

Assessment test results
(percent scoring at proficient or advanced level)
	Language	Math
NJASK-Grade 3	83.3%	90.4%
GEPA-Grade 8	NA	NA
HSPA-High School	NA	NA

SAT score averages
Pct tested	Math	Verbal	Writing
NA	NA	NA	NA

Teacher Qualifications
Avg. years of experience	17
Highly-qualified teachers one subject/all subjects	97.5%/97.5%
With emergency credentials	0.0%

No Child Left Behind
AYP, 2005-06 ... Meets Standards

Municipal Finance
State Aid Programs, 2008
Total aid	$2,051,843
CMPTRA	457,650
Energy tax receipts	1,437,410
Garden State Trust	156,783

General Budget, 2007
Total tax levy	$47,728,590
County levy	7,829,004
County taxes	6,221,582
County library	1,195,534
County health	0
County open space	411,887
School levy	24,702,155
Muni. levy	15,197,432
Misc. revenues	6,595,134

Taxes	2005	2006	2007
General tax rate per $100	2.73	2.88	1.02
County equalization ratio	51.5	43.18	114.65
Net valuation taxable	$1,497,333,183	$1,518,733,200	$4,702,561,453
State equalized value	$3,467,654,430	$4,072,227,317	$4,418,014,731

Burlington County
Lumberton Township

Demographics & Socio-Economic Characteristics
(2000 US Census, except as noted)

Population
1980*	5,236
1990*	6,705
2000	10,461
Male	4,990
Female	5,471
2006 (estimate)*	12,331
Population density	958.1

Race & Hispanic Origin, 2000
Race
White	8,192
Black/African American	1,438
American Indian/Alaska Native	24
Asian	354
Native Hawaiian/Pacific Islander	2
Other race	199
Two or more races	252
Hispanic origin, total	539
Mexican	46
Puerto Rican	337
Cuban	17
Other Hispanic	139

Age & Nativity, 2000
Under 5 years	873
18 years and over	7,524
21 years and over	7,262
65 years and over	1,158
85 years and over	156
Median age	35.6
Native-born	9,665
Foreign-born	676

Educational Attainment, 2000
Population 25 years and over	6,790
Less than 9th grade	4.5%
High school grad or higher	86.2%
Bachelor's degree or higher	30.9%
Graduate degree	9.6%

Income & Poverty, 1999
Per capita income	$25,789
Median household income	$60,571
Median family income	$70,329
Persons in poverty	381
H'holds receiving public assistance	69
H'holds receiving social security	747

Households, 2000
Total households	3,930
With persons under 18	1,630
With persons over 65	784
Family households	2,730
Single-person households	988
Persons per household	2.61
Persons per family	3.17

Labor & Employment
Total civilian labor force, 2006**	5,997
Unemployment rate	3.8%
Total civilian labor force, 2000	5,175
Unemployment rate	3.7%

Employed persons 16 years and over by occupation, 2000
Managers & professionals	2,217
Service occupations	526
Sales & office occupations	1,317
Farming, fishing & forestry	0
Construction & maintenance	336
Production & transportation	587
Self-employed persons	217

* US Census Bureau
** New Jersey Department of Labor

See Introduction for an explanation of all data sources.

General Information
Township of Lumberton
PO Box 1860
35 Municipal Drive
Lumberton, NJ 08048
609-267-3217

Website	www.lumbertontwp.com
Year of incorporation	1860
Land/water area (sq. miles)	12.87/0.17
Form of government	Township

Government
Legislative Districts
US Congressional	3
State Legislative	8

Local Officials, 2008
Mayor	Patrick Delany
Manager	Daniel Van Pelt
Clerk	Maureen Horton-Gross
Finance Dir.	Joanna Mustafa
Tax Assessor	Patty Sporer
Tax Collector	Leslie Nealon
Attorney	Michael Mouber
Building	Brad Regn
Comm Dev/Planning	NA
Engineering	Alaimo Group
Public Works	Steve Moorer
Police Chief	Marc Sano
Emerg/Fire Director	Tim Pearson

Housing & Construction
Housing Units, 2000*
Total	4,080
Median rent	$702
Median SF home value	$163,300

Permits for New Residential Construction
	Units	Value
Total, 2007	1	$124,000
Single family	1	$124,000
Total, 2006	31	$1,948,400
Single family	31	$1,948,400

Real Property Valuation, 2007
	Parcels	Valuation
Total	4,185	$1,432,650,700
Vacant	118	12,793,600
Residential	3,745	1,194,523,300
Commercial	147	115,446,100
Industrial	10	57,422,000
Apartments	8	30,929,800
Farm land	112	1,980,100
Farm homestead	45	19,555,800

Average Property Value & Tax, 2007
Residential value	$320,337
Property tax	$6,127
Tax credit/rebate	$951

Public Library
No public municipal library

Library statistics, 2006
Population served	NA
Full-time/total staff	NA/NA

	Total	Per capita
Holdings	NA	NA
Revenues	NA	NA
Expenditures	NA	NA
Annual visits	NA	NA
Internet terminals/annual users	NA/NA	

Taxes
	2005	2006	2007
General tax rate per $100	3.388	3.551	1.92
County equalization ratio	67.52	58.43	110.64
Net valuation taxable	$712,960,292	$740,300,400	$1,434,765,770
State equalized value	$1,220,195,605	$1,383,645,024	$1,509,851,020

Public Safety
Number of officers, 2006 28

Crime	2005	2006
Total crimes	364	359
Violent	24	29
Murder	0	0
Rape	1	1
Robbery	4	10
Aggravated assault	19	18
Non-violent	340	330
Burglary	55	47
Larceny	272	272
Vehicle theft	13	11
Domestic violence	102	158
Arson	5	14
Total crime rate	29.6	28.9
Violent	2.0	2.3
Non-violent	27.6	26.6

Public School District
(for school year 2006-07 except as noted)

Lumberton Township School District
33 Municipal Dr
Lumberton, NJ 08048
609-265-7709

Superintendent	Frank Logandro
Number of schools	4
Grade plan	K-8
Enrollment	1,740
Attendance rate, '05-06	96.1%
Dropout rate	NA
Students per teacher	10.9
Per pupil expenditure	$11,455
Median faculty salary	$51,226
Median administrator salary	$105,170
Grade 12 enrollment	NA
High school graduation rate	NA

Assessment test results
(percent scoring at proficient or advanced level)
	Language	Math
NJASK-Grade 3	91.4%	93.0%
GEPA-Grade 8	81.1%	76.5%
HSPA-High School	NA	NA

SAT score averages
Pct tested	Math	Verbal	Writing
NA	NA	NA	NA

Teacher Qualifications
Avg. years of experience	10
Highly-qualified teachers one subject/all subjects	100%/100%
With emergency credentials	0.9%

No Child Left Behind
AYP, 2005-06 . . . . Meets Standards

Municipal Finance
State Aid Programs, 2008
Total aid	$1,653,379
CMPTRA	60,898
Energy tax receipts	1,592,312
Garden State Trust	169

General Budget, 2007
Total tax levy	$27,442,525
County levy	5,432,584
County taxes	4,501,377
County library	413,176
County health	0
County open space	518,030
School levy	18,174,484
Muni. levy	3,835,457
Misc. revenues	6,312,813

©2008 Information Publications, Inc. All rights reserved. Photocopying prohibited. For additional copies, contact the publisher at www.informationpublications.com or (877)544-INFO (4636)

The New Jersey Municipal Data Book 279

Lyndhurst Township
Bergen County

Demographics & Socio-Economic Characteristics
(2000 US Census, except as noted)

Population
1980*	20,326
1990*	18,262
2000	19,383
Male	9,242
Female	10,141
2006 (estimate)*	19,732
Population density	4,243.4

Race & Hispanic Origin, 2000
Race
White	17,433
Black/African American	119
American Indian/Alaska Native	9
Asian	1,046
Native Hawaiian/Pacific Islander	1
Other race	397
Two or more races	378
Hispanic origin, total	1,744
Mexican	97
Puerto Rican	465
Cuban	273
Other Hispanic	909

Age & Nativity, 2000
Under 5 years	959
18 years and over	15,690
21 years and over	15,142
65 years and over	3,440
85 years and over	382
Median age	39.5
Native-born	15,904
Foreign-born	3,479

Educational Attainment, 2000
Population 25 years and over	14,263
Less than 9th grade	7.8%
High school grad or higher	81.4%
Bachelor's degree or higher	21.9%
Graduate degree	6.2%

Income & Poverty, 1999
Per capita income	$25,940
Median household income	$53,375
Median family income	$63,758
Persons in poverty	890
H'holds receiving public assistance	92
H'holds receiving social security	2,664

Households, 2000
Total households	7,877
With persons under 18	2,200
With persons over 65	2,564
Family households	5,205
Single-person households	2,269
Persons per household	2.46
Persons per family	3.06

Labor & Employment
Total civilian labor force, 2006**	10,985
Unemployment rate	5.2%
Total civilian labor force, 2000	10,363
Unemployment rate	5.3%

Employed persons 16 years and over by occupation, 2000
Managers & professionals	2,976
Service occupations	1,280
Sales & office occupations	3,313
Farming, fishing & forestry	0
Construction & maintenance	882
Production & transportation	1,358
Self-employed persons	429

* US Census Bureau
** New Jersey Department of Labor
§ State Fiscal Year July 1–June 30

General Information
Township of Lyndhurst
367 Valley Brook Ave
Lyndhurst, NJ 07071
201-804-2457

Website	www.lyndhurstnj.org
Year of incorporation	1917
Land/water area (sq. miles)	4.65/0.26
Form of government	Commission

Government
Legislative Districts
US Congressional	9
State Legislative	36

Local Officials, 2008
Mayor	Richard J. DiLascio
Manager/Admin	NA
Clerk	Helen Polito
Finance Dir	Deborah Ferrato
Tax Assessor	Denis McGuire
Tax Collector	Deborah Ferrato
Attorney	Gary C. Cucchiara
Building	Mark Sadonis
Comm Dev/Planning	NA
Engineering	Michael Neglia
Public Works	Matthew T. Ruzzo
Police Chief	James O'Connor
Emerg/Fire Director	Nicholas Marino

Housing & Construction
Housing Units, 2000*
Total	8,103
Median rent	$805
Median SF home value	$182,800

Permits for New Residential Construction
	Units	Value
Total, 2007	5	$1,190,055
Single family	3	$904,855
Total, 2006	20	$3,353,392
Single family	16	$2,933,892

Real Property Valuation, 2007
	Parcels	Valuation
Total	5,694	$3,468,663,900
Vacant	134	171,122,400
Residential	5,080	2,093,002,000
Commercial	328	469,160,100
Industrial	101	673,322,100
Apartments	51	62,057,300
Farm land	0	0
Farm homestead	0	0

Average Property Value & Tax, 2007
Residential value	$412,008
Property tax	$6,555
Tax credit/rebate	$1,013

Public Library
Lyndhurst Public Library
355 Valley Brook Ave
Lyndhurst, NJ 07071
201-804-2478

Director: Donna M. Romeo

Library statistics, 2006
Population served	19,383
Full-time/total staff	3/8

	Total	Per capita
Holdings	51,883	2.68
Revenues	$841,044	$43.39
Expenditures	$752,154	$38.80
Annual visits	113,040	5.83
Internet terminals/annual users	10/26,000	

Public Safety
Number of officers, 2006: 49

Crime	2005	2006
Total crimes	319	336
Violent	22	13
Murder	0	0
Rape	1	2
Robbery	11	3
Aggravated assault	10	8
Non-violent	297	323
Burglary	41	40
Larceny	211	257
Vehicle theft	45	26
Domestic violence	231	169
Arson	1	2
Total crime rate	16.3	17.3
Violent	1.1	0.7
Non-violent	15.2	16.6

Public School District
(for school year 2006-07 except as noted)

Lyndhurst Township School District
420 Fern Ave
Lyndhurst, NJ 07071
201-438-5683

Superintendent	Joseph Abate Jr
Number of schools	7
Grade plan	K-12
Enrollment	2,206
Attendance rate, '05-06	94.3%
Dropout rate	3.5%
Students per teacher	12.3
Per pupil expenditure	$12,608
Median faculty salary	$66,200
Median administrator salary	$117,345
Grade 12 enrollment	139
High school graduation rate	87.4%

Assessment test results
(percent scoring at proficient or advanced level)
	Language	Math
NJASK-Grade 3	88.7%	81.6%
GEPA-Grade 8	74.1%	78.2%
HSPA-High School	93.9%	82.8%

SAT score averages
Pct tested	Math	Verbal	Writing
70%	512	454	464

Teacher Qualifications
Avg. years of experience	13
Highly-qualified teachers one subject/all subjects	100%/100%
With emergency credentials	0.0%

No Child Left Behind
AYP, 2005-06: Meets Standards

Municipal Finance §
State Aid Programs, 2008
Total aid	$1,805,331
CMPTRA	725,133
Energy tax receipts	1,079,760
Garden State Trust	438

General Budget, 2007
Total tax levy	$55,238,412
County levy	5,568,773
County taxes	5,256,991
County library	0
County health	0
County open space	311,782
School levy	27,014,424
Muni. levy	22,655,215
Misc. revenues	8,828,785

Taxes	2005	2006	2007
General tax rate per $100	3.2	1.45	1.6
County equalization ratio	62.69	132.34	112.3
Net valuation taxable	$1,431,510,850	$3,464,760,600	$3,472,059,121
State equalized value	$2,590,969,864	$3,088,667,349	$3,367,437,409

Morris County
Madison Borough

Demographics & Socio-Economic Characteristics
(2000 US Census, except as noted)

Population
1980*	15,357
1990*	15,850
2000	16,530
Male	7,832
Female	8,698
2006 (estimate)*	16,016
Population density	3,813.3

Race & Hispanic Origin, 2000
Race
- White ... 14,826
- Black/African American ... 496
- American Indian/Alaska Native ... 21
- Asian ... 624
- Native Hawaiian/Pacific Islander ... 38
- Other race ... 256
- Two or more races ... 269
- Hispanic origin, total ... 987
  - Mexican ... 43
  - Puerto Rican ... 70
  - Cuban ... 30
  - Other Hispanic ... 844

Age & Nativity, 2000
- Under 5 years ... 981
- 18 years and over ... 13,126
- 21 years and over ... 11,333
- 65 years and over ... 2,157
- 85 years and over ... 301
- Median age ... 34.3
- Native-born ... 14,323
- Foreign-born ... 2,207

Educational Attainment, 2000
- Population 25 years and over ... 10,178
- Less than 9th grade ... 3.8%
- High school grad or higher ... 90.8%
- Bachelor's degree or higher ... 56.8%
- Graduate degree ... 26.0%

Income & Poverty, 1999
- Per capita income ... $38,416
- Median household income ... $82,847
- Median family income ... $101,798
- Persons in poverty ... 469
- H'holds receiving public assistance ... 59
- H'holds receiving social security ... 1,524

Households, 2000
- Total households ... 5,520
  - With persons under 18 ... 1,807
  - With persons over 65 ... 1,501
  - Family households ... 3,785
  - Single-person households ... 1,415
- Persons per household ... 2.53
- Persons per family ... 3.05

Labor & Employment
- Total civilian labor force, 2006** ... 8,082
  - Unemployment rate ... 2.4%
- Total civilian labor force, 2000 ... 9,199
  - Unemployment rate ... 12.5%

Employed persons 16 years and over by occupation, 2000
- Managers & professionals ... 4,256
- Service occupations ... 789
- Sales & office occupations ... 2,219
- Farming, fishing & forestry ... 12
- Construction & maintenance ... 228
- Production & transportation ... 545
- Self-employed persons ... 468

* US Census Bureau
** New Jersey Department of Labor

See Introduction for an explanation of all data sources.

General Information
Borough of Madison
Hartley Dodge Memorial
50 Kings Rd
Madison, NJ 07940
973-593-3042

- Website ... www.rosenet.org/gov
- Year of incorporation ... 1889
- Land/water area (sq. miles) ... 4.20/0.00
- Form of government ... Borough

Government
Legislative Districts
- US Congressional ... 11
- State Legislative ... 21

Local Officials, 2008
- Mayor ... Mary-Anna Holden
- Manager ... Raymond M. Codey
- Clerk ... Marilyn Schaefer
- Finance Dir ... Robert Kalafut
- Tax Assessor ... Lisa Baratto
- Tax Collector ... Francine DeAngelis
- Attorney ... Joseph Mezzacca Jr
- Building ... Russell Brown
- Planning ... Peter G. Steck
- Engineering ... Robert Vogel
- Public Works ... David Maines
- Police Chief ... Vincent Chirico
- Emerg/Fire Director ... Douglas Atchison

Housing & Construction
Housing Units, 2000*
- Total ... 5,641
- Median rent ... $1,036
- Median SF home value ... $362,400

Permits for New Residential Construction
	Units	Value
Total, 2007	30	$14,158,734
Single family	30	$14,158,734
Total, 2006	34	$14,134,501
Single family	32	$13,794,501

Real Property Valuation, 2007
	Parcels	Valuation
Total	4,532	$2,121,923,300
Vacant	75	16,966,900
Residential	4,188	1,692,930,600
Commercial	226	359,968,900
Industrial	6	3,422,000
Apartments	37	48,634,900
Farm land	0	0
Farm homestead	0	0

Average Property Value & Tax, 2007
- Residential value ... $404,234
- Property tax ... $9,476
- Tax credit/rebate ... $1,151

Public Library
Madison Public Library
39 Keep St
Madison, NJ 07940
973-377-0722

- Director ... Nancy S. Adamczyk

Library statistics, 2006
- Population served ... 16,530
- Full-time/total staff ... 6/12

	Total	Per capita
Holdings	139,642	8.45
Revenues	$1,530,643	$92.60
Expenditures	$1,542,826	$93.33
Annual visits	136,697	8.27
Internet terminals/annual users	35/16,110	

Taxes
	2005	2006	2007
General tax rate per $100	2.06	2.2	2.35
County equalization ratio	73.85	65.88	60.39
Net valuation taxable	$2,102,380,915	$2,105,477,500	$2,131,307,423
State equalized value	$3,191,227,861	$3,497,834,419	$3,669,134,554

Public Safety
Number of officers, 2006 ... 35

Crime
	2005	2006
Total crimes	186	184
Violent	12	18
Murder	0	0
Rape	1	1
Robbery	1	1
Aggravated assault	10	16
Non-violent	174	166
Burglary	58	24
Larceny	107	139
Vehicle theft	9	3
Domestic violence	32	35
Arson	1	0
Total crime rate	11.6	11.6
Violent	0.7	1.1
Non-violent	10.9	10.4

Public School District
(for school year 2006-07 except as noted)

Madison School District
359 Woodland Rd
Madison, NJ 07940
973-593-3100

- Superintendent ... Richard Noonan
- Number of schools ... 5
- Grade plan ... K-12
- Enrollment ... 2,277
- Attendance rate, '05-06 ... 95.5%
- Dropout rate ... 0.6%
- Students per teacher ... 10.4
- Per pupil expenditure ... $13,848
- Median faculty salary ... $64,340
- Median administrator salary ... $112,561
- Grade 12 enrollment ... 204
- High school graduation rate ... 98.1%

Assessment test results
(percent scoring at proficient or advanced level)
	Language	Math
NJASK-Grade 3	94.8%	95.4%
GEPA-Grade 8	91.0%	84.5%
HSPA-High School	97.8%	95.0%

SAT score averages
Pct tested	Math	Verbal	Writing
91%	569	560	561

Teacher Qualifications
- Avg. years of experience ... 10
- Highly-qualified teachers one subject/all subjects ... 100%/100%
- With emergency credentials ... 0.0%

No Child Left Behind
- AYP, 2005-06 ... Meets Standards

Municipal Finance
State Aid Programs, 2008
- Total aid ... $1,072,618
  - CMPTRA ... 384,578
  - Energy tax receipts ... 688,040
  - Garden State Trust ... 0

General Budget, 2007
- Total tax levy ... $49,962,940
  - County levy ... 8,447,672
    - County taxes ... 6,757,430
    - County library ... 0
    - County health ... 0
    - County open space ... 1,690,242
  - School levy ... 29,826,818
  - Muni. levy ... 11,688,450
- Misc. revenues ... 12,710,095

©2008 Information Publications, Inc. All rights reserved.

The New Jersey Municipal Data Book 281

Magnolia Borough
Camden County

Demographics & Socio-Economic Characteristics
(2000 US Census, except as noted)

Population
1980*	4,881
1990*	4,861
2000	4,409
Male	2,134
Female	2,275
2006 (estimate)*	4,379
Population density	4,514.4

Race & Hispanic Origin, 2000
Race
- White 3,395
- Black/African American 785
- American Indian/Alaska Native 10
- Asian 41
- Native Hawaiian/Pacific Islander 1
- Other race 68
- Two or more races 109
- Hispanic origin, total 179
  - Mexican 21
  - Puerto Rican 104
  - Cuban 12
  - Other Hispanic 42

Age & Nativity, 2000
- Under 5 years 298
- 18 years and over 3,318
- 21 years and over 3,164
- 65 years and over 563
- 85 years and over 39
- Median age 36.1
- Native-born 4,262
- Foreign-born 141

Educational Attainment, 2000
- Population 25 years and over 2,979
- Less than 9th grade 5.0%
- High school grad or higher 80.7%
- Bachelor's degree or higher 12.2%
- Graduate degree 2.7%

Income & Poverty, 1999
- Per capita income $19,032
- Median household income $43,728
- Median family income $50,791
- Persons in poverty 346
- H'holds receiving public assistance ... 30
- H'holds receiving social security ... 444

Households, 2000
- Total households 1,710
  - With persons under 18 599
  - With persons over 65 421
  - Family households 1,162
  - Single-person households 439
- Persons per household 2.57
- Persons per family 3.12

Labor & Employment
- Total civilian labor force, 2006** ... 2,707
  - Unemployment rate 8.6%
- Total civilian labor force, 2000 ... 2,482
  - Unemployment rate 7.9%

Employed persons 16 years and over by occupation, 2000
- Managers & professionals 626
- Service occupations 365
- Sales & office occupations 678
- Farming, fishing & forestry 0
- Construction & maintenance 302
- Production & transportation 316
- Self-employed persons 120

* US Census Bureau
** New Jersey Department of Labor

General Information
Borough of Magnolia
438 Evesham Ave W
Magnolia, NJ 08049
856-783-1520

- Website .... www.magnolia-nj.org
- Year of incorporation 1915
- Land/water area (sq. miles) 0.97/0.00
- Form of government .... Borough

Government
Legislative Districts
- US Congressional 1
- State Legislative 5

Local Officials, 2008
- Mayor .... Betty Ann Cowling-Carson
- Manager .... John D. Keenan Jr
- Clerk .... John D. Keenan Jr
- Finance Dir .... John Massanova
- Tax Assessor .... Thomas Davis
- Tax Collector .... Robin Sarlo
- Attorney .... Sal Siciliano
- Construction .... John Szczerbinski
- Comm Dev/Planning .... NA
- Engineering .... Bach Associates
- Public Works .... Steve Pacella
- Police Chief .... Rob Doyle
- Emerg/Fire Director .... Gary Riebel

Housing & Construction
Housing Units, 2000*
- Total 1,836
- Median rent $599
- Median SF home value $90,900

Permits for New Residential Construction
	Units	Value
Total, 2007	9	$765,279
Single family	9	$765,279
Total, 2006	6	$396,458
Single family	6	$396,458

Real Property Valuation, 2007
	Parcels	Valuation
Total	1,636	$159,912,200
Vacant	137	3,610,200
Residential	1,420	128,799,900
Commercial	71	15,849,300
Industrial	3	4,706,900
Apartments	5	6,945,900
Farm land	0	0
Farm homestead	0	0

Average Property Value & Tax, 2007
- Residential value $90,704
- Property tax $4,971
- Tax credit/rebate $969

Public Library
No public municipal library

Library statistics, 2006
- Population served .... NA
- Full-time/total staff .... NA/NA

	Total	Per capita
Holdings	NA	NA
Revenues	NA	NA
Expenditures	NA	NA
Annual visits	NA	NA
Internet terminals/annual users	NA/NA	

Taxes
	2005	2006	2007
General tax rate per $100	4.636	5.128	5.481
County equalization ratio	84.95	70.94	59.79
Net valuation taxable	$159,430,251	$159,518,800	$160,050,224
State equalized value	$224,739,570	$266,956,555	$288,788,205

Public Safety
Number of officers, 2006 12

Crime
	2005	2006
Total crimes	137	119
Violent	16	18
Murder	0	0
Rape	0	2
Robbery	5	1
Aggravated assault	11	15
Non-violent	121	101
Burglary	33	34
Larceny	72	55
Vehicle theft	16	12
Domestic violence	40	50
Arson	1	0
Total crime rate	31.2	27.1
Violent	3.6	4.1
Non-violent	27.6	23.0

Public School District
(for school year 2006-07 except as noted)

Magnolia Borough School District
420 N Warwick Rd
Magnolia, NJ 08049
856-783-6343

- Superintendent .... Warren Pross
- Number of schools 1
- Grade plan K-8
- Enrollment 460
- Attendance rate, '05-06 .... 95.1%
- Dropout rate .... NA
- Students per teacher 10.3
- Per pupil expenditure $11,754
- Median faculty salary $49,272
- Median administrator salary .. $70,000
- Grade 12 enrollment .... NA
- High school graduation rate .... NA

Assessment test results
(percent scoring at proficient or advanced level)

	Language	Math
NJASK-Grade 3	75.9%	84.5%
GEPA-Grade 8	71.2%	69.8%
HSPA-High School	NA	NA

SAT score averages
Pct tested	Math	Verbal	Writing
NA	NA	NA	NA

Teacher Qualifications
- Avg. years of experience 10
- Highly-qualified teachers
  one subject/all subjects 100%/100%
- With emergency credentials 0.0%

No Child Left Behind
AYP, 2005-06 .... Meets Standards

Municipal Finance
State Aid Programs, 2008
- Total aid $390,799
  - CMPTRA 0
  - Energy tax receipts 390,799
  - Garden State Trust 0

General Budget, 2007
- Total tax levy $8,771,911
  - County levy 1,887,090
  - County taxes 1,714,189
  - County library 119,331
  - County health 0
  - County open space 53,569
  - School levy 5,031,252
  - Muni. levy 1,853,569
  - Misc. revenues 2,071,131

Bergen County
Mahwah Township

Demographics & Socio-Economic Characteristics
(2000 US Census, except as noted)

Population
- 1980* 12,127
- 1990* 17,905
- 2000 24,062
  - Male 11,435
  - Female 12,627
- 2006 (estimate)* 24,560
- Population density 947.2

Race & Hispanic Origin, 2000
Race
- White 21,157
- Black/African American 519
- American Indian/Alaska Native 169
- Asian 1,518
- Native Hawaiian/Pacific Islander 7
- Other race 361
- Two or more races 331
- Hispanic origin, total 1,028
  - Mexican 136
  - Puerto Rican 264
  - Cuban 89
  - Other Hispanic 539

Age & Nativity, 2000
- Under 5 years 1,672
- 18 years and over 18,717
- 21 years and over 17,492
- 65 years and over 2,572
- 85 years and over 204
  - Median age 37.3
- Native-born 20,868
- Foreign-born 3,194

Educational Attainment, 2000
- Population 25 years and over 16,374
- Less than 9th grade 2.3%
- High school grad or higher 93.6%
- Bachelor's degree or higher 49.5%
- Graduate degree 17.1%

Income & Poverty, 1999
- Per capita income $44,709
- Median household income $79,500
- Median family income $94,484
- Persons in poverty 458
- H'holds receiving public assistance 71
- H'holds receiving social security 1,984

Households, 2000
- Total households 9,340
  - With persons under 18 2,955
  - With persons over 65 1,923
  - Family households 6,288
  - Single-person households 2,612
- Persons per household 2.43
- Persons per family 3.01

Labor & Employment
- Total civilian labor force, 2006** 13,321
  - Unemployment rate 3.9%
- Total civilian labor force, 2000 13,481
  - Unemployment rate 5.6%

Employed persons 16 years and over by occupation, 2000
- Managers & professionals 6,323
- Service occupations 1,181
- Sales & office occupations 3,932
- Farming, fishing & forestry 8
- Construction & maintenance 533
- Production & transportation 754
- Self-employed persons 777

* US Census Bureau
** New Jersey Department of Labor

See Introduction for an explanation of all data sources.

General Information
Township of Mahwah
475 Corporate Dr
Mahwah, NJ 07430
201-529-5757

- Website .... www.mahwahtwp.org
- Year of incorporation 1944
- Land/water area (sq. miles) 25.93/0.27
- Form of government .... Mayor-Council

Government
Legislative Districts
- US Congressional 5
- State Legislative 40

Local Officials, 2008
- Mayor .... Richard Martel
- Manager .... Brian Campion
- Clerk .... Kathrine Coletta
- Finance Dir .... Kenneth Sesholtz
- Tax Assessor .... Stuart Stolarz
- Tax Collector .... Elizabeth Villano
- Attorney .... Terry Paul Bottinelli
- Building .... Gary Montroy
- Planning .... Mara Winokur
- Engineering .... Kevin Boswell
- Public Works .... Stanley Spiech
- Police Chief .... James Batelli
- Emerg/Fire Director ..... Donald Stricker Jr

Housing & Construction
Housing Units, 2000*
- Total 9,577
- Median rent $1,160
- Median SF home value $334,100

Permits for New Residential Construction

	Units	Value
Total, 2007	23	$17,225,451
Single family	23	$17,225,451
Total, 2006	32	$16,865,362
Single family	32	$16,865,362

Real Property Valuation, 2007

	Parcels	Valuation
Total	9,923	$4,100,947,000
Vacant	470	93,175,400
Residential	9,196	3,264,954,200
Commercial	155	475,892,000
Industrial	66	228,921,000
Apartments	8	31,751,800
Farm land	18	506,400
Farm homestead	10	5,746,200

Average Property Value & Tax, 2007
- Residential value $355,279
- Property tax $6,746
- Tax credit/rebate $972

Public Library
Mahwah Public Library
100 Ridge Rd
Mahwah Township, NJ 07430
201-529-2972

- Director .... Kenneth W. Giaimo

Library statistics, 2006
- Population served 24,062
- Full-time/total staff 5/15

	Total	Per capita
Holdings	121,764	5.06
Revenues	$2,042,506	$84.89
Expenditures	$1,621,071	$67.37
Annual visits	239,620	9.96
Internet terminals/annual users	11/11,298	

Public Safety
- Number of officers, 2006 56

Crime	2005	2006
Total crimes	188	154
Violent	12	8
Murder	0	0
Rape	0	1
Robbery	2	0
Aggravated assault	10	7
Non-violent	176	146
Burglary	12	15
Larceny	150	116
Vehicle theft	14	15
Domestic violence	172	175
Arson	1	1
Total crime rate	7.6	6.3
Violent	0.5	0.3
Non-violent	7.1	5.9

Public School District
(for school year 2006-07 except as noted)

Mahwah Township School District
60 Ridge Rd
Mahwah, NJ 07430
201-529-6803

- Superintendent .... Charles Montesano
- Number of schools 6
- Grade plan K-12
- Enrollment 3,395
- Attendance rate, '05-06 .... 96.6%
- Dropout rate 1.4%
- Students per teacher 11.1
- Per pupil expenditure $14,628
- Median faculty salary $57,058
- Median administrator salary $115,000
- Grade 12 enrollment 215
- High school graduation rate 93.2%

Assessment test results
(percent scoring at proficient or advanced level)

	Language	Math
NJASK-Grade 3	88.7%	92.0%
GEPA-Grade 8	89.7%	90.2%
HSPA-High School	93.0%	87.8%

SAT score averages

Pct tested	Math	Verbal	Writing
94%	534	507	513

Teacher Qualifications
- Avg. years of experience 9
- Highly-qualified teachers
  - one subject/all subjects 100%/100%
- With emergency credentials 0.8%

No Child Left Behind
- AYP, 2005-06 .... Meets Standards

Municipal Finance
State Aid Programs, 2008
- Total aid $5,777,702
  - CMPTRA 0
  - Energy tax receipts 5,771,269
  - Garden State Trust 6,433

General Budget, 2007
- Total tax levy $77,951,343
  - County levy 11,657,979
    - County taxes 11,014,151
    - County library 0
    - County health 0
    - County open space 643,827
  - School levy 48,521,801
  - Muni. levy 17,771,563
- Misc. revenues 16,244,904

Taxes	2005	2006	2007
General tax rate per $100	1.69	1.79	1.9
County equalization ratio	79.36	70.42	64.07
Net valuation taxable	$4,088,426,805	$4,109,598,000	$4,105,452,839
State equalized value	$5,805,775,071	$6,418,751,769	$6,722,964,227

Manalapan Township
Monmouth County

Demographics & Socio-Economic Characteristics
(2000 US Census, except as noted)

Population
1980*	18,914
1990*	26,716
2000	33,423
Male	16,029
Female	17,394
2006 (estimate)*	37,169
Population density	1,206.0

Race & Hispanic Origin, 2000
Race
White	30,687
Black/African American	664
American Indian/Alaska Native	9
Asian	1,514
Native Hawaiian/Pacific Islander	5
Other race	177
Two or more races	367
Hispanic origin, total	1,183
Mexican	86
Puerto Rican	579
Cuban	143
Other Hispanic	375

Age & Nativity, 2000
Under 5 years	2,220
18 years and over	23,283
21 years and over	22,349
65 years and over	3,883
85 years and over	589
Median age	38.2
Native-born	29,956
Foreign-born	3,467

Educational Attainment, 2000
Population 25 years and over	21,286
Less than 9th grade	2.4%
High school grad or higher	92.5%
Bachelor's degree or higher	39.3%
Graduate degree	14.5%

Income & Poverty, 1999
Per capita income	$32,142
Median household income	$83,575
Median family income	$94,112
Persons in poverty	1,259
H'holds receiving public assistance	56
H'holds receiving social security	2,982

Households, 2000
Total households	10,781
With persons under 18	5,252
With persons over 65	2,800
Family households	9,001
Single-person households	1,607
Persons per household	3.09
Persons per family	3.45

Labor & Employment
Total civilian labor force, 2006**	18,389
Unemployment rate	3.5%
Total civilian labor force, 2000	15,892
Unemployment rate	3.4%

Employed persons 16 years and over by occupation, 2000
Managers & professionals	7,206
Service occupations	1,264
Sales & office occupations	4,897
Farming, fishing & forestry	23
Construction & maintenance	1,047
Production & transportation	922
Self-employed persons	1,041

‡ Main library for county
* US Census Bureau
** New Jersey Department of Labor

General Information
Township of Manalapan
120 Route 522
Manalapan, NJ 07726
732-446-3200

Website	www.twp.manalapan.nj.us
Year of incorporation	1848
Land/water area (sq. miles)	30.82/0.05
Form of government	Township

Government
Legislative Districts
US Congressional	6, 12
State Legislative	12

Local Officials, 2008
Mayor	Michelle Roth
Manager	Tara L. Lovrich
Clerk	Rose Ann Weeden
Finance Dir	Patricia Addario
Tax Assessor	Sharon Hartman
Tax Collector	Hope Lewis
Attorney	Kevin Kennedy
Building	Richard Hogan
Comm Dev/Planning	NA
Engineering	Greg Valesi
Public Works	Alan Spector
Police Chief	Stuart C. Brown
Emerg/Fire Director	Richard Hogan

Housing & Construction
Housing Units, 2000*
Total	11,066
Median rent	$1,124
Median SF home value	$257,100

Permits for New Residential Construction
	Units	Value
Total, 2007	227	$30,666,551
Single family	198	$27,584,123
Total, 2006	403	$51,694,461
Single family	282	$43,132,974

Real Property Valuation, 2007
	Parcels	Valuation
Total	14,717	$6,151,643,200
Vacant	1,324	200,229,100
Residential	12,754	5,485,094,000
Commercial	346	402,831,900
Industrial	9	24,603,500
Apartments	0	0
Farm land	185	2,296,200
Farm homestead	99	36,588,500

Average Property Value & Tax, 2007
Residential value	$429,603
Property tax	$7,065
Tax credit/rebate	$1,091

Public Library
Monmouth County Library‡
125 Symmes Dr
Manalapan, NJ 07726
732-431-7220

Director … Ken Sheinbaum

County Library statistics, 2006
Population served	399,613
Full-time/total staff	36/117

	Total	Per capita
Holdings	1,366,533	3.42
Revenues	$13,614,168	$34.07
Expenditures	$11,921,555	$29.83
Annual visits	2,235,563	5.59
Internet terminals/annual users	78/253,864	

Taxes
	2005	2006	2007
General tax rate per $100	3.528	3.607	1.645
County equalization ratio	53.04	48.39	101.64
Net valuation taxable	$2,448,575,455	$2,514,266,100	$6,157,351,118
State equalized value	$5,060,085,669	$5,837,550,667	$6,267,559,710

Public Safety
Number of officers, 2006 … 66

Crime	2005	2006
Total crimes	348	393
Violent	11	25
Murder	0	3
Rape	2	2
Robbery	3	7
Aggravated assault	6	13
Non-violent	337	368
Burglary	58	56
Larceny	263	296
Vehicle theft	16	16
Domestic violence	180	178
Arson	0	1
Total crime rate	9.4	10.7
Violent	0.3	0.7
Non-violent	9.1	10.0

Public School District
(for school year 2006-07 except as noted)

Manalapan-Englishtown Reg. School Dist.
54 Main St
Englishtown, NJ 07726
732-786-2500

Superintendent	John J. Marciante Jr
Number of schools	14
Grade plan	K-8
Enrollment	5,446
Attendance rate, '05-06	95.7%
Dropout rate	NA
Students per teacher	12.2
Per pupil expenditure	$11,340
Median faculty salary	$50,888
Median administrator salary	$92,939
Grade 12 enrollment	NA
High school graduation rate	NA

Assessment test results
(percent scoring at proficient or advanced level)
	Language	Math
NJASK-Grade 3	92.8%	93.7%
GEPA-Grade 8	91.8%	85.3%
HSPA-High School	NA	NA

SAT score averages
Pct tested	Math	Verbal	Writing
NA	NA	NA	NA

Teacher Qualifications
Avg. years of experience	9
Highly-qualified teachers one subject/all subjects	100%/100%
With emergency credentials	0.0%

No Child Left Behind
AYP, 2005-06 … Meets Standards

Municipal Finance
State Aid Programs, 2008
Total aid	$4,988,361
CMPTRA	335,299
Energy tax receipts	4,627,983
Garden State Trust	25,079

General Budget, 2007
Total tax levy	$101,261,706
County levy	16,336,841
County taxes	14,590,011
County library	835,236
County health	0
County open space	911,594
School levy	68,395,688
Muni. levy	16,529,177
Misc. revenues	14,323,577

Monmouth County
Manasquan Borough

Demographics & Socio-Economic Characteristics
(2000 US Census, except as noted)

Population
- 1980* 5,354
- 1990* 5,369
- 2000 6,310
  - Male 3,106
  - Female 3,204
- 2006 (estimate)* 6,199
  - Population density 4,492.0

Race & Hispanic Origin, 2000
Race
- White 6,177
- Black/African American 26
- American Indian/Alaska Native 7
- Asian 28
- Native Hawaiian/Pacific Islander 0
- Other race 30
- Two or more races 42
- Hispanic origin, total 283
  - Mexican 174
  - Puerto Rican 18
  - Cuban 11
  - Other Hispanic 80

Age & Nativity, 2000
- Under 5 years 391
- 18 years and over 4,808
- 21 years and over 4,623
- 65 years and over 942
- 85 years and over 113
  - Median age 39.0
- Native-born 6,021
- Foreign-born 289

Educational Attainment, 2000
Population 25 years and over 4,398
- Less than 9th grade 1.8%
- High school grad or higher 92.9%
- Bachelor's degree or higher 40.4%
- Graduate degree 13.2%

Income & Poverty, 1999
- Per capita income $32,898
- Median household income $63,079
- Median family income $73,670
- Persons in poverty 195
- H'holds receiving public assistance ... 46
- H'holds receiving social security ... 696

Households, 2000
- Total households 2,600
  - With persons under 18 810
  - With persons over 65 715
  - Family households 1,635
  - Single-person households 785
- Persons per household 2.43
- Persons per family 3.06

Labor & Employment
- Total civilian labor force, 2006** ... 3,584
  - Unemployment rate 2.4%
- Total civilian labor force, 2000 ... 3,328
  - Unemployment rate 2.4%

Employed persons 16 years and over by occupation, 2000
- Managers & professionals 1,289
- Service occupations 455
- Sales & office occupations 1,007
- Farming, fishing & forestry 9
- Construction & maintenance 214
- Production & transportation 273
- Self-employed persons 251

* US Census Bureau
** New Jersey Department of Labor

See Introduction for an explanation of all data sources.

General Information
Borough of Manasquan
201 E Main St
Manasquan, NJ 08736
732-223-0544
- Website .... www.manasquan-nj.com
- Year of incorporation 1887
- Land/water area (sq. miles) ... 1.38/1.15
- Form of government .... Borough

Government
Legislative Districts
- US Congressional 4
- State Legislative 10

Local Officials, 2008
- Mayor .... George Dempsey
- Manager .... John Trengrove
- Clerk .... Colleen Scimeca
- Finance Dir .... Joanne Madden
- Tax Assessor .... Robyn Palugiti
- Tax Collector .... NA
- Attorney .... Kenneth Fitzsimmons
- Building .... Sandy Ratz
- Comm Dev/Planning .... NA
- Engineering .... T&M Associates
- Public Works .... NA
- Police Chief .... Daniel Scimeca
- Emerg/Fire Director ..... Peter Mayer III

Housing & Construction
Housing Units, 2000*
- Total 3,531
- Median rent $808
- Median SF home value $265,300

Permits for New Residential Construction

	Units	Value
Total, 2007	32	$7,497,221
Single family	32	$7,497,221
Total, 2006	37	$8,845,643
Single family	37	$8,845,643

Real Property Valuation, 2007

	Parcels	Valuation
Total	3,177	$1,562,328,100
Vacant	130	26,716,700
Residential	2,840	1,391,130,600
Commercial	186	127,638,500
Industrial	13	8,349,900
Apartments	8	8,492,400
Farm land	0	0
Farm homestead	0	0

Average Property Value & Tax, 2007
- Residential value $489,835
- Property tax $7,007
- Tax credit/rebate $1,180

Public Library
Manasquan Public Library
55 Broad St
Manasquan, NJ 08736
732-223-1503
- Director .... Margo Petersen

Library statistics, 2006
- Population served 6,310
- Full-time/total staff 0/1

	Total	Per capita
Holdings	34,857	5.52
Revenues	$131,491	$20.84
Expenditures	$144,539	$22.91
Annual visits	46,521	7.37

- Internet terminals/annual users ... 2/2,151

Public Safety
- Number of officers, 2006 17

Crime	2005	2006
Total crimes	172	167
Violent	6	4
Murder	1	0
Rape	1	0
Robbery	0	1
Aggravated assault	4	3
Non-violent	166	163
Burglary	24	13
Larceny	140	150
Vehicle theft	2	0
Domestic violence	8	22
Arson	0	1
Total crime rate	27.4	26.9
Violent	1.0	0.6
Non-violent	26.4	26.3

Public School District
(for school year 2006-07 except as noted)

Manasquan School District
169 Broad St
Manasquan, NJ 08736
732-528-8800

- Superintendent .... Geraldine Margin
- Number of schools 2
- Grade plan K-12
- Enrollment 1,718
- Attendance rate, '05-06 .... 94.9%
- Dropout rate 0.6%
- Students per teacher 12.0
- Per pupil expenditure $12,038
- Median faculty salary $55,250
- Median administrator salary ... $119,346
- Grade 12 enrollment 248
- High school graduation rate 97.7%

Assessment test results
(percent scoring at proficient or advanced level)

	Language	Math
NJASK-Grade 3	89.3%	94.0%
GEPA-Grade 8	97.1%	91.3%
HSPA-High School	90.6%	82.3%

SAT score averages

Pct tested	Math	Verbal	Writing
99%	515	507	510

Teacher Qualifications
- Avg. years of experience 11
- Highly-qualified teachers
  one subject/all subjects 100%/100%
- With emergency credentials 0.0%

No Child Left Behind
- AYP, 2005-06 .... Meets Standards

Municipal Finance
State Aid Programs, 2008
- Total aid $523,430
  - CMPTRA 34,321
  - Energy tax receipts 489,105
  - Garden State Trust 4

General Budget, 2007
- Total tax levy $22,355,050
  - County levy 5,517,241
    - County taxes 4,844,878
    - County library 277,357
    - County health 92,284
    - County open space 302,722
  - School levy 11,822,383
  - Muni. levy 5,015,426
  - Misc. revenues 2,878,010

Taxes	2005	2006	2007
General tax rate per $100	1.368	1.429	1.431
County equalization ratio	96.38	87.95	77.71
Net valuation taxable	$1,528,308,179	$1,542,440,900	$1,562,791,260
State equalized value	$1,737,701,170	$1,985,380,189	$2,153,023,232

©2008 Information Publications, Inc. All rights reserved. Photocopying prohibited. For additional copies, contact the publisher at www.informationpublications.com or (877) 544-INFO (4636).

The New Jersey Municipal Data Book

Manchester Township — Ocean County

Demographics & Socio-Economic Characteristics
(2000 US Census, except as noted)

Population
1980*	27,987
1990*	35,976
2000	38,928
Male	16,459
Female	22,469
2006 (estimate)*	41,813
Population density	506.2

Race & Hispanic Origin, 2000
Race
White	36,724
Black/African American	1,190
American Indian/Alaska Native	45
Asian	338
Native Hawaiian/Pacific Islander	10
Other race	267
Two or more races	354
Hispanic origin, total	1,024
Mexican	62
Puerto Rican	590
Cuban	48
Other Hispanic	324

Age & Nativity, 2000
Under 5 years	1,019
18 years and over	34,744
21 years and over	34,114
65 years and over	21,210
85 years and over	3,645
Median age	67.7
Native-born	35,971
Foreign-born	2,989

Educational Attainment, 2000
Population 25 years and over	33,532
Less than 9th grade	7.2%
High school grad or higher	75.5%
Bachelor's degree or higher	12.7%
Graduate degree	4.1%

Income & Poverty, 1999
Per capita income	$22,409
Median household income	$29,525
Median family income	$43,363
Persons in poverty	2,102
H'holds receiving public assistance	396
H'holds receiving social security	15,035

Households, 2000
Total households	20,688
With persons under 18	2,242
With persons over 65	15,118
Family households	10,814
Single-person households	9,318
Persons per household	1.85
Persons per family	2.53

Labor & Employment
Total civilian labor force, 2006**	11,442
Unemployment rate	6.5%
Total civilian labor force, 2000	10,165
Unemployment rate	6.8%

Employed persons 16 years and over by occupation, 2000
Managers & professionals	2,597
Service occupations	1,683
Sales & office occupations	2,567
Farming, fishing & forestry	8
Construction & maintenance	1,155
Production & transportation	1,467
Self-employed persons	531

‡ Branch of county library
* US Census Bureau
** New Jersey Department of Labor
§ State Fiscal Year July 1–June 30

General Information
Township of Manchester
1 Colonial Dr
Manchester, NJ 08759
732-657-8121

Website	www.manchestertwp.com
Year of incorporation	1865
Land/water area (sq. miles)	82.60/0.29
Form of government	Mayor-Council

Government
Legislative Districts
US Congressional	4
State Legislative	9

Local Officials, 2008
Mayor	Michael Fressola
Manager	Constance Lauffer
Clerk	Marie Pellecchia
Finance Dir	William Garofalo
Tax Assessor	Martin Lynch
Tax Collector	Andrea Gaskill
Attorney	Steve Secare
Building	Michael Martin
Planning	Tom Thomas
Engineering	Charles Rooney
Public Works	Stephen Stanziano
Police Chief	William Brase
Public Safety Dir	William Brase

Housing & Construction
Housing Units, 2000*
Total	22,681
Median rent	$940
Median SF home value	$85,000

Permits for New Residential Construction
	Units	Value
Total, 2007	2	$287,691
Single family	2	$287,691
Total, 2006	1	$126,493
Single family	1	$126,493

Real Property Valuation, 2007
	Parcels	Valuation
Total	19,759	$2,096,382,381
Vacant	4,151	56,119,300
Residential	15,398	1,623,201,581
Commercial	140	139,220,200
Industrial	10	9,971,600
Apartments	31	266,171,600
Farm land	20	544,200
Farm homestead	9	1,153,900

Average Property Value & Tax, 2007
Residential value	$105,430
Property tax	$3,144
Tax credit/rebate	$927

Public Library
Manchester Branch Library‡
21 Colonial Dr
Manchester, NJ 08759
732-657-7600

Branch Librarian — Susan Scro

Library statistics, 2006
see Ocean County profile for library system statistics

Public Safety
Number of officers, 2006		67
Crime	**2005**	**2006**
Total crimes	361	335
Violent	14	19
Murder	0	0
Rape	2	2
Robbery	0	6
Aggravated assault	12	11
Non-violent	347	316
Burglary	69	72
Larceny	261	233
Vehicle theft	17	11
Domestic violence	247	245
Arson	6	13
Total crime rate	8.6	8.0
Violent	0.3	0.5
Non-violent	8.2	7.5

Public School District
(for school year 2006-07 except as noted)

Manchester Township School District
121 Route 539, Box 4100
Whiting, NJ 08759
732-350-5900

Superintendent	William E. DeFeo
Number of schools	5
Grade plan	K-12
Enrollment	3,260
Attendance rate, '05-06	95.1%
Dropout rate	2.5%
Students per teacher	10.4
Per pupil expenditure	$11,850
Median faculty salary	$48,496
Median administrator salary	$106,641
Grade 12 enrollment	255
High school graduation rate	92.5%

Assessment test results
(percent scoring at proficient or advanced level)
	Language	Math
NJASK-Grade 3	84.6%	89.9%
GEPA-Grade 8	72.9%	78.0%
HSPA-High School	90.7%	81.1%

SAT score averages
Pct tested	Math	Verbal	Writing
57%	512	471	483

Teacher Qualifications
Avg. years of experience	13
Highly-qualified teachers one subject/all subjects	100%/100%
With emergency credentials	0.0%

No Child Left Behind
AYP, 2005-06 — Meets Standards

Municipal Finance§
State Aid Programs, 2008
Total aid	$4,175,541
CMPTRA	926,851
Energy tax receipts	3,000,589
Garden State Trust	236,941

General Budget, 2007
Total tax levy	$62,612,929
County levy	13,384,252
County taxes	11,029,214
County library	1,307,160
County health	529,586
County open space	518,291
School levy	34,076,382
Muni. levy	15,152,295
Misc. revenues	14,641,052

Taxes
	2005	2006	2007
General tax rate per $100	2.759	2.838	2.982
County equalization ratio	60.73	54.56	48.68
Net valuation taxable	$1,991,302,044	$2,047,333,181	$2,099,812,765
State equalized value	$3,649,747,148	$4,209,480,200	$4,675,555,147

Salem County
Mannington Township

Demographics & Socio-Economic Characteristics
(2000 US Census, except as noted)

Population
1980*	1,740
1990*	1,693
2000	1,559
Male	763
Female	796
2006 (estimate)*	1,566
Population density	45.0

Race & Hispanic Origin, 2000
Race
White	1,179
Black/African American	326
American Indian/Alaska Native	8
Asian	6
Native Hawaiian/Pacific Islander	0
Other race	27
Two or more races	13
Hispanic origin, total	52
Mexican	12
Puerto Rican	23
Cuban	0
Other Hispanic	17

Age & Nativity, 2000
Under 5 years	86
18 years and over	1,207
21 years and over	1,182
65 years and over	365
85 years and over	78
Median age	42.7
Native-born	1,534
Foreign-born	25

Educational Attainment, 2000
Population 25 years and over	1,140
Less than 9th grade	10.2%
High school grad or higher	76.1%
Bachelor's degree or higher	20.6%
Graduate degree	6.0%

Income & Poverty, 1999
Per capita income	$24,262
Median household income	$52,625
Median family income	$62,500
Persons in poverty	98
H'holds receiving public assistance	17
H'holds receiving social security	185

Households, 2000
Total households	539
With persons under 18	173
With persons over 65	184
Family households	409
Single-person households	111
Persons per household	2.63
Persons per family	3.02

Labor & Employment
Total civilian labor force, 2006**	746
Unemployment rate	3.5%
Total civilian labor force, 2000	724
Unemployment rate	4.1%

Employed persons 16 years and over by occupation, 2000
Managers & professionals	269
Service occupations	70
Sales & office occupations	185
Farming, fishing & forestry	14
Construction & maintenance	52
Production & transportation	104
Self-employed persons	42

* US Census Bureau
** New Jersey Department of Labor

See Introduction for an explanation of all data sources.

General Information
Township of Mannington
491 Route 45
Mannington, NJ 08079
856-935-2359

Email	mannington@comcast.net
Year of incorporation	1701
Land/water area (sq. miles)	34.78/3.64
Form of government	Township

Government
Legislative Districts
US Congressional	2
State Legislative	3

Local Officials, 2008
Mayor	Donald C. Asay
Manager	Esther A. Mitchell
Clerk	Esther A. Mitchell
Finance Dir.	Donald A. Stiles
Tax Assessor	Donna Harris
Tax Collector	Lynne H. Stiles
Attorney	William L. Horner
Construction Officials	(state)
Planning	Rebecca G. Call
Engineering	Carl Gaskill
Public Works	John W. Dubois
Police Chief	NA
Emerg/Fire Director	S. Lee Butcher

Housing & Construction
Housing Units, 2000*
Total	573
Median rent	$613
Median SF home value	$115,400

Permits for New Residential Construction
	Units	Value
Total, 2007	4	$430,660
Single family	4	$430,660
Total, 2006	7	$1,312,350
Single family	7	$1,312,350

Real Property Valuation, 2007
	Parcels	Valuation
Total	1,286	$223,376,600
Vacant	222	3,587,000
Residential	408	68,537,100
Commercial	41	45,123,000
Industrial	4	52,645,400
Apartments	0	0
Farm land	433	7,591,300
Farm homestead	178	45,892,800

Average Property Value & Tax, 2007
Residential value	$195,273
Property tax	$3,816
Tax credit/rebate	$872

Public Library
No public municipal library

Library statistics, 2006
Population served	NA
Full-time/total staff	NA/NA

	Total	Per capita
Holdings	NA	NA
Revenues	NA	NA
Expenditures	NA	NA
Annual visits	NA	NA
Internet terminals/annual users	NA/NA	

Taxes
	2005	2006	2007
General tax rate per $100	3.082	2.019	2.021
County equalization ratio	70.91	118.69	118.69
Net valuation taxable	$124,321,529	$222,106,000	$224,172,116
State equalized value	$187,626,817	$187,926,698	$206,255,965

Public Safety
Number of officers, 2006		0

Crime	2005	2006
Total crimes	40	34
Violent	3	1
Murder	2	0
Rape	0	0
Robbery	0	0
Aggravated assault	1	1
Non-violent	37	33
Burglary	18	14
Larceny	17	18
Vehicle theft	2	1
Domestic violence	5	0
Arson	0	0
Total crime rate	25.4	21.8
Violent	1.9	0.6
Non-violent	23.5	21.1

Public School District
(for school year 2006-07 except as noted)

Mannington Township School District
495 Rt 45
Salem, NJ 08079
856-935-1078

Superintendent	Jean Rishel
Number of schools	1
Grade plan	K-8
Enrollment	154
Attendance rate, '05-06	96.5%
Dropout rate	NA
Students per teacher	9.5
Per pupil expenditure	$13,647
Median faculty salary	$53,550
Median administrator salary	$94,490
Grade 12 enrollment	NA
High school graduation rate	NA

Assessment test results
(percent scoring at proficient or advanced level)
	Language	Math
NJASK-Grade 3	81.3%	93.8%
GEPA-Grade 8	66.7%	93.4%
HSPA-High School	NA	NA

SAT score averages
Pct tested	Math	Verbal	Writing
NA	NA	NA	NA

Teacher Qualifications
Avg. years of experience	20
Highly-qualified teachers one subject/all subjects	100%/100%
With emergency credentials	0.0%

No Child Left Behind
AYP, 2005-06	Meets Standards

Municipal Finance
State Aid Programs, 2008
Total aid	$278,386
CMPTRA	0
Energy tax receipts	274,028
Garden State Trust	4,358

General Budget, 2007
Total tax levy	$4,528,932
County levy	1,806,981
County taxes	1,768,434
County library	0
County health	0
County open space	38,547
School levy	2,253,315
Muni. levy	468,635
Misc. revenues	746,431

Mansfield Township
Burlington County

Demographics & Socio-Economic Characteristics
(2000 US Census, except as noted)

Population
1980*	2,523
1990*	3,874
2000	5,090
Male	2,442
Female	2,648
2006 (estimate)*	8,047
Population density	370.5

Race & Hispanic Origin, 2000
Race
White	4,857
Black/African American	97
American Indian/Alaska Native	9
Asian	76
Native Hawaiian/Pacific Islander	2
Other race	11
Two or more races	38
Hispanic origin, total	93
Mexican	9
Puerto Rican	55
Cuban	4
Other Hispanic	25

Age & Nativity, 2000
Under 5 years	241
18 years and over	4,140
21 years and over	4,019
65 years and over	1,623
85 years and over	87
Median age	48.8
Native-born	4,824
Foreign-born	266

Educational Attainment, 2000
Population 25 years and over	3,816
Less than 9th grade	3.6%
High school grad or higher	85.6%
Bachelor's degree or higher	25.1%
Graduate degree	11.4%

Income & Poverty, 1999
Per capita income	$26,559
Median household income	$50,757
Median family income	$59,040
Persons in poverty	228
H'holds receiving public assistance	4
H'holds receiving social security	1,149

Households, 2000
Total households	2,077
With persons under 18	523
With persons over 65	1,067
Family households	1,561
Single-person households	469
Persons per household	2.45
Persons per family	2.86

Labor & Employment
Total civilian labor force, 2006**	2,460
Unemployment rate	5.2%
Total civilian labor force, 2000	2,105
Unemployment rate	4.4%

Employed persons 16 years and over by occupation, 2000
Managers & professionals	674
Service occupations	282
Sales & office occupations	563
Farming, fishing & forestry	14
Construction & maintenance	257
Production & transportation	222
Self-employed persons	112

* US Census Bureau
** New Jersey Department of Labor

General Information
Township of Mansfield
PO Box 249
Columbus, NJ 08022
609-298-0542

Website	www.mansfieldburlington.com
Year of incorporation	1688
Land/water area (sq. miles)	21.72/0.14
Form of government	Township

Government
Legislative Districts
US Congressional	4
State Legislative	8

Local Officials, 2008
Mayor	Arthur R. Puglia
Township Admin	Joseph Broski
Clerk	Linda Semus
Finance Dir	Joseph Monzo
Tax Assessor	Robin Bucchi
Tax Collector	Elaine Fortin
Attorney	Michael Magee
Building	Jeffrey Jones
Comm Dev/Planning	NA
Engineering	Leonard Faiola
Public Works	Jeffrey Jones
Public Safety Dir	Richard Bendel
Emerg/Fire Director	Sean Gable

Housing & Construction
Housing Units, 2000*
Total	2,122
Median rent	$706
Median SF home value	$153,800

Permits for New Residential Construction
	Units	Value
Total, 2007	40	$12,985,555
Single family	40	$12,985,555
Total, 2006	51	$7,762,494
Single family	51	$7,762,494

Real Property Valuation, 2007
	Parcels	Valuation
Total	4,060	$1,288,503,200
Vacant	318	45,735,400
Residential	3,300	1,094,648,400
Commercial	91	89,409,800
Industrial	2	5,301,200
Apartments	5	2,165,400
Farm land	221	4,218,900
Farm homestead	123	47,024,100

Average Property Value & Tax, 2007
Residential value	$333,530
Property tax	$6,052
Tax credit/rebate	$1,130

Public Library
No public municipal library

Library statistics, 2006
Population served	NA
Full-time/total staff	NA/NA

	Total	Per capita
Holdings	NA	NA
Revenues	NA	NA
Expenditures	NA	NA
Annual visits	NA	NA
Internet terminals/annual users	NA/NA	

Public Safety
Number of officers, 2006		10
Crime	**2005**	**2006**
Total crimes	127	146
Violent	10	5
Murder	1	0
Rape	0	0
Robbery	0	1
Aggravated assault	9	4
Non-violent	117	141
Burglary	11	8
Larceny	93	120
Vehicle theft	13	13
Domestic violence	31	26
Arson	0	0
Total crime rate	16.3	18.4
Violent	1.3	0.6
Non-violent	15.0	17.8

Public School District
(for school year 2006-07 except as noted)

Mansfield Township School District
200 Mansfield Rd East
Columbus, NJ 08022
609-298-2037

Superintendent	Diane Bacher
Number of schools	2
Grade plan	K-6
Enrollment	682
Attendance rate, '05-06	95.6%
Dropout rate	NA
Students per teacher	9.7
Per pupil expenditure	$11,999
Median faculty salary	$44,780
Median administrator salary	$102,980
Grade 12 enrollment	NA
High school graduation rate	NA

Assessment test results
(percent scoring at proficient or advanced level)
	Language	Math
NJASK-Grade 3	97.1%	98.0%
GEPA-Grade 8	NA	NA
HSPA-High School	NA	NA

SAT score averages
Pct tested	Math	Verbal	Writing
NA	NA	NA	NA

Teacher Qualifications
Avg. years of experience	6
Highly-qualified teachers one subject/all subjects	100%/100%
With emergency credentials	2.2%

No Child Left Behind
AYP, 2005-06	Meets Standards

Municipal Finance
State Aid Programs, 2008
Total aid	$666,315
CMPTRA	12,606
Energy tax receipts	653,709
Garden State Trust	0

General Budget, 2007
Total tax levy	$23,420,245
County levy	5,177,158
County taxes	4,289,861
County library	393,705
County health	0
County open space	493,592
School levy	16,079,140
Muni. levy	2,163,947
Misc. revenues	4,420,178

Taxes
	2005	2006	2007
General tax rate per $100	3.365	3.52	1.82
County equalization ratio	67.23	60.15	104.38
Net valuation taxable	$632,142,896	$649,514,415	$1,290,671,921
State equalized value	$1,050,944,133	$1,187,152,098	$1,305,662,095

Warren County
Mansfield Township

Demographics & Socio-Economic Characteristics
(2000 US Census, except as noted)

Population
- 1980* 5,780
- 1990* 7,154
- 2000 6,653
  - Male 3,237
  - Female 3,416
- 2006 (estimate)* 8,274
  - Population density 276.5

Race & Hispanic Origin, 2000
Race
- White 6,048
- Black/African American 300
- American Indian/Alaska Native 16
- Asian 81
- Native Hawaiian/Pacific Islander 0
- Other race 106
- Two or more races 102
- Hispanic origin, total 291
  - Mexican 25
  - Puerto Rican 63
  - Cuban 30
  - Other Hispanic 173

Age & Nativity, 2000
- Under 5 years 493
- 18 years and over 4,857
- 21 years and over 4,670
- 65 years and over 776
- 85 years and over 126
  - Median age 37.1
- Native-born 6,290
- Foreign-born 363

Educational Attainment, 2000
- Population 25 years and over 4,457
- Less than 9th grade 3.5%
- High school grad or higher 88.6%
- Bachelor's degree or higher 27.5%
- Graduate degree 9.3%

Income & Poverty, 1999
- Per capita income $26,277
- Median household income $61,763
- Median family income $76,102
- Persons in poverty 251
- H'holds receiving public assistance 30
- H'holds receiving social security 508

Households, 2000
- Total households 2,334
  - With persons under 18 961
  - With persons over 65 457
  - Family households 1,750
  - Single-person households 441
- Persons per household 2.76
- Persons per family 3.18

Labor & Employment
- Total civilian labor force, 2006** ... 4,021
  - Unemployment rate 4.2%
- Total civilian labor force, 2000 3,536
  - Unemployment rate 4.0%

Employed persons 16 years and over by occupation, 2000
- Managers & professionals 1,259
- Service occupations 476
- Sales & office occupations 882
- Farming, fishing & forestry 9
- Construction & maintenance 366
- Production & transportation 403
- Self-employed persons 363

* US Census Bureau
** New Jersey Department of Labor

See Introduction for an explanation of all data sources.

General Information
Township of Mansfield
100 Port Murray Rd
Port Murray, NJ 07865
908-689-6151
Website ..... www.mansfieldtownship-nj.gov
Year of incorporation 1754
Land/water area (sq. miles) 29.92/0.02
Form of government .... Township

Government
Legislative Districts
- US Congressional 5
- State Legislative 23

Local Officials, 2008
- Mayor .... George Baldwin
- Manager .... Charles Lee
- Clerk .... Dena Hrebenak
- Finance Dir .... Andrew Coppola
- Tax Assessor .... William Merdinger
- Tax Collector .... Carrie Rochelle
- Attorney .... Charles Lee
- Building .... Charles O'Connor
- Comm Dev/Planning .... NA
- Engineering .... Douglas Mace
- Public Works .... Brent Sliker
- Police Chief .... Douglas Ort
- Fire/Emergency Dir .... NA

Housing & Construction
Housing Units, 2000*
- Total 2,415
- Median rent $731
- Median SF home value $177,200

Permits for New Residential Construction

	Units	Value
Total, 2007	6	$1,445,750
Single family	6	$1,445,750
Total, 2006	7	$1,181,700
Single family	7	$1,181,700

Real Property Valuation, 2007

	Parcels	Valuation
Total	2,928	$651,627,600
Vacant	555	13,502,500
Residential	1,810	429,716,900
Commercial	53	89,207,400
Industrial	13	16,054,300
Apartments	4	49,799,900
Farm land	313	2,751,200
Farm homestead	180	50,595,400

Average Property Value & Tax, 2007
- Residential value $241,363
- Property tax $6,708
- Tax credit/rebate $1,163

Public Library
No public municipal library

Library statistics, 2006
- Population served .... NA
- Full-time/total staff .... NA/NA

	Total	Per capita
Holdings	NA	NA
Revenues	NA	NA
Expenditures	NA	NA
Annual visits	NA	NA
Internet terminals/annual users	NA/NA	

Taxes

	2005	2006	2007
General tax rate per $100	2.54	2.76	2.78
County equalization ratio	90.49	79.75	74.67
Net valuation taxable	$641,532,820	$643,081,600	$652,961,468
State equalized value	$804,429,868	$862,644,762	$933,029,035

Public Safety
Number of officers, 2006 15

Crime

	2005	2006
Total crimes	114	132
Violent	5	9
Murder	0	0
Rape	1	1
Robbery	0	1
Aggravated assault	4	7
Non-violent	109	123
Burglary	12	20
Larceny	96	94
Vehicle theft	1	9
Domestic violence	152	174
Arson	0	2
Total crime rate	13.7	16.0
Violent	0.6	1.1
Non-violent	13.1	14.9

Public School District
(for school year 2006-07 except as noted)

Mansfield Township School District
50 Port Murray Rd
Port Murray, NJ 07865
908-689-3212

- Superintendent .... Rita Seipp
- Number of schools 1
- Grade plan K-6
- Enrollment 704
- Attendance rate, '05-06 .... 95.5%
- Dropout rate .... NA
- Students per teacher 10.7
- Per pupil expenditure $10,290
- Median faculty salary $61,110
- Median administrator salary $92,671
- Grade 12 enrollment .... NA
- High school graduation rate .... NA

Assessment test results
(percent scoring at proficient or advanced level)

	Language	Math
NJASK-Grade 3	88.3%	90.7%
GEPA-Grade 8	NA	NA
HSPA-High School	NA	NA

SAT score averages

Pct tested	Math	Verbal	Writing
NA	NA	NA	NA

Teacher Qualifications
- Avg. years of experience 10
- Highly-qualified teachers
  - one subject/all subjects 100%/100%
- With emergency credentials 0.0%

No Child Left Behind
AYP, 2005-06 .... Meets Standards

Municipal Finance
State Aid Programs, 2008
- Total aid $1,098,886
  - CMPTRA 81,166
  - Energy tax receipts 986,555
  - Garden State Trust 31,165

General Budget, 2007
- Total tax levy $18,146,544
  - County levy 5,344,694
    - County taxes 4,363,317
    - County library 455,653
    - County health 0
    - County open space 525,723
  - School levy 10,486,633
  - Muni. levy 2,315,217
- Misc. revenues 3,446,811

Mantoloking Borough
Ocean County

Demographics & Socio-Economic Characteristics
(2000 US Census, except as noted)

Population
1980*	433
1990*	334
2000	423
Male	208
Female	215
2006 (estimate)*	451
Population density	1,025.0

Race & Hispanic Origin, 2000
Race
- White ... 413
- Black/African American ... 7
- American Indian/Alaska Native ... 0
- Asian ... 2
- Native Hawaiian/Pacific Islander ... 0
- Other race ... 1
- Two or more races ... 0

Hispanic origin, total ... 3
- Mexican ... 0
- Puerto Rican ... 0
- Cuban ... 0
- Other Hispanic ... 3

Age & Nativity, 2000
- Under 5 years ... 9
- 18 years and over ... 380
- 21 years and over ... 372
- 65 years and over ... 153
- 85 years and over ... 12
- Median age ... 58.0
- Native-born ... 345
- Foreign-born ... 24

Educational Attainment, 2000
- Population 25 years and over ... 322
- Less than 9th grade ... 0.0%
- High school grad or higher ... 99.1%
- Bachelor's degree or higher ... 59.9%
- Graduate degree ... 20.5%

Income & Poverty, 1999
- Per capita income ... $114,017
- Median household income ... $105,841
- Median family income ... $125,000
- Persons in poverty ... 3
- H'holds receiving public assistance ... 0
- H'holds receiving social security ... 104

Households, 2000
- Total households ... 207
- With persons under 18 ... 25
- With persons over 65 ... 111
- Family households ... 141
- Single-person households ... 63
- Persons per household ... 2.02
- Persons per family ... 2.45

Labor & Employment
- Total civilian labor force, 2006** ... 138
- Unemployment rate ... 0.0%
- Total civilian labor force, 2000 ... 137
- Unemployment rate ... 0.0%

Employed persons 16 years and over by occupation, 2000
- Managers & professionals ... 89
- Service occupations ... 0
- Sales & office occupations ... 39
- Farming, fishing & forestry ... 0
- Construction & maintenance ... 7
- Production & transportation ... 2
- Self-employed persons ... 25

* US Census Bureau
** New Jersey Department of Labor

General Information
Borough of Mantoloking
PO Box 247
Mantoloking, NJ 08738
732-899-6600

- Website ... www.mantoloking.org
- Year of incorporation ... 1911
- Land/water area (sq. miles) ... 0.44/0.22
- Form of government ... Borough

Government
Legislative Districts
- US Congressional ... 4
- State Legislative ... 10

Local Officials, 2008
- Mayor ... George Nebel
- Manager ... Irene Ryan
- Clerk ... Irene Ryan
- Finance Dir ... Michelle Swisher
- Tax Assessor ... James Anderson
- Tax Collector ... Michelle A. Swisher
- Attorney ... Edwin O'Malley Jr
- Building ... John Wardell
- Planning ... Russell Henshaw
- Engineering ... Thomas Guldin
- Public Works ... William Heckman
- Police Chief ... Mark Wright
- Emerg/Fire Director ... Douglas Popaca

Housing & Construction
Housing Units, 2000*
- Total ... 522
- Median rent ... $2,001
- Median SF home value ... $761,000

Permits for New Residential Construction
	Units	Value
Total, 2007	2	$1,920,000
Single family	2	$1,920,000
Total, 2006	1	$1,045,700
Single family	1	$1,045,700

Real Property Valuation, 2007
	Parcels	Valuation
Total	562	$982,719,100
Vacant	39	26,479,000
Residential	518	947,125,700
Commercial	5	9,114,400
Industrial	0	0
Apartments	0	0
Farm land	0	0
Farm homestead	0	0

Average Property Value & Tax, 2007
- Residential value ... $1,828,428
- Property tax ... $13,405
- Tax credit/rebate ... $1,179

Public Library
No public municipal library

Library statistics, 2006
- Population served ... NA
- Full-time/total staff ... NA/NA

	Total	Per capita
Holdings	NA	NA
Revenues	NA	NA
Expenditures	NA	NA
Annual visits	NA	NA
Internet terminals/annual users	NA/NA	

Taxes
	2005	2006	2007
General tax rate per $100	0.713	0.737	0.734
County equalization ratio	79.16	69.87	66.27
Net valuation taxable	$958,311,859	$975,442,800	$982,825,086
State equalized value	$1,371,564,132	$1,472,030,176	$1,587,953,942

Public Safety
Number of officers, 2006 ... 7

Crime
	2005	2006
Total crimes	13	15
Violent	0	0
Murder	0	0
Rape	0	0
Robbery	0	0
Aggravated assault	0	0
Non-violent	13	15
Burglary	1	2
Larceny	12	13
Vehicle theft	0	0
Domestic violence	1	1
Arson	0	0
Total crime rate	28.8	33.3
Violent	0.0	0.0
Non-violent	28.8	33.3

Public School District
(for school year 2006-07 except as noted)

Mantoloking School District
PO Box 881
Mantoloking, NJ 08738

No schools in district - sends students to Point Pleasant Beach schools

- Per pupil expenditure ... NA
- Median faculty salary ... NA
- Median administrator salary ... NA
- Grade 12 enrollment ... NA
- High school graduation rate ... NA

Assessment test results
(percent scoring at proficient or advanced level)

	Language	Math
NJASK-Grade 3	NA	NA
GEPA-Grade 8	NA	NA
HSPA-High School	NA	NA

SAT score averages
Pct tested	Math	Verbal	Writing
NA	NA	NA	NA

Teacher Qualifications
- Avg. years of experience ... NA
- Highly-qualified teachers one subject/all subjects ... NA/NA
- With emergency credentials ... NA

No Child Left Behind
- AYP, 2005-06 ... NA

Municipal Finance
State Aid Programs, 2008
- Total aid ... $156,520
- CMPTRA ... 0
- Energy tax receipts ... 156,520
- Garden State Trust ... 0

General Budget, 2007
- Total tax levy ... $7,205,294
- County levy ... 4,605,238
- County taxes ... 3,794,947
- County library ... 449,751
- County health ... 182,214
- County open space ... 178,326
- School levy ... 88,290
- Muni. levy ... 2,511,766
- Misc. revenues ... 1,141,454

Gloucester County
Mantua Township

Demographics & Socio-Economic Characteristics
(2000 US Census, except as noted)

Population
1980*	9,193
1990*	10,074
2000	14,217
Male	6,964
Female	7,253
2006 (estimate)*	14,974
Population density	941.8

Race & Hispanic Origin, 2000
Race
White	13,622
Black/African American	294
American Indian/Alaska Native	28
Asian	122
Native Hawaiian/Pacific Islander	0
Other race	40
Two or more races	111
Hispanic origin, total	179
Mexican	19
Puerto Rican	81
Cuban	12
Other Hispanic	67

Age & Nativity, 2000
Under 5 years	1,131
18 years and over	10,423
21 years and over	9,986
65 years and over	1,582
85 years and over	101
Median age	36.3
Native-born	13,784
Foreign-born	433

Educational Attainment, 2000
Population 25 years and over	9,517
Less than 9th grade	3.0%
High school grad or higher	85.7%
Bachelor's degree or higher	23.5%
Graduate degree	6.7%

Income & Poverty, 1999
Per capita income	$24,147
Median household income	$58,256
Median family income	$63,391
Persons in poverty	510
H'holds receiving public assistance	68
H'holds receiving social security	1,326

Households, 2000
Total households	5,265
With persons under 18	2,104
With persons over 65	1,145
Family households	3,947
Single-person households	1,111
Persons per household	2.69
Persons per family	3.14

Labor & Employment
Total civilian labor force, 2006**	9,401
Unemployment rate	5.1%
Total civilian labor force, 2000	7,934
Unemployment rate	4.5%

Employed persons 16 years and over by occupation, 2000
Managers & professionals	2,679
Service occupations	954
Sales & office occupations	2,230
Farming, fishing & forestry	15
Construction & maintenance	770
Production & transportation	926
Self-employed persons	362

‡ Main library for county
* US Census Bureau
** New Jersey Department of Labor

See Introduction for an explanation of all data sources.

General Information
Mantua Township
401 Main St
Mantua, NJ 08051
856-468-1500

Website	www.mantuatownship.com
Year of incorporation	1853
Land/water area (sq. miles)	15.90/0.01
Form of government	Township

Government
Legislative Districts
US Congressional	1, 2
State Legislative	3

Local Officials, 2008
Mayor	Timothy Chell
Township Admin	Michael Datz
Clerk	Shawn Menzies
Finance Dir	Gayle Tschopp
Tax Assessor	Sandra Elliot
Tax Collector	Lois Demure
Attorney	Michael Angelini
Building	James Gallagher
Planner	Timothy Kernan
Engineering	Jon Bryson
Public Works	Michael Datz
Police Chief	Graham Land
Emerg/Fire Director	(fire district)

Housing & Construction
Housing Units, 2000*
Total	5,411
Median rent	$656
Median SF home value	$123,200

Permits for New Residential Construction
	Units	Value
Total, 2007	2	$1,183,615
Single family	2	$1,183,615
Total, 2006	33	$6,916,788
Single family	13	$5,087,788

Real Property Valuation, 2007
	Parcels	Valuation
Total	6,100	$733,534,000
Vacant	540	16,885,400
Residential	5,121	617,292,200
Commercial	162	74,808,500
Industrial	7	7,217,800
Apartments	5	1,914,100
Farm land	176	1,325,000
Farm homestead	89	14,091,000

Average Property Value & Tax, 2007
Residential value	$121,187
Property tax	$5,501
Tax credit/rebate	$980

Public Library
Gloucester County Library‡
389 Wolfert Station Rd
Mullica Hill, NJ 08062
856-223-6000

Director: Robert S. Wetheral

County Library statistics, 2006
Population served	93,711
Full-time/total staff	11/41

	Total	Per capita
Holdings	212,851	2.27
Revenues	$4,021,551	$42.91
Expenditures	$3,762,771	$40.15
Annual visits	487,253	5.20
Internet terminals/annual users	67/73,356	

Public Safety
Number of officers, 2006: 28

Crime	2005	2006
Total crimes	331	324
Violent	11	31
Murder	0	0
Rape	1	6
Robbery	3	7
Aggravated assault	7	18
Non-violent	320	293
Burglary	51	60
Larceny	258	222
Vehicle theft	11	11
Domestic violence	203	196
Arson	2	6
Total crime rate	23.2	21.8
Violent	0.8	2.1
Non-violent	22.4	19.7

Public School District
(for school year 2006-07 except as noted)

Mantua Township School District
684 Main St, Simmerman Admin Bldg
Sewell, NJ 08080
856-468-2225

Superintendent	Steven Crispin
Number of schools	3
Grade plan	K-6
Enrollment	1,590
Attendance rate, '05-06	96.0%
Dropout rate	NA
Students per teacher	12.8
Per pupil expenditure	$9,966
Median faculty salary	$47,090
Median administrator salary	$94,593
Grade 12 enrollment	NA
High school graduation rate	NA

Assessment test results
(percent scoring at proficient or advanced level)
	Language	Math
NJASK-Grade 3	91.6%	93.3%
GEPA-Grade 8	NA	NA
HSPA-High School	NA	NA

SAT score averages
Pct tested	Math	Verbal	Writing
NA	NA	NA	NA

Teacher Qualifications
Avg. years of experience	12
Highly-qualified teachers one subject/all subjects	100%/100%
With emergency credentials	0.0%

No Child Left Behind
AYP, 2005-06: Meets Standards

Municipal Finance
State Aid Programs, 2008
Total aid	$1,564,984
CMPTRA	245,471
Energy tax receipts	1,319,513
Garden State Trust	0

General Budget, 2007
Total tax levy	$33,403,536
County levy	7,921,598
County taxes	6,822,362
County library	565,076
County health	0
County open space	534,159
School levy	19,582,974
Muni. levy	5,898,965
Misc. revenues	6,745,811

Taxes
	2005	2006	2007
General tax rate per $100	4.127	4.419	4.539
County equalization ratio	70.36	61.51	55.09
Net valuation taxable	$705,190,601	$714,706,500	$735,939,109
State equalized value	$1,146,464,967	$1,300,000,719	$1,446,085,487

Manville Borough
Somerset County

Demographics & Socio-Economic Characteristics
(2000 US Census, except as noted)

Population
1980*	11,278
1990*	10,567
2000	10,343
Male	5,072
Female	5,271
2006 (estimate)*	10,481
Population density	4,226.2

Race & Hispanic Origin, 2000
Race
White	9,928
Black/African American	47
American Indian/Alaska Native	7
Asian	136
Native Hawaiian/Pacific Islander	3
Other race	118
Two or more races	104
Hispanic origin, total	559
Mexican	46
Puerto Rican	121
Cuban	7
Other Hispanic	385

Age & Nativity, 2000
Under 5 years	516
18 years and over	8,203
21 years and over	7,905
65 years and over	1,826
85 years and over	143
Median age	39.5
Native-born	8,917
Foreign-born	1,390

Educational Attainment, 2000
Population 25 years and over	7,425
Less than 9th grade	8.3%
High school grad or higher	78.2%
Bachelor's degree or higher	13.7%
Graduate degree	3.7%

Income & Poverty, 1999
Per capita income	$23,293
Median household income	$51,258
Median family income	$61,151
Persons in poverty	394
H'holds receiving public assistance	88
H'holds receiving social security	1,386

Households, 2000
Total households	4,115
With persons under 18	1,209
With persons over 65	1,375
Family households	2,758
Single-person households	1,100
Persons per household	2.51
Persons per family	3.05

Labor & Employment
Total civilian labor force, 2006**	6,237
Unemployment rate	3.7%
Total civilian labor force, 2000	5,509
Unemployment rate	3.2%

Employed persons 16 years and over by occupation, 2000
Managers & professionals	1,369
Service occupations	788
Sales & office occupations	1,639
Farming, fishing & forestry	12
Construction & maintenance	646
Production & transportation	880
Self-employed persons	246

* US Census Bureau
** New Jersey Department of Labor

General Information
Borough of Manville
325 N Main St
Manville, NJ 08835
908-725-9478

Website	www.manvillenj.org
Year of incorporation	1929
Land/water area (sq. miles)	2.48/0.00
Form of government	Borough

Government
Legislative Districts
US Congressional	7
State Legislative	16

Local Officials, 2008
Mayor	Lillian M. Zuza
Manager	Gary Garwacke
Clerk	Philip Petrone
Finance Dir	Lori Majeski
Tax Assessor	Glenn Stives
Tax Collector	Lisa Gerickont
Attorney	Francis P. Linnus
Building	John Tamburini
Comm Dev/Planning	NA
Engineering	Gary Garwacke
Public Works	Philip Petrone
Police Chief	Mark Peltack
Emerg/Fire Director	Tom Collins

Housing & Construction
Housing Units, 2000*
Total	4,296
Median rent	$789
Median SF home value	$146,200

Permits for New Residential Construction
	Units	Value
Total, 2007	8	$1,009,076
Single family	5	$709,076
Total, 2006	8	$1,156,300
Single family	8	$1,156,300

Real Property Valuation, 2007
	Parcels	Valuation
Total	3,549	$1,155,249,700
Vacant	119	9,652,900
Residential	3,233	981,541,100
Commercial	146	113,509,400
Industrial	31	37,093,200
Apartments	20	13,453,100
Farm land	0	0
Farm homestead	0	0

Average Property Value & Tax, 2007
Residential value	$303,601
Property tax	$5,759
Tax credit/rebate	$1,044

Public Library
Manville Public Library
100 S Tenth Ave
Manville, NJ 08835
908-722-9722

Director..............Edward R. Smith

Library statistics, 2006
Population served	10,343
Full-time/total staff	1/4

	Total	Per capita
Holdings	51,562	4.99
Revenues	$343,690	$33.23
Expenditures	$400,809	$38.75
Annual visits	35,000	3.38
Internet terminals/annual users	6/11,648	

Taxes
	2005	2006	2007
General tax rate per $100	3.56	1.77	1.9
County equalization ratio	62.13	122.37	106.57
Net valuation taxable	$532,272,883	$1,158,783,200	$1,156,211,776
State equalized value	$945,422,528	$1,088,287,882	$1,150,006,934

Public Safety
Number of officers, 2006..............22

Crime	2005	2006
Total crimes	265	218
Violent	8	11
Murder	1	0
Rape	0	0
Robbery	3	2
Aggravated assault	4	9
Non-violent	257	207
Burglary	15	17
Larceny	219	164
Vehicle theft	23	26
Domestic violence	85	94
Arson	1	1
Total crime rate	25.4	21.0
Violent	0.8	1.1
Non-violent	24.7	19.9

Public School District
(for school year 2006-07 except as noted)

Manville Borough School District
410 Brooks Blvd
Manville, NJ 08835
908-231-8545

Superintendent	Donald J. Burkhardt
Number of schools	4
Grade plan	K-12
Enrollment	1,332
Attendance rate, '05-06	95.2%
Dropout rate	1.2%
Students per teacher	10.9
Per pupil expenditure	$11,790
Median faculty salary	$48,030
Median administrator salary	$106,169
Grade 12 enrollment	76
High school graduation rate	92.3%

Assessment test results
(percent scoring at proficient or advanced level)
	Language	Math
NJASK-Grade 3	78.2%	85.2%
GEPA-Grade 8	72.9%	64.5%
HSPA-High School	81.2%	65.7%

SAT score averages
Pct tested	Math	Verbal	Writing
72%	475	469	467

Teacher Qualifications
Avg. years of experience	6
Highly-qualified teachers one subject/all subjects	99.0%/99.0%
With emergency credentials	0.0%

No Child Left Behind
AYP, 2005-06.............Meets Standards

Municipal Finance
State Aid Programs, 2008
Total aid	$2,030,890
CMPTRA	1,341,175
Energy tax receipts	689,704
Garden State Trust	11

General Budget, 2007
Total tax levy	$21,930,433
County levy	3,349,892
County taxes	3,019,021
County library	0
County health	0
County open space	330,871
School levy	11,719,841
Muni. levy	6,860,701
Misc. revenues	6,459,922

Burlington County
Maple Shade Township

Demographics & Socio-Economic Characteristics
(2000 US Census, except as noted)

Population
1980*	20,525
1990*	19,211
2000	19,079
Male	9,339
Female	9,740
2006 (estimate)*	19,541
Population density	5,075.6

Race & Hispanic Origin, 2000
Race
White	15,868
Black/African American	1,376
American Indian/Alaska Native	30
Asian	1,164
Native Hawaiian/Pacific Islander	8
Other race	323
Two or more races	310
Hispanic origin, total	850
Mexican	154
Puerto Rican	446
Cuban	19
Other Hispanic	231

Age & Nativity, 2000
Under 5 years	1,072
18 years and over	15,382
21 years and over	14,835
65 years and over	2,930
85 years and over	315
Median age	36.5
Native-born	17,349
Foreign-born	1,730

Educational Attainment, 2000
Population 25 years and over	13,711
Less than 9th grade	4.6%
High school grad or higher	82.3%
Bachelor's degree or higher	21.4%
Graduate degree	7.1%

Income & Poverty, 1999
Per capita income	$23,812
Median household income	$45,426
Median family income	$53,912
Persons in poverty	1,009
H'holds receiving public assistance	120
H'holds receiving social security	2,125

Households, 2000
Total households	8,462
With persons under 18	2,207
With persons over 65	2,103
Family households	4,718
Single-person households	3,047
Persons per household	2.22
Persons per family	2.95

Labor & Employment
Total civilian labor force, 2006**	12,473
Unemployment rate	3.9%
Total civilian labor force, 2000	10,723
Unemployment rate	3.6%

Employed persons 16 years and over by occupation, 2000
Managers & professionals	3,403
Service occupations	1,462
Sales & office occupations	2,965
Farming, fishing & forestry	5
Construction & maintenance	909
Production & transportation	1,598
Self-employed persons	454

‡ Branch of county library
* US Census Bureau
** New Jersey Department of Labor

See Introduction for an explanation of all data sources.

General Information
Township of Maple Shade
200 N Stiles Ave
Maple Shade, NJ 08052
856-779-9610

Website	www.mapleshade.com
Year of incorporation	1945
Land/water area (sq. miles)	3.85/0.00
Form of government	Council-Manager

Government
Legislative Districts
US Congressional	1
State Legislative	7

Local Officials, 2008
Mayor	Louis A. Manchello
Manager	George Haeuber
Clerk	Andrea T. DeGolia
Finance Dir	Adriane McKendry
Tax Assessor	Karen McMahon
Tax Collector	Denise Lawler
Attorney	Eileen Fahey
Building	Ronald Bannon
Comm Dev/Planning	Rosemary Flaherty
Engineering	Jim Rudderman
Public Works	Jim Christy
Police Chief	Edmund Vernier
Emerg/Fire Director	William Riess

Housing & Construction
Housing Units, 2000*
Total	9,009
Median rent	$767
Median SF home value	$107,900

Permits for New Residential Construction
	Units	Value
Total, 2007	68	$3,863,085
Single family	10	$973,184
Total, 2006	77	$4,226,104
Single family	8	$794,976

Real Property Valuation, 2007
	Parcels	Valuation
Total	5,094	$1,590,686,100
Vacant	107	13,704,900
Residential	4,673	950,167,700
Commercial	268	337,908,500
Industrial	28	23,405,000
Apartments	18	265,500,000
Farm land	0	0
Farm homestead	0	0

Average Property Value & Tax, 2007
Residential value	$203,331
Property tax	$4,342
Tax credit/rebate	$915

Public Library
Maple Shade Branch Library‡
200 Stiles Ave
Maple Shade, NJ 08052
856-779-9767

Director .... Michael Bennett

Library statistics, 2006
see Burlington County profile for library system statistics

Public Safety
Number of officers, 2006 35

Crime
	2005	2006
Total crimes	459	496
Violent	38	35
Murder	1	0
Rape	3	6
Robbery	16	10
Aggravated assault	18	19
Non-violent	421	461
Burglary	115	84
Larceny	266	327
Vehicle theft	40	50
Domestic violence	106	136
Arson	2	2
Total crime rate	23.7	25.4
Violent	2.0	1.8
Non-violent	21.8	23.6

Public School District
(for school year 2006-07 except as noted)

Maple Shade Township School District
170 Frederick Ave.
Maple Shade, NJ 08052
856-779-1750

Superintendent	Cheryl L. Smith
Number of schools	4
Grade plan	K-12
Enrollment	2,084
Attendance rate, '05-06	93.4%
Dropout rate	1.0%
Students per teacher	11.4
Per pupil expenditure	$11,993
Median faculty salary	$51,454
Median administrator salary	$100,834
Grade 12 enrollment	142
High school graduation rate	96.6%

Assessment test results
(percent scoring at proficient or advanced level)
	Language	Math
NJASK-Grade 3	85.5%	92.3%
GEPA-Grade 8	64.1%	77.7%
HSPA-High School	84.7%	65.0%

SAT score averages
Pct tested	Math	Verbal	Writing
69%	469	450	456

Teacher Qualifications
Avg. years of experience	11
Highly-qualified teachers one subject/all subjects	99.5%/98.5%
With emergency credentials	0.0%

No Child Left Behind
AYP, 2005-06 .... Meets Standards

Municipal Finance
State Aid Programs, 2008
Total aid	$2,192,984
CMPTRA	671,715
Energy tax receipts	1,521,269
Garden State Trust	0

General Budget, 2007
Total tax levy	$34,011,107
County levy	6,196,451
County taxes	5,134,347
County library	471,241
County health	0
County open space	590,863
School levy	20,431,346
Muni. levy	7,383,310
Misc. revenues	5,069,090

Taxes
	2005	2006	2007
General tax rate per $100	3.748	2.007	2.14
County equalization ratio	72.55	124.2	107.18
Net valuation taxable	$822,970,817	$1,603,195,500	$1,592,773,167
State equalized value	$1,289,720,760	$1,497,825,632	$1,606,733,592

The New Jersey Municipal Data Book

©2008 Information Publications, Inc. All rights reserved. Photocopying prohibited. For additional copies, contact the publisher at www.informationpublications.com or (877)544-INFO (4636)

Maplewood Township

Essex County

Demographics & Socio-Economic Characteristics
(2000 US Census, except as noted)

Population
1980*	22,950
1990*	21,652
2000	23,868
Male	11,347
Female	12,521
2006 (estimate)*	22,759
Population density	5,911.4

Race & Hispanic Origin, 2000
Race
White	14,030
Black/African American	7,788
American Indian/Alaska Native	31
Asian	682
Native Hawaiian/Pacific Islander	7
Other race	373
Two or more races	957
Hispanic origin, total	1,248
Mexican	69
Puerto Rican	438
Cuban	97
Other Hispanic	644

Age & Nativity, 2000
Under 5 years	1,882
18 years and over	17,175
21 years and over	16,560
65 years and over	2,890
85 years and over	505
Median age	37.7
Native-born	19,614
Foreign-born	4,254

Educational Attainment, 2000
Population 25 years and over	15,987
Less than 9th grade	2.5%
High school grad or higher	91.9%
Bachelor's degree or higher	50.8%
Graduate degree	22.0%

Income & Poverty, 1999
Per capita income	$36,794
Median household income	$79,637
Median family income	$92,724
Persons in poverty	1,049
H'holds receiving public assistance	77
H'holds receiving social security	1,896

Households, 2000
Total households	8,452
With persons under 18	3,646
With persons over 65	2,136
Family households	6,379
Single-person households	1,720
Persons per household	2.81
Persons per family	3.27

Labor & Employment
Total civilian labor force, 2006**	13,593
Unemployment rate	4.2%
Total civilian labor force, 2000	12,848
Unemployment rate	3.9%

Employed persons 16 years and over by occupation, 2000
Managers & professionals	6,478
Service occupations	1,124
Sales & office occupations	3,263
Farming, fishing & forestry	0
Construction & maintenance	604
Production & transportation	883
Self-employed persons	823

* US Census Bureau
** New Jersey Department of Labor

General Information
Township of Maplewood
574 Valley St
Maplewood, NJ 07040
973-762-8120

Website	www.twp.maplewood.nj.us
Year of incorporation	1922
Land/water area (sq. miles)	3.85/0.00
Form of government	Township

Government
Legislative Districts
US Congressional	10
State Legislative	27

Local Officials, 2008
Mayor	Kenneth A. Pettis
Manager	Joseph Manning
Clerk	Elizabeth Fritzen
Finance Dir	Peter Fresulone
Tax Assessor	Edward Galante
Tax Collector	Peter Fresulone
Attorney	Roger Desiderio
Building	Robert Mittermaier
Comm Dev/Planning	NA
Engineering	Richard Calbi Jr
Public Works	Gary Lenci
Police Chief	Robert Cimino
Emerg/Fire Director	Dennis Carragher

Housing & Construction
Housing Units, 2000*
Total	8,615
Median rent	$950
Median SF home value	$222,700

Permits for New Residential Construction
	Units	Value
Total, 2007	14	$1,244,764
Single family	2	$278,864
Total, 2006	7	$580,679
Single family	2	$197,729

Real Property Valuation, 2007
	Parcels	Valuation
Total	7,264	$2,054,041,300
Vacant	41	4,189,600
Residential	6,872	1,841,838,200
Commercial	306	183,645,800
Industrial	33	13,710,500
Apartments	12	10,657,200
Farm land	0	0
Farm homestead	0	0

Average Property Value & Tax, 2007
Residential value	$268,021
Property tax	$11,319
Tax credit/rebate	$1,276

Public Library
Maplewood Memorial Library
51 Baker St
Maplewood, NJ 07040
973-762-1622

Director . . . . Jane E. Kennedy

Library statistics, 2006
Population served	23,868
Full-time/total staff	6/12

	Total	Per capita
Holdings	139,440	5.84
Revenues	$1,834,267	$76.85
Expenditures	$1,749,847	$73.31
Annual visits	295,382	12.38
Internet terminals/annual users	42/43,876	

Public Safety
Number of officers, 2006 66

Crime	2005	2006
Total crimes	779	598
Violent	85	67
Murder	0	0
Rape	2	3
Robbery	47	30
Aggravated assault	36	34
Non-violent	694	531
Burglary	87	74
Larceny	472	357
Vehicle theft	135	100
Domestic violence	70	52
Arson	16	3
Total crime rate	33.2	25.9
Violent	3.6	2.9
Non-violent	29.6	23.0

Public School District
(for school year 2006-07 except as noted)

South Orange-Maplewood School District
525 Academy St
Maplewood, NJ 07040
973-762-5600

Superintendent	Brian G. Osborne
Number of schools	18
Grade plan	K-12
Enrollment	6,087
Attendance rate, '05-06	95.1%
Dropout rate	0.5%
Students per teacher	11.1
Per pupil expenditure	$14,170
Median faculty salary	$55,758
Median administrator salary	$115,316
Grade 12 enrollment	454
High school graduation rate	95.8%

Assessment test results
(percent scoring at proficient or advanced level)
	Language	Math
NJASK-Grade 3	87.0%	90.5%
GEPA-Grade 8	75.4%	69.8%
HSPA-High School	89.2%	77.7%

SAT score averages
Pct tested	Math	Verbal	Writing
97%	513	500	503

Teacher Qualifications
Avg. years of experience	8
Highly-qualified teachers one subject/all subjects	100%/100%
With emergency credentials	0.5%

No Child Left Behind
AYP, 2005-06 . . . . Needs Improvement

Municipal Finance
State Aid Programs, 2008
Total aid	$2,353,375
CMPTRA	720,783
Energy tax receipts	1,632,592
Garden State Trust	0

General Budget, 2007
Total tax levy	$86,785,503
County levy	14,057,966
County taxes	13,696,762
County library	0
County health	0
County open space	361,204
School levy	50,248,738
Muni. levy	22,478,798
Misc. revenues	11,160,436

Taxes
	2005	2006	2007
General tax rate per $100	3.79	3.98	4.23
County equalization ratio	74.7	66.38	57.58
Net valuation taxable	$2,047,664,500	$2,047,983,000	$2,055,054,000
State equalized value	$3,084,761,223	$3,557,974,028	$3,792,155,742

Atlantic County | Margate City

Demographics & Socio-Economic Characteristics
(2000 US Census, except as noted)

Population
1980*	9,179
1990*	8,431
2000	8,193
Male	3,861
Female	4,332
2006 (estimate)*	8,601
Population density	6,100.0

Race & Hispanic Origin, 2000
Race
White	7,843
Black/African American	71
American Indian/Alaska Native	2
Asian	128
Native Hawaiian/Pacific Islander	6
Other race	75
Two or more races	68
Hispanic origin, total	222
Mexican	39
Puerto Rican	74
Cuban	13
Other Hispanic	96

Age & Nativity, 2000
Under 5 years	298
18 years and over	6,935
21 years and over	6,800
65 years and over	2,365
85 years and over	255
Median age	49.8
Native-born	7,586
Foreign-born	607

Educational Attainment, 2000
Population 25 years and over	6,668
Less than 9th grade	2.0%
High school grad or higher	88.3%
Bachelor's degree or higher	36.5%
Graduate degree	13.4%

Income & Poverty, 1999
Per capita income	$33,566
Median household income	$45,876
Median family income	$63,917
Persons in poverty	594
H'holds receiving public assistance	47
H'holds receiving social security	1,734

Households, 2000
Total households	3,984
With persons under 18	725
With persons over 65	1,707
Family households	2,303
Single-person households	1,440
Persons per household	2.06
Persons per family	2.67

Labor & Employment
Total civilian labor force, 2006**	4,366
Unemployment rate	5.1%
Total civilian labor force, 2000	3,981
Unemployment rate	5.6%

Employed persons 16 years and over by occupation, 2000
Managers & professionals	1,415
Service occupations	783
Sales & office occupations	1,198
Farming, fishing & forestry	0
Construction & maintenance	220
Production & transportation	142
Self-employed persons	361

* US Census Bureau
** New Jersey Department of Labor

See Introduction for an explanation of all data sources.

General Information
City of Margate
1 S Washington Ave
Margate City, NJ 08402
609-822-2605

Website	www.margate-nj.com
Year of incorporation	1909
Land/water area (sq. miles)	1.41/0.18
Form of government	Commission

Government
Legislative Districts
US Congressional	2
State Legislative	2

Local Officials, 2008
Mayor	Michael S. Becker
Manager/Admin	NA
Clerk	Thomas Hiltner
Finance Dir	Charles F. Beirne
Tax Assessor	Andy Bednarek
Tax Collector	Thomas D. Hiltner
Attorney	Mary Siracusa
Building	Jim Galantino
Comm Dev/Planning	NA
Engineering	Remington & Vernick
Public Works	Frank Ricciotti
Police Chief	David Wolfson
Emerg/Fire Director	John Kelley

Housing & Construction
Housing Units, 2000*
Total	7,006
Median rent	$739
Median SF home value	$189,300

Permits for New Residential Construction
	Units	Value
Total, 2007	49	$16,579,935
Single family	31	$12,481,533
Total, 2006	97	$21,605,521
Single family	54	$16,540,135

Real Property Valuation, 2007
	Parcels	Valuation
Total	6,903	$3,360,431,100
Vacant	236	60,952,800
Residential	6,471	3,202,948,900
Commercial	185	88,380,100
Industrial	0	0
Apartments	11	8,149,300
Farm land	0	0
Farm homestead	0	0

Average Property Value & Tax, 2007
Residential value	$494,970
Property tax	$5,837
Tax credit/rebate	$1,036

Public Library
Margate City Public Library
8100 Atlantic Ave
Margate, NJ 08402
609-822-4700

Director: James J. Cahill

Library statistics, 2006
Population served	8,193
Full-time/total staff	2/5

	Total	Per capita
Holdings	51,863	6.33
Revenues	$906,510	$110.64
Expenditures	$875,453	$106.85
Annual visits	113,120	13.81
Internet terminals/annual users	11/18,735	

Taxes
	2005	2006	2007
General tax rate per $100	1.124	1.204	1.18
County equalization ratio	127	102.56	88.06
Net valuation taxable	$3,274,070,521	$3,307,881,900	$3,361,487,250
State equalized value	$3,192,346,452	$3,757,583,765	$3,981,194,845

Public Safety
Number of officers, 2006		38

Crime	2005	2006
Total crimes	138	186
Violent	7	5
Murder	0	0
Rape	1	0
Robbery	0	0
Aggravated assault	6	5
Non-violent	131	181
Burglary	34	44
Larceny	90	133
Vehicle theft	7	4
Domestic violence	66	44
Arson	1	0
Total crime rate	16.0	21.5
Violent	0.8	0.6
Non-violent	15.2	20.9

Public School District
(for school year 2006-07 except as noted)

Margate City School District
8103 Winchester Ave
Margate City, NJ 08402
609-822-1686

Superintendent	Dominick A. Potena
Number of schools	3
Grade plan	K-8
Enrollment	593
Attendance rate, '05-06	94.4%
Dropout rate	NA
Students per teacher	9.7
Per pupil expenditure	$16,194
Median faculty salary	$73,140
Median administrator salary	$98,592
Grade 12 enrollment	NA
High school graduation rate	NA

Assessment test results
(percent scoring at proficient or advanced level)
	Language	Math
NJASK-Grade 3	97.0%	100.0%
GEPA-Grade 8	84.2%	82.5%
HSPA-High School	NA	NA

SAT score averages
Pct tested	Math	Verbal	Writing
NA	NA	NA	NA

Teacher Qualifications
Avg. years of experience	14
Highly-qualified teachers one subject/all subjects	100%/100%
With emergency credentials	0.0%

No Child Left Behind
AYP, 2005-06 ... Meets Standards

Municipal Finance
State Aid Programs, 2008
Total aid	$880,623
CMPTRA	0
Energy tax receipts	880,623
Garden State Trust	0

General Budget, 2007
Total tax levy	$39,639,687
County levy	10,588,384
County taxes	9,352,245
County library	0
County health	471,814
County open space	764,325
School levy	11,656,868
Muni. levy	17,394,435
Misc. revenues	5,267,763

The New Jersey Municipal Data Book

Marlboro Township

Monmouth County

Demographics & Socio-Economic Characteristics
(2000 US Census, except as noted)

Population
- 1980* 17,560
- 1990* 27,974
- 2000 36,398
  - Male 18,048
  - Female 18,350
- 2006 (estimate)* 39,843
- Population density 1,302.5

Race & Hispanic Origin, 2000
Race
- White 30,487
- Black/African American 752
- American Indian/Alaska Native 17
- Asian 4,612
- Native Hawaiian/Pacific Islander 5
- Other race 171
- Two or more races 354
- Hispanic origin, total 1,051
  - Mexican 123
  - Puerto Rican 350
  - Cuban 107
  - Other Hispanic 471

Age & Nativity, 2000
- Under 5 years 2,723
- 18 years and over 25,409
- 21 years and over 24,466
- 65 years and over 3,207
- 85 years and over 248
  - Median age 37.6
- Native-born 30,782
- Foreign-born 5,621

Educational Attainment, 2000
- Population 25 years and over 23,453
- Less than 9th grade 2.1%
- High school grad or higher 94.0%
- Bachelor's degree or higher 52.3%
- Graduate degree 22.6%

Income & Poverty, 1999
- Per capita income $38,635
- Median household income $101,322
- Median family income $107,894
- Persons in poverty 1,256
- H'holds receiving public assistance .. 74
- H'holds receiving social security . 2,313

Households, 2000
- Total households 11,478
  - With persons under 18 5,925
  - With persons over 65 2,245
  - Family households 10,167
  - Single-person households 1,110
  - Persons per household 3.15
  - Persons per family 3.38

Labor & Employment
- Total civilian labor force, 2006** . 20,455
  - Unemployment rate 3.0%
- Total civilian labor force, 2000 .. 17,945
  - Unemployment rate 3.3%

Employed persons 16 years and over by occupation, 2000
- Managers & professionals 9,569
- Service occupations 1,095
- Sales & office occupations 4,973
- Farming, fishing & forestry 0
- Construction & maintenance 724
- Production & transportation 993
- Self-employed persons 1,059

‡ Branch of county library
* US Census Bureau
** New Jersey Department of Labor

General Information
Township of Marlboro
1979 Township Dr
Marlboro, NJ 07746
732-536-0200

- Website .... www.marlboro-nj.gov
- Year of incorporation 1848
- Land/water area (sq. miles) 30.59/0.00
- Form of government .... Mayor-Council

Government
Legislative Districts
- US Congressional 6, 12
- State Legislative 12

Local Officials, 2008
- Mayor .... Jonathan L. Hornik
- Manager .... Alayne Shepler
- Clerk .... Alida Manco
- Finance Dir .... Ulrich Steinberg
- Tax Assessor .... Walter Kosul
- Tax Collector .... Shirley Giaquinto
- Attorney .... Jonathan Williams
- Building .... Joseph Labruzza
- Comm Dev/Planning .... NA
- Engineering .... Birdsall Engineering
- Public Works .... Robert DiMarco
- Police Chief .... Robert Holmes
- Fire/Emergency Dir .... NA

Housing & Construction
Housing Units, 2000*
- Total 11,896
- Median rent $1,334
- Median SF home value $286,300

Permits for New Residential Construction

	Units	Value
Total, 2007	69	$11,374,185
Single family	51	$10,931,685
Total, 2006	71	$18,134,600
Single family	71	$18,134,600

Real Property Valuation, 2007

	Parcels	Valuation
Total	14,131	$3,127,283,350
Vacant	914	53,984,300
Residential	12,728	2,839,037,100
Commercial	222	173,463,400
Industrial	28	40,301,700
Apartments	3	3,343,100
Farm land	152	786,550
Farm homestead	84	16,367,200

Average Property Value & Tax, 2007
- Residential value $222,870
- Property tax $9,134
- Tax credit/rebate $1,217

Public Library
Marlboro Library‡
1 Library Ct
Marlboro, NJ 07746
732-536-9406

- Branch Librarian .... Jennifer King

Library statistics, 2006
see Monmouth County profile for library system statistics

Public Safety
- Number of officers, 2006 74

Crime	2005	2006
Total crimes	365	418
Violent	17	16
Murder	1	0
Rape	0	1
Robbery	6	8
Aggravated assault	10	7
Non-violent	348	402
Burglary	66	73
Larceny	269	315
Vehicle theft	13	14
Domestic violence	163	184
Arson	3	9
Total crime rate	9.2	10.5
Violent	0.4	0.4
Non-violent	8.7	10.1

Public School District
(for school year 2006-07 except as noted)

Marlboro Township School District
1980 Township Dr
Marlboro, NJ 07746
732-972-2015

- Superintendent .... David Abbott
- Number of schools 8
- Grade plan K-8
- Enrollment 6,129
- Attendance rate, '05-06 .... 95.8%
- Dropout rate .... NA
- Students per teacher 12.5
- Per pupil expenditure $11,065
- Median faculty salary $51,993
- Median administrator salary .. $114,221
- Grade 12 enrollment .... NA
- High school graduation rate .... NA

Assessment test results
(percent scoring at proficient or advanced level)

	Language	Math
NJASK-Grade 3	93.3%	95.5%
GEPA-Grade 8	89.9%	84.9%
HSPA-High School	NA	NA

SAT score averages

Pct tested	Math	Verbal	Writing
NA	NA	NA	NA

Teacher Qualifications
- Avg. years of experience 8
- Highly-qualified teachers
  - one subject/all subjects 100%/100%
- With emergency credentials 0.9%

No Child Left Behind
- AYP, 2005-06 .... Meets Standards

Municipal Finance
State Aid Programs, 2008
- Total aid $3,032,832
  - CMPTRA 427,566
  - Energy tax receipts 2,605,266
  - Garden State Trust 0

General Budget, 2007
- Total tax levy $128,335,964
  - County levy 20,087,994
    - County taxes 17,639,976
    - County library 1,009,832
    - County health 336,005
    - County open space 1,102,181
  - School levy 90,600,429
  - Muni. levy 17,647,541
  - Misc. revenues 15,581,180

Taxes	2005	2006	2007
General tax rate per $100	3.84	4.037	4.099
County equalization ratio	51.62	47.36	42.7
Net valuation taxable	$3,017,281,871	$3,076,715,950	$3,131,514,009
State equalized value	$6,370,949,897	$7,209,924,440	$7,592,882,321

Monmouth County

Matawan Borough

Demographics & Socio-Economic Characteristics
(2000 US Census, except as noted)

Population
- 1980* 8,837
- 1990* 9,270
- 2000 8,910
  - Male 4,400
  - Female 4,510
- 2006 (estimate)* 8,781
  - Population density 3,851.3

Race & Hispanic Origin, 2000
Race
- White 7,337
- Black/African American 582
- American Indian/Alaska Native 2
- Asian 712
- Native Hawaiian/Pacific Islander ... 2
- Other race 110
- Two or more races 165
- Hispanic origin, total 575
  - Mexican 112
  - Puerto Rican 242
  - Cuban 51
  - Other Hispanic 170

Age & Nativity, 2000
- Under 5 years 562
- 18 years and over 6,900
- 21 years and over 6,627
- 65 years and over 935
- 85 years and over 90
  - Median age 36.4
- Native-born 7,641
- Foreign-born 1,336

Educational Attainment, 2000
- Population 25 years and over 6,256
- Less than 9th grade 3.9%
- High school grad or higher 88.4%
- Bachelor's degree or higher 30.4%
- Graduate degree 11.5%

Income & Poverty, 1999
- Per capita income $30,320
- Median household income $63,594
- Median family income $72,183
- Persons in poverty 485
- H'holds receiving public assistance ... 46
- H'holds receiving social security ... 831

Households, 2000
- Total households 3,531
  - With persons under 18 1,153
  - With persons over 65 715
- Family households 2,375
- Single-person households 904
- Persons per household 2.52
- Persons per family 3.07

Labor & Employment
- Total civilian labor force, 2006** ... 5,285
  - Unemployment rate 4.5%
- Total civilian labor force, 2000 ... 4,928
  - Unemployment rate 4.8%

Employed persons 16 years and over by occupation, 2000
- Managers & professionals 1,970
- Service occupations 596
- Sales & office occupations 1,322
- Farming, fishing & forestry 0
- Construction & maintenance 384
- Production & transportation 418
- Self-employed persons 225

‡ Joint library with Aberdeen Township
* US Census Bureau
** New Jersey Department of Labor

See Introduction for an explanation of all data sources.

General Information
Matawan Borough
201 Broad St
Matawan, NJ 07747
732-566-3898

- Website .... www.matawanborough.com
- Year of incorporation 1895
- Land/water area (sq. miles) ... 2.28/0.12
- Form of government .... Borough

Government
Legislative Districts
- US Congressional 6
- State Legislative 13

Local Officials, 2008
- Mayor .... Paul Buccellato
- Business Admin .... Fred Carr
- Clerk .... Jean Montfort
- Finance Dir .... Monica Antista
- Tax Assessor .... Eric Zanetti
- Tax Collector .... Peggy Warren
- Attorney .... Pasquale Menna
- Building .... John Quinn
- Planning .... Bill White
- Engineering .... Bill White
- Public Works .... Anthony Bucco
- Police Chief .... Robert McGowan
- Emerg/Fire Director ...... Glenn Turner

Housing & Construction
Housing Units, 2000*
- Total 3,640
- Median rent $808
- Median SF home value $178,500

Permits for New Residential Construction

	Units	Value
Total, 2007	4	$800,000
Single family	4	$800,000
Total, 2006	3	$720,500
Single family	3	$720,500

Real Property Valuation, 2007

	Parcels	Valuation
Total	2,600	$431,812,134
Vacant	136	4,178,775
Residential	2,300	333,933,659
Commercial	139	61,175,500
Industrial	9	4,481,200
Apartments	16	28,043,000
Farm land	0	0
Farm homestead	0	0

Average Property Value & Tax, 2007
- Residential value $145,189
- Property tax $7,666
- Tax credit/rebate $1,212

Public Library
Matawan-Aberdeen Public Library‡
165 Main St
Matawan, NJ 07747
732-583-9100

- Director .... Susan Pike

Library statistics, 2006
- Population served 26,364
- Full-time/total staff 3/6

	Total	Per capita
Holdings	96,193	3.65
Revenues	$957,222	$36.31
Expenditures	$837,766	$31.78
Annual visits	104,471	3.96
Internet terminals/annual users	14/15,294	

Public Safety
Number of officers, 2006 20

Crime	2005	2006
Total crimes	147	106
Violent	17	11
Murder	0	0
Rape	1	1
Robbery	7	6
Aggravated assault	9	4
Non-violent	130	95
Burglary	14	24
Larceny	103	63
Vehicle theft	13	8
Domestic violence	92	93
Arson	0	0
Total crime rate	16.5	12.0
Violent	1.9	1.2
Non-violent	14.6	10.8

Public School District
(for school year 2006-07 except as noted)

Matawan-Aberdeen Regional School District
One Crest Way
Aberdeen, NJ 07747
732-705-4003

- Superintendent .... Richard O'Malley
- Number of schools 14
- Grade plan K-12
- Enrollment 3,889
- Attendance rate, '05-06 .... 95.0%
- Dropout rate 0.4%
- Students per teacher 10.8
- Per pupil expenditure $14,180
- Median faculty salary $58,220
- Median administrator salary ... $115,224
- Grade 12 enrollment 232
- High school graduation rate 98.2%

Assessment test results
(percent scoring at proficient or advanced level)

	Language	Math
NJASK-Grade 3	87.7%	87.5%
GEPA-Grade 8	76.4%	70.5%
HSPA-High School	90.4%	70.8%

SAT score averages

Pct tested	Math	Verbal	Writing
82%	478	469	467

Teacher Qualifications
- Avg. years of experience 9
- Highly-qualified teachers
  - one subject/all subjects ... 99.0%/99.0%
- With emergency credentials 0.0%

No Child Left Behind
AYP, 2005-06 .... Meets Standards

Municipal Finance
State Aid Programs, 2008
- Total aid $1,833,917
- CMPTRA 63,546
- Energy tax receipts 1,770,371
- Garden State Trust 0

General Budget, 2007
- Total tax levy $22,837,059
- County levy 2,636,527
  - County taxes 2,437,770
  - County library 0
  - County health 46,443
  - County open space 152,314
- School levy 14,565,929
- Muni. levy 5,634,603
- Misc. revenues 3,778,219

Taxes

	2005	2006	2007
General tax rate per $100	4.721	5.013	5.28
County equalization ratio	57.23	49.18	42.73
Net valuation taxable	$429,613,084	$429,369,234	$432,543,706
State equalized value	$873,552,428	$1,005,643,015	$1,077,033,003

Maurice River Township
Cumberland County

Demographics & Socio-Economic Characteristics
(2000 US Census, except as noted)

Population
1980*	4,577
1990*	6,648
2000	6,928
Male	5,093
Female	1,835
2006 (estimate)*	8,083
Population density	86.5

Race & Hispanic Origin, 2000
Race
White	4,062
Black/African American	2,285
American Indian/Alaska Native	54
Asian	19
Native Hawaiian/Pacific Islander	1
Other race	307
Two or more races	200
Hispanic origin, total	634
Mexican	15
Puerto Rican	404
Cuban	51
Other Hispanic	164

Age & Nativity, 2000
Under 5 years	200
18 years and over	6,036
21 years and over	5,914
65 years and over	443
85 years and over	39
Median age	36.0
Native-born	6,710
Foreign-born	218

Educational Attainment, 2000
Population 25 years and over	5,704
Less than 9th grade	7.4%
High school grad or higher	62.8%
Bachelor's degree or higher	4.7%
Graduate degree	1.1%

Income & Poverty, 1999
Per capita income	$17,141
Median household income	$43,182
Median family income	$46,987
Persons in poverty	287
H'holds receiving public assistance	26
H'holds receiving social security	394

Households, 2000
Total households	1,332
With persons under 18	483
With persons over 65	327
Family households	1,012
Single-person households	258
Persons per household	2.68
Persons per family	3.03

Labor & Employment
Total civilian labor force, 2006**	1,990
Unemployment rate	4.2%
Total civilian labor force, 2000	1,777
Unemployment rate	5.7%

Employed persons 16 years and over by occupation, 2000
Managers & professionals	385
Service occupations	345
Sales & office occupations	328
Farming, fishing & forestry	11
Construction & maintenance	228
Production & transportation	379
Self-employed persons	72

* US Census Bureau
** New Jersey Department of Labor

General Information
Township of Maurice River
590 Main St
PO Box 218
Leesburg, NJ 08327
856-785-1120

Website	www.mauricerivertwp.org
Year of incorporation	1748
Land/water area (sq. miles)	93.41/2.31
Form of government	Township

Government
Legislative Districts
US Congressional	2
State Legislative	1

Local Officials, 2008
Mayor	Ronald D. Riggins Sr
Manager/Admin	NA
Clerk	J. Roy Oliver
Finance Dir	Sharon Lloyd
Tax Assessor	Michelle Sharp
Tax Collector	J. Roy Oliver
Attorney	Edward Duffy
Building	Gordon Gross
Comm Dev/Planning	NA
Engineering	Kent Schellinger
Public Works	NA
Police Chief	NA
Fire Official	Keith Mitchell

Housing & Construction
Housing Units, 2000*
Total	1,461
Median rent	$613
Median SF home value	$84,100

Permits for New Residential Construction
	Units	Value
Total, 2007	11	$1,703,010
Single family	11	$1,703,010
Total, 2006	14	$907,484
Single family	14	$907,484

Real Property Valuation, 2007
	Parcels	Valuation
Total	3,667	$142,529,900
Vacant	2,082	9,220,200
Residential	1,409	112,727,000
Commercial	64	7,867,400
Industrial	26	7,331,800
Apartments	2	391,500
Farm land	67	1,689,200
Farm homestead	17	3,302,800

Average Property Value & Tax, 2007
Residential value	$81,367
Property tax	$3,159
Tax credit/rebate	$796

Public Library
No public municipal library

Library statistics, 2006
Population served	NA
Full-time/total staff	NA/NA

	Total	Per capita
Holdings	NA	NA
Revenues	NA	NA
Expenditures	NA	NA
Annual visits	NA	NA
Internet terminals/annual users	NA/NA	

Taxes
	2005	2006	2007
General tax rate per $100	3.329	3.633	3.886
County equalization ratio	73.47	64.19	54.75
Net valuation taxable	$139,626,797	$140,563,800	$143,170,899
State equalized value	$217,521,105	$257,471,837	$289,689,671

Public Safety
Number of officers, 2006		0

Crime	2005	2006
Total crimes	41	51
Violent	6	6
Murder	0	0
Rape	0	0
Robbery	1	0
Aggravated assault	5	6
Non-violent	35	45
Burglary	10	11
Larceny	22	29
Vehicle theft	3	5
Domestic violence	34	14
Arson	1	1
Total crime rate	5.4	6.7
Violent	0.8	0.8
Non-violent	4.6	5.9

Public School District
(for school year 2006-07 except as noted)

Maurice River Township School District
South Delsea Drive, Drawer D
Port Elizabeth, NJ 08348
856-825-7411

Superintendent	John Saporito
Number of schools	1
Grade plan	K-8
Enrollment	390
Attendance rate, '05-06	94.0%
Dropout rate	NA
Students per teacher	9.1
Per pupil expenditure	$12,477
Median faculty salary	$45,974
Median administrator salary	$100,733
Grade 12 enrollment	NA
High school graduation rate	NA

Assessment test results
(percent scoring at proficient or advanced level)
	Language	Math
NJASK-Grade 3	94.8%	100.0%
GEPA-Grade 8	82.9%	70.7%
HSPA-High School	NA	NA

SAT score averages
Pct tested	Math	Verbal	Writing
NA	NA	NA	NA

Teacher Qualifications
Avg. years of experience	11
Highly-qualified teachers one subject/all subjects	97.0%/97.0%
With emergency credentials	0.0%

No Child Left Behind
AYP, 2005-06	Meets Standards

Municipal Finance
State Aid Programs, 2008
Total aid	$1,089,927
CMPTRA	168,924
Energy tax receipts	559,469
Garden State Trust	361,534

General Budget, 2007
Total tax levy	$5,559,145
County levy	2,599,636
County taxes	2,462,587
County library	0
County health	110,697
County open space	26,351
School levy	2,519,977
Muni. levy	439,533
Misc. revenues	2,917,289

Bergen County — Maywood Borough

Demographics & Socio-Economic Characteristics
(2000 US Census, except as noted)

Population
1980*	9,895
1990*	9,473
2000	9,523
Male	4,428
Female	5,095
2006 (estimate)*	9,374
Population density	7,210.8

Race & Hispanic Origin, 2000
Race
White	8,054
Black/African American	266
American Indian/Alaska Native	7
Asian	682
Native Hawaiian/Pacific Islander	1
Other race	315
Two or more races	198
Hispanic origin, total	1,115
Mexican	27
Puerto Rican	301
Cuban	106
Other Hispanic	681

Age & Nativity, 2000
Under 5 years	618
18 years and over	7,514
21 years and over	7,262
65 years and over	1,670
85 years and over	263
Median age	40.2
Native-born	7,728
Foreign-born	1,795

Educational Attainment, 2000
Population 25 years and over	7,053
Less than 9th grade	4.0%
High school grad or higher	87.6%
Bachelor's degree or higher	31.2%
Graduate degree	10.1%

Income & Poverty, 1999
Per capita income	$28,117
Median household income	$62,113
Median family income	$73,419
Persons in poverty	311
H'holds receiving public assistance	58
H'holds receiving social security	1,273

Households, 2000
Total households	3,710
With persons under 18	1,161
With persons over 65	1,239
Family households	2,626
Single-person households	923
Persons per household	2.56
Persons per family	3.09

Labor & Employment
Total civilian labor force, 2006**	5,422
Unemployment rate	3.6%
Total civilian labor force, 2000	5,116
Unemployment rate	3.5%

Employed persons 16 years and over by occupation, 2000
Managers & professionals	1,858
Service occupations	422
Sales & office occupations	1,864
Farming, fishing & forestry	4
Construction & maintenance	377
Production & transportation	413
Self-employed persons	253

* US Census Bureau
** New Jersey Department of Labor

See Introduction for an explanation of all data sources.

General Information
Borough of Maywood
15 Park Ave
Maywood, NJ 07607
201-845-2900

Website	www.maywoodnj.org
Year of incorporation	1894
Land/water area (sq. miles)	1.30/0.00
Form of government	Borough

Government
Legislative Districts
US Congressional	9
State Legislative	37

Local Officials, 2008
Mayor	Timothy J. Eustace
Manager/Admin	Thomas H. Richards
Clerk	Jean M. Pelligra
Finance Dir	Charles Cuccia
Tax Assessor	George Reggo
Tax Collector	Joseph Iannaconi Jr
Attorney	William Rupp
Building	James Mazzer
Comm Dev/Planning	NA
Engineering	Michael Neglia
Public Works	Fred Faul
Police Chief	David Pegg
Emerg/Fire Director	Henry Ahrens III

Housing & Construction
Housing Units, 2000*
Total	3,777
Median rent	$880
Median SF home value	$197,900

Permits for New Residential Construction
	Units	Value
Total, 2007	1	$329,200
Single family	1	$329,200
Total, 2006	2	$583,250
Single family	0	$325,700

Real Property Valuation, 2007
	Parcels	Valuation
Total	2,942	$615,936,100
Vacant	68	3,796,700
Residential	2,730	490,580,700
Commercial	102	48,204,400
Industrial	27	50,194,400
Apartments	15	23,159,900
Farm land	0	0
Farm homestead	0	0

Average Property Value & Tax, 2007
Residential value	$179,700
Property tax	$7,422
Tax credit/rebate	$1,179

Public Library
Maywood Public Library
459 Maywood Ave
Maywood, NJ 07607
201-845-2915

Director............Diane Rhodes

Library statistics, 2006
Population served	9,523
Full-time/total staff	1/4

	Total	Per capita
Holdings	69,257	7.27
Revenues	$532,437	$55.91
Expenditures	$515,792	$54.16
Annual visits	44,500	4.67
Internet terminals/annual users	24/13,300	

Public Safety
Number of officers, 2006	24

Crime	2005	2006
Total crimes	74	102
Violent	1	4
Murder	0	0
Rape	0	0
Robbery	0	1
Aggravated assault	1	3
Non-violent	73	98
Burglary	20	17
Larceny	47	78
Vehicle theft	6	3
Domestic violence	48	53
Arson	0	1
Total crime rate	7.8	10.8
Violent	0.1	0.4
Non-violent	7.7	10.4

Public School District
(for school year 2006-07 except as noted)

Maywood School District
452 Maywood Ave
Maywood, NJ 07607
201-845-9114

Superintendent	Robert Otnisky
Number of schools	2
Grade plan	K-8
Enrollment	860
Attendance rate, '05-06	95.9%
Dropout rate	NA
Students per teacher	12.2
Per pupil expenditure	$13,631
Median faculty salary	$50,063
Median administrator salary	$108,937
Grade 12 enrollment	NA
High school graduation rate	NA

Assessment test results
(percent scoring at proficient or advanced level)
	Language	Math
NJASK-Grade 3	88.1%	95.3%
GEPA-Grade 8	82.5%	88.7%
HSPA-High School	NA	NA

SAT score averages
Pct tested	Math	Verbal	Writing
NA	NA	NA	NA

Teacher Qualifications
Avg. years of experience	8
Highly-qualified teachers one subject/all subjects	98.5%/98.5%
With emergency credentials	0.0%

No Child Left Behind
AYP, 2005-06............Meets Standards

Municipal Finance
State Aid Programs, 2008
Total aid	$1,238,137
CMPTRA	106,079
Energy tax receipts	1,132,058
Garden State Trust	0

General Budget, 2007
Total tax levy	$25,455,090
County levy	2,461,982
County taxes	2,326,353
County library	0
County health	0
County open space	135,629
School levy	13,901,964
Muni. levy	9,091,144
Misc. revenues	4,193,684

Taxes
	2005	2006	2007
General tax rate per $100	3.64	3.88	4.13
County equalization ratio	59.24	52.51	45.69
Net valuation taxable	$617,665,199	$617,708,500	$616,354,245
State equalized value	$1,176,281,087	$1,352,428,946	$1,400,909,505

Medford Lakes Borough

Burlington County

Demographics & Socio-Economic Characteristics
(2000 US Census, except as noted)

Population
1980*	4,958
1990*	4,462
2000	4,173
Male	2,043
Female	2,130
2006 (estimate)*	4,161
Population density	3,438.8

Race & Hispanic Origin, 2000
Race
- White ... 4,103
- Black/African American ... 18
- American Indian/Alaska Native ... 5
- Asian ... 20
- Native Hawaiian/Pacific Islander ... 0
- Other race ... 4
- Two or more races ... 23
- Hispanic origin, total ... 41
  - Mexican ... 2
  - Puerto Rican ... 13
  - Cuban ... 18
  - Other Hispanic ... 8

Age & Nativity, 2000
- Under 5 years ... 261
- 18 years and over ... 3,106
- 21 years and over ... 2,988
- 65 years and over ... 516
- 85 years and over ... 31
- Median age ... 40.3
- Native-born ... 4,102
- Foreign-born ... 71

Educational Attainment, 2000
- Population 25 years and over ... 2,910
- Less than 9th grade ... 1.2%
- High school grad or higher ... 95.2%
- Bachelor's degree or higher ... 50.1%
- Graduate degree ... 14.0%

Income & Poverty, 1999
- Per capita income ... $31,382
- Median household income ... $77,536
- Median family income ... $83,695
- Persons in poverty ... 89
- H'holds receiving public assistance ... 7
- H'holds receiving social security ... 392

Households, 2000
- Total households ... 1,527
  - With persons under 18 ... 592
  - With persons over 65 ... 363
  - Family households ... 1,239
  - Single-person households ... 231
- Persons per household ... 2.73
- Persons per family ... 3.04

Labor & Employment
- Total civilian labor force, 2006** ... 13,504
  - Unemployment rate ... 2.4%
- Total civilian labor force, 2000 ... 2,346
  - Unemployment rate ... 1.5%

Employed persons 16 years and over by occupation, 2000
- Managers & professionals ... 1,124
- Service occupations ... 218
- Sales & office occupations ... 735
- Farming, fishing & forestry ... 0
- Construction & maintenance ... 96
- Production & transportation ... 137
- Self-employed persons ... 134

* US Census Bureau
** New Jersey Department of Labor

General Information
Borough of Medford Lakes
1 Cabin Circle
Medford Lakes, NJ 08055
609-654-8898

- Website ... www.medfordlakes.com
- Year of incorporation ... 1939
- Land/water area (sq. miles) ... 1.21/0.10
- Form of government ... Municipal Mgr 1923

Government
Legislative Districts
- US Congressional ... 3
- State Legislative ... 8

Local Officials, 2008
- Mayor ... Timothy S. Casey
- Manager ... Geoffrey D. Urbanik
- Clerk ... Mark J. McIntosh
- Finance Dir ... Donna A. Condo
- Tax Assessor ... Douglas Kolton
- Tax Collector ... Sharon Deviney
- Attorney ... Peter Lange Jr
- Building ... Thomas Heck
- Planning ... Debbie Klemas
- Engineering ... Alaimo Group
- Public Works ... Pat McCorriston Sr
- Police Chief ... Frank Martine
- Emerg/Fire Director ... Dennis Staples

Housing & Construction
Housing Units, 2000*
- Total ... 1,555
- Median rent ... $920
- Median SF home value ... $161,100

Permits for New Residential Construction
	Units	Value
Total, 2007	16	$2,194,974
Single family	16	$2,194,974
Total, 2006	16	$1,546,503
Single family	16	$1,546,503

Real Property Valuation, 2007
	Parcels	Valuation
Total	1,586	$231,853,400
Vacant	35	745,500
Residential	1,535	226,717,600
Commercial	16	4,390,300
Industrial	0	0
Apartments	0	0
Farm land	0	0
Farm homestead	0	0

Average Property Value & Tax, 2007
- Residential value ... $147,699
- Property tax ... $7,541
- Tax credit/rebate ... $1,227

Public Library
No public municipal library

Library statistics, 2006
- Population served ... NA
- Full-time/total staff ... NA/NA

	Total	Per capita
Holdings	NA	NA
Revenues	NA	NA
Expenditures	NA	NA
Annual visits	NA	NA
Internet terminals/annual users	NA/NA	

Public Safety
- Number of officers, 2006 ... 9

Crime	2005	2006
Total crimes	25	35
Violent	4	1
Murder	0	0
Rape	0	0
Robbery	0	0
Aggravated assault	4	1
Non-violent	21	34
Burglary	0	5
Larceny	18	29
Vehicle theft	3	0
Domestic violence	16	22
Arson	0	1
Total crime rate	5.9	8.4
Violent	1.0	0.2
Non-violent	5.0	8.1

Public School District
(for school year 2006-07 except as noted)

Medford Lakes Borough School District
135 Mudjekeewis Trail
Medford Lakes, NJ 08055
609-654-0991

- Superintendent ... James Lynch
- Number of schools ... 2
- Grade plan ... K-8
- Enrollment ... 525
- Attendance rate, '05-06 ... 96.1%
- Dropout rate ... NA
- Students per teacher ... 10.9
- Per pupil expenditure ... $11,231
- Median faculty salary ... $47,357
- Median administrator salary ... $88,252
- Grade 12 enrollment ... NA
- High school graduation rate ... NA

Assessment test results
(percent scoring at proficient or advanced level)

	Language	Math
NJASK-Grade 3	94.1%	94.2%
GEPA-Grade 8	94.8%	93.2%
HSPA-High School	NA	NA

SAT score averages
Pct tested	Math	Verbal	Writing
NA	NA	NA	NA

Teacher Qualifications
- Avg. years of experience ... 11
- Highly-qualified teachers
  - one subject/all subjects ... 100%/100%
- With emergency credentials ... 0.0%

No Child Left Behind
- AYP, 2005-06 ... Meets Standards

Municipal Finance
State Aid Programs, 2008
- Total aid ... $263,320
  - CMPTRA ... 0
  - Energy tax receipts ... 263,320
  - Garden State Trust ... 0

General Budget, 2007
- Total tax levy ... $11,849,307
  - County levy ... 1,885,704
    - County taxes ... 1,562,574
    - County library ... 143,390
    - County health ... 0
    - County open space ... 179,740
  - School levy ... 7,414,727
  - Muni. levy ... 2,548,877
- Misc. revenues ... 2,000,357

Taxes	2005	2006	2007
General tax rate per $100	4.686	4.941	5.11
County equalization ratio	63.44	56.13	51.65
Net valuation taxable	$231,932,824	$232,083,500	$232,075,420
State equalized value	$413,206,528	$449,498,733	$481,545,250

Burlington County

Medford Township

Demographics & Socio-Economic Characteristics
(2000 US Census, except as noted)

Population
1980*	17,471
1990*	20,526
2000	22,253
Male	10,779
Female	11,474
2006 (estimate)*	23,399
Population density	595.1

Race & Hispanic Origin, 2000
Race
White	21,527
Black/African American	170
American Indian/Alaska Native	26
Asian	327
Native Hawaiian/Pacific Islander	9
Other race	63
Two or more races	131
Hispanic origin, total	252
Mexican	37
Puerto Rican	99
Cuban	18
Other Hispanic	98

Age & Nativity, 2000
Under 5 years	1,416
18 years and over	16,279
21 years and over	15,684
65 years and over	2,387
85 years and over	430
Median age	40.0
Native-born	21,375
Foreign-born	878

Educational Attainment, 2000
Population 25 years and over	15,045
Less than 9th grade	1.2%
High school grad or higher	94.8%
Bachelor's degree or higher	49.9%
Graduate degree	18.5%

Income & Poverty, 1999
Per capita income	$38,641
Median household income	$83,059
Median family income	$97,135
Persons in poverty	410
H'holds receiving public assistance	67
H'holds receiving social security	1,720

Households, 2000
Total households	7,946
With persons under 18	3,188
With persons over 65	1,628
Family households	6,287
Single-person households	1,383
Persons per household	2.77
Persons per family	3.16

Labor & Employment
Total civilian labor force, 2006**	2,732
Unemployment rate	1.9%
Total civilian labor force, 2000	11,619
Unemployment rate	2.2%

Employed persons 16 years and over by occupation, 2000
Managers & professionals	6,249
Service occupations	1,007
Sales & office occupations	2,992
Farming, fishing & forestry	8
Construction & maintenance	559
Production & transportation	549
Self-employed persons	770

‡ Branch of county library
* US Census Bureau
** New Jersey Department of Labor

See Introduction for an explanation of all data sources.

General Information
Township of Medford
17 N Main St
Medford, NJ 08055
609-654-2608

Website	www.medfordtownship.com
Year of incorporation	1847
Land/water area (sq. miles)	39.32/0.49
Form of government	Council-Manager

Government
Legislative Districts
US Congressional	3
State Legislative	8

Local Officials, 2008
Mayor	Christopher Myers
Manager	Mike Achey
Clerk	Joyce Frenia
Finance Dir	Katherine Burger
Tax Assessor	Gilbert Goble
Tax Collector	Joan Schifferdecker
Attorney	Richard Hunt
Building	Richard Uschmann
Planning	(vacant)
Engineering	Christopher Noll
Public Works	George Snyder
Police Chief	James Kehoe
Emerg/Fire Director	Thomas Thorn

Housing & Construction
Housing Units, 2000*
Total	8,147
Median rent	$947
Median SF home value	$213,600

Permits for New Residential Construction
	Units	Value
Total, 2007	127	$8,652,738
Single family	7	$2,310,338
Total, 2006	10	$2,761,900
Single family	10	$2,761,900

Real Property Valuation, 2007
	Parcels	Valuation
Total	8,936	$1,770,357,900
Vacant	666	19,726,600
Residential	7,659	1,540,876,800
Commercial	327	148,084,500
Industrial	10	8,942,700
Apartments	7	29,815,900
Farm land	167	2,390,000
Farm homestead	100	20,521,400

Average Property Value & Tax, 2007
Residential value	$201,237
Property tax	$8,664
Tax credit/rebate	$1,145

Public Library
Pinelands Branch Library‡
39 Allen Ave
Medford, NJ 08055
609-654-6113

Branch Librarian: Judy Aley

Library statistics, 2006
see Burlington County profile for library system statistics

Public Safety
Number of officers, 2006		43
Crime	**2005**	**2006**
Total crimes	333	250
Violent	20	10
Murder	0	0
Rape	1	1
Robbery	8	1
Aggravated assault	11	8
Non-violent	313	240
Burglary	50	43
Larceny	252	192
Vehicle theft	11	5
Domestic violence	175	219
Arson	1	6
Total crime rate	14.1	10.6
Violent	0.8	0.4
Non-violent	13.3	10.2

Public School District
(for school year 2006-07 except as noted)

Medford Township School District
128 Route 70, Suite 1
Medford, NJ 08055
609-654-6416

Superintendent	Joesph J. Del Rossi
Number of schools	7
Grade plan	K-8
Enrollment	3,071
Attendance rate, '05-06	96.5%
Dropout rate	NA
Students per teacher	12.3
Per pupil expenditure	$12,643
Median faculty salary	$54,375
Median administrator salary	$106,700
Grade 12 enrollment	NA
High school graduation rate	NA

Assessment test results
(percent scoring at proficient or advanced level)
	Language	Math
NJASK-Grade 3	96.0%	96.0%
GEPA-Grade 8	92.3%	86.9%
HSPA-High School	NA	NA

SAT score averages
Pct tested	Math	Verbal	Writing
NA	NA	NA	NA

Teacher Qualifications
Avg. years of experience	7
Highly-qualified teachers one subject/all subjects	100%/100%
With emergency credentials	0.0%

No Child Left Behind
AYP, 2005-06 .... Meets Standards

Municipal Finance
State Aid Programs, 2008
Total aid	$2,629,165
CMPTRA	492,309
Energy tax receipts	2,053,916
Garden State Trust	10,178

General Budget, 2007
Total tax levy	$76,406,800
County levy	13,489,395
County taxes	11,177,843
County library	1,025,744
County health	0
County open space	1,285,809
School levy	53,555,867
Muni. levy	9,361,537
Misc. revenues	12,418,480

Taxes
	2005	2006	2007
General tax rate per $100	3.949	4.161	4.31
County equalization ratio	67.68	61.05	55.18
Net valuation taxable	$1,742,325,078	$1,761,434,200	$1,774,726,658
State equalized value	$2,853,931,332	$3,196,017,941	$3,382,269,731

Mendham Borough — Morris County

Demographics & Socio-Economic Characteristics
(2000 US Census, except as noted)

Population
- 1980* 4,899
- 1990* 4,890
- 2000 5,097
  - Male 2,410
  - Female 2,687
- 2006 (estimate)* 5,176
  - Population density 859.8

Race & Hispanic Origin, 2000
Race
- White 4,951
- Black/African American 23
- American Indian/Alaska Native 1
- Asian 72
- Native Hawaiian/Pacific Islander 3
- Other race 14
- Two or more races 33
- Hispanic origin, total 125
  - Mexican 11
  - Puerto Rican 23
  - Cuban 3
  - Other Hispanic 88

Age & Nativity, 2000
- Under 5 years 351
- 18 years and over 3,730
- 21 years and over 3,600
- 65 years and over 857
- 85 years and over 150
  - Median age 41.9
- Native-born 4,681
- Foreign-born 416

Educational Attainment, 2000
- Population 25 years and over 3,489
- Less than 9th grade 0.7%
- High school grad or higher 95.3%
- Bachelor's degree or higher 62.2%
- Graduate degree 27.8%

Income & Poverty, 1999
- Per capita income $48,629
- Median household income $110,348
- Median family income $129,812
- Persons in poverty 200
- H'holds receiving public assistance 0
- H'holds receiving social security 514

Households, 2000
- Total households 1,781
  - With persons under 18 666
  - With persons over 65 514
  - Family households 1,380
  - Single-person households 332
- Persons per household 2.72
- Persons per family 3.13

Labor & Employment
- Total civilian labor force, 2006** 2,486
  - Unemployment rate 1.5%
- Total civilian labor force, 2000 2,274
  - Unemployment rate 1.2%
- *Employed persons 16 years and over by occupation, 2000*
  - Managers & professionals 1,240
  - Service occupations 135
  - Sales & office occupations 728
  - Farming, fishing & forestry 14
  - Construction & maintenance 73
  - Production & transportation 57
- Self-employed persons 230

* US Census Bureau
** New Jersey Department of Labor

General Information
Borough of Mendham
2 W Main St
Mendham, NJ 07945
973-543-7152

- Website .... www.mendhamnj.org
- Year of incorporation 1906
- Land/water area (sq. miles) 6.02/0.02
- Form of government .... Borough

Government

Legislative Districts
- US Congressional 11
- State Legislative 16

Local Officials, 2008
- Mayor .... Neil Henry
- Manager .... Ellen Sandman
- Clerk .... Maureen Massey
- Finance Dir .... Susan Giordano
- Tax Assessor .... Scott Holzhauer
- Tax Collector .... Donna Cummins
- Attorney .... Fred Semrau
- Building .... Joseph Alicino
- Comm Dev/Planning .... NA
- Engineering .... Paul Ferriero
- Public Works .... Ken O'Brien
- Police Chief .... John Taylor
- Emerg/Fire Director .... Ed Tencza

Housing & Construction

Housing Units, 2000*
- Total 1,828
- Median rent $1,186
- Median SF home value $397,000

Permits for New Residential Construction

	Units	Value
Total, 2007	3	$3,021,200
Single family	3	$3,021,200
Total, 2006	2	$1,526,667
Single family	2	$1,526,667

Real Property Valuation, 2007

	Parcels	Valuation
Total	1,841	$1,598,179,940
Vacant	39	14,936,900
Residential	1,640	1,417,809,000
Commercial	84	121,984,300
Industrial	0	0
Apartments	4	2,475,000
Farm land	55	695,840
Farm homestead	19	40,278,900

Average Property Value & Tax, 2007
- Residential value $878,896
- Property tax $12,117
- Tax credit/rebate $1,261

Public Library
Mendham Borough Library
10 Hilltop Rd
Mendham, NJ 07945
973-543-4152

- Director .... Patricia Charney

Library statistics, 2006
- Population served 5,097
- Full-time/total staff 0/1

	Total	Per capita
Holdings	24,225	4.75
Revenues	$254,258	$49.88
Expenditures	$274,624	$53.88
Annual visits	27,040	5.31
Internet terminals/annual users		5/9,360

Taxes

	2005	2006	2007
General tax rate per $100	3.1	1.29	1.38
County equalization ratio	51.76	124.13	109.49
Net valuation taxable	$626,250,185	$1,599,198,000	$1,600,887,548
State equalized value	$1,269,254,530	$1,462,863,953	$1,525,363,801

Public Safety
- Number of officers, 2006 12

Crime	2005	2006
Total crimes	43	40
Violent	0	2
Murder	0	0
Rape	0	0
Robbery	0	0
Aggravated assault	0	2
Non-violent	43	38
Burglary	9	2
Larceny	34	36
Vehicle theft	0	0
Domestic violence	12	11
Arson	0	0
Total crime rate	8.3	7.7
Violent	0.0	0.4
Non-violent	8.3	7.3

Public School District
(for school year 2006-07 except as noted)

Mendham Borough School District
12 Hilltop Rd
Mendham, NJ 07945
973-543-2295

- Superintendent .... Janie P. Edmonds
- Number of schools 2
- Grade plan K-8
- Enrollment 729
- Attendance rate, '05-06 .... 96.2%
- Dropout rate .... NA
- Students per teacher 11.8
- Per pupil expenditure $12,257
- Median faculty salary $54,237
- Median administrator salary $119,600
- Grade 12 enrollment .... NA
- High school graduation rate .... NA

Assessment test results
(percent scoring at proficient or advanced level)

	Language	Math
NJASK-Grade 3	94.5%	95.9%
GEPA-Grade 8	93.8%	92.6%
HSPA-High School	NA	NA

SAT score averages

Pct tested	Math	Verbal	Writing
NA	NA	NA	NA

Teacher Qualifications
- Avg. years of experience 9
- Highly-qualified teachers
  - one subject/all subjects 98.0%/98.0%
- With emergency credentials 0.0%

No Child Left Behind
- AYP, 2005-06 .... Meets Standards

Municipal Finance

State Aid Programs, 2008
- Total aid $665,288
  - CMPTRA 28,690
  - Energy tax receipts 636,518
  - Garden State Trust 80

General Budget, 2007
- Total tax levy $22,071,691
  - County levy 3,475,886
    - County taxes 2,780,044
    - County library 0
    - County health 0
    - County open space 695,842
  - School levy 14,028,609
  - Muni. levy 4,567,196
  - Misc. revenues 1,927,371

Morris County — Mendham Township

Demographics & Socio-Economic Characteristics
(2000 US Census, except as noted)

Population
- 1980* 4,488
- 1990* 4,537
- 2000 5,400
  - Male 2,656
  - Female 2,744
- 2006 (estimate)* 5,596
  - Population density 313.3

Race & Hispanic Origin, 2000
Race
- White 5,179
- Black/African American 50
- American Indian/Alaska Native 5
- Asian 109
- Native Hawaiian/Pacific Islander 0
- Other race 19
- Two or more races 38
- Hispanic origin, total 82
  - Mexican 10
  - Puerto Rican 9
  - Cuban 12
  - Other Hispanic 51

Age & Nativity, 2000
- Under 5 years 423
- 18 years and over 3,674
- 21 years and over 3,569
- 65 years and over 582
- 85 years and over 44
  - Median age 40.3
- Native-born 4,993
- Foreign-born 407

Educational Attainment, 2000
- Population 25 years and over 3,467
- Less than 9th grade 0.9%
- High school grad or higher 97.9%
- Bachelor's degree or higher 71.3%
- Graduate degree 34.6%

Income & Poverty, 1999
- Per capita income $61,460
- Median household income $136,174
- Median family income $146,254
- Persons in poverty 96
- H'holds receiving public assistance 0
- H'holds receiving social security 406

Households, 2000
- Total households 1,788
  - With persons under 18 853
  - With persons over 65 382
  - Family households 1,539
  - Single-person households 198
- Persons per household 3.01
- Persons per family 3.27

Labor & Employment
- Total civilian labor force, 2006** 2,572
  - Unemployment rate 1.0%
- Total civilian labor force, 2000 2,355
  - Unemployment rate 1.1%

Employed persons 16 years and over by occupation, 2000
- Managers & professionals 1,405
- Service occupations 134
- Sales & office occupations 605
- Farming, fishing & forestry 0
- Construction & maintenance 110
- Production & transportation 75
- Self-employed persons 205

* US Census Bureau
** New Jersey Department of Labor

See Introduction for an explanation of all data sources.

General Information
Township of Mendham
Township Hall
PO Box 520
Brookside, NJ 07926
973-543-4555
- Website .... www.mendhamtownship.org
- Year of incorporation 1749
- Land/water area (sq. miles) 17.86/0.12
- Form of government .... Township

Government
Legislative Districts
- US Congressional 11
- State Legislative 25

Local Officials, 2008
- Mayor .... Phyllis Florek
- Administrator .... Stephen Mountain
- Municipal Clerk .... Ann Carlson
- Finance Dir. .... Jeffery Theriault
- Tax Assessor .... Scott Holzhauer
- Tax Collector .... NA
- Attorney .... Christopher Falcon
- Building .... Russell Heiney
- Comm Dev/Planning .... NA
- Engineering .... Thomas Lemanowicz
- Public Works .... NA
- Police Chief .... Thomas Costanza
- Emerg/Fire Dir. ...... Thomas Montgomery

Housing & Construction
Housing Units, 2000*
- Total 1,849
- Median rent $1,139
- Median SF home value $556,200

Permits for New Residential Construction

	Units	Value
Total, 2007	6	$4,777,580
Single family	6	$4,777,580
Total, 2006	13	$5,305,579
Single family	13	$5,305,579

Real Property Valuation, 2007

	Parcels	Valuation
Total	2,225	$2,130,523,750
Vacant	119	54,073,500
Residential	1,935	1,975,036,050
Commercial	7	11,198,500
Industrial	1	3,000
Apartments	0	0
Farm land	104	1,432,300
Farm homestead	59	88,780,400

Average Property Value & Tax, 2007
- Residential value $1,035,013
- Property tax $15,797
- Tax credit/rebate $1,347

Public Library
Mendham Township Library
Cherry Lane & Main St
Brookside, NJ 07926
973-543-4018
- Director .... Lee Tanen

Library statistics, 2006
- Population served 5,400
- Full-time/total staff 0/0

	Total	Per capita
Holdings	41,147	7.62
Revenues	$257,733	$47.73
Expenditures	$214,848	$39.79
Annual visits	39,102	7.24
Internet terminals/annual users	5/6,300	

Public Safety
Number of officers, 2006 15

Crime	2005	2006
Total crimes	47	50
Violent	4	1
Murder	0	0
Rape	0	0
Robbery	0	0
Aggravated assault	4	1
Non-violent	43	49
Burglary	4	5
Larceny	37	44
Vehicle theft	2	0
Domestic violence	4	5
Arson	0	0
Total crime rate	8.4	8.9
Violent	0.7	0.2
Non-violent	7.6	8.7

Public School District
(for school year 2006-07 except as noted)

Mendham Township School District
18 West Main St
Brookside, NJ 07926
973-543-7107

- Superintendent .... Christine Johnson
- Number of schools 2
- Grade plan K-8
- Enrollment 893
- Attendance rate, '05-06 .... 96.1%
- Dropout rate .... NA
- Students per teacher 9.8
- Per pupil expenditure $15,425
- Median faculty salary $52,829
- Median administrator salary $117,265
- Grade 12 enrollment .... NA
- High school graduation rate .... NA

Assessment test results
(percent scoring at proficient or advanced level)

	Language	Math
NJASK-Grade 3	94.2%	97.7%
GEPA-Grade 8	95.2%	90.5%
HSPA-High School	NA	NA

SAT score averages

Pct tested	Math	Verbal	Writing
NA	NA	NA	NA

Teacher Qualifications
- Avg. years of experience 9
- Highly-qualified teachers one subject/all subjects 100%/100%
- With emergency credentials 0.0%

No Child Left Behind
- AYP, 2005-06 .... Meets Standards

Municipal Finance
State Aid Programs, 2008
- Total aid $620,931
  - CMPTRA 3,677
  - Energy tax receipts 588,397
  - Garden State Trust 798

General Budget, 2007
- Total tax levy $32,548,265
  - County levy 5,084,452
    - County taxes 4,066,828
    - County library 0
    - County health 0
    - County open space 1,017,624
  - School levy 21,440,151
  - Muni. levy 6,023,662
- Misc. revenues 3,323,107

Taxes

	2005	2006	2007
General tax rate per $100	1.4	1.48	1.53
County equalization ratio	119.74	107.2	99.72
Net valuation taxable	$2,116,183,594	$2,121,231,650	$2,132,489,062
State equalized value	$1,974,051,860	$2,128,482,699	$2,192,059,627

Merchantville Borough
Camden County

Demographics & Socio-Economic Characteristics
(2000 US Census, except as noted)

Population
1980*	3,972
1990*	4,095
2000	3,801
Male	1,791
Female	2,010
2006 (estimate)*	3,806
Population density	6,343.3

Race & Hispanic Origin, 2000
Race
White	3,265
Black/African American	282
American Indian/Alaska Native	11
Asian	80
Native Hawaiian/Pacific Islander	0
Other race	108
Two or more races	55
Hispanic origin, total	208
Mexican	4
Puerto Rican	138
Cuban	7
Other Hispanic	59

Age & Nativity, 2000
Under 5 years	250
18 years and over	2,825
21 years and over	2,719
65 years and over	526
85 years and over	62
Median age	37.2
Native-born	3,651
Foreign-born	150

Educational Attainment, 2000
Population 25 years and over	2,531
Less than 9th grade	3.1%
High school grad or higher	81.8%
Bachelor's degree or higher	27.7%
Graduate degree	8.1%

Income & Poverty, 1999
Per capita income	$25,589
Median household income	$49,392
Median family income	$60,652
Persons in poverty	259
H'holds receiving public assistance	36
H'holds receiving social security	391

Households, 2000
Total households	1,524
With persons under 18	524
With persons over 65	398
Family households	946
Single-person households	488
Persons per household	2.48
Persons per family	3.19

Labor & Employment
Total civilian labor force, 2006**	2,186
Unemployment rate	3.2%
Total civilian labor force, 2000	2,026
Unemployment rate	3.3%

Employed persons 16 years and over by occupation, 2000
Managers & professionals	704
Service occupations	233
Sales & office occupations	644
Farming, fishing & forestry	0
Construction & maintenance	186
Production & transportation	193
Self-employed persons	150

‡ Branch of county library
* US Census Bureau
** New Jersey Department of Labor

General Information
Borough of Merchantville
1 W Maple Ave
Merchantville, NJ 08109
856-662-2474

Website	merchantvillenj.gov
Year of incorporation	1915
Land/water area (sq. miles)	0.60/0.00
Form of government	Borough

Government
Legislative Districts
US Congressional	1
State Legislative	7

Local Officials, 2008
Mayor	Frank North
Manager	John Fry
Clerk	Denise Brouse (Dep)
Finance Dir	Denise Moules
Tax Assessor	John Dymond
Tax Collector	John Fry
Attorney	Timothy Higgins
Building	William Joseph
Planning	Eric Schmidt
Engineering	Joe Brickley
Public Works	Daniel Beckett
Police Chief	Wayne Bauer
Emerg/Fire Director	Roy Adair

Housing & Construction
Housing Units, 2000*
Total	1,607
Median rent	$642
Median SF home value	$122,200

Permits for New Residential Construction
	Units	Value
Total, 2007	7	$621,096
Single family	7	$621,096
Total, 2006	10	$887,280
Single family	10	$887,280

Real Property Valuation, 2007
	Parcels	Valuation
Total	1,241	$157,475,000
Vacant	60	901,800
Residential	1,072	131,595,600
Commercial	84	16,167,600
Industrial	0	0
Apartments	25	8,810,000
Farm land	0	0
Farm homestead	0	0

Average Property Value & Tax, 2007
Residential value	$122,757
Property tax	$5,872
Tax credit/rebate	$1,019

Public Library
Merchantville Library‡
130 S Centre St
Merchantville, NJ 08109
856-665-3128

Branch Librarian	Mimi Cirillo

Library statistics, 2006
see Camden County profile for library system statistics

Public Safety
Number of officers, 2006	14

Crime	2005	2006
Total crimes	109	122
Violent	4	4
Murder	0	0
Rape	0	0
Robbery	1	2
Aggravated assault	3	2
Non-violent	105	118
Burglary	21	16
Larceny	79	100
Vehicle theft	5	2
Domestic violence	27	13
Arson	0	1
Total crime rate	28.6	31.9
Violent	1.0	1.0
Non-violent	27.5	30.9

Public School District
(for school year 2006-07 except as noted)

Merchantville School District
130 S Centre St
Merchantville, NJ 08109
856-663-1091

Chief School Admin	Christian Swanson
Number of schools	1
Grade plan	K-8
Enrollment	362
Attendance rate, '05-06	94.6%
Dropout rate	NA
Students per teacher	11.5
Per pupil expenditure	$13,277
Median faculty salary	$62,203
Median administrator salary	$90,449
Grade 12 enrollment	NA
High school graduation rate	NA

Assessment test results
(percent scoring at proficient or advanced level)
	Language	Math
NJASK-Grade 3	97.0%	97.1%
GEPA-Grade 8	60.5%	73.7%
HSPA-High School	NA	NA

SAT score averages
Pct tested	Math	Verbal	Writing
NA	NA	NA	NA

Teacher Qualifications
Avg. years of experience	23
Highly-qualified teachers one subject/all subjects	100%/100%
With emergency credentials	0.0%

No Child Left Behind
AYP, 2005-06	Meets Standards

Municipal Finance
State Aid Programs, 2008
Total aid	$412,082
CMPTRA	0
Energy tax receipts	412,082
Garden State Trust	0

General Budget, 2007
Total tax levy	$7,699,442
County levy	1,942,361
County taxes	1,763,210
County library	123,645
County health	0
County open space	55,506
School levy	4,073,599
Muni. levy	1,683,482
Misc. revenues	2,640,184

Taxes	2005	2006	2007
General tax rate per $100	4.408	4.65	4.784
County equalization ratio	79.5	70.4	57.91
Net valuation taxable	$163,279,412	$156,852,100	$160,970,463
State equalized value	$231,930,983	$275,047,368	$290,178,514

Middlesex County
Metuchen Borough

Demographics & Socio-Economic Characteristics
(2000 US Census, except as noted)

Population
- 1980* 13,762
- 1990* 12,804
- 2000 12,840
  - Male 6,137
  - Female 6,703
- 2006 (estimate)* 13,216
  - Population density 4,823.4

Race & Hispanic Origin, 2000
Race
- White 10,835
- Black/African American 681
- American Indian/Alaska Native 13
- Asian 928
- Native Hawaiian/Pacific Islander ... 0
- Other race 144
- Two or more races 239
- Hispanic origin, total 508
  - Mexican 50
  - Puerto Rican 188
  - Cuban 51
  - Other Hispanic 219

Age & Nativity, 2000
- Under 5 years 847
- 18 years and over 9,849
- 21 years and over 9,531
- 65 years and over 1,910
- 85 years and over 173
  - Median age 39.5
- Native-born 11,020
- Foreign-born 1,820

Educational Attainment, 2000
- Population 25 years and over .. 9,254
- Less than 9th grade 2.3%
- High school grad or higher 92.1%
- Bachelor's degree or higher 49.2%
- Graduate degree 19.8%

Income & Poverty, 1999
- Per capita income $36,749
- Median household income $75,546
- Median family income $85,022
- Persons in poverty 500
- H'holds receiving public assistance .. 40
- H'holds receiving social security .. 1,322

Households, 2000
- Total households 4,992
  - With persons under 18 1,726
  - With persons over 65 1,377
  - Family households 3,583
  - Single-person households .. 1,150
- Persons per household 2.57
- Persons per family 3.05

Labor & Employment
- Total civilian labor force, 2006** .. 7,770
  - Unemployment rate 4.9%
- Total civilian labor force, 2000 .. 7,058
  - Unemployment rate 4.4%

Employed persons 16 years and over by occupation, 2000
- Managers & professionals 3,593
- Service occupations 482
- Sales & office occupations ... 1,864
- Farming, fishing & forestry 0
- Construction & maintenance ... 282
- Production & transportation .. 523
- Self-employed persons 337

* US Census Bureau
** New Jersey Department of Labor

See Introduction for an explanation of all data sources.

General Information
Borough of Metuchen
500 Main St
Metuchen, NJ 08840
732-632-8540

- Website .... www.metuchennj.org
- Year of incorporation 1900
- Land/water area (sq. miles) 2.74/0.00
- Form of government .... Borough

Government
Legislative Districts
- US Congressional 6
- State Legislative 18

Local Officials, 2008
- Mayor .... Thomas Vahalla
- Administrator .... William Boerth
- Clerk .... Bozena Lacina
- Finance Dir .... Rebecca Cuthbert
- Tax Assessor .... Robert Sweeney
- Tax Collector .... NA
- Attorney .... David Frizell
- Building .... James Gyug
- Comm Dev/Planning .... NA
- Engineering .... Katherine Elliott
- Public Works Dir .... Fred Hall
- Police Chief .... James Keane
- Emerg/Fire Director ..... Timothy Gehy

Housing & Construction
Housing Units, 2000*
- Total 5,104
- Median rent $873
- Median SF home value $194,900

Permits for New Residential Construction

	Units	Value
Total, 2007	11	$1,426,700
Single family	9	$1,227,800
Total, 2006	9	$1,853,500
Single family	9	$1,853,500

Real Property Valuation, 2007

	Parcels	Valuation
Total	5,117	$966,427,600
Vacant	103	7,203,100
Residential	4,583	787,867,900
Commercial	356	113,813,500
Industrial	57	38,424,600
Apartments	18	19,118,500
Farm land	0	0
Farm homestead	0	0

Average Property Value & Tax, 2007
- Residential value $171,911
- Property tax $7,528
- Tax credit/rebate $1,116

Public Library
Metuchen Public Library
480 Middlesex Ave
Metuchen, NJ 08840
732-632-8526

- Director .... Melody B. Kokola

Library statistics, 2006
- Population served 12,840
- Full-time/total staff 4/5

	Total	Per capita
Holdings	76,507	5.96
Revenues	$740,603	$57.68
Expenditures	$701,082	$54.60
Annual visits	87,632	6.82
Internet terminals/annual users	10/13,900	

Public Safety
Number of officers, 2006 28

Crime	2005	2006
Total crimes	259	265
Violent	13	11
Murder	0	0
Rape	1	0
Robbery	4	2
Aggravated assault	8	9
Non-violent	246	254
Burglary	64	40
Larceny	168	201
Vehicle theft	14	13
Domestic violence	93	110
Arson	0	1
Total crime rate	19.4	19.8
Violent	1.0	0.8
Non-violent	18.4	19.0

Public School District
(for school year 2006-07 except as noted)

Metuchen School District
16 Simpson Place
Metuchen, NJ 08840
732-321-8700

- Superintendent .. Theresa Pollifrone-Sinatra
- Number of schools 4
- Grade plan K-12
- Enrollment 2,011
- Attendance rate, '05-06 .... 95.2%
- Dropout rate 0.5%
- Students per teacher 11.0
- Per pupil expenditure $13,942
- Median faculty salary $65,573
- Median administrator salary .. $102,031
- Grade 12 enrollment 138
- High school graduation rate ... 96.5%

Assessment test results
(percent scoring at proficient or advanced level)

	Language	Math
NJASK-Grade 3	93.7%	93.8%
GEPA-Grade 8	84.5%	83.8%
HSPA-High School	96.2%	91.1%

SAT score averages

Pct tested	Math	Verbal	Writing
92%	520	518	527

Teacher Qualifications
- Avg. years of experience 9
- Highly-qualified teachers
  - one subject/all subjects 100%/100%
- With emergency credentials 0.0%

No Child Left Behind
- AYP, 2005-06 .... Meets Standards

Municipal Finance
State Aid Programs, 2008
- Total aid $1,859,069
- CMPTRA 540,503
- Energy tax receipts 1,318,566
- Garden State Trust 0

General Budget, 2007
- Total tax levy $42,503,933
- County levy 6,389,036
  - County taxes 5,719,204
  - County library 0
  - County health 0
  - County open space 669,831
- School levy 28,056,178
- Muni. levy 8,058,720
- Misc. revenues 6,310,106

Taxes	2005	2006	2007
General tax rate per $100	3.82	4.13	4.38
County equalization ratio	56.63	49.61	43.65
Net valuation taxable	$957,841,188	$961,495,900	$970,679,061
State equalized value	$1,930,742,165	$2,207,598,007	$2,288,410,289

Middle Township
Cape May County

Demographics & Socio-Economic Characteristics
(2000 US Census, except as noted)

Population
- 1980* 11,373
- 1990* 14,771
- 2000 16,405
  - Male 7,908
  - Female 8,497
- 2006 (estimate)* 16,379
  - Population density 229.8

Race & Hispanic Origin, 2000
Race
- White 13,979
- Black/African American 1,781
- American Indian/Alaska Native 37
- Asian 236
- Native Hawaiian/Pacific Islander 4
- Other race 108
- Two or more races 260
- Hispanic origin, total 347
  - Mexican 27
  - Puerto Rican 173
  - Cuban 15
  - Other Hispanic 132

Age & Nativity, 2000
- Under 5 years 933
- 18 years and over 12,360
- 21 years and over 11,823
- 65 years and over 2,925
- 85 years and over 483
- Median age 39.8
- Native-born 15,906
- Foreign-born 499

Educational Attainment, 2000
- Population 25 years and over ... 11,252
- Less than 9th grade 6.0%
- High school grad or higher 77.8%
- Bachelor's degree or higher 16.5%
- Graduate degree 4.5%

Income & Poverty, 1999
- Per capita income $19,805
- Median household income $41,533
- Median family income $49,030
- Persons in poverty 1,580
- H'holds receiving public assistance 203
- H'holds receiving social security 2,081

Households, 2000
- Total households 6,009
  - With persons under 18 2,101
  - With persons over 65 1,797
  - Family households 4,216
  - Single-person households 1,481
  - Persons per household 2.58
  - Persons per family 3.08

Labor & Employment
- Total civilian labor force, 2006** ... 9,281
  - Unemployment rate 6.0%
- Total civilian labor force, 2000 ... 7,610
  - Unemployment rate 7.1%

Employed persons 16 years and over by occupation, 2000
- Managers & professionals 1,916
- Service occupations 1,672
- Sales & office occupations 1,811
- Farming, fishing & forestry 68
- Construction & maintenance 976
- Production & transportation 628
- Self-employed persons 568

* US Census Bureau
** New Jersey Department of Labor

General Information
Township of Middle
33 Mechanic St
Cape May Court House, NJ 08210
609-465-8732
- Website .... www.middletownship.com
- Year of incorporation 1723
- Land/water area (sq. miles) 71.27/11.83
- Form of government .... Township

Government
Legislative Districts
- US Congressional 2
- State Legislative 1

Local Officials, 2008
- Mayor .... F. Nate Doughty
- Manager .... James Alexis
- Clerk .... James Alexis
- Finance Dir .... Tracey Taverner
- Tax Assessor .... Joseph Ravitz
- Tax Collector .... Sandy Beasley
- Attorney .... James Pickering
- Building .... Ralph James
- Planning .... John Ludlam
- Engineering .... Vincent Orlando
- Public Works .... Richard Ceglarski
- Police Chief .... Joseph Evangelista
- Public Safety Dir ...... Susan De Lanzo

Housing & Construction
Housing Units, 2000*
- Total 7,510
- Median rent $677
- Median SF home value $116,200

Permits for New Residential Construction

	Units	Value
Total, 2007	220	$26,720,142
Single family	216	$26,400,142
Total, 2006	120	$17,957,954
Single family	120	$17,957,954

Real Property Valuation, 2007

	Parcels	Valuation
Total	11,730	$3,202,126,600
Vacant	3,330	244,668,000
Residential	7,725	2,317,353,400
Commercial	532	612,936,000
Industrial	4	5,552,100
Apartments	10	5,311,300
Farm land	76	1,265,900
Farm homestead	53	15,039,900

Average Property Value & Tax, 2007
- Residential value $299,871
- Property tax $3,419
- Tax credit/rebate $784

Public Library
No public municipal library

Library statistics, 2006
- Population served .... NA
- Full-time/total staff .... NA/NA

	Total	Per capita
Holdings	NA	NA
Revenues	NA	NA
Expenditures	NA	NA
Annual visits	NA	NA
Internet terminals/annual users	NA/NA	

Taxes

	2005	2006	2007
General tax rate per $100	2.81	2.91	1.15
County equalization ratio	58.35	47.13	112.66
Net valuation taxable	$1,075,205,749	$1,133,207,200	$3,208,981,699
State equalized value	$2,281,361,657	$2,747,659,774	$3,053,307,958

Public Safety
- Number of officers, 2006 51

Crime	2005	2006
Total crimes	709	859
Violent	84	100
Murder	0	1
Rape	3	4
Robbery	13	21
Aggravated assault	68	74
Non-violent	625	759
Burglary	140	154
Larceny	447	575
Vehicle theft	38	30
Domestic violence	268	235
Arson	13	9
Total crime rate	42.4	51.7
Violent	5.0	6.0
Non-violent	37.4	45.7

Public School District
(for school year 2006-07 except as noted)

Middle Township School District
216 S Main St
Cape May Court House, NJ 08210
609-465-1800
- Superintendent ...... Michael Kopakowski
- Number of schools 4
- Grade plan K-12
- Enrollment 2,876
- Attendance rate, '05-06 .... 93.0%
- Dropout rate 2.5%
- Students per teacher 11.0
- Per pupil expenditure $12,764
- Median faculty salary $52,155
- Median administrator salary ... $89,975
- Grade 12 enrollment 243
- High school graduation rate 89.0%

Assessment test results
(percent scoring at proficient or advanced level)

	Language	Math
NJASK-Grade 3	84.0%	90.9%
GEPA-Grade 8	70.4%	74.1%
HSPA-High School	84.8%	71.6%

SAT score averages

Pct tested	Math	Verbal	Writing
54%	511	493	479

Teacher Qualifications
- Avg. years of experience 12
- Highly-qualified teachers
  - one subject/all subjects ... 100%/100%
- With emergency credentials 0.0%

No Child Left Behind
- AYP, 2005-06 .... Needs Improvement

Municipal Finance
State Aid Programs, 2008
- Total aid $4,173,422
  - CMPTRA 0
  - Energy tax receipts 4,107,957
  - Garden State Trust 65,465

General Budget, 2007
- Total tax levy $36,588,912
  - County levy 5,434,170
    - County taxes 4,318,471
    - County library 829,808
    - County health 0
    - County open space 285,891
  - School levy 21,653,518
  - Muni. levy 9,501,223
- Misc. revenues 11,219,428

Middlesex County / Middlesex Borough

Demographics & Socio-Economic Characteristics
(2000 US Census, except as noted)

Population
- 1980* 13,480
- 1990* 13,055
- 2000 13,717
  - Male 6,682
  - Female 7,035
- 2006 (estimate)* 13,746
  - Population density 3,927.4

Race & Hispanic Origin, 2000
Race
- White 11,970
- Black/African American 461
- American Indian/Alaska Native 18
- Asian 570
- Native Hawaiian/Pacific Islander 3
- Other race 440
- Two or more races 255
- Hispanic origin, total 1,235
  - Mexican 48
  - Puerto Rican 244
  - Cuban 27
  - Other Hispanic 916

Age & Nativity, 2000
- Under 5 years 914
- 18 years and over 10,411
- 21 years and over 10,030
- 65 years and over 1,942
- 85 years and over 168
  - Median age 38.0
- Native-born 11,973
- Foreign-born 1,744

Educational Attainment, 2000
- Population 25 years and over 9,538
- Less than 9th grade 4.3%
- High school grad or higher 85.4%
- Bachelor's degree or higher 23.4%
- Graduate degree 6.3%

Income & Poverty, 1999
- Per capita income $27,834
- Median household income $60,723
- Median family income $70,343
- Persons in poverty 499
- H'holds receiving public assistance ... 65
- H'holds receiving social security .. 1,558

Households, 2000
- Total households 5,048
  - With persons under 18 1,849
  - With persons over 65 1,451
  - Family households 3,739
  - Single-person households 1,097
- Persons per household 2.71
- Persons per family 3.17

Labor & Employment
- Total civilian labor force, 2006** .. 7,989
  - Unemployment rate 3.2%
- Total civilian labor force, 2000 7,259
  - Unemployment rate 2.9%
- *Employed persons 16 years and over by occupation, 2000*
  - Managers & professionals 2,460
  - Service occupations 794
  - Sales & office occupations 2,148
  - Farming, fishing & forestry 0
  - Construction & maintenance 698
  - Production & transportation 947
- Self-employed persons 350

* US Census Bureau
** New Jersey Department of Labor

See Introduction for an explanation of all data sources.

General Information
Borough of Middlesex
1200 Mountain Ave
Middlesex, NJ 08846
732-356-7400

- Website .... www.middlesexboro-nj.gov
- Year of incorporation 1913
- Land/water area (sq. miles) 3.50/0.02
- Form of government .... Borough

Government
Legislative Districts
- US Congressional 6
- State Legislative 22

Local Officials, 2008
- Mayor .... Gerald D'Angelo
- Manager .... NA
- Clerk .... Kathleen Anello
- Finance Dir .... Andrea Corcoran
- Tax Assessor .... Frank Betts
- Tax Collector .... Tonya Hubosky
- Attorney .... Edward J. Johnson
- Building .... Matthew Imperato
- Comm Dev/Planning .... NA
- Engineering .... T&M Associates
- Public Works .... Jerry Schaefer
- Police Chief .... James Benson
- Emerg/Fire Director ...... Edward Winters

Housing & Construction
Housing Units, 2000*
- Total 5,130
- Median rent $830
- Median SF home value $164,200

Permits for New Residential Construction

	Units	Value
Total, 2007	8	$1,781,050
Single family	8	$1,781,050
Total, 2006	16	$2,896,390
Single family	10	$1,528,525

Real Property Valuation, 2007

	Parcels	Valuation
Total	4,702	$498,688,400
Vacant	175	5,099,700
Residential	4,173	386,724,700
Commercial	201	35,778,400
Industrial	148	61,240,600
Apartments	5	9,845,000
Farm land	0	0
Farm homestead	0	0

Average Property Value & Tax, 2007
- Residential value $92,673
- Property tax $6,206
- Tax credit/rebate $1,077

Public Library
Middlesex Public Library
1300 Mountain Ave
Middlesex, NJ 08846
732-356-6602

- Director .... May Lein Ho

Library statistics, 2006
- Population served 13,717
- Full-time/total staff 2/3

	Total	Per capita
Holdings	70,109	5.11
Revenues	$520,852	$37.97
Expenditures	$487,596	$35.55
Annual visits	54,200	3.95
Internet terminals/annual users		16/15,531

Public Safety
- Number of officers, 2006 31

Crime	2005	2006
Total crimes	109	174
Violent	7	11
Murder	0	1
Rape	0	0
Robbery	2	3
Aggravated assault	5	7
Non-violent	102	163
Burglary	15	31
Larceny	80	117
Vehicle theft	7	15
Domestic violence	64	46
Arson	2	0
Total crime rate	7.8	12.5
Violent	0.5	0.8
Non-violent	7.3	11.7

Public School District
(for school year 2006-07 except as noted)

Middlesex Borough School District
300 Kennedy Drive
Middlesex, NJ 08846
732-317-6000

- Superintendent .... James Baker
- Number of schools 5
- Grade plan K-12
- Enrollment 2,039
- Attendance rate, '05-06 .... 95.8%
- Dropout rate .... NA
- Students per teacher 10.4
- Per pupil expenditure $13,055
- Median faculty salary $51,880
- Median administrator salary $95,569
- Grade 12 enrollment 142
- High school graduation rate 100.0%

Assessment test results
(percent scoring at proficient or advanced level)

	Language	Math
NJASK-Grade 3	85.8%	89.6%
GEPA-Grade 8	76.8%	73.9%
HSPA-High School	85.8%	72.2%

SAT score averages

Pct tested	Math	Verbal	Writing
80%	499	467	474

Teacher Qualifications
- Avg. years of experience 9
- Highly-qualified teachers
  - one subject/all subjects 98.0%/96.5%
- With emergency credentials 1.2%

No Child Left Behind
- AYP, 2005-06 .... Meets Standards

Municipal Finance
State Aid Programs, 2008
- Total aid $2,279,503
  - CMPTRA 906,349
  - Energy tax receipts 1,373,154
  - Garden State Trust 0

General Budget, 2007
- Total tax levy $33,430,045
  - County levy 4,596,464
    - County taxes 4,114,863
    - County library 0
    - County health 0
    - County open space 481,601
  - School levy 19,627,218
  - Muni. levy 9,206,363
  - Misc. revenues 5,989,528

Taxes	2005	2006	2007
General tax rate per $100	5.85	6.33	6.7
County equalization ratio	40.12	35.28	31.4
Net valuation taxable	$496,611,033	$497,602,000	$499,199,384
State equalized value	$1,407,627,645	$1,585,290,374	$1,673,400,618

Middletown Township
Monmouth County

Demographics & Socio-Economic Characteristics[†]
(2000 US Census, except as noted)

Population
1980*	62,574
1990*	68,183
2000	66,327
Male	32,267
Female	34,060
2006 (estimate)*	67,578
Population density	1,643.4

Race & Hispanic Origin, 2000
Race
White	62,819
Black/African American	803
American Indian/Alaska Native	46
Asian	1,717
Native Hawaiian/Pacific Islander	17
Other race	353
Two or more races	572
Hispanic origin, total	2,265
Mexican	116
Puerto Rican	1,087
Cuban	188
Other Hispanic	874

Age & Nativity, 2000
Under 5 years	4,510
18 years and over	48,886
21 years and over	46,945
65 years and over	8,487
85 years and over	996
Median age	38.8
Native-born	62,069
Foreign-born	4,258

Educational Attainment, 2000
Population 25 years and over	44,664
Less than 9th grade	2.7%
High school grad or higher	90.7%
Bachelor's degree or higher	35.0%
Graduate degree	12.6%

Income & Poverty, 1999
Per capita income	$34,196
Median household income	$75,566
Median family income	$86,124
Persons in poverty	2,049
H'holds receiving public assistance	228
H'holds receiving social security	6,448

Households, 2000
Total households	23,236
With persons under 18	9,311
With persons over 65	6,165
Family households	18,109
Single-person households	4,397
Persons per household	2.84
Persons per family	3.27

Labor & Employment
Total civilian labor force, 2006**	36,171
Unemployment rate	3.4%
Total civilian labor force, 2000	33,728
Unemployment rate	3.4%

Employed persons 16 years and over by occupation, 2000
Managers & professionals	13,619
Service occupations	3,571
Sales & office occupations	9,952
Farming, fishing & forestry	66
Construction & maintenance	2,679
Production & transportation	2,710
Self-employed persons	1,587

[†] see Appendix C for American Community Survey data
* US Census Bureau
** New Jersey Department of Labor

General Information
Township of Middletown
1 Kings Highway
Middletown, NJ 07748
732-615-2000

Website	www.middletownnj.org
Year of incorporation	1693
Land/water area (sq. miles)	41.12/18.23
Form of government	Special Charter

Government
Legislative Districts
US Congressional	6, 12
State Legislative	13

Local Officials, 2008
Mayor	Gerard Scharfenberger
Township Admin	Frederick E. Jahn (Int)
Clerk	Heidi R. Abs
Finance Dir	Richard Wright
Tax Assessor	Charles Heck
Tax Collector	Robert Kapral
Attorney	Bernard Reilly
Building	Joseph Kachinsky
Planning	Anthony Mercantante
Engineering	Robert Bucco
Public Works	Lawrence Werger
Police Chief	Robert Oches
Fire Chief	William Kennelly Jr

Housing & Construction
Housing Units, 2000*
Total	23,841
Median rent	$836
Median SF home value	$210,700

Permits for New Residential Construction
	Units	Value
Total, 2007	241	$30,458,196
Single family	56	$15,071,507
Total, 2006	232	$31,431,559
Single family	197	$27,860,211

Real Property Valuation, 2007
	Parcels	Valuation
Total	24,115	$4,941,599,038
Vacant	1,352	52,305,760
Residential	21,949	4,195,008,178
Commercial	587	605,039,300
Industrial	2	1,152,500
Apartments	13	46,721,100
Farm land	136	487,100
Farm homestead	76	40,885,100

Average Property Value & Tax, 2007
Residential value	$192,322
Property tax	$7,036
Tax credit/rebate	$1,091

Public Library
Middletown Township Public Library
55 New Monmouth Rd
Middletown, NJ 07748
732-671-3700

Director... Susan O'Neal

Library statistics, 2006
Population served	66,327
Full-time/total staff	11/31

	Total	Per capita
Holdings	219,883	3.32
Revenues	$3,622,532	$54.62
Expenditures	$3,502,327	$52.80
Annual visits	585,321	8.82
Internet terminals/annual users	57/87,948	

Taxes
	2005	2006	2007
General tax rate per $100	3.429	3.558	3.659
County equalization ratio	52.94	47.4	42.59
Net valuation taxable	$4,909,216,446	$4,911,669,538	$4,948,064,387
State equalized value	$10,356,996,722	$11,539,217,832	$12,488,402,803

Public Safety
Number of officers, 2006... 103

Crime	2005	2006
Total crimes	743	862
Violent	40	55
Murder	0	0
Rape	1	3
Robbery	5	11
Aggravated assault	34	41
Non-violent	703	807
Burglary	105	120
Larceny	555	652
Vehicle theft	43	35
Domestic violence	245	365
Arson	4	4
Total crime rate	10.9	12.7
Violent	0.6	0.8
Non-violent	10.3	11.9

Public School District
(for school year 2006-07 except as noted)

Middletown Township School District
59 Tindall Rd
Middletown, NJ 07748
732-671-3850

Superintendent	Karen L. Bilbao
Number of schools	18
Grade plan	K-12
Enrollment	10,119
Attendance rate, '05-06	94.6%
Dropout rate	0.1%
Students per teacher	11.5
Per pupil expenditure	$12,798
Median faculty salary	$60,020
Median administrator salary	$117,335
Grade 12 enrollment	722
High school graduation rate	NA

Assessment test results
(percent scoring at proficient or advanced level)
	Language	Math
NJASK-Grade 3	92.1%	96.4%
GEPA-Grade 8	85.1%	83.8%
HSPA-High School	92.7%	81.8%

SAT score averages
Pct tested	Math	Verbal	Writing
NA	NA	NA	NA

Teacher Qualifications
Avg. years of experience	11
Highly-qualified teachers one subject/all subjects	100%/100%
With emergency credentials	0.0%

No Child Left Behind
AYP, 2005-06... Meets Standards

Municipal Finance
State Aid Programs, 2008
Total aid	$7,785,986
CMPTRA	936,999
Energy tax receipts	6,841,023
Garden State Trust	209

General Budget, 2007
Total tax levy	$181,026,677
County levy	29,592,650
County taxes	27,851,935
County library	0
County health	0
County open space	1,740,715
School levy	115,487,465
Muni. levy	35,946,561
Misc. revenues	24,832,795

Bergen County

Midland Park Borough

Demographics & Socio-Economic Characteristics
(2000 US Census, except as noted)

Population
- 1980* 7,381
- 1990* 7,047
- 2000 6,947
  - Male 3,388
  - Female 3,559
- 2006 (estimate)* 6,906
  - Population density 4,426.9

Race & Hispanic Origin, 2000
Race
- White 6,656
- Black/African American 30
- American Indian/Alaska Native 4
- Asian 154
- Native Hawaiian/Pacific Islander 1
- Other race 53
- Two or more races 49
- Hispanic origin, total 256
  - Mexican 13
  - Puerto Rican 50
  - Cuban 22
  - Other Hispanic 171

Age & Nativity, 2000
- Under 5 years 508
- 18 years and over 5,258
- 21 years and over 5,083
- 65 years and over 1,015
- 85 years and over 111
- Median age 38.8
- Native-born 6,381
- Foreign-born 566

Educational Attainment, 2000
- Population 25 years and over 4,867
- Less than 9th grade 3.4%
- High school grad or higher 93.1%
- Bachelor's degree or higher 38.9%
- Graduate degree 10.7%

Income & Poverty, 1999
- Per capita income $32,284
- Median household income $76,462
- Median family income $83,926
- Persons in poverty 141
- H'holds receiving public assistance ... 14
- H'holds receiving social security 742

Households, 2000
- Total households 2,613
  - With persons under 18 909
  - With persons over 65 739
  - Family households 1,884
  - Single-person households 617
- Persons per household 2.65
- Persons per family 3.19

Labor & Employment
- Total civilian labor force, 2006** .. 4,028
  - Unemployment rate 1.6%
- Total civilian labor force, 2000 3,806
  - Unemployment rate 1.7%

Employed persons 16 years and over by occupation, 2000
- Managers & professionals 1,625
- Service occupations 437
- Sales & office occupations 1,081
- Farming, fishing & forestry 0
- Construction & maintenance 344
- Production & transportation 253
- Self-employed persons 205

* US Census Bureau
** New Jersey Department of Labor

See Introduction for an explanation of all data sources.

General Information
Borough of Midland Park
280 Godwin Ave
Midland Park, NJ 07432
201-445-5720

- Website .... mpnj.com
- Year of incorporation 1894
- Land/water area (sq. miles) 1.56/0.00
- Form of government .... Borough

Government
Legislative Districts
- US Congressional 5
- State Legislative 40

Local Officials, 2008
- Mayor .... Joseph Monahan
- Manager .... Michelle Dugan
- Clerk .... Adeline Hanna
- Finance Dir .... Michelle Dugan
- Tax Assessor .... Marje Merolla
- Tax Collector .... Michelle Dugan
- Attorney .... Robert Regan
- Building .... John Wittekind
- Comm Dev/Planning .... NA
- Engineering .... Vollmer Associates
- Public Works .... Rudy Gnehm
- Police Chief .... John Casson
- Emerg/Fire Director .... Pete Hook

Housing & Construction
Housing Units, 2000*
- Total 2,650
- Median rent $1,044
- Median SF home value $256,500

Permits for New Residential Construction

	Units	Value
Total, 2007	3	$530,300
Single family	3	$530,300
Total, 2006	9	$1,504,600
Single family	4	$909,600

Real Property Valuation, 2007

	Parcels	Valuation
Total	2,414	$861,604,500
Vacant	41	6,433,100
Residential	2,196	685,923,900
Commercial	134	115,631,300
Industrial	39	42,033,700
Apartments	4	11,582,500
Farm land	0	0
Farm homestead	0	0

Average Property Value & Tax, 2007
- Residential value $312,352
- Property tax $8,689
- Tax credit/rebate $1,332

Public Library
Midland Park Mem Library
250 Godwin Ave
Midland Park, NJ 07432
201-444-2390

Director .... Jean M. Scott

Library statistics, 2006
- Population served 6,947
- Full-time/total staff 2/5

	Total	Per capita
Holdings	61,737	8.89
Revenues	$446,239	$64.23
Expenditures	$411,362	$59.21
Annual visits	53,122	7.65

Internet terminals/annual users 7/21,565

Public Safety
- Number of officers, 2006 13

Crime	2005	2006
Total crimes	51	43
Violent	3	3
Murder	0	0
Rape	0	0
Robbery	0	1
Aggravated assault	3	2
Non-violent	48	40
Burglary	9	4
Larceny	38	35
Vehicle theft	1	1
Domestic violence	25	22
Arson	0	0
Total crime rate	7.3	6.2
Violent	0.4	0.4
Non-violent	6.9	5.8

Public School District
(for school year 2006-07 except as noted)

Midland Park Borough School District
31 Highland Ave
Midland Park, NJ 07432
201-444-1400

- Superintendent ..... Nicholas Mamola (Int)
- Number of schools 2
- Grade plan K-12
- Enrollment 1,131
- Attendance rate, '05-06 .... 95.7%
- Dropout rate 0.3%
- Students per teacher 10.3
- Per pupil expenditure $14,397
- Median faculty salary $56,563
- Median administrator salary ... $118,408
- Grade 12 enrollment 74
- High school graduation rate 98.6%

Assessment test results
(percent scoring at proficient or advanced level)

	Language	Math
NJASK-Grade 3	92.5%	90.4%
GEPA-Grade 8	74.4%	68.0%
HSPA-High School	96.3%	81.3%

SAT score averages

Pct tested	Math	Verbal	Writing
102%	510	525	539

Teacher Qualifications
- Avg. years of experience 10
- Highly-qualified teachers
  - one subject/all subjects 98.5%/98.5%
- With emergency credentials 0.0%

No Child Left Behind
- AYP, 2005-06 .... Meets Standards

Municipal Finance
State Aid Programs, 2008
- Total aid $634,788
  - CMPTRA 120,147
  - Energy tax receipts 514,641
  - Garden State Trust 0

General Budget, 2007
- Total tax levy $23,996,004
  - County levy 2,466,587
    - County taxes 2,330,740
    - County library 0
    - County health 0
    - County open space 135,847
  - School levy 15,468,991
  - Muni. levy 6,060,426
- Misc. revenues 2,996,598

Taxes	2005	2006	2007
General tax rate per $100	2.54	2.67	2.79
County equalization ratio	83.42	74.28	64.06
Net valuation taxable	$855,006,629	$858,487,100	$862,570,429
State equalized value	$1,151,059,005	$1,341,027,291	$1,317,397,556

Milford Borough
Hunterdon County

Demographics & Socio-Economic Characteristics
(2000 US Census, except as noted)

Population
1980*	1,368
1990*	1,273
2000	1,195
Male	606
Female	589
2006 (estimate)*	1,219
Population density	1,060.0

Race & Hispanic Origin, 2000
Race
- White 1,166
- Black/African American 2
- American Indian/Alaska Native 2
- Asian 5
- Native Hawaiian/Pacific Islander 4
- Other race 1
- Two or more races 15

Hispanic origin, total 24
- Mexican 10
- Puerto Rican 2
- Cuban 1
- Other Hispanic 11

Age & Nativity, 2000
- Under 5 years 70
- 18 years and over 892
- 21 years and over 863
- 65 years and over 163
- 85 years and over 15
- Median age 38.7
- Native-born 1,163
- Foreign-born 32

Educational Attainment, 2000
- Population 25 years and over 846
- Less than 9th grade 3.1%
- High school grad or higher 88.5%
- Bachelor's degree or higher 26.2%
- Graduate degree 6.5%

Income & Poverty, 1999
- Per capita income $25,039
- Median household income $54,519
- Median family income $62,167
- Persons in poverty 44
- H'holds receiving public assistance 12
- H'holds receiving social security 133

Households, 2000
- Total households 469
- With persons under 18 165
- With persons over 65 122
- Family households 323
- Single-person households 127
- Persons per household 2.55
- Persons per family 3.11

Labor & Employment
- Total civilian labor force, 2006** 725
- Unemployment rate 6.2%
- Total civilian labor force, 2000 631
- Unemployment rate 3.6%

Employed persons 16 years and over by occupation, 2000
- Managers & professionals 197
- Service occupations 63
- Sales & office occupations 178
- Farming, fishing & forestry 0
- Construction & maintenance 79
- Production & transportation 91
- Self-employed persons 61

* US Census Bureau
** New Jersey Department of Labor

General Information
Borough of Milford
30 Water St
Milford, NJ 08848
908-995-4323

- Website .... www.milfordnj.org
- Year of incorporation 1911
- Land/water area (sq. miles) 1.15/0.07
- Form of government .... Borough

Government
Legislative Districts
- US Congressional 7
- State Legislative 23

Local Officials, 2008
- Mayor .... James A. Gallos
- Manager/Admin .... NA
- Clerk .... Karen Dysart
- Finance Dir .... Dawn Merante
- Tax Assessor .... David Gill
- Tax Collector .... Judy Holmberg
- Attorney .... Todd L. Bolig
- Building .... DCA
- Comm Dev/Planning .... NA
- Engineering .... Robert J. Clerico
- Public Works .... NA
- Police Chief .... NA
- Emerg/Fire Director .... Nathan Fleck

Housing & Construction
Housing Units, 2000*
- Total 484
- Median rent $794
- Median SF home value $153,800

Permits for New Residential Construction
	Units	Value
Total, 2007	0	$0
Single family	0	$0
Total, 2006	0	$0
Single family	0	$0

Real Property Valuation, 2007
	Parcels	Valuation
Total	528	$122,321,170
Vacant	51	2,034,300
Residential	416	94,823,600
Commercial	44	12,465,970
Industrial	4	8,318,800
Apartments	1	3,238,200
Farm land	8	31,800
Farm homestead	4	1,408,500

Average Property Value & Tax, 2007
- Residential value $229,124
- Property tax $6,560
- Tax credit/rebate $1,111

Public Library
Milford Public Library
40 Frenchtown-Milford Rd
Milford, NJ 08848
908-995-4072

Director .... Jennifer Locke

Library statistics, 2006
- Population served 1,195
- Full-time/total staff 0/1

	Total	Per capita
Holdings	21,031	17.60
Revenues	$61,504	$51.47
Expenditures	$60,132	$50.32
Annual visits	9,821	8.22

Internet terminals/annual users 1/1,048

Taxes
	2005	2006	2007
General tax rate per $100	2.55	2.62	2.87
County equalization ratio	87.58	83.87	74.68
Net valuation taxable	$118,377,206	$120,818,070	$122,552,705
State equalized value	$128,824,906	$151,900,421	$164,641,710

Public Safety
Number of officers, 2006 0

Crime	2005	2006
Total crimes	15	13
Violent	1	2
Murder	0	0
Rape	0	0
Robbery	1	0
Aggravated assault	0	2
Non-violent	14	11
Burglary	11	4
Larceny	70	7
Vehicle theft	4	0
Domestic violence	49	0
Arson	0	1
Total crime rate	12.4	10.7
Violent	0.8	1.6
Non-violent	11.6	9.1

Public School District
(for school year 2006-07 except as noted)

Milford Borough School District
7 Hillside Ave
Milford, NJ 08848
908-995-4349

- Chief School Admin .... Ed Stoloski
- Number of schools 1
- Grade plan K-8
- Enrollment 119
- Attendance rate, '05-06 .... 96.2%
- Dropout rate .... NA
- Students per teacher 7.9
- Per pupil expenditure $15,727
- Median faculty salary $43,140
- Median administrator salary $62,400
- Grade 12 enrollment .... NA
- High school graduation rate .... NA

Assessment test results
(percent scoring at proficient or advanced level)
	Language	Math
NJASK-Grade 3	NA	NA
GEPA-Grade 8	77.8%	83.3%
HSPA-High School	NA	NA

SAT score averages
Pct tested	Math	Verbal	Writing
NA	NA	NA	NA

Teacher Qualifications
- Avg. years of experience 10
- Highly-qualified teachers one subject/all subjects 100%/100%
- With emergency credentials 0.0%

No Child Left Behind
AYP, 2005-06 .... Meets Standards

Municipal Finance
State Aid Programs, 2008
- Total aid $190,276
- CMPTRA 0
- Energy tax receipts 190,276
- Garden State Trust 0

General Budget, 2007
- Total tax levy $3,508,786
- County levy 531,701
- County taxes 479,933
- County library 0
- County health 0
- County open space 51,768
- School levy 2,243,748
- Muni. levy 733,337
- Misc. revenues 962,612

Essex County / Millburn Township

Demographics & Socio-Economic Characteristics
(2000 US Census, except as noted)

Population
1980*	19,543
1990*	18,630
2000	19,765
Male	9,584
Female	10,181
2006 (estimate)*	19,153
Population density	2,041.9

Race & Hispanic Origin, 2000
Race
White	17,573
Black/African American	217
American Indian/Alaska Native	10
Asian	1,660
Native Hawaiian/Pacific Islander	6
Other race	85
Two or more races	214
Hispanic origin, total	404
Mexican	48
Puerto Rican	64
Cuban	35
Other Hispanic	257

Age & Nativity, 2000
Under 5 years	1,720
18 years and over	13,789
21 years and over	13,502
65 years and over	2,581
85 years and over	304
Median age	39.2
Native-born	16,866
Foreign-born	2,899

Educational Attainment, 2000
Population 25 years and over	13,190
Less than 9th grade	1.2%
High school grad or higher	96.6%
Bachelor's degree or higher	74.0%
Graduate degree	38.4%

Income & Poverty, 1999
Per capita income	$76,796
Median household income	$130,848
Median family income	$158,888
Persons in poverty	288
H'holds receiving public assistance	50
H'holds receiving social security	1,711

Households, 2000
Total households	7,015
With persons under 18	3,158
With persons over 65	1,784
Family households	5,604
Single-person households	1,224
Persons per household	2.82
Persons per family	3.19

Labor & Employment
Total civilian labor force, 2006**	9,490
Unemployment rate	2.1%
Total civilian labor force, 2000	8,956
Unemployment rate	1.8%

Employed persons 16 years and over by occupation, 2000
Managers & professionals	5,761
Service occupations	421
Sales & office occupations	2,167
Farming, fishing & forestry	0
Construction & maintenance	170
Production & transportation	280
Self-employed persons	799

* US Census Bureau
** New Jersey Department of Labor

See Introduction for an explanation of all data sources.

General Information
Township of Millburn
375 Millburn Ave
Millburn, NJ 07041
973-564-7000

Website	www.twp.millburn.nj.us
Year of incorporation	1857
Land/water area (sq. miles)	9.38/0.52
Form of government	Township

Government
Legislative Districts
US Congressional	11-Oct
State Legislative	21

Local Officials, 2008
Mayor	Sandra Haimoff
Manager	Timothy Gordon
Clerk	Joanne Monarque
Finance Dir	Jason Gabloff
Tax Assessor	Ernest Del Gurcio
Tax Collector	Gerald Viturello
Attorney	Christopher Falcon
Building	Steven Jones
Comm Dev/Planning	NA
Engineering	W. Thomas Watkinson
Public Works	Timothy Monahan
Police Chief	Paul Boegershausen
Emerg/Fire Director	J. Michael Roberts

Housing & Construction
Housing Units, 2000*
Total	7,158
Median rent	$1,114
Median SF home value	$549,000

Permits for New Residential Construction
	Units	Value
Total, 2007	15	$11,477,078
Single family	15	$11,477,078
Total, 2006	26	$15,093,990
Single family	26	$15,093,990

Real Property Valuation, 2007
	Parcels	Valuation
Total	6,538	$8,365,797,100
Vacant	82	50,171,400
Residential	6,174	6,700,006,700
Commercial	232	1,499,525,400
Industrial	30	46,886,300
Apartments	20	69,207,300
Farm land	0	0
Farm homestead	0	0

Average Property Value & Tax, 2007
Residential value	$1,085,197
Property tax	$17,080
Tax credit/rebate	$1,364

Public Library
Millburn Public Library
200 Glen Ave
Millburn, NJ 07041
973-376-1006

Director . . . . William R. Swinson

Library statistics, 2006
Population served	19,765
Full-time/total staff	9/17

	Total	Per capita
Holdings	115,113	5.82
Revenues	$2,812,558	$142.30
Expenditures	$2,586,726	$130.87
Annual visits	212,075	10.73

Internet terminals/annual users . . 16/184,827

Public Safety
Number of officers, 2006 53

Crime	2005	2006
Total crimes	645	781
Violent	22	17
Murder	0	0
Rape	0	1
Robbery	14	11
Aggravated assault	8	5
Non-violent	623	764
Burglary	43	66
Larceny	539	626
Vehicle theft	41	72
Domestic violence	75	92
Arson	0	1
Total crime rate	32.9	40.3
Violent	1.1	0.9
Non-violent	31.8	39.4

Public School District
(for school year 2006-07 except as noted)

Millburn Township School District
434 Millburn Ave
Millburn, NJ 07041
973-376-3600

Superintendent	Richard Brodow
Number of schools	7
Grade plan	K-12
Enrollment	4,581
Attendance rate, '05-06	94.7%
Dropout rate	NA
Students per teacher	10.5
Per pupil expenditure	$14,156
Median faculty salary	$69,000
Median administrator salary	$121,699
Grade 12 enrollment	300
High school graduation rate	100.0%

Assessment test results
(percent scoring at proficient or advanced level)
	Language	Math
NJASK-Grade 3	96.6%	97.7%
GEPA-Grade 8	95.4%	93.1%
HSPA-High School	97.6%	96.1%

SAT score averages
Pct tested	Math	Verbal	Writing
99%	628	597	605

Teacher Qualifications
Avg. years of experience	9
Highly-qualified teachers one subject/all subjects	99.0%/99.0%
With emergency credentials	0.0%

No Child Left Behind
AYP, 2005-06 . . . . Meets Standards

Municipal Finance
State Aid Programs, 2008
Total aid	$3,196,809
CMPTRA	154,941
Energy tax receipts	3,014,232
Garden State Trust	0

General Budget, 2007
Total tax levy	$131,776,030
County levy	31,837,996
County taxes	31,016,184
County library	0
County health	0
County open space	821,812
School levy	67,361,709
Muni. levy	32,576,326
Misc. revenues	11,321,819

Taxes
	2005	2006	2007
General tax rate per $100	2.05	2.12	1.58
County equalization ratio	85.08	78.37	102.18
Net valuation taxable	$5,962,668,369	$5,918,458,000	$8,372,472,024
State equalized value	$7,608,355,709	$8,116,490,969	$8,674,996,445

The New Jersey Municipal Data Book

Millstone Borough
Somerset County

Demographics & Socio-Economic Characteristics
(2000 US Census, except as noted)

Population
- 1980*..................................530
- 1990*..................................450
- 2000..................................410
  - Male..................................204
  - Female..............................206
- 2006 (estimate)*....................431
  - Population density............574.7

Race & Hispanic Origin, 2000
Race
- White..................................400
- Black/African American...........4
- American Indian/Alaska Native...0
- Asian....................................4
- Native Hawaiian/Pacific Islander...0
- Other race.............................0
- Two or more races..................2
- Hispanic origin, total.............13
  - Mexican................................0
  - Puerto Rican........................10
  - Cuban...................................0
  - Other Hispanic.......................3

Age & Nativity, 2000
- Under 5 years........................17
- 18 years and over.................331
- 21 years and over.................323
- 65 years and over..................70
- 85 years and over..................10
  - Median age........................45.6
- Native-born.........................398
- Foreign-born.........................19

Educational Attainment, 2000
- Population 25 years and over...........305
- Less than 9th grade..................2.0%
- High school grad or higher........91.5%
- Bachelor's degree or higher......39.0%
- Graduate degree......................16.4%

Income & Poverty, 1999
- Per capita income................$30,694
- Median household income........$76,353
- Median family income............$83,118
- Persons in poverty......................19
- H'holds receiving public assistance...2
- H'holds receiving social security...44

Households, 2000
- Total households.....................169
  - With persons under 18............47
  - With persons over 65..............51
  - Family households................127
  - Single-person households......32
- Persons per household............2.43
- Persons per family..................2.79

Labor & Employment
- Total civilian labor force, 2006**........270
  - Unemployment rate....................0.0%
- Total civilian labor force, 2000..........245
  - Unemployment rate....................2.0%

Employed persons 16 years and over by occupation, 2000
- Managers & professionals...........127
- Service occupations....................20
- Sales & office occupations...........51
- Farming, fishing & forestry............0
- Construction & maintenance.......23
- Production & transportation.......19
- Self-employed persons................21

* US Census Bureau
** New Jersey Department of Labor

General Information
Borough of Millstone
1353 Main St
Millstone, NJ 08844
908-281-6893

- Website............www.millstoneboro.org
- Year of incorporation...................1894
- Land/water area (sq. miles).......0.75/0.00
- Form of government................Borough

Government
Legislative Districts
- US Congressional.........................7
- State Legislative..........................16

Local Officials, 2008
- Mayor.....................Raymond Heck
- Manager/Admin........................NA
- Clerk........................Gregory Bonin
- Finance Dir.............Gregory Della Pia
- Tax Assessor............Marcia Sudano
- Tax Collector................Diane Wynn
- Attorney....................Steven Offen
- Building..................................NA
- Planning.............Carter Van Dyke
- Engineering...............James DeMuro
- Public Works............................NA
- Police Chief............................NA
- Fire/Emergency Dir...................NA

Housing & Construction
Housing Units, 2000*
- Total..173
- Median rent..........................$875
- Median SF home value......$205,400

Permits for New Residential Construction

	Units	Value
Total, 2007	1	$275,000
Single family	1	$275,000
Total, 2006	0	$0
Single family	0	$0

Real Property Valuation, 2007

	Parcels	Valuation
Total	185	$62,562,000
Vacant	11	415,200
Residential	156	58,332,700
Commercial	9	3,700,100
Industrial	0	0
Apartments	0	0
Farm land	9	114,000
Farm homestead	0	0

Average Property Value & Tax, 2007
- Residential value..................$373,928
- Property tax..........................$5,899
- Tax credit/rebate..................$1,069

Public Library
No public municipal library

Library statistics, 2006
- Population served......................NA
- Full-time/total staff..................NA/NA

	Total	Per capita
Holdings	NA	NA
Revenues	NA	NA
Expenditures	NA	NA
Annual visits	NA	NA
Internet terminals/annual users	NA	NA

Public Safety
Number of officers, 2006.................0

Crime	2005	2006
Total crimes	2	0
Violent	0	0
Murder	0	0
Rape	0	0
Robbery	0	0
Aggravated assault	0	0
Non-violent	2	0
Burglary	0	0
Larceny	1	0
Vehicle theft	1	0
Domestic violence	1	0
Arson	0	0
Total crime rate	4.6	0.0
Violent	0.0	0.0
Non-violent	4.6	0.0

Public School District
(for school year 2006-07 except as noted)

Millstone Borough School District
PO Box 854
Somerville, NJ 08876

No schools in district - sends students to Hillsborough schools

- Per pupil expenditure....................NA
- Median faculty salary...................NA
- Median administrator salary..........NA
- Grade 12 enrollment....................NA
- High school graduation rate..........NA

Assessment test results
(percent scoring at proficient or advanced level)

	Language	Math
NJASK-Grade 3	NA	NA
GEPA-Grade 8	NA	NA
HSPA-High School	NA	NA

SAT score averages

Pct tested	Math	Verbal	Writing
NA	NA	NA	NA

Teacher Qualifications
- Avg. years of experience..............NA
- Highly-qualified teachers
  - one subject/all subjects........NA/NA
- With emergency credentials..........NA

No Child Left Behind
- AYP, 2005-06.............................NA

Municipal Finance
State Aid Programs, 2008
- Total aid............................$78,728
  - CMPTRA...................................0
  - Energy tax receipts.............78,660
  - Garden State Trust...................68

General Budget, 2007
- Total tax levy.....................$987,800
  - County levy.......................174,997
    - County taxes...................141,532
    - County library..................17,967
    - County health............................0
    - County open space...........15,498
  - School levy.....................477,493
  - Muni. levy......................335,310
  - Misc. revenues................193,897

Taxes

	2005	2006	2007
General tax rate per $100	2.16	1.72	1.58
County equalization ratio	95.63	112.51	121.52
Net valuation taxable	$49,185,299	$58,070,800	$62,615,156
State equalized value	$51,422,163	$51,534,393	$55,193,293

Monmouth County
Millstone Township

Demographics & Socio-Economic Characteristics
(2000 US Census, except as noted)

Population
1980*	3,926
1990*	5,069
2000	8,970
Male	4,472
Female	4,498
2006 (estimate)*	10,064
Population density	273.8

Race & Hispanic Origin, 2000
Race
White	8,237
Black/African American	274
American Indian/Alaska Native	9
Asian	308
Native Hawaiian/Pacific Islander	3
Other race	55
Two or more races	84
Hispanic origin, total	315
Mexican	41
Puerto Rican	130
Cuban	35
Other Hispanic	109

Age & Nativity, 2000
Under 5 years	758
18 years and over	6,028
21 years and over	5,818
65 years and over	538
85 years and over	60
Median age	37.1
Native-born	8,374
Foreign-born	596

Educational Attainment, 2000
Population 25 years and over	5,624
Less than 9th grade	2.7%
High school grad or higher	92.2%
Bachelor's degree or higher	42.7%
Graduate degree	16.1%

Income & Poverty, 1999
Per capita income	$37,285
Median household income	$94,561
Median family income	$96,116
Persons in poverty	434
H'holds receiving public assistance	36
H'holds receiving social security	377

Households, 2000
Total households	2,708
With persons under 18	1,477
With persons over 65	366
Family households	2,426
Single-person households	204
Persons per household	3.28
Persons per family	3.46

Labor & Employment
Total civilian labor force, 2006**	4,638
Unemployment rate	1.9%
Total civilian labor force, 2000	4,337
Unemployment rate	2.5%

Employed persons 16 years and over by occupation, 2000
Managers & professionals	2,184
Service occupations	391
Sales & office occupations	1,138
Farming, fishing & forestry	37
Construction & maintenance	272
Production & transportation	207
Self-employed persons	356

* US Census Bureau
** New Jersey Department of Labor

See Introduction for an explanation of all data sources.

General Information
Township of Millstone
470 Stage Coach Rd
Millstone, NJ 08510
732-446-4249

Website	www.millstone.nj.us
Year of incorporation	1844
Land/water area (sq. miles)	36.76/0.42
Form of government	Township

Government
Legislative Districts
US Congressional	4
State Legislative	12

Local Officials, 2008
Mayor	Nancy A. Grbelja
Administrator	James Pickering Jr
Clerk	Maria Dellasala
Finance Dir	Annette Murphy
Tax Assessor	Thomas Davis
Tax Collector	Dawn Mitchell
Attorney	Duane Davison
Building	Henry Salerno
Planning	Pam D'Andrea
Engineering	Matt Shafai
Public Works	Ken Gann
Police Chief	NA
Fire Chief	Jim Carbin

Housing & Construction
Housing Units, 2000*
Total	2,797
Median rent	$941
Median SF home value	$319,500

Permits for New Residential Construction
	Units	Value
Total, 2007	16	$4,434,090
Single family	16	$4,434,090
Total, 2006	24	$7,354,500
Single family	24	$7,354,500

Real Property Valuation, 2007
	Parcels	Valuation
Total	4,120	$1,380,993,300
Vacant	383	41,914,200
Residential	2,989	1,210,892,100
Commercial	83	49,327,600
Industrial	4	3,925,900
Apartments	0	0
Farm land	424	4,262,400
Farm homestead	237	70,671,100

Average Property Value & Tax, 2007
Residential value	$397,261
Property tax	$10,123
Tax credit/rebate	$1,268

Public Library
No public municipal library

Library statistics, 2006
Population served	NA
Full-time/total staff	NA/NA

	Total	Per capita
Holdings	NA	NA
Revenues	NA	NA
Expenditures	NA	NA
Annual visits	NA	NA
Internet terminals/annual users	NA/NA	

Taxes
	2005	2006	2007
General tax rate per $100	2.315	2.331	2.549
County equalization ratio	81.89	73.55	67.28
Net valuation taxable	$1,322,024,153	$1,356,254,700	$1,383,072,039
State equalized value	$1,797,449,562	$2,017,993,414	$2,135,875,556

Public Safety
Number of officers, 2006 0

Crime
	2005	2006
Total crimes	80	112
Violent	7	4
Murder	0	0
Rape	1	0
Robbery	1	2
Aggravated assault	5	2
Non-violent	73	108
Burglary	21	27
Larceny	47	69
Vehicle theft	5	12
Domestic violence	19	8
Arson	1	2
Total crime rate	8.1	11.1
Violent	0.7	0.4
Non-violent	7.4	10.7

Public School District
(for school year 2006-07 except as noted)

Millstone Township School District
5 Dawson Court
Millstone Township, NJ 08535
732-446-0890

Superintendent	Mary Anne Donahue
Number of schools	2
Grade plan	K-8
Enrollment	1,678
Attendance rate, '05-06	95.5%
Dropout rate	NA
Students per teacher	11.7
Per pupil expenditure	$11,273
Median faculty salary	$48,250
Median administrator salary	$104,500
Grade 12 enrollment	NA
High school graduation rate	NA

Assessment test results
(percent scoring at proficient or advanced level)
	Language	Math
NJASK-Grade 3	93.9%	94.4%
GEPA-Grade 8	90.2%	82.4%
HSPA-High School	NA	NA

SAT score averages
Pct tested	Math	Verbal	Writing
NA	NA	NA	NA

Teacher Qualifications
Avg. years of experience	7
Highly-qualified teachers one subject/all subjects	100%/100%
With emergency credentials	0.0%

No Child Left Behind
AYP, 2005-06 .... Meets Standards

Municipal Finance
State Aid Programs, 2008
Total aid	$1,094,127
CMPTRA	19,160
Energy tax receipts	1,050,853
Garden State Trust	24,114

General Budget, 2007
Total tax levy	$35,243,624
County levy	5,638,026
County taxes	4,950,959
County library	283,425
County health	94,306
County open space	309,337
School levy	27,530,688
Muni. levy	2,074,910
Misc. revenues	6,102,406

Milltown Borough
Middlesex County

Demographics & Socio-Economic Characteristics
(2000 US Census, except as noted)

Population
1980*	7,136
1990*	6,968
2000	7,000
Male	3,377
Female	3,623
2006 (estimate)*	7,038
Population density	4,482.8

Race & Hispanic Origin, 2000
Race
White	6,570
Black/African American	53
American Indian/Alaska Native	11
Asian	215
Native Hawaiian/Pacific Islander	0
Other race	81
Two or more races	70
Hispanic origin, total	261
Mexican	16
Puerto Rican	67
Cuban	25
Other Hispanic	153

Age & Nativity, 2000
Under 5 years	387
18 years and over	5,399
21 years and over	5,200
65 years and over	1,098
85 years and over	121
Median age	39.9
Native-born	6,470
Foreign-born	530

Educational Attainment, 2000
Population 25 years and over	4,918
Less than 9th grade	4.4%
High school grad or higher	86.9%
Bachelor's degree or higher	27.2%
Graduate degree	7.4%

Income & Poverty, 1999
Per capita income	$29,996
Median household income	$68,429
Median family income	$77,869
Persons in poverty	158
H'holds receiving public assistance	34
H'holds receiving social security	799

Households, 2000
Total households	2,627
With persons under 18	882
With persons over 65	794
Family households	1,945
Single-person households	561
Persons per household	2.66
Persons per family	3.12

Labor & Employment
Total civilian labor force, 2006**	4,153
Unemployment rate	4.1%
Total civilian labor force, 2000	3,754
Unemployment rate	3.7%

Employed persons 16 years and over by occupation, 2000
Managers & professionals	1,393
Service occupations	475
Sales & office occupations	1,077
Farming, fishing & forestry	0
Construction & maintenance	336
Production & transportation	334
Self-employed persons	120

* US Census Bureau
** New Jersey Department of Labor

General Information
Borough of Milltown
39 Washington Ave
Milltown, NJ 08850
732-828-2100

Website	www.milltownnj.org
Year of incorporation	1889
Land/water area (sq. miles)	1.57/0.03
Form of government	Borough

Government
Legislative Districts
US Congressional	12
State Legislative	17

Local Officials, 2008
Mayor	Gloria Bradford
Manager	Denise Biancamono
Clerk	Michael Januszka
Finance Dir	Denise Biancamono
Tax Assessor	Eldo Magnani
Tax Collector	Diane Wagner
Attorney	Thomas Buck
Building	Vincent Lupo
Planning	Marcia Shiffman
Engineering	Michael McClelland
Public Works	Rich Williams
Police Chief	Raymond Geipel
Emerg/Fire Director	Brian Bush

Housing & Construction
Housing Units, 2000*
Total	2,670
Median rent	$753
Median SF home value	$178,400

Permits for New Residential Construction
	Units	Value
Total, 2007	4	$492,348
Single family	4	$492,348
Total, 2006	3	$369,261
Single family	3	$369,261

Real Property Valuation, 2007
	Parcels	Valuation
Total	2,547	$466,777,800
Vacant	54	5,353,100
Residential	2,387	396,133,800
Commercial	96	54,468,500
Industrial	5	8,927,400
Apartments	5	1,895,000
Farm land	0	0
Farm homestead	0	0

Average Property Value & Tax, 2007
Residential value	$165,955
Property tax	$6,444
Tax credit/rebate	$1,108

Public Library
Milltown Public Library
20 W Church St
Milltown, NJ 08850
732-247-2270

Director: Bonnie J. Sterling

Library statistics, 2006
Population served	7,000
Full-time/total staff	1/3

	Total	Per capita
Holdings	37,654	5.38
Revenues	$324,155	$46.31
Expenditures	$304,162	$43.45
Annual visits	59,280	8.47
Internet terminals/annual users	5/4,652	

Taxes
	2005	2006	2007
General tax rate per $100	3.54	3.77	3.89
County equalization ratio	60.17	54.89	48.73
Net valuation taxable	$465,740,454	$466,606,600	$467,046,467
State equalized value	$848,497,821	$957,824,244	$1,024,353,353

Public Safety
Number of officers, 2006	16

Crime	2005	2006
Total crimes	159	174
Violent	6	8
Murder	0	0
Rape	2	2
Robbery	1	2
Aggravated assault	3	4
Non-violent	153	166
Burglary	15	29
Larceny	130	128
Vehicle theft	8	9
Domestic violence	69	50
Arson	1	0
Total crime rate	22.2	24.4
Violent	0.8	1.1
Non-violent	21.4	23.3

Public School District
(for school year 2006-07 except as noted)

Milltown School District
80 Violet Terrace
Milltown, NJ 08850
732-214-2365

Superintendent	Linda A. Madison
Number of schools	2
Grade plan	K-8
Enrollment	680
Attendance rate, '05-06	95.9%
Dropout rate	NA
Students per teacher	10.2
Per pupil expenditure	$12,666
Median faculty salary	$42,783
Median administrator salary	$103,220
Grade 12 enrollment	NA
High school graduation rate	NA

Assessment test results
(percent scoring at proficient or advanced level)
	Language	Math
NJASK-Grade 3	90.8%	90.8%
GEPA-Grade 8	85.5%	80.5%
HSPA-High School	NA	NA

SAT score averages
Pct tested	Math	Verbal	Writing
NA	NA	NA	NA

Teacher Qualifications
Avg. years of experience	8
Highly-qualified teachers one subject/all subjects	100%/100%
With emergency credentials	0.0%

No Child Left Behind
AYP, 2005-06 .... Meets Standards

Municipal Finance
State Aid Programs, 2008
Total aid	$410,990
CMPTRA	151,189
Energy tax receipts	259,801
Garden State Trust	0

General Budget, 2007
Total tax levy	$18,135,657
County levy	2,763,912
County taxes	2,474,321
County library	0
County health	0
County open space	289,591
School levy	11,709,846
Muni. levy	3,661,899
Misc. revenues	4,438,834

Cumberland County

Millville City

Demographics & Socio-Economic Characteristics
(2000 US Census, except as noted)

Population
- 1980* 24,815
- 1990* 25,992
- 2000 26,847
  - Male 12,678
  - Female 14,169
- 2006 (estimate)* 28,194
- Population density 665.7

Race & Hispanic Origin, 2000
Race
- White 20,438
- Black/African American 4,025
- American Indian/Alaska Native 139
- Asian 216
- Native Hawaiian/Pacific Islander 8
- Other race 1,384
- Two or more races 637
- Hispanic origin, total 2,998
  - Mexican 168
  - Puerto Rican 2,392
  - Cuban 14
  - Other Hispanic 424

Age & Nativity, 2000
- Under 5 years 1,871
- 18 years and over 19,349
- 21 years and over 18,311
- 65 years and over 3,460
- 85 years and over 393
  - Median age 35.0
- Native-born 26,261
- Foreign-born 586

Educational Attainment, 2000
- Population 25 years and over 16,998
- Less than 9th grade 7.8%
- High school grad or higher 74.1%
- Bachelor's degree or higher 12.2%
- Graduate degree 3.2%

Income & Poverty, 1999
- Per capita income $18,632
- Median household income $40,378
- Median family income $46,093
- Persons in poverty 4,034
- H'holds receiving public assistance 555
- H'holds receiving social security 2,818

Households, 2000
- Total households 10,043
  - With persons under 18 3,978
  - With persons over 65 2,559
  - Family households 7,011
  - Single-person households 2,519
- Persons per household 2.65
- Persons per family 3.15

Labor & Employment
- Total civilian labor force, 2006** 14,220
  - Unemployment rate 8.3%
- Total civilian labor force, 2000 13,003
  - Unemployment rate 9.3%

Employed persons 16 years and over by occupation, 2000
- Managers & professionals 2,927
- Service occupations 2,345
- Sales & office occupations 2,884
- Farming, fishing & forestry 27
- Construction & maintenance 1,270
- Production & transportation 2,338
- Self-employed persons 606

---

* US Census Bureau
** New Jersey Department of Labor
§ State Fiscal Year July 1–June 30

See Introduction for an explanation of all data sources.

General Information
City of Millville
12 S High St
PO Box 609
Millville, NJ 08332
856-825-7000

- Website .... www.millvillenj.gov
- Year of incorporation 1866
- Land/water area (sq. miles) 42.35/2.19
- Form of government .... Commission

Government
Legislative Districts
- US Congressional 2
- State Legislative 1

Local Officials, 2008
- Mayor .... James Quinn
- Manager .... Lewis Thompson
- Clerk .... Lewis Thompson
- Finance Dir .... Maureen Mitchell
- Tax Assessor .... Brian Rosenberger
- Tax Collector .... Suzanne Olah
- Attorney .... Richard McCarthy
- Building .... Milton Truxton
- Planning .... Kim Ayres
- Engineering .... John Knoop
- Public Works .... W. James Parent
- Police Chief .... Ed Grennon (Actg)
- Emerg/Fire Director .... Kurt Hess

Housing & Construction
Housing Units, 2000*
- Total 10,652
- Median rent $589
- Median SF home value $86,700

Permits for New Residential Construction

	Units	Value
Total, 2007	224	$19,891,204
Single family	143	$12,793,604
Total, 2006	200	$19,082,794
Single family	191	$18,477,994

Real Property Valuation, 2007

	Parcels	Valuation
Total	10,003	$1,422,199,800
Vacant	1,303	45,028,600
Residential	7,999	997,000,000
Commercial	410	208,560,900
Industrial	70	122,092,900
Apartments	32	39,502,100
Farm land	137	1,368,900
Farm homestead	52	8,646,400

Average Property Value & Tax, 2007
- Residential value $124,910
- Property tax $3,736
- Tax credit/rebate $841

Public Library
Millville Public Library
210 Buck St
Millville, NJ 08332
856-825-7087

- Director .... Jennifer Druce

Library statistics, 2006
- Population served 26,847
- Full-time/total staff 2/4

	Total	Per capita
Holdings	54,923	2.05
Revenues	$696,088	$25.93
Expenditures	$673,135	$25.07
Annual visits	145,461	5.42

- Internet terminals/annual users 8/14,385

Taxes	2005	2006	2007
General tax rate per $100	2.34	2.826	2.993
County equalization ratio	128.52	102.86	86.55
Net valuation taxable	$1,352,978,038	$1,368,151,800	$1,427,591,878
State equalized value	$1,315,358,777	$1,586,676,514	$1,788,491,125

Public Safety
- Number of officers, 2006 78

Crime	2005	2006
Total crimes	1,739	1,775
Violent	241	240
Murder	1	8
Rape	18	8
Robbery	80	98
Aggravated assault	142	126
Non-violent	1,498	1,535
Burglary	316	398
Larceny	1,111	1,084
Vehicle theft	71	53
Domestic violence	817	1,056
Arson	1	14
Total crime rate	63.0	63.7
Violent	8.7	8.6
Non-violent	54.3	55.0

Public School District
(for school year 2006-07 except as noted)

Millville School District
110 N Third St, PO Box 5010
Millville, NJ 08332
856-327-7575

- Superintendent .... Shelly Schneider
- Number of schools 10
- Grade plan K-12
- Enrollment 6,400
- Attendance rate, '05-06 .... 92.0%
- Dropout rate 5.1%
- Students per teacher 10.6
- Per pupil expenditure $13,517
- Median faculty salary $54,253
- Median administrator salary $99,900
- Grade 12 enrollment 480
- High school graduation rate 80.1%

Assessment test results
(percent scoring at proficient or advanced level)

	Language	Math
NJASK-Grade 3	71.2%	68.6%
GEPA-Grade 8	52.7%	48.8%
HSPA-High School	77.1%	60.4%

SAT score averages

Pct tested	Math	Verbal	Writing
28%	470	464	453

Teacher Qualifications
- Avg. years of experience 11
- Highly-qualified teachers
  one subject/all subjects 100%/100%
- With emergency credentials 0.4%

No Child Left Behind
- AYP, 2005-06 .... Meets Standards

Municipal Finance§
State Aid Programs, 2008
- Total aid $5,071,163
- CMPTRA 1,537,458
- Energy tax receipts 3,482,630
- Garden State Trust 51,075

General Budget, 2007
- Total tax levy $42,695,791
- County levy 16,416,512
  - County taxes 15,546,447
  - County library 0
  - County health 702,773
  - County open space 167,293
- School levy 9,450,580
- Muni. levy 16,828,698
- Misc. revenues 12,787,398

Mine Hill Township
Morris County

Demographics & Socio-Economic Characteristics
(2000 US Census, except as noted)

Population
1980*	3,325
1990*	3,333
2000	3,679
Male	1,787
Female	1,892
2006 (estimate)*	3,666
Population density	1,226.1

Race & Hispanic Origin, 2000
Race
White	3,326
Black/African American	126
American Indian/Alaska Native	4
Asian	92
Native Hawaiian/Pacific Islander	3
Other race	66
Two or more races	62
Hispanic origin, total	319
Mexican	13
Puerto Rican	105
Cuban	19
Other Hispanic	182

Age & Nativity, 2000
Under 5 years	312
18 years and over	2,778
21 years and over	2,696
65 years and over	487
85 years and over	30
Median age	37.6
Native-born	3,257
Foreign-born	422

Educational Attainment, 2000
Population 25 years and over	2,626
Less than 9th grade	2.2%
High school grad or higher	90.9%
Bachelor's degree or higher	28.2%
Graduate degree	9.2%

Income & Poverty, 1999
Per capita income	$27,119
Median household income	$64,643
Median family income	$67,467
Persons in poverty	206
H'holds receiving public assistance	20
H'holds receiving social security	414

Households, 2000
Total households	1,365
With persons under 18	499
With persons over 65	349
Family households	1,041
Single-person households	264
Persons per household	2.70
Persons per family	3.08

Labor & Employment
Total civilian labor force, 2006**	2,078
Unemployment rate	4.3%
Total civilian labor force, 2000	1,885
Unemployment rate	3.4%

Employed persons 16 years and over by occupation, 2000
Managers & professionals	737
Service occupations	180
Sales & office occupations	524
Farming, fishing & forestry	7
Construction & maintenance	199
Production & transportation	173
Self-employed persons	28

* US Census Bureau
** New Jersey Department of Labor

General Information
Township of Mine Hill
10 Baker St
Mine Hill, NJ 07803
973-366-9031

Website	www.minehill.com
Year of incorporation	1923
Land/water area (sq. miles)	2.99/0.01
Form of government	Mayor-Council

Government
Legislative Districts
US Congressional	11
State Legislative	25

Local Officials, 2008
Mayor	Richard Leary
Manager	David J. Gilbride
Clerk	Patricia Korpos
Finance Dir	Janice Congleton
Tax Assessor	Joseph Ferraris
Tax Collector	NA
Attorney	Stephen N. Severud
Building	Steve Kaplan
Comm Dev/Planning	NA
Engineering	Paul Sterbenz
Public Works	NA
Police Chief	NA
Emerg/Fire Director	Carey Carroll

Housing & Construction
Housing Units, 2000*
Total	1,388
Median rent	$1,192
Median SF home value	$161,900

Permits for New Residential Construction
	Units	Value
Total, 2007	3	$399,400
Single family	3	$399,400
Total, 2006	3	$329,100
Single family	3	$329,100

Real Property Valuation, 2007
	Parcels	Valuation
Total	1,525	$535,608,700
Vacant	122	33,459,600
Residential	1,336	453,829,000
Commercial	56	28,979,800
Industrial	8	18,594,300
Apartments	1	722,300
Farm land	2	23,700
Farm homestead	0	0

Average Property Value & Tax, 2007
Residential value	$339,692
Property tax	$6,020
Tax credit/rebate	$1,093

Public Library
Mine Hill Public Library
10 Baker St
Mine Hill, NJ 07803
(973) 366-9217

Director.....NA

Library statistics, 2006
Population served	3,679
Full-time/total staff	NA/0

	Total	Per capita
Holdings	NA	NA
Revenues	NA	NA
Expenditures	NA	NA
Annual visits	NA	NA
Internet terminals/annual users	NA/NA	

Taxes
	2005	2006	2007
General tax rate per $100	3.86	1.71	1.78
County equalization ratio	57.66	119.1	103.37
Net valuation taxable	$224,358,342	$535,085,600	$536,052,138
State equalized value	$446,662,039	$518,070,390	$543,602,043

Public Safety
Number of officers, 2006.....0

Crime	2005	2006
Total crimes	55	35
Violent	0	2
Murder	0	0
Rape	0	1
Robbery	0	0
Aggravated assault	0	1
Non-violent	55	33
Burglary	18	8
Larceny	31	22
Vehicle theft	6	3
Domestic violence	17	9
Arson	1	0
Total crime rate	14.9	9.5
Violent	0.0	0.5
Non-violent	14.9	9.0

Public School District
(for school year 2006-07 except as noted)

Mine Hill Township School District
Canfield Ave
Mine Hill, NJ 07803
973-366-0590

Superintendent	Richard Bitondo
Number of schools	1
Grade plan	K-6
Enrollment	355
Attendance rate, '05-06	96.4%
Dropout rate	NA
Students per teacher	10.8
Per pupil expenditure	$11,944
Median faculty salary	$47,918
Median administrator salary	$50,805
Grade 12 enrollment	NA
High school graduation rate	NA

Assessment test results
(percent scoring at proficient or advanced level)

	Language	Math
NJASK-Grade 3	88.1%	95.3%
GEPA-Grade 8	NA	NA
HSPA-High School	NA	NA

SAT score averages
Pct tested	Math	Verbal	Writing
NA	NA	NA	NA

Teacher Qualifications
Avg. years of experience	12
Highly-qualified teachers one subject/all subjects	100%/100%
With emergency credentials	3.7%

No Child Left Behind
AYP, 2005-06.....Meets Standards

Municipal Finance
State Aid Programs, 2008
Total aid	$256,787
CMPTRA	0
Energy tax receipts	256,787
Garden State Trust	0

General Budget, 2007
Total tax levy	$9,499,116
County levy	1,245,951
County taxes	996,658
County library	0
County health	0
County open space	249,293
School levy	5,915,533
Muni. levy	2,337,633
Misc. revenues	1,820,526

Monmouth County / Monmouth Beach Borough

Demographics & Socio-Economic Characteristics
(2000 US Census, except as noted)

Population
- 1980* 3,318
- 1990* 3,303
- 2000 3,595
  - Male 1,684
  - Female 1,911
- 2006 (estimate)* 3,574
  - Population density 3,340.2

Race & Hispanic Origin, 2000
Race
- White 3,511
- Black/African American 19
- American Indian/Alaska Native 0
- Asian 31
- Native Hawaiian/Pacific Islander ... 0
- Other race 12
- Two or more races 22
- Hispanic origin, total 68
  - Mexican 5
  - Puerto Rican 23
  - Cuban 10
  - Other Hispanic 30

Age & Nativity, 2000
- Under 5 years 206
- 18 years and over 2,864
- 21 years and over 2,812
- 65 years and over 732
- 85 years and over 70
- Median age 44.6
- Native-born 3,382
- Foreign-born 213

Educational Attainment, 2000
- Population 25 years and over .. 2,737
- Less than 9th grade 2.2%
- High school grad or higher 94.3%
- Bachelor's degree or higher ... 48.8%
- Graduate degree 19.0%

Income & Poverty, 1999
- Per capita income $52,862
- Median household income $80,484
- Median family income $93,401
- Persons in poverty 68
- H'holds receiving public assistance ... 28
- H'holds receiving social security ... 497

Households, 2000
- Total households 1,633
  - With persons under 18 413
  - With persons over 65 538
  - Family households 976
  - Single-person households 574
- Persons per household 2.20
- Persons per family 2.89

Labor & Employment
- Total civilian labor force, 2006** ... 2,110
  - Unemployment rate 4.1%
- Total civilian labor force, 2000 ... 1,952
  - Unemployment rate 3.8%
- *Employed persons 16 years and over by occupation, 2000*
  - Managers & professionals 1,031
  - Service occupations 126
  - Sales & office occupations ... 507
  - Farming, fishing & forestry 0
  - Construction & maintenance .. 125
  - Production & transportation ... 89
- Self-employed persons 182

* US Census Bureau
** New Jersey Department of Labor

See Introduction for an explanation of all data sources.

General Information
Borough of Monmouth Beach
22 Beach Rd
Monmouth Beach, NJ 07750
732-229-2204
- Website .... www.monmouthbeach.us
- Year of incorporation 1906
- Land/water area (sq. miles) ... 1.07/0.85
- Form of government .... Commission

Government
Legislative Districts
- US Congressional 6
- State Legislative 11

Local Officials, 2008
- Mayor .... Susan Howard
- Administrator ...... Michael Corbally
- Clerk .... Joyce L. Escalante
- Finance Dir .... James Fuller
- Tax Assessor .... Timothy Anfuso
- Tax Collector .... James Fuller
- Attorney .... Dennis Collins
- Building .... Donald Clare Jr
- Comm Dev/Planning .... NA
- Engineering .... Edward Broberg
- Public Works .... Allen Miller
- Police Chief .... Richard White
- Emerg/Fire Director .... Richard White

Housing & Construction
Housing Units, 2000*
- Total 1,969
- Median rent $1,037
- Median SF home value $342,000

Permits for New Residential Construction

	Units	Value
Total, 2007	8	$4,801,214
Single family	8	$4,801,214
Total, 2006	7	$2,703,500
Single family	7	$2,703,500

Real Property Valuation, 2007

	Parcels	Valuation
Total	2,117	$1,240,248,200
Vacant	91	15,683,600
Residential	1,992	1,194,502,400
Commercial	34	30,062,200
Industrial	0	0
Apartments	0	0
Farm land	0	0
Farm homestead	0	0

Average Property Value & Tax, 2007
- Residential value $599,650
- Property tax $6,898
- Tax credit/rebate $1,064

Public Library
Monmouth Beach Library
18 Willow Ave
Monmouth Beach, NJ 07750
732-229-1187
- Director .... Nancy Leporatti

Library statistics, 2006
- Population served 3,595
- Full-time/total staff 0/0

	Total	Per capita
Holdings	40,072	11.15
Revenues	$96,781	$26.92
Expenditures	$100,811	$28.04
Annual visits	25,000	6.95
Internet terminals/annual users	2/5,000	

Public Safety
- Number of officers, 2006 10

Crime	2005	2006
Total crimes	42	35
Violent	0	4
Murder	0	0
Rape	0	0
Robbery	0	0
Aggravated assault	0	4
Non-violent	42	31
Burglary	4	1
Larceny	37	27
Vehicle theft	1	3
Domestic violence	3	4
Arson	0	1
Total crime rate	11.6	9.7
Violent	0.0	1.1
Non-violent	11.6	8.6

Public School District
(for school year 2006-07 except as noted)

Monmouth Beach School District
7 Hastings Place
Monmouth Beach, NJ 07750
732-222-6139

- Superintendent ...... Neil A. Frankenfield
- Number of schools 1
- Grade plan K-8
- Enrollment 308
- Attendance rate, '05-06 .... 95.7%
- Dropout rate .... NA
- Students per teacher 11.4
- Per pupil expenditure $12,391
- Median faculty salary $49,730
- Median administrator salary .. $84,059
- Grade 12 enrollment .... NA
- High school graduation rate ...... NA

Assessment test results
(percent scoring at proficient or advanced level)

	Language	Math
NJASK-Grade 3	97.6%	92.7%
GEPA-Grade 8	96.9%	93.8%
HSPA-High School	NA	NA

SAT score averages

Pct tested	Math	Verbal	Writing
NA	NA	NA	NA

Teacher Qualifications
- Avg. years of experience 8
- Highly-qualified teachers
  - one subject/all subjects ... 100%/100%
- With emergency credentials 0.0%

No Child Left Behind
- AYP, 2005-06 .... Meets Standards

Municipal Finance
State Aid Programs, 2008
- Total aid $374,447
  - CMPTRA 0
  - Energy tax receipts 374,447
  - Garden State Trust 0

General Budget, 2007
- Total tax levy $14,270,646
  - County levy 3,764,257
    - County taxes 3,361,755
    - County library 192,449
    - County health 0
    - County open space 210,053
  - School levy 7,046,309
  - Muni. levy 3,460,080
- Misc. revenues 2,575,761

Taxes

	2005	2006	2007
General tax rate per $100	1.019	1.107	1.151
County equalization ratio	130.14	101.74	88.79
Net valuation taxable	$1,223,756,327	$1,230,808,300	$1,240,583,960
State equalized value	$1,202,827,135	$1,386,566,779	$1,441,646,858

©2008 Information Publications, Inc. All rights reserved. Photocopying prohibited. For additional copies, contact the publisher at www.informationpublications.com or (877)544-INFO (4636)

The New Jersey Municipal Data Book

Monroe Township
Gloucester County

Demographics & Socio-Economic Characteristics
(2000 US Census, except as noted)

Population
1980*	21,639
1990*	26,703
2000	28,967
Male	13,988
Female	14,979
2006 (estimate)*	31,934
Population density	686.0

Race & Hispanic Origin, 2000
Race
White	24,573
Black/African American	3,231
American Indian/Alaska Native	72
Asian	356
Native Hawaiian/Pacific Islander	9
Other race	286
Two or more races	440
Hispanic origin, total	785
Mexican	96
Puerto Rican	486
Cuban	24
Other Hispanic	179

Age & Nativity, 2000
Under 5 years	1,908
18 years and over	21,540
21 years and over	20,553
65 years and over	3,737
85 years and over	331
Median age	37.1
Native-born	28,131
Foreign-born	836

Educational Attainment, 2000
Population 25 years and over	19,377
Less than 9th grade	4.4%
High school grad or higher	80.2%
Bachelor's degree or higher	15.9%
Graduate degree	4.0%

Income & Poverty, 1999
Per capita income	$20,488
Median household income	$50,037
Median family income	$56,810
Persons in poverty	1,769
H'holds receiving public assistance	174
H'holds receiving social security	3,029

Households, 2000
Total households	10,521
With persons under 18	3,996
With persons over 65	2,742
Family households	7,848
Single-person households	2,214
Persons per household	2.73
Persons per family	3.18

Labor & Employment
Total civilian labor force, 2006**	17,089
Unemployment rate	5.4%
Total civilian labor force, 2000	14,596
Unemployment rate	5.1%

Employed persons 16 years and over by occupation, 2000
Managers & professionals	3,692
Service occupations	2,237
Sales & office occupations	4,399
Farming, fishing & forestry	26
Construction & maintenance	1,588
Production & transportation	1,908
Self-employed persons	710

* US Census Bureau
** New Jersey Department of Labor

General Information
Township of Monroe
125 Virginia Ave
Williamstown, NJ 08094
856-728-9800

Website	www.monroetownshipnj.org
Year of incorporation	1859
Land/water area (sq. miles)	46.55/0.38
Form of government	Mayor-Council

Government
Legislative Districts
US Congressional	1
State Legislative	4

Local Officials, 2008
Mayor	Michael Gabbianelli
Manager	Kevin Heydel
Clerk	Susan McCormick
Finance Dir	Jeff Coles
Tax Assessor	Bruce Coyle
Tax Collector	Alma Alexander
Attorney	Charles Fiore
Building	Michael DePalma
Planning	Carolyn Farrell
Engineering	Adams, Rehmann & Heggan
Public Works	Vincent J. Agnesino
Police Chief	Domenic Christopher
Emerg/Fire Dir	Salvatore Tomarchio

Housing & Construction
Housing Units, 2000*
Total	11,069
Median rent	$621
Median SF home value	$114,200

Permits for New Residential Construction
	Units	Value
Total, 2007	142	$23,704,612
Single family	128	$22,787,782
Total, 2006	237	$31,222,272
Single family	237	$31,222,272

Real Property Valuation, 2007
	Parcels	Valuation
Total	13,350	$1,430,956,860
Vacant	2,201	45,113,600
Residential	10,256	1,205,875,900
Commercial	395	140,350,360
Industrial	16	6,271,100
Apartments	15	16,348,800
Farm land	328	1,811,100
Farm homestead	139	15,186,000

Average Property Value & Tax, 2007
Residential value	$117,466
Property tax	$5,600
Tax credit/rebate	$1,045

Public Library
Monroe Township Public Library
306 S Main St
Williamstown, NJ 08094
856-629-1212

Director	Elizabeth L. Lillie

Library statistics, 2006
Population served	28,967
Full-time/total staff	5/12

	Total	Per capita
Holdings	89,667	3.10
Revenues	$930,232	$32.11
Expenditures	$751,132	$25.93
Annual visits	179,948	6.21
Internet terminals/annual users	12/18,380	

Public Safety
Number of officers, 2006 ... 68

Crime	2005	2006
Total crimes	734	824
Violent	65	48
Murder	0	0
Rape	2	2
Robbery	18	17
Aggravated assault	45	29
Non-violent	669	776
Burglary	204	186
Larceny	432	536
Vehicle theft	33	54
Domestic violence	450	372
Arson	0	10
Total crime rate	23.7	26.2
Violent	2.1	1.5
Non-violent	21.6	24.7

Public School District
(for school year 2006-07 except as noted)

Monroe Township School District
75 E Academy St
Williamstown, NJ 08094
856-629-6400

Superintendent	Vincent Tarantino (Int)
Number of schools	6
Grade plan	K-12
Enrollment	5,986
Attendance rate, '05-06	94.6%
Dropout rate	4.1%
Students per teacher	13.3
Per pupil expenditure	$10,564
Median faculty salary	$48,774
Median administrator salary	$105,437
Grade 12 enrollment	437
High school graduation rate	89.9%

Assessment test results
(percent scoring at proficient or advanced level)
	Language	Math
NJASK-Grade 3	87.3%	91.0%
GEPA-Grade 8	73.8%	58.9%
HSPA-High School	88.3%	77.7%

SAT score averages
Pct tested	Math	Verbal	Writing
63%	481	456	444

Teacher Qualifications
Avg. years of experience	10
Highly-qualified teachers one subject/all subjects	100%/100%
With emergency credentials	0.0%

No Child Left Behind
AYP, 2005-06	Meets Standards

Municipal Finance
State Aid Programs, 2008
Total aid	$5,393,121
CMPTRA	831,470
Energy tax receipts	4,341,434
Garden State Trust	23,925

General Budget, 2007
Total tax levy	$68,463,201
County levy	14,564,763
County taxes	13,507,192
County library	0
County health	0
County open space	1,057,571
School levy	37,767,760
Muni. levy	16,130,678
Misc. revenues	15,723,507

Taxes	2005	2006	2007
General tax rate per $100	4.318	4.61	4.768
County equalization ratio	71.7	62.62	54.27
Net valuation taxable	$1,315,085,296	$1,369,209,660	$1,436,115,209
State equalized value	$2,100,104,273	$2,528,772,559	$2,851,700,740

Middlesex County

Monroe Township

Demographics & Socio-Economic Characteristics
(2000 US Census, except as noted)

Population
1980*	15,858
1990*	22,255
2000	27,999
Male	12,845
Female	15,154
2006 (estimate)*	34,907
Population density	832.3

Race & Hispanic Origin, 2000
Race
White	26,127
Black/African American	820
American Indian/Alaska Native	16
Asian	655
Native Hawaiian/Pacific Islander	24
Other race	189
Two or more races	168
Hispanic origin, total	666
Mexican	63
Puerto Rican	295
Cuban	57
Other Hispanic	251

Age & Nativity, 2000
Under 5 years	1,109
18 years and over	23,521
21 years and over	22,893
65 years and over	12,185
85 years and over	1,380
Median age	58.9
Native-born	25,737
Foreign-born	2,262

Educational Attainment, 2000
Population 25 years and over	22,394
Less than 9th grade	2.9%
High school grad or higher	90.0%
Bachelor's degree or higher	29.5%
Graduate degree	10.1%

Income & Poverty, 1999
Per capita income	$31,772
Median household income	$53,306
Median family income	$68,479
Persons in poverty	908
H'holds receiving public assistance	66
H'holds receiving social security	7,971

Households, 2000
Total households	12,536
With persons under 18	2,148
With persons over 65	8,107
Family households	8,233
Single-person households	4,006
Persons per household	2.15
Persons per family	2.70

Labor & Employment
Total civilian labor force, 2006**	12,876
Unemployment rate	5.3%
Total civilian labor force, 2000	10,058
Unemployment rate	5.0%

Employed persons 16 years and over by occupation, 2000
Managers & professionals	3,794
Service occupations	1,006
Sales & office occupations	2,945
Farming, fishing & forestry	34
Construction & maintenance	815
Production & transportation	961
Self-employed persons	617

* US Census Bureau
** New Jersey Department of Labor

See Introduction for an explanation of all data sources.

General Information
Township of Monroe
1 Municipal Plz
Monroe Township, NJ 08831
732-521-4400

Website	monroetwp.com
Year of incorporation	1838
Land/water area (sq. miles)	41.94/0.10
Form of government	Mayor-Council

Government
Legislative Districts
US Congressional	12
State Legislative	14

Local Officials, 2008
Mayor	Richard Pucci
Manager	Wayne Hamilton
Clerk	Sharon Doerfler
Finance Dir	George Lang
Tax Assessor	Mitchell Elias
Tax Collector	Dolores Schauer
Attorney	Joel Shain
Building	Robert Downey
Planning	Robert Tucker
Engineering	Ernest Feist
Public Works	Wayne Horbatt
Police Chief	John Kraivec
Fire/Emergency Dir	NA

Housing & Construction
Housing Units, 2000*
Total	13,259
Median rent	$877
Median SF home value	$174,100

Permits for New Residential Construction
	Units	Value
Total, 2007	416	$64,736,947
Single family	356	$61,194,946
Total, 2006	826	$95,480,576
Single family	459	$71,035,699

Real Property Valuation, 2007
	Parcels	Valuation
Total	19,664	$3,551,953,600
Vacant	2,603	177,657,500
Residential	16,286	2,850,401,400
Commercial	187	260,951,400
Industrial	46	198,931,000
Apartments	3	29,159,300
Farm land	370	3,944,000
Farm homestead	169	30,909,000

Average Property Value & Tax, 2007
Residential value	$175,102
Property tax	$5,479
Tax credit/rebate	$1,118

Public Library
Monroe Township Library
4 Municipal Plaza
Monroe Township, NJ 08831
732-521-5000

Director	Irene Goldberg

Library statistics, 2006
Population served	27,999
Full-time/total staff	7/18

	Total	Per capita
Holdings	125,575	4.48
Revenues	$2,231,375	$79.69
Expenditures	$2,376,007	$84.86
Annual visits	404,360	14.44
Internet terminals/annual users	19/25,166	

Public Safety
Number of officers, 2006 48

Crime	2005	2006
Total crimes	241	300
Violent	11	19
Murder	0	0
Rape	1	1
Robbery	2	1
Aggravated assault	8	17
Non-violent	230	281
Burglary	38	52
Larceny	185	217
Vehicle theft	7	12
Domestic violence	35	13
Arson	1	0
Total crime rate	7.4	8.8
Violent	0.3	0.6
Non-violent	7.1	8.3

Public School District
(for school year 2006-07 except as noted)

Monroe Township School District
423 Buckelew Ave
Monroe Township, NJ 08831
732-521-2111

Superintendent	Ralph Ferrie
Number of schools	6
Grade plan	K-12
Enrollment	4,924
Attendance rate, '05-06	95.7%
Dropout rate	1.0%
Students per teacher	10.4
Per pupil expenditure	$14,051
Median faculty salary	$45,000
Median administrator salary	$114,015
Grade 12 enrollment	331
High school graduation rate	95.2%

Assessment test results
(percent scoring at proficient or advanced level)
	Language	Math
NJASK-Grade 3	90.5%	93.1%
GEPA-Grade 8	87.2%	79.4%
HSPA-High School	87.8%	79.2%

SAT score averages
Pct tested	Math	Verbal	Writing
79%	522	495	490

Teacher Qualifications
Avg. years of experience	6
Highly-qualified teachers one subject/all subjects	99.5%/99.5%
With emergency credentials	0.0%

No Child Left Behind
AYP, 2005-06	Meets Standards

Municipal Finance
State Aid Programs, 2008
Total aid	$2,912,548
CMPTRA	420,050
Energy tax receipts	2,491,241
Garden State Trust	1,257

General Budget, 2007
Total tax levy	$111,291,796
County levy	20,815,978
County taxes	18,631,704
County library	0
County health	0
County open space	2,184,274
School levy	69,883,953
Muni. levy	20,591,865
Misc. revenues	18,199,820

Taxes
	2005	2006	2007
General tax rate per $100	2.92	2.99	3.13
County equalization ratio	61.83	56.34	48.47
Net valuation taxable	$3,105,831,277	$3,370,087,500	$3,556,604,685
State equalized value	$5,512,657,574	$6,958,094,964	$7,648,192,294

The New Jersey Municipal Data Book

Montague Township

Sussex County

Demographics & Socio-Economic Characteristics
(2000 US Census, except as noted)

Population
1980*	2,066
1990*	2,832
2000	3,412
Male	1,764
Female	1,648
2006 (estimate)*	3,904
Population density	88.7

Race & Hispanic Origin, 2000
Race
White	3,250
Black/African American	61
American Indian/Alaska Native	6
Asian	23
Native Hawaiian/Pacific Islander	0
Other race	37
Two or more races	35
Hispanic origin, total	112
Mexican	9
Puerto Rican	39
Cuban	12
Other Hispanic	52

Age & Nativity, 2000
Under 5 years	241
18 years and over	2,485
21 years and over	2,377
65 years and over	378
85 years and over	22
Median age	37.0
Native-born	3,278
Foreign-born	134

Educational Attainment, 2000
Population 25 years and over	2,262
Less than 9th grade	5.4%
High school grad or higher	80.2%
Bachelor's degree or higher	14.5%
Graduate degree	6.0%

Income & Poverty, 1999
Per capita income	$20,676
Median household income	$45,368
Median family income	$50,833
Persons in poverty	406
H'holds receiving public assistance	47
H'holds receiving social security	337

Households, 2000
Total households	1,286
With persons under 18	481
With persons over 65	281
Family households	911
Single-person households	298
Persons per household	2.65
Persons per family	3.14

Labor & Employment
Total civilian labor force, 2006**	1,875
Unemployment rate	7.9%
Total civilian labor force, 2000	1,638
Unemployment rate	5.7%

Employed persons 16 years and over by occupation, 2000
Managers & professionals	397
Service occupations	252
Sales & office occupations	441
Farming, fishing & forestry	0
Construction & maintenance	262
Production & transportation	193
Self-employed persons	147

* US Census Bureau
** New Jersey Department of Labor

General Information
Township of Montague
277 Clove Rd
Montague, NJ 07827
973-293-7300

Website	www.montaguenj.org
Year of incorporation	1759
Land/water area (sq. miles)	44.01/1.33
Form of government	Township

Government
Legislative Districts
US Congressional	5
State Legislative	24

Local Officials, 2008
Mayor	Joe Barbagallo
Manager/Admin	NA
Clerk	Diana Francisco
CFO	Gail Magura
Tax Assessor	Melissa Rockwell
Tax Collector	Fran Multari
Attorney	Bruce Padula
Building	Donald Stambough
Comm Dev/Planning	NA
Engineering	Jack O'Krepky
Public Works Foreman	Dave Behrman
Police Chief	NA
Emerg/Fire Director	David Coss

Housing & Construction
Housing Units, 2000*
Total	1,588
Median rent	$806
Median SF home value	$129,400

Permits for New Residential Construction
	Units	Value
Total, 2007	27	$4,171,807
Single family	27	$4,171,807
Total, 2006	35	$3,786,356
Single family	35	$3,786,356

Real Property Valuation, 2007
	Parcels	Valuation
Total	2,851	$220,493,010
Vacant	922	14,648,400
Residential	1,642	171,705,250
Commercial	60	21,961,400
Industrial	6	2,136,600
Apartments	2	420,000
Farm land	156	1,036,760
Farm homestead	63	8,584,600

Average Property Value & Tax, 2007
Residential value	$105,742
Property tax	$3,662
Tax credit/rebate	$846

Public Library
No public municipal library

Library statistics, 2006
Population served	NA
Full-time/total staff	NA/NA

	Total	Per capita
Holdings	NA	NA
Revenues	NA	NA
Expenditures	NA	NA
Annual visits	NA	NA
Internet terminals/annual users	NA/NA	

Taxes
	2005	2006	2007
General tax rate per $100	3.03	3.32	3.47
County equalization ratio	68.52	55.21	48.83
Net valuation taxable	$209,069,369	$215,149,060	$221,170,947
State equalized value	$378,680,255	$441,378,635	$469,911,838

Public Safety
Number of officers, 2006 0

Crime	2005	2006
Total crimes	88	75
Violent	6	4
Murder	0	0
Rape	1	1
Robbery	0	1
Aggravated assault	5	2
Non-violent	82	71
Burglary	13	8
Larceny	60	58
Vehicle theft	9	5
Domestic violence	19	6
Arson	1	1
Total crime rate	23.6	19.5
Violent	1.6	1.0
Non-violent	22.0	18.5

Public School District
(for school year 2006-07 except as noted)

Montague School District
475 Route 206
Montague, NJ 07827
973-293-7131

Chief School Admin	Janice Hodge
Number of schools	1
Grade plan	K-6
Enrollment	310
Attendance rate, '05-06	95.7%
Dropout rate	NA
Students per teacher	8.8
Per pupil expenditure	$14,150
Median faculty salary	$52,370
Median administrator salary	$81,504
Grade 12 enrollment	NA
High school graduation rate	NA

Assessment test results
(percent scoring at proficient or advanced level)
	Language	Math
NJASK-Grade 3	91.9%	91.9%
GEPA-Grade 8	NA	NA
HSPA-High School	NA	NA

SAT score averages
Pct tested	Math	Verbal	Writing
NA	NA	NA	NA

Teacher Qualifications
Avg. years of experience	14
Highly-qualified teachers one subject/all subjects	96.5%/96.5%
With emergency credentials	0.0%

No Child Left Behind
AYP, 2005-06 .... Meets Standards

Municipal Finance
State Aid Programs, 2008
Total aid	$501,250
CMPTRA	0
Energy tax receipts	308,634
Garden State Trust	192,616

General Budget, 2007
Total tax levy	$7,658,899
County levy	1,838,926
County taxes	1,502,550
County library	128,097
County health	49,547
County open space	158,732
School levy	4,955,039
Muni. levy	864,935
Misc. revenues	1,375,821

Essex County
Montclair Township

Demographics & Socio-Economic Characteristics
(2000 US Census, except as noted)

Population
- 1980* 38,321
- 1990* 37,729
- 2000 38,977
  - Male 18,053
  - Female 20,924
- 2006 (estimate)* 37,309
  - Population density 5,922.1

Race & Hispanic Origin, 2000
Race
- White 23,297
- Black/African American 12,497
- American Indian/Alaska Native ... 73
- Asian 1,228
- Native Hawaiian/Pacific Islander ... 14
- Other race 688
- Two or more races 1,180
- Hispanic origin, total 1,995
  - Mexican 183
  - Puerto Rican 584
  - Cuban 171
  - Other Hispanic 1,057

Age & Nativity, 2000
- Under 5 years 2,716
- 18 years and over 29,013
- 21 years and over 27,887
- 65 years and over 4,665
- 85 years and over 786
- Median age 37.5
- Native-born 33,389
- Foreign-born 5,679

Educational Attainment, 2000
- Population 25 years and over .. 26,652
- Less than 9th grade 3.0%
- High school grad or higher ... 92.0%
- Bachelor's degree or higher ... 57.4%
- Graduate degree 27.1%

Income & Poverty, 1999
- Per capita income $44,870
- Median household income ... $74,894
- Median family income $96,252
- Persons in poverty 2,149
- H'holds receiving public assistance ... 369
- H'holds receiving social security ... 3,197

Households, 2000
- Total households 15,020
  - With persons under 18 5,574
  - With persons over 65 3,271
  - Family households 9,682
  - Single-person households ... 4,396
- Persons per household 2.53
- Persons per family 3.16

Labor & Employment
- Total civilian labor force, 2006** 21,455
  - Unemployment rate 3.6%
- Total civilian labor force, 2000 21,484
  - Unemployment rate 5.0%

Employed persons 16 years and over by occupation, 2000
- Managers & professionals 11,898
- Service occupations 2,120
- Sales & office occupations ... 4,833
- Farming, fishing & forestry 0
- Construction & maintenance ... 561
- Production & transportation .. 1,002
- Self-employed persons 1,532

* US Census Bureau
** New Jersey Department of Labor

See Introduction for an explanation of all data sources.

General Information
Township of Montclair
205 Claremont Ave
Montclair, NJ 07042
973-744-1400

- Website .... www.montclairnjusa.org
- Year of incorporation 1979
- Land/water area (sq. miles) 6.30/0.00
- Form of government .... Council-Manager

Government
Legislative Districts
- US Congressional 8, 10
- State Legislative 34

Local Officials, 2008
- Mayor .... Edward Remsen
- Manager .... Joseph M. Hartnett
- Clerk .... Linda S. Wanat
- Finance Dir .... Gordon Stelter
- Tax Assessor .... Joan Kozeniesky
- Tax Collector .... Maureen Montesano
- Attorney .... Alan Trembulak
- Construction Official ... Robert Mcloughlin
- Planning .... Karen Kadus
- Engineering .... Kimberli Craft
- Public Works .... Steve Wood
- Police Chief .... David Sabagh
- Emerg/Fire Director .... Kevin Allen

Housing & Construction
Housing Units, 2000*
- Total 15,531
- Median rent $866
- Median SF home value $317,500

Permits for New Residential Construction

	Units	Value
Total, 2007	180	$18,374,075
Single family	11	$3,336,670
Total, 2006	277	$57,631,786
Single family	40	$8,504,947

Real Property Valuation, 2007

	Parcels	Valuation
Total	10,483	$7,406,314,800
Vacant	142	33,500,400
Residential	9,592	6,370,510,800
Commercial	582	701,678,900
Industrial	3	5,584,200
Apartments	164	295,040,500
Farm land	0	0
Farm homestead	0	0

Average Property Value & Tax, 2007
- Residential value $664,148
- Property tax $14,238
- Tax credit/rebate $1,371

Public Library
Montclair Public Library
50 S Fullerton Ave
Montclair, NJ 07042
973-744-0500

- Director .... David Hinkley

Library statistics, 2006
- Population served 38,977
- Full-time/total staff 14/35

	Total	Per capita
Holdings	231,601	5.94
Revenues	$4,005,902	$102.78
Expenditures	$3,827,839	$98.21
Annual visits	317,838	8.15
Internet terminals/annual users	... 40/58,915

Taxes

	2005	2006	2007
General tax rate per $100	5.09	5.36	2.15
County equalization ratio	49.92	45.16	107.33
Net valuation taxable	$2,775,430,506	$2,773,446,450	$7,415,062,627
State equalized value	$6,145,771,714	$6,853,658,398	$7,233,011,190

Public Safety
- Number of officers, 2006 108

Crime	2005	2006
Total crimes	1,080	1,090
Violent	121	92
Murder	0	1
Rape	2	1
Robbery	48	29
Aggravated assault	71	61
Non-violent	959	998
Burglary	214	251
Larceny	607	666
Vehicle theft	138	81
Domestic violence	185	196
Arson	5	1
Total crime rate	28.2	28.8
Violent	3.2	2.4
Non-violent	25.0	26.4

Public School District
(for school year 2006-07 except as noted)

Montclair School District
22 Valley Rd
Montclair, NJ 07042
973-509-4010

- Superintendent .... Frank R. Alvarez
- Number of schools 11
- Grade plan K-12
- Enrollment 6,621
- Attendance rate, '05-06 .... 95.3%
- Dropout rate .... NA
- Students per teacher 10.1
- Per pupil expenditure $14,358
- Median faculty salary $58,422
- Median administrator salary ... $109,886
- Grade 12 enrollment 459
- High school graduation rate ... 100.0%

Assessment test results
(percent scoring at proficient or advanced level)

	Language	Math
NJASK-Grade 3	89.8%	92.2%
GEPA-Grade 8	83.0%	73.6%
HSPA-High School	89.2%	74.5%

SAT score averages

Pct tested	Math	Verbal	Writing
92%	518	526	522

Teacher Qualifications
- Avg. years of experience 7
- Highly-qualified teachers
  - one subject/all subjects 99.5%/99.5%
- With emergency credentials 0.2%

No Child Left Behind
- AYP, 2005-06 .... Meets Standards

Municipal Finance
State Aid Programs, 2008
- Total aid $3,908,934
  - CMPTRA 1,206,743
  - Energy tax receipts 2,702,191
  - Garden State Trust 0

General Budget, 2007
- Total tax levy $158,963,363
  - County levy 27,146,736
    - County taxes 26,448,850
    - County library 0
    - County health 0
    - County open space 697,887
  - School levy 92,690,542
  - Muni. levy 39,126,085
  - Misc. revenues 20,116,710

Montgomery Township
Somerset County

Demographics & Socio-Economic Characteristics
(2000 US Census, except as noted)

Population
1980*	7,360
1990*	9,612
2000	17,481
Male	8,624
Female	8,857
2006 (estimate)*	23,243
Population density	712.5

Race & Hispanic Origin, 2000
Race
White	14,781
Black/African American	361
American Indian/Alaska Native	15
Asian	2,011
Native Hawaiian/Pacific Islander	2
Other race	80
Two or more races	231
Hispanic origin, total	387
Mexican	76
Puerto Rican	96
Cuban	47
Other Hispanic	168

Age & Nativity, 2000
Under 5 years	1,514
18 years and over	11,722
21 years and over	11,395
65 years and over	1,189
85 years and over	94
Median age	36.8
Native-born	14,934
Foreign-born	2,531

Educational Attainment, 2000
Population 25 years and over	11,032
Less than 9th grade	1.4%
High school grad or higher	97.3%
Bachelor's degree or higher	70.2%
Graduate degree	34.8%

Income & Poverty, 1999
Per capita income	$48,699
Median household income	$118,850
Median family income	$129,150
Persons in poverty	261
H'holds receiving public assistance	22
H'holds receiving social security	878

Households, 2000
Total households	5,803
With persons under 18	3,006
With persons over 65	839
Family households	4,783
Single-person households	823
Persons per household	2.99
Persons per family	3.33

Labor & Employment
Total civilian labor force, 2006**	9,813
Unemployment rate	2.4%
Total civilian labor force, 2000	8,711
Unemployment rate	2.1%

Employed persons 16 years and over by occupation, 2000
Managers & professionals	5,947
Service occupations	384
Sales & office occupations	1,714
Farming, fishing & forestry	21
Construction & maintenance	249
Production & transportation	217
Self-employed persons	446

‡ Branch of county library
* US Census Bureau
** New Jersey Department of Labor

General Information
Township of Montgomery
2261 Route 206
Belle Mead, NJ 08502
908-359-8211

Website	www.twp.montgomery.nj.us
Year of incorporation	1798
Land/water area (sq. miles)	32.62/0.00
Form of government	Township

Government
Legislative Districts
US Congressional	7
State Legislative	16

Local Officials, 2008
Mayor	Cecilia Xie Birge
Manager	Donato Nieman
Clerk	Donna Kukla
Finance Dir	Walter Sheppard
Tax Assessor	Eleanor Blake
Tax Collector	Randy Bahr
Attorney	Kristina Hadinger
Building	John Marold
Planning	Lori Savron
Engineering	Gail Smith
Public Works	Arthur Villano
Police Chief	Michael Beltranena
Fire/Emergency Dir	NA

Housing & Construction
Housing Units, 2000*
Total	6,130
Median rent	$1,196
Median SF home value	$348,500

Permits for New Residential Construction
	Units	Value
Total, 2007	6	$990,000
Single family	6	$990,000
Total, 2006	6	$189,900
Single family	6	$189,900

Real Property Valuation, 2007
	Parcels	Valuation
Total	7,240	$3,730,343,180
Vacant	401	41,316,700
Residential	6,328	3,224,294,000
Commercial	160	304,759,180
Industrial	1	3,112,900
Apartments	11	94,720,400
Farm land	233	2,131,700
Farm homestead	106	60,008,300

Average Property Value & Tax, 2007
Residential value	$510,460
Property tax	$12,314
Tax credit/rebate	$1,313

Public Library
served by Mary Jacobs Branch Library‡
64 Washington St
Rocky Hill, NJ 08553
609-924-7073

Branch Librarian............Helen Morris

Library statistics, 2006
see Somerset County profile
for library system statistics

Public Safety
Number of officers, 2006 32

Crime	2005	2006
Total crimes	218	244
Violent	4	4
Murder	0	0
Rape	0	2
Robbery	0	0
Aggravated assault	4	2
Non-violent	214	240
Burglary	46	69
Larceny	160	170
Vehicle theft	8	1
Domestic violence	52	62
Arson	4	1
Total crime rate	9.8	10.7
Violent	0.2	0.2
Non-violent	9.6	10.6

Public School District
(for school year 2006-07 except as noted)

Montgomery Township School District
1014 Route 601
Skillman, NJ 08558
609-466-7601

Superintendent	Samuel B. Stewart (Int)
Number of schools	5
Grade plan	K-12
Enrollment	5,226
Attendance rate, '05-06	97.1%
Dropout rate	0.1%
Students per teacher	11.7
Per pupil expenditure	$11,667
Median faculty salary	$50,915
Median administrator salary	$110,215
Grade 12 enrollment	366
High school graduation rate	100.0%

Assessment test results
(percent scoring at proficient or advanced level)
	Language	Math
NJASK-Grade 3	90.8%	94.3%
GEPA-Grade 8	94.4%	91.0%
HSPA-High School	97.3%	93.9%

SAT score averages
Pct tested	Math	Verbal	Writing
102%	596	579	580

Teacher Qualifications
Avg. years of experience	6
Highly-qualified teachers	
one subject/all subjects	100%/100%
With emergency credentials	1.1%

No Child Left Behind
AYP, 2005-06 .... Meets Standards

Municipal Finance
State Aid Programs, 2008
Total aid	$1,889,712
CMPTRA	123,162
Energy tax receipts	1,765,935
Garden State Trust	615

General Budget, 2007
Total tax levy	$90,088,750
County levy	15,745,362
County taxes	12,733,291
County library	1,617,004
County health	0
County open space	1,395,067
School levy	63,278,030
Muni. levy	11,065,358
Misc. revenues	17,269,069

Taxes	2005	2006	2007
General tax rate per $100	2.2	2.31	2.42
County equalization ratio	99.43	88.54	80
Net valuation taxable	$3,760,460,580	$3,741,595,852	$3,734,641,139
State equalized value	$4,247,188,367	$4,681,849,888	$4,859,619,031

Bergen County — Montvale Borough

Demographics & Socio-Economic Characteristics
(2000 US Census, except as noted)

Population
- 1980*............................ 7,318
- 1990*............................ 6,946
- 2000............................. 7,034
  - Male........................... 3,466
  - Female......................... 3,568
- 2006 (estimate)*.................. 7,308
  - Population density............ 1,840.8

Race & Hispanic Origin, 2000
Race
- White............................ 6,527
- Black/African American............. 31
- American Indian/Alaska Native....... 6
- Asian.............................. 377
- Native Hawaiian/Pacific Islander.... 0
- Other race.......................... 44
- Two or more races................... 49
- Hispanic origin, total............. 217
  - Mexican........................... 36
  - Puerto Rican...................... 41
  - Cuban............................. 36
  - Other Hispanic................... 104

Age & Nativity, 2000
- Under 5 years...................... 490
- 18 years and over................ 5,209
- 21 years and over................ 5,043
- 65 years and over.................. 884
- 85 years and over................... 75
- Median age........................ 39.7
- Native-born...................... 6,111
- Foreign-born....................... 923

Educational Attainment, 2000
- Population 25 years and over..... 4,818
- Less than 9th grade................ 0.9%
- High school grad or higher........ 95.0%
- Bachelor's degree or higher....... 55.3%
- Graduate degree................... 20.0%

Income & Poverty, 1999
- Per capita income............. $45,448
- Median household income....... $93,031
- Median family income......... $104,047
- Persons in poverty.................. 62
- H'holds receiving public assistance. 0
- H'holds receiving social security. 567

Households, 2000
- Total households................ 2,509
  - With persons under 18............ 984
  - With persons over 65............. 626
  - Family households.............. 2,000
  - Single-person households......... 437
- Persons per household............. 2.80
- Persons per family................ 3.18

Labor & Employment
- Total civilian labor force, 2006**. 3,922
  - Unemployment rate............... 2.8%
- Total civilian labor force, 2000. 3,698
  - Unemployment rate............... 2.8%

Employed persons 16 years and over by occupation, 2000
- Managers & professionals........ 1,989
- Service occupations................ 300
- Sales & office occupations...... 1,023
- Farming, fishing & forestry.......... 0
- Construction & maintenance........ 125
- Production & transportation....... 159
- Self-employed persons............. 169

* US Census Bureau
** New Jersey Department of Labor

See Introduction for an explanation of all data sources.

General Information
Borough of Montvale
12 Mercedes Dr
Montvale, NJ 07645
201-391-5700
- Website.................. www.montvale.org
- Year of incorporation............. 1894
- Land/water area (sq. miles)... 3.97/0.00
- Form of government............. Borough

Government
Legislative Districts
- US Congressional.................... 5
- State Legislative................... 39

Local Officials, 2008
- Mayor.................... Roger J. Fyfe
- Manager......... Maureen Iarossi-Alwan
- Clerk............ Maureen Iarossi-Alwan
- Finance Dir................. Carl Bello
- Tax Assessor......... Michael Leposky
- Tax Collector.......... Julia Piraino
- Attorney............... Philip Boggia
- Building............. Michael Tabback
- Planning................ John DePinto
- Engineering.......... Andrew Hipolit
- Public Works......... Robert Culvert
- Police Chief....... Joseph Marigliani
- Emerg/Fire Director.... Clinton Miller

Housing & Construction
Housing Units, 2000*
- Total............................ 2,590
- Median rent.................... $1,116
- Median SF home value......... $346,400

Permits for New Residential Construction

	Units	Value
Total, 2007	112	$16,877,950
Single family	112	$16,877,950
Total, 2006	54	$10,844,690
Single family	54	$10,844,690

Real Property Valuation, 2007

	Parcels	Valuation
Total	2,835	$2,300,479,000
Vacant	232	66,723,300
Residential	2,464	1,613,870,800
Commercial	121	589,973,300
Industrial	6	13,075,000
Apartments	1	14,553,000
Farm land	8	37,600
Farm homestead	3	2,246,000

Average Property Value & Tax, 2007
- Residential value............. $655,094
- Property tax.................... $9,491
- Tax credit/rebate............... $1,286

Public Library
Montvale Public Library
12 Mercedes Dr
Montvale, NJ 07645
201-391-5090
- Director............ Susan J. Ruttenber

Library statistics, 2006
- Population served............... 7,034
- Full-time/total staff.............. 1/2

	Total	Per capita
Holdings	74,817	10.64
Revenues	$673,317	$95.72
Expenditures	$616,346	$87.62
Annual visits	78,889	11.22
Internet terminals/annual users	...	19/35,000

Public Safety
- Number of officers, 2006........... 22

Crime	2005	2006
Total crimes	62	63
Violent	2	2
Murder	0	0
Rape	0	1
Robbery	0	1
Aggravated assault	2	0
Non-violent	60	61
Burglary	0	3
Larceny	56	55
Vehicle theft	4	3
Domestic violence	9	9
Arson	0	0
Total crime rate	8.5	8.6
Violent	0.3	0.3
Non-violent	8.2	8.3

Public School District
(for school year 2006-07 except as noted)

Montvale School District
47 Spring Valley Rd
Montvale, NJ 07645
201-391-1662

- Superintendent............. Susan King
- Number of schools................... 2
- Grade plan........................ K-8
- Enrollment...................... 1,007
- Attendance rate, '05-06.......... 96.2%
- Dropout rate...................... NA
- Students per teacher............. 10.4
- Per pupil expenditure......... $12,402
- Median faculty salary.......... $50,790
- Median administrator salary.. $117,907
- Grade 12 enrollment............... NA
- High school graduation rate....... NA

Assessment test results
(percent scoring at proficient or advanced level)

	Language	Math
NJASK-Grade 3	92.9%	90.4%
GEPA-Grade 8	95.9%	88.5%
HSPA-High School	NA	NA

SAT score averages

Pct tested	Math	Verbal	Writing
NA	NA	NA	NA

Teacher Qualifications
- Avg. years of experience............ 8
- Highly-qualified teachers
  - one subject/all subjects... 100%/100%
- With emergency credentials........ 0.0%

No Child Left Behind
- AYP, 2005-06.......... Meets Standards

Municipal Finance
State Aid Programs, 2008
- Total aid.................. $1,598,602
  - CMPTRA....................... 5,423
  - Energy tax receipts...... 1,593,179
  - Garden State Trust............... 0

General Budget, 2007
- Total tax levy............. $33,365,127
  - County levy............... 3,809,860
    - County taxes........... 3,600,106
    - County library................. 0
    - County health.................. 0
    - County open space......... 209,753
  - School levy.............. 20,896,176
  - Muni. levy................ 8,659,091
  - Misc. revenues............ 6,055,566

Taxes

	2005	2006	2007
General tax rate per $100	2.74	1.4	1.45
County equalization ratio	63.27	117.18	110.29
Net valuation taxable	$1,095,570,257	$2,262,446,400	$2,303,040,681
State equalized value	$1,920,368,549	$2,053,852,927	$2,125,754,113

©2008 Information Publications, Inc. All rights reserved. Photocopying prohibited. For additional copies, contact the publisher at www.informationpublications.com or (877)544-INFO (4636)

The New Jersey Municipal Data Book

Montville Township
Morris County

Demographics & Socio-Economic Characteristics
(2000 US Census, except as noted)

Population
1980*	14,290
1990*	15,600
2000	20,839
Male	10,138
Female	10,701
2006 (estimate)*	21,442
Population density	1,136.3

Race & Hispanic Origin, 2000
Race
White	17,703
Black/African American	193
American Indian/Alaska Native	9
Asian	2,619
Native Hawaiian/Pacific Islander	4
Other race	74
Two or more races	237
Hispanic origin, total	531
Mexican	69
Puerto Rican	158
Cuban	75
Other Hispanic	229

Age & Nativity, 2000
Under 5 years	1,435
18 years and over	15,597
21 years and over	15,126
65 years and over	2,256
85 years and over	233
Median age	38.9
Native-born	17,251
Foreign-born	3,588

Educational Attainment, 2000
Population 25 years and over	14,445
Less than 9th grade	1.9%
High school grad or higher	93.5%
Bachelor's degree or higher	51.2%
Graduate degree	20.4%

Income & Poverty, 1999
Per capita income	$43,341
Median household income	$94,557
Median family income	$105,394
Persons in poverty	794
H'holds receiving public assistance	78
H'holds receiving social security	1,403

Households, 2000
Total households	7,380
With persons under 18	2,858
With persons over 65	1,542
Family households	5,869
Single-person households	1,225
Persons per household	2.80
Persons per family	3.17

Labor & Employment
Total civilian labor force, 2006**	12,471
Unemployment rate	1.9%
Total civilian labor force, 2000	11,412
Unemployment rate	2.0%

Employed persons 16 years and over by occupation, 2000
Managers & professionals	6,023
Service occupations	686
Sales & office occupations	3,205
Farming, fishing & forestry	0
Construction & maintenance	638
Production & transportation	637
Self-employed persons	783

* US Census Bureau
** New Jersey Department of Labor

General Information
Township of Montville
195 Changebridge Rd
Montville, NJ 07045
973-331-3300

Website	www.montvillenj.org
Year of incorporation	1867
Land/water area (sq. miles)	18.87/0.26
Form of government	Special Charter

Government
Legislative Districts
US Congressional	11
State Legislative	26

Local Officials, 2008
Mayor	Art Daughtry
Manager	Frank Bastone
Clerk	Gertrude Atkinson
Finance Dir	Frances Vanderhoof
Tax Assessor	Thomas Lenhardt
Tax Collector	Francine Novak
Attorney	Martin Murphy
Building	Brian Laird
Planning	Linda White
Engineering	Anthony Barile Jr
Public Works	Thomas Mazzacaro
Police Chief	Richard Cook
Fire/Emergency Dir.	NA

Housing & Construction
Housing Units, 2000*
Total	7,541
Median rent	$1,186
Median SF home value	$346,600

Permits for New Residential Construction
	Units	Value
Total, 2007	16	$7,470,550
Single family	16	$7,470,550
Total, 2006	37	$14,677,802
Single family	37	$14,677,802

Real Property Valuation, 2007
	Parcels	Valuation
Total	7,769	$2,801,451,500
Vacant	374	51,034,900
Residential	6,967	2,300,050,300
Commercial	282	155,319,100
Industrial	81	236,326,800
Apartments	5	52,458,100
Farm land	40	172,700
Farm homestead	20	6,089,600

Average Property Value & Tax, 2007
Residential value	$330,062
Property tax	$9,990
Tax credit/rebate	$1,278

Public Library
Montville Township Public Library
90 Horseneck Rd
Montville, NJ 07045
973-402-0900

Director............ Patricia K. Anderson

Library statistics, 2006
Population served	20,839
Full-time/total staff	5/11

	Total	Per capita
Holdings	106,190	5.10
Revenues	$1,723,255	$82.69
Expenditures	$1,403,001	$67.33
Annual visits	154,529	7.42
Internet terminals/annual users	17/12,500	

Public Safety
Number of officers, 2006 42

Crime	2005	2006
Total crimes	237	239
Violent	10	8
Murder	0	1
Rape	0	0
Robbery	1	0
Aggravated assault	9	7
Non-violent	227	231
Burglary	27	41
Larceny	174	172
Vehicle theft	26	18
Domestic violence	102	91
Arson	1	2
Total crime rate	11.1	11.2
Violent	0.5	0.4
Non-violent	10.6	10.8

Public School District
(for school year 2006-07 except as noted)

Montville Township School District
328 Changebridge Rd
Pine Brook, NJ 07058
973-808-8580

Superintendent	Gary Bowen
Number of schools	7
Grade plan	K-12
Enrollment	4,182
Attendance rate, '05-06	96.0%
Dropout rate	0.2%
Students per teacher	12.0
Per pupil expenditure	$13,479
Median faculty salary	$56,050
Median administrator salary	$114,506
Grade 12 enrollment	272
High school graduation rate	98.6%

Assessment test results
(percent scoring at proficient or advanced level)
	Language	Math
NJASK-Grade 3	96.4%	95.7%
GEPA-Grade 8	92.0%	91.1%
HSPA-High School	92.3%	88.8%

SAT score averages
Pct tested	Math	Verbal	Writing
94%	576	543	541

Teacher Qualifications
Avg. years of experience	11
Highly-qualified teachers one subject/all subjects	98.0%/98.0%
With emergency credentials	0.0%

No Child Left Behind
AYP, 2005-06 .... Meets Standards

Municipal Finance
State Aid Programs, 2008
Total aid	$2,819,203
CMPTRA	81,922
Energy tax receipts	2,734,641
Garden State Trust	948

General Budget, 2007
Total tax levy	$84,901,061
County levy	12,095,267
County taxes	9,671,201
County library	0
County health	0
County open space	2,424,067
School levy	55,432,769
Muni. levy	17,373,025
Misc. revenues	10,286,403

Taxes
	2005	2006	2007
General tax rate per $100	2.74	2.9	3.03
County equalization ratio	64.64	59.71	54.54
Net valuation taxable	$2,792,190,798	$2,793,921,300	$2,805,003,955
State equalized value	$4,676,253,221	$5,126,582,793	$5,397,182,605

Bergen County

Moonachie Borough

Demographics & Socio-Economic Characteristics
(2000 US Census, except as noted)

Population
- 1980*......................................2,706
- 1990*......................................2,817
- 2000......................................2,754
  - Male....................................1,355
  - Female..................................1,399
- 2006 (estimate)*..........................2,797
  - Population density....................1,616.8

Race & Hispanic Origin, 2000
Race
- White.....................................2,359
- Black/African American.......................26
- American Indian/Alaska Native.................3
- Asian..183
- Native Hawaiian/Pacific Islander..............0
- Other race...................................81
- Two or more races...........................102
- Hispanic origin, total......................349
  - Mexican....................................22
  - Puerto Rican...............................88
  - Cuban......................................72
  - Other Hispanic............................167

Age & Nativity, 2000
- Under 5 years...............................131
- 18 years and over..........................2,179
- 21 years and over..........................2,090
- 65 years and over............................422
- 85 years and over.............................35
  - Median age.................................40.4
- Native-born...............................2,151
- Foreign-born................................603

Educational Attainment, 2000
- Population 25 years and over...............1,982
- Less than 9th grade........................10.0%
- High school grad or higher.................72.9%
- Bachelor's degree or higher................13.2%
- Graduate degree.............................3.2%

Income & Poverty, 1999
- Per capita income........................$24,654
- Median household income..................$50,571
- Median family income.....................$62,163
- Persons in poverty..........................104
- H'holds receiving public assistance..........19
- H'holds receiving social security..........322

Households, 2000
- Total households..........................1,041
  - With persons under 18.....................333
  - With persons over 65......................328
  - Family households.........................708
  - Single-person households..................289
- Persons per household.......................2.65
- Persons per family..........................3.27

Labor & Employment
- Total civilian labor force, 2006**........1,520
  - Unemployment rate.........................2.8%
- Total civilian labor force, 2000..........1,426
  - Unemployment rate.........................2.5%

Employed persons 16 years and over by occupation, 2000
- Managers & professionals....................312
- Service occupations.........................176
- Sales & office occupations..................513
- Farming, fishing & forestry...................0
- Construction & maintenance..................134
- Production & transportation.................255
- Self-employed persons........................66

* US Census Bureau
** New Jersey Department of Labor

See Introduction for an explanation of all data sources.

General Information
Borough of Moonachie
70 Moonachie Rd
Moonachie, NJ 07074
201-641-1813
- Website..............www.moonachie.us
- Year of incorporation................1910
- Land/water area (sq. miles).......1.73/0.00
- Form of government...............Borough

Government
Legislative Districts
- US Congressional............................9
- State Legislative..........................36

Local Officials, 2008
- Mayor...................Frederick Dressel
- Manager...............Anthony Ciannamea
- Clerk....................Supriya Sanyal
- Finance Dir................Paul Hansen
- Tax Assessor..............Paul Barbire
- Tax Collector.........Elizabeth Bassani
- Attorney...............Frank Migliorino
- Building..............Raymond Dressler
- Comm Dev/Planning..................NA
- Engineering............Kevin Boswell
- Public Works.......................NA
- Police Chief...........Michael McGahn
- Emerg/Fire Director......William Hunt

Housing & Construction
Housing Units, 2000*
- Total..............................1,074
- Median rent..........................$851
- Median SF home value............$192,900

Permits for New Residential Construction

	Units	Value
Total, 2007	7	$1,576,510
Single family	7	$1,576,510
Total, 2006	5	$970,950
Single family	5	$970,950

Real Property Valuation, 2007

	Parcels	Valuation
Total	800	$803,363,090
Vacant	23	11,736,800
Residential	597	229,588,690
Commercial	40	73,732,800
Industrial	140	488,304,800
Apartments	0	0
Farm land	0	0
Farm homestead	0	0

Average Property Value & Tax, 2007
- Residential value..................$384,571
- Property tax.........................$5,829
- Tax credit/rebate....................$1,037

Public Library
No public municipal library

Library statistics, 2006
- Population served.......................NA
- Full-time/total staff................NA/NA

	Total	Per capita
Holdings	NA	NA
Revenues	NA	NA
Expenditures	NA	NA
Annual visits	NA	NA

- Internet terminals/annual users.....NA/NA

Public Safety
- Number of officers, 2006....................19

Crime	2005	2006
Total crimes	96	91
Violent	3	2
Murder	0	0
Rape	0	0
Robbery	0	0
Aggravated assault	3	2
Non-violent	93	89
Burglary	11	10
Larceny	72	67
Vehicle theft	10	12
Domestic violence	37	26
Arson	0	0
Total crime rate	34.1	32.4
Violent	1.1	0.7
Non-violent	33.0	31.7

Public School District
(for school year 2006-07 except as noted)

Moonachie School District
20 W Park St
Moonachie, NJ 07074
201-641-5833

- Superintendent..............Mark Solimo
- Number of schools............................1
- Grade plan................................K-8
- Enrollment................................264
- Attendance rate, '05-06.................94.3%
- Dropout rate................................NA
- Students per teacher........................9.4
- Per pupil expenditure..................$15,946
- Median faculty salary..................$61,603
- Median administrator salary...........$85,000
- Grade 12 enrollment.........................NA
- High school graduation rate.................NA

Assessment test results
(percent scoring at proficient or advanced level)

	Language	Math
NJASK-Grade 3	65.4%	76.9%
GEPA-Grade 8	78.5%	92.9%
HSPA-High School	NA	NA

SAT score averages

Pct tested	Math	Verbal	Writing
NA	NA	NA	NA

Teacher Qualifications
- Avg. years of experience....................18
- Highly-qualified teachers
  - one subject/all subjects........100%/100%
- With emergency credentials...............0.0%

No Child Left Behind
- AYP, 2005-06.............Meets Standards

Municipal Finance
State Aid Programs, 2008
- Total aid........................$541,228
  - CMPTRA..............................0
  - Energy tax receipts............541,228
  - Garden State Trust...................0

General Budget, 2007
- Total tax levy................$12,192,961
  - County levy.................1,434,272
    - County taxes..............1,354,627
    - County library..................0
    - County health...................0
    - County open space............79,645
  - School levy.................6,127,472
  - Muni. levy..................4,631,217
- Misc. revenues.................2,529,713

Taxes	2005	2006	2007
General tax rate per $100	1.35	1.43	1.52
County equalization ratio	123.69	109.71	102.21
Net valuation taxable	$804,097,900	$803,280,460	$804,469,433
State equalized value	$732,930,362	$787,004,696	$831,541,623

The New Jersey Municipal Data Book

Moorestown Township
Burlington County

Demographics & Socio-Economic Characteristics
(2000 US Census, except as noted)

Population
1980*	15,596
1990*	16,116
2000	19,017
Male	8,974
Female	10,043
2006 (estimate)*	19,996
Population density	1,353.8

Race & Hispanic Origin, 2000
Race
White	16,962
Black/African American	1,082
American Indian/Alaska Native	30
Asian	621
Native Hawaiian/Pacific Islander	1
Other race	81
Two or more races	240
Hispanic origin, total	332
Mexican	49
Puerto Rican	140
Cuban	26
Other Hispanic	117

Age & Nativity, 2000
Under 5 years	1,218
18 years and over	13,797
21 years and over	13,363
65 years and over	3,120
85 years and over	557
Median age	40.9
Native-born	17,906
Foreign-born	1,111

Educational Attainment, 2000
Population 25 years and over	12,946
Less than 9th grade	2.7%
High school grad or higher	92.5%
Bachelor's degree or higher	52.5%
Graduate degree	23.2%

Income & Poverty, 1999
Per capita income	$42,154
Median household income	$78,826
Median family income	$94,844
Persons in poverty	634
H'holds receiving public assistance	71
H'holds receiving social security	2,048

Households, 2000
Total households	6,971
With persons under 18	2,697
With persons over 65	2,005
Family households	5,273
Single-person households	1,461
Persons per household	2.68
Persons per family	3.13

Labor & Employment
Total civilian labor force, 2006**	10,440
Unemployment rate	3.2%
Total civilian labor force, 2000	8,973
Unemployment rate	3.0%

Employed persons 16 years and over by occupation, 2000
Managers & professionals	4,877
Service occupations	599
Sales & office occupations	2,279
Farming, fishing & forestry	12
Construction & maintenance	347
Production & transportation	590
Self-employed persons	711

* US Census Bureau
** New Jersey Department of Labor

General Information
Township of Moorestown
111 W 2nd St
Moorestown, NJ 08057
856-235-0912

Website	www.moorestown.nj.us
Year of incorporation	1922
Land/water area (sq. miles)	14.77/0.16
Form of government	Council-Manager

Government
Legislative Districts
US Congressional	3
State Legislative	8

Local Officials, 2008
Mayor	Kevin E. Aberant
Manager	Christopher J. Schultz
Clerk	Patricia Hunt
Finance Dir	Thomas Merchel
Tax Assessor	Dennis DeKlerk
Tax Collector	Dorothy Samartino
Attorney	David M. Serlin
Building	Steven Holmes
Community Dev	Thomas Ford (Actg)
Engineering	Environmental Resolutions
Public Works	Kenneth Ewers
Police Chief	Harry Johnson
Fire Chief	W. Ruggiano

Housing & Construction
Housing Units, 2000*
Total	7,211
Median rent	$843
Median SF home value	$254,900

Permits for New Residential Construction
	Units	Value
Total, 2007	27	$5,962,400
Single family	24	$5,694,317
Total, 2006	57	$9,739,529
Single family	41	$9,356,715

Real Property Valuation, 2007
	Parcels	Valuation
Total	7,367	$1,933,902,200
Vacant	390	25,327,900
Residential	6,483	1,427,273,600
Commercial	248	268,290,700
Industrial	86	156,417,800
Apartments	23	39,709,200
Farm land	100	744,700
Farm homestead	37	16,138,300

Average Property Value & Tax, 2007
Residential value	$221,382
Property tax	$9,682
Tax credit/rebate	$1,095

Public Library
Moorestown Public Library
111 W Second St
Moorestown, NJ 08057
856-234-0333

Director.............Joseph Galbraith

Library statistics, 2006
Population served	19,017
Full-time/total staff	5/13

	Total	Per capita
Holdings	144,225	7.58
Revenues	$1,533,774	$80.65
Expenditures	$1,407,779	$74.03
Annual visits	111,579	5.87
Internet terminals/annual users	10/18,924	

Taxes
	2005	2006	2007
General tax rate per $100	4.02	4.227	4.379
County equalization ratio	57.9	52.23	47.57
Net valuation taxable	$1,918,047,214	$1,923,129,200	$1,941,169,706
State equalized value	$3,672,309,428	$4,050,655,867	$4,402,499,779

Public Safety
Number of officers, 2006 38

Crime	2005	2006
Total crimes	542	462
Violent	21	21
Murder	0	0
Rape	1	4
Robbery	13	6
Aggravated assault	7	11
Non-violent	521	441
Burglary	61	53
Larceny	436	379
Vehicle theft	24	9
Domestic violence	57	64
Arson	1	1
Total crime rate	27.0	23.1
Violent	1.0	1.0
Non-violent	26.0	22.0

Public School District
(for school year 2006-07 except as noted)

Moorestown Township School District
803 N Stanwick Rd
Moorestown, NJ 08057
856-778-6600

Superintendent	John Bach
Number of schools	6
Grade plan	K-12
Enrollment	4,382
Attendance rate, '05-06	95.7%
Dropout rate	0.2%
Students per teacher	11.6
Per pupil expenditure	$12,720
Median faculty salary	$54,986
Median administrator salary	$109,363
Grade 12 enrollment	298
High school graduation rate	97.7%

Assessment test results
(percent scoring at proficient or advanced level)
	Language	Math
NJASK-Grade 3	91.9%	95.0%
GEPA-Grade 8	88.3%	88.9%
HSPA-High School	95.5%	90.8%

SAT score averages
Pct tested	Math	Verbal	Writing
109%	561	550	546

Teacher Qualifications
Avg. years of experience	10
Highly-qualified teachers one subject/all subjects	100%/100%
With emergency credentials	0.0%

No Child Left Behind
AYP, 2005-06 .... Meets Standards

Municipal Finance
State Aid Programs, 2008
Total aid	$2,432,142
CMPTRA	734,319
Energy tax receipts	1,694,518
Garden State Trust	3,305

General Budget, 2007
Total tax levy	$84,898,408
County levy	15,870,751
County taxes	14,233,495
County library	0
County health	0
County open space	1,637,257
School levy	56,428,940
Muni. levy	12,598,717
Misc. revenues	11,357,793

Morris County
Morris Plains Borough

Demographics & Socio-Economic Characteristics
(2000 US Census, except as noted)
Population
1980*	5,305
1990*	5,219
2000	5,236
Male	2,512
Female	2,724
2006 (estimate)*	5,601
Population density	2,162.5

Race & Hispanic Origin, 2000
Race
White	4,865
Black/African American	70
American Indian/Alaska Native	3
Asian	226
Native Hawaiian/Pacific Islander	5
Other race	21
Two or more races	46
Hispanic origin, total	141
Mexican	28
Puerto Rican	31
Cuban	13
Other Hispanic	69

Age & Nativity, 2000
Under 5 years	379
18 years and over	4,003
21 years and over	3,913
65 years and over	848
85 years and over	127
Median age	40.7
Native-born	4,730
Foreign-born	506

Educational Attainment, 2000
Population 25 years and over	3,777
Less than 9th grade	1.9%
High school grad or higher	94.3%
Bachelor's degree or higher	51.0%
Graduate degree	21.5%

Income & Poverty, 1999
Per capita income	$36,553
Median household income	$84,806
Median family income	$98,333
Persons in poverty	124
H'holds receiving public assistance	0
H'holds receiving social security	573

Households, 2000
Total households	1,955
With persons under 18	679
With persons over 65	547
Family households	1,478
Single-person households	386
Persons per household	2.63
Persons per family	3.05

Labor & Employment
Total civilian labor force, 2006**	3,011
Unemployment rate	3.8%
Total civilian labor force, 2000	2,728
Unemployment rate	3.1%

Employed persons 16 years and over by occupation, 2000
Managers & professionals	1,496
Service occupations	235
Sales & office occupations	669
Farming, fishing & forestry	0
Construction & maintenance	147
Production & transportation	96
Self-employed persons	168

* US Census Bureau
** New Jersey Department of Labor

See Introduction for an explanation of all data sources.

General Information
Borough of Morris Plains
531 Speedwell Ave
Morris Plains, NJ 07950
973-538-2224
Website	www.morrisplainsboro.org
Year of incorporation	1926
Land/water area (sq. miles)	2.59/0.02
Form of government	Borough

Government
Legislative Districts
US Congressional	11
State Legislative	26

Local Officials, 2008
Mayor	Frank J. Druetzler
Manager/Admin	NA
Clerk	June Uhrin
Finance Dir	David Banks
Tax Assessor	Allan W. Adams
Tax Collector	Ana Thomas
Attorney	Gail Fraser
Building	Edward Easse
Planning	William Denzler
Municipal Engineer	Leon C. Hall
Public Works	Joseph Signorelli Jr
Police Chief	James Abbondanzo
Emerg/Fire Director	Michael Geary

Housing & Construction
Housing Units, 2000*
Total	1,994
Median rent	$1,045
Median SF home value	$282,500

Permits for New Residential Construction
	Units	Value
Total, 2007	51	$6,103,806
Single family	9	$4,061,892
Total, 2006	43	$6,096,324
Single family	11	$4,540,580

Real Property Valuation, 2007
	Parcels	Valuation
Total	2,221	$775,104,470
Vacant	189	4,862,500
Residential	1,933	455,050,570
Commercial	95	252,773,800
Industrial	3	52,005,000
Apartments	1	10,412,600
Farm land	0	0
Farm homestead	0	0

Average Property Value & Tax, 2007
Residential value	$235,412
Property tax	$7,157
Tax credit/rebate	$1,098

Public Library
Morris Plains Public Library
77 Glenbrook Rd
Morris Plains, NJ 07950
973-538-2599
Director............Camille Garretson (Int)

Library statistics, 2006
Population served	5,236
Full-time/total staff	0/0

	Total	Per capita
Holdings	23,376	4.46
Revenues	$113,504	$21.68
Expenditures	$98,668	$18.84
Annual visits	19,865	3.79
Internet terminals/annual users		3/4,889

Taxes
	2005	2006	2007
General tax rate per $100	2.79	2.88	3.05
County equalization ratio	60.15	57.34	48.41
Net valuation taxable	$780,183,032	$778,999,850	$776,136,704
State equalized value	$1,360,626,146	$1,610,225,277	$1,511,662,657

Public Safety
Number of officers, 2006	17

Crime	2005	2006
Total crimes	93	83
Violent	3	5
Murder	0	0
Rape	0	0
Robbery	1	2
Aggravated assault	2	3
Non-violent	90	78
Burglary	10	11
Larceny	79	60
Vehicle theft	1	7
Domestic violence	13	31
Arson	0	2
Total crime rate	16.7	14.7
Violent	0.5	0.9
Non-violent	16.2	13.9

Public School District
(for school year 2006-07 except as noted)

Morris Plains School District
500 Speedwell Ave
Morris Plains, NJ 07950
973-538-1650

Superintendent	Vicki Pede
Number of schools	2
Grade plan	K-8
Enrollment	617
Attendance rate, '05-06	96.4%
Dropout rate	NA
Students per teacher	10.4
Per pupil expenditure	$15,526
Median faculty salary	$48,053
Median administrator salary	$115,006
Grade 12 enrollment	NA
High school graduation rate	NA

Assessment test results
(percent scoring at proficient or advanced level)
	Language	Math
NJASK-Grade 3	95.5%	90.9%
GEPA-Grade 8	89.8%	88.5%
HSPA-High School	NA	NA

SAT score averages
Pct tested	Math	Verbal	Writing
NA	NA	NA	NA

Teacher Qualifications
Avg. years of experience	7
Highly-qualified teachers one subject/all subjects	95.5%/95.5%
With emergency credentials	2.4%

No Child Left Behind
AYP, 2005-06............Meets Standards

Municipal Finance
State Aid Programs, 2008
Total aid	$742,294
CMPTRA	121,132
Energy tax receipts	621,162
Garden State Trust	0

General Budget, 2007
Total tax levy	$23,596,552
County levy	3,818,433
County taxes	3,053,759
County library	0
County health	0
County open space	764,674
School levy	11,979,556
Muni. levy	7,798,563
Misc. revenues	3,374,427

©2008 Information Publications, Inc. All rights reserved. Photocopying prohibited. For additional copies, contact the publisher at www.informationpublications.com or (877)544-INFO (4636)

Morris Township — Morris County

Demographics & Socio-Economic Characteristics
(2000 US Census, except as noted)

Population
1980*	18,486
1990*	19,952
2000	21,796
Male	10,287
Female	11,509
2006 (estimate)*	21,374
Population density	1,356.2

Race & Hispanic Origin, 2000
Race
- White: 19,317
- Black/African American: 1,189
- American Indian/Alaska Native: 33
- Asian: 849
- Native Hawaiian/Pacific Islander: 3
- Other race: 199
- Two or more races: 206
- Hispanic origin, total: 830
  - Mexican: 62
  - Puerto Rican: 157
  - Cuban: 56
  - Other Hispanic: 555

Age & Nativity, 2000
- Under 5 years: 1,563
- 18 years and over: 16,846
- 21 years and over: 16,247
- 65 years and over: 3,356
- 85 years and over: 457
- Median age: 40.9
- Native-born: 19,460
- Foreign-born: 2,336

Educational Attainment, 2000
- Population 25 years and over: 15,565
- Less than 9th grade: 1.9%
- High school grad or higher: 95.1%
- Bachelor's degree or higher: 63.6%
- Graduate degree: 29.6%

Income & Poverty, 1999
- Per capita income: $54,782
- Median household income: $101,902
- Median family income: $116,866
- Persons in poverty: 802
- H'holds receiving public assistance: 49
- H'holds receiving social security: 2,075

Households, 2000
- Total households: 8,116
  - With persons under 18: 2,639
  - With persons over 65: 2,088
  - Family households: 5,953
  - Single-person households: 1,766
- Persons per household: 2.55
- Persons per family: 2.99

Labor & Employment
- Total civilian labor force, 2006**: 12,254
  - Unemployment rate: 3.3%
- Total civilian labor force, 2000: 11,579
  - Unemployment rate: 4.2%

Employed persons 16 years and over by occupation, 2000
- Managers & professionals: 6,956
- Service occupations: 736
- Sales & office occupations: 2,660
- Farming, fishing & forestry: 0
- Construction & maintenance: 407
- Production & transportation: 330
- Self-employed persons: 820

‡ Joint library with Morristown
* US Census Bureau
** New Jersey Department of Labor

General Information
Township of Morris
50 Woodland Ave
PO Box 7603
Convent Station, NJ 07961
973-326-7430

- Website: www.morristwp.com
- Year of incorporation: 1740
- Land/water area (sq. miles): 15.76/0.05
- Form of government: Township

Government
Legislative Districts
- US Congressional: 11
- State Legislative: 25

Local Officials, 2008
- Mayor: Robert E. Nace
- Manager: Fred Rossi
- Clerk: Cathleen Amelio
- Finance Dir: Julia Hasbrouck
- Tax Assessor: Sue Aceto
- Tax Collector: Audrey Adams
- Attorney: John Mills III
- Building: Albert Mastrobatista
- Comm Dev/Planning: NA
- Engineering: James Slate
- Public Works: James Stoia
- Police Chief: Timothy Quinn
- Emerg/Fire Director: Craig Goss

Housing & Construction
Housing Units, 2000*
- Total: 8,298
- Median rent: $1,040
- Median SF home value: $350,400

Permits for New Residential Construction

	Units	Value
Total, 2007	120	$7,821,290
Single family	120	$7,821,290
Total, 2006	18	$7,437,057
Single family	18	$7,437,057

Real Property Valuation, 2007

	Parcels	Valuation
Total	8,030	$3,815,501,350
Vacant	248	25,062,350
Residential	7,602	2,988,331,700
Commercial	142	594,323,600
Industrial	21	170,662,000
Apartments	4	31,165,000
Farm land	8	48,300
Farm homestead	5	5,908,400

Average Property Value & Tax, 2007
- Residential value: $393,616
- Property tax: $8,664
- Tax credit/rebate: $1,114

Public Library
Morristown & Morris Township Library‡
1 Miller Rd
Morristown, NJ 07960
973-538-6161

- Director: Susan H. Gulick

Library statistics, 2006
- Population served: 40,340
- Full-time/total staff: 13/22

	Total	Per capita
Holdings	225,615	5.59
Revenues	$2,811,352	$69.69
Expenditures	$2,683,358	$66.52
Annual visits	351,761	8.72

- Internet terminals/annual users: 28/60,500

Public Safety
- Number of officers, 2006: 44

Crime	2005	2006
Total crimes	173	219
Violent	22	38
Murder	0	0
Rape	0	4
Robbery	1	3
Aggravated assault	21	31
Non-violent	151	181
Burglary	25	31
Larceny	111	135
Vehicle theft	15	15
Domestic violence	71	78
Arson	2	0
Total crime rate	8.1	10.2
Violent	1.0	1.8
Non-violent	7.1	8.4

Public School District
(for school year 2006-07 except as noted)

Morris School District
31 Hazel St
Morristown, NJ 07960
973-292-2300

- Superintendent: Thomas Ficarra
- Number of schools: 18
- Grade plan: K-12
- Enrollment: 4,562
- Attendance rate, '05-06: 95.6%
- Dropout rate: 0.5%
- Students per teacher: 9.8
- Per pupil expenditure: $18,424
- Median faculty salary: $64,816
- Median administrator salary: $113,076
- Grade 12 enrollment: 321
- High school graduation rate: 95.3%

Assessment test results
(percent scoring at proficient or advanced level)

	Language	Math
NJASK-Grade 3	85.7%	89.0%
GEPA-Grade 8	76.9%	77.0%
HSPA-High School	80.3%	69.6%

SAT score averages

Pct tested	Math	Verbal	Writing
88%	534	533	526

Teacher Qualifications
- Avg. years of experience: 9
- Highly-qualified teachers one subject/all subjects: 100%/100%
- With emergency credentials: 0.6%

No Child Left Behind
- AYP, 2005-06: Meets Standards

Municipal Finance
State Aid Programs, 2008
- Total aid: $4,427,057
  - CMPTRA: 2,157,563
  - Energy tax receipts: 2,269,446
  - Garden State Trust: 48

General Budget, 2007
- Total tax levy: $84,081,495
  - County levy: 13,341,737
    - County taxes: 10,668,947
    - County library: 0
    - County health: 0
    - County open space: 2,672,790
  - School levy: 50,354,842
  - Muni. levy: 20,384,916
- Misc. revenues: 12,566,737

Taxes	2005	2006	2007
General tax rate per $100	2.06	2.13	2.21
County equalization ratio	82.16	75.78	68.24
Net valuation taxable	$3,836,370,667	$3,817,346,850	$3,819,837,079
State equalized value	$5,062,510,777	$5,597,988,850	$5,646,899,098

Morris County — Morristown Town

Demographics & Socio-Economic Characteristics
(2000 US Census, except as noted)

Population
1980*	16,614
1990*	16,189
2000	18,544
Male	9,302
Female	9,242
2006 (estimate)*	18,922
Population density	6,436.1

Race & Hispanic Origin, 2000
Race
- White 12,452
- Black/African American 3,144
- American Indian/Alaska Native ... 41
- Asian 700
- Native Hawaiian/Pacific Islander ... 12
- Other race 1,572
- Two or more races 623
- Hispanic origin, total 5,034
  - Mexican 139
  - Puerto Rican 286
  - Cuban 50
  - Other Hispanic 4,559

Age & Nativity, 2000
- Under 5 years 1,026
- 18 years and over 15,140
- 21 years and over 14,576
- 65 years and over 2,292
- 85 years and over 406
- Median age 35.0
- Native-born 12,528
- Foreign-born 6,016

Educational Attainment, 2000
- Population 25 years and over ... 13,604
- Less than 9th grade 7.6%
- High school grad or higher 83.0%
- Bachelor's degree or higher ... 39.3%
- Graduate degree 16.0%

Income & Poverty, 1999
- Per capita income $30,086
- Median household income $57,563
- Median family income $66,419
- Persons in poverty 2,069
- H'holds receiving public assistance .. 125
- H'holds receiving social security ... 1,565

Households, 2000
- Total households 7,252
- With persons under 18 1,875
- With persons over 65 1,574
- Family households 3,700
- Single-person households 2,805
- Persons per household 2.43
- Persons per family 3.19

Labor & Employment
- Total civilian labor force, 2006** ... 11,607
- Unemployment rate 3.4%
- Total civilian labor force, 2000 ... 10,747
- Unemployment rate 3.4%

Employed persons 16 years and over by occupation, 2000
- Managers & professionals 4,303
- Service occupations 2,226
- Sales & office occupations ... 2,144
- Farming, fishing & forestry 42
- Construction & maintenance 722
- Production & transportation ... 947
- Self-employed persons 387

‡ Joint library with Morris Township
* US Census Bureau
** New Jersey Department of Labor

See Introduction for an explanation of all data sources.

General Information
Town of Morristown
200 South St
PO Box 914
Morristown, NJ 07963
973-292-6600

- Website .... www.townofmorristown.org
- Year of incorporation 1865
- Land/water area (sq. miles) ... 2.94/0.06
- Form of government ...... Mayor-Council

Government
Legislative Districts
- US Congressional 11
- State Legislative 25

Local Officials, 2008
- Mayor .... Donald Crestiello
- Manager .... Michael Rogers
- Clerk .... Matthew Stechauner
- Finance Dir .... Bob Calise
- Tax Assessor .... Pat Aceto
- Tax Collector .... NA
- Attorney .... Jonathan Williams
- Building .... Fritz Reuss
- Planning .... Michael D'Altilio
- Engineering .... Jeffrey Hartke
- Public Works .... NA
- Police Chief .... Peter Demnitz
- Emerg/Fire Director ..... Robert Taylor

Housing & Construction
Housing Units, 2000*
- Total 7,615
- Median rent $914
- Median SF home value $224,400

Permits for New Residential Construction
	Units	Value
Total, 2007	130	$9,333,010
Single family	6	$1,480,482
Total, 2006	307	$54,295,400
Single family	2	$253,275

Real Property Valuation, 2007
	Parcels	Valuation
Total	4,222	$2,197,397,142
Vacant	229	55,989,100
Residential	3,377	1,194,136,942
Commercial	534	758,006,900
Industrial	10	11,665,100
Apartments	72	177,599,100
Farm land	0	0
Farm homestead	0	0

Average Property Value & Tax, 2007
- Residential value $353,609
- Property tax $8,058
- Tax credit/rebate $1,201

Public Library
Morristown & Morris Township Library‡
1 Miller Rd
Morristown, NJ 07960
973-538-6161

Director .... Susan H. Gulick

Library statistics, 2006
- Population served 40,340
- Full-time/total staff 13/22

	Total	Per capita
Holdings	225,615	5.59
Revenues	$2,811,352	$69.69
Expenditures	$2,683,358	$66.52
Annual visits	351,761	8.72
Internet terminals/annual users	28/60,500	

Taxes
	2005	2006	2007
General tax rate per $100	2.12	2.24	2.28
County equalization ratio	102.13	91.64	85.15
Net valuation taxable	$2,245,556,075	$2,197,622,042	$2,213,619,563
State equalized value	$2,450,410,383	$2,597,234,591	$2,897,676,843

Public Safety
Number of officers, 2006 59

Crime	2005	2006
Total crimes	971	835
Violent	142	107
Murder	0	0
Rape	4	3
Robbery	66	37
Aggravated assault	72	67
Non-violent	829	728
Burglary	196	111
Larceny	576	581
Vehicle theft	57	36
Domestic violence	233	259
Arson	4	3
Total crime rate	51.5	44.3
Violent	7.5	5.7
Non-violent	44.0	38.6

Public School District
(for school year 2006-07 except as noted)

Morris School District
31 Hazel St
Morristown, NJ 07960
973-292-2300

- Superintendent .... Thomas Ficarra
- Number of schools 18
- Grade plan K-12
- Enrollment 4,562
- Attendance rate, '05-06 .... 95.6%
- Dropout rate 0.5%
- Students per teacher 9.8
- Per pupil expenditure $18,424
- Median faculty salary $64,816
- Median administrator salary .. $113,076
- Grade 12 enrollment 321
- High school graduation rate 95.3%

Assessment test results
(percent scoring at proficient or advanced level)
	Language	Math
NJASK-Grade 3	85.7%	89.0%
GEPA-Grade 8	76.9%	77.0%
HSPA-High School	80.3%	69.6%

SAT score averages
Pct tested	Math	Verbal	Writing
88%	534	533	526

Teacher Qualifications
- Avg. years of experience 9
- Highly-qualified teachers one subject/all subjects 100%/100%
- With emergency credentials 0.6%

No Child Left Behind
AYP, 2005-06 .... Meets Standards

Municipal Finance
State Aid Programs, 2008
- Total aid $3,682,480
- CMPTRA 953,917
- Energy tax receipts 2,728,563
- Garden State Trust 0

General Budget, 2007
- Total tax levy $50,441,024
- County levy 6,171,245
- County taxes 4,935,357
- County library 0
- County health 0
- County open space 1,235,888
- School levy 23,599,652
- Muni. levy 20,670,127
- Misc. revenues 14,567,450

©2008 Information Publications, Inc. All rights reserved.

Mount Arlington Borough

Morris County

Demographics & Socio-Economic Characteristics
(2000 US Census, except as noted)

Population
1980*	4,251
1990*	3,630
2000	4,663
Male	2,216
Female	2,447
2006 (estimate)*	5,708
Population density	2,705.2

Race & Hispanic Origin, 2000
Race
White	4,263
Black/African American	85
American Indian/Alaska Native	9
Asian	178
Native Hawaiian/Pacific Islander	2
Other race	59
Two or more races	67
Hispanic origin, total	212
Mexican	16
Puerto Rican	68
Cuban	15
Other Hispanic	113

Age & Nativity, 2000
Under 5 years	310
18 years and over	3,634
21 years and over	3,526
65 years and over	496
85 years and over	30
Median age	37.9
Native-born	4,207
Foreign-born	456

Educational Attainment, 2000
Population 25 years and over	3,408
Less than 9th grade	2.4%
High school grad or higher	90.4%
Bachelor's degree or higher	35.9%
Graduate degree	11.2%

Income & Poverty, 1999
Per capita income	$32,222
Median household income	$67,213
Median family income	$79,514
Persons in poverty	153
H'holds receiving public assistance	22
H'holds receiving social security	392

Households, 2000
Total households	1,918
With persons under 18	576
With persons over 65	374
Family households	1,263
Single-person households	535
Persons per household	2.42
Persons per family	2.99

Labor & Employment
Total civilian labor force, 2006**	2,998
Unemployment rate	3.4%
Total civilian labor force, 2000	2,738
Unemployment rate	3.0%

Employed persons 16 years and over by occupation, 2000
Managers & professionals	999
Service occupations	276
Sales & office occupations	870
Farming, fishing & forestry	0
Construction & maintenance	266
Production & transportation	246
Self-employed persons	188

* US Census Bureau
** New Jersey Department of Labor

General Information
Borough of Mount Arlington
419 Howard Blvd
Mount Arlington, NJ 07856
973-398-6832

Website	www.ci.mount-arlington.nj.us
Year of incorporation	1890
Land/water area (sq. miles)	2.11/0.72
Form of government	Borough

Government
Legislative Districts
US Congressional	11
State Legislative	25

Local Officials, 2008
Mayor	Arthur R. Ondish
Manager	JoAnne Sendler
Clerk	Linda DeSantis
CFO	Joseph Kovalcik
Tax Assessor	John Marchione
Tax Collector	Patricia Simari
Attorney	Scarinci & Hollenbeck
Building	Sandor Nyari
Comm Dev/Planning	NA
Engineering	Daren Phil
Public Works	Paul Nelson
Police Chief	Richard Peterson
Emerg/Fire Director	Marc Feinberg

Housing & Construction
Housing Units, 2000*
Total	2,039
Median rent	$831
Median SF home value	$183,700

Permits for New Residential Construction
	Units	Value
Total, 2007	76	$4,838,477
Single family	19	$2,090,205
Total, 2006	94	$6,292,661
Single family	21	$2,301,115

Real Property Valuation, 2007
	Parcels	Valuation
Total	2,260	$692,031,300
Vacant	200	16,952,600
Residential	1,990	580,545,900
Commercial	46	71,623,100
Industrial	1	234,200
Apartments	7	22,663,200
Farm land	16	12,300
Farm homestead	0	0

Average Property Value & Tax, 2007
Residential value	$291,732
Property tax	$5,649
Tax credit/rebate	$931

Public Library
Mt Arlington Public Library
333 Howard Blvd
Mount Arlington, NJ 07856
973-398-1516

Director.................James Garland

Library statistics, 2006
Population served	4,256
Full-time/total staff	0/3

	Total	Per capita
Holdings	28,084	6.60
Revenues	$218,055	$51.23
Expenditures	$237,220	$55.74
Annual visits	25,000	5.87
Internet terminals/annual users	3/2,200	

Taxes
	2005	2006	2007
General tax rate per $100	1.78	1.81	1.94
County equalization ratio	101.75	91.85	82.05
Net valuation taxable	$628,328,490	$672,017,300	$692,720,330
State equalized value	$684,081,100	$819,790,869	$863,033,329

Public Safety
Number of officers, 2006	13

Crime	2005	2006
Total crimes	61	58
Violent	2	4
Murder	0	0
Rape	0	0
Robbery	1	0
Aggravated assault	1	4
Non-violent	59	54
Burglary	4	12
Larceny	54	38
Vehicle theft	1	4
Domestic violence	37	79
Arson	0	0
Total crime rate	11.9	10.9
Violent	0.4	0.8
Non-violent	11.5	10.1

Public School District
(for school year 2006-07 except as noted)

Mount Arlington School District
446 Howard Boulevard
Mount Arlington, NJ 07856
973-398-6400

Superintendent	Jane Mullins Jameson
Number of schools	2
Grade plan	K-8
Enrollment	405
Attendance rate, '05-06	96.1%
Dropout rate	NA
Students per teacher	9.8
Per pupil expenditure	$13,753
Median faculty salary	$49,079
Median administrator salary	$95,000
Grade 12 enrollment	NA
High school graduation rate	NA

Assessment test results
(percent scoring at proficient or advanced level)
	Language	Math
NJASK-Grade 3	86.0%	90.7%
GEPA-Grade 8	70.9%	66.0%
HSPA-High School	NA	NA

SAT score averages
Pct tested	Math	Verbal	Writing
NA	NA	NA	NA

Teacher Qualifications
Avg. years of experience	7
Highly-qualified teachers one subject/all subjects	100%/100%
With emergency credentials	0.0%

No Child Left Behind
AYP, 2005-06	Meets Standards

Municipal Finance
State Aid Programs, 2008
Total aid	$408,876
CMPTRA	47,607
Energy tax receipts	361,255
Garden State Trust	14

General Budget, 2007
Total tax levy	$13,413,604
County levy	2,011,662
County taxes	1,609,024
County library	0
County health	0
County open space	402,638
School levy	8,492,925
Muni. levy	2,909,017
Misc. revenues	4,856,909

Camden County

Mount Ephraim Borough

Demographics & Socio-Economic Characteristics
(2000 US Census, except as noted)

Population
- 1980* 4,863
- 1990* 4,517
- 2000 4,495
  - Male 2,173
  - Female 2,322
- 2006 (estimate)* 4,437
  - Population density 5,042.0

Race & Hispanic Origin, 2000
Race
- White 4,383
- Black/African American 18
- American Indian/Alaska Native 3
- Asian 28
- Native Hawaiian/Pacific Islander 1
- Other race 29
- Two or more races 33
- Hispanic origin, total 89
  - Mexican 5
  - Puerto Rican 67
  - Cuban 5
  - Other Hispanic 12

Age & Nativity, 2000
- Under 5 years 257
- 18 years and over 3,491
- 21 years and over 3,345
- 65 years and over 804
- 85 years and over 72
  - Median age 39.6
- Native-born 4,395
- Foreign-born 100

Educational Attainment, 2000
- Population 25 years and over 3,184
- Less than 9th grade 5.5%
- High school grad or higher 78.5%
- Bachelor's degree or higher 13.3%
- Graduate degree 3.4%

Income & Poverty, 1999
- Per capita income $21,150
- Median household income $44,824
- Median family income $59,468
- Persons in poverty 219
- H'holds receiving public assistance 39
- H'holds receiving social security 671

Households, 2000
- Total households 1,818
  - With persons under 18 541
  - With persons over 65 620
  - Family households 1,175
  - Single-person households 556
- Persons per household 2.46
- Persons per family 3.13

Labor & Employment
- Total civilian labor force, 2006** 2,484
  - Unemployment rate 5.6%
- Total civilian labor force, 2000 2,286
  - Unemployment rate 5.5%

Employed persons 16 years and over by occupation, 2000
- Managers & professionals 672
- Service occupations 218
- Sales & office occupations 669
- Farming, fishing & forestry 0
- Construction & maintenance 259
- Production & transportation 342
- Self-employed persons 53

‡ Branch of county library
* US Census Bureau
** New Jersey Department of Labor

See Introduction for an explanation of all data sources.

General Information
Borough of Mount Ephraim
121 S Black Horse Pike
Mount Ephraim, NJ 08059
856-931-1546
- Website .... www.mountephraim-nj.com
- Year of incorporation 1926
- Land/water area (sq. miles) 0.88/0.01
- Form of government .... Commission

Government
Legislative Districts
- US Congressional 1
- State Legislative 5

Local Officials, 2008
- Mayor .... Joseph E. Wolk
- Manager/Admin .... NA
- Clerk .... Michelle Le Viege
- Finance Dir .... Dean Siminera
- Tax Assessor .... Steve Kessler
- Tax Collector .... Marie Darlington
- Attorney .... Marrazzo & Platt
- Building .... Stephen Beach
- Comm Dev/Planning .... NA
- Engineering .... Remington & Vernick
- Public Works .... Joseph Ciano
- Police Chief .... Edward Dobleman
- Emerg/Fire Director .... Mario Scullan

Housing & Construction
Housing Units, 2000*
- Total 1,881
- Median rent $542
- Median SF home value $94,000

Permits for New Residential Construction

	Units	Value
Total, 2007	1	$206,776
Single family	1	$206,776
Total, 2006	2	$137,292
Single family	2	$137,292

Real Property Valuation, 2007

	Parcels	Valuation
Total	1,756	$173,015,100
Vacant	76	3,206,200
Residential	1,581	145,477,400
Commercial	88	20,247,000
Industrial	3	741,200
Apartments	8	3,343,300
Farm land	0	0
Farm homestead	0	0

Average Property Value & Tax, 2007
- Residential value $92,016
- Property tax $4,943
- Tax credit/rebate $963

Public Library
Mount Ephraim Library‡
130 Bell Rd
Mt. Ephraim, NJ 08059
856-931-6606
- Director .... Gloria Marsh

Library statistics, 2006
see Camden County profile
for library system statistics

Public Safety
- Number of officers, 2006 13

Crime	2005	2006
Total crimes	195	190
Violent	7	22
Murder	0	0
Rape	0	0
Robbery	3	10
Aggravated assault	4	12
Non-violent	188	168
Burglary	26	26
Larceny	146	126
Vehicle theft	16	16
Domestic violence	81	109
Arson	1	1
Total crime rate	43.6	42.5
Violent	1.6	4.9
Non-violent	42.1	37.6

Public School District
(for school year 2006-07 except as noted)

Mount Ephraim Borough School District
125 S Black Horse Pike
Mount Ephraim, NJ 08059
856-931-1634
- Superintendent .... Joseph G. Rafferty
- Number of schools 2
- Grade plan K-8
- Enrollment 452
- Attendance rate, '05-06 .... 94.0%
- Dropout rate .... NA
- Students per teacher 10.5
- Per pupil expenditure $11,689
- Median faculty salary $47,225
- Median administrator salary $112,847
- Grade 12 enrollment .... NA
- High school graduation rate .... NA

Assessment test results
(percent scoring at proficient or advanced level)

	Language	Math
NJASK-Grade 3	90.2%	95.2%
GEPA-Grade 8	83.7%	81.4%
HSPA-High School	NA	NA

SAT score averages

Pct tested	Math	Verbal	Writing
NA	NA	NA	NA

Teacher Qualifications
- Avg. years of experience 13
- Highly-qualified teachers
  one subject/all subjects 100%/100%
- With emergency credentials 0.0%

No Child Left Behind
- AYP, 2005-06 .... Meets Standards

Municipal Finance
State Aid Programs, 2008
- Total aid $342,349
  - CMPTRA 0
  - Energy tax receipts 342,349
  - Garden State Trust 0

General Budget, 2007
- Total tax levy $9,310,264
- County levy 2,007,367
  - County taxes 1,823,446
  - County library 126,937
  - County health 0
  - County open space 56,984
- School levy 4,886,164
- Muni. levy 2,416,734
- Misc. revenues 1,856,790

Taxes	2005	2006	2007
General tax rate per $100	4.456	5.008	5.372
County equalization ratio	80.06	67.94	60.83
Net valuation taxable	$171,510,075	$172,324,600	$173,312,920
State equalized value	$252,443,443	$283,592,977	$306,573,444

The New Jersey Municipal Data Book

Mount Holly Township
Burlington County

Demographics & Socio-Economic Characteristics
(2000 US Census, except as noted)

Population
1980*	10,818
1990*	10,639
2000	10,728
Male	5,356
Female	5,372
2006 (estimate)*	10,602
Population density	3,707.0

Race & Hispanic Origin, 2000
Race
White	7,368
Black/African American	2,314
American Indian/Alaska Native	45
Asian	147
Native Hawaiian/Pacific Islander	7
Other race	512
Two or more races	335
Hispanic origin, total	942
Mexican	71
Puerto Rican	638
Cuban	15
Other Hispanic	218

Age & Nativity, 2000
Under 5 years	706
18 years and over	7,905
21 years and over	7,467
65 years and over	1,335
85 years and over	153
Median age	35.0
Native-born	10,127
Foreign-born	618

Educational Attainment, 2000
Population 25 years and over	6,955
Less than 9th grade	4.5%
High school grad or higher	77.9%
Bachelor's degree or higher	18.6%
Graduate degree	4.2%

Income & Poverty, 1999
Per capita income	$19,672
Median household income	$43,284
Median family income	$52,000
Persons in poverty	1,023
H'holds receiving public assistance	180
H'holds receiving social security	1,095

Households, 2000
Total households	3,903
With persons under 18	1,430
With persons over 65	982
Family households	2,585
Single-person households	1,063
Persons per household	2.64
Persons per family	3.20

Labor & Employment
Total civilian labor force, 2006**	5,952
Unemployment rate	6.4%
Total civilian labor force, 2000	5,163
Unemployment rate	6.4%

Employed persons 16 years and over by occupation, 2000
Managers & professionals	1,317
Service occupations	839
Sales & office occupations	1,349
Farming, fishing & forestry	20
Construction & maintenance	452
Production & transportation	854
Self-employed persons	238

* US Census Bureau
** New Jersey Department of Labor

General Information
Township of Mount Holly
23 Washington St
Mount Holly, NJ 08060
609-267-0170

Website	www.mountholly.info
Year of incorporation	1931
Land/water area (sq. miles)	2.86/0.02
Form of government	Council-Manager

Government
Legislative Districts
US Congressional	3
State Legislative	7

Local Officials, 2008
Mayor	Brooke Tidswell
Manager	Kathleen D. Hoffman
Clerk	Kathleen D. Hoffman
Finance Dir.	Christina Chambers
Tax Assessor	Leo Midure
Tax Collector	Maryann Zanone
Attorney	Brian Guest
Building	Thomas Casey
Planning	Patrick Perinchief
Engineering	Richard Alaimo & Assoc
Public Works	Nick Troster
Police Chief	Steve Martin
Emerg/Fire Director	Ian Bruce

Housing & Construction
Housing Units, 2000*
Total	4,248
Median rent	$719
Median SF home value	$98,200

Permits for New Residential Construction
	Units	Value
Total, 2007	4	$674,000
Single family	4	$674,000
Total, 2006	2	$828,080
Single family	2	$828,080

Real Property Valuation, 2007
	Parcels	Valuation
Total	3,514	$314,978,300
Vacant	210	6,168,700
Residential	3,041	248,390,800
Commercial	208	44,018,800
Industrial	12	4,847,700
Apartments	39	11,395,400
Farm land	3	14,200
Farm homestead	1	142,700

Average Property Value & Tax, 2007
Residential value	$81,701
Property tax	$3,836
Tax credit/rebate	$841

Public Library
Mount Holly Public Library
307 High St
Mount Holly, NJ 08060
609-267-7111

Director .... T. Michael Eck

Library statistics, 2006
Population served	10,728
Full-time/total staff	0/1

	Total	Per capita
Holdings	11,879	1.11
Revenues	$39,597	$3.69
Expenditures	$98,194	$9.15
Annual visits	19,000	1.77
Internet terminals/annual users	7/4,000	

Taxes
	2005	2006	2007
General tax rate per $100	3.9	4.308	4.7
County equalization ratio	69.23	58.95	49.78
Net valuation taxable	$324,441,701	$316,642,200	$318,628,118
State equalized value	$550,367,601	$640,306,652	$703,290,644

Public Safety
Number of officers, 2006		26

Crime	2005	2006
Total crimes	400	390
Violent	41	55
Murder	0	0
Rape	0	0
Robbery	18	24
Aggravated assault	23	31
Non-violent	359	335
Burglary	48	55
Larceny	286	256
Vehicle theft	25	24
Domestic violence	295	342
Arson	0	2
Total crime rate	37.3	36.6
Violent	3.8	5.2
Non-violent	33.4	31.4

Public School District
(for school year 2006-07 except as noted)

Mount Holly Township School District
330 Levis Dr
Mount Holly, NJ 08060
609-267-7108

Superintendent	Dabid N. Gentile
Number of schools	3
Grade plan	K-8
Enrollment	1,064
Attendance rate, '05-06	93.7%
Dropout rate	NA
Students per teacher	9.4
Per pupil expenditure	$15,266
Median faculty salary	$69,760
Median administrator salary	$92,000
Grade 12 enrollment	NA
High school graduation rate	NA

Assessment test results
(percent scoring at proficient or advanced level)
	Language	Math
NJASK-Grade 3	73.8%	82.3%
GEPA-Grade 8	58.7%	63.3%
HSPA-High School	NA	NA

SAT score averages
Pct tested	Math	Verbal	Writing
NA	NA	NA	NA

Teacher Qualifications
Avg. years of experience	13
Highly-qualified teachers one subject/all subjects	100%/100%
With emergency credentials	0.0%

No Child Left Behind
AYP, 2005-06	Needs Improvement

Municipal Finance
State Aid Programs, 2008
Total aid	$1,896,152
CMPTRA	933,647
Energy tax receipts	962,488
Garden State Trust	17

General Budget, 2007
Total tax levy	$14,960,808
County levy	2,695,658
County taxes	2,233,734
County library	204,980
County health	0
County open space	256,945
School levy	9,074,037
Muni. levy	3,191,114
Misc. revenues	9,128,948

Burlington County
Mount Laurel Township

Demographics & Socio-Economic Characteristics
(2000 US Census, except as noted)

Population
1980*	17,614
1990*	30,270
2000	40,221
Male	18,983
Female	21,238
2006 (estimate)*	40,326
Population density	1,849.0

Race & Hispanic Origin, 2000
Race
White	35,034
Black/African American	2,785
American Indian/Alaska Native	38
Asian	1,529
Native Hawaiian/Pacific Islander	12
Other race	256
Two or more races	567
Hispanic origin, total	901
Mexican	110
Puerto Rican	407
Cuban	60
Other Hispanic	324

Age & Nativity, 2000
Under 5 years	2,460
18 years and over	30,916
21 years and over	30,015
65 years and over	5,905
85 years and over	413
Median age	38.9
Native-born	37,444
Foreign-born	2,777

Educational Attainment, 2000
Population 25 years and over	28,924
Less than 9th grade	2.2%
High school grad or higher	92.1%
Bachelor's degree or higher	42.1%
Graduate degree	14.1%

Income & Poverty, 1999
Per capita income	$32,245
Median household income	$63,750
Median family income	$76,288
Persons in poverty	1,243
H'holds receiving public assistance	96
H'holds receiving social security	4,311

Households, 2000
Total households	16,570
With persons under 18	5,279
With persons over 65	4,065
Family households	11,062
Single-person households	4,630
Persons per household	2.41
Persons per family	2.98

Labor & Employment
Total civilian labor force, 2006**	23,623
Unemployment rate	3.4%
Total civilian labor force, 2000	21,688
Unemployment rate	3.0%

Employed persons 16 years and over by occupation, 2000
Managers & professionals	10,417
Service occupations	1,930
Sales & office occupations	6,352
Farming, fishing & forestry	23
Construction & maintenance	1,015
Production & transportation	1,294
Self-employed persons	739

* US Census Bureau
** New Jersey Department of Labor

See Introduction for an explanation of all data sources.

General Information
Township of Mount Laurel
100 Mount Laurel Rd
Mount Laurel, NJ 08054
856-234-0001

Website	www.mountlaurel.com
Year of incorporation	1872
Land/water area (sq. miles)	21.81/0.12
Form of government	Council-Manager

Government
Legislative Districts
US Congressional	3
State Legislative	8

Local Officials, 2008
Mayor	John F. Drinkard
Manager	Debra Fourre
Clerk	Patricia Halbe
Finance Dir	Linda Lewis
Tax Assessor	Terry Paglione
Tax Collector	Brenda Kuhn
Attorney	Christopher Nor
Building	Raymond Holshue Jr
Comm Dev/Planning	NA
Engineering	William Long
Public Works	Everett Johnson
Police Chief	Dennis Moffett
Fire Chief	Robert Gallos

Housing & Construction
Housing Units, 2000*
Total	17,163
Median rent	$939
Median SF home value	$161,900

Permits for New Residential Construction
	Units	Value
Total, 2007	45	$10,140,473
Single family	45	$10,140,473
Total, 2006	38	$8,234,953
Single family	38	$8,234,953

Real Property Valuation, 2007
	Parcels	Valuation
Total	17,659	$3,355,926,500
Vacant	933	64,420,600
Residential	16,184	2,261,700,600
Commercial	413	871,521,900
Industrial	49	100,736,800
Apartments	7	51,942,000
Farm land	52	482,400
Farm homestead	21	5,122,200

Average Property Value & Tax, 2007
Residential value	$139,884
Property tax	$5,163
Tax credit/rebate	$943

Public Library
Mount Laurel Public Library
100 Walt Whitman Ave
Mount Laurel, NJ 08054
856-234-7319

Director . . . . Joan E. Bernstein

Library statistics, 2006
Population served	40,221
Full-time/total staff	8/11

	Total	Per capita
Holdings	120,182	2.99
Revenues	$1,879,368	$46.73
Expenditures	$1,755,458	$43.65
Annual visits	290,670	7.23
Internet terminals/annual users	26/109,775	

Public Safety
Number of officers, 2006		71
Crime	**2005**	**2006**
Total crimes	701	814
Violent	47	37
Murder	1	2
Rape	10	9
Robbery	18	15
Aggravated assault	18	11
Non-violent	654	777
Burglary	88	107
Larceny	532	648
Vehicle theft	34	22
Domestic violence	234	250
Arson	1	2
Total crime rate	17.2	20.0
Violent	1.2	0.9
Non-violent	16.1	19.1

Public School District
(for school year 2006-07 except as noted)

Mount Laurel Township School District
330 Moorestown-Mount Laurel Rd.
Mount Laurel, NJ 08054
856-235-3387

Superintendent	Antoinette Rath
Number of schools	8
Grade plan	K-8
Enrollment	4,516
Attendance rate, '05-06	95.9%
Dropout rate	NA
Students per teacher	11.4
Per pupil expenditure	$11,940
Median faculty salary	$53,350
Median administrator salary	$94,500
Grade 12 enrollment	NA
High school graduation rate	NA

Assessment test results
(percent scoring at proficient or advanced level)
	Language	Math
NJASK-Grade 3	93.6%	95.7%
GEPA-Grade 8	85.5%	78.7%
HSPA-High School	NA	NA

SAT score averages
Pct tested	Math	Verbal	Writing
NA	NA	NA	NA

Teacher Qualifications
Avg. years of experience	11
Highly-qualified teachers one subject/all subjects	99.5%/99.5%
With emergency credentials	0.0%

No Child Left Behind
AYP, 2005-06	Meets Standards

Municipal Finance
State Aid Programs, 2008
Total aid	$3,692,751
CMPTRA	447,381
Energy tax receipts	3,245,036
Garden State Trust	334

General Budget, 2007
Total tax levy	$124,149,663
County levy	23,183,217
County taxes	20,791,461
County library	0
County health	0
County open space	2,391,756
School levy	82,555,733
Muni. levy	18,410,713
Misc. revenues	19,249,000

Taxes
	2005	2006	2007
General tax rate per $100	3.407	3.532	3.694
County equalization ratio	70.15	63.24	56.21
Net valuation taxable	$3,273,254,101	$3,314,576,600	$3,363,391,074
State equalized value	$5,175,923,626	$5,905,077,433	$6,620,127,628

Mount Olive Township
Morris County

Demographics & Socio-Economic Characteristics
(2000 US Census, except as noted)

Population
1980*	18,748
1990*	21,282
2000	24,193
Male	12,119
Female	12,074
2006 (estimate)*	26,065
Population density	858.8

Race & Hispanic Origin, 2000
Race
White	20,974
Black/African American	918
American Indian/Alaska Native	40
Asian	1,452
Native Hawaiian/Pacific Islander	2
Other race	369
Two or more races	438
Hispanic origin, total	1,445
Mexican	102
Puerto Rican	466
Cuban	86
Other Hispanic	791

Age & Nativity, 2000
Under 5 years	2,108
18 years and over	17,525
21 years and over	16,896
65 years and over	1,542
85 years and over	123
Median age	34.1
Native-born	21,059
Foreign-born	3,134

Educational Attainment, 2000
Population 25 years and over	15,764
Less than 9th grade	2.4%
High school grad or higher	91.9%
Bachelor's degree or higher	36.5%
Graduate degree	11.2%

Income & Poverty, 1999
Per capita income	$28,691
Median household income	$64,515
Median family income	$75,189
Persons in poverty	735
H'holds receiving public assistance	67
H'holds receiving social security	1,267

Households, 2000
Total households	9,068
With persons under 18	3,696
With persons over 65	1,219
Family households	6,372
Single-person households	2,150
Persons per household	2.66
Persons per family	3.22

Labor & Employment
Total civilian labor force, 2006**	15,140
Unemployment rate	3.6%
Total civilian labor force, 2000	13,589
Unemployment rate	3.8%

Employed persons 16 years and over by occupation, 2000
Managers & professionals	5,728
Service occupations	1,403
Sales & office occupations	3,424
Farming, fishing & forestry	25
Construction & maintenance	1,031
Production & transportation	1,463
Self-employed persons	603

* US Census Bureau
** New Jersey Department of Labor

General Information
Township of Mount Olive
204 Flanders-Drakestown Rd
PO Box 450
Budd Lake, NJ 07828
973-691-0900
Website: www.mountolivetownship.com
Year of incorporation: 1871
Land/water area (sq. miles): 30.35/0.70
Form of government: Mayor-Council

Government
Legislative Districts
US Congressional	11
State Legislative	25

Local Officials, 2008
Mayor	David Scapicchio
Manager	Bill Sohl
Clerk	Lisa Lashway
Finance Dir.	Sherry Jenkins
Tax Assessor	John Marchione
Tax Collector	Rose Barsanti
Attorney	John Dorsey
Building	Gary Lindsay
Planning	Catherine Natafalusy
Engineering	Eugene Buczynski
Public Works	Tim Quinn
Police Chief	Mark Spitzer
Emerg/Fire Director	Fred Detoro Jr

Housing & Construction
Housing Units, 2000*
Total	9,311
Median rent	$800
Median SF home value	$197,800

Permits for New Residential Construction
	Units	Value
Total, 2007	31	$4,993,275
Single family	22	$3,562,178
Total, 2006	114	$15,588,415
Single family	64	$9,412,448

Real Property Valuation, 2007
	Parcels	Valuation
Total	7,832	$1,975,652,800
Vacant	1,090	74,085,600
Residential	6,217	1,237,440,800
Commercial	331	265,992,400
Industrial	61	250,998,400
Apartments	6	138,825,000
Farm land	94	1,102,900
Farm homestead	33	7,207,700

Average Property Value & Tax, 2007
Residential value	$199,144
Property tax	$7,961
Tax credit/rebate	$1,156

Public Library
Mount Olive Public Library
202 Flanders-Drakestown Rd
Flanders, NJ 07836
973-691-8686
Director: Rita L. Hilbert

Library statistics, 2006
Population served	24,193
Full-time/total staff	5/9

	Total	Per capita
Holdings	79,474	3.28
Revenues	$1,157,916	$47.86
Expenditures	$1,013,335	$41.89
Annual visits	268,001	11.08
Internet terminals/annual users	33/138,660	

Taxes
	2005	2006	2007
General tax rate per $100	3.54	3.79	4
County equalization ratio	70.6	59.7	53.81
Net valuation taxable	$1,985,836,832	$2,002,686,700	$1,978,562,802
State equalized value	$3,326,359,853	$3,724,907,741	$3,859,347,246

Public Safety
Number of officers, 2006 53

Crime	2005	2006
Total crimes	318	251
Violent	13	5
Murder	1	0
Rape	0	0
Robbery	1	2
Aggravated assault	11	3
Non-violent	305	246
Burglary	65	54
Larceny	227	169
Vehicle theft	13	23
Domestic violence	149	164
Arson	0	1
Total crime rate	12.4	9.7
Violent	0.5	0.2
Non-violent	11.9	9.5

Public School District
(for school year 2006-07 except as noted)

Mount Olive Township School District
89 Route 46
Budd Lake, NJ 07828
973-691-4008

Superintendent	Rosalie Lamonte
Number of schools	6
Grade plan	K-12
Enrollment	4,982
Attendance rate, '05-06	95.0%
Dropout rate	0.9%
Students per teacher	12.0
Per pupil expenditure	$13,378
Median faculty salary	$56,428
Median administrator salary	$108,181
Grade 12 enrollment	340
High school graduation rate	98.3%

Assessment test results
(percent scoring at proficient or advanced level)
	Language	Math
NJASK-Grade 3	87.3%	89.7%
GEPA-Grade 8	88.5%	81.2%
HSPA-High School	92.8%	85.9%

SAT score averages
Pct tested	Math	Verbal	Writing
82%	528	506	503

Teacher Qualifications
Avg. years of experience	8
Highly-qualified teachers one subject/all subjects	100%/100%
With emergency credentials	0.0%

No Child Left Behind
AYP, 2005-06 ..... Meets Standards

Municipal Finance
State Aid Programs, 2008
Total aid	$2,691,657
CMPTRA	618,202
Energy tax receipts	1,906,488
Garden State Trust	137,821

General Budget, 2007
Total tax levy	$79,093,624
County levy	8,600,756
County taxes	6,877,260
County library	0
County health	0
County open space	1,723,497
School levy	54,301,960
Muni. levy	16,190,908
Misc. revenues	9,934,785

The New Jersey Municipal Data Book

Morris County

Mountain Lakes Borough

Demographics & Socio-Economic Characteristics
(2000 US Census, except as noted)

Population
1980*	4,153
1990*	3,847
2000	4,256
Male	2,119
Female	2,137
2006 (estimate)*	4,343
Population density	1,626.6

Race & Hispanic Origin, 2000
Race
White	3,960
Black/African American	16
American Indian/Alaska Native	0
Asian	220
Native Hawaiian/Pacific Islander	3
Other race	22
Two or more races	35
Hispanic origin, total	72
Mexican	10
Puerto Rican	18
Cuban	11
Other Hispanic	33

Age & Nativity, 2000
Under 5 years	317
18 years and over	2,738
21 years and over	2,676
65 years and over	386
85 years and over	14
Median age	39.4
Native-born	3,839
Foreign-born	417

Educational Attainment, 2000
Population 25 years and over	2,624
Less than 9th grade	0.8%
High school grad or higher	98.4%
Bachelor's degree or higher	76.1%
Graduate degree	35.2%

Income & Poverty, 1999
Per capita income	$65,086
Median household income	$141,757
Median family income	$153,227
Persons in poverty	85
H'holds receiving public assistance	0
H'holds receiving social security	242

Households, 2000
Total households	1,330
With persons under 18	724
With persons over 65	266
Family households	1,187
Single-person households	122
Persons per household	3.20
Persons per family	3.41

Labor & Employment
Total civilian labor force, 2006**	1,980
Unemployment rate	0.6%
Total civilian labor force, 2000	1,819
Unemployment rate	1.0%

Employed persons 16 years and over by occupation, 2000
Managers & professionals	1,239
Service occupations	108
Sales & office occupations	356
Farming, fishing & forestry	0
Construction & maintenance	52
Production & transportation	46
Self-employed persons	156

* US Census Bureau
** New Jersey Department of Labor

See Introduction for an explanation of all data sources.

General Information
Borough of Mountain Lakes
400 Boulevard
Mountain Lakes, NJ 07046
973-334-3131

Website	www.mtnlakes.org
Year of incorporation	1924
Land/water area (sq. miles)	2.67/0.22
Form of government	Council-Manager

Government
Legislative Districts
US Congressional	11
State Legislative	24

Local Officials, 2008
Mayor	George B. Jackson
Manager	Joseph Tempesta
Clerk	Christina Whitaker
Finance Dir	Dana Mooney
Tax Assessor	Rick DelGuercio
Tax Collector	Dana Mooney
Attorney	Martin Murphy
Building	Rita Sharp
Comm Dev/Planning	NA
Engineering	Bill Ryden
Public Works	Mark Prusina
Police Chief	Robert Tovo
Emerg/Fire Director	Steve Butera

Housing & Construction
Housing Units, 2000*
Total	1,357
Median rent	$1,804
Median SF home value	$488,900

Permits for New Residential Construction
	Units	Value
Total, 2007	11	$3,910,034
Single family	11	$3,910,034
Total, 2006	8	$3,191,661
Single family	8	$3,191,661

Real Property Valuation, 2007
	Parcels	Valuation
Total	1,472	$1,473,816,100
Vacant	38	10,561,300
Residential	1,353	1,361,852,600
Commercial	75	98,174,600
Industrial	3	3,226,100
Apartments	0	0
Farm land	3	1,500
Farm homestead	0	0

Average Property Value & Tax, 2007
Residential value	$1,006,543
Property tax	$17,038
Tax credit/rebate	$1,454

Public Library
Mountain Lakes Public Library
9 Elm Rd
Mountain Lakes, NJ 07046
973-334-5095

Director .... Margaret J. Bulfer

Library statistics, 2006
Population served	4,256
Full-time/total staff	0/1

	Total	Per capita
Holdings	46,248	10.87
Revenues	$222,982	$52.39
Expenditures	$223,786	$52.58
Annual visits	25,548	6.00
Internet terminals/annual users	6/3,064	

Public Safety
Number of officers, 2006 14

Crime	2005	2006
Total crimes	70	86
Violent	1	2
Murder	0	0
Rape	1	1
Robbery	0	0
Aggravated assault	0	1
Non-violent	69	84
Burglary	23	22
Larceny	46	60
Vehicle theft	0	2
Domestic violence	0	1
Arson	1	1
Total crime rate	16.2	19.8
Violent	0.2	0.5
Non-violent	16.0	19.4

Public School District
(for school year 2006-07 except as noted)

Mountain Lakes School District
400 Boulevard
Mountain Lakes, NJ 07046
973-334-8280

Superintendent	John Kazmark
Number of schools	3
Grade plan	K-12
Enrollment	1,491
Attendance rate, '05-06	95.7%
Dropout rate	0.3%
Students per teacher	8.3
Per pupil expenditure	$18,652
Median faculty salary	$63,441
Median administrator salary	$114,307
Grade 12 enrollment	176
High school graduation rate	100.0%

Assessment test results
(percent scoring at proficient or advanced level)
	Language	Math
NJASK-Grade 3	94.5%	97.2%
GEPA-Grade 8	98.9%	96.6%
HSPA-High School	96.4%	91.0%

SAT score averages
Pct tested	Math	Verbal	Writing
94%	576	575	579

Teacher Qualifications
Avg. years of experience	11
Highly-qualified teachers one subject/all subjects	98.0%/98.0%
With emergency credentials	2.4%

No Child Left Behind
AYP, 2005-06 .... Meets Standards

Municipal Finance
State Aid Programs, 2008
Total aid	$512,026
CMPTRA	0
Energy tax receipts	512,026
Garden State Trust	0

General Budget, 2007
Total tax levy	$24,970,809
County levy	3,298,651
County taxes	2,638,644
County library	0
County health	0
County open space	660,007
School levy	17,534,925
Muni. levy	4,137,234
Misc. revenues	3,002,066

Taxes
	2005	2006	2007
General tax rate per $100	3.53	1.62	1.7
County equalization ratio	56.74	113.16	106.77
Net valuation taxable	$639,917,067	$1,474,084,000	$1,475,160,245
State equalized value	$1,293,807,252	$1,381,425,994	$1,407,254,762

©2008 Information Publications, Inc. All rights reserved. Photocopying prohibited. For additional copies, contact the publisher at www.informationpublications.com or (877)544-INFO (4636)

Mountainside Borough
Union County

Demographics & Socio-Economic Characteristics
(2000 US Census, except as noted)

Population
1980*	7,118
1990*	6,657
2000	6,602
Male	3,112
Female	3,490
2006 (estimate)*	6,644
Population density	1,652.7

Race & Hispanic Origin, 2000
Race
White	6,278
Black/African American	62
American Indian/Alaska Native	6
Asian	185
Native Hawaiian/Pacific Islander	4
Other race	18
Two or more races	49
Hispanic origin, total	199
Mexican	16
Puerto Rican	32
Cuban	48
Other Hispanic	103

Age & Nativity, 2000
Under 5 years	405
18 years and over	5,210
21 years and over	5,102
65 years and over	1,644
85 years and over	252
Median age	46.4
Native-born	5,726
Foreign-born	876

Educational Attainment, 2000
Population 25 years and over	4,931
Less than 9th grade	2.5%
High school grad or higher	92.6%
Bachelor's degree or higher	47.9%
Graduate degree	21.9%

Income & Poverty, 1999
Per capita income	$47,474
Median household income	$97,195
Median family income	$105,773
Persons in poverty	187
H'holds receiving public assistance	35
H'holds receiving social security	1,022

Households, 2000
Total households	2,434
With persons under 18	745
With persons over 65	990
Family households	1,925
Single-person households	436
Persons per household	2.60
Persons per family	2.95

Labor & Employment
Total civilian labor force, 2006**	3,089
Unemployment rate	2.5%
Total civilian labor force, 2000	2,952
Unemployment rate	2.5%

Employed persons 16 years and over by occupation, 2000
Managers & professionals	1,519
Service occupations	289
Sales & office occupations	794
Farming, fishing & forestry	0
Construction & maintenance	160
Production & transportation	116
Self-employed persons	235

* US Census Bureau
** New Jersey Department of Labor

General Information
Borough of Mountainside
1385 Route 22
Mountainside, NJ 07092
908-232-2400

Website	www.mountainside-nj.com
Year of incorporation	1895
Land/water area (sq. miles)	4.02/0.03
Form of government	Borough

Government
Legislative Districts
US Congressional	7
State Legislative	21

Local Officials, 2008
Mayor	Robert Viglianti
Manager	James Debbie Jr
Clerk	Martha DeJesus
Finance Dir	Jill Goode
Tax Assessor	Eldo Magnani
Tax Collector	NA
Attorney	John Post
Building	Jerry Eger
Planning	John Tomaine
Engineering	Mike Disko
Public Works	NA
Police Chief	James Debbie Jr
Emerg/Fire Director	Robert Farley

Housing & Construction
Housing Units, 2000*
Total	2,478
Median rent	$950
Median SF home value	$346,100

Permits for New Residential Construction
	Units	Value
Total, 2007	17	$5,247,151
Single family	17	$5,247,151
Total, 2006	17	$4,333,631
Single family	17	$4,333,631

Real Property Valuation, 2007
	Parcels	Valuation
Total	2,650	$486,617,000
Vacant	99	6,888,000
Residential	2,394	391,061,200
Commercial	104	61,692,600
Industrial	53	26,975,200
Apartments	0	0
Farm land	0	0
Farm homestead	0	0

Average Property Value & Tax, 2007
Residential value	$163,351
Property tax	$8,002
Tax credit/rebate	$1,150

Public Library
Mountainside Public Library
Constitution Plaza
Mountainside, NJ 07092
908-233-0115

Director .... Michael Banick

Library statistics, 2006
Population served	6,602
Full-time/total staff	2/3

	Total	Per capita
Holdings	57,235	8.67
Revenues	$609,492	$92.32
Expenditures	$640,491	$97.01
Annual visits	55,120	8.35
Internet terminals/annual users	11/14,829	

Public Safety
Number of officers, 2006 21

Crime	2005	2006
Total crimes	72	73
Violent	5	3
Murder	0	0
Rape	0	0
Robbery	1	0
Aggravated assault	4	3
Non-violent	67	70
Burglary	5	14
Larceny	53	49
Vehicle theft	9	7
Domestic violence	7	8
Arson	0	0
Total crime rate	10.8	11.0
Violent	0.8	0.5
Non-violent	10.1	10.6

Public School District
(for school year 2006-07 except as noted)

Mountainside School District
1497 Woodacres Dr
Mountainside, NJ 07092
908-232-3232

Superintendent	Richard O'Malley
Number of schools	2
Grade plan	K-8
Enrollment	761
Attendance rate, '05-06	98.6%
Dropout rate	NA
Students per teacher	10.0
Per pupil expenditure	$13,042
Median faculty salary	$50,731
Median administrator salary	$114,549
Grade 12 enrollment	NA
High school graduation rate	NA

Assessment test results
(percent scoring at proficient or advanced level)
	Language	Math
NJASK-Grade 3	92.6%	100.0%
GEPA-Grade 8	93.7%	87.3%
HSPA-High School	NA	NA

SAT score averages
Pct tested	Math	Verbal	Writing
NA	NA	NA	NA

Teacher Qualifications
Avg. years of experience	8
Highly-qualified teachers one subject/all subjects	100%/100%
With emergency credentials	0.0%

No Child Left Behind
AYP, 2005-06 .... Meets Standards

Municipal Finance
State Aid Programs, 2008
Total aid	$966,601
CMPTRA	133,590
Energy tax receipts	833,011
Garden State Trust	0

General Budget, 2007
Total tax levy	$23,854,085
County levy	6,526,899
County taxes	6,245,115
County library	0
County health	0
County open space	281,784
School levy	11,485,584
Muni. levy	5,841,602
Misc. revenues	4,212,868

Taxes
	2005	2006	2007
General tax rate per $100	4.412	4.61	4.899
County equalization ratio	30.5	27.19	26.19
Net valuation taxable	$483,573,794	$485,203,900	$486,939,472
State equalized value	$1,677,910,458	$1,852,968,092	$1,932,108,895

Atlantic County — Mullica Township

Demographics & Socio-Economic Characteristics
(2000 US Census, except as noted)

Population
- 1980*............................5,243
- 1990*............................5,896
- 2000.............................5,912
  - Male...........................2,975
  - Female.........................2,937
- 2006 (estimate)*..................6,080
- Population density................107.5

Race & Hispanic Origin, 2000
Race
- White............................4,764
- Black/African American.............371
- American Indian/Alaska Native.......16
- Asian..............................49
- Native Hawaiian/Pacific Islander.....7
- Other race........................509
- Two or more races.................196
- Hispanic origin, total............975
  - Mexican..........................86
  - Puerto Rican....................766
  - Cuban.............................3
  - Other Hispanic..................120

Age & Nativity, 2000
- Under 5 years....................354
- 18 years and over..............4,318
- 21 years and over..............4,105
- 65 years and over................630
- 85 years and over.................42
- Median age.......................37.0
- Native-born....................5,696
- Foreign-born.....................216

Educational Attainment, 2000
- Population 25 years and over...3,949
- Less than 9th grade..............9.9%
- High school grad or higher.....78.5%
- Bachelor's degree or higher....13.4%
- Graduate degree..................3.7%

Income & Poverty, 1999
- Per capita income.............$19,764
- Median household income.......$50,417
- Median family income..........$55,143
- Persons in poverty...............462
- H'holds receiving public assistance...27
- H'holds receiving social security...557

Households, 2000
- Total households..............2,044
  - With persons under 18..........842
  - With persons over 65...........474
  - Family households............1,537
  - Single-person households......396
- Persons per household...........2.87
- Persons per family..............3.30

Labor & Employment
- Total civilian labor force, 2006**...3,223
  - Unemployment rate..............5.7%
- Total civilian labor force, 2000...2,957
  - Unemployment rate..............6.3%

Employed persons 16 years and over by occupation, 2000
- Managers & professionals.........603
- Service occupations..............679
- Sales & office occupations.......680
- Farming, fishing & forestry.......49
- Construction & maintenance......478
- Production & transportation.....282
- Self-employed persons...........112

* US Census Bureau
** New Jersey Department of Labor

See Introduction for an explanation of all data sources.

General Information
Township of Mullica
PO Box 317
Elwood, NJ 08217
609-561-0064
- Website................mullicatownship.org
- Year of incorporation.................1838
- Land/water area (sq. miles).....56.58/0.36
- Form of government..............Township

Government
Legislative Districts
- US Congressional.......................2
- State Legislative......................2

Local Officials, 2008
- Mayor.................William Kennedy
- Manager/Admin.....................NA
- Clerk.................Kimberly Johnson
- Finance Dir............Dawn Stollenwerk
- Tax Assessor.............Gerard Mead
- Tax Collector...........Bert Cappuccio
- Attorney.............Norman Zlotnick
- Building.................John Holroyd
- Comm Dev/Planning...................NA
- Engineering.......Marathon Engineering
- Public Works............Pete Berenato
- Police Chief............Joseph Barbera
- Emerg/Fire Director.......Gary Franklin

Housing & Construction
Housing Units, 2000*
- Total............................2,176
- Median rent.......................$733
- Median SF home value..........$109,000

Permits for New Residential Construction

	Units	Value
Total, 2007	19	$3,079,100
Single family	19	$3,079,100
Total, 2006	29	$3,014,244
Single family	29	$3,014,244

Real Property Valuation, 2007

	Parcels	Valuation
Total	4,366	$283,041,100
Vacant	1,887	15,252,000
Residential	2,146	240,513,500
Commercial	85	15,680,800
Industrial	3	2,471,800
Apartments	2	515,400
Farm land	186	2,250,200
Farm homestead	57	6,357,400

Average Property Value & Tax, 2007
- Residential value.............$112,061
- Property tax...................$4,051
- Tax credit/rebate...............$837

Public Library
No public municipal library

Library statistics, 2006
- Population served..................NA
- Full-time/total staff...........NA/NA

	Total	Per capita
Holdings	NA	NA
Revenues	NA	NA
Expenditures	NA	NA
Annual visits	NA	NA
Internet terminals/annual users	NA/NA	

Taxes

	2005	2006	2007
General tax rate per $100	3.273	3.555	3.616
County equalization ratio	72.72	61.16	50.23
Net valuation taxable	$277,143,039	$279,433,200	$283,981,376
State equalized value	$453,144,276	$557,414,107	$598,956,545

Public Safety
- Number of officers, 2006..............14

Crime

Crime	2005	2006
Total crimes	68	93
Violent	17	12
Murder	0	0
Rape	0	1
Robbery	0	0
Aggravated assault	17	11
Non-violent	51	81
Burglary	8	25
Larceny	35	50
Vehicle theft	8	6
Domestic violence	44	39
Arson	1	1
Total crime rate	11.2	15.2
Violent	2.8	2.0
Non-violent	8.4	13.3

Public School District
(for school year 2006-07 except as noted)

Mullica Township School District
500 Elwood Rd, PO Box 318
Elwood, NJ 08217
609-561-3868

- Superintendent........Richard Goldberg
- Number of schools.....................3
- Grade plan.........................K-8
- Enrollment........................744
- Attendance rate, '05-06..........95.0%
- Dropout rate.......................NA
- Students per teacher..............10.6
- Per pupil expenditure..........$11,024
- Median faculty salary..........$57,293
- Median administrator salary....$86,200
- Grade 12 enrollment................NA
- High school graduation rate........NA

Assessment test results
(percent scoring at proficient or advanced level)

	Language	Math
NJASK-Grade 3	83.3%	87.5%
GEPA-Grade 8	84.2%	71.4%
HSPA-High School	NA	NA

SAT score averages

Pct tested	Math	Verbal	Writing
NA	NA	NA	NA

Teacher Qualifications
- Avg. years of experience.............13
- Highly-qualified teachers
  - one subject/all subjects.....100%/100%
- With emergency credentials.........1.8%

No Child Left Behind
- AYP, 2005-06...........Meets Standards

Municipal Finance
State Aid Programs, 2008
- Total aid.....................$591,639
  - CMPTRA.....................108,643
  - Energy tax receipts........410,461
  - Garden State Trust..........64,621

General Budget, 2007
- Total tax levy..............$10,266,268
  - County levy...............1,740,619
    - County taxes..........1,386,070
    - County library...........171,481
    - County health............69,874
    - County open space.......113,194
  - School levy..............5,739,651
  - Muni. levy...............2,785,997
- Misc. revenues.............2,198,216

National Park Borough
Gloucester County

Demographics & Socio-Economic Characteristics
(2000 US Census, except as noted)

Population
1980*	3,552
1990*	3,413
2000	3,205
Male	1,596
Female	1,609
2006 (estimate)*	3,215
Population density	3,215.0

Race & Hispanic Origin, 2000
Race
White	3,152
Black/African American	3
American Indian/Alaska Native	8
Asian	8
Native Hawaiian/Pacific Islander	1
Other race	17
Two or more races	16
Hispanic origin, total	46
Mexican	7
Puerto Rican	29
Cuban	3
Other Hispanic	7

Age & Nativity, 2000
Under 5 years	181
18 years and over	2,360
21 years and over	2,209
65 years and over	402
85 years and over	28
Median age	36.7
Native-born	3,177
Foreign-born	28

Educational Attainment, 2000
Population 25 years and over	2,065
Less than 9th grade	4.9%
High school grad or higher	76.7%
Bachelor's degree or higher	7.0%
Graduate degree	1.2%

Income & Poverty, 1999
Per capita income	$18,048
Median household income	$48,534
Median family income	$51,535
Persons in poverty	242
H'holds receiving public assistance	19
H'holds receiving social security	315

Households, 2000
Total households	1,111
With persons under 18	472
With persons over 65	292
Family households	865
Single-person households	207
Persons per household	2.86
Persons per family	3.24

Labor & Employment
Total civilian labor force, 2006**	1,966
Unemployment rate	6.5%
Total civilian labor force, 2000	1,652
Unemployment rate	5.4%

Employed persons 16 years and over by occupation, 2000
Managers & professionals	292
Service occupations	293
Sales & office occupations	396
Farming, fishing & forestry	4
Construction & maintenance	254
Production & transportation	324
Self-employed persons	26

* US Census Bureau
** New Jersey Department of Labor

General Information
Borough of National Park
7 S Grove Ave
National Park, NJ 08063
856-845-3891

Website	www.nationalparkboro.com
Year of incorporation	1892
Land/water area (sq. miles)	1.00/0.44
Form of government	Borough

Government
Legislative Districts
US Congressional	1
State Legislative	3

Local Officials, 2008
Mayor	Patricia Koloski
Manager	Robert Dougherty Jr
Clerk	Robert Dougherty Jr
Finance Dir	George Damminger
Tax Assessor	Roy Duffield
Tax Collector	Catherine Hull
Attorney	Kelly Conroy
Building	William Cattell
Comm Dev/Planning	NA
Engineering	Edwin Steck
Public Works	James Walker
Police Chief	Lin T. Couch
Emerg/Fire Director	Mark Gismondi

Housing & Construction
Housing Units, 2000*
Total	1,165
Median rent	$647
Median SF home value	$92,800

Permits for New Residential Construction
	Units	Value
Total, 2007	1	$129,000
Single family	1	$129,000
Total, 2006	3	$266,800
Single family	3	$266,800

Real Property Valuation, 2007
	Parcels	Valuation
Total	1,241	$97,669,200
Vacant	118	1,552,100
Residential	1,086	91,099,000
Commercial	33	4,382,300
Industrial	0	0
Apartments	4	635,800
Farm land	0	0
Farm homestead	0	0

Average Property Value & Tax, 2007
Residential value	$83,885
Property tax	$4,296
Tax credit/rebate	$885

Public Library
No public municipal library

Library statistics, 2006
Population served	NA
Full-time/total staff	NA/NA

	Total	Per capita
Holdings	NA	NA
Revenues	NA	NA
Expenditures	NA	NA
Annual visits	NA	NA
Internet terminals/annual users	NA/NA	

Taxes
	2005	2006	2007
General tax rate per $100	4.435	4.791	5.122
County equalization ratio	81.39	71.53	61.37
Net valuation taxable	$95,873,122	$97,425,400	$97,759,919
State equalized value	$134,032,045	$158,852,187	$182,786,566

Public Safety
Number of officers, 2006		7

Crime	2005	2006
Total crimes	66	62
Violent	10	5
Murder	0	1
Rape	0	0
Robbery	2	1
Aggravated assault	8	3
Non-violent	56	57
Burglary	12	18
Larceny	41	35
Vehicle theft	3	4
Domestic violence	20	25
Arson	1	0
Total crime rate	20.6	19.2
Violent	3.1	1.6
Non-violent	17.5	17.7

Public School District
(for school year 2006-07 except as noted)

National Park Borough School District
516 Lakehurst Ave
National Park, NJ 08063
856-845-6876

Superintendent	Ray Bider
Number of schools	1
Grade plan	K-6
Enrollment	307
Attendance rate, '05-06	94.6%
Dropout rate	NA
Students per teacher	12.3
Per pupil expenditure	$11,255
Median faculty salary	$55,700
Median administrator salary	$93,949
Grade 12 enrollment	NA
High school graduation rate	NA

Assessment test results
(percent scoring at proficient or advanced level)
	Language	Math
NJASK-Grade 3	81.6%	85.8%
GEPA-Grade 8	NA	NA
HSPA-High School	NA	NA

SAT score averages
Pct tested	Math	Verbal	Writing
NA	NA	NA	NA

Teacher Qualifications
Avg. years of experience	12
Highly-qualified teachers one subject/all subjects	100%/100%
With emergency credentials	0.0%

No Child Left Behind
AYP, 2005-06	Meets Standards

Municipal Finance
State Aid Programs, 2008
Total aid	$469,712
CMPTRA	0
Energy tax receipts	469,712
Garden State Trust	0

General Budget, 2007
Total tax levy	$5,006,682
County levy	945,446
County taxes	814,255
County library	67,441
County health	0
County open space	63,751
School levy	3,023,236
Muni. levy	1,038,000
Misc. revenues	1,731,309

Monmouth County
Neptune City Borough

Demographics & Socio-Economic Characteristics
(2000 US Census, except as noted)

Population
1980*	5,276
1990*	4,997
2000	5,218
Male	2,436
Female	2,782
2006 (estimate)*	5,150
Population density	5,659.3

Race & Hispanic Origin, 2000
Race
White	4,351
Black/African American	497
American Indian/Alaska Native	12
Asian	142
Native Hawaiian/Pacific Islander	0
Other race	110
Two or more races	106
Hispanic origin, total	277
Mexican	69
Puerto Rican	145
Cuban	11
Other Hispanic	52

Age & Nativity, 2000
Under 5 years	304
18 years and over	4,096
21 years and over	3,964
65 years and over	854
85 years and over	141
Median age	39.8
Native-born	4,801
Foreign-born	417

Educational Attainment, 2000
Population 25 years and over	3,771
Less than 9th grade	5.0%
High school grad or higher	82.0%
Bachelor's degree or higher	16.9%
Graduate degree	4.6%

Income & Poverty, 1999
Per capita income	$22,191
Median household income	$43,451
Median family income	$46,393
Persons in poverty	279
H'holds receiving public assistance	19
H'holds receiving social security	636

Households, 2000
Total households	2,221
With persons under 18	644
With persons over 65	582
Family households	1,331
Single-person households	743
Persons per household	2.29
Persons per family	2.96

Labor & Employment
Total civilian labor force, 2006**	2,831
Unemployment rate	4.2%
Total civilian labor force, 2000	2,640
Unemployment rate	4.1%

Employed persons 16 years and over by occupation, 2000
Managers & professionals	690
Service occupations	436
Sales & office occupations	675
Farming, fishing & forestry	7
Construction & maintenance	366
Production & transportation	359
Self-employed persons	54

* US Census Bureau
** New Jersey Department of Labor

See Introduction for an explanation of all data sources.

General Information
Borough of Neptune City
106 W Sylvania Ave
Neptune City, NJ 07753
732-776-7224

Website	www.neptunecitynj.com
Year of incorporation	1881
Land/water area (sq. miles)	0.91/0.00
Form of government	Borough

Government
Legislative Districts
US Congressional	6
State Legislative	11

Local Officials, 2008
Mayor	Thomas Arnone
Manager	Joel Popkin
Clerk	Joel Popkin
Finance Dir	W. Folk
Tax Assessor	Stephen Walters
Tax Collector	Joel Popkin
Attorney	Mark Aikins
Building	William Doolittle
Comm Dev/Planning	NA
Engineering	Matt Shafai
Public Works	Gerrit DeVos
Police Chief	William Geschke
Emerg/Fire Director	Brian McGrath

Housing & Construction
Housing Units, 2000*
Total	2,342
Median rent	$705
Median SF home value	$124,100

Permits for New Residential Construction
	Units	Value
Total, 2007	1	$189,000
Single family	1	$189,000
Total, 2006	1	$189,000
Single family	1	$189,000

Real Property Valuation, 2007
	Parcels	Valuation
Total	1,670	$431,534,300
Vacant	65	4,374,800
Residential	1,485	311,953,800
Commercial	103	75,532,100
Industrial	8	10,480,800
Apartments	9	29,192,800
Farm land	0	0
Farm homestead	0	0

Average Property Value & Tax, 2007
Residential value	$210,070
Property tax	$4,747
Tax credit/rebate	$928

Public Library
Neptune City Public Library
106 W Sylvania Ave
Neptune City, NJ 07753
732-988-8866

Director	Patricia Scott

Library statistics, 2006
Population served	5,218
Full-time/total staff	NA/0

	Total	Per capita
Holdings	NA	NA
Revenues	NA	NA
Expenditures	NA	NA
Annual visits	NA	NA
Internet terminals/annual users	NA/NA	

Taxes
	2005	2006	2007
General tax rate per $100	2.07	2.169	2.26
County equalization ratio	97.76	88.66	77.86
Net valuation taxable	$435,229,523	$430,228,300	$431,881,853
State equalized value	$490,897,274	$552,952,996	$4,110,043,516

Public Safety
Number of officers, 2006	16

Crime	2005	2006
Total crimes	192	177
Violent	19	17
Murder	0	0
Rape	1	2
Robbery	7	3
Aggravated assault	11	12
Non-violent	173	160
Burglary	35	30
Larceny	137	122
Vehicle theft	1	8
Domestic violence	61	48
Arson	0	1
Total crime rate	35.7	34.2
Violent	3.5	3.3
Non-violent	32.2	30.9

Public School District
(for school year 2006-07 except as noted)

Neptune City School District
210 W Sylvania Ave
Neptune City, NJ 07753
732-775-5319

Superintendent	Robert J. Shafer
Number of schools	1
Grade plan	K-8
Enrollment	392
Attendance rate, '05-06	94.4%
Dropout rate	NA
Students per teacher	10.3
Per pupil expenditure	$12,989
Median faculty salary	$45,310
Median administrator salary	$103,100
Grade 12 enrollment	NA
High school graduation rate	NA

Assessment test results
(percent scoring at proficient or advanced level)

	Language	Math
NJASK-Grade 3	72.7%	84.1%
GEPA-Grade 8	91.4%	80.0%
HSPA-High School	NA	NA

SAT score averages
Pct tested	Math	Verbal	Writing
NA	NA	NA	NA

Teacher Qualifications
Avg. years of experience	13
Highly-qualified teachers one subject/all subjects	100%/100%
With emergency credentials	0.0%

No Child Left Behind
AYP, 2005-06	Meets Standards

Municipal Finance
State Aid Programs, 2008
Total aid	$560,263
CMPTRA	95,750
Energy tax receipts	464,513
Garden State Trust	0

General Budget, 2007
Total tax levy	$9,759,179
County levy	1,526,523
County taxes	1,340,480
County library	76,743
County health	25,532
County open space	83,767
School levy	4,789,760
Muni. levy	3,442,896
Misc. revenues	2,190,489

Neptune Township — Monmouth County

Demographics & Socio-Economic Characteristics
(2000 US Census, except as noted)

Population
- 1980* 28,366
- 1990* 28,148
- 2000 27,690
  - Male 12,890
  - Female 14,800
- 2006 (estimate)* 28,163
- Population density 3,426.2

Race & Hispanic Origin, 2000
Race
- White 15,485
- Black/African American 10,567
- American Indian/Alaska Native 46
- Asian 325
- Native Hawaiian/Pacific Islander 12
- Other race 547
- Two or more races 708
- Hispanic origin, total 1,537
  - Mexican 296
  - Puerto Rican 791
  - Cuban 46
  - Other Hispanic 404

Age & Nativity, 2000
- Under 5 years 1,657
- 18 years and over 21,292
- 21 years and over 20,477
- 65 years and over 4,639
- 85 years and over 784
- Median age 39.4
- Native-born 25,663
- Foreign-born 2,027

Educational Attainment, 2000
- Population 25 years and over 19,450
- Less than 9th grade 4.8%
- High school grad or higher 84.0%
- Bachelor's degree or higher 23.5%
- Graduate degree 8.1%

Income & Poverty, 1999
- Per capita income $22,569
- Median household income $46,250
- Median family income $57,735
- Persons in poverty 3,150
- H'holds receiving public assistance 409
- H'holds receiving social security 3,314

Households, 2000
- Total households 10,907
  - With persons under 18 3,422
  - With persons over 65 3,062
  - Family households 6,802
  - Single-person households 3,437
- Persons per household 2.46
- Persons per family 3.14

Labor & Employment
- Total civilian labor force, 2006** .. 14,693
  - Unemployment rate 5.8%
- Total civilian labor force, 2000 13,943
  - Unemployment rate 7.1%
- Employed persons 16 years and over by occupation, 2000
  - Managers & professionals 4,769
  - Service occupations 2,086
  - Sales & office occupations 3,678
  - Farming, fishing & forestry 14
  - Construction & maintenance 976
  - Production & transportation 1,425
- Self-employed persons 611

* US Census Bureau
** New Jersey Department of Labor

General Information
Township of Neptune
PO Box 1125
Neptune, NJ 07754
732-988-5200

- Website .... www.neptuntownship.org
- Year of incorporation 1879
- Land/water area (sq. miles) 8.22/0.54
- Form of government .... Township

Government
Legislative Districts
- US Congressional 6
- State Legislative 11

Local Officials, 2008
- Mayor .... J. Randy Bishop
- Manager .... Philip Huhn
- Clerk .... Richard Cuttrell
- Finance Dir .... Michael Bascom
- Tax Assessor .... Bernard Haney
- Tax Collector .... Michael Bascom
- Attorney .... Gene Anthony
- Building .... William Doolittle
- Planning .... Martin Truscott
- Engineering .... Leann Hoffman
- Public Works .... Wayne Rode
- Police Chief .... Howard O'Neil
- Emerg/Fire Director ..... Kenneth Northrup

Housing & Construction
Housing Units, 2000*
- Total 12,217
- Median rent $658
- Median SF home value $138,100

Permits for New Residential Construction

	Units	Value
Total, 2007	108	$4,931,427
Single family	19	$4,664,032
Total, 2006	455	$15,687,215
Single family	8	$14,472,744

Real Property Valuation, 2007

	Parcels	Valuation
Total	10,548	$2,907,312,600
Vacant	384	34,456,100
Residential	9,595	2,304,877,600
Commercial	425	403,007,700
Industrial	61	70,921,400
Apartments	78	93,432,700
Farm land	3	16,100
Farm homestead	2	601,000

Average Property Value & Tax, 2007
- Residential value $240,229
- Property tax $5,018
- Tax credit/rebate $972

Public Library
Neptune Public Library
25 Neptune Blvd
Neptune, NJ 07753
732-775-8241

- Director .... Marian R. Bauman

Library statistics, 2006
- Population served 27,690
- Full-time/total staff 4/17

	Total	Per capita
Holdings	80,635	2.91
Revenues	$1,659,628	$59.94
Expenditures	$1,566,511	$56.56
Annual visits	75,216	2.72
Internet terminals/annual users	14/18,371	

Taxes

	2005	2006	2007
General tax rate per $100	1.908	2.013	2.089
County equalization ratio	98.36	84.26	76.04
Net valuation taxable	$2,912,345,753	$2,924,692,900	$2,912,721,639
State equalized value	$3,456,379,958	$3,852,152,565	$582,008,559

Public Safety
- Number of officers, 2006 73

Crime	2005	2006
Total crimes	1,598	1,540
Violent	151	161
Murder	0	1
Rape	4	8
Robbery	76	78
Aggravated assault	71	74
Non-violent	1,447	1,379
Burglary	264	251
Larceny	1,077	1,032
Vehicle theft	106	96
Domestic violence	474	370
Arson	8	14
Total crime rate	56.7	54.5
Violent	5.4	5.7
Non-violent	51.3	48.8

Public School District
(for school year 2006-07 except as noted)

Neptune Township School District
60 Neptune Blvd
Neptune, NJ 07753
732-776-2000

- Superintendent .... David Mooij
- Number of schools 8
- Grade plan K-12
- Enrollment 5,033
- Attendance rate, '05-06 .... 95.0%
- Dropout rate .... NA
- Students per teacher 12.5
- Per pupil expenditure $16,446
- Median faculty salary $53,038
- Median administrator salary $112,680
- Grade 12 enrollment 312
- High school graduation rate 99.6%

Assessment test results
(percent scoring at proficient or advanced level)

	Language	Math
NJASK-Grade 3	68.6%	75.0%
GEPA-Grade 8	60.7%	56.0%
HSPA-High School	74.4%	60.0%

SAT score averages

Pct tested	Math	Verbal	Writing
53%	444	435	436

Teacher Qualifications
- Avg. years of experience 9
- Highly-qualified teachers
  one subject/all subjects 100%/100%
- With emergency credentials 0.7%

No Child Left Behind
- AYP, 2005-06 .... Needs Improvement

Municipal Finance
State Aid Programs, 2008
- Total aid $6,395,038
  - CMPTRA 2,870,827
  - Energy tax receipts 3,524,211
  - Garden State Trust 0

General Budget, 2007
- Total tax levy $60,837,318
  - County levy 9,996,798
    - County taxes 9,243,163
    - County library 0
    - County health 176,063
    - County open space 577,572
  - School levy 30,773,257
  - Muni. levy 20,067,263
  - Misc. revenues 15,071,742

Morris County
Netcong Borough

Demographics & Socio-Economic Characteristics
(2000 US Census, except as noted)

Population
1980*	3,557
1990*	3,311
2000	2,580
Male	1,267
Female	1,313
2006 (estimate)*	3,292
Population density	3,919.0

Race & Hispanic Origin, 2000
Race
White	2,433
Black/African American	31
American Indian/Alaska Native	1
Asian	43
Native Hawaiian/Pacific Islander	0
Other race	37
Two or more races	35
Hispanic origin, total	184
Mexican	21
Puerto Rican	38
Cuban	12
Other Hispanic	113

Age & Nativity, 2000
Under 5 years	148
18 years and over	1,987
21 years and over	1,895
65 years and over	377
85 years and over	47
Median age	37.8
Native-born	2,311
Foreign-born	269

Educational Attainment, 2000
Population 25 years and over	1,817
Less than 9th grade	7.9%
High school grad or higher	84.8%
Bachelor's degree or higher	22.0%
Graduate degree	6.2%

Income & Poverty, 1999
Per capita income	$23,472
Median household income	$55,000
Median family income	$65,833
Persons in poverty	80
H'holds receiving public assistance	12
H'holds receiving social security	276

Households, 2000
Total households	1,008
With persons under 18	328
With persons over 65	283
Family households	681
Single-person households	265
Persons per household	2.56
Persons per family	3.10

Labor & Employment
Total civilian labor force, 2006**	1,559
Unemployment rate	3.3%
Total civilian labor force, 2000	1,425
Unemployment rate	2.9%

Employed persons 16 years and over by occupation, 2000
Managers & professionals	434
Service occupations	253
Sales & office occupations	370
Farming, fishing & forestry	0
Construction & maintenance	131
Production & transportation	196
Self-employed persons	96

*   US Census Bureau
** New Jersey Department of Labor

See Introduction for an explanation of all data sources.

General Information
Borough of Netcong
23 Maple Ave
Netcong, NJ 07857
973-347-0252

Website	www.netcong.org
Year of incorporation	1894
Land/water area (sq. miles)	0.84/0.06
Form of government	Borough

Government
Legislative Districts
US Congressional	11
State Legislative	24

Local Officials, 2008
Mayor	Joseph Nametko
Manager	Ralph Blakeslee
Clerk	Dolores Dalessandro
Finance Dir	Anna Madonna
Tax Assessor	Marvin Joss
Tax Collector	Dolores Dalessandro
Attorney	Anthony Bucco
Building	Barrie Krause
Comm Dev/Planning	NA
Engineering	Robert Guerin
Public Works	Bobby Olivo
Police Chief	Robert Weisert
Emerg/Fire Director	Shawn Bates

Housing & Construction
Housing Units, 2000*
Total	1,043
Median rent	$764
Median SF home value	$147,400

Permits for New Residential Construction
	Units	Value
Total, 2007	2	$251,554
Single family	2	$251,554
Total, 2006	4	$503,108
Single family	4	$503,108

Real Property Valuation, 2007
	Parcels	Valuation
Total	945	$343,299,500
Vacant	44	6,504,500
Residential	816	239,878,700
Commercial	76	43,595,500
Industrial	6	21,202,500
Apartments	3	32,118,300
Farm land	0	0
Farm homestead	0	0

Average Property Value & Tax, 2007
Residential value	$293,969
Property tax	$5,914
Tax credit/rebate	$1,066

Public Library
No public municipal library

Library statistics, 2006
Population served	NA
Full-time/total staff	NA/NA

	Total	Per capita
Holdings	NA	NA
Revenues	NA	NA
Expenditures	NA	NA
Annual visits	NA	NA
Internet terminals/annual users	NA/NA	

Taxes
	2005	2006	2007
General tax rate per $100	3.55	1.92	2.02
County equalization ratio	67.62	118	106.67
Net valuation taxable	$178,521,829	$343,530,700	$346,363,131
State equalized value	$293,863,093	$325,454,829	$334,882,208

Public Safety
Number of officers, 2006 9

Crime
	2005	2006
Total crimes	92	114
Violent	2	5
Murder	0	0
Rape	1	1
Robbery	0	2
Aggravated assault	1	2
Non-violent	90	109
Burglary	20	23
Larceny	61	75
Vehicle theft	9	11
Domestic violence	59	58
Arson	1	0
Total crime rate	27.9	34.6
Violent	0.6	1.5
Non-violent	27.3	33.1

Public School District
(for school year 2006-07 except as noted)

Netcong School District
26 College Rd
Netcong, NJ 07857
973-347-0020

Superintendent	Arthur DiBenedetto (Int)
Number of schools	1
Grade plan	K-8
Enrollment	295
Attendance rate, '05-06	95.1%
Dropout rate	NA
Students per teacher	9.3
Per pupil expenditure	$13,457
Median faculty salary	$63,925
Median administrator salary	$77,850
Grade 12 enrollment	NA
High school graduation rate	NA

Assessment test results
(percent scoring at proficient or advanced level)
	Language	Math
NJASK-Grade 3	80.0%	92.0%
GEPA-Grade 8	66.7%	81.8%
HSPA-High School	NA	NA

SAT score averages
Pct tested	Math	Verbal	Writing
NA	NA	NA	NA

Teacher Qualifications
Avg. years of experience	15
Highly-qualified teachers one subject/all subjects	100%/100%
With emergency credentials	0.0%

No Child Left Behind
AYP, 2005-06 .... Meets Standards

Municipal Finance
State Aid Programs, 2008
Total aid	$322,346
CMPTRA	0
Energy tax receipts	322,235
Garden State Trust	111

General Budget, 2007
Total tax levy	$6,968,441
County levy	779,538
County taxes	623,534
County library	0
County health	0
County open space	156,005
School levy	4,233,176
Muni. levy	1,955,727
Misc. revenues	1,469,159

New Brunswick City
Middlesex County

Demographics & Socio-Economic Characteristics
(2000 US Census, except as noted)

Population
1980*	41,442
1990*	41,711
2000	48,573
Male	24,085
Female	24,488
2006 (estimate)*	50,172
Population density	9,593.1

Race & Hispanic Origin, 2000
Race
White	23,701
Black/African American	11,185
American Indian/Alaska Native	224
Asian	2,584
Native Hawaiian/Pacific Islander	40
Other race	8,780
Two or more races	2,059
Hispanic origin, total	18,947
Mexican	7,364
Puerto Rican	3,178
Cuban	254
Other Hispanic	8,151

Age & Nativity, 2000
Under 5 years	3,394
18 years and over	38,824
21 years and over	31,338
65 years and over	3,146
85 years and over	389
Median age	23.6
Native-born	32,358
Foreign-born	16,215

Educational Attainment, 2000
Population 25 years and over	22,088
Less than 9th grade	21.6%
High school grad or higher	62.6%
Bachelor's degree or higher	19.2%
Graduate degree	7.5%

Income & Poverty, 1999
Per capita income	$14,308
Median household income	$36,080
Median family income	$38,222
Persons in poverty	11,454
H'holds receiving public assistance	741
H'holds receiving social security	2,396

Households, 2000
Total households	13,057
With persons under 18	4,576
With persons over 65	2,429
Family households	7,202
Single-person households	3,178
Persons per household	3.23
Persons per family	3.69

Labor & Employment
Total civilian labor force, 2006**	27,140
Unemployment rate	4.8%
Total civilian labor force, 2000	26,652
Unemployment rate	10.6%

Employed persons 16 years and over by occupation, 2000
Managers & professionals	5,929
Service occupations	5,327
Sales & office occupations	6,307
Farming, fishing & forestry	108
Construction & maintenance	1,099
Production & transportation	5,062
Self-employed persons	448

* US Census Bureau
** New Jersey Department of Labor

General Information
City of New Brunswick
City Hall
78 Bayard St
New Brunswick, NJ 08901
732 745 5004

Website	www.cityofnewbrunswick.org
Year of incorporation	1730
Land/water area (sq. miles)	5.23/0.52
Form of government	Mayor-Council

Government
Legislative Districts
US Congressional	6
State Legislative	17

Local Officials, 2008
Mayor	James Cahill
Manager	Thomas A. Loughlin III
Clerk	Daniel A. Torrisi
Finance Dir	Douglas A. Petix
Tax Assessor	Philip Duchesneau
Tax Collector	Marilyn Chetrancola
Attorney	William J. Hamilton Jr
Building	William Schrum
Planning	Glenn Patterson
Engineer	Thomas Guldin
Public Works	Steve Zarecki
Police Chief	Anthony Caputo
Emerg/Fire Director	Robert Rawls

Housing & Construction
Housing Units, 2000*
Total	13,893
Median rent	$837
Median SF home value	$122,600

Permits for New Residential Construction
	Units	Value
Total, 2007	270	$25,728,486
Single family	39	$3,126,189
Total, 2006	226	$27,153,868
Single family	19	$938,894

Real Property Valuation, 2007
	Parcels	Valuation
Total	7,245	$1,280,955,800
Vacant	896	19,678,400
Residential	5,416	623,475,500
Commercial	666	360,379,500
Industrial	96	144,186,100
Apartments	171	133,236,300
Farm land	0	0
Farm homestead	0	0

Average Property Value & Tax, 2007
Residential value	$115,117
Property tax	$5,260
Tax credit/rebate	$913

Public Library
New Brunswick Public Library
60 Livingston Ave
New Brunswick, NJ 08901
732-745-5108

Director........Robert Belvin

Library statistics, 2006
Population served	48,573
Full-time/total staff	7/19

	Total	Per capita
Holdings	89,748	1.85
Revenues	$1,667,548	$34.33
Expenditures	$1,636,232	$33.69
Annual visits	199,853	4.11
Internet terminals/annual users	22/27,689	

Public Safety
Number of officers, 2006		137
Crime	**2005**	**2006**
Total crimes	2,175	2,276
Violent	345	360
Murder	3	7
Rape	17	19
Robbery	204	207
Aggravated assault	121	127
Non-violent	1,830	1,916
Burglary	519	515
Larceny	1,111	1,194
Vehicle theft	200	207
Domestic violence	535	572
Arson	8	7
Total crime rate	43.5	45.4
Violent	6.9	7.2
Non-violent	36.6	38.2

Public School District
(for school year 2006-07 except as noted)

New Brunswick School District
268 Baldwin St, PO Box 2683
New Brunswick, NJ 08903
732-745-5300

Superintendent	Richard Kaplan
Number of schools	9
Grade plan	K-12
Enrollment	6,776
Attendance rate, '05-06	93.9%
Dropout rate	11.0%
Students per teacher	9.0
Per pupil expenditure	$17,470
Median faculty salary	$69,107
Median administrator salary	$108,657
Grade 12 enrollment	263
High school graduation rate	76.2%

Assessment test results
(percent scoring at proficient or advanced level)
	Language	Math
NJASK-Grade 3	58.4%	66.9%
GEPA-Grade 8	42.8%	40.2%
HSPA-High School	64.3%	50.2%

SAT score averages
Pct tested	Math	Verbal	Writing
68%	441	411	412

Teacher Qualifications
Avg. years of experience	8
Highly-qualified teachers one subject/all subjects	95.0%/94.5%
With emergency credentials	0.4%

No Child Left Behind
AYP, 2005-06 ....Needs Improvement

Municipal Finance
State Aid Programs, 2008
Total aid	$15,615,623
CMPTRA	12,551,883
Energy tax receipts	3,063,676
Garden State Trust	64

General Budget, 2007
Total tax levy	$59,807,624
County levy	9,250,403
County taxes	8,281,141
County library	0
County health	0
County open space	969,261
School levy	27,208,618
Muni. levy	23,348,603
Misc. revenues	45,221,789

Taxes	2005	2006	2007
General tax rate per $100	4.05	4.2	4.57
County equalization ratio	53.07	45.97	40.85
Net valuation taxable	$1,318,918,764	$1,280,532,100	$1,308,981,083
State equalized value	$2,869,085,847	$3,165,681,140	$3,548,101,678

Burlington County

New Hanover Township

Demographics & Socio-Economic Characteristics
(2000 US Census, except as noted)

Population
1980*	14,258
1990*	9,546
2000	9,744
Male	7,802
Female	1,942
2006 (estimate)*	9,479
Population density	425.4

Race & Hispanic Origin, 2000
Race
White	6,249
Black/African American	2,816
American Indian/Alaska Native	41
Asian	143
Native Hawaiian/Pacific Islander	8
Other race	259
Two or more races	228
Hispanic origin, total	1,890
Mexican	227
Puerto Rican	928
Cuban	77
Other Hispanic	658

Age & Nativity, 2000
Under 5 years	408
18 years and over	8,331
21 years and over	7,807
65 years and over	125
85 years and over	3
Median age	32.1
Native-born	9,498
Foreign-born	336

Educational Attainment, 2000
Population 25 years and over	6,700
Less than 9th grade	6.2%
High school grad or higher	74.1%
Bachelor's degree or higher	14.6%
Graduate degree	3.3%

Income & Poverty, 1999
Per capita income	$12,140
Median household income	$44,386
Median family income	$45,511
Persons in poverty	146
H'holds receiving public assistance	5
H'holds receiving social security	48

Households, 2000
Total households	1,162
With persons under 18	723
With persons over 65	41
Family households	991
Single-person households	159
Persons per household	3.14
Persons per family	3.46

Labor & Employment
Total civilian labor force, 2006**	1,071
Unemployment rate	3.6%
Total civilian labor force, 2000	950
Unemployment rate	3.4%

Employed persons 16 years and over by occupation, 2000
Managers & professionals	356
Service occupations	197
Sales & office occupations	216
Farming, fishing & forestry	0
Construction & maintenance	70
Production & transportation	79
Self-employed persons	38

* US Census Bureau
** New Jersey Department of Labor

See Introduction for an explanation of all data sources.

General Information
Township of New Hanover
2 Hockamick Rd
PO Box 159
Cookstown, NJ 08511
609-758-2172

Email	nhmc@comcast.net
Year of incorporation	1723
Land/water area (sq. miles)	22.28/0.10
Form of government	Township

Government
Legislative Districts
US Congressional	3
State Legislative	30

Local Officials, 2008
Mayor	Dennis Roohr
Manager	Jay Todd
Clerk	Jay Todd
Finance Dir	Dawn Robertson
Tax Assessor	Ed Burek
Tax Collector	Dawn Mitchell
Attorney	Anthony Drollas
Building	Alan Wilkins
Comm Dev/Planning	NA
Engineering	Richard Tangel
Public Works	NA
Police Chief	Gary Timmons
Emerg/Fire Director	Charles Wilkins

Housing & Construction
Housing Units, 2000*
Total	1,381
Median rent	$906
Median SF home value	$133,200

Permits for New Residential Construction
	Units	Value
Total, 2007	8	$726,166
Single family	8	$726,166
Total, 2006	21	$1,970,935
Single family	21	$1,970,935

Real Property Valuation, 2007
	Parcels	Valuation
Total	364	$55,121,700
Vacant	64	2,272,600
Residential	223	36,768,800
Commercial	24	12,141,500
Industrial	1	88,000
Apartments	0	0
Farm land	35	621,000
Farm homestead	17	3,229,800

Average Property Value & Tax, 2007
Residential value	$166,661
Property tax	$3,719
Tax credit/rebate	$783

Public Library
No public municipal library

Library statistics, 2006
Population served	NA
Full-time/total staff	NA/NA

	Total	Per capita
Holdings	NA	NA
Revenues	NA	NA
Expenditures	NA	NA
Annual visits	NA	NA
Internet terminals/annual users	NA/NA	

Taxes
	2005	2006	2007
General tax rate per $100	2.14	2.293	2.34
County equalization ratio	88.99	81.07	72.46
Net valuation taxable	$54,734,695	$54,003,400	$55,903,985
State equalized value	$67,515,351	$75,392,596	$83,721,948

Public Safety
Number of officers, 2006	4

Crime	2005	2006
Total crimes	14	21
Violent	1	1
Murder	0	0
Rape	0	0
Robbery	0	0
Aggravated assault	1	1
Non-violent	13	20
Burglary	0	10
Larceny	12	7
Vehicle theft	1	3
Domestic violence	7	8
Arson	0	0
Total crime rate	1.4	2.2
Violent	0.1	0.1
Non-violent	1.3	2.1

Public School District
(for school year 2006-07 except as noted)

New Hanover Township School District
122 Fort Dix St.
Wrightstown, NJ 08562
609-723-2139

Superintendent	Terri Sackett
Number of schools	2
Grade plan	K-8
Enrollment	162
Attendance rate, '05-06	95.4%
Dropout rate	NA
Students per teacher	8.1
Per pupil expenditure	$19,578
Median faculty salary	$49,327
Median administrator salary	$81,600
Grade 12 enrollment	NA
High school graduation rate	NA

Assessment test results
(percent scoring at proficient or advanced level)
	Language	Math
NJASK-Grade 3	75.0%	87.5%
GEPA-Grade 8	81.5%	70.4%
HSPA-High School	NA	NA

SAT score averages
Pct tested	Math	Verbal	Writing
NA	NA	NA	NA

Teacher Qualifications
Avg. years of experience	9
Highly-qualified teachers one subject/all subjects	94.0%/94.0%
With emergency credentials	0.0%

No Child Left Behind
AYP, 2005-06	Meets Standards

Municipal Finance
State Aid Programs, 2008
Total aid	$715,909
CMPTRA	297,872
Energy tax receipts	418,037
Garden State Trust	0

General Budget, 2007
Total tax levy	$1,307,463
County levy	323,385
County taxes	267,970
County library	24,590
County health	0
County open space	30,824
School levy	984,078
Muni. levy	0
Misc. revenues	2,307,364

The New Jersey Municipal Data Book

New Milford Borough — Bergen County

Demographics & Socio-Economic Characteristics
(2000 US Census, except as noted)

Population
1980*	16,876
1990*	15,990
2000	16,400
Male	7,900
Female	8,500
2006 (estimate)*	16,243
Population density	7,031.6

Race & Hispanic Origin, 2000
Race
White	12,888
Black/African American	429
American Indian/Alaska Native	19
Asian	2,420
Native Hawaiian/Pacific Islander	4
Other race	305
Two or more races	335
Hispanic origin, total	1,326
Mexican	47
Puerto Rican	328
Cuban	190
Other Hispanic	761

Age & Nativity, 2000
Under 5 years	1,050
18 years and over	12,895
21 years and over	12,512
65 years and over	2,888
85 years and over	404
Median age	39.9
Native-born	12,334
Foreign-born	4,066

Educational Attainment, 2000
Population 25 years and over	11,853
Less than 9th grade	4.6%
High school grad or higher	87.6%
Bachelor's degree or higher	32.4%
Graduate degree	11.2%

Income & Poverty, 1999
Per capita income	$29,064
Median household income	$59,118
Median family income	$77,216
Persons in poverty	543
H'holds receiving public assistance	98
H'holds receiving social security	1,870

Households, 2000
Total households	6,346
With persons under 18	1,996
With persons over 65	1,954
Family households	4,275
Single-person households	1,817
Persons per household	2.54
Persons per family	3.18

Labor & Employment
Total civilian labor force, 2006**	9,302
Unemployment rate	3.8%
Total civilian labor force, 2000	8,748
Unemployment rate	3.7%

Employed persons 16 years and over by occupation, 2000
Managers & professionals	3,509
Service occupations	830
Sales & office occupations	2,815
Farming, fishing & forestry	0
Construction & maintenance	589
Production & transportation	681
Self-employed persons	406

* US Census Bureau
** New Jersey Department of Labor

General Information
Borough of New Milford
930 River Rd
New Milford, NJ 07646
201-967-5044

Website: www.newmilfordboro.com
Year of incorporation: 1922
Land/water area (sq. miles): 2.31/0.00
Form of government: Borough

Government

Legislative Districts
US Congressional	5, 9
State Legislative	39

Local Officials, 2008
Mayor	Frank DeBari
Manager	Christine Demiris
Clerk	Christine Demiris
Finance Dir	Mark Polito
Tax Assessor	Barbara Potash
Tax Collector	Denise Amoroso
Attorney	S. Greg Moscaritolo
Building	James Taormino
Planning	Angelo DeCarlo
Engineering	Stephen Boswell
Public Works Dir	Mike Calamari (Asst)
Police Chief	Frank Papapietro
Emerg/Fire Director	Patrick Boselli

Housing & Construction

Housing Units, 2000*
Total	6,437
Median rent	$763
Median SF home value	$223,400

Permits for New Residential Construction
	Units	Value
Total, 2007	18	$3,677,591
Single family	13	$3,074,341
Total, 2006	25	$5,119,125
Single family	15	$3,912,625

Real Property Valuation, 2007
	Parcels	Valuation
Total	4,330	$1,945,676,500
Vacant	46	5,235,900
Residential	4,192	1,719,246,500
Commercial	76	88,932,700
Industrial	2	3,736,200
Apartments	14	128,525,200
Farm land	0	0
Farm homestead	0	0

Average Property Value & Tax, 2007
Residential value	$410,126
Property tax	$8,165
Tax credit/rebate	$1,284

Public Library
New Milford Public Library
200 Dahlia Ave
New Milford, NJ 07646
201-262-1221

Director: Terrie McColl

Library statistics, 2006
Population served	16,400
Full-time/total staff	4/9

	Total	Per capita
Holdings	66,375	4.05
Revenues	$860,802	$52.49
Expenditures	$852,036	$51.95
Annual visits	159,714	9.74
Internet terminals/annual users		5/8,119

Public Safety
Number of officers, 2006: 36

Crime	2005	2006
Total crimes	137	133
Violent	15	3
Murder	0	0
Rape	2	0
Robbery	5	1
Aggravated assault	8	2
Non-violent	122	130
Burglary	22	18
Larceny	97	110
Vehicle theft	3	2
Domestic violence	78	104
Arson	0	2
Total crime rate	8.4	8.2
Violent	0.9	0.2
Non-violent	7.4	8.0

Public School District
(for school year 2006-07 except as noted)

New Milford School District
145 Madison Ave
New Milford, NJ 07646
201-261-2952

Superintendent	Nicholas Brown
Number of schools	4
Grade plan	K-12
Enrollment	1,990
Attendance rate, '05-06	95.9%
Dropout rate	0.4%
Students per teacher	12.0
Per pupil expenditure	$12,273
Median faculty salary	$46,950
Median administrator salary	$101,766
Grade 12 enrollment	127
High school graduation rate	97.0%

Assessment test results
(percent scoring at proficient or advanced level)
	Language	Math
NJASK-Grade 3	92.3%	91.7%
GEPA-Grade 8	70.7%	70.8%
HSPA-High School	93.3%	78.4%

SAT score averages
Pct tested	Math	Verbal	Writing
89%	515	494	490

Teacher Qualifications
Avg. years of experience	6
Highly-qualified teachers one subject/all subjects	99.0%/96.5%
With emergency credentials	0.0%

No Child Left Behind
AYP, 2005-06: Meets Standards

Municipal Finance

State Aid Programs, 2008
Total aid	$2,077,219
CMPTRA	409,170
Energy tax receipts	1,666,286
Garden State Trust	1,763

General Budget, 2007
Total tax levy	$38,753,575
County levy	3,733,186
County taxes	3,527,694
County library	0
County health	0
County open space	205,493
School levy	23,147,645
Muni. levy	11,872,744
Misc. revenues	4,899,288

Taxes
	2005	2006	2007
General tax rate per $100	1.79	1.88	2
County equalization ratio	120.37	105.69	94.9
Net valuation taxable	$1,924,645,190	$1,933,795,000	$1,946,685,143
State equalized value	$1,821,028,659	$2,038,503,655	$2,119,328,186

Union County

New Providence Borough

Demographics & Socio-Economic Characteristics
(2000 US Census, except as noted)

Population
- 1980*.....................................12,426
- 1990*.....................................11,439
- 2000......................................11,907
  - Male......................................5,770
  - Female..................................6,137
- 2006 (estimate)*....................11,915
- Population density...............3,237.8

Race & Hispanic Origin, 2000
Race
- White.....................................10,689
- Black/African American...........105
- American Indian/Alaska Native....4
- Asian..905
- Native Hawaiian/Pacific Islander....3
- Other race..................................81
- Two or more races.................120
- Hispanic origin, total..............417
  - Mexican....................................37
  - Puerto Rican............................57
  - Cuban..44
  - Other Hispanic.......................279

Age & Nativity, 2000
- Under 5 years...........................934
- 18 years and over.................8,771
- 21 years and over.................8,545
- 65 years and over.................1,821
- 85 years and over...................212
  - Median age...............................39.0
- Native-born............................9,774
- Foreign-born..........................2,133

Educational Attainment, 2000
- Population 25 years and over......8,319
- Less than 9th grade..................2.3%
- High school grad or higher....95.1%
- Bachelor's degree or higher..58.1%
- Graduate degree......................27.6%

Income & Poverty, 1999
- Per capita income.................$42,995
- Median household income.......$90,964
- Median family income.........$105,013
- Persons in poverty....................212
- H'holds receiving public assistance....0
- H'holds receiving social security....1,275

Households, 2000
- Total households....................4,404
  - With persons under 18.........1,709
  - With persons over 65...........1,215
  - Family households................3,309
  - Single-person households.....944
- Persons per household...........2.67
- Persons per family..................3.13

Labor & Employment
- Total civilian labor force, 2006**....6,475
  - Unemployment rate................3.3%
- Total civilian labor force, 2000....6,189
  - Unemployment rate................3.3%

Employed persons 16 years and over by occupation, 2000
- Managers & professionals......3,601
- Service occupations................437
- Sales & office occupations...1,440
- Farming, fishing & forestry........0
- Construction & maintenance...314
- Production & transportation...195
- Self-employed persons...........368

* US Census Bureau
** New Jersey Department of Labor

See Introduction for an explanation of all data sources.

General Information
Borough of New Providence
360 Elkwood Ave
New Providence, NJ 07974
908-665-1400

- Website....................www.newprov.org
- Year of incorporation..................1899
- Land/water area (sq. miles).......3.68/0.00
- Form of government..................Borough

Government
Legislative Districts
- US Congressional..........................7
- State Legislative..........................21

Local Officials, 2008
- Mayor...........................John Thoms
- Manager..................Douglas Marvin
- Clerk...........................Wendi Barry
- Finance Dir................Ken DeRoberts
- Tax Assessor..............Pat Spychala
- Tax Collector............Monica Marino
- Attorney..................Carl Woodward
- Building........................Keith Lynch
- Comm Dev/Planning....................NA
- Engineering.............Andrew Hipolit
- Public Works...........James Johnston
- Police Chief.............Anthony Buccelli
- Emerg/Fire Director.......Craig Stapfer

Housing & Construction
Housing Units, 2000*
- Total......................................4,485
- Median rent...............................$941
- Median SF home value........$317,100

Permits for New Residential Construction

	Units	Value
Total, 2007	60	$9,607,338
Single family	25	$4,951,224
Total, 2006	65	$6,190,642
Single family	38	$2,337,642

Real Property Valuation, 2007

	Parcels	Valuation
Total	3,909	$1,290,943,265
Vacant	100	15,147,200
Residential	3,655	1,031,995,100
Commercial	129	133,726,485
Industrial	12	75,783,380
Apartments	13	34,291,100
Farm land	0	0
Farm homestead	0	0

Average Property Value & Tax, 2007
- Residential value..................$282,352
- Property tax..........................$10,114
- Tax credit/rebate...................$1,329

Public Library
New Providence Memorial Library
377 Elkwood Ave
New Providence, NJ 07974
908-665-0311

Director....................James K. Keehbler

Library statistics, 2006
- Population served.................11,907
- Full-time/total staff...................3/7

	Total	Per capita
Holdings	69,727	5.86
Revenues	$785,856	$66.00
Expenditures	$737,018	$61.90
Annual visits	142,263	11.95

Internet terminals/annual users.....8/8,728

Public Safety
Number of officers, 2006..............26

Crime	2005	2006
Total crimes	97	145
Violent	5	5
Murder	1	0
Rape	1	0
Robbery	0	0
Aggravated assault	3	5
Non-violent	92	140
Burglary	8	19
Larceny	77	120
Vehicle theft	7	1
Domestic violence	56	68
Arson	1	0
Total crime rate	8.1	12.2
Violent	0.4	0.4
Non-violent	7.7	11.8

Public School District
(for school year 2006-07 except as noted)

New Providence School District
356 Elkwood Ave
New Providence, NJ 07974
908-464-9050

- Superintendent.........David M. Miceli (Int)
- Number of schools.......................4
- Grade plan.............................K-12
- Enrollment..........................2,225
- Attendance rate, '05-06..........95.7%
- Dropout rate................................NA
- Students per teacher................11.1
- Per pupil expenditure..........$12,778
- Median faculty salary..........$58,430
- Median administrator salary....$118,388
- Grade 12 enrollment..................175
- High school graduation rate....100.0%

Assessment test results
(percent scoring at proficient or advanced level)

	Language	Math
NJASK-Grade 3	96.2%	98.4%
GEPA-Grade 8	92.8%	95.0%
HSPA-High School	96.9%	93.2%

SAT score averages

Pct tested	Math	Verbal	Writing
103%	581	552	554

Teacher Qualifications
- Avg. years of experience..............9
- Highly-qualified teachers
  one subject/all subjects........100%/100%
- With emergency credentials........0.0%

No Child Left Behind
- AYP, 2005-06..............Meets Standards

Municipal Finance
State Aid Programs, 2008
- Total aid.........................$1,706,689
  - CMPTRA..........................395,349
  - Energy tax receipts........1,311,340
  - Garden State Trust......................0

General Budget, 2007
- Total tax levy..................$46,355,460
  - County levy....................8,354,178
    - County taxes................7,993,827
    - County library......................0
    - County health.......................0
    - County open space..........360,352
  - School levy..................28,166,803
  - Muni. levy.....................9,834,479
- Misc. revenues..................5,976,382

Taxes	2005	2006	2007
General tax rate per $100	3.24	3.395	3.582
County equalization ratio	61.3	57.04	54.06
Net valuation taxable	$1,307,203,407	$1,300,153,880	$1,294,153,494
State equalized value	$2,213,348,132	$2,409,116,454	$2,543,936,986

The New Jersey Municipal Data Book

Newark City — Essex County

Demographics & Socio-Economic Characteristics[†]
(2000 US Census, except as noted)

Population
1980*	329,248
1990*	275,221
2000	273,546
Male	132,701
Female	140,845
2006 (estimate)*	281,402
Population density	11,823.6

Race & Hispanic Origin, 2000
Race
White	72,537
Black/African American	146,250
American Indian/Alaska Native	1,005
Asian	3,263
Native Hawaiian/Pacific Islander	135
Other race	38,430
Two or more races	11,926
Hispanic origin, total	80,622
Mexican	2,295
Puerto Rican	39,650
Cuban	2,962
Other Hispanic	35,715

Age & Nativity, 2000
Under 5 years	21,293
18 years and over	197,127
21 years and over	183,103
65 years and over	25,306
85 years and over	2,722
Median age	30.8
Native-born	207,489
Foreign-born	66,057

Educational Attainment, 2000
Population 25 years and over	164,298
Less than 9th grade	18.1%
High school grad or higher	57.9%
Bachelor's degree or higher	9.0%
Graduate degree	3.0%

Income & Poverty, 1999
Per capita income	$13,009
Median household income	$26,913
Median family income	$30,781
Persons in poverty	74,263
H'holds receiving public assistance	11,515
H'holds receiving social security	21,956

Households, 2000
Total households	91,382
With persons under 18	39,255
With persons over 65	19,077
Family households	61,999
Single-person households	24,331
Persons per household	2.85
Persons per family	3.43

Labor & Employment
Total civilian labor force, 2006**	106,352
Unemployment rate	8.5%
Total civilian labor force, 2000	108,256
Unemployment rate	16.1%

Employed persons 16 years and over by occupation, 2000
Managers & professionals	17,168
Service occupations	19,796
Sales & office occupations	24,985
Farming, fishing & forestry	134
Construction & maintenance	9,455
Production & transportation	19,281
Self-employed persons	2,707

[†] see Appendix C for American Community Survey data
* US Census Bureau
** New Jersey Department of Labor

General Information
City of Newark
920 Broad St
Newark, NJ 07102
973-733-6400

Website	www.ci.newark.nj.us
Year of incorporation	1836
Land/water area (sq. miles)	23.80/2.17
Form of government	Mayor-Council

Government
Legislative Districts
US Congressional	10, 13
State Legislative	27-29

Local Officials, 2008
Mayor	Cory A. Booker
Manager	Michelle L. Thomas (Actg)
Clerk	Robert P. Marasco
Finance Dir	Linda Landolfi (Actg)
Tax Assessor	Evelyn Laccitiello
Tax Collector	Michelle Jones
Attorney	Julien Neals
Building	Neil Midtgard
Planning/Comm Dev	Toni Griffin
Engineering	Bill Letona (Actg)
Public Works	NA
Police Chief	Anthony Campos
Emerg/Fire Director	David Giordano

Housing & Construction
Housing Units, 2000*
Total	100,141
Median rent	$586
Median SF home value	$119,000

Permits for New Residential Construction
	Units	Value
Total, 2007	959	$68,140,268
Single family	29	$5,443,263
Total, 2006	2,059	$164,085,874
Single family	100	$13,068,747

Real Property Valuation, 2007
	Parcels	Valuation
Total	41,291	$10,924,691,100
Vacant	4,889	451,084,700
Residential	28,770	4,931,192,800
Commercial	5,432	3,758,937,100
Industrial	957	1,065,273,000
Apartments	1,243	718,203,500
Farm land	0	0
Farm homestead	0	0

Average Property Value & Tax, 2007
Residential value	$171,401
Property tax	$4,252
Tax credit/rebate	$801

Public Library
Newark Public Library
5 Washington St
Newark, NJ 07101
973-733-7780

Director . . . . . Wilma J. Grey

Library statistics, 2006
Population served	273,546
Full-time/total staff	54/184

	Total	Per capita
Holdings	1,703,222	6.23
Revenues	$16,338,768	$59.73
Expenditures	$16,338,768	$59.73
Annual visits	663,065	2.42
Internet terminals/annual users	130/230,730	

Taxes
	2005	2006	2007
General tax rate per $100	2.3	2.49	2.49
County equalization ratio	94.69	81.43	70.68
Net valuation taxable	$10,900,573,643	$10,825,543,000	$11,001,867,400
State equalized value	$13,475,798,792	$15,438,960,530	$17,051,525,430

Public Safety
Number of officers, 2006	1,286

Crime	2005	2006
Total crimes	16,374	15,097
Violent	2,956	2,981
Murder	98	107
Rape	89	88
Robbery	1,328	1,360
Aggravated assault	1,441	1,426
Non-violent	13,418	12,116
Burglary	2,075	2,007
Larceny	5,582	4,951
Vehicle theft	5,761	5,158
Domestic violence	2,098	2,129
Arson	180	168
Total crime rate	58.4	53.8
Violent	10.5	10.6
Non-violent	47.8	43.2

Public School District
(for school year 2006-07 except as noted)

Newark School District
2 Cedar St
Newark, NJ 07102
973-733-7333

State District Superint	Marion Bolden
Number of schools	67
Grade plan	K-12
Enrollment	40,370
Attendance rate, '05-06	91.0%
Dropout rate	3.7%
Students per teacher	9.2
Per pupil expenditure	$17,237
Median faculty salary	$77,827
Median administrator salary	$109,823
Grade 12 enrollment	2,257
High school graduation rate	NA

Assessment test results
(percent scoring at proficient or advanced level)
	Language	Math
NJASK-Grade 3	63.1%	69.8%
GEPA-Grade 8	49.9%	35.3%
HSPA-High School	58.3%	39.7%

SAT score averages
Pct tested	Math	Verbal	Writing
NA	NA	NA	NA

Teacher Qualifications
Avg. years of experience	12
Highly-qualified teachers one subject/all subjects	93.5%/93.5%
With emergency credentials	0.9%

No Child Left Behind
AYP, 2005-06 . . . . Needs Improvement

Municipal Finance
State Aid Programs, 2008
Total aid	$107,081,098
CMPTRA	74,541,437
Energy tax receipts	32,539,661
Garden State Trust	0

General Budget, 2007
Total tax levy	$272,936,809
County levy	61,895,365
County taxes	60,286,973
County library	0
County health	0
County open space	1,608,393
School levy	94,774,264
Muni. levy	116,267,180
Misc. revenues	512,008,043

Gloucester County

Newfield Borough

Demographics & Socio-Economic Characteristics
(2000 US Census, except as noted)

Population
- 1980*..........................1,563
- 1990*..........................1,592
- 2000..........................1,616
  - Male..........................744
  - Female........................872
- 2006 (estimate)*..............1,664
  - Population density..........978.8

Race & Hispanic Origin, 2000
Race
- White........................1,537
- Black/African American...........21
- American Indian/Alaska Native....11
- Asian.............................9
- Native Hawaiian/Pacific Islander..0
- Other race.......................17
- Two or more races................21
- Hispanic origin, total...........62
  - Mexican.......................12
  - Puerto Rican..................32
  - Cuban..........................3
  - Other Hispanic................15

Age & Nativity, 2000
- Under 5 years....................93
- 18 years and over.............1,222
- 21 years and over.............1,169
- 65 years and over...............230
- 85 years and over................27
- Median age.....................38.8
- Native-born..................1,561
- Foreign-born.....................55

Educational Attainment, 2000
- Population 25 years and over..1,115
- Less than 9th grade............5.6%
- High school grad or higher...83.5%
- Bachelor's degree or higher..15.7%
- Graduate degree................3.7%

Income & Poverty, 1999
- Per capita income...........$21,063
- Median household income.....$51,875
- Median family income........$59,934
- Persons in poverty..............105
- H'holds receiving public assistance....9
- H'holds receiving social security...178

Households, 2000
- Total households................596
  - With persons under 18........221
  - With persons over 65.........163
  - Family households............471
  - Single-person households.....105
- Persons per household..........2.71
- Persons per family.............3.04

Labor & Employment
- Total civilian labor force, 2006**...1,046
  - Unemployment rate............5.4%
- Total civilian labor force, 2000....877
  - Unemployment rate............4.8%
- *Employed persons 16 years and over by occupation, 2000*
  - Managers & professionals.....229
  - Service occupations..........117
  - Sales & office occupations...248
  - Farming, fishing & forestry....2
  - Construction & maintenance...122
  - Production & transportation..117
- Self-employed persons...........47

* US Census Bureau
** New Jersey Department of Labor

See Introduction for an explanation of all data sources.

General Information
Borough of Newfield
18 Catawba Ave
PO Box 856
Newfield, NJ 08344
856-697-1100

- Website............www.newfieldboro.com
- Year of incorporation..............1924
- Land/water area (sq. miles).....1.70/0.00
- Form of government...............Borough

Government
Legislative Districts
- US Congressional...................2
- State Legislative..................4

Local Officials, 2008
- Mayor.................Joseph Curcio III
- Manager/Admin.....................NA
- Clerk...................Toni Van Camp
- Finance Dir..............Robert Scharle
- Tax Assessor............Timothy Mead
- Tax Collector......Lawrence Nightlinger
- Attorney.................John Eastlack
- Building..................John M. Eckler
- Comm Dev/Planning.................NA
- Engineering..Adams, Rehmann & Heggan
- Public Works......................NA
- Police Chief..........Michael Kappre
- Emerg/Fire Dir......Everett E. Marshall III

Housing & Construction
Housing Units, 2000*
- Total............................620
- Median rent.....................$711
- Median SF home value.........$103,200

Permits for New Residential Construction

	Units	Value
Total, 2007	2	$223,350
Single family	2	$223,350
Total, 2006	5	$558,373
Single family	5	$558,373

Real Property Valuation, 2007

	Parcels	Valuation
Total	780	$62,344,700
Vacant	136	2,706,700
Residential	576	51,390,900
Commercial	31	3,966,000
Industrial	10	2,727,700
Apartments	4	671,000
Farm land	17	105,500
Farm homestead	6	776,900

Average Property Value & Tax, 2007
- Residential value............$89,635
- Property tax..................$4,252
- Tax credit/rebate..............$920

Public Library
Newfield Public Library
115 Catawba Ave
Newfield, NJ 08344
856-697-0415

Manager................Susan Mounier

Library statistics, 2006
- Population served............1,616
- Full-time/total staff...........0/1

	Total	Per capita
Holdings	22,414	13.87
Revenues	$32,366	$20.03
Expenditures	$29,230	$18.09
Annual visits	14,687	9.09
Internet terminals/annual users	3/2,604	

Public Safety
Number of officers, 2006..........5

Crime	2005	2006
Total crimes	24	34
Violent	1	2
Murder	0	0
Rape	0	0
Robbery	0	0
Aggravated assault	1	2
Non-violent	23	32
Burglary	12	13
Larceny	9	18
Vehicle theft	2	1
Domestic violence	25	18
Arson	0	0
Total crime rate	14.5	20.5
Violent	0.6	1.2
Non-violent	13.9	19.3

Public School District
(for school year 2006-07 except as noted)

Newfield School District
1122 Almond Rd
Pittsgrove, NJ 08318

No schools in district

- Per pupil expenditure..............NA
- Median faculty salary..............NA
- Median administrator salary........NA
- Grade 12 enrollment................NA
- High school graduation rate........NA

Assessment test results
(percent scoring at proficient or advanced level)

	Language	Math
NJASK-Grade 3	NA	NA
GEPA-Grade 8	NA	NA
HSPA-High School	NA	NA

SAT score averages

Pct tested	Math	Verbal	Writing
NA	NA	NA	NA

Teacher Qualifications
- Avg. years of experience...........NA
- Highly-qualified teachers
  - one subject/all subjects......NA/NA
- With emergency credentials........NA

No Child Left Behind
- AYP, 2005-06.....................NA

Municipal Finance
State Aid Programs, 2008
- Total aid...................$105,420
- CMPTRA...........................0
- Energy tax receipts..........105,357
- Garden State Trust...............63

General Budget, 2007
- Total tax levy.............$2,965,695
- County levy..................711,216
  - County taxes..............612,528
  - County library.............50,732
  - County health...................0
  - County open space..........47,956
- School levy................1,609,315
- Muni. levy..................645,164
- Misc. revenues..............626,740

Taxes

	2005	2006	2007
General tax rate per $100	4.459	4.646	4.744
County equalization ratio	71.3	60.95	52.39
Net valuation taxable	$59,775,582	$60,848,300	$62,514,808
State equalized value	$98,073,145	$116,340,006	$130,136,128

Newton Town

Sussex County

Demographics & Socio-Economic Characteristics
(2000 US Census, except as noted)

Population
1980*	7,748
1990*	7,521
2000	8,244
Male	3,951
Female	4,293
2006 (estimate)*	8,337
Population density	2,689.4

Race & Hispanic Origin, 2000
Race
- White 7,582
- Black/African American 281
- American Indian/Alaska Native 11
- Asian 162
- Native Hawaiian/Pacific Islander 1
- Other race 96
- Two or more races 111
- Hispanic origin, total 313
  - Mexican 50
  - Puerto Rican 129
  - Cuban 20
  - Other Hispanic 114

Age & Nativity, 2000
- Under 5 years 522
- 18 years and over 6,271
- 21 years and over 5,992
- 65 years and over 1,284
- 85 years and over 225
  - Median age 37.6
- Native-born 7,569
- Foreign-born 675

Educational Attainment, 2000
- Population 25 years and over 5,690
- Less than 9th grade 4.7%
- High school grad or higher 83.6%
- Bachelor's degree or higher 19.2%
- Graduate degree 6.7%

Income & Poverty, 1999
- Per capita income $20,577
- Median household income $41,667
- Median family income $56,484
- Persons in poverty 882
- H'holds receiving public assistance 98
- H'holds receiving social security 1,049

Households, 2000
- Total households 3,258
  - With persons under 18 1,042
  - With persons over 65 892
  - Family households 1,942
  - Single-person households 1,093
- Persons per household 2.39
- Persons per family 3.12

Labor & Employment
- Total civilian labor force, 2006** 4,623
  - Unemployment rate 3.8%
- Total civilian labor force, 2000 4,152
  - Unemployment rate 3.3%

Employed persons 16 years and over by occupation, 2000
- Managers & professionals 1,318
- Service occupations 661
- Sales & office occupations 1,202
- Farming, fishing & forestry 0
- Construction & maintenance 303
- Production & transportation 532
- Self-employed persons 184

‡ Branch of county library
* US Census Bureau
** New Jersey Department of Labor

General Information
Town of Newton
39 Trinity St
Newton, NJ 07860
973-383-3521

- Website .... www.newtontownhall.com
- Year of incorporation 1864
- Land/water area (sq. miles) 3.10/0.01
- Form of government .... Council-Manager

Government

Legislative Districts
- US Congressional 5
- State Legislative 24

Local Officials, 2008
- Mayor .... Thea Unhoch
- Manager .... Eileen Kithcart
- Clerk .... Lorraine Read
- Finance Dir .... Dawn Babcock
- Tax Assessor .... Scott Holzhauer
- Tax Collector .... Linda Roth
- Attorney .... Sanford Hollander
- Construction/Code Enf .... Robert Bittle
- Community Dev Dir .... Debra Millikin
- Engineering .... Harold Pellow
- Public Works .... Kenneth Jaekel
- Police Chief .... John Tomasula
- Emerg/Fire Director .... Michael Teets

Housing & Construction

Housing Units, 2000*
- Total 3,425
- Median rent $697
- Median SF home value $136,100

Permits for New Residential Construction
	Units	Value
Total, 2007	0	$0
Single family	0	$0
Total, 2006	4	$276,200
Single family	0	$0

Real Property Valuation, 2007
	Parcels	Valuation
Total	2,341	$383,100,700
Vacant	70	4,424,200
Residential	1,975	249,313,600
Commercial	245	98,160,600
Industrial	12	10,126,000
Apartments	28	20,714,400
Farm land	9	48,600
Farm homestead	2	313,300

Average Property Value & Tax, 2007
- Residential value $126,266
- Property tax $6,102
- Tax credit/rebate $1,074

Public Library
Dennis Mem. Branch Library‡
101 Main St
Newton, NJ 07860
973-383-4810

- Branch Librarian .... Debbie Mole

Library statistics, 2006
see Sussex County profile for library system statistics

Public Safety
- Number of officers, 2006 24

Crime	2005	2006
Total crimes	194	146
Violent	13	8
Murder	0	0
Rape	0	0
Robbery	2	0
Aggravated assault	11	8
Non-violent	181	138
Burglary	16	9
Larceny	160	124
Vehicle theft	5	5
Domestic violence	82	112
Arson	1	0
Total crime rate	23.1	17.3
Violent	1.6	1.0
Non-violent	21.6	16.4

Public School District
(for school year 2006-07 except as noted)

Newton School District
57 Trinity St
Newton, NJ 07860
973-383-7392

- Chief School Admin .... Mark Miller
- Number of schools 3
- Grade plan K-12
- Enrollment 1,635
- Attendance rate, '05-06 .... 93.3%
- Dropout rate 0.7%
- Students per teacher 10.3
- Per pupil expenditure $12,143
- Median faculty salary $56,130
- Median administrator salary $108,543
- Grade 12 enrollment 204
- High school graduation rate 97.6%

Assessment test results
(percent scoring at proficient or advanced level)
	Language	Math
NJASK-Grade 3	83.9%	85.3%
GEPA-Grade 8	75.8%	69.6%
HSPA-High School	91.2%	78.2%

SAT score averages
Pct tested	Math	Verbal	Writing
75%	524	506	499

Teacher Qualifications
- Avg. years of experience 11
- Highly-qualified teachers
  - one subject/all subjects 100%/100%
- With emergency credentials 0.8%

No Child Left Behind
- AYP, 2005-06 .... Meets Standards

Municipal Finance

State Aid Programs, 2008
- Total aid $1,162,667
  - CMPTRA 178,351
  - Energy tax receipts 968,823
  - Garden State Trust 15,493

General Budget, 2007
- Total tax levy $18,751,963
  - County levy 2,984,432
    - County taxes 2,438,527
    - County library 207,878
    - County health 80,370
    - County open space 257,657
  - School levy 10,354,936
  - Muni. levy 5,412,595
- Misc. revenues 3,517,405

Taxes	2005	2006	2007
General tax rate per $100	4.23	4.58	4.84
County equalization ratio	68.09	58.28	53.04
Net valuation taxable	$379,632,623	$379,122,400	$388,020,571
State equalized value	$651,394,343	$719,329,158	$809,415,251

Bergen County

North Arlington Borough

Demographics & Socio-Economic Characteristics
(2000 US Census, except as noted)

Population
1980*	16,587
1990*	13,790
2000	15,181
Male	7,137
Female	8,044
2006 (estimate)*	15,077
Population density	5,843.8

Race & Hispanic Origin, 2000
Race
White	13,603
Black/African American	70
American Indian/Alaska Native	22
Asian	852
Native Hawaiian/Pacific Islander	2
Other race	348
Two or more races	284
Hispanic origin, total	1,605
Mexican	56
Puerto Rican	390
Cuban	241
Other Hispanic	918

Age & Nativity, 2000
Under 5 years	686
18 years and over	12,445
21 years and over	12,003
65 years and over	2,942
85 years and over	361
Median age	40.9
Native-born	11,880
Foreign-born	3,301

Educational Attainment, 2000
Population 25 years and over	11,252
Less than 9th grade	6.9%
High school grad or higher	82.1%
Bachelor's degree or higher	19.5%
Graduate degree	5.2%

Income & Poverty, 1999
Per capita income	$24,441
Median household income	$51,787
Median family income	$62,483
Persons in poverty	773
H'holds receiving public assistance	114
H'holds receiving social security	2,254

Households, 2000
Total households	6,392
With persons under 18	1,669
With persons over 65	2,186
Family households	4,129
Single-person households	1,977
Persons per household	2.37
Persons per family	3.00

Labor & Employment
Total civilian labor force, 2006**	8,335
Unemployment rate	4.0%
Total civilian labor force, 2000	7,851
Unemployment rate	4.0%

Employed persons 16 years and over by occupation, 2000
Managers & professionals	2,262
Service occupations	1,047
Sales & office occupations	2,654
Farming, fishing & forestry	0
Construction & maintenance	637
Production & transportation	939
Self-employed persons	301

* US Census Bureau
** New Jersey Department of Labor

See Introduction for an explanation of all data sources.

General Information
Borough of North Arlington
214 Ridge Rd
North Arlington, NJ 07031
201-991-6060

Website	www.northarlington.org
Year of incorporation	1896
Land/water area (sq. miles)	2.58/0.04
Form of government	Borough

Government
Legislative Districts
US Congressional	9
State Legislative	36

Local Officials, 2008
Mayor	Peter Massa
Manager	Terence M. Wall
Clerk	Terence M. Wall (Actg)
Finance Dir	Joseph Iannaconi Jr
Tax Assessor	Denis McGuire
Tax Collector	Joseph Iannaconi Jr
Attorney	Anthony D'Elia
Building	Robert Kairys
Planning	Joseph Bianchi
Engineering	Michael Neglia
Public Works	James McCabe
Police Chief	Louis Ghione
Emerg/Fire Director	Brian Heinzmann

Housing & Construction
Housing Units, 2000*
Total	6,529
Median rent	$763
Median SF home value	$183,300

Permits for New Residential Construction
	Units	Value
Total, 2007	2	$193,300
Single family	0	$0
Total, 2006	0	$202,600
Single family	0	$202,600

Real Property Valuation, 2007
	Parcels	Valuation
Total	4,078	$811,949,500
Vacant	56	11,312,000
Residential	3,745	668,415,300
Commercial	186	69,155,000
Industrial	54	25,807,200
Apartments	37	37,260,000
Farm land	0	0
Farm homestead	0	0

Average Property Value & Tax, 2007
Residential value	$178,482
Property tax	$7,604
Tax credit/rebate	$1,107

Public Library
North Arlington Public Library
210 Ridge Rd
North Arlington, NJ 07031
201-955-5640

Director.............. Stephanie M. Burke

Library statistics, 2006
Population served	15,181
Full-time/total staff	2/7

	Total	Per capita
Holdings	94,654	6.24
Revenues	$539,633	$35.55
Expenditures	$535,696	$35.29
Annual visits	75,600	4.98
Internet terminals/annual users	9/34,400	

Public Safety
Number of officers, 2006		32

Crime	2005	2006
Total crimes	268	266
Violent	13	15
Murder	0	0
Rape	1	3
Robbery	5	4
Aggravated assault	7	8
Non-violent	255	251
Burglary	41	35
Larceny	180	187
Vehicle theft	34	29
Domestic violence	111	100
Arson	3	1
Total crime rate	17.6	17.5
Violent	0.9	1.0
Non-violent	16.7	16.5

Public School District
(for school year 2006-07 except as noted)

North Arlington School District
222 Ridge Rd
North Arlington, NJ 07031
201-991-6800

Superintendent	Oliver Stringham
Number of schools	5
Grade plan	K-12
Enrollment	1,577
Attendance rate, '05-06	94.7%
Dropout rate	1.3%
Students per teacher	11.7
Per pupil expenditure	$12,157
Median faculty salary	$46,500
Median administrator salary	$121,513
Grade 12 enrollment	132
High school graduation rate	94.8%

Assessment test results
(percent scoring at proficient or advanced level)
	Language	Math
NJASK-Grade 3	90.1%	93.0%
GEPA-Grade 8	74.3%	72.9%
HSPA-High School	83.1%	66.2%

SAT score averages
Pct tested	Math	Verbal	Writing
71%	490	452	450

Teacher Qualifications
Avg. years of experience	8
Highly-qualified teachers one subject/all subjects	100%/100%
With emergency credentials	0.0%

No Child Left Behind
AYP, 2005-06 .... Meets Standards

Municipal Finance
State Aid Programs, 2008
Total aid	$1,361,041
CMPTRA	258,017
Energy tax receipts	1,103,024
Garden State Trust	0

General Budget, 2007
Total tax levy	$34,621,226
County levy	3,127,738
County taxes	2,955,638
County library	0
County health	0
County open space	172,100
School levy	18,855,448
Muni. levy	12,638,041
Misc. revenues	6,805,600

Taxes	2005	2006	2007
General tax rate per $100	3.65	3.76	4.27
County equalization ratio	61	52.18	47.41
Net valuation taxable	$805,206,400	$809,453,350	$812,629,529
State equalized value	$1,543,132,235	$1,708,214,379	$1,806,215,942

©2008 Information Publications, Inc. All rights reserved. Photocopying prohibited. For additional copies, contact the publisher at www.informationpublications.com or (877)544-INFO (4636)

North Bergen Township — Hudson County

Demographics & Socio-Economic Characteristics
(2000 US Census, except as noted)

Population
1980*	47,019
1990*	48,414
2000	58,092
Male	27,758
Female	30,334
2006 (estimate)*	57,237
Population density	11,007.1

Race & Hispanic Origin, 2000
Race
White	39,131
Black/African American	1,581
American Indian/Alaska Native	235
Asian	3,756
Native Hawaiian/Pacific Islander	28
Other race	9,023
Two or more races	4,338
Hispanic origin, total	33,260
Mexican	553
Puerto Rican	4,535
Cuban	7,635
Other Hispanic	20,537

Age & Nativity, 2000
Under 5 years	3,713
18 years and over	44,887
21 years and over	42,885
65 years and over	8,028
85 years and over	1,220
Median age	35.9
Native-born	30,990
Foreign-born	27,216

Educational Attainment, 2000
Population 25 years and over	39,719
Less than 9th grade	15.4%
High school grad or higher	68.7%
Bachelor's degree or higher	19.6%
Graduate degree	7.1%

Income & Poverty, 1999
Per capita income	$20,058
Median household income	$40,844
Median family income	$46,172
Persons in poverty	6,397
H'holds receiving public assistance	669
H'holds receiving social security	5,701

Households, 2000
Total households	21,236
With persons under 18	7,481
With persons over 65	5,809
Family households	14,242
Single-person households	5,890
Persons per household	2.70
Persons per family	3.33

Labor & Employment
Total civilian labor force, 2006**	27,384
Unemployment rate	5.5%
Total civilian labor force, 2000	27,526
Unemployment rate	8.1%

Employed persons 16 years and over by occupation, 2000
Managers & professionals	6,796
Service occupations	3,653
Sales & office occupations	7,958
Farming, fishing & forestry	29
Construction & maintenance	1,685
Production & transportation	5,168
Self-employed persons	1,257

* US Census Bureau
** New Jersey Department of Labor
§ State Fiscal Year July 1–June 30

General Information
Township of North Bergen
4233 Kennedy Blvd
North Bergen, NJ 07047
201-392-2000

Website	www.northbergen.org
Year of incorporation	1843
Land/water area (sq. miles)	5.20/0.42
Form of government	Commission

Government
Legislative Districts
US Congressional	9, 13
State Legislative	32

Local Officials, 2008
Mayor	Nicholas Sacco
Manager	Christopher Pianese
Clerk	Carol Ann Fontana
Finance Dir	Robert Pittfield
Tax Assessor	Paul Sadlon
Tax Collector	Denise Zambardino
Attorney	Herb Klitzner
Building	Brian Ribbaro
Planning	Brian Chewcaskie
Engineering	Dereck McGrath
Public Works	Frank Gargiulo
Police Chief	William Galvin
Emerg/Fire Director	Michael DeOrio

Housing & Construction
Housing Units, 2000*
Total	22,009
Median rent	$733
Median SF home value	$162,600

Permits for New Residential Construction
	Units	Value
Total, 2007	0	$0
Single family	0	$0
Total, 2006	32	$3,002,270
Single family	11	$1,587,770

Real Property Valuation, 2007
	Parcels	Valuation
Total	11,555	$2,475,206,100
Vacant	412	92,345,000
Residential	10,070	1,346,687,400
Commercial	694	583,305,400
Industrial	211	278,985,500
Apartments	168	173,882,800
Farm land	0	0
Farm homestead	0	0

Average Property Value & Tax, 2007
Residential value	$133,733
Property tax	$5,420
Tax credit/rebate	$915

Public Library
North Bergen Public Library
8411 Bergenline Ave
North Bergen, NJ 07047
201-869-4715

Director	Sai Rao

Library statistics, 2006
Population served	58,092
Full-time/total staff	4/8

	Total	Per capita
Holdings	231,954	3.99
Revenues	$1,218,750	$20.98
Expenditures	$1,002,158	$17.25
Annual visits	451,741	7.78
Internet terminals/annual users	45/51,870	

Public Safety
Number of officers, 2006 ... 120

Crime	2005	2006
Total crimes	1,342	1,035
Violent	132	121
Murder	0	1
Rape	12	4
Robbery	71	58
Aggravated assault	49	58
Non-violent	1,210	914
Burglary	189	166
Larceny	791	562
Vehicle theft	230	186
Domestic violence	571	597
Arson	5	1
Total crime rate	23.1	17.9
Violent	2.3	2.1
Non-violent	20.9	15.8

Public School District
(for school year 2006-07 except as noted)

North Bergen School District
7317 Kennedy Blvd
North Bergen, NJ 07047
201-295-2706

Superintendent	Robert Dandorph
Number of schools	7
Grade plan	K-12
Enrollment	7,509
Attendance rate, '05-06	94.1%
Dropout rate	2.1%
Students per teacher	13.1
Per pupil expenditure	$11,843
Median faculty salary	$60,275
Median administrator salary	$125,400
Grade 12 enrollment	426
High school graduation rate	90.6%

Assessment test results
(percent scoring at proficient or advanced level)
	Language	Math
NJASK-Grade 3	83.1%	90.9%
GEPA-Grade 8	75.7%	73.2%
HSPA-High School	87.1%	72.2%

SAT score averages
Pct tested	Math	Verbal	Writing
83%	449	434	432

Teacher Qualifications
Avg. years of experience	9
Highly-qualified teachers one subject/all subjects	99.0%/98.5%
With emergency credentials	0.2%

No Child Left Behind
AYP, 2005-06	Meets Standards

Municipal Finance§
State Aid Programs, 2008
Total aid	$8,757,880
CMPTRA	4,718,401
Energy tax receipts	4,039,479
Garden State Trust	0

General Budget, 2007
Total tax levy	$104,855,198
County levy	20,422,819
County taxes	19,917,551
County library	0
County health	0
County open space	505,268
School levy	38,722,318
Muni. levy	45,710,062
Misc. revenues	32,170,611

Taxes
	2005	2006	2007
General tax rate per $100	4.071	4.159	4.23
County equalization ratio	60.42	51.29	49.57
Net valuation taxable	$2,459,049,775	$2,487,457,100	$2,479,379,114
State equalized value	$4,794,403,929	$5,022,333,362	$5,487,571,552

Middlesex County — North Brunswick Township

Demographics & Socio-Economic Characteristics
(2000 US Census, except as noted)

Population
- 1980* 22,220
- 1990* 31,287
- 2000 36,287
  - Male 18,021
  - Female 18,266
- 2006 (estimate)* 39,852
- Population density 3,315.5

Race & Hispanic Origin, 2000
Race
- White 22,763
- Black/African American 5,542
- American Indian/Alaska Native 63
- Asian 5,152
- Native Hawaiian/Pacific Islander 10
- Other race 1,707
- Two or more races 1,050
- Hispanic origin, total 3,775
  - Mexican 522
  - Puerto Rican 1,316
  - Cuban 161
  - Other Hispanic 1,776

Age & Nativity, 2000
- Under 5 years 2,437
- 18 years and over 27,934
- 21 years and over 26,806
- 65 years and over 3,615
- 85 years and over 328
  - Median age 35.4
- Native-born 27,424
- Foreign-born 8,863

Educational Attainment, 2000
- Population 25 years and over 25,089
- Less than 9th grade 4.9%
- High school grad or higher 85.8%
- Bachelor's degree or higher 37.0%
- Graduate degree 14.3%

Income & Poverty, 1999
- Per capita income $28,431
- Median household income $61,325
- Median family income $70,812
- Persons in poverty 1,661
- H'holds receiving public assistance 377
- H'holds receiving social security 2,932

Households, 2000
- Total households 13,635
  - With persons under 18 4,817
  - With persons over 65 2,772
  - Family households 9,363
  - Single-person households 3,339
- Persons per household 2.58
- Persons per family 3.12

Labor & Employment
- Total civilian labor force, 2006** 22,635
  - Unemployment rate 4.2%
- Total civilian labor force, 2000 19,586
  - Unemployment rate 3.6%

Employed persons 16 years and over by occupation, 2000
- Managers & professionals 8,736
- Service occupations 1,763
- Sales & office occupations 5,365
- Farming, fishing & forestry 0
- Construction & maintenance 990
- Production & transportation 2,022
- Self-employed persons 816

* US Census Bureau
** New Jersey Department of Labor
§ State Fiscal Year July 1–June 30

See Introduction for an explanation of all data sources.

General Information
Township of North Brunswick
710 Hermann Rd
North Brunswick, NJ 08902
732-247-0922
- Website .... www.northbrunswickonline.com
- Year of incorporation 1779
- Land/water area (sq. miles) 12.02/0.23
- Form of government ... Mayor-Council-Admin

Government
Legislative Districts
- US Congressional 12
- State Legislative 17

Local Officials, 2008
- Mayor .... Francis Womack III
- Manager .... Robert Lombard
- Clerk .... Lisa Russo
- Finance Dir .... Ronald Amorino
- Tax Assessor .... Dianne Walker
- Tax Collector .... Laurie Hammarstrom
- Attorney .... Ronald Gordon
- Building .... Tom Paun
- Planning .... Tom Vigna
- Engineering .... CME Associates
- Public Works .... Glenn Sandor
- Police Chief .... Joseph Battaglia
- Emerg/Fire Director .... Craig Snediker

Housing & Construction
Housing Units, 2000*
- Total 13,932
- Median rent $907
- Median SF home value $179,400

Permits for New Residential Construction

	Units	Value
Total, 2007	28	$3,963,050
Single family	28	$3,963,050
Total, 2006	12	$1,896,476
Single family	12	$1,896,476

Real Property Valuation, 2007

	Parcels	Valuation
Total	11,036	$2,507,038,600
Vacant	929	55,827,300
Residential	9,615	1,513,303,500
Commercial	373	379,944,300
Industrial	57	351,718,700
Apartments	36	204,271,600
Farm land	18	177,600
Farm homestead	8	1,795,600

Average Property Value & Tax, 2007
- Residential value $157,446
- Property tax $6,662
- Tax credit/rebate $1,064

Public Library
North Brunswick Public Library
880 Hermann Rd
North Brunswick, NJ 08902
732-246-3545
- Director .... Cheryl McBride

Library statistics, 2006
- Population served 36,287
- Full-time/total staff 6/15

	Total	Per capita
Holdings	92,019	2.54
Revenues	$1,381,585	$38.07
Expenditures	$1,269,499	$34.98
Annual visits	176,021	4.85
Internet terminals/annual users		7/31,019

Public Safety
Number of officers, 2006 85

Crime	2005	2006
Total crimes	1,065	940
Violent	88	90
Murder	1	0
Rape	6	1
Robbery	44	34
Aggravated assault	37	55
Non-violent	977	850
Burglary	237	204
Larceny	642	582
Vehicle theft	98	64
Domestic violence	162	160
Arson	6	7
Total crime rate	27.4	23.7
Violent	2.3	2.3
Non-violent	25.1	21.4

Public School District
(for school year 2006-07 except as noted)

North Brunswick Township School District
Old Georges Rd, PO Box 6016
North Brunswick, NJ 08902
732-289-3030
- Superintendent .... Brian Zychowski
- Number of schools 6
- Grade plan K-12
- Enrollment 5,433
- Attendance rate, '05-06 .... 94.1%
- Dropout rate 2.5%
- Students per teacher 11.4
- Per pupil expenditure $12,570
- Median faculty salary $53,030
- Median administrator salary $103,394
- Grade 12 enrollment 419
- High school graduation rate 89.7%

Assessment test results
(percent scoring at proficient or advanced level)

	Language	Math
NJASK-Grade 3	88.2%	91.8%
GEPA-Grade 8	78.6%	75.8%
HSPA-High School	87.0%	76.7%

SAT score averages

Pct tested	Math	Verbal	Writing
78%	524	495	489

Teacher Qualifications
- Avg. years of experience 7
- Highly-qualified teachers
  - one subject/all subjects 100%/100%
- With emergency credentials 0.0%

No Child Left Behind
- AYP, 2005-06 .... Meets Standards

Municipal Finance§
State Aid Programs, 2008
- Total aid $5,764,182
- CMPTRA 1,521,125
- Energy tax receipts 4,238,404
- Garden State Trust 0

General Budget, 2007
- Total tax levy $106,224,654
- County levy 13,837,609
- County taxes 12,389,120
- County library 0
- County health 0
- County open space 1,448,489
- School levy 68,687,700
- Muni. levy 23,699,345
- Misc. revenues 20,856,106

Taxes

	2005	2006	2007
General tax rate per $100	3.74	4.07	4.24
County equalization ratio	69.52	62.05	54.2
Net valuation taxable	$2,462,025,809	$2,473,061,200	$2,510,462,561
State equalized value	$3,967,809,523	$4,566,652,231	$5,140,798,141

The New Jersey Municipal Data Book

North Caldwell Borough
Essex County

Demographics & Socio-Economic Characteristics
(2000 US Census, except as noted)

Population
1980*	5,832
1990*	6,706
2000	7,375
Male	3,999
Female	3,376
2006 (estimate)*	7,207
Population density	2,410.4

Race & Hispanic Origin, 2000
Race
White	5,873
Black/African American	1,070
American Indian/Alaska Native	2
Asian	347
Native Hawaiian/Pacific Islander	0
Other race	19
Two or more races	64
Hispanic origin, total	159
Mexican	19
Puerto Rican	21
Cuban	39
Other Hispanic	80

Age & Nativity, 2000
Under 5 years	431
18 years and over	5,673
21 years and over	5,441
65 years and over	801
85 years and over	48
Median age	37.3
Native-born	6,740
Foreign-born	635

Educational Attainment, 2000
Population 25 years and over	4,919
Less than 9th grade	0.7%
High school grad or higher	92.6%
Bachelor's degree or higher	58.2%
Graduate degree	29.1%

Income & Poverty, 1999
Per capita income	$48,249
Median household income	$117,395
Median family income	$125,465
Persons in poverty	75
H'holds receiving public assistance	0
H'holds receiving social security	507

Households, 2000
Total households	2,070
With persons under 18	904
With persons over 65	538
Family households	1,835
Single-person households	198
Persons per household	3.02
Persons per family	3.23

Labor & Employment
Total civilian labor force, 2006**	3,394
Unemployment rate	3.0%
Total civilian labor force, 2000	3,196
Unemployment rate	2.4%

Employed persons 16 years and over by occupation, 2000
Managers & professionals	1,967
Service occupations	141
Sales & office occupations	854
Farming, fishing & forestry	0
Construction & maintenance	79
Production & transportation	77
Self-employed persons	320

* US Census Bureau
** New Jersey Department of Labor

General Information
Borough of North Caldwell
Gould Ave
North Caldwell, NJ 07006
973-228-6410

Website	www.northcaldwell.org
Year of incorporation	1898
Land/water area (sq. miles)	2.99/0.00
Form of government	Borough

Government
Legislative Districts
US Congressional	11
State Legislative	27

Local Officials, 2008
Mayor	Melvin Levine
Manager	Joseph Kunz
Clerk	Francine Paserchia
Finance Dir.	Richard Mondelli
Tax Assessor	George Librizzi
Tax Collector	Richard Mondelli
Attorney	David Paris
Building	Ronald Young
Comm Dev/Planning	NA
Engineering	Frank Zichelli
Public Works	NA
Police Chief	Joseph Clark
Emerg/Fire Director	David Hicock

Housing & Construction
Housing Units, 2000*
Total	2,108
Median rent	$1,759
Median SF home value	$399,000

Permits for New Residential Construction
	Units	Value
Total, 2007	12	$3,227,400
Single family	12	$3,227,400
Total, 2006	9	$4,939,121
Single family	9	$4,939,121

Real Property Valuation, 2007
	Parcels	Valuation
Total	2,179	$370,767,800
Vacant	56	9,677,700
Residential	2,107	354,687,700
Commercial	12	5,563,900
Industrial	2	739,600
Apartments	0	0
Farm land	1	4,000
Farm homestead	1	94,900

Average Property Value & Tax, 2007
Residential value	$168,303
Property tax	$12,375
Tax credit/rebate	$1,315

Public Library
No public municipal library

Library statistics, 2006
Population served	NA
Full-time/total staff	NA/NA

	Total	Per capita
Holdings	NA	NA
Revenues	NA	NA
Expenditures	NA	NA
Annual visits	NA	NA
Internet terminals/annual users	NA/NA	

Taxes
	2005	2006	2007
General tax rate per $100	7.22	7.25	7.36
County equalization ratio	26.32	23.61	22.19
Net valuation taxable	$357,412,392	$366,184,776	$370,917,600
State equalized value	$1,513,817,840	$1,650,375,884	$1,747,406,162

Public Safety
Number of officers, 2006 16

Crime	2005	2006
Total crimes	61	51
Violent	5	1
Murder	0	0
Rape	0	0
Robbery	0	1
Aggravated assault	5	0
Non-violent	56	50
Burglary	7	8
Larceny	47	39
Vehicle theft	2	3
Domestic violence	2	5
Arson	0	2
Total crime rate	8.3	7.0
Violent	0.7	0.1
Non-violent	7.6	6.9

Public School District
(for school year 2006-07 except as noted)

North Caldwell School District
132 Gould Ave
North Caldwell, NJ 07006
973-228-6439

Superintendent	Linda Freda
Number of schools	2
Grade plan	K-6
Enrollment	648
Attendance rate, '05-06	95.9%
Dropout rate	NA
Students per teacher	10.0
Per pupil expenditure	$12,830
Median faculty salary	$48,227
Median administrator salary	$93,000
Grade 12 enrollment	NA
High school graduation rate	NA

Assessment test results
(percent scoring at proficient or advanced level)
	Language	Math
NJASK-Grade 3	90.4%	92.6%
GEPA-Grade 8	NA	NA
HSPA-High School	NA	NA

SAT score averages
Pct tested	Math	Verbal	Writing
NA	NA	NA	NA

Teacher Qualifications
Avg. years of experience	6
Highly-qualified teachers one subject/all subjects	100%/100%
With emergency credentials	0.0%

No Child Left Behind
AYP, 2005-06 ..... Meets Standards

Municipal Finance
State Aid Programs, 2008
Total aid	$593,979
CMPTRA	50,112
Energy tax receipts	543,867
Garden State Trust	0

General Budget, 2007
Total tax levy	$27,273,082
County levy	6,569,318
County taxes	6,400,497
County library	0
County health	0
County open space	168,821
School levy	16,162,502
Muni. levy	4,541,261
Misc. revenues	2,908,866

Passaic County
North Haledon Borough

Demographics & Socio-Economic Characteristics
(2000 US Census, except as noted)

Population
- 1980* 8,177
- 1990* 7,987
- 2000 7,920
  - Male 3,737
  - Female 4,183
- 2006 (estimate)* 9,039
  - Population density 2,627.6

Race & Hispanic Origin, 2000
Race
- White 7,526
- Black/African American 114
- American Indian/Alaska Native 5
- Asian 79
- Native Hawaiian/Pacific Islander 0
- Other race 75
- Two or more races 121
- Hispanic origin, total 308
  - Mexican 14
  - Puerto Rican 59
  - Cuban 36
  - Other Hispanic 199

Age & Nativity, 2000
- Under 5 years 436
- 18 years and over 6,360
- 21 years and over 6,055
- 65 years and over 1,551
- 85 years and over 246
  - Median age 40.5
- Native-born 6,858
- Foreign-born 1,062

Educational Attainment, 2000
- Population 25 years and over 5,580
- Less than 9th grade 4.9%
- High school grad or higher 88.1%
- Bachelor's degree or higher 33.8%
- Graduate degree 9.7%

Income & Poverty, 1999
- Per capita income $30,322
- Median household income $74,700
- Median family income $80,936
- Persons in poverty 298
- H'holds receiving public assistance . 21
- H'holds receiving social security .1,002

Households, 2000
- Total households 2,626
  - With persons under 18 807
  - With persons over 65 977
  - Family households 2,076
  - Single-person households 465
- Persons per household 2.79
- Persons per family 3.18

Labor & Employment
- Total civilian labor force, 2006** . 4,293
  - Unemployment rate 2.6%
- Total civilian labor force, 2000 .. 4,383
  - Unemployment rate 3.5%

Employed persons 16 years and over by occupation, 2000
- Managers & professionals 1,818
- Service occupations 725
- Sales & office occupations 996
- Farming, fishing & forestry 8
- Construction & maintenance 398
- Production & transportation 283
- Self-employed persons 241

* US Census Bureau
** New Jersey Department of Labor

See Introduction for an explanation of all data sources.

General Information
Borough of North Haledon
103 Overlook Ave
North Haledon, NJ 07508
973-427-7793
- Website .... www.northhaledon.com
- Year of incorporation 1901
- Land/water area (sq. miles) ... 3.44/0.03
- Form of government .... Borough

Government
Legislative Districts
- US Congressional 8
- State Legislative 35

Local Officials, 2008
- Mayor .... Randolph George
- Manager/Admin .... NA
- Clerk .... Renate Elatab
- Finance Dir .... Laura Leibowitz
- Tax Assessor .... Michael Barker
- Tax Collector .... NA
- Attorney .... Michael DeMarco
- Building .... Philip Cheff
- Planning .... Michael Kauker
- Engineering .... Boswell McClave
- Public Works .... NA
- Police Chief .... Robert Bracco
- Emerg/Fire Director ..... A.J. Ricciardi

Housing & Construction
Housing Units, 2000*
- Total 2,675
- Median rent $891
- Median SF home value $237,900

Permits for New Residential Construction

	Units	Value
Total, 2007	7	$1,195,621
Single family	7	$1,195,621
Total, 2006	9	$2,671,520
Single family	9	$2,671,520

Real Property Valuation, 2007

	Parcels	Valuation
Total	3,078	$441,542,300
Vacant	70	3,721,600
Residential	2,917	418,440,600
Commercial	83	16,998,300
Industrial	6	2,147,700
Apartments	0	0
Farm land	1	9,300
Farm homestead	1	224,800

Average Property Value & Tax, 2007
- Residential value $143,477
- Property tax $8,312
- Tax credit/rebate $1,274

Public Library
North Haledon Public Library
129 Overlook Ave
North Haledon, NJ 07508
973-427-6213
- Director .... Susan Serico

Library statistics, 2006
- Population served 7,920
- Full-time/total staff 1/2

	Total	Per capita
Holdings	29,973	3.78
Revenues	$447,776	$56.54
Expenditures	$382,807	$48.33
Annual visits	14,708	1.86
Internet terminals/annual users		6/1,590

Public Safety
Number of officers, 2006 18

Crime	2005	2006
Total crimes	52	66
Violent	2	6
Murder	0	0
Rape	0	0
Robbery	0	1
Aggravated assault	2	5
Non-violent	50	60
Burglary	14	24
Larceny	35	34
Vehicle theft	1	2
Domestic violence	54	38
Arson	1	0
Total crime rate	5.9	7.3
Violent	0.2	0.7
Non-violent	5.7	6.6

Public School District
(for school year 2006-07 except as noted)

North Haledon School District
515 High Mountain Rd
North Haledon, NJ 07508
973-427-8993

- Chief School Admin ...... Donna Cardiello
- Number of schools 2
- Grade plan K-8
- Enrollment 662
- Attendance rate, '05-06 .... 95.9%
- Dropout rate .... NA
- Students per teacher 11.9
- Per pupil expenditure $10,063
- Median faculty salary $52,420
- Median administrator salary .. $121,001
- Grade 12 enrollment .... NA
- High school graduation rate .... NA

Assessment test results
(percent scoring at proficient or advanced level)

	Language	Math
NJASK-Grade 3	85.1%	86.6%
GEPA-Grade 8	83.3%	79.2%
HSPA-High School	NA	NA

SAT score averages

Pct tested	Math	Verbal	Writing
NA	NA	NA	NA

Teacher Qualifications
- Avg. years of experience 9
- Highly-qualified teachers
  - one subject/all subjects 100%/100%
- With emergency credentials 0.0%

No Child Left Behind
- AYP, 2005-06 .... Meets Standards

Municipal Finance
State Aid Programs, 2008
- Total aid $689,523
  - CMPTRA 149,943
  - Energy tax receipts 534,325
  - Garden State Trust 4,127

General Budget, 2007
- Total tax levy $25,602,542
  - County levy 7,369,531
    - County taxes 7,220,551
    - County library 0
    - County health 0
    - County open space 148,980
  - School levy 11,365,661
  - Muni. levy 6,867,350
- Misc. revenues 3,306,630

Taxes	2005	2006	2007
General tax rate per $100	5.16	5.66	5.8
County equalization ratio	35.51	32.08	29.69
Net valuation taxable	$411,634,453	$437,451,400	$441,938,062
State equalized value	$1,283,149,791	$1,473,804,323	$1,561,719,312

North Hanover Township
Burlington County

Demographics & Socio-Economic Characteristics
(2000 US Census, except as noted)

Population
1980*	9,050
1990*	9,994
2000	7,347
Male	3,682
Female	3,665
2006 (estimate)*	7,577
Population density	437.0

Race & Hispanic Origin, 2000
Race
White	5,924
Black/African American	805
American Indian/Alaska Native	35
Asian	156
Native Hawaiian/Pacific Islander	4
Other race	160
Two or more races	263
Hispanic origin, total	423
Mexican	107
Puerto Rican	154
Cuban	21
Other Hispanic	141

Age & Nativity, 2000
Under 5 years	818
18 years and over	4,879
21 years and over	4,646
65 years and over	452
85 years and over	17
Median age	28.7
Native-born	6,967
Foreign-born	358

Educational Attainment, 2000
Population 25 years and over	4,156
Less than 9th grade	2.9%
High school grad or higher	87.0%
Bachelor's degree or higher	13.3%
Graduate degree	3.3%

Income & Poverty, 1999
Per capita income	$17,580
Median household income	$39,988
Median family income	$45,553
Persons in poverty	387
H'holds receiving public assistance	58
H'holds receiving social security	426

Households, 2000
Total households	2,498
With persons under 18	1,351
With persons over 65	350
Family households	2,020
Single-person households	388
Persons per household	2.94
Persons per family	3.29

Labor & Employment
Total civilian labor force, 2006**	3,497
Unemployment rate	5.1%
Total civilian labor force, 2000	3,000
Unemployment rate	4.8%

Employed persons 16 years and over by occupation, 2000
Managers & professionals	767
Service occupations	389
Sales & office occupations	827
Farming, fishing & forestry	27
Construction & maintenance	379
Production & transportation	467
Self-employed persons	236

* US Census Bureau
** New Jersey Department of Labor

General Information
Township of North Hanover
41 Schoolhouse Rd
Jacobstown, NJ 08562
609-758-2522

Website	www.northhanover.us
Year of incorporation	1905
Land/water area (sq. miles)	17.34/0.04
Form of government	Township

Government
Legislative Districts
US Congressional	3
State Legislative	30

Local Officials, 2008
Mayor	Michael Moscatiello
Manager/Admin	NA
Clerk	Monica L. Zur
Finance Dir	Kathleen Phelan
Tax Assessor	Donald Kosul
Tax Collector	Mary Picariello
Attorney	Mark Roselli
Building	Jeffrey Jones
Comm Dev/Planning	NA
Engineering	Remington & Vernick
Public Works	Wayne Wharton
Police Chief	Mark Keubler
Emerg/Fire Director	Chris Herbert

Housing & Construction
Housing Units, 2000*
Total	2,670
Median rent	$648
Median SF home value	$175,000

Permits for New Residential Construction
	Units	Value
Total, 2007	11	$2,019,932
Single family	11	$2,019,932
Total, 2006	15	$2,873,959
Single family	15	$2,873,959

Real Property Valuation, 2007
	Parcels	Valuation
Total	1,419	$231,917,777
Vacant	122	5,054,100
Residential	952	165,948,150
Commercial	66	29,440,250
Industrial	0	0
Apartments	10	7,346,300
Farm land	170	2,871,377
Farm homestead	99	21,257,600

Average Property Value & Tax, 2007
Residential value	$178,122
Property tax	$5,117
Tax credit/rebate	$909

Public Library
No public municipal library

Library statistics, 2006
Population served	NA
Full-time/total staff	NA/NA

	Total	Per capita
Holdings	NA	NA
Revenues	NA	NA
Expenditures	NA	NA
Annual visits	NA	NA
Internet terminals/annual users	NA/NA	

Public Safety
Number of officers, 2006	9

Crime
	2005	2006
Total crimes	92	82
Violent	14	5
Murder	0	0
Rape	3	0
Robbery	3	2
Aggravated assault	8	3
Non-violent	78	77
Burglary	17	20
Larceny	52	51
Vehicle theft	9	6
Domestic violence	36	52
Arson	1	0
Total crime rate	12.1	10.8
Violent	1.8	0.7
Non-violent	10.3	10.1

Public School District
(for school year 2006-07 except as noted)

North Hanover Township School District
331 Monmouth Rd
Wrightstown, NJ 08562
609-723-3050

Superintendent	Richard J. Carson
Number of schools	4
Grade plan	K-6
Enrollment	1,046
Attendance rate, '05-06	94.9%
Dropout rate	NA
Students per teacher	9.1
Per pupil expenditure	$14,113
Median faculty salary	$52,146
Median administrator salary	$98,201
Grade 12 enrollment	NA
High school graduation rate	NA

Assessment test results
(percent scoring at proficient or advanced level)
	Language	Math
NJASK-Grade 3	78.9%	82.8%
GEPA-Grade 8	NA	NA
HSPA-High School	NA	NA

SAT score averages
Pct tested	Math	Verbal	Writing
NA	NA	NA	NA

Teacher Qualifications
Avg. years of experience	10
Highly-qualified teachers one subject/all subjects	100%/100%
With emergency credentials	1.0%

No Child Left Behind
AYP, 2005-06 ..... Meets Standards

Municipal Finance
State Aid Programs, 2008
Total aid	$960,770
CMPTRA	91,277
Energy tax receipts	869,493
Garden State Trust	0

General Budget, 2007
Total tax levy	$6,797,567
County levy	1,854,965
County taxes	1,537,020
County library	141,076
County health	0
County open space	176,869
School levy	4,252,351
Muni. levy	690,250
Misc. revenues	2,695,180

Taxes
	2005	2006	2007
General tax rate per $100	2.625	2.808	2.929
County equalization ratio	71.48	60.96	52.44
Net valuation taxable	$219,617,043	$222,902,650	$232,407,963
State equalized value	$360,264,178	$425,751,605	$455,320,108

Somerset County
North Plainfield Borough

Demographics & Socio-Economic Characteristics
(2000 US Census, except as noted)

Population
1980*	19,108
1990*	18,820
2000	21,103
Male	10,409
Female	10,694
2006 (estimate)*	21,738
Population density	7,791.4

Race & Hispanic Origin, 2000
Race
White	13,307
Black/African American	2,824
American Indian/Alaska Native	59
Asian	1,064
Native Hawaiian/Pacific Islander	17
Other race	2,887
Two or more races	945
Hispanic origin, total	6,916
Mexican	332
Puerto Rican	787
Cuban	93
Other Hispanic	5,704

Age & Nativity, 2000
Under 5 years	1,654
18 years and over	15,664
21 years and over	14,959
65 years and over	1,996
85 years and over	282
Median age	33.7
Native-born	14,123
Foreign-born	6,980

Educational Attainment, 2000
Population 25 years and over	13,863
Less than 9th grade	8.3%
High school grad or higher	80.7%
Bachelor's degree or higher	26.5%
Graduate degree	9.3%

Income & Poverty, 1999
Per capita income	$22,791
Median household income	$55,322
Median family income	$62,875
Persons in poverty	1,340
H'holds receiving public assistance	112
H'holds receiving social security	1,413

Households, 2000
Total households	7,202
With persons under 18	2,899
With persons over 65	1,410
Family households	5,086
Single-person households	1,673
Persons per household	2.90
Persons per family	3.40

Labor & Employment
Total civilian labor force, 2006**	12,921
Unemployment rate	4.7%
Total civilian labor force, 2000	11,554
Unemployment rate	5.1%

Employed persons 16 years and over by occupation, 2000
Managers & professionals	3,386
Service occupations	1,389
Sales & office occupations	2,908
Farming, fishing & forestry	29
Construction & maintenance	955
Production & transportation	2,300
Self-employed persons	561

‡ Branch of county library
* US Census Bureau
** New Jersey Department of Labor

See Introduction for an explanation of all data sources.

General Information
Borough of North Plainfield
263 Somerset St
North Plainfield, NJ 07060
908-769-2900

Website	www.northplainfield.org
Year of incorporation	1885
Land/water area (sq. miles)	2.79/0.00
Form of government	Mayor-Council

Government
Legislative Districts
US Congressional	7
State Legislative	22

Local Officials, 2008
Mayor	Janice Allen
Manager	David Hollod
Clerk	Gloria Pflueger
Finance Dir	Patrick DeBlasio
Tax Assessor	Barbara A. Flaherty
Tax Collector	Catherine L. Park
Attorney	Eric Bernstein
Building	John Kapp
Comm Dev/Planning	NA
Engineering	Daniel Swayze
Public Works	James Rodino
Police Chief	William Parenti
Emerg/Fire Director	William F. Eaton

Housing & Construction
Housing Units, 2000*
Total	7,393
Median rent	$828
Median SF home value	$150,100

Permits for New Residential Construction
	Units	Value
Total, 2007	1	$233,300
Single family	1	$233,300
Total, 2006	2	$466,600
Single family	2	$466,600

Real Property Valuation, 2007
	Parcels	Valuation
Total	5,340	$837,224,425
Vacant	86	2,957,500
Residential	4,973	654,089,250
Commercial	242	117,655,575
Industrial	3	1,505,800
Apartments	36	61,016,300
Farm land	0	0
Farm homestead	0	0

Average Property Value & Tax, 2007
Residential value	$131,528
Property tax	$7,260
Tax credit/rebate	$1,191

Public Library
North Plainfield Branch Library‡
6 Rockview Ave
North Plainfield, NJ 07060
908-755-7909

Director....................Richard Stevens

Library statistics, 2006
see Somerset County profile for library system statistics

Public Safety
Number of officers, 2006 ... 46

Crime	2005	2006
Total crimes	580	615
Violent	59	46
Murder	1	2
Rape	1	1
Robbery	41	33
Aggravated assault	16	10
Non-violent	521	569
Burglary	121	177
Larceny	342	340
Vehicle theft	58	52
Domestic violence	235	212
Arson	0	0
Total crime rate	27.4	28.5
Violent	2.8	2.1
Non-violent	24.7	26.3

Public School District
(for school year 2006-07 except as noted)

North Plainfield Borough School District
33 Mountain Ave
North Plainfield, NJ 07060
908-769-6060

Superintendent	Marilyn E. Birnbaum
Number of schools	5
Grade plan	K-12
Enrollment	3,130
Attendance rate, '05-06	94.7%
Dropout rate	0.3%
Students per teacher	9.7
Per pupil expenditure	$13,259
Median faculty salary	$49,690
Median administrator salary	$124,275
Grade 12 enrollment	215
High school graduation rate	95.9%

Assessment test results
(percent scoring at proficient or advanced level)
	Language	Math
NJASK-Grade 3	61.7%	66.6%
GEPA-Grade 8	62.6%	48.4%
HSPA-High School	76.7%	55.6%

SAT score averages
Pct tested	Math	Verbal	Writing
60%	465	449	448

Teacher Qualifications
Avg. years of experience	7
Highly-qualified teachers one subject/all subjects	100%/100%
With emergency credentials	0.4%

No Child Left Behind
AYP, 2005-06 .... Needs Improvement

Municipal Finance
State Aid Programs, 2008
Total aid	$1,880,288
CMPTRA	711,870
Energy tax receipts	1,168,418
Garden State Trust	0

General Budget, 2007
Total tax levy	$46,241,209
County levy	6,201,707
County taxes	5,015,786
County library	636,706
County health	0
County open space	549,214
School levy	27,610,051
Muni. levy	12,429,451
Misc. revenues	5,934,509

Taxes	2005	2006	2007
General tax rate per $100	4.82	5.17	5.52
County equalization ratio	61.71	52.02	45.89
Net valuation taxable	$837,171,163	$838,203,325	$837,790,034
State equalized value	$1,609,325,573	$1,827,181,828	$1,936,344,626

North Wildwood City
Cape May County

Demographics & Socio-Economic Characteristics
(2000 US Census, except as noted)

Population
1980*	4,714
1990*	5,017
2000	4,935
Male	2,369
Female	2,566
2006 (estimate)*	4,803
Population density	2,713.6

Race & Hispanic Origin, 2000
Race
White	4,768
Black/African American	40
American Indian/Alaska Native	4
Asian	28
Native Hawaiian/Pacific Islander	1
Other race	38
Two or more races	56
Hispanic origin, total	96
Mexican	3
Puerto Rican	64
Cuban	0
Other Hispanic	29

Age & Nativity, 2000
Under 5 years	195
18 years and over	4,086
21 years and over	3,956
65 years and over	1,168
85 years and over	112
Median age	47.2
Native-born	4,706
Foreign-born	229

Educational Attainment, 2000
Population 25 years and over	3,807
Less than 9th grade	5.1%
High school grad or higher	82.3%
Bachelor's degree or higher	13.4%
Graduate degree	3.8%

Income & Poverty, 1999
Per capita income	$19,656
Median household income	$32,582
Median family income	$46,250
Persons in poverty	575
H'holds receiving public assistance	67
H'holds receiving social security	991

Households, 2000
Total households	2,309
With persons under 18	476
With persons over 65	869
Family households	1,394
Single-person households	804
Persons per household	2.14
Persons per family	2.73

Labor & Employment
Total civilian labor force, 2006**	2,756
Unemployment rate	11.5%
Total civilian labor force, 2000	2,285
Unemployment rate	13.7%

Employed persons 16 years and over by occupation, 2000
Managers & professionals	561
Service occupations	466
Sales & office occupations	624
Farming, fishing & forestry	12
Construction & maintenance	200
Production & transportation	110
Self-employed persons	108

* US Census Bureau
** New Jersey Department of Labor

General Information
City of North Wildwood
901 Atlantic Ave
North Wildwood, NJ 08260
609-522-2030
Website .... www.northwildwood.com
Year of incorporation 1917
Land/water area (sq. miles) 1.77/0.36
Form of government .... City

Government
Legislative Districts
US Congressional	2
State Legislative	1

Local Officials, 2008
Mayor	William J. Henfey
Manager	Ray Townsend
Clerk	Janet Harkins
Finance Dir.	Ross Versaggi
Tax Assessor	Louis Belasco
Tax Collector	Todd Burkey
Attorney	William Kaufmann
Building	Glenn Franzoi
Comm Dev/Planning	NA
Engineering	Ralph Petrella
Public Works	Harry Wozunk
Police Chief	Robert Matteucci
Emerg/Fire Director	Paul Evangelista

Housing & Construction
Housing Units, 2000*
Total	7,411
Median rent	$634
Median SF home value	$129,600

Permits for New Residential Construction
	Units	Value
Total, 2007	70	$7,488,795
Single family	10	$3,359,055
Total, 2006	308	$43,209,450
Single family	55	$8,294,780

Real Property Valuation, 2007
	Parcels	Valuation
Total	7,511	$3,477,802,700
Vacant	148	76,613,200
Residential	7,040	2,940,213,200
Commercial	238	393,328,300
Industrial	0	0
Apartments	85	67,648,000
Farm land	0	0
Farm homestead	0	0

Average Property Value & Tax, 2007
Residential value	$417,644
Property tax	$3,046
Tax credit/rebate	$923

Public Library
No public municipal library

Library statistics, 2006
Population served	NA
Full-time/total staff	NA/NA

	Total	Per capita
Holdings	NA	NA
Revenues	NA	NA
Expenditures	NA	NA
Annual visits	NA	NA
Internet terminals/annual users	NA/NA	

Taxes
	2005	2006	2007
General tax rate per $100	2.56	0.7	0.73
County equalization ratio	47.32	162.08	122.73
Net valuation taxable	$794,912,099	$3,392,027,250	$3,478,546,249
State equalized value	$1,975,918,715	$2,764,535,854	$3,093,498,284

Public Safety
Number of officers, 2006 30

Crime	2005	2006
Total crimes	344	366
Violent	26	15
Murder	0	0
Rape	2	4
Robbery	7	3
Aggravated assault	17	8
Non-violent	318	351
Burglary	43	50
Larceny	273	295
Vehicle theft	2	6
Domestic violence	59	72
Arson	1	0
Total crime rate	71.7	76.6
Violent	5.4	3.1
Non-violent	66.2	73.5

Public School District
(for school year 2006-07 except as noted)

North Wildwood City School District
1201 Atlantic Ave
North Wildwood, NJ 08260
609-522-6885

Superintendent	Michael Buccialia
Number of schools	1
Grade plan	K-8
Enrollment	316
Attendance rate, '05-06	93.2%
Dropout rate	NA
Students per teacher	6.9
Per pupil expenditure	$20,024
Median faculty salary	$49,304
Median administrator salary	$87,825
Grade 12 enrollment	NA
High school graduation rate	NA

Assessment test results
(percent scoring at proficient or advanced level)
	Language	Math
NJASK-Grade 3	88.6%	94.3%
GEPA-Grade 8	74.4%	62.8%
HSPA-High School	NA	NA

SAT score averages
Pct tested	Math	Verbal	Writing
NA	NA	NA	NA

Teacher Qualifications
Avg. years of experience	14
Highly-qualified teachers one subject/all subjects	100%/100%
With emergency credentials	0.0%

No Child Left Behind
AYP, 2005-06 .... Meets Standards

Municipal Finance
State Aid Programs, 2008
Total aid	$502,474
CMPTRA	0
Energy tax receipts	502,474
Garden State Trust	0

General Budget, 2007
Total tax levy	$25,371,914
County levy	5,353,959
County taxes	4,254,015
County library	818,363
County health	0
County open space	281,581
School levy	6,366,769
Muni. levy	13,651,186
Misc. revenues	7,900,335

Atlantic County / Northfield City

Demographics & Socio-Economic Characteristics
(2000 US Census, except as noted)

Population
- 1980* 7,795
- 1990* 7,305
- 2000 7,725
  - Male 3,679
  - Female 4,046
- 2006 (estimate)* 8,003
  - Population density 2,333.2

Race & Hispanic Origin, 2000
Race
- White 7,070
- Black/African American 205
- American Indian/Alaska Native 8
- Asian 193
- Native Hawaiian/Pacific Islander 6
- Other race 140
- Two or more races 103
- Hispanic origin, total 338
  - Mexican 18
  - Puerto Rican 90
  - Cuban 14
  - Other Hispanic 216

Age & Nativity, 2000
- Under 5 years 417
- 18 years and over 5,755
- 21 years and over 5,578
- 65 years and over 1,373
- 85 years and over 182
  - Median age 40.4
- Native-born 7,284
- Foreign-born 441

Educational Attainment, 2000
- Population 25 years and over 5,374
- Less than 9th grade 3.4%
- High school grad or higher 87.5%
- Bachelor's degree or higher 22.5%
- Graduate degree 5.0%

Income & Poverty, 1999
- Per capita income $25,059
- Median household income $56,875
- Median family income $62,896
- Persons in poverty 420
- H'holds receiving public assistance ... 21
- H'holds receiving social security 897

Households, 2000
- Total households 2,824
  - With persons under 18 1,068
  - With persons over 65 879
  - Family households 2,110
  - Single-person households 597
  - Persons per household 2.66
  - Persons per family 3.11

Labor & Employment
- Total civilian labor force, 2006** .. 4,340
  - Unemployment rate 3.1%
- Total civilian labor force, 2000 3,947
  - Unemployment rate 3.3%

Employed persons 16 years and over by occupation, 2000
- Managers & professionals 1,171
- Service occupations 1,104
- Sales & office occupations 959
- Farming, fishing & forestry 0
- Construction & maintenance 307
- Production & transportation 277
- Self-employed persons 247

* US Census Bureau
** New Jersey Department of Labor

See Introduction for an explanation of all data sources.

General Information
City of Northfield
1600 Shore Rd
Northfield, NJ 08225
609-641-2832
- Website .... www.cityofnorthfield.org
- Year of incorporation 1905
- Land/water area (sq. miles) 3.43/0.02
- Form of government .... City

Government
Legislative Districts
- US Congressional 2
- State Legislative 2

Local Officials, 2008
- Mayor .... Vincent Mazzeo
- Manager .... NA
- Clerk .... Carol A. Raph
- Finance Dir .... Marilyn Dolcy
- Tax Assessor .... Mark Sykes
- Tax Collector .... Cindy Ruffo
- Attorney .... Steven Scheffler
- Building .... Jerry Nuzzolo
- Comm Dev/Planning .... NA
- Engineering .... Matt Doran
- Public Works .... James Clark
- Police Chief .... Robert James
- Fire Chief .... Henry Martinelli

Housing & Construction
Housing Units, 2000*
- Total 2,922
- Median rent $783
- Median SF home value $128,100

Permits for New Residential Construction

	Units	Value
Total, 2007	23	$2,651,060
Single family	23	$2,651,060
Total, 2006	26	$3,102,432
Single family	26	$3,102,432

Real Property Valuation, 2007

	Parcels	Valuation
Total	3,572	$549,910,600
Vacant	245	15,766,600
Residential	3,112	414,370,800
Commercial	210	118,874,000
Industrial	0	0
Apartments	3	542,900
Farm land	1	3,600
Farm homestead	1	352,700

Average Property Value & Tax, 2007
- Residential value $133,223
- Property tax $5,445
- Tax credit/rebate $985

Public Library
Otto Bruyns Public Library
241 W Mill Rd
Northfield, NJ 08225
609-646-4476
- Director .... Margaret E. Derascavage

Library statistics, 2006
- Population served 7,725
- Full-time/total staff 0/1

	Total	Per capita
Holdings	31,108	4.03
Revenues	$316,642	$40.99
Expenditures	$212,070	$27.45
Annual visits	18,320	2.37

- Internet terminals/annual users 3/5,210

Taxes

	2005	2006	2007
General tax rate per $100	3.644	3.885	4.088
County equalization ratio	66.86	55.08	47.05
Net valuation taxable	$531,748,155	$543,709,800	$550,805,426
State equalized value	$965,410,594	$1,156,614,725	$1,213,754,553

Public Safety
- Number of officers, 2006 22

Crime	2005	2006
Total crimes	174	107
Violent	4	6
Murder	0	0
Rape	2	1
Robbery	2	3
Aggravated assault	0	2
Non-violent	170	101
Burglary	58	29
Larceny	106	68
Vehicle theft	6	4
Domestic violence	76	49
Arson	0	2
Total crime rate	21.6	13.3
Violent	0.5	0.7
Non-violent	21.1	12.6

Public School District
(for school year 2006-07 except as noted)

Northfield City School District
2000 New Rd
Northfield, NJ 08225
609-407-4000

- Superintendent .... Richard Stepura
- Number of schools 2
- Grade plan K-8
- Enrollment 1,078
- Attendance rate, '05-06 .... 95.7%
- Dropout rate .... NA
- Students per teacher 12.1
- Per pupil expenditure $9,689
- Median faculty salary $49,862
- Median administrator salary $94,082
- Grade 12 enrollment .... NA
- High school graduation rate .... NA

Assessment test results
(percent scoring at proficient or advanced level)

	Language	Math
NJASK-Grade 3	90.0%	95.1%
GEPA-Grade 8	83.5%	74.6%
HSPA-High School	NA	NA

SAT score averages

Pct tested	Math	Verbal	Writing
NA	NA	NA	NA

Teacher Qualifications
- Avg. years of experience 9
- Highly-qualified teachers
  - one subject/all subjects 100%/100%
- With emergency credentials 0.0%

No Child Left Behind
- AYP, 2005-06 .... Meets Standards

Municipal Finance
State Aid Programs, 2008
- Total aid $745,521
  - CMPTRA 119,785
  - Energy tax receipts 625,681
  - Garden State Trust 55

General Budget, 2007
- Total tax levy $22,511,549
  - County levy 3,252,028
    - County taxes 2,872,267
    - County library 0
    - County health 144,949
    - County open space 234,813
  - School levy 12,771,061
  - Muni. levy 6,488,460
- Misc. revenues 4,813,417

Northvale Borough — Bergen County

Demographics & Socio-Economic Characteristics
(2000 US Census, except as noted)

Population
1980*	5,016
1990*	4,563
2000	4,460
Male	2,222
Female	2,238
2006 (estimate)*	4,562
Population density	3,456.1

Race & Hispanic Origin, 2000
Race
White	3,698
Black/African American	34
American Indian/Alaska Native	3
Asian	627
Native Hawaiian/Pacific Islander	0
Other race	52
Two or more races	46
Hispanic origin, total	211
Mexican	3
Puerto Rican	36
Cuban	47
Other Hispanic	125

Age & Nativity, 2000
Under 5 years	256
18 years and over	3,458
21 years and over	3,328
65 years and over	713
85 years and over	70
Median age	40.2
Native-born	3,586
Foreign-born	866

Educational Attainment, 2000
Population 25 years and over	3,190
Less than 9th grade	4.3%
High school grad or higher	87.2%
Bachelor's degree or higher	29.6%
Graduate degree	10.8%

Income & Poverty, 1999
Per capita income	$28,206
Median household income	$72,500
Median family income	$81,153
Persons in poverty	171
H'holds receiving public assistance	31
H'holds receiving social security	512

Households, 2000
Total households	1,575
With persons under 18	572
With persons over 65	520
Family households	1,237
Single-person households	291
Persons per household	2.83
Persons per family	3.21

Labor & Employment
Total civilian labor force, 2006**	2,615
Unemployment rate	2.5%
Total civilian labor force, 2000	2,456
Unemployment rate	2.3%

Employed persons 16 years and over by occupation, 2000
Managers & professionals	987
Service occupations	343
Sales & office occupations	674
Farming, fishing & forestry	0
Construction & maintenance	258
Production & transportation	137
Self-employed persons	82

* US Census Bureau
** New Jersey Department of Labor

General Information
Borough of Northvale
116 Paris Ave
Northvale, NJ 07647
201-767-3330

Website	www.boroughofnorthvale.com
Year of incorporation	1916
Land/water area (sq. miles)	1.32/0.00
Form of government	Borough

Government
Legislative Districts
US Congressional	5
State Legislative	39

Local Officials, 2008
Mayor	John S. Hogan
Manager/Admin	NA
Clerk	Wanda Worner
Finance Dir	Shuaib Firozvi
Tax Assessor	John Guercio
Tax Collector	Suzanne Burroughs
Attorney	Paul Kaufman
Building	Nick Lepore
Comm Dev/Planning	NA
Engineering	Louis Raimondi
Public Works	Edward Keegan
Police Chief	Bruce Tietjen
Emerg/Fire Director	Briant Bodrato

Housing & Construction
Housing Units, 2000*
Total	1,596
Median rent	$871
Median SF home value	$246,100

Permits for New Residential Construction
	Units	Value
Total, 2007	79	$6,540,680
Single family	79	$6,540,680
Total, 2006	21	$3,442,112
Single family	21	$3,442,112

Real Property Valuation, 2007
	Parcels	Valuation
Total	1,639	$963,359,900
Vacant	73	14,898,400
Residential	1,422	692,867,700
Commercial	85	75,958,300
Industrial	59	179,635,500
Apartments	0	0
Farm land	0	0
Farm homestead	0	0

Average Property Value & Tax, 2007
Residential value	$487,249
Property tax	$8,651
Tax credit/rebate	$1,313

Public Library
Northvale Public Library
116 Paris Ave
Northvale, NJ 07647
201-768-4784

Director: Virginia Beckman

Library statistics, 2006
Population served	4,460
Full-time/total staff	0/4

	Total	Per capita
Holdings	37,984	8.52
Revenues	$274,988	$61.66
Expenditures	$257,207	$57.67
Annual visits	25,600	5.74
Internet terminals/annual users		3/8,435

Public Safety
Number of officers, 2006	14

Crime	2005	2006
Total crimes	30	29
Violent	0	1
Murder	0	0
Rape	0	0
Robbery	0	0
Aggravated assault	0	1
Non-violent	30	28
Burglary	5	6
Larceny	24	20
Vehicle theft	1	2
Domestic violence	18	25
Arson	0	0
Total crime rate	6.6	6.4
Violent	0.0	0.2
Non-violent	6.6	6.1

Public School District
(for school year 2006-07 except as noted)

Northvale School District
441 Tappan Rd
Northvale, NJ 07647
201-768-8484

Superintendent	Sylvan Hershey
Number of schools	2
Grade plan	K-8
Enrollment	577
Attendance rate, '05-06	96.8%
Dropout rate	NA
Students per teacher	11.9
Per pupil expenditure	$11,773
Median faculty salary	$64,776
Median administrator salary	$88,000
Grade 12 enrollment	NA
High school graduation rate	NA

Assessment test results
(percent scoring at proficient or advanced level)

	Language	Math
NJASK-Grade 3	86.1%	80.9%
GEPA-Grade 8	93.2%	89.2%
HSPA-High School	NA	NA

SAT score averages
Pct tested	Math	Verbal	Writing
NA	NA	NA	NA

Teacher Qualifications
Avg. years of experience	9
Highly-qualified teachers one subject/all subjects	100%/100%
With emergency credentials	0.0%

No Child Left Behind
AYP, 2005-06 .... Meets Standards

Municipal Finance
State Aid Programs, 2008
Total aid	$511,073
CMPTRA	0
Energy tax receipts	511,073
Garden State Trust	0

General Budget, 2007
Total tax levy	$17,113,623
County levy	1,712,660
County taxes	1,617,367
County library	0
County health	0
County open space	95,293
School levy	11,107,244
Muni. levy	4,293,719
Misc. revenues	3,138,948

Taxes
	2005	2006	2007
General tax rate per $100	3.28	3.42	1.78
County equalization ratio	59.95	55.37	102.32
Net valuation taxable	$475,861,687	$474,980,140	$963,926,829
State equalized value	$859,421,504	$937,266,641	$978,101,074

Bergen County   *Norwood Borough*

Demographics & Socio-Economic Characteristics
(2000 US Census, except as noted)

Population
1980*	4,413
1990*	4,858
2000	5,751
Male	2,704
Female	3,047
2006 (estimate)*	6,267
Population density	2,278.9

Race & Hispanic Origin, 2000
Race
White	4,478
Black/African American	48
American Indian/Alaska Native	1
Asian	1,092
Native Hawaiian/Pacific Islander	0
Other race	54
Two or more races	78
Hispanic origin, total	172
Mexican	9
Puerto Rican	26
Cuban	39
Other Hispanic	98

Age & Nativity, 2000
Under 5 years	320
18 years and over	4,269
21 years and over	4,104
65 years and over	896
85 years and over	186
Median age	40.8
Native-born	4,465
Foreign-born	1,286

Educational Attainment, 2000
Population 25 years and over	3,900
Less than 9th grade	2.8%
High school grad or higher	91.0%
Bachelor's degree or higher	42.8%
Graduate degree	14.2%

Income & Poverty, 1999
Per capita income	$40,039
Median household income	$92,447
Median family income	$100,329
Persons in poverty	271
H'holds receiving public assistance	15
H'holds receiving social security	436

Households, 2000
Total households	1,857
With persons under 18	799
With persons over 65	484
Family households	1,563
Single-person households	254
Persons per household	2.97
Persons per family	3.26

Labor & Employment
Total civilian labor force, 2006**	2,817
Unemployment rate	4.2%
Total civilian labor force, 2000	2,654
Unemployment rate	4.1%

Employed persons 16 years and over by occupation, 2000
Managers & professionals	1,288
Service occupations	291
Sales & office occupations	688
Farming, fishing & forestry	0
Construction & maintenance	161
Production & transportation	118
Self-employed persons	263

* US Census Bureau
** New Jersey Department of Labor

See Introduction for an explanation of all data sources.

General Information
Borough of Norwood
455 Broadway
Norwood, NJ 07648
201-767-7200

Website	www.norwoodboro.org
Year of incorporation	1905
Land/water area (sq. miles)	2.75/0.01
Form of government	Borough

Government
Legislative Districts
US Congressional	5
State Legislative	39

Local Officials, 2008
Mayor	James P. Barsa
Manager	Lorraine McMackin
Clerk	Lorraine McMackin
Finance Dir.	Maureen Neville
Tax Assessor	John Guercio
Tax Collector	Maureen Neville
Attorney	Andrew Fede
Building	Paul Renaud
Comm Dev/Planning	NA
Engineering	Michael J. Neglia
Public Works	NA
Police Chief	Jeffrey Krapels
Emerg/Fire Director	Richard Hess

Housing & Construction
Housing Units, 2000*
Total	1,888
Median rent	$1,086
Median SF home value	$345,100

Permits for New Residential Construction
	Units	Value
Total, 2007	15	$5,681,890
Single family	15	$5,681,890
Total, 2006	15	$3,921,189
Single family	15	$3,921,189

Real Property Valuation, 2007
	Parcels	Valuation
Total	1,954	$744,413,200
Vacant	71	7,443,800
Residential	1,787	634,462,200
Commercial	51	37,110,200
Industrial	43	55,799,600
Apartments	1	9,573,800
Farm land	1	23,600
Farm homestead	0	0

Average Property Value & Tax, 2007
Residential value	$355,043
Property tax	$10,596
Tax credit/rebate	$1,315

Public Library
Norwood Public Library
198 Summit St
Norwood, NJ 07648
201-768-9555

Director: Siobhan Koch

Library statistics, 2006
Population served	5,751
Full-time/total staff	1/3

	Total	Per capita
Holdings	43,210	7.51
Revenues	$416,404	$72.41
Expenditures	$295,836	$51.44
Annual visits	27,001	4.70
Internet terminals/annual users	3/14,006	

Public Safety
Number of officers, 2006		13
Crime	**2005**	**2006**
Total crimes	49	38
Violent	3	1
Murder	0	0
Rape	1	0
Robbery	0	0
Aggravated assault	2	1
Non-violent	46	37
Burglary	5	8
Larceny	41	28
Vehicle theft	0	1
Domestic violence	10	5
Arson	0	3
Total crime rate	7.9	6.1
Violent	0.5	0.2
Non-violent	7.4	5.9

Public School District
(for school year 2006-07 except as noted)

Norwood School District
177 Summit St
Norwood, NJ 07648
201-768-6363

Superintendent	Andrew Rose
Number of schools	1
Grade plan	K-8
Enrollment	641
Attendance rate, '05-06	96.5%
Dropout rate	NA
Students per teacher	12.0
Per pupil expenditure	$12,085
Median faculty salary	$53,000
Median administrator salary	$128,872
Grade 12 enrollment	NA
High school graduation rate	NA

Assessment test results
(percent scoring at proficient or advanced level)
	Language	Math
NJASK-Grade 3	91.0%	98.7%
GEPA-Grade 8	92.4%	93.8%
HSPA-High School	NA	NA

SAT score averages
Pct tested	Math	Verbal	Writing
NA	NA	NA	NA

Teacher Qualifications
Avg. years of experience	9
Highly-qualified teachers one subject/all subjects	100%/100%
With emergency credentials	0.0%

No Child Left Behind
AYP, 2005-06 .... Meets Standards

Municipal Finance
State Aid Programs, 2008
Total aid	$746,564
CMPTRA	25,148
Energy tax receipts	715,682
Garden State Trust	0

General Budget, 2007
Total tax levy	$22,236,582
County levy	2,762,136
County taxes	2,610,118
County library	0
County health	0
County open space	152,018
School levy	14,168,410
Muni. levy	5,306,036
Misc. revenues	2,730,066

Taxes
	2005	2006	2007
General tax rate per $100	2.76	2.87	2.99
County equalization ratio	65.88	58.33	49.11
Net valuation taxable	$726,919,386	$734,339,600	$745,106,346
State equalized value	$1,246,218,731	$1,496,071,641	$1,512,806,085

©2008 Information Publications, Inc. All rights reserved. Photocopying prohibited. For additional copies, contact the publisher at www.informationpublications.com or (877)544-INFO (4636)

Nutley Township
Essex County

Demographics & Socio-Economic Characteristics
(2000 US Census, except as noted)

Population
1980*	28,998
1990*	27,099
2000	27,362
Male	12,912
Female	14,450
2006 (estimate)*	27,011
Population density	8,015.1

Race & Hispanic Origin, 2000
Race
- White: 24,064
- Black/African American: 511
- American Indian/Alaska Native: 15
- Asian: 1,943
- Native Hawaiian/Pacific Islander: 10
- Other race: 480
- Two or more races: 339

Hispanic origin, total: 1,830
- Mexican: 72
- Puerto Rican: 585
- Cuban: 178
- Other Hispanic: 995

Age & Nativity, 2000
- Under 5 years: 1,510
- 18 years and over: 21,396
- 21 years and over: 20,686
- 65 years and over: 4,402
- 85 years and over: 476
- Median age: 39.3
- Native-born: 23,350
- Foreign-born: 4,012

Educational Attainment, 2000
- Population 25 years and over: 19,689
- Less than 9th grade: 4.4%
- High school grad or higher: 86.5%
- Bachelor's degree or higher: 32.9%
- Graduate degree: 10.5%

Income & Poverty, 1999
- Per capita income: $28,039
- Median household income: $59,634
- Median family income: $73,264
- Persons in poverty: 1,312
- H'holds receiving public assistance: 128
- H'holds receiving social security: 3,273

Households, 2000
- Total households: 10,884
- With persons under 18: 3,401
- With persons over 65: 3,261
- Family households: 7,371
- Single-person households: 3,036
- Persons per household: 2.51
- Persons per family: 3.11

Labor & Employment
- Total civilian labor force, 2006**: 15,447
- Unemployment rate: 3.9%
- Total civilian labor force, 2000: 14,709
- Unemployment rate: 3.8%

Employed persons 16 years and over by occupation, 2000
- Managers & professionals: 5,815
- Service occupations: 1,578
- Sales & office occupations: 4,460
- Farming, fishing & forestry: 0
- Construction & maintenance: 1,048
- Production & transportation: 1,254
- Self-employed persons: 736

* US Census Bureau
** New Jersey Department of Labor

General Information
Township of Nutley
1 Kennedy Dr
Nutley, NJ 07110
973-284-4951

- Website: nutleynj.org
- Year of incorporation: 1981
- Land/water area (sq. miles): 3.37/0.06
- Form of government: Commission

Government
Legislative Districts
- US Congressional: 8
- State Legislative: 36

Local Officials, 2008
- Mayor: Joanne Cocchiola
- Manager/Admin: NA
- Clerk: Evelyn Rosario
- Finance Dir: Rosemary Costa
- Tax Assessor: George Librizzi
- Tax Collector: Jodi De Maio
- Attorney: Kevin Harkins
- Building: William Spiezio
- Comm Dev/Planning: NA
- Engineering: Pennoni Associates
- Public Works: Michael Luzzi
- Police Chief: John Holland
- Emerg/Fire Director: Thomas Peters

Housing & Construction
Housing Units, 2000*
- Total: 11,118
- Median rent: $814
- Median SF home value: $190,500

Permits for New Residential Construction
	Units	Value
Total, 2007	42	$4,412,927
Single family	42	$4,412,927
Total, 2006	21	$2,409,802
Single family	21	$2,409,802

Real Property Valuation, 2007
	Parcels	Valuation
Total	8,936	$4,157,560,200
Vacant	155	27,407,900
Residential	8,229	3,320,422,800
Commercial	457	624,338,700
Industrial	27	22,841,600
Apartments	68	162,549,200
Farm land	0	0
Farm homestead	0	0

Average Property Value & Tax, 2007
- Residential value: $403,503
- Property tax: $8,757
- Tax credit/rebate: $1,321

Public Library
Nutley Public Library
93 Booth Dr
Nutley, NJ 07110
973-667-0405

Director: JoAnn A. Tropiano

Library statistics, 2006
- Population served: 27,362
- Full-time/total staff: 6/12

	Total	Per capita
Holdings	95,040	3.47
Revenues	$1,364,657	$49.87
Expenditures	$1,353,308	$49.46
Annual visits	146,428	5.35
Internet terminals/annual users	18/84,096	

Taxes
	2005	2006	2007
General tax rate per $100	15.66	2.05	2.18
County equalization ratio	14.85	107.89	97.93
Net valuation taxable	$518,053,700	$4,149,415,500	$4,163,063,500
State equalized value	$3,912,792,296	$4,242,650,566	$4,384,187,028

Public Safety
- Number of officers, 2006: 65

Crime
	2005	2006
Total crimes	402	478
Violent	24	39
Murder	1	0
Rape	0	3
Robbery	6	5
Aggravated assault	17	31
Non-violent	378	439
Burglary	102	94
Larceny	257	315
Vehicle theft	19	30
Domestic violence	163	141
Arson	1	12
Total crime rate	14.4	17.4
Violent	0.9	1.4
Non-violent	13.6	16.0

Public School District
(for school year 2006-07 except as noted)

Nutley School District
375 Bloomfield Ave
Nutley, NJ 07110
973-661-8798

- Superintendent: Joseph Zarra
- Number of schools: 7
- Grade plan: K-12
- Enrollment: 4,060
- Attendance rate, '05-06: 95.2%
- Dropout rate: 0.4%
- Students per teacher: 12.3
- Per pupil expenditure: $11,289
- Median faculty salary: $59,500
- Median administrator salary: $106,866
- Grade 12 enrollment: 322
- High school graduation rate: 95.8%

Assessment test results
(percent scoring at proficient or advanced level)
	Language	Math
NJASK-Grade 3	91.3%	94.1%
GEPA-Grade 8	83.1%	81.8%
HSPA-High School	92.7%	83.4%

SAT score averages
Pct tested	Math	Verbal	Writing
93%	516	499	499

Teacher Qualifications
- Avg. years of experience: 9
- Highly-qualified teachers one subject/all subjects: 100%/100%
- With emergency credentials: 0.0%

No Child Left Behind
- AYP, 2005-06: Meets Standards

Municipal Finance
State Aid Programs, 2008
- Total aid: $3,237,524
- CMPTRA: 1,109,323
- Energy tax receipts: 2,128,201
- Garden State Trust: 0

General Budget, 2007
- Total tax levy: $90,348,449
- County levy: 16,782,449
- County taxes: 16,351,145
- County library: 0
- County health: 0
- County open space: 431,304
- School levy: 42,343,045
- Muni. levy: 31,222,955
- Misc. revenues: 11,714,014

Bergen County

Oakland Borough

Demographics & Socio-Economic Characteristics
(2000 US Census, except as noted)

Population
- 1980* 13,443
- 1990* 11,997
- 2000 12,466
  - Male 6,090
  - Female 6,376
- 2006 (estimate)* 13,558
  - Population density 1,576.5

Race & Hispanic Origin, 2000
Race
- White 11,813
- Black/African American 97
- American Indian/Alaska Native 8
- Asian 337
- Native Hawaiian/Pacific Islander . 1
- Other race 87
- Two or more races 123
- Hispanic origin, total 483
  - Mexican 49
  - Puerto Rican 146
  - Cuban 62
  - Other Hispanic 226

Age & Nativity, 2000
- Under 5 years 970
- 18 years and over 9,294
- 21 years and over 9,012
- 65 years and over 1,584
- 85 years and over 193
  - Median age 38.9
- Native-born 11,316
- Foreign-born 1,150

Educational Attainment, 2000
- Population 25 years and over 8,707
- Less than 9th grade 2.6%
- High school grad or higher 92.5%
- Bachelor's degree or higher 41.4%
- Graduate degree 14.8%

Income & Poverty, 1999
- Per capita income $35,252
- Median household income $86,629
- Median family income $93,695
- Persons in poverty 206
- H'holds receiving public assistance . 57
- H'holds receiving social security . 959

Households, 2000
- Total households 4,255
  - With persons under 18 1,730
  - With persons over 65 992
  - Family households 3,567
  - Single-person households 545
- Persons per household 2.88
- Persons per family 3.15

Labor & Employment
- Total civilian labor force, 2006** . 7,260
  - Unemployment rate 2.8%
- Total civilian labor force, 2000 .. 6,847
  - Unemployment rate 2.9%

Employed persons 16 years and over by occupation, 2000
- Managers & professionals 3,151
- Service occupations 531
- Sales & office occupations 1,988
- Farming, fishing & forestry 0
- Construction & maintenance 580
- Production & transportation 399
- Self-employed persons 390

* US Census Bureau
** New Jersey Department of Labor

See Introduction for an explanation of all data sources.

General Information
Borough of Oakland
1 Municipal Plz
Oakland, NJ 07436
201-337-8111

- Website .... www.oakland-nj.org
- Year of incorporation 1902
- Land/water area (sq. miles) 8.60/0.15
- Form of government .... Borough

Government
Legislative Districts
- US Congressional 5
- State Legislative 40

Local Officials, 2008
- Mayor .... John P. Szabo Jr
- Manager .... Richard S. Kunze
- Clerk .... Lisa Duncan
- Finance Dir .... Raymond Herr
- Tax Assessor .... Scott Holzhauer
- Tax Collector .... Ellen Amorino
- Attorney .... Brian Chewcaskie
- Building .... Daniel Hagberg
- Comm Dev/Planning .... NA
- Engineering .... James Kelly
- Public Works .... Anthony Marcucilli
- Police Chief .... Edward Kasper
- Emerg/Fire Director .... Peter Sondervan

Housing & Construction
Housing Units, 2000*
- Total 4,345
- Median rent $1,173
- Median SF home value $245,300

Permits for New Residential Construction

	Units	Value
Total, 2007	11	$433,300
Single family	11	$433,300
Total, 2006	17	$2,079,300
Single family	17	$2,079,300

Real Property Valuation, 2007

	Parcels	Valuation
Total	4,819	$2,522,406,700
Vacant	193	45,082,600
Residential	4,415	2,128,715,000
Commercial	140	172,988,100
Industrial	59	172,016,600
Apartments	0	0
Farm land	8	25,800
Farm homestead	4	3,578,600

Average Property Value & Tax, 2007
- Residential value $482,529
- Property tax $9,202
- Tax credit/rebate $1,305

Public Library
Oakland Public Library
2 Municipal Plaza
Oakland, NJ 07436
210-337-3742

- Director .... Michele Reuty

Library statistics, 2006
- Population served 12,466
- Full-time/total staff 3/10

	Total	Per capita
Holdings	57,824	4.64
Revenues	$821,860	$65.93
Expenditures	$760,051	$60.97
Annual visits	20,800	1.67

Internet terminals/annual users 7/3,420

Public Safety
Number of officers, 2006 23

Crime	2005	2006
Total crimes	115	131
Violent	9	1
Murder	0	0
Rape	1	0
Robbery	1	1
Aggravated assault	7	0
Non-violent	106	130
Burglary	15	13
Larceny	89	116
Vehicle theft	2	1
Domestic violence	63	71
Arson	0	3
Total crime rate	8.4	9.6
Violent	0.7	0.1
Non-violent	7.7	9.5

Public School District
(for school year 2006-07 except as noted)

Oakland School District
315 Ramapo Valley Rd
Oakland, NJ 07436
201-337-6156

- Superintendent .... Richard Heflich
- Number of schools 4
- Grade plan K-8
- Enrollment 1,722
- Attendance rate, '05-06 .... 95.5%
- Dropout rate .... NA
- Students per teacher 11.0
- Per pupil expenditure $12,858
- Median faculty salary $57,978
- Median administrator salary .. $136,345
- Grade 12 enrollment .... NA
- High school graduation rate .... NA

Assessment test results
(percent scoring at proficient or advanced level)

	Language	Math
NJASK-Grade 3	95.4%	94.5%
GEPA-Grade 8	93.0%	90.6%
HSPA-High School	NA	NA

SAT score averages

Pct tested	Math	Verbal	Writing
NA	NA	NA	NA

Teacher Qualifications
- Avg. years of experience 8
- Highly-qualified teachers
  one subject/all subjects 100%/99.0%
- With emergency credentials 0.0%

No Child Left Behind
- AYP, 2005-06 .... Meets Standards

Municipal Finance
State Aid Programs, 2008
- Total aid $1,688,011
  - CMPTRA 323,796
  - Energy tax receipts 1,362,552
  - Garden State Trust 1,663

General Budget, 2007
- Total tax levy $48,192,774
  - County levy 4,697,744
    - County taxes 4,437,288
    - County library 0
    - County health 0
    - County open space 260,456
  - School levy 31,585,487
  - Muni. levy 11,909,544
- Misc. revenues 4,500,486

Taxes	2005	2006	2007
General tax rate per $100	1.67	1.8	1.91
County equalization ratio	120.33	105.95	97.29
Net valuation taxable	$2,524,648,350	$2,521,205,100	$2,526,995,660
State equalized value	$2,382,867,721	$2,595,141,591	$2,653,341,139

The New Jersey Municipal Data Book

Oaklyn Borough — Camden County

Demographics & Socio-Economic Characteristics
(2000 US Census, except as noted)

Population
1980*	4,223
1990*	4,430
2000	4,188
Male	2,036
Female	2,152
2006 (estimate)*	4,080
Population density	6,688.5

Race & Hispanic Origin, 2000
Race
White	4,017
Black/African American	48
American Indian/Alaska Native	9
Asian	40
Native Hawaiian/Pacific Islander	1
Other race	35
Two or more races	38
Hispanic origin, total	97
Mexican	2
Puerto Rican	75
Cuban	1
Other Hispanic	19

Age & Nativity, 2000
Under 5 years	247
18 years and over	3,233
21 years and over	3,114
65 years and over	703
85 years and over	85
Median age	38.0
Native-born	4,104
Foreign-born	64

Educational Attainment, 2000
Population 25 years and over	2,889
Less than 9th grade	4.8%
High school grad or higher	82.5%
Bachelor's degree or higher	19.3%
Graduate degree	5.5%

Income & Poverty, 1999
Per capita income	$24,157
Median household income	$44,364
Median family income	$55,434
Persons in poverty	271
H'holds receiving public assistance	29
H'holds receiving social security	563

Households, 2000
Total households	1,791
With persons under 18	516
With persons over 65	542
Family households	1,067
Single-person households	614
Persons per household	2.34
Persons per family	3.07

Labor & Employment
Total civilian labor force, 2006**	2,416
Unemployment rate	3.8%
Total civilian labor force, 2000	2,219
Unemployment rate	3.6%

Employed persons 16 years and over by occupation, 2000
Managers & professionals	696
Service occupations	251
Sales & office occupations	726
Farming, fishing & forestry	0
Construction & maintenance	271
Production & transportation	195
Self-employed persons	87

* US Census Bureau
** New Jersey Department of Labor

General Information
Borough of Oaklyn
500 White Horse Pike
Oaklyn, NJ 08107
856-858-2457

Website	www.oaklyn-nj.com
Year of incorporation	1905
Land/water area (sq. miles)	0.61/0.08
Form of government	Borough

Government
Legislative Districts
US Congressional	1
State Legislative	6

Local Officials, 2008
Mayor	Michael LaMaina
Manager/Admin	NA
Clerk	Marie Hawkins
Finance Dir	Janet LaBar
Tax Assessor	Anthony Leone
Tax Collector	Judy Pierce
Attorney	Timothy Higgins
Building	Dan Scriboni
Comm Dev/Planning	NA
Engineering	Key Engineers
Public Works	Rich Hawco
Police Chief	Jon Shelly
Emerg/Fire Director	Mark Quinter

Housing & Construction
Housing Units, 2000*
Total	1,893
Median rent	$540
Median SF home value	$98,200

Permits for New Residential Construction
	Units	Value
Total, 2007	1	$105,000
Single family	1	$105,000
Total, 2006	1	$105,000
Single family	1	$105,000

Real Property Valuation, 2007
	Parcels	Valuation
Total	1,453	$160,222,200
Vacant	19	1,156,200
Residential	1,341	134,829,500
Commercial	73	16,037,000
Industrial	1	169,000
Apartments	19	8,030,500
Farm land	0	0
Farm homestead	0	0

Average Property Value & Tax, 2007
Residential value	$100,544
Property tax	$5,223
Tax credit/rebate	$961

Public Library
Oaklyn Memorial Library
602 Newton Ave
Oaklyn, NJ 08107
856-858-8226

Director: Ann Marie Latini

Library statistics, 2006
Population served	4,188
Full-time/total staff	NA/0

	Total	Per capita
Holdings	NA	NA
Revenues	NA	NA
Expenditures	NA	NA
Annual visits	NA	NA
Internet terminals/annual users	NA/NA	

Taxes
	2005	2006	2007
General tax rate per $100	4.531	4.963	5.195
County equalization ratio	77.92	68.79	58.47
Net valuation taxable	$159,383,689	$159,915,300	$160,378,373
State equalized value	$231,696,015	$273,678,590	$301,325,722

Public Safety
Number of officers, 2006: 13

Crime	2005	2006
Total crimes	124	115
Violent	9	5
Murder	0	0
Rape	3	0
Robbery	3	2
Aggravated assault	3	3
Non-violent	115	110
Burglary	25	27
Larceny	87	80
Vehicle theft	3	3
Domestic violence	47	39
Arson	2	1
Total crime rate	30.0	27.9
Violent	2.2	1.2
Non-violent	27.9	26.7

Public School District
(for school year 2006-07 except as noted)

Oaklyn Borough School District
Kendall Boulevard
Oaklyn, NJ 08107
856-858-1731

Superintendent	Tommie Stringer
Number of schools	2
Grade plan	K-9
Enrollment	45
Attendance rate, '05-06	94.9%
Dropout rate	NA
Students per teacher	1.2
Per pupil expenditure	$11,931
Median faculty salary	$41,249
Median administrator salary	$87,172
Grade 12 enrollment	NA
High school graduation rate	NA

Assessment test results
(percent scoring at proficient or advanced level)
	Language	Math
NJASK-Grade 3	89.1%	89.1%
GEPA-Grade 8	62.8%	58.8%
HSPA-High School	NA	NA

SAT score averages
Pct tested	Math	Verbal	Writing
NA	NA	NA	NA

Teacher Qualifications
Avg. years of experience	12
Highly-qualified teachers one subject/all subjects	100%/100%
With emergency credentials	0.0%

No Child Left Behind
AYP, 2005-06: Meets Standards

Municipal Finance
State Aid Programs, 2008
Total aid	$287,025
CMPTRA	0
Energy tax receipts	287,025
Garden State Trust	0

General Budget, 2007
Total tax levy	$8,330,844
County levy	1,932,105
County taxes	1,755,075
County library	122,181
County health	0
County open space	54,849
School levy	4,007,239
Muni. levy	2,391,500
Misc. revenues	1,624,900

Cape May County

Ocean City

Demographics & Socio-Economic Characteristics
(2000 US Census, except as noted)

Population
1980*	13,949
1990*	15,512
2000	15,378
Male	7,129
Female	8,249
2006 (estimate)*	15,124
Population density	2,185.5

Race & Hispanic Origin, 2000
Race
White	14,389
Black/African American	663
American Indian/Alaska Native	18
Asian	86
Native Hawaiian/Pacific Islander	10
Other race	80
Two or more races	132
Hispanic origin, total	306
Mexican	60
Puerto Rican	140
Cuban	15
Other Hispanic	91

Age & Nativity, 2000
Under 5 years	529
18 years and over	12,862
21 years and over	12,510
65 years and over	3,989
85 years and over	580
Median age	47.8
Native-born	14,817
Foreign-born	561

Educational Attainment, 2000
Population 25 years and over	11,981
Less than 9th grade	2.6%
High school grad or higher	89.5%
Bachelor's degree or higher	33.5%
Graduate degree	10.3%

Income & Poverty, 1999
Per capita income	$33,217
Median household income	$44,158
Median family income	$61,731
Persons in poverty	1,031
H'holds receiving public assistance	80
H'holds receiving social security	2,962

Households, 2000
Total households	7,464
With persons under 18	1,370
With persons over 65	2,815
Family households	4,007
Single-person households	3,015
Persons per household	2.02
Persons per family	2.71

Labor & Employment
Total civilian labor force, 2006**	9,719
Unemployment rate	4.8%
Total civilian labor force, 2000	7,979
Unemployment rate	6.0%

Employed persons 16 years and over by occupation, 2000
Managers & professionals	2,871
Service occupations	1,427
Sales & office occupations	2,217
Farming, fishing & forestry	36
Construction & maintenance	499
Production & transportation	454
Self-employed persons	612

* US Census Bureau
** New Jersey Department of Labor

See Introduction for an explanation of all data sources.

General Information
City of Ocean
861 Asbury Ave
Ocean, NJ 08226
609-399-6111

Website	www.ocnj.us
Year of incorporation	1897
Land/water area (sq. miles)	6.92/4.16
Form of government	Mayor-Council

Government
Legislative Districts
US Congressional	2
State Legislative	1

Local Officials, 2008
Mayor	Salvatore Perillo
Business Admin	James Rutala
Clerk	Cindy Griffith
Finance Dir	John Hansen
Tax Assessor	Joseph Elliott
Tax Collector	Gary Hink
Attorney	Gerald Corcoran
Building	Patrick Newton
Planning	Randall Scheule
Engineering	Richard Carter
Public Works	Michael Rossbach
Police Chief	Robert Blevin
Emerg/Fire Director	Joseph Foglio

Housing & Construction
Housing Units, 2000*
Total	20,298
Median rent	$722
Median SF home value	$224,700

Permits for New Residential Construction
	Units	Value
Total, 2007	152	$36,906,997
Single family	64	$21,293,889
Total, 2006	286	$68,961,405
Single family	81	$33,523,665

Real Property Valuation, 2007
	Parcels	Valuation
Total	18,798	$8,246,103,400
Vacant	875	170,213,100
Residential	17,307	7,699,559,700
Commercial	574	349,838,900
Industrial	2	533,600
Apartments	40	25,958,100
Farm land	0	0
Farm homestead	0	0

Average Property Value & Tax, 2007
Residential value	$444,881
Property tax	$4,415
Tax credit/rebate	$880

Public Library
Ocean City Free Pub Library
1735 Simpson Ave
Ocean City, NJ 08226
609-399-2434

Director......Christopher Maloney

Library statistics, 2006
Population served	15,378
Full-time/total staff	4/8

	Total	Per capita
Holdings	118,635	7.71
Revenues	$3,312,270	$215.39
Expenditures	$2,673,722	$173.87
Annual visits	260,457	16.94
Internet terminals/annual users	25/2,868	

Public Safety
Number of officers, 2006......62

Crime	2005	2006
Total crimes	999	1,066
Violent	28	23
Murder	0	0
Rape	0	0
Robbery	13	4
Aggravated assault	15	19
Non-violent	971	1,043
Burglary	152	182
Larceny	805	853
Vehicle theft	14	8
Domestic violence	106	159
Arson	3	0
Total crime rate	64.4	69.5
Violent	1.8	1.5
Non-violent	62.6	68.0

Public School District
(for school year 2006-07 except as noted)

Ocean City School District
501 Atlantic Ave, Suite 1
Ocean City, NJ 08226
609-399-5150

Superintendent	Kathleen W. Taylor
Number of schools	3
Grade plan	K-12
Enrollment	2,114
Attendance rate, '05-06	94.6%
Dropout rate	1.1%
Students per teacher	9.3
Per pupil expenditure	$17,663
Median faculty salary	$81,874
Median administrator salary	$113,904
Grade 12 enrollment	362
High school graduation rate	94.0%

Assessment test results
(percent scoring at proficient or advanced level)
	Language	Math
NJASK-Grade 3	89.6%	89.9%
GEPA-Grade 8	85.4%	83.7%
HSPA-High School	92.4%	84.7%

SAT score averages
Pct tested	Math	Verbal	Writing
78%	522	501	493

Teacher Qualifications
Avg. years of experience	18
Highly-qualified teachers one subject/all subjects	97.5%/97.0%
With emergency credentials	0.0%

No Child Left Behind
AYP, 2005-06......Meets Standards

Municipal Finance
State Aid Programs, 2008
Total aid	$2,382,840
CMPTRA	0
Energy tax receipts	2,382,420
Garden State Trust	420

General Budget, 2007
Total tax levy	$81,869,977
County levy	22,596,417
County taxes	21,193,461
County library	0
County health	0
County open space	1,402,956
School levy	21,035,859
Muni. levy	38,237,701
Misc. revenues	18,069,280

Taxes	2005	2006	2007
General tax rate per $100	0.96	0.97	1
County equalization ratio	82.74	68.55	59.04
Net valuation taxable	$7,774,231,834	$8,010,568,600	$8,249,356,764
State equalized value	$11,340,965,476	$13,571,774,950	$13,365,922,948

Ocean Gate Borough

Ocean County

Demographics & Socio-Economic Characteristics
(2000 US Census, except as noted)

Population
- 1980* 1,385
- 1990* 2,078
- 2000 2,076
  - Male 977
  - Female 1,099
- 2006 (estimate)* 2,130
- Population density 4,840.9

Race & Hispanic Origin, 2000
Race
- White 2,004
- Black/African American 20
- American Indian/Alaska Native ... 3
- Asian 20
- Native Hawaiian/Pacific Islander ... 0
- Other race 11
- Two or more races 18
- Hispanic origin, total 49
  - Mexican 7
  - Puerto Rican 29
  - Cuban 1
  - Other Hispanic 12

Age & Nativity, 2000
- Under 5 years 144
- 18 years and over 1,536
- 21 years and over 1,462
- 65 years and over 300
- 85 years and over 28
- Median age 37.0
- Native-born 2,065
- Foreign-born 11

Educational Attainment, 2000
- Population 25 years and over ... 1,393
- Less than 9th grade 4.7%
- High school grad or higher ... 81.3%
- Bachelor's degree or higher ... 7.3%
- Graduate degree 0.6%

Income & Poverty, 1999
- Per capita income $19,239
- Median household income ... $41,067
- Median family income ... $50,847
- Persons in poverty 213
- H'holds receiving public assistance ... 9
- H'holds receiving social security ... 216

Households, 2000
- Total households 832
  - With persons under 18 ... 305
  - With persons over 65 221
  - Family households 547
  - Single-person households ... 234
- Persons per household 2.50
- Persons per family 3.06

Labor & Employment
- Total civilian labor force, 2006** ... 1,059
  - Unemployment rate 5.0%
- Total civilian labor force, 2000 ... 1,071
  - Unemployment rate 4.3%

Employed persons 16 years and over by occupation, 2000
- Managers & professionals ... 215
- Service occupations 171
- Sales & office occupations ... 318
- Farming, fishing & forestry ... 0
- Construction & maintenance ... 188
- Production & transportation ... 133
- Self-employed persons 45

* US Census Bureau
** New Jersey Department of Labor

General Information
Borough of Ocean Gate
801 Ocean Gate Ave
CN 100
Ocean Gate, NJ 08740
732-269-3166

- Website .... NA
- Year of incorporation 1918
- Land/water area (sq. miles) ... 0.44/0.00
- Form of government .... Borough

Government
Legislative Districts
- US Congressional 3
- State Legislative 9

Local Officials, 2008
- Mayor .... Paul J. Kennedy
- Manager/Admin .... NA
- Clerk .... Jodi Pellicano
- Finance Dir .... NA
- Tax Assessor .... Scott Pezarras
- Tax Collector ... Elizabeth V. Barger
- Attorney .... James Gluck
- Building .... Paul E. Butow Jr
- Comm Dev/Planning .... NA
- Engineering ...... Alan Dittenhofer
- Public Works .... George Althouse
- Police Chief .... Reece Fisher
- Emerg/Fire Director ... Gerald Barrett

Housing & Construction
Housing Units, 2000*
- Total 1,152
- Median rent $819
- Median SF home value ... $101,500

Permits for New Residential Construction
	Units	Value
Total, 2007	6	$1,328,600
Single family	6	$1,328,600
Total, 2006	3	$518,780
Single family	3	$518,780

Real Property Valuation, 2007
	Parcels	Valuation
Total	1,092	$258,052,900
Vacant	38	3,455,300
Residential	1,038	248,615,500
Commercial	13	4,683,100
Industrial	0	0
Apartments	3	1,299,000
Farm land	0	0
Farm homestead	0	0

Average Property Value & Tax, 2007
- Residential value $239,514
- Property tax $4,510
- Tax credit/rebate $904

Public Library
No public municipal library

Library statistics, 2006
- Population served .... NA
- Full-time/total staff .... NA/NA

	Total	Per capita
Holdings	NA	NA
Revenues	NA	NA
Expenditures	NA	NA
Annual visits	NA	NA
Internet terminals/annual users	NA/NA	

Taxes
	2005	2006	2007
General tax rate per $100	1.646	1.747	1.884
County equalization ratio	131.2	107.58	92.99
Net valuation taxable	$256,604,156	$256,650,000	$258,216,480
State equalized value	$238,524,034	$276,167,051	$280,138,518

Public Safety
- Number of officers, 2006 6

Crime
	2005	2006
Total crimes	40	57
Violent	6	6
Murder	0	0
Rape	0	0
Robbery	0	0
Aggravated assault	6	6
Non-violent	34	51
Burglary	8	12
Larceny	26	37
Vehicle theft	0	2
Domestic violence	35	45
Arson	0	0
Total crime rate	18.9	27.0
Violent	2.8	2.8
Non-violent	16.1	24.2

Public School District
(for school year 2006-07 except as noted)

Ocean Gate School District
126 W Arverne Ave, PO Box 478
Ocean Gate, NJ 08740
732-269-3023

- Superintendent .... Frank Vanalesti
- Number of schools 1
- Grade plan K-6
- Enrollment 147
- Attendance rate, '05-06 .... 93.3%
- Dropout rate .... NA
- Students per teacher 10.4
- Per pupil expenditure $13,425
- Median faculty salary $42,175
- Median administrator salary ... $87,550
- Grade 12 enrollment .... NA
- High school graduation rate ..... NA

Assessment test results
(percent scoring at proficient or advanced level)
	Language	Math
NJASK-Grade 3	100.0%	100.0%
GEPA-Grade 8	NA	NA
HSPA-High School	NA	NA

SAT score averages
Pct tested	Math	Verbal	Writing
NA	NA	NA	NA

Teacher Qualifications
- Avg. years of experience 13
- Highly-qualified teachers
  one subject/all subjects ... 100%/100%
- With emergency credentials 0.0%

No Child Left Behind
- AYP, 2005-06 .... Meets Standards

Municipal Finance
State Aid Programs, 2008
- Total aid $135,166
  - CMPTRA 0
  - Energy tax receipts 135,166
  - Garden State Trust 0

General Budget, 2007
- Total tax levy $4,862,269
  - County levy 862,321
    - County taxes 710,592
    - County library 84,217
    - County health 34,120
    - County open space 33,392
  - School levy 2,500,005
  - Muni. levy 1,499,943
- Misc. revenues 1,116,880

Monmouth County

Ocean Township

Demographics & Socio-Economic Characteristics
(2000 US Census, except as noted)

Population
1980*	23,570
1990*	25,058
2000	26,959
Male	12,983
Female	13,976
2006 (estimate)*	27,484
Population density	2,491.7

Race & Hispanic Origin, 2000
Race
White	22,738
Black/African American	1,529
American Indian/Alaska Native	40
Asian	1,689
Native Hawaiian/Pacific Islander	20
Other race	425
Two or more races	518
Hispanic origin, total	1,215
Mexican	148
Puerto Rican	335
Cuban	63
Other Hispanic	669

Age & Nativity, 2000
Under 5 years	1,698
18 years and over	20,088
21 years and over	19,285
65 years and over	3,275
85 years and over	294
Median age	38.4
Native-born	22,719
Foreign-born	4,240

Educational Attainment, 2000
Population 25 years and over	18,333
Less than 9th grade	2.4%
High school grad or higher	90.2%
Bachelor's degree or higher	39.1%
Graduate degree	16.1%

Income & Poverty, 1999
Per capita income	$30,581
Median household income	$62,058
Median family income	$74,572
Persons in poverty	1,350
H'holds receiving public assistance	118
H'holds receiving social security	2,439

Households, 2000
Total households	10,254
With persons under 18	3,822
With persons over 65	2,421
Family households	7,338
Single-person households	2,456
Persons per household	2.63
Persons per family	3.14

Labor & Employment
Total civilian labor force, 2006**	14,813
Unemployment rate	3.5%
Total civilian labor force, 2000	13,946
Unemployment rate	4.2%

Employed persons 16 years and over by occupation, 2000
Managers & professionals	5,559
Service occupations	1,696
Sales & office occupations	4,261
Farming, fishing & forestry	14
Construction & maintenance	824
Production & transportation	1,009
Self-employed persons	822

‡ Branch of county library
* US Census Bureau
** New Jersey Department of Labor

See Introduction for an explanation of all data sources.

General Information
Township of Ocean
399 Monmouth Rd
Oakhurst, NJ 07755
732-531-5000

Website	www.oceantwp.org
Year of incorporation	1849
Land/water area (sq. miles)	11.03/0.09
Form of government	Council-Manager

Government
Legislative Districts
US Congressional	6
State Legislative	11

Local Officials, 2008
Mayor	William Larkin
Manager	Andrew G. Brannen
Clerk	Vincent G. Buttiglieri
Finance Dir.	Stephen Gallagher
Tax Assessor	Edward Mullane
Tax Collector	Stephen Gallagher
Attorney	Martin J. Arbus
Building	Paul Vitale
Planning	Marianne Wilensky
Engineering	Peter Avakian
Public Works	Larry Iverson
Police Chief	Antonio Amodio
Fire Chiefs	M. Evans/S. Newman

Housing & Construction
Housing Units, 2000*
Total	10,756
Median rent	$689
Median SF home value	$198,900

Permits for New Residential Construction
	Units	Value
Total, 2007	67	$11,579,045
Single family	67	$11,579,045
Total, 2006	108	$16,754,115
Single family	108	$16,754,115

Real Property Valuation, 2007
	Parcels	Valuation
Total	9,270	$4,595,103,700
Vacant	667	115,614,800
Residential	8,209	3,647,007,700
Commercial	376	657,156,600
Industrial	0	0
Apartments	15	174,312,600
Farm land	2	3,200
Farm homestead	1	1,008,800

Average Property Value & Tax, 2007
Residential value	$444,338
Property tax	$7,700
Tax credit/rebate	$1,137

Public Library
Ocean Township Public Library‡
601 Deal Rd
Oakhurst, NJ 07755
732-531-5092

Branch Librarian.........Deborah Bagchi

Library statistics, 2006
see Monmouth County profile for library system statistics

Public Safety
Number of officers, 2006 62

Crime	2005	2006
Total crimes	762	800
Violent	35	43
Murder	0	0
Rape	6	5
Robbery	13	15
Aggravated assault	16	23
Non-violent	727	757
Burglary	102	102
Larceny	597	624
Vehicle theft	28	31
Domestic violence	185	175
Arson	1	3
Total crime rate	27.8	29.1
Violent	1.3	1.6
Non-violent	26.6	27.5

Public School District
(for school year 2006-07 except as noted)

Ocean Township School District
163 Monmouth Rd
Oakhurst, NJ 07755
732-531-5600

Superintendent	Thomas M. Pagano
Number of schools	10
Grade plan	K-12
Enrollment	4,318
Attendance rate, '05-06	95.6%
Dropout rate	0.1%
Students per teacher	11.4
Per pupil expenditure	$13,410
Median faculty salary	$62,280
Median administrator salary	$108,750
Grade 12 enrollment	326
High school graduation rate	99.1%

Assessment test results
(percent scoring at proficient or advanced level)
	Language	Math
NJASK-Grade 3	87.5%	90.7%
GEPA-Grade 8	81.6%	83.5%
HSPA-High School	91.1%	84.2%

SAT score averages
Pct tested	Math	Verbal	Writing
96%	525	502	496

Teacher Qualifications
Avg. years of experience	11
Highly-qualified teachers one subject/all subjects	100%/100%
With emergency credentials	0.0%

No Child Left Behind
AYP, 2005-06 ....Meets Standards

Municipal Finance
State Aid Programs, 2008
Total aid	$3,253,727
CMPTRA	597,051
Energy tax receipts	2,652,986
Garden State Trust	3,690

General Budget, 2007
Total tax levy	$79,685,943
County levy	14,731,485
County taxes	13,155,849
County library	753,211
County health	0
County open space	822,425
School levy	50,792,739
Muni. levy	14,161,719
Misc. revenues	13,935,625

Taxes
	2005	2006	2007
General tax rate per $100	1.58	1.674	1.733
County equalization ratio	120.12	94.96	83.55
Net valuation taxable	$4,512,324,619	$4,542,082,300	$4,598,474,695
State equalized value	$4,751,816,153	$5,440,101,338	$5,821,430,884

Ocean Township — Ocean County

Demographics & Socio-Economic Characteristics
(2000 US Census, except as noted)

Population
1980*	3,731
1990*	5,416
2000	6,450
Male	3,201
Female	3,249
2006 (estimate)*	8,241
Population density	396.2

Race & Hispanic Origin, 2000
Race
- White 6,278
- Black/African American 48
- American Indian/Alaska Native 10
- Asian 27
- Native Hawaiian/Pacific Islander 2
- Other race 23
- Two or more races 62
- Hispanic origin, total 200
  - Mexican 29
  - Puerto Rican 77
  - Cuban 32
  - Other Hispanic 62

Age & Nativity, 2000
- Under 5 years 373
- 18 years and over 4,807
- 21 years and over 4,585
- 65 years and over 888
- 85 years and over 87
- Median age 37.7
- Native-born 6,358
- Foreign-born 92

Educational Attainment, 2000
- Population 25 years and over 4,369
- Less than 9th grade 2.5%
- High school grad or higher 86.2%
- Bachelor's degree or higher 15.7%
- Graduate degree 5.0%

Income & Poverty, 1999
- Per capita income $22,830
- Median household income $46,461
- Median family income $55,379
- Persons in poverty 502
- H'holds receiving public assistance 23
- H'holds receiving social security 767

Households, 2000
- Total households 2,446
  - With persons under 18 885
  - With persons over 65 647
  - Family households 1,745
  - Single-person households 571
- Persons per household 2.61
- Persons per family 3.08

Labor & Employment
- Total civilian labor force, 2006** 3,121
  - Unemployment rate 6.4%
- Total civilian labor force, 2000 3,177
  - Unemployment rate 6.9%

Employed persons 16 years and over by occupation, 2000
- Managers & professionals 745
- Service occupations 568
- Sales & office occupations 685
- Farming, fishing & forestry 0
- Construction & maintenance 645
- Production & transportation 315
- Self-employed persons 222

‡ Branch of county library
* US Census Bureau
** New Jersey Department of Labor

General Information
Township of Ocean
50 Railroad Ave
Waretown, NJ 08758
609-693-3302

- Website .... www.townshipofocean.org
- Year of incorporation 1876
- Land/water area (sq. miles) 20.80/11.23
- Form of government .... Township

Government
Legislative Districts
- US Congressional 3
- State Legislative 9

Local Officials, 2008
- Mayor .... Daniel Van Pelt
- Manager/Admin .... Kenneth Mosca
- Clerk .... Diane B. Ambrosio
- Finance Dir .... Christine Thorne
- Tax Assessor .... Martin Lynch
- Tax Collector .... Kammie Verdolina
- Attorney .... Gregory McGuckin
- Building .... James McBrien
- Comm Dev/Planning .... NA
- Engineering .... Alaimo Group
- Public Works .... Kenneth Mosca
- Police Chief .... Kenneth Flatt
- Emerg/Fire Dir .... Matthew Ambrosino

Housing & Construction
Housing Units, 2000*
- Total 2,981
- Median rent $833
- Median SF home value $104,800

Permits for New Residential Construction

	Units	Value
Total, 2007	173	$49,293,890
Single family	173	$49,293,890
Total, 2006	201	$23,817,911
Single family	201	$23,817,911

Real Property Valuation, 2007

	Parcels	Valuation
Total	5,016	$1,219,916,200
Vacant	1,003	79,818,100
Residential	3,806	1,077,178,900
Commercial	118	60,019,100
Industrial	1	574,600
Apartments	0	0
Farm land	84	381,600
Farm homestead	4	1,943,900

Average Property Value & Tax, 2007
- Residential value $283,234
- Property tax $4,102
- Tax credit/rebate $837

Public Library
Waretown Branch Library‡
112 Main St
Waretown, NJ 08758
609-693-5133
Branch Librarian .... Kelly Ann Pernel

Library statistics, 2006
see Ocean County profile
for library system statistics

Public Safety
- Number of officers, 2006 19

Crime
	2005	2006
Total crimes	83	106
Violent	3	4
Murder	0	0
Rape	0	0
Robbery	0	0
Aggravated assault	3	4
Non-violent	80	102
Burglary	16	10
Larceny	63	92
Vehicle theft	1	0
Domestic violence	36	41
Arson	1	0
Total crime rate	11.1	13.6
Violent	0.4	0.5
Non-violent	10.7	13.0

Public School District
(for school year 2006-07 except as noted)

Ocean Township School District
64 Railroad Ave
Waretown, NJ 08758
609-693-3329

- Superintendent .... Donald Bochicchio
- Number of schools 2
- Grade plan K-6
- Enrollment 556
- Attendance rate, '05-06 .... 95.3%
- Dropout rate .... NA
- Students per teacher 9.1
- Per pupil expenditure $14,420
- Median faculty salary $50,800
- Median administrator salary $89,061
- Grade 12 enrollment .... NA
- High school graduation rate .... NA

Assessment test results
(percent scoring at proficient or advanced level)

	Language	Math
NJASK-Grade 3	85.9%	79.5%
GEPA-Grade 8	NA	NA
HSPA-High School	NA	NA

SAT score averages

Pct tested	Math	Verbal	Writing
NA	NA	NA	NA

Teacher Qualifications
- Avg. years of experience 14
- Highly-qualified teachers
  - one subject/all subjects 100%/100%
- With emergency credentials 0.0%

No Child Left Behind
- AYP, 2005-06 .... Meets Standards

Municipal Finance
State Aid Programs, 2008
- Total aid $768,481
- CMPTRA 42,563
- Energy tax receipts 701,694
- Garden State Trust 18,954

General Budget, 2007
- Total tax levy $17,688,435
  - County levy 4,095,314
    - County taxes 3,374,627
    - County library 400,016
    - County health 162,062
    - County open space 158,609
  - School levy 9,025,581
  - Muni. levy 4,567,539
- Misc. revenues 4,704,529

Taxes	2005	2006	2007
General tax rate per $100	1.362	1.417	1.449
County equalization ratio	134.07	105.41	92.46
Net valuation taxable	$1,093,513,551	$1,148,540,400	$1,221,267,417
State equalized value	$1,037,390,713	$1,243,587,870	$1,390,144,705

Monmouth County
Oceanport Borough

Demographics & Socio-Economic Characteristics
(2000 US Census, except as noted)

Population
1980*	5,888
1990*	6,146
2000	5,807
Male	2,875
Female	2,932
2006 (estimate)*	5,751
Population density	1,786.0

Race & Hispanic Origin, 2000
Race
White	5,558
Black/African American	114
American Indian/Alaska Native	4
Asian	46
Native Hawaiian/Pacific Islander	1
Other race	32
Two or more races	52
Hispanic origin, total	120
Mexican	24
Puerto Rican	39
Cuban	12
Other Hispanic	45

Age & Nativity, 2000
Under 5 years	347
18 years and over	4,384
21 years and over	4,104
65 years and over	827
85 years and over	82
Median age	40.5
Native-born	5,595
Foreign-born	220

Educational Attainment, 2000
Population 25 years and over	3,891
Less than 9th grade	3.1%
High school grad or higher	90.6%
Bachelor's degree or higher	35.7%
Graduate degree	10.8%

Income & Poverty, 1999
Per capita income	$33,356
Median household income	$71,458
Median family income	$85,038
Persons in poverty	149
H'holds receiving public assistance	7
H'holds receiving social security	635

Households, 2000
Total households	2,043
With persons under 18	762
With persons over 65	613
Family households	1,555
Single-person households	443
Persons per household	2.71
Persons per family	3.18

Labor & Employment
Total civilian labor force, 2006**	3,003
Unemployment rate	2.2%
Total civilian labor force, 2000	2,798
Unemployment rate	2.3%

Employed persons 16 years and over by occupation, 2000
Managers & professionals	1,221
Service occupations	223
Sales & office occupations	875
Farming, fishing & forestry	0
Construction & maintenance	221
Production & transportation	194
Self-employed persons	159

‡ Branch of county library
* US Census Bureau
** New Jersey Department of Labor

See Introduction for an explanation of all data sources.

General Information
Borough of Oceanport
222 Monmouth Blvd
PO Box 370
Oceanport, NJ 07757
732-222-8221

Website	www.oceanportboro.com
Year of incorporation	1920
Land/water area (sq. miles)	3.22/0.63
Form of government	Borough

Government
Legislative Districts
US Congressional	12
State Legislative	12

Local Officials, 2008
Mayor	Michael J. Mahon
Manager/Admin	NA
Clerk	Kimberly Jungfer
Finance Dir	Gregory Mayers
Tax Assessor	Helen Ward
Tax Collector	Cynthia Cortale
Attorney	John O. Bennett
Building	Walter Joyce
Planning/Zoning	Jeanne Smith (Bd Sec)
Engineering	William White
Public Works	Demitrio Zarate
Police Chief	Harold Sutton
Fire/Emergency Dir	NA

Housing & Construction
Housing Units, 2000*
Total	2,114
Median rent	$672
Median SF home value	$231,400

Permits for New Residential Construction
	Units	Value
Total, 2007	6	$1,996,784
Single family	6	$1,996,784
Total, 2006	10	$3,741,458
Single family	10	$3,741,458

Real Property Valuation, 2007
	Parcels	Valuation
Total	2,114	$1,335,556,300
Vacant	107	28,480,600
Residential	1,974	1,149,894,400
Commercial	30	156,003,000
Industrial	0	0
Apartments	1	669,800
Farm land	1	9,000
Farm homestead	1	499,500

Average Property Value & Tax, 2007
Residential value	$582,478
Property tax	$7,840
Tax credit/rebate	$1,138

Public Library
Oceanport Library‡
Monmouth Blvd & Myrtle Ave
Oceanport, NJ 07757
732-229-2626

Branch Librarian .... Michele Blake

Library statistics, 2006
see Monmouth County profile for library system statistics

Public Safety
Number of officers, 2006 15

Crime
	2005	2006
Total crimes	109	41
Violent	5	1
Murder	0	0
Rape	0	1
Robbery	0	0
Aggravated assault	5	0
Non-violent	104	40
Burglary	11	9
Larceny	92	27
Vehicle theft	1	4
Domestic violence	19	10
Arson	2	3
Total crime rate	18.7	7.1
Violent	0.9	0.2
Non-violent	17.8	6.9

Public School District
(for school year 2006-07 except as noted)

Oceanport Borough School District
29 Wolf Hill Ave
Oceanport, NJ 07757
732-544-8588

Superintendent	Andrew Orefice
Number of schools	2
Grade plan	K-8
Enrollment	693
Attendance rate, '05-06	95.2%
Dropout rate	NA
Students per teacher	10.7
Per pupil expenditure	$10,078
Median faculty salary	$45,310
Median administrator salary	$102,920
Grade 12 enrollment	NA
High school graduation rate	NA

Assessment test results
(percent scoring at proficient or advanced level)
	Language	Math
NJASK-Grade 3	85.5%	89.9%
GEPA-Grade 8	89.7%	87.5%
HSPA-High School	NA	NA

SAT score averages
Pct tested	Math	Verbal	Writing
NA	NA	NA	NA

Teacher Qualifications
Avg. years of experience	11
Highly-qualified teachers one subject/all subjects	98.0%/98.0%
With emergency credentials	0.0%

No Child Left Behind
AYP, 2005-06 .... Meets Standards

Municipal Finance
State Aid Programs, 2008
Total aid	$655,988
CMPTRA	75,275
Energy tax receipts	580,713
Garden State Trust	0

General Budget, 2007
Total tax levy	$17,985,010
County levy	3,392,683
County taxes	2,979,228
County library	170,539
County health	56,754
County open space	186,162
School levy	10,149,338
Muni. levy	4,442,989
Misc. revenues	2,055,864

Taxes
	2005	2006	2007
General tax rate per $100	3.291	1.306	1.346
County equalization ratio	51.65	121.39	108.17
Net valuation taxable	$491,851,779	$1,331,283,400	$1,336,274,205
State equalized value	$1,088,408,451	$1,231,436,704	$1,292,983,314

©2008 Information Publications, Inc. All rights reserved. Photocopying prohibited. For additional copies, contact the publisher at www.informationpublications.com or (877)544-INFO (4636)

The New Jersey Municipal Data Book 367

Ogdensburg Borough
Sussex County

Demographics & Socio-Economic Characteristics
(2000 US Census, except as noted)

Population
- 1980* 2,737
- 1990* 2,722
- 2000 2,638
  - Male 1,335
  - Female 1,303
- 2006 (estimate)* 2,623
- Population density 1,150.4

Race & Hispanic Origin, 2000
Race
- White 2,573
- Black/African American 4
- American Indian/Alaska Native 1
- Asian 19
- Native Hawaiian/Pacific Islander 0
- Other race 7
- Two or more races 34
- Hispanic origin, total 110
  - Mexican 33
  - Puerto Rican 38
  - Cuban 5
  - Other Hispanic 34

Age & Nativity, 2000
- Under 5 years 185
- 18 years and over 1,860
- 21 years and over 1,760
- 65 years and over 212
- 85 years and over 16
  - Median age 35.0
- Native-born 2,480
- Foreign-born 158

Educational Attainment, 2000
- Population 25 years and over 1,668
- Less than 9th grade 2.7%
- High school grad or higher 89.3%
- Bachelor's degree or higher 20.0%
- Graduate degree 5.9%

Income & Poverty, 1999
- Per capita income $24,305
- Median household income $60,313
- Median family income $70,521
- Persons in poverty 150
- H'holds receiving public assistance 5
- H'holds receiving social security 187

Households, 2000
- Total households 881
  - With persons under 18 400
  - With persons over 65 162
  - Family households 705
  - Single-person households 146
- Persons per household 2.99
- Persons per family 3.38

Labor & Employment
- Total civilian labor force, 2006** 1,597
  - Unemployment rate 3.7%
- Total civilian labor force, 2000 1,418
  - Unemployment rate 2.6%

Employed persons 16 years and over by occupation, 2000
- Managers & professionals 465
- Service occupations 152
- Sales & office occupations 406
- Farming, fishing & forestry 0
- Construction & maintenance 141
- Production & transportation 217
- Self-employed persons 43

* US Census Bureau
** New Jersey Department of Labor

General Information
Borough of Ogdensburg
14 Highland Ave
Ogdensburg, NJ 07439
973-827-3444

- Website .... (county website)
- Year of incorporation 1914
- Land/water area (sq. miles) ... 2.28/0.02
- Form of government .... Borough

Government
Legislative Districts
- US Congressional 5
- State Legislative 24

Local Officials, 2008
- Mayor .... James Sekelsky
- Manager/Admin .... NA
- Clerk .... Phyllis Drouin
- Finance Dir .... Linda Padula
- Tax Assessor .... Kathleen Keib
- Tax Collector .... Linda Pettenger
- Attorney .... John Ursin
- Building .... Jan Opt'Hof
- Comm Dev/Planning .... NA
- Engineering .... Eugene Buczynski
- Public Works .... Ken Smith
- Police Chief .... George Lott
- Emerg/Fire Director .... Eric Slater

Housing & Construction
Housing Units, 2000*
- Total 903
- Median rent $775
- Median SF home value $141,600

Permits for New Residential Construction

	Units	Value
Total, 2007	3	$548,250
Single family	3	$548,250
Total, 2006	7	$1,279,250
Single family	7	$1,279,250

Real Property Valuation, 2007

	Parcels	Valuation
Total	896	$116,904,350
Vacant	50	3,253,000
Residential	804	103,237,950
Commercial	29	7,386,800
Industrial	3	1,646,200
Apartments	3	734,700
Farm land	4	21,100
Farm homestead	3	624,600

Average Property Value & Tax, 2007
- Residential value $128,702
- Property tax $6,085
- Tax credit/rebate $1,078

Public Library
No public municipal library

Library statistics, 2006
- Population served .... NA
- Full-time/total staff .... NA/NA

	Total	Per capita
Holdings	NA	NA
Revenues	NA	NA
Expenditures	NA	NA
Annual visits	NA	NA
Internet terminals/annual users	NA/NA	

Public Safety
Number of officers, 2006 7

Crime	2005	2006
Total crimes	5	7
Violent	1	0
Murder	0	0
Rape	0	0
Robbery	0	0
Aggravated assault	1	0
Non-violent	4	7
Burglary	0	2
Larceny	3	5
Vehicle theft	1	0
Domestic violence	24	24
Arson	0	0
Total crime rate	1.9	2.7
Violent	0.4	0.0
Non-violent	1.5	2.7

Public School District
(for school year 2006-07 except as noted)

Ogdensburg Borough School District
100 Main St
Ogdensburg, NJ 07439
973-827-7126

- Chief School Admin .... John Petrelli
- Number of schools 1
- Grade plan K-8
- Enrollment 338
- Attendance rate, '05-06 .... 95.5%
- Dropout rate .... NA
- Students per teacher 9.5
- Per pupil expenditure $11,726
- Median faculty salary $46,328
- Median administrator salary $81,090
- Grade 12 enrollment .... NA
- High school graduation rate .... NA

Assessment test results
(percent scoring at proficient or advanced level)

	Language	Math
NJASK-Grade 3	87.5%	90.6%
GEPA-Grade 8	81.6%	79.0%
HSPA-High School	NA	NA

SAT score averages

Pct tested	Math	Verbal	Writing
NA	NA	NA	NA

Teacher Qualifications
- Avg. years of experience 17
- Highly-qualified teachers
  - one subject/all subjects ... 100%/100%
- With emergency credentials 0.0%

No Child Left Behind
- AYP, 2005-06 .... Meets Standards

Municipal Finance
State Aid Programs, 2008
- Total aid $108,406
  - CMPTRA 0
  - Energy tax receipts 94,725
  - Garden State Trust 13,681

General Budget, 2007
- Total tax levy $5,537,655
  - County levy 938,673
    - County taxes 766,971
    - County library 65,387
    - County health 25,292
    - County open space 81,023
  - School levy 2,865,819
  - Muni. levy 1,733,163
  - Misc. revenues 1,133,350

Taxes	2005	2006	2007
General tax rate per $100	4.37	4.5	4.73
County equalization ratio	65.42	59.25	51.19
Net valuation taxable	$115,381,319	$115,293,750	$117,122,064
State equalized value	$194,736,403	$225,496,501	$244,634,084

Middlesex County
Old Bridge Township

Demographics & Socio-Economic Characteristics[†]
(2000 US Census, except as noted)

Population
1980*	51,515
1990*	56,475
2000	60,456
Male	29,549
Female	30,907
2006 (estimate)*	65,661
Population density	1,723.8

Race & Hispanic Origin, 2000
Race
- White 48,049
- Black/African American 3,207
- American Indian/Alaska Native 94
- Asian 6,544
- Native Hawaiian/Pacific Islander ... 27
- Other race 1,133
- Two or more races 1,402

Hispanic origin, total 4,578
- Mexican 439
- Puerto Rican 2,002
- Cuban 377
- Other Hispanic 1,760

Age & Nativity, 2000
- Under 5 years 4,252
- 18 years and over 44,822
- 21 years and over 43,002
- 65 years and over 6,370
- 85 years and over 695
- Median age 36.5
- Native-born 49,341
- Foreign-born 11,115

Educational Attainment, 2000
- Population 25 years and over ... 40,677
- Less than 9th grade 3.5%
- High school grad or higher 88.4%
- Bachelor's degree or higher 29.5%
- Graduate degree 8.9%

Income & Poverty, 1999
- Per capita income $26,814
- Median household income $64,707
- Median family income $74,045
- Persons in poverty 2,547
- H'holds receiving public assistance ... 253
- H'holds receiving social security ... 4,765

Households, 2000
- Total households 21,438
-   With persons under 18 8,643
-   With persons over 65 4,524
-   Family households 15,959
-   Single-person households ... 4,527
- Persons per household 2.80
- Persons per family 3.30

Labor & Employment
- Total civilian labor force, 2006** ... 35,073
-   Unemployment rate 3.2%
- Total civilian labor force, 2000 ... 31,618
-   Unemployment rate 4.7%

Employed persons 16 years and over by occupation, 2000
- Managers & professionals 11,218
- Service occupations 3,373
- Sales & office occupations 9,469
- Farming, fishing & forestry 21
- Construction & maintenance ... 2,794
- Production & transportation ... 3,265
- Self-employed persons 1,097

[†] see Appendix C for American Community Survey data
* US Census Bureau
** New Jersey Department of Labor
§ State Fiscal Year July 1–June 30

See Introduction for an explanation of all data sources.

General Information
Township of Old Bridge
1 Old Bridge Plaza
Old Bridge, NJ 08857
732-721-5600

- Website .... www.oldbridge.com
- Year of incorporation 1976
- Land/water area (sq. miles) ... 38.09/2.57
- Form of government .... Mayor-Council

Government
Legislative Districts
- US Congressional 6, 12
- State Legislative 13

Local Officials, 2008
- Mayor .... James T. Phillips
- Manager .... Michael Jacobs
- Clerk .... Rose-Marie Saracino
- Finance Dir .... Himanshu Shah
- Tax Assessor .... Brian Enright
- Tax Collector .... Kathleen Silber
- Attorney .... Jerome J. Convery
- Building .... Alex Tucciarone
- Planning .... Ellen Ritchie
- Engineering .... James E. Cleary
- Public Works .... Rocco Donatelli
- Police Chief .... Thomas Collow
- Public Safety Dir ...... Michael Jacobs

Housing & Construction
Housing Units, 2000*
- Total 21,896
- Median rent $770
- Median SF home value $162,800

Permits for New Residential Construction
	Units	Value
Total, 2007	39	$5,751,506
Single family	29	$5,743,306
Total, 2006	270	$36,015,061
Single family	236	$33,566,570

Real Property Valuation, 2007
	Parcels	Valuation
Total	19,767	$3,335,270,600
Vacant	1,382	97,428,300
Residential	17,687	2,670,475,100
Commercial	461	329,575,900
Industrial	58	50,693,700
Apartments	25	177,960,400
Farm land	120	3,673,100
Farm homestead	34	5,464,100

Average Property Value & Tax, 2007
- Residential value $151,004
- Property tax $6,024
- Tax credit/rebate $1,037

Public Library
Old Bridge Public Library
1 Old Bridge Plaza
Old Bridge, NJ 08857
732-721-5600

- Director .... Margery Kirby Cyr

Library statistics, 2006
- Population served 60,456
- Full-time/total staff 8/17

	Total	Per capita
Holdings	166,581	2.76
Revenues	$2,163,736	$35.79
Expenditures	$2,116,499	$35.01
Annual visits	334,392	5.53
Internet terminals/annual users	15/53,000	

Taxes
	2005	2006	2007
General tax rate per $100	3.67	3.82	3.99
County equalization ratio	57.6	51.55	45.47
Net valuation taxable	$3,265,492,900	$3,304,444,000	$3,339,763,515
State equalized value	$6,334,612,803	$7,272,220,920	$7,837,444,066

Public Safety
Number of officers, 2006 104

Crime
	2005	2006
Total crimes	1,093	1,000
Violent	65	54
Murder	1	0
Rape	6	5
Robbery	27	18
Aggravated assault	31	31
Non-violent	1,028	946
Burglary	181	239
Larceny	754	625
Vehicle theft	93	82
Domestic violence	440	447
Arson	9	9
Total crime rate	17.0	15.4
Violent	1.0	0.8
Non-violent	16.0	14.6

Public School District
(for school year 2006-07 except as noted)

Old Bridge Township School District
4207 Route 516
Matawan, NJ 07747
732-290-3976

- Superintendent .... Simon M. Bosco
- Number of schools 15
- Grade plan K-12
- Enrollment 9,782
- Attendance rate, '05-06 .... 95.2%
- Dropout rate 0.8%
- Students per teacher 12.6
- Per pupil expenditure $11,984
- Median faculty salary $57,544
- Median administrator salary . $110,074
- Grade 12 enrollment 744
- High school graduation rate ... 96.4%

Assessment test results
(percent scoring at proficient or advanced level)
	Language	Math
NJASK-Grade 3	87.4%	91.8%
GEPA-Grade 8	81.6%	73.7%
HSPA-High School	92.8%	79.8%

SAT score averages
Pct tested	Math	Verbal	Writing
78%	502	483	489

Teacher Qualifications
- Avg. years of experience 10
- Highly-qualified teachers
    one subject/all subjects ... 99.5%/99.5%
- With emergency credentials 0.0%

No Child Left Behind
- AYP, 2005-06 ...... Needs Improvement

Municipal Finance[§]
State Aid Programs, 2008
- Total aid $8,032,976
-   CMPTRA 3,407,236
-   Energy tax receipts 4,607,109
-   Garden State Trust 18,631

General Budget, 2007
- Total tax levy $133,240,133
-   County levy 21,219,566
-     County taxes 18,996,422
-     County library 0
-     County health 0
-     County open space ... 2,223,143
-   School levy 84,967,283
-   Muni. levy 27,053,284
-   Misc. revenues 25,479,035

Old Tappan Borough
Bergen County

Demographics & Socio-Economic Characteristics
(2000 US Census, except as noted)

Population
1980*	4,168
1990*	4,254
2000	5,482
Male	2,632
Female	2,850
2006 (estimate)*	6,013
Population density	1,861.6

Race & Hispanic Origin, 2000
Race
White	4,533
Black/African American	33
American Indian/Alaska Native	3
Asian	857
Native Hawaiian/Pacific Islander	0
Other race	24
Two or more races	32
Hispanic origin, total	151
Mexican	14
Puerto Rican	28
Cuban	36
Other Hispanic	73

Age & Nativity, 2000
Under 5 years	346
18 years and over	4,004
21 years and over	3,844
65 years and over	798
85 years and over	110
Median age	41.0
Native-born	4,562
Foreign-born	920

Educational Attainment, 2000
Population 25 years and over	3,708
Less than 9th grade	1.8%
High school grad or higher	93.5%
Bachelor's degree or higher	49.4%
Graduate degree	18.3%

Income & Poverty, 1999
Per capita income	$48,367
Median household income	$102,127
Median family income	$106,772
Persons in poverty	94
H'holds receiving public assistance	16
H'holds receiving social security	519

Households, 2000
Total households	1,778
With persons under 18	780
With persons over 65	478
Family households	1,542
Single-person households	215
Persons per household	3.02
Persons per family	3.28

Labor & Employment
Total civilian labor force, 2006**	2,774
Unemployment rate	3.1%
Total civilian labor force, 2000	2,607
Unemployment rate	3.0%

Employed persons 16 years and over by occupation, 2000
Managers & professionals	1,389
Service occupations	188
Sales & office occupations	775
Farming, fishing & forestry	0
Construction & maintenance	86
Production & transportation	92
Self-employed persons	197

* US Census Bureau
** New Jersey Department of Labor

General Information
Borough of Old Tappan
227 Old Tappan Rd
Old Tappan, NJ 07675
201-664-1849

Website	www.oldtappan.net
Year of incorporation	1894
Land/water area (sq. miles)	3.23/0.85
Form of government	Borough

Government
Legislative Districts
US Congressional	5
State Legislative	39

Local Officials, 2008
Mayor	Victor Polce
Manager	Patrick O'Brien
Clerk	Jeanine Siek (Actg)
Finance Dir	Rebecca Overgaard
Tax Assessor	Irwin Sabin
Tax Collector	Rebecca Overgaard
Attorney	Allen Bell
Building	Peiro Abballe
Planning	Rea Epstein
Engineering	Thomas W. Skrable
Public Works	Arthur Lake
Police Chief	Joseph Fasulo
Emerg/Fire Director	Nicola Lepore

Housing & Construction
Housing Units, 2000*
Total	1,804
Median rent	$940
Median SF home value	$436,900

Permits for New Residential Construction
	Units	Value
Total, 2007	18	$7,981,372
Single family	18	$7,981,372
Total, 2006	35	$17,373,625
Single family	35	$17,373,625

Real Property Valuation, 2007
	Parcels	Valuation
Total	2,046	$1,264,632,700
Vacant	77	36,722,900
Residential	1,915	1,165,297,800
Commercial	50	61,889,900
Industrial	0	0
Apartments	1	331,800
Farm land	1	9,900
Farm homestead	2	380,400

Average Property Value & Tax, 2007
Residential value	$608,074
Property tax	$12,025
Tax credit/rebate	$1,383

Public Library
Old Tappan Public Library
56 Russell Ave
Old Tappan, NJ 07675
201-664-3499

Director	Susan Meeske

Library statistics, 2006
Population served	5,482
Full-time/total staff	1/2

	Total	Per capita
Holdings	52,270	9.53
Revenues	$556,885	$101.58
Expenditures	$375,421	$68.48
Annual visits	55,665	10.15
Internet terminals/annual users	3/6,344	

Public Safety
Number of officers, 2006 13

Crime
	2005	2006
Total crimes	39	34
Violent	0	4
Murder	0	0
Rape	0	0
Robbery	0	0
Aggravated assault	0	4
Non-violent	39	30
Burglary	4	3
Larceny	35	27
Vehicle theft	0	0
Domestic violence	4	6
Arson	0	0
Total crime rate	6.6	5.8
Violent	0.0	0.7
Non-violent	6.6	5.1

Public School District
(for school year 2006-07 except as noted)

Old Tappan School District
277 Old Tappan Rd, Demarest School
Old Tappan, NJ 07675
201-664-7231

Superintendent	William Ward
Number of schools	2
Grade plan	K-8
Enrollment	869
Attendance rate, '05-06	96.5%
Dropout rate	NA
Students per teacher	12.3
Per pupil expenditure	$13,182
Median faculty salary	$58,152
Median administrator salary	$114,700
Grade 12 enrollment	NA
High school graduation rate	NA

Assessment test results
(percent scoring at proficient or advanced level)
	Language	Math
NJASK-Grade 3	95.6%	98.9%
GEPA-Grade 8	97.2%	95.3%
HSPA-High School	NA	NA

SAT score averages
Pct tested	Math	Verbal	Writing
NA	NA	NA	NA

Teacher Qualifications
Avg. years of experience	8
Highly-qualified teachers one subject/all subjects	86.0%/86.0%
With emergency credentials	0.0%

No Child Left Behind
AYP, 2005-06 .... Meets Standards

Municipal Finance
State Aid Programs, 2008
Total aid	$1,674,571
CMPTRA	0
Energy tax receipts	1,636,031
Garden State Trust	0

General Budget, 2007
Total tax levy	$25,025,978
County levy	3,402,429
County taxes	3,215,248
County library	0
County health	0
County open space	187,181
School levy	18,244,949
Muni. levy	3,378,600
Misc. revenues	4,942,507

Taxes
	2005	2006	2007
General tax rate per $100	1.89	1.93	1.98
County equalization ratio	85.45	76.23	67.69
Net valuation taxable	$1,210,174,760	$1,241,755,700	$1,265,537,977
State equalized value	$1,587,530,841	$1,835,443,517	$1,901,179,807

Salem County

Oldmans Township

Demographics & Socio-Economic Characteristics
(2000 US Census, except as noted)

Population
1980*	1,847
1990*	1,683
2000	1,798
Male	909
Female	889
2006 (estimate)*	1,827
Population density	91.5

Race & Hispanic Origin, 2000
Race
White	1,561
Black/African American	173
American Indian/Alaska Native	5
Asian	3
Native Hawaiian/Pacific Islander	0
Other race	36
Two or more races	20
Hispanic origin, total	75
Mexican	27
Puerto Rican	29
Cuban	0
Other Hispanic	19

Age & Nativity, 2000
Under 5 years	98
18 years and over	1,355
21 years and over	1,292
65 years and over	213
85 years and over	22
Median age	39.1
Native-born	1,755
Foreign-born	43

Educational Attainment, 2000
Population 25 years and over	1,236
Less than 9th grade	5.6%
High school grad or higher	81.9%
Bachelor's degree or higher	10.9%
Graduate degree	3.2%

Income & Poverty, 1999
Per capita income	$22,495
Median household income	$57,589
Median family income	$64,091
Persons in poverty	146
H'holds receiving public assistance	7
H'holds receiving social security	179

Households, 2000
Total households	654
With persons under 18	235
With persons over 65	152
Family households	517
Single-person households	111
Persons per household	2.74
Persons per family	3.07

Labor & Employment
Total civilian labor force, 2006**	982
Unemployment rate	4.4%
Total civilian labor force, 2000	950
Unemployment rate	5.9%

Employed persons 16 years and over by occupation, 2000
Managers & professionals	230
Service occupations	96
Sales & office occupations	250
Farming, fishing & forestry	5
Construction & maintenance	111
Production & transportation	202
Self-employed persons	60

* US Census Bureau
** New Jersey Department of Labor

See Introduction for an explanation of all data sources.

General Information
Township of Oldmans
PO Box 416
Pedricktown, NJ 08067
856-299-0780

Website	oldmanstownship.com
Year of incorporation	1881
Land/water area (sq. miles)	19.97/0.33
Form of government	Township

Government
Legislative Districts
US Congressional	2
State Legislative	3

Local Officials, 2008
Mayor	Harry A. Moore
Manager/Admin	NA
Clerk	Susan Miller
Finance Dir	James Hackett
Tax Assessor	Michael Raio
Tax Collector	Margie L. Schieber
Attorney	John Hoffman
Building	Jeryl Goff
Comm Dev/Planning	NA
Engineering	John Bickel
Public Works	NA
Police Chief	NA
Emerg/Fire Director	Gary Moore

Housing & Construction
Housing Units, 2000*
Total	694
Median rent	$714
Median SF home value	$104,300

Permits for New Residential Construction
	Units	Value
Total, 2007	2	$125,000
Single family	2	$125,000
Total, 2006	5	$612,100
Single family	5	$612,100

Real Property Valuation, 2007
	Parcels	Valuation
Total	1,217	$111,599,840
Vacant	227	3,506,700
Residential	577	53,707,900
Commercial	35	5,218,400
Industrial	14	35,137,370
Apartments	0	0
Farm land	256	3,164,670
Farm homestead	108	10,864,800

Average Property Value & Tax, 2007
Residential value	$94,267
Property tax	$3,842
Tax credit/rebate	$863

Public Library
No public municipal library

Library statistics, 2006
Population served	NA
Full-time/total staff	NA/NA

	Total	Per capita
Holdings	NA	NA
Revenues	NA	NA
Expenditures	NA	NA
Annual visits	NA	NA
Internet terminals/annual users	NA/NA	

Taxes
	2005	2006	2007
General tax rate per $100	3.77	4.003	4.076
County equalization ratio	70.29	67.89	67.07
Net valuation taxable	$110,995,461	$111,370,740	$111,962,987
State equalized value	$163,493,093	$166,409,453	$189,291,266

Public Safety
Number of officers, 2006	0

Crime	2005	2006
Total crimes	55	52
Violent	1	3
Murder	0	0
Rape	0	0
Robbery	0	2
Aggravated assault	1	1
Non-violent	54	49
Burglary	11	16
Larceny	39	32
Vehicle theft	4	1
Domestic violence	16	3
Arson	3	0
Total crime rate	30.4	28.4
Violent	0.6	1.6
Non-violent	29.8	26.7

Public School District
(for school year 2006-07 except as noted)

Oldmans Township School District
10 Freed Rd
Pedricktown, NJ 08067
856-299-4240

Chief School Admin	Stephen Combs
Number of schools	1
Grade plan	K-8
Enrollment	220
Attendance rate, '05-06	95.1%
Dropout rate	NA
Students per teacher	8.9
Per pupil expenditure	$13,272
Median faculty salary	$66,244
Median administrator salary	$70,925
Grade 12 enrollment	NA
High school graduation rate	NA

Assessment test results
(percent scoring at proficient or advanced level)
	Language	Math
NJASK-Grade 3	92.8%	89.3%
GEPA-Grade 8	78.9%	89.5%
HSPA-High School	NA	NA

SAT score averages
Pct tested	Math	Verbal	Writing
NA	NA	NA	NA

Teacher Qualifications
Avg. years of experience	20
Highly-qualified teachers one subject/all subjects	100%/100%
With emergency credentials	0.0%

No Child Left Behind
AYP, 2005-06	Meets Standards

Municipal Finance
State Aid Programs, 2008
Total aid	$262,460
CMPTRA	0
Energy tax receipts	261,844
Garden State Trust	616

General Budget, 2007
Total tax levy	$4,563,608
County levy	1,579,475
County taxes	1,545,782
County library	0
County health	0
County open space	33,693
School levy	2,761,407
Muni. levy	222,726
Misc. revenues	1,155,263

The New Jersey Municipal Data Book

Oradell Borough
Bergen County

Demographics & Socio-Economic Characteristics
(2000 US Census, except as noted)

Population
1980*	8,658
1990*	8,024
2000	8,047
Male	3,849
Female	4,198
2006 (estimate)*	7,957
Population density	3,288.0

Race & Hispanic Origin, 2000
Race
White	7,248
Black/African American	39
American Indian/Alaska Native	3
Asian	651
Native Hawaiian/Pacific Islander	1
Other race	26
Two or more races	79
Hispanic origin, total	249
Mexican	12
Puerto Rican	72
Cuban	64
Other Hispanic	101

Age & Nativity, 2000
Under 5 years	509
18 years and over	6,020
21 years and over	5,852
65 years and over	1,337
85 years and over	182
Median age	41.5
Native-born	6,976
Foreign-born	1,071

Educational Attainment, 2000
Population 25 years and over	5,617
Less than 9th grade	1.8%
High school grad or higher	94.9%
Bachelor's degree or higher	51.8%
Graduate degree	21.4%

Income & Poverty, 1999
Per capita income	$39,520
Median household income	$91,014
Median family income	$102,842
Persons in poverty	193
H'holds receiving public assistance	17
H'holds receiving social security	784

Households, 2000
Total households	2,789
With persons under 18	1,097
With persons over 65	858
Family households	2,300
Single-person households	438
Persons per household	2.83
Persons per family	3.17

Labor & Employment
Total civilian labor force, 2006**	4,220
Unemployment rate	2.8%
Total civilian labor force, 2000	3,980
Unemployment rate	2.9%

Employed persons 16 years and over by occupation, 2000
Managers & professionals	2,189
Service occupations	234
Sales & office occupations	1,124
Farming, fishing & forestry	0
Construction & maintenance	124
Production & transportation	194
Self-employed persons	270

* US Census Bureau
** New Jersey Department of Labor

General Information
Borough of Oradell
355 Kinderkamack Rd
Oradell, NJ 07649
201-261-8200

Website	www.oradell.org
Year of incorporation	1922
Land/water area (sq. miles)	2.42/0.13
Form of government	Borough

Government
Legislative Districts
US Congressional	5
State Legislative	39

Local Officials, 2008
Mayor	Dianne Camelo Didio
Administrator	Wolfgang Albrecht Jr
Clerk	Laura J. Graham
Finance Dir	Roy Rossow
Tax Assessor	James Anzevino
Tax Collector	Roy Rossow
Attorney	Andrew P. Oddo
Building	Stephen A. Depken
Comm Dev/Planning	NA
Engineering	Boswell McClave
Public Works	Robert Stauffer
Police Chief	Rhynie Emanuel
Emerg/Fire Director	Kevin Burns

Housing & Construction
Housing Units, 2000*
Total	2,833
Median rent	$957
Median SF home value	$330,900

Permits for New Residential Construction
	Units	Value
Total, 2007	6	$3,095,955
Single family	6	$3,095,955
Total, 2006	5	$2,180,954
Single family	5	$2,180,954

Real Property Valuation, 2007
	Parcels	Valuation
Total	2,765	$839,971,000
Vacant	26	2,623,700
Residential	2,639	733,704,800
Commercial	94	99,879,500
Industrial	1	187,100
Apartments	5	3,575,900
Farm land	0	0
Farm homestead	0	0

Average Property Value & Tax, 2007
Residential value	$278,024
Property tax	$11,089
Tax credit/rebate	$1,435

Public Library
Oradell Public Library
375 Kinderkamack Rd
Oradell, NJ 07649
201-262-2613

Director ... Beth Zeigler

Library statistics, 2006
Population served	8,047
Full-time/total staff	3/6

	Total	Per capita
Holdings	70,195	8.72
Revenues	$744,309	$92.50
Expenditures	$776,927	$96.55
Annual visits	123,882	15.39
Internet terminals/annual users	13/3,720	

Public Safety
Number of officers, 2006 ... 22

Crime	2005	2006
Total crimes	63	74
Violent	2	4
Murder	0	0
Rape	0	0
Robbery	1	0
Aggravated assault	1	4
Non-violent	61	70
Burglary	20	16
Larceny	41	54
Vehicle theft	0	0
Domestic violence	34	24
Arson	0	1
Total crime rate	7.8	9.2
Violent	0.2	0.5
Non-violent	7.6	8.7

Public School District
(for school year 2006-07 except as noted)

Oradell School District
350 Prospect Ave
Oradell, NJ 07649
201-261-1153

Superintendent	Jeffrey S. Mohre
Number of schools	1
Grade plan	K-6
Enrollment	791
Attendance rate, '05-06	96.6%
Dropout rate	NA
Students per teacher	12.5
Per pupil expenditure	$11,553
Median faculty salary	$42,050
Median administrator salary	$107,860
Grade 12 enrollment	NA
High school graduation rate	NA

Assessment test results
(percent scoring at proficient or advanced level)
	Language	Math
NJASK-Grade 3	90.8%	96.3%
GEPA-Grade 8	NA	NA
HSPA-High School	NA	NA

SAT score averages
Pct tested	Math	Verbal	Writing
NA	NA	NA	NA

Teacher Qualifications
Avg. years of experience	8
Highly-qualified teachers one subject/all subjects	98.0%/98.0%
With emergency credentials	0.0%

No Child Left Behind
AYP, 2005-06 ... Meets Standards

Municipal Finance
State Aid Programs, 2008
Total aid	$1,035,032
CMPTRA	37,070
Energy tax receipts	983,862
Garden State Trust	0

General Budget, 2007
Total tax levy	$33,536,543
County levy	3,319,456
County taxes	3,136,144
County library	0
County health	0
County open space	183,312
School levy	21,944,365
Muni. levy	8,272,722
Misc. revenues	4,749,664

Taxes	2005	2006	2007
General tax rate per $100	3.56	3.78	3.99
County equalization ratio	55.79	49.38	45.93
Net valuation taxable	$837,944,713	$839,991,400	$840,814,283
State equalized value	$1,696,931,375	$1,829,554,273	$1,830,048,422

Essex County

Orange City Township

Demographics & Socio-Economic Characteristics
(2000 US Census, except as noted)

Population
1980*	31,136
1990*	29,925
2000	32,868
Male	15,199
Female	17,669
2006 (estimate)*	31,858
Population density	14,415.4

Race & Hispanic Origin, 2000
Race
White	4,337
Black/African American	24,685
American Indian/Alaska Native	113
Asian	415
Native Hawaiian/Pacific Islander	33
Other race	1,712
Two or more races	1,573
Hispanic origin, total	4,097
Mexican	387
Puerto Rican	538
Cuban	38
Other Hispanic	3,134

Age & Nativity, 2000
Under 5 years	2,810
18 years and over	23,760
21 years and over	22,469
65 years and over	3,562
85 years and over	504
Median age	32.5
Native-born	22,575
Foreign-born	10,293

Educational Attainment, 2000
Population 25 years and over	20,628
Less than 9th grade	10.0%
High school grad or higher	72.2%
Bachelor's degree or higher	16.7%
Graduate degree	6.3%

Income & Poverty, 1999
Per capita income	$16,861
Median household income	$35,759
Median family income	$40,852
Persons in poverty	6,078
H'holds receiving public assistance	885
H'holds receiving social security	2,699

Households, 2000
Total households	11,885
With persons under 18	4,783
With persons over 65	2,693
Family households	7,647
Single-person households	3,589
Persons per household	2.73
Persons per family	3.38

Labor & Employment
Total civilian labor force, 2006**	15,008
Unemployment rate	6.7%
Total civilian labor force, 2000	15,403
Unemployment rate	11.0%

Employed persons 16 years and over by occupation, 2000
Managers & professionals	3,513
Service occupations	3,170
Sales & office occupations	3,975
Farming, fishing & forestry	23
Construction & maintenance	1,061
Production & transportation	1,968
Self-employed persons	491

* US Census Bureau
** New Jersey Department of Labor
§ State Fiscal Year July 1–June 30

See Introduction for an explanation of all data sources.

General Information
City of Orange Township
29 N Day St
Orange, NJ 07050
973-266-4005

Website	www.ci.orange.nj.us
Year of incorporation	1981
Land/water area (sq. miles)	2.21/0.00
Form of government	Mayor-Council

Government
Legislative Districts
US Congressional	10
State Legislative	27

Local Officials, 2008
Mayor	Mims Hackett Jr
Manager	Jewel V. Thompson
Clerk	Dwight Mitchell
Finance Dir	Jack Kelly
Tax Assessor	Brigida Caruso
Tax Collector	David Marshall
Attorney	Marvin Braker
Building	Robert Corrado
Planning	Larry Samuels
Engineering	Richard W. Moody
Public Works	Robert Corrado
Police Chief	Aric D. Webster
Emerg/Fire Director	Allen Barnhardt

Housing & Construction
Housing Units, 2000*
Total	12,665
Median rent	$687
Median SF home value	$131,400

Permits for New Residential Construction
	Units	Value
Total, 2007	69	$4,984,136
Single family	18	$1,617,512
Total, 2006	72	$5,417,378
Single family	25	$2,511,985

Real Property Valuation, 2007
	Parcels	Valuation
Total	5,151	$1,615,555,200
Vacant	344	23,515,300
Residential	4,069	1,003,783,300
Commercial	518	277,150,500
Industrial	54	48,929,300
Apartments	166	262,176,800
Farm land	0	0
Farm homestead	0	0

Average Property Value & Tax, 2007
Residential value	$246,690
Property tax	$7,160
Tax credit/rebate	$1,193

Public Library
Orange Public Library
348 Main St
Orange, NJ 07050
973-673-0153

Director	Doris T. Walker

Library statistics, 2006
Population served	32,868
Full-time/total staff	4/13

	Total	Per capita
Holdings	207,317	6.31
Revenues	$926,256	$28.18
Expenditures	$907,311	$27.60
Annual visits	96,703	2.94
Internet terminals/annual users	16/47,078	

Public Safety
Number of officers, 2006		104
Crime	**2005**	**2006**
Total crimes	1,951	1,846
Violent	360	424
Murder	4	5
Rape	9	10
Robbery	217	266
Aggravated assault	130	143
Non-violent	1,591	1,422
Burglary	364	359
Larceny	635	630
Vehicle theft	592	433
Domestic violence	401	422
Arson	3	5
Total crime rate	60.2	57.5
Violent	11.1	13.2
Non-violent	49.1	44.3

Public School District
(for school year 2006-07 except as noted)

City Of Orange Township School District
451 Lincoln Ave
Orange, NJ 07050
973-677-4000

Superintendent	Nathan N. Parker
Number of schools	10
Grade plan	K-12
Enrollment	4,597
Attendance rate, '05-06	95.0%
Dropout rate	2.1%
Students per teacher	8.5
Per pupil expenditure	$14,290
Median faculty salary	$49,488
Median administrator salary	$94,764
Grade 12 enrollment	231
High school graduation rate	87.2%

Assessment test results
(percent scoring at proficient or advanced level)
	Language	Math
NJASK-Grade 3	75.1%	80.5%
GEPA-Grade 8	36.3%	25.5%
HSPA-High School	53.1%	24.6%

SAT score averages
Pct tested	Math	Verbal	Writing
82%	366	358	364

Teacher Qualifications
Avg. years of experience	6
Highly-qualified teachers one subject/all subjects	98.0%/98.0%
With emergency credentials	1.7%

No Child Left Behind
AYP, 2005-06	Needs Improvement

Municipal Finance§
State Aid Programs, 2008
Total aid	$9,669,549
CMPTRA	6,997,165
Energy tax receipts	2,672,384
Garden State Trust	0

General Budget, 2007
Total tax levy	$46,935,303
County levy	6,171,775
County taxes	6,013,024
County library	0
County health	0
County open space	158,752
School levy	9,013,468
Muni. levy	31,750,060
Misc. revenues	19,633,728

Taxes
	2005	2006	2007
General tax rate per $100	37.77	2.78	2.91
County equalization ratio	9.9	125.33	103.04
Net valuation taxable	$110,007,639	$1,638,734,300	$1,617,154,414
State equalized value	$1,304,954,199	$1,644,606,337	$1,769,745,433

Oxford Township
Warren County

Demographics & Socio-Economic Characteristics
(2000 US Census, except as noted)

Population
1980*	1,659
1990*	1,790
2000	2,307
Male	1,137
Female	1,170
2006 (estimate)*	2,622
Population density	441.4

Race & Hispanic Origin, 2000
Race
White	2,228
Black/African American	28
American Indian/Alaska Native	5
Asian	12
Native Hawaiian/Pacific Islander	0
Other race	15
Two or more races	19
Hispanic origin, total	80
Mexican	2
Puerto Rican	38
Cuban	4
Other Hispanic	36

Age & Nativity, 2000
Under 5 years	163
18 years and over	1,673
21 years and over	1,621
65 years and over	261
85 years and over	32
Median age	36.4
Native-born	2,223
Foreign-born	84

Educational Attainment, 2000
Population 25 years and over	1,568
Less than 9th grade	6.1%
High school grad or higher	82.1%
Bachelor's degree or higher	19.8%
Graduate degree	5.0%

Income & Poverty, 1999
Per capita income	$23,515
Median household income	$53,359
Median family income	$63,750
Persons in poverty	92
H'holds receiving public assistance	22
H'holds receiving social security	214

Households, 2000
Total households	886
With persons under 18	340
With persons over 65	209
Family households	618
Single-person households	233
Persons per household	2.60
Persons per family	3.18

Labor & Employment
Total civilian labor force, 2006**	1,400
Unemployment rate	7.5%
Total civilian labor force, 2000	1,219
Unemployment rate	6.8%

Employed persons 16 years and over by occupation, 2000
Managers & professionals	346
Service occupations	194
Sales & office occupations	281
Farming, fishing & forestry	4
Construction & maintenance	139
Production & transportation	172
Self-employed persons	63

* US Census Bureau
** New Jersey Department of Labor

General Information
Township of Oxford
11 Green St
PO Box 119
Oxford, NJ 07863
908-453-3098

Website	oxfordnj.org
Year of incorporation	1874
Land/water area (sq. miles)	5.94/0.08
Form of government	Township

Government
Legislative Districts
US Congressional	5
State Legislative	23

Local Officials, 2008
Mayor	Bonnie Riley
Manager/Admin	NA
Clerk	Sheila L. Oberly
Finance Dir	Dawn Stanchina
Tax Assessor	Richard Motyka
Tax Collector	Karen Lance
Attorney	Michael Lavery
Building	DCA
Planning	Peggy Housman
Engineering	Michael Finelli
Public Works	Lou Accetturo
Police Chief	Charles Lilly
Emerg/Fire Director	Richard Calabrese

Housing & Construction
Housing Units, 2000*
Total	938
Median rent	$665
Median SF home value	$125,200

Permits for New Residential Construction
	Units	Value
Total, 2007	5	$235,000
Single family	5	$235,000
Total, 2006	4	$166,500
Single family	4	$166,500

Real Property Valuation, 2007
	Parcels	Valuation
Total	1,153	$242,387,860
Vacant	199	5,426,300
Residential	855	214,930,200
Commercial	25	10,050,400
Industrial	4	5,973,400
Apartments	0	0
Farm land	52	239,860
Farm homestead	18	5,767,700

Average Property Value & Tax, 2007
Residential value	$252,804
Property tax	$5,667
Tax credit/rebate	$986

Public Library
Oxford Public Library
42 Washington Ave
Oxford, NJ 07863
908-453-2625

Librarian	Jean Docker

Library statistics, 2006
Population served	2,307
Full-time/total staff	NA/0

	Total	Per capita
Holdings	NA	NA
Revenues	NA	NA
Expenditures	NA	NA
Annual visits	NA	NA
Internet terminals/annual users	NA/NA	

Public Safety
Number of officers, 2006	4

Crime	2005	2006
Total crimes	19	15
Violent	1	1
Murder	0	0
Rape	0	0
Robbery	0	0
Aggravated assault	1	1
Non-violent	18	14
Burglary	9	3
Larceny	9	10
Vehicle theft	0	1
Domestic violence	11	24
Arson	0	0
Total crime rate	7.2	5.7
Violent	0.4	0.4
Non-violent	6.9	5.3

Public School District
(for school year 2006-07 except as noted)

Oxford Township School District
17 Kent St
Oxford, NJ 07863
908-453-4101

Chief School Admin	Robert Magnuson
Number of schools	1
Grade plan	K-8
Enrollment	318
Attendance rate, '05-06	95.4%
Dropout rate	NA
Students per teacher	10.7
Per pupil expenditure	$11,030
Median faculty salary	$42,612
Median administrator salary	$92,000
Grade 12 enrollment	NA
High school graduation rate	NA

Assessment test results
(percent scoring at proficient or advanced level)
	Language	Math
NJASK-Grade 3	88.0%	96.0%
GEPA-Grade 8	71.1%	70.2%
HSPA-High School	NA	NA

SAT score averages
Pct tested	Math	Verbal	Writing
NA	NA	NA	NA

Teacher Qualifications
Avg. years of experience	6
Highly-qualified teachers one subject/all subjects	100%/96.0%
With emergency credentials	0.0%

No Child Left Behind
AYP, 2005-06	Meets Standards

Municipal Finance
State Aid Programs, 2008
Total aid	$183,659
CMPTRA	0
Energy tax receipts	180,117
Garden State Trust	3,542

General Budget, 2007
Total tax levy	$5,455,549
County levy	1,410,921
County taxes	1,151,917
County library	120,256
County health	0
County open space	138,748
School levy	3,557,968
Muni. levy	486,660
Misc. revenues	1,925,630

Taxes	2005	2006	2007
General tax rate per $100	3.66	3.95	2.25
County equalization ratio	64.49	57.5	106
Net valuation taxable	$118,041,191	$117,911,708	$243,353,138
State equalized value	$205,289,028	$226,616,169	$238,414,200

Bergen County
Palisades Park Borough

Demographics & Socio-Economic Characteristics
(2000 US Census, except as noted)

Population
- 1980* 13,732
- 1990* 14,536
- 2000 17,073
  - Male 8,497
  - Female 8,576
- 2006 (estimate)* 19,306
  - Population density 15,955.4

Race & Hispanic Origin, 2000
Race
- White 8,241
- Black/African American 235
- American Indian/Alaska Native 32
- Asian 7,016
- Native Hawaiian/Pacific Islander 5
- Other race 991
- Two or more races 553
- Hispanic origin, total 2,813
  - Mexican 86
  - Puerto Rican 293
  - Cuban 279
  - Other Hispanic 2,155

Age & Nativity, 2000
- Under 5 years 1,152
- 18 years and over 13,761
- 21 years and over 13,182
- 65 years and over 2,061
- 85 years and over 222
  - Median age 35.6
- Native-born 7,348
- Foreign-born 9,725

Educational Attainment, 2000
- Population 25 years and over 12,173
- Less than 9th grade 11.4%
- High school grad or higher 79.3%
- Bachelor's degree or higher 30.6%
- Graduate degree 7.5%

Income & Poverty, 1999
- Per capita income $22,607
- Median household income $48,015
- Median family income $54,503
- Persons in poverty 1,659
- H'holds receiving public assistance ... 137
- H'holds receiving social security ... 1,373

Households, 2000
- Total households 6,247
  - With persons under 18 2,083
  - With persons over 65 1,537
  - Family households 4,445
  - Single-person households 1,429
- Persons per household 2.73
- Persons per family 3.20

Labor & Employment
- Total civilian labor force, 2006** ... 9,431
  - Unemployment rate 4.5%
- Total civilian labor force, 2000 ... 8,874
  - Unemployment rate 4.3%

Employed persons 16 years and over by occupation, 2000
- Managers & professionals 2,809
- Service occupations 1,405
- Sales & office occupations 2,498
- Farming, fishing & forestry 0
- Construction & maintenance 674
- Production & transportation 1,107
- Self-employed persons 482

* US Census Bureau
** New Jersey Department of Labor

See Introduction for an explanation of all data sources.

General Information
Borough of Palisades Park
275 Broad Ave
Palisades Park, NJ 07650
201-585-4100

- Website .... NA
- Year of incorporation 1899
- Land/water area (sq. miles) ... 1.21/0.06
- Form of government .... Borough

Government
Legislative Districts
- US Congressional 9
- State Legislative 37

Local Officials, 2008
- Mayor .... James Rotundo
- Manager/Admin .... David Lorenzo
- Clerk .... Martin A. Gobbo
- Finance Dir .... Roy Riggitano
- Tax Assessor .... Jim Anzevino
- Tax Collector .... Michael Apicella
- Attorney .... Joseph Mariniello
- Building .... Anthony Pollotta
- Comm Dev/Planning .... NA
- Engineering .... Steven Collazuol
- Public Works .... Mark Pasquali
- Police Chief .... Michael Vietri
- Emerg/Fire Director ..... Steven Killion

Housing & Construction
Housing Units, 2000*
- Total 6,386
- Median rent $903
- Median SF home value $231,700

Permits for New Residential Construction

	Units	Value
Total, 2007	76	$12,262,100
Single family	10	$2,117,500
Total, 2006	132	$21,959,450
Single family	44	$7,087,800

Real Property Valuation, 2007

	Parcels	Valuation
Total	3,720	$1,112,106,250
Vacant	86	15,457,200
Residential	3,316	868,270,100
Commercial	199	107,751,650
Industrial	40	51,577,700
Apartments	79	69,049,600
Farm land	0	0
Farm homestead	0	0

Average Property Value & Tax, 2007
- Residential value $261,843
- Property tax $7,885
- Tax credit/rebate $1,143

Public Library
Palisades Park Public Library
257 Second St
Palisades Park, NJ 07650
201-585-4150

- Director .... Megan Doyle

Library statistics, 2006
- Population served 17,073
- Full-time/total staff 1/5

	Total	Per capita
Holdings	53,637	3.14
Revenues	$652,529	$38.22
Expenditures	$623,571	$36.52
Annual visits	81,900	4.80
Internet terminals/annual users		13/13,680

Public Safety
Number of officers, 2006 31

Crime	2005	2006
Total crimes	133	180
Violent	25	16
Murder	0	0
Rape	2	0
Robbery	11	8
Aggravated assault	12	8
Non-violent	108	164
Burglary	31	48
Larceny	69	106
Vehicle theft	8	10
Domestic violence	88	75
Arson	0	1
Total crime rate	7.3	9.5
Violent	1.4	0.8
Non-violent	5.9	8.7

Public School District
(for school year 2006-07 except as noted)

Palisades Park School District
270 First St
Palisades Park, NJ 07650
201-947-3560

- Superintendent .... Mark Hayes
- Number of schools 3
- Grade plan K-12
- Enrollment 1,475
- Attendance rate, '05-06 .... 96.0%
- Dropout rate .... NA
- Students per teacher 10.2
- Per pupil expenditure $13,424
- Median faculty salary $47,400
- Median administrator salary $84,875
- Grade 12 enrollment 130
- High school graduation rate 97.3%

Assessment test results
(percent scoring at proficient or advanced level)

	Language	Math
NJASK-Grade 3	73.1%	85.0%
GEPA-Grade 8	70.5%	75.0%
HSPA-High School	86.5%	85.4%

SAT score averages

Pct tested	Math	Verbal	Writing
75%	502	459	455

Teacher Qualifications
- Avg. years of experience 7
- Highly-qualified teachers
  - one subject/all subjects 99.0%/99.0%
- With emergency credentials 1.4%

No Child Left Behind
- AYP, 2005-06 .... Meets Standards

Municipal Finance
State Aid Programs, 2008
- Total aid $1,216,900
  - CMPTRA 395,340
  - Energy tax receipts 821,560
  - Garden State Trust 0

General Budget, 2007
- Total tax levy $33,499,322
  - County levy 4,319,902
    - County taxes 4,081,008
    - County library 0
    - County health 0
    - County open space 238,894
  - School levy 17,891,557
  - Muni. levy 11,287,863
- Misc. revenues 6,747,240

Taxes

	2005	2006	2007
General tax rate per $100	2.91	2.96	3.02
County equalization ratio	57	50.18	46.75
Net valuation taxable	$982,964,792	$1,044,893,750	$1,112,429,021
State equalized value	$1,958,877,625	$2,235,399,181	$2,589,024,470

The New Jersey Municipal Data Book

Palmyra Borough
Burlington County

Demographics & Socio-Economic Characteristics
(2000 US Census, except as noted)

Population
1980*	7,085
1990*	7,056
2000	7,091
Male	3,421
Female	3,670
2006 (estimate)*	7,598
Population density	3,837.4

Race & Hispanic Origin, 2000
Race
White	5,743
Black/African American	1,017
American Indian/Alaska Native	21
Asian	99
Native Hawaiian/Pacific Islander	3
Other race	100
Two or more races	108
Hispanic origin, total	229
Mexican	19
Puerto Rican	146
Cuban	13
Other Hispanic	51

Age & Nativity, 2000
Under 5 years	413
18 years and over	5,508
21 years and over	5,296
65 years and over	960
85 years and over	86
Median age	38.0
Native-born	6,798
Foreign-born	293

Educational Attainment, 2000
Population 25 years and over	5,068
Less than 9th grade	3.2%
High school grad or higher	85.1%
Bachelor's degree or higher	21.8%
Graduate degree	6.1%

Income & Poverty, 1999
Per capita income	$23,454
Median household income	$51,150
Median family income	$57,192
Persons in poverty	295
H'holds receiving public assistance	45
H'holds receiving social security	705

Households, 2000
Total households	3,004
With persons under 18	894
With persons over 65	733
Family households	1,852
Single-person households	962
Persons per household	2.36
Persons per family	3.02

Labor & Employment
Total civilian labor force, 2006**	4,733
Unemployment rate	5.1%
Total civilian labor force, 2000	4,053
Unemployment rate	4.7%

Employed persons 16 years and over by occupation, 2000
Managers & professionals	1,258
Service occupations	485
Sales & office occupations	1,248
Farming, fishing & forestry	5
Construction & maintenance	394
Production & transportation	473
Self-employed persons	204

‡ Joint library with Riverton Borough
* US Census Bureau
** New Jersey Department of Labor

General Information
Borough of Palmyra
20 W Broad St
Palmyra, NJ 08065
856-829-6100

Website	www.boroughofpalmyra.com
Year of incorporation	1923
Land/water area (sq. miles)	1.98/0.44
Form of government	Borough

Government
Legislative Districts
US Congressional	1
State Legislative	7

Local Officials, 2008
Mayor	John J. Gural
Manager	Marianne Hulme
Clerk	Karen A. Gift
Finance Dir	Marianne Hulme
Tax Assessor	Karen Davis
Tax Collector	Marianne Hulme
Attorney	Ted Rosenburg
Building	Tracy Kilmer
Planning	Tracy Kilmer
Engineering	Land Engineering
Public Works	Brian McCleary
Police Chief	Richard K. Dreby
Emerg/Fire Director	Alan Zimmerman

Housing & Construction
Housing Units, 2000*
Total	3,219
Median rent	$818
Median SF home value	$110,500

Permits for New Residential Construction
	Units	Value
Total, 2007	10	$908,080
Single family	10	$908,080
Total, 2006	10	$738,947
Single family	10	$738,947

Real Property Valuation, 2007
	Parcels	Valuation
Total	3,109	$313,483,970
Vacant	141	3,926,400
Residential	2,778	270,920,370
Commercial	115	19,017,400
Industrial	25	6,250,400
Apartments	44	13,160,400
Farm land	6	209,000
Farm homestead	0	0

Average Property Value & Tax, 2007
Residential value	$97,524
Property tax	$4,223
Tax credit/rebate	$841

Public Library
Riverton Free Library‡
306 Main St
Riverton, NJ 08077
856-829-2476

Director..............Michael Robinson

Library statistics, 2006
Population served
Full-time/total staff............../

	Total	Per capita
Holdings		
Revenues		
Expenditures		
Annual visits		
Internet terminals/annual users........../		

Taxes
	2005	2006	2007
General tax rate per $100	3.687	4.002	4.33
County equalization ratio	73.24	64.8	56.77
Net valuation taxable	$313,959,790	$313,275,570	$313,815,715
State equalized value	$484,505,849	$552,200,487	$580,965,140

Public Safety
Number of officers, 2006		16

Crime	2005	2006
Total crimes	177	195
Violent	10	20
Murder	0	0
Rape	3	0
Robbery	4	9
Aggravated assault	3	11
Non-violent	167	175
Burglary	51	26
Larceny	101	131
Vehicle theft	15	18
Domestic violence	78	86
Arson	1	1
Total crime rate	23.1	25.5
Violent	1.3	2.6
Non-violent	21.8	22.9

Public School District
(for school year 2006-07 except as noted)

Palmyra Borough School District
301 Delaware Ave
Palmyra, NJ 08065
856-786-2963

Superintendent	Richard Perry
Number of schools	2
Grade plan	K-12
Enrollment	1,023
Attendance rate, '05-06	95.0%
Dropout rate	NA
Students per teacher	10.9
Per pupil expenditure	$11,732
Median faculty salary	$47,476
Median administrator salary	$94,851
Grade 12 enrollment	93
High school graduation rate	95.9%

Assessment test results
(percent scoring at proficient or advanced level)
	Language	Math
NJASK-Grade 3	97.1%	100.0%
GEPA-Grade 8	57.7%	70.5%
HSPA-High School	86.8%	62.3%

SAT score averages
Pct tested	Math	Verbal	Writing
69%	493	500	487

Teacher Qualifications
Avg. years of experience	12
Highly-qualified teachers one subject/all subjects	100%/100%
With emergency credentials	0.0%

No Child Left Behind
AYP, 2005-06............Meets Standards

Municipal Finance
State Aid Programs, 2008
Total aid	$612,888
CMPTRA	126,306
Energy tax receipts	486,582
Garden State Trust	0

General Budget, 2007
Total tax levy	$13,588,186
County levy	2,325,445
County taxes	1,926,955
County library	176,828
County health	0
County open space	221,662
School levy	7,217,835
Muni. levy	4,044,906
Misc. revenues	4,934,659

Bergen County

Paramus Borough

Demographics & Socio-Economic Characteristics
(2000 US Census, except as noted)

Population
1980*	26,474
1990*	25,067
2000	25,737
Male	12,497
Female	13,240
2006 (estimate)*	26,548
Population density	2,535.6

Race & Hispanic Origin, 2000
Race
White	20,380
Black/African American	291
American Indian/Alaska Native	12
Asian	4,434
Native Hawaiian/Pacific Islander	3
Other race	229
Two or more races	388
Hispanic origin, total	1,253
Mexican	60
Puerto Rican	211
Cuban	285
Other Hispanic	697

Age & Nativity, 2000
Under 5 years	1,331
18 years and over	19,755
21 years and over	19,117
65 years and over	5,531
85 years and over	824
Median age	42.9
Native-born	19,275
Foreign-born	6,462

Educational Attainment, 2000
Population 25 years and over	18,264
Less than 9th grade	5.8%
High school grad or higher	86.2%
Bachelor's degree or higher	38.7%
Graduate degree	14.3%

Income & Poverty, 1999
Per capita income	$29,295
Median household income	$76,918
Median family income	$84,406
Persons in poverty	803
H'holds receiving public assistance	21
H'holds receiving social security	2,809

Households, 2000
Total households	8,082
With persons under 18	3,182
With persons over 65	2,989
Family households	6,779
Single-person households	1,164
Persons per household	3.00
Persons per family	3.32

Labor & Employment
Total civilian labor force, 2006**	13,013
Unemployment rate	3.5%
Total civilian labor force, 2000	12,069
Unemployment rate	2.3%

Employed persons 16 years and over by occupation, 2000
Managers & professionals	5,206
Service occupations	1,073
Sales & office occupations	3,932
Farming, fishing & forestry	0
Construction & maintenance	736
Production & transportation	846
Self-employed persons	806

* US Census Bureau
** New Jersey Department of Labor

See Introduction for an explanation of all data sources.

General Information
Borough of Paramus
1 Jockish Sq
Paramus, NJ 07652
201-265-2100

Website	www.paramusborough.org
Year of incorporation	1922
Land/water area (sq. miles)	10.47/0.00
Form of government	Borough

Government
Legislative Districts
US Congressional	5
State Legislative	38

Local Officials, 2008
Mayor	James Tedesco III
Manager/Admin	NA
Clerk	Ian Shore
Finance Dir	Joseph Citro
Tax Assessor	James Anzevino
Tax Collector	Emil Hrabel
Attorney	John Ten Hove
Building	NA
Planning	Gary Pucci
Engineering	Boswell Engineering
Public Works	Brian Koenig
Police Chief	NA
Emerg/Fire Director	Tim Ferguson

Housing & Construction
Housing Units, 2000*
Total	8,209
Median rent	$1,483
Median SF home value	$284,800

Permits for New Residential Construction
	Units	Value
Total, 2007	25	$10,274,000
Single family	25	$10,274,000
Total, 2006	40	$18,503,171
Single family	40	$18,503,171

Real Property Valuation, 2007
	Parcels	Valuation
Total	8,683	$6,888,580,400
Vacant	114	155,672,300
Residential	8,123	3,673,674,200
Commercial	411	2,950,830,100
Industrial	26	89,876,200
Apartments	1	17,025,400
Farm land	4	22,400
Farm homestead	4	1,479,800

Average Property Value & Tax, 2007
Residential value	$452,215
Property tax	$7,279
Tax credit/rebate	$1,135

Public Library
Paramus Public Library
116 E Century Rd
Paramus, NJ 07652
201-599-1300

Director .... Leonard LoPinto

Library statistics, 2006
Population served	25,737
Full-time/total staff	10/26

	Total	Per capita
Holdings	126,337	4.91
Revenues	$2,881,063	$111.94
Expenditures	$2,708,527	$105.24
Annual visits	262,457	10.20
Internet terminals/annual users	33/86,000	

Public Safety
Number of officers, 2006	91

Crime	2005	2006
Total crimes	1,567	1,757
Violent	66	77
Murder	1	0
Rape	1	0
Robbery	28	34
Aggravated assault	36	43
Non-violent	1,501	1,680
Burglary	68	87
Larceny	1,356	1,487
Vehicle theft	77	106
Domestic violence	126	137
Arson	5	7
Total crime rate	58.9	66.2
Violent	2.5	2.9
Non-violent	56.4	63.3

Public School District
(for school year 2006-07 except as noted)

Paramus School District
145 Spring Valley Rd
Paramus, NJ 07652
201-261-7800

Superintendent	Eugene Westlake (Int)
Number of schools	8
Grade plan	K-12
Enrollment	4,293
Attendance rate, '05-06	97.4%
Dropout rate	0.4%
Students per teacher	10.7
Per pupil expenditure	$14,729
Median faculty salary	$52,390
Median administrator salary	$117,732
Grade 12 enrollment	340
High school graduation rate	98.2%

Assessment test results
(percent scoring at proficient or advanced level)
	Language	Math
NJASK-Grade 3	96.5%	95.9%
GEPA-Grade 8	89.4%	84.0%
HSPA-High School	92.8%	84.1%

SAT score averages
Pct tested	Math	Verbal	Writing
97%	542	513	520

Teacher Qualifications
Avg. years of experience	8
Highly-qualified teachers one subject/all subjects	99.5%/99.5%
With emergency credentials	0.0%

No Child Left Behind
AYP, 2005-06	Meets Standards

Municipal Finance
State Aid Programs, 2008
Total aid	$5,343,421
CMPTRA	1,681,066
Energy tax receipts	3,662,355
Garden State Trust	0

General Budget, 2007
Total tax levy	$110,966,343
County levy	15,435,898
County taxes	14,537,765
County library	0
County health	0
County open space	898,133
School levy	62,168,404
Muni. levy	33,362,041
Misc. revenues	17,113,381

Taxes	2005	2006	2007
General tax rate per $100	1.47	1.55	1.61
County equalization ratio	94.96	83.28	77.6
Net valuation taxable	$6,830,307,119	$6,837,927,200	$6,893,670,571
State equalized value	$8,201,617,578	$8,816,538,442	$9,210,730,155

©2008 Information Publications, Inc. All rights reserved. Photocopying prohibited. For additional copies, contact the publisher at www.informationpublications.com or (877)544-INFO (4636)

The New Jersey Municipal Data Book

Park Ridge Borough
Bergen County

Demographics & Socio-Economic Characteristics
(2000 US Census, except as noted)

Population
1980*	8,515
1990*	8,102
2000	8,708
Male	4,178
Female	4,530
2006 (estimate)*	8,945
Population density	3,440.4

Race & Hispanic Origin, 2000
Race
White	8,140
Black/African American	75
American Indian/Alaska Native	12
Asian	336
Native Hawaiian/Pacific Islander	2
Other race	64
Two or more races	79
Hispanic origin, total	463
Mexican	233
Puerto Rican	52
Cuban	38
Other Hispanic	140

Age & Nativity, 2000
Under 5 years	599
18 years and over	6,664
21 years and over	6,470
65 years and over	1,408
85 years and over	253
Median age	40.9
Native-born	7,510
Foreign-born	1,198

Educational Attainment, 2000
Population 25 years and over	6,293
Less than 9th grade	2.5%
High school grad or higher	91.4%
Bachelor's degree or higher	45.0%
Graduate degree	17.3%

Income & Poverty, 1999
Per capita income	$40,351
Median household income	$86,632
Median family income	$97,294
Persons in poverty	260
H'holds receiving public assistance	33
H'holds receiving social security	863

Households, 2000
Total households	3,161
With persons under 18	1,110
With persons over 65	839
Family households	2,389
Single-person households	673
Persons per household	2.67
Persons per family	3.12

Labor & Employment
Total civilian labor force, 2006**	4,750
Unemployment rate	1.6%
Total civilian labor force, 2000	4,480
Unemployment rate	1.5%

Employed persons 16 years and over by occupation, 2000
Managers & professionals	2,082
Service occupations	493
Sales & office occupations	1,365
Farming, fishing & forestry	0
Construction & maintenance	272
Production & transportation	200
Self-employed persons	295

* US Census Bureau
** New Jersey Department of Labor

General Information
Borough of Park Ridge
53 Park Ave
Park Ridge, NJ 07656
201-573-1800

Website	www.parkridgeboro.com
Year of incorporation	1894
Land/water area (sq. miles)	2.60/0.04
Form of government	Borough

Government
Legislative Districts
US Congressional	5
State Legislative	39

Local Officials, 2008
Mayor	Donald Ruschman
Manager	Gene Vinci
Clerk	Kelley R. O'Donnell
Finance Dir.	Ann Kilmartin
Tax Assessor	Robert Campora
Tax Collector	Ann Kilmartin
Attorney	John D'Anton
Building	Nick Saluzzi
Planning	Dave Mesiano
Engineering	Brooker Engineering
Public Works	William Beattie
Police Chief	NA
Emerg/Fire Director	Tom Derienzo

Housing & Construction
Housing Units, 2000*
Total	3,258
Median rent	$996
Median SF home value	$307,000

Permits for New Residential Construction
	Units	Value
Total, 2007	22	$5,396,861
Single family	12	$4,492,003
Total, 2006	51	$8,370,252
Single family	14	$5,053,920

Real Property Valuation, 2007
	Parcels	Valuation
Total	3,091	$1,717,710,400
Vacant	88	15,747,200
Residential	2,894	1,487,211,600
Commercial	97	197,808,300
Industrial	3	3,379,800
Apartments	9	13,563,500
Farm land	0	0
Farm homestead	0	0

Average Property Value & Tax, 2007
Residential value	$513,895
Property tax	$9,207
Tax credit/rebate	$1,255

Public Library
Park Ridge Library
51 Park Ave
Park Ridge, NJ 07656
201-391-5151

Director............Christina E. Doto

Library statistics, 2006
Population served	8,708
Full-time/total staff	1/2

	Total	Per capita
Holdings	64,088	7.36
Revenues	$630,211	$72.37
Expenditures	$563,066	$64.66
Annual visits	124,665	14.32
Internet terminals/annual users	10/5,095	

Public Safety
Number of officers, 2006............18

Crime	2005	2006
Total crimes	43	51
Violent	5	3
Murder	0	0
Rape	0	0
Robbery	1	1
Aggravated assault	4	2
Non-violent	38	48
Burglary	1	3
Larceny	35	42
Vehicle theft	2	3
Domestic violence	12	6
Arson	0	1
Total crime rate	4.8	5.7
Violent	0.6	0.3
Non-violent	4.2	5.4

Public School District
(for school year 2006-07 except as noted)

Park Ridge School District
2 Park Ave
Park Ridge, NJ 07656
201-573-6000

Superintendent	Patricia Johnson
Number of schools	3
Grade plan	K-12
Enrollment	1,353
Attendance rate, '05-06	97.1%
Dropout rate	0.5%
Students per teacher	10.8
Per pupil expenditure	$14,372
Median faculty salary	$58,936
Median administrator salary	$123,371
Grade 12 enrollment	69
High school graduation rate	97.0%

Assessment test results
(percent scoring at proficient or advanced level)
	Language	Math
NJASK-Grade 3	95.2%	97.1%
GEPA-Grade 8	88.0%	77.2%
HSPA-High School	95.3%	89.6%

SAT score averages
Pct tested	Math	Verbal	Writing
93%	550	538	539

Teacher Qualifications
Avg. years of experience	11
Highly-qualified teachers one subject/all subjects	100%/100%
With emergency credentials	0.0%

No Child Left Behind
AYP, 2005-06............Meets Standards

Municipal Finance
State Aid Programs, 2008
Total aid	$453,600
CMPTRA	93,707
Energy tax receipts	358,295
Garden State Trust	0

General Budget, 2007
Total tax levy	$30,798,412
County levy	3,660,814
County taxes	3,459,259
County library	0
County health	0
County open space	201,555
School levy	19,593,500
Muni. levy	7,544,098
Misc. revenues	3,956,875

Taxes	2005	2006	2007
General tax rate per $100	1.6	1.69	1.8
County equalization ratio	107	95.25	85.5
Net valuation taxable	$1,686,617,247	$1,704,534,500	$1,719,004,988
State equalized value	$1,770,726,769	$1,995,026,966	$2,007,028,357

Morris County
Parsippany-Troy Hills Township

Demographics & Socio-Economic Characteristics
(2000 US Census, except as noted)

Population
1980*	49,868
1990*	48,478
2000	50,649
Male	25,039
Female	25,610
2006 (estimate)*	51,839
Population density	2,165.4

Race & Hispanic Origin, 2000
Race
White	37,620
Black/African American	1,574
American Indian/Alaska Native	61
Asian	9,145
Native Hawaiian/Pacific Islander	28
Other race	963
Two or more races	1,258
Hispanic origin, total	3,535
Mexican	221
Puerto Rican	709
Cuban	228
Other Hispanic	2,377

Age & Nativity, 2000
Under 5 years	3,065
18 years and over	40,034
21 years and over	38,731
65 years and over	5,691
85 years and over	572
Median age	37.6
Native-born	37,064
Foreign-born	13,585

Educational Attainment, 2000
Population 25 years and over	36,644
Less than 9th grade	3.5%
High school grad or higher	89.9%
Bachelor's degree or higher	43.0%
Graduate degree	15.4%

Income & Poverty, 1999
Per capita income	$32,220
Median household income	$68,133
Median family income	$81,041
Persons in poverty	1,918
H'holds receiving public assistance	256
H'holds receiving social security	3,992

Households, 2000
Total households	19,624
With persons under 18	6,184
With persons over 65	4,141
Family households	13,160
Single-person households	5,321
Persons per household	2.53
Persons per family	3.13

Labor & Employment
Total civilian labor force, 2006**	31,083
Unemployment rate	3.1%
Total civilian labor force, 2000	29,230
Unemployment rate	2.9%

Employed persons 16 years and over by occupation, 2000
Managers & professionals	13,363
Service occupations	2,548
Sales & office occupations	8,115
Farming, fishing & forestry	18
Construction & maintenance	1,722
Production & transportation	2,623
Self-employed persons	1,304

* US Census Bureau
** New Jersey Department of Labor

See Introduction for an explanation of all data sources.

General Information
Township of Parsippany-Troy Hills
1001 Parsippany Blvd
Parsippany, NJ 07054
973-263-4350

Website	www.parsippany.net
Year of incorporation	1928
Land/water area (sq. miles)	23.94/1.48
Form of government	Mayor-Council

Government
Legislative Districts
US Congressional	11
State Legislative	26

Local Officials, 2008
Mayor	Michael M. Luther
Manager	Jasmine Lim
Clerk	Judith Silver
Finance Dir	Ruby Malcolm
Tax Assessor	Daniel Cassese
Tax Collector	Frank Ogrodnik
Attorney	Alfred C. DeCotiis
Building	Ed Corcoran
Comm Dev/Planning	NA
Engineering	Michael Pucilowski
Public Works	Greg Schneider
Police Chief	Michael Peckerman
Fire/Emergency Dir	NA

Housing & Construction
Housing Units, 2000*
Total	20,066
Median rent	$823
Median SF home value	$234,100

Permits for New Residential Construction
	Units	Value
Total, 2007	19	$3,530,871
Single family	19	$3,530,871
Total, 2006	68	$12,131,554
Single family	68	$12,131,554

Real Property Valuation, 2007
	Parcels	Valuation
Total	15,396	$7,577,700,200
Vacant	541	112,099,100
Residential	14,161	4,323,446,400
Commercial	599	2,433,467,700
Industrial	60	318,309,500
Apartments	33	390,048,000
Farm land	1	3,100
Farm homestead	1	326,400

Average Property Value & Tax, 2007
Residential value	$305,308
Property tax	$6,512
Tax credit/rebate	$1,070

Public Library
Parsippany-Troy Hills Public Library
449 Halsey Rd
Parsippany, NJ 07054
973-887-8907

Director ... Jayne Beline

Library statistics, 2006
Population served	50,649
Full-time/total staff	13/32

	Total	Per capita
Holdings	196,335	3.88
Revenues	$3,000,221	$59.24
Expenditures	$3,035,564	$59.93
Annual visits	396,091	7.82
Internet terminals/annual users	64/300,496	

Public Safety
Number of officers, 2006 ... 107

Crime	2005	2006
Total crimes	747	933
Violent	39	36
Murder	0	0
Rape	6	3
Robbery	6	9
Aggravated assault	27	24
Non-violent	708	897
Burglary	183	246
Larceny	476	575
Vehicle theft	49	76
Domestic violence	184	255
Arson	4	2
Total crime rate	14.5	18.1
Violent	0.8	0.7
Non-violent	13.7	17.4

Public School District
(for school year 2006-07 except as noted)

Parsippany-Troy Hills Township District
292 Parsippany Rd
Parsippany, NJ 07054
973-263-7250

Superintendent	LeRoy Seitz
Number of schools	13
Grade plan	K-12
Enrollment	6,856
Attendance rate, '05-06	96.1%
Dropout rate	0.8%
Students per teacher	10.2
Per pupil expenditure	$14,723
Median faculty salary	$61,445
Median administrator salary	$105,418
Grade 12 enrollment	536
High school graduation rate	NA

Assessment test results
(percent scoring at proficient or advanced level)
	Language	Math
NJASK-Grade 3	91.2%	96.4%
GEPA-Grade 8	81.9%	78.0%
HSPA-High School	89.3%	83.7%

SAT score averages
Pct tested	Math	Verbal	Writing
NA	NA	NA	NA

Teacher Qualifications
Avg. years of experience	9
Highly-qualified teachers one subject/all subjects	100%/100%
With emergency credentials	0.0%

No Child Left Behind
AYP, 2005-06 ... Meets Standards

Municipal Finance
State Aid Programs, 2008
Total aid	$5,815,772
CMPTRA	2,145,377
Energy tax receipts	3,614,055
Garden State Trust	1,162

General Budget, 2007
Total tax levy	$161,862,864
County levy	22,065,303
County taxes	17,645,135
County library	0
County health	0
County open space	4,420,168
School levy	103,009,828
Muni. levy	36,787,734
Misc. revenues	20,976,886

Taxes
	2005	2006	2007
General tax rate per $100	1.9	2.03	2.14
County equalization ratio	103.01	89.92	81.59
Net valuation taxable	$7,773,465,557	$7,665,305,500	$7,588,282,376
State equalized value	$8,644,868,280	$9,405,568,902	$9,692,069,591

©2008 Information Publications, Inc. All rights reserved. Photocopying prohibited. For additional copies, contact the publisher at www.informationpublications.com or (877)544-INFO (4636)

The New Jersey Municipal Data Book

Passaic City
Passaic County

Demographics & Socio-Economic Characteristics[†]
(2000 US Census, except as noted)

Population
1980*	52,463
1990*	58,041
2000	67,861
Male	33,852
Female	34,009
2006 (estimate)*	67,974
Population density	21,856.6

Race & Hispanic Origin, 2000
Race
White	24,044
Black/African American	9,385
American Indian/Alaska Native	531
Asian	3,740
Native Hawaiian/Pacific Islander	29
Other race	26,709
Two or more races	3,423
Hispanic origin, total	42,387
Mexican	13,346
Puerto Rican	9,122
Cuban	654
Other Hispanic	19,265

Age & Nativity, 2000
Under 5 years	6,525
18 years and over	46,962
21 years and over	43,331
65 years and over	5,513
85 years and over	757
Median age	28.6
Native-born	36,760
Foreign-born	31,101

Educational Attainment, 2000
Population 25 years and over	38,437
Less than 9th grade	23.2%
High school grad or higher	55.5%
Bachelor's degree or higher	13.7%
Graduate degree	5.1%

Income & Poverty, 1999
Per capita income	$12,874
Median household income	$33,594
Median family income	$34,935
Persons in poverty	14,249
H'holds receiving public assistance	1,238
H'holds receiving social security	4,274

Households, 2000
Total households	19,458
With persons under 18	9,532
With persons over 65	4,228
Family households	14,456
Single-person households	3,945
Persons per household	3.46
Persons per family	3.93

Labor & Employment
Total civilian labor force, 2006**	28,609
Unemployment rate	7.1%
Total civilian labor force, 2000	28,589
Unemployment rate	10.3%

Employed persons 16 years and over by occupation, 2000
Managers & professionals	4,608
Service occupations	4,452
Sales & office occupations	6,038
Farming, fishing & forestry	82
Construction & maintenance	1,857
Production & transportation	8,601
Self-employed persons	762

[†] see Appendix C for American Community Survey data
* US Census Bureau
** New Jersey Department of Labor
§ State Fiscal Year July 1–June 30

General Information
City of Passaic
330 Passaic St
Passaic, NJ 07055
973-365-5500

Website	www.cityofpassaic.com
Year of incorporation	1873
Land/water area (sq. miles)	3.11/0.10
Form of government	Mayor-Council

Government
Legislative Districts
US Congressional	8
State Legislative	36

Local Officials, 2008
Mayor	Samuel Rivera
Business Admin	Greg Hill
Clerk	Amada C. Curling
Finance Dir	Jose L. Agosto
Tax Assessor	Thomas Poalillo
Tax Collector	Carrie Malak
Attorney	Donald Scarinci
Building	John Miskovsky
Planning/Dev	Ronald Van Rensalier
Engineering	George Torres
Public Works	Theodore Evans
Police Chief	Daniel Paton
Emerg/Fire Director	Patrick Trentacost

Housing & Construction
Housing Units, 2000*
Total	20,194
Median rent	$677
Median SF home value	$153,000

Permits for New Residential Construction
	Units	Value
Total, 2007	75	$3,411,238
Single family	18	$1,956,040
Total, 2006	45	$3,056,782
Single family	9	$882,092

Real Property Valuation, 2007
	Parcels	Valuation
Total	8,156	$1,357,241,100
Vacant	251	7,989,700
Residential	6,220	805,216,400
Commercial	1,159	299,716,900
Industrial	120	92,631,000
Apartments	406	151,687,100
Farm land	0	0
Farm homestead	0	0

Average Property Value & Tax, 2007
Residential value	$129,456
Property tax	$7,244
Tax credit/rebate	$1,090

Public Library
Passaic Public Library
195 Gregory Ave
Passaic, NJ 07055
973-779-0474

Director............ Kathleen Mollica (Int)

Library statistics, 2006
Population served	67,861
Full-time/total staff	5/15

	Total	Per capita
Holdings	114,947	1.69
Revenues	$1,394,938	$20.56
Expenditures	$1,468,066	$21.63
Annual visits	117,936	1.74
Internet terminals/annual users	30/53,297	

Taxes
	2005	2006	2007
General tax rate per $100	4.71	5.25	5.6
County equalization ratio	60.53	50.11	41.71
Net valuation taxable	$1,355,558,400	$1,349,349,000	$1,362,112,700
State equalized value	$2,705,165,436	$3,240,818,124	$3,630,949,879

Public Safety
Number of officers, 2006 189

Crime
	2005	2006
Total crimes	2,303	2,325
Violent	684	647
Murder	4	5
Rape	6	3
Robbery	331	273
Aggravated assault	343	366
Non-violent	1,619	1,678
Burglary	363	394
Larceny	977	919
Vehicle theft	279	365
Domestic violence	725	698
Arson	12	8
Total crime rate	33.5	34.0
Violent	10.0	9.5
Non-violent	23.6	24.6

Public School District
(for school year 2006-07 except as noted)

Passaic City School District
101 Passaic Ave
Passaic, NJ 07055
973-470-5201

Chief School Admin	Robert Holster
Number of schools	18
Grade plan	K-12
Enrollment	12,247
Attendance rate, '05-06	92.7%
Dropout rate	8.3%
Students per teacher	11.0
Per pupil expenditure	$15,860
Median faculty salary	$51,970
Median administrator salary	$98,561
Grade 12 enrollment	510
High school graduation rate	69.2%

Assessment test results
(percent scoring at proficient or advanced level)
	Language	Math
NJASK-Grade 3	54.6%	64.7%
GEPA-Grade 8	42.6%	36.4%
HSPA-High School	57.7%	34.8%

SAT score averages
Pct tested	Math	Verbal	Writing
54%	408	395	383

Teacher Qualifications
Avg. years of experience	9
Highly-qualified teachers one subject/all subjects	98.5%/98.5%
With emergency credentials	0.5%

No Child Left Behind
AYP, 2005-06 .... Needs Improvement

Municipal Finance[§]
State Aid Programs, 2008
Total aid	$14,474,757
CMPTRA	11,302,047
Energy tax receipts	3,172,710
Garden State Trust	0

General Budget, 2007
Total tax levy	$76,218,316
County levy	16,557,387
County taxes	16,222,833
County library	0
County health	0
County open space	334,554
School levy	14,061,016
Muni. levy	45,599,913
Misc. revenues	29,206,393

Passaic County
Paterson City

Demographics & Socio-Economic Characteristics[†]
(2000 US Census, except as noted)

Population
- 1980* 137,970
- 1990* 140,891
- 2000 149,222
  - Male 72,473
  - Female 76,749
- 2006 (estimate)* 148,708
- Population density 17,619.4

Race & Hispanic Origin, 2000
Race
- White 45,913
- Black/African American 49,095
- American Indian/Alaska Native 901
- Asian 2,831
- Native Hawaiian/Pacific Islander ... 84
- Other race 41,184
- Two or more races 9,214
- Hispanic origin, total 74,774
  - Mexican 5,004
  - Puerto Rican 24,013
  - Cuban 858
  - Other Hispanic 44,899

Age & Nativity, 2000
- Under 5 years 12,578
- 18 years and over 104,785
- 21 years and over 97,577
- 65 years and over 12,399
- 85 years and over 1,356
- Median age 30.5
- Native-born 100,298
- Foreign-born 48,924

Educational Attainment, 2000
- Population 25 years and over 88,077
- Less than 9th grade 18.1%
- High school grad or higher 58.5%
- Bachelor's degree or higher 8.2%
- Graduate degree 2.8%

Income & Poverty, 1999
- Per capita income $13,257
- Median household income $32,778
- Median family income $35,420
- Persons in poverty 32,474
- H'holds receiving public assistance ... 3,874
- H'holds receiving social security ... 10,102

Households, 2000
- Total households 44,710
  - With persons under 18 21,997
  - With persons over 65 9,801
  - Family households 33,351
  - Single-person households 9,143
- Persons per household 3.25
- Persons per family 3.71

Labor & Employment
- Total civilian labor force, 2006** ... 59,433
  - Unemployment rate 8.6%
- Total civilian labor force, 2000 ... 60,463
  - Unemployment rate 13.1%

Employed persons 16 years and over by occupation, 2000
- Managers & professionals 8,774
- Service occupations 10,640
- Sales & office occupations 14,529
- Farming, fishing & forestry 84
- Construction & maintenance 4,114
- Production & transportation 14,404
- Self-employed persons 1,390

[†] see Appendix C for American Community Survey data
* US Census Bureau
** New Jersey Department of Labor
§ State Fiscal Year July 1–June 30

See Introduction for an explanation of all data sources.

General Information
City of Paterson
155 Market St
Paterson, NJ 07505
973-321-1500
- Website .... www.patcity.com
- Year of incorporation 1851
- Land/water area (sq. miles) 8.44/0.29
- Form of government .... Mayor-Council

Government
Legislative Districts
- US Congressional 8
- State Legislative 35

Local Officials, 2008
- Mayor .... Jose Torres
- Manager .... Eli Burgos
- Clerk .... Jane Williams-Warren
- Finance Dir .... Anthony Zambrano
- Tax Assessor .... J. Krieger
- Tax Collector .... Kathleen Gibson
- Attorney .... Susan Champion
- Building .... Salvatore Ianelli
- Planning .... Anthony DeFranco
- Engineering .... Frederick Margron
- Public Works .... Manny Ojeda
- Police Chief .... James Wittig
- Emerg/Fire Director .... Michael Postorino

Housing & Construction
Housing Units, 2000*
- Total 47,169
- Median rent $696
- Median SF home value $137,500

Permits for New Residential Construction

	Units	Value
Total, 2007	14	$866,600
Single family	8	$575,500
Total, 2006	0	$0
Single family	0	$0

Real Property Valuation, 2007

	Parcels	Valuation
Total	23,439	$9,374,065,900
Vacant	1,538	186,957,300
Residential	17,432	6,310,285,900
Commercial	3,445	1,736,768,700
Industrial	529	648,880,900
Apartments	495	491,173,100
Farm land	0	0
Farm homestead	0	0

Average Property Value & Tax, 2007
- Residential value $361,994
- Property tax $6,301
- Tax credit/rebate $964

Public Library
Paterson Free Public Library
250 Broadway
Paterson, NJ 07501
973-321-1223
- Director .... Cynthia Czesak

Library statistics, 2006
- Population served 149,222
- Full-time/total staff 8/46

	Total	Per capita
Holdings	214,990	1.44
Revenues	$2,480,025	$16.62
Expenditures	$2,394,401	$16.05
Annual visits	165,112	1.11
Internet terminals/annual users	53/82,975	

Public Safety
- Number of officers, 2006 457

Crime	2005	2006
Total crimes	5,880	6,037
Violent	1,445	1,672
Murder	20	15
Rape	32	37
Robbery	588	808
Aggravated assault	805	812
Non-violent	4,435	4,365
Burglary	1,413	1,361
Larceny	2,108	1,999
Vehicle theft	914	1,005
Domestic violence	2,082	1,577
Arson	13	17
Total crime rate	39.0	40.3
Violent	9.6	11.2
Non-violent	29.4	29.1

Public School District
(for school year 2006-07 except as noted)

Paterson School District
33-35 Church St
Paterson, NJ 07505
973-321-0980
- State District Superint .... Michael Glascoe
- Number of schools 38
- Grade plan K-12
- Enrollment 24,950
- Attendance rate, '05-06 .... 92.1%
- Dropout rate 2.8%
- Students per teacher 8.6
- Per pupil expenditure $16,914
- Median faculty salary $52,371
- Median administrator salary $103,257
- Grade 12 enrollment 1,285
- High school graduation rate .... NA

Assessment test results
(percent scoring at proficient or advanced level)

	Language	Math
NJASK-Grade 3	66.7%	68.3%
GEPA-Grade 8	46.1%	39.7%
HSPA-High School	56.3%	39.7%

SAT score averages

Pct tested	Math	Verbal	Writing
NA	NA	NA	NA

Teacher Qualifications
- Avg. years of experience 8
- Highly-qualified teachers
  - one subject/all subjects 94.5%/94.5%
- With emergency credentials 2.8%

No Child Left Behind
- AYP, 2005-06 .... Needs Improvement

Municipal Finance§
State Aid Programs, 2008
- Total aid $38,055,934
  - CMPTRA 30,508,644
  - Energy tax receipts 7,536,090
  - Garden State Trust 10,871

General Budget, 2007
- Total tax levy $163,426,735
  - County levy 35,867,310
    - County taxes 35,131,992
    - County library 0
    - County health 0
    - County open space 735,317
  - School levy 36,390,096
  - Muni. levy 91,169,329
- Misc. revenues 107,492,426

Taxes	2005	2006	2007
General tax rate per $100	24.99	26.3	1.75
County equalization ratio	11.58	9.52	129.64
Net valuation taxable	$574,851,402	$572,833,674	$9,388,617,332
State equalized value	$6,038,355,063	$7,188,708,575	$8,449,017,781

The New Jersey Municipal Data Book

Paulsboro Borough
Gloucester County

Demographics & Socio-Economic Characteristics
(2000 US Census, except as noted)

Population
1980*	6,944
1990*	6,577
2000	6,160
Male	2,885
Female	3,275
2006 (estimate)*	6,062
Population density	3,092.9

Race & Hispanic Origin, 2000
Race
White	3,915
Black/African American	1,949
American Indian/Alaska Native	15
Asian	20
Native Hawaiian/Pacific Islander	6
Other race	81
Two or more races	174
Hispanic origin, total	268
Mexican	36
Puerto Rican	159
Cuban	4
Other Hispanic	69

Age & Nativity, 2000
Under 5 years	463
18 years and over	4,387
21 years and over	4,138
65 years and over	854
85 years and over	86
Median age	34.3
Native-born	5,921
Foreign-born	239

Educational Attainment, 2000
Population 25 years and over	3,813
Less than 9th grade	7.2%
High school grad or higher	75.4%
Bachelor's degree or higher	6.0%
Graduate degree	1.9%

Income & Poverty, 1999
Per capita income	$16,368
Median household income	$35,569
Median family income	$41,359
Persons in poverty	1,084
H'holds receiving public assistance	77
H'holds receiving social security	714

Households, 2000
Total households	2,353
With persons under 18	908
With persons over 65	658
Family households	1,615
Single-person households	633
Persons per household	2.61
Persons per family	3.15

Labor & Employment
Total civilian labor force, 2006**	3,474
Unemployment rate	13.5%
Total civilian labor force, 2000	2,874
Unemployment rate	11.1%

Employed persons 16 years and over by occupation, 2000
Managers & professionals	395
Service occupations	488
Sales & office occupations	799
Farming, fishing & forestry	12
Construction & maintenance	281
Production & transportation	579
Self-employed persons	62

* US Census Bureau
** New Jersey Department of Labor

General Information
Borough of Paulsboro
1211 N Delaware St
Paulsboro, NJ 08066
856-423-1500

Website	www.paulsboronj.org
Year of incorporation	1904
Land/water area (sq. miles)	1.96/0.66
Form of government	Borough

Government
Legislative Districts
US Congressional	1
State Legislative	3

Local Officials, 2008
Mayor	John Burzichelli
Manager	John Salvatore
Clerk	Kathy VanScoy
Finance Dir	John Salvatore
Tax Assessor	Robyn Hammond
Tax Collector	Barbara Sockwell
Attorney	Michael Angelini
Building	Phil Zimm
Comm Dev/Planning	NA
Engineering	Remington & Vernick
Public Works	NA
Police Chief	Kenneth Ridinger
Emerg/Fire Dir	Michael Licciardello

Housing & Construction
Housing Units, 2000*
Total	2,628
Median rent	$570
Median SF home value	$78,600

Permits for New Residential Construction
	Units	Value
Total, 2007	3	$270,000
Single family	3	$270,000
Total, 2006	3	$740,800
Single family	3	$740,800

Real Property Valuation, 2007
	Parcels	Valuation
Total	2,342	$269,540,400
Vacant	204	2,803,100
Residential	1,979	140,390,700
Commercial	137	58,333,600
Industrial	8	61,126,500
Apartments	13	6,867,500
Farm land	1	19,000
Farm homestead	0	0

Average Property Value & Tax, 2007
Residential value	$70,940
Property tax	$2,869
Tax credit/rebate	$749

Public Library
Gill Memorial Library
145 E Broad St
Paulsboro, NJ 08066
856-432-5155

Librarian	Violet J. Valentin

Library statistics, 2006
Population served	6,160
Full-time/total staff	0/0

	Total	Per capita
Holdings	26,786	4.35
Revenues	$130,093	$21.12
Expenditures	$120,007	$19.48
Annual visits	11,707	1.90
Internet terminals/annual users	5/6,087	

Public Safety
Number of officers, 2006		20
Crime	2005	2006
Total crimes	329	283
Violent	43	52
Murder	0	0
Rape	1	1
Robbery	18	21
Aggravated assault	24	30
Non-violent	286	231
Burglary	60	54
Larceny	208	163
Vehicle theft	18	14
Domestic violence	172	130
Arson	5	2
Total crime rate	53.8	46.4
Violent	7.0	8.5
Non-violent	46.8	37.9

Public School District
(for school year 2006-07 except as noted)

Paulsboro School District
662 N Delaware St
Paulsboro, NJ 08066
856-423-5515

Superintendent	Frank Scambia
Number of schools	3
Grade plan	K-12
Enrollment	1,432
Attendance rate, '05-06	91.9%
Dropout rate	1.9%
Students per teacher	11.3
Per pupil expenditure	$13,143
Median faculty salary	$68,338
Median administrator salary	$98,426
Grade 12 enrollment	115
High school graduation rate	92.6%

Assessment test results
(percent scoring at proficient or advanced level)
	Language	Math
NJASK-Grade 3	71.1%	69.2%
GEPA-Grade 8	26.8%	38.7%
HSPA-High School	76.3%	53.5%

SAT score averages
Pct tested	Math	Verbal	Writing
61%	458	419	411

Teacher Qualifications
Avg. years of experience	14
Highly-qualified teachers one subject/all subjects	100%/100%
With emergency credentials	0.0%

No Child Left Behind
AYP, 2005-06	Meets Standards

Municipal Finance
State Aid Programs, 2008
Total aid	$527,230
CMPTRA	242,065
Energy tax receipts	285,165
Garden State Trust	0

General Budget, 2007
Total tax levy	$10,966,188
County levy	2,201,188
County taxes	2,041,367
County library	0
County health	0
County open space	159,821
School levy	4,637,900
Muni. levy	4,127,100
Misc. revenues	3,402,677

Taxes
	2005	2006	2007
General tax rate per $100	3.502	3.733	4.045
County equalization ratio	88.3	82.62	68.41
Net valuation taxable	$274,517,014	$268,806,500	$271,118,225
State equalized value	$332,264,602	$394,777,246	$484,538,585

Somerset County

Peapack & Gladstone Borough

Demographics & Socio-Economic Characteristics
(2000 US Census, except as noted)

Population
1980*	2,038
1990*	2,111
2000	2,433
Male	1,203
Female	1,230
2006 (estimate)*	2,480
Population density	427.6

Race & Hispanic Origin, 2000
Race
White	2,298
Black/African American	76
American Indian/Alaska Native	2
Asian	30
Native Hawaiian/Pacific Islander	0
Other race	17
Two or more races	10
Hispanic origin, total	92
Mexican	18
Puerto Rican	8
Cuban	3
Other Hispanic	63

Age & Nativity, 2000
Under 5 years	183
18 years and over	1,801
21 years and over	1,740
65 years and over	296
85 years and over	38
Median age	39.5
Native-born	2,138
Foreign-born	295

Educational Attainment, 2000
Population 25 years and over	1,694
Less than 9th grade	3.3%
High school grad or higher	92.9%
Bachelor's degree or higher	56.9%
Graduate degree	19.2%

Income & Poverty, 1999
Per capita income	$56,542
Median household income	$99,499
Median family income	$118,770
Persons in poverty	101
H'holds receiving public assistance	0
H'holds receiving social security	224

Households, 2000
Total households	840
With persons under 18	325
With persons over 65	202
Family households	647
Single-person households	152
Persons per household	2.71
Persons per family	3.11

Labor & Employment
Total civilian labor force, 2006**	1,343
Unemployment rate	2.9%
Total civilian labor force, 2000	1,318
Unemployment rate	5.0%

Employed persons 16 years and over by occupation, 2000
Managers & professionals	648
Service occupations	160
Sales & office occupations	331
Farming, fishing & forestry	9
Construction & maintenance	56
Production & transportation	48
Self-employed persons	94

‡ Branch of county library
* US Census Bureau
** New Jersey Department of Labor

See Introduction for an explanation of all data sources.

General Information
Borough of Peapack & Gladstone
1 School St
PO Box 218
Peapack, NJ 07977
908-234-2250

Website	www.peapack-gladstone-nj.gov
Year of incorporation	1912
Land/water area (sq. miles)	5.80/0.00
Form of government	Borough

Government
Legislative Districts
US Congressional	7
State Legislative	16

Local Officials, 2008
Mayor	William H. Horton
Manager	Margaret Gould
Clerk	Margaret Gould
Finance Dir	Mary Robinson
Tax Assessor	Edward Kerwin
Tax Collector	Mary Robinson
Attorney	Sharon Moore
Building	Joseph Alicino
Comm Dev/Planning	NA
Engineering	William Ryden
Public Works	John O'Neill
Police Chief	Gregory Skinner
Emerg/Fire Director	David Hill

Housing & Construction
Housing Units, 2000*
Total	871
Median rent	$1,132
Median SF home value	$461,500

Permits for New Residential Construction
	Units	Value
Total, 2007	6	$5,519,800
Single family	6	$5,519,800
Total, 2006	2	$1,173,150
Single family	2	$1,173,150

Real Property Valuation, 2007
	Parcels	Valuation
Total	948	$845,722,717
Vacant	39	13,285,800
Residential	725	574,460,600
Commercial	41	172,760,500
Industrial	1	7,920,000
Apartments	9	6,056,600
Farm land	99	470,917
Farm homestead	34	70,768,300

Average Property Value & Tax, 2007
Residential value	$850,104
Property tax	$13,479
Tax credit/rebate	$1,324

Public Library
Peapack Gladstone Branch‡
School St
Peapack, NJ 07977
908-234-0598

Branch Librarian . . . . Karen Pifher

Library statistics, 2006
see Somerset County profile
for library system statistics

Public Safety
Number of officers, 2006	9

Crime	2005	2006
Total crimes	9	14
Violent	0	1
Murder	0	0
Rape	0	0
Robbery	0	0
Aggravated assault	0	1
Non-violent	9	13
Burglary	3	4
Larceny	6	9
Vehicle theft	0	0
Domestic violence	2	2
Arson	0	0
Total crime rate	3.6	5.7
Violent	0.0	0.4
Non-violent	3.6	5.3

Public School District
(for school year 2006-07 except as noted)

Somerset Hills Regional School District
25 Olcott Ave
Bernardsville, NJ 07924
908-630-3011

Superintendent	Peter Miller
Number of schools	9
Grade plan	K-12
Enrollment	2,022
Attendance rate, '05-06	96.0%
Dropout rate	0.3%
Students per teacher	11.0
Per pupil expenditure	$15,675
Median faculty salary	$61,868
Median administrator salary	$132,115
Grade 12 enrollment	181
High school graduation rate	98.9%

Assessment test results
(percent scoring at proficient or advanced level)
	Language	Math
NJASK-Grade 3	94.4%	99.3%
GEPA-Grade 8	89.5%	86.2%
HSPA-High School	97.2%	92.7%

SAT score averages
Pct tested	Math	Verbal	Writing
91%	575	561	558

Teacher Qualifications
Avg. years of experience	10
Highly-qualified teachers one subject/all subjects	100%/100%
With emergency credentials	0.0%

No Child Left Behind
AYP, 2005-06 . . . . Meets Standards

Municipal Finance
State Aid Programs, 2008
Total aid	$317,916
CMPTRA	0
Energy tax receipts	317,858
Garden State Trust	58

General Budget, 2007
Total tax levy	$13,423,755
County levy	3,072,471
County taxes	2,484,897
County library	315,461
County health	0
County open space	272,113
School levy	6,502,139
Muni. levy	3,849,145
Misc. revenues	2,563,246

Taxes	2005	2006	2007
General tax rate per $100	1.76	1.66	1.59
County equalization ratio	100.61	99.46	93.27
Net valuation taxable	$756,473,045	$818,012,069	$846,611,057
State equalized value	$821,538,928	$906,492,977	$909,974,352

©2008 Information Publications, Inc. All rights reserved. Photocopying prohibited. For additional copies, contact the publisher at www.informationpublications.com or (877)544-INFO (4636)

The New Jersey Municipal Data Book

Pemberton Borough

Burlington County

Demographics & Socio-Economic Characteristics
(2000 US Census, except as noted)

Population
1980*	1,198
1990*	1,367
2000	1,210
Male	614
Female	596
2006 (estimate)*	1,381
Population density	2,340.7

Race & Hispanic Origin, 2000
Race
White	949
Black/African American	154
American Indian/Alaska Native	8
Asian	29
Native Hawaiian/Pacific Islander	0
Other race	33
Two or more races	37
Hispanic origin, total	104
Mexican	15
Puerto Rican	60
Cuban	2
Other Hispanic	27

Age & Nativity, 2000
Under 5 years	83
18 years and over	886
21 years and over	832
65 years and over	108
85 years and over	8
Median age	33.9
Native-born	1,130
Foreign-born	80

Educational Attainment, 2000
Population 25 years and over	767
Less than 9th grade	4.2%
High school grad or higher	83.7%
Bachelor's degree or higher	15.5%
Graduate degree	4.3%

Income & Poverty, 1999
Per capita income	$18,909
Median household income	$44,063
Median family income	$48,500
Persons in poverty	94
H'holds receiving public assistance	23
H'holds receiving social security	93

Households, 2000
Total households	470
With persons under 18	189
With persons over 65	82
Family households	317
Single-person households	124
Persons per household	2.56
Persons per family	3.06

Labor & Employment
Total civilian labor force, 2006**	758
Unemployment rate	5.0%
Total civilian labor force, 2000	648
Unemployment rate	4.3%

Employed persons 16 years and over by occupation, 2000
Managers & professionals	146
Service occupations	137
Sales & office occupations	163
Farming, fishing & forestry	0
Construction & maintenance	76
Production & transportation	98
Self-employed persons	49

* US Census Bureau
** New Jersey Department of Labor

General Information
Borough of Pemberton
50 Egbert St
Pemberton, NJ 08068
609-894-8222

Website	www.pembertonborough.us
Year of incorporation	1826
Land/water area (sq. miles)	0.59/0.02
Form of government	Borough

Government

Legislative Districts
US Congressional	3
State Legislative	8

Local Officials, 2008
Mayor	F. Lyman Simpkins
Manager/Admin	NA
Clerk	Donna Mull
Finance Dir	Donna Mull
Tax Assessor	Edward Burek
Tax Collector	Harold Griffin
Attorney	David M. Serlin
Building	Harry Wetterskog
Comm Dev/Planning	NA
Engineering	Richard Alaimo & Assoc
Public Works	Raymond Downs
Police Chief	Joseph Conlin
Emerg/Fire Director	Chas Bozoski

Housing & Construction

Housing Units, 2000*
Total	513
Median rent	$641
Median SF home value	$113,300

Permits for New Residential Construction
	Units	Value
Total, 2007	37	$4,242,729
Single family	37	$4,242,729
Total, 2006	56	$6,370,243
Single family	56	$6,370,243

Real Property Valuation, 2007
	Parcels	Valuation
Total	595	$53,547,600
Vacant	138	2,091,000
Residential	395	41,270,300
Commercial	46	7,293,000
Industrial	0	0
Apartments	10	2,753,800
Farm land	5	10,800
Farm homestead	1	128,700

Average Property Value & Tax, 2007
Residential value	$104,543
Property tax	$3,438
Tax credit/rebate	$862

Public Library
No public municipal library

Library statistics, 2006
Population served	NA
Full-time/total staff	NA/NA

	Total	Per capita
Holdings	NA	NA
Revenues	NA	NA
Expenditures	NA	NA
Annual visits	NA	NA
Internet terminals/annual users	NA/NA	

Taxes
	2005	2006	2007
General tax rate per $100	3.799	3.911	3.29
County equalization ratio	71.39	62.54	52.38
Net valuation taxable	$44,746,637	$46,281,700	$54,110,992
State equalized value	$71,548,828	$89,015,943	$102,675,520

Public Safety
Number of officers, 2006	7

Crime	2005	2006
Total crimes	53	40
Violent	4	6
Murder	0	0
Rape	0	3
Robbery	2	1
Aggravated assault	2	2
Non-violent	49	34
Burglary	11	9
Larceny	37	25
Vehicle theft	1	0
Domestic violence	26	33
Arson	0	0
Total crime rate	40.0	30.2
Violent	3.0	4.5
Non-violent	37.0	25.7

Public School District
(for school year 2006-07 except as noted)

Pemberton Borough School District
50 Egbert St
Pemberton, NJ 08068
609-894-2261

Superintendent	Charles Smith
Number of schools	NA
Grade plan	K-6
Enrollment	NA
Attendance rate, '05-06	93.6%
Dropout rate	NA
Students per teacher	7.7
Per pupil expenditure	
Median faculty salary	$54,195
Median administrator salary	$65,000
Grade 12 enrollment	NA
High school graduation rate	NA

Assessment test results
(percent scoring at proficient or advanced level)
	Language	Math
NJASK-Grade 3	NA	NA
GEPA-Grade 8	NA	NA
HSPA-High School	NA	NA

SAT score averages
Pct tested	Math	Verbal	Writing
NA	NA	NA	NA

Teacher Qualifications
Avg. years of experience	17
Highly-qualified teachers one subject/all subjects	100%/100%
With emergency credentials	0.0%

No Child Left Behind
AYP, 2005-06	Meets Standards

Municipal Finance

State Aid Programs, 2008
Total aid	$57,285
CMPTRA	0
Energy tax receipts	54,628
Garden State Trust	2,657

General Budget, 2007
Total tax levy	$1,779,359
County levy	433,136
County taxes	358,915
County library	32,936
County health	0
County open space	41,285
School levy	1,008,526
Muni. levy	337,697
Misc. revenues	887,303

Burlington County
Pemberton Township

Demographics & Socio-Economic Characteristics
(2000 US Census, except as noted)

Population
1980*	29,720
1990*	31,342
2000	28,691
Male	14,148
Female	14,543
2006 (estimate)*	28,831
Population density	467.4

Race & Hispanic Origin, 2000
Race
White	18,946
Black/African American	6,632
American Indian/Alaska Native	132
Asian	913
Native Hawaiian/Pacific Islander	23
Other race	828
Two or more races	1,217
Hispanic origin, total	2,477
Mexican	225
Puerto Rican	1,560
Cuban	44
Other Hispanic	648

Age & Nativity, 2000
Under 5 years	1,925
18 years and over	20,770
21 years and over	19,594
65 years and over	2,793
85 years and over	189
Median age	34.4
Native-born	26,607
Foreign-born	2,043

Educational Attainment, 2000
Population 25 years and over	18,049
Less than 9th grade	4.5%
High school grad or higher	80.0%
Bachelor's degree or higher	9.4%
Graduate degree	2.5%

Income & Poverty, 1999
Per capita income	$19,238
Median household income	$47,394
Median family income	$52,860
Persons in poverty	2,612
H'holds receiving public assistance	418
H'holds receiving social security	2,164

Households, 2000
Total households	10,050
With persons under 18	4,277
With persons over 65	2,009
Family households	7,484
Single-person households	2,048
Persons per household	2.80
Persons per family	3.22

Labor & Employment
Total civilian labor force, 2006**	15,037
Unemployment rate	5.8%
Total civilian labor force, 2000	13,931
Unemployment rate	6.1%

Employed persons 16 years and over by occupation, 2000
Managers & professionals	2,806
Service occupations	3,013
Sales & office occupations	3,769
Farming, fishing & forestry	51
Construction & maintenance	1,319
Production & transportation	2,129
Self-employed persons	566

* US Census Bureau
** New Jersey Department of Labor

See Introduction for an explanation of all data sources.

General Information
Township of Pemberton
500 Pemberton Browns Mills Rd
Pemberton, NJ 08068
609-894-8201

Website	www.pemberton-twp.com
Year of incorporation	1846
Land/water area (sq. miles)	61.68/0.82
Form of government	Mayor-Council

Government
Legislative Districts
US Congressional	3
State Legislative	8

Local Officials, 2008
Mayor	David A. Patriarca
Manager	Christopher Vaz
Clerk	Mary Ann Young
Finance Dir	Linda Eden
Tax Assessor	Maureen Francis
Tax Collector	Michelle Adams
Attorney	Andrew Bayer
Building	Robert Benasch
Comm Dev/Planning	NA
Engineering	Adams, Rehmann & Heggan
Public Works	Phil Sager
Police Chief	Robert Lewandowski
Fire/Emergency Dir	NA

Housing & Construction
Housing Units, 2000*
Total	10,778
Median rent	$670
Median SF home value	$98,300

Permits for New Residential Construction
	Units	Value
Total, 2007	31	$3,223,629
Single family	31	$3,223,629
Total, 2006	26	$2,344,288
Single family	26	$2,344,288

Real Property Valuation, 2007
	Parcels	Valuation
Total	11,572	$873,859,435
Vacant	3,050	19,737,250
Residential	7,983	757,657,050
Commercial	149	56,509,935
Industrial	5	4,323,800
Apartments	14	18,876,300
Farm land	249	2,923,900
Farm homestead	122	13,831,200

Average Property Value & Tax, 2007
Residential value	$95,187
Property tax	$3,237
Tax credit/rebate	$758

Public Library
No public municipal library

Library statistics, 2006
Population served	NA
Full-time/total staff	NA/NA

	Total	Per capita
Holdings	NA	NA
Revenues	NA	NA
Expenditures	NA	NA
Annual visits	NA	NA
Internet terminals/annual users	NA/NA	

Taxes
	2005	2006	2007
General tax rate per $100	3.244	3.319	3.41
County equalization ratio	77.01	66.29	57.08
Net valuation taxable	$851,697,405	$852,595,236	$876,162,692
State equalized value	$1,284,805,257	$1,496,215,906	$1,691,899,999

Public Safety
Number of officers, 2006 57

Crime
	2005	2006
Total crimes	779	774
Violent	109	75
Murder	1	2
Rape	17	4
Robbery	26	26
Aggravated assault	65	43
Non-violent	670	699
Burglary	191	250
Larceny	422	402
Vehicle theft	57	47
Domestic violence	412	570
Arson	11	11
Total crime rate	26.9	26.8
Violent	3.8	2.6
Non-violent	23.1	24.2

Public School District
(for school year 2006-07 except as noted)

Pemberton Township School District
One Egbert St, PO Box 228
Pemberton, NJ 08068
609-893-8141

Superintendent	Michael Gorman
Number of schools	11
Grade plan	K-12
Enrollment	5,226
Attendance rate, '05-06	93.2%
Dropout rate	2.8%
Students per teacher	9.0
Per pupil expenditure	$17,174
Median faculty salary	$68,578
Median administrator salary	$112,400
Grade 12 enrollment	294
High school graduation rate	91.3%

Assessment test results
(percent scoring at proficient or advanced level)
	Language	Math
NJASK-Grade 3	78.6%	82.6%
GEPA-Grade 8	54.4%	45.9%
HSPA-High School	76.7%	58.0%

SAT score averages
Pct tested	Math	Verbal	Writing
54%	470	467	459

Teacher Qualifications
Avg. years of experience	14
Highly-qualified teachers one subject/all subjects	100%/100%
With emergency credentials	0.0%

No Child Left Behind
AYP, 2005-06 . . . . Meets Standards

Municipal Finance
State Aid Programs, 2008
Total aid	$3,580,285
CMPTRA	1,521,280
Energy tax receipts	2,029,008
Garden State Trust	20,318

General Budget, 2007
Total tax levy	$29,794,856
County levy	6,414,421
County taxes	5,315,237
County library	487,759
County health	0
County open space	611,424
School levy	11,247,307
Muni. levy	12,133,128
Misc. revenues	10,887,220

The New Jersey Municipal Data Book

Pennington Borough
Mercer County

Demographics & Socio-Economic Characteristics
(2000 US Census, except as noted)

Population
1980*	2,109
1990*	2,537
2000	2,696
Male	1,293
Female	1,403
2006 (estimate)*	2,688
Population density	2,800.0

Race & Hispanic Origin, 2000
Race
White	2,560
Black/African American	71
American Indian/Alaska Native	0
Asian	27
Native Hawaiian/Pacific Islander	0
Other race	11
Two or more races	27
Hispanic origin, total	32
Mexican	4
Puerto Rican	4
Cuban	2
Other Hispanic	22

Age & Nativity, 2000
Under 5 years	173
18 years and over	1,922
21 years and over	1,859
65 years and over	405
85 years and over	51
Median age	41.3
Native-born	2,539
Foreign-born	157

Educational Attainment, 2000
Population 25 years and over	1,781
Less than 9th grade	0.4%
High school grad or higher	97.1%
Bachelor's degree or higher	69.5%
Graduate degree	33.0%

Income & Poverty, 1999
Per capita income	$45,843
Median household income	$90,366
Median family income	$107,089
Persons in poverty	64
H'holds receiving public assistance	0
H'holds receiving social security	269

Households, 2000
Total households	1,013
With persons under 18	417
With persons over 65	293
Family households	762
Single-person households	223
Persons per household	2.66
Persons per family	3.14

Labor & Employment
Total civilian labor force, 2006**	1,249
Unemployment rate	3.5%
Total civilian labor force, 2000	1,338
Unemployment rate	2.6%

Employed persons 16 years and over by occupation, 2000
Managers & professionals	837
Service occupations	60
Sales & office occupations	315
Farming, fishing & forestry	0
Construction & maintenance	43
Production & transportation	48
Self-employed persons	120

* US Census Bureau
** New Jersey Department of Labor

General Information
Borough of Pennington
30 N Main St
Pennington, NJ 08534
609-737-0276

Website	www.penningtonboro.org
Year of incorporation	1890
Land/water area (sq. miles)	0.96/0.00
Form of government	Borough

Government
Legislative Districts
US Congressional	12
State Legislative	15

Local Officials, 2008
Mayor	Anthony J. Persichilli
Manager	Eugene Dunworth Jr
Clerk	Betty Sterling
Finance Dir	Sandra Webb
Tax Assessor	Antoinette Sost
Tax Collector	Irene Billings
Attorney	Walter Bliss
Building	John Hall
Planning	Mary Mistretta
Engineering	Donald Fetzer
Public Works	William J. Wittkop
Police Chief	NA
Emerg/Fire Director	Dave Pinelli

Housing & Construction
Housing Units, 2000*
Total	1,040
Median rent	$881
Median SF home value	$283,800

Permits for New Residential Construction
	Units	Value
Total, 2007	1	$274,750
Single family	1	$274,750
Total, 2006	7	$1,177,082
Single family	7	$1,177,082

Real Property Valuation, 2007
	Parcels	Valuation
Total	979	$516,535,800
Vacant	58	3,324,400
Residential	859	452,711,100
Commercial	57	51,354,100
Industrial	2	7,417,400
Apartments	3	1,728,800
Farm land	0	0
Farm homestead	0	0

Average Property Value & Tax, 2007
Residential value	$527,021
Property tax	$10,239
Tax credit/rebate	$1,378

Public Library
Pennington Public Library
30 N Main St
Pennington, NJ 08534
609-737-0404

Director: Kathleen M. Doyle

Library statistics, 2006
Population served	2,696
Full-time/total staff	1/1

	Total	Per capita
Holdings	27,796	10.31
Revenues	$171,389	$63.57
Expenditures	$154,906	$57.46
Annual visits	24,500	9.09
Internet terminals/annual users	4/3,300	

Taxes
	2005	2006	2007
General tax rate per $100	4.04	1.88	1.95
County equalization ratio	57.44	118.19	107.89
Net valuation taxable	$228,041,075	$516,087,400	$518,248,052
State equalized value	$433,620,603	$480,436,224	$500,587,856

Public Safety
Number of officers, 2006		6

Crime	2005	2006
Total crimes	26	23
Violent	1	1
Murder	0	0
Rape	0	1
Robbery	0	0
Aggravated assault	1	0
Non-violent	25	22
Burglary	7	3
Larceny	18	19
Vehicle theft	0	0
Domestic violence	2	0
Arson	0	1
Total crime rate	9.6	8.5
Violent	0.4	0.4
Non-violent	9.2	8.2

Public School District
(for school year 2006-07 except as noted)

Hopewell Valley Regional School District
425 S Main St
Pennington, NJ 08534
609-737-4000

Chief School Admin	Judith Ferguson
Number of schools	18
Grade plan	K-12
Enrollment	4,036
Attendance rate, '05-06	96.2%
Dropout rate	0.5%
Students per teacher	10.6
Per pupil expenditure	$15,143
Median faculty salary	$109,814
Median administrator salary	$61,343
Grade 12 enrollment	284
High school graduation rate	97.9%

Assessment test results
(percent scoring at proficient or advanced level)
	Language	Math
NJASK-Grade 3	93.5%	92.9%
GEPA-Grade 8	88.7%	83.5%
HSPA-High School	97.1%	90.0%

SAT score averages
Pct tested	Math	Verbal	Writing
96%	562	557	585

Teacher Qualifications
Avg. years of experience	10
Highly-qualified teachers one subject/all subjects	100%/100%
With emergency credentials	0.0%

No Child Left Behind
AYP, 2005-06	Meets Standards

Municipal Finance
State Aid Programs, 2008
Total aid	$199,830
CMPTRA	0
Energy tax receipts	199,830
Garden State Trust	0

General Budget, 2007
Total tax levy	$10,068,398
County levy	2,246,673
County taxes	2,102,509
County library	0
County health	0
County open space	144,164
School levy	5,706,199
Muni. levy	2,115,527
Misc. revenues	1,055,890

Salem County | Penns Grove Borough

Demographics & Socio-Economic Characteristics
(2000 US Census, except as noted)

Population
- 1980*........................5,760
- 1990*........................5,228
- 2000.........................4,886
  - Male.......................2,252
  - Female.....................2,634
- 2006 (estimate)*.............4,797
  - Population density........5,158.1

Race & Hispanic Origin, 2000
Race
- White........................2,387
- Black/African American.......1,942
- American Indian/Alaska Native...18
- Asian...........................14
- Native Hawaiian/Pacific Islander...8
- Other race....................397
- Two or more races.............120
- Hispanic origin, total........845
  - Mexican.....................147
  - Puerto Rican................580
  - Cuban........................15
  - Other Hispanic..............103

Age & Nativity, 2000
- Under 5 years.................412
- 18 years and over...........3,275
- 21 years and over...........3,062
- 65 years and over.............576
- 85 years and over..............57
  - Median age..................30.9
- Native-born.................4,704
- Foreign-born..................176

Educational Attainment, 2000
- Population 25 years and over...2,803
- Less than 9th grade..........14.4%
- High school grad or higher...65.6%
- Bachelor's degree or higher...7.5%
- Graduate degree...............1.6%

Income & Poverty, 1999
- Per capita income..........$13,330
- Median household income....$26,227
- Median family income.......$34,076
- Persons in poverty...........1,020
- H'holds receiving public assistance...118
- H'holds receiving social security...606

Households, 2000
- Total households............1,827
  - With persons under 18......799
  - With persons over 65.......471
  - Family households........1,232
  - Single-person households...513
- Persons per household........2.67
- Persons per family...........3.26

Labor & Employment
- Total civilian labor force, 2006**...2,185
  - Unemployment rate..........13.1%
- Total civilian labor force, 2000...2,140
  - Unemployment rate..........15.3%

Employed persons 16 years and over by occupation, 2000
- Managers & professionals.....349
- Service occupations..........368
- Sales & office occupations...431
- Farming, fishing & forestry...24
- Construction & maintenance...150
- Production & transportation..490
- Self-employed persons.........73

‡ Joint library with Carneys Point
* US Census Bureau
** New Jersey Department of Labor

See Introduction for an explanation of all data sources.

General Information
Borough of Penns Grove
PO Box 527
Penns Grove, NJ 08069
856-299-0098
- Email.............pgclerk1@verizon.net
- Year of incorporation.........1894
- Land/water area (sq. miles)...0.93/0.00
- Form of government.........Borough

Government
Legislative Districts
- US Congressional..................2
- State Legislative.................3

Local Officials, 2008
- Mayor..............John A. Washington
- Manager/Admin....................NA
- Clerk.............Sharon R. Williams
- Finance Dir............Stephen Labb
- Tax Assessor........Marie Proccaci
- Tax Collector.........Tom Freeman
- Attorney.............Adam Telsey
- Building..............Jeryl Goff
- Planning.........Armondo Verdecchio
- Engineering........Mark Brunermer
- Public Works........Vass Wiggins
- Police Chief.......Gary Doubledee
- Emerg/Fire Director...Joseph Grasso

Housing & Construction
Housing Units, 2000*
- Total.........................2,075
- Median rent....................$526
- Median SF home value........$72,900

Permits for New Residential Construction
	Units	Value
Total, 2007	0	$0
Single family	0	$0
Total, 2006	1	$160,000
Single family	1	$160,000

Real Property Valuation, 2007
	Parcels	Valuation
Total	1,677	$90,373,600
Vacant	333	2,520,300
Residential	1,224	70,678,900
Commercial	108	15,001,100
Industrial	0	0
Apartments	12	2,173,300
Farm land	0	0
Farm homestead	0	0

Average Property Value & Tax, 2007
- Residential value.............$57,744
- Property tax...................$3,301
- Tax credit/rebate...............$848

Public Library
Penns Grove-Carneys Point Library‡
222 S Broad St
Penns Grove, NJ 08069
856-299-4255
- Director................Barbara Hunt

Library statistics, 2006
- Population served............12,570
- Full-time/total staff...........NA/0

	Total	Per capita
Holdings	NA	NA
Revenues	NA	NA
Expenditures	NA	NA
Annual visits	NA	NA
Internet terminals/annual users	NA/NA	

Taxes
	2005	2006	2007
General tax rate per $100	5.087	5.39	5.716
County equalization ratio	73.09	67.82	60.71
Net valuation taxable	$90,113,832	$88,691,000	$91,510,515
State equalized value	$132,872,061	$147,338,062	$168,495,434

Public Safety
- Number of officers, 2006..........16

Crime	2005	2006
Total crimes	300	279
Violent	57	46
Murder	0	0
Rape	2	0
Robbery	22	21
Aggravated assault	33	25
Non-violent	243	233
Burglary	49	59
Larceny	172	156
Vehicle theft	22	18
Domestic violence	86	105
Arson	1	1
Total crime rate	62.4	57.8
Violent	11.9	9.5
Non-violent	50.6	48.3

Public School District
(for school year 2006-07 except as noted)

Penns Grove-Carneys Pt. Reg. School Dist.
100 Iona Ave
Penns Grove, NJ 08069
856-299-4250
- Superintendent......Joseph A. Massare
- Number of schools...............10
- Grade plan.....................K-12
- Enrollment...................2,393
- Attendance rate, '05-06.......93.0%
- Dropout rate...................4.3%
- Students per teacher...........11.3
- Per pupil expenditure.......$12,045
- Median faculty salary.......$52,275
- Median administrator salary..$90,926
- Grade 12 enrollment............120
- High school graduation rate...85.8%

Assessment test results
(percent scoring at proficient or advanced level)

	Language	Math
NJASK-Grade 3	71.8%	83.0%
GEPA-Grade 8	44.0%	45.1%
HSPA-High School	75.7%	58.3%

SAT score averages
Pct tested	Math	Verbal	Writing
71%	427	419	412

Teacher Qualifications
- Avg. years of experience.......12
- Highly-qualified teachers
  - one subject/all subjects....99.5%/99.5%
- With emergency credentials....0.0%

No Child Left Behind
- AYP, 2005-06..........Meets Standards

Municipal Finance
State Aid Programs, 2008
- Total aid...................$325,175
  - CMPTRA.........................0
  - Energy tax receipts.......325,175
  - Garden State Trust..............0

General Budget, 2007
- Total tax levy............$5,230,490
  - County levy.............1,421,939
    - County taxes.........1,391,604
    - County library..............0
    - County health...............0
    - County open space......30,335
  - School levy.............2,158,775
  - Muni. levy..............1,649,776
- Misc. revenues...........3,831,893

Pennsauken Township
Camden County

Demographics & Socio-Economic Characteristics
(2000 US Census, except as noted)

Population
1980*	33,775
1990*	34,738
2000	35,737
Male	17,116
Female	18,621
2006 (estimate)*	35,443
Population density	3,365.9

Race & Hispanic Origin, 2000
Race
White	21,479
Black/African American	8,641
American Indian/Alaska Native	124
Asian	1,636
Native Hawaiian/Pacific Islander	7
Other race	2,954
Two or more races	896
Hispanic origin, total	5,126
Mexican	218
Puerto Rican	3,629
Cuban	32
Other Hispanic	1,247

Age & Nativity, 2000
Under 5 years	2,212
18 years and over	25,925
21 years and over	24,634
65 years and over	5,065
85 years and over	608
Median age	36.1
Native-born	32,881
Foreign-born	2,822

Educational Attainment, 2000
Population 25 years and over	22,983
Less than 9th grade	6.2%
High school grad or higher	77.2%
Bachelor's degree or higher	15.4%
Graduate degree	4.8%

Income & Poverty, 1999
Per capita income	$19,004
Median household income	$47,538
Median family income	$52,760
Persons in poverty	2,807
H'holds receiving public assistance	331
H'holds receiving social security	3,651

Households, 2000
Total households	12,389
With persons under 18	5,120
With persons over 65	3,436
Family households	9,097
Single-person households	2,865
Persons per household	2.83
Persons per family	3.34

Labor & Employment
Total civilian labor force, 2006**	18,081
Unemployment rate	5.8%
Total civilian labor force, 2000	16,881
Unemployment rate	5.4%

Employed persons 16 years and over by occupation, 2000
Managers & professionals	4,447
Service occupations	2,553
Sales & office occupations	4,967
Farming, fishing & forestry	5
Construction & maintenance	1,292
Production & transportation	2,699
Self-employed persons	542

* US Census Bureau
** New Jersey Department of Labor

General Information
Township of Pennsauken
5605 N Crescent Blvd
Pennsauken, NJ 08110
856-665-1000

Website	www.twp.pennsauken.nj.us
Year of incorporation	1892
Land/water area (sq. miles)	10.53/1.65
Form of government	Township

Government
Legislative Districts
US Congressional	1
State Legislative	7

Local Officials, 2008
Mayor	Jack Killion
Manager	Bob Cummings
Clerk	Gene Padalino
Finance Dir	Ronald Crane
Tax Assessor	John Dymond
Tax Collector	Daniel O'Brien
Attorney	Dave Luthman
Building	Gary Burgin
Planning	John Adams
Engineering	Dennis O'Rourke
Public Works	John Figueroa
Police Chief	John Coffey
Emerg/Fire Director	Jack Mattera

Housing & Construction
Housing Units, 2000*
Total	12,945
Median rent	$584
Median SF home value	$95,300

Permits for New Residential Construction
	Units	Value
Total, 2007	19	$1,788,930
Single family	19	$1,788,930
Total, 2006	38	$2,164,925
Single family	12	$1,068,450

Real Property Valuation, 2007
	Parcels	Valuation
Total	12,149	$1,613,332,900
Vacant	285	16,770,800
Residential	10,980	986,574,300
Commercial	798	486,458,700
Industrial	38	101,217,200
Apartments	48	22,311,900
Farm land	0	0
Farm homestead	0	0

Average Property Value & Tax, 2007
Residential value	$89,852
Property tax	$3,837
Tax credit/rebate	$843

Public Library
Pennsauken Free Public Library
5605 Crescent Blvd
Pennsauken, NJ 08110
856-665-5959

Director … John Patane

Library statistics, 2006
Population served	35,737
Full-time/total staff	4/9

	Total	Per capita
Holdings	116,029	3.25
Revenues	$945,951	$26.47
Expenditures	$912,502	$25.53
Annual visits	166,342	4.65
Internet terminals/annual users	9/38,500	

Taxes
	2005	2006	2007
General tax rate per $100	3.739	4.032	4.271
County equalization ratio	85.42	75.2	66.84
Net valuation taxable	$1,618,484,615	$1,616,967,900	$1,616,545,946
State equalized value	$2,152,240,180	$2,422,602,983	$2,783,862,650

Public Safety
Number of officers, 2006 … 93

Crime
	2005	2006
Total crimes	1,484	1,507
Violent	173	138
Murder	0	1
Rape	7	13
Robbery	74	49
Aggravated assault	92	75
Non-violent	1,311	1,369
Burglary	263	323
Larceny	888	911
Vehicle theft	160	135
Domestic violence	416	404
Arson	8	9
Total crime rate	41.7	42.4
Violent	4.9	3.9
Non-violent	36.8	38.5

Public School District
(for school year 2006-07 except as noted)

Pennsauken Township School District
1695 Hylton Rd
Pennsauken, NJ 08110
856-662-8505

Superintendent	James Chapman
Number of schools	10
Grade plan	K-12
Enrollment	5,404
Attendance rate, '05-06	93.7%
Dropout rate	6.2%
Students per teacher	12.0
Per pupil expenditure	$12,494
Median faculty salary	$61,925
Median administrator salary	$107,679
Grade 12 enrollment	390
High school graduation rate	84.2%

Assessment test results
(percent scoring at proficient or advanced level)
	Language	Math
NJASK-Grade 3	75.3%	77.8%
GEPA-Grade 8	55.7%	62.5%
HSPA-High School	73.5%	52.2%

SAT score averages
Pct tested	Math	Verbal	Writing
68%	434	422	419

Teacher Qualifications
Avg. years of experience	10
Highly-qualified teachers one subject/all subjects	98.5%/97.0%
With emergency credentials	0.0%

No Child Left Behind
AYP, 2005-06 … Needs Improvement

Municipal Finance
State Aid Programs, 2008
Total aid	$7,056,183
CMPTRA	2,036,282
Energy tax receipts	5,019,606
Garden State Trust	295

General Budget, 2007
Total tax levy	$69,040,486
County levy	16,142,938
County taxes	15,651,409
County library	0
County health	0
County open space	491,529
School levy	35,887,548
Muni. levy	17,010,000
Misc. revenues	17,690,000

Salem County | Pennsville Township

Demographics & Socio-Economic Characteristics
(2000 US Census, except as noted)

Population
1980*	13,848
1990*	13,794
2000	13,194
Male	6,337
Female	6,857
2006 (estimate)*	13,333
Population density	577.2

Race & Hispanic Origin, 2000
Race
White	12,756
Black/African American	127
American Indian/Alaska Native	21
Asian	127
Native Hawaiian/Pacific Islander	2
Other race	51
Two or more races	110
Hispanic origin, total	211
Mexican	45
Puerto Rican	102
Cuban	6
Other Hispanic	58

Age & Nativity, 2000
Under 5 years	758
18 years and over	10,134
21 years and over	9,689
65 years and over	2,047
85 years and over	189
Median age	39.3
Native-born	12,817
Foreign-born	428

Educational Attainment, 2000
Population 25 years and over	9,260
Less than 9th grade	4.4%
High school grad or higher	82.0%
Bachelor's degree or higher	13.6%
Graduate degree	2.6%

Income & Poverty, 1999
Per capita income	$22,717
Median household income	$47,250
Median family income	$57,340
Persons in poverty	653
H'holds receiving public assistance	131
H'holds receiving social security	1,789

Households, 2000
Total households	5,317
With persons under 18	1,730
With persons over 65	1,499
Family households	3,712
Single-person households	1,380
Persons per household	2.47
Persons per family	2.98

Labor & Employment
Total civilian labor force, 2006**	7,036
Unemployment rate	3.4%
Total civilian labor force, 2000	6,821
Unemployment rate	4.5%

Employed persons 16 years and over by occupation, 2000
Managers & professionals	1,843
Service occupations	936
Sales & office occupations	1,794
Farming, fishing & forestry	23
Construction & maintenance	754
Production & transportation	1,163
Self-employed persons	224

* US Census Bureau
** New Jersey Department of Labor

See Introduction for an explanation of all data sources.

General Information
Township of Pennsville
90 N Broadway
Pennsville, NJ 08070
856-678-3089
Website	www.pennsville.org
Year of incorporation	1965
Land/water area (sq. miles)	23.10/1.71
Form of government	Township

Government
Legislative Districts
US Congressional	2
State Legislative	3

Local Officials, 2008
Mayor	John Crawford
Manager	Jack Lynch
Clerk	Theresa Lappe
Finance Dir	John Willadsen
Tax Assessor	Randal Shidner
Tax Collector	Nancy McCarthy
Attorney	Walter Ray
Building	Tony Dariano
Comm Dev/Planning	NA
Engineering	Mark Brunermer
Public Works	Jack Lynch
Police Chief	Patrick McCaffery
Fire Chief	M. Ayares

Housing & Construction
Housing Units, 2000*
Total	5,623
Median rent	$640
Median SF home value	$103,700

Permits for New Residential Construction
	Units	Value
Total, 2007	12	$1,318,800
Single family	12	$1,318,800
Total, 2006	129	$12,625,005
Single family	28	$3,014,105

Real Property Valuation, 2007
	Parcels	Valuation
Total	5,926	$747,033,500
Vacant	829	15,202,700
Residential	4,614	476,106,900
Commercial	198	79,372,000
Industrial	3	150,155,900
Apartments	14	17,513,000
Farm land	216	2,027,200
Farm homestead	52	6,655,800

Average Property Value & Tax, 2007
Residential value	$103,464
Property tax	$4,266
Tax credit/rebate	$886

Public Library
Pennsville Public Library
190 S Broadway
Pennsville, NJ 08070
856-678-5473
Director .... Nancy Whitesell

Library statistics, 2006
Population served	13,194
Full-time/total staff	1/3

	Total	Per capita
Holdings	30,383	2.30
Revenues	$232,724	$17.64
Expenditures	$232,724	$17.64
Annual visits	19,720	1.49
Internet terminals/annual users		4/2,695

Taxes
	2005	2006	2007
General tax rate per $100	3.705	3.869	4.123
County equalization ratio	85.42	83.23	71.74
Net valuation taxable	$732,315,311	$738,555,300	$748,761,463
State equalized value	$879,869,411	$1,031,435,868	$1,170,611,549

Public Safety
Number of officers, 2006 24

Crime	2005	2006
Total crimes	408	396
Violent	19	14
Murder	0	0
Rape	0	0
Robbery	2	4
Aggravated assault	17	10
Non-violent	389	382
Burglary	65	86
Larceny	309	285
Vehicle theft	15	11
Domestic violence	268	240
Arson	3	4
Total crime rate	30.9	29.7
Violent	1.4	1.1
Non-violent	29.5	28.7

Public School District
(for school year 2006-07 except as noted)

Pennsville Township School District
30 Church St
Pennsville, NJ 08070
856-540-6210

Superintendent	Mark Jones
Number of schools	5
Grade plan	K-12
Enrollment	2,069
Attendance rate, '05-06	94.1%
Dropout rate	3.5%
Students per teacher	11.0
Per pupil expenditure	$12,481
Median faculty salary	$49,467
Median administrator salary	$86,763
Grade 12 enrollment	140
High school graduation rate	86.6%

Assessment test results
(percent scoring at proficient or advanced level)
	Language	Math
NJASK-Grade 3	80.6%	90.5%
GEPA-Grade 8	76.1%	80.0%
HSPA-High School	88.4%	70.3%

SAT score averages
Pct tested	Math	Verbal	Writing
77%	460	472	461

Teacher Qualifications
Avg. years of experience	11
Highly-qualified teachers one subject/all subjects	100%/100%
With emergency credentials	0.0%

No Child Left Behind
AYP, 2005-06 .... Meets Standards

Municipal Finance
State Aid Programs, 2008
Total aid	$6,798,773
CMPTRA	1,699,750
Energy tax receipts	5,098,747
Garden State Trust	276

General Budget, 2007
Total tax levy	$30,870,450
County levy	10,350,179
County taxes	10,129,366
County library	0
County health	0
County open space	220,813
School levy	17,412,656
Muni. levy	3,107,615
Misc. revenues	10,569,903

©2008 Information Publications, Inc. All rights reserved. Photocopying prohibited. For additional copies, contact the publisher at www.informationpublications.com or (877)544-INFO (4636)

Pequannock Township
Morris County

Demographics & Socio-Economic Characteristics
(2000 US Census, except as noted)

Population
- 1980* 13,776
- 1990* 12,844
- 2000 13,888
  - Male 6,688
  - Female 7,200
- 2006 (estimate)* 16,320
- Population density 2,308.3

Race & Hispanic Origin, 2000
Race
- White 13,416
- Black/African American 41
- American Indian/Alaska Native .. 17
- Asian 265
- Native Hawaiian/Pacific Islander .. 0
- Other race 69
- Two or more races 80
- Hispanic origin, total 408
  - Mexican 29
  - Puerto Rican 144
  - Cuban 42
  - Other Hispanic 193

Age & Nativity, 2000
- Under 5 years 947
- 18 years and over 10,293
- 21 years and over 9,912
- 65 years and over 1,956
- 85 years and over 206
- Median age 38.9
- Native-born 12,904
- Foreign-born 984

Educational Attainment, 2000
- Population 25 years and over ... 9,495
- Less than 9th grade 2.4%
- High school grad or higher .. 92.8%
- Bachelor's degree or higher . 37.5%
- Graduate degree 11.4%

Income & Poverty, 1999
- Per capita income $31,892
- Median household income .. $72,729
- Median family income $84,487
- Persons in poverty 414
- H'holds receiving public assistance .. 43
- H'holds receiving social security .. 1,460

Households, 2000
- Total households 5,026
  - With persons under 18 1,849
  - With persons over 65 1,414
  - Family households 3,828
  - Single-person households . 1,052
  - Persons per household 2.76
  - Persons per family 3.23

Labor & Employment
- Total civilian labor force, 2006** .. 7,946
  - Unemployment rate 4.0%
- Total civilian labor force, 2000 7,243
  - Unemployment rate 3.7%

Employed persons 16 years and over by occupation, 2000
- Managers & professionals ... 3,057
- Service occupations 701
- Sales & office occupations .. 2,263
- Farming, fishing & forestry 7
- Construction & maintenance .. 466
- Production & transportation .. 484
- Self-employed persons 358

* US Census Bureau
** New Jersey Department of Labor

General Information
Township of Pequannock
530 Newark Pompton Tpke
Pompton Plains, NJ 07444
973-835-5700
- Website ...... www.pequannocktownship.org
- Year of incorporation 1720
- Land/water area (sq. miles) ... 7.07/0.14
- Form of government ..... Council-Manager

Government
Legislative Districts
- US Congressional 11
- State Legislative 26

Local Officials, 2008
- Mayor .... Nicholas Kapotes
- Manager .... Kevin Boyle
- Clerk .... Dolores Sweeney
- Finance Dir .... David Hollberg
- Tax Assessor .... Robert Sweeney
- Tax Collector .... Lori Tarnogursky
- Attorney .... Michael Hubner
- Building .... Robert Grant
- Planning .... Eileen Banyra
- Engineering .... Fred Herrmann
- Public Works .... Bill Pereira
- Police Chief .... Brian Spring
- Emerg/Fire Director ... David Hollberg

Housing & Construction
Housing Units, 2000*
- Total 5,097
- Median rent $787
- Median SF home value .. $246,100

Permits for New Residential Construction

	Units	Value
Total, 2007	31	$2,814,885
Single family	5	$685,900
Total, 2006	286	$25,260,550
Single family	10	$2,660,550

Real Property Valuation, 2007

	Parcels	Valuation
Total	5,180	$2,803,064,800
Vacant	131	21,088,900
Residential	4,759	2,224,782,400
Commercial	230	257,880,100
Industrial	15	24,111,400
Apartments	3	263,282,000
Farm land	25	107,700
Farm homestead	17	11,812,300

Average Property Value & Tax, 2007
- Residential value $468,299
- Property tax $7,444
- Tax credit/rebate $1,165

Public Library
Pequannock Township Public Library
477 Newark Pompton Tpke
Pompton Plains, NJ 07444
973-825-7460
- Director .... Rosemary Garwood

Library statistics, 2006
- Population served 13,888
- Full-time/total staff 3/10

	Total	Per capita
Holdings	96,534	6.95
Revenues	$944,920	$68.04
Expenditures	$940,525	$67.72
Annual visits	136,942	9.86
Internet terminals/annual users	8/26,872	

Public Safety
- Number of officers, 2006 30

Crime	2005	2006
Total crimes	183	154
Violent	5	0
Murder	0	0
Rape	0	0
Robbery	3	0
Aggravated assault	2	0
Non-violent	178	154
Burglary	46	31
Larceny	125	110
Vehicle theft	7	13
Domestic violence	37	73
Arson	0	0
Total crime rate	12.0	9.9
Violent	0.3	0.0
Non-violent	11.7	9.9

Public School District
(for school year 2006-07 except as noted)

Pequannock Township School District
538 Newark-Pompton Turnpike
Pompton Plains, NJ 07444
973-616-6040
- Superintendent .... Larrie Reynolds
- Number of schools 5
- Grade plan K-12
- Enrollment 2,478
- Attendance rate, '05-06 ...... 95.9%
- Dropout rate .... NA
- Students per teacher 11.1
- Per pupil expenditure $12,364
- Median faculty salary $54,560
- Median administrator salary .. $114,864
- Grade 12 enrollment 204
- High school graduation rate .. 100.0%

Assessment test results
(percent scoring at proficient or advanced level)

	Language	Math
NJASK-Grade 3	92.4%	97.4%
GEPA-Grade 8	85.9%	89.9%
HSPA-High School	96.2%	86.2%

SAT score averages

Pct tested	Math	Verbal	Writing
95%	500	485	490

Teacher Qualifications
- Avg. years of experience 9
- Highly-qualified teachers
  - one subject/all subjects .. 99.5%/99.5%
- With emergency credentials 0.0%

No Child Left Behind
- AYP, 2005-06 .... Meets Standards

Municipal Finance
State Aid Programs, 2008
- Total aid $1,559,210
  - CMPTRA 386,393
  - Energy tax receipts .. 1,172,815
  - Garden State Trust 2

General Budget, 2007
- Total tax levy $44,589,666
  - County levy 6,549,373
    - County taxes 5,238,518
    - County library 0
    - County health 0
    - County open space 1,310,855
  - School levy 28,803,180
  - Muni. levy 9,237,113
- Misc. revenues 5,792,944

Taxes

	2005	2006	2007
General tax rate per $100	3.26	1.51	1.59
County equalization ratio	56.79	116.22	102.19
Net valuation taxable	$1,185,606,531	$2,755,178,700	$2,805,171,755
State equalized value	$2,318,354,578	$2,698,184,679	$2,813,324,285

Middlesex County
Perth Amboy City

Demographics & Socio-Economic Characteristics
(2000 US Census, except as noted)

Population
- 1980*........................38,951
- 1990*........................41,967
- 2000........................47,303
  - Male......................23,441
  - Female....................23,862
- 2006 (estimate)*.............48,607
  - Population density........10,168.8

Race & Hispanic Origin, 2000
Race
- White........................21,951
- Black/African American........4,749
- American Indian/Alaska Native...330
- Asian...........................723
- Native Hawaiian/Pacific Islander..60
- Other race...................16,834
- Two or more races.............2,656
- Hispanic origin, total.......33,033
  - Mexican....................3,056
  - Puerto Rican..............13,145
  - Cuban........................918
  - Other Hispanic............15,914

Age & Nativity, 2000
- Under 5 years................3,805
- 18 years and over...........33,831
- 21 years and over...........31,558
- 65 years and over............4,820
- 85 years and over..............599
- Median age....................31.2
- Native-born.................30,408
- Foreign-born................16,895

Educational Attainment, 2000
- Population 25 years and over...28,309
- Less than 9th grade............23.7%
- High school grad or higher.....55.7%
- Bachelor's degree or higher.....9.7%
- Graduate degree.................3.4%

Income & Poverty, 1999
- Per capita income............$14,989
- Median household income......$37,608
- Median family income.........$40,740
- Persons in poverty............8,190
- H'holds receiving public assistance..760
- H'holds receiving social security..3,694

Households, 2000
- Total households............14,562
  - With persons under 18......6,727
  - With persons over 65.......3,493
  - Family households.........10,768
  - Single-person households...2,993
- Persons per household..........3.20
- Persons per family.............3.63

Labor & Employment
- Total civilian labor force, 2006**....22,188
  - Unemployment rate............8.7%
- Total civilian labor force, 2000.....20,970
  - Unemployment rate...........10.8%

Employed persons 16 years and over by occupation, 2000
- Managers & professionals......3,267
- Service occupations...........3,252
- Sales & office occupations....4,667
- Farming, fishing & forestry......15
- Construction & maintenance....1,636
- Production & transportation...5,861
- Self-employed persons...........528

* US Census Bureau
** New Jersey Department of Labor
§ State Fiscal Year July 1–June 30

See Introduction for an explanation of all data sources.

General Information
City of Perth Amboy
260 High St
Perth Amboy, NJ 08861
732-826-0290

- Website.........www.ci.perthamboy.nj.us
- Year of incorporation..............1718
- Land/water area (sq. miles).....4.78/1.20
- Form of government.........Mayor-Council

Government
Legislative Districts
- US Congressional...................13
- State Legislative..................19

Local Officials, 2008
- Mayor....................Joseph Vas
- Manager...............Dianne Roman
- Clerk................Elaine M. Jasko
- Finance Dir................Jill Goldy
- Tax Assessor...........JoAnn Jimenez
- Tax Collector................(vacant)
- Attorney............Frank G. Capece
- Building................Vito Finetti
- Planning..............Michael Carr
- Engineering...........Michael Carr
- Public Works.......Kenneth Schwartz
- Police Chief.........Michael Kohut
- Emerg/Fire Director....Lawrence Cattano

Housing & Construction
Housing Units, 2000*
- Total.........................15,236
- Median rent.....................$732
- Median SF home value........$126,200

Permits for New Residential Construction

	Units	Value
Total, 2007	49	$3,877,995
Single family	21	$1,736,542
Total, 2006	201	$10,530,901
Single family	43	$3,021,600

Real Property Valuation, 2007

	Parcels	Valuation
Total	8,959	$3,575,020,400
Vacant	378	129,532,600
Residential	7,405	2,077,477,800
Commercial	888	530,427,300
Industrial	124	571,108,400
Apartments	164	266,474,300
Farm land	0	0
Farm homestead	0	0

Average Property Value & Tax, 2007
- Residential value............$280,551
- Property tax..................$5,824
- Tax credit/rebate..............$881

Public Library
Perth Amboy Public Library
196 Jefferson St
Perth Amboy, NJ 08861
732-826-2600

- Director................Patricia Gandy

Library statistics, 2006
- Population served............47,303
- Full-time/total staff...........3/12

	Total	Per capita
Holdings	167,103	3.53
Revenues	$1,176,582	$24.87
Expenditures	$1,152,790	$24.37
Annual visits	139,000	2.94

- Internet terminals/annual users...10/89,000

Taxes

	2005	2006	2007
General tax rate per $100	3.36	1.62	2.08
County equalization ratio	58.96	128.16	106.6
Net valuation taxable	$1,396,003,183	$3,576,828,200	$3,580,511,749
State equalized value	$2,777,563,038	$3,360,708,703	$3,730,246,923

Public Safety
- Number of officers, 2006............125

Crime	2005	2006
Total crimes	1,370	1,373
Violent	169	207
Murder	2	4
Rape	3	2
Robbery	59	95
Aggravated assault	105	106
Non-violent	1,201	1,166
Burglary	270	269
Larceny	779	737
Vehicle theft	152	160
Domestic violence	284	289
Arson	1	5
Total crime rate	28.1	28.1
Violent	3.5	4.2
Non-violent	24.6	23.9

Public School District
(for school year 2006-07 except as noted)

Perth Amboy School District
178 Barracks St
Perth Amboy, NJ 08861
732-376-6279

- Superintendent..........John M. Rodecker
- Number of schools................10
- Grade plan.....................K-12
- Enrollment....................9,536
- Attendance rate, '05-06........93.5%
- Dropout rate...................0.6%
- Students per teacher...........10.7
- Per pupil expenditure.......$14,535
- Median faculty salary.......$51,150
- Median administrator salary..$111,586
- Grade 12 enrollment.............463
- High school graduation rate....94.6%

Assessment test results
(percent scoring at proficient or advanced level)

	Language	Math
NJASK-Grade 3	74.9%	82.6%
GEPA-Grade 8	48.9%	42.1%
HSPA-High School	65.0%	47.1%

SAT score averages

Pct tested	Math	Verbal	Writing
57%	434	399	399

Teacher Qualifications
- Avg. years of experience..........7
- Highly-qualified teachers
  - one subject/all subjects....100%/100%
- With emergency credentials......0.3%

No Child Left Behind
- AYP, 2005-06........Needs Improvement

Municipal Finance§
State Aid Programs, 2008
- Total aid................$10,903,250
  - CMPTRA..................8,476,515
  - Energy tax receipts.....2,426,732
  - Garden State Trust..............3

General Budget, 2007
- Total tax levy...........$74,334,716
  - County taxes............9,831,409
    - County taxes..........8,800,944
    - County library................0
    - County health.................0
    - County open space.....1,030,464
  - School levy............18,708,510
  - Muni. levy.............45,794,797
- Misc. revenues...........32,770,935

©2008 Information Publications, Inc. All rights reserved. Photocopying prohibited. For additional copies, contact the publisher at www.informationpublications.com or (877)544-INFO (4636)

Phillipsburg Town

Warren County

Demographics & Socio-Economic Characteristics
(2000 US Census, except as noted)

Population
1980*	16,647
1990*	15,757
2000	15,166
Male	7,226
Female	7,940
2006 (estimate)*	14,831
Population density	4,605.9

Race & Hispanic Origin, 2000
Race
White	13,928
Black/African American	527
American Indian/Alaska Native	18
Asian	126
Native Hawaiian/Pacific Islander	2
Other race	306
Two or more races	259
Hispanic origin, total	816
Mexican	120
Puerto Rican	374
Cuban	30
Other Hispanic	292

Age & Nativity, 2000
Under 5 years	1,090
18 years and over	11,128
21 years and over	10,553
65 years and over	2,311
85 years and over	271
Median age	36.0
Native-born	14,537
Foreign-born	629

Educational Attainment, 2000
Population 25 years and over	9,913
Less than 9th grade	7.9%
High school grad or higher	71.3%
Bachelor's degree or higher	9.2%
Graduate degree	2.3%

Income & Poverty, 1999
Per capita income	$18,452
Median household income	$37,368
Median family income	$46,925
Persons in poverty	2,009
H'holds receiving public assistance	306
H'holds receiving social security	2,014

Households, 2000
Total households	6,044
With persons under 18	2,120
With persons over 65	1,751
Family households	3,945
Single-person households	1,793
Persons per household	2.49
Persons per family	3.08

Labor & Employment
Total civilian labor force, 2006**	8,375
Unemployment rate	6.6%
Total civilian labor force, 2000	7,320
Unemployment rate	5.9%

Employed persons 16 years and over by occupation, 2000
Managers & professionals	1,382
Service occupations	1,304
Sales & office occupations	2,032
Farming, fishing & forestry	9
Construction & maintenance	597
Production & transportation	1,566
Self-employed persons	238

* US Census Bureau
** New Jersey Department of Labor

General Information
Town of Phillipsburg
675 Corliss Ave
Phillipsburg, NJ 08865
908-454-5500

Website	www.phillipsburgnj.org
Year of incorporation	1861
Land/water area (sq. miles)	3.22/0.11
Form of government	Mayor-Council

Government

Legislative Districts
US Congressional	5
State Legislative	23

Local Officials, 2008
Mayor	Harry Wyant
Business Admin	Michele Broubalow
Clerk	Michele Broubalow
Finance Dir	Joseph Hriczak
Tax Assessor	Lydia Schmidt
Tax Collector	Joseph Hriczak
Attorney	Joel Kobert
Building	Kevin Duddy
Comm Dev/Planning	NA
Engineering	Stanley Schrek
Public Works	Dennis Viscomi
Police Chief	Edward Mirenda
Emerg/Fire Director	Richard Hay

Housing & Construction

Housing Units, 2000*
Total	6,651
Median rent	$600
Median SF home value	$90,000

Permits for New Residential Construction
	Units	Value
Total, 2007	25	$3,048,018
Single family	25	$3,048,018
Total, 2006	21	$2,453,496
Single family	21	$2,453,496

Real Property Valuation, 2007
	Parcels	Valuation
Total	5,048	$553,947,145
Vacant	168	6,473,400
Residential	4,478	400,550,634
Commercial	324	84,929,585
Industrial	39	43,137,350
Apartments	38	18,812,200
Farm land	1	43,976
Farm homestead	0	0

Average Property Value & Tax, 2007
Residential value	$89,449
Property tax	$3,342
Tax credit/rebate	$788

Public Library
Phillipsburg Public Library
200 Frost Ave
Phillipsburg, NJ 08865
908-454-3712

Director..............Ann DeRenzis

Library statistics, 2006
Population served	15,166
Full-time/total staff	4/12

	Total	Per capita
Holdings	117,311	7.74
Revenues	$1,302,209	$85.86
Expenditures	$1,363,522	$89.91
Annual visits	128,204	8.45
Internet terminals/annual users	15/25,376	

Public Safety
Number of officers, 2006.............35

Crime
	2005	2006
Total crimes	296	402
Violent	22	38
Murder	0	1
Rape	0	2
Robbery	8	21
Aggravated assault	14	14
Non-violent	274	364
Burglary	86	102
Larceny	159	227
Vehicle theft	29	35
Domestic violence	567	509
Arson	3	1
Total crime rate	19.6	26.9
Violent	1.5	2.5
Non-violent	18.2	24.4

Public School District
(for school year 2006-07 except as noted)

Phillipsburg School District
445 Marshall St
Phillipsburg, NJ 08865
908-454-3400

Superintendent	George Chando (Int)
Number of schools	6
Grade plan	K-12
Enrollment	3,355
Attendance rate, '05-06	93.4%
Dropout rate	3.8%
Students per teacher	9.1
Per pupil expenditure	$14,557
Median faculty salary	$55,998
Median administrator salary	$93,072
Grade 12 enrollment	415
High school graduation rate	86.9%

Assessment test results
(percent scoring at proficient or advanced level)
	Language	Math
NJASK-Grade 3	73.7%	76.8%
GEPA-Grade 8	59.0%	62.5%
HSPA-High School	83.5%	70.2%

SAT score averages
Pct tested	Math	Verbal	Writing
59%	525	505	495

Teacher Qualifications
Avg. years of experience	10
Highly-qualified teachers one subject/all subjects	99.5%/99.5%
With emergency credentials	0.0%

No Child Left Behind
AYP, 2005-06.........Needs Improvement

Municipal Finance

State Aid Programs, 2008
Total aid	$2,376,212
CMPTRA	1,382,803
Energy tax receipts	991,935
Garden State Trust	1,474

General Budget, 2007
Total tax levy	$20,777,460
County levy	5,691,271
County taxes	5,078,490
County library	0
County health	0
County open space	612,781
School levy	6,614,713
Muni. levy	8,471,476
Misc. revenues	7,122,621

Taxes
	2005	2006	2007
General tax rate per $100	3.32	3.45	3.74
County equalization ratio	75.36	65.21	55.53
Net valuation taxable	$554,463,875	$555,462,650	$556,129,342
State equalized value	$850,274,306	$1,002,997,093	$1,039,925,069

Salem County
Pilesgrove Township

Demographics & Socio-Economic Characteristics
(2000 US Census, except as noted)
Population
1980*	2,810
1990*	3,250
2000	3,923
Male	2,029
Female	1,894
2006 (estimate)*	4,534
Population density	129.9

Race & Hispanic Origin, 2000
Race
White	3,320
Black/African American	478
American Indian/Alaska Native	11
Asian	36
Native Hawaiian/Pacific Islander	2
Other race	42
Two or more races	34
Hispanic origin, total	117
Mexican	24
Puerto Rican	51
Cuban	0
Other Hispanic	42

Age & Nativity, 2000
Under 5 years	168
18 years and over	2,989
21 years and over	2,811
65 years and over	566
85 years and over	112
Median age	40.0
Native-born	3,864
Foreign-born	65

Educational Attainment, 2000
Population 25 years and over	2,709
Less than 9th grade	3.0%
High school grad or higher	87.7%
Bachelor's degree or higher	22.8%
Graduate degree	6.7%

Income & Poverty, 1999
Per capita income	$27,400
Median household income	$66,042
Median family income	$71,629
Persons in poverty	120
H'holds receiving public assistance	5
H'holds receiving social security	315

Households, 2000
Total households	1,216
With persons under 18	473
With persons over 65	317
Family households	995
Single-person households	181
Persons per household	2.91
Persons per family	3.24

Labor & Employment
Total civilian labor force, 2006**	1,967
Unemployment rate	4.0%
Total civilian labor force, 2000	1,895
Unemployment rate	4.2%

Employed persons 16 years and over by occupation, 2000
Managers & professionals	691
Service occupations	237
Sales & office occupations	396
Farming, fishing & forestry	24
Construction & maintenance	201
Production & transportation	266
Self-employed persons	228

‡ Joint library with Woodstown
* US Census Bureau
** New Jersey Department of Labor

See Introduction for an explanation of all data sources.

General Information
Township of Pilesgrove
1180 Route 40
Pilesgrove, NJ 08098
856-769-3222

Website	www.pilesgrovenj.org
Year of incorporation	1701
Land/water area (sq. miles)	34.91/0.14
Form of government	Township

Government
Legislative Districts
US Congressional	2
State Legislative	3

Local Officials, 2008
Mayor	Ernest A. Bickford
Manager	Maureen R. Abdill
Clerk	Maureen R. Abdill
Finance Dir	Ruth Moynihan
Tax Assessor	Randall Shidner
Tax Collector	NA
Attorney	William L. Horner
Building	John Holroyd
Comm Dev/Planning	NA
Engineering	James McKelvie
Public Works	NA
Police Chief	NA
Emerg/Fire Dir	Carlo Castagliuolo Jr

Housing & Construction
Housing Units, 2000*
Total	1,261
Median rent	$590
Median SF home value	$158,400

Permits for New Residential Construction
	Units	Value
Total, 2007	22	$4,386,482
Single family	22	$4,386,482
Total, 2006	22	$4,168,357
Single family	22	$4,168,357

Real Property Valuation, 2007
	Parcels	Valuation
Total	2,134	$483,491,700
Vacant	210	11,321,700
Residential	1,179	338,861,400
Commercial	66	47,711,700
Industrial	2	1,652,000
Apartments	4	7,466,300
Farm land	441	9,557,400
Farm homestead	232	66,921,200

Average Property Value & Tax, 2007
Residential value	$287,585
Property tax	$6,118
Tax credit/rebate	$1,046

Public Library
Woodstown-Pilesgrove Library‡
14 School Ln
Woodstown, NJ 08098
856-769-0098

Librarian............Betty Lou Wiest

Library statistics, 2006
Population served	7,059
Full-time/total staff	NA/0

	Total	Per capita
Holdings	NA	NA
Revenues	NA	NA
Expenditures	NA	NA
Annual visits	NA	NA
Internet terminals/annual users	NA/NA	

Taxes
	2005	2006	2007
General tax rate per $100	3.403	3.609	2.128
County equalization ratio	71.17	65.03	101.23
Net valuation taxable	$256,960,051	$268,269,000	$484,909,771
State equalized value	$395,140,783	$465,506,072	$476,874,556

Public Safety
Number of officers, 2006 0

Crime	2005	2006
Total crimes	71	102
Violent	2	9
Murder	0	0
Rape	0	0
Robbery	1	1
Aggravated assault	1	8
Non-violent	69	93
Burglary	19	24
Larceny	46	62
Vehicle theft	4	7
Domestic violence	23	10
Arson	1	2
Total crime rate	17.2	23.1
Violent	0.5	2.0
Non-violent	16.7	21.1

Public School District
(for school year 2006-07 except as noted)

Woodstown-Pilesgrove Reg. School District
135 East Ave
Woodstown, NJ 08098
856-769-1664

Superintendent	Robert Bumpus
Number of schools	6
Grade plan	K-12
Enrollment	1,621
Attendance rate, '05-06	95.6%
Dropout rate	0.4%
Students per teacher	11.2
Per pupil expenditure	$11,213
Median faculty salary	$47,555
Median administrator salary	$96,875
Grade 12 enrollment	157
High school graduation rate	99.1%

Assessment test results
(percent scoring at proficient or advanced level)
	Language	Math
NJASK-Grade 3	87.4%	86.3%
GEPA-Grade 8	80.2%	65.5%
HSPA-High School	88.6%	74.7%

SAT score averages
Pct tested	Math	Verbal	Writing
81%	493	494	484

Teacher Qualifications
Avg. years of experience	13
Highly-qualified teachers one subject/all subjects	100%/100%
With emergency credentials	0.0%

No Child Left Behind
AYP, 2005-06 ....Meets Standards

Municipal Finance
State Aid Programs, 2008
Total aid	$533,545
CMPTRA	0
Energy tax receipts	512,973
Garden State Trust	20,572

General Budget, 2007
Total tax levy	$10,315,132
County levy	4,514,377
County taxes	4,418,079
County library	0
County health	0
County open space	96,299
School levy	5,412,617
Muni. levy	388,137
Misc. revenues	2,300,500

©2008 Information Publications, Inc. All rights reserved. Photocopying prohibited. For additional copies, contact the publisher at www.informationpublications.com or (877)544-INFO (4636)

The New Jersey Municipal Data Book

Pine Beach Borough

Ocean County

Demographics & Socio-Economic Characteristics
(2000 US Census, except as noted)

Population
1980*	1,796
1990*	1,954
2000	1,950
Male	940
Female	1,010
2006 (estimate)*	2,032
Population density	3,277.4

Race & Hispanic Origin, 2000
Race
- White 1,919
- Black/African American 5
- American Indian/Alaska Native 1
- Asian 12
- Native Hawaiian/Pacific Islander 0
- Other race 4
- Two or more races 9
- Hispanic origin, total 46
  - Mexican 2
  - Puerto Rican 21
  - Cuban 11
  - Other Hispanic 12

Age & Nativity, 2000
- Under 5 years 101
- 18 years and over 1,507
- 21 years and over 1,454
- 65 years and over 337
- 85 years and over 38
- Median age 41.6
- Native-born 1,899
- Foreign-born 51

Educational Attainment, 2000
- Population 25 years and over 1,398
- Less than 9th grade 1.7%
- High school grad or higher 90.7%
- Bachelor's degree or higher 32.6%
- Graduate degree 11.5%

Income & Poverty, 1999
- Per capita income $26,487
- Median household income $57,366
- Median family income $67,404
- Persons in poverty 68
- H'holds receiving public assistance .. 2
- H'holds receiving social security . 259

Households, 2000
- Total households 767
- With persons under 18 254
- With persons over 65 247
- Family households 558
- Single-person households 172
- Persons per household 2.54
- Persons per family 3.01

Labor & Employment
- Total civilian labor force, 2006** .. 1,009
- Unemployment rate 4.2%
- Total civilian labor force, 2000 .. 1,015
- Unemployment rate 3.8%

Employed persons 16 years and over by occupation, 2000
- Managers & professionals 381
- Service occupations 136
- Sales & office occupations 268
- Farming, fishing & forestry 0
- Construction & maintenance 125
- Production & transportation 66
- Self-employed persons 54

* US Census Bureau
** New Jersey Department of Labor

General Information
Borough of Pine Beach
599 Pennsylvania Ave
PO Box 425
Pine Beach, NJ 08741
732-349-6425

- Website .... www.pinebeachborough.us
- Year of incorporation 1925
- Land/water area (sq. miles) 0.62/0.01
- Form of government .... Borough

Government
Legislative Districts
- US Congressional 3
- State Legislative 9

Local Officials, 2008
- Mayor .... Christopher J. Boyle
- Manager/Admin .... NA
- Clerk .... Charlene Carney
- Finance Dir .... Mary Jane Steib
- Tax Assessor .... Richard Kenny
- Tax Collector .... Christine Dehnz
- Attorney .... Steven Secare
- Building .... Anthony Avello
- Comm Dev/Planning .... NA
- Engineering .... John Mallon
- Public Works .... Steve Bortko
- Police Chief .... John Sgro
- Emerg/Fire Director ..... Thomas Haskell

Housing & Construction
Housing Units, 2000*
- Total 872
- Median rent $858
- Median SF home value $149,100

Permits for New Residential Construction
	Units	Value
Total, 2007	9	$1,485,875
Single family	9	$1,485,875
Total, 2006	16	$2,609,200
Single family	16	$2,609,200

Real Property Valuation, 2007
	Parcels	Valuation
Total	932	$292,422,300
Vacant	49	8,324,600
Residential	865	276,962,900
Commercial	18	7,134,800
Industrial	0	0
Apartments	0	0
Farm land	0	0
Farm homestead	0	0

Average Property Value & Tax, 2007
- Residential value $320,188
- Property tax $4,495
- Tax credit/rebate $875

Public Library
No public municipal library

Library statistics, 2006
- Population served .... NA
- Full-time/total staff .... NA/NA

	Total	Per capita
Holdings	NA	NA
Revenues	NA	NA
Expenditures	NA	NA
Annual visits	NA	NA
Internet terminals/annual users	NA/NA	

Taxes
	2005	2006	2007
General tax rate per $100	1.322	1.355	1.404
County equalization ratio	127.75	110.61	95.59
Net valuation taxable	$283,085,464	$288,886,400	$292,578,881
State equalized value	$255,931,167	$302,357,987	$315,198,921

Public Safety
- Number of officers, 2006 6

Crime
	2005	2006
Total crimes	32	27
Violent	0	0
Murder	0	0
Rape	0	0
Robbery	0	0
Aggravated assault	0	0
Non-violent	32	27
Burglary	3	4
Larceny	29	22
Vehicle theft	0	1
Domestic violence	12	23
Arson	0	0
Total crime rate	15.8	13.3
Violent	0.0	0.0
Non-violent	15.8	13.3

Public School District
(for school year 2006-07 except as noted)

Toms River Regional School District
1144 Hooper Ave
Toms River, NJ 08753
732-505-5510

- Superintendent .... Michael J. Ritacco
- Number of schools 72
- Grade plan K-12
- Enrollment 17,631
- Attendance rate, '05-06 .... 93.5%
- Dropout rate 3.5%
- Students per teacher 13.3
- Per pupil expenditure $10,065
- Median faculty salary $47,174
- Median administrator salary ... $111,050
- Grade 12 enrollment 1,315
- High school graduation rate .... NA

Assessment test results
(percent scoring at proficient or advanced level)

	Language	Math
NJASK-Grade 3	94.0%	95.0%
GEPA-Grade 8	81.0%	73.6%
HSPA-High School	87.0%	70.9%

SAT score averages
Pct tested	Math	Verbal	Writing
NA	NA	NA	NA

Teacher Qualifications
- Avg. years of experience 9
- Highly-qualified teachers
  - one subject/all subjects 99.5%/99.0%
- With emergency credentials 0.0%

No Child Left Behind
- AYP, 2005-06 .... Meets Standards

Municipal Finance
State Aid Programs, 2008
- Total aid $237,498
- CMPTRA 0
- Energy tax receipts 237,498
- Garden State Trust 0

General Budget, 2007
- Total tax levy $4,107,578
- County levy 950,562
- County taxes 783,306
- County library 92,836
- County health 37,612
- County open space 36,809
- School levy 1,864,473
- Muni. levy 1,292,543
- Misc. revenues 909,059

Camden County
Pine Hill Borough

Demographics & Socio-Economic Characteristics
(2000 US Census, except as noted)

Population
1980*	8,684
1990*	9,854
2000	10,880
Male	5,161
Female	5,719
2006 (estimate)*	11,275
Population density	2,869.0

Race & Hispanic Origin, 2000
Race
White	8,355
Black/African American	1,996
American Indian/Alaska Native	30
Asian	153
Native Hawaiian/Pacific Islander	2
Other race	132
Two or more races	212
Hispanic origin, total	396
Mexican	47
Puerto Rican	252
Cuban	16
Other Hispanic	81

Age & Nativity, 2000
Under 5 years	811
18 years and over	7,917
21 years and over	7,499
65 years and over	923
85 years and over	74
Median age	33.3
Native-born	10,530
Foreign-born	389

Educational Attainment, 2000
Population 25 years and over	6,959
Less than 9th grade	4.1%
High school grad or higher	80.7%
Bachelor's degree or higher	13.8%
Graduate degree	3.8%

Income & Poverty, 1999
Per capita income	$18,613
Median household income	$42,035
Median family income	$50,040
Persons in poverty	768
H'holds receiving public assistance	93
H'holds receiving social security	892

Households, 2000
Total households	4,214
With persons under 18	1,687
With persons over 65	743
Family households	2,742
Single-person households	1,172
Persons per household	2.58
Persons per family	3.18

Labor & Employment
Total civilian labor force, 2006**	6,366
Unemployment rate	6.4%
Total civilian labor force, 2000	5,844
Unemployment rate	5.9%

Employed persons 16 years and over by occupation, 2000
Managers & professionals	1,423
Service occupations	966
Sales & office occupations	1,732
Farming, fishing & forestry	4
Construction & maintenance	719
Production & transportation	653
Self-employed persons	237

* US Census Bureau
** New Jersey Department of Labor

See Introduction for an explanation of all data sources.

General Information
Borough of Pine Hill
45 W 7th Ave
Pine Hill, NJ 08021
856-783-7400

Website	www.pinehillboronj.com
Year of incorporation	1929
Land/water area (sq. miles)	3.93/0.03
Form of government	Borough

Government
Legislative Districts
US Congressional	1
State Legislative	6

Local Officials, 2008
Mayor	Fred Costantino
Manager/Admin	NA
Clerk	Loretta Buchanan
Finance Dir	Thomas Cardis
Tax Assessor	Michael Raio
Tax Collector	Diane May
Attorney	John Kearney
Building	Raymond Hallworth
Comm Dev/Planning	NA
Engineering	Robert Malissa
Public Works	William Buchanan
Police Chief	Kenneth Cheeseman
Emerg/Fire Director	Richard Wright Sr

Housing & Construction
Housing Units, 2000*
Total	4,444
Median rent	$627
Median SF home value	$88,500

Permits for New Residential Construction
	Units	Value
Total, 2007	27	$2,256,752
Single family	27	$2,256,752
Total, 2006	36	$2,790,888
Single family	36	$2,790,888

Real Property Valuation, 2007
	Parcels	Valuation
Total	3,371	$275,632,000
Vacant	278	7,996,500
Residential	3,018	244,952,000
Commercial	48	7,613,400
Industrial	3	772,800
Apartments	6	13,288,900
Farm land	12	33,300
Farm homestead	6	975,100

Average Property Value & Tax, 2007
Residential value	$81,325
Property tax	$4,802
Tax credit/rebate	$969

Public Library
No public municipal library

Library statistics, 2006
Population served	NA
Full-time/total staff	NA/NA

	Total	Per capita
Holdings	NA	NA
Revenues	NA	NA
Expenditures	NA	NA
Annual visits	NA	NA
Internet terminals/annual users	NA/NA	

Taxes
	2005	2006	2007
General tax rate per $100	5.11	5.763	5.905
County equalization ratio	73.87	64.35	55.08
Net valuation taxable	$272,574,180	$274,276,720	$276,080,556
State equalized value	$423,580,699	$498,461,189	$546,578,930

Public Safety
Number of officers, 2006		22

Crime	2005	2006
Total crimes	299	325
Violent	44	40
Murder	1	0
Rape	5	1
Robbery	6	13
Aggravated assault	32	26
Non-violent	255	285
Burglary	60	82
Larceny	180	183
Vehicle theft	15	20
Domestic violence	266	238
Arson	4	11
Total crime rate	26.6	28.7
Violent	3.9	3.5
Non-violent	22.7	25.2

Public School District
(for school year 2006-07 except as noted)

Pine Hill Borough School District
1003 Turnerville Rd
Pine Hill, NJ 08021
856-783-6900

Superintendent	Kenneth Koczur
Number of schools	4
Grade plan	K-12
Enrollment	2,215
Attendance rate, '05-06	92.8%
Dropout rate	6.2%
Students per teacher	10.8
Per pupil expenditure	$13,068
Median faculty salary	$69,774
Median administrator salary	$97,593
Grade 12 enrollment	209
High school graduation rate	83.6%

Assessment test results
(percent scoring at proficient or advanced level)
	Language	Math
NJASK-Grade 3	75.8%	87.8%
GEPA-Grade 8	63.2%	60.9%
HSPA-High School	81.9%	64.7%

SAT score averages
Pct tested	Math	Verbal	Writing
55%	473	468	448

Teacher Qualifications
Avg. years of experience	15
Highly-qualified teachers one subject/all subjects	97.0%/97.0%
With emergency credentials	0.0%

No Child Left Behind
AYP, 2005-06	Meets Standards

Municipal Finance
State Aid Programs, 2008
Total aid	$1,107,209
CMPTRA	407,907
Energy tax receipts	699,302
Garden State Trust	0

General Budget, 2007
Total tax levy	$16,300,462
County levy	3,521,667
County taxes	3,198,916
County library	222,754
County health	0
County open space	99,997
School levy	9,697,057
Muni. levy	3,081,738
Misc. revenues	3,731,384

Pine Valley Borough
Camden County

Demographics & Socio-Economic Characteristics
(2000 US Census, except as noted)

Population
- 1980*..23
- 1990*..19
- 2000...20
  - Male...12
  - Female..8
- 2006 (estimate)*.................................23
- Population density............................24.2

Race & Hispanic Origin, 2000
Race
- White..20
- Black/African American............................0
- American Indian/Alaska Native.....................0
- Asian...0
- Native Hawaiian/Pacific Islander..................0
- Other race..0
- Two or more races.................................0
- Hispanic origin, total............................0
  - Mexican...0
  - Puerto Rican....................................0
  - Cuban...0
  - Other Hispanic..................................0

Age & Nativity, 2000
- Under 5 years.....................................0
- 18 years and over................................15
- 21 years and over................................15
- 65 years and over.................................8
- 85 years and over.................................0
  - Median age...................................58.5
- Native-born......................................16
- Foreign-born......................................0

Educational Attainment, 2000
- Population 25 years and over.....................12
- Less than 9th grade............................0.0%
- High school grad or higher.....................83.3%
- Bachelor's degree or higher....................0.0%
- Graduate degree................................0.0%

Income & Poverty, 1999
- Per capita income..........................$23,981
- Median household income....................$31,875
- Median family income.......................$65,625
- Persons in poverty................................0
- H'holds receiving public assistance...............2
- H'holds receiving social security.................6

Households, 2000
- Total households..................................8
  - With persons under 18...........................2
  - With persons over 65............................5
  - Family households...............................7
  - Single-person households........................1
- Persons per household..........................2.50
- Persons per family.............................2.71

Labor & Employment
- Total civilian labor force, 2006**................0
  - Unemployment rate............................0.0%
- Total civilian labor force, 2000..................5
  - Unemployment rate............................0.0%

Employed persons 16 years and over by occupation, 2000
- Managers & professionals..........................2
- Service occupations...............................0
- Sales & office occupations........................2
- Farming, fishing & forestry.......................0
- Construction & maintenance........................0
- Production & transportation.......................1
- Self-employed persons.............................0

* US Census Bureau
** New Jersey Department of Labor

General Information
Borough of Pine Valley
1 Club Rd
Pine Valley, NJ 08021
856-783-7078

- Website.. NA
- Year of incorporation...........................1929
- Land/water area (sq. miles).........0.95/0.01
- Form of government.....................Commission

Government
Legislative Districts
- US Congressional...................................1
- State Legislative..................................6

Local Officials, 2008
- Mayor....................William Carson Jr
- Manager/Admin.......................NA
- Clerk..................Patricia M. Porter
- Finance Dir...........Patricia McCunney
- Tax Assessor............Sandra Elliott
- Tax Collector..........Patricia McCunney
- Attorney.................Joseph Betley
- Building..................Richard Wright
- Comm Dev/Planning..................NA
- Engineering........William Underwood
- Public Works........................NA
- Police Chief.............John Elder Jr
- Fire/Emergency Dir..................NA

Housing & Construction
Housing Units, 2000*
- Total..21
- Median rent...................................... NA
- Median SF home value....................$325,000

Permits for New Residential Construction

	Units	Value
Total, 2007	1	$456,100
Single family	1	$456,100
Total, 2006	0	$0
Single family	0	$0

Real Property Valuation, 2007

	Parcels	Valuation
Total	45	$37,942,200
Vacant	6	4,596,400
Residential	23	8,260,100
Commercial	16	25,085,700
Industrial	0	0
Apartments	0	0
Farm land	0	0
Farm homestead	0	0

Average Property Value & Tax, 2007
- Residential value...................$359,135
- Property tax...........................$5,234
- Tax credit/rebate.....................$1,125

Public Library
No public municipal library

Library statistics, 2006
- Population served........................NA
- Full-time/total staff..................NA/NA

	Total	Per capita
Holdings	NA	NA
Revenues	NA	NA
Expenditures	NA	NA
Annual visits	NA	NA
Internet terminals/annual users	NA/NA	

Taxes

	2005	2006	2007
General tax rate per $100	1.518	1.496	1.458
County equalization ratio	100	100	100
Net valuation taxable	$34,072,602	$36,902,200	$38,003,952
State equalized value	$33,368,526	$36,583,356	$37,292,838

Public Safety
Number of officers, 2006................4

Crime	2005	2006
Total crimes	0	0
Violent	0	0
Murder	0	0
Rape	0	0
Robbery	0	0
Aggravated assault	0	0
Non-violent	0	0
Burglary	0	0
Larceny	0	0
Vehicle theft	0	0
Domestic violence	0	0
Arson	0	0
Total crime rate	NA	NA
Violent	NA	NA
Non-violent	NA	NA

Public School District
(for school year 2006-07 except as noted)

Pine Valley School District
Pine Valley Golf Club, PO Box B
Clementon, NJ 08021

No schools in district

- Per pupil expenditure.......................
- Median faculty salary......................
- Median administrator salary...............
- Grade 12 enrollment........................NA
- High school graduation rate..............NA

Assessment test results
(percent scoring at proficient or advanced level)

	Language	Math
NJASK-Grade 3	NA	NA
GEPA-Grade 8	NA	NA
HSPA-High School	NA	NA

SAT score averages

Pct tested	Math	Verbal	Writing
NA	NA	NA	NA

Teacher Qualifications
- Avg. years of experience.................NA
- Highly-qualified teachers
  - one subject/all subjects..........NA/NA
- With emergency credentials..........NA

No Child Left Behind
- AYP, 2005-06...........................NA

Municipal Finance
State Aid Programs, 2008
- Total aid......................$2,586
- CMPTRA............................0
- Energy tax receipts..........2,586
- Garden State Trust...............0

General Budget, 2007
- Total tax levy................$553,914
  - County levy..................267,498
    - County taxes...............242,989
    - County library..............16,915
    - County health....................0
    - County open space...........7,594
  - School levy........................0
  - Muni. levy..................286,416
- Misc. revenues................123,361

Middlesex County

Piscataway Township

Demographics & Socio-Economic Characteristics
(2000 US Census, except as noted)

Population
1980*	42,223
1990*	47,089
2000	50,482
Male	24,979
Female	25,503
2006 (estimate)*	52,658
Population density	2,803.9

Race & Hispanic Origin, 2000
Race
- White ... 24,642
- Black/African American ... 10,254
- American Indian/Alaska Native ... 104
- Asian ... 12,519
- Native Hawaiian/Pacific Islander ... 13
- Other race ... 1,553
- Two or more races ... 1,397

Hispanic origin, total ... 4,002
- Mexican ... 185
- Puerto Rican ... 1,060
- Cuban ... 202
- Other Hispanic ... 2,555

Age & Nativity, 2000
- Under 5 years ... 3,127
- 18 years and over ... 39,430
- 21 years and over ... 35,541
- 65 years and over ... 4,374
- 85 years and over ... 361
- Median age ... 33.3
- Native-born ... 35,430
- Foreign-born ... 15,052

Educational Attainment, 2000
- Population 25 years and over ... 32,118
- Less than 9th grade ... 4.0%
- High school grad or higher ... 88.5%
- Bachelor's degree or higher ... 40.5%
- Graduate degree ... 16.6%

Income & Poverty, 1999
- Per capita income ... $26,321
- Median household income ... $68,721
- Median family income ... $75,218
- Persons in poverty ... 1,769
- H'holds receiving public assistance ... 259
- H'holds receiving social security ... 3,136

Households, 2000
- Total households ... 16,500
- With persons under 18 ... 6,264
- With persons over 65 ... 3,288
- Family households ... 12,325
- Single-person households ... 3,219
- Persons per household ... 2.84
- Persons per family ... 3.29

Labor & Employment
- Total civilian labor force, 2006** ... 30,202
- Unemployment rate ... 4.2%
- Total civilian labor force, 2000 ... 27,973
- Unemployment rate ... 5.7%

Employed persons 16 years and over by occupation, 2000
- Managers & professionals ... 12,068
- Service occupations ... 2,310
- Sales & office occupations ... 7,223
- Farming, fishing & forestry ... 12
- Construction & maintenance ... 1,545
- Production & transportation ... 3,230
- Self-employed persons ... 701

* US Census Bureau
** New Jersey Department of Labor
§ State Fiscal Year July 1–June 30

See Introduction for an explanation of all data sources.

General Information
Township of Piscataway
Municipal Complex
455 Hoes Lane
Piscataway, NJ 08854
732-562-2300

- Website ... www.piscatawaynj.org
- Year of incorporation ... 1693
- Land/water area (sq. miles) ... 18.78/0.20
- Form of government ... Mayor-Council

Government
Legislative Districts
- US Congressional ... 6
- State Legislative ... 17

Local Officials, 2008
- Mayor ... Brian C. Wahler
- Administrator ... Lyn Evers
- Clerk ... Ann Nolan
- Finance Dir ... Daniel Lamptey
- Tax Assessor ... Lisa Stephens
- Tax Collector ... NA
- Attorney ... James L. Clarkin III
- Building ... Joseph Hoff
- Planning ... John Donnelly
- Engineering ... Charles Carley
- Public Works ... Henry Zanetti Jr
- Police Chief ... Kevin Harris
- Emerg/Fire Director ... Robert Gorr

Housing & Construction
Housing Units, 2000*
- Total ... 16,946
- Median rent ... $829
- Median SF home value ... $170,800

Permits for New Residential Construction
	Units	Value
Total, 2007	22	$3,349,079
Single family	17	$3,154,548
Total, 2006	63	$7,487,249
Single family	31	$6,242,249

Real Property Valuation, 2007
	Parcels	Valuation
Total	13,816	$2,228,570,000
Vacant	468	30,884,600
Residential	12,871	1,422,113,800
Commercial	227	165,210,800
Industrial	198	509,869,700
Apartments	20	96,492,600
Farm land	16	216,900
Farm homestead	16	3,781,600

Average Property Value & Tax, 2007
- Residential value ... $110,646
- Property tax ... $6,125
- Tax credit/rebate ... $1,003

Public Library
Piscataway Township Libraries
500 Hoes Lane
Piscataway, NJ 08854
732-463-1633

Director ... Anne Roman

Library statistics, 2006
- Population served ... 50,482
- Full-time/total staff ... 10/25

	Total	Per capita
Holdings	193,286	3.83
Revenues	$2,973,859	$58.91
Expenditures	$2,900,388	$57.45
Annual visits	417,370	8.27
Internet terminals/annual users		18/90,489

Taxes
	2005	2006	2007
General tax rate per $100	4.83	5.02	5.54
County equalization ratio	45.58	38.97	34.23
Net valuation taxable	$2,263,104,481	$2,248,168,700	$2,236,016,835
State equalized value	$5,807,299,156	$6,575,747,444	$6,828,903,829

Public Safety
Number of officers, 2006 ... 92

Crime	2005	2006
Total crimes	861	894
Violent	60	75
Murder	0	0
Rape	5	4
Robbery	21	26
Aggravated assault	34	45
Non-violent	801	819
Burglary	154	180
Larceny	576	582
Vehicle theft	71	57
Domestic violence	291	323
Arson	7	13
Total crime rate	16.4	17.0
Violent	1.1	1.4
Non-violent	15.3	15.5

Public School District
(for school year 2006-07 except as noted)

Piscataway Township School District
1515 Stelton Rd, PO Box 1332
Piscataway, NJ 08855
732-572-2289

- Superintendent ... Robert L. Copeland
- Number of schools ... 10
- Grade plan ... K-12
- Enrollment ... 6,762
- Attendance rate, '05-06 ... 94.0%
- Dropout rate ... 0.8%
- Students per teacher ... 11.6
- Per pupil expenditure ... $12,869
- Median faculty salary ... $62,689
- Median administrator salary ... $110,759
- Grade 12 enrollment ... 480
- High school graduation rate ... 96.6%

Assessment test results
(percent scoring at proficient or advanced level)
	Language	Math
NJASK-Grade 3	82.6%	89.1%
GEPA-Grade 8	78.8%	73.6%
HSPA-High School	91.7%	83.5%

SAT score averages
Pct tested	Math	Verbal	Writing
95%	500	473	473

Teacher Qualifications
- Avg. years of experience ... 7
- Highly-qualified teachers one subject/all subjects ... 100%/100%
- With emergency credentials ... 0.0%

No Child Left Behind
AYP, 2005-06 ... Meets Standards

Municipal Finance§
State Aid Programs, 2008
- Total aid ... $7,511,765
- CMPTRA ... 2,485,211
- Energy tax receipts ... 5,026,553
- Garden State Trust ... 1

General Budget, 2007
- Total tax levy ... $123,769,833
- County levy ... 18,516,318
- County taxes ... 16,573,944
- County library ... 0
- County health ... 0
- County open space ... 1,942,374
- School levy ... 75,205,765
- Muni. levy ... 30,047,750
- Misc. revenues ... 18,742,420

©2008 Information Publications, Inc. All rights reserved. Photocopying prohibited. For additional copies, contact the publisher at www.informationpublications.com or (877)544-INFO (4636)

The New Jersey Municipal Data Book

Pitman Borough

Gloucester County

Demographics & Socio-Economic Characteristics
(2000 US Census, except as noted)

Population
- 1980* 9,744
- 1990* 9,365
- 2000 9,331
  - Male 4,338
  - Female 4,993
- 2006 (estimate)* 9,199
  - Population density 4,017.0

Race & Hispanic Origin, 2000
Race
- White 9,066
- Black/African American 85
- American Indian/Alaska Native 11
- Asian 58
- Native Hawaiian/Pacific Islander 1
- Other race 21
- Two or more races 89
- Hispanic origin, total 132
  - Mexican 36
  - Puerto Rican 49
  - Cuban 8
  - Other Hispanic 39

Age & Nativity, 2000
- Under 5 years 542
- 18 years and over 6,977
- 21 years and over 6,628
- 65 years and over 1,404
- 85 years and over 248
  - Median age 38.1
- Native-born 9,125
- Foreign-born 206

Educational Attainment, 2000
- Population 25 years and over 6,219
- Less than 9th grade 3.4%
- High school grad or higher 87.9%
- Bachelor's degree or higher 31.7%
- Graduate degree 10.3%

Income & Poverty, 1999
- Per capita income $22,133
- Median household income $49,743
- Median family income $59,419
- Persons in poverty 526
- H'holds receiving public assistance .. 32
- H'holds receiving social security .. 955

Households, 2000
- Total households 3,473
  - With persons under 18 1,263
  - With persons over 65 898
  - Family households 2,431
  - Single-person households 903
  - Persons per household 2.60
  - Persons per family 3.15

Labor & Employment
- Total civilian labor force, 2006** .. 5,515
  - Unemployment rate 6.5%
- Total civilian labor force, 2000 .. 4,892
  - Unemployment rate 9.6%

Employed persons 16 years and over by occupation, 2000
- Managers & professionals 1,891
- Service occupations 494
- Sales & office occupations 1,074
- Farming, fishing & forestry 4
- Construction & maintenance 452
- Production & transportation 507
- Self-employed persons 278

* US Census Bureau
** New Jersey Department of Labor

General Information
Borough of Pitman
110 S Broadway
Pitman, NJ 08071
856-589-3522

- Website .... www.pitman.org
- Year of incorporation 1905
- Land/water area (sq. miles) 2.29/0.03
- Form of government .... Borough

Government
Legislative Districts
- US Congressional 2
- State Legislative 4

Local Officials, 2008
- Mayor .... Micahael Batten
- Manager .... DawnMarie Human
- Clerk .... DawnMarie Human
- Finance Dir .... Stephen Considine
- Tax Assessor .... Ronald Fijalkowski
- Tax Collector .... Beth A. Walls
- Attorney .... Brian Duffield
- Building .... Jeffrey Kier
- Planning .... Henry Ryder
- Engineering .... Fralinger Engineering
- Public Works .... Chris Walsh
- Police Chief .... Scott Campbell
- Emerg/Fire Director ..... D. Clark Pierpont

Housing & Construction
Housing Units, 2000*
- Total 3,653
- Median rent $654
- Median SF home value $118,500

Permits for New Residential Construction
	Units	Value
Total, 2007	0	$0
Single family	0	$0
Total, 2006	1	$100,000
Single family	1	$100,000

Real Property Valuation, 2007
	Parcels	Valuation
Total	3,203	$380,951,700
Vacant	59	2,004,500
Residential	2,984	323,975,700
Commercial	140	24,195,400
Industrial	4	22,074,500
Apartments	12	8,501,800
Farm land	3	10,100
Farm homestead	1	189,700

Average Property Value & Tax, 2007
- Residential value $108,598
- Property tax $5,279
- Tax credit/rebate $971

Public Library
McCowan Memorial Library
15 Pitman Ave
Pitman, NJ 08071
856-589-1656

- Director .... Sharon Furgason

Library statistics, 2006
- Population served 9,331
- Full-time/total staff 1/5

	Total	Per capita
Holdings	46,717	5.01
Revenues	$335,273	$35.93
Expenditures	$310,650	$33.29
Annual visits	95,947	10.28
Internet terminals/annual users		6/7,757

Taxes
	2005	2006	2007
General tax rate per $100	4.137	4.549	4.862
County equalization ratio	74.6	65.59	57.59
Net valuation taxable	$379,133,910	$380,347,900	$381,311,418
State equalized value	$578,036,149	$660,838,571	$729,872,740

Public Safety
- Number of officers, 2006 16

Crime	2005	2006
Total crimes	128	152
Violent	5	3
Murder	0	1
Rape	0	0
Robbery	0	1
Aggravated assault	5	1
Non-violent	123	149
Burglary	5	10
Larceny	111	132
Vehicle theft	7	7
Domestic violence	108	103
Arson	0	1
Total crime rate	13.8	16.4
Violent	0.5	0.3
Non-violent	13.3	16.1

Public School District
(for school year 2006-07 except as noted)

Pitman School District
420 Hudson Ave
Pitman, NJ 08071
856-589-2145

- Superintendent .... Thomas Shulte
- Number of schools 5
- Grade plan K-12
- Enrollment 1,599
- Attendance rate, '05-06 .... 94.9%
- Dropout rate 1.4%
- Students per teacher 10.6
- Per pupil expenditure $12,939
- Median faculty salary $59,906
- Median administrator salary $97,403
- Grade 12 enrollment 124
- High school graduation rate 93.2%

Assessment test results
(percent scoring at proficient or advanced level)

	Language	Math
NJASK-Grade 3	89.9%	95.7%
GEPA-Grade 8	69.3%	75.4%
HSPA-High School	92.6%	85.3%

SAT score averages
Pct tested	Math	Verbal	Writing
79%	528	504	492

Teacher Qualifications
- Avg. years of experience 14
- Highly-qualified teachers
  - one subject/all subjects ... 100%/100%
- With emergency credentials 0.0%

No Child Left Behind
- AYP, 2005-06 .... Meets Standards

Municipal Finance
State Aid Programs, 2008
- Total aid $683,581
- CMPTRA 239,280
- Energy tax receipts 444,301
- Garden State Trust 0

General Budget, 2007
- Total tax levy $18,536,541
- County levy 3,667,886
  - County taxes 3,401,571
  - County library 0
  - County health 0
  - County open space 266,316
- School levy 10,548,663
- Muni. levy 4,319,992
- Misc. revenues 2,764,807

Salem County / Pittsgrove Township

Demographics & Socio-Economic Characteristics
(2000 US Census, except as noted)

Population
- 1980*..............................6,954
- 1990*..............................8,121
- 2000..............................8,893
  - Male.............................4,403
  - Female...........................4,490
- 2006 (estimate)*...................9,533
  - Population density...............211.0

Race & Hispanic Origin, 2000
Race
- White..............................7,838
- Black/African American..............715
- American Indian/Alaska Native........34
- Asian................................52
- Native Hawaiian/Pacific Islander......4
- Other race.........................115
- Two or more races..................135
- Hispanic origin, total.............303
  - Mexican............................25
  - Puerto Rican......................188
  - Cuban...............................1
  - Other Hispanic.....................89

Age & Nativity, 2000
- Under 5 years......................472
- 18 years and over................6,523
- 21 years and over................6,140
- 65 years and over................1,014
- 85 years and over..................108
  - Median age........................38.1
- Native-born.......................8,719
- Foreign-born........................174

Educational Attainment, 2000
- Population 25 years and over.....5,827
- Less than 9th grade................8.4%
- High school grad or higher........78.8%
- Bachelor's degree or higher.......16.4%
- Graduate degree....................4.4%

Income & Poverty, 1999
- Per capita income...............$21,624
- Median household income.........$56,687
- Median family income............$63,266
- Persons in poverty.................434
- H'holds receiving public assistance..46
- H'holds receiving social security..746

Households, 2000
- Total households................3,020
  - With persons under 18..........1,288
  - With persons over 65............667
  - Family households.............2,421
  - Single-person households........490
- Persons per household.............2.90
- Persons per family................3.23

Labor & Employment
- Total civilian labor force, 2006**...4,768
  - Unemployment rate................4.4%
- Total civilian labor force, 2000...4,656
  - Unemployment rate................6.3%

Employed persons 16 years and over by occupation, 2000
- Managers & professionals.........1,240
- Service occupations................637
- Sales & office occupations........983
- Farming, fishing & forestry........24
- Construction & maintenance........618
- Production & transportation.......863
- Self-employed persons.............275

* US Census Bureau
** New Jersey Department of Labor

See Introduction for an explanation of all data sources.

General Information
Township of Pittsgrove
989 Centerton Rd
Pittsgrove, NJ 08318
856-358-2300

- Website....... www.pittsgrovetownship.com
- Year of incorporation...............1769
- Land/water area (sq. miles)......45.19/0.74
- Form of government..............Township

Government
Legislative Districts
- US Congressional.......................2
- State Legislative......................3

Local Officials, 2008
- Mayor.......................Peter Voros
- Manager..............Deborah Turner-Fox
- Clerk..................Constance Garton
- Finance Dir................Donna Jacobs
- Tax Assessor...............Lisa Perella
- Tax Collector........Jennafer Hernandez
- Attorney..................Adam I. Telsey
- Building...................James Grasso
- Planning..................Nancy Huster
- Engineering............Mark Brunermer
- Public Works............Harry E. Snyder
- Public Safety Dir.......Harry E. Snyder
- Fire/Emergency Dir................NA

Housing & Construction
Housing Units, 2000*
- Total............................3,155
- Median rent......................$728
- Median SF home value..........$125,600

Permits for New Residential Construction

	Units	Value
Total, 2007	13	$2,293,860
Single family	13	$2,293,860
Total, 2006	30	$3,577,717
Single family	30	$3,577,717

Real Property Valuation, 2007

	Parcels	Valuation
Total	4,004	$592,496,300
Vacant	483	18,678,500
Residential	2,540	463,937,500
Commercial	79	53,041,200
Industrial	0	0
Apartments	0	0
Farm land	618	5,251,400
Farm homestead	284	51,587,700

Average Property Value & Tax, 2007
- Residential value................$182,551
- Property tax......................$5,151
- Tax credit/rebate..................$998

Public Library
No public municipal library

Library statistics, 2006
- Population served....................NA
- Full-time/total staff.............NA/NA

	Total	Per capita
Holdings	NA	NA
Revenues	NA	NA
Expenditures	NA	NA
Annual visits	NA	NA
Internet terminals/annual users	NA/NA	

Public Safety
- Number of officers, 2006...............0

Crime	2005	2006
Total crimes	84	164
Violent	6	8
Murder	0	0
Rape	1	1
Robbery	1	0
Aggravated assault	4	7
Non-violent	78	156
Burglary	36	51
Larceny	39	93
Vehicle theft	3	12
Domestic violence	37	3
Arson	2	2
Total crime rate	9.1	17.3
Violent	0.6	0.8
Non-violent	8.4	16.5

Public School District
(for school year 2006-07 except as noted)

Pittsgrove Township School District
1076 Almond Rd
Pittsgrove, NJ 08318
856-358-3094

- Superintendent........Henry Bermann (Int)
- Number of schools.....................4
- Grade plan........................K-12
- Enrollment......................1,920
- Attendance rate, '05-06..........94.6%
- Dropout rate......................0.8%
- Students per teacher..............12.6
- Per pupil expenditure..........$10,838
- Median faculty salary..........$56,680
- Median administrator salary...$74,727
- Grade 12 enrollment...............165
- High school graduation rate......93.6%

Assessment test results
(percent scoring at proficient or advanced level)

	Language	Math
NJASK-Grade 3	68.7%	76.7%
GEPA-Grade 8	68.8%	63.2%
HSPA-High School	84.0%	68.9%

SAT score averages

Pct tested	Math	Verbal	Writing
78%	453	452	443

Teacher Qualifications
- Avg. years of experience............15
- Highly-qualified teachers
  - one subject/all subjects......100%/99.0%
- With emergency credentials........0.0%

No Child Left Behind
- AYP, 2005-06..........Meets Standards

Municipal Finance
State Aid Programs, 2008
- Total aid.....................$829,409
  - CMPTRA.....................134,850
  - Energy tax receipts........675,031
  - Garden State Trust.........19,528

General Budget, 2007
- Total tax levy..............$16,766,893
  - County levy................6,387,027
    - County taxes............6,250,777
    - County library................0
    - County health.................0
    - County open space........136,249
  - School levy................8,698,366
  - Muni. levy.................1,681,501
- Misc. revenues..............2,314,899

Taxes

	2005	2006	2007
General tax rate per $100	2.582	2.75	2.822
County equalization ratio	109.56	97.72	87.44
Net valuation taxable	$573,778,274	$582,260,600	$594,170,863
State equalized value	$587,165,651	$667,712,610	$735,143,635

Plainfield City
Union County

Demographics & Socio-Economic Characteristics
(2000 US Census, except as noted)

Population
1980*	45,555
1990*	46,567
2000	47,829
Male	23,393
Female	24,436
2006 (estimate)*	47,353
Population density	7,839.9

Race & Hispanic Origin, 2000
Race
White	10,258
Black/African American	29,550
American Indian/Alaska Native	195
Asian	447
Native Hawaiian/Pacific Islander	46
Other race	5,156
Two or more races	2,177
Hispanic origin, total	12,033
Mexican	807
Puerto Rican	1,782
Cuban	145
Other Hispanic	9,299

Age & Nativity, 2000
Under 5 years	3,770
18 years and over	34,662
21 years and over	32,669
65 years and over	4,402
85 years and over	566
Median age	32.8
Native-born	36,502
Foreign-born	11,327

Educational Attainment, 2000
Population 25 years and over	29,821
Less than 9th grade	12.3%
High school grad or higher	70.6%
Bachelor's degree or higher	18.5%
Graduate degree	6.2%

Income & Poverty, 1999
Per capita income	$19,052
Median household income	$46,683
Median family income	$50,774
Persons in poverty	7,476
H'holds receiving public assistance	892
H'holds receiving social security	3,573

Households, 2000
Total households	15,137
With persons under 18	6,748
With persons over 65	3,195
Family households	10,898
Single-person households	3,194
Persons per household	3.10
Persons per family	3.49

Labor & Employment
Total civilian labor force, 2006**	25,513
Unemployment rate	6.4%
Total civilian labor force, 2000	24,966
Unemployment rate	7.9%

Employed persons 16 years and over by occupation, 2000
Managers & professionals	5,518
Service occupations	4,059
Sales & office occupations	6,272
Farming, fishing & forestry	33
Construction & maintenance	1,935
Production & transportation	5,180
Self-employed persons	639

* US Census Bureau
** New Jersey Department of Labor
§ State Fiscal Year July 1–June 30

General Information
City of Plainfield
515 Watchung Ave
Plainfield, NJ 07060
908-753-3000

Website	www.plainfield.com
Year of incorporation	1869
Land/water area (sq. miles)	6.04/0.00
Form of government	Special Charter

Government
Legislative Districts
US Congressional	6
State Legislative	22

Local Officials, 2008
Mayor	Sharon Robinson-Briggs
Manager	Marc Dashield
Clerk	Laddie Wyatt
Finance Dir	Sandra Cummings
Tax Assessor	Tracy Bennett
Tax Collector	Maria Glavan
Attorney	Daniel Williamson
Building	Joe Minarovich
Planning	Bill Nierstedt
Engineering	Robert Bucco
Public Works	Jennifer Wenson-Maier
Police Chief	NA
Emerg/Fire Director	Cecil Allen

Housing & Construction
Housing Units, 2000*
Total	16,180
Median rent	$726
Median SF home value	$137,500

Permits for New Residential Construction
	Units	Value
Total, 2007	7	$444,500
Single family	2	$89,500
Total, 2006	25	$2,650,902
Single family	18	$2,587,827

Real Property Valuation, 2007
	Parcels	Valuation
Total	10,275	$1,267,693,521
Vacant	333	7,787,900
Residential	9,125	1,029,309,321
Commercial	640	140,800,100
Industrial	63	25,268,200
Apartments	114	64,528,000
Farm land	0	0
Farm homestead	0	0

Average Property Value & Tax, 2007
Residential value	$112,801
Property tax	$6,393
Tax credit/rebate	$1,091

Public Library
Plainfield Public Library
800 Park Ave
Plainfield, NJ 07060
908-757-1111

Director: Joseph Hugh Da Rold

Library statistics, 2006
Population served	47,829
Full-time/total staff	7/20

	Total	Per capita
Holdings	180,002	3.76
Revenues	$2,357,447	$49.29
Expenditures	$1,996,617	$41.74
Annual visits	198,023	4.14
Internet terminals/annual users	27/71,708	

Taxes
	2005	2006	2007
General tax rate per $100	5.163	5.407	5.668
County equalization ratio	54.42	44.98	40.03
Net valuation taxable	$1,282,552,245	$1,270,415,621	$1,272,717,301
State equalized value	$2,686,535,913	$3,179,979,557	$3,480,060,844

Public Safety
Number of officers, 2006		153
Crime	**2005**	**2006**
Total crimes	2,094	2,189
Violent	517	571
Murder	15	10
Rape	16	12
Robbery	244	260
Aggravated assault	242	289
Non-violent	1,577	1,618
Burglary	371	495
Larceny	853	948
Vehicle theft	353	175
Domestic violence	755	692
Arson	16	18
Total crime rate	43.6	45.9
Violent	10.8	12.0
Non-violent	32.9	34.0

Public School District
(for school year 2006-07 except as noted)

Plainfield School District
504 Madison Ave
Plainfield, NJ 07060
908-731-4335

Superintendent	Peter D. Carter (Int)
Number of schools	13
Grade plan	K-12
Enrollment	6,699
Attendance rate, '05-06	93.4%
Dropout rate	1.7%
Students per teacher	9.5
Per pupil expenditure	$14,279
Median faculty salary	$55,755
Median administrator salary	$102,750
Grade 12 enrollment	421
High school graduation rate	85.4%

Assessment test results
(percent scoring at proficient or advanced level)
	Language	Math
NJASK-Grade 3	59.1%	64.0%
GEPA-Grade 8	31.1%	28.2%
HSPA-High School	62.1%	45.0%

SAT score averages
Pct tested	Math	Verbal	Writing
57%	390	381	375

Teacher Qualifications
Avg. years of experience	11
Highly-qualified teachers one subject/all subjects	97.0%/97.0%
With emergency credentials	1.5%

No Child Left Behind
AYP, 2005-06 .... Needs Improvement

Municipal Finance §
State Aid Programs, 2008
Total aid	$9,200,671
CMPTRA	5,947,294
Energy tax receipts	3,253,377
Garden State Trust	0

General Budget, 2007
Total tax levy	$72,132,106
County levy	11,129,435
County taxes	10,648,492
County library	0
County health	0
County open space	480,943
School levy	18,847,524
Muni. levy	42,155,148
Misc. revenues	25,398,762

Middlesex County
Plainsboro Township

Demographics & Socio-Economic Characteristics
(2000 US Census, except as noted)

Population
- 1980* 5,605
- 1990* 14,213
- 2000 20,215
  - Male 10,229
  - Female 9,986
- 2006 (estimate)* 21,213
  - Population density 1,791.6

Race & Hispanic Origin, 2000
Race
- White 11,765
- Black/African American 1,533
- American Indian/Alaska Native 20
- Asian 6,168
- Native Hawaiian/Pacific Islander 2
- Other race 275
- Two or more races 452
- Hispanic origin, total 937
  - Mexican 79
  - Puerto Rican 284
  - Cuban 77
  - Other Hispanic 497

Age & Nativity, 2000
- Under 5 years 1,428
- 18 years and over 15,239
- 21 years and over 14,873
- 65 years and over 853
- 85 years and over 83
- Median age 32.9
- Native-born 13,244
- Foreign-born 6,971

Educational Attainment, 2000
- Population 25 years and over 13,947
- Less than 9th grade 0.9%
- High school grad or higher 97.3%
- Bachelor's degree or higher 70.3%
- Graduate degree 31.7%

Income & Poverty, 1999
- Per capita income $38,982
- Median household income $72,097
- Median family income $88,783
- Persons in poverty 601
- H'holds receiving public assistance 57
- H'holds receiving social security 589

Households, 2000
- Total households 8,742
  - With persons under 18 2,991
  - With persons over 65 644
  - Family households 5,123
  - Single-person households 2,966
- Persons per household 2.30
- Persons per family 3.06

Labor & Employment
- Total civilian labor force, 2006** .. 13,684
  - Unemployment rate 2.5%
- Total civilian labor force, 2000 12,412
  - Unemployment rate 2.3%

Employed persons 16 years and over by occupation, 2000
- Managers & professionals 8,389
- Service occupations 619
- Sales & office occupations 2,479
- Farming, fishing & forestry 0
- Construction & maintenance 252
- Production & transportation 389
- Self-employed persons 316

* US Census Bureau
** New Jersey Department of Labor

See Introduction for an explanation of all data sources.

General Information
Township of Plainsboro
641 Plainsboro Rd
Plainsboro, NJ 08536
609-799-0909

- Website .... www.plainsboronj.com
- Year of incorporation 1919
- Land/water area (sq. miles) 11.84/0.41
- Form of government .... Township

Government
Legislative Districts
- US Congressional 12
- State Legislative 14

Local Officials, 2008
- Mayor .... Peter Cantu
- Manager .... Robert Sheehan
- Clerk .... Carol J. Torres
- Finance Dir .... Wendy Wulstein
- Tax Assessor .... (vacant)
- Tax Collector .... Mary Testori
- Attorney .... Michael Herbert
- Code Enforcement .... Tom Boyd
- Planning .... Lester Varga
- Engineering .... Mike McClelland
- Public Works .... Neil Blitz
- Police Chief .... Elizabeth Bondurant
- Emerg/Fire Director .... Brian Stultz

Housing & Construction
Housing Units, 2000*
- Total 9,133
- Median rent $942
- Median SF home value $257,100

Permits for New Residential Construction

	Units	Value
Total, 2007	11	$1,349,700
Single family	11	$1,349,700
Total, 2006	35	$4,068,700
Single family	35	$4,068,700

Real Property Valuation, 2007

	Parcels	Valuation
Total	5,831	$3,674,557,500
Vacant	479	58,854,000
Residential	5,152	2,050,076,100
Commercial	92	1,188,949,200
Industrial	4	61,420,800
Apartments	17	303,500,000
Farm land	69	942,200
Farm homestead	18	10,815,200

Average Property Value & Tax, 2007
- Residential value $398,625
- Property tax $8,203
- Tax credit/rebate $1,111

Public Library
Plainsboro Free Public Library
641 Plainsboro Rd
Plainsboro, NJ 08536
609-275-2897

- Director .... Jinny Baeckler

Library statistics, 2006
- Population served 20,215
- Full-time/total staff 4/9

	Total	Per capita
Holdings	95,472	4.72
Revenues	$1,339,991	$66.29
Expenditures	$1,195,125	$59.12
Annual visits	200,949	9.94
Internet terminals/annual users		8/65,127

Public Safety
- Number of officers, 2006 32

Crime	2005	2006
Total crimes	235	225
Violent	9	13
Murder	0	0
Rape	1	3
Robbery	3	1
Aggravated assault	5	9
Non-violent	226	212
Burglary	38	35
Larceny	178	163
Vehicle theft	10	14
Domestic violence	89	60
Arson	3	10
Total crime rate	11.0	10.5
Violent	0.4	0.6
Non-violent	10.6	9.9

Public School District
(for school year 2006-07 except as noted)

West Windsor-Plainsboro Reg. School Dist.
505 Village Rd West, PO Box 505
Princeton Junction, NJ 08550
609-716-5000

- Chief School Admin ...... Victoria Kniewel
- Number of schools 20
- Grade plan K-12
- Enrollment 9,509
- Attendance rate, '05-06 .... 96.8%
- Dropout rate 0.4%
- Students per teacher 11.4
- Per pupil expenditure $13,856
- Median faculty salary $64,345
- Median administrator salary $114,343
- Grade 12 enrollment 724
- High school graduation rate .... NA

Assessment test results
(percent scoring at proficient or advanced level)

	Language	Math
NJASK-Grade 3	96.6%	96.4%
GEPA-Grade 8	95.2%	92.2%
HSPA-High School	97.0%	94.2%

SAT score averages

Pct tested	Math	Verbal	Writing
NA	NA	NA	NA

Teacher Qualifications
- Avg. years of experience 13
- Highly-qualified teachers
  - one subject/all subjects 100%/100%
- With emergency credentials 0.3%

No Child Left Behind
- AYP, 2005-06 .... Meets Standards

Municipal Finance
State Aid Programs, 2008
- Total aid $2,117,932
  - CMPTRA 161,175
  - Energy tax receipts 1,956,692
  - Garden State Trust 65

General Budget, 2007
- Total tax levy $75,745,363
  - County levy 11,422,923
    - County taxes 10,226,067
    - County library 0
    - County health 0
    - County open space 1,196,856
  - School levy 52,960,598
  - Muni. levy 11,361,842
- Misc. revenues 8,338,497

Taxes	2005	2006	2007
General tax rate per $100	1.94	2	2.06
County equalization ratio	104.86	98.68	92.63
Net valuation taxable	$3,626,167,479	$3,649,446,500	$3,681,065,681
State equalized value	$3,674,673,165	$4,482,555,383	$3,783,419,991

©2008 Information Publications, Inc. All rights reserved. Photocopying prohibited. For additional copies, contact the publisher at www.informationpublications.com or (877)544-INFO (4636)

The New Jersey Municipal Data Book 401

Pleasantville City
Atlantic County

Demographics & Socio-Economic Characteristics
(2000 US Census, except as noted)

Population
- 1980* 13,435
- 1990* 16,027
- 2000 19,012
  - Male 8,925
  - Female 10,087
- 2006 (estimate)* 18,982
- Population density 3,284.1

Race & Hispanic Origin, 2000
Race
- White 4,755
- Black/African American 10,969
- American Indian/Alaska Native 54
- Asian 371
- Native Hawaiian/Pacific Islander .. 5
- Other race 2,084
- Two or more races 774
- Hispanic origin, total 4,158
  - Mexican 451
  - Puerto Rican 2,085
  - Cuban 61
  - Other Hispanic 1,561

Age & Nativity, 2000
- Under 5 years 1,481
- 18 years and over 13,234
- 21 years and over 12,481
- 65 years and over 2,124
- 85 years and over 373
- Median age 32.7
- Native-born 16,639
- Foreign-born 2,457

Educational Attainment, 2000
- Population 25 years and over .. 11,583
- Less than 9th grade 7.5%
- High school grad or higher 70.1%
- Bachelor's degree or higher ... 10.2%
- Graduate degree 3.1%

Income & Poverty, 1999
- Per capita income $17,668
- Median household income $36,913
- Median family income $40,016
- Persons in poverty 2,939
- H'holds receiving public assistance .. 286
- H'holds receiving social security .. 1,705

Households, 2000
- Total households 6,402
  - With persons under 18 2,838
  - With persons over 65 1,421
  - Family households 4,365
  - Single-person households 1,568
- Persons per household 2.90
- Persons per family 3.44

Labor & Employment
- Total civilian labor force, 2006** 9,149
  - Unemployment rate 8.0%
- Total civilian labor force, 2000 8,500
  - Unemployment rate 10.2%
- *Employed persons 16 years and over by occupation, 2000*
  - Managers & professionals 1,347
  - Service occupations 2,979
  - Sales & office occupations .. 1,979
  - Farming, fishing & forestry ... 33
  - Construction & maintenance ... 466
  - Production & transportation .. 833
- Self-employed persons 140

‡ Branch of county library
* US Census Bureau
** New Jersey Department of Labor

General Information
City of Pleasantville
18 N 1st St
Pleasantville, NJ 08232
609-484-3600
- Website .... www.pleasantville-nj.org
- Year of incorporation 1914
- Land/water area (sq. miles) 5.78/1.55
- Form of government .... City

Government
Legislative Districts
- US Congressional 2
- State Legislative 2

Local Officials, 2008
- Mayor .... Ralph Peterson Sr
- Manager .... Marvin D. Hopkins
- Clerk .... Gloria V. Griffin
- Finance Dir .... Ted Freedman
- Tax Assessor .... Brian Vigue
- Tax Collector .... Flor Roman
- Attorney .... Alfred Scerni Jr
- Building .... Kevin Cain
- Comm Dev/Planning .... NA
- Engineering ...... Remington & Vernick
- Public Works .... Robert Oglesby
- Police Chief .... Duane Comeaux
- Emerg/Fire Director ...... Leroy Borden

Housing & Construction
Housing Units, 2000*
- Total 7,042
- Median rent $715
- Median SF home value $86,500

Permits for New Residential Construction

	Units	Value
Total, 2007	94	$8,654,186
Single family	94	$8,654,186
Total, 2006	80	$7,210,448
Single family	54	$5,588,998

Real Property Valuation, 2007

	Parcels	Valuation
Total	5,978	$547,080,900
Vacant	454	13,511,000
Residential	5,065	360,720,700
Commercial	354	98,026,900
Industrial	81	47,897,700
Apartments	24	26,924,600
Farm land	0	0
Farm homestead	0	0

Average Property Value & Tax, 2007
- Residential value $71,218
- Property tax $3,180
- Tax credit/rebate $759

Public Library
Pleasantville Branch Library‡
132 W Washington Ave
Pleasantville, NJ 08232
609-641-1778
- Branch Librarian .... Pamela Saunders
- Library statistics, 2006
  see Atlantic County profile
  for library system statistics

Public Safety
- Number of officers, 2006 56

Crime	2005	2006
Total crimes	753	795
Violent	143	180
Murder	1	1
Rape	8	7
Robbery	56	75
Aggravated assault	78	97
Non-violent	610	615
Burglary	191	196
Larceny	366	365
Vehicle theft	53	54
Domestic violence	500	488
Arson	5	9
Total crime rate	39.4	41.8
Violent	7.5	9.5
Non-violent	31.9	32.3

Public School District
(for school year 2006-07 except as noted)

Pleasantville School District
900 W. Leeds Ave, PO Box 960
Pleasantville, NJ 08232
609-383-6800

- Superintendent .... Clarence Alston
- Number of schools 6
- Grade plan K-12
- Enrollment 3,423
- Attendance rate, '05-06 .... 93.1%
- Dropout rate 2.9%
- Students per teacher 7.2
- Per pupil expenditure $15,047
- Median faculty salary $46,199
- Median administrator salary .. $94,868
- Grade 12 enrollment 138
- High school graduation rate ... 85.2%

Assessment test results
(percent scoring at proficient or advanced level)

	Language	Math
NJASK-Grade 3	73.2%	76.1%
GEPA-Grade 8	33.6%	26.3%
HSPA-High School	53.2%	28.4%

SAT score averages

Pct tested	Math	Verbal	Writing
69%	376	349	359

Teacher Qualifications
- Avg. years of experience 6
- Highly-qualified teachers
  one subject/all subjects 100%/100%
- With emergency credentials 4.1%

No Child Left Behind
- AYP, 2005-06 .... Needs Improvement

Municipal Finance
State Aid Programs, 2008
- Total aid $2,473,741
  - CMPTRA 1,070,118
  - Energy tax receipts 1,403,372
  - Garden State Trust 251

General Budget, 2007
- Total tax levy $24,847,805
  - County levy 3,172,512
    - County taxes 2,525,188
    - County library 313,084
    - County health 127,574
    - County open space 206,666
  - School levy 7,569,370
  - Muni. levy 14,105,923
- Misc. revenues 10,400,754

Taxes	2005	2006	2007
General tax rate per $100	4.166	4.262	4.466
County equalization ratio	74.49	64.95	54.49
Net valuation taxable	$546,811,685	$540,682,600	$556,480,599
State equalized value	$841,896,359	$1,003,172,440	$1,188,199,311

Ocean County

Plumsted Township

Demographics & Socio-Economic Characteristics
(2000 US Census, except as noted)

Population
1980*	4,674
1990*	6,005
2000	7,275
Male	3,620
Female	3,655
2006 (estimate)*	8,122
Population density	202.9

Race & Hispanic Origin, 2000
Race
White	6,831
Black/African American	167
American Indian/Alaska Native	10
Asian	53
Native Hawaiian/Pacific Islander	1
Other race	99
Two or more races	114
Hispanic origin, total	280
Mexican	103
Puerto Rican	132
Cuban	17
Other Hispanic	28

Age & Nativity, 2000
Under 5 years	501
18 years and over	5,204
21 years and over	4,960
65 years and over	621
85 years and over	49
Median age	36.0
Native-born	6,940
Foreign-born	335

Educational Attainment, 2000
Population 25 years and over	4,720
Less than 9th grade	5.5%
High school grad or higher	84.2%
Bachelor's degree or higher	17.4%
Graduate degree	4.2%

Income & Poverty, 1999
Per capita income	$22,433
Median household income	$61,357
Median family income	$62,255
Persons in poverty	367
H'holds receiving public assistance	73
H'holds receiving social security	539

Households, 2000
Total households	2,510
With persons under 18	1,116
With persons over 65	465
Family households	2,002
Single-person households	400
Persons per household	2.90
Persons per family	3.22

Labor & Employment
Total civilian labor force, 2006**	3,827
Unemployment rate	3.3%
Total civilian labor force, 2000	3,871
Unemployment rate	3.2%

Employed persons 16 years and over by occupation, 2000
Managers & professionals	1,133
Service occupations	475
Sales & office occupations	1,028
Farming, fishing & forestry	43
Construction & maintenance	504
Production & transportation	563
Self-employed persons	182

‡ Branch of county library
* US Census Bureau
** New Jersey Department of Labor

See Introduction for an explanation of all data sources.

General Information
Township of Plumsted
121 Evergreen Rd
New Egypt, NJ 08533
609-758-2241

Website	www.plumsted.org
Year of incorporation	1845
Land/water area (sq. miles)	40.02/0.20
Form of government	Township

Government
Legislative Districts
US Congressional	4
State Legislative	30

Local Officials, 2008
Mayor	Ronald S. Dancer
Manager	Richard Kachmar
Clerk	Dorothy Hendrickson
Finance Dir	June Madden
Tax Assessor	Maureen Francis
Tax Collector	Danielle Peacock
Attorney	Gilmore & Monahan
Building	Glenn Riccardi
Comm Dev/Planning	NA
Engineering	John Mallon
Public Works	NA
Police Chief	Michael Lynch
Emerg/Fire Director	William Allen

Housing & Construction
Housing Units, 2000*
Total	2,628
Median rent	$697
Median SF home value	$150,800

Permits for New Residential Construction
	Units	Value
Total, 2007	21	$3,094,442
Single family	19	$3,053,442
Total, 2006	30	$3,391,799
Single family	30	$3,391,799

Real Property Valuation, 2007
	Parcels	Valuation
Total	3,097	$1,091,963,700
Vacant	336	36,630,500
Residential	2,395	925,185,000
Commercial	94	61,087,500
Industrial	8	9,030,500
Apartments	8	4,079,600
Farm land	147	2,272,700
Farm homestead	109	53,677,900

Average Property Value & Tax, 2007
Residential value	$390,920
Property tax	$5,149
Tax credit/rebate	$903

Public Library
Plumsted Branch Library‡
119 Evergreen Rd
New Egypt, NJ 08533
609-758-7888

Branch Librarian............Gigi Hayes

Library statistics, 2006
see Ocean County profile
for library system statistics

Taxes
	2005	2006	2007
General tax rate per $100	3.011	3.08	1.32
County equalization ratio	58.71	51.74	121.83
Net valuation taxable	$407,878,861	$411,827,100	$1,094,895,051
State equalized value	$788,324,045	$890,763,784	$973,220,759

Public Safety
Number of officers, 2006..............11

Crime	2005	2006
Total crimes	64	71
Violent	8	5
Murder	0	0
Rape	0	2
Robbery	0	0
Aggravated assault	8	3
Non-violent	56	66
Burglary	17	15
Larceny	34	36
Vehicle theft	5	15
Domestic violence	49	11
Arson	0	2
Total crime rate	8.0	8.8
Violent	1.0	0.6
Non-violent	7.0	8.2

Public School District
(for school year 2006-07 except as noted)

Plumsted Township School District
117 Evergreen Rd
New Egypt, NJ 08533
609-758-6800

Superintendent	Robert E. Smith (Int)
Number of schools	4
Grade plan	K-12
Enrollment	1,823
Attendance rate, '05-06	94.6%
Dropout rate	1.6%
Students per teacher	10.7
Per pupil expenditure	$10,116
Median faculty salary	$44,423
Median administrator salary	$99,750
Grade 12 enrollment	118
High school graduation rate	93.7%

Assessment test results
(percent scoring at proficient or advanced level)
	Language	Math
NJASK-Grade 3	83.5%	90.1%
GEPA-Grade 8	77.9%	85.7%
HSPA-High School	87.2%	78.2%

SAT score averages
Pct tested	Math	Verbal	Writing
58%	522	512	510

Teacher Qualifications
Avg. years of experience	4
Highly-qualified teachers one subject/all subjects	100%/100%
With emergency credentials	0.0%

No Child Left Behind
AYP, 2005-06............Meets Standards

Municipal Finance
State Aid Programs, 2008
Total aid	$584,829
CMPTRA	56,213
Energy tax receipts	519,565
Garden State Trust	8,930

General Budget, 2007
Total tax levy	$14,420,543
County levy	2,794,963
County taxes	2,303,176
County library	272,966
County health	110,591
County open space	108,230
School levy	10,421,155
Muni. levy	1,204,425
Misc. revenues	2,711,061

The New Jersey Municipal Data Book

Pohatcong Township
Warren County

Demographics & Socio-Economic Characteristics
(2000 US Census, except as noted)

Population
- 1980*..................................3,856
- 1990*..................................3,591
- 2000..................................3,416
  - Male................................1,693
  - Female..............................1,723
- 2006 (estimate)*......................3,410
- Population density....................255.8

Race & Hispanic Origin, 2000
Race
- White..................................3,348
- Black/African American.................15
- American Indian/Alaska Native..........1
- Asian..................................10
- Native Hawaiian/Pacific Islander.......0
- Other race............................22
- Two or more races.....................20
- Hispanic origin, total................69
  - Mexican..............................5
  - Puerto Rican........................20
  - Cuban................................5
  - Other Hispanic......................39

Age & Nativity, 2000
- Under 5 years........................221
- 18 years and over..................2,621
- 21 years and over..................2,538
- 65 years and over....................546
- 85 years and over.....................48
- Median age...........................39.8
- Native-born........................3,346
- Foreign-born..........................70

Educational Attainment, 2000
- Population 25 years and over.......2,428
- Less than 9th grade..................3.5%
- High school grad or higher..........86.1%
- Bachelor's degree or higher.........17.4%
- Graduate degree......................5.8%

Income & Poverty, 1999
- Per capita income.................$24,754
- Median household income...........$52,188
- Median family income..............$60,208
- Persons in poverty...................148
- H'holds receiving public assistance....5
- H'holds receiving social security...365

Households, 2000
- Total households..................1,341
  - With persons under 18.............434
  - With persons over 65..............399
  - Family households.................990
  - Single-person households..........295
- Persons per household...............2.54
- Persons per family..................2.99

Labor & Employment
- Total civilian labor force, 2006**.2,112
  - Unemployment rate..................3.7%
- Total civilian labor force, 2000...1,851
  - Unemployment rate..................2.9%

Employed persons 16 years and over by occupation, 2000
- Managers & professionals............629
- Service occupations.................236
- Sales & office occupations..........506
- Farming, fishing & forestry..........6
- Construction & maintenance.........243
- Production & transportation........177
- Self-employed persons..............146

* US Census Bureau
** New Jersey Department of Labor

General Information
Township of Pohatcong
50 Municipal Dr
Phillipsburg, NJ 08865
908-454-6121

- Website..............www.pohatcong.com
- Year of incorporation................1882
- Land/water area (sq. miles).....13.33/0.28
- Form of government.......Small Municipality

Government
Legislative Districts
- US Congressional......................5
- State Legislative....................23

Local Officials, 2008
- Mayor..................Stephen Babinsky
- Manager/Admin......................NA
- Clerk..................Wanda Kutzman
- Finance Dir............Peter Kowalick
- Tax Assessor.........Michael Schmidt
- Tax Collector........Carrie Rochelle
- Attorney.............Kevin Benbrook
- Building................Wayne Degan
- Comm Dev/Planning................NA
- Engineering...........Rich McIntyre
- Public Works.......................NA
- Police Chief............Paul Hager
- Emerg/Fire Director.....Don Freeman

Housing & Construction
Housing Units, 2000*
- Total..............................1,411
- Median rent.........................$717
- Median SF home value...........$135,100

Permits for New Residential Construction

	Units	Value
Total, 2007	8	$1,474,208
Single family	8	$1,474,208
Total, 2006	9	$1,448,763
Single family	9	$1,448,763

Real Property Valuation, 2007

	Parcels	Valuation
Total	1,732	$337,331,520
Vacant	129	6,702,800
Residential	1,229	203,357,900
Commercial	54	91,545,400
Industrial	5	5,636,800
Apartments	2	399,300
Farm land	203	2,566,920
Farm homestead	110	27,282,400

Average Property Value & Tax, 2007
- Residential value.................$172,248
- Property tax........................$5,652
- Tax credit/rebate..................$1,057

Public Library
No public municipal library

Library statistics, 2006
- Population served.....................NA
- Full-time/total staff..............NA/NA

	Total	Per capita
Holdings	NA	NA
Revenues	NA	NA
Expenditures	NA	NA
Annual visits	NA	NA
Internet terminals/annual users	NA/NA	

Taxes

	2005	2006	2007
General tax rate per $100	2.96	3.11	3.29
County equalization ratio	89.91	83.29	73.65
Net valuation taxable	$339,468,198	$338,776,270	$337,979,667
State equalized value	$407,573,776	$460,625,450	$490,528,368

Public Safety
Number of officers, 2006..............14

Crime	2005	2006
Total crimes	181	158
Violent	19	26
Murder	0	0
Rape	0	0
Robbery	0	1
Aggravated assault	19	25
Non-violent	162	132
Burglary	13	8
Larceny	145	114
Vehicle theft	4	10
Domestic violence	20	14
Arson	0	0
Total crime rate	52.8	46.3
Violent	5.5	7.6
Non-violent	47.3	38.7

Public School District
(for school year 2006-07 except as noted)

Pohatcong Township School District
240 Route 519
Phillipsburg, NJ 08865
908-859-8155

- Chief School Admin........Diane Mandry
- Number of schools.....................1
- Grade plan..........................K-8
- Enrollment..........................379
- Attendance rate, '05-06...........95.8%
- Dropout rate.........................NA
- Students per teacher...............11.8
- Per pupil expenditure...........$12,023
- Median faculty salary............$46,791
- Median administrator salary.....$80,000
- Grade 12 enrollment..................NA
- High school graduation rate..........NA

Assessment test results
(percent scoring at proficient or advanced level)

	Language	Math
NJASK-Grade 3	66.0%	66.0%
GEPA-Grade 8	75.6%	73.1%
HSPA-High School	NA	NA

SAT score averages

Pct tested	Math	Verbal	Writing
NA	NA	NA	NA

Teacher Qualifications
- Avg. years of experience..............11
- Highly-qualified teachers
  one subject/all subjects......100%/100%
- With emergency credentials..........0.0%

No Child Left Behind
- AYP, 2005-06............Meets Standards

Municipal Finance
State Aid Programs, 2008
- Total aid.......................$349,516
- CMPTRA...............................0
- Energy tax receipts.............335,602
- Garden State Trust..............13,914

General Budget, 2007
- Total tax levy................$11,089,715
- County levy....................2,808,440
  - County taxes.................2,292,328
  - County library................239,631
  - County health......................0
  - County open space............276,481
- School levy....................5,387,580
- Muni. levy.....................2,893,695
- Misc. revenues.................2,480,094

Ocean County
Point Pleasant Beach Borough

Demographics & Socio-Economic Characteristics
(2000 US Census, except as noted)

Population
- 1980*..5,415
- 1990*..5,112
- 2000...5,314
  - Male.......................................2,678
  - Female.....................................2,636
- 2006 (estimate)*............................5,398
- Population density......................3,748.6

Race & Hispanic Origin, 2000
Race
- White..5,098
- Black/African American......................28
- American Indian/Alaska Native...............18
- Asian...54
- Native Hawaiian/Pacific Islander..............1
- Other race....................................78
- Two or more races............................37
- Hispanic origin, total......................234
  - Mexican....................................120
  - Puerto Rican................................33
  - Cuban..8
  - Other Hispanic..............................73

Age & Nativity, 2000
- Under 5 years................................234
- 18 years and over..........................4,292
- 21 years and over..........................4,150
- 65 years and over..........................1,012
- 85 years and over............................141
- Median age..................................42.6
- Native-born................................5,008
- Foreign-born.................................306

Educational Attainment, 2000
- Population 25 years and over...............3,926
- Less than 9th grade........................3.8%
- High school grad or higher................87.1%
- Bachelor's degree or higher...............34.1%
- Graduate degree............................11.6%

Income & Poverty, 1999
- Per capita income........................$27,853
- Median household income..................$51,105
- Median family income.....................$61,250
- Persons in poverty..........................325
- H'holds receiving public assistance.........46
- H'holds receiving social security..........802

Households, 2000
- Total households..........................2,317
  - With persons under 18.....................570
  - With persons over 65......................742
  - Family households.......................1,317
  - Single-person households..................841
- Persons per household......................2.25
- Persons per family.........................2.96

Labor & Employment
- Total civilian labor force, 2006**........2,542
  - Unemployment rate........................3.7%
- Total civilian labor force, 2000..........2,617
  - Unemployment rate........................5.2%
- *Employed persons 16 years and over by occupation, 2000*
  - Managers & professionals..................918
  - Service occupations.......................396
  - Sales & office occupations................742
  - Farming, fishing & forestry................65
  - Construction & maintenance................206
  - Production & transportation...............153
- Self-employed persons.......................108

‡ Branch of county library
* US Census Bureau
** New Jersey Department of Labor

See Introduction for an explanation of all data sources.

General Information
Borough of Point Pleasant Beach
416 New Jersey Ave
Point Pleasant Beach, NJ 08742
732-892-1118
- Website........www.pointpleasantbeach.org
- Year of incorporation...................1886
- Land/water area (sq. miles).......1.44/0.28
- Form of government.................Borough

Government
Legislative Districts
- US Congressional.........................4
- State Legislative.......................10

Local Officials, 2008
- Mayor.................Vincent R. Barrella
- Manager ....Christine Riehl
- Clerk................Maryann Ellsworth
- Finance Dir..............Christine Riehl
- Tax Assessor..........Howard Carpenter
- Tax Collector ....Christine Riehl
- Attorney...................Sean Gertner
- Building..............Michael Gardner
- Comm Dev/Planning.................NA
- Engineering ....Raymond Savacool
- Public Works ....Robert Meany
- Police Chief................Daniel DePolo
- Emerg/Fire Director........John DeMillo

Housing & Construction
Housing Units, 2000*
- Total..............................3,558
- Median rent.........................$777
- Median SF home value...........$223,600

Permits for New Residential Construction

	Units	Value
Total, 2007	13	$3,123,800
Single family	10	$3,114,000
Total, 2006	19	$3,032,392
Single family	19	$3,032,392

Real Property Valuation, 2007

	Parcels	Valuation
Total	3,206	$2,558,562,100
Vacant	171	82,184,400
Residential	2,756	1,945,117,000
Commercial	270	510,319,100
Industrial	0	0
Apartments	9	20,941,600
Farm land	0	0
Farm homestead	0	0

Average Property Value & Tax, 2007
- Residential value $705,775
- Property tax $5,841
- Tax credit/rebate $995

Public Library
Point Pleasant Beach Branch‡
710 McLean Ave
Point Pleasant Beach, NJ 08742
732-892-4575
- Branch Librarian............Kathy Finnan

Library statistics, 2006
see Ocean County profile for library system statistics

Public Safety
- Number of officers, 2006................25

Crime	2005	2006
Total crimes	213	212
Violent	7	13
Murder	0	0
Rape	0	3
Robbery	3	1
Aggravated assault	4	9
Non-violent	206	199
Burglary	22	23
Larceny	176	172
Vehicle theft	8	4
Domestic violence	121	102
Arson	0	0
Total crime rate	39.4	39.3
Violent	1.3	2.4
Non-violent	38.1	36.9

Public School District
(for school year 2006-07 except as noted)

Point Pleasant Beach School District
299 Cooks Lane
Point Pleasant Beach, NJ 08742
732-899-8840
- Superintendent...........John A. Ravally
- Number of schools......................2
- Grade plan.........................K-12
- Enrollment..........................875
- Attendance rate, '05-06............93.9%
- Dropout rate.........................NA
- Students per teacher................10.1
- Per pupil expenditure............$12,937
- Median faculty salary............$51,181
- Median administrator salary.....$115,366
- Grade 12 enrollment................103
- High school graduation rate........92.8%

Assessment test results
(percent scoring at proficient or advanced level)

	Language	Math
NJASK-Grade 3	90.7%	86.1%
GEPA-Grade 8	89.9%	86.5%
HSPA-High School	94.9%	90.6%

SAT score averages

Pct tested	Math	Verbal	Writing
87%	530	500	514

Teacher Qualifications
- Avg. years of experience...............12
- Highly-qualified teachers
  - one subject/all subjects......100%/100%
- With emergency credentials...........0.0%

No Child Left Behind
- AYP, 2005-06...........Meets Standards

Municipal Finance
State Aid Programs, 2008
- Total aid......................$758,362
  - CMPTRA.....................35,089
  - Energy tax receipts............723,260
  - Garden State Trust 13

General Budget, 2007
- Total tax levy................$21,178,517
  - County levy 6,704,051
    - County taxes..............5,524,473
    - County library..............654,723
    - County health 265,258
    - County open space 259,597
  - School levy 9,899,757
  - Muni. levy 4,574,709
- Misc. revenues 7,281,309

Taxes	2005	2006	2007
General tax rate per $100	2.803	3.022	0.828
County equalization ratio	44.76	35.99	119.05
Net valuation taxable	$664,743,186	$670,946,300	$2,559,173,953
State equalized value	$1,847,021,912	$2,126,827,335	$2,344,690,735

Point Pleasant Borough
Ocean County

Demographics & Socio-Economic Characteristics
(2000 US Census, except as noted)

Population
1980*	17,747
1990*	18,177
2000	19,306
Male	9,279
Female	10,027
2006 (estimate)*	19,882
Population density	5,632.3

Race & Hispanic Origin, 2000
Race
White	18,887
Black/African American	56
American Indian/Alaska Native	27
Asian	105
Native Hawaiian/Pacific Islander	2
Other race	96
Two or more races	133
Hispanic origin, total	465
Mexican	171
Puerto Rican	117
Cuban	35
Other Hispanic	142

Age & Nativity, 2000
Under 5 years	1,150
18 years and over	14,729
21 years and over	14,193
65 years and over	2,883
85 years and over	412
Median age	39.4
Native-born	18,713
Foreign-born	593

Educational Attainment, 2000
Population 25 years and over	13,447
Less than 9th grade	2.6%
High school grad or higher	88.5%
Bachelor's degree or higher	27.8%
Graduate degree	7.7%

Income & Poverty, 1999
Per capita income	$25,715
Median household income	$55,987
Median family income	$64,798
Persons in poverty	616
H'holds receiving public assistance	86
H'holds receiving social security	2,079

Households, 2000
Total households	7,560
With persons under 18	2,566
With persons over 65	1,982
Family households	5,228
Single-person households	1,941
Persons per household	2.52
Persons per family	3.06

Labor & Employment
Total civilian labor force, 2006**	9,992
Unemployment rate	3.9%
Total civilian labor force, 2000	10,105
Unemployment rate	3.7%

Employed persons 16 years and over by occupation, 2000
Managers & professionals	3,511
Service occupations	1,532
Sales & office occupations	2,806
Farming, fishing & forestry	18
Construction & maintenance	1,017
Production & transportation	846
Self-employed persons	619

‡ Branch of county library
* US Census Bureau
** New Jersey Department of Labor

General Information
Borough of Point Pleasant
2233 Bridge Ave
PO Box 25
Point Pleasant, NJ 08742
732-892-3434

Website	www.ptboro.com
Year of incorporation	1920
Land/water area (sq. miles)	3.53/0.63
Form of government	Borough

Government
Legislative Districts
US Congressional	4
State Legislative	10

Local Officials, 2008
Mayor	Martin Konkus
Manager	David Maffei
Clerk	David Maffei
Finance Dir	Judith Block
Tax Assessor	John Butow
Tax Collector	Bernadine Pierce
Attorney	Jerry Dasti
Building	Michael Gardner
Planning	Robert Forsyth
Engineering	Schoor De Palma
Public Works	Dennis Sears
Police Chief	Raymond Hilling
Emerg/Fire Director	G. Donald Glover

Housing & Construction
Housing Units, 2000*
Total	8,350
Median rent	$859
Median SF home value	$160,100

Permits for New Residential Construction
	Units	Value
Total, 2007	93	$28,930,642
Single family	33	$5,265,595
Total, 2006	54	$5,960,971
Single family	38	$5,860,970

Real Property Valuation, 2007
	Parcels	Valuation
Total	8,090	$1,374,560,600
Vacant	223	22,958,900
Residential	7,546	1,230,660,600
Commercial	306	106,646,400
Industrial	0	0
Apartments	15	14,294,700
Farm land	0	0
Farm homestead	0	0

Average Property Value & Tax, 2007
Residential value	$163,088
Property tax	$5,815
Tax credit/rebate	$973

Public Library
Point Pleasant Branch Library‡
834 Beaver Dam Rd
Point Pleasant, NJ 08742
732-295-1555

Branch Librarian: Barbara Kaden

Library statistics, 2006
see Ocean County profile
for library system statistics

Public Safety
Number of officers, 2006	33

Crime	2005	2006
Total crimes	312	346
Violent	10	16
Murder	0	0
Rape	0	0
Robbery	2	2
Aggravated assault	8	14
Non-violent	302	330
Burglary	46	51
Larceny	249	269
Vehicle theft	7	10
Domestic violence	137	145
Arson	0	0
Total crime rate	15.7	17.4
Violent	0.5	0.8
Non-violent	15.2	16.6

Public School District
(for school year 2006-07 except as noted)

Point Pleasant Borough School District
2100 Panther Path
Point Pleasant, NJ 08742
732-701-1900

Superintendent	Robert Cilento
Number of schools	4
Grade plan	K-12
Enrollment	3,208
Attendance rate, '05-06	94.7%
Dropout rate	0.9%
Students per teacher	12.1
Per pupil expenditure	$10,115
Median faculty salary	$47,750
Median administrator salary	$108,032
Grade 12 enrollment	242
High school graduation rate	94.1%

Assessment test results
(percent scoring at proficient or advanced level)
	Language	Math
NJASK-Grade 3	95.3%	98.1%
GEPA-Grade 8	83.2%	81.8%
HSPA-High School	88.2%	74.6%

SAT score averages
Pct tested	Math	Verbal	Writing
77%	490	491	478

Teacher Qualifications
Avg. years of experience	8
Highly-qualified teachers one subject/all subjects	100%/100%
With emergency credentials	0.0%

No Child Left Behind
AYP, 2005-06	Meets Standards

Municipal Finance
State Aid Programs, 2008
Total aid	$1,576,741
CMPTRA	356,068
Energy tax receipts	1,220,673
Garden State Trust	0

General Budget, 2007
Total tax levy	$49,081,108
County levy	10,986,564
County taxes	9,053,473
County library	1,072,960
County health	434,704
County open space	425,427
School levy	27,085,313
Muni. levy	11,009,231
Misc. revenues	5,594,135

Taxes	2005	2006	2007
General tax rate per $100	3.22	3.4	3.566
County equalization ratio	51.76	44.6	38.92
Net valuation taxable	$1,351,395,959	$1,361,017,000	$1,376,424,076
State equalized value	$3,030,035,783	$3,499,062,668	$3,724,942,024

Passaic County
Pompton Lakes Borough

Demographics & Socio-Economic Characteristics
(2000 US Census, except as noted)

Population
1980*	10,660
1990*	10,539
2000	10,640
Male	5,119
Female	5,521
2006 (estimate)*	11,243
Population density	3,785.5

Race & Hispanic Origin, 2000
Race
White	9,896
Black/African American	129
American Indian/Alaska Native	20
Asian	322
Native Hawaiian/Pacific Islander	1
Other race	167
Two or more races	105
Hispanic origin, total	611
Mexican	180
Puerto Rican	148
Cuban	62
Other Hispanic	221

Age & Nativity, 2000
Under 5 years	738
18 years and over	8,061
21 years and over	7,754
65 years and over	1,425
85 years and over	146
Median age	37.2
Native-born	9,542
Foreign-born	1,098

Educational Attainment, 2000
Population 25 years and over	7,297
Less than 9th grade	5.0%
High school grad or higher	88.8%
Bachelor's degree or higher	28.4%
Graduate degree	7.9%

Income & Poverty, 1999
Per capita income	$26,802
Median household income	$65,648
Median family income	$74,701
Persons in poverty	343
H'holds receiving public assistance	34
H'holds receiving social security	1,159

Households, 2000
Total households	3,949
With persons under 18	1,424
With persons over 65	1,081
Family households	2,805
Single-person households	939
Persons per household	2.69
Persons per family	3.24

Labor & Employment
Total civilian labor force, 2006**	6,435
Unemployment rate	3.9%
Total civilian labor force, 2000	5,932
Unemployment rate	4.0%

Employed persons 16 years and over by occupation, 2000
Managers & professionals	2,225
Service occupations	648
Sales & office occupations	1,559
Farming, fishing & forestry	0
Construction & maintenance	604
Production & transportation	660
Self-employed persons	196

* US Census Bureau
** New Jersey Department of Labor

See Introduction for an explanation of all data sources.

General Information
Borough of Pompton Lakes
25 Lenox Ave
Pompton Lakes, NJ 07442
973-835-0143

Website	www.pomptonlakesgov.com
Year of incorporation	1895
Land/water area (sq. miles)	2.97/0.19
Form of government	Borough

Government
Legislative Districts
US Congressional	8
State Legislative	26

Local Officials, 2008
Mayor	Kenneth M. Cole
Manager	Lawrence Pollex
Clerk	Elizabeth Brandsness
Finance Dir	Lawrence Pollex
Tax Assessor	Michael Barker
Tax Collector	Gail Bado
Attorney	Joseph Ragno Jr
Building	Ron Van Dine
Comm Dev/Planning	NA
Engineering	Alaimo Group
Public Works	Ben Steltzer
Police Chief	William Smith (Actg)
Emerg/Fire Director	Dean Cioppa

Housing & Construction
Housing Units, 2000*
Total	4,024
Median rent	$933
Median SF home value	$180,100

Permits for New Residential Construction
	Units	Value
Total, 2007	7	$1,348,100
Single family	7	$1,348,100
Total, 2006	5	$1,111,000
Single family	5	$1,111,000

Real Property Valuation, 2007
	Parcels	Valuation
Total	3,947	$641,671,100
Vacant	57	3,264,900
Residential	3,711	548,511,400
Commercial	166	57,858,000
Industrial	5	17,498,600
Apartments	8	14,538,200
Farm land	0	0
Farm homestead	0	0

Average Property Value & Tax, 2007
Residential value	$147,807
Property tax	$7,857
Tax credit/rebate	$1,265

Public Library
Emanuel Einstein Public Library
333 Wanaque Ave
Pompton Lakes, NJ 07442
973-835-0482

Director . . . . Margaret M. Freathy

Library statistics, 2006
Population served	10,640
Full-time/total staff	1/1

	Total	Per capita
Holdings	38,809	3.65
Revenues	$452,147	$42.50
Expenditures	$371,592	$34.92
Annual visits	39,808	3.74
Internet terminals/annual users		3/3,276

Public Safety
Number of officers, 2006 25

Crime	2005	2006
Total crimes	114	108
Violent	8	6
Murder	1	0
Rape	0	0
Robbery	1	1
Aggravated assault	6	5
Non-violent	106	102
Burglary	19	24
Larceny	82	66
Vehicle theft	5	12
Domestic violence	49	59
Arson	0	0
Total crime rate	10.0	9.5
Violent	0.7	0.5
Non-violent	9.3	9.0

Public School District
(for school year 2006-07 except as noted)

Pompton Lakes School District
237 Van Ave
Pompton Lakes, NJ 07442
973-835-4334

Chief School Admin	Terrance Brennan
Number of schools	4
Grade plan	K-12
Enrollment	1,794
Attendance rate, '05-06	95.5%
Dropout rate	0.9%
Students per teacher	11.2
Per pupil expenditure	$13,701
Median faculty salary	$53,751
Median administrator salary	$124,200
Grade 12 enrollment	138
High school graduation rate	97.5%

Assessment test results
(percent scoring at proficient or advanced level)
	Language	Math
NJASK-Grade 3	92.5%	96.3%
GEPA-Grade 8	85.4%	72.0%
HSPA-High School	92.8%	82.2%

SAT score averages
Pct tested	Math	Verbal	Writing
75%	503	481	475

Teacher Qualifications
Avg. years of experience	10
Highly-qualified teachers one subject/all subjects	99.0%/99.0%
With emergency credentials	0.8%

No Child Left Behind
AYP, 2005-06 . . . . Meets Standards

Municipal Finance
State Aid Programs, 2008
Total aid	$1,353,397
CMPTRA	511,658
Energy tax receipts	799,755
Garden State Trust	41,984

General Budget, 2007
Total tax levy	$34,134,959
County tax	7,178,349
County taxes	7,033,293
County library	0
County health	0
County open space	145,056
School levy	19,394,649
Muni. levy	7,561,962
Misc. revenues	4,041,382

Taxes
	2005	2006	2007
General tax rate per $100	4.65	5.05	5.32
County equalization ratio	56.41	49.47	44.58
Net valuation taxable	$638,686,330	$640,743,500	$642,114,136
State equalized value	$1,291,057,873	$1,437,771,057	$1,521,711,647

Port Republic City
Atlantic County

Demographics & Socio-Economic Characteristics
(2000 US Census, except as noted)

Population
1980*	837
1990*	992
2000	1,037
Male	510
Female	527
2006 (estimate)*	1,234
Population density	161.9

Race & Hispanic Origin, 2000
Race
White	986
Black/African American	17
American Indian/Alaska Native	4
Asian	6
Native Hawaiian/Pacific Islander	0
Other race	7
Two or more races	17
Hispanic origin, total	11
Mexican	0
Puerto Rican	7
Cuban	0
Other Hispanic	4

Age & Nativity, 2000
Under 5 years	58
18 years and over	788
21 years and over	746
65 years and over	124
85 years and over	17
Median age	41.3
Native-born	985
Foreign-born	47

Educational Attainment, 2000
Population 25 years and over	707
Less than 9th grade	3.4%
High school grad or higher	90.5%
Bachelor's degree or higher	27.7%
Graduate degree	7.5%

Income & Poverty, 1999
Per capita income	$24,369
Median household income	$65,833
Median family income	$70,714
Persons in poverty	36
H'holds receiving public assistance	3
H'holds receiving social security	85

Households, 2000
Total households	365
With persons under 18	146
With persons over 65	92
Family households	289
Single-person households	61
Persons per household	2.82
Persons per family	3.17

Labor & Employment
Total civilian labor force, 2006**	626
Unemployment rate	3.3%
Total civilian labor force, 2000	578
Unemployment rate	4.2%

Employed persons 16 years and over by occupation, 2000
Managers & professionals	161
Service occupations	89
Sales & office occupations	153
Farming, fishing & forestry	7
Construction & maintenance	79
Production & transportation	65
Self-employed persons	64

* US Census Bureau
** New Jersey Department of Labor

General Information
City of Port Republic
143 Main St
Port Republic, NJ 08241
609-652-1501
Email.... portrepublic.cityclerk@comcast.net
Year of incorporation 1905
Land/water area (sq. miles) 7.62/1.05
Form of government.................City

Government
Legislative Districts
US Congressional	2
State Legislative	2

Local Officials, 2008
Mayor	Gary Giberson
Manager/Admin	NA
Clerk	Lucy Samuelsen
Finance Dir	Karen Thomas
Tax Assessor	Brian Vigue
Tax Collector	NA
Attorney	Sal Perillo
Building	Jay Haines
Comm Dev/Planning	NA
Engineering	Matthew Doran
Public Works	James Milton
Police Chief	NA
Emerg/Fire Director	John Yochim

Housing & Construction
Housing Units, 2000*
Total	389
Median rent	$790
Median SF home value	$155,700

Permits for New Residential Construction
	Units	Value
Total, 2007	3	$1,600,000
Single family	3	$1,600,000
Total, 2006	4	$1,800,000
Single family	4	$1,800,000

Real Property Valuation, 2007
	Parcels	Valuation
Total	589	$72,743,000
Vacant	118	2,660,500
Residential	447	66,616,900
Commercial	11	2,290,800
Industrial	0	0
Apartments	0	0
Farm land	7	76,100
Farm homestead	6	1,098,700

Average Property Value & Tax, 2007
Residential value	$149,483
Property tax	$4,596
Tax credit/rebate	$886

Public Library
No public municipal library

Library statistics, 2006
Population served	NA
Full-time/total staff	NA/NA

	Total	Per capita
Holdings	NA	NA
Revenues	NA	NA
Expenditures	NA	NA
Annual visits	NA	NA
Internet terminals/annual users	NA/NA	

Taxes
	2005	2006	2007
General tax rate per $100	2.815	2.969	3.075
County equalization ratio	63.73	57.6	51.64
Net valuation taxable	$68,987,910	$70,376,700	$73,058,758
State equalized value	$119,770,677	$136,629,846	$150,116,005

Public Safety
Number of officers, 2006 0

Crime	2005	2006
Total crimes	16	20
Violent	0	0
Murder	0	0
Rape	0	0
Robbery	0	0
Aggravated assault	0	0
Non-violent	16	20
Burglary	2	3
Larceny	11	17
Vehicle theft	3	0
Domestic violence	5	0
Arson	0	0
Total crime rate	14.0	16.8
Violent	0.0	0.0
Non-violent	14.0	16.8

Public School District
(for school year 2006-07 except as noted)

Port Republic School District
137 Pomona Ave
Port Republic, NJ 08241
609-652-7377

Chief School Admin	Janet Wilbraham
Number of schools	1
Grade plan	K-8
Enrollment	134
Attendance rate, '05-06	94.9%
Dropout rate	NA
Students per teacher	9.1
Per pupil expenditure	$12,634
Median faculty salary	$48,240
Median administrator salary	$60,248
Grade 12 enrollment	NA
High school graduation rate	NA

Assessment test results
(percent scoring at proficient or advanced level)
	Language	Math
NJASK-Grade 3	100.0%	85.7%
GEPA-Grade 8	76.5%	82.4%
HSPA-High School	NA	NA

SAT score averages
Pct tested	Math	Verbal	Writing
NA	NA	NA	NA

Teacher Qualifications
Avg. years of experience	10
Highly-qualified teachers one subject/all subjects	100%/100%
With emergency credentials	0.0%

No Child Left Behind
AYP, 2005-06 ....Meets Standards

Municipal Finance
State Aid Programs, 2008
Total aid	$220,602
CMPTRA	0
Energy tax receipts	218,211
Garden State Trust	2,391

General Budget, 2007
Total tax levy	$2,246,393
County levy	434,339
County taxes	345,678
County library	42,882
County health	17,473
County open space	28,306
School levy	1,352,425
Muni. levy	459,629
Misc. revenues	641,988

Mercer County

Princeton Borough

Demographics & Socio-Economic Characteristics
(2000 US Census, except as noted)

Population
1980*	12,035
1990*	12,016
2000	14,203
Male	7,380
Female	6,823
2006 (estimate)*	13,684
Population density	7,396.8

Race & Hispanic Origin, 2000
Race
White	11,399
Black/African American	908
American Indian/Alaska Native	40
Asian	1,060
Native Hawaiian/Pacific Islander	20
Other race	355
Two or more races	421
Hispanic origin, total	1,009
Mexican	340
Puerto Rican	113
Cuban	30
Other Hispanic	526

Age & Nativity, 2000
Under 5 years	446
18 years and over	12,774
21 years and over	9,644
65 years and over	1,321
85 years and over	264
Median age	24.7
Native-born	12,191
Foreign-born	2,012

Educational Attainment, 2000
Population 25 years and over	7,148
Less than 9th grade	4.8%
High school grad or higher	89.4%
Bachelor's degree or higher	60.1%
Graduate degree	39.6%

Income & Poverty, 1999
Per capita income	$27,292
Median household income	$67,346
Median family income	$102,957
Persons in poverty	656
H'holds receiving public assistance	16
H'holds receiving social security	811

Households, 2000
Total households	3,326
With persons under 18	780
With persons over 65	819
Family households	1,693
Single-person households	1,334
Persons per household	2.20
Persons per family	2.92

Labor & Employment
Total civilian labor force, 2006**	3,591
Unemployment rate	3.6%
Total civilian labor force, 2000	9,999
Unemployment rate	42.3%

Employed persons 16 years and over by occupation, 2000
Managers & professionals	3,620
Service occupations	1,076
Sales & office occupations	801
Farming, fishing & forestry	12
Construction & maintenance	133
Production & transportation	126
Self-employed persons	232

‡ Joint library with Princeton Township
* US Census Bureau
** New Jersey Department of Labor

See Introduction for an explanation of all data sources.

General Information
Borough of Princeton
PO Box 390
Princeton, NJ 08542
609-924-3118

Website	www.princetonboro.org
Year of incorporation	1813
Land/water area (sq. miles)	1.85/0.00
Form of government	Borough

Government
Legislative Districts
US Congressional	12
State Legislative	15

Local Officials, 2008
Mayor	Mildred T. Trotman
Manager	Robert W. Bruschi
Clerk	Andrea L. Quinty
Finance Dir	Sandra L. Webb
Tax Assessor	Neal Snyder
Tax Collector	NA
Attorney	Karen Cayci
Building	Martin Vogt
Comm Dev/Planning	NA
Engineering	Christopher Budzinski
Public Works	Wayne Carr
Police Chief	Anthony V. Federico
Emerg/Fire Director	Daniel Tomalin

Housing & Construction
Housing Units, 2000*
Total	3,495
Median rent	$920
Median SF home value	$343,500

Permits for New Residential Construction
	Units	Value
Total, 2007	14	$4,407,798
Single family	10	$3,783,298
Total, 2006	18	$5,935,977
Single family	14	$5,311,477

Real Property Valuation, 2007
	Parcels	Valuation
Total	2,457	$996,879,700
Vacant	151	17,898,200
Residential	2,064	719,124,000
Commercial	199	211,131,500
Industrial	0	0
Apartments	43	48,726,000
Farm land	0	0
Farm homestead	0	0

Average Property Value & Tax, 2007
Residential value	$348,413
Property tax	$13,656
Tax credit/rebate	$1,324

Public Library
Princeton Public Library‡
65 Witherspoon St
Princeton, NJ 08542
609-924-8822

Director ... Leslie Burger

Library statistics, 2006
Population served	30,230
Full-time/total staff	15/36

	Total	Per capita
Holdings	177,906	5.89
Revenues	$4,256,857	$140.82
Expenditures	$4,288,334	$141.86
Annual visits	867,377	28.69
Internet terminals/annual users	102/242,697	

Taxes
	2005	2006	2007
General tax rate per $100	3.63	3.69	3.92
County equalization ratio	54.69	51.13	44.33
Net valuation taxable	$1,000,992,410	$999,240,700	$999,506,688
State equalized value	$1,957,739,898	$2,257,511,679	$2,476,273,886

Public Safety
Number of officers, 2006		34
Crime	**2005**	**2006**
Total crimes	442	450
Violent	20	23
Murder	0	0
Rape	0	2
Robbery	10	11
Aggravated assault	10	10
Non-violent	422	427
Burglary	76	77
Larceny	333	339
Vehicle theft	13	11
Domestic violence	43	41
Arson	0	0
Total crime rate	32.5	33.3
Violent	1.5	1.7
Non-violent	31.1	31.6

Public School District
(for school year 2006-07 except as noted)

Princeton Regional School District
25 Valley Rd
Princeton, NJ 08540
609-806-4220

Superintendent	Judith A. Wilson
Number of schools	12
Grade plan	K-12
Enrollment	3,341
Attendance rate, '05-06	96.4%
Dropout rate	0.6%
Students per teacher	9.6
Per pupil expenditure	$16,809
Median faculty salary	$62,998
Median administrator salary	$122,094
Grade 12 enrollment	300
High school graduation rate	99.0%

Assessment test results
(percent scoring at proficient or advanced level)
	Language	Math
NJASK-Grade 3	89.1%	92.6%
GEPA-Grade 8	87.6%	87.2%
HSPA-High School	95.4%	90.5%

SAT score averages
Pct tested	Math	Verbal	Writing
98%	619	601	604

Teacher Qualifications
Avg. years of experience	8
Highly-qualified teachers one subject/all subjects	99.5%/99.5%
With emergency credentials	0.4%

No Child Left Behind
AYP, 2005-06 ... Meets Standards

Municipal Finance
State Aid Programs, 2008
Total aid	$1,304,945
CMPTRA	279,967
Energy tax receipts	1,024,975
Garden State Trust	3

General Budget, 2007
Total tax levy	$39,175,985
County levy	10,571,834
County taxes	9,893,383
County library	0
County health	0
County open space	678,451
School levy	18,708,414
Muni. levy	9,895,737
Misc. revenues	14,298,132

The New Jersey Municipal Data Book

Princeton Township — Mercer County

Demographics & Socio-Economic Characteristics
(2000 US Census, except as noted)

Population
1980*	13,683
1990*	13,198
2000	16,027
Male	7,750
Female	8,277
2006 (estimate)*	17,353
Population density	1,059.4

Race & Hispanic Origin, 2000
Race
White	12,807
Black/African American	852
American Indian/Alaska Native	20
Asian	1,599
Native Hawaiian/Pacific Islander	8
Other race	338
Two or more races	403
Hispanic origin, total	847
Mexican	309
Puerto Rican	70
Cuban	23
Other Hispanic	445

Age & Nativity, 2000
Under 5 years	821
18 years and over	12,121
21 years and over	11,804
65 years and over	2,463
85 years and over	228
Median age	40.8
Native-born	11,962
Foreign-born	4,065

Educational Attainment, 2000
Population 25 years and over	11,355
Less than 9th grade	2.6%
High school grad or higher	94.2%
Bachelor's degree or higher	75.9%
Graduate degree	48.2%

Income & Poverty, 1999
Per capita income	$56,360
Median household income	$94,580
Median family income	$123,098
Persons in poverty	897
H'holds receiving public assistance	45
H'holds receiving social security	1,482

Households, 2000
Total households	6,044
With persons under 18	2,121
With persons over 65	1,658
Family households	4,358
Single-person households	1,243
Persons per household	2.57
Persons per family	2.98

Labor & Employment
Total civilian labor force, 2006**	7,170
Unemployment rate	0.8%
Total civilian labor force, 2000	7,990
Unemployment rate	0.8%

Employed persons 16 years and over by occupation, 2000
Managers & professionals	5,629
Service occupations	676
Sales & office occupations	1,252
Farming, fishing & forestry	12
Construction & maintenance	113
Production & transportation	243
Self-employed persons	940

‡ Joint library with Princeton Borough
* US Census Bureau
** New Jersey Department of Labor

General Information
Township of Princeton
400 Witherspoon St
Princeton, NJ 08540
609-924-5176

Website	www.princetontwp.org
Year of incorporation	1838
Land/water area (sq. miles)	16.38/0.23
Form of government	Township

Government
Legislative Districts
US Congressional	12
State Legislative	15

Local Officials, 2008
Mayor	Phyllis Marchand
Manager	James Pascale
Clerk	Linda McDermott
Finance Dir.	Kathryn Monzo
Tax Assessor	Neal Snyder
Tax Collector	Kathryn Monzo
Attorney	Edwin Schmierer
Building	John Pettenati
Planning	Lee Solow
Engineering	Robert V. Kiser
Public Works	Donald Hansen
Police Chief	Mark V. Emann
Emerg/Fire Director	Rick McKee

Housing & Construction
Housing Units, 2000*
Total	6,224
Median rent	$748
Median SF home value	$417,000

Permits for New Residential Construction
	Units	Value
Total, 2007	11	$7,040,600
Single family	11	$7,040,600
Total, 2006	23	$11,066,520
Single family	23	$11,066,520

Real Property Valuation, 2007
	Parcels	Valuation
Total	5,460	$2,409,016,110
Vacant	377	45,850,100
Residential	4,899	2,085,805,700
Commercial	114	175,647,000
Industrial	2	5,180,100
Apartments	7	78,435,100
Farm land	44	345,410
Farm homestead	17	17,752,700

Average Property Value & Tax, 2007
Residential value	$427,900
Property tax	$14,858
Tax credit/rebate	$1,255

Public Library
Princeton Public Library‡
65 Witherspoon St
Princeton, NJ 08542
609-924-8822

Director: Leslie Burger

Library statistics, 2006
Population served	30,230
Full-time/total staff	15/36

	Total	Per capita
Holdings	177,906	5.89
Revenues	$4,256,857	$140.82
Expenditures	$4,288,334	$141.86
Annual visits	867,377	28.69
Internet terminals/annual users	102/242,697	

Taxes
	2005	2006	2007
General tax rate per $100	3.2	3.34	3.48
County equalization ratio	58.97	53.42	49.88
Net valuation taxable	$2,379,755,105	$2,397,049,510	$2,410,599,981
State equalized value	$4,454,801,769	$4,807,315,240	$5,078,540,899

Public Safety
Number of officers, 2006: 35

Crime
	2005	2006
Total crimes	190	183
Violent	15	16
Murder	0	0
Rape	3	4
Robbery	8	5
Aggravated assault	4	7
Non-violent	175	167
Burglary	57	35
Larceny	106	126
Vehicle theft	12	6
Domestic violence	25	45
Arson	1	0
Total crime rate	11.0	10.6
Violent	0.9	0.9
Non-violent	10.1	9.7

Public School District
(for school year 2006-07 except as noted)

Princeton Regional School District
25 Valley Rd
Princeton, NJ 08540
609-806-4220

Superintendent	Judith A. Wilson
Number of schools	12
Grade plan	K-12
Enrollment	3,341
Attendance rate, '05-06	96.4%
Dropout rate	0.6%
Students per teacher	9.6
Per pupil expenditure	$16,809
Median faculty salary	$62,998
Median administrator salary	$122,094
Grade 12 enrollment	300
High school graduation rate	99.0%

Assessment test results
(percent scoring at proficient or advanced level)
	Language	Math
NJASK-Grade 3	89.1%	92.6%
GEPA-Grade 8	87.6%	87.2%
HSPA-High School	95.4%	90.5%

SAT score averages
Pct tested	Math	Verbal	Writing
98%	619	601	604

Teacher Qualifications
Avg. years of experience	8
Highly-qualified teachers one subject/all subjects	99.5%/99.5%
With emergency credentials	0.4%

No Child Left Behind
AYP, 2005-06: Meets Standards

Municipal Finance
State Aid Programs, 2008
Total aid	$1,993,412
CMPTRA	235,937
Energy tax receipts	1,751,537
Garden State Trust	5,938

General Budget, 2007
Total tax levy	$83,701,112
County levy	22,619,780
County taxes	21,168,145
County library	0
County health	0
County open space	1,451,635
School levy	41,199,631
Muni. levy	19,881,701
Misc. revenues	13,775,691

Passaic County
Prospect Park Borough

Demographics & Socio-Economic Characteristics
(2000 US Census, except as noted)

Population
1980*	5,142
1990*	5,053
2000	5,779
Male	2,750
Female	3,029
2006 (estimate)*	5,720
Population density	11,916.7

Race & Hispanic Origin, 2000
Race
White	3,535
Black/African American	789
American Indian/Alaska Native	24
Asian	182
Native Hawaiian/Pacific Islander	4
Other race	792
Two or more races	453
Hispanic origin, total	2,211
Mexican	41
Puerto Rican	706
Cuban	43
Other Hispanic	1,421

Age & Nativity, 2000
Under 5 years	443
18 years and over	4,070
21 years and over	3,831
65 years and over	510
85 years and over	54
Median age	30.9
Native-born	3,955
Foreign-born	1,824

Educational Attainment, 2000
Population 25 years and over	3,433
Less than 9th grade	14.9%
High school grad or higher	68.3%
Bachelor's degree or higher	12.4%
Graduate degree	3.2%

Income & Poverty, 1999
Per capita income	$16,410
Median household income	$46,434
Median family income	$49,405
Persons in poverty	575
H'holds receiving public assistance	30
H'holds receiving social security	440

Households, 2000
Total households	1,822
With persons under 18	904
With persons over 65	380
Family households	1,432
Single-person households	309
Persons per household	3.17
Persons per family	3.56

Labor & Employment
Total civilian labor force, 2006**	2,946
Unemployment rate	6.3%
Total civilian labor force, 2000	2,712
Unemployment rate	6.1%

Employed persons 16 years and over by occupation, 2000
Managers & professionals	564
Service occupations	445
Sales & office occupations	818
Farming, fishing & forestry	0
Construction & maintenance	227
Production & transportation	492
Self-employed persons	34

* US Census Bureau
** New Jersey Department of Labor

See Introduction for an explanation of all data sources.

General Information
Borough of Prospect Park
106 Brown Ave
Prospect Park, NJ 07508
973-790-7902
Website	www.prospectpark.net
Year of incorporation	1901
Land/water area (sq. miles)	0.48/0.00
Form of government	Borough

Government
Legislative Districts
US Congressional	8
State Legislative	35

Local Officials, 2008
Mayor	Mohamed T. Khairullah
Manager/Admin	NA
Clerk	Yancy Wazirmas
Finance Dir	Stephen Sanzari
Tax Assessor	Rose Farrell
Tax Collector	Stephen Sanzari
Attorney	Schwartz, Simon et al
Building	David Heerema
Comm Dev/Planning	NA
Engineering	Boswell Engineering
Public Works	Ken Valt
Police Chief	Frank Franco
Emerg/Fire Director	R.J. Dansen

Housing & Construction
Housing Units, 2000*
Total	1,889
Median rent	$852
Median SF home value	$137,600

Permits for New Residential Construction
	Units	Value
Total, 2007	0	$0
Single family	0	$0
Total, 2006	0	$0
Single family	0	$0

Real Property Valuation, 2007
	Parcels	Valuation
Total	1,171	$180,873,350
Vacant	27	3,155,200
Residential	1,083	160,051,300
Commercial	59	14,911,150
Industrial	2	2,755,700
Apartments	0	0
Farm land	0	0
Farm homestead	0	0

Average Property Value & Tax, 2007
Residential value	$147,785
Property tax	$7,714
Tax credit/rebate	$1,085

Public Library
No public municipal library

Library statistics, 2006
Population served	NA
Full-time/total staff	NA/NA

	Total	Per capita
Holdings	NA	NA
Revenues	NA	NA
Expenditures	NA	NA
Annual visits	NA	NA
Internet terminals/annual users	NA/NA	

Public Safety
Number of officers, 2006	16

Crime	2005	2006
Total crimes	131	107
Violent	19	10
Murder	0	1
Rape	0	0
Robbery	6	2
Aggravated assault	13	7
Non-violent	112	97
Burglary	19	14
Larceny	84	72
Vehicle theft	9	11
Domestic violence	47	42
Arson	0	0
Total crime rate	22.6	18.6
Violent	3.3	1.7
Non-violent	19.3	16.8

Public School District
(for school year 2006-07 except as noted)

Prospect Park School District
290 North 8th St
Prospect Park, NJ 07508
973-720-1982
Chief School Admin	James F. Barriale
Number of schools	1
Grade plan	K-8
Enrollment	821
Attendance rate, '05-06	96.8%
Dropout rate	NA
Students per teacher	12.4
Per pupil expenditure	$10,590
Median faculty salary	$50,000
Median administrator salary	$93,839
Grade 12 enrollment	NA
High school graduation rate	NA

Assessment test results
(percent scoring at proficient or advanced level)
	Language	Math
NJASK-Grade 3	78.4%	78.5%
GEPA-Grade 8	71.1%	52.8%
HSPA-High School	NA	NA

SAT score averages
Pct tested	Math	Verbal	Writing
NA	NA	NA	NA

Teacher Qualifications
Avg. years of experience	7
Highly-qualified teachers one subject/all subjects	98.0%/98.0%
With emergency credentials	0.0%

No Child Left Behind
AYP, 2005-06	Meets Standards

Municipal Finance
State Aid Programs, 2008
Total aid	$195,658
CMPTRA	0
Energy tax receipts	195,658
Garden State Trust	0

General Budget, 2007
Total tax levy	$9,452,845
County levy	1,954,798
County taxes	1,915,321
County library	0
County health	0
County open space	39,477
School levy	4,742,493
Muni. levy	2,755,554
Misc. revenues	2,019,538

Taxes	2005	2006	2007
General tax rate per $100	4.43	4.92	5.22
County equalization ratio	61.55	52.85	46.08
Net valuation taxable	$180,574,550	$180,738,450	$181,097,450
State equalized value	$341,673,699	$392,465,739	$434,389,606

The New Jersey Municipal Data Book

Quinton Township
Salem County

Demographics & Socio-Economic Characteristics
(2000 US Census, except as noted)

Population
1980*	2,887
1990*	2,511
2000	2,786
Male	1,391
Female	1,395
2006 (estimate)*	2,864
Population density	118.5

Race & Hispanic Origin, 2000
Race
White	2,286
Black/African American	403
American Indian/Alaska Native	30
Asian	9
Native Hawaiian/Pacific Islander	0
Other race	20
Two or more races	38
Hispanic origin, total	42
Mexican	7
Puerto Rican	14
Cuban	1
Other Hispanic	20

Age & Nativity, 2000
Under 5 years	161
18 years and over	2,128
21 years and over	2,034
65 years and over	441
85 years and over	50
Median age	39.0
Native-born	2,737
Foreign-born	49

Educational Attainment, 2000
Population 25 years and over	1,931
Less than 9th grade	10.9%
High school grad or higher	72.1%
Bachelor's degree or higher	10.3%
Graduate degree	2.2%

Income & Poverty, 1999
Per capita income	$18,921
Median household income	$41,193
Median family income	$48,272
Persons in poverty	258
H'holds receiving public assistance	34
H'holds receiving social security	365

Households, 2000
Total households	1,074
With persons under 18	357
With persons over 65	324
Family households	779
Single-person households	244
Persons per household	2.56
Persons per family	3.02

Labor & Employment
Total civilian labor force, 2006**	1,311
Unemployment rate	5.3%
Total civilian labor force, 2000	1,294
Unemployment rate	8.8%

Employed persons 16 years and over by occupation, 2000
Managers & professionals	291
Service occupations	188
Sales & office occupations	267
Farming, fishing & forestry	17
Construction & maintenance	158
Production & transportation	259
Self-employed persons	63

* US Census Bureau
** New Jersey Department of Labor

General Information
Township of Quinton
885 Route 49
PO Box 65
Quinton, NJ 08072
856-935-2325

Website	(county website)
Year of incorporation	1873
Land/water area (sq. miles)	24.17/0.37
Form of government	Township

Government
Legislative Districts
US Congressional	2
State Legislative	3

Local Officials, 2008
Mayor	Joseph Donelson
Manager/Admin	NA
Clerk	Marty Uzdanovics
Finance Dir	Diane Bowman
Tax Assessor	Joseph Harasta
Tax Collector	Alice Howell
Attorney	Gary Salber
Building	Wayne Serfass
Comm Dev/Planning	NA
Engineering	T&M Associates
Public Works	NA
Police Chief	NA
Fire Chief	Patrick Foster

Housing & Construction
Housing Units, 2000*
Total	1,133
Median rent	$668
Median SF home value	$101,300

Permits for New Residential Construction
	Units	Value
Total, 2007	6	$793,000
Single family	6	$793,000
Total, 2006	13	$1,678,000
Single family	13	$1,678,000

Real Property Valuation, 2007
	Parcels	Valuation
Total	1,726	$121,069,600
Vacant	338	4,200,100
Residential	829	84,064,900
Commercial	55	10,807,600
Industrial	0	0
Apartments	1	302,600
Farm land	352	3,454,000
Farm homestead	151	18,240,400

Average Property Value & Tax, 2007
Residential value	$104,393
Property tax	$3,630
Tax credit/rebate	$872

Public Library
No public municipal library

Library statistics, 2006
Population served	NA
Full-time/total staff	NA/NA

	Total	Per capita
Holdings	NA	NA
Revenues	NA	NA
Expenditures	NA	NA
Annual visits	NA	NA
Internet terminals/annual users	NA/NA	

Public Safety
Number of officers, 2006: 0

Crime
	2005	2006
Total crimes	43	45
Violent	2	3
Murder	0	0
Rape	0	0
Robbery	1	0
Aggravated assault	1	3
Non-violent	41	42
Burglary	21	16
Larceny	15	20
Vehicle theft	5	6
Domestic violence	15	9
Arson	2	0
Total crime rate	15.2	15.7
Violent	0.7	1.0
Non-violent	14.5	14.7

Public School District
(for school year 2006-07 except as noted)

Quinton Township School District
Robinson St, PO Box 365
Quinton, NJ 08072
856-935-2379

Chief School Admin	Donna Agnew
Number of schools	1
Grade plan	K-8
Enrollment	346
Attendance rate, '05-06	95.3%
Dropout rate	NA
Students per teacher	10.2
Per pupil expenditure	$11,736
Median faculty salary	$56,057
Median administrator salary	$70,000
Grade 12 enrollment	NA
High school graduation rate	NA

Assessment test results
(percent scoring at proficient or advanced level)
	Language	Math
NJASK-Grade 3	71.9%	90.6%
GEPA-Grade 8	83.8%	73.0%
HSPA-High School	NA	NA

SAT score averages
Pct tested	Math	Verbal	Writing
NA	NA	NA	NA

Teacher Qualifications
Avg. years of experience	17
Highly-qualified teachers one subject/all subjects	100%/100%
With emergency credentials	0.0%

No Child Left Behind
AYP, 2005-06 .... Meets Standards

Municipal Finance
State Aid Programs, 2008
Total aid	$367,416
CMPTRA	0
Energy tax receipts	348,418
Garden State Trust	16,131

General Budget, 2007
Total tax levy	$4,231,156
County levy	1,558,983
County taxes	1,525,728
County library	0
County health	0
County open space	33,255
School levy	2,357,472
Muni. levy	314,701
Misc. revenues	1,358,844

Taxes
	2005	2006	2007
General tax rate per $100	3.2	3.379	3.477
County equalization ratio	86.17	79.56	73.75
Net valuation taxable	$119,319,569	$120,065,300	$121,695,748
State equalized value	$149,974,320	$163,455,029	$147,448,365

Union County

Rahway City

Demographics & Socio-Economic Characteristics
(2000 US Census, except as noted)

Population
1980*	26,723
1990*	25,325
2000	26,500
Male	12,639
Female	13,861
2006 (estimate)*	27,843
Population density	6,978.2

Race & Hispanic Origin, 2000
Race
White	15,950
Black/African American	7,173
American Indian/Alaska Native	42
Asian	950
Native Hawaiian/Pacific Islander	14
Other race	1,489
Two or more races	882
Hispanic origin, total	3,675
Mexican	424
Puerto Rican	887
Cuban	216
Other Hispanic	2,148

Age & Nativity, 2000
Under 5 years	1,660
18 years and over	20,170
21 years and over	19,300
65 years and over	3,836
85 years and over	430
Median age	37.1
Native-born	21,947
Foreign-born	4,553

Educational Attainment, 2000
Population 25 years and over	18,140
Less than 9th grade	6.7%
High school grad or higher	81.5%
Bachelor's degree or higher	18.6%
Graduate degree	5.5%

Income & Poverty, 1999
Per capita income	$22,481
Median household income	$50,729
Median family income	$61,931
Persons in poverty	1,864
H'holds receiving public assistance	342
H'holds receiving social security	3,019

Households, 2000
Total households	10,028
With persons under 18	3,448
With persons over 65	2,883
Family households	6,727
Single-person households	2,806
Persons per household	2.63
Persons per family	3.24

Labor & Employment
Total civilian labor force, 2006**	14,427
Unemployment rate	5.2%
Total civilian labor force, 2000	13,495
Unemployment rate	6.6%

Employed persons 16 years and over by occupation, 2000
Managers & professionals	3,862
Service occupations	1,683
Sales & office occupations	3,924
Farming, fishing & forestry	0
Construction & maintenance	1,206
Production & transportation	1,930
Self-employed persons	427

* US Census Bureau
** New Jersey Department of Labor
§ State Fiscal Year July 1–June 30

See Introduction for an explanation of all data sources.

General Information
City of Rahway
1 City Hall Plz
Rahway, NJ 07065
732-827-2000

Website	www.cityofrahway.com
Year of incorporation	1858
Land/water area (sq. miles)	3.99/0.05
Form of government	Mayor-Council

Government

Legislative Districts
US Congressional	10
State Legislative	22

Local Officials, 2008
Mayor	James Kennedy
Manager	Peter A. Pelissier
Clerk	Jean Kuc
Finance Dir.	F. Ruggiero
Tax Assessor	William Marbach
Tax Collector	Sally DiRini
Attorney	Louis N. Rainone
Building	Richard Watkins
Planner	Lenore Slothower
Engineering	Ludwig Bohler
Public Works	Anthony Deige
Police Chief	John Rodger
Emerg/Fire Director	William Young

Housing & Construction

Housing Units, 2000*
Total	10,381
Median rent	$732
Median SF home value	$142,600

Permits for New Residential Construction
	Units	Value
Total, 2007	273	$22,724,538
Single family	35	$3,284,726
Total, 2006	368	$16,171,533
Single family	61	$6,381,602

Real Property Valuation, 2007
	Parcels	Valuation
Total	7,915	$1,513,679,700
Vacant	303	11,736,500
Residential	7,070	949,849,700
Commercial	379	129,920,800
Industrial	89	377,740,700
Apartments	74	44,432,000
Farm land	0	0
Farm homestead	0	0

Average Property Value & Tax, 2007
Residential value	$134,349
Property tax	$6,159
Tax credit/rebate	$1,067

Public Library
Rahway Public Library
2 City Hall Plaza
Rahway, NJ 07065
732-340-1551

Director . . . . Gail Miller

Library statistics, 2006
Population served	26,500
Full-time/total staff	7/17

	Total	Per capita
Holdings	103,961	3.92
Revenues	$1,517,404	$57.26
Expenditures	$1,720,834	$64.94
Annual visits	134,952	5.09
Internet terminals/annual users	27/14,623	

Taxes
	2005	2006	2007
General tax rate per $100	4.139	4.354	4.585
County equalization ratio	60.39	51.62	47.35
Net valuation taxable	$1,495,515,100	$1,502,865,300	$1,517,592,096
State equalized value	$2,684,946,320	$3,178,630,541	$3,538,069,996

Public Safety
Number of officers, 2006 80

Crime	2005	2006
Total crimes	640	711
Violent	89	79
Murder	0	1
Rape	2	3
Robbery	46	48
Aggravated assault	41	27
Non-violent	551	632
Burglary	95	117
Larceny	376	433
Vehicle theft	80	82
Domestic violence	676	612
Arson	5	5
Total crime rate	23.2	25.8
Violent	3.2	2.9
Non-violent	20.0	22.9

Public School District
(for school year 2006-07 except as noted)

Rahway School District
Rahway Middle School, Kline Pl
Rahway, NJ 07065
732-396-1020

Superintendent	Frank R. Buglione
Number of schools	6
Grade plan	K-12
Enrollment	3,911
Attendance rate, '05-06	93.7%
Dropout rate	3.0%
Students per teacher	11.7
Per pupil expenditure	$11,423
Median faculty salary	$52,345
Median administrator salary	$107,253
Grade 12 enrollment	242
High school graduation rate	87.5%

Assessment test results
(percent scoring at proficient or advanced level)
	Language	Math
NJASK-Grade 3	68.6%	77.7%
GEPA-Grade 8	61.4%	57.8%
HSPA-High School	80.8%	60.3%

SAT score averages
Pct tested	Math	Verbal	Writing
78%	440	443	440

Teacher Qualifications
Avg. years of experience	7
Highly-qualified teachers one subject/all subjects	98.5%/98.5%
With emergency credentials	0.4%

No Child Left Behind
AYP, 2005-06 . . . . Meets Standards

Municipal Finance§

State Aid Programs, 2008
Total aid	$4,882,498
CMPTRA	2,851,740
Energy tax receipts	2,030,758
Garden State Trust	0

General Budget, 2007
Total tax levy	$69,571,695
County levy	11,292,714
County taxes	10,807,050
County library	0
County health	0
County open space	485,663
School levy	32,703,374
Muni. levy	25,575,607
Misc. revenues	17,190,236

Ramsey Borough

Bergen County

Demographics & Socio-Economic Characteristics
(2000 US Census, except as noted)

Population
1980*	12,899
1990*	13,228
2000	14,351
Male	6,928
Female	7,423
2006 (estimate)*	14,775
Population density	2,657.4

Race & Hispanic Origin, 2000
Race
White	13,148
Black/African American	112
American Indian/Alaska Native	14
Asian	840
Native Hawaiian/Pacific Islander	1
Other race	78
Two or more races	158
Hispanic origin, total	420
Mexican	82
Puerto Rican	81
Cuban	36
Other Hispanic	221

Age & Nativity, 2000
Under 5 years	1,088
18 years and over	10,474
21 years and over	10,173
65 years and over	1,614
85 years and over	171
Median age	38.6
Native-born	12,641
Foreign-born	1,710

Educational Attainment, 2000
Population 25 years and over	9,729
Less than 9th grade	2.0%
High school grad or higher	95.5%
Bachelor's degree or higher	54.5%
Graduate degree	19.9%

Income & Poverty, 1999
Per capita income	$41,964
Median household income	$88,187
Median family income	$104,036
Persons in poverty	276
H'holds receiving public assistance	62
H'holds receiving social security	1,193

Households, 2000
Total households	5,313
With persons under 18	2,054
With persons over 65	1,185
Family households	3,945
Single-person households	1,200
Persons per household	2.68
Persons per family	3.18

Labor & Employment
Total civilian labor force, 2006**	7,940
Unemployment rate	2.7%
Total civilian labor force, 2000	7,510
Unemployment rate	3.0%

Employed persons 16 years and over by occupation, 2000
Managers & professionals	3,917
Service occupations	505
Sales & office occupations	2,139
Farming, fishing & forestry	6
Construction & maintenance	411
Production & transportation	310
Self-employed persons	383

* US Census Bureau
** New Jersey Department of Labor

General Information
Borough of Ramsey
33 N Central Ave
Ramsey, NJ 07446
201-825-3400

Website	www.ramseynj.com
Year of incorporation	1908
Land/water area (sq. miles)	5.56/0.05
Form of government	Borough

Government
Legislative Districts
US Congressional	5
State Legislative	39

Local Officials, 2008
Mayor	Christopher Botta
Manager	Nicholas Saros
Clerk	Meredith Bendian
Finance Dir	Richard Mathieson
Tax Assessor	Angela Mattiace
Tax Collector	NA
Attorney	Peter Scandariato
Building	Robert Connell
Comm Dev/Planning	NA
Engineering	Harold Reed
Public Works	NA
Police Chief	Bryan Gurney
Emerg/Fire Director	Mike Scalione

Housing & Construction
Housing Units, 2000*
Total	5,400
Median rent	$1,120
Median SF home value	$329,700

Permits for New Residential Construction
	Units	Value
Total, 2007	29	$7,060,402
Single family	29	$7,060,402
Total, 2006	36	$8,101,646
Single family	36	$8,101,646

Real Property Valuation, 2007
	Parcels	Valuation
Total	5,482	$2,762,404,000
Vacant	186	35,772,800
Residential	5,046	2,155,684,500
Commercial	217	432,632,100
Industrial	27	123,671,100
Apartments	6	14,643,500
Farm land	0	0
Farm homestead	0	0

Average Property Value & Tax, 2007
Residential value	$427,207
Property tax	$9,607
Tax credit/rebate	$1,280

Public Library
Ramsey Free Public Library
30 Wyckoff Ave
Ramsey, NJ 07446
201-327-1445

Director.................Wendy B. Bloom

Library statistics, 2006
Population served	14,351
Full-time/total staff	4/7

	Total	Per capita
Holdings	101,367	7.06
Revenues	$1,125,221	$78.41
Expenditures	$963,279	$67.12
Annual visits	127,720	8.90
Internet terminals/annual users		9/19,780

Public Safety
Number of officers, 2006 33

Crime	2005	2006
Total crimes	154	182
Violent	9	15
Murder	0	1
Rape	0	0
Robbery	2	3
Aggravated assault	7	11
Non-violent	145	167
Burglary	11	19
Larceny	121	139
Vehicle theft	13	9
Domestic violence	68	69
Arson	0	1
Total crime rate	10.5	12.5
Violent	0.6	1.0
Non-violent	9.9	11.5

Public School District
(for school year 2006-07 except as noted)

Ramsey School District
266 E Main St
Ramsey, NJ 07446
201-785-2300

Superintendent	Roy Montesano
Number of schools	5
Grade plan	K-12
Enrollment	3,097
Attendance rate, '05-06	96.2%
Dropout rate	0.1%
Students per teacher	10.7
Per pupil expenditure	$13,792
Median faculty salary	$52,904
Median administrator salary	$124,847
Grade 12 enrollment	182
High school graduation rate	98.9%

Assessment test results
(percent scoring at proficient or advanced level)
	Language	Math
NJASK-Grade 3	97.8%	100.0%
GEPA-Grade 8	93.5%	90.5%
HSPA-High School	97.6%	95.2%

SAT score averages
Pct tested	Math	Verbal	Writing
97%	582	559	548

Teacher Qualifications
Avg. years of experience	8
Highly-qualified teachers one subject/all subjects	99.5%/99.5%
With emergency credentials	0.0%

No Child Left Behind
AYP, 2005-06 .... Meets Standards

Municipal Finance
State Aid Programs, 2008
Total aid	$1,987,354
CMPTRA	208,670
Energy tax receipts	1,778,684
Garden State Trust	0

General Budget, 2007
Total tax levy	$62,299,435
County levy	6,545,669
County taxes	6,184,786
County library	0
County health	0
County open space	360,884
School levy	42,061,181
Muni. levy	13,692,585
Misc. revenues	7,405,432

Taxes	2005	2006	2007
General tax rate per $100	2.04	2.14	2.25
County equalization ratio	95.16	84.78	76.99
Net valuation taxable	$2,725,566,472	$2,741,214,900	$2,770,445,552
State equalized value	$3,214,869,630	$3,568,621,487	$3,821,936,347

Morris County
Randolph Township

Demographics & Socio-Economic Characteristics
(2000 US Census, except as noted)

Population
1980*	17,828
1990*	19,974
2000	24,847
Male	12,317
Female	12,530
2006 (estimate)*	25,736
Population density	1,227.9

Race & Hispanic Origin, 2000
Race
White	21,293
Black/African American	572
American Indian/Alaska Native	15
Asian	2,272
Native Hawaiian/Pacific Islander	5
Other race	326
Two or more races	364
Hispanic origin, total	1,208
Mexican	130
Puerto Rican	257
Cuban	81
Other Hispanic	740

Age & Nativity, 2000
Under 5 years	1,885
18 years and over	17,469
21 years and over	16,902
65 years and over	1,817
85 years and over	172
Median age	36.5
Native-born	20,849
Foreign-born	3,998

Educational Attainment, 2000
Population 25 years and over	16,253
Less than 9th grade	1.3%
High school grad or higher	95.7%
Bachelor's degree or higher	59.4%
Graduate degree	25.7%

Income & Poverty, 1999
Per capita income	$43,072
Median household income	$97,589
Median family income	$115,722
Persons in poverty	356
H'holds receiving public assistance	49
H'holds receiving social security	1,398

Households, 2000
Total households	8,679
With persons under 18	3,929
With persons over 65	1,341
Family households	6,806
Single-person households	1,562
Persons per household	2.86
Persons per family	3.28

Labor & Employment
Total civilian labor force, 2006**	14,308
Unemployment rate	3.0%
Total civilian labor force, 2000	13,155
Unemployment rate	2.2%

Employed persons 16 years and over by occupation, 2000
Managers & professionals	7,575
Service occupations	957
Sales & office occupations	3,019
Farming, fishing & forestry	0
Construction & maintenance	584
Production & transportation	731
Self-employed persons	1,013

* US Census Bureau
** New Jersey Department of Labor

See Introduction for an explanation of all data sources.

General Information
Township of Randolph
502 Millbrook Ave
Randolph, NJ 07869
973-989-7100

Website	www.randolfnj.org
Year of incorporation	1806
Land/water area (sq. miles)	20.96/0.12
Form of government	Council-Manager

Government
Legislative Districts
US Congressional	11
State Legislative	25

Local Officials, 2008
Mayor	Allen Napoliello
Manager	John Lovell
Clerk	Donna M. Luciani
Finance Dir	Michael Soccio
Tax Assessor	Barbara Gothie
Tax Collector	Lisa Combes
Attorney	Ed Buzak
Building	Frank Howard
Planning	Darren Carney
Engineering	Steve Bury
Public Works	Bill Kerwick
Police Chief	Dean Kazaba
Emerg/Fire Director	Mark Absalon

Housing & Construction
Housing Units, 2000*
Total	8,903
Median rent	$875
Median SF home value	$329,800

Permits for New Residential Construction
	Units	Value
Total, 2007	6	$1,457,000
Single family	4	$1,333,000
Total, 2006	10	$3,200,800
Single family	10	$3,200,800

Real Property Valuation, 2007
	Parcels	Valuation
Total	7,915	$2,900,992,400
Vacant	336	35,793,800
Residential	7,189	2,400,450,300
Commercial	258	238,233,900
Industrial	50	114,961,900
Apartments	17	105,816,400
Farm land	42	185,300
Farm homestead	23	5,550,800

Average Property Value & Tax, 2007
Residential value	$333,611
Property tax	$9,804
Tax credit/rebate	$1,184

Public Library
Randolph Township Public Library
28 Calais Rd
Randolph, NJ 07869
973-895-3556

Director ... Anita S. Freeman

Library statistics, 2006
Population served	24,847
Full-time/total staff	4/9

	Total	Per capita
Holdings	106,873	4.30
Revenues	$1,522,738	$61.28
Expenditures	$1,521,171	$61.22
Annual visits	161,242	6.49
Internet terminals/annual users	21/62,400	

Taxes
	2005	2006	2007
General tax rate per $100	2.69	2.83	2.94
County equalization ratio	73.3	66.19	59.85
Net valuation taxable	$2,855,284,138	$2,878,129,200	$2,904,754,223
State equalized value	$4,313,769,660	$4,813,718,699	$4,978,028,627

Public Safety
Number of officers, 2006 ... 40

Crime	2005	2006
Total crimes	214	212
Violent	13	8
Murder	1	0
Rape	0	0
Robbery	2	6
Aggravated assault	10	2
Non-violent	201	204
Burglary	28	24
Larceny	168	170
Vehicle theft	5	10
Domestic violence	206	213
Arson	1	1
Total crime rate	8.3	8.2
Violent	0.5	0.3
Non-violent	7.8	7.9

Public School District
(for school year 2006-07 except as noted)

Randolph Township School District
25 School House Rd
Randolph, NJ 07869
973-361-0808

Superintendent	Max R. Riley
Number of schools	6
Grade plan	K-12
Enrollment	5,535
Attendance rate, '05-06	95.6%
Dropout rate	0.4%
Students per teacher	11.5
Per pupil expenditure	$11,477
Median faculty salary	$57,330
Median administrator salary	$104,083
Grade 12 enrollment	376
High school graduation rate	97.7%

Assessment test results
(percent scoring at proficient or advanced level)

	Language	Math
NJASK-Grade 3	95.9%	97.1%
GEPA-Grade 8	91.0%	81.3%
HSPA-High School	94.9%	90.0%

SAT score averages
Pct tested	Math	Verbal	Writing
98%	554	534	533

Teacher Qualifications
Avg. years of experience	9
Highly-qualified teachers one subject/all subjects	100%/100%
With emergency credentials	0.3%

No Child Left Behind
AYP, 2005-06 ... Meets Standards

Municipal Finance
State Aid Programs, 2008
Total aid	$2,412,249
CMPTRA	576,093
Energy tax receipts	1,819,612
Garden State Trust	0

General Budget, 2007
Total tax levy	$85,366,958
County levy	11,589,943
County taxes	9,270,686
County library	0
County health	0
County open space	2,319,257
School levy	57,518,177
Muni. levy	16,258,839
Misc. revenues	17,499,332

©2008 Information Publications, Inc. All rights reserved. Photocopying prohibited. For additional copies, contact the publisher at www.informationpublications.com or (877)544-INFO (4636)

The New Jersey Municipal Data Book

Raritan Borough
Somerset County

Demographics & Socio-Economic Characteristics
(2000 US Census, except as noted)

Population
1980*	6,128
1990*	5,798
2000	6,338
Male	3,042
Female	3,296
2006 (estimate)*	6,427
Population density	3,150.5

Race & Hispanic Origin, 2000
Race
White	5,561
Black/African American	59
American Indian/Alaska Native	5
Asian	518
Native Hawaiian/Pacific Islander	10
Other race	104
Two or more races	81
Hispanic origin, total	533
Mexican	43
Puerto Rican	63
Cuban	13
Other Hispanic	414

Age & Nativity, 2000
Under 5 years	460
18 years and over	4,922
21 years and over	4,757
65 years and over	1,026
85 years and over	128
Median age	37.6
Native-born	4,858
Foreign-born	1,480

Educational Attainment, 2000
Population 25 years and over	4,557
Less than 9th grade	10.0%
High school grad or higher	77.3%
Bachelor's degree or higher	27.0%
Graduate degree	9.1%

Income & Poverty, 1999
Per capita income	$26,420
Median household income	$51,122
Median family income	$59,962
Persons in poverty	406
H'holds receiving public assistance	47
H'holds receiving social security	715

Households, 2000
Total households	2,556
With persons under 18	817
With persons over 65	758
Family households	1,671
Single-person households	740
Persons per household	2.48
Persons per family	3.08

Labor & Employment
Total civilian labor force, 2006**	3,645
Unemployment rate	5.0%
Total civilian labor force, 2000	3,217
Unemployment rate	4.3%

Employed persons 16 years and over by occupation, 2000
Managers & professionals	1,132
Service occupations	457
Sales & office occupations	837
Farming, fishing & forestry	0
Construction & maintenance	271
Production & transportation	382
Self-employed persons	116

* US Census Bureau
** New Jersey Department of Labor

General Information
Borough of Raritan
22 1st St
Raritan, NJ 08869
908-231-1300

Website	www.raritanboro.org
Year of incorporation	1948
Land/water area (sq. miles)	2.04/0.00
Form of government	Borough

Government
Legislative Districts
US Congressional	11
State Legislative	16

Local Officials, 2008
Mayor	Jo-Ann Liptak
Manager	Daniel Jaxel
Clerk	Pamela Huefner
Finance Dir.	Carolyn Gara
Tax Assessor	Glen Stives
Tax Collector	Carolyn Gara
Attorney	Paul Rizzo
Building	Louis Gara
Comm Dev/Planning	NA
Engineering	Stanley Schrek
Public Works	Danny Laverde
Police Chief	(vacant)
Emerg/Fire Director	Carl Memoli

Housing & Construction
Housing Units, 2000*
Total	2,644
Median rent	$801
Median SF home value	$182,500

Permits for New Residential Construction
	Units	Value
Total, 2007	151	$15,217,685
Single family	5	$738,685
Total, 2006	133	$13,526,319
Single family	6	$886,819

Real Property Valuation, 2007
	Parcels	Valuation
Total	2,141	$1,140,143,929
Vacant	42	10,395,650
Residential	1,905	606,998,134
Commercial	175	215,552,677
Industrial	15	305,298,868
Apartments	4	1,898,600
Farm land	0	0
Farm homestead	0	0

Average Property Value & Tax, 2007
Residential value	$318,634
Property tax	$6,376
Tax credit/rebate	$1,038

Public Library
Raritan Public Library
54 E Somerset St
Raritan, NJ 08869
908-725-0413

Director: Jacqueline Widows

Library statistics, 2006
Population served	6,338
Full-time/total staff	0/2

	Total	Per capita
Holdings	51,579	8.14
Revenues	$429,190	$67.72
Expenditures	$239,402	$37.77
Annual visits	4,922	0.78
Internet terminals/annual users	4/1,917	

Taxes
	2005	2006	2007
General tax rate per $100	1.76	1.83	2.01
County equalization ratio	104.86	97.64	90.69
Net valuation taxable	$1,130,418,017	$1,148,334,789	$1,141,321,495
State equalized value	$1,157,740,697	$1,267,910,270	$1,255,461,316

Public Safety
Number of officers, 2006: 19

Crime	2005	2006
Total crimes	139	125
Violent	7	9
Murder	0	0
Rape	1	1
Robbery	2	4
Aggravated assault	4	4
Non-violent	132	116
Burglary	23	29
Larceny	105	83
Vehicle theft	4	4
Domestic violence	120	96
Arson	0	0
Total crime rate	21.7	19.6
Violent	1.1	1.4
Non-violent	20.6	18.2

Public School District
(for school year 2006-07 except as noted)

Bridgewater-Raritan Regional School Dist.
836 Newmans Ln, PO Box 6030
Bridgewater, NJ 08807
908-685-2777

Superintendent	Michael Schilder
Number of schools	22
Grade plan	K-12
Enrollment	9,176
Attendance rate, '05-06	96.1%
Dropout rate	0.5%
Students per teacher	10.4
Per pupil expenditure	$13,025
Median faculty salary	$51,364
Median administrator salary	$120,072
Grade 12 enrollment	644
High school graduation rate	98.6%

Assessment test results
(percent scoring at proficient or advanced level)
	Language	Math
NJASK-Grade 3	86.9%	94.2%
GEPA-Grade 8	88.6%	83.9%
HSPA-High School	93.3%	87.2%

SAT score averages
Pct tested	Math	Verbal	Writing
94%	568	529	529

Teacher Qualifications
Avg. years of experience	7
Highly-qualified teachers one subject/all subjects	99.5%/99.5%
With emergency credentials	0.3%

No Child Left Behind
AYP, 2005-06: Meets Standards

Municipal Finance
State Aid Programs, 2008
Total aid	$749,892
CMPTRA	178,620
Energy tax receipts	571,272
Garden State Trust	0

General Budget, 2007
Total tax levy	$22,836,772
County levy	3,857,651
County taxes	3,476,882
County library	0
County health	0
County open space	380,770
School levy	12,726,330
Muni. levy	6,252,791
Misc. revenues	2,769,928

Hunterdon County

Raritan Township

Demographics & Socio-Economic Characteristics
(2000 US Census, except as noted)

Population
1980*	8,292
1990*	15,616
2000	19,809
Male	9,606
Female	10,203
2006 (estimate)*	22,720
Population density	600.4

Race & Hispanic Origin, 2000
Race
White	18,466
Black/African American	244
American Indian/Alaska Native	17
Asian	693
Native Hawaiian/Pacific Islander	2
Other race	135
Two or more races	252
Hispanic origin, total	552
Mexican	86
Puerto Rican	173
Cuban	80
Other Hispanic	213

Age & Nativity, 2000
Under 5 years	1,431
18 years and over	14,010
21 years and over	13,570
65 years and over	1,770
85 years and over	251
Median age	37.4
Native-born	18,188
Foreign-born	1,621

Educational Attainment, 2000
Population 25 years and over	13,086
Less than 9th grade	1.8%
High school grad or higher	94.3%
Bachelor's degree or higher	48.3%
Graduate degree	17.7%

Income & Poverty, 1999
Per capita income	$38,919
Median household income	$85,996
Median family income	$96,336
Persons in poverty	399
H'holds receiving public assistance	69
H'holds receiving social security	1,169

Households, 2000
Total households	6,939
With persons under 18	3,083
With persons over 65	1,167
Family households	5,389
Single-person households	1,263
Persons per household	2.81
Persons per family	3.24

Labor & Employment
Total civilian labor force, 2006**	11,916
Unemployment rate	1.8%
Total civilian labor force, 2000	10,655
Unemployment rate	1.4%

Employed persons 16 years and over by occupation, 2000
Managers & professionals	5,508
Service occupations	945
Sales & office occupations	2,628
Farming, fishing & forestry	17
Construction & maintenance	686
Production & transportation	717
Self-employed persons	811

‡ Main library for county
* US Census Bureau
** New Jersey Department of Labor

See Introduction for an explanation of all data sources.

General Information
Township of Raritan
1 Municipal Dr
Flemington, NJ 08822
908-806-6100

Website	www.raritan-township.com
Year of incorporation	1838
Land/water area (sq. miles)	37.84/0.07
Form of government	Township

Government
Legislative Districts
US Congressional	7
State Legislative	23

Local Officials, 2008
Mayor	John W. King
Manager	Allan Pietrefesa
Clerk	Dorothy Gooditis
Finance Dir	Allan Pietrefesa
Tax Assessor	Marianne Busher
Tax Collector	Betty Kopp
Attorney	John Belardo
Building	Peter Ball
Planning	James Humphries
Engineering	Frederick Coppola
Public Works	Dirk Struening
Police Chief	Glenn S. Tabasko
Emerg/Fire Director	Mark Bishop

Housing & Construction
Housing Units, 2000*
Total	7,094
Median rent	$971
Median SF home value	$248,300

Permits for New Residential Construction
	Units	Value
Total, 2007	18	$4,138,604
Single family	18	$4,138,604
Total, 2006	49	$10,562,338
Single family	45	$10,207,538

Real Property Valuation, 2007
	Parcels	Valuation
Total	9,100	$4,282,470,800
Vacant	611	89,912,800
Residential	7,736	3,470,510,000
Commercial	272	517,905,600
Industrial	28	113,115,500
Apartments	5	12,686,700
Farm land	292	3,911,700
Farm homestead	156	74,428,500

Average Property Value & Tax, 2007
Residential value	$449,181
Property tax	$8,804
Tax credit/rebate	$1,115

Public Library
Hunterdon County Library‡
314 State Highway 12, Bldg #3
Flemington, NJ 08822
908-788-1444

Director: Mark Titus

County Library statistics, 2006
Population served	112,726
Full-time/total staff	19/53

	Total	Per capita
Holdings	459,749	4.08
Revenues	$7,054,381	$62.58
Expenditures	$5,973,091	$52.99
Annual visits	567,012	5.03
Internet terminals/annual users	24/42,017	

Public Safety
Number of officers, 2006	37

Crime	2005	2006
Total crimes	223	202
Violent	27	8
Murder	5	0
Rape	0	2
Robbery	2	3
Aggravated assault	20	3
Non-violent	196	194
Burglary	2	19
Larceny	12	164
Vehicle theft	0	11
Domestic violence	5	165
Arson	0	0
Total crime rate	10.0	8.9
Violent	1.2	0.4
Non-violent	8.8	8.6

Public School District
(for school year 2006-07 except as noted)

Flemington-Raritan Regional School Dist.
50 Court St
Flemington, NJ 08822
908-284-7575

Superintendent	Jack Farr
Number of schools	12
Grade plan	K-8
Enrollment	3,587
Attendance rate, '05-06	96.2%
Dropout rate	NA
Students per teacher	10.5
Per pupil expenditure	$12,736
Median faculty salary	$49,870
Median administrator salary	$108,184
Grade 12 enrollment	NA
High school graduation rate	NA

Assessment test results
(percent scoring at proficient or advanced level)
	Language	Math
NJASK-Grade 3	93.9%	96.4%
GEPA-Grade 8	89.1%	83.7%
HSPA-High School	NA	NA

SAT score averages
Pct tested	Math	Verbal	Writing
NA	NA	NA	NA

Teacher Qualifications
Avg. years of experience	11
Highly-qualified teachers one subject/all subjects	99.5%/99.5%
With emergency credentials	0.0%

No Child Left Behind
AYP, 2005-06 . . . . Meets Standards

Municipal Finance
State Aid Programs, 2008
Total aid	$2,811,370
CMPTRA	265,471
Energy tax receipts	2,540,926
Garden State Trust	4,973

General Budget, 2007
Total tax levy	$84,073,082
County levy	15,352,138
County taxes	12,848,211
County library	1,118,051
County health	0
County open space	1,385,875
School levy	58,064,946
Muni. levy	10,655,998
Misc. revenues	7,474,000

Taxes	2005	2006	2007
General tax rate per $100	3.21	3.44	1.96
County equalization ratio	58.25	53.98	93.08
Net valuation taxable	$2,195,501,325	$2,250,637,500	$4,289,462,305
State equalized value	$3,611,615,932	$4,156,262,795	$4,336,655,644

Readington Township
Hunterdon County

Demographics & Socio-Economic Characteristics
(2000 US Census, except as noted)

Population
1980*	10,855
1990*	13,400
2000	15,803
Male	7,782
Female	8,021
2006 (estimate)*	16,295
Population density	341.7

Race & Hispanic Origin, 2000
Race
White	15,035
Black/African American	120
American Indian/Alaska Native	10
Asian	405
Native Hawaiian/Pacific Islander	0
Other race	84
Two or more races	149
Hispanic origin, total	324
Mexican	34
Puerto Rican	103
Cuban	35
Other Hispanic	152

Age & Nativity, 2000
Under 5 years	1,171
18 years and over	11,618
21 years and over	11,279
65 years and over	1,542
85 years and over	147
Median age	39.0
Native-born	14,684
Foreign-born	1,119

Educational Attainment, 2000
Population 25 years and over	10,767
Less than 9th grade	1.4%
High school grad or higher	94.6%
Bachelor's degree or higher	48.2%
Graduate degree	18.8%

Income & Poverty, 1999
Per capita income	$41,000
Median household income	$95,356
Median family income	$106,343
Persons in poverty	255
H'holds receiving public assistance	72
H'holds receiving social security	1,174

Households, 2000
Total households	5,676
With persons under 18	2,221
With persons over 65	1,137
Family households	4,413
Single-person households	1,032
Persons per household	2.77
Persons per family	3.18

Labor & Employment
Total civilian labor force, 2006**	9,806
Unemployment rate	2.9%
Total civilian labor force, 2000	8,784
Unemployment rate	2.3%

Employed persons 16 years and over by occupation, 2000
Managers & professionals	4,476
Service occupations	565
Sales & office occupations	2,320
Farming, fishing & forestry	17
Construction & maintenance	532
Production & transportation	676
Self-employed persons	517

‡ Branch of county library
* US Census Bureau
** New Jersey Department of Labor

General Information
Township of Readington
509 County Road 523
Whitehouse Station, NJ 08889
908-534-4051

Website	www.readingtontwp.org
Year of incorporation	1730
Land/water area (sq. miles)	47.69/0.12
Form of government	Township

Government
Legislative Districts
US Congressional	7
State Legislative	23

Local Officials, 2008
Mayor	Thomas Aurema
Manager	Vita Mekovetz
Clerk	Vita Mekovetz
Finance Dir.	Vita Mekovetz
Tax Assessor	Mary Mastro
Tax Collector	Bonnie Holborow
Attorney	Sharon Dragan
Building	Michael Kovonuk
Comm Dev/Planning	NA
Engineering	Clay McEldowney
Public Works	Scott Jesseman
Police Chief	James Paganessi
Fire/Emergency Dir.	NA

Housing & Construction
Housing Units, 2000*
Total	5,794
Median rent	$937
Median SF home value	$289,700

Permits for New Residential Construction
	Units	Value
Total, 2007	40	$7,557,090
Single family	14	$5,409,090
Total, 2006	14	$12,720,328
Single family	14	$12,720,328

Real Property Valuation, 2007
	Parcels	Valuation
Total	7,092	$2,815,662,874
Vacant	476	36,031,500
Residential	5,529	2,137,249,000
Commercial	255	479,132,100
Industrial	15	21,709,500
Apartments	4	2,067,600
Farm land	487	4,665,174
Farm homestead	326	134,808,000

Average Property Value & Tax, 2007
Residential value	$388,054
Property tax	$9,633
Tax credit/rebate	$1,278

Public Library
Readington Township Library‡
105 Route 523
Whitehouse Station, NJ 08889
908-534-4421

Branch Librarian............ Karen Konn

Library statistics, 2006
see Hunterdon County profile for library system statistics

Public Safety
Number of officers, 2006 26

Crime
	2005	2006
Total crimes	140	167
Violent	5	14
Murder	0	0
Rape	0	3
Robbery	1	1
Aggravated assault	4	10
Non-violent	135	153
Burglary	37	35
Larceny	149	116
Vehicle theft	10	2
Domestic violence	164	64
Arson	1	4
Total crime rate	8.5	10.2
Violent	0.3	0.9
Non-violent	8.2	9.4

Public School District
(for school year 2006-07 except as noted)

Readington Township School District
52 Reddington Rd, PO Box 807
Whitehouse Station, NJ 08889
908-534-2195

Superintendent	Jorden Schiff
Number of schools	4
Grade plan	K-8
Enrollment	2,234
Attendance rate, '05-06	97.4%
Dropout rate	NA
Students per teacher	10.2
Per pupil expenditure	$13,061
Median faculty salary	$48,040
Median administrator salary	$104,500
Grade 12 enrollment	NA
High school graduation rate	NA

Assessment test results
(percent scoring at proficient or advanced level)
	Language	Math
NJASK-Grade 3	95.4%	96.6%
GEPA-Grade 8	88.8%	93.0%
HSPA-High School	NA	NA

SAT score averages
Pct tested	Math	Verbal	Writing
NA	NA	NA	NA

Teacher Qualifications
Avg. years of experience	9
Highly-qualified teachers one subject/all subjects	98.0%/98.0%
With emergency credentials	0.0%

No Child Left Behind
AYP, 2005-06 .... Meets Standards

Municipal Finance
State Aid Programs, 2008
Total aid	$1,885,540
CMPTRA	192,592
Energy tax receipts	1,686,901
Garden State Trust	6,047

General Budget, 2007
Total tax levy	$70,025,503
County levy	12,896,355
County taxes	10,792,479
County library	939,203
County health	0
County open space	1,164,673
School levy	46,871,425
Muni. levy	10,257,723
Misc. revenues	7,734,426

Taxes
	2005	2006	2007
General tax rate per $100	2.21	2.38	2.49
County equalization ratio	86.62	79.62	72.37
Net valuation taxable	$2,796,354,190	$2,813,339,275	$2,820,911,243
State equalized value	$3,282,105,857	$3,619,595,137	$3,831,917,130

Monmouth County
Red Bank Borough

Demographics & Socio-Economic Characteristics
(2000 US Census, except as noted)

Population
- 1980* 12,031
- 1990* 10,636
- 2000 11,844
  - Male 5,670
  - Female 6,174
- 2006 (estimate)* 11,850
- Population density 6,657.3

Race & Hispanic Origin, 2000
Race
- White 8,077
- Black/African American 2,375
- American Indian/Alaska Native 41
- Asian 259
- Native Hawaiian/Pacific Islander ... 10
- Other race 797
- Two or more races 285
- Hispanic origin, total 2,027
  - Mexican 1,171
  - Puerto Rican 296
  - Cuban 24
  - Other Hispanic 536

Age & Nativity, 2000
- Under 5 years 682
- 18 years and over 9,770
- 21 years and over 9,376
- 65 years and over 2,173
- 85 years and over 479
- Median age 37.5
- Native-born 10,073
- Foreign-born 1,771

Educational Attainment, 2000
- Population 25 years and over 8,737
- Less than 9th grade 8.7%
- High school grad or higher 81.6%
- Bachelor's degree or higher 31.9%
- Graduate degree 10.6%

Income & Poverty, 1999
- Per capita income $26,265
- Median household income $47,282
- Median family income $63,333
- Persons in poverty 1,363
- H'holds receiving public assistance .. 89
- H'holds receiving social security .. 1,582

Households, 2000
- Total households 5,201
  - With persons under 18 1,126
  - With persons over 65 1,478
  - Family households 2,504
  - Single-person households 2,233
- Persons per household 2.20
- Persons per family 2.99

Labor & Employment
- Total civilian labor force, 2006** .. 6,825
  - Unemployment rate 5.6%
- Total civilian labor force, 2000 .. 6,354
  - Unemployment rate 5.7%

Employed persons 16 years and over by occupation, 2000
- Managers & professionals 2,194
- Service occupations 1,166
- Sales & office occupations 1,788
- Farming, fishing & forestry 10
- Construction & maintenance 388
- Production & transportation 444
- Self-employed persons 333

* US Census Bureau
** New Jersey Department of Labor

See Introduction for an explanation of all data sources.

General Information
Borough of Red Bank
90 Monmouth St
Red Bank, NJ 07701
732-530-2740
- Website .... www.redbanknj.org
- Year of incorporation 1908
- Land/water area (sq. miles) 1.78/0.37
- Form of government .... Borough

Government
Legislative Districts
- US Congressional 6
- State Legislative 12

Local Officials, 2008
- Mayor .... Pasquale Menna
- Manager .... Stanley Sickels
- Clerk .... Carol Vivona
- Finance Dir .... Frank Mason
- Tax Assessor .... Mitchell Ellias
- Tax Collector .... Dale Connor
- Attorney .... Kenneth Pringle
- Building .... James Williams
- Planning .... Donna Barr
- Engineering ...... Richard Kosenski
- Public Works .... Gary Watson
- Police Chief .... Mark Fitzgerald
- Fire Chief .... Noel Blackwood (Vol)

Housing & Construction
Housing Units, 2000*
- Total 5,450
- Median rent $813
- Median SF home value $178,900

Permits for New Residential Construction

	Units	Value
Total, 2007	32	$5,556,043
Single family	7	$859,633
Total, 2006	53	$9,568,206
Single family	8	$1,114,667

Real Property Valuation, 2007

	Parcels	Valuation
Total	4,044	$2,228,466,300
Vacant	97	20,091,700
Residential	3,326	1,346,966,100
Commercial	542	659,393,500
Industrial	52	54,245,000
Apartments	27	147,770,000
Farm land	0	0
Farm homestead	0	0

Average Property Value & Tax, 2007
- Residential value $404,981
- Property tax $6,237
- Tax credit/rebate $1,076

Public Library
Red Bank Public Library
84 W Front St
Red Bank, NJ 07701
732-842-0690
- Director .... Deborah Griffin-Sadel

Library statistics, 2006
- Population served 11,844
- Full-time/total staff 3/7

	Total	Per capita
Holdings	47,676	4.03
Revenues	$813,236	$68.66
Expenditures	$655,162	$55.32
Annual visits	44,944	3.79
Internet terminals/annual users	12/9,191	

Public Safety
- Number of officers, 2006 41

Crime	2005	2006
Total crimes	297	377
Violent	29	50
Murder	0	0
Rape	2	5
Robbery	13	27
Aggravated assault	14	18
Non-violent	268	327
Burglary	18	36
Larceny	236	279
Vehicle theft	14	12
Domestic violence	132	143
Arson	0	0
Total crime rate	24.9	31.7
Violent	2.4	4.2
Non-violent	22.4	27.5

Public School District
(for school year 2006-07 except as noted)

Red Bank School District
76 Branch Ave
Red Bank, NJ 07701
732-758-1507

- Superintendent .... Laura C. Morana
- Number of schools 2
- Grade plan K-8
- Enrollment 857
- Attendance rate, '05-06 .... 95.2%
- Dropout rate .... NA
- Students per teacher 10.2
- Per pupil expenditure $13,411
- Median faculty salary $46,380
- Median administrator salary ... $98,500
- Grade 12 enrollment .... NA
- High school graduation rate .... NA

Assessment test results
(percent scoring at proficient or advanced level)

	Language	Math
NJASK-Grade 3	68.5%	79.3%
GEPA-Grade 8	51.0%	50.9%
HSPA-High School	NA	NA

SAT score averages

Pct tested	Math	Verbal	Writing
NA	NA	NA	NA

Teacher Qualifications
- Avg. years of experience 7
- Highly-qualified teachers
  - one subject/all subjects 100%/100%
- With emergency credentials 0.0%

No Child Left Behind
- AYP, 2005-06 .... Meets Standards

Municipal Finance
State Aid Programs, 2008
- Total aid $2,588,129
  - CMPTRA 329,770
  - Energy tax receipts 2,258,359
  - Garden State Trust 0

General Budget, 2007
- Total tax levy $34,476,987
  - County levy 5,629,004
    - County taxes 5,297,943
    - County library 0
    - County health 0
    - County open space 331,061
  - School levy 20,251,974
  - Muni. levy 8,596,010
- Misc. revenues 11,639,773

Taxes	2005	2006	2007
General tax rate per $100	3.223	3.428	1.541
County equalization ratio	61.22	50.44	102.35
Net valuation taxable	$965,104,265	$968,840,300	$2,238,531,929
State equalized value	$1,913,370,866	$2,145,416,879	$2,274,537,024

Ridgefield Borough
Bergen County

Demographics & Socio-Economic Characteristics
(2000 US Census, except as noted)

Population
1900*	10,294
1990*	9,996
2000	10,830
Male	5,240
Female	5,590
2006 (estimate)*	10,996
Population density	4,213.0

Race & Hispanic Origin, 2000
Race
White	8,217
Black/African American	83
American Indian/Alaska Native	9
Asian	1,887
Native Hawaiian/Pacific Islander	4
Other race	379
Two or more races	251
Hispanic origin, total	1,494
Mexican	30
Puerto Rican	244
Cuban	361
Other Hispanic	859

Age & Nativity, 2000
Under 5 years	567
18 years and over	8,465
21 years and over	8,192
65 years and over	1,853
85 years and over	230
Median age	39.5
Native-born	7,184
Foreign-born	3,646

Educational Attainment, 2000
Population 25 years and over	7,737
Less than 9th grade	7.3%
High school grad or higher	78.8%
Bachelor's degree or higher	26.0%
Graduate degree	6.7%

Income & Poverty, 1999
Per capita income	$25,558
Median household income	$54,081
Median family income	$66,330
Persons in poverty	709
H'holds receiving public assistance	88
H'holds receiving social security	1,356

Households, 2000
Total households	4,020
With persons under 18	1,385
With persons over 65	1,367
Family households	2,967
Single-person households	925
Persons per household	2.69
Persons per family	3.19

Labor & Employment
Total civilian labor force, 2006**	5,486
Unemployment rate	3.7%
Total civilian labor force, 2000	5,162
Unemployment rate	3.6%

Employed persons 16 years and over by occupation, 2000
Managers & professionals	1,787
Service occupations	770
Sales & office occupations	1,353
Farming, fishing & forestry	0
Construction & maintenance	480
Production & transportation	585
Self-employed persons	308

* US Census Bureau
** New Jersey Department of Labor
§ State Fiscal Year July 1–June 30

General Information
Borough of Ridgefield
604 Broad Ave
Ridgefield, NJ 07657
201-943-5215

Website	ridgefieldboro.com
Year of incorporation	1892
Land/water area (sq. miles)	2.61/0.26
Form of government	Borough

Government
Legislative Districts
US Congressional	9
State Legislative	38

Local Officials, 2008
Mayor	Anthony Suarez
Borough Admin	Roberta Stern
Clerk	Martin Gobbo
Finance Dir	NA
Tax Assessor	George Reggo
Tax Collector	Frank Berardo
Attorney	Douglas Doyle
Construction Official	Armand Marini III
Comm Dev/Planning	NA
Borough Engineer	Jenne & Associates
Public Works	Nick Gambardella
Police Chief	Richard Stoltenborg
Emerg/Fire Director	Joe Greco

Housing & Construction
Housing Units, 2000*
Total	4,120
Median rent	$903
Median SF home value	$239,100

Permits for New Residential Construction
	Units	Value
Total, 2007	22	$4,525,782
Single family	18	$3,904,914
Total, 2006	28	$4,932,273
Single family	18	$3,380,104

Real Property Valuation, 2007
	Parcels	Valuation
Total	2,910	$1,852,046,900
Vacant	101	66,466,100
Residential	2,500	1,246,000,800
Commercial	208	241,130,900
Industrial	87	231,860,300
Apartments	14	66,588,800
Farm land	0	0
Farm homestead	0	0

Average Property Value & Tax, 2007
Residential value	$498,400
Property tax	$6,795
Tax credit/rebate	$1,048

Public Library
Ridgefield Public Library
527 Morse Avenue
Ridgefield, NJ 07657
201-941-0192

Director	Jane Forte

Library statistics, 2006
Population served	10,830
Full-time/total staff	2/7

	Total	Per capita
Holdings	54,949	5.07
Revenues	$541,641	$50.01
Expenditures	$592,604	$54.72
Annual visits	21,840	2.02
Internet terminals/annual users	17/7,200	

Public Safety
Number of officers, 2006	27

Crime	2005	2006
Total crimes	103	120
Violent	7	12
Murder	0	0
Rape	0	0
Robbery	2	4
Aggravated assault	5	8
Non-violent	96	108
Burglary	18	28
Larceny	65	64
Vehicle theft	13	16
Domestic violence	36	10
Arson	0	0
Total crime rate	9.4	10.9
Violent	0.6	1.1
Non-violent	8.7	9.8

Public School District
(for school year 2006-07 except as noted)

Ridgefield School District
555 Chestnut St
Ridgefield, NJ 07657
201-945-9236

Superintendent	Richard Brockel
Number of schools	3
Grade plan	K-12
Enrollment	1,823
Attendance rate, '05-06	94.2%
Dropout rate	NA
Students per teacher	10.5
Per pupil expenditure	$14,326
Median faculty salary	$52,266
Median administrator salary	$104,623
Grade 12 enrollment	122
High school graduation rate	100.0%

Assessment test results
(percent scoring at proficient or advanced level)
	Language	Math
NJASK-Grade 3	85.0%	92.7%
GEPA-Grade 8	79.5%	69.9%
HSPA-High School	90.7%	80.2%

SAT score averages
Pct tested	Math	Verbal	Writing
87%	506	460	469

Teacher Qualifications
Avg. years of experience	9
Highly-qualified teachers one subject/all subjects	98.5%/98.5%
With emergency credentials	0.0%

No Child Left Behind
AYP, 2005-06	Meets Standards

Municipal Finance§
State Aid Programs, 2008
Total aid	$5,925,121
CMPTRA	0
Energy tax receipts	5,925,121
Garden State Trust	0

General Budget, 2007
Total tax levy	$25,266,745
County levy	3,449,757
County taxes	3,259,703
County library	0
County health	0
County open space	190,054
School levy	14,092,494
Muni. levy	7,724,494
Misc. revenues	10,795,995

Taxes	2005	2006	2007
General tax rate per $100	1.17	1.19	1.37
County equalization ratio	118.43	108.53	98.39
Net valuation taxable	$1,854,169,156	$1,849,861,600	$1,853,343,069
State equalized value	$1,708,439,285	$1,881,416,081	$2,066,699,202

Bergen County

Ridgefield Park Village

Demographics & Socio-Economic Characteristics
(2000 US Census, except as noted)

Population
1980*	12,738
1990*	12,454
2000	12,873
Male	6,150
Female	6,723
2006 (estimate)*	12,665
Population density	7,320.8

Race & Hispanic Origin, 2000
Race
White	10,067
Black/African American	528
American Indian/Alaska Native	28
Asian	1,011
Native Hawaiian/Pacific Islander	4
Other race	837
Two or more races	398
Hispanic origin, total	2,863
Mexican	64
Puerto Rican	491
Cuban	513
Other Hispanic	1,795

Age & Nativity, 2000
Under 5 years	755
18 years and over	9,995
21 years and over	9,615
65 years and over	1,655
85 years and over	163
Median age	37.2
Native-born	9,792
Foreign-born	3,081

Educational Attainment, 2000
Population 25 years and over	9,024
Less than 9th grade	5.1%
High school grad or higher	85.1%
Bachelor's degree or higher	26.1%
Graduate degree	8.3%

Income & Poverty, 1999
Per capita income	$24,290
Median household income	$51,825
Median family income	$62,414
Persons in poverty	865
H'holds receiving public assistance	83
H'holds receiving social security	1,280

Households, 2000
Total households	5,012
With persons under 18	1,588
With persons over 65	1,263
Family households	3,243
Single-person households	1,484
Persons per household	2.56
Persons per family	3.24

Labor & Employment
Total civilian labor force, 2006**	7,262
Unemployment rate	4.2%
Total civilian labor force, 2000	6,852
Unemployment rate	4.1%

Employed persons 16 years and over by occupation, 2000
Managers & professionals	2,115
Service occupations	848
Sales & office occupations	2,290
Farming, fishing & forestry	0
Construction & maintenance	517
Production & transportation	801
Self-employed persons	253

* US Census Bureau
** New Jersey Department of Labor

See Introduction for an explanation of all data sources.

General Information
Village of Ridgefield Park
234 Main St
Ridgefield Park, NJ 07660
201-641-4950

Website	www.ridgefieldpark.org
Year of incorporation	1892
Land/water area (sq. miles)	1.73/0.19
Form of government	Commission

Government
Legislative Districts
US Congressional	9
State Legislative	37

Local Officials, 2008
Mayor	George Fosdick
Manager/Admin	NA
Clerk	Sarah Warlikowski
Finance Dir	Paul Hansen
Tax Assessor	Arthur Carlson
Tax Collector	Sarah Warlikowski
Attorney	Martin Durkin
Building	Michael Landolfi
Planning	Fredrick Rosen
Engineering	Boswell Engineering
Public Works	Alan O'Grady
Police Chief	Robert Lee
Emerg/Fire Director	Eamonn Radburn

Housing & Construction
Housing Units, 2000*
Total	5,134
Median rent	$848
Median SF home value	$171,300

Permits for New Residential Construction
	Units	Value
Total, 2007	6	$680,400
Single family	6	$680,400
Total, 2006	4	$617,000
Single family	2	$337,000

Real Property Valuation, 2007
	Parcels	Valuation
Total	3,156	$872,173,050
Vacant	46	21,690,600
Residential	2,863	561,116,300
Commercial	166	189,720,250
Industrial	38	30,806,600
Apartments	43	68,839,300
Farm land	0	0
Farm homestead	0	0

Average Property Value & Tax, 2007
Residential value	$195,989
Property tax	$8,013
Tax credit/rebate	$1,238

Public Library
Ridgefield Park Public Library
107 Cedar St
Ridgefield Park, NJ 07660
201-641-0689

Director......... Eileen Mackesy-Karpoff

Library statistics, 2006
Population served	12,873
Full-time/total staff	1/5

	Total	Per capita
Holdings	47,408	3.68
Revenues	$671,083	$52.13
Expenditures	$640,591	$49.76
Annual visits	58,110	4.51
Internet terminals/annual users	8/12,611	

Public Safety
Number of officers, 2006 30

Crime	2005	2006
Total crimes	150	205
Violent	12	14
Murder	0	0
Rape	0	1
Robbery	2	3
Aggravated assault	10	10
Non-violent	138	191
Burglary	20	20
Larceny	104	152
Vehicle theft	14	19
Domestic violence	51	47
Arson	2	0
Total crime rate	11.7	16.1
Violent	0.9	1.1
Non-violent	10.8	15.0

Public School District
(for school year 2006-07 except as noted)

Ridgefield Park School District
712 Lincoln Ave
Ridgefield Park, NJ 07660
201-807-2638

Superintendent	John Richardson
Number of schools	4
Grade plan	K-12
Enrollment	2,078
Attendance rate, '05-06	95.0%
Dropout rate	1.4%
Students per teacher	10.9
Per pupil expenditure	$12,900
Median faculty salary	$56,513
Median administrator salary	$115,600
Grade 12 enrollment	195
High school graduation rate	94.0%

Assessment test results
(percent scoring at proficient or advanced level)
	Language	Math
NJASK-Grade 3	99.2%	98.5%
GEPA-Grade 8	74.0%	63.8%
HSPA-High School	87.0%	76.3%

SAT score averages
Pct tested	Math	Verbal	Writing
79%	464	433	442

Teacher Qualifications
Avg. years of experience	9
Highly-qualified teachers one subject/all subjects	100%/100%
With emergency credentials	0.0%

No Child Left Behind
AYP, 2005-06 .... Meets Standards

Municipal Finance
State Aid Programs, 2008
Total aid	$1,487,246
CMPTRA	536,209
Energy tax receipts	951,037
Garden State Trust	0

General Budget, 2007
Total tax levy	$35,690,530
County levy	2,799,148
County taxes	2,644,257
County library	0
County health	0
County open space	154,891
School levy	20,694,264
Muni. levy	12,197,118
Misc. revenues	5,786,468

Taxes	2005	2006	2007
General tax rate per $100	3.69	3.86	4.09
County equalization ratio	70.5	61.91	56.66
Net valuation taxable	$867,961,464	$875,107,290	$872,909,861
State equalized value	$1,401,972,967	$1,545,284,583	$1,642,628,848

©2008 Information Publications, Inc. All rights reserved. Photocopying prohibited. For additional copies, contact the publisher at www.informationpublications.com or (877)544-INFO (4636)

Ridgewood Village
Bergen County

Demographics & Socio-Economic Characteristics
(2000 US Census, except as noted)

Population
1980*	25,208
1990*	24,152
2000	24,936
Male	12,002
Female	12,934
2006 (estimate)*	24,639
Population density	4,255.4

Race & Hispanic Origin, 2000
Race
White	21,899
Black/African American	409
American Indian/Alaska Native	11
Asian	2,162
Native Hawaiian/Pacific Islander	0
Other race	148
Two or more races	307
Hispanic origin, total	942
Mexican	110
Puerto Rican	173
Cuban	134
Other Hispanic	525

Age & Nativity, 2000
Under 5 years	1,938
18 years and over	17,461
21 years and over	16,918
65 years and over	3,031
85 years and over	418
Median age	38.6
Native-born	20,931
Foreign-born	4,005

Educational Attainment, 2000
Population 25 years and over	16,407
Less than 9th grade	1.8%
High school grad or higher	95.9%
Bachelor's degree or higher	66.7%
Graduate degree	29.0%

Income & Poverty, 1999
Per capita income	$51,658
Median household income	$104,286
Median family income	$121,848
Persons in poverty	741
H'holds receiving public assistance	112
H'holds receiving social security	2,091

Households, 2000
Total households	8,603
With persons under 18	3,910
With persons over 65	2,101
Family households	6,777
Single-person households	1,592
Persons per household	2.87
Persons per family	3.30

Labor & Employment
Total civilian labor force, 2006**	12,055
Unemployment rate	2.8%
Total civilian labor force, 2000	11,791
Unemployment rate	3.1%

Employed persons 16 years and over by occupation, 2000
Managers & professionals	7,029
Service occupations	755
Sales & office occupations	2,973
Farming, fishing & forestry	0
Construction & maintenance	379
Production & transportation	290
Self-employed persons	965

* US Census Bureau
** New Jersey Department of Labor

General Information
Village of Ridgewood
131 N Maple Ave
Ridgewood, NJ 07450
201-670-5500

Website	ridgewoodnj.net
Year of incorporation	1894
Land/water area (sq. miles)	5.79/0.05
Form of government	Council-Manager

Government
Legislative Districts
US Congressional	5
State Legislative	40

Local Officials, 2008
Mayor	David Pfund
Manager	James Ten Hoeve
Clerk	Heather Mailander
Finance Dir	Stephen Sanzari
Tax Assessor	Michael Barker
Tax Collector	Mary Jo Gilmour
Attorney	Matthew Rogers
Building	Anthony Merlino
Comm Dev/Planning	NA
Engineering	Christopher Rutishauser
Public Works	Christopher Rutishauser
Police Chief	William Corcoran
Fire Chief	James Bombace

Housing & Construction
Housing Units, 2000*
Total	8,802
Median rent	$1,220
Median SF home value	$387,200

Permits for New Residential Construction
	Units	Value
Total, 2007	20	$5,579,355
Single family	18	$5,510,355
Total, 2006	34	$6,904,895
Single family	34	$6,904,895

Real Property Valuation, 2007
	Parcels	Valuation
Total	7,895	$3,947,869,700
Vacant	99	12,831,200
Residential	7,442	3,525,797,000
Commercial	327	349,937,500
Industrial	0	0
Apartments	27	59,304,000
Farm land	0	0
Farm homestead	0	0

Average Property Value & Tax, 2007
Residential value	$473,770
Property tax	$13,222
Tax credit/rebate	$1,386

Public Library
Ridgewood Public Library
125 N Maple Ave
Ridgewood, NJ 07450
201-670-5600

Director: Nancy K. Greene

Library statistics, 2006
Population served	24,936
Full-time/total staff	9/19

	Total	Per capita
Holdings	165,246	6.63
Revenues	$2,298,475	$92.17
Expenditures	$2,316,485	$92.90
Annual visits	327,234	13.12
Internet terminals/annual users	32/129,134	

Public Safety
Number of officers, 2006	44

Crime	2005	2006
Total crimes	260	248
Violent	11	10
Murder	0	0
Rape	1	0
Robbery	2	2
Aggravated assault	8	8
Non-violent	249	238
Burglary	54	42
Larceny	189	193
Vehicle theft	6	3
Domestic violence	84	89
Arson	1	2
Total crime rate	10.4	10.0
Violent	0.4	0.4
Non-violent	10.0	9.6

Public School District
(for school year 2006-07 except as noted)

Ridgewood Village School District
49 Cottage Place
Ridgewood, NJ 07451
201-670-2700

Superintendent	Timothy Brennan (Actg)
Number of schools	9
Grade plan	K-12
Enrollment	5,580
Attendance rate, '05-06	95.8%
Dropout rate	0.2%
Students per teacher	11.8
Per pupil expenditure	$13,571
Median faculty salary	$66,950
Median administrator salary	$124,700
Grade 12 enrollment	410
High school graduation rate	99.3%

Assessment test results
(percent scoring at proficient or advanced level)
	Language	Math
NJASK-Grade 3	97.7%	98.2%
GEPA-Grade 8	92.0%	90.8%
HSPA-High School	96.7%	94.5%

SAT score averages
Pct tested	Math	Verbal	Writing
99%	605	581	585

Teacher Qualifications
Avg. years of experience	9
Highly-qualified teachers one subject/all subjects	99.5%/99.5%
With emergency credentials	0.0%

No Child Left Behind
AYP, 2005-06 .... Meets Standards

Municipal Finance
State Aid Programs, 2008
Total aid	$2,531,906
CMPTRA	541,618
Energy tax receipts	1,990,278
Garden State Trust	10

General Budget, 2007
Total tax levy	$110,334,611
County levy	11,833,123
County taxes	11,181,717
County library	0
County health	0
County open space	651,406
School levy	72,400,666
Muni. levy	26,100,822
Misc. revenues	10,938,280

Taxes	2005	2006	2007
General tax rate per $100	2.56	2.67	2.8
County equalization ratio	75.34	67.73	60.79
Net valuation taxable	$3,902,027,619	$3,920,887,200	$3,953,480,368
State equalized value	$5,761,151,069	$6,454,891,621	$6,729,967,166

Passaic County
Ringwood Borough

Demographics & Socio-Economic Characteristics
(2000 US Census, except as noted)

Population
1980*	12,625
1990*	12,623
2000	12,396
Male	6,201
Female	6,195
2006 (estimate)*	12,814
Population density	507.5

Race & Hispanic Origin, 2000
Race
White	11,636
Black/African American	199
American Indian/Alaska Native	179
Asian	148
Native Hawaiian/Pacific Islander	1
Other race	83
Two or more races	150
Hispanic origin, total	527
Mexican	40
Puerto Rican	195
Cuban	61
Other Hispanic	231

Age & Nativity, 2000
Under 5 years	935
18 years and over	8,978
21 years and over	8,638
65 years and over	982
85 years and over	98
Median age	37.4
Native-born	11,322
Foreign-born	1,074

Educational Attainment, 2000
Population 25 years and over	8,192
Less than 9th grade	1.1%
High school grad or higher	91.5%
Bachelor's degree or higher	39.2%
Graduate degree	11.7%

Income & Poverty, 1999
Per capita income	$31,341
Median household income	$81,636
Median family income	$85,108
Persons in poverty	342
H'holds receiving public assistance	23
H'holds receiving social security	759

Households, 2000
Total households	4,108
With persons under 18	1,832
With persons over 65	691
Family households	3,446
Single-person households	496
Persons per household	3.00
Persons per family	3.28

Labor & Employment
Total civilian labor force, 2006**	7,457
Unemployment rate	3.8%
Total civilian labor force, 2000	6,877
Unemployment rate	3.8%

Employed persons 16 years and over by occupation, 2000
Managers & professionals	2,950
Service occupations	544
Sales & office occupations	1,878
Farming, fishing & forestry	0
Construction & maintenance	715
Production & transportation	531
Self-employed persons	500

* US Census Bureau
** New Jersey Department of Labor

See Introduction for an explanation of all data sources.

General Information
Borough of Ringwood
60 Margaret King Ave
Ringwood, NJ 07456
973-962-7037

Website	www.ringwoodnj.net
Year of incorporation	1918
Land/water area (sq. miles)	25.25/2.78
Form of government	Council-Manager

Government
Legislative Districts
US Congressional	5
State Legislative	40

Local Officials, 2008
Mayor	Walter Davison
Manager	Kelly A. Rohde (Actg)
Clerk	Kelley A. Rohde
Finance Dir	Gail Bado
Tax Assessor	Richard Motyka
Tax Collector	NA
Attorney	Richard Clemack
Building	William Fleck
Comm Dev/Planning	NA
Engineering	Jeffrey Yuhas
Public Works	Willard Bierwas
Police Chief	Bernard Lombardo
Fire/Emergency Dir	NA

Housing & Construction
Housing Units, 2000*
Total	4,221
Median rent	$1,137
Median SF home value	$193,400

Permits for New Residential Construction
	Units	Value
Total, 2007	19	$4,256,232
Single family	19	$4,256,232
Total, 2006	25	$5,490,445
Single family	25	$5,490,445

Real Property Valuation, 2007
	Parcels	Valuation
Total	4,714	$866,188,190
Vacant	272	34,966,300
Residential	4,310	784,304,460
Commercial	49	26,239,900
Industrial	25	17,824,100
Apartments	0	0
Farm land	46	133,030
Farm homestead	12	2,720,400

Average Property Value & Tax, 2007
Residential value	$182,097
Property tax	$8,478
Tax credit/rebate	$1,259

Public Library
Ringwood Public Library
30 Cannici Dr
Ringwood, NJ 07456
973-962-6256

Director: Andrea R. Cahoon

Library statistics, 2006
Population served	12,396
Full-time/total staff	1/3

	Total	Per capita
Holdings	75,619	6.10
Revenues	$627,807	$50.65
Expenditures	$629,276	$50.76
Annual visits	92,257	7.44
Internet terminals/annual users	35/18,912	

Public Safety
Number of officers, 2006: 23

Crime	2005	2006
Total crimes	80	70
Violent	8	7
Murder	0	0
Rape	0	2
Robbery	1	1
Aggravated assault	7	4
Non-violent	72	63
Burglary	17	14
Larceny	53	48
Vehicle theft	2	1
Domestic violence	70	79
Arson	1	1
Total crime rate	6.3	5.5
Violent	0.6	0.5
Non-violent	5.6	4.9

Public School District
(for school year 2006-07 except as noted)

Ringwood School District
121 Carletondale Rd
Ringwood, NJ 07456
973-962-7028

Chief School Admin	Patrick W. Martin
Number of schools	4
Grade plan	K-8
Enrollment	1,412
Attendance rate, '05-06	95.8%
Dropout rate	NA
Students per teacher	11.7
Per pupil expenditure	$12,991
Median faculty salary	$61,832
Median administrator salary	$98,726
Grade 12 enrollment	NA
High school graduation rate	NA

Assessment test results
(percent scoring at proficient or advanced level)
	Language	Math
NJASK-Grade 3	92.4%	97.9%
GEPA-Grade 8	87.5%	84.0%
HSPA-High School	NA	NA

SAT score averages
Pct tested	Math	Verbal	Writing
NA	NA	NA	NA

Teacher Qualifications
Avg. years of experience	13
Highly-qualified teachers one subject/all subjects	100%/100%
With emergency credentials	0.0%

No Child Left Behind
AYP, 2005-06 .... Meets Standards

Municipal Finance
State Aid Programs, 2008
Total aid	$2,148,393
CMPTRA	164,784
Energy tax receipts	1,895,992
Garden State Trust	37,768

General Budget, 2007
Total tax levy	$40,380,317
County levy	9,059,392
County taxes	8,875,522
County library	0
County health	0
County open space	183,870
School levy	22,861,756
Muni. levy	8,459,169
Misc. revenues	6,270,451

Taxes
	2005	2006	2007
General tax rate per $100	4.32	4.51	4.66
County equalization ratio	56.23	51.32	47.16
Net valuation taxable	$858,640,051	$861,318,490	$867,317,663
State equalized value	$1,673,109,998	$1,827,554,813	$1,978,276,677

River Edge Borough

Bergen County

Demographics & Socio-Economic Characteristics
(2000 US Census, except as noted)

Population
1980*	11,111
1990*	10,603
2000	10,946
Male	5,211
Female	5,735
2006 (estimate)*	10,862
Population density	5,747.1

Race & Hispanic Origin, 2000
Race
White	9,208
Black/African American	116
American Indian/Alaska Native	9
Asian	1,379
Native Hawaiian/Pacific Islander	1
Other race	89
Two or more races	144
Hispanic origin, total	581
Mexican	32
Puerto Rican	141
Cuban	113
Other Hispanic	295

Age & Nativity, 2000
Under 5 years	781
18 years and over	8,312
21 years and over	8,075
65 years and over	1,859
85 years and over	265
Median age	40.0
Native-born	8,602
Foreign-born	2,344

Educational Attainment, 2000
Population 25 years and over	7,807
Less than 9th grade	2.3%
High school grad or higher	93.6%
Bachelor's degree or higher	45.4%
Graduate degree	16.4%

Income & Poverty, 1999
Per capita income	$33,188
Median household income	$71,792
Median family income	$80,422
Persons in poverty	338
H'holds receiving public assistance	65
H'holds receiving social security	1,321

Households, 2000
Total households	4,165
With persons under 18	1,501
With persons over 65	1,331
Family households	3,105
Single-person households	947
Persons per household	2.62
Persons per family	3.11

Labor & Employment
Total civilian labor force, 2006**	5,846
Unemployment rate	3.0%
Total civilian labor force, 2000	5,498
Unemployment rate	2.9%

Employed persons 16 years and over by occupation, 2000
Managers & professionals	2,722
Service occupations	467
Sales & office occupations	1,600
Farming, fishing & forestry	0
Construction & maintenance	271
Production & transportation	281
Self-employed persons	298

* US Census Bureau
** New Jersey Department of Labor

General Information
Borough of River Edge
705 Kinderkamack Rd
River Edge, NJ 07661
201-599-6300

Website	www.riveredgenj.org
Year of incorporation	1930
Land/water area (sq. miles)	1.89/0.02
Form of government	Borough

Government
Legislative Districts
US Congressional	5
State Legislative	39

Local Officials, 2008
Mayor	Margaret Watkins
Manager	Alan Negreann
Clerk	Denise A. Dondiego
Finance Dir.	Alan Negreann
Tax Assessor	James Anzevino
Tax Collector	Zenab Bachok
Attorney	William Lindsley
Building	Robert Byrnes
Comm Dev/Planning	NA
Engineering	Robert Costa
Public Works	John Lynch
Police Chief	Thomas Cariddi
Emerg/Fire Director	Chris Weismann

Housing & Construction
Housing Units, 2000*
Total	4,210
Median rent	$969
Median SF home value	$252,700

Permits for New Residential Construction
	Units	Value
Total, 2007	22	$4,438,304
Single family	17	$2,258,404
Total, 2006	13	$3,655,372
Single family	8	$1,475,472

Real Property Valuation, 2007
	Parcels	Valuation
Total	3,393	$1,612,832,700
Vacant	34	7,055,300
Residential	3,218	1,402,078,700
Commercial	122	120,723,800
Industrial	4	12,088,000
Apartments	15	70,886,900
Farm land	0	0
Farm homestead	0	0

Average Property Value & Tax, 2007
Residential value	$435,699
Property tax	$9,671
Tax credit/rebate	$1,437

Public Library
River Edge Free Public Library
Elm & Tenney Aves
River Edge, NJ 07661
201-261-1663

Director	Daragh O'Connor

Library statistics, 2006
Population served	10,946
Full-time/total staff	4/8

	Total	Per capita
Holdings	87,012	7.95
Revenues	$772,952	$70.62
Expenditures	$756,480	$69.11
Annual visits	117,133	10.70
Internet terminals/annual users	5/8,346	

Public Safety
Number of officers, 2006 22

Crime
	2005	2006
Total crimes	121	130
Violent	4	7
Murder	0	0
Rape	2	1
Robbery	0	2
Aggravated assault	2	4
Non-violent	117	123
Burglary	35	22
Larceny	79	97
Vehicle theft	3	4
Domestic violence	76	56
Arson	1	0
Total crime rate	11.0	11.9
Violent	0.4	0.6
Non-violent	10.7	11.3

Public School District
(for school year 2006-07 except as noted)

River Edge School District
410 Bogert Rd
River Edge, NJ 07661
201-261-3404

Superintendent	Erika Steinbauer
Number of schools	2
Grade plan	K-6
Enrollment	1,126
Attendance rate, '05-06	96.6%
Dropout rate	NA
Students per teacher	13.0
Per pupil expenditure	$9,939
Median faculty salary	$52,097
Median administrator salary	$125,567
Grade 12 enrollment	NA
High school graduation rate	NA

Assessment test results
(percent scoring at proficient or advanced level)
	Language	Math
NJASK-Grade 3	92.7%	96.4%
GEPA-Grade 8	NA	NA
HSPA-High School	NA	NA

SAT score averages
Pct tested	Math	Verbal	Writing
NA	NA	NA	NA

Teacher Qualifications
Avg. years of experience	11
Highly-qualified teachers one subject/all subjects	96.0%/94.5%
With emergency credentials	0.0%

No Child Left Behind
AYP, 2005-06 . . . . Meets Standards

Municipal Finance
State Aid Programs, 2008
Total aid	$1,384,343
CMPTRA	276,710
Energy tax receipts	1,081,428
Garden State Trust	26,205

General Budget, 2007
Total tax levy	$35,954,530
County levy	3,266,655
County taxes	3,086,786
County library	0
County health	0
County open space	179,869
School levy	24,229,826
Muni. levy	8,458,049
Misc. revenues	6,258,617

Taxes
	2005	2006	2007
General tax rate per $100	1.93	2.09	2.22
County equalization ratio	113.06	99.95	90.22
Net valuation taxable	$1,619,016,446	$1,610,415,500	$1,619,895,547
State equalized value	$1,619,826,359	$1,792,032,609	$1,888,795,084

Bergen County

River Vale Township

Demographics & Socio-Economic Characteristics
(2000 US Census, except as noted)

Population
1980*	9,489
1990*	9,410
2000	9,449
Male	4,560
Female	4,889
2006 (estimate)*	9,751
Population density	2,390.0

Race & Hispanic Origin, 2000
Race
- White 8,724
- Black/African American 55
- American Indian/Alaska Native 0
- Asian 557
- Native Hawaiian/Pacific Islander 2
- Other race 41
- Two or more races 70
- Hispanic origin, total 304
  - Mexican 14
  - Puerto Rican 56
  - Cuban 74
  - Other Hispanic 160

Age & Nativity, 2000
- Under 5 years 654
- 18 years and over 6,876
- 21 years and over 6,657
- 65 years and over 1,263
- 85 years and over 123
  - Median age 40.3
- Native-born 8,361
- Foreign-born 1,088

Educational Attainment, 2000
- Population 25 years and over 6,454
- Less than 9th grade 1.4%
- High school grad or higher 94.3%
- Bachelor's degree or higher 48.5%
- Graduate degree 18.5%

Income & Poverty, 1999
- Per capita income $40,709
- Median household income $95,129
- Median family income $105,919
- Persons in poverty 261
- H'holds receiving public assistance 19
- H'holds receiving social security 815

Households, 2000
- Total households 3,275
  - With persons under 18 1,372
  - With persons over 65 866
  - Family households 2,677
  - Single-person households 503
- Persons per household 2.87
- Persons per family 3.22

Labor & Employment
- Total civilian labor force, 2006** 4,751
  - Unemployment rate 2.3%
- Total civilian labor force, 2000 4,468
  - Unemployment rate 2.3%

Employed persons 16 years and over by occupation, 2000
- Managers & professionals 2,295
- Service occupations 306
- Sales & office occupations 1,282
- Farming, fishing & forestry 0
- Construction & maintenance 190
- Production & transportation 293
- Self-employed persons 357

* US Census Bureau
** New Jersey Department of Labor

See Introduction for an explanation of all data sources.

General Information
Township of River Vale
406 Rivervale Rd
River Vale, NJ 07675
201-664-2346

- Website .... www.rivervalenj.org
- Year of incorporation 1906
- Land/water area (sq. miles) 4.08/0.23
- Form of government .... Mayor-Council

Government
Legislative Districts
- US Congressional 5
- State Legislative 39

Local Officials, 2008
- Mayor .... Joseph Blundo
- Business Admin .... Robert Gallione
- Clerk .... Karen Padva (Actg)
- Finance Dir .... Gennaro Rotella
- Tax Assessor .... Denis McGuire
- Tax Collector .... Lauren Roehrer
- Attorney .... Holly Schepisi
- Building .... Mike Sartori
- Comm Dev/Planning .... NA
- Engineering .... Dennis Harrington
- Public Works .... Rich Campanelli
- Police Chief .... Aaron Back
- Emerg/Fire Director .... Gerard Marsh

Housing & Construction
Housing Units, 2000*
- Total 3,312
- Median rent $1,119
- Median SF home value $350,300

Permits for New Residential Construction
	Units	Value
Total, 2007	18	$6,062,623
Single family	18	$6,062,623
Total, 2006	22	$3,981,678
Single family	22	$3,981,678

Real Property Valuation, 2007
	Parcels	Valuation
Total	3,404	$1,001,961,567
Vacant	69	14,660,850
Residential	3,293	937,134,067
Commercial	37	44,232,950
Industrial	0	0
Apartments	4	5,219,700
Farm land	0	0
Farm homestead	1	714,000

Average Property Value & Tax, 2007
- Residential value $284,714
- Property tax $10,957
- Tax credit/rebate $1,386

Public Library
River Vale Public Library
412 Rivervale Rd
River Vale, NJ 07675
201-391-2323

Director .... Holly Deni

Library statistics, 2006
- Population served 9,449
- Full-time/total staff 2/5

	Total	Per capita
Holdings	56,852	6.02
Revenues	$678,055	$71.76
Expenditures	$620,032	$65.62
Annual visits	106,080	11.23
Internet terminals/annual users	7/25,960	

Public Safety
Number of officers, 2006 20

Crime	2005	2006
Total crimes	62	43
Violent	3	4
Murder	0	0
Rape	0	0
Robbery	0	1
Aggravated assault	3	3
Non-violent	59	39
Burglary	5	1
Larceny	54	37
Vehicle theft	0	1
Domestic violence	18	27
Arson	0	0
Total crime rate	6.3	4.4
Violent	0.3	0.4
Non-violent	6.0	4.0

Public School District
(for school year 2006-07 except as noted)

River Vale School District
609 Westwood Ave
River Vale, NJ 07675
201-358-4020

- Superintendent .... David Verducci
- Number of schools 3
- Grade plan K-8
- Enrollment 1,357
- Attendance rate, '05-06 .... 96.2%
- Dropout rate .... NA
- Students per teacher 11.4
- Per pupil expenditure $12,196
- Median faculty salary $55,885
- Median administrator salary $137,687
- Grade 12 enrollment .... NA
- High school graduation rate .... NA

Assessment test results
(percent scoring at proficient or advanced level)
	Language	Math
NJASK-Grade 3	97.2%	98.6%
GEPA-Grade 8	93.6%	91.4%
HSPA-High School	NA	NA

SAT score averages
Pct tested	Math	Verbal	Writing
NA	NA	NA	NA

Teacher Qualifications
- Avg. years of experience 10
- Highly-qualified teachers
  - one subject/all subjects 100%/100%
- With emergency credentials 0.0%

No Child Left Behind
AYP, 2005-06 .... Meets Standards

Municipal Finance
State Aid Programs, 2008
- Total aid $961,879
  - CMPTRA 79,904
  - Energy tax receipts 858,616
  - Garden State Trust 0

General Budget, 2007
- Total tax levy $38,577,134
  - County levy 3,895,521
    - County taxes 3,681,039
    - County library 0
    - County health 0
    - County open space 214,482
  - School levy 26,832,236
  - Muni. levy 7,849,377
  - Misc. revenues 3,955,422

Taxes
	2005	2006	2007
General tax rate per $100	3.36	3.55	3.85
County equalization ratio	57.62	51.63	46.8
Net valuation taxable	$998,392,262	$1,002,087,367	$1,002,449,208
State equalized value	$1,933,744,455	$2,141,790,854	$2,239,507,902

The New Jersey Municipal Data Book   425

Riverdale Borough

Morris County

Demographics & Socio-Economic Characteristics
(2000 US Census, except as noted)

Population
1980*	2,530
1990*	2,370
2000	2,498
Male	1,211
Female	1,287
2006 (estimate)*	2,676
Population density	1,299.0

Race & Hispanic Origin, 2000
Race
White	2,333
Black/African American	27
American Indian/Alaska Native	1
Asian	68
Native Hawaiian/Pacific Islander	0
Other race	40
Two or more races	29
Hispanic origin, total	110
Mexican	15
Puerto Rican	39
Cuban	7
Other Hispanic	49

Age & Nativity, 2000
Under 5 years	152
18 years and over	1,911
21 years and over	1,827
65 years and over	302
85 years and over	21
Median age	37.2
Native-born	2,270
Foreign-born	228

Educational Attainment, 2000
Population 25 years and over	1,724
Less than 9th grade	2.1%
High school grad or higher	89.2%
Bachelor's degree or higher	30.9%
Graduate degree	8.4%

Income & Poverty, 1999
Per capita income	$31,187
Median household income	$71,083
Median family income	$79,557
Persons in poverty	132
H'holds receiving public assistance	7
H'holds receiving social security	241

Households, 2000
Total households	919
With persons under 18	313
With persons over 65	228
Family households	672
Single-person households	194
Persons per household	2.68
Persons per family	3.14

Labor & Employment
Total civilian labor force, 2006**	1,595
Unemployment rate	4.8%
Total civilian labor force, 2000	1,464
Unemployment rate	4.4%

Employed persons 16 years and over by occupation, 2000
Managers & professionals	506
Service occupations	120
Sales & office occupations	475
Farming, fishing & forestry	0
Construction & maintenance	157
Production & transportation	142
Self-employed persons	71

* US Census Bureau
** New Jersey Department of Labor

General Information
Borough of Riverdale
91 Newark-Pompton Turnpike
PO Box 6
Riverdale, NJ 07457
973-835-4060

Website	www.riverdalenj.com
Year of incorporation	1923
Land/water area (sq. miles)	2.06/0.01
Form of government	Borough

Government
Legislative Districts
US Congressional	11
State Legislative	26

Local Officials, 2008
Mayor	William Budesheim
Manager/Admin	NA
Clerk	Carol Talerico
Finance Dir.	Kenneth Sesholtz
Tax Assessor	Joseph De Stefano
Tax Collector	Maryann Murphy
Attorney	Robert Oostdyk
Building	Joseph Montemarano
Comm Dev/Planning	NA
Engineering	Paul Darmofalski
Public Works	Walter Mahon
Police Chief	Thomas Soules
Emerg/Fire Director	Michael Norton

Housing & Construction
Housing Units, 2000*
Total	940
Median rent	$951
Median SF home value	$210,200

Permits for New Residential Construction
	Units	Value
Total, 2007	6	$436,000
Single family	2	$36,000
Total, 2006	91	$7,220,600
Single family	12	$1,420,200

Real Property Valuation, 2007
	Parcels	Valuation
Total	1,874	$775,734,800
Vacant	342	61,518,300
Residential	1,403	505,020,000
Commercial	98	167,336,900
Industrial	24	39,583,100
Apartments	4	1,646,700
Farm land	2	5,600
Farm homestead	1	624,200

Average Property Value & Tax, 2007
Residential value	$360,145
Property tax	$5,105
Tax credit/rebate	$921

Public Library
Riverdale Public Library
93 Newark Pompton Tpke
Riverdale, NJ 07457
973-835-5044

Director. . . . . Abigail Sanner

Library statistics, 2006
Population served	2,498
Full-time/total staff	1/1

	Total	Per capita
Holdings	22,459	8.99
Revenues	$229,438	$91.85
Expenditures	$235,196	$94.15
Annual visits	20,080	8.04
Internet terminals/annual users	12/10,745	

Taxes
	2005	2006	2007
General tax rate per $100	1.26	1.3	1.42
County equalization ratio	126.81	106.11	96.09
Net valuation taxable	$663,440,749	$684,623,850	$782,494,435
State equalized value	$625,238,666	$720,293,341	$822,463,946

Public Safety
Number of officers, 2006 17

Crime	2005	2006
Total crimes	81	79
Violent	3	0
Murder	0	0
Rape	0	0
Robbery	0	0
Aggravated assault	3	0
Non-violent	78	79
Burglary	18	18
Larceny	58	53
Vehicle theft	2	8
Domestic violence	19	23
Arson	0	0
Total crime rate	30.8	30.0
Violent	1.1	0.0
Non-violent	29.6	30.0

Public School District
(for school year 2006-07 except as noted)

Riverdale School District
52 Newark-Pompton Turnpike
Riverdale, NJ 07457
973-839-1304

Superintendent	Betty Ann Wyks
Number of schools	1
Grade plan	K-8
Enrollment	266
Attendance rate, '05-06	96.4%
Dropout rate	NA
Students per teacher	8.4
Per pupil expenditure	$13,892
Median faculty salary	$46,770
Median administrator salary	$100,234
Grade 12 enrollment	NA
High school graduation rate	NA

Assessment test results
(percent scoring at proficient or advanced level)
	Language	Math
NJASK-Grade 3	90.0%	90.6%
GEPA-Grade 8	79.2%	83.4%
HSPA-High School	NA	NA

SAT score averages
Pct tested	Math	Verbal	Writing
NA	NA	NA	NA

Teacher Qualifications
Avg. years of experience	5
Highly-qualified teachers one subject/all subjects	100%/100%
With emergency credentials	0.0%

No Child Left Behind
AYP, 2005-06 . . . . Meets Standards

Municipal Finance
State Aid Programs, 2008
Total aid	$462,836
CMPTRA	0
Energy tax receipts	462,836
Garden State Trust	0

General Budget, 2007
Total tax levy	$11,091,107
County levy	1,947,010
County taxes	1,557,301
County library	0
County health	0
County open space	389,708
School levy	5,441,700
Muni. levy	3,702,398
Misc. revenues	3,057,541

Burlington County
Riverside Township

Demographics & Socio-Economic Characteristics
(2000 US Census, except as noted)
Population
1980*	7,941
1990*	7,974
2000	7,911
Male	3,936
Female	3,975
2006 (estimate)*	7,950
Population density	5,230.3

Race & Hispanic Origin, 2000
Race
White	7,137
Black/African American	351
American Indian/Alaska Native	11
Asian	33
Native Hawaiian/Pacific Islander	1
Other race	180
Two or more races	198
Hispanic origin, total	325
Mexican	37
Puerto Rican	150
Cuban	2
Other Hispanic	136

Age & Nativity, 2000
Under 5 years	515
18 years and over	5,931
21 years and over	5,638
65 years and over	1,089
85 years and over	126
Median age	35.6
Native-born	7,105
Foreign-born	806

Educational Attainment, 2000
Population 25 years and over	5,234
Less than 9th grade	9.8%
High school grad or higher	75.6%
Bachelor's degree or higher	11.5%
Graduate degree	3.0%

Income & Poverty, 1999
Per capita income	$18,758
Median household income	$43,358
Median family income	$52,479
Persons in poverty	642
H'holds receiving public assistance	59
H'holds receiving social security	867

Households, 2000
Total households	2,978
With persons under 18	1,091
With persons over 65	806
Family households	1,992
Single-person households	814
Persons per household	2.64
Persons per family	3.21

Labor & Employment
Total civilian labor force, 2006**	4,894
Unemployment rate	4.4%
Total civilian labor force, 2000	4,199
Unemployment rate	3.9%

Employed persons 16 years and over by occupation, 2000
Managers & professionals	804
Service occupations	570
Sales & office occupations	1,240
Farming, fishing & forestry	14
Construction & maintenance	651
Production & transportation	756
Self-employed persons	188

* US Census Bureau
** New Jersey Department of Labor

See Introduction for an explanation of all data sources.

General Information
Township of Riverside
PO Box 188
Riverside, NJ 08075
856-461-1460

Website	riversidetwp.org
Year of incorporation	1895
Land/water area (sq. miles)	1.52/0.10
Form of government	Township

Government
Legislative Districts
US Congressional	3
State Legislative	7

Local Officials, 2008
Mayor	George Conard Sr
Manager	Meghan Jack
Clerk	Susan M. Dydek
Finance Dir	Deborah Crowe
Tax Assessor	Carl Cicali
Tax Collector	Nancy Elmeaze
Attorney	George Saponaro
Building	Thomas Mahoney
Planning	Taylor Design Group
Engineering	Hugh Doherty
Public Works	Eric March
Police Chief	Paul Tursi
Fire Chief	Lawrence Winkelspecht

Housing & Construction
Housing Units, 2000*
Total	3,118
Median rent	$670
Median SF home value	$100,400

Permits for New Residential Construction
	Units	Value
Total, 2007	4	$342,610
Single family	4	$342,610
Total, 2006	11	$948,728
Single family	11	$948,728

Real Property Valuation, 2007
	Parcels	Valuation
Total	2,746	$450,375,550
Vacant	89	3,421,500
Residential	2,453	376,971,750
Commercial	162	43,081,900
Industrial	15	13,210,500
Apartments	27	13,689,900
Farm land	0	0
Farm homestead	0	0

Average Property Value & Tax, 2007
Residential value	$153,678
Property tax	$4,175
Tax credit/rebate	$883

Public Library
Riverside Public Library
10 Zurbrugg Way
Riverside, NJ 08075
856-461-6922

Director	Jean Bowker

Library statistics, 2006
Population served	7,911
Full-time/total staff	0/0

	Total	Per capita
Holdings	37,996	4.80
Revenues	$57,108	$7.22
Expenditures	$59,783	$7.56
Annual visits	11,813	1.49
Internet terminals/annual users	4/3,120	

Taxes
	2005	2006	2007
General tax rate per $100	2.334	2.551	2.72
County equalization ratio	127.29	107.59	93.85
Net valuation taxable	$451,887,327	$450,217,050	$452,606,662
State equalized value	$420,008,669	$482,020,345	$522,175,178

Public Safety
Number of officers, 2006		15

Crime	2005	2006
Total crimes	153	143
Violent	18	24
Murder	0	0
Rape	0	4
Robbery	5	4
Aggravated assault	13	16
Non-violent	135	119
Burglary	23	24
Larceny	102	89
Vehicle theft	10	6
Domestic violence	155	176
Arson	0	1
Total crime rate	19.1	17.9
Violent	2.2	3.0
Non-violent	16.9	14.9

Public School District
(for school year 2006-07 except as noted)

Riverside Township School District
112 E Washington St
Riverside, NJ 08075
856-461-1255

Superintendent	Robert Goldschmidt
Number of schools	3
Grade plan	K-12
Enrollment	1,444
Attendance rate, '05-06	93.6%
Dropout rate	2.4%
Students per teacher	11.6
Per pupil expenditure	$11,459
Median faculty salary	$54,712
Median administrator salary	$95,249
Grade 12 enrollment	96
High school graduation rate	89.3%

Assessment test results
(percent scoring at proficient or advanced level)
	Language	Math
NJASK-Grade 3	73.8%	84.1%
GEPA-Grade 8	59.8%	59.2%
HSPA-High School	79.5%	77.9%

SAT score averages
Pct tested	Math	Verbal	Writing
64%	451	440	428

Teacher Qualifications
Avg. years of experience	10
Highly-qualified teachers one subject/all subjects	95.0%/94.0%
With emergency credentials	0.0%

No Child Left Behind
AYP, 2005-06	Meets Standards

Municipal Finance
State Aid Programs, 2008
Total aid	$877,616
CMPTRA	198,119
Energy tax receipts	679,497
Garden State Trust	0

General Budget, 2007
Total tax levy	$12,295,108
County levy	2,042,366
County taxes	1,692,349
County library	155,303
County health	0
County open space	194,714
School levy	7,239,481
Muni. levy	3,013,261
Misc. revenues	3,185,811

Riverton Borough

Burlington County

Demographics & Socio-Economic Characteristics
(2000 US Census, except as noted)

Population
1980*	3,068
1990*	2,775
2000	2,759
Male	1,309
Female	1,450
2006 (estimate)*	2,715
Population density	4,113.6

Race & Hispanic Origin, 2000
Race
- White....................2,644
- Black/African American....49
- American Indian/Alaska Native....3
- Asian....23
- Native Hawaiian/Pacific Islander....0
- Other race....8
- Two or more races....32
- Hispanic origin, total....30
  - Mexican....4
  - Puerto Rican....8
  - Cuban....2
  - Other Hispanic....16

Age & Nativity, 2000
- Under 5 years....165
- 18 years and over....2,158
- 21 years and over....2,100
- 65 years and over....532
- 85 years and over....105
- Median age....41.8
- Native-born....2,687
- Foreign-born....72

Educational Attainment, 2000
- Population 25 years and over....2,036
- Less than 9th grade....2.4%
- High school grad or higher....89.8%
- Bachelor's degree or higher....36.2%
- Graduate degree....12.6%

Income & Poverty, 1999
- Per capita income....$30,223
- Median household income....$58,977
- Median family income....$68,125
- Persons in poverty....82
- H'holds receiving public assistance....9
- H'holds receiving social security....309

Households, 2000
- Total households....1,066
- With persons under 18....344
- With persons over 65....293
- Family households....746
- Single-person households....270
- Persons per household....2.48
- Persons per family....3.00

Labor & Employment
- Total civilian labor force, 2006**....1,605
- Unemployment rate....2.4%
- Total civilian labor force, 2000....1,382
- Unemployment rate....2.2%

Employed persons 16 years and over by occupation, 2000
- Managers & professionals....642
- Service occupations....84
- Sales & office occupations....381
- Farming, fishing & forestry....0
- Construction & maintenance....110
- Production & transportation....135
- Self-employed persons....121

‡ Joint library with Palmyra Borough
* US Census Bureau
** New Jersey Department of Labor

General Information
Borough of Riverton
505A Howard St
Riverton, NJ 08077
856-829-0120

- Website....www.riverton-nj.com
- Year of incorporation....1893
- Land/water area (sq. miles)....0.66/0.29
- Form of government....Borough

Government
Legislative Districts
- US Congressional....1
- State Legislative....7

Local Officials, 2008
- Mayor....Robert Martin
- Manager/Admin....NA
- Clerk....Mary Longbottom
- Finance Dir....Betty Boyle
- Tax Assessor....Tom Davis
- Tax Collector....Marianne E. Hulme
- Attorney....Bruce Gunn
- Building....Ed Schaefer
- Comm Dev/Planning....NA
- Engineering....Richard Arango
- Public Works....NA
- Police Chief....Robert Norcross
- Emerg/Fire Director....Scott Reed

Housing & Construction
Housing Units, 2000*
- Total....1,113
- Median rent....$695
- Median SF home value....$153,600

Permits for New Residential Construction
	Units	Value
Total, 2007	7	$1,132,400
Single family	7	$1,132,400
Total, 2006	6	$795,000
Single family	6	$795,000

Real Property Valuation, 2007
	Parcels	Valuation
Total	961	$131,331,100
Vacant	30	2,007,000
Residential	873	118,569,400
Commercial	45	6,448,900
Industrial	1	932,000
Apartments	12	3,373,800
Farm land	0	0
Farm homestead	0	0

Average Property Value & Tax, 2007
- Residential value....$135,818
- Property tax....$7,045
- Tax credit/rebate....$1,112

Public Library
Riverton Free Library‡
306 Main St
Riverton, NJ 08077
856-829-2476

Director....Michael Robinson

Library statistics, 2006
- Population served....
- Full-time/total staff...../

	Total	Per capita
Holdings		
Revenues		
Expenditures		
Annual visits		
Internet terminals/annual users		/

Public Safety
Number of officers, 2006....6

Crime	2005	2006
Total crimes	58	37
Violent	9	0
Murder	0	0
Rape	1	0
Robbery	3	0
Aggravated assault	5	0
Non-violent	49	37
Burglary	6	6
Larceny	42	31
Vehicle theft	1	0
Domestic violence	8	9
Arson	0	2
Total crime rate	21.1	13.5
Violent	3.3	0.0
Non-violent	17.8	13.5

Public School District
(for school year 2006-07 except as noted)

Riverton Borough School District
600 Fifth St
Riverton, NJ 08077
856-829-0087

- Superintendent....Mary Ellen Eck
- Number of schools....1
- Grade plan....K-8
- Enrollment....243
- Attendance rate, '05-06....96.2%
- Dropout rate....NA
- Students per teacher....9.3
- Per pupil expenditure....$13,140
- Median faculty salary....$54,617
- Median administrator salary....$83,277
- Grade 12 enrollment....NA
- High school graduation rate....NA

Assessment test results
(percent scoring at proficient or advanced level)

	Language	Math
NJASK-Grade 3	100.0%	100.0%
GEPA-Grade 8	68.1%	86.4%
HSPA-High School	NA	NA

SAT score averages
Pct tested	Math	Verbal	Writing
NA	NA	NA	NA

Teacher Qualifications
- Avg. years of experience....17
- Highly-qualified teachers one subject/all subjects....100%/100%
- With emergency credentials....0.0%

No Child Left Behind
- AYP, 2005-06....Meets Standards

Municipal Finance
State Aid Programs, 2008
- Total aid....$219,991
- CMPTRA....0
- Energy tax receipts....219,991
- Garden State Trust....0

General Budget, 2007
- Total tax levy....$6,818,289
- County levy....1,063,207
- County taxes....881,018
- County library....80,847
- County health....0
- County open space....101,342
- School levy....3,934,859
- Muni. levy....1,820,223
- Misc. revenues....1,548,706

Taxes	2005	2006	2007
General tax rate per $100	4.8	5.019	5.19
County equalization ratio	65.45	56.34	51.97
Net valuation taxable	$131,106,426	$131,330,500	$131,439,091
State equalized value	$232,705,761	$252,813,082	$271,341,159

428 The New Jersey Municipal Data Book

Mercer County
Robbinsville Township

Demographics & Socio-Economic Characteristics
(2000 US Census, except as noted)

Population
- 1980*...................................3,487
- 1990*...................................5,815
- 2000..................................10,275
  - Male..................................4,908
  - Female...............................5,367
- 2006 (estimate)*.....................11,906
  - Population density..................581.3

Race & Hispanic Origin, 2000
Race
- White..................................9,350
- Black/African American................297
- American Indian/Alaska Native.........14
- Asian...................................443
- Native Hawaiian/Pacific Islander........0
- Other race..............................57
- Two or more races.....................114
- Hispanic origin, total.................279
  - Mexican...............................29
  - Puerto Rican..........................95
  - Cuban.................................34
  - Other Hispanic.......................121

Age & Nativity, 2000
- Under 5 years..........................945
- 18 years and over...................7,590
- 21 years and over...................7,450
- 65 years and over.....................995
- 85 years and over......................61
- Median age............................37.3
- Native-born.........................9,382
- Foreign-born..........................893

Educational Attainment, 2000
- Population 25 years and over........7,241
- Less than 9th grade..................3.0%
- High school grad or higher..........92.3%
- Bachelor's degree or higher.........46.9%
- Graduate degree.....................15.3%

Income & Poverty, 1999
- Per capita income.................$35,529
- Median household income...........$71,377
- Median family income..............$90,878
- Persons in poverty....................381
- H'holds receiving public assistance...26
- H'holds receiving social security....863

Households, 2000
- Total households...................4,074
  - With persons under 18............1,519
  - With persons over 65..............765
  - Family households................2,815
  - Single-person households.........1,074
- Persons per household...............2.52
- Persons per family..................3.09

Labor & Employment
- Total civilian labor force, 2006**...5,176
  - Unemployment rate.................2.7%
- Total civilian labor force, 2000....5,605
  - Unemployment rate.................2.3%

Employed persons 16 years and over by occupation, 2000
- Managers & professionals...........3,144
- Service occupations..................344
- Sales & office occupations.........1,437
- Farming, fishing & forestry............0
- Construction & maintenance..........254
- Production & transportation.........296
- Self-employed persons...............204

‡ Branch of county library
* US Census Bureau
** New Jersey Department of Labor

See Introduction for an explanation of all data sources.

General Information
Robbinsville Township
(formerly Washington Township)
1 Washington Blvd, Suite 6
Robbinsville, NJ 08691
609-918-0002

- Website.............www.robbinsville-twp.org
- Year of incorporation................1860
- Land/water area (sq. miles)......20.48/0.02
- Form of government................Township

Government
Legislative Districts
- US Congressional........................4
- State Legislative......................30

Local Officials, 2008
- Mayor......................David Fried
- Administrator..........Mary Caffrey
- Clerk..................Michele Auletta
- Finance Dir............Deborah Bauer
- Tax Assessor...........Gregory Busa
- Tax Collector.........Janice Garcia
- Attorney..............Mark Roselli
- Building..............Robert Corby
- Planning..............Jack West
- Engineering...........Jack West
- Public Works.........Dino Colarocco
- Police Chief.........Martin Masseroni
- Emerg/Fire Director......Kevin Brink

Housing & Construction
Housing Units, 2000*
- Total.................................4,163
- Median rent...........................$788
- Median SF home value............$216,500

Permits for New Residential Construction

	Units	Value
Total, 2007	71	$14,141,500
Single family	71	$14,141,500
Total, 2006	84	$12,610,500
Single family	61	$8,610,500

Real Property Valuation, 2007

	Parcels	Valuation
Total	5,576	$2,577,721,667
Vacant	580	151,153,900
Residential	4,519	1,871,318,100
Commercial	163	266,412,000
Industrial	17	242,229,500
Apartments	1	9,849,500
Farm land	223	2,370,967
Farm homestead	73	34,387,700

Average Property Value & Tax, 2007
- Residential value..................$415,006
- Property tax.........................$8,275
- Tax credit/rebate...................$1,176

Public Library
Robbinsville Township Branch Library‡
42 Allentown Robbinsville Rd
Robbinsville, NJ 08691
609-259-2150
Branch Librarian.....Ann Marie Ehrenberg

Library statistics, 2006
see Mercer County profile
for library system statistics

Public Safety
- Number of officers, 2006..............26

Crime

	2005	2006
Total crimes	136	130
Violent	9	8
Murder	0	0
Rape	0	1
Robbery	3	2
Aggravated assault	6	5
Non-violent	127	122
Burglary	25	18
Larceny	90	95
Vehicle theft	12	9
Domestic violence	117	97
Arson	0	0
Total crime rate	11.9	11.2
Violent	0.8	0.7
Non-violent	11.1	10.5

Public School District
(for school year 2006-07 except as noted)

Robbinsville Township School District
155 Robbinsville-Edinburg Rd
Robbinsville, NJ 08691
609-632-0910

- Superintendent...............John Szabo
- Number of schools.....................3
- Grade plan.........................K-12
- Enrollment.......................2,498
- Attendance rate, '05-06.........98.1%
- Dropout rate........................NA
- Students per teacher..............13.5
- Per pupil expenditure..........$12,013
- Median faculty salary..........$47,556
- Median administrator salary..$102,096
- Grade 12 enrollment................NA
- High school graduation rate........NA

Assessment test results
(percent scoring at proficient or advanced level)

	Language	Math
NJASK-Grade 3	94.3%	94.8%
GEPA-Grade 8	85.3%	85.9%
HSPA-High School	94.7%	89.2%

SAT score averages

Pct tested	Math	Verbal	Writing
NA	NA	NA	NA

Teacher Qualifications
- Avg. years of experience..............8
- Highly-qualified teachers
  - one subject/all subjects....45.0%/44.5%
- With emergency credentials.........0.6%

No Child Left Behind
- AYP, 2005-06............Meets Standards

Municipal Finance
State Aid Programs, 2008
- Total aid.....................$1,686,907
  - CMPTRA..............................0
  - Energy tax receipts.........1,682,770
  - Garden State Trust.............4,137

General Budget, 2007
- Total tax levy...............$51,475,085
  - County levy.................11,263,478
    - County taxes..............9,702,873
    - County library..............895,178
    - County health....................0
    - County open space..........665,428
  - School levy.................30,247,963
  - Muni. levy..................9,963,644
  - Misc. revenues..............6,439,809

Taxes	2005	2006	2007
General tax rate per $100	4.25	4.51	2
County equalization ratio	57.69	52.16	116.41
Net valuation taxable	$936,560,490	$961,625,705	$2,581,417,305
State equalized value	$1,795,553,087	$2,113,939,477	$2,389,812,149

The New Jersey Municipal Data Book

Rochelle Park Township

Bergen County

Demographics & Socio-Economic Characteristics
(2000 US Census, except as noted)

Population
1980*	5,603
1990*	5,587
2000	5,528
Male	2,525
Female	3,003
2006 (estimate)*	6,027
Population density	5,740.0

Race & Hispanic Origin, 2000
Race
- White ... 4,980
- Black/African American ... 25
- American Indian/Alaska Native ... 2
- Asian ... 333
- Native Hawaiian/Pacific Islander ... 0
- Other race ... 112
- Two or more races ... 76
- Hispanic origin, total ... 474
  - Mexican ... 20
  - Puerto Rican ... 105
  - Cuban ... 68
  - Other Hispanic ... 281

Age & Nativity, 2000
- Under 5 years ... 312
- 18 years and over ... 4,497
- 21 years and over ... 4,359
- 65 years and over ... 1,319
- 85 years and over ... 320
- Median age ... 43.2
- Native-born ... 4,640
- Foreign-born ... 888

Educational Attainment, 2000
- Population 25 years and over ... 4,197
- Less than 9th grade ... 5.1%
- High school grad or higher ... 85.3%
- Bachelor's degree or higher ... 23.7%
- Graduate degree ... 7.6%

Income & Poverty, 1999
- Per capita income ... $25,054
- Median household income ... $60,818
- Median family income ... $74,016
- Persons in poverty ... 153
- H'holds receiving public assistance ... 41
- H'holds receiving social security ... 785

Households, 2000
- Total households ... 2,061
  - With persons under 18 ... 577
  - With persons over 65 ... 775
  - Family households ... 1,394
  - Single-person households ... 563
- Persons per household ... 2.52
- Persons per family ... 3.12

Labor & Employment
- Total civilian labor force, 2006** ... 2,966
  - Unemployment rate ... 4.4%
- Total civilian labor force, 2000 ... 2,784
  - Unemployment rate ... 4.1%

Employed persons 16 years and over by occupation, 2000
- Managers & professionals ... 1,002
- Service occupations ... 357
- Sales & office occupations ... 851
- Farming, fishing & forestry ... 0
- Construction & maintenance ... 152
- Production & transportation ... 307
- Self-employed persons ... 126

* US Census Bureau
** New Jersey Department of Labor

General Information
Township of Rochelle Park
151 W Passaic St
Rochelle Park, NJ 07662
201-587-7730

Website	rochelleparknj.gov
Year of incorporation	1929
Land/water area (sq. miles)	1.05/0.00
Form of government	Township

Government
Legislative Districts
- US Congressional ... 5
- State Legislative ... 37

Local Officials, 2008
Mayor	Joseph Scarpa
Manager	Michael Mariniello Jr
Clerk	Virginia De Maria
Finance Dir	Michael Mariniello Jr
Tax Assessor	James Tighe
Tax Collector	Roy Riggitano
Attorney	Joseph Rotolo
Building	Richard Bolan
Comm Dev/Planning	NA
Engineering	Kenneth Job
Public Works	Brian Koenig
Police Chief	Richard Zavinsky
Emerg/Fire Director	David Brown Jr

Housing & Construction
Housing Units, 2000*
- Total ... 2,111
- Median rent ... $842
- Median SF home value ... $190,600

Permits for New Residential Construction
	Units	Value
Total, 2007	8	$118,520
Single family	1	$32,100
Total, 2006	74	$2,526,327
Single family	4	$519,588

Real Property Valuation, 2007
	Parcels	Valuation
Total	2,010	$689,088,901
Vacant	53	8,087,901
Residential	1,802	415,706,800
Commercial	127	216,896,300
Industrial	23	24,498,800
Apartments	5	23,899,100
Farm land	0	0
Farm homestead	0	0

Average Property Value & Tax, 2007
- Residential value ... $230,692
- Property tax ... $5,722
- Tax credit/rebate ... $1,033

Public Library
Rochelle Park Public Library
151 W Passaic St
Rochelle Park, NJ 07662
201-587-7730

Director ... Judith Sands

Library statistics, 2006
- Population served ... 5,528
- Full-time/total staff ... 0/1

	Total	Per capita
Holdings	17,769	3.21
Revenues	$188,135	$34.03
Expenditures	$232,845	$42.12
Annual visits	31,768	5.75
Internet terminals/annual users	3/5,175	

Public Safety
Number of officers, 2006 ... 21

Crime	2005	2006
Total crimes	109	113
Violent	5	6
Murder	0	0
Rape	0	0
Robbery	3	0
Aggravated assault	2	6
Non-violent	104	107
Burglary	14	18
Larceny	85	83
Vehicle theft	5	6
Domestic violence	4	18
Arson	0	0
Total crime rate	19.0	19.3
Violent	0.9	1.0
Non-violent	18.1	18.3

Public School District
(for school year 2006-07 except as noted)

Rochelle Park School District
300 Rochelle Ave
Rochelle Park, NJ 07662
201-843-3120

Superintendent	C. Lauren Schoen
Number of schools	1
Grade plan	K-8
Enrollment	480
Attendance rate, '05-06	96.1%
Dropout rate	NA
Students per teacher	9.6
Per pupil expenditure	$13,502
Median faculty salary	$63,706
Median administrator salary	$103,515
Grade 12 enrollment	NA
High school graduation rate	NA

Assessment test results
(percent scoring at proficient or advanced level)
	Language	Math
NJASK-Grade 3	80.3%	82.0%
GEPA-Grade 8	82.5%	75.0%
HSPA-High School	NA	NA

SAT score averages
Pct tested	Math	Verbal	Writing
NA	NA	NA	NA

Teacher Qualifications
- Avg. years of experience ... 10
- Highly-qualified teachers
  - one subject/all subjects ... 100%/100%
- With emergency credentials ... 0.0%

No Child Left Behind
AYP, 2005-06 ... Meets Standards

Municipal Finance
State Aid Programs, 2008
- Total aid ... $761,733
  - CMPTRA ... 238,072
  - Energy tax receipts ... 523,661
  - Garden State Trust ... 0

General Budget, 2007
- Total tax levy ... $17,532,168
  - County levy ... 1,848,461
  - County taxes ... 1,744,716
  - County library ... 0
  - County health ... 0
  - County open space ... 103,745
  - School levy ... 8,889,109
  - Muni. levy ... 6,794,598
- Misc. revenues ... 3,507,041

Taxes	2005	2006	2007
General tax rate per $100	2.18	2.38	2.49
County equalization ratio	87.63	77.99	67.92
Net valuation taxable	$694,238,894	$672,743,300	$706,878,653
State equalized value	$890,163,988	$1,010,816,656	$1,140,633,000

Morris County
Rockaway Borough

Demographics & Socio-Economic Characteristics
(2000 US Census, except as noted)

Population
1980*	6,852
1990*	6,243
2000	6,473
Male	3,148
Female	3,325
2006 (estimate)*	6,410
Population density	3,067.0

Race & Hispanic Origin, 2000
Race
- White 5,680
- Black/African American 91
- American Indian/Alaska Native 13
- Asian 412
- Native Hawaiian/Pacific Islander 2
- Other race 193
- Two or more races 82

Hispanic origin, total 608
- Mexican 57
- Puerto Rican 158
- Cuban 16
- Other Hispanic 377

Age & Nativity, 2000
- Under 5 years 435
- 18 years and over 4,968
- 21 years and over 4,783
- 65 years and over 770
- 85 years and over 63
- Median age 37.8
- Native-born 5,476
- Foreign-born 997

Educational Attainment, 2000
- Population 25 years and over 4,552
- Less than 9th grade 3.4%
- High school grad or higher 89.7%
- Bachelor's degree or higher 28.7%
- Graduate degree 7.6%

Income & Poverty, 1999
- Per capita income $26,500
- Median household income $61,002
- Median family income $66,997
- Persons in poverty 322
- H'holds receiving public assistance 39
- H'holds receiving social security 476

Households, 2000
- Total households 2,445
- With persons under 18 881
- With persons over 65 585
- Family households 1,709
- Single-person households 582
- Persons per household 2.64
- Persons per family 3.16

Labor & Employment
- Total civilian labor force, 2006** 4,074
- Unemployment rate 5.3%
- Total civilian labor force, 2000 3,714
- Unemployment rate 4.6%

Employed persons 16 years and over by occupation, 2000
- Managers & professionals 1,278
- Service occupations 386
- Sales & office occupations 1,149
- Farming, fishing & forestry 13
- Construction & maintenance 254
- Production & transportation 463
- Self-employed persons 156

* US Census Bureau
** New Jersey Department of Labor

See Introduction for an explanation of all data sources.

General Information
Borough of Rockaway
1 E Main St
Rockaway, NJ 07866
973-627-2000

- Website .... www.rockawayborough.com
- Year of incorporation 1894
- Land/water area (sq. miles) 2.09/0.02
- Form of government .... Borough

Government
Legislative Districts
- US Congressional 11
- State Legislative 25

Local Officials, 2008
- Mayor .... Kathyann Snyder
- Manager/Admin .... NA
- Clerk .... Sheila Seifert
- Finance Dir .... John Doherty
- Tax Assessor .... Bernard Murdoch
- Tax Collector .... Donna Browne
- Attorney .... Edward Wacks
- Building .... Sam LoManto
- Comm Dev/Planning .... NA
- Engineering .... Michael Spillane
- Public Works .... Joseph Rossi
- Police Chief .... Douglas Scheer
- Emerg/Fire Director .... Joseph Giordano

Housing & Construction
Housing Units, 2000*
- Total 2,491
- Median rent $875
- Median SF home value $187,200

Permits for New Residential Construction
	Units	Value
Total, 2007	0	$0
Single family	0	$0
Total, 2006	0	$0
Single family	0	$0

Real Property Valuation, 2007
	Parcels	Valuation
Total	2,217	$765,476,300
Vacant	84	12,959,500
Residential	1,905	561,984,000
Commercial	190	138,492,700
Industrial	15	29,747,700
Apartments	23	22,292,400
Farm land	0	0
Farm homestead	0	0

Average Property Value & Tax, 2007
- Residential value $295,005
- Property tax $6,249
- Tax credit/rebate $1,067

Public Library
Rockaway Borough Library
82 E Main St
Rockaway, NJ 07866
973-627-5709

Director .... Edna Puleo

Library statistics, 2006
- Population served 6,473
- Full-time/total staff 1/1

	Total	Per capita
Holdings	35,902	5.55
Revenues	$274,871	$42.46
Expenditures	$271,416	$41.93
Annual visits	24,105	3.72
Internet terminals/annual users	2/5,625	

Public Safety
Number of officers, 2006 14

Crime	2005	2006
Total crimes	79	80
Violent	5	4
Murder	0	0
Rape	0	0
Robbery	1	0
Aggravated assault	4	4
Non-violent	74	76
Burglary	10	10
Larceny	57	59
Vehicle theft	7	7
Domestic violence	50	31
Arson	0	0
Total crime rate	12.3	12.5
Violent	0.8	0.6
Non-violent	11.5	11.8

Public School District
(for school year 2006-07 except as noted)

Rockaway Borough School District
103 E Main St
Rockaway, NJ 07866
973-625-8601

- Superintendent .... Emil Suarez
- Number of schools 2
- Grade plan K-8
- Enrollment 622
- Attendance rate, '05-06 .... 95.2%
- Dropout rate .... NA
- Students per teacher 12.4
- Per pupil expenditure $10,460
- Median faculty salary $50,963
- Median administrator salary $88,000
- Grade 12 enrollment .... NA
- High school graduation rate .... NA

Assessment test results
(percent scoring at proficient or advanced level)

	Language	Math
NJASK-Grade 3	85.1%	92.7%
GEPA-Grade 8	71.3%	75.3%
HSPA-High School	NA	NA

SAT score averages
Pct tested	Math	Verbal	Writing
NA	NA	NA	NA

Teacher Qualifications
- Avg. years of experience 10
- Highly-qualified teachers
  one subject/all subjects 100%/100%
- With emergency credentials 0.0%

No Child Left Behind
AYP, 2005-06 .... Meets Standards

Municipal Finance
State Aid Programs, 2008
- Total aid $604,828
- CMPTRA 172,148
- Energy tax receipts 432,680
- Garden State Trust 0

General Budget, 2007
- Total tax levy $16,232,135
- County levy 2,075,090
-   County taxes 1,659,355
-   County library 0
-   County health 0
-   County open space 415,735
- School levy 10,459,238
- Muni. levy 3,697,807
- Misc. revenues 2,449,319

Taxes
	2005	2006	2007
General tax rate per $100	1.94	2.02	2.12
County equalization ratio	106.66	96.36	88.01
Net valuation taxable	$767,065,591	$762,223,300	$766,256,440
State equalized value	$796,041,502	$866,918,580	$935,998,588

Rockaway Township
Morris County

Demographics & Socio-Economic Characteristics
(2000 US Census, except as noted)

Population
1980*	19,850
1990*	19,572
2000	22,930
Male	11,329
Female	11,601
2006 (estimate)*	25,789
Population density	602.3

Race & Hispanic Origin, 2000
Race
White	20,375
Black/African American	565
American Indian/Alaska Native	23
Asian	1,295
Native Hawaiian/Pacific Islander	4
Other race	367
Two or more races	301
Hispanic origin, total	1,440
Mexican	127
Puerto Rican	455
Cuban	109
Other Hispanic	749

Age & Nativity, 2000
Under 5 years	1,771
18 years and over	16,715
21 years and over	16,164
65 years and over	2,162
85 years and over	162
Median age	37.0
Native-born	19,892
Foreign-born	3,038

Educational Attainment, 2000
Population 25 years and over	15,488
Less than 9th grade	2.2%
High school grad or higher	93.0%
Bachelor's degree or higher	41.4%
Graduate degree	12.4%

Income & Poverty, 1999
Per capita income	$33,184
Median household income	$80,939
Median family income	$89,281
Persons in poverty	551
H'holds receiving public assistance	51
H'holds receiving social security	1,722

Households, 2000
Total households	8,108
With persons under 18	3,392
With persons over 65	1,586
Family households	6,381
Single-person households	1,376
Persons per household	2.82
Persons per family	3.21

Labor & Employment
Total civilian labor force, 2006**	14,614
Unemployment rate	2.5%
Total civilian labor force, 2000	12,706
Unemployment rate	3.3%

Employed persons 16 years and over by occupation, 2000
Managers & professionals	5,842
Service occupations	1,209
Sales & office occupations	3,469
Farming, fishing & forestry	0
Construction & maintenance	763
Production & transportation	1,004
Self-employed persons	603

* US Census Bureau
** New Jersey Department of Labor

General Information
Township of Rockaway
65 Mount Hope Rd
Rockaway, NJ 07866
973-627-7200
Website: www.rockawaytownship.org
Year of incorporation: 1844
Land/water area (sq. miles): 42.82/3.17
Form of government: Mayor-Council

Government
Legislative Districts
US Congressional	11
State Legislative	25

Local Officials, 2008
Mayor	Louis Sceusi
Manager	Gergory Poff II
Clerk	Mary Cilurso
Finance Dir	NA
Tax Assessor	Mark Burek
Tax Collector	Lorraine Benderoth
Attorney	Edward Buzak
Building	Andy Sanfilippo
Planning	Phyllis Hantman
Engineering	Jim Lutz
Public Works	Ed Hollenbeck
Police Chief	Walter Kimble
Emerg/Fire Director	Joe Mason

Housing & Construction
Housing Units, 2000*
Total	8,506
Median rent	$948
Median SF home value	$206,200

Permits for New Residential Construction
	Units	Value
Total, 2007	117	$14,873,128
Single family	21	$4,243,228
Total, 2006	42	$7,663,771
Single family	23	$6,109,882

Real Property Valuation, 2007
	Parcels	Valuation
Total	9,524	$2,899,883,300
Vacant	863	65,014,700
Residential	8,404	2,169,466,200
Commercial	162	450,806,800
Industrial	48	172,386,400
Apartments	9	38,686,200
Farm land	29	152,300
Farm homestead	9	3,370,700

Average Property Value & Tax, 2007
Residential value	$258,271
Property tax	$8,133
Tax credit/rebate	$1,202

Public Library
Rockaway Township Library
61 Mount Hope Rd
Rockaway, NJ 07866
973-627-2344
Director: Joy Kaufman

Library statistics, 2006
Population served	22,930
Full-time/total staff	2/2

	Total	Per capita
Holdings	128,052	5.58
Revenues	$1,406,384	$61.33
Expenditures	$1,099,449	$47.95
Annual visits	102,000	4.45
Internet terminals/annual users	20/50,000	

Taxes
	2005	2006	2007
General tax rate per $100	2.84	3.02	3.15
County equalization ratio	84.45	70.2	65.71
Net valuation taxable	$2,922,353,434	$2,921,491,000	$2,902,847,641
State equalized value	$4,162,896,630	$4,448,507,434	$4,471,197,469

Public Safety
Number of officers, 2006: 56

Crime	2005	2006
Total crimes	435	498
Violent	21	16
Murder	0	0
Rape	1	3
Robbery	9	6
Aggravated assault	11	7
Non-violent	414	482
Burglary	35	38
Larceny	363	424
Vehicle theft	16	20
Domestic violence	141	132
Arson	3	2
Total crime rate	17.2	19.5
Violent	0.8	0.6
Non-violent	16.4	18.9

Public School District
(for school year 2006-07 except as noted)

Rockaway Township School District
16 School Rd, PO Box 500
Hibernia, NJ 07842
973-627-8200

Superintendent	Gary J. Vitta
Number of schools	6
Grade plan	K-8
Enrollment	2,854
Attendance rate, '05-06	96.0%
Dropout rate	NA
Students per teacher	9.2
Per pupil expenditure	$14,891
Median faculty salary	$51,647
Median administrator salary	$120,311
Grade 12 enrollment	NA
High school graduation rate	NA

Assessment test results
(percent scoring at proficient or advanced level)
	Language	Math
NJASK-Grade 3	90.1%	93.4%
GEPA-Grade 8	85.3%	80.7%
HSPA-High School	NA	NA

SAT score averages
Pct tested	Math	Verbal	Writing
NA	NA	NA	NA

Teacher Qualifications
Avg. years of experience	7
Highly-qualified teachers one subject/all subjects	99.5%/99.5%
With emergency credentials	0.0%

No Child Left Behind
AYP, 2005-06: Meets Standards

Municipal Finance
State Aid Programs, 2008
Total aid	$2,230,456
CMPTRA	666,932
Energy tax receipts	1,273,457
Garden State Trust	115,650

General Budget, 2007
Total tax levy	$91,414,739
County levy	10,299,750
County taxes	8,235,638
County library	0
County health	0
County open space	2,064,112
School levy	60,229,412
Muni. levy	20,885,577
Misc. revenues	10,984,149

Bergen County

Rockleigh Borough

Demographics & Socio-Economic Characteristics
(2000 US Census, except as noted)

Population
1980*	192
1990*	270
2000	391
Male	191
Female	200
2006 (estimate)*	393
Population density	405.2

Race & Hispanic Origin, 2000
Race
- White: 351
- Black/African American: 13
- American Indian/Alaska Native: 1
- Asian: 15
- Native Hawaiian/Pacific Islander: 0
- Other race: 4
- Two or more races: 7

Hispanic origin, total: 19
- Mexican: 3
- Puerto Rican: 2
- Cuban: 6
- Other Hispanic: 8

Age & Nativity, 2000
- Under 5 years: 18
- 18 years and over: 288
- 21 years and over: 280
- 65 years and over: 125
- 85 years and over: 60
- Median age: 49.1
- Native-born: 319
- Foreign-born: 80

Educational Attainment, 2000
- Population 25 years and over: 277
- Less than 9th grade: 13.4%
- High school grad or higher: 78.7%
- Bachelor's degree or higher: 28.9%
- Graduate degree: 12.6%

Income & Poverty, 1999
- Per capita income: $48,935
- Median household income: $152,262
- Median family income: $157,816
- Persons in poverty: 68
- H'holds receiving public assistance: 3
- H'holds receiving social security: 15

Households, 2000
- Total households: 74
- With persons under 18: 29
- With persons over 65: 20
- Family households: 58
- Single-person households: 8
- Persons per household: 3.04
- Persons per family: 3.40

Labor & Employment
- Total civilian labor force, 2006**: 96
- Unemployment rate: 0.0%
- Total civilian labor force, 2000: 114
- Unemployment rate: 0.0%

Employed persons 16 years and over by occupation, 2000
- Managers & professionals: 68
- Service occupations: 9
- Sales & office occupations: 30
- Farming, fishing & forestry: 2
- Construction & maintenance: 3
- Production & transportation: 2
- Self-employed persons: 6

* US Census Bureau
** New Jersey Department of Labor

See Introduction for an explanation of all data sources.

General Information
Borough of Rockleigh
26 Rockleigh Rd
Rockleigh, NJ 07647
201-768-4217

- Website: www.rockleighnj.org
- Year of incorporation: 1923
- Land/water area (sq. miles): 0.97/0.00
- Form of government: Borough

Government
Legislative Districts
- US Congressional: 5
- State Legislative: 39

Local Officials, 2008
- Mayor: Nicholas Langella
- Manager: William J. McGuire
- Clerk: William J. McGuire
- Finance Dir: Anne Murphy
- Tax Assessor: Raymond Damiano
- Tax Collector: Anne Murphy
- Attorney: John Hall
- Building: William McGuire
- Comm Dev/Planning: NA
- Engineering: Neglia Engineering
- Public Works: NA
- Police Chief: Bruce Tietjen
- Emerg/Fire Director: Mike Malhame

Housing & Construction
Housing Units, 2000*
- Total: 80
- Median rent: $2,001
- Median SF home value: $937,500

Permits for New Residential Construction
	Units	Value
Total, 2007	0	$0
Single family	0	$0
Total, 2006	0	$0
Single family	0	$0

Real Property Valuation, 2007
	Parcels	Valuation
Total	100	$266,551,856
Vacant	11	10,274,956
Residential	73	149,236,700
Commercial	16	107,040,200
Industrial	0	0
Apartments	0	0
Farm land	0	0
Farm homestead	0	0

Average Property Value & Tax, 2007
- Residential value: $2,044,338
- Property tax: $12,240
- Tax credit/rebate: $1,353

Public Library
No public municipal library

Library statistics, 2006
- Population served: NA
- Full-time/total staff: NA/NA

	Total	Per capita
Holdings	NA	NA
Revenues	NA	NA
Expenditures	NA	NA
Annual visits	NA	NA
Internet terminals/annual users	NA/NA	

Taxes
	2005	2006	2007
General tax rate per $100	1.33	0.58	0.6
County equalization ratio	62.49	137.23	137.23
Net valuation taxable	$117,424,841	$274,233,300	$266,820,621
State equalized value	$200,110,499	$200,102,433	$212,508,478

Public Safety
Number of officers, 2006: 0

Crime
	2005	2006
Total crimes	8	11
Violent	1	2
Murder	0	0
Rape	0	0
Robbery	0	0
Aggravated assault	1	2
Non-violent	7	9
Burglary	1	2
Larceny	6	7
Vehicle theft	0	0
Domestic violence	0	0
Arson	0	0
Total crime rate	20.2	27.8
Violent	2.5	5.1
Non-violent	17.7	22.8

Public School District
(for school year 2006-07 except as noted)

Rockleigh Board of Education
Box 343
Closter, NJ 07624

No schools in district - sends students to Northvale and Northern Valley Regional schools (see Appendix D)

- Per pupil expenditure: NA
- Median faculty salary: NA
- Median administrator salary: NA
- Grade 12 enrollment: NA
- High school graduation rate: NA

Assessment test results
(percent scoring at proficient or advanced level)
	Language	Math
NJASK-Grade 3	NA	NA
GEPA-Grade 8	NA	NA
HSPA-High School	NA	NA

SAT score averages
Pct tested	Math	Verbal	Writing
NA	NA	NA	NA

Teacher Qualifications
- Avg. years of experience: NA
- Highly-qualified teachers one subject/all subjects: NA/NA
- With emergency credentials: NA

No Child Left Behind
- AYP, 2005-06: NA

Municipal Finance
State Aid Programs, 2008
- Total aid: $102,363
- CMPTRA: 0
- Energy tax receipts: 102,363
- Garden State Trust: 0

General Budget, 2007
- Total tax levy: $1,597,539
- County levy: 360,823
- County taxes: 340,879
- County library: 0
- County health: 0
- County open space: 19,943
- School levy: 390,707
- Muni. levy: 846,009
- Misc. revenues: 751,722

Rocky Hill Borough
Somerset County

Demographics & Socio-Economic Characteristics
(2000 US Census, except as noted)

Population
1980*	717
1990*	693
2000	662
Male	328
Female	334
2006 (estimate)*	678
Population density	1,011.9

Race & Hispanic Origin, 2000
Race
White	630
Black/African American	9
American Indian/Alaska Native	0
Asian	3
Native Hawaiian/Pacific Islander	4
Other race	6
Two or more races	10
Hispanic origin, total	26
Mexican	3
Puerto Rican	13
Cuban	3
Other Hispanic	7

Age & Nativity, 2000
Under 5 years	38
18 years and over	528
21 years and over	521
65 years and over	114
85 years and over	15
Median age	43.8
Native-born	585
Foreign-born	73

Educational Attainment, 2000
Population 25 years and over	523
Less than 9th grade	2.1%
High school grad or higher	96.0%
Bachelor's degree or higher	59.7%
Graduate degree	29.1%

Income & Poverty, 1999
Per capita income	$48,357
Median household income	$79,469
Median family income	$100,314
Persons in poverty	18
H'holds receiving public assistance	3
H'holds receiving social security	84

Households, 2000
Total households	284
With persons under 18	71
With persons over 65	89
Family households	190
Single-person households	79
Persons per household	2.33
Persons per family	2.82

Labor & Employment
Total civilian labor force, 2006**	429
Unemployment rate	3.0%
Total civilian labor force, 2000	386
Unemployment rate	2.6%

Employed persons 16 years and over by occupation, 2000
Managers & professionals	230
Service occupations	30
Sales & office occupations	70
Farming, fishing & forestry	0
Construction & maintenance	25
Production & transportation	21
Self-employed persons	40

‡ Branch of county library
* US Census Bureau
** New Jersey Department of Labor

General Information
Borough of Rocky Hill
PO Box 188
Rocky Hill, NJ 08553
609-924-7445
Website	www.rockyhill-nj.gov
Year of incorporation	1889
Land/water area (sq. miles)	0.67/0.00
Form of government	Borough

Government
Legislative Districts
US Congressional	7
State Legislative	16

Local Officials, 2008
Mayor	Edward P. Zimmerman
Manager/Admin	NA
Clerk	Donna M. Griffiths
Finance Dir	G. Ross Bobal
Tax Assessor	George Sopko
Tax Collector	Donna Griffiths
Attorney	Albert Cruz
Building	DCA
Comm Dev/Planning	NA
Engineering	Neil Van Cleef
Public Works	NA
Police Chief	NA
Emerg/Fire Director	Todd Harris

Housing & Construction
Housing Units, 2000*
Total	295
Median rent	$914
Median SF home value	$271,400

Permits for New Residential Construction
	Units	Value
Total, 2007	0	$0
Single family	0	$0
Total, 2006	0	$0
Single family	0	$0

Real Property Valuation, 2007
	Parcels	Valuation
Total	284	$62,214,800
Vacant	9	272,300
Residential	256	54,572,200
Commercial	13	3,451,000
Industrial	1	3,329,000
Apartments	2	569,400
Farm land	3	20,900
Farm homestead	0	0

Average Property Value & Tax, 2007
Residential value	$213,173
Property tax	$6,474
Tax credit/rebate	$1,031

Public Library
Mary Jacobs Branch Library‡
64 Washington St
Rocky Hill, NJ 08553
609-924-7073
Branch Librarian	Helen Morris

Library statistics, 2006
see Somerset County profile for library system statistics

Public Safety
Number of officers, 2006	0

Crime	2005	2006
Total crimes	4	3
Violent	1	0
Murder	0	0
Rape	0	0
Robbery	1	0
Aggravated assault	0	0
Non-violent	3	3
Burglary	2	1
Larceny	1	2
Vehicle theft	0	0
Domestic violence	0	1
Arson	0	0
Total crime rate	6.0	4.4
Violent	1.5	0.0
Non-violent	4.5	4.4

Public School District
(for school year 2006-07 except as noted)

Rocky Hill Borough School District
PO Box 270
Rocky Hill, NJ 08853

No schools in district

Per pupil expenditure	NA
Median faculty salary	NA
Median administrator salary	NA
Grade 12 enrollment	NA
High school graduation rate	NA

Assessment test results
(percent scoring at proficient or advanced level)
	Language	Math
NJASK-Grade 3	NA	NA
GEPA-Grade 8	NA	NA
HSPA-High School	NA	NA

SAT score averages
Pct tested	Math	Verbal	Writing
NA	NA	NA	NA

Teacher Qualifications
Avg. years of experience	NA
Highly-qualified teachers one subject/all subjects	NA/NA
With emergency credentials	NA

No Child Left Behind
AYP, 2005-06	NA

Municipal Finance
State Aid Programs, 2008
Total aid	$72,636
CMPTRA	0
Energy tax receipts	72,636
Garden State Trust	0

General Budget, 2007
Total tax levy	$1,892,197
County levy	452,895
County taxes	366,287
County library	46,499
County health	0
County open space	40,110
School levy	1,026,875
Muni. levy	412,427
Misc. revenues	568,009

Taxes	2005	2006	2007
General tax rate per $100	2.58	2.78	3.04
County equalization ratio	59.26	51.22	47.21
Net valuation taxable	$61,881,553	$62,039,800	$62,303,496
State equalized value	$120,815,215	$131,506,346	$134,752,765

Monmouth County

Roosevelt Borough

Demographics & Socio-Economic Characteristics
(2000 US Census, except as noted)

Population
- 1980*......................................835
- 1990*......................................884
- 2000......................................933
  - Male....................................449
  - Female..................................484
- 2006 (estimate)*..........................913
  - Population density....................465.8

Race & Hispanic Origin, 2000
Race
- White......................................830
- Black/African American.....................24
- American Indian/Alaska Native...............0
- Asian.......................................19
- Native Hawaiian/Pacific Islander.............1
- Other race..................................21
- Two or more races...........................38
- Hispanic origin, total......................42
  - Mexican....................................4
  - Puerto Rican..............................19
  - Cuban......................................0
  - Other Hispanic............................19

Age & Nativity, 2000
- Under 5 years...............................49
- 18 years and over..........................674
- 21 years and over..........................641
- 65 years and over..........................113
- 85 years and over...........................14
  - Median age...............................40.4
- Native-born................................848
- Foreign-born................................80

Educational Attainment, 2000
- Population 25 years and over...............584
- Less than 9th grade........................3.8%
- High school grad or higher................93.0%
- Bachelor's degree or higher...............44.2%
- Graduate degree...........................17.8%

Income & Poverty, 1999
- Per capita income......................$24,892
- Median household income.................$61,979
- Median family income....................$67,019
- Persons in poverty..........................40
- H'holds receiving public assistance..........2
- H'holds receiving social security...........80

Households, 2000
- Total households..........................337
  - With persons under 18...................138
  - With persons over 65.....................86
- Family households..........................258
- Single-person households....................63
- Persons per household......................2.77
- Persons per family........................3.17

Labor & Employment
- Total civilian labor force, 2006**..........538
  - Unemployment rate........................4.0%
- Total civilian labor force, 2000............496
  - Unemployment rate........................4.4%

Employed persons 16 years and over by occupation, 2000
- Managers & professionals...................221
- Service occupations.........................45
- Sales & office occupations..................97
- Farming, fishing & forestry..................0
- Construction & maintenance..................66
- Production & transportation.................45
- Self-employed persons.......................27

* US Census Bureau
** New Jersey Department of Labor

See Introduction for an explanation of all data sources.

General Information
Borough of Roosevelt
33 N Rochdale Ave
PO Box 128
Roosevelt, NJ 08555
609-448-0539

- Website......................................NA
- Year of incorporation......................1945
- Land/water area (sq. miles).........1.96/0.00
- Form of government.....................Borough

Government
Legislative Districts
- US Congressional..............................4
- State Legislative............................30

Local Officials, 2008
- Mayor............................Beth Battel
- Manager....................William Schmeling
- Clerk.............Krystyna Bieracka-Olejnik
- Treasurer........................A. Debevec
- Tax Assessor..............Michael L. Ticktin
- Tax Collector.........Salvatore Cannizzaro
- Attorney................Richard J. Shaklee
- Building......................Rick Bordeur
- Comm Dev/Planning....................NA
- Engineering................Carmela Robert
- Public Works.........................NA
- Police Chief.........................NA
- Emerg/Fire Director.........Kim Dexheimer

Housing & Construction
Housing Units, 2000*
- Total......................................351
- Median rent..............................$809
- Median SF home value..................$134,100

Permits for New Residential Construction

	Units	Value
Total, 2007	0	$0
Single family	0	$0
Total, 2006	1	$220,000
Single family	1	$220,000

Real Property Valuation, 2007

	Parcels	Valuation
Total	337	$95,836,500
Vacant	3	718,200
Residential	308	85,183,700
Commercial	3	1,183,700
Industrial	3	1,638,700
Apartments	1	2,101,400
Farm land	10	278,300
Farm homestead	9	4,732,500

Average Property Value & Tax, 2007
- Residential value....................$283,647
- Property tax..........................$5,737
- Tax credit/rebate......................$919

Public Library
No public municipal library

Library statistics, 2006
- Population served.........................NA
- Full-time/total staff..................NA/NA

	Total	Per capita
Holdings	NA	NA
Revenues	NA	NA
Expenditures	NA	NA
Annual visits	NA	NA
Internet terminals/annual users	NA/NA	

Taxes

	2005	2006	2007
General tax rate per $100	4.69	4.78	2.023
County equalization ratio	54.85	47.22	107.33
Net valuation taxable	$35,693,588	$36,308,910	$95,936,697
State equalized value	$75,589,979	$89,169,546	$89,391,635

Public Safety
- Number of officers, 2006....................0

Crime	2005	2006
Total crimes	4	4
Violent	1	1
Murder	0	0
Rape	0	0
Robbery	1	0
Aggravated assault	0	1
Non-violent	3	3
Burglary	2	1
Larceny	1	2
Vehicle theft	0	0
Domestic violence	1	0
Arson	0	0
Total crime rate	4.3	4.4
Violent	1.1	1.1
Non-violent	3.2	3.3

Public School District
(for school year 2006-07 except as noted)

Roosevelt Borough School District
School Lane, PO Box 160
Roosevelt, NJ 08555
609-448-2798

- Principal.....................Shari Payson
- Number of schools............................1
- Grade plan................................K-6
- Enrollment..................................91
- Attendance rate, '05-06..................96.7%
- Dropout rate...............................NA
- Students per teacher.......................10.4
- Per pupil expenditure..................$14,944
- Median faculty salary..................$41,746
- Median administrator salary............$70,122
- Grade 12 enrollment........................NA
- High school graduation rate................NA

Assessment test results
(percent scoring at proficient or advanced level)

	Language	Math
NJASK-Grade 3	100.0%	100.0%
GEPA-Grade 8	NA	NA
HSPA-High School	NA	NA

SAT score averages

Pct tested	Math	Verbal	Writing
NA	NA	NA	NA

Teacher Qualifications
- Avg. years of experience..................12
- Highly-qualified teachers
  - one subject/all subjects........100%/100%
- With emergency credentials.................0.0%

No Child Left Behind
- AYP, 2005-06..............Meets Standards

Municipal Finance
State Aid Programs, 2008
- Total aid...........................$76,697
- CMPTRA..................................0
- Energy tax receipts...................75,319
- Garden State Trust.....................1,378

General Budget, 2007
- Total tax levy....................$1,940,417
- County levy..........................245,540
  - County taxes.......................215,618
  - County library.....................12,343
  - County health.......................4,107
  - County open space..................13,472
- School levy.......................1,271,456
- Muni. levy..........................423,421
- Misc. revenues......................413,214

Roseland Borough
Essex County

Demographics & Socio-Economic Characteristics
(2000 US Census, except as noted)

Population
1980*	5,330
1990*	4,847
2000	5,298
Male	2,448
Female	2,850
2006 (estimate)*	5,400
Population density	1,491.7

Race & Hispanic Origin, 2000
Race
- White 4,950
- Black/African American 38
- American Indian/Alaska Native 2
- Asian 250
- Native Hawaiian/Pacific Islander 0
- Other race 23
- Two or more races 35
- Hispanic origin, total 121
  - Mexican 11
  - Puerto Rican 23
  - Cuban 12
  - Other Hispanic 75

Age & Nativity, 2000
- Under 5 years 314
- 18 years and over 4,207
- 21 years and over 4,107
- 65 years and over 1,044
- 85 years and over 92
  - Median age 44.0
- Native-born 4,694
- Foreign-born 604

Educational Attainment, 2000
- Population 25 years and over 3,988
- Less than 9th grade 2.4%
- High school grad or higher 92.2%
- Bachelor's degree or higher 46.5%
- Graduate degree 18.8%

Income & Poverty, 1999
- Per capita income $41,415
- Median household income $82,499
- Median family income $93,957
- Persons in poverty 88
- H'holds receiving public assistance 9
- H'holds receiving social security 794

Households, 2000
- Total households 2,142
  - With persons under 18 587
  - With persons over 65 768
  - Family households 1,525
  - Single-person households 550
- Persons per household 2.47
- Persons per family 2.99

Labor & Employment
- Total civilian labor force, 2006** 2,940
  - Unemployment rate 3.4%
- Total civilian labor force, 2000 2,760
  - Unemployment rate 2.7%

Employed persons 16 years and over by occupation, 2000
- Managers & professionals 1,416
- Service occupations 193
- Sales & office occupations 840
- Farming, fishing & forestry 0
- Construction & maintenance 161
- Production & transportation 75
- Self-employed persons 169

* US Census Bureau
** New Jersey Department of Labor

General Information
Borough of Roseland
19 Harrison Ave
Roseland, NJ 07068
973-226-8080

- Website .... www.roselandnj.org
- Year of incorporation 1908
- Land/water area (sq. miles) 3.62/0.00
- Form of government .... Borough

Government
Legislative Districts
- US Congressional 11
- State Legislative 27

Local Officials, 2008
- Mayor .... John Arvanites
- Manager .... Thomas Kaczynski
- Clerk .... Thomas Kaczynski
- Finance Dir .... Maureen Chumacas
- Tax Assessor .... Kevin Dillon
- Tax Collector .... Maureen Chumacas
- Attorney .... Paul Jemas
- Building .... Leonard Mendola
- Comm Dev/Planning .... NA
- Engineering .... Ralph Tango
- Public Works .... Gary Schall
- Police Chief .... Richard McDonough
- Emerg/Fire Director .... Kent Yates

Housing & Construction
Housing Units, 2000*
- Total 2,187
- Median rent $1,266
- Median SF home value $292,700

Permits for New Residential Construction
	Units	Value
Total, 2007	27	$4,965,018
Single family	21	$4,170,018
Total, 2006	36	$6,233,089
Single family	36	$6,233,089

Real Property Valuation, 2007
	Parcels	Valuation
Total	2,204	$259,673,741
Vacant	82	1,714,600
Residential	2,032	128,712,141
Commercial	63	108,117,400
Industrial	25	13,509,200
Apartments	1	7,616,900
Farm land	1	3,500
Farm homestead	0	0

Average Property Value & Tax, 2007
- Residential value $63,343
- Property tax $7,237
- Tax credit/rebate $1,050

Public Library
Roseland Free Public Library
20 Roseland Ave
Roseland, NJ 07068
973-226-8636

Director .... Judith Lind

Library statistics, 2006
- Population served 5,298
- Full-time/total staff 3/5

	Total	Per capita
Holdings	61,178	11.55
Revenues	$625,540	$118.07
Expenditures	$564,750	$106.60
Annual visits	52,000	9.82
Internet terminals/annual users	4/14,500	

Public Safety
Number of officers, 2006 27

Crime	2005	2006
Total crimes	62	44
Violent	2	1
Murder	0	0
Rape	0	0
Robbery	1	0
Aggravated assault	1	1
Non-violent	60	43
Burglary	16	7
Larceny	38	32
Vehicle theft	6	4
Domestic violence	32	30
Arson	1	0
Total crime rate	11.6	8.1
Violent	0.4	0.2
Non-violent	11.2	8.0

Public School District
(for school year 2006-07 except as noted)

Roseland School District
Noecker School, Passaic Ave
Roseland, NJ 07068
973-226-1296

- Superintendent .... Richard M. Sierchio
- Number of schools 1
- Grade plan K-6
- Enrollment 479
- Attendance rate, '05-06 .... 96.0%
- Dropout rate .... NA
- Students per teacher 12.6
- Per pupil expenditure $11,703
- Median faculty salary $58,500
- Median administrator salary $95,700
- Grade 12 enrollment .... NA
- High school graduation rate .... NA

Assessment test results
(percent scoring at proficient or advanced level)
	Language	Math
NJASK-Grade 3	92.3%	92.3%
GEPA-Grade 8	NA	NA
HSPA-High School	NA	NA

SAT score averages
Pct tested	Math	Verbal	Writing
NA	NA	NA	NA

Teacher Qualifications
- Avg. years of experience 11
- Highly-qualified teachers
  - one subject/all subjects 100%/100%
- With emergency credentials 0.0%

No Child Left Behind
AYP, 2005-06 .... Meets Standards

Municipal Finance
State Aid Programs, 2008
- Total aid $1,096,804
  - CMPTRA 58,828
  - Energy tax receipts 1,037,976
  - Garden State Trust 0

General Budget, 2007
- Total tax levy $29,694,793
  - County levy 7,798,881
    - County taxes 7,598,457
    - County library 0
    - County health 0
    - County open space 200,424
  - School levy 13,798,678
  - Muni. levy 8,097,234
  - Misc. revenues 5,269,912

Taxes	2005	2006	2007
General tax rate per $100	10.13	10.41	11.43
County equalization ratio	19.15	14.66	13.15
Net valuation taxable	$263,730,528	$254,991,241	$259,897,546
State equalized value	$1,798,980,409	$1,939,345,014	$1,993,115,140

Union County
Roselle Borough

Demographics & Socio-Economic Characteristics
(2000 US Census, except as noted)

Population
- 1980* 20,641
- 1990* 20,314
- 2000 21,274
  - Male 9,950
  - Female 11,324
- 2006 (estimate)* 21,158
- Population density 8,014.4

Race & Hispanic Origin, 2000
Race
- White 7,570
- Black/African American ... 10,917
- American Indian/Alaska Native ... 67
- Asian 577
- Native Hawaiian/Pacific Islander ... 15
- Other race 1,291
- Two or more races 837
- Hispanic origin, total 3,641
  - Mexican 597
  - Puerto Rican 876
  - Cuban 230
  - Other Hispanic 1,938

Age & Nativity, 2000
- Under 5 years 1,410
- 18 years and over 15,841
- 21 years and over 14,948
- 65 years and over 2,562
- 85 years and over 268
- Median age 35.3
- Native-born 16,396
- Foreign-born 4,878

Educational Attainment, 2000
- Population 25 years and over ... 14,017
- Less than 9th grade 6.2%
- High school grad or higher ... 77.6%
- Bachelor's degree or higher ... 17.3%
- Graduate degree 4.8%

Income & Poverty, 1999
- Per capita income $21,269
- Median household income ... $51,254
- Median family income ... $58,841
- Persons in poverty 1,582
- H'holds receiving public assistance ... 258
- H'holds receiving social security ... 2,024

Households, 2000
- Total households 7,520
  - With persons under 18 2,916
  - With persons over 65 1,984
  - Family households 5,223
  - Single-person households ... 1,895
- Persons per household 2.82
- Persons per family 3.41

Labor & Employment
- Total civilian labor force, 2006** ... 11,547
  - Unemployment rate 7.0%
- Total civilian labor force, 2000 ... 10,970
  - Unemployment rate 6.6%
- *Employed persons 16 years and over by occupation, 2000*
  - Managers & professionals ... 2,567
  - Service occupations 1,608
  - Sales & office occupations ... 3,456
  - Farming, fishing & forestry ... 5
  - Construction & maintenance ... 686
  - Production & transportation ... 1,925
- Self-employed persons 369

* US Census Bureau
** New Jersey Department of Labor
§ State Fiscal Year July 1–June 30

See Introduction for an explanation of all data sources.

General Information
Borough of Roselle
210 Chestnut St
Roselle, NJ 07203
908-245-5600

- Website .... www.boroughofroselle.com
- Year of incorporation 1894
- Land/water area (sq. miles) ... 2.64/0.01
- Form of government .... Borough

Government
Legislative Districts
- US Congressional 10
- State Legislative 20

Local Officials, 2008
- Mayor .... Garrett B. Smith
- Administrator .... Cheryl Fuller
- Clerk .... Rhona C. Bluestein
- Finance Dir .... Adrien Mapp
- Tax Assessor .... Pamela Steele
- Tax Collector .... Mary Testori
- Attorney .... Wilfredo Benitez
- Building .... Jeff Guy
- Comm Dev/Planning .... NA
- Engineering .... David Battaglia
- Public Works .... Louis Williams
- Police Chief .... (vacant)
- Fire Chief .... Paul Mucha (Dep)

Housing & Construction
Housing Units, 2000*
- Total 7,870
- Median rent $700
- Median SF home value $129,200

Permits for New Residential Construction

	Units	Value
Total, 2007	8	$688,956
Single family	3	$465,756
Total, 2006	4	$493,710
Single family	4	$493,710

Real Property Valuation, 2007

	Parcels	Valuation
Total	5,598	$784,256,500
Vacant	57	3,031,200
Residential	5,177	616,786,900
Commercial	227	78,788,300
Industrial	88	38,085,100
Apartments	49	47,565,000
Farm land	0	0
Farm homestead	0	0

Average Property Value & Tax, 2007
- Residential value $119,140
- Property tax $7,681
- Tax credit/rebate $1,341

Public Library
Roselle Free Public Library
104 W Fourth Ave
Roselle, NJ 07203
908-245-5809

- Director .... W. Keith McCoy

Library statistics, 2006
- Population served 21,274
- Full-time/total staff 2/7

	Total	Per capita
Holdings	53,250	2.50
Revenues	$676,766	$31.81
Expenditures	$664,246	$31.22
Annual visits	88,454	4.16
Internet terminals/annual users	4/32,131	

Public Safety
- Number of officers, 2006 56

Crime	2005	2006
Total crimes	623	501
Violent	76	87
Murder	0	1
Rape	2	4
Robbery	42	54
Aggravated assault	32	28
Non-violent	547	414
Burglary	147	109
Larceny	289	242
Vehicle theft	111	63
Domestic violence	222	163
Arson	2	0
Total crime rate	29.1	23.6
Violent	3.5	4.1
Non-violent	25.5	19.5

Public School District
(for school year 2006-07 except as noted)

Roselle Borough School District
710 Locust St
Roselle, NJ 07203
908-298-2040

- Superintendent of Schools . Elnardo Webster
- Number of schools 6
- Grade plan K-12
- Enrollment 2,850
- Attendance rate, '05-06 .... 93.8%
- Dropout rate 1.0%
- Students per teacher 10.1
- Per pupil expenditure $14,927
- Median faculty salary $46,856
- Median administrator salary ... $92,133
- Grade 12 enrollment 155
- High school graduation rate ... 96.3%

Assessment test results
(percent scoring at proficient or advanced level)

	Language	Math
NJASK-Grade 3	80.7%	85.0%
GEPA-Grade 8	43.7%	39.7%
HSPA-High School	71.4%	46.6%

SAT score averages

Pct tested	Math	Verbal	Writing
59%	383	391	404

Teacher Qualifications
- Avg. years of experience 5
- Highly-qualified teachers
  - one subject/all subjects ... 99.5%/99.5%
- With emergency credentials 0.0%

No Child Left Behind
- AYP, 2005-06 .... Needs Improvement

Municipal Finance §
State Aid Programs, 2008
- Total aid $2,978,575
  - CMPTRA 1,468,706
  - Energy tax receipts 1,509,869
  - Garden State Trust 0

General Budget, 2007
- Total tax levy $50,732,759
  - County levy 5,904,548
    - County taxes 5,649,286
    - County library 0
    - County health 0
    - County open space ... 255,262
  - School levy 22,354,904
  - Muni. levy 22,473,308
- Misc. revenues 9,799,601

Taxes	2005	2006	2007
General tax rate per $100	6.049	6.423	6.448
County equalization ratio	58.78	50.25	46.34
Net valuation taxable	$785,028,946	$787,791,000	$786,884,003
State equalized value	$1,454,295,936	$1,703,355,665	$1,818,456,399

Roselle Park Borough
Union County

Demographics & Socio-Economic Characteristics
(2000 US Census, except as noted)

Population
- 1980* 13,377
- 1990* 12,805
- 2000 13,281
  - Male 6,469
  - Female 6,812
- 2006 (estimate)* 13,124
- Population density 10,757.4

Race & Hispanic Origin, 2000
Race
- White 10,740
- Black/African American 322
- American Indian/Alaska Native 14
- Asian 1,214
- Native Hawaiian/Pacific Islander 2
- Other race 650
- Two or more races 339
- Hispanic origin, total 2,170
  - Mexican 242
  - Puerto Rican 423
  - Cuban 275
  - Other Hispanic 1,230

Age & Nativity, 2000
- Under 5 years 781
- 18 years and over 10,328
- 21 years and over 9,904
- 65 years and over 1,680
- 85 years and over 209
  - Median age 36.7
- Native-born 9,993
- Foreign-born 3,288

Educational Attainment, 2000
- Population 25 years and over 9,095
- Less than 9th grade 5.5%
- High school grad or higher 82.9%
- Bachelor's degree or higher 25.6%
- Graduate degree 7.7%

Income & Poverty, 1999
- Per capita income $24,101
- Median household income $53,717
- Median family income $63,403
- Persons in poverty 571
- H'holds receiving public assistance 96
- H'holds receiving social security ... 1,265

Households, 2000
- Total households 5,137
  - With persons under 18 1,665
  - With persons over 65 1,260
  - Family households 3,415
  - Single-person households 1,448
- Persons per household 2.58
- Persons per family 3.22

Labor & Employment
- Total civilian labor force, 2006** ... 7,881
  - Unemployment rate 4.8%
- Total civilian labor force, 2000 7,488
  - Unemployment rate 4.6%

Employed persons 16 years and over by occupation, 2000
- Managers & professionals 2,480
- Service occupations 1,036
- Sales & office occupations 2,190
- Farming, fishing & forestry 0
- Construction & maintenance 530
- Production & transportation 908
- Self-employed persons 224

* US Census Bureau
** New Jersey Department of Labor

General Information
Borough of Roselle Park
110 E Westfield Ave
Roselle Park, NJ 07204
908-245-6222
- Website .... www.rosellepark.net
- Year of incorporation 1901
- Land/water area (sq. miles) 1.22/0.00
- Form of government .... Borough

Government
Legislative Districts
- US Congressional 7
- State Legislative 21

Local Officials, 2008
- Mayor .... Joseph DeIorio
- Manager/Admin .... Doreen Cali
- Clerk .... Doreen Cali
- Finance Dir .... Kenneth Blum
- Tax Assessor .... Paul Endler
- Tax Collector .... NA
- Attorney .... Blake Johnstone
- Building .... Jerry Eger
- Comm Dev/Planning .... NA
- Engineering .... Neglia Engineering
- Public Works .... Frank Wirzbicki
- Police Chief .... Paul Morrison
- Emerg/Fire Director .... Robert Tobe

Housing & Construction
Housing Units, 2000*
- Total 5,258
- Median rent $785
- Median SF home value $157,700

Permits for New Residential Construction

	Units	Value
Total, 2007	13	$1,531,557
Single family	9	$762,957
Total, 2006	10	$848,370
Single family	10	$848,370

Real Property Valuation, 2007

	Parcels	Valuation
Total	3,585	$290,686,500
Vacant	33	521,000
Residential	3,315	234,150,900
Commercial	178	25,290,500
Industrial	24	5,797,800
Apartments	35	24,926,300
Farm land	0	0
Farm homestead	0	0

Average Property Value & Tax, 2007
- Residential value $70,634
- Property tax $7,341
- Tax credit/rebate $1,201

Public Library
Veteran's Memorial Library
404 Chestnut St
Roselle Park, NJ 07204
908-245-2456
- Director .... Susan Calantone

Library statistics, 2006
- Population served 13,281
- Full-time/total staff 1/4

	Total	Per capita
Holdings	77,160	5.81
Revenues	$555,279	$41.81
Expenditures	$453,922	$34.18
Annual visits	45,000	3.39
Internet terminals/annual users	10/16,000	

Public Safety
- Number of officers, 2006 35

Crime	2005	2006
Total crimes	229	231
Violent	24	8
Murder	1	0
Rape	0	0
Robbery	15	1
Aggravated assault	8	7
Non-violent	205	223
Burglary	36	35
Larceny	140	169
Vehicle theft	29	19
Domestic violence	77	77
Arson	2	0
Total crime rate	17.2	17.5
Violent	1.8	0.6
Non-violent	15.4	16.9

Public School District
(for school year 2006-07 except as noted)

Roselle Park School District
510 Chestnut St
Roselle Park, NJ 07204
908-245-1197
- Superintendent .... Patrick Spagnoletti
- Number of schools 5
- Grade plan K-12
- Enrollment 2,032
- Attendance rate, '05-06 .... 94.9%
- Dropout rate 0.9%
- Students per teacher 10.4
- Per pupil expenditure $11,758
- Median faculty salary $47,006
- Median administrator salary $91,075
- Grade 12 enrollment 170
- High school graduation rate 98.3%

Assessment test results
(percent scoring at proficient or advanced level)

	Language	Math
NJASK-Grade 3	88.7%	92.1%
GEPA-Grade 8	73.7%	68.6%
HSPA-High School	82.6%	77.1%

SAT score averages

Pct tested	Math	Verbal	Writing
85%	469	457	456

Teacher Qualifications
- Avg. years of experience 7
- Highly-qualified teachers
  - one subject/all subjects 98.5%/98.5%
- With emergency credentials 0.6%

No Child Left Behind
- AYP, 2005-06 .... Meets Standards

Municipal Finance
State Aid Programs, 2008
- Total aid $1,324,220
- CMPTRA 537,639
- Energy tax receipts 786,581
- Garden State Trust 0

General Budget, 2007
- Total tax levy $30,227,314
- County levy 4,322,284
  - County taxes 4,135,873
  - County library 0
  - County health 0
  - County open space 186,411
- School levy 16,875,449
- Muni. levy 9,029,581
- Misc. revenues 4,177,237

Taxes	2005	2006	2007
General tax rate per $100	9.096	9.725	10.394
County equalization ratio	28.98	25.85	23.48
Net valuation taxable	$290,771,295	$290,974,200	$290,832,123
State equalized value	$1,057,734,794	$1,239,408,724	$1,354,065,045

Morris County
Roxbury Township

Demographics & Socio-Economic Characteristics
(2000 US Census, except as noted)

Population
- 1980*.........................18,878
- 1990*.........................20,429
- 2000..........................23,883
  - Male........................11,674
  - Female......................12,209
- 2006 (estimate)*..............23,803
  - Population density........1,113.9

Race & Hispanic Origin, 2000
Race
- White.........................22,110
- Black/African American..........456
- American Indian/Alaska Native....35
- Asian............................855
- Native Hawaiian/Pacific Islander..17
- Other race......................162
- Two or more races...............248
- Hispanic origin, total........1,154
  - Mexican.......................77
  - Puerto Rican..................393
  - Cuban.........................103
  - Other Hispanic................581

Age & Nativity, 2000
- Under 5 years.................1,705
- 18 years and over............17,438
- 21 years and over............16,751
- 65 years and over.............2,363
- 85 years and over...............253
  - Median age....................37.5
- Native-born..................21,470
- Foreign-born..................2,413

Educational Attainment, 2000
- Population 25 years and over..16,150
- Less than 9th grade............3.3%
- High school grad or higher....90.0%
- Bachelor's degree or higher...33.9%
- Graduate degree...............10.0%

Income & Poverty, 1999
- Per capita income...........$30,174
- Median household income.....$72,982
- Median family income........$83,409
- Persons in poverty.............642
- H'holds receiving public assistance....107
- H'holds receiving social security...1,908

Households, 2000
- Total households..............8,364
  - With persons under 18.......3,524
  - With persons over 65........1,711
  - Family households...........6,534
  - Single-person households....1,501
- Persons per household..........2.84
- Persons per family.............3.25

Labor & Employment
- Total civilian labor force, 2006**....14,250
  - Unemployment rate............3.2%
- Total civilian labor force, 2000......13,018
  - Unemployment rate............3.0%

Employed persons 16 years and over by occupation, 2000
- Managers & professionals.....5,430
- Service occupations..........1,319
- Sales & office occupations...3,772
- Farming, fishing & forestry......9
- Construction & maintenance...1,121
- Production & transportation....974
- Self-employed persons..........701

* US Census Bureau
** New Jersey Department of Labor

See Introduction for an explanation of all data sources.

General Information
Roxbury Township
1715 US Highway 46
Ledgewood, NJ 07852
973-448-2000
- Website..............www.roxburynj.us
- Year of incorporation............1740
- Land/water area (sq. miles).....21.37/0.53
- Form of government.......Council-Manager

Government
Legislative Districts
- US Congressional...................11
- State Legislative..................25

Local Officials, 2008
- Mayor..................Timothy Smith
- Manager............Christopher Raths
- Clerk.............Betty Lou DeCroce
- Finance Dir...........Lisa Palmieri
- Tax Assessor..........Joseph McKeon
- Tax Collector......Maryann Albrecht
- Attorney............Tony Bucco Jr
- Building..............Rod Schmidt
- Planning.............Russell Stern
- Engineering.........Mike Kobylarz
- Public Works...........Rick Blood
- Police Chief............Mark Noll
- Fire Chief...........Adam Alberti

Housing & Construction
Housing Units, 2000*
- Total..........................8,550
- Median rent.....................$759
- Median SF home value........$207,400

Permits for New Residential Construction

	Units	Value
Total, 2007	40	$4,015,986
Single family	30	$3,980,586
Total, 2006	37	$4,119,796
Single family	29	$4,014,394

Real Property Valuation, 2007

	Parcels	Valuation
Total	8,728	$2,039,433,800
Vacant	447	34,695,400
Residential	7,780	1,611,457,800
Commercial	399	313,012,000
Industrial	44	64,614,100
Apartments	14	11,360,200
Farm land	31	231,800
Farm homestead	13	4,062,500

Average Property Value & Tax, 2007
- Residential value............$207,304
- Property tax..................$7,230
- Tax credit/rebate.............$1,135

Public Library
Roxbury Public Library
103 Main St
Succasunna, NJ 07876
973-584-2400
- Director............Mary C. Romance

Library statistics, 2006
- Population served.............23,883
- Full-time/total staff...........4/10

	Total	Per capita
Holdings	87,588	3.67
Revenues	$1,262,696	$52.87
Expenditures	$1,272,729	$53.29
Annual visits	252,050	10.55
Internet terminals/annual users	22/109,327	

Taxes
	2005	2006	2007
General tax rate per $100	3.2	3.35	3.49
County equalization ratio	66.39	58.24	54.2
Net valuation taxable	$2,048,814,719	$2,042,677,000	$2,044,763,921
State equalized value	$3,517,882,416	$3,774,462,641	$4,011,289,265

Public Safety
- Number of officers, 2006...........48

Crime	2005	2006
Total crimes	341	344
Violent	20	21
Murder	0	0
Rape	0	2
Robbery	5	9
Aggravated assault	15	10
Non-violent	321	323
Burglary	56	66
Larceny	250	232
Vehicle theft	15	25
Domestic violence	102	120
Arson	2	0
Total crime rate	14.3	14.4
Violent	0.8	0.9
Non-violent	13.5	13.5

Public School District
(for school year 2006-07 except as noted)

Roxbury Township School District
42 N Hillside Ave
Succasunna, NJ 07876
973-584-6867
- Superintendent.............Dennis Mack
- Number of schools..................7
- Grade plan......................K-12
- Enrollment....................4,499
- Attendance rate, '05-06.......96.1%
- Dropout rate...................0.9%
- Students per teacher...........11.6
- Per pupil expenditure.......$12,983
- Median faculty salary.......$57,494
- Median administrator salary.$98,000
- Grade 12 enrollment............360
- High school graduation rate..97.6%

Assessment test results
(percent scoring at proficient or advanced level)

	Language	Math
NJASK-Grade 3	88.3%	92.7%
GEPA-Grade 8	81.0%	78.1%
HSPA-High School	93.7%	78.5%

SAT score averages
Pct tested	Math	Verbal	Writing
85%	531	518	512

Teacher Qualifications
- Avg. years of experience..........12
- Highly-qualified teachers
  - one subject/all subjects....100%/100%
- With emergency credentials......0.0%

No Child Left Behind
- AYP, 2005-06..........Meets Standards

Municipal Finance
State Aid Programs, 2008
- Total aid..................$2,748,977
  - CMPTRA......................821,818
  - Energy tax receipts.......1,872,459
  - Garden State Trust...........19,910

General Budget, 2007
- Total tax levy.............$71,310,065
  - County levy...............9,023,553
    - County taxes............7,217,617
    - County library...................0
    - County health...................0
    - County open space.......1,805,936
  - School levy.............44,691,355
  - Muni. levy..............17,595,158
- Misc. revenues.............7,372,870

©2008 Information Publications, Inc. All rights reserved. Photocopying prohibited. For additional copies, contact the publisher at www.informationpublications.com or (877)544-INFO (4636)

Rumson Borough
Monmouth County

Demographics & Socio-Economic Characteristics
(2000 US Census, except as noted)

Population
- 1980* 7,623
- 1990* 6,701
- 2000 7,137
  - Male 3,457
  - Female 3,680
- 2006 (estimate)* 7,194
- Population density 1,378.2

Race & Hispanic Origin, 2000
Race
- White 6,978
- Black/African American 17
- American Indian/Alaska Native 4
- Asian 76
- Native Hawaiian/Pacific Islander ... 0
- Other race 26
- Two or more races 36
- Hispanic origin, total 99
  - Mexican 25
  - Puerto Rican 19
  - Cuban 20
  - Other Hispanic 35

Age & Nativity, 2000
- Under 5 years 528
- 18 years and over 4,862
- 21 years and over 4,729
- 65 years and over 914
- 85 years and over 92
- Median age 39.2
- Native-born 6,845
- Foreign-born 292

Educational Attainment, 2000
- Population 25 years and over ... 4,630
- Less than 9th grade 0.3%
- High school grad or higher 97.1%
- Bachelor's degree or higher 63.9%
- Graduate degree 24.9%

Income & Poverty, 1999
- Per capita income $73,692
- Median household income $120,865
- Median family income $140,668
- Persons in poverty 228
- H'holds receiving public assistance ... 12
- H'holds receiving social security ... 642

Households, 2000
- Total households 2,452
- With persons under 18 1,116
- With persons over 65 651
- Family households 1,989
- Single-person households 412
- Persons per household 2.91
- Persons per family 3.29

Labor & Employment
- Total civilian labor force, 2006** ... 3,283
- Unemployment rate 2.6%
- Total civilian labor force, 2000 3,047
- Unemployment rate 2.6%

Employed persons 16 years and over by occupation, 2000
- Managers & professionals 1,763
- Service occupations 154
- Sales & office occupations 844
- Farming, fishing & forestry 0
- Construction & maintenance 134
- Production & transportation 74
- Self-employed persons 204

* US Census Bureau
** New Jersey Department of Labor

General Information
Borough of Rumson
80 E River Rd
Rumson, NJ 07760
732-842-3300

- Website .... rumsonboro.com
- Year of incorporation 1907
- Land/water area (sq. miles) 5.22/2.01
- Form of government .... Borough

Government
Legislative Districts
- US Congressional 12
- State Legislative 11

Local Officials, 2008
- Mayor .... John E. Ekdahl
- Administrator .... Thomas S. Rogers
- Clerk .... Thomas S. Rogers
- Finance Dir .... Helen L. Graves
- Tax Assessor .... Peter Barnett
- Tax Collector .... Helen L. Graves
- Attorney .... Martin Barger
- Building .... Paul Reinhold Jr
- Planning .... Frederick Andre
- Engineering .... C. Bernard Blum Jr
- Public Works .... Mark T. Wellner
- Police Chief .... Rick Tobias
- Emerg/Fire Director ...... Joseph Ward

Housing & Construction
Housing Units, 2000*
- Total 2,610
- Median rent $1,187
- Median SF home value $455,300

Permits for New Residential Construction

	Units	Value
Total, 2007	36	$16,476,490
Single family	36	$16,476,490
Total, 2006	44	$21,377,575
Single family	44	$21,377,575

Real Property Valuation, 2007

	Parcels	Valuation
Total	2,580	$2,868,791,800
Vacant	84	41,876,500
Residential	2,417	2,715,256,600
Commercial	69	101,986,100
Industrial	0	0
Apartments	4	3,588,500
Farm land	5	32,400
Farm homestead	1	6,051,700

Average Property Value & Tax, 2007
- Residential value $1,125,438
- Property tax $15,629
- Tax credit/rebate $1,207

Public Library
Oceanic Free Library
109 Ave of Two Rivers
Rumson, NJ 07760
732-842-2692

- Director .... Ann Wissel

Library statistics, 2006
- Population served 7,137
- Full-time/total staff 1/1

	Total	Per capita
Holdings	20,964	2.94
Revenues	$147,517	$20.67
Expenditures	$161,610	$22.64
Annual visits	13,565	1.90
Internet terminals/annual users	3/1,415	

Public Safety
- Number of officers, 2006 17

Crime	2005	2006
Total crimes	70	89
Violent	4	2
Murder	0	0
Rape	0	0
Robbery	0	0
Aggravated assault	4	2
Non-violent	66	87
Burglary	17	23
Larceny	48	60
Vehicle theft	1	4
Domestic violence	4	22
Arson	0	2
Total crime rate	9.6	12.3
Violent	0.6	0.3
Non-violent	9.1	12.0

Public School District
(for school year 2006-07 except as noted)

Rumson Borough School District
Forrest Ave
Rumson, NJ 07760
732-842-4747

- Superintendent .... Roger A. Caruba
- Number of schools 2
- Grade plan K-8
- Enrollment 958
- Attendance rate, '05-06 .... 95.2%
- Dropout rate .... NA
- Students per teacher 10.9
- Per pupil expenditure $11,899
- Median faculty salary $53,440
- Median administrator salary .. $100,000
- Grade 12 enrollment .... NA
- High school graduation rate ...... NA

Assessment test results
(percent scoring at proficient or advanced level)

	Language	Math
NJASK-Grade 3	100.0%	96.7%
GEPA-Grade 8	95.4%	90.8%
HSPA-High School	NA	NA

SAT score averages

Pct tested	Math	Verbal	Writing
NA	NA	NA	NA

Teacher Qualifications
- Avg. years of experience 8
- Highly-qualified teachers
  - one subject/all subjects 100%/100%
- With emergency credentials 0.0%

No Child Left Behind
- AYP, 2005-06 .... Meets Standards

Municipal Finance
State Aid Programs, 2008
- Total aid $856,086
- CMPTRA 9,845
- Energy tax receipts 846,111
- Garden State Trust 130

General Budget, 2007
- Total tax levy $39,857,536
- County levy 9,523,930
  - County taxes 8,505,546
  - County library 486,919
  - County health 0
  - County open space 531,465
- School levy 22,273,805
- Muni. levy 8,059,801
- Misc. revenues 5,833,890

Taxes	2005	2006	2007
General tax rate per $100	1.323	1.358	1.389
County equalization ratio	102.71	90.19	81.15
Net valuation taxable	$2,777,584,506	$2,824,225,500	$2,870,060,583
State equalized value	$3,079,703,411	$3,481,455,773	$3,590,848,112

Camden County / Runnemede Borough

Demographics & Socio-Economic Characteristics
(2000 US Census, except as noted)

Population
- 1980* 9,461
- 1990* 9,042
- 2000 8,533
  - Male 4,103
  - Female 4,430
- 2006 (estimate)* 8,461
  - Population density 4,048.3

Race & Hispanic Origin, 2000

Race
- White 7,831
- Black/African American 321
- American Indian/Alaska Native 9
- Asian 132
- Native Hawaiian/Pacific Islander 1
- Other race 104
- Two or more races 135
- Hispanic origin, total 306
  - Mexican 81
  - Puerto Rican 170
  - Cuban 4
  - Other Hispanic 51

Age & Nativity, 2000
- Under 5 years 489
- 18 years and over 6,557
- 21 years and over 6,243
- 65 years and over 1,332
- 85 years and over 118
  - Median age 37.8
- Native-born 8,182
- Foreign-born 351

Educational Attainment, 2000
- Population 25 years and over 5,803
- Less than 9th grade 5.5%
- High school grad or higher 78.6%
- Bachelor's degree or higher 12.6%
- Graduate degree 3.4%

Income & Poverty, 1999
- Per capita income $19,143
- Median household income $41,126
- Median family income $50,127
- Persons in poverty 474
- H'holds receiving public assistance 17
- H'holds receiving social security ... 1,138

Households, 2000
- Total households 3,376
  - With persons under 18 1,145
  - With persons over 65 1,001
  - Family households 2,274
  - Single-person households 938
- Persons per household 2.52
- Persons per family 3.08

Labor & Employment
- Total civilian labor force, 2006** ... 4,807
  - Unemployment rate 6.5%
- Total civilian labor force, 2000 4,434
  - Unemployment rate 6.1%

Employed persons 16 years and over by occupation, 2000
- Managers & professionals 1,071
- Service occupations 662
- Sales & office occupations 1,376
- Farming, fishing & forestry 0
- Construction & maintenance 406
- Production & transportation 648
- Self-employed persons 149

* US Census Bureau
** New Jersey Department of Labor

See Introduction for an explanation of all data sources.

General Information
Borough of Runnemede
24 N Black Horse Pike
Runnemede, NJ 08078
856-939-5161

- Website .... www.runnemedenj.org
- Year of incorporation 1926
- Land/water area (sq. miles) 2.09/0.03
- Form of government .... Borough

Government

Legislative Districts
- US Congressional 1
- State Legislative 5

Local Officials, 2008
- Mayor .... Virginia Betteridge
- Manager/Admin .... NA
- Clerk .... Joyce Pinto
- Finance Dir .... Christie Melfi
- Tax Assessor .... Brian Schneider
- Tax Collector .... Joyce Pinto
- Attorney .... John S. Kennedy
- Building .... Chris Mecca
- Comm Dev/Planning .... NA
- Engineering .... Steven Bach
- Public Works .... Richard Batot
- Police Chief .... Mark Diano
- Emerg/Fire Director .... Patrick Moriarty

Housing & Construction

Housing Units, 2000*
- Total 3,510
- Median rent $598
- Median SF home value $97,800

Permits for New Residential Construction

	Units	Value
Total, 2007	7	$725,074
Single family	7	$725,074
Total, 2006	13	$1,447,213
Single family	13	$1,447,213

Real Property Valuation, 2007

	Parcels	Valuation
Total	2,870	$335,609,900
Vacant	93	3,211,700
Residential	2,588	255,372,400
Commercial	155	45,678,400
Industrial	13	13,049,700
Apartments	21	18,297,700
Farm land	0	0
Farm homestead	0	0

Average Property Value & Tax, 2007
- Residential value $98,676
- Property tax $4,805
- Tax credit/rebate $970

Public Library
Runnemede Public Library
Broadway & Black Horse Pike
Runnemede, NJ 08078
856-939-4688

Director .... Kathleen Vasinda

Library statistics, 2006
- Population served 8,533
- Full-time/total staff 1/3

	Total	Per capita
Holdings	22,294	2.61
Revenues	$320,496	$37.56
Expenditures	$238,023	$27.89
Annual visits	3,000	0.35
Internet terminals/annual users		6/2,391

Taxes

	2005	2006	2007
General tax rate per $100	4.491	4.742	4.87
County equalization ratio	82.47	70.84	63.11
Net valuation taxable	$334,052,693	$333,496,300	$336,731,321
State equalized value	$471,559,420	$529,666,038	$586,828,053

Public Safety
Number of officers, 2006 20

Crime	2005	2006
Total crimes	312	344
Violent	23	29
Murder	0	0
Rape	0	1
Robbery	4	6
Aggravated assault	19	22
Non-violent	289	315
Burglary	38	47
Larceny	235	250
Vehicle theft	16	18
Domestic violence	47	43
Arson	1	1
Total crime rate	36.7	40.4
Violent	2.7	3.4
Non-violent	34.0	37.0

Public School District
(for school year 2006-07 except as noted)

Runnemede Borough School District
505 W Third Ave
Runnemede, NJ 08078
856-931-5365

- Superintendent .... Joseph Sweeney
- Number of schools 3
- Grade plan K-8
- Enrollment 783
- Attendance rate, '05-06 .... 94.8%
- Dropout rate .... NA
- Students per teacher 10.0
- Per pupil expenditure $12,910
- Median faculty salary $57,000
- Median administrator salary $100,000
- Grade 12 enrollment .... NA
- High school graduation rate .... NA

Assessment test results
(percent scoring at proficient or advanced level)

	Language	Math
NJASK-Grade 3	84.1%	95.1%
GEPA-Grade 8	85.5%	87.8%
HSPA-High School	NA	NA

SAT score averages

Pct tested	Math	Verbal	Writing
NA	NA	NA	NA

Teacher Qualifications
- Avg. years of experience 20
- Highly-qualified teachers
  - one subject/all subjects 100%/100%
- With emergency credentials 0.0%

No Child Left Behind
- AYP, 2005-06 .... Meets Standards

Municipal Finance

State Aid Programs, 2008
- Total aid $961,895
  - CMPTRA 197,469
  - Energy tax receipts 764,426
  - Garden State Trust 0

General Budget, 2007
- Total tax levy $16,397,042
  - County levy 3,518,481
    - County taxes 3,411,763
    - County library 0
    - County health 0
    - County open space 106,718
  - School levy 9,143,036
  - Muni. levy 3,735,525
- Misc. revenues 2,855,539

©2008 Information Publications, Inc. All rights reserved. Photocopying prohibited. For additional copies, contact the publisher at www.informationpublications.com or (877)544-INFO (4636)

The New Jersey Municipal Data Book

Rutherford Borough   Bergen County

Demographics & Socio-Economic Characteristics
(2000 US Census, except as noted)

Population
1980*	19,068
1990*	17,790
2000	18,110
Male	8,699
Female	9,411
2006 (estimate)*	17,871
Population density	6,359.8

Race & Hispanic Origin, 2000
Race
White	14,849
Black/African American	489
American Indian/Alaska Native	8
Asian	2,054
Native Hawaiian/Pacific Islander	5
Other race	337
Two or more races	368
Hispanic origin, total	1,555
Mexican	88
Puerto Rican	348
Cuban	280
Other Hispanic	839

Age & Nativity, 2000
Under 5 years	946
18 years and over	14,349
21 years and over	13,818
65 years and over	2,637
85 years and over	328
Median age	38.8
Native-born	14,466
Foreign-born	3,644

Educational Attainment, 2000
Population 25 years and over	12,997
Less than 9th grade	3.7%
High school grad or higher	88.3%
Bachelor's degree or higher	40.3%
Graduate degree	14.0%

Income & Poverty, 1999
Per capita income	$30,495
Median household income	$63,820
Median family income	$78,120
Persons in poverty	668
H'holds receiving public assistance	111
H'holds receiving social security	1,970

Households, 2000
Total households	7,055
With persons under 18	2,165
With persons over 65	1,976
Family households	4,672
Single-person households	1,998
Persons per household	2.52
Persons per family	3.16

Labor & Employment
Total civilian labor force, 2006**	10,238
Unemployment rate	4.1%
Total civilian labor force, 2000	9,815
Unemployment rate	4.6%

Employed persons 16 years and over by occupation, 2000
Managers & professionals	4,191
Service occupations	984
Sales & office occupations	2,834
Farming, fishing & forestry	0
Construction & maintenance	603
Production & transportation	751
Self-employed persons	484

* US Census Bureau
** New Jersey Department of Labor

General Information
Borough of Rutherford
176 Park Ave
Rutherford, NJ 07070
201-460-3000

Website	www.rutherford-nj.com
Year of incorporation	1881
Land/water area (sq. miles)	2.81/0.12
Form of government	Borough

Government
Legislative Districts
US Congressional	9
State Legislative	36

Local Officials, 2008
Mayor	John F. Hipp
Manager	(vacant)
Clerk	Mary Kriston
Finance Dir	Ed Cortright
Tax Assessor	Joseph Nichols
Tax Collector	Caryn Miller
Attorney	Lane Biviano
Building	John Uhl
Comm Dev/Planning	NA
Engineering	Ralph Tango
Public Works	Christopher Seidler
Police Chief	(vacant)
Emerg/Fire Director	Christopher Seidler

Housing & Construction
Housing Units, 2000*
Total	7,214
Median rent	$832
Median SF home value	$218,300

Permits for New Residential Construction
	Units	Value
Total, 2007	1	$295,000
Single family	1	$295,000
Total, 2006	14	$3,330,600
Single family	10	$2,274,800

Real Property Valuation, 2007
	Parcels	Valuation
Total	5,400	$2,867,282,200
Vacant	86	51,284,700
Residential	5,001	2,243,829,900
Commercial	253	366,602,200
Industrial	24	94,820,600
Apartments	36	110,744,800
Farm land	0	0
Farm homestead	0	0

Average Property Value & Tax, 2007
Residential value	$448,676
Property tax	$8,772
Tax credit/rebate	$1,245

Public Library
Rutherford Public Library
150 Park Ave
Rutherford, NJ 07070
201-939-8600

Director: Jane Fisher

Library statistics, 2006
Population served	18,110
Full-time/total staff	5/14

	Total	Per capita
Holdings	101,193	5.59
Revenues	$1,355,311	$74.84
Expenditures	$1,403,569	$77.50
Annual visits	227,925	12.59
Internet terminals/annual users		11/33,874

Taxes
	2005	2006	2007
General tax rate per $100	3.71	1.77	1.96
County equalization ratio	58.25	115.44	102.15
Net valuation taxable	$1,252,104,081	$2,866,225,500	$2,881,009,587
State equalized value	$2,469,633,296	$2,819,199,566	$3,000,168,591

Public Safety
Number of officers, 2006		43

Crime	2005	2006
Total crimes	265	275
Violent	14	12
Murder	0	0
Rape	0	0
Robbery	6	2
Aggravated assault	8	10
Non-violent	251	263
Burglary	51	47
Larceny	170	189
Vehicle theft	30	27
Domestic violence	98	67
Arson	1	1
Total crime rate	14.7	15.3
Violent	0.8	0.7
Non-violent	13.9	14.6

Public School District
(for school year 2006-07 except as noted)

Rutherford School District
176 Park Ave
Rutherford, NJ 07070
201-939-1717

Superintendent	Leslie O'Keefe
Number of schools	5
Grade plan	K-12
Enrollment	2,456
Attendance rate, '05-06	95.6%
Dropout rate	0.2%
Students per teacher	10.9
Per pupil expenditure	$13,409
Median faculty salary	$62,382
Median administrator salary	$118,926
Grade 12 enrollment	192
High school graduation rate	99.5%

Assessment test results
(percent scoring at proficient or advanced level)
	Language	Math
NJASK-Grade 3	95.2%	96.3%
GEPA-Grade 8	90.2%	79.7%
HSPA-High School	92.7%	79.9%

SAT score averages
Pct tested	Math	Verbal	Writing
93%	529	507	493

Teacher Qualifications
Avg. years of experience	11
Highly-qualified teachers one subject/all subjects	100%/99.5%
With emergency credentials	0.0%

No Child Left Behind
AYP, 2005-06 .... Meets Standards

Municipal Finance
State Aid Programs, 2008
Total aid	$1,776,345
CMPTRA	524,798
Energy tax receipts	1,251,547
Garden State Trust	0

General Budget, 2007
Total tax levy	$56,325,461
County levy	5,135,080
County taxes	4,852,118
County library	0
County health	0
County open space	282,962
School levy	32,841,104
Muni. levy	18,349,278
Misc. revenues	7,353,324

Bergen County
Saddle Brook Township

Demographics & Socio-Economic Characteristics
(2000 US Census, except as noted)

Population
1980*	14,084
1990*	13,296
2000	13,155
Male	6,210
Female	6,945
2006 (estimate)*	13,625
Population density	5,009.2

Race & Hispanic Origin, 2000
Race
White	11,936
Black/African American	183
American Indian/Alaska Native	5
Asian	623
Native Hawaiian/Pacific Islander	0
Other race	223
Two or more races	185
Hispanic origin, total	825
Mexican	19
Puerto Rican	198
Cuban	87
Other Hispanic	521

Age & Nativity, 2000
Under 5 years	744
18 years and over	10,499
21 years and over	10,124
65 years and over	2,368
85 years and over	266
Median age	40.3
Native-born	11,043
Foreign-born	2,112

Educational Attainment, 2000
Population 25 years and over	9,703
Less than 9th grade	4.6%
High school grad or higher	85.3%
Bachelor's degree or higher	25.2%
Graduate degree	6.1%

Income & Poverty, 1999
Per capita income	$27,561
Median household income	$63,545
Median family income	$73,205
Persons in poverty	434
H'holds receiving public assistance	34
H'holds receiving social security	1,605

Households, 2000
Total households	5,062
With persons under 18	1,518
With persons over 65	1,645
Family households	3,579
Single-person households	1,263
Persons per household	2.58
Persons per family	3.11

Labor & Employment
Total civilian labor force, 2006**	1,424
Unemployment rate	3.0%
Total civilian labor force, 2000	6,953
Unemployment rate	5.2%

Employed persons 16 years and over by occupation, 2000
Managers & professionals	2,335
Service occupations	714
Sales & office occupations	2,187
Farming, fishing & forestry	0
Construction & maintenance	604
Production & transportation	752
Self-employed persons	272

* US Census Bureau
** New Jersey Department of Labor

See Introduction for an explanation of all data sources.

General Information
Township of Saddle Brook
93 Market St
Saddle Brook, NJ 07663
201-843-7100

Website	www.saddlebrooknj.gov
Year of incorporation	1955
Land/water area (sq. miles)	2.72/0.01
Form of government	Mayor-Council

Government
Legislative Districts
US Congressional	9
State Legislative	38

Local Officials, 2008
Mayor	Louis D'Arminio
Manager	Robert Elia
Clerk	Peter Lo Dico
Finance Dir	Thomas Kane
Tax Assessor	Arthur Carlson
Tax Collector	Michele Sanzari
Attorney	Anthony Suarez
Building	Ray Dressler
Comm Dev/Planning	NA
Engineering	Richard Moody
Public Works	Charles Cerone Sr
Police Chief	Robert Kugler
Fire Chief	Charles Cerone Jr (Vol)

Housing & Construction
Housing Units, 2000*
Total	5,161
Median rent	$887
Median SF home value	$198,600

Permits for New Residential Construction
	Units	Value
Total, 2007	189	$19,837,503
Single family	22	$2,666,029
Total, 2006	73	$4,351,364
Single family	38	$3,452,245

Real Property Valuation, 2007
	Parcels	Valuation
Total	4,418	$1,184,611,354
Vacant	66	9,961,800
Residential	4,143	775,970,000
Commercial	123	207,257,500
Industrial	79	161,843,754
Apartments	7	29,578,300
Farm land	0	0
Farm homestead	0	0

Average Property Value & Tax, 2007
Residential value	$187,297
Property tax	$6,179
Tax credit/rebate	$1,044

Public Library
Saddle Brook Public Library
340 Mayhill St
Saddle Brook, NJ 07663
201-843-3287

Director.................Alma J. Henderson

Library statistics, 2006
Population served	13,155
Full-time/total staff	2/2

	Total	Per capita
Holdings	58,903	4.48
Revenues	$737,987	$56.10
Expenditures	$675,923	$51.38
Annual visits	64,080	4.87
Internet terminals/annual users	11/18,020	

Taxes
	2005	2006	2007
General tax rate per $100	2.94	3.12	3.3
County equalization ratio	66.93	55.69	51.11
Net valuation taxable	$1,163,358,395	$1,167,242,754	$1,186,063,206
State equalized value	$2,088,989,756	$2,285,237,323	$2,444,957,120

Public Safety
Number of officers, 2006.............34

Crime
	2005	2006
Total crimes	428	317
Violent	9	7
Murder	0	0
Rape	0	1
Robbery	0	3
Aggravated assault	9	3
Non-violent	419	310
Burglary	45	45
Larceny	352	238
Vehicle theft	22	27
Domestic violence	41	61
Arson	1	1
Total crime rate	32.3	23.8
Violent	0.7	0.5
Non-violent	31.7	23.2

Public School District
(for school year 2006-07 except as noted)

Saddle Brook Township School District
355 Mayhill St
Saddle Brook, NJ 07663
201-843-2133

Superintendent	Harry A. Groveman
Number of schools	4
Grade plan	K-12
Enrollment	1,560
Attendance rate, '05-06	94.6%
Dropout rate	2.0%
Students per teacher	11.0
Per pupil expenditure	$12,533
Median faculty salary	$53,162
Median administrator salary	$112,484
Grade 12 enrollment	81
High school graduation rate	93.8%

Assessment test results
(percent scoring at proficient or advanced level)
	Language	Math
NJASK-Grade 3	77.5%	91.7%
GEPA-Grade 8	84.9%	77.2%
HSPA-High School	88.6%	73.6%

SAT score averages
Pct tested	Math	Verbal	Writing
113%	479	454	453

Teacher Qualifications
Avg. years of experience	11
Highly-qualified teachers one subject/all subjects	98.5%/98.5%
With emergency credentials	0.0%

No Child Left Behind
AYP, 2005-06............Meets Standards

Municipal Finance
State Aid Programs, 2008
Total aid	$1,849,346
CMPTRA	444,761
Energy tax receipts	1,404,585
Garden State Trust	0

General Budget, 2007
Total tax levy	$39,127,835
County levy	4,242,779
County taxes	4,008,768
County library	0
County health	0
County open space	234,011
School levy	22,966,002
Muni. levy	11,919,055
Misc. revenues	5,594,013

Saddle River Borough — Bergen County

Demographics & Socio-Economic Characteristics
(2000 US Census, except as noted)

Population
1980*	2,763
1990*	2,950
2000	3,201
Male	1,541
Female	1,660
2006 (estimate)*	3,786
Population density	760.2

Race & Hispanic Origin, 2000
Race
- White: 2,876
- Black/African American: 24
- American Indian/Alaska Native: 0
- Asian: 229
- Native Hawaiian/Pacific Islander: 1
- Other race: 26
- Two or more races: 45

Hispanic origin, total: 82
- Mexican: 12
- Puerto Rican: 18
- Cuban: 22
- Other Hispanic: 30

Age & Nativity, 2000
- Under 5 years: 165
- 18 years and over: 2,482
- 21 years and over: 2,400
- 65 years and over: 653
- 85 years and over: 127
- Median age: 46.9
- Native-born: 2,638
- Foreign-born: 563

Educational Attainment, 2000
- Population 25 years and over: 2,335
- Less than 9th grade: 2.8%
- High school grad or higher: 93.7%
- Bachelor's degree or higher: 60.6%
- Graduate degree: 31.9%

Income & Poverty, 1999
- Per capita income: $85,934
- Median household income: $134,289
- Median family income: $152,169
- Persons in poverty: 111
- H'holds receiving public assistance: 0
- H'holds receiving social security: 340

Households, 2000
- Total households: 1,118
- With persons under 18: 368
- With persons over 65: 378
- Family households: 927
- Single-person households: 159
- Persons per household: 2.77
- Persons per family: 3.05

Labor & Employment
- Total civilian labor force, 2006**: 7,380
- Unemployment rate: 5.3%
- Total civilian labor force, 2000: 1,344
- Unemployment rate: 3.2%

Employed persons 16 years and over by occupation, 2000
- Managers & professionals: 843
- Service occupations: 69
- Sales & office occupations: 304
- Farming, fishing & forestry: 0
- Construction & maintenance: 32
- Production & transportation: 53
- Self-employed persons: 182

* US Census Bureau
** New Jersey Department of Labor

General Information
Borough of Saddle River
100 E Allendale Rd
Saddle River, NJ 07458
201-327-2609

- Website: www.saddleriver.org
- Year of incorporation: 1894
- Land/water area (sq. miles): 4.98/0.00
- Form of government: Borough

Government

Legislative Districts
- US Congressional: 5
- State Legislative: 39

Local Officials, 2008
- Mayor: Conrad Caruso
- Manager: Charles Cuccia
- Clerk: Marie Macari
- Finance Dir: Charles Cuccia
- Tax Assessor: Stuart Stolarz
- Tax Collector: Linda Canavan
- Attorney: Harry Norton Jr
- Building: John Scialla
- Planning: Joseph Pera
- Engineering: Charles Wilde
- Public Works: NA
- Police Chief: Timothy McWilliams
- Emerg/Fire Director: Brian Yates

Housing & Construction

Housing Units, 2000*
- Total: 1,183
- Median rent: $1,451
- Median SF home value: $970,100

Permits for New Residential Construction
	Units	Value
Total, 2007	17	$12,909,448
Single family	17	$12,909,448
Total, 2006	21	$21,395,629
Single family	21	$21,395,629

Real Property Valuation, 2007
	Parcels	Valuation
Total	1,353	$2,130,715,800
Vacant	99	64,193,600
Residential	1,221	2,002,841,900
Commercial	18	54,552,400
Industrial	0	0
Apartments	0	0
Farm land	10	102,400
Farm homestead	5	9,025,500

Average Property Value & Tax, 2007
- Residential value: $1,641,001
- Property tax: $13,629
- Tax credit/rebate: $1,149

Public Library
No public municipal library

Library statistics, 2006
- Population served: NA
- Full-time/total staff: NA/NA

	Total	Per capita
Holdings	NA	NA
Revenues	NA	NA
Expenditures	NA	NA
Annual visits	NA	NA
Internet terminals/annual users	NA/NA	

Taxes
	2005	2006	2007
General tax rate per $100	0.78	0.8	0.84
County equalization ratio	97.67	91.74	87.3
Net valuation taxable	$2,004,522,124	$2,066,134,900	$2,131,618,846
State equalized value	$2,185,003,405	$2,367,477,230	$2,564,324,365

Public Safety
- Number of officers, 2006: 16

Crime
	2005	2006
Total crimes	18	25
Violent	1	1
Murder	0	0
Rape	0	0
Robbery	0	0
Aggravated assault	1	1
Non-violent	17	24
Burglary	4	8
Larceny	13	16
Vehicle theft	0	0
Domestic violence	2	12
Arson	0	0
Total crime rate	4.8	6.6
Violent	0.3	0.3
Non-violent	4.5	6.4

Public School District
(for school year 2006-07 except as noted)

Saddle River School District
97 E Allendale Rd
Saddle River, NJ 07458
201-327-0727

- Superintendent: David Goldblatt
- Number of schools: 1
- Grade plan: K-5
- Enrollment: 224
- Attendance rate, '05-06: 95.3%
- Dropout rate: NA
- Students per teacher: 9.3
- Per pupil expenditure: $16,149
- Median faculty salary: $57,635
- Median administrator salary: $130,200
- Grade 12 enrollment: NA
- High school graduation rate: NA

Assessment test results
(percent scoring at proficient or advanced level)
	Language	Math
NJASK-Grade 3	88.9%	97.2%
GEPA-Grade 8	NA	NA
HSPA-High School	NA	NA

SAT score averages
Pct tested	Math	Verbal	Writing
NA	NA	NA	NA

Teacher Qualifications
- Avg. years of experience: 8
- Highly-qualified teachers one subject/all subjects: 100%/100%
- With emergency credentials: 0.0%

No Child Left Behind
- AYP, 2005-06: Meets Standards

Municipal Finance

State Aid Programs, 2008
- Total aid: $494,819
- CMPTRA: 0
- Energy tax receipts: 494,819
- Garden State Trust: 0

General Budget, 2007
- Total tax levy: $17,703,817
- County levy: 4,417,113
- County taxes: 4,172,887
- County library: 0
- County health: 0
- County open space: 244,226
- School levy: 6,413,100
- Muni. levy: 6,873,603
- Misc. revenues: 2,733,989

Salem County

Salem City

Demographics & Socio-Economic Characteristics
(2000 US Census, except as noted)

Population
1980*	6,959
1990*	6,883
2000	5,857
Male	2,615
Female	3,242
2006 (estimate)*	5,784
Population density	2,216.1

Race & Hispanic Origin, 2000
Race
- White ... 2,194
- Black/African American ... 3,325
- American Indian/Alaska Native ... 35
- Asian ... 14
- Native Hawaiian/Pacific Islander ... 0
- Other race ... 81
- Two or more races ... 208

Hispanic origin, total ... 286
- Mexican ... 25
- Puerto Rican ... 191
- Cuban ... 8
- Other Hispanic ... 62

Age & Nativity, 2000
- Under 5 years ... 518
- 18 years and over ... 4,044
- 21 years and over ... 3,801
- 65 years and over ... 821
- 85 years and over ... 83
- Median age ... 33.5
- Native-born ... 5,761
- Foreign-born ... 45

Educational Attainment, 2000
- Population 25 years and over ... 3,385
- Less than 9th grade ... 12.1%
- High school grad or higher ... 67.8%
- Bachelor's degree or higher ... 7.9%
- Graduate degree ... 1.8%

Income & Poverty, 1999
- Per capita income ... $13,559
- Median household income ... $25,846
- Median family income ... $29,699
- Persons in poverty ... 1,531
- H'holds receiving public assistance ... 182
- H'holds receiving social security ... 791

Households, 2000
- Total households ... 2,383
-   With persons under 18 ... 901
-   With persons over 65 ... 647
-   Family households ... 1,464
-   Single-parent households ... 813
- Persons per household ... 2.43
- Persons per family ... 3.10

Labor & Employment
- Total civilian labor force, 2006** ... 2,227
-   Unemployment rate ... 8.2%
- Total civilian labor force, 2000 ... 2,209
-   Unemployment rate ... 10.3%

Employed persons 16 years and over by occupation, 2000
- Managers & professionals ... 403
- Service occupations ... 425
- Sales & office occupations ... 449
- Farming, fishing & forestry ... 0
- Construction & maintenance ... 201
- Production & transportation ... 503
- Self-employed persons ... 44

* US Census Bureau
** New Jersey Department of Labor

See Introduction for an explanation of all data sources.

General Information
City of Salem
17 New Market St
Salem, NJ 08079
856-935-0372

- Website ... www.salemcitynj.com
- Year of incorporation ... 1858
- Land/water area (sq. miles) ... 2.61/0.19
- Form of government ... City

Government
Legislative Districts
- US Congressional ... 2
- State Legislative ... 3

Local Officials, 2008
- Mayor ... Earl Gage
- Manager ... Barbara Wright
- Clerk ... Barbara Wright
- Finance Dir ... David Crescenzi
- Tax Assessor ... Marie Procacci
- Tax Collector ... David Crescenzi
- Attorney ... David Puma
- Building ... Wayne Serfass
- Comm Dev/Planning ... NA
- Engineering ... Albert Fralinger Jr
- Public Works ... Fred Mucci III
- Police Chief ... John Pelura III
- Emerg/Fire Director ... John Ayars

Housing & Construction
Housing Units, 2000*
- Total ... 2,863
- Median rent ... $444
- Median SF home value ... $74,300

Permits for New Residential Construction
	Units	Value
Total, 2007	1	$40,914
Single family	1	$40,914
Total, 2006	3	$122,742
Single family	3	$122,742

Real Property Valuation, 2007
	Parcels	Valuation
Total	1,990	$253,525,808
Vacant	267	5,065,500
Residential	1,551	155,733,400
Commercial	135	53,904,890
Industrial	15	20,213,818
Apartments	9	17,907,500
Farm land	9	165,800
Farm homestead	4	534,900

Average Property Value & Tax, 2007
- Residential value ... $100,494
- Property tax ... $2,899
- Tax credit/rebate ... $790

Public Library
Salem Free Public Library
112 W Broadway
Salem, NJ 08079
856-935-0526

- Director ... Jeffrey Dilks

Library statistics, 2006
- Population served ... 5,857
- Full-time/total staff ... 0/5

	Total	Per capita
Holdings	55,060	9.40
Revenues	$112,278	$19.17
Expenditures	$140,548	$24.00
Annual visits	12,000	2.05
Internet terminals/annual users		4/4,788

Taxes
	2005	2006	2007
General tax rate per $100	5.383	5.57	2.885
County equalization ratio	77.08	72.19	125.75
Net valuation taxable	$116,955,845	$114,542,875	$256,190,568
State equalized value	$162,011,144	$203,147,079	$255,281,149

Public Safety
Number of officers, 2006 ... 22

Crime	2005	2006
Total crimes	352	362
Violent	64	86
Murder	2	1
Rape	1	0
Robbery	22	28
Aggravated assault	39	57
Non-violent	288	276
Burglary	106	80
Larceny	165	185
Vehicle theft	17	11
Domestic violence	180	138
Arson	6	10
Total crime rate	60.8	62.3
Violent	11.1	14.8
Non-violent	49.8	47.5

Public School District
(for school year 2006-07 except as noted)

Salem City School District
205 Walnut St
Salem, NJ 08079
856-935-3800

- Superintendent ... A. Patrick Michel
- Number of schools ... 3
- Grade plan ... K-12
- Enrollment ... 1,497
- Attendance rate, '05-06 ... 92.2%
- Dropout rate ... 8.0%
- Students per teacher ... 8.2
- Per pupil expenditure ... $15,368
- Median faculty salary ... $47,700
- Median administrator salary ... $75,857
- Grade 12 enrollment ... 113
- High school graduation rate ... 80.1%

Assessment test results
(percent scoring at proficient or advanced level)

	Language	Math
NJASK-Grade 3	55.9%	66.0%
GEPA-Grade 8	38.4%	39.2%
HSPA-High School	76.2%	48.8%

SAT score averages
Pct tested	Math	Verbal	Writing
55%	433	432	422

Teacher Qualifications
- Avg. years of experience ... 5
- Highly-qualified teachers one subject/all subjects ... 96.5%/96.5%
- With emergency credentials ... 0.0%

No Child Left Behind
AYP, 2005-06 ... Meets Standards

Municipal Finance
State Aid Programs, 2008
- Total aid ... $1,223,477
-   CMPTRA ... 623,092
-   Energy tax receipts ... 600,385
-   Garden State Trust ... 0

General Budget, 2007
- Total tax levy ... $7,389,319
-   County levy ... 1,968,659
-     County taxes ... 1,926,660
-     County library ... 0
-     County health ... 0
-     County open space ... 41,999
-   School levy ... 2,446,661
-   Muni. levy ... 2,973,998
- Misc. revenues ... 4,424,790

Sandyston Township

Sussex County

Demographics & Socio-Economic Characteristics
(2000 US Census, except as noted)

Population
1980*	1,485
1990*	1,732
2000	1,825
Male	919
Female	906
2006 (estimate)*	1,924
Population density	45.2

Race & Hispanic Origin, 2000
Race
White	1,786
Black/African American	7
American Indian/Alaska Native	3
Asian	8
Native Hawaiian/Pacific Islander	2
Other race	1
Two or more races	18
Hispanic origin, total	24
Mexican	0
Puerto Rican	10
Cuban	5
Other Hispanic	9

Age & Nativity, 2000
Under 5 years	101
18 years and over	1,365
21 years and over	1,312
65 years and over	244
85 years and over	33
Median age	40.4
Native-born	1,761
Foreign-born	68

Educational Attainment, 2000
Population 25 years and over	1,249
Less than 9th grade	2.6%
High school grad or higher	87.4%
Bachelor's degree or higher	24.7%
Graduate degree	7.6%

Income & Poverty, 1999
Per capita income	$23,854
Median household income	$55,667
Median family income	$65,774
Persons in poverty	99
H'holds receiving public assistance	8
H'holds receiving social security	201

Households, 2000
Total households	693
With persons under 18	257
With persons over 65	183
Family households	504
Single-person households	158
Persons per household	2.63
Persons per family	3.12

Labor & Employment
Total civilian labor force, 2006**	1,069
Unemployment rate	4.1%
Total civilian labor force, 2000	954
Unemployment rate	3.2%

Employed persons 16 years and over by occupation, 2000
Managers & professionals	314
Service occupations	128
Sales & office occupations	240
Farming, fishing & forestry	2
Construction & maintenance	118
Production & transportation	121
Self-employed persons	84

* US Census Bureau
** New Jersey Department of Labor

General Information
Township of Sandyston
133 County Road 645
Sandyston, NJ 07826
973-948-3520
Website .... www.sandystontownship.com
Year of incorporation 1762
Land/water area (sq. miles) 42.61/0.70
Form of government .... Township

Government
Legislative Districts
US Congressional	5
State Legislative	24

Local Officials, 2008
Mayor	William Leppert
Manager/Admin	NA
Clerk	Betsy Cuneo
Finance Dir	Jessica Caruso
Tax Assessor	Robert W. Pastor
Tax Collector	Kelly Hahn
Attorney	Christopher Quinn
Building	John deJager
Planning	Sharon Yarosz
Engineering	Harold Pellow
Public Works	Alan Delea
Police Chief	NA
Emerg/Fire Director	Scott House

Housing & Construction
Housing Units, 2000*
Total	907
Median rent	$860
Median SF home value	$144,800

Permits for New Residential Construction
	Units	Value
Total, 2007	4	$1,172,700
Single family	4	$1,172,700
Total, 2006	6	$1,078,600
Single family	6	$1,078,600

Real Property Valuation, 2007
	Parcels	Valuation
Total	1,321	$269,884,300
Vacant	179	16,192,800
Residential	807	200,599,000
Commercial	52	19,816,200
Industrial	5	2,373,100
Apartments	0	0
Farm land	184	1,122,200
Farm homestead	94	29,781,000

Average Property Value & Tax, 2007
Residential value	$255,694
Property tax	$4,126
Tax credit/rebate	$847

Public Library
No public municipal library

Library statistics, 2006
Population served	NA
Full-time/total staff	NA/NA

	Total	Per capita
Holdings	NA	NA
Revenues	NA	NA
Expenditures	NA	NA
Annual visits	NA	NA
Internet terminals/annual users	NA/NA	

Taxes
	2005	2006	2007
General tax rate per $100	2.93	3.03	1.62
County equalization ratio	68.72	59.92	104.08
Net valuation taxable	$133,181,089	$134,212,400	$270,554,483
State equalized value	$222,264,835	$255,981,040	$286,655,454

Public Safety
Number of officers, 2006 0

Crime
	2005	2006
Total crimes	12	17
Violent	2	1
Murder	0	0
Rape	0	0
Robbery	0	1
Aggravated assault	2	0
Non-violent	10	16
Burglary	2	6
Larceny	6	9
Vehicle theft	2	1
Domestic violence	4	0
Arson	0	0
Total crime rate	6.3	8.9
Violent	1.0	0.5
Non-violent	5.2	8.3

Public School District
(for school year 2006-07 except as noted)

Sandyston-Walpack Township School Dist.
100 Route 560, PO Box 128
Layton, NJ 07851
973-948-4450

Chief School Admin	Glenn Sumpman
Number of schools	2
Grade plan	K-6
Enrollment	184
Attendance rate, '05-06	96.4%
Dropout rate	NA
Students per teacher	9.4
Per pupil expenditure	$13,157
Median faculty salary	$51,120
Median administrator salary	$110,000
Grade 12 enrollment	NA
High school graduation rate	NA

Assessment test results
(percent scoring at proficient or advanced level)
	Language	Math
NJASK-Grade 3	95.8%	95.8%
GEPA-Grade 8	NA	NA
HSPA-High School	NA	NA

SAT score averages
Pct tested	Math	Verbal	Writing
NA	NA	NA	NA

Teacher Qualifications
Avg. years of experience	10
Highly-qualified teachers one subject/all subjects	100%/100%
With emergency credentials	0.0%

No Child Left Behind
AYP, 2005-06 .... Meets Standards

Municipal Finance
State Aid Programs, 2008
Total aid	$345,712
CMPTRA	0
Energy tax receipts	199,615
Garden State Trust	146,097

General Budget, 2007
Total tax levy	$4,366,044
County levy	1,058,093
County taxes	864,549
County library	73,704
County health	28,503
County open space	91,337
School levy	2,910,966
Muni. levy	396,985
Misc. revenues	1,181,529

Middlesex County | Sayreville Borough

Demographics & Socio-Economic Characteristics
(2000 US Census, except as noted)

Population
- 1980* 29,969
- 1990* 34,986
- 2000 40,377
  - Male 19,803
  - Female 20,574
- 2006 (estimate)* 42,560
  - Population density 2,676.7

Race & Hispanic Origin, 2000
Race
- White 30,875
- Black/African American 3,481
- American Indian/Alaska Native 53
- Asian 4,265
- Native Hawaiian/Pacific Islander 8
- Other race 855
- Two or more races 840
- Hispanic origin, total 2,942
  - Mexican 105
  - Puerto Rican 1,365
  - Cuban 194
  - Other Hispanic 1,278

Age & Nativity, 2000
- Under 5 years 2,712
- 18 years and over 30,863
- 21 years and over 29,654
- 65 years and over 5,004
- 85 years and over 488
  - Median age 36.5
- Native-born 32,279
- Foreign-born 8,098

Educational Attainment, 2000
- Population 25 years and over 27,872
- Less than 9th grade 4.7%
- High school grad or higher 85.6%
- Bachelor's degree or higher 24.9%
- Graduate degree 7.4%

Income & Poverty, 1999
- Per capita income $24,736
- Median household income $58,919
- Median family income $66,266
- Persons in poverty 1,905
- H'holds receiving public assistance 220
- H'holds receiving social security 3,906

Households, 2000
- Total households 14,955
  - With persons under 18 5,505
  - With persons over 65 3,639
  - Family households 10,923
  - Single-person households 3,342
- Persons per household 2.68
- Persons per family 3.17

Labor & Employment
- Total civilian labor force, 2006** 23,252
  - Unemployment rate 4.1%
- Total civilian labor force, 2000 20,837
  - Unemployment rate 4.4%

Employed persons 16 years and over by occupation, 2000
- Managers & professionals 7,066
- Service occupations 2,360
- Sales & office occupations 6,232
- Farming, fishing & forestry 21
- Construction & maintenance 1,847
- Production & transportation 2,397
- Self-employed persons 656

* US Census Bureau
** New Jersey Department of Labor

See Introduction for an explanation of all data sources.

General Information
Borough of Sayreville
167 Main St
Sayreville, NJ 08872
732-390-7000
- Website .... www.sayreville.com
- Year of incorporation 1919
- Land/water area (sq. miles) 15.90/2.85
- Form of government .... Borough

Government
Legislative Districts
- US Congressional 6
- State Legislative 19

Local Officials, 2008
- Mayor .... Kennedy O'Brien
- Manager .... Jeffry Bertrand
- Clerk .... Theresa Farbaniec
- Finance Dir .... Wayne Kronowski
- Tax Assessor .... Joseph Kupsch Jr
- Tax Collector .... Donna Brodzinski
- Attorney .... Weiner-Lesniak
- Building .... Kirk Miick
- Planning .... John Misiewicz
- Engineering .... David Samuel
- Public Works .... Bernard Bailey
- Police Chief .... Edward Szkodny
- Fire Chief .... William Brugnoli

Housing & Construction
Housing Units, 2000*
- Total 15,235
- Median rent $795
- Median SF home value $153,400

Permits for New Residential Construction

	Units	Value
Total, 2007	21	$2,481,669
Single family	21	$2,481,669
Total, 2006	23	$3,218,639
Single family	23	$3,218,639

Real Property Valuation, 2007

	Parcels	Valuation
Total	13,020	$2,264,010,000
Vacant	634	64,708,000
Residential	11,900	1,703,734,200
Commercial	423	186,098,600
Industrial	38	151,582,300
Apartments	22	157,734,300
Farm land	2	8,700
Farm homestead	1	143,900

Average Property Value & Tax, 2007
- Residential value $143,171
- Property tax $5,450
- Tax credit/rebate $963

Public Library
Sayreville Public Library
1050 Washington Rd
Parlin, NJ 08859
732-727-0212
- Director .... Susan Kaplan

Library statistics, 2006
- Population served 40,377
- Full-time/total staff 4/12

	Total	Per capita
Holdings	101,952	2.53
Revenues	$1,489,057	$36.88
Expenditures	$1,304,984	$32.32
Annual visits	55,669	1.38
Internet terminals/annual users	9/33,472	

Public Safety
- Number of officers, 2006 87

Crime

	2005	2006
Total crimes	826	893
Violent	60	70
Murder	1	0
Rape	7	5
Robbery	20	13
Aggravated assault	32	52
Non-violent	766	823
Burglary	103	129
Larceny	582	603
Vehicle theft	81	91
Domestic violence	150	179
Arson	8	5
Total crime rate	19.4	20.8
Violent	1.4	1.6
Non-violent	18.0	19.1

Public School District
(for school year 2006-07 except as noted)

Sayreville School District
Lincoln St, PO Box 997
Sayreville, NJ 08872
732-525-5224

- Superintendent .... Frank Alfano
- Number of schools 7
- Grade plan K-12
- Enrollment 5,640
- Attendance rate, '05-06 .... 94.6%
- Dropout rate 1.6%
- Students per teacher 11.9
- Per pupil expenditure $11,422
- Median faculty salary $50,000
- Median administrator salary $108,955
- Grade 12 enrollment 367
- High school graduation rate 96.1%

Assessment test results
(percent scoring at proficient or advanced level)

	Language	Math
NJASK-Grade 3	88.5%	95.4%
GEPA-Grade 8	77.5%	74.0%
HSPA-High School	89.0%	76.8%

SAT score averages

Pct tested	Math	Verbal	Writing
77%	493	477	474

Teacher Qualifications
- Avg. years of experience 7
- Highly-qualified teachers
  - one subject/all subjects 100%/100%
- With emergency credentials 0.0%

No Child Left Behind
- AYP, 2005-06 .... Meets Standards

Municipal Finance
State Aid Programs, 2008
- Total aid $11,853,570
  - CMPTRA 206,740
  - Energy tax receipts 11,637,788
  - Garden State Trust 9,042

General Budget, 2007
- Total tax levy $86,316,237
  - County levy 14,394,064
    - County taxes 12,885,767
    - County library 0
    - County health 0
    - County open space 1,508,297
  - School levy 51,637,718
  - Muni. levy 20,284,455
  - Misc. revenues 28,104,915

Taxes	2005	2006	2007
General tax rate per $100	3.38	3.6	3.81
County equalization ratio	59.34	52.52	45.86
Net valuation taxable	$2,244,382,465	$2,247,165,500	$2,267,587,707
State equalized value	$4,273,386,262	$4,904,035,443	$5,373,620,401

©2008 Information Publications, Inc. All rights reserved. Photocopying prohibited. For additional copies, contact the publisher at www.informationpublications.com or (877)544-INFO (4636)

The New Jersey Municipal Data Book

Scotch Plains Township

Union County

Demographics & Socio-Economic Characteristics
(2000 US Census, except as noted)

Population
1980*	20,774
1990*	21,160
2000	22,732
Male	10,890
Female	11,842
2006 (estimate)*	23,246
Population density	2,560.1

Race & Hispanic Origin, 2000
Race
White	17,931
Black/African American	2,568
American Indian/Alaska Native	21
Asian	1,648
Native Hawaiian/Pacific Islander	3
Other race	216
Two or more races	345
Hispanic origin, total	895
Mexican	53
Puerto Rican	229
Cuban	106
Other Hispanic	507

Age & Nativity, 2000
Under 5 years	1,777
18 years and over	16,967
21 years and over	16,528
65 years and over	3,214
85 years and over	344
Median age	38.6
Native-born	19,155
Foreign-born	3,577

Educational Attainment, 2000
Population 25 years and over	15,911
Less than 9th grade	2.8%
High school grad or higher	92.0%
Bachelor's degree or higher	49.7%
Graduate degree	19.9%

Income & Poverty, 1999
Per capita income	$39,913
Median household income	$81,599
Median family income	$96,238
Persons in poverty	674
H'holds receiving public assistance	131
H'holds receiving social security	2,125

Households, 2000
Total households	8,349
With persons under 18	3,179
With persons over 65	2,262
Family households	6,291
Single-person households	1,737
Persons per household	2.71
Persons per family	3.16

Labor & Employment
Total civilian labor force, 2006**	12,389
Unemployment rate	2.7%
Total civilian labor force, 2000	11,822
Unemployment rate	2.6%

Employed persons 16 years and over by occupation, 2000
Managers & professionals	6,381
Service occupations	811
Sales & office occupations	3,139
Farming, fishing & forestry	0
Construction & maintenance	533
Production & transportation	656
Self-employed persons	567

* US Census Bureau
** New Jersey Department of Labor

General Information
Township of Scotch Plains
430 Park Ave
Scotch Plains, NJ 07076
908-322-6700

Website	www.scotchplainsnj.com
Year of incorporation	1917
Land/water area (sq. miles)	9.08/0.01
Form of government	Council-Manager

Government

Legislative Districts
US Congressional	7
State Legislative	22

Local Officials, 2008
Mayor	Martin Marks
Manager	Thomas Atkins
Clerk	Barbara Riepe
Finance Dir	Lori Majeski
Tax Assessor	Michael Ross
Tax Collector	NA
Attorney	Brian Levine
Building	Robert LaCosta
Comm Dev/Planning	NA
Engineering	Edward Gottko
Public Works	NA
Police Chief	Brian Mahoney
Emerg/Fire Director	Jonathan Ellis

Housing & Construction

Housing Units, 2000*
Total	8,479
Median rent	$985
Median SF home value	$258,800

Permits for New Residential Construction
	Units	Value
Total, 2007	33	$8,071,090
Single family	33	$8,071,090
Total, 2006	70	$13,363,937
Single family	70	$13,363,937

Real Property Valuation, 2007
	Parcels	Valuation
Total	7,853	$993,430,400
Vacant	273	7,007,200
Residential	7,294	887,625,400
Commercial	244	64,006,200
Industrial	26	5,737,800
Apartments	8	27,940,400
Farm land	4	14,500
Farm homestead	4	1,098,900

Average Property Value & Tax, 2007
Residential value	$121,776
Property tax	$9,901
Tax credit/rebate	$1,277

Public Library
Scotch Plains Public Library
1927 Bartle Ave
Scotch Plains, NJ 07076
908-322-5007

Director	Margaret B. Kolaya

Library statistics, 2006
Population served	22,732
Full-time/total staff	6/11

	Total	Per capita
Holdings	82,934	3.65
Revenues	$1,307,238	$57.51
Expenditures	$1,283,248	$56.45
Annual visits	139,146	6.12
Internet terminals/annual users	16/20,115	

Taxes
	2005	2006	2007
General tax rate per $100	7.478	7.775	8.131
County equalization ratio	28.71	25.91	24.23
Net valuation taxable	$974,583,717	$985,947,500	$994,137,196
State equalized value	$3,584,346,146	$4,069,906,196	$4,288,278,656

Public Safety
Number of officers, 2006		44
Crime	2005	2006
Total crimes	280	314
Violent	18	24
Murder	0	0
Rape	2	2
Robbery	7	10
Aggravated assault	9	12
Non-violent	262	290
Burglary	69	48
Larceny	176	224
Vehicle theft	17	18
Domestic violence	70	100
Arson	0	1
Total crime rate	12.2	13.5
Violent	0.8	1.0
Non-violent	11.4	12.5

Public School District
(for school year 2006-07 except as noted)

Scotch Plains-Fanwood School District
Evergreen Ave & Cedar St
Scotch Plains, NJ 07076
908-232-6161

Superintendent	Margaret W. Hayes
Number of schools	16
Grade plan	K-12
Enrollment	5,333
Attendance rate, '05-06	96.1%
Dropout rate	0.1%
Students per teacher	12.0
Per pupil expenditure	$12,673
Median faculty salary	$55,269
Median administrator salary	$116,675
Grade 12 enrollment	340
High school graduation rate	100.0%

Assessment test results
(percent scoring at proficient or advanced level)
	Language	Math
NJASK-Grade 3	93.6%	96.1%
GEPA-Grade 8	88.9%	85.7%
HSPA-High School	93.4%	87.8%

SAT score averages
Pct tested	Math	Verbal	Writing
105%	550	522	518

Teacher Qualifications
Avg. years of experience	8
Highly-qualified teachers one subject/all subjects	99.5%/99.5%
With emergency credentials	0.3%

No Child Left Behind
AYP, 2005-06	Meets Standards

Municipal Finance

State Aid Programs, 2008
Total aid	$2,915,301
CMPTRA	710,733
Energy tax receipts	2,204,568
Garden State Trust	0

General Budget, 2007
Total tax levy	$80,831,370
County levy	14,336,802
County taxes	13,720,697
County library	0
County health	0
County open space	616,105
School levy	51,971,797
Muni. levy	14,522,771
Misc. revenues	9,720,591

Monmouth County
Sea Bright Borough

Demographics & Socio-Economic Characteristics
(2000 US Census, except as noted)

Population
- 1980* 1,812
- 1990* 1,693
- 2000 1,818
  - Male 951
  - Female 867
- 2006 (estimate)* 1,799
- Population density 2,810.9

Race & Hispanic Origin, 2000
Race
- White 1,716
- Black/African American 32
- American Indian/Alaska Native 0
- Asian 41
- Native Hawaiian/Pacific Islander 0
- Other race 16
- Two or more races 13
- Hispanic origin, total 82
  - Mexican 37
  - Puerto Rican 16
  - Cuban 5
  - Other Hispanic 24

Age & Nativity, 2000
- Under 5 years 59
- 18 years and over 1,615
- 21 years and over 1,592
- 65 years and over 196
- 85 years and over 32
  - Median age 40.2
- Native-born 1,608
- Foreign-born 217

Educational Attainment, 2000
- Population 25 years and over 1,488
- Less than 9th grade 2.8%
- High school grad or higher 91.4%
- Bachelor's degree or higher 47.0%
- Graduate degree 18.5%

Income & Poverty, 1999
- Per capita income $45,066
- Median household income $65,563
- Median family income $72,031
- Persons in poverty 138
- H'holds receiving public assistance 21
- H'holds receiving social security 164

Households, 2000
- Total households 1,003
  - With persons under 18 127
  - With persons over 65 159
  - Family households 402
  - Single-person households 455
- Persons per household 1.81
- Persons per family 2.51

Labor & Employment
- Total civilian labor force, 2006** 1,303
  - Unemployment rate 5.0%
- Total civilian labor force, 2000 1,208
  - Unemployment rate 5.1%

Employed persons 16 years and over by occupation, 2000
- Managers & professionals 538
- Service occupations 114
- Sales & office occupations 341
- Farming, fishing & forestry 12
- Construction & maintenance 63
- Production & transportation 78
- Self-employed persons 56

* US Census Bureau
** New Jersey Department of Labor

See Introduction for an explanation of all data sources.

General Information
Borough of Sea Bright
1167 Ocean Ave
Sea Bright, NJ 07760
732-842-0099

- Website .... seabrightnj.org
- Year of incorporation 1889
- Land/water area (sq. miles) 0.64/0.49
- Form of government .... Borough

Government
Legislative Districts
- US Congressional 6
- State Legislative 11

Local Officials, 2008
- Mayor .... Maria D. Fernandes
- Manager/Admin .... NA
- Clerk .... Maryann M. Smeltzer
- Finance Dir .... Michael Bascom
- Tax Assessor .... Timothy Anfuso
- Tax Collector .... Patricia Spahr
- Attorney .... Scott Arnette
- Building .... Edward Wheeler
- Comm Dev/Planning .... NA
- Engineering .... David Hoder
- Public Works .... David Bahrle
- Police Chief .... William Moore
- Emerg/Fire Director .... John Jay Rock

Housing & Construction
Housing Units, 2000*
- Total 1,202
- Median rent $906
- Median SF home value $227,600

Permits for New Residential Construction

	Units	Value
Total, 2007	4	$1,821,092
Single family	4	$1,821,092
Total, 2006	8	$2,893,774
Single family	6	$2,293,774

Real Property Valuation, 2007

	Parcels	Valuation
Total	1,283	$519,796,800
Vacant	162	11,789,600
Residential	1,044	413,847,100
Commercial	71	88,605,000
Industrial	0	0
Apartments	6	5,555,100
Farm land	0	0
Farm homestead	0	0

Average Property Value & Tax, 2007
- Residential value $396,405
- Property tax $6,312
- Tax credit/rebate $946

Public Library
J.W. Ross/Sea Bright Library
1097 Ocean Ave
Sea Bright, NJ 07760
732-758-9554

- Director .... Joan Walsh

Library statistics, 2006
- Population served 1,818
- Full-time/total staff NA/0

	Total	Per capita
Holdings	NA	NA
Revenues	NA	NA
Expenditures	NA	NA
Annual visits	NA	NA
Internet terminals/annual users	NA/NA	

Public Safety
Number of officers, 2006 11

Crime	2005	2006
Total crimes	42	17
Violent	0	1
Murder	0	0
Rape	0	0
Robbery	0	0
Aggravated assault	0	1
Non-violent	42	16
Burglary	1	0
Larceny	41	16
Vehicle theft	0	0
Domestic violence	0	2
Arson	0	0
Total crime rate	23.1	9.5
Violent	0.0	0.6
Non-violent	23.1	8.9

Public School District
(for school year 2006-07 except as noted)

Sea Bright School District
PO Box 3125
Sea Bright, NJ 07760

No schools in district - sends students to Oceanport Borough and Shore Regional schools (see Appendix D)

- Per pupil expenditure .... NA
- Median faculty salary .... NA
- Median administrator salary .... NA
- Grade 12 enrollment .... NA
- High school graduation rate .... NA

Assessment test results
(percent scoring at proficient or advanced level)

	Language	Math
NJASK-Grade 3	NA	NA
GEPA-Grade 8	NA	NA
HSPA-High School	NA	NA

SAT score averages

Pct tested	Math	Verbal	Writing
NA	NA	NA	NA

Teacher Qualifications
- Avg. years of experience .... NA
- Highly-qualified teachers
  one subject/all subjects .... NA/NA
- With emergency credentials .... NA

No Child Left Behind
- AYP, 2005-06 .... NA

Municipal Finance
State Aid Programs, 2008
- Total aid $189,673
  - CMPTRA 0
  - Energy tax receipts 189,669
  - Garden State Trust 4

General Budget, 2007
- Total tax levy $8,281,616
  - County levy 2,358,097
    - County taxes 2,105,713
    - County library 120,629
    - County health 0
    - County open space 131,755
  - School levy 2,688,588
  - Muni. levy 3,234,932
  - Misc. revenues 1,331,840

Taxes	2005	2006	2007
General tax rate per $100	1.315	1.424	1.593
County equalization ratio	99.68	79.7	58.11
Net valuation taxable	$501,226,608	$513,096,300	$520,090,525
State equalized value	$628,891,604	$883,277,234	$859,888,235

Sea Girt Borough

Monmouth County

Demographics & Socio-Economic Characteristics
(2000 US Census, except as noted)

Population
1980*	2,650
1990*	2,099
2000	2,148
Male	1,001
Female	1,147
2006 (estimate)*	2,044
Population density	1,928.3

Race & Hispanic Origin, 2000
Race
White	2,129
Black/African American	2
American Indian/Alaska Native	0
Asian	6
Native Hawaiian/Pacific Islander	0
Other race	1
Two or more races	10
Hispanic origin, total	30
Mexican	3
Puerto Rican	7
Cuban	1
Other Hispanic	19

Age & Nativity, 2000
Under 5 years	96
18 years and over	1,716
21 years and over	1,678
65 years and over	591
85 years and over	87
Median age	50.3
Native-born	2,083
Foreign-born	65

Educational Attainment, 2000
Population 25 years and over	1,622
Less than 9th grade	1.0%
High school grad or higher	96.5%
Bachelor's degree or higher	58.6%
Graduate degree	23.3%

Income & Poverty, 1999
Per capita income	$63,871
Median household income	$86,104
Median family income	$102,680
Persons in poverty	75
H'holds receiving public assistance	4
H'holds receiving social security	400

Households, 2000
Total households	942
With persons under 18	199
With persons over 65	412
Family households	637
Single-person households	279
Persons per household	2.28
Persons per family	2.83

Labor & Employment
Total civilian labor force, 2006**	1,012
Unemployment rate	2.1%
Total civilian labor force, 2000	940
Unemployment rate	2.9%

Employed persons 16 years and over by occupation, 2000
Managers & professionals	520
Service occupations	76
Sales & office occupations	285
Farming, fishing & forestry	0
Construction & maintenance	14
Production & transportation	18
Self-employed persons	89

* US Census Bureau
** New Jersey Department of Labor

General Information
Borough of Sea Girt
4th Ave & Baltimore Blvd
Sea Girt, NJ 08750
732-449-9433

Website	www.seagirtboro.com
Year of incorporation	1917
Land/water area (sq. miles)	1.06/0.39
Form of government	Borough

Government
Legislative Districts
US Congressional	4
State Legislative	11

Local Officials, 2008
Mayor	Mark E. Clemmensen
Manager/Admin	NA
Clerk	Lorene K. Wright
Finance Dir	Christine L. Brown
Tax Assessor	Mary Lou Hartman
Tax Collector	Karen Brisden
Attorney	Joseph Brennan
Building	(Spring Lake Borough)
Comm Dev/Planning	NA
Engineering	Leon Avakian
Public Works	Kevin Thompson
Police Chief	Edward J. Sidley
Emerg/Fire Director	Tim Harmon

Housing & Construction
Housing Units, 2000*
Total	1,285
Median rent	$1,095
Median SF home value	$549,300

Permits for New Residential Construction
	Units	Value
Total, 2007	22	$11,420,554
Single family	22	$11,420,554
Total, 2006	27	$13,566,390
Single family	27	$13,566,390

Real Property Valuation, 2007
	Parcels	Valuation
Total	1,305	$1,927,154,900
Vacant	57	70,010,100
Residential	1,206	1,819,634,300
Commercial	42	37,510,500
Industrial	0	0
Apartments	0	0
Farm land	0	0
Farm homestead	0	0

Average Property Value & Tax, 2007
Residential value	$1,508,818
Property tax	$10,433
Tax credit/rebate	$1,296

Public Library
Sea Girt Library
The Plaza
Sea Girt, NJ 08750
732-449-1099

Librarian . . . . Anne Ryan

Library statistics, 2006
Population served	2,148
Full-time/total staff	NA/0

	Total	Per capita
Holdings	NA	NA
Revenues	NA	NA
Expenditures	NA	NA
Annual visits	NA	NA
Internet terminals/annual users	NA/NA	

Taxes
	2005	2006	2007
General tax rate per $100	0.633	0.669	0.692
County equalization ratio	127.78	112.5	101.75
Net valuation taxable	$1,912,007,914	$1,916,022,600	$1,927,456,756
State equalized value	$1,699,562,590	$1,883,361,440	$1,913,300,566

Public Safety
Number of officers, 2006 12

Crime	2005	2006
Total crimes	35	40
Violent	3	6
Murder	0	0
Rape	0	0
Robbery	1	0
Aggravated assault	2	6
Non-violent	32	34
Burglary	7	5
Larceny	25	28
Vehicle theft	0	1
Domestic violence	0	12
Arson	0	0
Total crime rate	16.7	19.3
Violent	1.4	2.9
Non-violent	15.3	16.4

Public School District
(for school year 2006-07 except as noted)

Sea Girt Borough School District
451 Bell Place
Sea Girt, NJ 08750
732-449-3422

Superintendent	Stephen LaValva
Number of schools	1
Grade plan	K-8
Enrollment	173
Attendance rate, '05-06	95.8%
Dropout rate	NA
Students per teacher	9.0
Per pupil expenditure	$15,399
Median faculty salary	$55,630
Median administrator salary	$120,662
Grade 12 enrollment	NA
High school graduation rate	NA

Assessment test results
(percent scoring at proficient or advanced level)
	Language	Math
NJASK-Grade 3	100.0%	94.5%
GEPA-Grade 8	93.3%	96.7%
HSPA-High School	NA	NA

SAT score averages
Pct tested	Math	Verbal	Writing
NA	NA	NA	NA

Teacher Qualifications
Avg. years of experience	12
Highly-qualified teachers one subject/all subjects	100%/100%
With emergency credentials	3.8%

No Child Left Behind
AYP, 2005-06 . . . . Meets Standards

Municipal Finance
State Aid Programs, 2008
Total aid	$226,386
CMPTRA	0
Energy tax receipts	226,386
Garden State Trust	0

General Budget, 2007
Total tax levy	$13,327,574
County levy	5,103,558
County taxes	4,557,852
County library	260,919
County health	0
County open space	284,787
School levy	3,832,116
Muni. levy	4,391,900
Misc. revenues	1,434,579

Cape May County

Sea Isle City

Demographics & Socio-Economic Characteristics
(2000 US Census, except as noted)

Population
1980*	2,644
1990*	2,692
2000	2,835
Male	1,354
Female	1,481
2006 (estimate)*	2,949
Population density	1,340.5

Race & Hispanic Origin, 2000
Race
- White ... 2,775
- Black/African American ... 8
- American Indian/Alaska Native ... 11
- Asian ... 10
- Native Hawaiian/Pacific Islander ... 1
- Other race ... 2
- Two or more races ... 28

Hispanic origin, total ... 30
- Mexican ... 15
- Puerto Rican ... 10
- Cuban ... 2
- Other Hispanic ... 3

Age & Nativity, 2000
- Under 5 years ... 94
- 18 years and over ... 2,391
- 21 years and over ... 2,340
- 65 years and over ... 768
- 85 years and over ... 78
- Median age ... 51.3
- Native-born ... 2,730
- Foreign-born ... 94

Educational Attainment, 2000
- Population 25 years and over ... 2,176
- Less than 9th grade ... 3.4%
- High school grad or higher ... 85.2%
- Bachelor's degree or higher ... 28.3%
- Graduate degree ... 9.8%

Income & Poverty, 1999
- Per capita income ... $28,754
- Median household income ... $45,708
- Median family income ... $62,847
- Persons in poverty ... 214
- H'holds receiving public assistance ... 0
- H'holds receiving social security ... 584

Households, 2000
- Total households ... 1,370
- With persons under 18 ... 235
- With persons over 65 ... 552
- Family households ... 795
- Single-person households ... 512
- Persons per household ... 2.07
- Persons per family ... 2.71

Labor & Employment
- Total civilian labor force, 2006** ... 1,677
- Unemployment rate ... 5.5%
- Total civilian labor force, 2000 ... 1,372
- Unemployment rate ... 6.5%

Employed persons 16 years and over by occupation, 2000
- Managers & professionals ... 445
- Service occupations ... 247
- Sales & office occupations ... 373
- Farming, fishing & forestry ... 0
- Construction & maintenance ... 141
- Production & transportation ... 77
- Self-employed persons ... 89

‡ Branch of county library
* US Census Bureau
** New Jersey Department of Labor

See Introduction for an explanation of all data sources.

General Information
City of Sea Isle
4416 Landis Ave
Sea Isle City, NJ 08243
609-263-4461

Website	sea-isle-city.nj.us
Year of incorporation	1907
Land/water area (sq. miles)	2.20/0.35
Form of government	Commission

Government
Legislative Districts
- US Congressional ... 2
- State Legislative ... 1

Local Officials, 2008
Mayor	Leonard Desiderio
Manager/Admin	George Savastano
Clerk	Theresa Tighe
Finance Dir	James Terruso
Tax Assessor	Joseph Berrodin Jr
Tax Collector	Paula Doll
Attorney	Paul Baldini
Building	Robert Bowman
Comm Dev/Planning	NA
Engineering	Andrew Previti
Public Works	John Manganaro
Police Chief	Michael Cook (Actg)
Emerg/Fire Director	John Mazurie

Housing & Construction
Housing Units, 2000*
- Total ... 6,622
- Median rent ... $717
- Median SF home value ... $280,100

Permits for New Residential Construction
	Units	Value
Total, 2007	88	$15,886,443
Single family	86	$15,584,643
Total, 2006	149	$27,760,716
Single family	149	$27,760,716

Real Property Valuation, 2007
	Parcels	Valuation
Total	6,678	$3,617,625,500
Vacant	481	114,391,100
Residential	6,042	3,410,254,600
Commercial	155	92,979,800
Industrial	0	0
Apartments	0	0
Farm land	0	0
Farm homestead	0	0

Average Property Value & Tax, 2007
- Residential value ... $564,425
- Property tax ... $3,585
- Tax credit/rebate ... $848

Public Library
Sea Isle City Branch Library‡
125 JF Kennedy Blvd
Sea Isle City, NJ 08243
609-263-8485

Branch Librarian ... Elizabeth Morris

Library statistics, 2006
see Cape May County profile for library system statistics

Public Safety
Number of officers, 2006 ... 24

Crime	2005	2006
Total crimes	317	315
Violent	17	18
Murder	0	0
Rape	0	0
Robbery	1	0
Aggravated assault	16	18
Non-violent	300	297
Burglary	24	16
Larceny	273	276
Vehicle theft	3	5
Domestic violence	24	23
Arson	0	0
Total crime rate	106.5	106.1
Violent	5.7	6.1
Non-violent	100.8	100.1

Public School District
(for school year 2006-07 except as noted)

Sea Isle City School District
4501 Park Rd
Sea Isle City, NJ 08243
609-263-8461

Chief School Admin	Stephen E. Derkoski
Number of schools	1
Grade plan	K-8
Enrollment	93
Attendance rate, '05-06	92.8%
Dropout rate	NA
Students per teacher	NA
Per pupil expenditure	NA
Median faculty salary	NA
Median administrator salary	NA
Grade 12 enrollment	NA
High school graduation rate	NA

Assessment test results
(percent scoring at proficient or advanced level)
	Language	Math
NJASK-Grade 3	NA	NA
GEPA-Grade 8	81.3%	81.3%
HSPA-High School	NA	NA

SAT score averages
Pct tested	Math	Verbal	Writing
NA	NA	NA	NA

Teacher Qualifications
- Avg. years of experience ... 19
- Highly-qualified teachers one subject/all subjects ... 91.5%/91.5%
- With emergency credentials ... 0.0%

No Child Left Behind
AYP, 2005-06 ... Meets Standards

Municipal Finance
State Aid Programs, 2008
- Total aid ... $303,893
- CMPTRA ... 0
- Energy tax receipts ... 302,852
- Garden State Trust ... 1,041

General Budget, 2007
- Total tax levy ... $22,987,129
- County levy ... 9,261,892
- County taxes ... 7,360,445
- County library ... 1,414,208
- County health ... 0
- County open space ... 487,239
- School levy ... 3,196,187
- Muni. levy ... 10,529,050
- Misc. revenues ... 5,739,472

Taxes	2005	2006	2007
General tax rate per $100	0.57	0.61	0.64
County equalization ratio	102.72	83.07	74.46
Net valuation taxable	$3,498,256,661	$3,552,214,800	$3,618,844,327
State equalized value	$4,211,215,434	$4,771,968,109	$4,866,234,292

The New Jersey Municipal Data Book

Seaside Heights Borough

Ocean County

Demographics & Socio-Economic Characteristics
(2000 US Census, except as noted)

Population
1980*	1,802
1990*	2,366
2000	3,155
Male	1,627
Female	1,528
2006 (estimate)*	3,242
Population density	5,314.8

Race & Hispanic Origin, 2000
Race
White	2,838
Black/African American	127
American Indian/Alaska Native	20
Asian	27
Native Hawaiian/Pacific Islander	0
Other race	37
Two or more races	106
Hispanic origin, total	306
Mexican	102
Puerto Rican	113
Cuban	5
Other Hispanic	86

Age & Nativity, 2000
Under 5 years	238
18 years and over	2,419
21 years and over	2,293
65 years and over	348
85 years and over	33
Median age	33.3
Native-born	2,917
Foreign-born	238

Educational Attainment, 2000
Population 25 years and over	2,052
Less than 9th grade	5.0%
High school grad or higher	76.3%
Bachelor's degree or higher	15.6%
Graduate degree	3.6%

Income & Poverty, 1999
Per capita income	$18,665
Median household income	$25,963
Median family income	$27,197
Persons in poverty	753
H'holds receiving public assistance	87
H'holds receiving social security	359

Households, 2000
Total households	1,408
With persons under 18	400
With persons over 65	260
Family households	692
Single-person households	564
Persons per household	2.17
Persons per family	2.93

Labor & Employment
Total civilian labor force, 2006**	1,526
Unemployment rate	6.9%
Total civilian labor force, 2000	1,590
Unemployment rate	7.5%

Employed persons 16 years and over by occupation, 2000
Managers & professionals	325
Service occupations	412
Sales & office occupations	374
Farming, fishing & forestry	10
Construction & maintenance	165
Production & transportation	184
Self-employed persons	61

* US Census Bureau
** New Jersey Department of Labor

General Information
Borough of Seaside Heights
PO Box 38
Seaside Heights, NJ 08751
732-793-9100

Website	www.seaside-heightsnj.org
Year of incorporation	1913
Land/water area (sq. miles)	0.61/0.15
Form of government	Borough

Government
Legislative Districts
US Congressional	3
State Legislative	10

Local Officials, 2008
Mayor	P. Kenneth Hershey
Manager	John Camera
Clerk	Diane B. Stabley
Finance Dir	Barbara Risley
Tax Assessor	Carey Rowe
Tax Collector	Christine Sierfeld
Attorney	George Gilmore
Building	James Erdman
Comm Dev/Planning	NA
Engineering	O'Donnell & Stanton
Public Works	Louis DiGuilio
Police Chief	Thomas Boyd
Emerg/Fire Director	William Rumbolo

Housing & Construction
Housing Units, 2000*
Total	2,840
Median rent	$635
Median SF home value	$124,400

Permits for New Residential Construction
	Units	Value
Total, 2007	27	$5,851,150
Single family	15	$2,159,150
Total, 2006	79	$12,675,000
Single family	74	$9,925,000

Real Property Valuation, 2007
	Parcels	Valuation
Total	1,968	$957,801,050
Vacant	108	47,218,000
Residential	1,636	542,856,200
Commercial	165	321,099,750
Industrial	0	0
Apartments	59	46,627,100
Farm land	0	0
Farm homestead	0	0

Average Property Value & Tax, 2007
Residential value	$331,819
Property tax	$3,440
Tax credit/rebate	$752

Public Library
No public municipal library

Library statistics, 2006
Population served	NA
Full-time/total staff	NA/NA

	Total	Per capita
Holdings	NA	NA
Revenues	NA	NA
Expenditures	NA	NA
Annual visits	NA	NA
Internet terminals/annual users	NA/NA	

Public Safety
Number of officers, 2006	23

Crime	2005	2006
Total crimes	337	348
Violent	87	93
Murder	0	0
Rape	5	3
Robbery	15	16
Aggravated assault	67	74
Non-violent	250	255
Burglary	63	54
Larceny	168	183
Vehicle theft	19	18
Domestic violence	241	355
Arson	1	0
Total crime rate	105.5	108.1
Violent	27.2	28.9
Non-violent	78.3	79.2

Public School District
(for school year 2006-07 except as noted)

Seaside Heights Borough School District
1200 Bay Blvd
Seaside Heights, NJ 08751
732-793-8485

Superintendent	Michael Ritacco
Number of schools	1
Grade plan	K-6
Enrollment	210
Attendance rate, '05-06	91.4%
Dropout rate	NA
Students per teacher	9.2
Per pupil expenditure	$13,443
Median faculty salary	$48,592
Median administrator salary	$1
Grade 12 enrollment	NA
High school graduation rate	NA

Assessment test results
(percent scoring at proficient or advanced level)
	Language	Math
NJASK-Grade 3	88.4%	96.0%
GEPA-Grade 8	NA	NA
HSPA-High School	NA	NA

SAT score averages
Pct tested	Math	Verbal	Writing
NA	NA	NA	NA

Teacher Qualifications
Avg. years of experience	15
Highly-qualified teachers one subject/all subjects	100%/100%
With emergency credentials	0.0%

No Child Left Behind
AYP, 2005-06	Meets Standards

Municipal Finance
State Aid Programs, 2008
Total aid	$180,334
CMPTRA	0
Energy tax receipts	180,334
Garden State Trust	0

General Budget, 2007
Total tax levy	$9,933,908
County levy	2,459,110
County taxes	2,026,419
County library	240,164
County health	97,301
County open space	95,225
School levy	4,778,953
Muni. levy	2,695,845
Misc. revenues	7,403,628

Taxes
	2005	2006	2007
General tax rate per $100	3.525	3.792	1.037
County equalization ratio	49	35.86	121.49
Net valuation taxable	$228,602,161	$230,871,000	$958,158,516
State equalized value	$637,485,112	$780,093,949	$873,307,749

Ocean County / Seaside Park Borough

Demographics & Socio-Economic Characteristics
(2000 US Census, except as noted)

Population
- 1980*......................................1,795
- 1990*......................................1,871
- 2000......................................2,263
  - Male....................................1,106
  - Female..................................1,157
- 2006 (estimate)*...........................2,302
  - Population density....................3,541.5

Race & Hispanic Origin, 2000
Race
- White.....................................2,213
- Black/African American.........................6
- American Indian/Alaska Native..................8
- Asian..14
- Native Hawaiian/Pacific Islander...............2
- Other race....................................4
- Two or more races............................16
- Hispanic origin, total.......................52
  - Mexican....................................7
  - Puerto Rican..............................18
  - Cuban......................................2
  - Other Hispanic............................25

Age & Nativity, 2000
- Under 5 years..............................107
- 18 years and over.........................1,938
- 21 years and over.........................1,889
- 65 years and over...........................568
- 85 years and over............................79
  - Median age...............................46.8
- Native-born...............................2,176
- Foreign-born.................................90

Educational Attainment, 2000
- Population 25 years and over..............1,819
- Less than 9th grade........................4.5%
- High school grad or higher................88.0%
- Bachelor's degree or higher...............33.8%
- Graduate degree...........................11.8%

Income & Poverty, 1999
- Per capita income.......................$30,090
- Median household income.................$45,380
- Median family income....................$58,636
- Persons in poverty..........................195
- H'holds receiving public assistance..........20
- H'holds receiving social security..........490

Households, 2000
- Total households..........................1,127
  - With persons under 18....................197
  - With persons over 65.....................404
  - Family households........................606
  - Single-person households.................437
- Persons per household......................2.01
- Persons per family.........................2.61

Labor & Employment
- Total civilian labor force, 2006**........1,140
  - Unemployment rate........................6.5%
- Total civilian labor force, 2000..........1,140
  - Unemployment rate........................5.7%

Employed persons 16 years and over by occupation, 2000
- Managers & professionals....................382
- Service occupations.........................149
- Sales & office occupations..................336
- Farming, fishing & forestry...................0
- Construction & maintenance..................121
- Production & transportation..................87
- Self-employed persons......................120

* US Census Bureau
** New Jersey Department of Labor

See Introduction for an explanation of all data sources.

General Information
Borough of Seaside Park
1701 N Ocean Ave
PO Box B
Seaside Park, NJ 08752
732-793-3700

- Website...............www.seasideparknj.org
- Year of incorporation......................1898
- Land/water area (sq. miles).......0.65/0.11
- Form of government..................Borough

Government
Legislative Districts
- US Congressional..............................3
- State Legislative............................10

Local Officials, 2008
- Mayor................Thomas E. Connors
- Administrator........Julie Horner-Keizer
- Clerk................Julie Horner-Keizer
- Finance Dir......................Ella Rice
- Tax Assessor..............Dennis Raftery
- Tax Collector..........Wendy Prior (Int)
- Attorney....................Steven Secare
- Building.............(Berkeley Township)
- Planning................John Vanna (Chr)
- Engineering..............CME Associates
- Public Works...............Joseph Dolci
- Police Chief..............Edward Dickson
- Fire Chief................John Lippincott

Housing & Construction
Housing Units, 2000*
- Total......................................2,811
- Median rent..................................$718
- Median SF home value.....................$215,100

Permits for New Residential Construction
	Units	Value
Total, 2007	15	$3,357,477
Single family	15	$3,357,477
Total, 2006	13	$3,741,951
Single family	13	$3,741,951

Real Property Valuation, 2007
	Parcels	Valuation
Total	2,002	$674,863,500
Vacant	42	11,585,500
Residential	1,893	618,805,700
Commercial	52	38,428,300
Industrial	0	0
Apartments	15	6,044,000
Farm land	0	0
Farm homestead	0	0

Average Property Value & Tax, 2007
- Residential value......................$326,892
- Property tax............................$6,467
- Tax credit/rebate........................$1,176

Public Library
No public municipal library

Library statistics, 2006
- Population served..........................NA
- Full-time/total staff...................NA/NA

	Total	Per capita
Holdings	NA	NA
Revenues	NA	NA
Expenditures	NA	NA
Annual visits	NA	NA

Internet terminals/annual users....NA/NA

Taxes
	2005	2006	2007
General tax rate per $100	1.691	1.832	1.979
County equalization ratio	76.17	62.93	53.46
Net valuation taxable	$679,901,640	$683,337,500	$675,104,221
State equalized value	$1,080,409,407	$1,278,496,767	$1,360,578,355

Public Safety
- Number of officers, 2006...................15

Crime
	2005	2006
Total crimes	75	87
Violent	4	1
Murder	0	0
Rape	0	1
Robbery	1	0
Aggravated assault	3	0
Non-violent	71	86
Burglary	11	10
Larceny	55	74
Vehicle theft	5	2
Domestic violence	25	18
Arson	0	0
Total crime rate	32.6	37.8
Violent	1.7	0.4
Non-violent	30.8	37.4

Public School District
(for school year 2006-07 except as noted)

Seaside Park Borough School District
Central & Fourth Avenues
Seaside Park, NJ 08752
732-793-0177

- Superintendent......Robert M. Gray Jr (Int)
- Number of schools............................1
- Grade plan................................K-6
- Enrollment..................................92
- Attendance rate, '05-06..................93.9%
- Dropout rate................................NA
- Students per teacher.......................6.8
- Per pupil expenditure..................$14,807
- Median faculty salary...................$41,340
- Median administrator salary.............$75,642
- Grade 12 enrollment.........................NA
- High school graduation rate.................NA

Assessment test results
(percent scoring at proficient or advanced level)
	Language	Math
NJASK-Grade 3	92.3%	92.3%
GEPA-Grade 8	NA	NA
HSPA-High School	NA	NA

SAT score averages
Pct tested	Math	Verbal	Writing
NA	NA	NA	NA

Teacher Qualifications
- Avg. years of experience...................20
- Highly-qualified teachers
  - one subject/all subjects......100%/100%
- With emergency credentials................0.0%

No Child Left Behind
- AYP, 2005-06............Meets Standards

Municipal Finance
State Aid Programs, 2008
- Total aid................................$250,080
  - CMPTRA.......................................0
  - Energy tax receipts....................250,080
  - Garden State Trust...........................0

General Budget, 2007
- Total tax levy........................$13,356,519
  - County levy.........................3,876,581
    - County taxes......................3,193,813
    - County library......................378,974
    - County health......................153,533
    - County open space.................150,261
  - School levy.........................4,878,387
  - Muni. levy..........................4,601,551
- Misc. revenues........................4,723,221

©2008 Information Publications, Inc. All rights reserved. Photocopying prohibited. For additional copies, contact the publisher at www.informationpublications.com or (877)544-INFO (4636)

The New Jersey Municipal Data Book   453

Secaucus Town
Hudson County

Demographics & Socio-Economic Characteristics
(2000 US Census, except as noted)

Population
1980*	13,719
1990*	14,061
2000	15,931
Male	7,879
Female	8,052
2006 (estimate)*	15,562
Population density	2,642.1

Race & Hispanic Origin, 2000
Race
White	12,512
Black/African American	709
American Indian/Alaska Native	18
Asian	1,880
Native Hawaiian/Pacific Islander	7
Other race	445
Two or more races	360
Hispanic origin, total	1,953
Mexican	47
Puerto Rican	521
Cuban	376
Other Hispanic	1,009

Age & Nativity, 2000
Under 5 years	825
18 years and over	12,866
21 years and over	12,430
65 years and over	2,571
85 years and over	311
Median age	39.5
Native-born	12,593
Foreign-born	3,246

Educational Attainment, 2000
Population 25 years and over	11,780
Less than 9th grade	6.2%
High school grad or higher	82.2%
Bachelor's degree or higher	29.1%
Graduate degree	10.5%

Income & Poverty, 1999
Per capita income	$31,684
Median household income	$59,800
Median family income	$72,568
Persons in poverty	1,149
H'holds receiving public assistance	81
H'holds receiving social security	1,934

Households, 2000
Total households	6,214
With persons under 18	1,718
With persons over 65	1,876
Family households	3,948
Single-person households	1,962
Persons per household	2.41
Persons per family	3.08

Labor & Employment
Total civilian labor force, 2006**	7,663
Unemployment rate	2.3%
Total civilian labor force, 2000	7,889
Unemployment rate	5.7%

Employed persons 16 years and over by occupation, 2000
Managers & professionals	3,032
Service occupations	673
Sales & office occupations	2,436
Farming, fishing & forestry	6
Construction & maintenance	550
Production & transportation	744
Self-employed persons	393

* US Census Bureau
** New Jersey Department of Labor

General Information
Town of Secaucus
1203 Paterson Plank Rd
Secaucus, NJ 07094
201-330-2000

Website	www.seacaucusnj.org
Year of incorporation	1917
Land/water area (sq. miles)	5.89/0.63
Form of government	Town

Government
Legislative Districts
US Congressional	9
State Legislative	32

Local Officials, 2008
Mayor	Dennis Elwell
Manager	David Drumeler
Clerk	Michael Marra
Finance Dir	Margaret Barkala
Tax Assessor	Michael Jaeger
Tax Collector	Alan Bartolozzi
Attorney	Frank Leanza
Building	Vincent Prieto
Comm Dev/Planning	NA
Engineering	Gerald Perricone
Public Works	Glenn Beckmeyer
Police Chief	Dennis Corcoran
Emerg/Fire Director	Robert Parisi

Housing & Construction
Housing Units, 2000*
Total	6,385
Median rent	$850
Median SF home value	$209,400

Permits for New Residential Construction
	Units	Value
Total, 2007	101	$12,050,834
Single family	48	$7,062,235
Total, 2006	55	$5,771,677
Single family	53	$5,557,435

Real Property Valuation, 2007
	Parcels	Valuation
Total	5,203	$2,540,213,775
Vacant	169	76,599,400
Residential	4,633	768,487,800
Commercial	234	765,539,075
Industrial	156	912,751,300
Apartments	11	16,836,200
Farm land	0	0
Farm homestead	0	0

Average Property Value & Tax, 2007
Residential value	$165,873
Property tax	$4,977
Tax credit/rebate	$862

Public Library
Secaucus Public Library
1379 Paterson Plank Rd
Secaucus, NJ 07094
201-330-2084

Director: Katherine Steffens

Library statistics, 2006
Population served	15,931
Full-time/total staff	2/11

	Total	Per capita
Holdings	79,233	4.97
Revenues	$1,358,069	$85.25
Expenditures	$1,432,597	$89.93
Annual visits	176,880	11.10
Internet terminals/annual users	52/62,000	

Taxes
	2005	2006	2007
General tax rate per $100	2.86	2.834	3.001
County equalization ratio	68.51	63.47	54.37
Net valuation taxable	$2,482,969,997	$2,521,402,875	$2,544,000,998
State equalized value	$3,912,037,178	$5,250,670,234	$5,601,437,675

Public Safety
Number of officers, 2006	60

Crime	2005	2006
Total crimes	705	732
Violent	24	21
Murder	0	0
Rape	0	0
Robbery	8	12
Aggravated assault	16	9
Non-violent	681	711
Burglary	43	37
Larceny	553	587
Vehicle theft	85	87
Domestic violence	171	223
Arson	1	3
Total crime rate	45.0	46.9
Violent	1.5	1.3
Non-violent	43.5	45.5

Public School District
(for school year 2006-07 except as noted)

Secaucus School District
20 Centre Ave, PO Box 1496
Secaucus, NJ 07096
201-974-2004

Superintendent	Constantino Scerbo
Number of schools	4
Grade plan	K-12
Enrollment	1,996
Attendance rate, '05-06	94.9%
Dropout rate	0.2%
Students per teacher	12.4
Per pupil expenditure	$14,442
Median faculty salary	$56,839
Median administrator salary	$130,980
Grade 12 enrollment	115
High school graduation rate	97.5%

Assessment test results
(percent scoring at proficient or advanced level)
	Language	Math
NJASK-Grade 3	85.1%	96.1%
GEPA-Grade 8	68.5%	68.0%
HSPA-High School	92.5%	78.4%

SAT score averages
Pct tested	Math	Verbal	Writing
92%	479	462	456

Teacher Qualifications
Avg. years of experience	11
Highly-qualified teachers one subject/all subjects	100%/100%
With emergency credentials	0.0%

No Child Left Behind
AYP, 2005-06	Meets Standards

Municipal Finance
State Aid Programs, 2008
Total aid	$2,396,413
CMPTRA	604,579
Energy tax receipts	1,791,804
Garden State Trust	30

General Budget, 2007
Total tax levy	$76,329,001
County levy	19,364,239
County taxes	18,893,056
County library	0
County health	0
County open space	471,182
School levy	28,982,354
Muni. levy	27,982,408
Misc. revenues	12,080,980

Burlington County

Shamong Township

Demographics & Socio-Economic Characteristics
(2000 US Census, except as noted)

Population
1980*	4,537
1990*	5,765
2000	6,462
Male	3,239
Female	3,223
2006 (estimate)*	6,873
Population density	153.4

Race & Hispanic Origin, 2000
Race
White	6,284
Black/African American	53
American Indian/Alaska Native	7
Asian	43
Native Hawaiian/Pacific Islander	0
Other race	20
Two or more races	55
Hispanic origin, total	68
Mexican	17
Puerto Rican	23
Cuban	9
Other Hispanic	19

Age & Nativity, 2000
Under 5 years	442
18 years and over	4,564
21 years and over	4,339
65 years and over	386
85 years and over	24
Median age	37.3
Native-born	6,330
Foreign-born	132

Educational Attainment, 2000
Population 25 years and over	4,134
Less than 9th grade	1.4%
High school grad or higher	92.3%
Bachelor's degree or higher	37.1%
Graduate degree	10.9%

Income & Poverty, 1999
Per capita income	$30,934
Median household income	$77,457
Median family income	$82,534
Persons in poverty	168
H'holds receiving public assistance	14
H'holds receiving social security	388

Households, 2000
Total households	2,132
With persons under 18	1,002
With persons over 65	292
Family households	1,821
Single-person households	243
Persons per household	3.03
Persons per family	3.29

Labor & Employment
Total civilian labor force, 2006**	4,178
Unemployment rate	3.0%
Total civilian labor force, 2000	3,586
Unemployment rate	2.7%

Employed persons 16 years and over by occupation, 2000
Managers & professionals	1,470
Service occupations	448
Sales & office occupations	1,014
Farming, fishing & forestry	5
Construction & maintenance	296
Production & transportation	256
Self-employed persons	245

* US Census Bureau
** New Jersey Department of Labor

See Introduction for an explanation of all data sources.

General Information
Township of Shamong
105 Willow Grove Rd
Shamong, NJ 08088
609-268-2377

Website	www.shamong.net
Year of incorporation	1852
Land/water area (sq. miles)	44.81/0.25
Form of government	Township

Government
Legislative Districts
US Congressional	2, 3
State Legislative	8

Local Officials, 2008
Mayor	Jonathan Shevelew
Manager	Susan Onorato
Clerk	Susan Onorato
Finance Dir.	Kathleen Phelan
Tax Assessor	James Renwick
Tax Collector	Kathryn Taylor
Attorney	Douglas L. Heinold
Building	Dan McGonigle
Comm Dev/Planning	NA
Engineering	Richard Arango
Public Works	NA
Police Chief	NA
Emerg/Fire Director	Michael Durham

Housing & Construction
Housing Units, 2000*
Total	2,175
Median rent	$764
Median SF home value	$191,900

Permits for New Residential Construction
	Units	Value
Total, 2007	13	$2,551,098
Single family	13	$2,551,098
Total, 2006	15	$2,924,532
Single family	15	$2,924,532

Real Property Valuation, 2007
	Parcels	Valuation
Total	2,494	$403,733,700
Vacant	223	5,262,250
Residential	1,951	372,814,200
Commercial	40	7,994,900
Industrial	7	1,370,200
Apartments	0	0
Farm land	181	1,532,950
Farm homestead	92	14,759,200

Average Property Value & Tax, 2007
Residential value	$189,708
Property tax	$7,059
Tax credit/rebate	$1,065

Public Library
No public municipal library

Library statistics, 2006
Population served	NA
Full-time/total staff	NA/NA

	Total	Per capita
Holdings	NA	NA
Revenues	NA	NA
Expenditures	NA	NA
Annual visits	NA	NA
Internet terminals/annual users	NA/NA	

Taxes
	2005	2006	2007
General tax rate per $100	3.405	3.566	3.729
County equalization ratio	66.53	60.64	53.97
Net valuation taxable	$400,234,661	$401,057,300	$404,819,378
State equalized value	$660,017,581	$744,293,991	$798,663,118

Public Safety
Number of officers, 2006 0

Crime	2005	2006
Total crimes	31	38
Violent	2	2
Murder	0	0
Rape	0	0
Robbery	0	0
Aggravated assault	2	2
Non-violent	29	36
Burglary	7	9
Larceny	19	22
Vehicle theft	3	5
Domestic violence	7	1
Arson	0	0
Total crime rate	4.5	5.5
Violent	0.3	0.3
Non-violent	4.2	5.2

Public School District
(for school year 2006-07 except as noted)

Shamong Township School District
295 Indian Mills Rd
Shamong, NJ 08088
609-268-0120

Superintendent	Thomas Christensen
Number of schools	2
Grade plan	K-8
Enrollment	943
Attendance rate, '05-06	95.8%
Dropout rate	NA
Students per teacher	11.4
Per pupil expenditure	$12,153
Median faculty salary	$67,293
Median administrator salary	$96,633
Grade 12 enrollment	NA
High school graduation rate	NA

Assessment test results
(percent scoring at proficient or advanced level)
	Language	Math
NJASK-Grade 3	97.6%	96.4%
GEPA-Grade 8	90.7%	88.2%
HSPA-High School	NA	NA

SAT score averages
Pct tested	Math	Verbal	Writing
NA	NA	NA	NA

Teacher Qualifications
Avg. years of experience	13
Highly-qualified teachers one subject/all subjects	100%/100%
With emergency credentials	0.0%

No Child Left Behind
AYP, 2005-06 ..... Meets Standards

Municipal Finance
State Aid Programs, 2008
Total aid	$762,116
CMPTRA	83,834
Energy tax receipts	507,709
Garden State Trust	170,303

General Budget, 2007
Total tax levy	$15,063,295
County tax	3,147,055
County taxes	2,607,788
County library	239,303
County health	0
County open space	299,964
School levy	11,835,254
Muni. levy	80,987
Misc. revenues	3,078,990

©2008 Information Publications, Inc. All rights reserved. Photocopying prohibited. For additional copies, contact the publisher at www.informationpublications.com or (877)544-INFO (4636)

The New Jersey Municipal Data Book

Shiloh Borough
Cumberland County

Demographics & Socio-Economic Characteristics
(2000 US Census, except as noted)

Population
1980*	604
1990*	408
2000	534
Male	251
Female	283
2006 (estimate)*	650
Population density	541.7

Race & Hispanic Origin, 2000
Race
- White 508
- Black/African American 14
- American Indian/Alaska Native 3
- Asian 0
- Native Hawaiian/Pacific Islander 0
- Other race 0
- Two or more races 9
- Hispanic origin, total 16
  - Mexican 7
  - Puerto Rican 9
  - Cuban 0
  - Other Hispanic 0

Age & Nativity, 2000
- Under 5 years 34
- 18 years and over 403
- 21 years and over 390
- 65 years and over 84
- 85 years and over 7
- Median age 39.8
- Native-born 528
- Foreign-born 8

Educational Attainment, 2000
- Population 25 years and over 341
- Less than 9th grade 4.4%
- High school grad or higher 76.8%
- Bachelor's degree or higher 14.1%
- Graduate degree 3.5%

Income & Poverty, 1999
- Per capita income $16,880
- Median household income $49,191
- Median family income $54,219
- Persons in poverty 31
- H'holds receiving public assistance 0
- H'holds receiving social security 49

Households, 2000
- Total households 194
- With persons under 18 72
- With persons over 65 59
- Family households 152
- Single-person households 35
- Persons per household 2.75
- Persons per family 3.09

Labor & Employment
- Total civilian labor force, 2006** 334
- Unemployment rate 5.0%
- Total civilian labor force, 2000 293
- Unemployment rate 5.1%

Employed persons 16 years and over by occupation, 2000
- Managers & professionals 71
- Service occupations 27
- Sales & office occupations 61
- Farming, fishing & forestry 8
- Construction & maintenance 45
- Production & transportation 66
- Self-employed persons 7

* US Census Bureau
** New Jersey Department of Labor

General Information
Borough of Shiloh
PO Box 349
900 Main St.
Shiloh, NJ 08353
856-455-3054
Email .... shilohclerk@verizon.net
Year of incorporation 1929
Land/water area (sq. miles) 1.20/0.00
Form of government .... Borough

Government
Legislative Districts
- US Congressional 2
- State Legislative 3

Local Officials, 2008
- Mayor .... Howard Scull Jr
- Manager/Admin .... NA
- Clerk .... Ronald Campbell Sr
- Finance Dir .... Teresa Delp
- Tax Assessor .... Lois Mazza
- Tax Collector .... Elizabeth Wallender
- Attorney .... Theodore Baker
- Building .... Andrew Jepson
- Comm Dev/Planning .... NA
- Engineering .... J. Michael Fralinger
- Public Works .... NA
- Police Chief .... NA
- Emerg/Fire Director .... Ronald Dubois

Housing & Construction
Housing Units, 2000*
- Total 204
- Median rent $558
- Median SF home value $97,600

Permits for New Residential Construction
	Units	Value
Total, 2007	2	$203,608
Single family	2	$203,608
Total, 2006	4	$407,214
Single family	4	$407,214

Real Property Valuation, 2007
	Parcels	Valuation
Total	241	$19,317,000
Vacant	7	171,800
Residential	186	16,437,700
Commercial	13	1,077,400
Industrial	0	0
Apartments	0	0
Farm land	25	334,400
Farm homestead	10	1,295,700

Average Property Value & Tax, 2007
- Residential value $90,477
- Property tax $3,315
- Tax credit/rebate $858

Public Library
No public municipal library

Library statistics, 2006
- Population served .... NA
- Full-time/total staff .... NA/NA

	Total	Per capita
Holdings	NA	NA
Revenues	NA	NA
Expenditures	NA	NA
Annual visits	NA	NA
Internet terminals/annual users	NA/NA	

Taxes
	2005	2006	2007
General tax rate per $100	3.625	4.05	3.667
County equalization ratio	89.12	75.87	63.72
Net valuation taxable	$19,094,488	$19,225,800	$19,430,642
State equalized value	$25,167,376	$30,304,108	$31,713,511

Public Safety
Number of officers, 2006 0

Crime
	2005	2006
Total crimes	2	8
Violent	0	2
Murder	0	0
Rape	0	0
Robbery	0	0
Aggravated assault	0	2
Non-violent	2	6
Burglary	1	2
Larceny	1	4
Vehicle theft	0	0
Domestic violence	1	0
Arson	0	0
Total crime rate	3.2	12.5
Violent	0.0	3.1
Non-violent	3.2	9.4

Public School District
(for school year 2006-07 except as noted)

Shiloh School District
Main St, PO Box 189
Shiloh, NJ 08353
856-451-5424

- Consulting Superintendent .... David Hitchner
- Number of schools .... NA
- Grade plan K-8
- Enrollment .... NA
- Attendance rate, '05-06 .... 96.8%
- Dropout rate .... NA
- Students per teacher 8.5
- Per pupil expenditure ....
- Median faculty salary $36,700
- Median administrator salary $26,000
- Grade 12 enrollment .... NA
- High school graduation rate .... NA

Assessment test results
(percent scoring at proficient or advanced level)
	Language	Math
NJASK-Grade 3	NA	NA
GEPA-Grade 8	NA	NA
HSPA-High School	NA	NA

SAT score averages
Pct tested	Math	Verbal	Writing
NA	NA	NA	NA

Teacher Qualifications
- Avg. years of experience 10
- Highly-qualified teachers one subject/all subjects 100%/100%
- With emergency credentials 0.0%

No Child Left Behind
AYP, 2005-06 .... Meets Standards

Municipal Finance
State Aid Programs, 2008
- Total aid $27,978
- CMPTRA 0
- Energy tax receipts 27,978
- Garden State Trust 0

General Budget, 2007
- Total tax levy $711,950
- County levy 301,729
- County taxes 285,826
- County library 0
- County health 12,846
- County open space 3,058
- School levy 318,906
- Muni. levy 91,315
- Misc. revenues 165,033

Ocean County

Demographics & Socio-Economic Characteristics
(2000 US Census, except as noted)

Population
1980*	1,427
1990*	1,352
2000	1,384
Male	666
Female	718
2006 (estimate)*	1,427
Population density	2,038.6

Race & Hispanic Origin, 2000
Race
White	1,333
Black/African American	4
American Indian/Alaska Native	10
Asian	12
Native Hawaiian/Pacific Islander	0
Other race	15
Two or more races	10
Hispanic origin, total	80
Mexican	52
Puerto Rican	5
Cuban	3
Other Hispanic	20

Age & Nativity, 2000
Under 5 years	47
18 years and over	1,179
21 years and over	1,146
65 years and over	372
85 years and over	45
Median age	50.5
Native-born	1,318
Foreign-born	77

Educational Attainment, 2000
Population 25 years and over	1,079
Less than 9th grade	2.4%
High school grad or higher	89.0%
Bachelor's degree or higher	25.4%
Graduate degree	9.4%

Income & Poverty, 1999
Per capita income	$27,870
Median household income	$42,098
Median family income	$60,417
Persons in poverty	114
H'holds receiving public assistance	3
H'holds receiving social security	291

Households, 2000
Total households	664
With persons under 18	111
With persons over 65	268
Family households	396
Single-person households	238
Persons per household	2.08
Persons per family	2.65

Labor & Employment
Total civilian labor force, 2006**	694
Unemployment rate	7.6%
Total civilian labor force, 2000	696
Unemployment rate	6.6%

Employed persons 16 years and over by occupation, 2000
Managers & professionals	219
Service occupations	128
Sales & office occupations	173
Farming, fishing & forestry	3
Construction & maintenance	77
Production & transportation	50
Self-employed persons	92

* US Census Bureau
** New Jersey Department of Labor

See Introduction for an explanation of all data sources.

Ship Bottom Borough

General Information
Borough of Ship Bottom
1621 Long Beach Blvd
Ship Bottom, NJ 08008
609-494-2171

Website	shipbottom.org
Year of incorporation	1947
Land/water area (sq. miles)	0.70/0.30
Form of government	Borough

Government
Legislative Districts
US Congressional	3
State Legislative	9

Local Officials, 2008
Mayor	William Huelsenbeck
Manager	T. Richard Bethea
Clerk	Kathleen Wells
Finance Dir	T. Richard Bethea
Tax Assessor	William Procacci
Tax Collector	T. Richard Bethea
Attorney	Christopher Conners
Building	Susan DeLuca
Comm Dev/Planning	NA
Engineering	Frank Little
Public Works	NA
Police Chief	Paul Sharkey
Emerg/Fire Director	Frederick Traut

Housing & Construction
Housing Units, 2000*
Total	2,218
Median rent	$783
Median SF home value	$236,000

Permits for New Residential Construction
	Units	Value
Total, 2007	20	$5,592,182
Single family	18	$5,426,682
Total, 2006	26	$5,151,671
Single family	24	$5,099,571

Real Property Valuation, 2007
	Parcels	Valuation
Total	2,014	$1,068,091,500
Vacant	73	26,689,500
Residential	1,791	918,975,200
Commercial	146	118,167,100
Industrial	0	0
Apartments	4	4,259,700
Farm land	0	0
Farm homestead	0	0

Average Property Value & Tax, 2007
Residential value	$513,107
Property tax	$4,793
Tax credit/rebate	$992

Public Library
No public municipal library

Library statistics, 2006
Population served	NA
Full-time/total staff	NA/NA

	Total	Per capita
Holdings	NA	NA
Revenues	NA	NA
Expenditures	NA	NA
Annual visits	NA	NA
Internet terminals/annual users	NA/NA	

Public Safety
Number of officers, 2006 11

Crime	2005	2006
Total crimes	95	93
Violent	8	7
Murder	0	0
Rape	0	0
Robbery	0	0
Aggravated assault	8	7
Non-violent	87	86
Burglary	14	25
Larceny	71	61
Vehicle theft	2	0
Domestic violence	9	6
Arson	2	1
Total crime rate	67.0	65.6
Violent	5.6	4.9
Non-violent	61.4	60.6

Public School District
(for school year 2006-07 except as noted)

Long Beach Island School District
200 Barnegat Ave
Surf City, NJ 08008
609-494-2341

Superintendent	Robert A. Garguilo
Number of schools	10
Grade plan	K-6
Enrollment	248
Attendance rate, '05-06	94.3%
Dropout rate	NA
Students per teacher	6.9
Per pupil expenditure	$21,956
Median faculty salary	$94,335
Median administrator salary	$68,857
Grade 12 enrollment	NA
High school graduation rate	NA

Assessment test results
(percent scoring at proficient or advanced level)
	Language	Math
NJASK-Grade 3	100.0%	90.0%
GEPA-Grade 8	NA	NA
HSPA-High School	NA	NA

SAT score averages
Pct tested	Math	Verbal	Writing
NA	NA	NA	NA

Teacher Qualifications
Avg. years of experience	19
Highly-qualified teachers one subject/all subjects	100%/100%
With emergency credentials	0.0%

No Child Left Behind
AYP, 2005-06 .... Meets Standards

Municipal Finance
State Aid Programs, 2008
Total aid	$269,692
CMPTRA	0
Energy tax receipts	269,692
Garden State Trust	0

General Budget, 2007
Total tax levy	$9,980,122
County levy	3,919,624
County taxes	3,363,028
County library	398,566
County health	0
County open space	158,031
School levy	3,072,112
Muni. levy	2,988,386
Misc. revenues	2,792,608

Taxes
	2005	2006	2007
General tax rate per $100	0.875	0.901	0.935
County equalization ratio	109.23	91.19	81.45
Net valuation taxable	$1,046,996,207	$1,046,285,000	$1,068,359,499
State equalized value	$1,148,148,050	$1,284,870,972	$1,325,772,467

The New Jersey Municipal Data Book

Shrewsbury Borough
Monmouth County

Demographics & Socio-Economic Characteristics
(2000 US Census, except as noted)

Population
1980*	2,962
1990*	3,096
2000	3,590
Male	1,781
Female	1,809
2006 (estimate)*	3,717
Population density	1,681.9

Race & Hispanic Origin, 2000
Race
- White ... 3,468
- Black/African American ... 19
- American Indian/Alaska Native ... 0
- Asian ... 60
- Native Hawaiian/Pacific Islander ... 0
- Other race ... 13
- Two or more races ... 30
- Hispanic origin, total ... 69
  - Mexican ... 16
  - Puerto Rican ... 13
  - Cuban ... 8
  - Other Hispanic ... 32

Age & Nativity, 2000
- Under 5 years ... 310
- 18 years and over ... 2,485
- 21 years and over ... 2,412
- 65 years and over ... 431
- 85 years and over ... 43
- Median age ... 38.4
- Native-born ... 3,325
- Foreign-born ... 265

Educational Attainment, 2000
- Population 25 years and over ... 2,367
- Less than 9th grade ... 2.7%
- High school grad or higher ... 91.0%
- Bachelor's degree or higher ... 48.7%
- Graduate degree ... 19.6%

Income & Poverty, 1999
- Per capita income ... $38,218
- Median household income ... $86,911
- Median family income ... $92,719
- Persons in poverty ... 37
- H'holds receiving public assistance ... 13
- H'holds receiving social security ... 290

Households, 2000
- Total households ... 1,207
  - With persons under 18 ... 567
  - With persons over 65 ... 301
  - Family households ... 1,016
  - Single-person households ... 156
- Persons per household ... 2.96
- Persons per family ... 3.27

Labor & Employment
- Total civilian labor force, 2006** ... 1,786
  - Unemployment rate ... 1.2%
- Total civilian labor force, 2000 ... 1,686
  - Unemployment rate ... 2.7%

Employed persons 16 years and over by occupation, 2000
- Managers & professionals ... 832
- Service occupations ... 137
- Sales & office occupations ... 516
- Farming, fishing & forestry ... 0
- Construction & maintenance ... 83
- Production & transportation ... 72
- Self-employed persons ... 152

‡ Branch of county library
* US Census Bureau
** New Jersey Department of Labor

General Information
Borough of Shrewsbury
419 Sycamore Ave
Shrewsbury, NJ 07702
732-741-4200

- Website ... www.shrewsburyboro.com
- Year of incorporation ... 1926
- Land/water area (sq. miles) ... 2.21/0.02
- Form of government ... Borough

Government
Legislative Districts
- US Congressional ... 12
- State Legislative ... 12

Local Officials, 2008
- Mayor ... Emilia Siciliano
- Manager ... Tom Seaman
- Clerk/Registrar ... Lynn Spillane
- Finance Dir ... Thomas Seaman
- Tax Assessor ... Stephen Walters
- Tax Collector ... Thomas Seaman
- Attorney ... Martin Barger
- Building ... Cary Costa
- Comm Dev/Planning ... NA
- Engineering ... David Cranmer
- Public Works ... Robert Wentway
- Police Chief ... John Wilson III
- Fire Chief ... Robert Wentway

Housing & Construction
Housing Units, 2000*
- Total ... 1,223
- Median rent ... $898
- Median SF home value ... $258,300

Permits for New Residential Construction
	Units	Value
Total, 2007	17	$3,647,907
Single family	17	$3,647,907
Total, 2006	18	$4,063,791
Single family	18	$4,063,791

Real Property Valuation, 2007
	Parcels	Valuation
Total	1,501	$805,956,900
Vacant	31	6,469,400
Residential	1,297	511,903,900
Commercial	171	286,794,000
Industrial	0	0
Apartments	0	0
Farm land	1	10,900
Farm homestead	1	778,700

Average Property Value & Tax, 2007
- Residential value ... $394,979
- Property tax ... $9,304
- Tax credit/rebate ... $1,255

Public Library
Eastern Branch Library‡
1001 Rte 35
Shrewsbury, NJ 07702
732-842-5995
- Branch Librarian ... Janet Kranis

Library statistics, 2006
see Monmouth County profile
for library system statistics

Public Safety
Number of officers, 2006 ... 16

Crime	2005	2006
Total crimes	98	79
Violent	3	9
Murder	0	0
Rape	0	1
Robbery	0	4
Aggravated assault	3	4
Non-violent	95	70
Burglary	16	16
Larceny	71	48
Vehicle theft	8	6
Domestic violence	10	6
Arson	0	0
Total crime rate	26.3	21.1
Violent	0.8	2.4
Non-violent	25.5	18.7

Public School District
(for school year 2006-07 except as noted)

Shrewsbury Borough School District
20 Obre Place
Shrewsbury, NJ 07702
732-747-0882

- Superintendent ... Lawrence Ambrosino
- Number of schools ... 1
- Grade plan ... K-8
- Enrollment ... 503
- Attendance rate, '05-06 ... 96.3%
- Dropout rate ... NA
- Students per teacher ... 10.3
- Per pupil expenditure ... $11,970
- Median faculty salary ... $52,455
- Median administrator salary ... $100,000
- Grade 12 enrollment ... NA
- High school graduation rate ... NA

Assessment test results
(percent scoring at proficient or advanced level)
	Language	Math
NJASK-Grade 3	92.3%	92.3%
GEPA-Grade 8	90.3%	83.9%
HSPA-High School	NA	NA

SAT score averages
Pct tested	Math	Verbal	Writing
NA	NA	NA	NA

Teacher Qualifications
- Avg. years of experience ... 11
- Highly-qualified teachers
  - one subject/all subjects ... 100%/97.5%
- With emergency credentials ... 0.0%

No Child Left Behind
- AYP, 2005-06 ... Meets Standards

Municipal Finance
State Aid Programs, 2008
- Total aid ... $470,320
  - CMPTRA ... 0
  - Energy tax receipts ... 470,320
  - Garden State Trust ... 0

General Budget, 2007
- Total tax levy ... $19,019,633
  - County levy ... 2,990,533
    - County taxes ... 2,670,764
    - County library ... 152,883
    - County health ... 0
    - County open space ... 166,886
  - School levy ... 10,185,018
  - Muni. levy ... 5,844,081
- Misc. revenues ... 2,142,723

Taxes	2005	2006	2007
General tax rate per $100	2.152	2.267	2.356
County equalization ratio	92.34	81.96	73.03
Net valuation taxable	$791,332,531	$794,670,600	$807,423,411
State equalized value	$965,510,653	$1,089,726,481	$1,147,105,317

Monmouth County
Shrewsbury Township

Demographics & Socio-Economic Characteristics
(2000 US Census, except as noted)

Population
1980*	995
1990*	1,098
2000	1,098
Male	530
Female	568
2006 (estimate)*	1,073
Population density	11,922.2

Race & Hispanic Origin, 2000
Race
- White....................733
- Black/African American....183
- American Indian/Alaska Native....0
- Asian....110
- Native Hawaiian/Pacific Islander....0
- Other race....31
- Two or more races....41
- Hispanic origin, total....73
  - Mexican....22
  - Puerto Rican....19
  - Cuban....0
  - Other Hispanic....32

Age & Nativity, 2000
- Under 5 years....82
- 18 years and over....872
- 21 years and over....838
- 65 years and over....119
- 85 years and over....16
- Median age....34.9
- Native-born....905
- Foreign-born....193

Educational Attainment, 2000
- Population 25 years and over....770
- Less than 9th grade....6.9%
- High school grad or higher....82.5%
- Bachelor's degree or higher....20.4%
- Graduate degree....5.7%

Income & Poverty, 1999
- Per capita income....$23,574
- Median household income....$36,875
- Median family income....$42,500
- Persons in poverty....96
- H'holds receiving public assistance....10
- H'holds receiving social security....90

Households, 2000
- Total households....521
  - With persons under 18....143
  - With persons over 65....102
  - Family households....255
  - Single-person households....206
- Persons per household....2.10
- Persons per family....2.89

Labor & Employment
- Total civilian labor force, 2006**....754
  - Unemployment rate....7.2%
- Total civilian labor force, 2000....689
  - Unemployment rate....7.0%

Employed persons 16 years and over by occupation, 2000
- Managers & professionals....192
- Service occupations....79
- Sales & office occupations....232
- Farming, fishing & forestry....0
- Construction & maintenance....48
- Production & transportation....90
- Self-employed persons....20

‡ Branch of county library
* US Census Bureau
** New Jersey Department of Labor

See Introduction for an explanation of all data sources.

General Information
Shrewsbury Township
1979 Crawford St
Shrewsbury Twp, NJ 07724
732-542-0675

- Website....NA
- Year of incorporation....1693
- Land/water area (sq. miles)....0.09/0.00
- Form of government....Township

Government
Legislative Districts
- US Congressional....12
- State Legislative....12

Local Officials, 2008
- Mayor....Albert Klose
- Manager/Admin....NA
- Clerk....Jan Delonardo
- Finance Dir....Adeline Schmidt
- Tax Assessor....Stephen Walters
- Tax Collector....Adeline Schmidt
- Attorney....Gene Anthony
- Code Enforcement....Joseph Muzetska
- Comm Dev/Planning....NA
- Engineering....Richard Maser
- Public Works....M. Willemsen/L. Delonardo
- Police Chief....(state)
- Fire Svcs....(Eatontown Fire Dept)

Housing & Construction
Housing Units, 2000*
- Total....546
- Median rent....$825
- Median SF home value....$61,100

Permits for New Residential Construction
	Units	Value
Total, 2007	0	$0
Single family	0	$0
Total, 2006	0	$0
Single family	0	$0

Real Property Valuation, 2007
	Parcels	Valuation
Total	391	$27,238,100
Vacant	0	0
Residential	122	9,103,800
Commercial	0	0
Industrial	0	0
Apartments	269	18,134,300
Farm land	0	0
Farm homestead	0	0

Average Property Value & Tax, 2007
- Residential value....$74,621
- Property tax....$4,130
- Tax credit/rebate....$720

Public Library
Eastern Branch Library‡
1001 Rte 35
Shrewsbury, NJ 07702
732-842-5995

- Branch Librarian....Janet Kranis

Library statistics, 2006
see Monmouth County profile for library system statistics

Public Safety
- Number of officers, 2006....0

Crime
	2005	2006
Total crimes	6	6
Violent	2	1
Murder	0	0
Rape	0	0
Robbery	0	0
Aggravated assault	2	1
Non-violent	4	5
Burglary	1	2
Larceny	3	3
Vehicle theft	0	0
Domestic violence	8	1
Arson	0	0
Total crime rate	5.5	5.6
Violent	1.8	0.9
Non-violent	3.7	4.6

Public School District
(for school year 2006-07 except as noted)

Tinton Falls School District
658 Tinton Ave
Tinton Falls, NJ 07724
732-460-2404

- Superintendent....John Russo
- Number of schools....6
- Grade plan....K-8
- Enrollment....1,576
- Attendance rate, '05-06....95.6%
- Dropout rate....NA
- Students per teacher....10.7
- Per pupil expenditure....$14,982
- Median faculty salary....$53,865
- Median administrator salary....$103,174
- Grade 12 enrollment....NA
- High school graduation rate....NA

Assessment test results
(percent scoring at proficient or advanced level)
	Language	Math
NJASK-Grade 3	88.7%	96.3%
GEPA-Grade 8	84.6%	79.0%
HSPA-High School	NA	NA

SAT score averages
Pct tested	Math	Verbal	Writing
NA	NA	NA	NA

Teacher Qualifications
- Avg. years of experience....12
- Highly-qualified teachers
  - one subject/all subjects....100%/100%
- With emergency credentials....0.0%

No Child Left Behind
- AYP, 2005-06....Meets Standards

Municipal Finance
State Aid Programs, 2008
- Total aid....$54,936
- CMPTRA....0
- Energy tax receipts....54,936
- Garden State Trust....0

General Budget, 2007
- Total tax levy....$1,509,625
- County levy....202,903
  - County taxes....181,208
  - County library....10,373
  - County health....0
  - County open space....11,322
- School levy....722,310
- Muni. levy....584,413
- Misc. revenues....228,276

Taxes
	2005	2006	2007
General tax rate per $100	4.965	5.095	5.535
County equalization ratio	46.46	43.26	36.21
Net valuation taxable	$27,304,436	$27,238,100	$27,278,537
State equalized value	$63,117,050	$75,269,951	$79,684,004

Somerdale Borough — Camden County

Demographics & Socio-Economic Characteristics
(2000 US Census, except as noted)

Population
1980*	5,900
1990*	5,440
2000	5,192
Male	2,541
Female	2,651
2006 (estimate)*	5,123
Population density	3,739.4

Race & Hispanic Origin, 2000
Race
- White 3,912
- Black/African American 917
- American Indian/Alaska Native 11
- Asian 168
- Native Hawaiian/Pacific Islander 1
- Other race 56
- Two or more races 127

Hispanic origin, total 202
- Mexican 14
- Puerto Rican 105
- Cuban 5
- Other Hispanic 78

Age & Nativity, 2000
- Under 5 years 274
- 18 years and over 4,033
- 21 years and over 3,868
- 65 years and over 801
- 85 years and over 64
- Median age 39.0
- Native-born 4,850
- Foreign-born 348

Educational Attainment, 2000
- Population 25 years and over 3,722
- Less than 9th grade 2.8%
- High school grad or higher 84.5%
- Bachelor's degree or higher 16.7%
- Graduate degree 6.9%

Income & Poverty, 1999
- Per capita income $21,259
- Median household income $46,898
- Median family income $54,200
- Persons in poverty 283
- H'holds receiving public assistance ... 64
- H'holds receiving social security 659

Households, 2000
- Total households 2,068
- With persons under 18 661
- With persons over 65 599
- Family households 1,380
- Single-person households 613
- Persons per household 2.51
- Persons per family 3.11

Labor & Employment
- Total civilian labor force, 2006** ... 2,984
- Unemployment rate 5.1%
- Total civilian labor force, 2000 2,743
- Unemployment rate 4.7%

Employed persons 16 years and over by occupation, 2000
- Managers & professionals 802
- Service occupations 367
- Sales & office occupations 765
- Farming, fishing & forestry 0
- Construction & maintenance 261
- Production & transportation 418
- Self-employed persons 92

* US Census Bureau
** New Jersey Department of Labor

General Information
Borough of Somerdale
105 Kennedy Blvd
Somerdale, NJ 08083
856-783-6320

- Website .... www.somerdale-nj.com
- Year of incorporation 1929
- Land/water area (sq. miles) ... 1.37/0.00
- Form of government .... Borough

Government
Legislative Districts
- US Congressional 1
- State Legislative 5

Local Officials, 2008
- Mayor .... Gary Passanante
- Administrator .... Victor Cantillo
- Clerk .... Regina J. White
- Finance Dir .... Victor Cantillo
- Tax Assessor .... Thomas Davis
- Tax Collector .... Virginia Knecht
- Attorney .... John Kearney
- Building .... Mike DePalma
- Comm Dev/Planning .... NA
- Engineering .... Charles Riebel Jr
- Public Works .... Donald Wharton
- Police Chief .... Anthony Campbell
- Emerg/Fire Director .... (vacant)

Housing & Construction
Housing Units, 2000*
- Total 2,168
- Median rent $544
- Median SF home value $97,700

Permits for New Residential Construction
	Units	Value
Total, 2007	2	$267,943
Single family	2	$267,943
Total, 2006	7	$819,300
Single family	7	$819,300

Real Property Valuation, 2007
	Parcels	Valuation
Total	1,942	$191,901,500
Vacant	100	1,729,600
Residential	1,684	147,447,900
Commercial	122	27,490,900
Industrial	29	8,351,300
Apartments	7	6,881,800
Farm land	0	0
Farm homestead	0	0

Average Property Value & Tax, 2007
- Residential value $87,558
- Property tax $4,769
- Tax credit/rebate $973

Public Library
No public municipal library

Library statistics, 2006
- Population served .... NA
- Full-time/total staff .... NA/NA

	Total	Per capita
Holdings	NA	NA
Revenues	NA	NA
Expenditures	NA	NA
Annual visits	NA	NA
Internet terminals/annual users	NA/NA	

Taxes
	2005	2006	2007
General tax rate per $100	4.811	5.196	5.447
County equalization ratio	83.63	72.76	61.49
Net valuation taxable	$191,938,059	$191,399,000	$192,194,865
State equalized value	$263,796,123	$311,686,371	$338,803,684

Public Safety
Number of officers, 2006 13

Crime
	2005	2006
Total crimes	162	171
Violent	20	23
Murder	0	0
Rape	1	3
Robbery	7	11
Aggravated assault	12	9
Non-violent	142	148
Burglary	26	32
Larceny	105	104
Vehicle theft	11	12
Domestic violence	23	28
Arson	0	1
Total crime rate	31.4	33.2
Violent	3.9	4.5
Non-violent	27.5	28.7

Public School District
(for school year 2006-07 except as noted)

Somerdale Borough School District
Park School, 301 Grace St
Somerdale, NJ 08083
856-783-2933

- Superintendent .... Debra L. Bruner
- Number of schools 1
- Grade plan K-8
- Enrollment 468
- Attendance rate, '05-06 .... 94.9%
- Dropout rate .... NA
- Students per teacher 10.5
- Per pupil expenditure $12,248
- Median faculty salary $47,796
- Median administrator salary $81,589
- Grade 12 enrollment .... NA
- High school graduation rate ...... NA

Assessment test results
(percent scoring at proficient or advanced level)

	Language	Math
NJASK-Grade 3	81.2%	83.1%
GEPA-Grade 8	61.2%	58.0%
HSPA-High School	NA	NA

SAT score averages
Pct tested	Math	Verbal	Writing
NA	NA	NA	NA

Teacher Qualifications
- Avg. years of experience 12
- Highly-qualified teachers
  one subject/all subjects ... 100%/100%
- With emergency credentials 0.0%

No Child Left Behind
AYP, 2005-06 .... Meets Standards

Municipal Finance
State Aid Programs, 2008
- Total aid $561,326
- CMPTRA 106,675
- Energy tax receipts 454,651
- Garden State Trust 0

General Budget, 2007
- Total tax levy $10,468,723
- County levy 2,202,377
- County taxes 2,000,560
- County library 139,289
- County health 0
- County open space 62,529
- School levy 5,779,389
- Muni. levy 2,486,957
- Misc. revenues 2,403,889

Atlantic County
Somers Point City

Demographics & Socio-Economic Characteristics
(2000 US Census, except as noted)

Population
1980*	10,330
1990*	11,216
2000	11,614
Male	5,460
Female	6,154
2006 (estimate)*	11,573
Population density	2,871.7

Race & Hispanic Origin, 2000
Race
White	9,948
Black/African American	814
American Indian/Alaska Native	29
Asian	368
Native Hawaiian/Pacific Islander	4
Other race	261
Two or more races	190
Hispanic origin, total	696
Mexican	132
Puerto Rican	332
Cuban	10
Other Hispanic	222

Age & Nativity, 2000
Under 5 years	699
18 years and over	8,899
21 years and over	8,571
65 years and over	1,748
85 years and over	245
Median age	38.4
Native-born	10,667
Foreign-born	947

Educational Attainment, 2000
Population 25 years and over	8,090
Less than 9th grade	3.8%
High school grad or higher	84.2%
Bachelor's degree or higher	19.8%
Graduate degree	5.1%

Income & Poverty, 1999
Per capita income	$22,229
Median household income	$42,222
Median family income	$51,868
Persons in poverty	799
H'holds receiving public assistance	97
H'holds receiving social security	1,391

Households, 2000
Total households	4,920
With persons under 18	1,564
With persons over 65	1,248
Family households	2,952
Single-person households	1,621
Persons per household	2.32
Persons per family	2.97

Labor & Employment
Total civilian labor force, 2006**	6,690
Unemployment rate	5.3%
Total civilian labor force, 2000	6,124
Unemployment rate	6.0%

Employed persons 16 years and over by occupation, 2000
Managers & professionals	1,569
Service occupations	1,691
Sales & office occupations	1,452
Farming, fishing & forestry	40
Construction & maintenance	573
Production & transportation	433
Self-employed persons	308

‡ Branch of county library
* US Census Bureau
** New Jersey Department of Labor

See Introduction for an explanation of all data sources.

General Information
City of Somers Point
1 W New Jersey Ave
Somers Point, NJ 08244
609-927-9088

Website	www.somerspoint-nj.com
Year of incorporation	1902
Land/water area (sq. miles)	4.03/1.14
Form of government	City

Government
Legislative Districts
US Congressional	2
State Legislative	1

Local Officials, 2008
Mayor	John L. Glasser Jr
Manager	W.E. Swain
Clerk	Carol Degrassi
Finance Dir.	John Hanson
Tax Assessor	Diane Hesley
Tax Collector	Lynn MacEwan
Attorney	Damon Tyner
Building	Burton Federman
Comm Dev/Planning	NA
Engineering	James Mott
Public Works	Guy Martin
Police Chief	Salvatore Armenia
Emerg/Fire Director	Frank Denan

Housing & Construction
Housing Units, 2000*
Total	5,402
Median rent	$639
Median SF home value	$122,000

Permits for New Residential Construction
	Units	Value
Total, 2007	19	$1,768,768
Single family	17	$1,465,268
Total, 2006	35	$3,926,539
Single family	21	$1,802,039

Real Property Valuation, 2007
	Parcels	Valuation
Total	4,200	$685,863,600
Vacant	180	11,367,900
Residential	3,731	465,068,900
Commercial	275	168,398,000
Industrial	0	0
Apartments	14	41,028,800
Farm land	0	0
Farm homestead	0	0

Average Property Value & Tax, 2007
Residential value	$124,650
Property tax	$4,787
Tax credit/rebate	$913

Public Library
Somers Point Branch Library‡
747 Shore Rd
Somers Point, NJ 08244
609-927-7113
Branch Librarian......Mary Jane Bolden

Library statistics, 2006
see Atlantic County profile for library system statistics

Public Safety
Number of officers, 2006 26

Crime	2005	2006
Total crimes	373	357
Violent	45	41
Murder	0	0
Rape	3	0
Robbery	14	18
Aggravated assault	28	23
Non-violent	328	316
Burglary	72	72
Larceny	251	237
Vehicle theft	5	7
Domestic violence	286	251
Arson	1	4
Total crime rate	31.8	30.5
Violent	3.8	3.5
Non-violent	28.0	27.0

Public School District
(for school year 2006-07 except as noted)

Somers Point School District
121 W New York Ave
Somers Point, NJ 08244
609-927-2053

Superintendent	Gerald Toscano
Number of schools	3
Grade plan	K-8
Enrollment	1,124
Attendance rate, '05-06	94.3%
Dropout rate	NA
Students per teacher	10.4
Per pupil expenditure	$11,009
Median faculty salary	$44,529
Median administrator salary	$100,949
Grade 12 enrollment	NA
High school graduation rate	NA

Assessment test results
(percent scoring at proficient or advanced level)
	Language	Math
NJASK-Grade 3	88.8%	82.9%
GEPA-Grade 8	72.8%	65.2%
HSPA-High School	NA	NA

SAT score averages
Pct tested	Math	Verbal	Writing
NA	NA	NA	NA

Teacher Qualifications
Avg. years of experience	7
Highly-qualified teachers one subject/all subjects	100%/100%
With emergency credentials	0.0%

No Child Left Behind
AYP, 2005-06 .... Meets Standards

Municipal Finance
State Aid Programs, 2008
Total aid	$1,239,315
CMPTRA	450,849
Energy tax receipts	788,462
Garden State Trust	4

General Budget, 2007
Total tax levy	$26,412,926
County levy	4,476,515
County taxes	3,550,496
County library	447,877
County health	182,499
County open space	295,643
School levy	14,485,130
Muni. levy	7,451,281
Misc. revenues	4,249,499

Taxes
	2005	2006	2007
General tax rate per $100	3.358	3.686	3.841
County equalization ratio	67.94	52.7	46.59
Net valuation taxable	$673,666,921	$678,596,100	$687,720,915
State equalized value	$1,278,305,353	$1,458,570,467	$1,556,398,566

Somerville Borough
Somerset County

Demographics & Socio-Economic Characteristics
(2000 US Census, except as noted)

Population
- 1980* 11,973
- 1990* 11,632
- 2000 12,423
  - Male 6,249
  - Female 6,174
- 2006 (estimate)* 12,550
- Population density 5,317.8

Race & Hispanic Origin, 2000
Race
- White 8,847
- Black/African American 1,606
- American Indian/Alaska Native 23
- Asian 913
- Native Hawaiian/Pacific Islander 3
- Other race 634
- Two or more races 397
- Hispanic origin, total 2,112
  - Mexican 278
  - Puerto Rican 402
  - Cuban 46
  - Other Hispanic 1,386

Age & Nativity, 2000
- Under 5 years 869
- 18 years and over 9,698
- 21 years and over 9,285
- 65 years and over 1,738
- 85 years and over 229
- Median age 35.6
- Native-born 9,674
- Foreign-born 2,807

Educational Attainment, 2000
- Population 25 years and over 8,603
- Less than 9th grade 6.6%
- High school grad or higher 81.9%
- Bachelor's degree or higher 31.5%
- Graduate degree 10.6%

Income & Poverty, 1999
- Per capita income $23,310
- Median household income $51,237
- Median family income $60,422
- Persons in poverty 926
- H'holds receiving public assistance ... 153
- H'holds receiving social security .. 1,430

Households, 2000
- Total households 4,743
  - With persons under 18 1,472
  - With persons over 65 1,210
  - Family households 2,891
  - Single-person households 1,489
- Persons per household 2.49
- Persons per family 3.15

Labor & Employment
- Total civilian labor force, 2006** .. 7,234
  - Unemployment rate 5.2%
- Total civilian labor force, 2000 ... 6,495
  - Unemployment rate 5.0%

Employed persons 16 years and over by occupation, 2000
- Managers & professionals 2,313
- Service occupations 1,015
- Sales & office occupations 1,601
- Farming, fishing & forestry 0
- Construction & maintenance 535
- Production & transportation 705
- Self-employed persons 281

* US Census Bureau
** New Jersey Department of Labor

General Information
Borough of Somerville
25 W End Ave
Somerville, NJ 08876
908-725-2300

- Website .... www.somervillenj.org
- Year of incorporation 1909
- Land/water area (sq. miles) 2.36/0.00
- Form of government .... Borough

Government
Legislative Districts
- US Congressional 11
- State Legislative 16

Local Officials, 2008
- Mayor .... Brian Gallagher
- Administrator .... Kevin Sluka
- Clerk .... Kevin Sluka
- Finance Dir .... Janet Kelk
- Tax Assessor .... Frank Betts
- Tax Collector .... Janet Kelk
- Attorney .... Jermy Solomon
- Building .... Frank Vuosa
- Planning .... Michael Cole
- Engineering .... NA
- Public Works .... Peter Hendershot
- Police Chief .... Dennis Manning
- Emerg/Fire Director .... Todd Starner

Housing & Construction
Housing Units, 2000*
- Total 4,882
- Median rent $822
- Median SF home value $156,700

Permits for New Residential Construction

	Units	Value
Total, 2007	12	$1,824,849
Single family	12	$1,824,849
Total, 2006	5	$764,735
Single family	5	$764,735

Real Property Valuation, 2007

	Parcels	Valuation
Total	3,176	$653,731,250
Vacant	66	5,053,500
Residential	2,653	394,527,400
Commercial	411	200,951,850
Industrial	14	11,352,900
Apartments	32	41,845,600
Farm land	0	0
Farm homestead	0	0

Average Property Value & Tax, 2007
- Residential value $148,710
- Property tax $7,180
- Tax credit/rebate $1,154

Public Library
Somerville Mem. Public Library
35 West End Ave
Somerville, NJ 08876
908-725-1336

- Director .... Melissa A. Banks

Library statistics, 2006
- Population served 12,423
- Full-time/total staff 4/6

	Total	Per capita
Holdings	58,640	4.72
Revenues	$712,725	$57.37
Expenditures	$688,094	$55.39
Annual visits	76,528	6.16
Internet terminals/annual users	12/14,132	

Public Safety
- Number of officers, 2006 32

Crime

	2005	2006
Total crimes	270	279
Violent	25	28
Murder	0	0
Rape	2	0
Robbery	14	20
Aggravated assault	9	8
Non-violent	245	251
Burglary	40	34
Larceny	196	199
Vehicle theft	9	18
Domestic violence	136	134
Arson	0	0
Total crime rate	21.7	22.4
Violent	2.0	2.2
Non-violent	19.7	20.1

Public School District
(for school year 2006-07 except as noted)

Somerville Borough School District
51 West Cliff St
Somerville, NJ 08876
908-218-4101

- Superintendent .... Carolyn F. Leary
- Number of schools 3
- Grade plan K-12
- Enrollment 2,167
- Attendance rate, '05-06 .... 95.9%
- Dropout rate 0.5%
- Students per teacher 10.8
- Per pupil expenditure $14,618
- Median faculty salary $55,600
- Median administrator salary $99,275
- Grade 12 enrollment 205
- High school graduation rate 96.4%

Assessment test results
(percent scoring at proficient or advanced level)

	Language	Math
NJASK-Grade 3	81.6%	89.5%
GEPA-Grade 8	78.9%	60.9%
HSPA-High School	88.1%	83.0%

SAT score averages

Pct tested	Math	Verbal	Writing
90%	549	525	527

Teacher Qualifications
- Avg. years of experience 10
- Highly-qualified teachers
  - one subject/all subjects ... 99.5%/99.5%
- With emergency credentials 0.0%

No Child Left Behind
- AYP, 2005-06 .... Meets Standards

Municipal Finance
State Aid Programs, 2008
- Total aid $1,803,799
  - CMPTRA 463,812
  - Energy tax receipts 1,338,958
  - Garden State Trust 1,029

General Budget, 2007
- Total tax levy $31,816,184
  - County levy 3,881,325
  - County taxes 3,498,240
  - County library 0
  - County health 0
  - County open space 383,085
  - School levy 19,045,230
  - Muni. levy 8,889,630
  - Misc. revenues 6,970,111

Taxes

	2005	2006	2007
General tax rate per $100	4.29	4.52	4.83
County equalization ratio	66.38	59.68	51.73
Net valuation taxable	$656,457,956	$652,299,900	$658,992,455
State equalized value	$1,099,963,063	$1,267,721,925	$1,426,107,217

Middlesex County

South Amboy City

Demographics & Socio-Economic Characteristics
(2000 US Census, except as noted)

Population
1980*	8,322
1990*	7,863
2000	7,913
Male	3,865
Female	4,048
2006 (estimate)*	7,865
Population density	5,074.2

Race & Hispanic Origin, 2000
Race
White	7,456
Black/African American	68
American Indian/Alaska Native	15
Asian	109
Native Hawaiian/Pacific Islander	2
Other race	135
Two or more races	128
Hispanic origin, total	534
Mexican	28
Puerto Rican	236
Cuban	21
Other Hispanic	249

Age & Nativity, 2000
Under 5 years	474
18 years and over	5,990
21 years and over	5,741
65 years and over	1,073
85 years and over	124
Median age	36.7
Native-born	7,204
Foreign-born	709

Educational Attainment, 2000
Population 25 years and over	5,393
Less than 9th grade	5.4%
High school grad or higher	81.1%
Bachelor's degree or higher	12.5%
Graduate degree	3.2%

Income & Poverty, 1999
Per capita income	$23,598
Median household income	$50,529
Median family income	$62,029
Persons in poverty	582
H'holds receiving public assistance	86
H'holds receiving social security	1,058

Households, 2000
Total households	2,967
With persons under 18	1,045
With persons over 65	839
Family households	2,042
Single-person households	768
Persons per household	2.65
Persons per family	3.22

Labor & Employment
Total civilian labor force, 2006**	4,287
Unemployment rate	4.6%
Total civilian labor force, 2000	3,893
Unemployment rate	4.2%

Employed persons 16 years and over by occupation, 2000
Managers & professionals	847
Service occupations	593
Sales & office occupations	1,258
Farming, fishing & forestry	0
Construction & maintenance	422
Production & transportation	610
Self-employed persons	108

* US Census Bureau
** New Jersey Department of Labor
§ State Fiscal Year July 1–June 30

See Introduction for an explanation of all data sources.

General Information
City of South Amboy
140 N Broadway
South Amboy, NJ 08879
732-727-4600

Website	www.southamboynj.com
Year of incorporation	1908
Land/water area (sq. miles)	1.55/1.15
Form of government	Mayor-Council

Government
Legislative Districts
US Congressional	6
State Legislative	19

Local Officials, 2008
Mayor	John O'Leary Jr
Business Admin	Camille Tooker
Clerk	Kathleen Vigilante
Finance Dir	Terance O'Neill
Tax Assessor	Brian Enright
Tax Collector	Joanne Katko
Attorney	John Lanza
Building	Thomas Kelly
Comm Dev/Planning	NA
Engineering	James E. Cleary
Public Works	Gerald Garnett
Police Chief	James Wallis
Emerg/Fire Director	James Larkin

Housing & Construction
Housing Units, 2000*
Total	3,110
Median rent	$767
Median SF home value	$138,500

Permits for New Residential Construction
	Units	Value
Total, 2007	2	$233,968
Single family	2	$233,968
Total, 2006	4	$467,936
Single family	4	$467,936

Real Property Valuation, 2007
	Parcels	Valuation
Total	2,945	$860,702,600
Vacant	179	34,233,600
Residential	2,598	717,832,100
Commercial	149	76,861,900
Industrial	11	25,962,200
Apartments	8	5,812,800
Farm land	0	0
Farm homestead	0	0

Average Property Value & Tax, 2007
Residential value	$276,302
Property tax	$4,741
Tax credit/rebate	$897

Public Library
Dowdell Public Library
100 Harold G Hoffman Plaza
South Amboy, NJ 08879
732-721-6060

Director . . . . Elaine R. Gaber

Library statistics, 2006
Population served	7,913
Full-time/total staff	1/3

	Total	Per capita
Holdings	76,109	9.62
Revenues	$309,480	$39.11
Expenditures	$289,613	$36.60
Annual visits	37,180	4.70
Internet terminals/annual users	17/4,966	

Taxes
	2005	2006	2007
General tax rate per $100	1.57	1.66	1.72
County equalization ratio	121.18	96.59	88.16
Net valuation taxable	$824,098,308	$839,830,400	$861,510,236
State equalized value	$853,192,161	$953,454,509	$1,029,863,829

Public Safety
Number of officers, 2006 29

Crime	2005	2006
Total crimes	152	147
Violent	17	13
Murder	0	2
Rape	0	0
Robbery	1	1
Aggravated assault	16	10
Non-violent	135	134
Burglary	28	32
Larceny	91	86
Vehicle theft	16	16
Domestic violence	84	72
Arson	3	1
Total crime rate	19.0	18.4
Violent	2.1	1.6
Non-violent	16.9	16.8

Public School District
(for school year 2006-07 except as noted)

South Amboy School District
240 John St
South Amboy, NJ 08879
732-525-2102

Superintendent	Robert Sheedy
Number of schools	2
Grade plan	K-12
Enrollment	1,117
Attendance rate, '05-06	95.7%
Dropout rate	1.2%
Students per teacher	10.1
Per pupil expenditure	$11,585
Median faculty salary	$53,259
Median administrator salary	$102,033
Grade 12 enrollment	78
High school graduation rate	87.6%

Assessment test results
(percent scoring at proficient or advanced level)
	Language	Math
NJASK-Grade 3	84.5%	97.6%
GEPA-Grade 8	69.6%	65.1%
HSPA-High School	79.8%	65.4%

SAT score averages
Pct tested	Math	Verbal	Writing
74%	483	467	445

Teacher Qualifications
Avg. years of experience	11
Highly-qualified teachers one subject/all subjects	99.0%/97.5%
With emergency credentials	1.1%

No Child Left Behind
AYP, 2005-06 . . . . Meets Standards

Municipal Finance §
State Aid Programs, 2008
Total aid	$4,445,465
CMPTRA	0
Energy tax receipts	4,445,465
Garden State Trust	0

General Budget, 2007
Total tax levy	$14,782,135
County levy	2,811,179
County taxes	2,516,620
County library	0
County health	0
County open space	294,558
School levy	7,623,641
Muni. levy	4,347,315
Misc. revenues	9,045,904

South Bound Brook Borough
Somerset County

Demographics & Socio-Economic Characteristics
(2000 US Census, except as noted)

Population
1980*	4,331
1990*	4,185
2000	4,492
Male	2,303
Female	2,189
2006 (estimate)*	4,524
Population density	5,800.0

Race & Hispanic Origin, 2000
Race
White	3,504
Black/African American	349
American Indian/Alaska Native	12
Asian	184
Native Hawaiian/Pacific Islander	2
Other race	295
Two or more races	146
Hispanic origin, total	1,028
Mexican	276
Puerto Rican	173
Cuban	3
Other Hispanic	576

Age & Nativity, 2000
Under 5 years	285
18 years and over	3,437
21 years and over	3,274
65 years and over	472
85 years and over	64
Median age	35.1
Native-born	3,495
Foreign-born	997

Educational Attainment, 2000
Population 25 years and over	3,061
Less than 9th grade	7.2%
High school grad or higher	78.5%
Bachelor's degree or higher	17.8%
Graduate degree	6.6%

Income & Poverty, 1999
Per capita income	$21,131
Median household income	$48,984
Median family income	$58,214
Persons in poverty	299
H'holds receiving public assistance	56
H'holds receiving social security	438

Households, 2000
Total households	1,632
With persons under 18	575
With persons over 65	364
Family households	1,104
Single-person households	409
Persons per household	2.75
Persons per family	3.31

Labor & Employment
Total civilian labor force, 2006**	2,754
Unemployment rate	6.1%
Total civilian labor force, 2000	2,426
Unemployment rate	5.3%

Employed persons 16 years and over by occupation, 2000
Managers & professionals	544
Service occupations	382
Sales & office occupations	688
Farming, fishing & forestry	17
Construction & maintenance	212
Production & transportation	454
Self-employed persons	49

* US Census Bureau
** New Jersey Department of Labor

General Information
Borough of South Bound Brook
12 Main St
South Bound Brook, NJ 08880
732-356-0258

Website	www.southboundbrook.com
Year of incorporation	1907
Land/water area (sq. miles)	0.78/0.00
Form of government	Borough

Government
Legislative Districts
US Congressional	7
State Legislative	16

Local Officials, 2008
Mayor	Terry G. Warrelmann
Administrator	Donald Kazar
Clerk	Donald Kazar
Finance Dir	Randy Bahr
Tax Assessor	Barbara Flaherty
Tax Collector	Randy Bahr
Attorney	William T. Cooper III
Building	William Boyle
Comm Dev/Planning	NA
Engineering	Maser Consulting
Public Works	Ken Pine
Police Chief	William King
Emerg/Fire Director	Matthew Tomaro

Housing & Construction
Housing Units, 2000*
Total	1,676
Median rent	$818
Median SF home value	$132,800

Permits for New Residential Construction
	Units	Value
Total, 2007	108	$8,605,582
Single family	57	$5,769,912
Total, 2006	115	$10,022,847
Single family	80	$8,081,774

Real Property Valuation, 2007
	Parcels	Valuation
Total	1,297	$164,350,867
Vacant	127	3,064,800
Residential	1,121	141,631,867
Commercial	39	11,418,800
Industrial	1	201,300
Apartments	9	8,034,100
Farm land	0	0
Farm homestead	0	0

Average Property Value & Tax, 2007
Residential value	$126,344
Property tax	$6,848
Tax credit/rebate	$1,165

Public Library
contracts with Bound Brook Library
402 E High St
Bound Brook, NJ 08805
732-356-0043

Director: Hannah Kerwin

Library statistics, 2006
Population served	NA
Full-time/total staff	NA/NA

	Total	Per capita
Holdings	NA	NA
Revenues	NA	NA
Expenditures	NA	NA
Annual visits	NA	NA
Internet terminals/annual users	NA/NA	

Public Safety
Number of officers, 2006: 13

Crime	2005	2006
Total crimes	6	4
Violent	2	0
Murder	0	0
Rape	0	0
Robbery	2	0
Aggravated assault	0	0
Non-violent	4	4
Burglary	1	2
Larceny	2	0
Vehicle theft	1	2
Domestic violence	43	0
Arson	0	0
Total crime rate	1.3	0.9
Violent	0.4	0.0
Non-violent	0.9	0.9

Public School District
(for school year 2006-07 except as noted)

South Bound Brook Borough School Dist.
122 Elizabeth St
South Bound Brook, NJ 08880
732-356-0018

Superintendent	Carol Rosevear
Number of schools	1
Grade plan	K-8
Enrollment	477
Attendance rate, '05-06	95.5%
Dropout rate	NA
Students per teacher	9.9
Per pupil expenditure	$12,858
Median faculty salary	$57,218
Median administrator salary	$105,517
Grade 12 enrollment	NA
High school graduation rate	NA

Assessment test results
(percent scoring at proficient or advanced level)
	Language	Math
NJASK-Grade 3	74.5%	72.3%
GEPA-Grade 8	72.0%	58.9%
HSPA-High School	NA	NA

SAT score averages
Pct tested	Math	Verbal	Writing
NA	NA	NA	NA

Teacher Qualifications
Avg. years of experience	15
Highly-qualified teachers one subject/all subjects	100%/97.5%
With emergency credentials	0.0%

No Child Left Behind
AYP, 2005-06: Meets Standards

Municipal Finance
State Aid Programs, 2008
Total aid	$329,889
CMPTRA	0
Energy tax receipts	329,725
Garden State Trust	164

General Budget, 2007
Total tax levy	$8,926,622
County levy	1,150,295
County taxes	930,318
County library	118,102
County health	0
County open space	101,874
School levy	5,280,796
Muni. levy	2,495,532
Misc. revenues	2,568,778

Taxes
	2005	2006	2007
General tax rate per $100	4.85	5.15	5.43
County equalization ratio	64.76	55.87	48.82
Net valuation taxable	$164,585,321	$165,320,667	$164,688,605
State equalized value	$294,586,220	$339,015,650	$362,823,109

Middlesex County

South Brunswick Township

Demographics & Socio-Economic Characteristics
(2000 US Census, except as noted)

Population
1980*	17,127
1990*	25,792
2000	37,734
Male	18,281
Female	19,453
2006 (estimate)*	40,570
Population density	992.9

Race & Hispanic Origin, 2000
Race
White	26,600
Black/African American	2,975
American Indian/Alaska Native	48
Asian	6,808
Native Hawaiian/Pacific Islander	14
Other race	518
Two or more races	771
Hispanic origin, total	1,918
Mexican	190
Puerto Rican	700
Cuban	141
Other Hispanic	887

Age & Nativity, 2000
Under 5 years	3,042
18 years and over	27,005
21 years and over	26,084
65 years and over	2,761
85 years and over	252
Median age	35.0
Native-born	29,578
Foreign-born	8,156

Educational Attainment, 2000
Population 25 years and over	24,872
Less than 9th grade	1.9%
High school grad or higher	93.3%
Bachelor's degree or higher	49.0%
Graduate degree	20.0%

Income & Poverty, 1999
Per capita income	$32,104
Median household income	$78,737
Median family income	$86,891
Persons in poverty	1,156
H'holds receiving public assistance	85
H'holds receiving social security	1,876

Households, 2000
Total households	13,428
With persons under 18	6,002
With persons over 65	2,031
Family households	10,083
Single-person households	2,627
Persons per household	2.80
Persons per family	3.27

Labor & Employment
Total civilian labor force, 2006**	23,457
Unemployment rate	3.2%
Total civilian labor force, 2000	20,797
Unemployment rate	3.4%

Employed persons 16 years and over by occupation, 2000
Managers & professionals	10,822
Service occupations	1,608
Sales & office occupations	5,268
Farming, fishing & forestry	0
Construction & maintenance	1,090
Production & transportation	1,305
Self-employed persons	757

* US Census Bureau
** New Jersey Department of Labor

See Introduction for an explanation of all data sources.

General Information
Township of South Brunswick
540 Ridge Road
PO Box 190
Monmouth Junction, NJ 08852
732-329-4000

Website	www.sbtnj.net
Year of incorporation	1779
Land/water area (sq. miles)	40.86/0.24
Form of government	Council-Manager

Government
Legislative Districts
US Congressional	12
State Legislative	14

Local Officials, 2008
Mayor	Frank Gambatese
Manager	Matthew U. Watkins
Clerk	Barbara Nyitrai
Finance Dir.	Joseph Monzo
Tax Assessor	Keith Fasanella
Tax Collector	Wendy Bukowski
Attorney	Donald Sears
Building	Jim Dowgin
Planning	Craig Marshall
Engineering	Jay Cornell
Public Works	Raymond Olsen
Police Chief	Raymond Hayducka
Emerg/Fire Director	Alan Laird

Housing & Construction
Housing Units, 2000*
Total	13,862
Median rent	$969
Median SF home value	$202,000

Permits for New Residential Construction
	Units	Value
Total, 2007	184	$25,906,318
Single family	184	$25,906,318
Total, 2006	145	$16,746,363
Single family	145	$16,746,363

Real Property Valuation, 2007
	Parcels	Valuation
Total	13,892	$3,922,934,100
Vacant	1,237	146,564,700
Residential	11,776	2,289,275,800
Commercial	324	304,252,400
Industrial	186	1,061,855,200
Apartments	20	100,011,800
Farm land	261	4,864,500
Farm homestead	88	16,109,700

Average Property Value & Tax, 2007
Residential value	$194,318
Property tax	$7,415
Tax credit/rebate	$1,062

Public Library
South Brunswick Pub Library
110 Kingston Lane
Monmouth Junction, NJ 08852
732-329-4000

Director	Chris Carbone

Library statistics, 2006
Population served	37,734
Full-time/total staff	13/24

	Total	Per capita
Holdings	147,213	3.90
Revenues	$2,589,472	$68.62
Expenditures	$2,560,956	$67.87
Annual visits	268,942	7.13
Internet terminals/annual users		36/76,860

Public Safety
Number of officers, 2006		82
Crime	2005	2006
Total crimes	546	630
Violent	31	31
Murder	0	0
Rape	1	2
Robbery	15	12
Aggravated assault	15	17
Non-violent	515	599
Burglary	112	142
Larceny	357	418
Vehicle theft	46	39
Domestic violence	127	175
Arson	1	1
Total crime rate	13.5	15.5
Violent	0.8	0.8
Non-violent	12.8	14.8

Public School District
(for school year 2006-07 except as noted)

South Brunswick Township School District
231 Black Horse Lane, PO Box 181
Monmouth Junction, NJ 08852
732-297-7800

Superintendent	Gary P. McCartney
Number of schools	10
Grade plan	K-12
Enrollment	8,790
Attendance rate, '05-06	95.3%
Dropout rate	0.7%
Students per teacher	11.2
Per pupil expenditure	$12,577
Median faculty salary	$52,857
Median administrator salary	$93,106
Grade 12 enrollment	669
High school graduation rate	96.7%

Assessment test results
(percent scoring at proficient or advanced level)
	Language	Math
NJASK-Grade 3	88.0%	93.2%
GEPA-Grade 8	89.8%	81.6%
HSPA-High School	95.6%	85.0%

SAT score averages
Pct tested	Math	Verbal	Writing
91%	550	517	527

Teacher Qualifications
Avg. years of experience	7
Highly-qualified teachers one subject/all subjects	100%/100%
With emergency credentials	0.0%

No Child Left Behind
AYP, 2005-06	Meets Standards

Municipal Finance
State Aid Programs, 2008
Total aid	$6,473,452
CMPTRA	0
Energy tax receipts	6,431,345
Garden State Trust	41,120

General Budget, 2007
Total tax levy	$149,997,731
County levy	23,278,566
County taxes	20,839,358
County library	0
County health	0
County open space	2,439,208
School levy	100,594,001
Muni. levy	26,125,164
Misc. revenues	23,639,685

Taxes
	2005	2006	2007
General tax rate per $100	3.36	3.57	3.82
County equalization ratio	65.09	57.64	48.53
Net valuation taxable	$3,800,163,189	$3,844,711,200	$3,930,649,851
State equalized value	$6,592,927,115	$7,931,601,455	$8,347,286,542

©2008 Information Publications, Inc. All rights reserved. Photocopying prohibited. For additional copies, contact the publisher at www.informationpublications.com or (877)544-INFO (4636)

The New Jersey Municipal Data Book

South Hackensack Township
Bergen County

Demographics & Socio-Economic Characteristics
(2000 US Census, except as noted)

Population
1980*	2,229
1990*	2,106
2000	2,249
Male	1,082
Female	1,167
2006 (estimate)*	2,313
Population density	3,257.7

Race & Hispanic Origin, 2000
Race
White	1,865
Black/African American	49
American Indian/Alaska Native	5
Asian	129
Native Hawaiian/Pacific Islander	7
Other race	142
Two or more races	52
Hispanic origin, total	339
Mexican	13
Puerto Rican	53
Cuban	22
Other Hispanic	251

Age & Nativity, 2000
Under 5 years	128
18 years and over	1,807
21 years and over	1,730
65 years and over	372
85 years and over	32
Median age	37.7
Native-born	1,640
Foreign-born	612

Educational Attainment, 2000
Population 25 years and over	1,664
Less than 9th grade	9.9%
High school grad or higher	75.9%
Bachelor's degree or higher	13.7%
Graduate degree	4.4%

Income & Poverty, 1999
Per capita income	$27,128
Median household income	$57,917
Median family income	$66,071
Persons in poverty	159
H'holds receiving public assistance	3
H'holds receiving social security	276

Households, 2000
Total households	811
With persons under 18	258
With persons over 65	268
Family households	594
Single-person households	187
Persons per household	2.77
Persons per family	3.27

Labor & Employment
Total civilian labor force, 2006**	1,255
Unemployment rate	5.2%
Total civilian labor force, 2000	1,178
Unemployment rate	4.9%

Employed persons 16 years and over by occupation, 2000
Managers & professionals	305
Service occupations	102
Sales & office occupations	421
Farming, fishing & forestry	0
Construction & maintenance	143
Production & transportation	149
Self-employed persons	51

* US Census Bureau
** New Jersey Department of Labor

General Information
Township of South Hackensack
227 Phillips Ave
South Hackensack, NJ 07606
201-440-1815

Website	www.southhackensacknj.org
Year of incorporation	1935
Land/water area (sq. miles)	0.71/0.02
Form of government	Township

Government
Legislative Districts
US Congressional	9
State Legislative	38

Local Officials, 2008
Mayor	Rosina Romano
Manager/Admin	NA
Clerk	Linda LoPiccolo
Finance Dir	L. D'Ambrosio
Tax Assessor	George Reggo
Tax Collector	Rosemarie Giotis
Attorney	John Carbone
Building	James Riley
Comm Dev/Planning	NA
Engineering	Boswell McClave
Public Works	Larry Paladino
Police Chief	Mike Frew
Emerg/Fire Director	Walter Peterson

Housing & Construction
Housing Units, 2000*
Total	830
Median rent	$984
Median SF home value	$183,600

Permits for New Residential Construction
	Units	Value
Total, 2007	0	$0
Single family	0	$0
Total, 2006	1	$200,000
Single family	1	$200,000

Real Property Valuation, 2007
	Parcels	Valuation
Total	795	$381,743,200
Vacant	58	5,227,400
Residential	515	117,567,400
Commercial	55	44,689,700
Industrial	167	214,258,700
Apartments	0	0
Farm land	0	0
Farm homestead	0	0

Average Property Value & Tax, 2007
Residential value	$228,286
Property tax	$6,924
Tax credit/rebate	$1,097

Public Library
No public municipal library

Library statistics, 2006
Population served	NA
Full-time/total staff	NA/NA

	Total	Per capita
Holdings	NA	NA
Revenues	NA	NA
Expenditures	NA	NA
Annual visits	NA	NA
Internet terminals/annual users	NA/NA	

Taxes
	2005	2006	2007
General tax rate per $100	2.61	2.95	3.12
County equalization ratio	84.48	76.71	67.71
Net valuation taxable	$384,936,698	$380,740,900	$382,057,348
State equalized value	$501,807,715	$562,668,193	$667,580,710

Public Safety
Number of officers, 2006 ... 17

Crime
	2005	2006
Total crimes	71	78
Violent	13	11
Murder	0	0
Rape	7	3
Robbery	1	2
Aggravated assault	5	6
Non-violent	58	67
Burglary	14	15
Larceny	33	38
Vehicle theft	11	14
Domestic violence	19	8
Arson	0	0
Total crime rate	30.5	33.6
Violent	5.6	4.7
Non-violent	24.9	28.9

Public School District
(for school year 2006-07 except as noted)

South Hackensack School District
Dyer Ave
South Hackensack, NJ 07606
201-440-2783

Superintendent	William DeFabiis
Number of schools	1
Grade plan	K-8
Enrollment	233
Attendance rate, '05-06	96.2%
Dropout rate	NA
Students per teacher	10.7
Per pupil expenditure	$16,105
Median faculty salary	$47,750
Median administrator salary	$111,829
Grade 12 enrollment	NA
High school graduation rate	NA

Assessment test results
(percent scoring at proficient or advanced level)
	Language	Math
NJASK-Grade 3	94.2%	100.0%
GEPA-Grade 8	88.5%	76.9%
HSPA-High School	NA	NA

SAT score averages
Pct tested	Math	Verbal	Writing
NA	NA	NA	NA

Teacher Qualifications
Avg. years of experience	7
Highly-qualified teachers one subject/all subjects	100%/100%
With emergency credentials	0.0%

No Child Left Behind
AYP, 2005-06 ... Meets Standards

Municipal Finance
State Aid Programs, 2008
Total aid	$422,128
CMPTRA	0
Energy tax receipts	422,128
Garden State Trust	0

General Budget, 2007
Total tax levy	$11,885,873
County levy	1,049,190
County taxes	991,465
County library	0
County health	0
County open space	57,725
School levy	5,814,509
Muni. levy	5,022,175
Misc. revenues	3,087,368

Gloucester County

South Harrison Township

Demographics & Socio-Economic Characteristics
(2000 US Census, except as noted)

Population
1980*	1,486
1990*	1,919
2000	2,417
Male	1,223
Female	1,194
2006 (estimate)*	2,956
Population density	187.1

Race & Hispanic Origin, 2000
Race
White	2,250
Black/African American	91
American Indian/Alaska Native	1
Asian	7
Native Hawaiian/Pacific Islander	1
Other race	53
Two or more races	14
Hispanic origin, total	83
Mexican	42
Puerto Rican	29
Cuban	2
Other Hispanic	10

Age & Nativity, 2000
Under 5 years	155
18 years and over	1,767
21 years and over	1,684
65 years and over	226
85 years and over	20
Median age	38.4
Native-born	2,307
Foreign-born	110

Educational Attainment, 2000
Population 25 years and over	1,604
Less than 9th grade	4.4%
High school grad or higher	86.3%
Bachelor's degree or higher	27.2%
Graduate degree	9.5%

Income & Poverty, 1999
Per capita income	$25,968
Median household income	$68,491
Median family income	$76,390
Persons in poverty	193
H'holds receiving public assistance	11
H'holds receiving social security	202

Households, 2000
Total households	800
With persons under 18	350
With persons over 65	166
Family households	663
Single-person households	107
Persons per household	2.94
Persons per family	3.25

Labor & Employment
Total civilian labor force, 2006**	1,412
Unemployment rate	4.0%
Total civilian labor force, 2000	1,246
Unemployment rate	4.3%

Employed persons 16 years and over by occupation, 2000
Managers & professionals	477
Service occupations	97
Sales & office occupations	298
Farming, fishing & forestry	11
Construction & maintenance	171
Production & transportation	139
Self-employed persons	100

* US Census Bureau
** New Jersey Department of Labor

General Information
Township of South Harrison
664 Harrisonville Rd
PO Box 113
Harrisonville, NJ 08039
856-769-3737

Website	www.southharrison-nj.org
Year of incorporation	1883
Land/water area (sq. miles)	15.80/0.02
Form of government	Township

Government
Legislative Districts
US Congressional	2
State Legislative	3

Local Officials, 2008
Mayor	Charles T. Tyson
Manager/Admin	Colleen Bianco
Clerk	Nancy Kearns
Finance Dir	Christie Melfi
Tax Assessor	Thomas Colavecchio
Tax Collector	Maria Berkett
Attorney	John C. Eastlack Jr
Building	Andy Haglen
Comm Dev/Planning	NA
Engineering	Steven Bach
Public Works	NA
Police Chief	Warren Mabey
Emerg/Fire Director	Keith Haney

Housing & Construction
Housing Units, 2000*
Total	829
Median rent	$656
Median SF home value	$188,900

Permits for New Residential Construction
	Units	Value
Total, 2007	26	$4,024,565
Single family	26	$4,024,565
Total, 2006	37	$7,940,499
Single family	37	$7,940,499

Real Property Valuation, 2007
	Parcels	Valuation
Total	1,353	$211,026,100
Vacant	152	6,337,100
Residential	831	168,446,600
Commercial	16	6,480,000
Industrial	0	0
Apartments	0	0
Farm land	217	2,781,000
Farm homestead	137	26,981,400

Average Property Value & Tax, 2007
Residential value	$201,888
Property tax	$7,313
Tax credit/rebate	$1,077

Public Library
No public municipal library

Library statistics, 2006
Population served	NA
Full-time/total staff	NA/NA

	Total	Per capita
Holdings	NA	NA
Revenues	NA	NA
Expenditures	NA	NA
Annual visits	NA	NA
Internet terminals/annual users	NA/NA	

Public Safety
Number of officers, 2006	5

Crime	2005	2006
Total crimes	27	33
Violent	1	3
Murder	0	0
Rape	0	0
Robbery	0	0
Aggravated assault	1	3
Non-violent	26	30
Burglary	15	6
Larceny	11	23
Vehicle theft	0	1
Domestic violence	9	2
Arson	0	1
Total crime rate	9.5	11.4
Violent	0.4	1.0
Non-violent	9.1	10.4

Public School District
(for school year 2006-07 except as noted)

South Harrison Township School District
904 Mullica Hill Rd, PO Box 112
Harrisonville, NJ 08039
856-769-0855

Chief School Admin	David Datz
Number of schools	1
Grade plan	K-6
Enrollment	312
Attendance rate, '05-06	95.8%
Dropout rate	NA
Students per teacher	12.1
Per pupil expenditure	$11,619
Median faculty salary	$45,293
Median administrator salary	$74,646
Grade 12 enrollment	NA
High school graduation rate	NA

Assessment test results
(percent scoring at proficient or advanced level)
	Language	Math
NJASK-Grade 3	92.8%	95.3%
GEPA-Grade 8	NA	NA
HSPA-High School	NA	NA

SAT score averages
Pct tested	Math	Verbal	Writing
NA	NA	NA	NA

Teacher Qualifications
Avg. years of experience	14
Highly-qualified teachers one subject/all subjects	100%/100%
With emergency credentials	0.0%

No Child Left Behind
AYP, 2005-06 .... Meets Standards

Municipal Finance
State Aid Programs, 2008
Total aid	$117,068
CMPTRA	0
Energy tax receipts	117,002
Garden State Trust	66

General Budget, 2007
Total tax levy	$7,661,247
County levy	2,066,229
County taxes	1,779,520
County library	147,388
County health	0
County open space	139,321
School levy	5,279,633
Muni. levy	315,386
Misc. revenues	1,692,017

Taxes	2005	2006	2007
General tax rate per $100	3.198	3.318	3.623
County equalization ratio	74.5	69.83	61.26
Net valuation taxable	$189,189,543	$197,900,700	$211,512,085
State equalized value	$270,928,746	$323,568,586	$353,254,457

South Orange Village Township — Essex County

Demographics & Socio-Economic Characteristics
(2000 US Census, except as noted)

Population
1980*	15,864
1990*	16,390
2000	16,964
Male	8,142
Female	8,822
2006 (estimate)*	16,371
Population density	5,744.2

Race & Hispanic Origin, 2000
Race
White	10,248
Black/African American	5,309
American Indian/Alaska Native	16
Asian	660
Native Hawaiian/Pacific Islander	5
Other race	266
Two or more races	460
Hispanic origin, total	837
Mexican	92
Puerto Rican	266
Cuban	60
Other Hispanic	419

Age & Nativity, 2000
Under 5 years	988
18 years and over	13,187
21 years and over	11,413
65 years and over	2,024
85 years and over	289
Median age	34.7
Native-born	14,095
Foreign-born	2,869

Educational Attainment, 2000
Population 25 years and over	10,351
Less than 9th grade	2.4%
High school grad or higher	93.4%
Bachelor's degree or higher	57.4%
Graduate degree	29.2%

Income & Poverty, 1999
Per capita income	$41,035
Median household income	$83,611
Median family income	$107,641
Persons in poverty	791
H'holds receiving public assistance	89
H'holds receiving social security	1,474

Households, 2000
Total households	5,522
With persons under 18	2,010
With persons over 65	1,464
Family households	3,768
Single-person households	1,393
Persons per household	2.69
Persons per family	3.26

Labor & Employment
Total civilian labor force, 2006**	8,730
Unemployment rate	4.5%
Total civilian labor force, 2000	9,422
Unemployment rate	4.2%

Employed persons 16 years and over by occupation, 2000
Managers & professionals	4,791
Service occupations	1,135
Sales & office occupations	2,411
Farming, fishing & forestry	0
Construction & maintenance	231
Production & transportation	462
Self-employed persons	704

* US Census Bureau
** New Jersey Department of Labor

General Information
Township of South Orange Village
Village Hall
101 S Orange Ave
South Orange, NJ 07079
973-378-7715

Website	www.sourthorange.org
Year of incorporation	1977
Land/water area (sq. miles)	2.85/0.00
Form of government	Special Charter

Government
Legislative Districts
US Congressional	8, 10
State Legislative	27

Local Officials, 2008
Mayor	Douglas Newman
Manager	John Gross
Clerk	Lynn Cucciniello
Finance Dir	John Gross
Tax Assessor	Ellen Foye Malgieri
Tax Collector	Aderonke Zaccheus
Attorney	Edwin Matthews
Building	Anthony Grenci
Comm Dev/Planning	NA
Engineering	Salvatore Renda
Public Works	Mario Luciani
Police Chief	James Chelel
Emerg/Fire Director	Jeff Markey

Housing & Construction
Housing Units, 2000*
Total	5,671
Median rent	$879
Median SF home value	$274,600

Permits for New Residential Construction
	Units	Value
Total, 2007	3	$1,642,230
Single family	0	$710,230
Total, 2006	14	$2,554,550
Single family	0	$2,409,550

Real Property Valuation, 2007
	Parcels	Valuation
Total	4,637	$1,014,214,000
Vacant	67	4,574,700
Residential	4,365	915,533,300
Commercial	174	68,231,400
Industrial	6	1,267,600
Apartments	25	24,607,000
Farm land	0	0
Farm homestead	0	0

Average Property Value & Tax, 2007
Residential value	$209,744
Property tax	$13,641
Tax credit/rebate	$1,438

Public Library
South Orange Public Library
65 Scotland Rd
South Orange, NJ 07079
973-762-0230

Director — Melissa Kopecky

Library statistics, 2006
Population served	16,964
Full-time/total staff	3/12

	Total	Per capita
Holdings	116,783	6.88
Revenues	$1,113,682	$65.65
Expenditures	$1,099,311	$64.80
Annual visits	103,955	6.13
Internet terminals/annual users	22/24,544	

Public Safety
Number of officers, 2006 — 55

Crime	2005	2006
Total crimes	634	480
Violent	80	52
Murder	0	1
Rape	2	1
Robbery	42	23
Aggravated assault	36	27
Non-violent	554	428
Burglary	87	74
Larceny	353	260
Vehicle theft	114	94
Domestic violence	55	49
Arson	1	0
Total crime rate	37.8	28.9
Violent	4.8	3.1
Non-violent	33.0	25.8

Public School District
(for school year 2006-07 except as noted)

South Orange-Maplewood School District
525 Academy St
Maplewood, NJ 07040
973-762-5600

Superintendent	Brian G. Osborne
Number of schools	18
Grade plan	K-12
Enrollment	6,087
Attendance rate, '05-06	95.1%
Dropout rate	0.5%
Students per teacher	11.1
Per pupil expenditure	$14,170
Median faculty salary	$55,758
Median administrator salary	$115,316
Grade 12 enrollment	454
High school graduation rate	95.8%

Assessment test results
(percent scoring at proficient or advanced level)
	Language	Math
NJASK-Grade 3	87.0%	90.5%
GEPA-Grade 8	75.4%	69.8%
HSPA-High School	89.2%	77.7%

SAT score averages
Pct tested	Math	Verbal	Writing
97%	513	500	503

Teacher Qualifications
Avg. years of experience	8
Highly-qualified teachers one subject/all subjects	100%/100%
With emergency credentials	0.5%

No Child Left Behind
AYP, 2005-06 — Needs Improvement

Municipal Finance
State Aid Programs, 2008
Total aid	$1,923,328
CMPTRA	354,302
Energy tax receipts	1,569,026
Garden State Trust	0

General Budget, 2007
Total tax levy	$66,095,066
County levy	10,407,968
County taxes	10,140,532
County library	0
County health	0
County open space	267,436
School levy	37,264,014
Muni. levy	18,423,085
Misc. revenues	13,195,797

Taxes
	2005	2006	2007
General tax rate per $100	5.82	6.17	6.51
County equalization ratio	49.19	42.92	38.28
Net valuation taxable	$1,004,248,560	$1,008,034,800	$1,016,298,304
State equalized value	$2,339,814,911	$2,635,875,327	$2,818,563,060

Middlesex County

South Plainfield Borough

Demographics & Socio-Economic Characteristics
(2000 US Census, except as noted)

Population
1980*	20,521
1990*	20,489
2000	21,810
Male	10,690
Female	11,120
2006 (estimate)*	22,795
Population density	2,726.7

Race & Hispanic Origin, 2000
Race
White	16,956
Black/African American	1,866
American Indian/Alaska Native	49
Asian	1,652
Native Hawaiian/Pacific Islander	1
Other race	759
Two or more races	527
Hispanic origin, total	1,888
Mexican	131
Puerto Rican	517
Cuban	99
Other Hispanic	1,141

Age & Nativity, 2000
Under 5 years	1,344
18 years and over	16,325
21 years and over	15,649
65 years and over	3,071
85 years and over	281
Median age	38.0
Native-born	18,589
Foreign-born	3,221

Educational Attainment, 2000
Population 25 years and over	14,940
Less than 9th grade	5.4%
High school grad or higher	84.3%
Bachelor's degree or higher	24.0%
Graduate degree	6.7%

Income & Poverty, 1999
Per capita income	$25,270
Median household income	$67,466
Median family income	$72,745
Persons in poverty	727
H'holds receiving public assistance	105
H'holds receiving social security	2,030

Households, 2000
Total households	7,151
With persons under 18	2,948
With persons over 65	2,049
Family households	5,858
Single-person households	1,094
Persons per household	3.01
Persons per family	3.35

Labor & Employment
Total civilian labor force, 2006**	12,450
Unemployment rate	3.4%
Total civilian labor force, 2000	11,348
Unemployment rate	3.1%

Employed persons 16 years and over by occupation, 2000
Managers & professionals	4,126
Service occupations	1,178
Sales & office occupations	3,065
Farming, fishing & forestry	5
Construction & maintenance	946
Production & transportation	1,671
Self-employed persons	465

* US Census Bureau
** New Jersey Department of Labor
§ State Fiscal Year July 1–June 30

See Introduction for an explanation of all data sources.

General Information
Borough of South Plainfield
2480 Plainfield Ave
South Plainfield, NJ 07080
908-754-9000

Website	www.southplainfieldnj.com
Year of incorporation	1926
Land/water area (sq. miles)	8.36/0.04
Form of government	Borough

Government
Legislative Districts
US Congressional	7
State Legislative	18

Local Officials, 2008
Mayor	Charles F. Butrico Jr
Manager	Glenn Cullen
Clerk	Joann Graf
Finance Dir	Glenn Cullen
Tax Assessor	Gary Toth
Tax Collector	Richard Lorentzen
Attorney	Joseph Sordillo
Building	John Pabst
Comm Dev/Planning	NA
Engineering	David Samuel
Public Works	Joseph Glowacki
Police Chief	John Ferraro
Fire Chief	L. DelNegro

Housing & Construction
Housing Units, 2000*
Total	7,307
Median rent	$976
Median SF home value	$165,800

Permits for New Residential Construction
	Units	Value
Total, 2007	15	$2,253,943
Single family	13	$2,074,843
Total, 2006	19	$3,506,589
Single family	17	$3,327,489

Real Property Valuation, 2007
	Parcels	Valuation
Total	8,082	$1,433,085,400
Vacant	365	18,675,700
Residential	7,151	861,041,900
Commercial	226	176,902,300
Industrial	325	354,383,000
Apartments	2	22,000,000
Farm land	13	82,500
Farm homestead	0	0

Average Property Value & Tax, 2007
Residential value	$120,409
Property tax	$5,282
Tax credit/rebate	$962

Public Library
South Plainfield Public Library
2484 Plainfield Ave
South Plainfield, NJ 07080
908-754-7885

Director	Sundra L. Randolph

Library statistics, 2006
Population served	21,810
Full-time/total staff	4/7

	Total	Per capita
Holdings	54,043	2.48
Revenues	$1,226,327	$56.23
Expenditures	$819,812	$37.59
Annual visits	72,804	3.34
Internet terminals/annual users	8/22,296	

Public Safety
Number of officers, 2006 55

Crime	2005	2006
Total crimes	504	518
Violent	39	27
Murder	1	0
Rape	0	0
Robbery	18	13
Aggravated assault	20	14
Non-violent	465	491
Burglary	77	84
Larceny	348	365
Vehicle theft	40	42
Domestic violence	115	144
Arson	2	6
Total crime rate	21.9	22.5
Violent	1.7	1.2
Non-violent	20.2	21.3

Public School District
(for school year 2006-07 except as noted)

South Plainfield School District
125 Jackson Ave
South Plainfield, NJ 07080
908-754-4620

Superintendent	Jose Negron
Number of schools	8
Grade plan	K-12
Enrollment	3,784
Attendance rate, '05-06	95.4%
Dropout rate	1.1%
Students per teacher	11.0
Per pupil expenditure	$12,496
Median faculty salary	$58,141
Median administrator salary	$96,366
Grade 12 enrollment	316
High school graduation rate	95.9%

Assessment test results
(percent scoring at proficient or advanced level)
	Language	Math
NJASK-Grade 3	88.7%	89.5%
GEPA-Grade 8	80.2%	78.8%
HSPA-High School	90.7%	79.9%

SAT score averages
Pct tested	Math	Verbal	Writing
82%	491	472	475

Teacher Qualifications
Avg. years of experience	10
Highly-qualified teachers one subject/all subjects	100%/100%
With emergency credentials	0.0%

No Child Left Behind
AYP, 2005-06 .... Meets Standards

Municipal Finance§
State Aid Programs, 2008
Total aid	$3,482,873
CMPTRA	1,069,908
Energy tax receipts	2,412,965
Garden State Trust	0

General Budget, 2007
Total tax levy	$62,986,357
County levy	10,157,378
County taxes	9,093,011
County library	0
County health	0
County open space	1,064,367
School levy	40,050,318
Muni. levy	12,778,662
Misc. revenues	10,615,092

Taxes
	2005	2006	2007
General tax rate per $100	4.05	4.31	4.39
County equalization ratio	48.96	44.61	40.71
Net valuation taxable	$1,409,031,502	$1,415,809,500	$1,435,804,761
State equalized value	$3,158,555,261	$3,480,753,789	$3,865,483,242

South River Borough
Middlesex County

Demographics & Socio-Economic Characteristics
(2000 US Census, except as noted)

Population
1980*	14,361
1990*	13,692
2000	15,322
Male	7,574
Female	7,748
2006 (estimate)*	15,822
Population density	5,630.6

Race & Hispanic Origin, 2000
Race
White	12,801
Black/African American	929
American Indian/Alaska Native	18
Asian	542
Native Hawaiian/Pacific Islander	8
Other race	587
Two or more races	437
Hispanic origin, total	1,480
Mexican	248
Puerto Rican	435
Cuban	53
Other Hispanic	744

Age & Nativity, 2000
Under 5 years	1,008
18 years and over	11,793
21 years and over	11,266
65 years and over	2,231
85 years and over	260
Median age	36.4
Native-born	11,290
Foreign-born	4,032

Educational Attainment, 2000
Population 25 years and over	10,547
Less than 9th grade	11.6%
High school grad or higher	76.5%
Bachelor's degree or higher	20.9%
Graduate degree	6.4%

Income & Poverty, 1999
Per capita income	$23,684
Median household income	$52,324
Median family income	$62,869
Persons in poverty	744
H'holds receiving public assistance	80
H'holds receiving social security	1,615

Households, 2000
Total households	5,606
With persons under 18	1,976
With persons over 65	1,624
Family households	3,985
Single-person households	1,306
Persons per household	2.72
Persons per family	3.23

Labor & Employment
Total civilian labor force, 2006**	8,758
Unemployment rate	6.6%
Total civilian labor force, 2000	7,920
Unemployment rate	6.1%

Employed persons 16 years and over by occupation, 2000
Managers & professionals	2,037
Service occupations	889
Sales & office occupations	2,141
Farming, fishing & forestry	0
Construction & maintenance	1,223
Production & transportation	1,148
Self-employed persons	341

* US Census Bureau
** New Jersey Department of Labor

General Information
Borough of South River
48 Washington St
South River, NJ 08882
732-257-1999

Website	www.southrivernj.org
Year of incorporation	1898
Land/water area (sq. miles)	2.81/0.13
Form of government	Borough

Government
Legislative Districts
US Congressional	12
State Legislative	18

Local Officials, 2008
Mayor	Raymond Eppinger
Manager	Andrew J. Salerno
Clerk	Patricia O'Connor
Finance Dir	Kanthiah Sivananthan
Tax Assessor	Michael Frangella
Tax Collector	Regina Baca
Attorney	Gary Schwartz
Building	NA
Planning	Thomas Sheehan
Engineering	David Samuel
Public Works	George Lyons
Police Chief	Wesley Bomba
Emerg/Fire Director	Peter Swecanski

Housing & Construction
Housing Units, 2000*
Total	5,769
Median rent	$745
Median SF home value	$149,600

Permits for New Residential Construction
	Units	Value
Total, 2007	18	$2,005,901
Single family	13	$1,654,234
Total, 2006	11	$1,028,411
Single family	6	$676,744

Real Property Valuation, 2007
	Parcels	Valuation
Total	4,928	$426,021,600
Vacant	275	3,317,000
Residential	4,410	367,922,900
Commercial	199	25,623,500
Industrial	28	19,514,000
Apartments	16	9,644,200
Farm land	0	0
Farm homestead	0	0

Average Property Value & Tax, 2007
Residential value	$83,429
Property tax	$4,874
Tax credit/rebate	$943

Public Library
South River Public Library
55 Appleby Ave
South River, NJ 08882
732-254-2488

Director............Andrea Londensky

Library statistics, 2006
Population served	15,322
Full-time/total staff	2/4

	Total	Per capita
Holdings	39,226	2.56
Revenues	$589,074	$38.45
Expenditures	$545,451	$35.60
Annual visits	55,710	3.64
Internet terminals/annual users	7/8,805	

Taxes
	2005	2006	2007
General tax rate per $100	5.17	5.53	5.85
County equalization ratio	35.21	30.89	26.72
Net valuation taxable	$427,361,228	$425,531,400	$426,314,982
State equalized value	$1,383,493,778	$1,592,887,531	$1,710,536,658

Public Safety
Number of officers, 2006 31

Crime	2005	2006
Total crimes	211	231
Violent	32	20
Murder	0	0
Rape	2	1
Robbery	10	4
Aggravated assault	20	15
Non-violent	179	211
Burglary	46	43
Larceny	127	159
Vehicle theft	6	9
Domestic violence	192	238
Arson	3	0
Total crime rate	13.2	14.4
Violent	2.0	1.2
Non-violent	11.2	13.1

Public School District
(for school year 2006-07 except as noted)

South River School District
15 Montgomery St
South River, NJ 08882
732-613-4000

Superintendent	Ronald Grygo
Number of schools	4
Grade plan	K-12
Enrollment	2,146
Attendance rate, '05-06	93.5%
Dropout rate	0.8%
Students per teacher	12.0
Per pupil expenditure	$9,920
Median faculty salary	$46,778
Median administrator salary	$99,953
Grade 12 enrollment	152
High school graduation rate	95.4%

Assessment test results
(percent scoring at proficient or advanced level)
	Language	Math
NJASK-Grade 3	82.0%	80.3%
GEPA-Grade 8	71.6%	70.0%
HSPA-High School	86.5%	73.9%

SAT score averages
Pct tested	Math	Verbal	Writing
70%	487	474	469

Teacher Qualifications
Avg. years of experience	6
Highly-qualified teachers one subject/all subjects	100%/100%
With emergency credentials	0.7%

No Child Left Behind
AYP, 2005-06 .... Meets Standards

Municipal Finance
State Aid Programs, 2008
Total aid	$1,054,043
CMPTRA	595,982
Energy tax receipts	458,061
Garden State Trust	0

General Budget, 2007
Total tax levy	$24,903,498
County levy	4,585,377
County taxes	4,104,828
County library	0
County health	0
County open space	480,548
School levy	13,393,933
Muni. levy	6,924,188
Misc. revenues	7,173,897

Ocean County
South Toms River Borough

Demographics & Socio-Economic Characteristics
(2000 US Census, except as noted)

Population
- 1980* 3,954
- 1990* 3,869
- 2000 3,634
  - Male 1,752
  - Female 1,882
- 2006 (estimate)* 3,716
  - Population density 3,203.4

Race & Hispanic Origin, 2000
Race
- White 2,637
- Black/African American 769
- American Indian/Alaska Native 5
- Asian 25
- Native Hawaiian/Pacific Islander 0
- Other race 91
- Two or more races 107
- Hispanic origin, total 337
  - Mexican 39
  - Puerto Rican 238
  - Cuban 5
  - Other Hispanic 55

Age & Nativity, 2000
- Under 5 years 253
- 18 years and over 2,467
- 21 years and over 2,306
- 65 years and over 328
- 85 years and over 22
  - Median age 31.9
- Native-born 3,513
- Foreign-born 95

Educational Attainment, 2000
- Population 25 years and over 2,201
- Less than 9th grade 5.9%
- High school grad or higher 74.0%
- Bachelor's degree or higher 5.6%
- Graduate degree 1.4%

Income & Poverty, 1999
- Per capita income $16,292
- Median household income $43,468
- Median family income $45,375
- Persons in poverty 452
- H'holds receiving public assistance 18
- H'holds receiving social security 294

Households, 2000
- Total households 1,073
  - With persons under 18 545
  - With persons over 65 252
  - Family households 902
  - Single-person households 134
- Persons per household 3.39
- Persons per family 3.63

Labor & Employment
- Total civilian labor force, 2006** 1,756
  - Unemployment rate 8.4%
- Total civilian labor force, 2000 1,773
  - Unemployment rate 8.0%

Employed persons 16 years and over by occupation, 2000
- Managers & professionals 274
- Service occupations 365
- Sales & office occupations 511
- Farming, fishing & forestry 9
- Construction & maintenance 236
- Production & transportation 237
- Self-employed persons 54

* US Census Bureau
** New Jersey Department of Labor

See Introduction for an explanation of all data sources.

General Information
Borough of South Toms River
144 Mill St
South Toms River, NJ 08757
732-349-0403

- Website .... NA
- Year of incorporation 1927
- Land/water area (sq. miles) 1.16/0.06
- Form of government .... Borough

Government
Legislative Districts
- US Congressional 3
- State Legislative 10

Local Officials, 2008
- Mayor .... Michael P. Keene
- Manager/Admin .... NA
- Clerk .... Elizabeth Silvestri
- Finance Dir .... Steve Gallagher
- Tax Assessor .... Dennis Raftery
- Tax Collector .... Barbara Herr
- Attorney .... Gregory McGuckin
- Building .... (county)
- Comm Dev/Planning .... NA
- Engineering .... Michael O'Donnell
- Public Works .... NA
- Police Chief .... Andrew Izatt
- Fire/Emergency Dir .... NA

Housing & Construction
Housing Units, 2000*
- Total 1,123
- Median rent $756
- Median SF home value $85,600

Permits for New Residential Construction

	Units	Value
Total, 2007	2	$174,308
Single family	2	$174,308
Total, 2006	5	$435,770
Single family	5	$435,770

Real Property Valuation, 2007

	Parcels	Valuation
Total	1,240	$280,569,800
Vacant	86	6,616,700
Residential	1,095	234,855,300
Commercial	58	38,731,000
Industrial	1	366,800
Apartments	0	0
Farm land	0	0
Farm homestead	0	0

Average Property Value & Tax, 2007
- Residential value $214,480
- Property tax $3,272
- Tax credit/rebate $739

Public Library
No public municipal library

Library statistics, 2006
- Population served .... NA
- Full-time/total staff .... NA/NA

	Total	Per capita
Holdings	NA	NA
Revenues	NA	NA
Expenditures	NA	NA
Annual visits	NA	NA
Internet terminals/annual users	NA/NA	

Public Safety
Number of officers, 2006 12

Crime

	2005	2006
Total crimes	109	95
Violent	7	7
Murder	0	0
Rape	0	1
Robbery	1	1
Aggravated assault	6	5
Non-violent	102	88
Burglary	27	21
Larceny	67	56
Vehicle theft	8	11
Domestic violence	80	66
Arson	1	0
Total crime rate	29.5	25.7
Violent	1.9	1.9
Non-violent	27.6	23.8

Public School District
(for school year 2006-07 except as noted)

Toms River Regional School District
1144 Hooper Ave
Toms River, NJ 08753
732-505-5510

- Superintendent .... Michael J. Ritacco
- Number of schools 72
- Grade plan K-12
- Enrollment 17,631
- Attendance rate, '05-06 .... 93.5%
- Dropout rate 3.5%
- Students per teacher 13.3
- Per pupil expenditure $10,065
- Median faculty salary $47,174
- Median administrator salary ... $111,050
- Grade 12 enrollment 1,315
- High school graduation rate .... NA

Assessment test results
(percent scoring at proficient or advanced level)

	Language	Math
NJASK-Grade 3	94.0%	95.0%
GEPA-Grade 8	81.0%	73.6%
HSPA-High School	87.0%	70.9%

SAT score averages

Pct tested	Math	Verbal	Writing
NA	NA	NA	NA

Teacher Qualifications
- Avg. years of experience 9
- Highly-qualified teachers
  - one subject/all subjects ... 99.5%/99.0%
- With emergency credentials 0.0%

No Child Left Behind
AYP, 2005-06 .... Meets Standards

Municipal Finance
State Aid Programs, 2008
- Total aid $251,280
  - CMPTRA 0
  - Energy tax receipts 251,280
  - Garden State Trust 0

General Budget, 2007
- Total tax levy $4,286,604
  - County levy 820,015
    - County taxes 675,656
    - County library 80,122
    - County health 32,455
    - County open space 31,781
  - School levy 1,567,866
  - Muni. levy 1,898,723
  - Misc. revenues 1,239,156

Taxes

	2005	2006	2007
General tax rate per $100	3.779	1.4	1.526
County equalization ratio	55.07	129.95	106.26
Net valuation taxable	$95,207,256	$279,254,100	$281,002,203
State equalized value	$213,086,965	$263,225,713	$287,342,926

Southampton Township
Burlington County

Demographics & Socio-Economic Characteristics
(2000 US Census, except as noted)

Population
1980*	8,008
1990*	10,202
2000	10,388
Male	4,856
Female	5,532
2006 (estimate)*	11,028
Population density	250.5

Race & Hispanic Origin, 2000
Race
- White 10,086
- Black/African American 125
- American Indian/Alaska Native 29
- Asian 65
- Native Hawaiian/Pacific Islander 0
- Other race 31
- Two or more races 52
- Hispanic origin, total 134
  - Mexican 34
  - Puerto Rican 63
  - Cuban 5
  - Other Hispanic 32

Age & Nativity, 2000
- Under 5 years 411
- 18 years and over 8,534
- 21 years and over 8,285
- 65 years and over 3,295
- 85 years and over 426
- Median age 49.7
- Native-born 9,977
- Foreign-born 356

Educational Attainment, 2000
- Population 25 years and over 7,951
- Less than 9th grade 3.9%
- High school grad or higher 83.7%
- Bachelor's degree or higher 18.0%
- Graduate degree 6.1%

Income & Poverty, 1999
- Per capita income $26,977
- Median household income $44,419
- Median family income $57,419
- Persons in poverty 399
- H'holds receiving public assistance 51
- H'holds receiving social security 2,303

Households, 2000
- Total households 4,574
- With persons under 18 1,001
- With persons over 65 2,284
- Family households 3,047
- Single-person households 1,369
- Persons per household 2.26
- Persons per family 2.79

Labor & Employment
- Total civilian labor force, 2006** 5,305
- Unemployment rate 5.3%
- Total civilian labor force, 2000 4,546
- Unemployment rate 4.9%

Employed persons 16 years and over by occupation, 2000
- Managers & professionals 1,382
- Service occupations 616
- Sales & office occupations 1,187
- Farming, fishing & forestry 14
- Construction & maintenance 494
- Production & transportation 628
- Self-employed persons 324

* US Census Bureau
** New Jersey Department of Labor

General Information
Township of Southampton
5 Retreat Rd
Southampton, NJ 08088
609-859-2736

- Website .... www.southamptonnj.org
- Year of incorporation 1845
- Land/water area (sq. miles) 44.03/0.24
- Form of government .... Township

Government
Legislative Districts
- US Congressional 3
- State Legislative 8

Local Officials, 2008
- Mayor .... James Young
- Manager .... Michael E. McFadden
- Clerk .... Michael E. McFadden
- Finance Dir .... Nancy Gower
- Tax Assessor .... Dennis DeKlerk
- Tax Collector .... Gwen Jobes
- Attorney .... George M. Morris
- Building .... Daniel McGonigle
- Comm Dev/Planning .... NA
- Engineering .... Richard Alaimo & Assoc
- Public Works .... Charles Oatman
- Police Chief .... NA
- Fire/Emergency Dir .... NA

Housing & Construction
Housing Units, 2000*
- Total 4,751
- Median rent $724
- Median SF home value $113,200

Permits for New Residential Construction
	Units	Value
Total, 2007	29	$5,572,939
Single family	29	$5,572,939
Total, 2006	68	$13,776,355
Single family	68	$13,776,355

Real Property Valuation, 2007
	Parcels	Valuation
Total	5,643	$746,254,400
Vacant	503	15,006,300
Residential	4,405	627,973,000
Commercial	149	48,950,300
Industrial	23	6,760,600
Apartments	0	0
Farm land	363	6,085,400
Farm homestead	200	41,478,800

Average Property Value & Tax, 2007
- Residential value $145,375
- Property tax $4,701
- Tax credit/rebate $1,071

Public Library
Keen Memorial Library
94 Main St
Vincentown, NJ 08088
609-859-3598

- Director .... Lynn French

Library statistics, 2006
- Population served 10,388
- Full-time/total staff 0/0

	Total	Per capita
Holdings	21,711	2.09
Revenues	$87,434	$8.42
Expenditures	$118,434	$11.40
Annual visits	11,290	1.09
Internet terminals/annual users	5/1,500	

Taxes
	2005	2006	2007
General tax rate per $100	3.005	3.189	3.239
County equalization ratio	76.16	66.15	59.88
Net valuation taxable	$720,109,519	$723,094,700	$748,341,530
State equalized value	$1,088,600,936	$1,209,777,711	$1,307,869,107

Public Safety
Number of officers, 2006 0

Crime	2005	2006
Total crimes	137	157
Violent	10	7
Murder	0	0
Rape	0	0
Robbery	1	0
Aggravated assault	9	7
Non-violent	127	150
Burglary	24	30
Larceny	85	98
Vehicle theft	18	22
Domestic violence	22	13
Arson	0	2
Total crime rate	12.5	14.4
Violent	0.9	0.6
Non-violent	11.6	13.7

Public School District
(for school year 2006-07 except as noted)

Southampton Township School District
177 Main St
Southampton, NJ 08088
609-859-2256

- Superintendent .... Michael Harris
- Number of schools 3
- Grade plan K-8
- Enrollment 799
- Attendance rate, '05-06 .... 95.2%
- Dropout rate .... NA
- Students per teacher 9.9
- Per pupil expenditure $13,447
- Median faculty salary $67,850
- Median administrator salary $98,628
- Grade 12 enrollment .... NA
- High school graduation rate .... NA

Assessment test results
(percent scoring at proficient or advanced level)

	Language	Math
NJASK-Grade 3	95.3%	98.9%
GEPA-Grade 8	77.9%	77.9%
HSPA-High School	NA	NA

SAT score averages
Pct tested	Math	Verbal	Writing
NA	NA	NA	NA

Teacher Qualifications
- Avg. years of experience 20
- Highly-qualified teachers one subject/all subjects 100%/100%
- With emergency credentials 0.0%

No Child Left Behind
- AYP, 2005-06 .... Meets Standards

Municipal Finance
State Aid Programs, 2008
- Total aid $1,616,146
- CMPTRA 115,758
- Energy tax receipts 1,379,672
- Garden State Trust 7,315

General Budget, 2007
- Total tax levy $24,200,665
- County levy 5,249,304
- County taxes 4,349,838
- County library 399,144
- County health 0
- County open space 500,322
- School levy 16,442,719
- Muni. levy 2,508,642
- Misc. revenues 3,322,336

The New Jersey Municipal Data Book

Sussex County / Sparta Township

Demographics & Socio-Economic Characteristics
(2000 US Census, except as noted)

Population
1980*	13,333
1990*	15,157
2000	18,080
Male	8,915
Female	9,165
2006 (estimate)*	19,348
Population density	517.5

Race & Hispanic Origin, 2000
Race
- White: 17,481
- Black/African American: 52
- American Indian/Alaska Native: 12
- Asian: 252
- Native Hawaiian/Pacific Islander: 5
- Other race: 81
- Two or more races: 197
- Hispanic origin, total: 459
  - Mexican: 81
  - Puerto Rican: 106
  - Cuban: 55
  - Other Hispanic: 217

Age & Nativity, 2000
- Under 5 years: 1,381
- 18 years and over: 12,544
- 21 years and over: 12,108
- 65 years and over: 1,491
- 85 years and over: 179
- Median age: 37.8
- Native-born: 16,841
- Foreign-born: 1,266

Educational Attainment, 2000
- Population 25 years and over: 11,764
- Less than 9th grade: 1.7%
- High school grad or higher: 94.8%
- Bachelor's degree or higher: 50.2%
- Graduate degree: 17.6%

Income & Poverty, 1999
- Per capita income: $36,910
- Median household income: $89,835
- Median family income: $100,658
- Persons in poverty: 279
- H'holds receiving public assistance: 29
- H'holds receiving social security: 1,226

Households, 2000
- Total households: 6,225
  - With persons under 18: 2,851
  - With persons over 65: 1,120
  - Family households: 5,032
  - Single-person households: 1,005
- Persons per household: 2.90
- Persons per family: 3.28

Labor & Employment
- Total civilian labor force, 2006**: 10,369
  - Unemployment rate: 2.8%
- Total civilian labor force, 2000: 9,248
  - Unemployment rate: 2.2%

Employed persons 16 years and over by occupation, 2000
- Managers & professionals: 4,520
- Service occupations: 760
- Sales & office occupations: 2,541
- Farming, fishing & forestry: 0
- Construction & maintenance: 539
- Production & transportation: 681
- Self-employed persons: 543

* US Census Bureau
** New Jersey Department of Labor

See Introduction for an explanation of all data sources.

General Information
Township of Sparta
65 Main St
Sparta, NJ 07871
973-729-4493

- Website: spartanj.net
- Year of incorporation: 1845
- Land/water area (sq. miles): 37.39/1.83
- Form of government: Council-Manager

Government
Legislative Districts
- US Congressional: 5, 11
- State Legislative: 24

Local Officials, 2008
- Mayor: Michael Spekhardt
- Manager: Henry Underhill
- Clerk: Miriam Tower
- Finance Dir: Michael Guerino
- Tax Assessor: Joseph Ferraris
- Tax Collector: NA
- Attorney: Clark Laddey
- Building: Jan Opt'Hof
- Comm Dev/Planning: NA
- Engineering: Charles Ryan
- Public Works: NA
- Police Chief: Ernest Reigstad
- Emerg/Fire Director: Peter Ruzycki

Housing & Construction
Housing Units, 2000*
- Total: 6,590
- Median rent: $777
- Median SF home value: $222,700

Permits for New Residential Construction
	Units	Value
Total, 2007	78	$15,676,403
Single family	54	$12,767,462
Total, 2006	105	$25,272,693
Single family	71	$18,656,693

Real Property Valuation, 2007
	Parcels	Valuation
Total	8,323	$2,382,516,600
Vacant	1,054	74,034,600
Residential	6,751	2,097,964,400
Commercial	252	151,153,000
Industrial	45	35,512,800
Apartments	3	4,700,400
Farm land	170	955,800
Farm homestead	48	18,195,600

Average Property Value & Tax, 2007
- Residential value: $311,246
- Property tax: $8,918
- Tax credit/rebate: $1,144

Public Library
Sparta Public Library
22 Woodport Rd
Sparta, NJ 07871
973-729-3101

- Director: Carol Boutilier

Library statistics, 2006
- Population served: 18,080
- Full-time/total staff: 2/8

	Total	Per capita
Holdings	72,800	4.03
Revenues	$1,094,628	$60.54
Expenditures	$1,016,107	$56.20
Annual visits	213,693	11.82
Internet terminals/annual users	11/20,841	

Taxes
	2005	2006	2007
General tax rate per $100	2.72	2.78	2.87
County equalization ratio	81.76	75.31	68.29
Net valuation taxable	$2,310,861,087	$2,355,745,200	$2,387,667,824
State equalized value	$3,068,465,127	$3,455,443,872	$3,645,359,933

Public Safety
Number of officers, 2006: 37

Crime	2005	2006
Total crimes	98	111
Violent	4	2
Murder	0	1
Rape	0	0
Robbery	1	1
Aggravated assault	3	0
Non-violent	94	109
Burglary	8	15
Larceny	85	93
Vehicle theft	1	1
Domestic violence	68	74
Arson	1	0
Total crime rate	5.1	5.7
Violent	0.2	0.1
Non-violent	4.9	5.6

Public School District
(for school year 2006-07 except as noted)

Sparta Township School District
18 Mohawk Ave
Sparta, NJ 07871
973-729-7886

- Chief School Admin: J. Thomas Morton
- Number of schools: 5
- Grade plan: K-12
- Enrollment: 4,027
- Attendance rate, '05-06: 94.4%
- Dropout rate: 0.3%
- Students per teacher: 12.4
- Per pupil expenditure: $11,836
- Median faculty salary: $64,170
- Median administrator salary: $108,932
- Grade 12 enrollment: 273
- High school graduation rate: 97.3%

Assessment test results
(percent scoring at proficient or advanced level)

	Language	Math
NJASK-Grade 3	93.4%	95.5%
GEPA-Grade 8	88.1%	84.4%
HSPA-High School	96.3%	89.5%

SAT score averages
Pct tested	Math	Verbal	Writing
101%	540	535	526

Teacher Qualifications
- Avg. years of experience: 9
- Highly-qualified teachers one subject/all subjects: 100%/100%
- With emergency credentials: 0.0%

No Child Left Behind
- AYP, 2005-06: Meets Standards

Municipal Finance
State Aid Programs, 2008
- Total aid: $1,656,289
  - CMPTRA: 449,048
  - Energy tax receipts: 1,136,245
  - Garden State Trust: 41,668

General Budget, 2007
- Total tax levy: $68,415,125
  - County levy: 13,214,920
    - County taxes: 11,605,613
    - County library: 0
    - County health: 382,931
    - County open space: 1,226,376
  - School levy: 41,929,287
  - Muni. levy: 13,270,918
- Misc. revenues: 9,644,874

Spotswood Borough
Middlesex County

Demographics & Socio-Economic Characteristics
(2000 US Census, except as noted)

Population
1980*	7,840
1990*	7,983
2000	7,880
Male	3,810
Female	4,070
2006 (estimate)*	8,179
Population density	3,525.4

Race & Hispanic Origin, 2000
Race
White	7,391
Black/African American	122
American Indian/Alaska Native	6
Asian	230
Native Hawaiian/Pacific Islander	1
Other race	58
Two or more races	72
Hispanic origin, total	345
Mexican	13
Puerto Rican	138
Cuban	55
Other Hispanic	139

Age & Nativity, 2000
Under 5 years	472
18 years and over	6,117
21 years and over	5,876
65 years and over	1,369
85 years and over	117
Median age	39.7
Native-born	7,259
Foreign-born	621

Educational Attainment, 2000
Population 25 years and over	5,650
Less than 9th grade	4.7%
High school grad or higher	83.2%
Bachelor's degree or higher	18.1%
Graduate degree	4.0%

Income & Poverty, 1999
Per capita income	$25,247
Median household income	$55,833
Median family income	$73,062
Persons in poverty	336
H'holds receiving public assistance	44
H'holds receiving social security	1,091

Households, 2000
Total households	3,099
With persons under 18	985
With persons over 65	1,047
Family households	2,163
Single-person households	821
Persons per household	2.54
Persons per family	3.10

Labor & Employment
Total civilian labor force, 2006**	4,572
Unemployment rate	4.0%
Total civilian labor force, 2000	4,146
Unemployment rate	3.6%

Employed persons 16 years and over by occupation, 2000
Managers & professionals	1,112
Service occupations	452
Sales & office occupations	1,246
Farming, fishing & forestry	0
Construction & maintenance	530
Production & transportation	656
Self-employed persons	147

* US Census Bureau
** New Jersey Department of Labor

General Information
Borough of Spotswood
77 Summerhill Rd
Spotswood, NJ 08884
732-251-0700

Website	www.spotswoodboro.com
Year of incorporation	1908
Land/water area (sq. miles)	2.32/0.17
Form of government	Mayor-Council

Government
Legislative Districts
US Congressional	12
State Legislative	18

Local Officials, 2008
Mayor	Barry Zagnit
Manager	Ronald Fasanello
Clerk	Patricia DeStefano
Finance Dir	Barbara Petren
Tax Assessor	Patricia Williams
Tax Collector	Sandra Conover
Attorney	Gary Schwartz
Building	Bob Simonelli
Comm Dev/Planning	NA
Engineering	CME Associates
Public Works	Jean Paul Mayer
Police Chief	Karl Martin
Fire Chief	Kevin Meade

Housing & Construction
Housing Units, 2000*
Total	3,158
Median rent	$704
Median SF home value	$155,100

Permits for New Residential Construction
	Units	Value
Total, 2007	16	$2,544,064
Single family	16	$2,544,064
Total, 2006	14	$2,273,026
Single family	14	$2,273,026

Real Property Valuation, 2007
	Parcels	Valuation
Total	2,845	$743,745,500
Vacant	262	8,467,900
Residential	2,518	635,438,000
Commercial	57	62,098,000
Industrial	5	30,471,100
Apartments	3	7,270,500
Farm land	0	0
Farm homestead	0	0

Average Property Value & Tax, 2007
Residential value	$252,358
Property tax	$6,198
Tax credit/rebate	$1,090

Public Library
Spotswood Public Library
548 Main St
Spotswood, NJ 08884
732-251-1515

Director .... Mary Faith Chmiel

Library statistics, 2006
Population served	7,880
Full-time/total staff	1/2

	Total	Per capita
Holdings	31,536	4.00
Revenues	$274,778	$34.87
Expenditures	$263,899	$33.49
Annual visits	43,199	5.48
Internet terminals/annual users	4/7,508	

Public Safety
Number of officers, 2006 19

Crime	2005	2006
Total crimes	98	115
Violent	7	5
Murder	0	0
Rape	0	0
Robbery	2	0
Aggravated assault	5	5
Non-violent	91	110
Burglary	11	19
Larceny	79	85
Vehicle theft	1	6
Domestic violence	55	65
Arson	0	1
Total crime rate	11.9	14.0
Violent	0.9	0.6
Non-violent	11.1	13.4

Public School District
(for school year 2006-07 except as noted)

Spotswood School District
105 Summerhill Rd
Spotswood, NJ 08884
732-723-2236

Superintendent	John Krewer
Number of schools	4
Grade plan	K-12
Enrollment	1,765
Attendance rate, '05-06	94.5%
Dropout rate	0.8%
Students per teacher	11.1
Per pupil expenditure	$12,112
Median faculty salary	$48,521
Median administrator salary	$98,708
Grade 12 enrollment	189
High school graduation rate	97.9%

Assessment test results
(percent scoring at proficient or advanced level)
	Language	Math
NJASK-Grade 3	90.5%	91.6%
GEPA-Grade 8	82.9%	82.9%
HSPA-High School	92.5%	88.1%

SAT score averages
Pct tested	Math	Verbal	Writing
75%	525	486	485

Teacher Qualifications
Avg. years of experience	8
Highly-qualified teachers one subject/all subjects	100%/100%
With emergency credentials	0.8%

No Child Left Behind
AYP, 2005-06 .... Meets Standards

Municipal Finance
State Aid Programs, 2008
Total aid	$782,119
CMPTRA	240,999
Energy tax receipts	541,120
Garden State Trust	0

General Budget, 2007
Total tax levy	$18,330,079
County levy	2,513,719
County taxes	2,250,340
County library	0
County health	0
County open space	263,380
School levy	10,937,941
Muni. levy	4,878,418
Misc. revenues	3,508,289

Taxes
	2005	2006	2007
General tax rate per $100	2.13	2.29	2.46
County equalization ratio	110.12	98.4	86.22
Net valuation taxable	$736,976,729	$736,841,700	$746,290,022
State equalized value	$748,960,090	$857,431,451	$917,135,643

Monmouth County

Spring Lake Borough

Demographics & Socio-Economic Characteristics
(2000 US Census, except as noted)

Population
1980*	4,215
1990*	3,499
2000	3,567
Male	1,650
Female	1,917
2006 (estimate)*	3,475
Population density	2,652.7

Race & Hispanic Origin, 2000
Race
White	3,523
Black/African American	12
American Indian/Alaska Native	0
Asian	10
Native Hawaiian/Pacific Islander	0
Other race	4
Two or more races	18
Hispanic origin, total	26
Mexican	5
Puerto Rican	11
Cuban	4
Other Hispanic	6

Age & Nativity, 2000
Under 5 years	205
18 years and over	2,790
21 years and over	2,725
65 years and over	897
85 years and over	133
Median age	47.7
Native-born	3,499
Foreign-born	68

Educational Attainment, 2000
Population 25 years and over	2,600
Less than 9th grade	0.5%
High school grad or higher	96.5%
Bachelor's degree or higher	59.5%
Graduate degree	26.6%

Income & Poverty, 1999
Per capita income	$59,445
Median household income	$89,885
Median family income	$103,405
Persons in poverty	91
H'holds receiving public assistance	4
H'holds receiving social security	602

Households, 2000
Total households	1,463
With persons under 18	359
With persons over 65	627
Family households	983
Single-person households	431
Persons per household	2.43
Persons per family	3.03

Labor & Employment
Total civilian labor force, 2006**	1,604
Unemployment rate	4.7%
Total civilian labor force, 2000	1,488
Unemployment rate	4.5%

Employed persons 16 years and over by occupation, 2000
Managers & professionals	757
Service occupations	142
Sales & office occupations	421
Farming, fishing & forestry	0
Construction & maintenance	67
Production & transportation	34
Self-employed persons	122

* US Census Bureau
** New Jersey Department of Labor

See Introduction for an explanation of all data sources.

General Information
Borough of Spring Lake
423 Warren Ave
Spring Lake, NJ 07762
732-449-0800

Website	springlakeboro.org
Year of incorporation	1892
Land/water area (sq. miles)	1.31/0.40
Form of government	Borough

Government
Legislative Districts
US Congressional	4
State Legislative	11

Local Officials, 2008
Mayor	Jennifer Naughton
Manager	Barry R. Lewis Jr
Clerk	Jane L. Gillespie
Finance Dir	Susan Schreck
Tax Assessor	Brian Enright
Tax Collector	Susan Schreck
Attorney	Joseph J. Colao Jr
Building	Sandy Ratz
Planning	Birdsall Svcs Group
Engineering	Leon S. Avakian Inc
Public Works	Frank Phillips
Police Chief	Robert Dawson Jr
Emerg/Fire Director	Edward Megill

Housing & Construction
Housing Units, 2000*
Total	1,930
Median rent	$1,420
Median SF home value	$638,200

Permits for New Residential Construction
	Units	Value
Total, 2007	22	$9,902,261
Single family	22	$9,902,261
Total, 2006	25	$11,862,886
Single family	25	$11,862,886

Real Property Valuation, 2007
	Parcels	Valuation
Total	2,037	$3,333,093,400
Vacant	58	62,810,300
Residential	1,874	3,116,649,200
Commercial	103	150,525,200
Industrial	1	599,100
Apartments	1	2,509,600
Farm land	0	0
Farm homestead	0	0

Average Property Value & Tax, 2007
Residential value	$1,663,100
Property tax	$10,706
Tax credit/rebate	$1,315

Public Library
Spring Lake Public Library
1501 3rd Ave
Spring Lake, NJ 07762
732-449-6654

Director: Kateri Quinn

Library statistics, 2006
Population served	3,567
Full-time/total staff	NA/0

	Total	Per capita
Holdings	NA	NA
Revenues	NA	NA
Expenditures	NA	NA
Annual visits	NA	NA
Internet terminals/annual users	NA/NA	

Public Safety
Number of officers, 2006: 14

Crime
	2005	2006
Total crimes	89	80
Violent	1	0
Murder	0	0
Rape	0	0
Robbery	0	0
Aggravated assault	1	0
Non-violent	88	80
Burglary	11	5
Larceny	77	68
Vehicle theft	0	7
Domestic violence	3	7
Arson	0	0
Total crime rate	25.0	22.8
Violent	0.3	0.0
Non-violent	24.7	22.8

Public School District
(for school year 2006-07 except as noted)

Spring Lake School District
411 Tuttle Ave, HW Mount School
Spring Lake, NJ 07762
732-449-6380

Superintendent	Patricia Wright
Number of schools	1
Grade plan	K-8
Enrollment	253
Attendance rate, '05-06	95.2%
Dropout rate	NA
Students per teacher	9.1
Per pupil expenditure	$17,887
Median faculty salary	$48,470
Median administrator salary	$94,742
Grade 12 enrollment	NA
High school graduation rate	NA

Assessment test results
(percent scoring at proficient or advanced level)
	Language	Math
NJASK-Grade 3	100.0%	100.0%
GEPA-Grade 8	91.4%	97.1%
HSPA-High School	NA	NA

SAT score averages
Pct tested	Math	Verbal	Writing
NA	NA	NA	NA

Teacher Qualifications
Avg. years of experience	10
Highly-qualified teachers one subject/all subjects	100%/100%
With emergency credentials	0.0%

No Child Left Behind
AYP, 2005-06: Meets Standards

Municipal Finance
State Aid Programs, 2008
Total aid	$349,217
CMPTRA	0
Energy tax receipts	349,217
Garden State Trust	0

General Budget, 2007
Total tax levy	$21,481,825
County levy	8,432,486
County taxes	7,936,512
County library	0
County health	0
County open space	495,974
School levy	6,374,301
Muni. levy	6,675,038
Misc. revenues	3,069,645

Taxes
	2005	2006	2007
General tax rate per $100	0.569	0.622	0.644
County equalization ratio	128.72	106.67	101.02
Net valuation taxable	$3,329,471,072	$3,313,985,400	$3,336,991,589
State equalized value	$3,121,281,590	$3,284,457,843	$3,496,974,483

©2008 Information Publications, Inc. All rights reserved. Photocopying prohibited. For additional copies, contact the publisher at www.informationpublications.com or (877)544-INFO (4636)

The New Jersey Municipal Data Book

Spring Lake Heights Borough
Monmouth County

Demographics & Socio-Economic Characteristics
(2000 US Census, except as noted)

Population
1980*	5,424
1990*	5,341
2000	5,227
Male	2,346
Female	2,881
2006 (estimate)*	5,106
Population density	3,868.2

Race & Hispanic Origin, 2000
White	5,085
Black/African American	58
American Indian/Alaska Native	1
Asian	19
Native Hawaiian/Pacific Islander	1
Other race	35
Two or more races	28
Hispanic origin, total	111
Mexican	15
Puerto Rican	29
Cuban	16
Other Hispanic	51

Age & Nativity, 2000
Under 5 years	215
18 years and over	4,347
21 years and over	4,239
65 years and over	1,545
85 years and over	210
Median age	48.3
Native-born	5,021
Foreign-born	206

Educational Attainment, 2000
Population 25 years and over	4,079
Less than 9th grade	4.1%
High school grad or higher	89.4%
Bachelor's degree or higher	38.5%
Graduate degree	12.0%

Income & Poverty, 1999
Per capita income	$35,093
Median household income	$51,330
Median family income	$64,345
Persons in poverty	392
H'holds receiving public assistance	19
H'holds receiving social security	1,088

Households, 2000
Total households	2,511
With persons under 18	472
With persons over 65	1,115
Family households	1,359
Single-person households	1,048
Persons per household	2.04
Persons per family	2.82

Labor & Employment
Total civilian labor force, 2006**	2,411
Unemployment rate	3.2%
Total civilian labor force, 2000	2,337
Unemployment rate	7.2%

Employed persons 16 years and over by occupation, 2000
Managers & professionals	977
Service occupations	341
Sales & office occupations	631
Farming, fishing & forestry	0
Construction & maintenance	101
Production & transportation	119
Self-employed persons	213

General Information
Borough of Spring Lake Heights
555 Brighton Ave
Spring Lake Heights, NJ 07762
732-449-3500

Website	www.springlakehts.com
Year of incorporation	1927
Land/water area (sq. miles)	1.32/0.02
Form of government	Borough

Government
Legislative Districts
US Congressional	4
State Legislative	11

Local Officials, 2008
Mayor	Elwood L. Malick
Manager	Theresa Casagrande
Clerk	Theresa Casagrande
Finance Dir.	Colleen Lapp
Tax Assessor	Mitchell Elias
Tax Collector	Mary Grace Neuhaus
Attorney	Fred Raffetto
Building	Sandy Ratz
Comm Dev/Planning	NA
Engineering	Peter Avakian
Public Works	Art Herner
Police Chief	Mark Steets
Emerg/Fire Director	Eric Bennett

Housing & Construction
Housing Units, 2000*
Total	2,950
Median rent	$877
Median SF home value	$218,600

Permits for New Residential Construction
	Units	Value
Total, 2007	20	$6,904,481
Single family	20	$6,904,481
Total, 2006	23	$3,648,647
Single family	23	$3,648,647

Real Property Valuation, 2007
	Parcels	Valuation
Total	2,262	$726,218,300
Vacant	43	4,561,900
Residential	2,131	607,776,300
Commercial	79	73,971,900
Industrial	0	0
Apartments	9	39,908,200
Farm land	0	0
Farm homestead	0	0

Average Property Value & Tax, 2007
Residential value	$285,207
Property tax	$5,176
Tax credit/rebate	$1,010

Public Library
No public municipal library

Library statistics, 2006
Population served	NA
Full-time/total staff	NA/NA

	Total	Per capita
Holdings	NA	NA
Revenues	NA	NA
Expenditures	NA	NA
Annual visits	NA	NA
Internet terminals/annual users	NA/NA	

Public Safety
Number of officers, 2006 12

Crime
	2005	2006
Total crimes	34	34
Violent	5	2
Murder	0	0
Rape	1	0
Robbery	0	0
Aggravated assault	4	2
Non-violent	29	32
Burglary	6	5
Larceny	23	26
Vehicle theft	0	1
Domestic violence	9	11
Arson	0	0
Total crime rate	6.6	6.6
Violent	1.0	0.4
Non-violent	5.6	6.2

Public School District
(for school year 2006-07 except as noted)

Spring Lake Heights Borough School Dist.
1110 Highway #71
Spring Lake Heights, NJ 07762
732-449-6149

Superintendent	Ruth Ziznewski
Number of schools	1
Grade plan	K-8
Enrollment	354
Attendance rate, '05-06	94.5%
Dropout rate	NA
Students per teacher	9.6
Per pupil expenditure	$11,463
Median faculty salary	$49,100
Median administrator salary	$81,200
Grade 12 enrollment	NA
High school graduation rate	NA

Assessment test results
(percent scoring at proficient or advanced level)
	Language	Math
NJASK-Grade 3	88.2%	94.1%
GEPA-Grade 8	82.4%	76.5%
HSPA-High School	NA	NA

SAT score averages
Pct tested	Math	Verbal	Writing
NA	NA	NA	NA

Teacher Qualifications
Avg. years of experience	11
Highly-qualified teachers one subject/all subjects	100%/100%
With emergency credentials	0.0%

No Child Left Behind
AYP, 2005-06 .... Meets Standards

Municipal Finance
State Aid Programs, 2008
Total aid	$492,621
CMPTRA	38,110
Energy tax receipts	454,511
Garden State Trust	0

General Budget, 2007
Total tax levy	$13,183,723
County levy	3,146,233
County taxes	2,809,819
County library	160,853
County health	0
County open space	175,561
School levy	6,783,320
Muni. levy	3,254,170
Misc. revenues	1,822,333

Taxes
	2005	2006	2007
General tax rate per $100	1.683	1.739	1.815
County equalization ratio	80.42	68.07	62.32
Net valuation taxable	$711,852,970	$720,269,200	$726,508,381
State equalized value	$1,045,766,079	$1,156,071,713	$1,204,831,962

* US Census Bureau
** New Jersey Department of Labor

Burlington County
Springfield Township

Demographics & Socio-Economic Characteristics
(2000 US Census, except as noted)

Population
1980*	1,691
1990*	3,028
2000	3,227
Male	1,614
Female	1,613
2006 (estimate)*	3,570
Population density	118.9

Race & Hispanic Origin, 2000
Race
- White 2,967
- Black/African American 104
- American Indian/Alaska Native 10
- Asian 85
- Native Hawaiian/Pacific Islander 0
- Other race 7
- Two or more races 54

Hispanic origin, total 57
- Mexican 5
- Puerto Rican 28
- Cuban 4
- Other Hispanic 20

Age & Nativity, 2000
- Under 5 years 180
- 18 years and over 2,394
- 21 years and over 2,310
- 65 years and over 346
- 85 years and over 28
- Median age 39.3
- Native-born 3,015
- Foreign-born 212

Educational Attainment, 2000
- Population 25 years and over 2,206
- Less than 9th grade 3.4%
- High school grad or higher 87.3%
- Bachelor's degree or higher 26.4%
- Graduate degree 8.3%

Income & Poverty, 1999
- Per capita income $29,322
- Median household income $69,268
- Median family income $72,292
- Persons in poverty 116
- H'holds receiving public assistance .. 5
- H'holds receiving social security .. 283

Households, 2000
- Total households 1,098
- With persons under 18 439
- With persons over 65 244
- Family households 907
- Single-person households 146
- Persons per household 2.93
- Persons per family 3.22

Labor & Employment
- Total civilian labor force, 2006** .. 1,980
- Unemployment rate 3.9%
- Total civilian labor force, 2000 .. 1,710
- Unemployment rate 3.8%

Employed persons 16 years and over by occupation, 2000
- Managers & professionals 600
- Service occupations 180
- Sales & office occupations 530
- Farming, fishing & forestry 15
- Construction & maintenance 153
- Production & transportation 167
- Self-employed persons 151

* US Census Bureau
** New Jersey Department of Labor

See Introduction for an explanation of all data sources.

General Information
Township of Springfield
2159 Jacksonville-Jobstown Rd
PO Box 119
Jobstown, NJ 08041
609-723-2464
Website .... www.springfieldtownship.org
Year of incorporation 1688
Land/water area (sq. miles) 30.03/0.01
Form of government .... Council-Manager

Government
Legislative Districts
- US Congressional 4
- State Legislative 8

Local Officials, 2008
- Mayor .... William Pettit Sr
- Manager .... J. Paul Keller
- Clerk .... Patricia Clayton
- Finance Dir .... Judith Schetler
- Tax Assessor .... Dennis Bianchini
- Tax Collector .... Caryn M. Hoyer
- Attorney .... Dennis McInerney
- Building .... Tom Casey
- Planning .... Carl Hintz
- Engineering .... Jeffrey Richter
- Public Works .... NA
- Police Chief .... (vacant)
- Fire/Emergency Dir .... NA

Housing & Construction
Housing Units, 2000*
- Total 1,138
- Median rent $541
- Median SF home value $185,400

Permits for New Residential Construction
	Units	Value
Total, 2007	2	$1,670,600
Single family	2	$1,670,600
Total, 2006	5	$1,318,246
Single family	5	$1,318,246

Real Property Valuation, 2007
	Parcels	Valuation
Total	1,691	$433,668,709
Vacant	103	7,222,300
Residential	1,012	321,869,600
Commercial	79	45,265,980
Industrial	0	0
Apartments	0	0
Farm land	336	6,777,679
Farm homestead	161	52,533,150

Average Property Value & Tax, 2007
- Residential value $319,184
- Property tax $7,256
- Tax credit/rebate $1,156

Public Library
No public municipal library

Library statistics, 2006
- Population served .... NA
- Full-time/total staff .... NA/NA

	Total	Per capita
Holdings	NA	NA
Revenues	NA	NA
Expenditures	NA	NA
Annual visits	NA	NA
Internet terminals/annual users	NA/NA	

Taxes
	2005	2006	2007
General tax rate per $100	1.999	2.163	2.28
County equalization ratio	116.48	102.34	90.55
Net valuation taxable	$429,773,825	$429,413,029	$434,707,402
State equalized value	$419,947,064	$475,337,530	$481,877,710

Public Safety
Number of officers, 2006 9

Crime
	2005	2006
Total crimes	44	76
Violent	4	4
Murder	0	0
Rape	0	0
Robbery	2	2
Aggravated assault	2	2
Non-violent	40	72
Burglary	13	24
Larceny	16	32
Vehicle theft	11	16
Domestic violence	9	10
Arson	0	1
Total crime rate	12.4	21.4
Violent	1.1	1.1
Non-violent	11.3	20.2

Public School District
(for school year 2006-07 except as noted)

Springfield Township School District
2146 Jacksonville Rd
Jobstown, NJ 08041
609-723-2479

- Superintendent .... Helena Sullivan
- Number of schools 1
- Grade plan K-6
- Enrollment 311
- Attendance rate, '05-06 .... 96.2%
- Dropout rate .... NA
- Students per teacher 11.4
- Per pupil expenditure $12,961
- Median faculty salary $51,759
- Median administrator salary .. $82,044
- Grade 12 enrollment .... NA
- High school graduation rate ..... NA

Assessment test results
(percent scoring at proficient or advanced level)
	Language	Math
NJASK-Grade 3	97.5%	100.0%
GEPA-Grade 8	NA	NA
HSPA-High School	NA	NA

SAT score averages
Pct tested	Math	Verbal	Writing
NA	NA	NA	NA

Teacher Qualifications
- Avg. years of experience 15
- Highly-qualified teachers
  one subject/all subjects ... 100%/100%
- With emergency credentials 0.0%

No Child Left Behind
AYP, 2005-06 .... Meets Standards

Municipal Finance
State Aid Programs, 2008
- Total aid $487,453
- CMPTRA 0
- Energy tax receipts 487,219
- Garden State Trust 234

General Budget, 2007
- Total tax levy $9,882,767
- County levy 2,012,052
-   County taxes 1,667,212
-   County library 153,003
-   County health 0
-   County open space 191,838
- School levy 6,343,390
- Muni. levy 1,527,324
- Misc. revenues 1,912,561

© 2008 Information Publications, Inc. All rights reserved. Photocopying prohibited. For additional copies, contact the publisher at www.informationpublications.com or (877)544-INFO (4636)

The New Jersey Municipal Data Book

Springfield Township — Union County

Demographics & Socio-Economic Characteristics
(2000 US Census, except as noted)

Population
1980*	13,955
1990*	13,420
2000	14,429
Male	6,805
Female	7,624
2006 (estimate)*	14,717
Population density	2,857.7

Race & Hispanic Origin, 2000
Race
White	12,946
Black/African American	537
American Indian/Alaska Native	3
Asian	676
Native Hawaiian/Pacific Islander	0
Other race	139
Two or more races	128
Hispanic origin, total	597
Mexican	20
Puerto Rican	78
Cuban	48
Other Hispanic	451

Age & Nativity, 2000
Under 5 years	893
18 years and over	11,463
21 years and over	11,164
65 years and over	2,972
85 years and over	390
Median age	42.1
Native-born	11,492
Foreign-born	2,937

Educational Attainment, 2000
Population 25 years and over	10,991
Less than 9th grade	3.9%
High school grad or higher	90.3%
Bachelor's degree or higher	46.7%
Graduate degree	16.8%

Income & Poverty, 1999
Per capita income	$36,754
Median household income	$73,790
Median family income	$85,725
Persons in poverty	453
H'holds receiving public assistance	30
H'holds receiving social security	1,981

Households, 2000
Total households	6,001
With persons under 18	1,707
With persons over 65	2,153
Family households	4,015
Single-person households	1,724
Persons per household	2.40
Persons per family	2.98

Labor & Employment
Total civilian labor force, 2006**	8,086
Unemployment rate	1.7%
Total civilian labor force, 2000	7,706
Unemployment rate	1.5%

Employed persons 16 years and over by occupation, 2000
Managers & professionals	3,771
Service occupations	749
Sales & office occupations	2,095
Farming, fishing & forestry	8
Construction & maintenance	438
Production & transportation	526
Self-employed persons	630

* US Census Bureau
** New Jersey Department of Labor

General Information
Township of Springfield
100 Mountain Ave
Springfield, NJ 07081
973-912-2200

Website	www.springfield-nj.com
Year of incorporation	1794
Land/water area (sq. miles)	5.15/0.00
Form of government	Township

Government
Legislative Districts
US Congressional	7
State Legislative	21

Local Officials, 2008
Mayor	Bart Fraenkel
Manager	Edward J. Fanning
Clerk	Kathleen Wisniewski
Treasurer	Kathleen Perez
Tax Assessor	Ed Galente
Tax Collector	Corinne Eckmann
Attorney	Bruce Bergen
Building	John Risso
Planning	Bob Michaels
Engineering	Todd Hay
Public Works	Ken Homlish
Police Chief	William Chisholm
Emerg/Fire Director	Wayne Masiello

Housing & Construction
Housing Units, 2000*
Total	6,204
Median rent	$1,018
Median SF home value	$250,500

Permits for New Residential Construction
	Units	Value
Total, 2007	93	$4,651,075
Single family	7	$1,394,329
Total, 2006	136	$6,503,176
Single family	8	$1,655,926

Real Property Valuation, 2007
	Parcels	Valuation
Total	5,199	$1,090,267,900
Vacant	85	7,820,400
Residential	4,784	761,625,100
Commercial	246	217,440,800
Industrial	66	49,452,500
Apartments	16	53,895,900
Farm land	2	33,200
Farm homestead	0	0

Average Property Value & Tax, 2007
Residential value	$159,203
Property tax	$8,335
Tax credit/rebate	$1,262

Public Library
Springfield Public Library
66 Mountain Ave
Springfield, NJ 07081
973-376-4930

Director	Susan Permahos

Library statistics, 2006
Population served	14,429
Full-time/total staff	5/7

	Total	Per capita
Holdings	86,642	6.00
Revenues	$978,431	$67.81
Expenditures	$948,855	$65.76
Annual visits	112,857	7.82
Internet terminals/annual users	21/30,189	

Taxes
	2005	2006	2007
General tax rate per $100	4.831	5.076	5.236
County equalization ratio	43.83	40.05	39.11
Net valuation taxable	$1,091,083,600	$1,087,255,800	$1,091,066,500
State equalized value	$2,532,103,968	$2,780,859,175	$2,992,752,222

Public Safety
Number of officers, 2006	41

Crime
	2005	2006
Total crimes	264	244
Violent	12	17
Murder	0	0
Rape	1	0
Robbery	6	9
Aggravated assault	5	8
Non-violent	252	227
Burglary	26	26
Larceny	172	172
Vehicle theft	54	29
Domestic violence	108	121
Arson	0	10
Total crime rate	17.9	16.6
Violent	0.8	1.2
Non-violent	17.0	15.4

Public School District
(for school year 2006-07 except as noted)

Springfield School District
PO Box 210
Springfield, NJ 07081
973-376-1025

Superintendent	Michael A. Davino
Number of schools	5
Grade plan	K-12
Enrollment	2,055
Attendance rate, '05-06	95.1%
Dropout rate	NA
Students per teacher	10.4
Per pupil expenditure	$14,459
Median faculty salary	$54,708
Median administrator salary	$105,504
Grade 12 enrollment	143
High school graduation rate	100.0%

Assessment test results
(percent scoring at proficient or advanced level)
	Language	Math
NJASK-Grade 3	86.8%	90.1%
GEPA-Grade 8	79.5%	79.1%
HSPA-High School	91.7%	82.7%

SAT score averages
Pct tested	Math	Verbal	Writing
93%	528	507	498

Teacher Qualifications
Avg. years of experience	6
Highly-qualified teachers one subject/all subjects	100%/100%
With emergency credentials	0.0%

No Child Left Behind
AYP, 2005-06	Meets Standards

Municipal Finance
State Aid Programs, 2008
Total aid	$2,249,518
CMPTRA	660,753
Energy tax receipts	1,588,765
Garden State Trust	0

General Budget, 2007
Total tax levy	$57,124,570
County levy	9,804,677
County taxes	9,383,078
County library	0
County health	0
County open space	421,599
School levy	29,853,559
Muni. levy	17,466,335
Misc. revenues	6,428,269

Ocean County

Stafford Township

Demographics & Socio-Economic Characteristics
(2000 US Census, except as noted)

Population
1980*	10,385
1990*	13,325
2000	22,532
Male	10,924
Female	11,608
2006 (estimate)*	25,819
Population density	554.9

Race & Hispanic Origin, 2000
Race
White	21,808
Black/African American	166
American Indian/Alaska Native	21
Asian	217
Native Hawaiian/Pacific Islander	7
Other race	114
Two or more races	199
Hispanic origin, total	542
Mexican	88
Puerto Rican	202
Cuban	55
Other Hispanic	197

Age & Nativity, 2000
Under 5 years	1,466
18 years and over	17,180
21 years and over	16,554
65 years and over	4,244
85 years and over	485
Median age	40.3
Native-born	21,533
Foreign-born	984

Educational Attainment, 2000
Population 25 years and over	16,012
Less than 9th grade	2.7%
High school grad or higher	84.9%
Bachelor's degree or higher	18.7%
Graduate degree	4.5%

Income & Poverty, 1999
Per capita income	$25,397
Median household income	$52,269
Median family income	$59,072
Persons in poverty	899
H'holds receiving public assistance	69
H'holds receiving social security	3,156

Households, 2000
Total households	8,535
With persons under 18	2,885
With persons over 65	2,756
Family households	6,433
Single-person households	1,755
Persons per household	2.61
Persons per family	3.01

Labor & Employment
Total civilian labor force, 2006**	12,508
Unemployment rate	4.3%
Total civilian labor force, 2000	10,559
Unemployment rate	4.6%

Employed persons 16 years and over by occupation, 2000
Managers & professionals	3,154
Service occupations	1,613
Sales & office occupations	2,913
Farming, fishing & forestry	35
Construction & maintenance	1,411
Production & transportation	948
Self-employed persons	772

‡ Branch of county library
* US Census Bureau
** New Jersey Department of Labor

See Introduction for an explanation of all data sources.

General Information
Township of Stafford
260 E Bay Ave
Manahawkin, NJ 08050
609-597-1000

Website	www.twp.stafford.nj.us
Year of incorporation	1750
Land/water area (sq. miles)	46.53/8.29
Form of government	Small Municipality

Government
Legislative Districts
US Congressional	3
State Legislative	9

Local Officials, 2008
Mayor	Carl W. Block
Manager	Paul Shives
Clerk	Bernadette Park
Finance Dir	Douglas Gannon
Tax Assessor	James Mancini
Tax Collector	Margaret Bevilacqua
Attorney	George Gilmore
Building	Robert Gaestel
Planning	Bonnie Flynn
Engineering	John Walsh
Public Works	Ronald Cop
Police Chief	Thomas Conroy
Emerg/Fire Director	Dean Clelland

Housing & Construction
Housing Units, 2000*
Total	11,522
Median rent	$848
Median SF home value	$139,100

Permits for New Residential Construction
	Units	Value
Total, 2007	141	$15,109,461
Single family	141	$15,109,461
Total, 2006	115	$18,378,006
Single family	115	$18,378,006

Real Property Valuation, 2007
	Parcels	Valuation
Total	14,812	$4,245,253,200
Vacant	2,047	164,068,700
Residential	12,328	3,671,707,400
Commercial	412	402,267,300
Industrial	1	1,116,400
Apartments	4	4,965,400
Farm land	16	60,100
Farm homestead	4	1,067,900

Average Property Value & Tax, 2007
Residential value	$297,825
Property tax	$5,089
Tax credit/rebate	$965

Public Library
Stafford Branch Library‡
129 N Main St
Manahawkin, NJ 08050
609-597-3381

Branch Librarian........ Sharon Osborn

Library statistics, 2006
see Ocean County profile for library system statistics

Public Safety
Number of officers, 2006 56

Crime
	2005	2006
Total crimes	573	508
Violent	41	21
Murder	0	4
Rape	2	0
Robbery	1	1
Aggravated assault	38	16
Non-violent	532	487
Burglary	76	42
Larceny	433	420
Vehicle theft	23	25
Domestic violence	147	155
Arson	4	6
Total crime rate	23.0	19.9
Violent	1.6	0.8
Non-violent	21.3	19.1

Public School District
(for school year 2006-07 except as noted)

Stafford Township School District
775 E Bay Ave
Manahawkin, NJ 08050
609-978-5700

Superintendent	Ronald L. Meinders
Number of schools	5
Grade plan	K-6
Enrollment	2,494
Attendance rate, '05-06	95.1%
Dropout rate	NA
Students per teacher	11.3
Per pupil expenditure	$12,231
Median faculty salary	$47,744
Median administrator salary	$79,222
Grade 12 enrollment	NA
High school graduation rate	NA

Assessment test results
(percent scoring at proficient or advanced level)
	Language	Math
NJASK-Grade 3	84.2%	91.8%
GEPA-Grade 8	NA	NA
HSPA-High School	NA	NA

SAT score averages
Pct tested	Math	Verbal	Writing
NA	NA	NA	NA

Teacher Qualifications
Avg. years of experience	10
Highly-qualified teachers one subject/all subjects	100%/100%
With emergency credentials	0.0%

No Child Left Behind
AYP, 2005-06 .... Meets Standards

Municipal Finance
State Aid Programs, 2008
Total aid	$3,405,915
CMPTRA	0
Energy tax receipts	3,112,332
Garden State Trust	57,086

General Budget, 2007
Total tax levy	$72,642,447
County levy	15,165,378
County taxes	12,497,001
County library	1,481,080
County health	600,052
County open space	587,245
School levy	32,750,639
Muni. levy	24,726,429
Misc. revenues	10,483,048

Taxes
	2005	2006	2007
General tax rate per $100	1.487	1.625	1.709
County equalization ratio	116.81	98.42	87.04
Net valuation taxable	$4,098,047,731	$4,195,433,600	$4,250,899,637
State equalized value	$4,163,836,345	$4,826,313,291	$5,052,309,775

©2008 Information Publications, Inc. All rights reserved. Photocopying prohibited. For additional copies, contact the publisher at www.informationpublications.com or (877) 544-INFO (4636)

Stanhope Borough

Sussex County

Demographics & Socio-Economic Characteristics
(2000 US Census, except as noted)

Population
1980*	3,638
1990*	3,393
2000	3,584
Male	1,700
Female	1,884
2006 (estimate)*	3,666
Population density	1,960.4

Race & Hispanic Origin, 2000
Race
White	3,353
Black/African American	48
American Indian/Alaska Native	2
Asian	55
Native Hawaiian/Pacific Islander	3
Other race	50
Two or more races	73
Hispanic origin, total	145
Mexican	9
Puerto Rican	52
Cuban	5
Other Hispanic	79

Age & Nativity, 2000
Under 5 years	249
18 years and over	2,686
21 years and over	2,588
65 years and over	268
85 years and over	23
Median age	36.8
Native-born	3,338
Foreign-born	183

Educational Attainment, 2000
Population 25 years and over	2,433
Less than 9th grade	0.9%
High school grad or higher	91.8%
Bachelor's degree or higher	32.3%
Graduate degree	7.5%

Income & Poverty, 1999
Per capita income	$27,535
Median household income	$63,059
Median family income	$73,203
Persons in poverty	77
H'holds receiving public assistance	4
H'holds receiving social security	239

Households, 2000
Total households	1,384
With persons under 18	501
With persons over 65	198
Family households	979
Single-person households	317
Persons per household	2.58
Persons per family	3.10

Labor & Employment
Total civilian labor force, 2006**	2,317
Unemployment rate	3.8%
Total civilian labor force, 2000	2,066
Unemployment rate	3.2%

Employed persons 16 years and over by occupation, 2000
Managers & professionals	813
Service occupations	173
Sales & office occupations	693
Farming, fishing & forestry	0
Construction & maintenance	125
Production & transportation	196
Self-employed persons	63

‡ Branch of county library
* US Census Bureau
** New Jersey Department of Labor

General Information
Borough of Stanhope
77 Main St
Stanhope, NJ 07874
973-347-0159

Email	stanhope@nac.net
Year of incorporation	1904
Land/water area (sq. miles)	1.87/0.34
Form of government	Borough

Government
Legislative Districts
US Congressional	11
State Legislative	24

Local Officials, 2008
Mayor	Diana Kuncken
Manager	Richard Stewart
Clerk	Robin Kline
Finance Dir	Richard Vitale
Tax Assessor	Maureen Kaman
Tax Collector	Kunjesh Trivedi
Attorney	Richard Stein
Building	Thomas Pershouse
Comm Dev/Planning	NA
Engineering	Omland Engineering
Public Works	William Storms
Police Chief	Steven Pittigher
Emerg/Fire Dir	Michael Donahue Sr

Housing & Construction
Housing Units, 2000*
Total	1,419
Median rent	$965
Median SF home value	$151,100

Permits for New Residential Construction
	Units	Value
Total, 2007	1	$228,500
Single family	1	$228,500
Total, 2006	3	$770,000
Single family	3	$770,000

Real Property Valuation, 2007
	Parcels	Valuation
Total	1,604	$432,094,600
Vacant	163	5,067,100
Residential	1,359	394,458,500
Commercial	58	23,181,600
Industrial	4	5,624,800
Apartments	9	3,744,200
Farm land	11	18,400
Farm homestead	0	0

Average Property Value & Tax, 2007
Residential value	$290,256
Property tax	$6,506
Tax credit/rebate	$1,098

Public Library
E. Louise Childs Branch Library‡
21 Sparta Rd
Stanhope, NJ 07874
973-770-1000

Branch Librarian......... Victoria Larson

Library statistics, 2006
see Sussex County profile for library system statistics

Public Safety
Number of officers, 2006		7

Crime	2005	2006
Total crimes	52	70
Violent	3	4
Murder	0	0
Rape	0	1
Robbery	1	1
Aggravated assault	2	2
Non-violent	49	66
Burglary	8	15
Larceny	38	49
Vehicle theft	4	2
Domestic violence	51	23
Arson	0	0
Total crime rate	14.0	18.9
Violent	0.8	1.1
Non-violent	13.2	17.8

Public School District
(for school year 2006-07 except as noted)

Stanhope Borough School District
24 Valley Rd
Stanhope, NJ 07874
973-347-0008

Chief School Admin	Nicholas P. Brown (Int)
Number of schools	1
Grade plan	K-8
Enrollment	405
Attendance rate, '05-06	96.1%
Dropout rate	NA
Students per teacher	10.8
Per pupil expenditure	$11,720
Median faculty salary	$46,313
Median administrator salary	$88,000
Grade 12 enrollment	NA
High school graduation rate	NA

Assessment test results
(percent scoring at proficient or advanced level)
	Language	Math
NJASK-Grade 3	85.2%	85.2%
GEPA-Grade 8	70.9%	73.0%
HSPA-High School	NA	NA

SAT score averages
Pct tested	Math	Verbal	Writing
NA	NA	NA	NA

Teacher Qualifications
Avg. years of experience	7
Highly-qualified teachers one subject/all subjects	100%/100%
With emergency credentials	0.0%

No Child Left Behind
AYP, 2005-06 .... Meets Standards

Municipal Finance
State Aid Programs, 2008
Total aid	$156,455
CMPTRA	0
Energy tax receipts	155,817
Garden State Trust	638

General Budget, 2007
Total tax levy	$9,695,537
County levy	1,664,189
County taxes	1,359,723
County library	115,916
County health	44,886
County open space	143,664
School levy	5,386,268
Muni. levy	2,645,079
Misc. revenues	1,222,958

Taxes
	2005	2006	2007
General tax rate per $100	5.14	2.11	2.25
County equalization ratio	52.56	119.68	106.19
Net valuation taxable	$168,931,999	$432,246,200	$432,571,360
State equalized value	$357,150,104	$407,530,051	$431,838,046

Sussex County

Stillwater Township

Demographics & Socio-Economic Characteristics
(2000 US Census, except as noted)

Population
1980*	3,887
1990*	4,253
2000	4,267
Male	2,105
Female	2,162
2006 (estimate)*	4,385
Population density	161.7

Race & Hispanic Origin, 2000
Race
White	4,180
Black/African American	7
American Indian/Alaska Native	9
Asian	20
Native Hawaiian/Pacific Islander	0
Other race	10
Two or more races	41
Hispanic origin, total	89
Mexican	4
Puerto Rican	31
Cuban	7
Other Hispanic	47

Age & Nativity, 2000
Under 5 years	265
18 years and over	3,072
21 years and over	2,909
65 years and over	360
85 years and over	32
Median age	37.2
Native-born	4,127
Foreign-born	140

Educational Attainment, 2000
Population 25 years and over	2,797
Less than 9th grade	2.5%
High school grad or higher	92.2%
Bachelor's degree or higher	27.1%
Graduate degree	8.4%

Income & Poverty, 1999
Per capita income	$24,933
Median household income	$63,750
Median family income	$71,563
Persons in poverty	120
H'holds receiving public assistance	0
H'holds receiving social security	324

Households, 2000
Total households	1,494
With persons under 18	653
With persons over 65	272
Family households	1,155
Single-person households	258
Persons per household	2.85
Persons per family	3.27

Labor & Employment
Total civilian labor force, 2006**	2,663
Unemployment rate	1.7%
Total civilian labor force, 2000	2,373
Unemployment rate	1.3%

Employed persons 16 years and over by occupation, 2000
Managers & professionals	793
Service occupations	236
Sales & office occupations	632
Farming, fishing & forestry	0
Construction & maintenance	387
Production & transportation	294
Self-employed persons	185

* US Census Bureau
** New Jersey Department of Labor

See Introduction for an explanation of all data sources.

General Information
Stillwater Township
964 Stillwater Rd
Newton, NJ 07860
973-383-9484

Website	www.stillwaternj.us
Year of incorporation	1824
Land/water area (sq. miles)	27.12/1.26
Form of government	Township

Government
Legislative Districts
US Congressional	5
State Legislative	24

Local Officials, 2008
Mayor	William Morrison
Manager	NA
Clerk	Susan Best
Finance Dir	Beth Barile
Tax Assessor	Penny Holenstein
Tax Collector	Donna Clouse
Attorney	Michael Garofalo
Building	Charles O'Connor
Comm Dev/Planning	NA
Engineering	Michael G. Vreeland
Public Works	Keith Whitehead
Police Chief	Anthony Kozlowski
Fire/Emergency Dir	NA

Housing & Construction
Housing Units, 2000*
Total	2,030
Median rent	$760
Median SF home value	$152,400

Permits for New Residential Construction
	Units	Value
Total, 2007	12	$1,718,179
Single family	12	$1,718,179
Total, 2006	14	$2,596,489
Single family	14	$2,596,489

Real Property Valuation, 2007
	Parcels	Valuation
Total	2,472	$247,016,300
Vacant	355	6,009,100
Residential	1,672	204,325,700
Commercial	46	8,930,700
Industrial	1	408,900
Apartments	0	0
Farm land	252	1,350,000
Farm homestead	146	25,991,900

Average Property Value & Tax, 2007
Residential value	$126,687
Property tax	$5,244
Tax credit/rebate	$989

Public Library
No public municipal library

Library statistics, 2006
Population served	NA
Full-time/total staff	NA/NA

	Total	Per capita
Holdings	NA	NA
Revenues	NA	NA
Expenditures	NA	NA
Annual visits	NA	NA
Internet terminals/annual users	NA/NA	

Taxes	2005	2006	2007
General tax rate per $100	3.73	3.98	4.14
County equalization ratio	59.5	50.13	45.16
Net valuation taxable	$244,394,774	$245,048,300	$247,402,880
State equalized value	$487,521,991	$543,065,869	$575,779,778

Public Safety
Number of officers, 2006 ... 5

Crime	2005	2006
Total crimes	51	30
Violent	2	1
Murder	0	0
Rape	1	0
Robbery	0	0
Aggravated assault	1	1
Non-violent	49	29
Burglary	3	2
Larceny	45	24
Vehicle theft	1	3
Domestic violence	4	3
Arson	0	0
Total crime rate	11.6	6.8
Violent	0.5	0.2
Non-violent	11.2	6.6

Public School District
(for school year 2006-07 except as noted)

Stillwater Township School District
PO Box 12
Stillwater, NJ 07875
973-383-6171

Chief School Admin	S. William Shelton
Number of schools	1
Grade plan	K-6
Enrollment	394
Attendance rate, '05-06	95.4%
Dropout rate	NA
Students per teacher	9.3
Per pupil expenditure	$13,663
Median faculty salary	$67,680
Median administrator salary	$98,548
Grade 12 enrollment	NA
High school graduation rate	NA

Assessment test results
(percent scoring at proficient or advanced level)
	Language	Math
NJASK-Grade 3	100.0%	100.0%
GEPA-Grade 8	NA	NA
HSPA-High School	NA	NA

SAT score averages
Pct tested	Math	Verbal	Writing
NA	NA	NA	NA

Teacher Qualifications
Avg. years of experience	19
Highly-qualified teachers one subject/all subjects	100%/100%
With emergency credentials	0.0%

No Child Left Behind
AYP, 2005-06 ... Meets Standards

Municipal Finance
State Aid Programs, 2008
Total aid	$362,977
CMPTRA	0
Energy tax receipts	275,543
Garden State Trust	87,434

General Budget, 2007
Total tax levy	$10,241,454
County levy	2,227,147
County taxes	1,819,757
County library	155,141
County health	60,009
County open space	192,240
School levy	6,317,384
Muni. levy	1,696,923
Misc. revenues	2,216,009

©2008 Information Publications, Inc. All rights reserved. Photocopying prohibited. For additional copies, contact the publisher at www.informationpublications.com or (877)544-INFO (4636)

The New Jersey Municipal Data Book

Stockton Borough
Hunterdon County

Demographics & Socio-Economic Characteristics
(2000 US Census, except as noted)

Population
1980*	643
1990*	629
2000	560
Male	262
Female	298
2006 (estimate)*	555
Population density	1,009.1

Race & Hispanic Origin, 2000
Race
- White: 552
- Black/African American: 0
- American Indian/Alaska Native: 0
- Asian: 5
- Native Hawaiian/Pacific Islander: 0
- Other race: 0
- Two or more races: 3

Hispanic origin, total: 3
- Mexican: 0
- Puerto Rican: 0
- Cuban: 1
- Other Hispanic: 2

Age & Nativity, 2000
- Under 5 years: 38
- 18 years and over: 441
- 21 years and over: 432
- 65 years and over: 83
- 85 years and over: 8
- Median age: 40.6
- Native-born: 549
- Foreign-born: 8

Educational Attainment, 2000
- Population 25 years and over: 415
- Less than 9th grade: 4.3%
- High school grad or higher: 86.7%
- Bachelor's degree or higher: 31.1%
- Graduate degree: 12.3%

Income & Poverty, 1999
- Per capita income: $25,712
- Median household income: $51,406
- Median family income: $65,000
- Persons in poverty: 11
- H'holds receiving public assistance: 5
- H'holds receiving social security: 77

Households, 2000
- Total households: 246
- With persons under 18: 71
- With persons over 65: 62
- Family households: 148
- Single-person households: 75
- Persons per household: 2.28
- Persons per family: 2.94

Labor & Employment
- Total civilian labor force, 2006**: 357
- Unemployment rate: 0.0%
- Total civilian labor force, 2000: 318
- Unemployment rate: 1.3%

Employed persons 16 years and over by occupation, 2000
- Managers & professionals: 125
- Service occupations: 30
- Sales & office occupations: 81
- Farming, fishing & forestry: 0
- Construction & maintenance: 29
- Production & transportation: 49
- Self-employed persons: 26

* US Census Bureau
** New Jersey Department of Labor

General Information
Borough of Stockton
2 S Main St
PO Box M
Stockton, NJ 08559
609-397-0070

- Email: stocktonclerk@aol.com
- Year of incorporation: 1898
- Land/water area (sq. miles): 0.55/0.06
- Form of government: Borough

Government
Legislative Districts
- US Congressional: 12
- State Legislative: 23

Local Officials, 2008
- Mayor: Stephen Giocondo
- Manager/Admin: NA
- Clerk: Michele Hovan
- CFO: Diane K. Schubach
- Tax Assessor: Michelle Trivieno
- Tax Collector: Carol Hettman
- Attorney: John Bennett
- Building: Edward Noval
- Comm Dev/Planning: NA
- Engineering: Dennis O'Neal
- Public Works: NA
- Police Chief: NA
- Emerg/Fire Director: Paul Steffanelli

Housing & Construction
Housing Units, 2000*
- Total: 258
- Median rent: $850
- Median SF home value: $188,500

Permits for New Residential Construction
	Units	Value
Total, 2007	2	$319,358
Single family	2	$319,358
Total, 2006	3	$479,037
Single family	3	$479,037

Real Property Valuation, 2007
	Parcels	Valuation
Total	263	$97,328,300
Vacant	21	3,205,700
Residential	205	77,901,000
Commercial	26	13,969,300
Industrial	1	364,000
Apartments	2	1,018,600
Farm land	6	24,600
Farm homestead	2	845,100

Average Property Value & Tax, 2007
- Residential value: $380,416
- Property tax: $5,743
- Tax credit/rebate: $993

Public Library
No public municipal library

Library statistics, 2006
- Population served: NA
- Full-time/total staff: NA/NA

	Total	Per capita
Holdings	NA	NA
Revenues	NA	NA
Expenditures	NA	NA
Annual visits	NA	NA
Internet terminals/annual users	NA/NA	

Taxes
	2005	2006	2007
General tax rate per $100	3.14	3.31	1.51
County equalization ratio	48.88	48.11	106.44
Net valuation taxable	$42,577,168	$42,319,500	$97,479,529
State equalized value	$82,770,544	$87,730,081	$89,697,921

Public Safety
Number of officers, 2006: 0

Crime	2005	2006
Total crimes	6	4
Violent	0	0
Murder	0	0
Rape	0	0
Robbery	0	0
Aggravated assault	0	0
Non-violent	6	4
Burglary	28	2
Larceny	105	2
Vehicle theft	2	0
Domestic violence	83	0
Arson	1	0
Total crime rate	10.7	7.1
Violent	0.0	0.0
Non-violent	10.7	7.1

Public School District
(for school year 2006-07 except as noted)

Stockton Borough School District
19 S Main St
Stockton, NJ 08559
609-397-2012

- Chief School Admin: Suzanne Ivans
- Number of schools: 1
- Grade plan: K-6
- Enrollment: 48
- Attendance rate, '05-06: 96.8%
- Dropout rate: NA
- Students per teacher: 8.9
- Per pupil expenditure: $11,468
- Median faculty salary: $31,800
- Median administrator salary: $55,368
- Grade 12 enrollment: NA
- High school graduation rate: NA

Assessment test results
(percent scoring at proficient or advanced level)
	Language	Math
NJASK-Grade 3	NA	NA
GEPA-Grade 8	NA	NA
HSPA-High School	NA	NA

SAT score averages
Pct tested	Math	Verbal	Writing
NA	NA	NA	NA

Teacher Qualifications
- Avg. years of experience: 10
- Highly-qualified teachers one subject/all subjects: 100%/100%
- With emergency credentials: 0.0%

No Child Left Behind
AYP, 2005-06: Meets Standards

Municipal Finance
State Aid Programs, 2008
- Total aid: $55,804
- CMPTRA: 0
- Energy tax receipts: 44,546
- Garden State Trust: 11,258

General Budget, 2007
- Total tax levy: $1,471,718
- County levy: 305,170
- County taxes: 255,397
- County library: 22,224
- County health: 0
- County open space: 27,548
- School levy: 926,744
- Muni. levy: 239,804
- Misc. revenues: 324,873

Cape May County
Stone Harbor Borough

Demographics & Socio-Economic Characteristics
(2000 US Census, except as noted)

Population
1980*	1,187
1990*	1,025
2000	1,128
Male	518
Female	610
2006 (estimate)*	1,039
Population density	731.7

Race & Hispanic Origin, 2000
Race
White	1,114
Black/African American	9
American Indian/Alaska Native	0
Asian	0
Native Hawaiian/Pacific Islander	0
Other race	2
Two or more races	3
Hispanic origin, total	5
Mexican	0
Puerto Rican	2
Cuban	0
Other Hispanic	3

Age & Nativity, 2000
Under 5 years	27
18 years and over	989
21 years and over	973
65 years and over	437
85 years and over	44
Median age	57.5
Native-born	1,104
Foreign-born	24

Educational Attainment, 2000
Population 25 years and over	954
Less than 9th grade	1.6%
High school grad or higher	93.9%
Bachelor's degree or higher	43.8%
Graduate degree	18.7%

Income & Poverty, 1999
Per capita income	$46,427
Median household income	$51,471
Median family income	$67,250
Persons in poverty	39
H'holds receiving public assistance	5
H'holds receiving social security	291

Households, 2000
Total households	596
With persons under 18	75
With persons over 65	317
Family households	331
Single-person households	240
Persons per household	1.89
Persons per family	2.50

Labor & Employment
Total civilian labor force, 2006**	600
Unemployment rate	5.1%
Total civilian labor force, 2000	486
Unemployment rate	4.9%

Employed persons 16 years and over by occupation, 2000
Managers & professionals	203
Service occupations	61
Sales & office occupations	146
Farming, fishing & forestry	3
Construction & maintenance	27
Production & transportation	22
Self-employed persons	49

‡ Branch of county library
* US Census Bureau
** New Jersey Department of Labor

See Introduction for an explanation of all data sources.

General Information
Borough of Stone Harbor
9508 2nd Ave
Stone Harbor, NJ 08247
609-368-5102

Website	www.stone-harbor.nj.us
Year of incorporation	1914
Land/water area (sq. miles)	1.42/0.57
Form of government	Borough

Government
Legislative Districts
US Congressional	2
State Legislative	1

Local Officials, 2008
Mayor	Suzanne Walters
Manager	Kenneth Hawk
Clerk	Suzanne Stanford
Finance Dir	James Nicola
Tax Assessor	Harry Supple Jr
Tax Collector	Kathryn McClure
Attorney	Michael Donohue
Building	Michael Koochembere
Comm Dev/Planning	NA
Engineering	Marc DeBlasio
Public Works	Greg Sheeran
Police Chief	William Toland
Emerg/Fire Director	Roger Stanford

Housing & Construction
Housing Units, 2000*
Total	3,428
Median rent	$669
Median SF home value	$445,300

Permits for New Residential Construction
	Units	Value
Total, 2007	34	$16,916,872
Single family	34	$16,916,872
Total, 2006	32	$15,008,231
Single family	32	$15,008,231

Real Property Valuation, 2007
	Parcels	Valuation
Total	3,151	$3,607,384,300
Vacant	78	87,413,600
Residential	2,872	3,397,754,700
Commercial	199	118,783,300
Industrial	0	0
Apartments	2	3,432,700
Farm land	0	0
Farm homestead	0	0

Average Property Value & Tax, 2007
Residential value	$1,183,062
Property tax	$5,982
Tax credit/rebate	$1,076

Public Library
Stone Harbor Branch Library‡
95th & Second Ave
Stone Harbor, NJ 08247
609-368-6809
Branch Librarian .. Geraldine M. Fridmann

Library statistics, 2006
see Cape May County profile for library system statistics

Public Safety
Number of officers, 2006		15

Crime	2005	2006
Total crimes	65	48
Violent	4	5
Murder	0	0
Rape	0	1
Robbery	0	0
Aggravated assault	4	4
Non-violent	61	43
Burglary	7	7
Larceny	54	35
Vehicle theft	0	1
Domestic violence	10	4
Arson	0	0
Total crime rate	59.8	45.2
Violent	3.7	4.7
Non-violent	56.1	40.5

Public School District
(for school year 2006-07 except as noted)

Stone Harbor School District
275 93rd St
Stone Harbor, NJ 08247
609-368-4413

Principal	David Rauenzahn
Number of schools	1
Grade plan	K-8
Enrollment	96
Attendance rate, '05-06	94.5%
Dropout rate	NA
Students per teacher	7.1
Per pupil expenditure	$17,652
Median faculty salary	$61,468
Median administrator salary	$52,894
Grade 12 enrollment	NA
High school graduation rate	NA

Assessment test results
(percent scoring at proficient or advanced level)
	Language	Math
NJASK-Grade 3	NA	NA
GEPA-Grade 8	NA	NA
HSPA-High School	NA	NA

SAT score averages
Pct tested	Math	Verbal	Writing
NA	NA	NA	NA

Teacher Qualifications
Avg. years of experience	18
Highly-qualified teachers one subject/all subjects	100%/91.5%
With emergency credentials	0.0%

No Child Left Behind
AYP, 2005-06 .... Meets Standards

Municipal Finance
State Aid Programs, 2008
Total aid	$224,416
CMPTRA	0
Energy tax receipts	224,416
Garden State Trust	0

General Budget, 2007
Total tax levy	$18,243,844
County levy	8,847,151
County taxes	7,030,840
County library	1,350,888
County health	0
County open space	465,423
School levy	1,969,219
Muni. levy	7,427,474
Misc. revenues	3,464,621

Taxes
	2005	2006	2007
General tax rate per $100	0.45	0.48	0.51
County equalization ratio	122	92.52	77.73
Net valuation taxable	$3,567,039,533	$3,584,070,000	$3,607,791,890
State equalized value	$3,855,425,349	$4,611,398,898	$4,770,187,175

©2008 Information Publications, Inc. All rights reserved. Photocopying prohibited. For additional copies, contact the publisher at www.informationpublications.com or (877)544-INFO (4636)

Stow Creek Township

Cumberland County

Demographics & Socio-Economic Characteristics
(2000 US Census, except as noted)

Population
1980*	1,365
1990*	1,437
2000	1,429
Male	703
Female	726
2006 (estimate)*	1,535
Population density	83.2

Race & Hispanic Origin, 2000
Race
White	1,335
Black/African American	50
American Indian/Alaska Native	23
Asian	3
Native Hawaiian/Pacific Islander	0
Other race	12
Two or more races	6
Hispanic origin, total	24
Mexican	2
Puerto Rican	12
Cuban	0
Other Hispanic	10

Age & Nativity, 2000
Under 5 years	74
18 years and over	1,093
21 years and over	1,044
65 years and over	207
85 years and over	12
Median age	40.7
Native-born	1,405
Foreign-born	29

Educational Attainment, 2000
Population 25 years and over	975
Less than 9th grade	5.9%
High school grad or higher	83.1%
Bachelor's degree or higher	18.9%
Graduate degree	5.8%

Income & Poverty, 1999
Per capita income	$20,925
Median household income	$52,500
Median family income	$58,583
Persons in poverty	96
H'holds receiving public assistance	9
H'holds receiving social security	149

Households, 2000
Total households	536
With persons under 18	182
With persons over 65	143
Family households	425
Single-person households	96
Persons per household	2.67
Persons per family	3.01

Labor & Employment
Total civilian labor force, 2006**	839
Unemployment rate	4.0%
Total civilian labor force, 2000	746
Unemployment rate	4.4%

Employed persons 16 years and over by occupation, 2000
Managers & professionals	231
Service occupations	94
Sales & office occupations	150
Farming, fishing & forestry	13
Construction & maintenance	98
Production & transportation	127
Self-employed persons	44

* US Census Bureau
** New Jersey Department of Labor

General Information
Township of Stow Creek
474 Macanippuck Rd
Bridgeton, NJ 08302
856-451-8822

Website	(county website)
Year of incorporation	1748
Land/water area (sq. miles)	18.45/0.42
Form of government	Township

Government
Legislative Districts
US Congressional	2
State Legislative	3

Local Officials, 2008
Mayor	Dale Cruzan Sr
Manager/Admin	NA
Clerk	Bruce Porter
Finance Dir	Ron Campbell
Tax Assessor	Donna Harris
Tax Collector	Roberta DiGiuseppi
Attorney	Thomas Farnoly
Building	Robert Young
Comm Dev/Planning	NA
Engineering	J. Michael Fralinger
Public Works	NA
Police Chief	NA
Emerg/Fire Director	Max Dilks

Housing & Construction
Housing Units, 2000*
Total	560
Median rent	$620
Median SF home value	$114,400

Permits for New Residential Construction
	Units	Value
Total, 2007	0	$0
Single family	0	$0
Total, 2006	3	$605,000
Single family	3	$605,000

Real Property Valuation, 2007
	Parcels	Valuation
Total	963	$78,142,800
Vacant	52	819,800
Residential	369	45,232,800
Commercial	16	3,212,900
Industrial	0	0
Apartments	0	0
Farm land	350	3,501,600
Farm homestead	176	25,375,700

Average Property Value & Tax, 2007
Residential value	$129,557
Property tax	$3,976
Tax credit/rebate	$860

Public Library
No public municipal library

Library statistics, 2006
Population served	NA
Full-time/total staff	NA/NA

	Total	Per capita
Holdings	NA	NA
Revenues	NA	NA
Expenditures	NA	NA
Annual visits	NA	NA
Internet terminals/annual users	NA/NA	

Taxes
	2005	2006	2007
General tax rate per $100	2.821	3.077	3.072
County equalization ratio	95.59	89.28	83.25
Net valuation taxable	$76,278,901	$76,229,100	$78,598,259
State equalized value	$85,437,837	$92,040,413	$85,754,880

Public Safety
Number of officers, 2006: 0

Crime
	2005	2006
Total crimes	8	19
Violent	0	1
Murder	0	0
Rape	0	0
Robbery	0	0
Aggravated assault	0	1
Non-violent	8	18
Burglary	3	11
Larceny	4	7
Vehicle theft	1	0
Domestic violence	9	1
Arson	0	0
Total crime rate	5.3	12.4
Violent	0.0	0.7
Non-violent	5.3	11.8

Public School District
(for school year 2006-07 except as noted)

Stow Creek Township School District
11 Gum Tree Corner Rd
Bridgeton, NJ 08302
856-455-1717

Chief School Admin	Donna Levick
Number of schools	1
Grade plan	K-8
Enrollment	145
Attendance rate, '05-06	95.2%
Dropout rate	NA
Students per teacher	10.2
Per pupil expenditure	$11,432
Median faculty salary	$38,175
Median administrator salary	$77,446
Grade 12 enrollment	NA
High school graduation rate	NA

Assessment test results
(percent scoring at proficient or advanced level)
	Language	Math
NJASK-Grade 3	NA	NA
GEPA-Grade 8	62.6%	62.5%
HSPA-High School	NA	NA

SAT score averages
Pct tested	Math	Verbal	Writing
NA	NA	NA	NA

Teacher Qualifications
Avg. years of experience	7
Highly-qualified teachers one subject/all subjects	86.5%/86.5%
With emergency credentials	0.0%

No Child Left Behind
AYP, 2005-06 .... Meets Standards

Municipal Finance
State Aid Programs, 2008
Total aid	$146,530
CMPTRA	0
Energy tax receipts	123,897
Garden State Trust	22,633

General Budget, 2007
Total tax levy	$2,411,936
County levy	938,128
County taxes	888,680
County library	0
County health	39,940
County open space	9,508
School levy	1,360,817
Muni. levy	112,991
Misc. revenues	705,083

Camden County
Stratford Borough

Demographics & Socio-Economic Characteristics
(2000 US Census, except as noted)

Population
1980*	8,005
1990*	7,614
2000	7,271
Male	3,544
Female	3,727
2006 (estimate)*	7,122
Population density	4,507.6

Race & Hispanic Origin, 2000
Race
- White 6,439
- Black/African American 480
- American Indian/Alaska Native 9
- Asian 173
- Native Hawaiian/Pacific Islander 1
- Other race 63
- Two or more races 106
- Hispanic origin, total 277
  - Mexican 105
  - Puerto Rican 92
  - Cuban 7
  - Other Hispanic 73

Age & Nativity, 2000
- Under 5 years 447
- 18 years and over 5,476
- 21 years and over 5,222
- 65 years and over 1,150
- 85 years and over 116
- Median age 37.7
- Native-born 6,885
- Foreign-born 386

Educational Attainment, 2000
- Population 25 years and over 4,910
- Less than 9th grade 4.5%
- High school grad or higher 86.3%
- Bachelor's degree or higher 20.0%
- Graduate degree 4.5%

Income & Poverty, 1999
- Per capita income $21,748
- Median household income $50,977
- Median family income $57,500
- Persons in poverty 327
- H'holds receiving public assistance 52
- H'holds receiving social security 802

Households, 2000
- Total households 2,736
  - With persons under 18 953
  - With persons over 65 747
  - Family households 1,907
  - Single-person households 705
- Persons per household 2.61
- Persons per family 3.18

Labor & Employment
- Total civilian labor force, 2006** 3,962
- Unemployment rate 4.1%
- Total civilian labor force, 2000 3,660
- Unemployment rate 3.7%

Employed persons 16 years and over by occupation, 2000
- Managers & professionals 1,288
- Service occupations 483
- Sales & office occupations 1,181
- Farming, fishing & forestry 13
- Construction & maintenance 271
- Production & transportation 289
- Self-employed persons 133

* US Census Bureau
** New Jersey Department of Labor

See Introduction for an explanation of all data sources.

General Information
Borough of Stratford
307 Union Ave
Stratford, NJ 08084
856-783-0600

- Website .... www.stratfordnj.org
- Year of incorporation 1925
- Land/water area (sq. miles) 1.58/0.00
- Form of government .... Borough

Government
Legislative Districts
- US Congressional 1
- State Legislative 5

Local Officials, 2008
- Mayor .... John Gentless
- Manager .... John Keenan Jr
- Clerk .... John Keenan Jr
- Finance Dir .... John Fabritiis
- Tax Assessor .... Richard Arrowood
- Tax Collector .... John Fabritiis
- Attorney .... Jeffrey Baron
- Building .... Chris Mecca
- Planning .... John Keenan Jr
- Engineering .... Joseph Schiavo
- Public Works .... Ken Ryker
- Police Chief .... Ronald Morello
- Emerg/Fire Director .... Stephen Gagliardi

Housing & Construction
Housing Units, 2000*
- Total 2,849
- Median rent $594
- Median SF home value $114,000

Permits for New Residential Construction
	Units	Value
Total, 2007	0	$0
Single family	0	$0
Total, 2006	2	$173,900
Single family	2	$173,900

Real Property Valuation, 2007
	Parcels	Valuation
Total	2,270	$285,584,900
Vacant	38	1,279,000
Residential	2,115	222,380,900
Commercial	106	50,205,800
Industrial	0	0
Apartments	11	11,719,200
Farm land	0	0
Farm homestead	0	0

Average Property Value & Tax, 2007
- Residential value $105,145
- Property tax $5,525
- Tax credit/rebate $1,022

Public Library
Stratford Public Library
303 Union Ave
Stratford, NJ 08084
856-783-0602

Director .... Ruth C. Roderick

Library statistics, 2006
- Population served 7,271
- Full-time/total staff 0/0

	Total	Per capita
Holdings	43,050	5.92
Revenues	$158,441	$21.79
Expenditures	$123,949	$17.05
Annual visits	17,224	2.37
Internet terminals/annual users		5/1,057

Public Safety
Number of officers, 2006 14

Crime	2005	2006
Total crimes	203	223
Violent	16	15
Murder	0	0
Rape	1	1
Robbery	6	7
Aggravated assault	9	7
Non-violent	187	208
Burglary	20	29
Larceny	158	169
Vehicle theft	9	10
Domestic violence	76	82
Arson	2	1
Total crime rate	28.2	31.0
Violent	2.2	2.1
Non-violent	26.0	29.0

Public School District
(for school year 2006-07 except as noted)

Stratford Borough School District
Yellin School, 111 Warwick Rd
Stratford, NJ 08084
856-783-2555

- Superintendent .... Albert K. Brown
- Number of schools 2
- Grade plan K-8
- Enrollment 851
- Attendance rate, '05-06 .... 95.4%
- Dropout rate .... NA
- Students per teacher 10.9
- Per pupil expenditure $11,635
- Median faculty salary $47,347
- Median administrator salary $87,808
- Grade 12 enrollment .... NA
- High school graduation rate .... NA

Assessment test results
(percent scoring at proficient or advanced level)

	Language	Math
NJASK-Grade 3	90.4%	89.1%
GEPA-Grade 8	82.7%	70.2%
HSPA-High School	NA	NA

SAT score averages
Pct tested	Math	Verbal	Writing
NA	NA	NA	NA

Teacher Qualifications
- Avg. years of experience 8
- Highly-qualified teachers
  - one subject/all subjects 100%/100%
- With emergency credentials 2.0%

No Child Left Behind
AYP, 2005-06 .... Meets Standards

Municipal Finance
State Aid Programs, 2008
- Total aid $823,688
  - CMPTRA 143,283
  - Energy tax receipts 680,405
  - Garden State Trust 0

General Budget, 2007
- Total tax levy $15,036,661
  - County levy 2,965,237
    - County taxes 2,875,358
    - County library 0
    - County health 0
    - County open space 89,879
  - School levy 9,192,493
  - Muni. levy 2,878,931
- Misc. revenues 2,889,989

Taxes
	2005	2006	2007
General tax rate per $100	4.594	4.991	5.225
County equalization ratio	81.5	71.02	63.7
Net valuation taxable	$286,714,550	$286,652,500	$286,151,557
State equalized value	$403,709,589	$450,631,471	$496,890,779

Summit City

Union County

Demographics & Socio-Economic Characteristics
(2000 US Census, except as noted)

Population
1980*	21,071
1990*	19,757
2000	21,131
Male	10,225
Female	10,906
2006 (estimate)*	21,103
Population density	3,488.1

Race & Hispanic Origin, 2000
Race
White	18,546
Black/African American	914
American Indian/Alaska Native	19
Asian	941
Native Hawaiian/Pacific Islander	3
Other race	360
Two or more races	348
Hispanic origin, total	2,150
Mexican	162
Puerto Rican	207
Cuban	159
Other Hispanic	1,622

Age & Nativity, 2000
Under 5 years	1,815
18 years and over	15,434
21 years and over	15,071
65 years and over	2,769
85 years and over	349
Median age	37.3
Native-born	17,262
Foreign-born	3,869

Educational Attainment, 2000
Population 25 years and over	14,517
Less than 9th grade	2.8%
High school grad or higher	92.4%
Bachelor's degree or higher	61.6%
Graduate degree	30.0%

Income & Poverty, 1999
Per capita income	$62,598
Median household income	$92,964
Median family income	$117,053
Persons in poverty	895
H'holds receiving public assistance	74
H'holds receiving social security	1,985

Households, 2000
Total households	7,897
With persons under 18	2,908
With persons over 65	2,054
Family households	5,610
Single-person households	1,887
Persons per household	2.67
Persons per family	3.18

Labor & Employment
Total civilian labor force, 2006**	11,000
Unemployment rate	2.5%
Total civilian labor force, 2000	10,473
Unemployment rate	2.5%

Employed persons 16 years and over by occupation, 2000
Managers & professionals	5,983
Service occupations	1,079
Sales & office occupations	2,287
Farming, fishing & forestry	11
Construction & maintenance	358
Production & transportation	498
Self-employed persons	761

* US Census Bureau
** New Jersey Department of Labor

General Information
City of Summit
512 Springfield Ave
Summit, NJ 07901
908-273-6400

Website	www.cityofsummit.org
Year of incorporation	1899
Land/water area (sq. miles)	6.05/0.02
Form of government	City

Government
Legislative Districts
US Congressional	7
State Legislative	21

Local Officials, 2008
Mayor	Jordan Glatt
Manager	Christopher Cotter
Clerk	David Hughes
Finance Dir.	Ronald Angelo
Tax Assessor	(vacant)
Tax Collector	Carolyn Brattlof
Attorney	Barry Osmun
Building	Tony Doyle
Comm Dev/Planning	NA
Engineering	Andy Hipolit
Public Works	Paul Cascais
Police Chief	Robert Lucid
Emerg/Fire Director	Joe Houck

Housing & Construction
Housing Units, 2000*
Total	8,146
Median rent	$1,078
Median SF home value	$469,200

Permits for New Residential Construction
	Units	Value
Total, 2007	12	$5,141,850
Single family	12	$5,141,850
Total, 2006	9	$2,062,155
Single family	9	$2,062,155

Real Property Valuation, 2007
	Parcels	Valuation
Total	6,569	$3,120,773,700
Vacant	72	10,419,600
Residential	6,053	2,481,875,600
Commercial	387	322,466,600
Industrial	10	234,816,200
Apartments	47	71,195,700
Farm land	0	0
Farm homestead	0	0

Average Property Value & Tax, 2007
Residential value	$410,024
Property tax	$13,553
Tax credit/rebate	$1,203

Public Library
Summit Free Public Library
75 Maple St
Summit, NJ 07901
908-273-0350

Director..................Glenn E. Devitt

Library statistics, 2006
Population served	21,131
Full-time/total staff	8/12

	Total	Per capita
Holdings	146,662	6.94
Revenues	$2,188,360	$103.56
Expenditures	$2,093,223	$99.06
Annual visits	237,200	11.23
Internet terminals/annual users	39/29,795	

Taxes
	2005	2006	2007
General tax rate per $100	2.915	3.102	3.306
County equalization ratio	51.73	46.81	44.02
Net valuation taxable	$3,067,049,487	$3,089,282,100	$3,123,755,824
State equalized value	$6,164,923,592	$7,021,561,142	$7,296,213,486

Public Safety
Number of officers, 2006 51

Crime	2005	2006
Total crimes	373	253
Violent	13	8
Murder	0	0
Rape	2	2
Robbery	2	2
Aggravated assault	9	4
Non-violent	360	245
Burglary	33	18
Larceny	291	215
Vehicle theft	36	12
Domestic violence	132	173
Arson	1	0
Total crime rate	17.5	11.9
Violent	0.6	0.4
Non-violent	16.9	11.6

Public School District
(for school year 2006-07 except as noted)

Summit City School District
14 Beekman Terrace
Summit, NJ 07901
908-918-2100

Superintendent	Carolyn Deacon
Number of schools	7
Grade plan	K-12
Enrollment	3,729
Attendance rate, '05-06	95.6%
Dropout rate	NA
Students per teacher	10.4
Per pupil expenditure	$13,883
Median faculty salary	$58,355
Median administrator salary	$120,293
Grade 12 enrollment	234
High school graduation rate	97.9%

Assessment test results
(percent scoring at proficient or advanced level)
	Language	Math
NJASK-Grade 3	93.5%	96.0%
GEPA-Grade 8	93.6%	89.9%
HSPA-High School	93.8%	89.4%

SAT score averages
Pct tested	Math	Verbal	Writing
96%	588	573	579

Teacher Qualifications
Avg. years of experience	9
Highly-qualified teachers one subject/all subjects	100%/100%
With emergency credentials	0.7%

No Child Left Behind
AYP, 2005-06 .... Meets Standards

Municipal Finance
State Aid Programs, 2008
Total aid	$3,899,322
CMPTRA	70,587
Energy tax receipts	3,828,735
Garden State Trust	0

General Budget, 2007
Total tax levy	$103,251,551
County levy	24,830,057
County taxes	23,761,759
County library	0
County health	0
County open space	1,068,298
School levy	53,877,623
Muni. levy	24,543,871
Misc. revenues	15,588,558

Ocean County

Surf City Borough

Demographics & Socio-Economic Characteristics
(2000 US Census, except as noted)

Population
1980*	1,571
1990*	1,375
2000	1,442
Male	685
Female	757
2006 (estimate)*	1,542
Population density	2,141.7

Race & Hispanic Origin, 2000
Race
White	1,414
Black/African American	2
American Indian/Alaska Native	3
Asian	5
Native Hawaiian/Pacific Islander	6
Other race	8
Two or more races	4
Hispanic origin, total	28
Mexican	15
Puerto Rican	1
Cuban	1
Other Hispanic	11

Age & Nativity, 2000
Under 5 years	39
18 years and over	1,263
21 years and over	1,230
65 years and over	492
85 years and over	58
Median age	53.4
Native-born	1,385
Foreign-born	46

Educational Attainment, 2000
Population 25 years and over	1,202
Less than 9th grade	3.2%
High school grad or higher	87.5%
Bachelor's degree or higher	26.0%
Graduate degree	6.4%

Income & Poverty, 1999
Per capita income	$26,632
Median household income	$38,190
Median family income	$50,268
Persons in poverty	107
H'holds receiving public assistance	2
H'holds receiving social security	352

Households, 2000
Total households	706
With persons under 18	102
With persons over 65	343
Family households	421
Single-person households	246
Persons per household	2.04
Persons per family	2.61

Labor & Employment
Total civilian labor force, 2006**	614
Unemployment rate	5.1%
Total civilian labor force, 2000	615
Unemployment rate	4.2%

Employed persons 16 years and over by occupation, 2000
Managers & professionals	191
Service occupations	91
Sales & office occupations	209
Farming, fishing & forestry	5
Construction & maintenance	45
Production & transportation	48
Self-employed persons	77

‡ Branch of county library
* US Census Bureau
** New Jersey Department of Labor

See Introduction for an explanation of all data sources.

General Information
Borough of Surf City
813 Long Beach Blvd
Surf City, NJ 08008
609-494-3064

Website	NA
Year of incorporation	1899
Land/water area (sq. miles)	0.72/0.20
Form of government	Borough

Government
Legislative Districts
US Congressional	3
State Legislative	9

Local Officials, 2008
Mayor	Leonard Connors Jr
Manager	Mary Madonna
Clerk	Mary Madonna
Finance Dir	David Pawlishak
Tax Assessor	William Procacci
Tax Collector	Grace T. DeGennaro
Attorney	Christopher Connors
Building	Frank Zappavigna
Comm Dev/Planning	NA
Engineering	Frank Little
Public Works	Edward Berg
Police Chief	William Collins
Emerg/Fire Director	B. Stasik

Housing & Construction
Housing Units, 2000*
Total	2,621
Median rent	$738
Median SF home value	$230,200

Permits for New Residential Construction
	Units	Value
Total, 2007	21	$7,462,775
Single family	21	$7,462,775
Total, 2006	19	$7,188,530
Single family	19	$7,188,530

Real Property Valuation, 2007
	Parcels	Valuation
Total	2,247	$1,490,391,900
Vacant	44	20,634,500
Residential	2,109	1,388,038,500
Commercial	94	81,718,900
Industrial	0	0
Apartments	0	0
Farm land	0	0
Farm homestead	0	0

Average Property Value & Tax, 2007
Residential value	$658,150
Property tax	$5,732
Tax credit/rebate	$1,104

Public Library
Long Beach Island Branch Library‡
217 S Central Ave
Surf City, NJ 08008
609-494-2480

Branch Librarian............Linda Feaster

Library statistics, 2006
see Ocean County profile for library system statistics

Taxes
	2005	2006	2007
General tax rate per $100	0.773	0.812	0.871
County equalization ratio	115.84	96.09	85.1
Net valuation taxable	$1,462,298,371	$1,470,594,800	$1,491,669,073
State equalized value	$1,521,800,782	$1,729,514,169	$1,786,391,438

Public Safety
Number of officers, 2006..............10

Crime
	2005	2006
Total crimes	48	42
Violent	4	1
Murder	0	0
Rape	0	0
Robbery	0	1
Aggravated assault	4	0
Non-violent	44	41
Burglary	5	3
Larceny	38	37
Vehicle theft	1	1
Domestic violence	8	3
Arson	0	0
Total crime rate	31.6	27.5
Violent	2.6	0.7
Non-violent	29.0	26.9

Public School District
(for school year 2006-07 except as noted)

Long Beach Island School District
200 Barnegat Ave
Surf City, NJ 08008
609-494-2341

Superintendent	Robert A. Garguilo
Number of schools	10
Grade plan	K-6
Enrollment	248
Attendance rate, '05-06	94.3%
Dropout rate	NA
Students per teacher	6.9
Per pupil expenditure	$21,956
Median faculty salary	$94,335
Median administrator salary	$68,857
Grade 12 enrollment	NA
High school graduation rate	NA

Assessment test results
(percent scoring at proficient or advanced level)
	Language	Math
NJASK-Grade 3	100.0%	90.0%
GEPA-Grade 8	NA	NA
HSPA-High School	NA	NA

SAT score averages
Pct tested	Math	Verbal	Writing
NA	NA	NA	NA

Teacher Qualifications
Avg. years of experience	19
Highly-qualified teachers one subject/all subjects	100%/100%
With emergency credentials	0.0%

No Child Left Behind
AYP, 2005-06............Meets Standards

Municipal Finance
State Aid Programs, 2008
Total aid	$181,006
CMPTRA	0
Energy tax receipts	181,006
Garden State Trust	0

General Budget, 2007
Total tax levy	$12,991,192
County levy	5,228,516
County taxes	4,486,029
County library	531,675
County health	0
County open space	210,811
School levy	4,452,676
Muni. levy	3,310,000
Misc. revenues	2,090,000

©2008 Information Publications, Inc. All rights reserved. Photocopying prohibited. For additional copies, contact the publisher at www.informationpublications.com or (877)544-INFO (4636)

The New Jersey Municipal Data Book

Sussex Borough
Sussex County

Demographics & Socio-Economic Characteristics
(2000 US Census, except as noted)

Population
1980*	2,418
1990*	2,201
2000	2,145
Male	1,025
Female	1,120
2006 (estimate)*	2,170
Population density	3,616.7

Race & Hispanic Origin, 2000
Race
White	2,066
Black/African American	24
American Indian/Alaska Native	2
Asian	26
Native Hawaiian/Pacific Islander	0
Other race	8
Two or more races	19
Hispanic origin, total	55
Mexican	6
Puerto Rican	28
Cuban	2
Other Hispanic	19

Age & Nativity, 2000
Under 5 years	133
18 years and over	1,632
21 years and over	1,552
65 years and over	273
85 years and over	27
Median age	36.1
Native-born	2,111
Foreign-born	34

Educational Attainment, 2000
Population 25 years and over	1,446
Less than 9th grade	4.2%
High school grad or higher	75.0%
Bachelor's degree or higher	10.7%
Graduate degree	2.5%

Income & Poverty, 1999
Per capita income	$18,866
Median household income	$36,172
Median family income	$45,250
Persons in poverty	235
H'holds receiving public assistance	45
H'holds receiving social security	250

Households, 2000
Total households	903
With persons under 18	287
With persons over 65	219
Family households	513
Single-person households	317
Persons per household	2.36
Persons per family	3.12

Labor & Employment
Total civilian labor force, 2006**	1,218
Unemployment rate	4.8%
Total civilian labor force, 2000	1,093
Unemployment rate	3.3%

Employed persons 16 years and over by occupation, 2000
Managers & professionals	184
Service occupations	238
Sales & office occupations	279
Farming, fishing & forestry	8
Construction & maintenance	111
Production & transportation	237
Self-employed persons	34

‡ Branch of county library
* US Census Bureau
** New Jersey Department of Labor

General Information
Borough of Sussex
2 Main St
Sussex, NJ 07461
973-875-4831

Website	(county website)
Year of incorporation	1902
Land/water area (sq. miles)	0.60/0.02
Form of government	Borough

Government
Legislative Districts
US Congressional	5
State Legislative	24

Local Officials, 2008
Mayor	Christian Parrott
Manager/Admin	NA
Clerk	Catherine Gleason
Finance Dir	Grant Rome
Tax Assessor	John Dyksen
Tax Collector	Terry Beshada
Attorney	John Ursin
Building	Ed Vandenberg
Planning	Thomas Heath
Engineering	Mike Simone
Public Works	Jeffrey Card
Police Chief	NA
Emerg/Fire Director	John Rome

Housing & Construction
Housing Units, 2000*
Total	961
Median rent	$667
Median SF home value	$122,500

Permits for New Residential Construction
	Units	Value
Total, 2007	7	$1,075,480
Single family	7	$1,075,480
Total, 2006	11	$2,403,598
Single family	8	$1,229,118

Real Property Valuation, 2007
	Parcels	Valuation
Total	591	$78,610,600
Vacant	47	1,015,800
Residential	461	52,863,000
Commercial	71	16,975,900
Industrial	2	464,900
Apartments	5	6,896,000
Farm land	4	21,100
Farm homestead	1	373,900

Average Property Value & Tax, 2007
Residential value	$115,231
Property tax	$4,581
Tax credit/rebate	$904

Public Library
Sussex-Wantage Branch Library‡
69 Route 639
Wantage, NJ 07461
973-875-3940

Branch Librarian ... Nancy Helmer

Library statistics, 2006
see Sussex County profile
for library system statistics

Public Safety
Number of officers, 2006 ... 0

Crime
	2005	2006
Total crimes	43	47
Violent	3	10
Murder	0	0
Rape	0	0
Robbery	0	1
Aggravated assault	3	9
Non-violent	40	37
Burglary	7	8
Larceny	24	25
Vehicle theft	9	4
Domestic violence	11	14
Arson	0	0
Total crime rate	19.7	21.5
Violent	1.4	4.6
Non-violent	18.3	16.9

Public School District
(for school year 2006-07 except as noted)

Sussex-Wantage Regional School District
31 Ryan Rd
Wantage, NJ 07461
973-875-3175

Superintendent	Edward Izbicki
Number of schools	6
Grade plan	K-8
Enrollment	1,668
Attendance rate, '05-06	94.8%
Dropout rate	NA
Students per teacher	10.6
Per pupil expenditure	$12,839
Median faculty salary	$56,080
Median administrator salary	$101,172
Grade 12 enrollment	NA
High school graduation rate	NA

Assessment test results
(percent scoring at proficient or advanced level)
	Language	Math
NJASK-Grade 3	87.2%	93.4%
GEPA-Grade 8	83.2%	68.1%
HSPA-High School	NA	NA

SAT score averages
Pct tested	Math	Verbal	Writing
NA	NA	NA	NA

Teacher Qualifications
Avg. years of experience	12
Highly-qualified teachers one subject/all subjects	100%/100%
With emergency credentials	0.0%

No Child Left Behind
AYP, 2005-06 ... Needs Improvement

Municipal Finance
State Aid Programs, 2008
Total aid	$134,130
CMPTRA	0
Energy tax receipts	134,130
Garden State Trust	0

General Budget, 2007
Total tax levy	$3,175,443
County levy	566,510
County taxes	462,883
County library	39,462
County health	15,258
County open space	48,908
School levy	2,079,243
Muni. levy	529,691
Misc. revenues	720,899

Taxes	2005	2006	2007
General tax rate per $100	3.58	3.84	3.98
County equalization ratio	72.55	62.28	57.41
Net valuation taxable	$79,468,917	$78,082,000	$79,881,585
State equalized value	$127,599,417	$137,430,730	$151,091,073

Gloucester County

Swedesboro Borough

Demographics & Socio-Economic Characteristics
(2000 US Census, except as noted)

Population
1980*	2,031
1990*	2,024
2000	2,055
Male	1,009
Female	1,046
2006 (estimate)*	2,043
Population density	2,798.6

Race & Hispanic Origin, 2000
Race
- White 1,581
- Black/African American 339
- American Indian/Alaska Native 1
- Asian 7
- Native Hawaiian/Pacific Islander 0
- Other race 69
- Two or more races 58
- Hispanic origin, total 175
- Mexican 10
- Puerto Rican 126
- Cuban 1
- Other Hispanic 38

Age & Nativity, 2000
- Under 5 years 153
- 18 years and over 1,492
- 21 years and over 1,406
- 65 years and over 258
- 85 years and over 38
- Median age 35.9
- Native-born 1,992
- Foreign-born 63

Educational Attainment, 2000
- Population 25 years and over 1,355
- Less than 9th grade 8.8%
- High school grad or higher 81.1%
- Bachelor's degree or higher 14.2%
- Graduate degree 4.9%

Income & Poverty, 1999
- Per capita income $20,857
- Median household income $49,286
- Median family income $58,721
- Persons in poverty 198
- H'holds receiving public assistance 28
- H'holds receiving social security 220

Households, 2000
- Total households 771
- With persons under 18 300
- With persons over 65 209
- Family households 529
- Single-person households 200
- Persons per household 2.66
- Persons per family 3.22

Labor & Employment
- Total civilian labor force, 2006** 1,190
- Unemployment rate 6.0%
- Total civilian labor force, 2000 1,006
- Unemployment rate 5.1%

Employed persons 16 years and over by occupation, 2000
- Managers & professionals 281
- Service occupations 108
- Sales & office occupations 295
- Farming, fishing & forestry 9
- Construction & maintenance 98
- Production & transportation 164
- Self-employed persons 26

‡ Joint library with Woolwich Township
* US Census Bureau
** New Jersey Department of Labor

See Introduction for an explanation of all data sources.

General Information
Borough of Swedesboro
PO Box 56
Swedesboro, NJ 08085
856-467-0202

- Website .... NA
- Year of incorporation 1902
- Land/water area (sq. miles) 0.73/0.03
- Form of government .... Borough

Government
Legislative Districts
- US Congressional 2
- State Legislative 3

Local Officials, 2008
- Mayor .... Thomas W. Fromm
- Manager/Admin .... NA
- Clerk .... Dolores Connors
- Finance Dir .... Jeff Coles
- Tax Assessor .... Horace Spoto
- Tax Collector .... Louis DeMore
- Attorney .... Timothy W. Chell
- Building .... Jim Sabetta
- Comm Dev/Planning .... NA
- Engineering .... Federici & Akin
- Public Works .... NA
- Police Chief .... William Dupper Jr
- Emerg/Fire Director .... Ed Barber

Housing & Construction
Housing Units, 2000*
- Total 860
- Median rent $642
- Median SF home value $98,400

Permits for New Residential Construction
	Units	Value
Total, 2007	77	$8,050,890
Single family	77	$8,050,890
Total, 2006	11	$2,029,097
Single family	11	$2,029,097

Real Property Valuation, 2007
	Parcels	Valuation
Total	965	$75,530,900
Vacant	248	4,352,800
Residential	626	54,978,500
Commercial	79	14,296,100
Industrial	4	902,800
Apartments	8	1,000,700
Farm land	0	0
Farm homestead	0	0

Average Property Value & Tax, 2007
- Residential value $87,825
- Property tax $4,248
- Tax credit/rebate $906

Public Library
Swedesboro Public Library‡
1442 Kings Hwy
Swedesboro, NJ 08085
856-467-0111

Director .... Marge Dombrosky

Library statistics, 2006
Population served
Full-time/total staff .... /

	Total	Per capita
Holdings		
Revenues		
Expenditures		
Annual visits		
Internet terminals/annual users		/

Taxes
	2005	2006	2007
General tax rate per $100	4.324	4.542	4.838
County equalization ratio	78.56	69.63	55.53
Net valuation taxable	$74,067,833	$72,739,800	$77,005,620
State equalized value	$106,373,450	$132,782,909	$152,054,664

Public Safety
Number of officers, 2006 7

Crime
	2005	2006
Total crimes	54	47
Violent	5	6
Murder	0	0
Rape	0	1
Robbery	0	3
Aggravated assault	5	2
Non-violent	49	41
Burglary	8	13
Larceny	38	27
Vehicle theft	3	1
Domestic violence	15	19
Arson	0	0
Total crime rate	26.3	22.9
Violent	2.4	2.9
Non-violent	23.9	20.0

Public School District
(for school year 2006-07 except as noted)

Swedesboro-Woolwich School District
15 Fredrick Blvd
Woolwich Twp, NJ 08085
856-241-1136

- Superintendent .... Richard Fisher
- Number of schools 6
- Grade plan K-6
- Enrollment 1,397
- Attendance rate, '05-06 .... 95.2%
- Dropout rate .... NA
- Students per teacher 11.4
- Per pupil expenditure $9,288
- Median faculty salary $42,590
- Median administrator salary $80,280
- Grade 12 enrollment .... NA
- High school graduation rate .... NA

Assessment test results
(percent scoring at proficient or advanced level)
	Language	Math
NJASK-Grade 3	89.1%	91.9%
GEPA-Grade 8	NA	NA
HSPA-High School	NA	NA

SAT score averages
Pct tested	Math	Verbal	Writing
NA	NA	NA	NA

Teacher Qualifications
- Avg. years of experience 4
- Highly-qualified teachers
  one subject/all subjects 100%/100%
- With emergency credentials 0.0%

No Child Left Behind
AYP, 2005-06 .... Meets Standards

Municipal Finance
State Aid Programs, 2008
- Total aid $151,673
- CMPTRA 0
- Energy tax receipts 151,659
- Garden State Trust 14

General Budget, 2007
- Total tax levy $3,725,080
- County levy 831,927
- County taxes 716,489
- County library 59,343
- County health 0
- County open space 56,095
- School levy 2,000,354
- Muni. levy 892,799
- Misc. revenues 1,126,427

The New Jersey Municipal Data Book

Tabernacle Township — Burlington County

Demographics & Socio-Economic Characteristics
(2000 US Census, except as noted)

Population
1980*	6,236
1990*	7,360
2000	7,170
Male	3,632
Female	3,538
2006 (estimate)*	7,337
Population density	148.3

Race & Hispanic Origin, 2000
Race
White	6,904
Black/African American	150
American Indian/Alaska Native	7
Asian	52
Native Hawaiian/Pacific Islander	0
Other race	22
Two or more races	35
Hispanic origin, total	106
Mexican	10
Puerto Rican	61
Cuban	8
Other Hispanic	27

Age & Nativity, 2000
Under 5 years	384
18 years and over	5,166
21 years and over	4,897
65 years and over	502
85 years and over	47
Median age	38.1
Native-born	7,012
Foreign-born	158

Educational Attainment, 2000
Population 25 years and over	4,651
Less than 9th grade	1.7%
High school grad or higher	92.7%
Bachelor's degree or higher	30.6%
Graduate degree	10.0%

Income & Poverty, 1999
Per capita income	$27,874
Median household income	$76,432
Median family income	$86,729
Persons in poverty	144
H'holds receiving public assistance	28
H'holds receiving social security	510

Households, 2000
Total households	2,346
With persons under 18	1,040
With persons over 65	389
Family households	2,011
Single-person households	268
Persons per household	3.03
Persons per family	3.28

Labor & Employment
Total civilian labor force, 2006**	4,628
Unemployment rate	2.2%
Total civilian labor force, 2000	3,994
Unemployment rate	2.0%

Employed persons 16 years and over by occupation, 2000
Managers & professionals	1,630
Service occupations	357
Sales & office occupations	1,147
Farming, fishing & forestry	12
Construction & maintenance	398
Production & transportation	369
Self-employed persons	233

* US Census Bureau
** New Jersey Department of Labor

General Information
Township of Tabernacle
163 Carranza Rd
Tabernacle, NJ 08088
609-268-1220

Website	www.townshipoftabernacle-nj.gov
Year of incorporation	1901
Land/water area (sq. miles)	49.46/0.06
Form of government	Township

Government
Legislative Districts
US Congressional	3
State Legislative	8

Local Officials, 2008
Mayor	Kimberly A. Brown
Administrator	Douglas Cramer
Clerk	LaShawn R. Barber
Finance Dir	Terry Henry
Tax Assessor	Dennis DeKlerk
Tax Collector	Susan Costales
Attorney	Peter C. Lange
Building	Frank Robert Perri
Comm Dev/Planning	NA
Engineering	Ray Worrell
Public Works	Douglas A. Cramer
Police Chief	NA
Emerg/Fire Director	Al Freeman

Housing & Construction
Housing Units, 2000*
Total	2,385
Median rent	$761
Median SF home value	$171,700

Permits for New Residential Construction
	Units	Value
Total, 2007	13	$3,682,948
Single family	13	$3,682,948
Total, 2006	11	$2,215,900
Single family	11	$2,215,900

Real Property Valuation, 2007
	Parcels	Valuation
Total	2,859	$727,452,800
Vacant	266	11,627,800
Residential	2,269	674,891,900
Commercial	56	19,572,400
Industrial	3	779,100
Apartments	0	0
Farm land	188	2,736,600
Farm homestead	77	17,845,000

Average Property Value & Tax, 2007
Residential value	$295,284
Property tax	$6,603
Tax credit/rebate	$1,093

Public Library
No public municipal library

Library statistics, 2006
Population served	NA
Full-time/total staff	NA/NA

	Total	Per capita
Holdings	NA	NA
Revenues	NA	NA
Expenditures	NA	NA
Annual visits	NA	NA
Internet terminals/annual users	NA/NA	

Public Safety
Number of officers, 2006	0

Crime	2005	2006
Total crimes	59	73
Violent	8	4
Murder	0	0
Rape	0	0
Robbery	2	0
Aggravated assault	6	4
Non-violent	51	69
Burglary	12	20
Larceny	35	44
Vehicle theft	4	5
Domestic violence	8	9
Arson	3	0
Total crime rate	8.0	9.9
Violent	1.1	0.5
Non-violent	6.9	9.4

Public School District
(for school year 2006-07 except as noted)

Tabernacle Township School District
132 New Rd
Tabernacle, NJ 08088
609-268-0153

Superintendent	Berenice Blum-Bart
Number of schools	2
Grade plan	K-8
Enrollment	895
Attendance rate, '05-06	95.7%
Dropout rate	NA
Students per teacher	11.5
Per pupil expenditure	$13,125
Median faculty salary	$66,655
Median administrator salary	$104,783
Grade 12 enrollment	NA
High school graduation rate	NA

Assessment test results
(percent scoring at proficient or advanced level)
	Language	Math
NJASK-Grade 3	93.8%	93.7%
GEPA-Grade 8	88.2%	75.6%
HSPA-High School	NA	NA

SAT score averages
Pct tested	Math	Verbal	Writing
NA	NA	NA	NA

Teacher Qualifications
Avg. years of experience	20
Highly-qualified teachers one subject/all subjects	100%/100%
With emergency credentials	0.0%

No Child Left Behind
AYP, 2005-06	Meets Standards

Municipal Finance
State Aid Programs, 2008
Total aid	$830,248
CMPTRA	66,289
Energy tax receipts	630,164
Garden State Trust	133,647

General Budget, 2007
Total tax levy	$16,290,705
County levy	3,269,357
County taxes	2,709,108
County library	248,596
County health	0
County open space	311,653
School levy	11,474,563
Muni. levy	1,546,785
Misc. revenues	2,284,461

Taxes	2005	2006	2007
General tax rate per $100	3.656	2.11	2.24
County equalization ratio	64.32	106.72	93.37
Net valuation taxable	$386,982,411	$722,019,900	$728,499,644
State equalized value	$673,364,209	$774,352,395	$837,584,103

Camden County

Tavistock Borough

Demographics & Socio-Economic Characteristics
(2000 US Census, except as noted)

Population
- 1980*....................................9
- 1990*...................................35
- 2000...................................24
  - Male...................................12
  - Female.................................12
- 2006 (estimate)*.......................26
  - Population density................104.0

Race & Hispanic Origin, 2000
Race
- White...................................22
- Black/African American.................2
- American Indian/Alaska Native.........0
- Asian....................................0
- Native Hawaiian/Pacific Islander......0
- Other race..............................0
- Two or more races......................0
- Hispanic origin, total..................0
  - Mexican...............................0
  - Puerto Rican..........................0
  - Cuban.................................0
  - Other Hispanic........................0

Age & Nativity, 2000
- Under 5 years...........................1
- 18 years and over......................15
- 21 years and over......................13
- 65 years and over.......................2
- 85 years and over.......................0
  - Median age.........................38.5
- Native-born............................22
- Foreign-born............................1

Educational Attainment, 2000
- Population 25 years and over............9
- Less than 9th grade..................0.0%
- High school grad or higher..........88.9%
- Bachelor's degree or higher.........33.3%
- Graduate degree.....................22.2%

Income & Poverty, 1999
- Per capita income.................$14,600
- Median household income...........$58,750
- Median family income..............$36,875
- Persons in poverty......................5
- H'holds receiving public assistance....1
- H'holds receiving social security.....1

Households, 2000
- Total households.........................7
  - With persons under 18.................4
  - With persons over 65..................2
  - Family households.....................7
  - Single-person households..............0
- Persons per household................3.43
- Persons per family...................3.43

Labor & Employment
- Total civilian labor force, 2006**....11
  - Unemployment rate.................0.0%
- Total civilian labor force, 2000........9
  - Unemployment rate.................0.0%

Employed persons 16 years and over by occupation, 2000
- Managers & professionals................4
- Service occupations.....................2
- Sales & office occupations..............0
- Farming, fishing & forestry.............0
- Construction & maintenance..............1
- Production & transportation.............2
- Self-employed persons...................4

* US Census Bureau
** New Jersey Department of Labor

See Introduction for an explanation of all data sources.

General Information
Borough of Tavistock
PO Box 8988
Turnersville, NJ 08012
856-429-0039

- Website..................www.tavistocknj.org
- Year of incorporation...................1921
- Land/water area (sq. miles)........0.25/0.00
- Form of government..............Commission

Government

Legislative Districts
- US Congressional........................1
- State Legislative.......................6

Local Officials, 2008
- Mayor....................George Buff III
- Manager...................Theresa Lappe
- Clerk.....................Theresa Lappe
- CFO..................Stephen J. Dringus Jr
- Tax Assessor..............Steven Kessler
- Tax Collector.......Patricia A. McCunney
- Attorney.............Thomas T. Booth Jr
- Building.............................NA
- Planning...............Larry Waetzman
- Engineering........Remington & Vernick
- Public Works........................NA
- Police Chief........................NA
- Fire/Emergency Dir..................NA

Housing & Construction

Housing Units, 2000*
- Total....................................7
- Median rent..........................$675
- Median SF home value............$137,500

Permits for New Residential Construction

	Units	Value
Total, 2007	NA	NA
Single family	NA	NA
Total, 2006	NA	NA
Single family	NA	NA

Real Property Valuation, 2007

	Parcels	Valuation
Total	5	$16,555,200
Vacant	0	0
Residential	3	4,550,000
Commercial	2	12,005,200
Industrial	0	0
Apartments	0	0
Farm land	0	0
Farm homestead	0	0

Average Property Value & Tax, 2007
- Residential value................$1,516,667
- Property tax........................$20,192
- Tax credit/rebate.......................$0

Public Library
No public municipal library

Library statistics, 2006
- Population served......................NA
- Full-time/total staff...............NA/NA

	Total	Per capita
Holdings	NA	NA
Revenues	NA	NA
Expenditures	NA	NA
Annual visits	NA	NA
Internet terminals/annual users	NA/NA	

Taxes	2005	2006	2007
General tax rate per $100	1.396	1.435	1.332
County equalization ratio	100	100	100
Net valuation taxable	$16,557,646	$16,555,200	$16,557,398
State equalized value	$10,201,248	$13,380,078	$14,969,380

Public Safety
Number of officers, 2006................0

Crime	2005	2006
Total crimes	2	0
Violent	0	0
Murder	0	0
Rape	0	0
Robbery	0	0
Aggravated assault	0	0
Non-violent	2	0
Burglary	0	0
Larceny	2	0
Vehicle theft	0	0
Domestic violence	0	0
Arson	0	0
Total crime rate	NA	NA
Violent	NA	NA
Non-violent	NA	NA

Public School District
(for school year 2006-07 except as noted)

Tavistock Borough School District
PO Box 8988
Turnersville, NJ 08012

No schools in district - sends students to Haddonfield Borough schools

- Per pupil expenditure.................NA
- Median faculty salary.................NA
- Median administrator salary..........NA
- Grade 12 enrollment...................NA
- High school graduation rate..........NA

Assessment test results
(percent scoring at proficient or advanced level)

	Language	Math
NJASK-Grade 3	NA	NA
GEPA-Grade 8	NA	NA
HSPA-High School	NA	NA

SAT score averages

Pct tested	Math	Verbal	Writing
NA	NA	NA	NA

Teacher Qualifications
- Avg. years of experience..............NA
- Highly-qualified teachers
  - one subject/all subjects.........NA/NA
- With emergency credentials...........NA

No Child Left Behind
- AYP, 2005-06..........................NA

Municipal Finance

State Aid Programs, 2008
- Total aid..........................$1,309
- CMPTRA..................................0
- Energy tax receipts................1,309
- Garden State Trust......................0

General Budget, 2007
- Total tax levy...................$220,437
  - County levy....................117,482
    - County taxes.................106,718
    - County library................7,429
    - County health.....................0
    - County open space.............3,335
  - School levy.....................12,015
  - Muni. levy......................90,940
- Misc. revenues.....................20,060

The New Jersey Municipal Data Book

Teaneck Township — Bergen County

Demographics & Socio-Economic Characteristics
(2000 US Census, except as noted)

Population
1980*	39,007
1990*	37,825
2000	39,260
Male	18,584
Female	20,676
2006 (estimate)*	39,610
Population density	6,547.1

Race & Hispanic Origin, 2000
Race
White	22,082
Black/African American	11,298
American Indian/Alaska Native	59
Asian	2,798
Native Hawaiian/Pacific Islander	11
Other race	1,633
Two or more races	1,379
Hispanic origin, total	4,103
Mexican	151
Puerto Rican	1,132
Cuban	329
Other Hispanic	2,491

Age & Nativity, 2000
Under 5 years	2,521
18 years and over	29,139
21 years and over	27,538
65 years and over	5,584
85 years and over	826
Median age	38.4
Native-born	29,825
Foreign-born	9,435

Educational Attainment, 2000
Population 25 years and over	26,054
Less than 9th grade	3.6%
High school grad or higher	89.7%
Bachelor's degree or higher	47.9%
Graduate degree	23.0%

Income & Poverty, 1999
Per capita income	$32,212
Median household income	$74,903
Median family income	$84,791
Persons in poverty	1,596
H'holds receiving public assistance	302
H'holds receiving social security	4,020

Households, 2000
Total households	13,418
With persons under 18	5,202
With persons over 65	4,075
Family households	10,071
Single-person households	2,838
Persons per household	2.86
Persons per family	3.34

Labor & Employment
Total civilian labor force, 2006**	20,717
Unemployment rate	3.7%
Total civilian labor force, 2000	20,106
Unemployment rate	4.7%

Employed persons 16 years and over by occupation, 2000
Managers & professionals	10,185
Service occupations	1,794
Sales & office occupations	5,137
Farming, fishing & forestry	0
Construction & maintenance	805
Production & transportation	1,230
Self-employed persons	1,268

* US Census Bureau
** New Jersey Department of Labor

General Information
Township of Teaneck
818 Teaneck Rd
Teaneck, NJ 07666
201-837-4811

Website	www.teanecknjgov.org
Year of incorporation	1895
Land/water area (sq. miles)	6.05/0.20
Form of government	Council-Manager

Government
Legislative Districts
US Congressional	9
State Legislative	37

Local Officials, 2008
Mayor	Elie Y. Katz
Manager	Helene Fall
Clerk	Lissette Aportela-Hernandez (Actg)
Finance Dir	Anthony Bianchi
Tax Assessor	James Tighe
Tax Collector	Milene Quijano
Attorney	Stanley Turitz
Construction Code Official	Steven Gluck
Comm Dev/Planning	NA
Engineering	Charles McKearnin
Public Works	Charles McKearnin
Police Chief	Fred Ahearn
Fire Chief	Robert Montgomery

Housing & Construction
Housing Units, 2000*
Total	13,719
Median rent	$873
Median SF home value	$208,800

Permits for New Residential Construction
	Units	Value
Total, 2007	4	$2,426,389
Single family	4	$2,426,389
Total, 2006	9	$1,812,500
Single family	9	$1,812,500

Real Property Valuation, 2007
	Parcels	Valuation
Total	11,879	$6,075,480,000
Vacant	133	25,474,400
Residential	11,284	5,242,322,900
Commercial	388	561,376,500
Industrial	16	46,853,000
Apartments	58	199,453,200
Farm land	0	0
Farm homestead	0	0

Average Property Value & Tax, 2007
Residential value	$464,580
Property tax	$9,960
Tax credit/rebate	$1,355

Public Library
Teaneck Public Library
840 Teaneck Rd
Teaneck, NJ 07666
201-837-4171

Director: Michael McCue

Library statistics, 2006
Population served	39,260
Full-time/total staff	7/23

	Total	Per capita
Holdings	131,350	3.35
Revenues	$2,538,286	$64.65
Expenditures	$2,538,427	$64.66
Annual visits	385,000	9.81
Internet terminals/annual users	4/35,000	

Public Safety
Number of officers, 2006: 100

Crime
	2005	2006
Total crimes	689	688
Violent	74	65
Murder	1	1
Rape	3	0
Robbery	37	27
Aggravated assault	33	37
Non-violent	615	623
Burglary	114	127
Larceny	446	451
Vehicle theft	55	45
Domestic violence	301	262
Arson	6	9
Total crime rate	17.3	17.4
Violent	1.9	1.6
Non-violent	15.4	15.7

Public School District
(for school year 2006-07 except as noted)

Teaneck School District
1 Merrison St
Teaneck, NJ 07666
201-833-5510

Superintendent	John Czeterko
Number of schools	7
Grade plan	K-12
Enrollment	4,148
Attendance rate, '05-06	95.0%
Dropout rate	1.3%
Students per teacher	10.5
Per pupil expenditure	$17,448
Median faculty salary	$72,629
Median administrator salary	$123,638
Grade 12 enrollment	373
High school graduation rate	97.1%

Assessment test results
(percent scoring at proficient or advanced level)
	Language	Math
NJASK-Grade 3	83.9%	85.7%
GEPA-Grade 8	76.4%	57.3%
HSPA-High School	84.0%	67.0%

SAT score averages
Pct tested	Math	Verbal	Writing
80%	480	468	470

Teacher Qualifications
Avg. years of experience	11
Highly-qualified teachers one subject/all subjects	99.5%/99.5%
With emergency credentials	0.0%

No Child Left Behind
AYP, 2005-06: Meets Standards

Municipal Finance
State Aid Programs, 2008
Total aid	$4,137,506
CMPTRA	1,100,087
Energy tax receipts	3,037,419
Garden State Trust	0

General Budget, 2007
Total tax levy	$130,357,925
County levy	10,425,278
County taxes	9,850,515
County library	0
County health	0
County open space	574,764
School levy	74,190,491
Muni. levy	45,742,156
Misc. revenues	15,199,912

Taxes
	2005	2006	2007
General tax rate per $100	4.38	4.64	2.15
County equalization ratio	58.15	52.37	106.17
Net valuation taxable	$2,636,350,451	$2,651,670,200	$6,080,678,681
State equalized value	$5,034,085,261	$5,690,561,461	$6,142,047,166

Bergen County / *Tenafly Borough*

Demographics & Socio-Economic Characteristics
(2000 US Census, except as noted)

Population
1980*	13,552
1990*	13,326
2000	13,806
Male	6,649
Female	7,157
2006 (estimate)*	14,390
Population density	3,121.5

Race & Hispanic Origin, 2000
Race
White	10,601
Black/African American	132
American Indian/Alaska Native	13
Asian	2,634
Native Hawaiian/Pacific Islander	3
Other race	193
Two or more races	230
Hispanic origin, total	642
Mexican	42
Puerto Rican	99
Cuban	98
Other Hispanic	403

Age & Nativity, 2000
Under 5 years	904
18 years and over	9,900
21 years and over	9,561
65 years and over	2,092
85 years and over	294
Median age	40.9
Native-born	9,862
Foreign-born	3,944

Educational Attainment, 2000
Population 25 years and over	9,173
Less than 9th grade	2.5%
High school grad or higher	93.5%
Bachelor's degree or higher	62.1%
Graduate degree	33.4%

Income & Poverty, 1999
Per capita income	$53,170
Median household income	$90,931
Median family income	$111,029
Persons in poverty	718
H'holds receiving public assistance	50
H'holds receiving social security	1,340

Households, 2000
Total households	4,774
With persons under 18	2,154
With persons over 65	1,399
Family households	3,868
Single-person households	801
Persons per household	2.86
Persons per family	3.21

Labor & Employment
Total civilian labor force, 2006**	6,953
Unemployment rate	3.7%
Total civilian labor force, 2000	6,559
Unemployment rate	3.6%

Employed persons 16 years and over by occupation, 2000
Managers & professionals	3,690
Service occupations	487
Sales & office occupations	1,650
Farming, fishing & forestry	8
Construction & maintenance	172
Production & transportation	314
Self-employed persons	621

* US Census Bureau
** New Jersey Department of Labor

General Information
Borough of Tenafly
100 Riveredge Rd
Tenafly, NJ 07670
201-568-6100

Website	www.tenaflynj.org
Year of incorporation	1894
Land/water area (sq. miles)	4.61/0.58
Form of government	Special Charter

Government
Legislative Districts
US Congressional	5
State Legislative	37

Local Officials, 2008
Mayor	Peter S. Rustin
Manager	Joseph Di Giacomo
Clerk	Nancy Hatten
Finance Dir	Karen Palermo
Tax Assessor	Carol Byrne
Tax Collector	Lily Tom
Attorney	William McClure
Building	Robert Byrnes Sr
Comm Dev/Planning	NA
Engineering	David Hals
Public Works	J. Robert Beutel
Police Chief	Michael Bruno
Emerg/Fire Director	Richard Philpott

Housing & Construction
Housing Units, 2000*
Total	4,897
Median rent	$1,186
Median SF home value	$403,600

Permits for New Residential Construction
	Units	Value
Total, 2007	185	$27,630,217
Single family	27	$11,893,383
Total, 2006	51	$17,698,550
Single family	29	$12,534,550

Real Property Valuation, 2007
	Parcels	Valuation
Total	4,606	$2,960,511,500
Vacant	133	25,324,900
Residential	4,276	2,721,651,500
Commercial	179	177,192,100
Industrial	11	8,507,700
Apartments	7	27,835,300
Farm land	0	0
Farm homestead	0	0

Average Property Value & Tax, 2007
Residential value	$636,495
Property tax	$15,467
Tax credit/rebate	$1,434

Public Library
Tenafly Public Library
100 Riveredge Rd
Tenafly, NJ 07670
201-568-8680

Director: Stephen R. Wechtler

Library statistics, 2006
Population served	13,806
Full-time/total staff	5/10

	Total	Per capita
Holdings	87,822	6.36
Revenues	$1,224,331	$88.68
Expenditures	$1,217,067	$88.15
Annual visits	85,500	6.19
Internet terminals/annual users	9/24,300	

Public Safety
Number of officers, 2006	38

Crime	2005	2006
Total crimes	111	107
Violent	7	1
Murder	0	0
Rape	0	0
Robbery	2	1
Aggravated assault	5	0
Non-violent	104	106
Burglary	20	22
Larceny	77	78
Vehicle theft	7	6
Domestic violence	22	31
Arson	2	2
Total crime rate	7.8	7.5
Violent	0.5	0.1
Non-violent	7.3	7.4

Public School District
(for school year 2006-07 except as noted)

Tenafly School District
500 Tenafly Rd
Tenafly, NJ 07670
201-816-4501

Superintendent	Morton Sherman
Number of schools	6
Grade plan	K-12
Enrollment	3,394
Attendance rate, '05-06	96.5%
Dropout rate	0.2%
Students per teacher	11.0
Per pupil expenditure	$14,857
Median faculty salary	$59,630
Median administrator salary	$130,200
Grade 12 enrollment	220
High school graduation rate	99.5%

Assessment test results
(percent scoring at proficient or advanced level)
	Language	Math
NJASK-Grade 3	97.6%	98.8%
GEPA-Grade 8	92.2%	93.5%
HSPA-High School	96.7%	96.7%

SAT score averages
Pct tested	Math	Verbal	Writing
106%	619	572	570

Teacher Qualifications
Avg. years of experience	9
Highly-qualified teachers one subject/all subjects	99.5%/99.5%
With emergency credentials	0.4%

No Child Left Behind
AYP, 2005-06 .... Meets Standards

Municipal Finance
State Aid Programs, 2008
Total aid	$1,521,138
CMPTRA	186,467
Energy tax receipts	1,334,189
Garden State Trust	482

General Budget, 2007
Total tax levy	$71,967,454
County levy	7,355,876
County taxes	6,950,939
County library	0
County health	0
County open space	404,937
School levy	46,538,389
Muni. levy	18,073,189
Misc. revenues	5,559,785

Taxes	2005	2006	2007
General tax rate per $100	2.15	2.3	2.43
County equalization ratio	93.25	83.24	73.27
Net valuation taxable	$2,876,948,670	$2,907,003,900	$2,961,681,275
State equalized value	$3,456,209,358	$3,968,812,048	$4,133,076,963

See Introduction for an explanation of all data sources.

Teterboro Borough
Bergen County

Demographics & Socio-Economic Characteristics
(2000 US Census, except as noted)

Population
1980*	19
1990*	22
2000	18
Male	9
Female	9
2006 (estimate)*	18
Population density	16.2

Race & Hispanic Origin, 2000
Race
White	15
Black/African American	0
American Indian/Alaska Native	0
Asian	0
Native Hawaiian/Pacific Islander	0
Other race	0
Two or more races	3
Hispanic origin, total	0
Mexican	0
Puerto Rican	0
Cuban	0
Other Hispanic	0

Age & Nativity, 2000
Under 5 years	3
18 years and over	12
21 years and over	11
65 years and over	1
85 years and over	0
Median age	33.0
Native-born	16
Foreign-born	0

Educational Attainment, 2000
Population 25 years and over	10
Less than 9th grade	0.0%
High school grad or higher	100.0%
Bachelor's degree or higher	50.0%
Graduate degree	0.0%

Income & Poverty, 1999
Per capita income	$72,613
Median household income	$44,167
Median family income	$43,750
Persons in poverty	0
H'holds receiving public assistance	0
H'holds receiving social security	3

Households, 2000
Total households	7
With persons under 18	3
With persons over 65	1
Family households	5
Single-person households	1
Persons per household	2.57
Persons per family	3.00

Labor & Employment
Total civilian labor force, 2006**	21
Unemployment rate	0.0%
Total civilian labor force, 2000	13
Unemployment rate	0.0%

Employed persons 16 years and over by occupation, 2000
Managers & professionals	3
Service occupations	0
Sales & office occupations	6
Farming, fishing & forestry	0
Construction & maintenance	4
Production & transportation	0
Self-employed persons	0

* US Census Bureau
** New Jersey Department of Labor

General Information
Borough of Teterboro
510 Route 46 W
Municipal Building
Teterboro, NJ 07608
201-288-1200

Website	NA
Year of incorporation	1917
Land/water area (sq. miles)	1.11/0.00
Form of government	Municipal Mgr 1923

Government
Legislative Districts
US Congressional	9
State Legislative	38

Local Officials, 2008
Mayor	John Watt
Manager	Paul Busch
Clerk	Nadine Conn
Finance Dir.	Rosemary McClave
Tax Assessor	James Hall
Tax Collector	Marion Semken
Attorney	David Bole
Building	Joseph Marra
Comm Dev/Planning	NA
Engineering	Boswell McClave
Public Works	John Fantacone
Police Chief	NA
Fire/Emergency Dir.	NA

Housing & Construction
Housing Units, 2000*
Total	8
Median rent	$738
Median SF home value	NA

Permits for New Residential Construction
	Units	Value
Total, 2007	0	$0
Single family	0	$0
Total, 2006	0	$0
Single family	0	$0

Real Property Valuation, 2007
	Parcels	Valuation
Total	83	$327,547,686
Vacant	7	930,600
Residential	7	1,080,700
Commercial	9	4,761,403
Industrial	59	319,750,783
Apartments	1	1,024,200
Farm land	0	0
Farm homestead	0	0

Average Property Value & Tax, 2007
Residential value	$154,386
Property tax	$1,664
Tax credit/rebate	$0

Public Library
No public municipal library

Library statistics, 2006
Population served	NA
Full-time/total staff	NA/NA

	Total	Per capita
Holdings	NA	NA
Revenues	NA	NA
Expenditures	NA	NA
Annual visits	NA	NA
Internet terminals/annual users	NA/NA	

Taxes
	2005	2006	2007
General tax rate per $100	1	1.01	1.08
County equalization ratio	113.11	93.29	80.53
Net valuation taxable	$314,726,170	$314,313,226	$328,200,779
State equalized value	$337,363,244	$495,505,736	$470,997,272

Public Safety
Number of officers, 2006		0

Crime	2005	2006
Total crimes	18	31
Violent	0	4
Murder	0	0
Rape	0	0
Robbery	0	0
Aggravated assault	0	4
Non-violent	18	27
Burglary	3	1
Larceny	7	24
Vehicle theft	8	2
Domestic violence	1	3
Arson	0	0
Total crime rate	NA	NA
Violent	NA	NA
Non-violent	NA	NA

Public School District
(for school year 2006-07 except as noted)

Teterboro School District
Municipal Building, Route 46
Teterboro, NJ 07608

No schools in district

Per pupil expenditure	NA
Median faculty salary	NA
Median administrator salary	NA
Grade 12 enrollment	NA
High school graduation rate	NA

Assessment test results
(percent scoring at proficient or advanced level)
	Language	Math
NJASK-Grade 3	NA	NA
GEPA-Grade 8	NA	NA
HSPA-High School	NA	NA

SAT score averages
Pct tested	Math	Verbal	Writing
NA	NA	NA	NA

Teacher Qualifications
Avg. years of experience	NA
Highly-qualified teachers one subject/all subjects	NA/NA
With emergency credentials	NA

No Child Left Behind
AYP, 2005-06	NA

Municipal Finance
State Aid Programs, 2008
Total aid	$123,717
CMPTRA	0
Energy tax receipts	123,717
Garden State Trust	0

General Budget, 2007
Total tax levy	$3,536,596
County levy	769,542
County taxes	727,091
County library	0
County health	0
County open space	42,451
School levy	99,129
Muni. levy	2,667,925
Misc. revenues	1,934,795

Hunterdon County
Tewksbury Township

Demographics & Socio-Economic Characteristics
(2000 US Census, except as noted)

Population
- 1980*..................................4,094
- 1990*..................................4,803
- 2000..................................5,541
  - Male..................................2,729
  - Female..................................2,812
- 2006 (estimate)*..................................6,088
  - Population density..................................192.5

Race & Hispanic Origin, 2000
Race
- White..................................5,365
- Black/African American..................................29
- American Indian/Alaska Native..................................0
- Asian..................................104
- Native Hawaiian/Pacific Islander..................................0
- Other race..................................15
- Two or more races..................................28
- Hispanic origin, total..................................85
  - Mexican..................................8
  - Puerto Rican..................................16
  - Cuban..................................15
  - Other Hispanic..................................46

Age & Nativity, 2000
- Under 5 years..................................373
- 18 years and over..................................4,091
- 21 years and over..................................3,989
- 65 years and over..................................623
- 85 years and over..................................43
  - Median age..................................42.6
- Native-born..................................5,268
- Foreign-born..................................273

Educational Attainment, 2000
- Population 25 years and over..................................3,886
- Less than 9th grade..................................1.7%
- High school grad or higher..................................95.7%
- Bachelor's degree or higher..................................58.9%
- Graduate degree..................................25.6%

Income & Poverty, 1999
- Per capita income..................................$65,470
- Median household income..................................$135,649
- Median family income..................................$150,189
- Persons in poverty..................................152
- H'holds receiving public assistance..................................0
- H'holds receiving social security..................................441

Households, 2000
- Total households..................................1,986
  - With persons under 18..................................747
  - With persons over 65..................................441
  - Family households..................................1,663
  - Single-person households..................................249
- Persons per household..................................2.79
- Persons per family..................................3.05

Labor & Employment
- Total civilian labor force, 2006**..................................3,152
  - Unemployment rate..................................2.4%
- Total civilian labor force, 2000..................................2,814
  - Unemployment rate..................................1.8%

Employed persons 16 years and over by occupation, 2000
- Managers & professionals..................................1,814
- Service occupations..................................193
- Sales & office occupations..................................559
- Farming, fishing & forestry..................................28
- Construction & maintenance..................................98
- Production & transportation..................................71
- Self-employed persons..................................382

* US Census Bureau
** New Jersey Department of Labor

See Introduction for an explanation of all data sources.

General Information
Township of Tewksbury
169 Old Turnpike Rd
Califon, NJ 07830
908-439-0022

- Website..................................www.tewksburytwp.net
- Year of incorporation..................................1755
- Land/water area (sq. miles)..................................31.63/0.02
- Form of government..................................Township

Government
Legislative Districts
- US Congressional..................................7
- State Legislative..................................24

Local Officials, 2008
- Mayor..................................William J. Voyce
- Manager..................................Jesse W. Landon
- Clerk..................................Roberta A. Brassard
- Finance Dir..................................Judie A. McGrorey
- Tax Assessor..................................Ann Marie Obiedzinski
- Tax Collector..................................Kay Winzenried
- Attorney..................................Michael S. Selvaggi
- Building..................................Charles Rogers
- Comm Dev/Planning..................................NA
- Engineering..................................Andrew Holt
- Public Works..................................Hayden Hull
- Police Chief..................................Russel O'Dell
- Emerg/Fire Director..................................Peter Melick

Housing & Construction
Housing Units, 2000*
- Total..................................2,052
- Median rent..................................$1,388
- Median SF home value..................................$461,200

Permits for New Residential Construction

	Units	Value
Total, 2007	13	$9,483,550
Single family	13	$9,483,550
Total, 2006	26	$6,003,313
Single family	7	$5,749,850

Real Property Valuation, 2007

	Parcels	Valuation
Total	3,034	$1,341,220,700
Vacant	159	14,424,900
Residential	1,920	1,040,886,800
Commercial	41	58,749,700
Industrial	1	2,733,000
Apartments	0	0
Farm land	568	3,638,400
Farm homestead	345	220,787,900

Average Property Value & Tax, 2007
- Residential value..................................$557,031
- Property tax..................................$12,432
- Tax credit/rebate..................................$1,331

Public Library
Tewksbury Township Library
31 Old Turnpike Rd
Oldwick, NJ 08858
908-439-3761

- Director..................................Judie Garey

Library statistics, 2006
- Population served..................................5,541
- Full-time/total staff..................................NA/0

	Total	Per capita
Holdings	NA	NA
Revenues	NA	NA
Expenditures	NA	NA
Annual visits	NA	NA
Internet terminals/annual users	NA/NA	

Taxes

	2005	2006	2007
General tax rate per $100	2.2	2.22	2.24
County equalization ratio	79.58	73.48	67.93
Net valuation taxable	$1,299,362,841	$1,320,803,900	$1,343,168,486
State equalized value	$1,650,823,073	$1,811,217,692	$1,872,287,627

Public Safety
Number of officers, 2006..................................11

Crime	2005	2006
Total crimes	28	37
Violent	1	3
Murder	0	0
Rape	0	1
Robbery	0	0
Aggravated assault	1	2
Non-violent	27	34
Burglary	2	11
Larceny	4	21
Vehicle theft	0	2
Domestic violence	1	8
Arson	0	0
Total crime rate	4.7	6.1
Violent	0.2	0.5
Non-violent	4.5	5.6

Public School District
(for school year 2006-07 except as noted)

Tewksbury Township School District
173 Old Turnpike Rd
Califon, NJ 07830
908-439-2010

- Superintendent..................................Gayle Carrick
- Number of schools..................................2
- Grade plan..................................K-8
- Enrollment..................................768
- Attendance rate, '05-06..................................96.1%
- Dropout rate..................................NA
- Students per teacher..................................10.3
- Per pupil expenditure..................................$14,441
- Median faculty salary..................................$54,495
- Median administrator salary..................................$101,963
- Grade 12 enrollment..................................NA
- High school graduation rate..................................NA

Assessment test results
(percent scoring at proficient or advanced level)

	Language	Math
NJASK-Grade 3	93.5%	100.0%
GEPA-Grade 8	88.0%	93.4%
HSPA-High School	NA	NA

SAT score averages

Pct tested	Math	Verbal	Writing
NA	NA	NA	NA

Teacher Qualifications
- Avg. years of experience..................................13
- Highly-qualified teachers
  - one subject/all subjects..................................100%/100%
- With emergency credentials..................................0.0%

No Child Left Behind
- AYP, 2005-06..................................Meets Standards

Municipal Finance
State Aid Programs, 2008
- Total aid..................................$681,494
  - CMPTRA..................................50,218
  - Energy tax receipts..................................630,848
  - Garden State Trust..................................428

General Budget, 2007
- Total tax levy..................................$29,976,869
  - County levy..................................6,574,109
    - County taxes..................................5,501,841
    - County library..................................478,777
    - County health..................................0
    - County open space..................................593,491
  - School levy..................................18,545,829
  - Muni. levy..................................4,856,931
- Misc. revenues..................................6,142,971

Tinton Falls Borough
Monmouth County

Demographics & Socio-Economic Characteristics
(2000 US Census, except as noted)

Population
1980*	7,740
1990*	12,361
2000	15,053
Male	7,157
Female	7,896
2006 (estimate)*	17,082
Population density	1,095.7

Race & Hispanic Origin, 2000
Race
- White: 11,862
- Black/African American: 1,963
- American Indian/Alaska Native: 36
- Asian: 747
- Native Hawaiian/Pacific Islander: 2
- Other race: 157
- Two or more races: 286

Hispanic origin, total: 707
- Mexican: 122
- Puerto Rican: 305
- Cuban: 49
- Other Hispanic: 231

Age & Nativity, 2000
- Under 5 years: 1,184
- 18 years and over: 11,215
- 21 years and over: 10,908
- 65 years and over: 1,633
- 85 years and over: 203
- Median age: 36.8
- Native-born: 13,557
- Foreign-born: 1,498

Educational Attainment, 2000
- Population 25 years and over: 10,457
- Less than 9th grade: 1.9%
- High school grad or higher: 92.7%
- Bachelor's degree or higher: 42.3%
- Graduate degree: 14.5%

Income & Poverty, 1999
- Per capita income: $31,520
- Median household income: $68,697
- Median family income: $79,773
- Persons in poverty: 577
- H'holds receiving public assistance: 61
- H'holds receiving social security: 1,173

Households, 2000
- Total households: 5,883
- With persons under 18: 2,145
- With persons over 65: 1,122
- Family households: 3,977
- Single-person households: 1,602
- Persons per household: 2.51
- Persons per family: 3.11

Labor & Employment
- Total civilian labor force, 2006**: 8,697
- Unemployment rate: 4.1%
- Total civilian labor force, 2000: 8,088
- Unemployment rate: 4.1%

Employed persons 16 years and over by occupation, 2000
- Managers & professionals: 3,570
- Service occupations: 869
- Sales & office occupations: 2,396
- Farming, fishing & forestry: 22
- Construction & maintenance: 376
- Production & transportation: 524
- Self-employed persons: 386

* US Census Bureau
** New Jersey Department of Labor

General Information
Borough of Tinton Falls
556 Tinton Ave
Tinton Falls, NJ 07724
732-542-3400

- Website: www.tintonfalls.com
- Year of incorporation: 1976
- Land/water area (sq. miles): 15.59/0.03
- Form of government: Mayor-Council

Government
Legislative Districts
- US Congressional: 12
- State Legislative: 12

Local Officials, 2008
- Mayor: Peter Maclearie
- Manager: W. Bryan Dempsey
- Clerk: Karen Mount-Taylor
- Finance Dir: Stephen Pfeffer
- Tax Assessor: Scott Imbriaco
- Tax Collector: Carol Hussey
- Attorney: James E. Berube Jr
- Building: Robert Corby
- Planning: W. Bryan Dempsey
- Engineering: Birdsall Engineering
- Public Works: John Bucciero
- Police Chief: Gerald M. Turning Sr
- Fire/Emergency Dir: NA

Housing & Construction
Housing Units, 2000*
- Total: 6,211
- Median rent: $1,198
- Median SF home value: $187,900

Permits for New Residential Construction
	Units	Value
Total, 2007	283	$23,178,339
Single family	59	$9,910,074
Total, 2006	154	$14,021,805
Single family	58	$8,408,963

Real Property Valuation, 2007
	Parcels	Valuation
Total	7,066	$1,279,158,300
Vacant	808	41,155,900
Residential	6,033	930,617,300
Commercial	153	191,731,300
Industrial	16	15,274,600
Apartments	3	97,242,400
Farm land	35	198,100
Farm homestead	18	2,938,700

Average Property Value & Tax, 2007
- Residential value: $154,281
- Property tax: $5,681
- Tax credit/rebate: $980

Public Library
Tinton Falls Public Library
664 Tinton Ave
Tinton Falls, NJ 07724
732-542-3110

Director: Rosemary Tunnicliffe

Library statistics, 2006
- Population served: 15,053
- Full-time/total staff: 0/1

	Total	Per capita
Holdings	46,702	3.10
Revenues	$146,221	$9.71
Expenditures	$137,316	$9.12
Annual visits	32,795	2.18
Internet terminals/annual users	2/1,700	

Taxes
	2005	2006	2007
General tax rate per $100	3.416	3.59	3.683
County equalization ratio	55.68	49.74	43.01
Net valuation taxable	$1,245,289,313	$1,259,348,700	$1,280,603,288
State equalized value	$2,503,597,332	$2,929,583,421	$3,226,755,881

Public Safety
Number of officers, 2006: 41

Crime	2005	2006
Total crimes	304	334
Violent	13	17
Murder	0	0
Rape	1	3
Robbery	4	7
Aggravated assault	8	7
Non-violent	291	317
Burglary	54	49
Larceny	210	252
Vehicle theft	27	16
Domestic violence	121	162
Arson	2	0
Total crime rate	18.8	19.3
Violent	0.8	1.0
Non-violent	18.0	18.4

Public School District
(for school year 2006-07 except as noted)

Tinton Falls School District
658 Tinton Ave
Tinton Falls, NJ 07724
732-460-2404

- Superintendent: Richard J. Wesler (Int)
- Number of schools: 6
- Grade plan: K-8
- Enrollment: 1,576
- Attendance rate, '05-06: 95.6%
- Dropout rate: NA
- Students per teacher: 10.7
- Per pupil expenditure: $14,982
- Median faculty salary: $53,865
- Median administrator salary: $103,154
- Grade 12 enrollment: NA
- High school graduation rate: NA

Assessment test results
(percent scoring at proficient or advanced level)
	Language	Math
NJASK-Grade 3	88.7%	96.3%
GEPA-Grade 8	84.6%	79.0%
HSPA-High School	NA	NA

SAT score averages
Pct tested	Math	Verbal	Writing
NA	NA	NA	NA

Teacher Qualifications
- Avg. years of experience: 12
- Highly-qualified teachers one subject/all subjects: 100%/100%
- With emergency credentials: 0.0%

No Child Left Behind
- AYP, 2005-06: Meets Standards

Municipal Finance
State Aid Programs, 2008
- Total aid: $1,917,404
- CMPTRA: 266,071
- Energy tax receipts: 1,651,115
- Garden State Trust: 218

General Budget, 2007
- Total tax levy: $47,152,414
- County levy: 8,030,509
- County taxes: 7,171,802
- County library: 410,564
- County health: 0
- County open space: 448,143
- School levy: 29,074,106
- Muni. levy: 10,047,799
- Misc. revenues: 10,252,470

Ocean County   Toms River Township

Demographics & Socio-Economic Characteristics[†]
(2000 US Census, except as noted)

Population
- 1980*..................................64,455
- 1990*..................................76,371
- 2000..................................89,706
  - Male................................43,160
  - Female..............................46,546
- 2006 (estimate)*.......................94,889
- Population density...................2,316.1

Race & Hispanic Origin, 2000
Race
- White..................................83,939
- Black/African American..................1,568
- American Indian/Alaska Native.............117
- Asian...................................2,207
- Native Hawaiian/Pacific Islander...........21
- Other race...............................850
- Two or more races......................1,004
- Hispanic origin, total..................4,070
  - Mexican................................720
  - Puerto Rican.........................1,764
  - Cuban..................................326
  - Other Hispanic.......................1,260

Age & Nativity, 2000
- Under 5 years..........................4,956
- 18 years and over.....................68,815
- 21 years and over.....................65,852
- 65 years and over.....................15,464
- 85 years and over......................1,708
- Median age..............................40.2
- Native-born...........................83,513
- Foreign-born...........................6,254

Educational Attainment, 2000
- Population 25 years and over..........62,453
- Less than 9th grade.....................3.2%
- High school grad or higher.............86.2%
- Bachelor's degree or higher............23.8%
- Graduate degree.........................8.0%

Income & Poverty, 1999
- Per capita income....................$25,010
- Median household income..............$54,776
- Median family income.................$62,561
- Persons in poverty.....................4,988
- H'holds receiving public assistance......608
- H'holds receiving social security.....11,254

Households, 2000
- Total households......................33,510
  - With persons under 18...............11,247
  - With persons over 65................10,409
  - Family households...................24,427
  - Single-person households.............7,619
- Persons per household...................2.62
- Persons per family......................3.09

Labor & Employment
- Total civilian labor force, 2006**....48,657
  - Unemployment rate.....................5.5%
- Total civilian labor force, 2000......43,541
  - Unemployment rate.....................4.6%

Employed persons 16 years and over by occupation, 2000
- Managers & professionals..............14,278
- Service occupations....................6,463
- Sales & office occupations............12,729
- Farming, fishing & forestry...............39
- Construction & maintenance.............4,206
- Production & transportation............3,831
- Self-employed persons..................2,373

† see Appendix C for American Community Survey data
‡ Branch of county library
* US Census Bureau
** New Jersey Department of Labor
§ State Fiscal Year July 1–June 30

See Introduction for an explanation of all data sources.

General Information
Township of Toms River
(formerly Dover Township)
33 Washington St
Toms River, NJ 08753
732-341-1000

- Website..........www.townshipofdover.com
- Year of incorporation.................1768
- Land/water area (sq. miles).....40.97/11.96
- Form of government..........Mayor-Council

Government
Legislative Districts
- US Congressional.........................3
- State Legislative.......................10

Local Officials, 2008
- Mayor...................Thomas Kelaher
- Business Admin........Robert Chankalian
- Clerk......................J. Mark Mutter
- Finance Dir............Christine Manolio
- Tax Assessor.............Glenn Seelhorst
- Tax Collector............Kathleen Adams
- Attorney.................Mark Troncone
- Building.................Pramod Pathak
- Comm Dev/Planning..................NA
- Engineering..............Frank Sadeghi
- Public Works.............Louis Amoruso
- Police Chief.........Michael Mastronardy
- Emerg/Fire Director.......John Lightbody

Housing & Construction
Housing Units, 2000*
- Total..............................41,116
- Median rent...........................$789
- Median SF home value............$149,900

Permits for New Residential Construction
	Units	Value
Total, 2007	450	$37,181,506
Single family	184	$24,063,756
Total, 2006	244	$39,748,316
Single family	244	$39,748,316

Real Property Valuation, 2007
	Parcels	Valuation
Total	41,160	$6,398,433,100
Vacant	1,632	129,449,300
Residential	37,881	5,218,276,300
Commercial	1,530	904,404,800
Industrial	44	54,448,300
Apartments	36	89,225,500
Farm land	22	100,600
Farm homestead	15	2,528,300

Average Property Value & Tax, 2007
- Residential value..................$137,767
- Property tax..........................$4,216
- Tax credit/rebate......................$882

Public Library
Toms River Branch Library[‡]
101 Washington St
Toms River, NJ 08753
732-349-6300

- Branch Librarian............Diane Tralka

Library statistics, 2006
see Ocean County profile
for library system statistics

Taxes
	2005	2006	2007
General tax rate per $100	2.975	3.052	3.061
County equalization ratio	51.43	44.23	38.71
Net valuation taxable	$6,291,172,914	$6,345,008,300	$6,413,452,768
State equalized value	$14,223,768,741	$16,407,971,572	$17,123,129,561

Public Safety
Number of officers, 2006..............165

Crime	2005	2006
Total crimes	1,984	2,075
Violent	133	112
Murder	2	0
Rape	9	12
Robbery	42	44
Aggravated assault	80	56
Non-violent	1,851	1,963
Burglary	316	312
Larceny	1,463	1,552
Vehicle theft	72	99
Domestic violence	733	698
Arson	13	17
Total crime rate	21.0	21.9
Violent	1.4	1.2
Non-violent	19.6	20.7

Public School District
(for school year 2006-07 except as noted)

Toms River Regional School District
1144 Hooper Ave
Toms River, NJ 08753
732-505-5510

- Superintendent..........Michael J. Ritacco
- Number of schools.........................72
- Grade plan..............................K-12
- Enrollment............................17,631
- Attendance rate, '05-06................93.5%
- Dropout rate...........................3.5%
- Students per teacher....................13.3
- Per pupil expenditure................$10,065
- Median faculty salary................$47,174
- Median administrator salary.........$111,050
- Grade 12 enrollment...................1,315
- High school graduation rate............NA

Assessment test results
(percent scoring at proficient or advanced level)

	Language	Math
NJASK-Grade 3	94.0%	95.0%
GEPA-Grade 8	81.0%	73.6%
HSPA-High School	87.0%	70.9%

SAT score averages
Pct tested	Math	Verbal	Writing
NA	NA	NA	NA

Teacher Qualifications
- Avg. years of experience................9
- Highly-qualified teachers
  - one subject/all subjects.....99.5%/99.0%
- With emergency credentials............0.0%

No Child Left Behind
- AYP, 2005-06............Meets Standards

Municipal Finance[§]
State Aid Programs, 2008
- Total aid.....................$10,918,744
- CMPTRA....................1,943,889
- Energy tax receipts...........8,973,283
- Garden State Trust...............1,572

General Budget, 2007
- Total tax levy.............$196,287,738
- County levy................51,513,661
  - County taxes.............42,449,776
  - County library............5,031,009
  - County health.............2,038,301
  - County open space........1,994,575
- School levy...............101,178,817
- Muni. levy.................43,595,260
- Misc. revenues.............37,211,940

©2008 Information Publications, Inc. All rights reserved. Photocopying prohibited. For additional copies, contact the publisher at www.informationpublications.com or (877)544-INFO (4636)

Totowa Borough
Passaic County

Demographics & Socio-Economic Characteristics
(2000 US Census, except as noted)

Population
1980*	11,448
1990*	10,177
2000	9,892
Male	4,672
Female	5,220
2006 (estimate)*	10,634
Population density	2,658.5

Race & Hispanic Origin, 2000
Race
White	9,239
Black/African American	111
American Indian/Alaska Native	2
Asian	224
Native Hawaiian/Pacific Islander	0
Other race	195
Two or more races	121
Hispanic origin, total	630
Mexican	5
Puerto Rican	253
Cuban	30
Other Hispanic	342

Age & Nativity, 2000
Under 5 years	444
18 years and over	8,085
21 years and over	7,808
65 years and over	2,113
85 years and over	257
Median age	42.7
Native-born	8,533
Foreign-born	1,313

Educational Attainment, 2000
Population 25 years and over	7,402
Less than 9th grade	11.9%
High school grad or higher	74.7%
Bachelor's degree or higher	17.8%
Graduate degree	4.1%

Income & Poverty, 1999
Per capita income	$26,561
Median household income	$60,408
Median family income	$69,354
Persons in poverty	398
H'holds receiving public assistance	0
H'holds receiving social security	1,369

Households, 2000
Total households	3,539
With persons under 18	1,028
With persons over 65	1,385
Family households	2,645
Single-person households	770
Persons per household	2.63
Persons per family	3.09

Labor & Employment
Total civilian labor force, 2006**	5,250
Unemployment rate	3.1%
Total civilian labor force, 2000	5,129
Unemployment rate	3.5%

Employed persons 16 years and over by occupation, 2000
Managers & professionals	1,330
Service occupations	702
Sales & office occupations	1,544
Farming, fishing & forestry	0
Construction & maintenance	539
Production & transportation	832
Self-employed persons	188

* US Census Bureau
** New Jersey Department of Labor

General Information
Borough of Totowa
537 Totowa Rd
Totowa, NJ 07512
973-956-1000

Website	www.totowanj.org
Year of incorporation	1898
Land/water area (sq. miles)	4.00/0.05
Form of government	Borough

Government
Legislative Districts
US Congressional	8
State Legislative	35

Local Officials, 2008
Mayor	John Coiro
Manager/Admin	NA
Clerk	Joseph Wassel
Finance Dir	J. Iandiorio
Tax Assessor	Curt Masklee
Tax Collector	Elaine Raddin
Attorney	Kristin M. Corrado
Building	Allan Burghardt
Comm Dev/Planning	NA
Engineering	Alaimo Group
Public Works	Doug Wright
Police Chief	Robert Coyle
Emerg/Fire Director	Larry Sperling

Housing & Construction
Housing Units, 2000*
Total	3,630
Median rent	$935
Median SF home value	$197,500

Permits for New Residential Construction
	Units	Value
Total, 2007	34	$6,310,224
Single family	34	$6,310,224
Total, 2006	47	$8,214,455
Single family	47	$8,214,455

Real Property Valuation, 2007
	Parcels	Valuation
Total	3,802	$1,171,716,200
Vacant	89	12,383,700
Residential	3,426	656,148,500
Commercial	221	312,149,700
Industrial	64	190,153,000
Apartments	0	0
Farm land	1	500
Farm homestead	1	550,800

Average Property Value & Tax, 2007
Residential value	$191,710
Property tax	$6,513
Tax credit/rebate	$1,062

Public Library
Dwight D. Eisenhower Library
537 Totowa Rd
Totowa, NJ 07512
973-790-3265

Director ... Joan A. Krautheim

Library statistics, 2006
Population served	9,892
Full-time/total staff	2/5

	Total	Per capita
Holdings	54,843	5.54
Revenues	$718,804	$72.67
Expenditures	$629,255	$63.61
Annual visits	47,692	4.82
Internet terminals/annual users	11/8,433	

Taxes
	2005	2006	2007
General tax rate per $100	3.09	3.21	3.4
County equalization ratio	59.68	56.04	50.95
Net valuation taxable	$1,176,878,670	$1,188,302,800	$1,173,139,182
State equalized value	$2,100,069,004	$2,333,856,557	$2,322,112,624

Public Safety
Number of officers, 2006	27

Crime	2005	2006
Total crimes	273	337
Violent	10	9
Murder	1	0
Rape	0	0
Robbery	1	6
Aggravated assault	8	3
Non-violent	263	328
Burglary	27	53
Larceny	210	235
Vehicle theft	26	40
Domestic violence	18	17
Arson	0	0
Total crime rate	26.4	31.8
Violent	1.0	0.8
Non-violent	25.4	31.0

Public School District
(for school year 2006-07 except as noted)

Totowa School District
10 Crews St
Totowa, NJ 07512
973-956-0010

Chief School Admin	Vincent Varcadipane
Number of schools	2
Grade plan	K-8
Enrollment	993
Attendance rate, '05-06	96.0%
Dropout rate	NA
Students per teacher	11.3
Per pupil expenditure	$13,702
Median faculty salary	$55,949
Median administrator salary	$107,494
Grade 12 enrollment	NA
High school graduation rate	NA

Assessment test results
(percent scoring at proficient or advanced level)
	Language	Math
NJASK-Grade 3	84.6%	84.7%
GEPA-Grade 8	76.1%	78.1%
HSPA-High School	NA	NA

SAT score averages
Pct tested	Math	Verbal	Writing
NA	NA	NA	NA

Teacher Qualifications
Avg. years of experience	8
Highly-qualified teachers one subject/all subjects	100%/100%
With emergency credentials	0.0%

No Child Left Behind
AYP, 2005-06 ... Meets Standards

Municipal Finance
State Aid Programs, 2008
Total aid	$1,721,595
CMPTRA	329,673
Energy tax receipts	1,391,922
Garden State Trust	0

General Budget, 2007
Total tax levy	$39,856,512
County levy	11,391,676
County taxes	11,160,028
County library	0
County health	0
County open space	231,648
School levy	18,989,821
Muni. levy	9,475,015
Misc. revenues	5,362,394

Mercer County

Trenton City

Demographics & Socio-Economic Characteristics[†]
(2000 US Census, except as noted)

Population
1980*	92,124
1990*	88,675
2000	85,403
Male	42,180
Female	43,223
2006 (estimate)*	83,923
Population density	10,956.0

Race & Hispanic Origin, 2000
Race
- White 27,802
- Black/African American 44,465
- American Indian/Alaska Native 300
- Asian 716
- Native Hawaiian/Pacific Islander 199
- Other race 9,190
- Two or more races 2,731
- Hispanic origin, total 18,391
  - Mexican 925
  - Puerto Rican 8,952
  - Cuban 200
  - Other Hispanic 8,314

Age & Nativity, 2000
- Under 5 years 6,468
- 18 years and over 61,757
- 21 years and over 58,165
- 65 years and over 9,716
- 85 years and over 1,201
- Median age 32.2
- Native-born 73,234
- Foreign-born 12,024

Educational Attainment, 2000
- Population 25 years and over 53,021
- Less than 9th grade 12.2%
- High school grad or higher 62.4%
- Bachelor's degree or higher 9.2%
- Graduate degree 3.5%

Income & Poverty, 1999
- Per capita income $14,621
- Median household income $31,074
- Median family income $36,681
- Persons in poverty 17,222
- H'holds receiving public assistance ... 2,255
- H'holds receiving social security 7,836

Households, 2000
- Total households 29,437
  - With persons under 18 11,659
  - With persons over 65 7,490
  - Family households 18,695
  - Single-person households 8,756
- Persons per household 2.75
- Persons per family 3.38

Labor & Employment
- Total civilian labor force, 2006** 39,915
  - Unemployment rate 10.7%
- Total civilian labor force, 2000 36,283
  - Unemployment rate 10.5%

Employed persons 16 years and over by occupation, 2000
- Managers & professionals 6,980
- Service occupations 8,390
- Sales & office occupations 8,973
- Farming, fishing & forestry 99
- Construction & maintenance 2,731
- Production & transportation 5,297
- Self-employed persons 936

[†] see Appendix C for American Community Survey data
* US Census Bureau
** New Jersey Department of Labor
§ State Fiscal Year July 1–June 30

See Introduction for an explanation of all data sources.

General Information
City of Trenton
319 E State St
Trenton, NJ 08608
609-989-3185

- Website .... www.trentonnj.org
- Year of incorporation 1792
- Land/water area (sq. miles) 7.66/0.49
- Form of government .... Mayor-Council

Government

Legislative Districts
- US Congressional 4, 12
- State Legislative 15

Local Officials, 2008
- Mayor .... Douglas H. Palmer
- Manager .... Jane Feigenbaum
- Clerk .... Juanita M. Joyner (Actg)
- Finance Dir .... Ronald Zilinski
- Tax Assessor .... Patricia Hice
- Tax Collector .... Ed Kirkendall
- Attorney .... R. Denise Lyles
- Building .... Leonard Pucciatti
- Planning .... Andrew Carten
- Engineering .... Sean Semple
- Public Works .... Eric Jackson
- Police Chief .... Joseph Santiago
- Emerg/Fire Director .... Henry Gliottone Jr (Actg)

Housing & Construction

Housing Units, 2000*
- Total 33,843
- Median rent $604
- Median SF home value $65,500

Permits for New Residential Construction
	Units	Value
Total, 2007	233	$25,205,960
Single family	13	$3,829,800
Total, 2006	5	$546,600
Single family	5	$546,600

Real Property Valuation, 2007
	Parcels	Valuation
Total	24,607	$1,950,196,475
Vacant	1,113	18,350,710
Residential	21,111	1,314,322,040
Commercial	2,135	530,827,025
Industrial	89	43,104,900
Apartments	159	43,591,800
Farm land	0	0
Farm homestead	0	0

Average Property Value & Tax, 2007
- Residential value $62,258
- Property tax $2,603
- Tax credit/rebate $743

Public Library
Trenton Public Library
120 Academy St
Trenton, NJ 08608
609-392-7188

- Director .... Larry Kroah (Asst)

Library statistics, 2006
- Population served 85,403
- Full-time/total staff 15/46

	Total	Per capita
Holdings	437,534	5.12
Revenues	$3,839,733	$44.96
Expenditures	$3,820,630	$44.74
Annual visits	481,448	5.64
Internet terminals/annual users	98/118,790	

Taxes
	2005	2006	2007
General tax rate per $100	4.06	4.1	4.19
County equalization ratio	94.59	82.25	68.32
Net valuation taxable	$1,918,990,947	$1,939,226,395	$1,963,159,141
State equalized value	$2,333,119,692	$2,853,742,822	$3,145,808,409

Public Safety
- Number of officers, 2006 359

Crime
	2005	2006
Total crimes	5,265	3,895
Violent	1,526	1,281
Murder	31	18
Rape	22	33
Robbery	808	633
Aggravated assault	655	597
Non-violent	3,739	2,614
Burglary	964	810
Larceny	2,097	1,340
Vehicle theft	678	464
Domestic violence	1,734	1,580
Arson	27	23
Total crime rate	61.7	46.0
Violent	17.9	15.1
Non-violent	43.8	30.9

Public School District
(for school year 2006-07 except as noted)

Trenton School District
108 North Clinton Ave
Trenton, NJ 08609
609-656-4900

- Superintendent .... Rodney Lofton
- Number of schools 21
- Grade plan K-12
- Enrollment 12,048
- Attendance rate, '05-06 .... 90.2%
- Dropout rate 1.3%
- Students per teacher 10.4
- Per pupil expenditure $14,968
- Median faculty salary $75,501
- Median administrator salary $112,563
- Grade 12 enrollment 584
- High school graduation rate .... NA

Assessment test results
(percent scoring at proficient or advanced level)
	Language	Math
NJASK-Grade 3	59.6%	62.9%
GEPA-Grade 8	37.3%	24.7%
HSPA-High School	51.2%	19.5%

SAT score averages
Pct tested	Math	Verbal	Writing
NA	NA	NA	NA

Teacher Qualifications
- Avg. years of experience 15
- Highly-qualified teachers
  - one subject/all subjects 95.5%/95.5%
- With emergency credentials 0.9%

No Child Left Behind
- AYP, 2005-06 .... Needs Improvement

Municipal Finance[§]

State Aid Programs, 2008
- Total aid $50,814,883
  - CMPTRA 44,198,465
  - Energy tax receipts 6,612,817
  - Garden State Trust 2,896

General Budget, 2007
- Total tax levy $82,085,146
  - County levy 13,846,295
    - County taxes 12,957,697
    - County library 0
    - County health 0
    - County open space 888,597
  - School levy 21,949,022
  - Muni. levy 46,289,829
- Misc. revenues 134,510,662

©2008 Information Publications, Inc. All rights reserved. Photocopying prohibited. For additional copies, contact the publisher at www.informationpublications.com or (877)544-INFO (4636)

The New Jersey Municipal Data Book   499

Tuckerton Borough — Ocean County

Demographics & Socio-Economic Characteristics
(2000 US Census, except as noted)

Population
- 1980* 2,472
- 1990* 3,048
- 2000 3,517
  - Male 1,749
  - Female 1,768
- 2006 (estimate)* 3,827
- Population density 1,045.6

Race & Hispanic Origin, 2000
Race
- White 3,408
- Black/African American 14
- American Indian/Alaska Native 10
- Asian 19
- Native Hawaiian/Pacific Islander 0
- Other race 19
- Two or more races 47
- Hispanic origin, total 109
  - Mexican 55
  - Puerto Rican 32
  - Cuban 4
  - Other Hispanic 18

Age & Nativity, 2000
- Under 5 years 209
- 18 years and over 2,708
- 21 years and over 2,579
- 65 years and over 591
- 85 years and over 62
  - Median age 39.2
- Native-born 3,349
- Foreign-born 94

Educational Attainment, 2000
- Population 25 years and over 2,408
- Less than 9th grade 4.4%
- High school grad or higher 84.6%
- Bachelor's degree or higher 13.5%
- Graduate degree 4.3%

Income & Poverty, 1999
- Per capita income $20,118
- Median household income $40,042
- Median family income $49,528
- Persons in poverty 273
- H'holds receiving public assistance 30
- H'holds receiving social security 569

Households, 2000
- Total households 1,477
  - With persons under 18 441
  - With persons over 65 452
  - Family households 921
  - Single-person households 467
- Persons per household 2.38
- Persons per family 3.02

Labor & Employment
- Total civilian labor force, 2006** 1,626
  - Unemployment rate 7.1%
- Total civilian labor force, 2000 1,634
  - Unemployment rate 6.3%

Employed persons 16 years and over by occupation, 2000
- Managers & professionals 435
- Service occupations 256
- Sales & office occupations 420
- Farming, fishing & forestry 15
- Construction & maintenance 236
- Production & transportation 169
- Self-employed persons 83

‡ Branch of county library
* US Census Bureau
** New Jersey Department of Labor

General Information
Borough of Tuckerton
140 E Main St
Tuckerton, NJ 08087
609-296-2701
- Website .... tuckertonborough.com
- Year of incorporation 1901
- Land/water area (sq. miles) 3.66/0.12
- Form of government .... Borough

Government
Legislative Districts
- US Congressional 3
- State Legislative 9

Local Officials, 2008
- Mayor .... Lewis Eggert
- Manager/Admin .... NA
- Clerk .... Grace Di Elmo
- Finance Dir .... Laura Giovene
- Tax Assessor .... Fredrick Millman
- Tax Collector .... E.J. Mary King
- Attorney .... Terry F. Brady
- Building .... Phil Read
- Comm Dev/Planning .... NA
- Engineering .... John Hess
- Public Works .... Carl R. Hewitt Jr
- Police Chief .... Charles Robinson
- Emerg/Fire Director ..... Tom McAndrew

Housing & Construction
Housing Units, 2000*
- Total 1,971
- Median rent $747
- Median SF home value $105,900

Permits for New Residential Construction

	Units	Value
Total, 2007	21	$3,304,524
Single family	16	$3,018,809
Total, 2006	16	$2,298,853
Single family	11	$2,013,138

Real Property Valuation, 2007

	Parcels	Valuation
Total	1,876	$423,978,200
Vacant	227	24,661,700
Residential	1,551	339,564,800
Commercial	95	38,634,000
Industrial	0	0
Apartments	3	21,117,700
Farm land	0	0
Farm homestead	0	0

Average Property Value & Tax, 2007
- Residential value $218,933
- Property tax $4,095
- Tax credit/rebate $848

Public Library
Tuckerton Branch Library‡
380 Bay Ave
Tuckerton, NJ 08087
609-296-1470
- Branch Librarian .... Rita Oakes

Library statistics, 2006
see Ocean County profile for library system statistics

Public Safety
- Number of officers, 2006 10

Crime	2005	2006
Total crimes	84	73
Violent	3	4
Murder	0	0
Rape	0	0
Robbery	1	0
Aggravated assault	2	4
Non-violent	81	69
Burglary	16	16
Larceny	62	48
Vehicle theft	3	5
Domestic violence	62	42
Arson	0	0
Total crime rate	23.3	19.3
Violent	0.8	1.1
Non-violent	22.5	18.3

Public School District
(for school year 2006-07 except as noted)

Tuckerton Borough School District
Marine St, PO Box 217
Tuckerton, NJ 08087
609-296-2858
- Superintendent Consultant . Robert M. Gray Jr
- Number of schools 1
- Grade plan K-6
- Enrollment 266
- Attendance rate, '05-06 .... 94.4%
- Dropout rate .... NA
- Students per teacher 8.0
- Per pupil expenditure $12,274
- Median faculty salary $41,474
- Median administrator salary $60,749
- Grade 12 enrollment .... NA
- High school graduation rate .... NA

Assessment test results
(percent scoring at proficient or advanced level)

	Language	Math
NJASK-Grade 3	90.9%	97.0%
GEPA-Grade 8	NA	NA
HSPA-High School	NA	NA

SAT score averages

Pct tested	Math	Verbal	Writing
NA	NA	NA	NA

Teacher Qualifications
- Avg. years of experience 9
- Highly-qualified teachers
  - one subject/all subjects 100%/100%
- With emergency credentials 0.0%

No Child Left Behind
- AYP, 2005-06 .... Meets Standards

Municipal Finance
State Aid Programs, 2008
- Total aid $362,066
- CMPTRA 0
- Energy tax receipts 361,905
- Garden State Trust 161

General Budget, 2007
- Total tax levy $7,941,577
- County levy 1,534,909
  - County taxes 1,264,723
  - County library 149,968
  - County health 60,756
  - County open space 59,462
- School levy 4,354,249
- Muni. levy 2,052,419
- Misc. revenues 1,654,186

Taxes	2005	2006	2007
General tax rate per $100	1.692	1.805	1.871
County equalization ratio	123.36	96.49	85.61
Net valuation taxable	$406,327,209	$420,024,500	$424,597,874
State equalized value	$421,108,103	$491,320,935	$530,791,238

Monmouth County
Union Beach Borough

Demographics & Socio-Economic Characteristics
(2000 US Census, except as noted)

Population
1980*	6,354
1990*	6,156
2000	6,649
Male	3,358
Female	3,291
2006 (estimate)*	6,631
Population density	3,527.1

Race & Hispanic Origin, 2000
Race
White	6,280
Black/African American	58
American Indian/Alaska Native	13
Asian	82
Native Hawaiian/Pacific Islander	0
Other race	90
Two or more races	126
Hispanic origin, total	538
Mexican	77
Puerto Rican	318
Cuban	49
Other Hispanic	94

Age & Nativity, 2000
Under 5 years	483
18 years and over	4,713
21 years and over	4,454
65 years and over	498
85 years and over	32
Median age	34.4
Native-born	6,310
Foreign-born	339

Educational Attainment, 2000
Population 25 years and over	4,167
Less than 9th grade	4.8%
High school grad or higher	79.0%
Bachelor's degree or higher	8.5%
Graduate degree	2.0%

Income & Poverty, 1999
Per capita income	$20,973
Median household income	$59,946
Median family income	$65,179
Persons in poverty	319
H'holds receiving public assistance	24
H'holds receiving social security	552

Households, 2000
Total households	2,143
With persons under 18	1,038
With persons over 65	388
Family households	1,722
Single-person households	332
Persons per household	3.09
Persons per family	3.44

Labor & Employment
Total civilian labor force, 2006**	3,682
Unemployment rate	5.6%
Total civilian labor force, 2000	3,418
Unemployment rate	5.5%

Employed persons 16 years and over by occupation, 2000
Managers & professionals	737
Service occupations	458
Sales & office occupations	948
Farming, fishing & forestry	0
Construction & maintenance	530
Production & transportation	557
Self-employed persons	89

* US Census Bureau
** New Jersey Department of Labor
§ State Fiscal Year July 1–June 30

See Introduction for an explanation of all data sources.

General Information
Borough of Union Beach
650 Poole Ave
Union Beach, NJ 07735
732-264-2277

Website	www.unionbeach.net
Year of incorporation	1925
Land/water area (sq. miles)	1.88/0.06
Form of government	Borough

Government
Legislative Districts
US Congressional	6
State Legislative	13

Local Officials, 2008
Mayor	Paul J. Smith Jr
Manager/Admin	NA
Clerk	Mary Sabik
Finance Dir	Joseph Faccone
Tax Assessor	George Lockwood
Tax Collector	NA
Attorney	John T. Lane Jr
Building	Robert Burlew
Comm Dev/Planning	NA
Engineering	Edward Broberg
Public Works	NA
Police Chief	Michael Kelly
Emerg/Fire Director	William Nealon

Housing & Construction
Housing Units, 2000*
Total	2,229
Median rent	$1,002
Median SF home value	$132,800

Permits for New Residential Construction
	Units	Value
Total, 2007	6	$504,287
Single family	6	$504,287
Total, 2006	10	$842,777
Single family	10	$842,777

Real Property Valuation, 2007
	Parcels	Valuation
Total	2,321	$447,159,200
Vacant	124	7,759,300
Residential	2,132	380,763,400
Commercial	59	14,017,100
Industrial	5	44,428,600
Apartments	1	190,800
Farm land	0	0
Farm homestead	0	0

Average Property Value & Tax, 2007
Residential value	$178,594
Property tax	$5,085
Tax credit/rebate	$940

Public Library
Union Beach Mem. Library
810 Union Ave
Union Beach, NJ 07735
732-264-3792

Director................NA

Library statistics, 2006
Population served	6,649
Full-time/total staff	NA/0

	Total	Per capita
Holdings	NA	NA
Revenues	NA	NA
Expenditures	NA	NA
Annual visits	NA	NA
Internet terminals/annual users	NA/NA	

Public Safety
Number of officers, 2006................16

Crime	2005	2006
Total crimes	80	47
Violent	10	6
Murder	0	0
Rape	1	0
Robbery	5	0
Aggravated assault	4	6
Non-violent	70	41
Burglary	10	13
Larceny	57	27
Vehicle theft	3	1
Domestic violence	64	61
Arson	0	0
Total crime rate	11.9	7.1
Violent	1.5	0.9
Non-violent	10.4	6.2

Public School District
(for school year 2006-07 except as noted)

Union Beach Borough School District
1207 Florance Ave
Union Beach, NJ 07735
732-264-5405

Superintendent	Arthur J. Waltz
Number of schools	1
Grade plan	K-8
Enrollment	826
Attendance rate, '05-06	94.3%
Dropout rate	NA
Students per teacher	11.6
Per pupil expenditure	$11,656
Median faculty salary	$48,280
Median administrator salary	$87,550
Grade 12 enrollment	NA
High school graduation rate	NA

Assessment test results
(percent scoring at proficient or advanced level)
	Language	Math
NJASK-Grade 3	78.7%	85.4%
GEPA-Grade 8	74.1%	81.2%
HSPA-High School	NA	NA

SAT score averages
Pct tested	Math	Verbal	Writing
NA	NA	NA	NA

Teacher Qualifications
Avg. years of experience	14
Highly-qualified teachers one subject/all subjects	95.0%/95.0%
With emergency credentials	1.8%

No Child Left Behind
AYP, 2005-06............Meets Standards

Municipal Finance§
State Aid Programs, 2008
Total aid	$746,663
CMPTRA	125,071
Energy tax receipts	621,592
Garden State Trust	0

General Budget, 2007
Total tax levy	$12,740,444
County levy	1,778,173
County taxes	1,561,478
County library	89,389
County health	29,744
County open space	97,563
School levy	6,200,048
Muni. levy	4,762,223
Misc. revenues	2,749,909

Taxes	2005	2006	2007
General tax rate per $100	2.502	2.627	2.847
County equalization ratio	92.08	79.67	69.38
Net valuation taxable	$440,980,606	$444,668,600	$447,508,698
State equalized value	$553,508,982	$641,307,897	$681,371,734

©2008 Information Publications, Inc. All rights reserved. Photocopying prohibited. For additional copies, contact the publisher at www.informationpublications.com or (877)544-INFO (4636)

Union City — Hudson County

Demographics & Socio-Economic Characteristics[†]
(2000 US Census, except as noted)

Population
1980*	55,593
1990*	58,012
2000	67,088
Male	33,639
Female	33,449
2006 (estimate)*	63,930
Population density	50,338.6

Race & Hispanic Origin, 2000
Race
White	39,167
Black/African American	2,442
American Indian/Alaska Native	467
Asian	1,441
Native Hawaiian/Pacific Islander	54
Other race	18,911
Two or more races	4,606
Hispanic origin, total	55,226
Mexican	2,752
Puerto Rican	7,388
Cuban	10,296
Other Hispanic	34,790

Age & Nativity, 2000
Under 5 years	4,945
18 years and over	50,117
21 years and over	47,197
65 years and over	6,694
85 years and over	739
Median age	32.5
Native-born	27,710
Foreign-born	39,378

Educational Attainment, 2000
Population 25 years and over	42,677
Less than 9th grade	24.9%
High school grad or higher	54.4%
Bachelor's degree or higher	12.5%
Graduate degree	5.4%

Income & Poverty, 1999
Per capita income	$13,997
Median household income	$30,642
Median family income	$32,246
Persons in poverty	14,244
H'holds receiving public assistance	1,495
H'holds receiving social security	4,894

Households, 2000
Total households	22,872
With persons under 18	9,473
With persons over 65	5,097
Family households	16,067
Single-person households	5,259
Persons per household	2.92
Persons per family	3.40

Labor & Employment
Total civilian labor force, 2006**	27,836
Unemployment rate	7.0%
Total civilian labor force, 2000	29,551
Unemployment rate	12.4%

Employed persons 16 years and over by occupation, 2000
Managers & professionals	4,436
Service occupations	4,969
Sales & office occupations	6,315
Farming, fishing & forestry	35
Construction & maintenance	2,038
Production & transportation	8,081
Self-employed persons	1,029

[†] see Appendix C for American Community Survey data
* US Census Bureau
** New Jersey Department of Labor
§ State Fiscal Year July 1–June 30

General Information
City of Union
3715 Palisade Ave
Union City, NJ 07087
201-348-5700

Website	www.ucnj.com
Year of incorporation	1925
Land/water area (sq. miles)	1.27/0.00
Form of government	Commission

Government
Legislative Districts
US Congressional	13
State Legislative	33

Local Officials, 2008
Mayor	Brian P. Stack
Manager/Admin	NA
Clerk	William Senande
Finance Dir	Douglas Gutch
Tax Assessor	Salvatore Bonaccorsi
Tax Collector	Sonia Schulman
Attorney	Donald Scarinci
Building	Martin Martinetti
Comm Dev/Planning	NA
Engineering	NA
Public Works	NA
Police Chief	Charles Everett
Emerg/Fire Svcs	North Hudson Regional

Housing & Construction
Housing Units, 2000*
Total	23,741
Median rent	$658
Median SF home value	$141,000

Permits for New Residential Construction
	Units	Value
Total, 2007	115	$11,379,840
Single family	1	$45,825
Total, 2006	47	$4,543,460
Single family	0	$0

Real Property Valuation, 2007
	Parcels	Valuation
Total	7,752	$1,423,671,200
Vacant	378	25,424,100
Residential	5,213	669,130,200
Commercial	1,358	432,436,500
Industrial	96	33,740,700
Apartments	707	262,939,700
Farm land	0	0
Farm homestead	0	0

Average Property Value & Tax, 2007
Residential value	$128,358
Property tax	$6,113
Tax credit/rebate	$918

Public Library
Union City Public Library
324 43rd St
Union City, NJ 07087
201-866-7500

Director	Rita Mann

Library statistics, 2006
Population served	67,088
Full-time/total staff	2/11

	Total	Per capita
Holdings	76,330	1.14
Revenues	$917,875	$13.68
Expenditures	$744,335	$11.09
Annual visits	90,000	1.34
Internet terminals/annual users	87/71,153	

Taxes
	2005	2006	2007
General tax rate per $100	4.682	4.796	5.107
County equalization ratio	60.21	49.69	42.02
Net valuation taxable	$1,417,116,686	$1,415,124,500	$1,430,722,422
State equalized value	$2,851,915,247	$3,375,701,896	$3,692,454,277

Public Safety
Number of officers, 2006	175

Crime	2005	2006
Total crimes	1,824	1,983
Violent	325	407
Murder	3	1
Rape	10	4
Robbery	178	214
Aggravated assault	134	188
Non-violent	1,499	1,576
Burglary	396	405
Larceny	836	931
Vehicle theft	267	240
Domestic violence	575	650
Arson	3	6
Total crime rate	27.6	30.4
Violent	4.9	6.2
Non-violent	22.7	24.2

Public School District
(for school year 2006-07 except as noted)

Union City School District
3912 Bergen Turnpike
Union City, NJ 07087
201-348-5851

Superintendent	Stanley Sanger
Number of schools	12
Grade plan	K-12
Enrollment	9,760
Attendance rate, '05-06	95.2%
Dropout rate	1.8%
Students per teacher	11.7
Per pupil expenditure	$14,657
Median faculty salary	$52,748
Median administrator salary	$121,922
Grade 12 enrollment	662
High school graduation rate	NA

Assessment test results
(percent scoring at proficient or advanced level)
	Language	Math
NJASK-Grade 3	78.3%	88.2%
GEPA-Grade 8	72.4%	67.5%
HSPA-High School	69.1%	58.3%

SAT score averages
Pct tested	Math	Verbal	Writing
NA	NA	NA	NA

Teacher Qualifications
Avg. years of experience	9
Highly-qualified teachers one subject/all subjects	99.5%/99.5%
With emergency credentials	0.0%

No Child Left Behind
AYP, 2005-06	Meets Standards

Municipal Finance[§]
State Aid Programs, 2008
Total aid	$17,804,859
CMPTRA	15,185,675
Energy tax receipts	2,619,184
Garden State Trust	0

General Budget, 2007
Total tax levy	$73,053,949
County levy	14,040,624
County taxes	13,696,228
County library	0
County health	0
County open space	344,397
School levy	16,125,529
Muni. levy	42,887,796
Misc. revenues	44,707,610

Hunterdon County

Union Township

Demographics & Socio-Economic Characteristics
(2000 US Census, except as noted)

Population
- 1980*................................3,971
- 1990*................................5,078
- 2000.................................6,160
  - Male...............................2,557
  - Female.............................3,603
- 2006 (estimate)*......................6,352
  - Population density.................334.8

Race & Hispanic Origin, 2000
Race
- White.................................5,041
- Black/African American.................823
- American Indian/Alaska Native...........11
- Asian...................................98
- Native Hawaiian/Pacific Islander.........1
- Other race..............................98
- Two or more races.......................88
- Hispanic origin, total.................316
  - Mexican................................15
  - Puerto Rican..........................159
  - Cuban..................................38
  - Other Hispanic........................104

Age & Nativity, 2000
- Under 5 years..........................278
- 18 years and over....................4,980
- 21 years and over....................4,842
- 65 years and over......................404
- 85 years and over.......................25
- Median age............................37.6
- Native-born..........................5,818
- Foreign-born...........................342

Educational Attainment, 2000
- Population 25 years and over.........4,591
- Less than 9th grade...................9.8%
- High school grad or higher...........77.1%
- Bachelor's degree or higher..........31.9%
- Graduate degree......................11.6%

Income & Poverty, 1999
- Per capita income..................$29,535
- Median household income............$81,089
- Median family income..............$102,146
- Persons in poverty......................69
- H'holds receiving public assistance......9
- H'holds receiving social security......287

Households, 2000
- Total households.....................1,666
  - With persons under 18................621
  - With persons over 65.................275
  - Family households..................1,163
  - Single-person households.............405
- Persons per household.................2.61
- Persons per family....................3.18

Labor & Employment
- Total civilian labor force, 2006**...2,665
  - Unemployment rate...................3.4%
- Total civilian labor force, 2000.....2,386
  - Unemployment rate...................3.0%

Employed persons 16 years and over by occupation, 2000
- Managers & professionals............1,272
- Service occupations....................157
- Sales & office occupations............565
- Farming, fishing & forestry..............9
- Construction & maintenance............174
- Production & transportation...........138
- Self-employed persons.................190

* US Census Bureau
** New Jersey Department of Labor

See Introduction for an explanation of all data sources.

General Information
Township of Union
140 Perryville Rd
Hampton, NJ 08827
908-735-8027

- Website............www.uniontwp-hcnj.org
- Year of incorporation................1853
- Land/water area (sq. miles)......18.97/1.62
- Form of government..............Township

Government
Legislative Districts
- US Congressional.........................7
- State Legislative.......................23

Local Officials, 2008
- Mayor....................Frank T. Mazza
- Manager/Admin......................NA
- Clerk....................Ella M. Ruta
- Finance Dir..............Grace Brennan
- Tax Assessor..............Robert Vance
- Tax Collector..............John Earley
- Attorney...................J. Peter Jost
- Building..............John W. Leonard
- Comm Dev/Planning..................NA
- Engineering.............John D. Reymann
- Public Works........................NA
- Police Chief........................NA
- Emerg/Fire Director.......Dan VanFossen

Housing & Construction
Housing Units, 2000*
- Total...............................1,725
- Median rent.........................$973
- Median SF home value............$285,200

Permits for New Residential Construction

	Units	Value
Total, 2007	21	$4,004,016
Single family	21	$4,004,016
Total, 2006	32	$6,171,968
Single family	32	$6,171,968

Real Property Valuation, 2007

	Parcels	Valuation
Total	2,161	$673,517,768
Vacant	153	21,461,753
Residential	1,686	501,947,100
Commercial	67	102,662,000
Industrial	6	14,192,100
Apartments	1	230,900
Farm land	155	1,072,715
Farm homestead	93	31,951,200

Average Property Value & Tax, 2007
- Residential value...................$300,111
- Property tax..........................$7,822
- Tax credit/rebate.....................$1,067

Public Library
No public municipal library

Library statistics, 2006
- Population served......................NA
- Full-time/total staff...............NA/NA

	Total	Per capita
Holdings	NA	NA
Revenues	NA	NA
Expenditures	NA	NA
Annual visits	NA	NA
Internet terminals/annual users	NA/NA	

Taxes

	2005	2006	2007
General tax rate per $100	2.34	2.49	2.61
County equalization ratio	76.61	69.87	64.55
Net valuation taxable	$656,558,506	$662,190,668	$674,912,841
State equalized value	$836,593,407	$920,236,400	$961,095,512

Public Safety
Number of officers, 2006................0

Crime

	2005	2006
Total crimes	40	41
Violent	3	3
Murder	0	0
Rape	0	0
Robbery	0	0
Aggravated assault	3	3
Non-violent	37	38
Burglary	5	6
Larceny	22	30
Vehicle theft	0	2
Domestic violence	25	0
Arson	0	0
Total crime rate	6.3	6.5
Violent	0.5	0.5
Non-violent	5.8	6.0

Public School District
(for school year 2006-07 except as noted)

Union Township School District
165 Perryville Rd
Hampton, NJ 08827
908-238-6013

- Superintendent..............Jeffrey Bender
- Number of schools........................2
- Grade plan............................K-8
- Enrollment............................600
- Attendance rate, '05-06..............96.0%
- Dropout rate...........................NA
- Students per teacher..................11.4
- Per pupil expenditure..............$13,195
- Median faculty salary..............$57,990
- Median administrator salary........$89,647
- Grade 12 enrollment....................NA
- High school graduation rate...........NA

Assessment test results
(percent scoring at proficient or advanced level)

	Language	Math
NJASK-Grade 3	94.6%	98.2%
GEPA-Grade 8	91.7%	87.5%
HSPA-High School	NA	NA

SAT score averages

Pct tested	Math	Verbal	Writing
NA	NA	NA	NA

Teacher Qualifications
- Avg. years of experience................10
- Highly-qualified teachers
  - one subject/all subjects.....92.5%/90.0%
- With emergency credentials...........0.0%

No Child Left Behind
- AYP, 2005-06.............Meets Standards

Municipal Finance
State Aid Programs, 2008
- Total aid........................$500,025
  - CMPTRA.........................67,679
  - Energy tax receipts............402,991
  - Garden State Trust..............29,355

General Budget, 2007
- Total tax levy................$17,591,750
  - County levy..................3,468,807
    - County taxes...............2,903,030
    - County library..............252,608
    - County health....................0
    - County open space...........313,169
  - School levy.................13,102,191
  - Muni. levy..................1,020,753
  - Misc. revenues..............2,950,774

Union Township
Union County

Demographics & Socio-Economic Characteristics
(2000 US Census, except as noted)

Population
1980*	50,184
1990*	50,024
2000	54,405
Male	25,446
Female	28,959
2006 (estimate)*	55,039
Population density	6,035.0

Race & Hispanic Origin, 2000
Race
- White 36,809
- Black/African American 10,752
- American Indian/Alaska Native 80
- Asian 4,201
- Native Hawaiian/Pacific Islander 13
- Other race 1,329
- Two or more races 1,221

Hispanic origin, total 4,861
- Mexican 113
- Puerto Rican 1,398
- Cuban 666
- Other Hispanic 2,684

Age & Nativity, 2000
- Under 5 years 2,994
- 18 years and over 42,286
- 21 years and over 39,998
- 65 years and over 9,427
- 85 years and over 1,391
- Median age 38.7
- Native-born 41,045
- Foreign-born 13,360

Educational Attainment, 2000
- Population 25 years and over 37,595
- Less than 9th grade 8.0%
- High school grad or higher 80.9%
- Bachelor's degree or higher 26.5%
- Graduate degree 8.4%

Income & Poverty, 1999
- Per capita income $24,768
- Median household income $59,173
- Median family income $68,707
- Persons in poverty 2,212
- H'holds receiving public assistance ... 439
- H'holds receiving social security 6,707

Households, 2000
- Total households 19,534
- With persons under 18 6,824
- With persons over 65 6,827
- Family households 14,164
- Single-person households 4,656
- Persons per household 2.71
- Persons per family 3.25

Labor & Employment
- Total civilian labor force, 2006** ... 28,978
- Unemployment rate 4.4%
- Total civilian labor force, 2000 27,371
- Unemployment rate 4.5%

Employed persons 16 years and over by occupation, 2000
- Managers & professionals 9,906
- Service occupations 3,150
- Sales & office occupations 8,130
- Farming, fishing & forestry 0
- Construction & maintenance 2,071
- Production & transportation 2,878
- Self-employed persons 1,089

---

* US Census Bureau
** New Jersey Department of Labor

General Information
Township of Union
1976 Morris Ave
Union, NJ 07083
908-688-2800

- Website .... uniontownship.com
- Year of incorporation 1808
- Land/water area (sq. miles) ... 9.12/0.00
- Form of government .... Township

Government
Legislative Districts
- US Congressional 7, 10
- State Legislative 20

Local Officials, 2008
- Mayor .... Clifton People Jr
- Manager .... Frank Bradley
- Clerk .... Eileen Birch
- Finance Dir .... Debra Cyburt
- Tax Assessor .... Paul Parsons
- Tax Collector .... Terri Magnusson
- Attorney .... Daniel Antonelli
- Building .... Richard Malanda
- Planning .... Phil Haderer
- Engineering .... Robert Bucco Jr
- Public Works .... Sergio Panunzio
- Police Chief .... Thomas Kraemer
- Emerg/Fire Director ..... Frederic Fretz

Housing & Construction
Housing Units, 2000*
- Total 20,001
- Median rent $844
- Median SF home value $172,900

Permits for New Residential Construction
	Units	Value
Total, 2007	12	$1,665,349
Single family	12	$1,665,349
Total, 2006	32	$5,687,421
Single family	22	$4,772,421

Real Property Valuation, 2007
	Parcels	Valuation
Total	17,261	$1,061,499,800
Vacant	182	4,417,900
Residential	16,109	739,367,800
Commercial	709	194,116,500
Industrial	210	102,058,600
Apartments	51	21,539,000
Farm land	0	0
Farm homestead	0	0

Average Property Value & Tax, 2007
- Residential value $45,898
- Property tax $6,631
- Tax credit/rebate $1,125

Public Library
Union Free Public Library
1980 Morris Ave
Union, NJ 07083
908-851-5450

Director .... Laurie D. Sansone

Library statistics, 2006
- Population served 54,405
- Full-time/total staff 8/21

	Total	Per capita
Holdings	211,281	3.88
Revenues	$2,186,147	$40.18
Expenditures	$2,187,152	$40.20
Annual visits	294,589	5.41
Internet terminals/annual users	31/51,238	

Taxes
	2005	2006	2007
General tax rate per $100	12.942	13.925	14.448
County equalization ratio	17.21	15.2	14.98
Net valuation taxable	$1,064,799,976	$1,063,091,600	$1,063,084,867
State equalized value	$6,304,321,942	$7,098,646,343	$7,710,370,833

Public Safety
Number of officers, 2006 135

Crime	2005	2006
Total crimes	1,776	1,744
Violent	174	154
Murder	1	2
Rape	14	2
Robbery	89	69
Aggravated assault	70	81
Non-violent	1,602	1,590
Burglary	199	233
Larceny	1,150	1,147
Vehicle theft	253	210
Domestic violence	335	292
Arson	9	0
Total crime rate	31.9	31.5
Violent	3.1	2.8
Non-violent	28.8	28.7

Public School District
(for school year 2006-07 except as noted)

Union Township School District
2369 Morris Ave
Union, NJ 07083
908-851-6420

- Superintendent ...... Theodore Jakubowski
- Number of schools 10
- Grade plan K-12
- Enrollment 7,901
- Attendance rate, '05-06 .... 94.6%
- Dropout rate 0.4%
- Students per teacher 12.6
- Per pupil expenditure $12,583
- Median faculty salary $56,828
- Median administrator salary .. $109,595
- Grade 12 enrollment 635
- High school graduation rate 98.6%

Assessment test results
(percent scoring at proficient or advanced level)
	Language	Math
NJASK-Grade 3	80.4%	85.8%
GEPA-Grade 8	64.3%	58.3%
HSPA-High School	82.4%	65.6%

SAT score averages
Pct tested	Math	Verbal	Writing
74%	466	444	443

Teacher Qualifications
- Avg. years of experience 9
- Highly-qualified teachers
  one subject/all subjects 99.0%/99.0%
- With emergency credentials 0.7%

No Child Left Behind
AYP, 2005-06 .... Meets Standards

Municipal Finance
State Aid Programs, 2008
- Total aid $7,505,624
- CMPTRA 2,557,557
- Energy tax receipts 4,948,067
- Garden State Trust 0

General Budget, 2007
- Total tax levy $153,584,445
- County levy 24,896,456
- County taxes 23,823,241
- County library 0
- County health 0
- County open space 1,073,215
- School levy 74,577,529
- Muni. levy 54,110,460
- Misc. revenues 22,311,141

Cumberland County
Upper Deerfield Township

Demographics & Socio-Economic Characteristics
(2000 US Census, except as noted)

Population
1980*	6,810
1990*	6,927
2000	7,556
Male	3,663
Female	3,893
2006 (estimate)*	8,000
Population density	257.2

Race & Hispanic Origin, 2000
Race
- White 5,725
- Black/African American 1,240
- American Indian/Alaska Native ... 61
- Asian 231
- Native Hawaiian/Pacific Islander ... 1
- Other race 138
- Two or more races 160

Hispanic origin, total 343
- Mexican 25
- Puerto Rican 267
- Cuban 6
- Other Hispanic 45

Age & Nativity, 2000
- Under 5 years 519
- 18 years and over 5,455
- 21 years and over 5,179
- 65 years and over 1,074
- 85 years and over 117
- Median age 37.5
- Native-born 7,314
- Foreign-born 242

Educational Attainment, 2000
- Population 25 years and over 4,910
- Less than 9th grade 5.3%
- High school grad or higher 81.1%
- Bachelor's degree or higher 15.6%
- Graduate degree 4.3%

Income & Poverty, 1999
- Per capita income $18,884
- Median household income $47,861
- Median family income $51,472
- Persons in poverty 1,032
- H'holds receiving public assistance ... 193
- H'holds receiving social security ... 930

Households, 2000
- Total households 2,757
- With persons under 18 1,088
- With persons over 65 783
- Family households 2,126
- Single-person households 551
- Persons per household 2.73
- Persons per family 3.12

Labor & Employment
- Total civilian labor force, 2006** ... 3,967
- Unemployment rate 5.1%
- Total civilian labor force, 2000 ... 3,576
- Unemployment rate 7.3%

Employed persons 16 years and over by occupation, 2000
- Managers & professionals 982
- Service occupations 508
- Sales & office occupations ... 938
- Farming, fishing & forestry .. 36
- Construction & maintenance ... 229
- Production & transportation .. 622
- Self-employed persons 255

* US Census Bureau
** New Jersey Department of Labor

See Introduction for an explanation of all data sources.

General Information
Township of Upper Deerfield
1325 State Highway 77
PO Box 5098
Seabrook, NJ 08302
856-451-3811
Website .... www.upperdeerfield.org
Year of incorporation 1922
Land/water area (sq. miles) 31.10/0.14
Form of government .... Township

Government
Legislative Districts
- US Congressional 2
- State Legislative 3

Local Officials, 2008
Mayor	Ralph A Cocove
Manager	Roy Spoltore
Clerk	Roy Spoltore
Finance Dir	Ruth Moynihan
Tax Assessor	Darlene Campbell
Tax Collector	Andrea Penny
Attorney	Theodore Baker
Building	Fred Froelich
Planning	Vicki Vagnarelli
Engineering	John Kakocha
Public Works	(vacant)
Police Chief	NA
Fire/Emergency Dir	David Smith

Housing & Construction
Housing Units, 2000*
- Total 2,881
- Median rent $535
- Median SF home value $116,000

Permits for New Residential Construction
	Units	Value
Total, 2007	58	$10,028,228
Single family	38	$7,552,154
Total, 2006	57	$10,895,161
Single family	40	$8,618,161

Real Property Valuation, 2007
	Parcels	Valuation
Total	3,635	$420,610,025
Vacant	402	11,888,625
Residential	2,447	284,568,300
Commercial	125	67,238,200
Industrial	2	11,644,500
Apartments	4	7,649,600
Farm land	442	7,051,500
Farm homestead	213	30,569,300

Average Property Value & Tax, 2007
- Residential value $118,473
- Property tax $4,183
- Tax credit/rebate $898

Public Library
No public municipal library

Library statistics, 2006
- Population served .... NA
- Full-time/total staff .... NA/NA

	Total	Per capita
Holdings	NA	NA
Revenues	NA	NA
Expenditures	NA	NA
Annual visits	NA	NA
Internet terminals/annual users	NA/NA	

Taxes
	2005	2006	2007
General tax rate per $100	3.214	3.425	3.532
County equalization ratio	88.3	79.56	73.2
Net valuation taxable	$399,407,924	$412,746,700	$421,881,678
State equalized value	$502,021,021	$565,189,395	$695,576,745

Public Safety
Number of officers, 2006 0

Crime
	2005	2006
Total crimes	196	262
Violent	16	22
Murder	0	0
Rape	0	0
Robbery	0	4
Aggravated assault	16	18
Non-violent	180	240
Burglary	43	67
Larceny	125	165
Vehicle theft	12	8
Domestic violence	60	6
Arson	2	0
Total crime rate	25.0	33.2
Violent	2.0	2.8
Non-violent	23.0	30.4

Public School District
(for school year 2006-07 except as noted)

Upper Deerfield Township School District
1369 Highway #77
Seabrook, NJ 08302
856-455-2267

- Superintendent .... Philip Exley
- Number of schools 3
- Grade plan K-8
- Enrollment 912
- Attendance rate, '05-06 ...... 94.5%
- Dropout rate .... NA
- Students per teacher 9.9
- Per pupil expenditure $13,752
- Median faculty salary $50,928
- Median administrator salary .. $93,101
- Grade 12 enrollment .... NA
- High school graduation rate .. NA

Assessment test results
(percent scoring at proficient or advanced level)
	Language	Math
NJASK-Grade 3	72.9%	78.1%
GEPA-Grade 8	70.9%	66.7%
HSPA-High School	NA	NA

SAT score averages
Pct tested	Math	Verbal	Writing
NA	NA	NA	NA

Teacher Qualifications
- Avg. years of experience 11
- Highly-qualified teachers
  one subject/all subjects 100%/100%
- With emergency credentials ... 1.5%

No Child Left Behind
AYP, 2005-06 .... Meets Standards

Municipal Finance
State Aid Programs, 2008
- Total aid $1,757,449
- CMPTRA 47,324
- Energy tax receipts 1,709,923
- Garden State Trust 202

General Budget, 2007
- Total tax levy $14,896,201
- County levy 5,802,288
-   County taxes 5,496,369
-   County library 0
-   County health 247,097
-   County open space 58,821
- School levy 9,093,913
- Muni. levy 0
- Misc. revenues 4,434,590

©2008 Information Publications, Inc. All rights reserved. Photocopying prohibited. For additional copies, contact the publisher at www.informationpublications.com or (877)544-INFO (4636)

The New Jersey Municipal Data Book

Upper Freehold Township
Monmouth County

Demographics & Socio-Economic Characteristics
(2000 US Census, except as noted)

Population
1980*	2,750
1990*	3,277
2000	4,282
Male	2,159
Female	2,123
2006 (estimate)*	6,573
Population density	140.3

Race & Hispanic Origin, 2000
Race
- White: 4,055
- Black/African American: 45
- American Indian/Alaska Native: 6
- Asian: 60
- Native Hawaiian/Pacific Islander: 0
- Other race: 36
- Two or more races: 80

Hispanic origin, total: 151
- Mexican: 57
- Puerto Rican: 54
- Cuban: 3
- Other Hispanic: 37

Age & Nativity, 2000
- Under 5 years: 342
- 18 years and over: 3,091
- 21 years and over: 2,990
- 65 years and over: 404
- 85 years and over: 40
- Median age: 38.4
- Native-born: 4,051
- Foreign-born: 231

Educational Attainment, 2000
- Population 25 years and over: 2,829
- Less than 9th grade: 3.1%
- High school grad or higher: 88.8%
- Bachelor's degree or higher: 36.3%
- Graduate degree: 9.6%

Income & Poverty, 1999
- Per capita income: $29,387
- Median household income: $71,250
- Median family income: $78,334
- Persons in poverty: 173
- H'holds receiving public assistance: 5
- H'holds receiving social security: 309

Households, 2000
- Total households: 1,437
- With persons under 18: 642
- With persons over 65: 287
- Family households: 1,199
- Single-person households: 168
- Persons per household: 2.96
- Persons per family: 3.24

Labor & Employment
- Total civilian labor force, 2006**: 2,443
- Unemployment rate: 1.8%
- Total civilian labor force, 2000: 2,285
- Unemployment rate: 2.7%

Employed persons 16 years and over by occupation, 2000
- Managers & professionals: 915
- Service occupations: 326
- Sales & office occupations: 538
- Farming, fishing & forestry: 69
- Construction & maintenance: 196
- Production & transportation: 179
- Self-employed persons: 169

* US Census Bureau
** New Jersey Department of Labor

General Information
Township of Upper Freehold
314 Route 539
PO Box 89
Cream Ridge, NJ 08514
609-758-7738

- Website: www.uftnj.com
- Year of incorporation: 1731
- Land/water area (sq. miles): 46.86/0.27
- Form of government: Township

Government
Legislative Districts
- US Congressional: 4
- State Legislative: 30

Local Officials, 2008
- Mayor: Stephen J. Alexander
- Manager: Barbara Bascom
- Clerk: Barbara Bascom
- Finance Dir.: Dianne Kelly
- Tax Assessor: Steve Walters
- Tax Collector: Barbara Pater
- Attorney: Granville D. Magee
- Building: Ron Gafgen
- Planning: Charles P. Newcomb
- Engineering: Glenn Gerken
- Public Works: John Haines
- Police Chief: (state)
- Fire/Emergency Dir.: Brad Carter

Housing & Construction
Housing Units, 2000*
- Total: 1,501
- Median rent: $743
- Median SF home value: $255,500

Permits for New Residential Construction
	Units	Value
Total, 2007	33	$11,650,887
Single family	33	$11,650,887
Total, 2006	59	$14,769,119
Single family	59	$14,769,119

Real Property Valuation, 2007
	Parcels	Valuation
Total	3,359	$1,318,008,300
Vacant	277	43,060,200
Residential	2,002	1,030,177,600
Commercial	56	46,029,500
Industrial	16	14,588,000
Apartments	1	427,900
Farm land	693	10,149,600
Farm homestead	314	173,575,500

Average Property Value & Tax, 2007
- Residential value: $519,755
- Property tax: $8,481
- Tax credit/rebate: $1,224

Public Library
No public municipal library

Library statistics, 2006
- Population served: NA
- Full-time/total staff: NA/NA

	Total	Per capita
Holdings	NA	NA
Revenues	NA	NA
Expenditures	NA	NA
Annual visits	NA	NA
Internet terminals/annual users	NA/NA	

Public Safety
Number of officers, 2006: 0

Crime	2005	2006
Total crimes	42	66
Violent	4	4
Murder	0	0
Rape	0	0
Robbery	0	0
Aggravated assault	4	4
Non-violent	38	62
Burglary	9	10
Larceny	25	49
Vehicle theft	4	3
Domestic violence	13	7
Arson	1	1
Total crime rate	7.0	9.9
Violent	0.7	0.6
Non-violent	6.3	9.3

Public School District
(for school year 2006-07 except as noted)

Upper Freehold Regional School District
27 High St
Allentown, NJ 08501
609-259-7292

- Superintendent: Richard Fitzpatrick
- Number of schools: 4
- Grade plan: K-12
- Enrollment: 2,280
- Attendance rate, '05-06: 95.1%
- Dropout rate: 0.2%
- Students per teacher: 11.8
- Per pupil expenditure: $11,552
- Median faculty salary: $51,966
- Median administrator salary: $101,891
- Grade 12 enrollment: 265
- High school graduation rate: 98.9%

Assessment test results
(percent scoring at proficient or advanced level)

	Language	Math
NJASK-Grade 3	93.3%	97.0%
GEPA-Grade 8	80.0%	82.5%
HSPA-High School	93.9%	84.3%

SAT score averages
Pct tested	Math	Verbal	Writing
81%	511	512	496

Teacher Qualifications
- Avg. years of experience: 8
- Highly-qualified teachers one subject/all subjects: 99.0%/99.0%
- With emergency credentials: 0.7%

No Child Left Behind
AYP, 2005-06: Meets Standards

Municipal Finance
State Aid Programs, 2008
- Total aid: $682,888
- CMPTRA: 41,166
- Energy tax receipts: 630,707
- Garden State Trust: 11,015

General Budget, 2007
- Total tax levy: $21,547,674
- County levy: 3,345,662
- County taxes: 2,987,937
- County library: 171,049
- County health: 0
- County open space: 186,675
- School levy: 16,194,364
- Muni. levy: 2,007,648
- Misc. revenues: 5,207,559

Taxes
	2005	2006	2007
General tax rate per $100	3.071	1.596	1.632
County equalization ratio	64.06	118.47	106.73
Net valuation taxable	$592,108,242	$1,278,462,600	$1,320,518,129
State equalized value	$1,006,815,579	$1,200,225,734	$1,287,243,526

Salem County

Upper Pittsgrove Township

Demographics & Socio-Economic Characteristics
(2000 US Census, except as noted)

Population
1980*	3,139
1990*	3,140
2000	3,468
Male	1,728
Female	1,740
2006 (estimate)*	3,620
Population density	89.6

Race & Hispanic Origin, 2000
Race
White	3,289
Black/African American	75
American Indian/Alaska Native	18
Asian	11
Native Hawaiian/Pacific Islander	0
Other race	45
Two or more races	30
Hispanic origin, total	109
Mexican	41
Puerto Rican	32
Cuban	0
Other Hispanic	36

Age & Nativity, 2000
Under 5 years	190
18 years and over	2,591
21 years and over	2,462
65 years and over	477
85 years and over	67
Median age	38.9
Native-born	3,342
Foreign-born	126

Educational Attainment, 2000
Population 25 years and over	2,299
Less than 9th grade	6.7%
High school grad or higher	81.9%
Bachelor's degree or higher	19.1%
Graduate degree	5.8%

Income & Poverty, 1999
Per capita income	$21,732
Median household income	$53,813
Median family income	$56,768
Persons in poverty	288
H'holds receiving public assistance	18
H'holds receiving social security	294

Households, 2000
Total households	1,207
With persons under 18	452
With persons over 65	299
Family households	960
Single-person households	204
Persons per household	2.80
Persons per family	3.13

Labor & Employment
Total civilian labor force, 2006**	1,777
Unemployment rate	1.9%
Total civilian labor force, 2000	1,728
Unemployment rate	3.2%

Employed persons 16 years and over by occupation, 2000
Managers & professionals	528
Service occupations	244
Sales & office occupations	410
Farming, fishing & forestry	36
Construction & maintenance	178
Production & transportation	277
Self-employed persons	136

* US Census Bureau
** New Jersey Department of Labor

See Introduction for an explanation of all data sources.

General Information
Township of Upper Pittsgrove
431 Route 77
Elmer, NJ 08318
856-358-8500

Website	NA
Year of incorporation	1846
Land/water area (sq. miles)	40.39/0.07
Form of government	Township

Government
Legislative Districts
US Congressional	2
State Legislative	3

Local Officials, 2008
Mayor	Jack Cimprich
Manager/Admin	NA
Clerk	Alan Newkirk
Finance Dir	Alan Newkirk
Tax Assessor	Edwin F. Kay
Tax Collector	Susan DeFrancesco
Attorney	John G. Hoffman
Building	NA
Planning	Linda S. Buzby
Engineering	J. Michael Fralinger
Public Works	Barry Foote
Police Chief	NA
Fire/Emergency Dir	NA

Housing & Construction
Housing Units, 2000*
Total	1,250
Median rent	$646
Median SF home value	$127,000

Permits for New Residential Construction
	Units	Value
Total, 2007	12	$1,609,850
Single family	12	$1,609,850
Total, 2006	6	$599,580
Single family	6	$599,580

Real Property Valuation, 2007
	Parcels	Valuation
Total	2,075	$340,258,750
Vacant	154	13,894,600
Residential	881	206,911,500
Commercial	54	24,884,000
Industrial	0	0
Apartments	0	0
Farm land	680	10,859,650
Farm homestead	306	83,709,000

Average Property Value & Tax, 2007
Residential value	$244,836
Property tax	$4,704
Tax credit/rebate	$899

Public Library
No public municipal library

Library statistics, 2006
Population served	NA
Full-time/total staff	NA/NA

	Total	Per capita
Holdings	NA	NA
Revenues	NA	NA
Expenditures	NA	NA
Annual visits	NA	NA
Internet terminals/annual users	NA/NA	

Taxes
	2005	2006	2007
General tax rate per $100	3.776	1.783	1.922
County equalization ratio	59.74	125.94	108.9
Net valuation taxable	$149,791,337	$338,706,250	$341,962,941
State equalized value	$267,915,108	$312,006,005	$323,796,912

Public Safety
Number of officers, 2006	0

Crime	2005	2006
Total crimes	63	62
Violent	4	3
Murder	0	0
Rape	1	0
Robbery	1	1
Aggravated assault	2	2
Non-violent	59	59
Burglary	24	21
Larceny	28	30
Vehicle theft	7	8
Domestic violence	15	5
Arson	0	1
Total crime rate	17.5	17.1
Violent	1.1	0.8
Non-violent	16.4	16.3

Public School District
(for school year 2006-07 except as noted)

Upper Pittsgrove Township School Dist.
235 Pine Tavern Rd
Monroeville, NJ 08343
856-358-8163

Superintendent	Robert Bazzel
Number of schools	1
Grade plan	K-8
Enrollment	434
Attendance rate, '05-06	95.1%
Dropout rate	NA
Students per teacher	12.1
Per pupil expenditure	$11,116
Median faculty salary	$49,685
Median administrator salary	$83,372
Grade 12 enrollment	NA
High school graduation rate	NA

Assessment test results
(percent scoring at proficient or advanced level)
	Language	Math
NJASK-Grade 3	84.7%	89.8%
GEPA-Grade 8	81.1%	84.9%
HSPA-High School	NA	NA

SAT score averages
Pct tested	Math	Verbal	Writing
NA	NA	NA	NA

Teacher Qualifications
Avg. years of experience	13
Highly-qualified teachers one subject/all subjects	96.5%/96.5%
With emergency credentials	0.0%

No Child Left Behind
AYP, 2005-06	Meets Standards

Municipal Finance
State Aid Programs, 2008
Total aid	$534,522
CMPTRA	0
Energy tax receipts	534,522
Garden State Trust	0

General Budget, 2007
Total tax levy	$6,570,729
County levy	2,947,480
County taxes	2,884,608
County library	0
County health	0
County open space	62,872
School levy	3,431,720
Muni. levy	191,529
Misc. revenues	1,598,651

©2008 Information Publications, Inc. All rights reserved. Photocopying prohibited. For additional copies, contact the publisher at www.informationpublications.com or (877)544-INFO (4636)

The New Jersey Municipal Data Book

Upper Saddle River Borough — Bergen County

Demographics & Socio-Economic Characteristics
(2000 US Census, except as noted)

Population
1980*	7,958
1990*	7,198
2000	7,741
Male	3,813
Female	3,928
2006 (estimate)*	8,531
Population density	1,612.7

Race & Hispanic Origin, 2000
Race
- White ... 7,063
- Black/African American ... 72
- American Indian/Alaska Native ... 2
- Asian ... 486
- Native Hawaiian/Pacific Islander ... 1
- Other race ... 40
- Two or more races ... 77

Hispanic origin, total ... 169
- Mexican ... 15
- Puerto Rican ... 33
- Cuban ... 37
- Other Hispanic ... 84

Age & Nativity, 2000
- Under 5 years ... 594
- 18 years and over ... 5,368
- 21 years and over ... 5,233
- 65 years and over ... 882
- 85 years and over ... 50
- Median age ... 40.1
- Native-born ... 6,801
- Foreign-born ... 940

Educational Attainment, 2000
- Population 25 years and over ... 5,147
- Less than 9th grade ... 1.3%
- High school grad or higher ... 96.6%
- Bachelor's degree or higher ... 59.9%
- Graduate degree ... 25.5%

Income & Poverty, 1999
- Per capita income ... $57,239
- Median household income ... $127,635
- Median family income ... $132,401
- Persons in poverty ... 52
- H'holds receiving public assistance ... 0
- H'holds receiving social security ... 585

Households, 2000
- Total households ... 2,497
- With persons under 18 ... 1,203
- With persons over 65 ... 609
- Family households ... 2,242
- Single-person households ... 210
- Persons per household ... 3.09
- Persons per family ... 3.27

Labor & Employment
- Total civilian labor force, 2006** ... 3,753
- Unemployment rate ... 4.3%
- Total civilian labor force, 2000 ... 3,523
- Unemployment rate ... 4.2%

Employed persons 16 years and over by occupation, 2000
- Managers & professionals ... 2,057
- Service occupations ... 123
- Sales & office occupations ... 986
- Farming, fishing & forestry ... 0
- Construction & maintenance ... 127
- Production & transportation ... 83
- Self-employed persons ... 319

* US Census Bureau
** New Jersey Department of Labor

General Information
Borough of Upper Saddle River
376 W Saddle River Rd
Upper Saddle River, NJ 07458
201-327-2196

- Website ... www.usrtoday.org
- Year of incorporation ... 1894
- Land/water area (sq. miles) ... 5.29/0.00
- Form of government ... Borough

Government
Legislative Districts
- US Congressional ... 5
- State Legislative ... 39

Local Officials, 2008
- Mayor ... Kenneth Gabbert
- Administrator ... Thoedore F. Preusch
- Clerk ... Rose Vido
- CFO ... Gene Leporiere
- Tax Assessor ... Marie Merolla
- Tax Collector ... Gene Leporiere
- Attorney ... Robert Regan
- Building ... James Dougherty
- Comm Dev/Planning ... NA
- Engineering ... Christopher Statile
- Public Works ... NA
- Police Chief ... Michael Fanning
- Fire Chief ... Erik Vierheilig

Housing & Construction
Housing Units, 2000*
- Total ... 2,560
- Median rent ... $1,929
- Median SF home value ... $603,900

Permits for New Residential Construction
	Units	Value
Total, 2007	15	$10,617,661
Single family	15	$10,617,661
Total, 2006	27	$15,316,330
Single family	27	$15,316,330

Real Property Valuation, 2007
	Parcels	Valuation
Total	2,760	$2,126,286,700
Vacant	71	17,674,000
Residential	2,614	1,891,001,200
Commercial	69	192,842,800
Industrial	4	6,217,700
Apartments	2	18,551,000
Farm land	0	0
Farm homestead	0	0

Average Property Value & Tax, 2007
- Residential value ... $723,413
- Property tax ... $13,837
- Tax credit/rebate ... $1,478

Public Library
Upper Saddle River Public Library
245 Lake St
Upper Saddle River, NJ 07458
201-327-2583

- Director ... Barbara Kruger

Library statistics, 2006
- Population served ... 7,741
- Full-time/total staff ... 3/4

	Total	Per capita
Holdings	66,422	8.58
Revenues	$1,007,968	$130.21
Expenditures	$933,288	$120.56
Annual visits	110,017	14.21
Internet terminals/annual users	16/22,545	

Public Safety
Number of officers, 2006 ... 18

Crime	2005	2006
Total crimes	46	42
Violent	8	5
Murder	0	0
Rape	1	0
Robbery	1	0
Aggravated assault	6	5
Non-violent	38	37
Burglary	7	10
Larceny	28	23
Vehicle theft	3	4
Domestic violence	7	39
Arson	0	2
Total crime rate	5.5	4.9
Violent	1.0	0.6
Non-violent	4.5	4.3

Public School District
(for school year 2006-07 except as noted)

Upper Saddle River School District
395 West Saddle River Rd
Upper Saddle River, NJ 07458
201-961-6502

- Superintendent ... Joyce Snider
- Number of schools ... 3
- Grade plan ... K-8
- Enrollment ... 1,347
- Attendance rate, '05-06 ... 96.2%
- Dropout rate ... NA
- Students per teacher ... 11.2
- Per pupil expenditure ... $13,445
- Median faculty salary ... $55,050
- Median administrator salary ... $103,390
- Grade 12 enrollment ... NA
- High school graduation rate ... NA

Assessment test results
(percent scoring at proficient or advanced level)

	Language	Math
NJASK-Grade 3	93.4%	97.1%
GEPA-Grade 8	94.8%	92.7%
HSPA-High School	NA	NA

SAT score averages
Pct tested	Math	Verbal	Writing
NA	NA	NA	NA

Teacher Qualifications
- Avg. years of experience ... 9
- Highly-qualified teachers one subject/all subjects ... 100%/100%
- With emergency credentials ... 0.0%

No Child Left Behind
AYP, 2005-06 ... Meets Standards

Municipal Finance
State Aid Programs, 2008
- Total aid ... $1,138,126
- CMPTRA ... 51,955
- Energy tax receipts ... 1,086,171
- Garden State Trust ... 0

General Budget, 2007
- Total tax levy ... $40,699,684
- County levy ... 5,419,480
- County taxes ... 5,120,675
- County library ... 0
- County health ... 0
- County open space ... 298,805
- School levy ... 28,473,409
- Muni. levy ... 6,806,795
- Misc. revenues ... 4,144,184

Taxes
	2005	2006	2007
General tax rate per $100	1.77	1.83	1.92
County equalization ratio	85.86	79.19	71.35
Net valuation taxable	$2,048,429,129	$2,097,873,100	$2,127,845,708
State equalized value	$2,586,727,022	$2,941,549,845	$3,079,565,233

Cape May County
Upper Township

Demographics & Socio-Economic Characteristics
(2000 US Census, except as noted)

Population
1980*	6,713
1990*	10,681
2000	12,115
Male	5,837
Female	6,278
2006 (estimate)*	11,363
Population density	179.9

Race & Hispanic Origin, 2000
Race
White	11,823
Black/African American	83
American Indian/Alaska Native	15
Asian	74
Native Hawaiian/Pacific Islander	7
Other race	23
Two or more races	90
Hispanic origin, total	155
Mexican	40
Puerto Rican	66
Cuban	2
Other Hispanic	47

Age & Nativity, 2000
Under 5 years	736
18 years and over	8,648
21 years and over	8,294
65 years and over	1,472
85 years and over	130
Median age	38.4
Native-born	11,800
Foreign-born	315

Educational Attainment, 2000
Population 25 years and over	7,928
Less than 9th grade	2.0%
High school grad or higher	91.2%
Bachelor's degree or higher	32.4%
Graduate degree	8.8%

Income & Poverty, 1999
Per capita income	$27,498
Median household income	$60,942
Median family income	$68,824
Persons in poverty	417
H'holds receiving public assistance	9
H'holds receiving social security	1,133

Households, 2000
Total households	4,266
With persons under 18	1,775
With persons over 65	1,053
Family households	3,365
Single-person households	744
Persons per household	2.84
Persons per family	3.23

Labor & Employment
Total civilian labor force, 2006**	7,582
Unemployment rate	2.0%
Total civilian labor force, 2000	6,149
Unemployment rate	2.5%

Employed persons 16 years and over by occupation, 2000
Managers & professionals	2,506
Service occupations	1,038
Sales & office occupations	1,415
Farming, fishing & forestry	43
Construction & maintenance	627
Production & transportation	368
Self-employed persons	546

‡ Branch of county library
* US Census Bureau
** New Jersey Department of Labor

See Introduction for an explanation of all data sources.

General Information
Upper Township
PO Box 205
Tuckahoe, NJ 08250
609-628-2011

Website	www.uppertownship.com
Year of incorporation	1723
Land/water area (sq. miles)	63.15/5.32
Form of government	Township

Government
Legislative Districts
US Congressional	2
State Legislative	1

Local Officials, 2008
Mayor	Richard Palombo
Manager/Admin	NA
Clerk	Wanda Gaglione
Finance Dir	Patricia Garbutt
Tax Assessor	Megan McAfee
Tax Collector	Susan Peifer
Attorney	Daniel J. Young
Building	Edward Kenney
Comm Dev/Planning	NA
Engineering	Paul Dietrich
Public Works	NA
Police Chief	NA
Fire/Emergency Dir	NA

Housing & Construction
Housing Units, 2000*
Total	5,472
Median rent	$827
Median SF home value	$161,700

Permits for New Residential Construction
	Units	Value
Total, 2007	14	$3,435,851
Single family	14	$3,435,851
Total, 2006	22	$5,180,790
Single family	22	$5,180,790

Real Property Valuation, 2007
	Parcels	Valuation
Total	7,307	$2,241,072,400
Vacant	1,340	116,926,300
Residential	5,560	1,899,588,000
Commercial	289	185,939,000
Industrial	1	25,986,700
Apartments	5	1,246,700
Farm land	81	520,000
Farm homestead	31	10,865,700

Average Property Value & Tax, 2007
Residential value	$341,702
Property tax	$3,796
Tax credit/rebate	$770

Public Library
Upper Cape Branch Library‡
2050 Rte 631
Petersburg, NJ 08270
609-628-2607

Branch Librarian...........Beth Dusman

Library statistics, 2006
see Cape May County profile for library system statistics

Public Safety
Number of officers, 2006.............0

Crime	2005	2006
Total crimes	171	198
Violent	7	5
Murder	0	0
Rape	1	1
Robbery	1	0
Aggravated assault	5	4
Non-violent	164	193
Burglary	40	52
Larceny	114	135
Vehicle theft	10	6
Domestic violence	62	13
Arson	0	1
Total crime rate	14.3	16.9
Violent	0.6	0.4
Non-violent	13.7	16.5

Public School District
(for school year 2006-07 except as noted)

Upper Township School District
525 Perry Rd.
Petersburg, NJ 08270
609-628-3513

Superintendent	Vincent Palmieri Jr
Number of schools	3
Grade plan	K-8
Enrollment	1,580
Attendance rate, '05-06	95.0%
Dropout rate	NA
Students per teacher	11.4
Per pupil expenditure	$12,418
Median faculty salary	$55,350
Median administrator salary	$96,029
Grade 12 enrollment	NA
High school graduation rate	NA

Assessment test results
(percent scoring at proficient or advanced level)
	Language	Math
NJASK-Grade 3	83.2%	97.3%
GEPA-Grade 8	81.6%	80.9%
HSPA-High School	NA	NA

SAT score averages
Pct tested	Math	Verbal	Writing
NA	NA	NA	NA

Teacher Qualifications
Avg. years of experience	16
Highly-qualified teachers one subject/all subjects	100%/98.0%
With emergency credentials	0.0%

No Child Left Behind
AYP, 2005-06............Meets Standards

Municipal Finance
State Aid Programs, 2008
Total aid	$6,771,173
CMPTRA	0
Energy tax receipts	6,670,703
Garden State Trust	94,941

General Budget, 2007
Total tax levy	$24,970,751
County levy	3,801,525
County taxes	3,020,598
County library	581,183
County health	0
County open space	199,744
School levy	21,169,226
Muni. levy	0
Misc. revenues	10,905,650

Taxes	2005	2006	2007
General tax rate per $100	2.55	1.05	1.12
County equalization ratio	60.79	132.85	110.55
Net valuation taxable	$895,903,081	$2,271,486,800	$2,248,016,808
State equalized value	$1,678,349,721	$2,061,564,657	$2,179,578,824

Ventnor City — Atlantic County

Demographics & Socio-Economic Characteristics
(2000 US Census, except as noted)

Population
- 1980* 11,704
- 1990* 11,005
- 2000 12,910
  - Male 6,152
  - Female 6,758
- 2006 (estimate)* 12,564
- Population density 5,871.0

Race & Hispanic Origin, 2000
Race
- White 9,953
- Black/African American 379
- American Indian/Alaska Native 24
- Asian 962
- Native Hawaiian/Pacific Islander 4
- Other race 1,210
- Two or more races 378
- Hispanic origin, total 2,213
  - Mexican 365
  - Puerto Rican 629
  - Cuban 44
  - Other Hispanic 1,175

Age & Nativity, 2000
- Under 5 years 721
- 18 years and over 10,328
- 21 years and over 9,996
- 65 years and over 2,550
- 85 years and over 309
- Median age 40.6
- Native-born 9,938
- Foreign-born 2,972

Educational Attainment, 2000
- Population 25 years and over 9,470
- Less than 9th grade 6.7%
- High school grad or higher 80.3%
- Bachelor's degree or higher 21.4%
- Graduate degree 7.7%

Income & Poverty, 1999
- Per capita income $22,631
- Median household income $42,478
- Median family income $52,701
- Persons in poverty 894
- H'holds receiving public assistance 107
- H'holds receiving social security 1,910

Households, 2000
- Total households 5,480
  - With persons under 18 1,403
  - With persons over 65 1,915
  - Family households 3,256
  - Single-person households 1,837
- Persons per household 2.35
- Persons per family 3.02

Labor & Employment
- Total civilian labor force, 2006** 7,160
  - Unemployment rate 5.7%
- Total civilian labor force, 2000 6,530
  - Unemployment rate 6.1%

Employed persons 16 years and over by occupation, 2000
- Managers & professionals 1,659
- Service occupations 2,329
- Sales & office occupations 1,452
- Farming, fishing & forestry 23
- Construction & maintenance 320
- Production & transportation 347
- Self-employed persons 330

‡ Branch of county library
* US Census Bureau
** New Jersey Department of Labor

General Information
City of Ventnor
6201 Atlantic Ave
Ventnor, NJ 08406
609-823-7900

- Website .... www.ventnorcity.org
- Year of incorporation 1903
- Land/water area (sq. miles) 2.14/1.40
- Form of government .... Commission

Government
Legislative Districts
- US Congressional 2
- State Legislative 2

Local Officials, 2008
- Mayor .... Tim Kreischer
- Administrator ...... Andrew McCrosson Jr
- Clerk .... Sandra M. Biagi
- Finance Dir .... Barry Ludy
- Tax Assessor .... William Johnson
- Tax Collector .... Julie Harron
- Attorney .... John Scott Abbott
- Building .... Jimmie Agnesino
- Comm Dev/Planning .... NA
- Engineering .... Richard Carter
- Public Works .... David Smith
- Police Chief .... Wayne Arnold
- Emerg/Fire Director .... Bert Sabo

Housing & Construction
Housing Units, 2000*
- Total 8,009
- Median rent $729
- Median SF home value $129,700

Permits for New Residential Construction
	Units	Value
Total, 2007	1	$5,915,245
Single family	1	$5,915,245
Total, 2006	2	$6,464,290
Single family	2	$6,464,290

Real Property Valuation, 2007
	Parcels	Valuation
Total	6,571	$2,671,345,000
Vacant	155	61,512,700
Residential	6,248	2,494,861,000
Commercial	134	95,650,000
Industrial	2	2,494,400
Apartments	32	16,826,900
Farm land	0	0
Farm homestead	0	0

Average Property Value & Tax, 2007
- Residential value $399,306
- Property tax $6,346
- Tax credit/rebate $972

Public Library
Ventnor Community Library‡
6500 Atlantic Ave
Ventnor City, NJ 08406
609-823-4614

Branch Librarian .... Ellen Eisen

Library statistics, 2006
see Atlantic County profile for library system statistics

Public Safety
- Number of officers, 2006 39

Crime
	2005	2006
Total crimes	305	335
Violent	15	18
Murder	0	0
Rape	3	2
Robbery	6	8
Aggravated assault	6	8
Non-violent	290	317
Burglary	85	103
Larceny	202	201
Vehicle theft	3	13
Domestic violence	338	346
Arson	0	0
Total crime rate	23.8	26.3
Violent	1.2	1.4
Non-violent	22.6	24.9

Public School District
(for school year 2006-07 except as noted)

Ventnor City School District
400 N Lafayette Ave
Ventnor, NJ 08406
609-487-7900

- Superintendent .... Carmine Bonanni
- Number of schools 2
- Grade plan K-8
- Enrollment 947
- Attendance rate, '05-06 .... 94.7%
- Dropout rate .... NA
- Students per teacher 9.9
- Per pupil expenditure $13,567
- Median faculty salary $66,456
- Median administrator salary $84,778
- Grade 12 enrollment .... NA
- High school graduation rate .... NA

Assessment test results
(percent scoring at proficient or advanced level)
	Language	Math
NJASK-Grade 3	71.4%	79.6%
GEPA-Grade 8	71.1%	65.4%
HSPA-High School	NA	NA

SAT score averages
Pct tested	Math	Verbal	Writing
NA	NA	NA	NA

Teacher Qualifications
- Avg. years of experience 9
- Highly-qualified teachers
  - one subject/all subjects 100%/100%
- With emergency credentials 0.0%

No Child Left Behind
- AYP, 2005-06 .... Meets Standards

Municipal Finance
State Aid Programs, 2008
- Total aid $788,137
  - CMPTRA 118,087
  - Energy tax receipts 670,050
  - Garden State Trust 0

General Budget, 2007
- Total tax levy $42,495,141
  - County levy 7,476,149
  - County taxes 5,839,901
  - County library 791,386
  - County health 322,470
  - County open space 522,392
  - School levy 17,133,097
  - Muni. levy 17,885,895
  - Misc. revenues 4,720,313

Taxes	2005	2006	2007
General tax rate per $100	2.766	1.421	1.59
County equalization ratio	73.16	128.29	102.52
Net valuation taxable	$1,289,108,275	$2,760,704,700	$2,674,012,188
State equalized value	$2,146,367,424	$2,695,478,584	$2,894,359,113

Sussex County

Vernon Township

Demographics & Socio-Economic Characteristics
(2000 US Census, except as noted)

Population
1980*	16,302
1990*	21,211
2000	24,686
Male	12,505
Female	12,181
2006 (estimate)*	25,453
Population density	372.2

Race & Hispanic Origin, 2000
Race
- White ... 23,837
- Black/African American ... 188
- American Indian/Alaska Native ... 22
- Asian ... 173
- Native Hawaiian/Pacific Islander ... 7
- Other race ... 195
- Two or more races ... 264

Hispanic origin, total ... 889
- Mexican ... 62
- Puerto Rican ... 352
- Cuban ... 85
- Other Hispanic ... 390

Age & Nativity, 2000
- Under 5 years ... 1,643
- 18 years and over ... 17,126
- 21 years and over ... 16,349
- 65 years and over ... 1,566
- 85 years and over ... 144
- Median age ... 35.4
- Native-born ... 23,431
- Foreign-born ... 1,255

Educational Attainment, 2000
- Population 25 years and over ... 15,485
- Less than 9th grade ... 2.0%
- High school grad or higher ... 92.8%
- Bachelor's degree or higher ... 25.3%
- Graduate degree ... 7.7%

Income & Poverty, 1999
- Per capita income ... $25,250
- Median household income ... $67,566
- Median family income ... $72,609
- Persons in poverty ... 717
- H'holds receiving public assistance ... 130
- H'holds receiving social security ... 1,384

Households, 2000
- Total households ... 8,368
  - With persons under 18 ... 3,932
  - With persons over 65 ... 1,168
  - Family households ... 6,607
  - Single-person households ... 1,359
- Persons per household ... 2.95
- Persons per family ... 3.35

Labor & Employment
- Total civilian labor force, 2006** ... 14,019
  - Unemployment rate ... 3.6%
- Total civilian labor force, 2000 ... 13,184
  - Unemployment rate ... 4.8%

Employed persons 16 years and over by occupation, 2000
- Managers & professionals ... 4,313
- Service occupations ... 1,559
- Sales & office occupations ... 3,554
- Farming, fishing & forestry ... 22
- Construction & maintenance ... 1,587
- Production & transportation ... 1,511
- Self-employed persons ... 788

‡ Branch of county library
* US Census Bureau
** New Jersey Department of Labor

See Introduction for an explanation of all data sources.

General Information
Township of Vernon
21 Church St
Vernon, NJ 07462
973-764-4055

- Website ... www.vernontwp.com
- Year of incorporation ... 1731
- Land/water area (sq. miles) ... 68.39/2.14
- Form of government ... Council-Manager

Government
Legislative Districts
- US Congressional ... 5
- State Legislative ... 24

Local Officials, 2008
- Mayor ... Austin Carew
- Manager ... Melinda Carlton
- Clerk ... Dennis Murray (Actg)
- Finance Dir ... Monica Goscicki
- Tax Assessor ... Lynne Schweighardt
- Tax Collector ... Terence Whalen
- Attorney ... Michael Witt
- Building ... Thomas Pinand
- Planning ... Lou Kneip
- Engineering ... Lou Kneip
- Public Works ... Dave Pullis
- Police Chief ... Roy Wherry
- Fire Chief ... Tom Davis

Housing & Construction
Housing Units, 2000*
- Total ... 9,994
- Median rent ... $930
- Median SF home value ... $150,800

Permits for New Residential Construction
	Units	Value
Total, 2007	28	$4,079,123
Single family	28	$4,079,123
Total, 2006	46	$8,368,495
Single family	46	$8,368,495

Real Property Valuation, 2007
	Parcels	Valuation
Total	13,644	$1,506,967,334
Vacant	2,378	49,982,114
Residential	10,610	1,315,066,200
Commercial	310	108,149,120
Industrial	22	9,085,600
Apartments	4	1,416,500
Farm land	200	1,638,100
Farm homestead	120	21,629,700

Average Property Value & Tax, 2007
- Residential value ... $124,576
- Property tax ... $5,129
- Tax credit/rebate ... $979

Public Library
Vernon Branch Library‡
66 Rte 94
Vernon, NJ 07462
973-827-8095

- Branch Librarian ... Jacqueline Oregero

Library statistics, 2006
see Sussex County profile for library system statistics

Public Safety
Number of officers, 2006 ... 34

Crime	2005	2006
Total crimes	326	502
Violent	12	10
Murder	1	1
Rape	0	0
Robbery	1	2
Aggravated assault	10	7
Non-violent	314	492
Burglary	27	43
Larceny	281	447
Vehicle theft	6	2
Domestic violence	172	163
Arson	0	3
Total crime rate	12.8	19.7
Violent	0.5	0.4
Non-violent	12.3	19.3

Public School District
(for school year 2006-07 except as noted)

Vernon Township School District
539 Route 515, PO Box 99
Vernon, NJ 07462
973-764-2900

- Chief School Admin ... Anthony J. Macerino
- Number of schools ... 6
- Grade plan ... K-12
- Enrollment ... 4,981
- Attendance rate, '05-06 ... 91.4%
- Dropout rate ... 0.2%
- Students per teacher ... 11.8
- Per pupil expenditure ... $12,573
- Median faculty salary ... $71,988
- Median administrator salary ... $101,538
- Grade 12 enrollment ... 452
- High school graduation rate ... 97.1%

Assessment test results
(percent scoring at proficient or advanced level)
	Language	Math
NJASK-Grade 3	89.4%	89.7%
GEPA-Grade 8	82.0%	72.4%
HSPA-High School	92.0%	80.5%

SAT score averages
Pct tested	Math	Verbal	Writing
78%	491	494	485

Teacher Qualifications
- Avg. years of experience ... 17
- Highly-qualified teachers one subject/all subjects ... 99.5%/99.5%
- With emergency credentials ... 0.3%

No Child Left Behind
- AYP, 2005-06 ... Meets Standards

Municipal Finance
State Aid Programs, 2008
- Total aid ... $2,839,916
- CMPTRA ... 355,948
- Energy tax receipts ... 2,039,080
- Garden State Trust ... 150,433

General Budget, 2007
- Total tax levy ... $62,275,825
- County levy ... 12,057,967
  - County taxes ... 10,125,137
  - County library ... 863,201
  - County health ... 0
  - County open space ... 1,069,630
- School levy ... 37,758,834
- Muni. levy ... 12,459,024
- Misc. revenues ... 8,674,341

Taxes	2005	2006	2007
General tax rate per $100	3.7	3.92	4.12
County equalization ratio	62.93	56.16	49.55
Net valuation taxable	$1,454,972,223	$1,475,740,560	$1,512,438,082
State equalized value	$2,590,762,505	$2,984,765,717	$3,235,840,167

Verona Township — Essex County

Demographics & Socio-Economic Characteristics
(2000 US Census, except as noted)

Population
1980*	14,166
1990*	13,597
2000	13,533
Male	6,376
Female	7,157
2006 (estimate)*	12,937
Population density	4,704.4

Race & Hispanic Origin, 2000
Race
White	12,585
Black/African American	207
American Indian/Alaska Native	3
Asian	462
Native Hawaiian/Pacific Islander	8
Other race	96
Two or more races	172
Hispanic origin, total	467
Mexican	38
Puerto Rican	127
Cuban	72
Other Hispanic	230

Age & Nativity, 2000
Under 5 years	888
18 years and over	10,490
21 years and over	10,236
65 years and over	2,614
85 years and over	385
Median age	41.4
Native-born	12,223
Foreign-born	1,310

Educational Attainment, 2000
Population 25 years and over	9,980
Less than 9th grade	2.6%
High school grad or higher	92.4%
Bachelor's degree or higher	49.5%
Graduate degree	18.4%

Income & Poverty, 1999
Per capita income	$41,202
Median household income	$74,619
Median family income	$97,673
Persons in poverty	441
H'holds receiving public assistance	38
H'holds receiving social security	1,921

Households, 2000
Total households	5,585
With persons under 18	1,694
With persons over 65	1,954
Family households	3,695
Single-person households	1,678
Persons per household	2.42
Persons per family	3.06

Labor & Employment
Total civilian labor force, 2006**	7,375
Unemployment rate	2.4%
Total civilian labor force, 2000	6,975
Unemployment rate	2.0%

Employed persons 16 years and over by occupation, 2000
Managers & professionals	3,514
Service occupations	676
Sales & office occupations	2,020
Farming, fishing & forestry	0
Construction & maintenance	271
Production & transportation	352
Self-employed persons	572

* US Census Bureau
** New Jersey Department of Labor

General Information
Township of Verona
600 Bloomfield Ave
Verona, NJ 07044
973-239-3220

Website	veronanj.org
Year of incorporation	1981
Land/water area (sq. miles)	2.75/0.02
Form of government	Council-Manager

Government
Legislative Districts
US Congressional	8
State Legislative	40

Local Officials, 2008
Mayor	Kenneth McKenna
Manager	Joseph A. Martin
Clerk	Jean McEnroe
Finance Dir	Dee Trimmer
Tax Assessor	Romeo Longo
Tax Collector	Dee Trimmer
Attorney	Paul J. Giblin
Building	Tom Jacobson
Comm Dev/Planning	NA
Engineering	James Helb
Public Works	James Helb
Police Chief	Douglas Huber
Emerg/Fire Director	Larry Burdett

Housing & Construction
Housing Units, 2000*
Total	5,719
Median rent	$867
Median SF home value	$237,900

Permits for New Residential Construction
	Units	Value
Total, 2007	9	$2,185,000
Single family	9	$2,185,000
Total, 2006	6	$1,743,750
Single family	6	$1,743,750

Real Property Valuation, 2007
	Parcels	Valuation
Total	5,108	$502,533,800
Vacant	82	3,488,700
Residential	4,823	441,457,500
Commercial	185	47,867,900
Industrial	6	2,098,100
Apartments	12	7,621,600
Farm land	0	0
Farm homestead	0	0

Average Property Value & Tax, 2007
Residential value	$91,532
Property tax	$8,319
Tax credit/rebate	$1,250

Public Library
Verona Public Library
17 Gould St
Verona, NJ 07044
973-857-4848

Director	James A. Thomas

Library statistics, 2006
Population served	13,533
Full-time/total staff	4/5

	Total	Per capita
Holdings	66,125	4.89
Revenues	$827,399	$61.14
Expenditures	$805,072	$59.49
Annual visits	49,997	3.69
Internet terminals/annual users	7/7,857	

Public Safety
Number of officers, 2006 31

Crime
	2005	2006
Total crimes	207	215
Violent	4	9
Murder	0	0
Rape	0	1
Robbery	2	0
Aggravated assault	2	8
Non-violent	203	206
Burglary	28	38
Larceny	157	146
Vehicle theft	18	22
Domestic violence	16	11
Arson	1	1
Total crime rate	15.5	16.4
Violent	0.3	0.7
Non-violent	15.2	15.7

Public School District
(for school year 2006-07 except as noted)

Verona Township School District
788 Bloomfield Ave
Verona, NJ 07044
973-239-2100

Superintendent	Earl T. Kim
Number of schools	6
Grade plan	K-12
Enrollment	2,047
Attendance rate, '05-06	95.8%
Dropout rate	0.5%
Students per teacher	11.5
Per pupil expenditure	$11,906
Median faculty salary	$57,965
Median administrator salary	$110,780
Grade 12 enrollment	153
High school graduation rate	98.7%

Assessment test results
(percent scoring at proficient or advanced level)
	Language	Math
NJASK-Grade 3	97.2%	97.2%
GEPA-Grade 8	87.7%	78.7%
HSPA-High School	93.5%	87.5%

SAT score averages
Pct tested	Math	Verbal	Writing
98%	542	524	519

Teacher Qualifications
Avg. years of experience	8
Highly-qualified teachers one subject/all subjects	98.5%/96.5%
With emergency credentials	4.2%

No Child Left Behind
AYP, 2005-06 ..... Meets Standards

Municipal Finance
State Aid Programs, 2008
Total aid	$1,487,010
CMPTRA	482,139
Energy tax receipts	1,004,871
Garden State Trust	0

General Budget, 2007
Total tax levy	$45,699,640
County levy	9,403,514
County taxes	9,161,643
County library	0
County health	0
County open space	241,871
School levy	25,085,853
Muni. levy	11,210,273
Misc. revenues	6,419,616

Taxes
	2005	2006	2007
General tax rate per $100	8.31	8.77	9.09
County equalization ratio	26.33	23.71	20.94
Net valuation taxable	$502,114,400	$503,160,200	$502,798,900
State equalized value	$2,117,732,602	$2,403,165,485	$2,558,991,169

Morris County
Victory Gardens Borough

Demographics & Socio-Economic Characteristics
(2000 US Census, except as noted)

Population
1980*	1,043
1990*	1,314
2000	1,546
Male	743
Female	803
2006 (estimate)*	1,523
Population density	10,153.3

Race & Hispanic Origin, 2000
Race
White	794
Black/African American	331
American Indian/Alaska Native	1
Asian	84
Native Hawaiian/Pacific Islander	0
Other race	236
Two or more races	100
Hispanic origin, total	783
Mexican	32
Puerto Rican	213
Cuban	2
Other Hispanic	536

Age & Nativity, 2000
Under 5 years	117
18 years and over	1,137
21 years and over	1,079
65 years and over	84
85 years and over	3
Median age	31.9
Native-born	979
Foreign-born	567

Educational Attainment, 2000
Population 25 years and over	984
Less than 9th grade	8.7%
High school grad or higher	70.1%
Bachelor's degree or higher	10.2%
Graduate degree	1.2%

Income & Poverty, 1999
Per capita income	$20,616
Median household income	$44,375
Median family income	$43,594
Persons in poverty	130
H'holds receiving public assistance	27
H'holds receiving social security	87

Households, 2000
Total households	564
With persons under 18	251
With persons over 65	65
Family households	382
Single-person households	142
Persons per household	2.74
Persons per family	3.21

Labor & Employment
Total civilian labor force, 2006**	912
Unemployment rate	4.2%
Total civilian labor force, 2000	827
Unemployment rate	3.3%

Employed persons 16 years and over by occupation, 2000
Managers & professionals	108
Service occupations	193
Sales & office occupations	241
Farming, fishing & forestry	0
Construction & maintenance	70
Production & transportation	188
Self-employed persons	14

* US Census Bureau
** New Jersey Department of Labor

See Introduction for an explanation of all data sources.

General Information
Borough of Victory Gardens
337 S Salem St
Victory Gardens, NJ 07801
973-366-5312

Website	NA
Year of incorporation	1951
Land/water area (sq. miles)	0.15/0.00
Form of government	Borough

Government
Legislative Districts
US Congressional	11
State Legislative	25

Local Officials, 2008
Mayor	Betty Simmons
Manager	Deborah Evans
Clerk	Deborah Evans
Finance Dir	Charles Wood
Tax Assessor	Mark Burec
Tax Collector	Lorraine Benderoth
Attorney	Philip Feintuch
Building	Russell Brown
Planning	Gail Frazer
Engineering	Leon Hall
Public Works	Eduardo Martinez
Police Chief	NA
Emerg/Fire Director	James Benton

Housing & Construction
Housing Units, 2000*
Total	588
Median rent	$834
Median SF home value	$117,100

Permits for New Residential Construction
	Units	Value
Total, 2007	0	$0
Single family	0	$0
Total, 2006	0	$0
Single family	0	$0

Real Property Valuation, 2007
	Parcels	Valuation
Total	322	$97,404,900
Vacant	3	104,800
Residential	292	76,478,800
Commercial	25	12,308,900
Industrial	0	0
Apartments	2	8,512,400
Farm land	0	0
Farm homestead	0	0

Average Property Value & Tax, 2007
Residential value	$261,914
Property tax	$4,452
Tax credit/rebate	$885

Public Library
No public municipal library

Library statistics, 2006
Population served	NA
Full-time/total staff	NA/NA

	Total	Per capita
Holdings	NA	NA
Revenues	NA	NA
Expenditures	NA	NA
Annual visits	NA	NA
Internet terminals/annual users	NA/NA	

Taxes
	2005	2006	2007
General tax rate per $100	4.09	1.83	1.7
County equalization ratio	38.73	99.39	98.66
Net valuation taxable	$39,775,297	$97,678,800	$97,474,423
State equalized value	$98,283,412	$99,073,534	$99,838,959

Public Safety
Number of officers, 2006 0

Crime	2005	2006
Total crimes	14	22
Violent	3	8
Murder	0	0
Rape	0	1
Robbery	0	3
Aggravated assault	3	4
Non-violent	11	14
Burglary	3	5
Larceny	7	7
Vehicle theft	1	2
Domestic violence	18	4
Arson	0	0
Total crime rate	9.1	14.4
Violent	2.0	5.2
Non-violent	7.2	9.2

Public School District
(for school year 2006-07 except as noted)

Victory Gardens School District
23 Franklin Rd
Dover, NJ 07801

No schools in district - sends students to Dover Town schools

Per pupil expenditure	NA
Median faculty salary	NA
Median administrator salary	NA
Grade 12 enrollment	NA
High school graduation rate	NA

Assessment test results
(percent scoring at proficient or advanced level)
	Language	Math
NJASK-Grade 3	NA	NA
GEPA-Grade 8	NA	NA
HSPA-High School	NA	NA

SAT score averages
Pct tested	Math	Verbal	Writing
NA	NA	NA	NA

Teacher Qualifications
Avg. years of experience	NA
Highly-qualified teachers one subject/all subjects	NA/NA
With emergency credentials	NA

No Child Left Behind
AYP, 2005-06 .... NA

Municipal Finance
State Aid Programs, 2008
Total aid	$37,916
CMPTRA	0
Energy tax receipts	37,916
Garden State Trust	0

General Budget, 2007
Total tax levy	$1,656,729
County levy	236,239
County taxes	188,970
County library	0
County health	0
County open space	47,269
School levy	874,442
Muni. levy	546,048
Misc. revenues	768,846

Vineland City — Cumberland County

Demographics & Socio-Economic Characteristics
(2000 US Census, except as noted)

Population
1980*	53,753
1990*	54,780
2000	56,271
Male	26,967
Female	29,304
2006 (estimate)*	58,271
Population density	848.3

Race & Hispanic Origin, 2000
Race
White	37,964
Black/African American	7,664
American Indian/Alaska Native	304
Asian	655
Native Hawaiian/Pacific Islander	43
Other race	7,881
Two or more races	1,760
Hispanic origin, total	16,880
Mexican	1,365
Puerto Rican	13,284
Cuban	232
Other Hispanic	1,999

Age & Nativity, 2000
Under 5 years	3,477
18 years and over	41,808
21 years and over	39,639
65 years and over	7,976
85 years and over	1,080
Median age	36.5
Native-born	51,686
Foreign-born	4,585

Educational Attainment, 2000
Population 25 years and over	37,333
Less than 9th grade	14.2%
High school grad or higher	67.8%
Bachelor's degree or higher	14.3%
Graduate degree	4.8%

Income & Poverty, 1999
Per capita income	$18,797
Median household income	$40,076
Median family income	$47,909
Persons in poverty	7,560
H'holds receiving public assistance	1,040
H'holds receiving social security	5,807

Households, 2000
Total households	19,930
With persons under 18	7,694
With persons over 65	5,488
Family households	14,201
Single-person households	4,731
Persons per household	2.70
Persons per family	3.17

Labor & Employment
Total civilian labor force, 2006**	28,972
Unemployment rate	6.5%
Total civilian labor force, 2000	27,593
Unemployment rate	10.7%

Employed persons 16 years and over by occupation, 2000
Managers & professionals	6,467
Service occupations	4,437
Sales & office occupations	6,045
Farming, fishing & forestry	488
Construction & maintenance	2,378
Production & transportation	4,818
Self-employed persons	1,211

* US Census Bureau
** New Jersey Department of Labor
§ State Fiscal Year July 1–June 30

General Information
City of Vineland
PO Box 1508
Vineland, NJ 08362
856-794-4000

Website	www.vinelandcity.org
Year of incorporation	1952
Land/water area (sq. miles)	68.69/0.29
Form of government	Mayor-Council

Government
Legislative Districts
US Congressional	2
State Legislative	1

Local Officials, 2008
Mayor	Perry Barse
Manager	Paul Trivellini
Clerk	Keith Petrosky
Finance Dir	Roxann Tosto
Tax Assessor	Donald Seifrit
Tax Collector	Carmen DiGiorgio
Attorney	Richard Tonetta
Building	Kevin Kirchner
Planning	Katheen Hicks
Engineering	David Battistini
Public Works	Joe Bond
Police Chief	Timothy Codispoti
Emerg/Fire Director	Robert Pagnini

Housing & Construction
Housing Units, 2000*
Total	20,958
Median rent	$638
Median SF home value	$97,200

Permits for New Residential Construction
	Units	Value
Total, 2007	218	$29,943,530
Single family	208	$28,068,630
Total, 2006	213	$26,354,186
Single family	195	$23,374,186

Real Property Valuation, 2007
	Parcels	Valuation
Total	19,217	$2,000,888,700
Vacant	1,670	36,537,000
Residential	15,003	1,392,716,400
Commercial	1,285	363,590,500
Industrial	149	118,462,300
Apartments	64	51,069,700
Farm land	640	4,126,800
Farm homestead	406	34,386,000

Average Property Value & Tax, 2007
Residential value	$92,615
Property tax	$3,546
Tax credit/rebate	$836

Public Library
Vineland Public Library
1058 E Landis Ave
Vineland, NJ 08360
856-794-4244

Director: Gloria G. Urban

Library statistics, 2006
Population served	56,271
Full-time/total staff	7/12

	Total	Per capita
Holdings	82,870	1.47
Revenues	$1,628,325	$28.94
Expenditures	$1,599,484	$28.42
Annual visits	213,866	3.80
Internet terminals/annual users	48/66,002	

Taxes
	2005	2006	2007
General tax rate per $100	3.597	3.839	3.832
County equalization ratio	70.51	64.04	56.12
Net valuation taxable	$1,869,730,783	$1,914,625,600	$2,008,948,291
State equalized value	$2,919,629,580	$3,420,685,806	$4,103,206,337

Public Safety
Number of officers, 2006	149

Crime	2005	2006
Total crimes	3,574	3,278
Violent	722	541
Murder	2	6
Rape	15	19
Robbery	198	167
Aggravated assault	507	349
Non-violent	2,852	2,737
Burglary	591	539
Larceny	2,088	2,068
Vehicle theft	173	130
Domestic violence	1,516	1,607
Arson	21	15
Total crime rate	61.6	56.4
Violent	12.4	9.3
Non-violent	49.2	47.1

Public School District
(for school year 2006-07 except as noted)

Vineland City School District
625 Plum St
Vineland, NJ 08360
856-794-6700

Superintendent	Charles Ottinger
Number of schools	21
Grade plan	K-12
Enrollment	9,641
Attendance rate, '05-06	92.5%
Dropout rate	4.5%
Students per teacher	9.1
Per pupil expenditure	$16,420
Median faculty salary	$49,662
Median administrator salary	$101,130
Grade 12 enrollment	592
High school graduation rate	NA

Assessment test results
(percent scoring at proficient or advanced level)
	Language	Math
NJASK-Grade 3	77.4%	85.4%
GEPA-Grade 8	57.3%	49.5%
HSPA-High School	67.5%	55.2%

SAT score averages
Pct tested	Math	Verbal	Writing
45%	485	470	465

Teacher Qualifications
Avg. years of experience	8
Highly-qualified teachers one subject/all subjects	97.5%/97.5%
With emergency credentials	1.3%

No Child Left Behind
AYP, 2005-06: Meets Standards

Municipal Finance§
State Aid Programs, 2008
Total aid	$7,745,707
CMPTRA	3,425,700
Energy tax receipts	4,297,219
Garden State Trust	17,795

General Budget, 2007
Total tax levy	$76,922,658
County levy	34,287,455
County taxes	33,924,116
County library	0
County health	0
County open space	363,338
School levy	20,330,766
Muni. levy	22,304,437
Misc. revenues	36,578,885

Camden County

Voorhees Township

Demographics & Socio-Economic Characteristics
(2000 US Census, except as noted)

Population
1980*	12,919
1990*	24,559
2000	28,126
Male	13,505
Female	14,621
2006 (estimate)*	29,391
Population density	2,533.7

Race & Hispanic Origin, 2000
Race
White	22,011
Black/African American	2,249
American Indian/Alaska Native	38
Asian	3,217
Native Hawaiian/Pacific Islander	8
Other race	156
Two or more races	447
Hispanic origin, total	694
Mexican	102
Puerto Rican	301
Cuban	52
Other Hispanic	239

Age & Nativity, 2000
Under 5 years	1,767
18 years and over	20,699
21 years and over	19,960
65 years and over	3,075
85 years and over	628
Median age	37.2
Native-born	24,364
Foreign-born	3,762

Educational Attainment, 2000
Population 25 years and over	18,961
Less than 9th grade	2.8%
High school grad or higher	91.2%
Bachelor's degree or higher	46.2%
Graduate degree	20.0%

Income & Poverty, 1999
Per capita income	$33,635
Median household income	$68,402
Median family income	$86,873
Persons in poverty	1,551
H'holds receiving public assistance	102
H'holds receiving social security	1,897

Households, 2000
Total households	10,489
With persons under 18	4,047
With persons over 65	1,969
Family households	7,072
Single-person households	2,826
Persons per household	2.60
Persons per family	3.23

Labor & Employment
Total civilian labor force, 2006**	16,504
Unemployment rate	3.2%
Total civilian labor force, 2000	14,938
Unemployment rate	3.2%

Employed persons 16 years and over by occupation, 2000
Managers & professionals	7,809
Service occupations	1,477
Sales & office occupations	3,902
Farming, fishing & forestry	29
Construction & maintenance	492
Production & transportation	745
Self-employed persons	870

‡ Main library for county
* US Census Bureau
** New Jersey Department of Labor

See Introduction for an explanation of all data sources.

General Information
Township of Voorhees
620 Berlin Rd
Voorhees, NJ 08043
856-429-7757

Website	www.voorhees-nj.com
Year of incorporation	1899
Land/water area (sq. miles)	11.60/0.03
Form of government	Township

Government
Legislative Districts
US Congressional	1
State Legislative	6

Local Officials, 2008
Mayor	Michael R. Mignogna
Administrator	Lawrence Spellman
Township Clerk	Jeanette Schelberg
CFO	Dean Ciminera
Tax Assessor	Michael Kane
Tax Collector	Jennifer Dukelow
Attorney	Howard Long
Building	Steve Murray
Comm Dev/Planning	NA
Engineering	Environmental Resolutions
Public Works	John Maurer
Police Chief	Keith Hummel
Emerg/Fire Director	James Pacifico

Housing & Construction
Housing Units, 2000*
Total	11,084
Median rent	$864
Median SF home value	$179,500

Permits for New Residential Construction
	Units	Value
Total, 2007	158	$10,885,376
Single family	80	$8,925,076
Total, 2006	74	$9,281,747
Single family	74	$9,281,747

Real Property Valuation, 2007
	Parcels	Valuation
Total	9,572	$3,843,181,678
Vacant	573	104,031,558
Residential	8,489	2,892,611,720
Commercial	445	676,297,900
Industrial	28	38,674,400
Apartments	17	129,149,500
Farm land	13	80,000
Farm homestead	7	2,336,600

Average Property Value & Tax, 2007
Residential value	$340,743
Property tax	$8,092
Tax credit/rebate	$1,195

Public Library
Camden County Library‡
203 Laurel Rd
Voorhees, NJ 08043
856-772-1636

Director . . . . Linda Devlin

County Library statistics, 2006
Population served	242,830
Full-time/total staff	31/76

	Total	Per capita
Holdings	433,872	1.79
Revenues	$9,967,299	$41.05
Expenditures	$8,724,690	$35.93
Annual visits	782,825	3.22
Internet terminals/annual users	124/169,050	

Public Safety
Number of officers, 2006 51

Crime
	2005	2006
Total crimes	897	886
Violent	44	59
Murder	0	0
Rape	5	6
Robbery	12	16
Aggravated assault	27	37
Non-violent	853	827
Burglary	124	124
Larceny	705	687
Vehicle theft	24	16
Domestic violence	193	237
Arson	4	6
Total crime rate	31.2	30.6
Violent	1.5	2.0
Non-violent	29.7	28.6

Public School District
(for school year 2006-07 except as noted)

Voorhees Township School District
329 Route 73
Voorhees, NJ 08043
856-751-8446

Superintendent	Raymond J. Brosel Jr
Number of schools	5
Grade plan	K-8
Enrollment	3,386
Attendance rate, '05-06	96.1%
Dropout rate	NA
Students per teacher	11.6
Per pupil expenditure	$13,189
Median faculty salary	$76,301
Median administrator salary	$122,312
Grade 12 enrollment	NA
High school graduation rate	NA

Assessment test results
(percent scoring at proficient or advanced level)
	Language	Math
NJASK-Grade 3	93.9%	94.7%
GEPA-Grade 8	89.6%	81.8%
HSPA-High School	NA	NA

SAT score averages
Pct tested	Math	Verbal	Writing
NA	NA	NA	NA

Teacher Qualifications
Avg. years of experience	19
Highly-qualified teachers one subject/all subjects	100%/97.0%
With emergency credentials	0.0%

No Child Left Behind
AYP, 2005-06 . . . . Meets Standards

Municipal Finance
State Aid Programs, 2008
Total aid	$2,870,735
CMPTRA	637,288
Energy tax receipts	2,228,634
Garden State Trust	4,813

General Budget, 2007
Total tax levy	$91,407,574
County levy	24,362,460
County taxes	22,112,136
County library	1,553,112
County health	0
County open space	697,213
School levy	52,840,823
Muni. levy	14,204,291
Misc. revenues	9,634,357

Taxes
	2005	2006	2007
General tax rate per $100	5.321	2.31	2.375
County equalization ratio	56.78	123.18	110.3
Net valuation taxable	$1,591,897,612	$3,872,245,800	$3,848,807,299
State equalized value	$3,082,683,215	$3,516,320,046	$3,938,476,294

©2008 Information Publications, Inc. All rights reserved. Photocopying prohibited. For additional copies, contact the publisher at www.informationpublications.com or (877)544-INFO (4636)

The New Jersey Municipal Data Book

Waldwick Borough

Bergen County

Demographics & Socio-Economic Characteristics
(2000 US Census, except as noted)

Population
1980*	10,802
1990*	9,757
2000	9,622
Male	4,683
Female	4,939
2006 (estimate)*	9,621
Population density	4,625.5

Race & Hispanic Origin, 2000
Race
White	8,918
Black/African American	57
American Indian/Alaska Native	4
Asian	435
Native Hawaiian/Pacific Islander	0
Other race	126
Two or more races	82
Hispanic origin, total	511
Mexican	36
Puerto Rican	105
Cuban	27
Other Hispanic	343

Age & Nativity, 2000
Under 5 years	734
18 years and over	7,170
21 years and over	6,963
65 years and over	1,459
85 years and over	114
Median age	38.1
Native-born	8,434
Foreign-born	1,188

Educational Attainment, 2000
Population 25 years and over	6,676
Less than 9th grade	2.2%
High school grad or higher	92.2%
Bachelor's degree or higher	36.7%
Graduate degree	9.8%

Income & Poverty, 1999
Per capita income	$30,733
Median household income	$75,532
Median family income	$82,208
Persons in poverty	199
H'holds receiving public assistance	59
H'holds receiving social security	1,018

Households, 2000
Total households	3,428
With persons under 18	1,316
With persons over 65	1,041
Family households	2,678
Single-person households	641
Persons per household	2.81
Persons per family	3.22

Labor & Employment
Total civilian labor force, 2006**	5,399
Unemployment rate	2.0%
Total civilian labor force, 2000	5,085
Unemployment rate	1.9%

Employed persons 16 years and over by occupation, 2000
Managers & professionals	2,153
Service occupations	623
Sales & office occupations	1,522
Farming, fishing & forestry	0
Construction & maintenance	384
Production & transportation	304
Self-employed persons	315

* US Census Bureau
** New Jersey Department of Labor

General Information
Borough of Waldwick
63 Franklin Turnpike
Waldwick, NJ 07463
201-652-5300

Website	www.waldwickpd.org
Year of incorporation	1919
Land/water area (sq. miles)	2.08/0.01
Form of government	Borough

Government
Legislative Districts
US Congressional	5
State Legislative	39

Local Officials, 2008
Mayor	Russell Litchult
Manager	Gary Kratz
Clerk	Paula Jaegge
Finance Dir.	MaryAnn Viviani
Tax Assessor	Angela Mattiace
Tax Collector	Maryann Viviani
Attorney	Thomas Herten
Building	Joseph Mysliwiec
Comm Dev/Planning	NA
Engineering	Dennis O'Brien
Public Works	Joseph Agugliaro
Police Chief	Mark Messner
Emerg/Fire Director	Joseph Alvarez

Housing & Construction
Housing Units, 2000*
Total	3,495
Median rent	$1,127
Median SF home value	$229,400

Permits for New Residential Construction
	Units	Value
Total, 2007	39	$5,831,841
Single family	28	$4,143,121
Total, 2006	13	$1,963,934
Single family	11	$1,613,934

Real Property Valuation, 2007
	Parcels	Valuation
Total	3,614	$1,549,465,300
Vacant	150	17,090,900
Residential	3,321	1,389,511,900
Commercial	123	112,990,300
Industrial	20	29,872,200
Apartments	0	0
Farm land	0	0
Farm homestead	0	0

Average Property Value & Tax, 2007
Residential value	$418,402
Property tax	$8,736
Tax credit/rebate	$1,351

Public Library
Waldwick Public Library
19 E Prospect St
Waldwick, NJ 07463
201-652-5104

Director ... Patricia Boyd

Library statistics, 2006
Population served	9,622
Full-time/total staff	2/4

	Total	Per capita
Holdings	48,693	5.06
Revenues	$628,051	$65.27
Expenditures	$591,601	$61.48
Annual visits	115,798	12.03
Internet terminals/annual users	6/26,301	

Taxes
	2005	2006	2007
General tax rate per $100	1.81	1.96	2.09
County equalization ratio	120.04	103.07	93.01
Net valuation taxable	$1,535,620,331	$1,537,323,400	$1,550,532,976
State equalized value	$1,489,880,985	$1,653,590,994	$1,698,739,748

Public Safety
Number of officers, 2006 ... 20

Crime	2005	2006
Total crimes	104	91
Violent	0	4
Murder	0	0
Rape	0	0
Robbery	0	2
Aggravated assault	0	2
Non-violent	104	87
Burglary	7	9
Larceny	95	78
Vehicle theft	2	0
Domestic violence	46	53
Arson	0	2
Total crime rate	10.8	9.4
Violent	0.0	0.4
Non-violent	10.8	9.0

Public School District
(for school year 2006-07 except as noted)

Waldwick School District
155 Summit Ave
Waldwick, NJ 07463
201-445-3131

Superintendent	Robert F. Penna
Number of schools	4
Grade plan	K-12
Enrollment	1,585
Attendance rate, '05-06	95.1%
Dropout rate	0.5%
Students per teacher	11.1
Per pupil expenditure	$13,920
Median faculty salary	$55,100
Median administrator salary	$122,000
Grade 12 enrollment	102
High school graduation rate	97.1%

Assessment test results
(percent scoring at proficient or advanced level)
	Language	Math
NJASK-Grade 3	94.3%	96.7%
GEPA-Grade 8	85.3%	83.9%
HSPA-High School	91.4%	87.6%

SAT score averages
Pct tested	Math	Verbal	Writing
91%	525	488	492

Teacher Qualifications
Avg. years of experience	7
Highly-qualified teachers one subject/all subjects	100%/100%
With emergency credentials	0.0%

No Child Left Behind
AYP, 2005-06 ... Meets Standards

Municipal Finance
State Aid Programs, 2008
Total aid	$2,993,739
CMPTRA	0
Energy tax receipts	2,993,729
Garden State Trust	10

General Budget, 2007
Total tax levy	$32,374,154
County levy	3,036,554
County taxes	2,869,420
County library	0
County health	0
County open space	167,134
School levy	22,018,483
Muni. levy	7,319,117
Misc. revenues	5,217,519

Monmouth County
Wall Township

Demographics & Socio-Economic Characteristics
(2000 US Census, except as noted)

Population
1980*	18,952
1990*	20,244
2000	25,261
Male	12,155
Female	13,106
2006 (estimate)*	25,997
Population density	849.0

Race & Hispanic Origin, 2000
Race
White	24,526
Black/African American	155
American Indian/Alaska Native	26
Asian	319
Native Hawaiian/Pacific Islander	9
Other race	80
Two or more races	146
Hispanic origin, total	391
Mexican	60
Puerto Rican	128
Cuban	43
Other Hispanic	160

Age & Nativity, 2000
Under 5 years	1,671
18 years and over	18,887
21 years and over	18,255
65 years and over	3,641
85 years and over	450
Median age	40.3
Native-born	24,243
Foreign-born	1,018

Educational Attainment, 2000
Population 25 years and over	17,618
Less than 9th grade	2.1%
High school grad or higher	91.6%
Bachelor's degree or higher	38.9%
Graduate degree	13.9%

Income & Poverty, 1999
Per capita income	$32,954
Median household income	$73,989
Median family income	$83,795
Persons in poverty	569
H'holds receiving public assistance	91
H'holds receiving social security	2,575

Households, 2000
Total households	9,437
With persons under 18	3,361
With persons over 65	2,508
Family households	6,931
Single-person households	2,140
Persons per household	2.64
Persons per family	3.14

Labor & Employment
Total civilian labor force, 2006**	13,703
Unemployment rate	3.0%
Total civilian labor force, 2000	12,820
Unemployment rate	4.0%

Employed persons 16 years and over by occupation, 2000
Managers & professionals	5,470
Service occupations	1,190
Sales & office occupations	3,395
Farming, fishing & forestry	56
Construction & maintenance	1,238
Production & transportation	954
Self-employed persons	955

‡ Branch of county library
* US Census Bureau
** New Jersey Department of Labor

See Introduction for an explanation of all data sources.

General Information
Township of Wall
2700 Allaire Rd
Wall Township, NJ 07719
732-449-8444

Website	www.wallnj.com
Year of incorporation	1851
Land/water area (sq. miles)	30.62/0.80
Form of government	Township

Government
Legislative Districts
US Congressional	4
State Legislative	11

Local Officials, 2008
Mayor	John P. Devlin
Manager	Joseph Verruni
Clerk	Lorraine Kubacz
Finance Dir.	Stephen Mayer
Tax Assessor	Denise Siegel
Tax Collector	Theresa Vola
Attorney	Mark G. Kitrich
Building	Paul Rabenda
Planning	John Hoffmann
Engineering	Matt Zahorsky
Public Works	Ken Critchlow
Police Chief	David Morris
Fire/Emergency Dir.	NA

Housing & Construction
Housing Units, 2000*
Total	9,957
Median rent	$818
Median SF home value	$234,700

Permits for New Residential Construction
	Units	Value
Total, 2007	35	$7,927,700
Single family	30	$7,887,700
Total, 2006	45	$5,148,319
Single family	45	$5,148,319

Real Property Valuation, 2007
	Parcels	Valuation
Total	10,683	$3,823,660,800
Vacant	666	115,329,600
Residential	9,171	2,886,261,800
Commercial	598	611,685,500
Industrial	87	149,710,800
Apartments	10	27,390,400
Farm land	89	956,400
Farm homestead	62	32,326,300

Average Property Value & Tax, 2007
Residential value	$316,104
Property tax	$7,220
Tax credit/rebate	$1,086

Public Library
Wall Public Library‡
2700 Allaire Rd
Wall, NJ 07719
732-449-8877

Branch Librarian	Pamela Sawall

Library statistics, 2006
see Monmouth County profile for library system statistics

Public Safety
Number of officers, 2006	71

Crime	2005	2006
Total crimes	429	522
Violent	34	27
Murder	0	0
Rape	1	0
Robbery	0	7
Aggravated assault	33	20
Non-violent	395	495
Burglary	81	121
Larceny	297	355
Vehicle theft	17	19
Domestic violence	207	163
Arson	1	2
Total crime rate	16.3	20.1
Violent	1.3	1.0
Non-violent	15.0	19.0

Public School District
(for school year 2006-07 except as noted)

Wall Township School District
18th Ave, PO Box 1199
Wall, NJ 07719
732-556-2000

Superintendent	James F. Habel
Number of schools	6
Grade plan	K-12
Enrollment	4,259
Attendance rate, '05-06	95.4%
Dropout rate	0.8%
Students per teacher	10.9
Per pupil expenditure	$12,565
Median faculty salary	$49,648
Median administrator salary	$120,514
Grade 12 enrollment	321
High school graduation rate	95.9%

Assessment test results
(percent scoring at proficient or advanced level)

	Language	Math
NJASK-Grade 3	92.1%	95.2%
GEPA-Grade 8	80.8%	76.7%
HSPA-High School	91.2%	82.1%

SAT score averages
Pct tested	Math	Verbal	Writing
87%	514	498	498

Teacher Qualifications
Avg. years of experience	8
Highly-qualified teachers one subject/all subjects	100%/100%
With emergency credentials	0.0%

No Child Left Behind
AYP, 2005-06	Meets Standards

Municipal Finance
State Aid Programs, 2008
Total aid	$4,375,636
CMPTRA	0
Energy tax receipts	4,344,607
Garden State Trust	22,240

General Budget, 2007
Total tax levy	$87,437,074
County levy	16,854,447
County taxes	14,800,263
County library	847,350
County health	281,956
County open space	924,879
School levy	51,867,165
Muni. levy	18,715,462
Misc. revenues	11,802,571

Taxes
	2005	2006	2007
General tax rate per $100	2.147	2.194	2.284
County equalization ratio	78.17	69.14	62.14
Net valuation taxable	$3,694,395,414	$3,776,393,800	$3,828,389,614
State equalized value	$5,343,354,663	$6,082,284,612	$6,777,064,627

©2008 Information Publications, Inc. All rights reserved. Photocopying prohibited. For additional copies, contact the publisher at www.informationpublications.com or (877)544-INFO (4636)

The New Jersey Municipal Data Book

Wallington Borough

Bergen County

Demographics & Socio-Economic Characteristics
(2000 US Census, except as noted)

Population
1980*	10,741
1990*	10,828
2000	11,583
Male	5,582
Female	6,001
2006 (estimate)*	11,430
Population density	11,430.0

Race & Hispanic Origin, 2000
Race
White	10,147
Black/African American	309
American Indian/Alaska Native	11
Asian	577
Native Hawaiian/Pacific Islander	2
Other race	269
Two or more races	268
Hispanic origin, total	776
Mexican	37
Puerto Rican	252
Cuban	66
Other Hispanic	421

Age & Nativity, 2000
Under 5 years	611
18 years and over	9,451
21 years and over	9,083
65 years and over	1,757
85 years and over	220
Median age	38.2
Native-born	6,849
Foreign-born	4,734

Educational Attainment, 2000
Population 25 years and over	8,434
Less than 9th grade	11.9%
High school grad or higher	72.4%
Bachelor's degree or higher	17.0%
Graduate degree	6.4%

Income & Poverty, 1999
Per capita income	$24,431
Median household income	$45,656
Median family income	$55,291
Persons in poverty	729
H'holds receiving public assistance	82
H'holds receiving social security	1,381

Households, 2000
Total households	4,752
With persons under 18	1,307
With persons over 65	1,342
Family households	3,043
Single-person households	1,415
Persons per household	2.44
Persons per family	3.05

Labor & Employment
Total civilian labor force, 2006**	6,658
Unemployment rate	6.0%
Total civilian labor force, 2000	6,269
Unemployment rate	5.9%

Employed persons 16 years and over by occupation, 2000
Managers & professionals	1,548
Service occupations	782
Sales & office occupations	1,711
Farming, fishing & forestry	0
Construction & maintenance	740
Production & transportation	1,118
Self-employed persons	272

* US Census Bureau
** New Jersey Department of Labor

General Information
Borough of Wallington
24 Union Blvd
Wallington, NJ 07057
973-777-0318

Website	www.wallingtonnj.org
Year of incorporation	1895
Land/water area (sq. miles)	1.00/0.04
Form of government	Borough

Government
Legislative Districts
US Congressional	9
State Legislative	36

Local Officials, 2008
Mayor	Walter Wargacki
Manager	Witold Baginski
Clerk	Witold Baginski
Finance Dir	Dorothy Siek
Tax Assessor	Stuart Stolarz
Tax Collector	Dorothy Siek
Attorney	Richard Cedzidlo
Building	Nick Melfi
Comm Dev/Planning	NA
Engineering	Kenneth Job
Public Works	NA
Police Chief	Anthony Benevento
Emerg/Fire Director	Raymond Dynes

Housing & Construction
Housing Units, 2000*
Total	4,906
Median rent	$756
Median SF home value	$201,800

Permits for New Residential Construction
	Units	Value
Total, 2007	23	$2,170,558
Single family	23	$2,170,558
Total, 2006	43	$3,857,500
Single family	43	$3,857,500

Real Property Valuation, 2007
	Parcels	Valuation
Total	2,439	$530,785,200
Vacant	93	6,491,400
Residential	2,127	385,742,700
Commercial	148	65,152,700
Industrial	38	29,627,700
Apartments	33	43,770,700
Farm land	0	0
Farm homestead	0	0

Average Property Value & Tax, 2007
Residential value	$181,355
Property tax	$6,514
Tax credit/rebate	$1,059

Public Library
JFK Memorial Library
92 Hathaway St
Wallington, NJ 07057
973-471-1692

Director.............Marianne R. Willms

Library statistics, 2006
Population served	11,583
Full-time/total staff	1/1

	Total	Per capita
Holdings	31,377	2.71
Revenues	$332,785	$28.73
Expenditures	$274,286	$23.68
Annual visits	11,363	0.98
Internet terminals/annual users	19/5,407	

Public Safety
Number of officers, 2006		24

Crime	2005	2006
Total crimes	202	170
Violent	11	11
Murder	0	0
Rape	0	0
Robbery	5	8
Aggravated assault	6	3
Non-violent	191	159
Burglary	23	33
Larceny	136	103
Vehicle theft	32	23
Domestic violence	39	20
Arson	3	0
Total crime rate	17.5	14.8
Violent	1.0	1.0
Non-violent	16.5	13.8

Public School District
(for school year 2006-07 except as noted)

Wallington School District
Jefferson School, Pine St
Wallington, NJ 07057
973-777-4421

Superintendent	Frank A. Cocchiola Jr
Number of schools	3
Grade plan	K-12
Enrollment	1,160
Attendance rate, '05-06	94.3%
Dropout rate	1.7%
Students per teacher	11.7
Per pupil expenditure	$11,058
Median faculty salary	$52,154
Median administrator salary	$104,605
Grade 12 enrollment	121
High school graduation rate	95.9%

Assessment test results
(percent scoring at proficient or advanced level)
	Language	Math
NJASK-Grade 3	84.1%	84.6%
GEPA-Grade 8	66.3%	68.9%
HSPA-High School	86.8%	92.7%

SAT score averages
Pct tested	Math	Verbal	Writing
59%	486	452	461

Teacher Qualifications
Avg. years of experience	10
Highly-qualified teachers one subject/all subjects	100%/100%
With emergency credentials	0.0%

No Child Left Behind
AYP, 2005-06 .... Meets Standards

Municipal Finance
State Aid Programs, 2008
Total aid	$862,506
CMPTRA	344,385
Energy tax receipts	518,121
Garden State Trust	0

General Budget, 2007
Total tax levy	$19,078,586
County levy	2,003,912
County taxes	1,893,656
County library	0
County health	0
County open space	110,255
School levy	10,969,528
Muni. levy	6,105,146
Misc. revenues	3,873,265

Taxes
	2005	2006	2007
General tax rate per $100	3.13	3.37	3.6
County equalization ratio	63.06	55.35	48.44
Net valuation taxable	$526,270,097	$527,209,300	$531,127,045
State equalized value	$950,804,150	$1,088,761,381	$1,200,127,559

Sussex County
Walpack Township

Demographics & Socio-Economic Characteristics
(2000 US Census, except as noted)

Population
1980*	150
1990*	67
2000	41
Male	20
Female	21
2006 (estimate)*	40
Population density	1.7

Race & Hispanic Origin, 2000
Race
- White 41
- Black/African American 0
- American Indian/Alaska Native 0
- Asian 0
- Native Hawaiian/Pacific Islander 0
- Other race 0
- Two or more races 0
- Hispanic origin, total 0
  - Mexican 0
  - Puerto Rican 0
  - Cuban 0
  - Other Hispanic 0

Age & Nativity, 2000
- Under 5 years 0
- 18 years and over 33
- 21 years and over 33
- 65 years and over 11
- 85 years and over 1
- Median age 49.3
- Native-born 37
- Foreign-born 0

Educational Attainment, 2000
- Population 25 years and over 37
- Less than 9th grade 0.0%
- High school grad or higher 62.2%
- Bachelor's degree or higher 0.0%
- Graduate degree 0.0%

Income & Poverty, 1999
- Per capita income $17,624
- Median household income $22,250
- Median family income $22,250
- Persons in poverty 0
- H'holds receiving public assistance 0
- H'holds receiving social security 14

Households, 2000
- Total households 20
  - With persons under 18 4
  - With persons over 65 7
  - Family households 12
  - Single-person households 8
- Persons per household 2.05
- Persons per family 2.75

Labor & Employment
- Total civilian labor force, 2006** 22
  - Unemployment rate 0.0%
- Total civilian labor force, 2000 18
  - Unemployment rate 0.0%

Employed persons 16 years and over by occupation, 2000
- Managers & professionals 0
- Service occupations 10
- Sales & office occupations 0
- Farming, fishing & forestry 0
- Construction & maintenance 8
- Production & transportation 0
- Self-employed persons 0

* US Census Bureau
** New Jersey Department of Labor

See Introduction for an explanation of all data sources.

General Information
Township of Walpack
Walpack Center
PO Box 94
Walpack, NJ 07881
908-841-9576

- Website .... (county website)
- Year of incorporation 1731
- Land/water area (sq. miles) 24.07/0.65
- Form of government .... Township

Government
Legislative Districts
- US Congressional 5
- State Legislative 24

Local Officials, 2008
- Mayor .... Raymond Fuller
- Manager/Admin .... NA
- Clerk .... Betsy Cuneo
- Finance Dir .... Michelle Lastarza
- Tax Assessor .... John Dykson
- Tax Collector .... Terry Beshada
- Attorney .... Michael Garofalo
- Building .... Greg Chontow
- Comm Dev/Planning .... NA
- Engineering .... NA
- Public Works .... NA
- Police Chief .... NA
- Fire/Emergency Dir .... NA

Housing & Construction
Housing Units, 2000*
- Total 34
- Median rent $400
- Median SF home value $275,000

Permits for New Residential Construction
	Units	Value
Total, 2007	0	$0
Single family	0	$0
Total, 2006	0	$0
Single family	0	$0

Real Property Valuation, 2007
	Parcels	Valuation
Total	30	$2,331,700
Vacant	7	85,100
Residential	8	645,250
Commercial	2	1,077,400
Industrial	0	0
Apartments	0	0
Farm land	9	101,950
Farm homestead	4	422,000

Average Property Value & Tax, 2007
- Residential value $88,938
- Property tax $695
- Tax credit/rebate $584

Public Library
No public municipal library

Library statistics, 2006
- Population served .... NA
- Full-time/total staff .... NA/NA

	Total	Per capita
Holdings	NA	NA
Revenues	NA	NA
Expenditures	NA	NA
Annual visits	NA	NA
Internet terminals/annual users	NA/NA	

Public Safety
Number of officers, 2006 0

Crime	2005	2006
Total crimes	1	3
Violent	0	1
Murder	0	0
Rape	0	0
Robbery	0	1
Aggravated assault	0	0
Non-violent	1	2
Burglary	1	2
Larceny	0	0
Vehicle theft	0	0
Domestic violence	0	0
Arson	0	0
Total crime rate	NA	NA
Violent	NA	NA
Non-violent	NA	NA

Public School District
(for school year 2006-07 except as noted)

Sandyston-Walpack Township School Dist.
100 Route 560, PO Box 128
Layton, NJ 07851
973-948-4450

- Chief School Admin .... Glenn Sumpman
- Number of schools 2
- Grade plan K-6
- Enrollment 184
- Attendance rate, '05-06 .... 96.4%
- Dropout rate .... NA
- Students per teacher 9.4
- Per pupil expenditure $13,157
- Median faculty salary $51,120
- Median administrator salary $110,000
- Grade 12 enrollment .... NA
- High school graduation rate .... NA

Assessment test results
(percent scoring at proficient or advanced level)

	Language	Math
NJASK-Grade 3	95.8%	95.8%
GEPA-Grade 8	NA	NA
HSPA-High School	NA	NA

SAT score averages
Pct tested	Math	Verbal	Writing
NA	NA	NA	NA

Teacher Qualifications
- Avg. years of experience 10
- Highly-qualified teachers
  - one subject/all subjects 100%/100%
- With emergency credentials 0.0%

No Child Left Behind
- AYP, 2005-06 .... Meets Standards

Municipal Finance
State Aid Programs, 2008
- Total aid $43,068
  - CMPTRA 0
  - Energy tax receipts 40,862
  - Garden State Trust 2,206

General Budget, 2007
- Total tax levy $18,727
  - County levy 9,868
    - County taxes 9,308
    - County library 794
    - County health 307
    - County open space 983
  - School levy 8,859
  - Muni. levy 0
- Misc. revenues 132,875

Taxes
	2005	2006	2007
General tax rate per $100	1.32	1.01	0.79
County equalization ratio	95.42	95.42	95.42
Net valuation taxable	$2,408,266	$2,331,700	$2,397,527
State equalized value	$2,523,859	$2,510,431	$2,509,445

Wanaque Borough
Passaic County

Demographics & Socio-Economic Characteristics
(2000 US Census, except as noted)

Population
1980*	10,025
1990*	9,711
2000	10,266
Male	4,956
Female	5,310
2006 (estimate)*	11,171
Population density	1,399.9

Race & Hispanic Origin, 2000
Race
White	9,308
Black/African American	155
American Indian/Alaska Native	35
Asian	372
Native Hawaiian/Pacific Islander	3
Other race	211
Two or more races	182
Hispanic origin, total	554
Mexican	69
Puerto Rican	179
Cuban	44
Other Hispanic	262

Age & Nativity, 2000
Under 5 years	689
18 years and over	7,765
21 years and over	7,470
65 years and over	1,233
85 years and over	247
Median age	37.6
Native-born	8,973
Foreign-born	1,293

Educational Attainment, 2000
Population 25 years and over	7,162
Less than 9th grade	6.2%
High school grad or higher	84.2%
Bachelor's degree or higher	22.3%
Graduate degree	7.7%

Income & Poverty, 1999
Per capita income	$25,403
Median household income	$66,113
Median family income	$71,127
Persons in poverty	330
H'holds receiving public assistance	64
H'holds receiving social security	841

Households, 2000
Total households	3,444
With persons under 18	1,401
With persons over 65	687
Family households	2,689
Single-person households	575
Persons per household	2.86
Persons per family	3.23

Labor & Employment
Total civilian labor force, 2006**	6,163
Unemployment rate	3.6%
Total civilian labor force, 2000	5,675
Unemployment rate	3.6%

Employed persons 16 years and over by occupation, 2000
Managers & professionals	1,712
Service occupations	871
Sales & office occupations	1,763
Farming, fishing & forestry	0
Construction & maintenance	473
Production & transportation	650
Self-employed persons	210

* US Census Bureau
** New Jersey Department of Labor

General Information
Borough of Wanaque
579 Ringwood Ave
Wanaque, NJ 07465
973-839-3000

Website	www.wanaqueborough.com
Year of incorporation	1918
Land/water area (sq. miles)	7.98/1.23
Form of government	Borough

Government
Legislative Districts
US Congressional	5
State Legislative	40

Local Officials, 2008
Mayor	Daniel Mahler
Manager	Thomas Carroll
Clerk	Katherine Falone
Finance Dir.	Mary Ann Brindisi
Tax Assessor	Brian Townsend
Tax Collector	Lynn Gordon
Attorney	Tony Fiorello
Building	Jeff Brusco
Planning	Richard Alaimo
Engineering	Mike Cristaldi
Public Works	Rick Crescente
Police Chief	Jack Reno
Emerg/Fire Director	Tad Skawinski

Housing & Construction
Housing Units, 2000*
Total	3,500
Median rent	$946
Median SF home value	$172,100

Permits for New Residential Construction
	Units	Value
Total, 2007	226	$19,586,620
Single family	4	$568,000
Total, 2006	231	$16,871,777
Single family	3	$331,250

Real Property Valuation, 2007
	Parcels	Valuation
Total	4,241	$562,941,184
Vacant	469	24,877,300
Residential	3,650	483,491,974
Commercial	99	42,143,720
Industrial	19	10,828,090
Apartments	4	1,600,100
Farm land	0	0
Farm homestead	0	0

Average Property Value & Tax, 2007
Residential value	$132,464
Property tax	$7,301
Tax credit/rebate	$1,189

Public Library
Wanaque Public Library
616 Ringwood Ave
Wanaque, NJ 07465
973-839-4434

Director: Richard L. Mariconda

Library statistics, 2006
Population served	10,266
Full-time/total staff	1/3

	Total	Per capita
Holdings	40,526	3.95
Revenues	$395,262	$38.50
Expenditures	$346,777	$33.78
Annual visits	20,000	1.95
Internet terminals/annual users	6/9,659	

Public Safety
Number of officers, 2006: 24

Crime	2005	2006
Total crimes	121	142
Violent	9	5
Murder	0	0
Rape	0	0
Robbery	4	0
Aggravated assault	5	5
Non-violent	112	137
Burglary	12	27
Larceny	95	101
Vehicle theft	5	9
Domestic violence	90	96
Arson	0	1
Total crime rate	11.6	13.4
Violent	0.9	0.5
Non-violent	10.7	12.9

Public School District
(for school year 2006-07 except as noted)

Wanaque School District
973 A Ringwood Ave
Haskell, NJ 07420
973-835-8202

Chief School Admin	Richard B. Weisenfeld
Number of schools	2
Grade plan	K-8
Enrollment	984
Attendance rate, '05-06	94.8%
Dropout rate	NA
Students per teacher	10.9
Per pupil expenditure	$12,710
Median faculty salary	$70,359
Median administrator salary	$107,478
Grade 12 enrollment	NA
High school graduation rate	NA

Assessment test results
(percent scoring at proficient or advanced level)
	Language	Math
NJASK-Grade 3	83.8%	84.1%
GEPA-Grade 8	83.3%	85.8%
HSPA-High School	NA	NA

SAT score averages
Pct tested	Math	Verbal	Writing
NA	NA	NA	NA

Teacher Qualifications
Avg. years of experience	12
Highly-qualified teachers one subject/all subjects	100%/100%
With emergency credentials	0.0%

No Child Left Behind
AYP, 2005-06: Meets Standards

Municipal Finance
State Aid Programs, 2008
Total aid	$1,165,606
CMPTRA	412,701
Energy tax receipts	743,785
Garden State Trust	7,889

General Budget, 2007
Total tax levy	$31,064,510
County levy	6,664,221
County taxes	6,529,336
County library	0
County health	0
County open space	134,885
School levy	18,021,313
Muni. levy	6,378,976
Misc. revenues	4,314,909

Taxes
	2005	2006	2007
General tax rate per $100	5.05	5.26	5.52
County equalization ratio	52.99	46.45	41.9
Net valuation taxable	$497,452,440	$518,907,284	$563,578,695
State equalized value	$1,070,941,744	$1,239,128,676	$1,387,533,751

Sussex County

Wantage Township

Demographics & Socio-Economic Characteristics
(2000 US Census, except as noted)

Population
1980*	7,268
1990*	9,487
2000	10,387
Male	5,113
Female	5,274
2006 (estimate)*	11,566
Population density	172.3

Race & Hispanic Origin, 2000
Race
White	10,086
Black/African American	67
American Indian/Alaska Native	6
Asian	70
Native Hawaiian/Pacific Islander	1
Other race	43
Two or more races	114
Hispanic origin, total	300
Mexican	23
Puerto Rican	130
Cuban	34
Other Hispanic	113

Age & Nativity, 2000
Under 5 years	701
18 years and over	7,337
21 years and over	6,975
65 years and over	916
85 years and over	97
Median age	36.3
Native-born	9,895
Foreign-born	492

Educational Attainment, 2000
Population 25 years and over	6,565
Less than 9th grade	4.0%
High school grad or higher	84.6%
Bachelor's degree or higher	19.5%
Graduate degree	7.7%

Income & Poverty, 1999
Per capita income	$22,488
Median household income	$58,440
Median family income	$65,339
Persons in poverty	508
H'holds receiving public assistance	102
H'holds receiving social security	826

Households, 2000
Total households	3,441
With persons under 18	1,592
With persons over 65	667
Family households	2,857
Single-person households	467
Persons per household	3.02
Persons per family	3.33

Labor & Employment
Total civilian labor force, 2006**	5,944
Unemployment rate	5.7%
Total civilian labor force, 2000	5,261
Unemployment rate	4.4%

Employed persons 16 years and over by occupation, 2000
Managers & professionals	1,597
Service occupations	759
Sales & office occupations	1,353
Farming, fishing & forestry	51
Construction & maintenance	658
Production & transportation	610
Self-employed persons	384

‡ Branch of county library
* US Census Bureau
** New Jersey Department of Labor

See Introduction for an explanation of all data sources.

General Information
Township of Wantage
888 Route 23
Wantage, NJ 07461
973-875-7192

Website	www.wantagewp.com
Year of incorporation	1754
Land/water area (sq. miles)	67.12/0.42
Form of government	Township

Government
Legislative Districts
US Congressional	5
State Legislative	24

Local Officials, 2008
Mayor	Parker Space
Administrator	Jim Doherty
Clerk	Jim Doherty
Finance Dir	Michelle Lastarza
Tax Assessor	Melissa Rockwell
Tax Collector	Marcia Snyder
Attorney	Mike Garofalo
Construction Official	Ed Vanderberg
Comm Dev/Planning	NA
Engineer	Harold Pellow
Public Works Supervisor	Claude Wagner
Police Chief	NA
Fire Chief	Leo Kinney

Housing & Construction
Housing Units, 2000*
Total	3,663
Median rent	$768
Median SF home value	$154,200

Permits for New Residential Construction
	Units	Value
Total, 2007	48	$7,138,933
Single family	33	$7,063,933
Total, 2006	80	$14,234,975
Single family	80	$14,234,975

Real Property Valuation, 2007
	Parcels	Valuation
Total	5,295	$1,424,042,411
Vacant	525	67,330,400
Residential	3,473	1,091,602,300
Commercial	142	105,338,862
Industrial	2	1,157,200
Apartments	3	5,978,200
Farm land	743	8,356,449
Farm homestead	407	144,279,000

Average Property Value & Tax, 2007
Residential value	$318,526
Property tax	$5,916
Tax credit/rebate	$1,029

Public Library
Sussex-Wantage Branch Library‡
69 Route 639
Wantage, NJ 07461
973-875-3940

Branch Librarian: Nancy Helmer

Library statistics, 2006
see Sussex County profile for library system statistics

Public Safety
Number of officers, 2006 0

Crime	2005	2006
Total crimes	115	112
Violent	11	12
Murder	0	0
Rape	2	0
Robbery	0	0
Aggravated assault	9	12
Non-violent	104	100
Burglary	28	26
Larceny	71	66
Vehicle theft	5	8
Domestic violence	22	9
Arson	1	7
Total crime rate	10.2	9.8
Violent	1.0	1.0
Non-violent	9.2	8.7

Public School District
(for school year 2006-07 except as noted)

Sussex-Wantage Regional School District
31 Ryan Rd
Wantage, NJ 07461
973-875-3175

Superintendent	Raymond Nazzaro (Int)
Number of schools	6
Grade plan	K-8
Enrollment	1,668
Attendance rate, '05-06	94.8%
Dropout rate	NA
Students per teacher	10.6
Per pupil expenditure	$12,839
Median faculty salary	$56,080
Median administrator salary	$101,172
Grade 12 enrollment	NA
High school graduation rate	NA

Assessment test results
(percent scoring at proficient or advanced level)

	Language	Math
NJASK-Grade 3	87.2%	93.4%
GEPA-Grade 8	83.2%	68.1%
HSPA-High School	NA	NA

SAT score averages
Pct tested	Math	Verbal	Writing
NA	NA	NA	NA

Teacher Qualifications
Avg. years of experience	12
Highly-qualified teachers one subject/all subjects	100%/100%
With emergency credentials	0.0%

No Child Left Behind
AYP, 2005-06 .... Needs Improvement

Municipal Finance
State Aid Programs, 2008
Total aid	$1,069,069
CMPTRA	382,937
Energy tax receipts	637,557
Garden State Trust	44,016

General Budget, 2007
Total tax levy	$26,507,667
County levy	5,249,661
County taxes	4,289,515
County library	365,609
County health	141,130
County open space	453,407
School levy	18,697,630
Muni. levy	2,560,376
Misc. revenues	3,578,560

Taxes	2005	2006	2007
General tax rate per $100	3.7	1.74	1.86
County equalization ratio	62.46	126.42	110.28
Net valuation taxable	$632,828,623	$1,422,032,104	$1,427,233,181
State equalized value	$1,092,025,234	$1,292,836,509	$1,396,169,750

Warren Township — Somerset County

Demographics & Socio-Economic Characteristics
(2000 US Census, except as noted)

Population
- 1980*: 9,805
- 1990*: 10,830
- 2000: 14,259
  - Male: 7,099
  - Female: 7,160
- 2006 (estimate)*: 15,816
  - Population density: 804.1

Race & Hispanic Origin, 2000
Race
- White: 12,303
- Black/African American: 180
- American Indian/Alaska Native: 5
- Asian: 1,521
- Native Hawaiian/Pacific Islander: 8
- Other race: 59
- Two or more races: 183
- Hispanic origin, total: 455
  - Mexican: 33
  - Puerto Rican: 66
  - Cuban: 76
  - Other Hispanic: 280

Age & Nativity, 2000
- Under 5 years: 1,019
- 18 years and over: 10,027
- 21 years and over: 9,708
- 65 years and over: 1,598
- 85 years and over: 151
  - Median age: 39.4
- Native-born: 12,018
- Foreign-born: 2,241

Educational Attainment, 2000
- Population 25 years and over: 9,396
- Less than 9th grade: 2.4%
- High school grad or higher: 93.4%
- Bachelor's degree or higher: 58.2%
- Graduate degree: 28.4%

Income & Poverty, 1999
- Per capita income: $49,475
- Median household income: $103,677
- Median family income: $121,264
- Persons in poverty: 299
- H'holds receiving public assistance: 17
- H'holds receiving social security: 1,046

Households, 2000
- Total households: 4,629
  - With persons under 18: 2,147
  - With persons over 65: 1,079
  - Family households: 3,937
  - Single-person households: 565
- Persons per household: 3.05
- Persons per family: 3.33

Labor & Employment
- Total civilian labor force, 2006**: 7,813
  - Unemployment rate: 2.0%
- Total civilian labor force, 2000: 6,936
  - Unemployment rate: 1.6%

Employed persons 16 years and over by occupation, 2000
- Managers & professionals: 3,947
- Service occupations: 554
- Sales & office occupations: 1,598
- Farming, fishing & forestry: 5
- Construction & maintenance: 345
- Production & transportation: 374
- Self-employed persons: 585

‡ Branch of county library
* US Census Bureau
** New Jersey Department of Labor

General Information
Township of Warren
46 Mountain Blvd
Warren, NJ 07059
908-753-8000

- Website: www.warrennj.org
- Year of incorporation: 1806
- Land/water area (sq. miles): 19.67/0.00
- Form of government: Township

Government
Legislative Districts
- US Congressional: 7
- State Legislative: 21

Local Officials, 2008
- Mayor: Gary DiNardo
- Manager: Mark Krane
- Clerk: Patricia DiRocco
- Finance Dir.: Shaw Boswell
- Tax Assessor: Edward Kerwin Jr
- Tax Collector: Loree Saums
- Attorney: John Belardo
- Building: Jeffrey Heiss
- Planning: John Chadwick
- Engineering: Christian Kastrud
- Public Works: Douglas Buro
- Police Chief: Russell Leffert
- Emerg/Fire Director: Timothy McGowan

Housing & Construction
Housing Units, 2000*
- Total: 4,718
- Median rent: $1,135
- Median SF home value: $427,200

Permits for New Residential Construction

	Units	Value
Total, 2007	38	$7,997,924
Single family	38	$7,997,924
Total, 2006	32	$5,090,982
Single family	32	$5,090,982

Real Property Valuation, 2007

	Parcels	Valuation
Total	5,907	$4,459,472,723
Vacant	619	115,876,200
Residential	4,941	3,550,591,500
Commercial	201	711,025,200
Industrial	11	45,402,300
Apartments	0	0
Farm land	87	234,623
Farm homestead	48	36,342,900

Average Property Value & Tax, 2007
- Residential value: $718,969
- Property tax: $11,795
- Tax credit/rebate: $1,275

Public Library
Warren Township Branch Library‡
42 Mountain Blvd
Warren, NJ 07059
908-754-5554

- Branch Director: Elaine Whiting

Library statistics, 2006
see Somerset County profile for library system statistics

Public Safety
- Number of officers, 2006: 28

Crime	2005	2006
Total crimes	108	107
Violent	5	3
Murder	0	0
Rape	3	0
Robbery	0	2
Aggravated assault	2	1
Non-violent	103	104
Burglary	9	13
Larceny	90	89
Vehicle theft	4	2
Domestic violence	25	3
Arson	0	1
Total crime rate	7.0	6.8
Violent	0.3	0.2
Non-violent	6.6	6.7

Public School District
(for school year 2006-07 except as noted)

Warren Township School District
213 Mount Horeb Rd
Warren, NJ 07059
732-560-8700

- Superintendent: James Crisfield
- Number of schools: 5
- Grade plan: K-8
- Enrollment: 2,216
- Attendance rate, '05-06: 96.2%
- Dropout rate: NA
- Students per teacher: 8.8
- Per pupil expenditure: $14,156
- Median faculty salary: $56,558
- Median administrator salary: $118,069
- Grade 12 enrollment: NA
- High school graduation rate: NA

Assessment test results
(percent scoring at proficient or advanced level)

	Language	Math
NJASK-Grade 3	95.2%	97.6%
GEPA-Grade 8	93.0%	88.3%
HSPA-High School	NA	NA

SAT score averages

Pct tested	Math	Verbal	Writing
NA	NA	NA	NA

Teacher Qualifications
- Avg. years of experience: 9
- Highly-qualified teachers one subject/all subjects: 100%/100%
- With emergency credentials: 0.0%

No Child Left Behind
- AYP, 2005-06: Meets Standards

Municipal Finance
State Aid Programs, 2008
- Total aid: $1,671,298
  - CMPTRA: 0
  - Energy tax receipts: 1,671,246
  - Garden State Trust: 52

General Budget, 2007
- Total tax levy: $73,256,542
  - County levy: 16,549,408
    - County taxes: 13,384,549
    - County library: 1,699,170
    - County health: 0
    - County open space: 1,465,689
  - School levy: 47,277,502
  - Muni. levy: 9,429,632
- Misc. revenues: 6,205,871

Taxes

	2005	2006	2007
General tax rate per $100	1.65	1.63	1.65
County equalization ratio	101.26	96.53	91.45
Net valuation taxable	$3,915,902,784	$4,196,000,263	$4,465,230,057
State equalized value	$4,317,899,199	$4,838,847,433	$4,917,070,906

Warren County
Washington Borough

Demographics & Socio-Economic Characteristics
(2000 US Census, except as noted)

Population
- 1980* 6,429
- 1990* 6,474
- 2000 6,712
  - Male 3,340
  - Female 3,372
- 2006 (estimate)* 6,841
  - Population density 3,490.3

Race & Hispanic Origin, 2000
Race
- White 6,138
- Black/African American 261
- American Indian/Alaska Native 8
- Asian 97
- Native Hawaiian/Pacific Islander 1
- Other race 108
- Two or more races 99
- Hispanic origin, total 280
  - Mexican 27
  - Puerto Rican 130
  - Cuban 18
  - Other Hispanic 105

Age & Nativity, 2000
- Under 5 years 444
- 18 years and over 4,932
- 21 years and over 4,716
- 65 years and over 715
- 85 years and over 97
  - Median age 35.2
- Native-born 6,120
- Foreign-born 592

Educational Attainment, 2000
- Population 25 years and over 4,414
- Less than 9th grade 4.3%
- High school grad or higher 83.4%
- Bachelor's degree or higher 22.7%
- Graduate degree 7.9%

Income & Poverty, 1999
- Per capita income $23,166
- Median household income $47,000
- Median family income $61,379
- Persons in poverty 375
- H'holds receiving public assistance 31
- H'holds receiving social security 654

Households, 2000
- Total households 2,724
  - With persons under 18 975
  - With persons over 65 578
  - Family households 1,685
  - Single-person households 862
- Persons per household 2.46
- Persons per family 3.15

Labor & Employment
- Total civilian labor force, 2006** 4,144
  - Unemployment rate 3.8%
- Total civilian labor force, 2000 3,629
  - Unemployment rate 3.3%

Employed persons 16 years and over by occupation, 2000
- Managers & professionals 1,176
- Service occupations 494
- Sales & office occupations 906
- Farming, fishing & forestry 0
- Construction & maintenance 399
- Production & transportation 534
- Self-employed persons 180

* US Census Bureau
** New Jersey Department of Labor

See Introduction for an explanation of all data sources.

General Information
Borough of Washington
100 Belvidere Ave
Washington, NJ 07882
908-689-3600
- Website .... www.washingtonboro-nj.org
- Year of incorporation 1868
- Land/water area (sq. miles) 1.96/0.00
- Form of government .... Council-Manager

Government
Legislative Districts
- US Congressional 5
- State Legislative 23

Local Officials, 2008
- Mayor .... Marianne Van Deursen
- Manager .... John Corica
- Clerk .... Kristine Blanchard
- Finance Dir .... Kay Stasyshan
- Tax Assessor .... Athan Efstathiou
- Tax Collector .... Kay Stasyshan
- Attorney .... Richard Cushing
- Building .... Chuck Herring
- Comm Dev/Planning .... NA
- Engineering .... Robert Miller
- Public Works .... NA
- Police Chief .... George Cortellesi
- Emerg/Fire Director .... Kurt Klausfelder

Housing & Construction
Housing Units, 2000*
- Total 2,876
- Median rent $697
- Median SF home value $119,000

Permits for New Residential Construction

	Units	Value
Total, 2007	12	$1,550,000
Single family	12	$1,550,000
Total, 2006	3	$135,300
Single family	3	$135,300

Real Property Valuation, 2007

	Parcels	Valuation
Total	2,200	$377,279,560
Vacant	77	5,960,300
Residential	1,915	282,165,460
Commercial	171	48,804,000
Industrial	14	16,823,900
Apartments	18	23,083,000
Farm land	4	5,300
Farm homestead	1	437,600

Average Property Value & Tax, 2007
- Residential value $147,496
- Property tax $5,850
- Tax credit/rebate $1,049

Public Library
Washington Public Library
20 W Carlton Ave
Washington, NJ 07882
908-689-0201
- Director .... Barbara A. Rose

Library statistics, 2006
- Population served 6,712
- Full-time/total staff 0/2

	Total	Per capita
Holdings	49,902	7.43
Revenues	$341,259	$50.84
Expenditures	$330,480	$49.24
Annual visits	33,752	5.03
Internet terminals/annual users	9/11,990	

Public Safety
- Number of officers, 2006 13

Crime

	2005	2006
Total crimes	137	184
Violent	8	9
Murder	0	1
Rape	0	0
Robbery	1	1
Aggravated assault	7	7
Non-violent	129	175
Burglary	29	37
Larceny	98	128
Vehicle theft	2	10
Domestic violence	164	126
Arson	0	6
Total crime rate	19.9	26.8
Violent	1.2	1.3
Non-violent	18.7	25.5

Public School District
(for school year 2006-07 except as noted)

Washington Borough School District
300 W Stewart St
Washington, NJ 07882
908-689-0241

- Superintendent .... Lance Rozsa
- Number of schools 2
- Grade plan K-6
- Enrollment 511
- Attendance rate, '05-06 .... 94.7%
- Dropout rate .... NA
- Students per teacher 9.3
- Per pupil expenditure $13,648
- Median faculty salary $54,817
- Median administrator salary $79,850
- Grade 12 enrollment .... NA
- High school graduation rate .... NA

Assessment test results
(percent scoring at proficient or advanced level)

	Language	Math
NJASK-Grade 3	78.0%	83.6%
GEPA-Grade 8	NA	NA
HSPA-High School	NA	NA

SAT score averages

Pct tested	Math	Verbal	Writing
NA	NA	NA	NA

Teacher Qualifications
- Avg. years of experience 14
- Highly-qualified teachers
  - one subject/all subjects 100%/100%
- With emergency credentials 0.0%

No Child Left Behind
- AYP, 2005-06 .... Meets Standards

Municipal Finance
State Aid Programs, 2008
- Total aid $647,109
  - CMPTRA 154,516
  - Energy tax receipts 492,593
  - Garden State Trust 0

General Budget, 2007
- Total tax levy $15,046,239
  - County levy 3,207,008
    - County taxes 2,861,487
    - County library 0
    - County health 0
    - County open space 345,521
  - School levy 8,029,288
  - Muni. levy 3,809,943
  - Misc. revenues 2,358,699

Taxes

	2005	2006	2007
General tax rate per $100	3.51	3.72	3.97
County equalization ratio	82.6	74.01	66.26
Net valuation taxable	$374,055,293	$373,195,160	$379,341,707
State equalized value	$505,411,827	$565,961,191	$584,553,362

The New Jersey Municipal Data Book

Washington Township — Bergen County

Demographics & Socio-Economic Characteristics
(2000 US Census, except as noted)

Population
1980*	9,550
1990*	9,245
2000	8,938
Male	4,291
Female	4,647
2006 (estimate)*	9,670
Population density	3,323.0

Race & Hispanic Origin, 2000
Race
White	8,229
Black/African American	88
American Indian/Alaska Native	4
Asian	498
Native Hawaiian/Pacific Islander	0
Other race	39
Two or more races	80
Hispanic origin, total	299
Mexican	21
Puerto Rican	85
Cuban	83
Other Hispanic	110

Age & Nativity, 2000
Under 5 years	606
18 years and over	6,905
21 years and over	6,730
65 years and over	1,512
85 years and over	92
Median age	41.8
Native-born	7,672
Foreign-born	1,266

Educational Attainment, 2000
Population 25 years and over	6,489
Less than 9th grade	2.3%
High school grad or higher	94.0%
Bachelor's degree or higher	44.8%
Graduate degree	16.6%

Income & Poverty, 1999
Per capita income	$39,248
Median household income	$83,694
Median family income	$88,017
Persons in poverty	216
H'holds receiving public assistance	19
H'holds receiving social security	994

Households, 2000
Total households	3,219
With persons under 18	1,147
With persons over 65	1,069
Family households	2,688
Single-person households	468
Persons per household	2.77
Persons per family	3.07

Labor & Employment
Total civilian labor force, 2006**	5,071
Unemployment rate	3.8%
Total civilian labor force, 2000	4,772
Unemployment rate	3.8%

Employed persons 16 years and over by occupation, 2000
Managers & professionals	2,341
Service occupations	388
Sales & office occupations	1,447
Farming, fishing & forestry	0
Construction & maintenance	260
Production & transportation	153
Self-employed persons	240

* US Census Bureau
** New Jersey Department of Labor

General Information
Township of Washington
350 Hudson Ave
Washington Township, NJ 07676
201-664-4404

Website	www.twpofwashington.us
Year of incorporation	1840
Land/water area (sq. miles)	2.91/0.05
Form of government	Mayor-Council

Government
Legislative Districts
US Congressional	5
State Legislative	39

Local Officials, 2008
Mayor	Rudolph J. Wenzel
Manager	Agnes Smith
Clerk	Mary Ann Ozment
Finance Dir.	Jacqueline Do
Tax Assessor	Raymond Damiano
Tax Collector	Joyce Campbell
Attorney	Kenneth Poller
Building	John Scialla
Comm Dev/Planning	NA
Engineering	Azzolina & Feury
Public Works	Robert Hamilton
Police Chief	William Cicchetti
Emerg/Fire Director	Jason Gugger

Housing & Construction
Housing Units, 2000*
Total	3,245
Median rent	$1,909
Median SF home value	$287,800

Permits for New Residential Construction
	Units	Value
Total, 2007	19	$3,417,042
Single family	13	$3,414,180
Total, 2006	21	$5,377,387
Single family	9	$5,371,665

Real Property Valuation, 2007
	Parcels	Valuation
Total	3,456	$1,907,386,100
Vacant	62	11,024,900
Residential	3,373	1,845,384,000
Commercial	21	50,977,200
Industrial	0	0
Apartments	0	0
Farm land	0	0
Farm homestead	0	0

Average Property Value & Tax, 2007
Residential value	$547,105
Property tax	$8,851
Tax credit/rebate	$1,305

Public Library
Washington Township Public Library
144 Woodfield Rd
Township of Washington, NJ 07676
201-664-4586

Director: Juliette L. Sobon

Library statistics, 2006
Population served	8,938
Full-time/total staff	2/4

	Total	Per capita
Holdings	43,090	4.82
Revenues	$593,405	$66.39
Expenditures	$591,437	$66.17
Annual visits	50,219	5.62
Internet terminals/annual users		7/3,158

Public Safety
Number of officers, 2006		24

Crime	2005	2006
Total crimes	41	37
Violent	1	5
Murder	0	2
Rape	0	0
Robbery	0	1
Aggravated assault	1	2
Non-violent	40	32
Burglary	7	1
Larceny	33	29
Vehicle theft	0	2
Domestic violence	13	11
Arson	0	0
Total crime rate	4.3	3.8
Violent	0.1	0.5
Non-violent	4.2	3.3

Public School District
(for school year 2006-07 except as noted)

Westwood Regional School District
701 Ridgewood Rd
Township of Washington, NJ 07676
201-664-2765

Superintendent	Geoffrey Zoeller
Number of schools	12
Grade plan	K-12
Enrollment	2,646
Attendance rate, '05-06	94.4%
Dropout rate	NA
Students per teacher	10.5
Per pupil expenditure	$14,584
Median faculty salary	$53,168
Median administrator salary	$113,163
Grade 12 enrollment	179
High school graduation rate	98.9%

Assessment test results
(percent scoring at proficient or advanced level)

	Language	Math
NJASK-Grade 3	87.1%	96.9%
GEPA-Grade 8	89.9%	80.1%
HSPA-High School	95.9%	82.8%

SAT score averages
Pct tested	Math	Verbal	Writing
92%	534	492	494

Teacher Qualifications
Avg. years of experience	8
Highly-qualified teachers one subject/all subjects	100%/100%
With emergency credentials	0.0%

No Child Left Behind
AYP, 2005-06	Meets Standards

Municipal Finance
State Aid Programs, 2008
Total aid	$882,893
CMPTRA	63,530
Energy tax receipts	819,363
Garden State Trust	0

General Budget, 2007
Total tax levy	$30,869,451
County levy	3,508,845
County taxes	3,315,080
County library	0
County health	0
County open space	193,765
School levy	19,310,909
Muni. levy	8,049,697
Misc. revenues	3,205,975

Taxes
	2005	2006	2007
General tax rate per $100	3.15	1.49	1.62
County equalization ratio	55.85	111.06	98.55
Net valuation taxable	$846,636,302	$1,909,368,500	$1,908,102,301
State equalized value	$1,702,123,647	$1,938,150,537	$1,992,348,341

Burlington County

Washington Township

Demographics & Socio-Economic Characteristics
(2000 US Census, except as noted)

Population
- 1980*.................................808
- 1990*.................................805
- 2000.................................621
  - Male...............................298
  - Female............................323
- 2006 (estimate)*...................651
- Population density................6.5

Race & Hispanic Origin, 2000
Race
- White.................................519
- Black/African American..........18
- American Indian/Alaska Native....0
- Asian....................................2
- Native Hawaiian/Pacific Islander....0
- Other race............................75
- Two or more races..................7
- Hispanic origin, total............106
  - Mexican..............................3
  - Puerto Rican........................96
  - Cuban..................................0
  - Other Hispanic......................7

Age & Nativity, 2000
- Under 5 years........................29
- 18 years and over.................439
- 21 years and over.................420
- 65 years and over.................151
- 85 years and over..................58
- Median age........................40.8
- Native-born.........................572
- Foreign-born...........................7

Educational Attainment, 2000
- Population 25 years and over....384
- Less than 9th grade.............21.1%
- High school grad or higher....55.7%
- Bachelor's degree or higher...12.2%
- Graduate degree..................2.9%

Income & Poverty, 1999
- Per capita income.............$13,977
- Median household income....$41,250
- Median family income........$42,188
- Persons in poverty..................68
- H'holds receiving public assistance....11
- H'holds receiving social security......46

Households, 2000
- Total households...................160
  - With persons under 18..........63
  - With persons over 65............48
- Family households.................113
- Single-person households........39
- Persons per household..........2.76
- Persons per family.................3.27

Labor & Employment
- Total civilian labor force, 2006**......198
  - Unemployment rate.............6.4%
- Total civilian labor force, 2000......174
  - Unemployment rate.............2.9%

Employed persons 16 years and over by occupation, 2000
- Managers & professionals.......34
- Service occupations................26
- Sales & office occupations......27
- Farming, fishing & forestry......30
- Construction & maintenance.....9
- Production & transportation....43
- Self-employed persons............10

* US Census Bureau
** New Jersey Department of Labor

See Introduction for an explanation of all data sources.

General Information
Washington Township
1018 River Rd
Egg Harbor City, NJ 08215
609-965-3242

- Website...............................NA
- Year of incorporation............1802
- Land/water area (sq. miles)....100.14/2.72
- Form of government..........Township

Government

Legislative Districts
- US Congressional.....................2
- State Legislative......................9

Local Officials, 2008
- Mayor....................Daniel James
- Manager/Admin.....................NA
- Clerk........................Paul Kain
- Finance Dir...........John Cicalese
- Tax Assessor..........Jay Renwick
- Tax Collector.......Victoria Boras
- Attorney..............Daniel Kehler
- Building..........................DCA
- Comm Dev/Planning..............NA
- Engineering..............Kris Kluk
- Public Works.......................NA
- Police Chief.........................NA
- Fire Chief............W. Homiller

Housing & Construction

Housing Units, 2000*
- Total.................................171
- Median rent........................$500
- Median SF home value......$95,000

Permits for New Residential Construction

	Units	Value
Total, 2007	2	$145,169
Single family	2	$145,169
Total, 2006	2	$97,446
Single family	2	$97,446

Real Property Valuation, 2007

	Parcels	Valuation
Total	499	$124,385,500
Vacant	130	4,798,600
Residential	308	91,834,900
Commercial	16	15,103,400
Industrial	3	2,399,900
Apartments	0	0
Farm land	22	1,654,400
Farm homestead	20	8,594,300

Average Property Value & Tax, 2007
- Residential value..............$306,187
- Property tax.......................$3,422
- Tax credit/rebate...................$744

Public Library
No public municipal library

Library statistics, 2006
- Population served.................NA
- Full-time/total staff..........NA/NA

	Total	Per capita
Holdings	NA	NA
Revenues	NA	NA
Expenditures	NA	NA
Annual visits	NA	NA
Internet terminals/annual users	NA/NA	

Taxes

	2005	2006	2007
General tax rate per $100	2.798	2.873	1.12
County equalization ratio	52.79	51.07	113.23
Net valuation taxable	$46,302,896	$46,469,150	$124,783,709
State equalized value	$90,665,549	$109,966,440	$132,316,228

Public Safety
Number of officers, 2006................0

Crime	2005	2006
Total crimes	10	17
Violent	1	0
Murder	0	0
Rape	0	0
Robbery	0	0
Aggravated assault	1	0
Non-violent	9	17
Burglary	2	3
Larceny	7	12
Vehicle theft	0	2
Domestic violence	0	0
Arson	0	2
Total crime rate	15.6	26.4
Violent	1.6	0.0
Non-violent	14.1	26.4

Public School District
(for school year 2006-07 except as noted)

Washington Township School District
2436 Route 563
Egg Harbor, NJ 08215

- Superintendent......Richard Goldberg
- Number of schools......................1
- Grade plan...........................K-8
- Enrollment............................71
- Attendance rate, '05-06.........95.0%
- Dropout rate..........................NA
- Students per teacher..............5.3
- Per pupil expenditure........$18,122
- Median faculty salary........$46,746
- Median administrator salary...$89,224
- Grade 12 enrollment................NA
- High school graduation rate......NA

Assessment test results
(percent scoring at proficient or advanced level)

	Language	Math
NJASK-Grade 3	NA	NA
GEPA-Grade 8	81.8%	63.7%
HSPA-High School	NA	NA

SAT score averages

Pct tested	Math	Verbal	Writing
NA	NA	NA	NA

Teacher Qualifications
- Avg. years of experience........14
- Highly-qualified teachers
  - one subject/all subjects......100%/100%
- With emergency credentials.....0.0%

No Child Left Behind
AYP, 2005-06............Meets Standards

Municipal Finance

State Aid Programs, 2008
- Total aid......................$1,233,223
  - CMPTRA...............................0
  - Energy tax receipts...........82,308
  - Garden State Trust..........1,128,350

General Budget, 2007
- Total tax levy.................$1,394,638
  - County levy....................469,330
    - County taxes................388,907
    - County library................35,688
    - County health......................0
    - County open space..........44,735
  - School levy....................925,308
  - Muni. levy..............................0
- Misc. revenues................1,637,778

Washington Township
Gloucester County

Demographics & Socio-Economic Characteristics
(2000 US Census, except as noted)

Population
1980*	27,878
1990*	41,960
2000	47,114
Male	22,834
Female	24,280
2006 (estimate)*	51,827
Population density	2,425.2

Race & Hispanic Origin, 2000
Race
White	42,497
Black/African American	2,286
American Indian/Alaska Native	39
Asian	1,558
Native Hawaiian/Pacific Islander	6
Other race	252
Two or more races	476
Hispanic origin, total	955
Mexican	138
Puerto Rican	464
Cuban	53
Other Hispanic	300

Age & Nativity, 2000
Under 5 years	2,901
18 years and over	33,571
21 years and over	31,831
65 years and over	4,233
85 years and over	491
Median age	36.0
Native-born	44,834
Foreign-born	2,280

Educational Attainment, 2000
Population 25 years and over	29,876
Less than 9th grade	2.0%
High school grad or higher	89.9%
Bachelor's degree or higher	30.4%
Graduate degree	8.8%

Income & Poverty, 1999
Per capita income	$25,705
Median household income	$66,546
Median family income	$74,661
Persons in poverty	1,518
H'holds receiving public assistance	145
H'holds receiving social security	3,435

Households, 2000
Total households	15,609
With persons under 18	7,198
With persons over 65	3,016
Family households	12,659
Single-person households	2,405
Persons per household	3.00
Persons per family	3.38

Labor & Employment
Total civilian labor force, 2006**	28,689
Unemployment rate	1.9%
Total civilian labor force, 2000	25,153
Unemployment rate	3.6%

Employed persons 16 years and over by occupation, 2000
Managers & professionals	9,895
Service occupations	3,025
Sales & office occupations	7,523
Farming, fishing & forestry	9
Construction & maintenance	1,713
Production & transportation	2,075
Self-employed persons	1,050

* US Census Bureau
** New Jersey Department of Labor

General Information
Washington Township
523 Egg Harbor Rd
Sewell, NJ 08080
856-589-0520

Website	www.twp.washington.nj.us
Year of incorporation	1836
Land/water area (sq. miles)	21.37/0.12
Form of government	Mayor-Council

Government
Legislative Districts
US Congressional	1
State Legislative	4

Local Officials, 2008
Mayor	Paul D. Moriarty
Manager	Jack Lipsett
Clerk	Jennica N. Bileci
Finance Dir	Mary Breslin
Tax Assessor	Leo Midure
Tax Collector	Penny Carre Morris
Attorney	John Eastlack
Building	Tom Krwawecz
Planning	Tom Krwawecz
Engineering	Remington & Vernick
Public Works	James McKeever
Police Chief	Rafael Muniz
Emerg/Fire Director	John Hoffman

Housing & Construction
Housing Units, 2000*
Total	16,020
Median rent	$833
Median SF home value	$140,700

Permits for New Residential Construction
	Units	Value
Total, 2007	16	$2,052,184
Single family	2	$931,184
Total, 2006	4	$1,509,925
Single family	4	$1,509,925

Real Property Valuation, 2007
	Parcels	Valuation
Total	17,514	$2,563,442,100
Vacant	507	34,918,100
Residential	16,113	2,089,670,700
Commercial	763	389,647,400
Industrial	12	5,945,200
Apartments	8	37,917,000
Farm land	78	640,300
Farm homestead	33	4,703,400

Average Property Value & Tax, 2007
Residential value	$129,715
Property tax	$5,684
Tax credit/rebate	$1,006

Public Library
Margaret E. Heggan Public Library
208 E Holly Ave
Hurffville, NJ 08080
856-589-3334

Director................Linda H. Snyder

Library statistics, 2006
Population served	47,114
Full-time/total staff	5/7

	Total	Per capita
Holdings	78,815	1.67
Revenues	$1,561,309	$33.14
Expenditures	$1,209,290	$25.67
Annual visits	162,641	3.45
Internet terminals/annual users	11/13,696	

Taxes
	2005	2006	2007
General tax rate per $100	3.995	4.186	4.382
County equalization ratio	67.79	59.57	53.11
Net valuation taxable	$2,517,398,028	$2,539,298,200	$2,567,559,483
State equalized value	$4,225,949,350	$4,785,694,009	$5,112,611,006

Public Safety
Number of officers, 2006 85

Crime	2005	2006
Total crimes	1,135	1,104
Violent	77	81
Murder	0	1
Rape	5	10
Robbery	26	27
Aggravated assault	46	43
Non-violent	1,058	1,023
Burglary	194	221
Larceny	803	734
Vehicle theft	61	68
Domestic violence	440	410
Arson	17	12
Total crime rate	22.3	21.7
Violent	1.5	1.6
Non-violent	20.8	20.1

Public School District
(for school year 2006-07 except as noted)

Washington Township School District
206 East Holly Ave
Sewell, NJ 08080
856-589-6644

Superintendent	Cheryl Simone
Number of schools	11
Grade plan	K-12
Enrollment	9,052
Attendance rate, '05-06	95.2%
Dropout rate	1.0%
Students per teacher	10.6
Per pupil expenditure	$12,847
Median faculty salary	$53,386
Median administrator salary	$111,170
Grade 12 enrollment	736
High school graduation rate	95.6%

Assessment test results
(percent scoring at proficient or advanced level)

	Language	Math
NJASK-Grade 3	92.2%	95.2%
GEPA-Grade 8	87.1%	79.9%
HSPA-High School	94.0%	82.7%

SAT score averages
Pct tested	Math	Verbal	Writing
80%	501	496	485

Teacher Qualifications
Avg. years of experience	13
Highly-qualified teachers one subject/all subjects	99.5%/99.5%
With emergency credentials	0.0%

No Child Left Behind
AYP, 2005-06 .... Meets Standards

Municipal Finance
State Aid Programs, 2008
Total aid	$4,105,020
CMPTRA	1,345,856
Energy tax receipts	2,759,164
Garden State Trust	0

General Budget, 2007
Total tax levy	$112,499,546
County levy	26,661,176
County taxes	24,725,344
County library	0
County health	0
County open space	1,935,833
School levy	64,373,558
Muni. levy	21,464,812
Misc. revenues	16,369,127

Morris County
Washington Township

Demographics & Socio-Economic Characteristics
(2000 US Census, except as noted)

Population
1980*	11,402
1990*	15,592
2000	17,592
Male	8,593
Female	8,999
2006 (estimate)*	18,691
Population density	416.7

Race & Hispanic Origin, 2000
Race
White	16,917
Black/African American	146
American Indian/Alaska Native	15
Asian	329
Native Hawaiian/Pacific Islander	9
Other race	62
Two or more races	114
Hispanic origin, total	389
Mexican	47
Puerto Rican	127
Cuban	62
Other Hispanic	153

Age & Nativity, 2000
Under 5 years	1,213
18 years and over	12,281
21 years and over	11,797
65 years and over	1,449
85 years and over	337
Median age	38.3
Native-born	16,537
Foreign-born	1,055

Educational Attainment, 2000
Population 25 years and over	11,313
Less than 9th grade	1.8%
High school grad or higher	96.3%
Bachelor's degree or higher	53.2%
Graduate degree	20.0%

Income & Poverty, 1999
Per capita income	$37,489
Median household income	$97,763
Median family income	$104,926
Persons in poverty	397
H'holds receiving public assistance	30
H'holds receiving social security	999

Households, 2000
Total households	5,755
With persons under 18	2,780
With persons over 65	960
Family households	4,874
Single-person households	701
Persons per household	3.02
Persons per family	3.31

Labor & Employment
Total civilian labor force, 2006**	9,903
Unemployment rate	3.2%
Total civilian labor force, 2000	9,048
Unemployment rate	2.7%

Employed persons 16 years and over by occupation, 2000
Managers & professionals	4,827
Service occupations	849
Sales & office occupations	2,178
Farming, fishing & forestry	18
Construction & maintenance	523
Production & transportation	406
Self-employed persons	634

* US Census Bureau
** New Jersey Department of Labor

See Introduction for an explanation of all data sources.

General Information
Washington Township
43 Schooleys Mountain Rd
Long Valley, NJ 07853
908-876-3315

Website	www.wtmorris.org
Year of incorporation	1798
Land/water area (sq. miles)	44.86/0.00
Form of government	Township

Government
Legislative Districts
US Congressional	11
State Legislative	24

Local Officials, 2008
Mayor	Kevin M. Walsh
Administrator	Dianne S. Gallets
Clerk	Dianne S. Gallets
Finance Dir.	Kevin Lifer
Tax Assessor	Dolores Pecorari
Tax Collector	Amy Monahan
Attorney	John Jansen
Building	Neil Ruggiero (Actg)
Comm Dev/Planning	NA
Engineering	Leon C. Hall
Public Works	NA
Police Chief	Michael Bailey
Fire/Emergency Dir.	Robert Drake

Housing & Construction
Housing Units, 2000*
Total	5,890
Median rent	$1,052
Median SF home value	$279,300

Permits for New Residential Construction
	Units	Value
Total, 2007	15	$3,801,090
Single family	15	$3,801,090
Total, 2006	25	$7,489,504
Single family	25	$7,489,504

Real Property Valuation, 2007
	Parcels	Valuation
Total	6,897	$1,718,916,500
Vacant	417	26,385,200
Residential	5,613	1,518,906,600
Commercial	166	56,861,500
Industrial	20	22,597,500
Apartments	5	20,332,800
Farm land	451	4,218,000
Farm homestead	225	69,614,900

Average Property Value & Tax, 2007
Residential value	$272,100
Property tax	$9,507
Tax credit/rebate	$1,201

Public Library
Washington Township Public Library
37 E Springtown Rd
Long Valley, NJ 07853
908-876-3596

Director................Virginia Scarlatelli

Library statistics, 2006
Population served	17,592
Full-time/total staff	4/7

	Total	Per capita
Holdings	84,801	4.82
Revenues	$1,003,934	$57.07
Expenditures	$1,034,540	$58.81
Annual visits	70,196	3.99
Internet terminals/annual users	14/20,532	

Public Safety
Number of officers, 2006............35

Crime	2005	2006
Total crimes	159	138
Violent	7	8
Murder	0	0
Rape	0	0
Robbery	0	0
Aggravated assault	7	8
Non-violent	152	130
Burglary	28	18
Larceny	122	102
Vehicle theft	2	10
Domestic violence	96	83
Arson	0	0
Total crime rate	8.6	7.4
Violent	0.4	0.4
Non-violent	8.2	7.0

Public School District
(for school year 2006-07 except as noted)

Washington Township School District
53 W Mill Rd
Long Valley, NJ 07853
908-876-4172

Superintendent	John Sakala (Int)
Number of schools	4
Grade plan	K-8
Enrollment	2,913
Attendance rate, '05-06	95.9%
Dropout rate	NA
Students per teacher	12.0
Per pupil expenditure	$12,576
Median faculty salary	$56,725
Median administrator salary	$115,363
Grade 12 enrollment	NA
High school graduation rate	NA

Assessment test results
(percent scoring at proficient or advanced level)
	Language	Math
NJASK-Grade 3	94.7%	97.4%
GEPA-Grade 8	90.4%	88.8%
HSPA-High School	NA	NA

SAT score averages
Pct tested	Math	Verbal	Writing
NA	NA	NA	NA

Teacher Qualifications
Avg. years of experience	9
Highly-qualified teachers one subject/all subjects	91.5%/91.5%
With emergency credentials	0.6%

No Child Left Behind
AYP, 2005-06............Meets Standards

Municipal Finance
State Aid Programs, 2008
Total aid	$1,829,185
CMPTRA	463,136
Energy tax receipts	1,347,469
Garden State Trust	17,781

General Budget, 2007
Total tax levy	$60,147,767
County levy	7,786,189
County taxes	6,228,198
County library	0
County health	0
County open space	1,557,991
School levy	42,375,558
Muni. levy	9,986,020
Misc. revenues	6,095,220

Taxes
	2005	2006	2007
General tax rate per $100	3.25	3.39	3.5
County equalization ratio	63.62	58.33	52.84
Net valuation taxable	$1,666,244,077	$1,690,287,800	$1,721,404,116
State equalized value	$2,856,581,651	$3,201,622,943	$3,327,277,751

The New Jersey Municipal Data Book

Washington Township
Warren County

Demographics & Socio-Economic Characteristics
(2000 US Census, except as noted)

Population
1980*	4,243
1990*	5,367
2000	6,248
Male	3,053
Female	3,195
2006 (estimate)*	6,981
Population density	397.1

Race & Hispanic Origin, 2000
Race
White	5,997
Black/African American	107
American Indian/Alaska Native	4
Asian	59
Native Hawaiian/Pacific Islander	0
Other race	31
Two or more races	50
Hispanic origin, total	135
Mexican	7
Puerto Rican	44
Cuban	21
Other Hispanic	63

Age & Nativity, 2000
Under 5 years	435
18 years and over	4,373
21 years and over	4,177
65 years and over	609
85 years and over	57
Median age	37.6
Native-born	5,994
Foreign-born	254

Educational Attainment, 2000
Population 25 years and over	4,049
Less than 9th grade	2.7%
High school grad or higher	90.8%
Bachelor's degree or higher	32.0%
Graduate degree	8.8%

Income & Poverty, 1999
Per capita income	$29,141
Median household income	$77,458
Median family income	$84,348
Persons in poverty	189
H'holds receiving public assistance	36
H'holds receiving social security	497

Households, 2000
Total households	2,099
With persons under 18	955
With persons over 65	442
Family households	1,740
Single-person households	297
Persons per household	2.95
Persons per family	3.26

Labor & Employment
Total civilian labor force, 2006**	3,751
Unemployment rate	5.2%
Total civilian labor force, 2000	3,271
Unemployment rate	4.5%

Employed persons 16 years and over by occupation, 2000
Managers & professionals	1,168
Service occupations	396
Sales & office occupations	949
Farming, fishing & forestry	15
Construction & maintenance	375
Production & transportation	220
Self-employed persons	142

* US Census Bureau
** New Jersey Department of Labor

General Information
Washington Township
350 Route 57 W
Washington, NJ 07882
908-689-7200

Website	www.washington-twp-warren.org
Year of incorporation	1849
Land/water area (sq. miles)	17.58/0.02
Form of government	Township

Government
Legislative Districts
US Congressional	5
State Legislative	23

Local Officials, 2008
Mayor	David Dempski
Manager/Admin	NA
Clerk	Mary Ann O'Neil
Finance Dir	Barbara Emery
Tax Assessor	Lydia Schmidt
Tax Collector	Evan Howell
Attorney	Michael B. Lavery
Building	Christopher Rose
Comm Dev/Planning	NA
Engineering	Michael Finelli
Public Works	Peter de Boer
Police Chief	James McDonald
Emerg/Fire Director	NA

Housing & Construction
Housing Units, 2000*
Total	2,174
Median rent	$822
Median SF home value	$185,400

Permits for New Residential Construction
	Units	Value
Total, 2007	12	$1,192,411
Single family	12	$1,192,411
Total, 2006	6	$1,142,950
Single family	6	$1,142,950

Real Property Valuation, 2007
	Parcels	Valuation
Total	2,932	$659,308,324
Vacant	279	12,837,300
Residential	2,263	549,201,899
Commercial	91	66,817,300
Industrial	6	3,501,200
Apartments	3	1,880,300
Farm land	195	2,359,325
Farm homestead	95	22,711,000

Average Property Value & Tax, 2007
Residential value	$242,542
Property tax	$7,083
Tax credit/rebate	$1,155

Public Library
No public municipal library

Library statistics, 2006
Population served	NA
Full-time/total staff	NA/NA

	Total	Per capita
Holdings	NA	NA
Revenues	NA	NA
Expenditures	NA	NA
Annual visits	NA	NA
Internet terminals/annual users	NA/NA	

Taxes
	2005	2006	2007
General tax rate per $100	2.62	2.78	2.93
County equalization ratio	92.13	83.89	76.25
Net valuation taxable	$627,661,363	$646,633,449	$660,917,555
State equalized value	$748,195,688	$849,627,389	$904,153,138

Public Safety
Number of officers, 2006		13

Crime	2005	2006
Total crimes	69	66
Violent	5	4
Murder	0	0
Rape	0	0
Robbery	0	0
Aggravated assault	5	4
Non-violent	64	62
Burglary	18	10
Larceny	45	52
Vehicle theft	1	0
Domestic violence	44	73
Arson	0	0
Total crime rate	10.1	9.5
Violent	0.7	0.6
Non-violent	9.4	8.9

Public School District
(for school year 2006-07 except as noted)

Washington Township School District
16 Castle St
Washington, NJ 07882
908-689-1119

Superintendent	Roger Jinks
Number of schools	2
Grade plan	K-6
Enrollment	674
Attendance rate, '05-06	95.4%
Dropout rate	NA
Students per teacher	12.0
Per pupil expenditure	$11,525
Median faculty salary	$60,365
Median administrator salary	$93,605
Grade 12 enrollment	NA
High school graduation rate	NA

Assessment test results
(percent scoring at proficient or advanced level)
	Language	Math
NJASK-Grade 3	89.3%	86.6%
GEPA-Grade 8	NA	NA
HSPA-High School	NA	NA

SAT score averages
Pct tested	Math	Verbal	Writing
NA	NA	NA	NA

Teacher Qualifications
Avg. years of experience	15
Highly-qualified teachers one subject/all subjects	100%/100%
With emergency credentials	0.0%

No Child Left Behind
AYP, 2005-06 .... Meets Standards

Municipal Finance
State Aid Programs, 2008
Total aid	$648,006
CMPTRA	87,427
Energy tax receipts	558,151
Garden State Trust	2,428

General Budget, 2007
Total tax levy	$19,300,572
County levy	5,301,369
County taxes	4,328,087
County library	451,895
County health	0
County open space	521,387
School levy	11,259,003
Muni. levy	2,740,200
Misc. revenues	2,687,514

Somerset County
Watchung Borough

Demographics & Socio-Economic Characteristics
(2000 US Census, except as noted)

Population
1980*	5,290
1990*	5,110
2000	5,613
Male	2,741
Female	2,872
2006 (estimate)*	6,284
Population density	1,043.9

Race & Hispanic Origin, 2000
Race
White	4,732
Black/African American	189
American Indian/Alaska Native	5
Asian	553
Native Hawaiian/Pacific Islander	5
Other race	40
Two or more races	89
Hispanic origin, total	168
Mexican	10
Puerto Rican	31
Cuban	27
Other Hispanic	100

Age & Nativity, 2000
Under 5 years	334
18 years and over	4,386
21 years and over	4,276
65 years and over	914
85 years and over	87
Median age	43.0
Native-born	4,754
Foreign-born	859

Educational Attainment, 2000
Population 25 years and over	4,144
Less than 9th grade	2.1%
High school grad or higher	93.9%
Bachelor's degree or higher	57.0%
Graduate degree	31.5%

Income & Poverty, 1999
Per capita income	$58,653
Median household income	$101,944
Median family income	$120,764
Persons in poverty	121
H'holds receiving public assistance	0
H'holds receiving social security	645

Households, 2000
Total households	2,098
With persons under 18	676
With persons over 65	558
Family households	1,618
Single-person households	399
Persons per household	2.62
Persons per family	3.00

Labor & Employment
Total civilian labor force, 2006**	3,003
Unemployment rate	3.0%
Total civilian labor force, 2000	2,699
Unemployment rate	3.7%

Employed persons 16 years and over by occupation, 2000
Managers & professionals	1,528
Service occupations	192
Sales & office occupations	570
Farming, fishing & forestry	0
Construction & maintenance	152
Production & transportation	157
Self-employed persons	288

‡ Branch of county library
* US Census Bureau
** New Jersey Department of Labor

General Information
Borough of Watchung
15 Mountain Blvd
Watchung, NJ 07069
908-756-0080

Website	watchungnj.com
Year of incorporation	1926
Land/water area (sq. miles)	6.02/0.02
Form of government	Borough

Government
Legislative Districts
US Congressional	7
State Legislative	21

Local Officials, 2008
Mayor	Albert Ellis
Manager	Laureen Fellin
Clerk	Laureen Fellin
Finance Dir	William Hance
Tax Assessor	Edward Kerwin
Tax Collector	Catherine Park
Attorney	Albert E. Cruz
Building	Edward Bennett
Planning	Heyer & Gruel
Engineering	Maser Consulting
Public Works	C. Gunther
Police Chief	Sean Whalen
Emerg/Fire Director	Stephen Peterson

Housing & Construction
Housing Units, 2000*
Total	2,155
Median rent	$854
Median SF home value	$429,400

Permits for New Residential Construction
	Units	Value
Total, 2007	9	$3,833,391
Single family	9	$3,833,391
Total, 2006	22	$4,650,055
Single family	14	$4,050,055

Real Property Valuation, 2007
	Parcels	Valuation
Total	2,212	$1,844,835,900
Vacant	213	43,352,700
Residential	1,904	1,415,883,400
Commercial	87	323,091,400
Industrial	7	7,348,400
Apartments	1	55,160,000
Farm land	0	0
Farm homestead	0	0

Average Property Value & Tax, 2007
Residential value	$743,636
Property tax	$11,959
Tax credit/rebate	$1,318

Public Library
Watchung Branch Library‡
12 Stirling Rd
Watchung, NJ 07060
908-561-0117

Branch Librarian......Douglas Poswencyk

Library statistics, 2006
see Somerset County profile for library system statistics

Public Safety
Number of officers, 2006.............28

Crime	2005	2006
Total crimes	433	317
Violent	7	6
Murder	0	0
Rape	2	0
Robbery	5	6
Aggravated assault	0	0
Non-violent	426	311
Burglary	9	13
Larceny	400	284
Vehicle theft	17	14
Domestic violence	56	37
Arson	0	0
Total crime rate	74.8	51.4
Violent	1.2	1.0
Non-violent	73.6	50.4

Public School District
(for school year 2006-07 except as noted)

Watchung Borough School District
One Parenty Way
Watchung, NJ 07069
908-755-8121

Superintendent	Mary Louise Malyska
Number of schools	2
Grade plan	K-8
Enrollment	682
Attendance rate, '05-06	96.0%
Dropout rate	NA
Students per teacher	10.4
Per pupil expenditure	$13,687
Median faculty salary	$49,620
Median administrator salary	$111,161
Grade 12 enrollment	NA
High school graduation rate	NA

Assessment test results
(percent scoring at proficient or advanced level)
	Language	Math
NJASK-Grade 3	92.0%	98.7%
GEPA-Grade 8	84.4%	88.3%
HSPA-High School	NA	NA

SAT score averages
Pct tested	Math	Verbal	Writing
NA	NA	NA	NA

Teacher Qualifications
Avg. years of experience	5
Highly-qualified teachers one subject/all subjects	100%/100%
With emergency credentials	0.0%

No Child Left Behind
AYP, 2005-06............Meets Standards

Municipal Finance
State Aid Programs, 2008
Total aid	$895,152
CMPTRA	98,596
Energy tax receipts	796,556
Garden State Trust	0

General Budget, 2007
Total tax levy	$29,692,053
County levy	6,929,589
County taxes	5,604,375
County library	711,488
County health	0
County open space	613,726
School levy	15,610,110
Muni. levy	7,152,355
Misc. revenues	5,377,669

Taxes	2005	2006	2007
General tax rate per $100	1.55	1.63	1.61
County equalization ratio	103.65	95.24	90.84
Net valuation taxable	$1,766,331,608	$1,769,386,700	$1,846,325,175
State equalized value	$1,854,611,096	$2,020,094,241	$1,936,090,680

See Introduction for an explanation of all data sources.

Waterford Township
Camden County

Demographics & Socio-Economic Characteristics
(2000 US Census, except as noted)

Population
1980*	8,126
1990*	10,940
2000	10,494
Male	5,255
Female	5,239
2006 (estimate)*	10,707
Population density	295.9

Race & Hispanic Origin, 2000
Race
White	9,733
Black/African American	439
American Indian/Alaska Native	22
Asian	94
Native Hawaiian/Pacific Islander	1
Other race	70
Two or more races	135
Hispanic origin, total	217
Mexican	24
Puerto Rican	127
Cuban	6
Other Hispanic	60

Age & Nativity, 2000
Under 5 years	635
18 years and over	7,793
21 years and over	7,407
65 years and over	854
85 years and over	72
Median age	36.1
Native-born	10,161
Foreign-born	324

Educational Attainment, 2000
Population 25 years and over	6,979
Less than 9th grade	4.3%
High school grad or higher	82.9%
Bachelor's degree or higher	12.8%
Graduate degree	3.5%

Income & Poverty, 1999
Per capita income	$21,676
Median household income	$59,075
Median family income	$63,693
Persons in poverty	590
H'holds receiving public assistance	44
H'holds receiving social security	779

Households, 2000
Total households	3,542
With persons under 18	1,491
With persons over 65	610
Family households	2,790
Single-person households	591
Persons per household	2.90
Persons per family	3.27

Labor & Employment
Total civilian labor force, 2006**	6,371
Unemployment rate	5.1%
Total civilian labor force, 2000	6,043
Unemployment rate	7.5%

Employed persons 16 years and over by occupation, 2000
Managers & professionals	1,585
Service occupations	822
Sales & office occupations	1,560
Farming, fishing & forestry	6
Construction & maintenance	894
Production & transportation	725
Self-employed persons	337

* US Census Bureau
** New Jersey Department of Labor

General Information
Township of Waterford
2131 Auburn Ave
Atco, NJ 08004
856-768-2300

Website	www.waterfordtwp.org
Year of incorporation	1695
Land/water area (sq. miles)	36.19/0.07
Form of government	Township

Government
Legislative Districts
US Congressional	2
State Legislative	6

Local Officials, 2008
Mayor	NA
Township Coord	Lawrence C. Ruocco
Clerk	Virginia Chandler
Finance Dir	Stephen A. Miller
Tax Assessor	Marie-Louise Procacci
Tax Collector	Mary Kennedy Nadzak
Attorney	John P. Maroccia
Construction	John Holroyd
Planning	Wendy M. Parducci (Chr)
Engineering	Christopher J. Noll
Public Works	Victor E. Pangia
Police Chief	John Knoll
Emerg/Fire Director	James Jankowski

Housing & Construction
Housing Units, 2000*
Total	3,671
Median rent	$725
Median SF home value	$116,500

Permits for New Residential Construction
	Units	Value
Total, 2007	24	$3,687,948
Single family	24	$3,687,948
Total, 2006	18	$2,982,244
Single family	18	$2,982,244

Real Property Valuation, 2007
	Parcels	Valuation
Total	4,461	$466,650,200
Vacant	515	11,499,800
Residential	3,531	402,157,300
Commercial	123	37,241,100
Industrial	5	1,225,400
Apartments	4	2,144,900
Farm land	205	1,551,900
Farm homestead	78	10,829,800

Average Property Value & Tax, 2007
Residential value	$114,433
Property tax	$5,446
Tax credit/rebate	$977

Public Library
Waterford Township Public Library
2204 Atco Ave
Atco, NJ 08004
856-767-7727

Director: Eva K. Lynch

Library statistics, 2006
Population served	10,494
Full-time/total staff	1/2

	Total	Per capita
Holdings	30,289	2.89
Revenues	$321,233	$30.61
Expenditures	$301,391	$28.72
Annual visits	11,500	1.10
Internet terminals/annual users	4/9,000	

Taxes
	2005	2006	2007
General tax rate per $100	4.18	4.484	4.76
County equalization ratio	75.53	66.81	58.11
Net valuation taxable	$457,779,934	$458,920,200	$467,672,601
State equalized value	$685,196,728	$790,891,193	$875,882,169

Public Safety
Number of officers, 2006		25

Crime	2005	2006
Total crimes	193	189
Violent	28	15
Murder	0	0
Rape	3	1
Robbery	3	5
Aggravated assault	22	9
Non-violent	165	174
Burglary	43	29
Larceny	107	134
Vehicle theft	15	11
Domestic violence	90	62
Arson	1	4
Total crime rate	18.1	17.6
Violent	2.6	1.4
Non-violent	15.5	16.2

Public School District
(for school year 2006-07 except as noted)

Waterford Township School District
1106 Old White Horse Pike
Waterford, NJ 08089
856-767-0331

Superintendent	Gary L. Dentino
Number of schools	3
Grade plan	K-6
Enrollment	921
Attendance rate, '05-06	94.9%
Dropout rate	NA
Students per teacher	10.2
Per pupil expenditure	$12,041
Median faculty salary	$66,868
Median administrator salary	$97,914
Grade 12 enrollment	NA
High school graduation rate	NA

Assessment test results
(percent scoring at proficient or advanced level)
	Language	Math
NJASK-Grade 3	81.0%	83.9%
GEPA-Grade 8	NA	NA
HSPA-High School	NA	NA

SAT score averages
Pct tested	Math	Verbal	Writing
NA	NA	NA	NA

Teacher Qualifications
Avg. years of experience	18
Highly-qualified teachers one subject/all subjects	100%/100%
With emergency credentials	0.0%

No Child Left Behind
AYP, 2005-06 .... Meets Standards

Municipal Finance
State Aid Programs, 2008
Total aid	$1,726,161
CMPTRA	363,383
Energy tax receipts	1,070,592
Garden State Trust	282,492

General Budget, 2007
Total tax levy	$22,256,994
County levy	5,293,878
County taxes	5,133,294
County library	0
County health	0
County open space	160,584
School levy	11,490,572
Muni. levy	5,472,544
Misc. revenues	3,892,366

Passaic County / Wayne Township

Demographics & Socio-Economic Characteristics
(2000 US Census, except as noted)

Population
1980*	46,474
1990*	47,025
2000	54,069
Male	25,699
Female	28,370
2006 (estimate)*	54,849
Population density	2,302.6

Race & Hispanic Origin, 2000
Race
White	48,687
Black/African American	895
American Indian/Alaska Native	54
Asian	3,066
Native Hawaiian/Pacific Islander	11
Other race	631
Two or more races	725
Hispanic origin, total	2,754
Mexican	164
Puerto Rican	726
Cuban	320
Other Hispanic	1,544

Age & Nativity, 2000
Under 5 years	3,313
18 years and over	41,543
21 years and over	39,201
65 years and over	8,765
85 years and over	1,236
Median age	40.0
Native-born	45,291
Foreign-born	8,824

Educational Attainment, 2000
Population 25 years and over	37,298
Less than 9th grade	4.4%
High school grad or higher	89.2%
Bachelor's degree or higher	41.5%
Graduate degree	15.4%

Income & Poverty, 1999
Per capita income	$35,349
Median household income	$83,651
Median family income	$95,114
Persons in poverty	1,443
H'holds receiving public assistance	155
H'holds receiving social security	5,528

Households, 2000
Total households	18,755
With persons under 18	6,801
With persons over 65	5,650
Family households	14,370
Single-person households	3,797
Persons per household	2.74
Persons per family	3.19

Labor & Employment
Total civilian labor force, 2006**	29,359
Unemployment rate	3.4%
Total civilian labor force, 2000	28,103
Unemployment rate	3.9%

Employed persons 16 years and over by occupation, 2000
Managers & professionals	12,791
Service occupations	2,614
Sales & office occupations	7,897
Farming, fishing & forestry	21
Construction & maintenance	1,627
Production & transportation	2,070
Self-employed persons	1,629

* US Census Bureau
** New Jersey Department of Labor

See Introduction for an explanation of all data sources.

General Information
Township of Wayne
475 Valley Rd
Wayne, NJ 07470
973-694-1800
Website: www.waynetownship.com
Year of incorporation: 1847
Land/water area (sq. miles): 23.82/1.37
Form of government: Mayor-Council

Government
Legislative Districts
US Congressional	8
State Legislative	40

Local Officials, 2008
Mayor	Christopher Vergano
Manager	Neal Bellet
Clerk	Katherine Pusterla
Finance Dir	Robert Miller
Tax Assessor	Dorothy Kreitz
Tax Collector	Carl Smith
Attorney	Mark Semeraro
Building	Joseph Albanese
Planning	John Szabo
Engineering	Fernando Zapata
Public Works	George Holzapfel
Police Chief	Donald Stouthamer
Emerg/Fire Director	John Babitz

Housing & Construction
Housing Units, 2000*
Total	19,218
Median rent	$943
Median SF home value	$284,800

Permits for New Residential Construction
	Units	Value
Total, 2007	17	$5,257,200
Single family	17	$5,257,200
Total, 2006	26	$5,722,745
Single family	26	$5,722,745

Real Property Valuation, 2007
	Parcels	Valuation
Total	17,878	$5,336,170,200
Vacant	478	66,003,100
Residential	16,721	3,814,643,700
Commercial	567	1,149,631,300
Industrial	85	207,547,100
Apartments	9	96,576,700
Farm land	11	91,200
Farm homestead	7	1,677,100

Average Property Value & Tax, 2007
Residential value	$228,140
Property tax	$9,058
Tax credit/rebate	$1,300

Public Library
Wayne Public Library
461 Valley Rd
Wayne, NJ 07470
973-694-4272
Director: Jody C. Treadway

Library statistics, 2006
Population served	54,069
Full-time/total staff	15/37

	Total	Per capita
Holdings	220,505	4.08
Revenues	$3,524,150	$65.18
Expenditures	$3,524,150	$65.18
Annual visits	290,112	5.37
Internet terminals/annual users	59/88,526	

Public Safety
Number of officers, 2006: 116

Crime	2005	2006
Total crimes	1,306	1,296
Violent	59	40
Murder	1	0
Rape	0	2
Robbery	19	21
Aggravated assault	39	17
Non-violent	1,247	1,256
Burglary	110	174
Larceny	1,044	1,004
Vehicle theft	93	78
Domestic violence	303	296
Arson	1	3
Total crime rate	23.6	23.5
Violent	1.1	0.7
Non-violent	22.5	22.8

Public School District
(for school year 2006-07 except as noted)

Wayne Township School District
50 Nellis Dr
Wayne, NJ 07470
973-633-3032

Chief School Admin	Cynthia Randina (Actg)
Number of schools	14
Grade plan	K-12
Enrollment	8,873
Attendance rate, '05-06	95.7%
Dropout rate	0.7%
Students per teacher	11.5
Per pupil expenditure	$12,894
Median faculty salary	$59,040
Median administrator salary	$112,987
Grade 12 enrollment	661
High school graduation rate	NA

Assessment test results
(percent scoring at proficient or advanced level)
	Language	Math
NJASK-Grade 3	89.6%	93.5%
GEPA-Grade 8	88.4%	84.0%
HSPA-High School	93.8%	89.8%

SAT score averages
Pct tested	Math	Verbal	Writing
NA	NA	NA	NA

Teacher Qualifications
Avg. years of experience	9
Highly-qualified teachers one subject/all subjects	99.5%/99.5%
With emergency credentials	0.0%

No Child Left Behind
AYP, 2005-06: Meets Standards

Municipal Finance
State Aid Programs, 2008
Total aid	$5,606,324
CMPTRA	1,196,436
Energy tax receipts	4,353,880
Garden State Trust	33,213

General Budget, 2007
Total tax levy	$212,186,389
County levy	53,914,620
County taxes	52,818,216
County library	0
County health	0
County open space	1,096,403
School levy	111,733,305
Muni. levy	46,538,464
Misc. revenues	24,835,401

Taxes
	2005	2006	2007
General tax rate per $100	3.53	3.77	3.98
County equalization ratio	59.94	55.06	48.89
Net valuation taxable	$5,384,588,548	$5,354,726,500	$5,343,989,098
State equalized value	$9,779,492,459	$10,961,230,873	$11,218,260,495

©2008 Information Publications, Inc. All rights reserved. Photocopying prohibited. For additional copies, contact the publisher at www.informationpublications.com or (877)544-INFO (4636)

Weehawken Township
Hudson County

Demographics & Socio-Economic Characteristics
(2000 US Census, except as noted)

Population
1980*	13,168
1990*	12,385
2000	13,501
Male	6,582
Female	6,919
2006 (estimate)*	12,649
Population density	14,881.2

Race & Hispanic Origin, 2000
Race
White	9,862
Black/African American	483
American Indian/Alaska Native	27
Asian	630
Native Hawaiian/Pacific Islander	14
Other race	1,882
Two or more races	603
Hispanic origin, total	5,487
Mexican	177
Puerto Rican	822
Cuban	1,182
Other Hispanic	3,306

Age & Nativity, 2000
Under 5 years	643
18 years and over	11,265
21 years and over	10,900
65 years and over	1,650
85 years and over	192
Median age	35.0
Native-born	8,272
Foreign-born	5,229

Educational Attainment, 2000
Population 25 years and over	10,010
Less than 9th grade	12.7%
High school grad or higher	76.0%
Bachelor's degree or higher	37.5%
Graduate degree	13.0%

Income & Poverty, 1999
Per capita income	$29,269
Median household income	$50,196
Median family income	$52,613
Persons in poverty	1,535
H'holds receiving public assistance	161
H'holds receiving social security	1,336

Households, 2000
Total households	5,975
With persons under 18	1,323
With persons over 65	1,250
Family households	3,061
Single-person households	2,126
Persons per household	2.26
Persons per family	3.02

Labor & Employment
Total civilian labor force, 2006**	7,773
Unemployment rate	4.1%
Total civilian labor force, 2000	7,854
Unemployment rate	5.8%

Employed persons 16 years and over by occupation, 2000
Managers & professionals	3,121
Service occupations	983
Sales & office occupations	2,152
Farming, fishing & forestry	5
Construction & maintenance	319
Production & transportation	818
Self-employed persons	458

* US Census Bureau
** New Jersey Department of Labor
§ State Fiscal Year July 1–June 30

General Information
Township of Weehawken
400 Park Ave
Weehawken, NJ 07086
201-319-6022

Website	www.weehawken-nj.us
Year of incorporation	1859
Land/water area (sq. miles)	0.85/0.66
Form of government	Council-Manager

Government
Legislative Districts
US Congressional	13
State Legislative	33

Local Officials, 2008
Mayor	Richard F. Turner
Manager	James V. Marchetti
Clerk	Rola Dahboul
Finance Dir.	Lisa Toscano
Tax Assessor	Paul Sadlon
Tax Collector	Joseph Fredericks
Attorney	Richard P. Venino
Building	Frank Tattoli
Comm Dev/Planning	NA
Engineering	Mayo, Lynch
Public Works	Robert Barsa
Police Chief	Thomas McGorty
Emerg/Fire Director	Jeffrey Welz

Housing & Construction
Housing Units, 2000*
Total	6,159
Median rent	$781
Median SF home value	$231,200

Permits for New Residential Construction
	Units	Value
Total, 2007	61	$11,191,496
Single family	10	$3,953,496
Total, 2006	30	$5,429,100
Single family	5	$2,182,800

Real Property Valuation, 2007
	Parcels	Valuation
Total	2,955	$1,090,888,140
Vacant	169	138,349,050
Residential	2,579	608,879,940
Commercial	65	236,164,100
Industrial	23	49,489,000
Apartments	119	58,006,050
Farm land	0	0
Farm homestead	0	0

Average Property Value & Tax, 2007
Residential value	$236,091
Property tax	$7,938
Tax credit/rebate	$926

Public Library
Weehawken Public Library
49 Hauxhurst Ave
Weehawken, NJ 07086
201-863-7823

Director: Phillip R. Greco

Library statistics, 2006
Population served	13,501
Full-time/total staff	1/13

	Total	Per capita
Holdings	46,341	3.43
Revenues	$734,498	$54.40
Expenditures	$972,708	$72.05
Annual visits	49,000	3.63
Internet terminals/annual users	18/18,360	

Taxes
	2005	2006	2007
General tax rate per $100	3.105	3.286	3.497
County equalization ratio	62.44	53.8	48.86
Net valuation taxable	$1,009,544,129	$1,037,375,723	$1,092,067,867
State equalized value	$1,876,476,076	$2,124,464,493	$2,233,404,282

Public Safety
Number of officers, 2006: 58

Crime	2005	2006
Total crimes	356	374
Violent	23	43
Murder	0	1
Rape	2	1
Robbery	11	18
Aggravated assault	10	23
Non-violent	333	331
Burglary	88	76
Larceny	189	220
Vehicle theft	56	35
Domestic violence	49	48
Arson	1	0
Total crime rate	27.0	28.9
Violent	1.7	3.3
Non-violent	25.2	25.6

Public School District
(for school year 2006-07 except as noted)

Weehawken Township School District
53 Liberty Place
Weehawken, NJ 07086
201-422-6126

Superintendent	Kevin McLellan
Number of schools	3
Grade plan	K-12
Enrollment	1,173
Attendance rate, '05-06	95.5%
Dropout rate	NA
Students per teacher	10.0
Per pupil expenditure	$14,199
Median faculty salary	$54,181
Median administrator salary	$123,263
Grade 12 enrollment	73
High school graduation rate	100.0%

Assessment test results
(percent scoring at proficient or advanced level)
	Language	Math
NJASK-Grade 3	87.1%	88.8%
GEPA-Grade 8	82.1%	78.6%
HSPA-High School	86.3%	72.6%

SAT score averages
Pct tested	Math	Verbal	Writing
89%	459	463	457

Teacher Qualifications
Avg. years of experience	14
Highly-qualified teachers one subject/all subjects	100%/100%
With emergency credentials	0.0%

No Child Left Behind
AYP, 2005-06: Meets Standards

Municipal Finance§
State Aid Programs, 2008
Total aid	$2,894,159
CMPTRA	2,137,045
Energy tax receipts	756,409
Garden State Trust	0

General Budget, 2007
Total tax levy	$38,180,084
County levy	9,310,933
County taxes	9,084,695
County library	0
County health	0
County open space	226,238
School levy	14,785,039
Muni. levy	14,084,113
Misc. revenues	16,146,334

Gloucester County
Wenonah Borough

Demographics & Socio-Economic Characteristics
(2000 US Census, except as noted)

Population
1980*	2,303
1990*	2,331
2000	2,317
Male	1,128
Female	1,189
2006 (estimate)*	2,333
Population density	2,405.2

Race & Hispanic Origin, 2000
Race
White	2,260
Black/African American	25
American Indian/Alaska Native	2
Asian	15
Native Hawaiian/Pacific Islander	0
Other race	0
Two or more races	15
Hispanic origin, total	17
Mexican	8
Puerto Rican	4
Cuban	1
Other Hispanic	4

Age & Nativity, 2000
Under 5 years	148
18 years and over	1,716
21 years and over	1,657
65 years and over	320
85 years and over	33
Median age	41.2
Native-born	2,281
Foreign-born	36

Educational Attainment, 2000
Population 25 years and over	1,584
Less than 9th grade	0.3%
High school grad or higher	97.2%
Bachelor's degree or higher	42.2%
Graduate degree	15.8%

Income & Poverty, 1999
Per capita income	$34,116
Median household income	$71,625
Median family income	$82,505
Persons in poverty	57
H'holds receiving public assistance	2
H'holds receiving social security	233

Households, 2000
Total households	844
With persons under 18	316
With persons over 65	211
Family households	652
Single-person households	166
Persons per household	2.70
Persons per family	3.13

Labor & Employment
Total civilian labor force, 2006**	1,414
Unemployment rate	5.0%
Total civilian labor force, 2000	1,233
Unemployment rate	7.4%

Employed persons 16 years and over by occupation, 2000
Managers & professionals	618
Service occupations	91
Sales & office occupations	266
Farming, fishing & forestry	4
Construction & maintenance	86
Production & transportation	77
Self-employed persons	82

* US Census Bureau
** New Jersey Department of Labor

See Introduction for an explanation of all data sources.

General Information
Borough of Wenonah
1 S West Ave
PO Box 66
Wenonah, NJ 08090
856-468-5228

Website	www.wenonahnj.us
Year of incorporation	1883
Land/water area (sq. miles)	0.97/0.00
Form of government	Borough

Government
Legislative Districts
US Congressional	1
State Legislative	3

Local Officials, 2008
Mayor	Thomas J. Capaldi
Manager/Admin	NA
Clerk	Karen L. Sweeney
CFO	Robert E. Scharle
Tax Assessor	Roy Duffield
Tax Collector	Lorraine Roberts
Attorney	Barry N. Lozuke
Building	Bob Kunkle
Comm Dev/Planning	NA
Engineering	Kreck, Wood & Hallowell
Public Works	Ken Trovarelli
Police Chief	Glenn Scheetz
Emerg/Fire Director	Andrew Sole III

Housing & Construction
Housing Units, 2000*
Total	860
Median rent	$665
Median SF home value	$161,600

Permits for New Residential Construction
	Units	Value
Total, 2007	6	$948,248
Single family	6	$948,248
Total, 2006	6	$870,653
Single family	6	$870,653

Real Property Valuation, 2007
	Parcels	Valuation
Total	868	$136,887,700
Vacant	37	1,147,100
Residential	819	133,534,800
Commercial	12	2,205,800
Industrial	0	0
Apartments	0	0
Farm land	0	0
Farm homestead	0	0

Average Property Value & Tax, 2007
Residential value	$163,046
Property tax	$8,207
Tax credit/rebate	$1,215

Public Library
Wenonah Public Library
101 E Mantua Ave
Wenonah, NJ 08090
856-468-6323

Director.................. Anne Zuber

Library statistics, 2006
Population served	2,317
Full-time/total staff	0/0

	Total	Per capita
Holdings	14,213	6.13
Revenues	$76,706	$33.11
Expenditures	$71,716	$30.95
Annual visits	3,085	1.33
Internet terminals/annual users	3/1,533	

Public Safety
Number of officers, 2006 6

Crime
	2005	2006
Total crimes	14	19
Violent	1	2
Murder	0	0
Rape	0	0
Robbery	1	0
Aggravated assault	0	2
Non-violent	13	17
Burglary	2	6
Larceny	10	11
Vehicle theft	1	0
Domestic violence	0	8
Arson	0	0
Total crime rate	6.0	8.1
Violent	0.4	0.9
Non-violent	5.6	7.3

Public School District
(for school year 2006-07 except as noted)

Wenonah School District
200 N Clinton Ave
Wenonah, NJ 08090
856-468-6000

Chief School Admin	Frank Vogel
Number of schools	1
Grade plan	K-6
Enrollment	234
Attendance rate, '05-06	96.0%
Dropout rate	NA
Students per teacher	10.6
Per pupil expenditure	$10,259
Median faculty salary	$48,833
Median administrator salary	$105,921
Grade 12 enrollment	NA
High school graduation rate	NA

Assessment test results
(percent scoring at proficient or advanced level)
	Language	Math
NJASK-Grade 3	80.7%	100.0%
GEPA-Grade 8	NA	NA
HSPA-High School	NA	NA

SAT score averages
Pct tested	Math	Verbal	Writing
NA	NA	NA	NA

Teacher Qualifications
Avg. years of experience	12
Highly-qualified teachers one subject/all subjects	100%/100%
With emergency credentials	0.0%

No Child Left Behind
AYP, 2005-06 .... Meets Standards

Municipal Finance
State Aid Programs, 2008
Total aid	$137,048
CMPTRA	0
Energy tax receipts	137,048
Garden State Trust	0

General Budget, 2007
Total tax levy	$6,897,174
County levy	1,405,877
County taxes	1,303,801
County library	0
County health	0
County open space	102,076
School levy	4,020,141
Muni. levy	1,471,156
Misc. revenues	1,187,066

Taxes
	2005	2006	2007
General tax rate per $100	4.302	4.744	5.034
County equalization ratio	71.41	61.93	53.7
Net valuation taxable	$136,070,523	$136,380,400	$137,030,600
State equalized value	$219,716,653	$254,129,682	$272,231,352

The New Jersey Municipal Data Book

West Amwell Township
Hunterdon County

Demographics & Socio-Economic Characteristics
(2000 US Census, except as noted)

Population
1980*	2,299
1990*	2,251
2000	2,383
Male	1,193
Female	1,190
2006 (estimate)*	2,944
Population density	135.5

Race & Hispanic Origin, 2000
Race
White	2,337
Black/African American	15
American Indian/Alaska Native	2
Asian	17
Native Hawaiian/Pacific Islander	0
Other race	1
Two or more races	11
Hispanic origin, total	17
Mexican	1
Puerto Rican	3
Cuban	1
Other Hispanic	12

Age & Nativity, 2000
Under 5 years	116
18 years and over	1,879
21 years and over	1,826
65 years and over	330
85 years and over	37
Median age	42.9
Native-born	2,274
Foreign-born	109

Educational Attainment, 2000
Population 25 years and over	1,782
Less than 9th grade	3.8%
High school grad or higher	89.6%
Bachelor's degree or higher	37.0%
Graduate degree	12.6%

Income & Poverty, 1999
Per capita income	$33,877
Median household income	$73,380
Median family income	$79,605
Persons in poverty	39
H'holds receiving public assistance	8
H'holds receiving social security	280

Households, 2000
Total households	949
With persons under 18	288
With persons over 65	245
Family households	697
Single-person households	202
Persons per household	2.51
Persons per family	2.93

Labor & Employment
Total civilian labor force, 2006**	1,584
Unemployment rate	2.8%
Total civilian labor force, 2000	1,411
Unemployment rate	2.2%

Employed persons 16 years and over by occupation, 2000
Managers & professionals	581
Service occupations	145
Sales & office occupations	353
Farming, fishing & forestry	19
Construction & maintenance	147
Production & transportation	135
Self-employed persons	154

* US Census Bureau
** New Jersey Department of Labor

General Information
Township of West Amwell
Township of West Amwell Municipal Offices
150 Rocktown-Lambertville Rd
Lambertville, NJ 08530
609-397-2054

Website	www.westamwelltwp.org
Year of incorporation	1846
Land/water area (sq. miles)	21.72/0.18
Form of government	Township

Government
Legislative Districts
US Congressional	12
State Legislative	23

Local Officials, 2008
Mayor	William J. Corboy
Manager/Admin	NA
Clerk	Lora L. Olsen
Finance Dir	Jane Luhrs
Tax Assessor	David Gill
Tax Collector	Catherine L. Park
Attorney	Phillip J. Faherty III
Building	Christopher Rose
Comm Dev/Planning	NA
Engineering	Robert J. Clerico
Public Works	Randy Hoagland
Police Chief	Stephen J. Bartzak
Emerg/Fire Director	Jeff Ent

Housing & Construction
Housing Units, 2000*
Total	984
Median rent	$865
Median SF home value	$198,800

Permits for New Residential Construction
	Units	Value
Total, 2007	9	$1,719,096
Single family	9	$1,719,096
Total, 2006	17	$3,081,611
Single family	17	$3,081,611

Real Property Valuation, 2007
	Parcels	Valuation
Total	1,571	$524,819,969
Vacant	170	11,716,700
Residential	913	386,011,700
Commercial	42	25,686,669
Industrial	7	11,864,400
Apartments	3	1,476,900
Farm land	289	2,493,300
Farm homestead	147	85,570,300

Average Property Value & Tax, 2007
Residential value	$444,889
Property tax	$7,935
Tax credit/rebate	$1,122

Public Library
No public municipal library

Library statistics, 2006
Population served	NA
Full-time/total staff	NA/NA

	Total	Per capita
Holdings	NA	NA
Revenues	NA	NA
Expenditures	NA	NA
Annual visits	NA	NA
Internet terminals/annual users	NA/NA	

Taxes
	2005	2006	2007
General tax rate per $100	1.56	1.71	1.79
County equalization ratio	102.72	89.27	87.07
Net valuation taxable	$508,423,351	$512,718,599	$525,595,942
State equalized value	$515,172,106	$555,930,162	$583,650,217

Public Safety
Number of officers, 2006 ... 5

Crime	2005	2006
Total crimes	39	29
Violent	1	5
Murder	0	0
Rape	0	1
Robbery	0	0
Aggravated assault	1	4
Non-violent	38	24
Burglary	12	4
Larceny	23	19
Vehicle theft	0	1
Domestic violence	22	20
Arson	0	0
Total crime rate	13.7	9.9
Violent	0.4	1.7
Non-violent	13.3	8.2

Public School District
(for school year 2006-07 except as noted)

West Amwell Township School District
1417 Route 179
Lambertville, NJ 08530
609-397-0819

Superintendent	Todd Fay
Number of schools	1
Grade plan	K-6
Enrollment	254
Attendance rate, '05-06	96.5%
Dropout rate	NA
Students per teacher	10.0
Per pupil expenditure	$13,172
Median faculty salary	$48,835
Median administrator salary	$80,000
Grade 12 enrollment	NA
High school graduation rate	NA

Assessment test results
(percent scoring at proficient or advanced level)
	Language	Math
NJASK-Grade 3	93.7%	91.7%
GEPA-Grade 8	NA	NA
HSPA-High School	NA	NA

SAT score averages
Pct tested	Math	Verbal	Writing
NA	NA	NA	NA

Teacher Qualifications
Avg. years of experience	10
Highly-qualified teachers one subject/all subjects	100%/100%
With emergency credentials	0.0%

No Child Left Behind
AYP, 2005-06 ... Meets Standards

Municipal Finance
State Aid Programs, 2008
Total aid	$357,767
CMPTRA	0
Energy tax receipts	275,334
Garden State Trust	60,813

General Budget, 2007
Total tax levy	$9,375,029
County levy	2,006,843
County taxes	1,679,530
County library	146,145
County health	0
County open space	181,168
School levy	6,535,608
Muni. levy	832,578
Misc. revenues	2,710,911

Essex County

West Caldwell Township

Demographics & Socio-Economic Characteristics
(2000 US Census, except as noted)

Population
1980*	11,407
1990*	10,422
2000	11,233
Male	5,330
Female	5,903
2006 (estimate)*	10,797
Population density	2,138.0

Race & Hispanic Origin, 2000
Race
White	10,541
Black/African American	100
American Indian/Alaska Native	4
Asian	432
Native Hawaiian/Pacific Islander	4
Other race	68
Two or more races	84
Hispanic origin, total	314
Mexican	23
Puerto Rican	85
Cuban	68
Other Hispanic	138

Age & Nativity, 2000
Under 5 years	813
18 years and over	8,463
21 years and over	8,241
65 years and over	2,142
85 years and over	376
Median age	41.0
Native-born	10,262
Foreign-born	971

Educational Attainment, 2000
Population 25 years and over	7,982
Less than 9th grade	1.7%
High school grad or higher	93.4%
Bachelor's degree or higher	48.1%
Graduate degree	18.2%

Income & Poverty, 1999
Per capita income	$38,345
Median household income	$83,396
Median family income	$94,379
Persons in poverty	227
H'holds receiving public assistance	48
H'holds receiving social security	1,353

Households, 2000
Total households	3,990
With persons under 18	1,469
With persons over 65	1,351
Family households	3,114
Single-person households	767
Persons per household	2.75
Persons per family	3.17

Labor & Employment
Total civilian labor force, 2006**	6,176
Unemployment rate	3.3%
Total civilian labor force, 2000	5,819
Unemployment rate	2.7%

Employed persons 16 years and over by occupation, 2000
Managers & professionals	2,819
Service occupations	596
Sales & office occupations	1,699
Farming, fishing & forestry	0
Construction & maintenance	325
Production & transportation	221
Self-employed persons	356

* US Census Bureau
** New Jersey Department of Labor

See Introduction for an explanation of all data sources.

General Information
Township of West Caldwell
30 Clinton Rd
West Caldwell, NJ 07006
973-226-2300

Website	www.westcaldwell.com
Year of incorporation	1904
Land/water area (sq. miles)	5.05/0.00
Form of government	Borough

Government
Legislative Districts
US Congressional	11
State Legislative	27

Local Officials, 2008
Mayor	Joseph Tempesta Jr
Administrator	Andy Katz
Clerk	Jock Watkins
Finance Dir	Lou Garbaccio
Tax Assessor	Richard Hamilton Jr
Tax Collector	Kathleen Bruchac
Attorney	Joseph Maddaloni
Building	Jock Watkins
Planning	Joe Dunn
Engineering	Benedict Martorana
Public Works	William Frint
Police Chief	Charles Tubbs
Fire Chief	Charles Holden

Housing & Construction
Housing Units, 2000*
Total	4,044
Median rent	$1,193
Median SF home value	$265,900

Permits for New Residential Construction
	Units	Value
Total, 2007	8	$1,769,762
Single family	8	$1,769,762
Total, 2006	5	$1,221,623
Single family	5	$1,221,623

Real Property Valuation, 2007
	Parcels	Valuation
Total	3,810	$1,132,723,800
Vacant	84	7,507,300
Residential	3,493	771,213,200
Commercial	155	163,515,800
Industrial	66	182,365,400
Apartments	6	8,040,700
Farm land	6	81,400
Farm homestead	0	0

Average Property Value & Tax, 2007
Residential value	$220,788
Property tax	$8,014
Tax credit/rebate	$1,202

Public Library
West Caldwell Public Library
30 Clinton Rd
West Caldwell, NJ 07006
973-226-5441

Director	April L. Judge

Library statistics, 2006
Population served	11,233
Full-time/total staff	5/9

	Total	Per capita
Holdings	63,131	5.62
Revenues	$1,112,394	$99.03
Expenditures	$977,041	$86.98
Annual visits	235,220	20.94
Internet terminals/annual users	14/13,242	

Public Safety
Number of officers, 2006 ... 29

Crime	2005	2006
Total crimes	116	116
Violent	9	4
Murder	0	0
Rape	0	0
Robbery	3	1
Aggravated assault	6	3
Non-violent	107	112
Burglary	13	10
Larceny	86	94
Vehicle theft	8	8
Domestic violence	38	44
Arson	1	1
Total crime rate	10.5	10.6
Violent	0.8	0.4
Non-violent	9.6	10.2

Public School District
(for school year 2006-07 except as noted)

Caldwell-West Caldwell School District
Harrison Bldg, Gray St
West Caldwell, NJ 07006
973-228-6979

Superintendent	Daniel Gerardi
Number of schools	12
Grade plan	K-12
Enrollment	2,638
Attendance rate, '05-06	96.6%
Dropout rate	0.1%
Students per teacher	11.6
Per pupil expenditure	$12,831
Median faculty salary	$52,270
Median administrator salary	$107,824
Grade 12 enrollment	190
High school graduation rate	100.0%

Assessment test results
(percent scoring at proficient or advanced level)
	Language	Math
NJASK-Grade 3	93.0%	91.2%
GEPA-Grade 8	80.0%	82.2%
HSPA-High School	96.3%	87.9%

SAT score averages
Pct tested	Math	Verbal	Writing
93%	541	529	535

Teacher Qualifications
Avg. years of experience	8
Highly-qualified teachers one subject/all subjects	100%/100%
With emergency credentials	0.0%

No Child Left Behind
AYP, 2005-06	Meets Standards

Municipal Finance
State Aid Programs, 2008
Total aid	$1,729,746
CMPTRA	334,658
Energy tax receipts	1,395,088
Garden State Trust	0

General Budget, 2007
Total tax levy	$41,136,787
County levy	8,848,303
County taxes	8,620,897
County library	0
County health	0
County open space	227,406
School levy	22,003,194
Muni. levy	10,285,290
Misc. revenues	7,167,789

Taxes
	2005	2006	2007
General tax rate per $100	3.42	3.5	3.63
County equalization ratio	62.1	56.79	50.53
Net valuation taxable	$1,115,842,700	$1,125,525,100	$1,133,389,100
State equalized value	$1,964,857,721	$2,228,162,743	$2,359,032,570

©2008 Information Publications, Inc. All rights reserved. Photocopying prohibited. For additional copies, contact the publisher at www.informationpublications.com or (877)544-INFO (4636)

The New Jersey Municipal Data Book

West Cape May Borough
Cape May County

Demographics & Socio-Economic Characteristics
(2000 US Census, except as noted)

Population
- 1980* 1,091
- 1990* 1,026
- 2000 1,095
  - Male 527
  - Female 568
- 2006 (estimate)* 1,007
- Population density 846.2

Race & Hispanic Origin, 2000
Race
- White 921
- Black/African American 159
- American Indian/Alaska Native 4
- Asian 0
- Native Hawaiian/Pacific Islander .. 0
- Other race 6
- Two or more races 5
- Hispanic origin, total 20
  - Mexican 7
  - Puerto Rican 7
  - Cuban 0
  - Other Hispanic 6

Age & Nativity, 2000
- Under 5 years 37
- 18 years and over 880
- 21 years and over 862
- 65 years and over 267
- 85 years and over 33
- Median age 46.3
- Native-born 1,043
- Foreign-born 52

Educational Attainment, 2000
- Population 25 years and over 870
- Less than 9th grade 4.7%
- High school grad or higher 83.1%
- Bachelor's degree or higher 31.8%
- Graduate degree 9.9%

Income & Poverty, 1999
- Per capita income $25,663
- Median household income $37,500
- Median family income $47,031
- Persons in poverty 81
- H'holds receiving public assistance 12
- H'holds receiving social security 213

Households, 2000
- Total households 507
  - With persons under 18 121
  - With persons over 65 202
  - Family households 302
  - Single-person households 178
- Persons per household 2.16
- Persons per family 2.80

Labor & Employment
- Total civilian labor force, 2006** 658
  - Unemployment rate 7.8%
- Total civilian labor force, 2000 536
  - Unemployment rate 9.0%

Employed persons 16 years and over by occupation, 2000
- Managers & professionals 197
- Service occupations 81
- Sales & office occupations 127
- Farming, fishing & forestry 8
- Construction & maintenance 56
- Production & transportation 19
- Self-employed persons 61

* US Census Bureau
** New Jersey Department of Labor

General Information
Borough of West Cape May
732 Broadway
West Cape May, NJ 08204
609-884-1005

- Website .... westcapemay.us
- Year of incorporation 1884
- Land/water area (sq. miles) ... 1.19/0.00
- Form of government .... Commission

Government
Legislative Districts
- US Congressional 2
- State Legislative 1

Local Officials, 2008
- Mayor .... Pamela Kaithern
- Manager/Admin .... NA
- Clerk .... Elaine Wallace
- Finance Dir .... John Hansen
- Tax Assessor .... Arthur Amonette
- Tax Collector .... Bruce Macleod
- Attorney .... Frank Corrado
- Building .... Bill Callahan
- Planning .... Gary Novak
- Engineering .... Ray Roberts
- Public Works .... Rob Flynn
- Police Chief .... Diane Sorantino
- Emerg/Fire Director ... Charles McPherson

Housing & Construction
Housing Units, 2000*
- Total 1,004
- Median rent $703
- Median SF home value $174,100

Permits for New Residential Construction

	Units	Value
Total, 2007	13	$3,590,411
Single family	13	$3,590,411
Total, 2006	7	$2,105,757
Single family	7	$2,105,757

Real Property Valuation, 2007

	Parcels	Valuation
Total	1,046	$507,289,300
Vacant	123	29,117,700
Residential	869	432,355,900
Commercial	34	40,776,000
Industrial	0	0
Apartments	2	1,189,500
Farm land	13	239,600
Farm homestead	5	3,610,600

Average Property Value & Tax, 2007
- Residential value $498,818
- Property tax $4,482
- Tax credit/rebate $940

Public Library
No public municipal library

Library statistics, 2006
- Population served .... NA
- Full-time/total staff .... NA/NA

	Total	Per capita
Holdings	NA	NA
Revenues	NA	NA
Expenditures	NA	NA
Annual visits	NA	NA
Internet terminals/annual users	NA/NA	

Taxes

	2005	2006	2007
General tax rate per $100	1.18	1.32	0.9
County equalization ratio	93.04	77.87	109.16
Net valuation taxable	$307,279,703	$309,783,400	$507,539,041
State equalized value	$394,606,014	$458,928,006	$488,215,593

Public Safety
- Number of officers, 2006 0

Crime	2005	2006
Total crimes	49	38
Violent	0	0
Murder	0	0
Rape	0	0
Robbery	0	0
Aggravated assault	0	0
Non-violent	49	38
Burglary	9	6
Larceny	40	31
Vehicle theft	0	1
Domestic violence	0	0
Arson	0	0
Total crime rate	45.9	36.6
Violent	0.0	0.0
Non-violent	45.9	36.6

Public School District
(for school year 2006-07 except as noted)

West Cape May School District
301 Moore St
West Cape May, NJ 08204
609-884-4614

- Chief School Admin ... Richard M. Strauss (Int)
- Number of schools 1
- Grade plan K-6
- Enrollment 49
- Attendance rate, '05-06 .... 93.4%
- Dropout rate .... NA
- Students per teacher 5.8
- Per pupil expenditure $18,741
- Median faculty salary $43,533
- Median administrator salary .. $22,500
- Grade 12 enrollment .... NA
- High school graduation rate ...... NA

Assessment test results
(percent scoring at proficient or advanced level)

	Language	Math
NJASK-Grade 3	NA	NA
GEPA-Grade 8	NA	NA
HSPA-High School	NA	NA

SAT score averages

Pct tested	Math	Verbal	Writing
NA	NA	NA	NA

Teacher Qualifications
- Avg. years of experience 12
- Highly-qualified teachers
  one subject/all subjects 100%/100%
- With emergency credentials 0.0%

No Child Left Behind
- AYP, 2005-06 .... Meets Standards

Municipal Finance
State Aid Programs, 2008
- Total aid $110,579
- CMPTRA 0
- Energy tax receipts 109,796
- Garden State Trust 783

General Budget, 2007
- Total tax levy $4,560,444
- County levy 886,358
- County taxes 704,390
- County library 135,339
- County health 0
- County open space 46,629
- School levy 2,475,051
- Muni. levy 1,199,035
- Misc. revenues 776,491

Gloucester County

West Deptford Township

Demographics & Socio-Economic Characteristics
(2000 US Census, except as noted)

Population
1980*	18,002
1990*	19,380
2000	19,368
Male	9,354
Female	10,014
2006 (estimate)*	21,763
Population density	1,368.7

Race & Hispanic Origin, 2000
Race
White	17,875
Black/African American	984
American Indian/Alaska Native	45
Asian	219
Native Hawaiian/Pacific Islander	4
Other race	82
Two or more races	159
Hispanic origin, total	341
Mexican	29
Puerto Rican	172
Cuban	9
Other Hispanic	131

Age & Nativity, 2000
Under 5 years	1,137
18 years and over	14,807
21 years and over	14,147
65 years and over	2,357
85 years and over	168
Median age	37.5
Native-born	18,995
Foreign-born	373

Educational Attainment, 2000
Population 25 years and over	13,226
Less than 9th grade	2.7%
High school grad or higher	85.7%
Bachelor's degree or higher	21.7%
Graduate degree	6.8%

Income & Poverty, 1999
Per capita income	$24,219
Median household income	$50,583
Median family income	$64,477
Persons in poverty	1,015
H'holds receiving public assistance	74
H'holds receiving social security	1,954

Households, 2000
Total households	7,719
With persons under 18	2,583
With persons over 65	1,700
Family households	5,129
Single-person households	2,115
Persons per household	2.49
Persons per family	3.07

Labor & Employment
Total civilian labor force, 2006**	12,892
Unemployment rate	5.0%
Total civilian labor force, 2000	10,862
Unemployment rate	4.2%

Employed persons 16 years and over by occupation, 2000
Managers & professionals	3,324
Service occupations	1,173
Sales & office occupations	3,158
Farming, fishing & forestry	25
Construction & maintenance	941
Production & transportation	1,789
Self-employed persons	331

* US Census Bureau
** New Jersey Department of Labor

See Introduction for an explanation of all data sources.

General Information
Township of West Deptford
400 Crown Point Rd
West Deptford, NJ 08086
856-845-4004

Website	www.westdeptford.com
Year of incorporation	1871
Land/water area (sq. miles)	15.90/1.86
Form of government	Township

Government
Legislative Districts
US Congressional	1
State Legislative	3

Local Officials, 2008
Mayor	Anna Docimo
Township Admin	Eric M. Campo
Clerk	Raymond Sherman
Finance Dir	Richard Giuliani
Tax Assessor	Alicia Melson
Tax Collector	George Damminger
Attorney	Michael Angelini
Building	Philip Zimm
Planning	Sandra Rost
Engineering	T&M Associates
Public Works	Edward J. Phelps
Police Chief	Craig Mangano
Fire Chief	J. Trautner

Housing & Construction
Housing Units, 2000*
Total	7,999
Median rent	$687
Median SF home value	$120,100

Permits for New Residential Construction
	Units	Value
Total, 2007	13	$2,068,415
Single family	13	$2,068,415
Total, 2006	83	$6,728,350
Single family	48	$4,574,850

Real Property Valuation, 2007
	Parcels	Valuation
Total	7,554	$1,412,654,500
Vacant	566	27,066,000
Residential	6,632	775,094,400
Commercial	282	302,230,900
Industrial	15	265,049,800
Apartments	11	41,600,100
Farm land	38	341,100
Farm homestead	10	1,272,200

Average Property Value & Tax, 2007
Residential value	$116,887
Property tax	$4,488
Tax credit/rebate	$858

Public Library
West Deptford Public Library
420 Crown Point Rd
Thorofare, NJ 08086
856-845-5593

Director........Marie Downes McDonald

Library statistics, 2006
Population served	19,368
Full-time/total staff	3/10

	Total	Per capita
Holdings	89,985	4.65
Revenues	$1,036,493	$53.52
Expenditures	$964,643	$49.81
Annual visits	134,916	6.97
Internet terminals/annual users	22/30,586	

Taxes
	2005	2006	2007
General tax rate per $100	3.462	3.618	3.84
County equalization ratio	77.97	65.55	59.66
Net valuation taxable	$1,402,042,348	$1,380,539,500	$1,447,494,592
State equalized value	$2,138,889,928	$2,351,621,764	$2,610,796,511

Public Safety
Number of officers, 2006 40

Crime
	2005	2006
Total crimes	498	582
Violent	33	42
Murder	0	1
Rape	6	11
Robbery	9	5
Aggravated assault	18	25
Non-violent	465	540
Burglary	113	93
Larceny	320	399
Vehicle theft	32	48
Domestic violence	246	291
Arson	5	8
Total crime rate	24.3	27.8
Violent	1.6	2.0
Non-violent	22.7	25.8

Public School District
(for school year 2006-07 except as noted)

West Deptford Township School District
675 Grove Rd, Suite 804
West Deptford, NJ 08066
856-848-4300

Superintendent	Edward Wasilewski Jr
Number of schools	5
Grade plan	K-12
Enrollment	3,332
Attendance rate, '05-06	94.5%
Dropout rate	3.0%
Students per teacher	13.6
Per pupil expenditure	$11,207
Median faculty salary	$59,285
Median administrator salary	$105,700
Grade 12 enrollment	266
High school graduation rate	90.7%

Assessment test results
(percent scoring at proficient or advanced level)
	Language	Math
NJASK-Grade 3	89.7%	90.1%
GEPA-Grade 8	76.6%	74.7%
HSPA-High School	91.0%	80.1%

SAT score averages
Pct tested	Math	Verbal	Writing
70%	498	478	473

Teacher Qualifications
Avg. years of experience	10
Highly-qualified teachers one subject/all subjects	100%/100%
With emergency credentials	0.0%

No Child Left Behind
AYP, 2005-06 .... Meets Standards

Municipal Finance
State Aid Programs, 2008
Total aid	$2,576,730
CMPTRA	830,954
Energy tax receipts	1,745,618
Garden State Trust	158

General Budget, 2007
Total tax levy	$55,578,499
County levy	13,327,935
County taxes	12,360,207
County library	0
County health	0
County open space	967,728
School levy	27,240,044
Muni. levy	15,010,520
Misc. revenues	15,616,779

©2008 Information Publications, Inc. All rights reserved. Photocopying prohibited. For additional copies, contact the publisher at www.informationpublications.com or (877)544-INFO (4636)

West Long Branch Borough — Monmouth County

Demographics & Socio-Economic Characteristics
(2000 US Census, except as noted)

Population
1980*	7,380
1990*	7,690
2000	8,258
Male	3,857
Female	4,401
2006 (estimate)*	8,312
Population density	2,876.1

Race & Hispanic Origin, 2000
Race
White	7,781
Black/African American	184
American Indian/Alaska Native	6
Asian	100
Native Hawaiian/Pacific Islander	3
Other race	41
Two or more races	143
Hispanic origin, total	241
Mexican	29
Puerto Rican	63
Cuban	20
Other Hispanic	129

Age & Nativity, 2000
Under 5 years	409
18 years and over	6,458
21 years and over	5,165
65 years and over	1,206
85 years and over	129
Median age	33.8
Native-born	7,676
Foreign-born	582

Educational Attainment, 2000
Population 25 years and over	4,722
Less than 9th grade	4.7%
High school grad or higher	87.1%
Bachelor's degree or higher	34.9%
Graduate degree	14.3%

Income & Poverty, 1999
Per capita income	$27,651
Median household income	$71,852
Median family income	$80,127
Persons in poverty	303
H'holds receiving public assistance	26
H'holds receiving social security	838

Households, 2000
Total households	2,448
With persons under 18	915
With persons over 65	889
Family households	1,860
Single-person households	522
Persons per household	2.77
Persons per family	3.25

Labor & Employment
Total civilian labor force, 2006**	3,434
Unemployment rate	4.4%
Total civilian labor force, 2000	4,169
Unemployment rate	14.7%

Employed persons 16 years and over by occupation, 2000
Managers & professionals	1,391
Service occupations	532
Sales & office occupations	1,120
Farming, fishing & forestry	0
Construction & maintenance	357
Production & transportation	156
Self-employed persons	244

* US Census Bureau
** New Jersey Department of Labor

General Information
Borough of West Long Branch
965 Broadway
West Long Branch, NJ 07764
732-229-1756

Website	www.westlongbranch.org
Year of incorporation	1908
Land/water area (sq. miles)	2.89/0.02
Form of government	Borough

Government
Legislative Districts
US Congressional	6
State Legislative	11

Local Officials, 2008
Mayor	Janet W. Tucci
Manager/Admin	NA
Clerk	Lori Cole
Finance Dir	Gail M. Watkins
Tax Assessor	Helen J. Ward
Tax Collector	Charlotte C. Rolly
Attorney	Gregory S. Baxter
Building	Michael Martin (Actg)
Comm Dev/Planning	NA
Engineering	T&M Associates
Public Works	Earl S. Reed Jr
Police Chief	Arthur N. Cosentino
Emerg/Fire Director	Michael Ciaglia

Housing & Construction
Housing Units, 2000*
Total	2,535
Median rent	$639
Median SF home value	$203,300

Permits for New Residential Construction
	Units	Value
Total, 2007	8	$591,500
Single family	3	$591,400
Total, 2006	6	$1,068,431
Single family	6	$1,068,431

Real Property Valuation, 2007
	Parcels	Valuation
Total	2,516	$1,357,877,100
Vacant	78	12,951,100
Residential	2,268	1,075,993,300
Commercial	159	262,126,700
Industrial	2	3,254,900
Apartments	2	1,907,600
Farm land	4	17,600
Farm homestead	3	1,625,900

Average Property Value & Tax, 2007
Residential value	$474,513
Property tax	$7,976
Tax credit/rebate	$1,202

Public Library
West Long Branch Public Library
95 Poplar Ave
West Long Branch, NJ 07764
732-222-5993

Director ... David M. Lisa

Library statistics, 2006
Population served	8,258
Full-time/total staff	1/3

	Total	Per capita
Holdings	42,283	5.12
Revenues	$419,087	$50.75
Expenditures	$324,065	$39.24
Annual visits	28,539	3.46
Internet terminals/annual users		7/8,270

Public Safety
Number of officers, 2006 ... 20

Crime	2005	2006
Total crimes	301	278
Violent	9	10
Murder	0	0
Rape	2	2
Robbery	2	2
Aggravated assault	5	6
Non-violent	292	268
Burglary	33	31
Larceny	252	231
Vehicle theft	7	6
Domestic violence	31	35
Arson	0	1
Total crime rate	36.5	33.6
Violent	1.1	1.2
Non-violent	35.4	32.3

Public School District
(for school year 2006-07 except as noted)

West Long Branch School District
135 Locust Ave
West Long Branch, NJ 07764
732-222-5900

Superintendent	Joan A. Kelly (Actg)
Number of schools	2
Grade plan	K-8
Enrollment	782
Attendance rate, '05-06	95.8%
Dropout rate	NA
Students per teacher	12.2
Per pupil expenditure	$12,010
Median faculty salary	$49,275
Median administrator salary	$112,310
Grade 12 enrollment	NA
High school graduation rate	NA

Assessment test results
(percent scoring at proficient or advanced level)
	Language	Math
NJASK-Grade 3	91.5%	92.8%
GEPA-Grade 8	77.6%	80.7%
HSPA-High School	NA	NA

SAT score averages
Pct tested	Math	Verbal	Writing
NA	NA	NA	NA

Teacher Qualifications
Avg. years of experience	11
Highly-qualified teachers one subject/all subjects	100%/100%
With emergency credentials	0.0%

No Child Left Behind
AYP, 2005-06 ... Meets Standards

Municipal Finance
State Aid Programs, 2008
Total aid	$946,220
CMPTRA	137,637
Energy tax receipts	808,583
Garden State Trust	0

General Budget, 2007
Total tax levy	$22,843,501
County levy	3,854,228
County taxes	3,442,108
County library	197,044
County health	0
County open space	215,076
School levy	13,773,566
Muni. levy	5,215,707
Misc. revenues	3,501,393

Taxes
	2005	2006	2007
General tax rate per $100	3.07	1.594	1.681
County equalization ratio	63.69	111.04	95.39
Net valuation taxable	$670,250,333	$1,357,047,700	$1,358,981,572
State equalized value	$1,210,275,069	$1,423,756,655	$1,463,073,787

Passaic County
West Milford Township

Demographics & Socio-Economic Characteristics
(2000 US Census, except as noted)

Population
- 1980*..................................22,750
- 1990*..................................25,430
- 2000..................................26,410
  - Male................................13,224
  - Female..............................13,186
- 2006 (estimate)*.....................28,144
- Population density..................373.1

Race & Hispanic Origin, 2000
Race
- White.................................25,110
- Black/African American..............326
- American Indian/Alaska Native......159
- Asian..................................269
- Native Hawaiian/Pacific Islander......4
- Other race............................160
- Two or more races....................382
- Hispanic origin, total...............893
  - Mexican..............................97
  - Puerto Rican........................305
  - Cuban................................97
  - Other Hispanic......................394

Age & Nativity, 2000
- Under 5 years.......................1,863
- 18 years and over..................19,222
- 21 years and over..................18,480
- 65 years and over...................2,212
- 85 years and over.....................251
- Median age............................37.0
- Native-born........................24,882
- Foreign-born........................1,528

Educational Attainment, 2000
- Population 25 years and over.......17,657
- Less than 9th grade...................2.6%
- High school grad or higher..........89.3%
- Bachelor's degree or higher.........27.2%
- Graduate degree.......................8.0%

Income & Poverty, 1999
- Per capita income..................$28,612
- Median household income............$74,124
- Median family income...............$80,264
- Persons in poverty..................1,085
- H'holds receiving public assistance..132
- H'holds receiving social security..1,702

Households, 2000
- Total households....................9,190
  - With persons under 18.............3,863
  - With persons over 65..............1,592
  - Family households.................7,186
  - Single-person households..........1,536
- Persons per household................2.84
- Persons per family...................3.23

Labor & Employment
- Total civilian labor force, 2006**...16,300
  - Unemployment rate...................4.5%
- Total civilian labor force, 2000....14,817
  - Unemployment rate...................4.3%

Employed persons 16 years and over by occupation, 2000
- Managers & professionals............5,003
- Service occupations.................1,533
- Sales & office occupations..........4,182
- Farming, fishing & forestry............19
- Construction & maintenance..........1,868
- Production & transportation.........1,575
- Self-employed persons.................913

* US Census Bureau
** New Jersey Department of Labor

See Introduction for an explanation of all data sources.

General Information
Township of West Milford
1480 Union Valley Rd
West Milford, NJ 07480
973-728-7000

- Website...............www.westmilford.org
- Year of incorporation................1834
- Land/water area (sq. miles).....75.44/4.97
- Form of government...Mayor-Council-Admin

Government

Legislative Districts
- US Congressional........................5
- State Legislative......................26

Local Officials, 2008
- Mayor.....................Bettina Bieri
- Manager.................Richard Kunze
- Clerk................Antoinette Battaglia
- Finance Dir............Arthur Magnotti
- Tax Assessor...........Brian Townsend
- Tax Collector..............Rita DeNivo
- Attorney..................Fred Semrau
- Building..................Kurt Wagner
- Planning.................William Drew
- Engineering..........Richard McFadden
- Public Works............Gerald Storms
- Police Chief..............Paul Costello
- Emerg/Fire Director..........Ed Steines

Housing & Construction

Housing Units, 2000*
- Total...............................9,909
- Median rent...........................$835
- Median SF home value..............$171,200

Permits for New Residential Construction

	Units	Value
Total, 2007	26	$6,516,790
Single family	26	$6,516,790
Total, 2006	36	$8,580,288
Single family	36	$8,580,288

Real Property Valuation, 2007

	Parcels	Valuation
Total	11,836	$1,511,622,700
Vacant	1,293	52,613,700
Residential	9,864	1,329,724,000
Commercial	282	90,219,000
Industrial	29	9,966,200
Apartments	1	550,000
Farm land	248	648,700
Farm homestead	119	27,901,100

Average Property Value & Tax, 2007
- Residential value.................$135,994
- Property tax........................$7,391
- Tax credit/rebate...................$1,190

Public Library
West Milford Township Library
1490 Union Valley Rd
West Milford, NJ 07480
973-728-2820

- Director...........Patricia Ann Hannon

Library statistics, 2006
- Population served..................26,410
- Full-time/total staff..................3/8

	Total	Per capita
Holdings	50,645	1.92
Revenues	$1,163,404	$44.05
Expenditures	$861,030	$32.60
Annual visits	87,360	3.31

- Internet terminals/annual users.....5/2,004

Taxes

	2005	2006	2007
General tax rate per $100	4.88	5.19	5.44
County equalization ratio	52.1	46.58	41.91
Net valuation taxable	$1,498,956,607	$1,504,617,300	$1,515,840,182
State equalized value	$3,218,026,207	$3,595,021,475	$3,803,218,990

Public Safety
Number of officers, 2006..............48

Crime	2005	2006
Total crimes	406	467
Violent	25	24
Murder	0	0
Rape	5	7
Robbery	1	3
Aggravated assault	19	14
Non-violent	381	443
Burglary	68	106
Larceny	299	327
Vehicle theft	14	10
Domestic violence	144	195
Arson	3	5
Total crime rate	14.4	16.6
Violent	0.9	0.9
Non-violent	13.5	15.7

Public School District
(for school year 2006-07 except as noted)

West Milford Township School District
46 Highlander Dr
West Milford, NJ 07480
973-697-1700

- Chief School Admin..........Glenn Kamp
- Number of schools......................8
- Grade plan..........................K-12
- Enrollment.........................4,386
- Attendance rate, '05-06.............95.1%
- Dropout rate.........................1.8%
- Students per teacher................11.8
- Per pupil expenditure.............$13,274
- Median faculty salary.............$63,025
- Median administrator salary.....$114,094
- Grade 12 enrollment..................323
- High school graduation rate........94.4%

Assessment test results
(percent scoring at proficient or advanced level)

	Language	Math
NJASK-Grade 3	91.3%	94.4%
GEPA-Grade 8	78.2%	74.3%
HSPA-High School	86.9%	79.3%

SAT score averages

Pct tested	Math	Verbal	Writing
67%	501	481	483

Teacher Qualifications
- Avg. years of experience..............10
- Highly-qualified teachers
  - one subject/all subjects.....99.5%/99.5%
- With emergency credentials............0.0%

No Child Left Behind
- AYP, 2005-06............Meets Standards

Municipal Finance

State Aid Programs, 2008
- Total aid.......................$3,874,572
  - CMPTRA...........................649,530
  - Energy tax receipts............2,334,539
  - Garden State Trust.............132,816

General Budget, 2007
- Total tax levy.................$82,385,741
  - County levy....................17,888,102
    - County taxes................17,526,476
    - County library....................0
    - County health....................0
    - County open space...........361,626
  - School levy...................45,366,540
  - Muni. levy....................19,131,099
  - Misc. revenues................12,584,840

West New York Town

Hudson County

Demographics & Socio-Economic Characteristics
(2000 US Census, except as noted)

Population
- 1980* 39,194
- 1990* 38,125
- 2000 45,768
  - Male 22,470
  - Female 23,298
- 2006 (estimate)* 46,398
  - Population density 45,488.2

Race & Hispanic Origin, 2000
Race
- White 27,503
- Black/African American 1,626
- American Indian/Alaska Native 305
- Asian 1,339
- Native Hawaiian/Pacific Islander 15
- Other race 11,515
- Two or more races 3,465
- Hispanic origin, total 36,038
  - Mexican 2,982
  - Puerto Rican 2,791
  - Cuban 8,991
  - Other Hispanic 21,274

Age & Nativity, 2000
- Under 5 years 3,049
- 18 years and over 35,562
- 21 years and over 33,621
- 65 years and over 5,828
- 85 years and over 614
  - Median age 34.0
- Native-born 15,937
- Foreign-born 29,831

Educational Attainment, 2000
- Population 25 years and over 30,669
- Less than 9th grade 25.7%
- High school grad or higher 54.4%
- Bachelor's degree or higher 16.4%
- Graduate degree 7.3%

Income & Poverty, 1999
- Per capita income $16,719
- Median household income $31,980
- Median family income $34,083
- Persons in poverty 8,635
- H'holds receiving public assistance ... 759
- H'holds receiving social security ... 4,149

Households, 2000
- Total households 16,719
  - With persons under 18 5,867
  - With persons over 65 4,613
  - Family households 11,042
  - Single-person households 4,593
- Persons per household 2.74
- Persons per family 3.30

Labor & Employment
- Total civilian labor force, 2006** ... 20,555
  - Unemployment rate 6.1%
- Total civilian labor force, 2000 ... 20,406
  - Unemployment rate 10.0%

Employed persons 16 years and over by occupation, 2000
- Managers & professionals 3,626
- Service occupations 3,686
- Sales & office occupations 4,828
- Farming, fishing & forestry 34
- Construction & maintenance 1,316
- Production & transportation 4,868
- Self-employed persons 858

* US Census Bureau
** New Jersey Department of Labor
§ State Fiscal Year July 1–June 30

General Information
Town of West New York
428 60th St
West New York, NJ 07093
201-295-5200
- Website .... www.westnewyorknj.org
- Year of incorporation 1898
- Land/water area (sq. miles) 1.02/0.31
- Form of government .... Commission

Government
Legislative Districts
- US Congressional 13
- State Legislative 33

Local Officials, 2008
- Mayor .... Silverio A. Vega
- Manager .... Nicholas Goldsack
- Clerk .... Carmela Riccie
- Finance Dir .... Darren Maloney
- Tax Assessor .... Salvatore Bonaccorsi
- Tax Collector .... Kerri Campen
- Attorney .... Daniel Horgan
- Building .... Franco Zanardelli
- Comm Dev/Planning .... NA
- Engineering .... PMK Group
- Public Works .... William Parkinson
- Police Chief .... Oscar Fernandez
- Emerg/Fire Director ... Brion McEldowney

Housing & Construction
Housing Units, 2000*
- Total 17,360
- Median rent $681
- Median SF home value $218,400

Permits for New Residential Construction

	Units	Value
Total, 2007	339	$55,371,242
Single family	0	$0
Total, 2006	413	$114,449,160
Single family	0	$0

Real Property Valuation, 2007

	Parcels	Valuation
Total	6,213	$949,940,700
Vacant	913	41,208,700
Residential	4,016	441,154,200
Commercial	732	234,873,100
Industrial	141	39,607,000
Apartments	411	193,097,700
Farm land	0	0
Farm homestead	0	0

Average Property Value & Tax, 2007
- Residential value $109,849
- Property tax $5,070
- Tax credit/rebate $872

Public Library
West New York Public Library
425 60th St
West New York, NJ 07093
201-295-5135
- Director .... Weiliang Lai

Library statistics, 2006
- Population served 45,768
- Full-time/total staff 2/14

	Total	Per capita
Holdings	70,263	1.54
Revenues	$642,244	$14.03
Expenditures	$642,244	$14.03
Annual visits	58,120	1.27
Internet terminals/annual users	38/51,850	

Taxes	2005	2006	2007
General tax rate per $100	4.689	4.826	4.962
County equalization ratio	56.66	47.08	39.66
Net valuation taxable	$929,118,780	$941,704,400	$950,480,860
State equalized value	$1,973,489,337	$2,375,063,610	$2,692,352,855

Public Safety
- Number of officers, 2006 126

Crime	2005	2006
Total crimes	1,029	1,021
Violent	168	186
Murder	3	3
Rape	8	5
Robbery	89	85
Aggravated assault	68	93
Non-violent	861	835
Burglary	227	215
Larceny	508	464
Vehicle theft	126	156
Domestic violence	278	272
Arson	0	1
Total crime rate	22.3	21.9
Violent	3.6	4.0
Non-violent	18.6	17.9

Public School District
(for school year 2006-07 except as noted)

West New york School District
6028 Broadway
West New York, NJ 07093
201-553-4000
- Superintendent .... Robert VanZanten
- Number of schools 9
- Grade plan K-12
- Enrollment 7,119
- Attendance rate, '05-06 .... 94.7%
- Dropout rate 0.5%
- Students per teacher 11.7
- Per pupil expenditure $15,142
- Median faculty salary $59,971
- Median administrator salary $118,277
- Grade 12 enrollment 327
- High school graduation rate 93.4%

Assessment test results
(percent scoring at proficient or advanced level)

	Language	Math
NJASK-Grade 3	75.5%	85.9%
GEPA-Grade 8	70.9%	74.2%
HSPA-High School	80.2%	70.8%

SAT score averages

Pct tested	Math	Verbal	Writing
77%	419	405	400

Teacher Qualifications
- Avg. years of experience 11
- Highly-qualified teachers
  - one subject/all subjects 100%/100%
- With emergency credentials 0.0%

No Child Left Behind
- AYP, 2005-06 .... Meets Standards

Municipal Finance §
State Aid Programs, 2008
- Total aid $8,038,312
  - CMPTRA 6,264,793
  - Energy tax receipts 1,773,519
  - Garden State Trust 0

General Budget, 2007
- Total tax levy $47,162,563
  - County levy 10,009,136
  - County taxes 9,765,322
  - County library 0
  - County health 0
  - County open space 243,814
  - School levy 13,307,428
  - Muni. levy 23,846,000
- Misc. revenues 30,202,719

Essex County
West Orange Township

Demographics & Socio-Economic Characteristics
(2000 US Census, except as noted)

Population
1980*	39,510
1990*	39,103
2000	44,943
Male	21,110
Female	23,833
2006 (estimate)*	43,536
Population density	3,592.1

Race & Hispanic Origin, 2000
Race
White	30,359
Black/African American	7,848
American Indian/Alaska Native	63
Asian	3,635
Native Hawaiian/Pacific Islander	17
Other race	1,584
Two or more races	1,437
Hispanic origin, total	4,514
Mexican	277
Puerto Rican	672
Cuban	214
Other Hispanic	3,351

Age & Nativity, 2000
Under 5 years	2,988
18 years and over	34,477
21 years and over	33,258
65 years and over	7,818
85 years and over	1,523
Median age	39.4
Native-born	33,369
Foreign-born	11,483

Educational Attainment, 2000
Population 25 years and over	31,694
Less than 9th grade	4.7%
High school grad or higher	86.3%
Bachelor's degree or higher	43.1%
Graduate degree	19.0%

Income & Poverty, 1999
Per capita income	$34,412
Median household income	$69,254
Median family income	$83,375
Persons in poverty	2,461
H'holds receiving public assistance	228
H'holds receiving social security	4,630

Households, 2000
Total households	16,480
With persons under 18	5,699
With persons over 65	5,053
Family households	11,682
Single-person households	4,050
Persons per household	2.66
Persons per family	3.19

Labor & Employment
Total civilian labor force, 2006**	23,447
Unemployment rate	4.0%
Total civilian labor force, 2000	22,909
Unemployment rate	4.4%

Employed persons 16 years and over by occupation, 2000
Managers & professionals	10,344
Service occupations	2,417
Sales & office occupations	6,116
Farming, fishing & forestry	22
Construction & maintenance	1,263
Production & transportation	1,738
Self-employed persons	1,514

* US Census Bureau
** New Jersey Department of Labor

See Introduction for an explanation of all data sources.

General Information
Township of West Orange
66 Main St
West Orange, NJ 07052
973-325-4155

Website	www.westorange.org
Year of incorporation	1979
Land/water area (sq. miles)	12.12/0.11
Form of government	Mayor-Council

Government
Legislative Districts
US Congressional	8, 10
State Legislative	27

Local Officials, 2008
Mayor	John McKeon
Administrator	John Sayers
Clerk	Joann Behar (Actg)
Finance Dir	Edward Coleman
Tax Assessor	Kevin Dillon
Tax Collector	Joseph Antonucci
Attorney	Richard Trenk
Building	Tom Tracy
Planning	Susan Borg
Engineering	Leonard Lepore
Public Works	Nick Salese
Police Chief	James Abbott
Fire Chief	Peter Smeraldo

Housing & Construction
Housing Units, 2000*
Total	16,901
Median rent	$857
Median SF home value	$209,200

Permits for New Residential Construction
	Units	Value
Total, 2007	101	$29,292,225
Single family	101	$29,292,225
Total, 2006	152	$25,316,440
Single family	152	$25,316,440

Real Property Valuation, 2007
	Parcels	Valuation
Total	13,973	$1,538,507,700
Vacant	559	24,025,500
Residential	12,899	1,217,999,700
Commercial	431	245,536,500
Industrial	40	9,457,200
Apartments	44	41,488,800
Farm land	0	0
Farm homestead	0	0

Average Property Value & Tax, 2007
Residential value	$94,426
Property tax	$10,754
Tax credit/rebate	$1,400

Public Library
West Orange Public Library
46 Mt Pleasant Ave
West Orange, NJ 07052
973-736-0198

Director .... Cynthia Chamberlin

Library statistics, 2006
Population served	44,943
Full-time/total staff	11/21

	Total	Per capita
Holdings	168,280	3.74
Revenues	$2,581,056	$57.43
Expenditures	$2,452,388	$54.57
Annual visits	238,174	5.30
Internet terminals/annual users	17/68,526	

Public Safety
Number of officers, 2006 111

Crime	2005	2006
Total crimes	1,174	1,159
Violent	93	83
Murder	0	0
Rape	0	0
Robbery	55	52
Aggravated assault	38	31
Non-violent	1,081	1,076
Burglary	191	197
Larceny	649	697
Vehicle theft	241	182
Domestic violence	221	183
Arson	2	1
Total crime rate	26.2	26.2
Violent	2.1	1.9
Non-violent	24.1	24.3

Public School District
(for school year 2006-07 except as noted)

West Orange School District
179 Eagle Rock Ave
West Orange, NJ 07052
973-669-5400

Superintendent	Jerry Tarnoff
Number of schools	11
Grade plan	K-12
Enrollment	6,330
Attendance rate, '05-06	94.7%
Dropout rate	2.8%
Students per teacher	9.0
Per pupil expenditure	$15,457
Median faculty salary	$61,330
Median administrator salary	$110,299
Grade 12 enrollment	437
High school graduation rate	95.1%

Assessment test results
(percent scoring at proficient or advanced level)

	Language	Math
NJASK-Grade 3	87.9%	89.0%
GEPA-Grade 8	74.0%	69.0%
HSPA-High School	86.0%	62.5%

SAT score averages
Pct tested	Math	Verbal	Writing
94%	486	472	468

Teacher Qualifications
Avg. years of experience	6
Highly-qualified teachers one subject/all subjects	100%/100%
With emergency credentials	0.2%

No Child Left Behind
AYP, 2005-06 .... Needs Improvement

Municipal Finance
State Aid Programs, 2008
Total aid	$5,755,773
CMPTRA	1,132,543
Energy tax receipts	4,617,908
Garden State Trust	105

General Budget, 2007
Total tax levy	$175,502,658
County levy	25,715,807
County taxes	25,054,887
County library	0
County health	0
County open space	660,920
School levy	103,746,403
Muni. levy	46,040,448
Misc. revenues	19,710,476

Taxes
	2005	2006	2007
General tax rate per $100	9.85	10.6	11.39
County equalization ratio	29.47	26.25	23.58
Net valuation taxable	$1,533,221,711	$1,529,967,300	$1,541,054,566
State equalized value	$5,840,844,613	$6,491,170,661	$6,914,081,906

West Paterson Borough
Passaic County

Demographics & Socio-Economic Characteristics
(2000 US Census, except as noted)

Population
1980*	11,293
1990*	10,982
2000	10,987
Male	5,288
Female	5,699
2006 (estimate)*	11,234
Population density	3,795.3

Race & Hispanic Origin, 2000
Race
White	9,507
Black/African American	347
American Indian/Alaska Native	9
Asian	421
Native Hawaiian/Pacific Islander	4
Other race	348
Two or more races	351
Hispanic origin, total	1,105
Mexican	38
Puerto Rican	355
Cuban	60
Other Hispanic	652

Age & Nativity, 2000
Under 5 years	669
18 years and over	8,834
21 years and over	8,527
65 years and over	1,680
85 years and over	144
Median age	38.1
Native-born	8,675
Foreign-born	2,312

Educational Attainment, 2000
Population 25 years and over	8,001
Less than 9th grade	9.3%
High school grad or higher	81.8%
Bachelor's degree or higher	25.2%
Graduate degree	8.2%

Income & Poverty, 1999
Per capita income	$29,758
Median household income	$60,273
Median family income	$67,292
Persons in poverty	368
H'holds receiving public assistance	79
H'holds receiving social security	1,289

Households, 2000
Total households	4,397
With persons under 18	1,286
With persons over 65	1,219
Family households	3,025
Single-person households	1,121
Persons per household	2.49
Persons per family	3.01

Labor & Employment
Total civilian labor force, 2006**	6,532
Unemployment rate	3.4%
Total civilian labor force, 2000	6,036
Unemployment rate	3.4%

Employed persons 16 years and over by occupation, 2000
Managers & professionals	2,305
Service occupations	705
Sales & office occupations	1,668
Farming, fishing & forestry	0
Construction & maintenance	423
Production & transportation	730
Self-employed persons	334

* US Census Bureau
** New Jersey Department of Labor

General Information
Borough of West Paterson
5 Brophy Ln
West Paterson, NJ 07424
973-345-8100

Website	www.westpaterson.com
Year of incorporation	1914
Land/water area (sq. miles)	2.96/0.14
Form of government	Small Municipality

Government
Legislative Districts
US Congressional	8
State Legislative	34

Local Officials, 2008
Mayor	Pat Lepore
Manager	Kevin Galland
Clerk	Kevin Galland
Finance Dir	Frederick J. Tomkins
Tax Assessor	Tim Henderson
Tax Collector	John McCluskey
Attorney	Albert Buglione
Building	Felix Esposito
Comm Dev/Planning	NA
Engineering	Vincent DeNave
Public Works	George Galbraith
Police Chief	Robert Reda
Emerg/Fire Director	Paul Salomone Jr

Housing & Construction
Housing Units, 2000*
Total	4,497
Median rent	$854
Median SF home value	$195,100

Permits for New Residential Construction
	Units	Value
Total, 2007	174	$22,612,022
Single family	90	$12,848,321
Total, 2006	209	$26,085,129
Single family	91	$11,968,751

Real Property Valuation, 2007
	Parcels	Valuation
Total	3,739	$811,675,577
Vacant	543	34,193,613
Residential	2,956	554,965,324
Commercial	200	150,161,360
Industrial	32	35,076,600
Apartments	7	37,277,000
Farm land	1	1,680
Farm homestead	0	0

Average Property Value & Tax, 2007
Residential value	$187,742
Property tax	$7,721
Tax credit/rebate	$1,204

Public Library
Alfred H. Baumann Library
7 Brophy Lane
West Paterson, NJ 07424
973-345-8120

Director ... Robert Lindsley

Library statistics, 2006
Population served	10,987
Full-time/total staff	0/3

	Total	Per capita
Holdings	44,624	4.06
Revenues	$504,757	$45.94
Expenditures	$423,537	$38.55
Annual visits	35,000	3.19
Internet terminals/annual users	8/3,859	

Taxes
	2005	2006	2007
General tax rate per $100	3.58	3.84	4.12
County equalization ratio	61.38	54.05	48.44
Net valuation taxable	$797,734,270	$804,892,162	$812,232,705
State equalized value	$1,475,919,093	$1,662,228,359	$1,779,377,152

Public Safety
Number of officers, 2006 ... 26

Crime	2005	2006
Total crimes	333	272
Violent	22	12
Murder	0	0
Rape	3	0
Robbery	3	6
Aggravated assault	16	6
Non-violent	311	260
Burglary	84	53
Larceny	206	188
Vehicle theft	21	19
Domestic violence	97	73
Arson	0	1
Total crime rate	29.5	24.2
Violent	1.9	1.1
Non-violent	27.5	23.1

Public School District
(for school year 2006-07 except as noted)

West Paterson School District
853 McBride Ave
West Paterson, NJ 07424
973-278-5535

Chief School Admin	Scott E. Rixtord
Number of schools	3
Grade plan	K-8
Enrollment	1,003
Attendance rate, '05-06	95.5%
Dropout rate	NA
Students per teacher	11.6
Per pupil expenditure	$12,295
Median faculty salary	$59,325
Median administrator salary	$101,353
Grade 12 enrollment	NA
High school graduation rate	NA

Assessment test results
(percent scoring at proficient or advanced level)
	Language	Math
NJASK-Grade 3	87.1%	86.5%
GEPA-Grade 8	76.2%	61.9%
HSPA-High School	NA	NA

SAT score averages
Pct tested	Math	Verbal	Writing
NA	NA	NA	NA

Teacher Qualifications
Avg. years of experience	8
Highly-qualified teachers one subject/all subjects	97.0%/94.0%
With emergency credentials	0.0%

No Child Left Behind
AYP, 2005-06 ... Meets Standards

Municipal Finance
State Aid Programs, 2008
Total aid	$1,057,745
CMPTRA	403,490
Energy tax receipts	647,581
Garden State Trust	0

General Budget, 2007
Total tax levy	$33,402,636
County levy	8,337,791
County taxes	8,169,125
County library	0
County health	0
County open space	168,666
School levy	16,889,855
Muni. levy	8,174,991
Misc. revenues	4,091,444

Cape May County

West Wildwood Borough

Demographics & Socio-Economic Characteristics
(2000 US Census, except as noted)

Population
1980*	360
1990*	453
2000	448
Male	217
Female	231
2006 (estimate)*	408
Population density	1,569.2

Race & Hispanic Origin, 2000
Race
- White 429
- Black/African American 0
- American Indian/Alaska Native 0
- Asian 1
- Native Hawaiian/Pacific Islander 0
- Other race 10
- Two or more races 8
- Hispanic origin, total 17
  - Mexican 1
  - Puerto Rican 15
  - Cuban 0
  - Other Hispanic 1

Age & Nativity, 2000
- Under 5 years 22
- 18 years and over 364
- 21 years and over 352
- 65 years and over 87
- 85 years and over 6
- Median age 47.3
- Native-born 449
- Foreign-born 0

Educational Attainment, 2000
- Population 25 years and over 348
- Less than 9th grade 4.0%
- High school grad or higher ... 69.0%
- Bachelor's degree or higher ... 5.2%
- Graduate degree 1.4%

Income & Poverty, 1999
- Per capita income $17,839
- Median household income .. $33,393
- Median family income $50,625
- Persons in poverty 29
- H'holds receiving public assistance ... 9
- H'holds receiving social security 95

Households, 2000
- Total households 202
  - With persons under 18 45
  - With persons over 65 70
  - Family households 118
  - Single-person households 74
- Persons per household 2.22
- Persons per family 2.92

Labor & Employment
- Total civilian labor force, 2006** ... 291
  - Unemployment rate 10.6%
- Total civilian labor force, 2000 234
  - Unemployment rate 12.0%

Employed persons 16 years and over by occupation, 2000
- Managers & professionals 34
- Service occupations 47
- Sales & office occupations 73
- Farming, fishing & forestry 0
- Construction & maintenance 31
- Production & transportation 21
- Self-employed persons 2

* US Census Bureau
** New Jersey Department of Labor

See Introduction for an explanation of all data sources.

General Information
Borough of West Wildwood
701 W Glenwood Ave
West Wildwood, NJ 08260
609-522-4845

- Website .... www.westwildwoodnj.com
- Year of incorporation 1920
- Land/water area (sq. miles) ... 0.26/0.09
- Form of government .... Commission

Government
Legislative Districts
- US Congressional 2
- State Legislative 1

Local Officials, 2008
- Mayor .... Christopher Fox
- Manager/Admin .... NA
- Clerk .... Dorothy Tomlin
- Finance Dir .... Judson Moore
- Tax Assessor .... Joseph Gallagher
- Tax Collector .... Dorothy Tomlin
- Attorney .... Ronald Stagliano
- Building .... Glenn Franzoi
- Comm Dev/Planning .... NA
- Engineering ...... John Feairheller Jr
- Public Works .... James Fox
- Police Chief .... Alan Fox
- Emerg/Fire Director ..... Daniel Spiegel

Housing & Construction
Housing Units, 2000*
- Total 775
- Median rent $765
- Median SF home value $87,600

Permits for New Residential Construction
	Units	Value
Total, 2007	2	$552,160
Single family	2	$552,160
Total, 2006	18	$3,371,000
Single family	16	$2,955,000

Real Property Valuation, 2007
	Parcels	Valuation
Total	945	$214,719,000
Vacant	179	26,530,900
Residential	753	181,235,700
Commercial	10	5,943,900
Industrial	0	0
Apartments	3	1,008,500
Farm land	0	0
Farm homestead	0	0

Average Property Value & Tax, 2007
- Residential value $240,685
- Property tax $3,457
- Tax credit/rebate $944

Public Library
No public municipal library

Library statistics, 2006
- Population served .... NA
- Full-time/total staff .... NA/NA

	Total	Per capita
Holdings	NA	NA
Revenues	NA	NA
Expenditures	NA	NA
Annual visits	NA	NA
Internet terminals/annual users	NA/NA	

Taxes
	2005	2006	2007
General tax rate per $100	1.39	1.44	1.44
County equalization ratio	113.85	89.03	73.98
Net valuation taxable	$201,571,529	$206,370,300	$214,772,552
State equalized value	$226,408,547	$279,015,384	$304,489,962

Public Safety
- Number of officers, 2006 6

Crime
	2005	2006
Total crimes	37	20
Violent	2	0
Murder	1	0
Rape	0	0
Robbery	0	0
Aggravated assault	1	0
Non-violent	35	20
Burglary	9	6
Larceny	25	14
Vehicle theft	1	0
Domestic violence	14	7
Arson	0	0
Total crime rate	88.1	48.4
Violent	4.8	0.0
Non-violent	83.3	48.4

Public School District
(for school year 2006-07 except as noted)

West Wildwood School District
701 W Glenwood Ave
West Wildwood, NJ 08260

No schools in district - sends students to North Wildwood schools

- Per pupil expenditure .... NA
- Median faculty salary .... NA
- Median administrator salary .... NA
- Grade 12 enrollment .... NA
- High school graduation rate .... NA

Assessment test results
(percent scoring at proficient or advanced level)

	Language	Math
NJASK-Grade 3	NA	NA
GEPA-Grade 8	NA	NA
HSPA-High School	NA	NA

SAT score averages
Pct tested	Math	Verbal	Writing
NA	NA	NA	NA

Teacher Qualifications
- Avg. years of experience .... NA
- Highly-qualified teachers
  - one subject/all subjects ..... NA/NA
- With emergency credentials .... NA

No Child Left Behind
- AYP, 2005-06 .... NA

Municipal Finance
State Aid Programs, 2008
- Total aid $49,810
- CMPTRA 0
- Energy tax receipts 49,810
- Garden State Trust 0

General Budget, 2007
- Total tax levy $3,084,854
- County levy 552,364
  - County taxes 438,959
  - County library 84,348
  - County health 0
  - County open space 29,056
- School levy 1,065,573
- Muni. levy 1,466,918
- Misc. revenues 613,597

©2008 Information Publications, Inc. All rights reserved.

The New Jersey Municipal Data Book

West Windsor Township — Mercer County

Demographics & Socio-Economic Characteristics
(2000 US Census, except as noted)

Population
1980*	8,542
1990*	16,021
2000	21,907
Male	10,858
Female	11,049
2006 (estimate)*	26,279
Population density	1,010.3

Race & Hispanic Origin, 2000
Race
White	15,670
Black/African American	605
American Indian/Alaska Native	17
Asian	4,986
Native Hawaiian/Pacific Islander	2
Other race	236
Two or more races	391
Hispanic origin, total	892
Mexican	177
Puerto Rican	152
Cuban	63
Other Hispanic	500

Age & Nativity, 2000
Under 5 years	1,541
18 years and over	14,939
21 years and over	14,470
65 years and over	1,349
85 years and over	110
Median age	37.0
Native-born	17,001
Foreign-born	4,906

Educational Attainment, 2000
Population 25 years and over	14,026
Less than 9th grade	1.5%
High school grad or higher	96.9%
Bachelor's degree or higher	73.9%
Graduate degree	39.0%

Income & Poverty, 1999
Per capita income	$48,511
Median household income	$116,335
Median family income	$127,877
Persons in poverty	548
H'holds receiving public assistance	63
H'holds receiving social security	961

Households, 2000
Total households	7,282
With persons under 18	3,730
With persons over 65	993
Family households	5,986
Single-person households	1,061
Persons per household	3.01
Persons per family	3.36

Labor & Employment
Total civilian labor force, 2006**	14,608
Unemployment rate	2.0%
Total civilian labor force, 2000	11,228
Unemployment rate	3.0%

Employed persons 16 years and over by occupation, 2000
Managers & professionals	7,731
Service occupations	487
Sales & office occupations	2,230
Farming, fishing & forestry	0
Construction & maintenance	175
Production & transportation	264
Self-employed persons	526

‡ Branch of county library
* US Census Bureau
** New Jersey Department of Labor

General Information
Township of West Windsor
271 Clarksville Rd
PO Box 38
West Windsor, NJ 08550
609-799-2400

Website	www.westwindsornj.org
Year of incorporation	1797
Land/water area (sq. miles)	26.01/0.32
Form of government	Mayor-Council

Government
Legislative Districts
US Congressional	12
State Legislative	14

Local Officials, 2008
Mayor	Shing-Fu Hsueh
Manager	Christopher R. Marion
Clerk	Sharon Young
Finance Dir	Joanne R. Louth
Tax Assessor	Steven Benner
Tax Collector	Rita Carr
Attorney	Michael Herbert
Building	Joseph Valeri
Planning	M. Patricia Ward
Engineering	Rob Korkuch (Actg)
Public Works	Alex Drummond (Actg)
Police Chief	Joseph Pica
Emerg/Fire Director	Jim Yates

Housing & Construction
Housing Units, 2000*
Total	7,450
Median rent	$1,198
Median SF home value	$333,800

Permits for New Residential Construction
	Units	Value
Total, 2007	62	$10,899,117
Single family	62	$10,899,117
Total, 2006	154	$11,451,838
Single family	154	$11,451,838

Real Property Valuation, 2007
	Parcels	Valuation
Total	8,719	$6,287,299,113
Vacant	679	150,314,710
Residential	7,645	4,394,359,300
Commercial	252	1,518,534,654
Industrial	10	78,378,900
Apartments	5	113,257,000
Farm land	97	1,627,749
Farm homestead	31	30,826,800

Average Property Value & Tax, 2007
Residential value	$576,496
Property tax	$11,424
Tax credit/rebate	$1,290

Public Library
West Windsor Branch Library‡
333 N Post Rd
Princeton Jnc, NJ 08550
609-799-0462
Branch Librarian: Kaija Greenberg

Library statistics, 2006
see Mercer County profile for library system statistics

Public Safety
Number of officers, 2006	45

Crime	2005	2006
Total crimes	535	563
Violent	13	17
Murder	0	1
Rape	4	1
Robbery	4	7
Aggravated assault	5	8
Non-violent	522	546
Burglary	74	53
Larceny	433	474
Vehicle theft	15	19
Domestic violence	55	57
Arson	1	1
Total crime rate	21.9	21.7
Violent	0.5	0.7
Non-violent	21.3	21.0

Public School District
(for school year 2006-07 except as noted)

West Windsor-Plainsboro Reg. School Dist.
505 Village Rd West, PO Box 505
Princeton Junction, NJ 08550
609-716-5000

Chief School Admin	Victoria Kniewel
Number of schools	20
Grade plan	K-12
Enrollment	9,509
Attendance rate, '05-06	96.8%
Dropout rate	0.4%
Students per teacher	11.4
Per pupil expenditure	$13,856
Median faculty salary	$64,345
Median administrator salary	$114,343
Grade 12 enrollment	724
High school graduation rate	NA

Assessment test results
(percent scoring at proficient or advanced level)
	Language	Math
NJASK-Grade 3	96.6%	96.4%
GEPA-Grade 8	95.2%	92.2%
HSPA-High School	97.0%	94.2%

SAT score averages
Pct tested	Math	Verbal	Writing
NA	NA	NA	NA

Teacher Qualifications
Avg. years of experience	13
Highly-qualified teachers one subject/all subjects	100%/100%
With emergency credentials	0.3%

No Child Left Behind
AYP, 2005-06 .... Meets Standards

Municipal Finance
State Aid Programs, 2008
Total aid	$2,926,930
CMPTRA	125,740
Energy tax receipts	2,796,067
Garden State Trust	5,123

General Budget, 2007
Total tax levy	$124,910,233
County levy	29,686,856
County taxes	25,574,013
County library	2,359,933
County health	0
County open space	1,752,909
School levy	75,680,378
Muni. levy	19,542,999
Misc. revenues	15,178,049

Taxes
	2005	2006	2007
General tax rate per $100	4.26	1.91	1.99
County equalization ratio	59.73	123.05	108.25
Net valuation taxable	$2,656,180,318	$6,289,299,663	$6,303,495,043
State equalized value	$5,038,278,297	$6,048,380,187	$6,220,359,254

Burlington County — Westampton Township

Demographics & Socio-Economic Characteristics
(2000 US Census, except as noted)

Population
- 1980* 3,383
- 1990* 6,004
- 2000 7,217
  - Male 3,418
  - Female 3,799
- 2006 (estimate)* 8,771
  - Population density 794.5

Race & Hispanic Origin, 2000
Race
- White 5,110
- Black/African American 1,535
- American Indian/Alaska Native 20
- Asian 219
- Native Hawaiian/Pacific Islander 3
- Other race 132
- Two or more races 198
- Hispanic origin, total 448
  - Mexican 24
  - Puerto Rican 296
  - Cuban 8
  - Other Hispanic 120

Age & Nativity, 2000
- Under 5 years 525
- 18 years and over 5,104
- 21 years and over 4,888
- 65 years and over 659
- 85 years and over 39
  - Median age 35.8
- Native-born 6,730
- Foreign-born 470

Educational Attainment, 2000
- Population 25 years and over 4,729
- Less than 9th grade 2.0%
- High school grad or higher 90.9%
- Bachelor's degree or higher 26.2%
- Graduate degree 6.9%

Income & Poverty, 1999
- Per capita income $26,594
- Median household income $63,973
- Median family income $69,656
- Persons in poverty 180
- H'holds receiving public assistance 12
- H'holds receiving social security 518

Households, 2000
- Total households 2,525
  - With persons under 18 1,158
  - With persons over 65 467
  - Family households 1,966
  - Single-person households 456
- Persons per household 2.83
- Persons per family 3.24

Labor & Employment
- Total civilian labor force, 2006** 4,331
  - Unemployment rate 3.5%
- Total civilian labor force, 2000 3,724
  - Unemployment rate 3.2%

Employed persons 16 years and over by occupation, 2000
- Managers & professionals 1,301
- Service occupations 521
- Sales & office occupations 1,208
- Farming, fishing & forestry 0
- Construction & maintenance 170
- Production & transportation 404
- Self-employed persons 108

* US Census Bureau
** New Jersey Department of Labor

See Introduction for an explanation of all data sources.

General Information
Township of Westampton
710 Rancocas Rd
Westampton, NJ 08060
609-267-1891

- Website .... www.westampton.com
- Year of incorporation 1850
- Land/water area (sq. miles) 11.04/0.12
- Form of government .... Township

Government

Legislative Districts
- US Congressional 3
- State Legislative 7

Local Officials, 2008
- Mayor .... Harry Adams
- Manager .... Donna Ryan
- Clerk .... Donna Ryan
- Finance Dir .... Robert Hudnell
- Tax Assessor .... Marie Procacci
- Tax Collector .... Carol Brown-Layou
- Attorney .... Christopher Baxter
- Building .... Gene Blair
- Comm Dev/Planning .... NA
- Engineering .... David Denton
- Public Works .... NA
- Police Chief .... Steven VanSciver
- Emerg/Fire Director .... Wylie Johnson

Housing & Construction

Housing Units, 2000*
- Total 2,581
- Median rent $1,112
- Median SF home value $127,300

Permits for New Residential Construction
	Units	Value
Total, 2007	31	$7,827,650
Single family	31	$7,827,650
Total, 2006	25	$6,597,876
Single family	25	$6,597,876

Real Property Valuation, 2007
	Parcels	Valuation
Total	3,484	$672,503,650
Vacant	197	11,196,200
Residential	3,085	456,815,600
Commercial	110	187,973,100
Industrial	2	11,261,400
Apartments	0	0
Farm land	68	1,043,250
Farm homestead	22	4,214,100

Average Property Value & Tax, 2007
- Residential value $148,384
- Property tax $4,584
- Tax credit/rebate $828

Public Library
No public municipal library

Library statistics, 2006
- Population served .... NA
- Full-time/total staff .... NA/NA

	Total	Per capita
Holdings	NA	NA
Revenues	NA	NA
Expenditures	NA	NA
Annual visits	NA	NA
Internet terminals/annual users	NA/NA	

Taxes
	2005	2006	2007
General tax rate per $100	2.852	3.034	3.09
County equalization ratio	72.11	65.98	59.78
Net valuation taxable	$622,307,010	$656,227,150	$673,846,216
State equalized value	$943,175,220	$1,099,184,157	$1,201,813,201

Public Safety
- Number of officers, 2006 22

Crime	2005	2006
Total crimes	214	250
Violent	23	20
Murder	0	0
Rape	3	3
Robbery	6	3
Aggravated assault	14	14
Non-violent	191	230
Burglary	25	24
Larceny	148	182
Vehicle theft	18	24
Domestic violence	86	108
Arson	0	0
Total crime rate	25.4	28.9
Violent	2.7	2.3
Non-violent	22.7	26.6

Public School District
(for school year 2006-07 except as noted)

Westampton Township School District
710 Rancocas Road
Westampton, NJ 08060
609-267-2053

- Superintendent .... Kenneth Hamilton
- Number of schools 2
- Grade plan K-8
- Enrollment 937
- Attendance rate, '05-06 .... 95.7%
- Dropout rate .... NA
- Students per teacher 11.0
- Per pupil expenditure $10,398
- Median faculty salary $47,238
- Median administrator salary $98,119
- Grade 12 enrollment .... NA
- High school graduation rate .... NA

Assessment test results
(percent scoring at proficient or advanced level)

	Language	Math
NJASK-Grade 3	84.6%	93.4%
GEPA-Grade 8	79.4%	77.4%
HSPA-High School	NA	NA

SAT score averages
Pct tested	Math	Verbal	Writing
NA	NA	NA	NA

Teacher Qualifications
- Avg. years of experience 7
- Highly-qualified teachers
  one subject/all subjects 93.5%/93.5%
- With emergency credentials 1.5%

No Child Left Behind
- AYP, 2005-06 .... Meets Standards

Municipal Finance

State Aid Programs, 2008
- Total aid $801,568
  - CMPTRA 72,272
  - Energy tax receipts 727,987
  - Garden State Trust 1,309

General Budget, 2007
- Total tax levy $20,817,782
  - County levy 4,730,244
    - County taxes 3,919,628
    - County library 359,701
    - County health 0
    - County open space 450,914
  - School levy 12,354,195
  - Muni. levy 3,733,344
- Misc. revenues 4,422,195

©2008 Information Publications, Inc. All rights reserved. Photocopying prohibited. For additional copies, contact the publisher at www.informationpublications.com or (877)544-INFO (4636)

Westfield Town — Union County

Demographics & Socio-Economic Characteristics
(2000 US Census, except as noted)

Population
- 1980* 30,447
- 1990* 28,870
- 2000 29,644
  - Male 14,209
  - Female 15,435
- 2006 (estimate)* 29,944
- Population density 4,449.3

Race & Hispanic Origin, 2000
Race
- White 26,675
- Black/African American 1,151
- American Indian/Alaska Native .. 27
- Asian 1,208
- Native Hawaiian/Pacific Islander .. 3
- Other race 185
- Two or more races 395
- Hispanic origin, total 836
  - Mexican 104
  - Puerto Rican 176
  - Cuban 103
  - Other Hispanic 453

Age & Nativity, 2000
- Under 5 years 2,369
- 18 years and over 21,235
- 21 years and over 20,704
- 65 years and over 4,015
- 85 years and over 528
- Median age 38.6
- Native-born 26,940
- Foreign-born 2,704

Educational Attainment, 2000
- Population 25 years and over .. 20,052
- Less than 9th grade 1.8%
- High school grad or higher 95.4%
- Bachelor's degree or higher ... 62.5%
- Graduate degree 29.8%

Income & Poverty, 1999
- Per capita income $47,187
- Median household income ... $98,390
- Median family income $112,145
- Persons in poverty 791
- H'holds receiving public assistance .. 93
- H'holds receiving social security .. 2,626

Households, 2000
- Total households 10,622
  - With persons under 18 4,454
  - With persons over 65 2,716
  - Family households 8,181
  - Single-person households ... 2,052
- Persons per household 2.77
- Persons per family 3.20

Labor & Employment
- Total civilian labor force, 2006** .. 15,764
  - Unemployment rate 2.7%
- Total civilian labor force, 2000 .. 14,907
  - Unemployment rate 2.2%
- *Employed persons 16 years and over by occupation, 2000*
  - Managers & professionals 8,811
  - Service occupations 1,102
  - Sales & office occupations ... 3,510
  - Farming, fishing & forestry 8
  - Construction & maintenance .. 484
  - Production & transportation .. 660
- Self-employed persons 942

* US Census Bureau
** New Jersey Department of Labor

General Information
Town of Westfield
425 E Broad St
Westfield, NJ 07090
908-789-4033

- Website .... www.westfieldnj.gov
- Year of incorporation 1903
- Land/water area (sq. miles) ... 6.73/0.02
- Form of government .... Special Charter

Government
Legislative Districts
- US Congressional 7
- State Legislative 21

Local Officials, 2008
- Mayor .... Andrew Skibitsky
- Manager .... James Gildea
- Clerk .... Claire Gray
- Finance Dir .... Liy-Huei Tsai
- Tax Assessor .... Ann Switzer
- Tax Collector .... Susan Noon
- Attorney .... Robert Cockren
- Building .... Steve Freedman
- Planning .... (private firm)
- Engineering .... Kenneth Marsh
- Public Works .... Claude Shafter
- Police Chief .... John Parizeau
- Emerg/Fire Director ...... Daniel Kelly

Housing & Construction
Housing Units, 2000*
- Total 10,819
- Median rent $1,048
- Median SF home value $346,000

Permits for New Residential Construction

	Units	Value
Total, 2007	54	$17,778,603
Single family	54	$17,778,603
Total, 2006	81	$20,798,335
Single family	81	$20,798,335

Real Property Valuation, 2007

	Parcels	Valuation
Total	9,785	$1,862,402,500
Vacant	262	13,582,300
Residential	9,084	1,649,131,600
Commercial	422	176,017,200
Industrial	4	1,988,100
Apartments	12	21,679,100
Farm land	1	4,200
Farm homestead	0	0

Average Property Value & Tax, 2007
- Residential value $181,542
- Property tax $11,487
- Tax credit/rebate $1,319

Public Library
Westfield Memorial Library
550 E Broad St
Westfield, NJ 07090
908-789-4090

- Director .... Philip Israel

Library statistics, 2006
- Population served 29,644
- Full-time/total staff 7/14

	Total	Per capita
Holdings	189,305	6.39
Revenues	$2,195,280	$74.05
Expenditures	$2,157,251	$72.77
Annual visits	257,422	8.68
Internet terminals/annual users	...	18/45,693

Taxes

	2005	2006	2007
General tax rate per $100	5.84	6.083	6.328
County equalization ratio	30.81	28.11	26.37
Net valuation taxable	$1,846,085,079	$1,849,664,900	$1,864,139,453
State equalized value	$6,245,213,393	$7,016,292,401	$7,535,727,649

Public Safety
- Number of officers, 2006 59

Crime	2005	2006
Total crimes	345	351
Violent	17	15
Murder	0	0
Rape	1	2
Robbery	5	6
Aggravated assault	11	7
Non-violent	328	336
Burglary	53	65
Larceny	266	259
Vehicle theft	9	12
Domestic violence	112	118
Arson	2	3
Total crime rate	11.5	11.7
Violent	0.6	0.5
Non-violent	10.9	11.2

Public School District
(for school year 2006-07 except as noted)

Westfield School District
302 Elm St
Westfield, NJ 07090
908-789-4420

- Superintendent .... William Foley
- Number of schools 9
- Grade plan K-12
- Enrollment 6,049
- Attendance rate, '05-06 .... 95.5%
- Dropout rate 0.2%
- Students per teacher 11.5
- Per pupil expenditure $12,391
- Median faculty salary $58,234
- Median administrator salary .. $112,551
- Grade 12 enrollment 434
- High school graduation rate 99.3%

Assessment test results
(percent scoring at proficient or advanced level)

	Language	Math
NJASK-Grade 3	95.6%	98.0%
GEPA-Grade 8	86.9%	88.2%
HSPA-High School	95.4%	92.6%

SAT score averages

Pct tested	Math	Verbal	Writing
103%	578	565	570

Teacher Qualifications
- Avg. years of experience 9
- Highly-qualified teachers
  - one subject/all subjects ... 100%/100%
- With emergency credentials 0.0%

No Child Left Behind
- AYP, 2005-06 .... Meets Standards

Municipal Finance
State Aid Programs, 2008
- Total aid $4,157,746
  - CMPTRA 1,449,357
  - Energy tax receipts 2,708,389
  - Garden State Trust 0

General Budget, 2007
- Total tax levy $117,952,551
  - County levy 24,654,622
    - County taxes 23,592,003
    - County library 0
    - County health 0
    - County open space 1,062,619
  - School levy 73,115,976
  - Muni. levy 20,181,953
  - Misc. revenues 15,838,776

Gloucester County

Westville Borough

Demographics & Socio-Economic Characteristics
(2000 US Census, except as noted)

Population
1980*	4,786
1990*	4,573
2000	4,500
Male	2,183
Female	2,317
2006 (estimate)*	4,458
Population density	4,643.8

Race & Hispanic Origin, 2000
Race
White	4,206
Black/African American	122
American Indian/Alaska Native	6
Asian	45
Native Hawaiian/Pacific Islander	1
Other race	58
Two or more races	62
Hispanic origin, total	133
Mexican	21
Puerto Rican	59
Cuban	2
Other Hispanic	51

Age & Nativity, 2000
Under 5 years	253
18 years and over	3,396
21 years and over	3,236
65 years and over	633
85 years and over	63
Median age	36.6
Native-born	4,398
Foreign-born	102

Educational Attainment, 2000
Population 25 years and over	3,033
Less than 9th grade	4.5%
High school grad or higher	75.5%
Bachelor's degree or higher	8.9%
Graduate degree	1.2%

Income & Poverty, 1999
Per capita income	$18,747
Median household income	$39,570
Median family income	$49,005
Persons in poverty	389
H'holds receiving public assistance	41
H'holds receiving social security	535

Households, 2000
Total households	1,812
With persons under 18	590
With persons over 65	471
Family households	1,126
Single-person households	577
Persons per household	2.48
Persons per family	3.15

Labor & Employment
Total civilian labor force, 2006**	2,845
Unemployment rate	6.0%
Total civilian labor force, 2000	2,388
Unemployment rate	5.0%

Employed persons 16 years and over by occupation, 2000
Managers & professionals	466
Service occupations	350
Sales & office occupations	707
Farming, fishing & forestry	0
Construction & maintenance	339
Production & transportation	406
Self-employed persons	108

* US Census Bureau
** New Jersey Department of Labor

See Introduction for an explanation of all data sources.

General Information
Borough of Westville
1035 Broadway
Westville, NJ 08093
856-456-0030

Website	www.westville-nj.com
Year of incorporation	1914
Land/water area (sq. miles)	0.96/0.39
Form of government	Borough

Government
Legislative Districts
US Congressional	1
State Legislative	5

Local Officials, 2008
Mayor	Michael K. Galbraith
Administrator	William J. Bittner Jr
Clerk	Christine A. Helder
Finance Dir	John A. Bruno Jr
Tax Assessor	Roy A. Duffield
Tax Collector	Christine A. Helder
Attorney	Timothy W. Chell
Building	Robert Kunkle
Land Use Official	Michael Sautter (Chr)
Engineering	Norman Rodgers
Public Works	Donna M. Domico
Police Chief	Frederick Lederer III
Emerg/Fire Director	Chuck Murtaugh

Housing & Construction
Housing Units, 2000*
Total	1,938
Median rent	$569
Median SF home value	$91,500

Permits for New Residential Construction
	Units	Value
Total, 2007	1	$92,304
Single family	1	$92,304
Total, 2006	6	$659,666
Single family	6	$659,666

Real Property Valuation, 2007
	Parcels	Valuation
Total	1,604	$161,231,300
Vacant	67	1,349,900
Residential	1,395	121,301,300
Commercial	103	21,150,400
Industrial	29	11,112,000
Apartments	10	6,317,700
Farm land	0	0
Farm homestead	0	0

Average Property Value & Tax, 2007
Residential value	$86,954
Property tax	$4,329
Tax credit/rebate	$868

Public Library
Westville Public Library
1035 Broadway
Westville, NJ 08093
856-456-0357

Director .... Gwen Carotenuto

Library statistics, 2006
Population served	4,500
Full-time/total staff	0/0

	Total	Per capita
Holdings	27,620	6.14
Revenues	$94,950	$21.10
Expenditures	$89,355	$19.86
Annual visits	9,829	2.18
Internet terminals/annual users		3/4,017

Taxes
	2005	2006	2007
General tax rate per $100	4.091	4.516	4.979
County equalization ratio	82.87	73.04	61.88
Net valuation taxable	$161,075,099	$160,791,900	$161,473,863
State equalized value	$220,529,982	$260,129,048	$285,002,895

Public Safety
Number of officers, 2006 10

Crime
	2005	2006
Total crimes	132	127
Violent	12	10
Murder	0	0
Rape	1	0
Robbery	1	2
Aggravated assault	10	8
Non-violent	120	117
Burglary	40	30
Larceny	70	72
Vehicle theft	10	15
Domestic violence	34	52
Arson	3	2
Total crime rate	29.5	28.4
Violent	2.7	2.2
Non-violent	26.8	26.2

Public School District
(for school year 2006-07 except as noted)

Westville School District
101 Birch St
Westville, NJ 08093
856-456-0235

Superintendent	Shannon M. Whalen
Number of schools	1
Grade plan	K-6
Enrollment	370
Attendance rate, '05-06	95.5%
Dropout rate	NA
Students per teacher	10.7
Per pupil expenditure	$11,650
Median faculty salary	$56,595
Median administrator salary	$94,000
Grade 12 enrollment	NA
High school graduation rate	NA

Assessment test results
(percent scoring at proficient or advanced level)
	Language	Math
NJASK-Grade 3	71.4%	81.7%
GEPA-Grade 8	NA	NA
HSPA-High School	NA	NA

SAT score averages
Pct tested	Math	Verbal	Writing
NA	NA	NA	NA

Teacher Qualifications
Avg. years of experience	19
Highly-qualified teachers one subject/all subjects	100%/100%
With emergency credentials	0.0%

No Child Left Behind
AYP, 2005-06 .... Meets Standards

Municipal Finance
State Aid Programs, 2008
Total aid	$332,712
CMPTRA	0
Energy tax receipts	332,712
Garden State Trust	0

General Budget, 2007
Total tax levy	$8,039,283
County levy	1,444,304
County taxes	1,339,437
County library	0
County health	0
County open space	104,866
School levy	4,315,979
Muni. levy	2,279,000
Misc. revenues	2,223,000

©2008 Information Publications, Inc. All rights reserved. Photocopying prohibited. For additional copies, contact the publisher at www.informationpublications.com or (877)544-INFO (4636)

The New Jersey Municipal Data Book

Westwood Borough

Bergen County

Demographics & Socio-Economic Characteristics
(2000 US Census, except as noted)

Population
1980*	10,714
1990*	10,446
2000	10,999
Male	5,218
Female	5,781
2006 (estimate)*	10,934
Population density	4,712.9

Race & Hispanic Origin, 2000
Race
- White ... 9,525
- Black/African American ... 629
- American Indian/Alaska Native ... 15
- Asian ... 483
- Native Hawaiian/Pacific Islander ... 1
- Other race ... 184
- Two or more races ... 162
- Hispanic origin, total ... 660
  - Mexican ... 135
  - Puerto Rican ... 113
  - Cuban ... 60
  - Other Hispanic ... 352

Age & Nativity, 2000
- Under 5 years ... 762
- 18 years and over ... 8,631
- 21 years and over ... 8,392
- 65 years and over ... 1,752
- 85 years and over ... 320
- Median age ... 38.6
- Native-born ... 9,317
- Foreign-born ... 1,682

Educational Attainment, 2000
- Population 25 years and over ... 8,052
- Less than 9th grade ... 4.8%
- High school grad or higher ... 88.1%
- Bachelor's degree or higher ... 37.4%
- Graduate degree ... 11.7%

Income & Poverty, 1999
- Per capita income ... $32,083
- Median household income ... $59,868
- Median family income ... $77,105
- Persons in poverty ... 474
- H'holds receiving public assistance ... 58
- H'holds receiving social security ... 1,315

Households, 2000
- Total households ... 4,485
  - With persons under 18 ... 1,348
  - With persons over 65 ... 1,279
  - Family households ... 2,878
  - Single-person households ... 1,395
- Persons per household ... 2.42
- Persons per family ... 3.08

Labor & Employment
- Total civilian labor force, 2006** ... 6,249
  - Unemployment rate ... 2.2%
- Total civilian labor force, 2000 ... 5,874
  - Unemployment rate ... 2.1%

Employed persons 16 years and over by occupation, 2000
- Managers & professionals ... 2,444
- Service occupations ... 839
- Sales & office occupations ... 1,678
- Farming, fishing & forestry ... 0
- Construction & maintenance ... 372
- Production & transportation ... 417
- Self-employed persons ... 311

* US Census Bureau
** New Jersey Department of Labor

General Information
Borough of Westwood
101 Washington Ave
Westwood, NJ 07675
201-664-7100

- Website ... www.westwoodnj.gov
- Year of incorporation ... 1894
- Land/water area (sq. miles) ... 2.32/0.00
- Form of government ... Borough

Government
Legislative Districts
- US Congressional ... 5
- State Legislative ... 39

Local Officials, 2008
- Mayor ... John Birkner Jr
- Administrator ... Robert S. Hoffmann
- Clerk ... Karen Hughes
- Finance Dir ... Raymond Herr
- Tax Assessor ... Barbara Potash
- Tax Collector ... Stephanie Stokes
- Attorney ... Russell Huntington
- Building ... Armand Marini
- Planning ... Jaymee Hodges
- Engineering ... Stephen Boswell
- Public Works ... Rick Woods
- Police Chief ... Frank Regino
- Emerg/Fire Director ... Robert Saul Jr

Housing & Construction
Housing Units, 2000*
- Total ... 4,610
- Median rent ... $996
- Median SF home value ... $239,300

Permits for New Residential Construction
	Units	Value
Total, 2007	7	$1,673,182
Single family	7	$1,673,182
Total, 2006	6	$1,027,800
Single family	6	$1,027,800

Real Property Valuation, 2007
	Parcels	Valuation
Total	3,458	$1,615,132,600
Vacant	105	11,763,500
Residential	3,055	1,208,785,300
Commercial	236	243,428,200
Industrial	34	39,439,400
Apartments	28	111,716,200
Farm land	0	0
Farm homestead	0	0

Average Property Value & Tax, 2007
- Residential value ... $395,674
- Property tax ... $7,997
- Tax credit/rebate ... $1,266

Public Library
Westwood Public Library
49 Park Ave
Westwood, NJ 07675
201-664-0583

Director ... Martha Urbiel

Library statistics, 2006
- Population served ... 10,999
- Full-time/total staff ... 2/6

	Total	Per capita
Holdings	45,355	4.12
Revenues	$710,335	$64.58
Expenditures	$705,195	$64.11
Annual visits	106,694	9.70
Internet terminals/annual users	11/21,900	

Taxes
	2005	2006	2007
General tax rate per $100	1.89	1.97	2.03
County equalization ratio	100.22	93.12	87.06
Net valuation taxable	$1,589,647,810	$1,609,472,600	$1,616,567,615
State equalized value	$1,707,096,016	$1,850,565,613	$1,938,277,082

Public Safety
Number of officers, 2006 ... 26

Crime	2005	2006
Total crimes	126	145
Violent	9	3
Murder	0	0
Rape	2	0
Robbery	2	1
Aggravated assault	5	2
Non-violent	117	142
Burglary	22	17
Larceny	92	118
Vehicle theft	3	7
Domestic violence	29	35
Arson	1	0
Total crime rate	11.4	13.2
Violent	0.8	0.3
Non-violent	10.6	12.9

Public School District
(for school year 2006-07 except as noted)

Westwood Regional School District
701 Ridgewood Rd
Township of Washington, NJ 07676
201-664-2765

- Superintendent ... Geoffrey Zoeller
- Number of schools ... 12
- Grade plan ... K-12
- Enrollment ... 2,646
- Attendance rate, '05-06 ... 94.4%
- Dropout rate ... NA
- Students per teacher ... 10.5
- Per pupil expenditure ... $14,584
- Median faculty salary ... $53,168
- Median administrator salary ... $113,163
- Grade 12 enrollment ... 179
- High school graduation rate ... 98.9%

Assessment test results
(percent scoring at proficient or advanced level)
	Language	Math
NJASK-Grade 3	87.1%	96.9%
GEPA-Grade 8	89.9%	80.1%
HSPA-High School	95.9%	82.8%

SAT score averages
Pct tested	Math	Verbal	Writing
92%	534	492	494

Teacher Qualifications
- Avg. years of experience ... 8
- Highly-qualified teachers one subject/all subjects ... 100%/100%
- With emergency credentials ... 0.0%

No Child Left Behind
AYP, 2005-06 ... Meets Standards

Municipal Finance
State Aid Programs, 2008
- Total aid ... $1,309,965
- CMPTRA ... 257,570
- Energy tax receipts ... 1,051,690
- Garden State Trust ... 0

General Budget, 2007
- Total tax levy ... $32,674,084
- County levy ... 3,391,190
  - County taxes ... 3,204,558
  - County library ... 0
  - County health ... 0
  - County open space ... 186,632
- School levy ... 18,888,235
- Muni. levy ... 10,394,659
- Misc. revenues ... 4,371,502

548 The New Jersey Municipal Data Book

Atlantic County / Weymouth Township

Demographics & Socio-Economic Characteristics
(2000 US Census, except as noted)

Population
1980*	1,260
1990*	1,957
2000	2,257
Male	1,085
Female	1,172
2006 (estimate)*	2,296
Population density	188.2

Race & Hispanic Origin, 2000
Race
White	2,076
Black/African American	108
American Indian/Alaska Native	9
Asian	18
Native Hawaiian/Pacific Islander	0
Other race	23
Two or more races	23
Hispanic origin, total	86
Mexican	24
Puerto Rican	42
Cuban	2
Other Hispanic	18

Age & Nativity, 2000
Under 5 years	141
18 years and over	1,694
21 years and over	1,628
65 years and over	387
85 years and over	29
Median age	39.4
Native-born	2,191
Foreign-born	59

Educational Attainment, 2000
Population 25 years and over	1,530
Less than 9th grade	5.6%
High school grad or higher	79.5%
Bachelor's degree or higher	14.2%
Graduate degree	4.4%

Income & Poverty, 1999
Per capita income	$18,987
Median household income	$45,882
Median family income	$49,800
Persons in poverty	115
H'holds receiving public assistance	29
H'holds receiving social security	297

Households, 2000
Total households	851
With persons under 18	283
With persons over 65	276
Family households	624
Single-person households	183
Persons per household	2.65
Persons per family	3.06

Labor & Employment
Total civilian labor force, 2006**	1,208
Unemployment rate	3.4%
Total civilian labor force, 2000	1,098
Unemployment rate	3.8%

Employed persons 16 years and over by occupation, 2000
Managers & professionals	255
Service occupations	228
Sales & office occupations	310
Farming, fishing & forestry	0
Construction & maintenance	139
Production & transportation	124
Self-employed persons	46

* US Census Bureau
** New Jersey Department of Labor

See Introduction for an explanation of all data sources.

General Information
Township of Weymouth
45 S Jersey Ave
Dorothy, NJ 08317
609-476-2633

Website	www.weymouthnj.org
Year of incorporation	1798
Land/water area (sq. miles)	12.20/0.37
Form of government	Township

Government

Legislative Districts
US Congressional	2
State Legislative	2

Local Officials, 2008
Mayor	Frank C. Craig
Manager	Bonnie Yearsley
Clerk	Bonnie Yearsley
Finance Dir	Ronald Trebing
Tax Assessor	Bernadette Leonardi
Tax Collector	Debra D'Amore
Attorney	James J. Carroll
Building	NA
Comm Dev/Planning	NA
Engineering	Fralinger Engineering
Public Works	Ronald Carroll
Police Chief	NA
Emerg/Fire Director	Robert Gibney

Housing & Construction

Housing Units, 2000*
Total	909
Median rent	$725
Median SF home value	$119,000

Permits for New Residential Construction
	Units	Value
Total, 2007	3	$322,160
Single family	3	$322,160
Total, 2006	3	$174,492
Single family	3	$174,492

Real Property Valuation, 2007
	Parcels	Valuation
Total	1,016	$93,845,600
Vacant	322	5,528,200
Residential	649	76,961,600
Commercial	34	9,393,600
Industrial	1	206,700
Apartments	2	1,439,900
Farm land	5	28,200
Farm homestead	3	287,400

Average Property Value & Tax, 2007
Residential value	$118,480
Property tax	$3,264
Tax credit/rebate	$677

Public Library
No public municipal library

Library statistics, 2006
Population served	NA
Full-time/total staff	NA/NA

	Total	Per capita
Holdings	NA	NA
Revenues	NA	NA
Expenditures	NA	NA
Annual visits	NA	NA
Internet terminals/annual users	NA/NA	

Taxes
	2005	2006	2007
General tax rate per $100	2.435	2.695	2.756
County equalization ratio	74.17	79.46	79.59
Net valuation taxable	$91,389,523	$91,904,500	$94,354,890
State equalized value	$115,013,243	$115,957,351	$133,907,442

Public Safety
Number of officers, 2006 ... 0

Crime	2005	2006
Total crimes	33	29
Violent	1	1
Murder	0	0
Rape	0	0
Robbery	0	0
Aggravated assault	1	1
Non-violent	32	28
Burglary	9	10
Larceny	19	17
Vehicle theft	4	1
Domestic violence	7	4
Arson	0	0
Total crime rate	14.2	12.5
Violent	0.4	0.4
Non-violent	13.8	12.0

Public School District
(for school year 2006-07 except as noted)

Weymouth Township School District
1202 Eleventh Ave
Dorothy, NJ 08317
609-476-2412

Administrative Principal	Donna Van Horn
Number of schools	1
Grade plan	K-8
Enrollment	258
Attendance rate, '05-06	95.2%
Dropout rate	NA
Students per teacher	10.2
Per pupil expenditure	$10,530
Median faculty salary	$43,338
Median administrator salary	$78,957
Grade 12 enrollment	NA
High school graduation rate	NA

Assessment test results
(percent scoring at proficient or advanced level)
	Language	Math
NJASK-Grade 3	88.5%	100.0%
GEPA-Grade 8	72.2%	83.4%
HSPA-High School	NA	NA

SAT score averages
Pct tested	Math	Verbal	Writing
NA	NA	NA	NA

Teacher Qualifications
Avg. years of experience	14
Highly-qualified teachers one subject/all subjects	100%/100%
With emergency credentials	0.0%

No Child Left Behind
AYP, 2005-06 ... Meets Standards

Municipal Finance

State Aid Programs, 2008
Total aid	$341,247
CMPTRA	0
Energy tax receipts	332,172
Garden State Trust	9,075

General Budget, 2007
Total tax levy	$2,599,495
County levy	365,013
County taxes	290,580
County library	36,000
County health	14,669
County open space	23,764
School levy	1,673,651
Muni. levy	560,831
Misc. revenues	795,420

The New Jersey Municipal Data Book

Wharton Borough
Morris County

Demographics & Socio-Economic Characteristics
(2000 US Census, except as noted)

Population
- 1980* 5,485
- 1990* 5,405
- 2000 6,298
  - Male 3,043
  - Female 3,255
- 2006 (estimate)* 6,211
- Population density 2,836.1

Race & Hispanic Origin, 2000
Race
- White 5,170
- Black/African American 277
- American Indian/Alaska Native 28
- Asian 198
- Native Hawaiian/Pacific Islander .. 0
- Other race 454
- Two or more races 171
- Hispanic origin, total 1,462
  - Mexican 147
  - Puerto Rican 391
  - Cuban 18
  - Other Hispanic 906

Age & Nativity, 2000
- Under 5 years 464
- 18 years and over 4,660
- 21 years and over 4,479
- 65 years and over 711
- 85 years and over 91
- Median age 35.7
- Native-born 5,430
- Foreign-born 868

Educational Attainment, 2000
- Population 25 years and over 4,218
- Less than 9th grade 5.1%
- High school grad or higher 80.9%
- Bachelor's degree or higher 22.7%
- Graduate degree 7.9%

Income & Poverty, 1999
- Per capita income $25,168
- Median household income $56,580
- Median family income $64,957
- Persons in poverty 517
- H'holds receiving public assistance .. 45
- H'holds receiving social security .. 607

Households, 2000
- Total households 2,328
  - With persons under 18 871
  - With persons over 65 558
  - Family households 1,599
  - Single-person households 616
- Persons per household 2.70
- Persons per family 3.28

Labor & Employment
- Total civilian labor force, 2006** .. 3,722
  - Unemployment rate 7.5%
- Total civilian labor force, 2000 .. 3,369
  - Unemployment rate 6.7%

Employed persons 16 years and over by occupation, 2000
- Managers & professionals 1,079
- Service occupations 379
- Sales & office occupations 990
- Farming, fishing & forestry 9
- Construction & maintenance 267
- Production & transportation 420
- Self-employed persons 94

* US Census Bureau
** New Jersey Department of Labor

General Information
Borough of Wharton
10 Robert St
Wharton, NJ 07885
973-361-8444

- Website .... www.whartonnj.com
- Year of incorporation 1902
- Land/water area (sq. miles) ... 2.19/0.03
- Form of government .... Borough

Government
Legislative Districts
- US Congressional 11
- State Legislative 25

Local Officials, 2008
- Mayor .... William Chegwidden
- Manager .... Jon Rheinhardt
- Clerk .... Gabrielle Voight-Cherna
- Finance Dir .... Jon Rheinhardt
- Tax Assessor .... Donald Sherman
- Tax Collector .... Susan Megletti
- Attorney .... George Johnson
- Building .... Rita Sharp
- Comm Dev/Planning .... NA
- Engineering .... CMX
- Public Works .... Walter Van Kirk
- Police Chief .... Anthony Fernandez
- Emerg/Fire Director ... Eugene Caulfield

Housing & Construction
Housing Units, 2000*
- Total 2,394
- Median rent $867
- Median SF home value $165,300

Permits for New Residential Construction

	Units	Value
Total, 2007	5	$899,600
Single family	5	$899,600
Total, 2006	4	$658,200
Single family	4	$658,200

Real Property Valuation, 2007

	Parcels	Valuation
Total	1,858	$351,623,200
Vacant	60	5,165,300
Residential	1,691	233,507,500
Commercial	77	38,138,900
Industrial	12	53,739,800
Apartments	15	20,922,300
Farm land	2	2,500
Farm homestead	1	146,900

Average Property Value & Tax, 2007
- Residential value $138,094
- Property tax $6,079
- Tax credit/rebate $1,062

Public Library
Wharton Public Library
15 S Main St
Wharton, NJ 07885
973-361-1333

- Director .... Nancy Kaminetsky

Library statistics, 2006
- Population served 6,298
- Full-time/total staff 2/2

	Total	Per capita
Holdings	29,975	4.76
Revenues	$427,511	$67.88
Expenditures	$251,364	$39.91
Annual visits	42,670	6.78
Internet terminals/annual users	12/9,795	

Taxes

	2005	2006	2007
General tax rate per $100	3.91	4.12	4.41
County equalization ratio	56.86	50.03	43.7
Net valuation taxable	$347,730,762	$347,496,300	$352,012,836
State equalized value	$695,044,497	$795,611,309	$868,595,068

Public Safety
- Number of officers, 2006 21

Crime	2005	2006
Total crimes	104	122
Violent	9	2
Murder	0	0
Rape	1	0
Robbery	4	0
Aggravated assault	4	2
Non-violent	95	120
Burglary	28	20
Larceny	64	96
Vehicle theft	3	4
Domestic violence	74	30
Arson	1	0
Total crime rate	16.7	19.6
Violent	1.4	0.3
Non-violent	15.2	19.3

Public School District
(for school year 2006-07 except as noted)

Wharton Borough School District
137 E Central Ave
Wharton, NJ 07885
973-361-2592

- Superintendent .... Richard Bitondo
- Number of schools 2
- Grade plan K-8
- Enrollment 746
- Attendance rate, '05-06 .... 95.3%
- Dropout rate .... NA
- Students per teacher 9.6
- Per pupil expenditure $12,708
- Median faculty salary $51,230
- Median administrator salary ... $93,753
- Grade 12 enrollment .... NA
- High school graduation rate .... NA

Assessment test results
(percent scoring at proficient or advanced level)

	Language	Math
NJASK-Grade 3	94.2%	91.3%
GEPA-Grade 8	78.4%	74.4%
HSPA-High School	NA	NA

SAT score averages

Pct tested	Math	Verbal	Writing
NA	NA	NA	NA

Teacher Qualifications
- Avg. years of experience 9
- Highly-qualified teachers
  - one subject/all subjects ... 98.5%/98.5%
- With emergency credentials 0.0%

No Child Left Behind
- AYP, 2005-06 .... Meets Standards

Municipal Finance
State Aid Programs, 2008
- Total aid $642,461
- CMPTRA 113,635
- Energy tax receipts 528,826
- Garden State Trust 0

General Budget, 2007
- Total tax levy $15,494,702
- County levy 1,937,348
- County taxes 1,549,718
- County library 0
- County health 0
- County open space 387,630
- School levy 11,152,764
- Muni. levy 2,404,590
- Misc. revenues 4,837,701

Warren County

White Township

Demographics & Socio-Economic Characteristics
(2000 US Census, except as noted)

Population
- 1980* 2,748
- 1990* 3,603
- 2000 4,245
  - Male 2,124
  - Female 2,121
- 2006 (estimate)* 5,825
  - Population density 212.8

Race & Hispanic Origin, 2000
Race
- White 4,090
- Black/African American 51
- American Indian/Alaska Native 8
- Asian 26
- Native Hawaiian/Pacific Islander 2
- Other race 14
- Two or more races 54
- Hispanic origin, total 90
  - Mexican 6
  - Puerto Rican 29
  - Cuban 11
  - Other Hispanic 44

Age & Nativity, 2000
- Under 5 years 236
- 18 years and over 3,299
- 21 years and over 3,160
- 65 years and over 772
- 85 years and over 55
  - Median age 41.5
- Native-born 4,029
- Foreign-born 216

Educational Attainment, 2000
- Population 25 years and over 3,086
- Less than 9th grade 4.3%
- High school grad or higher 81.4%
- Bachelor's degree or higher 22.4%
- Graduate degree 5.4%

Income & Poverty, 1999
- Per capita income $24,783
- Median household income $54,732
- Median family income $66,127
- Persons in poverty 201
- H'holds receiving public assistance ... 47
- H'holds receiving social security 610

Households, 2000
- Total households 1,668
  - With persons under 18 502
  - With persons over 65 562
  - Family households 1,179
  - Single-person households 420
- Persons per household 2.47
- Persons per family 2.98

Labor & Employment
- Total civilian labor force, 2006** ... 2,280
  - Unemployment rate 2.9%
- Total civilian labor force, 2000 ... 2,006
  - Unemployment rate 2.8%

Employed persons 16 years and over by occupation, 2000
- Managers & professionals 642
- Service occupations 282
- Sales & office occupations 514
- Farming, fishing & forestry 7
- Construction & maintenance 233
- Production & transportation 272
- Self-employed persons 151

* US Census Bureau
** New Jersey Department of Labor

See Introduction for an explanation of all data sources.

General Information
Township of White
555 County Road 519
Belvidere, NJ 07823
908-475-2093
Email .... clerk@whitetwp-nj.com
Year of incorporation 1913
Land/water area (sq. miles) 27.37/0.38
Form of government .... Township

Government
Legislative Districts
- US Congressional 5
- State Legislative 23

Local Officials, 2008
- Mayor .... Samuel Race
- Manager/Admin .... NA
- Clerk .... Kathleen Reinalda
- Finance Dir .... Kathleen Reinalda
- Tax Assessor .... Michelle Trivigno
- Tax Collector .... Susan Luthringer
- Attorney .... Brian Tipton
- Building .... Ralph Price
- Planning .... Maser Consulting
- Engineering .... Paul Sterbenz
- Public Works .... NA
- Police Chief .... NA
- Fire/Emergency Dir .... NA

Housing & Construction
Housing Units, 2000*
- Total 1,770
- Median rent $531
- Median SF home value $163,700

Permits for New Residential Construction

	Units	Value
Total, 2007	27	$3,049,307
Single family	27	$3,049,307
Total, 2006	75	$6,183,030
Single family	70	$5,922,207

Real Property Valuation, 2007

	Parcels	Valuation
Total	2,329	$621,390,282
Vacant	226	16,133,227
Residential	1,556	409,994,750
Commercial	81	39,688,000
Industrial	11	110,802,250
Apartments	6	6,112,100
Farm land	318	3,697,205
Farm homestead	131	34,962,750

Average Property Value & Tax, 2007
- Residential value $263,757
- Property tax $4,422
- Tax credit/rebate $936

Public Library
No public municipal library

Library statistics, 2006
- Population served .... NA
- Full-time/total staff .... NA/NA

	Total	Per capita
Holdings	NA	NA
Revenues	NA	NA
Expenditures	NA	NA
Annual visits	NA	NA
Internet terminals/annual users	NA/NA	

Taxes

	2005	2006	2007
General tax rate per $100	1.53	1.64	1.68
County equalization ratio	106.21	94.84	83.37
Net valuation taxable	$626,559,297	$618,065,082	$622,668,773
State equalized value	$660,648,774	$742,916,728	$775,982,745

Public Safety
Number of officers, 2006 0

Crime	2005	2006
Total crimes	31	49
Violent	2	4
Murder	0	0
Rape	0	0
Robbery	0	0
Aggravated assault	2	4
Non-violent	29	45
Burglary	12	13
Larceny	14	28
Vehicle theft	3	4
Domestic violence	17	0
Arson	0	0
Total crime rate	5.7	8.7
Violent	0.4	0.7
Non-violent	5.4	8.0

Public School District
(for school year 2006-07 except as noted)

White Township School District
565 County Route 519
Belvidere, NJ 07823
908-475-4773

- Chief School Admin .... Linda Heilman
- Number of schools 1
- Grade plan K-8
- Enrollment 438
- Attendance rate, '05-06 .... 96.0%
- Dropout rate .... NA
- Students per teacher 11.0
- Per pupil expenditure $12,055
- Median faculty salary $55,443
- Median administrator salary $80,000
- Grade 12 enrollment .... NA
- High school graduation rate .... NA

Assessment test results
(percent scoring at proficient or advanced level)

	Language	Math
NJASK-Grade 3	97.1%	91.4%
GEPA-Grade 8	85.5%	70.9%
HSPA-High School	NA	NA

SAT score averages

Pct tested	Math	Verbal	Writing
NA	NA	NA	NA

Teacher Qualifications
- Avg. years of experience 14
- Highly-qualified teachers
  - one subject/all subjects 100%/100%
- With emergency credentials 0.0%

No Child Left Behind
AYP, 2005-06 .... Meets Standards

Municipal Finance
State Aid Programs, 2008
- Total aid $390,166
  - CMPTRA 62,133
  - Energy tax receipts 287,110
  - Garden State Trust 27,481

General Budget, 2007
- Total tax levy $10,440,394
  - County levy 3,692,659
    - County taxes 2,851,684
    - County library 390,465
    - County health 0
    - County open space 450,511
  - School levy 6,312,638
  - Muni. levy 435,097
- Misc. revenues 2,578,517

The New Jersey Municipal Data Book

Wildwood City

Cape May County

Demographics & Socio-Economic Characteristics
(2000 US Census, except as noted)

Population
1980*	4,913
1990*	4,484
2000	5,436
Male	2,657
Female	2,779
2006 (estimate)*	5,309
Population density	4,115.5

Race & Hispanic Origin, 2000
Race
White	3,835
Black/African American	905
American Indian/Alaska Native	21
Asian	26
Native Hawaiian/Pacific Islander	8
Other race	481
Two or more races	160
Hispanic origin, total	958
Mexican	163
Puerto Rican	668
Cuban	9
Other Hispanic	118

Age & Nativity, 2000
Under 5 years	412
18 years and over	4,038
21 years and over	3,802
65 years and over	770
85 years and over	83
Median age	35.5
Native-born	5,294
Foreign-born	251

Educational Attainment, 2000
Population 25 years and over	3,531
Less than 9th grade	8.2%
High school grad or higher	66.3%
Bachelor's degree or higher	6.8%
Graduate degree	1.8%

Income & Poverty, 1999
Per capita income	$13,682
Median household income	$23,981
Median family income	$28,288
Persons in poverty	1,448
H'holds receiving public assistance	201
H'holds receiving social security	821

Households, 2000
Total households	2,333
With persons under 18	694
With persons over 65	625
Family households	1,273
Single-person households	891
Persons per household	2.30
Persons per family	3.06

Labor & Employment
Total civilian labor force, 2006**	3,095
Unemployment rate	17.2%
Total civilian labor force, 2000	2,644
Unemployment rate	21.4%

Employed persons 16 years and over by occupation, 2000
Managers & professionals	383
Service occupations	533
Sales & office occupations	599
Farming, fishing & forestry	33
Construction & maintenance	209
Production & transportation	322
Self-employed persons	169

* US Census Bureau
** New Jersey Department of Labor

General Information
City of Wildwood
4400 New Jersey Ave
Wildwood, NJ 08260
609-522-2444

Website	www.wildwoodnj.org
Year of incorporation	1912
Land/water area (sq. miles)	1.29/0.09
Form of government	Commission

Government
Legislative Districts
US Congressional	2
State Legislative	1

Local Officials, 2008
Mayor	Ernest Troiano Jr
Manager/Admin	NA
Clerk	Christopher Wood
Finance Dir	Jeanette Powers
Tax Assessor	Joseph Gallagher
Tax Collector	Faith Wilson
Attorney	Marcus Karavan
Building	Glenn Franzoi
Comm Dev/Planning	NA
Engineering	Mark DeBlasio
Public Works	Kevin Verity
Police Chief	Steve Long
Emerg/Fire Director	Conrad Johnson

Housing & Construction
Housing Units, 2000*
Total	6,488
Median rent	$526
Median SF home value	$84,000

Permits for New Residential Construction
	Units	Value
Total, 2007	97	$17,367,582
Single family	25	$6,046,452
Total, 2006	175	$23,873,580
Single family	61	$7,151,580

Real Property Valuation, 2007
	Parcels	Valuation
Total	5,249	$1,859,032,300
Vacant	314	79,387,600
Residential	4,074	1,070,892,300
Commercial	598	514,218,900
Industrial	6	5,766,900
Apartments	257	188,766,600
Farm land	0	0
Farm homestead	0	0

Average Property Value & Tax, 2007
Residential value	$262,860
Property tax	$4,066
Tax credit/rebate	$919

Public Library
No public municipal library

Library statistics, 2006
Population served	NA
Full-time/total staff	NA/NA

	Total	Per capita
Holdings	NA	NA
Revenues	NA	NA
Expenditures	NA	NA
Annual visits	NA	NA
Internet terminals/annual users	NA/NA	

Public Safety
Number of officers, 2006 46

Crime	2005	2006
Total crimes	620	531
Violent	75	78
Murder	1	0
Rape	4	4
Robbery	31	35
Aggravated assault	39	39
Non-violent	545	453
Burglary	142	110
Larceny	370	317
Vehicle theft	33	26
Domestic violence	126	49
Arson	0	2
Total crime rate	119.0	100.4
Violent	14.4	14.7
Non-violent	104.6	85.6

Public School District
(for school year 2006-07 except as noted)

Wildwood City School District
4300 Pacific Ave
Wildwood, NJ 08260
609-522-4157

Superintendent	Dennis Anderson
Number of schools	3
Grade plan	K-12
Enrollment	794
Attendance rate, '05-06	91.9%
Dropout rate	8.1%
Students per teacher	6.8
Per pupil expenditure	$19,449
Median faculty salary	$62,886
Median administrator salary	$91,695
Grade 12 enrollment	52
High school graduation rate	75.1%

Assessment test results
(percent scoring at proficient or advanced level)
	Language	Math
NJASK-Grade 3	77.5%	75.7%
GEPA-Grade 8	31.0%	52.4%
HSPA-High School	63.6%	45.3%

SAT score averages
Pct tested	Math	Verbal	Writing
58%	456	448	428

Teacher Qualifications
Avg. years of experience	15
Highly-qualified teachers one subject/all subjects	100%/100%
With emergency credentials	0.0%

No Child Left Behind
AYP, 2005-06 .... Meets Standards

Municipal Finance
State Aid Programs, 2008
Total aid	$1,195,626
CMPTRA	70,396
Energy tax receipts	1,125,230
Garden State Trust	0

General Budget, 2007
Total tax levy	$28,798,048
County levy	3,975,766
County taxes	3,159,229
County library	607,304
County health	0
County open space	209,233
School levy	9,362,913
Muni. levy	15,459,369
Misc. revenues	8,926,008

Taxes	2005	2006	2007
General tax rate per $100	1.42	1.51	1.55
County equalization ratio	134.57	102.98	89.55
Net valuation taxable	$1,727,550,881	$1,762,292,800	$1,861,748,849
State equalized value	$1,677,559,605	$1,970,999,716	$2,084,499,640

552 The New Jersey Municipal Data Book

Cape May County

Wildwood Crest Borough

Demographics & Socio-Economic Characteristics
(2000 US Census, except as noted)

Population
1980*	4,149
1990*	3,631
2000	3,980
Male	1,854
Female	2,126
2006 (estimate)*	3,979
Population density	3,460.0

Race & Hispanic Origin, 2000
Race
White	3,776
Black/African American	49
American Indian/Alaska Native	4
Asian	19
Native Hawaiian/Pacific Islander	0
Other race	88
Two or more races	44
Hispanic origin, total	168
Mexican	44
Puerto Rican	89
Cuban	1
Other Hispanic	34

Age & Nativity, 2000
Under 5 years	171
18 years and over	3,255
21 years and over	3,167
65 years and over	1,013
85 years and over	132
Median age	46.7
Native-born	3,746
Foreign-born	124

Educational Attainment, 2000
Population 25 years and over	2,955
Less than 9th grade	3.5%
High school grad or higher	79.5%
Bachelor's degree or higher	26.4%
Graduate degree	8.9%

Income & Poverty, 1999
Per capita income	$23,741
Median household income	$36,579
Median family income	$47,462
Persons in poverty	231
H'holds receiving public assistance	51
H'holds receiving social security	783

Households, 2000
Total households	1,833
With persons under 18	417
With persons over 65	755
Family households	1,114
Single-person households	634
Persons per household	2.17
Persons per family	2.76

Labor & Employment
Total civilian labor force, 2006**	2,301
Unemployment rate	13.4%
Total civilian labor force, 2000	1,908
Unemployment rate	15.4%

Employed persons 16 years and over by occupation, 2000
Managers & professionals	634
Service occupations	295
Sales & office occupations	475
Farming, fishing & forestry	5
Construction & maintenance	114
Production & transportation	91
Self-employed persons	160

‡ Privately owned
* US Census Bureau
** New Jersey Department of Labor

See Introduction for an explanation of all data sources.

General Information
Borough of Wildwood Crest
6101 Pacific Ave
Wildwood Crest, NJ 08260
609-522-3843
Website	www.wildwoodcrest.org
Year of incorporation	1910
Land/water area (sq. miles)	1.15/0.15
Form of government	Commission

Government
Legislative Districts
US Congressional	2
State Legislative	1

Local Officials, 2008
Mayor	Carl H. Groon
Manager	Kevin Yecco
Clerk	Kevin Yecco
Finance Dir	Stephen Ritchie
Tax Assessor	Jason Hesley
Tax Collector	Carolyn Hennessey
Attorney	Doreen Corino
Building	JCOW
Planning	Linda Adams
Engineering	Ralph Petrella
Public Works	Donald Twist
Police Chief	Thomas DePaul
Emerg/Fire Director	Albert Beers

Housing & Construction
Housing Units, 2000*
Total	4,862
Median rent	$610
Median SF home value	$147,600

Permits for New Residential Construction
	Units	Value
Total, 2007	9	$1,564,135
Single family	9	$1,522,145
Total, 2006	260	$31,525,403
Single family	66	$9,015,350

Real Property Valuation, 2007
	Parcels	Valuation
Total	5,035	$1,461,251,000
Vacant	212	45,946,400
Residential	4,641	1,200,459,700
Commercial	147	203,371,100
Industrial	0	0
Apartments	35	11,473,800
Farm land	0	0
Farm homestead	0	0

Average Property Value & Tax, 2007
Residential value	$258,664
Property tax	$3,390
Tax credit/rebate	$912

Public Library
Wildwood Crest Library‡
6301 Ocean Ave
Wildwood Crest, NJ 08260
609-522-0564
Director: William Smith

Library statistics, 2006
Population served
Full-time/total staff: /

	Total	Per capita
Holdings		
Revenues		
Expenditures		
Annual visits		
Internet terminals/annual users	/	

Public Safety
Number of officers, 2006: 22

Crime	2005	2006
Total crimes	220	204
Violent	2	5
Murder	0	0
Rape	0	0
Robbery	1	1
Aggravated assault	1	4
Non-violent	218	199
Burglary	53	56
Larceny	162	137
Vehicle theft	3	6
Domestic violence	82	76
Arson	0	0
Total crime rate	57.0	52.7
Violent	0.5	1.3
Non-violent	56.4	51.4

Public School District
(for school year 2006-07 except as noted)

Wildwood Crest School District
9100 Pacific Ave
Wildwood Crest, NJ 08260
609-729-3760

Superintendent	Dennis Anderson
Number of schools	1
Grade plan	K-8
Enrollment	274
Attendance rate, '05-06	95.5%
Dropout rate	NA
Students per teacher	7.3
Per pupil expenditure	$16,657
Median faculty salary	$74,100
Median administrator salary	$66,307
Grade 12 enrollment	NA
High school graduation rate	NA

Assessment test results
(percent scoring at proficient or advanced level)
	Language	Math
NJASK-Grade 3	96.2%	92.6%
GEPA-Grade 8	86.1%	91.7%
HSPA-High School	NA	NA

SAT score averages
Pct tested	Math	Verbal	Writing
NA	NA	NA	NA

Teacher Qualifications
Avg. years of experience	22
Highly-qualified teachers one subject/all subjects	100%/100%
With emergency credentials	0.0%

No Child Left Behind
AYP, 2005-06: Meets Standards

Municipal Finance
State Aid Programs, 2008
Total aid	$442,442
CMPTRA	0
Energy tax receipts	442,442
Garden State Trust	0

General Budget, 2007
Total tax levy	$19,152,757
County levy	4,492,522
County taxes	3,570,211
County library	685,973
County health	0
County open space	236,338
School levy	5,443,800
Muni. levy	9,216,435
Misc. revenues	7,705,904

Taxes
	2005	2006	2007
General tax rate per $100	1.25	1.27	1.32
County equalization ratio	84.2	70.93	62.31
Net valuation taxable	$1,311,305,112	$1,361,032,500	$1,461,561,623
State equalized value	$1,848,731,301	$2,184,635,099	$2,441,832,762

© 2008 Information Publications, Inc. All rights reserved. Photocopying prohibited. For additional copies, contact the publisher at www.informationpublications.com or (877)544-INFO (4636)

The New Jersey Municipal Data Book

Willingboro Township — Burlington County

Demographics & Socio-Economic Characteristics
(2000 US Census, except as noted)

Population
1980*	39,912
1990*	36,291
2000	33,008
Male	15,633
Female	17,375
2006 (estimate)*	33,045
Population density	4,297.1

Race & Hispanic Origin, 2000
Race
White	8,144
Black/African American	22,021
American Indian/Alaska Native	99
Asian	562
Native Hawaiian/Pacific Islander	12
Other race	866
Two or more races	1,304
Hispanic origin, total	1,998
Mexican	103
Puerto Rican	1,273
Cuban	46
Other Hispanic	576

Age & Nativity, 2000
Under 5 years	2,024
18 years and over	23,939
21 years and over	22,672
65 years and over	4,246
85 years and over	239
Median age	37.9
Native-born	30,299
Foreign-born	2,709

Educational Attainment, 2000
Population 25 years and over	21,431
Less than 9th grade	2.7%
High school grad or higher	87.2%
Bachelor's degree or higher	18.9%
Graduate degree	5.9%

Income & Poverty, 1999
Per capita income	$21,799
Median household income	$60,869
Median family income	$64,338
Persons in poverty	1,934
H'holds receiving public assistance	342
H'holds receiving social security	3,260

Households, 2000
Total households	10,713
With persons under 18	4,617
With persons over 65	3,086
Family households	8,780
Single-person households	1,607
Persons per household	3.07
Persons per family	3.36

Labor & Employment
Total civilian labor force, 2006**	17,139
Unemployment rate	5.9%
Total civilian labor force, 2000	16,077
Unemployment rate	7.0%

Employed persons 16 years and over by occupation, 2000
Managers & professionals	4,869
Service occupations	2,348
Sales & office occupations	4,574
Farming, fishing & forestry	31
Construction & maintenance	929
Production & transportation	2,207
Self-employed persons	505

* US Census Bureau
** New Jersey Department of Labor

General Information
Township of Willingboro
1 Salem Rd
Willingboro, NJ 08046
609-877-2200
Website: www.willingboro.org/twpindex.htm
Year of incorporation 1963
Land/water area (sq. miles) . . . 7.69/0.33
Form of government . . . . . Council-Manager

Government
Legislative Districts
US Congressional	3
State Legislative	7

Local Officials, 2008
Mayor	Jacqueline Jennings
Manager	Joanne Diggs
Clerk	Marie Annese
Finance Dir	Joanne Diggs
Tax Assessor	William Tantum
Tax Collector	NA
Attorney	Michael Armstrong
Building	Duane Wallace
Comm Dev/Planning	NA
Engineering	Remington & Vernick
Public Works	Richard Brevogel
Police Chief	(county)
Emerg/Fire Director	Tony Burnett

Housing & Construction
Housing Units, 2000*
Total	11,124
Median rent	$1,100
Median SF home value	$96,700

Permits for New Residential Construction
	Units	Value
Total, 2007	138	$642,319
Single family	1	$484,490
Total, 2006	1,657	$1,856,650
Single family	0	$2,500

Real Property Valuation, 2007
	Parcels	Valuation
Total	11,213	$1,110,112,600
Vacant	106	6,161,700
Residential	10,942	1,034,649,200
Commercial	152	60,626,100
Industrial	10	6,759,000
Apartments	1	1,767,300
Farm land	1	3,300
Farm homestead	1	146,000

Average Property Value & Tax, 2007
Residential value	$94,562
Property tax	$4,894
Tax credit/rebate	$1,009

Public Library
Willingboro Public Library
220 Willingboro Parkway
Willingboro, NJ 08046
609-877-6668
Director . . . . . . Christine H. King

Library statistics, 2006
Population served	33,008
Full-time/total staff	9/20

	Total	Per capita
Holdings	92,216	2.79
Revenues	$1,768,756	$53.59
Expenditures	$1,420,363	$43.03
Annual visits	155,671	4.72
Internet terminals/annual users	20/67,210	

Taxes
	2005	2006	2007
General tax rate per $100	4.37	5.18	5.18
County equalization ratio	73.09	62.17	56.03
Net valuation taxable	$1,088,105,440	$1,095,908,800	$1,113,114,323
State equalized value	$1,750,209,812	$1,959,228,610	$2,137,833,646

Public Safety
Number of officers, 2006 71

Crime	2005	2006
Total crimes	747	768
Violent	121	130
Murder	0	3
Rape	10	12
Robbery	49	56
Aggravated assault	62	59
Non-violent	626	638
Burglary	146	133
Larceny	428	434
Vehicle theft	52	71
Domestic violence	262	272
Arson	15	7
Total crime rate	22.6	23.2
Violent	3.7	3.9
Non-violent	18.9	19.3

Public School District
(for school year 2006-07 except as noted)

Willingboro Township School District
440 Beverly-Rancocas Rd
Willingboro, NJ 08046
609-835-8665

Superintendent	Ed Kern (Int)
Number of schools	8
Grade plan	K-12
Enrollment	4,977
Attendance rate, '05-06	92.8%
Dropout rate	4.0%
Students per teacher	11.4
Per pupil expenditure	$12,066
Median faculty salary	$49,984
Median administrator salary	$90,440
Grade 12 enrollment	248
High school graduation rate	96.0%

Assessment test results
(percent scoring at proficient or advanced level)
	Language	Math
NJASK-Grade 3	74.5%	74.4%
GEPA-Grade 8	50.3%	31.9%
HSPA-High School	71.2%	36.4%

SAT score averages
Pct tested	Math	Verbal	Writing
77%	420	413	403

Teacher Qualifications
Avg. years of experience	6
Highly-qualified teachers one subject/all subjects	100%/100%
With emergency credentials	0.7%

No Child Left Behind
AYP, 2005-06 . . . . . . Meets Standards

Municipal Finance
State Aid Programs, 2008
Total aid	$4,370,198
CMPTRA	2,100,432
Energy tax receipts	2,269,766
Garden State Trust	0

General Budget, 2007
Total tax levy	$57,609,534
County levy	7,714,477
County taxes	6,918,648
County library	0
County health	0
County open space	795,829
School levy	28,475,057
Muni. levy	21,420,000
Misc. revenues	13,546,900

Union County
Winfield Township

Demographics & Socio-Economic Characteristics
(2000 US Census, except as noted)

Population
1980*	1,785
1990*	1,576
2000	1,514
Male	691
Female	823
2006 (estimate)*	1,486
Population density	8,255.6

Race & Hispanic Origin, 2000
Race
White	1,468
Black/African American	5
American Indian/Alaska Native	3
Asian	2
Native Hawaiian/Pacific Islander	1
Other race	10
Two or more races	25
Hispanic origin, total	37
Mexican	3
Puerto Rican	16
Cuban	8
Other Hispanic	10

Age & Nativity, 2000
Under 5 years	76
18 years and over	1,198
21 years and over	1,156
65 years and over	241
85 years and over	35
Median age	38.9
Native-born	1,472
Foreign-born	42

Educational Attainment, 2000
Population 25 years and over	1,112
Less than 9th grade	3.7%
High school grad or higher	79.2%
Bachelor's degree or higher	8.0%
Graduate degree	1.9%

Income & Poverty, 1999
Per capita income	$21,565
Median household income	$37,000
Median family income	$47,167
Persons in poverty	113
H'holds receiving public assistance	12
H'holds receiving social security	233

Households, 2000
Total households	694
With persons under 18	191
With persons over 65	199
Family households	395
Single-person households	266
Persons per household	2.18
Persons per family	2.92

Labor & Employment
Total civilian labor force, 2006**	854
Unemployment rate	7.9%
Total civilian labor force, 2000	807
Unemployment rate	7.4%

Employed persons 16 years and over by occupation, 2000
Managers & professionals	140
Service occupations	142
Sales & office occupations	241
Farming, fishing & forestry	4
Construction & maintenance	90
Production & transportation	130
Self-employed persons	19

* US Census Bureau
** New Jersey Department of Labor

See Introduction for an explanation of all data sources.

General Information
Township of Winfield
12 Gulfstream Ave
Winfield, NJ 07036
908-925-3850

Website	www.winfield-nj.org
Year of incorporation	1941
Land/water area (sq. miles)	0.18/0.00
Form of government	Township

Government
Legislative Districts
US Congressional	7
State Legislative	22

Local Officials, 2008
Mayor	S. George Lowrey
Manager/Admin	NA
Clerk	Laura Reinertsen
Finance Dir	Sue Wright
Tax Assessor	Gary Toth
Tax Collector	Kimberley Allorto
Attorney	Frank Capece
Building	Gary Junkroft
Comm Dev/Planning	NA
Engineering	John Ziemian
Public Works	NA
Police Chief	Walter L. Berg
Emerg/Fire Director	Debra Daly

Housing & Construction
Housing Units, 2000*
Total	697
Median rent	$463
Median SF home value	$74,000

Permits for New Residential Construction
	Units	Value
Total, 2007	0	$0
Single family	0	$0
Total, 2006	0	$0
Single family	0	$0

Real Property Valuation, 2007
	Parcels	Valuation
Total	691	$1,382,200
Vacant	1	220,200
Residential	689	1,072,000
Commercial	1	90,000
Industrial	0	0
Apartments	0	0
Farm land	0	0
Farm homestead	0	0

Average Property Value & Tax, 2007
Residential value	$1,556
Property tax	$2,725
Tax credit/rebate	$829

Public Library
No public municipal library

Library statistics, 2006
Population served	NA
Full-time/total staff	NA/NA

	Total	Per capita
Holdings	NA	NA
Revenues	NA	NA
Expenditures	NA	NA
Annual visits	NA	NA
Internet terminals/annual users	NA/NA	

Public Safety
Number of officers, 2006		10
Crime	**2005**	**2006**
Total crimes	29	8
Violent	1	0
Murder	0	0
Rape	0	0
Robbery	0	0
Aggravated assault	1	0
Non-violent	28	8
Burglary	4	1
Larceny	23	6
Vehicle theft	1	1
Domestic violence	5	12
Arson	0	0
Total crime rate	19.2	5.3
Violent	0.7	0.0
Non-violent	18.5	5.3

Public School District
(for school year 2006-07 except as noted)

Winfield Township School District
7 1/2 Gulfstream Ave
Winfield, NJ 07036
908-486-7410

Superintendent	Alice D'Ambola
Number of schools	1
Grade plan	K-8
Enrollment	122
Attendance rate, '05-06	94.9%
Dropout rate	NA
Students per teacher	7.5
Per pupil expenditure	$15,924
Median faculty salary	$48,155
Median administrator salary	$88,860
Grade 12 enrollment	NA
High school graduation rate	NA

Assessment test results
(percent scoring at proficient or advanced level)
	Language	Math
NJASK-Grade 3	NA	NA
GEPA-Grade 8	NA	NA
HSPA-High School	NA	NA

SAT score averages
Pct tested	Math	Verbal	Writing
NA	NA	NA	NA

Teacher Qualifications
Avg. years of experience	12
Highly-qualified teachers one subject/all subjects	100%/100%
With emergency credentials	0.0%

No Child Left Behind
AYP, 2005-06 .... Meets Standards

Municipal Finance
State Aid Programs, 2008
Total aid	$59,228
CMPTRA	0
Energy tax receipts	59,228
Garden State Trust	0

General Budget, 2007
Total tax levy	$2,426,383
County levy	57,848
County taxes	55,363
County library	0
County health	0
County open space	2,486
School levy	1,430,010
Muni. levy	938,524
Misc. revenues	461,250

Taxes
	2005	2006	2007
General tax rate per $100	158.877	171.21	175.129
County equalization ratio	8.25	7.75	8.36
Net valuation taxable	$1,386,732	$1,382,200	$1,385,485
State equalized value	$15,289,217	$16,537,013	$16,536,778

Winslow Township
Camden County

Demographics & Socio-Economic Characteristics
(2000 US Census, except as noted)

Population
- 1980* 20,034
- 1990* 30,087
- 2000 34,611
  - Male 17,039
  - Female 17,572
- 2006 (estimate)* 38,612
- Population density 669.2

Race & Hispanic Origin, 2000
Race
- White 22,670
- Black/African American 10,154
- American Indian/Alaska Native 104
- Asian 449
- Native Hawaiian/Pacific Islander .. 10
- Other race 547
- Two or more races 677
- Hispanic origin, total 1,492
  - Mexican 217
  - Puerto Rican 958
  - Cuban 38
  - Other Hispanic 279

Age & Nativity, 2000
- Under 5 years 2,838
- 18 years and over 24,646
- 21 years and over 23,558
- 65 years and over 2,939
- 85 years and over 401
- Median age 34.4
- Native-born 33,353
- Foreign-born 1,306

Educational Attainment, 2000
- Population 25 years and over 22,366
- Less than 9th grade 6.3%
- High school grad or higher 82.2%
- Bachelor's degree or higher 18.6%
- Graduate degree 4.3%

Income & Poverty, 1999
- Per capita income $21,254
- Median household income $55,990
- Median family income $62,045
- Persons in poverty 2,007
- H'holds receiving public assistance 239
- H'holds receiving social security . 2,544

Households, 2000
- Total households 11,661
  - With persons under 18 5,354
  - With persons over 65 2,193
  - Family households 9,002
  - Single-person households 2,187
- Persons per household 2.87
- Persons per family 3.28

Labor & Employment
- Total civilian labor force, 2006** . 20,595
  - Unemployment rate 6.3%
- Total civilian labor force, 2000 .. 17,665
  - Unemployment rate 6.1%

Employed persons 16 years and over by occupation, 2000
- Managers & professionals 5,187
- Service occupations 2,484
- Sales & office occupations 4,699
- Farming, fishing & forestry 78
- Construction & maintenance 2,003
- Production & transportation 2,138
- Self-employed persons 811

‡ Branch of county library
* US Census Bureau
** New Jersey Department of Labor

General Information
Township of Winslow
125 S Route 73
Braddock, NJ 08037
609-567-0700

- Website .... www.winslowtownship.com
- Year of incorporation 1845
- Land/water area (sq. miles) 57.70/0.40
- Form of government .... Township

Government
Legislative Districts
- US Congressional 1
- State Legislative 6

Local Officials, 2008
- Mayor .... Sue Ann Metzner
- Manager .... Joseph Gallagher
- Clerk .... Deborah Puchakjian
- Finance Dir .... Steven Dringus
- Tax Assessor .... Stephen Kessler
- Tax Collector .... Constance Hegyi
- Attorney .... David C. Patterson
- Building .... Herb Leary
- Comm Dev/Planning ..... NA
- Engineering .... Environmental Resolutions
- Public Works .... Edward McGlinchey
- Police Chief .... Anthony Bello
- Emerg/Fire Director ... Michael Scardino

Housing & Construction
Housing Units, 2000*
- Total 12,413
- Median rent $738
- Median SF home value $112,800

Permits for New Residential Construction
	Units	Value
Total, 2007	146	$14,880,995
Single family	146	$14,880,995
Total, 2006	377	$39,458,623
Single family	377	$39,458,623

Real Property Valuation, 2007
	Parcels	Valuation
Total	15,445	$1,491,867,670
Vacant	2,063	41,017,800
Residential	12,318	1,284,205,000
Commercial	308	89,258,650
Industrial	15	20,132,300
Apartments	26	31,575,100
Farm land	506	4,226,000
Farm homestead	209	21,452,820

Average Property Value & Tax, 2007
- Residential value $104,227
- Property tax $4,741
- Tax credit/rebate $946

Public Library
South County Regional Library‡
35 Coopers Folly Rd
Atco, NJ 08004
856-753-2537

- Branch Librarian .... Nancy Bennett

Library statistics, 2006
see Camden County profile
for library system statistics

Public Safety
- Number of officers, 2006 76

Crime	2005	2006
Total crimes	994	1,017
Violent	199	186
Murder	0	1
Rape	8	8
Robbery	37	52
Aggravated assault	154	125
Non-violent	795	831
Burglary	238	246
Larceny	478	536
Vehicle theft	79	49
Domestic violence	538	584
Arson	13	14
Total crime rate	27.6	27.1
Violent	5.5	5.0
Non-violent	22.0	22.2

Public School District
(for school year 2006-07 except as noted)

Winslow Township School District
30 Cooper Folly Rd
Atco, NJ 08004
856-767-2850

- Superintendent .... Daniel Swirsky (Int)
- Number of schools 8
- Grade plan K-12
- Enrollment 6,242
- Attendance rate, '05-06 .... 94.2%
- Dropout rate 2.1%
- Students per teacher 10.6
- Per pupil expenditure $12,149
- Median faculty salary $59,978
- Median administrator salary $94,882
- Grade 12 enrollment 372
- High school graduation rate 84.2%

Assessment test results
(percent scoring at proficient or advanced level)
	Language	Math
NJASK-Grade 3	81.9%	80.0%
GEPA-Grade 8	61.5%	41.9%
HSPA-High School	85.0%	56.2%

SAT score averages
Pct tested	Math	Verbal	Writing
64%	447	448	444

Teacher Qualifications
- Avg. years of experience 11
- Highly-qualified teachers
  - one subject/all subjects 97.0%/97.0%
- With emergency credentials 0.0%

No Child Left Behind
- AYP, 2005-06 .... Needs Improvement

Municipal Finance
State Aid Programs, 2008
- Total aid $7,843,023
  - CMPTRA 391,631
  - Energy tax receipts 7,348,269
  - Garden State Trust 73,339

General Budget, 2007
- Total tax levy $68,032,361
  - County levy 18,745,465
    - County taxes 17,025,502
    - County library 1,187,071
    - County health 0
    - County open space 532,892
  - School levy 39,276,587
  - Muni. levy 10,010,309
- Misc. revenues 17,996,991

Taxes
	2005	2006	2007
General tax rate per $100	4.224	4.445	4.549
County equalization ratio	73.73	65.17	56.18
Net valuation taxable	$1,334,696,902	$1,426,640,470	$1,495,634,432
State equalized value	$2,048,023,480	$2,543,493,582	$2,924,416,077

Cape May County
Woodbine Borough

Demographics & Socio-Economic Characteristics
(2000 US Census, except as noted)
Population
1900* 1,009
1990* 2,678
2000 2,716
  Male 1,596
  Female 1,120
2006 (estimate)* 2,508
  Population density 313.5

Race & Hispanic Origin, 2000
Race
  White 1,450
  Black/African American 880
  American Indian/Alaska Native 6
  Asian 3
  Native Hawaiian/Pacific Islander 0
  Other race 299
  Two or more races 78
Hispanic origin, total 577
  Mexican 19
  Puerto Rican 478
  Cuban 5
  Other Hispanic 75

Age & Nativity, 2000
Under 5 years 249
18 years and over 1,993
21 years and over 1,895
65 years and over 283
85 years and over 26
  Median age 36.4
Native-born 2,680
Foreign-born 36

Educational Attainment, 2000
Population 25 years and over 1,765
Less than 9th grade 24.2%
High school grad or higher 58.1%
Bachelor's degree or higher 4.5%
Graduate degree 1.1%

Income & Poverty, 1999
Per capita income $13,335
Median household income $30,298
Median family income $31,786
Persons in poverty 383
H'holds receiving public assistance 82
H'holds receiving social security 209

Households, 2000
Total households 773
  With persons under 18 370
  With persons over 65 181
  Family households 558
  Single-person households 178
Persons per household 2.77
Persons per family 3.21

Labor & Employment
Total civilian labor force, 2006** 1,159
  Unemployment rate 7.1%
Total civilian labor force, 2000 954
  Unemployment rate 9.0%
Employed persons 16 years and over by occupation, 2000
  Managers & professionals 182
  Service occupations 290
  Sales & office occupations 176
  Farming, fishing & forestry 10
  Construction & maintenance 82
  Production & transportation 128
Self-employed persons 56

‡ Branch of county library
* US Census Bureau
** New Jersey Department of Labor

See Introduction for an explanation of all data sources.

General Information
Borough of Woodbine
501 Washington Ave
Woodbine, NJ 08270
609-861-2153
Website .... www.boroughofwoodbine.net
Year of incorporation 1903
Land/water area (sq. miles) 8.00/0.00
Form of government .... Borough

Government
Legislative Districts
US Congressional 2
State Legislative 1
Local Officials, 2008
Mayor .... William Pikolycky
Manager/Admin .... NA
Clerk .... Lisa Garrison
Finance Dir .... John Miller
Tax Assessor .... John Miller
Tax Collector .... Lisa Garrison
Attorney .... Paul Baldini
Building .... DCA
Planning .... Mike Zumpino
Engineering .... Bruce Graham
Public Works .... James Gurdgiel
Police Chief .... NA
Emerg/Fire Director .... Manuel Gonzalez

Housing & Construction
Housing Units, 2000*
Total 1,080
Median rent $463
Median SF home value $80,600

Permits for New Residential Construction
	Units	Value
Total, 2007	10	$548,062
Single family	10	$548,062
Total, 2006	18	$280,093
Single family	18	$280,093

Real Property Valuation, 2007
	Parcels	Valuation
Total	1,368	$177,144,400
Vacant	174	9,075,300
Residential	1,075	130,109,200
Commercial	62	23,161,300
Industrial	6	4,736,300
Apartments	2	5,061,400
Farm land	31	140,100
Farm homestead	18	4,860,800

Average Property Value & Tax, 2007
Residential value $123,486
Property tax $1,232
Tax credit/rebate $584

Public Library
Upper Cape Branch‡
801 Webster Ave
Woodbine, NJ 08270
609-463-6350
Librarian .... Deborah Poillon
Library statistics, 2006
see Cape May County profile for library system statistics

Public Safety
Number of officers, 2006 0

Crime	2005	2006
Total crimes	137	100
Violent	14	20
Murder	0	0
Rape	0	1
Robbery	1	5
Aggravated assault	13	14
Non-violent	123	80
Burglary	29	18
Larceny	85	54
Vehicle theft	9	8
Domestic violence	34	13
Arson	0	0
Total crime rate	52.4	38.9
Violent	5.4	7.8
Non-violent	47.0	31.1

Public School District
(for school year 2006-07 except as noted)

Woodbine School District
801 Webster Ave
Woodbine, NJ 08270
609-861-5174

Superintendent ..... Lynda Anderson-Towns
Number of schools 1
Grade plan K-8
Enrollment 236
Attendance rate, '05-06 .... 93.9%
Dropout rate .... NA
Students per teacher 10.9
Per pupil expenditure $13,397
Median faculty salary $63,812
Median administrator salary $77,500
Grade 12 enrollment .... NA
High school graduation rate .... NA

Assessment test results
(percent scoring at proficient or advanced level)

	Language	Math
NJASK-Grade 3	28.6%	46.7%
GEPA-Grade 8	54.5%	54.5%
HSPA-High School	NA	NA

SAT score averages
Pct tested	Math	Verbal	Writing
NA	NA	NA	NA

Teacher Qualifications
Avg. years of experience 21
Highly-qualified teachers
  one subject/all subjects 100%/100%
With emergency credentials 0.0%

No Child Left Behind
AYP, 2005-06 .... Meets Standards

Municipal Finance
State Aid Programs, 2008
Total aid $146,206
  CMPTRA 0
  Energy tax receipts 144,929
  Garden State Trust 662

General Budget, 2007
Total tax levy $1,780,461
  County levy 271,576
    County taxes 215,822
    County library 41,467
    County health 0
    County open space 14,287
  School levy 1,096,608
  Muni. levy 412,277
  Misc. revenues 2,596,981

Taxes	2005	2006	2007
General tax rate per $100	2.4	2.51	1
County equalization ratio	60.81	50.68	127.06
Net valuation taxable	$58,772,528	$59,070,200	$178,440,561
State equalized value	$115,967,893	$138,100,042	$166,991,045

©2008 Information Publications, Inc. All rights reserved. Photocopying prohibited. For additional copies, contact the publisher at www.informationpublications.com or (877)544-INFO (4636)

The New Jersey Municipal Data Book

Woodbridge Township
Middlesex County

Demographics & Socio-Economic Characteristics[†]
(2000 US Census, except as noted)

Population
1980*	90,074
1990*	93,086
2000	97,203
Male	48,640
Female	48,563
2006 (estimate)*	99,208
Population density	4,311.5

Race & Hispanic Origin, 2000
Race
White	68,848
Black/African American	8,507
American Indian/Alaska Native	167
Asian	14,054
Native Hawaiian/Pacific Islander	24
Other race	3,212
Two or more races	2,391
Hispanic origin, total	8,956
Mexican	390
Puerto Rican	3,838
Cuban	680
Other Hispanic	4,048

Age & Nativity, 2000
Under 5 years	6,161
18 years and over	75,460
21 years and over	72,777
65 years and over	13,005
85 years and over	1,042
Median age	37.1
Native-born	76,332
Foreign-born	20,871

Educational Attainment, 2000
Population 25 years and over	68,845
Less than 9th grade	5.2%
High school grad or higher	84.0%
Bachelor's degree or higher	26.8%
Graduate degree	8.9%

Income & Poverty, 1999
Per capita income	$25,087
Median household income	$60,683
Median family income	$68,492
Persons in poverty	4,565
H'holds receiving public assistance	643
H'holds receiving social security	9,953

Households, 2000
Total households	34,562
With persons under 18	12,405
With persons over 65	9,529
Family households	25,423
Single-person households	7,484
Persons per household	2.71
Persons per family	3.19

Labor & Employment
Total civilian labor force, 2006**	53,631
Unemployment rate	4.0%
Total civilian labor force, 2000	49,753
Unemployment rate	4.8%

Employed persons 16 years and over by occupation, 2000
Managers & professionals	17,681
Service occupations	4,982
Sales & office occupations	14,186
Farming, fishing & forestry	85
Construction & maintenance	4,000
Production & transportation	6,429
Self-employed persons	1,604

[†] see Appendix C for American Community Survey data
* US Census Bureau
** New Jersey Department of Labor
§ State Fiscal Year July 1–June 30

General Information
Township of Woodbridge
1 Main St
Woodbridge, NJ 07095
732-634-4500

Website	www.twp.woodbridge.nj.us
Year of incorporation	1669
Land/water area (sq. miles)	23.01/1.21
Form of government	Mayor-Council

Government
Legislative Districts
US Congressional	7, 13
State Legislative	19

Local Officials, 2008
Mayor	John E. McCormac
Manager	Robert M. Landolfi
Clerk	John M. Mitch
Finance Dir	Richard A. Cahill
Tax Assessor	Richard Duda
Tax Collector	Richard Lorentzen
Attorney	James Nolan Jr
Building	Lawrence Esoldo
Planning	Marta Lefsky
Engineering	Scott Thompson
Public Works	Dennis Henry
Police Chief	William Trenery
Fire/Emergency Dir	NA

Housing & Construction
Housing Units, 2000*
Total	35,298
Median rent	$879
Median SF home value	$158,100

Permits for New Residential Construction
	Units	Value
Total, 2007	0	$0
Single family	0	$0
Total, 2006	2	$376,200
Single family	2	$376,200

Real Property Valuation, 2007
	Parcels	Valuation
Total	28,732	$3,205,108,452
Vacant	1,012	63,547,752
Residential	26,408	1,977,848,800
Commercial	1,065	698,273,700
Industrial	167	283,852,700
Apartments	80	181,585,500
Farm land	0	0
Farm homestead	0	0

Average Property Value & Tax, 2007
Residential value	$74,896
Property tax	$5,308
Tax credit/rebate	$1,007

Public Library
Woodbridge Public Library
George Frederick Plaza
Woodbridge, NJ 07095
732-634-4450

Director	John Hurley

Library statistics, 2006
Population served	97,203
Full-time/total staff	23/71

	Total	Per capita
Holdings	445,580	4.58
Revenues	$5,944,520	$61.16
Expenditures	$5,961,826	$61.33
Annual visits	587,255	6.04
Internet terminals/annual users	21/47,564	

Taxes
	2005	2006	2007
General tax rate per $100	6.39	6.73	7.09
County equalization ratio	35.28	30.32	26.51
Net valuation taxable	$3,211,856,485	$3,213,780,952	$3,214,172,952
State equalized value	$10,593,194,212	$12,129,433,277	$13,464,599,563

Public Safety
Number of officers, 2006		201
Crime	**2005**	**2006**
Total crimes	3,162	3,117
Violent	311	267
Murder	2	0
Rape	17	17
Robbery	86	80
Aggravated assault	206	170
Non-violent	2,851	2,850
Burglary	347	415
Larceny	2,205	2,152
Vehicle theft	299	283
Domestic violence	829	986
Arson	19	15
Total crime rate	31.4	31.0
Violent	3.1	2.7
Non-violent	28.3	28.3

Public School District
(for school year 2006-07 except as noted)

Woodbridge Township School District
School St, PO Box 428
Woodbridge, NJ 07095
732-602-8550

Superintendent	Vincent S. Smith
Number of schools	24
Grade plan	K-12
Enrollment	13,431
Attendance rate, '05-06	94.8%
Dropout rate	0.8%
Students per teacher	11.7
Per pupil expenditure	$11,624
Median faculty salary	$59,826
Median administrator salary	$107,183
Grade 12 enrollment	1,065
High school graduation rate	NA

Assessment test results
(percent scoring at proficient or advanced level)
	Language	Math
NJASK-Grade 3	87.3%	94.6%
GEPA-Grade 8	75.1%	76.3%
HSPA-High School	89.6%	85.3%

SAT score averages
Pct tested	Math	Verbal	Writing
NA	NA	NA	NA

Teacher Qualifications
Avg. years of experience	10
Highly-qualified teachers one subject/all subjects	99.5%/99.5%
With emergency credentials	0.4%

No Child Left Behind
AYP, 2005-06	Meets Standards

Municipal Finance[§]
State Aid Programs, 2008
Total aid	$29,839,571
CMPTRA	6,922,686
Energy tax receipts	22,916,862
Garden State Trust	23

General Budget, 2007
Total tax levy	$227,800,761
County levy	34,916,879
County taxes	31,256,851
County library	0
County health	0
County open space	3,660,028
School levy	144,293,040
Muni. levy	48,590,842
Misc. revenues	50,393,592

Gloucester County — Woodbury City

Demographics & Socio-Economic Characteristics
(2000 US Census, except as noted)

Population
1980*	10,353
1990*	10,904
2000	10,307
Male	4,815
Female	5,492
2006 (estimate)*	10,410
Population density	5,004.8

Race & Hispanic Origin, 2000
Race
- White 7,467
- Black/African American 2,353
- American Indian/Alaska Native 23
- Asian 102
- Native Hawaiian/Pacific Islander 14
- Other race 132
- Two or more races 216

Hispanic origin, total 406
- Mexican 28
- Puerto Rican 235
- Cuban 17
- Other Hispanic 126

Age & Nativity, 2000
- Under 5 years 669
- 18 years and over 7,754
- 21 years and over 7,385
- 65 years and over 1,702
- 85 years and over 264
- Median age 37.0
- Native-born 10,030
- Foreign-born 277

Educational Attainment, 2000
- Population 25 years and over 6,842
- Less than 9th grade 6.4%
- High school grad or higher 80.3%
- Bachelor's degree or higher 21.9%
- Graduate degree 6.9%

Income & Poverty, 1999
- Per capita income $21,592
- Median household income $41,827
- Median family income $53,630
- Persons in poverty 1,324
- H'holds receiving public assistance 138
- H'holds receiving social security 1,305

Households, 2000
- Total households 4,051
  - With persons under 18 1,428
  - With persons over 65 1,199
  - Family households 2,588
  - Single-person households 1,283
- Persons per household 2.43
- Persons per family 3.08

Labor & Employment
- Total civilian labor force, 2006** 5,563
  - Unemployment rate 6.4%
- Total civilian labor force, 2000 4,670
  - Unemployment rate 5.4%

Employed persons 16 years and over by occupation, 2000
- Managers & professionals 1,592
- Service occupations 713
- Sales & office occupations 1,134
- Farming, fishing & forestry 12
- Construction & maintenance 335
- Production & transportation 634
- Self-employed persons 209

* US Census Bureau
** New Jersey Department of Labor

See Introduction for an explanation of all data sources.

General Information
City of Woodbury
33 Delaware St
Woodbury, NJ 08096
856-845-1300

- Website .... www.woodbury.nj.us
- Year of incorporation 1871
- Land/water area (sq. miles) 2.08/0.04
- Form of government .... City

Government
Legislative Districts
- US Congressional 1
- State Legislative 5

Local Officials, 2008
- Mayor .... Robert A. Curtis
- Manager .... Thomas Bowe
- Clerk .... Thomas Bowe
- Finance Dir .... Robert Law
- Tax Assessor .... Roy Duffield
- Tax Collector .... Lorraine Roberts
- Attorney .... James Pierson
- Building .... Robert Kunkle
- Planning .... Brian Bosworth
- Engineering .... Ted Wilkinson
- Public Works .... Michael Walsh
- Police Chief .... Reed Merinuk
- Emerg/Fire Director .... John Keuler Jr

Housing & Construction
Housing Units, 2000*
- Total 4,310
- Median rent $523
- Median SF home value $97,100

Permits for New Residential Construction
	Units	Value
Total, 2007	5	$774,881
Single family	5	$774,881
Total, 2006	12	$1,180,665
Single family	12	$1,180,665

Real Property Valuation, 2007
	Parcels	Valuation
Total	3,394	$371,955,900
Vacant	161	4,575,300
Residential	2,911	266,407,400
Commercial	298	86,964,300
Industrial	3	2,017,800
Apartments	21	11,991,100
Farm land	0	0
Farm homestead	0	0

Average Property Value & Tax, 2007
- Residential value $91,517
- Property tax $5,533
- Tax credit/rebate $1,014

Public Library
Woodbury Public Library
33 Delaware St
Woodbury, NJ 08096
856-845-2611

- Director .... Jean A. Wipf

Library statistics, 2006
- Population served 10,307
- Full-time/total staff 1/3

	Total	Per capita
Holdings	64,237	6.23
Revenues	$332,567	$32.27
Expenditures	$316,971	$30.75
Annual visits	50,665	4.92
Internet terminals/annual users	17/12,050	

Taxes
	2005	2006	2007
General tax rate per $100	5.339	5.767	6.047
County equalization ratio	76.4	67.51	59.63
Net valuation taxable	$375,825,278	$371,682,200	$375,017,643
State equalized value	$556,695,716	$626,736,897	$706,059,097

Public Safety
Number of officers, 2006 27

Crime
	2005	2006
Total crimes	597	712
Violent	42	55
Murder	0	0
Rape	7	5
Robbery	12	24
Aggravated assault	23	26
Non-violent	555	657
Burglary	75	100
Larceny	450	534
Vehicle theft	30	23
Domestic violence	200	200
Arson	0	3
Total crime rate	57.2	68.2
Violent	4.0	5.3
Non-violent	53.2	63.0

Public School District
(for school year 2006-07 except as noted)

Woodbury School District
25 N Broad St
Woodbury, NJ 08096
856-853-0123

- Superintendent .... Joseph Jones III
- Number of schools 4
- Grade plan K-12
- Enrollment 1,547
- Attendance rate, '05-06 .... 93.9%
- Dropout rate 0.7%
- Students per teacher 10.3
- Per pupil expenditure $14,518
- Median faculty salary $51,820
- Median administrator salary $98,072
- Grade 12 enrollment 74
- High school graduation rate 89.7%

Assessment test results
(percent scoring at proficient or advanced level)

	Language	Math
NJASK-Grade 3	76.3%	86.3%
GEPA-Grade 8	58.6%	65.4%
HSPA-High School	70.7%	53.2%

SAT score averages
Pct tested	Math	Verbal	Writing
80%	427	419	427

Teacher Qualifications
- Avg. years of experience 9
- Highly-qualified teachers
  one subject/all subjects 97.5%/96.5%
- With emergency credentials 0.0%

No Child Left Behind
AYP, 2005-06 .... Meets Standards

Municipal Finance
State Aid Programs, 2008
- Total aid $1,700,495
- CMPTRA 717,916
- Energy tax receipts 982,579
- Garden State Trust 0

General Budget, 2007
- Total tax levy $22,674,216
- County levy 3,475,455
  - County taxes 3,223,111
  - County library 0
  - County health 0
  - County open space 252,344
- School levy 12,028,611
- Muni. levy 7,170,150
- Misc. revenues 4,313,462

The New Jersey Municipal Data Book

Woodbury Heights Borough
Gloucester County

Demographics & Socio-Economic Characteristics
(2000 US Census, except as noted)

Population
1980*	3,460
1990*	3,392
2000	2,988
Male	1,437
Female	1,551
2006 (estimate)*	3,030
Population density	2,463.4

Race & Hispanic Origin, 2000
Race
White	2,879
Black/African American	46
American Indian/Alaska Native	8
Asian	30
Native Hawaiian/Pacific Islander	0
Other race	14
Two or more races	11
Hispanic origin, total	37
Mexican	2
Puerto Rican	23
Cuban	1
Other Hispanic	11

Age & Nativity, 2000
Under 5 years	179
18 years and over	2,207
21 years and over	2,113
65 years and over	396
85 years and over	29
Median age	38.3
Native-born	2,896
Foreign-born	92

Educational Attainment, 2000
Population 25 years and over	2,012
Less than 9th grade	4.1%
High school grad or higher	86.5%
Bachelor's degree or higher	22.9%
Graduate degree	7.8%

Income & Poverty, 1999
Per capita income	$24,001
Median household income	$63,266
Median family income	$70,167
Persons in poverty	121
H'holds receiving public assistance	14
H'holds receiving social security	284

Households, 2000
Total households	1,027
With persons under 18	421
With persons over 65	286
Family households	826
Single-person households	171
Persons per household	2.89
Persons per family	3.24

Labor & Employment
Total civilian labor force, 2006**	1,803
Unemployment rate	3.9%
Total civilian labor force, 2000	1,537
Unemployment rate	4.0%

Employed persons 16 years and over by occupation, 2000
Managers & professionals	439
Service occupations	162
Sales & office occupations	473
Farming, fishing & forestry	6
Construction & maintenance	175
Production & transportation	221
Self-employed persons	69

* US Census Bureau
** New Jersey Department of Labor

General Information
Borough of Woodbury Heights
500 Elm Ave
Woodbury Heights, NJ 08097
856-848-2832

Email	janetpz@bwhnj.com
Year of incorporation	1915
Land/water area (sq. miles)	1.23/0.00
Form of government	Borough

Government
Legislative Districts
US Congressional	1
State Legislative	5

Local Officials, 2008
Mayor	Harry W. Elton Jr
Manager/Admin	NA
Clerk	Janet Pizzi
Finance Dir	Sandra Kraus
Tax Assessor	Brian Schneider
Tax Collector	Sandra Kraus
Attorney	Barry Lozuke
Building	Robert Kunkle
Comm Dev/Planning	NA
Engineering	Mark Brunermer
Public Works	David Baresich
Police Chief	Leo Selb
Emerg/Fire Director	Robbie Conley

Housing & Construction
Housing Units, 2000*
Total	1,045
Median rent	$742
Median SF home value	$124,300

Permits for New Residential Construction
	Units	Value
Total, 2007	5	$373,582
Single family	5	$373,582
Total, 2006	9	$794,894
Single family	9	$794,894

Real Property Valuation, 2007
	Parcels	Valuation
Total	1,289	$194,248,300
Vacant	119	3,095,900
Residential	1,072	151,837,500
Commercial	84	29,895,900
Industrial	11	8,911,800
Apartments	3	507,200
Farm land	0	0
Farm homestead	0	0

Average Property Value & Tax, 2007
Residential value	$141,639
Property tax	$5,665
Tax credit/rebate	$1,041

Public Library
No public municipal library

Library statistics, 2006
Population served	NA
Full-time/total staff	NA/NA

	Total	Per capita
Holdings	NA	NA
Revenues	NA	NA
Expenditures	NA	NA
Annual visits	NA	NA
Internet terminals/annual users	NA/NA	

Taxes
	2005	2006	2007
General tax rate per $100	3.601	3.804	4
County equalization ratio	92.07	83.64	72.96
Net valuation taxable	$192,398,519	$193,492,500	$194,574,145
State equalized value	$230,031,706	$265,547,467	$290,205,415

Public Safety
Number of officers, 2006	7

Crime
	2005	2006
Total crimes	104	109
Violent	10	10
Murder	0	0
Rape	0	0
Robbery	4	4
Aggravated assault	6	6
Non-violent	94	99
Burglary	21	23
Larceny	68	71
Vehicle theft	5	5
Domestic violence	31	32
Arson	0	0
Total crime rate	34.6	36.1
Violent	3.3	3.3
Non-violent	31.2	32.8

Public School District
(for school year 2006-07 except as noted)

Woodbury Heights School District
100 Academy Ave
Woodbury Heights, NJ 08097
856-848-2610

Chief School Admin	Janie Haines
Number of schools	1
Grade plan	K-6
Enrollment	241
Attendance rate, '05-06	96.4%
Dropout rate	NA
Students per teacher	9.5
Per pupil expenditure	$11,751
Median faculty salary	$44,526
Median administrator salary	$105,000
Grade 12 enrollment	NA
High school graduation rate	NA

Assessment test results
(percent scoring at proficient or advanced level)
	Language	Math
NJASK-Grade 3	97.4%	94.8%
GEPA-Grade 8	NA	NA
HSPA-High School	NA	NA

SAT score averages
Pct tested	Math	Verbal	Writing
NA	NA	NA	NA

Teacher Qualifications
Avg. years of experience	9
Highly-qualified teachers one subject/all subjects	100%/100%
With emergency credentials	0.0%

No Child Left Behind
AYP, 2005-06	Meets Standards

Municipal Finance
State Aid Programs, 2008
Total aid	$268,090
CMPTRA	0
Energy tax receipts	268,090
Garden State Trust	0

General Budget, 2007
Total tax levy	$7,781,776
County levy	1,589,162
County taxes	1,368,651
County library	113,358
County health	0
County open space	107,153
School levy	4,292,641
Muni. levy	1,899,973
Misc. revenues	1,295,145

Bergen County

Woodcliff Lake Borough

Demographics & Socio-Economic Characteristics
(2000 US Census, except as noted)

Population
1980*	5,644
1990*	5,303
2000	5,745
Male	2,757
Female	2,988
2006 (estimate)*	5,953
Population density	1,787.7

Race & Hispanic Origin, 2000
Race
White	5,391
Black/African American	50
American Indian/Alaska Native	2
Asian	257
Native Hawaiian/Pacific Islander	0
Other race	11
Two or more races	34
Hispanic origin, total	134
Mexican	16
Puerto Rican	30
Cuban	28
Other Hispanic	60

Age & Nativity, 2000
Under 5 years	406
18 years and over	4,027
21 years and over	3,901
65 years and over	768
85 years and over	133
Median age	40.7
Native-born	5,162
Foreign-born	583

Educational Attainment, 2000
Population 25 years and over	3,791
Less than 9th grade	1.0%
High school grad or higher	96.1%
Bachelor's degree or higher	58.3%
Graduate degree	27.0%

Income & Poverty, 1999
Per capita income	$53,461
Median household income	$123,022
Median family income	$133,925
Persons in poverty	86
H'holds receiving public assistance	7
H'holds receiving social security	454

Households, 2000
Total households	1,824
With persons under 18	892
With persons over 65	451
Family households	1,605
Single-person households	193
Persons per household	3.08
Persons per family	3.31

Labor & Employment
Total civilian labor force, 2006**	2,859
Unemployment rate	1.5%
Total civilian labor force, 2000	2,692
Unemployment rate	1.4%

Employed persons 16 years and over by occupation, 2000
Managers & professionals	1,526
Service occupations	138
Sales & office occupations	810
Farming, fishing & forestry	0
Construction & maintenance	96
Production & transportation	83
Self-employed persons	271

* US Census Bureau
** New Jersey Department of Labor

See Introduction for an explanation of all data sources.

General Information
Borough of Woodcliff Lake
188 Pascack Rd
Woodcliff Lake, NJ 07677
201-391-4977

Website	www.wclnj.com
Year of incorporation	1910
Land/water area (sq. miles)	3.33/0.21
Form of government	Borough

Government
Legislative Districts
US Congressional	5
State Legislative	39

Local Officials, 2008
Mayor	Joseph T. La Paglia
Administrator	Edward Sandve
Clerk	Lorinda Sciara
CFO	Alyssa Mayer
Tax Assessor	Barbara Potash
Tax Collector	Lois Frezza
Attorney	Mark Madaio
Building	Nick Saluzzi
Planning	George Fry (Chr)
Engineering	Elliot Sachs
Public Works	Ed Barboni
Police Chief	Anthony Jannicelli
Fire Chief	Rob Kuehlke

Housing & Construction
Housing Units, 2000*
Total	1,842
Median rent	$1,258
Median SF home value	$450,700

Permits for New Residential Construction
	Units	Value
Total, 2007	18	$7,387,258
Single family	18	$7,387,258
Total, 2006	25	$8,702,913
Single family	25	$8,702,913

Real Property Valuation, 2007
	Parcels	Valuation
Total	2,008	$1,602,088,600
Vacant	90	20,990,400
Residential	1,863	1,205,649,800
Commercial	50	374,512,000
Industrial	0	0
Apartments	0	0
Farm land	2	5,600
Farm homestead	3	930,800

Average Property Value & Tax, 2007
Residential value	$646,613
Property tax	$12,747
Tax credit/rebate	$1,377

Public Library
No public municipal library

Library statistics, 2006
Population served	NA
Full-time/total staff	NA/NA

	Total	Per capita
Holdings	NA	NA
Revenues	NA	NA
Expenditures	NA	NA
Annual visits	NA	NA
Internet terminals/annual users	NA/NA	

Taxes
	2005	2006	2007
General tax rate per $100	1.75	1.87	1.98
County equalization ratio	94.83	87.18	73.96
Net valuation taxable	$1,552,518,524	$1,554,952,500	$1,603,445,695
State equalized value	$1,780,819,596	$2,104,218,231	$2,175,154,381

Public Safety
Number of officers, 2006	18

Crime	2005	2006
Total crimes	43	33
Violent	3	1
Murder	0	0
Rape	1	0
Robbery	0	0
Aggravated assault	2	1
Non-violent	40	32
Burglary	1	0
Larceny	39	31
Vehicle theft	0	1
Domestic violence	12	7
Arson	0	0
Total crime rate	7.3	5.6
Violent	0.5	0.2
Non-violent	6.8	5.4

Public School District
(for school year 2006-07 except as noted)

Woodcliff Lake School District
134 Woodcliff Ave
Woodcliff Lake, NJ 07677
201-391-6570

Superintendent	Peter Lisi
Number of schools	2
Grade plan	K-8
Enrollment	860
Attendance rate, '05-06	95.8%
Dropout rate	NA
Students per teacher	10.2
Per pupil expenditure	$14,054
Median faculty salary	$53,006
Median administrator salary	$115,407
Grade 12 enrollment	NA
High school graduation rate	NA

Assessment test results
(percent scoring at proficient or advanced level)
	Language	Math
NJASK-Grade 3	95.2%	96.5%
GEPA-Grade 8	95.3%	90.6%
HSPA-High School	NA	NA

SAT score averages
Pct tested	Math	Verbal	Writing
NA	NA	NA	NA

Teacher Qualifications
Avg. years of experience	8
Highly-qualified teachers one subject/all subjects	100%/100%
With emergency credentials	0.0%

No Child Left Behind
AYP, 2005-06	Meets Standards

Municipal Finance
State Aid Programs, 2008
Total aid	$684,246
CMPTRA	19,587
Energy tax receipts	653,473
Garden State Trust	0

General Budget, 2007
Total tax levy	$31,608,618
County levy	3,892,715
County taxes	3,675,670
County library	0
County health	0
County open space	217,044
School levy	20,683,798
Muni. levy	7,032,106
Misc. revenues	3,706,317

The New Jersey Municipal Data Book

Woodland Township
Burlington County

Demographics & Socio-Economic Characteristics
(2000 US Census, except as noted)

Population
1980*	2,285
1990*	2,063
2000	1,170
Male	582
Female	588
2006 (estimate)*	1,374
Population density	14.3

Race & Hispanic Origin, 2000
Race
White	1,147
Black/African American	7
American Indian/Alaska Native	1
Asian	4
Native Hawaiian/Pacific Islander	0
Other race	2
Two or more races	9
Hispanic origin, total	14
Mexican	2
Puerto Rican	6
Cuban	0
Other Hispanic	6

Age & Nativity, 2000
Under 5 years	57
18 years and over	868
21 years and over	824
65 years and over	90
85 years and over	7
Median age	38.4
Native-born	1,125
Foreign-born	35

Educational Attainment, 2000
Population 25 years and over	781
Less than 9th grade	4.5%
High school grad or higher	83.0%
Bachelor's degree or higher	18.4%
Graduate degree	6.1%

Income & Poverty, 1999
Per capita income	$26,126
Median household income	$59,271
Median family income	$65,972
Persons in poverty	33
H'holds receiving public assistance	8
H'holds receiving social security	76

Households, 2000
Total households	425
With persons under 18	164
With persons over 65	69
Family households	323
Single-person households	81
Persons per household	2.75
Persons per family	3.15

Labor & Employment
Total civilian labor force, 2006**	781
Unemployment rate	4.9%
Total civilian labor force, 2000	662
Unemployment rate	3.6%

Employed persons 16 years and over by occupation, 2000
Managers & professionals	181
Service occupations	91
Sales & office occupations	147
Farming, fishing & forestry	8
Construction & maintenance	118
Production & transportation	93
Self-employed persons	41

* US Census Bureau
** New Jersey Department of Labor

General Information
Township of Woodland
PO Box 388
Chatsworth, NJ 08019
609-726-1700

Website	NA
Year of incorporation	1866
Land/water area (sq. miles)	95.94/0.45
Form of government	Township

Government
Legislative Districts
US Congressional	3
State Legislative	8

Local Officials, 2008
Mayor	Robert DePetris
Manager	Maryalice Brown
Clerk	Maryalice Brown
Finance Dir	John Cicalese
Tax Assessor	Dennis DeKlerk
Tax Collector	Michele Adams
Attorney	Anthony Drollas
Building	Dan McGonigle
Comm Dev/Planning	NA
Engineering	Robert Callaway
Public Works	Matthew Henrich
Police Chief	(state)
Emergency Mgmt Dir	Stan Fayer

Housing & Construction
Housing Units, 2000*
Total	448
Median rent	$579
Median SF home value	$129,300

Permits for New Residential Construction
	Units	Value
Total, 2007	5	$683,732
Single family	5	$683,732
Total, 2006	5	$657,629
Single family	5	$657,629

Real Property Valuation, 2007
	Parcels	Valuation
Total	3,721	$168,848,500
Vacant	3,056	9,839,400
Residential	458	124,813,800
Commercial	20	5,817,000
Industrial	8	9,322,000
Apartments	0	0
Farm land	132	960,200
Farm homestead	47	18,096,100

Average Property Value & Tax, 2007
Residential value	$282,990
Property tax	$4,661
Tax credit/rebate	$883

Public Library
No public municipal library

Library statistics, 2006
Population served	NA
Full-time/total staff	NA/NA

	Total	Per capita
Holdings	NA	NA
Revenues	NA	NA
Expenditures	NA	NA
Annual visits	NA	NA
Internet terminals/annual users	NA/NA	

Taxes
	2005	2006	2007
General tax rate per $100	2.829	2.989	1.65
County equalization ratio	76.01	63.78	101.89
Net valuation taxable	$96,509,652	$95,777,305	$169,497,841
State equalized value	$151,316,482	$164,121,129	$172,803,195

Public Safety
Number of officers, 2006 0

Crime	2005	2006
Total crimes	50	64
Violent	2	18
Murder	0	1
Rape	0	0
Robbery	0	0
Aggravated assault	2	17
Non-violent	48	46
Burglary	14	20
Larceny	31	25
Vehicle theft	3	1
Domestic violence	1	0
Arson	0	1
Total crime rate	36.7	46.7
Violent	1.5	13.1
Non-violent	35.2	33.6

Public School District
(for school year 2006-07 except as noted)

Woodland Township School District
2 Giles Ave, PO Box 477
Chatsworth, NJ 08019
609-726-1230

Superintendent	William Randazzo
Number of schools	1
Grade plan	K-8
Enrollment	155
Attendance rate, '05-06	95.2%
Dropout rate	NA
Students per teacher	10.5
Per pupil expenditure	$15,588
Median faculty salary	$54,000
Median administrator salary	$72,266
Grade 12 enrollment	NA
High school graduation rate	NA

Assessment test results
(percent scoring at proficient or advanced level)
	Language	Math
NJASK-Grade 3	68.8%	75.1%
GEPA-Grade 8	63.2%	63.2%
HSPA-High School	NA	NA

SAT score averages
Pct tested	Math	Verbal	Writing
NA	NA	NA	NA

Teacher Qualifications
Avg. years of experience	19
Highly-qualified teachers one subject/all subjects	100%/100%
With emergency credentials	0.0%

No Child Left Behind
AYP, 2005-06 .... Meets Standards

Municipal Finance
State Aid Programs, 2008
Total aid	$1,314,744
CMPTRA	0
Energy tax receipts	130,676
Garden State Trust	711,711

General Budget, 2007
Total tax levy	$2,791,521
County levy	595,224
County taxes	576,075
County library	52,863
County health	0
County open space	66,286
School levy	2,196,297
Muni. levy	0
Misc. revenues	2,381,734

Camden County

Woodlynne Borough

Demographics & Socio-Economic Characteristics
(2000 US Census, except as noted)

Population
1980*	2,578
1990*	2,547
2000	2,796
Male	1,362
Female	1,434
2006 (estimate)*	2,718
Population density	12,354.5

Race & Hispanic Origin, 2000
Race
White	1,354
Black/African American	635
American Indian/Alaska Native	16
Asian	343
Native Hawaiian/Pacific Islander	0
Other race	324
Two or more races	124
Hispanic origin, total	576
Mexican	29
Puerto Rican	456
Cuban	5
Other Hispanic	86

Age & Nativity, 2000
Under 5 years	219
18 years and over	1,889
21 years and over	1,773
65 years and over	244
85 years and over	27
Median age	30.8
Native-born	2,401
Foreign-born	395

Educational Attainment, 2000
Population 25 years and over	1,679
Less than 9th grade	11.0%
High school grad or higher	69.3%
Bachelor's degree or higher	8.0%
Graduate degree	1.7%

Income & Poverty, 1999
Per capita income	$14,757
Median household income	$39,138
Median family income	$39,669
Persons in poverty	388
H'holds receiving public assistance	83
H'holds receiving social security	228

Households, 2000
Total households	912
With persons under 18	445
With persons over 65	197
Family households	684
Single-person households	189
Persons per household	3.07
Persons per family	3.52

Labor & Employment
Total civilian labor force, 2006**	1,450
Unemployment rate	6.4%
Total civilian labor force, 2000	1,321
Unemployment rate	5.4%

Employed persons 16 years and over by occupation, 2000
Managers & professionals	268
Service occupations	226
Sales & office occupations	353
Farming, fishing & forestry	0
Construction & maintenance	71
Production & transportation	332
Self-employed persons	29

‡ Branch of county library
* US Census Bureau
** New Jersey Department of Labor

See Introduction for an explanation of all data sources.

General Information
Borough of Woodlynne
200 Cooper Ave
Woodlynne, NJ 08107
856-962-8300

Website	www.woodlynnenj.com
Year of incorporation	1901
Land/water area (sq. miles)	0.22/0.02
Form of government	Borough

Government
Legislative Districts
US Congressional	1
State Legislative	5

Local Officials, 2008
Mayor	Jeraldo Fuentes
Manager	Jeraldo Fuentes
Clerk	Lavern Davis (Actg)
Finance Dir	Adriane McKendry
Tax Assessor	Bruce Coyle
Tax Collector	Paula Etschman
Attorney	Michael McKenna
Building	William Joseph
Planning	Cheryl Linthicum
Engineering	Steven Bach
Public Works	Robert Kenny
Police Chief	NA
Emerg/Fire Director	Kenneth Steward

Housing & Construction
Housing Units, 2000*
Total	1,012
Median rent	$635
Median SF home value	$56,800

Permits for New Residential Construction
	Units	Value
Total, 2007	0	$0
Single family	0	$0
Total, 2006	1	$80,300
Single family	1	$80,300

Real Property Valuation, 2007
	Parcels	Valuation
Total	931	$50,407,350
Vacant	18	298,800
Residential	876	45,584,000
Commercial	30	3,793,650
Industrial	0	0
Apartments	7	730,900
Farm land	0	0
Farm homestead	0	0

Average Property Value & Tax, 2007
Residential value	$52,037
Property tax	$3,707
Tax credit/rebate	$831

Public Library
Woodlynne Public Library‡
200 Cooper Ave
Woodlynne, NJ 08107
856-962-7172

Director..................Ann Vennell

Library statistics, 2006
see Camden County profile
for library system statistics

Public Safety
Number of officers, 2006 0

Crime	2005	2006
Total crimes	108	127
Violent	13	18
Murder	0	0
Rape	0	0
Robbery	4	4
Aggravated assault	9	14
Non-violent	95	109
Burglary	16	20
Larceny	66	69
Vehicle theft	13	20
Domestic violence	56	36
Arson	1	0
Total crime rate	39.2	46.3
Violent	4.7	6.6
Non-violent	34.5	39.7

Public School District
(for school year 2006-07 except as noted)

Woodlynne Borough School District
131 Elm Ave
Woodlynne, NJ 08107
856-962-8822

Superintendent	Patricia T. Doloughty
Number of schools	1
Grade plan	K-8
Enrollment	467
Attendance rate, '05-06	94.5%
Dropout rate	NA
Students per teacher	13.1
Per pupil expenditure	$10,302
Median faculty salary	$43,791
Median administrator salary	$91,776
Grade 12 enrollment	NA
High school graduation rate	NA

Assessment test results
(percent scoring at proficient or advanced level)
	Language	Math
NJASK-Grade 3	51.1%	60.4%
GEPA-Grade 8	33.3%	26.3%
HSPA-High School	NA	NA

SAT score averages
Pct tested	Math	Verbal	Writing
NA	NA	NA	NA

Teacher Qualifications
Avg. years of experience	6
Highly-qualified teachers one subject/all subjects	100%/100%
With emergency credentials	0.0%

No Child Left Behind
AYP, 2005-06 .... Meets Standards

Municipal Finance
State Aid Programs, 2008
Total aid	$121,384
CMPTRA	0
Energy tax receipts	121,384
Garden State Trust	0

General Budget, 2007
Total tax levy	$3,593,312
County levy	610,294
County taxes	554,365
County library	38,600
County health	0
County open space	17,328
School levy	1,734,234
Muni. levy	1,248,785
Misc. revenues	1,129,500

Taxes	2005	2006	2007
General tax rate per $100	6.568	6.924	7.125
County equalization ratio	79.68	68.71	58.18
Net valuation taxable	$50,350,552	$50,288,450	$50,438,045
State equalized value	$73,279,802	$86,471,169	$100,283,977

©2008 Information Publications, Inc. All rights reserved. Photocopying prohibited. For additional copies, contact the publisher at www.informationpublications.com or (877)544-INFO (4636)

Wood-Ridge Borough — Bergen County

Demographics & Socio-Economic Characteristics
(2000 US Census, except as noted)

Population
1980*	7,929
1990*	7,506
2000	7,644
Male	3,632
Female	4,012
2006 (estimate)*	7,594
Population density	6,903.6

Race & Hispanic Origin, 2000
Race
White	6,957
Black/African American	64
American Indian/Alaska Native	6
Asian	384
Native Hawaiian/Pacific Islander	1
Other race	135
Two or more races	97
Hispanic origin, total	556
Mexican	11
Puerto Rican	138
Cuban	87
Other Hispanic	320

Age & Nativity, 2000
Under 5 years	467
18 years and over	6,021
21 years and over	5,876
65 years and over	1,297
85 years and over	153
Median age	40.3
Native-born	6,481
Foreign-born	1,162

Educational Attainment, 2000
Population 25 years and over	5,590
Less than 9th grade	5.6%
High school grad or higher	84.4%
Bachelor's degree or higher	27.7%
Graduate degree	6.2%

Income & Poverty, 1999
Per capita income	$29,865
Median household income	$60,949
Median family income	$72,500
Persons in poverty	119
H'holds receiving public assistance	37
H'holds receiving social security	979

Households, 2000
Total households	3,024
With persons under 18	926
With persons over 65	952
Family households	2,138
Single-person households	781
Persons per household	2.53
Persons per family	3.07

Labor & Employment
Total civilian labor force, 2006**	4,348
Unemployment rate	3.2%
Total civilian labor force, 2000	4,086
Unemployment rate	3.3%

Employed persons 16 years and over by occupation, 2000
Managers & professionals	1,563
Service occupations	376
Sales & office occupations	1,227
Farming, fishing & forestry	0
Construction & maintenance	334
Production & transportation	452
Self-employed persons	219

* US Census Bureau
** New Jersey Department of Labor

General Information
Borough of Wood-Ridge
85 Humboldt St
Wood Ridge, NJ 07075
201-939-0202

Website	njwoodridge.org
Year of incorporation	1894
Land/water area (sq. miles)	1.10/0.00
Form of government	Borough

Government
Legislative Districts
US Congressional	9
State Legislative	36

Local Officials, 2008
Mayor	Paul Sarlo
Manager	Christopher W. Eilert
Clerk	Diane Thornley
Finance Dir	Nicholas Fargo
Tax Assessor	Stuart Stolarz
Tax Collector	Jacqueline Sharkey
Attorney	Paul Barbire
Building	Gary Ippolito
Comm Dev/Planning	NA
Engineering	Michael Neglia
Public Works	Richard Gennarelli
Police Chief	Joseph Rutigliano
Emerg/Fire Director	Tony Gentile

Housing & Construction
Housing Units, 2000*
Total	3,087
Median rent	$966
Median SF home value	$196,800

Permits for New Residential Construction
	Units	Value
Total, 2007	9	$2,216,330
Single family	9	$2,216,330
Total, 2006	13	$3,720,988
Single family	13	$3,720,988

Real Property Valuation, 2007
	Parcels	Valuation
Total	2,627	$781,166,400
Vacant	39	56,001,500
Residential	2,486	580,734,500
Commercial	66	38,193,700
Industrial	23	87,080,400
Apartments	13	19,156,300
Farm land	0	0
Farm homestead	0	0

Average Property Value & Tax, 2007
Residential value	$233,602
Property tax	$6,663
Tax credit/rebate	$1,088

Public Library
Wood-Ridge Memorial Library
231 Hackensack St
Wood-Ridge, NJ 07075
201-438-2455

Director: John J. Trause

Library statistics, 2006
Population served	7,644
Full-time/total staff	2/4

	Total	Per capita
Holdings	42,537	5.56
Revenues	$388,196	$50.78
Expenditures	$370,668	$48.49
Annual visits	67,392	8.82
Internet terminals/annual users	5/7,323	

Public Safety
Number of officers, 2006: 22

Crime	2005	2006
Total crimes	58	62
Violent	4	7
Murder	0	0
Rape	0	0
Robbery	2	2
Aggravated assault	2	5
Non-violent	54	55
Burglary	8	7
Larceny	36	43
Vehicle theft	10	5
Domestic violence	33	26
Arson	1	0
Total crime rate	7.6	8.1
Violent	0.5	0.9
Non-violent	7.1	7.2

Public School District
(for school year 2006-07 except as noted)

Wood-Ridge School District
89 Hackensack St
Wood-Ridge, NJ 07075
201-933-6778

Superintendent	Elaine Giugliano
Number of schools	3
Grade plan	K-12
Enrollment	1,126
Attendance rate, '05-06	95.6%
Dropout rate	0.5%
Students per teacher	13.0
Per pupil expenditure	$11,945
Median faculty salary	$53,657
Median administrator salary	$99,275
Grade 12 enrollment	106
High school graduation rate	96.5%

Assessment test results
(percent scoring at proficient or advanced level)
	Language	Math
NJASK-Grade 3	88.5%	91.5%
GEPA-Grade 8	75.0%	63.8%
HSPA-High School	87.7%	77.5%

SAT score averages
Pct tested	Math	Verbal	Writing
95%	513	491	486

Teacher Qualifications
Avg. years of experience	7
Highly-qualified teachers one subject/all subjects	97.0%/97.0%
With emergency credentials	0.0%

No Child Left Behind
AYP, 2005-06 … Meets Standards

Municipal Finance
State Aid Programs, 2008
Total aid	$860,703
CMPTRA	258,944
Energy tax receipts	601,759
Garden State Trust	0

General Budget, 2007
Total tax levy	$22,295,770
County levy	2,257,763
County taxes	2,133,350
County library	0
County health	0
County open space	124,413
School levy	11,502,777
Muni. levy	8,535,230
Misc. revenues	2,490,582

Taxes	2005	2006	2007
General tax rate per $100	2.44	2.67	2.86
County equalization ratio	77.98	71.02	63.91
Net valuation taxable	$735,037,403	$766,971,400	$781,729,040
State equalized value	$1,034,972,406	$1,200,694,298	$1,325,471,731

Salem County
Woodstown Borough

Demographics & Socio-Economic Characteristics
(2000 US Census, except as noted)

Population
1980*	3,250
1990*	3,154
2000	3,136
Male	1,459
Female	1,677
2006 (estimate)*	3,333
Population density	2,096.2

Race & Hispanic Origin, 2000
Race
White	2,667
Black/African American	405
American Indian/Alaska Native	6
Asian	23
Native Hawaiian/Pacific Islander	0
Other race	8
Two or more races	27
Hispanic origin, total	49
Mexican	12
Puerto Rican	14
Cuban	2
Other Hispanic	21

Age & Nativity, 2000
Under 5 years	183
18 years and over	2,360
21 years and over	2,270
65 years and over	517
85 years and over	66
Median age	37.9
Native-born	3,031
Foreign-born	105

Educational Attainment, 2000
Population 25 years and over	2,129
Less than 9th grade	2.8%
High school grad or higher	92.8%
Bachelor's degree or higher	31.6%
Graduate degree	9.8%

Income & Poverty, 1999
Per capita income	$24,182
Median household income	$44,533
Median family income	$56,328
Persons in poverty	171
H'holds receiving public assistance	10
H'holds receiving social security	434

Households, 2000
Total households	1,304
With persons under 18	435
With persons over 65	380
Family households	840
Single-person households	401
Persons per household	2.38
Persons per family	3.00

Labor & Employment
Total civilian labor force, 2006**	1,640
Unemployment rate	2.6%
Total civilian labor force, 2000	1,617
Unemployment rate	3.1%

Employed persons 16 years and over by occupation, 2000
Managers & professionals	634
Service occupations	227
Sales & office occupations	345
Farming, fishing & forestry	4
Construction & maintenance	87
Production & transportation	270
Self-employed persons	83

‡ Joint Library with Pilesgrove
* US Census Bureau
** New Jersey Department of Labor

See Introduction for an explanation of all data sources.

General Information
Borough of Woodstown
PO Box 286
Woodstown, NJ 08098
856-769-2200

Website	www.historicwoodstown.org
Year of incorporation	1882
Land/water area (sq. miles)	1.59/0.04
Form of government	Borough

Government
Legislative Districts
US Congressional	2
State Legislative	3

Local Officials, 2008
Mayor	Richard S. Pfeffer
Manager/Admin	NA
Clerk	Cynthia Dalessio
Finance Dir	James Hackett
Tax Assessor	Edwin Kay
Tax Collector	Elaine Urion
Attorney	George G. Rosenberger
Building	Joe Willie
Planning	Leah Furey
Engineering	Matthew Ecker
Public Works	Frank Mitchell
Police Chief	George Lacy
Emerg/Fire Director	Brian Facemayer

Housing & Construction
Housing Units, 2000*
Total	1,389
Median rent	$644
Median SF home value	$118,800

Permits for New Residential Construction
	Units	Value
Total, 2007	24	$2,017,525
Single family	24	$2,017,525
Total, 2006	25	$2,102,975
Single family	25	$2,102,975

Real Property Valuation, 2007
	Parcels	Valuation
Total	1,283	$151,783,100
Vacant	110	2,133,300
Residential	1,072	123,635,900
Commercial	78	17,780,400
Industrial	0	0
Apartments	10	8,103,200
Farm land	12	66,400
Farm homestead	1	63,900

Average Property Value & Tax, 2007
Residential value	$115,284
Property tax	$5,029
Tax credit/rebate	$947

Public Library
Woodstown-Pilesgrove Library‡
14 School Ln
Woodstown, NJ 08098
856-769-0098

Director	Ruth Fritz

Library statistics, 2006
Population served	7,059
Full-time/total staff	NA/0

	Total	Per capita
Holdings	NA	NA
Revenues	NA	NA
Expenditures	NA	NA
Annual visits	NA	NA
Internet terminals/annual users	NA/NA	

Taxes
	2005	2006	2007
General tax rate per $100	3.856	4.215	4.363
County equalization ratio	76.83	68.42	58.11
Net valuation taxable	$146,799,686	$147,001,000	$152,863,474
State equalized value	$214,556,688	$254,211,007	$278,006,300

Public Safety
Number of officers, 2006	9

Crime	2005	2006
Total crimes	58	67
Violent	1	4
Murder	0	0
Rape	0	0
Robbery	0	2
Aggravated assault	1	2
Non-violent	57	63
Burglary	7	14
Larceny	45	48
Vehicle theft	5	1
Domestic violence	49	41
Arson	1	0
Total crime rate	17.7	20.2
Violent	0.3	1.2
Non-violent	17.4	19.0

Public School District
(for school year 2006-07 except as noted)

Woodstown-Pilesgrove Reg. School District
135 East Ave
Woodstown, NJ 08098
856-769-1664

Superintendent	Robert Bumpus
Number of schools	6
Grade plan	K-12
Enrollment	1,621
Attendance rate, '05-06	95.6%
Dropout rate	0.4%
Students per teacher	11.2
Per pupil expenditure	$11,213
Median faculty salary	$47,555
Median administrator salary	$96,875
Grade 12 enrollment	157
High school graduation rate	99.1%

Assessment test results
(percent scoring at proficient or advanced level)
	Language	Math
NJASK-Grade 3	87.4%	86.3%
GEPA-Grade 8	80.2%	65.5%
HSPA-High School	88.6%	74.7%

SAT score averages
Pct tested	Math	Verbal	Writing
81%	493	494	484

Teacher Qualifications
Avg. years of experience	13
Highly-qualified teachers one subject/all subjects	100%/100%
With emergency credentials	0.0%

No Child Left Behind
AYP, 2005-06	Meets Standards

Municipal Finance
State Aid Programs, 2008
Total aid	$178,703
CMPTRA	0
Energy tax receipts	178,703
Garden State Trust	0

General Budget, 2007
Total tax levy	$6,668,680
County levy	2,465,506
County taxes	2,412,909
County library	0
County health	0
County open space	52,597
School levy	2,955,809
Muni. levy	1,247,365
Misc. revenues	2,053,957

©2008 Information Publications, Inc. All rights reserved. Photocopying prohibited. For additional copies, contact the publisher at www.informationpublications.com or (877)544-INFO (4636)

The New Jersey Municipal Data Book

Woolwich Township
Gloucester County

Demographics & Socio-Economic Characteristics
(2000 US Census, except as noted)

Population
1980*	1,129
1990*	1,459
2000	3,032
Male	1,505
Female	1,527
2006 (estimate)*	8,612
Population density	411.3

Race & Hispanic Origin, 2000
Race
White	2,763
Black/African American	138
American Indian/Alaska Native	0
Asian	34
Native Hawaiian/Pacific Islander	0
Other race	59
Two or more races	38
Hispanic origin, total	118
Mexican	26
Puerto Rican	65
Cuban	0
Other Hispanic	27

Age & Nativity, 2000
Under 5 years	309
18 years and over	2,081
21 years and over	2,001
65 years and over	206
85 years and over	21
Median age	33.8
Native-born	2,959
Foreign-born	73

Educational Attainment, 2000
Population 25 years and over	1,918
Less than 9th grade	4.0%
High school grad or higher	88.1%
Bachelor's degree or higher	29.2%
Graduate degree	11.6%

Income & Poverty, 1999
Per capita income	$29,503
Median household income	$83,790
Median family income	$87,111
Persons in poverty	88
H'holds receiving public assistance	8
H'holds receiving social security	151

Households, 2000
Total households	959
With persons under 18	496
With persons over 65	152
Family households	838
Single-person households	82
Persons per household	3.13
Persons per family	3.35

Labor & Employment
Total civilian labor force, 2006**	1,791
Unemployment rate	4.0%
Total civilian labor force, 2000	1,531
Unemployment rate	2.8%

Employed persons 16 years and over by occupation, 2000
Managers & professionals	664
Service occupations	123
Sales & office occupations	395
Farming, fishing & forestry	36
Construction & maintenance	127
Production & transportation	143
Self-employed persons	92

‡ Joint library with Swedesboro Borough
* US Census Bureau
** New Jersey Department of Labor

General Information
Township of Woolwich
121 Woodstown Rd
Woolwich Township, NJ 08085
856-467-2666

Website	www.woolwichtwp.org
Year of incorporation	1767
Land/water area (sq. miles)	20.94/0.24
Form of government	Township

Government
Legislative Districts
US Congressional	2
State Legislative	3

Local Officials, 2008
Mayor	Giuseppe Chila
Administrator	Jane DiBella
Clerk	Jane DiBella
Finance Dir	Merrie Schmidt
Tax Assessor	Bruce Komito
Tax Collector	Mary Folker
Attorney	Timothy Scaffidi
Building	James Sabetta
Comm Dev/Planning	NA
Engineering	Stan Bitgood
Public Works	Anthony Bertino
Police Chief	Russell Marino
Emerg/Fire Director	Ed Barber

Housing & Construction
Housing Units, 2000*
Total	1,026
Median rent	$763
Median SF home value	$194,800

Permits for New Residential Construction
	Units	Value
Total, 2007	86	$13,308,708
Single family	86	$13,308,708
Total, 2006	102	$14,458,449
Single family	102	$14,458,449

Real Property Valuation, 2007
	Parcels	Valuation
Total	3,470	$563,264,500
Vacant	476	20,050,700
Residential	2,553	466,470,800
Commercial	66	42,965,500
Industrial	1	633,900
Apartments	1	12,611,300
Farm land	259	5,113,700
Farm homestead	114	15,418,600

Average Property Value & Tax, 2007
Residential value	$180,686
Property tax	$7,554
Tax credit/rebate	$1,115

Public Library
Swedesboro Public Library‡
1442 Kings Hwy
Swedesboro, NJ 08085
856-467-0111

Director..............Marge Dombrosky

Library statistics, 2006
Population served	
Full-time/total staff	/

	Total	Per capita
Holdings		
Revenues		
Expenditures		
Annual visits		
Internet terminals/annual users	/	

Taxes
	2005	2006	2007
General tax rate per $100	3.773	3.96	4.181
County equalization ratio	66.02	59.96	53.86
Net valuation taxable	$436,394,102	$509,172,600	$564,546,727
State equalized value	$727,808,709	$946,674,886	$1,120,424,885

Public Safety
Number of officers, 2006		17

Crime	2005	2006
Total crimes	109	84
Violent	7	4
Murder	0	0
Rape	0	0
Robbery	2	1
Aggravated assault	5	3
Non-violent	102	80
Burglary	31	8
Larceny	65	70
Vehicle theft	6	2
Domestic violence	31	16
Arson	2	0
Total crime rate	17.8	11.1
Violent	1.1	0.5
Non-violent	16.7	10.6

Public School District
(for school year 2006-07 except as noted)

Swedesboro-Woolwich School District
15 Fredrick Blvd
Woolwich Twp, NJ 08085
856-241-1136

Superintendent	Richard Fisher
Number of schools	6
Grade plan	K-6
Enrollment	1,397
Attendance rate, '05-06	95.2%
Dropout rate	NA
Students per teacher	11.4
Per pupil expenditure	$9,288
Median faculty salary	$42,590
Median administrator salary	$80,280
Grade 12 enrollment	NA
High school graduation rate	NA

Assessment test results
(percent scoring at proficient or advanced level)
	Language	Math
NJASK-Grade 3	89.1%	91.9%
GEPA-Grade 8	NA	NA
HSPA-High School	NA	NA

SAT score averages
Pct tested	Math	Verbal	Writing
NA	NA	NA	NA

Teacher Qualifications
Avg. years of experience	4
Highly-qualified teachers one subject/all subjects	100%/100%
With emergency credentials	0.0%

No Child Left Behind
AYP, 2005-06 .... Meets Standards

Municipal Finance
State Aid Programs, 2008
Total aid	$527,911
CMPTRA	13,296
Energy tax receipts	513,762
Garden State Trust	853

General Budget, 2007
Total tax levy	$23,601,063
County levy	6,226,368
County taxes	5,362,402
County library	444,137
County health	0
County open space	419,829
School levy	14,060,625
Muni. levy	3,314,071
Misc. revenues	3,777,086

Burlington County

Wrightstown Borough

Demographics & Socio-Economic Characteristics
(2000 US Census, except as noted)

Population
- 1980* 3,031
- 1990* 3,843
- 2000 748
  - Male 364
  - Female 384
- 2006 (estimate)* 741
- Population density 421.0

Race & Hispanic Origin, 2000
Race
- White 373
- Black/African American 226
- American Indian/Alaska Native 4
- Asian 54
- Native Hawaiian/Pacific Islander 0
- Other race 54
- Two or more races 37
- Hispanic origin, total 84
  - Mexican 27
  - Puerto Rican 27
  - Cuban 1
  - Other Hispanic 29

Age & Nativity, 2000
- Under 5 years 58
- 18 years and over 526
- 21 years and over 496
- 65 years and over 64
- 85 years and over 5
- Median age 31.2
- Native-born 632
- Foreign-born 115

Educational Attainment, 2000
- Population 25 years and over 434
- Less than 9th grade 4.1%
- High school grad or higher 80.4%
- Bachelor's degree or higher 7.8%
- Graduate degree 1.4%

Income & Poverty, 1999
- Per capita income $14,489
- Median household income $27,500
- Median family income $29,375
- Persons in poverty 179
- H'holds receiving public assistance .. 11
- H'holds receiving social security 46

Households, 2000
- Total households 312
- With persons under 18 118
- With persons over 65 51
- Family households 182
- Single-person households 108
- Persons per household 2.37
- Persons per family 3.09

Labor & Employment
- Total civilian labor force, 2006** .. 420
  - Unemployment rate 6.0%
- Total civilian labor force, 2000 ... 364
  - Unemployment rate 6.9%

Employed persons 16 years and over by occupation, 2000
- Managers & professionals 46
- Service occupations 117
- Sales & office occupations 94
- Farming, fishing & forestry 0
- Construction & maintenance 21
- Production & transportation 61
- Self-employed persons 7

---
* US Census Bureau
** New Jersey Department of Labor

See Introduction for an explanation of all data sources.

General Information
Borough of Wrightstown
21 Saylors Pond Rd
Wrightstown, NJ 08562
609-723-4450
Email .... wrightstownclerk@comcast.net
Year of incorporation 1918
Land/water area (sq. miles) 1.76/0.00
Form of government .... Borough

Government
Legislative Districts
- US Congressional 3
- State Legislative 8

Local Officials, 2008
- Mayor .... Thomas Harper
- Manager/Admin .... NA
- Clerk .... Ellen Thorne
- Finance Dir .... Ron Ghrist
- Tax Assessor .... Douglas Kolton
- Tax Collector .... Lynn Davis
- Attorney .... Nicholas Costa
- Building .... Harry Case
- Planning .... Ragan Design Group
- Engineering .... Kluk Consultants
- Public Works .... NA
- Police Chief .... NA
- Emerg/Fire Director .... Joseph McFarland

Housing & Construction
Housing Units, 2000*
- Total 339
- Median rent $623
- Median SF home value $98,900

Permits for New Residential Construction

	Units	Value
Total, 2007	4	$423,600
Single family	4	$423,600
Total, 2006	5	$702,250
Single family	5	$702,250

Real Property Valuation, 2007

	Parcels	Valuation
Total	201	$25,636,450
Vacant	34	967,450
Residential	117	11,462,800
Commercial	39	9,565,100
Industrial	2	252,500
Apartments	7	3,376,150
Farm land	2	12,450
Farm homestead	0	0

Average Property Value & Tax, 2007
- Residential value $97,973
- Property tax $1,903
- Tax credit/rebate $542

Public Library
No public municipal library

Library statistics, 2006
- Population served .... NA
- Full-time/total staff .... NA/NA

	Total	Per capita
Holdings	NA	NA
Revenues	NA	NA
Expenditures	NA	NA
Annual visits	NA	NA
Internet terminals/annual users	NA/NA	

Taxes

	2005	2006	2007
General tax rate per $100	2.15	1.989	2.14
County equalization ratio	100.52	100.55	68.54
Net valuation taxable	$26,247,785	$24,774,400	$26,657,912
State equalized value	$26,104,212	$37,652,426	$33,472,665

Public Safety
Number of officers, 2006 0

Crime

	2005	2006
Total crimes	23	30
Violent	4	8
Murder	0	0
Rape	0	0
Robbery	1	1
Aggravated assault	3	7
Non-violent	19	22
Burglary	5	4
Larceny	12	15
Vehicle theft	2	3
Domestic violence	6	5
Arson	0	0
Total crime rate	30.7	40.2
Violent	5.3	10.7
Non-violent	25.4	29.5

Public School District
(for school year 2006-07 except as noted)

New Hanover Township School District
122 Fort Dix St
Wrightstown, NJ 08562
609-723-2139

- Superintendent .... Terri Sackett
- Number of schools 2
- Grade plan K-8
- Enrollment 162
- Attendance rate, '05-06 .... 95.4%
- Dropout rate .... NA
- Students per teacher 8.1
- Per pupil expenditure $19,578
- Median faculty salary $49,327
- Median administrator salary ... $81,600
- Grade 12 enrollment .... NA
- High school graduation rate .... NA

Assessment test results
(percent scoring at proficient or advanced level)

	Language	Math
NJASK-Grade 3	75.0%	87.5%
GEPA-Grade 8	81.5%	70.4%
HSPA-High School	NA	NA

SAT score averages

Pct tested	Math	Verbal	Writing
NA	NA	NA	NA

Teacher Qualifications
- Avg. years of experience 9
- Highly-qualified teachers
  - one subject/all subjects 94.0%/94.0%
- With emergency credentials 0.0%

No Child Left Behind
AYP, 2005-06 .... Meets Standards

Municipal Finance
State Aid Programs, 2008
- Total aid $105,881
  - CMPTRA 0
  - Energy tax receipts 105,881
  - Garden State Trust 0

General Budget, 2007
- Total tax levy $570,241
  - County levy 163,025
    - County taxes 135,079
    - County library 12,398
    - County health 0
    - County open space 15,548
  - School levy 407,216
  - Muni. levy 0
- Misc. revenues 1,891,800

The New Jersey Municipal Data Book

Wyckoff Township
Bergen County

Demographics & Socio-Economic Characteristics
(2000 US Census, except as noted)

Population
1980*	15,500
1990*	15,372
2000	16,508
Male	7,880
Female	8,628
2006 (estimate)*	17,167
Population density	2,620.9

Race & Hispanic Origin, 2000
Race
White	15,607
Black/African American	77
American Indian/Alaska Native	25
Asian	611
Native Hawaiian/Pacific Islander	2
Other race	74
Two or more races	112
Hispanic origin, total	376
Mexican	19
Puerto Rican	94
Cuban	62
Other Hispanic	201

Age & Nativity, 2000
Under 5 years	1,185
18 years and over	11,837
21 years and over	11,512
65 years and over	2,603
85 years and over	481
Median age	40.9
Native-born	14,978
Foreign-born	1,530

Educational Attainment, 2000
Population 25 years and over	11,122
Less than 9th grade	2.5%
High school grad or higher	93.8%
Bachelor's degree or higher	56.6%
Graduate degree	23.0%

Income & Poverty, 1999
Per capita income	$49,375
Median household income	$103,614
Median family income	$117,864
Persons in poverty	290
H'holds receiving public assistance	39
H'holds receiving social security	1,607

Households, 2000
Total households	5,541
With persons under 18	2,410
With persons over 65	1,573
Family households	4,634
Single-person households	819
Persons per household	2.89
Persons per family	3.22

Labor & Employment
Total civilian labor force, 2006**	8,046
Unemployment rate	2.8%
Total civilian labor force, 2000	7,574
Unemployment rate	2.8%

Employed persons 16 years and over by occupation, 2000
Managers & professionals	4,139
Service occupations	453
Sales & office occupations	2,109
Farming, fishing & forestry	5
Construction & maintenance	289
Production & transportation	364
Self-employed persons	691

* US Census Bureau
** New Jersey Department of Labor

General Information
Township of Wyckoff
340 Franklin Ave
Scott Plaza
Wyckoff, NJ 07481
201-891-7000

Website	www.wyckoff-nj.com
Year of incorporation	1926
Land/water area (sq. miles)	6.55/0.02
Form of government	Township

Government
Legislative Districts
US Congressional	5
State Legislative	40

Local Officials, 2008
Mayor	Richard C. Alnor
Manager	Robert Shannon Jr
Clerk	Joyce Santimauro
Finance Dir.	Diana McLeod
Tax Assessor	Pamela Steele
Tax Collector	Diana McLeod
Attorney	Robert Landel
Building	Thomas Gensheimer
Planning	J. Gordon Stanley
Engineering	Mark A. DiGennaro
Public Works	Scott Fisher
Police Chief	John W. Ydo
Emerg/Fire Director	David Murphy

Housing & Construction
Housing Units, 2000*
Total	5,638
Median rent	$1,114
Median SF home value	$417,500

Permits for New Residential Construction
	Units	Value
Total, 2007	23	$12,879,654
Single family	23	$12,879,654
Total, 2006	24	$12,134,960
Single family	24	$12,134,960

Real Property Valuation, 2007
	Parcels	Valuation
Total	5,791	$4,620,603,600
Vacant	100	39,559,500
Residential	5,528	4,326,701,800
Commercial	138	209,189,400
Industrial	18	40,155,000
Apartments	2	1,565,600
Farm land	2	27,000
Farm homestead	3	3,405,300

Average Property Value & Tax, 2007
Residential value	$782,880
Property tax	$10,469
Tax credit/rebate	$1,327

Public Library
Wyckoff Public Library
200 Woodland Ave
Wyckoff, NJ 07481
201-891-4866

Director	Judy Schmitt

Library statistics, 2006
Population served	16,508
Full-time/total staff	4/7

	Total	Per capita
Holdings	81,442	4.93
Revenues	$1,496,026	$90.62
Expenditures	$918,253	$55.62
Annual visits	147,133	8.91
Internet terminals/annual users	5/45,105	

Public Safety
Number of officers, 2006	26

Crime	2005	2006
Total crimes	108	115
Violent	11	4
Murder	0	0
Rape	0	0
Robbery	2	1
Aggravated assault	9	3
Non-violent	97	111
Burglary	12	18
Larceny	83	92
Vehicle theft	2	1
Domestic violence	52	49
Arson	1	0
Total crime rate	6.3	6.7
Violent	0.6	0.2
Non-violent	5.6	6.5

Public School District
(for school year 2006-07 except as noted)

Wyckoff Township School District
241 Morse Ave
Wyckoff, NJ 07481
201-848-5700

Superintendent	Janet Razze
Number of schools	5
Grade plan	K-8
Enrollment	2,384
Attendance rate, '05-06	96.2%
Dropout rate	NA
Students per teacher	11.6
Per pupil expenditure	$12,071
Median faculty salary	$60,481
Median administrator salary	$137,172
Grade 12 enrollment	NA
High school graduation rate	NA

Assessment test results
(percent scoring at proficient or advanced level)
	Language	Math
NJASK-Grade 3	93.2%	99.1%
GEPA-Grade 8	96.2%	90.3%
HSPA-High School	NA	NA

SAT score averages
Pct tested	Math	Verbal	Writing
NA	NA	NA	NA

Teacher Qualifications
Avg. years of experience	10
Highly-qualified teachers one subject/all subjects	99.5%/99.5%
With emergency credentials	0.0%

No Child Left Behind
AYP, 2005-06	Meets Standards

Municipal Finance
State Aid Programs, 2008
Total aid	$1,539,097
CMPTRA	281,648
Energy tax receipts	1,257,449
Garden State Trust	0

General Budget, 2007
Total tax levy	$61,872,380
County levy	8,040,897
County taxes	7,597,867
County library	0
County health	0
County open space	443,029
School levy	44,635,547
Muni. levy	9,195,936
Misc. revenues	6,785,774

Taxes
	2005	2006	2007
General tax rate per $100	2.58	1.26	1.34
County equalization ratio	58.93	114.6	104.59
Net valuation taxable	$2,147,223,666	$4,607,255,600	$4,626,761,443
State equalized value	$3,972,661,732	$4,410,683,587	$4,596,921,479

The New Jersey Municipal Data Book

2008

State & Municipal Profiles Series

County Profiles

[ip]
State &
Municipal
Profiles
Series

Atlantic County

Demographics & Socio-Economic Characteristics
(2006 American Community Survey, except as noted)

Population
1990*	224,327
2000*	252,552
2006	271,620
Male	131,331
Female	140,289
2007 (estimate)*	270,644
Population density	482.3

Race & Hispanic Origin, 2006
Race
- White 178,184
- Black/African American 44,553
- American Indian/Alaska Native 221
- Asian 17,984
- Native Hawaiian/Pacific Islander 40
- Two or more races 3,311

Hispanic origin, total 38,616
- Mexican 7,977
- Puerto Rican 15,042
- Cuban 623
- Other Hispanic 14,974

Age & Nativity, 2006
- Under 5 years 17,035
- 18 years and over 206,689
- 21 years and over 194,108
- 65 years and over 36,279
- 85 years and over 4,457
- Median age 38.0
- Native-born 230,747
- Foreign-born 40,873

Educational Attainment, 2006
- Population 25 years and over 183,027
- Less than 9th grade 5.0%
- High school grad or higher 85.8%
- Bachelor's degree or higher 23.5%
- Graduate degree 6.9%

Households, 2006
- Total households 103,504
  - With persons under 18 36,321
  - With persons over 65 25,869
  - Family households 67,704
  - Single-person households 30,929
- Persons per household 2.52
- Persons per family 3.13

Income & Poverty, 2006
- Per capita income $26,140
- Median household income $52,230
- Median family income $62,383
- Persons in poverty 9.2%
- H'holds receiving public assistance ... 3,125
- H'holds receiving social security 30,236

Labor & Employment, 2006*
- Total civilian labor force 139,700
  - Unemployment rate 5.7%

Employed persons 16 years and over by occupation, 2006
- Managers & professionals 33,829
- Service occupations 43,968
- Sales & office occupations 33,795
- Farming, fishing & forestry 1,063
- Construction & maintenance 11,934
- Production & transportation 10,064
- Self-employed persons 5,646

Civilian Labor Force Projections*
- 2009 140,900
- 2014 148,000
- 2020 156,400
- 2025 164,300

*US Census Bureau
**2006 American Community Survey
*** New Jersey Department of Labor
† sum of all municipalities in county

General Information
Atlantic County
1333 Atlantic Ave
Atlantic City, NJ 08401
609-345-6700

- Website .... www.aclink.org
- Year of formation 1837
- Land/water area (sq. miles) 561.1/110.4
- Class .... Fifth
- Government form .. County Executive Plan
- Number of Freeholders 9
- Number of municipalities 23

Government & Voters
Legislative Districts
- US Congressional 2
- State Legislative 1-2, 9

Registered Voters, November 2006
- Total 159,840
  - Democratic 33,781
  - Republican 37,556
  - Unaffiliated 88,466

County Officials, 2008
- County Executive .... Dennis Levinson
- Manager .... Gerald DelRosso
- Clerk .... Edward P. McGettigan
- Finance Dir .... George Boileau
- Tax Administrator .... Lois Finifter
- Surrogate .... James Carney
- Prosecutor .... Theodor Housel
- Public Works Dir .... Harry Tillett
- Planning/Dev Dir .... Joseph Maher
- Sheriff .... James McGettigan
- Fire Marshal .... Harold Swartz

County School District
6260 Old Harding Hwy
Mays Landing, NJ 08330
609-625-0004

- Superintendent .... Daniel Loggi
- Number of districts 26

Housing & Construction
Housing Units, 2006**
- Total 124,790
  - Single family units 71,083
  - Multiple family units 50,276
  - Owner-occupied units 70,698
  - Renter-occupied units 32,806
  - Vacant units 21,286
  - Median rent $896
  - Median SF home value $264,200

Permits for New Residential Construction
	Units	Value
Total, 2006	1,893	$224,611,774
Single family	1,536	$206,702,890
Total, 2007	1,137	$166,315,241
Single family	1,026	$158,841,839

Real Property Valuation, 2007†
	Parcels	Valuation
Total	136,814	31,377,673,400
Vacant	28,115	1,190,464,000
Residential	100,024	20,846,739,100
Farm land	1,655	17,817,900
Farm homestead	660	92,881,500
Non-residential	6,360	9,229,770,900
Commercial	5,802	8,795,040,700
Industrial	189	137,203,500
Apartments	369	297,526,700

Taxes†
	2005	2006	2007
Net valuation taxable	$25,152,364,169	$30,744,680,100	$31,428,365,455
State equalized value	$38,719,302,252	$49,966,321,696	57,370,738,179

Public Safety
Police Officers, 2006
- County officers 168
  - Sheriff's department 93
  - Prosecutors 75
- Municipal police 909

Crime
	2005	2006
Total crimes	12,200	12,012
Violent	1,396	1,471
Murder	16	30
Rape	84	82
Robbery	564	595
Aggravated assault	732	764
Non-violent	10,804	10,541
Burglary	1,855	2,001
Larceny	8,489	8,062
Vehicle theft	460	478
Domestic violence	5,795	5,378
Arson	76	62
Total crime rate	45.4	44.3
Violent	5.2	5.4
Non-violent	40.2	38.9

Public Library
Atlantic County Library
40 Farragut Avenue
Mays Landing, NJ 08330
(609) 625-2776

- Director .... William D. Paullin

Library statistics, 2006
- Population served 181,307

	Total	Per capita
Revenues	$7,939,215	$43.79
Expenditures	$7,421,052	$40.93
Holdings	673,896	3.72
Circulation	763,532	4.21
Annual visits	876,151	4.83

- Registered borrowers 60,315
- Reference transactions 28,730
- Hours open weekly 64
- Full-time/total staff 28/91
- Interlibrary loans
  - Provided/received 6,276/6,458
- Internet terminals 63
  - Annual users 114,465

State Income Tax, 2005
- Number of returns 118,079
  - Increase from previous year 3.6%
- Total income $5,841,716,000
  - Per capita $24,190
  - Increase from previous year 8.9%
- Net charged tax $157,868,000
  - Per capita $654
- Average taxable income $43,892
- Average income tax $1,337

County Finance
State Aid Programs, 2008†
- Total aid $35,714,499
  - CMPTRA 3,437,148
  - Energy tax receipts 31,366,311
  - Garden State Trust 638,681

General Budget, 2007†
- Total tax levy $830,916,416
  - County levy 143,082,346
    - County taxes 120,995,408
    - County library 7,797,468
    - County health 4,047,611
    - County open space 10,241,859
  - School levy 386,403,729
  - Muni. levy 301,430,341
- Misc. revenues 147,371,868

Bergen County

Demographics & Socio-Economic Characteristics
(2006 American Community Survey, except as noted)

Population
1990*	825,380
2000*	884,118
2006	904,037
Male	438,822
Female	465,215
2007 (estimate)*	895,744
Population density	3824.7

Race & Hispanic Origin, 2006
Race
White	672,604
Black/African American	51,504
American Indian/Alaska Native	1,146
Asian	125,373
Native Hawaiian/Pacific Islander	144
Two or more races	12,588
Hispanic origin, total	127,346
Mexican	7,826
Puerto Rican	23,868
Cuban	12,722
Other Hispanic	82,930

Age & Nativity, 2006
Under 5 years	51,560
18 years and over	700,348
21 years and over	670,492
65 years and over	132,341
85 years and over	19,865
Median age	40.8
Native-born	652,972
Foreign-born	251,065

Educational Attainment, 2006
Population 25 years and over	629,517
Less than 9th grade	5.0%
High school grad or higher	90.3%
Bachelor's degree or higher	42.7%
Graduate degree	15.8%

Households, 2006
Total households	333,469
With persons under 18	117,538
With persons over 65	93,402
Family households	233,826
Single-person households	85,759
Persons per household	2.68
Persons per family	3.26

Income & Poverty, 2006
Per capita income	$39,316
Median household income	$75,851
Median family income	$92,246
Persons in poverty	5.2%
H'holds receiving public assistance	3,922
H'holds receiving social security	95,109

Labor & Employment, 2006***
Total civilian labor force	477,000
Unemployment rate	3.9%

Employed persons 16 years and over by occupation, 2006
Managers & professionals	197,585
Service occupations	54,001
Sales & office occupations	140,328
Farming, fishing & forestry	359
Construction & maintenance	25,864
Production & transportation	35,974
Self-employed persons	26,833

Civilian Labor Force Projections***
2009	471,700
2014	480,000
2020	496,400
2025	507,400

*US Census Bureau
**2006 American Community Survey
*** New Jersey Department of Labor
† sum of all municipalities in county

General Information
Bergen County
1 Bergen County Plz
Hackensack, NJ 07601
201-336-6000

Website	www.co.bergen.nj.us
Year of formation	1683
Land/water area (sq. miles)	234.2/12.6
Class	First
Government form	County Executive Plan
Number of Freeholders	7
Number of municipalities	70

Government & Voters
Legislative Districts
US Congressional	5,9
State Legislative	32, 35-40

Registered Voters, November 2006
Total	500,899
Democratic	106,355
Republican	97,985
Unaffiliated	296,417

County Officials, 2008
County Executive	Dennis McNerney
Manager	Robert E. Laux
Clerk	Kathleen Donovan
Finance Dir	Alfred Dispoto
Tax Administrator	Robert Layton
Surrogate	Michael Dressler
Prosecutor	John Molinelli
Public Works Dir	Paul Juliano
Planning/Dev Dir	Farouk Ahmad
Sheriff	Leo McGuire
Fire Marshal	Bryan Hennig

County School District
1 Bergen County Plaza, 3rd Floor, Room 350
Hackensack, NJ 07601
201-336-6875

Superintendent	Aaron R. Graham
Number of districts	78

Housing & Construction
Housing Units, 2006**
Total	348,180
Single family units	186,606
Multiple family units	160,752
Owner-occupied units	226,828
Renter-occupied units	106,641
Vacant units	14,711
Median rent	$1,093
Median SF home value	$493,400

Permits for New Residential Construction
	Units	Value
Total, 2006	2,164	$469,835,747
Single family	1,096	$372,519,155
Total, 2007	2,887	$377,675,389
Single family	978	$344,481,010

Real Property Valuation, 2007†
	Parcels	Valuation
Total	269,385	141,092,630,212
Vacant	6,441	2,049,791,687
Residential	246,943	108,608,919,254
Farm land	78	857,300
Farm homestead	48	41,876,000
Non-residential	15,875	30,391,185,971
Commercial	11,414	18,901,677,834
Industrial	2,794	6,113,688,817
Apartments	1,667	5,375,819,320

Taxes†
	2005	2006	2007
Net valuation taxable	$109,204,537,237	$121,664,581,572	$141,301,209,895
State equalized value	$152,020,919,861	$170,543,198,365	180,207,616,315

Public Safety
Police Officers, 2006
County officers	664
Sheriff's department	457
Prosecutors	113
Municipal police	2,182

Crime
	2005	2006
Total crimes	13,657	13,683
Violent	1,022	952
Murder	7	7
Rape	46	34
Robbery	368	321
Aggravated assault	601	590
Non-violent	12,635	12,731
Burglary	1,858	2,006
Larceny	9,642	9,700
Vehicle theft	1,135	1,025
Domestic violence	4,729	4,664
Arson	53	67
Total crime rate	15.1	15.2
Violent	1.1	1.1
Non-violent	14.0	14.1

Public Library
No County Library
(Library statistics are the sum of all municipal libraries in the county)

Library statistics, 2006†
Population served 862,255

	Total	Per capita
Revenues	$56,535,435	$65.57
Expenditures	$52,332,601	$60.69
Holdings	4,363,188	5.06
Circulation	7,934,351	9.20
Annual visits	6,290,427	7.30

Registered borrowers	477,185
Reference transactions	715,322
Hours open weekly	NA
Number of libraries	62
Full-time/total staff	174/469
Interlibrary loans Provided/received	371,424/337,867
Internet terminals	653
Annual users	1,345,753

State Income Tax, 2005
Number of returns	382,889
Increase from previous year	2.2%
Total income	$36,342,373,000
Per capita	$45,553
Increase from previous year	7.8%
Net charged tax	$1,099,776,000
Per capita	$1,378
Average taxable income	$87,460
Average income tax	$2,872

County Finance
State Aid Programs, 2008†
Total aid	$115,613,548
CMPTRA	22,311,887
Energy tax receipts	93,076,866
Garden State Trust	50,096

General Budget, 2007†
Total tax levy	$2,880,279,810
County levy	311,817,549
County taxes	294,531,199
County library	0
County health	0
County open space	17,286,350
School levy	1,686,264,561
Muni. levy	882,197,701
Misc. revenues	418,859,720

Burlington County

Demographics & Socio-Economic Characteristics
(2006 American Community Survey, except as noted)

Population
- 1990*.............................395,066
- 2000*.............................423,394
- 2006..............................450,627
  - Male............................221,932
  - Female..........................228,695
- 2007 (estimate)*..................446,817
- Population density.................555.3

Race & Hispanic Origin, 2006
Race
- White..............................336,398
- Black/African American..............73,366
- American Indian/Alaska Native..........462
- Asian...............................18,007
- Native Hawaiian/Pacific Islander........58
- Two or more races...................9,431
- Hispanic origin, total..............23,254
  - Mexican...........................4,129
  - Puerto Rican......................9,654
  - Cuban...............................531
  - Other Hispanic....................8,940

Age & Nativity, 2006
- Under 5 years......................26,518
- 18 years and over.................346,717
- 21 years and over.................330,207
- 65 years and over..................57,433
- 85 years and over...................7,488
- Median age...........................38.6
- Native-born.......................410,741
- Foreign-born.......................39,886

Educational Attainment, 2006
- Population 25 years and over......308,053
- Less than 9th grade..................3.0%
- High school grad or higher..........89.7%
- Bachelor's degree or higher.........31.2%
- Graduate degree....................10.1%

Households, 2006
- Total households.................163,226
  - With persons under 18...........61,792
  - With persons over 65............38,808
  - Family households..............115,929
  - Single-person households........38,169
- Persons per household................2.68
- Persons per family...................3.18

Income & Poverty, 2006
- Per capita income................$30,349
- Median household income..........$68,090
- Median family income.............$79,285
- Persons in poverty...................5.9%
- H'holds receiving public assistance...2,063
- H'holds receiving social security...46,242

Labor & Employment, 2006*
- Total civilian labor force........245,700
- Unemployment rate....................4.1%

Employed persons 16 years and over by occupation, 2006
- Managers & professionals...........86,132
- Service occupations................31,977
- Sales & office occupations.........66,978
- Farming, fishing & forestry...........461
- Construction & maintenance.........17,567
- Production & transportation........20,875
- Self-employed persons..............10,780

Civilian Labor Force Projections*
- 2009..............................248,900
- 2014..............................260,200
- 2020..............................275,700
- 2025..............................286,100

*US Census Bureau
**2006 American Community Survey
*** New Jersey Department of Labor
† sum of all municipalities in county

See Introduction for an explanation of all data sources.

General Information
Burlington County
49 Rancocas Rd
County Office Bldg
Mount Holly, NJ 08060
609-265-5000
- Website..........www.co.burlington.nj.us
- Year of formation...................1694
- Land/water area (sq. miles)......804.6/14.9
- Class.............................Second
- Government form.......Freeholder Board
- Number of Freeholders..................5
- Number of municipalities..............40

Government & Voters
Legislative Districts
- US Congressional....................1-4
- State Legislative................7-9, 30

Registered Voters, November 2006
- Total............................247,266
  - Democratic.....................51,396
  - Republican.....................52,995
  - Unaffiliated..................142,816

County Officials, 2008
- County Executive.....................NA
- Manager.................Augustus Mosca
- Clerk................Wade Hale (Actg)
- Finance Dir..........................NA
- Tax Administrator.......Margaret Nuzzo
- Surrogate................George Kotch
- Prosecutor.............Robert Bernardi
- Public Works Dir...........Paul Wnek
- Planning/Dev Dir.......Steven Corcoran
- Sheriff................Jean Stanfield
- Fire Marshal..............Robert Rose

County School District
PO Box 6000
Mt. Holly, NJ 08060
609-265-5060
- Superintendent........Lester W. Ritchens
- Number of districts..................42

Housing & Construction
Housing Units, 2006**
- Total.............................172,352
  - Single family units.............109,704
  - Multiple family units............59,966
  - Owner-occupied units............128,053
  - Renter-occupied units............35,173
  - Vacant units......................9,126
- Median rent..........................$988
- Median SF home value............$259,300

Permits for New Residential Construction

	Units	Value
Total, 2006	2,784	$153,664,629
Single family	996	$145,912,103
Total, 2007	1,228	$135,460,307
Single family	850	$134,531,887

Real Property Valuation, 2007†

	Parcels	Valuation
Total	167,682	30,608,720,680
Vacant	15,492	604,178,900
Residential	141,598	23,772,113,269
Farm land	3,060	53,538,456
Farm homestead	1,470	393,197,050
Non-residential	6,062	5,785,693,005
Commercial	5,134	4,081,775,325
Industrial	592	861,250,630
Apartments	336	842,667,050

Taxes†

	2005	2006	2007
Net valuation taxable	$26,531,761,430	$28,215,475,850	$30,683,525,297
State equalized value	$40,667,753,763	$46,154,712,994	50,495,888,961

Public Safety
Police Officers, 2006
- County officers......................161
  - Sheriff's department...............73
  - Prosecutors........................88
- Municipal police....................806

Crime	2005	2006
Total crimes	8,667	8,878
Violent	824	795
Murder	6	13
Rape	85	80
Robbery	273	264
Aggravated assault	460	438
Non-violent	7,843	8,083
Burglary	1,443	1,528
Larceny	5,816	5,968
Vehicle theft	584	587
Domestic violence	3,598	3,795
Arson	62	79
Total crime rate	19.3	19.7
Violent	1.8	1.8
Non-violent	17.4	17.9

Public Library
Burlington County Library
5 Pioneer Dr, PO Box 6000
Mount Holly, NJ 08060
(609) 267-9660

- Director..................Gail Sweet

Library statistics, 2006
- Population served.................331,148

	Total	Per capita
Revenues	$11,572,549	$34.95
Expenditures	$9,375,059	$28.31
Holdings	1,043,996	3.15
Circulation	1,921,588	5.80
Annual visits	1,233,970	3.73

- Registered borrowers...............92,126
- Reference transactions...........322,163
- Hours open weekly...................68
- Full-time/total staff..............37/118
- Interlibrary loans
  - Provided/received...........6,704/5,897
- Internet terminals...................142
  - Annual users..................192,723

State Income Tax, 2005
- Number of returns................187,514
  - Increase from previous year......5.0%
- Total income............$12,630,611,000
  - Per capita....................$32,252
  - Increase from previous year......7.6%
- Net charged tax..............$360,956,000
  - Per capita.......................$922
- Average taxable income...........$60,711
- Average income tax................$1,925

County Finance
State Aid Programs, 2008†
- Total aid.....................$60,264,554
  - CMPTRA......................11,151,403
  - Energy tax receipts.........45,936,901
  - Garden State Trust..........2,320,159

General Budget, 2007†
- Total tax levy..............$1,016,452,841
  - County levy.................192,517,420
    - County taxes.............162,800,000
    - County library............11,089,980
    - County health...................0
    - County open space.........18,727,440
  - School levy.................646,832,466
  - Muni. levy..................177,102,956
- Misc. revenues................216,605,852

The New Jersey Municipal Data Book

Camden County

Demographics & Socio-Economic Characteristics
(2006 American Community Survey, except as noted)

Population
1990*	502,824
2000*	508,932
2006	517,001
Male	250,593
Female	266,408
2007 (estimate)*	513,769
Population density	2311.2

Race & Hispanic Origin, 2006
Race
White	345,113
Black/African American	97,253
American Indian/Alaska Native	1,385
Asian	23,789
Native Hawaiian/Pacific Islander	176
Two or more races	9,591
Hispanic origin, total	60,599
Mexican	8,748
Puerto Rican	34,942
Cuban	415
Other Hispanic	16,494

Age & Nativity, 2006
Under 5 years	33,539
18 years and over	387,684
21 years and over	367,034
65 years and over	62,686
85 years and over	8,939
Median age	37.0
Native-born	466,498
Foreign-born	50,503

Educational Attainment, 2006
Population 25 years and over	339,847
Less than 9th grade	6.1%
High school grad or higher	83.3%
Bachelor's degree or higher	26.9%
Graduate degree	9.7%

Households, 2006
Total households	189,498
With persons under 18	69,754
With persons over 65	44,787
Family households	129,949
Single-person households	49,316
Persons per household	2.68
Persons per family	3.25

Income & Poverty, 2006
Per capita income	$26,926
Median household income	$56,913
Median family income	$67,383
Persons in poverty	11.0%
H'holds receiving public assistance	5,981
H'holds receiving social security	51,550

Labor & Employment, 2006***
Total civilian labor force	271,600
Unemployment rate	5.1%

Employed persons 16 years and over by occupation, 2006
Managers & professionals	91,361
Service occupations	42,416
Sales & office occupations	71,185
Farming, fishing & forestry	173
Construction & maintenance	19,300
Production & transportation	26,967
Self-employed persons	12,624

Civilian Labor Force Projections***
2009	273,000
2014	279,200
2020	287,700
2025	293,400

*US Census Bureau
**2006 American Community Survey
*** New Jersey Department of Labor
† sum of all municipalities in county

General Information
Camden County
520 Market St
Camden, NJ 08102
856-225-5431

Website	www.co.camden.nj.us
Year of formation	1844
Land/water area (sq. miles)	222.3/5.3
Class	Second
Government form	Freeholder Board
Number of Freeholders	7
Number of municipalities	37

Government & Voters
Legislative Districts
US Congressional	1-3
State Legislative	4-7

Registered Voters, November 2006
Total	310,026
Democratic	88,985
Republican	34,343
Unaffiliated	186,567

County Officials, 2008
County Executive	NA
Manager	Ross Angilella
Clerk	James Beach
Finance Dir	Mark Lonetto
Tax Administrator	Sheri Garton
Surrogate	Patricia Jones
Prosecutor	Joshua M. Ottenberg (Actg)
Public Works Dir	Bob Kelly
Planning/Dev Dir	NA
Sheriff	Charles H. Billingham
Fire Marshal	Paul Hartstein

County School District
Forrest Hall, 509 Lakeland Rd
Blackwood, NJ 08012
856-401-2400

Superintendent	(vacant)
Number of districts	42

Housing & Construction
Housing Units, 2006**
Total	204,596
Single family units	113,391
Multiple family units	89,743
Owner-occupied units	134,155
Renter-occupied units	55,343
Vacant units	15,098
Median rent	$814
Median SF home value	$208,600

Permits for New Residential Construction
	Units	Value
Total, 2006	1,183	$113,361,833
Single family	872	$97,559,903
Total, 2007	1,190	$88,716,001
Single family	651	$76,109,001

Real Property Valuation, 2007†
	Parcels	Valuation
Total	180,001	23,387,251,361
Vacant	14,457	377,087,138
Residential	155,159	17,983,149,846
Farm land	831	6,737,500
Farm homestead	344	44,042,920
Non-residential	9,210	4,976,233,957
Commercial	7,964	3,688,845,313
Industrial	681	548,274,890
Apartments	565	739,113,754

Taxes†
	2005	2006	2007
Net valuation taxable	$20,476,422,500	$22,831,471,813	$23,468,795,316
State equalized value	$33,115,842,531	$37,486,792,605	41,409,021,714

Public Safety
Police Officers, 2006
County officers	340
Sheriff's department	151
Prosecutors	168
Municipal police	1,374

Crime	2005	2006
Total crimes	19,169	20,374
Violent	2,973	2,955
Murder	41	38
Rape	132	150
Robbery	1,104	1,222
Aggravated assault	1,696	1,545
Non-violent	16,196	17,419
Burglary	3,360	3,618
Larceny	11,027	11,796
Vehicle theft	1,809	2,005
Domestic violence	6,652	6,814
Arson	215	255
Total crime rate	37.1	39.3
Violent	5.8	5.7
Non-violent	31.4	33.6

Public Library
Camden County Library
203 Laurel Road, Echelon Urban Ctr
Voorhees, NJ 08043
(856) 772-1636

Director.....Linda Devlin

Library statistics, 2006
Population served.....242,830

	Total	Per capita
Revenues	$9,967,299	$41.05
Expenditures	$8,724,690	$35.93
Holdings	433,872	1.79
Circulation	1,427,213	5.88
Annual visits	782,825	3.22

Registered borrowers	73,809
Reference transactions	60,623
Hours open weekly	67
Full-time/total staff	31/76
Interlibrary loans Provided/received	5,191/4,668
Internet terminals	124
Annual users	169,050

State Income Tax, 2005
Number of returns	209,887
Increase from previous year	5.3%
Total income	$11,630,742,000
Per capita	$26,514
Increase from previous year	6.4%
Net charged tax	$285,639,000
Per capita	$651
Average taxable income	$49,553
Average income tax	$1,361

County Finance
State Aid Programs, 2008†
Total aid	$113,830,570
CMPTRA	61,168,478
Energy tax receipts	52,260,485
Garden State Trust	361,626

General Budget, 2007†
Total tax levy	$1,033,170,021
County levy	259,032,469
County taxes	243,271,733
County library	8,139,861
County health	0
County open space	7,620,875
School levy	561,175,938
Muni. levy	212,961,614
Misc. revenues	316,787,593

Cape May County

Demographics & Socio-Economic Characteristics
(2006 American Community Survey, except as noted)

Population
1990*	95,089
2000*	102,326
2006	97,724
Male	46,370
Female	51,354
2007 (estimate)*	96,422
Population density	377.8

Race & Hispanic Origin, 2006
Race
- White: 88,601
- Black/African American: 5,966
- American Indian/Alaska Native: 157
- Asian: 363
- Native Hawaiian/Pacific Islander: 0
- Two or more races: 1,215
- Hispanic origin, total: 3,965
  - Mexican: NA
  - Puerto Rican: NA
  - Cuban: NA
  - Other Hispanic: NA

Age & Nativity, 2006
- Under 5 years: 4,105
- 18 years and over: 78,089
- 21 years and over: 75,411
- 65 years and over: 20,020
- 85 years and over: 2,857
- Median age: 43.6
- Native-born: 94,483
- Foreign-born: 3,241

Educational Attainment, 2006
- Population 25 years and over: 71,155
- Less than 9th grade: 3.5%
- High school grad or higher: 87.2%
- Bachelor's degree or higher: 27.1%
- Graduate degree: 9.0%

Households, 2006
- Total households: 45,715
  - With persons under 18: 12,337
  - With persons over 65: 15,034
  - Family households: 27,865
  - Single-person households: 15,513
- Persons per household: 2.10
- Persons per family: 2.66

Income & Poverty, 2006
- Per capita income: $31,286
- Median household income: $50,024
- Median family income: $62,909
- Persons in poverty: 9.2%
- H'holds receiving public assistance: 1,054
- H'holds receiving social security: 17,203

Labor & Employment, 2006*
- Total civilian labor force: 58,900
- Unemployment rate: 7.0%

Employed persons 16 years and over by occupation, 2006
- Managers & professionals: 15,024
- Service occupations: 8,577
- Sales & office occupations: 10,437
- Farming, fishing & forestry: 127
- Construction & maintenance: 5,818
- Production & transportation: 3,641
- Self-employed persons: 3,072

Civilian Labor Force Projections*
- 2009: 55,300
- 2014: 55,800
- 2020: 56,900
- 2025: 57,900

*US Census Bureau
**2006 American Community Survey
*** New Jersey Department of Labor
† sum of all municipalities in county

See Introduction for an explanation of all data sources.

General Information
Cape May County
4 Moore Rd
Cape May Court House, NJ 08210
609-465-1000
- Website: www.capemaycountygov.net
- Year of formation: 1692
- Land/water area (sq. miles): 255.2/365.1
- Class: Sixth
- Government form: Freeholder Board
- Number of Freeholders: 5
- Number of municipalities: 16

Government & Voters
Legislative Districts
- US Congressional: 2
- State Legislative: 1

Registered Voters, November 2006
- Total: 66,593
  - Democratic: 9,281
  - Republican: 25,800
  - Unaffiliated: 31,490

County Officials, 2008
- County Executive: NA
- Administrator: Stephen O'Connor
- Clerk: Rita Marie Fulginiti
- Finance Dir: Edmund J. Grant Jr
- Tax Administrator: George R. Brown III
- Surrogate: W. Robert Hentges
- Prosecutor: Robert L. Taylor
- Public Works Dir: Dale Foster
- Planning/Dev Dir: NA
- Sheriff: John Callinan
- Fire/Emerg Dir: Frank McCall

County School District
4 Moore Rd
Cape May Court House, NJ 08210
609-465-1283
- Superintendent: Terrence J. Crowley
- Number of districts: 19

Housing & Construction
Housing Units, 2006**
- Total: 100,480
  - Single family units: 52,659
  - Multiple family units: 44,337
  - Owner-occupied units: 33,571
  - Renter-occupied units: 12,144
  - Vacant units: 54,765
  - Median rent: $901
  - Median SF home value: $348,000

Permits for New Residential Construction

	Units	Value
Total, 2006	1,580	$312,822,646
Single family	774	$190,031,006
Total, 2007	1,070	$193,294,657
Single family	614	$163,887,304

Real Property Valuation, 2007†

	Parcels	Valuation
Total	98,614	45,464,972,700
Vacant	9,154	1,608,684,900
Residential	84,419	39,763,195,800
Farm land	492	4,902,700
Farm homestead	188	61,200,600
Non-residential	4,361	4,026,988,700
Commercial	3,773	3,532,274,800
Industrial	19	42,575,600
Apartments	569	452,138,300

Taxes†

	2005	2006	2007
Net valuation taxable	$30,959,289,578	$39,149,670,150	$45,500,264,260
State equalized value	$43,138,710,236	$51,679,564,676	54,115,161,908

Public Safety
Police Officers, 2006
- County officers: 150
  - Sheriff's department: 121
  - Prosecutors: 29
- Municipal police: 342

Crime	2005	2006
Total crimes	4,792	5,043
Violent	310	333
Murder	2	1
Rape	14	18
Robbery	76	79
Aggravated assault	218	235
Non-violent	4,482	4,710
Burglary	899	888
Larceny	3,429	3,697
Vehicle theft	154	125
Domestic violence	1,303	1,185
Arson	19	20
Total crime rate	47.6	50.8
Violent	3.1	3.4
Non-violent	44.5	47.4

Public Library
Cape May County Library
30 Mechanic Street
Cape May Court House, NJ 08210
(609) 463-6350
- Director: Deborah Poillon

Library statistics, 2006
- Population served: 86,948

	Total	Per capita
Revenues	$9,257,692	$106.47
Expenditures	$6,174,698	$71.02
Holdings	368,230	4.24
Circulation	443,576	5.10
Annual visits	565,000	6.50

- Registered borrowers: 51,758
- Reference transactions: 51,000
- Hours open weekly: 74
- Full-time/total staff: 18/61
- Interlibrary loans Provided/received: 2,520/1,555
- Internet terminals: 54
  - Annual users: 64,909

State Income Tax, 2005
- Number of returns: 41,004
  - Increase from previous year: 4.3%
- Total income: $2,410,140,000
  - Per capita: $30,110
  - Increase from previous year: 14.6%
- Net charged tax: $80,525,000
  - Per capita: $1,006
- Average taxable income: $53,076
- Average income tax: $1,964

County Finance
State Aid Programs, 2008†
- Total aid: $21,217,089
  - CMPTRA: 528,046
  - Energy tax receipts: 20,145,620
  - Garden State Trust: 523,501

General Budget, 2007†
- Total tax levy: $374,867,813
  - County levy: 94,177,791
    - County taxes: 79,992,650
    - County library: 8,889,811
    - County health: 0
    - County open space: 5,295,329
  - School levy: 136,564,319
  - Muni. levy: 144,125,704
- Misc. revenues: 101,057,316

The New Jersey Municipal Data Book   575

Cumberland County

Demographics & Socio-Economic Characteristics
(2006 American Community Survey, except as noted)

Population
1990*	138,053
2000*	146,438
2006	154,823
Male	79,949
Female	74,874
2007 (estimate)*	155,544
Population density	317.9

Race & Hispanic Origin, 2006
Race
White	103,852
Black/African American	31,540
American Indian/Alaska Native	1,379
Asian	1,718
Native Hawaiian/Pacific Islander	0
Two or more races	2,624
Hispanic origin, total	35,185
Mexican	11,254
Puerto Rican	19,197
Cuban	313
Other Hispanic	4,421

Age & Nativity, 2006
Under 5 years	10,693
18 years and over	117,507
21 years and over	111,172
65 years and over	18,958
85 years and over	2,250
Median age	36.0
Native-born	140,007
Foreign-born	14,816

Educational Attainment, 2006
Population 25 years and over	103,298
Less than 9th grade	9.8%
High school grad or higher	72.6%
Bachelor's degree or higher	11.9%
Graduate degree	2.6%

Households, 2006
Total households	50,047
With persons under 18	19,983
With persons over 65	12,541
Family households	35,363
Single-person households	12,014
Persons per household	2.87
Persons per family	3.42

Income & Poverty, 2006
Per capita income	$19,722
Median household income	$47,443
Median family income	$57,204
Persons in poverty	15.3%
H'holds receiving public assistance	3,159
H'holds receiving social security	15,033

Labor & Employment, 2006***
Total civilian labor force	70,600
Unemployment rate	6.9%

Employed persons 16 years and over by occupation, 2006
Managers & professionals	16,143
Service occupations	12,318
Sales & office occupations	15,734
Farming, fishing & forestry	416
Construction & maintenance	6,762
Production & transportation	11,860
Self-employed persons	1,878

Civilian Labor Force Projections***
2009	71,700
2014	73,800
2020	76,900
2025	79,000

*US Census Bureau
**2006 American Community Survey
***New Jersey Department of Labor
† sum of all municipalities in county

General Information
Cumberland County
790 E Commerce St
Administration Bldg
Bridgeton, NJ 08302
856-453-2138

Website	www.co.cumberland.nj.us
Year of formation	1748
Land/water area (sq. miles)	489.3/187.3
Class	Third
Government form	Freeholder Board
Number of Freeholders	7
Number of municipalities	14

Government & Voters

Legislative Districts
US Congressional	2
State Legislative	13

Registered Voters, November 2006
Total	82,922
Democratic	16,000
Republican	13,234
Unaffiliated	53,655

County Officials, 2008
County Executive	NA
Manager	Ken Mecouch
Clerk	Gloria Noto
Finance Dir	Marcella D. Shepard
Tax Administrator	Patricia A. Belmont
Surrogate	Arthur J. Marchand
Prosecutor	Ronald Casella
Public Works Dir	Dan Orr
Planning/Dev Dir	Robert Brewer
Sheriff	Michael F. Barruzza
Fire Marshal	Robert Hoffman Jr

County School District
19 Landis Ave
Bridgeton, NJ 08302
856-451-0211

Superintendent	Daniel Mastrobuono
Number of districts	16

Housing & Construction

Housing Units, 2006**
Total	54,715
Single family units	35,848
Multiple family units	15,108
Owner-occupied units	33,336
Renter-occupied units	16,711
Vacant units	4,668
Median rent	$778
Median SF home value	$161,800

Permits for New Residential Construction
	Units	Value
Total, 2006	737	$84,238,864
Single family	693	$78,377,064
Total, 2007	679	$70,235,319
Single family	568	$66,831,105

Real Property Valuation, 2007†
	Parcels	Valuation
Total	59,937	5,381,134,850
Vacant	11,892	159,781,200
Residential	40,240	3,802,923,000
Farm land	3,028	35,972,800
Farm homestead	1,548	186,258,400
Non-residential	3,229	1,196,199,450
Commercial	2,752	781,644,850
Industrial	317	299,715,800
Apartments	160	114,838,800

Taxes†
	2005	2006	2007
Net valuation taxable	$5,137,949,473	$5,209,035,825	$5,405,826,973
State equalized value	$6,673,320,616	$7,770,530,909	9,110,946,900

Public Safety

Police Officers, 2006
County officers	82
Sheriff's department	52
Prosecutors	30
Municipal police	294

Crime
	2005	2006
Total crimes	7,338	7,441
Violent	1,363	1,243
Murder	8	15
Rape	51	50
Robbery	411	434
Aggravated assault	893	744
Non-violent	5,975	6,198
Burglary	1,336	1,533
Larceny	4,259	4,329
Vehicle theft	380	336
Domestic violence	3,290	3,353
Arson	38	44
Total crime rate	48.5	48.6
Violent	9.0	8.1
Non-violent	39.5	40.4

Public Library
Cumberland County Library
800 E. Commerce Street
Bridgeton, NJ 08302
(856) 453-2210

Director: Nancy J. Forester

Library statistics, 2006
Population served: 67,396

	Total	Per capita
Revenues	$1,288,403	$19.12
Expenditures	$1,232,694	$18.29
Holdings	113,489	1.68
Circulation	77,327	1.15
Annual visits	85,000	1.26

Registered borrowers	16,498
Reference transactions	9,800
Hours open weekly	60
Full-time/total staff	5/12
Interlibrary loans Provided/received	947/332
Internet terminals	31
Annual users	36,000

State Income Tax, 2005
Number of returns	57,562
Increase from previous year	7.1%
Total income	$2,436,243,000
Per capita	$19,739
Increase from previous year	8.1%
Net charged tax	$56,645,000
Per capita	$459
Average taxable income	$37,519
Average income tax	$984

County Finance

State Aid Programs, 2008†
Total aid	$23,737,030
CMPTRA	9,279,536
Energy tax receipts	13,306,106
Garden State Trust	1,146,395

General Budget, 2007†
Total tax levy	$192,615,379
County levy	78,815,627
County taxes	76,100,000
County library	0
County health	1,900,000
County open space	815,627
School levy	63,458,480
Muni. levy	50,341,272
Misc. revenues	81,457,984

Essex County

Demographics & Socio-Economic Characteristics
(2006 American Community Survey, except as noted)

Population
1990*	778,206
2000*	793,633
2006	786,147
Male	377,649
Female	408,498
2007 (estimate)*	776,087
Population density	6144.8

Race & Hispanic Origin, 2006
Race
White	334,699
Black/African American	323,306
American Indian/Alaska Native	2,661
Asian	33,772
Native Hawaiian/Pacific Islander	40
Two or more races	14,102
Hispanic origin, total	141,459
Mexican	5,648
Puerto Rican	53,643
Cuban	4,326
Other Hispanic	77,842

Age & Nativity, 2006
Under 5 years	57,958
18 years and over	581,677
21 years and over	547,449
65 years and over	90,877
85 years and over	12,706
Median age	36.0
Native-born	598,846
Foreign-born	187,301

Educational Attainment, 2006
Population 25 years and over	508,822
Less than 9th grade	8.9%
High school grad or higher	80.1%
Bachelor's degree or higher	30.6%
Graduate degree	12.2%

Households, 2006
Total households	278,863
With persons under 18	103,115
With persons over 65	65,561
Family households	183,054
Single-person households	83,854
Persons per household	2.73
Persons per family	3.42

Income & Poverty, 2006
Per capita income	$29,053
Median household income	$51,879
Median family income	$65,268
Persons in poverty	14.5%
H'holds receiving public assistance	10,349
H'holds receiving social security	71,934

Labor & Employment, 2006*
Total civilian labor force	370,600
Unemployment rate	5.8%

Employed persons 16 years and over by occupation, 2006
Managers & professionals	120,707
Service occupations	65,182
Sales & office occupations	95,777
Farming, fishing & forestry	222
Construction & maintenance	33,277
Production & transportation	40,151
Self-employed persons	20,878

Civilian Labor Force Projections*
2009	373,200
2014	382,700
2020	393,800
2025	404,300

*US Census Bureau
**2006 American Community Survey
*** New Jersey Department of Labor
† sum of all municipalities in county

See Introduction for an explanation of all data sources.

General Information
Essex County
465 Dr Martin Luther King Jr Blvd
Newark, NJ 07102
973-621-5100

Website	www.essexcountynj.org
Year of formation	1683
Land/water area (sq. miles)	126.3/3.3
Class	First
Government form	County Executive Plan
Number of Freeholders	9
Number of municipalities	22

Government & Voters
Legislative Districts
US Congressional	8-11, 13
State Legislative	21, 27-28, 34, 36, 40

Registered Voters, November 2006
Total	415,921
Democratic	150,399
Republican	41,137
Unaffiliated	224,297

County Officials, 2008
County Exec	Joseph DeVincenzo Jr
County Admin	Joyce Wilson Harley
Clerk	Christopher Durkin
Treasurer	Paul Hopkins II
Tax Administrator	Joan Codey Durkin
Surrogate	Joseph Brennan
Prosecutor	Paula Dow
Public Works Dir	Philip LiVecchi
Planning/Dev Dir	Philip LiVecchi
Sheriff	Armando Fontoura
Fire/Emerg Mgmt Dir	NA

County School District
7 Glenwood Ave, Suite 404
East Orange, NJ 07019
973-395-4677

Superintendent	Thomas Dowd
Number of districts	23

Housing & Construction
Housing Units, 2006**
Total	308,707
Single family units	106,682
Multiple family units	201,025
Owner-occupied units	133,992
Renter-occupied units	144,871
Vacant units	29,844
Median rent	$859
Median SF home value	$409,300

Permits for New Residential Construction
	Units	Value
Total, 2006	3,284	$392,801,103
Single family	654	$158,403,232
Total, 2007	1,862	$192,427,436
Single family	455	$112,390,881

Real Property Valuation, 2007†
	Parcels	Valuation
Total	176,821	56,530,473,241
Vacant	8,892	889,951,700
Residential	151,087	39,819,854,541
Farm land	17	143,900
Farm homestead	5	923,900
Non-residential	16,820	15,819,599,200
Commercial	12,143	10,107,854,100
Industrial	1,995	2,366,573,100
Apartments	2,682	3,345,172,000

Taxes†
	2005	2006	2007
Net valuation taxable	$35,083,477,855	$40,131,037,517	$56,674,138,715
State equalized value	$76,819,824,317	$86,661,310,831	93,148,280,922

Public Safety
Police Officers, 2006
County officers	578
Sheriff's department	391
Prosecutors	156
Municipal police	2,862

Crime	2005	2006
Total crimes	37,100	33,547
Violent	6,556	6,136
Murder	147	146
Rape	174	167
Robbery	3,191	2,990
Aggravated assault	3,044	2,833
Non-violent	30,544	27,411
Burglary	5,695	5,237
Larceny	14,944	13,838
Vehicle theft	9,905	8,336
Domestic violence	5,506	5,245
Arson	273	280
Total crime rate	46.6	42.4
Violent	8.2	7.8
Non-violent	38.3	34.7

Public Library
No County Library
(Library statistics are the sum of all municipal libraries in the county)

Library statistics, 2006†
Population served ... 784,096

	Total	Per capita
Revenues	$48,407,616	$61.74
Expenditures	$45,927,117	$58.57
Holdings	4,256,578	5.43
Circulation	3,131,537	3.99
Annual visits	3,710,829	4.73

Registered borrowers	342,060
Reference transactions	644,763
Hours open weekly	NA
Number of libraries	20
Full-time/total staff	173/470
Interlibrary loans Provided/received	47,098/73,138
Internet terminals	556
Annual users	1,024,309

State Income Tax, 2005
Number of returns	306,071
Increase from previous year	2.3%
Total income	$22,473,470,000
Per capita	$35,637
Increase from previous year	10.8%
Net charged tax	$660,874,000
Per capita	$1,048
Average taxable income	$67,470
Average income tax	$2,159

County Finance
State Aid Programs, 2008†
Total aid	$204,826,173
CMPTRA	129,926,918
Energy tax receipts	74,827,112
Garden State Trust	22,793

General Budget, 2007†
Total tax levy	$1,806,432,390
County levy	343,553,629
County taxes	334,701,235
County library	0
County health	0
County open space	8,852,394
School levy	858,938,770
Muni. levy	603,939,991
Misc. revenues	829,845,936

Gloucester County

Demographics & Socio-Economic Characteristics
(2006 American Community Survey, except as noted)

Population
1990*	230,082
2000*	254,673
2006	282,031
Male	137,558
Female	144,473
2007 (estimate)*	285,753
Population density	880.1

Race & Hispanic Origin, 2006
Race
White	238,991
Black/African American	27,447
American Indian/Alaska Native	381
Asian	6,416
Native Hawaiian/Pacific Islander	73
Two or more races	5,231
Hispanic origin, total	9,458
Mexican	1,493
Puerto Rican	5,410
Cuban	294
Other Hispanic	2,261

Age & Nativity, 2006
Under 5 years	15,874
18 years and over	216,600
21 years and over	202,586
65 years and over	32,647
85 years and over	3,501
Median age	37.5
Native-born	268,736
Foreign-born	13,295

Educational Attainment, 2006
Population 25 years and over	186,758
Less than 9th grade	3.3%
High school grad or higher	88.5%
Bachelor's degree or higher	26.1%
Graduate degree	7.9%

Households, 2006
Total households	99,275
With persons under 18	40,354
With persons over 65	22,837
Family households	72,503
Single-person households	23,084
Persons per household	2.79
Persons per family	3.31

Income & Poverty, 2006
Per capita income	$28,712
Median household income	$66,759
Median family income	$79,246
Persons in poverty	6.8%
H'holds receiving public assistance	1,889
H'holds receiving social security	25,488

Labor & Employment, 2006***
Total civilian labor force	153,000
Unemployment rate	4.7%

Employed persons 16 years and over by occupation, 2006
Managers & professionals	50,597
Service occupations	20,949
Sales & office occupations	42,648
Farming, fishing & forestry	326
Construction & maintenance	13,702
Production & transportation	17,221
Self-employed persons	6,290

Civilian Labor Force Projections***
2009	154,100
2014	161,200
2020	172,800
2025	181,100

*US Census Bureau
**2006 American Community Survey
*** New Jersey Department of Labor
† sum of all municipalities in county

General Information
Gloucester County
PO Box 337
Woodbury, NJ 08096
856-853-3200

Website	www.co.gloucester.nj.us
Year of formation	1686
Land/water area (sq. miles)	324.7/12.2
Class	Third
Government form	Freeholder Board
Number of Freeholders	7
Number of municipalities	24

Government & Voters

Legislative Districts
US Congressional	1-2
State Legislative	3-5

Registered Voters, November 2006
Total	173,834
Democratic	49,070
Republican	28,052
Unaffiliated	96,620

County Officials, 2008
Freeholder Director	Stephen Sweeney
Manager	Chad M. Bruner
Clerk	James Hogan
CFO/Treasurer	Gary Schwarz
Tax Administrator	Edward J. Burek
Surrogate	Helene Reed
Prosecutor	Sean Dalton
Public Works Dir	NA
Planning/Dev Dir	NA
Sheriff	Carmel Morino
Fire Marshal	William Reiger

County School District
1492 Tanyard Rd
Sewell, NJ 08080
856-468-6500

Superintendent	H. Mark Stanwood
Number of districts	30

Housing & Construction

Housing Units, 2006**
Total	105,502
Single family units	78,240
Multiple family units	24,985
Owner-occupied units	81,394
Renter-occupied units	17,881
Vacant units	6,227
Median rent	$828
Median SF home value	$226,900

Permits for New Residential Construction
	Units	Value
Total, 2006	1,141	$175,251,137
Single family	1,021	$169,613,387
Total, 2007	888	$147,968,203
Single family	855	$147,051,373

Real Property Valuation, 2007†
	Parcels	Valuation
Total	109,855	14,834,500,386
Vacant	12,745	381,086,987
Residential	88,414	10,890,647,450
Farm land	2,982	32,415,800
Farm homestead	1,287	187,403,300
Non-residential	4,427	3,342,946,849
Commercial	4,013	2,304,855,320
Industrial	222	795,434,329
Apartments	192	242,657,200

Taxes†
	2005	2006	2007
Net valuation taxable	$13,964,405,380	$14,270,861,336	$14,976,157,127
State equalized value	$21,382,135,336	$24,982,195,408	27,472,693,310

Public Safety

Police Officers, 2006
County officers	109
Sheriff's department	76
Prosecutors	33
Municipal police	593

Crime
	2005	2006
Total crimes	7,820	8,128
Violent	569	610
Murder	2	7
Rape	44	58
Robbery	178	192
Aggravated assault	345	353
Non-violent	7,251	7,518
Burglary	1,509	1,463
Larceny	5,341	5,651
Vehicle theft	401	404
Domestic violence	3,188	3,010
Arson	68	73
Total crime rate	28.8	29.4
Violent	2.1	2.2
Non-violent	26.7	27.1

Public Library
Gloucester County Library
389 Wolfert Station Road
Mullica Hill, NJ 08062
(856) 223-6000

Director: Robert S. Wetherall

Library statistics, 2006
Population served: 93,711

	Total	Per capita
Revenues	$4,021,551	$42.91
Expenditures	$3,762,771	$40.15
Holdings	212,851	2.27
Circulation	554,101	5.91
Annual visits	487,253	5.20

Registered borrowers	48,657
Reference transactions	21,533
Hours open weekly	69
Full-time/total staff	11/41
Interlibrary loans Provided/received	14,331/22,132
Internet terminals	67
Annual users	73,356

State Income Tax, 2005
Number of returns	116,378
Increase from previous year	7.9%
Total income	$6,729,930,000
Per capita	$26,752
Increase from previous year	9.8%
Net charged tax	$148,566,000
Per capita	$591
Average taxable income	$51,602
Average income tax	$1,277

County Finance

State Aid Programs, 2008†
Total aid	$31,419,598
CMPTRA	7,199,619
Energy tax receipts	23,971,013
Garden State Trust	52,674

General Budget, 2007†
Total tax levy	$623,604,581
County levy	145,732,944
County taxes	131,445,000
County library	3,996,540
County health	0
County open space	10,291,404
School levy	344,335,361
Muni. levy	133,536,276
Misc. revenues	133,530,484

Hudson County

Demographics & Socio-Economic Characteristics
(2006 American Community Survey, except as noted)

Population
1990*	553,099
2000*	608,975
2006	601,146
Male	298,253
Female	302,893
2007 (estimate)*	598,160
Population density	12808.6

Race & Hispanic Origin, 2006
Race
- White 339,879
- Black/African American 85,206
- American Indian/Alaska Native 3,115
- Asian 68,136
- Native Hawaiian/Pacific Islander 151
- Two or more races 7,996
- Hispanic origin, total 246,723
  - Mexican 17,114
  - Puerto Rican 50,100
  - Cuban 27,910
  - Other Hispanic 151,599

Age & Nativity, 2006
- Under 5 years 41,313
- 18 years and over 465,752
- 21 years and over 444,053
- 65 years and over 65,584
- 85 years and over 9,142
- Median age 35.7
- Native-born 357,885
- Foreign-born 243,261

Educational Attainment, 2006
- Population 25 years and over 411,884
- Less than 9th grade 11.7%
- High school grad or higher 77.6%
- Bachelor's degree or higher 30.5%
- Graduate degree 10.7%

Households, 2006
- Total households 223,451
  - With persons under 18 72,011
  - With persons over 65 46,933
  - Family households 137,082
  - Single-person households 69,463
- Persons per household 2.65
- Persons per family 3.37

Income & Poverty, 2006
- Per capita income $27,068
- Median household income $49,557
- Median family income $51,795
- Persons in poverty 15.2%
- H'holds receiving public assistance 7,193
- H'holds receiving social security ... 49,026

Labor & Employment, 2006***
- Total civilian labor force 294,100
- Unemployment rate 5.5%

Employed persons 16 years and over by occupation, 2006
- Managers & professionals 98,065
- Service occupations 56,673
- Sales & office occupations 78,563
- Farming, fishing & forestry 199
- Construction & maintenance 22,489
- Production & transportation 45,954
- Self-employed persons 13,887

Civilian Labor Force Projections***
- 2009 294,100
- 2014 295,100
- 2020 301,800
- 2025 302,400

*US Census Bureau
**2006 American Community Survey
*** New Jersey Department of Labor
† sum of all municipalities in county

See Introduction for an explanation of all data sources.

General Information
Hudson County
583 Newark Ave
Brennan Court House Building
Jersey City, NJ 07306
201-795-6000

- Website .... www.hudsoncountynj.org
- Year of formation 1840
- Land/water area (sq. miles) 46.7/15.7
- Class .... First
- Government form .. County Executive Plan
- Number of Freeholders 9
- Number of municipalities 12

Government & Voters

Legislative Districts
- US Congressional 9-10, 13
- State Legislative 31-33

Registered Voters, November 2006
- Total 284,072
  - Democratic 123,561
  - Republican 22,310
  - Unaffiliated 138,018

County Officials, 2008
- County Executive .... Thomas DeGise
- Manager .... Abraham Antun
- Clerk .... Barbara A. Netchert
- Finance Dir .... Wade Frazee
- Tax Administrator .... Donald Kenny
- Surrogate .... Donald DeLeo
- Prosecutor .... Edward DeFazio
- Public Works Dir .... NA
- Planning/Dev Dir .... Stephen Marks
- Sheriff .... Juan Perez
- Emerg Mgmt Dir .... Frank Pizzuta

County School District
595 Newark Ave
Jersey City, NJ 07306
201-319-3850

- Superintendent .... Robert Osak
- Number of districts 13

Housing & Construction

Housing Units, 2006**
- Total 251,211
  - Single family units 23,676
  - Multiple family units 227,208
  - Owner-occupied units 76,700
  - Renter-occupied units 146,751
  - Vacant units 27,760
  - Median rent $941
  - Median SF home value $387,100

Permits for New Residential Construction
	Units	Value
Total, 2006	4,275	$450,371,017
Single family	277	$32,231,367
Total, 2007	3,350	$70,105,925
Single family	158	$23,749,058

Real Property Valuation, 2007†
	Parcels	Valuation
Total	119,892	21,358,152,158
Vacant	10,288	901,237,668
Residential	94,048	11,608,951,179
Farm land	0	0
Farm homestead	0	0
Non-residential	15,556	8,847,963,311
Commercial	9,600	4,635,147,731
Industrial	1,851	2,541,247,130
Apartments	4,105	1,671,568,450

Taxes†
	2005	2006	2007
Net valuation taxable	$20,699,232,068	$21,147,492,189	$21,399,716,001
State equalized value	$48,159,722,307	$57,639,543,726	64,070,898,191

Public Safety

Police Officers, 2006
- County officers 301
  - Sheriff's department 197
  - Prosecutors 104
- Municipal police 1,984

Crime
	2005	2006
Total crimes	21,848	19,750
Violent	4,438	4,221
Murder	49	34
Rape	91	85
Robbery	2,253	2,193
Aggravated assault	2,045	1,909
Non-violent	17,410	15,529
Burglary	4,027	3,329
Larceny	10,044	9,422
Vehicle theft	3,339	2,778
Domestic violence	4,997	4,569
Arson	102	134
Total crime rate	36.0	32.7
Violent	7.3	7.0
Non-violent	28.7	25.7

Public Library
No County Library
(Library statistics are the sum of all municipal libraries in the county)

Library statistics, 2006†
- Population served 595,791

	Total	Per capita
Revenues	$18,356,990	$30.81
Expenditures	$17,691,906	$29.69
Holdings	1,421,625	2.39
Circulation	760,133	1.28
Annual visits	1,658,882	2.78

- Registered borrowers 279,617
- Reference transactions 637,679
- Hours open weekly .... NA
- Number of libraries 10
- Full-time/total staff 47/222
- Interlibrary loans
  - Provided/received 21,929/39,572
- Internet terminals 501
  - Annual users 504,680

State Income Tax, 2005
- Number of returns 251,814
- Increase from previous year 0.8%
- Total income $11,907,205,000
  - Per capita $25,356
  - Increase from previous year 6.9%
- Net charged tax $223,176,000
  - Per capita $475
- Average taxable income $43,398
- Average income tax $886

County Finance

State Aid Programs, 2008†
- Total aid $176,689,821
  - CMPTRA 92,122,341
  - Energy tax receipts 84,535,668
  - Garden State Trust 31,107

General Budget, 2007†
- Total tax levy $1,027,664,080
  - County levy 239,636,918
    - County taxes 233,775,687
    - County library 0
    - County health 0
    - County open space 5,861,231
  - School levy 356,247,173
  - Muni. levy 431,779,989
- Misc. revenues 620,741,432

©2008 Information Publications, Inc.

The New Jersey Municipal Data Book

Hunterdon County

Demographics & Socio-Economic Characteristics
(2006 American Community Survey, except as noted)

Population
1990*	107,776
2000*	121,989
2006	130,783
Male	64,852
Female	65,931
2007 (estimate)*	129,348
Population density	300.9

Race & Hispanic Origin, 2006
Race
White	120,038
Black/African American	2,502
American Indian/Alaska Native	0
Asian	5,010
Native Hawaiian/Pacific Islander	0
Two or more races	1,436
Hispanic origin, total	5,111
Mexican	597
Puerto Rican	897
Cuban	469
Other Hispanic	3,148

Age & Nativity, 2006
Under 5 years	6,848
18 years and over	100,383
21 years and over	96,016
65 years and over	14,237
85 years and over	2,146
Median age	41.4
Native-born	119,142
Foreign-born	11,641

Educational Attainment, 2006
Population 25 years and over	89,786
Less than 9th grade	2.7%
High school grad or higher	94.2%
Bachelor's degree or higher	46.4%
Graduate degree	18.2%

Households, 2006
Total households	45,428
With persons under 18	17,279
With persons over 65	9,158
Family households	33,218
Single-person households	10,077
Persons per household	2.77
Persons per family	3.30

Income & Poverty, 2006
Per capita income	$44,133
Median household income	$93,297
Median family income	$109,509
Persons in poverty	3.5%
H'holds receiving public assistance	302
H'holds receiving social security	10,391

Labor & Employment, 2006***
Total civilian labor force	73,100
Unemployment rate	3.3%

Employed persons 16 years and over by occupation, 2006
Managers & professionals	29,700
Service occupations	8,038
Sales & office occupations	19,871
Farming, fishing & forestry	76
Construction & maintenance	5,824
Production & transportation	3,887
Self-employed persons	6,049

Civilian Labor Force Projections***
2009	74,500
2014	78,000
2020	83,100
2025	86,400

*US Census Bureau
**2006 American Community Survey
*** New Jersey Department of Labor
† sum of all municipalities in county

General Information
Hunterdon County
PO Box 2900
71 Main St
Flemington, NJ 08822
908-788-1102

Website	www.co.hunterdon.nj.us
Year of formation	1714
Land/water area (sq. miles)	429.9/7.8
Class	Third
Government form	Freeholder Board
Number of Freeholders	5
Number of municipalities	26

Government & Voters
Legislative Districts
US Congressional	7, 12
State Legislative	23-24

Registered Voters, November 2006
Total	78,616
Democratic	9,749
Republican	28,427
Unaffiliated	40,411

County Officials, 2008
County Executive	NA
County Administrator	Cynthia J. Yard
Clerk	Mary Melfi
County Treasurer	Charles Balogh
Tax Administrator	Athan Efstathiou
Surrogate	Susan Hoffman
Prosecutor	J. Patrick Barnes
Roads, Bridges & Eng	John P. Glynn
Planning Dir	Sue Dziamara
Sheriff	Deborah Trout
Fire Marshal	George F. Wagner

County School District
10 Court St, PO Box 2900
Flemington, NJ 08822
908-788-1414

Superintendent	Frank Dragotta (Int)
Number of districts	31

Housing & Construction
Housing Units, 2006**
Total	48,540
Single family units	37,651
Multiple family units	10,629
Owner-occupied units	39,999
Renter-occupied units	5,429
Vacant units	3,112
Median rent	$1,045
Median SF home value	$475,300

Permits for New Residential Construction
	Units	Value
Total, 2006	350	$73,999,188
Single family	305	$72,628,625
Total, 2007	316	$55,281,128
Single family	211	$50,031,128

Real Property Valuation, 2007†
	Parcels	Valuation
Total	56,014	21,270,654,277
Vacant	3,894	395,874,176
Residential	41,199	16,342,308,285
Farm land	5,288	51,630,248
Farm homestead	3,260	1,567,752,000
Non-residential	2,373	2,913,089,568
Commercial	2,096	2,335,454,438
Industrial	155	443,136,650
Apartments	122	134,498,480

Taxes†
	2005	2006	2007
Net valuation taxable	$17,298,026,128	$18,428,098,995	$21,326,236,051
State equalized value	$21,163,094,853	$23,523,607,658	24,628,614,688

Public Safety
Police Officers, 2006
County officers	45
Sheriff's department	26
Prosecutors	19
Municipal police	175

Crime
	2005	2006
Total crimes	1,198	1,130
Violent	75	82
Murder	6	0
Rape	3	7
Robbery	7	14
Aggravated assault	59	61
Non-violent	1,123	1,048
Burglary	207	216
Larceny	852	780
Vehicle theft	64	52
Domestic violence	619	489
Arson	7	13
Total crime rate	9.2	8.7
Violent	0.6	0.6
Non-violent	8.7	8.0

Public Library
Hunterdon County Library
314 State Route 12, Bldg 3
Flemington, NJ 08822
(908) 788-1444

Director ... Mark Titus

Library statistics, 2006
Population served ... 112,726

	Total	Per capita
Revenues	$7,054,381	$62.58
Expenditures	$5,973,091	$52.99
Holdings	459,749	4.08
Circulation	953,015	8.45
Annual visits	567,012	5.03

Registered borrowers	119,556
Reference transactions	39,474
Hours open weekly	75
Full-time/total staff	19/53
Interlibrary loans Provided/received	566/2,185
Internet terminals	24
Annual users	42,017

State Income Tax, 2005
Number of returns	53,542
Increase from previous year	4.0%
Total income	$5,489,632,000
Per capita	$46,397
Increase from previous year	6.2%
Net charged tax	$199,364,000
Per capita	$1,685
Average taxable income	$93,516
Average income tax	$3,724

County Finance
State Aid Programs, 2008†
Total aid	$17,233,621
CMPTRA	870,566
Energy tax receipts	15,956,451
Garden State Trust	384,984

General Budget, 2007†
Total tax levy	$453,735,989
County levy	84,309,149
County taxes	70,858,000
County library	5,807,149
County health	0
County open space	7,644,000
School levy	312,809,932
Muni. levy	56,616,907
Misc. revenues	70,662,146

Mercer County

Demographics & Socio-Economic Characteristics
(2006 American Community Survey, except as noted)

Population
1990*	325,824
2000*	350,761
2006	367,605
Male	180,544
Female	187,061
2007 (estimate)*	365,449
Population density	1617.7

Race & Hispanic Origin, 2006
Race
White	241,856
Black/African American	72,257
American Indian/Alaska Native	760
Asian	30,494
Native Hawaiian/Pacific Islander	499
Two or more races	4,956
Hispanic origin, total	45,203
Mexican	5,719
Puerto Rican	15,313
Cuban	853
Other Hispanic	23,318

Age & Nativity, 2006
Under 5 years	22,261
18 years and over	282,821
21 years and over	265,503
65 years and over	43,608
85 years and over	5,956
Median age	36.9
Native-born	296,222
Foreign-born	71,383

Educational Attainment, 2006
Population 25 years and over	243,186
Less than 9th grade	6.0%
High school grad or higher	85.2%
Bachelor's degree or higher	38.8%
Graduate degree	17.3%

Households, 2006
Total households	127,216
With persons under 18	46,179
With persons over 65	30,519
Family households	86,654
Single-person households	33,491
Persons per household	2.78
Persons per family	3.36

Income & Poverty, 2006
Per capita income	$33,719
Median household income	$65,305
Median family income	$78,248
Persons in poverty	8.4%
H'holds receiving public assistance	2,526
H'holds receiving social security	34,220

Labor & Employment, 2006*
Total civilian labor force	201,800
Unemployment rate	4.2%

Employed persons 16 years and over by occupation, 2006
Managers & professionals	78,250
Service occupations	26,036
Sales & office occupations	44,043
Farming, fishing & forestry	346
Construction & maintenance	11,973
Production & transportation	15,879
Self-employed persons	10,031

Civilian Labor Force Projections*
2009	195,300
2014	201,600
2020	208,500
2025	213,100

*US Census Bureau
**2006 American Community Survey
*** New Jersey Department of Labor
† sum of all municipalities in county

See Introduction for an explanation of all data sources.

General Information
Mercer County
PO Box 8068
640 S Broad St
Trenton, NJ 08650
609-989-0318

Website	www.mercercounty.org
Year of formation	1838
Land/water area (sq. miles)	225.9/2.9
Class	Second
Government form	County Executive Plan
Number of Freeholders	7
Number of municipalities	13

Government & Voters

Legislative Districts
US Congressional	4, 12
State Legislative	12, 14-15, 30

Registered Voters, November 2006
Total	200,996
Democratic	50,898
Republican	26,343
Unaffiliated	123,668

County Officials, 2008
County Executive	Brian Hughes
Manager	Andrew A. Mair
Clerk	Paula Sollami-Covello
Finance Dir	David Miller
Tax Administrator	Martin Guhl
Surrogate	Diane Gerofsky
Prosecutor	Joseph L. Bocchini
Public Works Dir	NA
Planning/Dev Dir	NA
Sheriff	Kevin Larkin
Fire Marshal	George Lenhardt

County School District
1075 Old Trenton Rd
Trenton, NJ 08690
609-588-5884

Superintendent	(vacant)
Number of districts	11

Housing & Construction

Housing Units, 2006**
Total	139,888
Single family units	70,914
Multiple family units	68,394
Owner-occupied units	87,262
Renter-occupied units	39,954
Vacant units	12,672
Median rent	$958
Median SF home value	$314,300

Permits for New Residential Construction
	Units	Value
Total, 2006	847	$85,844,566
Single family	578	$70,544,291
Total, 2007	719	$76,162,024
Single family	465	$74,582,526

Real Property Valuation, 2007†
	Parcels	Valuation
Total	120,292	30,889,088,726
Vacant	6,442	628,451,279
Residential	105,484	22,266,730,390
Farm land	1,215	14,419,151
Farm homestead	580	386,887,750
Non-residential	6,571	7,592,600,156
Commercial	5,937	5,887,706,356
Industrial	286	969,111,000
Apartments	348	735,782,800

Taxes†
	2005	2006	2007
Net valuation taxable	$22,632,242,082	$29,175,585,406	$30,967,508,196
State equalized value	$38,497,371,705	$43,981,279,686	47,292,222,593

Public Safety

Police Officers, 2006
County officers	235
Sheriff's department	128
Prosecutors	107
Municipal police	931

Crime
	2005	2006
Total crimes	11,265	9,987
Violent	1,994	1,783
Murder	34	21
Rape	55	67
Robbery	1,011	867
Aggravated assault	894	828
Non-violent	9,271	8,204
Burglary	1,978	1,869
Larceny	6,214	5,510
Vehicle theft	1,079	825
Domestic violence	3,304	3,136
Arson	50	64
Total crime rate	30.8	27.3
Violent	5.5	4.9
Non-violent	25.4	22.4

Public Library
Mercer County Library
2751 Brunswick Pike
Lawrenceville, NJ 08648
(609) 989-6807

Director............Ellen O'Shea Brown

Library statistics, 2006
Population served.................143,288

	Total	Per capita
Revenues	$11,142,128	$77.76
Expenditures	$11,142,128	$77.76
Holdings	790,563	5.52
Circulation	1,635,406	11.41
Annual visits	1,125,704	7.86

Registered borrowers	63,576
Reference transactions	129,534
Hours open weekly	66
Full-time/total staff	47/114
Interlibrary loans Provided/received	3,823/2,385
Internet terminals	123
Annual users	740,529

State Income Tax, 2005
Number of returns	145,376
Increase from previous year	4.6%
Total income	$11,589,213,000
Per capita	$38,632
Increase from previous year	10.9%
Net charged tax	$387,649,000
Per capita	$1,292
Average taxable income	$73,165
Average income tax	$2,667

County Finance

State Aid Programs, 2008†
Total aid	$108,576,578
CMPTRA	59,977,944
Energy tax receipts	48,520,549
Garden State Trust	77,380

General Budget, 2007†
Total tax levy	$930,495,056
County levy	217,017,465
County taxes	193,980,795
County library	9,733,362
County health	0
County open space	13,303,308
School levy	505,877,823
Muni. levy	207,599,768
Misc. revenues	299,251,742

Middlesex County

Demographics & Socio-Economic Characteristics
(2006 American Community Survey, except as noted)

Population
1990*	671,780
2000*	750,162
2006	786,971
Male	388,591
Female	398,380
2007 (estimate)*	788,629
Population density	2546.4

Race & Hispanic Origin, 2006
Race
- White: 478,685
- Black/African American: 73,615
- American Indian/Alaska Native: 1,401
- Asian: 142,423
- Native Hawaiian/Pacific Islander: 0
- Two or more races: 14,697
- Hispanic origin, total: 132,920
  - Mexican: 21,481
  - Puerto Rican: 45,048
  - Cuban: 7,420
  - Other Hispanic: 58,971

Age & Nativity, 2006
- Under 5 years: 51,925
- 18 years and over: 603,021
- 21 years and over: 569,331
- 65 years and over: 94,090
- 85 years and over: 13,265
- Median age: 36.9
- Native-born: 565,033
- Foreign-born: 221,938

Educational Attainment, 2006
- Population 25 years and over: 527,538
- Less than 9th grade: 5.8%
- High school grad or higher: 86.5%
- Bachelor's degree or higher: 37.4%
- Graduate degree: 14.7%

Households, 2006
- Total households: 270,292
  - With persons under 18: 104,906
  - With persons over 65: 64,022
  - Family households: 195,172
  - Single-person households: 61,406
- Persons per household: 2.80
- Persons per family: 3.30

Income & Poverty, 2006
- Per capita income: $30,331
- Median household income: $72,669
- Median family income: $84,431
- Persons in poverty: 7.2%
- H'holds receiving public assistance: 3,968
- H'holds receiving social security: 66,947

Labor & Employment, 2006*
- Total civilian labor force: 427,700
- Unemployment rate: 4.3%

Employed persons 16 years and over by occupation, 2006
- Managers & professionals: 162,973
- Service occupations: 44,983
- Sales & office occupations: 114,996
- Farming, fishing & forestry: 69
- Construction & maintenance: 26,424
- Production & transportation: 46,827
- Self-employed persons: 14,815

Civilian Labor Force Projections*
- 2009: 423,900
- 2014: 432,600
- 2020: 447,600
- 2025: 460,600

*US Census Bureau
**2006 American Community Survey
*** New Jersey Department of Labor
† sum of all municipalities in county

General Information
Middlesex County
PO Box 1110
75 Bayard St
New Brunswick, NJ 08901
732-745-3000

- Website: www.co.middlesex.nj.us
- Year of formation: 1683
- Land/water area (sq. miles): 309.7/12.8
- Class: Second
- Government form: Freeholder Board
- Number of Freeholders: 7
- Number of municipalities: 25

Government & Voters
Legislative Districts
- US Congressional: 6-7, 12-13
- State Legislative: 13-14, 17-19, 22

Registered Voters, November 2006
- Total: 401,933
  - Democratic: 112,294
  - Republican: 43,678
  - Unaffiliated: 245,802

County Officials, 2008
- County Executive: NA
- Manager: Walter DeAngelo
- Clerk: Elaine Flynn
- Finance Dir: Albert P. Kuchinskas
- Tax Administrator: Irving Verosloff
- Surrogate: Kevin J. Hoagland
- Prosecutor: Bruce Kaplan
- Public Works Dir: David Campion
- Planning/Dev Dir: George Ververides
- Sheriff: Joseph C. Spicuzzo
- Fire Marshal: Michael Gallagher

County School District
1460 Livingston Ave, Bldg 400, 2nd Floor
North Brunswick, NJ 08902
732-249-2900

- Superintendent: Patrick Piegari
- Number of districts: 26

Housing & Construction
Housing Units, 2006**
- Total: 285,527
  - Single family units: 151,927
  - Multiple family units: 131,489
  - Owner-occupied units: 181,635
  - Renter-occupied units: 88,657
  - Vacant units: 15,235
  - Median rent: $1,087
  - Median SF home value: $365,000

Permits for New Residential Construction
	Units	Value
Total, 2006	2,567	$257,214,501
Single family	1,177	$180,170,204
Total, 2007	1,595	$150,604,078
Single family	873	$143,879,818

Real Property Valuation, 2007†
	Parcels	Valuation
Total	232,486	48,280,583,026
Vacant	13,936	1,175,083,302
Residential	206,027	31,507,022,624
Farm land	1,024	17,050,400
Farm homestead	405	105,311,500
Non-residential	11,094	15,476,115,200
Commercial	8,137	6,859,196,400
Industrial	2,132	6,291,600,000
Apartments	825	2,325,318,800

Taxes†
	2005	2006	2007
Net valuation taxable	$43,857,896,282	$46,444,919,492	$48,392,649,994
State equalized value	$88,317,049,132	$101,445,813,851	108,929,963,424

Public Safety
Police Officers, 2006
- County officers: 316
  - Sheriff's department: 186
  - Prosecutors: 130
- Municipal police: 1,638

Crime
	2005	2006
Total crimes	17,587	17,789
Violent	1,663	1,717
Murder	13	18
Rape	92	85
Robbery	639	641
Aggravated assault	919	973
Non-violent	15,924	16,072
Burglary	2,974	3,111
Larceny	11,391	11,476
Vehicle theft	1,559	1,485
Domestic violence	4,781	5,026
Arson	104	97
Total crime rate	22.4	22.5
Violent	2.1	2.2
Non-violent	20.3	20.4

Public Library
No County Library
(Library statistics are the sum of all municipal libraries in the county)

Library statistics, 2006†
- Population served: 748,337

	Total	Per capita
Revenues	$39,251,426	$52.45
Expenditures	$37,878,698	$50.62
Holdings	2,707,835	3.62
Circulation	5,463,634	7.30
Annual visits	4,683,314	6.26

- Registered borrowers: 350,355
- Reference transactions: 968,647
- Hours open weekly: NA
- Number of libraries: 24
- Full-time/total staff: 123/299
- Interlibrary loans
  - Provided/received: 51,104/55,033
- Internet terminals: 358
  - Annual users: 812,708

State Income Tax, 2005
- Number of returns: 330,194
  - Increase from previous year: 4.1%
- Total income: $20,457,080,000
  - Per capita: $29,393
  - Increase from previous year: 5.6%
- Net charged tax: $497,991,000
  - Per capita: $716
- Average taxable income: $55,673
- Average income tax: $1,508

County Finance
State Aid Programs, 2008†
- Total aid: $147,027,315
  - CMPTRA: 43,429,230
  - Energy tax receipts: 103,483,357
  - Garden State Trust: 101,521

General Budget, 2007†
- Total tax levy: $1,934,847,423
  - County levy: 293,236,400
    - County taxes: 262,500,000
    - County library: 0
    - County health: 0
    - County open space: 30,736,400
  - School levy: 1,176,205,385
  - Muni. levy: 465,405,638
- Misc. revenues: 425,554,467

Monmouth County

Demographics & Socio-Economic Characteristics
(2006 American Community Survey, except as noted)

Population
1990*	553,124
2000*	615,301
2006	635,285
Male	310,818
Female	324,467
2007 (estimate)*	642,030
Population density	1360.5

Race & Hispanic Origin, 2006
Race
- White... 523,224
- Black/African American... 48,488
- American Indian/Alaska Native... 1,393
- Asian... 32,998
- Native Hawaiian/Pacific Islander... 67
- Two or more races... 7,869
- Hispanic origin, total... 51,394
  - Mexican... 21,730
  - Puerto Rican... 16,227
  - Cuban... 1,403
  - Other Hispanic... 12,034

Age & Nativity, 2006
- Under 5 years... 37,990
- 18 years and over... 480,565
- 21 years and over... 455,893
- 65 years and over... 80,105
- 85 years and over... 11,353
- Median age... 39.8
- Native-born... 554,899
- Foreign-born... 80,386

Educational Attainment, 2006
- Population 25 years and over... 426,283
- Less than 9th grade... 3.3%
- High school grad or higher... 90.5%
- Bachelor's degree or higher... 39.3%
- Graduate degree... 14.8%

Households, 2006
- Total households... 229,938
  - With persons under 18... 82,883
  - With persons over 65... 56,544
  - Family households... 160,906
  - Single-person households... 58,203
- Persons per household... 2.72
- Persons per family... 3.31

Income & Poverty, 2006
- Per capita income... $36,767
- Median household income... $77,160
- Median family income... $94,866
- Persons in poverty... 5.8%
- H'holds receiving public assistance... 2,435
- H'holds receiving social security... 63,329

Labor & Employment, 2006***
- Total civilian labor force... 332,900
- Unemployment rate... 4.1%

Employed persons 16 years and over by occupation, 2006
- Managers & professionals... 133,281
- Service occupations... 47,313
- Sales & office occupations... 88,521
- Farming, fishing & forestry... 535
- Construction & maintenance... 24,895
- Production & transportation... 21,103
- Self-employed persons... 18,718

Civilian Labor Force Projections***
2009	339,000
2014	352,200
2020	368,000
2025	382,100

*US Census Bureau
**2006 American Community Survey
*** New Jersey Department of Labor
† sum of all municipalities in county

See Introduction for an explanation of all data sources.

General Information
Monmouth County
1 E Main St
Hall of Records
Freehold, NJ 07728
732-431-7310

- Website... www.visitmonmouth.com
- Year of formation... 1683
- Land/water area (sq. miles)... 471.9/193.2
- Class... Fifth
- Government form... Freeholder Board
- Number of Freeholders... 5
- Number of municipalities... 53

Government & Voters

Legislative Districts
- US Congressional... 4, 12
- State Legislative... 10-13, 30

Registered Voters, November 2006
- Total... 403,276
  - Democratic... 66,318
  - Republican... 77,326
  - Unaffiliated... 259,484

County Officials, 2008
- County Executive... NA
- County Administrator... Robert Czech
- Clerk... M. Claire French
- Finance Dir... Mark Acker
- Tax Administrator... Matthew Clark
- Surrogate... Rosemarie Peters
- Prosecutor... Luis Valentin
- Public Works Dir... John W. Tobia
- Planning/Dev Dir... NA
- Sheriff... Kim Guadagno
- Fire Marshal... Tim Smith

County School District
3680 State Highway 9, PO Box 1264
Freehold, NJ 07728
732-431-7816

- Superintendent... Carole K. Morris
- Number of districts... 57

Housing & Construction

Housing Units, 2006**
- Total... 253,372
  - Single family units... 168,320
  - Multiple family units... 81,938
  - Owner-occupied units... 177,418
  - Renter-occupied units... 52,520
  - Vacant units... 23,434
  - Median rent... $1,010
  - Median SF home value... $444,800

Permits for New Residential Construction
	Units	Value
Total, 2006	2,820	$352,945,169
Single family	1,517	$317,505,946
Total, 2007	2,105	$275,149,577
Single family	1,136	$266,816,196

Real Property Valuation, 2007†
	Parcels	Valuation
Total	235,366	87,161,767,972
Vacant	17,163	1,890,326,965
Residential	203,560	71,996,304,967
Farm land	2,705	28,791,400
Farm homestead	1,521	648,209,100
Non-residential	10,417	12,598,135,540
Commercial	8,897	9,933,979,740
Industrial	510	1,054,549,300
Apartments	1,010	1,609,606,500

Taxes†
	2005	2006	2007
Net valuation taxable	$65,515,271,859	$70,829,766,536	$87,315,329,030
State equalized value	$103,449,533,181	$117,866,660,069	126,074,912,133

Public Safety

Police Officers, 2006
- County officers... 536
  - Sheriff's department... 460
  - Prosecutors... 76
- Municipal police... 1,511

Crime
	2005	2006
Total crimes	13,826	13,993
Violent	1,240	1,431
Murder	8	16
Rape	76	71
Robbery	415	554
Aggravated assault	741	790
Non-violent	12,586	12,562
Burglary	2,157	2,192
Larceny	9,744	9,748
Vehicle theft	685	622
Domestic violence	5,353	5,403
Arson	55	89
Total crime rate	21.7	22.0
Violent	1.9	2.3
Non-violent	19.8	19.8

Public Library
Monmouth County Library
125 Symmes Drive
Manalapan, NJ 07726
(732) 431-7235

Director... Kenneth Sheinbaum

Library statistics, 2006
- Population served... 399,613

	Total	Per capita
Revenues	$13,614,168	$34.07
Expenditures	$11,921,555	$29.83
Holdings	1,366,533	3.42
Circulation	3,179,369	7.96
Annual visits	2,235,563	5.59

- Registered borrowers... 207,196
- Reference transactions... 470,404
- Hours open weekly... 68
- Full-time/total staff... 36/117
- Interlibrary loans
  - Provided/received... 8,852/5,810
- Internet terminals... 78
  - Annual users... 253,864

State Income Tax, 2005
- Number of returns... 266,809
  - Increase from previous year... 3.3%
- Total income... $23,652,126,000
  - Per capita... $41,405
  - Increase from previous year... 7.3%
- Net charged tax... $748,355,000
  - Per capita... $1,310
- Average taxable income... $81,043
- Average income tax... $2,805

County Finance

State Aid Programs, 2008†
- Total aid... $99,044,356
  - CMPTRA... 23,060,566
  - Energy tax receipts... 75,796,070
  - Garden State Trust... 137,712

General Budget, 2007†
- Total tax levy... $1,808,566,267
  - County levy... 317,688,375
    - County taxes... 286,504,000
    - County library... 11,527,743
    - County health... 1,752,756
    - County open space... 17,903,876
  - School levy... 1,096,824,514
  - Muni. levy... 394,053,378
- Misc. revenues... 345,569,989

©2008 Information Publications, Inc. All rights reserved. Photocopying prohibited. For additional copies, contact the publisher at www.informationpublications.com or (877)544-INFO (4636)

The New Jersey Municipal Data Book

Morris County

Demographics & Socio-Economic Characteristics
(2006 American Community Survey, except as noted)

Population
1990*	421,353
2000*	470,212
2006	493,160
Male	243,241
Female	249,919
2007 (estimate)*	488,475
Population density	1041.5

Race & Hispanic Origin, 2006
Race
- White 412,738
- Black/African American 15,151
- American Indian/Alaska Native 115
- Asian 42,389
- Native Hawaiian/Pacific Islander ... 2,255
- Two or more races 4,786

Hispanic origin, total 50,461
- Mexican 3,773
- Puerto Rican 11,491
- Cuban 1,166
- Other Hispanic 34,031

Age & Nativity, 2006
- Under 5 years 30,774
- 18 years and over 373,969
- 21 years and over 355,807
- 65 years and over 61,171
- 85 years and over 7,871
- Median age 40.0
- Native-born 400,758
- Foreign-born 92,402

Educational Attainment, 2006
- Population 25 years and over 334,910
- Less than 9th grade 2.8%
- High school grad or higher 92.8%
- Bachelor's degree or higher 47.1%
- Graduate degree 18.9%

Households, 2006
- Total households 174,256
  - With persons under 18 66,851
  - With persons over 65 40,584
  - Family households 128,209
  - Single-person households 39,555
- Persons per household 2.78
- Persons per family 3.30

Income & Poverty, 2006
- Per capita income $43,085
- Median household income $89,587
- Median family income $103,267
- Persons in poverty 3.9%
- H'holds receiving public assistance ... 1,872
- H'holds receiving social security ... 44,613

Labor & Employment, 2006***
- Total civilian labor force 274,000
  - Unemployment rate 3.3%

Employed persons 16 years and over by occupation, 2006
- Managers & professionals 121,658
- Service occupations 32,555
- Sales & office occupations 65,678
- Farming, fishing & forestry 282
- Construction & maintenance 16,823
- Production & transportation 17,746
- Self-employed persons 13,846

Civilian Labor Force Projections***
- 2009 275,400
- 2014 287,300
- 2020 301,500
- 2025 312,400

*US Census Bureau
**2006 American Community Survey
*** New Jersey Department of Labor
† sum of all municipalities in county

General Information
Morris County
PO Box 900
Morristown, NJ 07963
973-285-6000

- Website .... www.co.morris.nj.us
- Year of formation 1739
- Land/water area (sq. miles) ... 469.0/12.3
- Class .... Second
- Government form ...... Freeholder Board
- Number of Freeholders 7
- Number of municipalities 39

Government & Voters
Legislative Districts
- US Congressional 11
- State Legislative 26, 34-36, 40

Registered Voters, November 2006
- Total 298,824
  - Democratic 41,692
  - Republican 98,711
  - Unaffiliated 158,328

County Officials, 2008
- County Executive .... NA
- County Administrator ...... John Bonanni
- Clerk .... Joan Bramhall
- Finance Dir .... Glenn Roe
- Tax Administrator .... Ralph Meloro IV
- Surrogate .... John Pecoraro
- Prosecutor .... Robert A. Bianchi
- Public Works Dir ..... Stephen Hammond
- Planning, Dev & Tech Dir .... Walter Krich
- Sheriff .... Edward Rochford
- Fire Marshal .... Philip Wilk

County School District
Court House, PO Box 900
Morristown, NJ 07963
973-285-8332

- Superintendent .... Kathleen C. Serafino
- Number of districts 41

Housing & Construction
Housing Units, 2006**
- Total 183,501
  - Single family units 121,238
  - Multiple family units 61,810
  - Owner-occupied units 133,762
  - Renter-occupied units 40,494
  - Vacant units 9,245
  - Median rent $1,121
  - Median SF home value $488,900

Permits for New Residential Construction
	Units	Value
Total, 2006	1,670	$301,462,308
Single family	791	$202,635,791
Total, 2007	1,077	$175,975,134
Single family	682	$168,513,784

Real Property Valuation, 2007†
	Parcels	Valuation
Total	168,641	71,944,871,498
Vacant	9,980	1,334,469,750
Residential	148,375	54,814,294,479
Farm land	1,410	13,183,558
Farm homestead	719	574,707,200
Non-residential	8,157	15,208,216,511
Commercial	6,760	10,831,009,211
Industrial	1,003	2,557,634,300
Apartments	394	1,819,573,000

Taxes†
	2005	2006	2007
Net valuation taxable	$62,177,814,928	$70,984,491,271	$72,078,275,433
State equalized value	$88,095,915,466	$97,240,364,598	101,650,110,068

Public Safety
Police Officers, 2006
- County officers 370
  - Sheriff's department 267
  - Prosecutors 71
- Municipal police 1,089

Crime	2005	2006
Total crimes	6,953	6,908
Violent	486	450
Murder	2	1
Rape	31	28
Robbery	134	129
Aggravated assault	319	292
Non-violent	6,467	6,458
Burglary	1,360	1,210
Larceny	4,756	4,820
Vehicle theft	351	428
Domestic violence	2,461	2,599
Arson	39	22
Total crime rate	14.2	14.1
Violent	1.0	0.9
Non-violent	13.2	13.2

Public Library
Morris County Library
30 East Hanover Avenue
Whippany, NJ 07981
(973) 285-6934

- Director .... Joanne Kares

Library statistics, 2006
- Population served 470,212

	Total	Per capita
Revenues	$7,721,527	$16.42
Expenditures	$7,737,301	$16.45
Holdings	266,785	0.57
Circulation	587,937	1.25
Annual visits	268,126	0.57

- Registered borrowers 1,970
- Reference transactions 81,635
- Hours open weekly 69
- Full-time/total staff 27/78
- Interlibrary loans
  - Provided/received 59,357/146,209
- Internet terminals 76
- Annual users 204,374

State Income Tax, 2005
- Number of returns 211,230
  - Increase from previous year 3.5%
- Total income $22,558,008,000
  - Per capita $49,686
  - Increase from previous year 9.0%
- Net charged tax $824,235,000
  - Per capita $1,815
- Average taxable income $98,518
- Average income tax $3,902

County Finance
State Aid Programs, 2008†
- Total aid $60,957,692
  - CMPTRA 13,144,521
  - Energy tax receipts 46,489,830
  - Garden State Trust 735,825

General Budget, 2007†
- Total tax levy $1,608,353,861
  - County levy 232,661,665
    - County taxes 186,075,742
    - County library 0
    - County health 0
    - County open space 46,585,923
  - School levy 998,594,293
  - Muni. levy 377,097,903
- Misc. revenues 255,035,847

Ocean County

Demographics & Socio-Economic Characteristics
(2006 American Community Survey, except as noted)

Population
1990*	433,203
2000*	510,916
2006	562,335
Male	267,917
Female	294,418
2007 (estimate)*	565,493
Population density	888.7

Race & Hispanic Origin, 2006
Race
White	509,589
Black/African American	18,501
American Indian/Alaska Native	626
Asian	9,244
Native Hawaiian/Pacific Islander	296
Two or more races	6,148
Hispanic origin, total	36,822
Mexican	13,996
Puerto Rican	12,338
Cuban	962
Other Hispanic	9,526

Age & Nativity, 2006
Under 5 years	36,114
18 years and over	435,127
21 years and over	417,671
65 years and over	116,212
85 years and over	19,142
Median age	40.5
Native-born	519,518
Foreign-born	42,817

Educational Attainment, 2006
Population 25 years and over	393,009
Less than 9th grade	3.3%
High school grad or higher	88.0%
Bachelor's degree or higher	24.4%
Graduate degree	7.5%

Households, 2006
Total households	221,630
With persons under 18	68,716
With persons over 65	81,276
Family households	152,567
Single-person households	59,057
Persons per household	2.51
Persons per family	3.06

Income & Poverty, 2006
Per capita income	$27,638
Median household income	$54,820
Median family income	$67,911
Persons in poverty	8.8%
H'holds receiving public assistance	3,349
H'holds receiving social security	89,228

Labor & Employment, 2006***
Total civilian labor force	257,200
Unemployment rate	5.0%

Employed persons 16 years and over by occupation, 2006
Managers & professionals	84,909
Service occupations	40,446
Sales & office occupations	68,034
Farming, fishing & forestry	371
Construction & maintenance	31,035
Production & transportation	21,180
Self-employed persons	15,407

Civilian Labor Force Projections***
2009	272,400
2014	292,900
2020	307,200
2025	329,100

*US Census Bureau
**2006 American Community Survey
*** New Jersey Department of Labor
† sum of all municipalities in county

See Introduction for an explanation of all data sources.

General Information
Ocean County
PO Box 2191
Toms River, NJ 08754
732-244-2121

Website	www.co.ocean.nj.us
Year of formation	1850
Land/water area (sq. miles)	636.3/279.6
Class	Fifth
Government form	Freeholder Board
Number of Freeholders	5
Number of municipalities	33

Government & Voters

Legislative Districts
US Congressional	3-4
State Legislative	9-10, 30

Registered Voters, November 2006
Total	351,765
Democratic	48,975
Republican	82,372
Unaffiliated	220,332

County Officials, 2008
County Executive	NA
Manager	Alan W. Avery Jr
Clerk	Carl W. Block
Finance Dir	Julie N. Tarrant
Tax Admin	Lawrence Ozzie Vituscka
Surrogate	Jeffrey W. Moran
Prosecutor	Marlene Lynch Ford
Public Works Dir	William Santos
Planning/Dev Dir	David J. McKeon
Sheriff	William Polhemus
Fire Marshal	Daniel Mulligan

County School District
212 Washington St
Toms River, NJ 08753
732-929-2078

Superintendent	Bruce Greenfield
Number of districts	30

Housing & Construction

Housing Units, 2006**
Total	271,460
Single family units	203,635
Multiple family units	61,270
Owner-occupied units	183,953
Renter-occupied units	37,677
Vacant units	49,830
Median rent	$1,151
Median SF home value	$310,800

Permits for New Residential Construction
	Units	Value
Total, 2006	2,114	$341,607,209
Single family	2,079	$337,301,893
Total, 2007	2,145	$295,907,461
Single family	1,531	$281,090,908

Real Property Valuation, 2007†
	Parcels	Valuation
Total	274,833	66,962,225,829
Vacant	33,522	2,427,275,340
Residential	233,306	57,231,565,760
Farm land	482	5,298,527
Farm homestead	242	84,545,800
Non-residential	7,281	7,213,540,402
Commercial	6,523	5,369,591,202
Industrial	399	795,642,800
Apartments	359	1,048,306,400

Taxes†
	2005	2006	2007
Net valuation taxable	$52,045,082,824	$60,271,799,283	$67,050,661,857
State equalized value	$87,967,181,739	$101,281,498,360	107,636,225,899

Public Safety

Police Officers, 2006
County officers	200
Sheriff's department	128
Prosecutors	72
Municipal police	1,129

Crime
	2005	2006
Total crimes	10,840	11,470
Violent	772	803
Murder	2	9
Rape	49	47
Robbery	192	261
Aggravated assault	529	486
Non-violent	10,068	10,667
Burglary	1,777	2,142
Larceny	7,832	8,024
Vehicle theft	459	501
Domestic violence	5,591	5,733
Arson	82	91
Total crime rate	19.6	20.5
Violent	1.4	1.4
Non-violent	18.2	19.1

Public Library
Ocean County Library
101 Washington Street
Toms River, NJ 08753
(732) 349-6200

Director............Elaine H. McConnell

Library statistics, 2006
Population served 509,638

	Total	Per capita
Revenues	$28,066,096	$55.07
Expenditures	$27,935,381	$54.81
Holdings	1,209,656	2.37
Circulation	4,635,351	9.10
Annual visits	3,216,465	6.31

Registered borrowers	329,268
Reference transactions	1,495,871
Hours open weekly	68
Full-time/total staff	102/279
Interlibrary loans Provided/received	10,050/4,555
Internet terminals	205
Annual users	176,231

State Income Tax, 2005
Number of returns	234,630
Increase from previous year	5.3%
Total income	$12,495,737,000
Per capita	$25,509
Increase from previous year	8.4%
Net charged tax	$322,580,000
Per capita	$659
Average taxable income	$46,661
Average income tax	$1,375

County Finance

State Aid Programs, 2008†
Total aid	$66,066,547
CMPTRA	9,671,339
Energy tax receipts	54,992,523
Garden State Trust	964,499

General Budget, 2007†
Total tax levy	$1,285,823,192
County levy	317,212,648
County taxes	263,560,329
County library	30,615,559
County health	10,650,000
County open space	12,386,760
School levy	649,034,866
Muni. levy	319,575,678
Misc. revenues	249,138,747

The New Jersey Municipal Data Book

Passaic County

Demographics & Socio-Economic Characteristics
(2006 American Community Survey, except as noted)

Population
1990*	453,060
2000*	489,049
2006	497,093
Male	242,105
Female	254,988
2007 (estimate)*	492,115
Population density	2655.8

Race & Hispanic Origin, 2006
Race
White	293,218
Black/African American	60,066
American Indian/Alaska Native	686
Asian	22,959
Native Hawaiian/Pacific Islander	0
Two or more races	8,063
Hispanic origin, total	169,250
Mexican	26,463
Puerto Rican	42,272
Cuban	3,286
Other Hispanic	97,229

Age & Nativity, 2006
Under 5 years	37,153
18 years and over	366,623
21 years and over	345,236
65 years and over	58,149
85 years and over	9,857
Median age	36.0
Native-born	358,408
Foreign-born	138,685

Educational Attainment, 2006
Population 25 years and over	319,492
Less than 9th grade	10.9%
High school grad or higher	80.0%
Bachelor's degree or higher	23.5%
Graduate degree	8.0%

Households, 2006
Total households	159,398
With persons under 18	61,084
With persons over 65	36,818
Family households	113,339
Single-person households	39,087
Persons per household	3.03
Persons per family	3.65

Income & Poverty, 2006
Per capita income	$23,437
Median household income	$49,940
Median family income	$61,803
Persons in poverty	15.0%
H'holds receiving public assistance	3,371
H'holds receiving social security	40,737

Labor & Employment, 2006***
Total civilian labor force	240,300
Unemployment rate	5.6%

Employed persons 16 years and over by occupation, 2006
Managers & professionals	66,223
Service occupations	41,425
Sales & office occupations	67,257
Farming, fishing & forestry	54
Construction & maintenance	18,456
Production & transportation	40,137
Self-employed persons	9,673

Civilian Labor Force Projections***
2009	241,100
2014	246,400
2020	252,000
2025	259,300

*US Census Bureau
**2006 American Community Survey
*** New Jersey Department of Labor
† sum of all municipalities in county

General Information
Passaic County
401 Grand St
Administration Bldg
Paterson, NJ 07505
973-881-4000

Website	www.passaiccountynj.org
Year of formation	1837
Land/water area (sq. miles)	185.3/11.8
Class	Second
Government form	Freeholder Board
Number of Freeholders	7
Number of municipalities	16

Government & Voters

Legislative Districts
US Congressional	5, 8-9, 11
State Legislative	26, 34-36, 40

Registered Voters, November 2006
Total	253,611
Democratic	51,511
Republican	44,110
Unaffiliated	157,990

County Officials, 2008
County Executive	NA
Manager	Anthony DeNova
Clerk	Karen Brown
Finance Dir	Al Dispoto
Tax Administrator	James Murner Jr
Surrogate	Willam Bate
Prosecutor	James Avigliano
Public Works Dir	Steven J. Edmond
Planning/Dev Dir	Michael La Place
Sheriff	Jerry Speziale
Emerg Mgmt Dir	Robert Lyons

County School District
501 River St
Paterson, NJ 07524
973-569-2110

Superintendent	Robert Gilmartin
Number of districts	21

Housing & Construction

Housing Units, 2006**
Total	171,539
Single family units	71,361
Multiple family units	99,682
Owner-occupied units	87,811
Renter-occupied units	71,587
Vacant units	12,141
Median rent	$986
Median SF home value	$406,300

Permits for New Residential Construction
	Units	Value
Total, 2006	850	$94,758,952
Single family	375	$58,465,306
Total, 2007	755	$49,395,242
Single family	264	$46,916,594

Real Property Valuation, 2007†
	Parcels	Valuation
Total	123,748	30,219,744,215
Vacant	6,104	527,836,913
Residential	106,469	21,720,871,708
Farm land	319	959,974
Farm homestead	144	33,831,400
Non-residential	10,712	7,936,244,220
Commercial	8,103	4,921,895,530
Industrial	1,517	2,003,522,590
Apartments	1,092	1,010,826,100

Taxes†
	2005	2006	2007
Net valuation taxable	$21,335,720,331	$21,354,230,409	$30,268,051,426
State equalized value	$45,466,073,584	$51,774,568,393	55,623,705,991

Public Safety

Police Officers, 2006
County officers	777
Sheriff's department	688
Prosecutors	89
Municipal police	1,213

Crime
	2005	2006
Total crimes	13,898	14,249
Violent	2,512	2,666
Murder	29	23
Rape	61	59
Robbery	1,050	1,214
Aggravated assault	1,372	1,370
Non-violent	11,386	11,583
Burglary	2,600	2,761
Larceny	7,042	6,910
Vehicle theft	1,744	1,912
Domestic violence	4,652	4,105
Arson	35	39
Total crime rate	27.8	28.6
Violent	5.0	5.3
Non-violent	22.8	23.2

Public Library
No County Library
(Library statistics are the sum of all municipal libraries in the county)

Library statistics, 2006†
Population served	483,270

	Total	Per capita
Revenues	$16,812,471	$34.79
Expenditures	$15,819,433	$32.73
Holdings	1,286,424	2.66
Circulation	1,680,156	3.48
Annual visits	1,400,605	2.90

Registered borrowers	184,275
Reference transactions	318,959
Hours open weekly	NA
Number of libraries	15
Full-time/total staff	49/167
Interlibrary loans Provided/received	28,041/40,024
Internet terminals	255
Annual users	422,822

State Income Tax, 2005
Number of returns	205,170
Increase from previous year	2.6%
Total income	$10,747,008,000
Per capita	$24,962
Increase from previous year	8.3%
Net charged tax	$268,296,000
Per capita	$623
Average taxable income	$46,426
Average income tax	$1,308

County Finance

State Aid Programs, 2008†
Total aid	$88,069,308
CMPTRA	52,334,039
Energy tax receipts	34,592,159
Garden State Trust	299,132

General Budget, 2007†
Total tax levy	$1,094,192,591
County levy	258,421,280
County taxes	253,177,231
County library	0
County health	0
County open space	5,244,049
School levy	494,542,034
Muni. levy	341,229,278
Misc. revenues	253,918,960

Salem County

Demographics & Socio-Economic Characteristics
(2006 American Community Survey, except as noted)

Population
- 1990* 65,294
- 2000* 64,285
- 2006 66,595
  - Male 32,341
  - Female 34,254
- 2007 (estimate)* 66,016
- Population density 195.4

Race & Hispanic Origin, 2006
Race
- White 53,289
- Black/African American 10,104
- American Indian/Alaska Native .. 146
- Asian 315
- Native Hawaiian/Pacific Islander ... 0
- Two or more races 519
- Hispanic origin, total 3,167
  - Mexican .... NA
  - Puerto Rican .... NA
  - Cuban .... NA
  - Other Hispanic .... NA

Age & Nativity, 2006
- Under 5 years 4,237
- 18 years and over 51,339
- 21 years and over 48,820
- 65 years and over 9,224
- 85 years and over 1,581
- Median age 38.6
- Native-born 64,219
- Foreign-born 2,376

Educational Attainment, 2006
- Population 25 years and over ... 45,398
- Less than 9th grade 4.7%
- High school grad or higher 87.4%
- Bachelor's degree or higher 17.7%
- Graduate degree 4.3%

Households, 2006
- Total households 24,621
  - With persons under 18 8,446
  - With persons over 65 6,496
  - Family households 16,198
  - Single-person households 7,205
- Persons per household 2.67
- Persons per family 3.37

Income & Poverty, 2006
- Per capita income $25,547
- Median household income .. $58,164
- Median family income $70,448
- Persons in poverty 8.9%
- H'holds receiving public assistance .. 824
- H'holds receiving social security .. 7,604

Labor & Employment, 2006*
- Total civilian labor force 32,100
- Unemployment rate 5.0%

Employed persons 16 years and over by occupation, 2006
- Managers & professionals 9,637
- Service occupations 5,392
- Sales & office occupations 8,774
- Farming, fishing & forestry 80
- Construction & maintenance .. 3,607
- Production & transportation .. 4,894
- Self-employed persons 1,388

Civilian Labor Force Projections*
- 2009 32,800
- 2014 33,900
- 2020 35,100
- 2025 36,000

*US Census Bureau
**2006 American Community Survey
***New Jersey Department of Labor
† sum of all municipalities in county

See Introduction for an explanation of all data sources.

General Information
Salem County
94 Market St
Administration Bldg
Salem, NJ 08079
856-335-7510

- Website .... www.salemco.org
- Year of formation 1694
- Land/water area (sq. miles) ... 337.9/34.7
- Class .... Third
- Government form .... Freeholder Board
- Number of Freeholders 7
- Number of municipalities 15

Government & Voters

Legislative Districts
- US Congressional 2
- State Legislative 3

Registered Voters, November 2006
- Total 41,558
  - Democratic 9,391
  - Republican 7,320
  - Unaffiliated 24,838

County Officials, 2008
- County Executive .... NA
- Manager .... Earl Gage
- Clerk .... Gilda Gill
- Finance Dir .... Joanne Bell
- Tax Administrator ...... Linda Stewart
- Surrogate .... Nicki Burke
- Prosecutor .... John Lenahan
- Public Works Dir ..... Jeffrey Ridgeway Sr
- Planning/Dev Dir .... Amanda L. Jensen
- Sheriff .... Charles Miller III
- Fire Marshal .... John Turner Jr

County School District
94 Market St
Salem, NJ 08079
856-339-8611

- Superintendent .... Michael Elwell
- Number of districts 15

Housing & Construction

Housing Units, 2006**
- Total 27,304
  - Single family units 19,065
  - Multiple family units 7,294
  - Owner-occupied units 17,534
  - Renter-occupied units 7,087
  - Vacant units 2,683
  - Median rent $794
  - Median SF home value .. $184,000

Permits for New Residential Construction

	Units	Value
Total, 2006	298	$33,415,324
Single family	197	$23,804,424
Total, 2007	153	$19,550,637
Single family	148	$19,550,637

Real Property Valuation, 2007†

	Parcels	Valuation
Total	31,553	4,023,411,013
Vacant	4,428	103,380,800
Residential	19,907	2,573,431,625
Farm land	4,140	54,306,950
Farm homestead	1,847	356,916,850
Non-residential	1,231	935,374,788
Commercial	1,123	452,348,100
Industrial	50	414,362,788
Apartments	58	68,663,900

Taxes†

	2005	2006	2007
Net valuation taxable	$3,266,149,495	$3,629,370,280	$4,039,863,061
State equalized value	$4,246,589,649	$4,814,299,623	5,268,705,430

Public Safety

Police Officers, 2006
- County officers 150
  - Sheriff's department 133
  - Prosecutors 17
- Municipal police 104

Crime	2005	2006
Total crimes	1,780	1,872
Violent	188	208
Murder	5	2
Rape	5	1
Robbery	56	68
Aggravated assault	122	137
Non-violent	1,592	1,664
Burglary	442	463
Larceny	1,051	1,106
Vehicle theft	99	95
Domestic violence	814	663
Arson	21	22
Total crime rate	27.2	28.2
Violent	2.9	3.1
Non-violent	24.4	25.1

Public Library
No County Library
(Library statistics are the sum of all municipal libraries in the county)

Library statistics, 2006†
- Population served 40,064

	Total	Per capita
Revenues	$348,502	$8.70
Expenditures	$398,426	$9.94
Holdings	96,563	2.41
Circulation	58,848	1.47
Annual visits	37,417	0.93

- Registered borrowers 9,771
- Reference transactions 6,532
- Hours open weekly .... NA
- Number of libraries 5
- Full-time/total staff 1/8
- Interlibrary loans
  - Provided/received 731/1,412
- Internet terminals 13
  - Annual users 11,483

State Income Tax, 2005
- Number of returns 25,945
  - Increase from previous year .. 5.8%
- Total income $1,341,741,000
  - Per capita $24,248
  - Increase from previous year .. 9.3%
- Net charged tax $29,286,000
  - Per capita $529
- Average taxable income $46,163
- Average income tax $1,129

County Finance

State Aid Programs, 2008†
- Total aid $20,634,485
  - CMPTRA 2,697,283
  - Energy tax receipts 17,794,321
  - Garden State Trust 139,826

General Budget, 2007†
- Total tax levy $125,378,480
  - County levy 46,667,551
    - County taxes 45,672,026
    - County library 0
    - County health 0
    - County open space 995,526
  - School levy 63,494,544
  - Muni. levy 15,216,385
- Misc. revenues 52,324,767

The New Jersey Municipal Data Book

Somerset County

Demographics & Socio-Economic Characteristics
(2006 American Community Survey, except as noted)

Population
- 1990* 240,279
- 2000* 297,490
- 2006 324,186
  - Male 159,128
  - Female 165,058
- 2007 (estimate)* 323,552
  - Population density 1061.9

Race & Hispanic Origin, 2006
Race
- White 243,382
- Black/African American 27,536
- American Indian/Alaska Native 532
- Asian 40,655
- Native Hawaiian/Pacific Islander 0
- Two or more races 4,094
- Hispanic origin, total 38,412
  - Mexican 10,853
  - Puerto Rican 7,445
  - Cuban 954
  - Other Hispanic 19,160

Age & Nativity, 2006
- Under 5 years 21,726
- 18 years and over 242,247
- 21 years and over 232,466
- 65 years and over 36,558
- 85 years and over 6,304
  - Median age 39.2
- Native-born 256,189
- Foreign-born 67,997

Educational Attainment, 2006
- Population 25 years and over 219,782
- Less than 9th grade 3.5%
- High school grad or higher 92.6%
- Bachelor's degree or higher 48.4%
- Graduate degree 21.1%

Households, 2006
- Total households 114,164
  - With persons under 18 44,266
  - With persons over 65 25,066
  - Family households 84,065
  - Single-person households 24,715
- Persons per household 2.81
- Persons per family 3.32

Income & Poverty, 2006
- Per capita income $43,407
- Median household income $91,688
- Median family income $105,537
- Persons in poverty 4.4%
- H'holds receiving public assistance ... 1,181
- H'holds receiving social security ... 25,192

Labor & Employment, 2006***
- Total civilian labor force 179,900
  - Unemployment rate 3.5%

Employed persons 16 years and over by occupation, 2006
- Managers & professionals 85,091
- Service occupations 16,199
- Sales & office occupations 43,729
- Farming, fishing & forestry 237
- Construction & maintenance 9,800
- Production & transportation 12,241
- Self-employed persons 7,546

Civilian Labor Force Projections***
- 2009 179,200
- 2014 188,200
- 2020 197,700
- 2025 206,400

*US Census Bureau
**2006 American Community Survey
*** New Jersey Department of Labor
† sum of all municipalities in county

General Information
Somerset County
20 Grove Street
PO Box 3000
Somerville, NJ 08876
908-231-7000

- Website .... www.co.somerset.nj.us
- Year of formation 1688
- Land/water area (sq. miles) 304.7/0.4
- Class .... Second
- Government form .... Freeholder Board
- Number of Freeholders 5
- Number of municipalities 21

Government & Voters
Legislative Districts
- US Congressional 6-7, 11-12
- State Legislative 16-17, 21-22

Registered Voters, November 2006
- Total 167,501
  - Democratic 23,744
  - Republican 39,541
  - Unaffiliated 104,153

County Officials, 2008
- Freeholder Director .... Peter S. Palmer
- County Admin .... Richard E. Williams
- Clerk .... Brett A. Radi
- Finance Dir .... Brian Newman
- Tax Administrator .... William Linville
- Surrogate .... Frank G. Bruno
- Prosecutor .... Wayne J. Forrest
- Public Works Dir ..... Michael J. Amorosa
- Planning Dir .... Robert P. Bzik
- Sheriff .... Frank J. Provenzano
- OEM Director ...... LeRoy Gunzelman III

County School District
92 E Main St, PO Box 3000
Somerville, NJ 08876
908-541-5700

- Superintendent .... Trudy Doyle
- Number of districts 21

Housing & Construction
Housing Units, 2006**
- Total 120,063
  - Single family units 72,324
  - Multiple family units 47,512
  - Owner-occupied units 90,441
  - Renter-occupied units 23,723
  - Vacant units 5,899
  - Median rent $1,163
  - Median SF home value $457,000

Permits for New Residential Construction

	Units	Value
Total, 2006	1,058	$149,647,930
Single family	623	$108,774,149
Total, 2007	915	$120,431,294
Single family	578	$116,130,808

Real Property Valuation, 2007†

	Parcels	Valuation
Total	112,699	54,442,379,557
Vacant	6,088	752,777,200
Residential	99,426	42,463,520,557
Farm land	1,669	15,854,950
Farm homestead	898	1,044,164,200
Non-residential	4,618	10,166,062,650
Commercial	3,747	7,297,135,682
Industrial	650	2,157,179,068
Apartments	221	711,747,900

Taxes†

	2005	2006	2007
Net valuation taxable	$49,036,713,110	$53,183,937,868	$54,524,256,257
State equalized value	$55,171,930,705	$60,444,405,550	62,394,256,799

Public Safety
Police Officers, 2006
- County officers 239
  - Sheriff's department 183
  - Prosecutors 56
- Municipal police 626

Crime

	2005	2006
Total crimes	4,819	4,777
Violent	288	295
Murder	3	4
Rape	25	24
Robbery	137	145
Aggravated assault	123	122
Non-violent	4,531	4,482
Burglary	808	923
Larceny	3,435	3,248
Vehicle theft	288	311
Domestic violence	2,347	2,202
Arson	37	25
Total crime rate	15.2	14.9
Violent	0.9	0.9
Non-violent	14.3	14.0

Public Library
Somerset County Library
1 Vogt Drive
Bridgewater, NJ 08807
(908) 526-4016

- Director .... James M. Hecht

Library statistics, 2006
- Population served 176,402

	Total	Per capita
Revenues	$12,643,845	$71.68
Expenditures	$12,702,699	$72.01
Holdings	979,932	5.56
Circulation	2,443,300	13.85
Annual visits	1,060,418	6.01

- Registered borrowers 113,498
- Reference transactions 178,229
- Hours open weekly 69
- Full-time/total staff 53/128
- Interlibrary loans
  - Provided/received 6,566/4,503
- Internet terminals 113
  - Annual users 213,510

State Income Tax, 2005
- Number of returns 137,600
  - Increase from previous year 4.4%
- Total income $14,868,307,000
  - Per capita $49,951
  - Increase from previous year 7.3%
- Net charged tax $564,421,000
  - Per capita $1,896
- Average taxable income $99,846
- Average income tax $4,102

County Finance
State Aid Programs, 2008†
- Total aid $40,178,563
  - CMPTRA 7,828,882
  - Energy tax receipts 32,202,900
  - Garden State Trust 146,781

General Budget, 2007†
- Total tax levy $1,051,454,285
  - County levy 198,418,728
    - County taxes 167,500,000
    - County library 12,572,758
    - County health 0
    - County open space 18,345,970
  - School levy 660,821,120
  - Muni. levy 192,214,437
- Misc. revenues 158,218,056

Sussex County

Demographics & Socio-Economic Characteristics
(2006 American Community Survey, except as noted)

Population
- 1990*.........................130,943
- 2000*.........................144,166
- 2006..........................153,384
  - Male........................76,255
  - Female......................77,129
- 2007 (estimate)*..............151,478
  - Population density............290.6

Race & Hispanic Origin, 2006
Race
- White.........................144,127
- Black/African American..........2,557
- American Indian/Alaska Native........0
- Asian...........................2,882
- Native Hawaiian/Pacific Islander.....0
- Two or more races...............1,559
- Hispanic origin, total..........8,174
  - Mexican........................619
  - Puerto Rican.................2,396
  - Cuban..........................981
  - Other Hispanic...............4,178

Age & Nativity, 2006
- Under 5 years..................8,388
- 18 years and over.............115,899
- 21 years and over.............109,521
- 65 years and over.............15,059
- 85 years and over..............1,426
  - Median age.....................39.3
- Native-born..................143,981
- Foreign-born...................9,403

Educational Attainment, 2006
- Population 25 years and over..102,402
- Less than 9th grade............2.3%
- High school grad or higher....92.4%
- Bachelor's degree or higher...30.6%
- Graduate degree................10.4%

Households, 2006
- Total households..............54,811
  - With persons under 18......23,435
  - With persons over 65.......10,829
  - Family households..........43,314
  - Single-person households....9,346
- Persons per household...........2.75
- Persons per family..............3.11

Income & Poverty, 2006
- Per capita income...........$32,997
- Median household income.....$78,488
- Median family income........$86,501
- Persons in poverty..............4.8%
- H'holds receiving public assistance....853
- H'holds receiving social security....12,985

Labor & Employment, 2006***
- Total civilian labor force....85,300
  - Unemployment rate..............4.1%

Employed persons 16 years and over by occupation, 2006
- Managers & professionals.....31,694
- Service occupations..........10,228
- Sales & office occupations...24,317
- Farming, fishing & forestry.....277
- Construction & maintenance...9,962
- Production & transportation..6,617
- Self-employed persons........5,308

Civilian Labor Force Projections***
- 2009..........................87,600
- 2014..........................91,200
- 2020..........................96,600
- 2025..........................99,900

*US Census Bureau
**2006 American Community Survey
***New Jersey Department of Labor
† sum of all municipalities in county

See Introduction for an explanation of all data sources.

General Information
Sussex County
One Spring St
Administration Center
Newton, NJ 07860
973-579-0210

- Website..............www.sussex.nj.us
- Year of formation................1753
- Land/water area (sq. miles)....521.3/14.7
- Class............................Third
- Government form......Freeholder Board
- Number of Freeholders...............5
- Number of municipalities...........24

Government & Voters
Legislative Districts
- US Congressional................5, 11
- State Legislative..................24

Registered Voters, November 2006
- Total..........................88,672
  - Democratic...................8,884
  - Republican..................30,178
  - Unaffiliated................49,573

County Officials, 2008
- County Executive..................NA
- County Administrator....John H. Eskilson
- Clerk................Erma Gormley
- Finance Dir.............Bernard A. Re
- Tax Administrator.........Carol Dennis
- Surrogate............Nancy Fitzgibbons
- Prosecutor..............David Weaver
- Public Works Dir....................NA
- Planning/Dev Dir....................NA
- Sheriff................Robert Untig
- Fire Marshal......................NA

County School District
262 White Lake Rd
Sparta, NJ 07871
973-579-6996

- Superintendent..........Barry Worman
- Number of districts................27

Housing & Construction
Housing Units, 2006**
- Total..........................60,086
  - Single family units........48,838
  - Multiple family units......10,432
  - Owner-occupied units.......46,096
  - Renter-occupied units......8,715
  - Vacant units...............5,275
  - Median rent................$1,011
  - Median SF home value.....$332,400

Permits for New Residential Construction
	Units	Value
Total, 2006	603	$105,844,827
Single family	551	$96,887,147
Total, 2007	365	$64,223,469
Single family	326	$64,223,469

Real Property Valuation, 2007†
	Parcels	Valuation
Total	71,937	13,684,997,694
Vacant	9,814	418,601,914
Residential	54,278	11,318,102,014
Farm land	3,538	30,229,684
Farm homestead	1,774	497,170,600
Non-residential	2,533	1,420,893,482
Commercial	2,252	1,199,892,682
Industrial	195	157,424,500
Apartments	86	63,576,300

Taxes†
	2005	2006	2007
Net valuation taxable	$10,669,612,715	$12,207,798,955	$13,720,392,885
State equalized value	$17,141,051,415	$19,481,397,769	20,916,597,014

Public Safety
Police Officers, 2006
- County officers..................149
  - Sheriff's department..........118
  - Prosecutors....................31
- Municipal police................209

Crime
	2005	2006
Total crimes	1,791	1,902
Violent	89	98
Murder	1	2
Rape	7	7
Robbery	5	14
Aggravated assault	76	75
Non-violent	1,702	1,804
Burglary	230	288
Larceny	1,394	1,449
Vehicle theft	78	67
Domestic violence	987	989
Arson	7	15
Total crime rate	11.8	12.4
Violent	0.6	0.6
Non-violent	11.2	11.8

Public Library
Sussex County Library
125 Morris Turnpike
Newton, NJ 07860
(973) 948-3660

- Director..............Stanley Pollakoff

Library statistics, 2006
- Population served..............126,086

	Total	Per capita
Revenues	$4,742,094	$37.61
Expenditures	$4,673,761	$37.07
Holdings	321,551	2.55
Circulation	805,340	6.39
Annual visits	483,391	3.83

- Registered borrowers............60,771
- Reference transactions..........9,485
- Hours open weekly.................65
- Full-time/total staff............13/56
- Interlibrary loans
  - Provided/received........524/3,172
- Internet terminals................55
  - Annual users...............68,344

State Income Tax, 2005
- Number of returns..............61,819
  - Increase from previous year......5.1%
- Total income............$4,400,540,000
  - Per capita..................$32,109
  - Increase from previous year......7.1%
- Net charged tax............$121,579,000
  - Per capita.....................$887
- Average taxable income.........$63,551
- Average income tax.............$1,967

County Finance
State Aid Programs, 2008†
- Total aid..................$14,641,141
  - CMPTRA....................2,532,979
  - Energy tax receipts......10,595,398
  - Garden State Trust..........972,546

General Budget, 2007†
- Total tax levy............$396,335,609
  - County levy.............78,856,195
    - County taxes..........65,685,231
    - County library.........4,610,000
    - County health..........1,641,706
    - County open space......6,940,124
  - School levy...........240,034,170
  - Muni. levy.............77,445,244
- Misc. revenues..............63,101,619

Union County

Demographics & Socio-Economic Characteristics
(2006 American Community Survey, except as noted)

Population
1990*	493,819
2000*	522,541
2006	531,088
Male	258,111
Female	272,977
2007 (estimate)*	524,658
Population density	5079.0

Race & Hispanic Origin, 2006
Race
White	315,418
Black/African American	112,370
American Indian/Alaska Native	928
Asian	24,606
Native Hawaiian/Pacific Islander	563
Two or more races	7,508
Hispanic origin, total	130,477
Mexican	13,952
Puerto Rican	23,249
Cuban	7,896
Other Hispanic	85,380

Age & Nativity, 2006
Under 5 years	36,857
18 years and over	397,636
21 years and over	378,335
65 years and over	66,488
85 years and over	11,174
Median age	37.9
Native-born	369,954
Foreign-born	161,134

Educational Attainment, 2006
Population 25 years and over	351,772
Less than 9th grade	9.2%
High school grad or higher	82.0%
Bachelor's degree or higher	30.5%
Graduate degree	11.5%

Households, 2006
Total households	185,201
With persons under 18	74,409
With persons over 65	47,127
Family households	133,676
Single-person households	43,530
Persons per household	2.83
Persons per family	3.33

Income & Poverty, 2006
Per capita income	$31,364
Median household income	$62,260
Median family income	$74,223
Persons in poverty	7.7%
H'holds receiving public assistance	3,866
H'holds receiving social security	47,398

Labor & Employment, 2006***
Total civilian labor force	271,800
Unemployment rate	4.8%

Employed persons 16 years and over by occupation, 2006
Managers & professionals	85,608
Service occupations	42,906
Sales & office occupations	70,678
Farming, fishing & forestry	164
Construction & maintenance	18,738
Production & transportation	38,717
Self-employed persons	13,269

Civilian Labor Force Projections***
2009	273,600
2014	282,100
2020	291,100
2025	296,300

*US Census Bureau
**2006 American Community Survey
*** New Jersey Department of Labor
† sum of all municipalities in county

General Information
Union County
10 Elizabethtown Plz
Administration Bldg
Elizabeth, NJ 07207
908-527-4000

Website	www.unioncountynj.org
Year of formation	1857
Land/water area (sq. miles)	103.3/2.2
Class	Second
Government form	County Manager Plan
Number of Freeholders	9
Number of municipalities	21

Government & Voters
Legislative Districts
US Congressional	6-7, 10
State Legislative	20-22, 29

Registered Voters, November 2006
Total	271,112
Democratic	88,162
Republican	38,769
Unaffiliated	144,120

County Officials, 2008
County Executive	NA
Manager	George Devanney
Clerk	Joanne Rajoppi
Finance Dir	Lawrence Caroselli
Tax Administrator	Christopher Duryee
Surrogate	James LaCorte
Prosecutor	Theodore Romankow
Public Works Dir	Joseph Graziano
Parks/Comm Renewal	Alfred Faella
Sheriff	Ralph Froehlich
Emerg Serv Dir	Ben Laganga

County School District
300 North Ave E
Westfield, NJ 07090
908-654-9860

Superintendent	Carmen Centuolo
Number of districts	23

Housing & Construction
Housing Units, 2006**
Total	195,875
Single family units	101,609
Multiple family units	94,032
Owner-occupied units	114,852
Renter-occupied units	70,349
Vacant units	10,674
Median rent	$1,007
Median SF home value	$419,000

Permits for New Residential Construction
	Units	Value
Total, 2006	1,593	$151,828,051
Single family	549	$92,918,557
Total, 2007	1,131	$97,463,707
Single family	349	$73,360,911

Real Property Valuation, 2007†
	Parcels	Valuation
Total	142,325	23,917,567,850
Vacant	4,163	242,713,400
Residential	127,824	17,382,748,515
Farm land	9	157,520
Farm homestead	4	1,098,900
Non-residential	10,325	6,290,849,515
Commercial	7,652	2,991,009,785
Industrial	1,519	2,673,840,930
Apartments	1,154	625,998,800

Taxes†
	2005	2006	2007
Net valuation taxable	$23,947,228,345	$23,903,375,848	$23,952,106,354
State equalized value	$61,959,181,493	$70,964,438,449	76,528,105,229

Public Safety
Police Officers, 2006
County officers	574
Sheriff's department	169
Prosecutors	80
Municipal police	1,457

Crime
	2005	2006
Total crimes	16,204	15,599
Violent	2,033	2,138
Murder	36	37
Rape	76	75
Robbery	1,134	1,125
Aggravated assault	787	901
Non-violent	14,171	13,461
Burglary	2,118	2,263
Larceny	9,025	8,930
Vehicle theft	3,028	2,268
Domestic violence	4,193	4,096
Arson	52	55
Total crime rate	30.5	29.4
Violent	3.8	4.0
Non-violent	26.6	25.3

Public Library
No County Library
(Library statistics are the sum of all municipal libraries in the county)

Library statistics, 2006†
Population served		521,027
	Total	Per capita
Revenues	$26,097,165	$50.09
Expenditures	$25,355,223	$48.66
Holdings	2,221,049	4.26
Circulation	2,467,847	4.74
Annual visits	2,872,579	5.51
Registered borrowers		270,167
Reference transactions		334,548
Hours open weekly		NA
Number of libraries		20
Full-time/total staff		98/230
Interlibrary loans Provided/received		15,281/15,437
Internet terminals		420
Annual users		479,120

State Income Tax, 2005
Number of returns	223,801
Increase from previous year	3.3%
Total income	$15,943,474,000
Per capita	$34,500
Increase from previous year	7.3%
Net charged tax	$455,564,000
Per capita	$986
Average taxable income	$64,769
Average income tax	$2,036

County Finance
State Aid Programs, 2008†
Total aid	$114,935,731
CMPTRA	40,677,689
Energy tax receipts	74,258,041
Garden State Trust	1

General Budget, 2007†
Total tax levy	$1,393,424,438
County levy	249,338,317
County taxes	238,582,767
County library	0
County health	0
County open space	10,755,550
School levy	685,508,467
Muni. levy	458,577,654
Misc. revenues	325,227,005

Warren County

Demographics & Socio-Economic Characteristics
(2006 American Community Survey, except as noted)

Population
- 1990*........................91,607
- 2000*.......................102,437
- 2006........................110,919
  - Male......................53,809
  - Female....................57,110
- 2007 (estimate)*............109,737
  - Population density..........306.6

Race & Hispanic Origin, 2006
Race
- White.......................99,275
- Black/African American........3,873
- American Indian/Alaska Native....0
- Asian........................2,845
- Native Hawaiian/Pacific Islander....0
- Two or more races............1,052
- Hispanic origin, total..........NA
  - Mexican......................420
  - Puerto Rican...............1,598
  - Cuban........................457
  - Other Hispanic.............4,228

Age & Nativity, 2006
- Under 5 years................7,004
- 18 years and over...........84,214
- 21 years and over...........79,658
- 65 years and over...........13,879
- 85 years and over............2,246
- Median age....................38.9
- Native-born................101,069
- Foreign-born.................9,850

Educational Attainment, 2006
- Population 25 years and over..75,321
- Less than 9th grade...........3.1%
- High school grad or higher...87.9%
- Bachelor's degree or higher..27.1%
- Graduate degree...............6.6%

Households, 2006
- Total households............41,487
  - With persons under 18.....15,013
  - With persons over 65.......9,255
  - Family households.........29,811
  - Single-person households...9,672
- Persons per household.........2.64
- Persons per family............3.15

Income & Poverty, 2006
- Per capita income..........$29,060
- Median household income....$62,087
- Median family income.......$79,455
- Persons in poverty............5.6%
- H'holds receiving public assistance...1,061
- H'holds receiving social security....10,964

Labor & Employment, 2006*
- Total civilian labor force..60,400
  - Unemployment rate...........4.1%

Employed persons 16 years and over by occupation, 2006
- Managers & professionals....21,946
- Service occupations..........9,296
- Sales & office occupations..14,394
- Farming, fishing & forestry....581
- Construction & maintenance...5,501
- Production & transportation..6,423
- Self-employed persons........3,956

Civilian Labor Force Projections*
- 2009........................61,400
- 2014........................65,100
- 2020........................69,200
- 2025........................72,300

*US Census Bureau
**2006 American Community Survey
*** New Jersey Department of Labor
† sum of all municipalities in county

See Introduction for an explanation of all data sources.

General Information
Warren County
165 County Route 519 South
Belvidere, NJ 07823
908-475-6500

- Website............www.co.warren.nj.us
- Year of formation..............1824
- Land/water area (sq. miles)....357.9/4.9
- Class........................Third
- Government form......Freeholder Board
- Number of Freeholders............3
- Number of municipalities........22

Government & Voters
Legislative Districts
- US Congressional............5, 13
- State Legislative..............23

Registered Voters, November 2006
- Total.......................62,042
  - Democratic.................9,738
  - Republican................19,931
  - Unaffiliated..............32,353

County Officials, 2008
- Freeholder Director.......John DiMaio
- Admin/Freeholder Clerk.....Steve Marvin
- Clerk..................Patricia J. Kolb
- CFO..................Charles L. Houck
- Tax Administrator......Melissa Pritchett
- Surrogate................Susan Dickey
- Prosecutor..........Thomas S. Ferguson
- Supervisor of Roads....Frederick J. Miller
- Planning Dir...........David K. Dech
- Sheriff................Sal Simonetti
- Fire Marshal.............Joseph Lake

County School District
1501 Route 57
Washington, NJ 07782
908-689-0464

- Superintendent...........Thomas Gross
- Number of districts............25

Housing & Construction
Housing Units, 2006**
- Total.......................45,094
  - Single family units.......30,296
  - Multiple family units.....14,274
  - Owner-occupied units......30,818
  - Renter-occupied units.....10,669
  - Vacant units...............3,607
  - Median rent................$866
  - Median SF home value....$309,100

Permits for New Residential Construction

	Units	Value
Total, 2006	512	$57,138,556
Single family	452	$53,935,227
Total, 2007	261	$40,029,619
Single family	244	$40,029,619

Real Property Valuation, 2007†

	Parcels	Valuation
Total	45,902	10,279,856,324
Vacant	4,392	278,142,627
Residential	33,439	7,534,209,311
Farm land	3,993	38,050,682
Farm homestead	1,916	590,326,550
Non-residential	2,162	1,839,127,154
Commercial	1,817	1,040,506,204
Industrial	206	621,086,750
Apartments	139	177,534,200

Taxes†

	2005	2006	2007
Net valuation taxable	$8,937,084,483	$9,441,833,484	$10,308,312,140
State equalized value	$11,573,645,964	$12,837,907,870	13,620,394,720

Public Safety
Police Officers, 2006
- County officers................41
  - Sheriff's department.........19
  - Prosecutors..................22
- Municipal police..............160

Crime

	2005	2006
Total crimes	1,516	1,898
Violent	113	156
Murder	1	3
Rape	3	5
Robbery	11	32
Aggravated assault	98	116
Non-violent	1,403	1,742
Burglary	277	336
Larceny	1,049	1,300
Vehicle theft	77	106
Domestic violence	1,491	1,295
Arson	6	15
Total crime rate	13.8	17.2
Violent	1.0	1.4
Non-violent	12.8	15.8

Public Library
Warren County Library
199 Hardwick Street
Belvidere, NJ 07823
(908) 475-6322

- Director..........Thomas L. Carney

Library statistics, 2006
- Population served............64,903

	Total	Per capita
Revenues	$5,107,310	$78.69
Expenditures	$3,674,285	$56.61
Holdings	248,452	3.83
Circulation	587,321	9.05
Annual visits	330,000	5.08

- Registered borrowers.........39,926
- Reference transactions.......51,114
- Hours open weekly...............61
- Full-time/total staff.........7/37
- Interlibrary loans
  - Provided/received........8/4,821
- Internet terminals..............22
- Annual users................29,790

State Income Tax, 2005
- Number of returns...........44,318
  - Increase from previous year...4.1%
- Total income.........$2,703,500,000
  - Per capita...............$28,300
  - Increase from previous year...5.6%
- Net charged tax..........$68,643,000
  - Per capita..................$719
- Average taxable income.....$53,978
- Average income tax.........$1,549

County Finance
State Aid Programs, 2008†
- Total aid................$14,959,772
  - CMPTRA..................2,096,320
  - Energy tax receipts....12,129,562
  - Garden State Trust.......720,448

General Budget, 2007†
- Total tax levy..........$262,291,533
  - County levy............77,123,088
    - County taxes.........64,096,758
    - County library.......5,190,461
    - County health..............0
    - County open space....7,835,869
  - School levy...........144,768,670
  - Muni. levy.............40,399,775
- Misc. revenues............53,638,439

©2008 Information Publications, Inc. All rights reserved. Photocopying prohibited. For additional copies, contact the publisher at www.informationpublications.com or (877)544-INFO (4636)

The New Jersey Municipal Data Book

The New Jersey Municipal Data Book

2008

State & Municipal Profiles Series

Appendices

[ip]
State & Municipal Profiles Series

State of New Jersey Overview — Appendix A

Note to the reader:

These pages are extracted from the 2008 edition of the *Almanac of the 50 States*, also published by Information Publications. Please refer to that volume for similar information on each of the 50 States, the District of Columbia, and the United States in general. (ISBN: 978-0-929960-47-0, paper; 978-0-929960-48-3, hardcover.)

New Jersey 1

State Summary

Capital city .... Trenton
Governor .... Jon Corzine
    The State House
    PO Box 001
    Trenton, NJ 08625
    609-292-6000
Admitted as a state 1787
Area (square miles) 8,721
Population, 2007 (estimate) 8,685,920
Largest city .... Newark
    Population, 2006 281,402
Personal income per capita, 2006
    (in current dollars) $46,344
Gross domestic product, 2006 ($ mil) ... $453,177

Leading industries by payroll, 2005
Professional/Scientific/Technical, Health care/Social assistance, Wholesale trade

Leading agricultural commodities by receipts, 2005
Greenhouse/nursery, Horses/mules, Blueberries, Peaches, Dairy products

Geography & Environment

Total area (square miles) 8,721
    land 7,417
    water 1,304
Federally-owned land, 2004 (acres) 148,441
    percent 3.1%
Highest point .... High Point
    elevation (feet) 1,803
Lowest point .... Atlantic Ocean
    elevation (feet) .... sea level
General coastline (miles) 130
Tidal shoreline (miles) 1,792
Cropland, 2003 (x 1,000 acres) 528
Forest land, 2003 (x 1,000 acres) 1,605
Capital city .... Trenton
    Population 2000 85,403
    Population 2006 83,923
Largest city .... Newark
    Population 2000 273,546
    Population 2006 281,402

Number of cities with over 100,000 population
1990 4
2000 4
2006 4

State park and recreation areas, 2005
Area (x 1,000 acres) 397
Number of visitors (x 1,000) 15,791
Revenues ($1,000) $10,176
    percent of operating expenditures 27.6%

National forest system land, 2007
Acres 0

Demographics & Population Characteristics

Population
1980 7,364,823
1990 7,730,188
2000 8,414,347
2006 8,724,560
    Male 4,262,291
    Female 4,462,269
Living in group quarters, 2006 197,712
    percent of total 2.3%
2007 (estimate) 8,685,920
    persons per square mile of land 1,171.1
2008 (projected) 8,915,495
2010 (projected) 9,018,231
2020 (projected) 9,461,635
2030 (projected) 9,802,440

Population of Core-Based Statistical Areas (formerly Metropolitan Areas), x 1,000

	CBSA	Non-CBSA
1990	7,730	0
2000	8,414	0
2006	8,725	0

Change in population, 2000-2007
Number 271,573
    percent 3.2%
Natural increase (births minus deaths) 291,260
Net internal migration .... -377,159
Net international migration 376,519

Persons by age, 2006
Under 5 years 558,994
5 to 17 years 1,530,344
18 years and over 6,635,222
65 years and over 1,127,742
85 years and over 166,529
    Median age 38.2

Persons by age, 2010 (projected)
Under 5 years 587,220
18 and over 6,930,007
65 and over 1,231,585
    Median age 38.9

Race, 2006
One Race
    White 6,665,390
    Black or African American 1,264,681
    Asian 647,986
    American Indian/Alaska Native 27,970
    Hawaiian Native/Pacific Islander 6,878
Two or more races 111,655

Persons of Hispanic origin, 2006
Total Hispanic or Latino 1,364,699
    Mexican 186,918
    Puerto Rican 392,619
    Cuban 73,024

©2008 Information Publications, Inc. All rights reserved. Photocopying prohibited. For additional copies, contact the publisher at www.informationpublications.com or (877)544-INFO (4636)

The New Jersey Municipal Data Book

Appendix A

State of New Jersey Overview

Note to the reader:

These pages are extracted from the 2008 edition of the *Almanac of the 50 States*, also published by Information Publications. Please refer to that volume for similar information on each of the 50 States, the District of Columbia, and the United States in general. (ISBN: 978-0-929960-47-0, paper; 978-0-929960-46-3, hardcover.)

2   New Jersey

Persons of Asian origin, 2006
- Total Asian 652,378
  - Asian Indian 256,965
  - Chinese 129,896
  - Filipino 105,806
  - Japanese 16,681
  - Korean 86,356
  - Vietnamese 24,251

Marital status, 2006
- Population 15 years & over 7,006,178
  - Never married 2,222,005
  - Married 3,723,172
  - Separated 160,006
  - Widowed 483,310
  - Divorced 577,691

Language spoken at home, 2006
- Population 5 years and older 8,164,688
  - English only 5,907,177
  - Spanish 1,134,033
  - French 68,457
  - German 32,276
  - Chinese 104,226

Households & families, 2006
- Households 3,135,490
  - with persons under 18 years 1,146,672
  - with persons over 65 years 783,466
  - persons per household 2.72
- Families 2,180,404
  - persons per family 3.29
- Married couples 1,631,340
- Female householder,
  - no husband present 404,348
- One-person households 803,445

Nativity, 2006
- Number of residents born in state 4,573,613
  - percent of population 52.4%

Immigration & naturalization, 2006
- Legal permanent residents admitted 65,934
- Persons naturalized 39,801
- Non-immigrant admissions 771,060

Vital Statistics and Health

Marriages
- 2004 50,662
- 2005 49,305
- 2006 42,398

Divorces
- 2004 25,981
- 2005 25,343
- 2006 25,794

Health risks, 2006
- Percent of adults who are:
  - Smokers 18.0%
  - Overweight (BMI > 25) 59.9%
  - Obese (BMI > 30) 22.6%

Births
- 2005 113,776
  - Birthrate (per 1,000) 13.1
  - White 82,659
  - Black 19,990
  - Hispanic 27,959
  - Asian/Pacific Islander 10,949
  - Amer. Indian/Alaska Native 178
  - Low birth weight (2,500g or less) 8.2%
  - Cesarian births 36.3%
  - Preterm births 12.5%
  - To unmarried mothers 31.4%
  - Twin births (per 1,000) 41.8
  - Triplets or higher order (per 100,000) ... 288.7
- 2006 (preliminary) 115,006
  - rate per 1,000 .... 13.2

Deaths
- 2004
- All causes 71,371
  - rate per 100,000 .... 752.7
- Heart disease 20,560
  - rate per 100,000 .... 213.0
- Malignant neoplasms 17,208
  - rate per 100,000 .... 184.4
- Cerebrovascular disease 3,781
  - rate per 100,000 .... 39.2
- Chronic lower respiratory disease 3,031
  - rate per 100,000 .... 32.1
- Diabetes 2,595
  - rate per 100,000 .... 27.6
- 2005 (preliminary) 71,970
  - rate per 100,000 .... 745.9
- 2006 (provisional) 71,809

Infant deaths
- 2004 651
  - rate per 1,000 .... 5.7
- 2005 (provisional) 586
  - rate per 1,000 .... 5.1

Exercise routines, 2005
- None 29.2%
- Moderate or greater 45.9%
- Vigorous 25.5%

Abortions, 2004
- Total performed in state 32,642
  - rate per 1,000 women age 15-44 18
  - % obtained by out-of-state residents ... 4.8%

Physicians, 2005
- Total 26,918
  - rate per 100,000 persons 309

Community hospitals, 2005
- Number of hospitals 80
- Beds (x 1,000) 22.1
- Patients admitted (x 1,000) 1,110
- Average daily census (x 1,000) 16.2
- Average cost per day $1,797
- Outpatient visits (x 1 mil) 16.8

State of New Jersey Overview

Appendix A

Note to the reader:

These pages are extracted from the 2008 edition of the *Almanac of the 50 States*, also published by Information Publications. Please refer to that volume for similar information on each of the 50 States, the District of Columbia, and the United States in general. (ISBN: 978-0-929960-47-0, paper; 978-0-929960-48-7, hardcover.)

New Jersey 3

Disability status of population, 2006
- 5 to 15 years 5.3%
- 16 to 64 years 9.3%
- 65 years and over 36.5%

Education

Educational attainment, 2006
- Population over 25 years 5,871,240
  - Less than 9th grade 5.9%
  - High school graduate or more .. 86.1%
  - College graduate or more 33.4%
  - Graduate or professional degree .. 12.4%

Public school enrollment, 2005-06
- Total 1,395,602
  - Pre-kindergarten through grade 8 926,870
  - Grades 9 through 12 407,314

Graduating public high school seniors, 2004-05
- Diplomas (incl. GED and others) 86,502

SAT scores, 2007
- Average critical reading score 495
- Average writing score 494
- Average math score 510
- Percent of graduates taking test 82%

Public school teachers, 2006-07 (estimate)
- Total (x 1,000) 115.0
  - Elementary 44.4
  - Secondary 70.6
- Average salary $59,920
  - Elementary $58,866
  - Secondary $61,373

State receipts & expenditures for public schools, 2006-07 (estimate)
- Revenue receipts ($ mil) $21,167
- Expenditures
  - Total ($ mil) $21,096
  - Per capita $2,336
  - Per pupil $14,824

NAEP proficiency scores, 2007

	Reading Basic	Reading Proficient	Math Basic	Math Proficient
Grade 4	77.2%	43.1%	89.6%	51.8%
Grade 8	81.1%	39.0%	77.5%	40.4%

Higher education enrollment, fall 2005
- Total 75,443
  - Full-time men 25,388
  - Full-time women 26,707
  - Part-time men 9,601
  - Part-time women 13,747

Minority enrollment in institutions of higher education, 2005
- Black, non-Hispanic 53,971
- Hispanic 50,502
- Asian/Pacific Islander 32,409
- American Indian/Alaska Native 1,170

Institutions of higher education, 2005-06
- Total 59
  - Public 33
  - Private 26

Earned degrees conferred, 2004-05
- Associate's 14,726
- Bachelor's 31,987
- Master's 12,386
- First-professional 1,817
- Doctor's 1,142

Public Libraries, 2006
- Number of libraries 306
- Number of outlets 467
- Annual visits per capita 5.4
- Circulation per capita 6.4

State & local financial support for higher education, FY 2006
- Full-time equivalent enrollment (x 1,000) 228.1
- Appropriations per FTE $8,145

Social Insurance & Welfare Programs

Social Security benefits & beneficiaries, 2005
- Beneficiaries (x 1,000) 1,379
  - Retired & dependents 1,012
  - Survivors 169
  - Disabled & dependents 197
- Annual benefit payments ($ mil) ... $16,474
  - Retired & dependents $11,675
  - Survivors $2,565
  - Disabled & dependents $2,234
- Average monthly benefit
  - Retired & dependents $1,105
  - Disabled & dependents $1,023
  - Widowed $1,065

Medicare, July 2005
- Enrollment (x 1,000) 1,227
- Payments ($ mil) $9,860

Medicaid, 2004
- Beneficiaries (x 1,000) 119
- Payments ($ mil) $822

State Children's Health Insurance Program, 2006
- Enrollment (x 1,000) 120.9
- Expenditures ($ mil) $190.6

Persons without health insurance, 2006
- Number (x 1,000) 1,341
  - percent 15.5%
- Number of children (x 1,000) 277
  - percent of children 13.3%

Health care expenditures, 2004
- Total expenditures $50,384
  - per capita $5,807

The New Jersey Municipal Data Book

Appendix A — State of New Jersey Overview

Note to the reader:

These pages are extracted from the 2008 edition of the *Almanac of the 50 States*, also published by Information Publications. Please refer to that volume for similar information on each of the 50 States, the District of Columbia, and the United States in general. (ISBN: 978-0-929960-47-0, paper; 978-0-929960-46-3, hardcover.)

4 New Jersey

Federal and state public aid

State unemployment insurance, 2006
Recipients, first payments (x 1,000) 305
Total payments ($ mil) $1,775
Average weekly benefit $344

Temporary Assistance for Needy Families, 2006
Recipients (x 1,000) 1,157.4
Families (x 1,000) 472.1

Supplemental Security Income, 2005
Recipients (x 1,000) 152.4
Payments ($ mil) $763.4

Food Stamp Program, 2006
Avg monthly participants (x 1,000) 405.7
Total benefits ($ mil) $455.9

Housing & Construction

Housing units
Total 2005 (estimate) 3,443,194
Total 2006 (estimate) 3,472,643
Seasonal or recreational use, 2006 119,636
Owner-occupied, 2006 2,110,308
    Median home value $366,600
    Homeowner vacancy rate 1.6%
Renter-occupied, 2006 1,025,182
    Median rent $974
    Rental vacancy rate 7.3%
Home ownership rate, 2005 .... 70.1%
Home ownership rate, 2006 .... 69.0%

New privately-owned housing units
Number authorized, 2006 (x 1,000) 34.3
    Value ($ mil) $4,382.7
Started 2005 (x 1,000, estimate) 26.5
Started 2006 (x 1,000, estimate) 26.1

Existing home sales
2005 (x 1,000) 184.4
2006 (x 1,000) 154.1

Government & Elections

State officials 2008
Governor .... Jon Corzine
    Democratic, term expires 1/10
Lieutenant Governor .. (no Lieutenant Governor)
Secretary of State .... Nina Wells
Attorney General .... Anne Milgram
Chief Justice .... Stuart Rabner

Governorship
Minimum age 30
Length of term .... 4 years
Consecutive terms permitted 2
Who succeeds .... President of Senate

Local governments by type, 2002
Total 1,412
    County 21
    Municipal 324
    Township 242
    School District 549
    Special District 276

State legislature
Name .... Legislature
Upper chamber .... Senate
    Number of members 40
    Length of term .... 4 years
    Party in majority, 2008 .... Democratic
Lower chamber .... General Assembly
    Number of members 80
    Length of term .... 2 years
    Party in majority, 2008 .... Democratic

Federal representation, 2008 (110th Congress)
Senator .... Frank Lautenberg
    Party .... Democratic
    Year term expires 2009
Senator .... Robert Menendez
    Party .... Democratic
    Year term expires 2013
Representatives, total 13
    Democrats 7
    Republicans 6

Voters in November 2006 election (estimate)
Total 2,406,132
    Male 1,121,355
    Female 1,284,777
    White 2,036,979
    Black 266,563
    Hispanic 83,157
    Asian 96,283

Presidential election, 2004
Total Popular Vote 3,611,691
    Kerry 1,911,430
    Bush 1,670,003
Total Electoral Votes 15

Votes cast for US Senators
2004
Total vote (x 1,000) .... NA
Leading party .... NA
Percent for leading party .... NA
2006
Total vote (x 1,000) 102
Leading party .... Democratic
Percent for leading party 57.2%

Votes cast for US Representatives
2004
Total vote (x 1,000) 3,285
    Democratic 1,721
    Republican 1,515
Leading party .... Democratic
Percent for leading party 52.4%
2006
Total vote (x 1,000) 2,137
    Democratic 1,208
    Republican 903
Leading party .... Democratic
Percent for leading party 56.5%

State of New Jersey Overview

Appendix A

Note to the reader:

These pages are extracted from the 2008 edition of the *Almanac of the 50 States*, also published by Information Publications. Please refer to that volume for similar information on each of the 50 States, the District of Columbia, and the United States in general. (ISBN: 978 0 929960 17 0, paper; 978 0 929960 16 3, hardcover.)

New Jersey 5

State government employment, 2006
Full-time equivalent employees 156,768
Payroll ($ mil) $767.5

Local government employment, 2006
Full-time equivalent employees 354,987
Payroll ($ mil) $1,608.8

Women holding public office, 2008
US Congress 0
Statewide elected office 0
State legislature 34

Black public officials, 2002
Total 269
    US and state legislatures 18
    City/county/regional offices 162
    Judicial/law enforcement 0
    Education/school boards 89

Hispanic public officials, 2006
Total 109
    State executives & legislators 5
    City/county/regional offices 61
    Judicial/law enforcement 0
    Education/school boards 43

Governmental Finance

State government revenues, 2006
Total revenue (x $1,000) $57,610,331
  per capita $6,647.80
General revenue (x $1,000) $46,445,905
  Intergovernmental 11,378,454
  Taxes 26,266,187
    general sales 6,853,418
    individual income tax 10,506,565
    corporate income tax 2,508,428
  Current charges 4,682,195
  Miscellaneous 4,119,069

State government expenditure, 2006
Total expenditure (x $1,000) $54,073,301
  per capita $6,239.65
General expenditure (x $1,000) $43,349,868
  per capita, total $5,002.25
    Education 1,632.60
    Public welfare 1,442.60
    Health 92.11
    Hospitals 197.67
    Highways 301.83
    Police protection 61.54
    Corrections 164.02
    Natural resources 66.60
    Parks & recreation 52.12
    Governmental administration 204.17
    Interest on general debt 175.17

State debt & cash, 2006 ($ per capita)
Debt $5,515.84
Cash/security holdings $11,192.67

Federal government grants to state & local government, 2005 (x $1,000)
Total $11,124,122
by Federal agency
  Defense 68,094
  Education 890,179
  Energy 39,441
  Environmental Protection Agency 89,819
  Health & Human Services 6,397,656
  Homeland Security 33,108
  Housing & Urban Development 1,273,098
  Justice 130,135
  Labor 243,616
  Transportation 1,216,468
  Veterans Affairs 22,569

Crime & Law Enforcement

Crime, 2006 (rates per 100,000 residents)
Property crimes 199,958
  Burglary 39,433
  Larceny 135,801
  Motor vehicle theft 24,724
  Property crime rate 2,291.9
Violent crimes 30,672
  Murder 428
  Forcible rape 1,237
  Robbery 13,357
  Aggravated assault 15,650
  Violent crime rate 351.6
Hate crimes 802

Fraud and identity theft, 2006
Fraud complaints 11,284
  rate per 100,000 residents 129.3
Identity theft complaints 6,394
  rate per 100,000 residents 73.3

Law enforcement agencies, 2006
Total agencies 529
Total employees 36,456
  Officers 29,013
  Civilians 7,443

Prisoners, probation, and parole, 2006
Total prisoners 27,371
  percent change, 12/31/05 to 12/31/06 .... 0.0%
  in private facilities 9.5%
  in local jails 6.7%
Sentenced to more than one year 27,371
  rate per 100,000 residents 313
Adults on probation 132,636
Adults on parole 14,405

Prisoner demographics, June 30, 2005 (rate per 100,000 residents)
Male 1,019
Female 70
White 190
Black 2,352
Hispanic 630

Appendix A — State of New Jersey Overview

Note to the reader:

These pages are extracted from the 2008 edition of the *Almanac of the 50 States*, also published by Information Publications. Please refer to that volume for similar information on each of the 50 States, the District of Columbia, and the United States in general. (ISBN: 978-0-929960-47-0, paper; 978-0-929960-46-3, hardcover.)

6 New Jersey

Arrests, 2006
Total 388,116
  Persons under 18 years of age 60,840

Persons under sentence of death, 1/1/07
Total 11
  White 5
  Black 6
  Hispanic 0

State's highest court
Name .... Supreme Court
Number of members 7
Length of term .... 7 years
Intermediate appeals court? .... yes

Labor & Income

Civilian labor force, 2006 (x 1,000)
Total 4,490
  Men 2,428
  Women 2,063
  Persons 16-19 years 187
  White 3,473
  Black 599
  Hispanic 722

Civilian labor force as a percent of civilian non-institutional population, 2006
Total 66.6%
  Men 75.2
  Women 58.7
  Persons 16-19 years 38.1
  White 66.2
  Black 66.5
  Hispanic 70.6

Employment, 2006 (x 1,000)
Total 4,273
  Men 2,312
  Women 1,961
  Persons 16-19 years 162
  White 3,328
  Black 541
  Hispanic 676

Unemployment rate, 2006
Total 4.8%
  Men 4.8
  Women 4.9
  Persons 16-19 years 13.3
  White 4.2
  Black 9.7
  Hispanic 6.4

Full-time/part-time labor force, 2003 (x 1,000)
Full-time labor force, employed 3,454
Part-time labor force, employed 664
Unemployed, looking for
  Full-time work 222
  Part-time work 35
Mean duration of unemployment (weeks) ... 20.4
  Median 12.0

Labor unions, 2006
Membership (x 1,000) 770
  percent of employed 20.1%

Experienced civilian labor force by private industry, 2006
Total 3,340,229
  Natural resources & mining 12,073
  Construction 172,909
  Manufacturing 321,825
  Trade, transportation & utilities 864,235
  Information 97,150
  Finance 266,608
  Professional & business 596,296
  Education & health 522,312
  Leisure & hospitality 335,325
  Other 124,190

Experienced civilian labor force by occupation, May 2006
Management 185,110
Business & financial 200,310
Legal 32,750
Sales 418,290
Office & admin. support 761,070
Computers & math 119,890
Architecture & engineering 56,210
Arts & entertainment 44,720
Education 265,780
Social services 54,890
Health care practitioner & technical .. 201,670
Health care support 106,650
Maintenance & repair 147,460
Construction 144,050
Transportation & moving 318,750
Production 223,550
Farming, fishing & forestry 4,620

Hours and earnings of production workers on manufacturing payrolls, 2006
Average weekly hours 42.1
Average hourly earnings $16.55
Average weekly earnings $696.76

Income and poverty, 2006
Median household income $64,470
Personal income, per capita (current $) ... $46,344
  in constant (2000) dollars $40,455
Persons below poverty level 8.7%

Average annual pay
2006 .... $51,645
  increase from 2005 .... 4.4%

Federal individual income tax returns, 2005
Returns filed 4,152,741
Adjusted gross income ($1,000) ... $282,306,218
Total tax liability ($1,000) $42,460,858

Charitable contributions, 2004
Number of contributions 1,683.8
Total amount ($ mil) $5,533.7

State of New Jersey Overview

Appendix A

Note to the reader:

These pages are extracted from the 2008 edition of the *Almanac of the 50 States*, also published by Information Publications. Please refer to that volume for similar information on each of the 50 States, the District of Columbia, and the United States in general. (ISBN: 978-0-929960-47-0, paper; 978-0-929960-46-3, hardcover.)

New Jersey 7

Economy, Business, Industry & Agriculture

Fortune 500 companies, 2007 24
Bankruptcy cases filed, FY 2007 18,702

Patents and trademarks issued, 2007
Patents 3,185
Trademarks 2,691

Business firm ownership, 2002
Women-owned 185,197
   Sales ($ mil) $35,573
Black-owned 36,280
   Sales ($ mil) $3,202
Hispanic-owned 49,841
   Sales ($ mil) $7,245
Asian-owned 51,957
   Sales ($ mil) $18,495
Amer. Indian/Alaska Native-owned 2,645
   Sales ($ mil) $284
Hawaiian/Pacific Islander-owned 448
   Sales ($ mil) $37

Gross domestic product, 2006 ($ mil)
Total gross domestic product $453,177
   Agriculture, forestry, fishing and hunting 642
   Mining 226
   Utilities 8,917
   Construction 19,068
   Manufacturing, durable goods 13,915
   Manufacturing, non-durable goods .. 27,644
   Wholesale trade 36,464
   Retail trade 28,413
   Transportation & warehousing 13,119
   Information 21,541
   Finance & insurance 37,327
   Real estate, rental & leasing 78,182
   Professional and technical services.. 38,536
   Educational services 3,994
   Health care and social assistance .. 32,062
   Accommodation/food services 11,176
   Other services, except government .. 9,208
   Government 45,003

Establishments, payroll, employees & receipts, by major industry group, 2005

Total 242,128
   Annual payroll ($1,000) $166,018,238
   Paid employees 3,594,862
Forestry, fishing & agriculture 243
   Annual payroll ($1,000) $26,847
   Paid employees 751
Mining 110
   Annual payroll ($1,000) $137,556
   Paid employees 2,305
   Receipts, 2002 ($1,000) $379,558

Utilities 340
   Annual payroll ($1,000) $1,545,619
   Paid employees 18,164
   Receipts, 2002 ($1,000) .... NA
Construction 25,455
   Annual payroll ($1,000) $9,240,445
   Paid employees 175,322
   Receipts, 2002 ($1,000) $37,867,759
Manufacturing 9,575
   Annual payroll ($1,000) $15,352,555
   Paid employees 304,976
   Receipts, 2002 ($1,000) $96,599,807
Wholesale trade 16,347
   Annual payroll ($1,000) $17,375,975
   Paid employees 274,063
   Receipts, 2002 ($1,000) $256,925,492
Retail trade 35,263
   Annual payroll ($1,000) $11,303,325
   Paid employees 454,878
   Receipts, 2002 ($1,000) $102,153,833
Transportation & warehousing 7,228
   Annual payroll ($1,000) $6,443,091
   Paid employees 169,118
   Receipts, 2002 ($1,000) $16,421,043
Information 4,059
   Annual payroll ($1,000) $7,846,435
   Paid employees 122,177
   Receipts, 2002 ($1,000) .... NA
Finance & insurance 12,543
   Annual payroll ($1,000) $16,995,391
   Paid employees 216,384
   Receipts, 2002 ($1,000) .... NA
Professional, scientific & technical .. 31,669
   Annual payroll ($1,000) $20,504,746
   Paid employees 304,803
   Receipts, 2002 ($1,000) $36,005,523
Education 3,021
   Annual payroll ($1,000) $2,702,816
   Paid employees 84,880
   Receipts, 2002 ($1,000) $1,662,096
Health care & social assistance 24,772
   Annual payroll ($1,000) $19,367,540
   Paid employees 479,536
   Receipts, 2002 ($1,000) $38,708,974
Arts and entertainment 3,601
   Annual payroll ($1,000) $1,162,942
   Paid employees 46,240
   Receipts, 2002 ($1,000) $3,303,069
Real estate 9,584
   Annual payroll ($1,000) $2,841,714
   Paid employees 61,965
   Receipts, 2002 ($1,000) $12,262,786
Accommodation & food service 18,872
   Annual payroll ($1,000) $4,978,755
   Paid employees 274,639
   Receipts, 2002 ($1,000) $15,715,595

The New Jersey Municipal Data Book

Appendix A — State of New Jersey Overview

Note to the reader:

These pages are extracted from the 2008 edition of the *Almanac of the 50 States*, also published by Information Publications. Please refer to that volume for similar information on each of the 50 States, the District of Columbia, and the United States in general. (ISBN: 978-0-929960-47-0, paper; 978-0-929960-46-3, hardcover.)

8 New Jersey

Exports, 2006
Value of exported goods ($ mil) $27,002
    Manufactured $20,112
    Non-manufactured $1,862

Foreign direct investment in US affiliates, 2004
Property, plants & equipment ($ mil) ... $33,846
Employment (x 1,000) 219.7

Agriculture, 2006
Number of farms 9,800
Farm acreage (x 1,000) 790
    Acres per farm 81
Farm marketings and income ($ mil)
Total $923.9
    Crops $762.6
    Livestock $161.3
Net farm income $305.4

Principal commodities, in order by marketing receipts, 2005
Greenhouse/nursery, Horses/mules, Blueberries, Peaches, Dairy products

Federal economic activity in state
Expenditures, 2005 ($ mil)
    Total $58,617
        Per capita $6,735.11
    Defense $7,645
    Non-defense $50,972
Defense department, 2006 ($ mil)
    Payroll $2,004
    Contract awards $6,151
    Grants $77
Homeland security grants ($1,000)
    2006 .... $51,983
    2007 .... $61,109

FDIC-insured financial institutions, 2005
Number 131
Assets ($ billion) $139.7
Deposits ($ billion) $90.8

Fishing, 2006
Catch (x 1,000 lbs) 175,759
Value ($1,000) $145,850

Mining, 2006 ($ mil)
Total non-fuel mineral production $369
Percent of U.S. 0.57%

Communication, Energy & Transportation

Communication
Households with computers, 2003 .... 65.5%
Households with internet access, 2003 . 60.5%
High-speed internet providers 41
Total high-speed internet lines 3,392,607
    Residential 2,109,126
    Business 1,283,481
Wireless phone customers, 12/2006 .. 7,207,018

FCC-licensed stations (as of January 1, 2008)
TV stations 15
FM radio stations 97
AM radio stations 41

Energy
Energy consumption, 2004
    Total (trillion Btu) 2,630
    Per capita (million Btu) 303.2
By source of production (trillion Btu)
    Coal 113
    Natural gas 647
    Petroleum 1,270
    Nuclear electric power 282
    Hydroelectric power 0
By end-use sector (trillion Btu)
    Residential 626
    Commercial 617
    Industrial 484
    Transportation 903
Electric energy, 2005
    Primary source of electricity ...... Nuclear
    Net generation (billion kWh) 60.5
        percent from renewable sources ... 1.5%
    Net summer capability (million kW) . 17.5
    CO_2 emitted from generation 21.1
Natural gas utilities, 2005
    Customers (x 1,000) 2,775
    Sales (trillion Btu) 490
    Revenues ($ mil) $4,795
Nuclear plants, 2007 4
Total CO_2 emitted (million metric tons) .. 123.7
Energy spending, 2004 ($ mil) $27,060
    per capita $3,119
    Price per million Btu $14.07

Transportation, 2006
Public road & street mileage 38,561
    Urban 31,252
    Rural 7,309
    Interstate 431
Vehicle miles of travel (millions) .. 75,371
    per capita 8,697.2
Total motor vehicle registrations .. 5,957,988
    Automobiles 3,692,966
    Trucks 2,241,195
    Motorcycles 163,609
Licensed drivers 5,834,227
    19 years & under 244,542
Deaths from motor vehicle accidents ... 772
Gasoline consumed (x 1,000 gallons) . 4,281,216
    per capita 494.0

Commuting Statistics, 2006
Average commute time (min) 29.1
    Drove to work alone 71.9%
    Carpooled 9.3%
    Public transit 10.3%
    Walk to work 3.4%
    Work from home 3.2%

Municipalities by County — Appendix B

Atlantic County
Absecon City
Atlantic City
Brigantine City
Buena Borough
Buena Vista Township
Corbin City
Egg Harbor City
Egg Harbor Township
Estell Manor City
Folsom Borough
Galloway Township
Hamilton Township
Hammonton Town
Linwood City
Longport Borough
Margate City
Mullica Township
Northfield City
Pleasantville City
Port Republic City
Somers Point City
Ventnor City
Weymouth Township

Bergen County
Allendale Borough
Alpine Borough
Bergenfield Borough
Bogota Borough
Carlstadt Borough
Cliffside Park Borough
Closter Borough
Cresskill Borough
Demarest Borough
Dumont Borough
East Rutherford Borough
Edgewater Borough
Elmwood Park Borough
Emerson Borough
Englewood City
Englewood Cliffs Borough
Fair Lawn Borough
Fairview Borough
Fort Lee Borough
Franklin Lakes Borough
Garfield City
Glen Rock Borough
Hackensack City
Harrington Park Borough
Hasbrouck Heights Borough
Haworth Borough
Hillsdale Borough
Ho-Ho-Kus Borough

Bergen County, cont
Leonia Borough
Little Ferry Borough
Lodi Borough
Lyndhurst Township
Mahwah Township
Maywood Borough
Midland Park Borough
Montvale Borough
Moonachie Borough
New Milford Borough
North Arlington Borough
Northvale Borough
Norwood Borough
Oakland Borough
Old Tappan Borough
Oradell Borough
Palisades Park Borough
Paramus Borough
Park Ridge Borough
Ramsey Borough
Ridgefield Borough
Ridgefield Park Village
Ridgewood Village
River Edge Borough
River Vale Township
Rochelle Park Township
Rockleigh Borough
Rutherford Borough
Saddle Brook Township
Saddle River Borough
South Hackensack Township
Teaneck Township
Tenafly Borough
Teterboro Borough
Upper Saddle River Borough
Waldwick Borough
Wallington Borough
Washington Township
Westwood Borough
Woodcliff Lake Borough
Wood-Ridge Borough
Wyckoff Township

Burlington County
Bass River Township
Beverly City
Bordentown City
Bordentown Township
Burlington City
Burlington Township
Chesterfield Township

Burlington County, cont
Cinnaminson Township
Delanco Township
Delran Township
Eastampton Township
Edgewater Park Township
Evesham Township
Fieldsboro Borough
Florence Township
Hainesport Township
Lumberton Township
Mansfield Township
Maple Shade Township
Medford Township
Medford Lakes Borough
Moorestown Township
Mount Holly Township
Mount Laurel Township
New Hanover Township
North Hanover Township
Palmyra Borough
Pemberton Borough
Pemberton Township
Riverside Township
Riverton Borough
Shamong Township
Southampton Township
Springfield Township
Tabernacle Township
Washington Township
Westampton Township
Willingboro Township
Woodland Township
Wrightstown Borough

Camden County
Audubon Borough
Audubon Park Borough
Barrington Borough
Bellmawr Borough
Berlin Borough
Berlin Township
Brooklawn Borough
Camden City
Cherry Hill Township
Chesilhurst Borough
Clementon Borough
Collingswood Borough
Gibbsboro Borough
Gloucester City
Gloucester Township
Haddon Township
Haddon Heights Borough
Haddonfield Borough

Camden County, cont
Hi-Nella Borough
Laurel Springs Borough
Lawnside Borough
Lindenwold Borough
Magnolia Borough
Merchantville Borough
Mount Ephraim Borough
Oaklyn Borough
Pennsauken Township
Pine Hill Borough
Pine Valley Borough
Runnemede Borough
Somerdale Borough
Stratford Borough
Tavistock Borough
Voorhees Township
Waterford Township
Winslow Township
Woodlynne Borough

Cape May County
Avalon Borough
Cape May City
Cape May Point Borough
Dennis Township
Lower Township
Middle Township
North Wildwood City
Ocean City
Sea Isle City
Stone Harbor Borough
Upper Township
West Cape May Borough
West Wildwood Borough
Wildwood City
Wildwood Crest Borough
Woodbine Borough

Cumberland County
Bridgeton City
Commercial Township
Deerfield Township
Downe Township
Fairfield Township
Greenwich Township
Hopewell Township
Lawrence Township
Maurice River Township
Millville City
Shiloh Borough
Stow Creek Township
Upper Deerfield Township
Vineland City

Appendix B

Municipalities by County

Essex County
Belleville Township
Bloomfield Township
Caldwell Borough
Cedar Grove Township
East Orange City
Essex Fells Borough
Fairfield Township
Glen Ridge Borough
Irvington Township
Livingston Township
Maplewood Township
Millburn Township
Montclair Township
Newark City
North Caldwell Borough
Nutley Township
City of Orange Township
Roseland Borough
South Orange Village Township
Verona Township
West Caldwell Township
West Orange Township

Gloucester County
Clayton Borough
Deptford Township
East Greenwich Township
Elk Township
Franklin Township
Glassboro Borough
Greenwich Township
Harrison Township
Logan Township
Mantua Township
Monroe Township
National Park Borough
Newfield Borough
Paulsboro Borough
Pitman Borough
South Harrison Township
Swedesboro Borough
Washington Township
Wenonah Borough
West Deptford Township
Westville Borough
Woodbury City
Woodbury Heights Borough
Woolwich Township

Hudson County
Bayonne City
East Newark Borough
Guttenberg Town
Harrison Town
Hoboken City
Jersey City
Kearny Town
North Bergen Township
Secaucus Town
Union City
Weehawken Township
West New York Town

Hunterdon County
Alexandria Township
Bethlehem Township
Bloomsbury Borough
Califon Borough
Clinton Town
Clinton Township
Delaware Township
East Amwell Township
Flemington Borough
Franklin Township
Frenchtown Borough
Glen Gardner Borough
Hampton Borough
High Bridge Borough
Holland Township
Kingwood Township
Lambertville City
Lebanon Borough
Lebanon Township
Milford Borough
Raritan Township
Readington Township
Stockton Borough
Tewksbury Township
Union Township
West Amwell Township

Mercer County
East Windsor Township
Ewing Township
Hamilton Township
Hightstown Borough
Hopewell Borough
Hopewell Township
Lawrence Township

Mercer County, cont
Pennington Borough
Princeton Borough
Princeton Township
Robbinsville Township
 (formerly Washington)
Trenton City
West Windsor Township

Middlesex County
Carteret Borough
Cranbury Township
Dunellen Borough
East Brunswick Township
Edison Township
Helmetta Borough
Highland Park Borough
Jamesburg Borough
Metuchen Borough
Middlesex Borough
Milltown Borough
Monroe Township
New Brunswick City
North Brunswick Township
Old Bridge Township
Perth Amboy City
Piscataway Township
Plainsboro Township
Sayreville Borough
South Amboy City
South Brunswick Township
South Plainfield Borough
South River Borough
Spotswood Borough
Woodbridge Township

Monmouth County
Aberdeen Township
Allenhurst Borough
Allentown Borough
Asbury Park City
Atlantic Highlands Borough
Avon-by-the-Sea Borough
Belmar Borough
Bradley Beach Borough
Brielle Borough
Colts Neck Township
Deal Borough
Eatontown Borough
Englishtown Borough

Monmouth County, cont
Fair Haven Borough
Farmingdale Borough
Freehold Borough
Freehold Township
Hazlet Township
Highlands Borough
Holmdel Township
Howell Township
Interlaken Borough
Keansburg Borough
Keyport Borough
Lake Como Borough
Little Silver Borough
Loch Arbour Village
Long Branch City
Manalapan Township
Manasquan Borough
Marlboro Township
Matawan Borough
Middletown Township
Millstone Township
Monmouth Beach Borough
Neptune Township
Neptune City Borough
Ocean Township
Oceanport Borough
Red Bank Borough
Roosevelt Borough
Rumson Borough
Sea Bright Borough
Sea Girt Borough
Shrewsbury Borough
Shrewsbury Township
Spring Lake Borough
Spring Lake Heights Borough
Tinton Falls Borough
Union Beach Borough
Upper Freehold Township
Wall Township
West Long Branch Borough

Municipalities by County

Morris County
Boonton Town
Boonton Township
Butler Borough
Chatham Borough
Chatham Township
Chester Borough
Chester Township
Denville Township
Dover Town
East Hanover Township
Florham Park Borough
Hanover Township
Harding Township
Jefferson Township
Kinnelon Borough
Lincoln Park Borough
Long Hill Township
Madison Borough
Mendham Borough
Mendham Township
Mine Hill Township
Montville Township
Morris Township
Morris Plains Borough
Morristown Town
Mount Arlington Borough
Mount Olive Township
Mountain Lakes Borough
Netcong Borough
Parsippany-Troy Hills Township
Pequannock Township
Randolph Township
Riverdale Borough
Rockaway Borough
Rockaway Township
Roxbury Township
Victory Gardens Borough
Washington Township
Wharton Borough

Ocean County
Barnegat Township
Barnegat Light Borough
Bay Head Borough
Beach Haven Borough
Beachwood Borough
Berkeley Township
Brick Township
Eagleswood Township
Harvey Cedars Borough
Island Heights Borough

Ocean County, cont
Jackson Township
Lacey Township
Lakehurst Borough
Lakewood Township
Lavallette Borough
Little Egg Harbor Township
Long Beach Township
Manchester Township
Mantoloking Borough
Ocean Township
Ocean Gate Borough
Pine Beach Borough
Plumsted Township
Point Pleasant Borough
Point Pleasant Beach Borough
Seaside Heights Borough
Seaside Park Borough
Ship Bottom Borough
South Toms River Borough
Stafford Township
Surf City Borough
Toms River
Tuckerton Borough

Passaic County
Bloomingdale Borough
Clifton City
Haledon Borough
Hawthorne Borough
Little Falls Township
North Haledon Borough
Passaic City
Paterson City
Pompton Lakes Borough
Prospect Park Borough
Ringwood Borough
Totowa Borough
Wanaque Borough
Wayne Township
West Milford Township
West Paterson Borough

Salem County
Alloway Township
Carneys Point Township
Elmer Borough
Elsinboro Township
Lower Alloways Creek Township
Mannington Township
Oldmans Township
Penns Grove Borough

Salem County, cont
Pennsville Township
Pilesgrove Township
Pittsgrove Township
Quinton Township
Salem City
Upper Pittsgrove Township
Woodstown Borough

Somerset County
Bedminster Township
Bernards Township
Bernardsville Borough
Bound Brook Borough
Branchburg Township
Bridgewater Township
Far Hills Borough
Franklin Township
Green Brook Township
Hillsborough Township
Manville Borough
Millstone Borough
Montgomery Township
North Plainfield Borough
Peapack & Gladstone Borough
Raritan Borough
Rocky Hill Borough
Somerville Borough
South Bound Brook Borough
Warren Township
Watchung Borough

Sussex County
Andover Borough
Andover Township
Branchville Borough
Byram Township
Frankford Township
Franklin Borough
Fredon Township
Green Township
Hamburg Borough
Hampton Township
Hardyston Township
Hopatcong Borough
Lafayette Township
Montague Township
Newton Town
Ogdensburg Borough
Sandyston Township
Sparta Township
Stanhope Borough

Sussex County, cont
Stillwater Township
Sussex Borough
Vernon Township
Walpack Township
Wantage Township

Union County
Berkeley Heights Township
Clark Township
Cranford Township
Elizabeth City
Fanwood Borough
Garwood Borough
Hillside Township
Kenilworth Borough
Linden City
Mountainside Borough
New Providence Borough
Plainfield City
Rahway City
Roselle Borough
Roselle Park Borough
Scotch Plains Township
Springfield Township
Summit City
Union Township
Westfield Town
Winfield Township

Warren County
Allamuchy Township
Alpha Borough
Belvidere Town
Blairstown Township
Franklin Township
Frelinghuysen Township
Greenwich Township
Hackettstown Town
Hardwick Township
Harmony Township
Hope Township
Independence Township
Knowlton Township
Liberty Township
Lopatcong Township
Mansfield Township
Oxford Township
Phillipsburg Town
Pohatcong Township
Washington Borough
Washington Township
White Township

2006 American Community Survey Data

Appendix C

Note: The 2006 American Community Survey (ACS) collected demographic data for cities and counties with populations of at least 65,000 – in New Jersey's case, 20 out of 566 municipalities. For those municipalities, ACS data is included here as a measure of the civilian, non-institutional population.

Brick Township
Ocean County

Population
- Total 77,685
- Male 37,567
- Female 40,118

Race & Hispanic Origin
Race
- White .... NA
- Black/African American ... NA
- Amer. Indian/Alaskan Native .. NA
- Asian .... NA
- Pacific Islander .... NA
- Other Race .... NA
- Two or more races .... NA
- Hispanic origin, total ... NA
  - Mexican .... NA
  - Puerto Rican .... NA
  - Cuban .... NA
  - Other Hispanic .... NA

Age & Nativity
- Under 5 years 3,782
- 18 years and over 62,366
- 21 years and over 59,203
- 65 years and over 12,465
- 85 years and over 2,323
- Median age 39.6
- Native-born 73,341
- Foreign-born 4,344

Educational Attainment
- Population 25 years and over ... 55,310
  - Less than 9th grade 2.2%
  - High School grad or higher .. 90.4%
  - Bachelor's degree or higher . 28.3%
  - Graduate degree 7.6%

Households
- Total households 31,887
  - With persons under 18 ... 9,777
  - With persons over 65 9,368
  - Family households 21,319
  - Single person households .. 9,042
- Persons per household 2.42
- Persons per family 2.99

Income & Poverty
- Per capita income $30,632
- Median household income .. $62,023
- Median family income $79,496
- Persons in poverty 7.0%
- H'holds receiving public assistance .. 0
- H'holds receiving social security .. 10,457

Labor & Employment
- Total civilian labor force .. 43,913
  - Unemployment rate 4.5%

Employed persons 16 years and over by occupation,
- Managers & professionals ... 14,373
- Service occupations 6,178
- Sales & office occupations .. 11,680
- Farming, fishing & forestry .. 67
- Construction & maintenance .. 5,657
- Production & transportation .. 3,962
- Self-employed persons 2,106

Housing Units
- Total 35,369
  - Single family units 27,328
  - Multiple family units ... 7,849
  - Mobile home units 192
  - Owner-occupied units 26,203
  - Renter-occupied units ... 5,684
  - Vacant units 3,482
- Median SF home value $322,500
- Median rent $982

Camden City
Camden County

Population
- Total 73,838
- Male 35,712
- Female 38,126

Race & Hispanic Origin
Race
- White 9,750
- Black/African American ... 37,517
- Amer. Indian/Alaskan Native .. 562
- Asian 2,323
- Pacific Islander 0
- Other Race 21,526
- Two or more races 2,160
- Hispanic origin, total ... 30,530
  - Mexican 3,453
  - Puerto Rican 21,186
  - Cuban 0
  - Other Hispanic 5,891

Age & Nativity
- Under 5 years 6,383
- 18 years and over 50,229
- 21 years and over 46,914
- 65 years and over 5,980
- 85 years and over 998
- Median age 27.7
- Native-born 64,516
- Foreign-born 9,322

Educational Attainment
- Population 25 years and over ... 41,518
  - Less than 9th grade 19.0%
  - High School grad or higher .. 61.1%
  - Bachelor's degree or higher . 5.3%
  - Graduate degree 1.6%

Households
- Total households 24,271
  - With persons under 18 ... 11,505
  - With persons over 65 4,617
  - Family households 16,397
  - Single person households .. 6,362
- Persons per household 2.92
- Persons per family 3.58

Income & Poverty
- Per capita income $12,739
- Median household income .. $25,961
- Median family income $29,125
- Persons in poverty 35.6%
- H'holds receiving public assistance .. 3,044
- H'holds receiving social security .. 5,688

Labor & Employment
- Total civilian labor force .. 31,219
  - Unemployment rate 15.8%

Employed persons 16 years and over by occupation,
- Managers & professionals ... 5,168
- Service occupations 7,182
- Sales & office occupations .. 6,884
- Farming, fishing & forestry .. 0
- Construction & maintenance .. 2,128
- Production & transportation .. 4,930
- Self-employed persons 755

Housing Units
- Total 30,775
  - Single family units 4,034
  - Multiple family units ... 26,522
  - Mobile home units 219
  - Owner-occupied units 10,814
  - Renter-occupied units ... 13,457
  - Vacant units 6,504
- Median SF home value $77,100
- Median rent $636

Cherry Hill Township
Camden County

Population
- Total 71,621
- Male 34,258
- Female 37,363

Race & Hispanic Origin
Race
- White 58,379
- Black/African American ... 4,351
- Amer. Indian/Alaskan Native .. 48
- Asian 5,123
- Pacific Islander 0
- Other Race 2,407
- Two or more races 1,313
- Hispanic origin, total ... 3,608
  - Mexican .... NA
  - Puerto Rican .... NA
  - Cuban .... NA
  - Other Hispanic .... NA

Age & Nativity
- Under 5 years 5,022
- 18 years and over 54,932
- 21 years and over 52,581
- 65 years and over 12,993
- 85 years and over 2,402
- Median age 41.9
- Native-born 60,798
- Foreign-born 10,823

Educational Attainment
- Population 25 years and over ... 50,713
  - Less than 9th grade 1.5%
  - High School grad or higher .. 95.1%
  - Bachelor's degree or higher . 51.6%
  - Graduate degree 21.4%

Households
- Total households 26,752
  - With persons under 18 ... 8,967
  - With persons over 65 8,116
  - Family households 18,799
  - Single person households .. 6,204
- Persons per household 2.61
- Persons per family 3.13

Income & Poverty
- Per capita income $38,284
- Median household income .. $81,289
- Median family income $95,559
- Persons in poverty 4.7%
- H'holds receiving public assistance .. 369
- H'holds receiving social security .. 8,393

Labor & Employment
- Total civilian labor force .. 36,923
  - Unemployment rate 4.6%

Employed persons 16 years and over by occupation,
- Managers & professionals ... 18,101
- Service occupations 2,989
- Sales & office occupations .. 9,548
- Farming, fishing & forestry .. 0
- Construction & maintenance .. 1,929
- Production & transportation .. 2,643
- Self-employed persons 3,033

Housing Units
- Total 28,005
  - Single family units 19,791
  - Multiple family units ... 8,160
  - Mobile home units 54
  - Owner-occupied units 22,330
  - Renter-occupied units ... 4,422
  - Vacant units 1,253
- Median SF home value $301,700
- Median rent $1,123

Appendix C
2006 American Community Survey Data

Note: The 2006 American Community Survey (ACS) collected demographic data for cities and counties with populations of at least 65,000 – in New Jersey's case, 20 out of 566 municipalities. For those municipalities, ACS data is included here as a measure of the civilian, non-institutional population.

Clifton City
Passaic County

Population
- Total 79,349
  - Male 37,301
  - Female 42,048

Race & Hispanic Origin
- Race
  - White 52,878
  - Black/African American 2,388
  - Amer. Indian/Alaskan Native 281
  - Asian 6,286
  - Pacific Islander 0
  - Other Race 16,307
  - Two or more races 1,209
- Hispanic origin, total 21,492
  - Mexican 3,879
  - Puerto Rican 3,859
  - Cuban 97
  - Other Hispanic 13,657

Age & Nativity
- Under 5 years 4,618
- 18 years and over 62,565
- 21 years and over 58,842
- 65 years and over 11,081
- 85 years and over 1,762
  - Median age 39.0
- Native-born 51,503
- Foreign-born 27,846

Educational Attainment
- Population 25 years and over .. 54,695
  - Less than 9th grade 7.0%
  - High School grad or higher ... 85.2%
  - Bachelor's degree or higher .. 28.1%
  - Graduate degree 10.8%

Households
- Total households 28,235
  - With persons under 18 8,275
  - With persons over 65 7,894
  - Family households 19,503
  - Single person households 7,894
- Persons per household 2.78
- Persons per family 3.49

Income & Poverty
- Per capita income $24,446
- Median household income $51,756
- Median family income $61,781
- Persons in poverty 13.9%
- H'holds receiving public assistance .. 214
- H'holds receiving social security .. 8,522

Labor & Employment
- Total civilian labor force 39,943
  - Unemployment rate 5.2%

Employed persons 16 years and over by occupation,
- Managers & professionals 12,556
- Service occupations 5,374
- Sales & office occupations ... 11,031
- Farming, fishing & forestry 0
- Construction & maintenance ... 2,361
- Production & transportation .. 6,559
- Self-employed persons 763

Housing Units
- Total 29,837
  - Single family units 13,835
  - Multiple family units 16,002
  - Mobile home units 0
  - Owner-occupied units 17,316
  - Renter-occupied units 10,919
  - Vacant units 1,602
- Median SF home value $397,700
- Median rent $1,030

East Orange City
Essex County

Population
- Total 64,060
  - Male 29,918
  - Female 34,142

Race & Hispanic Origin
- Race
  - White 3,325
  - Black/African American 56,799
  - Amer. Indian/Alaskan Native 0
  - Asian 271
  - Pacific Islander 0
  - Other Race 2,597
  - Two or more races 1,068
- Hispanic origin, total 4,673
  - Mexican .... NA
  - Puerto Rican .... NA
  - Cuban .... NA
  - Other Hispanic .... NA

Age & Nativity
- Under 5 years 4,655
- 18 years and over 45,598
- 21 years and over 42,317
- 65 years and over 8,564
- 85 years and over 749
  - Median age 35.0
- Native-born 50,475
- Foreign-born 13,585

Educational Attainment
- Population 25 years and over .. 39,739
  - Less than 9th grade 5.4%
  - High School grad or higher ... 76.7%
  - Bachelor's degree or higher .. 16.1%
  - Graduate degree 5.8%

Households
- Total households 24,809
  - With persons under 18 8,781
  - With persons over 65 6,416
  - Family households 13,888
  - Single person households 9,982
- Persons per household 2.52
- Persons per family 3.50

Income & Poverty
- Per capita income $16,488
- Median household income $32,206
- Median family income $41,316
- Persons in poverty 30.3%
- H'holds receiving public assistance .. 1,177
- H'holds receiving social security .. 6,488

Labor & Employment
- Total civilian labor force 28,129
  - Unemployment rate 14.6%

Employed persons 16 years and over by occupation,
- Managers & professionals .... NA
- Service occupations .... NA
- Sales & office occupations .... NA
- Farming, fishing & forestry ...... NA
- Construction & maintenance ...... NA
- Production & transportation ..... NA
- Self-employed persons 907

Housing Units
- Total 29,020
  - Single family units 4,693
  - Multiple family units 24,104
  - Mobile home units 223
  - Owner-occupied units 6,559
  - Renter-occupied units 18,250
  - Vacant units 4,211
- Median SF home value $262,800
- Median rent $794

Edison Township
Middlesex County

Population
- Total 100,724
  - Male 51,192
  - Female 49,532

Race & Hispanic Origin
- Race
  - White 49,242
  - Black/African American 8,816
  - Amer. Indian/Alaskan Native ... 439
  - Asian 36,173
  - Pacific Islander 0
  - Other Race 3,982
  - Two or more races 2,072
- Hispanic origin, total 7,205
  - Mexican 2,335
  - Puerto Rican 1,861
  - Cuban 552
  - Other Hispanic 2,457

Age & Nativity
- Under 5 years 5,949
- 18 years and over 80,706
- 21 years and over 77,660
- 65 years and over 14,909
- 85 years and over 2,699
  - Median age 39.5
- Native-born 62,801
- Foreign-born 37,923

Educational Attainment
- Population 25 years and over .. 72,490
  - Less than 9th grade 5.3%
  - High School grad or higher ... 88.6%
  - Bachelor's degree or higher .. 47.3%
  - Graduate degree 21.2%

Households
- Total households 35,120
  - With persons under 18 11,915
  - With persons over 65 8,495
  - Family households 24,934
  - Single person households 8,340
- Persons per household 2.68
- Persons per family 3.22

Income & Poverty
- Per capita income $33,971
- Median household income $76,604
- Median family income $91,848
- Persons in poverty 5.6%
- H'holds receiving public assistance .. 148
- H'holds receiving social security .. 8,293

Labor & Employment
- Total civilian labor force 53,589
  - Unemployment rate 3.5%

Employed persons 16 years and over by occupation,
- Managers & professionals 26,000
- Service occupations 5,423
- Sales & office occupations ... 13,369
- Farming, fishing & forestry 0
- Construction & maintenance ... 1,998
- Production & transportation .. 4,909
- Self-employed persons 1,838

Housing Units
- Total 36,038
  - Single family units 18,141
  - Multiple family units 17,800
  - Mobile home units 97
  - Owner-occupied units 22,118
  - Renter-occupied units 13,002
  - Vacant units 918
- Median SF home value $392,900
- Median rent $1,178

2006 American Community Survey Data
Appendix C

Note: The 2006 American Community Survey (ACS) collected demographic data for cities and counties with populations of at least 65,000 – in New Jersey's case, 20 out of 566 municipalities. For those municipalities, ACS data is included here as a measure of the civilian, non-institutional population.

Elizabeth City
Union County

Population
- Total 125,337
  - Male 65,562
  - Female 63,775

Race & Hispanic Origin
Race
- White 58,912
- Black/African American 26,182
- Amer. Indian/Alaskan Native 326
- Asian 4,589
- Pacific Islander 472
- Other Race 36,764
- Two or more races 2,092
- Hispanic origin, total 73,354
  - Mexican 5,827
  - Puerto Rican 14,898
  - Cuban 4,700
  - Other Hispanic 47,929

Age & Nativity
- Under 5 years 11,230
- 18 years and over 96,798
- 21 years and over 91,738
- 65 years and over 13,250
- 85 years and over 1,639
  - Median age 33.4
- Native-born 62,941
- Foreign-born 66,396

Educational Attainment
- Population 25 years and over 82,898
  - Less than 9th grade 19.5%
  - High School grad or higher 65.2%
  - Bachelor's degree or higher 10.8%
  - Graduate degree 3.0%

Households
- Total households 42,693
  - With persons under 18 18,713
  - With persons over 65 9,100
  - Family households 29,885
  - Single person households 9,843
- Persons per household 2.98
- Persons per family 3.40

Income & Poverty
- Per capita income $18,209
- Median household income $42,412
- Median family income $43,285
- Persons in poverty 15.9%
- H'holds receiving public assistance . . . 1,711
- H'holds receiving social security 8,501

Labor & Employment
- Total civilian labor force 66,871
  - Unemployment rate 8.5%

Employed persons 16 years and over by occupation,
- Managers & professionals 10,286
- Service occupations 13,742
- Sales & office occupations 15,376
- Farming, fishing & forestry 0
- Construction & maintenance 6,255
- Production & transportation 15,535
- Self-employed persons 3,244

Housing Units
- Total 45,963
  - Single family units 6,741
  - Multiple family units 39,222
  - Mobile home units 0
  - Owner-occupied units 12,830
  - Renter-occupied units 29,863
  - Vacant units 3,270
- Median SF home value $385,100
- Median rent $894

Gloucester Township
Camden County

Population
- Total 71,042
  - Male 33,914
  - Female 37,128

Race & Hispanic Origin
Race
- White 55,555
- Black/African American 10,784
- Amer. Indian/Alaskan Native 83
- Asian 2,895
- Pacific Islander 0
- Other Race 458
- Two or more races 1,267
- Hispanic origin, total 1,597
  - Mexican . . . . NA
  - Puerto Rican . . . . NA
  - Cuban . . . . NA
  - Other Hispanic . . . . NA

Age & Nativity
- Under 5 years 4,455
- 18 years and over 51,631
- 21 years and over 48,584
- 65 years and over 6,835
- 85 years and over 427
  - Median age 35.7
- Native-born 66,925
- Foreign-born 4,117

Educational Attainment
- Population 25 years and over 44,350
  - Less than 9th grade 2.3%
  - High School grad or higher 89.0%
  - Bachelor's degree or higher 20.1%
  - Graduate degree 5.3%

Households
- Total households 24,377
  - With persons under 18 10,020
  - With persons over 65 4,792
  - Family households 17,888
  - Single person households 5,160
- Persons per household 2.89
- Persons per family 3.40

Income & Poverty
- Per capita income $26,150
- Median household income $62,453
- Median family income $73,226
- Persons in poverty 5.1%
- H'holds receiving public assistance 371
- H'holds receiving social security 5,712

Labor & Employment
- Total civilian labor force 39,000
  - Unemployment rate 7.2%

Employed persons 16 years and over by occupation,
- Managers & professionals 12,325
- Service occupations 4,833
- Sales & office occupations 11,930
- Farming, fishing & forestry 0
- Construction & maintenance 3,245
- Production & transportation 3,844
- Self-employed persons 1,090

Housing Units
- Total 24,697
  - Single family units 15,799
  - Multiple family units 8,608
  - Mobile home units 290
  - Owner-occupied units 18,717
  - Renter-occupied units 5,660
  - Vacant units 320
- Median SF home value $226,700
- Median rent $864

Hamilton Township
Mercer County

Population
- Total 90,072
  - Male 44,012
  - Female 46,060

Race & Hispanic Origin
Race
- White . . . . NA
- Black/African American . . . . NA
- Amer. Indian/Alaskan Native . . . . NA
- Asian . . . . NA
- Pacific Islander . . . . NA
- Other Race . . . . NA
- Two or more races . . . . NA
- Hispanic origin, total . . . . NA
  - Mexican . . . . NA
  - Puerto Rican . . . . NA
  - Cuban . . . . NA
  - Other Hispanic . . . . NA

Age & Nativity
- Under 5 years 5,075
- 18 years and over 69,298
- 21 years and over 66,029
- 65 years and over 14,249
- 85 years and over 2,439
  - Median age 42.1
- Native-born 74,310
- Foreign-born 15,762

Educational Attainment
- Population 25 years and over 60,717
  - Less than 9th grade 6.4%
  - High School grad or higher 86.2%
  - Bachelor's degree or higher 26.6%
  - Graduate degree 7.7%

Households
- Total households 31,886
  - With persons under 18 10,747
  - With persons over 65 9,416
  - Family households 22,864
  - Single person households 8,116
- Persons per household 2.80
- Persons per family 3.40

Income & Poverty
- Per capita income $27,861
- Median household income $66,574
- Median family income $75,546
- Persons in poverty 4.1%
- H'holds receiving public assistance 297
- H'holds receiving social security . . . 10,158

Labor & Employment
- Total civilian labor force 46,830
  - Unemployment rate 4.8%

Employed persons 16 years and over by occupation,
- Managers & professionals 16,564
- Service occupations 6,159
- Sales & office occupations 13,206
- Farming, fishing & forestry 0
- Construction & maintenance 3,999
- Production & transportation 4,671
- Self-employed persons 2,051

Housing Units
- Total 34,659
  - Single family units 23,731
  - Multiple family units 10,928
  - Mobile home units 0
  - Owner-occupied units 25,113
  - Renter-occupied units 6,773
  - Vacant units 2,773
- Median SF home value $270,400
- Median rent $888

Appendix C
2006 American Community Survey Data

Note: The 2006 American Community Survey (ACS) collected demographic data for cities and counties with populations of at least 65,000 – in New Jersey's case, 20 out of 566 municipalities. For those municipalities, ACS data is included here as a measure of the civilian, non-institutional population.

Jersey City
Hudson County

Population
Total........................242,845
  Male........................118,693
  Female......................124,152

Race & Hispanic Origin
Race
  White........................82,789
  Black/African American.......71,221
  Amer. Indian/Alaskan Native....500
  Asian........................45,827
  Pacific Islander...............151
  Other Race...................39,352
  Two or more races.............3,005
Hispanic origin, total........64,509
  Mexican......................4,717
  Puerto Rican................23,495
  Cuban........................1,095
  Other Hispanic..............35,202

Age & Nativity
Under 5 years.................18,481
18 years and over............183,730
21 years and over............174,162
65 years and over.............22,788
85 years and over..............2,782
  Median age....................34.8
Native-born..................154,148
Foreign-born.................88,697

Educational Attainment
Population 25 years and over......162,142
  Less than 9th grade............9.0%
  High School grad or higher....80.5%
  Bachelor's degree or higher...33.0%
  Graduate degree...............11.3%

Households
Total households.............90,020
  With persons under 18.......29,522
  With persons over 65........17,271
  Family households...........54,313
  Single person households....28,228
Persons per household..........2.67
Persons per family.............3.43

Income & Poverty
Per capita income...........$24,989
Median household income.....$43,426
Median family income........$43,372
Persons in poverty............20.0%
H'holds receiving public assistance...4,408
H'holds receiving social security....17,622

Labor & Employment
Total civilian labor force....127,708
  Unemployment rate............9.4%

Employed persons 16 years and over by occupation,
  Managers & professionals....40,404
  Service occupations.........24,599
  Sales & office occupations..29,381
  Farming, fishing & forestry......0
  Construction & maintenance...5,917
  Production & transportation.15,432
Self-employed persons.........5,793

Housing Units
Total........................102,579
  Single family units..........7,683
  Multiple family units.......94,809
  Mobile home units...............87
  Owner-occupied units........29,533
  Renter-occupied units.......60,487
  Vacant units................12,559
Median SF home value.......$359,100
Median rent....................$933

Lakewood Township
Ocean County

Population
Total.........................72,788
  Male........................35,817
  Female......................36,971

Race & Hispanic Origin
Race
  White...........................NA
  Black/African American..........NA
  Amer. Indian/Alaskan Native.....NA
  Asian...........................NA
  Pacific Islander................NA
  Other Race......................NA
  Two or more races...............NA
Hispanic origin, total............NA
  Mexican......................7,537
  Puerto Rican...................649
  Cuban...........................70
  Other Hispanic...............1,298

Age & Nativity
Under 5 years.................11,208
18 years and over.............46,341
21 years and over.............43,717
65 years and over.............10,988
85 years and over..............2,162
  Median age....................25.6
Native-born..................62,385
Foreign-born.................10,403

Educational Attainment
Population 25 years and over......37,644
  Less than 9th grade............6.1%
  High School grad or higher....87.0%
  Bachelor's degree or higher...25.4%
  Graduate degree................9.2%

Households
Total households.............22,615
  With persons under 18........9,792
  With persons over 65.........7,641
  Family households...........16,229
  Single person households.....5,565
Persons per household..........3.15
Persons per family.............3.81

Income & Poverty
Per capita income...........$15,810
Median household income.....$37,944
Median family income........$41,601
Persons in poverty............25.1%
H'holds receiving public assistance...1,293
H'holds receiving social security....8,336

Labor & Employment
Total civilian labor force....25,726
  Unemployment rate............6.6%

Employed persons 16 years and over by occupation,
  Managers & professionals.....8,565
  Service occupations..........4,440
  Sales & office occupations...6,100
  Farming, fishing & forestry....186
  Construction & maintenance...3,309
  Production & transportation..1,425
Self-employed persons.........1,921

Housing Units
Total........................25,126
  Single family units..........9,964
  Multiple family units.......15,124
  Mobile home units...............38
  Owner-occupied units........12,489
  Renter-occupied units.......10,126
  Vacant units.................2,511
Median SF home value.......$291,100
Median rent..................$1,305

Middletown Township
Monmouth County

Population
Total.........................69,870
  Male........................33,945
  Female......................35,925

Race & Hispanic Origin
Race
  White........................63,297
  Black/African American.......1,119
  Amer. Indian/Alaskan Native......0
  Asian........................2,600
  Pacific Islander.................0
  Other Race...................1,700
  Two or more races............1,154
Hispanic origin, total........3,584
  Mexican........................733
  Puerto Rican...................689
  Cuban...........................83
  Other Hispanic...............2,079

Age & Nativity
Under 5 years..................4,080
18 years and over.............52,336
21 years and over.............49,515
65 years and over.............10,095
85 years and over..............983
  Median age....................41.0
Native-born..................64,604
Foreign-born..................5,266

Educational Attainment
Population 25 years and over......47,030
  Less than 9th grade............1.7%
  High School grad or higher....94.1%
  Bachelor's degree or higher...36.7%
  Graduate degree...............14.5%

Households
Total households.............23,413
  With persons under 18........8,836
  With persons over 65.........6,850
  Family households...........17,524
  Single person households.....4,942
Persons per household..........2.97
Persons per family.............3.51

Income & Poverty
Per capita income...........$38,873
Median household income.....$88,873
Median family income.......$101,747
Persons in poverty.............3.1%
H'holds receiving public assistance......96
H'holds receiving social security....7,642

Labor & Employment
Total civilian labor force....35,555
  Unemployment rate............7.9%

Employed persons 16 years and over by occupation,
  Managers & professionals....14,812
  Service occupations..........4,173
  Sales & office occupations...9,015
  Farming, fishing & forestry......0
  Construction & maintenance...3,137
  Production & transportation..1,625
Self-employed persons.........1,363

Housing Units
Total........................24,627
  Single family units.........19,632
  Multiple family units........4,995
  Mobile home units................0
  Owner-occupied units........20,513
  Renter-occupied units........2,900
  Vacant units.................1,214
Median SF home value.......$441,200
Median rent..................$1,097

2006 American Community Survey Data

Appendix C

Note: The 2006 American Community Survey (ACS) collected demographic data for cities and counties with populations of at least 65,000 – in New Jersey's case, 20 out of 566 municipalities. For those municipalities, ACS data is included here as a measure of the civilian, non-institutional population.

Newark City
Essex County

Population
Total 266,736
  Male 131,772
  Female 134,964

Race & Hispanic Origin
Race
  White 59,018
  Black/African American 143,791
  Amer. Indian/Alaskan Native 1,282
  Asian 4,519
  Pacific Islander 40
  Other Race 51,237
  Two or more races 6,849
Hispanic origin, total 83,702
  Mexican 2,358
  Puerto Rican 39,404
  Cuban 1,613
  Other Hispanic 40,327

Age & Nativity
Under 5 years 20,118
18 years and over 196,208
21 years and over 182,653
65 years and over 24,856
85 years and over 2,422
  Median age 32.4
Native-born 194,942
Foreign-born 71,794

Educational Attainment
Population 25 years and over 166,151
  Less than 9th grade 17.0%
  High School grad or higher 65.5%
  Bachelor's degree or higher 11.9%
  Graduate degree 3.2%

Households
Total households 92,270
  With persons under 18 33,969
  With persons over 65 19,358
  Family households 57,772
  Single person households 29,701
Persons per household 2.75
Persons per family 3.47

Income & Poverty
Per capita income $16,077
Median household income $34,521
Median family income $40,958
Persons in poverty 24.2%
H'holds receiving public assistance .. 7,228
H'holds receiving social security .. 22,876

Labor & Employment
Total civilian labor force 125,556
  Unemployment rate 12.5%

Employed persons 16 years and over by occupation,
  Managers & professionals 20,480
  Service occupations 26,567
  Sales & office occupations 28,489
  Farming, fishing & forestry 85
  Construction & maintenance 15,627
  Production & transportation 18,557
Self-employed persons 4,575

Housing Units
Total 107,151
  Single family units 12,538
  Multiple family units 94,400
  Mobile home units 42
  Owner-occupied units 22,713
  Renter-occupied units 69,557
  Vacant units 14,881
Median SF home value $287,100
Median rent $787

Old Bridge Township
Middlesex County

Population
Total 60,338
  Male 29,640
  Female 30,698

Race & Hispanic Origin
Race
  White 48,174
  Black/African American 2,847
  Amer. Indian/Alaskan Native 154
  Asian 8,142
  Pacific Islander 0
  Other Race 205
  Two or more races 816
Hispanic origin, total .... NA
  Mexican .... NA
  Puerto Rican .... NA
  Cuban .... NA
  Other Hispanic .... NA

Age & Nativity
Under 5 years 4,209
18 years and over 47,119
21 years and over 45,068
65 years and over 6,534
85 years and over 707
  Median age 38.6
Native-born 46,567
Foreign-born 13,771

Educational Attainment
Population 25 years and over 42,495
  Less than 9th grade 1.9%
  High School grad or higher 91.9%
  Bachelor's degree or higher 34.0%
  Graduate degree 8.3%

Households
Total households 22,493
  With persons under 18 7,983
  With persons over 65 4,596
  Family households 16,851
  Single person households 4,868
Persons per household 2.66
Persons per family 3.10

Income & Poverty
Per capita income $33,647
Median household income $77,331
Median family income $87,049
Persons in poverty 3.0%
H'holds receiving public assistance 268
H'holds receiving social security ... 4,921

Labor & Employment
Total civilian labor force 36,223
  Unemployment rate 4.0%

Employed persons 16 years and over by occupation,
  Managers & professionals 13,331
  Service occupations 4,081
  Sales & office occupations 12,154
  Farming, fishing & forestry 0
  Construction & maintenance 2,172
  Production & transportation 3,051
Self-employed persons 1,261

Housing Units
Total 23,505
  Single family units 13,318
  Multiple family units 10,120
  Mobile home units 67
  Owner-occupied units 16,162
  Renter-occupied units 6,331
  Vacant units 1,012
Median SF home value $367,100
Median rent $949

Passaic City
Passaic County

Population
Total 56,665
  Male 29,154
  Female 27,511

Race & Hispanic Origin
Race
  White 21,782
  Black/African American 4,309
  Amer. Indian/Alaskan Native 0
  Asian 4,258
  Pacific Islander 0
  Other Race 25,325
  Two or more races 991
Hispanic origin, total 37,873
  Mexican 11,244
  Puerto Rican 7,279
  Cuban 983
  Other Hispanic 18,367

Age & Nativity
Under 5 years 5,605
18 years and over 39,896
21 years and over 37,440
65 years and over 4,436
85 years and over 947
  Median age 30.5
Native-born 29,657
Foreign-born 27,008

Educational Attainment
Population 25 years and over 34,057
  Less than 9th grade 20.9%
  High School grad or higher 66.2%
  Bachelor's degree or higher 19.4%
  Graduate degree 6.4%

Households
Total households 18,113
  With persons under 18 7,577
  With persons over 65 2,916
  Family households 11,772
  Single person households 5,199
Persons per household 3.10
Persons per family 4.00

Income & Poverty
Per capita income $13,366
Median household income $28,918
Median family income $33,595
Persons in poverty 23.5%
H'holds receiving public assistance 341
H'holds receiving social security ... 3,765

Labor & Employment
Total civilian labor force .... NA
  Unemployment rate .... NA

Employed persons 16 years and over by occupation,
  Managers & professionals .... NA
  Service occupations .... NA
  Sales & office occupations .... NA
  Farming, fishing & forestry .... NA
  Construction & maintenance .... NA
  Production & transportation .... NA
Self-employed persons 740

Housing Units
Total 19,633
  Single family units 2,579
  Multiple family units 17,054
  Mobile home units 0
  Owner-occupied units 4,344
  Renter-occupied units 13,769
  Vacant units 1,520
Median SF home value $385,300
Median rent $865

Appendix C

2006 American Community Survey Data

Note: The 2006 American Community Survey (ACS) collected demographic data for cities and counties with populations of at least 65,000 – in New Jersey's case, 20 out of 566 municipalities. For those municipalities, ACS data is included here as a measure of the civilian, non-institutional population.

Paterson City
Passaic County

Population
- Total.............................149,426
  - Male............................73,945
  - Female..........................75,481

Race & Hispanic Origin
Race
- White.............................36,302
- Black/African American............47,846
- Amer. Indian/Alaskan Native............0
- Asian..............................3,099
- Pacific Islander........................0
- Other Race........................59,664
- Two or more races..................2,515
- Hispanic origin, total............78,924
  - Mexican..........................9,818
  - Puerto Rican....................21,934
  - Cuban............................1,049
  - Other Hispanic..................46,123

Age & Nativity
- Under 5 years.....................12,928
- 18 years and over................107,320
- 21 years and over................100,512
- 65 years and over.................13,330
- 85 years and over..................1,606
  - Median age........................31.9
- Native-born......................98,477
- Foreign-born.....................50,949

Educational Attainment
- Population 25 years and over......91,243
  - Less than 9th grade..............16.8%
  - High School grad or higher.......69.1%
  - Bachelor's degree or higher.......7.8%
  - Graduate degree...................2.2%

Households
- Total households..................45,802
  - With persons under 18...........18,442
  - With persons over 65.............9,341
  - Family households...............31,928
  - Single person households........11,247
- Persons per household...............3.19
- Persons per family..................3.78

Income & Poverty
- Per capita income................$14,478
- Median household income..........$31,723
- Median family income.............$35,127
- Persons in poverty.................25.7%
- H'holds receiving public assistance...2,187
- H'holds receiving social security....10,392

Labor & Employment
- Total civilian labor force........68,644
  - Unemployment rate..................6.5%

Employed persons 16 years and over by occupation,
- Managers & professionals...........9,680
- Service occupations...............15,909
- Sales & office occupations........18,522
- Farming, fishing & forestry............0
- Construction & maintenance.........5,207
- Production & transportation.......14,874
- Self-employed persons..............2,496

Housing Units
- Total.............................51,538
  - Single family units...............8,653
  - Multiple family units............42,686
  - Mobile home units..................111
  - Owner-occupied units.............13,770
  - Renter-occupied units............32,032
  - Vacant units.....................5,736
- Median SF home value............$351,500
- Median rent.........................$957

Toms River Township
Ocean County

Population
- Total..............................96,571
  - Male............................47,659
  - Female..........................48,912

Race & Hispanic Origin
Race
- White.............................85,835
- Black/African American.............2,415
- Amer. Indian/Alaskan Native............0
- Asian..............................4,596
- Pacific Islander......................111
- Other Race........................2,010
- Two or more races..................1,604
- Hispanic origin, total.............7,010
  - Mexican..........................3,036
  - Puerto Rican.....................2,299
  - Cuban...............................31
  - Other Hispanic...................1,644

Age & Nativity
- Under 5 years......................4,958
- 18 years and over.................74,829
- 21 years and over.................72,178
- 65 years and over.................16,950
- 85 years and over..................2,013
  - Median age........................40.1
- Native-born......................87,442
- Foreign-born......................9,129

Educational Attainment
- Population 25 years and over......67,783
  - Less than 9th grade...............3.2%
  - High School grad or higher.......88.3%
  - Bachelor's degree or higher......26.5%
  - Graduate degree...................7.8%

Households
- Total households..................35,534
  - With persons under 18...........12,228
  - With persons over 65............11,105
  - Family households...............25,508
  - Single person households.........8,039
- Persons per household...............2.66
- Persons per family..................3.15

Income & Poverty
- Per capita income................$29,038
- Median household income..........$67,121
- Median family income.............$75,181
- Persons in poverty..................5.8%
- H'holds receiving public assistance.....489
- H'holds receiving social security....12,161

Labor & Employment
- Total civilian labor force........47,009
  - Unemployment rate..................6.6%

Employed persons 16 years and over by occupation,
- Managers & professionals..........16,330
- Service occupations...............6,693
- Sales & office occupations........12,266
- Farming, fishing & forestry...........85
- Construction & maintenance........4,882
- Production & transportation.......3,673
- Self-employed persons..............2,546

Housing Units
- Total.............................42,805
  - Single family units..............35,159
  - Multiple family units............6,460
  - Mobile home units................1,186
  - Owner-occupied units............30,324
  - Renter-occupied units............5,210
  - Vacant units.....................7,271
- Median SF home value............$345,100
- Median rent.......................$1,082

Trenton City
Mercer County

Population
- Total..............................83,581
  - Male............................42,080
  - Female..........................41,501

Race & Hispanic Origin
Race
- White.............................28,418
- Black/African American............42,744
- Amer. Indian/Alaskan Native..........234
- Asian................................305
- Pacific Islander........................0
- Other Race........................9,831
- Two or more races..................2,049
- Hispanic origin, total................NA
  - Mexican..........................3,079
  - Puerto Rican....................10,865
  - Cuban...............................76
  - Other Hispanic..................12,588

Age & Nativity
- Under 5 years......................6,110
- 18 years and over.................61,924
- 21 years and over.................58,899
- 65 years and over..................7,546
- 85 years and over....................669
  - Median age........................32.5
- Native-born......................67,935
- Foreign-born.....................15,646

Educational Attainment
- Population 25 years and over......53,673
  - Less than 9th grade..............11.4%
  - High School grad or higher.......66.7%
  - Bachelor's degree or higher.......9.9%
  - Graduate degree...................2.6%

Households
- Total households..................27,288
  - With persons under 18...........10,275
  - With persons over 65.............5,826
  - Family households...............16,145
  - Single person households.........8,607
- Persons per household...............2.92
- Persons per family..................3.72

Income & Poverty
- Per capita income................$15,933
- Median household income..........$32,548
- Median family income.............$36,247
- Persons in poverty.................21.3%
- H'holds receiving public assistance...1,920
- H'holds receiving social security.....7,686

Labor & Employment
- Total civilian labor force........40,731
  - Unemployment rate.................14.9%

Employed persons 16 years and over by occupation,
- Managers & professionals.............NA
- Service occupations..................NA
- Sales & office occupations...........NA
- Farming, fishing & forestry..........NA
- Construction & maintenance..........NA
- Production & transportation.........NA
- Self-employed persons..............1,450

Housing Units
- Total.............................32,675
  - Single family units..............5,254
  - Multiple family units...........27,376
  - Mobile home units....................0
  - Owner-occupied units............12,157
  - Renter-occupied units...........15,131
  - Vacant units.....................5,387
- Median SF home value............$126,300
- Median rent.........................$851

2006 American Community Survey Data
Appendix C

Note: The 2006 American Community Survey (ACS) collected demographic data for cities and counties with populations of at least 65,000 – in New Jersey's case, 20 out of 566 municipalities. For those municipalities, ACS data is included here as a measure of the civilian, non-institutional population.

Union City
Hudson County

Population
Total 67,556
   Male 33,543
   Female 34,013

Race & Hispanic Origin
Race
   White 51,040
   Black/African American 2,718
   Amer. Indian/Alaskan Native 54
   Asian 631
   Pacific Islander 0
   Other Race 11,526
   Two or more races 1,587
Hispanic origin, total .... NA
   Mexican 3,722
   Puerto Rican 7,199
   Cuban 7,840
   Other Hispanic 33,535

Age & Nativity
Under 5 years 5,383
18 years and over 50,279
21 years and over 47,671
65 years and over 7,660
85 years and over 978
   Median age 34.7
Native-born 29,561
Foreign-born 37,995

Educational Attainment
Population 25 years and over 43,919
   Less than 9th grade 23.5%
   High School grad or higher 62.0%
   Bachelor's degree or higher 16.9%
   Graduate degree 4.3%

Households
Total households 21,683
   With persons under 18 8,079
   With persons over 65 4,680
   Family households 15,547
   Single person households 5,039
Persons per household 3.09
Persons per family 3.63

Income & Poverty
Per capita income $16,991
Median household income $39,388
Median family income $42,866
Persons in poverty 17.3%
H'holds receiving public assistance .. 453
H'holds receiving social security . 4,749

Labor & Employment
Total civilian labor force 36,816
   Unemployment rate 8.7%

Employed persons 16 years and over by occupation,
   Managers & professionals .... NA
   Service occupations .... NA
   Sales & office occupations .... NA
   Farming, fishing & forestry ...... NA
   Construction & maintenance .... NA
   Production & transportation ...... NA
Self-employed persons 872

Housing Units
Total 23,953
   Single family units 1,134
   Multiple family units 22,819
   Mobile home units 0
   Owner-occupied units 4,569
   Renter-occupied units 17,114
   Vacant units 2,270
Median SF home value $405,700
Median rent $906

Woodbridge Township
Middlesex County

Population
Total 96,869
   Male 49,500
   Female 47,369

Race & Hispanic Origin
Race
   White 63,659
   Black/African American 8,253
   Amer. Indian/Alaskan Native 98
   Asian 15,948
   Pacific Islander 0
   Other Race 7,932
   Two or more races 979
Hispanic origin, total 15,108
   Mexican 1,043
   Puerto Rican 7,634
   Cuban 1,678
   Other Hispanic 4,753

Age & Nativity
Under 5 years 6,502
18 years and over 75,573
21 years and over 72,595
65 years and over 12,255
85 years and over 1,929
   Median age 38.5
Native-born 73,809
Foreign-born 23,060

Educational Attainment
Population 25 years and over 69,294
   Less than 9th grade 7.2%
   High School grad or higher 84.8%
   Bachelor's degree or higher 28.8%
   Graduate degree 9.3%

Households
Total households 33,255
   With persons under 18 13,122
   With persons over 65 8,655
   Family households 25,034
   Single person households 6,897
Persons per household 2.82
Persons per family 3.26

Income & Poverty
Per capita income $29,102
Median household income $77,019
Median family income $82,831
Persons in poverty 4.7%
H'holds receiving public assistance .. 407
H'holds receiving social security . 8,659

Labor & Employment
Total civilian labor force 50,879
   Unemployment rate 5.8%

Employed persons 16 years and over by occupation,
   Managers & professionals 18,309
   Service occupations 5,653
   Sales & office occupations 14,429
   Farming, fishing & forestry 0
   Construction & maintenance 3,691
   Production & transportation 5,833
Self-employed persons 1,692

Housing Units
Total 36,066
   Single family units 22,678
   Multiple family units 12,959
   Mobile home units 429
   Owner-occupied units 23,284
   Renter-occupied units 9,971
   Vacant units 2,811
Median SF home value $342,900
Median rent $1,110

The New Jersey Municipal Data Book

Supplemental School District Data

Appendix D

Additional Public School District Data
(for school year 2006-07 except where noted)

Black Horse Pike Regional High School District
580 Erial Rd
Blackwood, NJ 08012
Camden County
856-227-4106
http://www.bhprsd.org

Superintendent	Ralph E. Ross
Number of schools	3
Grade plan	9-12
Enrollment	4,262
Attendance rate, '05-06	92.9%
Dropout rate	1.5%
Students per teacher	13.1
Per pupil expenditure	$12,869
Median faculty salary	$45,326
Median administrator salary	$91,913
Grade 12 enrollment	956
High school graduation rate	NA

Assessment test results
(percent scoring at proficient or advanced level)

	Language	Math
ASK-Gr 3	NA	NA
GEPA-Gr 8	NA	NA
HSPA-High Schl	88.7%	71.4%

SAT score averages

Pct tested	Math	Verbal	Writing
NA	NA	NA	NA

Teacher Qualifications
Avg years of experience ... 9
Highly-qualified teachers
  one subject/all subjects ... 99.0%/99.0%
With emergency credentials ... 0.0%

No Child Left Behind
AYP, 2005-06 ... Needs Improvement

Carlstadt-East Rutherford Regional High School District
Paterson Ave & Cornelia St
East Rutherford, NJ 07073
Bergen County
201-935-4155
http://www.bectonhs.org

Superintendent	Samuel G. Feldman
Number of schools	1
Grade plan	9-12
Enrollment	523
Attendance rate, '05-06	93.8%
Dropout rate	0.2%
Students per teacher	10.6
Per pupil expenditure	$17,299
Median faculty salary	$70,146
Median administrator salary	$118,000
Grade 12 enrollment	124
High school graduation rate	99.2%

Assessment test results
(percent scoring at proficient or advanced level)

	Language	Math
ASK-Gr 3	NA	NA
GEPA-Gr 8	NA	NA
HSPA-High Schl	87.1%	69.5%

SAT score averages

Pct tested	Math	Verbal	Writing
75%	499	454	467

Teacher Qualifications
Avg years of experience ... 10
Highly-qualified teachers
  one subject/all subjects ... 100%/100%
With emergency credentials ... 0.0%

No Child Left Behind
AYP, 2005-06 ... Meets Standards

Central Regional School District
Forest Hills Parkway
Bayville, NJ 08721
Ocean County
732-269-1100
http://www.centralreg.k12.nj.us

Superintendent	David Trethaway
Number of schools	2
Grade plan	7-12
Enrollment	2,169
Attendance rate, '05-06	92.2%
Dropout rate	2.8%
Students per teacher	12.0
Per pupil expenditure	$13,542
Median faculty salary	$53,100
Median administrator salary	$97,798
Grade 12 enrollment	283
High school graduation rate	90.7%

Assessment test results
(percent scoring at proficient or advanced level)

	Language	Math
ASK-Gr 3	NA	NA
GEPA-Gr 8	73.4%	73.6%
HSPA-High Schl	85.8%	66.3%

SAT score averages

Pct tested	Math	Verbal	Writing
69%	469	461	453

Teacher Qualifications
Avg years of experience ... 8
Highly-qualified teachers
  one subject/all subjects ... 100%/100%
With emergency credentials ... 0.0%

No Child Left Behind
AYP, 2005-06 ... Needs Improvement

Clearview Regional High School District
420 Cedar Rd
Mullica Hill, NJ 08062
Gloucester County
856-223-2765
http://www.clearviewregional.edu

Superintendent	John Horchak III
Number of schools	2
Grade plan	7-12
Enrollment	2,391
Attendance rate, '05-06	94.8%
Dropout rate	0.8%
Students per teacher	12.9
Per pupil expenditure	$10,677
Median faculty salary	$49,500
Median administrator salary	$94,275
Grade 12 enrollment	347
High school graduation rate	96.6%

Assessment test results
(percent scoring at proficient or advanced level)

	Language	Math
ASK-Gr 3	NA	NA
GEPA-Gr 8	85.4%	80.9%
HSPA-High Schl	93.0%	81.9%

SAT score averages

Pct tested	Math	Verbal	Writing
78%	512	504	498

Teacher Qualifications
Avg years of experience ... 8
Highly-qualified teachers
  one subject/all subjects ... 100%/100%
With emergency credentials ... 0.0%

No Child Left Behind
AYP, 2005-06 ... Meets Standards

Cumberland Regional High School District
Love Lane, PO Box 5115
Seabrook, NJ 08302
Cumberland County
856-451-9400
http://www.crhsd.org

Superintendent	Katherine A. Kelk
Number of schools	1
Grade plan	9-12
Enrollment	1,385
Attendance rate, '05-06	93.0%
Dropout rate	3.7%
Students per teacher	12.2
Per pupil expenditure	$12,552
Median faculty salary	$60,069
Median administrator salary	$99,461
Grade 12 enrollment	289
High school graduation rate	84.8%

Assessment test results
(percent scoring at proficient or advanced level)

	Language	Math
ASK-Gr 3	NA	NA
GEPA-Gr 8	NA	NA
HSPA-High Schl	81.3%	68.9%

SAT score averages

Pct tested	Math	Verbal	Writing
49%	489	463	467

Teacher Qualifications
Avg years of experience ... 15
Highly-qualified teachers
  one subject/all subjects ... 100%/100%
With emergency credentials ... 0.0%

No Child Left Behind
AYP, 2005-06 ... Needs Improvement

Delaware Valley Regional High School
19 Senator Stout Rd
Frenchtown, NJ 08825
Hunterdon County
908-996-2131
http://www.dvrhs.k12.nj.us

Superintendent	Thomas Butler (Int)
Number of schools	1
Grade plan	9-12
Enrollment	952
Attendance rate, '05-06	96.6%
Dropout rate	0.4%
Students per teacher	10.9
Per pupil expenditure	$14,628
Median faculty salary	$55,955
Median administrator salary	$114,746
Grade 12 enrollment	233
High school graduation rate	97.9%

Assessment test results
(percent scoring at proficient or advanced level)

	Language	Math
ASK-Gr 3	NA	NA
GEPA-Gr 8	NA	NA
HSPA-High Schl	95.6%	86.4%

SAT score averages

Pct tested	Math	Verbal	Writing
83%	534	533	526

Teacher Qualifications
Avg years of experience ... 11
Highly-qualified teachers
  one subject/all subjects ... 100%/100%
With emergency credentials ... 0.0%

No Child Left Behind
AYP, 2005-06 ... Meets Standards

The New Jersey Municipal Data Book

Appendix D

Supplemental School District Data

Additional Public School District Data
(for school year 2006-07 except where noted)

Delsea Regional High School District
Fried Mill Rd, PO Box 405
Franklinville, NJ 08322
Gloucester County
856-694-0100
http://www.delsea.k12.nj.us

Superintendent	Frank Borelli
Number of schools	2
Grade plan	7-12
Enrollment	1,793
Attendance rate, '05-06	NA
Dropout rate	3.3%
Students per teacher	11.4
Per pupil expenditure	$13,453
Median faculty salary	$55,850
Median administrator salary	$97,232
Grade 12 enrollment	289
High school graduation rate	91.2%

Assessment test results
(percent scoring at proficient or advanced level)

	Language	Math
ASK-Gr 3	NA	NA
GEPA-Gr 8	72.3%	76.7%
HSPA-High Schl	91.9%	81.0%

SAT score averages

Pct tested	Math	Verbal	Writing
68%	502	475	477

Teacher Qualifications

Avg years of experience	12
Highly-qualified teachers one subject/all subjects	100%/100%
With emergency credentials	1.7%

No Child Left Behind

AYP, 2005-06	Meets Standards

Eastern Camden County Regional School District
Laurel Oak Rd, Box 2500
Voorhees, NJ 08043
Camden County
856-346-6740
http://www.eastern.k12.nj.us

Superintendent	Harold Melleby Jr
Number of schools	2
Grade plan	9-12
Enrollment	2,170
Attendance rate, '05-06	94.6%
Dropout rate	0.4%
Students per teacher	12.4
Per pupil expenditure	$13,583
Median faculty salary	$56,534
Median administrator salary	$110,681
Grade 12 enrollment	548
High school graduation rate	99.8%

Assessment test results
(percent scoring at proficient or advanced level)

	Language	Math
ASK-Gr 3	NA	NA
GEPA-Gr 8	NA	NA
HSPA-High Schl	93.8%	85.0%

SAT score averages

Pct tested	Math	Verbal	Writing
88%	550	541	538

Teacher Qualifications

Avg years of experience	10
Highly-qualified teachers one subject/all subjects	100%/100%
With emergency credentials	0.0%

No Child Left Behind

AYP, 2005-06	Meets Standards

Freehold Regional High School District
11 Pine St
Englishtown, NJ 07726
Monmouth County
732-792-7300
http://www.frhsd.com

Superintendent	James Wasser
Number of schools	6
Grade plan	9-12
Enrollment	11,527
Attendance rate, '05-06	93.9%
Dropout rate	0.3%
Students per teacher	13.0
Per pupil expenditure	$12,742
Median faculty salary	$57,400
Median administrator salary	$101,538
Grade 12 enrollment	2,819
High school graduation rate	NA

Assessment test results
(percent scoring at proficient or advanced level)

	Language	Math
ASK-Gr 3	NA	NA
GEPA-Gr 8	NA	NA
HSPA-High Schl	95.3%	88.9%

SAT score averages

Pct tested	Math	Verbal	Writing
NA	NA	NA	NA

Teacher Qualifications

Avg years of experience	9
Highly-qualified teachers one subject/all subjects	100%/100%
With emergency credentials	0.3%

No Child Left Behind

AYP, 2005-06	Needs Improvement

Gateway Regional School District
775 Tanyard Rd
Woodbury Heights, NJ 08096
Gloucester County
856-848-8172
http://www.gatewayhs.com

Superintendent	Joyce Stumpo
Number of schools	1
Grade plan	7-12
Enrollment	1,007
Attendance rate, '05-06	91.7%
Dropout rate	2.2%
Students per teacher	9.8
Per pupil expenditure	$14,549
Median faculty salary	$51,250
Median administrator salary	$94,000
Grade 12 enrollment	181
High school graduation rate	94.7%

Assessment test results
(percent scoring at proficient or advanced level)

	Language	Math
ASK-Gr 3	NA	NA
GEPA-Gr 8	71.6%	68.1%
HSPA-High Schl	86.5%	82.1%

SAT score averages

Pct tested	Math	Verbal	Writing
68%	503	478	462

Teacher Qualifications

Avg years of experience	9
Highly-qualified teachers one subject/all subjects	98.5%/98.5%
With emergency credentials	0.0%

No Child Left Behind

AYP, 2005-06	Meets Standards

Greater Egg Harbor Regional High School District
1824 Dr. Dennis Foreman Dr
Mays Landing, NJ 08330
Atlantic County
609-625-1456
http://www.gehrhsd.net

Superintendent	Adam Pfeffer
Number of schools	2
Grade plan	9-12
Enrollment	3,914
Attendance rate, '05-06	92.4%
Dropout rate	2.1%
Students per teacher	12.6
Per pupil expenditure	$12,710
Median faculty salary	$50,715
Median administrator salary	$94,081
Grade 12 enrollment	831
High school graduation rate	NA

Assessment test results
(percent scoring at proficient or advanced level)

	Language	Math
ASK-Gr 3	NA	NA
GEPA-Gr 8	NA	NA
HSPA-High Schl	85.9%	70.1%

SAT score averages

Pct tested	Math	Verbal	Writing
NA	NA	NA	NA

Teacher Qualifications

Avg years of experience	7
Highly-qualified teachers one subject/all subjects	100%/100%
With emergency credentials	0.0%

No Child Left Behind

AYP, 2005-06	Needs Improvement

Hanover Park Regional High School District
75 Mount Pleasant Avenue
East Hanover, NJ 07936
Morris County
973-887-0320
(no website)

Superintendent	Paul Arilotta
Number of schools	2
Grade plan	9-12
Enrollment	1,507
Attendance rate, '05-06	96.4%
Dropout rate	0.5%
Students per teacher	10.2
Per pupil expenditure	$16,471
Median faculty salary	$62,526
Median administrator salary	$121,400
Grade 12 enrollment	388
High school graduation rate	NA

Assessment test results
(percent scoring at proficient or advanced level)

	Language	Math
ASK-Gr 3	NA	NA
GEPA-Gr 8	NA	NA
HSPA-High Schl	95.2%	84.6%

SAT score averages

Pct tested	Math	Verbal	Writing
NA	NA	NA	NA

Teacher Qualifications

Avg years of experience	9
Highly-qualified teachers one subject/all subjects	100%/100%
With emergency credentials	0.0%

No Child Left Behind

AYP, 2005-06	Meets Standards

Supplemental School District Data

Appendix D

Additional Public School District Data
(for school year 2006-07 except where noted)

Henry Hudson Regional School
1 Grand Tour
Highlands, NJ 07732
Monmouth County
732-872-0900
http://www.henryhudsonreg.k12.nj.us

Superintendent	Kathryn A. Fedina
Number of schools	1
Grade plan	7-12
Enrollment	474
Attendance rate, '05-06	93.0%
Dropout rate	1.4%
Students per teacher	10.0
Per pupil expenditure	$17,348
Median faculty salary	$50,170
Median administrator salary	$102,903
Grade 12 enrollment	63
High school graduation rate	97.2%

Assessment test results
(percent scoring at proficient or advanced level)

	Language	Math
ASK-Gr 3	NA	NA
GEPA-Gr 8	67.1%	71.1%
HSPA-High Schl	88.6%	63.3%

SAT score averages

Pct tested	Math	Verbal	Writing
65%	470	487	464

Teacher Qualifications

Avg years of experience	7
Highly-qualified teachers one subject/all subjects	97.0%/94.5%
With emergency credentials	0.0%

No Child Left Behind
AYP, 2005-06 .... Meets Standards

High Point Regional School District
299 Pigeon Hill Rd
Sussex, NJ 07461
Sussex County
973-875-7204
http://www.hpregional.org

Chief School Admin	John W. Hannum
Number of schools	1
Grade plan	9-12
Enrollment	1,349
Attendance rate, '05-06	95.7%
Dropout rate	2.5%
Students per teacher	10.7
Per pupil expenditure	$14,329
Median faculty salary	$61,951
Median administrator salary	$98,449
Grade 12 enrollment	317
High school graduation rate	88.7%

Assessment test results
(percent scoring at proficient or advanced level)

	Language	Math
ASK-Gr 3	NA	NA
GEPA-Gr 8	NA	NA
HSPA-High Schl	91.5%	86.2%

SAT score averages

Pct tested	Math	Verbal	Writing
72%	525	503	493

Teacher Qualifications

Avg years of experience	9
Highly-qualified teachers one subject/all subjects	100%/100%
With emergency credentials	0.0%

No Child Left Behind
AYP, 2005-06 .... Meets Standards

Hopewell Valley Regional High School District
425 South Main St
Pennington, NJ 08534
Mercer County
609-737-4000
http://www.hvrsd.k12.nj.us

Chief School Admin	Judith Ferguson
Number of schools	6
Grade plan	K-12
Enrollment	4,036
Attendance rate, '05-06	96.2%
Dropout rate	0.5%
Students per teacher	10.6
Per pupil expenditure	$15,143
Median faculty salary	$61,343
Median administrator salary	$109,814
Grade 12 enrollment	284
High school graduation rate	97.9%

Assessment test results
(percent scoring at proficient or advanced level)

	Language	Math
ASK-Gr 3	93.5%	92.9%
GEPA-Gr 8	88.7%	83.5%
HSPA-High Schl	97.1%	90.0%

SAT score averages

Pct tested	Math	Verbal	Writing
96%	585	557	562

Teacher Qualifications

Avg years of experience	10
Highly-qualified teachers one subject/all subjects	100%/100%
With emergency credentials	0.0%

No Child Left Behind
AYP, 2005-06 .... Meets Standards

Hunterdon Central Regional High School
84 Route 31
Flemington, NJ 08822
Hunterdon County
908-782-5727
http://www.hcrhs.k12.nj.us

Superintendent	Lisa Brady
Number of schools	1
Grade plan	9-12
Enrollment	2,892
Attendance rate, '05-06	96.8%
Dropout rate	0.6%
Students per teacher	10.5
Per pupil expenditure	$17,780
Median faculty salary	$56,076
Median administrator salary	$115,249
Grade 12 enrollment	654
High school graduation rate	97.0%

Assessment test results
(percent scoring at proficient or advanced level)

	Language	Math
ASK-Gr 3	NA	NA
GEPA-Gr 8	NA	NA
HSPA-High Schl	95.6%	89.4%

SAT score averages

Pct tested	Math	Verbal	Writing
95%	553	544	546

Teacher Qualifications

Avg years of experience	8
Highly-qualified teachers one subject/all subjects	100%/100%
With emergency credentials	0.0%

No Child Left Behind
AYP, 2005-06 .... Meets Standards

Kingsway Regional School District
213 Kings Highway
Woolwich Twp, NJ 08085
Gloucester County
856-467-4600
http://www.kingsway.k12.nj.us

Superintendent	Ave Altersitz
Number of schools	2
Grade plan	7-12
Enrollment	2,039
Attendance rate, '05-06	94.1%
Dropout rate	NA
Students per teacher	12.4
Per pupil expenditure	$13,178
Median faculty salary	$43,355
Median administrator salary	$95,500
Grade 12 enrollment	371
High school graduation rate	98.2%

Assessment test results
(percent scoring at proficient or advanced level)

	Language	Math
ASK-Gr 3	NA	NA
GEPA-Gr 8	79.9%	79.0%
HSPA-High Schl	90.7%	81.9%

SAT score averages

Pct tested	Math	Verbal	Writing
74%	517	499	488

Teacher Qualifications

Avg years of experience	7
Highly-qualified teachers one subject/all subjects	100%/100%
With emergency credentials	0.0%

No Child Left Behind
AYP, 2005-06 .... Meets Standards

Kittatinny Regional High School
77 Halsey Rd
Newton, NJ 07860
Sussex County
973-383-1800
http://www.krhs.net

Chief School Admin	Robert G. Walker
Number of schools	1
Grade plan	7-12
Enrollment	1,243
Attendance rate, '05-06	96.0%
Dropout rate	1.2%
Students per teacher	10.5
Per pupil expenditure	$14,295
Median faculty salary	$64,755
Median administrator salary	$106,002
Grade 12 enrollment	216
High school graduation rate	96.2%

Assessment test results
(percent scoring at proficient or advanced level)

	Language	Math
ASK-Gr 3	NA	NA
GEPA-Gr 8	86.9%	86.3%
HSPA-High Schl	94.6%	91.5%

SAT score averages

Pct tested	Math	Verbal	Writing
82%	511	500	485

Teacher Qualifications

Avg years of experience	9
Highly-qualified teachers one subject/all subjects	99.0%/99.0%
With emergency credentials	0.0%

No Child Left Behind
AYP, 2005-06 .... Meets Standards

The New Jersey Municipal Data Book

Appendix D

Supplemental School District Data

Additional Public School District Data
(for school year 2006-07 except where noted)

Lakeland Regional High School
205 Conklintown Rd
Wanaque, NJ 07465
Passaic County
973-835-1900
http://www.lakeland.k12.nj.us

Chief School Admin	Albert Guazzo
Number of schools	1
Grade plan	9-12
Enrollment	1,128
Attendance rate, '05-06	95.2%
Dropout rate	1.7%
Students per teacher	10.9
Per pupil expenditure	$16,325
Median faculty salary	$69,400
Median administrator salary	$111,500
Grade 12 enrollment	261
High school graduation rate	91.3%

Assessment test results
(percent scoring at proficient or advanced level)

	Language	Math
ASK-Gr 3	NA	NA
GEPA-Gr 8	NA	NA
HSPA-High Schl	90.8%	83.6%

SAT score averages

Pct tested	Math	Verbal	Writing
79%	493	503	504

Teacher Qualifications

Avg years of experience	12
Highly-qualified teachers one subject/all subjects	100%/100%
With emergency credentials	0.0%

No Child Left Behind

AYP, 2005-06 .... Meets Standards

Lenape Regional High School District
93 Willow Grove Rd
Shamong, NJ 08088
Burlington County
609-268-2000
http://www.lr.k12.nj.us

Superintendent	Emily Capella
Number of schools	4
Grade plan	9-12
Enrollment	7,447
Attendance rate, '05-06	94.2%
Dropout rate	0.6%
Students per teacher	10.8
Per pupil expenditure	$14,956
Median faculty salary	$56,594
Median administrator salary	$124,300
Grade 12 enrollment	1,793
High school graduation rate	NA

Assessment test results
(percent scoring at proficient or advanced level)

	Language	Math
ASK-Gr 3	NA	NA
GEPA-Gr 8	NA	NA
HSPA-High Schl	92.8%	87.1%

SAT score averages

Pct tested	Math	Verbal	Writing
NA	NA	NA	NA

Teacher Qualifications

Avg years of experience	9
Highly-qualified teachers one subject/all subjects	100%/100%
With emergency credentials	0.0%

No Child Left Behind

AYP, 2005-06 .... Meets Standards

Lenape Valley Regional High School District
28 Sparta Rd, PO Box 578
Stanhope, NJ 07874
Sussex County
973-347-7600
http://www.lvhs.org

Chief School Admin	Paul A. Palek Jr
Number of schools	1
Grade plan	9-12
Enrollment	809
Attendance rate, '05-06	95.1%
Dropout rate	2.7%
Students per teacher	10.4
Per pupil expenditure	$13,621
Median faculty salary	$63,000
Median administrator salary	$105,600
Grade 12 enrollment	161
High school graduation rate	92.3%

Assessment test results
(percent scoring at proficient or advanced level)

	Language	Math
ASK-Gr 3	NA	NA
GEPA-Gr 8	NA	NA
HSPA-High Schl	92.2%	81.2%

SAT score averages

Pct tested	Math	Verbal	Writing
85%	501	491	500

Teacher Qualifications

Avg years of experience	14
Highly-qualified teachers one subject/all subjects	100%/100%
With emergency credentials	0.0%

No Child Left Behind

AYP, 2005-06 .... Meets Standards

Long Beach Island School District
200 Barnegat Avenue
Surf City, NJ 08008
Ocean County
609-494-2341
http://www.lbischools.org

Superintendent	Robert A. Garguilo
Number of schools	2
Grade plan	K-6
Enrollment	248
Attendance rate, '05-06	94.3%
Dropout rate	NA
Students per teacher	6.9
Per pupil expenditure	$21,956
Median faculty salary	$68,857
Median administrator salary	$94,335
Grade 12 enrollment	NA
High school graduation rate	NA

Assessment test results
(percent scoring at proficient or advanced level)

	Language	Math
ASK-Gr 3	100%	90.0%
GEPA-Gr 8	NA	NA
HSPA-High Schl	NA	NA

SAT score averages

Pct tested	Math	Verbal	Writing
NA	NA	NA	NA

Teacher Qualifications

Avg years of experience	19
Highly-qualified teachers one subject/all subjects	100%/100%
With emergency credentials	0.0%

No Child Left Behind

AYP, 2005-06 .... Meets Standards

Lower Cape May Regional School District
687 Route 9
Cape May, NJ 08204
Cape May County
609-884-3475
http://www.lcmrschools.com

Superintendent	Jack Pfizenmayer
Number of schools	2
Grade plan	7-12
Enrollment	1,762
Attendance rate, '05-06	91.5%
Dropout rate	4.0%
Students per teacher	10.7
Per pupil expenditure	$13,695
Median faculty salary	$63,120
Median administrator salary	$91,617
Grade 12 enrollment	249
High school graduation rate	84.4%

Assessment test results
(percent scoring at proficient or advanced level)

	Language	Math
ASK-Gr 3	NA	NA
GEPA-Gr 8	67.7%	63.8%
HSPA-High Schl	86.0%	69.5%

SAT score averages

Pct tested	Math	Verbal	Writing
56%	500	481	472

Teacher Qualifications

Avg years of experience	13
Highly-qualified teachers one subject/all subjects	99.0%/99.0%
With emergency credentials	0.0%

No Child Left Behind

AYP, 2005-06 .... Needs Improvement

Mainland Regional High School
1301 Oak Avenue
Linwood, NJ 08221
Atlantic County
609-927-2461
http://mainlandregional.net

Superintendent	Russell Dever
Number of schools	1
Grade plan	9-12
Enrollment	1,622
Attendance rate, '05-06	92.9%
Dropout rate	1.8%
Students per teacher	11.2
Per pupil expenditure	$12,533
Median faculty salary	$67,300
Median administrator salary	$103,378
Grade 12 enrollment	395
High school graduation rate	93.3%

Assessment test results
(percent scoring at proficient or advanced level)

	Language	Math
ASK-Gr 3	NA	NA
GEPA-Gr 8	NA	NA
HSPA-High Schl	93.1%	84.6%

SAT score averages

Pct tested	Math	Verbal	Writing
82%	521	509	507

Teacher Qualifications

Avg years of experience	12
Highly-qualified teachers one subject/all subjects	100%/100%
With emergency credentials	0.0%

No Child Left Behind

AYP, 2005-06 .... Meets Standards

Supplemental School District Data

Additional Public School District Data
(for school year 2006-07 except where noted)

Monmouth Regional High School District
One Norman J. Field Way
Tinton Falls, NJ 07724
Monmouth County
732-542-1170
http://www.monreghs.k12.nj.us

Superintendent.......... James W. Cleary
Number of schools..................... 1
Grade plan........................ 9-12
Enrollment...................... 1,200
Attendance rate, '05-06 .... 97.6%
Dropout rate....................... 1.0%
Students per teacher................. 9.1
Per pupil expenditure........... $19,944
Median faculty salary............ $57,450
Median administrator salary...... $98,609
Grade 12 enrollment................ 280
High school graduation rate 96.0%

Assessment test results
(percent scoring at proficient or advanced level)

	Language	Math
ASK-Gr 3	NA	NA
GEPA-Gr 8	NA	NA
HSPA-High Schl	91.0%	73.3%

SAT score averages

Pct tested	Math	Verbal	Writing
84%	504	488	482

Teacher Qualifications
Avg years of experience 12
Highly-qualified teachers
  one subject/all subjects...... 100%/100%
With emergency credentials 0.0%

No Child Left Behind
AYP, 2005-06 .... Needs Improvement

Morris Hills Regional School District
10 Knoll Dr
Rockaway, NJ 07866
Morris County
973-664-2291
http://www.mhrd.k12.nj.us

Superintendent............ Ernest Palestis
Number of schools..................... 2
Grade plan........................ 9-12
Enrollment...................... 2,731
Attendance rate, '05-06 .... 96.3%
Dropout rate....................... 0.5%
Students per teacher................ 10.1
Per pupil expenditure........... $16,597
Median faculty salary............ $67,450
Median administrator salary..... $125,592
Grade 12 enrollment................ 645
High school graduation rate .... NA

Assessment test results
(percent scoring at proficient or advanced level)

	Language	Math
ASK-Gr 3	NA	NA
GEPA-Gr 8	NA	NA
HSPA-High Schl	88.8%	80.5%

SAT score averages

Pct tested	Math	Verbal	Writing
NA	NA	NA	NA

Teacher Qualifications
Avg years of experience 8
Highly-qualified teachers
  one subject/all subjects...... 100%/100%
With emergency credentials 0.0%

No Child Left Behind
AYP, 2005-06 .... Meets Standards

North Hunterdon/Voorhees Regional High School District
1445 State Route 31
Annandale, NJ 08801
Hunterdon County
908-735-2846
http://www.nhvweb.net

Superintendent....... Charles M. Shaddow
Number of schools..................... 2
Grade plan........................ 9-12
Enrollment...................... 2,964
Attendance rate, '05-06 .... 97.1%
Dropout rate....................... 0.6%
Students per teacher................ 10.6
Per pupil expenditure........... $16,543
Median faculty salary............ $54,770
Median administrator salary..... $105,800
Grade 12 enrollment................ 669
High school graduation rate .... NA

Assessment test results
(percent scoring at proficient or advanced level)

	Language	Math
ASK-Gr 3	NA	NA
GEPA-Gr 8	NA	NA
HSPA-High Schl	96.1%	91.1%

SAT score averages

Pct tested	Math	Verbal	Writing
NA	NA	NA	NA

Teacher Qualifications
Avg years of experience 9
Highly-qualified teachers
  one subject/all subjects...... 100%/100%
With emergency credentials 0.0%

No Child Left Behind
AYP, 2005-06 .... Meets Standards

North Warren Regional School District
10 Noe Rd, PO Box 410
Blairstown, NJ 07825
Warren County
908-362-9342
http://www.northwarren.org

Superintendent...... Catherine Mozak (Int)
Number of schools..................... 1
Grade plan........................ 7-12
Enrollment...................... 1,112
Attendance rate, '05-06 .... 93.3%
Dropout rate....................... 1.3%
Students per teacher................ 11.6
Per pupil expenditure........... $13,051
Median faculty salary............ $49,658
Median administrator salary...... $97,844
Grade 12 enrollment................ 163
High school graduation rate 91.8%

Assessment test results
(percent scoring at proficient or advanced level)

	Language	Math
ASK-Gr 3	NA	NA
GEPA-Gr 8	75.8%	69.9%
HSPA-High Schl	95.6%	80.1%

SAT score averages

Pct tested	Math	Verbal	Writing
77%	491	493	478

Teacher Qualifications
Avg years of experience 11
Highly-qualified teachers
  one subject/all subjects...... 100%/100%
With emergency credentials 1.3%

No Child Left Behind
AYP, 2005-06 .... Meets Standards

Northern Burlington County Regional High School District
160 Mansfield Rd East
Columbus, NJ 08022
Burlington County
609-298-3900
http://www.nburlington.com

Superintendent............ James Sarruda
Number of schools..................... 2
Grade plan........................ 7-12
Enrollment...................... 1,774
Attendance rate, '05-06 .... 94.4%
Dropout rate....................... 0.5%
Students per teacher................. 9.7
Per pupil expenditure........... $14,221
Median faculty salary............ $51,534
Median administrator salary...... $90,434
Grade 12 enrollment................ 281
High school graduation rate 97.7%

Assessment test results
(percent scoring at proficient or advanced level)

	Language	Math
ASK-Gr 3	NA	NA
GEPA-Gr 8	78.4%	73.1%
HSPA-High Schl	92.8%	82.2%

SAT score averages

Pct tested	Math	Verbal	Writing
80%	509	503	505

Teacher Qualifications
Avg years of experience 8
Highly-qualified teachers
  one subject/all subjects...... 100%/100%
With emergency credentials 0.8%

No Child Left Behind
AYP, 2005-06 .... Meets Standards

Northern Highlands Regional High School
298 Hillside Avenue
Allendale, NJ 07401
Bergen County
201-327-8700
http://www.northernhighlands.org

Superintendent........... Robert McGuire
Number of schools..................... 1
Grade plan........................ 9-12
Enrollment...................... 1,269
Attendance rate, '05-06 .... 99.5%
Dropout rate....................... 0.2%
Students per teacher................ 10.2
Per pupil expenditure........... $16,039
Median faculty salary............ $62,212
Median administrator salary..... $116,581
Grade 12 enrollment................ 316
High school graduation rate 99.4%

Assessment test results
(percent scoring at proficient or advanced level)

	Language	Math
ASK-Gr 3	NA	NA
GEPA-Gr 8	NA	NA
HSPA-High Schl	97.7%	93.0%

SAT score averages

Pct tested	Math	Verbal	Writing
NA	578	556	572

Teacher Qualifications
Avg years of experience 9
Highly-qualified teachers
  one subject/all subjects...... 100%/100%
With emergency credentials 0.0%

No Child Left Behind
AYP, 2005-06 .... Meets Standards

Appendix D

Supplemental School District Data

Additional Public School District Data
(for school year 2006-07 except where noted)

Northern Valley Regional High School District
162 Knickerbocker Rd
Demarest, NJ 07627
Bergen County
201-768-2200
http://www.nvnet.org

Superintendent	Jan Furman
Number of schools	2
Grade plan	9-12
Enrollment	2,453
Attendance rate, '05-06	96.5%
Dropout rate	0.0%
Students per teacher	9.0
Per pupil expenditure	$15,312
Median faculty salary	$75,636
Median administrator salary	$141,143
Grade 12 enrollment	551
High school graduation rate	NA

Assessment test results
(percent scoring at proficient or advanced level)

	Language	Math
ASK-Gr 3	NA	NA
GEPA-Gr 8	NA	NA
HSPA-High Schl	97.0%	92.2%

SAT score averages

Pct tested	Math	Verbal	Writing
NA	NA	NA	NA

Teacher Qualifications
Avg years of experience 9
Highly-qualified teachers
  one subject/all subjects 100%/99.5%
With emergency credentials 1.1%

No Child Left Behind
AYP, 2005-06 .... Needs Improvement

Pascack Valley Regional High School District
46 Akers Avenue
Montvale, NJ 07645
Bergen County
201-358-7005
http://www.pascack.k12.nj.us

Superintendent	Benedict Tantillo
Number of schools	2
Grade plan	9-12
Enrollment	1,832
Attendance rate, '05-06	94.5%
Dropout rate	0.2%
Students per teacher	11.0
Per pupil expenditure	$18,892
Median faculty salary	$75,040
Median administrator salary	$128,166
Grade 12 enrollment	425
High school graduation rate	NA

Assessment test results
(percent scoring at proficient or advanced level)

	Language	Math
ASK-Gr 3	NA	NA
GEPA-Gr 8	NA	NA
HSPA-High Schl	96.8%	92.0%

SAT score averages

Pct tested	Math	Verbal	Writing
NA	NA	NA	NA

Teacher Qualifications
Avg years of experience 8
Highly-qualified teachers
  one subject/all subjects 100%/100%
With emergency credentials 0.0%

No Child Left Behind
AYP, 2005-06 .... Meets Standards

Passaic County Manchester Regional High School
70 Church St
Haledon, NJ 07508
Passaic County
973-389-2820
http://www.mrhs.net

Chief School Admin	Raymond Kwak
Number of schools	1
Grade plan	9-12
Enrollment	793
Attendance rate, '05-06	95.0%
Dropout rate	8.1%
Students per teacher	11.2
Per pupil expenditure	$18,142
Median faculty salary	$52,850
Median administrator salary	$108,757
Grade 12 enrollment	171
High school graduation rate	84.7%

Assessment test results
(percent scoring at proficient or advanced level)

	Language	Math
ASK-Gr 3	NA	NA
GEPA-Gr 8	NA	NA
HSPA-High Schl	75.2%	56.5%

SAT score averages

Pct tested	Math	Verbal	Writing
52%	461	445	441

Teacher Qualifications
Avg years of experience 6
Highly-qualified teachers
  one subject/all subjects 100%/98.0%
With emergency credentials 0.0%

No Child Left Behind
AYP, 2005-06 .... Meets Standards

Passaic Valley Regional High School District
East Main St
Little Falls, NJ 07424
Passaic County
973-890-2560
http://www.pvhs.k12.nj.us

Chief School Admin	Viktor Joganow
Number of schools	1
Grade plan	9-12
Enrollment	1,313
Attendance rate, '05-06	93.7%
Dropout rate	1.1%
Students per teacher	11.9
Per pupil expenditure	$13,523
Median faculty salary	$57,331
Median administrator salary	$99,707
Grade 12 enrollment	331
High school graduation rate	96.8%

Assessment test results
(percent scoring at proficient or advanced level)

	Language	Math
ASK-Gr 3	NA	NA
GEPA-Gr 8	NA	NA
HSPA-High Schl	91.9%	79.9%

SAT score averages

Pct tested	Math	Verbal	Writing
78%	494	469	477

Teacher Qualifications
Avg years of experience 9
Highly-qualified teachers
  one subject/all subjects 100%/100%
With emergency credentials 0.0%

No Child Left Behind
AYP, 2005-06 .... Meets Standards

Pinelands Regional School District
520 Nugentown Rd, PO Box 248
Tuckerton, NJ 08087
Ocean County
609-296-3106
http://www.pinelandsregional.org

Superintendent	Detlef Kern
Number of schools	2
Grade plan	7-12
Enrollment	1,895
Attendance rate, '05-06	89.2%
Dropout rate	4.5%
Students per teacher	9.2
Per pupil expenditure	$13,822
Median faculty salary	$46,600
Median administrator salary	$103,217
Grade 12 enrollment	269
High school graduation rate	89.4%

Assessment test results
(percent scoring at proficient or advanced level)

	Language	Math
ASK-Gr 3	NA	NA
GEPA-Gr 8	69.6%	65.3%
HSPA-High Schl	82.9%	72.6%

SAT score averages

Pct tested	Math	Verbal	Writing
54%	495	489	464

Teacher Qualifications
Avg years of experience 7
Highly-qualified teachers
  one subject/all subjects 100%/100%
With emergency credentials 0.0%

No Child Left Behind
AYP, 2005-06 .... Meets Standards

Ramapo Indian Hills Regional High School District
131 Yawpo Avenue
Oakland, NJ 07436
Bergen County
201-416-8100
http://www.rih.org

Superintendent	Paul Saxton
Number of schools	2
Grade plan	9-12
Enrollment	2,283
Attendance rate, '05-06	94.1%
Dropout rate	0.4%
Students per teacher	11.1
Per pupil expenditure	$17,399
Median faculty salary	$51,278
Median administrator salary	$111,140
Grade 12 enrollment	577
High school graduation rate	NA

Assessment test results
(percent scoring at proficient or advanced level)

	Language	Math
ASK-Gr 3	NA	NA
GEPA-Gr 8	NA	NA
HSPA-High Schl	95.4%	85.8%

SAT score averages

Pct tested	Math	Verbal	Writing
NA	NA	NA	NA

Teacher Qualifications
Avg years of experience 7
Highly-qualified teachers
  one subject/all subjects 100%/100%
With emergency credentials 0.0%

No Child Left Behind
AYP, 2005-06 .... Meets Standards

Supplemental School District Data

Appendix D

Additional Public School District Data
(for school year 2006-07 except where noted)

Rancocas Valley Regional High School
520 Jacksonville Rd
Mount Holly, NJ 08060
Burlington County
609-267-0830
http://www.rancocasvalley.k12.nj.us

Superintendent........Michael Moskalski
Number of schools.....................2
Grade plan.........................9-12
Enrollment......................2,367
Attendance rate, '05-06...........94.2%
Dropout rate.......................1.8%
Students per teacher...............16.0
Per pupil expenditure...........$11,922
Median faculty salary...........$49,400
Median administrator salary......$85,374
Grade 12 enrollment.................550
High school graduation rate..........NA

Assessment test results
(percent scoring at proficient or advanced level)

	Language	Math
ASK-Gr 3	NA	NA
GEPA-Gr 8	NA	NA
HSPA-High Schl	84.8%	77.9%

SAT score averages

Pct tested	Math	Verbal	Writing
73%	492	487	475

Teacher Qualifications
Avg years of experience.................6
Highly-qualified teachers
  one subject/all subjects......100%/100%
With emergency credentials..........0.0%

No Child Left Behind
AYP, 2005-06.........Needs Improvement

Red Bank Regional High School District
101 Ridge Rd
Little Silver, NJ 07739
Monmouth County
732-842-8000
http://www.redbankregional.k12.nj.us

Superintendent......Edward D. Westervelt
Number of schools.....................1
Grade plan.........................9-12
Enrollment......................1,110
Attendance rate, '05-06...........93.0%
Dropout rate.......................0.3%
Students per teacher................9.2
Per pupil expenditure...........$18,324
Median faculty salary...........$53,280
Median administrator salary......$91,975
Grade 12 enrollment.................262
High school graduation rate.......96.5%

Assessment test results
(percent scoring at proficient or advanced level)

	Language	Math
ASK-Gr 3	NA	NA
GEPA-Gr 8	NA	NA
HSPA-High Schl	91.3%	85.2%

SAT score averages

Pct tested	Math	Verbal	Writing
80%	498	500	504

Teacher Qualifications
Avg years of experience.................8
Highly-qualified teachers
  one subject/all subjects......100%/100%
With emergency credentials..........0.0%

No Child Left Behind
AYP, 2005-06.........Needs Improvement

River Dell Regional High School District
136 Woodland Avenue
River Edge, NJ 07661
Bergen County
201-599-7206
http://www.riverdell.k12.nj.us

Superintendent...........Patrick Fletcher
Number of schools.....................2
Grade plan.........................7-12
Enrollment......................1,493
Attendance rate, '05-06...........96.0%
Dropout rate.......................0.3%
Students per teacher...............11.2
Per pupil expenditure...........$14,456
Median faculty salary...........$62,995
Median administrator salary.....$120,000
Grade 12 enrollment.................240
High school graduation rate.......98.8%

Assessment test results
(percent scoring at proficient or advanced level)

	Language	Math
ASK-Gr 3	NA	NA
GEPA-Gr 8	87.4%	84.3%
HSPA-High Schl	95.7%	89.0%

SAT score averages

Pct tested	Math	Verbal	Writing
97%	556	529	525

Teacher Qualifications
Avg years of experience.................8
Highly-qualified teachers
  one subject/all subjects......100%/100%
With emergency credentials..........0.0%

No Child Left Behind
AYP, 2005-06............Meets Standards

Rumson-Fair Haven Regional High School District
74 Ridge Rd
Rumson, NJ 07760
Monmouth County
732-842-5456
http://www.rfh.k12.nj.us

Superintendent...............Peter Righi
Number of schools.....................1
Grade plan.........................9-12
Enrollment........................997
Attendance rate, '05-06...........93.2%
Dropout rate.......................0.3%
Students per teacher...............11.0
Per pupil expenditure...........$15,443
Median faculty salary...........$60,360
Median administrator salary......$98,622
Grade 12 enrollment.................242
High school graduation rate.......98.8%

Assessment test results
(percent scoring at proficient or advanced level)

	Language	Math
ASK-Gr 3	NA	NA
GEPA-Gr 8	NA	NA
HSPA-High Schl	97.2%	92.2%

SAT score averages

Pct tested	Math	Verbal	Writing
NA	553	543	545

Teacher Qualifications
Avg years of experience.................7
Highly-qualified teachers
  one subject/all subjects......100%/100%
With emergency credentials..........0.0%

No Child Left Behind
AYP, 2005-06............Meets Standards

Shore Regional High School District
Monmouth Park Highway
West Long Branch, NJ 07764
Monmouth County
732-222-9300
http://shoreregional.org

Superintendent......Leonard G. Schnappauf
Number of schools.....................1
Grade plan.........................9-12
Enrollment........................748
Attendance rate, '05-06...........95.2%
Dropout rate........................NA
Students per teacher...............11.5
Per pupil expenditure...........$16,739
Median faculty salary...........$57,800
Median administrator salary.....$100,181
Grade 12 enrollment.................174
High school graduation rate........100%

Assessment test results
(percent scoring at proficient or advanced level)

	Language	Math
ASK-Gr 3	NA	NA
GEPA-Gr 8	NA	NA
HSPA-High Schl	90.9%	81.2%

SAT score averages

Pct tested	Math	Verbal	Writing
96%	506	499	505

Teacher Qualifications
Avg years of experience................10
Highly-qualified teachers
  one subject/all subjects......100%/100%
With emergency credentials..........1.8%

No Child Left Behind
AYP, 2005-06............Meets Standards

South Hunterdon Regional High School
301 Mount Airy-Harbourton Rd
Lambertville, NJ 08530
Hunterdon County
609-397-2060
http://www.shrhs.org

Superintendent.........Nancy Gartenberg
Number of schools.....................1
Grade plan.........................7-12
Enrollment........................341
Attendance rate, '05-06...........94.9%
Dropout rate.......................0.4%
Students per teacher................6.5
Per pupil expenditure...........$23,061
Median faculty salary...........$56,742
Median administrator salary......$93,123
Grade 12 enrollment..................59
High school graduation rate.......96.7%

Assessment test results
(percent scoring at proficient or advanced level)

	Language	Math
ASK-Gr 3	NA	NA
GEPA-Gr 8	79.7%	72.4%
HSPA-High Schl	91.5%	76.6%

SAT score averages

Pct tested	Math	Verbal	Writing
84%	517	519	518

Teacher Qualifications
Avg years of experience.................8
Highly-qualified teachers
  one subject/all subjects......100%/100%
With emergency credentials..........0.0%

No Child Left Behind
AYP, 2005-06............Meets Standards

Appendix D

Supplemental School District Data

Additional Public School District Data
(for school year 2006-07 except where noted)

Southern Regional School District
105 Cedar Bridge Rd
Manahawkin, NJ 08050
Ocean County
609-597-9481
http://www.srsd.org

Superintendent.............Craig Henry
Number of schools......................2
Grade plan........................7-12
Enrollment.......................3,272
Attendance rate, '05-06..........93.7%
Dropout rate......................2.0%
Students per teacher..............11.4
Per pupil expenditure..........$14,812
Median faculty salary..........$57,257
Median administrator salary...$109,974
Grade 12 enrollment................676
High school graduation rate......92.8%

Assessment test results
(percent scoring at proficient or advanced level)

	Language	Math
ASK-Gr 3	NA	NA
GEPA-Gr 8	81.0%	71.2%
HSPA-High Schl	92.4%	81.6%

SAT score averages

Pct tested	Math	Verbal	Writing
71%	502	483	479

Teacher Qualifications
Avg years of experience...............11
Highly-qualified teachers
  one subject/all subjects......100%/100%
With emergency credentials..........0.0%

No Child Left Behind
AYP, 2005-06............Meets Standards

Sterling High School District
501 South Warwick Rd
Somerdale, NJ 08083
Camden County
856-784-1287
http://www.sterling.k12.nj.us

Superintendent..........Jack L. McCulley
Number of schools......................1
Grade plan........................9-12
Enrollment.........................973
Attendance rate, '05-06..........94.8%
Dropout rate......................2.0%
Students per teacher..............11.6
Per pupil expenditure..........$13,798
Median faculty salary..........$53,400
Median administrator salary....$89,250
Grade 12 enrollment................193
High school graduation rate......94.3%

Assessment test results
(percent scoring at proficient or advanced level)

	Language	Math
ASK-Gr 3	NA	NA
GEPA-Gr 8	NA	NA
HSPA-High Schl	86.2%	73.7%

SAT score averages

Pct tested	Math	Verbal	Writing
73%	496	487	486

Teacher Qualifications
Avg years of experience................7
Highly-qualified teachers
  one subject/all subjects......100%/96.5%
With emergency credentials..........1.3%

No Child Left Behind
AYP, 2005-06............Meets Standards

Wallkill Valley Regional High School
10 Grumm Rd
Hamburg, NJ 07419
Sussex County
973-827-4100
http://wallkill.k12.nj.us

Superint/Principal......Joseph DiPasquale
Number of schools......................1
Grade plan........................9-12
Enrollment.........................877
Attendance rate, '05-06..........95.1%
Dropout rate......................3.3%
Students per teacher..............12.1
Per pupil expenditure..........$14,786
Median faculty salary..........$76,165
Median administrator salary...$107,099
Grade 12 enrollment................215
High school graduation rate......90.3%

Assessment test results
(percent scoring at proficient or advanced level)

	Language	Math
ASK-Gr 3	NA	NA
GEPA-Gr 8	NA	NA
HSPA-High Schl	90.4%	74.5%

SAT score averages

Pct tested	Math	Verbal	Writing
67%	516	504	498

Teacher Qualifications
Avg years of experience...............14
Highly-qualified teachers
  one subject/all subjects......100%/100%
With emergency credentials..........1.4%

No Child Left Behind
AYP, 2005-06............Meets Standards

Warren Hills Regional School District
89 Bowerstown Rd
Washington, NJ 07882
Warren County
908-689-3143
http://www.warrenhills.org

Superintendent............Peter Merluzzi
Number of schools......................2
Grade plan........................7-12
Enrollment.......................2,161
Attendance rate, '05-06..........93.5%
Dropout rate......................3.0%
Students per teacher..............12.1
Per pupil expenditure..........$13,930
Median faculty salary..........$61,760
Median administrator salary...$109,150
Grade 12 enrollment................358
High school graduation rate......90.8%

Assessment test results
(percent scoring at proficient or advanced level)

	Language	Math
ASK-Gr 3	NA	NA
GEPA-Gr 8	75.8%	64.8%
HSPA-High Schl	89.4%	81.1%

SAT score averages

Pct tested	Math	Verbal	Writing
72%	511	504	493

Teacher Qualifications
Avg years of experience...............11
Highly-qualified teachers
  one subject/all subjects......100%/100%
With emergency credentials..........1.5%

No Child Left Behind
AYP, 2005-06.........Needs Improvement

Watchung Hills Regional High School
108 Stirling Rd
Warren, NJ 07059
Somerset County
908-647-4800
http://www.whrhs.org

Superintendent......Frances C. Stromsland
Number of schools......................1
Grade plan........................9-12
Enrollment.......................2,008
Attendance rate, '05-06..........96.5%
Dropout rate......................0.4%
Students per teacher..............11.0
Per pupil expenditure..........$14,649
Median faculty salary..........$59,285
Median administrator salary...$103,305
Grade 12 enrollment................454
High school graduation rate......98.1%

Assessment test results
(percent scoring at proficient or advanced level)

	Language	Math
ASK-Gr 3	NA	NA
GEPA-Gr 8	NA	NA
HSPA-High Schl	95.9%	90.5%

SAT score averages

Pct tested	Math	Verbal	Writing
98%	551	536	534

Teacher Qualifications
Avg years of experience................8
Highly-qualified teachers
  one subject/all subjects......100%/100%
With emergency credentials..........0.0%

No Child Left Behind
AYP, 2005-06............Meets Standards

West Essex Regional School District
West Greenbrook Rd
North Caldwell, NJ 07006
Essex County
973-582-1600
http://www.westex.org

Superintendent......Mario Cardinale (Int)
Number of schools......................2
Grade plan........................7-12
Enrollment.......................1,615
Attendance rate, '05-06..........93.9%
Dropout rate......................0.2%
Students per teacher..............10.7
Per pupil expenditure..........$16,420
Median faculty salary..........$65,978
Median administrator salary....$95,842
Grade 12 enrollment................237
High school graduation rate......99.2%

Assessment test results
(percent scoring at proficient or advanced level)

	Language	Math
ASK-Gr 3	NA	NA
GEPA-Gr 8	91.1%	88.3%
HSPA-High Schl	92.6%	84.7%

SAT score averages

Pct tested	Math	Verbal	Writing
89%	554	516	532

Teacher Qualifications
Avg years of experience................7
Highly-qualified teachers
  one subject/all subjects......95.0%/93.0%
With emergency credentials..........0.0%

No Child Left Behind
AYP, 2005-06............Meets Standards

Supplemental School District Data

Appendix D

Additional Public School District Data
(for school year 2006-07 except where noted)

West Morris Regional High School District
10 South Four Bridges Rd
Chester, NJ 07930
Morris County
908-879-6404
http://www.wmchs.org

Superintendent.........Anthony diBattista
Number of schools......................2
Grade plan......................... 9-12
Enrollment 2,525
Attendance rate, '05-06 .... 95.3%
Dropout rate.......................0.4%
Students per teacher 10.6
Per pupil expenditure $15,827
Median faculty salary............ $57,765
Median administrator salary...... $125,025
Grade 12 enrollment.................592
High school graduation rate ....NA

Assessment test results
(percent scoring at proficient or advanced level)

	Language	Math
ASK-Gr 3	NA	NA
GEPA-Gr 8	NA	NA
HSPA-High Schl	98.1%	93.2%

SAT score averages

Pct tested	Math	Verbal	Writing
NA	NA	NA	NA

Teacher Qualifications
Avg years of experience 9
Highly-qualified teachers
  one subject/all subjects...... 100%/98.5%
With emergency credentials 0.0%

No Child Left Behind
AYP, 2005-06 ....Meets Standards

©2008 Information Publications, Inc. All rights reserved. Photocopying prohibited. For additional copies, contact the publisher at www.informationpublications.com or (877)544-INFO (4636)

The New Jersey Municipal Data Book

County Comparative Tables

Appendix E

Population 2007

1.	Bergen County	895,744
2.	Middlesex County	788,629
3.	Essex County	776,087
4.	Monmouth County	642,030
5.	Hudson County	598,160
6.	Ocean County	565,493
7.	Union County	524,658
8.	Camden County	513,769
9.	Passaic County	492,115
10.	Morris County	488,475
11.	Burlington County	446,817
12.	Mercer County	365,449
13.	Somerset County	323,552
14.	Gloucester County	285,753
15.	Atlantic County	270,644
16.	Cumberland County	155,544
17.	Sussex County	151,478
18.	Hunterdon County	129,348
19.	Warren County	109,737
20.	Cape May County	96,422
21.	Salem County	66,016

(estimate)

Land Area

1.	Burlington County	804.6
2.	Ocean County	636.3
3.	Atlantic County	561.1
4.	Sussex County	521.3
5.	Cumberland County	489.3
6.	Monmouth County	471.9
7.	Morris County	469.0
8.	Hunterdon County	429.9
9.	Warren County	357.9
10.	Salem County	337.9
11.	Gloucester County	324.7
12.	Middlesex County	309.7
13.	Somerset County	304.7
14.	Cape May County	255.2
15.	Bergen County	234.2
16.	Mercer County	225.9
17.	Camden County	222.3
18.	Passaic County	185.3
19.	Essex County	126.3
20.	Union County	103.3
21.	Hudson County	46.7

(square miles)

Unemployment Rate 2006

1.	Cape May County	7.0%
2.	Cumberland County	6.9
3.	Essex County	5.8
4.	Atlantic County	5.7
5.	Passaic County	5.6
6.	Hudson County	5.5
7.	Camden County	5.1
8.	Ocean County	5.0
9.	Salem County	5.0
10.	Union County	4.8
11.	Gloucester County	4.7
12.	Middlesex County	4.3
13.	Mercer County	4.2
14.	Burlington County	4.1
15.	Monmouth County	4.1
16.	Sussex County	4.1
17.	Warren County	4.1
18.	Bergen County	3.9
19.	Somerset County	3.5
20.	Hunterdon County	3.3
21.	Morris County	3.3

Income per capita 2006

1.	Hunterdon County	$44,133
2.	Somerset County	43,407
3.	Morris County	43,085
4.	Bergen County	39,316
5.	Monmouth County	36,767
6.	Mercer County	33,719
7.	Sussex County	32,997
8.	Union County	31,364
9.	Cape May County	31,286
10.	Burlington County	30,349
11.	Middlesex County	30,331
12.	Warren County	29,060
13.	Essex County	29,053
14.	Gloucester County	28,712
15.	Ocean County	27,638
16.	Hudson County	27,068
17.	Camden County	26,926
18.	Atlantic County	26,140
19.	Salem County	25,547
20.	Passaic County	23,437
21.	Cumberland County	19,722

Median Home Value 2006

1.	Bergen County	$493,400
2.	Morris County	488,900
3.	Hunterdon County	475,300
4.	Somerset County	457,000
5.	Monmouth County	444,800
6.	Union County	419,000
7.	Essex County	409,300
8.	Passaic County	406,300
9.	Hudson County	387,100
10.	Middlesex County	365,000
11.	Cape May County	348,000
12.	Sussex County	332,400
13.	Mercer County	314,300
14.	Ocean County	310,800
15.	Warren County	309,100
16.	Atlantic County	264,200
17.	Burlington County	259,300
18.	Gloucester County	226,900
19.	Camden County	208,600
20.	Salem County	184,000
21.	Cumberland County	161,800

(specified owner-occupied homes)

Crime Rate 2006

1.	Cape May County	50.8
2.	Cumberland County	48.6
3.	Atlantic County	44.3
4.	Essex County	42.4
5.	Camden County	39.3
6.	Hudson County	32.7
7.	Gloucester County	29.4
8.	Union County	29.4
9.	Passaic County	28.6
10.	Salem County	28.2
11.	Mercer County	27.3
12.	Middlesex County	22.5
13.	Monmouth County	22.0
14.	Ocean County	20.5
15.	Burlington County	19.7
16.	Warren County	17.2
17.	Bergen County	15.2
18.	Somerset County	14.9
19.	Morris County	14.1
20.	Sussex County	12.4
21.	Hunterdon County	8.7

(rate per 1,000 residents)

The New Jersey Municipal Data Book

Municipal Comparative Tables

Population, 2006 (estimate)

#	Municipality	County	Population
1.	Newark City	Essex	281,402
2.	Jersey City	Hudson	241,789
3.	Paterson City	Passaic	148,708
4.	Elizabeth City	Union	126,179
5.	Edison Township	Middlesex	99,523
6.	Woodbridge Township	Middlesex	99,208
7.	Toms River Township	Ocean	94,889
8.	Hamilton Township	Mercer	90,559
9.	Trenton City	Mercer	83,923
10.	Clifton City	Passaic	79,606
11.	Camden City	Camden	79,318
12.	Brick Township	Ocean	78,232
13.	Cherry Hill Township	Camden	71,586
14.	Lakewood Township	Ocean	69,606
15.	Passaic City	Passaic	67,974
16.	Middletown Township	Monmouth	67,578
17.	East Orange City	Essex	67,247
18.	Gloucester Township	Camden	65,687
19.	Old Bridge Township	Middlesex	65,661
20.	Union City	Hudson	63,930
21.	Franklin Township	Somerset	60,273
22.	Bayonne City	Hudson	58,844
23.	Vineland City	Cumberland	58,271
24.	Irvington Township	Essex	58,024
25.	North Bergen Township	Hudson	57,237
26.	Union Township	Union	55,039
27.	Wayne Township	Passaic	54,849
28.	Piscataway Township	Middlesex	52,658
29.	Jackson Township	Ocean	52,305
30.	Parsippany-Troy Hills Township	Morris	51,839
31.	Washington Township	Gloucester	51,827
32.	Howell Township	Monmouth	50,548
33.	New Brunswick City	Middlesex	50,172
34.	Perth Amboy City	Middlesex	48,607
35.	East Brunswick Township	Middlesex	47,649
36.	Plainfield City	Union	47,353
37.	Evesham Township	Burlington	46,711
38.	West New York Town	Hudson	46,398
39.	Bloomfield Township	Essex	45,372
40.	Bridgewater Township	Somerset	44,818
41.	Hackensack City	Bergen	43,671
42.	West Orange Township	Essex	43,536
43.	Berkeley Township	Ocean	42,577
44.	Sayreville Borough	Middlesex	42,560
45.	Manchester Township	Ocean	41,813
46.	South Brunswick Township	Middlesex	40,570
47.	Mount Laurel Township	Burlington	40,326
48.	Atlantic City	Atlantic	39,958
49.	Linden City	Union	39,874
50.	Hoboken City	Hudson	39,853
51.	North Brunswick Township	Middlesex	39,852
52.	Marlboro Township	Monmouth	39,843
53.	Teaneck Township	Bergen	39,610
54.	Egg Harbor Township	Atlantic	38,793
55.	Winslow Township	Camden	38,612
56.	Hillsborough Township	Somerset	38,110
57.	Kearny Town	Hudson	38,008
58.	Montclair Township	Essex	37,309
59.	Manalapan Township	Monmouth	37,169
60.	Fort Lee Borough	Bergen	37,008
61.	Ewing Township	Mercer	36,916
62.	Galloway Township	Atlantic	36,205
63.	Pennsauken Township	Camden	35,443
64.	Monroe Township	Middlesex	34,907
65.	Belleville Township	Essex	34,444
66.	Freehold Township	Monmouth	33,953
67.	Willingboro Township	Burlington	33,045
68.	Long Branch City	Monmouth	32,314
69.	Lawrence Township	Mercer	32,081
70.	Monroe Township	Gloucester	31,934
71.	Orange City Township	Essex	31,858
72.	Fair Lawn Borough	Bergen	31,246
73.	Deptford Township	Gloucester	30,216
74.	Westfield Town	Union	29,944
75.	Garfield City	Bergen	29,644
76.	Voorhees Township	Camden	29,391
77.	Pemberton Township	Burlington	28,831
78.	Livingston Township	Essex	28,413
79.	Millville City	Cumberland	28,194
80.	Neptune Township	Monmouth	28,163
81.	West Milford Township	Passaic	28,144
82.	Rahway City	Union	27,843
83.	Englewood City	Bergen	27,824
84.	Ocean Township	Monmouth	27,484
85.	Bernards Township	Somerset	27,140
86.	Nutley Township	Essex	27,011
87.	East Windsor Township	Mercer	26,926
88.	Paramus Borough	Bergen	26,548
89.	Lacey Township	Ocean	26,300
90.	West Windsor Township	Mercer	26,279
91.	Bergenfield Borough	Bergen	26,194
92.	Mount Olive Township	Morris	26,065
93.	Wall Township	Monmouth	25,997
94.	Stafford Township	Ocean	25,819
95.	Rockaway Township	Morris	25,789
96.	Randolph Township	Morris	25,736
97.	Vernon Township	Sussex	25,453
98.	Ridgewood Village	Bergen	24,639
99.	Mahwah Township	Bergen	24,560
100.	Hamilton Township	Atlantic	24,423
101.	Bridgeton City	Cumberland	24,389
102.	Lodi Borough	Bergen	24,310
103.	Roxbury Township	Morris	23,803
104.	Medford Township	Burlington	23,399
105.	Scotch Plains Township	Union	23,246
106.	Montgomery Township	Somerset	23,243
107.	Cliffside Park Borough	Bergen	22,970
108.	South Plainfield Borough	Middlesex	22,795
109.	Maplewood Township	Essex	22,759
110.	Raritan Township	Hunterdon	22,720
111.	Cranford Township	Union	22,369
112.	Carteret Borough	Middlesex	22,264
113.	Jefferson Township	Morris	21,963
114.	Burlington Township	Burlington	21,787
115.	West Deptford Township	Gloucester	21,763
116.	North Plainfield Borough	Somerset	21,738
117.	Hillside Township	Union	21,684
118.	Montville Township	Morris	21,442
119.	Morris Township	Morris	21,374
120.	Plainsboro Township	Middlesex	21,213

The New Jersey Municipal Data Book

Appendix F

Municipal Comparative Tables

Population, 2006 (estimate)

Municipality	County	Population
121. Barnegat Township	Ocean	21,192
122. Roselle Borough	Union	21,158
123. Summit City	Union	21,103
124. Hazlet Township	Monmouth	20,936
125. Lower Township	Cape May	20,785
126. Little Egg Harbor Township	Ocean	20,283
127. Moorestown Township	Burlington	19,996
128. Point Pleasant Borough	Ocean	19,882
129. Lyndhurst Township	Bergen	19,732
130. Maple Shade Township	Burlington	19,541
131. Glassboro Borough	Gloucester	19,360
132. Sparta Township	Sussex	19,348
133. Palisades Park Borough	Bergen	19,306
134. Millburn Township	Essex	19,153
135. Pleasantville City	Atlantic	18,982
136. Morristown Town	Morris	18,922
137. Elmwood Park Borough	Bergen	18,805
138. Washington Township	Morris	18,691
139. Dover Town	Morris	18,387
140. Aberdeen Township	Monmouth	18,382
141. Hawthorne Borough	Passaic	18,166
142. Hopewell Township	Mercer	17,968
143. Rutherford Borough	Bergen	17,871
144. Dumont Borough	Bergen	17,365
145. Princeton Township	Mercer	17,353
146. Delran Township	Burlington	17,283
147. Wyckoff Township	Bergen	17,167
148. Lindenwold Borough	Camden	17,160
149. Tinton Falls Borough	Monmouth	17,082
150. Franklin Township	Gloucester	16,853
151. Holmdel Township	Monmouth	16,834
152. Denville Township	Morris	16,671
153. Asbury Park City	Monmouth	16,546
154. Middle Township	Cape May	16,379
155. South Orange Village Township	Essex	16,371
156. Pequannock Township	Morris	16,320
157. Readington Township	Hunterdon	16,295
158. New Milford Borough	Bergen	16,243
159. Madison Borough	Morris	16,016
160. Hopatcong Borough	Sussex	15,884
161. South River Borough	Middlesex	15,822
162. Warren Township	Somerset	15,816
163. Secaucus Town	Hudson	15,562
164. Cinnaminson Township	Burlington	15,449
165. Ocean City	Cape May	15,124
166. North Arlington Borough	Bergen	15,077
167. Branchburg Township	Somerset	15,049
168. Mantua Township	Gloucester	14,974
169. Phillipsburg Town	Warren	14,831
170. Ramsey Borough	Bergen	14,775
171. Springfield Township	Union	14,717
172. Clark Township	Union	14,650
173. Haddon Township	Camden	14,484
174. Tenafly Borough	Bergen	14,390
175. Highland Park Borough	Middlesex	14,175
176. Clinton Township	Hunterdon	14,082
177. Eatontown Borough	Monmouth	14,022
178. Collingswood Borough	Camden	13,961
179. Harrison Town	Hudson	13,942
180. Middlesex Borough	Middlesex	13,746
181. Hanover Township	Morris	13,737
182. Princeton Borough	Mercer	13,684
183. Fairview Borough	Bergen	13,628
184. Saddle Brook Township	Bergen	13,625
185. Berkeley Heights Township	Union	13,575
186. Hammonton Town	Atlantic	13,572
187. Oakland Borough	Bergen	13,558
188. Pennsville Township	Salem	13,333
189. Metuchen Borough	Middlesex	13,216
190. Roselle Park Borough	Union	13,124
191. Verona Township	Essex	12,937
192. Brigantine City	Atlantic	12,886
193. Cedar Grove Township	Essex	12,848
194. Ringwood Borough	Passaic	12,814
195. Ridgefield Park Village	Bergen	12,665
196. Weehawken Township	Hudson	12,649
197. Florham Park Borough	Morris	12,605
198. Ventnor City	Atlantic	12,564
199. Somerville Borough	Somerset	12,550
200. Lumberton Township	Burlington	12,331
201. New Providence Borough	Union	11,915
202. Robbinsville Township	Mercer	11,906
203. Red Bank Borough	Monmouth	11,850
204. Harrison Township	Gloucester	11,849
205. Little Falls Township	Passaic	11,829
206. Florence Township	Burlington	11,637
207. East Hanover Township	Morris	11,633
208. Hasbrouck Heights Borough	Bergen	11,621
209. Colts Neck Township	Monmouth	11,587
210. Somers Point City	Atlantic	11,573
211. Wantage Township	Sussex	11,566
212. Haddonfield Borough	Camden	11,515
213. Gloucester City	Camden	11,482
214. Wallington Borough	Bergen	11,430
215. Glen Rock Borough	Bergen	11,396
216. Freehold Borough	Monmouth	11,394
217. Upper Township	Cape May	11,363
218. Franklin Lakes Borough	Bergen	11,340
219. Pine Hill Borough	Camden	11,275
220. Pompton Lakes Borough	Passaic	11,243
221. West Paterson Borough	Passaic	11,234
222. Bellmawr Borough	Camden	11,193
223. Wanaque Borough	Passaic	11,171
224. Southampton Township	Burlington	11,028
225. Ridgefield Borough	Bergen	10,996
226. Westwood Borough	Bergen	10,934
227. River Edge Borough	Bergen	10,862
228. Lincoln Park Borough	Morris	10,856
229. West Caldwell Township	Essex	10,797
230. Beachwood Borough	Ocean	10,744
231. Guttenberg Town	Hudson	10,717
232. Little Ferry Borough	Bergen	10,715
233. Waterford Township	Camden	10,707
234. Totowa Borough	Passaic	10,634
235. Mount Holly Township	Burlington	10,602
236. Keansburg Borough	Monmouth	10,573
237. Manville Borough	Somerset	10,481
238. Bordentown Township	Burlington	10,469
239. Woodbury City	Gloucester	10,410
240. Chatham Township	Morris	10,279

The New Jersey Municipal Data Book

Municipal Comparative Tables

Appendix F

Population, 2006 (estimate)

Municipality	County	Population
241. Bound Brook Borough	Somerset	10,225
242. Millstone Township	Monmouth	10,064
243. Hillsdale Borough	Bergen	10,053
244. River Vale Township	Bergen	9,751
245. Burlington City	Burlington	9,715
246. Kinnelon Borough	Morris	9,681
247. Washington Township	Bergen	9,670
248. Edgewater Borough	Bergen	9,628
249. Waldwick Borough	Bergen	9,621
250. Pittsgrove Township	Salem	9,533
251. New Hanover Township	Burlington	9,479
252. Hackettstown Town	Warren	9,478
253. Maywood Borough	Bergen	9,374
254. Pitman Borough	Gloucester	9,199
255. North Haledon Borough	Passaic	9,039
256. Audubon Borough	Camden	8,981
257. Park Ridge Borough	Bergen	8,945
258. East Rutherford Borough	Bergen	8,931
259. Leonia Borough	Bergen	8,799
260. Long Hill Township	Morris	8,785
261. Matawan Borough	Monmouth	8,781
262. Westampton Township	Burlington	8,771
263. Closter Borough	Bergen	8,730
264. Byram Township	Sussex	8,656
265. Woolwich Township	Gloucester	8,612
266. Margate City	Atlantic	8,601
267. Boonton Town	Morris	8,600
268. Upper Saddle River Borough	Bergen	8,531
269. Runnemede Borough	Camden	8,461
270. Bedminster Township	Somerset	8,449
271. Lopatcong Township	Warren	8,439
272. Cresskill Borough	Bergen	8,437
273. Chatham Borough	Morris	8,390
274. Haledon Borough	Passaic	8,358
275. Newton Town	Sussex	8,337
276. West Long Branch Borough	Monmouth	8,312
277. Hardyston Township	Sussex	8,283
278. Mansfield Township	Warren	8,274
279. Ocean Township	Ocean	8,241
280. Spotswood Borough	Middlesex	8,179
281. Plumsted Township	Ocean	8,122
282. Bogota Borough	Bergen	8,108
283. Maurice River Township	Cumberland	8,083
284. Butler Borough	Morris	8,074
285. Absecon City	Atlantic	8,065
286. Mansfield Township	Burlington	8,047
287. Northfield City	Atlantic	8,003
288. Upper Deerfield Township	Cumberland	8,000
289. Carneys Point Township	Salem	7,981
290. Edgewater Park Township	Burlington	7,968
291. Oradell Borough	Bergen	7,957
292. Riverside Township	Burlington	7,950
293. Berlin Borough	Camden	7,910
294. Chester Township	Morris	7,890
295. South Amboy City	Middlesex	7,865
296. Kenilworth Borough	Union	7,741
297. Fairfield Township	Essex	7,707
298. Bernardsville Borough	Somerset	7,688
299. Bloomingdale Borough	Passaic	7,604
300. Palmyra Borough	Burlington	7,598
301. Wood-Ridge Borough	Bergen	7,594
302. North Hanover Township	Burlington	7,577
303. Buena Vista Township	Atlantic	7,487
304. Keyport Borough	Monmouth	7,471
305. Clayton Borough	Gloucester	7,469
306. Caldwell Borough	Essex	7,373
307. Haddon Heights Borough	Camden	7,365
308. Linwood City	Atlantic	7,354
309. Tabernacle Township	Burlington	7,337
310. Emerson Borough	Bergen	7,318
311. Montvale Borough	Bergen	7,308
312. Fanwood Borough	Union	7,211
313. North Caldwell Borough	Essex	7,207
314. Rumson Borough	Monmouth	7,194
315. Stratford Borough	Camden	7,122
316. Milltown Borough	Middlesex	7,038
317. Barrington Borough	Camden	7,004
318. Washington Township	Warren	6,981
319. Dunellen Borough	Middlesex	6,940
320. Glen Ridge Borough	Essex	6,908
321. Midland Park Borough	Bergen	6,906
322. Shamong Township	Burlington	6,873
323. Green Brook Township	Somerset	6,854
324. Washington Borough	Warren	6,841
325. East Greenwich Township	Gloucester	6,788
326. Fairfield Township	Cumberland	6,783
327. Allendale Borough	Bergen	6,713
328. Eastampton Township	Burlington	6,697
329. Mountainside Borough	Union	6,644
330. Union Beach Borough	Monmouth	6,631
331. Upper Freehold Township	Monmouth	6,573
332. Andover Township	Sussex	6,552
333. Chesterfield Township	Burlington	6,451
334. Jamesburg Borough	Middlesex	6,429
335. Raritan Borough	Somerset	6,427
336. Rockaway Borough	Morris	6,410
337. Union Township	Hunterdon	6,352
338. Lebanon Township	Hunterdon	6,292
339. Watchung Borough	Somerset	6,284
340. Norwood Borough	Bergen	6,267
341. Wharton Borough	Morris	6,211
342. Manasquan Borough	Monmouth	6,199
343. Logan Township	Gloucester	6,177
344. Hainesport Township	Burlington	6,161
345. Little Silver Borough	Monmouth	6,089
346. Tewksbury Township	Hunterdon	6,088
347. Mullica Township	Atlantic	6,080
348. Paulsboro Borough	Gloucester	6,062
349. Carlstadt Borough	Bergen	6,037
350. Rochelle Park Township	Bergen	6,027
351. Old Tappan Borough	Bergen	6,013
352. Blairstown Township	Warren	5,982
353. Woodcliff Lake Borough	Bergen	5,953
354. Belmar Borough	Monmouth	5,923
355. Dennis Township	Cape May	5,907
356. Fair Haven Borough	Monmouth	5,885
357. White Township	Warren	5,825
358. Englewood Cliffs Borough	Bergen	5,793
359. Salem City	Salem	5,784
360. Independence Township	Warren	5,770

©2008 Information Publications, Inc. All rights reserved. Photocopying prohibited. For additional copies, contact the publisher at www.informationpublications.com or (877)544-INFO (4636)

The New Jersey Municipal Data Book 629

Appendix F

Municipal Comparative Tables

Population, 2006 (estimate)

Municipality	County	Population
361. Oceanport Borough	Monmouth	5,751
362. Prospect Park Borough	Passaic	5,720
363. Mount Arlington Borough	Morris	5,708
364. Frankford Township	Sussex	5,680
365. Morris Plains Borough	Morris	5,601
366. Mendham Township	Morris	5,596
367. Commercial Township	Cumberland	5,419
368. Berlin Township	Camden	5,405
369. Roseland Borough	Essex	5,400
370. Point Pleasant Beach Borough	Ocean	5,398
371. Holland Township	Hunterdon	5,310
372. Wildwood City	Cape May	5,309
373. Hightstown Borough	Mercer	5,300
374. Greenwich Township	Warren	5,229
375. Hampton Township	Sussex	5,213
376. Franklin Borough	Sussex	5,210
377. Mendham Borough	Morris	5,176
378. Neptune City Borough	Monmouth	5,150
379. Somerdale Borough	Camden	5,123
380. Demarest Borough	Bergen	5,106
381. Spring Lake Heights Borough	Monmouth	5,106
382. Alexandria Township	Hunterdon	5,089
383. Highlands Borough	Monmouth	4,987
384. Greenwich Township	Gloucester	4,972
385. Clementon Borough	Camden	4,922
386. Harrington Park Borough	Bergen	4,916
387. Brielle Borough	Monmouth	4,852
388. North Wildwood City	Cape May	4,803
389. Penns Grove Borough	Salem	4,797
390. Bradley Beach Borough	Monmouth	4,784
391. Hopewell Township	Cumberland	4,756
392. Delaware Township	Hunterdon	4,730
393. Atlantic Highlands Borough	Monmouth	4,614
394. Northvale Borough	Bergen	4,562
395. East Amwell Township	Hunterdon	4,557
396. Pilesgrove Township	Salem	4,534
397. South Bound Brook Borough	Somerset	4,524
398. Westville Borough	Gloucester	4,458
399. Egg Harbor City	Atlantic	4,454
400. Mount Ephraim Borough	Camden	4,437
401. Boonton Township	Morris	4,396
402. Stillwater Township	Sussex	4,385
403. Magnolia Borough	Camden	4,379
404. Mountain Lakes Borough	Morris	4,343
405. Flemington Borough	Hunterdon	4,267
406. Garwood Borough	Union	4,233
407. Delanco Township	Burlington	4,224
408. Medford Lakes Borough	Burlington	4,161
409. Ho-Ho-Kus Borough	Bergen	4,095
410. Allamuchy Township	Warren	4,093
411. Oaklyn Borough	Camden	4,080
412. Kingwood Township	Hunterdon	4,043
413. Bethlehem Township	Hunterdon	4,008
414. Wildwood Crest Borough	Cape May	3,979
415. Bordentown City	Burlington	3,953
416. Montague Township	Sussex	3,904
417. Cranbury Township	Middlesex	3,899
418. Elk Township	Gloucester	3,867
419. Tuckerton Borough	Ocean	3,827
420. Cape May City	Cape May	3,809
421. Lambertville City	Hunterdon	3,808
422. Merchantville Borough	Camden	3,806
423. Buena Borough	Atlantic	3,804
424. Saddle River Borough	Bergen	3,786
425. High Bridge Borough	Hunterdon	3,763
426. Shrewsbury Borough	Monmouth	3,717
427. South Toms River Borough	Ocean	3,716
428. Mine Hill Township	Morris	3,666
429. Stanhope Borough	Sussex	3,666
430. Upper Pittsgrove Township	Salem	3,620
431. Monmouth Beach Borough	Monmouth	3,574
432. Springfield Township	Burlington	3,570
433. Green Township	Sussex	3,558
434. Hamburg Borough	Sussex	3,554
435. Long Beach Township	Ocean	3,498
436. Spring Lake Borough	Monmouth	3,475
437. Haworth Borough	Bergen	3,433
438. Pohatcong Township	Warren	3,410
439. Harding Township	Morris	3,363
440. Fredon Township	Sussex	3,361
441. Woodstown Borough	Salem	3,333
442. Netcong Borough	Morris	3,292
443. Seaside Heights Borough	Ocean	3,242
444. Deerfield Township	Cumberland	3,231
445. National Park Borough	Gloucester	3,215
446. Franklin Township	Warren	3,189
447. Knowlton Township	Warren	3,180
448. Franklin Township	Hunterdon	3,152
449. Alloway Township	Salem	3,066
450. Woodbury Heights Borough	Gloucester	3,030
451. South Harrison Township	Gloucester	2,956
452. Liberty Township	Warren	2,954
453. Sea Isle City	Cape May	2,949
454. Lawrence Township	Cumberland	2,944
455. West Amwell Township	Hunterdon	2,944
456. Quinton Township	Salem	2,864
457. Harmony Township	Warren	2,860
458. Lawnside Borough	Camden	2,800
459. Moonachie Borough	Bergen	2,797
460. Lavallette Borough	Ocean	2,752
461. Woodlynne Borough	Camden	2,718
462. Riverton Borough	Burlington	2,715
463. Belvidere Town	Warren	2,701
464. Pennington Borough	Mercer	2,688
465. Riverdale Borough	Morris	2,676
466. Lakehurst Borough	Ocean	2,674
467. Beverly City	Burlington	2,651
468. Ogdensburg Borough	Sussex	2,623
469. Oxford Township	Warren	2,622
470. Clinton Town	Hunterdon	2,605
471. Lafayette Township	Sussex	2,524
472. Woodbine Borough	Cape May	2,508
473. Peapack & Gladstone Borough	Somerset	2,480
474. Gibbsboro Borough	Camden	2,451
475. Alpha Borough	Warren	2,437
476. Alpine Borough	Bergen	2,429
477. Wenonah Borough	Gloucester	2,333
478. South Hackensack Township	Bergen	2,313
479. Seaside Park Borough	Ocean	2,302
480. Weymouth Township	Atlantic	2,296

Municipal Comparative Tables

Appendix F

Population, 2006 (estimate)

Municipality	County	Population
481. Brooklawn Borough	Camden	2,294
482. Frelinghuysen Township	Warren	2,218
483. East Newark Borough	Hudson	2,217
484. Sussex Borough	Sussex	2,170
485. Avon-by-the-Sea Borough	Monmouth	2,166
486. Ocean Gate Borough	Ocean	2,130
487. Avalon Borough	Cape May	2,125
488. Essex Fells Borough	Essex	2,071
489. Sea Girt Borough	Monmouth	2,044
490. Swedesboro Borough	Gloucester	2,043
491. Pine Beach Borough	Ocean	2,032
492. Helmetta Borough	Middlesex	2,023
493. Hopewell Borough	Mercer	2,022
494. Glen Gardner Borough	Hunterdon	1,992
495. Hope Township	Warren	1,974
496. Folsom Borough	Atlantic	1,948
497. Sandyston Township	Sussex	1,924
498. Laurel Springs Borough	Camden	1,923
499. Lower Alloways Creek Township	Salem	1,914
500. Chesilhurst Borough	Camden	1,879
501. Island Heights Borough	Ocean	1,877
502. Allentown Borough	Monmouth	1,847
503. Englishtown Borough	Monmouth	1,841
504. Lebanon Borough	Hunterdon	1,830
505. Oldmans Township	Salem	1,827
506. Sea Bright Borough	Monmouth	1,799
507. Lake Como Borough	Monmouth	1,752
508. Estell Manor City	Atlantic	1,720
509. Downe Township	Cumberland	1,675
510. Newfield Borough	Gloucester	1,664
511. Hampton Borough	Hunterdon	1,658
512. Chester Borough	Morris	1,651
513. Hardwick Township	Warren	1,631
514. Eagleswood Township	Ocean	1,614
515. Bass River Township	Burlington	1,570
516. Mannington Township	Salem	1,566
517. Farmingdale Borough	Monmouth	1,563
518. Surf City Borough	Ocean	1,542
519. Stow Creek Township	Cumberland	1,535
520. Victory Gardens Borough	Morris	1,523
521. Frenchtown Borough	Hunterdon	1,491
522. Winfield Township	Union	1,486
523. Ship Bottom Borough	Ocean	1,427
524. Pemberton Borough	Burlington	1,381
525. Woodland Township	Burlington	1,374

Municipality	County	Population
526. Elmer Borough	Salem	1,370
527. Beach Haven Borough	Ocean	1,366
528. Bay Head Borough	Ocean	1,260
529. Port Republic City	Atlantic	1,234
530. Milford Borough	Hunterdon	1,219
531. Longport Borough	Atlantic	1,088
532. Elsinboro Township	Salem	1,073
533. Shrewsbury Township	Monmouth	1,073
534. Audubon Park Borough	Camden	1,071
535. Califon Borough	Hunterdon	1,052
536. Deal Borough	Monmouth	1,044
537. Stone Harbor Borough	Cape May	1,039
538. Hi-Nella Borough	Camden	1,007
539. West Cape May Borough	Cape May	1,007
540. Far Hills Borough	Somerset	928
541. Roosevelt Borough	Monmouth	913
542. Greenwich Township	Cumberland	893
543. Bloomsbury Borough	Hunterdon	881
544. Interlaken Borough	Monmouth	881
545. Branchville Borough	Sussex	839
546. Barnegat Light Borough	Ocean	833
547. Wrightstown Borough	Burlington	741
548. Allenhurst Borough	Monmouth	701
549. Rocky Hill Borough	Somerset	678
550. Andover Borough	Sussex	654
551. Washington Township	Burlington	651
552. Shiloh Borough	Cumberland	650
553. Fieldsboro Borough	Burlington	577
554. Stockton Borough	Hunterdon	555
555. Corbin City	Atlantic	530
556. Mantoloking Borough	Ocean	451
557. Millstone Borough	Somerset	431
558. West Wildwood Borough	Cape May	408
559. Rockleigh Borough	Bergen	393
560. Harvey Cedars Borough	Ocean	389
561. Loch Arbour Village	Monmouth	274
562. Cape May Point Borough	Cape May	230
563. Walpack Township	Sussex	40
564. Tavistock Borough	Camden	26
565. Pine Valley Borough	Camden	23
566. Teterboro Borough	Bergen	18

Appendix F — Municipal Comparative Tables

Unemployment Rate, 2006

#	Municipality	County	Unemp Rt
1.	Wildwood City	Cape May	17.2%
2.	Paulsboro Borough	Gloucester	13.5
3.	Wildwood Crest Borough	Cape May	13.4
4.	Penns Grove Borough	Salem	13.1
5.	North Wildwood City	Cape May	11.5
6.	Asbury Park City	Monmouth	10.7
7.	Camden City	Camden	10.7
8.	Trenton City	Mercer	10.7
9.	West Wildwood Borough	Cape May	10.6
10.	Hi-Nella Borough	Camden	9.7
11.	Beverly City	Burlington	9.5
12.	Bridgeton City	Cumberland	9.4
13.	Clementon Borough	Camden	9.1
14.	Fairfield Township	Cumberland	9.1
15.	Egg Harbor City	Atlantic	8.7
16.	Perth Amboy City	Middlesex	8.7
17.	Gloucester City	Camden	8.6
18.	Magnolia Borough	Camden	8.6
19.	Paterson City	Passaic	8.6
20.	Dover Town	Morris	8.5
21.	Newark City	Essex	8.5
22.	Atlantic City	Atlantic	8.4
23.	Lindenwold Borough	Camden	8.4
24.	Lower Township	Cape May	8.4
25.	South Toms River Borough	Ocean	8.4
26.	Carteret Borough	Middlesex	8.3
27.	Millville City	Cumberland	8.3
28.	Chesilhurst Borough	Camden	8.2
29.	Salem City	Salem	8.2
30.	Pleasantville City	Atlantic	8.0
31.	Montague Township	Sussex	7.9
32.	Winfield Township	Union	7.9
33.	Lawnside Borough	Camden	7.8
34.	West Cape May Borough	Cape May	7.8
35.	Beach Haven Borough	Ocean	7.7
36.	East Orange City	Essex	7.6
37.	Keansburg Borough	Monmouth	7.6
38.	Ship Bottom Borough	Ocean	7.6
39.	Haledon Borough	Passaic	7.5
40.	Oxford Township	Warren	7.5
41.	Wharton Borough	Morris	7.5
42.	Hillside Township	Union	7.4
43.	Cape May City	Cape May	7.3
44.	Fairview Borough	Bergen	7.2
45.	Hammonton Town	Atlantic	7.2
46.	Lakehurst Borough	Ocean	7.2
47.	Shrewsbury Township	Monmouth	7.2
48.	Dunellen Borough	Middlesex	7.1
49.	Passaic City	Passaic	7.1
50.	Tuckerton Borough	Ocean	7.1
51.	Woodbine Borough	Cape May	7.1
52.	Fieldsboro Borough	Burlington	7.0
53.	Franklin Township	Gloucester	7.0
54.	Irvington Township	Essex	7.0
55.	Roselle Borough	Union	7.0
56.	Union City	Hudson	7.0
57.	Bogota Borough	Bergen	6.9
58.	Carneys Point Township	Salem	6.9
59.	Seaside Heights Borough	Ocean	6.9
60.	Commercial Township	Cumberland	6.8
61.	Elizabeth City	Union	6.8%
62.	Orange City Township	Essex	6.7
63.	Phillipsburg Town	Warren	6.6
64.	South River Borough	Middlesex	6.6
65.	Manchester Township	Ocean	6.5
66.	National Park Borough	Gloucester	6.5
67.	Pitman Borough	Gloucester	6.5
68.	Runnemede Borough	Camden	6.5
69.	Seaside Park Borough	Ocean	6.5
70.	Vineland City	Cumberland	6.5
71.	Buena Borough	Atlantic	6.4
72.	Garfield City	Bergen	6.4
73.	Glassboro Borough	Gloucester	6.4
74.	Mount Holly Township	Burlington	6.4
75.	Ocean Township	Ocean	6.4
76.	Pine Hill Borough	Camden	6.4
77.	Plainfield City	Union	6.4
78.	Washington Township	Burlington	6.4
79.	Woodbury City	Gloucester	6.4
80.	Woodlynne Borough	Camden	6.4
81.	Alpha Borough	Warren	6.3
82.	Boonton Town	Morris	6.3
83.	Bradley Beach Borough	Monmouth	6.3
84.	Delanco Township	Burlington	6.3
85.	Estell Manor City	Atlantic	6.3
86.	Freehold Borough	Monmouth	6.3
87.	Loch Arbour Village	Monmouth	6.3
88.	Prospect Park Borough	Passaic	6.3
89.	Winslow Township	Camden	6.3
90.	Lebanon Township	Hunterdon	6.2
91.	Milford Borough	Hunterdon	6.2
92.	Absecon City	Atlantic	6.1
93.	Branchville Borough	Sussex	6.1
94.	Lawrence Township	Cumberland	6.1
95.	South Bound Brook Borough	Somerset	6.1
96.	West New York Town	Hudson	6.1
97.	Berkeley Township	Ocean	6.0
98.	Jersey City	Hudson	6.0
99.	Middle Township	Cape May	6.0
100.	Swedesboro Borough	Gloucester	6.0
101.	Wallington Borough	Bergen	6.0
102.	Westville Borough	Gloucester	6.0
103.	Wrightstown Borough	Burlington	6.0
104.	Andover Borough	Sussex	5.9
105.	Atlantic Highlands Borough	Monmouth	5.9
106.	Burlington City	Burlington	5.9
107.	Highlands Borough	Monmouth	5.9
108.	Lebanon Borough	Hunterdon	5.9
109.	Willingboro Township	Burlington	5.9
110.	Neptune Township	Monmouth	5.8
111.	Pemberton Township	Burlington	5.8
112.	Pennsauken Township	Camden	5.8
113.	Alexandria Township	Hunterdon	5.7
114.	Hopatcong Borough	Sussex	5.7
115.	Little Egg Harbor Township	Ocean	5.7
116.	Mullica Township	Atlantic	5.7
117.	Ventnor City	Atlantic	5.7
118.	Wantage Township	Sussex	5.7
119.	Florence Township	Burlington	5.6
120.	Mount Ephraim Borough	Camden	5.6

Municipal Comparative Tables

Unemployment Rate, 2006

#	Municipality	County	Unemp Rt
121.	Red Bank Borough	Monmouth	5.6%
122.	Union Beach Borough	Monmouth	5.6
123.	Bayonne City	Hudson	5.5
124.	Belleville Township	Essex	5.5
125.	Belvidere Town	Warren	5.5
126.	Bloomsbury Borough	Hunterdon	5.5
127.	Kearny Town	Hudson	5.5
128.	Knowlton Township	Warren	5.5
129.	Long Beach Township	Ocean	5.5
130.	North Bergen Township	Hudson	5.5
131.	Sea Isle City	Cape May	5.5
132.	Toms River Township	Ocean	5.5
133.	Alloway Township	Salem	5.4
134.	Bound Brook Borough	Somerset	5.4
135.	Clayton Borough	Gloucester	5.4
136.	Hackensack City	Bergen	5.4
137.	Harrison Town	Hudson	5.4
138.	Linden City	Union	5.4
139.	Monroe Township	Gloucester	5.4
140.	Newfield Borough	Gloucester	5.4
141.	Downe Township	Cumberland	5.3
142.	Edgewater Park Township	Burlington	5.3
143.	Monroe Township	Middlesex	5.3
144.	Quinton Township	Salem	5.3
145.	Rockaway Borough	Morris	5.3
146.	Saddle River Borough	Bergen	5.3
147.	Somers Point City	Atlantic	5.3
148.	Southampton Township	Burlington	5.3
149.	Beachwood Borough	Ocean	5.2
150.	East Rutherford Borough	Bergen	5.2
151.	Elk Township	Gloucester	5.2
152.	Galloway Township	Atlantic	5.2
153.	Hampton Borough	Hunterdon	5.2
154.	Lafayette Township	Sussex	5.2
155.	Long Branch City	Monmouth	5.2
156.	Lyndhurst Township	Bergen	5.2
157.	Mansfield Township	Burlington	5.2
158.	Rahway City	Union	5.2
159.	Somerville Borough	Somerset	5.2
160.	South Hackensack Township	Bergen	5.2
161.	Washington Township	Warren	5.2
162.	Bay Head Borough	Ocean	5.1
163.	Franklin Borough	Sussex	5.1
164.	Hardyston Township	Sussex	5.1
165.	Keyport Borough	Monmouth	5.1
166.	Mantua Township	Gloucester	5.1
167.	Margate City	Atlantic	5.1
168.	North Hanover Township	Burlington	5.1
169.	Palmyra Borough	Burlington	5.1
170.	Somerdale Borough	Camden	5.1
171.	Stone Harbor Borough	Cape May	5.1
172.	Surf City Borough	Ocean	5.1
173.	Upper Deerfield Township	Cumberland	5.1
174.	Waterford Township	Camden	5.1
175.	Collingswood Borough	Camden	5.0
176.	Island Heights Borough	Ocean	5.0
177.	Ocean Gate Borough	Ocean	5.0
178.	Pemberton Borough	Burlington	5.0
179.	Raritan Borough	Somerset	5.0
180.	Sea Bright Borough	Monmouth	5.0
181.	Shiloh Borough	Cumberland	5.0%
182.	Wenonah Borough	Gloucester	5.0
183.	West Deptford Township	Gloucester	5.0
184.	Belmar Borough	Monmouth	4.9
185.	Clifton City	Passaic	4.9
186.	Elmwood Park Borough	Bergen	4.9
187.	Lacey Township	Ocean	4.9
188.	Lakewood Township	Ocean	4.9
189.	Metuchen Borough	Middlesex	4.9
190.	Woodland Township	Burlington	4.9
191.	Deerfield Township	Cumberland	4.8
192.	Egg Harbor Township	Atlantic	4.8
193.	Hamilton Township	Atlantic	4.8
194.	Helmetta Borough	Middlesex	4.8
195.	Kenilworth Borough	Union	4.8
196.	Lake Como Borough	Monmouth	4.8
197.	Liberty Township	Warren	4.8
198.	Lodi Borough	Bergen	4.8
199.	New Brunswick City	Middlesex	4.8
200.	Ocean City	Cape May	4.8
201.	Riverdale Borough	Morris	4.8
202.	Roselle Park Borough	Union	4.8
203.	Sussex Borough	Sussex	4.8
204.	North Plainfield Borough	Somerset	4.7
205.	Spring Lake Borough	Monmouth	4.7
206.	Blairstown Township	Warren	4.6
207.	Bloomfield Township	Essex	4.6
208.	Buena Vista Township	Atlantic	4.6
209.	Englewood City	Bergen	4.6
210.	Guttenberg Town	Hudson	4.6
211.	Hamburg Borough	Sussex	4.6
212.	Hope Township	Warren	4.6
213.	Jamesburg Borough	Middlesex	4.6
214.	Little Ferry Borough	Bergen	4.6
215.	South Amboy City	Middlesex	4.6
216.	Barnegat Township	Ocean	4.5
217.	Bellmawr Borough	Camden	4.5
218.	Brick Township	Ocean	4.5
219.	Byram Township	Sussex	4.5
220.	Cliffside Park Borough	Bergen	4.5
221.	Clinton Township	Hunterdon	4.5
222.	Hazlet Township	Monmouth	4.5
223.	Little Falls Township	Passaic	4.5
224.	Matawan Borough	Monmouth	4.5
225.	Palisades Park Borough	Bergen	4.5
226.	South Orange Village Township	Essex	4.5
227.	West Milford Township	Passaic	4.5
228.	Eagleswood Township	Ocean	4.4
229.	East Newark Borough	Hudson	4.4
230.	Harrison Township	Gloucester	4.4
231.	Jackson Township	Ocean	4.4
232.	Oldmans Township	Salem	4.4
233.	Pittsgrove Township	Salem	4.4
234.	Riverside Township	Burlington	4.4
235.	Rochelle Park Township	Bergen	4.4
236.	Union Township	Union	4.4
237.	West Long Branch Borough	Monmouth	4.4
238.	Berlin Borough	Camden	4.3
239.	Brigantine City	Atlantic	4.3
240.	Interlaken Borough	Monmouth	4.3

Appendix F — Municipal Comparative Tables

Unemployment Rate, 2006

#	Municipality	County	Unemp Rt
241.	Mine Hill Township	Morris	4.3%
242.	Stafford Township	Ocean	4.3
243.	Upper Saddle River Borough	Bergen	4.3
244.	Avon-by-the-Sea Borough	Monmouth	4.2
245.	Bordentown City	Burlington	4.2
246.	Burlington Township	Burlington	4.2
247.	Chester Borough	Morris	4.2
248.	Franklin Township	Somerset	4.2
249.	Highland Park Borough	Middlesex	4.2
250.	Mansfield Township	Warren	4.2
251.	Maplewood Township	Essex	4.2
252.	Maurice River Township	Cumberland	4.2
253.	Neptune City Borough	Monmouth	4.2
254.	North Brunswick Township	Middlesex	4.2
255.	Norwood Borough	Bergen	4.2
256.	Pine Beach Borough	Ocean	4.2
257.	Piscataway Township	Middlesex	4.2
258.	Ridgefield Park Village	Bergen	4.2
259.	Victory Gardens Borough	Morris	4.2
260.	Audubon Park Borough	Camden	4.1
261.	Bass River Township	Burlington	4.1
262.	Cinnaminson Township	Burlington	4.1
263.	Hasbrouck Heights Borough	Bergen	4.1
264.	Milltown Borough	Middlesex	4.1
265.	Monmouth Beach Borough	Monmouth	4.1
266.	Rutherford Borough	Bergen	4.1
267.	Sandyston Township	Sussex	4.1
268.	Sayreville Borough	Middlesex	4.1
269.	Stratford Borough	Camden	4.1
270.	Tinton Falls Borough	Monmouth	4.1
271.	Weehawken Township	Hudson	4.1
272.	Corbin City	Atlantic	4.0
273.	Demarest Borough	Bergen	4.0
274.	Dennis Township	Cape May	4.0
275.	East Greenwich Township	Gloucester	4.0
276.	Eatontown Borough	Monmouth	4.0
277.	Edgewater Borough	Bergen	4.0
278.	Franklin Township	Hunterdon	4.0
279.	Gibbsboro Borough	Camden	4.0
280.	Greenwich Township	Gloucester	4.0
281.	Holland Township	Hunterdon	4.0
282.	Laurel Springs Borough	Camden	4.0
283.	North Arlington Borough	Bergen	4.0
284.	Pequannock Township	Morris	4.0
285.	Pilesgrove Township	Salem	4.0
286.	Roosevelt Borough	Monmouth	4.0
287.	South Harrison Township	Gloucester	4.0
288.	Spotswood Borough	Middlesex	4.0
289.	Stow Creek Township	Cumberland	4.0
290.	West Orange Township	Essex	4.0
291.	Woodbridge Township	Middlesex	4.0
292.	Woolwich Township	Gloucester	4.0
293.	Chesterfield Township	Burlington	3.9
294.	Mahwah Township	Bergen	3.9
295.	Maple Shade Township	Burlington	3.9
296.	Nutley Township	Essex	3.9
297.	Point Pleasant Borough	Ocean	3.9
298.	Pompton Lakes Borough	Passaic	3.9
299.	Springfield Township	Burlington	3.9
300.	Woodbury Heights Borough	Gloucester	3.9
301.	Bordentown Township	Burlington	3.8%
302.	Ewing Township	Mercer	3.8
303.	Fair Lawn Borough	Bergen	3.8
304.	Frankford Township	Sussex	3.8
305.	Green Township	Sussex	3.8
306.	Haworth Borough	Bergen	3.8
307.	Howell Township	Monmouth	3.8
308.	Kingwood Township	Hunterdon	3.8
309.	Lumberton Township	Burlington	3.8
310.	Morris Plains Borough	Morris	3.8
311.	New Milford Borough	Bergen	3.8
312.	Newton Town	Sussex	3.8
313.	Oaklyn Borough	Camden	3.8
314.	Ringwood Borough	Passaic	3.8
315.	Stanhope Borough	Sussex	3.8
316.	Washington Borough	Warren	3.8
317.	Washington Township	Bergen	3.8
318.	Allentown Borough	Monmouth	3.7
319.	Bergenfield Borough	Bergen	3.7
320.	Boonton Township	Morris	3.7
321.	Colts Neck Township	Monmouth	3.7
322.	Lambertville City	Hunterdon	3.7
323.	Linwood City	Atlantic	3.7
324.	Longport Borough	Atlantic	3.7
325.	Manville Borough	Somerset	3.7
326.	Ogdensburg Borough	Sussex	3.7
327.	Pohatcong Township	Warren	3.7
328.	Point Pleasant Beach Borough	Ocean	3.7
329.	Ridgefield Borough	Bergen	3.7
330.	Teaneck Township	Bergen	3.7
331.	Tenafly Borough	Bergen	3.7
332.	Edison Township	Middlesex	3.6
333.	Flemington Borough	Hunterdon	3.6
334.	Haddon Heights Borough	Camden	3.6
335.	Haddon Township	Camden	3.6
336.	Maywood Borough	Bergen	3.6
337.	Montclair Township	Essex	3.6
338.	Mount Olive Township	Morris	3.6
339.	New Hanover Township	Burlington	3.6
340.	Princeton Borough	Mercer	3.6
341.	Vernon Township	Sussex	3.6
342.	Wanaque Borough	Passaic	3.6
343.	Brielle Borough	Monmouth	3.5
344.	Deptford Township	Gloucester	3.5
345.	East Brunswick Township	Middlesex	3.5
346.	East Hanover Township	Morris	3.5
347.	Englewood Cliffs Borough	Bergen	3.5
348.	Freehold Township	Monmouth	3.5
349.	Hampton Township	Sussex	3.5
350.	High Bridge Borough	Hunterdon	3.5
351.	Lincoln Park Borough	Morris	3.5
352.	Manalapan Township	Monmouth	3.5
353.	Mannington Township	Salem	3.5
354.	Ocean Township	Monmouth	3.5
355.	Paramus Borough	Bergen	3.5
356.	Pennington Borough	Mercer	3.5
357.	Westampton Township	Burlington	3.5
358.	Aberdeen Township	Monmouth	3.4
359.	Barnegat Light Borough	Ocean	3.4
360.	Barrington Borough	Camden	3.4

Municipal Comparative Tables — Appendix F

Unemployment Rate, 2006

#	Municipality	County	Unemp Rt
361.	Brooklawn Borough	Camden	3.4%
362.	Cherry Hill Township	Camden	3.4
363.	Elmer Borough	Salem	3.4
364.	Englishtown Borough	Monmouth	3.4
365.	Hightstown Borough	Mercer	3.4
366.	Jefferson Township	Morris	3.4
367.	Middletown Township	Monmouth	3.4
368.	Morristown Town	Morris	3.4
369.	Mount Arlington Borough	Morris	3.4
370.	Mount Laurel Township	Burlington	3.4
371.	Pennsville Township	Salem	3.4
372.	Roseland Borough	Essex	3.4
373.	South Plainfield Borough	Middlesex	3.4
374.	Union Township	Hunterdon	3.4
375.	Wayne Township	Passaic	3.4
376.	West Paterson Borough	Passaic	3.4
377.	Weymouth Township	Atlantic	3.4
378.	Carlstadt Borough	Bergen	3.3
379.	Delran Township	Burlington	3.3
380.	East Amwell Township	Hunterdon	3.3
381.	Fairfield Township	Essex	3.3
382.	Greenwich Township	Cumberland	3.3
383.	Hainesport Township	Burlington	3.3
384.	Morris Township	Morris	3.3
385.	Netcong Borough	Morris	3.3
386.	New Providence Borough	Union	3.3
387.	Plumsted Township	Ocean	3.3
388.	Port Republic City	Atlantic	3.3
389.	West Caldwell Township	Essex	3.3
390.	Frelinghuysen Township	Warren	3.2
391.	Hillsborough Township	Somerset	3.2
392.	Merchantville Borough	Camden	3.2
393.	Middlesex Borough	Middlesex	3.2
394.	Moorestown Township	Burlington	3.2
395.	Old Bridge Township	Middlesex	3.2
396.	Roxbury Township	Morris	3.2
397.	South Brunswick Township	Middlesex	3.2
398.	Spring Lake Heights Borough	Monmouth	3.2
399.	Voorhees Township	Camden	3.2
400.	Washington Township	Morris	3.2
401.	Wood-Ridge Borough	Bergen	3.2
402.	Berlin Township	Camden	3.1
403.	Bloomingdale Borough	Passaic	3.1
404.	Butler Borough	Morris	3.1
405.	East Windsor Township	Mercer	3.1
406.	Franklin Township	Warren	3.1
407.	Frenchtown Borough	Hunterdon	3.1
408.	Green Brook Township	Somerset	3.1
409.	Little Silver Borough	Monmouth	3.1
410.	Long Hill Township	Morris	3.1
411.	Northfield City	Atlantic	3.1
412.	Old Tappan Borough	Bergen	3.1
413.	Parsippany-Troy Hills Township	Morris	3.1
414.	Totowa Borough	Passaic	3.1
415.	Bridgewater Township	Somerset	3.0
416.	Denville Township	Morris	3.0
417.	Evesham Township	Burlington	3.0
418.	Fair Haven Borough	Monmouth	3.0
419.	Fort Lee Borough	Bergen	3.0
420.	Glen Ridge Borough	Essex	3.0
421.	Hopewell Township	Cumberland	3.0%
422.	Lavallette Borough	Ocean	3.0
423.	Livingston Township	Essex	3.0
424.	Marlboro Township	Monmouth	3.0
425.	North Caldwell Borough	Essex	3.0
426.	Randolph Township	Morris	3.0
427.	River Edge Borough	Bergen	3.0
428.	Rocky Hill Borough	Somerset	3.0
429.	Saddle Brook Township	Bergen	3.0
430.	Shamong Township	Burlington	3.0
431.	Wall Township	Monmouth	3.0
432.	Watchung Borough	Somerset	3.0
433.	Alpine Borough	Bergen	2.9
434.	Dumont Borough	Bergen	2.9
435.	Fanwood Borough	Union	2.9
436.	Hackettstown Town	Warren	2.9
437.	Haddonfield Borough	Camden	2.9
438.	Hardwick Township	Warren	2.9
439.	Hawthorne Borough	Passaic	2.9
440.	Peapack & Gladstone Borough	Somerset	2.9
441.	Readington Township	Hunterdon	2.9
442.	White Township	Warren	2.9
443.	Andover Township	Sussex	2.8
444.	Avalon Borough	Cape May	2.8
445.	Deal Borough	Monmouth	2.8
446.	Eastampton Township	Burlington	2.8
447.	Glen Rock Borough	Bergen	2.8
448.	Hoboken City	Hudson	2.8
449.	Leonia Borough	Bergen	2.8
450.	Montvale Borough	Bergen	2.8
451.	Moonachie Borough	Bergen	2.8
452.	Oakland Borough	Bergen	2.8
453.	Oradell Borough	Bergen	2.8
454.	Ridgewood Village	Bergen	2.8
455.	Sparta Township	Sussex	2.8
456.	West Amwell Township	Hunterdon	2.8
457.	Wyckoff Township	Bergen	2.8
458.	Allendale Borough	Bergen	2.7
459.	Allenhurst Borough	Monmouth	2.7
460.	Bedminster Township	Somerset	2.7
461.	Florham Park Borough	Morris	2.7
462.	Garwood Borough	Union	2.7
463.	Gloucester Township	Camden	2.7
464.	Greenwich Township	Warren	2.7
465.	Harrington Park Borough	Bergen	2.7
466.	Hillsdale Borough	Bergen	2.7
467.	Ramsey Borough	Bergen	2.7
468.	Scotch Plains Township	Union	2.7
469.	Robbinsville Township	Mercer	2.7
470.	Westfield Town	Union	2.7
471.	Bernards Township	Somerset	2.6
472.	Clinton Town	Hunterdon	2.6
473.	Cranford Township	Union	2.6
474.	Far Hills Borough	Somerset	2.6
475.	Folsom Borough	Atlantic	2.6
476.	Hopewell Township	Mercer	2.6
477.	Lower Alloways Creek Township	Salem	2.6
478.	North Haledon Borough	Passaic	2.6
479.	Rumson Borough	Monmouth	2.6
480.	Woodstown Borough	Salem	2.6

©2008 Information Publications, Inc. All rights reserved. Photocopying prohibited. For additional copies, contact the publisher at www.informationpublications.com or (877)544-INFO (4636)

Appendix F — Municipal Comparative Tables

Unemployment Rate, 2006

#	Municipality	County	Unemp Rt
481.	Chatham Borough	Morris	2.5%
482.	Cresskill Borough	Bergen	2.5
483.	Essex Fells Borough	Essex	2.5
484.	Glen Gardner Borough	Hunterdon	2.5
485.	Harding Township	Morris	2.5
486.	Holmdel Township	Monmouth	2.5
487.	Mountainside Borough	Union	2.5
488.	Northvale Borough	Bergen	2.5
489.	Plainsboro Township	Middlesex	2.5
490.	Rockaway Township	Morris	2.5
491.	Summit City	Union	2.5
492.	Branchburg Township	Somerset	2.4
493.	Farmingdale Borough	Monmouth	2.4
494.	Harmony Township	Warren	2.4
495.	Madison Borough	Morris	2.4
496.	Manasquan Borough	Monmouth	2.4
497.	Medford Lakes Borough	Burlington	2.4
498.	Montgomery Township	Somerset	2.4
499.	Riverton Borough	Burlington	2.4
500.	Tewksbury Township	Hunterdon	2.4
501.	Verona Township	Essex	2.4
502.	Caldwell Borough	Essex	2.3
503.	Chester Township	Morris	2.3
504.	Franklin Lakes Borough	Bergen	2.3
505.	Logan Township	Gloucester	2.3
506.	River Vale Township	Bergen	2.3
507.	Secaucus Town	Hudson	2.3
508.	Berkeley Heights Township	Union	2.2
509.	Delaware Township	Hunterdon	2.2
510.	Hamilton Township	Mercer	2.2
511.	Kinnelon Borough	Morris	2.2
512.	Lopatcong Township	Warren	2.2
513.	Oceanport Borough	Monmouth	2.2
514.	Tabernacle Township	Burlington	2.2
515.	Westwood Borough	Bergen	2.2
516.	Allamuchy Township	Warren	2.1
517.	Clark Township	Union	2.1
518.	Closter Borough	Bergen	2.1
519.	Cranbury Township	Middlesex	2.1
520.	Millburn Township	Essex	2.1
521.	Sea Girt Borough	Monmouth	2.1
522.	Bethlehem Township	Hunterdon	2.0
523.	Lawrence Township	Mercer	2.0
524.	Upper Township	Cape May	2.0
525.	Waldwick Borough	Bergen	2.0
526.	Warren Township	Somerset	2.0%
527.	West Windsor Township	Mercer	2.0
528.	Medford Township	Burlington	1.9
529.	Millstone Township	Monmouth	1.9
530.	Montville Township	Morris	1.9
531.	Upper Pittsgrove Township	Salem	1.9
532.	Washington Township	Gloucester	1.9
533.	Audubon Borough	Camden	1.8
534.	Emerson Borough	Bergen	1.8
535.	Hanover Township	Morris	1.8
536.	Raritan Township	Hunterdon	1.8
537.	Upper Freehold Township	Monmouth	1.8
538.	Springfield Township	Union	1.7
539.	Stillwater Township	Sussex	1.7
540.	Fredon Township	Sussex	1.6
541.	Midland Park Borough	Bergen	1.6
542.	Park Ridge Borough	Bergen	1.6
543.	Bernardsville Borough	Somerset	1.5
544.	Elsinboro Township	Salem	1.5
545.	Mendham Borough	Morris	1.5
546.	Woodcliff Lake Borough	Bergen	1.5
547.	Chatham Township	Morris	1.4
548.	Independence Township	Warren	1.4
549.	Cedar Grove Township	Essex	1.2
550.	Shrewsbury Borough	Monmouth	1.2
551.	Hopewell Borough	Mercer	1.0
552.	Mendham Township	Morris	1.0
553.	Princeton Township	Mercer	0.8
554.	Mountain Lakes Borough	Morris	0.6
555.	Ho-Ho-Kus Borough	Bergen	0.5
556.	Califon Borough	Hunterdon	0
557.	Cape May Point Borough	Cape May	0
558.	Harvey Cedars Borough	Ocean	0
559.	Mantoloking Borough	Ocean	0
560.	Millstone Borough	Somerset	0
561.	Pine Valley Borough	Camden	0
562.	Rockleigh Borough	Bergen	0
563.	Stockton Borough	Hunterdon	0
564.	Tavistock Borough	Camden	0
565.	Teterboro Borough	Bergen	0
566.	Walpack Township	Sussex	0

Municipal Comparative Tables

Appendix F

Crime Rate, 2006 (per 1,000 residents)

#	Municipality	County	Crime Rate
1.	Avalon Borough	Cape May	145.8
2.	Atlantic City	Atlantic	132.7
3.	Cape May Point Borough	Cape May	122.9
4.	Seaside Heights Borough	Ocean	108.1
5.	Brooklawn Borough	Camden	107.1
6.	Sea Isle City	Cape May	106.1
7.	Wildwood City	Cape May	100.4
8.	Beach Haven Borough	Ocean	98.4
9.	Camden City	Camden	81.4
10.	Asbury Park City	Monmouth	78.5
11.	Cape May City	Cape May	77.4
12.	North Wildwood City	Cape May	76.6
13.	Irvington Township	Essex	76.2
14.	Ocean City	Cape May	69.5
15.	Woodbury City	Gloucester	68.2
16.	Paramus Borough	Bergen	66.2
17.	Long Beach Township	Ocean	65.9
18.	Ship Bottom Borough	Ocean	65.6
19.	Loch Arbour Village	Monmouth	65.5
20.	Millville City	Cumberland	63.7
21.	Salem City	Salem	62.3
22.	Belmar Borough	Monmouth	61.7
23.	Bridgeton City	Cumberland	58.4
24.	Penns Grove Borough	Salem	57.8
25.	Orange City Township	Essex	57.5
26.	Vineland City	Cumberland	56.4
27.	Neptune Township	Monmouth	54.5
28.	Avon-by-the-Sea Borough	Monmouth	53.9
29.	Newark City	Essex	53.8
30.	Wildwood Crest Borough	Cape May	52.7
31.	Deptford Township	Gloucester	52.1
32.	Middle Township	Cape May	51.7
33.	Watchung Borough	Somerset	51.4
34.	Fairfield Township	Essex	49.8
35.	Clementon Borough	Camden	49.4
36.	Harvey Cedars Borough	Ocean	49.2
37.	Hamilton Township	Atlantic	49.0
38.	Lindenwold Borough	Camden	48.6
39.	West Wildwood Borough	Cape May	48.4
40.	Secaucus Town	Hudson	46.9
41.	Woodland Township	Burlington	46.7
42.	East Orange City	Essex	46.6
43.	Paulsboro Borough	Gloucester	46.4
44.	Pohatcong Township	Warren	46.3
45.	Woodlynne Borough	Camden	46.3
46.	Trenton City	Mercer	46.0
47.	Elizabeth City	Union	45.9
48.	Plainfield City	Union	45.9
49.	East Rutherford Borough	Bergen	45.4
50.	Eatontown Borough	Monmouth	45.4
51.	New Brunswick City	Middlesex	45.4
52.	Stone Harbor Borough	Cape May	45.2
53.	Barnegat Light Borough	Ocean	45.0
54.	Morristown Town	Morris	44.3
55.	Jersey City	Hudson	44.2
56.	Mount Ephraim Borough	Camden	42.5
57.	Pennsauken Township	Camden	42.4
58.	Glassboro Borough	Gloucester	42.2
59.	Lawnside Borough	Camden	42.1
60.	Pleasantville City	Atlantic	41.8
61.	Deal Borough	Monmouth	41.2
62.	Bradley Beach Borough	Monmouth	40.6
63.	Bay Head Borough	Ocean	40.5
64.	Runnemede Borough	Camden	40.4
65.	Millburn Township	Essex	40.3
66.	Paterson City	Passaic	40.3
67.	Commercial Township	Cumberland	40.2
68.	Wrightstown Borough	Burlington	40.2
69.	Absecon City	Atlantic	39.9
70.	Point Pleasant Beach Borough	Ocean	39.3
71.	Woodbine Borough	Cape May	38.9
72.	Seaside Park Borough	Ocean	37.8
73.	Little Falls Township	Passaic	37.5
74.	Berlin Township	Camden	37.4
75.	Mount Holly Township	Burlington	36.6
76.	West Cape May Borough	Cape May	36.6
77.	Linden City	Union	36.2
78.	Woodbury Heights Borough	Gloucester	36.1
79.	Buena Borough	Atlantic	35.3
80.	Elk Township	Gloucester	34.8
81.	Hillside Township	Union	34.8
82.	Keansburg Borough	Monmouth	34.7
83.	Netcong Borough	Morris	34.6
84.	Lawrence Township	Mercer	34.2
85.	Neptune City Borough	Monmouth	34.2
86.	Passaic City	Passaic	34.0
87.	Egg Harbor Township	Atlantic	33.9
88.	South Hackensack Township	Bergen	33.6
89.	West Long Branch Borough	Monmouth	33.6
90.	Mantoloking Borough	Ocean	33.3
91.	Princeton Borough	Mercer	33.3
92.	Somerdale Borough	Camden	33.2
93.	Upper Deerfield Township	Cumberland	33.2
94.	Cherry Hill Township	Camden	33.1
95.	Lake Como Borough	Monmouth	32.4
96.	Moonachie Borough	Bergen	32.4
97.	Bloomfield Township	Essex	32.0
98.	Clayton Borough	Gloucester	32.0
99.	Merchantville Borough	Camden	31.9
100.	Totowa Borough	Passaic	31.8
101.	Red Bank Borough	Monmouth	31.7
102.	Union Township	Union	31.5
103.	Stratford Borough	Camden	31.0
104.	Woodbridge Township	Middlesex	31.0
105.	Beverly City	Burlington	30.7
106.	Collingswood Borough	Camden	30.7
107.	Audubon Park Borough	Camden	30.6
108.	Glen Ridge Borough	Essex	30.6
109.	Voorhees Township	Camden	30.6
110.	Long Branch City	Monmouth	30.5
111.	Somers Point City	Atlantic	30.5
112.	Union City	Hudson	30.4
113.	Longport Borough	Atlantic	30.3
114.	Pemberton Borough	Burlington	30.2
115.	Chesilhurst Borough	Camden	30.0
116.	Riverdale Borough	Morris	30.0
117.	Hoboken City	Hudson	29.9
118.	Pennsville Township	Salem	29.7
119.	Haddon Township	Camden	29.3
120.	Lawrence Township	Cumberland	29.2

The New Jersey Municipal Data Book

Appendix F

Municipal Comparative Tables

Crime Rate, 2006 (per 1,000 residents)

Municipality	County	Crime Rate	Municipality	County	Crime Rate
121. Belleville Township	Essex	29.1	181. Lacey Township	Ocean	24.4
122. Ocean Township	Monmouth	29.1	182. Milltown Borough	Middlesex	24.4
123. Audubon Borough	Camden	29.0	183. Cinnaminson Township	Burlington	24.3
124. Greenwich Township	Gloucester	28.9	184. Bellmawr Borough	Camden	24.2
125. Harrison Town	Hudson	28.9	185. Haddonfield Borough	Camden	24.2
126. Laurel Springs Borough	Camden	28.9	186. West Paterson Borough	Passaic	24.2
127. Lumberton Township	Burlington	28.9	187. Ewing Township	Mercer	24.0
128. South Orange Village Township	Essex	28.9	188. Galloway Township	Atlantic	24.0
129. Weehawken Township	Hudson	28.9	189. Burlington City	Burlington	23.9
130. Westampton Township	Burlington	28.9	190. Saddle Brook Township	Bergen	23.8
131. Gloucester City	Camden	28.8	191. North Brunswick Township	Middlesex	23.7
132. Montclair Township	Essex	28.8	192. Egg Harbor City	Atlantic	23.6
133. Pine Hill Borough	Camden	28.7	193. Hightstown Borough	Mercer	23.6
134. North Plainfield Borough	Somerset	28.5	194. Roselle Borough	Union	23.6
135. Berlin Borough	Camden	28.4	195. East Hanover Township	Morris	23.5
136. Oldmans Township	Salem	28.4	196. Hamilton Township	Mercer	23.5
137. Westville Borough	Gloucester	28.4	197. Wayne Township	Passaic	23.5
138. Freehold Township	Monmouth	28.3	198. Green Brook Township	Somerset	23.3
139. Hackensack City	Bergen	28.3	199. Beachwood Borough	Ocean	23.2
140. Corbin City	Atlantic	28.2	200. Dennis Township	Cape May	23.2
141. Carlstadt Borough	Bergen	28.1	201. Elsinboro Township	Salem	23.2
142. Kearny Town	Hudson	28.1	202. Willingboro Township	Burlington	23.2
143. Perth Amboy City	Middlesex	28.1	203. Moorestown Township	Burlington	23.1
144. Edgewater Park Township	Burlington	27.9	204. Pilesgrove Township	Salem	23.1
145. Oaklyn Borough	Camden	27.9	205. Fairfield Township	Cumberland	23.0
146. Rockleigh Borough	Bergen	27.8	206. Flemington Borough	Hunterdon	23.0
147. West Deptford Township	Gloucester	27.8	207. Keyport Borough	Monmouth	22.9
148. Bass River Township	Burlington	27.5	208. Swedesboro Borough	Gloucester	22.9
149. Gloucester Township	Camden	27.5	209. Spring Lake Borough	Monmouth	22.8
150. Surf City Borough	Ocean	27.5	210. Delanco Township	Burlington	22.7
151. Lakewood Township	Ocean	27.4	211. Dover Town	Morris	22.7
152. Magnolia Borough	Camden	27.1	212. Hi-Nella Borough	Camden	22.7
153. Winslow Township	Camden	27.1	213. Fairview Borough	Bergen	22.6
154. Freehold Borough	Monmouth	27.0	214. Hainesport Township	Burlington	22.6
155. Ocean Gate Borough	Ocean	27.0	215. South Plainfield Borough	Middlesex	22.5
156. Manasquan Borough	Monmouth	26.9	216. Somerville Borough	Somerset	22.4
157. Phillipsburg Town	Warren	26.9	217. Gibbsboro Borough	Camden	21.9
158. Elmer Borough	Salem	26.8	218. Guttenberg Town	Hudson	21.9
159. Pemberton Township	Burlington	26.8	219. Toms River Township	Ocean	21.9
160. Washington Borough	Warren	26.8	220. West New York Town	Hudson	21.9
161. Clifton City	Passaic	26.7	221. Burlington Township	Burlington	21.8
162. Washington Township	Burlington	26.4	222. Mannington Township	Salem	21.8
163. Hackettstown Town	Warren	26.3	223. Mantua Township	Gloucester	21.8
164. Ventnor City	Atlantic	26.3	224. Washington Township	Gloucester	21.7
165. Monroe Township	Gloucester	26.2	225. West Windsor Township	Mercer	21.7
166. West Orange Township	Essex	26.2	226. Margate City	Atlantic	21.5
167. Edison Township	Middlesex	26.1	227. Sussex Borough	Sussex	21.5
168. Maplewood Township	Essex	25.9	228. Bloomsbury Borough	Hunterdon	21.4
169. Rahway City	Union	25.8	229. Springfield Township	Burlington	21.4
170. South Toms River Borough	Ocean	25.7	230. Elmwood Park Borough	Bergen	21.1
171. Allenhurst Borough	Monmouth	25.5	231. Franklin Township	Gloucester	21.1
172. Palmyra Borough	Burlington	25.5	232. Shrewsbury Borough	Monmouth	21.1
173. Greenwich Township	Warren	25.4	233. Dunellen Borough	Middlesex	21.0
174. Maple Shade Township	Burlington	25.4	234. Manville Borough	Somerset	21.0
175. Bound Brook Borough	Somerset	25.3	235. Downe Township	Cumberland	20.9
176. Carneys Point Township	Salem	25.0	236. Sayreville Borough	Middlesex	20.8
177. Englewood City	Bergen	24.8	237. Hopewell Township	Cumberland	20.5
178. Little Egg Harbor Township	Ocean	24.8	238. Newfield Borough	Gloucester	20.5
179. Lower Township	Cape May	24.5	239. Butler Borough	Morris	20.3
180. Buena Vista Township	Atlantic	24.4	240. Woodstown Borough	Salem	20.2

Municipal Comparative Tables — Appendix F

Crime Rate, 2006 (per 1,000 residents)

Municipality	County	Crime Rate
241. Edgewater Borough	Bergen	20.1
242. Wall Township	Monmouth	20.1
243. Cranbury Township	Middlesex	20.0
244. Mount Laurel Township	Burlington	20.0
245. Stafford Township	Ocean	19.9
246. Brick Township	Ocean	19.8
247. Metuchen Borough	Middlesex	19.8
248. Mountain Lakes Borough	Morris	19.8
249. Vernon Township	Sussex	19.7
250. Livingston Township	Essex	19.6
251. Raritan Borough	Somerset	19.6
252. Wharton Borough	Morris	19.6
253. Carteret Borough	Middlesex	19.5
254. Montague Township	Sussex	19.5
255. Rockaway Township	Morris	19.5
256. East Brunswick Township	Middlesex	19.3
257. Folsom Borough	Atlantic	19.3
258. Haddon Heights Borough	Camden	19.3
259. Rochelle Park Township	Bergen	19.3
260. Sea Girt Borough	Monmouth	19.3
261. Tinton Falls Borough	Monmouth	19.3
262. Tuckerton Borough	Ocean	19.3
263. National Park Borough	Gloucester	19.2
264. Logan Township	Gloucester	19.0
265. Stanhope Borough	Sussex	18.9
266. Kenilworth Borough	Union	18.7
267. Prospect Park Borough	Passaic	18.6
268. Eagleswood Township	Ocean	18.5
269. Mansfield Township	Burlington	18.4
270. South Amboy City	Middlesex	18.4
271. Bordentown Township	Burlington	18.3
272. Franklin Borough	Sussex	18.3
273. Andover Borough	Sussex	18.2
274. Brigantine City	Atlantic	18.2
275. Hamburg Borough	Sussex	18.2
276. Parsippany-Troy Hills Township	Morris	18.1
277. Alpha Borough	Warren	17.9
278. North Bergen Township	Hudson	17.9
279. Riverside Township	Burlington	17.9
280. Garfield City	Bergen	17.7
281. Lambertville City	Hunterdon	17.7
282. Bayonne City	Hudson	17.6
283. Englewood Cliffs Borough	Bergen	17.6
284. Waterford Township	Camden	17.6
285. North Arlington Borough	Bergen	17.5
286. Roselle Park Borough	Union	17.5
287. Nutley Township	Essex	17.4
288. Point Pleasant Borough	Ocean	17.4
289. Teaneck Township	Bergen	17.4
290. Berkeley Township	Ocean	17.3
291. Frenchtown Borough	Hunterdon	17.3
292. Lyndhurst Township	Bergen	17.3
293. Newton Town	Sussex	17.3
294. Pittsgrove Township	Salem	17.3
295. Cedar Grove Township	Essex	17.2
296. Farmingdale Borough	Monmouth	17.2
297. Highlands Borough	Monmouth	17.2
298. East Greenwich Township	Gloucester	17.1
299. Upper Pittsgrove Township	Salem	17.1
300. Highland Park Borough	Middlesex	17.0
301. Piscataway Township	Middlesex	17.0
302. Upper Township	Cape May	16.9
303. Hammonton Town	Atlantic	16.8
304. Port Republic City	Atlantic	16.8
305. Springfield Township	Union	16.6
306. West Milford Township	Passaic	16.6
307. Pitman Borough	Gloucester	16.4
308. Verona Township	Essex	16.4
309. Evesham Township	Burlington	16.3
310. Franklin Township	Somerset	16.3
311. Hampton Borough	Hunterdon	16.2
312. Ridgefield Park Village	Bergen	16.1
313. Mansfield Township	Warren	16.0
314. Quinton Township	Salem	15.7
315. Fair Lawn Borough	Bergen	15.6
316. Harrison Township	Gloucester	15.6
317. South Brunswick Township	Middlesex	15.5
318. Old Bridge Township	Middlesex	15.4
319. Aberdeen Township	Monmouth	15.3
320. Rutherford Borough	Bergen	15.3
321. Bridgewater Township	Somerset	15.2
322. Hasbrouck Heights Borough	Bergen	15.2
323. Mullica Township	Atlantic	15.2
324. Delran Township	Burlington	14.9
325. East Windsor Township	Mercer	14.8
326. Frankford Township	Sussex	14.8
327. Wallington Borough	Bergen	14.8
328. Clark Township	Union	14.7
329. Deerfield Township	Cumberland	14.7
330. Morris Plains Borough	Morris	14.7
331. Chester Borough	Morris	14.5
332. Lodi Borough	Bergen	14.5
333. Roxbury Township	Morris	14.4
334. South River Borough	Middlesex	14.4
335. Southampton Township	Burlington	14.4
336. Victory Gardens Borough	Morris	14.4
337. Hazlet Township	Monmouth	14.3
338. Hawthorne Borough	Passaic	14.2
339. Far Hills Borough	Somerset	14.1
340. Spotswood Borough	Middlesex	14.0
341. Estell Manor City	Atlantic	13.9
342. Holmdel Township	Monmouth	13.9
343. Hampton Township	Sussex	13.8
344. Hardyston Township	Sussex	13.8
345. Greenwich Township	Cumberland	13.7
346. Atlantic Highlands Borough	Monmouth	13.6
347. Ocean Township	Ocean	13.6
348. Riverton Borough	Burlington	13.5
349. Scotch Plains Township	Union	13.5
350. Hanover Township	Morris	13.4
351. Lakehurst Borough	Ocean	13.4
352. Wanaque Borough	Passaic	13.4
353. East Newark Borough	Hudson	13.3
354. Knowlton Township	Warren	13.3
355. Northfield City	Atlantic	13.3
356. Pine Beach Borough	Ocean	13.3
357. Haledon Borough	Passaic	13.2
358. Westwood Borough	Bergen	13.2
359. Allentown Borough	Monmouth	12.9
360. Cranford Township	Union	12.9

Appendix F

Municipal Comparative Tables

Crime Rate, 2006 (per 1,000 residents)

Municipality	County	Crime Rate
361. Linwood City	Atlantic	12.7
362. Middletown Township	Monmouth	12.7
363. Garwood Borough	Union	12.5
364. Middlesex Borough	Middlesex	12.5
365. Ramsey Borough	Bergen	12.5
366. Rockaway Borough	Morris	12.5
367. Shiloh Borough	Cumberland	12.5
368. Weymouth Township	Atlantic	12.5
369. Stow Creek Township	Cumberland	12.4
370. Independence Township	Warren	12.3
371. Rumson Borough	Monmouth	12.3
372. New Providence Borough	Union	12.2
373. Fieldsboro Borough	Burlington	12.0
374. Lebanon Borough	Hunterdon	12.0
375. Lopatcong Township	Warren	12.0
376. Matawan Borough	Monmouth	12.0
377. River Edge Borough	Bergen	11.9
378. Summit City	Union	11.9
379. Barnegat Township	Ocean	11.8
380. Branchville Borough	Sussex	11.8
381. Jackson Township	Ocean	11.8
382. Eastampton Township	Burlington	11.7
383. Westfield Town	Union	11.7
384. Chatham Borough	Morris	11.6
385. Jefferson Township	Morris	11.6
386. Lavallette Borough	Ocean	11.6
387. Madison Borough	Morris	11.6
388. Denville Township	Morris	11.5
389. Blairstown Township	Warren	11.4
390. South Harrison Township	Gloucester	11.4
391. Franklin Township	Warren	11.3
392. Bogota Borough	Bergen	11.2
393. Montville Township	Morris	11.2
394. Robbinsville Township	Mercer	11.2
395. High Bridge Borough	Hunterdon	11.1
396. Little Ferry Borough	Bergen	11.1
397. Millstone Township	Monmouth	11.1
398. Woolwich Township	Gloucester	11.1
399. Florence Township	Burlington	11.0
400. Jamesburg Borough	Middlesex	11.0
401. Mountainside Borough	Union	11.0
402. Mount Arlington Borough	Morris	10.9
403. Ridgefield Borough	Bergen	10.9
404. Lafayette Township	Sussex	10.8
405. Maywood Borough	Bergen	10.8
406. North Hanover Township	Burlington	10.8
407. Alloway Township	Salem	10.7
408. Hope Township	Warren	10.7
409. Manalapan Township	Monmouth	10.7
410. Milford Borough	Hunterdon	10.7
411. Montgomery Township	Somerset	10.7
412. Howell Township	Monmouth	10.6
413. Medford Township	Burlington	10.6
414. Princeton Township	Mercer	10.6
415. West Caldwell Township	Essex	10.6
416. Bordentown City	Burlington	10.5
417. Brielle Borough	Monmouth	10.5
418. Marlboro Township	Monmouth	10.5
419. Plainsboro Township	Middlesex	10.5
420. Barrington Borough	Camden	10.4
421. Dumont Borough	Bergen	10.4
422. Franklin Lakes Borough	Bergen	10.4
423. Little Silver Borough	Monmouth	10.3
424. Morris Township	Morris	10.2
425. Readington Township	Hunterdon	10.2
426. Fort Lee Borough	Bergen	10.1
427. Allamuchy Township	Warren	10.0
428. Cliffside Park Borough	Bergen	10.0
429. Ridgewood Village	Bergen	10.0
430. Pequannock Township	Morris	9.9
431. Tabernacle Township	Burlington	9.9
432. Upper Freehold Township	Monmouth	9.9
433. West Amwell Township	Hunterdon	9.9
434. Bloomingdale Borough	Passaic	9.8
435. Wantage Township	Sussex	9.8
436. Bergenfield Borough	Bergen	9.7
437. Hillsborough Township	Somerset	9.7
438. Leonia Borough	Bergen	9.7
439. Monmouth Beach Borough	Monmouth	9.7
440. Mount Olive Township	Morris	9.7
441. Oakland Borough	Bergen	9.6
442. Hopatcong Borough	Sussex	9.5
443. Mine Hill Township	Morris	9.5
444. Palisades Park Borough	Bergen	9.5
445. Pompton Lakes Borough	Passaic	9.5
446. Sea Bright Borough	Monmouth	9.5
447. Washington Township	Warren	9.5
448. Waldwick Borough	Bergen	9.4
449. Allendale Borough	Bergen	9.3
450. Bedminster Township	Somerset	9.2
451. Demarest Borough	Bergen	9.2
452. Lebanon Township	Hunterdon	9.2
453. Oradell Borough	Bergen	9.2
454. Hillsdale Borough	Bergen	9.1
455. Bernardsville Borough	Somerset	8.9
456. Englishtown Borough	Monmouth	8.9
457. Fanwood Borough	Union	8.9
458. Mendham Township	Morris	8.9
459. Raritan Township	Hunterdon	8.9
460. Sandyston Township	Sussex	8.9
461. Monroe Township	Middlesex	8.8
462. Plumsted Township	Ocean	8.8
463. Andover Township	Sussex	8.7
464. Florham Park Borough	Morris	8.7
465. Frelinghuysen Township	Warren	8.7
466. White Township	Warren	8.7
467. Franklin Township	Hunterdon	8.6
468. Island Heights Borough	Ocean	8.6
469. Montvale Borough	Bergen	8.6
470. Pennington Borough	Mercer	8.5
471. Closter Borough	Bergen	8.4
472. Medford Lakes Borough	Burlington	8.4
473. Delaware Township	Hunterdon	8.3
474. Lower Alloways Creek Township	Salem	8.3
475. Colts Neck Township	Monmouth	8.2
476. New Milford Borough	Bergen	8.2
477. Randolph Township	Morris	8.2
478. Liberty Township	Warren	8.1
479. Roseland Borough	Essex	8.1
480. Wenonah Borough	Gloucester	8.1

Municipal Comparative Tables — Appendix F

Crime Rate, 2006 (per 1,000 residents)

Municipality	County	Crime Rate
481. Wood-Ridge Borough	Bergen	8.1
482. Lincoln Park Borough	Morris	8.0
483. Manchester Township	Ocean	8.0
484. Boonton Town	Morris	7.8
485. Mendham Borough	Morris	7.7
486. Branchburg Township	Somerset	7.6
487. Clinton Town	Hunterdon	7.6
488. Essex Fells Borough	Essex	7.6
489. Tenafly Borough	Bergen	7.5
490. Washington Township	Morris	7.4
491. Belvidere Town	Warren	7.3
492. Fair Haven Borough	Monmouth	7.3
493. Kinnelon Borough	Morris	7.3
494. North Haledon Borough	Passaic	7.3
495. Harmony Township	Warren	7.1
496. Oceanport Borough	Monmouth	7.1
497. Stockton Borough	Hunterdon	7.1
498. Union Beach Borough	Monmouth	7.1
499. Glen Gardner Borough	Hunterdon	7.0
500. Hopewell Township	Mercer	7.0
501. North Caldwell Borough	Essex	7.0
502. Caldwell Borough	Essex	6.8
503. Stillwater Township	Sussex	6.8
504. Warren Township	Somerset	6.8
505. Berkeley Heights Township	Union	6.7
506. Maurice River Township	Cumberland	6.7
507. Wyckoff Township	Bergen	6.7
508. Chester Township	Morris	6.6
509. Fredon Township	Sussex	6.6
510. Saddle River Borough	Bergen	6.6
511. Spring Lake Heights Borough	Monmouth	6.6
512. Emerson Borough	Bergen	6.5
513. Glen Rock Borough	Bergen	6.5
514. Union Township	Hunterdon	6.5
515. Bernards Township	Somerset	6.4
516. Boonton Township	Morris	6.4
517. Northvale Borough	Bergen	6.4
518. Mahwah Township	Bergen	6.3
519. Byram Township	Sussex	6.2
520. Green Township	Sussex	6.2
521. Midland Park Borough	Bergen	6.2
522. Norwood Borough	Bergen	6.1
523. Tewksbury Township	Hunterdon	6.1
524. Chesterfield Township	Burlington	6.0
525. Long Hill Township	Morris	6.0
526. Hopewell Borough	Mercer	5.9
527. Clinton Township	Hunterdon	5.8
528. Old Tappan Borough	Bergen	5.8
529. Oxford Township	Warren	5.7
530. Park Ridge Borough	Bergen	5.7
531. Peapack & Gladstone Borough	Somerset	5.7
532. Sparta Township	Sussex	5.7
533. Shrewsbury Township	Monmouth	5.6
534. Woodcliff Lake Borough	Bergen	5.6
535. Ringwood Borough	Passaic	5.5
536. Shamong Township	Burlington	5.5
537. Winfield Township	Union	5.3
538. Harding Township	Morris	5.1
539. Hardwick Township	Warren	5.0
540. Upper Saddle River Borough	Bergen	4.9
541. Califon Borough	Hunterdon	4.7
542. Kingwood Township	Hunterdon	4.7
543. Chatham Township	Morris	4.5
544. Alexandria Township	Hunterdon	4.4
545. East Amwell Township	Hunterdon	4.4
546. River Vale Township	Bergen	4.4
547. Rocky Hill Borough	Somerset	4.4
548. Roosevelt Borough	Monmouth	4.4
549. Helmetta Borough	Middlesex	3.9
550. Alpine Borough	Bergen	3.8
551. Holland Township	Hunterdon	3.8
552. Washington Township	Bergen	3.8
553. Bethlehem Township	Hunterdon	3.5
554. Ho-Ho-Kus Borough	Bergen	3.4
555. Interlaken Borough	Monmouth	3.4
556. Cresskill Borough	Bergen	3.3
557. Ogdensburg Borough	Sussex	2.7
558. Haworth Borough	Bergen	2.3
559. Harrington Park Borough	Bergen	2.2
560. New Hanover Township	Burlington	2.2
561. South Bound Brook Borough	Somerset	0.9
562. Millstone Borough	Somerset	0.0
563. Pine Valley Borough	Camden	NA
564. Tavistock Borough	Camden	NA
565. Teterboro Borough	Bergen	NA
566. Walpack Township	Sussex	NA

Appendix F

Municipal Comparative Tables

Land Area (square miles)

#	Municipality	County	Area
1.	Hamilton Township	Atlantic	111.28
2.	Washington Township	Burlington	100.14
3.	Jackson Township	Ocean	100.06
4.	Woodland Township	Burlington	95.94
5.	Maurice River Township	Cumberland	93.41
6.	Galloway Township	Atlantic	90.49
7.	Lacey Township	Ocean	84.00
8.	Manchester Township	Ocean	82.60
9.	Bass River Township	Burlington	75.88
10.	West Milford Township	Passaic	75.44
11.	Middle Township	Cape May	71.27
12.	Vineland City	Cumberland	68.69
13.	Vernon Township	Sussex	68.39
14.	Egg Harbor Township	Atlantic	67.35
15.	Wantage Township	Sussex	67.12
16.	Upper Township	Cape May	63.15
17.	Pemberton Township	Burlington	61.68
18.	Dennis Township	Cape May	61.35
19.	Howell Township	Monmouth	60.91
20.	Hopewell Township	Mercer	58.11
21.	Winslow Township	Camden	57.70
22.	Mullica Township	Atlantic	56.58
23.	Franklin Township	Gloucester	56.01
24.	Hillsborough Township	Somerset	54.69
25.	Estell Manor City	Atlantic	53.57
26.	Downe Township	Cumberland	50.76
27.	Tabernacle Township	Burlington	49.46
28.	Little Egg Harbor Township	Ocean	49.11
29.	Readington Township	Hunterdon	47.69
30.	Upper Freehold Township	Monmouth	46.86
31.	Lower Alloways Creek Township	Salem	46.78
32.	Franklin Township	Somerset	46.77
33.	Monroe Township	Gloucester	46.55
34.	Stafford Township	Ocean	46.53
35.	Pittsgrove Township	Salem	45.19
36.	Washington Township	Morris	44.86
37.	Shamong Township	Burlington	44.81
38.	Southampton Township	Burlington	44.03
39.	Montague Township	Sussex	44.01
40.	Berkeley Township	Ocean	42.90
41.	Rockaway Township	Morris	42.82
42.	Sandyston Township	Sussex	42.61
43.	Millville City	Cumberland	42.35
44.	Fairfield Township	Cumberland	42.29
45.	Monroe Township	Middlesex	41.94
46.	Buena Vista Township	Atlantic	41.36
47.	Hammonton Town	Atlantic	41.26
48.	Middletown Township	Monmouth	41.12
49.	Toms River Township	Ocean	40.97
50.	South Brunswick Township	Middlesex	40.86
51.	Jefferson Township	Morris	40.63
52.	Upper Pittsgrove Township	Salem	40.39
53.	Plumsted Township	Ocean	40.02
54.	Hamilton Township	Mercer	39.45
55.	Medford Township	Burlington	39.32
56.	Freehold Township	Monmouth	38.45
57.	Old Bridge Township	Middlesex	38.09
58.	Raritan Township	Hunterdon	37.84
59.	Lawrence Township	Cumberland	37.47
60.	Sparta Township	Sussex	37.39
61.	Millstone Township	Monmouth	36.76
62.	Delaware Township	Hunterdon	36.74
63.	Hardwick Township	Warren	36.48
64.	Waterford Township	Camden	36.19
65.	Kingwood Township	Hunterdon	35.23
66.	Pilesgrove Township	Salem	34.91
67.	Mannington Township	Salem	34.78
68.	Barnegat Township	Ocean	34.67
69.	Frankford Township	Sussex	34.11
70.	Alloway Township	Salem	32.85
71.	Montgomery Township	Somerset	32.62
72.	Commercial Township	Cumberland	32.46
73.	Bridgewater Township	Somerset	32.45
74.	Hardyston Township	Sussex	32.09
75.	Lebanon Township	Hunterdon	31.69
76.	Tewksbury Township	Hunterdon	31.63
77.	Colts Neck Township	Monmouth	31.43
78.	Upper Deerfield Township	Cumberland	31.10
79.	Blairstown Township	Warren	31.02
80.	Manalapan Township	Monmouth	30.82
81.	Wall Township	Monmouth	30.62
82.	Marlboro Township	Monmouth	30.59
83.	Mount Olive Township	Morris	30.35
84.	Edison Township	Middlesex	30.12
85.	Springfield Township	Burlington	30.03
86.	Clinton Township	Hunterdon	30.00
87.	Mansfield Township	Warren	29.92
88.	Hopewell Township	Cumberland	29.90
89.	Evesham Township	Burlington	29.54
90.	Chester Township	Morris	29.33
91.	East Amwell Township	Hunterdon	28.68
92.	Lower Township	Cape May	28.22
93.	Alexandria Township	Hunterdon	27.54
94.	White Township	Warren	27.37
95.	Stillwater Township	Sussex	27.12
96.	Bedminster Township	Somerset	26.47
97.	Brick Township	Ocean	26.23
98.	West Windsor Township	Mercer	26.01
99.	Mahwah Township	Bergen	25.93
100.	Ringwood Borough	Passaic	25.25
101.	Lakewood Township	Ocean	24.82
102.	Knowlton Township	Warren	24.78
103.	Hampton Township	Sussex	24.62
104.	Cherry Hill Township	Camden	24.25
105.	Quinton Township	Salem	24.17
106.	Walpack Township	Sussex	24.07
107.	Bernards Township	Somerset	24.00
108.	Franklin Township	Warren	23.99
109.	Parsippany-Troy Hills Township	Morris	23.94
110.	Wayne Township	Passaic	23.82
111.	Harmony Township	Warren	23.81
112.	Newark City	Essex	23.80
113.	Holland Township	Hunterdon	23.70
114.	Frelinghuysen Township	Warren	23.43
115.	Gloucester Township	Camden	23.22
116.	Pennsville Township	Salem	23.10
117.	Woodbridge Township	Middlesex	23.01
118.	Franklin Township	Hunterdon	22.88
119.	Logan Township	Gloucester	22.62
120.	New Hanover Township	Burlington	22.28

The New Jersey Municipal Data Book

Municipal Comparative Tables

Land Area (square miles)

Appendix F

Municipality	County	Area
121. Lawrence Township	Mercer	22.14
122. East Brunswick Township	Middlesex	21.95
123. Mount Laurel Township	Burlington	21.81
124. Mansfield Township	Burlington	21.72
125. West Amwell Township	Hunterdon	21.72
126. Chesterfield Township	Burlington	21.41
127. Roxbury Township	Morris	21.37
128. Washington Township	Gloucester	21.37
129. Byram Township	Sussex	21.07
130. Randolph Township	Morris	20.96
131. Woolwich Township	Gloucester	20.94
132. Bethlehem Township	Hunterdon	20.84
133. Ocean Township	Ocean	20.80
134. Allamuchy Township	Warren	20.54
135. Robbinsville Township	Mercer	20.48
136. Harding Township	Morris	20.44
137. Branchburg Township	Somerset	20.26
138. Andover Township	Sussex	20.18
139. Oldmans Township	Salem	19.97
140. Independence Township	Warren	19.84
141. Warren Township	Somerset	19.67
142. Elk Township	Gloucester	19.63
143. Harrison Township	Gloucester	19.13
144. Union Township	Hunterdon	18.97
145. Montville Township	Morris	18.87
146. Piscataway Township	Middlesex	18.78
147. Hope Township	Warren	18.50
148. Stow Creek Township	Cumberland	18.45
149. Greenwich Township	Cumberland	18.16
150. Lafayette Township	Sussex	18.02
151. Holmdel Township	Monmouth	17.97
152. Kinnelon Borough	Morris	17.89
153. Mendham Township	Morris	17.86
154. Fredon Township	Sussex	17.76
155. Washington Township	Warren	17.58
156. Carneys Point Township	Salem	17.50
157. Deptford Township	Gloucester	17.50
158. North Hanover Township	Burlington	17.34
159. Deerfield Township	Cumberland	16.84
160. Princeton Township	Mercer	16.38
161. Eagleswood Township	Ocean	16.37
162. Green Township	Sussex	16.18
163. Mantua Township	Gloucester	15.90
164. Sayreville Borough	Middlesex	15.90
165. West Deptford Township	Gloucester	15.90
166. South Harrison Township	Gloucester	15.80
167. Morris Township	Morris	15.76
168. East Windsor Township	Mercer	15.65
169. Tinton Falls Borough	Monmouth	15.59
170. Ewing Township	Mercer	15.33
171. Jersey City	Hudson	14.92
172. Moorestown Township	Burlington	14.77
173. East Greenwich Township	Gloucester	14.75
174. Livingston Township	Essex	13.88
175. Burlington Township	Burlington	13.47
176. Cranbury Township	Middlesex	13.41
177. Pohatcong Township	Warren	13.33
178. Bernardsville Borough	Somerset	12.93
179. Lumberton Township	Burlington	12.87
180. Elsinboro Township	Salem	12.27
181. Elizabeth City	Union	12.22
182. Weymouth Township	Atlantic	12.20
183. West Orange Township	Essex	12.12
184. Denville Township	Morris	12.11
185. Long Hill Township	Morris	12.08
186. North Brunswick Township	Middlesex	12.02
187. Plainsboro Township	Middlesex	11.84
188. Liberty Township	Warren	11.80
189. Voorhees Township	Camden	11.60
190. Atlantic City	Atlantic	11.35
191. Clifton City	Passaic	11.30
192. Egg Harbor City	Atlantic	11.11
193. Westampton Township	Burlington	11.04
194. Ocean Township	Monmouth	11.03
195. Hopatcong Borough	Sussex	10.96
196. Linden City	Union	10.81
197. Hanover Township	Morris	10.66
198. Greenwich Township	Warren	10.55
199. Pennsauken Township	Camden	10.53
200. Paramus Borough	Bergen	10.47
201. Fairfield Township	Essex	10.45
202. Florence Township	Burlington	9.71
203. Franklin Lakes Borough	Bergen	9.45
204. Millburn Township	Essex	9.38
205. Chatham Township	Morris	9.33
206. Greenwich Township	Gloucester	9.32
207. Glassboro Borough	Gloucester	9.21
208. Kearny Town	Hudson	9.14
209. Union Township	Union	9.12
210. Scotch Plains Township	Union	9.08
211. Camden City	Camden	8.82
212. Bloomingdale Borough	Passaic	8.80
213. Oakland Borough	Bergen	8.60
214. Bordentown Township	Burlington	8.51
215. Paterson City	Passaic	8.44
216. Boonton Township	Morris	8.42
217. South Plainfield Borough	Middlesex	8.36
218. Folsom Borough	Atlantic	8.27
219. Neptune Township	Monmouth	8.22
220. East Hanover Township	Morris	8.16
221. Woodbine Borough	Cape May	8.00
222. Wanaque Borough	Passaic	7.98
223. Corbin City	Atlantic	7.89
224. Willingboro Township	Burlington	7.69
225. Trenton City	Mercer	7.66
226. Port Republic City	Atlantic	7.62
227. Buena Borough	Atlantic	7.61
228. Cinnaminson Township	Burlington	7.60
229. Florham Park Borough	Morris	7.43
230. Clayton Borough	Gloucester	7.18
231. Lopatcong Township	Warren	7.08
232. Pequannock Township	Morris	7.07
233. Ocean City	Cape May	6.92
234. Lincoln Park Borough	Morris	6.73
235. Westfield Town	Union	6.73
236. Delran Township	Burlington	6.64
237. Wyckoff Township	Bergen	6.55
238. Hainesport Township	Burlington	6.52
239. Brigantine City	Atlantic	6.43
240. Alpine Borough	Bergen	6.36

©2008 Information Publications, Inc. All rights reserved. Photocopying prohibited. For additional copies, contact the publisher at www.informationpublications.com or (877)544-INFO (4636).

Appendix F — Municipal Comparative Tables

Land Area (square miles)

Municipality	County	Area
241. Montclair Township	Essex	6.30
242. Berkeley Heights Township	Union	6.26
243. Bridgeton City	Cumberland	6.22
244. Summit City	Union	6.05
245. Teaneck Township	Bergen	6.05
246. Plainfield City	Union	6.04
247. Mendham Borough	Morris	6.02
248. Watchung Borough	Somerset	6.02
249. Oxford Township	Warren	5.94
250. Eatontown Borough	Monmouth	5.92
251. Secaucus Town	Hudson	5.89
252. Peapack & Gladstone Borough	Somerset	5.80
253. Ridgewood Village	Bergen	5.79
254. Pleasantville City	Atlantic	5.78
255. Eastampton Township	Burlington	5.75
256. Absecon City	Atlantic	5.72
257. Bayonne City	Hudson	5.63
258. Hazlet Township	Monmouth	5.62
259. Ramsey Borough	Bergen	5.56
260. Aberdeen Township	Monmouth	5.54
261. Bloomfield Township	Essex	5.32
262. Long Beach Township	Ocean	5.31
263. Upper Saddle River Borough	Bergen	5.29
264. New Brunswick City	Middlesex	5.23
265. Long Branch City	Monmouth	5.22
266. Rumson Borough	Monmouth	5.22
267. North Bergen Township	Hudson	5.20
268. Fair Lawn Borough	Bergen	5.17
269. Springfield Township	Union	5.15
270. West Caldwell Township	Essex	5.05
271. Saddle River Borough	Bergen	4.98
272. Englewood City	Bergen	4.92
273. Far Hills Borough	Somerset	4.86
274. Cranford Township	Union	4.82
275. Perth Amboy City	Middlesex	4.78
276. Lyndhurst Township	Bergen	4.65
277. Tenafly Borough	Bergen	4.61
278. Green Brook Township	Somerset	4.58
279. Franklin Borough	Sussex	4.49
280. Carteret Borough	Middlesex	4.36
281. Clark Township	Union	4.34
282. Cedar Grove Township	Essex	4.22
283. Avalon Borough	Cape May	4.21
284. Madison Borough	Morris	4.20
285. Hackensack City	Bergen	4.12
286. River Vale Township	Bergen	4.08
287. Somers Point City	Atlantic	4.03
288. Mountainside Borough	Union	4.02
289. Totowa Borough	Passaic	4.00
290. Rahway City	Union	3.99
291. Montvale Borough	Bergen	3.97
292. Carlstadt Borough	Bergen	3.95
293. Lindenwold Borough	Camden	3.94
294. East Orange City	Essex	3.93
295. Pine Hill Borough	Camden	3.93
296. Maple Shade Township	Burlington	3.85
297. Maplewood Township	Essex	3.85
298. Linwood City	Atlantic	3.83
299. East Rutherford Borough	Bergen	3.81
300. Hackettstown Town	Warren	3.70
301. New Providence Borough	Union	3.68
302. Tuckerton Borough	Ocean	3.66
303. Roseland Borough	Essex	3.62
304. Berlin Borough	Camden	3.58
305. Point Pleasant Borough	Ocean	3.53
306. Middlesex Borough	Middlesex	3.50
307. North Haledon Borough	Passaic	3.44
308. Northfield City	Atlantic	3.43
309. Hawthorne Borough	Passaic	3.40
310. Nutley Township	Essex	3.37
311. Belleville Township	Essex	3.34
312. Woodcliff Lake Borough	Bergen	3.33
313. Berlin Township	Camden	3.25
314. Old Tappan Borough	Bergen	3.23
315. Oceanport Borough	Monmouth	3.22
316. Phillipsburg Town	Warren	3.22
317. Closter Borough	Bergen	3.17
318. Allendale Borough	Bergen	3.12
319. Passaic City	Passaic	3.11
320. Newton Town	Sussex	3.10
321. Bellmawr Borough	Camden	3.03
322. Burlington City	Burlington	3.00
323. Mine Hill Township	Morris	2.99
324. North Caldwell Borough	Essex	2.99
325. Hillsdale Borough	Bergen	2.98
326. Pompton Lakes Borough	Passaic	2.97
327. Irvington Township	Essex	2.96
328. West Paterson Borough	Passaic	2.96
329. Morristown Town	Morris	2.94
330. Edgewater Park Township	Burlington	2.91
331. Washington Township	Bergen	2.91
332. Bergenfield Borough	Bergen	2.90
333. West Long Branch Borough	Monmouth	2.89
334. Mount Holly Township	Burlington	2.86
335. South Orange Village Township	Essex	2.85
336. Haddonfield Borough	Camden	2.83
337. Rutherford Borough	Bergen	2.81
338. South River Borough	Middlesex	2.81
339. Hillside Township	Union	2.79
340. North Plainfield Borough	Somerset	2.79
341. Little Silver Borough	Monmouth	2.77
342. Beachwood Borough	Ocean	2.76
343. Little Falls Township	Passaic	2.75
344. Norwood Borough	Bergen	2.75
345. Verona Township	Essex	2.75
346. Metuchen Borough	Middlesex	2.74
347. Glen Rock Borough	Bergen	2.72
348. Saddle Brook Township	Bergen	2.72
349. Haddon Township	Camden	2.69
350. Dover Town	Morris	2.68
351. Mountain Lakes Borough	Morris	2.67
352. Elmwood Park Borough	Bergen	2.65
353. Roselle Borough	Union	2.64
354. Ridgefield Borough	Bergen	2.61
355. Salem City	Salem	2.61
356. Park Ridge Borough	Bergen	2.60
357. Morris Plains Borough	Morris	2.59
358. North Arlington Borough	Bergen	2.58
359. Fort Lee Borough	Bergen	2.53
360. Delanco Township	Burlington	2.49

Municipal Comparative Tables

Appendix F

Land Area (square miles)

Municipality	County	Area
361. Cape May City	Cape May	2.48
362. Manville Borough	Somerset	2.48
363. Oradell Borough	Bergen	2.42
364. Chatham Borough	Morris	2.41
365. High Bridge Borough	Hunterdon	2.41
366. Somerville Borough	Somerset	2.36
367. Boonton Town	Morris	2.35
368. Spotswood Borough	Middlesex	2.32
369. Westwood Borough	Bergen	2.32
370. New Milford Borough	Bergen	2.31
371. Pitman Borough	Gloucester	2.29
372. Matawan Borough	Monmouth	2.28
373. Ogdensburg Borough	Sussex	2.28
374. Lodi Borough	Bergen	2.26
375. Emerson Borough	Bergen	2.24
376. Orange City Township	Essex	2.21
377. Shrewsbury Borough	Monmouth	2.21
378. Gibbsboro Borough	Camden	2.20
379. Gloucester City	Camden	2.20
380. Sea Isle City	Cape May	2.20
381. Wharton Borough	Morris	2.19
382. Cresskill Borough	Bergen	2.14
383. Kenilworth Borough	Union	2.14
384. Ventnor City	Atlantic	2.14
385. Garfield City	Bergen	2.13
386. Mount Arlington Borough	Morris	2.11
387. Englewood Cliffs Borough	Bergen	2.09
388. Rockaway Borough	Morris	2.09
389. Runnemede Borough	Camden	2.09
390. Butler Borough	Morris	2.08
391. Waldwick Borough	Bergen	2.08
392. Woodbury City	Gloucester	2.08
393. Demarest Borough	Bergen	2.07
394. Riverdale Borough	Morris	2.06
395. Raritan Borough	Somerset	2.04
396. Freehold Borough	Monmouth	2.00
397. Dumont Borough	Bergen	1.99
398. Palmyra Borough	Burlington	1.98
399. Haworth Borough	Bergen	1.96
400. Paulsboro Borough	Gloucester	1.96
401. Roosevelt Borough	Monmouth	1.96
402. Washington Borough	Warren	1.96
403. Clementon Borough	Camden	1.89
404. River Edge Borough	Bergen	1.89
405. Union Beach Borough	Monmouth	1.88
406. Stanhope Borough	Sussex	1.87
407. Harrington Park Borough	Bergen	1.86
408. Princeton Borough	Mercer	1.85
409. Highland Park Borough	Middlesex	1.84
410. Collingswood Borough	Camden	1.83
411. Brielle Borough	Monmouth	1.78
412. Red Bank Borough	Monmouth	1.78
413. North Wildwood City	Cape May	1.77
414. Wrightstown Borough	Burlington	1.76
415. Ho-Ho-Kus Borough	Bergen	1.74
416. Moonachie Borough	Bergen	1.73
417. Ridgefield Park Village	Bergen	1.73
418. Chesilhurst Borough	Camden	1.72
419. Bound Brook Borough	Somerset	1.71
420. Alpha Borough	Warren	1.70
421. Newfield Borough	Gloucester	1.70
422. Fair Haven Borough	Monmouth	1.67
423. Barrington Borough	Camden	1.61
424. Woodstown Borough	Salem	1.59
425. Stratford Borough	Camden	1.58
426. Milltown Borough	Middlesex	1.57
427. Glen Gardner Borough	Hunterdon	1.56
428. Midland Park Borough	Bergen	1.56
429. Haddon Heights Borough	Camden	1.55
430. South Amboy City	Middlesex	1.55
431. Chester Borough	Morris	1.54
432. Hampton Borough	Hunterdon	1.54
433. Little Ferry Borough	Bergen	1.53
434. Riverside Township	Burlington	1.52
435. Hasbrouck Heights Borough	Bergen	1.51
436. Leonia Borough	Bergen	1.51
437. Audubon Borough	Camden	1.49
438. Andover Borough	Sussex	1.46
439. Point Pleasant Beach Borough	Ocean	1.44
440. Asbury Park City	Monmouth	1.43
441. Stone Harbor Borough	Cape May	1.42
442. Essex Fells Borough	Essex	1.41
443. Keyport Borough	Monmouth	1.41
444. Margate City	Atlantic	1.41
445. Lawnside Borough	Camden	1.40
446. Manasquan Borough	Monmouth	1.38
447. Clinton Town	Hunterdon	1.37
448. Somerdale Borough	Camden	1.37
449. Fanwood Borough	Union	1.34
450. Belvidere Town	Warren	1.32
451. Northvale Borough	Bergen	1.32
452. Spring Lake Heights Borough	Monmouth	1.32
453. Spring Lake Borough	Monmouth	1.31
454. Maywood Borough	Bergen	1.30
455. Wildwood City	Cape May	1.29
456. Frenchtown Borough	Hunterdon	1.28
457. Glen Ridge Borough	Essex	1.28
458. Hoboken City	Hudson	1.28
459. Union City	Hudson	1.27
460. Atlantic Highlands Borough	Monmouth	1.24
461. Hightstown Borough	Mercer	1.23
462. Woodbury Heights Borough	Gloucester	1.23
463. Deal Borough	Monmouth	1.22
464. Harrison Town	Hudson	1.22
465. Roselle Park Borough	Union	1.22
466. Medford Lakes Borough	Burlington	1.21
467. Palisades Park Borough	Bergen	1.21
468. Shiloh Borough	Cumberland	1.20
469. Caldwell Borough	Essex	1.19
470. West Cape May Borough	Cape May	1.19
471. Haledon Borough	Passaic	1.16
472. Hamburg Borough	Sussex	1.16
473. South Toms River Borough	Ocean	1.16
474. Milford Borough	Hunterdon	1.15
475. Wildwood Crest Borough	Cape May	1.15
476. Lambertville City	Hunterdon	1.13
477. Teterboro Borough	Bergen	1.11
478. Wood-Ridge Borough	Bergen	1.10
479. Keansburg Borough	Monmouth	1.08
480. Flemington Borough	Hunterdon	1.07

The New Jersey Municipal Data Book

Appendix F

Municipal Comparative Tables

Land Area (square miles)

Municipality	County	Area
481. Monmouth Beach Borough	Monmouth	1.07
482. Sea Girt Borough	Monmouth	1.06
483. Rochelle Park Township	Bergen	1.05
484. Dunellen Borough	Middlesex	1.04
485. Belmar Borough	Monmouth	1.02
486. West New York Town	Hudson	1.02
487. National Park Borough	Gloucester	1.00
488. Wallington Borough	Bergen	1.00
489. Beach Haven Borough	Ocean	0.98
490. Califon Borough	Hunterdon	0.97
491. Magnolia Borough	Camden	0.97
492. Rockleigh Borough	Bergen	0.97
493. Wenonah Borough	Gloucester	0.97
494. Cliffside Park Borough	Bergen	0.96
495. Pennington Borough	Mercer	0.96
496. Westville Borough	Gloucester	0.96
497. Pine Valley Borough	Camden	0.95
498. Penns Grove Borough	Salem	0.93
499. Bordentown City	Burlington	0.92
500. Lakehurst Borough	Ocean	0.92
501. Bloomsbury Borough	Hunterdon	0.91
502. Neptune City Borough	Monmouth	0.91
503. Mount Ephraim Borough	Camden	0.88
504. Elmer Borough	Salem	0.87
505. Lebanon Borough	Hunterdon	0.87
506. Edgewater Borough	Bergen	0.85
507. Fairview Borough	Bergen	0.85
508. Helmetta Borough	Middlesex	0.85
509. Weehawken Township	Hudson	0.85
510. Jamesburg Borough	Middlesex	0.84
511. Netcong Borough	Morris	0.84
512. Lavallette Borough	Ocean	0.80
513. South Bound Brook Borough	Somerset	0.78
514. Bogota Borough	Bergen	0.76
515. Highlands Borough	Monmouth	0.76
516. Millstone Borough	Somerset	0.75
517. Swedesboro Borough	Gloucester	0.73
518. Barnegat Light Borough	Ocean	0.72
519. Surf City Borough	Ocean	0.72
520. South Hackensack Township	Bergen	0.71
521. Ship Bottom Borough	Ocean	0.70
522. Hopewell Borough	Mercer	0.69
523. Rocky Hill Borough	Somerset	0.67
524. Garwood Borough	Union	0.66
525. Riverton Borough	Burlington	0.66
526. Seaside Park Borough	Ocean	0.65
527. Sea Bright Borough	Monmouth	0.64
528. Pine Beach Borough	Ocean	0.62
529. Allentown Borough	Monmouth	0.61
530. Oaklyn Borough	Camden	0.61
531. Seaside Heights Borough	Ocean	0.61
532. Island Heights Borough	Ocean	0.60
533. Merchantville Borough	Camden	0.60
534. Sussex Borough	Sussex	0.60
535. Bay Head Borough	Ocean	0.59
536. Bradley Beach Borough	Monmouth	0.59
537. Branchville Borough	Sussex	0.59
538. Pemberton Borough	Burlington	0.59
539. Beverly City	Burlington	0.58
540. Englishtown Borough	Monmouth	0.57
541. Harvey Cedars Borough	Ocean	0.55
542. Stockton Borough	Hunterdon	0.55
543. Farmingdale Borough	Monmouth	0.53
544. Prospect Park Borough	Passaic	0.48
545. Brooklawn Borough	Camden	0.47
546. Laurel Springs Borough	Camden	0.47
547. Mantoloking Borough	Ocean	0.44
548. Ocean Gate Borough	Ocean	0.44
549. Avon-by-the-Sea Borough	Monmouth	0.43
550. Longport Borough	Atlantic	0.38
551. Interlaken Borough	Monmouth	0.35
552. Cape May Point Borough	Cape May	0.29
553. Fieldsboro Borough	Burlington	0.27
554. Allenhurst Borough	Monmouth	0.26
555. West Wildwood Borough	Cape May	0.26
556. Lake Como Borough	Monmouth	0.25
557. Tavistock Borough	Camden	0.25
558. Hi-Nella Borough	Camden	0.23
559. Woodlynne Borough	Camden	0.22
560. Guttenberg Town	Hudson	0.19
561. Winfield Township	Union	0.18
562. Audubon Park Borough	Camden	0.15
563. Victory Gardens Borough	Morris	0.15
564. East Newark Borough	Hudson	0.10
565. Loch Arbour Village	Monmouth	0.10
566. Shrewsbury Township	Monmouth	0.09

Federal and State Representatives

Appendix G

Federal Representatives, 110th Congress

U.S. Senate

Frank R. Lautenberg (Democratic) – term ends 2009
Robert Menendez (Democratic) – term ends 2013

U.S. House of Representatives

District	Name	Party
1.	Robert E. Andrews	Democratic
2.	Frank A. LoBiondo	Republican
3.	Jim Saxton	Republican
4.	Christopher H. Smith	Republican
5.	Scott Garrett	Republican
6.	Frank Pallone Jr	Democratic
7.	Mike Ferguson	Republican
8.	Bill Pascrell Jr	Democratic
9.	Steven R. Rothman	Democratic
10.	Donald M. Payne	Democratic
11.	Rodney P. Frelinghuysen	Republican
12.	Rush D. Holt	Democratic
13.	Albio Sires	Democratic

Appendix G

Federal and State Representatives

New Jersey State Legislature, 2008-09 Session

Each of New Jersey's 40 legislative districts elects 1 member of the State Senate and 2 members of the General Assembly.

District	Senate	Assembly 1	Assembly 2
1.	Jeff Van Drew (D)	Nelson T. Albano (D)	Matthew W. Milam (D)
2.	Jim Whelan (D)	John F. Amodeo (R)	Vincent J. Polistina (D)
3.	Stephen M. Sweeney (D)	John J. Burzichelli (D)	Douglas H. Fisher (D)
4.	Fred H. Madden Jr (D)	Sandra Love (D)	Paul D. Moriarty (D)
5.	Dana L. Redd (D)	Nilsa Cruz-Perez (D)	Joseph J. Roberts Jr (D)
6.	John H. Adler (D)	Louis D. Greenwald (D)	Pamela R. Lampitt (D)
7.	Diane B. Allen (R)	Herb Conway Jr (D)	Jack Conners (D)
8.	Philip E. Haines (R)	Dawn Marie Addiego (R)	Scott Rudder (R)
9.	Christopher J. Connors (R)	Brian E. Rumpf (R)	Daniel M. Van Pelt (R)
10.	Andrew R. Ciesla (R)	James W. Holzapfel (R)	David W. Wolfe (R)
11.	Sean T. Kean (R)	Mary Pat Angelini (R)	David P. Rible (R)
12.	Jennifer Beck (R)	Caroline Casagrande (R)	Declan J. O'Scanlon Jr (R)
13.	Joseph M. Kyrillos Jr (R)	Amy H. Handlin (R)	Samuel D. Thompson (R)
14.	Bill Baroni (R)	Wayne P. DeAngelo (D)	Linda R. Greenstein (D)
15.	Shirley K. Turner (D)	Reed Gusciora (D)	Bonnie Watson Coleman (D)
16.	Christopher Bateman (R)	Peter J. Biondi (R)	Denise M. Coyle (R)
17.	Bob Smith (D)	Upendra J. Chivukula (D)	Joseph V. Egan (D)
18.	Barbara Buono (D)	Peter J. Barnes III (D)	Patrick J. Diegnan Jr (D)
19.	Joseph F. Vitale (D)	Joseph Vas (D)	John S. Wisniewski (D)
20.	Raymond J. Lesniak (D)	Neil M. Cohen (D)	Joseph Cryan (D)
21.	Thomas H. Kean Jr (R)	Jon M. Bramnick (R)	Eric Munoz (R)
22.	Nicholas P. Scutari (D)	Jerry Green (D)	Linda Stender (D)
23.	Leonard Lance (R)	Michael J. Doherty (R)	Marcia A. Karrow (R)
24.	Steven V. Oroho (R)	Gary R. Chiusano (R)	Alison Littell McHose (R)
25.	Anthony R. Bucco (R)	Michael Patrick Carroll (R)	Richard A. Merkt (R)
26.	Joseph Pennacchio (R)	Alex DeCroce (R)	Jay Webber (R)
27.	Richard J. Codey (D)	Mila M. Jasey (D)	John F. McKeon (D)
28.	Ronald L. Rice (D)	Ralph R. Caputo (D)	Cleopatra G. Tucker (D)
29.	M. Teresa Ruiz (D)	Albert Coutinho (D)	L. Grace Spencer (D)
30.	Robert W. Singer (R)	Ronald S. Dancer (R)	Joseph R. Malone III (R)
31.	Sandra B. Cunningham (D)	Anthony Chiappone (D)	L. Harvey Smith (D)
32.	Nicholas J. Sacco (D)	Vincent Prieto (D)	Joan M. Quigley (D)
33.	Brian P. Stack (D)	Ruben J. Ramos Jr. (D)	Caridad Rodriguez (D)
34.	Nia H. Gill (D)	Thomas P. Giblin (D)	Sheila Y. Oliver (D)
35.	John A. Girgenti (D)	Elease Evans (D)	Nellie Pou (D)
36.	Paul A. Sarlo (D)	Frederick Scalera (D)	Gary S. Schaer (D)
37.	Loretta Weinberg (D)	Gordon M. Johnson (D)	Valerie Vainieri Huttle (D)
38.	Robert M. Gordon (D)	John M. Voss (D)	Connie Wagner (D)
39.	Gerald Cardinale (R)	John E. Rooney (R)	Charlotte Vandervalk (R)
40.	Kevin J. O'Toole (R)	Scott T. Rumana (R)	David C. Russo (R)

ORDER FORM

S=NJ08 Book

Title	Qty	Edition	Price	Extended Price	Standing Order YES	NO
State & Municipal Profiles Series						
Almanac of the 50 States 2008		Hardcover	$89		☐	☐
Almanac of the 50 States 2008		Paperback	$79		☐	☐
California Cities, Towns & Counties 2008		CD	$119		☐	☐
California Cities, Towns & Counties 2008		Paperback	$119		☐	☐
Connecticut Municipal Profiles 2008		CD	$85		☐	☐
Connecticut Municipal Profiles 2008		Paperback	$85		☐	☐
Florida Cities, Towns & Counties 2008		CD	$119		☐	☐
Florida Cities, Towns & Counties 2008		Paperback	$119		☐	☐
Massachusetts Municipal Profiles 2008		CD	$109		☐	☐
Massachusetts Municipal Profiles 2008		Paperback	$109		☐	☐
The New Jersey Municipal Data Book 2008		CD	$119		☐	☐
The New Jersey Municipal Data Book 2008		Paperback	$119		☐	☐
North Carolina Cities, Towns & Counties 2008		CD	$119		☐	☐
North Carolina Cities, Towns & Counties 2008		Paperback	$119		☐	☐
Essential Topics Series						
Energy, Transportation & the Environment: A Statistical Sourcebook and Guide to Government Data 2008		Paperback	$77		☐	☐
American Profiles Series						
Black Americans: A Statistical Sourcebook and Guide to Government Data 2008		Paperback	$77		☐	☐
Hispanic Americans: A Statistical Sourcebook and Guide to Government Data 2008		Paperback	$77		☐	☐
Asian Americans: A Statistical Sourcebook and Guide to Government Data 2008		Paperback	$77		☐	☐

Offer and prices valid until 12/31/08

Purchase orders accepted from libraries, government agencies, and educational institutions.
Prepayment required from all other organizations.

Order Subtotal: _____
(Required ONLY for shipments to California) CA Sales Tax: _____
Shipping & Handling: _____
Total: _____

Please complete the following shipping and billing information. If paying by credit card or PO please call **(877)544-4636** or fax your completed order form to **(877)544-4635**. To pay by check, please mail this form and your payment to the address below.

Information Publications, Inc.
2995 Woodside Rd., Suite 400-182
Woodside, CA 94062

U.S. Ground Shipping Rates

Order Subtotal	Shipping & Handling
$0-$89	$7
$90-$119	$9
$120-$240	$14
$241-$400	$19
$401-$500	$22
>$500	Call

Call for Int'l or Express Shipping Rates

Shipping Information (UPS/FedEx tracking number sent via email)

Organization Name			
Shipping Contact			
Address (No PO Boxes, please)			
City		State	Zip
Email Address (req'd if want tracking #)		Phone #	

Payment Information (mark choice)

	☐ Check	☐ Credit Card ☐ Visa ☐ MC ☐ AMEX	☐ Purchase Order (attach PO to this form)
	Check #	CC#	PO #
		Exp Date	

☐ Check if same as Shipping Address

Credit Card Billing Information

Name on Credit Card			
Billing Address of Credit Card			
City		State	Zip
Signature			

2995 Woodside Rd., Suite 400-182
Woodside, CA 94062

WWW.INFORMATIONPUBLICATIONS.COM

Toll Free Phone 877-544-INFO (4636)
Toll Free Fax 877-544-4635

• Since 1980, A Trusted Ready Reference Resource for Easy-To-Use Federal, State and Local Information •

ORDER FORM

S=NJ08 Book

Title	Qty	Edition	Price	Extended Price	Standing Order YES	NO
State & Municipal Profiles Series						
Almanac of the 50 States 2008		Hardcover	$89		☐	☐
Almanac of the 50 States 2008		Paperback	$79		☐	☐
California Cities, Towns & Counties 2008		CD	$119		☐	☐
		Paperback	$119		☐	☐
Connecticut Municipal Profiles 2008		CD	$85		☐	☐
		Paperback	$85		☐	☐
Florida Cities, Towns & Counties 2008		CD	$119		☐	☐
		Paperback	$119		☐	☐
Massachusetts Municipal Profiles 2008		CD	$109		☐	☐
		Paperback	$109		☐	☐
The New Jersey Municipal Data Book 2008		CD	$119		☐	☐
		Paperback	$119		☐	☐
North Carolina Cities, Towns & Counties 2008		CD	$119		☐	☐
		Paperback	$119		☐	☐
Essential Topics Series						
Energy, Transportation & the Environment: A Statistical Sourcebook and Guide to Government Data 2008		Paperback	$77		☐	☐
American Profiles Series						
Black Americans: A Statistical Sourcebook and Guide to Government Data 2008		Paperback	$77		☐	☐
Hispanic Americans: A Statistical Sourcebook and Guide to Government Data 2008		Paperback	$77		☐	☐
Asian Americans: A Statistical Sourcebook and Guide to Government Data 2008		Paperback	$77		☐	☐

Offer and prices valid until 12/31/08

Order Subtotal _____
(Required ONLY for shipments to California) CA Sales Tax _____
Shipping & Handling _____
Total _____

Purchase orders accepted from libraries, government agencies, and educational institutions.
Prepayment required from all other organizations.

Please complete the following shipping and billing information. If paying by credit card or PO please call **(877)544-4636** or fax your completed order form to **(877)544-4635**. To pay by check, please mail this form and your payment to the address below.

Information Publications, Inc.
2995 Woodside Rd., Suite 400-182
Woodside, CA 94062

U.S. Ground Shipping Rates

Order Subtotal	Shipping & Handling
$0-$89	$7
$90-$119	$9
$120-$240	$14
$241-$400	$19
$401-$500	$22
>$500	Call

Call for Int'l or Express Shipping Rates

Shipping Information (UPS/FedEx tracking number sent via email)

Organization Name		
Shipping Contact		
Address (No PO Boxes, please)		
City	State	Zip
Email Address (req'd if want tracking #)	Phone #	

Payment Information (mark choice)

	☐ Check	☐ Credit Card ☐ Visa ☐ MC ☐ AMEX	☐ Purchase Order (attach PO to this form)
	Check #	CC#	PO #
		Exp Date	

☐ Check if same as Shipping Address

Credit Card Billing Information

Name on Credit Card		
Billing Address of Credit Card		
City	State	Zip
Signature		

2995 Woodside Rd., Suite 400-182
Woodside, CA 94062
WWW.INFORMATIONPUBLICATIONS.COM

Toll Free Phone 877-544-INFO (4636)
Toll Free Fax 877-544-4635

• Since 1980, A Trusted Ready Reference Resource for Easy-To-Use Federal, State and Local Information •